GUN TRADER'S GUIDE™

Forty-Fifth Edition

A Comprehensive, Fully Illustrated Guide to Modern Collectible Firearms with Current Market Values

Edited by Robert A. Sadowski

Skyhorse Publishing

Skyhorse Publishing books may be purchased in bulk at special discounts for sales promotion, corporate gifts, fund-raising, or educational purposes. Special editions can also be created to specifications. For details, contact the Special Sales Department, Skyhorse Publishing, 307 West 36th Street, 11th Floor, New York, NY 10018 or info@skyhorsepublishing.com.

Skyhorse® and Skyhorse Publishing® are registered trademarks of Skyhorse Publishing, Inc.®, a Delaware corporation.

Visit our website at www.skyhorsepublishing.com.

10 9 8 7 6 5 4 3 2 1

Library of Congress Cataloging-in-Publication Data is available on file.

Cover design by Brian Peterson

Print ISBN: 978-1-5107-7731-6
Ebook ISBN: 978-1-5107-7732-3

Printed in the United States of America

Contents

Introduction

This is the forty-fifth edition of the *Gun Trader's Guide* (GTG). Welcome to the best source for popular gun values.

We all know "hokey religions and ancient weapons are no match for a good blaster at your side, kid." This year, there was a phenomenal pistol brought to auction by Rock Island Auction Company in August 2022, and the story of this pistol...or rather, the BlasTech DL-44 heavy blaster, starts a long time ago in a galaxy far, far away. Yes, this is the iconic, incredibly historic, and only surviving DL-44 Heavy Blaster Pistol originally used by Harrison Ford starring as Han Solo in the filming and promotion of the 1977 epic *Star Wars: Episode IV - A New Hope*.

The only surviving BlasTech DL-44 heavy blaster from the original Star Wars movie sold for $1,057,500. (Courtesy Rock Island Auction Company.)

A London prop company took on the job to outfit George Lucas' characters with prop weapons for the movie. The budget was tight so readily available surplus firearms were modified with accessories and what Lucas and his team called "greebles," which was the term used to describe all the small mechanical looking parts on the exteriors and interiors of the spacecraft. The little details made the movie more believable. Greebles are what helped to make the props used on screen almost unrecognizable. Early science fiction movies were often over-polished and over-sanitized, and the vision Lucas had was the "used future" concept. The more grimy and well used, the more believable. For the char-

acters, gear, vehicles, and settings to be more credible, Lucas relied heavily on the equipment the characters used and the vehicles they traveled in having a "lived in" or well-used appearance.

From Han Solo's perspective, the Blaster provided plenty of power and got Han out of trouble. (Courtesy Rock Island Auction Company.)

Modified surplus weapons worked well too. The BlasTech E-11 blasters carried by most Stormtroopers were modified Sterling L2A3 submachine guns. The BlasTech DLT-19 Heavy Blaster Rifle, also carried by the Emperor's army, were altered MG34 machine guns used during World War II. Even a modified Lewis gun became the BlasTech T-21. But the BlasTech DL-44 heavy blaster is the most famous, especially when we see what the blaster is capable of in the famous "cantina" standoff scene between Han Solo and the bounty hunter Greedo. Solo uses the blaster in numerous shootouts with Imperial thugs. This prop pistol has achieved icon status in pop culture as much as Dirty Harry's Smith & Wesson Model 29 .44 Magnum revolver, Rambo's M60 machine gun, James Bond's Walther PPK, Quigley's Sharps 1874 rifle, and *Miami Vice* Sonny Crockett's Dornaus & Dixon Bren Ten pistol all have.

In actuality, the BlasTech DL-44 heavy blaster is a modified Mauser C96 pistol, also known as a "Broomhandle" Mauser for its narrow grip shaped like a broom. Three Mauser C96 pistols were modified into DL-44 blasters for the film. A vintage German Hensoldt scope was attached to a

In the hands of Han Solo, the Blaster quickly became an iconic weapon in the Star Wars franchise. (Courtesy Rock Island Auction Company.)

Mauser C96 pistol, which had the barrel shortened and a MG81 flash hider attached. The prop fired real blanks in the action scenes to help synchronize special effects and to aid actors in their reactions. After filming, the guns were stripped back to their original condition and refinished for use in future films. Of the three BlasTech DL-44 heavy blasters created for the film, only one survived.

A Hensoldt-Wetzlar Ziel Dialyt 3x scope was attached to the Mauser alone with a MG81 flash hider to give the pistol a lethal and well-used look. (Courtesy Rock Island Auction Company.)

The Mauser C96 is a semi-automatic pistol produced from 1896 to 1937. A distinct characteristic of the C96 is the internal box magazine in front of the trigger guard. These were one of the first successful and reliable semi-automatic pistol designs and were chambered in 7.63x25mm Mauser and later in 9mm. China and Spain made copies. The pistol was used in the Spanish-American War, the Boxer Rebellion, World War I, World War II, and numerous conflicts throughout the 20th century.

An example of a Chinese Shansei C96, Type 17 Pistol, chambered in .45 ACP. About 9,000 of these pistols were produced in China. The Chinese characters translate to "Type Semiautomatic Pistol." (Courtesy Historic Investments LLC)

Winston Churchill used a Mauser C96 during the Second Boer War. Lawrence of Arabia carried one during his time in the Middle East. Indian revolutionary Ram Prasad Bismil used a Mauser pistol as did Chinese communist general, Zhu De, during his Nanchang Uprising and later conflicts. Zhu's gun is in the Beijing war museum.

Many Mauser C96 pistols were equipped with a wood shoulder stock that was marked with a matching number. The wood stock doubled as a holster. (Courtesy Rock Island Auction Company.)

An example of a Spanish produced knockoff of the C96 type Broomhandle Mauser pistol chambered in 7.63x25mm Mauser. (Courtesy Rock Island Auction Company.)

If you want to dig into the history of the Mauser C96 pistols, detailed descriptions and values for different variants can be found on page 132.

CURRENT AND UP-TO-DATE

GTG is the definitive source for making informed decisions on selling and purchasing used firearms. This is why more than 2 million copies have been sold in the book's lifetime. We at *GTG* take buying and selling firearms as serious business. Whether you are buying a used shotgun for duck hunting, trading in your old concealed carry pistol for something better, or trying to figure out the value of a wall hanger.

GTG is revised annually to ensure information is both current and detailed. In the past fifty some years, *GTG* has grown to over six hundred pages and thousands of firearm listings. *GTG* is one of the most complete identification and price guides of modern smokeless-powder rifles, shotguns, and handguns manufactured from the late 19th century to the present. We ensure the information is current and up-to-date. Not every gun ever manufactured can be listed in a book of this size, but every effort has been made to include popular makes and models.

EASY-TO-USE FORMAT

GTG's reference guide format is simple and straightforward. Three tabbed sections—handguns, rifles, and shotguns—make it fast and easy to find the model in question. Entries are alphabetized by manufacturer and model with specifications that include:

- Manufacturer
- Model Name / Number
- Caliber or Gauge
- Barrel Length
- Overall Length
- Weight
- Distinguishing features
- Variations of different models
- Dates of manufacture (when they can be accurately determined)
- Date of discontinuation (if applicable)

- Current value for condition
- Photos (or illustrations)

ACCURATE GUN VALUES

Values shown are based on national averages obtained by conferring with knowledgeable gun dealers, traders, collectors, online auction sites, and auctioneers around the country. The listed values accurately reflect the nationwide average at the time of publication. Keep in mind that the stated values are averages based on a wide spectrum of variables. No price given in any such catalog should be considered the one and only value for a particular firearm. Value is ultimately determined by the buyer and seller. Supply and demand also dictate price.

In the case of rare or one-of-a-kind items, such as the Winchester Model 1873 One of One Thousand rifle or the Parker AA1 Special shotgun in 28 gauge, where little trading takes place, active gun collectors were consulted to obtain current market values.

In researching data, some manufacturers' records were unavailable and at times information was unobtainable. Some early firearms manufacturers' production records have been destroyed in fires, lost, or were simply not maintained accurately. These circumstances resulted in some minor deviations in the presentation format of certain model listings. For example, production dates may not be listed when manufacturing records are unclear or unavailable. As an alternative, approximate dates of manufacture may be listed to reflect the availability of guns from a manufacturer or distributor. These figures may represent disposition dates indicating when that particular model was shipped to a distributor or importer. Frequently, and especially with foreign manufacturers, production records are unavailable. Therefore, availability information is often based on importation records that reflect domestic distribution only.

This is meant to explain the procedure and policy used regarding these published dates and to establish the distinction between production dates, which are based on manufacturers' records, and availability dates, which are based on distribution records in the absence of recorded production data.

ACKNOWLEDGMENTS

The publisher wishes to express special thanks to the many collectors, dealers, manufacturers, shooting editors, firearm companies and distributors' public relations and production personnel, research personnel, and other industry professionals who provide us with updates throughout the year. We are especially grateful for their assistance and cooperation. Special thanks to Rock Island Auctions (rockislandauction.com), Remington (remarms.com), and Historic Investments (investmentsinarms.com) for the use of photos.

Finally, thank you for your comments and suggestions. We appreciate and value your input.

Send comments, queries, or suggestions to: info@skyhorsepublishing.com

Collector Notes: Top 5 Pump-Action Shotguns

The pump-action shotgun is an original American design. The first successful pump-action shotgun was the Winchester Model 1893 designed by John Browning. That gun evolved into the Winchester Model 1897 (page 588) and was produced from 1897 to 1957. Over a million of these external hammer shotguns were built and used by the military, law enforcement, and hunters. Originals and knock-offs are still used today mostly in cowboy action shooting competitions. This is a classic and almost made it to the top-5 list. The Remington Model 31 (pages 546-547) is another sought after shotgun due to its smooth cycling action. It debuted in 1931 with less than 200,000 built, which is a drop in the bucket compared to the top-5 guns. The honorable mention is also given to the Winchester Model 42 (page 587) in .410. It is similar to a scaled down Model 12.

This is my Top 5 list. All are best-selling pumps manufactured in the millions so there are plenty of used models on the market and some are still manufactured today.

#5: WINCHESTER MODEL 12

Winchester introduced the Model 12 in 1912 and had them in production until 1964. It was Winchester's first hammerless shotgun. More than 1.9 million of these slick-operating pumps were built. It was initially chambered in 20 gauge only; 12 and 16 gauge came in 1913 and the 28 gauge in 1934. Go to pages 584-585 for more details and values.

#4: ITHACA MODEL 37

This is another classic pump gun that shucks empties via the bottom of the receiver, not to the side like its contemporaries. Introduced in 1937 during the depths of the Great Depression, the Model 37 was adopted by the military and law enforcement as well as hunters. Due to high production costs and competition from inexpensive foreign-made pump guns, the company went belly up in 2005, but interest has never really petered out for this beloved pump. New production re-started in 2007. I have a 16-gauge with a straight grip stock manufactured by the original Ithaca Gun Company that I wouldn't part with for anything. Go to pages 501-503 for more on older guns and recent manufactured guns.

#3: BENELLI NOVA

Yes, the Nova is not American-made, but it took Benelli to give the pump gun a modern makeover in 1999. Not only does the Nova look modern but it also has great ergonomics. The forend is extra long so there will be no pinched hands on the rearward pump. Unique to this pump is a magazine cutoff button on the bottom of the forend that allows the user to eject the round in the chamber and the shells in the magazine tube remain in place. This pump uses a one-piece receiver and buttstock made of steel-reinforced polymer so it is nearly impervious to the elements. Sure, it is bit heavy for pheasant hunting, so use it for ducks and turkey. The Nova reintroduced the pump-action to the newer generation that was raised with polymer-stock shotguns. Check out the values and models on pages 443-444.

#2: MOSSBERG MODEL 500/590

The Model 500 and Model 590 pumps are the workhorses of pump-action shotguns. They are not the most beautiful guns, but they are affordable and ultra reliable. My first pump-action was a Model 500 combo 12 gauge with a bird barrel and slug barrel. Mossberg offers these guns outfitted to take on tactical duties with Special Purpose variants and Field models perfect for upland birds, ducks, deer, and turkey. The ability to swap barrels makes it versatile. I have used countless Mossberg pumps and have never had any issues with them. Over 11,000,000 million Model 500 pumps have been built since it was introduced in 1961. The Military uses the 590A1, a beefed up version of Model 590. Did I mention how affordable they are? For details, model variants, and values, go to pages 526-530.

#1: REMINGTON MODEL 870

The Model 870 is perhaps the premier American-made pump-action shotgun that knocked the Winchester Model 12 off its pedestal. Introduced in 1951, when tail fins were still standard equipment on sedans, the Model 870 was innovative, had a smooth action, though not as silky as a Winchester Model 12, and proved itself reliable and adaptable. The Model 870 was the first pump-action shotgun to incorporate dual-action bars for enhanced reliability. With the ability to swap barrels, the 870 is suited for any situation: 18-in. for home defense, 20-in. for turkey, 28-in. for pheasant, and 30-in. for trap. In 2020, Remington went bankrupt, but that didn't keep Big Green down. In 2021, the new RemArms company announced production of the classic Model 870. For values and variants, go to pages 547-552.

The Remington Model 870 Wingmaster is available again and is perhaps the definitive example of the American-made pump-action shotgun with style, reliability, and performance. (Courtesy RemArms)

How to Use *GTG*

Are you planning on buying or selling a used rifle, shotgun, or handgun? Perhaps you just want to establish the value of a favorite rifle, shotgun, or handgun in your collection. No matter what your interest in collectible modern, smokeless-powder firearms, today's enthusiast inevitably turns to the *Gun Trader's Guide* (*GTG*) to determine specifications, date of manufacture, and the average value (in the United States) of a specific modern firearm.

Opening the book, the collector asks him- or herself the first obvious question: "How much is my used gun worth?" Values contained in this book should be considered retail; that is, the average price a collector anywhere in the United States may expect to pay for a firearm in similar condition. Don't leap to the conclusion that your firearm will bring top dollar! There is no right or wrong price for any collectible firearm. The listings shown here are based on national averages and may be higher or lower depending on where you live and the strength of the market in your area. There is a market for everything from folk art to Star Wars action figures, but the range of values can be extreme and only items in perfect condition will bring top dollar.

Many variables must be considered when buying or selling a used gun. Scarcity, demand, geographic location, and the buyer's position. The condition of the gun ultimately governs the selling price. Sentiment often shades the value of a particular gun in the seller's mind, but the market value of Grandpa's old .30- 30 cannot be logically cataloged nor effectively marketed—except possibly to someone else in the family!

GRANDPA'S DEER GUN

To illustrate how the price of a particular gun may fluctuate, let us consider the popular Winchester Model 94 (it was discontinued in 2006, after 110 years of continuous production, then reintroduced in 2010) and see what its value might be.

The Model 1894 (or Model 94) is a lever-action, solid-frame repeater. Round or octagon barrels of twenty-six inches were standard when the rifle was first introduced in 1894. However, half-octagon barrels were offered for a slight increase in price. Various magazine lengths were also available.

Fancy grade versions in all calibers were available featuring a checkered walnut pistol grip stock and forearm.

In addition, Winchester produced this model in a carbine style with a saddle ring on the left side of the receiver. The carbine had a twenty-inch round barrel and a full or half magazine. Some carbines were supplied with standard-grade barrels while others were made of nickel steel. Trapper models were also available with shorter fourteen-, sixteen-, or eighteen-inch barrels.

In later years, the Rifle and Trapper models were discontinued, and only the carbine remained. Eventually, the saddle ring was eliminated from this model and the carbine butt stock was replaced with a shotgun-type butt stock and shortened forend.

After World War II, the finish on Winchester Model 94 carbines

Many firearms are inherited from avid hunters or shooters. Since such firearms were used, they will not have as high a value as firearms in new or mint condition.

changed to strictly hot caustic bluing; thus, prewar models usually demand a premium over postwar models.

In 1964 (a turning point for many American firearms manufacturers), beginning with serial number 2,700,000, the action on the Winchester Model 94 was redesigned for easier manufacture. Many collectors and firearms enthusiasts considered this and other design changes to be inferior to former models. Therefore, the term pre-'64 has become the watchword for collectors when it comes to setting values on Winchester-made firearms. This will likely be the case in the future, as the now-discontinued models 70, 94, and 1300 Winchester reach the collectible market.

SCARCE AND VALUABLE

Whether this evaluation is correct or not is unimportant. The justification for an immediate increase in the value of pre-'64 models was that they were no longer available. This diminished availability placed them in the scarce class, making them more desirable to collectors.

Shortly after the 1964 transition, Winchester began producing Model 94 commemorative models in great numbers, which added confusion to the concept of limited production. Increased availability adversely affected the annual appreciation and price stability of these commemorative models. The negative response generated by this marketing practice was increased when Winchester was sold in the 1980s. The name of this long-established American firearms manufacturer was changed to U.S. Repeating Arms Company, which manufactured the Model 94 in standard, carbine, and big-bore models until 2006. Later, the Angle-Eject model was introduced, a design change that allowed for the mounting of scope sights directly above the action. Currently the Model 94 in various configurations are in production in Japan; originals were built in New Haven, Connecticut.

With the above facts in mind, let's explore *GTG* to establish the approximate value of your particular Model 94. We will assume that you recently inherited the rifle, which has "Winchester Model 94" inscribed on the barrel. Turn to the "Rifle" section of the book and look under "Winchester." The index at the back of the book is another way to locate your rifle.

The listings in the *GTG* are arranged within each manufacturer's entry, first by model numbers in consecutive order followed by model names in alphabetical order. At first glance, you see that there are two model designations that may apply: the original designation (Model 1894) or the revised, shorter designation (Model 94). Which of these designations applies to your recently acquired Winchester?

The next step in the process is to try to match the appearance of your model with an illustration in the book. The photos may all look alike at first glance, but close evaluation and careful attention to detail will enable you to eliminate models that are not applicable. Further examination of your gun might reveal a curved or crescent-shaped butt plate. By careful observation of your gun's characteristics and close visual comparison of the photographic examples, you may logically conclude that your gun is the Winchester Model 94 Lever-Action Carbine. (Please note that the guns shown in the *GTG* are not always shown in proportion to one another; that is, a carbine barrel might not appear to be shorter than a rifle barrel.)

You have now tentatively determined your model, but to be sure, you should read through the specifications for that model and establish that the barrel on the pictured rifle is twenty inches long and round, octagonal, or half-octagonal.

Upon measuring you find that the barrel on your rifle is approximately twenty inches, and it is round. Additionally, your rifle is marked .32 W.S. The caliber offerings listed in the specifications include .32 W.S., so you are further convinced that this is your gun. You may read on to determine that this rifle was manu-

Winchester Model 94 Lever Action Saddle Ring Carbine with 20-in. round barrel, walnut stock, chambered in .32 W.S. (Winchester Special), and manufactured in 1927. This example rates GOOD (Gd). (Courtesy of Rock Island Auctions)

factured from 1894 to 1937. After that date, only the shorter-barreled carbine was offered by Winchester, and then only in .25-35, .30-30, and .38-55.

At this point, you know you have a Winchester Model 94 manufactured before World War II. You read the value and take the rifle to your dealer to initiate a sale.

Here is a look at some of the trades you may encounter for Grandpa's deer rifle:

WHAT TO EXPECT

Since the rifle rates Gd, this means there are/may be some minor replacement parts, the metal is smoothly rusted or lightly pitted in places, and the stock is lightly scratched, bruised or minor cracks repaired. It is also in good working order. However, keep in mind that the dealer is in business to make a profit. If he pays you the full value of the gun, he will have to charge more than this when he sells it to make a reasonable profit.

Therefore, expect a reputable dealer to offer you less than the published value for the gun in its present condition. The exact amount will vary for a variety of reasons. For example, if the dealer already has a dozen or so of the same model on his shelf and they do not sell well, his offer will be considerably lower. On the other hand, if the dealer does not have any of this model in stock and knows several collectors who want it, chances are his offer will be considerably higher.

Maybe you think refinishing the rifle will increase the value. Even when a collectible firearm has been expertly refinished to excellent condition, it is no longer original, and a rule of thumb is to deduct 50 percent from the value listed in this book. If the job is poorly done, deduct 80 percent or more.

TOP-DOLLAR OPTIONS

One alternative for getting top dollar for your gun is to go online and list it with one of several online gun auction websites, and sell the firearm directly to a private collector. Many collectors have a special interest in certain models, manufacturers, or product lines and will happily pay full price and sometimes more for a hard-to-find piece. However, this approach may prove time-consuming, frustrating, and expensive. Online auction websites charge fees, and you have to package and ship the firearm to your buyer's FFL dealer. In addition, there may be federal and local restrictions on the sale of firearms in your area, so be sure to check with the local police chief or sheriff before you proceed with a private sale.

STANDARDS OF CONDITION

The condition of a firearm is an important factor in determining its value. In some rare and unusual models, a variation in condition from excellent to very good can mean a value difference of 50 percent or more. Therefore, you must be able to determine the gun's condition before you can accurately evaluate the value of the firearm.

Several sets of value standards have been used in gun trading, but the National Rifle Association Standards of Condition of Modern Firearms is the most popular, with the condition established as a percentage of original finish remaining on the wood and metal of the firearm.

Here's a look at how these standards are applied:

EXCELLENT

For the purpose of assigning comparative values as a basis for trading, firearms listed in this book are assumed to be in excellent (Ex) condition if they have 95 percent or more remaining original finish, no noticeable marring

of wood or metal, and the bore has no pits or rust.

To the novice, this translates to meaning a practically new gun, almost as though it had just been removed from its shipping box. The trained eye, however, will see the difference between new in the box (NiB) or mint condition and merely excellent.

VERY GOOD

Any other defects, no matter how minor, diminish the value. For example, if more than 5 percent of the original finish is gone and there are minor surface dents or scratches, regardless of how small, the gun is no longer in excellent condition. Instead, it is considered to be in very good condition, provided the gun is in perfect working order. Despite the minor defects, the gun will still look relatively new to the untrained buyer.

GOOD

If the gun is in perfect working condition and functions properly but has minor wear on working surfaces (perhaps some deep scratches on the wood or metal), the gun is considered to be in good (Gd) condition, one grade below very good according to NRA standards. Again, the price shown in this book for that particular firearm must be reduced to reflect its true value.

The two remaining NRA conditions fall under the headings of fair and poor. These guns normally have little value unless they are of historical importance or an aficionado simply must have them to complete his collection. The value of such guns is then determined by the price the buyer is willing to pay.

In any case, do not sell any gun until you have researched its history and value. Many plain-looking guns have sold for thousands of dollars for a variety of reasons. Many an innocent widow has given away her deceased husband's guns without knowing that they were of extremely high value. Avoid buyers who are in a hurry to make a purchase or who quickly offer what seems to be more money than the gun is worth. Not every gun is priceless, but many of them are nearly so!

GTG offers multiplication factors to use for firearms in other than excellent condition. These factors are listed below. Be aware that the figures given are simply another rough means of establishing value.

For guns in other-than-excellent condition, multiply the price shown in this book for the model in question by the following factors:

Multiplication Factors:

Condition	X	Factor
Mint or New (NiB)		1.25
Excellent (Ex)		1.00
Very Good (VG)		.85
Good (Gd)		.68
Fair		.45
Poor		.15

UNIQUE SERIAL NUMBERS

The serial number on a firearm can increase the value if it is unique, and consecutive serial numbers can boost value to a set of firearms.

PROVENANCE

Provenance means place or source of origin. In gun trading, it means who owned the gun and to a certain extent, when or where the gun was used. Beware of Jesse James six-shooters or else I may want to sell you the Brooklyn Bridge. Make sure the gun has documentation stating prior ownership. It can mean the difference between a really valuable firearm or a really expensive fake.

PARTING THOUGHTS

Remember, the word "guide" in *GTG* should be taken literally. This book is meant to be a reference only and is not the gospel of the collectible trade. We sincerely hope, however, that you find this publication useful when you decide to buy or sell a used collectible modern firearm.

Also, keep in mind that gun values vary from region to region. For example, lever-action deer rifles are more popular among collectors and hunters in the east, while bolt-action bean field rifles bring higher prices in the south and west. For this reason, we recommend that you attend regional gun shows, auctions, and look online to develop a better understanding of local gun values and pricing. And, whenever you travel, check the prices of guns you're familiar with to compare their values in other parts of the country. The difference can be surprising!

Finally, beware of guns that have been refinished or refurbished by amateurs or even expert gunsmiths. A century-old gun that looks brand new has probably been refinished and will actually be worth far less than a time-worn original. Every new screw, pin, or spring added to an original firearm diminishes its value—the worn, pitted original parts of a firearm enhance its value far more than modern replacements. Refinishing a gun may improve its looks and satisfy the final owner, but it will lose collectible value that will never be recovered.

ABBREVIATIONS USED IN GTG:

ACP = Automatic Colt Pistol
Adj. = Adjustable
AE = Action Express
Auto. = Automatic
Avail. = Available
Bbl. = Barrel
C = Cylinder choke
c. = Circa
Cal. = caliber
DA = Double Action
Disc. = Discontinued
Eject. = Ejector
F = Full choke
FN = Fabrique Nationale
Ga. = Gauge
H&H = Holland & Holland
IC = Improved Cylinder choke
in. = inch

L.H. = Left hand
lbs. = Pounds
Imp. = imported
LC = Long Colt
LR = Long Rifle
M = Modified choke
M&P = Military & Police
Mag. = Magnum
Mfg. = Manufactured
mm = Millimeter
NiB = New in Box
NM = National Match
O/U = Over-and-under
Reintro. = Reintroduced
Rem. = Remington
Rnd. = Round
S/N = serial number
S/S = side-by-side

SA = Single Action
SK = Skeet choke
SL = Self Loading
Spl. = Special
STW = Shooting Times Westerner
Syn. = Synthetic
TH = Target Hammer
TT = Target Trigger
UCC = Usel Caseless Cartridge
Vent. = Ventilated
VR = Vent rib
w/ = with
w/o = without
Wby. = Weatherby
Win. = Winchester
WMR = Winchester Magnum Rimfire
WRF = Winchester Rimfire

Colt Model 1911
Semi-Automatic Pistol

Adopted by the U.S. Ordnance Department in 1911, the Colt semi-automatic pistol was originally manufactured by Colt and the government's Springfield Armory. In 1917, with the US entry into World War I, the government contracted with Colt for one million pistols and contracts were signed for the production of a total of two million more pistols with Remington-UMC, North American Arms, Savage, Winchester, National Cash Register Co., Burroughs Adding Machine, Lamston Monotype, and Caron Bros. A total of 629,000 pistols were completed by the war's end in1918. Production was resumed in 1924 with a series of design modifications introduced during the inter-war period resulting in the Model 1911 A1. From the onset of World War II until its end in 1945 Colt, Remington UMC, Remington-Rand, Ithaca, Singer, and Union Switch and Signal Company manufactured nearly 2 million M1911A1s.

NRA Perfect Condition is 100 percent original condition. This Colt 1911 has all original parts and commands the same price with or without the box. The frame and receiver are in perfect condition with no wear or damage. The checkering on the grip is in "as new" condition and the wood shows no wear, scratches, or stains.

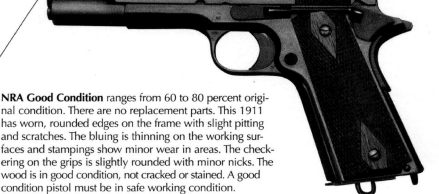

NRA Good Condition ranges from 60 to 80 percent original condition. There are no replacement parts. This 1911 has worn, rounded edges on the frame with slight pitting and scratches. The bluing is thinning on the working surfaces and stampings show minor wear in areas. The checkering on the grips is slightly rounded with minor nicks. The wood is in good condition, not cracked or stained. A good condition pistol must be in safe working condition.

NRA Fair Condition ranges from 20 to 60 percent original condition. This Model 1911 is in well-worn condition with the frame retaining only 40 percent of its original finish. Some major and minor parts have been replaced and scratches and pitting from rust and corrosion are evident on the frame and slide. Serial numbers and other markings are shallow and difficult to identify. While the grips on this pistol are not badly scratched or soiled, they show worn checkering and several large and small dents. The gun must function and shoot properly.

Winchester Model 94

Winchester produced approximately 2,550,000 Model 94 lever action rifles between 1894 and 1962. The Model 94 was manufactured in both rifle and carbine versions with several configurations that included pistol- and straight-grip stocks, various grades of wood, and several different barrel lengths and magazine capacities. Crescent and shotgun style buttstocks and takedown barrels were also offered. The Model 94 was produced in 25-35, 30, 30-30, 32-40 and 38-55 calibers.

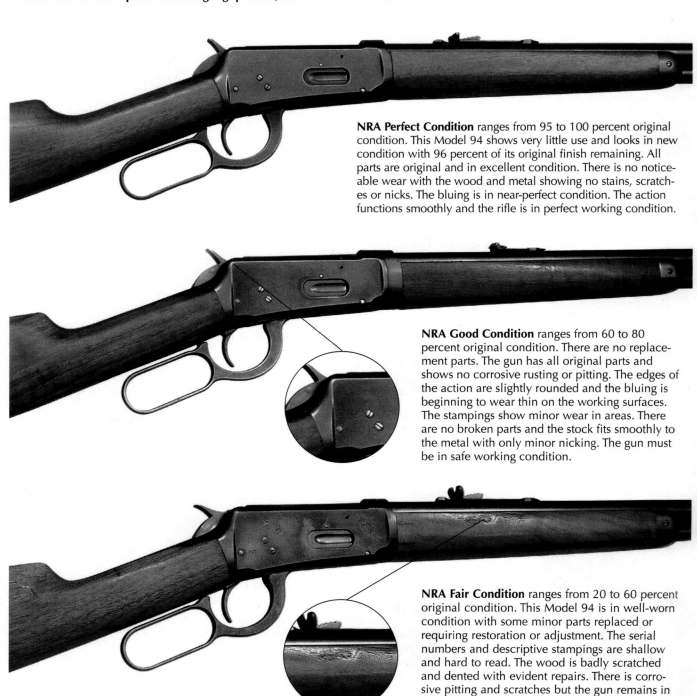

NRA Perfect Condition ranges from 95 to 100 percent original condition. This Model 94 shows very little use and looks in new condition with 96 percent of its original finish remaining. All parts are original and in excellent condition. There is no noticeable wear with the wood and metal showing no stains, scratches or nicks. The bluing is in near-perfect condition. The action functions smoothly and the rifle is in perfect working condition.

NRA Good Condition ranges from 60 to 80 percent original condition. There are no replacement parts. The gun has all original parts and shows no corrosive rusting or pitting. The edges of the action are slightly rounded and the bluing is beginning to wear thin on the working surfaces. The stampings show minor wear in areas. There are no broken parts and the stock fits smoothly to the metal with only minor nicking. The gun must be in safe working condition.

NRA Fair Condition ranges from 20 to 60 percent original condition. This Model 94 is in well-worn condition with some minor parts replaced or requiring restoration or adjustment. The serial numbers and descriptive stampings are shallow and hard to read. The wood is badly scratched and dented with evident repairs. There is corrosive pitting and scratches but the gun remains in safe firing condition.

Winchester Model 12

When introduced in 1912, the hammerless Model 12 slide-action shotgun was offered only in 20-gauge with a 2½-inch chamber. In 1914 12- and 16-gauge versions were introduced followed by a 28-gauge in 1937. The Model 12 was available with various chokes and with walnut, straight or pistol grip stock and forearm. Winchester sold more than 1,900,000 Model 1912s during the shotgun's 51-year history.

NRA Perfect Condition is 100 percent original condition. This Model 12 is in NIB condition and has not been previously sold at retail. The shotgun shows no signs of use and retains 100 percent of its original finish. All parts are original and in new condition.

NRA Good Condition ranges from 60 to 80 percent original condition. This gun has all original parts in good condition. There is no corrosive pitting or rusting and the action displays only slightly rounded edges. The gun retains 70 percent of its original finish with bluing beginning to wear on the working surfaces. The stock fits smoothly to the metal and has only minor nicking. The shotgun must be in good working order.

NRA Fair Condition ranges from 20 to 60 percent original condition. Showing a well-worn condition, this gun may require minor parts to be replaced or adjusted. The serial numbers and descriptive stamping are shallow and difficult to read. The wood is badly scratched and dented with evident repairs. Corrosive pitting and scratches in the metal, while considerable, do not render the gun unsafe.

The Art of Gun Trading

No matter if you are trading baseball cards, action figures, or fine firearms, there is an art and a science to the process that beginners often fail to realize and seasoned experts rely on. In other words, if you do not know what you are doing, you can expect to be burned—badly, in some cases.

GUN TRADING BASICS

As is the case when selling any collectible item, there is no substitute for research.

The first step in shrewd gun trading is to know your firearm, its condition, and its value in your market—meaning your part of the country. A Marlin .30/30 lever-action rifle, for example, will not carry as high a value in California, Georgia, or Texas as it will in Pennsylvania, Maine, New York, or elsewhere in the east, where short-range brush-country guns are most popular.

Next, study the NRA Standards of Condition (see pages xi–xiii) and get a feel for such terms as New In Box, Excellent, and Good and what they mean to a collector.

DICKERING HOW-TO

When it comes to "horse trading" there are no rules, but the conflict is always the same: Each party wants to come out of the deal a winner.

Below are a few tips for the new gun trader to consider.

DON'T SAY TOO MUCH

Present the gun to the prospective buyer and let him or her make all the comments and ask all the questions.

DECIDE ON A PRICE

This requires a little of the poker player's panache. If you name a price and the buyer pounces on it, then you came in too low. But set the price too high and he or she might walk away.

The right price will keep a buyer interested, which is why knowing your gun and its value is important.

DON'T LIE OR EMBELLISH

Gun collectors generally know their guns as well as anyone and are quick to spot a fraud. If your gun is not in its original condition, has been refurbished, or is not what it appears to be, be honest and say so. If you don't know the answer to an important question, take the time to find out.

KNOW WHEN TO QUIT

Trust your instincts when a buyer seems overeager to buy your gun, tells you its value is much less than you know it is worth, or tries to tell you the gun is illegal, a fake, or otherwise not what you say it is. If you feel that you are being tricked—while either buying or selling—back away, do more research, and come back with new knowledge and a different offer.

LEARN AS YOU GO

If you spend time buying and selling guns, or any collectible for that matter, you are going to make some great sales and unfortunately, you are also going to be beaten in price by a buyer or dealer who has been in the game longer than you have. Generally, the best advice is to never sell a gun for less than you paid for it. Good research will keep you from selling a $10,000 gun for $100—it happens!—or from paying thousands more than a gun is worth, which also happens.

The ultimate value of a firearm depends on the rarity of the model, the region, and the buyer's needs; rare, unusual, or one-of-a-kind guns can be worth substantially more than the standard model. It's in your best interest to find out what kind of gun you have and what it is worth before you offer it for sale.

Courtesy of NSSF.org

Gun Shows

The best classroom for learning about the value and condition of used firearms is the weekend gun show. Dealers from the region and often across the country will attend to show, sell, buy, trade, and talk about new and used guns of every make and model. Some dealers specialize in firearms made by a specific manufacturer while some deal in just one model of firearm. Others may offer custom guns while others offer a variety of collectibles including swords, knives, and ancient weaponry.

Attending gun shows is a chance to see a wide variety of firearms, their condition, and their value at the local level. This is the place to really learn about guns and how their value is determined. Most dealers will gladly explain the nuances of gun condition, why perfectly refurbished firearms are worth so much less than a rusted, beat-up original, and what makes one firearm worth so much while another seemingly similar model is worth so much less.

GUN SHOW ETIQUETTE

Unless otherwise noted, all gun shows in the United States are open to the public. There are security requirements that must be met and procedures that must be followed. In general, anyone attending a gun show may bring guns for appraisal, sale, or trade. Laws vary from state to state, so be sure to check with show promoters or local law enforcement before bringing a gun.

Most guns shows are well attended, often crowded, and sales can be brisk. If a particular dealer or booth is overrun with customers, come back later to talk. There are always slow periods at gun shows, such as early in the day, lunchtime, and just before closing.

In general, do not bring a gun to a show and expect to get top dollar for it. Show dealers often work in volume sales and may have a dozen or more of your model on the table.

Specialty guns, of course, will draw any dealer's attention, and once in a while you will get far more than you expected from a particular firearm. However, it is best to see what the dealer is willing to give you and compare that to the prices listed in the *GTG* and other collectible gun books. If he or she is offering you a higher price than you expected, then conduct some more research because you may have a unique and valuable model.

In most cases, there will be too much diversion to allow you to make a serious sale or trade. If you are feeling rushed or pressured, move on to another dealer. Don't be rushed into a sale.

WORK THE CROWD

While huge crowds at gun shows can be a hindrance, you can use the crowd to your advantage by carrying your locked and tagged for-sale gun with you as you move around the booths. There will be gun buyers, dealers, and fans in the crowd who may stop you to discuss your firearm. A buyer who needs a particular piece to complete his collection could easily offer you more than the gun is listed for, more than the dealer offered, and more than you ever expected to get for it.

Even if you do not make a sale, you can make valuable contacts for future transactions.

Gun shows are ongoing events that occur weekly, monthly, or annually in towns and cities around the country. Some shows are sponsored by the same organizations in the same location each time, so it is easy to keep track of them.

For a complete, updated list of gun shows near you, go to gunshows-usa.com for a listing of all the gun shows scheduled in every state. Google "gun shows" and you will find both local and national shows.

Online Buying and Selling

There is not a facet of our lives that isn't touched by technology. Auction websites such as gunbroker.com, gunsamerica.com, and others offer a vast selection of firearms you can buy and sell using your computer.

Online auction websites enable sellers to reach buyers they might not have normally reached. If you are a private individual with a gun to sell, all you need to do is create an account, type in a description, take a few digital pictures of the item, and list it. It's that simple and that easy.

All the same federal, state, and local gun laws apply when selling and purchasing a gun online as when purchasing a gun at a brick-and-mortar retailer. In fact, the transfer of the firearm is the same. When a buyer purchases a firearm the buyer must provide the seller with a copy of their gun shop's FFL (Federal Firearms License) or arrange to have the seller ship the firearm to one of the FFL located near the buyer that is listed on the website. The seller then ships the gun to the gun shop with the FFL holder—not directly to the buyer—and the buyer then fills out the necessary state and local paperwork to take transfer of the gun. Gun shops usually charge the buyer a fee to transfer the gun. It is up to the buyer to be aware of state and local laws.

Auction sites charge a small percentage of the sale to all sellers. The fee is only charged if the seller actually sells the gun through an auction. There is no charge to list a firearm. When setting up an account with online auction websites, a seller needs to provide a credit card. Once an auction closes with a sale, the fee is automatically charged to the seller's credit card.

Finding a specific firearm is easy for buyers because of search functionality built into auction websites. Once a user has an account, they can click off search options to zero in on a specific manufacturer, model, caliber, barrel length, magazine capacity, and other criteria. The user then has the ability to save the search and have e-mail alerts sent to their e-mail inbox with search results.

Most sellers and buyers online strive to ensure all parties are satisfied with the transaction. Like any aspect in a buying and selling situation, there are some who will try to take advantage. Do your due diligence and contact the seller prior to making a bid, get as much information as you can about the item, and finally look at the seller's rating. Most sellers do their best to keep their rating high, and most will be willing to go the distance to satisfy a customer.

The auction websites have a system in place to deal with buyer and seller protection. Like in anything, the old dictum "buyer beware" applies. If the deal seems too good to be true, then it probably is. Move on.

With online auctions, there is an excitement about bidding against other buyers—remember your budget, and remember what the firearm is worth. You do not want to get caught up in a bidding frenzy and overpay. On the other hand, you may be inclined to pay slightly more for an item that is rare in your geographic area or for an item that is no longer manufactured. Technology has opened up gun trading 24/7/365.

TYPES OF ONLINE AUCTIONS

Basic: The seller's starting price is the amount the seller is willing to take for the item.

Dutch: A seller is auctioning two or more identical items, and a buyer bids on the per-item cost. If you bid $1 and there are ten items, the total price is $10.

Absolute or Penny: Starts out at $.01 with no reserve with the item selling for the last bid after the auction closes.

Reserve: A seller has a minimum reserve price set for the item. This amount is hidden.

HANDGUNS

A.A. (Azanza y Arrizabalaga) — Eibar, Spain

M1916 PISTOL . . . . **NiB $240 Ex $140 Gd $100**
Semiauto blowback-operated pistol. Caliber: 7.65mm, 9-rnd. magazine. 3.25-in. bbl. Wood grip, blued finish. Made 1916.

REIMS PISTOL. . . . . **NiB $190 Ex $120 Gd $95**
Semiauto blowback-operated pistol. Caliber: 6.25mm or 7.65mm. Similar to M1906 Browning pistol. Made 1914.

A.A. ARMS — Monroe, NC

AP-9 SERIES
Semiauto recoil-operated pistol w/polymer integral grip/frame design. Fires from a closed bolt. Caliber: 9mm Parabellum. 10- or 20-rnd. magazine, 3-, 5- or 11-in. bbl., 11.8 in. overall w/5-in. bbl., Weight: 3.5 lbs. Fixed blade, protected post front sight adjustable for elevation, winged square notched rear. Matte phosphate/blue or nickel finish. Checkered polymer grip/frame. Made 1988-99.
AP9 model (pre-94 w/ventilated bbl.,
  shroud) . . . . **NiB $445 Ex $369 Gd $267**
AP9 Mini model
  (post-94 w/o bbl., shroud) . . . . . . **NiB $265 Ex $250 Gd $195**
AP9 Target model
  (pre-94 w/11-in. bbl.) . . . . **NiB $550 Ex $425 Gd $315**
Nickel finish, add **$40**

ACCU-TEK — Chino, CA

MODEL AT-9 AUTO PISTOL
Caliber: 9mm Para. 8-rnd. magazine, Double action only. 3.2-in. bbl., 6.25 in. overall. Weight: 28 oz. Fixed blade front sight, adj. rear w/3-dot system. Firing pin block with no External safety. Stainless or black over stainless finish. Checkered black nylon grips. Announced 1992, but made 1995-99.
Satin stainless model. . . . . **NiB $347 Ex $275 Gd $210**
Matte black stainless. . . . . **NiB $311 Ex $250 Gd $200**

MODEL AT-25 AUTO PISTOL
Similar to Model AT380 except chambered .25 ACP, 7-rnd. magazine. Made 1992-96.
Lightweight w/aluminum frame . . . **NiB $164 Ex $135 Gd $115**
Bright stainless (disc. 1991) . . . . . . **NiB $164 Ex $135 Gd $115**
Satin stainless model. . . . . **NiB $164 Ex $135 Gd $115**
Matte black stainless. . . . . **NiB $164 Ex $135 Gd $115**

MODEL AT-32 AUTO PISTOL
Similar to AT-380 except chambered .32 ACP. Made 1990-2003.
Lightweight w/aluminum
  Frame (disc. 1991) . . . . **NiB $215 Ex $160 Gd $110**
Satin stainless model. . . . . **NiB $215 Ex $160 Gd $110**
Matte black stainless. . . . . **NiB $225 Ex $170 Gd $120**

MODEL AT-40 DA AUTO PISTOL
Caliber: .40 S&W. 7-rnd. magazine, 3.2-in. bbl., 6.25 in. overall. Weight: 28 oz. Fixed blade front sight, adj. rear w/3-dot system.

Arrizabalaga Hijos De C 1916

Firing pin block with no External safety. Stainless or black over stainless finish. Checkered black nylon grips. Announced 1992, but made 1995-96.
Satin stainless model. . . . . **NiB $290 Ex $166 Gd $129**
Matte black stainless. . . . . **NiB $295 Ex $177 Gd $140**

MODEL AT-380 AUTO PISTOL
Caliber: .380 ACP. Five-round magazine, 2.75-in. bbl., 5.6 in. overall. Weight: 20 oz. External hammer w/slide safety. Grooved black composition grips. Alloy or stainless frame w/steel slide. Black, satin aluminum or stainless finish. Made 1992-2003.
Standard alloy frame (disc. 1992) . . . . . . **NiB $291 Ex $165 Gd $145**
AT-380II Satin stainless
  (Avail. 1990). . . . . **NiB $291 Ex $165 Gd $145**
Matte black stainless . . . . **NiB $279 Ex $188 Gd $129**

MODELS BL-9, BL-380 . . . . **NiB $200 Ex $155 Gd $130**
Ultra compact DAO Semiauto pistols. Calibers: .380 ACP, 9mm Para. 5-rnd. magazine, 3-in. bbl., 5.6 in. overall. Weight: 24 oz. Fixed sights. Carbon steel frame and slide w/black finish. Polymer grips. Made 1997-99.

MODELS CP-9, CP-40, CP-45
Compact, double action only, Semiauto pistols. Calibers: 9mm Parabellum, .40 S&W, .45 ACP, 8-, 7- or 6-rnd. magazine, 3.2-in. bbl., 6.25 in. overall. Weight: 28 oz. Fixed blade front sight, adj. rear w/3-dot system. Firing-pin block with no External safety. Stainless or black/stainless finish. Checkered black nylon grips. Made 1997-2002 (CP-9), 1999 (CP-40), 1996 (CP-45).
Black stainless model . . . . **NiB $255 Ex $190 Gd $140**
Satin stainless model. . . . . **NiB $255 Ex $190 Gd $140**

MODEL HC-380 AUTO PISTOL . . . . . **NiB $280 Ex $235 Gd $220**
Caliber: .380 ACP. 13-rnd. magazine, 2.75-in. bbl., 6 in. overall. Weight: 28 oz. External hammer w/slide safety. Checkered black composition grips. Stainless finish. Made 1993-2003, Reintro. 2007.

MODEL XL-9SS . . . . **NiB $240 Ex $165 Gd $120**
Caliber: 9mm. 5-rnd. magazine, 3-in. bbl. Weight: 24 oz. DOA. Textured black composition grips. Stainless finish. Made 1999-2003.

Accu-Tek Model AT .380

Accu-Tek Model
BL-9

Accu-Tek HC-380SS

Action Arms AT-84 with
Prototype of Model AT-84P
in background

ACTION ARMS — Philadelphia, PA

See also listings under CZ pistols. Action Arms stopped import-ing firearms in 1994.

AT-84S DA AUTOMATIC PISTOL. . .NiB $580 Ex $410 Gd $330
Caliber: 9mm Para. 15-rnd. magazine, 4.75-in. bbl., 8 in. overall. Weight: 35 oz. Fixed front sight, drift-adj. rear. Checkered walnut grips. Blued finish. Made in Switzerland from 1988 to 1989.

AT-84P DA AUTO PISTOL. . . . . NiB $510 Ex $365 Gd $320
Compact version of the Model AT-84. Only a few prototypes were manufactured in 1985.

AT-88P DA AUTO PISTOL. . . . . NiB $530 Ex $479 Gd $377
Compact version of the AT-88S w/3.7-in. bbl. Only a few proto-types of this model were manufactured in 1985.

Note: *The AT-88 pistol series was later manufactured by Sphinx-Muller as the AT-2000 series.*

AT-88S DA AUTOMATIC. . . . . . NiB $555 Ex $400 Gd $340
Calibers: 9mm Para. or .41 AE, 10-rnd. magazine, 4.6-in. bbl., 8.1 in. overall. Weight: 35.3 oz. Fixed blade front sight, adj. rear. Checkered walnut grips. Imported 1989 to 1991.

ADVANTAGE ARMS — St. Paul, MN

MODEL 422 DERRINGER. . . . . NiB $175 Ex $115 Gd $110
Hammerless, top-break, 4-bbl., derringer w/rotating firing pin. Calibers: .22 LR and .22 Mag., 4-rnd. capacity, 2.5 in. bbl., 4.5 in. overall. Weight: 15 oz. Fixed sights. Walnut grips. Blued, nickel or PDQ matte black finish. Made 1985-87.

S. A. ALKARTASUNA FABRICA DE ARMAS — Guernica, Spain

"RUBY" AUTOMATIC PISTOL . NiB $355 Ex $283 Gd $225
Caliber: .32 Automatic (7.65mm), 9-rnd. magazine, 3.63-in. bbl., 6.38 in. overall. Weight: About 34 oz. Fixed sights. Blued finish. Checkered wood or hard rubber grips. Made 1917-22.

Note: *Mfd. by a number of Spanish firms, the Ruby was a secondary standard service pistol of the French Army in World Wars I and II. Specimens made by Alkartasuna bear the "Alkar" trademark.*

AMERICAN ARMS — Kansas City, MO

Importer of Spanish and Italian shotguns, pistols, and rifles. Acquired by TriStar Sporting Arms, Ltd., in 2000.

BISLEY SA REVOLVER. . . . . NiB $490 Ex $400 Gd $315
Uberti reproduction of Colt's Bisley. Caliber: .45 LC, 6-rnd. cylinder, 4.75-, 5.5- or 7.7-in. bbl., Case-hardened steel frame. Fixed blade front sight, grooved top strap rear. Hammer block safety. Imported from 1997 to 1998

CX-22 CLASSIC DA AUTOMATIC PISTOL
Similar to Model PX-22 except w/8-rnd. magazine, 3.33-in. bbl., 6.5 in. overall. Weight: 22 oz. Made 1990-95.
CX-22 Classic . . . . NiB $200 Ex $145 Gd $125
CXC-22 w/chrome
  Slide (disc. 1990) . . . . NiB $195 Ex $140 Gd $120

EP-380 DA AUTOMATIC PISTOL NiB $410 Ex $299 Gd $160
Caliber: .380 Automatic. 7-rnd. magazine, 3.5-in. bbl., 6.5 in. overall. Weight: 25 oz. Fixed front sight, square notch adj. rear. Stainless finish. Checkered wood grips. Made 1989-91.

ESCORT DA AUTO PISTOL. . . . NiB $315 Ex $225 Gd $155
Caliber: .380 ACP, 7-rnd. magazine, 3.38-in. bbl., 6.13 in. overall. Weight: 19 oz. Fixed, low-profile sights. Stainless steel

frame, slide, and trigger. Nickel-steel bbl., Soft polymer grips. Loaded chamber indicator. Made 1995-97.

MATEBA AUTO REVOLVER . . . Nib $4010 EX $3010 GD $2010
Unique combination action design allows both slide and cylinder to recoil together causing cylinder to rotate. Single or double action. Caliber: .357 Mag, 6-rnd. cylinder, 4- or 6-in. bbl., 8.77 in. overall w/4-in. bbl., Weight: 2.75 lbs. Steel/alloy frame. Ramped blade front sight, adjustable rear. Blue finish. Smooth walnut grips. Imported from 1997-99.

P-98 CLASSIC DA AUTO . . . . . NiB $215 Ex $140 Gd $105
Styled after Walther P-38. Caliber: .22 LR, 8-rnd. magazine, 5-in. bbl., 8.25 in. overall. Weight: 25 oz. Fixed front sight, square notch adj. rear. Blued finish. Serrated black polymer grips. Made 1989-96.

PK-22 CLASSIC DA AUTO . . . . NiB $190 Ex $145 Gd $120
Styled after Walther PPK. Caliber: .22 LR. 8-rnd. magazine, 3.33-in. bbl., 6.33 in. overall. Weight: 22 oz. Fixed front sight, V-notch rear. Blued finish. Checkered black polymer grips. Made 1989-96.

PX-22 DA AUTOMATIC PISTOL NiB $245 Ex $177 Gd $155
Caliber: .22 LR. 7-rnd. magazine, 2.75-in. bbl., 5.33 in. overall. Weight: 15 oz. Fixed front sight, V-notch rear. Blued finish. Checkered black polymer grips. Made 1989-96.

PX-25 DA AUTOMATIC PISTOL NiB $255 Ex $220 Gd $190
Same general specifications as the Model PX-22 except chambered for .25 ACP. Made 1991-92.

REGULATOR SA REVOLVER
Similar in appearance to the Colt Single-Action Army. Calibers: .357 Mag., .44-.40, .45 Long Colt. Six-round cylinder, 4.75- or 7.5-in. bbl., blade front sight, fixed rear. Brass trigger guard/backstrap on Standard model. Casehardened steel on Deluxe model. Made by Uberti from 1992 to 2000.
Standard model. . . . . NiB $279 Ex $210 Gd $125
Standard combo set (45 LC/.45 ACP
& .44-.40/.44 Spec.). . . . . NiB $445 Ex $375 Gd $275
Deluxe model . . . . NiB $375 Ex $315 Gd $225
Deluxe combo set (.45 LC/.45
ACP & .44-40/.44 Spl.). . . . . . NiB $445 Ex $389 Gd $260
Stainless steel . . . . NiB $425 Ex $355 Gd $250

BUCKHORN SA REVOLVER
Similar to Regulator model except chambered .44 Mag. w/4.75-, 6- or 7.7-in. bbl., Fixed or adjustable sights. Hammer block safety. Made by Uberti, 1993 to 1996.
w/standard sights . . . . NiB $425 Ex $315 Gd $255
w/adjustable sights, add $40

SPECTRE DA AUTO PISTOL
Blowback action, fires closed bolt. Calibers: 9mm Para., .40 S&W, .45 ACP, 30-rnd. magazine, 6-in. bbl., 13.75 in. overall. Weight: 4 lbs. 8 oz. Adj. post front sight, fixed U-notch rear. Black nylon grips. Matte black finish. Imported 1990 to 1994.
9mm Para. . . . . NiB $545 Ex $450 Gd $260
.40 S&W (disc. 1991) . . . . NiB $515 Ex $400 Gd $300
.45 ACP. . . . . NiB $560 Ex $445 Gd $315

454 SSA REVOLVER . . . . NiB $795 Ex $680 Gd $530
SSA chambered 454. 6-rnd. cylinder, 6-in. solid raised rib or 7.7-in. top-ported bbl., satin nickel finish, adj. rear sight. Hammer block safety. Made by Uberti, 1996 to 1997.

Mateba Auto Revolver

**American Arms
Regulator Deluxe Model**

WOODMASTER SA AUTO PISTOL . . .NiB $300 Ex $250 Gd $195
Caliber: .22 LR. 10-rnd. magazine, 5.88-in. bbl., 10.5 in. overall. Weight: 31 oz. Fixed front sight, square-notch adj. rear. Blued finish. Checkered wood grips. Disc. 1989.

AMERICAN CLASSIC — Philippines
Manufactured in Philippines and currently imported by TriStar Arms, North Kansas City, MO, previously imported by Eagle Imports, Wanamassa, NJ.

AMIGO SERIES . . . . NiB $714 Ex $690 Gd $610
Similar to Classic II except compact. Semiauto. SA. Caliber: .45 ACP; 8-rnd. magazine. 3.5 in.-bbl. Frame: steel. Sights: fixed, Novak style. Finish: blue, duotone, hard chrome. Grip: textured hardwood. Length: 7.25 in. Weight: 32.45 oz. Imported from 2011 to 2022.
hard chrome or duotone finish, add $70

COMMANDER SERIES . . . . NiB $624 Ex $560 Gd $510
1911 Commander platform. Semiauto. SA. Caliber: .45 ACP; 8-rnd. magazine. 5-in. bbl. Frame: steel. Sights: fixed, Novak style. Finish: blue, duotone, hard chrome. Grip: textured hardwood. Length: 7.5-in. Weight: 35.2 oz. Imported from 2011 to date.
hard chrome or duotone finish, add $70

CLASSIC SERIES . . . . NiB $589 Ex $520 Gd $480
1911 platform. Semiauto. SA. Caliber: .45 ACP; 8-rnd. magazine. 5-in. bbl. Frame: steel. Sights: fixed, GI style. Finish: matte blue. Grip: textured hardwood. Length: 8.25-in. Weight: 36.9 oz. Imported from 2010 to date.

CLASSIC II SERIES . . . . .NIB $609 EX $580 GD $510
1911 platform. Semiauto. SA. Caliber: 9mm or .45 ACP; 8-rnd. magazine. 5-in. bbl. Frame: steel. Sights: fixed, Novak style. Finish: blue, duotone, hard chrome. Grip: textured hardwood. Length: 8.37 in. Weight: 37.28 oz. Imported from 2010 to date.
hard chrome or duotone finish, add $70

TROPHY SERIES. . . . . NIB $819 EX $780 GD $710
Similar to Classic II except ambi. safety, fiber optic front sight, beavertail. Imported from 2011 to date.

American Derringer
Model 3

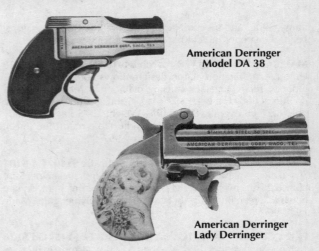

American Derringer
Model DA 38

American Derringer
Lady Derringer

AMERICAN DERRINGER CORPORATION — Waco, TX

MODEL 1 STAINLESS
Single-action similar to the Remington O/U derringer, 2-shot capacity. More than 60 calibers from .22 LR to .45-70, 3-in. bbl., 4.82 in. overall, weight: 15 oz. Automatic bbl., selection. Satin or high-polished stainless steel. Rosewood grips. Made 1980 to date.

.45 Colt, .44-40 Win., .44 Special, .410	NiB $575	Ex $420	Gd $300
.45-70, .44 Mag., 41 Mag., .30-30 Win., .223 Rem.	NiB $650	Ex $550	Gd $458
.357 Max., .357 Mag., .45 Win. Mag., 9mm Para.	NiB $655	Ex $555	Gd $460
.38 Special, .38 Super, .32 Mag., .22 LR, .22 WRM	NiB $655	Ex $560	Gd $455

MODEL 2 STEEL "PEN" PISTOL
Calibers: .22 LR, .25 Auto, .32 Auto. Single-shot, 2-in. bbl., 5.6 in. overall (4.2 in. in pistol format). Weight: 5 oz. Stainless finish. Made 1993-94.

.22 LR	NiB $510	Ex $430	Gd $337
.25 Auto	NiB $610	Ex $530	Gd $430
.32 Auto	NiB $760	Ex $580	Gd $480

MODEL 3 STAINLESS STEEL ... NiB $640 Ex $480 Gd $290
Single-shot. Calibers: .32 Mag. or .38 Special. 2.5-in. bbl., 4.9 in. overall. Weight: 8.5 oz. Rosewood grips. Made 1984-95.

MODEL 4 DOUBLE DERRINGER
Calibers: .357 Mag., .357 Max., .44 Mag., .45 LC, .45 ACP (upper bbl., and 3-in. .410 shotshell (lower bbl.). 4.1-in. bbl, 6 in. overall. Weight: 16.5 oz. Stainless steel. Staghorn grips. Made 1984 to date. (.44 Mag.and .45-70 disc. 2003.)

.357 Mag., .357 Max.	NiB $670	Ex $525	Gd $345
.44 Mag., .45 LC, .45 ACP	NiB $770	Ex $555	Gd $489
Engraved, add			$150

MODEL 4 ALASKAN SURVIVAL
MODEL .... NiB $730 Ex $570 Gd $340
Similar specifications as Model 4 except upper bbl., chambered for .45-70 or 3-in. .410 and .45 LC lower bbl. Also available in .45 Auto, .45 LC, .44 Special, .357 Mag. and .357 Max. Made 1985 to date.

MODEL 6 .... NiB $785 Ex $625 Gd $499
Caliber: .22 Mag., .357 Mag., .45 LC, .45 ACP or .45 LC/.410 or .45 Colt. Bbl.: 6 in., 8.2 in. overall. Weight: .22 oz. Satin or high-polished stainless steel w/rosewood grips. Made 1986 to date.
Engraved, add $150

MODEL 7
Similar as Model 1 except w/high-strength aircraft aluminum used to reduce its weight to 7.5 oz. Made 1986 to date. (.44 Special disc. then reintroduced in 2008.)

.22 LR, .22 WMR	NiB $580	Ex $440	Gd $280
.44 Special, add			$150

MODEL 8 .... NiB $730 Ex $530 Gd $280
Calibers: .45 LC/.410, 8-in. bbl., 9.8 in. overall. Weight: 24 oz. Rosewood grips. New 1997.
Engraved (Made 1997-98), add $1000

MODEL 10
Similar as the Model 7 except chambered for .38 Special, .45 ACP or .45 LC with aluminum grip frame

.38 Special or .45 ACP	NiB $559	Ex $365	Gd $295
.45 LC	NiB $500	Ex $395	Gd $279

MODEL 11 .... NiB $559 Ex $490 Gd $369
Same general specifications as Model 7 except with a matte gray finish only, weight: 11 oz. Made 1980-2003.

25 AUTOMATIC PISTOL
Calibers: .25 ACP or .250 Mag. Bbl.: 2.1 in., 4.4 in. overall. Weight: 15.5 oz. Smooth rosewood grips. Limited production.

blued (est. production 50)	NiB $650	Ex $540	Gd $385
.25 ACP stainless (est. production 400)	NiB $510	Ex $425	Gd $380
.250 Mag. stainless (est. production 100)	NiB $675	Ex $530	Gd $407

DA 38 DOUBLE ACTION DERRINGER
Hammerless, double action, double bbl (o/u). Calibers: .22LR, .357 Mag., .38 Special, 9mm Para., .40 S&W. 3-in. bbls., satin stainless with aluminum grip frame. DA trigger, hammerblock thumb safety. Weight: 14.5 oz. Made 1990 to date.

.22LR (1996-03), .38 Special, 9mm Para.,	NiB $580	Ex $415	Gd $230
.357 Mag. or .40 cal. (Disc. 2012)	NiB $630	Ex $445	Gd $265
Lady Derringer (faux ivory grips, made 1992-94), add			$20

COP DA DERRINGER .... NiB $660 Ex $510 Gd $291
Hammerless, double-action, 4-bbl., derringer. Caliber: .22 rimfire, .357 Mag. 3.15-in. bbl., 5.5 in. overall. Weight: 16 oz. Blade front sight, open notched rear. Rosewood grips. Intro. 1990, disc. 1994.

LM-5 AUTOMATIC PISTOL
Calibers: .25 ACP, .32 H&R Mag. or .380 Automatic. Bbl.: 2 in., 3 in. overall. Weight: 15 oz. Stainless steel construction, smooth wood grips. Limited production.

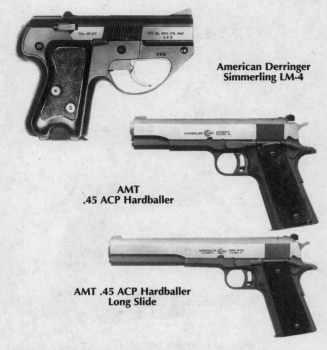

American Derringer Simmerling LM-4

AMT .45 ACP Hardballer

AMT .45 ACP Hardballer Long Slide

.25 ACP or .32 H&R Mag. . . . . NiB $650 Ex $540 Gd $385
.380 Automatic (Disc. 1999). . . NiB $425 Ex $380 Gd $300

LADY DERRINGER . . . . NiB $769 Ex $610 Gd $499
Similar specifications as Model 1 except w/custom-tuned action fitted w/scrimshawed synthetic ivory grips. Calibers: .32 H&R Mag., .32 Special, .38 Special (additional calibers on request). Deluxe Grade engraved and highly polished w/French fitted jewelry box. Made 1991 to date.
**Deluxe Engraved (Disc. 1994) . NiB $699 Ex $470 Gd $355
Gold Engraved (Disc. 1994)** . . . . **Rare
Lady II (aluminum frame,
   made 1999-03)**. . . . . NiB $400 Ex $350 Gd $255

SEMMERLING LM-4
Manually operated repeater. Calibers: .45 ACP or 9mm, 4-rnd. (.45 ACP) or 6-rnd. magazine (9mm), 3.6-in. bbl., 5.2 in. overall. Weight: 24 oz. Made 1997 to date. Limited availability.
Blued or Stainless steel   . . . NiB $3830 Ex $3200 Gd $2020

TEXAS COMMEMORATIVE . . . NiB $580 Ex $350 Gd $300
Similar to Model 1 except w/solid brass frame, stainless bbls. and stag grips. Calibers: .22 LR, .32 Mag., .38 Special, .44-40 Win. or .45 LC. Made 1991 to date.

125TH ANNIVERSARY
Same general specifications as Model 1 except w/solid brass frame, stainless bbls. and stag grips. Calibers: .38 Special, .44-40 Win. or .45 LC. Disc. 1993. Limited production.
.38 Special . . . . NiB $337 Ex $320 Gd $295
.44-40 Win. or .45 LC. . . . . . . NiB $400 Ex $395 Gd $375

AMERICAN FIREARMS MFG. CO., INC. — San Antonio, TX

25 AUTO PISTOL
Caliber: .25 Auto. 8-rnd. magazine, 2.1-in. bbl., 4.4 in. overall. Weight: 14.5 oz. Fixed sights. Stainless or blued ordnance steel. Smooth walnut grips. Made 1966-74.
Stainless steel model. . . . . NiB $215 Ex $190 Gd $110

Blued steel model . . . . NiB $200 Ex $145 Gd $110

AMERICAN DERRINGER . . . . NiB $210 Ex $140 Gd $95
O/U bbl. Caliber: .38 Spl. Made 1972-74.

380 AUTO PISTOL . . . . NiB $735 Ex $540 Gd $389
Caliber: .380 Auto. 8-rnd. magazine, 3.5-in. bbl., 5.5 in. overall. Weight: 20 oz. Stainless steel. Smooth walnut grips. Made 1972-74.

AMT (ARCADIA MACHINE & TOOL) —Trademark owed by Crusader Gun Company Houston, TX
Previously Galena Industries, Strugis, SD; and Irwindale Arms, Inc., Irwindale, CA

NOTE: *The AMT Backup II automatic pistol was introduced in 1993 as a continuation of the original .380 Backup with a double action trigger and a redesigned double safety. AMT Backup and Automag II line of handguns is currently marketed by High Standard Manufacturing, Houston, TX.*

45 ACP HARDBALLER. . . . . . . NiB $545 Ex $430 Gd $345
Colt 1991 style. Caliber: .45 ACP, 7-rnd. magazine, 5-in. bbl., 8.5 in. overall. Weight: 39 oz. Adj. or fixed sights. Serrated matte slide rib w/loaded chamber indicator. Extended combat safety, adj. trigger and long grip safety. Wraparound Neoprene grips. Stainless steel. Made 1978-2001.
Long slide conversion kit (disc. 1997), add. $315

45 ACP HARDBALLER LONG SLIDE
Similar to the standard Hardballer except w/7-in. bbl. and slide. Also chambered for .400 Cor-Bon. Made 1980-2001
.45 ACP long slide. . . . . NiB $529 Ex $435 Gd $320
**.400 Cor-Bon long
   slide (Intro.1998)** . . . . NiB $535 Ex $425 Gd $300
5-in. conversion kit (disc. 1997), add $315

**45 ACP STANDARD GOVERNMENT MODEL
AUTO PISTOL**. . . . . NiB $460 Ex $395 Gd $339
Caliber: .45 ACP, 7-rnd. magazine, 5-in. bbl., 8.5 in. overall. Weight: 38 oz. Fixed sights. Wraparound Neoprene grip. Made 1979 to date.

**AUTOMAG II SEMIAUTOMATIC
PISTOL**. . . . . NiB $850 Ex $575 Gd $360
Caliber: .22 Mag., 7- or 9-rnd. magazine, bbl. lengths: 3.38, 4.5-, 6-in.. Weight: 32 oz. Fully adj. Millett sights. Stainless finish. Smooth black composition grips. Made 1986-2001, reintro. 2004.

**AUTOMAG III SEMIAUTOMATIC
PISTOL** . . . . NiB $600 Ex $495 Gd $365
Calibers: .30 M1 or 9mm Win. Mag., 8-rnd. magazine., 6.38-in. bbl., 10.5 in. overall. Weight: 43 oz. Millet adj. sights. Stainless finish. Carbon fiber grips. Made 1992-2001.

**AUTOMAG IV SEMIAUTOMATIC
PISTOL** . . . . NiB $610 Ex $520 Gd $395
Calibers: 10mm or .45 Win. Mag., 8- or 7-rnd. magazine, 6.5- or 8.63-in. bbl., 10.5 in. overall. Weight: 46 oz. Millet adj. sights. Stainless finish. Carbon fiber grips. Made 1992-2001.

**AUTOMAG V SEMIAUTOMATIC
PISTOL** . . . . NiB $1000 Ex $855 Gd $775
Caliber: .50 A.E., 5-rnd. magazine, 7-in. bbl., 10.5 in. overall. Weight: 46 oz. Custom adj. sights. Stainless finish. Carbon fiber grips. Made 1994-95.

BACKUP (SMALL FRAME) AUTOMATIC PISTOL
Caliber: .22 LR, .380 ACP, 8-rnd. (.22LR) or 5-rnd. (.380 ACP) magazine, 2.5-in. bbl., 5 in. overall. Weight: 18 oz. (.380 ACP). Open sights. Carbon fiber or walnut grips. Stainless steel finish. Made 1990-87.
.22 LR (disc. 1987) . . . . NiB $495 Ex $335 Gd $188
.380 ACP (disc. 2000, reintro.
   2004, disc. 2010). . . . . NiB $450 Ex $305 Gd $171

BACKUP II . . . . NiB $300 Ex $260 Gd $200
Caliber: .380 ACP, 5-rnd. magazine, 2.5-in. bbl., 5 in. overall. Weight: 18 oz. Single action. Open sights. Stainless steel finish. Carbon-fiber grips. Made 1993-98.

BACKUP (LARGE FRAME) DAO AUTO PISTOL
Calibers: .357 SIG, .38 Super, 9mm Para., .40 Cor-Bon, .40 S&W, .45 ACP. Six-round (.357 SIG, .38 Super 9mm) or 5-rnd. (.40 Cor-Bon, .40 S&W, .45 ACP) magazine, 2.5-in. bbl., 5.75-in. overall. Weight: 23 oz. Double action only. Open fixed sights. Stainless steel finish. Carbon fiber grips. Made 1992 to date.
.357 SIG, .38 Super, 9mm.40 S&W,
   .45 ACP . . . . NiB $560 Ex $430 Gd $300
.40 Cor-Bon (disc. 2010). . . . . . NiB $660 Ex $440 Gd $400

BULL'S EYE TARGET MODEL . NiB $695 Ex $550 Gd $415
Similar to the standard Hardballer. Caliber: .40 S&W, 8-rnd. magazine, 5-in. bbl., 8.5 in. overall. Weight: 38 oz. Millet adjustable sights. Wide adj. trigger. Wraparound Neoprene grips. Made 1990-91.

JAVELINA . . . . NiB $570 Ex $550 Gd $420
Caliber: 10mm, 8-rnd. magazine, 7-in. bbl., 10.5 in. overall. Weight: 48 oz. Long grip safety, beveled magazine well, wide adj. trigger. Millet adj. sights. Wraparound Neoprene grips. Stainless finish. Made 1991-93.

LIGHTNING AUTO PISTOL
Caliber: .22 LR. 10-rnd. magazine, 5-, 6.5-, 8.5-, 10-in. bbl., 10.75 in. overall (6.5-in. bbl.). Weight: 45 oz. (6.5-in. bbl.). Millett adj. sights. Checkered rubber grips. Stainless finish. Made 1984-87.
Standard model. . . . . NiB $455 Ex $315 Gd $210
Bull's-Eye model
   (6.5-in. bull bbl.) . . . . NiB $520 Ex $355 Gd $240

ON DUTY DA PISTOL
Calibers: .40 S&W, 9mm Para., .45 ACP. 15-rnd. (9mm), 13-shot (.40 S&W) or 9-rnd. (.45 ACP) magazine, 4.5-in. bbl., 7.75 in. overall. Weight: 32 oz. Hard anodized aluminum frame. Stainless steel slide and bbl., Carbon fiber grips. Made 1991-94.
9mm or .40 S&W . . . . NiB $465 Ex $316 Gd $235
.45 ACP. . . . . NiB $515 Ex $400 Gd $265

SKIPPER AUTO PISTOL. . . . . . NiB $465 Ex $359 Gd $325
Calibers: .40 S&W or .45 ACP, 7-rnd. magazine, 4.25-in. bbl., 7.5 in. overall. Weight: 33 oz. Millet adj. sights. Walnut grips. Matte finish stainless. Made 1990-92.

ANSCHUTZ — Ulm, Germany
Mfd. by J.G. Anschutz GmbH Jagd und Sportwaffenfabrik.
Currently imported by Champion's Choice, La Vergne, TN; previously imported by Accuracy International, Boseman, MT and AcuSport Corporation, Bellefontaine, OH

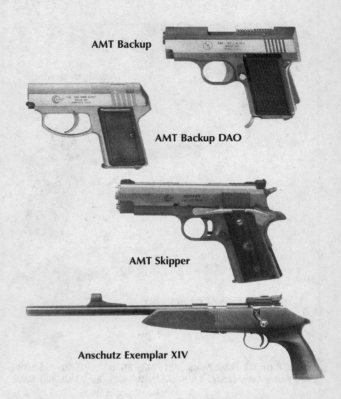

AMT Backup

AMT Backup DAO

AMT Skipper

Anschutz Exemplar XIV

MODEL 17LP . . . . NiB $660 Ex $500 Gd $340
Similar to model 64P except in .17 HRM caliber, 4-rnd. magazine. Imported from 2003 to 2004.

MODEL 64P
Calibers: .22 LR or .22 WMR, 5- or 4-rnd. magazine, 10-in. bbl., 64MS action w/two-stage trigger. Target sights optional. Rynite black synthetic stock. Imported from 1998 to 2003.
.22 LR . . . . NiB $580 Ex $430 Gd $225
.22 WMR (disc 2001) . . . . NiB $638 Ex $473 Gd $247
w/tangent sights, add $100

EXEMPLAR (1416P/1451P) BOLT-ACTION PISTOL
Caliber: .22 LR, single-shot or 5-rnd. magazine, 7- or 10-in. bbl., 19 in. overall (10-in. bbl.). Weight: 3.33 lbs. Match 64 action. Slide safety. Hooded ramp post front sight, adjustable open notched rear. European walnut contoured grip. Exemplar made from 1987-95 and 1400 series made from 1997. Disc. 1997.

Note: *The .22 WMR chambering was advertised but never manufactured.*
Exemplar w/7- or 10-in. bbl. . . . . NiB $510 Ex $405 Gd $310
Left-hand model (disc. 1997) . . NiB $620 Ex $505 Gd $410
Model 1451P (single-shot) . . . . NiB $530 Ex $425 Gd $330
Model 1416P (5-rnd. repeater) NiB $1150 Ex $869 Gd $610

EXEMPLAR HORNET . . . . NiB $900 Ex $815 Gd $700
Based on the Anschutz Match 54 action, tapped and grooved for scope mounting with no open sights. Caliber: .22 Hornet, 5-rnd. magazine, 10-in. bbl., 20 in. overall. Weight: 4.35 lbs. Checkered European walnut grip. Winged safety. Made 1990-95.

EXEMPLAR XIV . . . . NiB $560 Ex $560 Gd $465
Same general specifications as the standard Exemplar bolt-action pistol except w/14-in. bbl., weight: 4.15 lbs. Made 1989-95.

ARCHON FIREARMS — Las Vegas, NV

Importer/Distributor Las Vegas, NV.

Archon Firearms Type B

TYPE B . . . . **NiB $800 Ex $790 Gd $610**
Semiauto. Striker-fired, polymer frame. Caliber: 9mm, 15-rnd. magazine, 4.3-in. bbl., 7.6 in. overall. Reversable magazine release. Finish: Matte black. Grip: Textured polymer. Sights: Fiber optic front. AF-Speedlock mechanism, flat trigger. Previous imported as the STRYK B pistol. Imported from 2017 to date.

AREX — Solvinia

Currently imported by FIME Group, Las Vegas, NV.

REX DELTA . . . . **NiB $345 Ex $305 Gd $255**
Semiauto. Striker-fired, polymer frame. Caliber: 9mm, 17-rnd. magazine, 4-in. bbl., 7 in. overall. Ambi. slide stop, magazine release and safety. Finish: Matte black. Grip: Modular grip straps. Sights: Low profile steel. Imported from 2019 to date.

REX DELTA GEN.2. . . . . **NiB $540 Ex $480 Gd $400**
Similar to Rex Delta except w/enhanced grip frame w/modular grip back straps. Three sizes: M-compact slide/frame, L-longslide/full frame, X-crossover compact slide/full frame. Sights: Low profile steel, optic ready. Imported from 2021 to date.

REX ZERO 1 . . . . **NiB $580 Ex $510 Gd $430**
Semiauto. DA/SA. Caliber: 9mm, 17-rnd. magazine, 4.3-in. bbl., 7.7 in. overall. Ambidextrous slide stop, magazine release and safety. Matte black finish, checkered synthetic grips. Imported from 2016 to present.
Alpha (competition ready, adj. sights, 5-in. bbl.), add . . **$350**
Compact, add **$30**
Tactical (threaded bbl.), add **$175**

ARMALITE, INC. — Genesco, IL

Formerly Costa Mesa, CA., currently Genesco, IL.

AR-24 AUTOMATIC PISTOL . . . **NiB $500 Ex $380 Gd $300**
Full size automatic, mfg. by Sarzsilmaz in Turkey. Caliber: 9mm Para, 15-rnd. magazine, 4.67-in. bbl., 8.3 in. overall. Parkerized finish, checkered synthetic grips. Imported from 2007 to 2013.
AR-24-15C (adj. rear sight) . . . **NiB $560 Ex $430 Gd $375**
AR-24K-13 (3.89-in. bbl.) . . . . . **NiB $500 Ex $400 Gd $380**
**AR-24K-13C (adj. rear sight,
3.89-in. bbl.)** . . . . **NiB $560 Ex $430 Gd $375**

ARMSCOR (Arms Corp.)—Manila, Philippines

Currently imported by Armscor Precision Int'l. Pahrump, NV. Previously Imported by K.B.I., Harrisburg, PA., 1991–95 by Ruko Products, Inc., Buffalo NY., Armscor Precision, San Mateo, CA. Formerly Squires Bingham Mfg. Inc. Also mfg. and distributes Rock Island Armory pistols.

MODEL M1911-A1 . . . . **NiB $360 Ex $320 Gd $275**
Semiauto pistol. 1911 style. Caliber: .45 ACP. Eight-round magazine, 5-in. bbl., 8.75 in. overall. Weight: 38 oz. Blade front sight, drift adjustable rear w/3-dot system. Skeletonized tactical hammer and trigger. Extended slide release and beavertail grip safety. Parkerized finish. Checkered composition or wood stocks. Imported from 1996 to 1997. Reintro. 2001 to 2008.
Two-tone finish, add **$50**
Stainless, add **$95**
**Commander model
(4-in. bbl., disc. 1991)** . . . . . . **NiB $370 Ex $300 Gd $220**
**Officer model
(3.5-in. bbl., disc. 1991)** . . . . . **NiB $380 Ex $350 Gd $265**

**MODEL M1911-A1
MEDALLION SERIES** . . . . **NiB $450 Ex $360 Gd $285**
Caliber: 9mm Para., .40 S&W, .45ACP. Standard or Tactical, blue finish standard. Bbl.: 5 in. Custom model with match barrel, checkered wood Pachmayr grips. Disc. 1991.
Two-tone finish (Tactical), add **$200**
Chrome (Tactical), add **$250**

M200 DC/TC DA REVOLVER . . . .**NiB $240 Ex $160 Gd $110**
Caliber: .38 Special. Six-round cylinder, 2.5-, 4-, or 6-in. bbl.; 7.3, 8.8, or 11.3 in. overall. Weight: 22, 28, or 34 oz. Ramp front and fixed rear sights. Checkered mahogany or rubber grips. made from 1996 to1999, 2001to 2014, and 2015 to date.
**M202A (no bbl. shroud,
disc. 1991)** . . . . **NiB $180 Ex $110 Gd $95**
**M206 (2.8-in. bbl., w/and
w/o hammer spur)** . . . . **NiB $250 Ex $203 Gd $170**
M210 (4-in. bbl., disc. 1991) . . . **NiB $200 Ex $170 Gd $140**

STK100 . . . . **NiB $499 Ex $409 Gd $380**
Semiauto. Striker-fired, metal frame. Caliber: 9mm, 17-rnd. magazine, 4.5-in. bbl., 7.9 in. overall. Reversable magazine release. Finish: Matte black. Sights: Fixed, optic ready. Compatible w/ Glock magazines. Imported 2021 to date.

MODEL 202A REVOLVER . . . . . **NiB $180 Ex $110 Gd $95**
Caliber: .38 Special. Similar to Model 200 (DC) revolver except does not have bbl. shroud. Disc. 1991.

MODEL 206 REVOLVER. . . . . . . **NiB $250 Ex $203 Gd $170**
Caliber: .38 Special. Similar to Model 200 (DC) revolver except has a 2.87-in. bbl. Weight: 24 oz. Disc. 1991.

MODEL 210 REVOLVER. . . . . . **NiB $200 Ex $170 Gd $135**
Caliber: .38 Special. Similar to Model 200 (DC) except has a 4-in. ventilated rib bbl., adj. rear sight. Weight: 28 oz. Disc. 1991.

ASAI AG — Advanced Small Arms Industries Solothurn, Switzerland

Currently imported by Magnum Research Inc., Minneapolis, MN. See listings under Magnum Research Pistols

ASTRA — Guernica, Spain

Manufactured by Unceta y Compania.Currently not imported to U.S., previously imported by E.A.A. Corporation, Sharpes, FL.

MODEL 357 DA REVOLVER . . . **NiB $330 Ex $299 Gd $230**
Caliber: .357 Magnum. Six-round cylinder. 3-, 4-, 6-, 8.5-in. bbl., 11.25 in. overall (w/ 6-in. bbl.). Weight: 42 oz. (w/ 6-in.

Astra Model 44 DA

Astra Model 3003 Pocket

Astra Model 4000 Falcon

bbl.). Ramp front sight, adj. rear sight. Blued finish. Checkered wood grips. Imported from 1972 to 1988.

MODEL 44 DA REVOLVER
Similar to Astra .357 except chambered for .44 Magnum. Six- or 8.5-in. bbl., 11.5 in. overall (6-in. bbl.). Weight: 44 oz. (6-in. bbl.). Imported from 1980 to 1993.
Blued finish (disc. 1987) . . . . . . NiB $460 Ex $290 Gd $245
Stainless finish (disc. 1993) . . . . NiB $380 Ex $320 Gd $255

MODEL 41 DA REVOLVER . . . . NiB $460 Ex $295 Gd $235
Same general specifications as Model 44 except in .41 Mag. Imported from 1980-85.

MODEL 45 DA REVOLVER . . . . NiB $460 Ex $275 Gd $215
Similar to Astra .357 except chambered for .45 LC or .45 ACP. Six- or 8.5-in. bbl., 11.5 in. overall (w/ 6-in. bbl.). Weight: 44 oz. (6-in. bbl.). Imported from 1980-87.

MODEL 200 FIRECAT
VEST POCKET AUTO PISTOL . . NiB $320 Ex $260 Gd $205
Caliber: .25 Automatic (6.35mm). Six-round magazine, 2.25-in. bbl., 4.38 in. overall. Weight: 11.75 oz. Fixed sights. Blued finish. Plastic grips. Made 1920 to date. U.S. importation disc. in 1968.

MODEL 202 FIRECAT
VEST POCKET AUTO PISTOL . . NiB $590 Ex $475 Gd $400
Same general specifications as the Model 200 except chromed and engraved w/pearl grips. U.S. importation disc. 1968.

MODEL 300 . . . . NiB $910 Ex $410 Gd $260
Caliber: .32 ACP or .380 ACP. Made 1923-46.
Nazis Mfg.(S/N range 350,001-630,475), add **100%**

MODEL 400 AUTO PISTOL . . . NiB $725 Ex $595 Gd $350
Caliber: 9mm Bayard Long (.38 ACP, 9mm Browning Long, 9mm Glisenti, 9mm Para. and 9mm Steyr cartridges may be used interchangeably in this pistol because of its chamber design). Nine-round magazine., 6-in. bbl., 10 in. overall. Weight: 35 oz. Fixed sights. Blued finish. Plastic grips. Made 1922-45.
Note: *This pistol, as well as Astra Models 600 and 3000, is a modification of the Browning Model 1912.*
Nazis Mfg. (S/N range 92,850-98,850), add **100%**

MODEL 600 MIL./POLICE-TYPE
AUTO PISTOL . . . . NiB $565 Ex $425 Gd $300
Calibers: .32 Automatic (7.65mm), 9mm Para. Magazine: 10-rnd. (.32 cal.) or 8-rnd. (9mm)., 5.25-in. bbl., 8 in. overall. Weight: About 33 oz. Fixed sights. Blued finish. Checkered wood or plastic grips. Made 1944-45.
Nazis markings, add **100%**

MODEL 700 . . . . NIB $1510 EX $1130 GD $830
Similar to F/N Browning Model 1910. Caliber: .32 ACP. 12-rnd. magazine. 3.75-in. brrl. Grip:checkered hard rubber.

MODEL 800 CONDOR
MILITARY AUTO PISTOL . . NiB $1860 Ex $1754 Gd $1512
Similar to Models 400 and 600 except has an external hammer. Caliber: 9mm Para. Eight-round magazine, 5.25-in. bbl., 8.25 in. overall. Weight: 32.5 oz. Fixed sights. Blued finish. Plastic grips. Imported from 1958 to 1965.

MODEL 900 . . . . NiB $3510 EX $2010 GD $1010
Similar to Mauser Broomhandle. Caliber: 7.63 Mauser. Mfg. from 1928 to 1936.
Matching stock, add **$1,500**

MODEL 902 (20-RND.
MAGAZINE) . . . . NiB $20,000 Ex $15,000 Gd $11,000

MODEL 2000 CAMPER
AUTOMATIC PISTOL . . . . NiB $395 Ex $279 Gd $215
Same as Model 2000 Cub except chambered for .22 Short only, has 4-in. bbl., overall length, 6.25 in., weight: 11.5 oz. Imported from 1955 to 1960.

MODEL 2000 CUB
POCKET AUTO PISTOL . . . . . . NiB $363 Ex $297 Gd $214
Calibers: .22 Short, .25 Auto. Six-round magazine, 2.25-in. bbl., 4.5 in. overall. Weight: About 11 oz. Fixed sights. Blued or chromed finish. Plastic grips. Made 1954 to date. U.S. importation disc. 1968.

MODEL 3000
POCKET AUTO PISTOL . . . . . . NiB $860 Ex $654 Gd $467
Calibers: .22 LR, .32 Automatic (7.65mm), .380 Auto (9mm Short). Ten-round magazine (.22 cal.), 7-rnd. (.32 cal.), 6-rnd. (.380 cal.). Four-in. bbl., 6.38 in. overall. Weight: About 22 oz. Fixed sights. Blued finish. Plastic grips. Made 1947-56.

MODEL 3003
POCKET AUTO PISTOL . . . . NiB $2420 Ex $1419 Gd $880
Same general specifications as the Model 3000 except chromed and engraved w/pearl grips. Disc. 1956.

MODEL 4000
FALCON AUTO PISTOL . . . . . . NiB $675 Ex $495 Gd $320
Similar to Model 3000 except has an External hammer. Calibers: .22 LR, .32 Automatic (7.65mm), .380 Auto (9mm Short). Ten-round magazine (.22 LR), 8-rnd. (.32 Auto), 7-rnd. (.380 Auto), 3.66-in. bbl., 6.5-in. overall. Weight: 20 oz. (.22 cal.) or 24.75 oz. (.32 and .380). Fixed sights. Blued finish. Plastic grips. Made 1956-71.
Model 4002 (light engraved) . . . NiB $1210 Ex $660 Gd $480
Model 4003 (deep engraved) . . . NiB $2410 Ex $1310 Gd $810

CONSTABLE DA AUTO PISTOL
Calibers: .22 LR, .32 Automatic (7.65mm), .380 Auto (9mm Short). Magazine capacity: 10-rnd. (.22 LR), 8-rnd. (.32), 7-rnd. (.380). 3.5-in. bbl., 6.5 in. overall. Weight: about 24 oz. Blade front sight, windage adj. rear. Blued or chromed finish. Imported from 1965 to 1992.
Stainless finish. . . . . NiB $330 Ex $290 Gd $229
Blued engraved finish . . . . NiB $560 Ex $419 Gd $297
Chrome finish (disc. 1990), add **$15**

Astra Cadix DA

Astra Constable DA

Auto-Ordnance 1927 A-1 Deluxe w/drum magazine

MODEL A-60 . . . . .NiB $415 Ex $285 Gd $210
Similar to the Constable except in .380 only, w/13-rnd. magazine and slide-mounted ambidExtrous safety. Blued finish only. Imported from 1980 to 1991.

MODEL A-70 COMPACT AUTO PISTOL
Calibers: 9mm Para., .40 S&W. Eight-round (9mm) or 7-rnd. (.40 S&W) magazine, 3.5-in. bbl., 6.5 in. overall. Blued, nickel or stainless finish. Weight: 29.3 oz. Imported 1992–96.
Blued finish. . . . . NiB $360 Ex $295 Gd $210
Nickel finish . . . . NiB $390 Ex $345 Gd $229
Stainless finish. . . . . NiB $510 Ex $430 Gd $372

MODEL A-75 ULTRALIGHT . . . NiB $360 Ex $299 Gd $234
Similar to the standard Model 75 except 9mm only w/24-oz. aluminum alloy frame. Imported from 1994 to 1997.

MODEL A-80 AUTO PISTOL . . .NiB $410 Ex $404 Gd $265
Calibers: 9mm Para., .38 Super, .45 ACP. 15-rnd. or 9-rnd. (.45 ACP). magazine. Bbl.: 3.75 in., 7 in. overall. Weight: 36 oz. Imported from 1982 to 1989.

MODEL A-90 DA
AUTOMATIC PISTOL . . . . NiB $460 Ex $400 Gd $245
Calibers: 9mm Para., .45 ACP. 15-rnd. (9mm) or 9-rnd. (.45 ACP) magazine, 3.75-in. bbl., 7 in. overall. Weight: about 40 oz. Fixed sights. Blued finish. Checkered plastic grips. Imported 1985 to 1990.

MODEL A-100 DA AUTO PISTOL
Same general specifications as the Model A-90 except selective double action chambered for 9mm Para., .40 S&W or .45 ACP. Imported from 1991 to 1997.
Blued finish. . . . . NiB $410 Ex $310 Gd $249
Nickel finish . . . . NiB $451 Ex $340 Gd $287
For night sights, add $100

CADIX DA REVOLVER
Calibers: .22 LR, .38 Special. Nine-round (.22 LR) or 5-rnd. (.38 cal.) cylinder. Four- or 6-in. bbl., Weight: About 27 oz. (6-in. bbl.). Ramp front sight, adj. rear sight. Blued finish. Plastic grips. Imported from 1960-68.
Standard model. . . . . .NiB $275 Ex $229 Gd $160
Lightly engraved model. . . . . . .NiB $380 Ex $255 Gd $200
Heavily engraved model (shown) . .NiB $700 Ex $515 Gd $395

MODEL A-75 DECOCKER AUTO PISTOL
Similar to the Model 70 except in 9mm, .40 S&W and .45 ACP w/ decocking system and contoured pebble-tExtured grips. Imported from 1993-97.
Blued finish, 9mm or .40 S&W . . . .NiB $395 Ex $320 Gd $235
Nickel finish, 9mm or .40 S&W . . .NiB $405 Ex $330 Gd $245
Stainless, 9mm or .40 S&W . . . . NiB $410 Ex $305 Gd $197

Blued finish, .45 ACP . . . . NiB $395 Ex $315 Gd $235
Nickel finish, .45 ACP. . . . . NiB $405 Ex $350 Gd $275
Stainless, .45 ACP. . . . . NiB $420 Ex $365 Gd $290

AUTAUGA ARMS — Prattville, AL

MODEL 32 (MK II)
DAO AUTOMATIC PISTOL . . . . NiB $330 Ex $309 Gd $267
Caliber: .32 ACP. Six-round magazine, 2-in. bbl., weight: 11.36 oz. Double action only. Stainless steel. Black polymer grips. Made 1996-2000.

AUTO MAG — Loris, SC
Previously Pasadena, CA, from 1970-72. Purchased by Auto Mag Ltd., Co. in 2015.

Note: Auto Mag Corporation was in business from 1970 thru 1972 when they declared bankruptcy. Some 3,000 pistol were mfg. during this period. From 1973 thru 1983 about 6,000 pistols were mfg. by a variety of companies—TDE, OMC, Thomas Oil Company, High Standard, and AMT.

ORIGINAL . . . . NiB $3500 Ex $3000 Gd $2750
Semiauto. Short recoil action. Calibers: .44 AMP, .357 AMP, .41 JMP, 7-rnd. magazine. Barrel: 6.5- or 8.5-in. VR. Length: 11.5 in. Weight: 57 oz. Sights Adj. target. Finish: Stainless steel. Grips: Checkered plastic. Made 1970-73.
TDE North Hollywood mfg.
  (.44 AMP) . . . . NiB $3250 Ex $3000 Gd $2750
TDE North Hollywood mfg.
  (.357 AMP) . . . . NiB $2950 Ex $2750 Gd $2500
TDE El Monte mfg. (.44 AMP). . NiB $2750 Ex $2500 Gd $2355
TDE El Monte mfg.
  (.357 AMP) . . . . NiB $2250 Ex $2100 Gd $1855
High Standard mfg. . . . . NiB $2250 Ex $2100 Gd $1855
TDE/OCM mfg. . . . . NiB $3150 Ex $2855 Gd $1855
AMT mfg. . . . . NiB $2255 Ex $2110 Gd $1855

- CURRENT MFG. -

Classic model (.44 AMP, G10 or Hogue wood grip,
  2017-date) . . . . NiB $2980 Ex $2610 Gd $2030
Founder's model (.44 AMP, 8.5-in. bbl., wood grip,
  2017-20) . . . . NiB $3410 Ex $2955 Gd $2310

AUTO-ORDNANCE CORPORATION — Greeley, PA
Previously Worcester, MA, West Hurley, New York. Purchased by Kahr Arms in 1999.

1911 A1 GOVERNMENT AUTO . . . NiB $460 Ex $375 Gd $300
Copy of Colt 1911 A1 Semiauto pistol. Calibers: 9mm Para., .38 Super, 10mm, .45 ACP. 9-rnd. (9mm, .38 Super) or 7-rnd. 10mm, .45 ACP) magazine. 5-in. bbl., 8.5 in. overall. Weight: 39 oz. Fixed blade front sight, rear adj. Blued, satin nickel or Duo-Tone finish. Checkered plastic grips. Made 1983-99.

1911 A1 WWII/1911A1 GI SPECS .NiB $590 Ex $525 Gd $300
Similar to 1911 A1 Government model except w/parkerized or matte black finish, checkered plastic or wood. 1992 to date.
1911 A1 100th Anniversary (laser engraved), add **20%**
Commander model (4.25-in. bbl.,
  2018-date) . . . . NiB $460 Ex $375 Gd $300

GRADING: **NiB** = New in Box   **Ex** = Excellent or NRA 95%   **Gd** = Good or NRA 68%

1911A1 .40 S&W PISTOL.....NiB $460 Ex $399 Gd $309
Similar to the Model 1911 A1 except has 4.5-in. bbl., w/7.75-in. overall length. Eight-round magazine, weight: 37 oz. Blade front and adj. rear sights w/3-dot system. Checkered black rubber wraparound grips. Made 1991–93.

1911 A1 "THE GENERAL".....NiB $390 Ex $351 Gd $253
Caliber: .45 ACP. Seven-round magazine, 4.5-in. bbl., 7.75 in. overall. Weight: 37 oz. Blued nonglare finish. Made 1992-99.

1927 A-1 DELUXE SEMIAUTO PISTOL
Similar to Thompson Model 1928A submachine gun except has no provision for automatic firing and does not have detachable buttstock. Caliber: .45 ACP, 5-, 15-, 20- and 30-rnd. detachable box magazines. 30-rnd. drum also available. 13-in. finned bbl., 26 in. overall. Weight: About 6.75 lbs. Adj. rear sight, blade front. Blued finish. Walnut grips. Made 1977-94, reintro. 2008.
w/box magazine . . . . NiB $1260 Ex $1078 Gd $764
w/drum magazine, add $200

ZG-51 PIT BULL PISTOL.....NiB $390 Ex $325 Gd $288
Caliber: .45 ACP. Seven-round magazine, 3.5-in. bbl., 7 in. overall. Weight: 32 oz. Fixed front sight, square-notch rear. Blued finish. Checkered plastic grips. Made 1991-99.

1911A1 SPECIAL EDITIONS
Similar to 1911A1 GI Specs but commemorative models featuring engraving and special finishes.
100th Anniversary . . . . NiB $530 Ex $420 Gd $335
75th Anniversary Iwo Jima. . NiB $1245 Ex $1200 Gd $1000
Bootlegger . . . . NiB $1105 Ex $955 Gd $755
Fly Girls of WWII . . . . NiB $1055 Ex $930 Gd $720
Liberty "Don't Tread On Me" . NiB $1105 Ex $955 Gd $755
Promises Kept . . . . NiB $1055 Ex $930 Gd $720
Revolution Special . . . . NiB $1055 Ex $930 Gd $720
Squadron Special . . . . NiB $1055 Ex $930 Gd $720
Trump 2020 . . . . NiB $1055 Ex $930 Gd $720
Victory Girls WWII . . . . NiB $1055 Ex $930 Gd $720

Auto-Ordnance
ZG-51 Pit Bull

LES BAER — Le Claire, IA
Previously Hilldale, Illinois.

1911 CONCEPT SERIES AUTOMATIC PISTOL
Similar to Government 1911 built on steel or alloy full-size or compact frame. Caliber: .45 ACP. Seven-round magazine, 4.25- or 5-in. bbl. Weight: 34 to 37 oz. Adjustable low mount combat or BoMar target sights. Blued, matte black, Two-Tone or stainless finish. Checkered wood grips. Made 1996 to date.
Concept models I & II . . . . . NiB $1780 Ex $1360 Gd $980
Concept
    models III, IV & VII . . . . . NiB $1930 Ex $1310 Gd $960
Concept
    models V, VI & VIII . . . . . . NiB $1960 Ex $1310 Gd $960
Concept models IX & X. . . . . NiB $1960 Ex $1310 Gd $960

1911 MONOLITH . . . . NiB $2425 Ex $2105 Gd $1585
4.24- or 5-in. bbl. and full dust cover. Caliber: .45 ACP, .400 CorBon, .40 S&W, 9x23, 9mm, or .38 Super. BoMar sights, Commander-style hammer, speed trigger. Finish: Blued. Weight: 37 oz.
Commanche model . . . . NiB $2485 Ex $2165 Gd $1895
Commanche
    Heavyweight model . . . . . NiB $2525 Ex $2195 Gd $1655
Heavyweight model . . . . NiB $2475 Ex $2165 Gd $1625
Tactical Illuminator model . . . NiB $1855 Ex $1505 Gd $805

1911 PREMIER II SERIES AUTOMATIC PISTOL
Similar to the Concept series except also chambered for .38 Super, 9x23 Win., .400 Cor-Bon and .45 ACP. 5- or 6-in. bbl. Weight: 37 to .40 oz. Made 1996 to date.
9x23 w/5-in. bbl. . . . . NiB $2280 Ex $1680 Gd $1360
.400 Cor-Bon
    w/5-in. bbl. . . . . NiB $2080 Ex $1480 Gd $1160
.45 ACP w/5-in. bbl. . . . . . . NiB $1880 Ex $1280 Gd $960
.45 ACP S/S
    w/5-in. bbl. . . . . NiB $1960 Ex $1360 Gd $1040
.45/.400
    combo w/5-in. bbl. . . . . . NiB $2470 Ex $1870 Gd $1550
.38 Super w/6-in. bbl. . . . . . NiB $2560 Ex $1980 Gd $1460
.400 Cor-Bon
    w/6-in. bbl. . . . . NiB $2210 Ex $1630 Gd $1110
.45 ACP w/6-in. bbl. . . . . . . NiB $2110 Ex $1530 Gd $1010

S.R.P. AUTOMATIC PISTOL
Similar to F.B.I. Contract "Swift Response Pistol" built on a (customer-supplied) Para-Ordance over-sized frame or a 1911 full-size or compact frame. Caliber: .45 ACP. Seven-round magazine, 4.25-in. or 5-in. bbl., weight: 37 oz. Ramp front and fixed rear sights, w/Tritium Sight insert.
Government
    or Commanche model . . . NiB $2510 Ex $1910 Gd $1360

1911 ULTIMATE MASTER COMBAT SERIES
Model 1911 in Combat Competition configuration. Calibers: .38 Super, 9x23 Win., .400 Cor-Bon and .45 ACP. Five- or 6-in. NM bbl., weight: 37 to 40 oz. Made 1996 to date.

.38 or 9x23 w/5-in. bbl. . . . NiB $2660 Ex $2080 Gd $1630
.400 Cor-Bon w/5-in. bbl.. . NiB $2610 Ex $2030 Gd $1580
.45 ACP w/5-in. bbl. . . . . . . NiB $2560 Ex $1980 Gd $1530
.38 or 9x23 w/6-in. bbl. . . . NiB $2680 Ex $2025 Gd $1495
.400 Cor-Bon w/6-in. bbl. . . NiB $2630 Ex $2060 Gd $1450
.45 ACP w/6-in. bbl. . . . . . . NiB $2630 Ex $2060 Gd $1580
Ultimate "Steel Special"
    (.38 Super Bianchi SPS) . . . NiB $2855 Ex $2310 Gd $1661
Ultimate "PARA" (.38, 9x23
    or .45 IPSC comp) . . . . . . NiB $2871 Ex $2326 Gd $1650
w/Triple-Port Compensator, add $150

1911 CUSTOM CARRY SERIES AUTOMATIC PISTOL
Model 1911 in Combat Carry configuration built on steel or alloy full-size or compact frame. 4.5- or 5-in. NM bbl., chambered for .45 ACP. Weight: 34 to 37 oz.
Custom carry (steel frame
    w/4.24- or 5-in. bbl.) . . . . NiB $1880 Ex $1280 Gd $960
Custom carry (alloy frame
    w/4.24-in. bbl.) . . . . NiB $1980 Ex $1380 Gd $1060

BAUER FIREARMS CORP. — Fraser, MI

25 AUTOMATIC PISTOL.....NiB $230 Ex $180 Gd $130
Stainless steel. Caliber: .25 Automatic. Six-round magazine, 2.13-in. bbl., 4 in. overall. Weight: 10 oz. Fixed sights. Checkered walnut or simulated pearl grips. Made 1972-84.

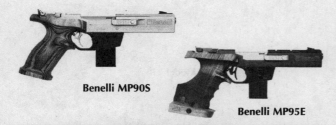

Benelli MP90S

Benelli MP95E

POCKET AUTOMATIC PISTOL . NiB $272 Ex $227 Gd $191
Caliber: .32 Automatic (7.65mm). Seven-round magazine, 2.9-in. bbl., 5.5 in. overall. Weight: 22 oz. Fixed sights. Blued finish. Serrated wood or hard rubber grips. Made by Becker and Hollander 1915 to 1920, by Stenda-Werke circa 1920 to 1925.

Note: *Essentially the same pistol was manufactured w/the Stenda version as the "Leonhardt" by H. M. Gering and as the "Menta" by August Menz.*

BAYARD — Herstal, Belgium
Mfd. by Anciens Etablissements Pieper.

**MODEL 1908 POCKET
AUTOMATIC PISTOL . . . . NiB $455 Ex $300 Gd $195**
Calibers: .25 Automatic (6.35mm). .32 Automatic (7.65mm), .380 Automatic (9mm Short). Six-round magazine, 2.25-in. bbl., 4.88 in. overall. Weight: About 16 oz. Fixed sights. Blued finish. Hard rubber grips. Intro. 1908. Disc. 1923.

**MODEL 1923 POCKET
.25 AUTOMATIC PISTOL . . . . . NiB $480 Ex $300 Gd $170**
Caliber: .25 Automatic (6.35mm). 2.13-in. bbl., 4.31 in. overall. Weight: 12 oz. Fixed sights. Blued finish. Checkered hard-rubber grips. Intro. 1923. Disc. 1930.

**MODEL 1923 POCKET
AUTOMATIC PISTOL . . . . NiB $780 Ex $350 Gd $230**
Calibers: .32 Automatic (7.65mm), .380 Automatic (9mm Short). Six-round magazine, 3.31-in. bbl., 5.5 in. overall. Weight: About 19 oz. Fixed sights. Blued finish. Checkered hard-rubber grips. Intro. 1923. Disc. 1940. .380 ACP, add $80

**MODEL 1930 POCKET
.25 AUTOMATIC PISTOL . . . . . NiB $480 Ex $255 Gd $195**
This is a modification of the Model 1923, which it closely resembles.

BEEMAN PRECISION ARMS, INC. — Santa Rosa, CA

P08 SEMIAUTOMATIC PISTOL . . . NiB $420 Ex $335 Gd $245
Luger toggle action. Caliber: .22 LR. 10-rnd. magazine, 3.8-in. bbl., 7.8 in. overall. Weight: 25 oz. Fixed sights. Blued finish. Checkered hardwood grips. Imported from 1969 to 1991.

MINI P08 PISTOL . . . . NiB $470 Ex $375 Gd $295
Caliber: Same general specifications as P08 except shorter 3.5-in. bbl., 7.4 in. overall. Weight: 20 oz. Imported 1986 to 1991.

SP METALLIC SILHOUETTE PISTOLS
Caliber: .22 LR. Single-shot. Bbl. lengths: 6-, 8-, 10- or 15-in. Adj. rear sight. Receiver contoured for scope mount. Walnut target grips w/adj. palm rest. Models SP made 1985-86 and SPX 1993-94.

	NiB	Ex	Gd
SP Standard w/8-or 10-in. bbl.	$285	$235	$172
SP Standard w/12-in. bbl.	$330	$266	$191
SP Standard w/15-in. bbl.	$344	$286	$200
SP Deluxe w/8-or 10-in. bbl.	$346	$276	$199
SP Deluxe w/12-in. bbl.	$355	$291	$209
SP Deluxe w/15-in. bbl.	$374	$306	$215
SPX Standard w/10-in. bbl.	$679	$548	$387
SPX Deluxe w/10-in. bbl.	$925	$744	$524

BEHOLLA — Suhl, Germany
Mfd. by both Becker and Holländer and Stenda-Werke GmbH.

BENELLI — Urbino, Italy
Imported by Larry's Guns in Gray, ME since 2003. Previously imported by EEA in Sharpes, FL; Sile Dist. New York, NY; Saco, Arlington, VA.

MP90S WORLD CUP TARGET PISTOL
Semiauto blowback action. Calibers: .22 Short, .22 LR, .32 W.C. Five-round magazine, 4.33-in. fixed bbl. 6.75 in. overall. Weight: 36 oz. Post front sight, adjustable rear. Blue finish. Anatomic shelf-style grip. Imported 1992 to 2001, reintro. 2003.

	NiB	Ex	Gd
.22 LR	$1700	$1230	$995
.22 Short, disc. 1995	$1314	$1155	$984

.32 S&W, add $160
w/conversion kit, add $80

MODEL B-76 . . . . NiB $1110 Ex $610 Gd $410
Semiauto, SA/DA. Cal.: 9 mm Para. Bbl.: 4.25 in. 8-rnd. mag. Weight: 34 oz. Disc. 1990.

MODEL B-765 TARGET. . . . . . . NiB $1500 Ex $930 Gd $710
Cal.: 9 mm Para. Similar to B-76 model but w/5.5-in. bbl., target grips, adj. rear sight. Disc. 1990.

MODEL B-77 . . . . NiB $405 Ex $309 Gd $220
Semiauto, SA/DA. Cal.: .32 ACP. Bbl.: Steel, 4.25 in. 8-rnd. mag. Disc. 1995.

MODEL B-80 . . . . NiB $425 Ex $315 Gd $245
Semiauto, SA/DA. Cal.: .30 Luger. Bbl.: Steel, 4.25 in. 8-rnd. mag. Weight: 34 oz. Disc. 1995.

B-80s Target, add $126

MODEL B-82 . . . . NiB $813 Ex $551 Gd $414
Limited production Italian police model; serial no. with "D" suffix. Cal.: .30 Luger, .32 ACP, 9 mm Ultra.

MODEL MP3S. . . . . NiB $660 Ex $380 Gd $300
Semiauto, target model. Cal.: .32 S&W Long Wadcutter. Bbl.: 5.5 in. High gloss blued finish, target grips. Adj. rear sight. Disc. 1995.

MP95E SPORT TARGET PISTOL
Similar to the MP90S except w/5- or 9-rnd. magazine, 4.25- in. bbl., Blue or chrome finish. Checkered target grip. Imported from 1994 to date.
.22 LR . . . . NiB $1020 Ex $760 Gd $530
.32 WC, add $205
Chrome, add. $80

BERETTA USA CORP. — Accokeek, MD
Beretta firearms are manufactured by Fabbrica D'Armi Pietro Beretta S. p. A. in Gardone Val Trompia (Brescia), Italy. This prestigious firm has been in business since 1526. In 1977, Beretta U.S.A. Corp., a manufacturing and importing facility, opened in Accokeek, MD. (Previously imported by Garcia Corp., J.L. Galef & Son, Inc. and Berben Corporation.) Note: Beretta holdings also owns additional firearms companies including: Benelli, Franchi, Sako, Stoeger, Tikka and Uberti.

MODEL 20 DA AUTO PISTOL. . .NiB $257 Ex $203 Gd $136
Caliber: .25 ACP. Eight-round magazine, 2.5-in. bbl., 4.9 in. overall. Weight: 10.9 oz. Plastic or walnut grips. Fixed sights. Made 1984-85.

MODEL 21 DA AUTO PISTOL
Calibers: .22 LR and .25 ACP. Seven-round (.22 LR) or 8-rnd. (.25 ACP) magazine, 2.5-in. bbl., 4.9 in. overall. Weight: About 12 oz. Blade front sight, V-notch rear. Walnut grips. Made 1985 to date. Model 21EL disc. 2000.
Blued finish. . . . . .NiB $285 Ex $210 Gd $165
Nickel finish (.22 LR only) . . . .NiB $300 Ex $225 Gd $177
Model 21EL engraved model. . .NiB $375 Ex $310 Gd $230

MODEL 70 AUTOMATIC
PISTOL . . . . NiB $278 Ex $199 Gd $131
Improved version of Model 1935. Steel or lightweight alloy. Calibers: .32 Auto (7.65mm), .380 Auto (9mm Short). Eight-round (.32) or 7-rnd. (.380) magazine, 3.5-in. bbl., 6.5 in. overall. Weight: Steel, 22.25 oz.; alloy, 16 oz. Fixed sights. Blued finish. Checkered plastic grips. Made 1959–85.

Note: *Formerly marketed in U.S. as "Puma" (alloy model in .32) and "Cougar" (steel model in .380). Disc.*

MODEL 70S . . . . .NiB $420 Ex $288 Gd $210
Similar to Model 70T except chambered for .22 Auto and .380 Auto. Longer bbl. guide and safety lever blocking hammer. Front blade and rear sight fixed on breechblock. Weight: 1 lb., 7 oz. Made 1977-85.

MODEL 70T AUTOMATIC
PISTOL . . . . NiB $330 Ex $255 Gd $200
Similar to Model 70. Caliber: .32 Automatic (7.65mm). Nine-round magazine, 6-in. bbl., 9.5-in. overall. Weight: 19 oz. adj. rear sight, blade front sight. Blued finish. Checkered plastic grips. Intro. in 1959. Disc.

MODEL 71 AUTOMATIC
PISTOL . . . . .NiB $360 Ex $280 Gd $220
Similar to alloy Model 70. Caliber: .22 LR. Six-in. bbl., 8-rnd. magazine, Adj. rear sight frame. Single action. Made 1959-89. Note: Formerly marketed in U.S. as the "Jaguar Plinker."

MODEL 72 . . . . .NiB $360 Ex $240 Gd $190
Same as Model 71 except has 6-in. bbl., weight: 18 oz. Intro. in 1959. Disc. Note: Formerly marketed in U.S as "Jaguar Plinker."

MODEL 76 AUTO TARGET PISTOL
Caliber: .22 LR. 10-rnd. magazine, 6-in. bbl., 8.8 in. overall. Weight: 33 oz. adj. rear sight, front sight w/interchangeable blades. Blued finish. Checkered plastic or wood grips. Made 1966-85. Note: Formerly marketed in the U.S. as the "Sable."
Model 76 w/plastic grips . . . . .NiB $800 Ex $660 Gd $510
Model 76W w/wood grips, add $40

MODEL 81 DA AUTO PISTOL. . .NiB $341 Ex $247 Gd $199
Caliber: .32 Automatic (7.65mm). 12-rnd. magazine, 3.8-in. bbl., 6.8 in. overall. Weight: 23.5 oz. Fixed sights. Blued finish. Plastic grips. Made principally for the European market 1975 to 1984, w/similar variations as the Model 84.

MODEL 82W DA AUTO
PISTOL . . . . .NiB $330 Ex $231 Gd $178
Caliber: .32 ACP. Similar to the Model 81 except with a slimmer-profile frame designed to accept a single column 9-rnd. magazine. Matte black finish. Importation disc. 1984.

MODEL 84 DA AUTO PISTOL. . .NiB $325 Ex $222 Gd $173
Same as Model 81 except made in caliber .380 Automatic w/13-rnd. magazine, 3.82-in. bbl., 6.8 in. overall. Weight: 23 oz. Fixed front and rear sights. Made 1975-82.

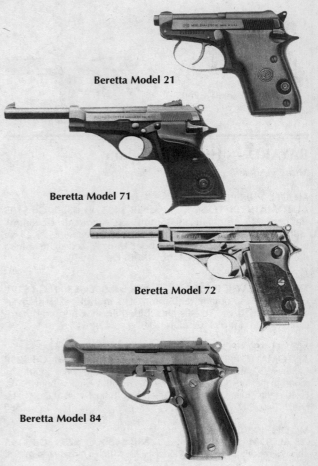

Beretta Model 21

Beretta Model 71

Beretta Model 72

Beretta Model 84

MODEL 84B DA AUTO
PISTOL . . . . .NiB $335 Ex $230 Gd $184
Improved version of Model 84 w/strengthened frame and slide, and firing-pin block safety added. AmbidExtrous reversible magazine release. Blued or nickel finish. Checkered black plastic or wood grips. Other specifications same. Made circa 1982 to 1984.

MODEL 84(BB) DA AUTO PISTOL
Improved version of Model 84B w/further-strengthened slide, frame and recoil spring. Caliber: .380 ACP. 13-rnd. magazine, 3.82-in. bbl., 6.8 in. overall. Weight: 23 oz. Checkered black plastic or wood grips. Blued or nickel finish. Notched rear and blade front sight. Made circa 1984-94.
Blued w/plastic grips . . . . .NiB $393 Ex $241 Gd $152
Blued w/wood grips . . . . .NiB $446 Ex $372 Gd $270
Nickel finish w/wood grips. . . . NiB $630 Ex $493 Gd $383

MODEL 84 CHEETAH SEMIAUTO PISTOL
Similar to the Model 84 BB except with required design changes as mandated by regulation, including reduced magazine capacity (10-rnd. magazine) and marked as 9mm short (.380) as a marketing strategy to counter increased availability of 9mm chamberings from other manufacturers. Made 1994–2002,, reintro. 2004.
Blued w/plastic grips . . . . .NiB $700 Ex $520 Gd $360
Blued w/wood grips . . . . .NiB $667 Ex $551 Gd $367
Nickel finish w/wood grips. . . .NiB $735 Ex $498 Gd $372

MODEL 85 DA AUTO PISTOL .NiB $660 Ex $460 Gd $330
Similar to the Model 84 except designed with a slimmer-profile frame to accept a single column 8-rnd. magazine, no

Beretta Model 85

Beretta Model 86 Cheetah

ambidextrous magazine release. Matte black finish. Weight: 21.8 oz. Introduced in 1977 following the Model 84.

MODEL 85B DA AUTO PISTOL NiB $430 Ex $330 Gd $210
Improved version of the Model 85. Imported from 1982-85.

MODEL 85BB DA PISTOL
Improved version of the Model 85B w/strengthened frame and slide. Caliber: .380 ACP. Eight-round magazine, 3.82 in. bbl., 6.8 in. overall. Weight: 21.8 oz. Blued or nickel finish. Checkered black plastic or wood grips. Imported from 1985 to 1994.
Blued finish w/plastic grips. . . . NiB $520 Ex $395 Gd $280
Blued finish w/wood grips . . . . NiB $530 Ex $404 Gd $295
Nickel finish w/wood grips . . . . NiB $582 Ex $430 Gd $315

MODEL 85 CHEETAH SEMIAUTO PISTOL
Similar to the Model 85BB except with required design changes as mandated by regulation and marked as 9mm short (.380). Made 1994 to date.
Blued finish w/plastic grips. . . . NiB $656 Ex $470 Gd $310
Blued finish w/wood grips . . . . NiB $680 Ex $490 Gd $330
Nickel finish w/wood grips . . . . NiB $719 Ex $525 Gd $393

MODEL 85F DA PISTOL
Similar to the Model 85BB except has re-contoured trigger guard and manual ambidextrous safety w/decocking device. Matte black Bruniton finish. Imported in 1990 only.
plastic grips. . . . . NiB $390 Ex $315 Gd $255
wood grips . . . . NiB $420 Ex $344 Gd $283

MODEL 86 CHEETAH . . . . NiB $660 Ex $500 Gd $410
Caliber: .380 auto. Eight-round magazine, 4.4- in. bbl., 7.3 in. overall. Weight: 23.3 oz. Bruniton finish w/wood grips. Made 1986-89. (Reintroduced 1990 in the Cheetah series.)

MODEL 87 CHEETAH AUTOMATIC PISTOL
Similar to the Model 85 except in .22 LR w/8- or 10- rnd. magazine (Target) and optional Extended 6-in. bbl. (Target in single action). Overall length: 6.8 to 8.8 in. Weight: 20.1 oz. to 29.4 oz (Target). Checkered wood grips. Made 1987 to date.
Blued finish
   (double-action) . . . . NiB $830 Ex $660 Gd $480
Target model
   (single action) . . . . NiB $930 Ex $760 Gd $580

MODEL 89 GOLD STANDARD TARGET
AUTOMATIC PISTOL . . . . NiB $640 Ex $420 Gd $330
Caliber: .22 LR. Eight-round magazine, 6-in. bbl., 9.5 in. over-all. Weight: 41 oz. Adj. target sights. Blued finish. Target-style walnut grips. Made 1988-2000.

MODEL 90 DA AUTO PISTOL . NiB $280 Ex $235 Gd $195
Caliber: .32 Auto (7.65mm). Eight-round magazine, 3.63-in. bbl., 6.63 in. overall. Weight: 19.5 oz. Fixed sights. Blued fin-ish. Checkered plastic grips. Made 1969-83.

NOTE: *The Model 92 has been in production since 1976 and has many model variations. In 1985, the U.S. Military adopted the 92FS as the M9 as the replacement for the M1911A1. The Model 92F reflects changes to the model during U.S. Military testing. The Model 92FS has an enlarged hammer pin due to U.S. Military requirement discovered during testing.*

MODEL 90-TWO TYPE F . . . . . NiB $600 Ex $460 Gd $400
Similar to 92F. Caliber: 9mm Para or .40 S&W, DA/SA, 4.9-in. bbl., 8.5 in. overall. Weight: 32.5 oz. Fixed sights. Blued finish. Wrap around grip in two sizes. Accessory rail w/cover. Made 2006-09.

MODEL 92 (1ST SERIES) . . . . . . NiB $860 Ex $630 Gd $400
Caliber: 9mm Para. 15-rnd. magazine, 4.9-in. bbl., 8.5 in. overall. DA/SA trigger. Weight: 33.5 oz. Fixed sights. Blued finish. Plastic grips. Initial production of 5,000 made in 1976.

MODEL 92S (2ND SERIES) . . . . NiB $700 Ex $400 Gd $260
Revised version of Model 92 w/ambidextrous slide-mounted safety modification intended for both commercial and mili-tary production. Evolved to Model 92S-1 for U.S. Military trials. Made 1980-85.

MODEL 92SB-P
(3RD SERIES) . . . . NiB $610 Ex $410 Gd $345
Same general specifications as standard Model 92 except has slide-mounted safety and repositioned magazine release. Made 1981-85.

MODEL 92D . . . . NiB $560 Ex $360 Gd $260
Same general specifications as Model 92F except DAO only w/ bobbed hammer and 3-dot sight. Made 1992-98.
w/Tritium sights, add $100
Centurian . . . . Nib $470 Ex $310 Gd $220

MODEL 92F COMPACT . . . . . . NiB $630 Ex $560 Gd $279
Caliber: 9mm Para. 12-rnd. magazine, 4.3-in. bbl., 7.8 in. over-all. Weight: 31.5 oz. Wood grips. Square-notched rear sight, blade front integral w/slide. Made 1990-93.

MODEL 92F COMPACT L TYPE M
Same general specifications as the original 92F Compact except 8-rnd. magazine, Weight: 30.9 oz. Bruniton matte fin-ish. Made 1998–2003.
Bruniton finish . . . . NiB $660 Ex $580 Gd $390
Inox finish. . . . . NiB $656 Ex $583 Gd $393
w/Tritium sights, add $100

MODEL 92F
Same general specifications as Model 92 except w/slide-mounted safety and repositioned magazine release. Replaced Model 92SB. Blued or stainless finish. Made 1992–98.
Blued finish. . . . . NiB $630 Ex $493 Gd $341
Stainless finish. . . . . NiB $619 Ex $477 Gd $325
Model 92F-EL gold, add $200
Deluxe (engraved, gold or
   silver plate, 1993) . . . . NiB $5760 Ex $3760 Gd $2180

MODEL 92FS

Calibers: 9mm, 15- rnd. magazine, 4.9- in. bbl., 8.5 in. overall. Weight: 34.4 oz. Ambidextrous safety/decock lever. Chrome-lined bore w/combat trigger guard. Bruniton finish w/plastic grips or Inox finish w/rubber grips. Made 1999 to date. This model was adopted as the standard-issue sidearm by the U.S. Armed Forces in 1985 and renamed the M9.

matte black Bruniton finish. . . . NiB $600 Ex $460 Gd $360
olive drab finish (made 2004), add. $50
Inox finish. . . . . .NiB $680 Ex $470 Gd $360
Inox Tactical. . . . . NiB $700 Ex $490 Gd $380
w/ checkered wood grips, add $25
w/B-lok (made 2003), add $25
470th Anniversary (made 1999) . . . NiB $1960 Ex $1110 Gd $800
"Desert Storm" edition (made 1991-92). . . .NiB $630 Ex $500 Gd $450
92A1 (mfg. in Italy, 2010-present)NiB $660 Ex $480 Gd $360
Billenium (SAO, 2002-03). . . . NiB $1760 Ex $1110 Gd $760
Steel I (steel frame, 2004-05) . . NiB $1510 Ex $930 Gd $760
Year 2000 (laminated grips,
      2000 only). . . . . NiB $620 Ex $460 Gd $360
"United We Stand" (2001-02) . . NiB $630 Ex $490 Gd $380
"Operation Enduring Freedom"
      (2003 only) . . . . NiB $630 Ex $490 Gd $380
M9 . . . . NiB $580 Ex $450 Gd $360
M9A1 (accesory rail) . . . . NiB $660 Ex $490 Gd $370
M9A3 (modular grips) . . . . . . NiB $1000 Ex $810 Gd $630
M9 Limited Edition (gold inscribed) . . . NiB $610 Ex $430 Gd $320
M9 Limited Edition Deluxe
      (gold inscribed/plated) . . . . . . NiB $700 Ex $480 Gd $370
M9 20th Anniversary . . . . NiB $560 Ex $420 Gd $340
M9 25th Anniversary . . . . NiB $580 Ex $450 Gd $360
Compact (4.3-in. brrl., 1999-2003). . . NiB $580 Ex $420 Gd $340
Compact stainless (2000-03), add. $45
Compact stainless w/rail (2013-16), add $60

MODEL 92FS BORDER MARSHAL . . .NiB $675 Ex $485 Gd $460

Similar to 92F except commericial equivilent of I.N.S. gov't. contract pistol. Made 1999-2000.

MODEL 92FS BRIGADIER

Similar to 92FS except w/heavier slide and rubber wrap around grips. Made 1999-2005; reintro. 2015 to date.
Matte black Bruniton . . . . .NiB $660 Ex $556 Gd $395
Inox. .NiB $700 Ex $630 Gd $477

MODEL 92FS CENTURION

Similar to 92FS except w/compact barrel/slide and full size frame. Wood or plastic grips. Made 1999-2005; reintro. 2015 to date.
Matte black Bruniton . . . . .NiB $525 Ex $400 Gd $340

MODEL 92FS VERTEC. . . . . . . .NiB $680 Ex $400 Gd $290

Similar to 92FS except w/straight backstrap, thin grip panels, short-reach trigger, and accessory rail. Made 2002-05.

MODEL 92G-SD . . . . NiB $960 Ex $590 Gd $460

Similar to 92F except w/srping loaded decocking lever, accessory rail, 10-rnd. magazine, Tritium sights. Made 2003-05.

MODEL 92G ELITE IA. . . . . . . .NiB $730 Ex $500 Gd $360

Similar to 92FS Brigadier except w/4.7-in. stainless bbl. Made 1999-2005.
Elite II (made 2000-05). . . . . . .NiB $820 Ex $540 Gd $390

MODEL 96 DA

Similar to Model 92F except in .40 S&W. 10-rnd. magazine (9-rnd. in Compact model). Made 1992-98.
Model 96 D (DAO). . . . . .NiB $475 Ex $355 Gd $300
Model 96 Centurion (compact) NiB $550 Ex $460 Gd $310

w/Tritium sights, add $110
w/Tritium sights system, add. $115
Border Marshal (commercial version
      of INS issue, 1999-2000). . . . . NiB $680 Ex $485 Gd $380
Brigadier (heavy slide, 1995-2005) . . . NiB $670 Ex $450 Gd $340
Brigadier stainless, add. $20
Combat (tuned trigger,
      mfg.Itly, 1997-2001) . . . . NiB $1360 Ex $910 Gd $630
Custom Carry (4.3-in.
      brrl., 1999-2000). . . . . NiB $560 Ex $410 Gd $340
Steel 1 (steel frame, 2004-05) . . . NiB $1230 Ex $960 Gd $760
Stock (competition
      set up, 1997-99) . . . . NiB $1200 Ex $870 Gd $610
Vertec (straight grip, 2002-05). . . NiB $640 Ex $450 Gd $350
Vertec stainless (2002-03), add. $40

MODEL 101 . . . . NiB $270 Ex $200 Gd $155

Same as Model 70T except caliber .22 LR, has 10-rnd. magazine, Intro. in 1959. Disc.

MODEL 318 AUTO PISTOL . . . . .NiB $280 Ex $200 Gd $155

Caliber: .25 Automatic (6.35mm). Eight-round magazine, 2.5-in. bbl., 4.5 in. overall. Weight: 14 oz. Fixed sights. Blued finish. Plastic grips. Made 1934 to c. 1939.
Model 319 (blue/engraved), add. $140
Model 320 (nickel/engraved), add $210
Model 321 (gold/engraved), add. $300

Beretta Model 92F

**Beretta Model 92
Compact L Type M**

**Beretta Model 92FS
Brigadier Inox**

Beretta Model 96

**Beretta Model 949
Olimpionico**

**Beretta Model 950BS
Jetfire**

MODEL 418 AUTO PISTOL . . . . . **NiB $270 Ex $200 Gd $155**
Similar to Model 318 but with loaded chamber indicator and grip safety. Made 1937-61.
Model 419 (blue/engraved), add **$140**
Model 420 (nickel/engraved), add **$210**
Model 421 (gold/engraved), add **$300**

MODEL 949 OLYMPIC TARGET . . **NiB $708 Ex $577 Gd $456**
Calibers: .22 Short, .22 LR. Five-round magazine, 8.75-in. bbl., 12.5 in. overall. Weight: 38 oz. Target sights. Adj. bbl., weight. Muzzle brake. Checkered walnut grips w/thumbrest. Made 1959-64.

MODEL 950B JETFIRE. . . . . **NiB $160 Ex $110 Gd $90**
Same general specifications as Model 950CC except caliber .25 Auto, has 7-rnd. magazine, Made 1959 to date.

MODEL 950BS JETFIRE
Calibers: .25 ACP or .22 Short (disc.1992). Seven- or 8-rnd. magazine, 2.4- or 4- in. bbl. Weight: 9.9 oz. Fixed blade front and V-notch rear sights. Matte Blue or Inox (Stainless) finish. Checkered black plastic grips. Made 1987-2002.
Blued finish . . . . **NiB $185 Ex $120 Gd $90**
Nickel finish . . . . **NiB $225 Ex $173 Gd $147**
Inox finish . . . . **NiB $257 Ex $204 Gd $160**
w/4-in. bbl., (.22 Short) . . . . . . **NiB $256 Ex $207 Gd $157**

MODEL 950CC MINX. . . . . **NiB $140 Ex $126 Gd $104**
Caliber: .22 Short. Six-round magazine, hinged 2.38-in. bbl., 4.75 in. overall. Weight: 11 oz. Fixed sights. Blued finish. Plastic

grips. Made 1959-64. Note: Formerly marketed in the U.S. as "Minx M2."
Special model (4-in. brrl., Minx M4), add **$20**

**MODEL 951 (1951) BRIGADIER
MILITARY AUTO PISTOL** . . . . . **NiB $580 Ex $400 Gd $300**
Caliber: 9mm Para. Eight-round magazine, 4.5-in. bbl., 8 in. overall. Weight: 31 oz. Fixed sights. Blued finish. Plastic grips. Made from 1952 to date. Note: Was standard pistol of the Italian Armed Forces, also used by Egyptian and Israeli armies and by the police in Nigeria. Egyptian and Israeli models usually command a premium. Formerly marketed in the U.S. as the "Brigadier."

MODEL 1915 AUTO PISTOL. . . **NiB $1587 Ex $1386 Gd $1087**
Calibers: 9mm Glisenti and .32 ACP (7.65mm). Eight-round magazine, 4-in. bbl., 6.7 in. overall (9mm), 5.7 in. (.32 ACP). Weight: 30 oz. (9mm), 20 oz. (.32 ACP). Fixed sights. Blued finish. Wood grips. Made 1915-22. An improved postwar 1915/1919 version in caliber .32 ACP was later offered for sale in 1922 as the Model 1922.

MODEL 1919 . . . . **NiB $380 Ex $280 Gd $210**
Caliber: .25 ACP. 8-rnd. magazine.

MODEL 1923 AUTO PISTOL. . . **NiB $2136 Ex $2094 Gd $1669**
Caliber: 9mm Glisenti (Luger). Eight-round magazine, 4-in. bbl., 6.5 in. overall. Weight: 30 oz. Fixed sights. Blued finish. Plastic grips. Made circa 1923 to 1936.

MODEL 1926 . . . . **NIB $360 EX $280 GD $200**
Similar to Model 1919 except w/ wood grips.

MODEL 1931 . . . . **NIB $330 EX $255 GD $180**
Similar to Model 1919 except .32 ACP.

MODEL 1934 AUTO PISTOL
Caliber: .380 Automatic (9mm Short). Seven-round magazine, 3.38-in. bbl., 5.88 in. overall. Weight: 24 oz. Fixed sights. Blued finish. Plastic grips. Official pistol of the Italian Armed Forces. Wartime pieces not as well made and finished as commercial models. Made 1934-59.
**Commercial model
(deluxe, post-WWII)** . . . . **NiB $3510 Ex $2100 Gd $1333**
WWII model . . . . **NiB $660 Ex $380 Gd $260**

MODEL 1935 AUTO PISTOL
Caliber: .32 ACP (7.65mm). Eight-round magazine, 3.5-in. bbl., 5.75 in. overall. Weight: 24 oz. Fixed sights. Blued finish. Plastic grips. A roughly-finished version of this pistol was produced during WW II. Made 1935-59.
Commercial model . . . . **NiB $1806 Ex $1465 Gd $1078**
**Deluxe Commercial model (engraved,
gold plated, cased)** . . . . . **NiB $3510 Ex $2000 Gd $1500**
War model . . . . **NiB $500 Ex $383 Gd $299**

MODEL 3032 TOMCAT
Caliber: .32 ACP. Seven-round magazine, 2.45-in. bbl., 5 in. overall. Weight: 14.5 oz. Fixed sights. Blued or stainless finish. Made 1996 to date.
Matte blue . . . . **NiB $329 Ex $262 Gd $180**
Polished blue. . . . . **NiB $386 Ex $329 Gd $252**
Stainless . . . . **NiB $412 Ex $365 Gd $252**

MODEL 8000/8040/8045 COUGAR
Calibers: 9mm, .40 S&W and .45 Auto. Eight- or 10-shot magazine, 3.6 to 3.7- in. bbl., 7- to 7.2 in. overall. Weight: 32 to 32.6 oz. Short recoil action w/rotating barrel. Fixed

sights w/3-dot Tritium system. Textured black grips. Matte black Bruniton w/alloy frame. Made 1995-2005.

8000 Cougar D (9mm DAO)... NiB $715 Ex $649 Gd $400
8000 Cougar F (9mm DA)..... NiB $750 Ex $644 Gd $388
8040 Cougar D (.40 S&W DAO) NiB $685 Ex $618 Gd $373
8040 Cougar F (.40 S&W DA) . NiB $685 Ex $618 Gd $373
8045 Cougar D (.45 Auto DAO) NiB $736 Ex $637 Gd $400
8045 Cougar F (.357 Sig SA/DA) NiB $685 Ex $536 Gd $386

MODEL 8000/8040/8045 MINI COUGAR

Calibers: 9mm, .40 S&W and .45 Auto. Six- 8- or 10-rnd. magazine, 3.6- to 3.7- in. bbl., 7 in. overall. Weight: 27.4 to 30.4 oz. Fixed sights w/3-dot Tritium system. AmbidExtrous safety/decocker lever. Matte black Bruniton finish w/anodized aluminum alloy frame. Made 1995-2008.

8000 Mini Cougar D (9mm DAO) .. NiB $654 Ex $577 Gd $326
8000 Mini Cougar F (9mm DA)..... NiB $654 Ex $577 Gd $326
8040 Mini Cougar D (.40 S&W DAO) ... NiB $654 Ex $577 Gd $326
8040 Mini Cougar F (.40 S&W DA)... NiB $654 Ex $577 Gd $326
8045 Mini Cougar D (.45 Auto DAO) ... NiB $654 Ex $577 Gd $326
8045 Mini Cougar F (.45 Auto DA) ... NiB $654 Ex $577 Gd $326

MODEL 9000S SUBCOMPACT PISTOL SERIES

Calibers: 9mm, .40 S&W. 10-rnd. magazine, 3.5- in. bbl., 6.6 in. overall. Weight: 25.7 to 27.5 oz. Single/double and double-action only. Front and rear dovetail sights w/3- dot system. Chrome-plated bbl. w/Techno-polymer frame. Geometric locking system w/tilt barrel. Made 2000–05.

Type D (9mm) .... NiB $432 Ex $366 Gd $304
Type D (.40 S&W).......... NiB $432 Ex $366 Gd $304
Type F (9mm) .... NiB $432 Ex $366 Gd $304
Type F (.40 S&W) .... NiB $432 Ex $366 Gd $304

APX .... NiB $485 Ex $405 Gd $255
Striker-fired polymer-frame. Caliber: 9mm or .40 S&W, 14- (.40 S&W) or 17-rnd (9mm) magazine capacity. Barrel: 4.25-in. Striker deactivation button, trigger safety and ring-pin block safety. Weight: 29 oz. Modular interchangeable grip inserts. Finish: matte black, OD Green, FDE or Wolf Gray. 2017-date.
Carry model (3-in. bbl.) .... NiB $485 Ex $405 Gd $255
Centurion model (3.7-in. bbl.) .. NiB $485 Ex $405 Gd $255
Combat model (threaded bbl.) .. NiB $636 Ex $555 Gd $405
RDO model (optic ready) ..... NiB $560 Ex $480 Gd $330

NANO .... NiB $ 370 Ex $280 Gd $200
Semiauto. Striker fired. Caliber: 9mm. 6-rnd. magazine. 3.07-in. bbl. Frame: polymer with removable trigger group. Grip: texture polymer; black, pink or FDE. Sights: low-profile,fixed. Length: 5.63 in. Weight: 19.8 oz. Made 2011 to date.

PICO .... NiB $270 Ex $200 Gd $180
Semiauto. Striker fired. Caliber: .380 ACP, 6-rnd magazine. 2.7-in. bbl. Frame: polymer with removable trigger group.

Beretta APX

**Beretta
Model 3032 Tomcat**

**Beretta
Model 8000 Cougar D**

Beretta PX4 Storm

Grip: texture polymer, black. Sights: low-profile, fixed. Length: 5.1 in. Weight: 11.5 oz. Made 2013 to date.

PX4 STORM.............. NiB $575 Ex $490 Gd $440
SA/DA Semiauto pistol. Rotating bbl. system. Polymer frame. Calibers: 9mm, .40 S&W or .45 ACP. 9-17 rnd. magazine. Bbl lengths: 3.2 or 4 in. Finish: matte black, Pronox or Super Luminova. Made 2005 to date.
Inox finish, add 90%
Storm Special Duty .... NiB $1145 Ex $980 Gd $830

LARAMIE SA REVOLVER .... NiB $1030 Ex $760 Gd $550
Reproduction of S&W Model 1870 Schofield. Calibers: .38 Special, .45 Long Colt. 6-rnd. cylinder, Bbl length: 5, 6.5 in. Blued finish. Built by Uberti from 2005 to 2008.

STAMPEDE SA REVOLVER

Calibers: .357 Magnum, .44-40, .45 Long Colt. 6-rnd. cylinder, Bbl length: 4.75, 5.5, 7.5 in. Built by Uberti from 2003-11.
Blued finish .... NiB $490 Ex $345 Gd $265
Brushed nickel finish........ NiB $510 Ex $355 Gd $275
Deluxe finish............... NiB $520 Ex $425 Gd $325

Beretta Stampede

Bernardelli Model 60 Pocket

Bernardelli Model 68

finish. Bakelite or pearl grips. This model, like its .22-caliber counterpart, was known as the "Baby" Bernardelli. Disc. 1970.

MODEL 69 TARGET PISTOL . . . NiB $693 Ex $570 Gd $383
Caliber: .22 LR. 10-rnd. magazine, 5.9-in. bbl., 9 in. overall. Weight: 2.2 lbs. Fully adj. target sights. Blued finish. Stippled right- or left-hand wraparound walnut grips. Made 1987 to date. This was previously Model 100; not imported to the U.S.

MODEL 80 . . . . NiB $204 Ex $128 Gd $92
Calibers: .22 LR, .32 ACP (7.65mm), .380 Auto (9mm Short). Magazine capacity: 10-rnd. (.22), 8-rnd. (.32), 7-rnd. (.380). 3.5-in. bbl., 6.5 in. overall. Weight: 25.6 oz. adj. rear sight, white dot front sight. Blued finish. Plastic thumbrest grips. Note: Model 80 is a modification of Model 60 designed to conform w/U.S. import regulations. Made 1968-88.

MODEL 90 SPORT TARGET . . . NiB $245 Ex $199 Gd $148
Same as Model 80 except has 6-in. bbl., 9 in. overall, weight: 26.8 oz. Made 1968 1990.

MODEL 100 TARGET PISTOL . . NiB $428 Ex $362 Gd $291
Caliber: .22 LR. 10-rnd. magazine, 5.9-in. bbl., 9 in. overall. Weight: 37.75 oz. Adj. rear sight, interchangeable front sights. Blued finish. Checkered walnut thumbrest grips. Made 1969-86. Note: Formerly Model 69.

MODEL AMR AUTO PISTOL . . . NiB $433 Ex $321 Gd $270
Simlar to Model USA except w/6-in. bbl. and target sights. Imported from 1992 to 1994.

"BABY" AUTOMATIC PISTOL . NiB $321 Ex $235 Gd $179
Calibers: .22 Short, .22 Long. Five-round magazine, 2.13-in. bbl., 4.13 in. overall. Weight: 9 oz. Fixed sights. Blued finish. Bakelite grips. Made 1949-68.

MODEL P010 . . . . NiB $712 Ex $520 Gd $341
Caliber: .22 LR. Five- and 10-rnd. magazine, 5.9-in. bbl. w/7.5-in. sight radius. Weight: 40 oz. Interchangeable front sight, adj. rear. Blued finish. Textured walnut grips. Made 1988-92 and 1995 to 1997.

P018 COMPACT MODEL . . . . . NiB $571 Ex $461 Gd $385
Slightly smaller version of the Model P018 standard DA automatic except has 14-rnd. magazine and 4-in. bbl., 7.68 in. overall. Weight: 33 oz. Walnut grips only. Imported from 1987 to 1996.

P018 DOUBLE-ACTION AUTOMATIC PISTOL
Caliber: 9mm Para. 16-rnd. magazine, 4.75-in. bbl., 8.5 in. overall. Weight: 36 oz. Fixed combat sights. Blued finish. Checkered plastic or walnut grips. Imported from 1987 to 1996.
w/plastic grips . . . . NiB $510 Ex $405 Gd $305
w/walnut grips . . . . NiB $551 Ex $428 Gd $342

P-ONE DA AUTO PISTOL
Caliber: 9mm Para. or .40 S&W. 10- or 16-rnd. magazine, 4.8-in. bbl., 8.35 in. overall. Weight: 34 oz. Blade front sight, adjustable rear w/3-dot system. Matte black or chrome finish. Checkered walnut or black plastic grips. Imported from 1993 to 1997.
Model P-One blue finish . . . . . . NiB $622 Ex $525 Gd $357
Model P-One chrome finish . . . NiB $693 Ex $556 Gd $393
w/walnut grips, add $50

Old west finish . . . . NiB $515 Ex $405 Gd $305
Bisley model . . . . NiB $510 Ex $355 Gd $275

U22 NEOS . . . . NiB $295 Ex $240 Gd $210
SA Semiauto pistol. .22 LR w/10-rnd. magazine. Bbl length: 4.5 or 6 in. Modular design. Finishes: aqua, black/blue or gray. Weight: 31.5-36 oz. made from 2002 to date.
DLX (adj. trigger, interchangable sights) add $40

BERNARDELLI, VINCENZO S.P.A. — Gardone V. T. (Brescia), Italy

MODEL 60 POCKET . . . . NiB $300 Ex $247 Gd $190
Calibers: .22 LR, .32 Auto (7.65mm), .380 Auto (9mm Short). Eight-round magazine (.22 and .32), 7-rnd. (.380). 3.5-in. bbl., 6.5 in. overall. Weight: About 25 oz. Fixed sights. Blued finish. Bakelite grips. Made 1959-90.

MODEL 68 AUTOMATIC PISTOL . . .NiB $200 Ex $180 Gd $92
Caliber: 6.35. Five- and 8-rnd. magazine, 2.13-in. bbl., 4.13 in. overall. Weight: 10 oz. Fixed sights. Blued or chrome

Bernardelli P018

Bersa Model 85

P-ONE PRACTICAL VB AUTO PISTOL
Similar to Model P One except chambered for 9x21mm w/2-, 4- or 6-port compensating system for IPSC competition. Imported 1993 to 1997.
Model P One
   Practical (2 port) . . . . NiB $1148 Ex $1068 Gd $785
Model P One
   Practical (4 port) . . . . NiB $1259 Ex $1054 Gd $782
Model P One
   Practical (6 port) . . . . NiB $1678 Ex $1393 Gd $995
w/chrome finish, add $75

SPORTER AUTOMATIC PISTOL . NiB $332 Ex $245 Gd $133
Caliber .22 LR. Eight-round magazine, bbl., lengths: 6-, 8- and 10-in., 13 in. overall (10-in. bbl.). weight: About 30 oz. (10-in. bbl.) Target sights. Blued finish. Walnut grips. Made 1949-68.

MODEL USA AUTO PISTOL
Single-action, blowback. Calibers: .22 LR, .32 ACP, .380 ACP. Seven-round magazine or 10-rnd. magazine (.22 LR). 3.5-in. bbl., 6.5 in. overall. Weight: 26.5 oz. Ramped front sight, adjustable rear. Blue or chrome finish. Checkered black bakelite grips w/thumbrest. Imported from 1991 to 1997.
Model USA blue finish . . . . NiB $420 Ex $330 Gd $265
Model USA chrome finish . . . . . NiB $469 Ex $385 Gd $219

VEST POCKET
AUTOMATIC PISTOL . . . . NiB $275 Ex $199 Gd $148
Caliber: .25 Auto (6.35mm). Five- or 8-rnd. magazine, 2.13-in. bbl., 4.13 in. overall. Weight: 9 oz. Fixed sights. Blued finish. Bakelite grips. Made 1945-68.

BERGMANN-BAYNARD — Herstal, Belgium
Manufactured by Avciens Establishment Pieper (AEP).

MODEL 1908 STANDARD
COMMERCIAL . . . . NiB $3400 Ex $2760 Gd $910
Semiauto. Caliber: 9mm Bergmann-Baynard; 6- or 10-rnd., detachable magazine forward of trigger guard. 4-in. bbl.

Sights: blade front, tangent rear. Grip: Checkered wood, lanyard loop. Blued finish. Note: Knight logo on magazine well indicates a commercial Belgian 1908 pistol. Mfg. from 1908-14.
w/slotted grip for stock, add 25%

MODEL 1910 STANDARD
COMMERCIAL . . . . NiB $2755 Ex $2210 Gd $810
Similar to Model 1908 Standard Commercial except w/cutouts in magazine well.

BERSA — Argentina
Currently imported by Eagle Imports, Wanamassa, NJ. Previously by Interarms & Outdoor Sports.

MODEL 83 DA AUTO PISTOL
Similar to the Model 23 except for the following specifications: Caliber: .380 ACP. Seven-round magazine, 3.5-in. bbl., Front blade sight integral on slide, square-notch rear adj. for windage. Blued or satin nickel finish. Custom wood grips. Imported from 1988 to 1994.
Blued finish . . . . NiB $300 Ex $201 Gd $126
Satin nickel . . . . NiB $321 Ex $271 Gd $194

MODEL 85 DA AUTO PISTOL
Same general specifications as Model 83 except 13-rnd. magazine, Imported from 1988 to 1994.
Blued finish . . . . NiB $355 Ex $235 Gd $128
Satin nickel . . . . NiB $377 Ex $286 Gd $179

MODEL 86 DA AUTO PISTOL
Same general specifications as Model 85 except available in matte blued finish and w/Neoprene grips. Imported from 1992 to 1994.
Matte blued finish . . . . NiB $347 Ex $270 Gd $219
Nickel finish . . . . NiB $362 Ex $262 Gd $199

MODEL 95 (THUNDER 380) DA AUTOMATIC PISTOL
Caliber: .380 ACP. Seven-round magazine, 3.5-in. bbl., weight: 23 oz. Grip: checkered polymer panels or wrap around rubber. Blade front and rear notch sights. Imported from 1995 to date.
Blued finish . . . . NiB $280 Ex $214 Gd $158
Nickel finish . . . . NiB $300 Ex $204 Gd $143
Thunder Combat series (smaller beavertail, 8- or
   15-rnd. magazine), add $10
Thunder Plus series (15-rnd. magazine), add $10
Thunder Conceal Carry series (bobbed hammer), add . . . $10

MODEL 97 AUTO PISTOL . . . . NiB $360 Ex $332 Gd $219
Caliber: .380 ACP. Seven-round magazine, 3.3-in. bbl., 6.5 in. overall. Weight: 28 oz. Intro. 1982. Disc.

MODEL 223 . . . . NiB $255 EX $168 GD $125
Same general specifications as Model 383 except in .22 LR w/10-rnd. magazine capacity. Disc. 1987.

MODEL 224 . . . . NiB $255 EX $168 GD $125
Similar to Model 223 except 4-in. bbl., weight: 26 oz. Front blade sight, square-notched rear adj. for windage. Blued finish. Checkered nylon or custom wood grips. Made 1984. SA. disc. 1986.

MODEL 225 . . . . NiB $255 EX $168 GD $125
Similar to Model 224 except 5-in. brrl.

MODEL 226 . . . . NiB $255 EX $168 GD $125
Similar as Model 224 but w/6-in. bbl. Disc. 1987.

Bersa Thunder .380

MODEL 383 AUTO PISTOL
Caliber: .380 Auto. Seven-round magazine, 3.5-in. bbl. Front blade sight integral on slide, square-notched rear sight adj. for windage. Custom wood grips on double-action, nylon grips on single action. Blued or satin nickel finish. Made 1984. SA. disc. 1989.
Double-action . . . . NiB $235 Ex $150 Gd $102
Single-action . . . . NiB $219 Ex $158 Gd $122

MODEL 622 AUTO PISTOL . . . NiB $204 Ex $138 Gd $100
Caliber: .22 LR. Seven-round magazine, 4- or 6-in. bbl., 7 or 9 in. overall. Weight: 2.25 lbs. Blade front sight, square-notch rear adj. for windage. Blued finish. Nylon grips. Made 1982-87.

MODEL 644 AUTO PISTOL . . . NiB $286 Ex $240 Gd $168
Caliber: .22 LR. 10-rnd. magazine, 3.5-in. bbl., weight: 26.5 oz. 6.5 in. overall. Adj. rear sight, blade front. Contoured black nylon grips. Made 1980-88.

MODEL BPCC . . . . NiB $390 Ex $310 Gd $230
Semiauto. Striker-fired. Caliber: .380 ACP, 9mm or .40 S&W; 8-rnd. magazine. 3.3-in bbl. Frame: polymer. Sights: fixed, 3-dot. Finish: numerous. Grip: textured polymer. Length: 6.83-in. Weight: 21.5 oz. Made 2010 to date.

THUNDER PRO . . . . NiB $470 Ex $360 Gd $260
Semiauto. DA/SA. Caliber: 9mm, .40 S&W, or .45 ACP.; 13-, 17, or 7-rnd. magazine. 4.25-in. bbl. Frame: alloy. Sights: fixed, low-profile. Finish: two-tone or matte black. Grip: textured polymer. Length: 7.56-in. Weight: 30.7 oz. Made 2004 to date.
Ultra Compact model (3.2-in. bbl.), subtract $10
XT model (adj. sights) add, ... $20

THUNDER 9 AUTO PISTOL . . . NiB $408 Ex $272 Gd $168
Caliber: 9mm Para. 15-rnd. magazine, 4-in. bbl., 7.38 in. overall. Weight: 30 oz. Blade front sight, adj. rear w/3-dot system. AmbidExtrous safety and decocking device. Matte blued finish. Checkered black polymer grips. Made 1993-96.

THUNDER .22 (MODEL 23)
Caliber: .22 LR, 10-rnd. magazine, 3.5-in. bbl., 6.63 in. overall. Weight: 24.5 oz. Notched-bar dovetailed rear, blade integral w/slide front. Black polymer grips. Made 1988-98, reintro. 2012.
Blued finish . . . . NiB $254 Ex $214 Gd $168
Nickel finish . . . . NiB $260 Ex $220 Gd $177

THUNDER 380
Caliber: .380 ACP. Seven-round magazine, 3.5-in. bbl., 6.63 in. overall. Weight: 25.75 oz. Notched-bar dovetailed rear, blade integral w/slide front. Blued, satin nickel, or Duo-Tone finish. Made 1995-98.

Blued finish . . . . NiB $306 Ex $230 Gd $183
Satin nickel finish . . . . NiB $333 Ex $255 Gd $204
Duo-Tone finish . . . . NiB $306 Ex $230 Gd $168

THUNDER .380 PLUS AUTO PISTOL
Same as Thunder 380 except has 10-rnd. magazine and weight: 26 oz. Made 1995-97.
Matte finish . . . . NiB $306 Ex $230 Gd $168
Satin nickel finish . . . ., . . NiB $321 Ex $245 Gd $194
Duo-Tone finish, add. $40

BOBERG ARMS CORP — White Bear Lake, MN
Boberg purchased by Bond Arms in 2016.

MODEL XR9-S . . . . NiB $980 Ex $860 Gd $660
DAO. Semiauto. Reverse feed system. Caliber: 9mm; 6-rnd. magazine. 3.5-in. bbl. Frame: polymer. Sights: fixed, low-profile, 3-dot. Finish: two-tone. Grip: textured polymer. Length: 8.3-in. Weight: 17.4 oz. Made 2013-16.
L model (4.2-in. bbl.), add $10

MODEL XR45-S . . . . NiB $1060 Ex $810 Gd $810
Similar to XR9-S except in .45 ACP. Made 2014-16.

BOND ARMS INC — Granbury, TX
Established 1995.

TEXAS DEFENDER . . . . NiB $430 Ex $330 Gd $260
O/U derringer with optional barrels in the following calibers: .22 LR, .22 WMR, .32 H&R Mag., .327 Fed. Mag., .380 ACP. .38 Spl., .357 Mag., 9mm, .40 S&W, .44-40, .44 Spl., .45 ACP, .45 LC/.410 gauge. Break action. SA spit trigger. Grips: checkered rosewood. Made 1995 to present.
Backup (2.5-in. brrl., rubber grip,
    2014-present) . . . . NiB $430 Ex $330 Gd $260
Bond Mini (2.5-in. brrl.,
    2012-present) . . . . NiB $410 Ex $310 Gd $230
Century 2000 Defender (2.5- or
    3-in. brrl., 1995-present) . . . . NiB $445 Ex $335 Gd $245
Cowboy Defender (3-in. brrl.,
    1995-present) . . . . NiB $430 Ex $330 Gd $260
Mama Bear (2.5-in. brrl.,
    2015-present) . . . . NiB $410 Ex $310 Gd $230
Papa Bear (2.5-in. brrl.,
    2015-present) . . . . NiB $430 Ex $330 Gd $260
Patriot (3-in. brrl., extended grip,
    2015-present) . . . . NiB $520 Ex $390 Gd $290
Ranger (4.25-in. brrl., extended grip,
    2008-15) . . . . NiB $630 Ex $480 Gd $350
Ranger II (4.25-in. brrl., extended grip, trigger
    guard, 2011-present) . . . . NiB $630 Ex $480 Gd $350
Snake Slayer (3-in. brrl., extended grip,
    2005-present) . . . . NiB $490 Ex $370 Gd $280

Bond Arms Texas Defender

Snake Slayer IV (4.25-in. brrl., extended grip,
2005-present) . . . . NiB $530 Ex $400 Gd $300
Super Defender (3-in. brrl.,
2003-04) . . . . NiB $305 Ex $230 Gd $170
Texas Defender (3-in. bbl., trigger guard,
20 oz., 1995-date) . . . . NiB $540 Ex $465 Gd $355
Texas Ranger Special (3-in. brrl., trigger guard,
limited ed. 2012) . . . . NiB $1200 Ex $920 Gd $800
USA Defender (3-in. brrl.,
2012-15) . . . . NiB $515 Ex $390 Gd $290

BULLPUP . . . . NiB $955 Ex $830 Gd $655
Similar to Boberg Arms XR9. Caliber: 9mm, 7-rnd magazine capacity. Barrel: 4.35-in. Reverse feed system. Weight: 17.5 oz. Grip: engraved rosewood. 2017-date.

BREN 10 — Huntington Beach, CA

Original mfg. by Dornaus & Dixon Ent., Inc. (1983-86) in Huntington Beach, CA.

Bren 10

STANDARD . . . . NiB $2460 Ex $1880 Gd $980
Semiauto. Selective DA trigger. Caliber: 10mm; 11-rnd. magazine. 5-in. bbl. Sights: fixed, low-profile, 3-dot. Finish: two-tone. Serial number prefix: 83SM. Made 1984-86.
Military/Police model (DA/SA trigger, Serial # prefix: 83MP,
Made 1984–86.), add $200
Special Forces Model D (DA/SA trigger, 4-in. brrl., dark finish,
Serial # prefix: SFD, Made 1986.), add $225
Special Forces Model L (DA/SA trigger, 4-in. brrl., light finish,
Serial # prefix: SFL, Made 1986.), add $225

- Recent mfg. by Vltor Mfg. (2010-11) -
SM SERIES . . . . NiB $1100 Ex $880 Gd $660
Semiauto. DA/SA trigger. Caliber: 10mm or .45 ACP; 10- or 15-rnd. magazine. 5-in. bbl. Sights: fixed, low-profile, 3-dot. Finish: blue slide/stainless frame. Rare, few manufactured. Made 2010-11.
SMV Series (stainless frame/hard chrome slide), add $80

BROLIN ARMS — La Verne, CA

"LEGEND SERIES" SA AUTOMATIC PISTOL
Caliber: .45 ACP. Seven-round magazine, 4- or 5-in. bbl., weight: 32-36 oz. Walnut grips. Single action, full size, compact, or full size frame compact slide. Matte blued finish. Lowered and flared ejection port. Made 1995-98.
Model L45 . . . . NiB $469 Ex $398 Gd $306
Model L45C . . . . NiB $487 Ex $366 Gd $305
Model L45T . . . . NiB $487 Ex $366 Gd $305

"PATRIOT SERIES" SA AUTOMATIC PISTOL
Caliber: .45 ACP. Seven-round magazine, 3.25- and 4-in. bbl., weight: 33-37 oz. Wood grips. Fixed rear sights. Made 1996-97.

Model P45 . . . . NiB $627 Ex $469 Gd $301
Model P45C (disc. 1997) . . . . . NiB $638 Ex $479 Gd $311
Model P45T (disc. 1997) . . . . . . NiB $658 Ex $551 Gd $372

"PRO-STOCK AND PRO-COMP" SA PISTOL
Caliber: .45 ACP. Eight-round magazine, 4- or 5-in. bbl., weight: 37 oz. Single action, blued or two-tone finish. Wood grips. Bomar adjustable sights. Made 1996-97.
Model Pro comp . . . . NiB $872 Ex $663 Gd $566
Model Pro stock . . . . NiB $714 Ex $551 Gd $475

TAC SERIES
Caliber: .45 ACP. Eight-round magazine, 5-in. bbl., 8.5 in. overall. Weight: 37 oz. Low profile combat or Tritium sights. Beavertail grip safety. Matte blue, chrome or two-tone finish. Checkered wood or contoured black rubber grips. Made 1997-98.
Model TAC 11 service . . . . NiB $643 Ex $510 Gd $398
Model TAC 11 compact . . . . . . NiB $653 Ex $531 Gd $419
w/Tritium sights, add $100

BANTAM MODEL . . . . NiB $403 Ex $283 Gd $ 204
Caliber: 9mmPara., .40 S&W. Single or double-action, super compact size, concealed hammer, all steel construction; 3-dot sights; royal blue or matte finish. Manufactured 1999 only.

BRONCO — Eibar, Spain

Manufactured by Echave y Arizmendi.

**MODEL 1918 POCKET
AUTOMATIC PISTOL** . . . . NiB $180 Ex $129 Gd $92
Caliber: .32 ACP (7.65mm). Six-round magazine 2.5-in. bbl., 5 in. overall. Weight: 20 oz. Fixed sights. Blued finish. Hard rubber grips. Made circa 1918- to 1925.

VEST POCKET AUTO PISTOL . . . NiB $165 Ex $128 Gd $66
Caliber: .25 ACP, 6-rnd. magazine, 2.13-in. bbl., 4.13 in. over-all. Weight: 11 oz. Fixed sights. Blued finish. Hard rubber grips. Made 1919-35.

BROWNING — Morgan, UT

The following Browning pistols have been manufactured by Fabrique Nationale d'Armes de Guerre (now Fabrique Nationale Herstal) of Herstal, Belgium, by Arms Technology Inc. of Salt Lake City and by J. P. Sauer & Sohn of Eckernforde, W. Germany. See also FN Browning and J.P. Sauer & Sohn listings.

1911-22 SERIES . . . . NiB $599 EX $530 GD $520
1911 style platform. Semiauto. SA. Caliber: .22 LR, 10-rnd. magazine. 4.25-in. bbl. Frame: alloy. Sights: fixed. Finish:

**Browning
Model 25 Automatic**

**Browning
BDA .380 Nickel Finish**

**Browning
Buck Mark 5.5 Field**

**Browning
Buck Mark Bullseye**

**Browning
Buck Mark Plus**

**Browning
BDM 9mm DA**

matte black. Grip: checkered walnut. Length: 7.37 in. Weight: 15 oz. Made 2011 to date.
Compact (3.62-in. bbl.)...... NiB $599 Ex $530 Gd $520
Black Label Series.......... NiB $639 Ex $600 Gd $580
Black Label Series Compact
   (3.62-in. bbl.) .... NiB $639 Ex $600 Gd $580
Black Label Series Suppressor Ready, add............. $90

.25 AUTOMATIC PISTOL
Same general specifications as FN Browning Baby (see separate listing). Standard Model, blued finish, hard rubber grips. Light Model, nickel-plated, Nacrolac pearl grips. Renaissance Model, nickel-plated, Nacrolac pearl grips. Made by FN 1955-69.
Standard model............NiB $587 Ex $534 Gd $283
Lightweight model ....NiB $592 Ex $540 Gd $294
Renaissance model ....NiB $1121 Ex $867 Gd $539

.32 AND .380 AUTOMATIC PISTOL, 1955 TYPE
Same general specifications as FN Browning .32 (7.65mm) and .380 Pocket Auto. Standard Model, Renaissance Engraved Model as furnished in .25 Automatic. Made by FN 1955-69.
Standard model (.32 ACP)..... NiB $507 Ex $386 Gd $291
Standard model (.380 ACP).... NiB $454 Ex $376 Gd $283
Renaissance model ....NiB $1121 Ex $918 Gd $740

.380 AUTOMATIC PISTOL, 1971 TYPE
Same as .380 Automatic, 1955 Type except has longer slide, 4.44-in. bbl., is 7.06 in. overall, weight: 23 oz. Rear sight adj. for windage and elevation, plastic thumbrest grips. Made 1971-75.
Standard model............NiB $509 Ex $387 Gd $294
Renaissance model ....NiB $1132 Ex $913 Gd $616

BDA .380 DA AUTOMATIC PISTOL
Caliber: .380 Auto. 10- or 13-rnd. magazine, bbl. length: 3.81 in., 6.75 in. overall. Weight: 23 oz. Fixed blade front sight, square-notch drift-adj. rear sight. Blued or nickel finish. Smooth walnut grips. Made 1982-97 by Beretta.
Blued finish .... NiB $730 Ex $454 Gd $284
Nickel finish, add............................... $80

BDA DA AUTOMATIC PISTOL
Similar to SIG-Sauer P220. Calibers: 9mm Para., .38 Super Auto, .45 Auto. Nine-round magazine (9mm and .38), 7-rnd. (.45 cal), 4.4-in. bbl., 7.8 in. overall. Weight: 29.3 oz. Fixed sights. Blued finish. Plastic grips. Made 1977-80 by J. P. Sauer.
9mm, .45 ACP.............NiB $900 Ex $550 Gd $380
.38 Super ....NiB $1180 Ex $710 Gd $530

BDM SERIES AUTOMATIC PISTOLS
Calibers: 9mm Para., 10-rnd. magazine, 4.73-in. bbl., 7.85 in. overall. Weight: 31 oz., windage adjustable sights w/3-dot system. Low profile removable blade front sights. Matte blued, Bi-Tone or silver chrome finish. Selectable shooting mode and decocking safety lever. Made 1991-97.
Standard ....NiB $622 Ex $499 Gd $333
Practical ....NiB $598 Ex $490 Gd $373
Silver Chrome finish ....NiB $693 Ex $509 Gd $384

BLACK LABEL 1911-380 SERIES ... NiB $560 EX $460 GD $330
1911 style platform. Semiauto. SA. Caliber: .380 ACP, 8-rnd. magazine. 4.25-in. bbl. Frame: alloy. Sights: fixed. Finish: matte black. Grip: checkered polymer. Length: 7.5 in. Weight: 17.5 oz. Made 2015 to date. Pro models disc. 2020.
Compact (3.62-in. bbl.)........ NiB $530 Ex $410 Gd $370
Medallion Pro Series
   (rosewood grips, 2017-present) . NiB $660 Ex $480 Gd $380
Pro Series (G10 grips, 2016-20) .... NiB $680 Ex $510 Gd $380
Pro Series w/ rail, add $75
Pro Series Compact
   (3.62-in. bbl.) .... NiB $660 Ex $480 Gd $380
Pro Series Compact w/ rail, add....................$20

BUCK MARK AUTOMATIC PISTOL
Caliber: .22 LR. 10-rnd. magazine, 5.5-in. bbl., 9.5 in. overall. Weight: 32 oz. Black molded grips. Adj. rear sight. Blued or nickel finish. Made 1985 to date.
Blued finish................NiB $342 Ex $221 Gd $143
Nickel finish ....NiB $403 Ex $285 Gd $203

BUCK MARK BULLSEYE
Same general specifications as the standard Buck Mark 22 except w/7.25-in. fluted barrel, 11.83 in. overall. Weight: 36 oz. Adjustable target trigger. Undercut post front sight, click-adjustable Pro-Target rear. Laminated, Rosewood, black rubber or composite grips. Made 1996-2006.
Standard model (composite grips).. NiB $487 Ex $344 Gd $249
Target model...............NiB $475 Ex $316 Gd $219

BUCK MARK
BULLSEYE TARGET .... NiB $487 Ex $344 Gd $249
Caliber: .22 LR. 10-rnd. magazine, 7.25-in. fluted bbl., 11.83 in. overall. Weight: 31 oz. Rosewood wrap- around finger groove grips w/matte blued finish. Made 1996-2005.

BUCK MARK CAMPER . . . . NiB $300 Ex $210 Gd $150
Similar to Buckmark except w/5.5-in. heavy bbl., matte blued or satin nickel finish. Black polymer grips. Made 1999-2012.
Stainless . . . . NiB $320 Ex $230 Gd $17
Camper UFX (2013-present) . . . . NiB $300 Ex $200 Gd $155
Camper UFX stainless (2013-present), add $30
Camper URX stainless (gold trigger, 2016-present), add $80

BUCK MARK CHALLENGER . . NiB $345 Ex $220 Gd $165
Similar to Buckmark except w/smaller grip. 5.5-in. bbl., matte blued finish. Made 1999-2010.
Micro Challenge (4-in. bbl.). . . . NiB $300 Ex $210 Gd $155

BUCK MARK 5.5 FIELD . . . . . . NiB $487 Ex $344 Gd $249
Similar to Buck Mark 5.5 Target except w/standard sights. Made 1991-2011.

BUCK MARK 5.5 TARGET
Caliber: .22 LR. 10-rnd. magazine, 5.5-in. bbl., 9.6 in. overall. Weight: 35.5 oz. Pro target sights. Wrap-around walnut or contoured finger groove grips. Made 1990-2009.
Matte blue finish. . . . . NiB $455 Ex $374 Gd $223
Nickel finish (1994 to date) . . . NiB $499 Ex $395 Gd $245
Gold finish (1991-99) . . . . NiB $385 Ex $270 Gd $184

BUCK MARK HUNTER . . . . NiB $385 EX $255 GD $200
7.25-in. brrl., Adj. sights, wood grip. Made 2015 to present.

BUCK MARK LITE SPLASH URX . . . NiB $375 Ex $235 Gd $200
Similar to Buck Mark except w/5.5- or 7.25-in. rnd. aluminum bbl. sleeve. TruGlo fibrtr optic sights. Made 2006-09.

BUCK MARK MICRO
Same general specifications as standard Buck Mark except w/4-in. bbl., 8 in. overall. Weight: 32 oz. Molded composite grips. Ramp front sight, Pro Target rear sight. URX grip introduced in 2007. Made 1992-2013.
Blued finish. . . . . NiB $367 Ex $271 Gd $181
Nickel finish . . . . NiB $418 Ex $321 Gd $244
Stainless finish. . . . . NiB $367 Ex $271 Gd $181

BUCK MARK MICRO PLUS
Same specifications as the Buck Mark Micro except ambidextrous, laminated wood grips. Made 1996-2001.
Blued finish. . . . . NiB $285 Ex $234 Gd $192
Nickel finish . . . . NiB $382 Ex $321 Gd $204

BUCK MARK PLUS
Same general specifications as standard Buck Mark except for black molded, impregnated hardwood grips. Made 1987-2007.
Blued finish. . . . . NiB $383 Ex $321 Gd $204
Nickel finish . . . . NiB $404 Ex $329 Gd $223
Plus UDX (2010-present) . . . . . . NiB $440 Ex $285 Gd $225
Plus UDX stainless (2010-present), add $30
Field Plus UDX (2010-present) . . NiB $400 Ex $280 Gd $210
Plus Practical UDX (2017-present) . . . NiB $385 Ex $310 Gd $200
Plus UDX Rosewood (2016-present) . . . NiB $440 Ex $285 Gd $225

BUCK MARK SILHOUETTE. . . . NiB $544 Ex $372 Gd $220
Similar to standard Buck Mark except for 9.88-in. bbl. Weight: 53 oz. Target sights mounted on full-length scope base, and laminated hardwood grips and forend. Made 1987-99.

BUCK MARK UNLIMITED
SILHOUETTE. . . . . NiB $547 Ex $431 Gd $285
Same general specifications as standard Buck Mark Silhouette except w/14-in. bbl., 18.69 in. overall. Weight: 64 oz.

**Browning
Buck Mark Silhouette**

**Browning
Buck Mark 5.5 Target**

**Browning
Buck Mark Micro Plus**

**Browning Challenger
Standard Model**

**Browning Challenger
Renaissance Model**

**Browning
Challenger III Sporter**

**Browning
9mm Hi-Power w/Molded Grips**

**Browning
9mm Hi-Power AmbidExtrous Safety**

**Browning
Hi-Power Captain**

Interchangeable post front sight and Pro Target rear. Nickel finish. Made 1991-99.

BUCK MARK VARMINT
AUTO PISTOL. . . . . NiB $346 Ex $282 Gd $230
Same general specifications as standard Buck Mark except for 9.88-in. bbl. Weight: 48 oz. No sights, full-length scope base, and laminated hardwood grips. Made 1987-99.

CHALLENGER AUTOMATIC PISTOL
Semiauto pistol. Caliber: .22 LR. 10-rnd. magazine, bbl. lengths: 4.5 and 6.75-in. 11.44 in. overall (w/ 6.75-in. bbl.). Weight: 38 oz. (6.75-in. bbl.). Removable blade front sight, screw adj. rear. Standard finish, blued, also furnished gold inlaid (Gold model) and engraved and chrome-plated (Renaissance model). Checkered walnut grips. Finely figured and carved grips on Gold and Renaissance models. Standard made by FN 1962-75, higher grades. Intro. 1971. Disc.
Standard model. . . . . NiB $790 Ex $610 Gd $480
Gold model. . . . . NiB $3500 Ex $1955 Gd $1742
Renaissance model . . . . NiB $3400 Ex $1910 Gd $1744

CHALLENGER II . . . . NiB $480 Ex $380 Gd $210
Same general specifications as Challenger Standard model w/6.75-in. bbl. except changed grip angle and impregnated hardwood grips. Original Challenger design modified for lower production costs. Made by ATI from 1976 to 1983.

CHALLENGER III . . . . NiB $430 Ex $305 Gd $180
Same general description as Challenger II except has 5.5 in. bull bbl., alloy frame and new sight system. Weight: 35 oz. Made 1982-84. Sporter Model w/6.75-in. bbl. Made 1982-85.

HI-POWER AUTOMATIC PISTOL
Same general specifications as FN Browning Model 1935 except chambered for 9mm Para., .30 Luger or .40 S&W. 10- or 13-rnd. magazine, 4.63-in. bbl., 7.75 in. overall. Weight: 32 oz. (9mm) or 35 oz. (.40 S&W). Fixed sights, also available w/rear sight adj. for windage and elevation, and ramp front sight. AmbidExtrous safety added after 1989. Standard model blued, chrome-plated or Bi-Tone finish. Checkered walnut, contour-molded Polyamide or wraparound rubber grips. Renaissance Engraved model chrome-plated, w/Nacrolac pearl grips. Made by FN from 1954 to 1988, assembled in Portugal 1989-2017. Disc. 2018.
Standard model (mfg. 1954-88,
   fixed sights, 9mm). . . . . NiB $1030 Ex $780 Gd $430
Standard model (mfg. 1989-2017,
   fixed sights, 9mm). . . . . NiB $910 Ex $689 Gd $510
Standard model, fixed sights,
   .40 S&W (intro. 1995). . . . . . NiB $784 Ex $683 Gd $582
Standard model,
   .30 Luger (1986-89) . . . . NiB $942 Ex $702 Gd $489
Renaissance model,
   fixed sights . . . . NiB $3900 Ex $3651 Gd $2688
w/adjustable rear sight, add $75
w/ambidextrous safety, add $110
w/moulded grips, deduct $50
w/tangent rear sight (1965-78), add* $315
w/T-Slot grip & tangent sight (1965-78), add* $620
*Check with FN to certify serial number.

HI-POWER CAPTAIN . . . . NiB $980 Ex $760 Gd $430
Similar to the standard Hi-Power except fitted w/adj. 500-meter tangent rear sight and rounded hammer. Made 1993-2000.

Browning
Hi-Power Mark III

Browning
Hi-Power Practical

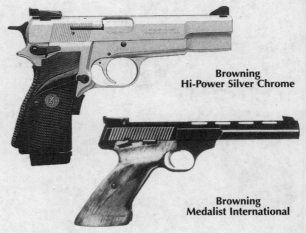

Browning
Hi-Power Silver Chrome

Browning
Medalist International

HI-POWER MARK III . . . . **NiB $880 Ex $510 Gd $398**
Calibers: 9mm or .40 S&W. 10-rnd. magazine, 4.75-in. bbl.,
7.75 in. overall. Weight: 32 oz. Fixed sights with molded grips.
Durable non-glare matte blue or black epoxy finish. Made
1985-2000; reintro. 2002 to 2017.

HI-POWER PRACTICAL
Similar to standard Hi-Power except has silver-chromed
frame and blued slide w/Commander-style hammer. Made
1991-2006.
w/fixed sights . . . . **NiB $960 Ex $710 Gd $430**
w/adj. sights, add **$50**

HI-POWER SILVER CHROME . . **NiB $960 Ex $710 Gd $430**
Calibers: 9mm or .40 S&W. 10-rnd. magazine, 4.75-in. bbl.,
7.75 in. overall. Weight: 36 oz. Adjustable sights with Pachmayer
grips. Silver-chromed finish. Made 1991-2000.

HI-POWER 9MM CLASSIC
Limited Edition 9mm Hi-Power, w/silver-gray finish, high-grade
engraving and finely-checkered walnut grips w/double border.
Proposed production of the Classic was 5000 w/less than half
that number produced. Gold Classic limited to 500 w/two-
thirds proposed production in circulation. Made 1985-86.
Gold classic . . . . **NiB $4610 Ex $3110 Gd $3000**
Standard classic . . . . **NiB $2460 Ex $1510 Gd $1000**

INTERNATIONAL MEDALIST EARLY MODEL
TARGET PISTOL . . . . **NiB $1300 Ex $860 Gd $610**
Modification of Medalist to conform w/International Shooting
Union rules. 5.9-in. bbl., Smaller grip with no forearm. Weight:
42 oz. Made 1970-73. Subtract 30% for post 1974 models.

MEDALIST AUTOMATIC TARGET PISTOL
Caliber: .22 LR. 10-rnd. magazine, 6.75-in. bbl. w/VR,
11.94 in. overall. Weight: 46 oz. Removable blade front
sight, click-adj. micrometer rear. Standard finish, blued
also furnished gold-inlaid (Gold Model) and engraved and
chrome-plated (Renaissance Model). Checkered walnut
grips w/thumbrest (for right- or left-handed shooter). Finely
figured and carved grips on Gold and Renaissance Models.
Made by FN from 1962 to 1975. Higher grades. Intro. 1971.
Standard model. . . . . **NiB $1860 Ex $1160 Gd $830**
Gold model. . . . . **NiB $4600 Ex $2800 Gd $2000**
Renaissance model . . . . **NiB $5660 Ex $3510 Gd $3000**

NOMAD AUTOMATIC PISTOL. . . **NiB $610 Ex $410 Gd $330**
Caliber: .22 LR. 10-rnd. magazine, bbl. lengths: 4.5 and 6.75-
in., 8.94 in. overall (4.5-in. bbl.). Weight: 34 oz. (w/ 4.5-in.
bbl.). Removable blade front sight, screw adj. rear. Blued finish.
Plastic grips. Made by FN from 1962 to 1974.

PRO-9/PRO-40 . . . . **NiB $555 Ex $455 Gd $345**
Mfg. by FHN USA. DA/SA trigger Caliber: 9mm or .40 S&W,
16- (9mm) or 14-rnd (.40 S&W) magazine. Barrel: 4-in. Grips:
Textured composite, with modular backstrap inserts. Weight:

30 oz. Finish: black polymer frame, stainless steel slide. Mfg.
2003-06.

RENAISSANCE 9MM, .25 AUTO AND .380 AUTO (1955)
ENGRAVED, CASED SET . . . **NiB $9600 Ex $6610 Gd $5000**
One pistol of each of the three models in a special walnut or black
vinyl carrying case, all chrome-plated w/Nacrolac pearl grips.
Made by FN from 1954 to 1969. Options and engraving varies.

BRYCO ARMS INC. — Irvine, CA
Distributed by Jennings Firearms. Inc. Carson City, NV.

MODELS J22, J25 AUTO PISTOL
Calibers: .22 LR, .25 ACP. Six-round magazine, 2.5-in. bbl.,
about 5 in. overall. Weight: 13 oz. Fixed sights. Chrome, satin
nickel or black Teflon finish. Walnut, grooved black Cycolac or
resin-impregnated wood grips. Made 1981-85.
Model J-22 (disc. 1985) . . . . **NiB $73 Ex $56 Gd $45**
Model J-25 (disc. 1995) . . . . **NiB $123 Ex $90 Gd $75**

MODELS M25, M32, M38 AUTO PISTOL
Calibers: .25 ACP, .32 ACP, .380 ACP. Six-round magazine,
2.81-in. bbl., 5.31 in. overall. Weight: 11oz. to 15 oz. Fixed
sights. Chrome, satin nickel or black Teflon finish. Walnut,
grooved, black Cycolac or resin-impregnated wood grips.
Made 1988-2000.
Model M25 (disc.). . . . . **NiB $119 Ex $92 Gd $74**
Model M32 . . . . **NiB $143 Ex $102 Gd $77**
Model M38 . . . . **NiB $147 Ex $108 Gd $91**

MODEL M48 AUTO PISTOL. . . . **NiB $128 Ex $102 Gd $81**
Calibers: .22 LR, .32 ACP, .380 ACP. Seven-round magazine, 4-in. bbl., 6.69 in. overall. Weight: 20 oz. Fixed sights.
Chrome, satin nickel or black Teflon finish. Smooth wood or
black Teflon grips. Made 1989-95.

**Browning
Medalist Automatic Target**

**Budischowsky
Model TP-70**

MODEL M58. . . . . NiB $132 Ex $108 Gd $90
Caliber: .380 ACP. 10-rnd. magazine, 3.75-in. bbl., 5.5 in. overall. Weight: 30 oz. Fixed sights. Chrome, satin nickel, blued or black Teflon finish. Smooth wood or black Teflon grips. Made 1993-95.

MODEL M59 AUTO PISTOL. . . . NiB $128 Ex $102 Gd $82
Caliber: 9mm Para. 10-rnd. magazine, 4-in. bbl., 6.5 in. overall. Weight: 33 oz. Fixed sights. Chrome, satin nickel, blued or black Teflon finish. Smooth wood or black Teflon grips. Made 1994-96.

MODEL NINE . . . . NiB $171 Ex $136 Gd $112
Similar to Bryco/Jennings Model M59 except w/redesigned slide w/loaded chamber indicator and frame mounted ejector. Weight: 30 oz. Made 1997-2003.

MODEL 5 AUTO PISTOL . . . . NiB $102 Ex $69 Gd $46
Caliber: .380 ACP, 9mm Para.; 10- or 12-shot magazine. Bbl: 3.25 in. Blue or nickel finish, black synthetic grips. Weight: 36 oz. Disc. 1995.

BUDISCHOWSKY — Mt. Clemens, MI

Mfd. by Norton Armament Corporation

TP-70 DA AUTOMATIC PISTOL
Calibers: .22 LR, .25 Auto. Six-round magazine, 2.6-in. bbl., 4.65 in. overall. Weight: 12.3 oz. Fixed sights. Stainless steel. Plastic grips. Made 1973-77.
.22 LR . . . . NiB $487 Ex $361 Gd $372
.25 ACP . . . . NiB $362 Ex $249 Gd $192

BUSHMASTER FIREARMS — Huntsville, AL

Formerly Ilion, NY, and Windham, Maine. Purchased by Freedom Group Inc. 2011. Part of Remington bankruptcy in 2020; purchased by Franklin Armory Holdings.

BUSHMASTER PISTOL . . . . NIB $630 EX $460 GD $380
AK-47 design except 11.5-in. bbl. 1986-88.

CARBON-15 SERIES
AR-15 type. Semiauto. Lightweight carbon fiber upper and lower. Caliber: 5.56 NATO. 7.25-in. bbl. w/flash hider. Grip: A2 style. Sights: ghost ring. Made 2003-12.
P21S . . . . NiB $730 Ex $560 Gd $410
P97S . . . . NiB $700 Ex $530 Gd $380
9mm . . . . NiB $790 Ex $630 Gd $480

PIT VIPER AP-21 . . . . NiB $730 Ex $560 Gd $410
AR-15 type. Semiauto. Alloy upper and lower. Caliber: 5.56 NATO. 7.25-in. bbl. w/flash hider. Grip: A2 style. Sights: ghost ring. Made 2011 only.

XM-15 SERIES
AR-15 type. Semiauto. Alloy upper and lower. Caliber: 5.56 NATO. 7- or 10.5-in. bbl. w/flash hider. Made 2013-15.
Enhanced Patrolman's
(Magpul MOE grip) . . . . NiB $1000 Ex $760 Gd $560
Patrolman's (A2 grip) . . . . NiB $830 Ex $610 Gd $460

CALICO LIGHT WEAPONS SYSTEM — Hillsboro, OR

MODEL 110 AUTO PISTOL . . . NiB $580 Ex $576 Gd $486
Caliber: .22 LR. 100-rnd. magazine, 6-in. bbl., 17.9 in. overall. Weight: 3.75 lbs. Adj. post front sight, fixed U-notch rear. Black finish aluminum frame. Molded composition grip. Made 1986-94.

MODEL M-950 AUTO PISTOL . NiB $780 Ex $660 Gd $362
Caliber: 9mm Para. 50- or 100-rnd. magazine, 7.5-in. bbl., 14 in. overall. Weight: 2.25 lbs. Adj. post front sight, fixed U-notch rear. Glass-filled polymer grip. Made 1989-94.

CANIK — Turkey
See Century Arms.

CARACAL — Abu Dhabi, UAE

MODEL C . . . . NiB $560 Ex $460 Gd $340
Semiauto. Striker-fire. Glock style trigger safety. Caliber: 9mm, 15-rnd. magazine, 3.5-in. bbl., 6.6 in. overall. Weight: 24.6 oz. Fixed sights. Finish: Matte black. Polymer frame. Made 2006 to date.
Model SC (3.3-in. bbl., 13-rnd.) . . . NiB $560 Ex $460 Gd $340
Model F (4.1-in. bbl., 18-rnd.) . . . . NiB $560 Ex $460 Gd $340

Caracal Model F

CENTURY ARMS — Delray Beach, FL

Formerly Century Arms International, importer of military surplus firearms. In 2015 named changed to Century Arms with continued import of new firearms and U.S.-made AK-47 platform firearms.

TP9 (CANIK55) . . . . NiB $350 Ex $320 Gd $300
Similar to Walther P99 platform. Semiauto. DAO. Caliber: 9mm, 17-rnd. magazine, 4.07-in. bbl., 6.75 in. overall. Weight: 29 oz. Fixed sights. Finish: Matte black. Polymer frame. Made 2013-15.
**TP9v2 (Imported from
2015 to present)** . . . . NiB $350 Ex $320 Gd $300

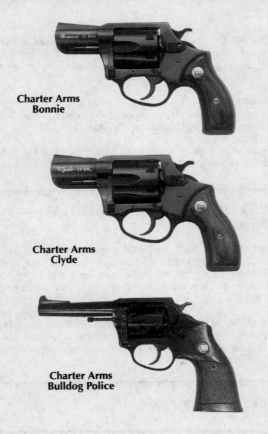

**Charter Arms
Bonnie**

**Charter Arms
Clyde**

**Charter Arms
Bulldog Police**

PAP M85 NP . . . . **NiB $630 Ex $560 Gd $370**
Similar to AK-47 platform. Semiauto. Caliber: 5.56x45mm, 30-rnd. magazine, 10-in. bbl., 19.7 in. overall. Weight: 6.4 lbs. Fixed sights. Finish: blued. Krinkov style muzzle brake and hinged dust cover. Stamped receiver. Made in U.S. from 2013 to date.

PAP M92 PV . . . . **NiB $530 Ex $550 Gd $350**
Similar to AK-47 platform. Semiauto. Caliber: 7.62x39mm, 30-rnd. magazine, 10-in. bbl., 19.7 in. overall. Weight: 6.4 lbs. Fixed sights. Finish: blued. Krinkov style muzzle brake. Stamped receiver. Made in U.S. from 2013 to date.

CHARLES DALY — Dayton, OH
See Daly, Charles.

CHARTER ARMS — Shelton, CT

Formerly Charter 2000 and ChartArmsms Corp. (Ansonia, CT). Established in 1962 Charter Arms has gone through several names changes. Models name and features are similar; recent manufacture noted.

MODEL 40 AUTOMATIC PISTOL . **NiB $283 Ex $224 Gd $171**
Caliber: .22 LR. Eight-round magazine, 3.3-in. bbl., 6.3 in. overall. Weight: 21.5 oz. Fixed sights. Checkered walnut grips. Stainless steel finish. Made 1985-86.

**MODEL 79K DA
AUTOMATIC PISTOL** . . . . **NiB $362 Ex $286 Gd $230**
Calibers: .380 or .32 Auto. Seven-round magazine, 3.6-in. bbl.,

6.5 in. overall. Weight: 24.5 oz. Fixed sights. Checkered walnut grips. Stainless steel finish. Made 1985-86.

BONNIE AND CLYDE SET . . . . **NiB $454 Ex $342 Gd $297**
Matching pair of shrouded 2.5-in. bbl., revolvers chambered for .32 Magnum (Bonnie) and .38 Special (Clyde). Blued finish w/scrolled name on bbls. Made 1989-90 and 1999.

BULLDOG .44 DA REVOLVER
SA/DA revolver. Caliber: .44 Special. Five-round cylinder, 2.5- or 3-in. bbl., 7 or 7.5 in. overall. Weight: 19 or 19.5 oz. Fixed sights. Blued, nickel-plated or stainless finish. Checkered walnut Bulldog or square buttgrips. Made 1973-96.
**Blued finish/
  Pocket Hammer (2.5-in.)** . . . . **NiB $260 Ex $192 Gd $134**
**Blued finish/Bulldog grips
  (3-in. disc. 1988)** . . . . **NiB $244 Ex $206 Gd $147**
Electroless nickel. . . . . **NiB $274 Ex $223 Gd $146**
**Stainless steel/
  Bulldog grips (disc. 1992).** . . . **NiB $220 Ex $193 Gd $132**
Neoprene grips/Pocket Hammer. . **NiB $242 Ex $203 Gd $148**

NOTE: *In 1999 the Bulldog was reintroduced. Similar to other Bulldog models but w/2.5-in. barrel, shrouded ejector rod, blued finish, and checkered rubber grips. Other older model were also reintroduced as noted. Recent models offered in numerous color finishes and patterns.*

- Recent Manufacture (1999 to date) -
Standard . . . . **NiB $409 Ex $355 Gd $315**
stainless finish, add. **$20**
Classic. . . . . **NiB $436 Ex $400 Gd $395**
DAO . . . . **NiB $426 Ex $370 Gd $345**
**On Duty (shrouded hammer,
  stainless finish)** . . . . **NiB $432 Ex $380 Gd $355**
Police (4.2-in. bbl., stainless) . . . . **NiB $408 Ex $360 Gd $320**
**Target (4.2-in. bbl., adj. sights,
  stainless)** . . . . **NiB $475 Ex $420 Gd $370**
**Boomer (DAO, stainless finish, ported bbl., no sights,
  2016-present)** . . . . **NiB $380 Ex $280 Gd $210**

BULLDOG .357 DA REVOLVER. . . **NiB $214 Ex $169 Gd $129**
Caliber: .357 Magnum. Five-round cylinder, 6-in. bbl., 11 in. overall. Weight: 25 oz. Fixed sights. Blued finish. Square, checkered walnut grips. Made 1977-96.

BULLDOG NEW POLICE DA REVOLVER
Same general specifications as Bulldog Police except chambered for .44 Special. Five-round cylinder, 2.5- or 3.5-in. bbl. Made 1990-92.
Blued finish. . . . . **NiB $263 Ex $201 Gd $148**
Stainless finish (2.5-in. bbl. only) . . **NiB $202 Ex $166 Gd $114**

BULLDOG POLICE DA REVOLVER
Caliber: .38 Special or .32 H&R Magnum. Six-round cylinder, 4-in. bbl., 8.5 in. overall. Weight: 20.5 oz. Adj. rear sight, ramp front. Blued or stainless finish. Square checkered walnut grips. Made 1976-93. No shroud on new models.
Blued finish. . . . . **NiB $272 Ex $204 Gd $158**
Stainless finish. . . . . **NiB $234 Ex $194 Gd $147**
.32 H&R Magnum (disc.1992) . . . **NiB $270 Ex $204 Gd $142**

BULLDOG PUG DA REVOLVER
Caliber: .44 Special. Five-round cylinder, 2.5 in. bbl., 7.25 in. overall. Weight: 20 oz. Blued or stainless finish. Fixed ramp front sight, fixed square-notch rear. Checkered Neoprene or walnut grips. Made 1988-93.

HANDGUNS

Charter Arms Bulldog Pug

Charter Arms Bulldog Target

Charter Arms Explorer II

Blued finish. . . . . NiB $262 Ex $224 Gd $183
Stainless finish. . . . . NiB $224 Ex $172 Gd $121

BULLDOG TARGET. . . . . NiB $207 Ex $134 Gd $102
Calibers: .357 Magnum, .44 Special (latter intro. in 1977). 4- or 5-in. bbl., 8.5 in. overall. Weight: 20.5 oz. in .357. Adj. rear sight, ramp front. Blued finish. Square checkered walnut grips. Made 1976-92, reintro. 2009.
Stainless steel . . . . NiB $420 Ex $320 Gd $200

BULLDOG TRACKER . . . . NiB $207 Ex $134 Gd $102
DA reviolver. Caliber: .357 Mag. Five-round cylinder, 2.5-, 4- or 6-in. bbl., 11 in. overall (6-in. bbl.). Weight: 21 oz. (2.5-in. bbl.). Adj. rear sight, ramp front. Checkered walnut grips. Blued finish. 4- or 6-in. bbl., Disc.1986. Reintro. 1989 to 1992.

CHIC LADY SERIES. . . . . NIB $360 EX $320 GD $230
Revolver. Lightweight aluminum frame. Trigger: DAO or DA/SA. Caliber: .38 Spl. 2-in. bbl. Grip: checkered rubber. Numerous colored finishes. Made 2012 to present.

EXPLORER II SEMIAUTO SURVIVAL PISTOL
Caliber: .22 LR, 8-rnd. magazine, 6-, 8- or 10-in. bbl., 13.5 inchesoverall (6-in. bbl.). Weight: 28 oz. finishes: Black, heat cured, semigloss textured enamel or silvertone anticorrosion. Disc. 1987.
Standard model. . . . . NiB $158 Ex $100 Gd $66
Silvertone (w/optional
  6- or 10-in. bbl.) . . . . NiB $143 Ex $123 Gd $83

MAG PUG. . . . . NiB $397 Ex $345 Gd $305
SImilar to Bulldog .357 except w/2.5-in. bbl. w/ejector shroud and rubber grips. Made 2001 to date.

OFF-DUTY DA REVOLVER
Calibers: .22 LR or .38 Special. Six-round (.22 LR) or 5-rnd. (.38 Special) cylinder. Two-in. bbl., 6.25 in. overall. Weight: 16 oz. Fixed rear sight, Partridge-type front sight. Plain walnut grips. Matte black, nickel or stainless steel finish. Made 1992-96.
Matte black finish . . . . NiB $185 Ex $153 Gd $112
Nickel finish . . . . NiB $230 Ex $194 Gd $150
Stainless steel . . . . NiB $260 Ex $194 Gd $128

- Recent Manufacture (1999 to date) -
Standard (2-in. bbl., hammerless, aluminum frame, matte black finish). . . . . NiB $419 Ex $360 Gd $315
two-tone finish, add $20

ON DUTY. . . . . NiB $402 Ex $355 Gd $310
SImilar to Mag Pug or Undercover depending on caliber except w/shrouded hammer. Matte stainless finsih. Made 2009 to date.

PATHFINDER DA REVOLVER
Calibers: .22 LR, .22 WMR. Six-round cylinder, bbl. lengths: 2-, 3-, 6-in., 7.13 in. overall (in 3-in. bbl.), and regular grips. Weight: 18.5 oz. (3-in. bbl.). Adj. rear sight, ramp front. Blued or stainless finish. Plain walnut regular, checkered Bulldog or square buttgrips. Made 1970 to date. Note: Originally designated "Pocket Target," name was changed in 1971 to "Pathfinder." Grips changed in 1984.
Blued finish. . . . . NiB $203 Ex $148 Gd $112
Stainless finish. . . . . NiB $240 Ex $192 Gd $128

- Recent Manufacture (1999 to date) -
Standard (2-in. bbl., .22 LR or .22 Mag., 6-shot cylinder, stainless finish) . . . . NiB $365 Ex $320 Gd $280
two-tone colores finish, add $20

PATRIOT. . . . . NiB $345 Ex $305 Gd $255
SImilar to Bulldog .357 except in .327 Federal. Made 2009-12.

PITBULL DA REVOLVER
Calibers: 9mm, .357 Magnum, .38 Special. Five-round cylinder, 2.5-, 3.5- or 4-in. bbl., 7 in. overall (2.5-in. bbl.). Weight: 21.5 to 25 oz. All stainless steel frame. Fixed ramp front sight, fixed square-notch rear. Checkered Neoprene grips. Blued or stainless finish. Made 1989-91.
Blued finish. . . . . NiB $261 Ex $223 Gd $137
Stainless finish. . . . . NiB $270 Ex $ 230 Gd $143

- Recent Manufacture (2010 to date) -
Standard (2-in. bbl., 9mm, .40 S&W or .45 ACP, 5-shot cylinder, stainless finish) . . . . NiB $502 Ex $420 Gd $380
.40 S&W or .45 ACP, deduct. $10

PROFESSIONAL . . . . NiB $375 Ex $340 Gd $300
DA/SA revolver. Caliber: .32 H&R Magnum, 7-rnd capacity. Barrel: 3 in. Grip: Smooth walnut. Sights: Fixed rear, LitePipe front. Finish: stainless steel. Mfg. on the large frame. Made 2019 to date.

SOUTHPAW . . . . NiB $419 Ex $365 Gd $330
SImilar to Undercover except true left hand design. Made 2008 to date.

UNDERCOVER DA REVOLVER
Caliber: .38 Special. Five-round cylinder,. bbl., lengths: 2-, 3-, 4-in., 6.25 in. overall (2-in. bbl.), and regular grips. Weight: 16 oz. (2-in. bbl.). Fixed sights. Plain walnut, checkered Bulldog or square buttgrips. Made 1965-96.
Blued or nickel-plated finish. . . NiB $216 Ex $120 Gd $101
Stainless finish. . . . . NiB $281 Ex $230 Gd $148

- Recent Manufacture (1999 to date) -
Standard (2-in. bbl., blued finish). . NiB $346 Ex $290 Gd $255
stainless finish, add. $10
DAO (2-in. bbl., blued finish) . . NiB $352 Ex $300 Gd $265

UNDERCOVER DA REVOLVER
Same general specifications as standard Undercover except chambered for .32 H&R Magnum or .32 S&W Long, has 6-rnd. cylinder and 2.5-in. bbl.

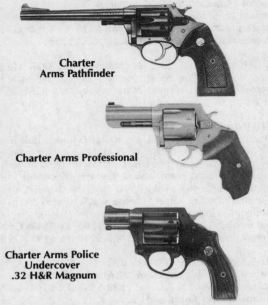

Charter Arms Pathfinder

Charter Arms Professional

Charter Arms Police Undercover .32 H&R Magnum

.32 H&R Magnum (blued).....	NiB $316	Ex $253	Gd $170
.32 H&R Magnum nickel......	NiB $212	Ex $171	Gd $109
.32 H&R Magnum (stainless)..	NiB $332	Ex $268	Gd $187
.32 S&W Long (blued) disc. 1989...	NiB $303	Ex $225	Gd $179

UNDERCOVER LITE .... NiB $397 Ex $345 Gd $305
SImilar to Undercover except w/aluminum frame. Caliber: .38 Special. Five-round cylinder,. bbl., lengths: 2-in. Rubber grips. Weight: 12 oz. Fixed sights. Matte aluminum finsh. Made 1991 to date.
colored finishes, add $20
.32 H&R Magnum (dicon. 2012... NiB $345 Ex $260 Gd $180

UNDERCOVER POCKET POLICE DA REVOLVER
Same general specifications as standard Undercover except has 6-rnd. cylinder and pocket-type hammer. Blued or stainless steel finish. Made 1969-81.
Blued finish. . . . . NiB $342 Ex $283 Gd $ 214
Stainless steel . . . . NiB $356 Ex $290 Gd $219

UNDERCOVER POLICE DA REVOLVER
Same general specifications as standard Undercover except has 6-rnd. cylinder. Made 1984-89. Reintroduced 1993.
Blued . . . . NiB $390 Ex $ 279 Gd $204
Stainless, add $20

UNDERCOVERETTE
DA REVOLVER . . . . NiB $179 Ex $130 Gd $101
Same as Undercover except w/2-in. bbl., caliber .32 S&W Long, 6-rnd. cylinder, blued finish only. Weight: 16.5 oz. Made 1972-83.
- Recent Manufacture (1999 to date) -
Standard (2-in. bbl., .32 H&R Mag.,
   stainless finish) . . . . NiB $375 Ex $330 Gd $290
two-tone colores finish, add $20

CHIAPPA FIREARMS LTD. — DAYTON, OH
Chiappa owns ARMI SPORT REPLICA FIREARMS MFG. and manufactures Cimarron, Legacy Sports, Taylor's & Co. Imported currently, manufactured in Italy.

1892 MARE'S LEG. . . . . NiB $515 Ex $460 Gd $360
Lever-action pistol. SA. Caliber: .357 Mag., .44 Mag., or .45 Long Colt, 4-rnd. magazine. 9- or 12-in. bbl. Sights: adj rear.

Finish: case-hardened receiver, blue bbl. Imported from 2013 to date.

1911-45 CUSTOM . . . . NiB $560 Ex $450 Gd $340
1911 full size platform. Semiauto. SA. Caliber: .45 ACP, 8-rnd. magazine. 5-in. bbl. Sights: Novak style. Grip: checkered olive wood. Finish: black. Imported from 2013 to date.

1911-22 STANDARD. . . . . NiB $278 Ex $230 Gd $200
1911 style. Semiauto. SA. Caliber: .22 LR, 10-rnd. magazine. 5-in. bbl. Sights: fixed front, adj. rear. Grip: checkered wood. Finish: black, OD/black, tan/black. Length: 8.6 in. Weight: 33 oz. Imported from 2010 to date.
Compact model, add. $50
Custom model, add. $100
Target model, add $30

MFOUR PISTOL . . . . NiB $515 Ex $460 Gd $360
AR15 style. Semiauto, blowback. SA. Caliber: .22 LR, 10- or 28-rnd. magazine. 6-in. bbl. Sights: adj. Imported from 2011 to 2013.

M9 . . . . NiB $520 Ex $320 Gd $240
Beretta M9 style. Semiauto. DA/SA. Caliber: 9mm, 10- or 15-rnd. magazine. 4.9-in. bbl. Sights: fixed. Grip: checkered polymer or wood. Finish: black. Imported from 2013 to 2015.

M9-22 STANDARD . . . . NiB $370 Ex $320 Gd $240
Beretta M9 style. Semiauto. DA/SA. Caliber: .22 LR, 10-rnd. magazine. 5-in. bbl. Sights: fixed front, adj. rear. Grip: checkered polymer or wood. Finish: black. Length: 8.6 in. Weight: 37 oz. Imported from 2013 to date.
checkered wood grip, add $25

RHINO SERIES
Revolver. Bore aligns with bottom chamber of cylinder. DA/SA. Caliber: .357 Mag., 9mm, or .40 S&W, 6-rnd. cylinder. 2-, 4-, 5-, or 6-in. bbl. Frame: aluminum. Sights: fixed front, adj. rear. Grip: checkered wood or rubber. Finish: black or nickel. Weight: 24-33.2 oz. depending on bbl. length. Imported from 2010 to date.
200D (2-in. bbl., rubber grip). . NiB $990 Ex $880 Gd $660
200DS (2-in. bbl., wood grip). . NiB $990 Ex $880 Gd $660
200DS Polymer
   (2-in. bbl., wood grip,
   polymer frame) . . . . NiB $750 Ex $660 Gd $510
30DS (.357 Mag., 3-in. bbl., rubber or wood grip,
   2018-date) . . . . NiB $930 Ex $815 Gd $630
30DS X (.357 Mag., 3-in. bbl., G10 grip, stainless,
   2020-date) . . . . NiB $1255 Ex $1100 Gd $855
30 SAR (.357 Mag., SAO
   3-in. bbl., rubber grip,
   stainless, 2018-date) . . . . . . NiB $1255 Ex $1100 Gd $855
40DS (4-in. bbl., wood grip). . NiB $1073 Ex $960 Gd $710
50DS (5-in. bbl., wood grip). NiB $1075 Ex $960 Gd $710
60DS (6-in. bbl., wood grip). . NiB $1099 Ex $980 Gd $720
Charging Rhino Gen II
   (improved trigger) . . . . NiB $1624 Ex $1580 Gd $1400

CIMARRON F.A. CO. — Fredricksburg, TX
Currently imports, distrbutes and retails black powder and cartridge firearms manufactured by Armi-Sport, Chiappa, Pedersoli, Pietta, and Uberti.

1851 NAVY RICHARDS-MASON . .NiB $515 EX $455 GD $355
Reproduction of Colt Richards-Mason Navy open-top conversion SA revolver. Caliber: .38 Spl., 6-rnd. cylinder. Barrel: 4.75-5.5- or 7.5-in. octagon. Finish: Charcoal blue, blued or nickel. Mfg. Uberti, imported 2003-date.

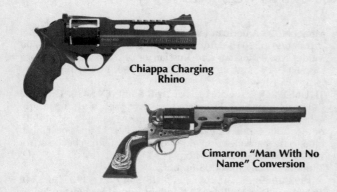

Chiappa Charging Rhino

Cimarron "Man With No Name" Conversion

Made 1984-93. Mfg. by Uberti. See listing under Uberti. Imported 2002 to date.

Buntline . . . . NiB $415 Ex $330 Gd $220
Bisley . . . . NiB $615 Ex $500 Gd $440

BIG IRON . . . . NiB $430 Ex $355 Gd $280
SAA-style revolver. Caliber: .357 Mag. or .45 LC., 6-rnd. cylinder. Barrel: 4.7-in. Finish: Case hard frame, blue bbl./cylinder. Grip: Smooth wood. Sights: Fixed. Brass backstrap/trigger guard. Made 2011-15.

BLACK EL DIABLO . . . . NiB $690 Ex $610 Gd $470
SAA Frontier-style revolver. Caliber: .45 LC., 6-rnd. cylinder. Barrel: 4.7-in. Grip: Smooth wood. Sights: Fixed. Made 2012-16.

BUCKHORN SERIES
SAA revolver. Caliber: .44 Mag. Barrel: 4.7-, 6- or 7.5-in. Sights: Fixed. Steel or brass backstrap. Disc. 1993.
Standard model. . . . . NiB $360 Ex $315 Gd $245
**Buntline model (.44-40 or .44 Mag., 18-in. bbl., adj.
  or fixed sights, disc. 1989)** . . . NiB $375 Ex $330 Gd $255
**Convertible model (.44-40 and .44
  Mag. cylinders, disc. 1989)** . . . NiB $375 Ex $330 Gd $255
**Target model (.44 Mag., adj. sights,
  disc. 1993)** . . . . NiB $375 Ex $330 Gd $255

EL MALO SERIES. . . . . NiB $520 Ex $455 Gd $355
SAA-style revolver. Caliber: .357 Mag. or .45 LC., 6-rnd. cylinder. Barrel: 4.7-, 5.5- or 7.5-in., octagon. Finish: Case hard Pre-War frame, blue bbl./cylinder. Grip: Smooth wood. Sights: Fixed. Made 2016-date.
**El Malo 2 model (Army or Thunderer grip,
  2019-date)** . . . . NiB $555 Ex $485 Gd $380

EL PISTOLERO SA REVOLVER . . NiB $444 Ex $336 Gd $260
Calibers: .22 LR, .357 Mag., .45 Colt. Six-round cylinder, 4.75-5.5- or 7.5-in. bbl., polished brass backstrap and triggerguard. Otherwise, same as Colt Single-Action Army revolver w/parts being interchangeable. Mfg. Uberti and Pietta, imported 1997-98, 2007-13, reintro. 2017.

EVIL ROY SAA . . . . NiB $740 EX $630 GD $530
Calibers: .38 Spl./.357 Mag., .44-40, .45 Colt. 6-rnd. cylinder, 4.75- or 5.5-in. bbl., tuned action, wide sights, smooth or checkered wood grip. Case hardened frame, blue grip frame. Engraved with Evil Roy signature. Made 2005 to date.

FRONTIER SIX SHOOTER. . . . . NiB $730 Ex $580 Gd $450
Calibers: .22 LR, .22 Mag., .38 Spl./.357 Mag., .38-40, .44 Spl., .44-40 or .45 Long Colt. 6-rnd. cylinder, 4.75-, 5.5- or 7.5-in. bbl., steel backstrap. Original Colt-like finish. Made 2008-10.
Sheriff's model (3- or 4-in. bbl.). . . NiB $400 Ex $300 Gd $220
Target model (adj. rear sight) . . NiB $360 Ex $270 Gd $200

FRONTIER SAA. . . . . NiB $500 Ex $430 Gd $380
Mfg. by Pietta. Calibers: .357 Mag., .44-40, .45 Colt. 6-rnd. cylinder. 3.5-, 4.75-, 5.5-, or 7.5-in. bbl. Finish: blue or charcoal blue. Imported from 2011 to date.
**George S. Patton model (.45 LC, 4.7- or 5.5-in. bbl.,
  faux ivory grip, laser engraved, nickel
  finish)** . . . . NiB $725 Ex $635 Gd $495
**Short Stroke model (short stroke hammer, checkered
  wood grip, blued or stainless,
  Pietta, 2014-16)** . . . . NiB $505 Ex $430 Gd $320
**Teddy Roosevelt model (.45 LC, 7.5-in. bbl., faux ivory grip,
  laser engraved, nickel finish)** . . NiB $770 Ex $675 Gd $525
**Texas Ranger model (.45 LC, 4.7-in. bbl., faux ivory grip,
  laser engraved, nickel finish)** . . NiB $770 Ex $675 Gd $525

**1858 NEW MODEL ARMY/NAVY
  CONVERSION** . . . . NiB $515 Ex $455 Gd $355
Reproduction of Remington 1858 New Model Army/Navy conversion SA revolver. Caliber: .38 Spl., .44-40, or .45 LC, 6-rnd. cylinder. Barrel: 5.5-, 7.3- or 8-in., octagon. Finish: Nickel or blued. Brass trigger guard. Mfg. Uberti, imported 2007-date.

1860 ARMY RICHARDS-MASON. . NiB $515 Ex $455 Gd $355
Reproduction of Colt Richards-Mason Army open-top conversion SA revolver. Caliber: .38 Spl., .44 Spl., .45 LC, 6-rnd. cylinder. Barrel: 4.75- 5.5- or 8-in. Finish: Charcoal blue or blued. Mfg. Uberti, imported 2003-date.
**Richrads Transition, Type II model (Richards ejector,
  Richards-Mason conversion).** . . NiB $585 Ex $515 Gd $400

1862 POCKET CONVERSION. . . . NiB $515 Ex $455 Gd $355
Open-top conversion SA revolver. Caliber: .380 ACP, 6-rnd. cylinder. Barrel: 6-in. Finish: Charcoal blue. Imported 2018-date.

1872 OPEN-TOP SA REVOLVER. . . NiB $510 Ex $345 Gd $270
Reproduction of Colt Navy and Army open-top conversion revolvers. Calibers: .38 Long Colt, .38 Spl., .44-40, .44 Spl., 44 Russian, .45 Schofield or .45 Long Colt. Six-round cylinder, 4.75- 5.5- or 7.5-in. bbl., brass backstrap and triggerguard, blued finish. Made 1999 to date.
Silver plated backstrap (2010) . . . . NiB $550 Ex $385 Gd $310
Engraved, add $1000

1875 OUTLAW. . . . . NiB $535 Ex $470 Gd $365
Reproduction of Remington 1875 SA revolver. Caliber: .357 Mag., .44-40, or .45 LC, 6-rnd. cylinder. Barrel: 5.5-, 7.3- or 8-in. Finish: Nickel or blued. Disc. 1993, reintro. 2010-date.

MODEL 1890 . . . . NiB $545 Ex $480 Gd $370
Reproduction of Remington 1890 SA revolver. Caliber: .357 Mag., .44-40, or .45 LC. 6-rnd. cylinder. Barrel: 5.5-in. Finish: Nickel or blued. Lanyard ring. Disc. 1993, reintro. 2010-date.

BAD BOY . . . . NiB $630 Ex $550 Gd $430
SAA revolver. Calibers: 10mm or .44 Mag. 5-rnd. cylinder. Barrel: 6- or 8-in. octagon. Pre-war frame, Army grip. Grip: Smooth wood. Sights: Adj. Made 2017-date.

BADLAND SA REVOLVER. . . . . . NiB $280 Ex $210 Gd $180
Calibers: .357 Mag., .45 Colt. 6-rnd. cylinder, 4.75-in. bbl., brass backstrap and triggerguard, wood grip. Made 2005-07.

BADLAND SA REVOLVER. . . . . . NiB $400 Ex $315 Gd $200
Calibers: .44 Spl./.44 Mag. 6-rnd. cylinder, 4.75-, 6- or 7.5-in. bbl., brass or steel backstrap and triggerguard, wood grip.

"HAND OF GOD" HOLY
SMOKER . . . . NiB $760 Ex $660 Gd $580
Hollywood Series. Mfg. by Pietta or Uberti. Calibers: .45 Colt. 6-rnd. cylinder, 4.75- in. bbl., blue finish, one-piece walnut grip with gold cross inlay on both sides. Made 2005-14.

JUDGE ROY BEAN
COMMEMORATIVE . . . . . . NiB $1600 Ex $1400 Gd $1100
Disc. 1996.

LIGHTNING . . . . NiB $500 Ex $430 Gd $380
Patterned after Colt Lightning revolver with bird's head grip expect SA. Mfg. by Uberti. Calibers: .22 LR, .38 Colt, .38 Spl., or .41 Colt. 6-rnd. cylinder, 3.5-, 4.75-, 5.5-, or 6.5-in. bbl., blue finish, one-piece smooth walnut grip. Made 1999-2001, reintro. 2003.

"MAN WITH NO NAME"
CONVERSION . . . . NiB $817 Ex $690 Gd $590
Hollywood Series. Mfg. by Uberti. Navy cartridge conversion. Calibers: .38 Spl. 6-rnd. cylinder, 7.5-in. bbl., Finish: case-hardened and blue, brass grip frame and trigger guard. Grip: one-piece walnut with silver rattlesnake inlay.

"MAN WITH NO NAME" . . . . . . NiB $680 Ex $550 Gd $380
Hollywood Series. Mfg. by Uberti. Calibers: .45 Colt. 6-rnd. cylinder, 4.75- or 5.5-in. bbl., blue finish, one-piece walnut grip with silver rattlesnake inlay.

MODEL P . . . . NiB $550 Ex $480 Gd $420
Patterned after Colt Model P revolver. Calibers: .32-20, .38-40, .357 Mag., .44-40 or .45 Colt. 6-rnd. cylinder. 4.75-, 5.5-, or 7.5-in. bbl. Available with pinched frame, Old Model or Pre-War models. Finish: blue, charcoal blue. Imported from 1996 to date.
Model P Jr. (smaller frame size) . . . NiB $450 Ex $390 Gd $340
Model P Jr. Black Stallion
(.22 LR/.22 WMR) . . . . NiB $520 Ex $460 Gd $390

NEW SHERIFF . . . . NiB $515 Ex $455 Gd $355
Mfg. by Pietta or Uberti. Calibers: .357 Mag., .44-40 or .45 Colt. 6-rnd. cylinder. 3.5-in. bbl. Finish: case-hardened and blue. Grip: smooth walnut. With ejector rod. Imported from 2011 to date.

PISTOLEER . . . . NiB $445 Ex $385 Gd $305
SAA-style revolver. Caliber: .357 Mag. or .45 LC., 6-rnd. cylinder. Barrel: 4.7-in. Finish: Blued. Grip: Smooth wood w/ Cimarron medallion. Sights: Fixed. Steel or nickel plated backstrap/trigger guard. Imported 2021-date.

PLINKERTON . . . . NiB $180 Ex $155 Gd $130
Mfg. by Chiappa. Calibers: .22 LR. 6-rnd. cylinder. 4.75-in. bbl. Finish: matte black. Grip: Checkered black plastic or wood. Sights: Fixed. Mfg. Chiappa, imported 2007-15, reintro. 2020.

"ROOSTER SHOOTER" . . . . . . NiB $780 Ex $580 Gd $430
Hollywood Series. Mfg. by Pietta or Uberti. Calibers: .357 Mag., .44-40, or .45 Colt. 6-rnd. cylinder. 4.75-in. bbl., antique finish, one-piece faux ivory grip with finger grooves. Imported from 2010 to date.

SCHOFIELD MODEL NO. 3 . . . NiB $735 Ex $550 Gd $410
Patterned after Smith & Wesson Schofield revolver. Mfg. by San Marco or Uberti. Calibers: .38 Spl., .38-40, .44 Russian, .44 Spl., .44-40, .45 Schofield, .45 ACP, or .45 Colt. 6-rnd. cylinder. 3.5- (Wells Fargo model), 5-, or 7-in. bbl. Finish: blue, case hardened, or nickel. Grip: checkered or smooth walnut. Mfg. Armi San Marco. Imported from 1996-99. Current mfg. Uberti, 2007-date.
Armi San Marco mfg. . . . . NiB $735 Ex $550 Gd $410
Uberti mfg . . . . NiB $1035 Ex $910 Gd $710

Model No. 3 American (.44 Spl., .44-40, or .45 LC, 1st Model frame/grip, 2019-date) . . . . . NiB $1025 Ex $900 Gd $700
Model No. 3 Russian (.44 Russian or .45 Colt, trigger guard spur) . . . . NiB $960 Ex $710 Gd $500

THUNDERER . . . . NiB $500 EX $430 Gd $380
Patterned after Colt Thundered revolver with bird's head grip expect SA. Mfg. by Uberti. Calibers: .357 Mag., .44 Spl., .44-40, or .45 Colt. 6-rnd. cylinder. 3.5-, 4.75-, or 5.5-in. bbl. Finish: blue, case hardened, stainless, or nickel. Grip: checkered or smooth walnut. Imported from 1994 to date.
Thunderer Long Tom (7.5-in. bbl.,
1997-2009) . . . . NiB $540 Ex $390 Gd $340
Thunderer Doc Holliday (3.5-in. bbl., shoulder holster, knife, 2008-present) . . . . NiB $1370 Ex $1210 Gd $940

THUNDERBALL . . . . NiB $500 Ex $440 Gd $340
Similar to Thunderer w/ bird's head grip. Mfg. by Pietta. Calibers: .357 Mag. or .45 Colt. 6-rnd. cylinder. 3.5- or 4.75-in. bbl. w/ejector rod. Finish: blue or stainless. Imported 2011 to date.

U.S.V. ARTILLERY
"ROUGH RIDER" . . . . NiB $520 Ex $390 Gd $290
Patterned after Colt U.S. Artillery revolver. Mfg. by Pietta or Uberti. Calibers: .45 Colt. 6-rnd. cylinder. 5.5-in. bbl. Finish: blue, and case hardened. Grip: smooth walnut with cartouche. Imported from 1996 to date.

U.S. 7TH CAVALRY CUSTER
MODEL. . . . . NiB $520 Ex $460 Gd $310
Patterned after Colt U.S. Military cavalry contract revolver. Mfg. by Pietta or Uberti. Calibers: .45 Colt. 6-rnd. cylinder. 7.5-in. bbl. Finish: blue, and case hardened. Grip: one-piece smooth walnut with cartouche. Imported from 1990 to date.

WYATT EARP BUNTLINE . . . . . . NiB $790 Ex $690 Gd $540
SAA-style revolver. Caliber: .45 LC., 6-rnd. cylinder. Barrel: 10-in. Finish: Case hardened. Grip: Smooth wood w/silver badge medallion. Sights: Fixed. Mfg. by Uberti and Pietta, imported 2002-date.

MODEL 1911 SERIES . . . . NiB $490 EX $430 GD $335
1911 type. Semiauto. Caliber: .45 ACP. 5-in. bbl. Grip: checkered wood. Finish; blue, parkerized, nickel. Sights: fixed. Made by Chiappa. Imported 2011 to present.
Wild Bunch (WWI replica
w/ shoulder holster) . . . . NiB $820 Ex $720 Gd $555

COLT'S MANUFACTURING CO., INC. — Hartford, CT

CZG (Česká zbrojovka Group SE), owner of CZ, acquired Colt Holding Company LLC in February 2021. Previously Colt Industries, Firearms Division. Production of some Colt handguns spans the period before World War II to the postwar years. Values shown for these models are for earlier production. Those manufactured c. 1946 and later generally are less desirable to collectors and values are approximately 30 percent lower.

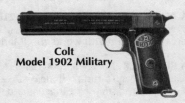

Colt Model 1902 Military

Colt 1903 Early Hammer

Colt Model 1903 Pocket Hammerless

NOTE: *For ease in finding a particular firearm, Colt handguns are grouped into three sections: Automatic Pistols, Single-Shot Pistols & Derringers, and Revolvers. For a complete listing, please refer to the Index.*

- AUTOMATIC PISTOLS -

MODEL 1900 .38 AUTOMATIC PISTOL
Caliber: .38 ACP (modern high-velocity cartridges should not be used in this pistol). Seven-round magazine, 6-in. bbl., 9 in. overall. Weight: 35 oz. Fixed sights. Blued finish. Hard rubber and plain or checkered walnut grips. Sharp-spur hammer. Combination rear sight and safety unique to the Model 1900 (early production). In mid-1901 a solid rear sight was dovetailed into the slide. (S/N range 1-4274) Made 190003. Note: 250 models were sold to the military (50 Navy and 200 Army).
Early commercial model
  (w/sight/safety) . . . NiB $15,810 Ex $14,586 Gd $11,220
Late commercial model
  (w/dovetailed sight). . . NiB $15,810 Ex $14,586 Gd $11,220
Army Model w/U.S. inspector marks (1st Series - S/N 90-150
  w/inspector mark J.T.T) . . . NiB $32,130 Ex $27,540 Gd $22,185
  (2nd Series - S/N 1600-1750
  w/inspector mark R.A.C.). . . NiB $11,577 Ex $9736 Gd $6700
Navy model (Also marked
  w/USN-I.D. number) . . . NiB $18,967 Ex $13,107 Gd $10,200

MODEL 1902 MILITARY .38 AUTOMATIC PISTOL
Caliber: .38 ACP (modern high-velocity cartridges should not be used in this pistol). Eight-round magazine, 6-in. bbl., 9 in. overall. Weight: 37 oz. Fixed sights w/blade front and V-notch rear. Blued finish. Checkered hard rubber grips. Round back hammer, changed to spur type in 1908. No safety but fitted w/standard military swivel. About 18,000 produced with split S/N ranges. The government contract series (15,001-15,200) and the commercial sales series (15,000 receding to 11,000) and (30,200-47,266). Made 1902-29.
Early military model (w/front
  slide serrations) . . . . NiB $5760 Ex $4510 Gd $3528
Late military model (w/rear
  slide serrations) . . . . NiB $6115 Ex $3732 Gd $2525
Marked "U.S. ARMY"
  (S/N 15,001-15,200). . . NiB $19,635 Ex $17,340 Gd $15,402

MODEL 1902 SPORTING
.38 AUTOMATIC PISTOL . . NiB $5750 Ex $4250 Gd $2500
Caliber: .38 ACP (modern high-velocity cartridges should not be used in this pistol). Seven-round magazine, 6-in. bbl., 9 in. overall. Weight: 35 oz. Fixed sights w/blade front and V-notch rear. Blued finish. Checkered hard rubber grips. Round back hammer was standard but some spur hammers were installed during late production. No safety and w/o swivel as found on military model. Total production about 7,500 w/split S/N ranges (4275-10,999) and (30,000-30,190) Made 1902-08.

MODEL 1903 POCKET .32 AUTOMATIC PISTOL FIRST ISSUE (TYPE I) - COMMERCIAL SERIES
Caliber: .32 Auto. Eight-round magazine, 4-in. bbl., 7 in. overall. Weight: 23 oz. Fixed sights. Blued or nickel finish. Checkered hard rubber grips. Hammerless (concealed hammer). Slide lock and grip safeties. Fitted w/barrel bushing but early models have no magazine safety. Total production of the Model 1903 reached 572,215. The First Issue maded 1903-08 (S/N range 1-72,000).
Blued finish. . . . . NiB $2016 Ex $1102 Gd $587
Nickel finish. . . . . NiB $2420 Ex $990 Gd $602

MODEL 1903 POCKET .32 AUTOMATIC PISTOL SECOND ISSUE (TYPE II) - COMMERCIAL SERIES
Same as First Issue but w/3.75-in. bbl. and small Extractor. Made 1908-10 (S/N range 72,001 -105,050).
Blued finish. . . . . NiB $1638 Ex $910 Gd $474
Nickel finish. . . . . NiB $1965 Ex $1092 Gd $498

MODEL 1903 POCKET .32 AUTOMATIC PISTOL, THIRD ISSUE (TYPE III) - COMMERCIAL SERIES
Caliber: .32 Auto. Similar to Second Issue w/3.75-in. bbl. except with integral bbl. bushing and locking lug at muzzle end of bbl. Production occurred 1910 to 1926 (S/N range 105,051-468,096).
Blued finish. . . . . NiB $1260 Ex $710 Gd $440
Nickel finish. . . . . NiB $1512 Ex $1234 Gd $918

MODEL 1903 POCKET .32 AUTOMATIC PISTOL FOURTH ISSUE - COMMERCIAL SERIES
Caliber: .32 Auto. Similar to Third Issue except a slide lock safety change was made when a Tansley-style disconnector was added on all pistols above S/N 468,097, which prevents firing of cartridge in chamber when the magazine is removed. Blued or nickel finish. Checkered walnut grips. These design changes were initiated 1926 to 1945 (S/N range 105,051-554,446).
Blued finish . . . . NiB $1260 Ex $1020 Gd $804
Nickel finish . . . . NiB $1512 Ex $1132 Gd $945

MODEL 1903 POCKET HAMMER .38 AUTOMATIC PISTOL
Caliber: .38 ACP (modern high-velocity cartridges should not be used in this pistol). Similar to Model 1902 Sporting .38 but w/ shorter frame, slide and 4.5-in. bbl. Overall dimension reduced to 7.5 in. Weight: 31 oz. Fixed sights w/blade front and V-notch rear. Blued finish. Checkered hard rubber grips. Round back hammer, changed to spur type in 1908. No safety. (S/N range 16,001-47,226 with some numbers above 30,200 assigned to 1902 Military). Made 1903-29.
Early model
  (round hammer) . . . . NiB $6513 Ex $3588 Gd $1612
Late model (spur hammer). . . NiB $5010 Ex $2760 Gd $1240

MODEL 1903 POCKET HAMMERLESS (CONCEALED HAMMER) .32 AUTOMATIC PISTOL - MILITARY
Caliber: .32 ACP. Eight-round magazine, Similar to Model 1903 Pocket .32 except concealed hammer and equipped w/ magazine safety. Parkerized or blued finish. (S/N range with "M" prefix M1-M200,000) Made 1941-45.
Blued service model (marked
  "U.S. Property") . . . . NiB $3615 Ex $1815 Gd $1290
Parkerized service model (marked
  "U.S. Property") . . . . NiB $2410 Ex $1210 Gd $860
Blued documented
  Officer's model. . . . . NiB $3100 Ex $2710 Gd $1860
Parkerized documented
  Officer's model. . . . . NiB $3010 Ex $2010 Gd $1310

GRADING: **NiB** = New in Box   **Ex** = Excellent or NRA 95%   **Gd** = Good or NRA 68%

**Colt
Model 1905 Military**

**Colt
Model 1908 Pocket 25**

**Colt Model 1911
Commercial**

MODEL 1905 .45 AUTOMATIC PISTOL
Caliber: .45 (Rimless) Automatic. Seven-round magazine, 5-in. bbl., 8 in. overall. Weight: 32.5 oz. Fixed sights w/blade front and V-notch rear. Blued finish. Checkered walnut, hard rubber or pearl grips. Predecessor to Model 1911 Auto Pistol and contributory to the development of the .45 ACP cartridge. (S/N range 1-6100) Made 1905-11.
Commercial model . . . . NiB $7510 Ex $5100 Gd $3010
w/slotted backstrap
(500 produced). . . . . . . NiB $11,265 Ex $7650 Gd $4515
w/shoulder stock/holster, add. . . . .$7650 to $10,200

MODEL 1905 .45 (1907)
CONTRACT PISTOL . NiB $26,285 Ex $17,850 Gd $10,535
Variation of the Model 1905 produced to U.S. Military specifications, including loaded chamber indicator, grip safety and lanyard loop. Only 201 were produced, but 200 were delivered and may be identified by the chief inspector's initials "K.M." (S/N range 1-201) Made 1907-08.

MODEL 1908 VEST POCKET .25 HAMMERLESS
Caliber: .25 Auto. Six-round magazine, 2-in. bbl., 4.5 in. overall. Weight: 13 oz. Flat-top front, square-notch rear sight in groove. Blued, nickel or Parkerized finish. Checkered hard rubber grips on early models, checkered walnut on later type, special pearl grips illustrated. Both a grip safety and slide lock safety are included on all models. The Tansley-style safety disconnector was added in 1916 at pistol No. 141000. (S/N range 1-409,061) Made 1908-46.
Blued finish. . . . . NiB $860 Ex $610 Gd $430
Nickel finish, add $350
Marked "U.S. Property"
(w/blued finish) . . . . NiB $4810 Ex $3410 Gd $2210

MODEL 1908 POCKET .380 . . .NiB $1660 EX $1210 GD $810
Similar to Pocket .32 Auto w/3.75-in. bbl. except chambered for

.380 Auto w/seven-round magazine. Weight: 23 oz. Blue, nickel or Parkerized finish. (S/N range 1-138,009) Made 1908-45.
First Issue - Type I (made 1908-11, w/bbl., lock and bushing, w/S/N 1-6,250)
Second Issue - Type II (made 1911-28, w/o bbl., lock and bushing, w/S/N 6,251-92,893)
Third Issue - Type III (made 1928-45, w/safety disconnector, w/S/N 92,894-138,009)
Parkerized service model (Marked "U.S. Property" made 1942-45, w/S/N "M" prefix.). . .NiB $3010 Ex $2260 Gd $1310
Documented officer's model (service model w/military assignment papers) . . . . . NiB $4010 Ex $3260 Gd $2310

NOTE: *During both World Wars, Colt licensed other firms to make 1911 pistols under government contract, including Ithaca Gun Co., North American Arms Co., Ltd. (Canada), Remington-Rand Co., Remington-UMC, Singer Sewing Machine Co., and Union Switch & Signal Co. M1911 also produced at Springfield Armory.*

MODEL 1911 AUTOMATIC PISTOL (COMMERCIAL)
Caliber: .45 Auto. Seven-round magazine, 5-in. bbl., 8.5 in. overall. Weight: 39 oz. Fixed sights. Blued finish on Commercial model. Parkerized or similar finish on most military pistols. Checkered walnut grips (early production), plastic grips (later production). Checkered, arched mainspring housing and longer grip safety spur adopted in 1923 on M1911A1. C-series.
Model 1911 commercial (mfg. 1912-25, S/N range: C1-C138532). . . . . NiB $15,300 Ex $13,255 Gd $11,424
Model 1911A1 commercial Pre-WWII ("C" prefix serial number, mfg. 1925-42, S/N range: C138533-C215000) . . . . NiB $3886 Ex $3172 Gd $2240
Model 1911A1 commercial Post-WWII (changed to "C" suffix S/N in 1950, mfg. 1946-70). . NiB $3886 Ex $3172 Gd $2240

MODEL 1911 U.S. MILITARY GOVERNMENT
These are U.S. Military pistols made between 1912 through 1918 by a variety of manufacturers. Typical characteristics include: Straight mainspring housing, checkered wood grips, lanyard loop, and long trigger.
Colt manufacture
(mfg. 1912) . . . . NiB $10,353 Ex $8975 Gd $6849
(mfg. 1913-15) . . . . NiB $5500 Ex $4800 Gd $4300
(mfg. 1916) . . . . NiB $5700 Ex $5100 Gd $4300
(mfg. 1917-18, blue finish) . . . . NiB $4760 Ex $3300 Gd $2100
(mfg. 1917-18, black Army finish) . . . . .NiB $4760 Ex $3300 Gd $2100
(mfg. 1919-25) . . . . NiB $4760 Ex $3300 Gd $2100
Marine Model M1911 type (stamped: "MODEL OF 1911 U.S. ARMY" on r. of slide) NiB $7510 Ex $6000 Gd $3600
Navy Model M1911 type (stamped: "MODEL OF 1911 U.S. NAVY" on right of slide) . . . NiB $10,600 Ex $6100 Gd $3300
North American Arms Co. manufacture (1918)
under 100 produced. . . NiB $36,000 Ex $29,580 Gd $24,990
Remington-UMC manufacture (1918-19)
S/N range: 1-21676. . . . . . . NiB $8600 Ex $5600 Gd $3100
Springfield manufacture (1914-15)
S/N ranges: 72751-83855, 102597-107596, 113497-120566, 125567-133186. . . . . NiB $7600 Ex $5800 Gd $3100

MODEL 1911 FOREIGN MILITARY CONTRACTS
Simialr to U.S. Military M1911s except exported to foreign goverments.
Argentine type (Arg. seal stamped on top of slide, S/N w/"C" prefix, mfg. 1914-19) . . . NiB $3900 Ex $3600 Gd $3200
British type (stamped: "CALIBRE 455", mfg. 1915-19) . . . . NiB $5800 Ex $4800 Gd $3000

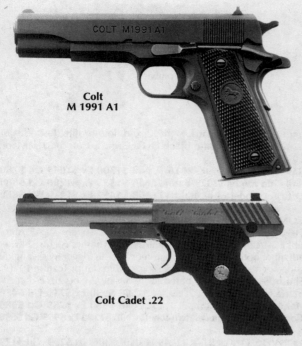

**Colt
M 1991 A1**

Colt Cadet .22

Norwegian 1914 type (w/extended slide release,
mfg. 1918-47).........NiB $2400 Ex $1900 Gd $1600
Russian type (w/Cyrillis markings on left side of receiver,
mfg. 1916-17).........NiB $8800 Ex $4600 Gd $4100

M1911 SERIES 70 WWI MODEL 1918
REPRODUCTION..............NiB $1500 Ex $950 Gd $700
Reproduction of Model 1911 (see above) w/black finish, original WWI rollmarks. Made 2008-09.

M1911 MODEL O SERIES 70
REPRODUCTION............... NiB $1600 Ex $950 Gd $700
Reproduction of Model 1911 (see above) w/original 1911 U.S. Military rollmarks, carbonia blue finish. Made 2003-09.

MODEL 1911A1 U.S. MILITARY GOVERNMENT
These are U.S. Military pistols made between 1924 through 1945 by a variety of manufacturers. Simialr to M1911 except w/arched main spring housing, blued or parkerized (mot common) finsih, cheched plastic grips, short trigger, longer grip safety, finger groove cut out in frame.
Colt manufacture........ NiB $4600 Ex $3900 Gd $3000
Ithaca manufacture...... NiB $2300 Ex $1900 Gd $1600
Remington-Rand manufacture..NiB $2600 Ex $2200 Gd $200
Singer manufacture.. NiB $65,900 Ex $50,015 Gd $40,455
Union Switch &
Signal manufacture...... NiB $6227 Ex $5247 Gd $4047

MODEL 1911A1 FOREIGN MILITARY CONTRACTS
Simialr to U.S. Military M1911A1s except exported to foreign goverments.
Argentine contract (stamped w/Argentine crest and
"Model 1927")........NiB $1600 Ex $1400 Gd $1200
Argentine manufacture (stamped w/crest and two lines on r.
side of slide: "EJERCITO ARGENTINO / SIST. COLT. CAL.
11.25mm M 1927")....NiB $1500 Ex $1300 Gd $1100
Brazilian contract (stamped w/crest and two lines on
right side of slide: "EXERCITO BRASILEIRIO / 1937", mfg.
1937-41)..............NiB $4900 Ex $4100 Gd $3800

Mexican contract (stamped w/seal and one line on right
side of "EJERCITO NACIONAL", S/N w/"C" prefix
mfg. 1921-27)........NiB $3900 Ex $3000 Gd $2700

M1911A1 MODEL O SERIES 70 WWII
REPRODUCTION..............NiB $1610 Ex $910 Gd $600
Reproduction of Model 1911A1 (see above) w/pakerized finish, original WWII rollmarks. Made 2001-04.

1991 SERIES GOVERNEMNT MODEL SERIES 70 MODEL O
Reissue of Series 70 action. Caliber: .38 Super, .45 ACP. Seven-round magazine, 5-in. bbl., 8.5 in. overall. Weight: 39 oz. Fixed blade front sight, square notch rear. Blued or stainless finish. Made 2003 to date.
Blued......................NiB $1080 Ex 900 Gd $600
Stainless ....NiB $1120 Ex $940 Gd $650
.38 Super (stainless) ....NiB $800 Ex $700 Gd $600
.38 Super (bright stainless) ...NiB $1200 Ex $900 Gd $600

1991 SERIES GOVERNMENT MODEL SERIES 80 MODEL O
Similar to Series 80 model except w/9mm or .45 ACP. Seven-round magazine, 5-in. bbl., 8.5 in. overall. Weight: 39 oz. Fixed sights. Rollmarked "Colt M1991A1" on slide. Blued, stainless or parkerized finish. Made 1991 to date.
Blued......................NiB $975 Ex $600 Gd $300
Parkerized..................NiB $975 Ex $600 Gd $300
Stainless ....NiB $1040 Ex $750 Gd $380
Commander model..........NiB $995 Ex $560 Gd $380
Officer's Compact model .....NiB $620 Ex $430 Gd $380

CADET AUTOMATIC PISTOL
Caliber: 22 LR. 10-rnd. magazine, 4.5-in. VR bbl., 8.63 in. overall. Weight: 33.5 oz. Blade front sight, dovetailed rear. Stainless finish. TExtured black polymer grips w/Colt medallion. Made 1993-95. **Note:** The Cadet Model name was disc. under litigation but the manufacturer continued to produce this pistol configuration as the Model "Colt 22". For this reason the "Cadet" model will command premiums.

ACE AUTOMATIC PISTOL
Caliber: .22 LR (regular or high speed). 10-rnd. magazine. Built on the same frame as the Government Model .45 Auto w/same safety features, etc. Hand-honed action, target bbl., adj. rear sight. 4.75-in. bbl., 8.25. in. overall. Weight: 38 oz. Made 1930-40.
Commercial model ....NiB $4650 Ex $3783 Gd $3264
Service model (1938-42)...NiB $7710 Ex $5498 Gd $4769
Post-War model (1978-89) ..NiB $2010 Ex $1260 Gd $800

ALL AMERICAN
MODEL 2000 DA PISTOL..... NiB $785 Ex $566 Gd $408
Hammerless Semiauto w/blued slide and polymer or alloy receiver fitted w/roller-bearing trigger. Caliber: 9mm Para. 15-rnd. magazine, 4.5-in. bbl., 7.5 in. overall. Weight: 29 oz. (Polymer) or 33 oz (Alloy). Fixed blade front sight, square-notch rear w/3-dot system. Matte blued slide w/black polymer or anodized aluminum receiver. Made 1992-94.
Aluminum frame, add..........................$100

AUTOMATIC .25 PISTOL
As a result of the 1968 Firearms Act restricting the importation of the Colt Pocket Junior that was produced in Spain, Firearms International was contracted by Colt to manufacture a similar blowback action with the same Exposed hammer configuration. Both the U.S. and Spanish-made .25 automatics were recalled to correct an action malfunction. Returned firearms were fitted with a rebounding firing pin to prevent accidental

**Colt All American
Model 2000**

**Colt Series 70 Combat
Commander**

discharges. Caliber: .25 ACP. Six-round magazine, 2.25-in. bbl., 4.5 in. overall. Weight: 12.5 oz. Integral blade front, square-notch rear sight groove. Blued finish. Checkered wood grips w/Colt medallion. Made 1970-75.

Model as issued. . . . . NiB $386 Ex $316 Gd $198
Model recalled & refitted . . . . . NiB $386 Ex $316 Gd $198

COLT 22 SPORT . . . . NiB $430 Ex $260 Gd $200
Semiauto. SA. Caliber: .22 LR, 10-rnd. magazine. 4.5-in. VR bbl. Weight: 33.5 oz. Sights: fixed. Finish: stainless. Pachmayr rubber grips. Made 1994-98.

COLT 22 TARGET . . . . NiB $430 Ex $260 Gd $200
Similar to Colt 22 model except w/6-in. VR bbl. Weight: 40.5 oz. Sights: adj. rear. Made 1995-99.

CHALLENGER. . . . . NiB $1100 Ex $800 Gd $400
Similar as Second Series Woodsman Target model but 4.5- or 6-in. bbl., 9 to 10.5 in. overall. Weight: 30 oz. (4.5-in. bbl.) or 31.5 oz. (6-in. bbl.) Blued finish. Checkered plastic grips. Made 1950-55.

COMMANDER (pre-Series 70) AUTOMATIC PISTOL
Same basic design as Government Model except w/shorter 4.25-in. bbl., and a special lightweight "Coltalloy" receiver and mainspring housing. Calibers: .45 Auto, .38 Super Auto, 9mm Para. Seven-round magazine (.45 cal.), nine-round (.38 Auto and 9mm), 8 in. overall. Weight: 26.5 oz. Fixed sights. Round spur hammer. Improved safety lock. Blued finish. Checkered plastic or walnut grips. Made 1950-69.

9mm Para. . . . . NiB $1350 Ex $1000 Gd $700
.38 Super, .45 ACP . . . . NiB $1450 Ex $1150 Gd $900

SERIES 70 COMBAT COMMANDER AUTOMATIC PISTOL
Similar to Lightweight Commander except w/steel frame, blued or nickel-plated finish. Made 1971-80.

9mm Para. . . . . NiB $736 Ex $590 Gd $444
.38 Super, .45 ACP . . . . NiB $852 Ex $691 Gd $486

SERIES 70 LIGHTWEIGHT COMMANDER AUTOMATIC PISTOL
Same as Commander except w/blued or nickel-plated finish. Made 1970-83.

9mm Para. . . . . NiB $1350 Ex $1000 Gd $700
.38 Super, .45 ACP . . . . NiB $1150 Ex $870 Gd $620

COMBAT ELITE SERIES
1911 Series 80 platform. Cal.: 9mm or .45 Auto. Bbl.: 5-in. Match Grade. Stainless steel frame w/under cut trigger guard. Sights: Fixed, low profile. Round spur hammer, wide angled serrations, checkered front grip strap. Finish: Two-tone. Grip: Textured G10. Made 2018-date.

Gov't. model (5-in. bbl.) . . . . . NiB $1355 Ex $1110 Gd $830
Commander model (4.2-in. bbl.) . . NiB $1355 Ex $1110 Gd $830
Defender model (3-in. bbl.) . . NiB $1355 Ex $1110 Gd $830

COMBAT UNIT SERIES
1911 Series 80 platform. CCO and CCU models. Cal.: 9mm or .45 Auto. Bbl.: 5-in. Match Grade. Stainless steel frame w/

under cut trigger guard. Sights: Fixed, low profile. Round spur hammer. Finish: Matte black DLC. Grip: Textured G10. Made 2016, 2019-date.

Rail Gun model (disc. 2016) . . NiB $1300 Ex $1055 Gd $780
Rail Gun model (2019-date) . . NiB $1555 Ex $1280 Gd $880
Officers model (3-in. bbl.) . . . NiB $1455 Ex $1210 Gd $860

COMPETITION SERIES
1911 Series 70 platform. Cal.: 9mm, .38 Super, or .45 Auto. Bbl.: 5-in. Match Grade. Stainless steel frame. Sights: Novak adj. fiber optic. Round spur hammer, 3-hole trigger, wide angled slide serrations, dual recoil spring system. Grip: Textured G10. Finish: Stainless, matte blued, or two-tone. Made 2016-date.

matte blued finish. . . . . NiB $930 Ex $710 Gd $450
stainless finish. . . . . NiB $980 Ex $755 Gd $480
Competition Plus model (two-tone) . . NiB $1180 Ex $955 Gd $630

CONVERSION UNIT—.22-.45 . . . NiB $306 Ex $255 Gd $179
Converts Service Ace .22 to National Match .45 Auto. Unit consists of match-grade slide assembly and bbl., bushing, recoil spring, recoil spring guide and plug, magazine and slide stop. Made 1938-42.

CONVERSION UNIT — .45-.22 . . NiB $617 Ex $489 Gd $362
Converts Government Model .45 Auto to a .22 LR target pistol. Unit consists of slide assembly, bbl., floating chamber (as in Service Ace), bushing, ejector, recoil spring, recoil spring guide and plug, magazine and slide stop. The component parts differ and are not interchangable between post war, series 70, series 80, ACE I and ACE II units. Made 1938-84.

DEFENDER. . . . . NiB $1100 Ex $700 Gd $480
Caliber: 9mm, .40 S&W or .45 ACP. 3-in. bbl. 7-rnd. magazine, Three-dot, sights. rubber finger-groove wrap around grips. Matte stainless finish. Made 1998 to date.

Defender Plus (2002-03) . . . . . NiB $880 Ex $660 Gd $5801

DELTA ELITE
Caliber: 10mm. Five-in. bbl., 8.5 in. overall. Eight-round magazine, Weight: 38 oz. Checkered Neoprene combat grips w/ Delta medallion. Three-dot, high-profile front and rear combat sights. Blued or stainless finish. Made 1987-96.

First Edition
(500 Ltd. edition) . . . . NiB $975 Ex $784 Gd $551
Blued finish. . . . . NiB $923 Ex $626 Gd $468
Matte stainless finish. . . . . NiB $975 Ex $784 Gd $551
Ultra bright stainless finish, add $100

DELTA ELITE SERIES
Current mfg., updated model similar to earlier Delta Elite. Made 2008 to date.

matte stainless to two-tone finish . . NiB $1180 Ex $955 Gd $630
Rail model (Picatinny rail,
matte stainless) . . . . NiB $1275 Ex $1030 Gd $680

DELTA GOLD CUP SEMIAUTO PISTOL
Same general specifications as Delta Elite except w/Accro adjustable rear sight. Made 1989-93; 1995-96.

Colt National Match

Colt MK II/Series 90 Double Eagle

Colt MK IV/ Series 80 .380

Blued finish (disc. 1991) . . . . . **NiB $997 Ex $693 Gd $474**
Stainless steel finish . . . . **NiB $1076 Ex $792 Gd $576**

GOLD CUP TROPHY NATIONAL
MATCH .45 AUTO . . . . **NiB $1250 Ex $900 Gd $640**
Similar to MK IV Series 80 Gold Cup National Match except w/aluminum trigger, Bo-Mar raer adj. sight, black checkered rubber wrap around grips, 7 or 8-rnd. magazine. Weight: 39 oz. Made 1997-2010.

GOLD CUP SERIES
Current mfg. 1911 Series 70 platform. Cal.: 9mm, .38 Super, or .45 Auto. Bbl.: 5-in. Match Grade. Stainless steel frame. Bomar adj rear, fiber optic front. Round spur hammer, 3-hole trigger, wide angled slide serrations. Grip: Textured blue G10. Finish: Matte stainless. Made 2019-date.
9mm or .45 Auto . . . . **NiB $1180 Ex $955 Gd $630**
.38 Super . . . . **NiB $1215 Ex $985 Gd $650**

GOLD CUP NATION
MATCH SERIES . . . . **NiB $1299 Ex $1160 Gd $890**
Current mfg. 1911 Series 70 platform. Cal.: 9mm or .45 Auto. Bbl.: 5-in. Match Grade. Steel frame. Sights: Adj. target. Spur hammer, 3-hole adj. trigger, fine angled slide serrations. Grip: Checkered rosewood w/medallion. Finish: Blued. Made 2016-date.

GOLD CUP TROPHY SERIES
Current mfg. 1911 Series 70 platform. Cal.: 9mm, .38 Super, or .45 Auto. Bbl.: 5-in. Match Grade. Stainless steel frame w/ magwell. Sights: Adj rear, fiber optic front. Round spur hammer, 3-hole trigger, wide angled slide serrations, dual recoil spring system. Grip: Textured G10. Finish: Matte stainless. Made 2016-date.
9mm or .45 Auto . . . . **NiB $1655 Ex $1330 Gd $880**
.38 Super . . . . **NiB $1705 Ex $1369 Gd $910**

GOVERNMENT MODEL 1911/1911A1
See Colt Model 1911.

HUNTSMAN . . . . **NiB $900 Ex $650 Gd $350**
Similar to Third Series Woodsman Traget and Sport models, except 4.5- or 6-in. bbl., fixed rear sight, no automatic slide stop. Early versions had black plastic grips. Later versions, beginning in 1960, had walnut stocks. No thumbrest. Made 1955-77.

MK I & II/SERIES 90 DOUBLE EAGLE
COMBAT COMMANDER . . . . **NiB $860 Ex $500 Gd $380**
SA/DA trigger. Calibers: .40 S&W, .45 ACP. Seven-round magazine, 4.25-in. bbl., 7.75 in. overall. Weight: 36 oz. Fixed blade front sight, square-notch rear. Checkered Xenoy grips. Stainless finish. Made 1991-96.

MK II/SERIES 90 DOUBLE EAGLE SEMIAUTO
PISTOL . . . . **NiB $860 Ex $510 Gd $380**
SA/DA trigger. Calibers: .38 Super, 9mm, 10mm, .45 ACP. Seven-round magazine. Five-in. bbl., 8.5 in. overall. Weight: 39 oz. Fixed or Accro adj. sights. Matte stainless finish. Checkered Xenoy grips. Made 1990-96.
.38 Super, 9mm, add $100
10mm, add $25

MK II/SERIES 90 DOUBLE EAGLE
OFFICER'S MODEL . . . . **NiB $860 Ex $510 Gd $380**
Same general specifications as Double Eagle except chambered for .45 ACP only, 3.5-in. bbl., 7.25 in. overall. Weight: 35 oz. Also available in lightweight (25 oz.) w/blued finish (same price). Made 1990-91.

MK II/MK III NATIONAL MATCH
MID-RANGE . . . . **NiB $1241 Ex $1020 Gd $704**
Similar to Gold Cup National Match .45 Auto except chambered for .38 Special Mid Range. Five-round magazine, Made 1961-74.

MK IV/SERIES 70 COMBAT COMMANDER
Same general specifications as the Lightweight Commander except made 1970-83.
Blued finish . . . . **NiB $1020 Ex $903 Gd $750**
Nickel finish . . . . **NiB $1193 Ex $974 Gd $815**

MK IV/SERIES 70 GOLD CUP
NATIONAL MATCH . . . . **NiB $1743 Ex $1356 Gd $1153**
Match version of MK IV/Series '70 Government Model. Caliber: .45 Auto only. Flat mainspring housing. Accurizor bbl., and bushing. Solid rib, Colt-Elliason adj. rear sight undercut front sight. Adj. trigger, target hammer. 8.75 in. overall. Weight: 38.5 oz. Blued finish. Checkered walnut grips. Made 1970-84.

MK IV/SERIES 70
GOVERNMENT . . . . **NiB $1120 Ex $815 Gd $570**
Calibers: .45 Auto, .38 Super Auto, 9mm Para. Seven-round magazine in .45, 9-rnd. in .38 and 9mm. Five-in. bbl., 8.38 in. overall. Weight: 38 oz., (.45); 39 oz. in .38 and 9mm. Fixed rear sight and ramp front sight. Blued or nickel-plated finish. Checkered walnut grips. Made 1970-84.

MK IV/SERIES 80 .380 GOVERNMENT AUTOMATIC
PISTOL
Caliber: .380 ACP, 3.29-in. bbl., 6.15 in. overall. Weight: 21.8 oz. Composition grips. Fixed sights. Made since 1983 to 1996.
Blued finish (disc.1997) . . . . . **NiB $1132 Ex $918 Gd $712**
Bright nickel (disc.1995) . . . . . **NiB $1181 Ex $974 Gd $729**
Satin nickel Coltguard (disc.1989) NiB$1219 Ex$1016 Gd$751
Stainless finish. . . . . **NiB $1173 Ex $974 Gd $755**

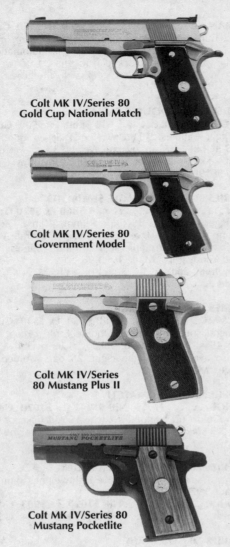

Colt MK IV/Series 80 Gold Cup National Match

Colt MK IV/Series 80 Government Model

Colt MK IV/Series 80 Mustang Plus II

Colt MK IV/Series 80 Mustang Pocketlite

MK IV/SERIES 80 COMBAT COMMANDER
Simialr specifications as MK IV/Series 80 Governemnt except w/ steel frame, 4.25-in. bbl. Made 1983-93.

Blued finish (disc.1996)	NiB $950	Ex $620	Gd $470
Satin nickel (disc.1987)	NiB $975	Ex $650	Gd $580
Stainless finish (disc.1998)	NiB $860	Ex $570	Gd $450
Two-tone finish (disc.1998)	NiB $810	Ex $600	Gd $450
Gold Cup (disc.1993)	NiB $1200	Ex $930	Gd $830

MK IV/SERIES 80 COMBAT
GOVERNMENT . . . . NiB $960 Ex $670 Gd $480
Same general specifications as MK IV/Series 80 Government except w/matte black finish. Calibers: .45 ACP. Made 1983-98.

Combat Elite (.38 Super)	NiB $980	Ex $700	Gd $600
Combat Target (adj. sights)	NiB $770	Ex $530	Gd $460

MK IV/SERIES 80 GOLD CUP NATIONAL MATCH
Same general specifications as Match Series 70 except w/ additional finishes and "pebbled" wraparound Neoprene grips. Made 1983-96.

Blued finish	NiB $1071	Ex $714	Gd $490
Bright blued finish	NiB $1071	Ex $714	Gd $490
Stainless finish	NiB $1148	Ex $867	Gd $638

MK IV/SERIES 80 GOVERNMENT MODEL
Similar specifications as Government Model Series 70 except w/firing pin safety feature. Made 1983-97.

Blued finish	NiB $1117	Ex $755	Gd $520
Nickel finish	NiB $1150	Ex $800	Gd $570
Stain nickel/blue finish	NiB $1150	Ex $800	Gd $570
Matte stainless finish	NiB $1100	Ex $730	Gd $490
Bright stainless finish	NiB $1410	Ex $1010	Gd $580

MK IV/SERIES 80 LIGHT-
WEIGHT COMMANDER . . . . NiB $1071 Ex $714 Gd $490
Updated version of the MK IV/Series 70.

MK IV/SERIES 80
MUSTANG .380 AUTOMATIC
Caliber: .380 ACP. Five- or 6-rnd. magazine, 2.75-in. bbl., 5.5 in. overall. Weight: 18.5 oz. Blued, nickel or stainless finish. Black composition grips. Made 1983-98.

Blued finish	NiB $638	Ex $437	Gd $296
Nickel finish (disc.1994)	NiB $770	Ex $479	Gd $308
Satin nickel Coltguard (disc.1988)	NiB $740	Ex $474	Gd $306
Stainless finish	NiB $709	Ex $397	Gd $306

MK IV/SERIES 80 MUSTANG PLUS II
Caliber: .380 ACP, 7-rnd. magazine, 2.75-in. bbl., 5.5 in. overall. Weight: 20 oz. Blued or stainless finish w/checkered black composition grips. Made 1988-96.

Blued finish	NiB $693	Ex $407	Gd $302
Stainless finish	NiB $693	Ex $407	Gd $302

MK IV/SERIES 80 MUSTANG POCKETLITE
Same general specifications as the Mustang 30 except weight: 12.5 oz. w/aluminum alloy receiver. Blued, chrome or stainless finish. Optional wood grain grips. 1987-97.

Blued finish	NiB $683	Ex $405	Gd $305
Lady Elite (two-tone) finish	NiB $683	Ex $405	Gd $305
Stainless finish	NiB $683	Ex $405	Gd $305
Teflon/stainless finish	NiB $683	Ex $405	Gd $305

MUSTANG XSP . . . . NiB $580 Ex $480 Gd $355
Similar to Mustang Pocketlite model except w/polymer grip frame. 2013-15.

MK IV/SERIES 80 OFFICER'S ACP AUTOMATIC PISTOL
Caliber: .45 ACP, 3.63-in. bbl., 7.25 in. overall. 6-rnd. magazine. Weight: 34 oz. Made 1984-98.

Blued finish (disc.1996)	NiB $605	Ex $500	Gd $357
Matte finish (disc.1991)	NiB $581	Ex $474	Gd $349
Satin nickel finish (disc.1985)	NiB $669	Ex $544	Gd $378
Stainless steel (disc.1997)	NiB $630	Ex $514	Gd $367
Lightweight (disc.1997)	NiB $900	Ex $710	Gd $520
Conceal Carry (disc.1998)	NiB $900	Ex $710	Gd $520
General's Officer (disc.1996)	NiB $1350	Ex $1040	Gd $680

MK IV/SERIES 80 SA LIGHTWEIGHT CONCEALED
CARRY OFFICER . . . . NiB $741 Ex $581 Gd $415
Caliber: .45 ACP. Seven-round magazine, 4.25-in. bbl., 7.75 in. overall. Weight: 35 oz. Aluminum alloy receiver w/stainless slide. Dovetailed low-profile sights w/3-dot system. Matte stainless finish w/blued receiver. Wraparound black rubber grip w/finger grooves. Made in 2000.

MK IV/SERIES 80 SPECIAL COMBAT GOVERNMENT
SEMIAUTO PISTOL . . . . NiB $2100 Ex $1450 Gd $800
Calibers: .38 Super or .45 ACP, 5-in. bbl., custom tuned for competition. Blued, hard crome or two-tone finsh. Made 1992 to date.

Colt MK IV/Series 80 Officer's ACP

Colt Pocket Junior

Colt Super Match .38

Carry (1992-00, reintro. 1996) ... NiB $2095 Ex $1450 Gd $800
CMC Marine Pistol .... NiB $2160 Ex $1200 Gd $820

MK IV/SERIES 90 DEFENDER
SA LIGHTWEIGHT .... NiB $918 Ex $576 Gd $398
Caliber: .45 ACP. Seven-round magazine, 3-in. bbl., 6.75 in. over-all. Weight: 22.5 oz. Aluminum alloy receiver w/ stainless slide. Dovetailed low-profile sights w/3-dot system. Matte stainless finish w/Nickel-Teflon receiver. Wraparound black rubber grip w/finger grooves. Made since 1998.

MK IV/SERIES 90
PONY DAO PISTOL .... NiB $772 Ex $567 Gd $396
Caliber: .380 ACP. Six-round magazine, 2.75-in. bbl., 5.5 in. overall. Weight: 19 oz. Ramp front sight, dovetailed rear. Stainless finish. Checkered black composition grips. Made 1997-98.

MK IV/SERIES 90
PONY POCKETLITE .... NiB $794 Ex $577 Gd $396
Similar to standard weight Pony Model except w/aluminum frame. Brushed stainless and Teflon finish. Made 1997-99.

NATIONAL MATCH (PRE-WWWII)
Identical to the Government Model .45 Auto but w/hand-honed action, match-grade bbl., adj. rear and ramp front sights or fixed sights. Made 1932-40.
w/adjustable sights ..... NiB $10,000 Ex $8000 Gd $4300
w/fixed sights .... NiB $8500 Ex $7000 Gd $4000

NATIONAL MATCH (WWII & POST-WWII)
AUTOMATIC PISTOL ..... NiB $2500 Ex $1600 Gd $900
Similar to Pre-WWII National Match except in .45 Auto only. Made 1957-70.

NEW AGENT .... NiB $1080 Ex $800 Gd $500
Series 80 system. Similar to Defender except in 9mm or .45 ACP w/trench style sights, hammerless. Made 2008-13.

NRA CENTENNIAL .45 GOLD CUP
NATIONAL MATCH .... NiB $1321 Ex $1024 Gd $841
Only 2500 produced in 1971.

POCKET JUNIOR MODEL
AUTOMATIC PISTOL .... NiB $464 Ex $344 Gd $260
Made in Spain by Unceta y Cia (Astra). Calibers: .22 Short, .25 Auto. Six-round magazine, 2.25 in. bbl., 4.75 in. over-all. Weight: 12 oz. Fixed sights. Checkered walnut grips. Note: In 1980, this model was subject to recall to correct an action malfunction. Returned firearms were fitted with a rebounding firing pin to prevent accidental discharges. Made 1958-68.

RAIL GUN SERIES
1911 Series 80 platform. Cal.: 9mm or .45 Auto. Bbl.: 5-in. Match Grade. Stainless steel frame w/Picatinny rail. Sights: Novak, low profile. Round spur hammer, 3-hole trigger, wide slide serrations. Grip: Checkered rosewood. Finish: Stainless, two-tone, or Cerakote. Made 2009-18.
two-tone finish .... NiB $1030 Ex $900 Gd $630
Cerakote stainless FDE finish .. NiB $1480 Ex $1230 Gd $880
Lightweight model
(aluminum frame) .... NiB $1130 Ex $1030 Gd $830
Lightweight Commander
model (aluminum frame,
4.2-in. bbl.) .... NiB $1130 Ex $1030 Gd $830
M45A1 Close Quarter
Battle model .... NiB $1655 Ex $1330 Gd $880
Stainless Commander model
(4.2-in. bbl.) .... NiB $1030 Ex $900 Gd $630

SUPER .38 AUTOMATIC PISTOL
Identical to Government Model .45 Auto except for caliber and magazine capacity. Caliber: .38 Automatic. Nine-round magazine, Made 1928-70.
Pre-war .... NiB $6125 Ex $4429 Gd $3010
Post-war .... NiB $2709 Ex $2199 Gd $2008

SUPER MATCH .38 AUTOMATIC PISTOL
Identical to Super .38 Auto but w/hand-honed action, match grade bbl., adjustable rear sight and ramp front sight or fixed sights. Made 1933-46.
w/adjustable sights ..... NiB $11,595 Ex $6125 Gd $3162
w/fixed sights .... NiB $10,125 Ex $5125 Gd $2125

TARGETSMAN MODEL .... NiB $950 Ex $700 Gd $400
Similar to Third Series Woodsman Target model except w/ 6-in. bbl. only, economy adj. rear sight, lacks automatic slide stop. Grip: Early versions had black plastic stocks, later versions, beginning in 1960, had walnut stocks, standard with left panel thumbrest. Made 1959-77.

TRADITIONAL SERIES
1911 Series 70 platform. Cal.: 9mm, .38 Super, or .45 Auto. Bbl.: 5-in. Match Grade. Steel frame. Sights: Fixed GI-style. Spur hammer, solid trigger, fine vertical slide serrations. Grip: Checkered rosewood. Finish: Stainless, blued, or Royal Blue. Made 2018-date.

GRADING: NiB = New in Box **Ex** = Excellent or NRA 95% **Gd** = Good or NRA 68%

Colt Targetsman

Colt Woodsman Match Target First Series

Colt Woodsman Target Model First Series (pencil bbl. 1915-22)

Colt Woodsman Target Model Firts Series (straight taper bbl. 1934-37)

blued finish. . . . . NiB $799 Ex $750 Gd $680
stainless finish. . . . . NiB $899 Ex $850 Gd $780
royal blue finish (wood grip
    w/medallion) . . . . NiB $1499 Ex $1350 Gd $950

USMC M45 CQBP . . . . NiB $1995 Ex $1500 Gd $1000
Caliber: .45 ACP. Same general specifications as MK IV/Series 80 Rail Gun except w/Cerakote desert tan finish, stainless barrel, G10 grips. Made 2013 to date.

WILEY CLAPP SERIES
1911 platform similar to other models. Made 2019-date.
CCO model (Series 70) . . . . . . NiB $1130 Ex $1030 Gd $830
Gov't. 1911 model (Series 70) . . NiB $1130 Ex $1030 Gd $830
Lightweight Commander model
    (Series 70). . . . . NiB $1130 Ex $1030 Gd $830
Stainless Commander model
    (Series 70). . . . . NiB $1200 Ex $1055 Gd $860

COLT AUTOMATIC TARGET PISTOL
(PRE-WOODSMAN) . . . . . . NiB $3000 Ex $2000 Gd $700
Semiauto. SA. Caliber: .22 LR (reg. velocity). 10-rnd. magazine w/ bottom release. 6-5/8-in. bbl., 10.5 in. overall. Weight: 28 oz. Adj. front and rear sights. Blued finish. Checkered walnut grips. Serial number range: 1-54000. Made 1915-22.

NOTE: *The earliest model of what would come to be known as the Woodsman originally came in only one version and*

was known simply as *"Colt Automatic Target Pistol."* Usually called *Pre-Woodsman* by collectors today. Note: The mainspring housing of this model is not strong enough to permit safe use of high-speed cartridges. Change to a new heat-treated mainspring housing was made at pistol No. 83,790. Many of the old models were converted by installation of new housings. The new housing may be distinguished from the earlier type by the checkering in the curve under the breech. The new housing is grooved straight across, while the old type bears a diagonally-checkered oval.

FIRST SERIES WOODSMAN TARGET
MODEL. . . . . NiB $2600 Ex $1500 Gd $500
Similar to late pre-Woodsman except "THE WOODSMAN" is marked on side of receiver. Made 1927-47.

NOTE: *There are three series of Woodsman pistols, corresponding to three basic frame designs. First Series refers to all those built on the S frame as it existed prior to and during World War Two. Second Series includes all versions built on the second S frame design from late 1947 until mid 1955, and Third Series means the third S frame design as used from 1955 to the end of regular production in 1977. Each series had a Sport Model w/a 4-1/2 in. rnd. barrel, a Target Model w/a 6 or 6-5/8 in. rnd. barrel, and a Match Target Model with a heavy, flat sided barrel. The very similar Challenger, Huntsman, and Targetsman were made during the post-WWII years only.*

FIRST SERIES WOODSMAN MATCH TARGET
MODEL. . . . . NiB $4500 Ex $2600 Gd $1500
Same basic design as other First Series Woodsman Target model. Caliber: .22 LR. 10-rnd. magazine, 6-5/8-in. bbl. slightly tapered w/flat sides, 11 in. overall. Weight: 36 oz. Adjustable rear sight. Blued finish. Checkered walnut one-piece grip w/ extended sides known as "Elephant Ear" grips. Made 1938-43.

FIRST SERIES WOODSMAN SPORT
MODEL . . . . NiB $2800 Ex $1700 Gd $600
Similar as Firts Series Woodsman Target model except has 4.5-in. bbl., fixed front sight. Weight: 27 oz., 8.5 in. overall. Note: Some of the early Sport Models had a lighter, medium weight barrel, and some of the later pre-WWII Sport Models had an optional elevation adjustable front sight. Made 1933-47.

NOTE: *The Second Series Woodsmans are the only models that have a push button thumb magazine release, similar to Colt Government Model 1911 pistols.*

SECOND SERIES WOODSMAN MATCH TARGET
MODEL. . . . . NiB $2400 Ex $1600 Gd $800
Same basic design as First Series Woodsman Target model except: Caliber: .22 LR (reg. or high speed). 10-rnd. magazine. 4.5- or 6-in. bbl. Grips: plastic with left panel thumbrest. Made 1947-55.

SECOND SERIES WOODSMAN SPORT
MODEL. . . . . NiB $2100 Ex $453 Gd $316
Same as Second Series Match Target model except w/4.5-in. bbl., 9 in. overall. Weight: 36 oz. Grips: standard was plastic, before mid-1949 no thumbrest, after mid-1949 left panel thumbrest. Made 1948-55.

SECOND SERIES WOODSMAN TARGET
MODEL. . . . . NiB $1900 Ex $800 Gd $750
Same as Second Series Woodsman Match Target model except 6-in. bbl. only, 9 in. overall. Weight: 30 oz. Grips: standard with plastic and left panel thumbrest. Made 1948-55.

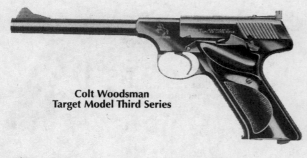

**Colt Woodsman
Target Model Third Series**

**Colt Woodsman
Sport Model Third Series**

**Colt World War II
D-Day Invasion
Commemorative**

**Colt World
War II
50th Anniversary
Commemorative**

NOTE: *The Third Series replaced the Second Series in mid 1955. The most obvious change was the replacement of the push button magazine release with a snap catch at the butt. The Challenger was replaced in the third series with the very similar Huntsman.*

THIRD SERIES WOODSMAN TARGET

MODEL . . . . **NiB $1400 Ex $950 Gd $500**
Same basic design as Second Series Woodsman Target model but w/6-in. bbl. only. Grip: early versions had black plastic stocks,

later versions, beginning in 1960, had walnut stocks. NOTE: All Second and Third Series Target models were standard with left panel thumbrest. Made 1955-77.

THIRD SERIES WOODSMAN SPORT

MODEL . . . . **NiB $1450 Ex $1000 Gd $500**
Same basic design as Third Series Woodsman Target model but w/4.5-in. bbl. only. Grip: standard with left panel thumbrest, early versions had black plastic stocks, later versions, beginning in 1960, had walnut stocks. Made 1955-77.

THIRD SERIES WOODSMAN MATCH TARGET

MODEL . . . . **NiB $900 Ex $650 Gd $350**
Same basic design as Third Series Woodsman Target model but w/4.5- or 6-in. bbl. Grip: early versions had black plastic stocks, later versions, beginning in 1960, had walnut stocks. NOTE: All Second and Third Series Target models were standard with left panel thumbrest. Made 1955-77.

WORLD WAR I 50TH ANNIVERSARY
COMMEMORATIVE SERIES

Limited production replica of Model 1911 .45 Auto engraved w/battle scenes, commemorating Battles at Chateau Thierry, Belleau Wood Second Battle of the Marne, Meuse Argonne. In special presentation display cases. Production: 7,400 Standard model, 75 Deluxe, 25 Special Deluxe grade. Match numbered sets offered. Made 1967-69. Values indicated are for commemoratives in new condition.
Standard grade . . . . **NiB $1046 Ex $780 Gd $638**
Deluxe grade . . . . **NiB $2152 Ex $1743 Gd $1220**
Special Deluxe grade . . . . . **NiB $4687 Ex $3890 Gd $2448**

WORLD WAR II COMMEMORATIVE

.45 AUTO . . . . **NiB $1047 Ex $774 Gd $562**
Limited production replica of Model 1911A1 .45 Auto engraved w/respective names of locations where historic engagements occurred during WW II, as well as specific issue and theater identification. European model has oak leaf motif on slide, palm leaf design frames the Pacific issue. Cased. 11,500 of each model were produced. Made in 1970. Value listed is for gun in new condition.

WORLD WAR II 50TH ANNIVERSARY

COMMEMORATIVE . . . . . . **NiB $2647 Ex $2064 Gd $1629**
Same general specifications as the Colt World War II Commemorative .45 Auto except slightly different scroll engraving, 24-karat gold-plate trigger, hammer, slide stop, magazine catch, magazine catch lock, safety lock and four grip screws. Made in 1995 only.

WORLD WAR II D-DAY

INVASION COMMEMORATIVE . . **NiB $1550 Ex $1436 Gd $1138**
High-luster and highly decorated version of the Colt Model 1911A1. Caliber: .45 ACP. Same general specifications as the Colt Model 1911 except for 24-karat gold-plated hammer, trigger, slide stop, magazine catch, magazine catch screw, safety lock and four grip screws. Also has scrolls and inscription on slide. Made 1991 only.

WORLD WAR II GOLDEN ANNIVERSARY V-J DAY

TRIBUTE .45 AUTO . . . . **NiB $2662 Ex $2239 Gd $1658**
Basic Colt Model 1911A1 design w/highly-polished bluing and decorated w/specialized tributes to honor V-J Day. Two 24-karat gold scenes highlight the slide. 24-karat gold-plated hammer. Checkered wood grips w/gold medallion on each side. Made 1995.

**Colt
Camp Perry First Issue**

**Colt
Camp Perry Second Issue**

XSE SERIES MODEL O SEMIAUTO PISTOL
Caliber: .45 Auto. 8-rnd. magazine, 4.24- or 5-in. bbl. Novak sights, front/rear slide serrations, extanded ambi. thumb safety. Checkered rosewood grips. Made 2000-15.

Combat Elite . . . . NiB $1100 Ex $700 Gd $500
Commander . . . . NiB $1200 Ex $730 Gd $530
Government . . . . NiB $1100 Ex $700 Gd $500
Ligthweight Commander. . . . . NiB $1100 Ex $700 Gd $500
Ligthweight Government . . . . NiB $1100 Ex $700 Gd $500
Rail Gun . . . . NiB $1200 Ex $730 Gd $530

- SINGLE-SHOT PISTOLS & DERRINGERS -

CAMP PERRY MODEL SINGLE-
SHOT PISTOL, FIRST ISSUE . . . NiB $2410 Ex $1960 Gd $1660
Built on Officers' Model frame. Caliber: .22 LR (embedded head chamber for high-speed cartridges after 1930). 10 in. bbl., 13.75 in. overall. Weight: 34.5 oz. Adj. target sights. Hand-finished action. Blued finish. Checkered walnut grips. Made 1926-34.

CAMP PERRY MODEL
SECOND ISSUE . . . . NiB $3374 Ex $2744 Gd $2324
Same general specifications as First Issue except has shorter hammer fall and 8-in. bbl., 12 in. overall. Weight: 34 oz. Made 1934-41 (about 440 produced).

CIVIL WAR CENTENNIAL MODEL PISTOL
Single-shot replica of Colt Model 1860 Army Revolver. Caliber: .22 Short. Six-in. bbl., weight: 22 oz. Blued finish w/gold-plated frame, grip frame, and trigger guard, walnut grips. Cased. 24,114 were produced. Made in 1961.

Single pistol . . . . NiB $362 Ex $265 Gd $204
Pair w/consecutive
  serial numbers . . . . NiB $689 Ex $541 Gd $408

DERRINGER NO. 4
Replica of derringer No. 3 (1872 Thuer Model). Single-shot w/ sideswing bbl., Caliber: .22 Short, 2.5-in. bbl., 4.9 in. overall. Weight: 7.75 oz. Fixed sights. Gold-plated frame w/blued bbl., and walnut grips or completely nickel- or gold-plated w/ simulated ivory or pearl grips. Made 1959-63. 112,000 total production. (S/N w/D or N suffix)

Single pistol (gun only) . . . . NiB $128 Ex $88 Gd $61
Single pistol (cased w/accessories). . . NiB $408 Ex $281 Gd $189

DERRINGER NO. 4 COMMEMORATIVE MODELS
Limited production version of .22 derringers issued, w/ appropriate inscription, to commemorate historical events. Additionally, non-firing models (w/unnotched bbls.) were furnished in books, picture frames and encased in plExiglass as singles or in cased pairs.
No. 4 Presentation Derringers
  (Non-firing w/accessories) . . . . NiB $408 Ex $281 Gd $189

Ltd. Ed. Book Series(w/nickel-plated
  derringers) . . . . NiB $388 Ex $255 Gd $143
1st Presentation Series
  (Leatherette covered metal case) . . NiB $408 Ex $281 Gd $189
2nd Presentation Series
  (Single wooden case) . . . . NiB $408 Ex $281 Gd $189
2nd Presentation Series
  (Paired wooden case) . . . . NiB $423 Ex $291 Gd $198
1961 Issue Geneseo, Illinois,
  125th Anniversary (104 produced) . . NiB $729 Ex $556 Gd $388
1962 Issue Fort McPherson, Nebraska, Centennial
  (300 produced). . . . . NiB $729 Ex $556 Gd $388

LORD AND LADY DERRINGERS (NO. 5)
Same as Derringer No. 4. Lord model with blued bbl., w/gold-plated frame and walnut grips. Lady model is gold-plated w/ simulated pearl grips. Sold in cased pairs. Made 1970-72. (S/N w/Der suffix)

Lord derringer, pair in case. . . . NiB $577 Ex $408 Gd $301
Lady derringer, pair in case. . . . NiB $577 Ex $408 Gd $301
Lord and Lady derringers,
  one each, in case . . . . NiB $577 Ex $408 Gd $301

ROCK ISLAND ARSENAL
CENTENNIAL PISTOL. . . . . NiB $520 Ex $489 Gd $332
Limited production (550 pieces) version of Civil War Centennial Model single-shot .22 pistol, made Exclusively for Cherry's Sporting Goods, Geneseo, Illinois, to commemorate the centennial of the Rock Island Arsenal in wIllinois. Cased. Made in 1962.

NOTE: *This section of Colt handguns contains only revolvers (single action and double action) by model name in alphabetical order. For automatic pistols or single-shot pistols and derringers, please see the two sections that precede this. For a complete listing, refer to the Index.*

- REVOLVERS -

MODEL 1877 LIGHTNING. . . NiB $4500 Ex $3264 Gd $2973
DA revolver w/fixed cyiInder. Also called Thunderer Model. Calibers: .38 and .41 centerfire. Six-round cylinder, bbl. lengths: 2.5-, 3.5-, 4.5- and 6-in. without ejector, 4.5- and 6-in. w/ejector, 8.5 in. overall (3.5-in. bbl.). Weight: 23 oz. (.38 cal., w/3.5-in. bbl.) Fixed sights. Blued or nickel finish. Hard rubber bird's-head grips. Made 1877-1909.

MODEL 1877
THUNDERER . . . . NiB $4760 Ex $3210 Gd $2260
Similar to Lightning except in .41 Colt only. Made 1877-1909.

MODEL 1878 . . . . NiB $6010 Ex $5100 Gd $3250
DA. Calibers: .32-20, .38 Colt, .38-40, .41 LC, .44 Russian, .44 S&W, .44-40, .45 LC, .450 Eley, .455 Eley or .476 Eley.

Colt Agent First Issue

Colt Banker's Special

Colt Anaconda

Colt Lightning/Thunderer 1877-1912

Colt Model 1877 Lightning

Six-round fixed cylinder. Bbl. Lengths: 2.5-, 3.5-, 4- w/o ejector rod and 4.75-, 5.5-, 7.5-, 8.5-, 9-, 10- or 12-in. w/ejctor rod. Fixed sights. Finish: blued, case hardened or nickel. Checkered hard rubber bird's-head grips. Made 1878-1905.

.38 DS II REVOLVER . . . . NiB $660 Ex $430 Gd $230
Similar to Detective Special. Caliber: .38 Special or .357 Mag. Six-round cylinder, 2-in. bbl., 7 in. overall. Weight: 21 oz. Ramp front sight, fixed notch rear. Satin stainless finish. Black rubber combat grip w/finger grooves. Made 1997-98.

.38 SF-VI . . . . NiB $660 Ex $560 Gd $430
DA. Caliber: .38 Special only. Six-round cylinder, 2- or 4-in. bbl. Ramp front sight, fixed notch rear. Finish: Satin, polished or black. Grip: black rubber. Made 1995-96.

AGENT FIRST ISSUE . . . . NiB $890 Ex $710 Gd $510
Same as Cobra, first issue except has short-grip frame .38 Special only, weight: 14 oz. Made 1955-72.

AGENT (LW) SECOND ISSUE . . NiB $810 Ex $530 Gd $430
Same as Colt Agent, first issue except has shrouded ejector rod and alloy frame. Made 1973-86.

AIRCREWMAN . . . . NiB $4510 Ex $2760 Gd $1130
DA revolver made for U.S. Air Force. Caliber: .38 Special only. Six-round swing-out cylinder, 2-in. bbl. Aluminum frame. Weight: 11 oz. Fixed sights. Grip: checkered walnut that overlapped the frame above the grip w/silver U.S. Air Force medallions. Satmped "Property of U.S. Air Force" on back strap and an U.S. Air Force issue number on the butt. S/N range: 2,901LW to about 7,775LW. Made 1951.

ANACONDA DA REVOLVER
Calibers: .44 Mag., .45 Colt., bbl. lengths: 4, 6 or 8 in.; 11.63 in. overall (w/ 6-in. bbl.). Weight: 53 oz. (6-in. bbl.). Adj. white outline rear sight, red insert ramp-style front. Matte stainless or Realtree gray camo finish. Black Neoprene combat grips w/ finger grooves. Made 1990-99 and 2002-06.

Matte stainless . . . . NiB $1910 Ex $1760 Gd $1260
4-in. bbl., add $100
Realtree gray camo
  finish (disc. 1996) . . . . NiB $2260 Ex $2110 Gd $1360
Custom model
  (.44 Mag. w/ported bbl.) . NiB $2260 Ex $2110 Gd $1360
First Edition model (Ltd. Edition
  1000, 1990 only) . . . . NiB $3510 Ex $3010 Gd $1999
Hunter model
  (.44 Mag. w/2x scope) . . . NiB $2260 Ex $2110 Gd $1360

- Recent MFG -

Anaconda (bright stainless, 6- or 8-in. bbl.,
  2021-date) . . . . NiB $1499 Ex $1399 Gd $1300

ANACONDA TITANIUM DA REVOLVER
Same general specifications as the standard Anaconda except chambered .44 Mag. only w/titanium-plated finish, gold-plated trigger, hammer and cylinder release. Limited edition of 1,000 distributed by American Historical Foundation w/personalized inscription. Made in 1996.
One of 1000 . . . . NiB $2744 Ex $2242 Gd $1624
Presentation case, add $255

GRADING: **NiB** = New in Box   **Ex** = Excellent or NRA 95%   **Gd** = Good or NRA 68%

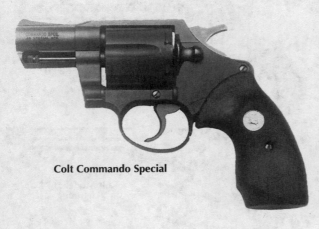

Colt Commando Special

**Colt Cobra
Round Butt First Issue**

COBRA (ROUND BUTT)
FIRST ISSUE . . . . **NiB $1260 Ex $960 Gd $660**
Similar to Detective Special model except w/Colt-alloy light-weight frame. Two-in. bbl., calibers: .22 LR, .38 Special, .38 New Police, .32 New Police. Weight: 15 oz., (.38 cal.). Blued finish. Checkered plastic or walnut grips. Made 1950-72.
.22 LR, add **20%**
nickel finish, add **20%**

COBRA SECOND ISSUE . . . . . . **NiB $860 Ex $760 Gd $530**
Similar to Cobra First Issue except w/shrouded ejector rod. Made 1973-81.
Cobra (new mfg. 2017-date) . . . . **NiB $620 Ex $560 Gd $410**
Combat Cobra (1986-87) . . . **NiB $3900 Ex $2800 Gd $1800**

COBRA (SQUARE BUTT)
FIRST ISSUE . . . . **NiB $1260 Ex $960 Gd $660**
Similar to Cobra First Issue except w/4-in. bbl., Calibers: .38 Special, .38 New Police, .32 New Police. Weight: 17 oz. in .38 caliber. Blued finish. Checkered plastic or walnut grips. Early models.

COBRA (RECENT MFG.) . . . . . . **NiB $630 Ex $505 GD $405**
New linear leaf main spring. Bbl.: 2-in. Caliber: .38 Special +P. Sight: Fiber optic front. Weight: 25 oz. Finish: Matte stainless. Grip: Hogue rubber. Made 2017 to date.

COMMANDO SPECIAL . . . . . . **NiB $760 Ex $510 Gd $330**
Similar to Detective Special. Caliber: .38 Special. Six-round cylinder, 2-in. bbl., 6.88 in. overall. Weight: 21.5 oz. Fixed sights. Low-luster blued finish. Rubber grips. Made 1984-86.

COURIER . . . . **NiB $1510 Ex $1210 Gd $600**
Aluminum "D" frame, similar to Cobra. Caliber: .22 LR or .32 S&W. Six-round swing-out cylinder, 3-in. bbl. Fixed sights. Bright blue-black anodized finish. Checkered wood grips. Made 1953-56.

ARMY SPECIAL
DA REVOLVER . . . . **NiB $1399 Ex $1000 Gd $760**
.41-caliber frame. Calibers: .32-20, .38 Special (.41 Colt). Six-round cylinder, right revolution. Bbl., lengths: 4-, 4.5, 5-, and 6-in., 9.25 in. overall (4-in. bbl.). Weight: 32 oz. (4-in. bbl.). Fixed sights. Blued or nickel-plated finish. Hard rubber grips. Made 1908-27. Note: This model has a some-what heavier frame than the New Navy, which it replaced. S/N begin w/300,000. The heavy .38 Special High velocity loads should not be used in .38 Special arms of this model. Made 1908-27.

BANKER'S SPECIAL DA REVOLVER
This is the Police Positive w/a 2-in. bbl., otherwise specifications same as that model, rounded butt intro. in 1933. Calibers: .22 LR (embedded head-cylinder for high speed cartridges intro. 1933), .38 New Police. 6.5 in. overall. Weight: 23 oz. (.22 LR), 19 oz. (.38). Made 1926-40.
.38 caliber . . . . **NiB $2260 Ex $1860 Gd $1260**
.22 caliber . . . . **NiB $3210 Ex $2510 Gd $1860**

BOA . . . . **NiB $9500 Ex $8510 Gd $5510**
DA. Uses Mark V action. Caliber: .357 Mag. 4- or 6-in. bbl. w/ full ejector shroud. Lew Horton distributor. Made 1985.
Two gun set . . . . **NiB $22,500 Ex $18,510 Gd $12,520**

**Colt
Detective Special First Issue**

DETECTIVE SPECIAL DA REVOLVER, FIRST ISSUE
Similar to Police Positive Special except w/2-in. bbl., otherwise specifications same as that model, rounded butt intro. 1933. .38 Special only in pre-war issue. Blued or nickel-plated finish. Weight: 17 oz. 6.75 in. overall. Made 1927-46.
Blued finish . . . . NiB $2155 Ex $1855 Gd $1630
Nickel finish, add 20%

DETECTIVE SPECIAL SECOND ISSUE
Similar to Detective special first issue except w/2- or 3-in. bbl., and also chambered .32 New Police, .38 New Police. Wood, plastic or over-sized grips. Post-WWII manufacture, made 1947-72.
Blued finish . . . . NiB $1355 Ex $1155 Gd $955
Nickel finish, add 20%
w/three-in. bbl., add 15%

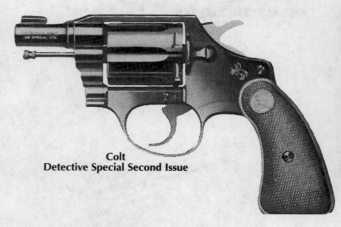

**Colt
Detective Special Second Issue**

DETECTIVE SPECIAL THIRD ISSUE
"D" frame, shrouded ejector rod. Caliber: .38 Special. Six-round cylinder, 2-in. bbl., 6.88 in. overall. Weight: 21.5 oz. Fixed rear sight, ramp front. Blued or nickel-plated finish. Checkered walnut wraparound grips. Made 1973-86.
Blued finish . . . . NiB $980 Ex $860 Gd $760
Nickel finish . . . . NiB $571 Ex $464 Gd $342
w/three-in. bbl., add $90

DETECTIVE SPECIAL DA REVOLVER, FOURTH ISSUE
Similar to Detective Special, Third Issue except w/alloy frame. Blued or chrome finish. Wraparound black neoprene grips w/ Colt medallion. Made 1993-95.
Blued finish . . . . NiB $700 Ex $662 Gd $596
Chrome finish, add 10%
DAO model
   (bobbed hammer) . . . . NiB $855 Ex $730 Gd $610

DIAMONDBACK DA REVOLVER
"D" frame, shrouded ejector rod. Calibers: .22 LR, .22 WRF, .38 Special. Six-round cylinder, 2.5-, 4- or 6-in. bbl., w/VR, 9 in. overall (w/ 4-in. bbl). Weight: 31.75 oz. (.22 cal., 4-in. bbl.), 28.5 oz. (.38 cal.). Ramp front sight, adj. rear. Blued or nickel finish. Checkered walnut grips. Made 1966-84.
Blued finish . . . . NiB $1460 Ex $1310 Gd $1000
Nickel finish, add 20%
2.5-in. brrl., add $800
.22 rimfire . . . . NiB $1760 Ex $1460 Gd $1110
.22 LR w/2.5-in. bb., ... NiB $3520 Ex $3170 Gd $2260
.22 LR, nickel finish, add $500

**Colt
Diamondback**

Extra interchangeable cylinder, add 10%
(K and P serial number suffix), add $100

FRONTIER SCOUT REVOLVER COMMEMORATIVE MODELS
Limited production versions of Frontier Scout issued, w/appropriate inscription, to commemorate historical events. Cased, in new condition.
1961 ISSUES
Kansas Statehood Centennial (6201 produced) . . . NiB $536
Pony Express Centennial
   (1007 produced) . . . . NiB $638

1962 ISSUES
Columbus, Ohio, Sesquicentennial
   (200 produced) . . . . NiB $638
Fort Findlay, Ohio,
   Sesquicentennial (130 produced) . . . . NiB $913
Fort Findlay Cased Pair, .22 Long
   Rifle and .22 Magnum (20 produced) . . . . NiB $2627
New MExico Golden Anniversary . . . . NiB $638
West Virginia Statehood
   Centennial (3452 produced) . . . . NiB $6130

1963 ISSUES
Arizona Territorial Centennial
   (5355 produced) . . . . NiB $638

DA ARMY (1878) . . . . NiB $6140 Ex $4524 Gd $3177
Also called DA Frontier. Similar in appearance to the smaller Lightning Model but has heavier frame of different shape, rnd. disc on left side of frame, lanyard loop in butt. Calibers: .38-40, .44-40, .45 Colt. Six-round cylinder, bbl. lengths: 3.5- and 4-in. (w/o ejector), 4.75-, 5.5- and 7.5-in. w/ejector. 12.5 in. overall (7.5-in. bbl.). Weight: 39 oz. (.45 cal., 7.5-in. bbl.). Fixed sights. Hard rubber bird's-head grips. Blued or nickel finish. Made 1878-1905.

FRONTIER SCOUT REVOLVER
SA Army replica, smaller scale. Calibers: .22 Short, Long, LR or .22 WMR (interchangeable cylinder available). Six-round cylinder, 4.75-in. bbl., 9.9 in. overall. Weight: 24 oz. Fixed sights. Plastic grips. Originally made w/bright alloy frame. Since 1959 w/steel frame and blued finish or all-nickel finish w/composition, wood or Staglite grips. Made 1958-71.
(Q or F serial number suffix) . . NiB $500 Ex $330 Gd $220
wood grips, add 50%
Buntline model, add 20%

Colt Idaho Territorial Centennial 1963 Issue

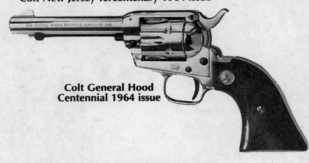

Colt New Jersey Tercentenary 1964 issue

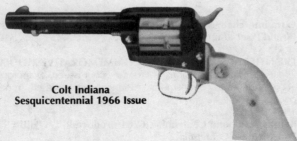

Colt General Hood Centennial 1964 issue

Colt Indiana Sesquicentennial 1966 Issue

Battle of Gettysburg Centennial
   (1019 produced) . . . . NiB $638
Carolina Charter Tercentenary (300 produced) . . NiB $2270
Fort Stephenson, Ohio,
   Sesquicentennial (200 produced) . . . . NiB $638
General John Hunt Morgan Indiana Raid . . . . NiB $689
Idaho Territorial Centennial (902 produced) . . . . . NiB $638

1964 ISSUES
California Gold Rush (500 produced) . . . . NiB $638
Chamizal Treaty (450 produced) . . . . NiB $638
General Hood Centennial (1503 produced) . . . . . NiB $638
Montana Territorial Centennial (2300 produced) . . NiB $638

Nevada "Battle Born" (981 produced) . . . . NiB $597
Nevada Statehood Centennial (3984 produced) . . NiB $2678
New Jersey Tercentenary (1001 produced) . . . . NiB $577
St. Louis Bicentennial (802 produced) . . . . NiB $638
Wyoming Diamond Jubilee (2357 produced) . . . . . NiB $638

1965 ISSUES
Appomattox Centennial (1001 produced) . . . . NiB $577
Forty-Niner Miner (500 produced) . . . . NiB $638
General Meade Campaign (1197 produced) . . . . . NiB $1647
Kansas Cowtown Series—Wichita (500 produced) . . . . . . NiB $577
Old Fort Des Moines Reconstruction (700 prod.). NiB $2280
Oregon Trail (1995 produced) . . . . NiB $638
St. Augustine Quadricentennial (500 produced) . . . NiB $638

1966 ISSUES
Colorado Gold Rush (1350 produced) . . . . NiB $638
Dakota Territory (1000 produced) . . . . NiB $638
Indiana Sesquicentennial (1500 produced) . . . . . . NiB $638
Kansas Cowtown Series—Abilene (500 produced) . . NiB $577
Kansas Cowtown Series—Dodge City
   (500 produced) . . . . NiB $577
Oklahoma Jubilee (1343 produced) . . . . NiB $638

1967 ISSUES
Alamo (4500 produced) . . . . NiB $577
Kansas Cowtown Series—Coffeyville
   (500 produced) . . . . NiB $561
Kansas Trail Series—Chisholm Trail (500 produced) NiB $577
Lawman Series—Bat Masterson (3000 produced) . . NiB $570

1968 ISSUES
Kansas Cowtown Series—Santa Fe
   Trail (501 produced) . . . . NiB $577
Kansas Trail Series—Pawnee Trail (501 produced) . NiB $577
Lawman Series—Pat Garrett (3000 produced) . . . . NiB $638
Nebraska Centennial (7001 produced) . . . . NiB $577

1969 ISSUES
Alabama Sesquicentennial (3001 produced) . . . . . . NiB $577
Arkansas Territory Sesquicentennial
   (3500 produced) . . . . NiB $561
California Bicentennial (5000 produced) . . . . NiB $577
General Nathan Bedford Forrest (3000 produced) . . . NiB $577
Golden Spike (11,000 produced) . . . . NiB $577
Kansas Trail Series—Shawnee Trail
   (501 produced) . . . . NiB $577
Lawman Series—Wild Bill Hickock
   (3000 produced) . . . . NiB $638

1970 ISSUES
Kansas Fort Series—Fort Larned (500 produced) . . . NiB $577
Kansas Fort Series—Fort Hays (500 produced) . . . NiB $577
Kansas Fort Series—Fort Riley (500 produced) . . . . NiB $577
Lawman Series—Wyatt Earp (3000 produced) . . . NiB $780
Maine Sesquicentennial (3000 produced) . . . . NiB $577

Missouri Sesquicentennial
   (3000 produced) . . . . NiB $577

1971 ISSUES
Kansas Fort Series—Fort Scott (500 produced) . . . . NiB $577

1972 ISSUES
Florida Territory Sesquicentennial
   (2001 produced) . . . . NiB $638

1973 ISSUES
Arizona ranger (3001 produced) . . . . NiB $638

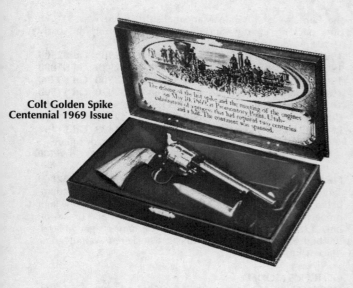

**Colt Golden Spike
Centennial 1969 Issue**

KING COBRA REVOLVER
Caliber: .357 Mag., bbl. lengths: 2.5-, 4-, 6- or 8-in., 9 in. overall (w/ 4-in. bbl.). Weight: 42 oz., average. Matte stainless steel or blued finish. Black Neoprene combat grips. Made 1986 to date. 2.5-in. bbl. and "Ultimate" bright or blued finish. Made 1988-92.

Blued.	NiB $1760	Ex $1460	Gd $1110
Matte stainless, add			$200
Ultimate bright stainless, add			15%
2.5-in. bbl., add			20%

KING COBRA (RECENT MFG.) . NiB $775 Ex $700 GD $400
New linear leaf main spring. Bbl.: 3-in. Caliber: .357 Mag.; 6-rnd. cylinder. Sight: blade front/groove rear. Weight: 34 oz. Finish: Matte stainless. Grip: Hogue Overmolded rubber. Made 2019 to date.

Carry DAO (2-in. bbl.)	NiB $775	Ex $655	Gd $400
Carry DAO (2-in. bbl., bobbed hammer)	NiB $775	Ex $655	Gd $400
Target (4.25-in. bbl., wood grip).	NiB $880	Ex $755	Gd $520

LAWMAN MK III DA REVOLVER
Shrouded ejector rod on 2-in. bbl., only. Caliber: .357 Magnum. Six-round cylinder, bbl. lengths: 2-, 4-in. 9.38 in. overall (w/4-in. bbl.), Weight: (w/ 4-in. bbl.), 35 oz. Fixed rear sight, ramp front. Service trigger and hammer or target trigger and wide-spur hammer. Blued or nickel-plated finish. Checkered walnut service or target grips. Made 1969-83.

Blued finish.	NiB $850	Ex $760	Gd $380
Nickel finish, add			$50
MK V (shrouded ejector, 1984-91), add			5%

**Colt King Cobra
(1988-92 MFG.)**

MAGNUM CARRY
DA REVOLVER . . . . NiB $2510 Ex $1760 Gd $730
Similar to Model DS II except chambered for .357 Magnum. Made 1999 only.

MARINE CORPS MODEL 1905 DA REVOLVER
General specifications same as New Navy Second Issue except has rnd. butt, was supplied only in .38 caliber (.38 Short & Long Colt, .38 Special) w/6-in. bbl. (S/N range 10,001-10,926) Made 1905-09.

Marine Corps model	NiB $4600	Ex $3800	Gd $2230
Marked "USMC", add.			35%

METROPOLITAN MK III . . . . . . NiB $660 Ex $530 Gd $430
Same as Official Police MK III except has 4-in. bbl. w/service or target grips. Weight: 36 oz. Made 1969-72.

NEW NAVY (1889) DA, FIRST ISSUE
Also called New Army. Calibers: .38 Short & Long Colt, .41 Short & Long Colt. Six-round cylinder, left revolution. Bbl. lengths: 3-, 4.5- and 6-in., 11.25 in. overall (w/ 6-in. bbl.). Weight: 32 oz. w/6-in. bbl. Fixed sights, knife-blade and V-notch. Blued or nickel-plated finish. Walnut or hard rubber grips. Made 1889-1994. Note: This model, which was adopted by both the Army and Navy, was Colt's first revolver of the solid frame, swing-out cylinder type. It lacks the cylinder-locking notches found on later models made on this .41 frame; ratchet on the back of the cylinder is held in place by a double projection on the hand.

First issue	NiB $2760	Ex $2260	Gd $1460
First issue w/3-in. bbl., add.			40%
Navy contract (marked U.S.N. on butt, S/N range: 1-1500), add.			70%

**Colt Lawman
MK V**

FRONTIER SCOUT
SA .22 REVOLVER . . . . NiB $532 Ex $342 Gd $235
Same as Peacemaker .22 except has flat-top frame, adj. rear sight, ramp front sight. Made 1971-76; reintro. 1982-86.

GRADING: **NiB** = New in Box   **Ex** = Excellent or NRA 95%   **Gd** = Good or NRA 68%

Colt New Navy

Colt New Service

NEW NAVY (1892) DA, SECOND ISSUE
Also called New Army. General specifications same as First Issue except double cylinder notches and double locking bolt. Calibers: .38 Special added in 1904 and .32-20 in 1905. Made 1892-1907. Note: The heavy .38 Special High Velocity loads should not be used in .38 Special arms of this model.
Second issue . . . . NiB $2160 Ex $1760 Gd $1020

NEW POCKET . . . . NiB $1460 Ex $1150 Gd $900
DA/SA. Caliber: .32 Short & Long Colt. Six-round cylinder. bbl. lengths: 2.5, 3.5- and 6-in. 7.5 in. overall w/3.5-in. bbl., Weight: 16 oz., w/3.5-in. bbl. Fixed sights, knife-blade and V-notch. Blued or nickel finish. Rubber grips. Made 1893-1905.

NEW POLICE . . . . NiB $1360 Ex $800 Gd $410
DA/SA. Built on New Pocket frame but w/larger grip. Calibers: .32 Colt New Police, .32 Short & Long Colt. Bbl. lengths: 2.5-, 4- and 6-in.; 8.5 in. overall (w/ 4-in. bbl.). Weight: 17 oz., w/4-in. bbl. Fixed knife-blade front sight, V-notch rear. Blued or nickel finish. Rubber grips. Made 1896-1907.

NEW POLICE TARGET . . . . . NiB $2260 Ex $1660 Gd $840
Target version of the New Police except w/target sights. Six-in. bbl., blued finish only. Made 1896-1905.

NEW SERVICE DA REVOLVER
Calibers: .38 Special, .357 Magnum (intro. 1936), .38-40, .44-40, .44 Russian, .44 Special, .45 Auto, .45 Colt, .450 Eley, .455 Eley, .476 Eley. Six-round cylinder, bbl. lengths: 4-, 5- and 6-in. in .38 Special and .357 Magnum, 4.5-, 5.5- and 7.5 in. in other calibers; 9.75 in. overall (w/ 4.5-in. bbl.). Weight: 39 oz. (.45 cal. w/4.5-in. bbl.). Fixed sights. Blued or nickel finish. Checkered walnut grips. Made 1898-42. Note: More than 500,000 of this model in caliber .45 Auto (designated "Model 1917 Revolver") were purchased by the U.S. Gov't. during WW I. These arms were later sold as surplus to National Rifle Association members through

the Director of Civilian Marksmanship. Price was $16.15 plus packing charge. Supply Exhausted during the early 1930s. Made 1898-1927.

1909 Army . . . . NiB $3760	Ex $2900	Gd $2500
1909 Navy . . . . NiB $4000	Ex $2920	Gd $1880
1909 USMC . . . . NiB $4100	Ex $3700	Gd $3200
1917 Army . . . . NiB $3760	Ex $2920	Gd $1500
1917 Commercial . . . . NiB $1700	Ex $1070	Gd $660
Commercial model . . . . NiB $3260	Ex $2760	Gd $1900
RNWMP/RCMP model . . . . NiB $2160	Ex $1483	Gd $1197

Shooting Master (various calibers, 6-in. bbl., rnd. or square butt, checkered grips straps)...NiB $2510 Ex $1900 Gd $1700

NEW SERVICE TARGET . . . . NiB $3500 Ex $3350 Gd $2800
Target version of the New Service. Calibers: Originally chambered for .44 Russian, .450 Eley, .455 Eley and .476 Eley, later models in .44 Special, .45 Colt and .45 Auto. Six- or 7.5-in. bbl., 12.75 in. overall (7.5-in. bbl.). Adj. target sights. Hand-finished action. With blued finish. Checkered walnut grips. Made 1900-40.

OFFICER'S MODEL
FIRST ISSUE . . . . NiB $1960 Ex $1499 Gd $1260
DA/SA. Caliber: .38 Spl. or .38 LC. Six-in. bbl., flat top frame, hand-finished action, adj. target sights. Checkered with walnut grips w/o medalion. Made 1904-08.

OFFICER'S MODEL SECOND
ISSUE . . . . NiB $1860 Ex $1550 Gd $1150
Similar to Officer's Modle First Issue except using improved Army Special action and more bbl. lengths: 4-, 4.5-, 5-, 6- and 7.5-in.. Made 1908-26.

OFFICER'S MODEL TARGET THIRD
ISSUE . . . . NiB $1460 Ex $1250 Gd $1000
Calibers: .22 LR (intro. 1930, embedded head-cylinder for high-speed cartridges after 1932), .32 Police Positive (made 1932-42), .38 Special. Six-round cylinder, bbl. lengths: 4-, 4.5-, 5-, 6- and 7.5-in. (in .38 Special) or 6-in. only (.22 LR and .32 PP), 11.25 in. overall (6-in. bbl. in .38 Special). Adj. target sights. Blued finish. Checkered walnut grips. Hand-finished action. General features same as Army Special and Official Police of same date. Made 1908-49 (w/exceptions noted).

.38 caliber . . . . NiB $1130	Ex $930	Gd $653
.32 caliber . . . . NiB $1744	Ex $1426	Gd $984
.22 caliber . . . . NiB $1232	Ex $1018	Gd $729

w/shorter bbls. (4-, 4.5- or 5-in.), add 50%

OFFICER'S MODEL SPECIAL
(FOURTH ISSUE) . . . . NiB $1530 Ex $1130 Gd $830
Post WWII model. Similar Officers' Model Third Issue excpt w/ extra heavy, nontapered bbl. Redesigned hammer. Ramp front sight, "Coltmaster" rear sight adj. for windage and elevation. Blued finish. Checkered plastic reddish-brown "Coltwood" grips. Made 1949-52.

OFFICER'S MODEL MATCH
(FIFTH ISSUE) . . . . NiB $1510 Ex $980 Gd $810
Same general design as Officers' Model Special except w/ tapered heavy bbl., wide hammer spur, Adjustable rear sight ramp front sight, large target grips of checkered walnut w/ medalion. Calibers: .22 LR, .22 Mag., .38 Special. Six-in. bbl., 11.25 in. overall. Weight: 43 oz. (in .22 cal.), 39 oz. (.38 cal.). Blued finish. Made 1953-69.
.22 Mag., add $1000

Colt Officers' Match

**Colt
Officers' Target Second Issue**

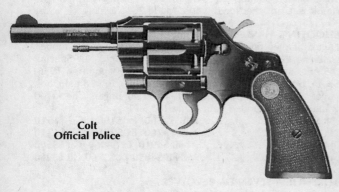

**Colt
Official Police**

**Colt
Peacekeeper**

OFFICER'S MODEL MATCH MK III
(SIXTH ISSUE) . . . . **NiB $2960 Ex $1960 Gd $1210**
Similar to Officers' Model Match Fifth Issue except .38 Special only. Made 1969-71.

OFFICIAL POLICE DA REVOLVER
Calibers: .22 LR (intro. 1930, embedded head-cylinder for high-speed cartridges after 1932), .32-20 (disc. 1942), .38

Special, .41 Long Colt (disc. 1930). Six-round cylinder, bbl. lengths: 4-, 5-, and 6-in. or 2-in. and 6-in. heavy bbl. in .38 Special only; .22 LR w/4- and 6-in. bbls. only; 11.25 in. over-all. Weight: 36 oz. (standard 6-in. bbl.) in .38 Special. Fixed sights. Blued or nickel-plated finish. Checkered walnut grips on all revolvers of this model except some of postwar production had checkered plastic grips. Made 1927-69. Note: This model is a refined version of the Army Special, which it replaced in 1928 at about serial number 520,000. The Commando .38 Special was a wartime adaptation of the Official Police made to government specifications. Commando can be identified by its sandblasted blued finish and stamped "COLT COMMANDO". Serial numbers start w/number 1-50,000 (made 1942-45). Marshal Model marked "COLT MARSHAL" has S/N w/"M" suffix (made 1954-56).
Commercial model
  (pre-war) . . . . **NiB $1160 Ex $770 Gd $560**
Commercial model (post-war) . . . **NiB $960 Ex $700 Gd $550**
Commando model . . . . **NiB $1950 Ex $1700 Gd $1450**
Marshal model . . . . **NiB $2510 Ex $1750 Gd $1500**

OFFICIAL POLICE MK III . . . . . **NiB $660 Ex $510 Gd $460**
"J" frame, without shrouded ejector rod. Caliber: .38 Special. Six-round cylinder. bbl., lengths: 4-, 5-, 6-in., 9.25 in. overall w/4-in. bbl., weight: 34 oz. (4-in. bbl.). Fixed rear sight, ramp front. Service trigger and hammer or target trigger and wide-spur hammer. Blued or nickel-plated finish. Checkered walnut service grips. Made 1969-75.

PEACEKEEPER DA REVOLVER . . **NiB $1010 Ex $780 Gd $460**
Caliber: .357 Mag. Six-round cylinder, 4- or 6-in. bbl., 11.25 in. overall (6-in. bbl.). Weight: 46 oz. (w/ 6-in. bbl.). Adj. white outline rear sight, red insert ramp-style front. Non-reflective matte blued finish. Made 1985-89.

PEACEMAKER .22 SECOND AMENDMENT
COMMEMORATIVE . . . . **NiB $660 Ex $544 Gd $286**
Caliber: .22, revolver w/7.5-in. bbl., nickel-plated frame, bbl. ejector rod assembly, hammer and trigger, blued cylinder, backstrap and trigger guard. Black pearlite grips. bbl., inscribed "The Right to Keep and Bear Arms." Presentation case. Limited edition of 3000 issued in 1977. Top value is for revolver in new condition.

PEACEMAKER 22 SCOUT . . . . . **NiB $760 Ex $460 Gd $310**
SA. Calibers: .22 LR and .22 WMR. Furnished w/cylinder for each caliber, 6-rnd.. Bbl.: 4.38-, 6- or 7.5-in., 11.25 in. overall (w/ 6-in. bbl.). Weight: 30.5 oz. (w/ 6-in. bbl.). Fixed sights. Black composite grips. Made 1971-76.

POCKET POSITIVE FIRST & SECOND ISSUES
DA/SA. General specifications same as New Pocket except this model has positive lock feature (see Police Positive). Calibers: .32 Short & Long Colt (disc. 1914), .32 Colt New Police (.32 S&W Short & Long). Fixed sights, flat top and square notch. Blue or nickel finish. Made 1905-40.
Blue finish . . . . **NiB $1300 Ex $1000 Gd $760**
Nickel finish, add **20%**

POLICE POSITIVE FIRST ISSUE
Improved version of the New Police w/the "Positive Lock," which prevents the firing pin coming in contact w/the cartridge except when the trigger is pulled. Calibers: .32 Short & Long Colt (disc. 1915), .32 Colt New Police (.32 S&W Short & Long), .38 New Police (.38 S&W). Six-round cylinder, bbl. lengths: 2.5- (.32 cal. only), 4- 5- and 6-in.; 8.5 in. overall (w/ 4-in.

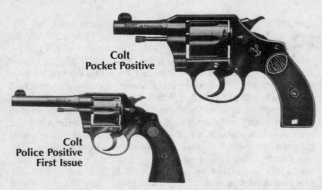

**Colt
Pocket Positive**

**Colt
Police Positive
First Issue**

bbl.). Weight 20 oz. (w/ 4-in. bbl.). Fixed sights. Blued or nickel finish. Rubber or checkered walnut grips. Made 1907-27.
Blue finish. . . . . **NiB $1010 Ex $660 Gd $400**
Nickel finish, add **20%**

POLICE POSITIVE SECOND ISSUE
Same as Detective Special second issue except has 4-in. bbl., 9 in. overall, weight: 26.5 oz. Intro. in 1977. Note: Original Police Positive (First Issue) has a shorter frame, is not chambered for .38 Special. Made 1928-47.
Blue finish. . . . . **NiB $1005 Ex $655 Gd $390**

POLICE POSITIVE SPECIAL FIRST & SECOND ISSUES
DA REVOLVER . . . . **NiB $910 Ex $560 Gd $420**
Based on the Police Positive w/frame lengthened to permit longer cylinder. Calibers: .32-20 (disc. 1942), .38 Special, .32 New Police and .38 New Police (intro. 1946). Six-round cylinder; bbl. lengths: 4-(only length in current production), 5- and 6-in.; 8.75 in. overall (w/ 4-in. bbl.). Weight: 23 oz. (w/ 4-in. bbl. in .38 Special). Fixed sights. Checkered grips of hard rubber, plastic or walnut. Made 1907-27 (First Issue) and 1928 to 1946 (Second Issue).

POLICE POSITIVE SPECIAL THIRD & FOURTH ISSUES
Based on Detective Special Second Issue but w/4-, 5- or 6-in. bbl. in .38 Spl. only. Made 1947-76 (Third Issue), 1977 to 1978 (Fourth Issue).
Third Issue . . . . **NiB $980 Ex $760 Gd $480**
Fourth Issue, subtract **10%**

POLICE POSITIVE MK V FIFTH ISSUE
DA REVOLVER . . . . **NiB $900 Ex $660 Gd $510**
.38 Spl. only. 4-in. bbl. w/ejector shroud. Finish: blued. Grips: rubber. Made 1994-95.

POLICE POSITIVE TARGET FIRST AND SECOND ISSUES
DA REVOLVER . . . . **NiB $1310 Ex $1110 Gd $860**
Target version of the Police Positive. Calibers: .22 LR (intro. 1910, embedded-head cylinder for high-speed cartridges after 1932), .22 WRF (1910-35), .32 Short & Long Colt, (1915), .32 New Police (.32 S&W Short & Long). Six-in. bbl., blued finish only, 10.5 in. overall. Weight: 26 oz. in .22 cal. Adj. target sights. Hard rubber grips until 1923 then checkered walnut grips. Second Issue had heavier fram. Made 1907-25 (First Issue), 1926 to 1941 (Second Issue).
Second Issue, deduct **10%**

PYTHON DA REVOLVER
"I" frame, shrouded ejector rod. Calibers: .357 Magnum, .38 Special. Six-round cylinder, 2.5-, 4-, 6- or 8-in. VR bbl., 11.25 in. overall (w/ 6-in. bbl.). Weight: 44 oz. (6-in. bbl.). Adj. rear sight, ramp front. Blued, nickel or stainless finish. Checkered walnut target grips. Made 1955-96. Ultimate stainless finish made in 1985.

**Blued or Royal Blued finish
  (mfg. 1955-69)** . . . . **NiB $3510 Ex $2660 Gd $1510**
Blued finish (mfg. 1970-96), subtract **$400**
Nickel finish . . . . **NiB $3860 Ex $3260 Gd $2260**
Stainless finish. . . . . **NiB $3510 Ex $3160 Gd $1960**
Ultimate stainless finish . . . **NiB $3960 Ex $3510 Gd $2510**
2.5-in. bbl., add **100%**
Elite model (mfg. 2002-06). . **NiB $3760 Ex $3260 Gd $2260**
**Grizzly model (ported bbl.,
  non-fluted cylinder,
  Pachmayer grips)** . . . . **NiB $4000 Ex $3610 Gd $3260**
Hunter model (w/2x scope) NiB $4500 Ex $3900 Gd $2960
Silhouette model (w/2x scope) . . . **NiB $4160 Ex $3760 Gd $3060**
**Ten Pointer model (w/3x scope, carrying case, two sets
  of grips, 8-in. bbl.)** . . . . . **NiB $3760 Ex $3260 Gd $2760**
**Whitetailer model (w/2x scope, 8-in. bbl., aluminum
  case)** . . . . **NiB $2520 Ex $2270 Gd $1610**
**Whitetailer II model (w/1.5-4x
  scope, 8-in. bbl., bright
  satinless finish)** . . . . **NiB $2260 Ex $2010 Gd $1960**
**Ultimate model (custom shop tuned, two sets of sights, two
  sets of grips, 1991-93)** . . **NiB $3960 Ex $3510 Gd $2510**
Ultimate stainless, add **$100**

PYTHON (RECENT MFG.) . . . **NiB $1355 Ex $1220 GD $900**
Bbl.: 3-, 4.2- or 6-in. VR. Caliber: .357 Mag.; 6-rnd. cylinder. Sight: blade front/adj. rear. Weight: 42 or 46 oz. Finish: bright stainless. Grip: checkered wood. Made 2020 to date.

SHOOTING MASTER
Deluxe target revolver based on the New Service model. Calibers: Originally made only in .38 Special, .44 Special, .45 Auto and .45 Colt added in 1933, .357 Magnum in 1936. Six-in. bbl., 11.25 in. overall. Weight: 44 oz., in (.38 cal.), adj. target sights. Hand-finished action. Blued finish. Checkered walnut grips. Rounded butt. Made 1932-41.
.38 Special . . . . **NiB $2760 Ex $1960 Gd $1510**
.357 Mag. . . . . **NiB $3260 Ex $2810 Gd $1710**
.44 Special . . . . **NiB $4910 Ex $4060 Gd $3500**
.45 ACP or .45LC . . . . **NiB $4850 Ex $3760 Gd $3260**

THREE-FIFTY-SEVEN DA REVOLVER
Heavy frame. Caliber: .357 Magnum. Six-shot cylinder, 4 or 6-in. bbl. Quickdraw ramp front sight, Accro rear sight. Blued finish. Checkered walnut grips. 9.25 or 11.25 in. overall. Weight: 36 oz. (4-in. bbl.), 39 oz. (6 in. bbl.). Made 1953-61.
**w/standard hammer and
  service grips** . . . . **NiB $711 Ex $601 Gd $431**
**w/wide-spur hammer and
  target grips** . . . . **NiB $733 Ex $612 Gd $444**

TROOPER DA REVOLVER
Similar specifications as Officers' Model Match except has 4-in. bbl. w/quick-draw ramp front sight, weight: 34 oz. Claiber: .22 LR, .38 Spl. or .357 Mag. Made 1953-69.
**w/standard hammer and
  service grips** . . . . **NiB $810 Ex $710 Gd $635**
**w/wide-spur hammer and
  target grips** . . . . **NiB $835 Ex $735 Gd $660**

TROOPER MK III . . . . **NiB $660 Ex $330 Gd $225**
DA revolver. "J" frame, shrouded ejector rod. Calibers: .22 LR, .22 Magnum, .38 Special, .357 Magnum. Six-round cylinder. bbl. lengths: 4-, 6-in. 9.5 in. overall (w/ 4-in. bbl.). Weight: 39 oz. (4-in. bbl.). Adj. rear sight, ramp front. Target trigger and hammer. Blued or nickel-plated finish. Checkered walnut target grips. Made 1969-78.
Nickel finish, add **20%**

**Colt
Police Positive Target**

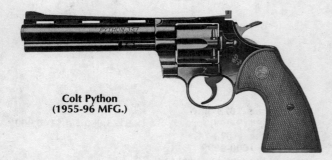

**Colt Python
(1955-96 MFG.)**

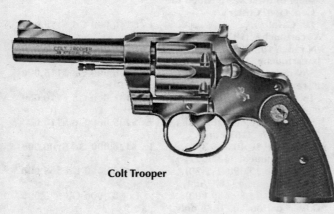

Colt Trooper

Colt Trooper MK V

TROOPER MK V REVOLVER
Re-engineered Mark III for smoother, faster action. Caliber: .357 Magnum. Six-round cylinder, bbl. lengths: 4-, 6-, 8-in. w/ VR. Adj. rear sight, ramp front, red insert. Checkered walnut grips. Made 1982-86.
Blued finish. . . . . **NiB $660 Ex $310 Gd $240**
Nickel finish, add **20%**

VIPER DA REVOLVER . . . . . **NiB $3510 Ex $3160 Gd $2260**
Same as Cobra, Second Issue except has 4-in. bbl., 9 in. overall, weight: 20 oz. Made 1977-84.

SINGLE ACTION ARMY (SAA) REVOLVER
Also called Frontier Six-Shooter and Peacemaker. Available in more than 30 calibers including: .22 Rimfire (Short, Long, LR), .22 WRF, .32 Rimfire, .32 Colt, .32 S&W, .32-20, .38 Colt, .38 S&W, .38 Special, .357 Magnum, .38-40, .41 Colt, .44 Rimfire, .44 Russian, .44 Special, .44-40, .45 Colt, .45 Auto, .450 Boxer, 450 Eley, .455 Eley, .476 Eley. Six-round cylinder. Bbl. lengths: 4.75, 5 .5 and 7.5 in. w/ejector or 3 and 4 in. w/o ejector. 10.25 in. overall (w/ 4.75-in. bbl.). Weight: 36 oz. (.45 cal. w/4.75-in. bbl.). Fixed sights. Also made in Target Model w/flat top-strap and target sights. Blued finish w/casehardened frame or nickel-plated. One-piece smooth walnut or checkered black rubber grips. Note: S.A. Army Revolvers w/serial numbers above 165,000 (circa 1896) are adapted to smokeless powder and cylinder pin screw was changed to spring catch at about the same time. The "First Generation" of SA Colts included both blackpowder and smokeless configurations and were manufactured from 1873 to 1940. Production resumed in 1955 w/serial number 1001SA and continued through 1975 to complete the second series, which is referred to as the "Second Generation." In 1976, the "Third Generation" of production began and continues to date. However, several serial number rollovers occurred at 99,999. For Example, in 1978 the "SA" suffix became an "SA" prefix and again in 1993, when the serial number SA99,999 was reached, the serialization format was changed again to include both an "S" prefix and an "A" suffix. Although the term "Fourth Generation" is frequently associated with this rollover, no series change actually occurred, therefore, the current production is still a "Third Generation" series. Current calibers: .357 Magnum, .44 Special, .45 Long Colt.

Note: *In the previous section the GTG deviates from the observed practice of listing only the value of firearms produced after 1900. This deliberate departure from the standard format is intended to provide a general reference and establish proper orientation for the reader, because the Colt SSA had its origins in the last quarter of the 19th century. Consequently, antique firearms produced prior to 1898 have been listed as a preface and introduction to the first series of production (what is now recognized as "1st Generation") in order to systematically demonstrate the progressive and sequential development of the multi-generation Colt SAA. Therefore, the previous general values have been provided to establish a point of reference to allow a more comprehensive Examination of the evolution of the Colt SAA. However, please note that the following values apply only to original models, not to similar S.A.A. revolvers of more recent manufacture.*

1st Generation (mfg. 1873-1940)
SAA (COMMERICAL). . . . . **Ex $250,000 Gd $10,000**
Variation of the SAA military model developed for commercial market.
Pinched frame (1873 only,
S/N range 1-160). . . . . **Ex $250,000 Gd $175,000**
Early black powder cartridge
(1873-77, S/N range 160-22,000). . . **Ex $90,000 Gd $70,000**
Large bore rimfire (1875-1940). . . . **Ex $75,000 Gd $60,000**
Small bore rimfire (1875-80) . . . . . . **Ex $40,000 Gd $25,000**

SAA (U.S. MILITARY). . . . . **Ex $175,000 Gd $11,000**
Original SAA revolver model developed for U.S. military.

NOTE: Total number of SAA revolvers sold to the U.S. Military was 37,063 and each revolver was stamped with the initials,

---

GRADING: **NiB** = New in Box   **Ex** = Excellent or NRA 95%   **Gd** = Good or NRA 68%

Colt SA Army — 125th Anniversary

Colt 150th Anniversary Deluxe

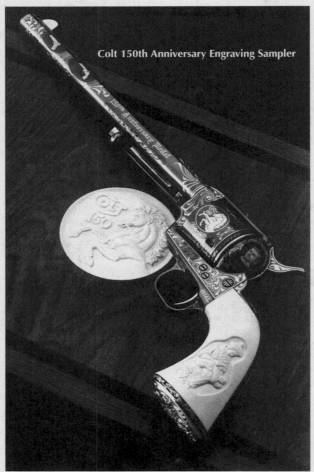

Colt 150th Anniversary Engraving Sampler

"A" cartouche (1873 only,
S/N range 179-999) . . . . Ex $175,000 Gd $140,000
"A" cartouche (1873-74,
S/N range 1000-9999,
some of these were issued to
Gen. Geo. Custer's
7th Cavalry) . . . . Ex $140,000 Gd $115,000
"A" cartouche (1874-75,
S/N range 10,000-15,000) . . . . . . Ex $120,000 Gd $100,000
"L" cartouche (1875 only,
S/N range 15,000-16,500) . . . . Ex $140,000 Gd $115,000
"J" cartouche (1875 only, S/N range
16,800-18,450) . . . . Ex $135,000 Gd $110,000
"J" cartouche ("J", 1875 only,
S/N range 16,800-18,450) . . . . Ex $135,000 Gd $110,000
"C" cartouche (1875 only,
S/N range 16,400-19,350) . . . . Ex $120,000 Gd $100,000
"J.T.C." cartouche (1876-77,
S/N range 30,690-35,570) . . . . . . Ex $80,000 Gd $65,000
"H.N." cartouche (1877 only,
S/N range 36,800-39,880) . . . . . . Ex $87,000 Gd $70,000
"D.F.C." cartouche (1878 only,
S/N range 41,000-42,300) . . . . . . Ex $75,000 Gd $50,000
"D.F.C." cartouche (1880-87,
S/N range 53,000-121,000) . . . . . . Ex $55,000 Gd $46,000
"R.A.C." cartouche (1890-91,
S/N range 131,187-140,361) . . . . Ex $45,000 Gd $42,000
Artillery model (refurbished military models w/5.5-in.
bbl., refurbished 1896-1903, higher value for:
Rough Rider documented, matching serial numbers,
New York State Militia model) . . . . . . Ex $18,000-$30,000

SAA BISLEY . . . . **NiB $10,000 Ex $8600 Gd $7600**
Variation of the SAA commercial developed for target shooting
w/modified grips, trigger and hammer. Made 1894-1915.
Flattop Target Bisley (w/flattop frame, adj. rear sight,
7.5-in. bbl., mfg. 1894-1913) . . . **NiB $20,000 Ex $18,000
Gd $15,000**

**SAA FLATTOP
TARGET** . . . . **NiB $25,000 Ex $20,000 Gd $16,500**
Similar to the SAA Commercial model developed for target shoot-
ing w/flattop frame w/adj. rear sight. 925 mfg. Made 1888-96.

SAA LONG FLUTE . . . . . **NiB $17,600 Ex $9,999 Gd $6,200**
Similar to the SAA Commercial model except w/modified
long fluted cylinders from 1878 DA revolvers. Made 1913-15.

cartouche, of a U.S. Ordnance inspectors. Inspectors of
early models are O.W. Ainsworth (A), S.B. Lewis (L), W.W.
Johnson (J), and A.P. Casey (C). Later model inspectors are
John T. Cleveland (J.T.C.), Henry Nettleton (H.N.), David F.
Clark (D.F.C.), and Rinaldo A. Carr (R.A.C.). Depending on
the inspector, some models have more value. These revolvers
are typically well used. Caliber: .45 LC. Barrel: 7.5-in. Finish:
Blued. Grip: oil finished, smooth walnut.

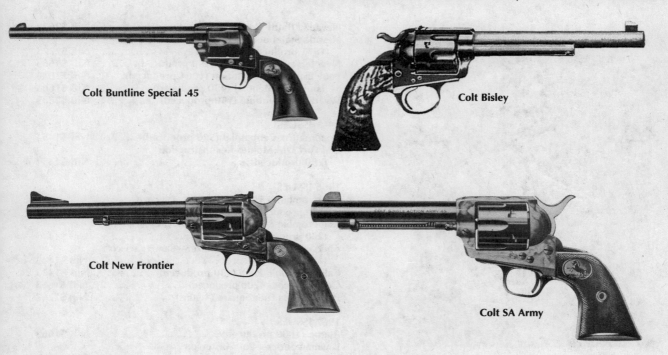

Colt Buntline Special .45

Colt Bisley

Colt New Frontier

Colt SA Army

SAA SHERIFF . . . . **EX $95,000 TO $25,500**
Similar to the SAA commercial model except commercial model w/o an ejector rod. Also referred to as Banker Special or Shopkeeper model.

2nd Generation (mfg. 1956-75)
SAA (STANDARD MODEL)
Variation of the 1st Gen. SAA commercial w/slight changes to mechanism. Calibers: .38 Spl., .357 Mag., .44 Spl. or .45 LC. Bbl. length: 4.75-, 5.5- or 7.5-in. Finish: blued or nickel.
.38 Spl. . . . . NiB $3000 Ex $2600 Gd $1800
.357 Mag. . . . . NiB $2600 Ex $2000 Gd $1250
.44 Spl. . . . . NiB $3260 Ex $2650 Gd $1900
.45 LC . . . . NiB $3200 Ex $2950 Gd $2600
4.75-in. bbl., add 15%
nickel finish, add. 10%
factory engraved w/ factory letter, add 75-100%

BUNTLINE SPECIAL . . . . . . NiB $2448 Ex $1960 Gd $1260
Same as standard 2nd Gen. SAA except w/12-in. bbl., caliber .45 Long Colt only. Made 1957-75.

NEW FRONTIER . . . . NiB $1420 Ex $1220 Gd $1120
Similar to 2nd Gen. SAA except w/adj. rear sight and ramp blade front sight. Calibers: .38 Spl., .357 Mag., .44 Spl. or .45 LC. Bbl. length: 4.75-, 5.5- or 7.5-in. Finish: blued or nickel. Grip: smooth walnut w/medalion. Made 1961-75.
.38 Spl., add 270%
4.75-in. bbl., add 50%
5.5-in. bbl., add 25%
Buntline (12-in. bbl.,
   .45 LC) . . . . NiB $2520 Ex $2200 Gd $1895

SA SHERIFF'S MODEL .45
Limited edition replica of Storekeeper's Model in caliber .45 Colt, made Exclusively for Centennial Arms Corp. Chicago, Illinois. Numbered "1SM." Blued finish w/casehardened frame or nickel-plated. Walnut grips. Made in 1961.

Blued finish
   (478 produced) . . . . NiB $2760 Ex $1780 Gd $1454
Nickel finish
   (25 produced) . . . . NiB $7860 Ex $4210 Gd $3010

3rd Generation (mfg.1976-Present)
SAA (STANDARD MODEL) . . . NiB $1800 Ex $1300 Gd $1000
Variation of the 2nd Gen. SAA standard w/slight changes to mechanism. Calibers: .32-20, .38-40, .38 Spl., .357 Mag., .44 Spl., .44-40 or .45 LC. Bbl. length: 4-, 4.75-, 5-, 5.5- or 7.5-in. Finish: blued or nickel. Grip: smooth wood or black plastic w/ eagle.
.38 Spl., add 25%
nickel finish, add. 20%
black powder frame (pre-1996), add. 15%
factory ivory grip, add 70%
Frontier Six Shooter
   (.44-40, 2008-10) . . . . NiB $1800 Ex $1300 Gd $1000
factory Class A engraving, add $1200
factory Class B engraving, add $2400
factory Class C engraving, add $3500
factory Class D engraving, add $4700

BUNTLINE SPECIAL . . . . NiB $1400 Ex $1070 Gd $900
Same as standard 3rd Gen. SAA except w/12-in. bbl. Caliber: .44-40 or .45 Long Colt. Blued and case hardened finish. Grip: smooth walnut.

NEW FRONTIER . . . . NiB $1560 Ex $1120 Gd $900
Similar to 2nd Gen. New Frontier except w/adj. rear sight and ramp blade front sight. Calibers: .357 Mag., .44 Spl., .44-40 or .45 LC. Bbl. length: 4.75-, 5.5- or 7.5-in. Finish: blued. Grip: smooth walnut w/medalion. Made 1978-81 and 2008-10, reintro. 2011 to date.
New Frontier
   Buntline (12-in. bbl.,
   .45 LC) . . . . NiB $2520 Ex $2200 Gd $1895

Colt U.S. Bicentennial Commemorative Set

SHERIFF MODEL . . . . NiB $1500 Ex $1160 Gd $900
Same as standard 2nd Gen. Sheriff except w/3-in. bbl. w/o
ejector rod. Caliber .44 Spl., .44-40 or .45 LC. Finish: blued
and case hardened, royal blue or nickel.
extra convertible cylinder, add 10%
factory ivory grip, add 70%
nickel finish, add. 10%
Royal blue finish, deduct 15%

STOREKEEPERS MODEL . . . . NiB $1900 Ex $1200 Gd $900
Similar to 3rd Gen. Sheriff except w/4-in. bbl. w/o ejector
rod. Caliber: .45 LC only. Finish: blued and case hardened or
nickel. Grips: ivory. Made: 1984-85 and 2008-10.
nickel finish, add. 10%

SAA 125TH ANNIVERSARY . . . NiB $1668 Ex $1438 Gd $1239
Limited production deluxe version of SAA issued in commemo-
ration of Colt's 125th Anniversary. Caliber: .45 Long Colt., 7.5-
in. bbl., cold-plated frame trigger, hammer, cylinder pin, ejector
rod tip, and grip medallion. Presentation case w/anniversary
medallion. Serial numbers "50AM." 7368 were made in 1961.

SAA COMMEMORATIVE MODELS
Limited production versions of SAA .45 issued, w/appropriate
inscription to commemorate historical events. Cased. Note: Values
indicated are for commemorative revolvers in new condition.

1963 ISSUES
Arizona Territorial Centennial (1280 produced) . . NiB $1663
West Virginia Statehood Centennial
   (600 produced) . . . . NiB $1663

1964 ISSUES
Chamizal Treaty (50 produced) . . . . NiB $1867
Colonel Sam Colt Sesquicentennial
   Presentation (4750 produced) . . . . NiB $1663
Deluxe Presentation (200 produced) . . . . NiB $3621
Special Deluxe Presentation (50 produced) . . . . . NiB $5687
Montana Territorial Centennial (851 produced) . . NiB $1724

Nevada "Battle Born" (100 produced) . . . . NiB $2672
Nevada Statehood Centennial
   (1877 produced) . . . . NiB $2275
New Jersey Tercentenary (250 produced) . . . . . . NiB $1663
Pony Express Presentation (1004 produced) . . . . . NiB $1836
St. Louis Bicentennial (450 produced) . . . . NiB $1663
Wyatt Earp Buntline (150 produced) . . . . NiB $2809

1965 ISSUES
Appomattox Centennial (500 produced) . . . . NiB $1454
Old Fort Des Moines Reconstruction
   (200 produced) . . . . NiB $1454

1966 ISSUES
Abercrombie & Fitch Trailblazer—Chicago
   (100 produced) . . . . NiB $1423
Abercrombie & Fitch Trailblazer—New York
   (200 produced) . . . . NiB $1423
Abercrombie & Fitch Trailblazer—San Francisco
   (100 produced) . . . . NiB $1423
California Gold Rush (130 produced) . . . . NiB $1423
General Meade (200 produced) . . . . NiB $1663
Pony Express Four Square (4 guns) . . . . NiB $7268

1967 ISSUES
Alamo (1000 produced) . . . . NiB $1663
Lawman Series—Bat Masterson
   (500 produced) . . . . NiB $1760
1968 ISSUES
Lawman Series—Pat Garrett (500 produced) . . . . . . NiB $1663

1969 ISSUES
Lawman Series—Wild Bill Hickok
   (500 produced) . . . . NiB $1663

1970 ISSUES
Lawman Series—Wyatt Earp (501 produced) . . . . . NiB $2907
Texas Ranger (1000 produced) . . . . NiB $2351

1971 ISSUES
NRA Centennial, .357 or .45 (5001 produced) . . . . NiB $1525

1975 ISSUES
Peacemaker Centennial .45 (1501 produced) . . . NiB $1872
Peacemaker Centennial .44-40
   (1501 produced) . . . . NiB $1872
Peacemaker Centennial Cased Pair
   (501 produced) . . . . NiB $1872
Missouri Sesquicentennial
   (501 produced) . . . . NiB $1627

1979 ISSUES
Ned Buntline .45 (3000 produced) . . . . NiB $1367

1986 ISSUES
Colt 150th Anniversary (standard) . . . . NiB $2064
Colt 150th Anniversay (engraved) . . . . NiB $3647

U.S. BICENTENNIAL COMMEMORATIVE SET . . . NiB $3290
Replica Colt 3rd Model Dragoon revolver w/accessories, Colt SA
Army revolver, and Colt Python revolver. Matching roll-engraved
unfluted cylinders, blued finish and rosewood grips w/Great
Seal of the United States silver medallion. Dragoon revolver
has silver grip frame. Serial numbers 0001 to 1776. All revolvers in set have same number. Deluxe drawer-style presentation
case of walnut w/book compartment containing a reproduction
of "Armsmear." Issued in 1976. Value is for revolvers in new
condition.

SAA COWBOY REVOLVER . . . . **NiB $1200 Ex $860 Gd $660**
SA variant designed for "Cowboy Action Shooting" with transfer-bar safety system. Caliber: .45 Colt. Six-round cylinder, 5.5-in. bbl., 11 in. overall. Weight: 42 oz. Blade front sight, fixed V-notch rear. Blued finish w/color casehardened frame. Grip: Smooth walnut or checkered plastic. Made 1999-2003.

COONAN, INC. — Blaine, MN

Formerly Coonan Arms in Maplewood, Minnesota and St. Paul, Minnesota.

MODEL .357 MAGNUM SEMIAUTO PISTOL
Caliber: .357 Mag. Seven-round magazine, 5- or 6-in. bbl., 8.3 in. overall (w/ 5-in. bbl.). Weight: 42 oz. Front ramp interchangeable sight, fixed rear sight, adj. for windage. Black walnut grips. Made 1983-99; reintro. 2010.
Model A w/o grip
safety (disc. 1991) . . . . **NiB $1221 Ex $1056 Gd $869**
Model B w/5-in. bbl., ... **NiB $944 Ex $703 Gd $500**
Model B w/6-in. bbl., ... **NiB $714 Ex $601 Gd $437**
Model B w/5-in. compensated bbl.,
   Classic. . . . . **NiB $1336 Ex $1122 Gd $923**
Model B w/6-in.
   compensated bbl . . . . **NiB $1016 Ex $789 Gd $561**
Classic (2010-present) . . . . . . **NiB $1310 Ex $1150 Gd $800**

.357 MAGNUM CADET COMPACT
Similar to the standard .357 Magnum model except w/3.9-in. bbl., on compact frame. Six-round (Cadet), 7- or 8-rnd. magazine (Cadet II). Weight: 39 oz., 7.8 in. overall. Made 1993-99; reintro. 2016.
Cadet model . . . . **NiB $897 Ex $653 Gd $497**
Cadet II model . . . . **NiB $897 Ex $653 Gd $497**
Compact (2016-present) . . . . . **NiB $1460 Ex $1120 Gd $860**

CZ (CESKA ZBROJOVKA), INC. — Uhersky Brod, Czech Republic

Formerly Strakonice, Czechoslovakia. Mfd. by Ceska Zbrojovka-Nardoni Podnik formerly Bohmische Waffenfabrik A. G. Currently imported by CZ-USA, Kansas City, KS. Previously by Magnum Research and Action Arms. Vintage importation is by Century International Arms. Also, see Dan Wesson Firearms listings.

CZ P-01. . . . . **NiB $550 Ex $406 Gd $305**
Caliber: 9mm Para. Based on CZ-75 design but with improved metals, aluminum alloy frame, hammer forged bbl. (3.8 in.), checkered rubber grips, matte black polycoat finish. Imported 2003.

CZ P-07

CZ P-06. . . . . **NiB $580 Ex $460 Gd $350**
Similar to P-01 except in .40 S&W. Imported 2008 to 2016.

CZ P-07 DUTY . . . . **NiB $440 Ex $330 Gd $270**
Caliber: 9mm Para. or .40 S&W. Polymer frame in black or OD green, 3.8-in. bbl. Made 2009-13.
Urban Gray Suppressor Ready, add **$20**

CZ P-09 DUTY . . . . **NiB $530 Ex $480 GD $400**
Semiauto. DA/SA. Full size version of CZ P-09. Caliber: 9mm or .40 S&W; 15- or 14-rnd. magazine depending on caliber. 4.5-in. bbl. Frame: polymer. Sights: fixed 3-dot. Finish: matte black. Grip: textured polymer. Made 2013 to date.
P-09 FDE (FDE finish) add, ... **$60**
Urban Gray Suppressor Ready, add **$20**

CZ P-10 C . . . . **NiB $445 Ex $395 GD $255**
Semiauto. Striker-fire. Caliber: 9mm; 15- or 10-rnd. magazine. 4.02-in. bbl. Frame: polymer. Sights: metal fixed 3-dot. Finish: matte black, FDE, OD green, or urban grey. Grip: textured polymer. Made 2017 to date.
F model (4.5-in. bbl.,
   19-rnd. mag.) . . . . **NiB $575 Ex $520 Gd $300**
S model (3.5-in. bbl.,
   12-rnd. mag.) . . . . **NiB $500 Ex $480 Gd $300**
Suppressor Ready model, add **$20**
Optics-Ready model, add **$30**

CZ 2075 RAMI . . . . **NiB $520 Ex $380 Gd $270**
Caliber: 9mm Para. or .40 S&W. Polymer or alloy frame in black, 3-in. bbl. Polymer frame made 2006-11. Alloy frame made 2005-present.

CZ 40B . . . . **NiB $430 Ex $372 Gd $321**
Caliber: .40 S&W. M1911-style frame, CZ-75B operating mechanism; single or double-action; black polycoat finish. Fixed sights; 10-rnd. mag.

MODEL 27 AUTO PISTOL . . . . **NiB $653 Ex $555 Gd $385**
Caliber: .32 Automatic (7.65mm). Eight-round magazine, 4-in. bbl., 6 in. overall. Weight: 23.5 oz. Fixed sights. Blued finish. Plastic grips. Made 1927-51. Note: After the German occupation (March 1939), Models 27 and 38 were marked w/manufacturer code "fnh." Designation of Model 38 was changed to "Pistole 39(t)."

MODEL 38 AUTO PISTOL (VZ SERIES)
Caliber: .380 Automatic (9mm). Nine-round magazine, 3.75-in. bbl., 7 in. overall. Weight: 26 oz. Fixed sights. Blued finish. Plastic grips. After 1939 designated as T39. Made 1938-45.

CZ 2075 Rami P shown w/ extended magazine

CZ DAO model . . . . NiB $518 Ex $442 Gd $358
CZ SA/DA model . . . . NiB $1451 Ex $1144 Gd $825

MODEL 50 DA . . . . NiB $460 Ex $330 Gd $255
Similar to Walther Model PP except w/frame-mounted safety and trigger guard not hinged. Caliber: .32 ACP (7.65mm), 8-rnd. magazine, 3.13-in. bbl., 6.5 in. overall. Weight: 24.5 oz. Fixed sights. Blued finished. Intro. in 1950. disc.
Note: "VZ50" is the official designation of this pistol used by the Czech National Police ("New Model .006" was the Export designation but very few were released).

MODEL 52 . . . . NiB $248 Ex $202 Gd $137
Roller-locking breech system. Calibers: 7.62mm or 9mm Para. Eight-round magazine, 4.7-in. bbl., 8.1 in. overall. Weight: 31 oz. Fixed sights. Blued finish. Grooved composition grips. Made 1952-56.

MODEL 70 . . . . NiB $260 Ex $200 Gd $160
Similar to Model 50 but redesigned to improve function and dependability. Made 1962-83.

CZ-75 SERIES
DA/SA or DAO. Calibers: 9mm Para. or .40 S&W w/selective action mode. 10-, 13- or 15-rnd. magazine, 3.9-in. bbl., (Compact) or 4.75-in. bbl., (Standard), 8 in. overall (Standard). Weight: 35 oz. Fixed sights. Blued, nickel, Two-Tone or black polymer finish. Checkered wood or high-impact plastic grips. Made 1975 to date.
Black polymer finish . . . . NiB $459 Ex $385 Gd $284
High-polish blued finish . . . . . NiB $526 Ex $453 Gd $347
Matte blued finish . . . . NiB $499 Ex $398 Gd $295
Nickel finish . . . . NiB $541 Ex $442 Gd $330
Two-tone finish . . . . NiB $530 Ex $431 Gd $325
w/.22 Kadet conversion, add $281
Compact model, add. $65
Champion (1999-04,
** 2006-09)** . . . . NiB $1430 Ex $1055 Gd $610

CZ-75 SP-01 ACCUSHADOW . . NiB $1480 Ex $1300 Gd $930
Semi-auto. DA/SA trigger. Caliber: 9mm. Barrel: 4.6-in. Undercut trigger guard, ambi. safety. Sights: target, fully adj. Grip: thin black aluminum. Finish: black polycoat. 2013-14.
AccuShadow 2 model (2018–date) . . NiB $1855 Ex $1630 Gd $1265

CZ-75 SP-01 SHADOW SERIES
Similar to SP-01 series except custom shop competition modifications.
Target model (2010–14) . . . . . NiB $1180 Ex $1000 Gd $705
Target II model (2015–date) . . . NiB $1470 Ex $1285 Gd $1000

CZ-75 TS CZECHMATE . . . . . . NiB $2970 Ex $2600 Gd $2020
Semi-auto designed for competition. SAO trigger. Caliber: 9mm, 20- or 26-rnd. magazine. Barrel: 5.2-in. Undercut trigger guard, ambi. safety. Sights: target, fully adj. Grip: checkered thin aluminum. Finish: black polycoat. 2011 to date.

CZ-75 SHADOW SERIES
Competition variant of the CZ-75 except w/DA/SA or SAO trigger and Model 85 style trigger. Caliber: 9mm Para. Made 2011-13.
DA/SA. . . . . NiB $920 Ex $730 Gd $580
SAO . . . . NiB $850 Ex $660 Gd $460
CTS LS-P (long slide, disc. 2013) . . NiB $1300 Ex $1030 Gd $780

SHADOW 2 SERIES
Semi-auto. DA/SA (Black & Blue) or SAO (SA). Caliber: 9mm, 17-rnd. magazine. Barrel: 4.8-in. Undercut trigger guard, ambi.

CZ-75 Shadow

CZ-83

safety. Sights: Target, fully adj. Grip: checkered blue aluminum. Finish: black polycoat. 2018 to date.
Black & Blue model . . . . NiB $1155 Ex $1010 Gd $780
SA model . . . . NiB $1155 Ex $1010 Gd $780
Orange model (orange aluminum grip,
** DA/SA, 2020-date)** . . . . NiB $1030 Ex $900 Gd $705
Urban Grey model (urban grey finish,
** DA/SA, 2017-date)** . . . . NiB $1155 Ex $1010 Gd $780

TACTICAL SPORT . . . . NiB $1130 Ex $980 Gd $730
Semi-auto. DA/SA (Black & Blue) or SAO (SA). Caliber: 9mm or .40 S&W. Barrel: 5.3-in. Ambi. safety. Grip: Checkered wood. Sights: target, fully adj. Finish: dual tone. 2006-18.
Orange model (orange grip, SAO trigger,
** 2016-date)** . . . . NiB $1570 Ex $1680 Gd $1070

CZ-75 SP-01 PHANTOM . . . . . NiB $530 Ex $380 Gd $280
Caliber: 9mm Para. Polymer black frame. Made 2009-13.

CZ-75 B
Similar to CZ-75 except w/firing pin safety block. Made 1998 to date.
Military (2000-02) . . . . NiB $370 Ex $275 Gd $230
Target SA (2010) . . . . NiB $1055 Ex $800 Gd $530

CZ-82 . . . . NiB $407 Ex $306 Gd $221
Similar to the standard CZ-83 model except chambered in 9x18 Makarov. This model currently is the Czech military sidearm since 1983.

CZ-83
Calibers: .32 ACP, .380 ACP. 15-rnd. (.32 ACP) or 13-rnd. (.380 ACP) magazine, 3.75-in. bbl., 6.75 in. overall. Weight: 26.5 oz. Fixed sights. Blued (standard); chrome and nickel (optional special edition) w/brushed, matte or polished finish. Checkered black plastic grips. Made 1985-2012.
Standard finish . . . . NiB $434 Ex $357 Gd $221
Special edition . . . . NiB $580 Ex $453 Gd $322
Engraved . . . . NiB $1234 Ex $1017 Gd $718

CZ 97B

CZ 100

CZ VZ 61 Skorpion

805 BREN S1 . . . . **NIB $1700 EX $1500 GD $1000**
Piston system, semiauto. Caliber: 5.56 NATO or .300 Blackout, 30-rnd. magazine. Barrel: 16.2-in. threaded. Top and bottom accessory Picatinny rails. Finish black or Flat Dark Earth. 2015–16.

BREN 2 MS . . . . **NIB $1700 EX $1500 GD $1000**
Similar to 805 Bren S1 except w/polymer frame. Caliber: 5.56 NATO or 7.62x39mm. 2018 to date.

SCORPION EVO 3 S1 . . . . **NiB $850 Ex $790 Gd $700**
Semiauto. SA. Caliber: 9mm; 20-rnd. magazine. 7.72-in. bbl. Frame: polymer. Sights: low profile adj. aperture. Finish: matte black. Grip: textured polymer, adj. for reach. Weight: 5 lbs. Length: 16 in. Made 2015 to date.

DUO POCKET PISTOL . . . . **NiB $328 Ex $252 Gd $174**
Caliber: .25 Automatic (6.35mm). Six-round magazine, 2.13 in. bbl., 4.5 in. overall. Weight: 14-.5 oz. Fixed sights. Blued or nickel finish. Plastic grips. Made circa 1926-60.

DAEWOO — Seoul, Korea

Mfd. by Daewoo Precision Industries Ltd. Imported by Daewoo Precision Industries, Southhampton, PA, Previously by Nationwide Sports Distributors and KBI, Inc.

DH40 AUTO PISTOL . . . . **NiB $357 Ex $255 Gd $172**
Caliber: .40 S&W. 12-rnd. magazine, 4.25-in. bbl., 7 in. overall. Weight: 28 oz. Blade front sight, dovetailed rear w/3-dot system. Blued finish. Checkered composition grips. DH/DP series feature a patented "fastfire" action w/5-6 lb. trigger pull. Made 1994-96.

DH45 AUTO PISTOL . . . . **NiB $346 Ex $248 Gd $189**
Caliber: .45 ACP. 13-rnd. magazine, 5-in. bbl., 8.1 in. over all. Weight: 35 oz. Blade front sight, dovetailed rear w/3-dot system. Blued finish. Checkered composition grips. Announced 1994, but not imported.

DP51 AUTO PISTOL . . . . **NiB $330 Ex $221 Gd $148**
Caliber: 9mm Para. 13-rnd. magazine, 4.1-in. bbl., 7.5 in. overall. Weight: 28 oz. Blade front and square-notch rear sights. Matte black finish. Checkered composition grips. Made 1991-96.

DP52 AUTO PISTOL . . . . **NiB $330 Ex $255 Gd $172**
Caliber: .22 LR. 10-rnd. magazine, 3.8-in. bbl., 6.7 in. overall. Weight: 23 oz. Blade front sight, dovetailed rear w/3-dot system. Blued finish. Checkered wood grips. Made 1994-96.

Daewoo DH40

CZ-85
Same as CZ-75 except w/ambi. slide release and safety. Calibers: 9mm Para., 7.65mm. Made 1986 to date.
Black polymer finish . . . . **NiB $560 Ex $388 Gd $274**
High-polish blued finish, add **50%**
Combat model (adj. sights,
1992-2016) . . . . **NiB $560 Ex $430 Gd $360**

CZ-97 B . . . . **NiB $629 Ex $540 Gd $344**
Similar to CZ-75 except chambered for the .45 ACP cartridge. 10-rnd. magazine, Frame-mounted thumb safety that allows single-action, cocked-and-locked carry. Made 1998 to date.

CZ-100 . . . . **NiB $488 Ex $398 Gd $265**
DA Semiauto. Caliber: 9mm, .40 S&W. 10-rnd. magazine, 3.8-in. bbl., Weight: 25 oz. Polymer grips w/fixed low-profile sights. Made 1996-2007. Reintro. 2009.

VZ 45 POCKET PISTOL . . . . . . **NiB $328 Ex $241 Gd $183**
Caliber: .25 Auto (6.35mm). Eight-round magazine, 2.5-in. bbl., 5 in. overall. Weight: 15 oz. Fixed sights. Blued finish. Plastic grips. Made 1945-52.

CZ VZ 61 SKORPION . . . . **NiB $599 Ex $340 Gd $300**
Semiauto version of VZ 61 Skorpion submachine gun. Caliber: .32 ACP. 20-rnd. magazine, 4.5-in. bbl. Made 2009-10.

DAKOTA — Santa Ana, CA

Trademark name of E.MF. Company for single action revolvers. Manufactured by Armi Jager in Italy from about 1975 to 1985. Uberti manufactured revolvers under the Dakota trademark from 1992 thru 2008.

MODEL 1873 SA REVOLVER
Calibers: .22 LR, .22 Mag., .357 Mag., .45 Long Colt, .30 M1 carbine, .38-40, .32-20, .44-40. Bbl. lengths: 3.5, 4.75, 5.5, 7.5 in. Blued or nickel finish. Engraved models avail.

Standard model . . . . NiB $347 Ex $305 Gd $229
Nickel finish, add 40%

BISLEY SA REVOLVER
Calibers: .44-40, .45 Long Colt, .357 Mag, 5.5- or 7.5-in. bbl., disc. 1992. Reintroduced 1994.

Standard model . . . . NiB $459 Ex $378 Gd $272
Engraved model . . . . NiB $638 Ex $509 Gd $283

HARTFORD SA REVOLVER
Calibers: .22 LR, .32-20, .357 Mag., .38-40, .44-40, .44 Special, .45 Long Colt. These are Exact replicas of the original Colts w/steel backstraps, trigger guards and forged frames. Blued or nickel finish. Imported from 1990 to 2008.

Standard model . . . . NiB $444 Ex $367 Gd $274
Engraved model . . . . NiB $734 Ex $546 Gd $499
Hartford Artillery, U.S. Cavalry models . . . . NiB $484 Ex $401 Gd $267

SHERIFF'S MODEL . . . . NiB $437 Ex $377 Gd $271
SA revolver. Calibers: .32-20, .357 Mag., .38-40, .44 Special, .44-40, .45 LC. 3.5-in. bbl. Reintroduced 1994.

TARGET SA REVOLVER . . . . . . NiB $478 Ex $351 Gd $279
SA revolver. Calibers: .45 Long Colt, .357 Mag., .22 LR; 5.5- or 7.5-in. bbl. Polished, blued finish, casehardened frame. Walnut grips. Ramp front, blade target sight, adj. rear sight.

DALY, CHARLES — Dayton, OH

Mfd. by Flli. Pietta (SAA models) Armscor (1911 series) and Bul Transmark (M-5 series).

MODEL 1873 CLASSIC SERIES NiB $520 Ex $370 Gd $315
SA revolver based on Colt SAA. Caliber: .357 Mag. or .45 LC. 6-rnd. cylinder. Bbbl. length: 4.75-, 5.5- or 7.5-in. Brass or steel backstrap/trigger guard. Imported from 2004 to 2007.
Birdshead model (birdshead grip, .45 LC only), add $30
Lightning model, add $30
Sonora model (matte blue finish), add $100

**Dakota Hartford
Engraved Model**

MODEL 1911-A1 SERIES . . . . . NiB $480 Ex $420 Gd $360
SA Semiauto. 1911 style. Various bbl. lenghts depending on model.Caliber: .38 Super, .40 S&W or .45 ACP. 8- or 10-rnd. magazine, 5-in. bbl. Weight: 39.5 oz. Blued finish. Imported from 1998 to 2008.

Satinless finish, add $100
Target model, add $80
Empire ECMT Custom Match model, add $275
Commander model . . . . NiB $480 Ex $420 Gd $360
Officer's model . . . . NiB $480 Ex $420 Gd $360
Polymer Frame PC model . . . . . NiB $470 Ex $410 Gd $350

MODEL M1911-A1 FIELD FS AUTOMATIC PISTOL
Caliber: .45 ACP. Eight- or 10-rnd. magazine (Hi-Cap), 5-in. bbl., 8.75 in. overall. Weight: 38 oz. Blade front sight, drift adjustable rear w/3-dot system. Skeletonized tactical hammer and trigger. Extended slide release and beavertail grip safety. Matte blue, stainless or Duo finish. Checkered composition or wood stocks. Imported from 1999 to 2000.

Matte blue (Field FS) . . . . NiB $525 Ex $479 Gd $326
Stainless (Empire EFS) . . . . NiB $560 Ex $459 Gd $361
Duo (Superior FS) . . . . NiB $653 Ex $497 Gd $363
w/.22 conversion kit, add $204

MODEL DDA
10-45 FS PISTOL . . . . NiB $455 Ex $400 Gd $345
SA/DA Semiauto polymer pistol. Calibers: .40 S&W or .45 ACP. 10-rnd. magazine. 4.3-in. bbl. Weight: 28.5 oz. Finish: matte black or two-tone. Imported from 2000 to 2002.

FIELD HP HI-POWER . . . . NiB $390 Ex $340 Gd $295
Similar to Browning HP pistol. 9mm. 10- or 13-rnd. magazine. 4.75-in. bbl. Finish: matte blued. Made in U.S. from 2003 to 2006.
Hard Chrome finish, add $100

M-5 FS
SEMIAUTO PISTOL . . . . NiB $670 Ex $585 Gd $505
Based on 1911 pistol w/polymer frame. Caliber: 9mm, .40 S&W or .45 ACP. 10-, 14- or 17-rnd. magazine. 3.1-, 4.2- or 5-in. bbl. Finish: blued or chrome. Weight: 31-33 oz. Imported from 2004 to 2009.
IPSC model (2004-07) . . . . . . NiB $1255 Ex $1100 Gd $945

DAN WESSON — Kansas City, KS

Currently owned by CZ-USA. Listsing below are for recent production of pistols and revolvers. Also see Wesson Fireams Company for older production revolvers.

MODEL 44-AGS (ALASKA GUIDE SPECIAL)
REVOLVER . . . . NiB $1295 Ex $1080 Gd $960
Caliber: .445 Super Mag., 6-shot cylinder. 4-in. heavy w/VR bbl. Finish: black teflon. Grip: rubber finger groove. Made 2002-04, and 2006-07.

MODEL 715 SEREIS . . . . NiB $710 Ex $630 Gd $560
Small frame revolver. Caliber: .357 Mag., 6-shot cylinder. 2.5-, 4-, 6-, 8-, or 10-in. heavy w/VR interchangeable bbls. Finish: stainless. Grip: rubber finger groove. Made 2002-04, and 2011-12.
2011-12 mfg. (6-in. bbl.) . . . . NiB $1168 Ex $1030 Gd $910

MODEL 741 SEREIS . . . . NiB $830 Ex $730 Gd $660
Large frame revolver. Caliber: .44 Mag., 6-shot cylinder. 4-, 6-, 8-, or 10-in. heavy w/VR interchangeable bbls. Finish: stainless. Grip: rubber finger groove. Made 2002-04.

Dan Wesson ECP

MODEL 7445 SEREIS . . . . **NiB $830 Ex $730 Gd $660**
Supermag frame revolver. Caliber: .445 Super Mag., 6-shot
cylinder. 4-, 6-, 8-, or 10-in. heavy w/VR interchangeable bbls.
Finish: stainless. Grip: rubber finger groove. Made 2002-04,
and 2006-07.

- Recent CZ USA Manufacture (2005 to date) -

MODEL 7460 SERIES . . . . **NiB $1070 Ex $810 Gd $730**
Supermag frame revolver. Caliber: .45 ACP, .45 Auto Rim, .445
Super Mag., .45 Win. Mag., or .450 Rowland, 6-shot cylinder.
Made 1999.

A2 SERIES
1911 platform. GI style. Caliber: .45 ACP, 8-rnd. magazine.
5-in. bbl. Finish: matte blue or parkerized. Grip: Double diamond checkered wood. 2017-date.
Full-Size model . . . . **NiB $1155 Ex $1005 Gd $780**
Commander model
  (4.25-in. bbl., 2017-19) . . . . **NiB $1155 Ex $1005 Gd $780**

BRUIN
1911 platform, long slide. Caliber: 10mm or .45 ACP, 8- or
9-rnd. magazine. 6.3-in. bbl. Finish: two-tone bronze/black.
Grip: G10. 2016-date.
.45 ACP cal . . . . **NiB $1790 Ex $1555 Gd $1220**
10mm cal . . . . **NiB $2020 Ex $1785 Gd $1450**

CCO BOBTAIL
1911 platform, bobtail frame. Caliber: 10mm or .45 ACP, 8- or
9-rnd. magazine. 4.2-in. bbl. Finish: matte. Grip: double diamond checkered wood. 2005-09, reintroduce. 2016 to date.
.45 ACP cal . . . . **NiB $1455 Ex $1280 Gd $990**
10mm cal . . . . **NiB $1485 Ex $1785 Gd $1450**

DISCRETION SERIES
1911 platform. Similar to Pointman series, except 5.75-in. bbl.
suppressor ready. Accessory rail, slide with relief cuts. Caliber:
9mm or .45 ACP. Sights: fixed tall. Grips: Textured G10. 2016-
20.
Full Size model . . . . **NiB $1855 Ex $1355 Gd $1055**
Commander model
  (4.25-in. bbl.) . . . . **NiB $1855 Ex $1355 Gd $1055**

DWX SERIES
Hybrid semiauto pistol built using Dan Wesson 1911 SA trigger
control group and frame of a CZ-75 pistol. Caliber: 9mm or .40
S&W, 19- (9mm) or 15-rnd. (.40 S&W) mag. Barrel: 5 in. Grips:
checkered red aluminum. Sights: fixed fiber-optic front/adjust-
able rear. Length: 8.52 in. overall. Weight: 43 oz. unloaded.
Finish: black Duty Coat, flat red aluminum trigger. Compatible
with CZ P-09 and CZ P-10 F magazines, bull bbl. and full dust
cover with accessory rail, oversized controls.

Full-Size model (5-in. bbl.) . . **NiB $1700 Ex $1680 Gd $1400**
Compact model (4-in. bbl.). . **NiB $1700 Ex $1680 Gd $1400**

ECO
1911 platform, Officer size frame. Caliber: 9mm or .45 ACP,
8- or 9-rnd. magazine. 3.5-in. bbl. Matte black or OD green
finish. G10 grip. Tritium night sights. 2012–19.
.45 ACP cal . . . . **NiB $1430 Ex $1255 Gd $985**
9mm cal . . . . **NiB $1390 Ex $1215 Gd $945**

ECP
1911 platform, Officer size frame w/bobtail. Caliber: 9mm
or .45 ACP, 8- or 9-rnd. magazine. Barrel: 4-in. heavy match.
Black duty finish. Weight: 29 oz. G10 grip. Fixed low-profile
sights. 2018-date.
.45 ACP cal . . . . **NiB $1370 Ex $1205 Gd $955**
9mm cal . . . . **NiB $1345 Ex $1180 Gd $930**

ELITE SERIES
1911 platform designed for competition. Caliber: 9mm, .38
Super, .40 S&W, 10mm, or .45 ACP, double-stack magazine.
Barrel: 5-in. Accessory rail, ambi. safety. Adj. sights. Textured
G10 grips. 2014-19.
Chaos model (9mm, 5-in. bbl.) . . **NiB $3255 Ex $2855 Gd $2215**
Fury model (9mm or 10mm,
  5.5-in. bbl.) . . . . **NiB $4180 Ex $3655 Gd $2830**
Havoc model (9mm or .38 Super, 4.5- or 5-in. bbl., optic-
ready) . . . . **NiB $3655 Ex $3210 Gd $2480**
Mayham model (.40 S&W, 6-in. bbl.,
  fiber-optic sights). . . . . **NiB $3330 Ex $2930 Gd $2255**
Titan model (10mm, 4.75-in. bbl.,
  tritium sights) . . . . **NiB $3255 Ex $2855 Gd $2215**

EZ-10 RAZORBACK
. . . . **NiB $1355 Ex $1180 Gd $930**
1911 platform. Caliber: 10mm, 8-rnd. magazine. Barrel: 5-in.
match. Brushed stainless finish. Checkered cocobolo grip. Adj.
sights. 2012–18.

GUARDIAN
1911 platform, Commander size frame w/bobtail. Caliber:
9mm, .38 Super, or .45 ACP, 8- or 9-rnd. magazine. 4.25-in.
barrel. Black duty finish. Weight: 29 oz. Checkered cocobolo
grip. Tritium night sights. 2010-date.
.45 ACP cal . . . . **NiB $1415 Ex $1240 Gd $990**
9mm or .38 Super cal . . . . **NiB $1355 Ex $1180 Gd $930**

KODIAK
. . . . **NiB $1995 Ex $1755 Gd $1355**
1911 platform, long slide. Caliber: 10mm, 8-rnd. magazine.
6-in. bbl. Stainless finish. G10 grip. Adj. rear, fiber optic front
sights. 2019-date.

COMMANDER
CLASSIC BOBTAIL. . . . . **NiB $1050 Ex $780 Gd $610**
1911 platform. Caliber: 10mm or .45 Auto. 4.25-in. bbl.,
bobbed frame. Series 70. Made 2005-09.

GLOBAL . . . . **NiB $1000 Ex $790 Gd $610**
1911 platform. Caliber: 10mm or .45 Auto. 5- or 6-in. bbl., accessory rail or full length dust cover frame. Series 70. Made 2005.

PATRIOT . . . . **NiB $830 Ex $660 Gd $480**
1911 platform. Caliber: 10mm or .45 Auto. 4.25- or 5-in. bbl.,
blued or stainless. Series 70. Made 2001-05.

POINTMAN SEVEN . . . . **NiB $1050 Ex $780 Gd $610**
1911 platform. Caliber: .40 S&W, 10mm or .45 Auto. 5-in.
bbl., blued or stainless, adj. target sights. Series 70. Made
2005-09.

GRADING: **NiB** = New in Box   **Ex** = Excellent or NRA 95%   **Gd** = Good or NRA 68%

Davis Industries Model P-32

PM POINTMAN . . . . **NIB $730 EX $655 GD $505**
1911 platform. Caliber: 10mm or .45 Auto. 5-in. bbl. Bomar adj. rear sights. Blued or stainless finish. Series 70. Disc. 2005.

POINTMAN SERIES
Similar to Pointman Seven series. Caliber: 9mm, .38 Super or .45 Auto. 5-in. bbl. Adj. rear sights. Stainless finish. Checkered cocobolo grip. Weight: 38.5 oz. 2015-date.
PM-7 model (.45 ACP) . . . . NiB $1380 Ex $1205 Gd $930
PM-9 model (9mm) . . . . NiB $1390 Ex $1215 Gd $940
PM-38 model (.38 Super) . . . . NiB $1380 Ex $1205 Gd $930
PM-45 model (.45 ACP) . . . . . . NiB $1390 Ex $1215 Gd $940

SILVERBACK . . . . **NIB $1605 EX $1405 GD $1005**
1911 platform. Caliber: 9mm, 10mm or .45 ACP; 8- or 9-rnd. magazine. Barrel: 5-in. Black duty finish. Textured G10 grip. Tritium night sights. 2015-17.

SPECIALIST SERIES
1911 platform. Caliber: 9mm, 10mm or .45 ACP, 8- or 9-rnd. magazine. Barrel: 5-in. Accessory rail, ambi. safety. Tritium night sights. G10 VZ Operator II grip. Brushed stainless finish. 2012-date.
Full-Size model (5-in. bbl.) . . NiB $1480 Ex $1300 Gd $1005
Commander model (9mm or .45 ACP,
 4.25-in. bbl.) . . . . NiB $1480 Ex $1300 Gd $1005
Distressed finish, add. $230

TCP . . . . **NiB $1455 Ex $1280 Gd $780**
1911 platform. Caliber: 9mm or .45 Auto. Barrel: 5-in. match. Aluminum frame with magwell. Fixed combat sights. G10 grip. Black duty finish. 2018-date.

VALKYRIE SERIES . . . . **NiB $1720 Ex $1505 Gd $1170**
1911 platform, Full and Commander size. Caliber: 9mm, 10mm, or .45 ACP, 7- or 8-rnd. magazine. Barrel: 4.5- or 4.25-in. Tritium night sights. G10 grip. Black duty finish. 2015-17.

VALOR SERIES
1911 platform, Full and Commander size. Caliber: 9mm or .45 ACP, 7- or 8-rnd. magazine. Barrel: 4.5- or 4.25-in. Adj. or Heine Ledge Straight sights. G10 grips. Matte black or matte stainless finish. 2008-18, reintro. 2020.
2008-18 model . . . . NiB $1455 Ex $1280 Gd $990
current model . . . . NiB $1590 Ex $1390 Gd $1085
Commander model (2016-18) . NiB $1455 Ex $1280 Gd $990

V-BOB SERIES . . . . **NiB $1580 Ex $1385 Gd $1080**
1911 platform, Commander size w/Bobtail frame. Caliber: 9mm or .45 ACP, 7- or 8-rnd. magazine. Barrel: 4.25-in. Tritium night sights. Black G10 grips. Matte stainless or black duty finish. 2020-date.
Two-tone finish . . . . NiB $1590 Ex $1390 Gd $1085
Commander model
 (black or stainless, 2010-18) NiB $1505 Ex $1320 Gd $1030

VIGIL SERIES . . . . **NIB $1105 EX $980 GD $755**
1911 platform, Full or Commander size frame. Caliber: 9mm or .45 ACP, 7- or 8-rnd. magazine. Barrel: 4.25- or 5-in. Tritium night sights. Cocobolo grips. Black duty finish. 2018-date.
CCO model (subcompact frame) . .NiB $1105 Ex $980 Gd $755
Suppressor-ready model. . . . . . NiB $1205 Ex $1080 Gd $855

WRAITH . . . . **NIB $1470 EX $1285 GD $1000**
1911 platform, Full-size frame. Caliber: 9mm, 10mm or .45 ACP, 7- or 8-rnd. magazine. 5.75-in. threaded barrel. Tritium night tall sights. G10 grips. Distressed duty finish. 2018-20.

DAVIS INDUSTRIES, INC. — Chino, CA

MODEL D DERRINGER
Single-action double derringer. Calibers: .22 LR, .22 Mag., .25 ACP, .32 Auto, .32 H&R Mag., 9mm, .38 Special. Two-round capacity, 2.4-in. or 2.75-in. bbl., 4 in. overall (2.4-in. bbl.). Weight: 9 to 11.5 oz. Laminated wood grips. Black Teflon or chrome finish. Made 1987-2001.
.22 LR or .25 ACP . . . . NiB $192 Ex $109 Gd $88
.22 Mag., .32 H&R
 Mag., .38 Spec. . . . . NiB $204 Ex $128 Gd $91
.32 Auto . . . . NiB $214 Ex $115 Gd $91
9mm Para. . . . . NiB $170 Ex $122 Gd $96

LONG BORE DERRINGER . . . . . NiB $219 Ex $122 Gd $97
Similar to Model D except in calibers .22 Mag., .32 H&R Mag., .38 Special, 9mm Para. 3.75-in. bbl., weight: 16 oz. Made 1995-2001.

MODEL P-32. . . . . NiB $152 Ex $101 Gd $78
Caliber: .32 Auto. Six-round magazine, 2.8-in. bbl., 5.4 in. overall. Weight: 22 oz. Black Teflon or chrome finish. Laminated wood grips. Made 1987-2001.

MODEL P-380. . . . . NiB $192 Ex $115 Gd $89
Caliber: .380 Auto. Five-round magazine, 2.8-in. bbl., 5.4 in. overall. Weight: 22 oz. Black Teflon or chrome finish. Made 1990-2001.

DESERT INDUSTRIES, INC. — Las Vegas, NV

Previously Steel City Arms, Inc.

DOUBLE DEUCE DA PISTOL . . NiB $360 Ex $286 Gd $225
Caliber: .22 LR. Six-round magazine, 2.5-in. bbl., 5.5 in. overall. Weight: 15 oz. Matte-finish stainless steel. Rosewood grips.

TWO-BIT SPECIAL PISTOL . . . . NiB $380 Ex $326 Gd $237
Similar to the Double Deuce model except chambered in .25 ACP w/5-shot magazine.

DETONICS FIREARMS IND. — Phoenix, AZ
Founded in the mid 1970s, previously Detonics Mfg. Co. (1976-87), New Detonics (1987-92), Detonics USA (2004-07) and currently Detonics Defense. Located previously in Bellevue, WA., currently Milstadt, IL.

COMBATMASTER
Calibers: .45 ACP, .451 Detonics Mag. Six-round magazine, 3.5-in. bbl., 6.75 in. overall. Combat-type w/fixed or adjustable sights. Checkered walnut grip. Stainless steel. Disc. 1992.
MK I, matte stainless,
 fixed sights (disc. 1981) . . . . NiB $1097 Ex $963 Gd $893

Detonics Combatmaster

MK II polished finish,
(disc. 1979). . . . . NiB $1494 Ex $1370 Gd $1133
MK III chrome, (disc. 1980) . . . NiB $551 Ex $443 Gd $328
MK IV polished blued,
adj. sights, (disc. 1981). . . . . NiB $612 Ex $500 Gd $373
MK V matte stainless,
fixed sights, (disc. 1985). . . . . NiB $762 Ex $621 Gd $499
MK VI polished stainless, fixed
sights, (disc. 1985) . . . . NiB $831 Ex $666 Gd $509
MK VI in .451 Magnum,
(disc. 1986). . . . . NiB $1199 Ex $979 Gd $695
MK VII matte stainless steel,
no sights, (disc. 1985) . . . . . NiB $1037 Ex $845 Gd $591
MK VII in .451 Magnum,
(disc. 1980) . . . . NiB $1380 Ex $1131 Gd $806

DTX. . . . . NIB $1000 EX $730 GD $510
SAO. Semiauto. Caliber: 9mm or.40 S&W. Semiauto. 4.5-in.
bbl. Made 2011-14.

NEMESIS HT . . . . NIB $1920 EX $1440 GD $1040
SA. Semiauto. Caliber: .40 S&W. 5-in. bbl. Magazine: 9-rnd.
Finish: Cerakote. Weight: 38 oz. Made 2011-14.

POCKET 9 . . . . NiB $668 Ex $541 Gd $426
Calibers: 9mm Para., .380. Six-round magazine, three-in. bbl.,
5.88 in. overall. Fixed sights. Double- and single-action trigger
mechanism. Disc. 1986.

SCOREMASTER. . . . . NiB $1550 Ex $1257 Gd $1120
Calibers: .45 ACP, .451 Detonics Mag. Seven-round magazine.
Five- or 6-in. heavyweight match bbl., 8.75 in. overall. Weight:
47 oz. Stainless steel construction, self-centering bbl., system.
Disc. 1992.

SERVICEMASTER. . . . . NiB $1117 Ex $780 Gd $530
Caliber: .45 ACP. Seven-round magazine, 4.25-in. bbl.,
weight: 39 oz. Interchangeable front sight, Millett rear sight.
Disc. 1986.

SERVICEMASTER II . . . . NiB $1117 Ex $780 Gd $530
Same general specifications as standard Service Master except
comes in polished stainless steel w/self-centering bbl., system.
Disc. 1992.

DIAMONDBACK FIREARMS — COCOA, FL

DB9. NiB $431 Ex $380 Gd $280
Semiauto. Striker fire. Caliber: 9mm, 6-rnd. magazine. 3-in.
bbl. Frame: polymer. Sights: fixed. Finish: matte black, FDE,
pink, or two-tone. Grip: textured polymer. Weight: 11 oz.
Length: 5.6 in. Made 2011 to date.
FDE or pink, add. $10
Two-tone, add. $30

MODEL DB FS 9 . . . . NiB $483 Ex $400 Gd $380
Semiauto. Striker fire. Caliber: 9mm, 15-rnd. magazine. 4.75-
in. bbl. Frame: polymer. Sights: fixed. Finish: matte black. Grip:
textured polymer. Weight: 21.5 oz. Length: 7.8 in. Made 2014
to date.

MODEL DB15PODG7 . . . . NiB $914 Ex $890 Gd $810
AR15 platform. Semiauto. SA. Caliber: 5.56 NATO, 30-rnd. magazine. 7.5-in. bbl. Frame: forged aluminum. Sights: none. Finish:
matte black. Grip: textured polymer. Made 2014 to date.

MODEL DB380. . . . . NiB $394 Ex $430 Gd $330
Similar to DB9 except chambered in .380 ACP.

MODEL DBAM29 . . . . NiB $300 Ex $290 Gd $170
Semiauto. Striker fire. Caliber: 9mm, 15-, or 21-rnd. magazine.
3.5-in. bbl. Frame: polymer. Sights: fixed. Finish: matte black.
Grip: textured polymer. Weight: 22 oz. Length: 6.5 in. Made 2019
to date.

DOUBLETAP DEFENSE — ST. LOUIS, MO

DOUBLETAP. . . . . NIB $460 EX $390 GD $330
O/U derringer, break action, dbl. bbl. DAO. Caliber: 9mm or
.45 ACP. 3-in. bbl., allows bbls. to be swapped. Frame: aluminum. Sights: fixed. Finish: matte black. Grip: textured aluminum w/storage for 2 extra cartridges. Weight: 15 oz. Length:
5.5 in. Made 2012 to date.
Ported brls., add $70
Titanium frame, add $240

DOWNSIZER CORPORATION — Santee, CA

MODEL WSP DAO PISTOL. . . . NiB $420 Ex $381 Gd $264
Single-round, tip-up pistol. Calibers: .22 Mag., .32 Mag., .380
ACP. 9mm Parabellum, .357 Mag., .40 S&W, .45 ACP. Six-
round cylinder, 2.10-in. bbl. w/o Extractor, 3.25 in. overall.
Weight: 11 oz. No sights. Stainless finish. Synthetic grips.
Made 1994-2007.

DREYSE — Sommerda, Germany

*Mfd. by Rheinische Metallwaren und Maschinenfabrik
("Rheinmetall").*

MODEL 1907 . . . . NiB $273 Ex $224 Gd $179
Caliber: .32 Auto (7.65mm). Eight-round magazine, 3.5-in.
bbl., 6.25 in. overall. Weight: About 24 oz. Fixed sights. Blued
finish. Hard rubber grips. Made circa 1907 to 1914.

VEST POCKET . . . . NiB $357 Ex $293 Gd $204
Conventional Browning type. Caliber: .25 Auto (6.35mm).
Six-round magazine, 2-in. bbl., 4.5 in. overall. Weight: About
14 oz. Fixed sights. Blued finish. Hard rubber grips. Made
1909-14.

Dreyse Model 1907

DWM — Berlin, Germany
Mfd. by Deutsche Waffen-und-Munitionsfabriken.

POCKET AUTOMATIC PISTOL...NiB $1050 Ex $918 Gd $713
Similar to the FN Browning Model 1910. Caliber: .32 Automatic (7.65mm). 3.5-in. bbl., 6 in. overall. Weight: About 21 oz. Blued finish. Hard rubber grips. Made circa 1921 to 1931.

ED BROWN — Perry, MT

Manufacturer of custom 1911 style pistols.

CLASS A LTD............NiB $2312 Ex $2152 Gd $1041
Caliber: .38 Super, 9mm, 9x23, .45 ACP. Seven-round magazine, 4.25- or 5-in. bbl., weight: 34-39 oz. Rubber checkered or optional Hogue Exotic wood grip. M1911 style single action pistol. Fixed front and rear Novak Lo-mount or fully adjustable sights.

CLASSIC CUSTOM.......NiB $3231 Ex $2553 Gd $1527
Caliber: .45 ACP. Seven-round magazine, 4.25- or 5-in. bbl., weight: 39 oz. Exotic Hogue wood grip w/modified ramp or post front and rear adjustable sights.

EXECUTIVE.............NiB $2430 EX $1760 GD $1310
Similar to Classic Custom series except stainless steel. Made 2004 to present.

COMMANDER BOBTAIL ... NiB $2360 EX $1770 GD $1310
Similar to Classic Custom series except w/ rounded butt. Made 2003 to present.

SPECIAL FORCES ....NiB $2430 Ex $1918 Gd $1437
Caliber: .45 ACP. Seven-round magazine, 4.25- or 5-in. bbl., weight: 34-39 oz. Rubber checkered, optional exotic wood grips. Single action M1911 style pistol.

E.M.F. Co., In. — Santa Anna, CA
Importer, distributor, and retailer of numerous reproduction and new deisgn pistols and revolvers. See Davide Pedersoli & Co. (Sharps rifle reproductions), F.A.P F.LLI. Pietta (single action revolvers), and Uberti. (lever action rifles). Great Western is a trademark of E.M.F. for a series of single action revolvers.

GREAT WESTERN II SEREIS
Patterned after 1873 SAA revolver. Mfg: Pietta,Italy. Calibers: .22 LR, .357 Mag., .44-40, .44 Mag., .45 Long Colt Bbl. lengths: 3.5, 4.75, 5.5, 7.5 in. Blued or nickel finish. Engraved models avail.

Custom 1873 model..........NiB $730 Ex $530 Gd $330
Alchimista I and II models, deduct.................$200
Alchimista III model, deduct......................$150
Buntline model, deduct..........................$200
California model, deduct $250
Deluxe Sheriff model, add $10
Express Agent model, deduct $200
Pony Express model, deduct $150

ENFIELD — Enfield Lock, Middlesex, England
Mfd. by Rheinische Metallwaren und Manufactured by Royal Small Arms Factory.

**Enfield
(British Service) No. 2 MK 1 Revolver**

NO. 2 MK 1 DA REVOLVER ... NiB $1110 Ex $860 Gd $660
British Military Service. Webley pattern. Hinged frame. Double action. Caliber: .380 British Service (.38 S&W w/200-grain bullet). Six-round cylinder, 5-in. bbl., 10.5 in. overall. Weight: About 27.5 oz. Fixed sights. Blued finish. Vulcanite grips. First issued in 1932, this was the standard revolver of the British Army in WW II. Now obsolete. Note: This model was also produced w/spurless hammer as No. 2 Mk 1* and Mk 1**, deduct $200 except for H.A.C. mfg., add 100%.

ENTREPRISE ARMS — Irwindale, CA

ELITE SERIES SA AUTO PISTOL...NiB $661 Ex $498 Gd $401
Single action M1911 style pistol. Caliber: .45 ACP. 10-rnd. magazine, 3.25-, 4.25-, 5-in. bbl., (models P325, P425, P500). Weight: 36-40 oz. Ultraslim checkered grips, Tactical 2 high profile sights w/3-dot system. Lightweight adjustable trigger. Blued or matte black oxide finish. Made 1997 to date.

MEDALIST SA AUTOMATIC PISTOL
Similar to Elite model except machined to match tolerances and target configuration. Caliber: .45 ACP, .40 S&W. 10-rnd. magazine, 5-in. compensated bbl. w/dovetail front and fully adjustable rear Bo-Mar sights. Weight: 40 oz. Made 1997 to date.
.40 S&W model............NiB $1015 Ex $862 Gd $689
.45 ACP model ....NiB $893 Ex $740 Gd $577

TACTICAL SA AUTOMATIC PISTOL
Similar to Elite model except in combat carry configuration. De-horned frame and slide w/ambidExtrous safety. Caliber: .45 ACP. 10-rnd. magazine, 3.25-, 4.25-, 5-in. bbl., weight: 36-40 oz. Tactical 2 Ghost Ring or Novak Lo-mount sights.
Tactical 2 ghost
ring sights.................NiB $917 Ex $724 Gd $571
Novak Lo-Mount............NiB $917 Ex $724 Gd $571
Tactical plus model..........NiB $917 Ex $724 Gd $571

BOXER ....NiB $1243 Ex $1122 Gd $831
Similar to Medalist model except w/profiled slide configuration and fully adjustable target sights. weight: 42 oz. Made 1997 to date.

TOURNAMENT SHOOTER MODEL SA AUTOMATIC PISTOL
Similar to Elite model except in IPSC configuration. Caliber: .45 ACP, .40 S&W. 10-rnd. magazine, 5-in. compensated bbl., w/dovetail front and fully adjustable rear Bo-Mar sights. Weight: 40 oz. Made 1997 to date.
TSM I model ....NiB $2145 Ex $1986 Gd $1637
TSM II model ....NiB $1834 Ex $1687 Gd $1331
TSM III model...........NiB $2575 Ex $1403 Gd $1661

ERMA-WERKE — Dachau, Germany

MODEL ER-772...........NiB $1132 Ex $1071 Gd $655
Revolver. Caliber: .22 LR. Six-round cylinder, 6-in. bbl., 12 in. overall. Weight: 47.25 oz. Adjustable micrometer rear

**Erma
Model ER-772 Match Revolver**

**Erma-Werke
Model KGP69**

sight and front sight blade. Adjustable trigger. Interchangeable walnut sporter or match grips. Polished blued finish. Made 1991-94.

MODEL ER-773 MATCH . . . . . . NiB $957 Ex $831 Gd $587
Same general specifications as Model 772 except chambered for .32 S&W. Made 1991-95.

MODEL ER-777 MATCH . . . . . . NiB $923 Ex $785 Gd $623
Revolver. Caliber: .357 Magnum. Six-round cylinder. 4- or 5.5-in. bbl., 9.7 to 11.3 in. overall. Weight: 43.7 oz. (w/ 5.5-in. bbl.). Micrometer adj. rear sight. Checkered walnut sporter or match-style grip (interchangeable). Made 1991-95.

MODEL ESP-85A COMPETITION PISTOL
Calibers: .22 LR and .32 S&W Wadcutter. Eight- or 5-rnd. magazine, 6-in. bbl., 10 in. overall. Weight: 40 oz. Adj. rear sight, blade front sight. Checkered walnut grip w/thumbrest. Made 1991-97.
Match model. . . . . NiB $1280 Ex $1128 Gd $716
Chrome match . . . . NiB $1540 Ex $1330 Gd $998
Sporting model . . . . NiB $1251 Ex $1049 Gd $735
Conversion unit .22 LR . . . . NiB $1566 Ex $1212 Gd $1030
Conversion unit .32 S&W . . NiB $1566 Ex $1212 Gd $1030

**MODEL KGP68
AUTOMATIC PISTOL** . . . . NiB $484 Ex $306 Gd $239
Luger type. Calibers: .32 Auto (7.65mm), .380 Auto (9mm Short). Six-round magazine (.32 Auto), 5-rnd. (.380 Auto), 4-in. bbl., 7.38 in. overall. Weight: 22.5 oz. Fixed sights. Blued finish. Checkered walnut grips. Made 1968-93.

**MODEL KGP69
AUTOMATIC PISTOL** . . . . NiB $357 Ex $291 Gd $214
Luger type. Caliber: .22 LR. Eight-round magazine, 4-in. bbl., 7.75 in. overall. Weight: 29 oz. fixed sights. Blued finish. Checkered walnut grips. Imported from 1969 to 1993.

EUROPEAN AMERICAN ARMORY (EAA) — Rockledge, FL

See also listings under Astra Pistols.

EUROPEAN 32 AND 380. . . . . . . NiB $150 Ex $120 Gd $85
Semiauto. Calibers: .32 ACP (SA only), .380 ACP (SA or DA), 3.85-in. bbl., 7.38 overall, 7-rnd. magazine, Weight: 26 oz.

Blade front sight, drift-adj. rear. Blued, chrome, blue/chrome, blue/gold, Duo-Tone or Wonder finish. Imported 1991 to 2001.
.32 ACP, deduct 10%
Chrome, add 10%

BIG BORE BOUNTY HUNTER SA REVOLVER
Calibers: .357 Mag., .41 Mag., .44-40, .44 Mag., .45 Colt. Bbl. lengths: 4.63, 5.5, 7.5 in. Blade front and grooved topstrap rear sights. Blued or chrome finish w/color casehardened or gold-plated frame. Smooth walnut grips. Imported 1992.
Blued finish . . . . NiB $430 Ex $320 Gd $230
w/color-casehardened frame, add 10%
Blued w/gold-plated frame, add 15%
Chrome finish, add 20%
Gold-plated frame, add. 15%

BOUNTY HUNTER SA REVOLVER
Calibers: .22 LR, .22 Mag. Bbl. lengths: 4.75, 6 or 9 in. Blade front and dovetailed rear sights. Blued finish or blued w/gold-plated frame. European hardwood grips. Imported from 1997 to date.
Blued finish (4.75-in. bbl.) . . . . NiB $320 Ex $235 Gd $155
.22 LR/.22 WRF combo, add. 10%

EA22 TARGET . . . . NiB $398 Ex $281 Gd $214
Caliber: .22 LR. 12-rnd. magazine, 6-in. bbl., 9.10 in. overall. Weight: 40 oz. Ramp front sight, fully adj. rear. Blued finish. Checkered walnut grips w/thumbrest. Made 1991-94.

**European American Armory
Big Bore Bounty Hunter shown
w/optional scope**

European American Armory Witness

**European American Armory
Windicator Target**

GRADING: **NiB** = New in Box **Ex** = Excellent or NRA 95% **Gd** = Good or NRA 68%

FAB 92 AUTO PISTOL . . . . **NiB $340 Ex $260 Gd $190**
Similar to the Witness model except chambered in 9mm only w/slide-mounted safety and no cock-and-lock provision. Standard and compact sizes. Imported 1992 to 1995.

SAR B6 SERIES
Semiauto. Polymer frame, DA/SA trigger. Caliber: 9mm; 13-, 16- or 17-rnd. magazine. 4.5-in. barrel. Fixed sights. Weight: 24 oz. Matte black finish. Textured polymer grip. Accessory rail. 2013-17.
Full-Size model . . . . **NiB $345 Ex $305 Gd $265**
Competitor model
  (4.75-in. bbl., adj. sights) . . . . **NiB $705 Ex $605 Gd $480**
Pavona model (3.8-in. bbl.) . . . . . **NiB $355 Ex $305 Gd $265**

SAR K2 SERIES
Semiauto. Steel frame, DA/SA trigger. Caliber: 9mm, .40 S&W, 10mm and .45 ACP; double stack magazine. Barrel: 4.5-in. Adj. rear sights. Weight: 40 oz. Blued or stainless steel finish. Textured polymer grip. Accessory rail. 2011-17.
Full-Size model . . . . **NiB $395 Ex $340 Gd $255**
P model (3.8-in. bbl.) . . . . **NiB $370 Ex $330 Gd $255**

SARGUN . . . . **NiB $545 Ex $435 Gd $335**
Semiauto. SA. Caliber: 9mm, .40 S&W or .45 ACP; 17- or 15-rnd. magazine depending on caliber. 4.5-in. bbl. Frame: polymer. Sights: low profile adj. Finish: matte black, two-tone. Grip: textured polymer. Weight: 30.5 oz. Length: 7.8 in. Ambidextrous controls. Imported from Turkey from 2013 to date.

WINDICATOR STANDARD . . . . **NiB $300 Ex $220 Gd $145**
Revolver. DA/SA. Calibers: .22 LR, .22 WRF, .32 H&R Mag., .38 Special. Two-, 4- or 6-in. bbl., blade front sight, fixed or adj. rear. Blued finish. European hardwood grips w/finger grooves. Imported 1991 to date.
.22 LR combo, add **$80**
.357 Mag, add. **$100**

WINDICATOR TACTICAL GRADE REVOLVER
Similar to the Windicator Standard model except chambered in .38 Special only. Two- or 4-in. bbl., fixed sights. Available w/ compensator. Imported from 1991-93.
Tactical revolver . . . . **NiB $229 Ex $185 Gd $109**
w/compensator, add **$60**

WINDICATOR TARGET
REVOLVER . . . . **NiB $444 Ex $381 Gd $255**
Calibers: .22 LR, .38 Special, .357 Magnum. Eight-round cylinder in .22 LR, 6-rnd. in .38 Special and .357 Magnum. Six-in. bbl. w/bbl. weights. 11.8 in. overall. Weight: 50.2 oz. Interchangeable blade front sight, fully adj. rear. Walnut competition-style grips. Imported from 1991-93.

WITNESS DA AUTO PISTOL
Similar to the Brno CZ-75 w/a cocked-and-locked system. Double or single action. Calibers: 9mm Para. .38 Super, .40 S&W, 10mm; .41 AE and .45 ACP. 16-rnd. magazine (9mm), 12 shot (.38 Super/.40 S&W), or 10-rnd. (10mm/.45 ACP), 4.75-in. bbl., 8.10 in. overall. Weight: 35.33 oz. Blade front sight, rear sight adj. for windage w/3-dot sighting system. Steel or polymer frame. Blued, satin chrome, blue/chrome, stainless or Wonder finish. Checkered rubber grips. EA Series imported 1991 to date.
9mm blue . . . . **NiB $475 Ex $337 Gd $249**
9mm chrome or blue/chrome. . **NiB $475 Ex $337 Gd $249**
9mm stainless . . . . **NiB $469 Ex $337 Gd $283**
9mm Wonder finish . . . . **NiB $500 Ex $356 Gd $265**
.38 Super and .40 S&W blued . **NiB $475 Ex $337 Gd $237**
.38 Super and .40 S&W chrome
  or blue/chrome . . . . **NiB $469 Ex $388 Gd $273**
.38 Super and .40 S&W
  stainless . . . . **NiB $546 Ex $425 Gd $292**
.38 Super and .40 S&W
  Wonder finish . . . . **NiB $577 Ex $340 Gd $296**
10mm, .41 AE and .45 ACP
  blued . . . . **NiB $474 Ex $346 Gd $235**
10mm, .41 AE and .45 ACP
  chrome or blue/chrome . . . **NiB $546 Ex $437 Gd $316**
10mm, .41 AE and .45 ACP
  stainless . . . . **NiB $577 Ex $464 Gd $337**
10mm, .41 AE and
  .45 ACP Wonder finish . . . . **NiB $562 Ex $439 Gd $321**

WITNESS COMPACT DA AUTO PISTOL (L SERIES)
Similar to the standard Witness series except more compact w/ 3.625-in. bbl., and polymer or steel frame. Weight: 30 oz. Matte blued or Wonder finish. Imported 1999 to date.
9mm blue . . . . **NiB $468 Ex $330 Gd $235**
9mm Wonder finish . . . . **NiB $468 Ex $330 Gd $235**
.38 Super and .40 S&W blued . **NiB $468 Ex $330 Gd $235**
.38 Super and .40 S&W Wonder
  finish. . . . . **NiB $468 Ex $330 Gd $235**
10mm, .41 AE and .45 ACP
  blued . . . . **NiB $549 Ex $369 Gd $273**
10mm, .41 AE and .45 ACP
  Wonder fin. . . . . **NiB $549 Ex $369 Gd $273**
w/ported bbl., add **$50**

WITNESS CARRY COMP
Double/Single action. Calibers: .38 Super, 9mm Parabellum, .40 S&W, 10mm, .45 ACP. 10-, 12- or 16-rnd. magazine, 4.25-in. bbl., w/1-in. compensator. Weight: 33 oz., 8.10 in. overall. Black rubber grips. Post front sight, drift adjustable rear w/3-dot system. Matte blue, Duo-Tone or Wonder finish. Imported 1992 to 2004.
9mm, .40 S&W . . . . **NiB $453 Ex $359 Gd $273**
.38 Super, 10mm, .45 ACP . . . . **NiB $453 Ex $359 Gd $273**
w/Duo-Tone finish (disc.), add **$40**
w/Wonder finish, add **$20**

WITNESS LIMITED CLASS . . . . **NiB $909 Ex $734 Gd $559**
Single action. Semiauto. Calibers: .38 Super, 9mm Parabellum, .40 S&W, .45 ACP. 10-rnd. magazine, 4.75-in. bbl., Weight: 37 oz. Checkered competition-style walnut grips. Long slide w/post front sight, fully adj. rear. Matte blue finish. Imported 1994 to 1998.

WITNESS SUBCOMPACT DA AUTO PISTOL
Calibers: 9mm Para., .40 S&W, 41 AE, .45 ACP. 13-rnd. magazine in 9mm, 9-rnd. in .40 S&W, 3.66-in. bbl., 7.25 in. overall. Weight: 30 oz. Blade front sight, rear sight adj. for windage. Blued, satin chrome or blue/chrome finish. Imported from 1995 to 1997.
9mm blue . . . . **NiB $408 Ex $281 Gd $204**
9mm chrome or blue/chrome. . **NiB $453 Ex $306 Gd $225**
.40 S&W blue . . . . **NiB $453 Ex $306 Gd $225**
.40 S&W chrome or
  blue/chrome. . . . . **NiB $497 Ex $366 Gd $229**
.41 AE blue . . . . **NiB $525 Ex $429 Gd $308**
.41 AE chrome or blue/chrome. . . . **NiB $577 Ex $448 Gd $319**
.45 ACP blued. . . . . **NiB $525 Ex $336 Gd $308**
.45 ACP chrome
  or blue/chrome. . . . . **NiB $500 Ex $439 Gd $321**

WITNESS TARGET PISTOLS
Similar to standard Witness model except fitted w/2- or 3-port compensator, competition frame and S/A target trigger.

Feather Guardian Angel Derringer

FEG Mark II AP-.22

SP607 . . . . NiB $985 Ex $804 Gd $658
Similar to Model FAS 601 except chambered for .22 LR, w/ removable bbl. weights. Imported 1995 to date.

FEATHER INDUSTRIES — Boulder, CO

GUARDIAN ANGEL DERRINGER
Double-action over/under derringer w/interchangeable drop-in loading blocks. Calibers: .22 LR, .22 WMR, 9mm, .38 Spec. Two-round capacity, 2-in. bbl., 5 in. overall. weight: 12 oz. Stainless steel. Checkered black grip. Made 1988-95.
.22 LR, .22 WMR . . . . NiB 165 Ex $101 Gd $81
9mm, .38 Special (disc. 1989) . . . NiB $233 Ex $189 Gd $150

FEG (FEGYVERGYAN) — Budapest, Soroksariut, Hungary

Currently imported by KBI, Inc. Previously by Century International Arms and Interarms.

MARK II AP-22 DA
AUTO PISTOL . . . . NiB $240 Ex $219 Gd $179
Caliber: .22 LR. 8-rnd. magazine, 3.4-in. bbl., Weight: 23 oz. Drift-adj. sights. Double action, all-steel pistol. Imported 1997 to 1998.

MARK II AP-380 DA AUTO
PISTOL . . . . NiB $240 Ex $219 Gd $179
Caliber: .380. 7-rnd. magazine, 3.9-in. bbl., weight 27 oz. Drift-adj. sights. Double action, all-steel pistol. Imported 1997 to 1998.

MARK II APK-380 DA AUTO
PISTOL . . . . NiB $240 Ex $219 Gd $179
Caliber: .380. 7-rnd. magazine, 3.4-in. bbl., weight: 25 oz. Drift-adj. sights. Double action, all-steel pistol. Imported 1997 to 1998.

MODEL GKK-9 (92C) . . . . NiB $430 Ex $330 Gd $204
Improved version of the double-action FEG Model MBK. Caliber: 9mm Para. 14-rnd. magazine, 4-in. bbl., 7.4 in. overall. Weight: 34 oz. Blade front sight, rear sight adj. for windage. Checkered wood grips. Blued finish. Imported from 1992 to 1993.
GKK-40 (.40 S&W, 1995-96). . . . NiB $305 Ex $225 Gd $175

MODEL GKK-45 . . . . NiB $302 Ex $225 Gd $175
Improved version of the double-action FEG Model MBK. Caliber: .45 ACP. Eight-round magazine, 4.1-in. bbl., 7.75 in. overall. Weight: 36 oz. Blade front sight, adj. rear sight w/3-dot system. Checkered walnut grips. Blued or chrome finish. Imported 1993 to 1996.

MODEL MBK-9HP . . . . NiB $469 Ex $306 Gd $281
Similar to the double-action Browning Hi-Power. Caliber: 9mm Para. 14-rnd. magazine, 4.6-in. bbl., 8 in. overall. Weight: 36 oz. Blade front sight, rear sight adj. for windage. Checkered wood grips. Blued finish. Imported 1992 to 1993.

MODEL PA-63 AUTO PISTOL . . . . Ex $175 Gd $95
Hungary's military pistol. Similar to the Walther PP. Caliber: 9x18mm Makarov. 7-rnd. magazine, 3.95-in. bbl., 6.9 in. overall. Weight: 21 oz. Fixed sights. Two-tone finish; blued slide natutal aluminum frame. Checkered plasic grips. Military surplus.

Calibers: 9mm Para., 9x21, .40 S&W, 10mm and .45 ACP, 5.25-in. match bbl., 10.5 in. overall. Weight: 38 oz. Square post front sight, fully adj. rear or drilled and tapped for scope. Blued or hard chrome finish. Low-profile competition grips. Imported 1992 to date.
Silver Team (blued w/2-port
  compensator) . . . . NiB $895 Ex $785 Gd $561
Gold Team (chrome
  w/3-port compensator) . . . NiB $1810 Ex $1632 Gd $1331

WITNESS P SERIES
Similar to standard Witness model except w/polymer frame. Caliber: 9mm, .40 S&W, 10mm, and .45 ACP; double stack magazine. Barrel: 4.5-in. Adj. rear sights. Weight: 30.4 oz. Matte black finish. Textured polymer grip. Accessory rail. 2014-date.
Full-Size model . . . . NiB $505 Ex $455 Gd $370
Carry model (3.6-in. bbl.) . . . . . . NiB $590 Ex $480 Gd $370
Compact model
  (3.6-in. bbl., shorter frame). . . NiB $505 Ex $455 Gd $370
Match model (4.75-in. bbl., extended magwell and mag
  release, SA trigger) . . . . NiB $705 Ex $605 Gd $480

WITNESS PAVONA . . . . NIB $430 EX $380 GD $280
Similar to Witness P series except chambered in .380 ACP, 9mm, .40 S&W, 10mm, and .45 ACP; double stack magazine. DA/SA trigger. Barrel: 3.6-in. Fixed sights. Weight: 25 oz. Various finish colors. Textured polymer grip. Accessory rail. 2014-date.

FAS — Malino, Italy
Currently imported by Nygord Precision Products. Previously by Beeman Precision Arms and Osborne's, Cheboygan, MI.

OP601 SEMIAUTO MATCH TARGET PISTOL
Caliber: .22 Short. Five-round top-loading magazine, 5.6-in. ported and ventilated bbl., 11 in. overall. Weight: 41.5 oz. Removable, adj. trigger group. Blade front sight, open-notch fully adj. rear. Stippled walnut wraparound or adj. target grips.
Right-hand model . . . . NiB $1030 Ex $930 Gd $714
Left-hand model, add 10%

602 SEMIAUTO MATCH TARGET PISTOL
Similar to Model FAS 601 except chambered for .22 LR. Weight: 37 oz.
Right-hand model . . . . NiB $900 Ex $705 Gd $581
Left-hand model, add 10%

CF603 . . . . NiB $980 Ex $816 Gd $647
Similar to Model FAS 601 except chambered for .32 S&W (wadcutter).

MODEL PJK-9HP . . . . **NiB $430 Ex $340 Gd $280**
Similar to the single-action Browning Hi-Power. Caliber: 9mm Para. 13-rnd. magazine, 4.75-in. bbl., 8 in. overall. Weight: 21 oz. Blade front sight, rear sight adj. for windage w/3-dot system. Checkered walnut or rubber grips. Blued or chrome finish. Imported 1992 to 2003.
chrome finish, add **$50**

MODEL PSP-25 . . . . **NiB $318 Ex $205 Gd $155**
Similar to the Browning .25. Caliber: .25 ACP. Six-round magazine, 2.1-in. bbl., 4.1 in. overall. Weight: 9.5 oz. Fixed sights. Checkered composition grips. Blued or chrome finish.
chrome finish, add **15%**

MODEL SMC-22 . . . . **NiB $222 Ex $130 Gd $79**
Same general specifications as SMC-380 except in .22 LR. Eight-round magazine, 3.5-in. bbl., 6.1 in. overall. Weight: 18.5 oz. Blade front sight, rear sight adj. for windage. Checkered composition grips w/thumbrest. Blued finish.

MODEL SMC-380 . . . .**NiB $222 Ex $130 Gd $79**
Similar to the Walther DA PPK w/alloy frame. Caliber: .380 ACP. Six-round magazine, 3.5-in. bbl., 6.1 in. overall. Weight: 18.5 oz. Blade front sight, rear sight adj. for windage. Checkered composition grips w/ thumbrest. Blued finish. Imported 1993 to 1997.

MODEL SMC-918 . . . .**NiB $203 Ex $120 Gd $90**
Same general specifications as SMC-380 except chambered in 9x18mm Makarov. Imported from 1994 to 1997.

TOKAGYPT 58 . . . . **NIB $910 EX $810 GD $410**
Similar to Soviet TT pistol except 9MM. Grip: brown plastic. Finish: blued. Made 1952. Military sidearm.
Firebird (commercial variant) . . . **NiB $480 Ex $365 Gd $255**
Super 12 (9mm or 7.62x25mm,
   black plastic grip) . . . . **NiB $480 Ex $365 Gd $255**

FIALA OUTFITTERS, INC. — New York, NY

REPEATING PISTOL . . . .**NiB $689 Ex $479 Gd $365**
Hand-operated, not Semiauto. Caliber: .22 LR. 10-rnd. magazine, bbl. lengths: 3-, 7.5- and 20-in. 11.25 in. overall (w/ 7.5-in. bbl.). Weight: 31 oz. (w/ 7.5-in. bbl.). Target sights. Blued finish. Plain wood grips. Shoulder stock was originally supplied for use w/20-in. bbl. Made 1920-23. Value shown is for pistol w/one bbl., no shoulder stock. Three bbl. cased sets start at $3,030.

F.I.E. CORPORATION — Hialeah, FL

The F.I.E. Corporation became QFI (Quality Firearms Corp.) of Opa Locka, Fl., about 1990, when most of F.I.E.'s models were discontinued.

MODEL A27 "THE BEST" . . . . . . **NiB $140 Ex $95 Gd $55**
Semiauto. Caliber: .25 ACP. Six-round magazine, 2.5-in. bbl., 6.75 in. overall. Weight: 13 oz. Fixed sights. Checkered walnut grip. Discontinued in 1990.

ARMINIUS DA STANDARD REVOLVER
Calibers: .22 LR, .22 combo w/interchangeable cylinder, .32 S&W, .38 Special, .357 Magnum. Six, 7 or 8 rounds depending on caliber. Swing-out cylinder. bbl. lengths: 2-, 3-, 4, 6-in. VR on calibers other than .22, 11 in. overall (w/ 6-in. bbl.). Weight: 26 to 30 oz. Fixed or micro-adj. sights.

F.I.E. Model A27

F.I.E. Arminius

F.I.E. Titan II

Checkered plastic or walnut grips. Blued finish. Made in Germany. Disc.
.22 LR . . . .**NiB $130 Ex $89 Gd $67**
.22 Combo . . . .**NiB $198 Ex $148 Gd $101**
.32 S&W . . . .**NiB $207 Ex $149 Gd $101**
.38 Special . . . .**NiB $161 Ex $95 Gd $70**
.357 Magnum . . . .**NiB $240 Ex $179 Gd $135**

BUFFALO SCOUT SA REVOLVER
Calibers: .22 LR, .22 WRF, .22 combo w/interchangeable cylinder. 4.75-in. bbl., 10 in. overall. Weight: 32 oz. Adjustable sights. Blued or chrome finish. Smooth walnut or black checkered nylon grips. Made in Italy. Disc.
Blued standard . . . .**NiB $84 Ex $62 Gd $40**
Chrome standard . . . .**NiB $91 Ex $62 Gd $40**
convertible model . . . .**NiB $91 Ex $62 Gd $40**

HOMBRE SA REVOLVER . . . . . .**NiB $230 Ex $179 Gd $105**
Calibers: .357 Magnum, .44 Magnum, .45 Colt. Six-round cylinder. bbl. lengths: 6 or 7.5 in., 11 in. overall (w/ -in. bbl.). Weight: 45 oz. (6-in. bbl.). Fixed sights. Blued bbl., w/color-casehardened receiver. Smooth walnut grips. Made 1979-90.

SUPER TITAN II . . . . **NiB $138 Ex $95 Gd $70**
Caliber: .32 ACP or .380 ACP, 3.25-in. bbl., weight: 28 oz. Blued or chrome finish. Disc. 1990.

TEXAS RANGER . . . . **NiB $97 Ex $75 Gd $55**
Revolver. SA. Calibers: .22 LR, .22 WRF, .22 combo w/ interchangeable cylinder. bbl., lengths: 4.75-, 6.5-, 9-in. 10 in. overall (w/ 4.75-in. bbl.). Weight: 32 oz. (w/ 4.75-in. bbl.). Fixed sights. Blued finish. Smooth walnut grips. Made 1983-90.

LITTLE RANGER . . . . **NiB $97 Ex $75 Gd $55**
Same as the Texas Ranger except w/3.25-in. bbl. and bird's-head grips. Made 1986-90.

TITAN TIGER DA REVOLVER . . . . . **NiB $78 Ex $47 Gd $35**
Caliber: .38 Special. Six-round cylinder, 2- or 4-in. bbl., 8.25 in. overall (w/ 4-in. bbl.). Weight: 30 oz. (4-in. bbl.). Fixed sights. Blued finish. Checkered plastic or walnut grips. Made in the U.S. Disc. 1990.

**Firearms International
Model D**

**FN Browning
1900 Pocket**

**Firearms
International Regent**

**FN Browning 1910
Pocket**

TITAN II SEMIAUTO

Caiibers: .22 LR, .32 ACP, .380 ACP. 10-rnd. magazine, integral tapered post front sight, windage-adjustable rear sight. European walnut grips. Blued or chrome finish. Disc. 1990.

.22 LR in blue . . . . NiB $140 Ex $108 Gd $88
.32 ACP or .380 ACP blued. . . . NiB $211 Ex $170 Gd $128
.32 ACP or .380 ACP chrome. . . NiB $221 Ex $176 Gd $141

MODEL TZ75. . . . . NiB $387 Ex $302 Gd $214
Semiauto. Similar to CZ-75. DA/SA. Caliber: 9mm. 15-rnd. magazine, 4.5-in. bbl., 8.25 in. overall. Weight: 35 oz. Ramp front sight, windage-adjustable rear sight. European walnut or black rubber grips. Imported from 1988 to 1990.
Satin chrome, add. 10%

YELLOW ROSE. . . . . NiB $140 Ex $93 Gd $59
Same general specifications as the Buffalo Scout except in .22 combo w/interchangeable cylinder and plated in 24-karat gold. Limited Edition w/scrimshawed ivory polymer grips and American walnut presentation case. Made 1987-90.
Limited Edition . . . . NiB $292 Ex $229 Gd $188

FIREARMS INTERNATIONAL CORP. — Washington, D.C.

MODEL D AUTOMATIC PISTOL NiB $219 Ex $179 Gd $95
Caliber: .380 Automatic. Six-round magazine, 3.3-in. bbl., 6.13 in. overall. Weight: 19.5 oz. Blade front sight, windage-adjustable rear sight. Blued, chromed, or military finish. Checkered walnut grips. Made 1974-77.

REGENT DA REVOLVER . . . . . . NiB $189 Ex $130 Gd $101
Calibers: .22 LR, .32 S&W Long. Eight-round cylinder (.22 LR), or 7-rnd. (.32 S&W). Bbl. lengths: 3-, 4-, 6-in. (.22 LR) or 2.5-, 4-in. (.32 S&W). Weight: 28 oz.(w/ 4-in. bbl.). Fixed sights. Blued finish. Plastic grips. Made 1966-72.

FN BROWNING — Liege, Belgium.

Mfd. by Fabrique Nationale Herstal

See also Browning handguns.

6.35MM POCKET AUTO PISTOL
See FN Browning Baby Auto Pistol.

MODEL 1900 POCKET
AUTO PISTOL. . . . . NiB $1200 Ex $900 Gd $600
Caliber: .32 Automatic (7.65mm). Seven-round magazine, 4-in. bbl., 6.75 in. overall. Weight: 22 oz. Fixed sights. Blued finish. Hard rubber grips. Made 1899-1910.
Imperial Russian contract model, add $1200
Imperial German contract model, add $110

MODEL 1903 MILITARY AUTO PISTOL
Caliber: 9mm Browning Long. Seven-round magazine, 5-in. bbl., 8 in. overall. Weight: 32 oz. Fixed sights. Blued finish. Hard rubber grips. Note: Aside from size, this pistol is of the same basic design as the Colt Pocket .32 and .380 Automatic pistols. Made 1903-39.

Standard. . . . . NiB $2000 Ex $1500 Gd $1000
w/slotted backstrap. . . . . . . NiB $4000 Ex $3000 Gd $2000
**w/slotted backstrap, shoulder stock
and extended magazine** . . NiB $5525 Ex $5270 Gd $4790

MODEL 1910 (MODEL 1955 OR 1910/55)
POCKET AUTO PISTOL . . . . . . NiB $710 Ex $510 Gd $260
Calibers: .32 Auto (7.65mm), .380 Auto (9mm). Seven-round magazine (.32 cal.), or 6-rnd. (.380 cal.), 3.5-in. bbl., 6 in. overall. Weight: 20.5 oz. Fixed sights. Blued finish. Hard rubber grips. Made 1910-83.

MODEL 1922 (10/22) POLICE/MILITARY AUTO
Calibers: .32 Auto (7.65mm), .380 Auto (9mm). Nine-round magazine (.32 cal.), or 8-rnd. (.380 cal.), 4.5-in. bbl., 7 in. overall. Weight: 25 oz. Fixed sights. Blued finish. Hard rubber grips. Made 1922-59.
Commercial model . . . . NiB $530 Ex $380 Gd $280
Military contract, add. $120
w/Nazis proofs, add. . . .10% . . . NiB $414 Ex $326 Gd $265

MODEL 1935 MILITARY HI-POWER PISTOL
Variation of the Browning-Colt .45 Auto design. Caliber: 9mm Para.13-rnd. magazine, 4.63-in. bbl., 7.75 in. overall. Weight: About 35 oz. Adjustable rear sight and fixed front, or both fixed. Blued finish (Canadian manufacture Parkerized). Checkered walnut or plastic grips. Note: Above specifications in general apply to both the original FN production and the pistols made by John Inglis Company of Canada for the Chinese government. A smaller version, w/shorter bbl. and slide and 10-rnd. magazine, was made by FN for the Belgian and Rumanian Governments about 1937 to 1940. Both types were made at the FN plant during the German occupation of Belgium.
**Pre-war commercial
(w/fixed sights)** . . . . NiB $2760 Ex $1710 Gd $960
**Pre-war commercial
(w/tangent sight only)**. . . . NiB $2040 Ex $1347 Gd $712
**Pre-war commercial
(w/tangent sight, slotted
backstrap)** . . . . NiB $3014 Ex $2652 Gd $1448
**Pre-war Belgian military
contract** . . . . NiB $6510 Ex $5010 Gd $3510
**Pre-war Foreign military
contract** . . . . Ex $2410-$3710
**War production Waffenamt Proofed (w/fixed sights,
no slotted backstrap)** . . . . . NiB $1210 Ex $710 Gd $510
**War production Waffenamt Proofed (w/tangent sight,
no slotted backstrap)** . . . NiB $2260 Ex $1660 Gd $1010
**War production Waffenamt Proofed (w/tangent sight and
slotted backstrap)** . . . . . . NiB $5210 Ex $4410 Gd $2910
**Post-war/BAC marked
(w/fixed sights)** . . . . NiB $660 Ex $577 Gd $430

FN Browning 1935 Military Hi-Power

FN Browning 1922 Police/Military

FN America FNS-40

FN FNP-9

FN Browning Baby

Post-war/BAC marked
(w/tangent sight only) . . . . . . NiB $1310 Ex $910 Gd $660
Post-war/BAC marked (w/tangent sight,
slotted backstrap) . . . . . . NiB $1510 Ex $1110 Gd $756
Inglis manufacture Canadian military
(w/fixed sights) . . . . NiB $1015 Ex $743 Gd $571
Inglis manufacture Canadian military
(w/fixed sight, slotted) . . . . NiB $1960 Ex $1494 Gd $1021
Inglis manufacture Canadian military
(w/tangent sight, slotted) . . . NiB $1533 Ex $1235 Gd $884
Inglis manufacture Canadian military
(marked w/Inglis logo) . . . . NiB $3510 Ex $2749 Gd $1760
Inglis manufacture Chinese military contract
(w/tangent sight, slotted) . . NiB $3500 Ex $2754 Gd $1876
w/issue wooden holster, add. $500

BABY AUTO PISTOL . . . . NiB $780 Ex $480 Gd $300
Caliber: .25 Automatic (6.35mm). Six-round magazine, 2.13-in. bbl., 4 in. overall. Weight: 10 oz. Fixed sights. Blued finish. Hard rubber grips. Made 1931-83.
BAC marked, deduct $100

FN AMERICA (FNH USA) — Liege, Belgium

Herstal Group owns U.S. Repeating Arms Company (Winchester) and Browning Arms Company. FN America is the American subsidiary of FN Herstal; FNH USA, located in McLean, Virginia, is current U.S. headquarters.

FIVE-SEVEN . . . . NiB $1180 Ex $880 Gd $680
Semiauto. SA. Caliber: 5.7x28mm, 10- or 20-rnd. 4.8-in. bbl. Frame: polymer. Sights: adj. rear. Finish: matte black, two-tone, or FDE. Grip: textured polymer. Ambi. safety. Imported from 2000 to date.

FN HIGH POWER . . . . NiB $1269 EX $1200 GD $1100
Semiauto. Reintroduction of 1935 FN pistol. Caliber: 9mm. Magazine: 17-rnd. Bbl: 4.7-in. Sights: Fixed, steel similar to FN 509. Weight: 40 os. Grip: Textured G10. Finish: matte black, FDE, stainless. New take-down design. Made 2022-date.
stainless, add $100

FNP SERIES . . . . NiB $580 Ex $440 Gd $345
Semiauto. DA/SA. Caliber: 9mm, 10- or 16-rnd. 4-in. bbl. Frame: polymer. Sights: low profile fixed. Finish: matte black, two-tone, or FDE. Grip: textured polymer w/inserts. Ambidextrous decocker. Imported from 2006 to 2011. FNP-40 (.40 S&W), FNP-357 (.357 SIG), and FNP-45 (.45 Auto) have similar features and value.
FNP-9M (3.8-in. bbl.), deduct $20
FNP-45 Competition (2011-12), add $300
FNP-45 Tactical (2010-12), add $400

FNS SERIES . . . . NiB $530 Ex $410 Gd $310
Semiauto. Striker fire. Caliber: 9mm or .40 S&W; 17-rnd. (9mm) magazine; 4-in. bbl. Frame: polymer. Sights: low profile fixed. Finish: matte black or two-tone. Grip: textured polymer w/interchangeable backstraps. Ambidextrous slide stop and magazine release. Manufactured in Fredericksburg, VA, from 2011-18. FNS-40 (.40 S&W) has similar features and value.
FNS-9 Compact (3.6-in. bbl.) . . NiB $575 Ex $500 Gd $370
FNS-9 Longslide (5-in. bbl.), add $50
FNS-40 Compact (3.6-in. bbl.,
2015-18) . . . . NiB $530 Ex $470 Gd $350
FNS-40 Longslide (5-in. bbl., 2013-18), add $50

FNX-9 . . . . NiB $620 Ex $475 Gd $355
Semiauto. DA/SA. Caliber: 9mm, 10- or 17-rnd. 4-in. bbl. Frame: polymer w/replaceable steel inserts. Sights: 3-dot fixed. Finish: two-tone, or FDE. Grip: textured polymer w/inserts. Ambidextrous decocker. Imported from 2010 to date.
FNX-40 (.40 S&W) . . . . NiB $620 Ex $475 Gd $355

FNX-45 . . . . NiB $700 Ex $555 Gd $425
Semiauto. DA/SA. Caliber: .45 ACP, 10- or 12-rnd. 4.5-in. bbl. Frame: polymer w/replaceable steel inserts. Sights: 3-dot fixed. Finish: matte black, two-tone, or FDE. Grip: textured polymer w/inserts. Ambidextrous decocker. Imported from 2012 to date.
Tactical (threaded bbl., 15-rnd. magazine, optic ready,
high-profile sights) . . . . NiB $1140 Ex $900 Gd $425

FN 15 . . . . NiB $1410 Ex $1280 Gd $1055
Semiauto. AR-15 style. Caliber: .5.56 or 300 BLK. Magazine: 30-rnd. Bbl: 10.5-in. (5.56), 12-in. (300 BLK) w/ A2 flash hider. Sights: optic ready. Weight: 5.2 lbs. Furniture: SBX-K brace, Magpul MOE grip, Midwest Inst. M-LOK rail. Finish: matte black. Made 2018-19.

FN 502 TACTICAL SERIES . . . . . . NiB $519 Ex $480 Gd $430
Semiauto. SAO. Caliber: .22 LR. Magazine: 10- or 15-rnd. Bbl: 4.6-in. threaded. Sights: Suppressor-height, fixed front/rear, optic ready. Weight: 23.7 ozs. Grip: Textured polymer Finish: matte black or FDE. Fits most FN 509 Tactical holsters, ambi controls, manual safety. Made 2022-date.

FN 503 . . . . NiB $549 Ex $500 Gd $310
Semiauto. Striker fire. Caliber: 9mm, 6- or 8-rnd. 3.1-in. bbl. Frame: polymer. Sights: low profile fixed. Finish: matte black. Weight: 21 oz. Imported from 2020 to date.

FN 509 SERIES
Semiauto. Striker fire. Caliber: 9mm, 17-rnd. 4-in. bbl. Frame: polymer w/interchangeable back straps. Sights: 3-dot fixed. Finish: matte black or FDE. Ambidextrous slide stop and magazine release. Weight: 26.9 oz. Imported from 2017 to date.
Full-size . . . . NiB $1049 Ex $1000 Gd $810
Midsize (shorter grip) . . . . NiB $799 Ex $710 Gd $510
Midsize MRD (4-in. bbl., optic ready,
2020-date) . . . . NiB $705 Ex $655 Gd $505
Compact MRD (3.7-in. bbl., optic ready,
2019-date) . . . . NiB $799 Ex $710 Gd $510
Compact Tactical (4.3-in. threaded bbl.,
optic ready, 2020-date) . . . . . . NiB $900 Ex $800 Gd $600

LS Edge (5-in. bbl., flat trigger, optic ready,
2021-date) . . . . NiB $1355 Ex $1180 Gd $930
Tactical (4.5-in. threaded bbl., optic mount,
full size grip) . . . . NiB $679 Ex $610 Gd $410

FOREHAND & WADSWORTH — Worcester, MA

See listings of comparable Harrington & Richardson and Iver Johnson revolvers for values.

FORT WORTH FIREARMS — Fort Worth, TX

MATCH MASTER STANDARD . . . NiB $499 Ex $283 Gd $225
Semiauto. Caliber: .22LR. Equipped w/3 7/8-, 4 1/2-, 5 1/2-, 7 1/2- or 10-in. bull bbl., double Extractors, includes upper push button and standard magazine release, angled grip, low profile frame. Made 1995-2000.

MATCH MASTER DOVETAIL . . . . NiB $500 Ex $408 Gd $321
Similar to Match Master except has 3 7/8-, 4 1/2-, or 5 1/2-in. bbl. with dovetail rib.

MATCH MASTER DELUXE . . . . NiB $581 Ex $464 Gd $367
Similar to Match master Standard except has Weaver rib on bbl.
w/10-in. bbl., add. $128

SPORT KING . . . . NiB $601 Ex $321 Gd $270
Semiauto. Caliber: .22 LR. Equipped w/4 1/2- or 5 1/2-in. bbl., blued finish, military grips, drift sights, 10 rnd. magazine. Made 1995-2000.

CITATION . . . . NiB $439 Ex $319 Gd $265
Semiauto. Caliber: .22 LR. Equipped w/5 1/2-in. bull bbl. or 7 1/2-in. fluted bbl., military grips, 10-rnd. magazine.

TROPHY . . . . NiB $433 Ex $332 Gd $270
Semiauto. Caliber: .22 LR. Equipped w/5 1/2- or 7 1/2- in. bull bbl. blued finish, military grips, 10-rnd. magazine.
w/LH action (5 1/2-in. bbl. only), add $65

VICTOR . . . . NiB $499 Ex $398 Gd $301
Semiauto. Caliber: .22LR. Equipped w/3 7/8-, 4 1/2- (VR or Weaver rib), 8- (Weaver rib) or 10-in. (Weaver rib) bbls.; blued finish, military grips, 10-rnd. magazine.
w/4 1/2- or 4 1/2-in. Weaver rib bbls, add $100
w/8- or 10-in. Weaver rib bbls, add $190

OLYMPIC . . . . NiB $668 Ex $525 Gd $410
Semiauto. Caliber: .22 LR or Short. Equipped w/6 1/2-in. fluted bbl., blued finish, military grips, 10-rnd. magazine.

SHARPSHOOTER . . . . NiB $499 Ex $365 Gd $259
Semiauto. Caliber: .22 LR. Equipped w/5 1/2-in. bull bbl.,blued finish, military grips, 10-rnd. magazine.

LE FRANCAIS — St. Etienne, France

Produced by Manufacture Francaise d'Armes et Cycles.

ARMY MODEL
AUTOMATIC PISTOL . . . . . NiB $3010 Ex $1700 Gd $1005
Similar in operation to the Le Francais .25 Automatics. Caliber: 9mm Browning Long. Eight-round magazine, 5-in. bbl., 7.75 in. overall. Weight: About 34 oz. Fixed sights. Blued finish. Checkered walnut grips. Made 1928-38.

Freedom Arms
Model 83 Varmint

POLICEMAN MODEL
AUTOMATIC PISTOL . . . . NiB $410 Ex $260 Gd $185
DA. Hinged bbl., Caliber: .25 Automatic (6.35mm). Seven-round magazine, 3.5-in. bbl., 6 in. overall. Weight: About 12 oz. Fixed sights. Blued finish. Hard rubber grips. Introduced in 1914. disc.

STAFF OFFICER MODEL
AUTOMATIC PISTOL . . . . NiB $360 Ex $255 Gd $180
Caliber: .25 Automatic. Similar to the "Policeman" model except no cocking-piece head, barrel, is about an in. shorter and weight is an ounce less. Made 1914-66.

FREEDOM ARMS — Freedom, WY

MODEL 83 FIELD GRADE
SA REVOLVER . . . . NiB $2060 Ex $1420 Gd $870
Calibers: .22LR, .357 Mag., .41 Mag., .44 Mag., .454 Casull, .475 Linebaugh, .50 AE or .500 Wyoming Express. Five-round cylinder, bbl. lengths: 4.75-, 6-, 7.5-, 9- or 10-in. Adj. sight or fixed. Impregnated hardwood grips. Brushed matte stainless steel finish. Made 1988 to date.
.22 LR (10-in. bbl., Made 1991 to present) add $300

MODEL 83 FIELD GRADE HUNTER PACK
SA REVOLVER . . . . NiB $1160 Ex $900 Gd $710
Similar to Model 83 Field Grade except calibers: .357 Mag., .44 Mag., or .454 Casull only. 7.5-in. bbl., sling studs. Made 1990-93.

MODEL 83 PREMIER GRADE
SA REVOLVER . . . . NiB $2430 Ex $1680 Gd $1000
Calibers: .357 Mag., .41 Mag., .44 Mag., .454 Casull, .475 Linebaugh, .50 AE or .500 Wyoming Express.Adjustable sight or fixed. Impregnated hardwood grips. Brushed bright stainless steel finish. Made 1983 to date.

MODEL 83 PREMIER GRADE HUNTER PACK
SA REVOLVER . . . . NiB $1400 Ex $930 Gd $760
Similar to Model 83 Field Grade except calibers: .357 Mag., .44 Mag., or .454 Casull only. 7.5-in. bbl., sling studs. Made 1990-93.

MODEL 83 RIMFIRE VARMINT GRADE
SA REVOLVER . . . . NiB $1530 Ex $1430 Gd $930
Calibers: .22 LR. Bbl. length: 5.6- or 7.5-in. 5-shot. Adjustable sights. Brushed matte stainless finish. Hardwood grips. Made 1991-2005.

MODEL 83 SILHOUETTE GRADE (RIMFIRE)
SA REVOLVER . . . . NiB $2260 Ex $1610 Gd $1160
Calibers: .22 LR. Bbl. lengths: 5.13 or 10 in. 5-shot. Adjustable competition silhouette sights. Brushed or matte stainless finish. Black Micarta grips. Made 1991 to date.

MODEL 83 SILHOUETTE GRADE (CENTERFIRE)
SA REVOLVER . . . . NiB $1610 Ex $1080 Gd $835
Calibers: .357 Mag., .41 Mag., or .44 Mag. Bbl. lengths: 9- or 10-in. Removable blade front sight w/hood, adjustable rear. Brushed matte stainless finish. Wood grips.
.454 Casull . . . . NiB $1600 Ex $1080 Gd $850

MODEL 97 PREMIER GRADE SA REVOLVER
Calibers: .17 HMR, .22 LR, .224-32 F.A., .327 Fed., .32 H&R Mag., .357 Mag., .41 Mag. or .45 LC. Five- or 6-rnd. cylinder, 4.25, 5, 5.5, 6 or 7.5-in. bbl., removable front blade with adjustable or fixed rear sight. Hardwood or black Micarta grips. Satin stainless finish. Made 1997 to date.
Premier grade 97 . . . . NiB $1880 Ex $1220 Gd $890
w/extra cylinder, add $225
w/fixed sights, deduct $150

MODEL U.S. DEPUTY MARSHAL
SA REVOLVER . . . . NiB $1330 Ex $780 Gd $540
Bbl. lengths: 3-in. Adj. or fixed sights. No ejector rod. Brushed matte stainless. Made 1990-93.

MODEL FA-L-22LR
MINI-REVOLVER . . . . NiB $204 Ex $159 Gd $103
Caliber: .22 LR, 1.75-in. contoured bbl., partial high-gloss stainless steel finish. Bird's-head-type grips. Disc. 1987.

MODEL FA-S-22LR
MINI-REVOLVER . . . . NiB $214 Ex $189 Gd $105
Caliber: .22 LR. One-inch contoured bbl., partial high-gloss stainless steel finish. Disc. 1988.
w/1.75-in. bbl . . . . NiB $204 Ex $159 Gd $103
w/3-in. bbl . . . . NiB $237 Ex $165 Gd $128

MODEL FA-S-22M
MINI-REVOLVER . . . . NiB $189 Ex $135 Gd $101
Same general specifications as Model FA-S-22LR except in caliber .22 WMR. Disc. 1988.

FRENCH MILITARY PISTOLS — Cholet, France
Manufactured originally by Société Alsacienne de Constructions Mécaniques (S.A.C.M.). Currently made by Manufacture d'Armes Automatiques, Lotissement Industriel des Pontots, Bayonne.

MODEL 1935A
AUTOMATIC PISTOL . . . . NiB $260 Ex $210 Gd $170
Caliber: 7.65mm Long. Eight-round magazine, 4.3-in. bbl., 7.6 in. overall. Weight: 26 oz. Two-lug locking system similar to the Colt U.S. M1911A1. Fixed sights. Blued finish. Checkered grips. Made 1935-45. Note: This pistol was used by French troops during WW II and in Indo-China 1945 to 1954.
w/WWII Waffenamt proof marks, add 50%

French Military MAB P-15

Frommer Stop

MODEL 1935S
AUTOMATIC PISTOL . . . . NiB $370 Ex $300 Gd $220
Similar to Model 1935A except 4.1-in. bbl., 7.4 in. overall and 28 oz. Single-step lug locking system.

MODEL 1950
AUTOMATIC PISTOL . . . . NiB $1300 Ex $910 Gd $600
Caliber: 9mm Para. Nine-round magazine, 4.4-in. bbl., 7.6 in. overall. Weight: 30 oz. Fixed sights, tapered post front and U-notched rear. Similar in design and function to the U.S. .45 service automatic except no bbl. bushing.

MODEL MAB P-8
AUTOMATIC PISTOL . . . . NiB $576 Ex $464 Gd $342
Similar to Model MAB P-15 except w/8-rnd. magazine,

MODEL MAB P-15
AUTOMATIC PISTOL . . . . NiB $710 Ex $480 Gd $370
Caliber: 9mm Para. 15-rnd. magazine, 4.5-in. bbl., 7.9 in. overall. Weight: 38 oz. Fixed sights, tapered post front and U-notched rear.
F1 Target model (adj. sights, 6-in. bbl.), add $1000

FROMMER — Budapest, Hungary
Manufactured by Fémáru-Fegyver-és Gépgyár R.T.

MODEL 1937
. . . . NiB $500 Ex $305 Gd $220
Semiauto. Caliber: .32 ACP or .380 ACP. 8-rnd magazine. Bbl. Length: 3.9-in. Grips: walnut with vertical grooves. Weight: 27 oz.
w/WWII Waffenamt proof marks, add 50%

LILIPUT POCKET
AUTOMATIC PISTOL . . . . NiB $420 Ex $220 Gd $110
Caliber: .25 ACP (6.35mm). Six-round magazine, 2.14-in. bbl., 4.33 in. overall. Weight: 10.13 oz. Fixed sights. Blued finish. Hard rubber grips. Made during early 1920s. Note: Although similar in appearance to the Stop and Baby, this pistol is designed for blowback operation.

STOP POCKET
AUTOMATIC PISTOL . . . . NiB $414 Ex $321 Gd $165
Locked-breech action, outside hammer. Calibers: .32 ACP (7.65mm), .380 ACP. Seven-round (.32 cal.) or 6-rnd. (.380 cal.) magazine, 3.88-in. bbl., 6.5 in. overall. Weight: About 21 oz. Fixed sights. Blued finish. Hard rubber grips. Made 1912 -20.

**Galesi
Model 6 Pocket**

BABY POCKET
AUTOMATIC PISTOL . . . . NiB $321 Ex $262 Gd $143
Similar to Stop model except has 2-in. bbl., 4.75 in. overall. Weight 17.5 oz. Magazine capacity is one round less than Stop Model. Intro. shortly after WW I.

GALENA INDUSTRIES INC. — Sturgis, SD
Galena Industries purchased the rights to use the AMT trademark in 1998. Many, but not all, original AMT designs were included in the transaction.

AMT BACKUP . . . . NiB $474 EX $291 GD $219
Caliber: .380 (small frame, 2.5-in. bbl. only), .38 Super, .357 Sig, .40 S&W, .400 CorBon, .45 ACP, 9mm; magazine capacity: 5 or 6 rounds. Double action, 3-in. bbl., weight: 18 oz. (in .380), or 23 oz.
.38 Super, .357 Sig, .400 CorBon, add. $75

AUTOMAG II SEMI AUTO . . . . NiB $831 Ex $587 Gd $321
Caliber: .22 WMR, 9-rnd. magazine (except 7-rnd. in 3.38-in. bbl.); 3.38- 4.5- or 6-in. bbls.; weight: About 32 oz.

AUTOMAG III . . . . NiB $561 Ex $500 Gd $377
Similar to Automag II except chambered for the .30 Carbine cartridge, 6.38-in. bbl., stainless steel finish, weight: About 43 oz.

AUTOMAG IV. . . . . NiB $561 Ex $500 Gd $377
Caliber: .45 Winchester Magnum; 7-rnd. magazine, 6.5-in. bbl., weight: 46 oz.

AUTOMAG .440 CORBON. . . . . NiB $816 Ex $689 Gd $571
Semiauto, 7.5-in. bbl., 5-rnd. magazine, checkered walnut grips, matte black finish, weight: 46 oz. Intro. in 2000.

COMMANDO. . . . . NiB $474 Ex $326 Gd $220
Similar to Hardballer model except caliber: .40 S&W, 4-in. bbl., 8-rnd. magazine capacity, stainless steel finish, weight: About 38 ounces.

HARDBALLER II . . . . NiB $505 Ex $347 Gd $235
Based on the Colt Model 1911 frame. Caliber: .45 ACP, .40 S&W, .400 CorBon, 7-rnd. magazine capacity, 5-in. bbl., weight: About 38 oz.

HARDBALLER II LONGSLIDE. . . NiB $530 Ex $431 Gd $342
Similar to Hardballer model except caliber: .45 ACP, 7-in. bbl., 7-rnd. magazine capacity, stainless steel finish, weight: About 46 ounces.

HARDBALLER ACCELERATOR . . NiB $587 Ex $437 Gd $332
Similar to Hardballer model except caliber: .400 CorBon, 7-in. bbl., 7-rnd. magazine capacity, stainless steel finish, weight: About 46 ounces.

GALESI — Collebeato (Brescia), Italy
Manufactured by Industria Armi Galesi.

MODEL 6
POCKET AUTOMATIC . . . . NiB $170 Ex $120 Gd $95
Calibers: .22 Long, .25 Automatic (6.35mm). Six-round magazine, 2.25-in. bbl., 4.38 in. overall. Weight: About 11 oz. Fixed sights. Blued finish. Plastic grips. Made 1930 disc.
chrome engraved finish, add. $120

MODEL 9 POCKET AUTOMATIC. . . NiB $200 Ex $150 Gd $105
Calibers: .22 LR, .32 Auto (7.65mm), .380 Auto (9mm Short). Eight-round magazine, 3.25-in. bbl., 5.88 in. overall. Weight: About 21 oz. Fixed sights. Blued finish. Plastic grips. Made 1930 disc.

Note: *Specifications vary, but those shown for .32 ACP are common.*

chrome engraved finish, add. $200

GIRSAN — Giresun, Turkey

Mfg. of pistols currently imported by Zenith Firearms, Afton, VA.

MC 14. . . . . NiB $379 Ex $350 Gd $300
Semiauto. DA/SA. Caliber: .380 ACP, 13-rnd. magazine. 3.4-in. bbl. Frame: alloy. Sights: fixed. Finish: matte black. Grip: textured polymer. Ambidextrous thumb safety. Imported from 2016 to date.

MC 28 SAC. . . . . NiB $320 Ex $330 Gd $280
Semiauto. Striker fired. Caliber: 9mm, 15-rnd. magazine. 3.8 or 4.25-in. bbl. Frame: polymer. Sights: fixed. Finish: numerous. Grip: textured polymer. Imported from 2016 to date.

MC 39. . . . . NiB $450 Ex $430 Gd $370
Beretta 92 style platform. Semiauto. DA/SA. Caliber: 9mm, 15-rnd. magazine. 4.3 or 4.92-in. bbl. Frame: alloy. Sights: fixed. Finish: matte black. Grip: textured polymer. Ambidextrous thumb safety. Imported from 2016 to date.

MC 1911 S . . . . NiB $480 Ex $460 Gd $390
1911 style platform. Semiauto. SA. Caliber: .45 ACP, 8-rnd. magazine. 4.36- or 5-in. bbl. Frame: alloy. Sights: fixed. Finish: matte black. Grip: checkered wood. Accessory rail. Imported from 2016 to date.

GLISENTI — Carcina (Brescia), Italy

Mfd. by Societa Siderurgica Glisenti.

MODEL 1910 ITALIAN
MILITARY AUTOMATIC . . . . NiB $1755 Ex $1255 Gd $805
Caliber: 9mm Glisenti. 7-rnd. magazine, 4-in. bbl., 8.5 in. overall. Weight: About 32 oz. Fixed sights. Blued finish. Hard rubber or plastic grips. Adopted 1910 and used through WWII.

BRIXIA MODEL . . . . NiB $2255 Ex $1255 Gd $755
Similar to Glisenti Model 1910 except mass produced using simplified mfg. techniques for the civilian market.

GRADING: **NiB** = New in Box   **Ex** = Excellent or NRA 95%   **Gd** = Good or NRA 68%

**Glock Model 19
GEN1**

SOSSO MODEL . . . . **EXTREMELY RARE**
Experimental Semiauto. Cal.: 9 mm Para. Double action (marked "Sosso"), later single action. Mag.: 19 or 21 rounds. Made by FNA. Fewer than 10 made.

GLOCK, INC. — Austria

Manufactured in Austria and since 2005 in Smyrna, Georgia.

NOTE: *Generation 1 (GEN1) models were produced from 1986 to 1988 with a pepple texture grip; Generation 2 (GEN2) models were produced from 1988 to 1997 with a checkered grenade type grip texture with horizontal serrations on the front and back grips straps; Generation 3 (GEN3) models were first produced from 1995 to 2014 w/finger grooves in the front grip strap and thumbrests, they then transitioned into finger grooves with thumbrests and checkered finished frame with a front accessory rail. Generation 4 (GEN4) production began from 2010 to date and have interchangable backstraps. Generation 5 (GEN5) have been produced from 2017 to date with "Less Aggressive" Polymid Traction Rough Textured Frame, SF (Short Frame) includes interchangeable frame backstraps, ambidextrous slide stop levers, a grip with no finger grooves, flared magazine well, recessed thumb rests and rails, reversible enlarged magazine catch. The "C" suffix added to model numbers indicated a compensated model, add $20. All use a striker-fired system and generally differ in bbl. length, overal size, caliber and magazine capacity. Except where noted, models with Meprolight sights add $80, Trijicon sights add $100, Internal Locking System (ILS) add $20, adj. sights add $20, Glock night sights add $40, threaded bbl. (TB) add $100, and MOS add $100.*

MODEL 17 AND 17C
(GEN1, GEN2, GEN3) . . . . NiB $475 Ex $400 Gd $301
Caliber: 9mm Parabellum. 10-, 17- or 19-rnd. magazine, 4.5-in. bbl., 7.2 in. overall. Weight: 22 oz w/o magazine. Polymer frame, steel bbl., slide and springs. Fixed or adj. rear sights. Matte, nonglare finish. Imported from 1985 to date.
GEN4 variant, add $60
GEN4 MOS variant (2015 to present), add. $120
GEN4 TB variant (2014 to present), add. $100
GEN5 variant, add $80

MODEL 17L
(GEN1, GEN2, GEN3) . . . . NiB $620 Ex $577 Gd $396
Similar to Model 17 except w/long slide and 6-in. bbl., 8.85 in. overall., weight: 23.35 oz. Imported 1988 to 1999, GEN3 1998 to date.

w/ported bbl., (early production), add $75
w/adjustable sights, add $50

MODEL 19 AND 19C
(GEN1, GEN2, GEN3) . . . . NiB $430 Ex $395 Gd $255
Similar to Model 17 except compact version w/4-in. bbl., 6.85 in. overall. weight: 21 oz. Imported from 1988 to date.
GEN4 variant, add $60
GEN4 MOS variant (2015 to present), add. $120
GEN4 TB variant (2014 to present), add. $100
GEN5 variant, add $80

MODEL 20
AND 20C (GEN2, GEN3). . . . . NiB $510 Ex $400 Gd $360
Caliber: 10mm. 15-rnd., hammerless, 4.6-in. bbl., 7.59 in. overall. Weight: 26.3 oz. Fixed sights. Matte, non-glare finish. Made 1990 to date.
GEN3 SF variant (2015 to present), add. $20
GEN4 variant, add $60

MODEL 21 AND 21C
(GEN2, GEN3) . . . . NiB $510 Ex $400 Gd $360
Caliber: .45 ACP. 13-rnd. magazine, 7.59 in. overall. Weight: 25.2 oz. Imported from 1990 to date.
GEN3 SF variant (2015 to present), add. $20
GEN3 SF TB variant (2015 to present), add $120
GEN4 variant, add $60

MODEL 22
AND 22C (GEN2, GEN3). . . . . NiB $480 Ex $400 Gd $340
Similar to Model 17 except chambered for .40 S&W. 15-rnd. magazine, 7.4 in. overall. Imported from 1990 to date.
GEN4 variant, add $25
GEN5 variant, add $60

MODEL 23 AND 23C
(GEN2, GEN3) . . . . NiB $480 Ex $400 Gd $310
Same general specifications as Model 19 except chambered for .40 S&W. 13-rnd. magazine, 6.97 in. overall, fixed sights. Imported from 1990 to date.
GEN4 variant, add $25
GEN5 variant, add $60

MODEL 24 AND 24C
(GEN2, GEN3) . . . . NiB $630 Ex $480 Gd $360
Caliber: .40 S&W, 10- and 15-rnd. magazine, 6.02-in. bbl., 8.85 in. overall. Weight: 26.5 oz., fixed sights. Made 1994 to present.
w/adjustable sights, add $75

MODEL 26 (GEN3) . . . . NiB $480 Ex $400 Gd $330
Similar to Model 17 except w/10-rnd. magazine, 3.47-in. bbl., 6.3 in. overall. Weight: 19.77 oz., fixed sights. Imported from 1995 to date.
Gen4 variant, add. $25
GEN5 variant, add $80

MODEL 27 (GEN3). . . . . NIB $480 EX $400 GD $360
Similar to the Model 22 except w/10-rnd. magazine, 3.5-in. bbl., Weight: 21.7 oz. Fixed sights. Imported from 1995 to date.
GEN4 variant, add $25
GEN5 variant, add $60

MODEL 29 (GEN2, GEN3) . . . NiB $480 Ex $410 Gd $360
Similar to the Model 20 except w/10-rnd. magazine, 3.8-in. bbl., weight: 27.1 oz. Fixed sights. Imported from 1997 to date.
GEN4 variant, add $60

MODEL 30 (GEN3) . . . . NiB $500 Ex $420 Gd $360
Similar to the Model 21 except subcompact. 10-rnd. magazine, 3.8-in. bbl., weight: 26.5 oz. Imported from 1997 to date.
GEN3 SF variant (2015 to present), add $20
GEN3 30S variant (2008 to present), add $20
GEN4 variant, add $60

MODEL 31 AND 31C
(GEN2, GEN3) . . . . NiB $480 Ex $400 Gd $360
Caliber: .357 SIG. 10- 15- or 17-rnd. magazine, 4.49-in. bbl., weight: 23.28 oz., fixed sights. Imported from 1998 to date.
GEN4 variant, add $60

Model 32 (GEN2, GEN3) . . . . . NiB $480 Ex $300 Gd $360
Similar to Model 31 except w/10- 13- or 15-rnd. magazine, 4.02-in. bbl., weight: 21.52 oz. Imported from 1998 to date.
Model 32C . . . . NiB $648 Ex $485 Gd $395
GEN4 variant, add $60

MODEL 33 (GEN2, GEN3) . . . NiB $480 Ex $400 Gd $286
Similar to Model 31 except w/ 9- or 11-rnd. magazine, 3.46-in. bbl. Weight: 19.75 oz. Imported from 1998 to date.
GEN4 variant, add $60

MODEL 34 (GEN3) . . . . NiB $600 Ex $470 Gd $377
Similar to Model 17 except w/longer slide and extended slide-stop lever and magazine release. 10-, 17- or 19-rnd. magazine, 5.31-in. bbl. Weight: 22.9 oz., adj. sights. Imported from 1998 to date.
GEN4 variant, add $60
GEN4 MOS variant (2015 to present), add. $120

MODEL 35 (GEN3) . . . . NiB $600 Ex $470 Gd $362
Similar to Model 34 except .40 S&W. Imported from 1998 to date.
GEN4 variant, add $60
GEN4 MOS variant (2015 to present), add. $120

MODEL 36 (GEN3) . . . . NiB $500 Ex $400 Gd $350
Similar to Model 30 except w/6-rnd. single stack magazine. Weight: 20.11 oz. Imported from 1999 to date.

MODEL 37 (GEN3) . . . . NiB $580 Ex $430 Gd $330
Similar to Model 17 except chambered in .45 G.A.P. Made 2003 to date.
GEN4 variant, add $60

MODEL 38 (GEN3) . . . . NiB $540 Ex $380 Gd $300
Similar to Model 37 except more compact w/4-in. bbl. Made 2005 to date.
GEN4 variant, add $60

MODEL 39 (GEN3) . . . . NiB $540 Ex $380 Gd $300
Similar to Model 37 except more sub-compact w/3.4-in. bbl. Made 2005 to date.
GEN4 variant, add $60

MODEL 41
AND 41 MOS (GEN4) . . . . NiB $680 Ex $500 Gd $340
Similar to Model 21 except w/long slide and 5.3-in. bbl. Made 2014 to date.

MODEL 42 (GEN4) . . . . NiB $480 Ex $370 Gd $300
Caliber: .380 ACP; 6-rnd. single stack magazine. 3.25-in. bbl. Weight: 13.7 oz. Made 2014 to date.

MODEL 43 (GEN4) . . . . NiB $545 Ex $435 Gd $340
Caliber: 9mm; 6-rnd. single stack magazine. 3.39-in. bbl. Weight: 17.9 oz. Made 2015 to date.

MODEL 43X. . . . . NiB $520 Ex $435 GD $355
Similar to G43 except w/longer grip, silver nPVD slide (early mfg.) or black nPVD (current mfg.) w/forward serrations. Caliber: 9mm; 10-rnd. single stack magazine. Bbl.: 3.41-in. Weight: 18.7 oz. Made 2019 to date.

MODEL 44 (GEN5) . . . . NiB $380 Ex $360 Gd $300
Similar in size as G19 model. Caliber: .22 LR; 10-rnd. single stack magazine. 4.02-in. bbl. Weight: 14.6 oz. Made 2019 to date.

MODEL 48. . . . . NiB $520 Ex $435 Gd $355
Similar to G43X except w/longer 4.17-in. bbl. Weight: 20.7 oz. Made 2019 to date.

DESERT STORM
COMMEMORATIVE . . . . . . NiB $1525 Ex $1375 Gd $1225
Same specifications as Model 17 except "Operation Desert Storm, January 16-February 27, 1991" engraved on side of slide w/list of coalition forces. Limited issue of 1,000 guns. Made in 1991.

GRAND POWER — Slovenská L'upča, Slovakia

Manufactured in Slovenia. Previously imported by Eagle Imports, Wanamassa, New Jersey. In 2002 STI partnered with Grand Power and imported GP 6 (K100 MK6) pistols in 2008.

K22S SERIES . . . . NiB $528 Ex $480 Gd $400
Semiauto. DA/SA. Caliber: .22 LR; 10-rnd. magazine. 5-in. bbl. threaded. Frame: steel. Sights: fixed, low-profile. Finish: black. Grip: textured polymer w/modular backstraps. Length: 8-in. Weight: 24.5 oz. Imported from 2016 to date.
K22 X-TRIM (scalloped slide) . . . NiB $788 Ex $700 Gd $680

K100 SERIES . . . . NiB $629 Ex $600 Gd $580
Semiauto. Rotary locking bbl. system. DA/SA. Caliber: 9mm; 15-rnd. magazine. 4.3-in. bbl. Frame: steel. Sights: fixed, low-profile. Finish: black. Grip: textured polymer w/modular backstraps. Length: 8-in. Weight: 26.1 oz. Imported from 2014 to date.
X-Caliber (2014-date) . . . . NiB $788 Ex $700 Gd $680
X-Trim (2014-date) . . . . NiB $560 Ex $500 Gd $470

**Grand Power Model
K100 X-Caliber**

P1 SERIES . . . . NiB $629 Ex $600 Gd $580
Similar to K100 except more compact w/3.7-in. bbl. Imported from 2014 to date.

P1 Ultra (scalloped slide) . . . . . NiB $789 Ex $740 Gd $680
P11 (sub compact) . . . . NiB $615 Ex $570 Gd $500
CP 380 (similar to P11
   except .380 ACP). . . . . NiB $528 Ex $480 Gd $400

P40 SERIES . . . . NiB $819 Ex $780 Gd $690
Similar to K100 except chambered in .40 S&W. Imported from 2014 to date.

P45 SERIES . . . . NiB $819 Ex $780 Gd $690
Similar to K100 except chambered in .45 ACP. Imported from 2014 to date.

Q100 SERIES. . . . . NiB $574 Ex $540 Gd $500
Semiauto. Rotary locking bbl. system. Striker fire. Caliber: 9mm; 15-rnd. magazine. 4.3-in. bbl. Frame: steel. Sights: fixed, low-profile. Finish: black. Grip: textured polymer w/modular backstraps. Length: 8-in. Weight: 26.1 oz. Imported from 2016 to date.

GREAT WESTERN

NOTE: *Trademark of single action revolvers imported by E.M.F. Company manufactured by FAP F.LLI Pietta in Italy. See E.M.F. Company.*

GREAT WESTERN ARMS CO. — North Hollywood, CA

NOTE: *Values shown are for improved late model revolvers early Great Westerns are variable in quality and should be evaluated accordingly. It should also be noted that, beginning about July 1956, these revolvers were offered in kit form. Values of guns assembled from these kits will, in general, be of less value than factory-completed weapons.*

DOUBLE BBL. DERRINGER. . . . . NiB $610 Ex $510 Gd $360
Replica of Remington Double Derringer. Caliber: .38 S&W, .38 S&W Spl. Double bbls. (superposed), 3-in. bbl. Overall length: 5 in. Fixed sights. Blued finish. Checkered black plastic grips. Made 1953-62 in various configurations.

FRONTIER SIX SHOOTER. . . . . NiB $810 Ex $610 Gd $410
Replica of the Colt SAA revolver. Calibers: .22 LR, .22 WMR, .357 Magnum, .38 Special, .44 Special, .44 Magnum .45 Colt. Six-round cylinder, bbl. lengths: 4.75-, 5.5 and 7.5-in. Weight: 40 oz. in .22 cal. w/5.5-in. bbl. Overall length: 11.13 in.

w/5.5-in. bbl. Fixed sights. Blued finish. Imitation stag grips. Made 1951-62.

rimfire caliber, deduct $200

SHERIFF'S MODEL . . . . NiB $1010 Ex $910 Gd $810
Reportedly made from old Colt parts inventory. Cal.: .45 Long Colt. Blue, nickel, or case-colored finish. Plastic staghorn grips.

FAST DRAW MODEL . . . . NiB $760 Ex $660 Gd $560
Similar to Frontier model. Bbl.: 4.75 in. Brass backstrap and trigger guard; blue finish; plastic staghorn grips. Longer, turned-up hammer spur.

TARGET MODEL. . . . . NiB $710 Ex $616 Gd $474
Similar to Frontier model. Cal.: .22 LR. Adj. rear sights, Micro front blade. Blue or case colored frame. Bbl.: Various lengths.

DEPUTY MODEL . . . . NiB $1010 Ex $910 Gd $810
Cal.: .22 LR, .38 Spl., .357 Mag. Bbl.: 4 in. Deluxe blue finish, walnut grips. Adj. rear sight. Fewer than 100 made.

GRENDEL, INC. — Rockledge, FL

MODEL P-10 . . . . NiB $260 Ex $180 Gd $160
Hammerless, blow-back action. DAO with no external safety. Caliber: .380 ACP. 10-rnd. box magazine integrated in grip. Three-in. bbl., 5.3 in. overall. Weight: 15 oz. Matte blue, nickel or green Teflon finish. Made 1988-91.
Nickel or green finish, add $20

MODEL P-12. . . . . NIB $260 EX $180 GD $160
Semiauto. Caliber: .380 ACP. 11-rnd. Zytel magazine, 3-in. bbl., 5.3 in. overall. Weight: 13 oz. Fixed sights. Polymer DuPont ST-800 grip. Made 1991-95.
Standard model. . . . . NiB $214 Ex $135 Gd $105
Electroless nickel, add. $20

MODEL P-30. . . . . NiB $355 Ex $255 Gd $210
Semiauto. Caliber: .22 WMR. 30-rnd. magazine, 5-or 8-in. bbl., 8.5 in. overall w/5-in. bbl., weight: 21 oz. Blade front sight, fixed rear sight. Made 1991-95.
w/8-in. bbl., add $40

MODEL P-31. . . . . NiB $455 Ex $430 Gd $285
Caliber: .22 WMR. 30-rnd. Zytel magazine, 11-in. bbl., 17.3 in. overall. Weight: 48 oz. Adjustable blade front sight, fixed rear. Checkered black polymer DuPont ST-800 grip and forend. Made 1991-95.

**Great Westerm Arms Co.
Frontier Six Shooter**

Grendel Model P-12

H&R 1871, INC. — Gardner, MA

NOTE: *In 1991, H&R 1871, Inc. was formed from the residual of the parent company, Harrington & Richardson, and then took over the New England Firearms facility. H&R 1871 produced firearms under both their logo and the NEF brand name until 1999, when the Marlin Firearms Company acquired the assets of H&R 1871. See listings under Harrington & Richardson, Inc.*

HÄMMERLI — Ulm/Donau, Germany

Currently trademark of Walther. Previously imported by Sigarms, Inc., Exeter, NH. Previously by Hammerli, USA; Beeman Precision Arms & Mandall Shooting Supplies. Previously manufactured in Lenzburg, Switzerland.

FP-10 FREE PISTOL . . . . NiB $1530 Ex $955 Gd $755
Caliber: .22 LR. Imported 2000 to 2004.

MODEL 33MP FREE PISTOL . . NiB $964 EX $863 GD $577
System Martini single-shot action, set trigger. Caliber: .22 LR. 11.5-in. octagon bbl., 16.5 in. overall. Weight: 46 oz. Micrometer rear sight, interchangeable front sights. Blued finish. Walnut grips, forearm. Imported from 1933 to 1949.

FP-60 . . . . NiB $2070 Ex $1455 Gd $1055
Caliber: .22 LR. Brrl.: 12.75-in. Imported 2005 to date.

MODEL 100 FREE PISTOL
Same general specifications as Model 33MP. Improved action and sights, redesigned stock. Standard model has plain grips and forearm, deluxe model has carved grips and forearm. Imported 1950 to 1956.
Standard model. . . . . NiB $938 Ex $775 Gd $556
Deluxe model . . . . NiB $1020 Ex $893 Gd $612

MODEL 101 . . . . NiB $913 Ex $791 Gd $612
Similar to Model 100 except has heavy rnd. bbl. w/matte finish, improved action and sights, adj. grips. Weight: About 49 oz. Imported from 1956 to 1960.

MODEL 102
Same as Model 101 except bbl., has highly polished blued finish. Deluxe model (illustrated) has carved grips and forearm. Made 1956-60.
Standard model. . . . . NiB $928 Ex $760 Gd $561
Deluxe model . . . . NiB $1035 Ex $791 Gd $602

MODEL 103 . . . . NiB $969 Ex $826 Gd $536
Same as Model 101 except has lighter octagon bbl. (as in Model 100) w/highly polished blued finish, grips and forearm of select French walnut. Weight: About 46 oz. Imported 1956 to 1960.

MODEL 104 . . . . NiB $804 Ex $673 Gd $439
Similar to Model 102 except has lighter rnd. bbl., improved action redesigned grips and forearm. Weight: 46 oz. Imported 1961 to 1965.

MODEL 105 . . . . NiB $960 Ex $779 Gd $500
Similar to Model 103 except has improved action, redesigned grips and forearm. Imported from 1961 to 1965.

MODEL 106 . . . . NiB $933 Ex $796 Gd $464
Similar to Model 104 except has improved trigger and grips. Made 1966-71.

MODEL 107
Similar to Model 105 except has improved trigger and stock. Deluxe model (illustrated) has engraved receiver and bbl., carved grips and forearm. Imported from 1966 to 1971.
Standard model. . . . . NiB $1034 Ex $831 Gd $462
Deluxe model . . . . NiB $1025 Ex $826 Gd $474

MODEL 120 HEAVY BARREL
Same as Models 120-1 and 120-2 except has 5.7-in. heavy bbl., weight: 41 oz. Avail. w/standard or adj. grips. 1,000 made. Imported from 1972.
w/standard grips . . . . NiB $800 Ex $590 Gd $388
w/adj. grips, add $300

MODEL 120-1 SINGLE-
SHOT FREE PISTOL . . . . NiB $658 Ex $536 Gd $385
Side lever-operated bolt action. Adj. single-stage or two-stage trigger. Caliber: .22 LR, 9.9-in. bbl., 14.75 in. overall. Weight: 44 oz. Micrometer rear sight, front sight on high ramp. Blued finish bbl., and receiver, lever and grip frame anodized aluminum. Checkered walnut thumbrest grips. Imported from 1972 to date.

Hämmerli
Model 102 Deluxe

Hämmerli
Model 107 Deluxe

Hämmerli
Model 120 Heavy Barrel

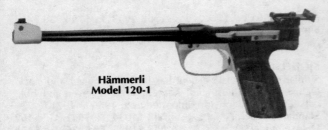

**Hämmerli
Model 120-1**

**Hämmerli
Model 150**

MODEL 120-2 . . . . **NiB $734 Ex $648 Gd $377**
Same as Model 120-1 except has hand-contoured grips w/adj. palm rest (available for right or left hand). Imported from 1972 to date.

MODELS 150/151 FREE PISTOLS
Improved Martini-type action w/lateral-action cocking lever. Set trigger adj. for weight, length and angle of pull. Caliber: .22 LR, 11.3-in. rnd. free-floating bbl., 15.4 in. overall. Weight: 43 oz. (w/Extra weights, 49.5 oz.). Micrometer rear sight, front sight on high ramp. Blued finish. Select walnut forearm and grips w/adj. palm shelf. Imported 1972-93.
Model 150 (disc. 1989) . . . . **NiB $1938 Ex $1709 Gd $1020**
Model 151 (disc. 1993) . . . . **NiB $1938 Ex $1709 Gd $1020**

MODEL 152 ELECTRONIC PISTOL
Same general specifications as Model 150 except w/electronic trigger. Made 1990-92
Right hand . . . . **NiB $1812 Ex $1700 Gd $1036**
w/adj. grips, add **$306**

MODELS 160/162 FREE PISTOLS
Caliber: .22 LR. Single-shot. 11.31-in. bbl., 17.5 in. overall. Weight: 46.9 oz. Interchangeable front sight blades, fully adj. match rear. Match-style stippled walnut grips w/adj. palm shelf and poly-carbon fiber forend. Imported from 1993 to 2002.
Model 160 w/mechanical set trigger
   (disc. 2000) . . . . **NiB $1812 Ex $1681 Gd $1005**
Model 162 w/electronic
   trigger . . . . **NiB $1982 Ex $1622 Gd $1132**

MODEL 206 . . . . **NiB $680 Ex $530 Gd $400**
Semiauto. Caliber: .22 Short to LR. Bbl. Len.: 7.06-in. w/ muzzle brake. Grip: walnut. Imported from 1962 to 1969.

MODEL 207 . . . . **NiB $730 Ex $560 Gd $430**
Similar to Model 206 except w/adj. grip heel.

MODEL 208 STANDARD
AUTO PISTOL . . . . **NiB $1802 Ex $1488 Gd $959**
Caliber: .22 LR. Eight-round magazine, 5.9-in. bbl., 10 in. overall. Weight: 35 oz. (bbl. weight adds 3 oz.). Micrometer rear sight, ramp front. Blued finish. Checkered walnut grips w/ adj. heel plate. Imported from 1966 to 1988.

MODEL 208S
TARGET PISTOL . . . . **NiB $2540 Ex $2232 Gd $2066**
Semiauto. Caliber: .22 LR. Eight-round magazine, 6-in. bbl., 10.2 in. overall. Weight: 37.3 oz. Micrometer rear sight, ramp front sight. Blued finish. Stippled walnut grips w/adj. heel plate. Imported from 1988 to 2000.

MODEL 211 . . . . **NiB $1601 Ex $1458 Gd $847**
Same as Model 208 except w/standard thumbrest grips. Imported from 1966 to 1990.

MODEL 212 HUNTER . . . . **NiB $2146 Ex $1816 Gd $1436**
Caliber: .22 LR, 4.88-in. bbl., 8.5 in. overall. Weight: 31 oz. Blade front sight, square-notched fully adj. rear. Blued finish. Checkered walnut grips. Imported 1984-93.

MODEL 215 . . . . **NiB $2368 Ex $2035 Gd $1734**
Similar to the Model 208 except w/heavier bbl. and fewer deluxe features. Imported from 1990 to 1993.

MODEL 230-1 RAPID FIRE
AUTO PISTOL . . . . **NiB $755 Ex $576 Gd $478**
Caliber: .22 Short. Five-round magazine, 6.3-in. bbl., 11.6 in. overall. Weight: 44 oz. Micrometer rear sight, post front. Blued finish. Smooth walnut thumbrest grips. Imported from 1970 to 1983.

MODEL 230-2 RAPID FIRE
AUTO PISTOL . . . . **NiB $785 Ex $601 Gd $444**
Same as Model 230-1 except has checkered walnut grips w/ adj. heel plate. Imported from 1970 to 1983.

MODEL 232 RAPID FIRE
AUTO PISTOL . . . . **NiB $1454 Ex $1256 Gd $780**
Caliber: .22 Short. Six-round magazine, 5.1-in. ported bbl., 10.5 in. overall. Weight: 44 oz. Fully adj. target sights. Blued finish. Stippled walnut wraparound target grips. Imported 1984 to 1993.

**Hämmerli
Model 215**

**Hämmerli
International Model 206**

**Hämmerli
Model 232 Rapid Fire**

MODEL SP 20 . . . . **NiB $1750 Ex $1330 Gd $930**
Semiauto. Caliber: .22 LR or .32 S&W. Alloy receiver is various
finishes. Imported from 1998 to 2008.

MODEL SP 20 RSR . . . . **NiB $1435 Ex $1125 Gd $925**
Semiauto. Caliber: .22 LR or .32 S&W. Composite receiver.
Imported from 2002 to 2005.

MODEL PL-20 TRAILSIDE . . . . . . **NiB $400 Ex $310 Gd $260**
Semiauto. Caliber: .22 LR. Bbl. Len.: 4.5- or 6-in. Imported
from 1999 to 2006.
Competition model, add **$180**

**INTERNATIONAL MODEL 206
AUTO PISTOL** . . . . **NiB $709 Ex $469 Gd $306**
Calibers: .22 Short, .22 LR. Six-round (.22 Short) or 8-rnd. (.22
LR) magazine, 7.1-in. bbl. w/muzzle brake, 12.5 in. overall.
Weight: 33 oz. (.22 Short), 39 oz. (.22 LR) (supplementary
weights add 5 and 8 oz.). Micrometer rear sight, ramp front.
Blued finish. Standard thumbrest grips. Imported from 1962
to 1969.

**INTERNATIONAL MODEL 207
AUTO PISTOL** . . . . **NiB $760 Ex $621 Gd $469**
Same as Model 206 except has grips w/adj. heel plate, weight:
2 oz. more. Made 1962-69.

**INTERNATIONAL MODEL 209
AUTO PISTOL** . . . . **NiB $825 Ex $672 Gd $562**
Caliber: .22 Short. Five-round mag., 4.75-in. bbl., w/muzzle
brake and gas-escape holes, 11 in. overall. Weight: 39 oz.
(interchangeable front weight adds 4 oz.). Micrometer rear
sight, post front. Blued finish. Standard thumbrest grips of
checkered walnut. Imported from 1966 to 1970.

INTERNATIONAL MODEL 210 . . **NiB $827 Ex $676 Gd $530**
Same as Model 209 except has grips w/adj. heel plate, is
0.8-in. longer and weighs 1 ounce more. Made 1966-70.
Model 280 Target Pistol Carbon-reinforced synthetic frame
and bbl., housing. Calibers: .22 LR, .32 S&W Long WC. Six-
round (.22 LR) or 5-rnd. (.32 S&W) magazine, 4.5-in. bbl. w/
interchangeable metal or carbon fiber counterweights. 11.88
in. overall. Weight: 39 oz. Micro-adj. match sights w/inter-
changeable elements. Imported from 1988 to 2000.
.22 LR . . . . **NiB $1550 Ex $1295 Gd $627**
.32 S&W Long WC . . . . **NiB $1729 Ex $1550 Gd $842**
.22/.32 Conversion kit, add **$816**

VIRGINIAN SA REVOLVER . . . **NiB $780 Ex $602 Gd $ 440**
Similar to Colt Single-Action Army except has base pin
safety system (SWISSAFE). Calibers: .357 Magnum, .45
Colt. Six-round cylinder. 4.63-, 5.5- or 7.5-in. bbl., 11 in.
overall (w/ 5.5-in. bbl.). Weight: 40 oz. (w/ 5.5-in. bbl.).

Fixed sights. Blued bbl. and cylinder, casehardened frame,
chrome-plated grip frame and trigger guard. One-piece
smooth walnut stock. Imported from 1973 to 1976 by
Interarms, AlExandria, Va.

**WALTHER OLYMPIA MODEL 200 AUTOMATIC
PISTOL, 1952-TYPE** . . . . **NiB $704 Ex $598 Gd $479**
Similar to 1936 Walther Olympia Funfkampf model. Calibers:
.22 Short, .22 LR. Six-round (.22 Short) or 10-rnd. (.22 LR) magazine, 7.5-in. bbl., 10.7 in. overall. Weight: 27.7 oz. (.22 Short,
light alloy breechblock), 30.3 oz. (.22 LR). Supplementary
weights provided. Adj. target sights. Blued finish. Checkered
walnut thumbrest grips. Imported 1952 to 1958.

**WALTHER OLYMPIA
MODEL 200,1958-TYPE** . . . . . . **NiB $780 Ex $632 Gd $530**
Same as Model 200 1952 type except has muzzle brake, 8-rnd.
magazine (.22 LR). 11.6 in. overall. Weight: 30 oz. (.22 Short),
33 oz. (.22 LR). Imported 1958 to 1963.

**WALTHER OLYMPIA
MODEL 201** . . . . **NiB $704 Ex $546 Gd $437**
Same as Model 200,1952-Type except has 9.5-in. bbl. Imported
from 1955 to 1957.

**WALTHER
OLYMPIA MODEL 202** . . . . **NiB $780 Ex $632 Gd $530**
Same as Model 201 except has grips w/adjustable heel plate.
Imported from 1955 to 1957.

WALTHER OLYMPIA MODEL 203
Same as corresponding Model 200 (1955 type lacks muzzle
brake) except has grips w/adjustable heel plate. Imported
1955 to 1963.
1955 type . . . . **NiB $794 Ex $638 Gd $479**
1958 type . . . . **NiB $842 Ex $709 Gd $475**

**Hämmerli
International Model 210**

**Hämmerli-Walther
Olympia Model 203 1958-Type**

**Hämmerli-Walther
Olympia Model 205**

**SIG-Hämmerli
Model P240 Target**

WALTHER OLYMPIA MODEL 204
American model. Same as corresponding Model 200 (1956-Type lacks muzzle brake) except in .22 LR only, has slide stop and micrometer rear sight. Imported from 1956 to 1963.
1956-type . . . . **NiB $760 Ex $606 Gd $464**
1958-type . . . . **NiB $816 Ex $680 Gd $556**

WALTHER OLYMPIA MODEL 205
American model. Same as Model 204 except has grips w/ adjustable heel plate. Imported from 1956 to 1963.
1956-type . . . . **NiB $842 Ex $714 Gd $610**
1958-type . . . . **NiB $893 Ex $727 Gd $556**

MODEL P240 TARGET AUTO PISTOL
Calibers: .32 S&W Long (wadcutter), .38 Special (wadcutter). Five-round magazine, 5.9-in. bbl., 10 in. overall. Weight: 41 oz. Micrometer rear sight, post front. Blued finish/smooth walnut thumbrest grips. Accessory .22 LR conversion unit available. Imported from 1975 to 1986.
.32 S&W Long. . . . . **NiB $1540 Ex $1329 Gd $755**
.38 Special . . . . **NiB $2545 Ex $2353 Gd $2025**
.22 LR conversion unit, add **$561**

HARRINGTON & RICHARDSON, INC. —
Gardner, MA
Formerly Harrington & Richardson Arms Co. of Worcester, Mass. One of the oldest and most distinguished manufacturers of handguns, rifles and shotguns, H&R suspended operations on January 24, 1986. In 1987, New England Firearms was established as an independent company producing selected H&R models under the NEF logo. In 1991, H&R 1871, Inc., was formed from the residual of the parent company and then took over the New England Firearms facility. H&R 1871 produced firearms under both its logo and the NEF brand name until 1999, when the Marlin Firearms Company acquired the assets of H&R 1871.

NOTE: *For ease in finding a particular firearm, H&R handguns are grouped into Automatic/Single-Shot Pistols, followed by Revolvers. For a complete listing, please refer to the index.*

- AUTOMATIC/SINGLE-SHOT PISTOLS -

SELF LOADING .25 PISTOL . . . **NiB $587 Ex $405 Gd $290**
Semiauto. Modified Webley & Scott design. Caliber: .25 Auto. Six-round magazine, 2-in. bbl., 4.5 in. overall. Weight: 12 oz. Fixed sights. Blued finish. Black hard rubber grips. Made 1912-16.

SELF LOADING .32 PISTOL . . . **NiB $562 Ex $321 Gd $205**
Semiauto. Modified Webley & Scott design. Caliber: .32 Auto. Eight-round magazine, 3.5-in. bbl., 6.5 in. overall. Weight: About 20 oz. Fixed sights. Blued finish. Black hard rubber grips. Made 1916-24.

USRA MODEL SINGLE-SHOT
TARGET PISTOL . . . . **NiB $2000 Ex $1810 Gd $1010**
Hinged frame. Caliber: .22 LR, bbl. lengths: 7-, 8- and 10-in. Weight: 31 oz. w/10-in. bbl., Adj. target sights. Blued finish. Checkered walnut grips. Made 1928-41.

- REVOLVERS -

MODEL 4 (1904) . . . . **NiB $255 Ex $180 Gd $90**
DA/SA. Revolver. Solid frame. Calibers: .32 S&W Long, .38 S&W. Six-round cylinder (.32 cal.), or 5-rnd. (.38 cal.), bbl. Lengths: 2.5-, 4.5- and 6-in. Weight: About 16 oz. (in .32 cal.) Fixed sights. Blued or nickel finish. Hard rubber grips. Made 1904-41.

MODEL 5 (1905) . . . . **NiB $237 Ex $159 Gd $77**
DA/SA. Revolver. Solid frame. Caliber: .32 S&W. Five-round cylinder, bbl., lengths: 2.5-,4.5- and 6-in. Weight: About 11 oz. Fixed sights. Blued or nickel finish. Hard rubber grips. Made 1905-41.

MODEL 6 (1906) . . . . **NiB $198 Ex $115 Gd $75**
DA/SA. Revolver. Solid frame. Caliber: .22 LR. Seven-round cylinder, bbl. lengths: 2.5, 4.5- and 6-in. Weight: About 10 oz. Fixed sights. Blued or nickel finish. Hard rubber grips. Made 1906-41.

.22 SPECIAL DA . . . . **NiB $351 Ex $197 Gd $101**
Heavy hinged frame. Calibers: .22 LR, .22 Mag. Nine-round cylinder, 6-in. bbl., weight: 23 oz. Fixed sights, front gold-plated. Blued finish. Checkered walnut grips. Recessed safety cylinder on later models for high-speed ammunition. Disc. prior to 1942.

MODEL 199 SPORTSMAN
SA Revolver . . . . **NiB $347 Ex $291 Gd $158**
Hinged frame. Caliber: .22 LR. Nine-round cylinder, 6-in. bbl., 11 in. overall. Weight: 30 oz. Adj. target sights. Blued finish. Checkered walnut grips. Disc. 1951.

MODEL 504 DA . . . . **NiB $255 Ex $189 Gd $143**
Caliber: .32 H&R Magnum. Five-round cylinder, 4- or 6-in. bbl., (square butt), 3- or 4-in. bbl., rnd. butt. Made 1984-86.

Harrington & Richardson SL .32

Harrington & Richardson USRA Model Single-Shot Target Pistol

MODEL 532 DA . . . .**NiB $179 Ex $129 Gd $88**
Caliber: .32 H&R Magnum. Five-round cylinder, 2.5- or 4-in. bbl., weight: Approx. 20 and 25 oz. respectively. Fixed sights. American walnut grips. Lustre blued finish. Made 1984-86.

MODEL 586 DA . . . .**NiB $290 Ex $188 Gd $130**
Caliber: .32 H&R Magnum. Five-round cylinder. bbl. lengths: 4.5, 5.5, 7.5, 10 in. Weight: 30 oz. average. Adj. rear sight, blade front. Walnut finished hardwood grips. Made 1984-86.

MODEL 603 TARGET . . . .**NiB $219 Ex $158 Gd $115**
Similar to Model 903 except in .22 WMR. Six-round capacity w/unfluted cylinder. Made 1980-83.

MODEL 604 TARGET . . . .**NiB $219 Ex $158 Gd $115**
Similar to Model 603 except w/6-in. bull bbl., weight: 38 oz. Made 1980-83.

MODEL 622/623 DA . . . .**NiB $170 Ex $128 Gd $79**
Solid frame. Caliber: .22 Short, Long, LR, 6-rnd. cylinder. bbl. lengths: 2.5-, 4-, 6-in. Weight: 26 oz. (w/ 4-in. bbl.). Fixed sights. Blued finish. Plastic grips. Made 1957-86. Note: Model 623 is same except chrome or nickel finish.

MODEL 632/633
GUARDSMAN DA REVOLVER . .**NiB $171 Ex $128 Gd $79**
Solid Frame. Caliber: .32 S&W Long. Six-round cylinder, bbl. lengths: 2.5- and 4-in. Weight: 19 oz. (w/ 2.5-in. bbl.). Fixed sights. Blued or chrome finish. Checkered Tenite grips (round butt on 2.5-in., square butt on 4-in.). Made 1953-86. Note: Model 633 is the same except for chrome or nickel finish.

MODEL 649/650 DA . . . .**NiB $265 Ex $158 Gd $95**
Solid frame. Side loading and ejection. Convertible model w/ two 6-rnd. cylinders. Calibers: .22 LR, .22 WMR. 5.5-in. bbl., Weight: 32 oz. Adj. rear sight, blade front. Blued finish. One-piece, Western-style walnut grip. Made 1976-86. Note: Model 650 is same except nickel finish.

MODEL 666 DA . . . .**NiB $151 Ex $104 Gd $64**
Solid frame. Convertible model w/two 6-rnd. cylinders. Calibers: .22 LR, .22 WMR. Six-in. bbl., weight: 28 oz. Fixed sights. Blued finish. Plastic grips. Made 1976-78.

MODEL 676 DA . . . .**NiB $283 Ex $200 Gd $104**
Solid frame. Side loading and ejection. Convertible model w/ two 6-rnd. cylinders. Calibers: .22 LR, .22 WMR, bbl. lengths: 4.5, 5.5, 7.5, 12-in. Weight: 32 oz. (w/ 5.5-in. bbl.). Adj. rear sight, blade front. Blued finish, color-casehardened frame. One-piece, Western-style walnut grip. Made 1976-80.

MODEL 686 DA . . . .**NiB $306 Ex $205 Gd $128**
Caliber: .22 LR and .22 WMR. Six-round magazine, 4.5, 5.5, 7.5, 10 or 12-in. bbl. Adj. rear sight, ramp and blade front. Blued, color-casehardened frame. Weight: 31 oz. (w/ 4.5-in. bbl.). Made 1980-86.

MODEL 732/733 DA . . . .**NiB $198 Ex $129 Gd $83**
Solid frame, swing-out 6-rnd. cylinder. Calibers: .32 S&W, .32 S&W Long. bbl., lengths: 2.5 and 4-in. Weight: 26 oz. (w/ 4-in. bbl.). Fixed sights (windage adj. rear on 4-in. bbl. model). Blued finish. Plastic grips. Made 1958-86. Note: Model 733 is the same except with nickel finish.

MODEL 826 DA . . . .**NiB $200 Ex $135 Gd $88**
Caliber: .22 WMR. Six-round magazine, 3-in. bull bbl., ramp and blade front sight, adj. rear. American walnut grips. Weight: 28 oz. Made 1981-83.

MODEL 829/830 DA
Same as Model 826 except in .22 LR caliber. Nine rnd. capacity. Made 1981-83.
Model 829, blued . . . .**NiB $189 Ex $143 Gd $94**
Model 830, nickel. . . . .**NiB $181 Ex $135 Gd $90**

MODEL 832/833 DA
Same as Model 826 except in .32 SW Long. Blued or nickel finish. Made 1981-83.
Model 832, blued . . . .**NiB $199 Ex $112 Gd $77**
Model 833, nickel. . . . .**NiB $199 Ex $112 Gd $77**

MODEL 900/901 DA . . . .**NiB $179 Ex $105 Gd $70**
Solid frame, snap-out cylinder. Calibers: .22 Short, Long, LR. Nine-round cylinder, bbl. lengths: 2.5, 4, and 6-in. Weight: 26 oz. (w/ 6-in. bbl.). Fixed sights. Blued finish. Cycolac grips. Made 1962-73. Note: Model 901 (disc. in 1963) is the same except has chrome finish and white Tenite grips.

MODEL 903 TARGET . . . .**NiB $240 Ex $177 Gd $112**
Caliber: .22 LR. Nine rnd. capacity. SA/DA, 6-in. target-weight flat-side bbl., swing-out cylinder. Weight: 35 oz. Blade front sight, adj. rear. American walnut grips. Made 1980-83.

**Harrington & Richardson
.22 Special**

**Harrington & Richardson
Model 622**

**Harrington & Richardson
Model 199 Sportsman**

**Harrington & Richardson
Model 649**

MODEL 904 TARGET .... NiB $265 Ex $177 Gd $116
Similar to Model 903 except 4 or 6-in. bull bbl. Weight: 32 oz. w/4-in. bbl. Made 1980-86.

MODEL 905 TARGET .... NiB $270 Ex $183 Gd $137
Same as Model 904 except w/4-in. bbl. only. Nickel finish. Made 1981-83.

**MODEL 922 DA REVOLVER
FIRST ISSUE** .... NiB $232 Ex $189 Gd $148
Solid frame. Caliber: .22 LR. Nine-round cylinder, 10-in. octagon bbl., (early model) or 6-in., rnd. bbl. (later production). Weight: 26 oz. (w/ 6-in. bbl.). Fixed sights. Blued finish. Checkered walnut grips. Safety cylinder on later models. Disc. prior to 1942.

**MODEL 922/923 DA REVOLVER,
SECOND ISSUE** .... NiB $220 Ex $112 Gd $88
Solid frame. Caliber: .22 LR. Nine-round cylinder, bbl. lengths: 2.5, 4, and 6-in. Weight: 24 oz. (w/ 4-in. bbl.). Fixed sights. Blued finish. Plastic grips. Made 1950-86. Note: Second Issue Model 922 has a different frame from that of the First Issue. Model 923 is same as Model 922, Second Issue except for nickel finish.

MODEL 925 DEFENDER ...... NiB $255 Ex $148 Gd $110
DA. Hinged frame. Caliber: .38 S&W. Five-round cylinder, 2.5-in. bbl., weight: 22 oz. Adj. rear sight, fixed front. Blued finish. One-piece wraparound grip. Made 1964-78.

MODEL 926 DA .... NiB $255 Ex $158 Gd $110
Hinged frame. Calibers: .22 LR, .38 S&W. Nine-round (.22 LR) or 5-rnd. (.38) cylinder, 4-in. bbl., weight: 31 oz. Adj. rear sight, fixed front. Blued finish. Checkered walnut grips. Made 1968-78.

**MODEL 929/930
SIDEKICK DA REVOLVER** ..... NiB $219 Ex $130 Gd $95
Caliber: .22 LR. Solid frame, swing-out 9-rnd. cylinder, bbl. lengths: 2.5-, 4-, 6-in. Weight: 24 oz. (w/ 4-in. bbl.). Fixed sights. Blued finish. Checkered plastic grips. Made 1956-86. Note: Model 930 is same except with nickel finish.

**MODEL 939/940 ULTRA SIDEKICK
DA REVOLVER** .... NiB $290 Ex $187 Gd $112
Solid frame, swing-out 9-rnd. cylinder. Safety lock. Calibers: .22 Short, Long, LR. Flat-side 6-in. bbl. w/VR. Weight: 33 oz. Adj. rear sight, ramp front. Blued finish. Checkered walnut grips. Made 1958-86, reintroduced by H&R 1871 in 1992. Note: Model 940 is same except has rnd. bbl.

**MODEL 949/950 FORTY-NINER
DA REVOLVER** .... NiB $270 Ex $190 Gd $110
Solid frame. Side loading and ejection. Calibers: .22 Short, Long, LR. Nine-round cylinder, 5.5- or 7.5 in. bbl., weight: 31 to 38 oz. Adj. rear sight, blade front. Blued or nickel finish. One-piece, Western-style walnut grip. Made 1960-86, reintroduced by H&R 1871 in 1992 to 1999. Note: Model 950 is same except has nickel finish.

MODEL 976 DA .... NiB $310 Ex $197 Gd $109
Same as Model 949 except has color-casehardened frame, 7.5-in. bbl. Weight: 36 oz. Intro. 1977. Disc.

**MODEL 999 SPORTSMAN DA REVOLVER,
FIRST ISSUE** .... NiB $499 Ex $316 Gd $200
Hinged frame. Calibers: .22 LR, .22 Mag. Same specifications as Model 199 Sportsman Single Action. Disc. before 1942.

**MODEL 999 SPORTSMAN DA REVOLVER
SECOND ISSUE** .... NiB $464 Ex $309 Gd $197
Hinged frame. Caliber: .22 LR. Nine-round cylinder, 6-in. bbl. w/VR. Weight: 30 oz. Adj. sights. Blued finish. Checkered walnut grips. Made 1950-86.

**(NEW) MODEL 999 SPORTSMAN
DA REVOLVER** .... NiB $499 Ex $316 Gd $197
Hinged frame. Caliber: .22 Short, Long, LR. Nine-round cylinder. Six-in. bbl. w/VR. Weight: 30 oz. Blade front sight adj. for elevation, square-notched rear adj. for windage. Blued finish. Checkered hardwood grips. Reintroduced by H&R 1871 in 1992.

AMERICAN DA .... NiB $245 Ex $115 Gd $79
Solid frame. Calibers: .32 S&W Long, .38 S&W. Six-round (.32 cal.) or 5-rnd. (.38 cal.) cylinder, bbl. lengths: 2.5-,4.5- and 6-in. Weight: About 16 oz. Fixed sights. Blued or nickel finish. Hard rubber grips. Disc. prior to 1942.

AUTOMATIC EJECTING
DA REVOLVER . . . . NiB $231 Ex $174 Gd $120
Hinged frame. Calibers: .32 S&W Long, .38 S&W. Six-round (.32 cal.) or 5-rnd. (.38 cal.) cylinder, bbl. lengths: 3.25-, 4-, 5- and 6-in. Weight: 16 oz. (.32 cal.), 15 oz. (.38 cal.). Fixed sights. Blued or nickel finish. Black hard rubber grips. Disc. prior to 1942.

BOBBY DA . . . . NiB $316 Ex $219 Gd $160
Hinged frame. Calibers: .32 S&W, .38 S&W. Six-round cylinder (.32 cal.) or 5-rnd. (.38 cal.). Four-in. bbl., 9 in. overall. Weight: 23 oz. Fixed sights. Blued finish. Checkered walnut grips. Disc. 1946. Note: Originally designed and produced for use by London's bobbies.

DEFENDER .38 DA . . . . NiB $346 Ex $219 Gd $110
Hinged frame. Based on the Sportsman design. Caliber: .38 S&W. Bbl. lengths: 4- and 6-in., 9 in. overall (w/ 4-in. bbl.). Weight: 25 oz. w/4-in. bbl. Fixed sights. Blued finish. Black plastic grips. Disc. 1946. Note: This model was manufactured during WW II as an arm for plant guards, auxiliary police, etc.

EXPERT MODEL DA . . . . NiB $499 Ex $283 Gd $110
Same specifications as .22 Special except has 10-in. bbl., weight: 28 oz. Disc. prior to 1942.

HAMMERLESS DA,
LARGE FRAME . . . . NiB $206 Ex $137 Gd $115
Hinged frame. Calibers: .32 S&W Long 38 S&W. Six-round (.32 cal.), or 5-rnd. (.38 cal.) cylinder, bbl. lengths: 3.25, 4, and 6-in. Weight: About 17 oz. Fixed sights. Blued or nickel finish. Hard rubber grips. Disc. prior to 1942.

**Harrington & Richardson
Model 903**

**Harrington & Richardson
Model 925**

HAMMERLESS DA,
SMALL FRAME . . . . NiB $189 Ex $130 Gd $101
Hinged frame. Calibers: .22 LR, .32 S&W. Seven-round (.22 cal.) or 5-rnd. (.32 cal.) cylinder, bbl. lengths: 2, 3, 4, 5 and 6-in. Weight: About 13 oz. Fixed sights. Blued or nickel finish. Hard rubber grips. Disc. prior to 1942.

HUNTER MODEL DA . . . . NiB $601 Ex $410 Gd $309
Solid frame. Caliber: .22 LR. Nine-round cylinder, 10-in. octagon bbl., weight: 26 oz. Fixed sights. Blued finish. Checkered walnut grips. Safety cylinder on later models. Note: An earlier Hunter Model was built on the smaller 7-rnd. frame. Disc. prior to 1942.

NEW DEFENDER DA . . . . NiB $346 Ex $244 Gd $189
Hinged frame. Caliber: .22 LR. Nine-round cylinder, 2-in. bbl., 6.25 in. overall. Weight: 23 oz. Adj. sights. Blued finish. Checkered walnut grips, rnd. butt. Note: Basically, this is the Sportsman DA w/a short bbl., Disc. prior to 1942.

PREMIER DA . . . . NiB $306 Ex $198 Gd $109
Small hinged frame. Calibers: .22 LR, .32 S&W. Seven-round (.22 LR) or 5-rnd. (.32) cylinder. Bbl. Lengths: 2, 3, 4, 5, and 6-in. Weight: 13 oz. (in .22 LR), 12 oz. (in .32 S&W). Fixed sights. Blued or nickel finish. Black hard rubber grips. Disc. prior to 1942.

STR 022
BLANK REVOLVER . . . . NiB $143 Ex $90 Gd $70
Caliber: .22 RF blanks. Nine-round cylinder, 2.5-in. bbl. Weight: 19 oz. Satin blued finish.

STR 032
BLANK REVOLVER . . . . NiB $148 Ex $95 Gd $75
Same general specifications as STR 022 except chambered for .32 S&W blank cartridges.

TARGET MODEL DA . . . . NiB $237 Ex $166 Gd $120
Small hinged frame. Calibers: .22 LR, .22 W.R.F. Seven-round cylinder, 6-in. bbl., weight: 16 oz. Fixed sights. Blued finish. Checkered walnut grips. Disc. prior to 1942.

TRAPPER MODEL DA . . . . NiB $388 Ex $219 Gd $130
Solid frame. Caliber: .22 LR. Seven-round cylinder, 6-in. octagon bbl., weight: 12.5 oz. Fixed sights. Blued finish. Checkered walnut grips. Safety cylinder on later models. Disc. prior to 1942.

ULTRA SPORTSMAN . . . . NiB $321 Ex $219 Gd $165
SA. Hinged frame. Caliber: .22 LR. Nine-round cylinder, 6-in. bbl., weight: 30 oz. Adj. target sights. Blued finish.

**Harrington & Richardson
Model 922, First Issue**

Harrington & Richardson Model 939

Harrington & Richardson Trapper

Harrington & Richardson Model 950

Harrington & Richardson Vest Pocket

Harrington & Richardson Model 999, Second Issue

Checkered walnut grips. This model has short action, wide hammer spur, cylinder is length of a .22 LR cartridge. Disc. prior to 1942.

VEST POCKET DA. . . . . NiB $138 Ex $95 Gd $70
Solid frame. Spurless hammer. Calibers: .22 Rimfire, .32 S&W. Seven-round (.22 cal.) or 5-rnd. (.32 cal.) cylinder, 1.13-in. bbl., weight: About 9 oz. Blued or nickel finish. Hard rubber grips. Disc. prior to 1942.

YOUNG AMERICA DA . . . . NiB $241 Ex $109 Gd $81
Solid frame. Calibers: .22 Long, .32 S&W. Seven-round (.22 cal.) or 5-rnd. (.32 cal.) cylinder. Bbl. lengths: 2-, 4.5- and 6-in. Weight: About 9 oz. Fixed sights. Blued or nickel finish. Hard rubber grips. Disc. prior to 1942.

HARTFORD ARMS & EQUIPMENT CO. — Hartford, CT

Hartford pistols were the forebearer of the original High Standard line. High Standard Mfg. Corp. acquired Hartford Arms & Equipment Co. in 1932. The High Standard Model B is essentially the same as the Hartford Automatic.

Harrington & Richardson Hammerless, Small Frame

AUTOMATIC TARGET PISTOL. . .NiB $800 Ex $660 Gd $440
Caliber. .22 LR. 10-rnd. magazine, 6.75-in. bbl., 10.75 in. overall. Weight: 31 oz. Target sights. Blued finish. Black rubber grips. This gun closely resembles the early Colt Woodsman and High Standard pistols. Made 1929-30.
.22 Short model . . . . NiB $2810 Ex $2110 Gd $1510

REPEATING PISTOL . . . . .EXTREMELY RARE
Check for authenticity. This model is a hand-operated repeating pistol similar to the Fiala and Schall pistols Made 1929-30.

SINGLE-SHOT TARGET PISTOL . . .NiB $910 Ex $710 Gd $530
Similar in appearance to the Hartford Automatic except manually operated. Caliber: .22 LR, 6.75-in. bbl., 10.75 in. overall. Weight: 38 oz. Target sights. Mottled frame and slide, blued bbl., Black rubber or walnut grips. Made 1929-30.
Target model (10-in. bbl) . . . NiB $3010 Ex $2510 Gd $1810

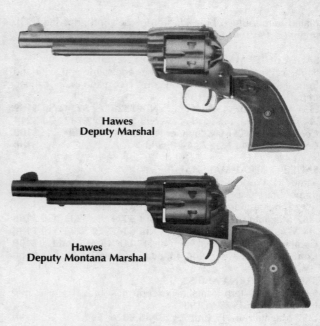

Hawes
Deputy Marshal

HASKELL MANUFACTURING — Lima, OH
See listings under Hi-Point.

Hawes
Deputy Montana Marshal

HAWES FIREARMS — Van Nuys, CA

DEPUTY MARSHAL SA REVOLVER
Calibers: .22 LR, also .22 WMR in two-cylinder combination. Six-round cylinder, 5.5-in. bbl., 11 in. overall. Weight: 34 oz. Adj. rear sight, blade front. Blued finish. Plastic or walnut grips. Imported 1973 to 1981.
.22 LR (plastic grips). . . . . .NiB $219 Ex $120 Gd $88
Combination, .22 LR/.22 WMR, add. $50
Walnut grips, add $20

DEPUTY DENVER MARSHAL
Same as Deputy Marshal SA except has brass frame. Imported 1973 to 1981.
.22 LR (plastic grips). . . . . .NiB $265 Ex $212 Gd $110
Combination, .22 LR/.22 WMR, add. $50
Walnut grips add $10

DEPUTY MONTANA MARSHAL
Same as Deputy Marshal except has brass grip frame. Walnut grips only. Imported from 1973 to 1981.
.22 LR .NiB $283 Ex $198 Gd $118
Combination, .22 LR/.22 WMR, add. $50

Hawes Sauer Chief
Marshal

DEPUTY SILVER CITY MARSHAL
Same as Deputy Marshal except has chrome-plated frame, brass grip frame, blued cylinder and bbl., Imported from 1973 to 1981.
.22 LR (plastic grips). . . . . .NiB $281 Ex $209 Gd $158
Combination, .22 LR/.22 WMR, add. $50
Walnut grips, add $15

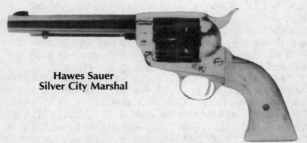

Hawes Sauer
Montana Marshal .22

DEPUTY TEXAS MARSHAL
Same as Deputy Marshal except has chrome finish. Imported 1973 to 1981.
.22 LR (plastic grips). . . . . .NiB $293 Ex $205 Gd $110
Combination, .22 LR/.22 WMR, add. $50
Walnut grips, add $15

FAVORITE SINGLE-SHOT
TARGET PISTOL. . . . . NiB $219 Ex $128 Gd $90
Replica of Stevens No. 35. Tip-up action. Caliber: .22 LR. Eight-in. bbl., 12 in. overall. Weight: 24 oz. Target sights. Chrome-

Hawes Sauer
Silver City Marshal

plated frame. Blued bbl., Plastic or rosewood grips (add $5).
Imported 1972- to 1976.

SAUER CHIEF MARSHAL SA TARGET REVOLVER
Same as Western Marshal except has adjustable rear sight and
front sight, oversized rosewood grips. Not made in .22 caliber.
Imported from 1973 to 1981.

.357 Magnum or .45 Colt . . . . . NiB $326 Ex $254 Gd $189
.44 Magnum . . . . NiB $362 Ex $282 Gd $214
Combination .357 Mag./9mm or .45 LC/.45 ACP, add $100
Combination .44 Mag./.44-40, add $100

SAUER FEDERAL MARSHAL
Same as Western Marshal except has color-casehardened
frame, brass grip frame, one-piece walnut grip. Not made in
.22 caliber. Imported from 1973 to 1981.

.357 Magnum or .45 Colt . . . . . NiB $321 Ex $235 Gd $198
.44 Magnum . . . . NiB $362 Ex $235 Gd $198
Combination .357 Mag./9mm or .45 LC/.45 ACP, add . . $100
Combination .44 Mag./.44-40, add $100

SAUER MONTANA MARSHAL
Same as Western Marshal except has brass grip frame.
Imported from 1973 to 1981.

.357 Magnum or .45 Colt . . . . . NiB $326 Ex $270 Gd $190
.44 Magnum . . . . NiB $357 Ex $281 Gd $214
.357 Mag./9mm or .45 LC/.45 ACP, add $100
Combination .44 Mag./.44-40, add $100
.22 LR . . . . NiB $306 Ex $240 Gd $180
Combination .22 LR/.22 WMR, add $50

SAUER SILVER CITY MARSHAL
Same as Western Marshal except has nickel plated frame, brass
grip frame, blued cylinder and barrel, pearlite grips. Imported
from 1973 to 1981.

.44 Magnum . . . . NiB $377 Ex $289 Gd $219
.357 Mag./9mm or .45 LC/.45 ACP, add $100
Combination .44 Mag./.44-40, add $100

SAUER TEXAS MARSHAL
Same as Western Marshal except nickel plated, has pearlite
grips. Imported from 1973 to 1981.

.357 Magnum or .45 Colt . . . . . NiB $362 Ex $270 Gd $204
.44 Magnum . . . . NiB $365 Ex $303 Gd $214
.357 Mag./9mm or
   .45 LC/.45 ACP, add $100
Combination
   .44 Mag./.44-40, add $100
.22 LR . . . . NiB $321 Ex $244 Gd $189
Combination .22 LR/.22 WMR, add $50

SAUER WESTERN MARSHAL SA REVOLVER
Calibers: .22 LR (disc.), .357 Magnum, .44 Magnum, .45 Auto.
Also in two-cylinder combinations: .22 WMR (disc.), 9mm
Para., .44-40, .45 Auto. Six-round cylinder, bbl. lengths: 5.5-
in. (disc.), 6-in., 11.75 in. overall (w/ 6-in. bbl.). Weight: 46
oz. Fixed sights. Blued finish. Originally furnished w/simulated
stag plastic grips. Recent production has smooth rosewood
grips. Made 1968 by J. P. Sauer & Sohn, Eckernforde, Germany.
Imported from 1973 to 1981.

.357 Magnum or .45 LC . . . . . . NiB $357 Ex $265 Gd $200
.44 Magnum . . . . NiB $377 Ex $290 Gd $219
.357 Mag./9mm or .45 LC/.45 ACP, add $100
Combination .44 Mag./.44-40, add $100
.22 LR . . . . NiB $281 Ex $198 Gd $160
Combination .22 LR/.22 WMR, add $50

HECKLER & KOCH — Oberndorf am Neckar, Germany, and Columbus, GA; Asburn, VA; and Newington, NH; formerly Chantilly, VA

MODEL HK4 DA AUTO PISTOL
Calibers: .380 Automatic (9mm Short), .22 LR, .25 Automatic
(6.35mm), .32 Automatic (7.65mm) w/conversion kits. Seven-
round magazine (.380 Auto), 8-rnd. in other calibers, 3.4-in.
bbl., 6.19 in. overall. Weight: 18 oz. Fixed sights. Blued finish.
Plastic grip. Disc. 1984.

.22 LR or .380 units to kit . . . . . NiB $536 Ex $388 Gd $265
.25 ACP or .32 ACP units to kit . . . . NiB $536 Ex $377 Gd $255
.380 units to kit w/.22
   conversion unit . . . . NiB $530 Ex $357 Gd $225
.380 units to kit w/.22, .25, .32
   conversion units . . . . NiB $530 Ex $357 Gd $225

MODEL HK45 . . . . NiB $1025 EX $800 GD $550
Semiauto. DA/SA. Caliber: .45 ACP; 10-rnd. magazine. 4.53-
in. bbl. w/O-ring. Frame: polymer. Sights: low-profile, 3-dot.
Finish: black. Grip: textured polymer w/grip panels. Length:
8.3-in. Weight: 31.2 oz. Imported from 2008 to date.
Tactical (DA/SA or DAO, thread bbl.,
   intro. 2013) . . . . NiB $1225 Ex $930 Gd $680
Compact
   (3.9-in. bbl., intro. 2008) . . NiB $1025 Ex $800 Gd $550
Compact Tactical (3.9-in. threaded bbl.,
   intro. 2011) . . . . NiB $1225 Ex $930 Gd $680

MARK 23 . . . . NiB $2060 Ex $1530 Gd $1100
Short-recoil Semiauto pistol w/polymer frame and steel slide.
Caliber: .45 ACP. 10-rnd. magazine, 5.87-in. bbl., 9.65 in.
overall. Weight: 43 oz. Seven interchangeable rear sight adjustment units w/3-dot system. Developed primarily in response to
specifications by the Special Operations Command (SOCOM).
Imported from 1996 to date.

MODEL P7 K3 DA AUTO PISTOL
Caliber: .380 ACP. Eight-round magazine, 3.8 in.-bbl., 6.3 in.
overall. Weight: About 26 oz. Adj. rear sight. Imported 1988
to 1994.

.380 Cal. . . . . NiB $2200 Ex $1785 Gd $1250
.22 LR conversion kit add, ... $1500
.32 ACP conversion kit add, ... $1000

MODEL P7 M8 . . . . NiB $2250 Ex $1750 Gd $1175
Squeeze-cock SA Semiauto. Caliber: 9mm Para. Eight-round
magazine, 4.13-in. bbl., 6.73 in. overall. Weight: 29.9 oz.
Matte black or nickel finish. Adjustable rear sight. Imported
from 1985 to 2005.

MODEL P7 M10. . . . . NiB $3200 Ex $2500 Gd $1880
Caliber: .40 S&W. Nine-round magazine, 4.2-in. bbl., 6.9 in.
overall. Weight: 43 oz. Fixed front sight blade, adj. rear w/3-
dot system. Imported from 1992 to 1994.
Nickel finish add, ... 20%

MODEL P7 M13. . . . . NiB $3200 Ex $2500 Gd $1880
Caliber: 9mm. 13-rnd. magazine, 4.13-in. bbl., 6.65 in.
overall. Weight: 34.42 oz. Matte black finish. Adj. rear sight.
Imported 1985 to 1994.

MODEL P7 (PSP). . . . . .NiB $1200 Ex $900 Gd $720
Caliber: 9mm Para. Eight-round magazine, 4.13-in. bbl., 6.54 in. overall. DA. Weight: About 33.5 oz. Blued finish. Imported 1983 to 1985 and 1990 with limited availability.
European model, add 15%

MODEL P9 AND P9S
Semiauto. DA/SA (P9) or SAO (P9S) trigger. Calibers: 9mm or .45 ACP. Nine-round (9mm) or 7-rnd. (.45 Auto) magazine. Four-in. bbl., 7.63 in. overall. Weight: 32 ounces. Fixed sights. Blued finish. Contoured plastic grips. Disc. 1986.
9mm . . . . .NiB $950 Ex $800 Gd $530
.45 ACP, add 20%

MODEL P9S TARGET COMPETITION KIT
Same as Model P9S Target except w/extra 5.5-in. bbl. and bbl. weights. Also available w/walnut competition grip.
w/standard grip . . . . .NiB $3000 Ex $2300 Gd $1810
w/competition grip. . . . . . .NiB $4000 Ex $3000 Gd $2000

MODEL P30. . . . . NiB $950 Ex $680 Gd $480
Semiauto. DA/SA. Caliber: 9mm or .40 S&W; 15 or 13-rnd. magazine. 3.85-in. bbl. Frame: polymer. Sights: low-profile, 3-dot. Finish: black. Grip: textured polymer w/grip panels. Length: 7.12-in. Weight: 26 oz. Imported from 2007 to date.
P30SK (3.27-in. bbl.). . . . . .NiB $950 Ex $660 Gd $450
P30L (4.45-in. bbl.). . . . . .NiB $950 Ex $660 Gd $450

MODEL P2000. . . . . NiB $700 Ex $560 Gd $450
Semiauto. DA/SA, DAO or LEM trigger. Caliber: 9mm, .357 SIG (2005-12) or .40 S&W; 12 or 13-rnd. magazine. 3.66-in. bbl. Frame: polymer. Sights: low-profile, 3-dot. Finish: black. Grip: textured polymer w/ modular backstrap. Length: 6.85-in. Weight: 24.96 oz. Imported from 2004 to date.
SK (3.26-in. bbl., 2005 to date) . .NiB $700 Ex $560 Gd $450

MODEL SP5K. . . . . NiB $2500 Ex $2100 Gd $1600
Semiauto commercial version of H&K MP5. SA. Caliber: 9mm; 10 or 30-rnd. magazine. 4.53-in. bbl. Frame: polymer. Sights: fixed front, adj. rear. Finish: black. Grip: textured polymer. Length: 13.9-in. Weight: 4.2 lbs. Imported from 2016 to date.

MODEL SP89 . . . . .NiB $4960 Ex $4160 Gd $3740
Semiauto, recoil-operated, delayed roller-locked bolt system. Caliber: 9mm Para. 15-rnd. magazine, 4.5-in. bbl., 13 in. overall. Weight: 68 oz. Hooded front sight, adj. rotary-aperture rear. Imported 1989 to 1993.

MODEL USP . . . . NiB $840 Ex $610 Gd $460
Polymer integral grip/frame design w/recoil reduction system. Calibers: 9mm Para., .40 S&W or .45 ACP. 15-rnd. (9mm) or 13-rnd. (.40 S&W and .45ACP) magazine, 4.13- or 4.25-in. bbl., 6.88 to 7.87 in. overall. Weight: 26.5-30.4 oz. Blade front sight, adj. rear w/3-dot system. Matte black finish. Stippled black polymer grip. Available in SA/DA or DAO. Imported 1993 to date.
Stainless finish, deduct $130
w/Tritium sights, add $100
w/LEM trigger, add $60
.45 ACP caliber, add $60

MODEL USP COMPACT. . . . . . . NiB $860 Ex $660 Gd $450
Similar to USP model except w/10-rnd. magazine, 4.25-in. bbl., 7.64 in. overall. Weight: 25.5 oz. Imported from 1993 to date.

Heckler & Koch
Mark 23

Heckler & Koch
Model HK4

Heckler &
Koch VP9

Heckler & Koch
Model P7 (PSP)

Heckler & Koch
USP45

Heckler & Koch
Model P9

Heckler & Koch
Model USP45
Compact 50th
Anniversary

Heckler & Koch
Model USP Expert

Heckler & Koch
Model USP Tactical

Stainless slide finish, deduct $130
w/LEM trigger, add $60
.45 ACP caliber, add $60
50th Anniversary (1 of 1,000). . NiB $1199 Ex $947 Gd $709

MODEL USP TACTICAL . . . . . NiB $1200 Ex $910 Gd $530
Similar to USP model except w/threaded 4.8-in. bbl., match grade trigger, adj. sights. Imported from 2015 to date.

**MODEL USP CUSTOM
COMBAT**. . . . . NiB $1160 Ex $880 Gd $610
Similar to USP model except w/9mm or .40 S&W caliber, DA/SA trigger, Novak sights. Made 2009 only.

**MODEL US COMBAT
COMPETITION**. . . . . NiB $1260 Ex $940 Gd $710
Similar to USP model except w/4.25-in. bbl., 9mm or .40 S&W caliber, DA/SA or LEM trigger. Imported 2007 to 2010.

GRADING: **NiB** = New in Box   **Ex** = Excellent or NRA 95%   **Gd** = Good or NRA 68%

Heckler & Koch
Model VP 7OZ

MODEL US COMPETITION . . . NiB $1130 Ex $860 Gd $630
Similar to USP Combat Competition model except w/LEM match trigger. Imported 2007 to 2008.

MODEL USP EXPERT . . . . NiB $1230 Ex $930 Gd $680
Similar to USP model except w/5.2-in. bbl. Weight: 30 oz. Adjustable 3-dot target sights. Short recoil modified Browning action w/recoil reduction system. Reinforced polymer frame w/integral grips and match-grade slide. Imported from 1999 to 2009 reintro. 2013.

MODEL USP ELITE . . . . NiB $1380 Ex $1010 Gd $810
Similar to USP model except w/long slide variant in 9mm or .45 ACP caliber, DA/SA trigger, adj. sights. Imported 2003 to 2009.

MODEL USP MATCH . . . . . . NiB $2160 Ex $1580 Gd $1050
Similar to USP Elite except w/6.02-in. bbl. w/bbl. weight, .45 ACP, adj. sights. Imported 1997 to 1998.

MODEL VP9. . . . . NIB $650 EX $510 GD $410
Semiauto. Striker-fired. Caliber: 9mm; 10 or 15-rnd. magazine. 4.0-in. bbl. Frame: polymer. Sights: fixed, low-profile, 3-dot. Finish: black. Grip: textured polymer w/modular grip panels. Length: 7.3-in. Weight: 25.56 oz. Imported from 2014 to date.
VP40 (.40 S&W, intro. 2015) . . NiB $650 Ex $510 Gd $410

MODEL VP 70Z . . . . NiB $760 Ex $610 Gd $510
Caliber: 9mm Para. 18-rnd. magazine, 4.5-in. bbl., 8 in. overall. Weight: 32.5 oz. DA Fixed sights. Blued slide, polymer receiver and grip. Disc. 1986.

HELWAN
See listings under Interarms.

HEIZER DEFENSE — PEVELY, MO

**MODEL PS1 POCKET
SHOTGUN. . . . . NiB $350 Ex $280 Gd $230**
Single-shot derringer, break action. DAO. Caliber: .45 ACP/410 gauge. 3.25-in. bbl. Frame: stainless steel. Sights: fixed. Finish: matte stainless. Grip: textured aluminum w/storage for 2 extra cartridges. Weight: 21 oz. Length: 4.6 in. Made 2013 to date.
**Hedy Jane model
(.45 ACP/.410 bore) . . . . NiB $355 Ex $280 Gd $230
PAR1 (5.56 caliber). . . . . NiB $350 Ex $380 Gd $230
PAK1 (7.62x39mm caliber). . . . NiB $350 Ex $380 Gd $230**

HENRY REPEATING ARMS — BAYONNE, NJ

MARE'S LEG RIMFIRE . . . . NiB $400 Ex $320 Gd $265
Lever-action pistol. SA. Caliber: .22 S/L/LR, 10-rnd. magazine. 12.8-in. bbl. Sights: adj rear. Finish: blue. Grip: smooth wood. Made 2011 to date.

MARE'S LEG PISTOL CENTERFIRE . . . . NiB $870 Ex $610 Gd $455
Lever-action pistol. SA. Caliber: .357 Mag., .44 Mag., or .45 Long Colt, 5-rnd. magazine. 12.9-in. bbl. Sights: adj rear. Finish: blue or brass receiver, blue bbl. Made 2011 to date.

HERITAGE MANUFACTURING — Opa Locka, FL

Acquired by Taurus Int'l. in 2012

MODEL H-25 AUTO PISTOL
Caliber: .25 ACP. Six-round magazine, 2.5-in. bbl., 4.63 in. overall. Weight: 12 oz. Fixed sights. Blued or chrome finish. Made 1995-99.
**Blued. NiB $136 Ex $95 Gd $75
Nickel, add $20**

BIG BORE ROUGH RIDER SERIES
SA revolver. Cal.: .357 Mag., .44-40, .44 Mag., or .45 LC; 6-rnd. cylinder. Bbl.: 4.7-, 5.5- or 7.5 ins. Weight: 32-34 oz. Sights: Fixed blade front, groove rear. Finish: Blued, chrome, nickel or case colored. Grip: Smooth walnut. Made 1992-2021.
**blued. NiB $440 Ex $380 Gd $305
case colored . . . . NiB $445 Ex $385 Gd $310
chrome . . . . NiB $460 Ex $400 Gd $325
nickel . . . . NiB $510 Ex $415 Gd $375**

ROUGH RIDER SA REVOLVER
Calibers: .22 LR, .22 Mag. Six-rnd. cylinder. bbl. lengths: 2.75, 3.75, 4.75, 6.5 or 9 ins. Weight: 31-38 oz. Sights: Fixed or adj. High-polished blued finish or faux case hardened. Grips: Smooth or checkered walnut, faux pearl, faux ivory. Made 1993 to date.
**.22 LR . . . . NiB $200 Ex $115 Gd $95
.22 LR/.22 Mag. combo . . . . . . NiB $250 Ex $170 Gd $110**

**9-Shot model (4.7- or 6.5-in. bbl.,
9-rnd. cylinder). . . . . NiB $220 Ex $205 Gd $120
16" model (16-in. bbl.). . . . . NiB $200 Ex $170 Gd $90
Barkeep model (2- or 3-in. bbl.) . . NiB $195 Ex $120 Gd $90
Bird Head Model (bird head grip,
3.5- or 4-in. bbl.) . . . . NiB $200 Ex $170 Gd $90
Tactical Cowboy model (6.5-in. threaded bbl.,
optic Picatinny rail) . . . . NiB $210 Ex $195 Gd $100**

SENTRY DA REVOLVER
Calibers: .22 LR, .22 Mag., .32 Mag., 9mm or .38 Special. Six- or 8-rnd. (rimfire) cylinder, 2- or 4-in. bbl., 6.25 in. overall (2-in. bbl.). Ramp front sight, fixed rear. Blued or nickel finish. Checkered polymer grips. Made 1993-97.
**Blued. . . . . NiB $131 Ex $95 Gd $75
Nickel, add $15**

STEALTH DA AUTO PISTOL . . . NiB $241 Ex $179 Gd $101
Calibers: 9mm, .40 S&W. 10-rnd. magazine, 3.9-in. bbl., weight: 20.2 oz. Gas-delayed blowback, double action only. AmbidExtrous trigger safety. Blade front sight, drift-adj. rear.

**Heritage Mfg. Rough Rider shown
w/ birds head grip**

**Heritage Mfg.
Sentry**

Black chrome or stainless slide. Black polymer grip frame. Made 1996-2000.

HI-POINT FIREARMS — Mansfield, OH

MODEL JS-9 AUTO PISTOL . . . . NiB $158 Ex $101 Gd $75
Caliber: 9mm Para. Eight-round magazine, 4.5-in. bbl., 7.75 in. overall. Weight: 39 oz. Fixed low-profile sights w/3-dot system. Matte blue, matte black or chrome finish. Checkered synthetic grips. Made 1990-2000.

**MODEL JS-9 COMPETITION
PISTOL (STALLARD) . . . . NiB $151 Ex $90 Gd $69**
Similar to standard JS-9 except w/4-in. compensated bbl. w/ shortened slide and adj. sights. 10-rnd. magazine, 7.25 in. overall. Weight: 30 oz. Made 1998-2006.

**MODEL JS-9/C-9 COMPACT PISTOL
(BEEMILLER) . . . . NiB $148 Ex $90 Gd $75**
Similar to standard JS-9 except w/3.5-in. bbl. and shortened slide w/alloy or polymer frame. 6.72 in. overall. Weight: 29 oz. or 32 oz. Three-dot-style sights. JS-9 made from 1993 to 2000, C-9 1993 date.

MODEL CF-380 . . . . NiB $158 Ex $88 Gd $61
Caliber: .380 ACP. Eight-round magazine, 3.5-in. bbl., 6.72 in. overall. Weight: 32 oz. Three-dot sights. Made 1994 to date.

**MODEL JS-40/JC-40 AUTO PISTOL
(IBERIA) . . . . NiB $171 Ex $110 Gd $75**
Similar to Model JS-9mm except in caliber .40 S&W.

**MODEL JS-45/JH-45 AUTO PISTOL
(HASKELL). . . . . NiB $150 Ex $101 Gd $70**
Similar to Model JS-9mm except in caliber .45 ACP w/7-rnd. magazine and two-tone Polymer finish.

J. C. HIGGINS

See Sears, Roebuck & Company.

HIGH STANDARD SPORTING FIREARMS
— East Hartford, CT

Formerly High Standard Mfg. Co., Hamden, Connecticut. A long-standing producer of sporting arms, High Standard disc. its operations in 1984. See new High Standard models under separate entry, HIGH STANDARD MFG. CO., INC.

**Hi-Point Model
C-9**

**Hi-Point Model
JS-9**

GRADING: NiB = New in Box   **Ex =** Excellent or NRA 95%   **Gd =** Good or NRA 68%

NOTE: *For ease in finding a particular firearm, High Standard handguns are grouped into three sections: Automatic pistols, derringers and revolvers. For a complete listing, please refer to the Index.*

- AUTOMATIC PISTOLS -

MODEL A
HAMMERLESS. . . . . .NiB $847 Ex $748 Gd $497
Caliber: .22 LR. 10-rnd. magazine, bbl. lengths: 4.5-, 6.75-in. 11.5 in. overall (6.75-in. bbl.). Weight: 36 oz. (in 6.75-in. bbl.). Adj. target sights. Blued finish. Checkered walnut grips. Made 1938-42.

MODEL B
AUTOMATIC PISTOL . . . . .NiB $668 Ex $444 Gd $367
Original Standard pistol. Hammerless. Caliber: .22 LR. 10-rnd. magazine, bbl. lengths: 4.5-, 6.75-in., 10.75 in. overall (w/ 6.75-in. bbl.). Weight: 33 oz. (6.75-in. bbl.). Fixed sights. Blued finish. Hard rubber grips. Made 1932-42.

MODEL C
AUTOMATIC PISTOL . . . . .NiB $979 Ex $826 Gd $549
Same as Model B except in .22 Short. Made 1935-42.

MODEL D
AUTOMATIC PISTOL . . . . . . .NiB $1020 Ex $774 Gd $544
Same general specifications as Model A but heavier bbl., weight: 40 oz. (6.75-in. bbl.). Made 1937-42.

DURA-MATIC . . . . .NiB $362 Ex $301 Gd $204
Takedown. Caliber: .22 LR. 10-rnd. magazine, 4.5 or 6.5 in. interchangeable bbl., 10.88 in. overall (6.5-in. bbl.). Weight: 35 oz. (in 6.5-in. bbl.). Fixed sights. Blued finish. Checkered grips. Made 1952-70.

MODEL E
AUTOMATIC PISTOL . . . . . .NiB $1275 Ex $1051 Gd $929
Same general specifications as Model A but w/Extra heavy bbl. and thumbrest grips. Weight: 42 oz. (6.75-in. bbl.). Made 1937-42.

FIELD-KING AUTOMATIC PISTOL FIRST MODEL
Same general specifications as Sport-King but w/heavier bbl. and target sights. Late model 6.75-in. bbls. have recoil stabilizer and lever take-down feature. Weight: 43 oz. (6.75-in. bbl.). Made 1951-58.
w/one bbl. . . . . .NiB $683 Ex $529 Gd $408
w/both bbls., add $204

FIELD-KING AUTOMATIC PISTOL SECOND MODEL
Same general specifications as First Model Field-King but w/ button take-down and marked FK 100 or FK 101.
w/one bbl. . . . . .NiB $852 Ex $588 Gd $324
w/both bbls., add $204

FLITE-KING AUTOMATIC PISTOL — FIRST MODEL
Same general specifications as Sport-King except in .22. Short w/aluminum alloy frame and slide and marked FK 100 or FK 101. Weight: 26 oz. (6.5-in. bbl.). Made 1953-58.
w/one bbl. . . . . .NiB $668 Ex $469 Gd $342
w/both bbls. . . . . .NiB $872 Ex $660 Gd $546

FLITE-KING AUTOMATIC PISTOL — SECOND MODEL
Same as Flite-King—First Model except w/steel frame and marked in the 102 or 103 series. Made 1958-66.

Model 102 . . . . .NiB $556 Ex $398 Gd $265
Model 103 . . . . .NiB $536 Ex $388 Gd $219

MODEL G-380
AUTOMATIC PISTOL . . . . .NiB $668 Ex $571 Gd $408
Lever takedown. Visible hammer. Thumb safety. Caliber: .380 Automatic. Six-round magazine, 5-in. bbl., weight: 40 oz. Fixed sights. Blued finish. Checkered plastic grips. Made 1943-50.

MODEL G-B AUTOMATIC PISTOL
Lever takedown. Hammerless. Interchangeable bbls. Caliber: .22 LR. 10-rnd. magazine, bbl. lengths: 4.5, 6.75 in., 10.75 in. overall (w/ 6.75-in. bbl.). Weight: 36 oz. (w/ 6.75-in. bbl.). Fixed sights. Blued finish. Checkered plastic grips. Made 1948-51.
w/one bbl. . . . . .NiB $689 Ex $500 Gd $365
w/both bbls. . . . . .NiB $893 Ex $704 Gd $576

MODEL G-D AUTOMATIC PISTOL
Lever takedown. Hammerless. Interchangeable bbls. Caliber: .22 LR. 10-rnd. magazine, bbl. lengths: 4.5, 6.75 in. 11.5 in. overall (w/ 6.75-in. bbl.). Weight: 41 oz. (6.75-in. bbl.). Target sights. Blued finish. Checkered walnut grips. Made 1948-51.
w/one bbl. . . . . .NiB $1076 Ex $917 Gd $709
w/both bbls. . . . . .NiB $1275 Ex $1048 Gd $898

High Standard
Model A

High Standard
Model B

High Standard
Model D

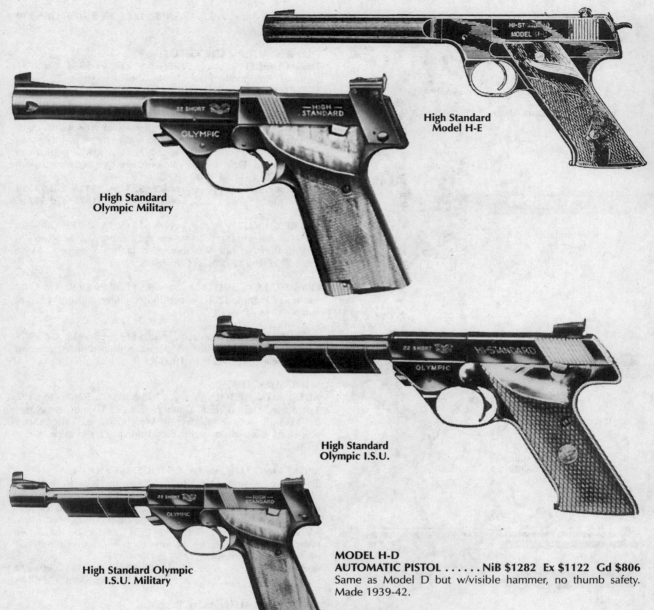

High Standard
Model H-E

High Standard
Olympic Military

High Standard
Olympic I.S.U.

High Standard Olympic
I.S.U. Military

MODEL G-E AUTOMATIC PISTOL
Same general specifications as Model G-D but w/Extra heavy bbl. and thumbrest grips. Weight: 44 oz. (w/ 6.75-in. bbl.). Made 1949-51.
w/one bbl. . . . . NiB $1488 Ex $1266 Gd $1015
w/both bbls. . . . . NiB $1692 Ex $1470 Gd $1200

MODEL H-A
AUTOMATIC PISTOL . . . . . . NiB $2230 Ex $1355 Gd $859
Same as Model A but w/visible hammer, no thumb safety. Made 1939-42.

MODEL H-B
AUTOMATIC PISTOL . . . . NiB $816 Ex $590 Gd $433
Same as Model B but w/visible hammer, no thumb safety. Made 1940-42.

MODEL H-D
AUTOMATIC PISTOL . . . . . . NiB $1282 Ex $1122 Gd $806
Same as Model D but w/visible hammer, no thumb safety. Made 1939-42.

MODEL H-DM
AUTOMATIC PISTOL . . . . NiB $663 Ex $524 Gd $429
Also called H-D Military. Same as Model H-D but w/thumb safety. Made 1941-51.

MODEL H-E
AUTOMATIC PISTOL . . . . . NiB $2275 Ex $2142 Gd $1197
Same as Model E but w/visible hammer, no thumb safety. Made 1939-42.

OLYMPIC AUTOMATIC PISTOL FIRST MODEL (G-O)
Same general specifications as Model G-E but in .22 Short w/ light alloy slide. Made 1950-51.
w/one bbl. . . . . NiB $1785 Ex $1153 Gd $629
w/both bbls, add. $408

OLYMPIC AUTOMATIC SECOND MODEL
Same general specifications as Supermatic but in .22 Short w/ light alloy slide. Weight: 39 oz. (6.75-in. bbl.). Made 1951-58.

GRADING: NiB = New in Box   Ex = Excellent or NRA 95%   Gd = Good or NRA 68%

High Standard Dura-Matic

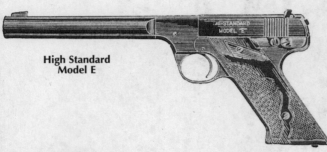

High Standard Model E

High Standard G-380

High Standard Model G-B

High Standard Model H-A

w/one bbl. . . . . NiB $1325 Ex $1076 Gd $730
w/both bbls, add. $306

OLYMPIC AUTOMATIC PISTOL,
THIRD MODEL. . . . . NiB $1213 Ex $984 Gd $734
Same as Supermatic Trophy w/bull bbl. except in .22 Short. Made 1963-66.

OLYMPIC COMMEMORATIVE
Limited edition of Supermatic Trophy Military issued to commemorate the only American-made rimfire target pistol ever to win an Olympic gold medal. Highly engraved w/Olympic rings inlaid in gold. Deluxe presentation case. Two versions issued: In 1972 (.22 LR) and 1980 (.22 Short).
1972 issue. . . . . NiB $6523 Ex $5416 Gd $3550
1980 issue. . . . . NiB $2243 Ex $1877 Gd $1215

OLYMPIC I.S.U . . . . NiB $1316 Ex $1020 Gd $798
Same as Supermatic Citation except caliber .22 Short, 6.75- or 8-in. tapered bbl. w/stabilizer, detachable weights. Made 1958-77. Eight-in. bbl. disc. in 1966.

OLYMPIC I.S.U. MILITARY . . . NiB $1120 Ex $940 Gd $702
Same as Olympic I.S.U. except has military grip and bracket rear sight. Intro. in 1965. Disc.

OLYMPIC MILITARY . . . . NiB $1142 Ex $932 Gd $755
Same as Olympic — Third Model except has military grip and bracket rear sight. Made in 1965.

SHARPSHOOTER
AUTOMATIC PISTOL . . . . NiB $385 Ex $267 Gd $197
Takedown. Hammerless. Caliber: .22 LR. 10-rnd. magazine, 5.5-in. bull bbl., 9 in. overall. Weight: 42 oz. Micrometer rear sight, blade front sight. Blued finish. Plastic grips. Made 1971-83.

SPORT-KING AUTOMATIC PISTOL FIRST MODEL
Takedown. Hammerless. Interchangeable barrels. Caliber: .22 LR. 10-rnd. magazine, bbl. lengths: 4.5-, 6.75-in. 11.5 in. overall (w/ 6.75-in. barrel). Weight: 39 oz. (w/ 6.75-in. barrel). Fixed sights. Blued finish. Checkered plastic thumbrest grips. Made 1951-58. Note: 1951 to 1954 production has lever takedown as in "G" series. Later version (illustrated at left) has push-button takedown.
w/one bbl. . . . . NiB $388 Ex $306 Gd $220
w/both bbls. . . . . NiB $590 Ex $500 Gd $408

SPORT-KING AUTOMATIC PISTOL
SECOND MODEL. . . . . NiB $357 Ex $279 Gd $204
Caliber: .22 LR. 10-rnd. magazine, 4.5- or 6.75 in. interchangeable bbl. 11.25 in. overall (w/ 6.75-in. barrel). Weight: 42 oz. (w/ 6.75-in. barrel). Fixed sights. Blued finish. Checkered grips. Made 1958-70.

SPORT-KING AUTOMATIC PISTOL
THIRD MODEL. . . . . NiB $305 Ex $204 Gd $135
Similar to Sport-King — Second Model with same general specifications for weight and length. Blued or nickel finish. Introduced in 1974. Disc.

SPORT-KING LIGHTWEIGHT
Same as standard Sport-King except lightweight has forged aluminum alloy frame. Weight: 30 oz. w/6.75-in. bbl. Made 1954-65.
w/one bbl. . . . . NiB $590 Ex $380 Gd $255
w/both bbls. . . . . NiB $791 Ex $602 Gd $453

SUPERMATIC AUTOMATIC PISTOL

Takedown. Hammerless. Interchangeable bbls. Caliber: .22 LR. 10-rnd. magazine, bbl. lengths: 4.5-, 6.75-in. Late model 6.75-in. bbl. have recoil stabilizer feature. Weight: 43 oz. (w/ 6.75-in. barrel) 11.5 in. overall (w/ 6.75-in. barrel). Target sights. Elevated serrated rib between sights. Adjustable bbl. weights add 2 or 3 oz. Blued finish. Checkered plastic thumb-rest grips. Made 1951-58.

w/one bbl. . . . . NiB $872 Ex $683 Gd $509
w/both bbls. . . . . NiB $1070 Ex $893 Gd $714

SUPERMATIC CITATION

Same as Supermatic Tournament except 6.75-, 8- or 10-in. tapered bbl. with stabilizer and two removable weights. Also furnished with Tournament's 5.5-in. bull barrel, adjustable trigger pull, recoil-proof click-adjustable rear sight (barrel-mounted on 8- and 10-in. barrels), checkered walnut thumbrest grips on bull bbl. model. Currently manufactured with only bull barrel. Made 1958-66.

w/5.5-in. bull bbl. . . . . NiB $893 Ex $612 Gd $377
w/6.75-in. tapered bbl. . . . . NiB $893 Ex $612 Gd $377
w/8-in. tapered bbl. . . . . NiB $1066 Ex $760 Gd $536
w/10-in. tapered bbl. . . . . NiB $1099 Ex $811 Gd $571

SUPERMATIC CITATION MILITARY

Same as Supermatic Citation except has military grip and bracket rear sight as in Supermatic Trophy. Made 1965-73.

w/bull bbl. . . . . NiB $897 Ex $581 Gd $499
w/fluted bbl. . . . . NiB $964 Ex $806 Gd $602

SUPERMATIC TOURNAMENT. . . . . NiB $734 Ex $587 Gd $362

Takedown. Caliber: .22 LR. 10-rnd. magazine, interchangeable 5.5-in. bull or 6.75-in. heavy tapered bbl., notched and drilled for stabilizer and weights. 10 in. overall (w/ 5.5-in. bbl.). Weight: 44 oz. (5.5-in. bbl.). Click adj. rear sight, undercut ramp front. Blued finish. Checkered grips. Made 1958-66.

SUPERMATIC TOURNAMENT

MILITARY . . . . NiB $1305 Ex $997 Gd $836
Same as Supermatic Tournament except has military grip. Made 1965-71.

SUPERMATIC TROPHY

Same as Supermatic Citation except w/5.5-in. bull bbl., or 7.25-in. fluted bbl., w/detachable stabilizer and weights, Extra magazine, High-luster blued finish, checkered walnut thumbrest grips. Made 1963-66.

w/bull bbl. . . . . NiB $1305 Ex $1090 Gd $638
w/fluted bbl. . . . . NiB $1305 Ex $1090 Gd $638

SUPERMATIC TROPHY MILITARY

Same as Supermatic Trophy except has military grip and bracket rear sight. Made 1965-84.

w/bull bbl. . . . . NiB $1357 Ex $1060 Gd $760
w/fluted bbl. . . . . NiB $1408 Ex $1120 Gd $813

THE VICTOR AUTOMATIC . . . NiB $3299 Ex $2798 Gd $2550

Takedown. Caliber: .22 LR. 10-rnd. magazine, 4.5-in. solid or VR and 5.5-in. VR, interchangeable bbl. 9.75 in. overall (w/ 5.5-in. bbl.). Weight: 52 oz. (w/ 5.5-in. bbl.). Rib mounted target sights. Blued finish. Checkered walnut thumbrest grips. Standard or military grip configuration. Made 1972-84 (standard-grip model made 1974-75).

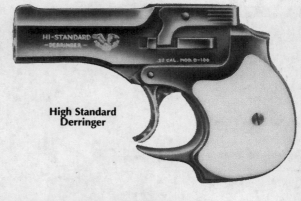

**High Standard
Derringer**

**High Standard
Double-Nine — Steel Frame**

**High Standard
Kit Gun**

- DERRINGERS -

DERRINGER

Hammerless, double action, two-round, double bbl. (over/under). Calibers: .22 Short, Long, LR or .22 Magnum Rimfire, 3.5-in. bbls., 5 in. overall. Weight: 11 oz. Standard model has blued or nickel finish w/plastic grips. Presentation model is goldplated in walnut case. Standard model made from 1963 (.22 S-L-LR) and 1964 (.22 MRF) to 1984. Gold model, made 1965-83.

Standard model (blue) . . . . . . NiB $332 Ex $225 Gd $204
Standard model (nickel) . . . . . . NiB $332 Ex $225 Gd $204
Standard model
   (Electroless nickel). . . . . NiB $337 Ex $291 Gd $230
Gold Presentation
   One Derringer. . . . . NiB $541 Ex $362 Gd $286
Silver Presentation
   One Derringer. . . . . NiB $592 Ex $431 Gd $342
Presentation Set, Matched pair, consecutive
   numbers (1965 only) . . . . NiB $1392 Ex $1180 Gd $836

GRADING: **NiB** = New in Box   **Ex** = Excellent or NRA 95%   **Gd** = Good or NRA 68%

High Standard Longhorn
Steel Frame

High Standard Sport-King
Automatic — First Model

High Standard
Sentinel

High Standard Sport-King
Automatic — Second Model

High Standard
Sentinel I

High Standard Supermatic

High Standard
Sentinel Mark II

High Standard
Sentinel Snub

- REVOLVERS -

CAMP GUN . . . . **NiB $270 Ex $220 Gd $189**
Same as Sentinel Mark I/Mark IV except has 6-in. bbl., adj. rear sight, target-style checkered walnut grips. Caliber: .22 LR or .22 WMR. Made 1976-83.

DOUBLE-NINE DA REVOLVER —ALUMINUM FRAME
Western-style version of Sentinel. Blued or nickel finish w/ simulated ivory, ebony or stag grips, 5.5-in. bbl., 11 in. overall. Weight: 27.25 oz. Made 1959-71.
Blue model . . . . **NiB $255 Ex $190 Gd $150**

High Standard Victor
Solid Rib Barrel

High Standard
Supermatic Citation Bull Barrel

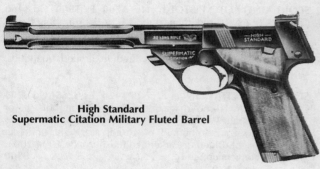

High Standard
Supermatic Citation Military Fluted Barrel

High Standard
Supermatic Tournament Bull Barrel

High Standard Mfg. Co.
10-X Supermatic Citation
(current mfg.)

DOUBLE-NINE—STEEL FRAME
Similar to Double-Nine—Aluminum Frame, w/same general specifications except w/steel frame and has Extra cylinder for .22 WMR, walnut grips. Intro. in 1971. Disc.
Blue model . . . . NiB $291 Ex $225 Gd $179
Nickel model. . . . . NiB $306 Ex $225 Gd $190

DOUBLE-NINE DELUXE . . . . . . NiB $326 Ex $240 Gd $198
Same as Double-Nine Steel Frame except has adj. target rear sight. Intro. in 1971. Disc.

DURANGO
Similar to Double-Nine—Steel Frame except .22 LR only, available w/4.5- or 5.5-in. bbl. Made 1971-73.
Blue model . . . . NiB $275 Ex $189 Gd $150
Nickel model. . . . . NiB $301 Ex $219 Gd $170

HIGH SIERRA DA REVOLVER
Similar to Double-Nine—Steel Frame except has 7-in. octagon bbl., w/gold-plated grip frame, fixed or adj. sights. Made 1973-83.
w/fixed sights . . . . NiB $352 Ex $286 Gd $214
w/adj. sights . . . . NiB $362 Ex $306 Gd $230

HOMBRE
Similar to Double-Nine—Steel Frame except .22 LR only, lacks single-action type ejector rod and tube, has 4.5-in. bbl. Made 1971-73.
Blue model . . . . NiB $281 Ex $204 Gd $143
Nickel model. . . . . NiB $306 Ex $220 Gd $165

KIT GUN DA REVOLVER . . . . . NiB $275 Ex $214 Gd $150
Solid frame, swing-out cylinder. Caliber: .22 LR. Nine-round cylinder, 4-in. bbl., 9 in. overall. Weight: 19 oz. Adj. rear sight, ramp front. Blued finish. Checkered walnut grips. Made 1970-73.

LONGHORN ALUMINUM FRAME
Similar to Double-Nine—Aluminum Frame except has Longhorn hammer spur, 4.5-, 5.5- or 9.5-in. bbl., Walnut, simulated pearl or simulated stag grips. Blued finish. Made 1960-71.
w/4.5- or 5.5-in. bbl. . . . . NiB $357 Ex $254 Gd $190
w/9.5-in. bbl . . . . NiB $357 Ex $254 Gd $190

LONGHORN STEEL FRAME
Similar to Double-Nine — Steel Frame except has 9.5-in. bbl. w/fixed or adj. sights. Made 1971-83
w/fixed sights . . . . NiB $362 Ex $270 Gd $204
w/adj. sights . . . . NiB $377 Ex $316 Gd $229

NATCHEZ . . . . NiB $418 Ex $270 Gd $209
Similar to Double-Nine — Aluminum Frame except 4.5-in. bbl., 10 in. overall, weight: 25.25 oz., blued finish, simulated ivory bird's-head grips. Made 1961-66.

POSSE . . . . NiB $281 Ex $180 Gd $148
Similar to Double-Nine — Aluminum Frame except 3.5-in. bbl., 9 in. overall, weight: 23.25 oz. Blued finish, brass-grip frame and trigger guard, walnut grips. Made 1961-66.

GRADING: NiB = New in Box   Ex = Excellent or NRA 95%   Gd = Good or NRA 68%

SENTINEL DA REVOLVER
Solid frame, swing-out cylinder. Caliber: .22 LR. Nine-round cylinder, 3- 4- or 6-in. bbl. Nine in. overall (w/ 4-in.-bbl.). Weight: 19 oz. (w/ 4-in. bbl.). Fixed sights. Aluminum frame. Blued or nickel finish. Checkered grips. Made 1955-56.

Blue model	NiB $302	Ex $156	Gd $120
Blue/green model	NiB $577	Ex $439	Gd $319
Gold model	NiB $555	Ex $397	Gd $317
Nickel model	NiB $270	Ex $214	Gd $158
Pink model	NiB $536	Ex $306	Gd $180

SENTINEL DELUXE
Same as Sentinel except w/4- or 6-in. bbl., wide trigger, drift-adj. rear sight, two-piece square-butt grips. Made 1957-74. Note: Designated Sentinel after 1971.

Blue model	NiB $270	Ex $170	Gd $128
Nickel model	NiB $296	Ex $189	Gd $160

SENTINEL IMPERIAL
Same as Sentinel except has onyx-black or nickel finish, two-piece checkered walnut grips, ramp front sight. Made 1962-65.

Blue model	NiB $270	Ex $179	Gd $130
Nickel model	NiB $281	Ex $189	Gd $143

SENTINEL MARK 1 DA REVOLVER
Steel frame. Caliber: .22 LR. Nine-round cylinder, bbl. lengths: 2-, 3-, 4-in., 6.88 in. overall (w/ 2-in. bbl.). Weight: 21.5 oz. (2-in. bbl.). Ramp front sight, fixed or adj. rear. Blued or nickel finish. Smooth walnut grips. Made 1974-83.

Blue model	NiB $265	Ex $219	Gd $179
Nickel model	NiB $296	Ex $255	Gd $190
w/adj. sights	NiB $337	Ex $270	Gd $225

SENTINEL MARK II
DA REVOLVER . . . . NiB $326 Ex $255 Gd $179
Caliber: .357 Magnum. Six-round cylinder, bbl. lengths: 2.5-, 4-, 6-in., 9 in. overall w/4-in. bbl., weight: 38 oz. (w/ 4-in. bbl.). Fixed sights. Blued finish. Walnut service or combat-style grips. Made 1974-76.

SENTINEL MARK III . . . . NiB $326 Ex $255 Gd $175
Same as Sentinel Mark II except has ramp front and adj. rear sights. Weight: 40 oz. (w/ 4-in. bbl.). Blued finish. Made 1974-76.

SENTINEL MARK IV
Same as Sentinel Mark I except in .22 WMR. Made 1974-83.

Blue model	NiB $301	Ex $230	Gd $175
Nickel model	NiB $326	Ex $265	Gd $198
w/adj. sights	NiB $352	Ex $255	Gd $220

SENTINEL SNUB
Same as Sentinel Deluxe except w/2.75-in. bbl., (7.25 in. overall, weight: 15 oz.), checkered bird's head-type grips. Made 1957-74.

Blued finish	NiB $255	Ex $190	Gd $148
Nickel finish	NiB $274	Ex $160	Gd $109

HIGH STANDARD MFG. CO., INC. — Houston, TX
In 1993, High Standard acquired original assets and moved to Houston, Texas. The first Texas-manufactured firearms began shipping in March 1994 to 2018.

DURAMATIC PLINKER . . . . NiB $460 Ex $360 Gd $260
Semiauto. SA trigger. Caliber: .22 LR, 10-rnd. magazine. Bbl. Len.: 4.5-in. Sights: adj. Grip: Black plastic. Weight: 44 oz. Made 2013-16.

PLINKER . . . . NiB $460 Ex $360 Gd $260
Semiauto. SA trigger. Caliber: .22 LR, 10-rnd. magazine. Bbl. Len.: 4-, 6- or 8-in. Sights: adj. Made 2011 only.

OLYMPIC SERIES AUTOMATIC PISTOL
Same specifications as the 1958 I.S.U. issue. See listing under previous High Standard Section.

I.S.U. model	NiB $560	Ex $390	Gd $255
Military model	NiB $900	Ex $605	Gd $405
Rapid Fire model	NiB $930	Ex $630	Gd $430
Trophy Space Gun model	NiB $1160	Ex $880	Gd $630

SPORT KING AUTO PISTOL . . . NiB $760 Ex $580 Gd $460
Caliber: .22 LR. 10-rnd. magazine, 4.5- or 6.75-in. bbl., 8.5 or 10.75 in. overall. Weight: 44 oz. (w/ 4.5-in. bbl.), 46 oz. (w/ 6.75-in. bbl.). Fixed sights, slide mounted. Checkered walnut grips. Parkerized finish. Manufactured in limited quantities. Disc. 2013.

SUPERMATIC CITATION . . . . . NiB $420 Ex $265 Gd $205
Caliber: .22 LR. 10-rnd. magazine, 5.5- or 7.75-in. bbl., 9.5 or 11.75 in. overall. Weight: 44 oz. (w/ 5.5-in. bbl.), 46 oz. (w/ 7.75-in. bbl.). Frame-mounted, micro-adj. rear sight, undercut ramp front sight. Blued or Parkerized finish. Made 1994-2003.
.22 Short conversion, add $300

SUPERMATIC CITATION MS. . . NiB $855 Ex $580 Gd $380
Similar to the Supermatic Citation except has 10-in. bbl., 14 in. overall. Scope mount base. Weight: 49 oz. Made 1994-2016.

SUPERMATIC CITATION 10X. . . NiB $1160 Ex $860 Gd $610
Caliber: .22 LR. 10-rnd. magazine, 5.5-in. bbl., Finish: blue. Weight: 45 oz. Made 1994-2016.
Bob Shea tuned, add $300

SUPERMATIC TOURNAMENT. . . NiB $900 Ex $660 Gd $480
Caliber: .22 LR. 10-rnd. magazine, bbl. lengths: 4.5, 5.5, or 6.75 in., overall length: 8.5, 9.5 or 10.75 in. Weight: 43, 44 or 45 oz. depending on bbl. length. Micro-adj. rear sight, undercut ramp front sight. Checkered walnut grips. Parkerized finish. Made 1995-97.

SUPERMATIC TROPHY . . . . NiB $950 Ex $710 Gd $510
Caliber: .22 LR. 10-rnd. magazine, 5.5 or 7.25-in. bbl., 9.5 or 11.25 in. overall. Weight: 44 oz. (w/ 5.5-in. bbl.). Micro-adj. rear sight, undercut ramp front sight. Checkered walnut grips w/ thumbrest. Blued or Parkerized finish. Made 1994-2018.
.22 Short conversion kit, add $400

VICTOR . . . . NiB $850 Ex $660 Gd $480
Caliber: .22 LR.10-rnd. magazine, 4.5- or 5.5-in. ribbed bbl., 8.5 or 9.5 in. overall. Weight: 45 oz. (w/ 4.5-in. bbl.), 46 oz. (w/ 5.5-in. bbl.). Micro-adj. rear sight, post front. Checkered walnut grips. Blued or Parkerized finish. Made 1994-2018.
.22 Short conversion kit, add $400

VICTOR 10X AUTO PISTOL . . NiB $1230 Ex $1080 Gd $555
Caliber: .22 LR. 10-rnd. magazine, 5.5-in. bbl., 9.5 in. overall. Weight: 45 oz. Checkered walnut grips. Blued finish. Made 1994-2018.
Shea model
(built by Bob Shea) . . . . NiB $1455 Ex $1180 Gd $855

HONOR DEFENSE, LLC — Gainesville, GA

HONOR GUARD SERIES
Semiauto. Polymer frame, striker-fire. Caliber: 9mm, 7- or 8-rnd. magazine. Bbl.: 3.2-in. Weight: 22 oz. Blued finish. Grips: Textured polymer. Made 2015 to present.
Sub-Compact model . . . . **NiB $455 Ex $370 Gd $305**
Sub-Compact Long-Slide model
(3.8-in. bbl.) . . . . **NiB $455 Ex $370 Gd $305**

HOPKINS & ALLEN ARMS CO. — Norwich, CT

See listings of comparable Harrington & Richardson and Iver Johnson models for values.

Honor Defense Honor Guard Long-Slide

INGRAM — Powder Springs, GA

See listings under M.A.C. (Military Armament Corp.)

Note: *Military Armament Corp. ceased production of the select-fire automatic, M10 (9mm & .45 ACP) and M11 (.380 ACP) in 1977. Commercial production resumed on Semiauto versions under the M.A.C. banner until 1982.*

INLAND MANUFACTURING — Dayton, Ohio

MODEL 1911A1 . . . . **NiB $800 Ex $705 Gd $555**
Similar to US Military 1911A1 pistol. Semiauto. SA. Caliber: .45 ACP; 7-rnd. magazine. 5.0-in. bbl. Frame: steel. Sights: fixed. Finish: parkerized. Grip: checkered polymer. Length: 8.5 in. Weight: 39 oz. Made 2014 to date.
Custom Carry model, add **$200**
National Match model . . . . . . **NiB $1280 Ex $1120 Gd $870**

MODEL M1 ADVISOR . . . . . **NIB $1030 EX $810 GD $610**
Similar to US Military M1 Carbine pistol. Semiauto. SA. Caliber: .30 Carbine; 15-rnd. magazine. 12 in. bbl. Receiver: steel. Sights: fixed front, adj. rear. Finish: parkerized. Grip: smooth wood. Length: 19.75 in. Weight: 4.4 lbs. Made 2015 to date.

INTERARMS — Alexandria, VA

Importer and distributor from 1956 to 1999. Imported a variety of brands and models from FEG, Hammerli, Helwan, Howa, Rossi, and Walther. Also see those brand listings.

HELWAN BRIGADIER . . . . **NiB $355 Ex $280 Gd $230**
Semiauto. Caliber: 9mm, 8-rnd. magazine, 4.25-in. bbl., 8 in. overall. Weight: 32 oz. Blade front sight, dovetailed rear. Blued finish. Grooved plastic grips. Imported from 1987 to 1995.

VIRGINIAN DRAGOON SA REVOLVER
Calibers: .357 Magnum, .44 Magnum, .45 Colt. Six-round cylinder. Bbls.: 5- (not available in .44 Magnum), 6-, 7.5-, 8.38-in. (latter only in .44 Magnum w/adj. sights), 11.88 in. overall w/(6-in. bbl.). Weight: 48 oz. (w/ 6-in. bbl.). Fixed sights or micrometer rear and ramp front sights. Blued finish w/color-casetreated frame. Smooth walnut grips. SWISSAFE base pin safety system. Mfg. by Interarms Industries Inc., Midland, VA. from 1977 to 1984.
Standard Dragoon . . . . **NiB $388 Ex $281 Gd $214**
Engraved Dragoon . . . . **NiB $785 Ex $530 Gd $362**
Deputy model . . . . **NiB $377 Ex $274 Gd $179**
Stainless . . . . **NiB $398 Ex $265 Gd $165**

VIRGINIAN REVOLVER
SILHOUETTE MODEL . . . . **NiB $385 Ex $274 Gd $244**
Same general specifications as regular model except designed in stainless steel w/untapered bull bbl., lengths of 7.5, 8.38 and 10.5 in. Made 1985-86.

VIRGINIAN SA REVOLVER . . . . **NiB $388 Ex $270 Gd $265**
Similar to Colt Single Action Army except has base pin safety system. Imported from 1973-76. (See also listing under Hämmerli.)

INTRATEC U.S.A., INC. — Miami, FL

CAT-380, CAT-9 AND CAT-45 . . . **NiB $330 Ex $240 Gd $185**
Semiauto. Blowback action w/polymer frame. Caliber: 9mm Par Eight-round magazine, 3 or 3.25-in. bbl., 7.7 in. overall. Weight: 18 oz. Grips: textured black polymer. Matte black finish. Made 1993-2000.

MODEL PROTEC-25 DAO SEMIAUTO
Caliber: .25 ACP. 10-rnd. magazine, 2.5-in. bbl., 5 in. overall. Weight: 14 oz. Wraparound composition grips. Black Teflon, satin grey or Tec-Kote finish. Disc. 2000.
standard . . . . **NiB $128 Ex $88 Gd $61**
w/satin or Tec-Kote, add **$5**

MODEL TEC-DC9 . . . . **NiB $480 Ex $380 Gd $280**
Semiauto. Caliber: 9mm 20- or 36-rnd. magazine, 5-in. bbl., weight: 50-51 oz. Open fixed front sight, adj. rear. Military nonglare blued or stainless finish.
w/Tec Kote finish, add **$20**
w/stainless finish, add **$75**

MODEL TEC-DC9M . . . . **NiB $500 Ex $430 Gd $330**
Same specifications as Model Tec-9 except has 3-in. bbl. without shroud and 20-rnd. magazine, blued or stainless finish.
w/stainless finish, add **$75**

TEC-22 . . . . **NiB $380 Ex $280 Gd $210**
Caliber: .22 LR. 10/.22-type 30-rnd. magazine, 4-in. bbl., 11.19 in. overall. Weight: 30 oz. Protected post front sight, adj. rear sight. Matte black or Tec-Kote finish. Made 1991-94.

Tec-22T (threaded bbl.), add. $20
Tec-22TK Tec-Kote, add. $50

TEC-38 DERRINGER . . . . NiB $115 Ex $90 Gd $70
Calibers: .22 Mag., .32 H&R Mag., .357 Mag., .38 Special.
Two-round capacity, 3-in. blued bbl., 4.63 in. overall. Weight:
13 oz. Fixed sights. Synth. black frame. Double-action. Made
1986-88.

**Interarms/Helwan
Brigadier**

ISRAEL ARMS — Kfar Sabs, Israel

Imported by Israel Arms International, Houston, TX.

**BUL-M5 LOCKED BREECH (2000)
AUTO PISTOL** . . . . NiB $398 Ex $235 Gd $148
Similar to the M1911 U.S. Government model. Caliber: .45
ACP. Seven-round magazine, 5-in. bbl., 8.5 in. overall. Weight:
38 oz. Blade front and fixed, low-profile rear sights.

KAREEN MK II (1500) AUTO PISTOL
Single-action only. Caliber: 9mm Para. 10-rnd. magazine, 4.75-
in. bbl., 8 in. overall. Weight: 33.6 oz. Blade front sight, rear
adjustable for windage. TExtured black composition or rubber-
ized grips. Blued, two-tone, matte black finish. Imported from
1997 to 1998.
Blued or matte black finish. . . . . NiB $386 Ex $301 Gd $219
Two-tone finish . . . . NiB $556 Ex $386 Gd $304
Meprolite sights, add $50

**KAREEN MK II COMPACT
(1501) AUTO PISTOL** . . . . NiB $386 Ex $290 Gd $204
Similar to standard Kareen MKII except w/3.85-in. bbl., 7.1 in.
overall. Weight: 32 oz. Imported 1999 to 2000.

GOLAN MODEL (2500) AUTO PISTOL
Single or double action. Caliber: 9mm Para., .40 S&W. 10-rnd.
magazine, 3.85-in. bbl., 7.1 in. overall. Weight: 34 oz. Steel
slide and alloy frame w/ambidExtrous safety and decocking
lever. Matte black finish. Imported 1999.
9mm Para. . . . . NiB $954 Ex $755 Gd $536
.40 S&W . . . . NiB $954 Ex $755 Gd $536

**GAL MODEL
(5000) AUTO PISTOL** . . . . NiB $437 Ex $289 Gd $220
Caliber: .45 ACP. Eight-round magazine, 4.25-in. bbl., 7.25 in.
overall. Weight: 42 oz. Low profile 3-dot sights. Combat-style
black rubber grips. Imported from 1999 to 2001.

**Interarms Virginian
SA Revolver**

JAPANESE MILITARY PISTOLS — Tokyo, Japan

Manufactured by Government Plant.

**TYPE 14 (1925)
AUTOMATIC PISTOL** . . . . . . NiB $1500 Ex $1100 Gd $900
Modification of the Nambu Model 1914, changes chiefly
intended to simplify mass production. Standard rnd. trigger
guard or oversized guard for use w/gloves. Caliber: 8mm
Nambu. Eight-round magazine, 4.75-in. bbl., 9 in. overall.
Weight: About 29 oz. Fixed sights. Blued finish. Grooved wood
grips. Intro. 1925 and mfd. through WW II.
mfg. 1930-39, deduct 30%
mfg. 1939-45, deduct 70%

TYPE 26 REVOLVER . . . . NiB $1586 Ex $1120 Gd $779
DAO. Top-break frame. Caliber: 9mm Japanese. Six-round
cylinder w/automatic Extractor/ejector, 4.7-in. bbl., adopted by

Intratec TEC-DC9

the Japanese Army from 1893 to 1914, replaced by the Model
14 Automatic Pistol but remained in service through World
War II. Made 1893-1945.

**TYPE 94 (1934)
AUTOMATIC PISTOL** . . . . NiB $780 Ex $464 Gd $342
Poorly designed and constructed, this pistol is unsafe and
can be fired merely by applying pressure on the sear, which
is Exposed on the left side. Caliber: 8mm Nambu. Six-round

110

magazine, 3.13-in. bbl., 7.13 in. overall. Weight: About 27 oz. Fixed sights. Blued finish. Hard rubber or wood grips. Intro. in 1934, principally for Export to Latin American countries, production continued thru WW II.

BABY NAMBU (TYPE B) . . . . NiB $4500 Ex $3380 Gd $2480
Similar to Model 1904 except smaller frame, caliber: 7mm Nambu, 3.25-in. bbl. Grips: wood. Made 1909-29.

NAMBU MODEL
1904 AUTOMATIC PISTOL NiB $3500 Ex $2300 Gd $2000
Original Japanese service pistol, resembles Luger in appearance and Glisenti in operation. Caliber: 8mm Nambu. 8-rnd. magazine, 4.7-in. bbl., 9 in. overall. Weight: About 30 oz. Fixed front sight, adj. rear sight. Blued finish. Checkered wood grips. Made 1904-25.

Japanese
Type 14 (1925)

Japanese
Model 26 DAO Revolver

JENNINGS FIREARMS INC. — Irvine, CA

Currently Manufactured by Bryco Arms, Irvine, California. Previously by Calwestco, Inc. & B.L. Jennings. See additional listings under Bryco Arms.

MODEL J-22 AUTO PISTOL. . . . . . . NiB $66 Ex $40 Gd $30
Calibers: .22 LR, .25 ACP. Six-round magazine, 2.5-in. bbl., about 5 in. overall. Weight: 13 oz. Fixed sights. Chrome, satin nickel or black Teflon finish. Walnut, grooved black Cycolac or resin-impregnated wood grips. Made 1981-85 under Jennings and Calwestco logos; disc. 1985 by Bryco Arms.

JERICO — Tel Aviv, Israel

Trademark and manufactured by IWI Ltd., imported by IWI USA in Harrisburg, PA. First imported into the US in 1990 by K.B.I. Also imported under various names: Uzi Eagle (O.F. Mossberg), Baby Eagle (Magnum Research), and Desert Eagle Pistol (Magnum Research)

MODEL 941 SERIES
Semiauto. DA/SA. Caliber: 9mm or .40 S&W, 10-rnd. magazine, 4.4-in. bbl., Made 1900 to present.
PL model (polymer frame) . . . . . NiB $480 Ex $380 Gd $300
PS model (steel frame) . . . . NiB $580 Ex $460 Gd $330

Japanese Type 94 (1934)

IVER JOHNSON ARMS, INC. — Jacksonville, AR

Operation of this company dates back to 1871, when Iver Johnson and Martin Bye partnered to manufacture metallic cartridge revolvers. Johnson became the sole owner and changed the name to Iver Johnson's Arms & Cycle Works, which it was known as for almost 100 years. Modern management shortened the name, and after several owner changes the firm was moved from Massachusetts, its original base, to Jacksonville, Arkansas. In 1987, the American Military Arms Corporation (AMAC) acquired the operation, which subsequently ceased in 1993.

NOTE: *For ease in finding a particular firearm, Iver Johnson handguns are divided into two sections: Automatic Pistols (below) and Revolvers, which follow. For the complete handgun listing, please refer to the Index.*

Jennings Model J-22

- AUTOMATIC PISTOLS -

9MM DA AUTOMATIC......NiB $474 Ex $357 Gd $265
Caliber: 9mm. Six-round magazine, 3-in. bbl., 6.5 in. overall. Weight: 26 oz. Blade front sight, adj. rear. Smooth hardwood grip. Blued or matte blued finish. Intro. 1986.

COMPACT .25 ACP.........NiB $273 Ex $190 Gd $148
Bernardelli V/P design. Caliber: .25 ACP. Five-round magazine, 2.13-in. bbl., 4.13 in. overall. Weight: 9.3 oz. Fixed sights. Checkered composition grips. Blued slide, matte blued frame and color-casehardened trigger. Made 1991-93.

ENFORCER................NiB $893 Ex $643 Gd $431
Caliber: .30 U.S. Carbine. Five-, 15-, or 30-rnd. magazine, 9.5-in. bbl., weight: 5.5 lbs. Adj. sights. Walnut stock. Made 1986.

I.J. SUPER ENFORCER.......NiB $893 Ex $643 Gd $431
Caliber: .30 U.S. Carbine. Fifteen- or 30-rnd. magazine, 9.5-in. bbl., 17 in. overall. Weight: 4 pounds. Adj. peep rear sight, blade front. American walnut stock. Made 1978-93.

PONY AUTOMATIC PISTOL
Caliber: .380 Auto. Six-round magazine, 3.1-in. bbl., 6.1 in. overall. Blue, matte blue, nickel finish or stainless. Weight: 20 oz. Wooden grips. Smallest of the locked breech automatics. Made 1982-88. Reintro. 1989-91.
Blue or matte blue finish .....NiB $434 Ex $342 Gd $270
Nickel finish ....NiB $464 Ex $345 Gd $290
Deluxe finish...............NiB $464 Ex $377 Gd $281

Jericho 941 PL

MODEL TP-22 DA
AUTOMATIC...............NiB $316 Ex $219 Gd $160
Calibers: .22 LR, Seven-round magazine, 2.85-in. bbl., 5.39 in. overall. Blued finish. Weight: 14.46 oz. Made 1982-89.

MODEL TP25 DA
POCKET PISTOL............NiB $271 Ex $190 Gd $143
Double-action automatic. Caliber: .25 ACP. Seven-round magazine, 3-in. bbl., 5.5 in. overall. Weight: 12 oz. Black plastic grips and blued finish. Made 1981-82.

TRAILSMAN AUTOMATIC PISTOL
Caliber: .22 LR. 10-rnd. magazine, 4.5 or 6-in. bbl., 8.75 in. overall (w/ 4.5-in. bbl.). Weight: 46 oz. Fixed target-type sights. Checkered composition grips. Made 1985-91.
Standard model.............NiB $306 Ex $220 Gd $160
Deluxe model ....NiB $321 Ex $230 Gd $170

- REVOLVERS -

MODEL 55
TARGET DA REVOLVER ......NiB $237 Ex $160 Gd $115
Solid frame. Caliber: .22 LR. Eight-round cylinder, bbl. lengths: 4.5-, 6-in. 10.75 in. overall (w/ 6-in. bbl.). Weight: 30.5 oz. (w/ 6-in. bbl.). Fixed sights. Blued finish. Walnut grips. Note: Original model designation was 55; changed to 55A when loading gate was added in 1961. Made 1955-60.

MODEL 55-S REVOLVER......NiB $265 Ex $165 Gd $110
Same general specifications as the Model 55 except for 2.5-in. bbl. and small, molded pocket-size grip.

MODEL 56
BLANK REVOLVER ....NiB $128 Ex $81 Gd $55
Solid frame. Caliber: .22 blanks only. Eight-round cylinder, 2.5-in. solid bbl., 6.75 in. overall. Weight: 10 oz.

MODEL 57A
TARGET DA REVOLVER ......NiB $255 Ex $143 Gd $101
Solid frame. Caliber: .22 LR. Eight-round cylinder, bbl. lengths: 4.5, and 6-in. 10.75 in. overall. Weight: 30.5 oz. w/6-in. bbl. Adj. sights. Blued finish. Walnut grips. Note: Original model designation was 57, changed to 57A when loading gate was added in 1961. Made 1961-78.

MODEL 66 TRAILSMAN
DA REVOLVER ....NiB $306 Ex $209 Gd $160
Hinged frame. Rebounding hammer. Caliber: .22 LR. Eight-round cylinder, 6-in. bbl., 11 in. overall. Weight: 34 oz. Adj. sights. Blued finish. Walnut grips. Made 1985-91.

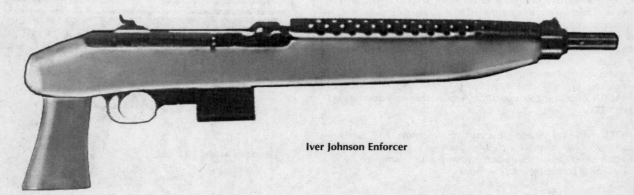

Iver Johnson Enforcer

MODEL 67
VIKING DA REVOLVER . . . . . . NiB $273 Ex $165 Gd $110
Hinged frame. Caliber: .22 LR. Eight-round cylinder, bbl. lengths: 4.5- and 6-in., 11 in. overall (w/ 6-in. bbl.). Weight: 34 oz. (w/ 6-in. bbl.). Adj. sights. Walnut grips w/thumbrest. Made 1964-78.

MODEL 67S VIKING
SNUB REVOLVER . . . . NiB $286 Ex $189 Gd $179
DA. Hinged frame. Calibers: .22 LR, .32 S&W Short and Long, .38 S&W. Eight-round cylinder in .22, 5-rnd. in .32 and .38 calibers; 2.75-in. bbl. Weight: 25 oz. Adj. sights. Tenite grips. Made 1964-78.

MODEL 1900 DA REVOLVER . . . . NiB $158 Ex $90 Gd $65
Solid frame. Calibers: .22 LR, .32 S&W, .32 S&W Long, .38 S&W. Seven-round cylinder in .22 cal., 6-rnd. (.32 S&W), 5-rnd. (.32 S&W Long, .38 S&W); bbl. lengths: 2.5-, 4.5- and 6-in. Weight: 12 oz. (in .32 S&W w/2.5-in. bbl.). Fixed sights. Blued or nickel finish. Hard rubber grips. Made 1900-41.

MODEL 1900
TARGET DA REVOLVER . . . . . . NiB $222 Ex $175 Gd $135
Solid frame. Caliber: .22 LR. Seven-round cylinder, bbl. lengths: 6- and 9.5-in. Fixed sights. Blued finish. Checkered walnut grips. (This earlier model does not have counterbored chambers as in the Target Sealed 8. Made 1925-42.)

AMERICAN BULLDOG DA REVOLVER
Solid frame. Calibers: .22 LR, .22 WMR, .38 Special. Six-round cylinder in .22, 5-rnd. in .38. Bbl. lengths: 2.5-, 4-in. 9 in. overall (w/ 4-in. bbl.). Weight: 30 oz. (w/ 4-in. bbl.). Adj. sights. Blued or nickel finish. Plastic grips. Made 1974-76.
.38 Special . . . . NiB $464 Ex $286 Gd $204
Other calibers . . . . NiB $464 Ex $286 Gd $204

ARMSWORTH MODEL 855 SA . . . NiB $464 Ex $290 Gd $198
Hinged frame. Caliber: .22 LR. Eight-round cylinder, 6-in. bbl., 10.75 in. overall. Weight: 30 oz. Adj. sights. Blued finish. Checkered walnut one-piece grip. Adj. finger rest. Made 1955-57.

CADET DA REVOLVER . . . . NiB $255 Ex $165 Gd $101
Solid frame. Calibers: .22 LR, .22 WMR, .32 S&W Long, .38 S&W, .38 Special. Six- or 8-rnd. cylinder in .22, 5-rnd. in other calibers, 2.5-in. bbl., 7 in. overall. Weight: 22 oz. Fixed sights. Blued finish or nickel finish. Plastic grips. Note: Loading gate added in 1961, .22 cylinder capacity changed from 8 to 6 rounds in 1975. Made 1955-77.

CATTLEMAN SA REVOLVER . . . NiB $369 Ex $301 Gd $170
Patterned after the Colt Army SA revolver. Calibers: .357 Magnum, .44 Magnum, .45 Colt. Six-round cylinder. Bbl. lengths: 4.75-, 5.5- (not available in .44), 6- (.44 only), 7.25-in. Weight: About 41 oz. Fixed sights. Blued bbl., and cylinder color-casehardened frame, brass grip frame. One-piece walnut grip. Made by Aldo Uberti, Brescia, Italy, from 1973 to 1978.
.44 Magnum, add $50

CATTLEMAN BUCKHORN SA REVOLVER
Same as standard Cattleman except has adj. rear and ramp front sights. Bbl. lengths: 4.75- (.44 only), 5.75- (not available in .44), 6- (.44 only), 7.5- or 12-in. bbl., weight: About 44 oz. Made 1973-78.
.357 Magnum or .45
  Colt w/12-in. bbl. . . . . NiB $439 Ex $326 Gd $219

**Iver Johnson
Model TP**

**Iver Johnson
Model 55 Target**

**Iver Johnson
Model 55-S**

**Iver Johnson
Model 56 Blank Revolver**

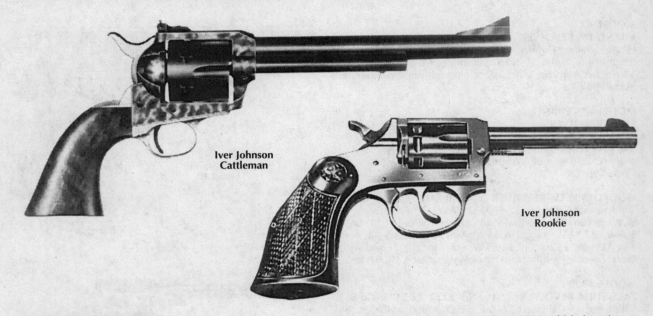

Iver Johnson Cattleman

Iver Johnson Rookie

.357 Magnum or .45
Colt w/5.75- or 7.5-in. bbl. . . **NiB $342 Ex $255 Gd $158**
.44 Magnum, w/12-in. bbl. . . . . . **NiB $459 Ex $367 Gd $279**
.44 Magnum, other bbls . . . . **NiB $439 Ex $326 Gd $219**

CATTLEMAN BUNTLINE SA REVOLVER
Same as Cattleman Buckhorn except has 18-in. bbl., walnut shoulder stock w/brass fittings. Weight: About 56 oz. Made 1973-78.
.44 Magnum . . . . **NiB $443 Ex $332 Gd $225**
Other calibers . . . . **NiB $443 Ex $332 Gd $225**

CATTLEMAN
TRAIL BLAZER . . . . **NiB $377 Ex $274 Gd $189**
Similar to Cattleman Buckhorn except .22 caliber has interchangeable .22 LR and .22 WMR cylinders, 5.5- or 6.5-in. bbl., weight: About 40 oz. Made 1973-78.

CHAMPION 822
.22 TARGET SA . . . . **NiB $499 Ex $326 Gd $175**
Hinged frame. Caliber: .22 LR. Eight-round cylinder. Single action. Counterbored chambers as in Sealed 8 model, 6-in. bbl., 10.75 in. overall. Weight: 28 oz. Adj. target sights. Blued finish. Checkered walnut grips, adj. finger rest. Made 1938-48.

DELUXE TARGET. . . . . **NiB $305 Ex $225 Gd $175**
Same as Sportsman except has adj. sights. Made 1975-76.

PROTECTOR SEALED 8
DA REVOLVER . . . . **NiB $453 Ex $337 Gd $204**
Hinged frame. Caliber: .22 LR. Eight-round cylinder, 2.5-in. bbl., 7.25 in. overall. Weight: 20 oz. Fixed sights. Blued finish. Checkered walnut grips. Made 1933-49.

ROOKIE DA REVOLVER . . . . . . **NiB $270 Ex $204 Gd $90**
Solid frame. Caliber: .38 Special. Five-round cylinder, 4-in. bbl., 9-in. overall. Weight: 30 oz. Fixed sights. Blued or nickel finish. Plastic grips. Made 1975-77.

SAFETY HAMMER
DA REVOLVER . . . . **NiB $342 Ex $170 Gd $105**
Hinged frame. Calibers: .22 LR, .32 S&W, .32 S&W Long, .38 S&W. Seven-round cylinder in .22 cal.,or 6-rnd. (.32 S&W Long), 5-rnd. (.32 S&W, .38 S&W). bbl. lengths: 2, 3, 3.25, 4, 5 or 6 in. Weight w/4-in. bbl.: 15 oz. (.22, .32 S&W), 19.5 oz. (.32 S&W Long) or 19 oz. (.38 S&W). Fixed sights. Blued or nickel finish. Hard rubber, rnd. butt grips or square butt, rubber or walnut grips available. Note: .32 S&W Long and .38 S&W models built on heavy frame. Made 1892-1950.

SAFETY HAMMERLESS
DA REVOLVER . . . . **NiB $337 Ex $219 Gd $129**
Similar to the Safety Hammer Model except w/shrouded hammerless frame. Made 1895-1950.

SIDEWINDER
DA REVOLVER . . . . **NiB $281 Ex $179 Gd $110**
Solid frame. Caliber: .22 LR. Six- or 8-rnd. cylinder, bbl. lengths: 4.75, 6 in.; 11.25 in. overall (w/ 6-in. bbl.). Weight: 31 oz. (w/ 6-in. bbl.). Fixed sights. Blued or nickel finish w/ plastic staghorn grips or color-casehardened frame w/walnut grips. Note: Cylinder capacity changed from 8 to 6 rounds in 1975. Made 1961-78

SIDEWINDER "S" . . . . **NiB $281 Ex $179 Gd $110**
Same as Sidewinder except has interchangeable cylinders in .22 LR and .22 WMR, adj. sights. Intro. 1974. Disc.

SPORTSMAN
DA REVOLVER . . . . **NiB $222 Ex $165 Gd $109**
Solid frame. Caliber: .22 LR. Six-round cylinder. Bbl. lengths: 4.75-, 6-in., 10.75 in. overall (w/ 6-in. bbl.). Weight: 30.5 oz. (w/ 6-in. bbl.). Fixed sights. Blued finish. Plastic grips. Made 1974-76.

SUPERSHOT .22 DA
REVOLVER . . . . **NiB $273 Ex $175 Gd $119**
Hinged frame. Caliber: .22 LR. Seven-round cylinder, 6-in. bbl. Fixed sights. Blued finish. Checkered walnut grips. This earlier model does not have counterbored chambers as in the Supershot Sealed 8. Made 1929-49.

SUPERSHOT 9
DA REVOLVER . . . . **NiB $273 Ex $175 Gd $119**
Same as Supershot Sealed 8 except has nine non-counterbored chambers. Made 1929-49.

SUPERSHOT
MODEL 844 DA . . . . **NiB $336 Ex $204 Gd $129**
Hinged frame. Caliber: .22 LR. Eight-round cylinder, bbl. lengths: 4.5- or 6-in., 9.25 in. overall (w/ 4.5-in. bbl.). Weight: 27 oz. (4.5-in. bbl.). Adj. sights. Blued finish. Checkered walnut one-piece grip. Made 1955-56.

SUPERSHOT SEALED
8 DA REVOLVER . . . . **NiB $316 Ex $180 Gd $140**
Hinged frame. Caliber: .22 LR. Eight-round cylinder, 6-in. bbl., 10.75 in. overall. Weight: 24 oz. Adj. target sights. Blued finish. Checkered walnut grips. Postwar model does not have adj. finger rest as earlier version. Made 1931-57.

SWING-OUT DA REVOLVER
Calibers: .22 LR, .22 WMR, .32 S&W Long, .38 Special. Six-round cylinder in .22, 5-rnd. in .32 and .38. Two, 3-, 4-in. plain bbl., or 4- 6-in. VR bbl., 8.75 in. overall (w/ 4-in. bbl.). Fixed or adj. sights. Blue or nickel finish. Walnut grips. Made in 1977.
w/plain barrel, fixed sights . . . . **NiB $220 Ex $158 Gd $115**
w/VR, adj. sights . . . . **NiB $204 Ex $148 Gd $110**

TARGET 9 DA REVOLVER . . . . . **NiB $265 Ex $180 Gd $135**
Same as Target Sealed 8 except has nine non-counterbored chambers. Made 1929-46.

TARGET SEALED
8 DA REVOLVER . . . . **NiB $273 Ex $166 Gd $135**
Solid frame. Caliber: .22 LR. Eight-round cylinder, bbl. lengths: 6- and 10-in. 10.75 in. overall (w/ 6-in. bbl.). Weight: 24 oz. (w/ 6-in. bbl.). Fixed sights. Blued finish. Checkered walnut grips. Made 1931-57.

TRIGGER-COCKING
SA TARGET . . . . **NiB $321 Ex $239 Gd $187**
Hinged frame. First pull on trigger cocks hammer, second pull releases hammer. Caliber: .22 LR. Eight-round cylinder, counterbored chambers, 6-in. bbl., 10.75 in. overall. Weight: 24 oz. Adj. target sights. Blued finish. Checkered walnut grips. Made 1940-47.

Iver Johnson
Model 67 Viking

Iver Johnson
Model 67S Viking Snub

Iver Johnson
Safety Hammer

KAHR ARMS — Greeley, PA
Formerly Pearl River, New York. Manufacturing in Worcester, MA.

K SERIES
Semiauto. DAO. Steel frame. Caliber: 9mm, .40 S&W, or .45 ACP. Seven-round magazine, 3.5-in. bbl., 6 in. overall. Weight: 24 oz. Fixed sights. Matte black, electroless nickel, Birdsong Black-T or matte stainless finish. Wraparound textured polymer or hardwood grips. Made 1994-2003. K40 .40 S&W models discontinued 2020.
Duo-Tone finish . . . . **NiB $587 Ex $464 Gd $321**
Electroless nickel finish . . . . . . **NiB $657 Ex $577 Gd $395**
Black-T finish . . . . **NiB $740 Ex $602 Gd $464**
Matte stainless finish . . . . **NiB $785 Ex $631 Gd $453**
Kahr Lady K9 model . . . . **NiB $530 Ex $345 Gd $270**
Elite model . . . . **NiB $836 Ex $610 Gd $399**
Tritium Night Sights, add **$100**
KP45 Model (.45 ACP), add **$100**
E9 model (economy version, made 1997,
reintro. 2003), deduct **$100**

CT SERIES . . . . **NiB $390 Ex $295 Gd $215**
Semiauto. DA/SA. Polymer frame. Caliber: .380, 9mm or .40 S&W, 8-rnd. magazine (9mm), 4-in. bbl. Made 2015 to present. CT40 .40 S&W discontinued 2020.

CT380 (.380 caliber), deduct **10%**

P SERIES . . . . **NiB $660 Ex $510 Gd $365**
Semiauto. DA/SA. Polymer frame. Caliber: .380, 9mm or .40 S&W, 6-rnd. magazine, 2.5-in. bbl. Made 2010 to present.
P380 (.380 caliber), deduct **15%**
P40 (.40 S&W caliber), deduct **10%**
P45 (.45 ACP caliber), add **5%**

PM SERIES. . . . . **NiB $690 Ex $520 Gd $380**
Semiauto. DA/SA. Polymer frame. Caliber: 9mm, .40 S&W or .45 Auto; 6- or 7-rnd. magazine; 3-in. bbl. Weight: 16 oz. Made 2003 to present.
PM40 (.40 S&W caliber), deduct **5%**
PM45 (.45 ACP caliber), add **10%**

CW SERIES . . . . **NiB $390 Ex $300 Gd $220**
Semiauto. DAO. Caliber: .380, 9mm, .40 S&W, .45 ACP. Seven-round magazine (9mm Para), 3.6-in. bbl., 6 in. overall. Weight: 15.8 oz. Fixed sights. Textured black polymer frame, matte stainless steel slide. Made 2005-present (9mm), 2008-20 (.40 S&W), 2005-present (.45 ACP), 2013-present (.380).
.380 caliber, deduct **5%**

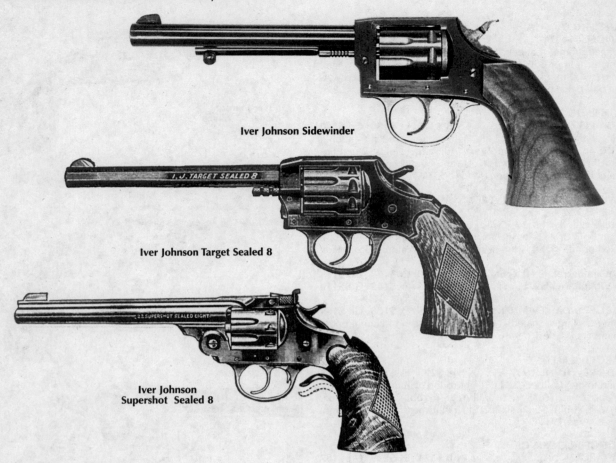

Iver Johnson Sidewinder

Iver Johnson Target Sealed 8

**Iver Johnson
Supershot Sealed 8**

CM SERIES . . . . **NiB $400 Ex $350 Gd $250**
Semiauto. DAO. Caliber: .380, 9mm, .40 S&W, .45 ACP. Six-round magazine (9mm Para), 3-in. bbl., 6 in. overall. Weight: 15.8 oz. Fixed sights. Textured black polymer frame, matte stainless steel slide. Made 2011-present (9mm), 2012-20 (.40 S&W), 2013-present (.380, .45 ACP).

MK MICRO SERIES . . . . **NiB $650 Ex $520 Gd $430**
Semiauto. DAO. Caliber: 9mm Para., .40 S&W. Six-round magazine (9mm para), 3-in. bbl., 5.5 in. overall. Weight: 15.8 oz. Fixed sights., Matte stainless steel slide and frame. Made 1998-99 (9mm para), intro. 1999 (.40 S&W).
MK40 Micro (.40 S&W, 2000-20), add **$100**

T SERIES . . . . **NiB $730 Ex $560 Gd $405**
Semiauto. DAO. Caliber: 9mm Para., .40 S&W. 8-rnd. magazine (9mm para), 4-in. bbl., 6.5 in. overall. Weight: 26 oz. Fixed sights., Matte stainless steel slide and frame, wood grips. Made 2002-present (9mm para), 2004-20. (.40 S&W).

TP SERIES . . . . **NiB $700 Ex $615 Gd $480**
Similar to T series except polymer frame and matte stainless steel slide. TP9 (9mm, 2004-14, reintro. 2017-20), TP40 (.40 S&W, 2006-14, reintro. 2017-20), TP45 (.45 Auto, 2007-14, reintro. 2017-20).
TP9 Gen2 (4-in. bbl., 2015-17), add **18%**
TP9 Gen2 (5-in. bbl., 2015-17), add **20%**
TP9 Gen2 (6-in. bbl., 2015-17), add **90%**
TP40, deduct **15%**
TP45, deduct **15%**

TP45 Gen2 (5-in. bbl., 2015-17), add **20%**
TP45 Gen2 (6-in. bbl., 2015-17), add **90%**

KBI, INC — Harrisburg, PA

MODEL PSP-25 AUTO PISTOL . . . . **NiB $308 Ex $244 Gd $157**
Caliber: .25 ACP. Six-round magazine, 2.13-in. bbl., 4.13 in. overall. Weight: 9.5 oz. All-steel construction w/dual safety system. Made 1994.

KEL-TEC CNC INDUSTRIES, INC. — Cocoa, FL

P-11 . . . . **NiB $290 Ex $200 Gd $160**
Semiauto. DAO. Caliber: 9mm. 10-rnd. magazine, 3.1- in. bbl., 5.6 in. overall. Weight: 14 oz. Blade front sight, drift adjustable rear. Aluminum frame w/steel slide. Checkered black, gray, or green polymer grips. Matte blue, nickel, stainless steel or Parkerized finish. Made 1995-2019.
Parkerized finish, add **$75**
Nickel finish (disc. 1995) add **$75**
Stainless finish, (1996 to date) add **$75**
Tritium Night Sights, add **$90**
.40 S&W conversion kit, add **$204**

CP33 . . . . **NIB $505 EX $530 GD $330**
Semiauto, polymer frame. Cal.: .22 LR; 33-rnd magazine. Bbl.: 5.5 in. threaded. Textured polymer grips. Optic ready. 10.6 in. overall. Weight: 1.5 lbs. Matte black finish. Mfg. 2019-date.

Kahr Model K9

Kel-Tec Model P-11

PLR-16 . . . . **NiB $590 Ex $460 Gd $350**
M-16-type gas operated. Cal.: .223 Rem., 10-rnd. mag. Bbl.: 9.2 in. Upper w/Picatinny accessory rail. Black composite frame. Weight: 3.2 lbs.

P15 . . . . **NiB $425 Ex $400 Gd $330**
Semiauto, polymer frame. Cal.: 9mm; 15-rnd magazine. Bbl.: 4 in. Textured polymer grips. Fixed sights. 6.6 in. overall. Weight: 14 oz. Matte black finish. Mfg. 2022-date.

P17 . . . . **NiB $175 Ex $155 Gd $130**
Semiauto, polymer frame. Caliber: .22 LR; 16-rnd magazine. Barrel: 3.8 in. Textured polymer grips. Fixed sights. 6.7 in. overall. Weight: 11.2 oz. Matte black finish.

PLR-22 . . . . **NiB $335 Ex $265 Gd $170**
Similar to PLR-16 except in .22 LR; 26-rnd. mag. Weight: 2.8 lbs.

PF-9 . . . . **NiB $290 Ex $198 Gd $143**
Similar to P-11, cal.: 9 mm Para. Bbl.: 3.1 in. 7-rnd. mag., lower accessory rail. Black finish. Weight: 12.7 oz. Limited production in 2006, reintro. 2008-19.
Parkerized finish, add $50
Hard chrome finish, add $65

PMR-30 . . . . **NiB $500 Ex $370 Gd $300**
Cal.: .22 Mag. Bbl.: 4.3 in. 30-rnd. mag, blowback action, manual safety. Picatinny accessory rail. Steel slide and bbl., fiber optic sights. Weight: 19.5 oz. Made 2010 to date.

KIMBER MANUFACTURING, INC. — Troy, AL

Formerly Kimber of America, Inc.

- REVOLVERS -

K6S SERIES
Revolver, DAO. Caliber: .357 Magnum; 6-shot cylinder. Barrel: 2- or 3-in. Sights: fixed low profile. Stainless steel frame finish. Rubber or walnut grips. Weight: 23 oz. 2016-date.
Stainless model . . . . **NiB $745 Ex $655 Gd $605**
First Edition model (2-in. bbl., bright stainless finish,
   pau ferro grip, 2016-17) . . . . . **NiB $990 Ex $855 Gd $680**
CDP model (2-in. bbl., Tritium sights,
   rosewood grip) . . . . **NiB $990 Ex $855 Gd $680**
DC model (2-in. bbl., Tritium sights, G10 or
   Crimson Trace laser grip) . . . . **NiB $990 Ex $855 Gd $680**
DCR model (2-in. bbl., fiber optic sights,
   rosewood grip) . . . . **NiB $955 Ex $880 Gd $680**
TLE model (2- or 3-in. bbl., Tritium sights,
   G10 finger groove grip) . . . . . . **NiB $855 Ex $755 Gd $580**
Royal Special Edition (2-in. bbl., 3-dot sights,
   G10 ivory grip, blued) . . . . . **NiB $1455 Ex $1280 Gd $990**

K6S DASA SERIES
Revolver, DA/SA trigger. Caliber: .357 Magnum; 6-shot cylinder. Barrel: 2-, 3- or 4-in. Fixed low profile or adj. target sights. Stainless steel frame. Extended walnut grip. Weight: 23 to 29 oz. 2019-date.
Stainless model (2- or 3-in. bbl.) . . **NiB $830 Ex $730 Gd $565**
Combat model (4-in. bbl.,
   fixed sights) . . . . **NiB $845 Ex $740 Gd $575**
Target model (4-in. bbl.,
   adj. sights) . . . . **NiB $845 Ex $740 Gd $575**

P-32 . . . . **NiB $270 Ex $195 Gd $145**
Semiauto. DAO. Cal.: .32 ACP. Internal block safety. 7-rnd. mag. Bbl.: 2.68 in.; Parkerized, blue, or chrome finish. Choice of ivory or colored grips. Weight: 6.6 oz. Made 1999 to present.

P-3AT . . . . **NiB $280 Ex $180 Gd $95**
Similar to P-32 except. .380 ACP. Bbl.: 2.76 in. 6-rnd. mag. Black composite frame with Parkerized steel slide. Weight: 8.3 oz. Mfg. 2003-19.

P-40 . . . . **NiB $290 Ex $175 Gd $88**
Semiauto, double-action. 9- or 10-rnd. mag. Composite frame with steel slide. Bbl.: 3.3 in. Parkerized, blue, or chrome finish. Made 1999-2001.
Parkerized finish, add $50
Hard chrome finish, add $70

P50 . . . . **NiB $905 Ex $805 Gd $600**
Semiauto, polymer frame. Cal.: 5.7x28mm; 50-rnd magazine. Bbl.: 9.6 in. Textured polymer grips. Optic ready. 15 in. overall. Weight: 3.2 lbs. Matte black finish. Mfg. 2021-date.

Kimber Model Classic .45

Texas Edition (2-in. bbl., engraved,
G10 ivory grip) . . . . **NiB $1155 Ex $1010 Gd $785**

- *SEMIAUTO PISTOLS* -

MODEL CLASSIC .45

Similar to Government 1911 built on steel, polymer or alloy full-size or compact frame. Caliber: .45 ACP. Seven-, 8-, 10- or 14-rnd. magazine, 4- or 5-in. bbl., 7.7 or 8.75 in. overall. Weight: 28 oz. (Compact LW), 34 oz. (Compact or Polymer) or .38 oz. (Custom FS). McCormick low-profile combat or Kimber adj. target sights. Blued, matte black oxide or stainless finish. Checkered custom wood or black synthetic grips. Made 1994-2001. NOTE: Early Kimber 1911 pistols were called "Classic" models. The "Classic" was dropped in 1989.

Custom (matte black) . . . . **NiB $882 Ex $599 Gd $431**
Custom Royal (polished blue) . . . . **NiB $774 Ex $612 Gd $443**
Custom stainless (satin stainless) . . . **NiB $737 Ex $577 Gd $439**
Custom Target (matte black) . . . **NiB $755 Ex $581 Gd $453**
Target Gold Match
(polished blue) . . . . **NiB $1020 Ex $755 Gd $587**
Target stainless Match
(polished stainless) . . . . **NiB $852 Ex $669 Gd $474**
Polymer (matte black) . . . . **NiB $852 Ex $669 Gd $474**
Polymer Stainless
(satin stainless slide) . . . . **NiB $967 Ex $784 Gd $577**
Polymer Target
(matte black slide) . . . . **NiB $918 Ex $744 Gd $536**
Compact (matte black) . . . . **NiB $644 Ex $541 Gd $377**
Compact stainless
(satin stainless) . . . . **NiB $714 Ex $559 Gd $437**
Compact LW (matte
black w/alloy frame) . . . . **NiB $733 Ex $577 Gd $408**

SERIES II MODELS

Similar to Classic 1911 models except includes firing pin block safety and denoted with "II" following all model names. Size configurations vary per model and include from smallest to largest: Micro (2.75-in. bbl., micro frame), Ultra (3-in. bbl., short frame), Ultra+ (3-in. bbl., full size frame), Compact (4-in. bbl., short frame), Pro (4-in. bbl., full size frame), Custom (5-in. bbl., full size frame). Made 2001 to date.

Aegis II (intro. 2006) . . . . . . **NiB $1200 Ex $1140 Gd $840**
CDP II (intro. 2000) . . . . **NiB $1150 Ex $1095 Gd $805**
Compact II . . . . **NiB $960 Ex $912 Gd $500**
Covert II (intro. 2007) . . . . . **NiB $1450 Ex $1100 Gd $650**
Crimson Cary II
(laser grip) . . . . **NiB $1050 Ex $900 Gd $735**

Custom II . . . . **NiB $730 Ex $525 Gd $330**
Custom II Stainless . . . . **NiB $855 Ex $655 Gd $365**
Custom Royal II . . . . **NiB $1900 Ex $1000 Gd $580**
Eclipse II (intro. 2002) . . . . **$1100 Ex $1045 Gd $570**
Gold Match II . . . . **NiB $1300 Ex $1000 Gd $580**
Master Carry II (intro. 2013) . . . . **NiB $1330 Ex $1265 Gd $931**
Micro Carry
(intro. 2013, .380 ACP) . . . . **NiB $580 Ex $475 Gd $375**
Raptor II (intro. 2004) . . . . . **NiB $1300 Ex $1235 Gd $910**
Super Carry II (intro. 2010) . . . . **NiB $1350 Ex $1285 Gd $945**
Tactical II (intro. 2003) . . . . . **NiB $1130 Ex $1075 Gd $795**
Ultra Carry II (intro. 1999) . . . . **NiB $800 Ex $760 Gd $560**
Custom Royal II . . . . **NiB $1900 Ex $1000 Gd $580**

EVO SP Series . . . . **NiB $730 Ex $640 Gd $505**
Semiauto. Micro compact striker fire. Caliber: 9mm, 7-rnd magazine. Barrel: 3.16-in. Steel slide, alloy frame. Weight: 19 oz. Length: 6.1-in. Stainless slide, black frame. 2018 to date.
CDP model (gray frame/black slide,
rosewood grip) . . . . **NiB $805 Ex $705 Gd $555**
CS model (gray finish,
black G10 grip) . . . . **NiB $900 Ex $790 Gd $615**
Raptor model (silver finish,
scale texture wood grip) . . . . . . **NiB $855 Ex $755 Gd $580**
Select model (black or stainless finish, black or
brown nylon grip) . . . . **NiB $515 Ex $455 Gd $355**
TLE model (black finish,
green G10 grip) . . . . **NiB $790 Ex $690 Gd $555**

MODEL R7 MAKO . . . . **NiB $590 Ex $500 Gd $480**
Semiauto. triker firer. Cal.: 9mm, 10-, 11- and 12-rnd. magazine. Bbl.: 3.3-in. bbl. Frame: Polymer. Sights: Steel fixed, 3-dot; optic ready. Finish: Matte black. Weight: 19.5 oz. Length: 6.2 in. Made 2022 to date.

MODEL MICRO SERIES

Scaled down 1911-style. Semiauto. SA. Caliber: .380 ACP, 7-rnd magazine. 2.75-in. bbl. Frame: aluminum. Sights: steel fixed. Finish: numerous. Grip: numerous. Weight: 13 oz. Length: 5.6 in. Made 2012 to date.

Laser grip, add **$200**
Bel Air (turquoise frame/stainless slide,
ivory micarta grip) . . . . **NiB $802 Ex $790 Gd $690**
Carry Advocate
(two-tone finish, brown or purple grip) . **NiB $714 Ex $700**
Gd $680
Crimson Carry (two-tone finish,
laser grip) . . . . **NiB $839 Ex $800 Gd $710**
CDP (two-tone, rosewood grip) **NiB $869 Ex $800 Gd $610**
DC (matte black, rosewood grip) . . . **NiB $877 Ex $810 Gd $710**
Diamond (matte stainless frame/engraved slide,
ivory micarta grip) . . . . **NiB $1013 Ex $1000 Gd $980**
Raptor (matte black,
zebrawood grip) . . . . **NiB $815 Ex $800 Gd $780**
Raptor Stainless
(stainless finish) . . . . **NiB $842 Ex $810 Gd $790**
RCP (matte black,
rosewood grip) . . . . **NiB $775 Ex $710 Gd $680**
Sapphire (stainless frame/blue engraved slide,
blue G10 grip) . . . . **NiB $1013 Ex $1000 Gd $980**
Stainless (stainless finish, rosewood
grip) . . . . **NiB $597 Ex $560 Gd $500**
Two-Tone (rosewood grip) . . . . **NiB $597 Ex $580 Gd $500**

MODEL MICRO 9 SERIES

Similar to Micro except in 9mm, 6-rnd. magazine. Made 2015 to date.

Kimber Micro 9 Stainless

Kolibri Pistol (smallest commercial centerfire pistol)

Kimber Solo Carry

Crimson Carry (two-tone finish,
laser grip) . . . . **NiB $894 Ex $870 Gd $720**
Stainless (stainless finish,
rosewood grip) . . . . **NiB $654 Ex $610 Gd $570**
Two-Tone finish
(rosewood grip) . . . . **NiB $654 Ex $610 Gd $570**

MODEL SOLO SERIES
Hammerless design. Semiauto. DAO striker firer. Caliber: .380 ACP, 7-rnd magazine. 2.7-in. bbl. Frame: aluminum. Sights: steel fixed, 3-dot. Finish: numerous. Grip: numerous. Weight: 17 oz. Length: 5.6 in. Made 2012-17.
Laser grip, add **$200**
Carry (black frame/stainless slide,
black checkered synthetic) . . . **NiB $815 Ex $800 Gd $770**
CDP LG (two-tone, laser grip) . . . **NiB $1223 Ex $1100 Gd $920**
Crimson Carry (two-tone finish,
laser grip) . . . . **NiB $1073 Ex $1000 Gd $960**
DC (matte black, black checkered
micarta) . . . . **NiB $904 Ex $890 Gd $800**
Sapphire (stainless frame/blue engraved slide,
blue G10 grip) . . . . **NiB $1291 Ex $1200 Gd $990**
Stainless (stainless finish, black
checkered synthetic) . . . . . . **NiB $815 Ex $800 Gd $770**

KOLIBRI — Austria-Hungary
Smallest commercially available centerfire Semiauto pistol.

KOLIBRI PISTOL . . . . **NiB $2500 Ex $1940 Gd $1490**
Calibers: 2.7mm Kolibri Car Pistol or 2.7x9mm Kolibri w/5-rnd. magazine. Bbls: 1.25-in. Overall Len.: 3-in. Weight: 7.7 oz. Finish: blued or nickel. Grips: checkered wood or plastic. Imported 1914 to 1938.
w/original case, add **$310**

KORTH — Lollar, Germany
Previously Ratzeburg, Germany. Currently imported by Korth USA (Earl's Repair Service, Tewkberry, MA). Previously by Keng's Firearms Specialty, Inc., Beeman Precision Arms; Osborn Beeman Precision Arms; Osborne's and Mandall Shooting Supply.

REVOLVERS COMBAT, SPORT, TARGET
Calibers: .357 Mag. and .22 LR w/interchangeable combination cylinders of .357 Mag./9mm Para. or .22 LR/.22 WMR also .22 Jet, .32 S&W and .32 H&R Mag. Bbls: 2.5-, 3-, 4-in. (combat) and 5.25- or 6-in. (target). Weight: 33 to 42 oz. Blued, stainless, matte silver or polished silver finish. Checkered walnut grips. Imported 1967 to date.
Standard rimfire model . . . . **NiB $4590 Ex $2735 Gd $1895**
Standard centerfire model . **NiB $6899 Ex $5100 Gd $4029**
ISU Match Target model . . . **NiB $7429 Ex $5433 Gd $3329**
Custom stainless finish, add **$485**
Matte silver finish, add **$689**
Polished silver finish, add **$950**

SEMIAUTO PISTOL
Calibers: 30 Luger, 9mm Para., .357 SIG, .40 S&W, 9x21mm. 10- or 14-rnd. magazine, 4- or 5-in. bbl., all-steel construction,

Korth Sport Model

recoil-operated. Ramp front sight, adj. rear. Blued, stainless, matte silver or polished silver finish. Checkered walnut grips. Limited import from 1988 .

Standard model . . . . NiB $6495 Ex $5040 Gd $3934
Matte silver finish, add $332
Polished silver finish, add $791

KRISS USA — Chesapeake, VA

North American extension of the Switzerland based KRISS Group.

MODEL VECTOR SPD . . . . . NiB $1230 EX $930 GD $680
Semiauto. Multi-caliber platform. Closed bolt delayed blow-beck system design for minimal recoil. Caliber: 9mm or .45 ACP, 17- or 15-rnd 9mm, 13- or 25-rnd .45 ACP, uses Glock magazine. 5.5-in. bbl., threaded muzzle. Frame: polymer. Sights: flip-up adj. Finish: matte black. Grip: textured polymer. Weight: 5.9 lbs. Length: 16.75 in. Imported from 2011 to date.

Alpine, FDE, or ODG finish, add $70
Gen II models, add 10%

LAHTI — Sweden & Finland

Mfd. by Husqvarna Vapenfabriks A. B. Huskvarna, Sweden, and Valtion Kivaar Tedhas ("VKT") Jyväskyla, Finland.

MODEL 40 AND L-35
Caliber: 9mm Para. Eight-round magazine, 4.75-in. bbl., weight: About 46 oz. Fixed sights. Blued finish. Plastic grips. Specifications given are those of the Swedish Model 40 but also apply in general to the Finnish Model L-35, which differs only slightly. A considerable number of Swedish Lahti pistols were imported and sold in the U.S. The Finnish model, somewhat better made, is rare. Four variation of L-35 were built. Finnish Model L-35 adopted 1935. Swedish Model 40 adopted 1940, mfd. through 1944.

Finnish L-35 model (1st Variation,
S/N range: 1001-3700) . . . . NiB $5255 Ex $3755 Gd $2500
(2nd Variation, S/N range: 3701-4700), deduct 15%
(3rd Variation, S/N range: 4701-6800), deduct 90%
(4th Variation, S/N range: 6801-9100), deduct 100%
Swedish 40 model . . . . NiB $850 Ex $430 Gd $360

L.A.R. MANUFACTURING, INC. — West Jordan, UT

MARK I GRIZZLY WIN. MAG. . . . . NiB $1255 Ex $1010 Gd $710
Similar to 1911 platform. Calibers: .357 Mag., .45 ACP, .45 Win. Mag. Seven-round magazine. Bbl. Len.: 5.4-, 6.5-,

Lahti Automatic Pistol

8- or 10-in. 10.5 in. overall. Weight: 48 oz. Fully adj. sights. Checkered rubber combat-style grips. Blued finish. Made 1983-99, 8- or 10-in. bbl. made 1987-99.

chrome finish, add $200
w/conversion unit, add $700
MK II model (fixed sights), deduct $200

MARK IV GRIZZLY . . . . NiB $1755 Ex $1355 Gd $605
Same general specifications as the Mark I except chambered for .44 Magnum, 5.5- or 6.5-in. bbl., beavertail grip safety, matte blued finish. Made 1991-99.

MARK V . . . . NiB $2455 Ex $1955 Gd $1505
Similar to the Mark I except chambered in .50 Action Express. Six-round magazine, 5.4- or 6.5-in. bbl., 10.6 in. overall (w/ 5.4-in. bbl.). Weight: 56 oz. Checkered walnut grips. Made 1993-99.

LASERAIM TECHNOLOGIES, INC. — Little Rock, AR

SERIES I SA AUTO PISTOL
Calibers: .40 S&W, .45 ACP, 10mm. Seven or 8- rnd. magazine, 3.875- or 5.5-in. dual-port compensated bbl., 8.75 or 10.5 in. overall. Weight: 46 or 52 oz. Fixed sights w/Laseraim or adjustable Millet sights. Textured black composition grips. Extended slide release, ambidExtrous safety and beveled magazine well. Stainless or matte black Teflon finish. Made 1993-99.

Series I w/adjustable sights . . . . NiB $362 Ex $255 Gd $188
Series I w/fixed sights . . . . NiB $362 Ex $255 Gd $188
Series I w/fixed sights (HotDot) . . NiB $479 Ex $270 Gd $203
Series I Dream Team (RedDot) . . NiB $479 Ex $ 270 Gd $203
Series I Illusion (Laseraim) . . . . NiB $479 Ex $270 Gd $203

L.A.R. Mark I Grizzly

**Laseraim
Series II**

SERIES II SA AUTO PISTOL
Similar to Series I except w/stainless finish and no bbl., compensator. Made 1993-96.
Series II w/adjustable sights . . . NiB $530 Ex $365 Gd $265
Series II w/fixed sights . . . . NiB $530 Ex $365 Gd $265
Series II Dream Team . . . . NiB $602 Ex $437 Gd $279
Series II Illusion . . . . NiB $540 Ex $439 Gd $321

SERIES III SA AUTO PISTOL
Similar to Series II except w/serrated slide and 5-in. compensated bbl., only. Made 1994. Disc.
Series III w/adjustable sights . . NiB $632 Ex $536 Gd $398
Series III w/fixed sights. . . . . . . NiB $632 Ex $599 Gd $362

VELOCITY SERIES SA AUTO PISTOL
Similar to Series I except chambered for .357 Sig. or .400 Cor-Bon, 3.875-in. unported bbl., (compact) or 5.5-in. dual-port compensated bbl. Made 1993-99.
Compact model (unported). . . . NiB $362 Ex $290 Gd $204
Government model (ported). . . NiB $362 Ex $290 Gd $204
w/wireless laser (HotDot), add. $175

LIGNOSE — Suhl, Germany
Aktien-Gesellschaft "Lignose" Abteilung

The following Lignose pistols were manufactured from 1920 to the mid-1930s. They were also marketed under the Bergmann name.

EINHAND MODEL 2A
POCKET AUTO PISTOL . . . . . . NiB $400 Ex $230 Gd $170
As the name implies, this pistol is designed for one-hand operation, pressure on a "trigger" at the front of the guard retracts the slide. Caliber: .25 Auto. (6.35 mm). Six-round magazine, 2-in. bbl., 4.75 in. overall. Weight: About 14 oz. Blued finish. Hard rubber grips.

MODEL 2 POCKET
AUTO PISTOL. . . . . NiB $330 Ex $220 Gd $175
Conventional Browning type. Same general specifications as Einhand Model 2A but lacks the one-hand operation.

EINHAND MODEL
3A POCKET AUTO PISTOL. . . . NiB $479 Ex $369 Gd $270
Same as the Model 2A except has longer grip, 9-rnd. magazine, weight: About 16 oz.

LLAMA — Vitoria, Spain

Manufactured by Gabilondo y Cia, Vitoria, Spain, imported by S.G.S., Wanamassa, New Jersey.

NOTE: *For ease in finding a particular Llama handgun, the listings are divided into two groupings: Automatic Pistols (below) and Revolvers, which follow. For a complete listing of Llama handguns, please refer to the index.*

-AUTOMATIC PISTOLS -

MODEL IIIA
AUTOMATIC PISTOL . . . . NiB $337 Ex $170 Gd $109
Caliber: .380 Auto. Seven-round magazine, 3.69-in. bbl., 6.5 in. overall. Weight: 23 oz. Adj. target sights. Blued finish. Plastic grips. Intro. 1951. Disc.

Lignose Model 3A

MODELS IIIA, XA, XV DELUXE
Same as standard Model IIIA, XA and XV except engraved w/blued or chrome finish and simulated pearl grips.
Chrome-engraved finish . . . . . . NiB $365 Ex $306 Gd $219
Blue-engraved finish . . . . NiB $356 Ex $290 Gd $204

MODEL VIII
AUTOMATIC PISTOL . . . . NiB $377 Ex $306 Gd $255
Caliber: .38 Super. Nine-round magazine, 5-in. bbl., 8.5 in. overall. Weight: 40 oz. Fixed sights. Blued finish. Wood grips. Intro. in 1952. Disc.

MODELS VIII, IXA, XI DELUXE
Same as standard Models VIII, IXA and XI except finish (chrome engraved or blued engraved) and simulated pearl grips. Disc. 1984.
Chrome-engraved finish . . . . . . NiB $377 Ex $290 Gd $190
Blue-engraved finish . . . . NiB $377 Ex $290 Gd $190

MODEL IXA
AUTOMATIC PISTOL . . . . NiB $377 Ex $290 Gd $190
Same as model VIII except .45 Auto, 7-rnd. magazine,

MODEL XA
AUTOMATIC PISTOL . . . . NiB $377 Ex $290 Gd $190
Same as model IIIA except .32 Auto, 8-rnd. magazine,

MODEL XI
AUTOMATIC PISTOL . . . . NiB $377 Ex $290 Gd $190
Same as model VIII except 9mm Para.

MODEL XV
AUTOMATIC PISTOL . . . . NiB $321 Ex $255 Gd $170
Same as model XA except .22 LR.

MODELS BE-IIIA,
BE-XA, BE-XV . . . . NiB $530 Ex $332 Gd $235
Same as models IIIA, XA and XV except w/blued-engraved finish. Made 1977-84.

MODELS BE-VIII,
BE-IXA, BE-XI DELUXE . . . . NiB $530 Ex $398 Gd $281
Same as models VIII, IXA and XI except w/blued-engraved finish. Made 1977-84.

MODELS C-IIIA, C-XA, C-XV . . NiB $408 Ex $365 Gd $259
Same as models IIIA, XA and XV except in satin chrome.

MODELS C-VIII, C-IXA, C-XI . . NiB $475 Ex $357 Gd $244
Same as models VIII, IXA and XI except in satin chrome.

**MODELS CE-IIIA,
CE-XA, CE-XV** . . . . NiB $398 Ex $347 Gd $230
Same as models IIIA, XA and XV except w/chrome engraved finish. Made 1977-84.

**MODELS CE-VIII,
CE-IXA, CE-XI** . . . . NiB $475 Ex $357 Gd $244
Same as models VIII, IXA and XI, w/except chrome engraved finish. Made 1977-84.

**COMPACT FRAME
AUTO PISTOL** . . . . NiB $345 Ex $270 Gd $204
Calibers: 9mm Para., .38 Super, .45 Auto. Seven-, 8- or 9-rnd. magazine, 5-in. bbl., 7.88 in. overall. Weight: 34 oz. Blued, satin-chrome or Duo-Tone finishes. Made 1986-97. Duo-Tone disc. 1993.

**DUO-TONE LARGE
FRAME AUTO PISTOL** . . . . NiB $449 Ex $368 Gd $305
Caliber: .45 ACP. Seven-round magazine, 5-in. bbl., 8.5 in. overall. Weight: 36 oz. Adj. rear sight. Blued finished w/satin chrome. Polymer black grips. Made 1991-93.

**DUO-TONE SMALL
FRAME AUTO PISTOL** . . . . NiB $306 Ex $209 Gd $150
Calibers: .22 LR, .32 and .380 Auto. Seven- or 8-rnd. magazine, 3.69 in. bbl., 6.5 in. overall. Weight: 23 oz. Square-notch rear sight, Partridge-type front. Blued finish w/chrome. Made 1990-93.

MODEL G-IIIA DELUXE . . . NiB $2520 Ex $1944 Gd $1659
Same as Model IIIA except gold damascened w/simulated pearl grips. Disc. 1982.

LARGE-FRAME AUTOMATIC PISTOL (IXA)
Caliber: .45 Auto. 7-rnd. magazine, 5-in. bbl., weight: 2 lbs., 8 oz. Adj. rear sight, Partridge-type front. Walnut grips or teakwood on satin chrome model. Later models w/polymer grips.
Blued finish. . . . . NiB $369 Ex $258 Gd $198
Satin chrome finish . . . . NiB $538 Ex $444 Gd $290

**M-82 DA
AUTOMATIC PISTOL** . . . . NiB $587 Ex $398 Gd $270
Caliber: 9mm Para. 15-rnd. magazine, 4.25-in. bbl., 8 in. overall. Weight: 39 oz. Drift-adj. rear sight. Matte blued finish. Matte black polymer grips. Made 1988-93.

**M-87 COMPETITION
PISTOL** . . . . NiB $1029 Ex $816 Gd $634
Caliber: 9mm Para. 15-rnd. magazine, 5.5-in. bbl., 9.5 in. overall. Weight: 40 oz. Low-profile combat sights. Satin nickel finish. Matte black grip panels. Built-in ported compensator to minimize recoil and muzzle rise. Made 1989-93.

MICRO-MAX SA AUTOMATIC PISTOL
Caliber: .380 ACP. Seven-round magazine, 3.125-in. bbl., weight: 23 oz. Blade front sight, drift adjustable rear w/3-dot system. Matte blue or satin chrome finish. Checkered polymer grips. Imported from 1997 to 2005.

**Llama Model IIIA
Deluxe Chrome Engraved First Issue**

Llama Model XA First Issue

Llama Model Compact

Matte blue finish. . . . . NiB $281 Ex $204 Gd $165
Satin chrome finish . . . . NiB $288 Ex $230 Gd $219

MINI-MAX SA AUTOMATIC PISTOL
Calibers: 9mm, .40 S&W or .45 ACP. Six- or 8-rnd. magazine, 3.5-in. bbl., 8.3 in. overall. Weight: 35 oz. Blade front sight,

Llama Model C-XI

Llama Comanche I

Llama M-82 DA Auto

Llama MINI-MAX II

MINI-MAX II SA AUTOMATIC PISTOL
Cal: .45 ACP only. 10-rnd. mag., 3.625 in. bbl., 7.375 in. overall. Wt: 37 oz. Blade front sight, drift adj. rear w/3-dot system. Shortened bbl. and grip. Matte and Satin Chrome finish. Imp. 2005.
Matte blue finish............NiB $290 Ex $225 Gd $170
Satin chrome finish..........NiB $316 Ex $255 Gd $189

MAX-I SA AUTOMATIC PISTOL
Calibers: 9mm or .45 ACP. 7- or 9-rnd. magazine, 4.25- to 5.125 in. bbl., weight: 34 or 36 oz. Blade front sight, drift adj. rear w/3-dot system. Matte blue, Duo-Tone or satin chrome finish. Checkered black rubber grips. Imported from 1995 to 1999. Reintroduced 2016 to date.
Duo-Tone finish ....NiB $306 Ex $265 Gd $198
Matte blue finish............NiB $301 Ex $240 Gd $189
Satin chrome finish..........NiB $316 Ex $270 Gd $219

MAX-II SA AUTOMATIC PISTOL
Same as the MAX-I w/4.25 bbl. except w/10-rnd. mag. Weight 40 oz., made 2005.
Matte blue finish............NiB $306 Ex $265 Gd $198
Satin chrome finish..........NiB $332 Ex $270 Gd $219

OMNI 45 DOUBLE-ACTION
AUTOMATIC PISTOL ....NiB $437 Ex $291 Gd $220
Caliber: .45 Auto. Seven-round magazine, 4.25-in. bbl., 7.75 in. overall. Weight: 40 oz. Adj. rear sight, ramp front. Highly polished deep blued finish. Made 1984-86.

OMNI 9MM DOUBLE-ACTION
AUTOMATIC. ....NiB $469 Ex $347 Gd $290
Same general specifications as .45 Omni except chambered for 9mm w/13-rnd. magazine. Made 1983-86.

SINGLE-ACTION
AUTOMATIC PISTOL ....NiB $485 Ex $386 Gd $270
Calibers: .38 Super, 9mm, .45 Auto. Nine-round magazine (7-rnd. for .45 Auto), 5-in. bbl., 8.5 in. overall. Weight: 2 lbs., 8 oz. Intro. in 1981.

SMALL-FRAME AUTOMATIC PISTOL
Calibers: .380 Auto (7-rnd. magazine), .22 RF (8-rnd. magazine), 3.69-in. bbl., weight: 23 oz. Partridge-blade front sight, adj. rear. Blued or satin-chrome finish. Disc. 1997.
Blued finish.................NiB $255 Ex $204 Gd $165
Satin-chrome finish..........NiB $270 Ex $220 Gd $175

drift adjustable rear w/3-dot system. Matte blue, Duo-Tone or satin chrome finish. Checkered polymer grips. Imported 1996 to 2005. Reintroduced 2016 to date.
Duo-Tone finish ....NiB $290 Ex $204 Gd $158
Matte blue finish............NiB $306 Ex $220 Gd $170
Satin chrome finish..........NiB $326 Ex $240 Gd $190
Stainless (disc.) ....NiB $359 Ex $301 Gd $235

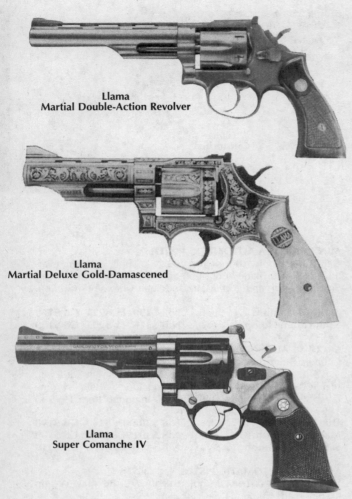

**Llama
Martial Double-Action Revolver**

**Llama
Martial Deluxe Gold-Damascened**

**Llama
Super Comanche IV**

Lorcin Model L-380

COMANCHE III . . . . NiB $306 Ex $219 Gd $144
Caliber: .357 Magnum. Six-round cylinder, 4-in. bbl., 9.25 in. overall. Weight: 36 oz. Adj. rear sight, ramp front. Blued finish. Checkered walnut grips. Made 1975-95. Note: Prior to 1977, this model was designated "Comanche."

COMANCHE III CHROME . . . . NiB $362 Ex $270 Gd $204
Same gen. specifications as Comanche III except has satin chrome finish, 4- or 6-in. bbl. Made 1975-95.

SUPER COMANCHE IV . . . . . . NiB $388 Ex $301 Gd $204
Caliber: .44 Magnum. Six-round cylinder, 6-in. bbl., 11.75 in. overall. Weight: 50 oz. Adj. rear sight, ramp front. Polished deep blued finish. Checkered walnut grips. Disc. 1998.

SUPER COMANCHE V . . . . NiB $362 Ex $270 Gd $214
Caliber: .357 Mag. Six-round cylinder, 4-, 6- or 8.5-in. bbl., weight: 48 oz. Ramped front blade sight, click-adj. Rear. Made 1980-88.

LORCIN ENGINEERING CO., INC. — Mira Loma, CA

**MODEL L-22
SEMIAUTO PISTOL** . . . . NiB $120 Ex $90 Gd $70
Caliber: 22 LR. Nine-round magazine, 2.5-in. bbl., 5.25 in. overall. Weight: 16 oz. Blade front sight, fixed notch rear w/3-dot system. Black Teflon or chrome finish. Black, pink or pearl composition grips. Made 1990-98.

MODEL L-25, LT-.25 SEMIAUTO PISTOL
Caliber: 25 ACP. Seven-round magazine, 2.4-in. bbl., 4.8 in. overall. Weight: 12 oz. (LT-25) or 14.5 oz. (L-25). Blade front sight, fixed rear. Black Teflon or chrome finish. Black, pink or pearl composition grips. Made 1989-98.
Model L-25 . . . . NiB $89 Ex $61 Gd $40
Model LT-25 . . . . NiB $79 Ex $50 Gd $35
Model Lady Lorcin . . . . NiB $81 Ex $55 Gd $35

**MODEL L-32
SEMIAUTO PISTOL** . . . . NiB $90 Ex $65 Gd $50
Caliber: 32 ACP. Seven-round magazine, 3.5-in. bbl., 6.6 in. overall. Weight: 27 oz. Blade front sight, fixed notch rear. Black Teflon or chrome finish. Black composition grips. Made 1992-98.

- REVOLVERS -

**MARTIAL DOUBLE-
ACTION REVOLVER** . . . . NiB $255 Ex $170 Gd $120
Calibers: .22 LR, .38 Special. Six-round cylinder, bbl. lengths: 4-in. (.38 Special only) or 6-in.; 11.25 in. overall (w/6-in. bbl.). Weight: About 36 oz. w/6-in. bbl. Target sights. Blued finish. Checkered walnut grips. Made 1969-76.

MARTIAL DOUBLE-ACTION DELUXE
Same as standard Martial except w/satin chrome, chrome-engraved, blued engraved or gold damascened finish. Simulated pearl grips. Made 1969-76.
Satin-chrome finish . . . . NiB $306 Ex $225 Gd $165
Chrome-engraved finish . . . . . . NiB $581 Ex $431 Gd $286
Blue-engraved finish . . . . NiB $638 Ex $453 Gd $332
Gold-damascened finish . . . NiB $2810 Ex $2647 Gd $2299

COMANCHE I . . . . NiB $270 Ex $204 Gd $160
Same general specifications as Martial .22. Made 1977-82.

COMANCHE II . . . . NiB $265 Ex $189 Gd $150
Same general specifications as Martial .38. Made 1977-82.

MODEL L-380 SEMIAUTO PISTOL

Caliber: .380 ACP. Seven- or 10-rnd. magazine, 3.5-in. bbl., 6.6 in. overall. Weight: 23 oz. Blade front sight, fixed notch rear. Matte Black finish. Grooved black composition grips. Made 1994-98.

Model L-380 (10-rnd.) . . . . **NiB $158 Ex $95 Gd $65**
Model L-380 (13-rnd.) . . . . **NiB $128 Ex $90 Gd $61**

MODEL L9MM SEMIAUTO PISTOL

Caliber: 9mm Parabellum. 10- or 13-rnd. magazine, 4.5-in. bbl., 7.5 in. overall. Weight: 31 oz. Blade front sight, fixed notch rear w/3-dot system. Black Teflon or chrome finish. Black composition grips. Made 1992-98.

Model L-9mm (7-rnd.) . . . . **NiB $158 Ex $95 Gd $65**
Model L-9mm (10-rnd.) . . . . **NiB $158 Ex $95 Gd $65**

O/U DERRINGER . . . . **NiB $198 Ex $105 Gd $70**
Caliber: .38 Special/.357 Mag., .45LC. Two-round derringer. 3.5-in. bbls. 6.5 in. overall. Weight: 12 oz. Blade front sight, fixed notch rear. Stainless finish. Black composition grips. Made 1996-98.

LUGER — Manufactured by Deutsche Waffen und Munitionsfabriken (DWM), Berlin, Germany

1900 AMERICAN EAGLE . . **NiB $6900 Ex $6555 Gd $4830**
Caliber: 7.65 mm. Eight-round magazine; thin, 4.75-in.; tapered bbl.; 9.5 in. overall. Weight: 32 oz. Fixed rear sight, dovetailed front sight. Grip safety. Checkered walnut grips. Early-style toggle, narrow trigger, wide guard, no stock lug. American Eagle over chamber. Estimated 12,000 production.

1900 COMMERCIAL . . . . . . **NiB $6910 Ex $6565 Gd $4837**
Same specifications as Luger 1900 American Eagle except DWM on early-style toggle, no chamber markings. Estimated 5,500 production.

1900 SWISS COMMERCIAL . . . **NiB $5760 Ex $4760 Gd $3510**
Same specifications as Luger 1900 American Eagle except Swiss cross in sunburst over chamber. Estimated 2,000 production.
w/unrelived grip frame, add **66%**
Swiss Military model, add **8%**
Swiss Military model w/unrelived grip frame, add **74%**

1902 AMERICAN EAGLE . . . . . **NiB $14,760 Ex $11,860 Gd $7110**
Caliber: 9mm Para. Eight-round magazine, 4-in. heavy tapered bbl., 8.75 in. overall. Weight: 30 oz. Fixed rear sight, dovetailed front sight. Grip safety. Checkered walnut grips. American Eagle over chamber, DWM on early-style toggle, narrow trigger, wide guard, no stock lug. Estimated 700 production.

1902 CARBINE . . . . **NiB $18,510 Ex $15,010 Gd $9510**
Caliber: 7.65mm. Eight-round magazine, 11.75-in. tapered bbl., 16.5 in. overall. Weight: 46 oz. Adj. 4-position rear sight, long ramp front sight. Grip safety. Checkered walnut grips and forearm. DWM on early-style toggle, narrow trigger, wide guard, no chamber markings, stock lug. Estimated 2,500 production.
w/issued stock and matching numbers, add, ... **20%**
w/original stock and non-matching numbers, deduct . . . **20%**

1902 COMMERCIAL . . . . . . **NiB $11,760 Ex $9260 Gd $6760**
Same basic specifications as Luger 1902 Cartridge Counter except DWM on early-style toggle, narrow trigger, wide guard,

**Luger 1900
American Eagle**

no chamber markings, no stock lug. Referred to as a "fat Barrel" model. Estimated 400 production.

1902 AMERICAN EAGLE CARTRIDGE
COUNTER . . . . **NiB $40,000 Ex $30,000 Gd $20,000**
Same basic specifications as Luger 1902 Cartridge Counter except American Eagle over chamber, DWM on early-style toggle, narrow trigger, wide guard, no stock lug. Estimated 700 production.

1904 GL "BABY" . . . . **EXTREMELY RARE**
Caliber: 9mm Para. Seven-round magazine, 3.25-in. bbl., 7.75 in. overall. Weight: Approx. 20 oz. Serial number 10077B. "GL" marked on rear of toggle. Georg Luger's personal sidearm. Only four are believed to exist.

1904 NAVAL (REWORKED) . . . . **EXTEMELY RARE**
Caliber: 9mm Para. Eight-round magazine, bbl., length altered to 4 in., 8.75 in. overall. Weight: 30 oz. Adj. two-position rear sight, dovetailed front sight. Thumb lever safety. Checkered walnut grips. Heavy tapered bbl., DWM on new-style toggle w/lock, 1902 over chamber. w/or without grip safety and stock lug. Estimated 800 production. Untouched original (rare) worth $50,000.

1907 U.S. ARMY TEST TRIALS (11.35MM) . . . **EXTREMELY RARE**
Caliber: .45 ACP. Six-round magazine, 5-in. bbl., 9.75 in. overall. Weight: 36 oz. Fixed rear sight, dovetailed front sight. Grip safety. Checkered walnut grips. GL monogram on rear toggle link, larger frame w/altered trigger guard and trigger, no proofs, no markings over chamber. No stock lug. Only three were known to be made. Note: This version of the Luger pistol is the most valuable next to the "GL" Baby Luger.

1906 AMERICAN EAGLE
(7.65MM) . . . . **NiB $3160 Ex $2630 Gd $1680**
Caliber: 7.65mm. Eight-round magazine, thin 4.75-in. tapered bbl., 9.5 in. overall. Weight: 32 oz. Fixed rear sight, dovetailed front sight. Grip safety. Checkered walnut grips. DWM on new-style toggle, American Eagle over chamber. No stock lug. Estimated 8,000 production.

1906 AMERICAN EAGLE (9MM) . . . **NiB $4600 Ex $4370 Gd $2000**
Same basic specifications as the 7.65mm 1906 except in 9mm Para. w/4-in. barrel, 8.75 in. overall, weight: 30 oz. Estimated 3,500 production.

1906/24 BERN (7.65MM) . . **NiB $2360 Ex $2010 Gd $1260**
Same basic specifications as the 7.65mm 1906 American Eagle except checkered walnut grips w/.38-in. borders, Swiss Cross on new-style toggle, Swiss proofs, no markings over chamber, no stock lug. Estimated 17,874 production.

GRADING: **NiB** = New in Box **Ex** = Excellent or NRA 95% **Gd** = Good or NRA 68%

1906 BRAZILIAN (7.65MM) . . . . NiB $4510 Ex $3510 Gd $2855
Same general specifications as the 7.65mm 1906 American Eagle except w/Brazilian proofs, no markings over chamber, no stock lug. Estimated 5,000 produced.

1908 BOLIVIAN . . . . NiB $6510 Ex $5510 Gd $5010
Same basic specifications as the 9mm 1906 American Eagle except w/4-in. bbl.

1906 COMMERCIAL . . . . . . NiB $2880 Ex $2310 Gd $1500
Calibers: 7.65mm or 9mm. Same specifications as the 1906 American Eagle versions (above) except no chamber markings and no stock lug. Estimated production: 5,000 (7.65mm) and 3,000 (9mm).
9mm model, add **44%**

1906 DUTCH . . . . NiB $3110 Ex $2810 Gd $1860
Caliber: 9mm Para. Same specifications as the 9mm 1906 American Eagle except tapered bbl., w/proofs, no markings over chamber, no stock lug. Arsenal rework. Estimated 4,000 production.
Original finish, add **50%**

**1906 LOEWE
AND COMPANY** . . . . **EXTREMELY RARE**
Caliber: 7.65mm. Eight-round magazine, 6-in. tapered bbl., 10.75 in. overall. Weight: 35 oz. Adj. two-position rear sight, dovetailed front sight. Grip safety. Checkered walnut grips. Loewe & Company over chamber, Naval proofs, DWM on new-style toggle, no stock lug. Estimated production unknown.

1906 NAVY
Caliber: 9mm Para. Eight-round magazine, 6-in. tapered bbl., 10.75 in. overall. Weight: 35 oz. Adj. two-position rear sight, dovetailed front sight. Grip safety and thumb safety w/lower marking (1st issue), higher marking (2nd issue). Checkered walnut grips. No chamber markings, DWM on new-style toggle w/o lock, but w/stock lug. Est. production: 9,000 (lst issue); 2,000 (2nd issue).
First issue . . . . NiB $6000 Ex $5260 Gd $3510
Second issue, add **20%**

1906 NAVY COMMERCIAL . . NiB $5600 Ex $5320 Gd $2350
Same as the 1906 Navy except lower marking on thumb safety, no chamber markings. DWM on new-style toggle, w/stock lug and commercial proofs. Estimated 3,000 production.

1906 PORTUGUESE ARMY . . NiB $3400 Ex $3230 Gd $1720
Same specifications as the 7.65mm 1906 American Eagle except w/Portuguese proofs, crown and crest over chamber. No stock lug. Estimated 3,500 production.

**1906 PORTUGUESE
NAVAL** . . . . NiB $7000 Ex $6000 Gd $5000
Same as the 9mm 1906 American Eagle except w/Portuguese proofs, crown and anchor over chamber, no stock lug.

1906 RUSSIAN . . . . . NiB $17,600 Ex $15,767 Gd $12,890
Same general specifications as the 9mm 1906 American Eagle except thumb safety has markings concealed in up position, DWM on new-style toggle, DWM bbl., proofs, crossed rifles over chamber. Estimated production unknown.

1906 SWISS COMMERCIAL . . . NiB $3000 Ex $2709 Gd $2100
Same general specifications as the 7.65mm 1906 American Eagle Luger except Swiss Cross in sunburst over chamber, no stock lug. Estimated 10,300 production.

1906 SWISS (REWORK) . . . NiB $3750 Ex $3250 Gd $2000
Same basic specifications as the 7.65mm 1906 Swiss except in bbl. lengths of 3.63, 4 and 4.75 in., overall length 8.38 in. (w/ 4-in. bbl.). Weight 32 oz. (w/ 4-in. bbl). DWM on new-style toggle, bbl., w/serial number and proof marks, Swiss Cross in sunburst or shield over chamber, no stock lug. Estimated production unknown.

1906 SWISS POLICE . . . . . . NiB $2760 Ex $2160 Gd $1560
Same general specifications as the 7.65mm 1906 Swiss except DWM on new-style toggle, Swiss Cross in matted field over chamber, no stock lug. Estimated 10,300 production.

1908 BULGARIAN . . . . NiB $4500 Ex $3855 Gd $3400
Caliber: 9mm Para. Eight-round magazine, 4-in. tapered bbl., 8.75 in. overall. Weight: 30 oz. Fixed rear sight dovetailed front sight. Thumb safety w/lower marking concealed. Checkered walnut grips. DWM chamber marking, no proofs, crown over shield on new-style toggle lanyard loop, no stock lug. Estimated production 10,000.

1908 COMMERCIAL . . . . . . NiB $2920 Ex $2610 Gd $2155
Same basic specifications as the 1908 Bulgarian except higher marking on thumb safety. No chamber markings, commercial proofs, DWM on new-style toggle, no stock lug. Estimated 500 production.

1908 ERFURT MILITARY . . . NiB $2555 Ex $2055 Gd $1824
Caliber: 9mm Para. Eight-round magazine, 4-in. tapered bbl., 8.75 in. overall. Weight: 30 oz. Fixed rear sight dovetailed front sight. Thumb safety w/higher marking concealed. Checkered walnut grips. Serial number and proof marks on barrel, crown and Erfurt on new-style toggle, dated chamber, but no stock lug. Estimated production unknown.

1908 MILITARY
Same general specifications as the 9mm 1908 Erfurt Military Luger except first and second issue have thumb safety w/ higher marking concealed, serial number on bbl., no chamber markings, proofs on frame, DWM on new-style toggle but no stock lug. Estimated production: 10,000 (first issue) and 5000 (second issue). Third issue has serial number and proof marks on barrel, dates over chamber, DWM on new-style toggle but no stock lug. Estimated 3,000 production.
First issue . . . . NiB $2460 Ex $2160 Gd $1645
Second issue . . . . NiB $2010 Ex $1605 Gd $1320
Third issue . . . . NiB $2299 Ex $1897 Gd $1645

1908 NAVY . . . . NiB $8405 Ex $79849 Gd $3475
Same basic specifications as the 9mm 1908 military Lugers except w/6-in. bbl, adj. two-position rear sight, no chamber markings, DWM on new-style toggle, w/stock lug. Estimated 26,000 production.

1908 NAVY (COMMERCIAL) . . . NiB $6600 Ex $6270 Gd $4620
Same specifications as the 1908 Naval Luger except no chamber markings or date. Commercial proofs, DWM on new-style toggle, w/stock lug. Estimated 1,900 produced.

1914 ERFURT ARTILLERY . . . NiB $4670 Ex $4435 Gd $3040
Caliber: 9mm Para. Eight-shot magazine, 8-in. tapered bbl., 12.75 in. overall. Weight: 40 oz. Artillery rear sight, Dovetailed front sight. Thumb safety w/higher marking concealed. Checkered walnut grips. Serial number and proof marks on barrel, crown and Erfurt on new-style toggle, dated chamber, w/stock lug. Estimated production unknown.

1914 ERFURT MILITARY...NiB $2170 Ex $2061 Gd $1190
Same specifications as the 1914 Erfurt Artillery except w/4-in. bbl., and corresponding length, weight, etc.; fixed rear sight. Estimated 3,000 production.

1914 NAVY............NiB $6000 Ex $5700 Gd $3000
Same specifications as 9mm 1914 Lugers except has 6-in. bbl. w/corresponding length and weight, adj. two-position rear sight. Dated chamber, DWM on new-style toggle, w/stock lug. Estimated 40,000 produced.

1914 Crown-Erfurt Artillery Luger

1914–1918 DWM ARTILLERY...NiB $3600 Ex $3090 Gd $1997
Caliber: 9mm Para. Eight-shot magazine, 8-in. tapered bbl., 12.75 in. overall. Weight: 40 oz. Artillery rear sight, dovetailed front sight. Thumb safety w/higher marking concealed. Checkered walnut grips. Serial number and proof marks on barrel, DWM on new-style toggle, dated chamber, w/stock lug. Estimated 3,000 production.

1914–1918 DWM MILITARY....NiB $2200 Ex $1899 Gd $1100
Same specifications as the 9mm 1914-18 DWM Artillery except w/4-in. tapered bbl., and corresponding length, weight, etc., and fixed rear sight. Production unknown.

1920 CARBINE
Caliber: 7.65mm. Eight-round magazine, 11.75-in. tapered bbl., 15.75 in. overall. Weight: 44 oz. Four-position rear sight, long ramp front sight. Grip (or thumb) safety. Checkered walnut grips and forearm. Serial numbers and proof marks on barrel, no chamber markings, various proofs, DWM on new-style toggle, w/stock lug. Estimated production unknown.
gun only ....NiB $7430 Ex $7058 Gd $3000
w/shoulder stock, add..........................35%

1920 NAVY CARBINE.....NiB $4800 Ex $4560 Gd $3360
Caliber: 7.65mm. Eight-round magazine, 11.75-in. tapered bbl., 15.75 in. overall. Two-position sliding rear sight. Naval military proofs and no forearm. Production unknown.

1920 COMMERCIAL......NiB $1450 Ex $1250 Gd $1018
Calibers: 7.65mm, 9mm Para. Eight-round magazine, 3.63-, 3.75-, 4-, 4.75-, 6-, 8-, 10-, 12-, 16-, 18- or 20-in. tapered bbl., overall length: 8.375 to 24.75 in. Weight: 30 oz. (w/ 3.63-in. bbl.). Varying rear sight configurations, dovetailed front sight. Thumb safety. Checkered walnut grips. Serial numbers and proof marks on barrel, no chamber markings, various proofs, DWM or crown over Erfurt on new-style toggle, w/stock lug. Production not documented.

1920 POLICE ....NiB $1410 Ex $1200 Gd $931
Same specifications as 9mm 1920 DWM w/some dated chambers, various proofs, DWM or crown over Erfurt on new-style

toggle, identifying marks on grip frame, w/stock lug. Estimated 3,000 production.

1923 COMMERICAL......NiB $1600 Ex $1520 Gd $1120
Calibers: 7.65mm and 9mm Para. Eight-round magazine, 3.63, 3.75, 4, 6, 8, 12 or 16-in. tapered bbl., overall length: 8.38 in. (w/ 3.63-in. bbl.). Weight: 30 oz. (w/ 3.63-in. bbl.). Various rear sight configurations, dovetailed front sight. Thumb lever safety. Checkered walnut grips. DWM on new-style toggle, serial number and proofs on barrel, no chamber markings, w/stock lug. Estimated 15,000 production.

1923 DUTCH COMMERICAL ...NiB $2320 Ex $2088 Gd $1872
Same basic specifications as 1923 Commercial Luger w/ same caliber offerings, but only 3.63 or 4-in. bbl. Fixed rear sight, thumb lever safety w/arrow markings. Production unknown.

1923 KRIEGHOFF
COMMERCIAL ....NiB $2340 Ex $2223 Gd $1638
Same specifications as 1923 Commercial Luger, w/same caliber offerings but bbl., lengths of 3.63, 4, 6, and 8 in. "K" marked on new-style toggle. Serial number, proofs and Germany on barrel. No chamber markings, but w/ stock lug. Production unknown.

1923 SAFE AND LOADED...NiB $2460 Ex $2337 Gd $1722
Same caliber offerings, bbl., lengths and specifications as the 1923 Commercial except thumb lever safety, "safe" and "loaded" markings, w/stock lug. Estimated 10,000 production.

1923 STOEGER
Same general specifications as the 1923 Commercial Luger with the same caliber offerings and bbl., lengths of 3.75, 4, 6, 8 and up to 24 in. Thumb lever safety. DWM on new-style toggle, serial number and/or proof marks on barrel. American Eagle over chamber but no stock lug. Estimated production less than 1000 (also see Stoeger listings). Note: Qualified appraisals should be obtained on all Stoeger Lugers with bbl. lengths over 8 in. to ensure accurate values.
3.75-, 4-, or 6-in. bbl......NiB $5660 Ex $5377 Gd $2730
8-in. bbl................NiB $6350 Ex $6035 Gd $2255

1926 "BABY"
PROTOTYPE ......NiB $112,750 Ex $90,295 Gd $62,355
Calibers: 7.65mm Browning and 9mm Browning (short). Five-round magazine, 2.31-in. bbl., about 6.25 in. overall.

Luger 1923 Stoeger

Small-sizedframe and toggle assembly. Prototype for a Luger "pocket pistol," but never manufactured commercially. Checkered walnut grips, slotted for safety. Only four known to exist, but as many as a dozen could have been made.

1929 SWISS . . . . NiB $2017 Ex $1486 Gd $989
Caliber: 7.65mm. Eight-round magazine, 4.75-in. tapered bbl., 9.5 in. overall. Weight: 32 oz. Fixed rear sight, dovetailed front sight. Long grip safety and thumb lever w/S markings. Stepped receiver and straight grip frame. Checkered plastic grips. Swiss Cross in shield on new-style toggle. Serial numbers and proofs on barrel, no markings over chamber and no stock lug. Estimated 1,900 production.

1934 KRIEGHOFF COMMERCIAL
(SIDE FRAME) . . . . NiB $ 7100 Ex $6350 Gd $2895
Caliber: 7.65mm or 9mm Para. Eight-round magazine, bbl. lengths: 4, 6, and 8 in., overall length: 8.75 (w/ 4-in. bbl.). Weight: 30 oz. (w/ 4-in. bbl.). Various rear sight configurations w/dovetailed front sight. Thumb lever safety. Checkered brown plastic grips. Anchor w/H K Krieghoff Suhl on new-style toggle, but no chamber markings. Tapered bbl., w/serial number and proofs; w/stock lug. Estimated 1,700 production.

1934 KRIEGHOFF S CODE MODELS
Caliber: 9mm Para. Eight-round magazine, 4-in. tapered bbl., 8.75 in. overall. Weight: 30 oz. Fixed rear sight, dovetailed front sight. Thumb lever safety. Anchor w/H K Krieghoff Suhl on new-style toggle, S dated chamber, bbl., proofs and stock lug. Early model: Checkered walnut or plastic grips. Estimated 2,500 production. Late model: Checkered brown plastic grips. Estimated 1,200 production.
Early model . . . . NiB $4660 Ex $4077 Gd $2976
Late model . . . . NiB $4460 Ex $3900 Gd $1464

1934 BYF . . . . NiB $2170 Ex $1950 Gd $1000
Caliber: 9mm Para. Eight-round magazine, 4-in. tapered bbl., 8.75 in. overall. Weight: 30 oz. Fixed rear sight, dovetailed front sight. Thumb lever safety. Checkered walnut or plastic grips. "byf" on new-style toggle, serial number and proofs on bbl., 41-42 dated chamber and w/stock lug. Estimated 3,000 productlon.

1934 MAUSER S/42 K . . . . . NiB $7950 Ex $6800 Gd $3500
Caliber: 9mm Para. Eight-round magazine, 4-in. tapered bbl., 8.75 in. overall. Weight: 30 oz. Fixed rear sight dovetailed front sight. Thumb lever safety. Checkered walnut or plastic grips. "42" on new-style toggle, serial number and proofs on barrel,

Luger 1929 Swiss

1939-40 dated chamber markings and w/stock lug. Estimated 10,000 production.

1934 MAUSER S/42
(DATED) . . . . NiB $2244 Ex $2117 Gd $1599
Same specifications as Luger 1934 Mauser 42 except 41 dated chamber markings and w/stock lug. Production unknown.

1934 MAUSER BANNER
(MILITARY) . . . . NiB $4190 Ex $3455 Gd $3097
Same specifications as Luger 1934 Mauser 42 except Mauser in banner on new-style toggle, tapered bbl., w/serial number and proofs usually, dated chamber markings and w/stock lug. Production unknown.

1934 MAUSER BANNER
COMMERCIAL . . . . NiB $4400 Ex $3760 Gd $3156
Same specifications as Luger 1934 Mauser 42 except checkered walnut grips. Mauser in banner on new-style toggle, tapered bbl., usually w/serial number and proofs, no chamber markings, but w/ stock lug. Production unknown.

1934 MAUSER
BANNER DUTCH . . . . NiB $3787 Ex $3375 Gd $3099
Same specifications as Luger 1934 Mauser 42 except checkered walnut grips. Mauser in banner on new-style toggle, tapered bbl., w/caliber, 1940 dated chamber markings and w/stock lug. Production unknown.

1934 MAUSER LATVIAN . . . NiB $3260 Ex $2355 Gd $1989
Caliber: 7.65mm. Eight-round magazine, 4-in. tapered bbl., 8.75 in. overall. Weight: 30 oz. Fixed square-notched rear sight, dovetailed Partridge front sight. Thumb lever safety. Checkered walnut stocks. Mauser in banner on new-style toggle, 1937 dated chamber markings and w/stock lug. Production unknown.

1934 MAUSER
(OBERNDORF) . . . . NiB $3155 Ex $2535 Gd $1733
Same as 1934 Mauser 42 except checkered walnut grips. Oberndorf 1934 on new-style toggle, tapered bbl., w/proofs and caliber, Mauser banner over chamber and w/stock lug (also see Mauser).

1934 SIMSON-S TOGGLE . . . NiB $4459 Ex $4188 Gd $3799
Same as 1934 Mauser 42 except checkered walnut grips, "S" on new-style toggle, tapered bbl., w/proofs and S/N, no chamber markings; w/stock lug. Estimated 10,000 production.

42 MAUSER
BANNER (BYF) . . . . NiB $3877 Ex $3078 Gd $2689
Same specifications as Luger 1934 Mauser 42 except weight: 32 oz. Mauser in banner on new-style toggle, tapered bbl., w/serial number and proofs usually, dated chamber markings and w/stock lug. Estimated 3,500 production.

ABERCROMBIE AND
FITCH . . . . NiB $5465 Ex $4876 Gd $2879
Calibers: 7.65mm and 9mm Para. Eight-round magazine, 4.75-in. tapered bbl., 9.5 in. overall. Weight: 32 oz. Fixed rear sight, dovetailed front sight. Grip safety. Checkered walnut grips. DWM on new-style toggle Abercrombie & Fitch markings on barrel, Swiss Cross in sunburst over chamber, no stock lug. Est. 100 production.

DUTCH ROYAL

AIR FORCE . . . . **NiB $3324 Ex $2190 Gd $998**
Caliber: 9mm Para. Eight-round magazine, 4-in. tapered bbl., 8.75 in. overall. Weight: 30 oz. Fixed rear sight dovetailed front sight. Grip safety and thumb safety w/markings and arrow. Checkered walnut grips. DWM on new-style toggle, bbl., dated w/serial number and proofs, no markings over chamber, no stock lug. Estimated 4,000 production.

DWM (G DATE) . . . . **NiB $2189 Ex $1953 Gd $1645**
Caliber: 9mm Para. Eight-round magazine, 4-in. tapered bbl., 8.75 in. overall. Weight: 30 oz. Fixed rear sight, dovetailed front sight. Thumb lever safety. Checkered walnut grips. DWM on new-style toggle, serial number and proofs on barrel, G (1935 date) over chamber and w/stock lug. Production unknown.

DWM AND ERFURT . . . . **NiB $1357 Ex $1134 Gd $876**
Caliber: 9mm Para. Eight-round magazine, 4- or 6-in. tapered bbl., overall length: 8.75 or 10.75 in. Weight: 30 or 38 oz. Fixed rear sight, dovetailed front sight. Thumb safety. Checkered walnut grips. Serial numbers and proof marks on barrel, double dated chamber, various proofs, DWM or crown over Erfurt on new-style toggle and w/stock lug. Production unknown.

KRIEGHOFF 36 . . . . **NiB $4550 Ex $3799 Gd $1899**
Caliber: 9mm Para. Eight-round magazine, 4-in. tapered bbl., 8.75 in. overall. Weight: 30 oz. Fixed rear sight, dovetailed front sight. Thumb lever safety. Checkered brown plastic grips. Anchor w/H K Krieghoff Suhl on new-style toggle, 36 dated chamber, serial number and proofs on bbl. and w/stock lug. Estimated 700 production.

KRIEGHOFF DATED (1936 - 1945)
Same specifications as Luger Krieghoff 36 except 1936-45 dated chamber, bbl. proofs. Est. 8,600 production.
1936, 1937 and 1940 . . . . . **NiB $5500 Ex $4779 Gd $2735**
1938 and 1941 . . . . **NiB $6500 Ex $5779 Gd $2735**
1942 thru 1943, add **60%**
1945, add **110%**

KRIEGHOFF (GRIP SAFETY) . . . **NiB $4977 Ex $3965 Gd $2790**
Same specifications as Luger Krieghoff 36 except grip safety and thumb lever safety. No chamber markings, tapered bbl., w/serial number, proofs and caliber, no stock lug. Production unknown.

MAUSER BANNER

(GRIP SAFETY) . . . . **NiB $2874 Ex $2050 Gd $1465**
Caliber: 7.65mm. Eight-round magazine, 4.75-in. tapered bbl., 9.5 in. overall. Weight: 30 oz. Fixed rear sight, dovetailed front sight. Grip safety and thumb lever safety. Checkered walnut grips. Mauser in banner on new-style toggle, serial number and proofs on barrel, 1939 dated chamber markings, but no stock lug. Production unknown.

MAUSER BANNER 42

(DATED) . . . . **NiB 2170 Ex $1196 Gd $100**
Caliber: 9mm Para. Eight-round magazine, 4-in. tapered bbl., 8.75 in. overall. Weight: 30 oz. Fixed rear sight, dovetailed front sight. Thumb lever safety. Checkered walnut or plastic grips. Mauser in banner on new-style toggle serial number and proofs on bbl., (usually) 1942 dated chamber markings and stock lug. Production unknown.

MAUSER BANNER

(SWISS PROOF) . . . . **NiB $3460 Ex $2830 Gd $1540**
Same specifications as Luger Mauser Banner 42 except checkered walnut grips and 1939 dated chamber.

MAUSER FREISE . . . . **NiB $4960 Ex $4090 Gd $2866**
Same specifications as Mauser Banner 42 except checkered walnut grips, tapered bbl. w/proofs on sight block and Freise above chamber. Production unknown.

S/42

Caliber: 9mm Para. Eight-round magazine, 4-in. tapered barrel. 8.75 in. overall. Weight: 30 oz. Fixed rear sight, dovetailed front sight. Thumb lever safety. Checkered walnut grips. S/42 on new-style toggle, serial number and proofs on bbl. and w/ stock lug. Dated Model: Has dated chamber; estimated 3000 production. G Date: Has G (1935 date) over chamber; estimated 3000 production. K Date: Has K (1934 date) over chamber; production unknown.
Dated model . . . . **NiB $2960 Ex $2150 Gd $1360**
G date model . . . . **NiB $3010 Ex $2460 Gd $1630**
K date model . . . . **NiB $9010 Ex $7860 Gd $5610**

RUSSIAN COMMERCIAL . . . **NiB $3146 Ex $2548 Gd $1713**
Caliber: 7.65mm. Eight-round magazine, 3.63-in. tapered bbl., 8.38 in. overall. Weight: 30 oz. Fixed rear sight, dovetailed front sight. Thumb lever safety. Checkered walnut grips. DWM on new-style toggle, Russian proofs on barrel, no chamber markings but w/stock lug. Production unknown.

SIMSON AND COMPANY . . . **NiB $3960 Ex $3510 Gd $2510**
Calibers: 7.65mm and 9mm Para. Eight-round magazine, Weight: 32 oz. Fixed rear sight, dovetailed front sight. Thumb lever safety. Checkered walnut grips. Simson & Company Suhl on new-style toggle, serial number and proofs on barrel, date over chamber and w/stock lug. Estimated 12,000 production.
Military dated
  9mm w/1925 date . . . . . . **NiB $7510 Ex $6510 Gd $4510**
S Code, undated . . . . **NiB $6510 Ex $5660 Gd $2389**

VICKERS-DUTCH . . . . **NiB $4375 Ex $3968 Gd $3316**
Caliber: 9mm Para. Eight-round magazine, 4-in. tapered bbl., 8.75 in. overall. Weight: 30 oz. Fixed rear sight, dovetailed front sight. Grip safety and thumb lever w/arrow markings. Checkered walnut grips (coarse). Vickers LTD on new-style toggle, no chamber markings, dated bbl. but no stock lug. Estimated 10,000 production.

LUNA FREE PISTOL — Zella-Mehlis, Germany

Originally mfd. by Ernst Friedr. Buchel and later by Udo Anschutz.

MODEL 200 FREE PISTOL . . **NiB $1198 Ex $1027 Gd $784**
Single-shot. System Aydt action. Set trigger. Caliber: .22 LR. Eleven-in. bbl., weight: 40 oz. Target sights. Blued finish. Checkered and carved walnut grip and forearm; improved design w/adj. hand base on later models of Udo Anschutz manufacture. Made prior to WWII.

M.A.C. (Military Armament Corp.) — Ducktown, TN

INGRAM MODEL 10 AUTO PISTOL
Select fire (NFA-Title II-Class III) SMG based on Ingram M10 blowback system using an open bolt design with or without telescoping stock. Calibers: 9mm or .45 ACP. Cyclic rate: 750 RPM (9mm) or 900 RPM (.45 ACP). 32- or 30-rnd. magazine,

**Luna Model 200
Free Pistol**

MAC 10

5.75-in. threaded bbl. (to accept muzzle brake) bbl. Extension or suppressor, 10.5 in. overall w/o stock or 10.6 (w/telescoped stock) and 21.5 (w/Extended stock). Weight: 6.25 pounds. Front protected post sight, fixed aperture rear sight.

9mm model . . . . NiB $1113 Ex $920 Gd $669
ACP model . . . . NiB $998 Ex $877 Gd $668
w/bbl. extension, add $255
w/suppressor, add $587

INGRAM MODEL 10A1S SEMIAUTO
Similar to the Model 10 except (Class I) Semiauto w/closed bolt design to implement an interchangable component system to easily convert to fire 9mm and .45 ACP.

9mm model . . . . NiB $408 Ex $332 Gd $225
.45 ACP model . . . . NiB $431 Ex $342 Gd $235
w/bbl. extension, add $204
w/fake suppressor, add $225

INGRAM MODEL 11 SEMIAUTO
Similar to the Model 10A1 except (Class I) Semiauto chambered .380 ACP.

.380 ACP model . . . . NiB $862 Ex $714 Gd $536
w/bbl. extension, add $204
w/fake suppressor, add $225

MAC — Philippines

Manufactured in Philippines and imported by Eagle Imports, Wanamassa, New Jersey. Series-70 style.

1911 BOBCUT SERIES . . . . NiB $978 Ex $910 Gd $870
Similar 1911 Classic except w/4.35-in. bbl. and bobcat frame.

1911 CLASSIC SERIES . . . . NiB $609 Ex $570 Gd $500
1911 platform. Semiauto. SA. Caliber: .45 ACP; 8-rnd. magazine. 5 in. bbl. Frame: steel. Sights: adj. rear, fiber optic front. Finish: blue, black chrome, hard chrome. Grip: textured hardwood. Length: 8.88 in. Weight: 40.56 oz. Beavertail, magwell. Imported from 2011 to date.
hard chrome or black chrome finish, add $70

1911 BULLSEYE SERIES . . . . NiB $1219 Ex $1180 Gd $1000
Similar 1911 Classic except w/6-in. bbl.
hard chrome finish, add $70

3011 SSD SERIES . . . . NiB $1215 Ex $570 Gd $500
1911 platform. Semiauto. SA. Caliber: .40 S&W or .45 ACP; 14-rnd. magazine. 5-in. bbl. Frame: steel. Sights: adj. rear, fiber optic front. Finish: deep blue, hard chrome. Grip: checkered aluminum. Length: 8.91 in. Weight: 46.54 oz. Beavertail, magwell funnel.
3011 SSD Tactical (accessory rail), add $90

MAGNUM RESEARCH, INC. (MRI) —
Minneapolis, MN
Originally mfd. by IMI (Isreal Military Industries). MRI purchased by Kahr Arms in 2010.

**BABY EAGLE
SEMIAUTO** . . . . NiB $577 Ex $479 Gd $365
DA. Calibers: 9mm, .40 S&W, .41 AE. 15-shot magazine (9mm), 9-rnd. magazine (.40 S&W), 10-rnd. magazine (.41 AE), 4.75-in. bbl., 8.15 in. overall. Weight: 35.4 oz. Combat sights. Matte blued finish. Imported from 1991-96 and 1999 to 2007.
Baby Eagle II (w/accessory rail,
   2008-present) . . . . NiB $565 Ex $430 Gd $330
Baby Eagle III (polymer frame,
   2015-present) . . . . NiB $550 Ex $430 Gd $330
Baby Eagle III (steel frame, 2015-present), add $40

**BFR LONG CYLINDER
REVOVER** . . . . NiB $1050 Ex $780 Gd $550
SA. Calibers: .30-30 Win., .444 Marlin, .45 LC/.410, .450 Marlin, .45-70 Gov't., .460 S&W Mag., and .50 S&W Mag. 5-rnd. cylinder, bbl. lengths: 7.5- or 10-in. Stainless finish. Weight: 4-4.4 lbs.Rubber grips. Made 1999 to date.

**BFR SHORT
CYLINDER REVOVER** . . . . NiB $1050 Ex $780 Gd $550
SA. Calibers: .44 Mag., .454 Casull, .475 Linebaugh, and .480 Ruger, 5-rnd. cylinder, bbl. lengths: 5-, or 7.5-in. Stainless finish. Rubber grips. Weight: 3.2-4.4 lbs. Made 1999 to date.

DESERT EAGLE MK VII SEMIAUTO
Gas-operated. Calibers: .357 Mag., .41 Mag., .44 Mag., .50 Action Express (AE). Eight- or 9-rnd. magazine, 6-in. standard bbl., or 10- and 14-in. w/polygonal bbl., 10.6 in. overall (w/ 6-in. bbl.). Weight: 52 oz. (w/alum. alloy frame) to 67 oz. (w/steel frame). Fixed or adj. combat sights. Combat-type trigger guard. finish: Military black oxide, nickel, chrome, stainless or blued. Wraparound rubber grips. Made 1983-95 and 1998 to 2001.
.357 standard (steel)
   or alloy (6-in. bbl.) . . . . NiB $903 Ex $658 Gd $562
.357 stainless steel (6-in. bbl.) . . . . . NiB $940 Ex $704 Gd $536
.41 Mag. standard (steel) or alloy
   (6-in. bbl.) . . . . NiB $1099 Ex $831 Gd $638

Magnum Research Model Desert Eagle Mark XIX shown w/optional Leupold scope

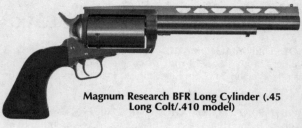

Magnum Research BFR Long Cylinder (.45 Long Colt/.410 model)

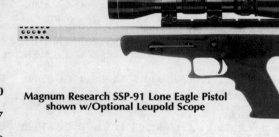

Magnum Research SSP-91 Lone Eagle Pistol shown w/Optional Leupold Scope

.41 Mag. stainless steel
(6-in. bbl.) . . . . NiB $1145 Ex $984 Gd $780
.44 Mag. standard (steel) or alloy
(6-in. bbl.) . . . . NiB $1015 Ex $798 Gd $567
.44 Mag. stainless steel
(6-in. bbl.) . . . . NiB $991 Ex $806 Gd $559
.50 AE Magnum standard . . . . NiB $1135 Ex $968 Gd $689
For 10-in. bbl., add . . . . NiB $204 Ex $148 Gd $110
For 14-in. bbl., add . . . . NiB $225 Ex $175 Gd $128

DESERT EAGLE MARK XIX SEMIAUTO PISTOL
Interchangeable component system based on .50-caliber frame. Calibers: .357 Mag., .44 Mag., .50 AE. Nine-, 8-, 7-rnd. magazine, 6- or 10-in. bbl. w/dovetail design and cross slots to accept scope rings. Weight: 70.5 oz. (6-in. bbl.) or 79 oz. 10.75 or 14.75 in. overall. Sights: Post front and adjustable rear. Blue, chrome or nickel finish; available brushed, matte or polished. Hogue soft rubber grips. Made 1995-98.

.357 Mag. and .44 Mag.
(w/6-in. bbl.) . . . . NiB $1400 Ex $1150 Gd $900
.50 AE (w/6-in. bbl.) . . . . . . NiB $1435 Ex $1164 Gd $989
w/10-in. bbl., add $100
Two caliber conversion (bbl., bolt & mag.), add $444
XIX Platform System (three-caliber conversion kit
w/six bbls.) . . . . NiB $4335 Ex $3799 Gd $3260
XIX6 System (two-caliber conversion kit
w/two 6-in. bbls.) . . . . NiB $2675 Ex $2254 Gd $1969
XIX10 System (two-caliber conversion
kit w/two 10-in. bbls.) . . . . . NiB $2150 Ex $1720 Gd $1196
Custom shop finish, add $20%
24K gold finish, add $40%

MICRO DESERT EAGLE. . . . . . . NiB $470 Ex $380 Gd $265
DAO. Calibers: .380 ACP. 6-shot magazine, 2-2-in. bbl. Weight: 14 oz. Imported from 2009 to 2013.

(ASAI) MODEL ONE PRO .45 PISTOL
Calibers: .45 ACP or .400 COR-BON, 3.75- in. bbl., 7.04 or 7.83 (IPSC Model) in. overall. Weight: 23.5 (alloy frame) or 31.1 oz. 10-rnd. magazine. Short recoil action. SA or DA mode w/de-cocking lever. Steel or alloy grip-frame. Textured black polymer grips. Imported from 1998.
Model 1P45 . . . . NiB $740 Ex $567 Gd $399
Model 1C45/400 (compensator kit), add $204
Model 1C400NC (400 conversion kit), add $150

MOUNTAIN EAGLE SEMIAUTO
Caliber: .22 LR. 15-rnd. polycarbonate resin magazine, 6.5-in. injection-molded polymer and steel bbl., 10.6 in. overall. Weight: 21 oz. Ramp blade front sight, adj. rear. Injection-molded, checkered and textured grip. Matte black finish. Made 1992-96.
Standard, w/6-in. bb. . . . . NiB $214 Ex $160 Gd $143
Compact, w/4.5-in. bbl. . . . . . . NiB $190 Ex $143 Gd $110
Target, w/8-in. bbl. . . . . NiB $240 Ex $150 Gd $120

MR SERIES
. . . . NiB $480 Ex $380 Gd $300
Similar to Walther P99. Calibers: 9mm or .40 S&W. 15-rnd. magazine (9mm), 11-rnd. magazine (.40 S&W), 4.5-in. bbl. Made 2009-13.

SSP-91 LONE EAGLE PISTOL
Single-shot action w/interchangeable rotating breech bbl., assembly. Calibers: .22 LR, .22 Mag., .22 Hornet, .22-250, .223 Rem., .243 Win., 6mm BR, 7mm-08, 7mm BR, .30-06, .30-30, .308 Win., .35 Rem., .357 Mag., .44 Mag., .444 Marlin. 14-in. interchangeable bbl. assembly, 15 in. overall. Weight: 4.5 lbs. Black or chrome finish. Made 1991-2001.
Black finish . . . . NiB $434 Ex $321 Gd $165
Chrome finish . . . . NiB $464 Ex $342 Gd $186
Extra 14-in. bbl., black finish $150
Extra 14-in. bbl., chrome finish, ... $175
Ambidextrous stock assembly (only) $220
w/muzzle brake, add $408
w/open sights, add $45

GRADING: **NiB** = New in Box   **Ex** = Excellent or NRA 95%   **Gd** = Good or NRA 68%

MAUSER — Oberndorf, Germany, Waffenfabrik Mauser of Mauser-Werke A.G.

MODEL 80-SA AUTOMATIC. . . NiB $577 Ex $395 Gd $255
Caliber: 9mm Para. 13-rnd. magazine, 4.66-in. bbl., 8 in. overall. Weight: 31.5 oz. Blued finish. Hardwood grips. Made 1992-96.

MODEL 90-DA AUTOMATIC . . NiB $530 Ex $354 Gd $234
Caliber: 9mm Para. 14-rnd. magazine, 4.66-in. bbl., 8 in. overall. Weight: 35 oz. Blued finish. Hardwood grips. Made 1992-96.
DAC Compact model, add $10

MODEL 1898 "BROOMHANDLE" MILITARY AUTO PISTOL
Caliber: 7.63mm Mauser, but also chambered for 9mm Mauser and 9mm Para. w/the latter being identified by a large red "9" in the grips. 10-rnd. box magazine, 5.25-in. bbl., 12 in. overall. Weight: 45 oz. Adj. rear sight. Blued finish. Walnut grips. Made 1897-1939. Note: Specialist collectors recognize a number of variations at significantly higher values. Price here is for more common commercial and military types with original finish.
Commercial model (pre-war). . . NiB $3520 Ex $2735 Gd $1096
Commercial model
 (wartime) . . . . NiB $3015 Ex $2512 Gd $1040
Red 9 Commercial model
 (fixed sight). . . . . NiB $3265 Ex $2979 Gd $1049
Red 9 WWI Contract
 (tangent sight). . . . . NiB $3300 Ex $2670 Gd $1300
w/stock sssembly
 (matching S/N), add $1300

MODEL HSC DA AUTO PISTOL
Calibers: .32 Auto (7.65mm), .380 Auto (9mm Short). Eight-round (.32) or 7-rnd. (.380) magazine, 3.4-in. bbl., 6.4 in. overall. Weight: 23.6 oz. Fixed sights. Blued or nickel finish. Checkered walnut grips. Made 1938-45 and 1968-96.
Military model
 (low grip screw) . . . . NiB $6200 Ex $5110 Gd $2820
Commercial model (wartime) . . . NiB $536 Ex $398 Gd $249
Nazi military model (pre-war) . . . NiB $1148 Ex $974 Gd $632
Nazi military model (wartime) . . . .NiB $600 Ex $499 Gd $270
French production (postwar) . . . . NiB $474 Ex $398 Gd $239

Mauser production (postwar) . . . NiB $497 Ex $377 Gd $235
Recent importation
 (Armes De Chasse) . . . . .NiB $478 Ex $398 Gd $270
Recent importation
 (Interarms) . . . . .NiB $388 Ex $289 Gd $230
Recent importation
 (European Amer. Arms). . . . .NiB $328 Ex $196 Gd $115
Recent importation
 (Gamba, USA) . . . . .NiB $431 Ex $316 Gd $194
American Eagle model
 (1 of 5000) . . . . .NiB $562 Ex $433 Gd $319

LUGER LANGE PISTOL 08
Caliber: 9mm Para. Eight-in. bbl., Checkered grips. Blued finish. Accessorized w/walnut shoulder stock, front sight tool, spare magazine, leather case. Currently in production. Commemorative version made in limited quantities w/ivory grips and 14-carat gold monogram plate.
Commemorative model
 (100 produced). . . . . NiB $2855 Ex $2330 Gd $1875
Commemorative matched
 pair. . . . . NiB $5423 Ex $4412 Gd $3099
Cartridge counter model. . . NiB $4010 Ex $2907 Gd $2017
Carbine model (w/matching
 buttstock) . . . . NiB $8025 Ex $6309 Gd $3718

PARABELLUM LUGER AUTO PISTOL
Similar to commercial model. P-08 and Swiss pattern with grip safety. Calibers: 7.65mm Luger, 9mm Para. Eight-round magazine, bbl. lengths: 4-, 6-in., 8.75 in. overall (w/ 4-in. bbl.). Weight: 30 oz. (w/ 4-in. bbl.). Fixed sights. Blued finish. Checkered walnut grips. Imported 1970s. Note: Pistols of this

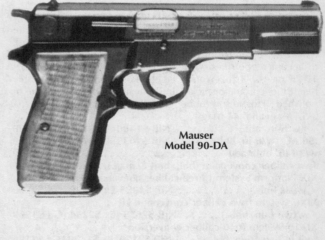

Mauser
Model 90-DA

Mauser HSc
(Interarm Import)

Mauser Model 1898
Broomhandle Military

model sold in the U.S. have the American Eagle stamped on the receiver.
Standard model (blue) . . . . . NiB $1603 Ex $1230 Gd $704

POCKET MODEL 1910 AUTO PISTOL
Caliber: .25 Auto (6.35mm). Nine-round magazine, 3.1-in. bbl., 5.4 in. overall. Weight: 15 oz. Fixed sights. Blued finish. Checkered walnut or hard rubber grips. Made 1910-34.
Model 1910 (standard) . . . . . . NiB $691 Ex $461 Gd $306
Model 1910 (w/side latch) . . . . NiB $546 Ex $431 Gd $309

POCKET MODEL 1914 . . . . . . NiB $691 Ex $485 Gd $314
Similar to Pocket Model 1910. Caliber: .32 Auto (7.65mm). Eight-round magazine, 3.4-in. bbl., 6 in. overall. Weight: 21 oz. Fixed sights. Blued finish. Checkered walnut or hard rubber grips. Made 1914-34

POCKET MODEL 1934 . . . . NiB $816 Ex $595 Gd $410
Similar to Pocket Models 1910 and 1914 in the respective calibers. Chief difference is in the more streamlined, one-piece grips. Made 1934-39.

WTP MODEL I AUTO PISTOL . NiB $779 Ex $610 Gd $413
"Westentaschen-Pistole" (Vest Pocket Pistol). Caliber: .25 Automatic (6.35mm). Six-round magazine, 2.5-in. bbl., 4 in. overall. Weight: 11.5 oz. Blued finish. Hard rubber grips. Made 1922-37.

WTP MODEL II
AUTO PISTOL . . . . NiB $1398 Ex $1137 Gd $895
Similar to Model I but smaller and lighter. Caliber: .25 Automatic (6.35mm). Six-round magazine, 2-in. bbl., 4 in. overall. Weight: 9.5 oz. Blued finish. Hard rubber grips. Made 1938-40.

MERWIN HULBERT & CO. — New York, NY

FIRST MODEL
FRONTIER ARMY . . . . NiB $9679 Ex $8023 Gd $6029
SA .44 caliber, 7.5-in. bbl. Square butt, open top, scoop flutes on cylinder, two screws above trigger guard.

SECOND MODEL
FRONTIER ARMY . . . . NiB $8617 Ex $7608 Gd $6138
Similar to First Model except one screw above trigger guard.

SECOND MODEL
POCKET ARMY . . . . NiB $7740 Ex $ 6487 Gd $5009
Similar to Second Model except has bird's-head butt instead of square butt, 3.5- or 7-in. (scarce) bbl. Some models may be marked "Pocket Army."

Merwin Hulbert Frontier Model

THIRD MODEL
FRONTIER ARMY . . . . NiB $6995 Ex $3429 Gd $2152
Caliber: .44, 7-in. rnd. bbl. with no rib, single action. Square butt, top strap, usually has conventional fluting on cylinder but some have scoop flutes.

THIRD MODEL DA
FRONTIER ARMY . . . . NiB $6775 Ex $5254 Gd $4890
Similar to Third Model Frontier Army SA except is double action.

THIRD MODEL
POCKET ARMY . . . . NiB $7610 Ex $5366 Gd $4997
Caliber: .44, 3.5- or 7.5-in. bbl. with no rib. Single action, bird's-head butt, top strap.

THIRD MODEL
POCKET ARMY DA . . . . NiB $6648 Ex $5096 Gd $3930
Similar to Third Model Pocket Army SA except DA.

FOURTH MODEL
FRONTIER ARMY . . . . NiB $9010 Ex $8188 Gd $4992
Caliber: .44, 3.5- 5- or 7-in. unique ribbed bbl. Single action, square butt, top strap, conventional flutes on cylinder.

FOURTH MODEL FRONTIER
ARMY DA . . . . NiB $8189 Ex $5883 Gd $5409
Similar to Fourth Model Frontier Army SA DA.

NOTE: *The following handguns are foreign copies of Merwin Hulbert Co. guns and may be marked as such, or as "Sistema Merwin Hulbert," but rarely with the original Hopkins & Allen markings. These guns will usually bring half or less of a comparable genuine Merwin Hulbert product.*

FIRST POCKET MODEL . . . NiB $2270 Ex $1996 Gd $1416
Caliber: .38 Special, 5-rnd. cylinder (w/cylinder pin Exposed at front of frame), single action. Spur trigger; round loading hole in recoil shield, no loading gate.

SECOND POCKET MODEL . . . NiB $1815 Ex $1595 Gd $1416
Similar to First Pocket Model except has sliding loading gate.

THIRD POCKET MODEL . . . . NiB $1633 Ex $1270 Gd $1111
Similar to First Pocket Model except has enclosed cylinder pin.

THIRD POCKET MODEL W/TRIGGER
GUARD . . . . NiB $1517 Ex $1319 Gd $1133
Similar to First Pocket Model except w/conventional trigger guard.

SMALL FRAME
POCKET MODEL . . . . NiB $1360 Ex $1120 Gd $601
Caliber: .38 Spec., 5-rnd. cylinder, DA, may have hammer spur.

SMALL FRAME
POCKET MODEL 32 . . . . NiB $1377 Ex $1190 Gd $979
Similar to Medium Frame Pocket Model except .32 caliber, 7-rnd. cylinder, double action.

TIP-UP MODEL 22 . . . . NiB $1579 Ex $1367 Gd $1056
Similar to S&W Model One except .22 caliber, 7-rnd. cylinder, spur trigger. Scarce.

Mitchell Arms
Citation II

MITCHELL ARMS, INC. — Santa Ana, CA

MODEL 1911 GOLD SIGNATURE
Caliber: .45 ACP. Eight-round mag, 5-in. bbl., 8.75 in. overall.
Weight: 39 oz. Interchangeable blade front sight, drift-adj.
combat or fully adj. rear. Smooth or checkered walnut grips.
Made 1994-96.

Blued model w/fixed sights. . . . NiB $512 Ex $393 Gd $301
Blued model w/adj. sights. . . . . NiB $554 Ex $456 Gd $412
Stainless model w/fixed sights . . . NiB $709 Ex $549 Gd $464
Stainless model w/adj. sights . . . . NiB $755 Ex $601 Gd $530

ALPHA MODEL AUTO PISTOL
Dual action w/interchangeable trigger modules. Caliber:
.45 ACP. Eight-round magazine, 5-in. bbl., 8.75 in. overall.
Weight: 39 oz. Interchangeable blade front sight, drift-adj.
rear. Smooth or checkered walnut grips. Blued or stainless
finish. Made in 1994. Advertised in 1995 but not manufactured.

AMERICAN EAGLE
LUGER PISTOL . . . . NiB $900 Ex $678 Gd $369
Stainless-steel re-creation of the American Eagle Parabellum
auto pistol. Caliber: 9mm Para. Seven-round magazine,
4-in. bbl., 9.6 in. overall. Weight: 26.6 oz. Blade front sight,
fixed rear. Stainless finish. Checkered walnut grips. Made
1993-94.

CITATION II AUTO PISTOL . . . NiB $433 Ex $309 Gd $228
Re-creation of the High Standard Supermatic Citation Military.
Caliber: .22 LR. 10-rnd. magazine, 5.5-in. bull bbl. or 7.25

fluted bbl., 9.75 in. overall (5.5-in. bbl.). Weight: 44.5 oz.
Ramp front sight, slide-mounted micro-adj. rear. Satin blued
or stainless finish. Checkered walnut grips w/thumbrest. Made
1992-96.

OLYMPIC I.S.U. . . . . NiB $659 Ex $556 Gd $434
Similar to the Citation II model except chambered in .22 Short,
6.75-in. rnd. tapered bbl. w/stabilizer and removable counterweights. Made 1992-96.

SHARPSHOOTER I . . . . NiB $362 Ex $288 Gd $212
Re-creation of the High Standard Sharpshooter. Caliber: .22 LR.
10-rnd. magazine, 5-in. bull bbl., 10.25 in. overall. Weight:
42 oz. Ramp front sight, slide-mounted micro-adj. rear. Satin
blued or stainless finish. Checkered walnut grips w/thumbrest.
Made 1992-96.

SA SPORT KING II . . . . NiB $304 Ex $226 Gd $170
Caliber: .22 LR. 10-rnd. magazine, 4.5- or 6.75-in. bbl., 9 or
11.25 in. overall. Weight: 39 or 42 oz. Checkered walnut or
black plastic grips. Blade front sight and drift adjustable rear.
Made 1993-94.

SA ARMY REVOLVER
Calibers: .357 Mag., .44 Mag., .45 Colt/.45 ACP. Six-round
cylinder. bbl., lengths: 4.75, 5.5, 7.5 in., weight: 40-43 oz.
Blade front sight, grooved top strap or adj. rear. Blued or nickel
finish w/color-casehardened frame. Brass or steel backstrap/
trigger guard. Smooth one-piece walnut grips. Imported from
1987-94 and 1997. Disc.

w/blued finish . . . . NiB $431 Ex $319 Gd $235
w/nickel finish . . . . NiB $464 Ex $398 Gd $303
w/steel backstrap . . . . NiB $541 Ex $422 Gd $317
.45 Combo
  w/blued finish. . . . . NiB $544 Ex $429 Gd $346
.45 Combo
  w/nickel finish . . . . NiB $601 Ex $562 Gd $433

TROPHY II . . . . NiB $464 Ex $337 Gd $270
Similar to the Citation II model except w/gold-plated trigger
and gold-filled markings. Made 1992-96.

VICTOR II AUTO PISTOL . . . . . NiB $544 Ex $419 Gd $342
Re-creation of the High Standard Victor w/full-length VR.
Caliber: .22 LR. 10-rnd. magazine, 4.5- or 5.5-in. bbl., 9.75
in. overall (w/ 5.5-in. bbl.). Weight: 52 oz. (w/ 5.5-in. bbl.).
Rib-mounted target sights. Satin blued or stainless finish.
Checkered walnut grips w/thumbrest. Made 1992-96.

Mitchell Arms
Sharpshooter II

Mitchell Arms
Victor II

GUARDIAN ANGEL
DERRINGER . . . . **NiB $158 Ex $120 Gd $101**
Hammerless, double-action O/U derringer w/interchangeable drop-in breech block. Calibers: .22 LR, .22 WRM. Two-round capacity. Two-in. bbl., 5 in. overall. Weight: 12 oz. Blue, nickel or gold finish. Blade front and fixed rear sights. Checkered black grips. Made 1996-97.

GUARDIAN II. . . . . **NiB $327 Ex $235 Gd $169**
Caliber: .38 Special, Six-round cylinder, 2-, 4- or 6-in. bbl., 8.5 in. overall (w/ 4-in. bbl.). Weight: 32 oz (w/ 4-in. bbl.). Blade ramp front and fixed rear sights. Checkered combat or target grips. Blued finish. Made in 1995.

GUARDIAN III . . . . **NiB $369 Ex $272 Gd $181**
Same specifications as Guardian II model except w/adjustable rear sights. Made in 1995.

TITAN II DA . . . . **NiB $295 Ex $259 Gd $175**
Caliber: .357 Mag. Six-round cylinder. 2-, 4- or 6-in. bbl., 7.75 in. overall (w/ 4-in. bbl.). Weight: 38 oz (w/ 4-in. bbl.). Blade front and fixed rear sights. Crane mounted cylinder release. Blued or stainless finish. Made in 1995.

TITAN III DA. . . . . **NiB $345 Ex $204 Gd $119**
Same specification as the Titan II except w/adjustable rear sight. Made in 1995.

MKE Kirikkale

MKE — Ankara, Turkey
Manufactured by Makina ve Kimya Endüstrisi Kurumu.

KIRIKKALE DA
AUTOMATIC PISTOL . . . . **NiB $399 Ex $283 Gd $212**
Similar to Walther PP. Calibers: .32 Auto (7.65mm), .380 Auto (9mm Short). Seven-round magazine, 3.9-in. bbl., 6.7 in. overall. Weight: 24 oz. Fixed sights. Blued finish. Checkered plastic grips. Made 1948-88. Note: This is a Turkish Army standard service pistol.

**MOA Maximum
Carbine Pistol**

MOA CORPORATION — Dayton, OH

MAXIMUM . . . . **NiB $930 Ex $730 Gd $530**
Single shot. Calibers: .22 Hornet to .454 Casull Mag. Armoloy, Chromoloy or stainless falling block action fitted w/blued or stainless 8.75-, 10- or 14-in. Douglas bbl., weight: 60-68 oz. Smooth walnut grips. Made 1986.
Carbine model (18-in. bbl.), add $20
w/stainless bbl., add $390
w/extra blued bbl., add $300

**Mossberg Brownie
"Pepperbox" Pistol**

O.F. MOSSBERG & SONS, INC. — North Haven, CT

BROWNIE "PEPPERBOX" PISTOL **NiB $816 Ex $562 Gd $375**
Hammerless, top-break, double-action, four bbls. w/revolving firing pin. Caliber: .22 LR, 2.5-in. bbls., weight: 14 oz. Blued finish. Serrated grips. Approximately 37,000 made from 1919-32.

MODEL 715P PISTOL . . . . **NiB $308 Ex $270 Gd $260**
Semiauto. Uses a Model 702 Plinkster barreled action. Caliber: .22 LR, 10- or 20-rnd. magazine. 6-in. bbl. Weight: 48 oz. Blued finish. Polymer grips. Made 2014-18.
w/red dot optic, add $45
Duck Commander, add $100

MODEL MC1SC . . . . **NiB $425 Ex $400 Gd $300**
Semiauto. Polymer frame, striker-fire. Caliber: 9mm, 6- or 7-rnd. magazine. Bbl.: 3.4-in. Weight: 48 oz. Blued finish. Grips: Textured polymer. Sights: 3-dot. Made 2019 to present.
MC2c (2019 to date) . . . . **NiB $425 Ex $400 Gd $300**

NAMBU
See Listings under Japanese Military Pistols.

NAVY ARMS COMPANY — Martinsburg, WV
Since 1956, importer of numerous reproduction revolvers manufactured by Davide Pedersoli & Co., F.A.P F.LLI. Pietta, A. Uberti, and C. Navy Arms. Previously sold C&R military firearms.

MODEL 1873 SA REVOLVER

Calibers: .44-40, .45 Colt. Six-round cylinder, bbl. lengths: 3, 4.75, 5.5, 7.5 in., 10.75 in. overall (w/ 5.5-in. bbl.). Weight: 36 oz. Blade front sight, grooved topstrap rear. Blued w/color-casehardened frame or nickel finish. Smooth walnut grips. Made 1991-2009.

Blued finish w/brass backstrap	NiB $468	Ex $357	Gd $235
U.S. Artillery model w/5-in. bbl.	NiB $544	Ex $386	Gd $270
U.S. Cavalry model w/7-in. bbl	NiB $544	Ex $386	Gd $270
Bisley model	NiB $536	Ex $359	Gd $225
Sheriff's model (disc. 1998)	NiB $434	Ex $356	Gd $220

MODEL 1875 SCHOFIELD REVOLVER

Replica of S&W Model 3, top-break single-action w/auto ejector. Calibers: .44-40 or .45 LC. Six-round cylinder, 5- or 7-in. bbl., 10.75 or 12.75 in. overall. Weight: 39 oz. Blade front sight, square-notched rear. Polished blued finish. Smooth walnut grips. Made 1999-2009.

Cavalry model (7-in. bbl.)	NiB $668	Ex $544	Gd $336
Deluxe Cavalry model (engraved)	NiB $1720	Ex $1398	Gd $1176
Wells Fargo model (5-in. bbl.)	NiB $840	Ex $636	Gd $447
Deluxe Wells Fargo model (engraved)	NiB $1479	Ex $1266	Gd $1122
Hideout model (3.5-in. bbl.)	NiB $748	Ex $590	Gd $398

1875 REMINGTON

SA REVOLVER . . . . **NiB $398 Ex $283 Gd $194**
Replica of Remington Model 1875. Calibers: .357 Magnum, .44-40, .45 Colt. Six-round cylinder, 7.5-in. bbl., 13.5 in. overall. Weight: About 48 oz. Fixed sights. Blued or nickel finish. Smooth walnut grips. Made in Italy c.1955-80 and 1994 to 2000. Originally marketed in the U.S. as Replica Arms Model 1875 (that firm was acquired by Navy Arms Co).

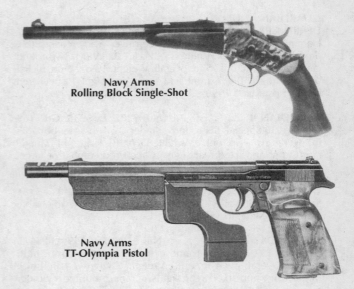

**Navy Arms
Rolling Block Single-Shot**

**Navy Arms
TT-Olympia Pistol**

**Navy Arms
Model 1875 Schofield**

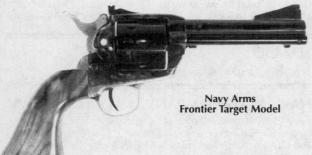

**Navy Arms
Frontier Target Model**

FRONTIER SA REVOLVER . . . . . **NiB $397 Ex $290 Gd $224**
Calibers: .22 LR, .22 WMR, .357 Mag., .45 Colt. Six-round cylinder, bbl. lengths: 4.5-, 5.5-, 7.5-in., 10.25 in. overall (w/ 4.5-in. bbl.). Weight: About 36 oz. (w/ 4.5-in. bbl.). Fixed sights. Blued bbl., and cylinder, color-casehardened frame, brass grip frame. One-piece smooth walnut grip. Imported from 1975 to 1979.

FRONTIER TARGET MODEL . . . **NiB $416 Ex $312 Gd $225**
Same as standard Frontier except has adj. rear sight and ramp front sight. Imported from 1975 to 1979.

BUNTLINE FRONTIER . . . . **NiB $569 Ex $467 Gd $342**
Same as Target Frontier except has detachable shoulder stock and 16.5-in. bbl. Calibers: .357 Magnum and .45 Colt only. Made 1975-79.

LUGER AUTOMATIC . . . . **NiB $166 Ex $112 Gd $88**
Caliber: .22 LR, standard or high velocity. 10-rnd. magazine, bbl. length: 4.5 in., 8.9 in. overall. Weight: 1 lb., 13.5 oz. Square blade front sight w/square notch, stationary rear sight. Walnut checkered grips. Non-reflecting black finish. Made 1986-88.

ROLLING BLOCK

SINGLE-SHOT PISTOL . . . . **NiB $418 Ex $345 Gd $231**
Calibers: .22 LR, .22 Hornet, .357 Magnum. Eight-in. bbl., 12 in. overall. Weight: About 40 oz. Adjustable sights. Blued bbl., color-casehardened frame, brass trigger guard. Smooth walnut grip and forearm. Imported from 1965 to 1980.

TT-OLYMPIA PISTOL. . . . . **NiB $283 Ex $214 Gd $170**
Reproduction of the Walther Olympia Target Pistol. Caliber: .22 LR. Eight in. overall 4.6-in. bbl., weight: 28 oz. Blade front sight, adj. rear. Blued finish. Checkered hardwood grips. Imported 1992 to 1994.

NEW ENGLAND FIREARMS — Gardner, MA

In 1987, New England Firearms was established as an independent company producing select H&R models under the NEF logo. In 1991, H&R 1871, Inc. was formed from the residual of the parent company and took over the New England Firearms

New England Firearms
Model R73 Revolver

facility. H&R 1871 produced firearms under both their logo and the NEF brand name until 1999, when the Marlin Firearms Company acquired the assets of H&R 1871. Purchased by Freedom Group in 2008.

MODEL R73 REVOLVER . . . . NiB $158 Ex $98 Gd $67
Caliber: .32 H&R Mag. Five-round cylinder, 2.5- or 4-in. bbl., 8.5 in. overall (w/ 4-in. bbl.). Weight: 26 oz. (w/ 4 in. bbl.). Fixed or adjustable sights. Blued or nickel finish. Walnut-finish hardwood grips. Made 1988-99.

MODEL R92 REVOLVER . . . . NiB $137 Ex $90 Gd $64
Same general specifications as Model R73 except chambered for .22 LR. Nine-round cylinder. Weight: 28 oz. w/4 in. bbl., Made 1988-99.

MODEL 832 STARTER PISTOL . . NiB $148 Ex $101 Gd $75
Calibers: .22 Blank, .32 Blank. Nine- and 5-rnd. cylinders, respectively. Push-pin swing-out cylinder. Solid wood grips w/ NEF medallion insert.

ULTRA REVOLVER . . . . NiB $170 Ex $109 Gd $70
Calibers: .22 LR, .22 Mag. Nine-round cylinder in .22 LR, 6-rnd. cylinder in .22 Mag., 4- or 6-in. ribbed bull bbl., 10.75 in. overall (w/ 6-in. bbl.). Weight: 36 oz. (w/ 6-in. bbl.). Blade front sight, adj. square-notched rear. Blued or nickel finish. Walnut-finish hardwood grips. Made 1989-99.

LADY ULTRA REVOLVER . . . . . NiB $169 Ex $144 Gd $106
Same basic specifications as the Ultra except in .32 H&R Mag. w/5-rnd. cylinder and 3-in. ribbed bull bbl., 7.5 in. overall. Weight: 31 oz. Made 1992-99.

NORTH AMERICAN ARMS — Provo, UT

MODEL .22LR . . . . NiB $175 Ex $149 Gd $70
Same as Model 22S except chambered for .22 LR., is 3.88-in. overall, weight: 4.5 oz. Made 1975 to date.

MODEL 22S MINI REVOLVER . . NiB $170 Ex $150 Gd $70
Single-Action. Caliber: .22 Short. Five-round cylinder, 1.13-in. bbl., 3.5-in. overall. Weight: 4 oz. Fixed sights. Stainless steel. Plastic grips. Made 1975 to date.

MODEL 450 MAGNUM EXPRESS
Single-Action. Calibers: .450 Magnum Express, .45 Win. Mag. Five-round cylinder, 7.5- or 10.5-in. bbl., matte or polished stainless steel finish. Walnut grips. Presentation case. Disc. 1984.
Matte stainless model . . . . . . NiB $1259 Ex $1066 Gd $808
Polished stainless model . . . . NiB $1528 Ex $1234 Gd $856
w/10-in. bbl., add $281
w/combo cylinder, add $255

BLACK WIDOW REVOLVER
SA. Calibers: .22 LR., .22 WMR. Five-round cylinder, 2-in. heavy vent bbl., 5.88-in. overall. Weight: 8.8 oz. Fixed or adj. sights. Full-size black rubber grips. Stainless steel brush finish. Made 1990 to date.
Adj. sight model . . . . NiB $257 Ex $188 Gd $135
Adj. sight combo model, add $45
Fixed sight model . . . . NiB $257 Ex $188 Gd $135
Fixed sight combo model, add $40

GUARDIAN DAO PISTOL . . . . NiB $377 Ex $286 Gd $198
Caliber: .25 ACP, .32 ACP or .380. Six-round magazine (.32 ACP), 2-in. bbl., 4.4 in. overall. Weight: 13.5 oz. Fixed sights. Black synthetic grips. Stainless steel. Made 1997 to date.

MINI-MASTER TARGET REVOLVER
SA. Calibers: .22 LR., .22 WMR. Five-round cylinder, 4-in. heavy VR bbl., 7.75-in. overall. Weight: 10.75 oz. Fixed or adj. sights. Black rubber grips. Stainless steel brush finish. Made 1990 to date.
Adj. sight model . . . . NiB $270 Ex $214 Gd $165
Adj. sight combo model, add $35
Fixed sight model . . . . NiB $270 Ex $214 Gd $165
Fixed sight combo model, add $35

New England Firearms
Model 832 Starter Pistol

North American Arms
Model .22 LR

GRADING: **NiB** = New in Box   **Ex** = Excellent or NRA 95%   **Gd** = Good or NRA 68%

NORWEGIAN MILITARY PISTOLS — Manufactured by Kongsberg Vaapenfabrikk, Government Arsenal at Kongsberg, Norway

MODEL 1912 . . . . **NiB $2885 Ex $2289 Gd $1588**
Same as the model 1914 except has conventional slide stop. Only 500 were made.

MODEL 1914
AUTOMATIC PISTOL . . . . **NiB $511 Ex $378 Gd $283**
Similar to Colt Model 1911 .45 Automatic w/same general specifications except has lengthened slide stop. Made 1919-46.

OLYMPIC ARMS, INC. — Olympia, WA

OA-93 AR SEMIAUTO PISTOL
AR-15 style receiver with no buffer tube or charging handle. Caliber: .223 Rem. or 7.62x39mm. Five-, 20- or 30-rnd. detachable magazine, 6-, 9- or 14-in. stainless steel bbl., 15.75 in. overall w/6-in. bbl., weight: 4 lbs., 3 oz. Flattop upper with no open sights. VortEx flash suppressor. A2 stowaway pistol grip and forward pistol grip. Made 1993-94. Note: All post-ban versions of OA-93 style weapons are classified by BATF as "Any Other Weapon" and must be transferred by a Class III dealer. Values listed here are for limited-production, pre-ban guns.
(.223 Rem.) . . . . **NiB $1134 Ex $871 Gd $687**
(7.62x39mm) . . . . **NiB $2234 Ex $1669 Gd $1378**

OA-96 AR SEMIAUTO
PISTOL . . . . **NiB $904 Ex $804 Gd $637**
Similar to Model OA-93 AR except w/6.5-in. bbl. only chambered for .223 Rem. Additional compliance modifications include a fixed (nonremovable) well-style magazine and no forward pistol grip. Made 1996-2000.

WHITNEY WOLVERINE . . . . . . **NiB $294 Ex $265 Gd $235**
Similar to original Whitney Wolverine from 1950s except w/polymer frame and ventalated rib. .22 LR, 10-rnd. magazine. Finish: black, pink, desert tan, coyote brown. Weight: 19.2 oz. Made 2010-18.

Olympic Arms OA-93

**Ortgies
Pocket Automatic Pistol**

ORTGIES PISTOLS — Erfurt, Germany

Manufactured by Deutsche Werke A.G.

POCKET
AUTOMATIC PISTOL . . . . **NiB $399 Ex $305 Gd $225**
Calibers: .32 Auto (7.65mm), .380 Auto (9mm). Seven-round magazine (.380 cal.), 8-rnd. (.32 cal.), 3.25-in. bbl., 6.5-in. overall. Weight: 22 oz. Fixed sights. Blued finish. Plain walnut grips. Made in 1920's.

VEST POCKET
AUTOMATIC PISTOL . . . . **NiB $365 Ex $289 Gd $203**
Caliber: .25 Auto (6.35mm). Six-round magazine, 2.75-in. bbl., 5.19 in. overall. Weight: 13.5 oz. Fixed sights. Blued finish. Plain walnut grips. Made in 1920's.

PARA USA, INC. — Pineville, NC

Purchased by Freedom Group in 2012. Previously Para-Ordnance in Ontario, Canada. Manufacturing stopped in 2015.

Note: *Para-Ord pistols are based on the 1911 platform in single-stack and double-stack magazine variants. The standard model was the P series chambered in 9mm, .40 S&W, 10mm or .45 ACP. Barrel lengths from 3-, 3.5-, 4.25- or 5-in. Finishes were matte black or stainless. Custom-tuned and fully accessorized "Limited Edition" versions of standard "P" Models. Enhanced-grip frame and serrated slide fitted w/match-grade bbl., and full-length recoil spring guide system. Beavertail grip safety and skeletonized hammer. Ambidextrous safety and trigger-stop adjustment. Fully adjustable or contoured low-mount sights.*

P SERIES AUTO PISTOL
Calibers: 9mm, .40 S&W, 10mm or .45 ACP. 10-rnd. magazine, Bbl.: 3.5-, 4.25- or 5-in. Weight: 24 oz. (alloy frame) or 31 oz. (steel frame). Ramp front sight and drift adjustable rear w/3-dot system. Matte black, Duo-Tone or stainless finish.
Model P10 (1997-02) . . . . **NiB $630 Ex $540 Gd $413**
Model P12 (.40 S&W or .45 ACP,
    compact model, 1990-03) . . . **NiB $760 Ex $581 Gd $464**
Model P13 (4.25-in. bbl., 1993-03) . . **NiB $760 Ex $577 Gd $447**
Model P14 (5-in. bbl., 1990-03) . . . **NiB $690 Ex $536 Gd $410**
Model P15 (.40 S&W, 4.25-in. bbl.,
    1996-99) . . . . **NiB $630 Ex $475 Gd $380**

Model P16 (.40 S&W, 5-in. bbl.,
1995-02) . . . . NiB $630 Ex $475 Gd $380
Model P18 (9mm, 5-in. bbl.,
1998-03) . . . . NiB $810 Ex $610 Gd $450

EXPERT SERIES AUTO PISTOL
Calibers: 9mm or .45 ACP. Single stack magazine, 5-in. bbl.
Weight: 39 oz. (steel frame). Fiber optic front sight, 2-dot rear.
Polymer grips. Finish: black nitride.
Black nitride (2013-15) . . . . NiB $570 Ex $430 Gd $315
Stainless (2013-15) . . . . NiB $610 Ex $455 Gd $330
Carry model (3-in. bbl., 2013-15) . . . . . NiB $680 Ex $505 Gd $370
Commander model
(4.25-in. bbl., 2013-15) . . . . . . NiB $680 Ex $505 Gd $370
10.45 model (.45 ACP,
5-in. bbl., 2013-15) . . . . NiB $755 Ex $670 Gd $405
14.45 model (.45 ACP, 5-in. bbl., double
stack magazine, 2012-15) . . . . NiB $680 Ex $505 Gd $370

ELITE SERIES AUTO PISTOL
Calibers: 10mm or .45 ACP, 6-, 7-, 8- or 9-rnd. magazine, 3-,
3.5-, 4.25-, 5- or 6-in. bbl.Fiber optic front sight, adj. rear or
night sights. Textured G10 grips. Matte black or tow-tone finish.
Made 2013-15.
Elite (.45 ACP, 5-in. bbl.,
8-rnd. magazine) . . . . NiB $805 Ex $605 Gd $445
Elite Carry (.45 ACP, 3-in. bbl.,
6-rnd. magazine) . . . . NiB $805 Ex $605 Gd $400
Elite Commander (.45 ACP, 4.25-in. bbl.,
8-rnd. magazine) . . . . NiB $805 Ex $605 Gd $400
Elite LS Hunter (10mm,
6-in. bbl.) . . . . NiB $1055 Ex $800 Gd $580
Elite Pro (.45 ACP, 5-in. bbl.) . . NiB $1055 Ex $800 Gd $580
Elite Officer (.45 ACP, 3.5-in. bbl.,
7-rnd. magazine) . . . . NiB $805 Ex $605 Gd $400
Elite Target (.45 ACP, 5-in. bbl.,
8-rnd. magazine) . . . . NiB $855 Ex $645 Gd $480

CUSTOM SERIES AUTO PISTOL
Caliber: 9mm, .40 S&W or .45 ACP. 8-, 10-, 14-, 16- or 18-rnd.
magazine. Alloy or steel frame. Fiber optic front sight, adj. rear.
G10 grips. Made 2013-15.
Executive Agent (.45 ACP, 3-in. bbl.,
bobtail frame) . . . . NiB $1190 Ex $900 Gd $655
Executive Carry (.45 ACP, 3-in. bbl.,
bobtail frame) . . . . NiB $1190 Ex $900 Gd $655
Pro Custom 10.45 (.45 ACP, 5-in. bbl.,
stainless) . . . . NiB $1230 Ex $930 Gd $680
Pro Custom 14.45 (.45 ACP, 5-in. bbl., stainless, 14-rnd.
magazine) . . . . NiB $1230 Ex $930 Gd $680
Pro Custom 16.40 (.40 S&W, 5-in. bbl., stainless,
16-rnd. magazine) . . . . NiB $1230 Ex $930 Gd $680
Pro Custom 18.9 (9mm, 5-in. bbl., stainless,
16-rnd. magazine) . . . . NiB $1230 Ex $930 Gd $680
Pro Comp (9mm or .40 S&W, 5-in. bbl., stainless,
single stack magazine) . . . . . . NiB $1110 Ex $830 Gd $605
Tomasie Custom (.40 S&W, 5-in. bbl., stainless,
16-rnd. magazine) . . . . NiB $1705 Ex $1280 Gd $940

S SERIES
Similar to P-Series pistols except with competition features.
Caliber: .40 S&W or .45 ACP.
S10 Limited (1999-02) . . . . NiB $770 Ex $580 Gd $420
S12 Limited (1999-03) . . . . NiB $900 Ex $675 Gd $500
S13 Limited (1999-03) . . . . NiB $900 Ex $675 Gd $500
S14 Limited (1999-03) . . . . NiB $855 Ex $640 Gd $460
S16 Limited (1998-03) . . . . NiB $855 Ex $640 Gd $460

Para-Ordnance
PXT LDA SSP

Para-Ordnance
P-14 Auto Pistol

PXT LDA DOUBLE STACK SERIES
Similar to PXT LDA single stack series except w/double stack
magazine capacity.
Carry (.45 ACP, 3.25-in. bbl.,
12-rnd. magazine) . . . . NiB $1055 Ex $790 Gd $580
Tac-Four (.45 ACP, 4.25-in. bbl.,
12-rnd. magazine) . . . . NiB $965 Ex $740 Gd $530
Tac-Forty (.40 S&W, 4.25-in. bbl.,
15-rnd. magazine) . . . . NiB $930 Ex $730 Gd $530
Tac-Five (9mm, 5-in. bbl.,
18-rnd. magazine) . . . . NiB $1055 Ex $790 Gd $580
Covert Black Nite-Tac (.45 ACP, 5-in. bbl.,
accessory rail, 2006-08) . . . . NiB $1000 Ex $735 Gd $530
Hi-Capacity (.45 ACP, stainless,
disc. 2008) . . . . NiB $1000 Ex $735 Gd $530
Hi-Capacity Limited (.45 ACP, stainless,
disc. 2009) . . . . NiB $1080 Ex $780 Gd $590

PXT LDA SINGLE STACK SERIES
DAO w/spurless hammer. Caliber: 9mm, .45 GAP or .45 ACP.
Single stack magazine, 3-, 3.5- or 4.25-in. bbl.
Carry (.45 ACP, 3-in. bbl., stainless) . . NiB $1030 Ex $775 Gd $570
Carry (.45 GAP, 3-in. bbl., disc. 2008) . . NiB $980 Ex $740 Gd $540
Carry (9mm, 3-in. bbl., matte black,
2006-11) . . . . NiB $910 Ex $680 Gd $500
CCO (.45 ACP, 3.5-in. bbl., matte black,
disc. 2008) . . . . NiB $1010 Ex $755 Gd $555
CCO (.45 GAP, 3.5-in. bbl.,
2006-08) . . . . NiB $980 Ex $740 Gd $540
CCO Companion Black Watch (.45 ACP, 3.5-in. bbl.,
stainless) . . . . NiB $980 Ex $740 Gd $540
CCW (.45 ACP, 4.25-in. bbl., matte black,
disc. 2008) . . . . NiB $1010 Ex $755 Gd $555
Companion (.45 ACP, 3.5-in. bbl., stainless,
2011-12) . . . . NiB $900 Ex $655 Gd $470
Companion II (.45 ACP, 4.25-in. bbl., stainless,
2011-12) . . . . NiB $755 Ex $530 Gd $380
Covert Black Carry
(.45 ACP, 3-in. bbl.) . . . . NiB $1030 Ex $775 Gd $570
Covert Black Nite-Tac (.45 ACP, 5-in. bbl.,
stainless, 2006-08) . . . . NiB $1010 Ex $755 Gd $555

Hawg 9 (9mm, 3-in. bbl., 3-dot sights,
2013-15) . . . . NiB $880 Ex $660 Gd $485
Limited (.45 ACP, 5-in. bbl., blue
or stainless) . . . . NiB $940 Ex $705 Gd $505
PDA (9mm, 3-in. bbl., matte black,
2008-11) . . . . NiB $1130 Ex $830 Gd $610
PDA (.45 ACP, 3-in. bbl., matte black,
2008-11) . . . . NiB $1155 Ex $855 Gd $630
SSP (.45 ACP, 5-in. bbl., stainless,
disc. 2009) . . . . NiB $1030 Ex $775 Gd $570

PXT SINGLE STACK SERIES AUTO PISTOL
Caliber: 9mm Para., .38 Super or .45 ACP. Eight- or 9-rnd. (9mm Para) magazine, 3-, 3.5-, 4.25-, 5- or 6-in. bbl., 8.5 in. overall (5-in. bbl.). Weight: 30 oz. (5-in. bbl.). Steel or stainless frame. Blade front sight, adj. rear w/3-dot system. Textured composition grips. Matte black alloy or steel finish. Made 2004-15.
1911 OPS (disc. 2008) . . . . NiB $980 Ex $931 Gd $450
1911 LTC (intro. 2009) . . . . NiB $780 Ex $741 Gd $330
1911 Wild Bunch (intro. 2011) . . . NiB $660 Ex $550 Gd $340
GI Expert (intro. 2009) . . . . NiB $580 Ex $440 Gd $355
Slim Hawg (.45 ACP, 3-in. bbl.) . . . NiB $860 Ex $670 Gd $400
Black Ops (.45 ACP, 5-in. bbl., night sights,
2012-15) . . . . NiB $1080 Ex $830 Gd $630
Black Ops 14.45 (.45 ACP, 5-in. bbl., night sights, double
stack magazine, 2012-15) . . . NiB $1110 Ex $830 Gd $630
Black Ops Combat (.45 ACP, 5.5-in.
threaded bbl., night sights, double stack magazine,
2013-15) . . . . NiB $1130 Ex $830 Gd $630
Black Ops Recon (9mm or .45 ACP, 4.25-in. bbl.,
night sights, double stack magazine,
2013-15) . . . . NiB $1110 Ex $830 Gd $630
Limited (.45 ACP, 5-in. bbl., wood grips, single stack
magazine, 2011 only) . . . . . . NiB $1155 Ex $855 Gd $630
SSP (.38 Super or .45 ACP, 5-in. bbl., 2004-08
and 2012-15). . . . . NiB $780 Ex $555 Gd $380

PXT HIGH CAPACITY SERIES AUTO PISTOL
Similar to PXT Single Stack series except 10-, 14-, or 18-rnd. magazine. Made 2004-15.
P14.45 (.45 ACP) . . . . NiB $880 Ex $650 Gd $410
P18.9 (9mm Para) . . . . NiB $1030 Ex $840 Gd $470
Warthog (.45 ACP) . . . . NiB $900 Ex $700 Gd $400
Hawg 7 (.45 ACP, 3.5-in. bbl.,
2011-13) . . . . NiB $780 Ex $580 Gd $430
Lite Hawg 7 (accessory rail,
disc. 2008) . . . . NiB $995 Ex $745 Gd $550
Hawg 9 (9mm, 3-in. bbl., 3-dot sights,
2013-15). . . . . NiB $880 Ex $660 Gd $485
Lite Hawg 9 (accessory rail, disc.
2008) . . . . NiB $995 Ex $745 Gd $550
Nite Hawg (.45 ACP, 3-in. bbl., night sights,
disc. 2015) . . . . NiB $1000 Ex $750 Gd $550
Big Hawg (.45 ACP, 5-in. bbl.,
disc. 2015) . . . . NiB $880 Ex $670 Gd $485
Super Hawg (.45 ACP, 6-in. bbl.,
2008-10) . . . . NiB $1255 Ex $940 Gd $690

PHOENIX ARMS — Ontario, CA

MODEL HP22/HP25 SA
AUTO PISTOLS . . . . NiB $170 Ex $95 Gd $66
Caliber: .22 LR, .25 ACP. 10-rnd. magazine, 3-in. bbl., 5.5 in. overall. Weight: 20 oz. Checkered synthetic grips. Blade front sight, adj. rear. Blue, chrome or nickel finish. Made 1994 to date.

MODEL HP RANGE-MASTER TARGET SA
AUTO PISTOL . . . . NiB $170 Ex $95 Gd $66
Similar to Model HP .22 except w/5.5-in. target bbl. and Extended magazine, Ramp front sight, adj. notch rear on VR. Checkered synthetic grips. Blue or satin nickel finish. Made 1998 to date.

MODEL HP RANGE-MASTER DELUXE TARGET
SA AUTO PISTOL . . . . NiB $204 Ex $165 Gd $110
Similar to Model HP Rangemaster Target model except w/dual-2000 laser sight and custom wood grips. Made 1998 to date.

RAVEN SA AUTO PISTOL . . . . NiB $88 Ex $61 Gd $45
Caliber: .25 ACP. Six-round magazine, 2.5 in. bbl., 4.75 in. overall. Weight: 15 oz. Ivory, pink pearl, or black slotted stocks. Fixed sights. Blue, chrome or nickel finish. Made 1993-98.

PLAINFIELD MACHINE COMPANY — Dunellen, NJ
This firm disc. operation about 1982.

MODEL 71 AUTOMATIC PISTOL
Calibers: .22 LR, .25 Automatic w/conversion kit available. 10-rnd. magazine (.22 LR) or 8-round (.25 Auto), 2.5-in. bbl., 5.13 in. overall. Weight: 25 oz. Fixed sights. Stainless steel frame/slide. Checkered walnut grips. Made 1970-82.
.22 LR or .25 Auto . . . . NiB $200 Ex $177 Gd $128
w/conversion kit . . . . NiB $222 Ex $188 Gd $119

MODEL 72 AUTOMATIC PISTOL
Same as Model 71 except has aluminum slide, 3.5-in. bbl., 6 in. overall. Made 1970-82
.22 LR or .25 Auto only . . . . . . NiB $220 Ex $177 Gd $101
w/conversion kit . . . . NiB $235 Ex $166 Gd $128

Plainfield Model 71

Plainfield Model 72

Polish Military P-83 Wanad

RADOM — Radom, Poland
Manufactured by the Polish Arsenal.

P-35 AUTOMATIC PISTOL
Variation of the Colt Government Model .45 Auto. Caliber: 9mm Para. Eight-round magazine, 4.75-in. bbl., 7.75 in. overall. Weight: 29 oz. Fixed sights. Blued finish. Plastic grips. Made 1935 thru WWII.

Commercial model
  (Polish Eagle) . . . . NiB $4599 Ex $4370 Gd $2555
Nazi military model
  (w/slotted backstrap) . . . . . NiB $1629 Ex $1199 Gd $877
Nazi military model
  (w/takedown lever) . . . . . . NiB $1300 Ex $1000 Gd $431
Nazi military model
  (No takedown lever or slot) . . NiB $459 Ex $356 Gd $232
Nazi military model (Parkerized), add $357

POLISH MILITARY PISTOLS — Radom, Poland
Manufactured at Lucznik Arms Factory.

MODEL P-64. . . . . NiB n/a Ex $250 Gd $125
SA/DA. Similar to Walther PPK. Caliber: 9x18mm Makarov. 3.3-in. bbl., 22 oz. Military surplus. Made 1965 to date.

MODEL P-83 WANAD . . . . NiB n/a Ex $350 Gd $220
SA/DA. Caliber: 9x18mm Makarov. 8-rnd. magazine. 3.5-in. bbl., 26 oz. Military surplus. Made 1983 to date.

PROFESSIONAL ORDNANCE, INC. — Lake Havasu City, AZ

MODEL CARBON-15 TYPE 20
SEMIAUTO PISTOL. . . . . NiB $944 Ex $819 Gd $581
Similar to Carbon-15 Type 97 except w/unfluted barrel. Weight: 40 oz. Matte black finish. Made 1999-2000.

MODEL CARBON-15 TYPE 97
SEMIAUTO PISTOL. . . . . NiB $1030 Ex $927 Gd $588
AR-15 operating system w/recoil reduction system. Caliber: .223 Rem. 10-rnd. magazine, 7.25-in. fluted bbl., 20 in. overall. Weight: 46 oz. Ghost ring sights. Carbon-fiber upper and lower receivers w/Chromoly bolt carrier. Matte black finish. Checkered composition grip. Made 1996-2003.

Radom P-35

RANDALL FIREARMS COMPANY — Sun Valley, CA
The short-lived Randall firearms Company (1982 to 1984) was a leader in the production of stainless steel semi-autimatic handguns, particularly in left-handed configurations. Prices shown are for production models. Add 50% for prototype models (t-prefix on serial numbers) and $125 for guns with serial numbers below 2000. Scare models (C311, C332, etc., made in lots of four pieces or less) valued substantially higher to avid collectors.

MODEL A111 . . . . NiB $791 Ex $479 Gd $316
Caliber: .45 Auto. Barrel: 5 in. Round-slide top; right-hand model. Sights: Fixed. Total production: 3,431 pieces.

MODEL A112 . . . . NiB $920 Ex $689 Gd $581
Calibers: 9mm. Barrel: 5 in. Round-slide top; right-hand model. Sights: Fixed.

MODEL A121 . . . . NiB $734 Ex $643 Gd $377
Caliber: .45 Auto. Barrel: 5 in. Flat-slide top; right-hand model. Sights: Fixed.

MODEL A211 . . . . NiB $785 Ex $571 Gd $479
Caliber: .45 Auto. Barrel: 4.25 in. Round-slide top; right-hand model. Sights: Fixed.

MODEL A232 . . . . NiB $1560 Ex $1357 Gd $1100
Caliber: 9mm. Barrel: 4.25 in. Flat-slide top; right-hand model. Sights: Fixed.

MODEL A331 . . . . NiB $1808 Ex $1566 Gd $1234
Caliber: .45 Auto. Barrel: 4.25 in. Flat-slide top; right-hand model. Sights: Fixed.

MODEL B111 . . . . NiB $1270 Ex $1124 Gd $890
Caliber: .45 Auto. Barrel: 5 in. Round-slide top; left-hand model. Sights: Fixed. Toatal production: 297 pieces

MODEL B131 . . . . NiB $1470 Ex $1326 Gd $1152
Caliber: .45 Auto. Barrel: 5 in. Flat-slide top; left-hand model. Sights: Millet. Total production: 225 pieces.

MODEL B311 . . . . NiB $1632 Ex $1418 Gd $1206
Caliber: .45 Auto. Barrel: 4.25 in. Round-slide top; left-hand model. Sights: Fixed. Total production: 52 pieces.

MODEL B312 LEMAY . . . . . NiB $5170 Ex $1669 Gd $3090
Caliber: 9mm. Barrel: 4.25 in. Round-slide top; left-hand model. Sights: Fixed. Total production: 9 pieces.

MODEL B331 . . . . NiB $1800 Ex $1589 Gd $1356
Caliber: .45 Auto. Barrel: 4.25 in. Flat-slide top; left-hand model. Sights: Millet. Total production: 45 pieces.

RECORD-MATCH PISTOLS — Zella-Mehlis, Germany. Manufactured by Udo Anschütz

MODEL 200 FREE PISTOL . . . NiB $1039 Ex $760 Gd $616
Basically the same as Model 210 except w/different stock design and conventional set trigger, spur trigger guard. Made prior to WW II.

MODEL 210 FREE PISTOL . . NiB $1355 Ex $1206 Gd $919
System Martini action, set trigger w/button release. Caliber: .22 LR. Single-shot, 11-in. bbl., weight: 46 oz. Target sights micrometer rear. Blued finish. Carved and checkered walnut forearm and stock w/adj. hand base. Also made w/dual action (Model 210A); weight 35 oz. Made prior to WWII.

REISING ARMS CO. — Hartford, CT

TARGET AUTOMATIC PISTOL . . . NiB $1132 Ex $862 Gd $587
Hinged frame. Outside hammer. Caliber: .22 LR. 12-rnd. magazine, 6.5-in. bbl., fixed sights. Blued finish. Hard rubber grips. Made 1921-24.

REMINGTON ARMS COMPANY — Madison, NC

Manufacturing in Ilion, New York; Lonoke, AR; and Mayfield, KY. Owned by the Freedom Group. Purchased by Roundhill Group after 2020 Remington bankruptcy.

MODEL 51 AUTOMATIC PISTOL
Calibers: .32 Auto, .380 Auto. Seven-round magazine, 3.5-in. bbl., 6.63 in. overall. Weight: 21 oz. Fixed sights. Blued finish. Hard rubber grips. Made 1918-26.
.32 ACP . . . . NiB $887 Ex $780 Gd $453
.380 ACP . . . . NiB $899 Ex $790 Gd $495

MODEL 95 DOUBLE DERRINGER
SA. Caliber: 41 Short Rimfire. Three-inch double bbls. (superposed), 4.88 in. overall. Early models have long hammer spur and two-armed Extractor, but later guns have short hammer spur and sliding Extractor (a few have no Extractor). Fixed blade front sight and grooved rear. finish: Blued, blued w/nickel-plated frame or fully nickel-plated; also w/factory engraving. Grips: Walnut, checkered hard rubber, pearl, ivory. Weight: 11 oz. Made 1866-1935. Approximately 150,000 were manufactured. Note: Duringthe 70 years of its production, serial numbering of this model was repeated two or three times. Therefore, aside from hammer and Extractor differences between the earlier and later models, the best clue to the age of a Double Derringer is the stamping of the company's name on the top of the bbl., or side rib. Prior to 1888, derringers were stamped "E. Remington & Sons, Ilion, N.Y." on one side rib and "Elliot's Patent Dec. 12, 1865" on the other (Type I-early & mid-production) and on the top rib (Type I-late production). In 1888-1911, "Remington Arms Co., Ilion, N.Y." and patent date were stamped on the top rib

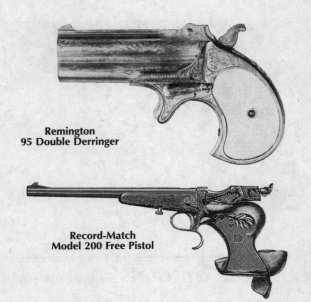

Remington
95 Double Derringer

Record-Match
Model 200 Free Pistol

(Type II) and from 1912-35 "Remington Arms - U.M.C. Co., Ilion, N.Y." and patent date were stamped on the top rib.
Model 95 (Early Type I,
 w/o Extractor) . . . . NiB $6600 Ex $5000 Gd $3800
Model 95 (Mid Type I,
 w/Extractor) . . . . NiB $11,000 Ex $8000 Gd $4000
Model 95 (Late Type I,
 w/Extractor) . . . . NiB $5000 Ex $4219 Gd $1000
M95 (TYPE II
 produced 1888-1911) . . . . NiB $3700 Ex $2588 Gd $909
Model 95 (Type III,
 produced 1912-35) . . . . . NiB $3600 Ex $3000 Gd $1099
Factory-engraved model w/ivory
 or pearl grips, add 40%

NEW MODEL SINGLE-SHOT TARGET PISTOL
Also called Model 1901 Target. Rolling-block action. Calibers: .22 Short & Long, .25 Stevens, .32 S&W, .44 S&W Russian. 10-in. half-octagon bbl., 14 in. overall. Weight: 45 oz. (.22 cal.). Target sights. Blued finish. Checkered walnut grips and forearm. Made 1901-09.
Model 1901 (.22 caliber) . . NiB $3750 Ex $2550 Gd $1203
Model 1901
 (.25 Stevens, .32 S&W) . . NiB $3449 Ex $2988 Gd $1380
Model 1901 (.44 Russian) . . NiB $3969 Ex $2709 Gd $1190

MODEL XP-100
SINGLE-SHOT PISTOL. . . . . . . NiB $984 Ex $622 Gd $464
Bolt action. Caliber: 221 Rem. Fireball. 10.5-in. VR bbl., 16.75 in. overall. Weight: 3.75 lbs. Adj. rear sight, blade front, receiver drilled and tapped for scope mounts. Blued finish. One-piece brown nylon stock. Made 1963-88.

MODEL XP-100
CUSTOM PISTOL. . . . . NiB $1096 Ex $755 Gd $596
Bolt-action, single-shot, long-range pistol. Calibers: .223 Rem., 7mm-08 or .35 Rem. 14.5-in. bbl., standard contour or heavy. Weight: About 4.25 lbs. 1986–94.

MODEL XP-100 SILHOUETTE . NiB $984 Ex $622 Gd $464
Same general specifications as Model XP-100 except chambered for 7mm BR Rem. and 35 Rem. 14.75-in. bbl., weight: 4.13 lbs. Made 1987-92.

MODEL XP-100
VARMINT SPECIAL . . . . NiB $984 Ex $622 Gd $464
Bolt-action, single-shot, long-range pistol. Calibers: .223 Rem., 7mm BR. 14.5-in. bbl., 21.25 in. overall. Weight: About 4.25 lbs. One-piece Du Pont nylon stock w/universal grips. Made 1986-92.

MODEL XP-100R
CUSTOM REPEATER
Same general specifications as Model XP-100 Custom except 4- or 5- rnd. repeater chambered for .22-250, .223 Rem., .250 Savage, 7mm-08 Rem., .308 Win., .35 Rem. and .350 Rem. Mag. Kevlar-reinforced synthetic or fiberglass stock w/blind magazine and sling swivel studs. Made 1992-94 and from 1998 to 1999.
w/fiberglass stock . . . . NiB $984 Ex $622 Gd $464
KS model
  (kevlar stock) . . . . NiB $984 Ex $622 Gd $464

MODEL 700 CP . . . . NiB $1169 Ex $1111 Gd $850
Uses Model 700 action. Bolt-action. Calibers: .223 Rem., .300 BLK, .308 Win. and 6.5 Creedmoor; 10-rnd. magazine. X-Mark Pro trigger, M-LOK handguard, and SBA3 arm brace. Bbl.: 10.5- to 12.5-in. depending on caliber. Made 2020 only.

NOTE: *The following Remington derringers were produced from the mid-1860s through the mid-1930s. The Zig-Zag model is reputed to be the first cartridge handgun ever produced at the Remington plant. Few if any Remington derringers Exiswt in "new" or "in box" condition, therefore, guns in 90-percent condition command top price.*

ZIG-ZAG DERRINGER . . . . NiB $6155 Ex $5875 Gd $4145
Caliber: .22S, L, LR. Six shot, six-barrel (rotating) cluster. 3-in. bbl., blued, ring trigger. Two-piece rubber grips. Fewer than 1,000 pieces produced from 1861 to 1863.

ELIOT'S FIVE-SHOT
DERRINGER . . . . NiB $1897 Ex $1268 Gd $1091
Caliber: .22S, L, LR. Five shot, five-barrel fixed cluster. 3-in. bbl., ring trigger, blue and/or nickel finish. Two-piece rubber, walnut, ivory or pearl grips.

ELIOT'S FOUR-SHOT
DERRINGER . . . . NiB $5000 Ex $4275 $3795
Caliber: .32. Four shot, four-barrel fixed cluster. 3-3/8 in. bbl., ring trigger, blue and/or nickel finish. Two-piece rubber, walnut, ivory or pearl grips. Approx. 25,000 pieces (.22 and .32) produced.

VEST POCKET
DERRINGER . . . . NiB $3255 Ex $2920 Gd $2635
Caliber: .22, .30, .32, .41 rimfire. Two shot, various bbl. lengths, blue or nickel finish. Two-piece walnut grips. Spur trigger. Made 1865-88.

OVER AND UNDER
DERRINGER . . . . NiB $6270 Ex $4720 Gd $3955
Caliber: .41 rimfire. Two shot, 3-in. super imposed bbl., spur trigger, blue and/or nickel finish. Two-piece rubber, walnut, ivory or pearl grips. Oscillating firing pin. Produced 1866-1934. Also known as Double Derringer or Model 95. Type 1 and variatitons bear maker's name, patent data stamped between the barrels, with or without Extractor. Types Two and Three marked "Remington Arms Company, Ilion, NY. Type Four marked on top of barrel, "Remington Arms-U.M.C. Co. Ilion, NY."

MODEL 1866
ROLLING BLOCK PISTOL . . . NiB $6210 Ex $4329 Gd $3144
Caliber: .50 rimfire. Single-shot, 8-1/2 in. round, blue finish. Walnut grip and forearm. Spur trigger. Made 1866-67. Mistakenly designated as Model 1865 Navy. Top values are for military-marked, pristine pieces. Very few of these guns remain in original condition.

MODEL 1870 NAVY
ROLLING BLOCK PISTOL . . . NiB $4225 Ex $3199 Gd $1905
Caliber: .50 centerfire. Single shot, 7-in. rnd. bbl. Standard trigger with trigger guard, walnut grip and forearm. Approx. 6,400 pieces made from 1870-75. Modified for the Navy from Model 1866. Higher values are for 8--in. commercial version without proof marks.

RIDER'S
MAGAZINE PISTOL . . . . NiB $3577 Ex $2885 Gd $2389
Caliber: .32. Five shot, 3-in. octagon bbl. blued (add 50 percent for case-hardened receiver). Walnut, rosewood, ivory or pearl grips. Spur trigger. Made 1871-88.

ELIOT'S VEST POCKET SINGLE-SHOT
DERRINGER . . . . NiB $3387 Ex $1109 Gd $879
Caliber: .41 rimfire. Single-shot, 2-1/2-in. rnd. bbl., blue and/or nickel finish. Also known as "Mississippi Derringer." Two-piece walnut grips. Spur trigger. Approx. 10,000 made from 1867 to 1888.

MODEL 1890 SINGLE-ACTION
REVOLVER . . . . NiB $15,210 Ex $14,070 Gd $7680
Caliber: .41 centerfire. Six shot, 5-3/4 or 7-1/2-in. rnd. bbl., blue or nickel finish. Standard trigger with trigger guard. Two-piece ivory or pearl grips with Remington monogram. nickel finish valued about 15 percent less.

MODEL 1911
REMINGTON UMC . . . . . NiB $7000 Ex $5550 Gd $1650
Caliber: .45 ACP. WWII military contract production. Blued finish. Made 1918-19, with serial numbers 1 to 21,676.

MODEL 1911A1
REMINGTON RAND . . . . NiB $2500 Ex $2079 Gd $1086
Caliber: .45 ACP. Parkerized finish. Two-piece walnut grips. Made 1943-45 by Remington Rand Co., not Remington Arms Co.

MODEL 1911 R1 . . . . NiB $774 Ex $660 Gd $510
1911 platform. Semiauto. SA. Caliber: .45 ACP; 7-rnd. magazine. 5.0-in. bbl. Frame: steel. Sights: fixed. Finish: high polish blue. Grip: checkered double diamond walnut. Length: 8.5 in. Weight: 38.5 oz. Made 2014-20.
Carry model (extended beavertail, ambi.
  safety) . . . . NiB $1067 Ex $1000 Gd $880
Carry Commander model (4.25-in. bbl., extended beaver-
  tail, ambi. safety) . . . . NiB $1067 Ex $1000 Gd $880
Carry Commander CT model
  (4.25-in. bbl., laser grip) . . NiB $1350 Ex $1100 Gd $880
Commander model
  (4.25-in. bbl.) . . . . NiB $774 Ex $660 Gd $510
Enhanced model (extended beavertail, ambi.
  safety) . . . . NiB $837 Ex $790 Gd $700
Enhanced stainless model (extended beavertail, ambi.
  safety, stainless) . . . . NiB $990 Ex $880 Gd $750

Enhanced threaded bbl. model (extended beavertail, ambi.
  safety, thread bbl.) . . . . NiB $959 Ex $960 Gd $850
Stainless model (stainless) . . . NiB $837 Ex $790 Gd $700

GRADING: **NiB** = New in Box   **Ex** = Excellent or NRA 95%   **Gd** = Good or NRA 68%   **143**

MODEL R51 . . . . **NiB $405 Ex $330 Gd $280**
Semiauto. Caliber: 9mm; 7-rnd. magazine. 3.4-in. bbl. Frame: aluminum. Sights: fixed. Finish: matte black. Grip: checkered polymer. Length: 6.6 in. Weight: 22 oz. Made 2014; rereleased 2016–20.

MODEL RM380 . . . . **NiB $380 Ex $310 Gd $235**
Semiauto. DAO. Caliber: .380 ACP; 6-rnd. magazine. 2.9-in. bbl. Frame: aluminum. Sights: fixed. Finish: matte black. Grip: checkered polymer. Length: 5.27 in. Made 2016–20.

RG (RÖHM GESELLSCHAFT)—Germany

Imported by R.G. Industries, Miami, FL., then manufactured until 1986.

MODEL 23 . . . . **NiB $115 Ex $88 Gd $70**
SA/DA. 6-rnd. magazine, swing-out cylinder. Caliber: .22 LR. 1.75- or 3.38-in. bbl., Overall length: 5.13 and 7.5 in. Weight: 16-17 oz. Fixed sights. Blued or nickel finish. Disc. 986.

RG Model 23

MODEL 38S
SA/DA. Caliber: .38 Special. Six-round magazine, swing-out cylinder. Three- or 4-in. bbl., overall length: 8.25 and 9.25 in. Weight: 32-34 oz. Windage-adj. rear sight. Blued finish. Disc. 1986.
w/plastic grips . . . . **NiB $177 Ex $140 Gd $101**
w/wood grips . . . . **NiB $212 Ex $130 Gd $95**

ROCK ISLAND ARMORY (RIA) — Philippines
Currently the trademark of Armscor.

NOTE: *Numerous 1911 platform pistols in a variety of series. See each series for features but generally as follows. Calibers: 9mm, .38 Super, .40 S&W, 10mm or .45 ACP; single or double stack magazines. Bbl. Lengths: 3.5-, 4.25-, 5-in. bbl. Fiber optic or post front sight, adj. rear or fixed sights. Grips: smooth wood, checkered rubber or textured G10 grips. Finish: parkerized. Made 1996 to present. Models are designated CS (compact frame, 3.5-in. bbl.), MS (commander size frame, 4.2-in. bbl.), and FS (full size frame, 5-in. bbl.).*

BBR SERIES
Compact 1911 configuration. Caliber: .380, 7-rnd. magazine. Barrel: 3.78 in. Finish: Parkerized. Sights: Fixed. Grip: Checkered rubber. Imported 2016 to date.
Standard Model . . . . **NiB $405 Ex $355 Gd $280**
3.10 model (.45 ACP, 10-rnd. mag., 3.1-in. bbl., 2020 to date) . . . . **NiB $605 Ex $505 Gd $405**

GI SERIES
Standard 1911 military configuration. Parkerized. Fixed sights. Wood grip, 9mm, .38 Super, or .45 Auto.
CS model (3.5-in. bbl.) . . . . **NiB $475 Ex $340 Gd $255**

FS model (5-in. bbl.) . . . . **NiB $465 Ex $335 Gd $255**
MS model (4.25-in. bbl.) . . . . **NiB $465 Ex $335 Gd $255**

LI380. . . . . **NiB $299 Ex $270 Gd $210**
Semiauto. DAO trigger, metal frame. Caliber: .380 Auto, 8-rnd. magazine, 3.5-in. bbl., 6.5 in. overall. Finish: Black anodized. Grip: Textured polymer. Sights: Fixed. Mfg. 2023 to date.

MAPP SERIES
Semiauto. DA/SA trigger. Polymer frame. Integrated front sight, snag free rear sight, 9mm w/ 10- or 15-rnd. magazine.
CS model (3.5-in. bbl.) . . . . **NiB $455 Ex $335 Gd $255**
FS model (4.6-in. bbl.) . . . . **NiB $455 Ex $335 Gd $255**
MS model (3.7-in. bbl.). . . . . **NiB $455 Ex $335 Gd $255**

PRO MATCH SERIES
Fiber optic front sight, single or double stack magazine.
Pro Ultra Match model (10mm or .45 ACP, 6-in. bbl., single-stack magazine, accessory rail) . . **NiB $1000 Ex $780 Gd $580**
Pro Ultra Match HC (9mm, .40 S&W or .45 ACP, double-stack magazine, 5- or 6-in. bbl.) . . **NiB $770 Ex $580 Gd $405**

RIA 5.0 . . . . **NiB $1,298 Ex $1,100 Gd $990**
Semiauto. Striker-fired, metal frame. Caliber: 9mm, 17-rnd. magazine, 4.9-in. bbl., 8.1 in. overall. Finish: Black anodized. Grip: Textured nylon. Sights: Fixed or factory mounted red dot optic. RVS recoil system. Mfg. 2023 to date.

ROCK STANDARD SERIES
Upgraded sights, skeletonized hammer and trigger, ambidextrous safety, 7- or 8-rnd. magazine.
CS model (.45 ACP,) . . . . **NiB $555 Ex $430 Gd $330**
FS model (9mm or .45 ACP, checkered rubber grip) . . . . . . **NiB $530 Ex $380 Gd $280**
MS model (.45 ACP,) . . . . **NiB $530 Ex $380 Gd $280**

ROCK ULTRA SERIES
Fiber optic front sight, skeletonized hammer and trigger, ambidextrous safety.
CS model (.45 ACP, 7-rnd. magazine) . . . . **NiB $690 Ex $530 Gd $455**
CS Warrior model (.45 ACP, G10 grips) . . . . **NiB $730 Ex $585 Gd $455**
FS model (9mm, .40 S&W, 10mm or .45 ACP, 8- or 9-rnd. magazine) . . . . . . **NiB $680 Ex $530 Gd $455**
MS model (9mm, .40 S&W, 10mm or .45 ACP, 8-rnd. magazine) . . . . **NiB $680 Ex $530 Gd $455**

STK100 . . . . **NiB $599 Ex $575 Gd $500**
Semiauto. Striker-fired, metal frame. Caliber: 9mm, 17-rnd. magazine, 4.5-in. bbl., 7.0 in. overall. Finish: Black anodized. Grip: Textured aluminum. Sights: Fixed steel, optic ready. 1911 style trigger guard. Compatible with Glock magazines. Slide cuts. Imported from 2021 to date.

TAC SERIES
Full dust cover, accessory rail, fiber optic front sight/adj. rear, skeletonized hammer and trigger, ambidextrous safety, G10 grip. .40 Auto disc., 7-, 8-, or 9-rnd. magazines depending on caliber.
Standard FS model (.45 ACP, 8-rnd. magazine) . . . . **NiB $530 Ex $380 Gd $280**
Ultra CS model (9mm or .45 ACP,) . . . . **NiB $720 Ex $570 Gd $490**
Ultra FS model (.40 S&W, 10mm or .45 ACP,) . . . . **NiB $705 Ex $555 Gd $480**
Ultra MS model (9mm, .40 S&W, or .45 ACP,) . . . . **NiB $720 Ex $570 Gd $490**

TCM SERIES

Caliber: .22 TCM. Accessory rail, fiber optic front sight/adj. rear, skeletonized hammer and trigger, ambi safety, G10 grip.

Rock Premium FS model (5-in. bbl.,
17-rnd. magazine) . . . . NiB $815 Ex $715 Gd $555
Rock Ultra CS model (3.62-in. bbl.,
8-rnd. magazine, 2016-19) . . . NiB $740 Ex $585 Gd $455
Rock Ultra CCO model (4.25-in. bbl.,
disc. 2016) . . . . NiB $745 Ex $585 Gd $455
Rock Ultra FS model (5-in. bbl., 10-rnd.
magazine, disc. 2019) . . . . . . NiB $730 Ex $585 Gd $455
Standard MS model (4.25-in. bbl., 17-rnd.
magazine, 2020-date) . . . . . . NiB $640 Ex $555 Gd $430
TAC Ultra FS model (5-in. bbl., 10-rnd.
magazine, disc. 2019) . . . . . . NiB $785 Ex $620 Gd $490

XT SERIES

1911 configuration except blowback action. Caliber: .22 LR, 10- or 15-rnd. magazine. Barrel: 5 in. Finish: Parkerized. Sights: Fixed. Grip: Checkered rubber. Imported from 2011 to 2018 and 2020 to date.

Standard Model . . . . NiB $520 Ex $470 Gd $380
Standard Combo model
(.22 LR/.45 ACP) . . . . NiB $770 Ex $690 Gd $590
TAC model (.22 LR, optic ready,
2014-16) . . . . NiB $540 Ex $455 Gd $370
22 Magnum (.22 Magnum, 14-rnd. mag., 2014-18, reintro.
2020 to date) . . . . NiB $520 Ex $470 Gd $380
22 Magnum Target (.22 Magnum, 14-rnd. mag., adj. sights,
2014-18, reintro. 2020 to date) . . NiB $520 Ex $470 Gd $380
22 Magnum Pro (.22 Magnum, 14-rnd. mag., optic ready,
2014-18, reintro. 2020 to date) . . NiB $520 Ex $470 Gd $380

ROHRBAUGH FIREARMS — Long Island, NY

Purchased by Remington in January 2014.

MODEL R9 . . . . NiB $1349 Ex $1300 Gd $1200
Semiauto. DAO. Caliber: .380 ACP or 9mm, 6-rnd magazine. 2.9-in. bbl. Frame: aluminum. Sights: fixed. Finish: matte black or two-tone. Grip: smooth polymer. Weight: 13.5 oz. Length: 5.2 in. Made 2002-14.

Rohrbaugh 380

ROSSI — Sáo Leopoldo, Brazil

Manufactured by Amadeo Rossi S.A., imported by BrazTech, Int'l., in Miami, Florida; previously by Interarms, Alexandria, VA.

MODEL 31 DA REVOLVER . . . . NiB $144 Ex $78 Gd $62
Caliber: .38 Special. Five-round cylinder, 4-in. bbl., weight: 20 oz. Blued or nickel finish. Disc. 1985.

MODEL 51 DA REVOLVER . . . . NiB $147 Ex $82 Gd $61
Caliber: .22 LR. Six-round cylinder, 6-in. bbl., weight: 28 oz. Blued finish. Disc. 1985.

MODEL 68 . . . . NiB $177 Ex $147 Gd $101
Caliber: .38 Special. Five-round magazine, 2- or 3-in. bbl., overall length: 6.5 and 7.5 in. Weight: 21-23 oz. Blued finish. Nickel finish available w/3-in. bbl. Disc. 1998.

MODEL 84 DA REVOLVER . . NiB $209 Ex $160 Gd $110
Caliber: .38 Special. 6-rnd. cylinder, 3-in. bbl., 8-in. overall. Weight: 27.5 oz. Stainless steel finish. Imported 1984 to 1986.

MODEL 85 DA REVOLVER . . NiB $209 Ex $160 Gd $110
Same as Model 84 except has VR. Imported 1985-86.

MODEL 88 DA REVOLVER
Caliber: .38 Special. Five-round cylinder, 2- or 3-in. bbl., weight: 21 oz. Stainless steel finish. Imported from 1988 to 98.
Model 88 (disc.) . . . . NiB $219 Ex $180 Gd $148
Model 88 Lady Rossi
(round butt) . . . . NiB $225 Ex $189 Gd $152

MODEL 88/2 DA REVOLVER NiB $219 Ex $180 Gd $140
Caliber: .38 Special. Five-round cylinder, 2- or 3-in. bbl., 6.5 in. overall. Weight: 21 oz. Stainless steel finish. Imported 1985 to 1987.

MODEL 89 DA REVOLVER . . . NiB $184 Ex $110 Gd $75
Caliber: .32 S&W. Six-round cylinder, 3-in. bbl., 7.5 in. overall. Weight: 17 oz. Stainless steel finish. Imported 1989 to 1990.

MODEL 94 DA REVOLVER . . . NiB $175 Ex $109 Gd $88
Caliber: .38 Special. Six-round cylinder, 3-in. bbl., 8 in. overall. Weight: 29 oz. Imported from 1985 to 1988.

MODEL 95 (951) REVOLVER NiB $219 Ex $175 Gd $141
Caliber: .38 Special. 6-rnd. cylinder, 3-in. bbl., 8-in. overall. Weight: 27.5 oz. VR. Blued finish. Imported 1985 to 1990.

MODEL 351/352 REVOLVERS
Caliber: .38 Special. Five-round cylinder, 2-in. bbl., 6.87 in. overall. Weight: 22 oz. Ramp front and rear adjustable sights. Stainless or matte blued finish. Imported 1999 to date.
Model 351 (matte blue finish) NiB $362 Ex $255 Gd $186
Model 352 (stainless finish) . NiB $437 Ex $326 Gd $265

MODEL 461/462 REVOLVERS
Caliber: .357 Magnum. Six-round cylinder, 2-in. heavy bbl., 6.87 in. overall. Weight: 26 oz. Rubber grips w/ serrated ramp front sight. Stainless or matte blued finish. Imported 1999 to date.
Model 461 (matte blue finish) NiB $365 Ex $265 Gd $188
Model 462 (stainless finish) . NiB $439 Ex $290 Gd $219

MODEL 511 DA REVOLVER . . NiB $195 Ex $170 Gd $75
Similar to the Model 51 except in stainless steel. Imported 1986 to 1990.

MODEL 515 DA REVOLVER . . NiB $214 Ex $105 Gd $70
Calibers: .22 LR, .22 Mag. Six-round cylinder, 4-in. bbl., 9 in. overall. Weight: 30 oz. Red ramp front sight, adj. square-notched rear. Stainless finish. Checkered hardwood grips. Imported from 1994 to 1998.

MODEL 518 DA REVOLVER . . NiB $214 Ex $105 Gd $70
Similar to the Model 515 except in caliber .22 LR. Imported from 1993 to 1998.

MODEL 677 DA REVOLVER . NiB $225 Ex $180 Gd $128
Caliber: .357 Mag. Six-round cylinder, 2-in. bbl., 6.87 in. overall. Weight: 26 oz. Serrated front ramp sight, channel rear. Matte blue finish. Contoured rubber grips. Imported 1997-98.

Rossi Cyclops

Rossi 971 VRC

MODEL 720 DA REVOLVER. NiB $235 Ex $170 Gd $141
Caliber: .44 Special. Five-round cylinder, 3-in. bbl., 8 in. overall. Weight: 27.5 oz. Red ramp front sight, adj. square-notched rear. Stainless finish. Checkered Neoprene combat-style grips. Imported from 1992 to 1998.

MODEL 841 DA REVOLVER. NiB $319 Ex $225 Gd $160
Same general specifications as Model 84 except has 4-in. bbl., (9 in. overall), weight: 30 oz. Imported 1985-86.

MODEL 851 DA REVOLVER. NiB $336 Ex $259 Gd $158
Same general specifications as Model 85 except w/3-or 4-in. bbl., 8 in. overall (w/ 3-in. bbl.). Weight: 27.5 oz. (w/ 3-in. bbl.). Red ramp front sight, adj. square-notched rear. Stainless finish. Checkered hardwood grips. Imported from 2001 to 2009 to date.

MODEL 877 DA REVOLVER . . . NiB $230 Ex $160 Gd $110
Same general specifications as Model 677 except stainless steel. Made 1996 to date.

MODEL 941 DA REVOLVER . . . . NiB $214 Ex $109 Gd $82
Caliber: .38 Special. Six-round cylinder, 4-in. bbl., 9 in. overall. Weight: 30 oz. Blued finish. Imported from 1985-86.

MODEL 951 DA REVOLVER . . . . NiB $214 Ex $109 Gd $82
Previous designation M95 w/same general specifications.

MODEL 971 DA REVOLVER
Caliber: .357 Magnum. Six-round cylinder, 2.5-, 4- or 6-in. bbl., 9 in. overall (w/ 4-in. bbl.). Weight: 36 oz. (w/ 4-in. bbl.). Blade front sight, adj. square-notched rear. Blued or stainless finish. Checkered hardwood grips. Imported from 1988 to 1998.
Blued finish. . . . . NiB $219 Ex $166 Gd $129
Stainless finish. . . . . NiB $240 Ex $175 Gd $101
w/compensated bbl., add $25

MODEL 971 VRC
DA REVOLVER . . . . NiB $321 Ex $270 Gd $175
Same general specifications as Model 971 stainless except w/ventilated rib and compensated bbl. Made 1988-98.

MODEL 972 . . . . NiB $380 Ex $330 Gd $260
Similar to Model 971 except stainless steel, 6-in. bbl. Imported from 2001 to date.

CYCLOPS DA REVOLVER . . . . . NiB $425 Ex $362 Gd $274
Caliber: .357 Mag. Six-round cylinder, 6- or 8-in. compensated slab-sided bbl., 11.75 or 13.75 in. overall. Weight: 44 oz. or 51 oz. Undercut blade front sight, fully adjustable rear. B-Square scope mount and rings. Stainless steel finish. Checkered rubber grips. Made 1997-98.

DA REVOLVER . . . . NiB $220 Ex $170 Gd $124
Calibers: .22 LR, .32 S&W Long, .38 Special. 5-rnd. (.38) or 6-rnd. cylinder (other calibers), bbl. lengths: 3-, 6-in. Weight: 22 oz. (3-in. bbl.). Adj. Rear sight, ramp front. Blued or nickel finish. Wood or plastic grips. Imported from 1965-91.

MATCHED PAIR . . . . NiB $380 Ex $330 Gd $260
Single-shot, break action w/interchangeable bbls. SA. Caliber: .22 LR or .45 Long Colt/410 gauge. 11-in. bbl. Frame: steel. Sights: fixed front, adj. rear. Finish: blue. Grip: textured rubber. Made 2012 to date.

RANCH HAND . . . . NiB $597 Ex $500 Gd $380
Lever-action Mare's Leg style pistol. SA. Caliber: .357 Mag., .44 Mag., or .45 Long Colt, 6-rnd. magazine. 12-in. bbl. Sights: adj rear. Finish: blue. Made 2010-16.

SPORTSMAN'S .22 . . . . NiB $279 Ex $219 Gd $170
Caliber: .22 LR. Six-round magazine, 4-in. bbl., 9 in. overall. Weight: 30 oz. Stainless steel finish. Disc. 1991.

RUBY — Manufactured by Gabilondo y Urresti, Eibar, Spain, and others

7.65MM AUTOMATIC PISTOL . . . NiB $342 Ex $255 Gd $129
Secondary standard service pistol of the French Army in world wars I and II. Essentially the same as the Alkartasuna (see separate listing). Other manufacturers: Armenia Elgoibarresa y Cia., Eceolaza y Vicinai y Cia., Hijos de Angel Echeverria y Cia., Bruno Salaverria y Cia., Zulaika y Cia., all of Eibar, Spain-Gabilondo y Cia., Elgoibar Spain; Ruby Arms Company, Guernica, Spain. Made 1914-22.

RUGER — Southport, CT

Manufactured by Sturm, Ruger & Co. Rugers made in 1976 are designated "Liberty" in honor of the U.S. Bicentennial and bring a premium of approximately 25% in value over regular models.

NOTE: *For ease in finding a particular Ruger handgun, the listings are divided into two groups: Automatic/Single-Shot Pistols (below) and Revolvers, which follow. For a complete listing, please refer to the index.*

- AUTOMATIC/SINGLE-SHOT PISTOLS -

22 CHARGER . . . . NiB $330 Ex $230 Gd $180
Uses Ruger 10/22 action. Caliber: .22 LR, 10-in. bbl., black/grey laminated pistol grip and forend, bipod, matte black finish. Made 2008-12.

22 CHARGER (RECENT MFG.) . NiB $270 Ex $235 Gd $150
Uses Ruger 10/22 action. Caliber: .22 LR, 10-in. threaded bbl. Stock: laminated or polymer. Grip: AR15 A2 style. Finish: matte black. Made 2015 to date.
Takedown (quick take down) . . . NiB $355 Ex $300 Gd $230

PC CHARGER . . . . NiB $799 Ex $750 Gd $480
Uses Ruger PC Carbine action. Takedown. Caliber: 9mm, 17-rnd. Bbl.: 6.5-in. threaded. M-LOK handguard. Interchangeable magazine well. Finish: matte black. Made 2020 to date.

Ruger Charger (2015-date MFG.)

AMERICAN SERIES
Semiauto. Striker fired. Caliber: 9mm or .45 ACP, 10 or 17-rnd magazine. 4.2- or 4.5-in. bbl. Frame: polymer. Sights: fixed. Finish: matte black. Grip: modular polymer inserts. Weight: 30-31.5 oz. Length: 7.5-8 in. Made 2016 to date.

Duty (4.25-in. bbl.) . . . . NiB $480 Ex $360 Gd $280
Compact (3.5-in. bbl.) . . . . NiB $480 Ex $360 Gd $280
Competition (5-in. bbl.) . . . . NiB $480 Ex $360 Gd $280

HAWKEYE SINGLE-SHOT
PISTOL . . . . NiB $2555 Ex $2427 Gd $1000
Built on a SA revolver frame w/cylinder replaced by a swing-out breechblock and fitted w/a bbl., w/integral chamber. Caliber: .256 Magnum. 8.5-in. bbl., 14.5 in. overall. Weight: 45 oz. Blued finish. Ramp front sight, click adj. rear. Smooth walnut grips. Made 1963-65 (3,300 produced).

MARK I TARGET MODEL AUTOMATIC PISTOL
Caliber: .22 LR. 10-rnd. magazine, 5.25- and 6.88-in. heavy tapered or 5.5-in. untapered bull bbl., 10.88 in. overall (w/ 6.88-in. bbl.). Weight: 42 oz. (in 5.5- or 6.88-in. bbl.). Undercut target front sight, adj. rear. Blued finish. Hard rubber grips or checkered walnut thumbrest grips. Made 1952-82.

Standard model . . . . NiB $877 Ex $791 Gd $612
w/red medallion . . . . NiB $975 Ex $859 Gd $712
Walnut grips, add $434

MARK II AUTOMATIC PISTOL
Caliber: .22 LR, standard or high velocity 10-rnd. magazine, 4.75- or 6-in. tapered bbl., 8.31 in. overall (w/ 4.75-in. bbl.). Weight: 36 oz. Fixed front sight, square notch rear. Blued or stainless finish. Made 1982-2004.

Blued. . . . . NiB $265 Ex $305 Gd $158
Stainless . . . . NiB $321 Ex $265 Gd $204
Bright stainless (ltd. prod.
    5,000 in 1982) . . . . NiB $590 Ex $479 Gd $346

MARK II 22/45 AUTOMATIC PISTOL
Same general specifications as Ruger Mark II .22 LR except w/blued or stainless receiver and bbl., in four lengths: 4-in. tapered w/adj. sights (P4), 4.75-in. tapered w/fixed sights (KP4), 5.25-in. tapered w/adj. sights (KP 514) and 5.5-in. bull (KP 512). Fitted w/Zytel grip frame of the same design as the Model 1911 45 ACP. Made 1993-2004.

Model KP4 (4.75-in. bbl.) . . . . . NiB $255 Ex $177 Gd $140
Model KP512, KP514
    (w/5.5- or 5.25-in. bbl.) . . . . . NiB $365 Ex $229 Gd $126
Model P4, P512
    (Blued w/4- or 5.5-in. bbl.) . . NiB $270 Ex $216 Gd $160

MARK II BULL BBL. MODEL
Same as standard Mark II except for bull bbl. (5.5- or 10-in.). Weight: About 2.75 lbs.

Blued finish. . . . . NiB $319 Ex $237 Gd $175
Stainless finish (intro. 1985) . . . NiB $430 Ex $379 Gd $128

MARK II GOVERNMENT MODEL AUTO PISTOL
Civilian version of the Mark II used by U.S. Armed Forces. Caliber: .22LR. 10-rnd. magazine, 6.88-in. bull bbl., 11.13 in. overall. Weight: 44 oz. Blued or stainless finish. Made 1986-99.

Blued model (MK687G
    commercial) . . . . NiB $430 Ex $280 Gd $170
Stainless steel model
    (KMK678G commercial) . . . . NiB $480 Ex $330 Gd $180
w/U.S. markings (military model). . . NiB $1260 Ex $760 Gd $380
w/Competition Slabside bbl.
    (1992-2004) . . . . NiB $480 Ex $330 Gd $180

Ruger Mark II

Ruger Mark II 22/45

MARK II TARGET MODEL
Caliber: .22 LR. 10-rnd. magazine, 4-, 5.5- and 10-in. bull bbl. or 5.25- and 6.88-in. heavy tappered bbl., weight: 38 oz. to 52 oz. 11.13 in. overall (w/ 6.88-in. bbl.). Made 1982-2004.

Blued. . . . . NiB $375 Ex $303 Gd $128
Stainless steel . . . . NiB $444 Ex $377 Gd $290

MARK III AUTOMATIC PISTOL
Similar to Mark II pistol except w/magazine button on left side grip, tapered bolt ears, and improved ejection port. Made 2005 to date.

Blued. . . . . NiB $389 Ex $190 Gd $120

MARK III TARGET AUTOMATIC PISTOL
Same as Mark III pistol except w/tapered barrel, adj. rear sight, laminated grips. Made 2005 to date.

Blued. . . . . NiB $460 Ex $240 Gd $180
Stainless steel . . . . NiB $569 Ex $290 Gd $190
Government Competition . . . . . NiB $659 Ex $350 Gd $250

MARK III 22/45 AUTOMATIC PISTOL
Similar to Mark II 22/45 pistol except w/Mark III improvements. Made 2005-12.

Blued. . . . . NiB $345 Ex $260 Gd $180
Stainless steel, add $20
Hunter (fluted bbl.), add. $90
Lite (2012 to date) . . . . NiB $480 Ex $335 Gd $280
Target (5.5- or 6.87-in. bull bbl.) . . . NiB $430 Ex $325 Gd $240
Threaded bbl. (2011 to date), add $80

MARK IV AUTOMATIC PISTOL
Same as Mark III pistol except w/one-button take down feature. Made 2016 to date. NOTE: 22/45 models have a polymer 1911-style grip.

Standard (blue, 4.75- or 6-in. tapered bbl.,
    fixed sights) . . . . NiB $449 Ex $400 Gd $305
Competition (stainless, 6.8-in. slab side bbl., adj. sights,
    wood grip) . . . . NiB $749 Ex $690 Gd $400

Hunter (stainless, 6.8-in. fluted bbl., fiber optic sight, wood grip) . . . . NiB $769 Ex $700 Gd $410

Tactical (blue, 5.5-in. threaded bull bbl., target sights, picatinny rails). . . . . NiB $569 Ex $500 Gd $310

Target (blue or stainless, 5.5-in. bull bbl., target sights) . . NiB $529 Ex $500 Gd $310

Target (10-in. bull bbl.), add $110

22/45 (blue, 5.5-in. bull bbl., target sights) . . . . NiB $409 Ex $380 Gd $205

22/45 Lite (various finishes, lightweight ventilated receiver, 4.4-in. threaded bbl.) . . . NiB $559 Ex $500 Gd $370

22/45 Tactical (blue, 5.5-in. threaded bull bbl., target sights, picatinny rails) . . . . NiB $529 Ex $500 Gd $350

MODEL LCP . . . . NiB $379 Ex $230 Gd $150
DOA. Caliber: .380 ACP, 6- or 7-rnd. magazine, 2.75 in. bbl. Weight: 9.4 oz. Fixed sights. Made 2008 to date.
w/Crimsontrace sight, add $150
w/LaserMax sight, add $75
Stainless steel slide finish . . . . . NiB $429 Ex $225 Gd $175

MODEL LCP II SERIES . . . . NiB $349 Ex $300 Gd $180
DOA. Caliber: .22 LR (10-rnd. mag.) or .380 Auto (6-rnd. mag.) 2.75 in. bbl. Polymer frame. Finish: blue. Weight: 11.2 oz. Fixed sights. Lite Rack slide. Made 2016 to date.

MODEL LC9 PISTOL . . . . NiB $379 Ex $230 Gd $150
DAO. Caliber: 9mm. 7- or 9-rnd. magazine, 3.12 in. bbl. Weight: 17.1 oz. Fixed 3-dot sights. Blued finish. Made 2011 to date.
w/Crimsontrace sight, add $150
w/LaserMax sight, add $75

MODEL LC380 PISTOL . . . . . . NiB $379 Ex $230 Gd $150
Similar to LC9 pistol except chambered in .380 ACP. Blued finish. Made 2013 to date.
w/Crimsontrace sight, add $150
w/LaserMax sight, add $75

MODEL P-85 AND P-85 MK II
Semiauto. Caliber: 9mm. DA, recoil-operated. 15-rnd. capacity, 4.5 in. bbl., 7.84 in. overall. Weight: 32 oz. Fixed rear sight, square-post front. Available w/decocking levers, ambidExtrous safety or in DA only. Blued or stainless finish. Made 1987-92.
Blued finish. . . . . NiB $350 Ex $270 Gd $220
Stainless steel finish, add $50

MODEL P-89 AUTOMATIC PISTOL
Caliber: 9mm. DA w/slide-mounted safety levers. 15-rnd. magazine, 4.5-in. bbl., 7.84 in. overall. Weight: 32 oz. Square-post front sight, adj. rear w/3-dot system. Blued or stainless steel finish. Grooved black Xenoy grips. Made 1992-2007.
P-89 blued . . . . NiB $434 Ex $321 Gd $225
P-89 stainless . . . . NiB $546 Ex $453 Gd $388

MODEL P-89 DAC/DAO AUTO PISTOLS
Similar to the standard Model P-89 except the P-89 DAC has ambidextrous decocking levers. The P-89 DAO operates in double-action-only mode. Made 1991-2009.
P-89 DAC blued . . . . NiB $431 Ex $316 Gd $225
P-89 DAC/DAO stainless . . . . . NiB $530 Ex $431 Gd $316

MODEL P-90, KP90 DA AUTOMATIC PISTOL
Caliber: .45 ACP. Seven-round magazine, 4.5-in. bbl., 7.88 in. overall. Weight: 33.5 oz. Square-post front sight adj. square-notched rear w/3-dot system. Grooved black Xenoy composition grips. Blued or stainless finish. DAC model has ambidExtrous decocking levers. Made 1991-2010.

Ruger P-89

Ruger P-90

Ruger P-93
Compact

Ruger P-97

blued. . . . . NiB $530 Ex $342 Gd $240
DAC (decocker) . . . . NiB $530 Ex $342 Gd $240
DAC stainless . . . . NiB $536 Ex $367 Gd $270
DAC (decocker) . . . . NiB $536 Ex $367 Gd $270

MODEL P-91 DA AUTOMATIC PISTOL
Same general specifications as the Model P-90 except chambered for .40 S&W w/12-rnd. double-column magazine, Made 1992-94.
DAC (decockers) . . . . NiB $444 Ex $289 Gd $225
DAO (DA only) . . . . NiB $444 Ex $289 Gd $225

MODEL P-93D AUTO PISTOL
Similar to the standard Model P-89 except w/3.9-in. bbl., (7.3 in. overall). Weight: 31 oz. Stainless steel finish. Made 1993-2004.
DAC (decocker) (disc. 1994) . . . NiB $444 Ex $289 Gd $225
Stainless . . . . NiB $485 Ex $357 Gd $283

MODEL P-94 AUTOMATIC PISTOL
Similar to the Model P-91 except w/4.25-in. bbl., Calibers: 9mm or .40 S&W. Blued or stainless steel finish. Made 1994-2004.

DAC (S/S decocker) . . . . NiB $444 Ex $289 Gd $225
DAO (S/S dble. action only) . . . NiB $444 Ex $289 Gd $225
DAC (Blued decocker) . . . . NiB $444 Ex $289 Gd $225
DAO (blued dble. action only). . . NiB $395 Ex $290 Gd $198

MODEL P-95PR AUTO PISTOL
Caliber: 9mm Parabellum. 10-rnd. magazine, 3.9-in. bbl., 7.3 in. overall. Weight: 27 oz. Square-post front sight, drift adjustable rear w/3-dot system. Molded polymer grip-frame fitted w/ stainless or chrome-moly slide. AmbidExtrous decocking levers (P-95D) or double action only (DAO). Matte black or stainless finish. Made 1997 to date.

P-95 blued . . . . NiB $444 Ex $289 Gd $225
KP-95PR stainless . . . . NiB $398 Ex $270 Gd $190

MODEL P-97D AUTOMATIC PISTOL
Caliber: .45 ACP. Eight-round magazine, 4.5- in. bbl., 7.25 in. overall. Weight: 30.5 oz. Square-post front sight adj. square-notched rear w/3-dot system. Grooved black Xenoy composition grips. Blued or stainless finish. DAC model has ambidExtrous decocking levers. Made 2002-04.

DAO stainless . . . . NiB $444 Ex $289 Gd $225
DAC (decockers) . . . . NiB $377 Ex $306 Gd $219

MODEL P-345 AUTOMATIC PISTOL
SA/DA. Caliber: .45 ACP. 8-rnd. magazine, 4.25-in. bbl. Black polymer frame w/rail, blued steel slide. Weight: 29 oz. Fixed sights. Ambidextrous safety or decocking levers. Made 2005-12.

blued. NiB $490 Ex $340 Gd $225
decocker . . . . NiB $520 Ex $350 Gd $230

MODEL P-944 . . . . NiB $450 Ex $300 Gd $220
Similar to Model P-94 except in .40 S&W, ambidextrous safety and blued finish. Many variations of safety type, decocker or DAO. Made 1999-2010.

Stainless finish, add. $50

MODEL SR22 . . . . NiB $399 Ex $265 Gd $230
SA/DA. Caliber: .22 LR. 10-rnd. magazine, 3.25-in. bbl. Polymer frame, steel slide w/front/rear serrations. Weight: 17.5 oz. 3-dot adj. sights. Blued finish. Two backstrap inserts. Made 2012 to date.

Threaded barrel, add. $50
Two-tone finish, add $30
w/4.5-in. bbl., add $10

MODEL SR9/SR40/SR45 . . . . . NiB $480 Ex $355 Gd $230
Striker fired system. Caliber: 9mm. 10- or 17-rnd. magazine, 4.1-in. bbl. Polymer frame w/reversible backstrap. Weight: 26.5 oz. 3-dot low profile sights. Black stainless, brushed stainless, or OD green finish. Made 2007-18. **NOTE:** SR40 (.40 S&W) and SR45 (.45 Auto) have similar features and values.

9E model (economy version), subtract $100
OD green finish (2009-10), add $20
SR9C (3.5-in. bbl., 2010-18) . . . . NiB $480 Ex $355 Gd $280

MODEL SR1911 SERIES
1911 platform. Caliber: .45 ACP. 5-in. bbl., 7- and 8-rnd. magazine. Stainless steel, checkered cocobola grips. Navak 3-dot sights. Made 2011 to date.

Full-size. . . . . NiB $790 Ex $500 Gd $330

Commander model
(4.25-in. bbl.) . . . . NiB $829 Ex $470 Gd $330
Lightweight Commander model (9mm or .45 ACP,
aluminum receiver) . . . . NiB $829 Ex $630 Gd $460
Officer-Style (3.6-in. bbl., 9mm,
7-rnd. mag.) . . . . NiB $979 Ex $900 Gd $680
Target model (Bomar adj. sights,
2016-present) . . . . NiB $870 Ex $660 Gd $480

RUGER-57. . . . . NiB $799 Ex $700 Gd $550
Semiauto. Polymer frame, striker-fire, Caliber: 5.7x28mm, 20-rnd. magazine. Bbl.: 4.9-in. Weight: 24.5 oz. Finish: blued. Grips: textured polymer. Sights: adj. rear/fiber optic front. Mfg. from 2020 to date.

STANDARD MODEL AUTOMATIC PISTOL
Caliber: .22 LR. Nine-round magazine, 4.75- or 6-in. bbl., 8.75 in. overall (w/ 4.75-in. bbl.). Weight: 36 oz. (w/ 4.75 in. bbl.). Fixed sights. Blued finish. Hard rubber or checkered walnut grips. Made 1949-52. Known as the "Red Eagle Automatic," this early type is now a collector's item. Note: After the death of Alexander Sturm in 1951, the color of the eagle on the grip medallion was changed from red to black as a memorial. Made 1952-81.

w/red eagle medallion . . . . NiB $689 Ex $536 Gd $431
w/black eagle medallion. . . . . . . NiB $430 Ex $379 Gd $170
Walnut grips, add $40

SECURITY-9 SERIES
Semiauto. Polymer frame, striker-fire, Secure Action similar to LCP II. Caliber: 9mm, 15-rnd. magazine. Bbl.: 4-in. Weight: 23.8 oz. Finish: Blued. Grips: Textured polymer. Sights: Snag free, low profile. Made 2017 to present.

Standard model. . . . . NiB $370 Ex $300 Gd $250
Compact model . . . . NiB $370 Ex $300 Gd $250
w/Viridian E-Series Red Laser, add $100
w/Hogue slip-on grip, add $20

- REVOLVERS -

BEARCAT, SUPER
(OLD MODEL) . . . . NiB $602 Ex $365 Gd $291
Same general specifications as Bearcat except has steel frame. Weight: 25 oz. Made 1971-74.

NEW MODEL BEARCAT
Single action. Same general specifications as Super Bearcat except all steel frame and trigger guard. Interlocked mechanism and transfer bar. Calibers: .22 LR and .22WMR. Interchangeable 6-rnd. cylinders (disc. 1996). Smooth walnut stocks w/Ruger medallion. Made 1994 to date.

Convertible model (disc.
1996 after factory recall) . . NiB $1555 Ex $955 Gd $680
Blued (.22 LR only) . . . . NiB $545 Ex $410 Gd $300
Stainless, add $45

BISLEY, LARGE FRAME
Single action. Calibers: .357 Mag., .41 Mag. .44 Mag., .45 Long Colt. 7.5-in. bbl., 13 in. overall. Weight: 48 oz. Non-fluted or fluted cylinder, no engraving. Ramp front sight, adj. rear. Satin blued or stainless. Made 1986 to date.

Blued finish. . . . . NiB $485 Ex $365 Gd $270
Vaquero/Bisley (blued w/case
colored fr.) . . . . NiB $612 Ex $474 Gd $398
Vaquero/Bisley (stainless
steel) . . . . NiB $587 Ex $434 Gd $357
w/ivory grips, add $50

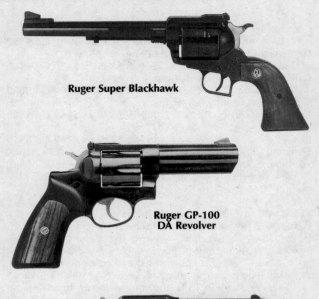

Ruger Super Blackhawk

Ruger LCR

Ruger GP-100
DA Revolver

Ruger Bearcat SA
(Old Model)

Ruger Bisley
Colt .45 Long (New Model)

BISLEY SINGLE-SIX, SMALL FRAME
Single action. Calibers: .22 LR and .32 Mag. Six-round cylinder, 6.5-in. bbl., 11.5 in. overall. Weight: 41 oz. Fixed rear sight, blade front. Blue finish. Goncalo Alves grips. Made 1986 to date.
.22 caliber . . . . NiB $485 Ex $365 Gd $270
.32 H&R Mag. . . . . NiB $693 Ex $601 Gd $479

BLACKHAWK CONVERTIBLE (OLD MODEL)
Same as Blackhawk except has Extra cylinder. Caliber combinations: .357 Magnum and 9mm Para., .45 Colt and .45 Automatic. Made 1967-72.
.357/9mm combo (early w/o
  prefix S/N) . . . . .NiB $556 Ex $437 Gd $290
.357/9mm combo (late
  w/prefix S/N) . . . . NiB $556 Ex $437 Gd $290
.45 LC/.45 ACP combo
  (1967-85 & 1999 to date) . . . NiB $556 Ex $437 Gd $290

BLACKHAWK (OLD MODEL)
Single action. Calibers: .30 Carbine, .357 Mag., .41 Mag., .45 Colt. Six-round cylinder, bbl. lengths: 4.63-in. (.357, .41, .45 caliber), 6.5-in. (.357, .41 caliber), 7.5-in. (.30, .45 caliber). 10.13 in. overall (.357 Mag. w/4.63-in. bbl.). Weight: 38 oz.

(.357 w/4.63-in. bbl.). Ramp front sight, adj. rear. Blued finish. Checkered hard rubber or smooth walnut grips. Made 1955-62.
.30 Carbine, .357 Mag. . . . . NiB $510 Ex $432 Gd $325
.41 Mag. . . . . NiB $760 Ex $660 Gd $265
.45 Colt . . . . NiB $875 Ex $532 Gd $255

BLACKHAWK SA "FLAT-TOP" (OLD MODEL)
Similar to standard Blackhawk except w/"Flat Top" cylinder strap. Calibers: .357 Mag. or .44 Mag. Six-round fluted cylinder, 4.625-, 6.5-, 7.5- or 10-in. bbl., adj. rear sight, ramp front. Blued finish. Black rubber or smooth walnut grips. Made 1955-62.
.357 Mag. (w/4.625-in.
  bbl.) . . . . NiB $1235 Ex $1148 Gd $975
.357 Mag. (w/6.5-in. bbl.) . . . . NiB $479 Ex $342 Gd $198
.357 Mag. (w/10-in. bbl.) . . . . NiB $2540 Ex $1650 Gd $1030
.44 Mag. (w/fluted cylinder/4.625-in.
  bbl.) . . . . NiB $1336 Ex $1270 Gd $1030
.44 Mag. (w/fluted cylinder/ 6.5-in.
  bbl.) . . . . NiB $1020 Ex $666 Gd $408
.44 Mag. (w/fluted cylinder/ 10-in.
  bbl.) . . . . NiB $2540 Ex $1945 Gd $1779

GP-100 SERIES
DA/SA. Caliber: .22 LR, .327 Fed. Mag., .357 Mag., 10mm or .44 Spl.; 5- or 6-rnd. capacity. Bbl.: 2.5-, 3-, 4.2-, 5- or 6--in. full lug or standard. Overall length: 9.38 or 11.38 in.. Grip: Hougue mongrip, rubber grip w/wood inserts or wood. Sights: adj. or fixed. Made 1986 to date. NOTE: There are numerous distributor variations offerd by Talo, Davidson, and Lipsey's and these receive a higher premium.
Blued. . . . . NiB $769 Ex $700 Gd $400
Stainless . . . . NiB $829 Ex $800 Gd $440
Rubber grip w/hardwood insert, add $30

GP-100 MATCH CHAMPION . . . NiB $830 Ex $725 Gd $460
Similar to GP-100 except tuned for competition w/slab side, half under lug 4.25-in. bbl. Matte stainless finish. Caliber: .357 Mag. or 10mm. Grip: Hogue stippled hardwood. Sights: adj. or fixed. Made 2014 to date.
9mm model. . . . . NiB $2540 Ex $1945 Gd $1779

SUPER GP 100 . . . . NiB $1549 Ex $1500 Gd $800
DA/SA. Uses Super Redhawk frame, tuned action. Caliber: .357 Mag. or 9mm; 8-rnd. capacity. Bbl.: 5.5-in. w/vented shroud, half lug. Grip: Hogue hardwood. Sights: adj. rear/fiber optic front. Made 2019 to date.

LCR . . . . NiB $490 Ex $370 Gd $300
DAO. Caliber: .22 LR, .22 WMR, .38 Spl.+P, or .357 Mag. Hammless design, polymer fire control housing, monolithic aluminum frame, stainless cylinder, 1.87-in. bbl., fixed sights, Hogue rubber grip. Made 2010 to date.
.357 Mag., add. $80

Ruger Blackhawk High-Gloss Stainless
(New Model) .357 Magnum

Ruger New Model Blackhawk Convertible

Ruger Single-Six SSM
(New Model)

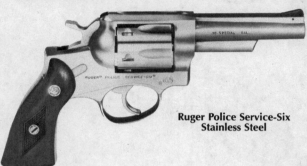

Ruger Police Service-Six
Stainless Steel

Ruger Super Blackhawk
(New Model)

.44 Mag.); 10.5-in. in .44 Mag; 10.38 in. overall (.357 Mag. w/4.63-in. bbl.). Weight: 40 oz. (.357 w/4.63-in. bbl.). Adj. rear sight, ramp front. Blued finish or stainless steel; latter only in .357 or .45 LC. Smooth walnut grips. Made 1973 to date.

Blued finish. . . . . NiB $464 Ex $326 Gd $203
High-gloss stainless (.357 Mag.,
     .45 LC) . . . . NiB $459 Ex $316 Gd $190
Satin stainless (.357 Mag.,
     .45 LC) . . . . NiB $418 Ex $332 Gd $265
.357 Maximum SRM (1984-85) . . . NiB $452 Ex $357 Gd $226

NEW MODEL BLACKHAWK BISLEY
Similar to New Model Blackhawk except w/Bisley shaped grip and hammer, fluted or unfluted cylinder. Made 1986 to date.
Blued finish. . . . . NiB $799 Ex $430 Gd $320
Unfluted cylinder, add $120

NEW MODEL BLACKHAWK CONVERTIBLE
Same as New Model Blackhawk except has Extra cylinder. Blued finish only. Caliber combinations: .357 Magnum/9mm Para., .44 Magnum/.44-40, .45 Colt/.45 ACP. (Limited Edition Buckeye Special .32-20/.32 H&R Mag. or .38-40/10mm). Made 1973-85. Reintro. 1999.
.32-20/.32 H&R Mag. (1989-90) . . . NiB $556 Ex $386 Gd $259
.38-40/10mm (1990-91) . . . . . NiB $556 Ex $386 Gd $259
.357/9mm combo . . . . NiB $556 Ex $386 Gd $259
.44/.44-40 combo (disc.1982) . NiB $834 Ex $579 Gd $389
.45 LC/.45 ACP combo (disc. 1985) . . NiB $556 Ex $386 Gd $259

Ruger Super Single-Six
Convertible (New Model)

Crimson Trace laser grips, add. $280
LCRX model (external hammer, 2014-present), add $50
LCRX model (3-in. bbl., 2015-present), add $20

NEW MODEL BLACKHAWK SA REVOLVER
Safety transfer bar mechanism. SA. Calibers: .30 Carbine, .357 Magnum, .357 Maximum, .41 Magnum, .44 Magnum, .44 Special, .45 Colt. Six-round cylinder, bbl. lengths: 4.63-in. (.357, .41, .45 Colt); 5.5 in. (.44 Mag., .44 Spec.); 6.5-in. (.357, .41, .45 Long Colt); 7.5-in. (.30, .45, .44 Special,

NEW MODEL SUPER SINGLE-SIX SSM
SA REVOLVER. . . . . NiB $555 Ex $480 Gd $209
Same general specifications as standard Single-Six except chambered for .32 H&R Magnum cartridge. Bbl. lengths: 4.63, 5.5, 6.5 or 9.5 in.

NEW MODEL SUPER BLACKHAWK SA REVOLVER
Safety transfer bar mechanism. SA. Caliber: .44 Magnum. Six-round cylinder, 5.5-in., 7.5-in. and 10.5-in. bull bbl. 13.38

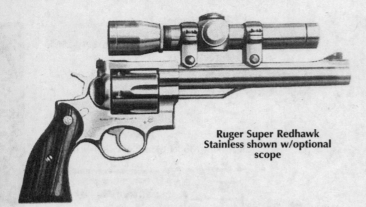

Ruger Super Redhawk Stainless shown w/optional scope

Ruger Super Redhawk Stainless

Ruger Single-Six (Old Model)

in. overall. Weight: 48 oz. Adj. rear sight, ramp front. Blued and stainless steel finish. Smooth walnut grips. Made 1973 to date, 5.5-in. bbl. made from 1973 to date.

Blued finish	NiB $570	Ex $477	Gd $281
High-gloss stainless (1994-96)	NiB $580	Ex $486	Gd $290
Satin stainless steel	NiB $570	Ex $480	Gd $295
Stainless steel Hunter (intro. 2002)	NiB $780	Ex $490	Gd $295

NEW MODEL SUPER BLACKHAWK BISLEY
Similar to New Model Super Blackhawk except w/Bisley shaped grip and hammer, fluted or unfluted cylinder. Made 1986 to date.

Blued finish	NiB $729	Ex $330	Gd $260
Stainless Hunter model	NiB $859	Ex $480	Gd $340

NEW MODEL SUPER SINGLE-SIX CONVERTIBLE
Safety transfer bar mechanism. SA. Calibers: .22 LR and .22 WMR. Interchangeable 6-rnd. cylinders. Bbl. lengths: 4.63, 5.5, 6.5, 9.5 in. 10.81 in. overall (w/ 4.63 in. bbl.). Weight: 33 oz. (w/ 4.63-in. bbl.). Adj. rear sight, ramp

front. Blued finish or stainless steel; latter only w/5.5- or 6.5-in. bbl., smooth walnut grips. Made 1994-2004.

Blued finish	NiB $500	Ex $306	Gd $190
Stainless steel	NiB $530	Ex $316	Gd $219
Stainless steel Hunter (intro. 2002)	NiB $660	Ex $560	Gd $295
Stainless steel Hunter 17 HMR/.17 Mach 2 (2005-06)	NiB $760	Ex $560	Gd $295

NEW MODEL VAQUERO
NiB $590 Ex $431 Gd $316
Similar to Vaquero except w/smaller pre-1962 XR-3 style grip frame, reverse indexing cylinder, recontoured hammer, beveled cylinder, cresent shaped ejector rod. Blued w/case-color or bright stainless finish. Checkered rubber or smooth rosewood grips. Made 2005 to date.

NEW MODEL VAQUERO BISLEY
NiB $655 Ex $440 Gd $315
Similar to New Model Vaquero except w/Bisley shaped grip and hammer, fluted cylinder. Made 2009 to date.

POLICE SERVICE-SIX
Same general specifications as Speed-Six except has square butt. Stainless steel models and 9mm Para. caliber available w/ only 4-in. bbl., Made 1971-88.

.38 Special, blued finish	NiB $434	Ex $306	Gd $230
.38 Special, stainless steel	NiB $345	Ex $290	Gd $270
.357 Magnum or 9mm Para., blued finish	NiB $444	Ex $309	Gd $235
.357 Magnum, stainless steel	NiB $439	Ex $306	Gd $225

REDHAWK
DA/SA. Calibers: .357 Mag., .41 Mag., .45 LC, .44 Mag. Six-round cylinder, 5.5-and 7.5-in. bbl., 11 and 13 in. overall, respectively. Weight: About 52 oz. Adj. rear sight, interchangeable front sights. Stainless finish. Made 1979-2009; .357 Mag. disc. 1986. Alloy steel model w/blued finish intro. in 1986 in .41 Mag. and .44 Mag. calibers.

Blued finish	NiB $620	Ex $450	Gd $270
Stainless steel	NiB $789	Ex $499	Gd $300

SUPER REDHAWK
DA/SA. Calibers: .44 Mag., .454 Casull and .480 Ruger. Six-round cylinder, 7.5- to 9.5- in. bbl., 13 to 15 in. overall. Weight: 53 to 58 oz. Integral scope mounting system w/stainless rings. Adjustable rear sight. Cushioned grip panels. Made 1987 to date.

Model .44 Mag. 7.5- in. bbl., stainless	NiB $795	Ex $546	Gd $434
Model .44 Mag. 9.5- in. bbl., stainless	NiB $830	Ex $577	Gd $444
Model .454 Casull & .480 Ruger Stainless/target gray stainless	NiB $862	Ex $590	Gd $474
Alaskan (intro. 2005)	NiB $880	Ex $590	Gd $480

SECURITY-SIX
DA/SA. Caliber: .357 Magnum, handles .38 Special. Six-round cylinder, bbl. lengths: 2.25-, 4-, 6-in., 9.25 in. overall (w/ 4-in. bbl.). Weight: 33.5 oz. (w/ 4-in. bbl.). Adj. rear sight, ramp front. Blued finish or stainless steel. Square butt. Checkered walnut grips. Made 1971-85.

Blued finish	NiB $410	Ex $280	Gd $214
Stainless steel	NiB $420	Ex $300	Gd $265

SINGLE-SIX REVOLVER (OLD MODEL)
Calibers: .22 LR, .22 WMR. Six-round cylinder. bbl., lengths: 4.63, 5.5, 6.5, 9.5 in., 10.88 in. overall (w/ 5.5-in. bbl.). Weight: About 35 oz. Fixed sights. Blued finish. Checkered hard rubber or smooth walnut grips. Made 1953-73. Note: Pre-

Ruger Single-Six Fixed Sight

Ruger Vaquero Stainless Steel

Ruger Speed-Six Stainless Steel

1956 model w/flat loading gate is worth about twice as much as later version.
Standard . . . . **NiB $879 Ex $602 Gd $439**
Convertible (w/two cylinders,
 .22 LR/.22 WMR) . . . . **NiB $561 Ex $398 Gd $272**

SINGLE-SIX - LIGHTWEIGHT. . . **NiB $1086 Ex $816 Gd $530**
Same general specifications as Single-Six except has 4.75-in. bbl., lightweight alloy cylinder and frame, 10 in. overall length, weight: 23 oz. Made in 1956.

SINGLE-NINE . . . . **NiB $639 Ex $380 Gd $280**
Same general specifications as New Model Single-Six except chambered in .22 WMR, 9-rnd. cylinder, 6.5-in. bbl. Stainless steel. Made in 2013 to date.

SINGLE-TEN . . . . **NiB $639 Ex $370 Gd $270**
Same general specifications as New Model Single-Six except w/10-rnd. cylinder, 5.5-in. bbl. Stainless steel. Made in 2012 to date.

SP101. . . . .**NiB $610 Ex $455 Gd $345**
DA/SA. Calibers: .22 LR, .32 Mag., 9mm, .38 Special+P, .357 Mag. Five- or 6-rnd. cylinder, 2.25-, 3.06- or 4-in. bbl., weight:

25-34 oz. Stainless steel finish. Cushioned grips. Made 1989 to date.
.22 LR (8-rnd. capacity), add **$30**
9mm, add **$300**
High gloss stainless (1996-97), add. **$40**

SPEED-SIX
DA/SA. Calibers: .38 Special, .357 Magnum, 9mm Para. Six-round cylinder, 2.75-, 4-in. bbl., (9mm available only w/2.75-in. bbl.). 7.75 in. overall (2.75-in. bbl.). Weight: 31 oz. (w/ 2.75-in. bbl.). Fixed sights. Blued or stainless steel finish; latter available in .38 Special (w/ 2.75 in. bbl.), .357 Magnum and 9mm w/either bbl., Round butt. Checkered walnut grips. Made 1973-87.
blued finish . . . . **NiB $450 Ex $305 Gd $190**
stainless steel, add **$25**
9mm Para., blued finish, add **$300**
9mm Para., stainless steel, add **$325**

SUPER BLACKHAWK (OLD MODEL)
SA w/heavy frame and unfluted cylinder. Caliber: .44 Magnum. Six-round cylinder. 6.5- or 7.5-in. bbl., Adj. rear sight, ramp front. Steel or brass grip frame w/square-back trigger guard. Smooth walnut grips. Blued finish. Made 1956-73.
w/6.5-in. bbl., ... **NiB $1316 Ex $1148 Gd $918**
w/7.5-in. bbl., ... **NiB $806 Ex $385 Gd $281**
w/brass gripframe . . . . **NiB $1599 Ex $1316 Gd $1153**

VAQUERO . . . . NiB $590 Ex $431 Gd $316
SA. Calibers: .357 Mag., .44-40, .44 Magnum, .45 Colt. Six-round cylinder. Bbl. lengths: 4.625, 5.5, 7.5 in., 13.63 in. overall (w/ 7.5-in. bbl.). Weight: 41 oz. (w/ 7.5-in. bbl.). Blade front sight, grooved topstrap rear. Blued w/color casehardened frame or polished stainless finish. Smooth rosewood grips w/ Ruger medallion. Made 1993-2004.
Bisley (Bisley-shaped grip and
 hammer, 1999-04) . . . . **NiB $575 Ex $460 Gd $230**

WRANGLER . . . . NiB $220 Ex $200 Gd $100
SA. Alloy frame and trigger guard. Interlocked mechanism and transfer bar. Calibers: .22 LR; 6-rnd. unfluted cylinder. Finish: Cerakote black, silver, or burnt bronze. Grip: checkered synthetic. Sights: fixed. Made 2019 to date.
Birdshead model (birdshead grip, 3.7-in. bbl.,
 2022-date) . . . .**NiB $230 Ex $210 Gd $110**

RUSSIAN SERVICE PISTOLS —
Manufactured by Government plants at Tula and elsewhere

Note: *Tokarev-type pistols have also been made in Hungary, Poland, Yugoslavia, People's Republic of China, N. Korea.*

MODEL TT30 TOKAREV SERVICE AUTOMATIC
Modified Colt-Browning type. Caliber: 7.62mm Russian Auto (also uses 7.63mm Mauser Auto cartridge). Eight-round magazine, 4.5-in. bbl., 7.75 in. overall. Weight: About 29 oz. Fixed sights. Made 1930 to mid-1950s. Note: A slightly modified version, model TT33, w/improved locking system and different disconnector was adopted in 1933.
TT30 . . . . **NiB $2400 Ex $1810 Gd $1325**
TT33 . . . . **NiB $1210 Ex $910 Gd $665**
Recent imports
 (distinguished by importer
 marks). . . . .**NiB $220 Ex $160 Gd $120**

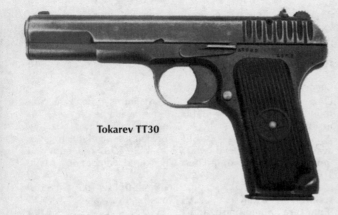

Tokarev TT30

Sako Model .22-.32 Olympic

Sauer 1930 Pocket

Russian Service Pistols Nagant M1895

MODEL PM MAKAROV PISTOL

Double-action, blowback design. Semiauto. Caliber: 9x18mm Makarov. Eight-round magazine, 3.8-in. bbl., 6.4 in. overall. Weight: 26 oz. Blade front sight, square-notched rear. Checkered composition grips. Numerous examples exist from former Eastern Bloc countries such as Bulgaria and East Germany as well as China.

Standard Service Model PM
(Pistole Makarov) . . . . **NiB $600   Ex $400   Gd $255**
Recent non-Russian imports (distinguished
   by importer marks) . . . . **NiB $434   Ex $306   Gd $170**

NAGANT M1895 . . . . **NiB $330 Ex $230 Gd $150**
Revolver. DA/SA or SAO. Caliber: 7.62x38mmR. 7-rnd. capacity. 4.5-in. bbl., 10.5 in. overall. Weight: 28.8 oz. Blade front sight, rear square-notched. Cylinder moves forward on firing to seal chamber and barrel. In service from 1895 to present.

SAKO — Riihimaki, Finland

Manufactured by Oy Sako Ab.

.22-.32 OLYMPIC PISTOL (TRIACE)

Calibers: .22 LR, .22 Short, .32 S&W Long. Five-round magazine, 6- or 8.85- (.22 Short) in. bbl., weight: About 46 oz. (.22 LR); 44 oz. (.22 Short); 48 oz. (.32). Steel frame. ABS plastic, anatomically designed grip. Non-reflecting matte black upper surface and chromium-plated slide. Equipped w/carrying case and tool set. Limited importation from 1983 to 1989.

Sako .22 or .32
   Single pistol . . . . **NiB $1355   Ex $1240   Gd $1090**
Sako Triace, triple-barrel set
   w/wooden grip . . . . **NiB $2647   Ex $2279   Gd $2045**

SAUER — Germany

Manufactured through WW II by J. P. Sauer & Sohn, Suhl, Germany. Now manufactured by J. P. Sauer & Sohn, GmbH, Ecmernförde, West Germany. Also see listings under Sig Sauer for automatic pistols, Hawes for single action revolvers.

MODEL 1913 POCKET PISTOL . . **NiB $342   Ex $240   Gd $179**
Semiauto pistol. Caliber: .32 ACP (7.65mm). Seven-round magazine, 3-in. bbl., 5.88 in. overall. Weight: 22 oz. Fixed sights. Blued finish. Black hard rubber grips. Made 1913-30.

MODEL 1930 POCKET AUTOMATIC PISTOL

Authority Model (Behorden Model). Successor to Model 1913, has improved grip and safety. Caliber: .32 Auto (7.65mm). Seven-round magazine, 3-in. bbl., 5.75 in. overall. Weight: 22 oz. Fixed sights. Blued finish. Black hard rubber grips. Made 1930-38. Note: Some pistols made w/indicator pin showing when cocked. Also mfd. w/dual slide and receiver; this type weight: about 7 oz. less than the standard model.

Steel model . . . . **NiB $455   Ex $290   Gd $203**
Dural (alloy) model, rare . . . . **Ex $3500-$5500**

MODEL 38H DA AUTOMATIC PISTOL

Calibers: .25 Auto (6.35mm), .32 Auto (7.65mm), .380 Auto (9mm). Specifications shown are for .32 Auto model. Seven-round magazine, 3.25-in. bbl., 6.25 in. overall. Weight: 20 oz. Fixed sights. Blued finish. Black plastic grips. Also made in dual model weighing about 6 oz. less. Made 1938-45. Note: This pistol, designated Model .38, was mfd. during WW II for military use. Wartime models are inferior in design to earlier production, as some lack safety lever.

Savage Model 101

Savage Model 1907

**Sears/J.C. Higgins
Model 88 DA Revolver**

.22 caliber rare . . . . Ex $2500-$7500
.32 ACP . . . . NiB $643 Ex $410 Gd $281
.32 ACP (w/Nazi proofs), add 10%

POCKET 25 (1913) . . . . NiB $360 Ex $286 Gd $214
Smaller version of Model 1913, issued about same time as .32 caliber model. Caliber: .25 Auto (6.35mm). Seven-round magazine. 2.5-in. bbl., 4.25 in. overall. Weight: 14.5 oz. Fixed sights. Blued finish. Black hard rubber grips. Made 1913-30.

SAVAGE ARMS — Utica, NY

MODEL 101 SA SINGLE-SHOT
PISTOL . . . . NiB $275 Ex $220 Gd $140
Barrel integral w/swing-out cylinder. Calibers: .22 Short, Long, LR. 5.5-in. bbl. Weight: 20 oz. Blade front sight, slotted rear, adj. for windage. Blued finish. Grips of compressed, impregnated wood. Made 1960-68.

MODEL 501/502F "STRIKER" SERIES PISTOLS
Calibers: .22 LR., and .22 WMR. 5- or 10- rnd. magazine, 10-in. bbl., 19 in. overall. Weight: 4 lbs. Drilled and tapped sights for scope mount (installed). AmbidExtrous rear grip. Made 2000-05.
Model 501F, .22 LR. . . . . NiB $240 Ex $206 Gd $165
Model 502F, .22 WMR . . . . NiB $301 Ex $190 Gd $158

MODEL 510/516 "STRIKER" SERIES PISTOLS
Calibers: .223 Rem., .22-250 Rem., .243 Win., 7mm-08 Rem., .260 Rem., and .308 Win. Three-round magazine, 14-in. bbl., 22.5 in. overall. Drilled and tapped for scope mounts. Left hand bolt with right hand ejection. Stainless steel finish. Made 1998-2005.
Model 510F. . . . . NiB $495 Ex $395 Gd $235
Model 516FSAK . . . . NiB $546 Ex $474 Gd $230
Model 516FSS . . . . NiB $546 Ex $474 Gd $230
Model 516FSAK . . . . NiB $704 Ex $468 Gd $408
Model 516BSS . . . . NiB $755 Ex $500 Gd $437

MODEL 1907 AUTOMATIC PISTOL
Caliber: .32 ACP, 10-rnd. magazine, 3.25-in. bbl., 6.5 in. overall. Weight: 19 oz. Checkered hard rubber or steel grips marked "Savage Quality," circling an Indian-head logo. Optional pearl grips. Blue, nickel, silver or gold finish. Made 1910-17.
Blued model (.32 ACP) . . . . . . NiB $710 Ex $655 Gd $330
Blued model (.380 ACP) . . . . . NiB $1000 Ex $830 Gd $555

MODEL 1915 AUTOMATIC PISTOL
Same general specifications as the Savage Model 1907 except the Model 1915 is hammerless and has a grip safety. It is also chambered for both the .32 and .380 ACP. Made froim 1915 to 1917.
.32 ACP . . . . NiB $1410 Ex $1160 Gd $660
.380 ACP . . . . NiB $1810 Ex $1610 Gd $1110

U.S. ARMY TEST MODEL . . NiB $35,000 Ex $30,000 Gd $17,500
Caliber: .45 ACP, Seven-round magazine w/exposed hammer. An enlarged version of the Model 1910 manufactured for military trials between 1907 and 1911. Note: Most "Trial Pistols" were refurbished and resold as commercial models. Values are for original Government Test Issue models.

MODEL 1917 AUTOMATIC PISTOL
Same specifications as 1907 Model except has spur-type hammer and redesigned, heavier grip. Mfg. 1917 to 1928.
.32 ACP . . . . NiB $610 Ex $530 Gd $279
.380 ACP . . . . NiB $860 Ex $730 Gd $430

STANCE. . . . . NiB $440 Ex $390 Gd $290
Semiauto. Cal.: 9mm, 7-, 8- and 10-rnd. magazine, 3.2-in. bbl., 6.2 in overall. Weight: 21.9 oz. Frame: polymer w/modular back straps, removable chassis. Sights: Orange dot front, U-notch rear. Finish: matte black, black/gray, black/FDE. Ambi. controls. Made 2022 to date.

SCCY INDUSTRIES — Daytona Beach, FL

CPX-1 . . . . NiB $290 Ex $220 Gd $160
Semiauto. DAO. Caliber: 9mm, 10-rnd magazine. 3.1-in. bbl. Frame: polymer with thumb safety. Sights: fixed. Finish: matte black, pink, purple, FDE, and many other colors. Grip: textured polymer. Weight: 15 oz. Length: 5.7 in. Made 2013 to date.

CPX-2 . . . . NiB $270 Ex $210 Gd $155
Similar to CPX-1 except w/o thumb safety. Made 2011 to date.

SEARS, ROEBUCK & COMPANY — Chicago, IL

J.C. HIGGINS MODEL 80
AUTO PISTOL. . . . . NiB $281 Ex $165 Gd $109
Caliber: .22 LR. 10-rnd. magazine, 4.5- or 6.5-in. interchangeable bbl., 10.88 in. overall (w/ 6.5-in. bbl.). Weight: 41 oz. (w/

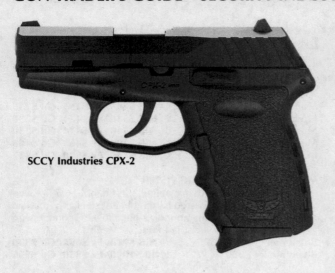

SCCY Industries CPX-2

Seecamp LWS .380

6.5-in. bbl.). Fixed Partridge sights. Blued finish. Checkered grips w/thumbrest.

J.C. HIGGINS MODEL 88
DA REVOLVER . . . . **NiB $209 Ex $105 Gd $75**
Caliber: .22 LR. Nine-round cylinder, 4- or 6-in. bbl., 9.5 in. (w/ 4-in. bbl.). Weight: 23 oz. (w/ 4-in. bbl.). Fixed sights. Blued or nickel finish. Checkered plastic grips.

J.C. HIGGINS RANGER
DA REVOLVER . . . . **NiB $219 Ex $137 Gd $88**
Caliber: .22 LR. Nine-round cylinder, 5.5-in. bbl., 10.75 in. overall. Weight: 28 oz. Fixed sights. Blued or chrome finish. Checkered plastic grips.

SECURITY INDUSTRIES OF AMERICA — Little Ferry, NJ
MODEL PM 357
DA REVOLVER . . . . **NiB $255 Ex $198 Gd $160**
Caliber: .357 Magnum. Five-round cylinder, 2.5-in. bbl., 7.5 in. overall. Weight: 21 oz. Fixed sights. Stainless steel. Walnut grips. Made 1975. Disc.

MODEL PPM357
DA REVOLVER . . . . **NiB $255 Ex $198 Gd $160**
Caliber: .357 Magnum. Five-round cylinder, 2-in. bbl., 6.13 in. overall. Weight: 18 oz. Fixed sights. Stainless steel. Walnut grips. Made in 1975. Note: Spurless hammer was disc. in 1975; this model has the same conventional hammer as other Security revolvers.

MODEL PSS 38 DA REVOLVER . . . **NiB $197 Ex $112 Gd $90**
Caliber: .38 Special. Five-round cylinder, 2-in. bbl., 6.5 in. overall. Weight: 18 oz. Fixed sights. Stainless steel. Walnut grips. Intro. 1973. disc.

R. F. SEDGLEY. INC. — Philadelphia, PA
BABY HAMMERLESS
EJECTOR REVOLVER . . . . **NiB $704 Ex $556 Gd $290**
DA. Solid frame. Folding trigger. Caliber: .22 Long. Six-round cylinder, 4 in. overall. Weight: 6 oz. Fixed sights. Blued or nickel finish. Rubber grips. Made 1930-39.

L. W. SEECAMP, INC. — Milford, CT
LWS .25 DAO PISTOL . . . . **NiB $439 Ex $398 Gd $281**
Caliber: .25 ACP. Seven-round magazine, 2-in. bbl., 4.125 in. overall. Weight: 12 oz. Checkered black polycarbonate grips. Matte stainless finish. No sights. Made 1981-85.

LWS .32 DAO PISTOL
Caliber: .32 ACP. Six-round magazine, 2-in. bbl., 4.25 in. overall. Weight: 12.9 oz. Ribbed sighting plane with no sights. Checkered black LExon grips. Stainless steel. Made 1985 to date. Limited production results in inflated resale values.
Matte stainless finish. . . . . **NiB $464 Ex $398 Gd $272**
Polished stainless finish, add **$128**

LWS .380
DAO PISTOL . . . . **NiB $795 Ex $650 Gd $470**
Similar to LWS 32 except chambered in .380 ACP. Made 2000 to date.

SHERIDAN PRODUCTS, INC. — Racine, WI
KNOCKABOUT
SINGLE-SHOT PISTOL . . . . **NiB $305 Ex $189 Gd $108**
Tip-up type. Caliber: .22 LR, Long, Short; 5-in. bbl., 6.75 in. overall. Weight: 24 oz. Fixed sights. Checkered plastic grips. Blued finish. Made 1953-60.

SIG ARMS AG — Neuhausen am Rheinfall, Switzerland
See also listings under SIG-Sauer.

P210 DANISH MILITARY . . . . . . **NiB $3500 Ex $3000 Gd $2000**
Danish military version of the P210. Early models had wood grips; later models with black plastic grips. 1949–62.

MODEL P210 SERIES
Semiauto. Calibers: .22 LR, 7.65mm Luger, 9mm Para. Eight-round magazine, 4.75-in. bbl., 8.5 in. overall. Weight: 33 oz. (.22 cal.) or 35 oz. (7.65mm, 9mm). Fixed sights. Polished blued finish. Checkered wood grips. Made 1949-86.
P210-1 . . . . **NiB $2500 Ex $1510 Gd $1010**

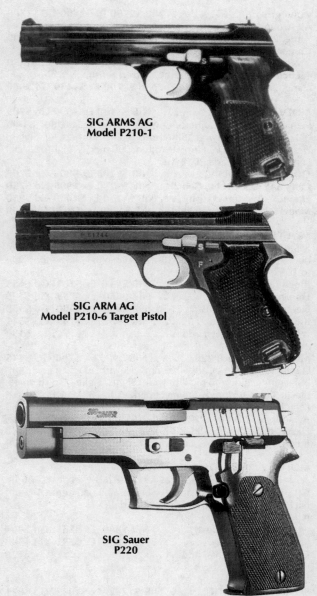

**SIG ARMS AG
Model P210-1**

**SIG ARM AG
Model P210-6 Target Pistol**

**SIG Sauer
P220**

**P210-2 (matte finish, wood or plastic grips,
1987-2002)** . . . . **NiB $1810 Ex $1510 Gd $755**
**P210-5 (matte finish, wood or rubber grips, bottom or side
magazine release, 1997-2007)** . . . . **NiB $2955 Ex $2510
Gd $1255**
**P210-6 (matte finish, wood grips, bottom or side magazine
release)** . . . . **NiB $2010 Ex $1830 Gd $1130**

SIG SAUER — Neuhausen, Switzerland and Exeter, NH

Manufactured by J. P. Sauer & Sohn of Germany, SIG of Switzerland, and other manufacturers. In Oct. 2007, SIG Arms changed its name to Sig Sauer. NOTE: Early SIG models will be marked "W. Germany" or "Germany" and if in Ex condition add 10% to value. All recent models are marked Exeter, NH.

MODEL MOSQUITO . . . . **NiB $408 Ex $350 Gd $270**
Similar to P226 except chambered in .22 LR. Finish: numerous finish options. Weight: 24.6 oz. Made 2005-14.
Sporter model (long slide, disc. 2012), add **$80**
Pink, FDE, or OD green finish, add **$20**
Threaded bbl., add **$30**

MODEL P210 LEGEND . . . . . **NiB $2180 Ex $1710 Gd $1255**
Semiauto. SAO. Caliber: 9mm, 8-rnd. magazine, 5-in. bbl., 8.5 in. overall. Weight: 35 oz. 3-dot, fixed sights. Black nitron finish. Checkered wood grips. Made 2011-14.
**Target model (5-in. bbl., adj. sights,
    wood target grips)** . . . . **NiB $1355 Ex $1185 Gd $925**

MODEL P220 DA/DAO AUTOMATIC PISTOL
Calibers: 22LR, 7.65mm, 9mm Para., .38 Super, .45 ACP. Seven-round in .45 ACP, 9-rnd. in other calibers, 4.4-in. bbl., 8 in. overall. Weight: 26.5 oz. (9mm). Fixed sights. Blue, electroless nickel, K-Kote, Duo/nickel or Ilaflon finish. Alloy frame. Checkered plastic grips. Imported from 1976 to date. Note: Also sold in U.S. as Browning BDA.
Blue finish . . . . **NiB $918 Ex $734 Gd $499**
Duo/nickel finish . . . . **NiB $1030 Ex $712 Gd $523**
Nickel finish . . . . **NiB $988 Ex $784 Gd $546**
K-Kote finish . . . . **NiB $974 Ex $693 Gd $474**
Ilaflon finish . . . . **NiB $969 Ex $689 Gd $507**
.22 LR conversion kit, add **$434**
w/Siglite sights, add **$100**

MODEL P220 CARRY . . . . . . **NiB $1108 Ex $930 Gd $730**
Compact version of the P220 full size w/3.9-in. bbl. Made 2007 to date.
Stainless finish, add **$200**
Elite (Siglite sights, Nitron finish, 2009-12), add **$300**
**Equinox (two-tone slide, Siglite sights,
    blackwood grip), add** **$100**
SAS (SIG Anti-Snag treatment), add **$50**

**MODEL P220 COMPACT
NITRON** . . . . **NiB $1170 Ex $950 Gd $710**
Subcompact version of the P220 full size w/3.9-in. bbl., shorter frame, DA/SA or SAO trigger. Made 2007-15.
two-tone finish, add **$80**
SAS (SIG Anti-Snag treatment) NiB $1170 Ex $950 Gd $710

**MODEL P220 SPORT
AUTOMATIC** . . . . **NiB $1415 Ex $1119 Gd $1016**
Similar to Model P220 except .45 ACP only w/4.5-in. compensated bbl., 10-rnd. magazine, adj. target sights. Weight: 46.1 oz. Stainless finish. Made 1999 to date.

MODEL P224 NITRON . . . . . . **NiB $1108 Ex $890 Gd $630**
Compact version of the P229. Caliber: 9mm, .40 S&W or .357 SIG; 10-, 12-, or 15-rnd. magazine depending on caliber. Finish: Nitron. Grip: E2 style textured polymer. Weight: 29.0 oz. Length: 6.7 in. DA/SA or DAK trigger. Made 2012-15.
Equinox (night sights, G10 grip), add **$100**
**Extreme (black and grey Hogue Piranha grip,
    Siglite sights, short reset trigger), add** **$80**
Nickel (nickel slide, black frame finish), add **$20**

MODEL P225 DA AUTOMATIC
Caliber: 9mm Para. Eight-round magazine, 3.85-in. bbl., 7 in. overall. Weight: 26.1 oz. Blue, nickel, K-Kote, Duo/nickel or Ilaflon finish. Disc. 1998.
Blued finish . . . . **NiB $628 Ex $556 Gd $431**
Duo/nickel finish . . . . **NiB $669 Ex $588 Gd $500**
Nickel finish . . . . **NiB $700 Ex $612 Gd $478**

SIG Sauer
P225

SIG Sauer P230

K-Kote finish . . . . NiB $700 Ex $612 Gd $478
w/Siglite sights, add $128

MODEL P225-A1 . . . . NiB $1122 EX $990 GD $890
Reintroduction of the P225 with ergonomic enhancements.
Finish: Nitron. Grip: checkered G10. Weight: 30.5 oz. Length:
6.9 in. Made 2015–19.
**Model P225-A1 Classic (blued finish, checkered American
hardwood grip)** . . . . NiB $1079 Ex $900 Gd $880

MODEL P226 DA/DAO AUTOMATIC
Caliber: .357 SIG, 9mm Para., .40 S&W, 10- or 15-rnd.
magazine, 4.4-in. bbl., 7.75 in. overall. Weight: 29.5 oz. Alloy
frame. Blue, electroless nickel, K-Kote, Duo/nickel or Nitron
finish. Imported from 1983 to date.
Blued finish . . . . NiB $882 Ex $724 Gd $444
Duo/nickel finish . . . . NiB $898 Ex $809 Gd $496
Nickel finish . . . . NiB $804 Ex $659 Gd $478
K-Kote finish . . . . NiB $804 Ex $639 Gd $485
**Nitron finish
(blackened stainless)** . . . . NiB $826 Ex $658 Gd $479
w/Siglite sights, add $100

MODEL P226 X SERIES
Design evolution of the P226 X-Five series. Made 2014 to date.
All Around (DA/SA trigger) . . . NiB $2250 Ex $1960 Gd $1600
**Classic (SAO trigger,
wood grip)** . . . . NiB $2680 Ex $2400 Gd $1860
**Entry (SAO trigger,
polymer grip, fixed sights)** . NiB $1760 Ex $1560 Gd $1210
**Match (SAO trigger,
laminated grips, adj. sights)** NiB $1730 Ex $1510 Gd $1110
**Open (SAO trigger, G10 grips, 5-in.
compensated bbl.)** . . . . NiB $4850 Ex $4460 Gd $3560
**Super Match (5- or 6-in. bbl.,
adj. sights)** . . . . NiB $3040 Ex $2710 Gd $2260
**Tactical (SAO trigger,
Nitron finish)** . . . . NiB $1680 Ex $1500 Gd $1130

MODEL P226 X-FIVE SERIES
Similar to P226 except customized by SIG Mastershop. Calibers:
9mm or .40 S&W. 5-in. bbl. Sights: adj. Trigger: adj. SA. Grips: checkered wood or polymer. Weight: 47.2 oz. Made 2005-12.

wood grips . . . . NiB $2750 Ex $2400 Gd $1700
**All Around (ergonomic grip frame,
mfg. 2007 to 2012)** . . . . NiB $1700 Ex $1430 Gd $980
**Competition (polymer grips,
mfg. 2007 to 2012)** . . . . . . NiB $1980 Ex $1730 Gd $1250
**Tactical (ergonomic grip frame, Nitron finish,
mfg. 2007 to 2012)** . . . . NiB $1700 Ex $1430 Gd $980

MODEL P227 . . . . NiB $1108 Ex $800 Gd $700
Semiauto. DA/SA. Caliber: .45 ACP; 10-rnd. magazine. 4.4-in.
bbl. Frame: alloy w/picatinny rail. Sights: contrast or Siglite.
Finish: matte black. Grip: textured polymer. Weight: 32 oz.
Length: 7.7 in. Made 2013-18.
Carry (3.9-in. bbl.) . . . . NiB $1108 Ex $800 Gd $700
Carry SAS (3.9-in. bbl., Gen 2) . . NiB $1150 Ex $995 Gd $750
Equinox (two-tone finish) . . . . NiB $1250 Ex $1050 Gd $950
Model P227R (threaded bbl.) . . . NiB $1230 Ex $1050 Gd $950

MODEL P228
Same general specifications as Model P226 except w/3.86-in.
bbl., 7.13 in. overall. 10- or 13-rnd. magazine, Imported 1990
to 1997; reintro. 2004-06.
Blued finish . . . . NiB $831 Ex $709 Gd $455
Duo/nickel finish . . . . NiB $860 Ex $755 Gd $499
Electroless nickel finish . . . . NiB $895 Ex $780 Gd $530
K-Kote finish . . . . NiB $882 Ex $743 Gd $541
w/Siglite night sights, add $130

MODEL M11-A1 (P228) . . . . . . NiB $900 EX $790 GD $615
Semiauto. DA/SA. Caliber: 9mm; 15-rnd. magazine. 3.9-in.
bbl. Frame: alloy w/o picatinny rail. Sights: Siglite. Finish: matte
black. Grip: textured polymer marked P228. Weight: 32 oz.
Length: 7.1 in. Commercial version of M11 Issued to US Naval
Aviation built on the P229. Made 2013 to date.
Desert (FDE finish), add $100
threaded bbl., add. $120

MODEL P229 DA/DAO AUTOMATIC
Same general specifications as Model P228 except w/3.86-in.
bbl., 10- or 12-rnd. magazine, weight: 32.5 oz. Nitron or Satin
Nickel finish. Imported from 1991 to date.
**Nitron finish
(Blackened stainless)** . . . . NiB $860 Ex $755 Gd $464
Satin nickel finish . . . . NiB $890 Ex $791 Gd $500
For Siglite nite sights, add $128

MODEL P229
SPORT AUTOMATIC . . . . NiB $1292 Ex $1035 Gd $871
Similar to Model P229 except .357 SIG only w/4.5-in. compensated bbl., adj. target sights. Weight: 43.6 oz. Stainless
finish. Made 1998-2003. Reintroduced 2003 to 2005.

MODEL P230 DA AUTOMATIC PISTOL
Calibers: .22 LR, .32 Auto (7.65mm), .380 Auto (9mm Short),
9mm Ultra. 10-rnd. magazine in .22, 8-rnd. in .32, 7-rnd. in
9mm; 3.6-in. bbl., 6.6 in. overall. Weight: 18.2 oz. or 22.4
oz. (steel frame). Fixed sights. Blued or stainless finish. Plastic
grips. Imported 1976 to 1996.
Blued finish . . . . NiB $530 Ex $408 Gd $308
Stainless finish (P230SL) . . . . . . NiB $602 Ex $500 Gd $367

MODEL P232 SERIES
DA/SA or DAO. Caliber: .380 ACP. Seven-round magazine,
3.6-in. bbl., 6.6 in. overall. Weight: 16.2 oz. or 22.4 oz. (steel
frame). DA/SA or DAO. Blade front and notch rear drift adjustable sights. Alloy or steel frame. Automatic firing pin lock and
heelmounted magazine release. Blue, Duo or stainless finish.
Stippled black composite stocks. Imported 1997 to 2014.

Blued finish. . . . . NiB $730 Ex $655 Gd $480
Duo finish. . . . . NiB $760 Ex $685 Gd $510
Stainless finish. . . . . NiB $800 Ex $655 Gd $455
w/Siglite night sights, add. $65

MODEL P238 SERIES
Semiauto. SA. Caliber: .380 ACP; 6-rnd. magazine. 2.7-in. bbl. Frame: alloy. Sights: Siglite. Finish: matte black. Grip: textured grooved polymer. Weight: 15.2 oz. Length: 5.5 in. Numerous finishes available. Made 2009 to date.

Nitron. . . . . NiB $555 Ex $480 Gd $345
Blackwood (two-tone finish), add. $100
Desert (FDE finish, rubber grip), add $65
Diamond Plate (two-tone, diamond plate engraving, 2011-
   13), add $35
Edge (stainless steel slide, black G10 grip), add $105
Engraved (engraved slide, rosewood grip), add. $150
Equinox (two-tome, black wood grip), add. $85
Extreme (7+1 capacity), add. $90
HD (stainless frame, black controls, G10 grip, 2015 only),
   add $130
HDW (stainless frame, black controls, rosewood grip, 2015
   only), add $130
HD Nickel (nickel finish, blackwood
   grip, 2015-16), add. $160
Lady (red cerakote finish, gold engraving, rosewood grip,
   2011-15), add. $100
Nightmare (stainless slide, black frame,
   black G10 grip), add. $65
Polished (polished finish, engraved, pearlite grip), add. . $100
Rainbow (rainbow finish, rosewood grip), add. $85
Rosewood (checkered rosewood grip), add $100
SAS (snag-free frame, brown wood grip), add $85
Scorpion (FDE finish, G10 grip, 2012-16), add. $100
Spartan (bronze finish, MOLON LABE engraving), add . $300
Stainless (stainless finish, G10 or rosewood grip,
   2010-13), add. $130
Tactical Laser (two-tone finish, laser sight,
   2010-12), add. $175
Tribal Rosewood (two-tone finish, tribal engraving, rosewood
   grip, 2014-15), add. $115
Tribal Two-Tone (two-tone finish, tribal engraving,
   2014-15), add. $115
Trigger Guard Laser (Nitron finish, laser sight,
   2015 only), add $130

MODEL P239 SERIES
DA/SA or DAO. Semiauto. Caliber: .357 SIG, 9mm Parabellum or .40 S&W. Seven- or 8-rnd. magazine, 3.6-in. bbl., 6.6 in. overall. Weight: 28.2 oz. Double/single action or double action only. Blade front and notch rear adjustable sights. Alloy frame w/stainless slide. AmbidExtrous frame- mounted magazine release. Matte black or Duo finish. Stippled black composite stocks. Made 1996 to date.

Matte black finish . . . . NiB $590 Ex $524 Gd $301
DAO finish . . . . NiB $638 Ex $530 Gd $365
w/Siglite night sights, add $128

MODEL P245. . . . . NiB $845 Ex $700 Gd $690
Semiauto. DA/SA. Caliber: .45 ACP; 6 and 8-rnd. magazine. 3.9-in. bbl. Frame: alloy. Sights: contrast. Finish: blue, two-tone. Grip: textured polymer. Weight: 30 oz. Made 1999-2006.

MODEL P250 SERIES
Semiauto. Striker fire. Caliber: 9mm, .357 SIG, .40 S&W, .45ACP; 17-, 14- or 10-rnd. magazine depending on caliber. 4.7-in. bbl. Frame: polymer, modular grip frames allows trigger group to be swapped from frame sizes. Sights: contrast or

Siglite. Finish: matte black. Grip: textured polymer. Weight: 29.4 oz. Made 2008-13, reintro. 2015–16.

Full-size. . . . . NiB $420 Ex $400 Gd $290
Compact, add $90
Compact Diamond, add $80
Subcompact, add $110
TacPac (compact frame, holster), add. $100

MODEL P290RS. . . . . NiB $570 Ex $495 Gd $450
Semiauto. DAO. Caliber: 9mm; 6- or 8-rnd. magazine. 2.9-in. bbl. Frame: polymer. Sights: contrast or Siglite. Finish: matte black also numerous finishes available. Grip: textured polymer. Weight: 29.4 oz. Made 2011 to date.

MODEL P320 SERIES
Semiauto. SFO or DAO. Caliber: 9mm or .40 S&W; 17- or 14-rnd. magazine depending on caliber. 4.7-in. bbl. Frame: polymer w/modular grip panels. Sights: contrast or Siglite. Finish: matte black. Grip: textured polymer. Weight: 29.4 oz. Made 2014 to date. AXG models have metal modular frame with G10 or wood grips and optic ready, 2021-date.
AXG Classic (curved trigger,
   3.9-in. bbl., Nitron,
   wood grip) . . . . NiB $1200 Ex $1100 Gd $900
AXG Equinox (flat trigger,
   3.9-in. bbl., two-tone,
   G10 grip) . . . . NiB $1200 Ex $1100 Gd $900
AXG Pro (flat trigger, 4.7-in. bbl., magwell,
   G10 grip) . . . . NiB $1200 Ex $1100 Gd $900
AXG Scorpion (flat trigger, 3.9-in. bbl., FDE,
   G10 grip) . . . . NiB $1400 Ex $1300 Gd $950
Nitron. . . . . NiB $600 Ex $530 Gd $400
Carry Nitron (3.9-in. bbl.) . . . . . NiB $600 Ex $530 Gd $400
Compact (3.9-in. bbl.). . . . . NiB $600 Ex $530 Gd $400
Subcompact (3.6-in. bbl.) . . . . . . NiB $600 Ex $530 Gd $400
RPX models (factory mounted red dot), add. $100

MODEL P320 XSERIES
Similar to P320 series except XGrip frame module w/extended beavertail, magwell, flat trigger. Caliber: 9mm. Spectre series has flat trigger, lightened slide, some w/gold accents; 2021-date.
XCarry (3.9-in. bbl., 17-rnd. mag.,
   matte black) . . . . NiB $700 Ex $690 Gd $600
XCompact (3.6-in. bbl., 15-rnd. mag.,
   matte black) . . . . NiB $700 Ex $690 Gd $600
XFive (full size, 5-in. bull bbl., 21-rnd. mag., matte black,
   removable extended magwell) NiB $760 Ex $700 Gd $580
XFull (full size, 4.7-in. bbl., 17-rnd. mag., matte black
   or coyote tan) . . . . NiB $760 Ex $700 Gd $580
Compact Spectre (3.9-in. bbl.,
   Nitron) . . . . NiB $1100 Ex $1000 Gd $890
Spectre Comp (4.7-in. bbl.,
   gold accents). . . . . NiB $1100 Ex $1000 Gd $890
Carry Spectre (3.9-in. bbl.,
   gold accents). . . . . NiB $1100 Ex $1000 Gd $890

P365 SERIES
Semi-auto. Striker fire. Caliber: 9mm w/10- (flush), 12- or 13-rnd. magazine. Bbl.: 3.1 in. Overall: 5.8 in. Weight: 17.8 oz. Receiver: Polymer. Sight: SIG X-RAY3 day/night sights. Finish: Matte black. Made 2018 to date.

380 (.380 Auto, 3.1-in. bbl.,
   curved trigger) . . . . NiB $510 Ex $455 Gd $355
Nitron. . . . . NiB $580 Ex $500 Gd $450
SAS (FT Bullseye sights,
   ported bbl./slide) . . . . NiB $580 Ex $500 Gd $450
XL (3.7-in. bbl., flat trigger, extended grip,
   12-rnd. mag.) . . . . NiB $590 Ex $510 Gd $460

XL RomeoZero (3.7-in. bbl., flat trigger, extended grip, 12-rnd. mag., red dot sight) . . . NiB $680 Ex $600 Gd $560
XL Spectre (3.7-in. bbl., flat gold trigger, extended grip, lightened slide) . . . . NiB $590 Ex $520 Gd $410
XL Spectre Comp (5.6-in. bbl. w/comp, flat gold trigger, extended grip, lightened slide) . . NiB $600 Ex $530 Gd $420

MODEL P320-M17 . . . . NiB $600 Ex $585 Gd $460
Commercial version of the US Military M17 and M18 pistols. Semiauto. Striker-fire. Caliber: 9mm; 17- or 21-rnd. magazine. 4.7-in. bbl. Frame: polymer w/modular grip panels. Sights: Siglite. Finish: coyote tan. Grip: textured polymer. Weight: 29.6 oz. Manual thumb safety. Made 2018 to date.
P320-M18 (3.9-in. bbl.) . . . . NiB $600 Ex $585 Gd $460

MODEL P938 SERIES
Similar to P238 except chambered in 9mm. 6- or 7-rnd. magazine. Numerous finishes and grip styles. Made 2012-20.
Nitron . . . . NiB $655 Ex $600 Gd $405
Aluminum (black aluminum grips, 2013–15), add $75
Blackwood (two-tone finish), add $20
BRG (black rubber finger groove grip), add $30
Edge (custom PVD coating), add $45
Equinox (polished two-tone), add $45
Extreme (two-tone), add $45
Nightmare (black finish, G10 grips), add $40
SAS (Sig Night Sights, wood grips), add $45
Scorpion (FDE finish, G10 grips, 2014–15), add. $125

MODEL P400 . . . . NiB $1414 Ex $1120 Gd $990
AR15 style gas system. Semiauto. Caliber: 5.56; 30-rnd. magazine. 9.0-in. bbl. Frame: forged aluminum. Sights: flip-up, adj. Finish: matte black. Grip: textured polymer. Weight: 6.5 lbs. Includes SB15 stabilizing brace. Made 2014-15.
Elite (SBX brace) . . . . NiB $1656 Ex $1500 Gd $1375

MODEL P516 . . . . NiB $1754 Ex $1480 Gd $1275
AR15 style except short stroke piston system. Semiauto. Caliber: 5.56; 10-rnd. magazine. 5.7- or 10.0-in. bbl. Frame: forged aluminum. Sights: flip-up, adj. Finish: matte black. Grip: textured polymer. Weight: 6.5 lbs. Includes SB15 stabilizing brace. Made 2010-15.

MODEL P522 . . . . NiB $467 Ex $420 Gd $380
Blow-back system. Semiauto. Caliber: .22 LR; 10- or 25-rnd. magazine. 10.6-in. bbl. Frame: polymer. Sights: adj. Finish: matte black. Grip: textured polymer. Weight: 6.5 lbs. Made 2010 only, reintro. 2014-15.

MODEL P556 SERIES
Semiauto. AR15 style system. Cal.: 5.56 NATO; 30-rnd. magazine. 10.0-in. bbl. w/A2 style flash suppressor. Frame: forged aluminum. Sights: Picatinny top rail. Finish: matte black. Grip: Textured polymer. Weight: 6.3 lbs.Made 2009-10.
Standard . . . . NiB $1830 Ex $1655 Gd $1310
Lightweight (polymer lower,
   2010-13) . . . . NiB $1080 Ex $955 Gd $730
xi (polymer rail, flip up sights, w/ or w/o brace,
   2014-16) . . . . NiB $1420 Ex $1255 Gd $970
xi SWAT (aluminum rail, flip up sights, w/brace,
   2014-16) . . . . NiB $1530 Ex $1355 Gd $1055

MODEL P716 . . . . NiB $2252 Ex $2000 Gd $1890
AR15 style except short stroke piston system. Semiauto. Caliber: 7.62x51mm NATO; 10-rnd. magazine. 12.5-in. bbl. Frame: forged aluminum. Sights: flip-up, adj. Finish: matte black. Grip: textured polymer. Weight: 8.6 lbs. Includes SB15 stabilizing brace. Disc. 2015.

MODEL SP2022 . . . . NiB $640 Ex $550 Gd $480
Semiauto. DA/SA. Caliber: 9mm or .40 S&W; 10-, 12-, or 15-rnd. magazine depending on caliber. 3.9-in. bbl. Frame: polymer. Sights: contrast or Siglite. Finish: matte black. Grip: textured polymer. Weight: 29.0 oz. Made 2011 to date.
Two-tone, add $90
Nitron TB (threaded bbl.), add $100
FDE (FDE finish), add $60
TacPac (holster), add. $100

MODEL 1911 GSR CARRY SERIES
Similar to 1911 GSR except w/4-in. bbl. Made 2007-12, reintro. 2015 only.
Nitron or two-tone
   finish, 2007-12 . . . . NiB $1130 Ex $980 Gd $730
Fastback (fastback frame,
   mfg. 2012 only) . . . . NiB $1170 Ex $1130 Gd $730
Nightmare (black finish w/
   stainless controls) . . . . NiB $1240 Ex $1180 Gd $860
Scorpion (FDE finish) . . . . NiB $1210 Ex $1170 Gd $850
Spartan "Molon Labe"
   (bronze finish), add $300
CarryTacops (accessory rail, ambi.
   safety, Ergo TX grip, mfg. 2012 only), deduct. $90
Threaded bbl., add $60

MODEL 1911 GSR COMPACT SERIES
Similar to 1911 GSR Carry except w/4-in. bbl. and short frame. Made 2007-09.
Nitron or two-tone finish,
   2007-09 . . . . NiB $1170 Ex $980 Gd $730
Compact C3 (two-tone finish) . . . NiB $1040 Ex $930 Gd $730
Compact RCS (dehorned treatment), add. $50

MODEL 1911 GSR . . . . NiB $1140 Ex $990 Gd $880
1911 style platform w/SIG styling on slide. Semiauto. SA. Caliber:.40 S&W or .45 ACP; 8-rnd. magazine. 5-in. match grade bbl. Sights: Novak or low-profile. Finish: numerous. Grip: numerous material and textures. Weight: 41.0 oz. Made 2004-15.
Desert (desert tan finish), deduct $10
Extreme (G-10 grips, mfg. 2012 only), deduct $80
Fastback (bobtail frame, mfg. 2012 only), deduct. $80
Max (competition ready), add. $500
Nightmare (bobtail frame), add $200
POW-MIA (engraved, mfg. 2012 only), add $300
Railed Tacpac (accessory rail, holster, mag. pouch), add. . . $100
STX (two-tone finish), add $100
Scorpion (FED finish), add $200
Spartan "Molon Labe" (bronze finish), add $400
Stainless (.45 ACP only, disc. 2013), add $90
TTT (.45 ACP only, two-tone finish, disc. 2012), add $90
Tacops (accessory rail, ambi. safety, Ergo TX grip), add . . . $100
Target (Nitron or stainless finish, 2011-12), add. $90
XO (.45 ACP only, Nitron or stainless finish), deduct. . . . $50
Threaded bbl., add $50

MODEL 1911 MATCH ELITE. . . . NiB $1140 Ex $990 Gd $860
Similar to 1911 Traditional except chambered in 9mm, .40 S&W or .45 ACP; 8-rnd. magazine. 5-in. bbl. Sights: adj. target. Finish: stainless or two-tone. Grip: Hogue wood. Made 2011-12.

MODEL 1911 TRADITIONAL STAINLESS SERIES
Similar to 1911 Traditional except stainless steel construction and chambered in 9mm, .38 Super, .40 S&W or .45 ACP. Made 2014-15.

Stainless Match Elite . . . . NiB $1170 Ex $1030 Gd $780
Nightmare (fastback frame). . . NiB $1240 Ex $1090 Gd $830
Scorpion (FDE finish) . . . . . . NiB $1210 Ex $1080 Gd $830

MODEL 1911 TRADITIONAL . . . NIB $1140 Ex $990 Gd $860
1911 full size style platform w/traditional slide styling. Semiauto. SA. Caliber: .40 S&W or .45 ACP; 8-rnd. magazine. 5-in. bbl. Sights: low-profile Siglite. Finish: reverse two-tone. Grip: Hogue wood. Weight: 41.0 oz. Made 2011-12.
Compact (3.9-in. bbl.,
  2011-12). . . . . NiB $1140 Ex $990 Gd $860
Tacops. . . . . NiB $1220 Ex $930 Gd $760

MODEL 1911-22 . . . . NIB $460 EX $400 Gd $320
Similar to a full size 1911platform except chambered in .22 LR. Semiauto. SA. Caliber: .40 S&W or .45 ACP; 8-rnd. magazine. 5-in. bbl. Sights: low-profile Siglite. Finish: black, camo, FDE or OD green. Grip: Hogue rosewood. Weight: 34 oz. Made 2011-14.

SMITH & WESSON — Springfield, MA

NOTE: *For ease in locating a particular S&W handgun, the listings are divided into two groupings: Automatic/Single-Shot Pistols (below) and Revolvers (page 168). For a complete handgun listing, please refer to the index.*

In 1957 S&W started to use a number system for each model. Models with a dash followed by a one, two or three digit number indicate a model that has had a design and/or production change, i.e.: Model 29-2 indicates this Model 29 was produced during the second design and/or production change. To determine the model number of a revolver, swing out the cylinder and where the yoke meets the frame the model name is stamped.

Since 1990 S&W's Performance Center has been building or modfiying existing guns. Many handguns have come out of the shop and it is difficult to keep an accurate accounting of all models and variants. Note that guns from the Performance Center in the past decade are marked with the Performance Center logo on the frame. Champion and Pros Series handguns are designed in collaboration with professional competition shooters. Since 2007, S&W began the Classics Series reissuing revolvers with aestetics of classic revolver models.

- AUTOMATIC/SINGLE-SHOT PISTOLS -

MODEL 35 (1913) . . . . NiB $979 Ex $780 Gd $469
Semiauto. SA. Caliber: 35 S&W Auto. 7-rnd. magazine, 3.5-in. bbl., (hinged to frame). 6.5 in. overall. Weight: 25 oz. Fixed sights. Blued or nickel finish. Plain walnut grips. Made 1913-21.

MODEL 32 . . . . NiB $3097 Ex $2315 Gd $1699
Semiauto. SA. Caliber: .32 Automatic. Same general specifications as .35 caliber model, but bbl. is fastened to the receiver instead of hinged. Made 1924-37.

MODEL 22A SPORT SERIES
Semiauto. SA. Caliber: .22 LR. 10-rnd. magazine, 4-, 5.5- or 7-in. standard (A-series) or bull bbl., (S-series). Single action. Eight, 9.5 or 11 in. overall. Weight: 28 oz. to 33 oz. Partridge front sight, fully adjustable rear. Alloy frame w/stainless slide. Blued finish. Black polymer or Dymondwood grips. Made 1997-2014.
Model 22A (w/4-in. bbl.) . . . . . NiB $255 Ex $190 Gd $105
Model 22A (w/5.5-in. bbl.). . . . NiB $265 Ex $204 Gd $120

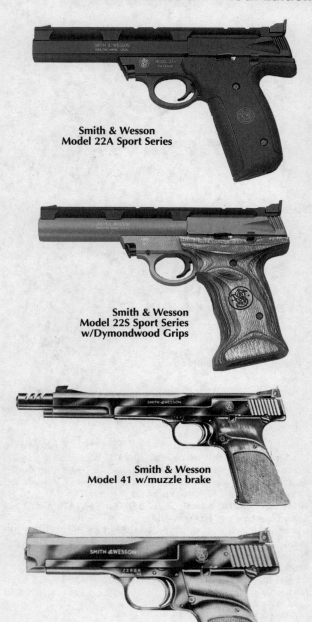

Smith & Wesson
Model 22A Sport Series

Smith & Wesson
Model 22S Sport Series
w/Dymondwood Grips

Smith & Wesson
Model 41 w/muzzle brake

Smith & Wesson
Model 41

Model 22A (w/7-in. bbl.) . . . . . NiB $265 Ex $204 Gd $120
Model 22S (w/5.5-in. bbl.) . . . . NiB $362 Ex $290 Gd $214
Model 22S (w/7-in. bbl.). . . . . . NiB $395 Ex $337 Gd $265
w/bull bbl., add $65
w/Dymondwood grips, add $100

MODEL 39
Semiauto. DA/SA. Calibers: 9mm Para. Eight-round magazine, 4-in. bbl. Overall length: 7.44-in. Steel or alloy frames. Weight: 26.5 oz. (w/alloy frame). Click adjustable rear sight, ramp front. Blued or nickel finish. Checkered walnut grips. Made

**Smith & Wesson
Model 52**

**Smith & Wesson
Model 59**

1954-82. Note: Between 1954 and 1966, 927 pistols were produced w/steel instead of alloy. In 1970, Model 39-1 w/alloy frame and steel slide. In 1971, Model 39-2 was introduced as an improved version of the original Model 39 w/modified Extractor. Model 39 (early production) 1954-70.
First series (S/N 1000-2600) ... NiB $1566 Ex $1418 Gd $1299
9mm blue (w/steel frame & slide,
   produced 1966) .... NiB $1866 Ex $1618 Gd $1299
9mm blue (w/alloy frame) .... NiB $622 Ex $437 Gd $225
Nickel finish, add $45
Models 39-1, 39-2 (late production, 1970-82),
   9mm blue (w/alloy frame) ... NiB $534 Ex $331 Gd $220
Nickel finish, add $50

MODEL 41
Semiauto. SA. Caliber: .22 LR, .22 Short (not interchangeably). 10-rnd. magazine, bbl. lengths: 5-, 5.5-, 7.75-in.; latter has detachable muzzle brake, 12 in. overall (w/ 7.75-in. bbl.). Weight: 43.5 oz. (w/ 7.75-in. bbl.). Click adj. rear sight, undercut Partridge front. Blued finish. Checkered walnut grips w/ thumbrest. 1957 to date.
.22 LR model .... NiB $1200 Ex $870 Gd $529
.22 Short model (w/counter-
   weights & muzzle brake) ...NiB $2700 Ex $1299 Gd $1120
w/Extended sight, add $128
w/muzzle brake, add $50

MODEL 46 .... NiB $1800 Ex $1600 Gd $1155
Semiauto. SA. Caliber: .22 LR. 10-rnd. magazine, bbl. lengths: 5-, 5.5-, 7-in. 10.56 in. overall (w/ 7-in. bbl.). Weight: 42 oz. (w/ 7-in. bbl.). Click adj. rear sight, undercut Partridge front. Blued finish. Molded nylon grips w/thumbrest. Only 4,000 produced. Made 1957-66.

MODEL 52 .38 MASTER AUTO
Caliber: .38 Special (midrange wadcutter only). Five-round magazine, 5-in. bbl., overall length: 8.63 in. Weight: 41 oz. Micrometer click rear sight, Partridge front on ramp base. Blued finish. Checkered walnut grips. Made 1961-63.
Model 52 (1961-63) .... NiB $1109 Ex $915 Gd $546
Model 52-1 (1963-71) .... NiB $1029 Ex $915 Gd $546
Model 52-2 (1971-93) .... NiB $1029 Ex $915 Gd $546
Model 52-A USA
   Marksman (fewer
      than 100 mfg.) .... NiB $3820 Ex $3470 Gd $3139

MODEL 59 9MM DA AUTO
Similar specifications as Model 39 except has 14-rnd. staggered column magazine, checkered nylon grips. Made 1971-81.
Model 59, blue .... NiB $549 Ex $431 Gd $290
Model 59, nickel .... NiB $600 Ex $444 Gd $326
Model 59 (early production
   w/smooth grip frame) .... NiB $1647 Ex $1508 Gd $1015

MODEL 61 ESCORT POCKET AUTOMATIC PISTOL
Caliber: .22 LR. Five-round magazine, 2.13-in. bbl., 4.69 in. overall. Weight: 14 oz. Fixed sights. Blued or nickel finish. Checkered plastic grips. Made 1970-74.
Model 61, blue .... NiB $380 Ex $270 Gd $165
Model 61, nickel .... NiB $431 Ex $316 Gd $220

MODEL 410 .... NiB $561 Ex $444 Gd $244
Semiauto. DA/SA. Caliber: .40 S&W. 10-rnd. magazine, 4-in. bbl., 7.5 in. overall. Weight: 28.5 oz. Alloy frame w/steel slide. Post front sight, fixed rear w/3-dot system. Matte blue finish. Checkered synthetic grips w/straight backstrap. Made 1996-2007.

MODEL 411 .... NiB $530 Ex $433 Gd $386
Similar to S&W Model 915 except in caliber .40 S&W. 11-rnd. magazine, made 1994-96.

MODEL 422 .... NIB $455 EX $280 GD $155
Semiauto. SA. Caliber: .22 LR. 10-rnd. magazine, 4.5- or 6-in. bbl., 7.5 in. overall (w/ 4.5-in. bbl.). Weight: 22-23.5 oz. Fixed or adjustable sights. Checkered plastic or walnut grips. Blued finish. Made 1987-96.
Target model .... NiB $455 Ex $405 Gd $305

MODEL 439
Semiauto. DA/SA. Caliber: 9mm Para. Two 8-rnd. magazines, 4-in. bbl., 7.44 in. overall. Alloy frame. Weight: 30 oz. Serrated ramp square front sight, square notch rear. Checkered walnut grips. Blued or nickel finish. Made 1979-88.
Model 439, blue .... NiB $530 Ex $368 Gd $306
Model 439, nickel .... NiB $529 Ex $386 Gd $316
w/adjustable sights, add $40

MODEL 457 .... NiB $571 Ex $434 Gd $265
Semiauto. DA/SA. Caliber: .45 ACP. Seven-round magazine, 3.75-in. bbl., 7.25 in. overall. Weight: 29 oz. Alloy frame w/ steel slide. Post front sight, fixed rear w/3-dot system. Bobbed hammer. Matte blue finish. Wraparound synthetic grip w/ straight backstrap. Made 1996-2006.

MODEL 459
Semiauto. DA/SA. Caliber: 9mm Para. Two 14-rnd. magazines, 4-in. bbl., 7.44 in. overall. Alloy frame. Weight: 28 oz. Blued or nickel finish. Made 1979-87.

**Smith & Wesson
Model 422**

**Smith & Wesson
Model 439**

**Smith & Wesson
Model 459**

**Smith & Wesson
Model 469**

Model 459, blue . . . . NiB $485 Ex $431 Gd $319
Model 459, nickel. . . . . NiB $527 Ex $475 Gd $377
FBI Model (brushed finish) . . . . NiB $733 Ex $599 Gd $437

MODEL 469 (MINI) . . . . NiB $485 Ex $388 Gd $270
Semiauto. DA/SA. Caliber: 9mm Para. Two 12-rnd. magazines, 3.5-in. bbl., 6.88 in. overall. Weight: 26 oz. Yellow ramp front sight, dovetail mounted square-notch rear. Sandblasted blued finish. Optional ambidExtrous safety. Made 1982-88.

MODEL 539 DA AUTOMATIC
Similar to Model 439 except w/steel frame. Caliber: 9mm Para. Two 8-rnd. magazines, 4-in. bbl., 7.44 in. overall. Weight: 36 oz. Blued or nickel finish. Made 1980-83.
Model 539, blue . . . . NiB $590 Ex $486 Gd $368
Model 539, nickel. . . . . NiB $601 Ex $530 Gd $408
w/adjustable sights, add $50

MODEL 559 DA AUTOMATIC
Similar to Model 459 except w/steel frame. Caliber: 9mm Para. Two 14-rnd. magazines, 4-in. bbl., 7.44 in. overall. Weight: 39.5 oz. Blued or nickel finish. (3750 produced) Made 1980-83.
Model 559, blue . . . . NiB $612 Ex $536 Gd $408
Model 559, nickel. . . . . NiB $648 Ex $561 Gd $444
w/adjustable sights, add $50

MODEL 622 . . . . NiB $330 EX $205 GD $155
Same general specifications as Model 422 except w/stainless finish. Made 1989-96.
Target model . . . . NiB $480 Ex $405 Gd $330

MODEL 639 AUTOMATIC . . . . NiB $530 Ex $377 Gd $304
Caliber: 9mm Para. Stainless. Two 12-rnd. magazines, 3.5-in. bbl., 6.9 in. overall. Weight: 36 oz. Made 1986-88.

MODEL 645 DA AUTOMATIC
Caliber: .45 ACP. Eight-round. 5-in. bbl., overall length: 8.5 in. Weight: Approx. 38 oz. Red ramp front, fixed rear sights. Stainless. Made 1986-88.
Model 645 (w/fixed sights) . . . . NiB $601 Ex $433 Gd $346
Model 645 (w/adjustable sights)NiB $638 Ex $464 Gd $366

MODEL 659 9MM AUTOMATIC
DA. Similar to S&W Model 459 except weight: 39.5 oz. and finish is satin stainless steel finish. Made 1983-88.
Model 659 (w/fixed
   sights) . . . . NiB $517 Ex $419 Gd $326
Model 659 (w/adjustable
   sights) . . . . NiB $528 Ex $444 Gd $356

MODEL 669 AUTOMATIC . . . . NiB $559 Ex $345 Gd $274
Caliber: 9mm. 12-rnd. magazine, 3.5 in. bbl., 6.9 in. overall. Weight: 26 oz. Serrated ramp front sight w/red bar, fixed rear. Non-glare stainless steel finish. Made 1986-88.

MODEL 745 AUTOMATIC PISTOL
Caliber: .45 ACP. Eight-round magazine, 5-in. bbl., 8.63 in. overall. Weight: 38.75 oz. Fixed sights. Blued slide, stainless frame. Checkered walnut grips. Similar to the model 645, but w/o DA capability. Made 1987-90.
w/standard competition
   features. . . . . NiB $760 Ex $549 Gd $433
IPSC Commemorative
   (first 5,000). . . . . NiB $798 Ex $638 Gd $429

Smith & Wesson
Model 639

Smith & Wesson
Model 745

Smith & Wesson
Model 645

Smith & Wesson
Model 1026

Smith & Wesson
Model 659

MODEL 908/910 AUTO PISTOLS

Caliber: 9mm Parabellum. Double action. Eight-round (Model 908), 9-rnd. (Model 909) or 10-rnd. (Model 910) magazine; 3.5- or 4-in. bbl.; 6.83 or 7.38 in. overall. Weight: 26 oz. to 28.5 oz. Post front sight, fixed rear w/3-dot system. Matte blue steel slide w/alloy frame. Delrin synthetic wrap-around grip w/straight backstrap. Made 1994 to date.
Model 908 . . . . NiB $541 Ex $397 Gd $272

Model 909 (disc 1996) . . . . NiB $479 Ex $347 Gd $239
Model 910 . . . . NiB $497 Ex $348 Gd $255

MODEL 915 AUTO PISTOL . . . NiB $434 Ex $306 Gd $220
DA. Caliber: 9mm Para. 15-rnd. magazine, 4-in. bbl., 7.5 in. overall. Weight: 28.5 oz. Post front sight, fixed square-notched rear w/3-dot system. Xenoy wraparound grip. Blued steel slide and alloy frame. Made 1992-94.

MODEL 1000 SERIES DA AUTO
Caliber: 10mm. Nine-round magazine, 4.25- or 5-in. bbl., 7.88 or 8.63 in. overall. Weight: About 38 oz. Post front sight, adj. or fixed square-notched rear w/3-dot system. One-piece Xenoy wraparound grips. Stainless slide and frame. Made 1990-94.
Model 1006 (fixed sights,
    5-in. bbl.) . . . . NiB $724 Ex $530 Gd $433
Model 1006 (adj. sights,
    5-in. bbl.) . . . . NiB $740 Ex $544 Gd $479
Model 1026 (fixed sights, 5-in.
    bbl., decocking lever) . . . . . . NiB $724 Ex $530 Gd $433
Model 1066 (fixed
sights, 4.25 in. bbl.) . . . . NiB $678 Ex $530 Gd $362
Model 1076 (fixed sights, 4.25 in. bbl., frame-mounted
    decocking lever, ... NiB $730 Ex $536 Gd $439
Model 1076 (same as above
    w/Tritium night sight) . . . . . . NiB $730 Ex $536 Gd $439
Model 1086 (same as model
    1076 in DA only) . . . . NiB $760 Ex $544 Gd $429

MODEL 2206. . . . . .NiB $355 EX $305 GD $140
Similar to Model 422 except w/stainless-steel slide and frame, weight: 35-39 oz. Partridge front sight on adj. sight model; post w/white dot on fixed sight model. Plastic grips. Made 1990-96.
Target model . . . . .NiB $405 Ex $330 Gd $180

MODEL 2213 SPORTSMAN . . . NiB $305 Ex $305 Gd $135
Semiauto. SA. Caliber: .22 LR. Eight-round magazine, 3-in. bbl., 6.13 in. overall. Weight: 18 oz. Partridge front sight, fixed square-notched rear w/3-dot system. Black synthetic molded grips. Stainless steel slide w/alloy frame. Made 1992-99.

MODEL 2214 SPORTSMAN . . . NiB $405 Ex $330 Gd $150
Same general specifications as Model 2214 except w/blued slide and matte black alloy frame. Made 1990-99.

MODEL 3904/3906 DA AUTO PISTOL
Caliber: 9mm. Eight-round magazine, 4-in. bbl., 7.5 in. overall. Weight: 25.5 oz. (Model 3904) or 34 oz. (Model 3906). Fixed or adj. sights. Delrin one-piece wraparound checkered grips. Alloy frame w/blued carbon steel slide (Model 3904) or satin stainless (Model 3906). Made 1989-91.
Model 3904 w/adj. sights . . . . .NiB $536 Ex $362 Gd $287
Model 3904 w/fixed sights . . . .NiB $497 Ex $328 Gd $249
Model 3904 w/Novak LC sight . . .NiB $536 Ex $362 Gd $287
Model 3906 w/adj. sights . . . . .NiB $576 Ex $497 Gd 431
Model 3906 w/Novak LC
  sight . . . . .NiB $546 Ex $499 Gd $366

MODEL 3913/3914 DA AUTOMATIC
Caliber: 9mm Parabellum (Luger). Eight-round magazine, 3.5-in. bbl., 6.88 in. overall. Weight: 25 oz. Post front sight, fixed or adj. square-notched rear. One-piece Xenoy wraparound grips w/straight backstrap. Alloy frame w/stainless or blued slide. Made 1990-99.
Model 3913 stainless . . . . .NiB $577 Ex $449 Gd $346
Model 3913LS Lady Smith stainless
  w/contoured trigger guard . . .NiB $755 Ex $588 Gd $479
Model 3913TSW (intro. 1998) . . .NiB $739 Ex $596 Gd $479
Model 3914 blued compact
  (disc 1995) . . . . .NiB $559 Ex $467 Gd $386

MODEL 3953/3954 DA AUTO PISTOL
Same general specifications as Model 3913/3914 except double action only. Made 1990-2002.
Model 3953 stainless,
  double action only . . . . .NiB $590 Ex $444 Gd $396
Model 3954 blued, double
  action only (disc. 1992) . . . . .NiB $530 Ex $431 Gd $340

MODEL 4000 SERIES DA AUTO
Caliber: .40 S&W. 11-rnd. magazine, 4-in. bbl., 7.88 in. overall. Weight: 28-30 oz. w/alloy frame or 36 oz. w/stainless frame. Post front sight, adj. or fixed square-notched rear w/2 white dots. Straight backstrap. One-piece Xenoy wraparound grips. Blued or stainless finish. Made between 1991 to 1993.
Model 4003 stainless w/alloy
  frame . . . . .NiB $658 Ex $498 Gd $388
Model 4003 TSW w/
  S&W Tactical options . . . . . .NiB $870 Ex $779 Gd $608
Model 4004 blued w/alloy
  frame . . . . .NiB $601 Ex $449 Gd $397

Model 4006 stainless
  frame, fixed sights. . . . . . . .NiB $711 Ex $562 Gd $431
Model 4006 stainless
  frame, Adj. sights . . . . .NiB $744 Ex $634 Gd $498
Model 4006 TSW w/
  S&W Tactical options . . . . . .NiB $855 Ex $760 Gd $475
Model 4013 stainless frame,
  fixed sights . . . . .NiB $622 Ex $419 Gd $377
Model 4013 TSW w/
  S&W Tactical options . . . . . .NiB $855 Ex $760 Gd $475
Model 4014 blued, fixed sights
  (disc. 1993). . . . . .NiB $581 Ex $419 Gd $398
Model 4026 w/decocking
  Lever (disc. 1994). . . . . .NiB $659 Ex $562 Gd $449
Model 4043 DA only, stainless
  w/alloy frame . . . . .NiB $693 Ex $580 Gd $497
Model 4044 DA only,
  blued w/alloy frame . . . . . . .NiB $569 Ex $448 Gd $346
Model 4046 DA only, stainless
  frame, fixed sights. . . . . . . .NiB $739 Ex $668 Gd $499
Model 4046 TSW w/
  S&W Tactical options . . . . . .NiB $700 Ex $632 Gd $485
Model 4046 DA only, stainless
  frame, Tritium night sight . . .NiB $724 Ex $634 Gd $475

**Smith & Wesson
Model 3906**

**Smith & Wesson
Model 3953**

**Smith & Wesson
Model 4013**

**Smith & Wesson
Model 4046**

MODEL 4013/4014 SERIES
Caliber: .40 S&W. Eight-round capacity, 3.5-in. bbl., 7 in. overall. Weight: 26 oz. Post front sight, fixed Novak LC rear w/3-dot system. One-piece Xenoy wraparound grips. Stainless or blued slide w/alloy frame. Made 1991–96.

Model 4013 w/stainless slide
  (disc. 1996)..............NiB $643 Ex $536 Gd $327
Model 4013 Tactical w/stainless
  slide ....NiB $860 Ex $693 Gd $588
Model 4014 w/blued slide
  (disc. 1993)..............NiB $587 Ex $464 Gd $328

MODEL 4053/4054 SERIES
Same general specifications as Model 4013/4014 except double action only. Alloy frame fitted w/blued steel slide. Made 1991-97.

Model 4053 DA only w/stainless
  slide ....NiB $668 Ex $530 Gd $458
Model 4053 TSW w/ S&W
  Tactical options..........NiB $760 Ex $648 Gd $541
Model 4054 DA only w/blued slide
(disc. 1992)................NiB $709 Ex $464 Gd $378

MODEL 4500 SERIES DA AUTOMATIC
Caliber: .45 ACP. Six-, 7- or 8-rnd. magazine, bbl. lengths: 3.75, 4.25 or 5 in.; 7.13 to 8.63 in. overall. Weight: 34.5 to 38.5 oz. Post front sight, fixed Novak LC rear w/3-dot system or adj. One-piece Xenoy wraparound grips. Satin stainless finish. Made 1991-97.

Model 4505 w/fixed sights,
  5-in. bbl..................NiB $693 Ex $597 Gd $386
Model 4505 w/Novak LC sight,
  5-in. bbl..................NiB $653 Ex $578 Gd $431

Model 4506 w/fixed sights,
  5-in. bbl..............NiB $744 Ex $581 Gd $523
Model 4506 w/Novak LC sight,
  5-in. bbl..............NiB $755 Ex $590 Gd $500
Model 4513T (TSW) w/3.75-in.
  bbl.Tactical Combat ....NiB $781 Ex $633 Gd $499
Model 4516 w/3.75-in. bbl. ....NiB $724 Ex $622 Gd $479
Model 4526 w/5-in. bbl., alloy frame,
  decocking lever, fixed sights ...NiB $734 Ex $590 Gd $500
Model 4536, decocking lever ...NiB $734 Ex $590 Gd $500
Model 4546, w/3.75-in. bbl.,
  DA only ....NiB $734 Ex $590 Gd $500
Model 4553T (TSW) w/3.75-in.
  bbl. Tactical Combat.......NiB $780 Ex $665 Gd $459
Model 4556, w/3.75-in. bbl.,
  DA only ....NiB $700 Ex $601 Gd $397
Model 4563 TSW w/4.25-in. bbl.
  Tactical Combat ....NiB $779 Ex $658 Gd $499
Model 4566 w/4.25-in. bbl., ambidextrous
  safety, fixed sights.........NiB $693 Ex $536 Gd $453
Model 4566 TSW w/4.25-in.
  bbl. Tactical Combat.......NiB $693 Ex $536 Gd $453
Model 4576 w/4.25-in. bbl.,
  decocking lever...........NiB $691 Ex $607 Gd $449
Model 4583T TSW w/4.25-in. bbl.
  Tactical Combat ....NiB $780 Ex $665 Gd $459
Model 4586 w/4.25-in. bbl.,
  DA only ....NiB $780 Ex $610 Gd $500
Model 4586 TSW w/4.25-in. bbl.
  Tactical Combat ....NiB $734 Ex $590 Gd $500

MODEL 5900 SERIES DA AUTOMATIC
Caliber: 9mm. 15-rnd. magazine, 4-in. bbl., 7.5 in. overall. Weight: 26-38 oz. Fixed or adj. sights. One-piece Xenoy wraparound grips. Alloy frame w/stainless-steel slide (Model 5903) or blued slide (Model 5904) stainless-steel frame and slide (Model 5906). Made 1990-97.

Model 5903 w/adjustable
  sights ....NiB $693 Ex $556 Gd $386
Model 5903 w/Novak LC rear
  sight ....NiB $780 Ex $691 Gd $386
Model 5903 TSW w/4-in. bbl.,
  Tactical Combat ....NiB $767 Ex $658 Gd $497
Model 5904 w/adjustable
  sights ....NiB $581 Ex $468 Gd $376
Model 5904 w/Novak LC rear
  sight ....NiB $599 Ex $474 Gd $398
Model 5905 L/C Adjustable
  Sights ....NiB $693 Ex $549 Gd $398
Model 5905 w/Novak LC rear
  sight ....NiB $733 Ex $634 Gd $464
Model 5906 w/adjustable
  sights ....NiB $658 Ex $544 Gd $439
Model 5906 w/Novak LC rear
  sight ....NiB $658 Ex $544 Gd $439
Model 5906 w/Tritium night
  sight ....NiB $755 Ex $650 Gd $562
Model 5906 TSW w/4-in. bbl.,
  Tactical Combat ....NiB $862 Ex $733 Gd $544
Model 5924 w/anodized frame,
  blued slide ....NiB $659 Ex $508 Gd $337
Model 5926 w/stainless frame,
  decocking lever...........NiB $644 Ex $543 Gd $444
Model 5943 w/alloy frame/
  stainless slide, DA only.....NiB $601 Ex $444 Gd $351
Model 5943 TSW w/4-in. bbl.,
  DA only ....NiB $650 Ex $546 Gd $429

Model 5944 w/alloy frame/
blued slide, DA only . . . . NiB $689 Ex $556 Gd $456
Model 5946 w/stainless frame/slide,
DA only . . . . NiB $658 Ex $534 Gd $376
Model 5946 TSW w/4-in. bbl.,
DA only . . . . NiB $774 Ex $632 Gd $337

MODEL 6900 COMPACT SERIES
Double action. Caliber: 9mm. 12-rnd. magazine, 3.5-in. bbl. 6.88 in. overall. Weight: 26.5 oz. AmbidExtrous safety. Post front sight, fixed Novak LC rear w/3-dot system. Alloy frame w/ blued carbon steel slide (Model 6904) or stainless steel slide (Model 6906). Made 1989-97.
Model 6904 . . . . NiB $601 Ex $499 Gd $377
Model 6906 (fixed sights) . . . . . NiB $621 Ex $546 Gd $499
Model 6906 (Tritium night
sight) . . . . NiB $843 Ex $621 Gd $500
Model 6926 (decocking lever) . . . NiB $691 Ex $587 Gd $374
Model 6944 (DA only) . . . . NiB $612 Ex $546 Gd $342
Model 6946
(DA only, fixed sights) . . . . . . NiB $709 Ex $577 Gd $395
Model 6946 (Tritium night
sight) . . . . NiB $709 Ex $544 Gd $433

M&P9/M&P357/M&P40/M&P45 . . NiB $569 Ex $320 Gd $270
Striker fired action. Caliber: 9mm. 10- or 17-rnd. magazine, 4.25-in. bbl., polymer frame w/three interchangeable grip inserts and accessory rail, low profile fixed sights, w/ or w/o thumb safety. Weight: 24 oz. Black Melonite finish. Made 2006-19. NOTE: M&P40 (.40 S&W), M&P357 (.357 SIG), and M&P45 (.45 Auto) have similar values.
M&P9L (5-in. bbl.,
discont. 2010) . . . . NiB $575 Ex $400 Gd $330
M&P9 Compact (3.5-in. bbl.) . . NiB $569 Ex $320 Gd $270
M&P9 JG (Julie Goloski-Golob design collaboration,
discont. 2012) . . . . NiB $465 Ex $330 Gd $280
M&P9 VTAC (Viking Tactics design collaboration, 4.5-in. bbl.
w/full size frame, FDE finish) . . NiB $799 Ex $430 Gd $330

M&P9 C.O.R.E.
AUTOMATIC PISTOL . . . . NiB $729 Ex $480 Gd $350
Similar to M&P9 or M&P40 except set up for competition w/ optic mount, fixed 3-dot sights. Made 2013 to date.

M&P9 PRO SERIES
AUTOMATIC PISTOL . . . . NiB $699 Ex $410 Gd $310
Similar to M&P9 except w/5-in. bbl., fiber optic Novak sights, optic ready. Made 2012 to date.

M&P9/M&P40/M&P45 M2.0 SERIES
Similar to M&P9 except full-length steel chassis, a rough textured grip, and uses improved trigger system of the Pro series. Armornite or FDE finish. **NOTE:** M&P40 M2.0 (.40 S&W) and M&P40 M2.0 (.45 Auto) models have similar values. Made 2017 to date.
No thumb safety . . . . NiB $500 Ex $400 Gd $250
w/thumb safety . . . . NiB $500 Ex $400 Gd $250

Smith & Wesson
M&P9 M2.0

Compact (3.6- or 4-in. bbl., 15-rnd. mag.) NiB $569 Ex $500 Gd $450
Compact Threaded bbl. (4.6-in. bbl., 15-rnd. mag.) NiB $569 Ex $500 Gd $450
Subcompact (3.6-in. bbl., 12-rnd. mag.) . . NiB $569 Ex $500 Gd $450
w/Crimson Trace laser (green or red), add $190
Performance Center (ported bbl./slide, 4.25- or 5-in. bbl., C.O.R.E.) . . . . NiB $735 Ex $700 Gd $550

M&P BODYGUARD . . . . NiB $380 Ex $240 Gd $185
DAO. Caliber: .380 ACP. 6-nd. magazine, 2.75-in. bbl., polymer frame w/ or w/o manual thumb safety. Weight: 11.9 oz. Black Melonite finish. Made 2014 to date.
w/Crimson Trace laser (green or red), add $190
engraved model, add $20

M&P SHIELD . . . . NiB $449 Ex $280 Gd $210
Similar to M&P9 and M&P40 except sub-compact variant w/3.1-in. bbl., 6-, 7- or 8-rnd. single stack magazine. Weight: 19 oz. Black Melonite finish. Made 2012 to date.
w/Crimson Trace laser (green or red), add $190

M&P9 SHIELD M2.0 SERIES
Similar to M&P9 Shield except w/M2.0 improvements like more grip texture, front slide serrations, refined trigger. **NOTE:** M&P40 Shield M2.0 (.40 S&W) and M&P40 Shield M2.0 (.45 Auto) models have similar values. Made 2019 to date.
No thumb safety . . . . NiB $479 Ex $400 Gd $250
w/thumb safety . . . . NiB $479 Ex $400 Gd $250
w/Crimson Trace laser (green or red), add $190
w/Tritium night sights, add $90
Performance Center Ported . . . . . NiB $565 Ex $510 Gd $450

M&P380 SHIELD EZ SERIES . . . . . NiB $399 EX $340 GD $290
Semi-auto. Striker-fire. Caliber: .380 ACP; 8-rnd. magazine. 3.6-in. bbl. Weight: 18.5 oz. Finish: Black Armorite. Polymer frame w/textured grip and grip safety, accessory rail. Sights: 3-dot. Easy rack slide. Made 2019 to date.
w/manual thumb safety . . . . NiB $399 Ex $340 Gd $290
w/Crimson Trace laser (green or red), add $190
Performance Center (ported bbl./slide; gold, silver or black accents) . . . . NiB $517 Ex $500 Gd $390

M&P9 SHIELD EZ SERIES . . . . . . NiB $479 Ex $400 Gd $350
Similar to M&P380 EZ except chambered in 9mm. 8-rnd. magazine. 3.6-in. bbl. Weight: 23 oz. Made 2019 to date.
w/manual thumb safety . . . . NiB $479 Ex $400 Gd $350
w/Crimson Trace laser (green or red), add $190

SIGMA SW380 . . . . NiB $536 Ex $357 Gd $290
Caliber: .380 ACP. DAO. Six-round magazine, 3-in. bbl., weight: 14 oz. Black integral polymer gripframe w/checkered back and front straps. Fixed channel sights. Polymer frame w/ hammerless steel slide. Made 1994-96.

SIGMA W9/SW40 SERIES AUTOMATIC PISTOL
Caliber: 9mm Parabellum. Double action only. 10-rnd. magazine, 3.25-, 4- or 4.5-in. bbl., weight: 17.9 oz. to 24.7 oz. Polymer frame w/hammerless steel slide. Post front sight and drift adjustable rear w/3-dot system. Gray or black integral polymer gripframe w/checkered back and front straps. Made 1994-96. **NOTE:** SW40 series (.40 S&W) has similar values and features, mfg. 1994-98.
Model SW9C (compact w/3.25-in.
bbl.) . . . . NiB $500 Ex $425 Gd $326

**Smith & Wesson
Sigma SW9**

**Model SW9F (blue slide w/4.5-in.
   bbl.)** . . . . NiB $500 Ex $425 Gd $326
**Model SW9M (compact w/3.25-in.
   bbl.)** . . . . NiB $342 Ex $255 Gd $165
**Model SW9P (3.7-in.
   ported bbl.).** . . . . NiB $340 Ex $255 Gd $165
**Model SW9V (stainless slide w/4-in.
   bbl.)** . . . . NiB $408 Ex $304 Gd $229
Tritium night sight, add. $25

MODEL SW22 VICTORY. . . . . . . NiB $409 EX $380 Gd $310
Semiauto. SA. Caliber:.22 LR; 10-rnd. magazine. 5.5-in. bbl.
Sights: fiber optic front, adj. rear. Finish: stainless. Grip: textured polymer. Weight: 36.0 oz. Made 2016 to date.
Threaded bbl., add $20
Camo finish, add. $10
w/fluted steel or carbon fiber bbl . . NiB $580 EX $500 Gd $400

**MODEL 1891 SINGLE-SHOT TARGET PISTOL,
FIRST MODEL**
Hinged frame. Calibers: .22 LR, .32 S&W, .38 S&W. Bbl.
lengths: 6-, 8- and 10-in., approx. 13.5 in. overall (w/ 10-in.
bbl.). Weight: About 25 oz. Target sights, bbl. catch rear adj. for
windage and elevation. Blued finish. Square butt, hard rubber
grips. Made 1893-1905. Note: This model was available also
as a combination arm w/accessory .38 revolver bbl. and cylinder enabling conversion to a pocket revolver. It has the frame
of the .38 SA revolver Model 1891 w/side flanges, hand and
cylinder stop slots.
Single-shot pistol, .22 LR . . NiB $2890 Ex $2643 Gd $2425
**Single-shot pistol, .32 S&W
   or .38 S&W.** . . . . NiB $2320 Ex $1996 Gd $1748
**Combination set, revolver
and single-shot barrel . . . . .** NiB $3635 Ex $3145 Gd $2869

**MODEL 1891 SINGLE-SHOT TARGET PISTOL,
SECOND MODEL** . . . . NiB $2797 Ex $2466 Gd $1580
Similar to the First Model except side flanges, hand and stop
slots eliminated, cannot be converted to revolver, redesigned
rear sight. Caliber: .22 LR only, 10-in. bbl. only. Made 1905-09.

PERFECTED SINGLE-SHOT TARGET PISTOL
Similar to Second Model except has double-action lockwork.
Caliber: .22 LR only, 10-in. bbl. Checkered walnut grips,
Extended square-butt target type. Made 1909-23. Note: In
1920 and thereafter, this model was made w/barrels having

**Smith & Wesson
Model 1**

bore diameter of .223 instead of .226 and tight, short chambering. The first group of these pistols was produced for the
U.S. Olympic Team of 1920, thus the designation Olympic
Model.
Pre-1920 type . . . . NiB $2314 Ex $1945 Gd $1566
Olympic model. . . . . NiB $2665 Ex $2380 Gd $2235

**STRAIGHT LINE SINGLE-SHOT
TARGET PISTOL** . . . . NiB $3345 Ex $3267 Gd $3095
Frame shaped like that of an automatic pistol, bbl. swings to
the left on pivot for Extracting and loading, straight-line trigger
and hammer movement. Caliber: .22 LR. 10-in. bbl., 11.25 in.
overall. Weight: 34 oz. Target sights. Blued finish. Smooth walnut grips. Supplied in metal case w/screwdriver and cleaning
rod. Made 1925-36.

- REVOLVERS -

**MODEL .22 HAND EJECTOR
FIRST MODEL.** . . . . NiB $2670 Ex $2000 Gd $1289
First Model. Forerunner of the .32 Hand Ejector and Regulation
Police models, this was the first S&W revolver of the solid-
frame, swing-out cylinder type. Top strap of this model is longer
than those of later models, and it lacks the usual S&W cylinder
latch. Caliber: .22 Long. Bbl., lengths: 3.25-, 4.25-, and 6-in.
Fixed sights. Blued or nickel finish. Round butt, hard rubber
stocks. Made 1896-1903.

NO. 3 SA FRONTIER . . . . . NiB $5170 Ex $4350 Gd $3095
Caliber: .44-40 WCF. Bbl., lengths: 4-, 5- and 6.5-in. Fixed
or target sights. Blued or nickel finish. Round, hard rubber or
checkered walnut grips. Made 1885-1908.

NO. 3 SA (NEW MODEL). . NiB $7245 Ex $6095 Gd $4270
Hinged frame. Six-round cylinder. Caliber: .44 S&W Russian.
Bbl., lengths: 4-, 5-, 6-, 6.5-, 7.5- and 8-in. Fixed or target
sights. Blued or nickel finish. Round, hard rubber or checkered walnut grips. Made 1878-1908. Note: Value shown is
for standard model. Specialist collectors recognize numerous
variations w/a range of higher values.
**Performance Center Schofield Model of 2000
   (modern repro)** . . . . NiB $1800

NO. 3 SA TARGET. . . . . NiB $6996 Ex $3890 Gd $3175
Hinged frame. Six-round cylinder. Calibers: .32/.44 S&W,
.38/.44 S&W Gallery & Target. 6.5-in. bbl. only. Fixed or target
sights. Blued or nickel finish. Round, hard rubber or checkered
walnut grips. Made 1887-1910.

MODEL 10 .38 MILITARY & POLICE DA
Also called Hand Ejector Model of 1902, Hand Ejector Model
of 1905, Model K. Manufactured substantially in its present
form since 1902, this model has undergone numerous changes, most of them minor. Round- or square-butt models, the latter intro. in 1904. Caliber: .38 Special. Six-round cylinder, bbl.
lengths: 2-(intro. 1933), 4-, 5-, 6- and 6.5-in. (latter disc. 1915)
also 4-in. heavy bbl., (intro. 1957); 11.13 in. overall (square-
butt model w/6-in. bbl.). Round-butt model is 1/4-in. shorter,
weight: About 1/2 oz. less. Fixed sights. Blued or nickel finish.
Checkered walnut grips, hard rubber available in round-butt
style. Current Model 10 has short action. Made 1902 to date.
Note: S&W Victory Model, wartime version of the M & P .38,
was produced for the U.S. Government from 1940 to the end of
the war. A similar revolver, designated .38/200 British Service
Revolver, was produced for the British Government during the
same period. These arms have either brush-polish or sandblast
blued finish, and most of them have plain, smooth walnut
grips, lanyard swivels.

Smith & Wesson Model 12 (Two-inch Barrel)

Smith & Wesson Model 10 (Two-inch Barrel)

Smith & Wesson Model 14

Smith & Wesson Model 13 (Heavy Barrel)

Model of 1902 (1902-05) . . . . . NiB $639 Ex $536 Gd $362
Model of 1905 (1905-40) . . . . NiB $1165 Ex $910 Gd $602
.38/200 British Service
 (1940-45) . . . . NiB $1165 Ex $910 Gd $602
Victory Model (1942-45) . . . . . NiB $643 Ex $529 Gd $425
Model of 1944 (1945-48) . . . . NiB $785 Ex $431 Gd $319
Model 10 (1948-date) . . . . NiB $530 Ex $437 Gd $319

MODEL 10 .38 MILITARY
& POLICE HEAVY BARREL . . . . NiB $632 Ex $499 Gd $337
Same as standard Model 10 except has heavy 4-in. bbl., weight: 34 oz. Made 1957-86.

MODEL 10 CLASSICS SERIES . . NiB $632 Ex $499 Gd $337
Recent manufacture of Model 10 except chambered in .38 Spl.+P and w/heavy 4-in. bbl., fixed sights, blued finish, checkered wood grips. Made 2010 to date.

MODEL 12 .38 M&P
AIRWEIGHT . . . . NiB $544 Ex $388 Gd $290
Same as standard Military & Police except has light alloy frame, f8rnished w/2- or 4-in. bbl. only, weight: 18 oz. (w/2-in. bbl.). Made 1952-86.

MODEL 12/13 (AIR FORCE MODEL)
DA REVOLVER . . . . NiB $536 Ex $439 Gd $265
Special "Air Force" Model designed with alloy cylinder and frame to be used as a "Survival Weapon" for air crews. Athough this weapon was actually a first-series Model 12, the Air Force stamped "M13" on the top strap. Issued 1953 but recalled for function problems in 1954.

MODEL 13 (.357 M&P) . . . . . . NiB $500 Ex $430 Gd $190
Same as Model 10 .38 Military & Police Heavy bbl. except chambered for .357 Mag. and .38 Spl. w/3- or 4-in. bbl. Round or square butt configuration. Made 1974-98.

K-38 TARGET MASTERPIECE & MODEL 14
DA/SA or SAO. K-frame, squ. butt. Calibers: .38 Spl. 6-rnd. cylinder. Bbl.: 6-in. narrow rib. Click adj. rear sight, Partridge front. Blued finish. Checkered walnut grips.
K-38 Target Masterpiece
 (1946-57) . . . . NiB $930 Ex $830 Gd $630
Model 14 (6- or 8.3-in. bbl.,
 1947-81) . . . . NiB $655 Ex $380 Gd $250
SA only model, add. $100
Model 14 (full lug 6-in. bbl.,
 1991-99) . . . . NiB $605 Ex $430 Gd $380
Model 14 (Classic series,
 blue or nickel, 2009-11) . . . . . NiB $700 Ex $455 Gd $340

MODELS 15 (K-38) & 18 (K-22) COMBAT MASTERPIECE
Same as K-22 and K-38 Masterpiece but w/2- (.38) or 4-in. bbl., and Baughman quick-draw front sight. 9.13 in. overall w/4-in. bbl., Weight: 34 oz. (.38 cal.). Made 1950-99.
Model 15 . . . . NiB $805 Ex $602 Gd $456
Model 18 (disc. 1985) . . . . NiB $691 Ex $523 Gd $487
w/target options TH & TT, add $50
Model 15 (Classics Series,
 4-in. bbl., 2010-11) . . . . NiB $780 Ex $560 Gd $270

K-32 HAND EJECTOR/TARGET/MASTERPIECE & MODEL 16
SA/DA. K-frame, squ. butt. Calibers: .32 S&W Long, 6-rnd. cylinder. Bbl.: 6-in. Weight: 34 oz. Click adj. rear sight, Partridge front. Blued finish. Checkered walnut grip.
K-32 (1st model, K-32 Target, 5 screw,
 diamond around screw grip screw,
 1936-41) . . . . NiB $18,500 Ex $15,000 Gd $10,500
K-32 Masterpiece (5 screw,
 1947-57) . . . . NiB $3255 Ex $2805 Gd $2005
Model 16 (1947-74) . . . . NiB $3130 Ex $2755 Gd $1530
Model 16-2 Masterpiece (.32 H&R Mag.,
 full lug bbl., 1990-92) . . . . . . NiB $1055 Ex $880 Gd $530

K-22 MASTERPIECE & MODEL 17
DA/SA. Caliber: 22 LR. 6-rnd. cylinder, Bbl.: 6-in. 11.13 in. overall. Weight: 38 oz. Partridge-type front sight, S&W micrometer click rear. Checkered walnut Service grips with S&W momogram. S&W blued finish.
K-22 Outdoorsman (1st model, 1931–40) . . . . NiB $2155 Ex $1855 Gd $1380
K-22 Masterpiece (2nd model, micrometer-adj. rear
 sight, short action, anti-backlash trigger, 1,000 mfg.,
 1940–41) . . . . NiB $4955 Ex $4510 Gd $3310
K-22 Masterpiece (3rd model, K prefix, micrometer rear
 sight, short action,
 ribbed bbl., 1946–57) . . . . . . NiB $1010 Ex $855 Gd $705
Model 17 (1996–98) . . . . NiB $755 Ex $555 Gd $380
Model 17 (4-, 6- or 8.3-in. full lug, 6- or 10-rnd. cylinder,
 1990–99) . . . . NiB $755 Ex $555 Gd $380
Model 17 (Classics Series, 6-in. bbl.,
 2009–11) . . . . NiB $780 Ex $560 Gd $270

K-22 COMBAT MASTERPIECE & MODEL 18
Similar to K-22 Masterpiece/Model 17 except w/4-in. bbl., adj. sights, blued finish, checkered wood grips. Made 1949-86.
K-22 Combat Masterpiece (pre Model 18, 4-in. bbl.,
 1949–57) . . . . NiB $1010 Ex $855 Gd $705
Model 18 (1949–57) . . . . NiB $1010 Ex $805 Gd $505
Model 18 (Classics Series,
 4-in. bbl., 2009–11) . . . . NiB $700 Ex $560 Gd $360

MODEL 19 .357 COMBAT MAGNUM
DA/SA. Caliber: .357 Magnum. Six-round cylinder, bbl. lengths: 2.5 (round butt), 4, or 6 in., 9.5 in. overall (w/ 4-in. bbl.). Weight: 35 oz. (w/ 4-in. bbl.). Click adj. rear sight, ramp front. Blued or nickel finish. Target grips of checkered Goncalo Alves. Made 1956 to date (2.5- and 6-in. bbls. were disc. in 1991).
Model 19 (first issue) . . . . NiB $1110 Ex $955 Gd $705
Model 19-3 (mfg. 1994–99) . . . . NiB $655 Ex $500 Gd $250
w/target options TH & TT, add $75
nickel finish, add. $20
Model 19 (Classic, 2019–date) . . NiB $740 Ex $690 Gd $480

MODEL 20 HEAVY DUTY/.38/44 HEAVY DUTY
DA/SA. Caliber: .38 Special. Six-round cylinder, bbl. lengths: 4, 5 and 6.5 in.;10.38 in. overall (w/ 5-in. bbl.). Weight: 40 oz. (w/ 5-in. bbl.). Fixed sights. Blued or nickel finish. Checkered

Smith & Wesson Model 15

Smith & Wesson Model 18 (See Model 15 for description)

Smith & Wesson Model 17 K-22

Smith & Wesson Model 19 (Round Butt)

Smith & Wesson Model 19 (Square Butt)

Smith & Wesson Model 20

Smith & Wesson Model 22

Smith & Wesson Model 22/32 Kit Gun

walnut grips. Short action after 1948. Made 1930-56 and from 1957 to 67.

Pre-World War II . . . . **NiB $1970 Ex $1770 Gd $525**
Post-war . . . .**NiB $2270 Ex $1620 Gd $910**

MODEL 21 (.44 HAND EJECTOR 4TH MODEL)

Postwar version of the 1926 Model 44 Military. Model of 1950. Caliber: .44 Spl., 6-rnd. cylinder. Bbl.: 4-, 5- and 6.5-in. 11.75 in. overall (w/6.5-in. bbl.) Weight: 39.5 oz. (w/6.5-in. bbl.). Fixed front sight w/square-notch rear sight; target model has micrometer click rear sight adj. for windage and elevation. Checkered walnut grips w/S&W monogram. Blued or nickel finish. Made 1950-67. **NOTE:** Renamed the Model 20 in 1957.

Model 21 (4- or 5-in. bbl.). . . . .NiB $2979 Ex $2035 Gd $809
Model 21 (6.5-in. bbl.), add 50%
Model 21-4 Thunder Ranch Special (4-in. bbl., rnd. butt,
   2004–06) . . . . NiB $755 Ex $680 Gd $455

.45 HAND EJECTOR

Model of 1917. DA/SA. Caliber: .45 Auto using 3-cartridge half-moon clip or .45 Auto Rim, without clip. 6-rnd. cylinder, 5.5-in. bbl., 10.75 in. overall. Weight: 36.25 oz. Fixed sights. Blued finish (blue-black finish on commercial model, brush polish on military). Checkered walnut grips (commercial model, smooth on military). Made under U.S. Government contract 1917-19 and produced commercially 1919-41. **Note:** About 175,000 of these revolvers were produced during WW I. The DCM sold these to NRA members during the 1930s at $16.15 each.

Commercial model . . . . . . .NiB $2500 Ex $2168 Gd $1870
Military model . . . . .NiB $1860 Ex $1640 Gd $1389
Brazilian Contract model (1937 stamped on sideplate) . . NiB $1450 Ex $1270 Gd $805

.45 HAND EJECTOR & MODEL 22

Postwar version of the 1917 Army w/same general specifications except redesigned hammer. Made 1950-67.

.45 Hand Ejector Model (1950 Army,
   1951–66) . . . . NiB $1810 Ex $1410 Gd $610
Model 22 (Classics Series, 4- or 5.5-in. bbl.,
   2007–10) . . . . NiB $855 Ex $655 Gd $420
Model 22 Model of 1917 (Classics Series, lanyard loop,
   5.5-in. bbl., 2008–12). . . . . . . NiB $780 Ex $655 Gd $420
Model 22-4 Thunder Ranch Special (4-in. bbl., sq. butt,
   2005–14) . . . . NiB $780 Ex $655 Gd $420

.22/.32 HAND EJECTOR
DA/SA. Also known as the "Bekeart Model." Design based upon ".32 Hand Ejector." Caliber: .22 LR (recessed head cylinder for high-speed cartridges intro. 1935). Six-round cylinder, 6-in. bbl., 10.5 in. overall. Weight: 23 oz. Adj. target sights. Blued finish. Checkered walnut grips. Made 1911-53. **Note:** In 1911, San Francisco gun dealer Phil Bekeart, who suggested this model, received 292 pieces. These are the true "Bekeart Model" revolvers and are marked with separate identification numbers on the base of the wooden grip.

.22/.32 Standard Model .... NiB $1580 Ex $1330 Gd $875
.22/.32 (early prod. 1-3000), add.................. 20%
.22/.32 Bekeart model, add 100%

.22/.32 KIT GUN
Same as .22/.32 Hand Ejector except has 2- or 4-in. bbl., round grips, 6- or 8-in. overall, weight: 19-21oz.
Pre-war (mfg. 1935–41) .... NiB $4010 Ex $3010 Gd $2010
Post-war (mfg. 1946–52)...... NiB $1010 Ex $710 Gd $380

MODEL 23 .38-44 OUTDOORSMAN
Similar to Model 20 except w/adj. micrometer-click rear sight. Finish: blue. Bbl.: 6.5-in. Weight: 41.75 oz. **NOTE:** 1950 transition model has ribbed barrel, redesigned hammer. Made 1946–67.
Post-war (1946–49)........ NiB $1555 Ex $1355 Gd $955
Marked Model 23. .... NiB $2255 Ex $1955 Gd $1505

MODEL 24 (1950 TARGET)
Postwar version of the .44 Hand Ejector Fourth Model. .44 Special w/4-, 5- or 6.5-in. ribbed bbl., redesigned hammer, micrometer click rear sight. Satin or polished blue finish. Made 1950-67. Model 24 reintroduced in 1983 only.
Model 24 (1950 w/6.5-in.
  bbl...................NiB $2310 Ex $1696 Gd $897
Model 24 (1950) w/4-in. bbl., add. 20%
Model 24 (1950) w/5-in. bbl., add................ 100%
w/polished blue finish, add....................... 25%
w/nickel finish, add 65%
Model 24-3 (7,500 produced
  in 1983-84) ....NiB $855 Ex $755 Gd $410
Model 24-6 (Classics Series,
  6.5-in. bbl., 2006–12)...... NiB $770 Ex $645 Gd $420

MODEL 25 (1955 TARGET MODEL)
Same as Model 24-1950 Target, but chambered for .45 ACP, .45 Auto Rim or .45 LC w/4-, 6-, 6.5-or 8.3-in. pinned bbl. Made 1955-99 in several variations. Note: In 1961, the .45 ACP was designated Model 25-2, and in 1978 the .45 LC was designated Model 25-5.
.45 ACP or .45 Auto Rim...... NiB $930 Ex $810 Gd $480
.45 LC early production ... NiB $3680 Ex $3155 Gd $2310
w/pinned bbl. (mfg. until 1982), add $150
early 4 screw model, add....................... 50%
Model 25-5 (.45 LC w/4-in.
  bbl., 1978–91) ....NiB $910 Ex $780 Gd $500
Model 25 (Classic Series,
  2008-date) .... NiB $800 Ex $680 Gd $420

MODEL 26 (1950 .45 LIGHT TARGET BARREL)
Similar to 1950 Model Target except w/lighter bbl. **Note:** Lighter profile was not well received. Only 2,768 produced. Mfg. 1950–60.
.45 ACP or .45 Auto Rim.....NiB $4010 Ex $3510 Gd $2010

.357 REGISTERED MAGNUM AND MODEL 27 SERIES
DA/SA. N-frame. Caliber: .357 Mag. 6-rnd. cylinder, bbl. lengths: 3.5-, 4-, 5-, 6-, 6.5-and 8.38-in., 11.38 in. overall (w/ 6-in. bbl.).

**Smith & Wesson
Model 22/32 Target Revolver**

Weight: 44 oz. (w/ 6-in. bbl.). Adj. target sights, Baughman quick-draw ramp front sight on 3.5-in. bbl., Blued or nickel finish. Checkered walnut grips. The .357 Registered Magnum was made from 1935-94. **Note:** Until 1938, the .357 Registered Magnum was custom made in any bbl. length from 3.5- to 8.75 in. Each of these revolvers was accompanied by a registration certificate and has its registration number stamped on the inside of the yoke along with the prefix "REG"; this was discontinued in 1939. Postwar magnums have a redesigned hammer w/shortened fall and the S&W micrometer click rear sight. The Model 27 has had 7 engineering changes. Recessed cylinders were discontinued in 1981; pinned barrels were discontinued in 1982.
Pre-war model
  (REG prefix on yoke)...... NiB $7000 Ex $6000 Gd $5500
Pre-war model (w/o REG
  prefix, 1938–41)....... NiB $6810 Ex $4880 Gd $3580
Post-war model (S prefix,
  1947–57) .... NiB $1730 Ex $1480 Gd $1090
Model 27 (4 screw)........ NiB $1255 Ex $1055 Gd $655
Model 27 (3 screw)........ NiB $1255 Ex $1055 Gd $655
Model 27 (3.5- or 5-in. bbl.), add.................. 50%
Model 27 (8.3-in. bbl.), add 10%
Model 27 (Classic Series, 4- or 6-in. bbl.,
  2008-date) .... NiB $800 Ex $680 Gd $420

HIGHWAY PATROLMAN & MODEL 28
DA/SA. N-frame, 5 screw, square butt. Similar to Model 27 but plain version designed for law enforcement. Caliber: .357 Magnum. Six-round cylinder, bbl. lengths: 4- or 6-in. 1954–57. The Highway Patrolman was renamed the Model 28 in 1957 and was mfg. until 1986.
Early model (pinned bbl.,
  recessed cylinder, 5 screw) NiB $1010 Ex $880 Gd $635
Model 28 (mfg. 1954–57)...... NiB $855 Ex $780 Gd $455
Model 28 (mfg. 1957–86)...... NiB $500 Ex $405 Gd $280

MODEL 29 SERIES
DA/SA. N-frame. Caliber: .44 Magnum. Six-round cylinder. bbl., lengths: 4-, 5-, 6.5-, 8.38-in. 11.88 in. overall (w/ 6.5-in. bbl.). Weight: 47 oz. (w/ 6.5-in. bbl.). Click adj. rear sight, ramp front. Blued or nickel finish. Checkered Goncalo Alves target grips. Pre Model 29, 5 screw, were mfg. from 1956-58; Model 29, 4 screw, were mfg. 1957-61; dash Model 29, 3 screw, 1961-99. The Model 29 had 10 engineering changes.
3-Screw Model 29-1 (1961) NiB $4510 Ex $3410 Gd $1755
4-Screw model (1957-58)... NiB $2200 Ex $1693 Gd $880
5-Screw model (1956-57).. NiB $4255 Ex $3710 Gd $1810
Model 29-2 (S prefix, 1962–69)NiB $1810 Ex $1530 Gd $980
Model 29-2 (N prefix, 1970–83)NiB $1555 Ex $855 Gd $480
Model 29-3 and higher dash
  models (1984–99).......... NiB $855 Ex $730 Gd $470
Model 29 (Classic Series,
  1991–94) .... NiB $755 Ex $605 Gd $355
Model 29 (Classic Series,
  2008–date) .... NiB $800 Ex $680 Gd $420

Smith & Wesson Model 23

Smith & Wesson Model 24 Target

Smith & Wesson Model 25 Target

Smith & Wesson Model 27

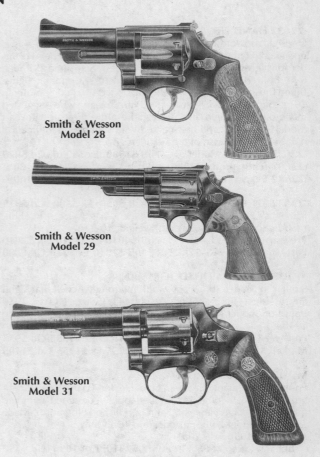

Smith & Wesson Model 28

Smith & Wesson Model 29

Smith & Wesson Model 31

Model 29 Classic Hunter (6-in.
bbl., 1987) . . . . NiB $1255 Ex $755 Gd $410
Model 29 Magna Classic (7.5-in. full lug
bbl., 1990) . . . . NiB $1510 Ex $910 Gd $510
Model 29 Silhouette (10.63-in.
bbl., 1983–91) . . . . NiB $1510 Ex $1010 Gd $455

MODEL 30 & .32 HAND
EJECTOR . . . . NiB $554 Ex $469 Gd $356
DA/SA. I-frame. Caliber: .32 S&W Long. Six-round cylinder, bbl. lengths: 2- (intro. 1949), 3-, 4- and 6-in., 8 in. overall (w/ 4-in. bbl.). Weight: 18 oz. (w/ 4-in. bbl.). Fixed sights. Blued or nickel finish. Round, checkered walnut or hard rubber grips. Made 1903-76.

MODELS 31 & 33 REGULATION POLICE
Same basic type as .32 Hand Ejector except has square buttgrips. Calibers: .32 S&W Long (Model 31) .38 S&W (Model 33). Six-round cylinder in .32 cal., 5-rnd. in .38 caliber. Bbl., lengths: 2- (intro. 1949), 3-, 4- and 6-in. in .32 cal., 4-in. only in .38 cal., 8.5 in. overall (w/ 4-in. bbl.). Weight: 18 oz. (.38 cal. w/4-in. bbl.), 18.75 oz. (.32 cal. w/4-in. bbl.). Fixed sights. Blued or nickel finish. Checkered walnut grips. Made 1917. Model 33 disc. in 1974; Model 31 disc. in 1992.

Model 31 . . . . NiB $546 Ex $306 Gd $255
Model 33 . . . . NiB $448 Ex $283 Gd $198

.32 DOUBLE ACTION SERIES. . NiB $430 Ex $385 Gd $300
Break-top action. Hinged frame. Caliber: .32 S&W. 5-rnd. cylinder, bbl. lengths: 3-, 3.5- and 6-in. Fixed sights. Blued or nickel finish. Hard rubber grips. Made 1880-1919 and five model variations. Note: Value shown applies generally to the several varieties. exception is the rare first issue of 1880 (identified by squared sideplate and serial no. 1 to 30) valued up to $2,500.

MODEL 32 TERRIER . . . . NiB $455 Ex $380 Gd $155
DA/SA. Caliber: .38 S&W. Five-round cylinder, 2-in. bbl., 6.25 in. overall. Weight: 17 oz. Fixed sights. Blued or nickel finish. Checkered walnut or hard rubber grips. Built on .32 Hand Ejector frame. Made 198-74.

MODEL 33 (.38 REGULATION
POLICE) . . . . NiB $480 Ex $390 Gd $200
DA/SA. I-frame. Caliber: .38 S&W; 5-rnd. cylinder. Bbl.: 4-in. Square butt. Grip: walnut. Mfg. 1953–74.

MODEL 34 . . . . NiB $905 Ex $755 Gd $355
DA/SA. Model of 1953 22/32 Kit Gun. J-frame. Caliber: .22 LR. 6-rnd. cylinder, 2- or 4-in. bbl. and rnd. or square grips, blued or nickel finish. Made 1953-91.

MODEL 35 . . . . NiB $1505 Ex $1105 Gd $505
Same general specifications as previous Model 34 except has micrometer-click rear sight. Magna type target grips. Weight: 25 oz. Made 1953-73.

**Smith & Wesson
Model 32**

**Smith & Wesson
Model 34**

**Smith & Wesson
Model 36**

**Smith & Wesson
Model 37**

.38 CHIEFS SPECIAL & MODEL 36

Based on .32 Hand Ejector w/J-frame lengthened to permit longer cylinder for .38 Spl. cartridge. Caliber: .38 Spl. 5-rnd. cylinder. Bbl.: lengths: 2- or 3-in., 6.5 in. overall (w/ 2-in. bbl.). Weight: 19 oz. Fixed sights. Blued or nickel finish. Checkered walnut grips, rnd. or square butt. **NOTE:** .38 Chiefs Special mfg. from 1950–57. Model 36 mfg. 1958 to date. The Model 36 has had 10 engineering changes.

Model 36 Chiefs Special
 Classics . . . . **NiB $655 Ex $540 Gd $505**
Nickel finish, add $20
Early model (5-screw, small trigger
 guard, S/N 1-2500) . . . .**NiB $900 Ex $610 Gd $365**
Model 36 Ladysmith
 (1990-2008) . . . .**NiB $680 Ex $490 Gd $190**
Model 36 Target (target sights,
 1955) . . . .**NiB $1380 Ex $1010 Gd $505**
Model 36 (Classic Series) . . . . . .**NiB $769 Ex $700 Gd $500**
Model 50 (target sights,
 1,100 mfg., 1955-75) . . . . . .**NiB $1155 Ex $855 Gd $505**

.38 CHIEFS SPECIAL AIRWEIGHT &

MODEL 37 . . . .**NiB $1000 Ex $630 Gd $430**
Same general specifications as .38 Chiefs Special and Model 36 except has light alloy frame, weight: 12.5 oz. w/2-in. bbl., blued finish only. Made 1954-95. The Model 37 has had 3 engineering changes.
Model 37 Chiefs Special Airweight
 (target sights, 1955) . . . .**NiB $555 Ex $455 Gd $195**

BODYGUARD AIRWEIGHT & MODEL 38

Shrouded hammer. Light alloy J-frame. Caliber: .38 Spl. 5-rnd. cylinder, 2- or 3-in. bbl., 6.38 in. overall (w/2-in. bbl.). Weight: 14.5 oz. Fixed sights. Blued or nickel finish. Checkered walnut grips. Bodyguard Airweight mfg. 1955-57. Model 38 was discontinued in 1999.
Early model (pinned bbl. &
 recessed cyl., pre-1981) . . . .**NiB $855 Ex $780 Gd $555**
Model 38 . . . .**NiB $455 Ex $350 Gd $205**
Model 38 (nickel finish), add $20

.38 DOUBLE ACTION SERIES. . **NiB $500 Ex $355 Gd $210**

Break-top action. Hinged frame. Caliber: .38 S&W. Five-round cylinder, bbl. lengths: 4-, 4.25-, 5-, 6-, 8- and 10-in. Fixed sights. Blued or nickel finish. Hard rubber grips. Made 1880-1911 and four model variations. **Note:** Value shown applies generally to the several varieties. exceptions are the first issue of 1880 (identified by squared sideplate and serial no. 1 to 4,000) and the 8- and 10-in. bbl. models of the third issue (1884 to 1995).

MODEL .38 MILITARY & POLICE SEREIS

Military & Police — First Model. Resembles Colt New Navy in general appearance, lacks bbl., lug and locking bolt common to all later S&W hand ejector models. Caliber: .38 Long Colt. Six-round cylinder, bbl. lengths: 4-, 5-, 6- and 6.5-in., 11.5 in. overall (w/ 6.5-in. bbl.). Fixed sights. Blued or nickel finish. Round, checkered walnut or hard rubber grips. Made 1899-1902.
Standard model
 (civilian issue) . . . .**NiB $1870 Ex $1322 Gd $1132**
Army Model (marked U.S.
 Army Model, 1000 issued) NiB $3610 Ex $3310 Gd $2510
Navy Model (marked USN,
 1000 issued) . . . .**NiB $3610 Ex $3310 Gd $2510**
Second Model (.38 Spl.,
 1902–03) . . . .**NiB $1480 Ex $1280 Gd $910**
Model of 1905 (1905–06) . . . .**NiB $1410 Ex $1230 Gd $855**

**Smith & Wesson
Model 38 Bodyguard Airweight**

.38 Military & Police (post-war, squ. butt, K-frame, 5 screw, 1946–57)..........NiB $510 Ex $410 Gd $290

.38 DOUBLE ACTION
PERFECTED..............NiB $880 Ex $480 Gd $280
Break-top action. Hinged frame. Similar to earlier .38 Double Action Model but heavier frame, side latch as in solid-frame models, improved lockwork. Caliber: .38 S&W. 5-rnd. cylinder, bbl. lengths: 3.25, 4, 5 and 6 in. Fixed sights. Blued or nickel finish. Hard rubber grips. Made 1909-20.

CENTENNIAL & MODEL 40 SERIES
Similar to .38 Chiefs Special but has Safety Hammerless-type mechanism w/grip safety. 2-in. bbl. Weight: 19 oz. Mfg. 1952–57 was named for S&W's 100th anniversary; renamed Model 40 in 1957–74; Model 40-1 Classics mfg. 2007–12. The Model 40 had 1 engineering change.
Centennial model...........NiB $755 Ex $630 Gd $555
Model 40 or 40-1...........NiB $650 Ex $430 Gd $320

CENTENNIAL AIRWEIGHT & MODEL 42 SERIES
Same as standard Centennial/Model 40 model except has light alloy frame, weight: 13 oz. Made 1954-74.
**Centennital
   Airweight model**..........NiB $810 Ex $730 Gd $630
Model 42 ....NiB $600 Ex $430 Gd $330
Model 42 (nickel finish), add.....................$650
**Model 42-1 (Classics series,
   .38 Spl. +P, 2009–10)**.......NiB $640 Ex $430 Gd $330

MODEL 43 ....NiB $1000 Ex $610 Gd $355
Same as .22/32 Kit Gun Aitweight except has light alloy frame, square grip. Furnished w/3.5-in. bbl., weight: 14.25 oz. Made 1954-74.

MODEL 43C CENTENNIAL .... NiB $530 Ex $280 Gd $165
Similar to Centennial/Model 40 but .22 LR; 8-rnd. cylinder. J-frame. 2-in. bbl. Weight: 11 oz. Made from 2010 to date.

DOUBLE ACTION FIRST MODEL
Also called Wesson Favorite (lightweight model), Frontier (caliber .44-40). Break-top action. Hinged frame. 6-rnd. cylinder. Calibers: .44 S&W Russian, .38-40, .44-40. Bbl. lengths: 4-, 5-, 6- and 6.5-in. Weight: 37.5 oz. (w/ 6.5-in. bbl.). Fixed sights. Blued or nickel finish. Hard rubber grips. Made 1881-1913.

**Standard model (.44 S&W
   Russian)** ....NiB $4500 Ex $1910 Gd $1010
**Standard model (.38-40,
   1900-10)**...............NiB $6030 Ex $5095 Gd $1479
**Frontier model (.44-40,
   1886–1913)** ....NiB $4500 Ex $1910 Gd $1010
**Favorite model (.44 S&W Russian,
   1882–83)** .... NiB $10,000 Ex $8200 Gd $7500

.44 HAND EJECTOR MODEL SERIES
First Model, New Century, also called "Triple Lock" because of its third cylinder lock at the crane. Six-round cylinder. Calibers: .44 S&W Special, .450 Eley, .455 Mark II. Bbl. lengths: 4-, 5-, 6.5- and 7.5-in. Weight: 39 oz. (w/ 6.5-in. bbl.). Fixed sights. Blued or nickel finish. Checkered walnut grips. Made 1907-66. Second Model is basically the same as New Century except crane lock ("Triple Lock" feature) and Extractor rod casing eliminated. Calibers: .44 S&W Special .44-40 Win. .45 Colt. Bbl. lengths: 4-, 5-, 6.5- and 7.5-in.; 11.75 in. overall (w/ 6.5-in. bbl.). Weight: 38 oz. (w/ 6.5-in. bbl.). Fixed sights. Blued or nickel finish. Checkered walnut grips. First Model mfg. from 1908–17, Second Model w/o "Triple Lock" feature mfg. 1915–40, Third Model w/o "Triple Lock" feature mfg. 1926–41.
First Model (w/triple lock, 1908-17)
**Second Model
   (w/o triple lock, 1915-37)**.. NiB $2380 Ex $2055 Gd $2810
Third Model (1926–41)..... NiB $3680 Ex $2310 Gd $2610
Third Model Target (target sights, 1926–41) ... NiB $9500 Ex $8550 Gd $6500

MODEL 45 (.22 MILITARY & POLICE)
Training gun. K-frame. Caliber: .22 LR, 6-rnd. cylinder. Bbl.: 4- or 6-in. Fixed sights. Blued. Made 1948–78.
4-in. bbl ....NiB $2610 Ex $2410 Gd $1010
6-in. bbl., add 50%

MODEL 48 (K-22 MRF MASTERPIECE)
Caliber: .22 MRF. and .22 LR, 6-rnd. cylinder. Bbl.: 4-, 6- or 8.3-in. 11.13 in. overall (w/ 6-in. bbl.). Weight: 39 oz. Adj. rear sight, ramp front. Made 1959-86.
w/4- or 6-in. bbl. ....NiB $1210 Ex $910 Gd $455
w/8.3-in. bbl. ....NiB $1310 Ex $1010 Gd $555
w/target options TH & TT, add $75
**Model 48 (Classic Series,
   2010–date)** .... NiB $780 Ex $590 Gd $380

MODEL 49 BODYGUARD.....NIB $455 EX $355 GD $230
Same as Model 38 Bodyguard Airweight except w/steel frame, weight: 20.5 oz. Made 1959-96.
nickel finish, add................................$25

MODEL 51 ....NiB $955 Ex $755 Gd $380
Same as Model 34 except chambered for .22 WMR 3.5-in. bbl., weight: 24 oz. Made 1960-74.

MODEL 53 .22 REM. JET
DA/SA. Caliber: .22 Rem. Jet C.F. Magnum. 6-rnd. cylinder (inserts permit use of .22 Short, Long, or LR cartridges). Bbl.: 4-, 6-, or 8.38-in., 11.25 in. overall (w/ 6-in. bbl.). Weight: 40 oz. (w/ 6-in. bbl.). Micrometer-click rear sight ramp front. Checkered walnut grips. Made 1960-74. This model had 1 engineering change.
4 screw ....NiB $1855 Ex $1255 Gd $680
3 screw ....NiB $1705 Ex $1055 Gd $380
w/rnd. butt, add 20%

**Smith & Wesson
Model 48**

**Smith & Wesson
Model 49 Bodyguard**

**Smith & Wesson
Model 57**

**Smith & Wesson
Model 60**

MODEL 56. . . . . NiB $5755 Ex $4505 Gd $3505
USAF issue. Caliber: .38 Spl., 6-rnd. cylinder. Bbl.: 2-in. Fixed sights, non serrated. Blued. Marked "U.S." on backstrap. Made 1963 only.

MODEL 57
SA/DA. N-frame. Caliber: 41 Mag. 6-rnd. cylinder. Bbl.: 4-, 6-, 5-, 8.38-in. Weight: 40 oz. (w/ 6-in. bbl.). Micrometer click rear sight, ramp front. Target grips of checkered Goncalo Alves. Made 1964-93.

N prefix. . . . . NiB $755 Ex $555 Gd $405
S prefix . . . . NiB $1605 Ex $1105 Gd $805
8.3-in. bbl., add 5%
nickel finish, add. 25%
Model 57 (Classic Series,
    2009–date) . . . . NiB $800 Ex $540 Gd $520

**MODEL 58 (.41
MILITARY & POLICE) . . . . NiB $905 Ex $755 Gd $505**
SA/DA. N-frame. Caliber: 41 Mag. 6-rnd. cylinder, 4-in. bbl. 9.25 in. overall. Weight: 41 oz. Fixed sights. Checkered walnut grips. Made 1964-82.
Model 58 (Classic Series, 2008-11). . NiB $780 Ex $530 Gd $420

MODEL 60 SERIES
DA/SA. Stainless version of Model 36. Caliber: .38 Spl. or .357 Mag. 5-rnd. cylinder, bbl. length: 2, 2.1 or 3 in., 6.5 or 7.5 in. overall. Weight: 19 to 23 oz. Square-notch rear sight, ramp front. Satin finish stainless steel.
.38 Spl. (1965–96) . . . . NiB $505 Ex $430 Gd $255
.357 Mag. (1996–date) . . . . NiB $530 Ex $330 Gd $225
Ladysmith .38 Spl. or .357 Mag.,
    1990–date) . . . . NiB $555 Ex $335 Gd $225
Pro Series (.38 Spl. or .357 Mag., 3-in. bbl.,
    2007–date) . . . . NiB $615 Ex $440 Gd $330

MODEL 63 . . . . NiB $855 Ex $580 Gd $430
Similar to Model 34 Kit Gun. Caliber: .22 LR. 6-rnd. cylinder, 2- or 4-in. bbl., 6.5 or 8.5 in. overall. Weight: 19 to 24.5 oz. Adj. rear sight, ramp front. Stainless steel. Checkered walnut or synthetic grips. Disc. 1998.
Model 63 (stainless, 3- or 5-in. bbl., 8-rnd. cylinder, 2008–date). . . . . NiB $630 Ex $480 Gd $355

**MODEL 64 MILITARY &
POLICE . . . . NiB $520 Ex $280 Gd $155**
Same as standard Model 10 except satin-finished stainless steel, square butt w/4-in. heavy bbl. or rnd. butt w/2-in. bbl. Made 1970 to date.

MODEL 65. . . . . NiB $455 Ex $405 Gd $205
Same as Model 13 except satin-finished stainless steel. Made 1974-2004.
Ladysmith 1992–04. . . . . NiB $480 Ex $280 Gd $155

**MODEL 66 COMBAT
MAGNUM . . . . NiB $655 EX $530 GD $380**
Same as Model 19 except satin-finished stainless steel. Made 1971 to date.
w/target options TH & TT, add $65
Model 66 Combat Magnum
    (Classic Series, 2014–date) . . . NiB $605 Ex $355 Gd $230

**MODEL 67 COMBAT
MASTERPIECE . . . . NiB $505 Ex $280 Gd $180**
Same as Model 15 except satin-finished stainless steel available only w/4-in. bbl. Made 1972-88 and from 1991-98.

Smith & Wesson Model 63

Smith & Wesson Model 64

Smith & Wesson Model 66 Combat Magnum

Smith & Wesson Model 67 Combat Masterpiece

MODEL 68 COMBAT MAGNUM. . . . . NiB $955 Ex $600 Gd $230
Same as Model 66 except w/4- or 6-in. bbl., chambered for .38 Spl. Made to accommodate CA Highway Patrol because they were not authorized to carry .357 Magnums. Made 1976-83. (7,500 produced)

MODEL 69 COMBAT MAGNUM NiB $755 Ex $355 Gd $230
DA/SA. L-frame. Caliber: .44 Mag., 5-rnd. cylinder. Bbl.: 2.75- or 4.25-in. Adj. sights. Matte stainless. Rubber grip. Made 2014–date.

MODEL 242 AIRLITE TI CENTENNIAL. . . . . NiB $500 Ex $300 Gd $220
DAO. Caliber: .38 Spl.+P. 7-rnd. titanium cylinder, 2.5-in. bbl., alloy L-frame. Uncle Mike's boot grip. Made 1990 only.

MODEL 296 AIRLITE TI CENTENNIAL. . . . . NiB $650 Ex $400 Gd $260
DAO. Caliber: .44 Spl. 5-rnd. titanium cylinder, 2.5-in. bbl., alloy L-frame. Uncle Mike's boot grip. Made 1990 only.

MODEL 310 NIGHTGUARD . . NiB $895 Ex $540 Gd $360
SA/DA. Caliber: .40 S&W or 10mm. 6-rnd. stainless cylinder, 2.5-in. bbl., scandium alloy N-frame. Fixed sights. Pachmayr grip. Made 2009-10.

MODEL 315 NIGHTGUARD . . . NiB $895 Ex $540 Gd $360
SA/DA. Caliber: .40 S&W or 10mm. 6-rnd. stainless cylinder, 2.5-in. bbl., scandium alloy N-frame. Fixed sights. Pachmayr grip. Made 2009-10.

MODEL 317 AIRLITE DA REVOLVER
Caliber: .22 LR. Eight-round cylinder, 1.88- or 3-in. bbl., 6.3 or 7.2 in. overall. Weight: 9.9 oz. or 11 oz. Ramp front sight, notched frame rear. Aluminum, carbon fiber, stainless and titanium construction. Brushed aluminum finish. Synthetic or Dymondwood grips. Made 1997 to date.
w/1.88-in. bbl. . . . . NiB $590 Ex $380 Gd $306
w/3-in. bbl. . . . . NiB $683 Ex $453 Gd $356
w/Dymondwood grips, add $100

MODEL 325 NIGHTGUARD . . . NiB $830 Ex $430 Gd $350
SA/DA. Caliber: .45 ACP. 6-rnd. stainless cylinder, 2.5-in. bbl., alloy N-frame. Fixed sights. Weight: 26.5 oz. Pachmayr rubber grip. Made 2008-12.

MODEL 325 PD-AIRLITE SC. . . . . NiB $800 Ex $490 Gd $340
SA/DA. Caliber: .45 ACP. 6-rnd. titanium cylinder, 2.5- or 4-in. bbl., scandium alloy N-frame. Weight: 21.5-25 oz. Hogue rubber grip. Made 2004-07.

MODEL 327 NIGHTGUARD . . . NiB $830 Ex $430 Gd $350
SA/DA. Caliber: .357 Mag. 8-rnd. stainless cylinder, 2.5-in. bbl., alloy N-frame. Fixed sights. Weight: 28 oz. Pachmayr rubber grip. Made 2008-12.

MODEL 327 PD-AIRLITE SC. . . . . NiB $960 Ex $460 Gd $320
SA/DA. Caliber: .357 Mag. 8-rnd. titanium cylinder, 4-in. bbl., scandium alloy N-frame. Fixed sights. Weight: 28 oz. Wood grip. Made 2008-09.

MODEL 329 NIGHTGUARD . . . . NiB $830 Ex $430 Gd $350
SA/DA. Caliber: .44 Mag. 6-rnd. stainless cylinder, 2.5-in. bbl., alloy N-frame. Fixed sights. Weight: 28 oz. Pachmayr rubber grip. Made 2008-12.

MODEL 329
PD-AIRLITE SC . . . . NiB $1160 Ex $530 Gd $350
SA/DA. Caliber: .44 Mag. 6-rnd. titanium cylinder, 4-in. bbl., scandium alloy N-frame. Fixed sights. Weight: 28 oz. Wood grip. Made 2003 to date.

MODEL 331 AIRLITE TI
CHIEFS SPECIAL . . . . NiB $675 Ex $465 Gd $310
SA/DA. Caliber: .32 H&R Mag. 6-rnd. titanium cylinder, 1.87-in. bbl., alloy J-frame. Fixed sights. Weight: 28 oz. Wood or Uncle Mike's grip. Made 1999-2003.

MODEL 332 AIRLITE TI
CENTENNIAL . . . . NiB $575 Ex $455 Gd $310
DAO. Caliber: .32 H&R Mag. 6-rnd. titanium cylinder, 1.87-in. bbl., alloy J-frame. Fixed sights. Weight: 28 oz. Uncle Mike's grip. Made 1999-2003.

MODEL 337 AIRLITE TI
CHIEFS SPECIAL . . . . NiB $675 Ex $465 Gd $310
SA/DA. Caliber: .38 Spl.+P. 5-rnd. titanium cylinder, 1.87-in. bbl., alloy J-frame. Fixed sights. Weight: 12 oz. Made 1999-2003.

MODEL 337 AIRLITE TI
KIT GUN . . . . NiB $600 Ex $350 Gd $290
SA/DA. Caliber: .38 Spl.+P. 5-rnd. cylinder, 3.12-in. bbl., J-frame. Fixed sights. Weight: 12 oz. Made 2000-03.

MODEL 337 PD AIRLITE TI . . . NiB $585 Ex $345 Gd $315
SA/DA. Caliber: .38 Spl.+P. 5-rnd. titanium cylinder, 1.87-in. bbl., alloy J-frame. Fixed sights. Weight: 10.7 oz. Made 2000-03.

MODEL 340 AIRLITE SC
CENTENNIAL . . . . NiB $775 Ex $410 Gd $350
DAO. Caliber: .357 Mag. 5-rnd. titanium cylinder, 1.87-in. bbl., alloy J-frame. Fixed sights. Weight: 10.7 oz. Made 2001-08.

MODEL 340 PD-AIRLITE SC
CENTENNIAL . . . . NiB $775 Ex $410 Gd $350
DAO. Caliber: .357 Mag. 5-rnd. titanium cylinder, 1.87-in. bbl., alloy J-frame. HiViz fixed sights. Weight: 10.7 oz. Made 2000 to date.

MODEL 340 M&P
CENTENNIAL . . . . NiB $869 Ex $500 Gd $280
DAO. Caliber: .357 Mag. 5-rnd. stainless cylinder, 1.87-in. bbl., alloy J-frame. HiViz fixed sights. Weight: 10.7 oz. Made 2007 to date.

MODEL 342 AIRLITE TI
CENTINNIAL . . . . NiB $575 Ex $355 Gd $310
DAO. Caliber: .38 Spl.+P. 5-rnd. titanium cylinder, 1.87-in. bbl., alloy J-frame. Fixed sights. Weight: 12 oz. Made 1999-2003.

MODEL 342 PD AIRLITE TI
CENTINNIAL . . . . NiB $575 Ex $355 Gd $310
DAO. Caliber: .38 Spl.+P. 5-rnd. titanium cylinder, 1.87-in. bbl., alloy J-frame. Fixed sights. Weight: 10.8 oz. Made 1999-2003.

MODEL 351 PD AIRLITE SC
CHIEF'S SPECIAL . . . . NiB $759 Ex $400 Gd $310
SA/DA. Caliber: .22 WMR. 7-rnd. cylinder, 1.87-in. bbl., alloy J-frame. Fixed sights. Weight: 10.6 oz. Made 2004 to date.

MODEL 351 PD AIRLITE
CENTINNIAL . . . . NiB $689 Ex $375 Gd $300
DAO. Caliber: .22 WMR. 7-rnd. cylinder, 1.87-in. bbl., alloy J-frame. Fixed sights. Weight: 11 oz. Made 2010 to date.

MODEL 357 PD . . . . NiB $815 Ex $405 Gd $345
SA/DA. Caliber: .41 Mag. 6-rnd. titanium cylinder, 4-in. bbl., scandium alloy N-frame. HiViz front, adj. rear sights. Weight: 27.5 oz. Ahrends wood grip. Made 2005-07.

MODEL 357 NIGHTGUARD . . NiB $895 Ex $430 Gd $355
SA/DA. Caliber: .41 Mag. 6-rnd. stainless cylinder, 2.5-in. bbl., alloy N-frame. Fixed sights. Weight: 29.7 oz. Rubber grip. Made 2010 only.

MODEL 360 AIRLITE SC
CHIEF'S SPECIAL . . . . NiB $780 Ex $410 Gd $345
SA/DA. Caliber: .357 Mag. 5-rnd. titanium cylinder, 1.87-in. bbl., alloy J-frame. Fixed sights. Weight: 12 oz. Hogue rubber grip. Made 2001-07.
Kit Gun model (3.1-in. bbl.) . . . NiB $775 Ex $440 Gd $330

MODEL 360 PD AIRLITE SC
CHIEF'S SPECIAL . . . . NiB $1020 Ex $400 Gd $345
SA/DA. Caliber: .357 Mag. 5-rnd. titanium cylinder, 1.87-in. bbl., alloy J-frame. Fixed sights. Weight: 12 oz. Hogue rubber grip. Matte grey finish. Made 2002 to date.

MODEL 360 M&P
CHIEF'S SPECIAL . . . . NiB $1020 Ex $400 Gd $345
SA/DA. Caliber: .357 Mag. 5-rnd. stainless cylinder, 1.87-in. bbl., scandium alloy J-frame. Fixed sights. Weight: 13.3 oz. Rubber grip. Matte black finish. Made 2007-10.

MODEL 386 AIRLITE SC
MOUNTAIN LITE . . . . NiB $660 Ex $3700 Gd $325
SA/DA. Caliber: .357 Mag. 7-rnd. titanium cylinder, 2.5- or 3.1-in. bbl., scandium alloy L-frame. HiViz front, adj. rear sights. Weight: 18.5 oz. Rubber grip. Matte black finish. Made 2001-07.

MODEL 386 PD-AIRLITE SC . . . NiB $1020 Ex $400 Gd $345
SA/DA. Caliber: .357 Mag. 7-rnd. titanium cylinder, 2.5-in. bbl., scandium alloy L-frame. Adj. sights. Weight: 17.5 oz. Hogue rubber grip. Matte grey finish. Made 2001-05.

MODEL 386 SC/S . . . . NiB $780 Ex $390 Gd $340
SA/DA. Caliber: .357 Mag. 7-rnd. stainless cylinder, 2.5-in. bbl., scandium alloy L-frame. Adj. sights. Weight: 21.2 oz. Made 2007-08.

MODEL 386 NIGHTGUARD . . NiB $750 Ex $460 Gd $410
SA/DA. Caliber: .357 Mag. 7-rnd. stainless cylinder, 2.5-in. bbl., alloy L-frame. Fixed sights. Weight: 24.5 oz. Made 2008-12.

MODEL 386 XL HUNTER
AIRLITE SC . . . . NiB $795 Ex $430 Gd $380
SA/DA. Caliber: .357 Mag. 7-rnd. stainless cylinder, 6-in. bbl., alloy L-frame. Fixed sights. Weight: 30 oz. Matte black finish. Made 2010-12.

MODEL 396 AIRLITE TI
MOUNTAIN LITE . . . . NiB $625 Ex $360 Gd $320
SA/DA. Caliber: .44 Spl. 5-rnd. titanium cylinder, 3.1-in. bbl., alloy L-frame. Adj. sights. Weight: 18 oz. Matte grey finish. Made 2001-04.

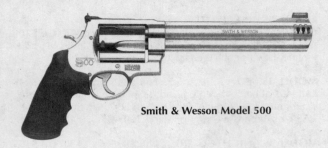

Smith & Wesson Model 500

MODEL 396 NIGHTGUARD. . . NiB $825 Ex $480 Gd $430
SA/DA. Caliber: .44 Spl. 5-rnd. stainless cylinder, 2.5-in. bbl., alloy L-frame. Fixed sights. Weight: 24.2 oz. Made 2008-09.

MODEL 431 AIRWEIGHT . . . . NiB $525 Ex $355 Gd $300
SA/DA. Caliber: .32 H&R Mag. 6-rnd. cylinder, 2-in. bbl., J-frame. Fixed sights. Blued finish. Made 2004-05.

**MODEL 431 CENTENNIAL
AIRWEIGHT. . . . . NiB $5505 Ex $380 Gd $310**
DAO. Caliber: .32 H&R Mag. 6-rnd. cylinder, 2-in. bbl., J-frame. Fixed sights. Blued finish. Made 2004-05.

MODEL 438 AIRWEIGHT . . . . NiB $525 Ex $355 Gd $300
SA/DA. Caliber: .38 Spl.+P. 5-rnd. cylinder, 1.87-in. bbl., J-frame. Fixed sights. Weight: 15 oz. Matte black finish. Made 2004-05.

**MODEL 442 AIRWEIGHT
CENTINNIAL. . . . . NiB $470 Ex $220 Gd $180**
DAO. Caliber: .38 Spl.+P. 5-rnd. cylinder, 1.87-in. bbl., J-frame. Fixed sights. Weight: 15 oz. Matte black, blued, or nickel finish. Made 1993 to date.
442 Pro Series (moon clips). . . . NiB $499 Ex $230 Gd $190

MODEL 469 V/XVR . . . . NiB $1370 Ex $700 Gd $600
SA/DA. Caliber: .460 S&W Mag. 5-rnd. cylinder, 5- or 8.5-in. bbl., X-frame. HiViz adj. sights. Matte stainless finish. Made 2005 to date.

MODEL 500
Caliber: .500 S&W Magnum. Uses S&W's largest revolver frame: X-frame. 5-rnd. cylinder, bbl. lengths: 4, 6.5 and 8.38 in., ported bbl., overall length: 15 in. (8.38-in. bbl.). Weight: 71.9 oz. (8.38-in. bbl.). Interchangeable front sight, micrometer-click adj. rear. Synthetic grip. Satin stainless finish. Made 2003 to date.
w/6- or 8.38-in. bbl. . . . . NiB $1299 Ex $740 Gd $459
w/4-in. bbl., add $70
w/factory HI-VIZ sights (8.38-in. bbl.), add $70

MODEL 520 . . . . NiB $930 Ex $705 Gd $455
DA/SA. Caliber: .357 Mag. Six-round cylinder. N-Frame w/4-in. bbl. Weight: 40 oz. Fixed sights. In 1980, 3,000 pieces were made for the N.Y. State Police but that agency did not purchase those firearms, so they were sold commercially.
**Model 520 (recent mfg., L-frame,
    2005–06) . . . . NiB $500 Ex $380 Gd $300**

**MODEL 547 MILITARY &
POLICE . . . . NiB $1010 Ex $580 Gd $355**
Caliber: 9mm. 6-rnd. cylinder. Bbl.: 3- or 4-in., 7.31 in. overall. Weight: 32 oz. Square-notch rear sight, ramp front. Mfg. 1980-85.

**MODEL 581 DISTINGUISHED
SERVICE MAGNUM . . . . .NiB $755 Ex $570 Gd $420**
SA/DA. Caliber: .357 Mag. 6-rnd. cylinder, 4-in. full lug bbl., L-frame, fixed sights, blued or nickel finish. Mfg. 1981-92.
Nickel finish, add $25

MODEL 586 DISTINGUISHED COMBAT MAGNUM
Caliber: .357 Magnum. Six-round cylinder, bbl. lengths: 4, 6 and 8.38 in., overall length: 9.75 in. (w/ 4-in. bbl.). Weight: 42, 46, 53 oz., respectively. Red ramp front sight, micrometer-click adj. rear. Checkered grip. Blued or nickel finish. Made 1980-99.
Blued finish. . . . . NiB $655 Ex $455 Gd $305
Nickel finish, add 5%
w/adjustable front sight, add $50
**Model 586 (Classic Series,
    2008-date) . . . . NiB $620 Ex $355 Gd $215**

MODEL 610 CLASSIC . . . . . . .NIB $830 EX $705 GD $480
SA/DA. Caliber: .40 S&W/10mm. 6-rnd. fluted or unfluted cylinder. 4-, 5- or 6.5-in. full lug bbl. N-frame, Adj. sights, stainless finish. Made 1990; 1998 to 2004; 2009-date.
**Model 610 (recent mfg.,
    2009–date) . . . . NiB $730 Ex $530 Gd $355**

**MODEL 617 K-22
MASTERPIECE. . . . . .NiB $755 Ex $530 Gd $405**
SA/DA. Caliber: .22 LR. 6- or 10-rnd. cylinder. 4-, 6- or 8.37-in. full lug bbl. K-frame, Adj. sights, matte stainless finish, Hogue rubber grips. Made 1990 to date.
w/8.38-in. bbl., add $55
w/10-rnd. aluminum cylinder, add 15%
w/6-rnd. cylinder, deduct 5%

MODEL 619. . . . . NiB $450 Ex $230 Gd $190
SA/DA. Caliber: .357 Mag. 7-rnd. cylinder. 5-in. bbl. L-frame, fixed sights, matte stainless finish, rubber grips. Made 2005-06.

MODEL 620 . . . . NiB $590 Ex $390 Gd $275
SA/DA. Caliber: .357 Mag. 7-rnd. cylinder. 4-in. bbl., L-frame, adj. sights, matte stainless finish, rubber grips. Made 2005-09.

MODEL 624 . . . . NiB $750 Ex $530 Gd $460
SA/DA. Caliber: .44 Spl. 6-rnd. cylinder. 4- or 6.5-in. bbl., N-frame, adj. sights, matte stainless finish. Made 1986-87.

MODEL 625 . . . . NiB $730 Ex $630 Gd $455
Model of 1988/Model of 1989. Same general specifications as Model 25 except 3-, 4- or 5-in. bbl., round-butt Pachmayr grips and satin stainless steel finish. Made 1989-2007.

MODEL 625 JM . . . . .NiB $800 Ex $555 Gd $430
SA/DA. Caliber: .45 ACP. 6-rnd. cylinder. 3-, 4- or 5-in. full lug bbl., N-frame, adj. sights, matte stainless finish, made in colaboration with competitive shooter Jerry Miculek. Made 1988 to date.

MODEL 627 . . . . .NiB $1755 Ex $1310 Gd $880
SA/DA. Caliber: .357 Mag. unfluted 6-rnd. cylinder, 5.5-in. full lug bbl., N-frame, adj. sights, satin stainless steel finish. Made 1989-97.

MODEL 627 . . . . .NiB $605 Ex $430 Gd $305
Recent mfg. SA/DA. Caliber: .357 Mag. 8-rnd. cylinder. 4-in. bbl., N-frame, adj. sights, satin stainless steel finish. Made 2008-09.
**Pro Series (.38 Spl. or .357 Mag., 8-rnd. cylider, 4-in. bbl.,
    2008–date) . . . . NiB $780 Ex $530 Gd $430**

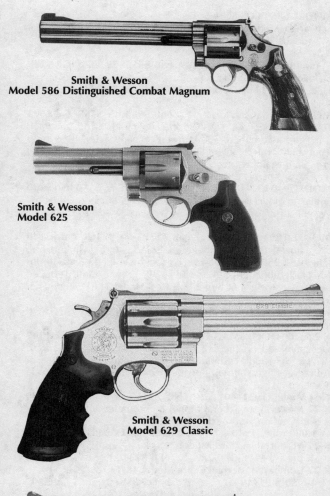

**Smith & Wesson
Model 586 Distinguished Combat Magnum**

**Smith & Wesson
Model 625**

**Smith & Wesson
Model 629 Classic**

**Smith & Wesson
Model 629**

MODEL 629

Same as Model 29 except in stainless steel. Pinned bbl. variants also have recessed chambers, mfg. 1979–82. Non-pinned barrels made 1982–date. Model 629 Classic had full under lug barrel, mfg. 1990–date.

Pinned bbl. (1979–82) . . . . NiB $855 Ex $730 Gd $605
Pinned bbl. (4-in. bbl.,
   1979–82) . . . . NiB $905 Ex $780 Gd $530
Model 629 . . . . NiB $730 Ex $530 Gd $405
Model 629 Backpacker (3-in. bbl.,
   Hogue rubber grip). . . . . NiB $705 Ex $655 Gd $530
Classic. . . . . NiB $755 Ex $630 Gd $405
Classic DX (2 sets go grips,
   1992–2002) . . . . NiB $1155 Ex $755 Gd $580

Magna Classic (1,800 mfg.,
   1990 only) . . . . NiB $1255 Ex $805 Gd $655
Deluxe (3- or 6.5-in. full lug bbl.,
   wood grip, 2017–date) . . . . . . NiB $780 Ex $540 Gd $430

MODEL 631 . . . . NIB $800 EX $659 GD $246
Similar to Model 31 except chambered for .32 H&R Mag. 2-in. bbl. Fixed sights. Goncalo Alves combat grips. Mfg. 1990–92.
Ladysmith, (rosewood grip) . . . NiB $605 Ex $455 Gd $255

MODEL 632 CENTENNIAL . . . . NIB $605 EX $355 GD $200
Same general specifications as Model 640 except chambered for .32 H&R Mag. 2- or 3-in. bbl., weight: 15.5 oz. Stainless slide w/alloy frame. Fixed sights. Santoprene combat grips. Made 1991-92.
w/3-in. bbl., add $120
Pro Series (2.1- or 3-in. ported bbl.,
   2009–12) . . . . NiB $605 Ex $555 Gd $380

**MODEL 637 CHIEFS SPECIAL AIRWEIGHT
DA REVOLVER** . . . . NiB $360 Ex $280 Gd $195
Same general specifications as Model 37 except w/alloy frame and stainless cylinder. 560 made in 1991 and reintroduced in 1996.
Pro Series (2.1-in. bbl., 2009–10) . . NiB $540 Ex $420 Gd $335
w/LaserMax, add $65
w/CrimsonTrace laser grip, add $200

**MODEL 638 BODYGUARD
AIRWEIGHT** . . . . NiB $360 Ex $280 Gd $195
Similar to Model 38 except w/alloy frame and stainless cylinder. 1,200 made in 1990 and reintroduced in 1998.
w/LaserMax, add $65
w/CrimsonTrace laser grip, add $200

MODEL 640 CENTENNIAL . . . . . NiB $530 Ex $380 Gd $270
DAO. Caliber: .38 Spl. or .357 Mag., 5-rnd. cylinder, 1.7-, 2.1- or 3-in. bbl., 6.31 in. overall. Weight: 20-22 oz. Fixed sights. Stainless finish. Smooth hardwood service grips. Made 1991 to date.

**MODEL 642 CENTENNIAL AIRWEIGHT
DAO REVOLVER** . . . . NiB $360 Ex $280 Gd $195
Same general specifications as Model 640 except w/stainless steel/aluminum alloy frame and finish. Weight 15.8 oz. Santoprene combat grips. Made 1990-93 and reintroduced 1996.
Ladysmith . . . . NiB $390 Ex $300 Gd $220
2.1-in. bbl. w/ PowerPort (2009-10), add $150
Pro Series (cylinder cut for full moon clips,
   mfg. 2010-date), ... NiB $390 Ex $300 Gd $220
642 CT (CrimsonTrace grip,
   2004–date) . . . . NiB $520 Ex $370 Gd $290
642 LaserMax (laser, 2015–16). . NiB $530 Ex $320 Gd $230

MODEL 646 . . . . NIB $900 EX $570 GD $470
DA/SA. L-frame. Caliber: .40 S&W., 6-rnd. cylinder. Bbl.: 4-in. Adj. sights. Matte stainless, titanium cylinder. Mfg. 2000–03.

MODEL 647 . . . . NIB $1010 EX $680 GD $555
DA/SA. K-frame. Caliber: .17 HMR., 6-rnd. cylinder. Bbl.: 8.3-in. full lug. Adj. sights. Stainless. Mfg. 1989–96.

MODEL 648 . . . . NiB $1010 Ex $680 Gd $555
DA/SA. K-frame. Caliber: .22 WMR., 6-rnd. cylinder. Bbl.: 6-in. w/full lug. Adj. sights. Stainless. Grip: Hogue rubber. Mfg. 1989–96.
642-2 (.22 WMR, 2003–05) . . . . NiB $855 Ex $500 Gd $405

Smith & Wesson
Model 640

Smith & Wesson
Model 642 Centennial Airweight

MODEL 649 BODYGUARD . . . NiB $590 Ex $305 Gd $170
Similar to Model 49 except w/stainless frame and finish. Made 1986 to date.

MODEL 650 . . . . NiB $1210 Ex $755 Gd $605
DA/SA. J-frame. Caliber: .22 Mag. 6-rnd. cylinder, 3-in. bbl., 7 in. overall. Weight: 23.5 oz. Serrated ramp front sight, fixed square-notch rear. Round butt, checkered walnut mono-grammed grips. Stainless steel finish. Made 1983-87.

MODEL 651 . . . . NiB $1210 EX $755 GD $555
DA/SA. J-frame. Caliber: .22 Mag. Rimfire. 6-rnd. cylinder, Bbl.: 3- or 4-in. 7 and 8.63 in., respectively, overall. Weight: 24.5 oz. Adj. rear sight, ramp front. Made 1983-87, 1990–98. Note: .22 LR cylinder available during early production.
w/extra cylinder, add 50%

MODEL 657 . . . . NiB $730 EX $530 GD $420
DA/SA. N-frame. Caliber: 41 Mag. 6-rnd. unfluted cylinder. Bbl.: 2.2-, 4-, 6-, 7.5- or 8.3-in. 9.6, 11.4, and 13.9 in. overall. Weight: 44.2, 48 and 52.5 oz. Serrated black ramp front sight on ramp base click rear, adj. for windage and elevation. Satin finished stainless steel. Made 1986-2008.

MODEL 681 DISTINGUISHED
SERVICE MAGNUM . . . . NiB $430 Ex $280 Gd $180
DA/SA. L-frame. Caliber: .357 Mag., 6-rnd. cylinder. Bbl.: 4-in. Fixed sights. Stainless. Mfg. 1980–92.

MODEL 686 DISTINGUISHED
SERVICE MAGNUM . . . . NiB $620 EX $355 GD $255
DA/SA. L-frame. Caliber: .357 Mag., 6-rnd. cylinder. Bbl.: full lug 2.5-, 4-, 6-, or 8.3-in. Fixed or adj. sights. Finish: stainless. Grip: rubber or wood. Mfg. 1980–date.
SSR Pro Series (4- or 5-in. bbl.,
** 2007–date) . . . . NiB $755 Ex $520 Gd $355**

MODEL 686 PLUS SERIES
Similar to Model 686 Distinguished Combat Magnum except w/7-rnd. cylinder and 3-, 5- or 7-in. bbl. Made 2017 to date.
3-5-7 Magnum
** (unfluted cylider) . . . . NiB $655 Ex $370 Gd $280**
Deluxe (fluted cylinder,
** 3- or 6-in. bbl.) . . . . NiB $655 Ex $370 Gd $280**

MODEL 696 . . . . NiB $955 Ex $755 Gd $605
DA/SA. Caliber: .44 S&W Special. L-Frame. 5-rnd. cylinder, 3-in. shrouded bbl., 8.38 in. overall. Weight: 48 oz. Red ramp front sight, micrometer-click adj. rear. Checkered synthetic grip. Satin stainless steel. Mfg. 1997–2002.

MODEL 940 CENTENNIAL . . . . . NiB $880 Ex $580 Gd $330
Similar to Model 640 except chambered for 9mm. 2- or 3-in. bbl., Weight: 23-25 oz. Santoprene combat grips. Made 1991-98.

MODEL 1891 . . . . NiB $2779 Ex $2465 Gd $2190
SA. Hinged frame. Caliber: .38 S&W. 5-rnd. cylinder, bbl. lengths: 3.25, 4, 5 and 6-in. Fixed sights. Blued or nickel finish. Hard rubber grips. Made 1891-1911. Note: Until 1906, an accessory single-shot target bbl. (see Model 1891 Single-Shot Target Pistol) was available for this revolver.
w/extra .22 single-shot bbl. . . NiB $5300 Ex $4220 Gd $3690

K-22 OUTDOORSMAN DA NiB $2552 Ex $1906 Gd $1392
Design based on the .38 Military & Police Target. Caliber: .22 LR. Six-round cylinder, 11.13 in. overall. Weight: 35 oz. Adj. target sights. Blued finish. Checkered walnut grip. Made 1931 -40.
First Model (1931–40) . . . . . NiB $2155 Ex $1855 Gd $1380
K-22 Masterpiece Second Model (micrometer-adj. rear sight,
** short action, anti-backlash trigger,**
** 1,000 mfg., 1940–41) . . . . NiB $4955 Ex $4510 Gd $3310**
K-22 Masterpiece Third Model
** (K prefix, 1946–57) . . . . NiB $1010 Ex $855 Gd $705**
K-22 Combat Masterpiece (pre Model 18,
** 4-in. bbl., 1949–57) . . . . NiB $1010 Ex $855 Gd $705**

K-32 AND K-38 HEAVY MASTERPIECES
Same as K32 and K38 Masterpiece but w/heavy bbl. Weight: 38.5 oz. Made 1950-53. Note: All K32 and K38 revolvers made after September 1953 have heavy bbls. and the "Heavy Masterpiece" designation was disc. Values for Heavy Masterpiece models are the same as shown for Models 14 and 16. (See separate listing).

K-32 TARGET
DA REVOLVER . . . . NiB $18,600 Ex $15,400 Gd $9900
Same as .38 Military & Police Target except chambered for .32 S&W Long cartridge, slightly heavier bbl., weight: 34 oz. Only 98 produced. Made 1938-40.

LADY SMITH (MODEL M HAND EJECTOR) DA REVOLVER
Caliber: .22 LR. Seven-round cylinder, bbl. length: 2.25-, 3-, 3.5- and 6-in. (Third Model only), approximately 7 in. overall w/3.5-in. bbl., weight: About 9.5 oz. Fixed sights, adj. target sights available on Third Model. Blued or nickel finish. Round butt, hard rubber grips on First and Second models; checkered walnut or hard rubber square buttgrips on Third Model. First Model —1902-06: Cylinder locking bolt operated by button on left side of frame, no bbl., lug and front locking bolt. Second Model —1906-11: Rear cylinder latch eliminated, has bbl. lug, forward cylinder lock w/draw-bolt fastening. Third Model —1911-21: Same as Second Model except has square grips, target sights and 6-in. bbl. available. Note: Legend has it that a

straight-laced D.B. Wesson ordered discontinuance of the Lady Smith when he learned of the little revolver's reputed popularity w/ladies of the evening. The story, which undoubtedly has enhanced the appeal of this model to collectors, is not true: The Lady Smith was disc. because of difficulty of manufacture and high frequency of repairs.

First model . . . . NiB $3140 Ex $2130 Gd $1696
Second model . . . . NiB $2315 Ex $1779 Gd $1015
Third model, w/fixed sights,
   2.25- or 3.5-in. bbl. . . . . NiB $2315 Ex $1779 Gd $1015
Third model, w/fixed sights,
   6-in. bbl. . . . . NiB $2315 Ex $1779 Gd $1015
Third model, w/adj. sights,
   6-in. bbl. . . . . NiB $2215 Ex $1888 Gd $934

REGULATION POLICE
DA (I Frame) . . . . NiB $811 Ex $602 Gd $434
Calibers: .32 S&W (6-rnd.) or .38 S&W (5-rnd.) built on .32 Hand Ejector frames. Two-, 3-, 3.25-, 4-, 4.25- or 6-in. bbl., weight: 20-24 oz. Fixed sights. Blue or nickel finish. Checkered walnut grips. Made 1917-57. Note: After 1957 "J" Frames replaced the older "I" Frames and designations changed to Model 31 and 33 respectively.
Regulation Police, .32 S&W . . NiB $1097 Ex $920 Gd $599
Regulation Police, .38 S&W . . NiB $1097 Ex $920 Gd $599

REGULATION POLICE TARGET DA
Target version of the Regulation Police w/standard features of that model. Calibers: .32 S&W Long or .38 S&W. 6-in. bbl., 10.25 in. overall. Weight: 20 oz. Adjustable target sights. Blue or nickel finish. Checkered walnut grips. Made about 1917 to 1957.
Regulation Police Target,
   .32 S&W . . . . NiB $2600 Ex $2470 Gd $780
Regulation Police Target,
   .38 S&W (pre-war) . . . . . . NiB $3000 Ex $2855 Gd $900

SAFETY HAMMERLESS . . . . NiB $1396 Ex $1178 Gd $1024
Also called New Departure Double Action. Hinged frame. Calibers: .32 S&W, .38 S&W. Five-round cylinder, bbl. lengths: 2, 3- and 3.5-in. (.32 cal.) or 2-, 3.25-, 4-, 5- and 6-in. (.38 cal.); 6.75 in. overall (.32 cal. w/3-in. bbl.) or 7.5 in. (.38 cal. w/3.25-in. bbl.). Weight: 14.25 oz. (.32 cal. w/3-in. bbl.) or 18.25 oz. (.38 cal. 2.5-in. bbl.). Fixed sights. Blued or nickel finish. Hard rubber grips. Made 1888-1937 (.32 cal.); 1887 to 1941 (.38 cal. w/various minor changes.)

TEXAS RANGER
COMMEMORATIVE . . . . NiB $658 Ex $359 Gd $270
Issued to honor the 150th anniversary of the TExas Rangers. Model 19 .357 Combat Magnum w/4-in. bbl., sideplate stamped w/TExas Ranger Commemorative Seal, smooth Goncalo Alves grips. Special Bowie knife in presentation case. 8,000 sets made in 1973. Top value is for set in new condition.

SPHINX ENGINEERING S.A. — Matten b. Interlaken, Switzerland

North American extension of the Switzerland based KRISS Group based in Chesapeake, VA.

MODEL AT-380 DA PISTOL
Caliber: .380 ACP. 10-rnd. magazine, 3.27- in. bbl., 6.03 in. overall. Weight: 25 oz. Stainless steel frame w/blued slide or Palladium finish. Slide latch w/ambidExtrous magazine release. Imported from 1993 to 1996.

Smith & Wesson
Model 696

Smith & Wesson
Model K-22 Outdoorsman

Smith & Wesson
Lady Smith First Model

Smith & Wesson
Regulation Police Target

Smith & Wesson
Safety Hammerless

Sphinx Model AT2000S w/optional scope

Two-tone (w/blued slide) . . . . . NiB $474 Ex $336 Gd $240
w/Palladium finish . . . . NiB $561 Ex $431 Gd $336

NOTE: *The AT-88 pistol series was previously manufactured by ITM in Switzerland and imported by Action Arms before Sphinx-Muller resumed production of these firearms, now designated as the AT-2000 series.*

MODEL 2000S DA AUTOMATIC PISTOL
Calibers: 9mm Parabellum, .40 S&W. 15- or 11-rnd. magazine respectively, 4.53-in. bbl., (S-standard), 3.66-in. bbl., (P-compact), 3.34-in. bbl., (H-subcompact), 8.25 in. overall. Weight: 36.5 oz. Fixed sights w/3-dot system. Stainless frame w/blued slide or Palladium finish. AmbidExtrous safety. Checkered walnut or neoprene grips. Imported 1993 to 1996.
Standard model. . . . . NiB $990 Ex $903 Gd $581
Compact model . . . . NiB $890 Ex $755 Gd $536
Sub-compact model . . . . NiB $890 Ex $755 Gd $536
.40 S&W, add $50
Palladium finish, add. $100

MODEL AT2000C/2000CS COMPETITOR
Similar to the Model AT2000S except also chambered for 9x21mm. 10-rnd. magazine, 5.31-in. compensated bbl., 9.84 in. overall. Weight: 40.56 oz. Fully adjustable BoMar or ProPoint sights. Made 1993-96.
w/Bomar sight . . . . NiB $1844 Ex $1599 Gd $1418
w/ProPoint sight . . . . NiB $2254 Ex $1923 Gd $1690

MODEL AT2000GM/GMS GRAND MASTER
Similar to the AT2000C except single action only w/square trigger guard and Extended beavertail grip. Imported 1993-96.
w/BoMar sight . . . . NiB $1872 Ex $1624 Gd $1375
w/ProPoint sight . . . . NiB $2179 Ex $1919 Gd $1699

SPD STANDARD . . . . NiB $1295 EX $1100 GD $830
Semiauto. DA/SA. Caliber: 9mm; 10- or 17-rnd. magazine. 4.5-in. bbl. Sights: fiber optic front, adj. rear or fixed white dot. Finish: matte black. Grip: textured polymer w/modular grip inserts. Length: 8.3-in. Weight: 31.6 oz. Made 2012 to date.
SPD Compact (3.7-in. bbl.) . . . . . NiB $999 Ex $980 Gd $900
SPD Subcompact (3.1-in. bbl.) . . . NiB $949 Ex $900 Gd $880

SPRINGFIELD ARMORY — Geneseo, IL
Formerly U.S. Government run Springfield Armory in Springfield, Massachusetts. Springfield Armory name purchased in 1974 for commercial/civilian manufacturing.

911 SERIES
Semiauto. SA trigger w/exposed hammer. Mini 1911 style platform. Caliber: .380 ACP or 9mm w/6- (flush) or 7-rnd. magazine. Bbl.: 3-in. Receiver: Aluminum. Grips: Textured G10 Made 2017 to date.
Nitride finish. . . . . NiB $500 Ex $480 Gd $400

Two-Tone finish. . . . . NiB $530 Ex $510 Gd $430
.380 ACP models, subtract $100
w/Laser grip, add $30

MODEL M1911 SERIES AUTO PISTOL
Springfield builds the "PDP" (Personal Defense Pistol) Series based on the self-loading M 1911-A1 pistol (military specifications model) as adopted for a standard service weapon by the U.S. Army. With enhancements and modifications they produce a full line of firearms including Ultra-Compacts, Lightweights, Match Grade and Competition Models. For values see specific models.

MODEL 1911-A1 GOVERNMENT
Calibers: 9mm Para., .38 Super, .40 S&W, 10mm or .45 ACP., 7-, 8-, 9- or 10-rnd. magazine, 4- or 5-in. bbl., 8.5 in. overall. Weight: 36 oz. Fixed combat sights. Blued, Parkerized or Duo-Tone finish. Checkered walnut grips. Note: This is an Exact duplicate of the Colt M1911-A1 that was used by the U.S. Armed Forces as a service weapon.
Blued finish. . . . . NiB $453 Ex $347 Gd $265
Parkerized finish . . . . NiB $453 Ex $347 Gd $265

MODEL 1911-A1 (PRE '90 SERIES)
Calibers: 9mm Parabellum, .38 Super, 10mm, .45 ACP. Seven-, 8-, 9- or 10-rnd. magazine, bbl. length: 3.63, 4, 4.25 or 5 in., 8.5 in. overall. Weight: 36 oz. Fixed combat sights. Blued, Duo-Tone or Parkerized finish. Checkered walnut stocks. Made 1985-90.
Government model (blued). . . . NiB $453 Ex $347 Gd $265
Government model
  (Parkerized) . . . . NiB $621 Ex $436 Gd $362
Bullseye model (wadcutter) . NiB $1474 Ex $1345 Gd $866
Combat Commander model
  (blued) . . . . NiB $474 Ex $386 Gd $321
Combat Commander model
  (Parkerized) . . . . NiB $650 Ex $475 Gd $353
Commander model (blued). . . . NiB $479 Ex $306 Gd $219
Commander model
  (Duo-Tone) . . . . NiB $567 Ex $473 Gd $397
Commander model
  (Parkerized) . . . . NiB $650 Ex $536 Gd $386
Compact model (blued) . . . . . NiB $ 470 Ex $347 Gd $265
Compact model (Duo-Tone) . . . NiB $559 Ex $500 Gd $434
Compact model (Parkerized). . . NiB $668 Ex $500 Gd $342
Defender model (blued) . . . . . . NiB $546 Ex $434 Gd $290
Defender model (Parkerized) . . NiB $704 Ex $556 Gd $377
Defender model
  (Custom Carry) . . . . NiB $540 Ex $429 Gd $326
National Match model
  (Hardball) . . . . NiB $829 Ex $709 Gd $546
Trophy Master (Competition) NiB $1355 Ex $1265 Gd $918
Trophy Master
  (Distinguished) . . . . NiB $2152 Ex $2030 Gd $1234
Trophy Master (Expert) . . . . NiB $1723 Ex $1528 Gd $1322

MODEL 1911-A1 (CUSTOM LOADED SERIES)
1911 style operating system w/steel or alloy frame. Calibers: 9mm Parabellum, .38 Super, .40 S&W, 10mm, .45 ACP. Seven-, 8-, 9- or 10-rnd. magazine, bbl. length: 3.63, 4, 4.25 or 5 in.; 8.5 in. overall. Weight: 28 oz. to 36 oz. Fixed combat sights. Blued, Duo-Tone, Parkerized or stainless finish. Checkered composition or walnut stocks. Made 1990-98.
Mil-Spec model (blued). . . . . . NiB $595 Ex $419 Gd $340
Mil-Spec model (Parkerized). . . NiB $809 Ex $644 Gd $444
Standard model (blued) . . . . . . NiB $879 Ex $689 Gd $499
Standard model (Parkerized). . NiB $1068 Ex $998 Gd $826
Standard model (stainless) . . . . NiB $806 Ex $699 Gd $497
Trophy model (blued) . . . . . . NiB $1440 Ex $1240 Gd $989
Trophy model (Hi-Tone) . . . NiB $1437 Ex $1245 Gd $1029
Trophy model (stainless) . . . . . NiB $709 Ex $577 Gd $429

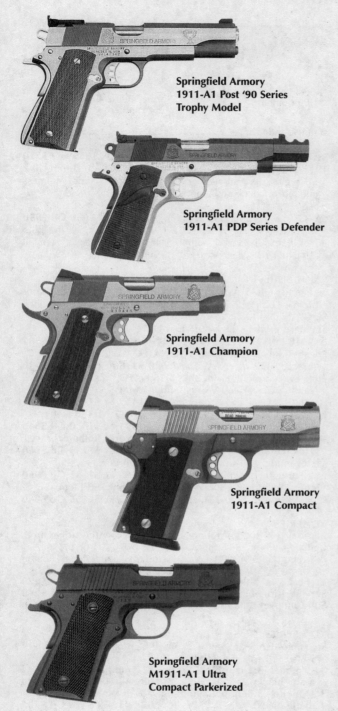

**Springfield Armory
1911-A1 Post '90 Series
Trophy Model**

**Springfield Armory
1911-A1 PDP Series Defender**

**Springfield Armory
1911-A1 Champion**

**Springfield Armory
1911-A1 Compact**

**Springfield Armory
M1911-A1 Ultra
Compact Parkerized**

.45 ACP Champion Comp
(blued) . . . . NiB $780 Ex $562 Gd $431
.45 ACP Compact Comp HC
(blued) . . . . NiB $602 Ex $453 Gd $398
.380 Sup Factory Comp (blued) NiB $740 Ex $546 Gd $431
.45 ACP Factory Comp (blued) NiB $866 Ex $780 Gd $544
.380 Sup Factory Comp HC
(blued) . . . . NiB $740 Ex $546 Gd $398
.45 ACP Factory Comp HC
(blued) . . . . NiB $733 Ex $789 Gd $556

MODEL M1911-A1 CHAMPION
Calibers: .380 ACP, 9mm Para., .45 ACP. Six- or 7-rnd. magazine, 4-in. bbl. Weight: 26.5 to 33.4 oz. Low profile post front sight and drift adjustable rear w/3-dot sighting system. Commander-style hammer and slide. Checkered walnut grips. Blue, Bi-Tone, Parkerized or stainless finish. Made 1992-2002.
.380 ACP standard
(disc. 1995) . . . . NiB $850 Ex $807 Gd $479
.45 ACP (parkerized or blued) NiB $700 Ex $665 Gd $480
.45 ACP (Bi-Tone) (B/H Model) NiB $912 Ex $790 Gd $386
.45 ACP (stainless) . . . . NiB $742 Ex $707 Gd $522
.45 ACP Super Tuned (1997-99) NiB $850 Ex $807 Gd $479

MODEL M1911-A1 COMPACT
Similar to the standard M1911 w/champion length slide on a steel or alloy frame w/a shortened grip. Caliber: .45 ACP. Six- or 7-rnd. magazine (10+ law enforcement only), 4-in. bbl. weight: 26.5 to 32 oz. Low profile sights w/3-dot system. Checkered walnut grips. Matte blue, Duo-Tone or Parkerized finish. Made 1991-96.
Compact (Parkerized) . . . . NiB $464 Ex $380 Gd $290
Compact (blued) . . . . NiB $464 Ex $380 Gd $290
Compact (Duo-Tone) . . . . NiB $577 Ex $500 Gd $434
Compact (stainless) . . . . NiB $556 Ex $376 Gd $270
Compact Comp (ported) . . . . . . NiB $882 Ex $792 Gd $587
High capacity (blued) . . . . NiB $595 Ex $369 Gd $321
High capacity (stainless) . . . . . . NiB $831 Ex $638 Gd $499

MODEL M1911-A1 ULTRA COMPACT
Similar to M1911 Compact except chambered for .380 ACP or .45 ACP. 6- or 7-rnd. magazine, 3.5-in. bbl., weight: 22 oz. to 30 oz. Matte Blue, Bi-Tone, Parkerized (military specs) or stainless finish. Made 1995-2003.
.380 ACP Ultra (disc. 1996) . . . NiB $740 Ex $585 Gd $388
.45 ACP Ultra (Parkerized
or blued) . . . . NiB $740 Ex $585 Gd $388
.45 ACP Ultra (Bi-Tone) . . . . . . NiB $844 Ex $709 Gd $500
.45 ACP (stainless) . . . . NiB $740 Ex $585 Gd $388
.45 ACP ultra high capacity
(Parkerized) . . . . NiB $740 Ex $585 Gd $388
.45 ACP ultra high capacity
(blued) . . . . NiB $780 Ex $615 Gd $499
.45 ACP ultra high capacity
(stainless) . . . . NiB $780 Ex $615 Gd $499
.45 ACP V10 ultra comp
(Parkerized) . . . . NiB $979 Ex $806 Gd $495
.45 ACP V10 ultra comp
(blued) . . . . NiB $979 Ex $806 Gd $495
.45 ACP V10 ultra comp
(stainless) . . . . NiB $979 Ex $806 Gd $495
.45 ACP V10 ultra (super
tuned) . . . . NiB $1090 Ex $974 Gd $577

MODEL 1911-A1 TRP (TACITCAL RESPONSE PISTOL)
SA AUTO PISTOL . . . . NiB $1620 Ex $1460 Gd $780
1911 style operating system w/steel frame. Caliber: .45 ACP. Seven-round magazine, bbl. length: 5 in.; 8.5 in. overall. Weight: 36 oz. Fixed combat sights. Black Armory Kote or stainless finish. Checkered front strap, composition stocks. Made 2008 to date.

MODEL 1911-A1 PDP SERIES
PDP Series (Personal Defense Pistol). Calibers: .38 Super, .40 S&W, .45 ACP. Seven-, 8-, 9-, 10-, 13- or 17-rnd. magazine, bbl. length: 4, 5, 5.5 or 5.63 in., 9 to 11 in. overall w/compensated bbl. Weight: 34.5 oz. to 42.8 oz. Post front sight, adjustable rear w/3-dot system. Blued, Duo-Tone, Parkerized or stainless finish. Checkered composition or walnut stocks. Made 1991-98.
Defender model (blued) . . . . . . NiB $910 Ex $780 Gd $586
Defender model (Duo-Tone) . . . NiB $910 Ex $780 Gd $586
Defender model (Parkerized) . . NiB $910 Ex $780 Gd $586

GRADING: **NiB** = New in Box   **Ex** = Excellent or NRA 95%   **Gd** = Good or NRA 68%

MODEL 1911-A1 LONG SLIDE CUSTOM LOADED
SA AUTO PISTOL . . . . **NiB $1100 Ex $960 Gd $480**
1911 style operating system w/steel frame. Caliber: .45 ACP or .45 Super. Seven-round magazine, bbl. length: 6 in.; 8.5 in. overall. Weight: 36 oz. Fixed combat sights. Black Armory Kote or stainless finish. Checkered wood stocks. Made 2001-12.

MODEL EMP (ENHANCED
MICRO PISTOL). . . . . **NiB $1175 EX $800 GD $600**
Similar to 1911-style Semiauto except in 9mm Parabellum or .40 S&W, and 3-in. bull bbl.

FIRECAT . . . . **NIB $556 EX $408 GD $289**
Calibers: 9mm, .40 S&W. Eight-round magazine (9mm) or 7-rnd. magazine (.40 S&W), 3.5-in. bbl., 6.5 in. overall. Weight: 25.75 oz. Fixed sights w/3-dot system. Checkered walnut grip. Matte blued finish. Made 1991-93.

HELLCAT . . . . **NiB $520 EX $480 GD $400**
Semiauto. Striker-fire. Polymer frame. Caliber: 9mm; 11- or 13-rnd. mag. .Bbl.: 3-in. Overall length: 6 in. Weight: 18.6 w/13-rnd. mag. Finish: balck or FDE. Sights: tritium dot. Made 2019 to date.
OSP (Optical Sight Pistol), add $30
RDP model (Hex red dot, Gen 2 trigger,
    self indexing compensator) . . . **NiB $960 Ex $850 Gd $730**
Pro OSP model (optic ready,
    full-size grip) . . . . **NiB $630 Ex $580 Gd $480**

PANTHER AUTO PISTOL . . . . . **NiB $606 Ex $453 Gd $346**
Calibers: 9mm, .40 S&W. 15-rnd. magazine (9mm) or 11-round magazine (.40 S&W), 3.8-in. bbl., 7.5 in. overall. Weight: 28.95 oz. Blade front sight, rear adj. for windage w/3-dot system. Checkered walnut grip. Matte blued finish. Made 1991-93.

MODEL P9 DA COMBAT SERIES
Calibers: 9mm, .40 S&W, .45 ACP. Magazine capacity: 15-rnd. (9mm), 11-rnd. (.40 S&W) or 10-rnd. (.45 ACP), 3.66-in. bbl., (Compact and Sub-Compact), or 4.75-in. bbl., (Standard), 7.25 or 8.1 in. overall. Weight: 32 to 35 oz. Fixed sights w/3-dot system. Checkered walnut grip. Matte blued, Parkerized, stainless or Duo-Tone finish. Made 1990-94.
Compact model (9mm,
    Parkerized) . . . .**NiB $464 Ex $342 Gd $279**
Sub-Compact model (9mm,
    Parkerized) . . . .**NiB $433 Ex $309 Gd $235**
Standard model (9mm,
    Parkerized) . . . .**NiB $498 Ex $377 Gd $304**
w/blued finish, add $50
w/Duo-Tone finish, add $100
w/stainless finish, add $128
.40 S&W, add $35
.45 ACP add $50

MODEL P9 COMPETITION SERIES
Same general specifications as Model P9 except in target configuration w/5-in. bbl., (LSP Ultra) or 5.25-in. bbl. Factory Comp model w/dual port compensator system, Extended safety and magazine release.
Factory Comp model
    (9mm Bi-Tone) . . . . **NiB $648 Ex $444 Gd $337**
Factory Comp model
    (9mm stainless) . . . . **NiB $733 Ex $431 Gd $281**
IPSC Ultra model
    (9mm Bi-Tone) . . . . **NiB $689 Ex $431 Gd $270**
LSP Ultra model (9mm stainless) . .**NiB $785 Ex $580 Gd $425**
.40 S&W, .45 ACP: add $128

MODEL RANGE OFFICER. . . . . **NiB $800 Ex $680 Gd $460**
Similar to 1911-style Semiauto except in 9mm Parabellum or .45 ACP only, 5-in. match bbl., adj. sights. Finish: blued or stainless finish. Mfg. 2011-21.

**Springfield Armory
P9 Combat**

**Springfield Armory
Panther**

stainless, add. $100

MODEL RONIN . . . . **NiB $710 EX $655 GD $510**
1911-style semiauto. Caliber: 9mm, .45 ACP or 10mm. Bbl: 5-in. Sights: tactical white-dot. Finish: blued slide, stainless frame. Grip: checkered wood laminate. 2020 to date.

SA-35 . . . . **NiB $695 Ex $680 Gd $590**
Semiauto. FN Hi-Power clone. Cal.: 9mm; 15-rnd. magazine. Bbl.: 4.7-in. Grip: Checkered walnut. Sights: White dot front, serrated tactical rack rear. Weight: 31.5 ozs. Steel frame. Mfg. 2022-date.

SAINT SERIES
Semiauto. AR-15 type action. Cal.: 5.56 NATO, .300 BLK, or .308 Win. Bbl.: 7.2- or 9.5-in. w/flash hider. Brace: SB Tactical SBX-K. Sights: Optic ready.
Standard model (7.2- or 9.5-in. bbl.,
    2018-20) . . . .**NiB $765 Ex $655 Gd $505**
Edge model (10.5-in. bbl., 5.56 NATO, Maxim Defense CQB
    brace, 2020-22) . . . .**NiB $1180 Ex $930 Gd $730**
Edge Evac model (7.5-in. bbl., 5.56 NATO,
    folding Gear Head Works Tailhook brace,
    2020-21) . . . .**NiB $1475 Ex $1165 Gd $915**
Edge PDW model (5.5-in. bbl., 5.56 NATO, Maxim Defense
    SCW brace, 2020-22) . . . . .**NiB $1355 Ex $1070 Gd $840**
Victor model (7.5-in. bbl., Gear Head Works Tailhook brace,
    Hex red dot, 2020-date) . . .**NiB $1255 Ex $1155 Gd $960**
Victor model (7.5-in. bbl., Magpul BTR brace,
    2020-date) . . . .**NiB $1255 Ex $1155 Gd $960**
Victor .308 model (.308 Win., 10.35-in. bbl., SB Tactical
    SBA3 brace, 2020-22) . . . . .**NiB $1255 Ex $1155 Gd $960**

XD SERIES
Based on HS 2000 pistol manufactured in Croatia. Striker fired. Calibers: 9mm, .357 SIG, .40 S&W, .45 ACP or .45 G.A.P. Polymer frame. 9-, 10-, 12- or 15-rnd. magazine depending on caliber. Matte black or bi-tone finish. Imported 2002 to date.
Tactical 5-in. bbl. . . . .**NiB $480 Ex $400 Gd $270**
Service 4-in. bbl.. . . . .**NiB $465 Ex $330 Gd $240**
Sub-Compact 3-in. bbl.. . . . .**NiB $465 Ex $330 Gd $240**

XD-E SERIES
Semiauto. DA/SA trigger w/exposed hammer. Caliber: 9mm or .45 ACP. Polymer frame. Made 2018-21.
3.3" model (3.3-in. bbl., 8- or 9-rnd. (9mm) mag.,
    matte black) . . . .**NiB $440 Ex $420 Gd $380**
3.3" model (3.8-in. bbl., 9mm only, 8- or 9-rnd. mag.,
    matte black) . . . .**NiB $440 Ex $420 Gd $380**
4.5" model (4.5-in. bbl., 9mm only, 8- or 9-rnd. mag.,
    matte black) . . . .**NiB $540 Ex $520 Gd $500**

XD-S . . . . **NiB $530 Ex $405 Gd $320**
Similar to XD and XD(M) series except with single stack magazine, 3.3- or 4-in. bbl., fiber optic sights. Finish: blued or two-tone. Made 2013 to date.
two-tone, add $100
laser sight, add $100

XD M 2 SERIES
Similar to XD and XD(M) series except with modified grip and Grip Zone w/3 grip texture types, fiber optic sights.

Tactical (5-in. bbl.) . . . . NiB $555 Ex $430 Gd $340
Service (4-in. bbl.) . . . . NiB $515 Ex $370 Gd $240
Sub-Compact (3- or 3.5-in. bbl.). . . NiB $500 Ex $370 Gd $240

XD(M) SERIES . . . . NiB $555 Ex $420 Gd $340
Similar to XD series except w/modular backstraps, diagonal slide serrations. Striker fired. Calibers: 9mm, .40 S&W, or .45 ACP. Bbl. lengths: 3.8- or 4.5-in. Made 2008 to date.
Compact . . . . NiB $555 Ex $420 Gd $320
Competition . . . . NiB $655 Ex $530 Gd $350
OSP (Optical Sight Pistol), add $125
Threaded bbl., add $20

S.P.S. — Spain

Manufactured in Spain and imported by Eagle Imports, Wanamassa, New Jersey. Series-70 style.

SPS PANTERA SERIES . . . . NiB $1480 Ex $1120 Gd $820
1911 platform. Semiauto. SA. Caliber: 9mm, .40 S&W, or.45 ACP; 12, 16-, or 21-rnd. magazine depending on caliber. 5-in. bbl. Frame: steel. Sights: adj. rear, fiber optic front. Finish: blue, black chrome, hard chrome. Grip: glass filled nylon. Length: 8.71 in. Weight: 36.68 oz. Beavertail, magwell. Competition ready. Imported from 2011 to date.

SPS VISTA . . . . NiB $2180 Ex $1630 Gd $1200
Similar to Pantera except chambered in 9mm or .38 Super, 5.5-in. bbl. w/compensator, optic mount. Designed for IPSC, USPSA, and IDPA competition.

STALLARD ARMS — Mansfield, OH
See listings under Hi-Point.

STAR — Eibar, Spain
Manufactured by Star, Bonifacio Echeverria, S.A.

MODEL 30M DA AUTO PISTOL . . NiB $431 Ex $288 Gd $189
Caliber: 9mm Para. 15-rnd. magazine, 4.38-in. bbl., 8 in. overall. Weight: 40 oz. Steel frame w/combat features. Adj. sights. Checkered composition grips. Blued finish. Made 1984-91.

**MODEL 30PK DA
AUTO PISTOL** . . . . NiB $431 Ex $288 Gd $189
Same gen. specifications as Star Model 30M except 3.8-in. bbl., weight: 30 oz. Alloy frame. Made 1984-89.

MODEL 31P DA AUTO PISTOL
Same general specifications as Model 30M except removable backstrap houses complete firing mechanism. Weight: 39.4 oz. Made 1990-94.
Blued finish. . . . . NiB $431 Ex $288 Gd $189
Starvel finish, add $50

MODEL 31 PK DA AUTO PISTOL . . . NiB $431 Ex $288 Gd $189
Same general specifications as Model 31P except w/alloy frame. Weight: 30 oz. Made 1990-97.

MODEL A AUTOMATIC PISTOL . .NiB $365 Ex $259 Gd $169
Modification of the Colt Government Model .45 Auto, which it closely resembles, but lacks grip safety. Caliber: .38 Super. Eight-round magazine, 5-in. bbl., 8 in. overall. Weight: 35 oz. Fixed sights. Blued finish. Checkered grips. Made 1934-97. (No longer imported.)

MODELS AS, BS, PS . . . . NiB $500 Ex $380 Gd $279
Same as Models A, B and P except have magazine safety. Made in 1975.

MODEL B . . . . NiB $498 Ex $365 Gd $259
Same as Model A except in 9mm Para. Made 1934-75.

MODEL BKM . . . . NiB $398 Ex $306 Gd $225
Similar to Model BM except has aluminum frame weight: 25.6 oz. Made 1976-92.

**MODEL BKS STARLIGHT
AUTOMATIC PISTOL** . . . . NiB $431 Ex $279 Gd $209
Light alloy frame. Caliber: 9mm Para. Eight-round magazine, 4.25-in. bbl., 7 in. overall. Weight: 25 oz. Fixed sights. Blued or chrome finish. Plastic grips. Made 1970-81.

MODEL BM AUTOMATIC PISTOL
Caliber: 9mm. Eight-round magazine, 3.9-in. bbl., 6.95 in. overall. Weight: 34.5 oz. Fixed sights. Checkered walnut grips. Blued or Starvel finish. Made 1976-92.
Blued finish. . . . . NiB $367 Ex $279 Gd $220
Starvel finish . . . . NiB $380 Ex $304 Gd $240

**MODEL CO POCKET
AUTOMATIC PISTOL** . . . . NiB $316 Ex $217 Gd $126
Caliber: .25 Automatic (6.35mm), 2.75-in. bbl., 4.5 in. overall. Weight: 13 oz. Fixed sights. Blued finish. Plastic grips. Made 1941-97.

**MODEL CU STARLET
POCKET PISTOL** . . . . NiB $291 Ex $198 Gd $124
Light alloy frame. Caliber: .25 Auto (6.35mm). Eight-round magazine, 2.38-in. bbl., 4.75 in. overall. Weight: 10.5 oz. Fixed sights. Blued or chrome-plated slide w/frame anodized in black, blue, green, gray or gold. Plastic grips. Made 1957-97. (U.S. importation disc. 1968.)

**MODEL F
AUTOMATIC PISTOL** . . . . NiB $362 Ex $268 Gd $130
Caliber: .22 LR. 10-rnd. magazine, 4.5-in. bbl., 7.5 in. overall. Weight: 25 oz. Fixed sights. Blued finish. Plastic grips. Made 1942-67.

**MODEL F
OLYMPIC RAPID-FIRE** . . . . NiB $556 Ex $408 Gd $230
Caliber: .22 Short. Nine-round magazine, 7-in. bbl., 11.06 in. overall. Weight: 52 oz. w/weights. Adj. target sight. Adj. 3-piece bbl. weight. Aluminum alloy slide. Muzzle brake. Plastic grips. Made 1942-67.

MODEL FM. . . . . NiB $362 Ex $279 Gd $171
Similar to Model FR except has heavier frame w/web in front of trigger guard, 4.25-in. heavy bbl., Weight: 32 oz. Made 1972-91.

MODEL FR . . . . NiB $362 Ex $279 Gd $171
Similar to Model F w/same general specifications but restyled, has slide stop and adj. rear sight. Made 1967-72.

MODEL FR SPORT . . . . NiB $398 Ex $306 Gd $229
Same as Model FR except has 6-in. bbl., weight: 28 oz. Also avail. in chrome finish. Made 1967-91.

MODEL FS . . . . NiB $362 Ex $309 Gd $165
Same as regular Model F but w/6-in. bbl. and adj. sights. Weight: 27 oz. Made 1942-67.

**MODEL HK LANCER
AUTOMATIC PISTOL**. . . . . NiB $319 Ex $225 Gd $249
Similar to Starfire w/same general specifications except .22 LR. Made 1955-68.

Star Model 30M

Star Model 30PK

Star Model AS

Star Model BKS

Star Model F

Star Model F
Olympic Rapid-Fire

Star
Model PD

MODEL HN
AUTOMATIC PISTOL . . . . **NiB $431 Ex $279 Gd $220**
Caliber: .380 Auto (9mm Short). Six-round magazine, 2.75-in. bbl., 5.56 in. overall. Weight: 20 oz. Fixed sights. Blued finish. Plastic grips. Made 1934-41.

MODEL H . . . . **NiB $357 Ex $281 Gd $165**
Same as Model HN except .32 Auto (7.65mm), 7-rnd. magazine, weight: 20 oz. Made 1934-41.

MODEL I
AUTOMATIC PISTOL . . . . **NiB $398 Ex $302 Gd $177**
Caliber: .32 Auto (7.65mm). Nine-round magazine, 4.81-in. bbl., 7.5 in. overall. Weight: 24 oz. Fixed sights. Blued finish. Plastic grips. Made 1934-36.

MODEL IN. . . . . **NiB $434 Ex $290 Gd $175**
Same as Model I except caliber .380 Auto (9mm Short), 8-rnd. magazine, weight: 24.5 oz. Made 1934-36.

MODEL M MILITARY
AUTOMATIC PISTOL . . . . **NiB $398 Ex $337 Gd $219**
Modification of the Model M without grip safety. Calibers: 9mm Bergmann (Largo), .45 ACP, 9mm Para. Eight-round magazine except 7-shot in .45 caliber, 5-in. bbl., 8.5 in. overall. Weight: 36 oz. Fixed sights. Blued finish. Checkered grips. Made 1934-39.

MODELS M40, M43, M45 FIRESTAR AUTO PISTOLS
Calibers: 9mm, .40 S&W, .45 ACP. Seven-round magazine (9mm) or 6-rnd. (other calibers). 3.4-in. bbl., 6.5 in. overall. Weight: 30.35 oz. Blade front sight, adj. rear w/3-dot system. Checkered rubber grips. Blued or Starvel finish. Made 1990-97.
M40 blued (.40 S&W) . . . . NiB $367 Ex $289 Gd $232
M40 Starvel (.40 S&W) . . . . NiB $398 Ex $304 Gd $239
M43 blued (9mm) . . . . NiB $365 Ex $294 Gd $237

M43 Starvel (9mm) . . . . NiB $398 Ex $304 Gd $239
M45 blued (.45 ACP) . . . . NiB $357 Ex $270 Gd $120
M45 Starvel (.45 ACP) . . . . NiB $377 Ex $290 Gd $143

MEGASTAR AUTOMATIC PISTOL
Calibers: 10mm, .45 ACP. 12-rnd. magazine, 4.6-in. bbl., 8.44 in. overall. Weight: 47.6 oz. Blade front sight, adj. rear. Checkered composition grip. finishes: Blued or Starvel. Made 1992-97.
Blued finish, 10mm or .45 ACP . . . NiB $500 Ex $397 Gd $274
Starvel finish, 10mm or .45 ACP . . . NiB $544 Ex $416 Gd $305

MODEL P . . . . NiB $464 Ex $345 Gd $283
Same as Model A except caliber .45 Auto, has 7-rnd. magazine. Made 1934-75.

MODEL PD AUTOMATIC PISTOL
Caliber: .45 Auto. Six-round magazine, 3.75-in. bbl., 7 in. overall. Weight: 25 oz. Adj. rear sight, ramp front. Blued or Starvel finish. Checkered walnut grips. Made 1975-92.
Blued finish . . . . NiB $398 Ex $304 Gd $224
Starvel finish . . . . NiB $422 Ex $342 Gd $270

MODEL S . . . . NiB $319 Ex $220 Gd $159
Same as Model SI except caliber .380 Auto (9mm), 7-rnd. magazine, weight: 19 oz. Made 1941-65.

MODEL SI
AUTOMATIC PISTOL . . . . NiB $316 Ex $225 Gd $130
Reduced-size modification of the Colt Government Model .45 Auto, lacks grip safety. Caliber: .32 Auto (7.65mm). Eight-round magazine, 4-in. bbl., 6.5 in. overall. Weight: 20 oz. Fixed sights. Blued finish. Plastic grips. Made 1941-65.

STARFIRE DK
AUTOMATIC PISTOL . . . . NiB $453 Ex $337 Gd $255
Light alloy frame. Caliber: .380 Automatic (9mm Short). Seven-round magazine, 3.13-in. bbl. 5.5 in. overall. Weight: 14.5 oz. Fixed sights. Blued or chrome-plated slide w/frame anodized in black, blue, green, gray or gold. Plastic grips. Made 1957-97. U.S. importation disc. 1968.

MODEL SUPER A
AUTOMATIC PISTOL . . . . NiB $499 Ex $431 Gd $220
Caliber: .38 Super. Improved version of Model A but has disarming bolt permitting easier takedown, cartridge indicator, magazine safety, take-down magazine, improved sights w/luminous spots for aiming in darkness. This is the standard service pistol of the Spanish Armed Forces, adopted 1946.

MODEL SUPER B AUTOMATIC PISTOL
Caliber: 9mm Para. Similar to Model B except w/improvements described under Model Super A. Made 1946-90.
Super blued finish . . . . NiB $453 Ex $342 Gd $225
Starvel finish . . . . NiB $456 Ex $366 Gd $249

MODELS SUPER M, SUPER P . . NiB $852 Ex $685 Gd $478
Calibers: .45 ACP, 9mm Parabellum or 9mm Largo, (Super M) and 9mm Parabellum (Super P). Improved versions of the Models M & P w/same general specifications, but has disarming bolt permitting easier takedown, cartridge indicator, magazine safety, take-down magazine, improved sights w/luminous spots for aiming in darkness.

MODELS SUPER SI, SUPER S . . NiB $332 Ex $239 Gd $274
Same general specifications as the regular Model SI and S except w/improvements described under Super Star. Made 1946-72.

MODEL SUPER SM . . . . NiB $398 Ex $386 Gd $204
Similar to Model Super S except has adj. rear sight, wood grips. Made 1973-81.

SUPER TARGET MODEL . . . NiB $1595 Ex $1396 Gd $1309
Same as Super Star model except w/adj. target sight. (Disc.)

ULTRASTAR DA
AUTOMATIC PISTOL . . . . NiB $365 Ex $290 Gd $200
Calibers: 9mm Parabellum or .40 S&W. Nine-round magazine, 3.57-in. bbl., 7 in. overall. Weight: 26 oz. Blade front, adjustable rear w/3-dot system. Polymer frame. Blue metal finish. Checkered black polymer grips. Imported from 1994 to 1997.

STENDA-WERKE — Suhl, Germany

POCKET AUTOMATIC PISTOL . NiB $337 Ex $279 Gd $160
Essentially the same as the Beholla (see listing of that pistol for specifications). Made circa 1920-.25. Note: This pistol may be marked "Beholla" along w/the Stenda name and address.

STERLING ARMS CORPORATION — Gasport, NY

MODEL 283 TARGET 300
AUTO PISTOL . . . . NiB $189 Ex $109 Gd $90
Caliber: .22 LR. 10-rnd. magazine, bbl. lengths: 4.5-, 6- 8-in. 9 in. overall w/4.5-in. bbl., Weight: 36 oz. w/4.52-in. bbl. Adj. sights. Blued finish. Plastic grips. Made 1970-71.

MODEL 284 TARGET 300L . . . . . NiB $179 Ex $115 Gd $90
Same as Model 283 except has 4.5- or 6-in. Luger-type bbl. Made 1970-71.

MODEL 285 HUSKY . . . . NiB $179 Ex $115 Gd $90
Same as Model 283 except has fixed sights, 4.5-in. bbl only. Made 1970-71.

MODEL 286 TRAPPER . . . . NiB $129 Ex $115 Gd $90
Same as Model 284 except w/fixed sights. Made 1970-71.

MODEL 287 PPL-.380
AUTOMATIC PISTOL . . . . NiB $179 Ex $115 Gd $90
Caliber: .380 Auto. Six-round magazine, 1-in. bbl., 5.38 in. overall. Weight: 22.5 oz. Fixed sights. Blued finish. Plastic grips. Made 1971-72.

MODEL 300
AUTOMATIC PISTOL . . . . NiB $150 Ex $90 Gd $75
Caliber: .25 Auto. Six-round magazine, 2.33-in. bbl., 4.5 in. overall. Weight: 13 oz. Fixed sights. Blued or nickel finish. Plastic grips. Made 1972-83.

MODEL 300S . . . . NiB $179 Ex $115 Gd $90
Same as Model 300 except in stainless steel. Made 1976-83.

MODEL 302 . . . . NiB $179 Ex $115 Gd $90
Same as Model 300 except in .22 LR. Made 1973-83.

MODEL 302S . . . . NiB $179 Ex $115 Gd $90
Same as Model 302 except in stainless steel. Made 1976-83.

MODEL 400 DA
AUTOMATIC PISTOL . . . . NiB $309 Ex $214 Gd $129
Caliber: .380 Auto. Seven-round magazine, 3.5-in. bbl., 6.5 in. overall. Weight: 24 oz. Adj. rear sight. Blued or nickel finish. Checkered walnut grips. Made 1975-83.

MODEL 400S . . . . NiB $309 Ex $214 Gd $129
Same as Model 400 except stainless steel. Made1977-83.

**Sterling
Model 285 Husky**

**Sterling
Model 286 Trapper**

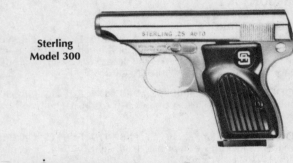

**Sterling
Model 300**

**Sterling Model
400**

MODEL 450 DA AUTO PISTOL . . NiB $309 Ex $214 Gd $129
Caliber: .45 Auto. Eight-round magazine, 4-in. bbl., 7.5 in. overall. Weight: 36 oz. Adj. rear sight. Blued finish. Smooth walnut grips. Made 1977-83.

**MODEL PPL-22
AUTOMATIC PISTOL . . . . NiB $309 Ex $214 Gd $129**
Caliber: .22 LR. 10-rnd. magazine, 1-in. bbl., 5.5 in. overall. Weight: About 24 oz. Fixed sights. Blued finish. Wood grips. Only 382 made in 1970-71.

J. STEVENS ARMS & TOOL CO. —
Chicopee Falls, MA

This firm was established in Civil War era by Joshua Stevens, for whom the company was named. In 1999 Savage Arms began manufacture of Stevens designs.

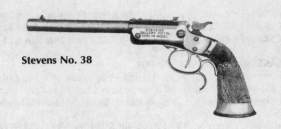

Stevens No. 38

**NO. 10 SINGLE-SHOT
TARGET PISTOL . . . . NiB $249 Ex $207 Gd $160**
Caliber: .22 LR. 8-in. bbl., 11.5 in. overall. Weight: 37 oz. Target sights. Blued finish. Hard rubber grips. In External appearance this arm resembles an automatic pistol but it has a tip-up action. Made 1919-39.

**NO. 35 OFFHAND MODEL SINGLE-SHOT
TARGET PISTOL . . . . NiB $377 Ex $301 Gd $255**
Tip-up action. Caliber: .22 LR. Bbl. lengths: 6, 8, 10, 12.25 in. Weight: 24 oz. w/6-in. bbl. Target sights. Blued finish. Walnut grips. Note: This pistol is similar to the earlier "Gould" model. Made 1907-39.

**NO. 35 OFFHAND SINGLE-SHOT
PISTOL/SHOTGUN. . . . . NiB $377 Ex $301 Gd $255**
Same general specifications as the standard No. 35 pistol except chambered for the .410 shotshell. Six-, 8-, 10-, or 12-in. half-ocatagonal bbl., iron frame either blued, nickel plated, or casehardened. BATF Class 3 license required to purchase. Made 1923-42.

NO. 36 SINGLE-SHOT PISTOL . . NiB $842 Ex $577 Gd $439
Tip-up action. Calibers: .22 Short and LR, .22 WRF, .25 Stevens, .32 Short Colt, .38 Long Colt, .44 Russian. 10- or 12-in. half-octagonal bbl., iron or brass frame w/nickel plated finish. Blued bbl. Checkered walnut grips. Made 1880-1911.

NO. 37 SINGLE-SHOT PISTOL . . . NiB $1020 Ex $836 Gd $544
Similar specifications to the No. 38 except the finger spur on the trigger guard has been omitted. Made 1889-1919.

NO. 38 SINGLE-SHOT PISTOL NiB $536 Ex $437 Gd $247
Tip-up action. Calibers: .22 Short and LR, .22 WRF, .25 Stevens, .32 Stevens, .32 Short Colt. Iron or brass frame. Checkered grips. Made 1884-1903.

**NO. 41 TIP-UP
SINGLE-SHOT PISTOL . . . . NiB $342 Ex $281 Gd $204**
Tip-up action. Caliber: .22 Short, 3.5-in. half-octagonal bbl. Blued metal parts w/optional nickel frame. Made 1896 to1915.

Stevens No. 10

Stevens No. 35

STEYR DAIMLER PUCH A.G. — Steyr, Austria

STEYR-HAHN (M12) AUTOMATIC PISTOL
Caliber: 9mm Steyr. Eight-round fixed magazine, charger loaded; 5.1-in. bbl., 8.5 in. overall. Weight: 35 oz. Fixed sights. Blued finish. Checkered wood grips. Made 1911-19. Adopted by the Austro-Hungarian Army in 1912. Note: Confiscated by the Germans in 1938, an estimated 250,000 of these pistols were converted to 9mm Para. and stamped w/an identifying "08" on the left side of the slide. Mfd. by Osterreichische Waffenfabrik-Gesellschaft.
Commercial model (9mm Steyr) . . **NiB $544 Ex $468 Gd $377**
**Military model (9mm Steyr-Austro
  -Hungarian Army)** . . . . **NiB $568 Ex $479 Gd $229**
**Military model (9mm Parabellum
  Conversion marked "08")** . . **NiB $1033 Ex $879 Gd $498**

STEYR ARMS — Steyr, Austria

GB SEMIAUTO PISTOL
Caliber: 9mm Para. 18-rnd. magazine, 5.4-in. bbl., 8.9 in. overall. Weight: 2.9 lbs. Post front sight, fixed, notched rear. Double, gas-delayed, blow-back action. Made 1981-88.
Commercial model . . . . **NiB $680 Ex $530 Gd $337**
**Military model
  (Less than 1000 imported)** . . **NiB $800 Ex $652 Gd $377**

C-A1 SERIES . . . . **NiB $560 Ex $500 Gd $400**
Similar to M-A1 series pistol but with smaller frame and 12 or 17-rnd. magazine.

L-A1 SERIES . . . . **NiB $560 Ex $500 Gd $400**
Similar to M-A1 series pistol but with full size frame, 4.5-in. bbl., 12 or 17-rnd. magazine.

M SERIES . . . . **NiB $610 Ex $510 Gd $410**
Semiauto. DAO. Caliber: 9mm, .40 S&W or .357 SIG; 10-rnd. magazine. Sights: trapezoidal. Weight: 28 oz. Polymer frame. Finish: matte black. One of the first pistols to use an integrate safety lock. Made 1999-2002.

M-A1 SERIES . . . . **NiB $560 Ex $500 Gd $400**
Updated Model M series. Semiauto. Striker firer. Caliber: 9mm, .40 S&W or .357 SIG; 10-, 12-, or 15-rnd. magazine depending on caliber. 3.5- or 4-in. bbl. Sights: trapezoidal. Weight: 27 oz. Polymer frame. Finish: matte black. One of the first pistols to use an integrate safety lock. Made 2004-99, reintro. 2010.

S-A1 SERIES . . . . **NiB $560 Ex $500 Gd $400**
Similar to M-A1 series pistol but with smaller frame and 10-rnd. magazine.

MODEL SPP . . . . **NiB $895 Ex $810 Gd $610**
Semiauto. SA. Caliber: 9mm; 15- or 30-rnd. magazine. 5.9-in. bbl. Weight: 44 oz. Polymer construction. Made 1992-93.

STACCATO 2011 (STI INTERNATIONAL) — Georgetown, TX

Note: *STI changed names to Staccato 2011 in 2019 and ceased mfg. single-stack 1911 style pistols. Previous STI uses a numerical code with model names to designate bbl. length, i.e. Lawman 5.0 features a 5-in. bbl. STI produces two platform types: 1911 single stack metal frame and 2011 double stack wide body polymer/steel frame. Magazine capacity as follows: 1911 style pistols have a 6- or 7-rnd. (.45 ACP); 7- or 8-rnd. (.40 S&W/10mm Auto); 8-, 9- or 10-rnd. (9mm) magazine. 2011 platform pistols have a 10-, 12-, or 14-rnd. (.45 ACP); 12-, 14-, 17-, or 22-rnd. (.40 S&W/10mm Auto); and 15-, 17-, 20-, or 26-rnd. (9mm/.38 Super) magazine.*

—2011 SERIES—

MODEL APERIO . . . . **NiB $2199 Ex $1630 Gd $1030**
Semiauto. SA. 2011 style platform. Caliber: 9mm, .40 S&W, or .45 ACP. 5-in. island bbl. Weight: 38 oz. Polymer/steel wide body frame. Sights: fiber optic front, adj. Bomar rear. Finish: blue. Made 2010 to date.

MODEL DVC 3-GUN . . . . . **NiB $2999 Ex $2150 Gd $1550**
Semiauto. SA. 2011 style platform. Caliber: 9mm. 5.4-in. bushing bbl. Polymer/steel wide body frame. Sights: adj. rear, fiber optic front. Finish: black. Made 2015 to date.

MODEL DVC CLASSIC . . . **NiB $2799 Ex $2150 Gd $1550**
Semiauto. SA. Colt 1911 style platform. Caliber: 9mm, .40 S&W or .45 ACP. 5.4-in. bushing bbl. Steel frame. Sights: adj. rear, fiber optic front. Grips: VZ Operator II. Finish: hard chrome. Made 2015 to date.

MODEL DVC LIMITED . . . **NiB $2999 Ex $2150 Gd $1550**
Semiauto. SA. 2011 style platform. Caliber: 9mm or .40 S&W. 5-in. bull bbl. Weight: 41 oz. Polymer/steel wide body frame. Sights: adj. Bomar rear, ramped front. Finish: hard chrome. Slide and dust cover cuts. Made 2015 to date.

MODEL DVC OPEN . . . . . **NiB $3999 Ex $32150 Gd $2550**
Semiauto. SA. 2011 style platform. Caliber: 9mm or .38 Super. 5-in. trubor bbl. Weight: 48 oz. Polymer/steel wide body frame. Sights: C-More red dot. Finish: hard chrome. Made 2015 to date.

—1911 SERIES—

MODEL DUTY ONE . . . . . . **NiB $1380 Ex $1030 Gd $655**
Semiauto. SA. 1911 style platform. Caliber: 9mm, .40 S&W, or .45 ACP. 3-, 4-, 5-in. bushing bbl. Steel frame. Sights: tritium. Finish: matte blue. Grip: textured G10. Made 2013-19.

MODEL DUTY CT . . . . **NiB $1288 Ex $955 Gd $610**
Semiauto. SA. 1911 style platform. Caliber: 9mm, .40 S&W, or .45 ACP. 5-in. bull bbl. Steel frame w/ rail. Sights: fixed. Finish: matte blue. Made 2006-08.

MODEL EAGLE . . . . **NiB $1899 Ex $1590 Gd $1000**
Semiauto. SA. 2011 style platform. Caliber: 9mm or .40 S&W. 5- or 6-in. bushing bbl. Polymer/steel wide body frame. Sights: ramped front, ledge rear. Finish: matte blue. Made 1998-2019.

MODEL EDGE . . . . **NiB $2199 Ex $1630 Gd $1030**
Semiauto. SA. 2011 style platform. Caliber: 9mm, .38 Super, .40 S&W, or .45 ACP. 5-in. bull bbl. Polymer/steel wide body frame. Sights: fiber optic front, adj. Bomar rear. Finish: blue. Made 1998-2019.

MODEL ELECTRA . . . . **NiB $1399 Ex $1090 Gd $700**
Semiauto. SA. 1911 style platform. Caliber: 9mm or .45 ACP. 3-in. bull bbl. Aluminum frame. Sights: tritium front/rear. Grips: textured G10. Finish: two-tone. Made 2010-19.

MODEL ESCORT . . . . **NiB $1299 Ex $930 Gd $580**
Semiauto. SA. 1911 style platform. Caliber: 9mm or .45 ACP. 3.24-in. bull bbl. Aluminum frame. Sights: fixed white dot. Grips: ultra thin cocobolo. Finish: two-tone. Made 2009-19.

MODEL EXECUTIVE . . . . . **NiB $2699 Ex $1980 Gd $1245**
Semiauto. SA. 2011 style platform. Caliber: 9mm, .40 S&W, or .45 ACP. 5-in. bull bbl. Polymer/steel wide body frame. Sights: fiber optic front, adj. Bomar rear. Finish: hard chrome. Made 2001-19.

MODEL G.I. . . . . **NiB $874 Ex $660 Gd $420**
Semiauto. SA. 1911 style platform. Caliber: .45 ACP. 5-in. bushing bbl. Steel frame. Sights: G.I. style fixed. Grips: smooth wood. Finish: matte blue. Made 2010-15.

MODEL GP6 . . . . **NiB $660 Ex $555 Gd $405**
Semiauto. DA/SA. Mfg. by Grand Power. Caliber: 9mm. 4.25-in. bbl. Steel frame. Sights: adj. Weight: 26.1 oz. Finish: blued. Made 2009-12.

MODEL GM. . . . . **NiB $3680 Ex $3740 Gd $1730**
Semiauto. SA. 2011 style platform. Caliber: 9mm or .38 Super. 5.5-in. Trubor bbl. w/ compensator. Weight: 44.6 oz. Polymer/steel wide body frame. Sights: C-More red dot. Finish: blue/hard chrome. Made 2012-19.

MODEL GUARDIAN . . . . **NiB $1299 Ex $880 Gd $550**
Semiauto. SA. 1911 style platform. Caliber: 9mm or .45 ACP. 3.9-in. bull bbl. Steel frame. Sights: fixed white dot. Grips: ultra thin cocobolo. Finish: two-tone. Discontinued 2019.

MODEL GUARDIAN 2011 . **NiB $1899 Ex $1480 Gd $890**
Semiauto. SA. 2011 style platform. Caliber: 9mm. 3.9-in. bull bbl. Polymer/steel wide body frame. Sights: fixed white dot. Finish: two-tone. Made 2016-19.

MODEL HAWK . . . . **NiB $1899 Ex $1480 Gd $890**
Semiauto. SA. 1911 style platform. Caliber: various. 4.3-in. bbl. Aluminum or steel frame. Made 1993-99.

MODEL HEX TACTICAL SS
Semiauto. SA. Caliber: 9mm or .45 ACP. 4- or 5-in. bushing bbl. Steel frame. Sights: ledge rear, fiber optic front. Grips: VZ Alien (1911) or black (2011). Finish: black cerakote. Made 2016-19.
1911 platform . . . . **NiB $2099 Ex $1950 Gd $1350**
2011 platform . . . . **NiB $2599 Ex $1950 Gd $1350**

MODEL LAWMAN . . . . **NiB $1299 Ex $930 Gd $580**
Semiauto. SA. 1911 style platform. Caliber: 9mm or .45 ACP. 3-, 4.15-, or 5-in. bull (3-in.) or bushing bbl. Steel frame. Sights: ramped front, TAS rear. Grips: textured G10. Finish: black cerakote. Made 2005-19.

MODEL LEGEND . . . . **NiB $1299 Ex $930 Gd $580**
Semiauto. SA. 1911 style platform. Caliber: 9mm, .38 Super, .40 S&W, or .45 ACP. 5-in. bull bbl. Steel frame. Sights: competition. Finish: blued or hard chrome. Made 2007-15.

MODEL MARAUDER . . . . . . **NiB $2399 Ex $1580 Gd $990**
Semiauto. SA. 2011 style platform. Caliber: 9mm. 5-in. bushing bbl. Polymer/steel wide body frame. Sights: fiber optic front, TAS rear. Finish: black cerakote. Made 2014-19.

MODEL MATCH MASTER . **NiB $2999 Ex $2370 Gd $1500**
Semiauto. SA. 2011 style platform. Caliber: 9mm or .38 Super. 4.26-in. trubor bbl. Polymer/steel wide body frame. Sights: C-More red dot. Finish: blue. Made 2009 to date.

MODEL NEMESIS . . . . **NiB $870 Ex $730 Gd $455**
Semiauto. SA. 1911 style platform. Caliber: 7x23mm. 2.5-in. bbl. Steel frame. Made 2010-11.

MODEL NIGHT HAWK . . . . **NiB $2136 Ex $1400 Gd $860**
Semiauto. SA. 2011 style platform. Caliber: .45 ACP. 4.3-in. bbl. Polymer/steel wide body frame. Finish: blued. Made 1997-99.

MODEL NITRO 10. . . . . **NiB $1599 Ex $1130 Gd $710**
Semiauto. SA. 1911 style platform. Caliber: 10mm Auto. 5-in. bull or bushing bbl. Steel frame. Sights: ramped front, ledge rear. Grips: textured G10. Finish: blued. Disc. 2019.

MODEL OFF DUTY . . . . **NiB $1599 Ex $1130 Gd $710**
Semiauto. SA. 1911 style platform. Caliber: 9mm or .45 ACP. 3-in. bbl. Steel frame. Sights: ramped front, ledge rear. Grips: cocobolo. Finish: blued or hard chrome. Made 2009-13.

MODEL PERFECT 10 . . . . . **NiB $2699 Ex $1955 Gd $1230**
Semiauto. SA. 2011 style platform. Caliber: 10mm Auto. 6-in. bull bbl. Polymer/steel wide body frame. Sights: competition front, adj. Bomar rear. Finish: blue. Made 2009-19.

MODEL RANGE MASTER . . **NiB $1599 Ex $1210 Gd $755**
Semiauto. SA. 1911 style platform. Caliber: 9mm or .45 ACP. 5-in. bull bbl. Steel frame. Sights: competition front, LPA rear. Grips: textured cocobolo. Finish: matte blue. Made 2005-19.

MODEL RANGER II . . . . **NiB $1181 Ex $880 Gd $555**
Semiauto. SA. 1911 style platform. Caliber: 9mm, .40 S&W, or .45 ACP. 3.9- or 4.15-in. bull bbl. Steel frame. Sights: fixed. Weight: 29- oz. Grips: checkered double diamond mahogany. Finish: blued or hard chrome. Made 2001-15.

MODEL ROGUE . . . . **NiB $1025 Ex $830 Gd $580**
Semiauto. SA. 1911 style platform. Caliber: 9mm. 3-in. bull bbl. Aluminum frame. Sights: integral sights. Weight: 21 oz. Finish: two-tone. Made 2009-15.

MODEL SENTINEL . . . . **NiB $2099 Ex $1780 Gd $1130**
Semiauto. SA. 1911 style platform. Caliber: 9mm or .45 ACP. 5-in. bushing bbl. Steel frame. Sights: ramped tritium front, TAS tritium rear. Grips: textured G10. Finish: hard chrome. Made 2007-08.

MODEL SENTINEL PREMIER . . . . . **NiB $2099 Ex $1780 Gd $1130**
Semiauto. SA. 1911 style platform. Caliber: 9mm or .45 ACP. 5-in. bushing bbl. Steel frame. Sights: tritium. Finish: hard chrome. Made 2009-19.

MODEL SENTRY . . . . **NiB $1755 Ex $1310 Gd $830**
Semiauto. SA. 1911 style platform. Caliber: 9mm, .40 S&W or .45 ACP. 5-in. bushing bbl. Steel frame. Sights: adj. Weight: 35.3 oz. Grips: checkered cocobolo. Finish: blued or hard chrome. Made 2009-15.

MODEL SHADOW . . . . **NiB $1475 Ex $1100 Gd $700**
Semiauto. SA. 1911 style platform. Caliber: 9mm, .40 S&W or .45 ACP. 3-in. bull bbl. Aluminum frame. Sights: tritium. Weight: 23.4 oz. Grips: ultra thin G10. Finish: matte black. Made 2010-15.

MODEL SPARTAN . . . . **NiB $745 Ex $580 Gd $635**
Semiauto. SA. 1911 style platform. Caliber: 9mm or .45 ACP. 3-, 4-, or 5-in. bull bbl. Commander size steel frame. Sights: fixed. Weight: 32.7 oz. Grips: checkered double diamond mahogany. Finish: parkerized. Made 2012-19.

MODEL STEEL MASTER . . . **NiB $2999 Ex $2370 Gd $1500**
Semiauto. SA. 2011 style platform. Caliber: 9mm. 4.26-in. trubor bbl. Polymer/steel wide body frame. Sights: C-More red dot. Finish: blue. Made 2009 to date.

MODEL TACTICAL . . . . **NiB $2099 Ex $1580 Gd $990**
Semiauto. SA. 2011 style platform. Caliber: 9mm, .40 S&W, or .45 ACP. 4-, 4.15-, or 5-in. bull bbl. Polymer/steel wide body frame. Sights: ramped front, ledge rear. Finish: black cerakote. Made 2014-19.

MODEL TACTICAL SS . . . . . **NiB $1899 Ex $1460 Gd $950**
Semiauto. SA. 1911 style platform. Caliber: 9mm or .45 ACP. 3.75-, 4.15-, or 5-in. thrd. bull bbl. Steel frame. Sights: ramped front, ledge rear. Grips: textured G10. Finish: black cerakote. Made 2013-19.

MODEL TARGET MASTER . . **NiB $1799 Ex $1360 Gd $860**
Semiauto. SA. 1911 style platform. Caliber: 9mm or .45 ACP. 6-in. bull bbl. Steel frame. Sights: aristocrat front, tri-setrear. Grips: textured cocobolo. Finish: blue. Disc. 2019.

MODEL TEXICAN . . . . **NiB $1344 Ex $1010 Gd $610**
Revolver. SA. Colt SAA style platform. Caliber: .45 LC, 6-shot cylinder. 5.5-in. bbl. Steel frame. Sights: fixed. Grips: textured hard rubber. Weight: 36 oz. Finish: case hardened frame; blue bbl., cylinder, backstrap and trigger guard. Made 2007-10.

MODEL TROJAN . . . . NiB $1299 Ex $910 Gd $580
Semiauto. SA. 1911 style platform. Caliber: 9mm, .38 Super, .40 S&W, or .45 ACP. 5-in. bushing bbl. Steel frame. Sights: fixed rear, fiber optic front. Grips: cocobolo. Finish: blued. Made 1999-2019.
Model Trojan Lite (aluminum frame), add. $100

MODEL TRUBOR. . . . . NiB $2899 Ex $2370 Gd $1500
Semiauto. SA. 2011 style platform. Caliber: 9mm or .38 Super. 5-in. trubor bbl. Polymer/steel wide body frame. Sights: C-More red dot. Finish: blue. Made 1999-2019.

MODEL TRUSIGHT . . . . NiB $1985 Ex $1530 Gd $910
Semiauto. SA. 2011 style platform. Caliber: 9mm, .40 S&W, or .45 ACP. 5-in. bull bbl. w/ expansion chamber. Polymer/steel wide body frame. Sights: adj. competition. Finish: blued, polished slide. Made 2006-09.

MODEL USPSA
DOUBLE STACK. . . . . NIB $2425 EX $2010 GD $1210
Semiauto. SA. 2011 style platform. Caliber: 9mm, .40 S&W or .45 ACP. 5-in. bushing bbl. Polymer/steel wide body frame. Sights: adj. competition. Weight: 38.3 oz. Finish: blued. Made 2009-12.

MODEL USPSA
SINGLE STACK. . . . . NiB $1976 Ex $1500 Gd $930
Semiauto. SA. 1911 style platform. Caliber: 9mm, .38 Super, .40 S&W or .45 ACP. 5-in. bushing bbl. Steel frame. Sights: adj. competition. Weight: 38.3 oz. Finish: blued. Made 2009-15.

STOEGER — Accokeek, MD
Current brand owned by Beretta.

COUGAR . . . . NiB $390 Ex $280 Gd $220
Copy of Beretta 8000 series. Semiauto. DA/SA. Calibers: 9mm, .40 S&W and .45 Auto. 8-, 11- or 10-rnd. magazine, 3.6 to 3.7-in. bbl., 7- to 7.2 in. overall. Weight: 32 to 32.6 oz. Short recoil action w/rotating barrel. Fixed sights. Textured black grips. Matte black Bruniton or two-tone. Made 2007–16.
.45 Auto, add $30
Cougar Compact (9mm, 3.6-in. bbl.,
 13-rnd. mag., 2011–16) . . . . . . NiB $390 Ex $280 Gd $220

PRO SERIES 95 SERIES
Copy of High Standard target pistol series. Semiauto. SA. Calibers: .22 LR, 10-rnd. magazine, 5.5 or 7.2-in VR, bull or fluted bbl. Weight: 45 to 47 oz. Adj. target sights. Pachmayr rubber grip. Finish: stainless. Made 1995–96.
Bull bbl . . . . NiB $445 Ex $340 Gd $280
Fluted bbl . . . . NiB $460 Ex $345 Gd $280
VR bbl. . . . . NiB $520 Ex $370 Gd $290

STR-9 . . . . NiB $400 Ex $350 Gd $200
Semiauto. Striker-fire. Calibers: 9mm, 15-rnd. magazine, 4.1-in. bbl., 7.4 in. overall. Weight: 24 oz. Fixed sights. Polymer frame w/textured black grips. Matte black. Made 2019–date.
STR-9 Compact (3.8-in. bbl., 10-rnd. mag.,
 2020–date) . . . . NiB $330 Ex $300 Gd $200

STOEGER LUGERS — South Hackensack, NJ
Formerly manufactured by Stoeger Industries, So. Hackensack, New Jersey; later by Classic Arms, Union City, New Jersey.

AMERICAN EAGLE LUGER
Caliber: 9mm Para. 7-rnd. magazine, 4- or 6-in. bbl., 8.25 in. overall (w/ 4-in. bbl.). or 10.25 in. (w/ 6-in. bbl.). Weight: 30 or 32 oz. Checkered walnut grips. Stainless steel w/brushed or matte black finish. Intro. 1994. Disc.

Model P-08 stainless (4-in.
 bbl.) . . . . NiB $955 Ex $730 Gd $455
Navy model (6-in. bbl.). . . . . . . NiB $1035 Ex $810 Gd $535
w/matte black finish, add $85

STANDARD LUGER . . . . NiB $299 Ex $270 Gd $195
Caliber: .22 LR. 10-rnd. magazine, 4.5- or 5.5-in. bbl., 8.88 in. overall (w/ 4.5-in. bbl.). Weight: 29.5 oz. (w/ 4.5-in. bbl.). Fixed sights. Black finish. Smooth wood grips. Made 1969-86.

STEEL FRAME LUGER . . . . NiB $299 Ex $270 Gd $195
Caliber: .22 LR. 10-rnd. magazine, 4.5-in. bbl., 8.88 in. overall. Blued finish. Checkered wood grips. Features one piece forged and machined steel frame. Made 1980-86.

TARGET LUGER
.22 AUTO PISTOL . . . . NiB $310 Ex $280 Gd $200
Same as Standard Luger .22 except has target sights 9.38 in. overall w/4.5-in. bbl., Checkered wood grips. Made 1975-86.

SWISS SERVICE PISTOLS

Note: *Produced by SIG, Neuhausen, Switzerland; also see SIG and SIG Sauer.*

M49 . . . . NiB $3500 Ex $3000 Gd $2010
Semiauto. SA. 9mm Parabellum; 8-rnd magazine. 4.75-in. bbl. Frame-mounted manual safety. Finish: blued. Adopted 1949, in service thru 1975. Note: The Model P 210 was adopted by the Swiss Military as the Model M49. Early models had serrated wood grips, later models had checkered black plastic grips.

TARGA PISTOLS — Italy
Manufactured by Armi Tanfoglio Guiseppe.

MODEL GT26S AUTO PISTOL . . . NiB $166 Ex $98 Gd $79
Caliber: .25 ACP. Six-round magazine, 2.5-in. bbl., 4.63 in. overall. Weight: 15 oz. fixed sights. Checkered composition grips. Blued or chrome finish. Disc. 1990.

**Stoeger
American Eagle Luger P08 Stainless**

**Stoeger
Standard Luger .22**

MODEL GT32 AUTO PISTOL
Caliber: .32 ACP. Six-round magazine, 4.88-in. bbl., 7.38 in. overall. Weight: 26 oz. fixed sights. Checkered composition or walnut grips. Blued or chrome finish.
Blued finished . . . . NiB $166 Ex $109 Gd $88
Chrome finish . . . . NiB $179 Ex $118 Gd $89

MODEL GT380 AUTOMATIC PISTOL
Same as the Targa GT32 except chambered for .380 ACP.
Blued finish . . . . NiB $179 Ex $118 Gd $89
Chrome finish . . . . NiB $197 Ex $137 Gd $101

MODEL GT380XE
AUTOMATIC PISTOL . . . . NiB $220 Ex $165 Gd $101
Caliber: .380 ACP. 11-rnd. magazine, 3.75-in. bbl., 7.38 in. overall. Weight: 28 oz. Fixed sights. Blued or satin nickel finish. Smooth wooden grips. Made 1980-90.

TAURUS INT'L. MFG. — Porto Alegre, Brazil
Manufactured by FORJAS TAURUS S.A. Porto Alegre, Brazil; imported Miami, FL.

NOTE: *For ease in locating a particular Taurus handgun, the listings are divided into two groupings: Automatic Pistols (page 195) and Revolvers (below). For a complete handgun listing, please refer to the index.*

- REVOLVERS -

MODEL GAUCHO. . . . . NiB $425 Ex $285 Gd $245
SA. Colt SAA reproduction. Caliber: .357 Mag., .44-40, or .45 LC. Six-round cylinder, 4.75-, 5.5-, 7.5- or 12-in. bbl. Blued, case color, matte or bright stainless finish. Made 2005-07.

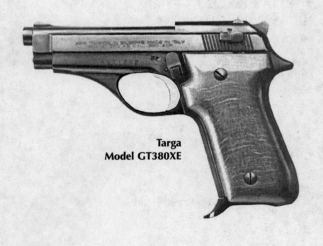

**Targa
Model GT380XE**

Taurus MODEL 45-410 "THE JUDGE"

MODEL 17C . . . . NiB $300 Ex $190 Gd $170
SA/DA. Caliber: .17 HMR or .17 Mach 2. 8-rnd. cylinder, 2-, 4-, 5-in. bbl. Adj. sights, rubber grips. Blued finish. Made 2003-07.
Ultra-Lite (2-in. bbl.) . . . . NiB $340 Ex $200 Gd $180
Polished stainless finish . . . . . . NiB $330 Ex $195 Gd $175

MODEL 17IB . . . . NiB $295 Ex $185 Gd $170
SA/DA. Caliber: .17 HMR or .17 Mach 2. 8- or 9-rnd. cylinder, 1.75-in. bbl. Adj. sights, rubber grips. Blued finish. Made 2005-07.
Matte stainless finish . . . . NiB $330 Ex $195 Gd $175

MODEL 17 TRACKER . . . . NiB $481 Ex $265 Gd $225
SA/DA. Caliber: .17 HMR. 7-rnd. cylinder, 4-, 6.5-, 8.6-in. VR bbl. Adj. sights, rubber grips. Made 2003 to date.
Matte stainless, add $50
Two-tone finish, add $50
Silhoutte model (12-in. bbl., optic mount,
    discont. 2004) . . . . NiB $320 Ex $205 Gd $185

MODEL 21T TRACKER . . . . NiB $330 Ex $205 Gd $185
SA/DA. Caliber: .218 Bee. 7-rnd. cylinder, 6.5-in. VR bbl. Adj. sights, rubber grips. Made 2003-05.

MODEL 22H
RAGING HORNET . . . . NiB $800 Ex $530 Gd $455
SA/DA. Caliber: .22 Hornet. 8-rnd. cylinder, 10-in. VR bbl. Adj. sights, optic mount, rubber grips. Made 1999-2004.

MODEL 30C RAGING THIRTY
HUNTER . . . . NiB $800 Ex $530 Gd $455
SA/DA. Caliber: .30 Carbine. 8-rnd. cylinder, 12-in. VR full lug bbl. Adj. sights, optic mount, adj. trigger, rubber grips. Made 2003-04.
Silhoutte model (12-in. half lug bbl., optic mount,
    discont. 2004) . . . . NiB $795 Ex $525 Gd $450

MODEL 44 . . . . NIB $433 EX $327 GD $220
Caliber: .44 Mag. 6-rnd. cylinder, 4-, 6.5-, or 8.38-in. bbl. Weight: 44.75 oz., 52.5 or 57.25 oz. Brazilian hardwood grips. Blued or stainless steel finish. Mfg. 1994 to 2004.
Model 44SS (stainless) . . . . NiB $655 Ex $490 Gd $370

MODEL 44C TRACKER . . . . NiB $646 Ex $430 Gd $380
SA/DA. Caliber: .44 Mag. 5-rnd. cylinder, 4-in. ported bbl. Blued or matte stainless finish. Made 2005 to date.

MODEL 45-410 "THE JUDGE" . . . . NiB $610 Ex $355 Gd $300
SA/DA. Caliber: .45 LC/.410 3-in. chamber. 5-rnd. cylinder, 2.5-, 3-, 6.5-in. bbl. Blued or matte stainless finish. Made 2006 to date.
Ultra-Lite . . . . NiB $580 Ex $400 Gd $355

MODEL 45-410 "THE JUDGE"
PUBLIC DEFENDER . . . . NiB $610 Ex $355 Gd $300
SA/DA. Caliber: .45 LC/.410 2.5-in. chamber. 5-rnd. stainless or titanium cylinder, 2-in. bbl. smaller hammer. Blued or matte stainless finish. Made 2009 to date.
Ultra-Lite . . . . NiB $580 Ex $400 Gd $355
Polymer frame . . . . NiB $550 Ex $400 Gd $355

MODEL 65 DA REVOLVER
Caliber: .357 Magnum. 6-rnd. cylinder, 3- or 4-in. bbl., weight: 32 oz. Front ramp sight, square notch rear. Checkered walnut target grip. Royal blued or satin nickel finish. Imported 1992 to 1997 and from 1999 to date.
Blue finish . . . . NiB $398 Ex $289 Gd $171
Stainless finish . . . . NiB $427 Ex $351 Gd $212

MODEL 66 DA REVOLVER
Calibers: .357 Magnum, .38 Special. Six-round cylinder, 3-, 4- and 6-in. bbl., weight: 35 oz. Serrated ramp front sight, rear click adj. Checkered walnut grips. Royal blued or nickel finish. Imported 1992-97 and from 1999 to date.

Taurus Model 44

**Taurus
Model 76 Target**

Taurus Model 80

Taurus Model 82

Blue finish................NiB $500 Ex $351 Gd $212
Model 66SS Stainless finish....NiB $550 Ex $398 Gd $229

MODEL 73 DA REVOLVER ....NiB $211 Ex $121 Gd $101
Caliber: .32 Long. Six-round cylinder, 3-in. heavy bbl., weight: 20 oz. Checkered grips. Blued or satin nickel finish. Disc. 1993.

MODEL 76 TARGET ....NiB $244 Ex $279 Gd $118
Caliber: .32 S&W Long. Six-round cylinder, 3-in. bbl., 8.25 in. overall. Weight: 20 oz. Adj. rear sight, ramp front. Blued or nickel finish. Checkered walnut grips. Made 1971-90.

MODEL 80 DA REVOLVER
Caliber: .38 Special. Six-round cylinder, bbl. lengths: 3, 4 in., 9.25 in. overall (w/ 4-in. bbl). Weight: 30 oz. (w/ 4-in. bbl.) Fixed sights. Blued or nickel finish. Checkered walnut grips. Made 1996-97.
Blued finish................NiB $214 Ex $140 Gd $98
Model 80SS Stainless finish....NiB $431 Ex $337 Gd $258

MODEL 82 HEAVY BARREL
Same as Model 80 except has heavy bbl., weight: 33 oz. w/4-in. bbl., Made 1971 to date.
Blued finish................NiB $366 Ex $290 Gd $212
Model 82SS Stainless finish
(intro. 1993) ....NiB $437 Ex $327 Gd $259

MODEL 83 HEAVY BBL. TARGET GRADE
Same as Model 84 except has heavy bbl., weight: 34.5 oz. Made 1977 to date.
Blued finish................NiB $255 Ex $160 Gd $105
Model 83SS Stainless finish....NiB $281 Ex $198 Gd $128

**MODEL 84 TARGET
GRADE REVOLVER** ....NiB $312 Ex $235 Gd $170
Copy of S&W Model 15. Made 1971-89.

MODEL 85 DA REVOLVER
Caliber: .38 Special. Five-round cylinder, 2- or 3-in. bbl., weight: 21 oz. Fixed sights. Checkered walnut grips. Blued, satin nickel or stainless-steel finish. Model 85CH is the same as the standard version except for concealed hammer. Made 1997-2012.
Blued or satin nickel finish ....NiB $377 Ex $302 Gd $143
Stainless steel finish ....NiB $437 Ex $362 Gd $189
Titanium Ultra-Lightweight....NiB $540 Ex $370 Gd $320

**MODEL 85PLYB2
"PROTECTOR PLY"** ....NiB $355 Ex $230 Gd $210
SA/DA. Caliber: .38 Spl.+P. Five-round blued or matte stainless cylinder, 1.25- or 1.75-in. VR bbl., polymer frame. Weight: 16.5 oz. Fixed fiber optic sights. Made 2011-12.

MODEL VIEW (85VTA) ....NiB $390 Ex $320 Gd $255
Revolver. DAO. Caliber: .38 Spl., 5-shot cylinder. 1.41-in. bbl. Weight: 8 oz. Unique clear Lexan side plate, stainless frame, bobbed hammer, small checkered polymer grip. Sights: fixed. Finish: matte stainless, gold color hammer. Made 2014 only.

**MODEL 86 CUSTOM TARGET
DA REVOLVER** ....NiB $275 Ex $205 Gd $165
Caliber: .38 Special. Six-round cylinder, 6-in. bbl., 11.25 in. overall. Weight: 34 oz. Adj. rear sight, Partridge-type front. Blued finish. Checkered walnut grips. Made 1971-94.

MODEL 94 DA REVOLVER
Same as Model 74 except .22 LR. w/9-rnd. cylinder, 3- or 4-in. bbl., weight: 25 oz. Blued or stainless finish. Made 1971 to date.
Blued finish................NiB $362 Ex $306 Gd $219
Model 94SS Stainless finish....NiB $386 Ex $348 Gd $255

MODEL 96 TARGET SCOUT...NiB $301 Ex $209 Gd $112
Same as Model 86 except in .22 LR. Made 1971-98.

MODEL 380 IB ....NiB $433 Ex $310 Gd $205
Revolver. DAO. Caliber: .380 ACP, 5-shot cylinder. 1.75-in. bbl. Weight: 15.5 oz. Bobbed hammer. Sights: fixed. Finish: blued. Made 2012 to date.

MODEL 425 SERIES
DA/SA. Caliber: .41 Mag. 5-rnd. cylinder. Bbl.: 4-in. full lug Weight: 38 oz. Sights: ramp front/adj. rear. Stainless or titanium frame. Grip: ribbed rubber.
425SS (stainless frame,
2000–12) ....NiB $520 Ex $405 Gd $300

Taurus Model 84

Taurus Model 85 Concealed Hammer

Taurus Model 86

Taurus Model 85 w/Spur Hammer

425T (titanium frame, 24.3 oz., 2000–06) . . . . NiB $630 Ex $495 Gd $385

MODELS 431/441
DA/SA. Caliber: .44 Spl. 5-rnd. cylinder. Bbl.: 2-, 3- or 4-in. Sights: fixed. Stainless or blue. Mfg. 1993–97.
431 (blued) . . . . NiB $270 Ex $205 Gd $165
431SS (stainless) . . . . NiB $320 Ex $225 Gd $175
441SS (stainless, adj. sights) . . . . NiB $380 Ex $270 Gd $205

MODEL 444 RAGING BULL . . . . NiB $630 Ex $495 Gd $385
DA/SA. Caliber: .44 Mag. 6-rnd. cylinder. Bbl.: 6- or 8.3-in. VR, ported. Sights: adj. Blue. Mfg. 1999–date.
Stainless, add $70
Ultra-Lite (titanium frame), add $30

MODEL 445 . . . . NiB $300 EX $220 GD $175
DA/SA. Caliber: .44 Spl. 5-rnd. cylinder, 2-in. bbl., 6.75 in. overall. Weight: 28.25 oz. Serrated ramp front sight, notched frame rear. Standard or concealed hammer. Santoprene I grips. Blue or stainless finish. Imported from 1997 to 2003.
w/conceal hammer, blued . . . . NiB $300 Ex $220 Gd $175
Stainless . . . . NiB $315 Ex $225 Gd $175
w/conceal hammer, stainless. . NiB $315 Ex $225 Gd $175
Ultra-Lite (ported bbl.). . . . . NiB $400 Ex $305 Gd $225
Ultra-Lite Conceal Carry (titanium frame, ported bbl.). . . . . NiB $375 Ex $270 Gd $205
445T (titanium frame, ported bbl., 1999–2002) . . . . NiB $505 Ex $400 Gd $300

MODEL 450 . . . . NiB $430 Ex $320 Gd $245
DA/SA. Caliber: .45 LC. 5-rnd. cylinder. Bbl.: 6- or 8.3-in. VR, ported. Sights: adj. Stainless. Mfg. 1999–2002.
450T (titanium frame) . . . . NiB $505 Ex $400 Gd $300

MODEL 454 RAGING BULL . . NiB $862 EX $730 GD $587
Caliber: .454 Casull. 5-rnd. cylinder, ported 6.5- or 8.4-in. VR bbl., 12 in. overall (w/6.5-in. bbl.). Weight: 53 or 63 oz. Partridge front sight, micrometer adj. rear. Santoprene or walnut grips. Blue or stainless finish. Imported 1997 to date.
Stainless finish. . . . . NiB $940 Ex $700 Gd $495

MODEL 455 TRACKER . . . . NiB $455 Ex $350 Gd $265
DA/SA. Caliber: .45 Auto. 5-rnd. cylinder. Bbl.: 2-, 4- or 6-in. ported. Sights: adj. Stainless. Mfg. 2002–04.
Titanium frame. . . . . NiB $530 Ex $430 Gd $330

MODEL 460 TRACKER . . . . NiB $450 Ex $345 Gd $265
DA/SA. Caliber: .45 LC. 5-rnd. cylinder. Bbl.: 4- or 6.5-in. VR ported. Sights: adj. Stainless. Mfg. 2003–04.
Titanium frame. . . . . NiB $570 Ex $460 Gd $355

MODEL 465 RAGING BULL . . . NiB $755 Ex $580 Gd $445
DA/SA. Caliber: .460 S&W Mag. 5-rnd. cylinder. Bbl.: 2.5-, 4-, 6.5- or 10-in. ported. Sights: fixed or adj. Stainless. Mfg. 2006.

MODEL 480 RUGER
RAGING BULL . . . . NiB $530 Ex $430 Gd $330
DA/SA. Caliber: .480 Ruger. 5-rnd. cylinder. Bbl.: 5-, 6.5- or 8.3-in. VR. Sights: fixed or adj. Stainless. Mfg. 2001–05.

MODEL 492 . . . . NiB $370 EX $310 GD $280
Similar to Model 856 except chambered in .22 LR or .22 WMR; 8-rnd. cylinder. Bbl.: 2- or 3-in. Serrated ramp front sight, adj. rear. Matte blued or matte stainless finish. Black rubber grip. Made 2020–date.

MODEL 500 RAGING BULL . . . NiB $780 Ex $600 Gd $455
DA/SA. Caliber: .500 S&W Mag. 5-rnd. cylinder. Bbl.: 2.5-, 4-, 6.5- or 10-in. ported. Sights: fixed or adj. Stainless. Mfg. 2005–07.

MODEL 513 RAGING
JUDGE MAGNUM . . . . NiB $855 Ex $655 Gd $480
DA/SA. Caliber: .45 LC, .454 Casual and .410 bore. 6-rnd. non-fluted cylinder. Bbl.: 3- or 6.5-in. VR or ported. Sights: fixed or adj. Blued. Mfg. 2011-13.
Stainless. . . . . NiB $930 Ex $690 Gd $490
Ultra-Lite (2011–12) . . . . NiB $830 Ex $635 Gd $470
Ultra-Lite SS (stainless, 2011–12). . . . . NiB $890 Ex $680 Gd $490

MODEL 590 TRACKER . . . . NiB $365 Ex $265 Gd $205
DA/SA. Caliber: 5mm Rem. Rimfire Mag., 9-rnd. cylinder. Bbl.: 6.5-in. Sights: adj. Blued. Mfg. 2008–11.
Stainless. . . . . NiB $405 Ex $315 Gd $245

MODEL 605. . . . . NiB $305 Ex $235 Gd $185
DA/SA. Small frame. Caliber: .357 Mag., 5-shot cylinder. 2-, 2.2- or 3-in. bbl. Sights: fixed. Finish: blued. Made 2011–date.
605SS (stainless) . . . . NiB $315 Ex $245 Gd $195
605T (titanium frame, 2005-06) NiB $540 Ex $345 Gd $185
605 Protector (polymer frame, Protector Ply, 2011–date) . . . . NiB $305 Ex $235 Gd $185
605 Protector (stainless cylinder, polymer frame, Protector Ply, 2012-date) . . . . NiB $315 Ex $245 Gd $195

MODEL 606. . . . . NiB $290 Ex $220 Gd $175
DA/SA. Medium frame. Caliber: .357 Mag., 6-shot cylinder. 2- or 2.2-in. bbl. Sights: fixed. Finish: blued. Mfg. 1997–98.
606SS (stainless) . . . . NiB $315 Ex $225 Gd $175

MODEL 607. . . . . **NiB $340 Ex $240 Gd $185**
DA/SA. Medium frame. Caliber: .357 Mag., 7-shot cylinder. 4- or 6.5-in. VR bbl. Sights: adj. Blued. Mfg. 1995–97.
607SS (stainless) . . . . **NiB $380 Ex $270 Gd $205**

MODEL 608. . . . . **NiB $360 Ex $265 Gd $205**
DA/SA. Large frame. Caliber: .357 Mag., 8-shot cylinder. 3-, 4-, 6.5-, 8.3-in. VR bbl. Sights: adj. Blued. Mfg. 1996–2004.
608SS (stainless) . . . . **NiB $565 Ex $445 Gd $335**

MODEL 617 . . . . **NiB $420 Ex $315 Gd $245**
DA/SA. Medium frame. Caliber: .357 Mag., 7-shot cylinder. 2-in. bbl. Sights: fixed. Blued. Grip: rubber. Mfg. 1998–2012.
617SS (stainless) . . . . **NiB $480 Ex $355 Gd $265**
617ULT (aluminum frame,
2001–02) . . . .**NiB $460 Ex $350 Gd $265**
617T (titanium frame, 1999–06) NiB $555 Ex $455 Gd $355

MODEL 627 TRACKER. . . . . **NiB $555 Ex $455 Gd $355**
DA/SA. Medium frame. Caliber: .357 Mag., 7-shot cylinder. 4- or 6.5-in. VR ported bbl. Sights: adj. Finish: stainless. Grip: rubber. Mfg. 2000–date.
627T Tracker (titanium frame,
2000–06) . . . . **NiB $615 Ex $490 Gd $385**

MODEL 650 CIA . . . . **NiB $420 Ex $315 Gd $245**
DAO. Small frame. Caliber: .38 Spl. +P., 5-shot cylinder. 2-in. bbl. Sights: fixed. Finish: blued. Grip: rubber. Weight: 24 oz. Made 2001–date.
650 CIA SS (stainless, 2001–12) NiB $420 Ex $315 Gd $245

MODEL 651 PROTECTOR . . . . . **NiB $370 Ex $270 Gd $205**
DAO. Small frame. Caliber: .357 Mag., 5-shot cylinder. 2-in. bbl. Sights: fixed. Finish: blued. Grip: rubber. Weight: 25 oz. Made 2003–12.
651SS Protector (stainless,
2003–12) . . . . **NiB $405 Ex $315 Gd $245**
651T Protector (titanium frame,
2004–06) . . . . **NiB $515 Ex $405 Gd $300**

MODEL 669/669VR DA REVOLVER
Caliber: .357 Mag. Six-round cylinder, 4- or 6-in. solid-rib bbl. w/ejector shroud Model 669VR has VR bbl., weight: 37 oz. w/4-in. bbl., Serrated ramp front sight, micro-adj. rear. Royal blued or stainless finish. Checkered Brazilian hardwood grips. Made 1989-98.
Blued finish. . . . . **NiB $283 Ex $214 Gd $165**
Stainless finish. . . . . **NiB $362 Ex $286 Gd $240**
Model 669VR, blued finish . . . . **NiB $301 Ex $225 Gd $175**
Model 669VR, stainless finish . . **NiB $362 Ex $286 Gd $255**

MODEL 692/992 SERIES
DA/SA. Medium frame. Caliber: .22 LR/.22 WMR, 9-shot (992) or .357 Mag./9mm, 7-shot (692). Dual cylinders w/button on frames allows cylinders to be swapped. Standard 1.5-, 3- or 4- or VR 6.5-in. bbl. Sights: adj. Finish: stainless or blue. Grip: ribbed rubber. Model 992 mfg. 2011–date, Model 692 mfg. 2018–date.
992 (blue, 4- or 6.5-in. bbl.). . . . **NiB $495 Ex $450 Gd $300**
992 (stainless, 4- or 6.5-in. bbl.). **NiB $541 Ex $500 Gd $440**
692 (blue, standard 1-, ported 3- or 6.5-in.
VR ported bbl.). . . . . **NiB $639 Ex $600 Gd $500**
692 (stainless; standard 1-, ported 3- or 6.5-in.
VR ported bbl.). . . . . **NiB $690 Ex $620 Gd $520**

MODEL 741/761 DA REVOLVER
Caliber: .32 H&R Mag. Six-round cylinder, 3- or 4-in. solid-rib bbl. w/ejector shroud. Weight: 20 oz. w/3-in. bbl., Serrated ramp front sight, micro-adj. rear. Blued or stainless finish. Checkered Brazilian hardwood grips. Made 1991-97.
Blued finish. . . . . **NiB $225 Ex $129 Gd $90**
Stainless finish . . . . **NiB $291 Ex $204 Gd $150**
Model 761(6-in. bbl.,
34 oz., blued finish) . . . . **NiB $281 Ex $204 Gd $143**

**Taurus
Model 669**

MODEL 856 SERIES
DA/SA. Caliber: .38 Spl. +P; 6-rnd. cylinder. Barrel: 2-in. Weight: 22 oz. Serrated ramp front sight, groove rear. Matte blued or matte stainless finish. Black rubber grips. Made 2008-12, reintro. 2018-date.
Blue finish. . . . . **NiB $355 Ex $305 Gd $225**
Stainless finish. . . . . **NiB $400 Ex $340 Gd $260**
Concealed Hammer model . . . . . **NiB $320 Ex $270 Gd $195**
Defender model (3-in. bbl., stainless steel or light weight
frame, VZ or Altamont grip) . . . . **NiB $370 Ex $330 Gd $255**
Ultra-Lite model (15.7 oz.
light weight frame) . . . . **NiB $320 Ex $270 Gd $195**
w/night sights, add **$25**

MODEL 941 TARGET REVOLVER
Caliber: .22 Magnum. Eight-round cylinder. Solid-rib bbl. w/ ejector shroud. Micro-adj. rear sight. Brazilian hardwood grips. Blued or stainless finish.
Blued finish. . . . . **NiB $357 Ex $306 Gd $204**
Stainless finish. . . . . **NiB $408 Ex $365 Gd $274**

- AUTOMATIC PISTOLS -

CURVE. . . . . **NiB $392 Ex $300 Gd $250**
Semiauto. DAO. Caliber: .380 ACP, 6-rnd. magazine. 2.5-in. bbl. Weight: 10.2 oz. Unique polymer frame curved to fit body when carry. Finish: blued. Carry clip. Integrated laser and light. Made 2015–18.

MODEL 22 PLY . . . . **NiB $285 Ex $177 Gd $101**
DAO. Caliber: .22 LR. 8-rnd. magazine, tip-up 2.3-in. bbl., polymer frame. Weight: 10.8 oz. Fixed sights. Made 2012 to date.

MODEL 25 PLY . . . . **NiB $285 Ex $177 Gd $101**
Similar to Model 22 PLY model except chambered in .25 ACP. Made 2012–15.

MODEL G2 MILLENIUM . . . . . **NiB $280 EX $240 GD $195**
Semiauto. DA/SA. Polymer frame w/Picatinny rail. Caliber: 9mm or .40 S&W; 6- or 7-rnd. magazine. Barrel: 3.25-in. Fixed 3-dot sights. Matte black finish. Weight: 22 oz. Mfg. 2013-18.

MODEL G2C. . . . . **NiB $280 EX $240 GD $195**
Semiauto. Striker-fired. Polymer frame w/Picatinny rail. Caliber: 9mm or .40 S&W; G2S has 6- or 7-rnd. magazine, G2C has 10- or 12-rnd. Barrel: 3.25-in. Fixed 3-dot sights. Matte black finish. Weight: 22 oz. Mfg. 2018-date. Model G2S is slightly smaller; 2018-date.
G2S. . . . . **NiB $255 Ex $225 Gd $175**

MODEL G3. . . . . **NiB $305 EX $255 GD $205**
Semiauto. SA w/restrike trigger. Polymer frame w/Picatinny rail. Caliber: 9mm; 10-, 15- or 17-rnd. magazine. Barrel: 4-in. Fixed 3-dot sights. Matte black, OD green or tan finish. Weight: 22 oz. Mfg. 2020-date.
G3C (3.2-in. bbl.) . . . . **NiB $270 Ex $235 Gd $180**
G3X (3.2-in. bbl., full size frame). .**NiB $340 Ex $300 Gd $280**
G3XL (4-in. bbl., compact frame) . . **NiB $340 Ex $300 Gd $280**

MODEL GX4 SERIES
Semiauto. Striker-fire. Cal.: 9mm; 11-rnd. magazine. 3-in. bbl. Frame: Polymer. Sights: Steel fixed white-dot. Finish: Matte black or coyote/black. Grip: Textured polymer. Weight: 18.7 oz. Made 2021-date.
Standrad . . . . **NiB $410 Ex $390 Gd $300**
T.O.R.O. (red dot ready, 2022-date). . **NiB $420 Ex $400 Gd $320**

MODEL PT-22 . . . . NiB $285 Ex $177 Gd $101
SA/DA. Caliber: .22 LR. Nine-round magazine, 2.75-in. bbl., weight: 12.3 oz. Fixed open sights. Brazilian hardwood grips. Blued finish. Made 1991-2015.

MODEL PT-24/7 . . . . NiB $455 Ex $300 Gd $260
DAO. Caliber: 9mm, .40 S&W or .45 ACP. 10-, 12-, 15, or 17-rnd. magazine, 4-in. bbl. Polymer frame w/blued or stainless slide. 3-dot sights. Acessory rail. Made 2004-05.

**MODEL PT-24/7
PRO FULL SIZE** . . . . NiB $420 Ex $290 Gd $240
SA with DA second strike trigger. Caliber: 9mm, .40 S&W or .45 ACP. 10-, 12-, 15, or17-rnd. magazine, 4-in. bbl. Polymer frame w/blued or stainless slide. 3-dot sights. Acessory rail. Made 2006-10.

Taurus
Model PT-22

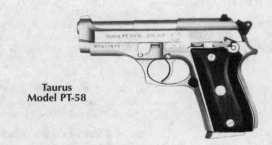

Taurus
Model PT-58

Taurus
Model PT-92AF

Taurus Curve

Taurus
Model PT-908

Pro Compact (3.1-in. bbl.) . . . . NiB $420 Ex $280 Gd $250
Pro Long Slide (5.2-in. bbl.) . . . NiB $450 Ex $295 Gd $255

MODEL PT-24/7 G2 . . . . NiB $530 Ex $300 Gd $260
SA with DA second strike trigger. Caliber: 9mm, .40 S&W or .45 ACP. 10-, 12-, 15, or17-rnd. magazine, 4-in. bbl. Polymer frame w/interchangeable backstraps, ambidextrous controls, blued or stainless slide. 3-dot sights. Acessory rail. Made 2011 to date.
Compact (3.1-in. bbl.) . . . . NiB $530 Ex $300 Gd $260

MODEL PT-24/7 OSS . . . . NiB $480 Ex $330 Gd $290
Similar to PT-24/7 Pro Full Size except w/5.25-in. bbl. and tan or black polymer frame. Made 2007-10.

MODEL PT-25 . . . . NiB $285 Ex $170 Gd $92
Same general specifications as Model PT 22 except in .25 ACP w/eight-round magazine. Made 1992-2015.

MODEL PT-58 . . . . NiB $408 Ex $332 Gd $240
Caliber: .380 ACP. Twelve-round magazine, 4-in. bbl., 7.2 in. overall. Weight: 30 oz. Blade front sight, rear adj. for windage w/3-dot sighting system. Blued, satin nickel or stainless finish. Made 1988-96.

MODEL PT-92AF
SA/DA. Similar to Beretta M92 SB-F. Caliber: 9mm Para. 15-rnd. magazine, 5-in. bbl., 8.5 in. overall. Weight: 24 oz. Blade front sight, notched bar rear. Smooth Brazilian walnut grips. Blued, satin nickel or stainless finish. Made 1991 to date.
Blued finish. . . . . NiB $670 Ex $377 Gd $286
Satin nickel finish . . . . NiB $720 Ex $418 Gd $319
Stainless finish. . . . . NiB $679 Ex $398 Gd $306
Deluxe (blue/gold or
  stainless/gold) . . . . NiB $520 Ex $390 Gd $300

MODEL PT-92AFC COMPACT PISTOL
Same general specs as Model PT-92AF except w/13-rnd. magazine, 4.25-in. bbl., 7.5 in. overall. Weight: 31 oz. Made 1991-96
Blued finish. . . . . NiB $362 Ex $283 Gd $214
Satin nickel finish . . . . NiB $408 Ex $328 Gd $266
Stainless finish. . . . . NiB $434 Ex $346 Gd $220

**MODEL PT-99AF
SEMIAUTO PISTOL** . . . . NiB $530 Ex $437 Gd $301
Same general specifications as Model PT-92AF except rear sight is adj. for elevation and windage, and finish is blued or satin nickel.

MODEL PT-100 DA AUTOMATIC PISTOL
Caliber: .40 S&W. Eleven-round magazine, 5-in. bbl., weight: 34 oz. Fixed front sight, adj. rear w/3-dot system. Smooth hardwood grip. Blued, satin nickel or stainless finish. Made 1991-97.
Blued finish. . . . . NiB $500 Ex $444 Gd $362
Satin finish . . . . NiB $546 Ex $469 Gd $377
Stainless finish. . . . . NiB $536 Ex $444 Gd $367

MODEL PT-101 DA AUTOMATIC PISTOL
Same general specifications as Model 100 except w/microm-eter click adj. sights. Made 1992-96.
Blued finish. . . . . NiB $536 Ex $444 Gd $367
Satin nickel finish . . . . NiB $576 Ex $453 Gd $367
Stainless finish. . . . . NiB $536 Ex $444 Gd $367

MODEL PT-111 MILLENNIUM DAO PISTOL
Caliber: 9mm Parabellum. 10-rnd. magazine, 3.12-in. bbl., 6 in. overall. Weight: 19.1 oz. Fixed low-profile sights w/3-dot system. Black polymer grip/frame. Blue or stainless slide. Imported from 1998 to 2004.
Blue finish. . . . . NiB $362 Ex $265 Gd $130
Stainless finish. . . . . NiB $380 Ex $286 Gd $185

MODEL PT-132 . . . . NiB $355 Ex $265 Gd $210
Semiauto. DAO. Caliber: .32 ACP, 10-rnd. magazine. 4-in. bbl. Weight: 16 oz. Polymer frame.Finish: blued or stainless steel. Made 2001-04.

MODEL PT-132 MILLENNIUM

PRO . . . . NIB $375 Ex $300 Gd $225
Similar to PT-132 expect DA/SA trigger, Heinie sights. Made 2005-11.

MODEL PT-138 . . . . NIB $350 Ex $255 Gd $180
Similar to PT-132 except .380 ACP. Made 1998-2004.
PT-140 (.40 S&W, 1999-2004) . NiB $350 Ex $255 Gd $180
PT-145 (.45 ACP, 2000-03) . . . . NiB $400 Ex $315 Gd $245

MODEL PT-138 MILLENNIUM

PRO . . . . NIB $395 Ex $300 Gd $230
Similar to PT-132 Millennium Pro except .380 ACP. Made 2005-11.
PT-140 Millennium Pro

   (.40 S&W, 2003-12) . . . . NiB $395 Ex $290 Gd $215
PT-145 Millennium Pro

   (.45 ACP, 2003-12) . . . . NiB $395 Ex $290 Gd $215

MODEL PT-609 . . . . NIB $535 Ex $435 Gd $330
Semiauto. DA/SA. Caliber: 9mm, 13-rnd. magazine. 3.25-in. bbl. Weight: 19.7 oz. Polymer frame. Made 2007-10.

MODEL PT-709 SLIM . . . . NIB $316 Ex $300 Gd $200
Semiauto. DA/SA w/ Strike Two capability. Caliber: 9mm, 7-rnd. magazine. 3-in. bbl. Weight: 19 oz. Polymer frame. Sights: fixed. Finish: black or stainless. Made 2008-12, reintro. 2014.

MODEL PT-732 TCP . . . . NIB $295 Ex $300 Gd $200
Semiauto. DAO. Caliber: .32 ACP, 6-rnd. magazine. 3.3-in. bbl. Weight: 10.2 oz. Polymer frame. Sights: fixed. Finish: black or pink. Made 2011-12.
Model PT-7328 TCP (.380 ACP) . . . NiB $356 Ex $260 Gd $175

MODEL PT-740 SLIM . . . . NIB $316 Ex $300 Gd $200
Similar to PT-709 SLIM except in .40 S&W, 6-rnd. magazine. Made 2011-17.

MODEL PT-809 . . . . NIB $486 Ex $350 Gd $225
Semiauto. DA/SA w/ Strike Two capability. Caliber: 9mm, 17-rnd. magazine. 4-in. bbl. Weight: 30.2 oz. Polymer frame w/ accessory rail. Ambidextrous 3-position safety. External hammer. Sights: Novak fixed. Finish: black tennifer. Made 2007-16.
Model PT-809 Compact

   (3.5-in. bbl.) . . . . NiB $486 Ex $350 Gd $225
Model PT-840 (.40 S&W) . . . . . NiB $486 Ex $350 Gd $225
Model PT-840 Compact

   (3.5-in. bbl.) . . . . NiB $486 Ex $350 Gd $225
Model PT-845 (.45 ACP) . . . . . . NiB $486 Ex $350 Gd $225

MODEL PT-908 SEMIAUTO PISTOL
Caliber: 9mm Para. Eight-round magazine, 3.8-in. bbl., 7 in. overall. Weight: 30 oz. Post front sight, drift-adj. combat rear w/3-dot system. Blued, satin nickel or stainless finish. Made 1993-97.
Blued finish . . . . NiB $357 Ex $286 Gd $204
Satin nickel finish . . . . NiB $388 Ex $316 Gd $205
Stainless finish . . . . NiB $431 Ex $321 Gd $265

MODEL PT-911 COMPACT SEMIAUTO PISTOL
Caliber: 9mm Parabellum. 10-rnd. magazine, 3.75-in. bbl., 7.05 in. overall. Weight: 28.2 oz. Fixed low-profile sights w/3-dot system. Santoprene II grips. Blue or stainless finish. Imported from 1997 to 2010.
Blued finish . . . . NiB $546 Ex $408 Gd $270
Stainless finish . . . . NiB $546 Ex $408 Gd $270

MODEL PT-938 COMPACT SEMIAUTO PISTOL
Caliber: 380 ACP. 10-rnd. magazine, 3.72-in. bbl., 6.75 in. overall. Weight: 27 oz. Fixed low-profile sights w/3-dot system. Santoprene II grips. Blue or stainless finish. Imported 1997 to 2005.
Blue finish . . . . NiB $499 Ex $357 Gd $265
Stainless finish . . . . NiB $469 Ex $377 Gd $286

MODEL PT-940 COMPACT SEMIAUTO PISTOL
Caliber: .40 S&W. 10-rnd. magazine, 3.75-in. bbl., 7.05 in. overall. Weight: 28.2 oz. Fixed low-profile sights w/3-dot system. Santoprene II grips. Blue or stainless finish. Imported from 1996-2010.
Blue finish . . . . NiB $546 Ex $437 Gd $290
Stainless finish . . . . NiB $571 Ex $499 Gd $316

MODEL PT-945 COMPACT SEMIAUTO PISTOL
Caliber: .45 ACP. Eight-round magazine, 4.25-in. bbl., 7.48 in. overall. Weight: 29.5 oz. Fixed low-profile sights w/3-dot system. Santoprene II grips. Blue or stainless finish. Imported from 1995-2010.
Blue finish . . . . NiB $601 Ex $530 Gd $377
Stainless finish . . . . NiB $587 Ex $437 Gd $316

MODEL PT-957 . . . . NiB $523 Ex $365 Gd $240
Similar to PT-945 except in .357 SIG. Made 1999-2003.

MODEL PT-1911 . . . . NiB $729 Ex $555 Gd $370
Semiauto. SA. Colt 1911 style platform. Caliber: .38 Super, 9mm, .40 S&W or .45 ACP; 8- (.40 S&W, .45 ACP) or 9- (.38 Super, 9mm) rnd. magazine. 5-in. bbl. Weight: 32 oz. Steel or aluminum frame, steel slide w/ front/rear serrations. Sights: Heinie fixed. Grips: wood. Finish: blued or two-tone. Made 2005 to date.

MODEL PT-1911 COMPACT (4.25-IN. BBL.) . . . NiB $490 Ex $360 Gd $275
stainless finish, add $180
PT-1911FS (fixed sights, .45 ACP only) NiB $685 Ex $460 Gd $355

MODEL PT-1911B-1 . . . . NiB $834 Ex $750 Gd $600
Similar to PT-1911 except with accessory rail. Made 2009-11.

MODEL PT-2011 DT INTEGRAL NiB $570 Ex $420 Gd $290
Semiauto. DA/SA w/ trigger safety. Caliber: .380 ACP or 9mm; 11- (.380 ACP) or 13/15- (9mm) rnd. magazine. 3.2-in. bbl. Weight: 21-24 oz. Aluminum frame, steel slide. Sights: adj. rear. Grips: black polymer. Finish: matte black or stainless. Made 2012 only.

MODEL PT-2011 DT HYBRID . NiB $585 Ex $430 Gd $290
Similar to Model PT-2011 DT Integral except 9mm or .40 S&W. Made 2012-13.

MODEL PT-2045 . . . . NiB $570 Ex $420 Gd $290
Semiauto. DA/SA. Caliber: .45 ACP; 12-rnd. magazine. 4.2-in. bbl. Weight: 32 oz. Combined features of 800 series, 24/7 series and 24/7 OSS series. Made in 2009 only.

MODEL SPECTRUM . . . . NiB $250 Ex $205 Gd $165
Semiauto. Striker-fire. Caliber: .380 ACP, 6- or 7-rnd. magazine. 2.8-in. bbl. Weight: 10 oz. Polymer frame w/soft touch panels. Sights: low profile, fixed. Finish: various colors. Mfg. 2017-19, reintro. 2021-date.

MODEL TH9/TH40 SERIES
Semiauto. DA/SA, hammer-fire. Caliber: 9mm (17-rnd.) or .40 S&W (15-rnd.). 4.2-in. bbl. Weight: 28.2 oz. Polymer frame w/ interchangeable backstraps. Sights: Novak low profile, fixed. Finish: various colors. TH9 denotes 9mm pistols, TH40 denotes .40 S&W. Made 2018–date.
Full-size . . . . NiB $300 Ex $270 Gd $165
Compact size (3.5-in. bbl.,

   smaller grip). . . . . NiB $300 Ex $270 Gd $165

MODEL TX22 . . . . NiB $305 Ex $270 Gd $165
Semiauto. Striker-fire, Taurus Pitman Trigger system w/trigger safety. Caliber: .22 LR, 10-rnd. magazine. 4.1-in. bbl. Weight: 17.3 oz. Polymer frame. Sights: adj. 3-dot. Finish: various colors. W/ or w/o manual thumb safety. Made 2019–date.
Competition (5.2-in. bbl.,

   red dot ready). . . . . NiB $530 Ex $500 Gd $450
Competition SCR (5.2-in. bbl., red dot ready, TandemKross

   Game Changer PRO comp) . . NiB $580 Ex $550 Gd $500

GRADING: **NiB** = New in Box   **Ex** = Excellent or NRA 95%   **Gd** = Good or NRA 68%

TEXAS ARMS — Waco, TX

DEFENDER DERRINGER...... NiB $306 Ex $218 Gd $120
Calibers: 9mm, .357 Mag., .44 Mag., .45 ACP, .45 Colt/.410. Three-in. bbl., 5 in. overall. Weight: 21 oz. Blade front sight, fixed rear. Matte gun-metal gray finish. Smooth grips. Made 1993-99.

TEXAS LONGHORN ARMS — Richmond, TX

"THE JEZEBEL" PISTOL....... NiB $337 Ex $265 Gd $200
Top-break, single-shot. Caliber: .22 Short, Long or LR. Six-inch half-round bbl., 8 in. overall. Weight: 15 oz. Bead front sight, adj. rear. One-piece walnut grip. Stainless finish. Intro. in 1987.

SA REVOLVER CASED SET
Set contains one each of the Texas Longhorn Single Actions. Each chambered in the same caliber and w/the same serial number. Intro. in 1984.
Standard set .... NiB $1620 Ex $1400 Gd $1000
Engraved set .... NiB $1820 Ex $1615 Gd $1219

**SOUTH TEXAS ARMY LIMITED
EDITION SA REVOLVER**... NiB $1840 Ex $1418 Gd $1120
Calibers: All popular centerfire pistol calibers. Six-round cylinder, 4.75-in. bbl.,10.25 in. overall. Weight: 40 oz. Fixed sights. Color casehardened frame. One-piece deluxe walnut grips. Blued bbl., Intro. in 1984.

**SESQUICENTENNIAL
SA REVOLVER**.......... NiB $2613 Ex $2114 Gd $1489
Same as South Texas Army Limited Edition except engraved and nickel-plated w/one-piece ivory grip. Intro. in 1986.

**TEXAS BORDER SPECIAL
SA REVOLVER**........... NiB $1744 Ex $1316 Gd $954
Same as South Texas Army Limited Edition except w/3.5-in. bbl. and bird's-head grips. Intro. in 1984.

**WEST TEXAS FLAT TOP
TARGET SA REVOLVER**..... NiB $1633 Ex $1316 Gd $896
Same as South TExas Army Limited Edition except w/choice of bbl. lengths from 7 .5 to 15 in. Same special features w/flat-top style frame and adj. rear sight. Intro. in 1984.

THOMPSON — West Hurley, NY

Manufactured by Auto-Ordnance Corporation; owned by Kahr Arms. Also see Auto-Ordnance handgun section.

MODEL 1927A-5 .... NiB $1071 Ex $855 Gd $668
Similar to Thompson Model 1928A submachine gun except has no provision for automatic firing, does not have detachable buttstock. Caliber: .45 Auto, 20-rnd. detachable box magazine (5-, 15- and 30-rnd. box magazines, 39-rnd. drum also available), 13-in. finned bbl., overall length: 26 in. Weight: About 6.75 lbs. Adj. rear sight, blade front. Blued finish. Walnut grips. Intro. in 1977.

THOMPSON/CENTER ARMS — Rochester, NH
Acquired by Smith & Wesson in 2006.

CONTENDER SINGLE-SHOT PISTOL
Break frame, underlever action. Calibers: (rimfire) .22 LR. .22 WMR, 5mm RRM; (standard centerfire), .218 Bee, .22 Hornet, .22 Rem. Jet, .221 Fireball, .222 Rem., .25-35, .256 Win. Mag., .30 M1 Carbine, .30-30, .38 Auto, .38 Special .357 Mag./Hot Shot, 9mm Para., .45 Auto, .45 Colt, .44 Magnum/Hot Shot; (wildcat centerfire) .17 Ackley Bee, .17 Bumblebee, .17 Hornet, .17 K Hornet, .17 Mach IV, .17-.222, .17-.223, .22 K Hornet, .30 Herrett, .357 Herrett, .357-4 B&D. Interchangeable

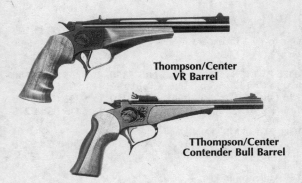

**Thompson/Center
VR Barrel**

**TThompson/Center
Contender Bull Barrel**

bbls.: 8.75- or 10-in. standard octagon (.357 Mag., .44 Mag. and .45 Colt available w/detachable choke for use w/Hot Shot cartridges); 10-in. w/VR and detachable internal choke tube for Hot Shots, .357 and .44 Magnum only; 10-in. bull bbl., .30 or .357 Herrett only. 13.5 in. overall w/10-in. bbl., Weight: 43 oz. (w/standard 10-in. bbl.). Adj. rear sight, ramp front; VR model has folding rear sight, adj. front; bull bbl., available w/or w/o sights. Lobo 1.5/ scope and mount (add $40 to value). Blued finish. Receiver photoengraved. Checkered walnut thumbrest grip and forearm (pre-1972 model has different grip w/silver grip cap). Made 1967 to date, w/the following revisions and variations.
Standard model............ NiB $419 Ex $321 Gd $204
VR model .... NiB $439 Ex $342 Gd $230
Bull bbl. model, w/sights ..... NiB $434 Ex $326 Gd $214
Bull bbl. model, without sights .. NiB $431 Ex $316 Gd $204
Extra standard bbl, add........................... $255
Extra VR or bull bbl, add......................... $306

CONTENDER BULL BARREL... NiB $408 Ex $321 Gd $204
Caliber offerings of the bull bbl. version Expanded in 1973 and 1978, making it the Contender model w/the widest range of caliber options: .22 LR, .22 Win. Mag., .22 Hornet, .223 Rem., 7mm T.C.U., 7x30 Waters, .30 M1 Carbine, .30-30 Win., .32 H&R Mag., .32-20 Win., .357 Rem. Max., .357 Mag., 10mm Auto, .44 Magnum, .445 Super Magnum. 10-in. heavy bbl., Partridge-style iron sights. Contoured Competitor grip. Blued finish.

**CONTENDER INTERNAL
CHOKE MODEL** .... NiB $434 Ex $347 Gd $225
Originally made in 1968-69 w/octagonal bbl., this Internal Choke version in .45 Colt/.410 caliber only was reintroduced in 1986 w/10-in. bull bbl. VR also available. Fixed iron rear sight, bead front. Detachable choke screws into muzzle. Blued finish. Contoured American black walnut Competitor grip, also since 1986, has nonslip rubber insert permanently bonded to back of grip.
w/bull bbl, add................................. $50
w/VR, add $61

**CONTENDER OCTAGON
BARREL**.................. NiB $388 Ex $290 Gd $204
The original Contender design, this octagonal bbl., version began to see the discontinuance of caliber offerings in 1980. Now it is available in .22 LR only, 10-in. octagonal bbl., Partridge-style iron sights. Contoured Competitor grip. Blued finish.

CONTENDER STAINLESS
Similar to the standard Contender models except stainless steel w/blued sights. Black Rynite forearm and ambidExtrous finger-groove grip. Made 2006 to date.
Standard SS model (10-in. bbl.) ...NiB $469 Ex $386 Gd $306
SS Super 14................. NiB $377 Ex $291 Gd $143
SS Super 16................. NiB $377 Ex $291 Gd $143

CONTENDER SUPER (14 IN./16 IN.)
Calibers: .22 LR, .222 Rem., .223 Rem., 6mm T.C.U., 6.5mm T.C.U., 7mm T.C.U., 7x30 Waters, .30 Herrett, .30-30 Win., .357 Herrett, .357 Rem. Max., .35 Rem., 10mm Auto, .44 Mag., .445 Super Mag. 14- or 16.25-in. bull bbl., 18 or 20.25 in. overall. Weight: 43-65 oz. Partridge-style ramp front sight, adj. target rear. Blued finish. Made 1978-97.

Super 14	NiB $380	Ex $306	Gd $204
Super 16	NiB $380	Ex $306	Gd $204

CONTENDER TC ALLOY II
Calibers: .22 LR, .223 Rem., .357 Magnum, .357 Rem. Max., .44 Magnum, 7mm T.C.U., .30-30 Win., .45 Colt/.410 (w/ internal choke), .35 Rem. and 7-30 Waters (14-in. bbl.). 10- or 14-in. bull bbl. or 10-in. VR bbl. (w/internal choke). All metal parts permanently electroplated w/T/C Alloy II, which is harder than stainless steel, ensuring smoother action, 30 percent longer bbl. life. Other design specifications the same as late model Contenders. Made 1986-89.

w/10-in. bull bbl.	NiB $377	Ex $306	Gd $214
w/VR bbl. and choke	NiB $464	Ex $377	Gd $286
Super 14	NiB $388	Ex $306	Gd $219

ENCORE SINGLE-SHOT PISTOL
Similar to the standard Contender models except w/10-, 12- or 15-in. bbl., Calibers: .22-250 Rem., .223 Rem., .243 Win., .260 Rem., .270 Win., 7mm BR Rem., 7mm-08 Rem., 7.62x39mm, .308 Win., .30-06 Spfd., .44 Rem. Mag., .444 Marlin, .45-70 Govt., .45 LC/410. Blue or stainless finish. Walnut or composition, ambidExtrous finger-groove grip. Hunter Model w/2.5-7x pistol scope. Note: Encore bbls. are not interchangeable with Contenter models. Made 1998 to date.

w/10-in. bbl. (blue, disc.)	NiB $561	Ex $499	Gd $270
w/12-in. bbl., blued	NiB $561	Ex $499	Gd $270
w/15-in. bbl., blued	NiB $576	Ex $464	Gd $286
Hunter model w/2,5-7x scope	NiB $755	Ex $546	Gd $365
Encore model (stainless finish), add			$25

G2 CONTENDER SINGLE-SHOT PISTOL
Similar to the Contender model except w/12- or 14-in. bbl., various rimfire and centerfire calibers. Walnut grip. Note: older Contender bbls. are compatiable with G2 Contenter models. Made 2002-12.

Blued finish	NiB $650	Ex $400	Gd $350
Stainless finish	NiB $695	Ex $425	Gd $370

PRO-HUNTER SINGLE-SHOT
PISTOL . . . . NiB $655 Ex $430 Gd $360
Similar to the Contender model except w/15-in. fluted stainless steel bbl., various calibers. Walnut or composite grip. Made 2006-12.

TISAS — Trabzon, Turkey
Est. 1993. Mfg. of pistols currently imported by Zenith Firearms, Afton, VA.

ZIG M 45 . . . . NiB $500 Ex $480 Gd $450
1911 style platform. Semiauto. SA. Caliber: .45 ACP, 8-rnd. magazine. 4-in. bbl. Frame: alloy. Sights: fixed. Finish: matte black. Grip: checkered wood. Ambidextrous thumb safety. Imported from 2016 to date.

Zig PC 1911 (5-in. brrl., rail)	NiB $550	Ex $510	Gd $490
Zig PCS 1911			
(matte stainless, rail)	NiB $550	Ex $510	Gd $490
Zig PCS 9 (matte stainless,			
rail, 9mm)	NiB $550	Ex $510	Gd $490

ZIGNA FC . . . . NiB $550 EX $510 Gd $490

Semiauto. DA/SA. Caliber: 9mm, 15-rnd. magazine. 4.6-in. bbl. Frame: alloy. Sights: fixed. Finish: matte stainless. Grip: textured polymer. Ambidextrous thumb safety. Imported from 2016 to date.

Tisas Zigna KC (4.1-in. brrl.) . . . NiB $550 Ex $510 Gd $490

FATIH 13 . . . . NiB $400 EX $380 GD $300
Beretta style open slide. Semiauto. DA/SA. Caliber: .380 ACP, 13-rnd. magazine. 3.9-in. bbl. Frame: alloy. Sights: fixed. Finish: matte black. Grip: textured polymer. Ambidextrous thumb safety. Imported from 2016 to date.

UBERTI — Ponte Zanano, Italy
Manufactured by Aldo Uberti, imported by Uberti USA, Inc. Manufactures many reproduction revolvers for a variety of companies including EMF, Taylor's & Co., and Cimarron Firearms.

1851 NAVY CONVERSION . . NiB $569 Ex $470 Gd $260
Revolver. SA. Replica of Colt 1851 Navy Conversion. Caliber: .38 Spl., 6-shot cylinder. 4.75-, 5.5-, or 7.5-in. bbl. Finish: case-hardened frame; blued bbl., cylinder; and brass trigger guard and backstrap. Octagon bbl., ejector rod. Grips: 1-piece smooth walnut. Sights: fixed. Made 2007 to date.

1860 ARMY CONVERSION . . NiB $589 Ex $480 Gd $265
Revolver. SA. Replica of Colt 1860 Army Conversion. Caliber: .38 Spl. or .45 LC, 6-shot cylinder. 4.75-, 5.5-, or 8-in. bbl. Overall length: 13.8-in. Weight: 41.6 oz. Finish: case-hardened frame; blued bbl., cylinder, backstrap and trigger guard. Round bbl. Grips: 1-piece smooth walnut. Sights: fixed. Made 2007 to date.

1871 NAVY OPEN-TOP . . . . . NiB $539 Ex $470 Gd $260
Revolver. SA. Replica of Colt 1871 Navy Open-Top. Caliber: .38 Spl. or .45 LC, 6-shot cylinder. 4.75-, 5.5-, or 7.5-in. bbl. Finish: case-hardened frame; blued bbl., cylinder; and brass backstrap trigger guard. Round bbl., ejector rod. Grips: 1-piece smooth walnut. Sights: fixed. Made 2002 to date.

1871 ROLLING BLOCK
TARGET PISTOL . . . . NiB $418 Ex $321 Gd $230
Single shot. Calibers: .22 LR, .22 Magnum, .22 Hornet and .357 Magnum; 9.5-in. bbl., 14 in. overall. Weight: 44 oz. Ramp front sight, fully adjustable rear. Smooth walnut grip and forearm. Color casehardened frame w/brass trigger guard. Blued half-octagon or full rnd. barrel. Made 2002-06.

1872 ARMY OPEN-TOP . . . . . . NiB $569 Ex $475 Gd $265
Revolver. SA. Replica of Colt 1872 Army Open-Top. Caliber: .38 Spl. or .45 LC, 6-shot cylinder. 7.5-in. bbl. Finish: case-hardened frame; blued bbl., cylinder, backstrap and trigger guard. Round bbl. Grips: 1-piece smooth walnut. Sights: fixed. Made 2002 to date.

1873 CATTLEMAN SA REVOLVER
Calibers: .357 Magnum, .38-40, .44-40, .44 Special, .45 Long Colt, .45 ACP. Six-round cylinder, Bbl length: 3.5, 4.5, 4.75, 5.5, 7.5 or 18 in.; 10.75 in. overall (5.5-in. bbl.). Weight: 38 oz. (5.5-in. bbl.). Color casehardened steel frame w/steel or brass back strap and trigger guard. Nickel-plated or blued bbl. and cylinder. First issue imported from 1997 to 2004; new models from 2002 to date.

First issue	NiB $459	Ex $386	Gd $235
Bisley	NiB $459	Ex $386	Gd $235
Bisley (flattop)	NiB $459	Ex $386	Gd $235
Buntline (reintroduced 1992)	NiB $500	Ex $395	Gd $244
Quick Draw	NiB $459	Ex $386	Gd $235
Sabre (bird head)	NiB $459	Ex $386	Gd $235

**Uberti
Rolling Block Target**

**Uberti
Model 1873 Cattleman**

**Uberti
Cattleman Buntline Target**

Sheriff's model . . . . NiB $459 Ex $386 Gd $235
Convertible cylinder, add $75
Stainless steel, add $150
Steel backstrap and trigger guard, add $75
Target sights, add $75

1873 HORSEMAN . . . . NiB $549 Ex $400 Gd $255
Revolver. SA. Replica of Colt 1873 SAA. Caliber: .22 LR, .38
Spl., .44 Mag. or .45 LC, 6-shot cylinder. 4.75, 5.5-, or 7.5-in.
bbl. Finish: case-hardened frame; blued bbl., cylinder, backstrap and trigger guard. Grips: 1-piece smooth walnut. Sights:
fixed. Coil main spring, wide trigger, transfer bar safety system.
Made 2013 to date.

1875 NO. 3 TOP BREAK . . . . . NiB $1079 Ex $800 Gd $500
Revolver. SA. Replica of S&W No. 3. Caliber: .38 Spl., .44-40
or .45 LC, 6-shot cylinder. 3.5-, 5, or 7-in. bbl. Finish: case-
hardened, blued or nickel. Grips: 2-piece smooth walnut or
pearl. Sights: fixed. Made 2005 to date.
nickel finish, add. $300

1875 REMINGTON OUTLAW
Replica of Model 1875 Remington. Calibers: .357 Mag., .44-
40, .45 ACP, .45 Long Colt. Six-round cylinder, 5.5- to 7.5-in.
bbl., 11.75 to13.75 in. overall. Weight: 44 oz. (w/ 7.5 in. bbl).
Color casehardened steel frame w/steel or brass back strap and
trigger guard. Blue or nickel finish.
Blue finish. . . . . NiB $479 Ex $366 Gd $219
Nickel finish (disc. 1995) . . . . . NiB $541 Ex $473 Gd $321
Convertible cylinder
  (.45 LC/.45 ACP), add $50
Target model (adj. rear sight,
  1987-89) . . . . NiB $479 Ex $366 Gd $219

1890 REMINGTON POLICE
Similar to Model 1875 Remington except without the web
under the ejector housing.
Blue Model . . . . NiB $464 Ex $346 Gd $198
Nickel finish (disc. 1995) . . . . . NiB $862 Ex $704 Gd $345
Convertible Cylinder (.45 LC/.45 ACP), add. $50

NO. 3 RUSSIAN TOP BREAK. NiB $1079 Ex $800 Gd $500
Similar to 1875 No. 3 Top Break except .44 Russian or .45 LC
only. 6.5-in. bbl. Finish: case-hardened/blued or nickel. Grips:
2-piece smooth walnut. Sights: fixed. Trigger spur. Made 2005
to date.
nickel finish, add. $300

BIRD'S HEAD . . . . NiB $569 Ex $420 Gd $265
Similar to new model Cattleman except bird's head grip.
Caliber: .357 Mag. or .45 LC, 6-shot cylinder. 3.5-, 4.75, or
5.5-in. bbl. Finish: case-hardened frame; blued bbl., cylinder,
backstrap and trigger guard. Grips: 1-piece smooth walnut.
Sights: fixed. Made 1997 to date.

BISLEY . . . . NiB $609 Ex $445 Gd $280
Similar to new model Cattleman except Replica of Colt Bisley.
Caliber: .357 Mag. or .45 LC, 6-shot cylinder. 4.75, 5.5-, or
7.5-in. bbl. Finish: case-hardened frame; blued bbl., cylinder,
backstrap and trigger guard. Grips: 1-piece smooth walnut.
Sights: fixed. Made 1997 to date.

**REMINGTON 1858
NEW ARMY CONVERSION. . . NiB $589 Ex $480 Gd $265**
Revolver. SA. Replica of Remington 1858 New Army Conversion.
Caliber: .45 LC, 6-shot cylinder. 8-in. bbl. Overall length: 13.8-
in. Weight: 41.6 oz. Finish: blued. Octagon bbl. Grips: 2-piece
smooth walnut. Sights: fixed. Made 2007 to date.

STALLION . . . . NiB $449 Ex $350 Gd $220
Revolver. SA. Replica of Colt SAA. Caliber: .22 LR or .38 Spl.,
6-shot cylinder. 4.75 or 5.5-in. bbl. Finish: case-hardened
frame; blued bbl. and cylinder; brass backstrap and trigger
guard. Round bbl. Grips: 1-piece smooth walnut. Sights: fixed.
Made 1999 to date.
conversion model (.22 LR/.22 Mag.), add. $70
steel backstrap and trigger guard, add $50
Stallion Target (adj. sights), add $70

STALLION 10-SHOT . . . . NiB $499 Ex $325 Gd $210
Similar to Stallion except .22 LR only, 10-shot cylinder. Made
2010 to date.
Stallion Target 10-Shot (adj. sights), add. $70

ULTRA LIGHT ARMS, INC — Granville, WV

MODEL 20 SERIES PISTOLS
Calibers: .22-250 thru .308 Win. Five-round magazine, 14-in.
bbl., weight: 4 lbs. Composite Kevlar, graphite reinforced
stock. Benchrest grade action available in right- or left-hand
models. Timney adjustable trigger w/three function safety.
Bright or matte finish. Made 1987-99.
Model 20 Hunter's Pistol
  (disc. 1989) . . . . NiB $1295 Ex $1057 Gd $974
Model 20 Reb Pistol
  (disc. 1999). . . . . NiB $1508 Ex $1345 Gd $1199

UNIQUE — Hendaye, France
*Manufactured by Manufacture d'Armes des Pyrénées.
Currently imported by Nygord Precision Products, previously
by Beeman Precision Arms.*

**MODEL B/CF
AUTOMATIC PISTOL . . . . NiB $220 Ex $115 Gd $70**
Calibers: .32 ACP, .380 ACP. 9-rnd. (.32) or 8-rnd. (.38) maga-
zine, 4-in. bbl., 6.6 in. overall. Weight: 24.3 oz. Blued finish.
Plain or thumbrest plastic grips. Intro. in 1954. Disc.

MODEL D2 . . . . **NiB $326 Ex $219 Gd $177**
Same as Model D6 except has 4.5-in. bbl., 7.5 in. overall, weight: 24.5 oz. Made 1954. Disc.

MODEL D6
AUTOMATIC PISTOL . . . . **NiB $332 Ex $239 Gd $118**
Caliber: .22 LR. 10-rnd. magazine, 6-in. bbl., 9.25 in. overall. Weight: About 26 oz. Adj. sights. Blued finish. Plain or thumbrest plastic grips. Intro. in 1954. Disc.

MODEL DES/32U RAPID FIRE PISTOL
Caliber: .32 S&W Long (wadcutter). Five- or 6-rnd. magazine, 5.9-in. bbl., weight: .40.2 oz. Blade front sight, micro-adj. rear. Trigger adj. for weight and position. Blued finish. Stippled handrest grips. Imported from 1990 to date.
Right-hand model . . . . NiB $1418 Ex $1316 Gd $1155
Left-hand model . . . . NiB $1486 Ex $1366 Gd $1220

MODEL DES/69-U STANDARD MATCH PISTOL
Caliber: .22 LR. Five-round magazine, 5.9-in. bbl., w/250 gm counterweight. 10.6 in. overall. Trigger adjusts for position and pull. Weight: 35.3 oz. Blade front sight, micro-adj. rear. Checkered walnut thumbrest grips w/adj. handrest. Blued finish. Imported from 1969 to 1999.
Right-hand model . . . . NiB $1234 Ex $1138 Gd $909
Left-hand model . . . . NiB $1240 Ex $1144 Gd $941

MODEL DES 823U RAPID FIRE
MATCH AUTOMATIC PISTOL NiB $1122 Ex $950 Gd $836
Caliber: .22 Short. Five-round magazine, 5.9-in. bbl., 10.4 in. overall. Weight: 43 oz. Click adj. rear sight blade front. Checkered walnut thumbrest grips w/adj. handrest. Trigger adj. for length of pull. Made 1974-98.

KRIEGSMODELL L
AUTOMATIC PISTOL . . . . **NiB $362 Ex $255 Gd $180**
Caliber: .32 Auto (7.65mm). Nine-round magazine, 3.2-in. bbl., 5.8 in. overall. Weight: 26.5 oz. Fixed sights. Blued finish. Plastic grips. Mfd. during German occupation of France 1940 to 194545. Note: Bears the German military acceptance marks and may have grips marked "7.65m/m 9 SCHUSS."

MODEL L
AUTOMATIC PISTOL . . . . **NiB $283 Ex $204 Gd $149**
Calibers: .22 LR, .32 Auto (7.65mm), .380 Auto (9mm Short). 10-rnd. magazine in .22, 7 in .32, 6 in .380; 3.3-in. bbl.; 5.8 in. overall. Weight: 16.5 oz. (.380 Auto w/light alloy frame), 23 oz. (w/steel frame). Fixed sights. Blued finish. Plastic grips. Intro. in 1955. Disc.

MODEL MIKROS POCKET
AUTOMATIC PISTOL . . . . **NiB $225 Ex $150 Gd $97**
Calibers: .22 Short, .25 Auto (6.35mm). Six-round magazine, 2.25-in. bbl., 4.44 in. overall. Weight: 9.5 oz. (light alloy frame), 12.5 oz. (steel frame.). Fixed sights. Blued finish. Plastic grips. Intro. in 1957. Disc.

MODEL RR
AUTOMATIC PISTOL . . . . **NiB $218 Ex $109 Gd $68**
Postwar commercial version of WWII Kriegsmodell w/same general specifications. Intro. in 1951. Disc.

MODEL 2000-U MATCH PISTOL
Caliber: .22 Short. Designed for U.I.T. rapid fire competition. Five-round top-inserted magazine, 5.5-in. bbl., w/five vents for recoil reduction. 11.4 in. overall. Weight: 43.4 oz. Special light alloy frame, solid steel slide and shock absorber. Stippled French walnut w/adj. handrest. Imported from 1990 to 1996.

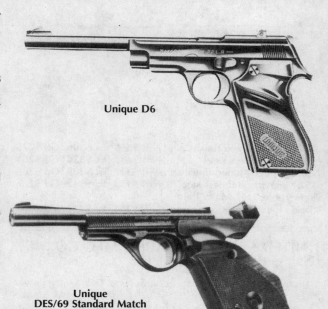

Unique D6

**Unique
DES/69 Standard Match**

**Unique
Model DES/VO Rapid Fire Match**

**Unique
Mikros Pocket**

Right-hand model . . . . NiB $1367 Ex $1199 Gd $1122
Left-hand model . . . . NiB $1398 Ex $1250 Gd $1196

UNITED STATES ARMS CORPORATION — Riverhead, NY

ABILENE SA REVOLVER
Safety Bar action. Calibers: .357 Mag., .41 Mag., .44 Mag., .45 Colt and .357/9mm convertible model w/two cylinders. Six-round cylinder, bbl. lengths: 4.63-, 5.5-, 6.5-in., 7.5- and 8.5-in. in .44 Mag. only. Weight: About 48 oz. Adj. rear sight, ramp front. Blued finish or stainless steel. Smooth walnut grips. Made 1976-83.

U.S. Arms Corp. Abilene

Universal Enforcer (3000)

.44 Magnum, blued finish . . . . . NiB $365 Ex $306 Gd $225
Magnum, stainless steel . . . . . . NiB $437 Ex $336 Gd $265
Other calibers, blued finish . . . NiB $327 Ex $209 Gd $200
.357 Magnum, stainless steel . . NiB $433 Ex $342 Gd $266
Convertible, .357 Mag./9mm
  Para., blued finish. . . . . NiB $362 Ex $224 Gd $207

UNITED STATES FIRE ARMS MFG CO., INC. — Hartford, CT

Manufacturer of high quality reproduction Colt SAA revolver and Colt 1911 pistols from 1995 to 2012. The facility was once located in the old Colt factory building. Ceased production of replica Colts in 2011 and launched the polymer ZIP .22 rimfire. Company closed in 2017.

1910 COMMERCIAL MODEL
AUTOMATIC PISTOL . . . . . . NiB $1650 Ex $1300 Gd $800
Full size 1911-style pistol. Caliber: .45 ACP, 7-rnd. magazine, 5-in. bbl., 8.3 in. overall. High polish Armory Blue finish, checkered walnut grips. Made 2006-09.
1911 Military Model (similar
  Colt 1911 rollmarks). . . . NiB $1650 Ex $1300 Gd $800
1911 Super 38 (.38 Super) . NiB $1650 Ex $1300 Gd $800

SINGLE ACTION ARMY REVOLVER
PREMIUM GRADE . . . . NiB $910 Ex $660 Gd $400
Calibers: .22 LR, .22 WMR, .32-20, .357 Mag., .38 Special, .38-40, .41 Colt, .44-40, .44 Special, .45 Long Colt, .45 ACP. Six-round cylinder, Bbl length: 3, 4, 4.75, 5.5, 7.5 or 10 in. Dome Blue, Old Armory, Bone Case or nickel finish.
Flat Top (adj. sights) . . . . NiB $1509 Ex $1186 Gd $710
U.S. Pre-War. . . . . NiB $1400 Ex $1000 Gd $610
New Buntline Special (16-in. bbl.,
  skeleton stock) . . . . NiB $1900 Ex $1550 Gd $990

**Uzi
Semiauto Pistol**

Bisley . . . . NiB $1560 Ex $1210 Gd $710
Sheriff's Model . . . . NiB $1060 Ex $900 Gd $500
Rodeo (matte finish) . . . . NiB $700 Ex $500 Gd $350
Cowboy (Dome Blue finish,
  brown rubber grips) . . . . NiB $775 Ex $600 Gd $400
Omni-Potent (Bisley grip) . . . NiB $1500 Ex $1060 Gd $675

MODEL ZIP . . . . NiB $269 Ex $200 Gd $190
Semiauto. SA. Caliber: .22 LR, comparable w/ Ruger 10/22 magazine. 5.25-in. bbl. Length: 7.75 in. Weight: 15.2 oz. Unique polymer frame/grip. Sights: none, rail. Finish: black or gray. Made 2013-17.

UNIVERSAL FIREARMS CORPORATION — Hialeah, FL

This company was purchased by Iver Johnson Arms in the mid-1980s, when the Enforcer listed below was disc. An improved version was issued under the Iver Johnson name (see separate listing).

ENFORCER (3000)
SEMIAUTO PISTOL. . . . . NiB $479 Ex $337 Gd $265
M-1 Carbine-type action. Caliber: 30 Carbine. Five-, 15- or 30-rnd. clip magazine, 10.25-in. bbl., 17.75 in. overall. Weight: 4.5 lbs. (w/ 30-rnd. magazine). Adj. rear sight, blade front. Blued finish. Walnut stock w/pistol grip and handguard. Made 1964-83.

UZI — Israel

Manufactured by Israel Military Industries, Israel currently imported by UZI America.

SEMIAUTO PISTOL. . . . . NiB $1044 Ex $855 Gd $658
Caliber: 9mm Para. 20-rnd. magazine, 4.5-in. bbl., about 9.5 in. overall. Weight: 3.8 lbs. Front post-type sight, rear open-type, both adj. Disc. in 1993.

"EAGLE" SERIES SEMIAUTO DA PISTOL
Caliber: 9mm Parabellum, .40 S&W, .45 ACP (Short Slide). 10-rnd. magazine, 3.5-, 3.7- and 4.4-in. bbl., weight: 32 oz. to 35 oz. Blade front sight, drift adjustable tritium rear. Matte blue finish. Black synthetic grips. Imported from 1997 to 1998.
Compact model (DA or DAO) . . . NiB $540 Ex $406 Gd $317
Polymer compact model . . . . . NiB $540 Ex $496 Gd $317
Full-size model . . . . NiB $540 Ex $496 Gd $317
Short slide model . . . . NiB $540 Ex $496 Gd $317

WALTHER — Manufactured by German, French, Swiss and U.S. firms

The following Walther pistols were made before and during World War II by Waffenfabrik Walther, Zella-Mehlis (Thür.), Germany.

MODEL 1

AUTOMATIC PISTOL . . . . NiB $900 Ex $581 Gd $316
Caliber: .25 Auto (6.35mm). Six-round. 2.1-in. bbl., 4.4 in. overall. Weight: 12.8 oz. Fixed sights. Blued finish. Checkered hard rubber grips. Intro. in 1908.

MODEL 2 AUTOMATIC PISTOL

Caliber: .25 Auto (6.35mm). Six-round magazine, 2.1-in. bbl., 4.2 in. overall. Weight: 9.8 oz. Fixed sights. Blued finish. Checkered hard rubber grips. Intro. in 1909.
Standard model. . . . . NiB $663 Ex $468 Gd $227
Pop-up sight model . . . . NiB $1950 Ex $1345 Gd $1188

MODEL 3

AUTOMATIC PISTOL . . . . . NiB $4010 Ex $3286 Gd $1005
Caliber: .32 Auto (7.65mm). Six-round magazine, 2.6-in. bbl., 5 in. overall. Weight: 16.6 oz. Fixed sights. Blued finish. Checkered hard rubber grips. Intro. in 1910.

MODEL 4

AUTOMATIC PISTOL . . . . NiB $556 Ex $425 Gd $235
Caliber: .32 Auto (7.65mm). Eight-round magazine, 3.5-in. bbl., 5.9 in. overall. Weight: 18.6 oz. Fixed sights. Blued finish. Checkered hard rubber grips. Made 1910-18.

MODEL 5

AUTOMATIC PISTOL . . . . NiB $660 Ex $541 Gd $204
Improved version of Model 2 w/same general specifications, distinguished chiefly by better workmanship and appearance. Intro. in 1913.

Walther Model 5

Walther Model 8

Walther Model 9

MODEL 6

AUTOMATIC PISTOL . . . . . NiB $9570 Ex $7933 Gd $5420
Caliber: 9mm Para. Eight-round magazine, 4.75-in. bbl., 8.25 in. overall. Weight: 34 oz. Fixed sights. Blued finish. Checkered hard rubber grips. Made 1915-17. Note: The 9mm Para. cartridge is too powerful for the simple blow-back system of this pistol, so firing is not recommended.

MODEL 7

AUTOMATIC PISTOL . . . . NiB $759 Ex $553 Gd $301
Caliber: .25 Auto. (6.35mm). Eight-round magazine, 3-in. bbl., 5.3 in. overall. Weight: 11.8 oz. Fixed sights. Blued finish. Checkered hard rubber grips. Made 1917-18.

MODEL 8

AUTOMATIC PISTOL . . . . NiB $770 Ex $639 Gd $240
Caliber: .25 Auto. (6.35mm). Eight-round magazine, 2.88-in. bbl., 5.13 in. overall. Weight: 12.38 oz. Fixed sights. Blued finish. Checkered plastic grips. Made 1920-45.

MODEL 8 LIGHTWEIGHT

AUTOMATIC PISTOL . . . . NiB $733 Ex $530 Gd $422
Same as standard Model Eight except about 25 percent lighter due to use of aluminum alloys.

MODEL 9 VEST POCKET

AUTOMATIC PISTOL . . . . NiB $779 Ex $577 Gd $396
Caliber: .25 Auto (6.35mm). Six-round magazine, 2-in. bbl., 3.94 in. overall. Weight: 9 oz. Fixed sights. Blued finish. Checkered plastic grips. Made 1921-45.

MODEL HP DOUBLE-ACTION AUTOMATIC

Prewar commercial version of the P38 marked with an "N" proof over an "Eagle" or "Crown." The "HP" is an abbreviation of "Heeres Pistole" (Army Pistol). Caliber: 9mm Para. 8-rnd. magazine, 5-in. bbl., 8.38 in. overall. Weight: About 34.5 oz. Fixed sights. Blued finish. Checkered wood or plastic grips. The Model HP is distinguished by its notably fine material and workmanship. Made 1937-44. (S/N range 1000-25900)
**First production (Swedish Trials
model H1000-H2000). . . . . NiB $3595 Ex $2765 Gd $2064**
**Standard commercial production
    (2000-24,000). . . . . NiB $2152 Ex $1825 Gd $1743**
**War production - marked "P38"
    (24,000-26,000) . . . . NiB $1722 Ex $1550 Gd $1289**
w/Nazi proof "Eagle/359," add $270

OLYMPIA FUNFKAMPF

MODEL AUTOMATIC . . . . . NiB $3266 Ex $2430 Gd $2220
Caliber: .22 LR. 10-rnd. magazine, 9.6-in. bbl., 13 in. overall. Weight: 33 oz., less weight. Set of 4 detachable weights. Adj. target sights. Blued finish. Checkered grips. Intro. in 1936.

OLYMPIA HUNTING

MODEL AUTOMATIC . . . . . NiB $2762 Ex $2430 Gd $2220
Same general specifications as Olympia Sport Model but w/4-in. bbl., Weight: 28.5 oz.

OLYMPIA RAPID

FIRE AUTO. . . . . NiB $2550 Ex $1620 Gd $1244
Caliber: .22 Short. Six-round magazine, 7.4-in. bbl., 10.7 in. overall. Weight: (without 12.38 oz. detachable muzzle weight,) 27.5 oz. Adj. target sights. Blued finish. Checkered grips. Made 1936-40.

OLYMPIA SPORT

MODEL AUTOMATIC . . . . . NiB $2090 Ex $1398 Gd $1269
Caliber: .22 LR. 10-rnd. magazine, 7.4-in. bbl., 10.7 in. overall. Weight: 30.5 oz., less weight. Adj. target sights. Blued

finish. Checkered grips. Set of four detachable weights was supplied at Extra cost. Made about 1936 to 1940.

P38 MILITARY DA AUTOMATIC
Modification of the Model HP adopted as an official German Service arm in 1938 and produced throughout WW II by Walther (code "ac"), Mauser (code "byf") and a few other manufacturers. General specifications and appearance same as Model HP, but w/a vast difference in quality, the P38 being a mass-produced military pistol. Some of the late wartime models were very roughly finished and tolerances were quite loose.

War Production w/Walther banner (1940)
Zero S/N 1st issue
    (S/N 01-01,000)........ NiB $8130 Ex $6160 Gd $2445
Zero S/N. 2nd issue
    (S/N 01,000-03,500).... NiB $6515 Ex $5125 Gd $2309
Zero S/N. 3rd issue
    (S/N 03,500-013,000)... NiB $3130 Ex $2112 Gd $1021

WALTHER CONTRACT PISTOLS (LATE 1940-44)
"480" code Series
    (S/N 1-7,600) .... NiB $5745 Ex $3937 Gd $1590
"ac" code Ser. w/no date
    (S/N 7,350-9,700)...... NiB $6079 Ex $4390 Gd $2244
"ac" code Ser. w/.40 below
    code (S/N 9,700-9,900A) NiB $4435 Ex $3866 Gd $1879
"ac40" code inline Ser.
    (S/N 1-9,900B)........ NiB $2360 Ex $1966 Gd $909
"ac" code Ser. w/41 below code
    (S/N 1-4,5001) .... NiB $1897 Ex $1633 Gd $974
"ac" code Ser. w/42 below code
    (S/N 4,500I-9,300K)..... NiB $1610 Ex $1364 Gd $869
"ac" code Ser. w/43 date
    (inline or below)......... NiB $831 Ex $633 Gd $478
"ac" code Ser. w/45
    (inline or below)......... NiB $780 Ex $599 Gd $439

MAUSER CONTRACT PISTOLS (LATE 1942-44)
"byf" code Ser. w/42 date
    (19,000 prod.) .... NiB $1418 Ex $1023 Gd $816
"bcf" code Ser. w/43, 44 or 45 date
    (inline or below) .... NiB $984 Ex $744 Gd $612
"svw" code Ser. (French prod. w/Nazi
    proofs) .... NiB $1316 Ex $1066 Gd $693
"svw" code Ser. (French prod.
    w/star proof) .... NiB $576 Ex $500 Gd $376

SPREEWERKE CONTRACT PISTOLS (LATE 1942-45)
"cyq" code 1st Ser. w/Eagle over
    359 (500 prod.) .... NiB $1866 Ex $1598 Gd $1135
"cyq" code Standard Ser.
    (300,000 prod.) .... NiB $989 Ex $590 Gd $478
"cyq" code "0" Ser.
    (5,000 prod.) .... NiB $1132 Ex $741 Gd $562

Walther P38

MODEL PP DA AUTOMATIC PISTOL
Polizeipistole (Police Pistol). Calibers: .22 LR (5.6mm), .32 Auto (7.65mm), .380 Auto (9mm). Eight-round magazine, (7-rnd. in .380), 3.88-in. bbl., 6.94 in. overall. Weight: 23 oz. Fixed sights. Blued finish. Checkered plastic grips. 1929-45. Post-War production and importation 1963 to 2000.

NOTE: *Pre-War models were mfg. from 1929–1940. The "Crown N" proof was used until 1939; then the "Eagle N" proof for Nazi commercial until 1945. Serial numbers start at about 750,000 in 1929 and go to 1,000,000 in the late 1930s; these PP serial numbers were mixed with PPK serial numbers. Serial numbers then started again w/100,000P through to 396,000P by 1945. Verchromt models had a dull gray finish; very few were produced. Imported police surplus guns are stamped on the frame with importer's name. The value of these PP models in 30% less.*

PRE-WAR COMMERICAL MODEL WITH CROWN "N" PROOF
.22 LR cal. .... NiB $1755 Ex $1355 Gd $855
.32 ACP cal. .... NiB $1010 Ex $1755 Gd $480
.380 ACP cal. .... NiB $2010 Ex $1755 Gd $1210
w/Dural alloy frame, add 15%
w/Verchromt finish,
    .32 ACP or .380 ACP .... NiB $3560 Ex $2533 Gd $907
A.F.Stoeger Contract,
    .32 ACP.............. NiB $2550 Ex $1656 Gd $691
Allemagne French
    contract, .32 ACP....... NiB $1489 Ex $1189 Gd $712
w/bottom release mag.
    (.32 ACP) .... NiB $1755 Ex $1255 Gd $755
w/bottom release mag.
    (.380 ACP) .... NiB $2010 Ex $2330 Gd $1655

NOTE: *Wartime models are inferior in quality to prewar commercial pistols. AC markings indicate a late production, no left side of slide markings. NSKK markings indicate Nationalsozialistisches Kraftfahrkorps or Transportation Corp. R.R.Z. markings indicate Reichs Rundfunk Zenhale or German Radio Broadcasting, these are rare. PDM markings indicate Polizei, Direktion Munchen or Munich Police Directorate. RFV mark indicates Reichsfinzverwaltung or Reich Finance Office. RJ marking indicates Reichjustizminsterium or Reich Justice Ministry. SA markings indicates Strum Abteilung or leaders of Nazi party. Panagraph or pantagraph slide models have the serial number rollmarked on the frame and in front of the slide serrations. Verchromt models had a plating that gave the PPK a dull gray appearance; very few were produced.*

WARTIME MODEL WITH EAGLE "N" PROOF
.32 ACP cal. (w/Waffenampt
    proofs) .... NiB $1355 Ex $1010 Gd $555
.32 ACP cal. (w/Eagle "C" or "Eagle F" Nazi Police
    markings) .... NiB $2010 Ex $1755 Gd $1010
.32 cal. (w/Eagle "F"
    markings) .... NiB $910 Ex $780 Gd $555
.22 LR cal. (w/Eagle "N" Nazi markings) ..... NiB $1510 Ex $1255 Gd $805
.32 cal. (w/NSKK markings)..NiB $5510 Ex $4510 Gd $2510
.32 cal. (w/RFV markings) ..NiB $2510 Ex $2010 Gd $1010
w/RJ markings, .32 ACP .... NiB $2510 Ex $2210 Gd $1110
w/SA markings,
    .22 LR or .32 ACP....... NiB $3260 Ex $2655 Gd $1680
.380 cal. (w/Waffenampt
    proofs) .... NiB $3510 Ex $3010 Gd $2010

NOTE: *Post-War PP models were similar to Pre-War models. Imported from 1963 to 2000. All German mfg. except where* noted that Manurhin, a manufacturer in France, produced a licensed version of the PP from 1952 to 1986.

POST-WAR COMMERCIAL MODELS
.22 LR . . . . NiB $810 Ex $655 Gd $380
.32 ACP . . . . NiB $655 Ex $505 Gd $300
.380 ACP . . . . NiB $755 Ex $605 Gd $355
Manurhin mfg., all calibers . . . . NiB $580 Ex $505 Gd $405

MODEL PP SPORT DA AUTOMATIC PISTOL
Target version of the Model PP. Caliber: .22 LR. Eight-round magazine, 5.75- to 7.75 in. bbl. w/adjustable sights. Blue or nickel finish. Checkered plastic grips w/thumbrest. Made 1953-70.

Walther manufacture . . . . NiB $1233 Ex $730 Gd $464
Manurhin manufacture . . . . NiB $990 Ex $834 Gd $561
C Model (comp./SA) . . . . NiB $1294 Ex $920 Gd $668
w/nickel finish, add $204
w/matched bbl., weights, add $100

MODEL PP DELUXE ENGRAVED
These elaborately engraved models are available in blued finish, silver- or gold-plated.

Blued finish . . . . NiB $1430 Ex $1130 Gd $840
Chrome finish . . . . NiB $1455 Ex $1130 Gd $790
Silver-plated . . . . NiB $1755 Ex $1210 Gd $890
Gold-plated . . . . NiB $1955 Ex $1510 Gd $1030
w/ivory grips, add $300
w/presentation case, add $500
.22 caliber, add 5%

MODEL PP LIGHTWEIGHT
Same as standard Model PP except about 25 percent lighter due to use of aluminum alloys (Dural). Values 40 percent higher. (See individual listings).

MODEL PP SUPER
DA PISTOL . . . . NiB $1066 Ex $831 Gd $623
Caliber: 9x18mm. Seven-round magazine, 3.6-in. bbl., 6.9 in. overall. Weight: 30 oz. Fixed sights. Blued finish. Checkered plastic grips. Made 1973-79.

MODEL PP 7.65MM
PRESENTATION . . . . NiB $2100 Ex $1596 Gd $1214
Made of soft aluminum alloy in green-gold color, these pistols were not intended to be fired.

MODEL PPK DOUBLE-ACTION AUTOMATIC PISTOL
Polizeipistole Kriminal (Police Pistol - Detective). Calibers: .22 LR (5.6mm), .25 Auto (6.35mm), .32 Auto (7.65mm), .380 Auto (9mm). Seven-round magazine, (6-rnd. in .380), 3.25-in. bbl., 5.88 in. overall. Weight: 19 oz. Fixed sights. Blued finish. Checkered plastic grips.

NOTE: After both World Wars, the Walther manufacturing facility was required to cease the production of "restricted" firearms as part of the armistice agreements. Following WW II, Walther moved its manufacturing facility from the original location in Zella/Mehilis, Germany to Ulm/Donau. In 1950, the firm Manufacture de Machines du Haut Rhine at Mulhouse, France was licensed by Walther and started production of PP and PPK models at the Manurhin facility in 1952. The MK II Walthers as produced at Manurhin were imported into the U.S. until 1968 when CGA importation requirements restricted the PPK firearm configuration from further importation. As a result, Walther developed the PPK/S to conform to the new regulations and licensed Interarms to produce the firearm in the U.S. from 1986-99. From 1984-86, Manurhin imported PP and

PPK/S type firearms under the Manurhin logo. Additional manufacturing facilities (both licensed & unlicensed) that produced PP and PPK type firearms were established after WW II in various locations and other countries including: China, France, Hungary, Korea, Romania and Turkey. In 1996, Walther was sold to UmarEx Sportwaffen GmbH and manufacturing facilities were relocated in Arnsberg, Germany. In 1999, Walther formed a partnership with Smith and Wesson and selected Walther firearms were licensed for production in the U.S.

NOTE: "K" and "W" suffix variants had either a "K" or a "W" following the serial number. The "K" which started in 1938 is common, but the "W" is less common and fetches more. A 7-digit serial number was used prior to the "K" suffix. It is unclear and has been lost as to what the suffixes stand for or why Walther created them.

COMMERCIAL MODEL (PREWAR MFG 1930–40)
NOTE: Pre-War production was 1930-40. Finishes included blue, nickel, chrome or gold.

.22 cal. . . . . NiB $2560 Ex $1735 Gd $1509
.25 cal. . . . . NiB $15,000 Ex $10,000 Gd $4500
.32 cal. . . . . NiB $1755 Ex $1255 Gd $705
.380 cal. . . . . NiB $4530 Ex $2505 Gd $1505
w/7-digit serial number . . . . NiB $2255 Ex $1755 Gd $1010
w/"K" suffix (.32 ACP) . . . . . NiB $2510 Ex $2020 Gd $1210
w/"W" suffix (.32 ACP) . . . . . NiB $1510 Ex $1255 Gd $855
w/90 degree safety . . . . NiB $2010 Ex $1510 Gd $930
w/bottom release magazine latch, add 60%

NOTE: Wartime production models were manufactured 1940–45. Early models had a 90-degree safety lever that was changed to 60 degrees on later models. Pre-1940 models were marked with "Crown N" proof; after April 1940 models were marked with "Eagle N" proof mark, which was the standard Nazi commercial proof mark. The proof mark is located on the right side of the slide below the ejection port and on the bbl. breech block. There were numerous proof marks and markings used for specific government agencies. DRP mark is Deutsche Reichspost or German Postal Service. PDM mark is Polizeidirekton Munchen or Munich Police Department. RFV mark indicates Reichsfinzverwaltung or Reich Finance Office. RZM mark on left side of slide is for the Reichzeugmeisterel or Reich Purchasing Office. Party Leader pistols have black or brown grips that have a large Nazi Eagle clutching a Swastika encircled by a wreath at the top on both sides in lieu of the Walther banner. These pistols were presented to high ranking Nazi officers of the NSDAP for meritorious service to the Nazi Party. Paragraph or pantagraph slide models have the serial number rollmarked on the frame and in front of the slide serrations. Verchromt models had a plating that gave the PPK a dull gray appearance; very few were produced.

COMMERCIAL, POLICE AND MILITARY MODELS (WARTIME MFG 1940-45)

POLICE & MILITARY MODELS
w/"Eagle C" proof (.32 ACP,
Nazi Police issue) . . . . NiB $2255 Ex $1755 Gd $905

**Walther PP
(Prewar)**

w/"Eagle F" proof (.32 ACP,
aluminum frame) . . . . NiB $3005 Ex $2505 Gd $1505
w/DRP mark (.32 ACP) . . . . . NiB $3255 Ex $2855 Gd $1630
w/PDM mark (.32 ACP,
bottom release mag) . . . . . NiB $3505 Ex $3010 Gd $1630
w/RFV mark (.32 ACP) . . . . . NiB $3505 Ex $3010 Gd $1630
w/RZM mark (.32 ACP) . . . . . NiB $3205 Ex $2755 Gd $1755
Pantagraph variation . . . . . . NiB $2255 Ex $1830 Gd $1255
Party Leader (.32 ACP) . . . . . NiB $8510 Ex $6810 Gd $3655
w/Waffenamt proof
(.32 ACP) . . . . NiB $2810 Ex $2155 Gd $1210
w/Verchromt finish
(.32 ACP) . . . . NiB $4510 Ex $3855 Gd $2555
w/Verchromt finish
(.380 ACP) . . . . NiB $6765 Ex $5780 Gd $3830
w/Dural frame (.22 LR) . . . . . NiB $3510 Ex $3010 Gd $1910
w/Dural frame (.32 ACP) . . . . NiB $2510 Ex $1755 Gd $955
w/Dural frame (.380 ACP) . . NiB $6010 Ex $4810 Gd $2810

COMMERCIAL MODEL (POST-WAR MFG 1945-68)
.22 cal. (German manufacture) . . . NiB $1076 Ex $945 Gd $411
.32 cal. (German manufacture) . . . NiB $850 Ex $601 Gd $383
.380 cal. (German manufacture) . . NiB $1091 Ex $591 Gd $498
.22 cal. (French manufacture) . . NiB $2212 Ex $924 Gd $538
.32 cal. (French manufacture) . . NiB $857 Ex $651 Gd $437
.380 cal. (French manufacture) . . NiB $1173 Ex $839 Gd $452
.22, .32 or .380 cal. (other foreign
manuf.) . . . . NiB $332 Ex $281 Gd $201

COMMERCIAL MODEL (U.S. PRODUCTION 1986-2001)
.380 cal. (w/blue finish) . . . . . . NiB $658 Ex $499 Gd $403
.380 cal. (w/nickel finish) . . . . . NiB $658 Ex $499 Gd $403
.32 or .380 Cal. (stainless steel) . . NiB $658 Ex $499 Gd $403
(U.S. PRODUCTION 1996-99 by Emco, Gadsden, AL)
.32 and .380 cal. (stainless finish) . . NiB $480 Ex $605 Gd $370
(U.S. PRODUCTION 2001-12 by S&W)
.380 cal. (blued or stainless finish) . . NiB $455 Ex $355 Gd $300
(U.S. PRODUCTION 2019-date by Walther Arms, Forth Smith, AR)
.380 cal. (blued or stainless finish) . . NiB $630 Ex $580 Gd $400

MODEL PPK DELUXE ENGRAVED
These elaborately engraved models are available in blued finish, chrome-, silver- or gold-plated.
Blued finish . . . . NiB $1932 Ex $1543 Gd $1199
Chrome-plated . . . . NiB $3087 Ex $2156 Gd $1779
Silver-plated . . . . NiB $2234 Ex $1789 Gd $1418
Gold-plated . . . . NiB $2567 Ex $1979 Gd $1598
w/ivory grips, add $306
w/Presentation case, add $791
.22 cal, add $75
.25 cal, add $128
.380 cal, add $110

MODEL PPK LIGHTWEIGHT
Same as standard Model PPK except about 25 percent lighter due to aluminum alloys. Values 50 percent higher.

MODEL PPK 7.65MM
PRESENTATION . . . . NiB $1856 Ex $1418 Gd $966
Made of soft aluminum alloy in green-gold color, these pistols were not intended to be fired.

MODEL PPK/S DA AUTOMATIC PISTOL
Designed to meet the requirements of the U.S. Gun Control Act of 1968, this model has the frame of the PP and the shorter slide and bbl., of the PPK. Overall length: 6.1 in. Weight: 23 oz. Other specifications are the same as those of standard PPK except steel frame only. German, French and U.S. production

1971 to date. U.S. version made by Interarms 1978-99, Smith & Wesson production from 2002-09.
.22 cal. (German manufacture) . . NiB $1336 Ex $1016 Gd $660
.32 cal. (German manufacture) . . NiB $997 Ex $789 Gd $497
.380 cal. (German
manufacture) . . . . NiB $1321 Ex $997 Gd $577
.22 cal. (French manufacture) . . . NiB $968 Ex $760 Gd $561
.32 cal. (French manufacture) . . . NiB $973 Ex $781 Gd $577
.380 cal. (French manufacture) . . . . NiB $944 Ex $632 Gd $500
(U.S. PRODUCTION 1983-99 by Emco, Gadsden, AL)
.32 and .380 cal.
(stainless finish) . . . . NiB $755 Ex $605 Gd $400
(U.S. PRODUCTION 2001-12 by S&W)
.380 cal. (blued or
stainless finish) . . . . NiB $455 Ex $355 Gd $300
(U.S. PRODUCTION 2019-date by Walther Arms,
Forth Smith, AR)
.380 cal. (blued or
stainless finish) . . . . NiB $630 Ex $580 Gd $400
.22 LR cal. (blued or
stainless finish) . . . . NiB $340 Ex $300 Gd $295

NOTE: *Interarms (Interarmco) acquired a license from Walther in 1978 to manufacturer PP and PPK models at the Ranger Manufacturing Co., Inc. in Gadsden, Alabama. In 1988 the Ranger facility was licensed as EMCO and continued to produce Walther firearms for Interarms until 1996. From 1996-99, Black Creek in Gadsden, Alabama, produced Walther pistols for Interarms. From 2002-12, Smith & Wesson acquired manufacturing rights for Walther firearms at the Black Creek facility. In 2012 Walther Arms, Inc. located in Fort Smith, AR, imports all Walther products.*

MODELS PPK/S DELUXE ENGRAVED
These elaborately engraved models are available in blued finish, chrome-, silver- or gold-plated.
Blued finish . . . . NiB $1634 Ex $1216 Gd $1094
Chrome-plated . . . . NiB $1552 Ex $1268 Gd $976
Silver-plated . . . . NiB $1755 Ex $1296 Gd $966
Gold-plated . . . . NiB $1889 Ex $1566 Gd $1034

NOTE: *The following Walther pistols are now manufactured by Carl Walther, Waffenfabrik, Ulm/Donau, Germany.*

SELF-LOADING
SPORT PISTOL . . . . NiB $866 Ex $856 Gd $546
Caliber: .22 LR. 10-rnd. magazine, bbl. lengths: 6- and 9-in. 9.88 in. overall w/6-in. bbl. Target sights. Blued finish. One-piece, wood or plastic grips, checkered. Intro. in 1932.

MODEL FREE PISTOL . . . . . NiB $1533 Ex $1367 Gd $1159
Single-Shot. Caliber: .22 LR. 11.7-in. heavy bbl., Weight: 48 oz. Adj. grips and target sights w/electronic trigger. Importation disc. 1991.

MODEL GSP TARGET AUTOMATIC PISTOL
Calibers: .22 LR, .32 S&W Long Wadcutter. Five-round magazine, 4.5-in. bbl., 11.8 in. overall. Weights: 44.8 oz. (.22 cal.) or 49.4 oz. (.32 cal.). Adj. target sights. Black finish. Walnut thumbrest grips w/adj. handrest. Made 1969-94.
.22 LR . . . . NiB $1598 Ex $1432 Gd $889
.32 S&W Long Wadcutter . . NiB $2773 Ex $2513 Gd $2122
Conversion unit. .22 Short or .22 LR, add $1071

MODEL OSP RAPID
FIRE TARGET PISTOL . . . . . NiB $1744 Ex $1509 Gd $1345
Caliber: .22 Short. Five-round magazine, 4.5-in. bbl., 11.8 in. overall. Weight: 42.3 oz. Adj. target sights. Black finish. Walnut

Walther Free Pistol

Walther P38K

Walther P1

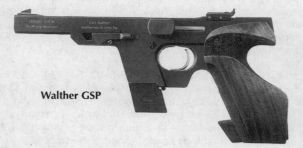

Walther GSP

Walther P99

Walther P88

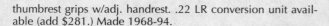

Walther P5

Walther TPH

thumbrest grips w/adj. handrest. .22 LR conversion unit available (add $281.) Made 1968-94.

MODEL P4 (P38-LV) . . . . NiB $855 Ex $712 Gd $448
Similar to P38 except has an uncocking device instead of a manual safety. Caliber: 9mm Para. 4.3-in. bbl., 7.9 in. overall. Other general specifications same as for current model P38. Made 1974-82.

MODEL P5 . . . . NiB $1955 Ex $1510 Gd $1030
Alloy frame w/frame-mounted decocking levers. Caliber: 9mm Para. Eight-round magazine, 3.5-in. bbl., 7 in. overall. Weight: 28 oz. blued finish. Checkered walnut or synthetic grips. Made 1997 to date.
P5 Compact (3.1-in. bbl.,
** 1987-date) . . . . NiB $2500 Ex $2000 Gd $1000**

MODEL P1
Postwar commercial version of the P38, has light alloy frame. Calibers: .22 LR, 7.65mm Luger, 9mm Para. Eight-round magazine, bbl., lengths: 5.1-in. in .22 caliber, 4.9- in. in 7.65mm and 9mm, 8.5 in. overall. Weight: 28.2 oz. Fixed sights. Nonreflective black finish. Checkered plastic grips. Made 1957-89. Note: The "P1" was W. German Armed Forces official pistol.
.22 LR . . . . NiB $805 Ex $644 Gd $433
Other calibers . . . . NiB $806 Ex $610 Gd $398

MODEL P38 DELUXE ENGRAVED
Elaborately engraved, available in blued or chrome-, silver- or gold-plated finish.
Blued finish . . . . NiB $2077 Ex $1566 Gd $1028
Chrome-plated . . . . NiB $1776 Ex $1432 Gd $998
Silver-plated . . . . NiB $1712 Ex $1429 Gd $1043
Gold-plated . . . . NiB $1987 Ex $1603 Gd $1163

MODEL P38K . . . . NiB $3210 Ex $2410 Gd $1080
Short-barreled version of current P38, the "K" standing for "kurz" (meaning short). Same general specifications as standard model except 2.8-in. bbl., 6.3 in. overall, weight: 27.2 oz. Front sight is slide mounted. Caliber: 9mm Para. Made 1974-80.

MODEL P88 . . . . NiB $1132 Ex $988 Gd $774
DA/SA. Caliber: 9mm Para. 15-rnd. magazine, 4-in. bbl., 7.38 in. overall. Weight: 31.5 oz. Blade front sight, adj. rear. Checkered black synthetic grips. External hammer w/ambidExtrous decocking levers. Alloy frame w/matte blued steel slide. Made 1987-93.

MODEL P88 DA COMPACT
Similar to the standard P88 Model except w/10- or 13-rnd. magazine, 3.8-in. bbl., 7.1 in. overall. Weight: 29 oz. Imported from 1993 to 2003.
Model P88
** (early importation) . . . . NiB $1088 Ex $975 Gd $648**
Model P88
** (post 1994 importation) . . . . NiB $1088 Ex $975 Gd $648**

MODEL P99 . . . . NiB $756 Ex $576 Gd $486
Calibers: 9mm Para., .40 S&W or 9x21mm. 10-rnd. magazine, 4-in. bbl., 7.2 in. overall. Weight: 22-25 oz. AmbidExtrous magazine release, decocking lever and 3-function safety. Interchangeable front post sight, micro-adj. rear. Polymer grip-frame w/blued slide. Imported from 1995 to date.

MODEL TP . . . . NiB $955 Ex $755 Gd $355
Semiauto. SA. Updated Model 9. Light alloy frame. Cal.: .22 LR, .25 ACP; 6-rnd. magazine. Bbl.: 2.6-in. Overall: 5.38 in. Weight: 12 oz. Fixed sights. Blued finish. Checkered plastic grips. Heel magazine release. Made 1961-71.
.25 ACP, subtract. $200

MODEL TPH
DA/SA. Light alloy frame. Calibers: .22 LR, .25 ACP (6.35mm). Six-round magazine, 2.25-in. bbl., 5.38 in. overall. Weight: 14 oz. Fixed sights. Blued finish. Checkered plastic grips. Made 1968 to date. Note: Few Walther-made models reached the U.S. because of import restrictions. A U.S.-made version was mfd. by Interarms from 1986 to 1999.
German model . . . . NiB $1770 Ex $1540 Gd $880
U.S. model . . . . NiB $900 Ex $800 Gd $655

NOTE: *The Walther Olympia Model pistols were manufactured 1952-63 by Hämmerli AG Jagd-und Sportwaffenfabrik, Lenzburg, Switzerland, and marketed as "Hämmerli-Walther." See Hämmerli listings for specific data.*

OLYMPIA MODEL 200 AUTO PISTOL,
1952 TYPE . . . . NiB $729 Ex $612 Gd $453
Similar to 1936 Walther Olympia Funfkampf Model.
Note: For Hammerli-Walther Models—200, 201, 202, 203, 204, and 205—see listings under Hammerli Section.

- CURRENT MFG. -

MODEL CCP . . . . NiB $450 Ex $240 Gd $190
Semiauto. Striker-fire. Caliber: 9mm Parabellum, 8-rnd. magazine. 3.54-in. bbl. Weight: 22.3 oz. Steel slide, polymer frame w/ ergonomic Walther grip, accessory rail. Sights: low profile adj. Finish: black or stainless. Features SOFTCOIL gas-delay blowback system. Made 2014–18.
CCP M2 (tool-less takedown,
    2018-date) . . . . NiB $465 Ex $405 Gd $315

MODEL CREED . . . . NiB $355 Ex $330 Gd $255
Semiauto. Short recoil action. Pre-cocked DA trigger. Cal.: 9mm, 16-rnd. magazine. Bbl.: 4-in. Weight: 27 oz. Polymer frame, steel slide. Ambi. magazine release. Mfg. 2016-18.

MODEL P22 . . . . NiB $380 Ex $280 Gd $180
Semiauto. DA/SA. Caliber: .22 LR, 10-rnd. magazine. 3.4- or 5-in. bbl. Weight: 17 or 20 oz. Polymer frame, steel slide. Sights: adj. rear. Finish: matte black slide/green frame, black slide/black frame, or nickel slide/black frame. Made 2002-20.
laser sight, add $30
nickel finish, add. $65
Military model
    (black slide/tan frame). . . . . NiB $380 Ex $280 Gd $180
Tactical model (3.25-in. thrd. bbl.). . NiB $450 Ex $350 Gd $255
Target model (5-in. bbl.) . . . . . . NiB $480 Ex $380 Gd $230

PDP SERIES
Semiauto. Striker-fired. Polymer frame w/accessory rail. Caliber: 9mm. Capacity: 15 rnd. magazine. Barrel: 4- or 4.5-in. Textured polymer grip, modular backstrap. 3-dot sight, optic ready. Length: 7.5 in. overall. Weight: 24.4 oz. unloaded. Black finish. Mfg. 2021-date.
Compact model (4-in. bbl.). . . . . NiB $650 Ex $600 Gd $540
Full Size model (4.5-in. bbl.). . . . NiB $650 Ex $600 Gd $540

MODEL PK380 . . . . NiB $399 Ex $355 Gd $230
Semiauto. DA/SA. Caliber: .380 ACP, 8-rnd. magazine. 43.6-in. bbl. Weight: 21 oz. Steel slide, polymer frame. Ambidextrous slide safety. Sights: fixed 3-dot. Finish: black or nickel slide, black frame. Accessory rail. Made 2009 to date.
nickel finish, add. $50
laser sight, add $50

MODEL PPQ . . . . NiB $600 Ex $530 Gd $385
Semiauto. Striker-fire. Caliber: 9mm Parabellum or .40 S&W, 15/12 (9mm) or 17/14 (.40) rnd. magazine. 4-in. bbl. Weight: 24.5 oz. Steel slide, polymer frame with interchangeable backstraps. Ambidextrous slide and magazine release. Sights: adjustable. Finish: black. Loaded-chamber indicator, accessory rail, Quick Defense Trigger (Glock style). Mfg. 2011-12.

MODEL PPQ M2. . . . . NiB $555 Ex $430 Gd $330
Similar to PPQ except w/4-, 4.1- (.40 S&W only), 4.6- (thread bbl., 9mm only), or 5-in. bbl. Ambidextrous magazine release button. Sights: low-profile combat. Finish: black. Made 2013 to date.
5-in. bbl. model, add $105
PPQ M2 Navy (4.6-in. thrd. bbl.), add $55
PPQ M2 .22 LR. . . . . NiB $430 Ex $340 Gd $260
PPQ M2 SD Tactical .22 LR . . . NiB $450 Ex $350 Gd $260
PPQ M2 Sub-Compact (3.5-in. bbl.,
    10-rnd. mag.) . . . . NiB $475 Ex $410 Gd $320
PPQ M2 Sub-Compact LE (3.5-in. bbl., night sights,
    10-rnd. mag.) . . . . NiB $485 Ex $420 Gd $330
PPQ M2 Sub-Compact XS NS (3.5-in. bbl., night sights,
    10-rnd. mag.) . . . . NiB $485 Ex $420 Gd $330

MODEL Q4 SERIES
Similar to PPQ M2 except w/4.6-in. threaded bbl. Caliber: 9mm w/15-rnd. magazine. Weight: 25 oz. Receiver: Polymer. Sights: Adj. rear, fiber optic front. Ambi. slide stop and paddle style mag. release. Finish: Matte black.
M1 . . . . NiB $699 Ex $600 Gd $470
M2 (button style mag.
    release) . . . . NiB $699 Ex $600 Gd $470

MODEL Q4 STEEL FRAME SERIES
Similar to PPQ M2 except w/steel frame. 4-in. bbl. Caliber: 9mm w/15-rnd. magazine. Weight: 39.7 oz. Receiver: steel. Sights: fixed. Ambi. slide stop and button style mag. release. Finish: Matte black. Mfg. 2020–date.
Steel Frame . . . . NiB $1260 Ex $1100 Gd $900
Steel Frame OR (Adj. rear, fiber optic front/
    optic ready) . . . . NiB $1499 Ex $1400 Gd $900

MODEL Q5 MATCH SERIES
Similar to PPQ M2 except w/5-in. bbl. Caliber: 9mm w/15-rnd. magazine. Weight: 27.9 oz. Receiver: Polymer or steel. Lightened slide cuts. Sights: Adj. rear, fiber optic front. Finish: Matte black, blue trigger. Made 2016 to date.
polymer receiver. . . . . NiB $755 Ex $605 Gd $455
Steel Frame model (steel frame,
    2019 to date). . . . . NiB $1455 Ex $1280 Gd $1000
Steel Frame Pro model (steel frame, removable extended mag
    well, 2019 to date) . . . . . . NiB $1580 Ex $1385 Gd $1080

MODEL PPS CLASSIC . . . . **NiB $530 Ex $455 Gd $355**
Semiauto. Striker-fire. Caliber: 9mm Parabellum or .40
S&W, 6/7/8 (9mm) or 5/6/7 (.40) rnd. magazine. 3.2-in. bbl.
Weight: 21 oz. Steel slide, polymer frame with interchangeable backstraps. Ambidextrous magazine release. Sights:
fixed. Finish: black. Cocking indicator, accessory rail, Glock
style trigger, 3 magazine sizes. Mfg. 2008-18.

MODEL PPS M2 . . . . **NiB $465 Ex $405 Gd $315**
Similar to PPS except push-button magazine release, ergonomic Walther grip, no accessory rail. Made 2016 to date.

MODEL PPX . . . . **NiB $450 Ex $400 Gd $265**
Semiauto. DAO, hammer fired. Caliber: 9mm Parabellum or
.40 S&W, 16- (9mm) or 14- (.40) rnd. magazine. 4- or 4.6-in.
bbl. Weight: 21 oz. Steel slide, polymer frame. Ambidextrous
magazine release, slide stop. Sights: low profile 3-dot fixed
polymer. Finish: black. Accessory rail. Made 2013–16.

MODEL SP22 SERIES
Semiauto. SA. Caliber: .22 LR, 10-rnd. magazine. 4-in. bbl.
Weight: 27 oz. Steel slide, polymer frame. Sights: adj. target.
Made 2008–2010.
M1 . . . . **NiB $335 Ex $270 Gd $205**
M2 (6-in. bbl.) . . . . **NiB $355 Ex $325 Gd $255**
M3 (top and bottom
  accessory rails) . . . . **NiB $430 Ex $355 Gd $265**
M4 (6-in. match bbl., 32.2 oz.,
  wood target grip.) . . . . **NiB $680 Ex $605 Gd $455**

WARNER — Norwich, CT
Warner Arms Corp. or Davis-Warner Arms Co.

**INFALLIBLE POCKET
AUTOMATIC PISTOL** . . . . **NiB $507 Ex $356 Gd $253**
Caliber: .32 Auto. Seven-round magazine, 3-in. bbl., 6.5 in.
overall. Weight: About 24 oz. Fixed sights. Blued finish. Hard
rubber grips. Made 1917-19.

WEBLEY & SCOTT LTD. — London and Birmingham, England

**MODEL 1909 9MM MILITARY
& POLICE AUTOMATIC** . . . **NiB $2090 Ex $1465 Gd $1288**
Caliber: 9mm Browning Long. Eight-round magazine, 8 in.
overall. Weight: 32 oz. Fixed sights. Blued finish. Checkered
Vulcanite grips. Made 1909-30.

**MODEL 1907 HAMMER
AUTOMATIC** . . . . **NiB $1006 Ex $866 Gd $207**
Caliber: .25 Automatic. Six-round magazine, overall length:
4.75 in. Weight: 11.75 oz. No sights. Blued finish. Checkered
Vulcanite grips. Made 1906-40.

**MODEL 1912 HAMMERLESS
AUTOMATIC** . . . . **NiB $1500 Ex $1306 Gd $1233**
Caliber: .25 Automatic. Six-round magazine, overall length:
4.25 in., weight: 9.75 oz. Fixed sights. Blued finish. Checkered
Vulcanite grips. Made 1909-40.

**MARK I 455
AUTOMATIC PISTOL** . . . . . **NiB $2505 Ex $1988 Gd $1600**
Caliber: .455 Webley Auto. Seven-round magazine, 5-in. bbl.,
8.5 in. overall. Weight: About 39 oz. Fixed sights. Blued finish.

**Webley 9MM
Military Police Automatic**

**Webley Mark III
38 Military & Police Revolver**

**Webley-Fosbery Automatic
Revolver**

Checkered Vulcanite grips. Made 1913-31. Reissued during
WWII. Total production about 9,300. Note: Mark I No. 2 is
same pistol w/adj. rear sight and modified manual safety.

**MARK III 38 MILITARY & POLICE
DA REVOLVER** . . . . **NiB $974 Ex $789 Gd $633**
Hinged frame. DA. Caliber: .38 S&W. Six-round cylinder, bbl.
lengths: 3- and 4-in. 9.5 in. overall (w/ 4-in. bbl.). Weight: 21
oz. (w/ 4-in. bbl.). Fixed sights. Blued finish. Checkered walnut
or Vulcanite grips. Made 1897-1945.

**MARK IV 22 CALIBER
TARGET REVOLVER** . . . . **NiB $806 Ex $691 Gd $386**
Same frame and general appearance as Mark IV .38. Caliber:
.22 LR. Six-round cylinder, 6-in. bbl., 10.13 in. overall. Weight:
34 oz. Target sights. Blued finish. Checkered grips. Disc. in
1945.

**MARK IV 38 MILITARY & POLICE
DA REVOLVER** . . . . **NiB $806 Ex $691 Gd $386**
Identical in appearance to the double-action Mark IV .22 w/
hinged frame except chambered for .38 S&W. Six-round cylinder, bbl. length: 3-, 4- and 5-in.; 9.13 in. overall (w/ 5-in.
bbl.). Weight: 27 oz. (w/ 5-in. bbl.). Fixed sights. Blued finish.
Checkered grips. Made 1929-57.

**MARK VI NO. 1 BRITISH SERVICE
DA REVOLVER** . . . . **NiB $691 Ex $567 Gd $478**
Hinged frame. Caliber: 455 Webley. Six-round cylinder, bbl.
lengths: 4-, 6- and 7.5-in.; 11.25 in. overall (w/ 6-in. bbl.).
Weight: 38 oz. (w/ 6-in. bbl.). Fixed sights. Blued finish.
Checkered walnut or Vulcanite grips. Made 1915-47.

MARK VI 22
TARGET REVOLVER . . . . **NiB $1266 Ex $1096 Gd $909**
Same frame and general appearance as the Mark VI 455. Caliber: .22 LR. Six-round cylinder, 6-in. bbl., 11.25 in. overall. Weight: 40 oz. Target sights. Blued finish. Checkered walnut or Vulcanite grips. Disc. in 1945.

METROPOLITAN POLICE
AUTOMATIC PISTOL . . . . . **NiB $1629 Ex $1528 Gd $1266**
Calibers: .32 Auto, .380 Auto. Eight-round (.32) or 7-rnd. (.380) magazine, 3.5-in. bbl., 6.25 in. overall. weight: 20 oz. Fixed sights. Blued finish. Checkered Vulcanite grips. Made 1906-40 (.32) and 1908 to 1920 (.380).

R.I.C. MODELS DA REVOLVER **NiB $950 Ex $700 Gd $500**
Royal Irish Constabulary or Bulldog Model. Solid frame. Caliber: .455 Webley. Five-round cylinder, 2.25-in. bbl., weight: 21 oz. Fixed sights. Blued finish. Checkered walnut or vulcanite grips. Made 1897-1939.

SEMIAUTO
SINGLE-SHOT PISTOL . . . . . **NiB $1090 Ex $ 916 Gd $617**
Similar in appearance to the Webley Metropolitan Police Automatic, this pistol is "Semiauto" in the sense that the fired case is Extracted and ejected and the hammer cocked as in a blow-back automatic pistol; it is loaded singly and the slide manually operated in loading. Caliber: .22 Long, 4.5- or 9-in. bbl., 10.75 in. overall (w/ 9-in. bbl.). Weight: 24 oz. (w/ 9-in. bbl.). Adj. sights. Blued finish. Checkered Vulcanite grips. Made 1911-27.

SINGLE-SHOT
TARGET PISTOL . . . . **NiB $1588 Ex $1469 Gd $1190**
Hinge frame. Caliber: .22 LR. 10-in. bbl., 15 in. overall. Weight: 37 oz. Fixed sights on earlier models, current production has adj. rear sight. Blued finish. Checkered walnut or Vulcanite grips. Made 1909.

WEBLEY-FOSBERY AUTOMATIC REVOLVER
Hinged frame. Recoil action revolves cylinder and cocks hammer. Caliber: 455 Webley. Six-round cylinder, 6-in. bbl., 12 in. overall. Weight: 42 oz. Fixed or adjustable sights. Blued finish. Checkered walnut grips. Made 1901-39. Note: A few were produced in caliber .38 Colt Auto w/an 8-shot cylinder (very rare).
1901 model. . . . . **NiB $12,600 Ex $8600 Gd $5500**
1902 model .38
  Colt (8-rnd.), add **300%**
1903 model. . . . . **NiB $10,000 Ex $7600 Gd $4600**
Target model w/adjustable sights, add **20%**

WESSON FIREARMS CO., INC. — Palmer, MA
Renamed Dan Wesson Firearms, Inc. Acquired by CZ-USA in 2005 and renamed Dan Wesson. Also see Dan Wesson for current production.

NOTE: *Models with a three digit model number that begins with a "7" are starinless steel models.*

MODEL 8 SERVICE
Same general specifications as Model 14 except caliber .38 Special. Made 1971-75. Values same as for Model 14.

MODEL 8-2 SERVICE
Similar as Model 14-2 except caliber .38 Special. Made 1975 to date. Values same as for Model 14-2.

MODEL 9 TARGET
Same as Model 15 except caliber .38 Special. Made 1971-75. Values same as for Model 15.

MODEL 9-2 TARGET
Same as Model 15-2 except caliber .38 Special. Made 1975 to date. Values same as for Model 15-2.

MODEL 9-2H HEAVY BARREL
Same general specifications as Model 15-2H except caliber .38 Special. Made 1975 to date. Values same as for Model 15-2H. Disc. 1983.

MODEL 9-2HV VR HEAVY BARREL
Same as Model 15-2HV except caliber .38 Special. Made 1975 to date. Values same as for Model 15-2HV.

MODEL 9-2V VR
Same as Model 15-2V except caliber .38 Special. Made 1975 to date. Values same as for Model 15-2H.

MODEL 11 SERVICE DA REVOLVER
Caliber: .357 Magnum. Six-round cylinder. bbl. lengths: 2.5-, 4-, 6-in. interchangeable bbl. assemblies, 9 in. overall (w/ 4-in. bbl.). Weight: 38 oz. (w/ 4-in. bbl.). Fixed sights. Blued finish. Interchangeable grips. Made 1970-71. Note: The Model 11 has an External bbl. nut.
w/one bbl. assembly and grip . . **NiB $274 Ex $180 Gd $101**
Extra bbl. assembly, add **$75**
Extra grip, add **$50**

MODEL 12 TARGET
Same general specifications as Model 11 except has adj. sights. Made 1970-71.
w/one-bbl. assembly and grip . . **NiB $290 Ex $204 Gd $135**
Extra bbl. assembly, add **$75**
Extra grip, add **$50**

MODEL 14 SERVICE DA REVOLVER
Caliber: .357 Magnum. Six-round cylinder, bbl. length: 2.25-, 3.75, 5.75-in.; interchangeable bbl. assemblies, 9 in. overall (w/ 3.75-in. bbl.). Weight: 36 oz. (w/ 3.75-in. bbl.). Fixed sights. Blued or nickel finish. Interchangeable grips. Made 1971-75. Note: Model 14 has recessed bbl. nut.
w/one-bbl.
  assembly and grip . . . . **NiB $225 Ex $158 Gd $101**
Extra bbl. assembly, add **$61**
Extra grip, add **$25**

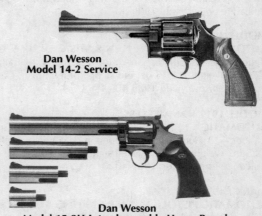

**Dan Wesson
Model 14-2 Service**

**Dan Wesson
Model 15-2H Interchangeable Heavy Barrels**

MODEL 14-2 SERVICE DA REVOLVER

Caliber: .357 Magnum. Six-round cylinder, bbl. lengths: 2.5-, 4-, 6-, 8-in.; interchangeable bbl. assemblies, 9.25 in. overall (w/ 4-in. bbl.) Weight: 34 oz. (w/ 4-in. bbl.). Fixed sights. Blued finish. Interchangeable grips. Made 1975-95. Note: Model 14-2 has recessed bbl. nut.

w/one bbl. assembly
(8 in.) and grip . . . . .NiB $270 Ex $204 Gd $158
w/one bbl. assembly
(other lengths) and grip . . . . NiB $270 Ex $204 Gd $158
Extra bbl. assembly, 8 in., add $75
Extra bbl. assembly,other lengths, add $75
Extra grip, add $50

MODEL 15 TARGET

Same general specifications as Model 14 except has adj. sights. Made 1971-75.
w/one bbl. assembly and grip. . NiB $306 Ex $230 Gd $190
Extra bbl. assembly, add $75
Extra grip, add $50

MODEL 15-2 TARGET

Same general specifications as Model 14-2 except has adj. rear sight and interchangeable blade front; also avail. w/10-, 12- or 15-in. bbl., Made 1975-95.
w/one bbl. assembly (8 in.) and grip. . . . NiB $362 Ex $289 Gd $187
w/one bbl. assembly (10 in.)
and grip . . . . NiB $362 Ex $289 Gd $187
w/one bbl. assembly
(12 in.)/grip. Disc. . . . . .NiB $362 Ex $289 Gd $187
w/one bbl. assembly
(15 in.)/grip. Disc. . . . . .NiB $362 Ex $289 Gd $187
w/one-bbl. assembly
(other lengths)/grip. . . . . . . .NiB $244 Ex $159 Gd $133
Extra bbl. assembly, add $75
Extra grip, add $50

MODEL 15-2H HEAVY BARREL

Same as Model 15-2 except has heavy bbl., assembly weight: w/ 4-in. bbl., 38 oz. Made 1975-83.
w/one bbl. assembly . . . . NiB $500 Ex $345 Gd $235
Extra bbl. assembly, add $75
Extra grip, add $50

MODEL 15-2HV VR HEAVY BARREL

Same as Model 15-2 except has VR heavy bbl. assembly; weight: (w/4-in. bbl.) 37 oz. Made 1975-95.
w/one bbl. assembly
(8 in.) and grip . . . . .NiB $303 Ex $240 Gd $162
w/one bbl. assembly
(10 in.) and grip . . . . .NiB $303 Ex $240 Gd $162
w/one bbl. assembly
(12 in.) and grip . . . . .NiB $303 Ex $240 Gd $162
w/one bbl. assembly
(15 in.) and grip . . . . .NiB $321 Ex $273 Gd $192
w/one bbl. assembly
(other lengths) and grip . . . . NiB $198 Ex $241 Gd $163
Extra bbl. assembly (8 in.), add. $75
Extra bbl. assembly (10 in.), add. $75
Extra bbl. assembly (12 in.), add. $75
Extra bbl. assembly (15 in.), add. $75
Extra bbl. assembly (other lengths), add $75
Extra grip, add $50

MODEL 15-2V VR

Same as Model 15-2 except has VR bbl. assembly, weight: 35 oz. (w/ 4-in. bbl.). Made 1975 to date. Values same as for 15-2H.

HUNTER PACS

Dan Wesson Hunter Pacs are offered in all Magnum calibers and include heavy VR 8-in. shrouded bbl., Burris scope mounts, bbl. changing tool in a case.

	NiB	Ex	Gd
HP22M-V	$893	$660	$473
HP22M-2	$733	$612	$447
HP722M-V	$843	$632	$439
HP722M-2	$806	$612	$408
HP32-V	$785	$571	$395
HP32-2	$691	$530	$425
HP732-V	$816	$597	$434
HP732-2	$755	$608	$449
HP15-V	$755	$608	$449
HP15-2	$780	$601	$437
HP715-V	$831	$654	$479
HP715-2	$755	$657	$478
HP41-V	$688	$556	$425
HP741-V	$841	$689	$495
HP741-2	$739	$607	$439
HP44-V	$884	$700	$536
HP44-2	$739	$607	$439
HP744-V	$933	$781	$576
HP744-2	$897	$738	$546
HP40-V	$616	$497	$366
HP40-2	$827	$691	$496
HP740-V	$988	$816	$590
HP740-2	$918	$729	$526
HP375-V	$595	$500	$356
HP375-2	$944	$786	$590
HP45-V	$734	$626	$439

WHITNEY FIREARMS COMPANY — Hartford, CT

NOTE: *Since 2004 the Whitney Wolverine design is currently manufactured by Olympic Arms, Olympia, WA. Also see Olympic Arms.*

WOLVERINE AUTOMATIC PISTOL

Dural frame/shell contains all operating components. Caliber: .22 LR. 10-rnd. magazine, 4.63-in. bbl., 9 in. overall. Weight: 23 oz. Partridge-type sights. Blued or nickel finish. Plastic grips. Made 1955-62.
Blue finish. . . . . .NiB $680 Ex $575 Gd $383
Nickel finish . . . . .NiB $1330 Ex $1080 Gd $610

WICHITA ARMS — Wichita, Kansas

CLASSIC PISTOL

Caliber: Chambered to order. Bolt-action, single-shot. 11.25-in. octagonal bbl., 18 in. overall. Weight: 78 oz. Open micro sights. Custom-grade checkered walnut stock. Blued finish. Made 1980-97.
Standard . . . . .NiB $3310 Ex $2546 Gd $2245

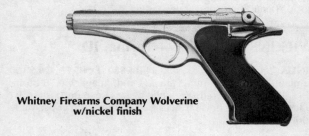

**Whitney Firearms Company Wolverine
w/nickel finish**

Wilkinson Arms
Linda

Witchta Arms
International Model

Zastava M88A

SHERRY.................NiB $274 Ex $188 Gd $126
Semiauto. Caliber: .22 LR. 8-rnd. magazine, 2.13-in. bbl., 4.38
in. overall. Weight: 9.25 oz. Crossbolt safety. Fixed sights. Blued
or blue-gold finish. Checkered composition grips. Made 2000-05.

DIANE.....................NiB $160 Ex $97 Gd $55
Semiauto. Caliber: .25 ACP, 6-rnd. magazine, 2.125-in. bbl.
Weight: 77 oz. Rear peep sight w/blade front. Blued finish.
Checkered composition grips. Made 2000-05.

ZASTAVA ARMS — Serbia

NOTE: *Established in 1853, Zastava firearms have been
imported into the U.S. by Century Arms International, EAA,
Remington and others.*

CZ999...................NiB $475 Ex $420 Gd $265
Semiauto. DA/SA. Caliber: 9mm, 10- or 15-rnd. magazine,
4.25-in. bbl., 7.8 in. overall. Weight: 33.5 oz. Fixed sight. Finish:
matte black. Checkered polymer grips. Made 2013 to date.
CZ999 Compact (3.5-in. bbl.)..NiB $475 Ex $420 Gd $265

M57....................NiB $310 Ex $300 Gd $180
Similar to Soviet TT. Semiauto. SA. Caliber: 7.62x25mm
Tokarev, 9-rnd. magazine, 4.5-in. bbl., 7.9 in. overall. Weight:
31 oz. Fixed sight. Finish: blued. Polymer grips. Manual safety.
Made 2013 to date.

M70A....................NiB $310 Ex $300 Gd $180
Similar to Soviet TT. Semiauto. SA. Caliber: 9mm, 9-rnd. maga-
zine, 4.5-in. bbl., 7.9 in. overall. Weight: 31 oz. Fixed sight.
Finish: blued. Polymer grips. Manual safety. Made 2013 to date.

M88.....................NiB $310 Ex $300 Gd $180
Semiauto. SA. Caliber: 9mm, 9-rnd. magazine, 3.8-in. bbl., 6.9
in. overall. Weight: 29.9 oz. Fixed sight. Finish: blued. Polymer
grips. Manual safety. Made 2013 to date.

**Presentation grade
(engraved)** ....NiB $5379 Ex $3916 Gd $2166

HUNTER PISTOL ....NiB $1433 Ex $1096 Gd $872
Bolt-action, single-shot. Calibers: .22 LR, .22 WRF, 7mm Super
Mag., 7-30 Waters, .30-30 Win., .32 H&R Mag., .357 Mag.,
.357 Super Mag. 10.5-in. bbl., 16.5 in. overall, weight: 60 oz.
No sights (scope mount only). Stainless steel finish. Walnut
stock. Made 1983-94.

INTERNATIONAL PISTOL.....NiB $733 Ex $567 Gd $453
Top-break, single-shot. SA. Calibers: 7-30 Waters, 7mm Super
Mag., 7R (.30-30 Win. necked to 7mm), .30-30 Win. .357 Mag.,
.357 Super Mag., .32 H&R Mag., .22 Mag., .22 LR. 10- and
14-in. bbl. (10.5 in. for centerfire calibers). Weight: 50-71 oz.
Partridge front sight, adj. rear. Walnut forend and grips.

MK-40 SILHOUETTE......NiB $1613 Ex $1407 Gd $1206
Calibers: .22-250, 7mm IHMSA, .308 Win. Bolt-action, single-
shot. 13-in. bbl., 19.5 in. overall. Weight: 72 oz. Wichita
Multi-Range sight system. Aluminum receiver w/blued bbl.,
gray Fiberthane glass stock. Made 1981-94.

SILHOUETTE PISTOL ....NiB $1587 Ex. $1453 Gd $1356
Calibers: .22-250, 7mm IHMSA 308 Win. Bolt-action, single-shot.
14.94-in. bbl., 21.38 in. overall. Weight: 72 oz. Wichita Multi-
Range sight system. Blued finish. Walnut or gray Fiberthane glass
stock. Walnut center or rear grip. Made 1979-94.

WILKINSON ARMS — Parma, ID

LINDA.....................NiB $680 Ex $557 Gd $360
Semiauto. Caliber: 9mm Para. 31-rnd. magazine, 8.25-in.
bbl., 12.25 in. overall. Weight: 77 oz. Rear peep sight w/
blade front. Blued finish. Checkered composition grips. Made
2000-05.

ZENITH FIREARMS — Afton, VA

*Importer of H&K-licensed mfg. pistols, TISAS pistols and Girsan
pistols all mfg. in Turkey.*

Model MKE Z-5RS....... NiB $1800 Ex $1700 Gd $1650
Licensed version of H&K MP5 except Semiauto. SA. Caliber:
9mm; 10 or 30-rnd. magazine. 8.9-in. bbl. Frame: polymer.
Sights: fixed front, adj. rear. Finish: black. Grip: textured poly-
mer. Length: 19.9-in. Weight: 5.5 lbs. Imported 2016 to date.
w/SB Tactical Stabilizing Brace, add.................$200
MKE Z-5P (5.8-in. bbl.)....NiB $1800 Ex $1700 Gd $1650
MKE Z-5K (4.6-in. bbl.)....NiB $1750 Ex $1650 Gd $1600

RIFLES

A.A. ARMS — Monroe, NC

AR-9 . . . . .NiB $805 Ex $641 Gd $439
Semiauto recoil-operated rifle w/side-folding metal stock design. Fires from a closed bolt. Caliber: 9mm Parabellum. 20-rnd. magazine. 16.25-in. bbl., 33 in. overall. Weight: 6.5 lbs. Fixed blade, protected postfront sight adjustable for elevation, winged square notched rear. Matte phosphate/blue or nickel finish. Checkered polymer grip/frame. Made 1991-94 (banned).

ACCURACY INTERNATIONAL LTD. (AI) — Hampshire, England

Currently U.S. office Fredericksburg, VA; formerly Orchard Park, NY.

AE MODEL . . . . .NiB $3330 Ex $2780 Gd $1710
Similar to AWP Model. Caliber: .243 Win., .260 Rem., or 6.5 Creedmoor, 5-rnd. magazine. 20- or 24-in. bbl. Weight: 8.5 lbs. Imported 2002 to present.

AW MODEL . . . . .NiB $5510 Ex $4010 Gd $2855
Bolt-action. Caliber: .243 Win., .260 Rem., 6.5 Creedmoor, .300 Win. Mag., or .338 Lapua Mag. 10-rnd. magazine. 20-, 24-, 26- or 27-in. bbl. Weight: 14 lbs. Imported 1995 to present.

AWP MODEL . . . . .NiB $4255 Ex $3155 Gd $2155
Similar to AW model except 20- or 24-in. bbl. w/o muzzle device. Weight: 15 lbs. Imported 1995 to 2007.

AW50 MODEL . . . . .NiB $12,500 Ex $10,600 Gd $9000
Bolt-action. Caliber: .50 BMG. 5-rnd. magazine. 27-in. bbl. w/ muzzle brake. Weight: 30 lbs. Imported 1998 to 2012.

AWM MODEL . . . . .NiB $5600 Ex $4680 Gd $2955
Bolt-action. Caliber: .300 Win. Mag. or .338 Lapua Mag. 5-rnd. magazine. 20-, 24-, 26- or 27-in. bbl. w/ or w/o muzzle brake. Weight: 15.5 lbs. Imported 1995 to 2009.

AX MODEL . . . . .NiB $6010 Ex $4610 Gd $3355
Bolt-action. Caliber: .243 Win., .260 Rem., 6.5 Creedmoor, .308 Win., or .338 Lapua Mag. 10-rnd. magazine. 20-, 24-, 26- or 27-in. bbl. Folding chassis. Finish: black, green or dark earth.

AXMC MODEL . . . . .NiB $6500 Ex $6000 Gd $5500
Bolt-action, multi-caliber system. Caliber: .308 Win., .300 Win. Mag. or .338 Lapua Mag. 10-rnd. magazine. 20-, 24-, 26- or 27-in. bbl. Weight: 14.6 lbs. Folding chassis. Finish: black, green or pale brown. Imported 2014 to present.

ACTION ARMS — Philadelphia, PA

MODEL B SPORTER
SEMIAUTO CARBINE . . . . .NiB $650 Ex $572 Gd $380
Similar to Uzi Carbine (see separate listing) except w/thumbhole stock. Caliber: 9mm Parabellum, 10-rnd. magazine. 16-in. bbl. Weight: 8.75 lbs. Post front sight; adj. rear. Imported 1994.

TIMBER WOLF REPEATING RIFLE
Calibers: .357 Mag./.38 Special and .44 Mag. slide-action. Tubular magazine holds 10 and 8 rnd., respectively. 18.5-in. bbl. 36.5 in. overall. Weight: 5.5 lbs. Fixed blade front sight; adj. rear. Receiver w/integral scope mounts. Checkered walnut stock. Imported from 1989 to 1993, later by I.M.I. Israel.
Blued model . . . . .NiB $338 Ex $271 Gd $190
Chrome model, add $75
.44 Mag., add $126

ALPHA ARMS, INC. — Dallas, TX

CUSTOM BOLT-ACTION RIFLE . NiB $1707 Ex $1335 Gd $876
Calibers: .17 Rem. thru .338 Win. Mag. Right or left-hand action in three action lengths w/three-lug locking system and 60-degree bolt rotation. 20- or 24-in. bbl. Weight: 6 to 7 lbs. No sights. Presentation-grade California Claro walnut stock w/ hand-rubbed oil finish, custom inletted sling swivels and ebony forend tip. Made 1984-87.

ALASKAN BOLT-ACTION RIFLE . . NiB $1706 Ex $1337 Gd $869
Similar to Custom model but w/stainless-steel bbl. and receiver w/all other parts coated w/Nitex. Weight: 6.75 to 7.25 lbs. Open sights w/bbl-band sling swivel. Classic-style Alpha wood stock w/Niedner-style steel grip cap and solid recoil pad. Made 1985-87.

GRAND SLAM
BOLT-ACTION RIFLE. . . . . .NiB $1322 Ex $1065 Gd $795
Same as Custom model but has Alphawood (fiberglass and wood) classic-style stock featuring Niedner-style grip cap. Wt: 6.5 lbs. Left-hand models same value. Made 1985 to 1987.custom Bolt-Action Rifle Same as Custom Rifle except designed on Mauser-style action w/claw extractor drilled and tapped for scope. Originally designated Alpha Model 1. Calibers: .243, 7mm-08, .308 original chambering (1984 to 1985) up to .338 Win. Mag. in standard model; .338 thru .458 Win. Mag. in Big Five model (1987). Teflon-coated trigger guard/floorplate assembly. Made 1984-87.
Jaguar Grade I . . . . .NiB $1035 Ex $855 Gd $624
Jaguar Grade II . . . . .NiB $1268 Ex $684 Gd $707
Jaguar Grade III . . . . .NiB $1319 Ex $1046 Gd $756
Jaguar Grade IV . . . . .NiB $1424 Ex $1056 Gd $755
Big Five model . . . . .NiB $1717 Ex $1198 Gd $977

AMERICAN ARMS — N. Kansas City, MO

1860 HENRY. . . . . .NiB $926 Ex $698 Gd $530
Replica of 1860 Henry rifle. Calibers: .44-40 or .45 LC. 24.25-in. half-octagonal bbl. 43.75 in. overall. Weight: 9.25 lbs. Brass frame and appointments. Straight-grip walnut buttstock. Imported 1999 to 2000.

Action Arms Timber Wolf

Alpha Arms Custom

Accuracy International AE

Alpha Arms Jaguar

1866 WINCHESTER
Replica of 1866 Winchester. Calibers: .44-40 or .45 LC. 19-in. rnd. tapered bbl. (carbine) or 24.25-in. tapered octagonal bbl. (rifle). 38 to 43.25 in. overall. Weight: 7.75 or 8.15 lbs. Brass frame, elevator and buttplate. Walnut buttstock and forend. Imported 1999 to 2000.
Carbine . . . . NiB $743 Ex $625 Gd $409
Rifle . . . . NiB $743 Ex $625 Gd $409

1873 WINCHESTER
Replica of 1873 Winchester rifle. Calibers: .44-40 or .45 LC. 24.25-in. tapered octagonal bbl. w/tubular magazine. Color casehardened steel frame w/brass elevator and ejection port cover. Walnut buttstock w/steel buttplate. Imported 1999 to 2000.
Standard model. . . . . NiB $876 Ex $710 Gd $419
Deluxe model . . . . NiB $1141 Ex $924 Gd $640

1874 SHARPS
Replica of 1874 Sharps rifle. Calibers: .45-70 or .45-120 22 or 28-in. bbl. w/tubular magazine. Color case-hardened steel frame, single trigger. Walnut buttstock w/steel buttplate. Imported 1999–2000.
Cavalry Carbine model (22-in.
  rnd bbl.) . . . . .NiB $630 Ex $530 Gd $365
Frontier Carbine model
  (22-in. bbl.) . . . . NiB $620 Ex $525 Gd $365
Sporting Rifle model (28-in.
  octagon bbl.) . . . . NiB $640 Ex $540 Gd $365

Deluxe Sporting Rifle model (28-in. octagon bbl.,
  brown finish), add. $25

AMERICAN SPIRIT ARMS CORP. — Scottsdale, AZ

Manufacturer from 1998 thru 2005; last located in Tempe, AZ.

A2 CAR CARBINE . . . . NiB $1041 Ex $703 Gd $544
Caliber: 9mm Parabellum. Forged receiver, non-collapsible stock. Bbl.: 16-in. Wilson w/o muzzle brake, bird cage flash hider (pre-ban) or muzzle brake (post-ban).

ASA 24-IN. MATCH RIFLE . . NiB $1806 Ex $1106 Gd $789
Caliber: .308 Win. Bbl.: 24-in. stainless steel match w/ or w/o fluting/porting. Side-charging handle; pistol grip. Introduced 2002.

ASA A2 RIFLE . . . . NiB $926 Ex $633 Gd $509
Caliber: .223 Rem. A2 receiver; 20-in. National Match barrel. Intro. 1999.

ASA BULL BARREL A2 RIFLE . . NiB $989 Ex $733 Gd $535
Similar to Flattop Rifle except has A2 upper receiver with carrying handle and sights. Introduced 1999.

ASA BULL BARREL FLATTOP NiB $1043 Ex $709 Gd $533
Semiauto. Caliber: .223 Rem. Patterned after AR-15. Forged steel lower receiver, aluminum flattop upper receiver, 24-in. stainless bull barrel, free-floating aluminum hand guard, includes Harris bipod.

ASA CARBINE . . . . **NiB $1077 Ex $707 Gd $589**
Caliber: .223 Rem. or Short. Side-charging, flattop receiver; M4 hand guard; 16-in. National Match bbl. w/slotted muzzle brake.

ASA M4 RIFLE . . . . **NiB $944 Ex $679 Gd $482**
Caliber: .223 Rem. Non-collapsible stock, M4 hand guard, 16-in. bbl. w/muzzle brake; aluminum flattop upper receiver.

ASA TACTICAL RIFLE . . . . . . **NiB $1788 Ex $1096 Gd $780**
Caliber: .308 Win. Bbl.: 16-in. stainless steel regular or match; side-charging handle; pistol grip.
Match (w/fluted bbl. match trigger, chrome finish) Add $525

BULL BARREL A2 INVADER . . **NiB $1032 Ex $710 Gd $544**
Caliber: .223 Rem. Similar to ASA 24-in. bull bbl. rifle except has 16-in. stainless steel bbl. Introduced 1999.

DCM SERVICE RIFLE . . . . **NiB $1412 Ex $915 Gd $618**
Caliber: .223 Rem. Bbl.: 20-in. stainless steel match type with free-floating shroud. National Match front and rear sights; match trigger; pistol grip.

FLATTOP CAR RIFLE . . . . **NiB $1041 Ex $703 Gd $544**
Caliber: 9mm Parabellum. Similar to A2 CAR Rifle except flattop design w/o sights. Introduced 2002.

LIMITED MATCH RIFLE . . . . . **NiB $1411 Ex $909 Gd $579**
Caliber: .223 Rem. Bbl.: 16-in. fluted stainless steel match with round shroud. National Match front and rear sights; match trigger.

OPEN MATCH RIFLE . . . . . . **NiB $1471 Ex $1097 Gd $745**
Caliber: .223 Rem. Bbl.: 16-in. fluted and ported stainless steel match with round shroud. Flattop without sights, forged upper and lower receiver, match trigger. Introduced 2001.

POST-BAN CARBINE . . . . **NiB $909 Ex $690 Gd $482**
Caliber: .223 Rem. Wilson 16-in. National Match bbl.; non-collapsible stock. Introduced 1999.

AMERICAN WESTERN ARMS, INC. (AWA)— Delray Beach, FL

Importer of replica Old West firearms manufactured in Italy, from 1999–2000. Similar calibers and features as other Italian-made cowboy replicas.

1892 CARBINE/RIFLE . . . . **NiB $630 Ex $530 Gd $365**
Replica of 1892 Winchester.

LIGHTNING CARBINE/RIFLE . . . **NiB $750 Ex $630 Gd $465**
Replica of Colt pump-action.
Limited Edition model (engraved chrome receiver), add . . **$335**

AMT (ARCADIA MACHINE & TOOL) — Irwindale, CA (1998)

BOLT-ACTION REPEATING RIFLE
Winchester-type push-feed or Mauser-type controlled-feed short-, medium- or long-action. Calibers: .223 Remi., .22-250 Rem., .243 A, .243 Win., 6mm PPC, .25-06 Rem., 6.5x08, .270 Win., 7x57 Mauser, 7mm-08 Rem., 7mm Rem. Mag., 7.62x39mm, .308 Win., .30-06, .300 Win. Mag., .338 Win. Mag., .375 H&H, .416 Rem., .416 Rigby, .458 Win. Mag. 22- to 28-in. number 3 contour bbl. Weight:

7.75 to 8.5 lbs. Sights: None furnished; drilled and tapped for scope mounts. Classic composite or Kevlar stock. Made 1996-97.
Standard model . . . . **NiB $899 Ex $720 Gd $531**
Deluxe model . . . . **NiB $1087 Ex $830 Gd $529**

BOLT-ACTION SINGLE-SHOT RIFLE
Winchester-type cone breech push-feed or Mauser-type controlled-feed action. Calibers: .22 Hornet, .22 PPC, .222 Rem., .223 Rem., .22-250 Rem., .243 A, .243 Win., 6mm PPC, 6.5x08, .270 Win., 7mm-08 Rem., .308 Win. 22- to 28-in. #3 contour bbl. Weight: 7.75 to 8.5 lbs. Sights: None furnished; drilled and tapped for scope mounts. Classic composite or Kevlar stock. Made from1996.
Standard model . . . . **NiB $865 Ex $733 Gd $520**
Deluxe model . . . . **NiB $1077 Ex $744 Gd $500**

CHALLENGER AUTOLOADING TARGET RIFLE SERIES I, II & III
Similar to Small Game Hunter except w/McMillan target fiberglass stock. Caliber: .22 LR. 10-rnd. magazine. 16.5-, 18-, 20- or 22-in. bull bbl. Drilled and tapped for scope mount; no sights. Stainless steel finish. Made 1994-98.bull bbl. Drilled and tapped for scope mount; no sights. Stainless steel finish. Made 1994-98.
Challenger I Standard . . . . **NiB $822 Ex $577 Gd $409**
Challenger II w/muzzle brake . . **NiB $926 Ex $755 Gd $554**
Challenger III w/bbl extension NiB $976 Ex $588 Gd $452
w/jeweled trigger, add **$227**

LIGHTNING 25/22
AUTOLOADING RIFLE . . . . **NiB $316 Ex $237 Gd $170**
Caliber: .22 LR. 25-rnd. magazine. 18-in. tapered or bull bbl. Weight: 6 lbs. 37 in. overall. Sights: Adj. rear; ramp front. Folding stainless-steel stock w/matte finish. Made 1986 to 1993.

MAGNUM HUNTER RIFLE . . . **NiB $495 Ex $455 Gd $240**
Similar to Lightning Small Game Hunter II model except chambered in .22 WRF w/22-in. match-grade bbl. Made 1995-98.

SMALL GAME HUNTER SERIES
Similar to AMT 25/22 except w/conventional matte black fiberglass/nylon stock. 10-rnd. rotary magazine. 22-in. bbl. 40.5 in. overall. Weight: 6 lbs. Grooved for scope; no sights. Made 1986-94 (Series I), and 1993 (Series II).
Hunter I . . . . **NiB $333 Ex $218 Gd $155**
Hunter II (w/22-in.
heavy target bbl.) . . . . **NiB $269 Ex $223 Gd $159**

ANSCHUTZ — Ulm, Germany

Currently imported by Anschutz North America in Trussville, AL, previously by Merkel USA. Anschutz models 1407 ISU, 1408-ED, 1411, 1413, 1418, 1432, 1433, 1518 and 1533 were marketed in the U.S. by Savage Arms. Further, Anschutz models 1403, 1416, 1422D, 1441, 1516 and 1522D were sold as Savage/Anschutz with Savage model designations (see also listings under Savage Arms).

MODEL 54.18MS . . . . **NiB $1300 Ex $899 Gd $469**
Silhouette model. Bolt-action, single-shot, Caliber: .22 LR. 22-in. bbl. European hardwood stock w/cheekpiece. Stipple-checkered forend and Wundhammer swell pistol-grip. Receiver grooved, drilled and tapped for scope blocks. Weight: 8.4 lbs. Imported 1982 to 1997.

MODEL 54.18MS-REP REPEATING RIFLE
Same as model 54.18MS except w/repeating action and 5-rnd. magazine. 22- to 30-in. bbl. 41-49 in. overall. Avg. weight:

RIFLES

Anschutz Model 54.18MS-REP

Anschutz Model 1416D

Anschutz Model 1418

7 lbs., 12 oz. Hardwood or synthetic gray thumbhole stock. Imported from 1989 to 1997.

Standard MS-REP model .... **NiB $2050 Ex $1569 Gd $880**
Left-hand model .... **NiB $2070 Ex $1579 Gd $790**

MODEL 54.30 .... **NiB $2300 Ex $2255 Gd $1610**
Silhouette model. Bolt-action. Caliber: .22 LR. 25.9-in. bbl. Imported from 2015 to present.

MODEL 64S BOLT-ACTION SINGLE-SHOT RIFLE
Silhouette model. Bolt-action, single-shot. Caliber: .22 LR. 26-in. bbl. Checkered European hardwood stock w/Wundhammer swell pistol-grip and adj. buttplate. Single-stage trigger. Aperture sights. Weight: 8.25 lbs. Imported from 1963 to 1981.
Standard (left or right hand) ... **NiB $480 Ex $370 Gd $250**

MODEL 64MS BOLT-ACTION SINGLE-SHOT RIFLE
Silhouette model. Bolt-action, single-shot. Caliber: .22 LR. 21.25-in. bbl. European hardwood silhouette-style stock w/cheekpiece. Forend base and Wundhammer swell pistol-grip, stipple-checkered. Adj. two-stage trigger. Receiver grooved, drilled and tapped for scope blocks. Weight: 8 lbs. Imported from 1982 to 1996.
Standard or Featherweight
(disc. 1988) .... **NiB $1133 Ex $780 Gd $620**
Left-hand model .... **NiB $1133 Ex $780 Gd $620**

MODEL 64MPR BOLT-ACTION REPEATER
Similar to Anschutz Model 64MS except repeater w/5-rnd. magazine. Imported from 1996.
Standard model .... **NiB $930 Ex $655 Gd $455**
Left-hand model, add **$50**

MODEL 520/61 SEMIAUTO ..NiB $300 EX $270 GD $167
Caliber: .22 LR. 10-rnd. magazine. 24-in. bbl. Sights: Folding leaf rear, hooded ramp front. Receiver grooved for scope mounting. Rotary-style safety. Monte Carlo stock and beavertail forend, checkered. Weight: 6.5 lbs. Imported from 1982 to 1983.

MODEL 525 AUTOLOADER
Caliber: .22 LR. 10-rnd. magazine. 20- or 24-in. bbl. 39 to 43 in. overall. Weight: 6.1 to 6.5 lbs. Adj. folding rear sight; hooded ramp front. Checkered European hardwood Monte Carlo style buttstock and beavertail forend. Sling swivel studs. Imported 1984 to 1995.
Carbine model (disc. 1986) ... **NiB $430 Ex $324 Gd $227**
Rifle model (24-in. bbl.) ...... **NiB $500 Ex $443 Gd $319**

MODEL 1403B .... **NiB $855 Ex $745 Gd $440**
A lighter-weight model designed for Biathlon competition. Caliber: .22 LR. 21.5-in. bbl. Adj. two-stage trigger. Adj. grooved wood buttplate, stipple-checkered deep thumb-rest flute and straight pistol-grip. Weight: 9 lbs. w/sights. Imported from 1990 to 1992.

MODEL 1403D MATCH SINGLE-SHOT TARGET RIFLE
Caliber: .22 LR. 25-in. bbl. 43 in. overall. Weight: 8.6 lbs. No sights, receiver grooved for Anschutz target sights. Walnut-finished hardwood target stock w/adj. buttplate. Importation disc. 1992.
Standard model .... **NiB $707 Ex $567 Gd $417**
w/match sights .... **NiB $988 Ex $779 Gd $555**

MODEL 1407 I.S.U. MATCH 54 RIFLE
Bolt-action, single-shot, caliber: .22 LR. 26.88-in. bbl. Scope bases. Receiver grooved for Anschutz sights. Single-stage adj. trigger. Select walnut target stock w/deep forearm for position shooting,adj. buttplate, hand stop and swivel. Weight: 10 lbs. Imported 1970 to 1981.
Standard model .... **NiB $653 Ex $535 Gd $291**
Left-hand model .... **NiB $653 Ex $535 Gd $291**
w/international sights, add **$75**

MODEL 1408 .... **NiB $466 Ex $408 Gd $370**
Bolt-action, single-shot, caliber: .22 LR. 23.5-in. bbl. w/sliding weights. No metallic sights. Receiver drilled and tapped for scope-sight bases. Single-stage adj. trigger. Oversize bolt knob. Select walnut stock w/thumbhole, adj. comb and buttplate. Weight: 9.5 lbs. Intro. 1976. Disc. Add $175 for ED model.

MODEL 1411 MATCH 54 RIFLE
Bolt-action, single-shot. Caliber: .22 LR. 27.5-in. extra heavy bbl. w/mounted scope bases. Receiver grooved for Anschutz sights. Single-stage adj. trigger. Select walnut target stock w/ cheekpiece (adj. in 1973 and later production), full pistol-grip, beavertail forearm, adj. buttplate, hand stop and swivel. Model 1411-L has left-hand stock. Weight: 11 lbs. Disc.
w/Non-adj. cheekpiece .... **NiB $678 Ex $423 Gd $269**

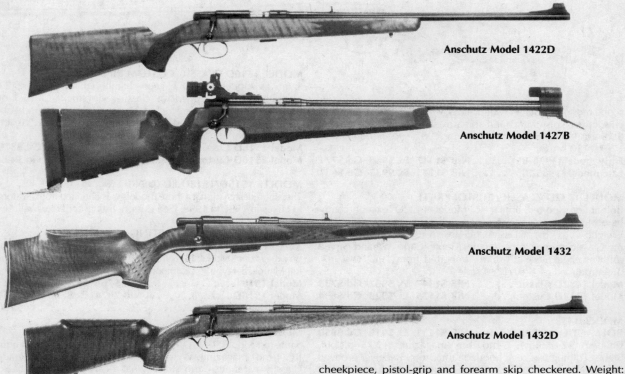

Anschutz Model 1422D

Anschutz Model 1427B

Anschutz Model 1432

Anschutz Model 1432D

w/adj. cheekpiece . . . . NiB $703 Ex $532 Gd $402
w/Anschutz International Sight set, add $300

MODEL 1413 SUPER MATCH 54 RIFLE
Freestyle international target rifle w/specifications similar to those of Model 1411, except w/special stock w/thumbhole, adj. pistol grip, adj. cheekpiece in 1973 and later production, adj. hook buttplate, adj. palmrest. Model 1413-L has left-hand stock. Weight: 15.5 lbs. Disc.
w/non-adj. cheekpiece . . . . NiB $830 Ex $733 Gd $400
w/adj. cheekpiece . . . . NiB $704 Ex $572 Gd $399
w/Anschutz International sight set, add $300

MODEL 1416D . . . . NiB $790 Ex $577 Gd $368
Bolt-action sporter. Caliber: .22 LR. 22.5-in. bbl. Sights: Folding leaf rear; hooded ramp front. Receiver grooved for scope mounting. Select European stock w/cheekpiece, skip-checkered pistol grip and forearm. Weight: 6 lbs. Imported 1982 to 2007.

MODEL 1416D CLASSIC/CUSTOM SPORTERS
Same as Model 1416D except w/American classic-style stock (Classic) or modified European-style stock w/Monte Carlo roll-over cheekpiece and Schnabel forend (Custom). Weight: 5.5 lbs. (Classic); 6 lbs. (Custom). Imported 1986 to 2007.
Model 1416D Classic . . . . NiB $995 Ex $549 Gd $380
Model 1416D Classic,
  "True" left-hand . . . . NiB $1095 Ex $577 Gd $419
Model 1416D Custom. . . . . NiB $980 Ex $750 Gd $380
Model 1416D fiberglass (1991-92)NiB $760 Ex $623 Gd $445

MODEL 1418 BOLT-ACTION
SPORTER. . . . . NiB $452 Ex $352 Gd $200
Caliber: .22 LR. 5- or 10-rnd. magazine. 19.75-in. bbl. Sights: Folding leaf rear; hooded ramp front. Receiver grooved for scope mounting. Select walnut stock, Mannlicher type w/ cheekpiece, pistol-grip and forearm skip checkered. Weight: 5.5 lbs. Intro. 1976. Disc.

MODEL 1418D BOLT-ACTION
SPORTER. . . . . NiB $1008 Ex $886 Gd $533
Caliber: .22 LR. 5- or 10-rnd. magazine. 19.75-in. bbl. European walnut Monte Carlo stock, Mannlicher type w/ cheekpiece, pistolgrip and forend skip-line checkered, buffalo horn Schnabel tip. Weight: 5.5 lbs. Imported from 1982 to 1995 and 1998 to 2003.

MODEL 1422D CLASSIC/CUSTOM RIFLE
Bolt-action sporter. Caliber: .22 LR. Five-rnd. removable straight-feed clip magazine. 24-in. bbl. Sights: Folding leaf rear; hooded ramp front. Select European walnut stock, classic type (Classic); Monte Carlo w/hand-carved rollover cheekpiece (Custom). Weight: 7.25 lbs. (Classic) 6.5 lbs. (Custom). Imported 1982 to 1989.
Model 1422D Classic . . . . NiB $833 Ex $670 Gd $432
Model 1422D Custom. . . . . NiB $896 Ex $833 Gd $479

MODEL 1427B
BIATHLON RIFLE . . . . NiB $1943 Ex $1377 Gd $937
Bolt-action clip repeater. Caliber: .22 LR. 21.5-in. bbl. Two-stage trigger w/wing-type safety. Hardwood stock w/deep fluting, pistol grip and deep forestock with adj. hand stop rail. Target sights w/adjustable weights. Advertised in 1981 but imported from 1982 to date as Model 1827B.

MODEL 1430D MATCH . . . . . . NiB $976 Ex $650 Gd $429
Improved version of Model 64S. Bolt-action, single-shot. Caliber: .22 LR. 26-in. medium-heavy bbl. Walnut Monte Carlo stock w/cheekpiece, adj. buttplate, deep midstock tapered to forend. Pistol-grip and contoured thumb groove w/stipple checkering. Single-stage adj. trigger. Target sights. Weight: 8.38 lbs. Imported 1982 to 1990.

MODEL 1432 BOLT-ACTION SPORTER
Caliber: .22 Hornet. 5-rnd. box magazine. 24-in. bbl. Sights: Folding leaf rear, hooded ramp front. Receiver grooved for

Anschutz Model 1707

scope mounting. Select walnut stock w/Monte Carlo comb and cheekpiece, pistol-grip and forearm skip-checkered. Weight: 6.75 lbs. Imported from 1974 to 1987. (Reintroduced as 1707/1730 series)
Early model (1974-85) ...... **NiB $1347 Ex $988 Gd $721**
Late model (1985-87) .... **NiB $1145 Ex $933 Gd $631**

MODEL 1432D CLASSIC/CUSTOM RIFLE
Bolt-action sporter similar to Model 1422D except chambered for Caliber: .22 Hornet. 4-rnd. magazine. 23.5-in. bbl. Weight: 7.75 lbs. (Classic); 6.5 lbs. (Custom). Classic stock on Classic model; fancy-grade Monte Carlo w/hand-carved rollover cheekpiece (Custom). Imported from 1982 to 1987. (Reintroduced as 1707/1730 series)
Model 1432D Classic .... **NiB $1347 Ex $982 Gd $733**
Model 1432D Custom. ...... **NiB $1175 Ex $923 Gd $634**

MODEL 1433
BOLT-ACTION SPORTER .... **NiB $1131 Ex $916 Gd $650**
Caliber: .22 Hornet. 5-rnd. box magazine. 19.75-in. bbl. Sights: Folding leaf rear, hooded ramp front. Receiver grooved for scope mounting. Single-stage or double-set trigger. Select walnut Mannlicher stock; cheekpiece, pistol-grip and forearm skip-checkered. Weight: 6.5 lbs. Imported from 1976 to 1986.

MODEL 1448D .... **NiB $421 Ex $324 Gd $236**
Similar to Model 1449 except chambered for Caliber: .22 LR. w/22.5-in. smooth bore bbl. and no sights. Walnut-finished hardwood stock. Imported from 1999 to 2001.

MODEL 1449D YOUTH SPORTER NiB $300 Ex $233 Gd $177
Bolt-action sporter version of Model 2000. Caliber: .22 LR. 5-rnd. box magazine. 16.25-in. bbl. Weight: 3.5 lbs. Hooded ramp front sight, addition. Walnut-finished hardwood stock. Imported from 1990 to 1991.

MODEL 1450B TARGET RIFLE . **NiB $703 Ex $533 Gd $397**
Biathlon rifle developed on 2000 Series action. 19.5-in. bbl. Weight: 5.5 lbs. Adj. buttplate. Target sights. Imported 1993 to 1994.

MODEL 1451 E/R SPORTER/TARGET
Bolt-action, single-shot (1451E) or repeater (1451R). Caliber: .22 LR. 22- or 22.75-in. bbl. w/o sights. Select hardwood stock w/stippled pistolgrip and vented forearm. beavertail forend, adj. cheekpiece, and deep thumb flute. Weight: 6.5 lbs. Imported from 1996 to 2001.
Model 1451E (disc. 1997) .... **NiB $487 Ex $370 Gd $254**
Model 1451R .... **NiB $479 Ex $455 Gd $310**

MODEL 1451D CLASSIC/CUSTOM RIFLE
Same as Model 1451R except w/walnut-finished hardwood stock (Classic) or modified European-style walnut stock w/Monte Carlo rollover cheekpiece and Schnabel forend (Custom). Weight: 5 lbs. Imported from 1998 to 2001.
Model 1451D Classic (Super) . . **NiB $367 Ex $288 Gd $199**
Model 1451D Custom. .... **NiB $488 Ex $455 Gd $321**

MODEL 1451 ST- R RIFLE. .... **NiB $499 Ex $454 Gd $342**
Same as Model 1451R except w/two-stage trigger and walnut-finished hardwood uncheckered stock. Imported 1996 to 2001.

MODEL 1516D CLASSIC/CUSTOM RIFLE
Same as Model 1416D except chambered for Caliber: .22 Magnum RF, with American classic-style stock (Classic) or modified European-style stock w/Monte Carlo rollover cheekpiece and Schnabel forend (Custom). Weight: 5.5 lbs. (Classic), 6 lbs. (Custom). Imported from1986 to 2003.
Model 1516D Classic .... **NiB $704 Ex $572 Gd $379**
Model 1516D Custom. .... **NiB $639 Ex $600 Gd $423**

MODELS 1516D/1518D LUXUS RIFLES
The alpha designation for these models was changed from Custom to Luxus in 1996 to 1998. (See Custom listings for Luxus values.)

MODELS 1518/1518D SPORTING RIFLES
Same as Model 1418 except chambered for .22 Magnum RF, 4-rnd. box magazine. Model 1518 intro. 1976. Disc. Model 1518D has full Mannlicher-type stock. Imported from 1982 to 2001.
Model 1518 .... **NiB $766 Ex $650 Gd $423**
Model 1518D .... **NiB $974 Ex $788 Gd $544**
w/set trigger, add **$150**

MODEL 1522D CLASSIC/CUSTOM RIFLE
Same as Model 1422D except chambered for .22 Magnum RF, 4-rnd. magazine. Weight: 6.5 lbs. (Custom). Fancy-grade Classic or Monte Carlo stock w/hand-carved rollover cheekpiece. Imported 1982 to 1989. (Reintroduced as 1707D/1730D series)
Model 1522D Classic .... **NiB $1197 Ex $869 Gd $633**
Model 1522D Custom. ...... **NiB $1197 Ex $869 Gd $633**

MODEL 1532D CLASSIC/CUSTOM RIFLE
Same as Model 1432D except chambered for .222 Rem. Three-rnd. mag. Weight: 6.5 lbs. (Custom). Classic stock on Classic Model; fancy-grade Monte Carlo stock w/handcarved rollover cheekpiece (Custom). Imported from 1982 to 1989. (Reintroduced as 1707D/174 D0 series)
Model 1532D Classic .... **NiB $1019 Ex $795 Gd $448**
Model 1532D Custom. ...... **NiB $1297 Ex $996 Gd $698**

MODEL 1533 .... **NiB $1090 Ex $844 Gd $589**
Same as Model 1433 except chambered for .222 Rem. Three-shot box magazine. Imported from 1976 to 1994.

MODEL 1707 SERIES BOLT-ACTION REPEATER
Match 54 Sporter. Calibers: .22 LR, .22 Mag., .22 Hornet, .222 Rem. Five-shot removable magazine 24-in. bbl. 43 in. overall. Weight: 7.5 lbs. Folding leaf rear sight, hooded ramp front. Select European walnut stock w/cheekpiece and Schnabel forend tip. Imported from 1989 to 2001.
Standard Model 1707
Bavarian — rimfire cal. ...... **NiB $1018 Ex $933 Gd $580**
Standard Model 1707
Bavarian — centerfire cal. . . **NiB $1342 Ex $1056 Gd $697**
Model 1707D Classic (Classic stock, 6.75 lbs.)
  rimfire cal. .... **NiB $1179 Ex $994 Gd $698**
Model 1707D
  Classic — centerfire cal.. . **NiB $1279 Ex $1044 Gd $748**
Model 1707D
  Custom — rimfire cal. .... **NiB $1094 Ex $893 Gd $633**
Model 1707D
  Custom — centerfire cal. **NiB $1332 Ex $1088 Gd $775**
Model 1707D Graphite Cust. (McMillan graphite reinforced
  stock, 22-in. bbl., intro. 1991) ..... **NiB $1156 Ex $985 Gd $641**

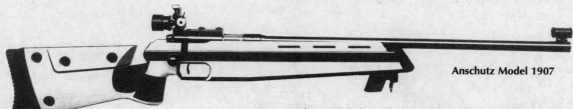

Anschutz Model 1907

Select walnut and gold trigger, add $200
Model 1707 FWT (featherweight, 6.5 lbs.) –
rimfire cal. . . . . NiB $1122 Ex $909 Gd $641
Model 1707 FWT — centerfire
cal. . . . . NiB $1289 Ex $1136 Gd $703

MODEL 1733D MANNLICHER. .NiB $1370 Ex $1168 Gd $860
Same as Model 1707D except w/19-in. bbl. and Mannlicher-
style stock. 39 in. overall. Weight: 6.25 lbs. Imported from
1993 to 1995 (Reintroduced in 1998, disc. 2001).

MODEL 1740 MONTE CARLO SPORTER
Caliber: .22 Hornet or .222 Rem. Three and 5-rnd. magazines
respectively. 24-in. bbl. 43.25 in. overall. Weight: 6.5 lbs.
Hooded ramp front, folding leaf rear. Drilled and tapped for
scope mounts. Select European walnut stock w/roll-over cheek-
piece, checkered grip and forend. Imported from 1998 to 2006.
Model 1740 Classic
(Meistergrade) . . . . NiB $1504 Ex $1237 Gd $866
Model 1740 Custom . . . . NiB $1370 Ex $1089 Gd $733

MODEL 1743 MONTE CARLO
SPORTER. . . . . NiB $1370 Ex $1132 Gd $769
Similar to Model 1740 except w/Mannlicher full stock.
Imported from 1997 to 2001.

MODEL 1807 ISU
STANDARD MATCH . . . . NiB $1359 Ex $1094 Gd $708
Bolt-action single-shot. Caliber: 22 LR. 26-in. bbl. Improved
Super Match 54 action. Two-stage match trigger. Removable
cheekpiece, adj. buttplate, thumbpiece and forestock w/
stipple-checkered. Weight: 10 lbs. Imported 1982 to 1988.
(Reintroduced as 1907 ISU)

MODEL 1808ED SUPER RUNNING TARGET
Bolt-action single-shot. Caliber: .22 LR. 23.5-in. bbl. w/sliding
weights. Improved Super Match 54 action. Heavy beavertail
forend w/adj.cheekpiece and buttplate. Adj. single-stage trigger. Weight: 9.5 lbs. Imported from 1982 to 1998.
Right-hand model . . . . NiB $1677 Ex $1328 Gd $869
Left-hand model . . . . NiB $1688 Ex $1377 Gd $973

MODEL 1808MS-R
METALLIC SILHOUETTE . . . . NiB $2021 Ex $1565 Gd $932
Bolt-action repeater. Caliber: .22 LR. 19.2-in. bbl. w/o sights.
Thumbhole Monte Carlo stock w/grooved forearm enhanced w/
"Anschutz" logo. Weight: 8.2 lbs. Imported from 1998 to date.

MODEL 1810 SUPER MATCH II . . . . NiB $1979 Ex $1440 Gd $937
A less detailed version of the Super Match 1813 model.
Tapered forend w/deep receiver area. Select European hardwood stock. Weight: 13.5 lbs. Imported from 1982 to 1988
(reintroduced as 1910 series).

MODEL 1811 PRONE MATCH. . . NiB $1843 Ex $1623 Gd $877
Bolt-action single-shot. Caliber: .22 LR. 27.5-in. bbl. Improved
Super Match 54 action. Select European hardwood stock w/

beavertail forend, adj. cheekpiece, and deep thumb flute.
Thumb groove and pistol grip w/stipple checkering. Adj. buttplate. Weight: 11.5 lbs. Imported 1982 to 1988. (Reintroduced
as 1911 Prone Match)

MODEL 1813 SUPER MATCH . . . NiB $2281 Ex $1951 Gd $869
Bolt-action single-shot. Caliber: .22 LR. 27.5-in. bbl. Improved
Super Match 54 action w/light firing pin, one-point adj. trigger.
European walnut thumbhole stock, adj. palm rest, forend and
pistol grip stipple checkered. Adj. cheekpiece and hook buttplate. Weight: 15.5 lbs. Imported 1979 to 1988. Reintroduced
as 1913 Super Match.

MODEL 1827B BIATHLON RIFLE
Bolt-action clip repeater. Caliber: .22 LR. 21.5-in. bbl. 42.5 in.
overall. Weight: 8.5 to 9 lbs. Slide safety. Adj. target sight set
w/snow caps. European walnut stock w/cheekpiece, stippled
pistol grip and forearm w/adj. weights. Fortner straight pull bolt
option offered in 1986. Imported from 1982 to date.
Model 1827B w/Sup. Mat. 54
action . . . . NiB $2359 Ex $2153 Gd $1020
Model 1827B, left-hand . . . NiB $2101 Ex $1716 Gd $1224
Model 1827BT w/Fortner
Option, right-hand . . . . . NiB $2467 Ex $2261 Gd $1032
Model 1827BT, left-hand . . NiB $2604 Ex $2127 Gd $1513
Model 1827BT w/laminated stock, add $175
w/stainless steel bbl., add $205

MODEL 1903D MATCH SINGLE-SHOT TARGET RIFLE
Caliber: .22 LR. 25.5-in. bbl. 43.75 in. overall. Weight: 8.5
lbs. No sights; receiver grooved, drilled and tapped for scope
mounts. Blonde or walnut-finished hardwood stock w/adj.
cheekpiece, stippled grip and forend. Left-hand version.
Imported 1987 to 1993.
Right-hand model
(Reintroduced as 1903D) . . . NiB $1006 Ex $844 Gd $544
Left-hand model . . . . NiB $1108 Ex $866 Gd $633

MODEL 1907 ISU INTERNATIONAL MATCH RIFLE
Updated version of Model 1807 w/same general specifications
as Model 1913 except w/26-in. bbl. 44.5 in. overall. Weight:
11 lbs. Designed for ISU 3-position competition. Fitted w/
vented beechwood or walnut, blonde or color-laminated stock.
Imported from 1989 to date.
Right-hand model . . . . NiB $1544 Ex $1353 Gd $838
Left-hand model . . . . NiB $1730 Ex $1415 Gd $1012
w/laminated stock, add $135
w/walnut stock, add $100
w/stainless steel bbl., add $130

MODEL 1910 INTERNATIONAL SUPER MATCH RIFLE
Updated version of Model 1810 w/same general specifications
Model 1913 except w/less-detailed hardwood stock w/tapered
forend. Weight: 13.5 lbs. Imported from 1989 to 1998.
Right-hand model . . . . NiB $2566 Ex $2077 Gd $1103
Left-hand model . . . . NiB $2560 Ex $2097 Gd $1506

MODEL 1911 PRONE MATCH RIFLE
Updated version of Model 1811 w/same general specifications
Model 1913 except w/specialized prone match hardwood

Anschutz Model 2013

Anschutz Achiever

stock w/beavertail forend. Weight: 11.5 lbs. Imported from 1989 to date.
Right-hand model . . . . **NiB $1854 Ex $1764 Gd $849**

MODEL 1912
LADIES' SPORT RIFLE . . . . . **NiB $2695 Ex $1855 Gd $1355**
Similar to the Model 1907 designed for ISU 3-position competition w/same general U.I.T. specifications except w/shorter dimensions to accomodate smaller competitors. Weight: 11.4 lbs. Imported from 1999 to date.

MODEL 1913
STANDARD RIFLE . . . . **NiB $1611 Ex $1235 Gd $909**
Similar to 1913 Super Match w/economized appointments. Imported from 1997 to date.

MODEL 1913 SUPER MATCH RIFLE
Bolt-action single-shot Super Match (updated version of Model 1813). Caliber: .22 LR. 27.5-in. bbl. Weight: 14.2 lbs. Adj. two- stage trigger. Vented International thumbhole stock w/adj. cheek- piece, hand and palm rest, fitted w/10-way butthook. Imported from 1989 to date.
Right-hand model . . . . **NiB $3310 Ex $1989 Gd $879**
Left-hand model . . . . **NiB $2370 Ex $1909 Gd $1343**
W/laminated stock, add $150
W/stainless steel bbl., add $175

MODEL 2007 ISU STANDARD RIFLE
Bolt-action single-shot. Caliber: .22 LR. 19.75-in. bbl. 43.5 to 44.5 in. overall. Weight: 10.8 lbs. Two-stage trigger. Standard ISU stock w/adj. cheekpiece. Imported from 1992 to date.
Right-hand model . . . . **NiB $1997 Ex $1529 Gd $909**
Left-hand model . . . . **NiB $2040 Ex $1719 Gd $1244**
W/stainless steel bbl., add $175

MODEL 2013
LADIES' SPORT RIFLE . . . . . . **NiB $2197 Ex $2021 Gd $933**
Similar to the Model 2007 designed for ISU 3-position competition w/same general U.I.T. specifications except w/shorter dimensions to accomodate smaller competitors. Weight: 11.4 lbs. Imported from 1999 to date.

MODEL 2013
BENCHREST RIFLE (BR-50) . . **NiB $1889 Ex $1624 Gd $877**
Bolt-action single-shot. Caliber: .22 LR. 19.6-in. bbl. 43 in. overall. Weight: 10.3 lbs. Adjustable trigger for single or two-stage function. Benchrest-configuration stock. Imported 1999 to date.

MODEL 2013
SILHOUETTE RIFLE . . . . **NiB $2187 Ex $1675 Gd $944**
Bolt-action single-shot. Caliber: .22 LR. 20-in. bbl. 45.5 in. overall. Weight: 11.5 lbs. Two-stage trigger. Thumbhole black synthetic or laminated stock w/adj. cheekpiece, hand and palm rest. Imported from 1994 to date.

MODEL 2013 (BR-50) SUPER MATCH FREE RIFLE
Silhouette model. Bolt-action single-shot. Caliber: .22 LR. 19.75- or 27.1-in. bbl. 43 to 50.1 in. overall. Weight: 15.5 lbs. Two-stage trigger. International thumbhole, black synthetic or laminated stock w/adj. cheekpiece, hand and palm rest; fitted w/10-way butthook. Imported from 1994 to 1998.
Right-hand model . . . . **NiB $2260 Ex $1380 Gd $910**
w/laminated stock, add $300

ACHIEVER BOLT-ACTION RIFLE . . **NiB $422 Ex $337 Gd $219**
Caliber: .22 LR. 5-rnd. magazine. Mark 2000-type repeating action. 19.5-in. bbl. 36.5 in. overall. Weight: 5 lbs. Adj. open rear sight; hooded ramp front. Plain European hardwood target-style stock w/vented forend and adj. buttplate. Imported 1987 to 1995.

ACHIEVER ST-SUPER TARGET . . **NiB $559 Ex $431 Gd $269**
Same as Achiever except single-shot w/22-in. bbl. and adj. stock. 38.75 in. overall. Weight: 6.5 lbs. Target sights. Imported since 1994 to 1995.

BR-50 BENCH REST RIFLE . . . **NiB $2755 Ex $2110 Gd $1400**
Single-shot. Caliber: .22 LR. 19.75-in. bbl. (23 in. w/muzzle weight). 37.75-42.5 in. overall. Weight: 11 lbs. Grooved receiver, no sights. Walnut-finished hardwood or synthetic benchrest stock w/adj. cheekpiece. Imported from 1994 to 1997. (Reintroduced as Model 2013 BR-50)

KADETT BOLT-ACTION
REPEATING RIFLE . . . . **NiB $370 Ex $241 Gd $198**
Caliber: .22 LR. 5-rnd. detachable box magazine. 22-in. bbl. 40 in. overall. Weight: 5.5 lbs. Adj. folding leaf rear sight; hooded ramp front. Checkered European hardwood stock w/ walnut-finish. Imported 1987.

MARK 2000 MATCH . . . . **NiB $448 Ex $355 Gd $221**
Takedown, bolt-action single-shot. Caliber: .22 LR. 26-in. heavy bbl. Walnut stock w/deep-fluted thumb-groove, Wundhammer swell pistol grip, beavertail forend. Adj. buttplate, single-stage adj. trigger. Weight: 8 lbs. Imported from 1982 to 1988.

Armalite AR-180

Armalite AR-7

Armi Jager AP-74 Wood Stock

ARMALITE, INC. — Geneseo, IL

Formerly Hollywood, California. Armalite was in Costa Mesa, California from 1959-73. Following the acquisition by Eagle Arms in 1995, production resumed under the Armalite, Inc. logo in Geneseo, IL. Purchased in 2013 by Strategic Armory Corps.

Production by ARMALITE (1959–1973)

AR-7 EXPLORER SURVIVAL

RIFLE . . . . NiB $410 Ex $345 Gd $290
Takedown. Semiauto. Caliber: .22 LR. Eight-rnd. box magazine. 16-in. cast aluminum bbl. w/steel liner. Sights: Peep rear; blade front. Brown or multi color plastic stock, recessed to stow barrel, action, and magazine. Weight: 2.75 lbs. Will float stowed or assembled. Made 1959-73 by Armalite; from 1974-90 by Charter Arms; from 1990-97 by Survival Arms, Cocoa, FL.; from 1997 to date by Henry Repeating Arms Co., Brooklyn, NY.
Custom (deluxe walnut stock, 1964-70), deduct $75

AR-180 SEMIAUTO RIFLE

Commercial version of full automatic AR-18 Combat Rifle. Gas-operated. Semiauto. Caliber: .223 Rem. (5.56mm). 5-, 20-, 30-rnd. magazines. 18.25-in. bbl. w/flash hider/muzzle brake. Sights: Flip-up "L" type rear, adj. for windage; post front, adj. for elevation. Accessory: 3x scope and mount (add $60 to value). Folding buttstock of black nylon, rubber buttplate and pistol grip, heat dissipating fiberglass forend (hand guard), swivels, sling. 38 in. overall, 28.75 in. folded. Weight: 6.5 lbs. Note: Made by Armalite Inc. 1969 to 1972, manufactured for Armalite by Howa Machinery Ltd., Nagoya, Japan, from 1972 to 1973; by Sterling Armament Co. Ltd., Dagenham, Essex, England, from 1976 to 1994. Importation disc, mfg. by Armalite-Costa.
mfg. Costa Mesa . . . . NiB $2189 Ex $1543 Gd $1043
mfg. by Howa . . . . NiB $2109 Ex $1535 Gd $990
mfg. by Sterling . . . . NiB $1809 Ex $1404 Gd $933
w/3x scope and mount, add $250

Production by ARMALITE, Inc. (1995–present)

AR-10 Series

Gas-operated. Semiauto action. Calibers: .243 Win. or .308 Win. (7.62 x 51mm). 10-rnd. magazine. 16- or 20-in. bbl.

35.5 or 39.5 in. overall. Weight: 9 to 9.75 lbs. Post front sight, adj. aperature rear. Black or green composition stock. Made 1995-2013.
AR-10 A2 (Std. carbine) . . . . NiB $1330 Ex $1088 Gd $707
AR-10 A2 (Std. rifle) . . . . NiB $1330 Ex $1088 Gd $707
AR-10 A4 (carbine) . . . . NiB $1320 Ex $1000 Gd $780
AR-10 A4 (SPR rifle) . . . . NiB $1320 Ex $1000 Gd $780
AR-10 AB (.308 Win.,
**   1999-2008) . . . . NiB $1455 Ex $1130 Gd $850**

AR-10 T (TARGET) . . . . NiB $1400 Ex $1100 Gd $835
Similar to AR-10A except in National Match configuration w/three-slot short Picatinny rail system and case deflector. Additional calibers: .260 Rem., .300 RUM, 7mm-08 Rem., .338 Fed. 16- or 24-in. bbl. Weight: 8.25 to 10.4 lbs. Composite stock and handguard. No sights. Optional National Match carry handle and detachable front sight. Made 1995 to date.
AR-10 T (Carbine) . . . . NiB $1630 Ex $1210 Gd $930

MODEL AR-50 SS

BOLT-ACTION RIFLE . . . . . . NiB $3198 Ex $2645 Gd $1370
Caliber: .50 BMG. 31-in. bbl. w/muzzle brake. 59 in. overall. Weight: 41 lbs. Modified octagonal-form receiver, drilled and slotted for scope rail. Single-stage trigger. Triple front-locking bolt lug w/spring-loaded plunger for automatic ejection. Magnesium phosphate steel, hard-anodized aluminum finish. Made 1999 to date.

M15 SERIES

Gas-operated Semiauto w/A2-style forward-assist mechanism and push-type pivot pin for easy takedown. Caliber: .223 Rem., 5.56 NATO or 6.8 SPC. 7-rnd. magazine. 16-, 20- or 24-in. bbl. Weight: 7-9.2 lbs. Composite or retractable stock. Fully adj. sights. Black anodized finish. Made 1995 to date.
M-15A2 (Carbine) . . . . NiB $927 Ex $800 Gd $647
M-15A2 (Service Rifle) . . . . NiB $989 Ex $845 Gd $655
M-15A2 (National Match) . . . NiB $1350 Ex $1123 Gd $770
M-15A2 (Golden Eagle
**   heavy bbl.) . . . . NiB $1332 Ex $1086 Gd $730**
M-15A2 M4C (retractable stock,
**   disc. 1997) . . . . NiB $1299 Ex $1021 Gd $698**
M-15A4 (Action Master,
**   disc. 1997) . . . . NiB $1139 Ex $934 Gd $670**
M-15A4 (Predator) . . . . NiB $1140 Ex $1020 Gd $670

M-15A4 S.P. R. (Special Purpose
  Rifle)....................NiB $956 Ex $799 Gd $535
M-15A4 (S.P. Carbine) ....NiB $875 Ex $720 Gd $463
M-15A4T (Eagle Eye Carbine)...NiB $1326 Ex $1090 Gd $775
M-15A4T (Eagle Eye Rifle) ..NiB $1377 Ex $1030 Gd $755

ARMI JAGER — Turin, Italy

AP-74 SEMIAUTO RIFLE
Styled after U.S. M16 military rifle. Caliber: .22 LR, .32 Auto
(pistol cartridge). Detachable clip magazine; capacity: 14 rnd.
caliber .22 LR, 9 rnd. .32 ACP. 20-in. bbl. w/flash suppressor.
Weight: 6.5 lbs. M16 type sights. Stock, pistol-grip and forearm
of black plastic, swivels and sling. Intro. 1974. Disc.
.22 LR. ....NiB $359 Ex $290 Gd $200
.32 Auto ....NiB $379 Ex $322 Gd $209
Commando model .... NiB $322 Ex $248 Gd $166
Wood stock model..................NiB $448 Ex $380 Gd $250

ARMSCOR (Arms Corp.) — Manila,
Philippines *Imported by Armscor Precision Int'l.*

MODEL 20 SEMIAUTOMATIC RIFLE
Caliber: .22 LR. 15-rnd. magazine. 21-in. bbl. 39.75 in. overall.
Weight: 6.5 lbs. Sights: Hooded front; adj. rear. Checkered or
plain walnut finished mahogany stock. Blued finish. Imported
1990 to 1991. (Reinstated by Ruko in the M series.)
Model 20 (checkered stock) .... NiB $167 Ex $130 Gd $97
Model 20C (carbine-style stock) NiB $144 Ex $122 Gd $98
Model 20P (plain stock) .... NiB $126 Ex $100 Gd $78

MODEL 1600 SEMIAUTOMATIC RIFLE
Caliber: .22 LR. 15-rnd. magazine. 19.5-in. bbl. 38 in. overall.
Weight: 6 lbs. Sights: Post front; aperture rear. Plain mahogany
stock. Matte black finish. Imported 1987 to 1991. (Reinstated
by Ruko in the M series.)
Standard model............ NiB $180 Ex $155 Gd $100
Retractable stock model ...... NiB $190 Ex $167 Gd $110

MODEL AK22 SEMIAUTOMATIC RIFLE
Caliber: .22 LR. 15- or 30-rnd. magazine. 18.5-in. bbl. 36
in. overall. Weight: 7 lbs. Sights: Post front; adj. rear. Plain
mahogany stock. Matte black finish. Imported 1987 to 1991.
Standard model............ NiB $179 Ex $150 Gd $110
Folding stock model .... NiB $269 Ex $220 Gd $166

MODEL M14 SERIES BOLT-ACTION RIFLE
Caliber: .22 LR. 10-rnd. magazine. 23-in. bbl. Weight: 6.25
lbs. Open sights. Walnut or mahogany stock. Imported 1991
to 1997.
M14P Standard model .... NiB $129 Ex $98 Gd $70
M14D Deluxe model
  (checkered stock, disc. 1995) ...NiB $149 Ex $110 Gd $90

MODEL M20 SERIES SEMIAUTOMATIC RIFLE
Caliber: .22 LR. 10- or 15-rnd. magazine. 18.25- or 20.75-in.
bbl. Weight:5.5 to 6.5 lbs. 38 to 40.5 in. overall. Hooded front
sight w/windage adj. rear. Walnut finished mahogany stock.
Imported 1990 to 1997.
M20C (carbine model) .... NiB $144 Ex $109 Gd $80
M20P (standard model) .... NiB $128 Ex $100 Gd $78
M20S Sporter Deluxe (w/checkered
  mahogany stock)........... NiB $167 Ex $150 Gd $97
M20SC Super Classic (w/checkered
  walnut stock) .... NiB $281 Ex $227 Gd $108

MODEL M1400 BOLT-ACTION RIFLE
Similar to Model 14P except w/checkered stock w/Schnabel
forend. Weight: 6 lbs. Imported from 1990 to 1997.

M1400LW (Lightweight, disc. 1992)... NiB $239 Ex $199 Gd $137
M1400S (Sporter) .... NiB $177 Ex $150 Gd $100
M1400SC (Super Classic) ..... NiB $300 Ex $255 Gd $179

MODEL M1500 BOLT-ACTION RIFLE
Caliber: .22 Mag. 5-rnd. magazine. 21.5-in. bbl. Weight: 6.5
lbs. Open sights. Checkered mahogany stock. Imported 1991
to 1997.
M1500 (standard) .... NiB $198 Ex $137 Gd $105
M1500LW (Euro-style walnut
  stock, disc. 1992) .... NiB $219 Ex $188 Gd $135
M1500SC (Monte Carlo stock) ... NiB $224 Ex $190 Gd $140

MODEL M1600 SEMIAUTOMATIC RIFLE
Rimfire replica of Armalite Model AR 180 (M16) except
chambered for Caliber .22 LR. 15-rnd. magazine. 18-in.
bbl. Weight: 5.25 lbs. Composite or retractable buttstock w/
composite handguard and pistol grip. Carrying handle w/adj.
aperture rear sight and protected post front. Black anodized
finish. Imported from 1991 to 1997.
M-1600 (standard w/fixed stock)... NiB $190 Ex $149 Gd $110
M-1600R (retractable stock)... NiB $200 Ex $161 Gd $120

MODEL M1800 BOLT-ACTION RIFLE
Caliber: .22 Hornet. 5-rnd. magazine. 22-in. bbl. Weight: 6.6
lbs. Checkered hardwood or walnut stock. Sights: Post front;
adj. rear. Imported from 1996 to 1997.
M-1800 (standard) .... NiB $310 Ex $233 Gd $175
M-1800SC (checkered walnut stock) ... NiB $400 Ex $327 Gd $255

MODEL M2000
Similar to Model 20P except w/checkered mahogany stock and
adj. sights. Imported from 1991 to 1997.
M2000S (standard) .... NiB $177 Ex $139 Gd $100
M2000SC (w/checkered
  walnut stock) .... NiB $279 Ex $220 Gd $167

ARMSCORP USA, INC.— Baltimore, MD
*Importer and re-manufacturer of military style rifles,
1986-2006. Currently deals in parts only.*

M-14 SERIES SEMIAUTOMATIC RIFLE
Rebuilt M-14 civilian style rifles using Nornico or USGI parts.
Caliber: .308 Win.
M-14 (Nornico parts, 1991–92) NiB $1230 Ex $1155 Gd $880
M-14 (USGI parts, 1986–2006) .. NiB $1930 Ex $1410 Gd $1130
M-14 National Match (USGI parts,
  premium bbl.,1993–96) .... NiB $2055 Ex $1655 Gd $1130
M-14 NMR (1987–2006) .... NiB $2680 Ex $2130 Gd $1210
M-21 Match Rifle (match built,
  1 MOA guarantee) ...... NiB $3480 Ex $2910 Gd $1655

T-48 FAL SERIES SEMIAUTOMATIC RIFLE
Rebuilt FAL style civilian rifles. Caliber: .308 Win.
Israeli Pattern model (21-in.
  heavy or standard bbl., 1990–92) .. NiB $1655 Ex $1480
  Gd $1080
L1A1 Pattern model (Disc.
  1992) .... NiB $1680 Ex $1510 Gd $1110
Bush model (18-in. bbl.,Disc.
  1990).................... NiB $1630 Ex $1455 Gd $1030

FAL SERIES SEMIAUTOMATIC RIFLE
Rebuilt FAL style civilian rifles w/Armscoprp forged receiver.
Caliber: .308 Win. Mfg. 1987–89.
FAL model (21-in. bbl.) ... NiB $1810 Ex $1580 Gd $1130
FAL Bush model (18-in. bbl.) NiB $2210 Ex $2155 Gd $1755
FAL Para model (18-in. bbl.,
  folding metal stock) .... NiB $2410 Ex $2155 Gd $1750

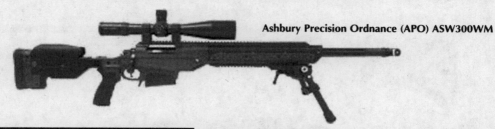

Ashbury Precision Ordnance (APO) ASW300WM

ARNOLD ARMS — Arlington, WA

AFRICAN SAFARI
Calibers: .243 to .458 Win. Mag. and proprietary cartridges. 22- to 26-in. bbl. Weight: 7-9 lbs. Scope mount standard or w/optional M70 Express sights. Chrome-moly in four finishes. "A" and "AA" Fancy Grade English walnut stock with number 5 standard wraparound checkering pattern. Ebony forend tip. Made 1994-2001.

w/ "A" Grade English
walnut stock, blue finish	NiB $4732	Ex $3841	Gd $2690
Std. polish	NiB $4969	Ex $4000	Gd $2821
Hi-Luster	NiB $5189	Ex $4290	Gd $2950
Stainless steel matte	NiB $4733	Ex $3847	Gd $2993

w/ "AA" Grade English walnut stock,
C-M matte blue finish	NiB $4707	Ex $3810	Gd $2688
Std. polish	NiB $4988	Ex $4037	Gd $2835
Hi-Luster	NiB $5188	Ex $4200	Gd $2969
Stainless steel matte finish	NiB $4707	Ex $3875	Gd $2710

ALASKAN TROPHY
Calibers: .300 Magnum to .458 Win. Magnum. 24- to 26-in. bbl. Weight: 7-9 lbs. Scope mount w/Express sights standard. Stainless steel or chrome-moly Apollo action w/fibergrain or black synthetic stock. Barrel band on 357 H&H and larger magnums. Made 1996-2000.
Matte finish	NiB $3330	Ex $2689	Gd $1900
Std. polish	NiB $3559	Ex $2900	Gd $2044
Stainless steel	NiB $3386	Ex $2744	Gd $1935

ARSENAL Inc. — Las Vegas, NV

Exclusive importer and manufacturer of Bulgarian Arsenal commercial AK platform rifles since 2001.

SAM-5 series . . . . NiB $720 Ex $540 Gd $400
AK-47 platform. Semiauto. SA. Caliber: .223 Rem., 30-rnd. magazine. 16.3-in. bbl. Furniture: black or green polymer. Sights: adj. front/rear. Finish: blued. Weight: 8 lbs. Made 2003-09.

SAM-7 S . . . . NiB $1400 Ex $1060 Gd $770
AK-47 platform. Semiauto. SA. Caliber: 7.62x39mm, 30-rnd. magazine. Milled receiver. Made 2003-11.
SAM-7 Classic (blonde wood furniture, 2001-02
  reintro. 2007) . . . . NiB $1800 Ex $1260 Gd $900
SAM-7 A1 (front sight block w/bayonet lug,
  2007-09) . . . . NiB $860 Ex $640 Gd $470
SAM-7 A1R (front sight block w/bayonet lug,
  scope rail, 2007-09), add $70
SAM-7 R (14mm muzzle threads, bayonet
  lug, 2012 to date) . . . . NiB $1760 Ex $1260 Gd $910
SAM-7 SF (U.S. mfg., folding stock, Krinkov handguard,
  2007-09 reintro. 2013) . . . NiB $1410 Ex $1060 Gd $780
SAM-7 SFK (U.S. mfg., polymer furniture,
  folding stock, Krinkov handguard, 2007–11
  reintro. 2013) . . . . NiB $2780 Ex $2060 Gd $1510

SA RPK-3R . . . . NiB $2260 Ex $1760 Gd $1260
RPK style platform. Semiauto. SA. Caliber: 5.45x39mm, 45-rnd. magazine. 22.3-in. heavy bbl. w/folding bi-pod.

Furniture: wood w/paddle style buttstock. Milled receiver. Mfg. 2011 only.
SA RPK-5 R (.223 Rem.; 2003-05, 2007-11
  reintro. 2013) . . . . . NiB $2130 Ex $1600 Gd $1180
SA RPK-7 (7.62x39mm;
  2003-05, 2007-09) . . . NiB $1000 Ex $750 Gd $550

SAS M-7 CLASSIC . . . . NiB $1760 Ex $1260 Gd $1000
AK-47 platform Russian style. Semiauto. SA. U.S. mfg. Caliber: 7.62x39mm, 30-rnd. magazine. Stock: metal underfolding. Furniture: blonde wood. Made 2001-02, reintro. 2007 to date.
SAM-7 (blonde wood furniture, underfolder, Bulgarian
  style, 2004-07) . . . . . . NiB $1080 Ex $810 Gd $600

SLR-101 S . . . . NiB $600 Ex $510 Gd $410
AK style platform. Semiauto. SA. Caliber: 7.62x39mm, 30-rnd. magazine. Furniture: OD green or black polymer. Stamped receiver. Mfg. 2003-05 reintro. 2013.
Recent models after 2013, add $300
SLR-101 SB/SG (Furniture: OD green or black polymer,
  2004-05) . . . . NiB $730 Ex $660 Gd $410

SLR-104 SERIES . . . . NiB $960 Ex $720 Gd $530
AK-74 style platform. Semiauto. SA 2-stage trigger. Caliber: 5.45x39mm, 30-rnd. magazine. 16.25-in. bbl. Furniture: black polymer w/side folding stock. Stamped receiver. Made 2013 to date.

SLR-105 SERIES . . . . NiB $700 Ex $610 Gd $480
AK-74 style platform. Semiauto. SA. Caliber: 5.45x39mm, 30-rnd. magazine. 16.25-in. bbl. Furniture: black polymer NATO style buttstock. Stamped receiver. Made 2007-09.

SLR-106 SERIES . . . . NiB $910 Ex $680 Gd $500
AK-74 style platform. Semiauto. SA. Caliber: 5.56x45mm, 30-rnd. magazine. 16.25-in. bbl. Furniture: black or desert sand polymer w/side folding buttstock. Stamped receiver. Mfg. 2007-13.

SLR-107 SERIES . . . . NiB $910 Ex $680 Gd $500
AK-47 style platform. Semiauto. SA. Caliber: 7.62x39mm, 30-rnd. magazine. 16.25-in. bbl. Furniture: black or desert sand polymer w/side folding wire or solid buttstock. Stamped receiver. Made 2008 to date.

ASHBURY PRECISION ORDNANCE (APO) — Charlottesville, VA

Mfg. of high quality precision tactical rifles, ASW (Asymmetric Warrior Series) series and TCR (Tactical Competition Rifle) series. Since 1995.

ASW50 . . . . NiB $12,575 Ex $10,000 Gd $6755
Bolt action. McMillan action. Caliber: .50 BMG., 5-rnd. magazine. 27- or 29-in. bbl. w/muzzle brake. Stock: fully adjustable. Finish: black, FDE, OD green, nordic gray. Weight: 25.75 lbs.

ASW338LM . . . . NiB $8555 Ex $7110 Gd $4610
Bolt action. Surgeon action. Caliber: .338 LM., 10-rnd. magazine. 20- or 27-in. bbl. w/AAC muzzle brake. Stock: fully

RIFLES

A-Square Hannibal

Steyr-Mannlicher Model 90

adjustable. Finish: black, FDE, OD green, nordic gray. Weight: 17 lbs.
ASW300 model (.300 Win. Mag.) NiB $8500 Ex $7830 Gd $4610
ASW308 (.308 Win.) . . . . NiB $7010 Ex $6210 Gd $4010
ASW6.5CM (6.5 Creedmoor) NiB $7010 Ex $6210 Gd $4010
ASW223 (.223 Rem.) . . . . . . NiB $7010 Ex $6210 Gd $4010

TCR338 . . . . NiB $7300 Ex $5755 Gd $3555
Bolt action. Surgeon action. Caliber: .338 Norma Mag., 5-rnd. magazine. 27-in. bbl. w/muzzle brake. Stock: fully adjustable. Finish: black, FDE, OD green, nordic gray. Weight: 14 lbs.
TCR300 model (.300 Win.
Mag., 24-in. bbl.) . . . NiB $7300 Ex $5755 Gd $3510
TCR308 (.308 Win.,
24-in. bbl.) . . . . NiB $7300 Ex $5755 Gd $3510
TCR6.5 (6.5 Creedmoor) NiB $7300 Ex $5755 Gd $3510
TCR223 (.223 Rem.,
20- or 22-in. bbl.) . . . NiB $6330 Ex $5110 Gd $3310
TCR260 (.260 Rem.,
24-in. bbl.) . . . . NiB $6330 Ex $5110 Gd $3310

A-SQUARE COMPANY INC. — Glenrock, WY

CAESAR BOLT-ACTION RIFLE Custom rifle built on Remington's 707 receiver. Calibers: Same as Hannibal, Groups I, II and III. 20- to 26-in. bbl. Weight: 8.5 to 11 lbs. Express 3-leaf rear sight, ramp front. Synthetic or classic Claro oil-finished walnut stock w/flush detachable swivels and Coil-Chek recoil system. Three-way adj. target trigger; 3-position safety. Right- or left-hand. Made 1986-2012.
Synthetic stock model . . . . NiB $3512 Ex $2790 Gd $1947
Walnut stock model . . . . . . NiB $4044 Ex $2379 Gd $1756

GENGHIS KHAN BOLT-ACTION RIFLE
Custom varmint rifle developed on Winchester's M70 receiver; fitted w/heavy tapered bbl. and Coil-Chek stock. Calibers: .22-250 Rem., .243 Win., .25-06 Rem., 6mm Rem. Weight: 8-8.5 lbs. Made 1995-2012.
Synthetic stock model . . . . . NiB $3566 Ex $2312 Gd $2044
Walnut stock model . . . . . . NiB $3482 Ex $2854 Gd $2023

HAMILCAR BOLT-ACTION RIFLE
Similar to Hannibal Model except lighter. Calibers: .25-06, .257 Wby., 6.5x55 Swedish, .270 Wby., 7x57, 7mm Rem., 7mm STW, 7mm Wby., .280 Rem., .30-06, .300 Win., .300 Wby., .338-06, 9.3x62. Weight: 8-8.5 lbs. Made 1994-2012.
Synthetic stock model . . . . . NiB $3554 Ex $2909 Gd $2011
Walnut stock model . . . . . . NiB $3508 Ex $2866 Gd $2009

HANNIBAL BOLT-ACTION RIFLE
Custom rifle built on reinforced P-17 Enfield receiver. Calibers: Group I: 30-06; Group II: 7mm Rem. Mag., .300 Win. Mag.,

.416 Taylor, .425 Express, .458 Win. Mag.; Group III: .300 H&H, .300 Wby. Mag., 8mm Rem. Mag., .340 Wby. Mag., .375 H&H, .375 Wby. Mag., .404 Jeffery, .416 Hoffman, .416 Rem Mag., .450 Ackley, .458 Lott; Group IV: .338 A-Square Mag., .375 A-Square Mag., .378 Wby. Mag., .416 Rigby, .416 Wby. Mag., .460 Short Square Mag., .500 A-Square Mag. 20- to 26-in. bbl. Weight: 9 to 11.75 lbs. Express 3-leaf rear sight, ramp front. Classic Claro oil-finished walnut stock or synthetic stock w/flush detachable swivels and Coil-Chek recoil system. Adj. trigger w/2-position safety. Made 1986-2012.
Synthetic stock model . . . . . NiB $3614 Ex $2870 Gd $1921
Walnut stock model . . . . . . NiB $3707 Ex $2795 Gd $2021

AUSTRIAN MILITARY — Steyr, Austria
Manufactured at Steyr Armory.

MODEL 90
STEYR-MANNLICHER . . . . NiB $337 Ex $189 Gd $139
Straight-pull bolt action. Caliber: 8mm. 5-rnd. magazine. Open sights. 10-in. bayonet. Cartridge clip forms part of the magazine mechanism. Some of these rifles were provided with a laced canvas hand guard, others were of wood.
Carbine model (19.5-in. bbl.) . . . NiB $339 Ex $228 Gd $139

MODEL 95 STEYR-MANNLICHER
SERVICE RIFLE . . . . NiB $299 Ex $190 Gd $137
Straight-pull bolt action. Caliber: 8x50R Mannlicher (many of these rifles were altered during World War II to use the 7.9mm German service ammunition). 5-rnd. Mannlicher-type box magazine. 30-in. bbl. Weight: 8.5 lbs. Sights: Blade front; rear adj. for elevation. Military-type full stock.
Carbine model (19.5-in. bbl.) . . . NiB $329 Ex $250 Gd $141

AUTO-ORDNANCE CORPORATION — Worcester, MA
A division of Kahr Arms. Since 1999, Auto-Ordnance owns the original 1927 Thompson sub-machine gun trademark and mfg. semiauto-only models.

M-1 CARBINE . . . . NiB $780 Ex $690 Gd $485
M-1 Carbine style platform. Semiauto. SA. Caliber: .30 Carbine, 15-rnd. magazine. 18-in. bbl. Stock: smooth walnut. Finish: parkerized. Made 2004 to date.
Paratrooper model
(folding wire buttstock) . . . . . . NiB $840 Ex $720 Gd $500
Tactical model (folding polymer buttstock,
2008-12) . . . . NiB $660 Ex $440 Gd $330

THOMPSON 22-27A-3 . . . . NiB $997 Ex $754 Gd $498
Similar as Deluxe Model 27A-1 except 22 LR w/lightweight alloy receiver, weight 6.5 lbs. Magazines include 5-, 20-, 30- and 50-rnd. box types, 80-rnd. drum. Made 1977-94.

**Auto-Ordnance
Thompson Model 27A-1
Deluxe**

THOMPSON 27A-1
DELUXE. . . . . **NiB $1280 Ex $1130 Gd $755**
Same as Standard Model 27A-1 except w/finned bbl. w/ compensator, adj. rear sight, pistol-grip forestock. Caliber: .22 LR, l0mm (1991 to 1993) or 45 ACP. Weight: 11.5 lbs. Made 1976-99.
.22 LR (Limited production). . . **NiB $1190 Ex $1000 Gd $770**
10-rnd. stick magazine, add $70
20- or 30-rnd. stick magazine, add. $80
10-rnd. drum magazine, add $200
50-rnd. drum magazine, add $300
100-rnd. drum magazine, add $600
Violin carrying case, add $227
Hard carrying case, add $200
Detacable stock/horizontal grip (2007), add $440
Hard Chrome model (2016). . . . . NiB $2610 Ex $2310 Gd $1510
Titanium Gold model (2016). . . NiB $2610 Ex $2310 Gd $1510

THOMPSON 27A-1 STANDARD
SEMIAUTO CARBINE . . . . **NiB $689 Ex $641 Gd $440**
Similar to Thompson submachine gun ("Tommy Gun") except has no provision for automatic firing. Caliber: .45 ACP. 20-rnd. detachable box magazine (5-,15- and 30-rnd. box magazines, 39-rnd. drum also available). 16-in. plain bbl. Weight: 14 lbs. Sights: Aperture rear; blade front. Walnut buttstock, pistol grip and grooved forearm, sling swivels. Made 1976-86.

**THOMPSON
27A-1C LIGHTWEIGHT** . . . . . **NiB $1090 Ex $900 Gd $707**
Similar to Model 27A-1 except w/lightweight alloy receiver. Weight: 9.25 lbs. Made 1984 to date.

THOMPSON M1 . . . . **NiB $1210 Ex $1080 Gd $710**
Similar to Model 27A-1 except in M-1 configuration w/side cocking lever and horizontal forearm. Weight: 11.5 lbs. Made 1986 to date.
M1-C (lightweight). . . . . **NiB $1080 Ex $860 Gd $570**

**THOMPSON
27A-1 COMMANDO** . . . . . . **NiB $1220 Ex $1090 Gd $720**
Similar to Model 27A-1 except parkerized finish and black stock. 13 lbs. Made 1997 to date.

BAIKAL — Izhevsk, Russia
Imported by RWC, Tullytown, PA. Formerly imported by EAA, Corp., Rockledge, Florida.

IZH-18MN SINGLE SHOT . . . . **NiB $250 Ex $190 Gd $110**
Boxlock, break action. Caliber: .222 Rem., .223 Rem., .243 Win., .270 Win., 7.62x39mm, .308 Win., .30-06, or .45-70. 23.5-in. bbl., 40 in. overall. Matte blue finish, checkered walnut stock. Imported from 2003 to 2009.

IZH-94 O/U EXPRESS . . . . . . **NiB $455 Ex $400 Gd $300**
Double barrel, boxlock, break action, extractors. Caliber: .22 Rem., .223 Rem., 30-06, .308 Win., 6.5x55mm or 7.62x39mm.

24-in. bbl. Matte blue finish, checkered walnut stock. Imported from 2001–04.

MP161K SEMIAUTOMATIC . . . **NiB $380 Ex $330 Gd $210**
Caliber: .17 HMR, .22 LR or .22 WMR. 10-rnd. magazine. 19.5-in. bbl., 39 in. overall. Matte blue finish, polymer thumb-hole stock. Imported from 2009 to date.
.17 HMR or .22 WMR, add. 20%

MP221 SIDE BY SIDE . . . . **NiB $990 Ex $870 Gd $555**
Double barrel, boxlock, break action. Caliber: .223 Rem., .270 Win., .30-06, .308 Win., or .45-70. 23.5-in. bbl., 40 in. overall. Matte blue finish, checkered walnut stock. Imported from 2003 to 2009, reintro. 2011 to date.

BALLARD ARMS, INC. — Onsted, MI
Formerly Ballard Rifle LLC, Cody, WY. Mfg. reproduction Ballard and Winchester High Wall rifles from 1996–2009.

1-1/2 HUNTER'S RIFLE. . . . **NiB $3200 Ex $2440 Gd $1833**
Calibers: Seven calibers from .22 LR to .50-70. Single trigger, S-style lever action; uncheckered stock. Weight: 10.5 lbs.

1-3/4 FAR WEST RIFLE . . . . **NiB $2902 Ex $2045 Gd $1471**
Calibers: Eight calibers from .32-40 WCF to .50-90 SS. Patterned after original Ballard Far West model. 30 or 32-in. bbl., standard or heavyweight octagon; double set triggers; ring-style lever. Weight: 9.75 to 10.5 lbs.

NO. 5 PACIFIC . . . . **NiB $3208 Ex $2460 Gd $1996**
Calibers: Nine calibers between .32-40 WCF and .50-90 SS. Similar to No. 1-3/4 Far West model but with under-barrel wiping rod.

NO. 4-1/2 MID-RANGE . . . **NiB $2900 Ex $2080 Gd $1765**
Calibers: Five calibers between .32-40 WCF and .45-110. Designed for black powder silhouette shooting. 30 or 32-in. bbl., half-octagonal heavyweight; single or double set triggers; pistol grip stock; full loop lever; hard rubber Ballard buttplate; Vernier tang sight. Weight: 10.75 to 11.5 lbs.

NO. 7 LONG-RANGE. . . . . **NiB $3369 Ex $2390 Gd $1479**
Caliber: Five calibers between .40-65 Win. and .45-110. Similar to No. 4-1/2 Mid-Range Rifle; designed for long-range shooting. 32 or 34-in. half-octagon standard or heavyweight bbl.

MODEL 1885
HIGH WALL RIFLE . . . . **NiB $3190 Ex $2444 Gd $1954**
Calibers: Various. Exact replica of Winchester Model 1885 (parts are interchangeable). 30 or 32-in. bbl., octagon, case-colored receiver, uncheckered straight-grip stock and forearm. Weight: Approx. 9 lbs. Introduced 2001.
Deluxe model, add $1717
Sporting model, add $250
Shuetzen model, add $400

BANSNER'S ULTIMATE RIFLES, LLC — Adamstown, PA

Established in 1981 in Adamstown, Pennsylvania, as Basner's Gunsmithing Specialties. Company name changed in 2000.

HIGH TECH SERIES . . . . NiB $1032 Ex $790 Gd $641
Calibers: Various. Steel or stainless steel action with factory bbl. Bansner's synthetic stock and Pachmayer decelerator pad.
Stainless steel model, add. $300

SAFARI HUNTER . . . . NiB $6200 Ex $4396 Gd $2398
Calibers: Various dangerous game calibers. Based on Model 70 Classic action; muzzle brake; Lilja Precision stainless steel barrel; synthetic stock; matte black Teflon metal finish. Introduced 2003.

ULTIMATE ONE . . . . NiB $5540 Ex $3766 Gd $3060
Calibers: Various. Bolt-action, modeled on Winchester M70 and Remington 707 actions. Various metal finishes; muzzle brake; custom trigger; custom stock; Pachmayer decelerator pad; custom scope mounts and bases.
Three-position safety, add. $250

WORLD SLAM LIMITED EDITION
RIFLE. . . . . NiB $5345 Ex $3850 Gd $2300
Calibers: Various. Customized Model 707 action; fluted bold body. jeweled trigger. three-position safety; synthetic stock. Only 25-50 of limited edition models were made beginning in 2003.

BARRETT FIREARMS MFG., INC. — Murfreesboro, TN

MODEL 82A . . . . NiB $5000 Ex $3955 Gd $3455
Semiauto. Caliber: .50 BMG. 11-rnd. detachable box magazine. Bbl.: 33 to 37 in. Made 1982-87.

MODEL 82A1
SEMIAUTOMATIC RIFLE. . . NiB $9125 Ex $7010 Gd $5500
Caliber:.416 Barrett or .50 BMG. 10-rnd. detachable box magazine. 29-in. recoiling bbl. w/muzzle brake. 57 in. overall. Weight: 28.5 lbs. Open iron sights and 10x scope. Composit stock w/Sorbothance recoil pad and self-leveling bipod. Blued finish. Made in various configurations from 1985 to date.
Cerakote tan finish, add $200

MODEL 90 . . . . NiB $3530 Ex $3099 Gd $2020
Caliber: .50 BMG. Five round magazine. 29-in. match bbl. 45 in. overall. Weight: 22 lbs. Composite stock w/retractable bipod. Made 1990-95.

MODEL 95 BOLT-ACTION . . NiB $6260 Ex $4890 Gd $3530
Similar to Model 90 bullpup except w/improved muzzle brake and extendable bipod. Made 1995 to date.

MODEL 98B BOLT-ACTION. . . NiB $4410 Ex $4400 Gd $2530
Caliber: .338 Lapua Mag. 20-, 26-, or 27-in. bbl. Weight: 13.5 lbs. 10-rnd. magazine. Muzzle brake, adj. stock. Made 2009-16.

MODEL 99 . . . . NiB $3610 Ex $2830 Gd $2180
Bolt action. Single shot. Caliber:.416 Barrett or .50 BMG. 29- or 32-in. bbl. w/muzzle brake. Picatinny optic rail. Bipod. Finish: black, brown, silver or tan. Weight: 23-24 lbs. Made 1999 to date.
fluted bbl., add $150

MODEL 107A1 . . . . NiB $12,285 Ex $11,000 Gd $7500
Semiauto. Caliber: .50 BMG, 10-rnd. magazine. 20- or 29-in. bbl. w/muzzle brake. Picatinny optic rail. Bipod. Finish: black, brown, gray, OD green or tan. Weight: 31 lbs. Made 2011 to date.

MODEL M4468. . . . . NiB $2400 Ex $1707 Gd $1000
AR-style rifle. Caliber: 6.8 SPC. 16-in. bbl. Weight: 8 lbs. 5-, 10-, 30-rnd. magazine. Made 2005-08.

FIELDCARFT . . . . NiB $1700 Ex $1490 Gd $1130
Bolt action. Forbes style action. Calibers: .243 Win., .22-250, .25-06, 6mm Creedmoor, 6.5 Creedmoor, 6.5x55 Swede, .270, 7mm-08, .308 Win., or .30-06. Barrel: 18- to 24-in. Weight: 5-6 lbs. Sights: Optic ready. Finish: Stainless steel. Stock: Carbon fiber. Lightweight hunting rifle. Made 2017-19.

MODEL MRAD . . . . NiB $5700 Ex $4800 Gd $3755
Bolt action. Modular design for multiple caliber conversions. Caliber: 6.5 Creedmoor, .260 Rem., .308 Win., 7mm Rem. Mag., or .300 Win. Mag. 17- thru 27-in. bbl. w/muzzle brake. Picatinny optic rail, aluminum receiver, folding stock. Finish: black, brown, burnt bronze, OD green or FDE. Weight: 23-24 lbs. Made 2011 to date.
fluted bbl., add $150

MRAD SMR. . . . . NiB $4260 Ex $3730 Gd $2900
Bolt action. Calibers: 6.5 Creedmoor, .308 Win., .300 PRC, .300 Win. Mag., .300 Norma Mag., .338 Lapua Mag., .338 Norma Mag, 10-rnd. magazine. Barrel: 17- to 24-in. fluted. Weight: 10.6-12.3 lbs. Sights: Optic ready. Finish: Black, tungsten gray or FDE. Stock: Fixed. Adj, trigger. Made 2020-date.

MODEL REC7 . . . . NiB $1960 Ex $1500 Gd $1080
AR-style rifle. Action: direct gas impingement. Single-stage trigger. Caliber: 5.56 NATO or 6.8 SPC. 16-in. bbl. Weight: 7.62 lbs. 30-rnd. magazine. Made 2008-13.

MODEL REC7 DI . . . . . NiB $1630 Ex $1430 Gd $930
Similar to Rec7 Gen II but with gas piston system, also in .300 BLK, 2016–date.

MODEL REC7 GEN II . . . . NiB $2130 Ex $1555 Gd $1100
AR-style rifle. Single-stage trigger. Caliber: 5.56 NATO or 6.8 SPC. 16-in. bbl. Handguard: KeyMod. 30-rnd. magazine. Finish: black, grey, FDE or OD green. Sights: flip up. Made 2014 to date.
DMR model (18-in. bbl.,
  2016–date). . . . . NiB $2380 Ex $2080 Gd $1210
Flyweight model (16-in. bbl., 6.1 lbs.,
  2016–date) . . . . NiB $1880 Ex $1655 Gd $1025

MODEL REC10. . . . . NiB $2655 EX $2380 GD $1980
Semiauto. AR10-style carbine. Caliber: .308 Win., 20-rnd. magazine. Barrel: 16-in. w/flash hider. Handguard: BRS M-LOK. Stock: Magpul MOE-SL. Finish: black, grey, or FDE. Sights: Magpul MBUS flip up. Weight: 8.3 lbs. Made 2019 to date.

BEEMAN PRECISION ARMS INC. — Santa Rosa, CA

Since 1993 all European firearms imported by Beeman have been distributed by Beeman Outdoor Sports, Div., Roberts Precision Arms, Inc., Santa Rosa, CA.

WEIHRAUCH HW MODELS 60J AND
60J-ST BOLT-ACTION RIFLES
Calibers: .22 LR (60J-ST), .222 Rem. (60J). 22.8-in. bbl. 41.7 in. overall. Weight: 6.5 lbs. Sights: Hooded blade front; open adj. rear. Blued finish. Checkered walnut stock w/cheekpiece. Made from 1988 to 1994.
Model 60J . . . . NiB $835 Ex $746 Gd $615
Model 60J-ST . . . . NiB $655 Ex $539 Gd $398

**Beretta 501
Bolt-Action Sporter**

Beretta AR-70

WEIHRAUCH HW MODEL 60M
SMALL BORE RIFLE . . . . **NiB $690 Ex $579 Gd $389**
Caliber: .22 LR. Single-shot. 26.8-in. bbl. 45.7 in. overall.
Weight: 10.8 lbs. Adj. trigger w/push-button safety. Sights:
Hooded blade front on ramp, precision aperture rear. Target-
style stock w/stippled forearm and pistol grip. Blued finish.
Made 1988-94.

WEIHRAUCH HW MODEL 660
MATCH RIFLE . . . . **NiB $1023 Ex $855 Gd $445**
Caliber: .22 LR. 26-in. bbl. 45.3 in. overall. Weight: 10.7 lbs.
Adj. match trigger. Sights: globe front, precision aperture rear.
Match-style walnut stock w/adj. cheekpiece and buttplate.
Made 1988-94.

FEINWERKBAU MODEL 2600 SERIES TARGET RIFLE
Caliber: .22 LR. Single-shot. 26.3-in. bbl. 43.7 in. overall.
Weight: 10.6 lbs. Match trigger w/fingertip weight adjustment dial.
Sights: Globe front; micrometer match aperture rear. Laminated
hardwood stock w/adj. cheekpiece. Made 1988-94.
Standard Model 2600 (left-hand) NiB $1733 Ex $1360 Gd $944
Standard Model 2600
   (right-hand) . . . . **NiB $1560 Ex $1239 Gd $816**
Free Rifle Model 2602
   (left-hand) . . . . **NiB $2196 Ex $1755 Gd $1024**
Free Rifle Model 2602
   (right-hand) . . . . **NiB $2196 Ex $1755 Gd $1024**

BELGIAN MILITARY — Belgium

*Mfd. by Fabrique Nationale D'Armes de Guerre, Herstal, Belgium;
Fabrique D'Armes de L'Etat, Lunich, Belgium. Hopkins & Allen
Arms Co. of Norwich, Conn., as well as contractors in Birmingham,
England, also produced these guns during World War I.*

MODEL 1889 MAUSER
MILITARY RIFLE . . . . **NiB $279 Ex $230 Gd $156**
Caliber: 7.65mm Belgian Service (7.65mm Mauser). 5-rnd.
projecting box magazine. 30.75-in. bbl. w/jacket. Weight: 8.5
lbs. Adj. rear sight, blade front. Straight-grip military stock.
This, and the carbine version, was the principal weapon of the
Belgian Army at the start of WWII. Made 1889 to c.1935.

MODEL 1916 MAUSER CARBINE . . . **NiB $300 Ex $240 Gd $190**
Same as Model 1889 Rifle except w/20.75-in. bbl. Weighs 8 lbs.
and has minor differences in the rear sight graduations, lower
band closer to the muzzle and swivel plate on side of buttstock.

MODEL 1935 MAUSER
MILITARY RIFLE . . . . **NiB $370 Ex $292 Gd $169**
Same general specifications as F.N. Model 1924; minor dif-
ferences. Caliber: 7.65mm Belgian Service. Mfd. by Fabrique
Nationale D'Armes de Guerre.

MODEL 1936 MAUSER
MILITARY RIFLE . . . . **NiB $378 Ex $290 Gd $166**
An adaptation of Model 1889 w/German M/98-type bolt,
Belgian M/89 protruding box magazine. Caliber: 7.65mm
Belgian Service. Mfd. by Fabrique Nationale D'Armes de Guerre.

BENELLI — Urbino, Itay

Imported by Benelli USA, Accokeek, MD.

LUPO SERIES
Bolt action. Cal.: .243 Win., .270 Win., 6.5 Creedmoor, .308
Win., .30-06, or .300 Win. Mag.; detachable magazine. Bbl.:
22- or 24-in. free floated, threaded. Finish: Matte blue. Stock:
Adj. black synthetic. Sights: Optic ready. Weight: 6.9-7.1 lbs.
Adj. trigger.   Imported from 2002 to date.
Standard model. . . . . **NiB $1455 Ex $1280 Gd $990**
**BE.S.T. model (BE.S.T. finish, walnut
or camo stock, 2022-date)** . . **NiB $1699 Ex $1499 Gd $1100**

R1 SEMIAUTOMATIC . . . . **NiB $910 Ex $700 Gd $500**
Caliber: .270 WSM, .308 Win., .30-06, .300 WSM, .300 Win.
Mag. or .338 Win. Mag. 20-, 22- or 24-in. bbl. Matte black
finish, checkered walnut or polymer stock. Designated Argo in
Europe. Imported from 2002 to date.
ComforTech stock, add **$125**

BENTON & BROWN FIREARMS, INC. — Fort Worth, TX

MODEL 93 BOLT-ACTION RIFLE
Similar to Blaser Model R84 (the B&B rifle is built on the Blaser
action, see separate listing) with an interchangeable bbl. system.
Calibers: .243 Win., 6mm Rem., .25-06, .257 Wby., .264 Win.,
.270 Win., .280 Rem., 7mm Rem Mag., .30-06, .308, .300 Wby.,
.300 Win. Mag., .338 Win., .375 H&H. 22- or 24-in. bbl. 41 or
43 in. overall. Bbl.-mounted scope rings and one-piece base; no
sights. Two-piece walnut or fiberglass stock. Made 1993–96.
Walnut stock model . . . . . . **NiB $1896 Ex $1744 Gd $1012**
Fiberglass stock model add **$227**
Extra bbl. assembly, add **$525**
Extra bolt assembly, add **$450**

BERETTA U.S.A. CORP. — Accokeek, MD

*Manufactured by Fabbrica D'Armi Pietro Beretta, S.P.A.,
Gardone Val Trompia (Brescia), Italy.*

455 SIDE BY SIDE EXPRESS DOUBLE RIFLE
Sidelock action w/removable sideplates. Calibers: .375 H&H,
.458 Win. Mag., .470 NE, .500 NE (3 in.), .416 Rigby. Bbls.:
23.5 or 25.5-in. Weight: 11 lbs. Double triggers. Sights: Blade
front; V-notch folding leaf rear. Checkered European walnut
forearm and buttstock w/recoil pad. Color casehardened
receiver w/blued bbls. Various grades of engraving. Custom
built. Made 1990 to date.
Model 455 . . . . **NiB $100,000**
Model 455EELL . . . . **NiB $150,000**

500 BOLT-ACTION SPORTER
Centerfire bolt-action rifle w/Sako A I short action. Calibers:
.222 Rem., .223 Rem. Five round magazine. 23.63-in. bbl.
Weight: 6.5 lbs. Available w/ or w/o iron sights. Tapered dove-
tailed receiver. European walnut stock. Disc. 1998.
Standard model. . . . . **NiB $560 Ex $455 Gd $355**
DL model . . . . **NiB $1400 Ex $1288 Gd $909**
EELL model . . . . **NiB $1555 Ex $1465 Gd $990**
w/iron sights, add **10%**

501 BOLT-ACTION SPORTER
Same as Model 500 except w/Sako A II medium action.
Calibers: .243 Win., .308 Win. Weight: 7.5 lbs. Disc. 1986.
Standard . . . . **NiB $600 Ex $466 Gd $420**

RIFLES

DL model . . . . NiB $1400 Ex $1097 Gd $944
501 EELL (engraved) . . . . NiB $1560 Ex $1329 Gd $989
w/iron sights, add 10%

502 BOLT-ACTION SPORTER
Same as Model 500 except w/Sako A III long action. Calibers: .270 Win., 7mm Rem. Mag., .30/06, 375 H&H. Weight: 8.5 lbs. Disc. 1986.
Standard model. . . . . NiB $630 Ex $534 Gd $460
DL model . . . . NiB $1500 Ex $1299 Gd $980
502 EELL (engraved) . . . . . . NiB $1580 Ex $1347 Gd $1088
w/iron sights, add 10%

AR-70 . . . . NiB $1930 Ex $1788 Gd $1077
Semiauto. Caliber: .223 Rem. (5.56mm). 30-rnd. magazine. 17.75-in. bbl. Weight: 8.25 lbs. Sights: Rear peep adj. for windage and elevation; blade front. High-impact synthetic buttstock. Imported 1984-89.

ARX 100. . . . . NIB $1400 Ex $1380 Gd $1030
Semiauto. Ambidextrous controls. Caliber: 5.56 NATO. 16-in. quick-change bbl. Receiver: polymer. Weight: 6.75 lbs. Compatible w/AR15-style 30-rnd. magazine. Made 2013 to date.

ARX 160. . . . . NIB $530 EX $380 GD $920
Similar to ARX 100 except in .22 LR. Made 2013 to date.

CX4 STORM. . . . . NIB $700 EX $560 GD $460
Semiauto. SA. Calibers: 9mm, .40 S&W or .45 ACP. 16.6-in. quick-change bbl. Receiver: polymer w/thumbhole stock. Weight: 5.6 lbs. Compatible w/CX4 Storm magazines. Made 2003 to date.

EXPRESS S686/S689 SILVER SABLE O/U RIFLE
Calibers: .30-06 Spfld., 9.3x74R, and .444 Marlin. 24-in. bbl. Weight: 7.7 lbs. Drilled and tapped for scope mount. European-style cheek rest and ventilated rubber recoil pad. Imported 1995.
Model S686/S689 Silver
   Sable II. . . . . NiB $4010 Ex $3800 Gd $2244
Model S689 Gold Sable . . . NiB $7755 Ex $5329 Gd $3144
Model S686/S689 EELL
   Diamond Sable . . . . . . NiB $10,510 Ex $9765 Gd $6479
w/extra bbl. set, add $350
w/detachable claw mounts, add $645

EXPRESS SSO O/U EXPRESS DOUBLE RIFLE
Sidelock. Calibers: .375 H&H Mag., .458 Win. Mag., 9.3 x 74R. 23-24- or 25.5-in. blued bbls. Weight: 11 lbs. Double triggers. Express sights w/blade front and V-notch folding leaf rear. Optional Zeiss scope w/claw mounts. Color casehardened receiver w/scroll engraving, game scenes and gold inlays on higher grades. Checkered European walnut forearm and buttstock w/cheekpiece and recoil pad. Imported 1985 to 1989.
Model SS0 (disc. 1989) NiB $15,800 Ex $10,600 Gd $6545
Model SS05 (disc. 1990) NiB $18600 Ex $14,300 Gd $7600
Model SS06 Custom . . . . NiB $75,000
Model SS06 EELL Gold Custom. . . . . NiB $125,000
Extra bbl. assembly, add $7070
Claw mounts, add. $800

MATO . . . . NiB $980 Ex $733 Gd $533
Calibers: .270 Win., .280 Rem., 7mm Rem. Mag, .300 Win. Mag., .338 Win. Mag., .375 H&H. 23.6-in. bbl. Weight: 8 lbs. Adjustable trigger. Drop-out box magazine. Drilled and tapped for scope w/ or w/o adj. sights. Walnut or synthetic stock. Manufactured based on Mauser 98 action. Made 1997-2002.

Deluxe model . . . . NiB $2015 Ex $1723 Gd $976
.375 H&H w/iron sights, add $350

SMALL BORE SPORTING CARBINE/TARGET RIFLE
Semiauto w/bolt handle in raised or conventional single-shot bolt-action w/handle in lowered position. Caliber: .22 LR. Four, 5-, 8-, 10- or 20-rnd. magazines. 20.5-in. standard or heavy bbl. Sights: 3-leaf folding rear, partridge front. Target or sporting stock w/checkered pistol grip and forend and sling swivels. Weight: 5.5 to 6 lbs.
Sporter model (Super Sport X) . NiB $460 Ex $355 Gd $256
Target model (Olympia X). . . . . NiB $340 Ex $520 Gd $345

BERGARA — Bergara, Spain

Black Powder Products (BPI) in Lawrenceville, GA, which owns CVA trademark, imports Bergara rifles and barrels.

B-14 SERIES
Bolt action. Caliber: .22-250, .243, 6.5 Creedmoor, 6.5 PRC, .270 Win, 7mm-08, 7mm Rem. Mag., .308 Win, .30-06, .300 Win Mag., .300 PRC, and .450 Bushmaster; detachable or box magazine. Wood, synthetic, or chassis stock. Barrel: 20-, 22-, 24-in. various contours depending on model. Weight: 7-10 lbs. depending on model. Adj. trigger. Mfg. 2015-date.
BMP model (20-, 22 or 24-in. bbl., BMP chassis stock w/
   adj. comb and LOP) . . . . NiB $980 Ex $855 Gd $680
HMR model (20-, 22 or 24-in. threaded bbl., composite stock
   w/adj. comb and LOP) . . . . . . NiB $980 Ex $855 Gd $680
Hunter model (straight comb synthetic stock;
   22 or 24-in. bbl.) . . . . NiB $730 Ex $630 Gd $480
R model (.22 LR, 18-in. bbl.,
   HMR stock). . . . . NiB $980 Ex $855 Gd $680
Ridge model (straight comb synthetic stock;
   18-, 20-, 22 or 24-in. bbl.) . . . NiB $755 Ex $645 Gd $480
Sporter Varmint model (.308, black synthetic stock,
   24-in. heavy bbl.) . . . . NiB $805 Ex $705 Gd $555
Timber model (Monte Carlo wood stock,
   fixed magazine, matte blue) . . NiB $805 Ex $705 Gd $555
Woodsman model (wood stock, fixed or detachable
   magazine, blued, disc.) . . . . . . NiB $805 Ex $705 Gd $555

BC15 LONG RANGE
HUNTER. . . . . NIB $3805 EX $3405 GD $2555
Bolt action. Caliber: .300 Win. Mag. or .300 Rem. Ultra Mag.; detachable or box magazine. McMillan A3 Sporter stock. Barrel: 24-in. Adj. Timney or Shilen trigger. Mfg. 2013-15.

BCR13 SPORT HUNTER . . . . NIB $3255 EX $2980 GD $2260
Bolt action. Caliber: .270 Win, .308 Win, .30-06. McMillan A3 Sporter stock. Barrel: 22-in. Adj. Timney or Shilen trigger. Mfg. 2013-15.

BCR17 MEDIUM
TACTICAL . . . . NIB $3805 EX $3405 GD $2555
Bolt action. Caliber: .308 Win. McMillan A1-3 stock. Barrel: 22-in. Adj. Timney or Shilen trigger. Mfg. 2013-15.
w/chassis stock (APO Sporter
   Modular chassis stock) . . . NiB $4205 Ex $3830 Gd $2880

BCR19 HEAVY TACTICAL . . NIB $4205 EX $3830 GD $2880
Bolt action. Caliber: .308 Win. or .300 Win. Mag. McMillan A4 stock. Barrel: 26-in. Adj. Timney or Shilen trigger. Mfg. 2013-15.

BCR22 MOUNTAIN
HUNTER. . . . . NIB $2755 EX $2410 GD $1855
Bolt action. Cal.: Various short action calibers. Bbl.: 18-in. tapered. Stock: Fiberglass. Weight: 6.5-7 lbs. Adj. Timney trigger. Disc. 2017.

BCR23 SPORT HUNTER . . . NIB $3505 EX $2905 GD $2105
Bolt action. Caliber: Various calibers. McMillan Hunter stock. Barrel: 22- or 24-in. Adj. Timney trigger. Mfg. 2015-18.

**BCR24 VARMINT
HUNTER . . . .** NIB $3605 EX $3005 GD $2205
Bolt action. Caliber: .22-250, .222, .223, .234, 6mm Creedmoor, 6.5 Creedmoor, .260, .308,. McMillan Remington Varmint stock. Barrel: 24-in. Adj. Timney trigger. Mfg. 2016-18.

**BCR25 LONG RANGE
HUNTER . . . .** NIB $3755 EX $3155 GD $2330
Bolt action. Caliber: Various calibers. McMillan A3 stock. Barrel: 24-in. Adj. Timney trigger. Mfg. 2015-18.

BCR27 COMPETITION . . . . NIB $4455 EX $3730 GD $2755
Bolt action. Caliber: Various calibers. McMillan A3-5 stock. Barrel: 26-in. w/Dead Air muzzle brake. Adj. Timney trigger. Mfg. 2016-18.

**BCR28 COMPETITION
CHASSIS . . . .** NIB $3705 EX $3255 GD $2505
Bolt action. Caliber: Various calibers. Magpul PRS stock. Barrel: 26-in. w/Dead Air muzzle brake. Adj. Timney trigger. Mfg. 2016-17.

BCR29 HEAVY TACTICAL . . NIB $4455 EX $3730 GD $2755
Bolt action. Caliber: Various calibers. Magpul PRS stock. Barrel: 24-in. w/Dead Air muzzle brake. Adj. Timney trigger. Disc. 2018.

**BCR30 HEAVY TACTICAL
CHASSIS . . . .** NIB $4305 EX $3605 GD $2655
Bolt action. Caliber: Various calibers. Accuracy International AX stock. Barrel: 24-in. w/Dead Air muzzle brake. Adj. Timney trigger. Mfg. 2016-18.

BMR . . . . NIB $480 EX $430 GD $330
Bolt action. Cal.: .17 HMR, .22 LR, or .22 WMR. Bbl.: 18- or 20-in. w/match chamber, threaded. Stock: Composite. Weight: 5.5-5.8 lbs. Bergara Performance Trigger. Mfg. 2021-date.
Carbon model (carbon fiber bbl.) NiB $580 Ex $505 Gd $405

**BX-11 TAKEDOWN
HUNTER . . . .** NIB $4755 EX $4155 GD $3255
Bolt action. Caliber: Various calibers. Accuracy International AX stock. Barrel: 24-in. w/Dead Air muzzle brake. Adj. Timney trigger. Mfg. 2016-18.

BXR SERIES
Semiauto. Cal.: .22 LR, 10-rnd. rotary magazine. Bbl.: 16.5-in. carbon fiber or fluted steel, threaded. Sights: Optic ready. Stock: Synthetic. Weight: 4.7-5.2 lbs. Bergara BXR Trigger. Mfg. 2019-date.
steel bbl . . . . NIB $480 EX $430 GD $330
carbon fiber bbl . . . . NIB $570 EX $520 GD $420

HEAVY TACTICAL . . . . NIB $4755 EX $4155 GD $3255
Bolt action. Caliber: .243, .270, .308 Win., .30-06 or .300 Win. Mag; detachable magazine. Walnut or black synthetic stock. Barrel: 22- or 24-in. Weight: 6.6 lbs. Mfg. 2013-17.

MOUNTAIN HUNTER SERIES
Bolt action. Caliber: .243, .270 Win, 7mm-08, .308 Win, .30-06 and .300 Win Mag. Lightweight fiberglass stock. Barrel: 18- or 20-in. Weight: 5.8 lbs. Adj. Timney trigger. Mfg. 2014-15.
Standard model. . . . . NiB $3505 Ex $3070 Gd $2380
**BCR22 model (18-in. bbl., fiberglass stock,
fixed magazine) . . . .** NiB $2755 Ex $2405 Gd $1855

PREMIER SERIES
Bolt action. Caliber: .22-250, .243, 6.5 Creedmoor, 6.5 PRC, .270 Win, .28 Nosler, 7mm-08, 7mm Rem. Mag., .308 Win, .30-06, .300 Win Mag., .300 PRC, .450 Bushmaster; 5-rnd. detachable or fixed magazine. Various stocks. Barrel: 20-, 24- or 26-in. w/threaded muzzle. Weight: 8.5-8.75 lbs. Mfg. 2016-date.
Standard model. . . . . NiB $3505 Ex $3070 Gd $2380
**Approach model (Grayboe fiberglass
stock) . . . .** NiB $1670 Ex $1460 Gd $1130
**Classic model (walnut Monte Carlo
stock, 2016-18)) . . . .** NiB $2055 Ex $1800 Gd $1405
**Highlander model (composite stock,
fixed magazine) . . . .** NiB $1605 Ex $1405 Gd $1105
**HMR Pro model (HMR stock, AICS
detachable magazine). . . . .** NiB $1455 Ex $1280 Gd $990
**Long Range model (carbon
fiber stock, detachable
magazine, 2017-18) . . . . . .** NiB $2555 Ex $2230 Gd $1730
**LRP model (XLR Element
chassis, 2016-19) . . . .** NiB $1710 Ex $1500 Gd $1155
**LRP 2.0 model (XLR Element
3.0 chassis, 2020-date) . . .** NiB $1710 Ex $1500 Gd $1155
**LRP Elite model (ORIAS chassis, Magpul
PRS stock, 2016-18) . . . . .** NiB $2610 Ex $2280 Gd $1755
**Mountain model (carbon fiber
stock, disc. 2019) . . . .** NiB $1870 Ex $1630 Gd $1280
**Mountain 2.0 model (AG carbon
fiber stock, 2020-date) . . .** NiB $1830 Ex $1610 Gd $1380
**Ridgeback model (adj. fiberglass
stock, 2019-date) . . . .** NiB $1710 Ex $1510 Gd $1155
**Stalker model (fiberglass
stock, 2016-18). . . . .** NiB $1870 Ex $1630 Gd $1280

WILDERNESS SERIES
Bolt action. Cal.: 6.4 Creedmoor, 6.5 PRC, 7mm-08, .308 Win., .28 Nosler, .300 PRC, or .300 Win. Mag. Bbl.: 20-, 24-, or 26-in. threaded. Stock: Composite. Weight: 7.1-9.9 lbs. Bergara Performance Trigger, B-14 action. Mfg. 2020-date.
**HMR model (composite
HMR stock) . . . .** NiB $1080 Ex $955 Gd $730
Hunter model (synthetic stock). . NiB $770 Ex $680 Gd $530
**Ridge model (synthetic stock,
Omni muzzle brake). . . . . . .** NiB $830 Ex $730 Gd $565
**Terrain model (composite stock,
Omni muzzle brake). . . . . . .** NiB $1030 Ex $910 Gd $710

VINCENZO BERNARDELLI — Brescia, Italy

Currently headquartered in Brescia, Italy, Bernardelli arms were manufactured from 1721 to 1997 in Gardone, Italy. Imported and distributed by Armsport, Inc., Miami, Florida. Also handled by Magnum Research, Inc., Quality Arms, Inc., Armes De Chasse, Stoeger and Action Arms.

CARBINA .22 . . . . NiB $580 Ex $300 Gd $170
Semiauto. Caliber: .22 rimfire. Blow-back action. Imported from 1990 to 1997.

EXPRESS VB . . . . NiB $5768 Ex $4755 Gd $3690
Double barrel. Calibers: Various. Side-by-side sidelock action. Ejectors, double triggers. Imported from 1990 to1997.
Deluxe model (w/double triggers), add $1125

EXPRESS 2000. . . . . NiB $2707 Ex $2025 Gd $1580
Calibers: .30-06, 7x65R, 8x57JRS, 9.3x74R. Over/under box-lock design. Single or double triggers, extractors. Checkered walnut stock and forearm. Imported from 1994 to 1997.
Single trigger, add $200

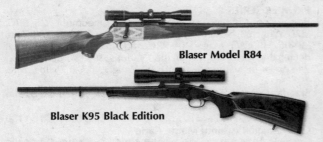

Blaser Model R84

Blaser K95 Black Edition

**British Military No. 5
Mark 1 "Jungle Carbine"**

MINERVA EXPRESS . . . . . . NiB $5200 Ex $3890 Gd $4098
Caliber: Various. Exposed hammers. Extractors, double triggers. Moderate engraving. Imported from 1995 to 1997.

MODEL 120 . . . . NiB $2120 Ex $1587 Gd $1100
Combination gun; over-under boxlock; 12 gauge over .22 Hornet, .222 Rem., 5.6x50R Mag., .243 Win., 6.5x57R, .270 Win., 7x57R, .308 Win., .30-06, 6.5x55, 7x65R, 8x57JRS, 9.3x74R. Iron sights. Checkered walnut stock and forearm. Double triggers, automatic ejectors or extractors. Ventilated recoil pad. Engraved action. Made in Italy. Discontinued.

MODEL 190 . . . . NiB $1489 Ex $1129 Gd $1069
Combination gun; over-under boxlock. Calibers: 12, 16 or 20 ga. Over .222 Rem., .243 Win., .30-06, .308 Win., 5.6x50R Mag., .5.6x57R, 6.5x55, 6.5x57R, 7x57R, 7x65R, 8x57JRS, 9.3x74R. Iron sights. Checkered walnut stock. Double triggers; extractors. Made in Italy. Introduced in 1969, discontinued 1989.

MODEL 2000 . . . . NiB $2713 Ex $1866 Gd $1390
Combination gun; over-under boxlock action. Calibers: 12, 16 or 20 ga. Over .222 Rem., .22 Hornet, 5.6x50R Mag., .243 Win., 6.5x55, 6.5x57R, .270 Win., 7x57R, .308 Win., .30-06, 8x57JRS, 9.3x74R. Bbl: 23 in. Sights: Blade front, open rear. Hand checkered, oil-finished select European walnut stock, double-set triggers, auto ejectors. Silvered, engraved action. Made in Italy. Introduced in 1990, disconti nued 1991.
Extra bbl. assembly, add $595

BLASER U.S.A., INC. — Fort Worth, TX

Manufactured by Blaser Jagdwaffen GmbH, Germany, imported by Sigarms, Exeter, NH; Autumn Sales, Inc., Fort Worth, Texas. All rifles are highly customizable by customer. Contact Blaser directly on the more luxurious models.

MODEL BL 820. . . . . NiB $1560 Ex $1080 Gd $810
Single-shot. Action: falling block. Calibers: various. Imported 1982 to 1989.

MODEL K77 A . . . . NiB $2010 Ex $1480 Gd $1110
Single-shot. Break action. Calibers: various. 22.6- or 24-in. bbl. Stock: Checkered walnut. Weight: 5.5 lbs. Imported 1988 to 1990.

MODEL K95 Series
Single-shot. Break action. Calibers: various. 22- or 25-in. bbl. Stock: Checkered walnut. Imported from 2000 to date.
Jaeger . . . . NiB $4480 Ex $3900 Gd $2430
Luxus (Grade 4 wood stock) . . . NiB $5180 Ex $4510 Gd $2810
Stutzen Luxus
    (engraved receiver) . . . . NiB $8210 Ex $7155 Gd $4510

MODEL R8 PROFESSIONAL SERIES BOLT-ACTION REPEATER
Improved version of R93. Various calibers, stock configurations, and bbl lengths. Imported from 2011 to date.
Classic Sporter (wood stock) . . . . NiB $3255 Ex $2830 Gd $1660
Professional Hunter
    (dangerous game calibers) . . . NiB $7155 Ex $6210 Gd $3830

Professional Success
    (thumbhole stock) . . . . NiB $3930 Ex $3380 Gd $1780

MODEL R84 BOLT-ACTION RIFLE
Calibers: .22-250, .243, 6mm Rem., .25-06, .270, .280 Rem., .30-06- .257 Wby. Mag., .264 Win. Mag., 7mm Rem Mag., .300 Win. Mag., .300 Wby. Mag., .338 Win. Mag., .375 H&H. Interchangeable bbls. w/standard or Magnum bolt assemblies. Bbl. length: 23 in. (standard); 24 in. (Magnum). 41 to 42 in. overall. Weight: 7 to 7.25 lbs. No sights. Bbl.-mounted scope system. Two-piece Turkish walnut stock w/solid black recoil pad. Imported from 1989 to 1994.
Standard . . . . NiB $2245 Ex $1725 Gd $1190
Deluxe (engraved
    game scene) . . . . NiB $2400 Ex $2021 Gd $1200
Super Deluxe
    (Gold and silver inlays) . . NiB $2449 Ex $1990 Gd $1590
Left-hand model, add $150
Extra bbl. assembly, add $600

MODEL R93 SAFARI SERIES BOLT-ACTION REPEATER
Similar to Model R-84 except restyled action w/straight-pull bolt, unique safety and searless trigger mechanism. Additional chamberings: 6.5x55, 7x57, .308, .416 Rem. Optional open sights. Imported 1994 to 1998.
Safari . . . . NiB $3598 Ex $2277 Gd $1844
Safari Deluxe . . . . NiB $3943 Ex $4134 Gd $3297
Safari Super Deluxe . . . . NiB $4854 Ex $4326 Gd $3458
Extra bbl. assembly, add $600

MODEL R93 CLASSIC SERIES BOLT-ACTION REPEATER
Similar to Model R-93 Safari except w/expanded model variations. Imported from 1998 to 2002.
Attache (Premium wood,
    fluted bbl.) . . . . NiB $5890 Ex $4550 Gd $3250
Classic
    (.22-250 to .375 H&H) . . NiB $2600 Ex $1860 Gd $1510
Classic Safari
    (.416 Rem.) . . . . NiB $3580 Ex $2660 Gd $1830
LRS 2 (long range sporter) . . . . NiB $3960
    Ex $2810 Gd $1730
Luxus. . . . . NiB $4160 Ex $2860 Gd $1860
LX (.22-250 to .416 Rem.) . . NiB $1799 Ex $1445 Gd $996
Octagon . . . . NiB $7110 Ex $5000 Gd $3260
Prestige (2002-10) . . . . NiB $2980 Ex $2130 Gd $1510
Professional
    (green synthetic stock. . . . NiB $2860 Ex $2060 Gd $1300
Stutzen (octagon brrl . . . . . . NiB $6580 Ex $5260 Gd $3960
Synthetic (.22-250
    to .375 H&H) . . . . NiB $1908 Ex $1235 Gd $855
Extra bbl. assembly, add $600

MODEL S2 . . . . NiB $7360 Ex $5860 Gd $4560
Side-by-side. Action: Boxlock. Calibers: various. 22.6- or 24-in. bbl. Stock: Checkered Turkish walnut. Weight: 7.7 lbs. Imported from 2004 to 2005, reintro. 2007 to date.
Safari (dangerous game
    calibers) . . . . NiB $10,160 Ex $8010 Gd $6310

BRITISH MILITARY — England

Manufactured at Royal Small Arms Factory, Enfield Lock, Middlesex, England, private contractors.

Brno Model 2

Brno Model 21H
Bolt-Action Sporting Rifle

Brno Model 22F

Brno Model-ZKM 611

RIFLE NO. 1 MK III* . . . . NiB $910 Ex $800 Gd $510
Short magazine Lee-Enfield (S.M.L.E.). Bolt action. Caliber:
.303 British. 10-rnd. box magazine. 25.25-in. bbl. Weight:
8.75 lbs. Sights: Adj. rear; blade front w/guards. Two-piece,
full-length military stock. Note: The earlier Mark III (approved
1907) is virtually the same as Mark III (adopted 1918) except
for sights and different magazine cut-off that was eliminated
on the latter.
H.T. Sniper (factory scope) . . NiB $7510 Ex $6010 Gd $4755

**S.M.L.E. MK V (RIFLE
NO. 1 MK V).** . . . . NiB $1810 Ex $1610 Gd $1055
NOTE: Similar to Rifle No. 1 MK III and III* except w/ receiver
mounted aperture sights.

**RIFLE NO. 3 MK I
(PATTERN 1914 RIFLE)** . . . . . NiB $1355 Ex $1010 Gd $755
Modified Mauser-type bolt action. Except for caliber .303 British
and long-range sight, this rifle is the same as U.S. Model 1917
Enfield. See listing of the latter for general specifications.
**T (sniper configuration
w/scope)** . . . . NiB $9255 Ex $7510 Gd $6010

RIFLE NO. 4 MK I AND I* . . . . . NiB $1355 Ex $1005 Gd $805
Post-World War I modification of the S.M.L.E. intended to simplify mass production. General specifications same as Rifle No.
1 Mark III except w/aperture rear sight and minor differences in
construction and weighs 9.25 lbs.
**T (sniper configuration
w/scope)** . . . . NiB $8510 Ex $6255 Gd $4655

**RIFLE NO. 4 MK
1/2 AND 1/3.** . . . . NiB $1105 Ex $855 Gd $680
Modification of the S.M.L.E. Caliber: .303 British. 10-rnd. box
magazine. 23-in. bbl. Weight: 6.75 lbs. Sights: Micrometer
click rear peep; blade front. One-piece military-type stock w/
recoil pad. Made post WWII.

RIFLE NO. 5 MK I . . . . NiB $905 Ex $680 Gd $500
Jungle Carbine. Modification of the S.M.L.E. similar to Light
Rifle No. 4 Mark I except w/20.5-in. bbl. w/flash hider, carbine-type stock. Made during WWII, originally designed for
use in the Pacific Theater.

BRNO SPORTING RIFLES — Brno, Czech Republic

*Manufactured by Ceska Zbrojovka; Imported by Euro-Imports,
El Cajon, California, previously by Bohemia Arms & Magnum
Research. See also CZ rifles.*

MODEL I (ZKM 451) . . . . NiB $689 Ex $615 Gd $437
Bolt action. Caliber: .22 LR. Five round detachable magazine.
22.75-in. bbl. Weight: 6 lbs. Sights: three-leaf open rear;
hooded ramp front. Sporting stock w/checkered pistol grip,
swivels. Made 1945 to 1957.

MODEL 2 (ZKM 452) . . . . NiB $641 Ex $543 Gd $444
Same as Model I except w/deluxe grade stock. Made 1949-57.

MODEL 3 (ZKM 455) . . . . NiB $641 Ex $567 Gd $495
Same as Model I except w/heavy bbl. and target stock. Made
1948-56.

MODEL 4 (ZKM 456) . . . . NiB $700 Ex $587 Gd $488
Same as Model 3 except w/improved target trigger mechanism.
Made 1956 to 1962.

MODEL 5 (ZKM 573) . . . . NiB $755 Ex $633 Gd $456
Same as Model I except w/improved trigger mechanism. Made
1957-78.

**MODEL 21H BOLT-ACTION
SPORTING RIFLE** . . . . NiB $1590 Ex $1325 Gd $1009
Mauser-type action. Calibers: 6.5x57mm, 7x57mm 8x57mm.
Five round box magazine. 20.5-in. bbl. Double set trigger.
Weight: 6.75 lbs. Sights: Two-leaf open rear-hooded ramp
front. Half-length sporting stock w/cheekpiece, checkered
pistol-grip and forearm, swivels. Made 1946-55.

MODEL 22F . . . . NiB $1408 Ex $1010 Gd $679
Same as Model 21H except w/full-length Mannlicher-type
stock, weight: 6 lbs., 14 oz. Disc.

MODEL 98 STANDARD
Calibers: .243 Win., .270 Win., .30-06, .308 Win., .300 Win.
Mag., 7x57mm, 7x64mm, or 9.3x62mm. 23.8-in. bbl. Overall
34.5 in. Weight: 7.25 lbs. Checkered walnut stock w/Bavarian
cheekpiece. Imported from 1998. Disc.
Standard calibers . . . . NiB $630 Ex $439 Gd $300
**Calibers .300 Win., Mag.,
9.3x62mm** . . . . NiB $580 Ex $469 Gd $386
w/single set trigger, add $150

MODEL 98 MANNLICHER
Similar to Model 98 Standard except full length stock and set
triggers. Imported from 1998. Disc.
Standard calibers . . . . NiB $830 Ex $545 Gd $390
Calibers .300 Win. Mag., 9.3x62mm . . . NiB $910 Ex $600 Gd $445

ZKB-110 SINGLE-SHOT
Calibers: .22 Hornet, .222 Rem., 5.6x52R, 5.6x50 Mag.,
6.5x57R, 7x57R, and 8x57JRS. 23.8-in. bbl. Weight: 6.1 lbs.
Walnut checkered buttstock and forearm w/Bavarian cheek-
piece. Imported from 1998 to 2003.
Standard model. . . . . NiB $230 Ex $175 Gd $130
Lux model, add $70
Calibers 7x57R and 8x57 JRS, add $50
w/interchangeable 12 ga. shotgun bbl., add $150

ZOM-451 . . . . NiB $220 Ex $165 Gd $120
Straight pull bolt action. Caliber: .22 LR. Imported by Century
Arms 1998. Disc.

ZKM-451. . . . . NiB $600 Ex $450 Gd $330
Bolt action. Caliber: .22 LR. Imported 1995 to 2000.

ZKM-456 LUX SPORTER. . . . . . . NiB $320 Ex $240 Gd $180
Bolt action. Caliber: .22 LR, 5- or 10-rnd. magazine. Imported
1992 to 1998.

RIFLES

Brown Precision High Country Youth Rifle

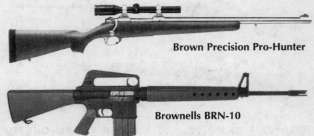

Brown Precision Pro-Hunter

Brownells BRN-10

HORNET SPORTER (ZKM 465). . .NiB $1278 Ex $1043 Gd $689
Miniature Mauser action. Caliber: .22 Hornet. Five-rnd. detachable box magazine. 23-in. bbl. Double set trigger. Weight: 6.25 lbs. Sights: Three-leaf open rear hooded ramp front. Sporting stock w/checkered pistol grip and forearm, swivels. Made 1949-74. Note: This rifle was also marketed in U.S. as "Z-B Mauser Varmint Rifle." (Reintroduced as Model ZKB 689)

ZKB 689 . . . . NiB $482 Ex $345 Gd $296
Bolt action. Calibers: .22 Hornet, .222 Rem. Five-rnd. detachable box magazine. 23.5-in. bbl. Weight: 5.75 lbs. Double-set triggers. Adj. open rear sight, hooded ramp front. Walnut stock. Imported 1985–92.

ZKM 611 SEMIAUTO RIFLE
Caliber: .17 HMR or .22 WMR. Six-rnd. magazine. 20-in. bbl. 37 in. overall. Weight: 6.2 lbs. Hooded front sight; mid-mounted rear sight. Checkered walnut or beechwood stock. Single thumbscrew takedown. Grooved receiver for scope mounting. Imported from 2006 to date.
Standard beechwood model . . . NiB $800 Ex $655 Gd $389
Deluxe walnut model . . . . NiB $960 Ex $780 Gd $328

BROWN PRECISION INC. — Los Molinos, CA

MODEL 7 SUPER LIGHT
SPORTER . . . . NiB $1128 Ex $1086 Gd $775
Lightweight sporter built on a Remington Model 7 barreled action w/18-in. factory bbl. Weight: 5.25 lbs. Kevlar stock. Made 1984-92.

HIGH COUNTRY BOLT-ACTION SPORTER
Custom sporting rifles built on Blaser, Remington 707, Ruger 77 and Winchester 70 actions. Calibers: .243 Win., .25-06, .270 Win., 7mm Rem. Mag., .308 Win., .30-06. Five-rnd. magazine (4-rnd. in 7mm Mag.). 22- or 24-in. bbl. Weight: 6.5 lbs. Fiberglass stock w/recoil pad, sling swivels. No sights. Made 1975-92.
Standard High Country . . . . . NiB $1624 Ex $1043 Gd $855
Custom High Country . . . . . NiB $5430 Ex $4955 Gd $3130
Left-hand action, add $250
Stainless bbl., add $250
70, 77 or Blaser actions, add $150
70 SG action, add $400

HIGH COUNTRY
YOUTH RIFLE. . . . . NiB $1336 Ex $1023 Gd $688
Similar to standard Model 7 Super Light except w/Kevlar or graphite stock, scaled-down to youth dimensions. Calibers: .223, .243, 6mm, 7mm-08, .308. Made 1993-2000.

PRO-HUNTER BOLT-ACTION RIFLE
Custom sporting rifle built on Remington 707 or Winchester 70 SG action fitted w/match-grade Shilen bbl. chambered in customer's choice of caliber. Matte blued, nickel or Teflon finish. Express-style rear sight hooded ramp front. Synthetic stock. Made 1989 to date.
Standard Pro-Hunter. . . . . . NiB $5480 Ex $4580 Gd $2710
Pro-Hunter Elite (1993 to date) . . . NiB $6855 Ex $5810 Gd $3380
Pro-Hunter w/Rem 40X action, add $650

PRO-VARMINTER BOLT-ACTION RIFLE
Custom varminter built on a Remington 700 or 40X action fitted w/Shilen stainless steel benchrest bbl. Varmint or benchrest-style stock. Made 1993 to date.

Standard Pro-Varminter . . . NiB $4580 Ex $4110 Gd $2555
w/Rem 40X action, add $650

SELECTIVE TARGET MODEL. . NiB $1044 Ex $835 Gd $590
Tactical law-enforcement rifle built on a Remington 707V action. Caliber: .308 Win. 20-, 22- or 24-in. bbl. Synthetic stock. Made 1989-92.

TACTICAL ELITE RIFLE . . . . NiB $4566 Ex $3290 Gd $1977
Similar to Selective Target Model except fitted w/select match-grade Shilen benchrest heavy stainless bbl. Calibers: .223, .308, .300 Win. Mag. Black or camo Kevlar/graphite composite fiberglass stock w/adj. buttplate. Non-reflective black Teflon metal finish. Made 1997 to date.

BROWNELLS, INC. — Grinnell, IA

Gun parts and accessories company.

BRN-10 . . . . NiB $1399 Ex $1299 Gd $1100
Replica of Armalite AR-10 prototype with trigger-style charging handle located under the carry handle. Semiauto. Direct Impingement gas-operated action. Caliber: 7.62mm NATO. 20-rnd. detachable magazine. Bbl.: 20-in. w/duckbill flash hider. Overall: 41 in. Weight: 9 lbs. Sights: Post front, adj. aperature rear. Stock: Brown polymer. Made 2018 to 2019.
BRN-10B (black furniture, Portugese
style flash hider) . . . . NiB $1399 Ex $1299 Gd $1100

RETRO M16 SERIES BRN-16A1 . . NiB $1299 Ex $1050 Gd $990
Replica of Colt Model M16A1. Semiauto. Direct Impingement gas-operated action. Caliber: 5.56mm NATO. 20-rnd. detachable magazine. Bbl.: 20-in. w/A1 flash hider. Overall: 40 in. Weight: 6.8 lbs. Sights: Post front, adj. aperature rear. Stock: Black polymer, triangular handguard. Made 2018-19.
BRN-601 (replica of Colt
model 601) . . . . NiB $1299 Ex $1050 Gd $990
BRN-605 (replica of Colt
model 605). . . . . NiB $1299 Ex $1050 Gd $990
BRN-PROTO (replica of
AR-15 prototype). . . . . . . NiB $1499 Ex $1200 Gd $1000
XBRN16E1 (replica of Colt
model XM16E1). . . . . NiB $1299 Ex $1050 Gd $990
XBRN177E2 (Replica of Colt Model
XM177E2 carbine) . . . . . NiB $1299 Ex $1050 Gd $990

BROWNING — Morgan, UT
Manufactured for Browning by Fabrique Nationale d'Armes de Guerre (now Fabrique Nationale Herstal), Herstal, Belgium; Miroku Firearms Mfg. Co., Tokyo, Japan; A.T.I., Salt Lake City, UT; Oy Sako Ab, Riihimaki, Finland.

.22 AUTOMATIC RIFLE, GRADE I
Similar to discontinued Remington Model 241A. Autoloading. Take-down. Calibers: .22 LR. .22 Short (not interchangeably). Tubular magazine in buttstock holds 11 LR. 16 Short. Bbl.

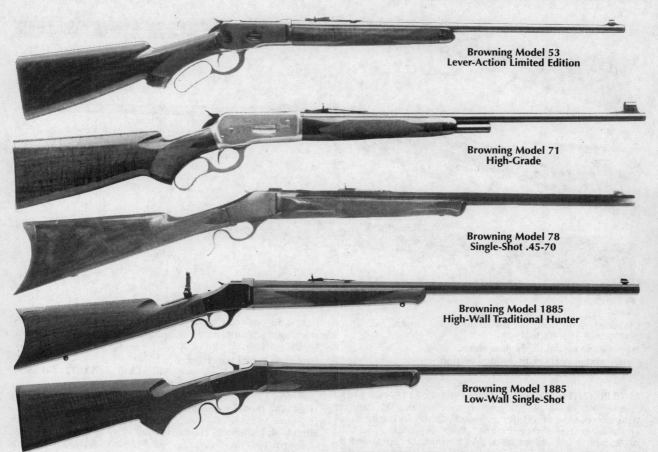

Browning Model 53
Lever-Action Limited Edition

Browning Model 71
High-Grade

Browning Model 78
Single-Shot .45-70

Browning Model 1885
High-Wall Traditional Hunter

Browning Model 1885
Low-Wall Single-Shot

lengths: 19.25 in. (.22 LR), 22.25 in. (.22 Short). Weight: 4.75 lbs. (.22 LR); 5 lbs. (.22 Short). Receiver scroll engraved. Open rear sight, bead front. Checkered pistol-grip buttstock, semi-beavertail forearm. Made 1956-72 by FN; from 1972 to date by Miroku. Note: Illustrations are of rifles manufactured by FN.
FN manufacture . . . . NiB $899 Ex $500 Gd $265
Miroku manufacture . . . . NiB $650 Ex $398 Gd $327

.22 AUTOMATIC RIFLE, GRADE II
Same as Grade I except satin chrome-plated receiver engraved w/small game animal scenes, gold-plated trigger select walnut stock and forearm. .22 LR only. Made 1972 to 1984.
FN manufacture . . . . NiB $1700 Ex $1355 Gd $980
Miroku manufacture . . . . NiB $900 Ex $705 Gd $530

.22 AUTOMATIC RIFLE, GRADE III
Same as Grade I except satin chrome-plated receiver elaborately hand-carved and engraved w/dog and game-bird scenes, scrolls and leaf clusters: gold-plated trigger, extra-fancy walnut stock and forearm, skip-checkered. .22 LR only. Made 1972-84.
FN manufacture . . . . NiB $3500 Ex $2930 Gd $2280
Miroku manufacture . . . . . . NiB $1655 Ex $1380 Gd $1000

.22 AUTOMATIC, GRADE VI. . NiB $1400 Ex $1230 Gd $955
Same general specifications as standard .22 Automatic except for engraving, high-grade stock w/checkering and glossy finish. Made by Miroku from 1986 to date.

MODEL 52 BOLT-ACTION RIFLE . . . NiB $955 Ex $700 Gd $443
Limited edition of Winchester Model 52C Sporter. Caliber: .22 LR. Five-rnd. magazine. 24-in. bbl. Weight: 7 lbs. Micro-Motion trigger. No sights. Checkered select walnut stock w/

rosewood forend and metal grip cap. Blued finish. 5000 made from 1991 to 1992.

MODEL 53 LEVER-ACTION RIFLE . . . NiB $930 Ex $800 Gd $720
Limited edition of Winchester Model 53. Caliber: .32-20. Seven-rnd. tubular half-magazine. 22-in. bbl. Weight: 6.5 lbs. Adj. rear sight, bead front. Select walnut checkered pistol-grip stock w/high-gloss finish. Classic-style forearm. Blued finish. 5000 made in 1990.

MODEL 65 GRADE I LEVER-ACTION
RIFLE . . . . NiB $730 Ex $445 Gd $370
Caliber: .218 Bee. 7-rnd. tubular half-magazine. 24-in. bbl. Weight: 6.75 lbs. Sights: Adj. buckhorn-style rear, hooded bead front. Select walnut pistol-grip stock w/high-gloss finish. Semibeavertail forearm. Limited edition of 3500 made in 1989.
High Grade model (engraved and gold-plated
animals on grayed receiver, only
1,500 produced) . . . . . . NiB $1055 Ex $930 Gd $820

MODEL 71 GRADE I CARBINE . . . NiB $880 Ex $640 Gd $455
Replica of Winchester Model 71 except carbine w/20-in. rnd. bbl. and weighs 8 lbs. Limited edition of 4000 made in 1986 to 1987.
High Grade model (20-in. rnd bbl., limited edition of 3,000
made. 1986–88) . . . . NiB $1332 Ex $1123 Gd $765

MODEL 71 GRADE I
RIFLE . . . . NiB $916 Ex $710 Gd $497
Replica of Winchester 71 lever action. Caliber: .348 Win. 4-rnd. magazine. 24-in. rnd. bbl. Weight: 8 lbs., 2 oz. Open buckhorn sights. Select walnut straight grip stock w/satin finish.

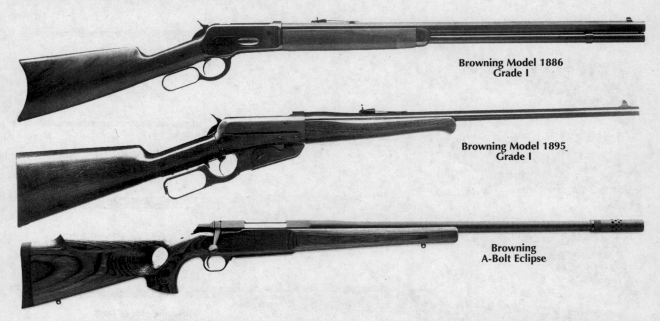

Browning Model 1886
Grade I

Browning Model 1895
Grade I

Browning
A-Bolt Eclipse

Classic-style forearm, flat metal buttplate. Limited edition of 3000 made in 1986 to 1987.

High Grade model (high gloss stock,
    engraved gray receiver, limited edition
    of 3,000 made. 1986–87) .. NiB $1430 Ex $1180 Gd $880

M-78 BICENTENNIAL SET... NiB $1980 Ex $1555 Gd $1210
Special Model 78 .45-70 w/same specifications as standard type, except sides of receiver engraved w/bison and eagle, scroll engraving on top of receiver, lever, both ends of bbl. and buttplate; high-grade walnut stock and forearm. Accompanied by an engraved hunting knife and stainless steel commemorative medallion, all in an alder wood presentation case. Each item in set has matching serial number beginning with "1776" and ending with numbers 1 to 1,000. Edition limited to 1,000 sets. Made in 1976.

MODEL B-78 SINGLE-SHOT RIFLE
Falling-block lever-action similar to Winchester 1885 High Wall single-shot rifle. Calibers: .22-250, 6mm Rem., .243 Win., .25-06, 7mm Rem. Mag., .30-06, .45-70 Govt. 26-in. octagon or heavy rnd. bbl.; 24-in. octagon bull bbl. on .45-70 model. Weight: 7.75 lbs. w/octagon bbl.; w/round bbl., 8.5 lbs.; .45-70, 8.75 lbs. Furnished w/o sights except .45-70 model w/open rear sight, blade front. Checkered fancy walnut stock and forearm. .45-70 model w/straight-grip stock and curved buttplate; others have Monte Carlo comb and cheekpiece, pistol-grip w/cap, recoil pad. Made 1973-83 by Miroku. Reintroduced in 1985 as Model 1885.
All calibers except .45-70.. NiB $1500 Ex $1274 Gd $1010
.45-70 .... NiB $970 Ex $766 Gd $523

MODEL 1885 SINGLE-SHOT RIFLE
Calibers: .22 Hornet, .223, .243, (Low Wall); .357 Mag., .44 Mag., .45 LC (L/W Traditional Hunter); .22-250, .223 Rem., .270 Win., 7mm Rem. Mag., .30-06, .454 Casull Mag., .45.70 (High Wall); .30.30 Win., .38-55 WCF, .45 Govt. (H/W Traditional Hunter); .40-65, .45 Govt. and .45.90 (BPCR). 24-, 28-, 30 or 34-in. rnd., octagonal or octagonal and rnd. bbl. 39.5, 43.5, 44.25 or 46.125 in. overall. Weight: 6.25, 8.75, 9, 11, or 11.75 lbs. respectively. Blued or color casehardened receiver. Gold-colored adj. trigger. Drilled and tapped for scope mounts w/no sights or vernier tang rear sight w/globe

front and open sights on .45-70 Govt. Walnut straight-grip stock and Schnabel forearm w/cut checkering and high-gloss or oil finish. Made 1985-2001.
Low Wall model w/o sights
    (Intro. 1995) .... NiB $1230 Ex $1075 Gd $680
Low Wall Traditional Hunter model
    (Intro. 1998) .... NiB $1450 Ex $990 Gd $575
High Wall model w/o sights
    (Intro. 1985) .... NiB $1610 Ex $1380 Gd $810
High Wall Traditional Hunter model
    (Intro. 1997) .... NiB $1390 Ex $1020 Gd $770
BPCR model w/o
    ejector (Intro. 1996).... NiB $1933 Ex $1442 Gd $1041
BPCR Creedmoor Model .45-90
    (Intro. 1998) .... NiB $1933 Ex $1442 Gd $1041

MODEL 1886 MONTANA
CENTENNIAL RIFLE ...... NiB $2255 Ex $1855 Gd $1600
Same general specifications as Model 1886 High Grade lever-action except w/specially engraved receiver designating Montana Centennial; also different stock design. Made in 1986 in limited issue by Miroku.

MODEL 1886 GRADE I ... NiB $2155 Ex $1755 Gd $1555
Lever action. Caliber: .45-70 Govt., 8-rnd. magazine. 26-in. octagonal bbl. 45 in. overall. Weight: 9 lbs., 5 oz. Deep blued finish on receiver. Open buckhorn sights. Straight-grip walnut stock. Classic-style forearm. Metal buttplate. Satin finish. Made in 1986 in limited issue 7000 by Miroku.
High Grade model (receiver is grayed,
    steel embellished w/scroll; elk and American
    bison engraving, high-gloss stock, limited edition
    of 3,000 mfg. 1986) ...... NiB $2410 Ex $2155 Gd $1680

MODEL 1886 HIGH-GRADE
LEVER-ACTION CARBINE . NiB $2210 Ex $1780 Gd $1555
Same general specifications as the Model 1886 Grade I rifle except 22-in. rnd. bbl., saddle ring, crescent butt plate. Made 1992–93 in limited issue of 7,000 by Miroku.
High Grade model (receiver is grayed w/
    elk and bear engraving, high-grade stock,
    limited edition of 3,000 mfg.
    1992–93) .... NiB $2410 Ex $2155 Gd $1680

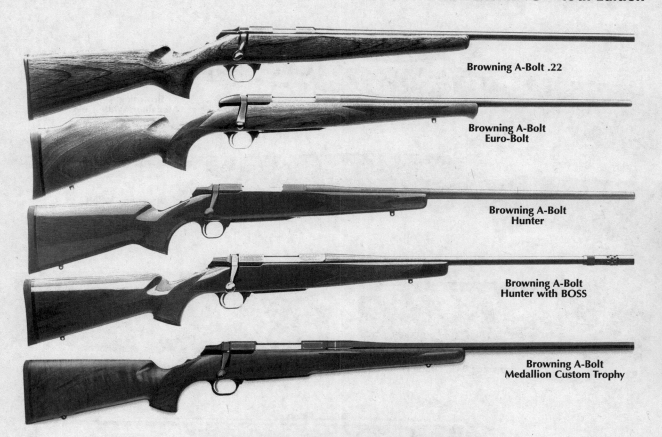

Browning A-Bolt .22

Browning A-Bolt
Euro-Bolt

Browning A-Bolt
Hunter

Browning A-Bolt
Hunter with BOSS

Browning A-Bolt
Medallion Custom Trophy

MODEL 1895 GRADE I
LEVER-ACTION RIFLE. . . . . NiB $979 Ex $911 Gd $765
Caliber: .30-06, .30-40 Krag. Four round magazine. 24-in.
rnd. bbl. 42 in. overall. Weight: 8 lbs. French walnut stock and
Schnabel forend. Sights: Rear buckhorn; gold bead on elevated
ramp front. Made in 1984 in limited issue of 8,000 (2,000
chambered for .30-40 Krag and 6,000 chambered for .30-06).
Mfd. by Miroku.
High Grade model (engraved receiver and Grade III French
walnut stock w/fine checkering, limited issue of 1000 in
each caliber, 1985) . . . . . NiB $1630 Ex $1379 Gd $1000

MODEL ACERA. . . . . NiB $896 Ex $800 Gd $660
Straight pull action. Calibers: .30-06 or .300 Win. Mag.
Detachable magazine. 22- or 24-in. bbl. Weight: 7 lbs.
Finish: gloss blue. Stock: checkered walnut. Made 1999-2000.
NOTE: The A-Bolt was mfg. from 1985 to 1993 and replaced by
the A-Bolt II series in 1994. The Series II incorporates an anit-
bind non-rotating bolt sleeve and improved trigger. The A-Bolt
III was introduced in 2013 and made to date.

NOTE: *On A-Bolt series I and Series II rifles add $100 for
BOSS muzzle device, $100 for left-hand models, $75 for
iron sights, and $30 for WSM calibers.*

MODEL A-BOLT .22 RIFLE
Calibers: .22 LR, .22 Magnum. Five- and 15-rnd. magazines.
22-in. rnd. bbl. 40.25 in. overall. Weight: 5 lbs., 9 oz. Gold-
colored adj. trigger. Laminated walnut stock w/checkering.
Rosewood forend grip cap; pistol grip. With or w/o sights.
Ramp front and adj. folding leaf rear on open sight model. 22
LR made 1985-96; 22 Magnum, 1990 to 1996.

Grade I .22 LR . . . . NiB $575 Ex $340 Gd $255
Grade I .22 Magnum. . . . . NiB $600 Ex $423 Gd $269
Deluxe Grade Gold Medallion. . . NiB $620 Ex $479 Gd $354

MODEL A-BOLT ECLIPSE II BOLT RIFLE
Similar as Hunter Grade except fitted w/gray and black laminated thumbhole stock. Available in both short and long action
w/two bbl. configurations w/BOSS. Mfd. by Miroku 1996
to 2006.
w/standard bbl.. . . . . NiB $1110 Ex $855 Gd $430
Varmint w/heavy bbl.. . . . . NiB $810 Ex $660 Gd $380
M-1000
    Target (.300 Win. Mag.) . . . NiB $1055 Ex $805 Gd $405

MODEL A-BOLT EURO-BOLT RIFLE
Same general specifications as Hunter Grade except w/check-
ered satin-finished walnut stock. W/continental-style cheekpiece, palm-swell grip and Schnabel forend. Mannlicher-style
spoon bolt handle and contoured bolt shroud. 22- or 26-in.
bbl. w/satin blued finish. Weight: 6.8 to 7.4 lbs. Calibers: .22-
250 Rem., .243 Win., .270 Win., .30.06, .308 Win., 7mm Rem.
Mag. Mfd. by Miroku 1993 to 1994; 1994 to 1996 (Euro-Bolt II).
Euro-Bolt. . . . . NiB $679 Ex $536 Gd $369
Euro-Bolt II . . . . NiB $755 Ex $640 Gd $470

MODEL A-BOLT HUNTER GRADE RIFLE
Calibers: .22 Hornet, .223 Rem., .22-250 Rem., .243 Win.,
.257 Roberts, 7mm-08 Rem., .308 Win., (short action) .25-06
Rem., .270 Win., .280 Rem., .284 Win., .30-06, 7mm Rem.
Mag., .300 Win. Mag., .338 Win. Mag. Four-rnd. magazine
(standard), 3-rnd. (magnum). 22-in. bbl. (standard), 24-in.
(magnum). Weight: 7.5 lbs. (standard), 8.5 lbs. (magnum).

GRADING: **NiB** = New in Box   **Ex** = Excellent or NRA 95%   **Gd** = Good or NRA 68%

Browning A-Bolt Medallion White Gold

Browning A-Bolt Medallion

Browning BAR, Grade IV

Browning BAR, Grade V

Browning BAR Mark II Safari

Browning ShortTrac

With or w/o sights. Classic-style walnut stock. Produced in two action lengths w/nine locking lugs, fluted bolt w/60 degree rotation. Mfd. by Miroku from 1985 to 1993; from 1994 to 2007 (Hunter II).

Hunter . . . . .NiB $495 Ex $430 Gd $269
Hunter II. . . . . .NiB $830 Ex $635 Gd $380
Hunter Micro . . . . .NiB $596 Ex $395 Gd $317

MODEL A-BOLT MEDALLION GRADE RIFLE
Same as Hunter Grade except w/high-gloss deluxe stock rosewood grip cap and forend; high-luster blued finish. Also in .375 H&H w/open sights. Left-hand models available in long action only. Mfd. by Miroku from 1988 to 1993; from 1994 to 2009 (Medallion II). Bighorn Sheep Ltd. Ed.

.270 Win. (600 made 1986) . NiB $1412 Ex $1096 Gd $790
Gold Medallion Deluxe Grade . . . NiB $679 Ex $500 Gd $346
Gold Medallion II Deluxe
    Grade . . . . .NiB $670 Ex $525 Gd $380

Medallion, Standard Grade . . .NiB $633 Ex $488 Gd $354
Medallion II, Standard Grade . .NiB $780 Ex $630 Gd $355
Medallion, .375 H&H . . . . .NiB $999 Ex $770 Gd $488
Medallion II, .375 H&H . . . . .NiB $1012 Ex $790 Gd $497
Micro Medallion . . . . .NiB $690 Ex $557 Gd $367
Micro Medallion II . . . . .NiB $530 Ex $470 Gd $310
Pronghorn Antelope Ltd. Ed. 243 Win.
    (500 made 1987) . . . . . . .NiB $1266 Ex $1139 Gd $923

MODEL A-BOLT STALKER RIFLE
Same general specifications as Model A-Bolt Hunter Rifle except w/checkered graphite-fiberglass composite stock and matte blued or stainless metal. Non-glare matte finish of all exposed metal surfaces. 3 models: Camo Stalker orig. w/multicolored laminated wood stock, matte blued metal; Composite Stalker w/graphite-fiberglass stock, matte blued metal; w/composite stock, stainless metal. Made by Miroku from 1987 to 1993; 1994 to date. (Stalker II).

Camo Stalker (orig. laminated stock) NiB $480 Ex $430 Gd $255
Composite Stalker . . . . NiB $530 Ex $430 Gd $255
Composite Stalker II . . . . NiB $600 Ex $530 Gd $305
Stainless Stalker . . . . NiB $630 Ex $530 Gd $335
Stainless Stalker II . . . . NiB $890 Ex $630 Gd $330
Stainless Stalker (.375 H&H), add $100

MODEL A-BOLT
VARMINT II RIFLE . . . . NiB $720 Ex $605 Gd $340
Same general specifications as Stalker model except w/22-in. heavy bbl. w/BOSS system and varmint-style black laminated wood stock. Calibers: .22-250, .223 or .308. No sights. Bright blue or satin finish. Made by Miroku from 2002 to 2008.

MODEL AB3 SERIES
Similar to A-Bolt II series. Made 2013 to date.
Composite Stalker (black
  composite stock) . . . . NiB $500 Ex $400 Gd $340
Hunter (satin checkered walnut stock,
matte blue) . . . . NiB $555 Ex $430 Gd $355
Micro Stalker (13-in. LOP) . . . . . NiB $500 Ex $400 Gd $340

MODEL B-92 LEVER-ACTION
RIFLE . . . . NiB $605 Ex $530 Gd $345
Calibers: .357 Mag. and .44 Rem. Mag. 11-rnd. magazine. 20-in. rnd. bbl. 37.5 in. overall. Weight: 5.5 to 6.4 lbs. Seasoned French walnut stock w/high gloss finish. Cloverleaf rear sight; steel post front. Made from1979 to 1989 by Miroku.

BAR AUTOMATIC RIFLE, GRADE I,
STANDARD CALIBERS . . . . . . NiB $805 Ex $ 623 Gd $455
Gas-operated Semiauto. Calibers: .243 Win., .270 Win., .280 Rem., .308 Win., .30-06. Four-rnd. box magazine. 22-in. bbl. Weight: 7.5 lbs. Folding leaf rear sight, hooded ramp front. French walnut stock and forearm checkered, QD swivels. Made 1967-92 by FN.

BAR, GRADE I, MAGNUM
CALIBERS . . . . NiB $809 Ex $733 Gd $590
Same as BAR in standard calibers, except w/24-in. bbl. 7mm Rem. Mag. or .300 Win. Mag. .338 Win. Mag. w/3-rnd. box magazine and recoil pad. Weight: 8.5 lbs. Made 1969 to 1992 by FN.

BAR, GRADE II
Same as Grade I except receiver engraved w/big-game heads (deer and antelope on standard-caliber rifles, ram and grizzly on Magnum-caliber) and scrollwork, higher grade wood. Made 1967 to 1974 by FN.
Standard calibers . . . . NiB $1229 Ex $976 Gd $657
Magnum calibers . . . . NiB $1338 Ex $875 Gd $617

BAR, GRADE III
Same as Grade I except receiver of grayed steel engraved w/ big-game heads (deer and antelope on standard-caliber rifles, moose and elk on Magnum-caliber) framed in fine-line scroll-work, gold-plated trigger, stock and forearm of highly figured French walnut, hand-checkered and carved. Made 1971-74 by FN.
Standard calibers . . . . NiB $1554 Ex $993 Gd $591
Magnum calibers . . . . NiB $1617 Ex $1230 Gd $725

BAR, GRADE IV
Same as Grade I except receiver of grayed steel engraved w/full detailed rendition of running deer and antelope on standard-caliber rifles, moose and elk on Magnum-caliber gold-plated trigger, stock and forearm of highly figured French walnut, hand checkered and carved. Made frm 1971 to 1986 by FN.
Standard calibers . . . . NiB $2490 Ex $1546 Gd $1110
Magnum calibers . . . . NiB $2669 Ex $1721 Gd $1300

BAR, GRADE V
Same as Grade I except receiver w/complete big-game scenes executed by a master engraver and inlaid w/18K gold (deer and antelope on standard-caliber rifles, moose and elk on Magnum caliber), gold-plated trigger, stock and forearm of finest French walnut, intricately hand-checkered and carved. Made 1971-74 by FN.
Standard calibers . . . . NiB $6457 Ex $4707 Gd $2897
Magnum calibers . . . . NiB $6844 Ex $5110 Gd $3194

BAR MARK II SAFARI AUTOMATIC RIFLE
Same general specifications as standard BAR Semiauto rifle, except w/redesigned gas and buffer systems, new bolt release lever, and engraved receiver. Made 1993 to date.
Standard calibers . . . . NiB $1130 Ex $990 Gd $770
Magnum calibers . . . . NiB $1230 Ex $1090 Gd $870
Lightweight (alloy receiver
  w/20-in. bbl.) . . . . NiB $765 Ex $588 Gd $380
BAR Mk II Grade III
  (intro. 1996) . . . . NiB $3520 Ex $2377 Gd $1290
BAR Mk II Grade IV
  (intro. 1996) . . . . NiB $3609 Ex $2303 Gd $1829
W/BOSS option, add $75
W/open sights, add $25

BAR MARK III SERIES
Same general specifications as BAR Shorttrac and Longtrac semiauto rifles, except w/engraved satin nickel aluminum alloy receiver, polymer trigger guard/floorplate, and shim adj. Made 2016 to date.
standard calibers . . . . NiB $1145 Ex $1010 Gd $780
magnum calibers . . . . NiB $1245 Ex $1110 Gd $880
Camo (Mossy Oak camo
  finish, 2017-date) . . . . NiB $1245 Ex $1090 Gd $855
DBM (.308 Win., 18-in. fluted bbl., black composite
  camo stock, 2017-date) . . . NiB $1335 Ex $1160 Gd $905
DBM Wood (.308 Win., 18-in. fluted bbl.,
  wood stock, 2019-date) . . . NiB $1355 Ex $1180 Gd $910
Hell's Canyon Speed (composite
  camo stock, 2019-date) . . . NiB $1415 Ex $1240 Gd $965

BAR LONGTRAC . . . . NiB $1000 Ex $855 Gd $630
Similar to BAR Shorttrac except in .270 Win., .30-06, .300 Win. Mag., or 7mm Rem. Made in Belgium from 2004-15.
WSM calibers, add $120
Stalker (matte black finish,
  composite stock) . . . . NiB $1055 Ex $880 Gd $655
Camo, add $100

BAR SHORTTRAC . . . . NiB $1055 Ex $930 Gd $730
Semiautomatc. Gas operated. Calibers: .243 Win., .270 WSM, .300 WSM, .308 Win., 7mm-08, 7mm WSM or .325 WSM. 3- or 4-rnd. detacable magazine. 22- or 23-in. bbl. Weight: 6.6-7.25 lbs. Stock: satin or oil finish walnut. Finish: black or stain nickel. Made in Belgium from 2004-15.
WSM calibers, add $120
Stalker (matte black finish,
  composite stock) . . . . NiB $1055 Ex $930 Gd $730
Camo, add $100

BAR 22 AUTOMATIC RIFLE
Semiauto. Caliber: .22 LR. Tubular magazine holds 15 rnd. 20.25-in. bbl. Weight: 6.25 lbs. Sights: Folding-leaf rear, gold bead front on ramp. Receiver grooved for scope mounting. French walnut pistol-grip stock and forearm checkered. Made 1977-85.
Grade I . . . . NiB $700 Ex $630 Gd $455
Grade II . . . . NiB $1255 Ex $980 Gd $730

RIFLES

GRADING: NiB = New in Box   Ex = Excellent or NRA 95%   Gd = Good or NRA 68%

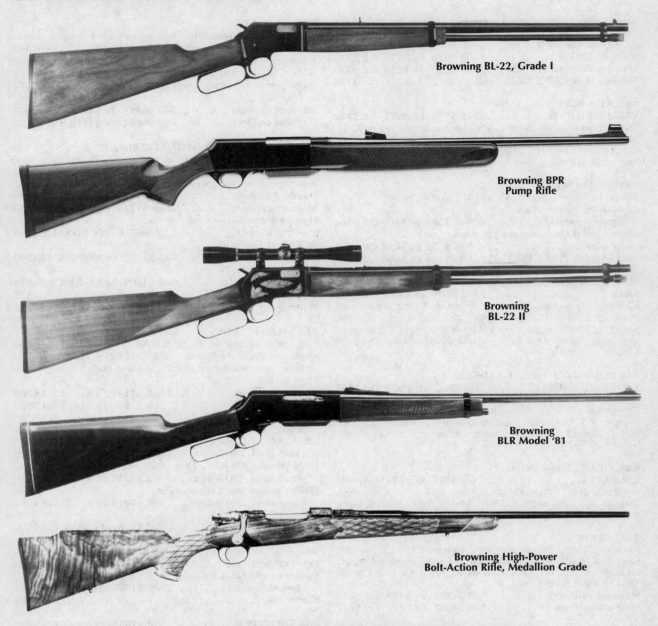

Browning BL-22, Grade I

Browning BPR Pump Rifle

Browning BL-22 II

Browning BLR Model '81

Browning High-Power Bolt-Action Rifle, Medallion Grade

BBR LIGHTNING . . . . **NiB $606 Ex $495 Gd $400**
Bolt-action rifle w/short bolt throw of 60 degrees. Calibers: .25-06 Rem., .270 Win., .30-06, 7mm Rem. Mag., .300 Win. Mag. 24-in. bbl. Weight: 8 lbs. Made 1979-84.

BL-17 GRADE I . . . . **NiB $425 Ex $380 Gd $290**
Similar to BL-22 except .17 Mach 2. Made 2005 to date.
Grade II, add **$50**
Grade II Field Octagon, add **$330**

BL-22 LEVER-ACTION REPEATING RIFLE
Short-throw lever-action. Caliber: .22 LR, Long, Short. Tubular magazine holds 15 LR, 17 Long 22 Short rounds. 20-in. bbl. Weight: 5 lbs. Sights: Folding leaf rear; bead front. Receiver grooved for scope mounting. Walnut straight-grip stock and forearm, bbl. band. Made 1970 to date by Miroku.
Grade I . . . . **NiB $455 Ex $390 Gd $290**
Grade II (w/scroll engraving) . . **NiB $555 Ex $480 Gd $310**

BLR LEVER-ACTION REPEATING RIFLE
Calibers: (short action only) .243 Win., .308 Win., .358 Win. Four round detachable box magazine. 20-in. bbl. Weight: 7 lbs. Sights: Windage and elevation adj. open rear; hooded ramp front. Walnut straight-grip stock and forearm, checkered, bbl. band, recoil pad. Made in 1966 by BAC/USA; from 1969 to 1973 by FN; from 1974 to 1980 by Miroku. Note: USA manufacture of this model was limited to prototypes and pre-production guns only and may be identified by the "MADE IN USA" roll stamp on the bbl.
FN model . . . . **NiB $930 Ex $830 Gd $530**
Miroku model . . . . **NiB $780 Ex $680 Gd $430**
USA model . . . . **NiB $1000 Ex $880 Gd $600**

BLR LIGHTNING MODEL
Lightweight version of the Browning BLR '81 w/forged alloy receiver and redesigned trigger group. Calibers: Short Action—.22-250 Rem., .223 Rem., .243 Win., 7mm-08 Rem., .308

Browning T-Bolt T-2

Browning X-Bolt Hell's Canyon Speed

Win.; Long Action— .270 Win., 7mm Rem. Mag., .30-06, .300 Win. Mag. Three or 4-rnd. detachable box magazine. 20-, 22- or 24-in. bbl. Weight: 6.5 to 7.75 lbs. Pistol-grip style walnut stock and forearm, cut checkering and recoil pad. Made by Miroku from 1995 to 2002.
Short action model . . . . NiB $630 Ex $586 Gd $390
Long action model . . . . NiB $655 Ex $596 Gd $400

BLR MODEL '81
Redesigned version of the Browning BLR. Calibers: .222-50 Rem., .243 Win., .308 Win., .358 Win; Long Action— .270 Win., 7mm Rem. Mag., .30-06. Fourround detachable box magazine. 20-in. bbl. Weight: 7 lbs. Walnut straight-grip stock and forearm, cut checkering, recoil pad. Made by Miroku from 1981 to 1995; Long Action intro. 1991. Disc. 1995.
Short action model . . . . NiB $780 Ex $592 Gd $396
Long action model . . . . NiB $850 Ex $505 Gd $390

MODEL BLR LIGHTWEIGHT '81 LEVER-ACTION REPEATER
Improved BLR '81 series. Made 2003 to date.
Short Action model . . . . NiB $850 Ex $745 Gd $580
Long Action model . . . . NiB $890 Ex $780 Gd $610
Takedown model, add $270
Magnum calibers, add $70

BPR-22 PUMP RIFLE
Hammerless slide-action repeater. Specifications same as for BAR-.22, except also available chambered for .22 Magnum RF; magazine capacity, 11 rnd. Made 1977-82 by Miroku.
Grade I . . . . NiB $605 Ex $555 Gd $320
Grade II . . . . NiB $905 Ex $755 Gd $455

BPR PUMP RIFLE
Slide-action repeater based on proven BAR designs w/forged alloy receiver and slide that cams down to clear bbl. and receiver. Calibers: .243 Win., .308 Win., .270 Win., .30-06, 7mm Rem. Mag. .300 Win. Mag. Three or 4-rnd. detachable box magazine. 22- or 24-in. bbl. w/ramped front sight and open adj. rear. Weight: 7.2 to 7.4 lbs. Made 1997-2001 by Miroku.
standard calibers. . . . . NiB $755 Ex $655 Gd $380
magnum calibers add $50

EXPRESS RIFLE . . . . NiB $6010 Ex $5600 Gd $4800
Custom shop. Superposed Superlight action. Calibers: .270, .30-06 or 9.3x74R. O/U barrels 24-in. Stock: straight grip. Single trigger. Weight: 6.8 lbs. Cased. Made in Belgium. Discontinued 1986.
Grade I . . . . NiB $7600 Ex $6600 Gd $5600

HIGH-POWER BOLT-ACTION RIFLE, MEDALLION GRADE . . . . NiB $3877 Ex $3488 Gd $1967
Same as Safari Grade except receiver and bbl. scroll engraved, ram's head engraved on floorplate; select walnut stock w/rosewood forearm tip, grip cap. Made 1961-74.

HIGH-POWER BOLT-ACTION RIFLE, OLYMPIAN GRADE . . . . . NiB $3831 Ex $3435 Gd $1925
Same as Safari Grade except bbl. engraved; receiver, trigger guard and floorplate satin chrome-plated and engraved w/game scenes appropriate to caliber; finest figured walnut stock w/rosewood forearm tip and grip cap, latter w/18K-gold medallion. Made 1961-74.

HIGH-POWER BOLT-ACTION RIFLE SAFARI GRADE, MEDIUM ACTION . . NiB $1443 Ex $988 Gd $733
Same as Standard except medium action. Calibers: .22-250, .243 Win., .264 Win. Mag., .284 Win. Mag., .308 Win. Bbl.: 22-in. lightweight bbl.; .22-250 and .243 also available w/24-in. heavy bbl. Weight: 6 lbs., 12 oz. w/lightweight bbl.; 7 lbs. 13 oz. w/heavy bbl. Made 1963 to 1974 by Sako.

HIGH-POWER BOLT-ACTION RIFLE, SAFARI GRADE, SHORT ACTION . . . . NiB $1722 Ex $933 Gd $747
Same as Standard except short action. Calibers: .222 Rem., .222 Rem. Mag. 22-in. lightweight or 24-in. heavy bbl. No sights. Weight: 6 lbs., 2 oz. w/lightweight bbl.; 7.5 lbs. w/heavy bbl. Made 1963-74 by Sako.

HIGH-POWER BOLT-ACTION RIFLE, SAFARI GRADE, STANDARD ACTION . . . . . . NiB $1523 Ex $1133 Gd $944
Mauser-type action. Calibers: .270 Win., .30-06, 7mm Rem. Mag., .300 H&H Mag., .300 Win. Mag., .308 Norma Mag. .338 Win. Mag., .375 H&H Mag., .458 Win. Mag. Cartridge capacity: 6 rnd. in .270, .30-06; 4 in Magnum calibers. Bbl. length: 22 in., in .270, .30-06; 24 in., in Magnum calibers. Weight: 7 lbs., 2 oz., in .270, .30-06; 8.25 lbs. in Mag. calibers. Folding leaf rear sight, hooded ramp front. Checkered stock w/pistol grip, Monte Carlo cheekpiece, QD swivels; recoil pad on Magnum models. Made 1959-74 by FN.

T-BOLT T-1 .22 REPEATING RIFLE
Straight-pull bolt action. Caliber: .22 LR. Five round clip magazine. 24-in. bbl. Peep rear sight w/ramped blade front. Plain walnut stock w/pistol grip and laquered finish. Weight: 6 lbs. Also left-hand model. Made 1965-74 by FN.
Right-hand model . . . . NiB $650 Ex $469 Gd $300
Left-hand model . . . . NiB $675 Ex $512 Gd $409

T-BOLT T-2
Same as T-1 Model except w/checkered fancy figured walnut stock. Made 1966-74 by FN. (Reintroduced briefly during the late 1980's with oil-finished stock)

GRADING: NiB = New in Box Ex = Excellent or NRA 95% Gd = Good or NRA 68%

BSA
Model 12/15 Martini

BSA
Model 15 Martini

Original model . . . . NiB $909 Ex $579 Gd $289
Reintroduced model . . . . NiB $589 Ex $433 Gd $266

T-BOLT SPORTER/TARGET. . . . . NiB $620 Ex $520 Gd $330
Similar as T-2 model except w/chambered in .17 HMR, .22 LR
or .22 WMR. Barrel: 22 in. free floated. 10-rnd. helix rotary
magazine. Finish: blued. Stock: walnut or composite. Made
2006–date.

F.N. BROWNING FAL SEMIAUTO RIFLE
Same as F.N. FAL Semiauto Rifle. See F.N. listing for specifica-
tions. Sold by Browning for a brief period c. 1960.
F.N. FAL standard
    model (G-series) . . . . NiB $4977 Ex $3677 Gd $2928
F.N. FAL lightweight
    model (G-series) . . . . NiB $5310 Ex $4400 Gd $3090
F.N. FAL heavy bbl.
    model (G-series) . . . . NiB $7175 Ex $6230 Gd $4956
BAC FAL model . . . . NiB $5320 Ex $4952 Gd $4915

X-BOLT HUNTER . . . . NiB $910 Ex $800 Gd $750
Bolt-action, short and long actions. Similar calibers as A-Bolt
series except w/adj. 22- or 26-in. free float bbl. Feather trigger.
3- or 4-rnd. detachable magazine. Stock: Satin walnut. Finish:
low luster blue. Weight: 6.5-7 lbs. Optic ready. Made 2008 to
date.
Eclipse Hunter (laminated thumbhole stock,
    matte blue finish) . . . . NiB $870 Ex $770 Gd $370
Micro Hunter (youth stock) . . NiB $1020 Ex $860 Gd $770
RMEF Special Hunter, add $150
Composite Stalker
    (composite stock) . . . . NiB $730 Ex $505 Gd $380
Eclipse Target (laminated thumbhole stock,
    matte blue finish) . . . . NiB $900 Ex $590 Gd $390
Eclipse Varmint (laminated thumbhole stock,
    heavy bbl.) . . . . NiB $900 Ex $590 Gd $390
Hell's Canyon Long Range (composite stock,
    burnt bronze finish) . . . . NiB $1030 Ex $705 Gd $305
Hell's Canyon Long Range McMillian
    (McMillian Game Scout composite
    stock, 2018-date) . . . . NiB $1955 Ex $1710 Gd $1330
Hell's Canyon Max Long Range (A-TACS AU camo composite
    stock, 2021-date) . . . . NiB $1230 Ex $1080 Gd $840
Hell's Canyon Speed (composite stock,
    burnt bronze finish) . . . . NiB $1000 Ex $705 Gd $505
Hunter Long Range (walnut
    stock, 2020-date) . . . . NiB $1955 Ex $1710 Gd $1330
Long Range Hunter (carbon fiber
    stock, disc. 2016) . . . . NiB $1220 Ex $1055 Gd $820
Max Varmint (adj. Max stock,
    2019-date) . . . . NiB $1180 Ex $1030 Gd $810
Medallion (high gloss
    walnut stock) . . . . NiB $880 Ex $580 Gd $380
Medallion Safari (high gloss walnut
    stock) . . . . NiB $1630 Ex $1080 Gd $830

Micro Composite (composite
    stock, 2018-date) . . . . NiB $880 Ex $770 Gd $600
Micro Hunter (laminate wood
    stock, 2009-14) . . . . NiB $755 Ex $655 Gd $505
Micro Midas . . . . NiB $730 Ex $505 Gd $380
Mountain Pro (26-in. spiral fluted bbl., carbon
    fiber stock, 2022-date) . . . NiB $2520 Ex $2450 Gd $1400
Pro (composite stock,
    2018-date) . . . . NiB $2680 Ex $2550 Gd $1800
Pro McMillian (composite
    stock, 2018-date) . . . . NiB $2680 Ex $2550 Gd $1800
Pro Long Range (26-in. skip fluted heavy bbl., carbon
    fiber stock, 2022-date) . . . NiB $2240 Ex $2150 Gd $1900
RMEF Special White Gold
    Medlallion . . . . NiB $1205 Ex $830 Gd $605
Stainless Stalker (composite stock,
    matte stainless) . . . . NiB $955 Ex $680 Gd $480
Varmint Stalker (composite stock,
    heavy bbl.) . . . . NiB $930 Ex $630 Gd $430
Varmint Stalker Camo (Mossy
    Oak finish composite stock,
    heavy bbl.) . . . . NiB $780 Ex $530 Gd $380
White Gold Medlallion (stainless bbl., walnut
    stock) . . . . NiB $1130 Ex $780 Gd $580

BSA GUNS LTD. — Birmingham, England
*Previously imported by Samco Global Arms, BSA Guns Ltd
and Precision Sports. Importation into the U.S. stopped in
1987.*

MODEL 12 MARTINI SINGLE-SHOT
TARGET RIFLE. . . . . NiB $766 Ex $567 Gd $433
Caliber .22 LR. 29-in. bbl. Weight: 8.75 lbs. Parker-Hale
Model 7 rear sight and Model 2 front sight. Straight-grip
stock, checkered forearm. Note: This model was also available w/open sights or w/BSA No. 20 and 30 sights. Made
before WWII.

MODEL 12/15
MARTINI HEAVY . . . . NiB $765 Ex $544 Gd $379
Same as Standard Model 12/15 except w/extra heavy bbl.,
weighs 11 lbs.

MODEL 12/15 MARTINI SINGLE-SHOT
TARGET RIFLE. . . . . NiB $650 Ex $479 Gd $355
Caliber: .22 LR. 29-in. bbl. Weight: 9 lbs. Parker-Hale No.
PH-7A rear sight and No. FS-22 front sight. Target stock w/high
comb and cheekpiece, beavertail forearm. Note: This is a post-
WWII model; however, a similar rifle, the BSA-Parker Model
12/15, was produced c. 1938.

BSA CFT Target

BSA
Martini-International ISU Match

BSA
Monarch Deluxe Varmint

MODEL 13 MARTINI SINGLE-SHOT
TARGET RIFLE. . . . . NiB $756 Ex $579 Gd $443
Caliber: .22 LR. Lighter version of the No.12 w/same general specifications except w/25-in. bbl., weighs 6.5lbs. Made before WWII.

MODEL 13 SPORTING RIFLE
Same as No. 13 Target except fitted w/Parker-Hale "Sportarget" rear sight and bead front sight. Also available in .22 Hornet. Made before WWII.
.22 Long Rifle . . . . NiB $756 Ex $579 Gd $443
.22 Hornet . . . . NiB $976 Ex $800 Gd $579

MODEL 15 MARTINI SINGLE-SHOT
TARGET RIFLE. . . . . NiB $765 Ex $577 Gd $338
Caliber: .22 LR. 29-in. bbl. Weight: 9.5 lbs. BSA No. 30 rear sight and No. 20 front sight. Target stock w/cheekpiece and pistol-grip, long, semi-beavertail forearm. Made before WWII.

CENTURION MATCH
RIFLE. . . . . NiB $810 Ex $680 Gd $430
Same general specifications as Model 15 except w/Centurion match bbl. Made before WWII.

CF-2 . . . . NiB $543 Ex $399 Gd $265
Mauser-type action. Calibers: 7mm Rem. Mag., .300 Win. Mag. Three-rnd. magazine. 23.6-in. bbl. Weight: 8 lbs. Sights: Adj. rear; hooded ramp front. Checkered walnut stock w/ Monte Carlo comb, rollover cheekpiece, rosewood forend tip, recoil pad, sling swivels. Made 1975 to 1987.

CF-2 STUTZEN RIFLE . . . . NiB $700 Ex $630 Gd $455
Calibers: .222 Rem., .22-250, .243 Win., .270 Win., .308 Win. .30-06. Four round capacity (5 in 222 Rem.). 20.6-in. bbl. 41.5 in. (approx.) overall length. Weight: 7.5 to 8 lbs. Williams front and rear sights. Hand-finished European walnut stock. Monte Carlo cheekpiece and Wundhammer palm swell. Double-set triggers. Importation disc. 1987.

CFT TARGET RIFLE . . . . NiB $680 Ex $600 Gd $380
Single-shot bolt action. Caliber: 7.62mm. 26.5-in. bbl. About 47.5 in. overall. Weight: 11 lbs., incl. accessories. Bbl. and action weight: 6 lbs., 12 oz. Importation disc. 1987.

MAJESTIC DELUXE FEATHERWEIGHT HUNTING RIFLE
Mauser-type action. Calibers: .243 Win., .270 Win., .308 Win., .30-06, .458 Win. Mag. Four round magazine. 22-in. bbl. w/ BESA recoil reducer. Weight: 6.25 lbs.; 8.75 lbs. in 458. Folding leaf rear sight, hooded ramp front. Checkered European-style walnut stock w/cheekpiece, pistol-grip, Schnabel forend, swivels, recoil pad. Made 1959-65.
.458 Win. Mag. caliber . . . . NiB $650 Ex $508 Gd $380
Other calibers. . . . . NiB $506 Ex $433 Gd $298

MAJESTIC DELUXE STANDARD
WEIGHT . . . . NiB $508 Ex $332 Gd $255
Same as Featherweight model except heavier bbl. w/o recoil reducer. Calibers: .22 Hornet, .222 Rem., .243 Win., 7x57mm, .308 Win., .30-06. Weight: 7.25 to 7.75 lbs. Disc.
.22 Hornet caliber, add $400

MARTINI-INTERNATIONAL ISU
MATCH RIFLE. . . . . NiB $944 Ex $708 Gd $577
Similar to MK III, but modified to meet International Shooting Union "Standard Rifle" specifications. 28-in. standard weight bbl. Weight: 10.75 lbs. Redesigned stock and forearm, latter attached to bbl. w/"V" section alloy strut. Intro. 1968. Disc.

MARTINI-INTERNATIONAL MATCH RIFLE SINGLE-SHOT
HEAVY PATTERN . . . . NiB $866 Ex $630 Gd $443
Caliber: .22 LR. 29-in. heavy bbl. Weight: 14 lbs. Parker-Hale "International" front and rear sights. Target stock w/full cheekpiece and pistol-grip, broad beavertail forearm, handstop, swivels. Right- or left-hand models. Made 1950-53.

GRADING: **NiB** = New in Box   **Ex** = Excellent or NRA 95%   **Gd** = Good or NRA 68%

Bushmaster Carbon-15 Model 4

Bushmaster ACR Basic

MARTINI-INTERNATIONAL MATCH
RIFLE — LIGHT PATTERN. . . . . NiB $775 Ex $584 Gd $455
Same general specifications as Heavy Pattern except w/26-in. lighter weight bbl. Weight: 11 lbs. Disc.

MARTINI-INTERNATIONAL MK II
MATCH RIFLE. . . . . NiB $1043 Ex $720 Gd $630
Same general specifications as original model. Heavy and Light Pattern. Improved trigger mechanism and ejection system. Redesigned stock and forearm. Made 1953-59.

MARTINI-INTERNATIONAL MK III
MATCH RIFLE. . . . . NiB $1044 Ex $812 Gd $613
Same general specifications as MK II Heavy Pattern. Longer action frame w/I-section alloy strut to which forearm is attached; bbl. is fully floating. Redesigned stock and forearm. Made 1959 to 1967.

MONARCH DELUXE BOLT-ACTION
HUNTING RIFLE . . . . NiB $580 Ex $530 Gd $360
Same as Majestic Deluxe Standard Weight model except w/ redesigned stock of U.S. style w/contrasting hardwood forend tip and grip cap. Calibers: .222 Rem., .243 Win., .270 Win., 7mm Rem. Mag., .308 Win., .30-06. 22-in. bbl. Weight: 7 to 7.25 lbs. Made 1965 to 1974.

MONARCH DELUXE VARMINT
RIFLE. NiB $480 Ex $430 Gd $300
Same as Monarch Deluxe except w/24-in. heavy bbl. and weighs 9 lbs. Calibers: .222 Rem., .243 Win.

BUSHMASTER FIREARMS — Ilion, NY
Quality Parts Company. Currently Ilion, NY, formerly Windham, Maine. Purchased by Freedom Group Inc. 2011. Part of the Remington bankruptcy in 2020. Franklin Armory Holdings bought the Bushmaster brand and some related assets.

.308 SERIES. . . . . NiB $1430 Ex $1080 Gd $800
Similar to M4 except in .308 Win. 16- or 20-in. bbl. 2004-05.

ACR SERIES
Gas piston system. Modular system. Semiauto. Caliber: 5.56 NATO. 16- or 18.5-in. bbl. w/flash hider. Stock: polymer, adj., folding or fixed. Ambidextrous controls. Made 2010-20.

Basic Folder . . . . NiB $1830 Ex $1580 Gd $1160
A-TACS, add $100
DMR (18.5-in. bbl.). . . . . NiB $2180 Ex $1910 Gd $1120
**Enhanced (aluminum
  handguard). . . . . NiB $1995 Ex $1690 Gd $1040**
**Patrol Carbine (ratchet-style suppressor
  mount, 2010-16) . . . . NiB $2100 Ex $1580 Gd $1160**
**Special Purpose Carbine (ratchet-style
  suppressor mount, 6-position stock,
  2011-16). . . . . NiB $2380 Ex $1780 Gd $1310**
**ORC (optic ready carbine,
  2008-13). . . . . NiB $930 Ex $710 Gd $530**

—*Currrent Mfg.*—

**ARC Carbine model (450 Bushmaster, 5-rnd.
  magazine, 2022-date). . . . . NiB $1950 Ex $1850 Gd $1750**

AK CARBINE. . . . . NiB $996 Ex $760 Gd $560
Similar to XM-15 except AK-style muzzle brake. 2008-10.

BA30. . . . . NiB $1799 Ex $1699 Gd $1500
Bolt action, ambi. straight pull. Cal.: 6.5 Creedmoor or .308 Win., 10-rnd. magazine. Bbl.: 18- or 24-in. free floated w/ Snake Charmer muzzle brake. Aluminum chassis, adj. stock w/BFT rail and pistol grip. Finish: Anodized black. Made 2022-date.

BA50 . . . .   NiB $5000 Ex $4510 Gd $3010
Bolt action. Caliber .50 BMG. Barrel: 22- or 30-in. free floated w/AAC muzzle device. 10-rnd. magazine. Aluminum chassis stock. Finish: anodized black. Weight: 20 lbs. (22-in. bbl.), 27 lbs. (30-in. bbl.) Made 2009–20.

CARBON-15 SERIES
AR15 platform. Semiauto. lightweight carbon fiber upper/lower receivers. Caliber: 5.56 NATO. 16-in. bbl. Weight: 3.9 lbs.
.22 LR (.22 LR, discont. 2009) . . . NiB $660 Ex $460 Gd $310
9mm (9mm, 2006-12). . . . . NiB $780 Ex $660 Gd $430
Flat Top (2006-16). . . . . NiB $800 Ex $610 Gd $460
Model 4 (M4 style, 2005-13) . . . NiB $800 Ex $610 Gd $460

ORC (2005-16) . . . . NiB $730 Ex $560 Gd $410
R21 . . . . NiB $830 Ex $630 Gd $460
R97/97S (2003-10) . . . . NiB $1080 Ex $810 Gd $380
Top Loading (top-loading internal
  magazine, 2006-10) . . . . NiB $880 Ex $660 Gd $480

DCM COMPETITION . . . . NiB $1100 Ex $960 Gd $710
Similar to M4 except w/20-in. extra heavy bbl., enhanced trigger. 1998-05.
DCM-XR (2008-10) . . . . NiB $980 Ex $730 Gd $560

DISSIPATOR CARBINE . . . . NiB $996 Ex $760 Gd $560
Similar to XM-15 except w/gas block located behind front sight. Made 2004 to 2010.

GAS PISTON CARBINE . . . . . . NiB $1330 Ex $1030 Gd $830
Similar to XM-15 except w/gas piston system. Made 2008 to 2010.

HUNTER . . . . NiB $1200 Ex $910 Gd $660
Similar to M4 except in .308 Win. and 20-in. fluted bbl. 2011-13.

M4 SERIES
AR15 platform. Semiauto. Caliber: 5.56 NATO. 16-in. bbl. w/ birdcage muzzle device. Stock: polymer, 6-position. Weight: 6.5 lbs. Made 2009-20.
Patrolman's Carbine . . . . NiB $780 Ex $690 Gd $490
A3 Patrolman's Carbine, add. $75
MOE/A-TACS . . . . NiB $930 Ex $860 Gd $630
A.R.M.S. Carbine . . . . NiB $880 Ex $755 Gd $455

MOE SERIES
Similar to XM-15 except w/Magpul MOE furniture. Made 2011-20.
Dissipator . . . . NiB $930 Ex $860 Gd $630
.223 Mid-Length . . . . NiB $930 Ex $860 Gd $630
.308 Mid-Length . . . . NiB $1320 Ex $980 Gd $730

ORC (Optic Ready Carbine) Series
Similar to M4 series except in 5.56 NATO and 7.62 NATO, 16- or 18-in. bbl.
ORC carbine . . . . NiB $930 Ex $855 Gd $510
ORC Gas Piston carbine . . . . NiB $995 Ex $880 Gd $560

PREDATOR . . . . NiB $980 Ex $890 Gd $580
Similar to M4 except w/20-in. fluted varmint bbl. Made 2006-13.

VARMINTER . . . . NiB $980 Ex $890 Gd $680
Similar to M4 except w/24-in. extra heavy bbl. Made 2002-13.

V-MATCH COMPETITION . . . . . NiB $930 Ex $710 Gd $530
Similar to M4 except w/20-, 24- or 26-in. bbl. Made 1994-2010.

M17S BULLPUP . . . . NiB $755 Ex $655 Gd $430
Caliber: .223. 21.5-in. bbl. Weight: 8.2 lbs. Polymer stocks. Handle w/fixed open sights w/Weaver-type rail for any optics. Semiauto, self-compensating short stroke gas piston. Forward trigger/grip w/rear chamber. Bullpup style. Alloy receiver. Synthetic lower receiver is hinged to upper w/hinged takedown system. Accepts M-16 type magazines. Made 1992-2005.

VARMINTER . . . . NiB $4255 Ex $3725 Gd $2355
Bolt action. Caliber 5.56 NATO. Barrel: 24-in. free floated. 4-rnd. internal magazine. Stock: Hogue Overmolded. Sights: TrackingPoint 3-21x scope w/laser range finder. Weight: 10.2 lbs. Made 2014–15.

XM10 SERIES
Similar to XM15 series except chambered in 7.62 NATO. 16-, 18- or 18.5-in. bbl. Weight: 7.7-9 lbs.
Enhanced ORC model (Magpul
  PRS stock, 2014–16) . . . . . NiB $1355 Ex $1210 Gd $820
DMR model (Magpul
  PRS stock, 2014–20) . . . . . . NiB $1710 Ex $1510 Gd $955
ORC Gen 1 model (16- or 18-in.
  heavy bbl., 2011–15,
  reintroduced 2017–20) . . . . NiB $1055 Ex $955 Gd $630

XM15 E2S SERIES
AR15 style platform. Caliber: .223. 16-, 20-, 24- or 26-in. bbl. Weight: 7 to 8.6 lbs. Polymer stocks. Adjustable sights w/dual flip-up aperture; optional flattop rail accepts scope. Direct gas-operated w/rotating bolt. Forged alloy receiver. All steel-coated w/manganese phosphate. Accepts M-16 type magazines. Made 1989-2020.
Carbine . . . . NiB $1210 Ex $989 Gd $750
Target Rifle . . . . NiB $1244 Ex $1018 Gd $707

—*Currrent Mfg.*—

450 Bravo Zulu model(450 Bushmaster,
2022-date) . . . . NiB $1300 Ex $1200 Gd $1100
450 Bushmaster model (450 Bushmaster, A2 fixed
stock, 2022-date) . . . . NiB $1300 Ex $1200 Gd $1100
Bravo Zulu model (2022-date) . . NiB $1160 Ex $1060 Gd $960
Bravo Zulu BFSIII model
(binary trigger, 2022-date) . . NiB $1390 Ex $1290 Gd $1190
Bravo Zulu SBR model
(11.5-in. bbl., 2022-date) . . . NiB $1500 Ex $1400 Gd $1300
M4 Patrolman's model (carry
handle, 2022-date) . . . . NiB $1000 Ex $900 Gd $800
M4 Patrolman's BFSIII model
(binary trigger, 2022-date) . . NiB $1260 Ex $1160 Gd $1060
M4 Patrolman's Flat Top
model (2022-date) . . . . NiB $950 Ex $900 Gd $880
ORC model (optic ready,
2022-date) . . . . NiB $880 Ex $780 Gd $680
QRC model (2022-date) . . . . NiB $880 Ex $780 Gd $680
QRC Pro model (2022-date) . . . . NiB $940 Ex $840 Gd $740
QRC BFSIII model (binary
trigger, 2022-date) . . . . NiB $1190 Ex $1090 Gd $990
QRC Pro BFSIII model (binary
trigger, 2022-date) . . . . NiB $1250 Ex $1150 Gd $1050

CABELA'S, INC. — Sidney, NE
Cabela's is a sporting goods dealer and catalog company headquartered in Sidney, Nebraska. Cabela's imports black powder cartridge Sharps replicas, revolvers and other reproductions and replicas manufactured in Italy by A. Uberti, Pedersoli, Pietta and others. Cabela's also includes private label rifles manufactured by Ruger, Winchester, Cooper, and others. Look to those manufacturers for comparable models and values.

RIFLES

CALICO LIGHT WEAPONS SYSTEMS — Cornelius, OR

Formerly Bakersville, California.

LIBERTY 50/100 SEMIAUTO RIFLE

Retarded blowback action. Caliber: 9mm. 50- or 100-rnd. helical-feed magazine. 16.1-in. bbl. 34.5 in. overall. Weight: 7 lbs. Adjustable post front sight and aperture rear. Ambidextrous rotating safety. Glass-filled polymer or thumbhole-style wood stock. Made 1995 to 2001; reintro. 2007.

Model Liberty 50 . . . . NiB $800 Ex $668 Gd $410
Model Liberty 100 . . . . NiB $909 Ex $869 Gd $495

Calico M-100

MODEL M-100 SEMIAUTO SERIES

Similar to the Liberty 100 Model except chambered for .22 LR. Weight: 5 lbs. 34.5 in. overall. Folding or glass-filled polymer stock and forearm. Made 1986-94; reintro. 2007.

w/folding stock (disc. 1994) . . . NiB $600 Ex $355 Gd $300
FS w/fixed stock disc. 1996 . . . NiB $400 Ex $379 Gd $320

MODEL M-105 SEMIAUTO

SPORTER. . . . . NiB $688 Ex $492 Gd $333
Similar to the Liberty 100 Model except fitted w/walnut buttstock and forearm. Made 1989-94.

MODEL M-900 SEMIAUTO CARBINE

Caliber: 9mm Parabellum. 50- or 100-rnd. magazine. 16.1-in. bbl. 28.5 in. overall. Weight: 3.7 lbs. Post front sight adj. for windage and elevation, fixed notch rear. Collapsible steel buttstock and glass-filled polymer grip. Matte black finish. Made 1989-90, 1992 to 1993 and 2007.

w/folding stock (disc. 1994) . . . NiB $808 Ex $497 Gd $338
FS w/fixed stock (intro. 1996) . . . NiB $677 Ex $533 Gd $390

MODEL M-951 TACTICAL CARBINE

Similar to Model 900 except w/long compensator and adj. forward grip. Made 1990-94.

Model 951 . . . . NiB $725 Ex $533 Gd $445
Model 951-S . . . . NiB $725 Ex $533 Gd $445

CANADIAN MILITARY — Quebec, Canada

Manufactured by Ross Rifle Co.

MODEL 1907 MARK II ROSS

MILITARY RIFLE . . . . NiB $409 Ex $299 Gd $277
Straight-pull bolt action. Caliber: .303 British. Five-rnd. box magazine. 28-in. bbl. Weight: 8.5 lbs. Sights: adj. rear; blade front. Military-type full stock. Note: The Ross was originally issued as a Canadian service rifle in 1907. There were several variations; it was the official weapon at the start of WWI, but has been obsolete for many years. For Ross sporting rifle, see listing under Ross Rifle company.

Canadian Military 1907 Mark II Ross Rifle

Century International Arms Tantal Sporter

Century International Arms VZ 2008 Sporter

Century International Arms Degtyarev DP28

Century International Arms Sterling SA

CENTURY INTERNATIONAL ARMS, INC. — Delray Beach, FL

Importer of military surplus and sporting firearms as well as manufacturer of firearms.

CENTURION M38/M96 BOLT-ACTION SPORTER

Sporterized Swedish M38/96 Mauser action. Caliber: 6.5x55mm. Five-rnd. magazine. 24-in. bbl. 44 in. overall. Adj. rear sight. Blade front. Black synthetic or checkered European hardwood Monte Carlo stock. Holden Ironsighter see-through scope mount. Imported from 1987 to date.

w/hardwood stock . . . . NiB $277 Ex $190 Gd $133
w/synthetic stock . . . . NiB $280 Ex $198 Gd $144

CENTURION M98 BOLT-ACTION SPORTER

Sporterized VZ24 or 98 Mauser action. Calibers: .270 Win., 7.62x39mm, .308 Win., .30-06. Five round magazine. 22-in. bbl. 44 in. overall. Weight: 7.5 lbs. W/Millet or Weaver scope base(s), rings and no iron sights. Classic or Monte Carlo laminated hardwood, black synthetic or checkered European hardwood stock. Imported from 1992 to date.

**M98 Action W/black
synthetic stock (w/o rings) . .** NiB $300 Ex $220 Gd $167
**M98 Action W/hardwood Stock
(w/o rings) . . . .** NiB $290 Ex $190 Gd $126
**VZ24 action w/laminated
hardwood stock (Elite) . . . . .** NiB $355 Ex $289 Gd $188
VZ24 action w/black synthetic stock NiB $338 Ex $269 Gd $175
w/Millet base and rings, add. $45

CENTURION P-14 SPORTER
Sporterized P-14 action. Caliber: 7mm Rem. Mag., .300 Win. Mag. Five-rnd. magazine. 24-in. bbl. 43.4 in. overall. Weight: 8.25 lbs. Weaver-type scope base. Walnut stained hardwood or fiberglass stock. Imported from 1987 to date.
w/hardwood stock . . . . NiB $269 Ex $211 Gd $157
w/fiberglass stock . . . . NiB $299 Ex $223 Gd $167

CETME SPORTER . . . . NiB $754 Ex $577 Gd $387
Semiauto. Cal.: .308 Win. Bbl.: 19.5 in. 20-rnd. mag. Blue or Mossy Oak Break-Up camo finish, wood or synthetic stock w/pistol grip. Vented forearm. Weight: 9.7 lbs.

DEGTYAREV DP28 . . . . NiB $4125 Ex $3155 Gd $2390
Semiauto, top-mounted magazine. Cal.: 7.62x54R. Gas operated. Full stock. 47- to 50-rnd. mag. Weight: 10 lbs. Disc.
DPM 28 (pistol grip) . . . . . . NiB $3970 Ex $3289 Gd $2410
DPX Tank Model . . . . NiB $3970 Ex $3289 Gd $2410

ENFIELD SPORTER 4 BOLT-ACTION RIFLE
Sporterized Lee-Enfield action. Caliber: .303 British. 10-rnd. magazine. 25.25-in. bbl. 44.5 in. overall. Blade front sight, adj. aperture rear. Sporterized beechwood military stock or checkered walnut Monte Carlo stock. Blued finish. Imported from 1987. Disc.
w/sporterized military stock . . . . NiB $169 Ex $128 Gd $90
w/checkered walnut stock . . . . NiB $223 Ex $190 Gd $135

GAMESTALKER . . . . NiB $1399 Ex $1088 Gd $946
Cal.: .243 WSSM, .25 WSSM, .300 WSSM. Bbl.: 22 in., stainless steel, flattop upper, free-floating aluminum hand guard. ACE skeleton stock with ERGO Sure Grip. 100% camo. Weight: 7 lbs.

G-3 SPORTER . . . . NiB $866 Ex $633 Gd $425
Semiauto. Cal.: .308 Win. Made G3 parts, American-made receiver with integrated scope rail. Bbl.: 19 in. 20-rnd. mag. Pistol grip stock, matte black finish. Weight: 9.3 pounds. Imported 1999 to 2006.

GP 1975 . . . . NiB $650 Ex $440 Gd $300
Cal.: 7.62x39mm. Bbl.: 16.25 in. Black synthetic furniture, U.S.-made receiver and bbl. Weight: 7.4 lbs.

GP WASR-10. . . . . NiB $555 Ex $370 Gd $244
AK-47 type by Romarm. Cal.: 7.62x39mm. Bbl.: 16.25 in. Wood stock and forearm, 5- and 10-rnd. mag. Weight: 7.5 lbs.
High-Cap series. . . . . NiB $529 Ex $345 Gd $221

GOLANI SPORTER. . . . . NiB $835 Ex $650 Gd $456
Made in Israel. Cal.: .223 Rem. Bbl.: 21 in. Folding stock, opt. bayonet lug., 35-rnd. mag. Weight: 8 lbs. Disc.

L1A1 FAL SPORTER . . . . NiB $944 Ex $749 Gd $588
Sporterized L1A1 FAL Semiauto. Caliber: .308 Win. 20.75-in. bbl. 41 in. overall. Weight: 9.75 lbs. Protected front post sight,

adj. aperture rear. Matte blued finish. Black or camo Bell & Carlson thumbhole sporter stock w/rubber buttpad. Imported from 1988-98.

L1A1/R1A1 SPORTER . . . . NiB $1044 Ex $835 Gd $229
Modeled after British L1A1. Cal.: .308 Win. Bbl.: 22.5 in. Carrying handle, synthetic furn. 20-rnd. mag. Folding rear sight. Weight: 9.5 lbs.

M-14 SPORTER . . . . NiB $460 Ex $338 Gd $255
Sporterized M-14 gas operated Semiauto action. Caliber: .308 Win. 10-rnd. magazine. 22-in. bbl. 41 in. overall. Weight: 8.25 lbs. Blade front sight, adj. aperture rear sight. Parkerized finish. Walnut stock w/rubber recoil pad. Forged receiver. Imported from 1991 Disc.

M-76 SNIPER . . . . NiB $1956 Ex $1538 Gd $967
Semiauto version of Yugoslav M76. Cal.: 8mm Mauser. Bbl.: 21.5 in. U.S.-made receiver. Includes scope, mount and 10-rnd. mag. Weight: 11.3 lbs. Disc.

MODEL B-82 . . . . NiB $835 Ex $600 Gd $380
Limited production Italian police model; serial no. with "D" suffix. Cal.: .30 Luger, .32 ACP, 9 mm Ultra.

PAR 1 . . . . NiB $439 Ex $300 Gd $218
AK-47 receiver, made by PAR. Cal.: 7.62x39mm; 10-rnd. mag. Bbl.: 20.9 in. Weight: 7.6 lbs. Imported 2002 to 2009.
PAR 3 (.223 Rem.) . . . . NiB $439 Ex $300 Gd $218

S.A.R. 1 . . . . NiB $835 Ex $600 Gd $380
AK-47-type by Romarm. Cal.: 7.62x39mm. Bbl.: 16 in. Wood stock and forearm. Includes one 10 and one 30-rnd. double-stack magazine. Disc. 2003.
S.A.R. 2 (5.45x39mm). . . . . NiB $835 Ex $600 Gd $380
S.A.R. 3 (.223 Rem.) . . . . NiB $835 Ex $600 Gd $380

STERLING SA . . . . NiB $745 Ex $560 Gd $380
Semiauto version of Sterling sub-machine gun. Cal.: 9mm Para., 34-rnd. mag. Bbl.: 16 in. U.S.-made receiver and bbl., crinkle finish; folding stock. Disc.

TANTAL SPORTER. . . . . NiB $735 Ex $555 Gd $455
Cal.: 5.45x39mm. Bbl.: 18 in., flash hider. Folding wire stock. Parkerized finish. Includes extra mag. Weight: 8 lbs.

TIGER DRAGUNOV . . . . . . NiB $5000 Ex $4800 Gd $4000
Russian SVD Semiauto sniper rifle. Caliber: 7.62x54R. Five-rnd. magazine. 21-in. bbl. 43 in. overall. Weight: 8.5 lbs. Blade front sight, open rear adj. for elevation. Blued finish. European laminated hardwood thumbhole stock. 4x range-finding scope w/lighted reticle and sunshade. Quick detachable scope mount. Imported from 1994 to 1995.

VZ 2008 SPORTER . . . . NiB $865 Ex $645 Gd $465
Copy of the Czech V258. Cal.: 7.62x39mm. Bbl.: 16.25 in.; steel receiver w/matte finish; wood or plastic stock. Weight: 7 lbs. Disc.

CHARTER ARMS CORPORATION —
Shelton, CT

AR-7 EXPLORER SURVIVAL RIFLE. . . NiB $139 Ex $120 Gd $99
Same as Armalite AR-7, except w/black, instead of brown, "wood grain" plastic stock. See listing of that rifle for specifications. Made 1973-90.

RIFLES

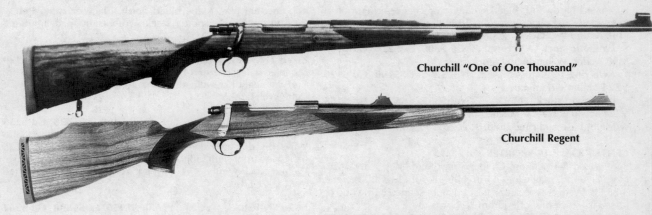

Churchill "One of One Thousand"

Churchill Regent

FIELD KING . . . . **NiB $305 Ex $265 Gd $170**
Bolt action. Mauser style action. Calibers: .243 Win., .25-06 Rem., .270 Win., .308 Win. or .30-06. 4-rnd internal magazine. 18- or 22-in. bbl. Finish: blued or stainless. Stock: black fiberglass. Made 2000–02.

CHIAPPA FIREARMS USA — Dayton, OH
Importer and manufacturer located in Italy since 1958.

—*Lever-Action Models*—

1886 SERIES
Replica of Winchester Model 1886. Caliber: .45-70. Barrel: 16-, 18.5-, 22- or 26-in.
Carbine Hunter model
  (22-in. rnd. bbl.) . . . . **NiB $1480 Ex $1280 Gd $780**
Classic Carbine model (22-in. rnd.
  bbl., caseharden receiver) . . . . . **NiB $1480 Ex $1280 Gd $780**
Kodiak model (18.5-in. half octagon bbl., brushed nickel)
  . . . . **NiB $1555 Ex $1255 Gd $880**
Kodiak Traditional model (18.5-in. full octagon bbl.,
  caseharden receiver) . . . . . . **NiB $1355 Ex $1280 Gd $780**
Rifle model (26-in. octagon bbl.,
  caseharden receiver) . . . . . **NiB $1555 Ex $1330 Gd $830**
Rifle Deluxe model (checkered walnut),
  add **$175**
Skinner model (16-in. rnd. bbl.,
  matte blue) . . . . **NiB $1430 Ex $1255 Gd $755**
Trapper model (16-in. rnd. bbl., optic ready, matte blue,
  disc.) . . . . **NiB $1210 Ex $1055 Gd $710**

1892 SERIES
Replica of Winchester Model 1892. Caliber: .38-40 Win., .357 Mag., .44-40 Win., .44 Mag., or .45 LC. Barrel: 16-, 20-, or 24-in.

Chiappa Little Badger (in folded position)

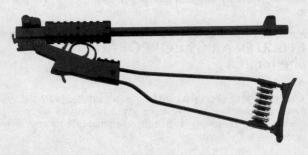

Carbine model (20-in. rnd. bbl.) **NiB $1255 Ex $1080 Gd $730**
Rifle model (20- or 24-in.
  octagon bbl.) . . . . **NiB $1255 Ex $1080 Gd $730**
Takedown Rifle model (24-in.
  octagon bbl.) . . . . **NiB $1355 Ex $1180 Gd $830**
Trapper Classic model (16-in.
  rnd. bbl., blued) . . . . **NiB $1200 Ex $1030 Gd $710**
Trapper Skinner model (16-in. rnd. bbl.,
  optic ready, matte blue) . . . . . **NiB $1310 Ex $1110 Gd $755**

LA332 TAKEDOWN . . . . . . **NiB $400 Ex $340 Gd $210**
Replica of Marlin Model 39 lever-action rifle. Cal.: .22 LR. Bbl.: 18.5-in. Finish: matte blue or case color. Stock: straight grip wood.
Deluxe (pistol grip wood stock) . . . **NiB $555 Ex $485 Gd $305**
Kodiak Cub (matte chrome) . . . . . **NiB $730 Ex $640 Gd $405**

SPENCER
Replica of Spencer repeating rifles. Cal.: .44-40 WCF, .45 Schofield, .45 Long Colt, or .56-50. Bbl.: 20-, 22-, 30- or 33-in. Blue finish, color case hardened frame. Stock: oil finished walnut.
Carbine (20- or 22-in.
  rnd. bbl.) . . . . **NiB $1780 Ex $1510 Gd $880**
Rifle (30- or 33-in.
  octagon bbl.) . . . . **NiB $1880 Ex $1610 Gd $980**

—*Single-Shot Models*—

LITTLE BADGER. . . . . **NiB $180 Ex $155 Gd $110**
Folding survival rifle. Caliber: .17 HMR, .22 LR, or .22 WMR. Barrel: 16.5-in. Finish: blued. Stock: wire steel. Sights: Adj. rear, blade front.
Deluxe model (wood stock), add **$50**

LITTLE SHARPS SERIES
Scaled down replica of Sharps Model 1874. Caliber: .17 HMR, .22 LR, .22 WMR, .22 Hornet, .218 Bee, .30-30 Win., .38-55 Win., .44-40 Win., or .45 LC. Barrel: 24- or 26-in. octagon. Finish: case color receiver, blued barrel. Stock: straight grip, smooth wood. Sights: Adj. tang mounted diopter rear, adj. blade front.
Classic model . . . . **NiB $1280 Ex $1120 Gd $710**
Hunter model (.17 Hornet, 24-in. bbl., disc. 2015) . . . . **NiB $980 Ex $845 Gd $580**
Target model (.17 Hornet, 26-in. bbl., disc. 2015) . . . . . **NiB $1130 Ex $980 Gd $630**

SHARPS SERIES
Replica of Sharps Model 1874. Caliber: .38-55, .45-70, .45-90, .45-110, or .50-70. Barrel: 22- thru 34-in. octagon or rnd. Finish: case color receiver, blued barrel. Stock: straight grip, smooth wood. Sights: Adj. tang mounted diopter rear, adj. blade front.

Cimarron 1883 Burgess Rifle

Cimarron Adobe Walls Falling Block Rifle

Cimarron 1876 Centennial Sporting Rifle

Cimarron 1892 Carbine El Dorado

Berdan model (.45-70, 30-in. rnd.
  bbl., dbl. triggers) . . . . NiB $1455 Ex $1230 Gd $755
Business model (.45-70, 28-in. octagon
  bbl., dbl. triggers) . . . . NiB $1300 Ex $1340 Gd $715
Cavalry model (.45-70 or .50-70,
  22-in. rnd. bbl.) . . . . NiB $1300 Ex $1340 Gd $715
Creedmoor model (.45-70, 34-in.
  bbl., disc. 2014) . . . . NiB $1500 Ex $1315 Gd $830
Down Under model (multilple
  calibers, 34-in. octagon bbl.,
  dbl. triggers, pewter accents) . . . NiB $1655 Ex $1455 Gd $930
Sporting model (.45-70,
  32-in. octagon bbl.,
  dbl. triggers) . . . . NiB $1300 Ex $1340 Gd $715

—Semiautomatic Models—

M1-22
Replica of M1 Carbine. Caliber: .22 LR, 10-rnd. magazine.
Barrel: 18-in. Finish: blued. Stock: polymer or wood. Sights:
Adj. rear, blade front. Weight: 5.5 lbs.
Wood stock . . . . NiB $380 Ex $355 Gd $310
polymer stock, deduct $100

M1-9
Replica of M1 Carbine. Caliber: 9mm, 10-rnd. magazine.
Barrel: 19-in. Finish: blued. Stock: polymer or wood. Sights:
Adj. rear, blade front. Weight: 6.3 lbs.
Wood stock . . . . NiB $590 Ex $530 Gd $365
polymer stock, deduct $80

MFOUR-22 GEN II SERIES
Replica of M4 AR15 style Carbine. Caliber: .22 LR, 10- or
28-rnd. magazine. Barrel: 16-in. Finish: matte black. Stock: adj.
polymer. Sights: Adj. rear/front. Weight: 5.5 lbs.
Rifle model . . . . NiB $455

CHIPMUNK RIFLES — Milltown, PA

*Formerly Prospect, Oregon. Manufactured by Rogue Rifle
Company, formerly Oregon Arms Company and Chipmunk
Manufacturing, Inc.*

BARRACUDA . . . . NiB $175 Ex $135 Gd $100
Similar to Standard model except w/thumbhole stock and
Picatinny rail, no sights.

STANDARD RIFLE . . . . NiB $140 Ex $100 Gd $75
Bolt action. Single shot. Calibers: .17 HMR, .17 Mach 2, .22
LR. or .22 WMR. 16.13-in. standard or 18.13-in. bull bbl.
Weight: 2.5 lbs. (standard) or 4 lbs. (Bull bbl.) Peep sight rear;
ramp front. Plain or checkered American walnut, laminated or
black hardwood stock. Made 1982-2007.
w/laminated stock, add. $5
w/checkered walnut stock, add $20
.17 HMR, .17 Mach 2 or .22 WMR, add $20

E.J. CHURCHILL — England

*Manufactured in High Wycombe, England, imported by Elliot
Brothers, Chapin, SC.*

HIGHLANDER . . . . NiB $439 Ex $367 Gd $298
Calibers: .243 Win., .25-06 Rem., .270 Win., .308 Win.,
.30-06, 7mm Rem. Mag., .300 Win. Mag. Four round magazine (standard); 3-rnd. (magnum). Bbl. length: 22-in. (standard); 24-in. (magnum). 42.5 to 44.5 in. overall. Weight: 7.5
lbs. Adj. rear sight, blade front. Checkered European walnut
pistol-grip stock. Imported from 1986 to 1991.

**"ONE OF ONE
THOUSAND"** . . . . NiB $4220 Ex $2535 Gd $1966
Made for Interarms to commemorate that firm's 20th anniversary. Mauser-type action. Calibers: .270, 7mm Rem. Mag.,
.308, .30-06, .300 Win. Mag., .375 H&H Mag., .458 Win.
Mag. Five round magazine (3-rnd. in Magnum calibers).
24-in. bbl. Weight: 8 lbs. Classic-style French walnut stock w/
cheekpiece, black forend tip, checkered pistol grip and forearm, swivel-mounted recoil pad w/cartridge trap, pistol-grip
cap w/trap for extra front sight, barrel-mounted sling swivel.
Limited issue of 1,000 rifles made in 1973. See illustration
previous page.

REGENT BOLT-ACTION RIFLE . . . NiB $577 Ex $423 Gd $290
Calibers: .243 Win., .25-06 Rem., .270 Win., .308 Win.,
.30-06, 7mm Rem. Mag., .300 Win. Mag. Four round
magazine. 22-in. rnd. bbl. 42.5 in. overall. Weight: 7.5 lbs.
Ramp front sight w/gold bead; adj. rear. Hand-checkered
Monte Carlo-style stock of select European walnut; recoil
pad. Made 1986-88.

CIMARRON ARMS — Fredericksburg, TX

*Importer of reproductions and replicas manufactured in Italy
by A. Uberti, Pedersoli, Pietta and others.*

1860 HENRY SERIES
Reproduction of 1860 Henry lever-action repeating rifle w/
original Henry loading system. Cal.: .44-40 WCF, .44 Spl., or
.45 LC. Bbl.: 22- or 24-in. Rec.: Brass or case hardened steel.
Finish: In-the-white, blue, charcoal blue, or antique. NOTE:
Civil War models include military inspector's marks and cartouche, military-type sling swivels. Mfg. by Uberti, imported
1993-date.
antique finish . . . . NiB $1545 Ex $1380 Gd $1120
blue finish . . . . NiB $1345 Ex $1180 Gd $920
charcoal blue finish. . . . . NiB $1475 Ex $1310 Gd $1050
in-the-white finish. . . . . NiB $1395 Ex $1230 Gd $970
Civil War model,
  antique finish . . . . NiB $1680 Ex $1495 Gd $1210

RIFLES

Civil War model,
blue finish. . . . . NiB $1480 Ex $1295 Gd $1010
Civil War model, charcoal
blue finish. . . . . NiB $1610 Ex $1425 Gd $1140
Civil War model,
in-the-white finish. . . . . NiB $1550 Ex $1365 Gd $1080
w/ standard engraving add $2550
w/standard engraving, deluxe wood, add $3150
w/Lincoln hand engraving (disc. 2009), add. $4500
w/Lincoln hand engraving,
deluxe wood (disc. 2009), add $5000

1866 YELLOWBOY LEVER-ACTION
Replica of Winchester 1866 lever-action repeating rifle. Cal.: .22 LR, .22 WMR, .32-20 WCF, .38 Spl., .38-55 WCF, .44 Spl., .44-40 WCF, or .45 LC. Bbl.: 19-in. rnd. Stock: Smooth walnut. Brass receiver, saddle ring. Mfg. by Uberti, imported 1993-date.
Carbine model . . . . NiB $1130 Ex $990 Gd $770
Pawnee Carbine model (19-in. rnd. bbl., brass tacks
in stock, 1989-date) . . . . NiB $1255 Ex $1100 Gd $855
Red Cloud model (19-in. rnd. bbl., brass tacks in stock,
engraved receiver, disc. 1989) . . NiB $955 Ex $830 Gd $630
Short Rifle model (20-in.
octagon bbl., 2000-date). . . . . NiB $1145 Ex $1010 Gd $780
Sporting Rifle model (24-in.
octagon bbl., 1993-date). . . . . NiB $1145 Ex $1010 Gd $780
Trapper model (16-in. rnd.
bbl., 2002-date) . . . . NiB $1110 Ex $970 Gd $755
w/A-engraving, add. $2025
w/B-engraving, add. $2500
w/C-engraving, add. $3000

1873 CARBINE/RIFLE SERIES
Reproduction of Winchester 1873 lever-action repeating rifle. Cal.: .22 LR, .22 Mag., .32-20 WCF, .357 Mag., .38-40 WCF, .44 Spl., .44-40 WCF, or .45 LC. Bbl.: 16- to 30-in. rnd., octagon or half rnd./octagon. Finish: Blued or case hardened. Stock: Smooth or checkered wood, straight or pistol grip. Saddle ring.
Evil Roy model (20-in. bbl.,
tuned action, 2005-07) . . . . . NiB $1755 Ex $1510 Gd $1130
Evil Roy Texas Brush Popper model (18-in.
half octagon/rnd. bbl., straight or pistol grip,
tuned action, 2010-13) . . . . . NiB $1710 Ex $1455 Gd $1055
Larry Crow model (20-in. bbl.,
tuned action, 2005-07) . . . . . NiB $1855 Ex $1580 Gd $1155
Long Range Sporting Rifle model (30-in. octagon bbl., straight
or pistol grip, 1990-date). . . . . NiB $1255 Ex $1100 Gd $855
Saddle Rifle model (18-in.
octagon bbl., 2017-date) . . . . . NiB $1265 Ex $1110 Gd $855
Saddle Ring Carbine model (19-in.
rnd. bbl., 1993-date) . . . . NiB $1225 Ex $1080 Gd $835
Short Rifle model (20-in.
octagon bbl., 1990-date) . . . . . NiB $1200 Ex $1055 Gd $830
Sporting Rifle model (24-in. octagon bbl., straight or
pistol grip, 1990-date) . . . . NiB $1200 Ex $1055 Gd $830
Texas Brush Popper model (18-in. half octagon/rnd. bbl., straight
or pistol grip, 1990-date). . . . . NiB $1320 Ex $1160 Gd $900
Trapper Carbine model (16-in. rnd.
bbl., 1990-date). . . . . NiB $1180 Ex $1030 Gd $810
U.S. Marshall Carbine model (.44 Mag.,
18-in. rnd. bbl., 2018-20) . . . . NiB $1255 Ex $1100 Gd $855
U.S. Marshall Indian Territory Carbine model
(18-in. rnd. bbl., 2019-date) . . NiB $1290 Ex $1130 Gd $880
One of 1000 engraved model NiB $2409 Ex $2033 Gd $1354

SHARPS MODEL 1874 SERIES
Reproduction of Sharps Model 1874 falling block, single-shot rifle. Cal.: .38-55 WCF, .45-70 Gov't., .45-90 Win., .45-110, or

.50-90. Bbl.: 22- to 34-in., rnd. or octagon. Stock: Checkered or smooth walnut. Double set triggers. Mfg. by Armi-Sport or Pedersoli, imported 1997-date.
Big 50 Long Range model (mfg. Pedersoli, .50-90, 34-in. bbl.,
2004-20). . . . . NiB $2590 Ex $2255 Gd $1755
Billy Dixon Sporting model (mfg. Armi-Sport, deluxe wood,
1997-date) . . . . NiB $1400 Ex $1225 Gd $960
Billy Dixon Sporting model (mfg. Pedersoli, deluxe wood,
1997-date) . . . . NiB $1930 Ex $1690 Gd $1320
Billy Dixon Officer's model (mfg. Pedersoli, 26-in. bbl.,
2015-16). . . . . NiB $2055 Ex $1800 Gd $1400
Business model (mfg. Pedersoli, 32-in. bbl., shotgun style
butt, 2017-date) . . . . NiB $1345 Ex $1180 Gd $1310
Little Rascal Mini Sharps model (mfg. Armi-Sport,
.22lr, .22 Hornet, .30-30, .38-55
or .45 LC; 2011-15) . . . . NiB $1155 Ex $955 Gd $710
McNelly Carbine model (mfg. Armi-Sport, 22-in. rnd. bbl.;
2017-18). . . . . NiB $1345 Ex $1180 Gd $890
McNelly Carbine model (mfg. Armi-Sport,
.45-70 or .50-70, 22-in. rnd. bbl., engraved
"T*S" on bbl., 2004-date). . NiB $1355 Ex $1185 Gd $930
Professional Hunter model (mfg. Pedersoli, .45-70, 32-in.
bbl., 2005-14). . . . . NiB $1355 Ex $1155 Gd $880
Pride Of The Plains II model (mfg. Armi-Sport, w/ or w/o
telescopic sight, 2008-09). . NiB $1255 Ex $1080 Gd $830
Pride Of The Plains II model (mfg.
Pedersoli, nickel receiver, Creedmoor
sight, 2004-date). . . . . NiB $1920 Ex $1680 Gd $1310
Quigley Rifle From Down Under II model
(mfg. Armi-Sport, 34-in. octagon
bbl., 2000-date) . . . . NiB $1560 Ex $1365 Gd $1060
Quigley Rifle From Down Under II
model (mfg. Pedersoli, 34-in. octagon
bbl., 2000-date) . . . . NiB $2035 Ex $1780 Gd $1385
Rocky Mountain II model (mfg. Armi-Sport, .45-70, 30-in.
octagon bbl., silver receiver, ptional 6x Malcolm
rifle scope, 2010-14) . . . . . NiB $1500 Ex $1280 Gd $880
w/scope, add $650
Slotter & Co. model (mfg. Pedersoli, .45-70, 34-in. octagon/
rnd. bbl., 2011-date). . . . . . NiB $2140 Ex $1880 Gd $1455
Sporting model (mfg. Armi-Sport, 32-in.
bbl., 2019-date) . . . . NiB $1270 Ex $1110 Gd $870
Sporting #1 model (mfg. Pedersoli,
.40-65 or .45-70, 32-in.
octagon bbl., 2000-02) . . . . . NiB $1110 Ex $980 Gd $730
Sporting #1 Silhouette model (mfg.
Pedersoli, .45-70 or .50-70, 32-in.
octagon bbl., 2003-18) . . . NiB $1500 Ex $1315 Gd $1020
U.S.A. Shooting Team Creedmoor model
(mfg. Armi-Sport, .45-70, 34-in.
rnd. bbl., disc. 2014) . . . . . NiB $1380 Ex $1180 Gd $910

1883 BURGESS RIFLE . . . . . NiB $1310 Ex $1130 Gd $855
Reproduction of Colt Burgess lever action. Caliber: .45 Long Colt. Bbl.: 20 or 25 ½ in. Reproduction. Mfg. Uberti, imported 2010-16.

LIGHTNING RIFLE . . . . . . NiB $1488 Ex $1088 Gd $755
Reproduction of Colt Lightning Rifle. Cal.: .357 Mag., .44-40 WCF or .45 Long Colt. Bbl.: rnd.; 20 or 24 in.; octagon: 20, 24, or 26 in. Blue or case-colored frame. Imported 2006-12.
W/octagon bbl., add. $150
Color case-hardened frame, add. $300

ROLLING BLOCK SERIES
Reproduction of Remington Rolling Block single-shot rifle. Caliber: .45-70 Gov't. Barrel: 30-in., octagon. Finish: Blued. Stock: Checkered walnut. Sights: Fixed. Imported 1989-90.

**Model 1871 Rolling Block Baby (.22 LR,
.22 WMR, .22 Hornet or .357 Mag.;
22-in. bbl.; disc 1990)** . . . . . . NiB $500 Ex $455 Gd $330
**Adobe Walls model
(double set triggers, silver
nose cap, 2004-date)** . . . . NiB $1515 Ex $1330 Gd $1030
**Deluxe Sporting Rifle model
(high grade wood stock)** . . . . . NiB $930 Ex $830 Gd $655
**Long Range Creedmoor model (30-in.
tapered octagon bbl.)** . . . . . NiB $1380 Ex $1230 Gd $860
Sporting Rifle model . . . . NiB $830 Ex $730 Gd $555

BABY CARBINE . . . . NiB $379 Ex $290 Gd $195
Remington repro. Caliber: .22 LR, .22 Hornet, .22 Mag. Or
.357 Mag. Bbl: 22 in. Walnut stock and forearm. Brass trigger
guard and buttplate. Disc. 1990.
Deluxe model . . . . NiB $785 Ex $580 Gd $338

1860 SPENCER RIFLE . . . . .NiB $1560 Ex $1154 Gd $933
By Armi Sport. Cal.: 56-50. Bbl.: 30 in. Plain walnut stock and
forearm. Case hardened receiver, trigger guard and hammer.
Three barrel bands. Imported 2008-12.

**1865 SPENCER
REPEATING RIFLE** . . . . .NiB $1680 Ex $1470 Gd $1145
By Armi Sport. Cal.: .44-40 WCF, .45 Schofield, .45 Long
Colt, .56-50. Bbl.: 20 or 30 in. (in 56-50 only, disc. 2009).
Blue finish, color case hardened frame. Straight grip walnut
stock. Imported 2005 to date.
w/30-in. bbl., add $200

SPRINGFIELD TRAPDOOR SERIES
Reproduction of Springfield Trapdoor single-shot carbine. Caliber:
.45-70. Barrel: 22-in. rnd. Finish: Case Hardened. Stock: Straight
grip, smooth walnut. Barrel band. 2013-date.
Cavalry Carbine model . . . . . . NiB $1440 Ex $1255 Gd $980
**Billy Dixon Trapdoor Carbine model
(mfg. Pedersoli, .45-70, 26-in.
rnd. bbl., 2019-22)** . . . . . . NiB $2410 Ex $2110 Gd $1635

1876 RIFLE SERIES
Reproduction of Winchester 1876 lever-action, repeating rifle.
Cal.: .40-60 WCF, .45-60 WCF, .45-70 WCF,.50-95 WCF. Bbl.: 20-
to 28-in., octagon. Finish: Blue or case hardened. Sight: Iron. Stock:
Smooth walnut, straight grip. Mfg. Uberti, imported 2006-date.
Centennial Sporting model . . NiB $1530 Ex $1340 Gd $1040
**Crossfire Carbine model (.45-60 WCF or .45-75,
22-in. rnd. bbl., full length fore end w/bbl. band,
2010-21)** . . . . NiB $1675 Ex $1465 Gd $1140
**N.W.M.P. Carbine model (.45-60 WCF or .45-75, 22-in. rnd.
bbl., full length fore end w/bbl. band, Canadian N.W.M.P.
model, 2010-date)** . . . . NiB $1675 Ex $1465 Gd $1140
**Presidio Carbine model (.50-95, 22-in. rnd. bbl., half mag.,
2017-date)** . . . . NiB $1455 Ex $1465 Gd $1130
**Tom Horn Rifle model (.45-60,
28-in. octagon bbl., aperture
rear sight, 2017-date)** . . . . NiB $1575 Ex $1380 Gd $1080

1885 HIGH-WALL RIFLE . . . . NiB $1169 Ex $977 Gd $749
Cal.: .30-40 Krag, .348 Win., .38-55 Win., .405 Win., .40-65
WCF, .45-70 Gov't., .45-90 WCF, .45-120 WCF. Bbl.: 28 or 30
in., octagon. Case hardened finish frame. Iron sights standard
or optional aperture rear and globe front offered.
Pedersoli mfg. . . . . NiB $2378 Ex $1956 Gd $1100

1885 LOW-WALL RIFLE . . . . . NiB $1077 Ex $800 Gd $654
Cal.: .22 LR, .22 Hornet, .22 Mag., .30-30 Win., .32-20 WCF,
.357 Mag., .38-40 WCF, .44 Mag., .38-55, .44-40 WCF, .45-

70 Gov't., .45 Long Colt. Bbl.: 30 in. Hand checkered walnut
stock, single- or double-set trigger.
Deluxe model, add $200
Standard custom engraving, add. $1750
Double set triggers, add $400

1886 CARBINE/RIFLE SERIES
Reproduction of Winchester 1886 lever-action, repeating rifle.
Cal.: .45-70 Gov't. Bbl.: 22- to 26-in., octagon. Finish: Case
hardened. Sight: Iron. Stock: Smooth or checkered walnut,
straight or pistol grip. Mfg. Armi-Sport, imported 2011-date.
Carbine model (straight grip) . . NiB $1365 Ex $1190 Gd $900
**Deluxe Rifle model (straight grip,
checkered stock)** . . . . NiB $1585 Ex $1410 Gd $1120
**Deluxe Rifle model (pistol grip,
checkered stock)** . . . . NiB $2135 Ex $1960 Gd $1670
Rifle model (straight grip) . . . . NiB $1455 Ex $1280 Gd $990
Rifle model (pistol grip) . . . . . NiB $1835 Ex $1660 Gd $1370

1892 CARBINE/RIFLE SERIES
Reproduction of Winchester 1892 lever-action, repeating rifle.
Cal.: .357 Mag., .44 Mag., .44-40 WCF, or .45 LC. Bbl.: 20-
or 24-in., rnd. or octagon. Solid or take-down frame. Stock:
Smooth walnut. Finish: Case colored. Saddle ring w/20-in. bbl.
only.Mfg. Armi-Sport, imported 2005-13, reintro. 2015-date.
Rifle model . . . . NiB $1235 Ex $1080 Gd $840
take-down frame, add. $200
Carbine model (20-in. rnd. bbl.) . . NiB $1235 Ex $866 Gd $650
**Cogburn Carbine model (.45 LC, 20-in. rnd. bbl., big loop
lever, 2017-date)** . . . . NiB $1255 Ex $1110 Gd $855
**El Dorado Carbine model (.357 Mag. or .45 LC, 20-in. rnd. bbl.,
big loop lever, disc. 2017)** . . . . . NiB $1010 Ex $880 Gd $680

1894 CARBINE/RIFLE SERIES
Reproduction of Winchester 1894 lever-action, repeating rifle.
Cal.: .30-30 or .38-55. Bbl.: 20- or 26-in., rnd. or octagon.
Stock: Smooth walnut. Finish: Case colored or blued. Mfg.
Armi-Sport, imported 2005-13, reintro. 2019-date.
Carbine model (20-in. rnd. bbl.) . . NiB $1085 Ex $950 Gd $740
**Rifle model (24.2- or 26-in. octagon bbl.,
2019-date)** . . . . NiB $1085 Ex $950 Gd $740
**Short Rifle model (20-in. octagon bbl.,
2021-date)** . . . . NiB $1085 Ex $950 Gd $740

MODEL 71 SERIES
Reproduction of Winchester Model 71 lever-action, repeat-
ing rifle. Cal.: .348 Win. or .45-70. Bbl.: 24-in., rnd. Stock:
Checkered walnut w/pistol grip. Finish: Case colored or blued.
Imported 2015-18.
Classic model (blued) . . . . . . NiB $1730 Ex $1515 Gd $1180
**Hogzilla Killa model (.45-70, 19-in. rnd. bbl.,
2015-17)** . . . . NiB $1580 Ex $1330 Gd $955
**Premium model (case hardened,
2015-date)** . . . . NiB $1680 Ex $1470 Gd $1145

CLERKE RECREATION PRODUCTS —
Santa Monica, CA

DELUXE HIGH-WALL . . . . .NiB $337 Ex $290 Gd $219
Same as standard model, except w/adj. trigger, half-octagon bbl.,
select wood, stock w/cheekpiece and recoil pad. Made 1972-74.

HIGH-WALL SINGLE-SHOT RIFLE . .NiB $310 Ex $234 Gd $177
Falling-block lever-action similar to Winchester 1885 High Wall
S.S. Color casehardened investment-cast receiver. Calibers:
.222 Rem., .22-250, .243 Rem., 6mm Rem., .25-06, .270 Win.,
7mm Rem. Mag., .30-06, .45-70 Govt. 26-in. medium-weight

RIFLES

bbl. Weight: 8 lbs. Furnished w/o sights. Checkered walnut pistol-grip stock and Schnabel forearm. Made 1972-74.

CLIFTON ARMS — Medina, TX

SCOUT BOLT-ACTION RIFLE
Custom rifle built on the Dakota 76, Ruger 77 or Winchester 70 action. Shilen match-grade barrel cut and chambered to customer's specification. Clifton composite stock fitted and finished to customer's preference. Made 1992-97.

	NiB	Ex	Gd
African Scout	$3175	$2690	$2310
Pseudo Scout	$3160	$2211	$1589
Standard Scout	$3122	$2520	$1443
Super Scout	$3145	$2175	$1590

COLT'S MFG. CO., INC. — West Hartford, CT

NOTE: *AR-15 model rifles are the Semiauto version of the U.S. Military M16 model and divided into three types: Pre-ban manufactured from 1963 to 1989, Pre-ban manufactured from 1989 to 10/13/1994, and Post-ban from 10/12/1994 to present. Receivers were stamped with model names—Colt Carbine, Government Model, Match Target, SP1, Sporter II, and Sporter Match H-Bar. Pre-ban made from 1963 to 1989.*

AR-15 SP1 . . . . NiB $2110 EX $1855 GD $1605
Commercial version of U.S. M16 rifle. Gas-operated. Takedown. Caliber: .223 Rem. (5.56mm). 20-rnd. magazine w/spacer to reduce capacity to 5 rnd. 20-in. bbl. w/flash suppressor. Sights: Rear peep w/windage adjustment in carrying handle; front adj. for windage. 3x scope and mount optional. Black molded buttstock of high-impact synthetic material, rubber buttplate. Barrel surrounded by handguard of black fiberglass w/heat-reflecting inner shield. Swivels, black web sling strap. Weight: w/o accessories, 6.3 lbs. Made 1964-94.
Carbine (16-in. bbl., collapsible stock), add $800
Delta H-Bar model (20-in. heavy bbl.,
    removable cheek piece, 3-9x rubber armored
    scope, 1987-91) . . . . Nib $2305 Ex $1930 Gd $1580
H-Bar model (20-in.
    heavy bbl.) . . . . Nib $2055 Ex $1755 Gd $1405
Government Model
    (20-in. bbl.). . . . . Nib $2255 Ex $1955 Gd $1455
Sporter II (20-in. bbl.). . . . . . Nib $1880 Ex $1480 Gd $1180
Sporter II Carbine
    (16-in. bbl.). . . . . Nib $2230 Ex $1855 Gd $1530

Pre-ban made from 1989 to 1994.

AR-15 MATCH H-BAR . . . . NiB $1755 Ex $1455 Gd $1155
Brrl.: 20-in. heavy H-Bar style. Fixed stock.
Delta H-Bar (Furnished w/3-9x rubber armored
    scope and removeable cheekpiece.
    1987-91.). . . . . NiB $2455 Ex $2155 Gd $1855

AR-15 GOVERNMENT CARBINE . . NiB $2280 Ex $2030 Gd $1755
Caliber: .223 Rem., Five-rnd. magazine. 16-in. bbl. w/flash suppressor and bayonet lug. 35 in. overall. Weight: 5.8 lbs. Two-position telescoping aluminum buttstock; sling swivels. Made 1988-94.

AR-15 COLT CARBINE . . . . NiB $2155 Ex $1855 Gd $1630
Similar to Government Carbine model except w/o bayonet lug. Made 1985-88.

AR-15 9MM CARBINE . . . . NiB $2255 Ex $1990 Gd $1176
Semiauto. Caliber: 9mm NATO. 20-rnd. detachable magazine. Bbl.: 16-in. w/bayonet lug. Weight: 6.3 lbs. Adj. rear and front sights. 2-position adj. buttstock. Ribbed round handguard. Made 1985-86.
w/o bayonet lug (1992-94) . . NiB $1955 Ex $1655 Gd $1380

AR-15 TARGET COMPETITION
H-BAR . . . . NiB $1855 Ex $1555 Gd $1205
Caliber: .223 Rem. 20-in. heavy bbl., Flat-top receiver w/ detachable carry handle. Weight: 8.5 lbs.

AR-15 COMPETITION H-BAR . . NiB $1955 Ex $1655 Gd $1355
Similar to Target Competition H-BAR Model except made by Colt Custom Shop.

AR-15 SPORTER LIGHTWEIGHT . . . NiB $1655 Ex $1355 GD $1005
Similar to Government Carbine Model except w/o bayonet lug or adj. stock.
7.62x39mm (1992-94) . . . . NiB $1855 Ex $1555 Gd $1280

AR-15 SPORTER TARGET . . . NiB $1755 Ex $1455 Gd $1155
Similar to Match H-Bar model except w/reduced bbl. diameter. Weight: 7.5 lbs.

AR-15 TACTICAL CARBINE . . . NiB $2980 Ex $2280 Gd $1910
Smilar to Government Carbine except flattop reciever, 16-in. heavt bbl., bayonet lug, 4-position adj. stock. Very rare variant. S/N range up to 134. Made 1994 only.
S/N range 135 and up . . . . NiB $1255 Ex $955 Gd $755

Post-ban made from 1994 to present.

AR-15 MILITARY CLASSICS SERIES
Semiauto. Caliber: 5.56 NATO. US Property Marked rollmarks. 2016-date.
M16A1 Retro Reissue model (20-in. bbl.,
    fixed A2 stock, triangular handguard,
    carry handle) . . . . NiB $2499 Ex $2200 Gd $1760
M4A1 SOCOM Carbine model (14.5-in. bbl. w/pinned
    extended flash hider,
    M4 furniture) . . . . NiB $1499 Ex $1355 Gd $1210
XM177E2 Retro Carbine model (11.5-in. bbl. w/pinned extended
flash hider, carry handle) . . . NiB $2599 Ex $2310 Gd $2110

EXPANSE M4. . . . . NiB $705 Ex $655 Gd $505
Semiauto. Caliber: 5.56 NATO. 16.1-in. free floated bbl. 2016-17.

EXPERT SERIES
Semiauto. Caliber: 5.56 NATO. 18-in. mid-weight bbl., MagPul furniture. Made 2013-15.
CRE-16 (16-in. bbl.) . . . . NiB $1380 Ex $1055 Gd $755
CRE-16 Gen2 (16-in. H-Bar
    style bbl.) . . . . NiB $1380 Ex $1055 Gd $755
CRE-16 Gen3 (Wylde chamber,
    16-in. H-Bar style bbl.) . . . . NiB $1455 Ex $1130 Gd $855
CRE-18 . . . . NiB $1380 Ex $1055 Gd $755
CRE-18 Gen2 (stainless H-Bar
    style bbl.) . . . . NiB $1380 Ex $1055 Gd $755
CRE-18 Gen3 (Wylde chamber, stainless
    H-Bar style bbl.) . . . . NiB $1455 Ex $1130 Gd $855

MARKSMAN SERIES
Semiauto. Caliber: .223 Rem. 16-in. mid-weight bbl., MagPul furniture, competition match trigger. Made 2013-19.
CRX-16 (16-in. bbl., fixed stock,
    2013-16) . . . . NiB $1205 Ex $955 Gd $720

Colt AR-15 Government Model (pre-ban 1963-89)

Colt AR-15 Delta H-BAR (pre-ban 1963-89)

Colt AR-15 Sporter II Carbine (pre-ban 1963-89)

Colt AR-15 SP1 (pre-ban 1963-1989)

Colt Stagecoach

Colteer 1-.22

Colteer .22 Autoloader

CRX-16 Gen2 (16-in. H-Bar
style bbl.) . . . . NiB $1030 Ex $805 Gd $600
CRX-16 Gen3 (Hogue stock,
16-in.) . . . . NiB $1055 Ex $820 Gd $630
CRZ-16 (16-in. H-Bar style bbl.,
Hogue stock) . . . . NiB $855 Ex $655 Gd $520

MATCH TARGET SERIES
Semiauto. Caliber: .223 Rem. 20-in. bbl., quick detach carry
handle, Picatinny rail.
Competition H-Bar (1992-2013) NiB $980 Ex $730 Gd $540
Competition H-Bar II
(1995-2012) . . . . NiB $955 Ex $705 Gd $530
H-Bar (1986-2010) . . . . NiB $1030 Ex $805 Gd $600
Lightweight (16-in. bbl.,
1991-2002) . . . . NiB $900 Ex $700 Gd $520
M4 Carbine (.223 Rem., 7.62x39mm or 9mm;
16-in. bbl.; 2002-13) . . . . NiB $955 Ex $705 Gd $530

PRO SERIES
Semiauto. Caliber: .223 Rem., 6.5 Grendel, 6.5 Creedmoor,
or .308 Win. 16-in. heavy-weight bbl., MagPul CRT stock and
MOE grip, Geissele 2-stage trigger. Made 2013-19.

CRB-16 (300 BLK) . . . . NiB $1530 Ex $1080 Gd $780
CRP-16 (5.56 NATO) . . . . NiB $1630 Ex $1230 Gd $900
CRP-18 Gen2 (.223 Rem.,
18-in. bbl.) . . . . NiB $1730 Ex $1300 Gd $930
CRP-18 3-Gun model (18-in. bbl.,
2013-15) . . . . NiB $1730 Ex $1300 Gd $930
CRP-18 Gen2 3-Gun model (Wylde chamber, 18-in. bbl.,
Hogue grip, M-LOK rail) . . . . NiB $1730 Ex $1300 Gd $930
CRP-18LV (lightweight varmint model, 18-in. bbl.,
2013-15) . . . . NiB $1630 Ex $1230 Gd $900
CRP-20 (.223 Rem., 20-in. bbl.,
2013-15) . . . . NiB $1630 Ex $1230 Gd $900
CRP-20VR (varmint model, .223 Rem.,
20-in. bbl.) . . . . NiB $1630 Ex $1230 Gd $900
CRG-20 (6.5 Grendel, 20-in. bbl.,
2013 only) . . . . NiB $1405 Ex $1010 Gd $780
CRC-22 (6.5 Creedmoor, 22-in. fluted
bbl., 2014-15) . . . . NiB $2555 Ex $1805 Gd $1255
CLR-16 (.308 Win.,
M-LOK rail) . . . . NiB $1955 Ex $1455 Gd $1055
CLR-16 Gen2 (.308 Win.) . . . NiB $2000 Ex $1500 Gd $1100

GRADING: **NiB** = New in Box   **Ex** = Excellent or NRA 95%   **Gd** = Good or NRA 68%

CLR-20 (.308 Win., 20-in. match bbl., Geissele
2-stage trigger) . . . . NiB $2555 Ex $1930 Gd $1405
CLR-20 Gen2 (.308 Win., 20-in. match bbl., Geissele 2-stage
trigger, M-LOK rail). . . . . . NiB $2480 Ex $1780 Gd $1255

LE6920 SERIES
Semiauto. Caliber: 5.56 NATO. 16-in. bbl. w/bayonet lug.
AE (ambidextrous controls, flattop, BUIS, adj. stock,
2014-16) . . . . NiB $1230 Ex $930 Gd $680
M4 Carbine (flattop, BUIS, adj.
stock, 2012-19) . . . . NiB $880 Ex $655 Gd $520
MP-R (flattop, BUIS, Magpul adj. stock, Troy rail,
2012-15) . . . . NiB $1130 Ex $855 Gd $630
OEM1 (flattop, BUIS, no furniture,
2015-18) . . . . NiB $710 Ex $545 Gd $420
SOCOM (flattop, BUIS, adj. stock, Knights Armament rail,
2012-14) . . . . NiB $1400 Ex $1055 Gd $780

LE6940 SERIES
Semiauto. Caliber: 5.56 NATO. 16-in. free floated bbl. w/
bayonet lug.
M4 MONOLITHIC (flattop, BUIS, adj. stock,
2012-19) . . . . NiB $1205 Ex $955 Gd $705
P (flattop, BUIS, Magpul adj. stock,
2012-15) . . . . NiB $1755 Ex $1330 Gd $980
AE-3G (Piston system, flattop, ambidextrous controls, BUIS,
adj. stock, 2014-15) . . . . . . NiB $1655 Ex $1255 Gd $930

LE6960-CCU . . . . NiB $1155 Ex $1010 Gd $810
Semiauto. Caliber: 5.56 NATO. 16.1-in. free floated bbl. w/
Magpul furniture. 2016-17.

LE6720 . . . . NiB $1180 Ex $1055 Gd $810
Semiauto. Caliber: 5.56 NATO. 16.1-in. free floated bbl. w/
Magpul ACS stock, Troy rail. 2014-16.

M4 SERIES
Semiauto. Caliber: 5.56 NATO. 16.1-in. free floated bbl. Sights:
Iron or optic ready. 2016-date.
Carbine model (M4 buttstock/handguard,
Magpul MBUS) . . . . NiB $1099 Ex $980 Gd $890
Trooper model (Centurion Arms M-LOK free-floated rail,
M4 buttstock) . . . . NiB $1049 Ex $970 Gd $880
Enhanced Patrol Rifle model (extended rail, Magpul MBUS,
B5 Bravo buttstock) . . . . NiB $1399 Ex $1280 Gd $1190
Monolithic model (one-piece rail/upper, Magpul MBUS, M4
buttstock) . . . . NiB $1399 Ex $1280 Gd $1190
OEM 1 model (barreled action,
font sight, no furniture) . . . . . . NiB $849 Ex $720 Gd $670
OEM 2 model (barreled action,
optic ready, no furniture) . . . . . NiB $849 Ex $720 Gd $670

M4 MAGPUL SERIES
Semiauto. Caliber: 5.56 NATO. 16.1-in. free floated bbl. Sights:
Irons, optic ready. 2016-date.
SL Black model (black Magpul MOE SL
buttstock/pistol grip). . . . . NiB $1199 Ex $980 Gd $890
SL Gray model (gray Magpul
MOE SL buttstock/pistol grip). . NiB $1199 Ex $980 Gd $890

M.A.R.C. 901 MONOLITHIC . . NiB $1810 Ex $1560 Gd $1210
Semiauto. monolithic upper receiver. Caliber: .308 Win. 16- or
18-in. heavy free floated bbl. VLTOR adj. stock, BUIS, ambidextrous controls. Made 2015-17.
Carbine model . . . . NiB $1255 Ex $1110 Gd $860

SPORTER CARBINE. . . . . NiB $1000 Ex $780 Gd $605
Semiauto. Caliber: .223 Rem. 16-in. bbl. adj. stock, disc. 2011.

Coltsman 1961 Custom

Coltsman 1961 Standard

Colt-Sauer Grand African

Colt-Sauer Short Action

TACTICAL ELITE . . . . NiB $1655 Ex $1255 Gd $905
Semiauto. Caliber: .223 Rem. 20-in. heavy bbl. Made by Colt
Custom Shop 1996-97.

TARGET GOVERNMENT. . . . . . . NiB $930 Ex $705 Gd $555
Semiauto. Caliber: .223 Rem. 20-in. bbl. fixed stock,
disc. 2002.
w/.22 LR conversion kit, add $200

LIGHTNING MAGAZINE RIFLE - LARGE FRAME
Similar to Medium Frame model except w/large frame to
accommodate larger calibers: .38-56, .44-60, .45-60, .45-
65, .45-85, or .50-95 Express. Standard 22-in. (carbine &
baby carbine) or 28-in. rnd. or octagonal bbl. (rifle). Note:
Additional bbl. lengths optional. Weight: 8 to 10.5 lbs. Sights:
Open rear; bead or blade front. Walnut stock and checkered
forearm. Made 1887 to 1994. (6,496 produced)
Rifle . . . . NiB $11,765 Ex $7390 Gd $3469
Carbine . . . . NiB $10,576 Ex $7798 Gd $4479
Baby Carbine . . . . NiB $14,475 Ex $9077 Gd $5796
.50-95 Express, add. 40%

LIGHTNING MAGAZINE RIFLE - MEDIUM FRAME
Slide-action w/12-rnd. tubular magazine Carbine & Baby
Carbine) or 15-rnd. tubular magazine (rifle). Calibers: .32-20,
.38-40, .44-40. Standard 20-in. (Carbine & Baby Carbine) or
26-in. rnd. or octagonal bbl.(rifle). Note: Additional bbl. lengths
optional. Weight: 5.5 lbs. (Baby Carbine), 6.25 lbs. (carbine) or
7 to 9 lbs. (rifle). Sights: Open rear; bead or blade front. Walnut
stock and checkered forearm. Blue finish w/color casehardened
hammer. Made 1884-1902. (89,777 produced)
Rifle . . . . NiB $6096 Ex $3822 Gd $2274
Carbine . . . . NiB $7778 Ex $4966 Gd $2988
Baby Carbine . . . . NiB $9380 Ex $5246 Gd $4012
Military model w/bayonet
lug & sling swivels . . . . . NiB $5250 Ex $3844 Gd $2691

LIGHTNING MAGAZINE RIFLE - SMALL FRAME
Similar to Medium Frame model except w/smaller frame
and chambered for .22 caliber only. Standard 24-in. rnd. or
octagonal bbl. w/half magazine. Note: Additional bbl. lengths
optional. Weight: 6 lbs. Sights: Open rear; bead or blade
front. Walnut stock and checkered forearm. Made 1884-1902.
(89,912 produced)
Standard Rifle model . . . . . NiB $5599 Ex $4125 Gd $2889
W/Deluxe or optional features, add 25%

STAGECOACH .22
AUTOLOADER . . . . **NiB $395 Ex $298 Gd $200**
Same as Colteer .22 Autoloader except w/engraved receiver, saddle ring, 16.5-in. bbl. Weight: 4 lbs., 10 oz. Made 1965-75.

COLTEER 1-.22 SINGLE-SHOT
BOLT-ACTION RIFLE . . . . **NiB $403 Ex $397 Gd $159**
Caliber: .22 LR. Long, Short. 20- or 22-in. bbl. Sights: Open rear; ramp front. Pistol-grip stock w/Monte Carlo comb. Weight: 5 lbs. Made 1957-67.

.22 AUTOLOADER
. . . . **NiB $390 Ex $288 Gd $227**
Caliber: .22 LR. 15-rnd. tubular magazine. 19.38-in. bbl. Sights: Open rear; hooded ramp front. Straight-grip stock, Western carbine-style forearm w/bbl. band. Weight: 4.75 lbs. Made 1964 to 1975.

CUSTOM BOLT-ACTION SPORTING
RIFLE . . . . **NiB $600 Ex $498 Gd $338**
FN Mauser action, side safety, engraved floorplate. Calibers: .30-06, .300 H&H Mag. Five round box magazine. 24-in. bbl., rampfront sight. Fancy walnut stock. Monte Carlo comb, cheekpiece, pistol-grip, checkered, QD swivels. Weight: 7.25 lbs. Made 1957 to 1961.

DELUXE RIFLE
. . . . **NiB $977 Ex $798 Gd $569**
FN Mauser action. Same as Custom model, except plain floorplate, plainer wood and checkering. Made 1957-61. Value shown is for rifle as furnished by manufacturer w/o rear sight.

1957 SERIES RIFLES
Sako medium action. Calibers: .243, .308. Weight: 6.75 lbs. Other specifications similar to those of models w/FN actions. Made 1957-61.
Standard . . . . **NiB $755 Ex $486 Gd $417**
Custom . . . . **NiB $944 Ex $697 Gd $488**
Deluxe . . . . **NiB $944 Ex $697 Gd $488**

1961 MODEL CUSTOM RIFLE **NiB $733 Ex $568 Gd $422**
Sako action. Calibers: .222, .222 Mag., .223, .243, .264, .270, .308, .30-06, .300 H&H. 23-, 24-in. bbl. Sights: Folding leaf rear; hooded ramp front. Fancy French walnut stock w/ Monte Carlo comb, rosewood forend tip and grip cap skip checkering, recoil pad, sling swivels. Weight: 6.5 - 7.5 lbs. Made 1963-65.

1961 MODEL, STANDARD RIFLE . . . **NiB $744 Ex $578 Gd $432**
Same as Custom model except plainer, American walnut stock. Made 1963-65.

STANDARD RIFLE
. . . . **NiB $689 Ex $533 Gd $390**
FN Mauser action. Same as Deluxe model except in .243, .30-06, .308, .300 Mag. and stock w/o cheekpiece, bbl. length 22 in. Made 1957-61. Value shown is for rifle as furnished by manufacturer w/o rear sight.

COLT-SAUER DRILLINGS *See Colt shotgun listings.*

GRAND AFRICAN . . . . **NiB $2656 Ex $1966 Gd $1049**
Same specifications as standard model except .458 Win. Mag., weight: 9.5 lbs. Sights: Adj. leaf rear; hooded ramp front. Magnum-style stock of Bubinga. Made 1973-85.

GRAND ALASKAN . . . . **NiB $2606 Ex $1989 Gd $1008**
Same specifications as standard model except .375 H&H, weight: 8.5 lbs. Sights: Adj. leaf rear; hooded ramp front. Magnum-style stock of walnut.

Commando Arms Mark 45

MAGNUM
. . . . **NiB $2506 Ex $1923 Gd $778**
Same specifications as standard model except calibers 7mm Rem. Mag., .300 Win. Mag., .300 Weatherby. Weight: 8.5 lbs. Made 1973-85.

SHORT ACTION
. . . . **NiB $2390 Ex $1613 Gd $766**
Same specifications as standard model except shorter action chambered for the following calibers: .22-250, .243 Win., .308 Win. and similar length cartridges. Weight: 7.5 1bs.; 8.25 lbs. (.22-250). Drilled and tapped for scope mount. No front or rear open sights. Made 1973-88.

SPORTING RIFLE, STANDARD
MODEL . . . . **NiB $2077 Ex $1405 Gd $766**
Sauer 80 non-rotating bolt action. Calibers: .25-06, .270 Win., .30-06. Three-rnd. detachable box magazine. 24-in. bbl. Weight: 7.75 lbs., 8.5 lbs. (.25-06). Furnished w/o sights. American walnut stock w/Monte Carlo cheekpiece, checkered pistol grip and forearm, rosewood forend tip and pistol-grip cap, recoil pad. Made 1973-88.

COMMANDO ARMS — Knoxville, TN

Formerly Volunteer Enterprises, Inc.

MARK III SEMIAUTO CARBINE
Blow-back action, fires from closed bolt. Caliber: .45 ACP. 15- or 30-rnd. magazine. 16.5-in. bbl. w/cooling sleeve and muzzle brake. Weight: 8 lbs. Sights: peep rear; blade front. "Tommy Gun" style stock and forearm or grip. Made l969-76.
w/horizontal forearm . . . . **NiB $510 Ex $399 Gd $277**

MARK 9
Same specifications as Mark III and Mark 45 except caliber 9mm Luger. Made 1976-81.
w/horizontal forearm . . . . **NiB $545 Ex $439 Gd $333**
w/vertical foregrip . . . . **NiB $650 Ex $565 Gd $389**

MARK 45
Same specifications as Mark III. Has redesigned trigger housing and magazines. Made 1976-88.
w/horizontal forearm . . . . **NiB $499 Ex $438 Gd $293**
w/vertical foregrip . . . . **NiB $596 Ex $484 Gd $341**

CONTINENTAL ARMS CORP. — New York, NY
Manufactured in Belgium for Continental Arms Corp., New York, New York.

DOUBLE RIFLE
Calibers: .270, .303 Sav., .30-40, .348 Win., .30-06, .375 H&H, .400 Jeffrey, .465, .470, .475 No. 2, .500, .600. Side-by-side. Anson-Deeley reinforced boxlock action w/triple bolting lever work. Two triggers. Non-automatic safety. 24- or 26-in. bbls. Sights: Express rear; bead front. Checkered cheekpiece stock and forend. Weight: From 7 lbs., depending on caliber. Imported from 1956 to 1975.

.270 to .348 Win. . . . . NiB $5077 Ex $3966 Gd $3095
.375 H&H & larger calibers, add 60%

COOPER FIREARMS OF MONTANA, INC. — Stevensville, MT (Previously COOPER ARMS)

MODEL 21

Similar to Model 36C except in calibers .17 Rem., .17 Mach IV, .221 Fireball, .222, .223, 6x45, 6x47. 24-in. stainless or chrome-moly bbl. 43.5 in. overall. Weight: 8.75 lbs. Made 1994 to date.

21 Benchrest.	NiB $1513	Ex $1207	Gd $943
21 Classic	NiB $2223	Ex $1766	Gd $1007
21 Custom Classic	NiB $2178	Ex $1859	Gd $1032
21 Western Classic	NiB $3030	Ex $1956	Gd $1043
21 Varminter.	NiB $1408	Ex $976	Gd $800
21 Varmint Extreme	NiB $1944	Ex $1244	Gd $976

MODEL 22

Bolt-action, single-shot. Calibers: .22 BR. .22-250 Rem., .220 Swift, .243 Win., 6mm PPC, 6.5x55mm, 25-06 Rem., 7.62x39mm 26-in. bbl, 45.63 in. overall. Weight: 8 lbs., 12 oz. Single-stage trigger. AAA Claro walnut stock. Made 1999 to date.

22 Benchrest.	NiB $1533	Ex $1377	Gd $1079
22 Classic	NiB $2176	Ex $1312	Gd $755
22 Custom Classic.	NiB $1370	Ex $1244	Gd $879
22 Western Classic	NiB $2244	Ex $1359	Gd $954
22 Varminter.	NiB $1468	Ex $934	Gd $650
22 Pro-Varmint Extreme	NiB $2011	Ex $1143	Gd $836
22 Black Jack	NiB $1895	Ex $1154	Gd $846

MODEL 36 RF/BR 50 . . . . . . NiB $1608 Ex $1266 Gd $880
Bolt action. Caliber: .22 LR. Bolt-action. Single-shot. 22-in. bbl. 40.5 in. overall. Weight: 6.8 lbs. No sights. Fully-adj. match-grade trigger. Stainless barrel. McMillan benchrest stock. Three mid-bolt locking lugs. Made 1993-99.

MODEL 36 CF

Bolt action. Calibers: .17 CCM, .22 CCM, .22 Hornet. Four-rnd. mag. 23.75 in. bbl. 42.5 in. overall. Weight: 7 lbs. Walnut or synthetic stock. Made 1992-94.

Marksman	NiB $1635	Ex $880	Gd $654
Sportsman	NiB $730	Ex $544	Gd $343
Classic Grade	NiB $1863	Ex $1154	Gd $866
Custom Grade	NiB $1744	Ex $937	Gd $665
Custom Classic Grade.	NiB $1706	Ex $1266	Gd $876

MODEL 36 RF

Similar to Model 36CF except in caliber .22 LR. Five round magazine. Weight: 6.5-7 lbs. Made 1992-94.

BR-50 (22-in. stainless bbl.). . . .	NiB $1755	Ex $1139	Gd $768
Custom Grade.	NiB $1756	Ex $906	Gd $675
Custom Classic Grade.	NiB $1670	Ex $951	Gd $688
Featherweight	NiB $1617	Ex $988	Gd $709

MODEL 36 TRP-1 SERIES

Similar to Model 36RF except in target configuration w/ ISU or silhouette-style stock. Made 1992-93.

TRP-1 (ISU single-shot).	NiB $944	Ex $778	Gd $533
TRP-1S (Silhouette)	NiB $944	Ex $778	Gd $533

MODEL 38 SINGLE SHOT

Similar to Model 36CF except in calibers .17 or .22 CCM w/3-rnd. magazine. Weight: 8 lbs. Walnut or synthetic stock. Made 1992 -93.

Standard Sporter.	NiB $1544	Ex $1023	Gd $688
Classic Grade	NiB $2239	Ex $1836	Gd $989

Custom Grade.	NiB $3035	Ex $1997	Gd $977
Custom Classic Grade.	NiB $1570	Ex $1267	Gd $855

MODEL 40 CLASSIC BOLT-ACTION RIFLE

Calibers: .17 CCM, .17 Ackley Hornet, .22 Hornet, .22K Hornet, .22 CCM, 4- or 5-rnd. magazine. 23.75-in. bbl. Checkered oil-finished AAA Claro walnut stock. Made 1995-96.

Classic.	NiB $1644	Ex $1233	Gd $886
Custom Classic	NiB $1844	Ex $1450	Gd $1139
Classic Varminter	NiB $1844	Ex $1450	Gd $1139

CUMBERLAND MOUNTAIN ARMS — Winchester, TN

PLATEAU RIFLE

Falling block action w/underlever. Calibers: .40-65, and .45-70. 32-in. rnd. bbl. 48 in. overall. Weight: 10.5 lbs. American walnut stock. Bead front sight, adj. buckhorn rear. Blued finish. Lacquer finish walnut stock w/crescent buttplate. Made 1993-99.

Standard model.	NiB $1133	Ex $829	Gd $631
Deluxe model, add			$375

CZ (CESKA ZBROJOVKA), INC. (CZ-USA) — Uherský Brod, Moravia, Czech Republic

Formerly Strankonice, Czechoslovakia, currently CZ-USA Kansas City, Kansas, formerly Czechpoint, Inc. See also listings under Brno Sporting Rifles and Springfield, Inc.

ZKK 600 . . . . NiB $613 Ex $479 Gd $350
Bolt action. Calibers: .270 Win., 7x57, 7x64, .30-06. Five round magazine. 23.5-in. bbl. Weight: 7.5 lbs. Adj. folding-leaf rear sight, hooded ramp front. Pistol-grip walnut stock. Imported from 1990 to 1995.
Deluxe model . . . . NiB $688 Ex $554 Gd $400

ZKK 601 . . . . NiB $570 Ex $495 Gd $443
Similar to Model ZKK 600 except w/short action in calibers .223 Rem., .243 Win., .308 Win. 43 in. overall. Weight: 6 lbs., 13 oz. Checkered walnut pistol-grip stock w/Monte Carlo cheekpiece. Imported from 1990 to 1995.
Deluxe model . . . . NiB $641 Ex $567 Gd $423

ZKK 602 . . . . NiB $727 Ex $650 Gd $468
Similar to Model ZKK 600 except w/Magnum action in calibers .300 Win. Mag., 8x68S, .375 H&H, .458 Win. Mag. 25-in. bbl. 45.5 in. overall. Weight: 9.25 lbs. Imported from 1990 to 1997.
Deluxe model . . . . NiB $896 Ex $744 Gd $505

452 (ZKM-452) . . . . NiB $360 Ex $338 Gd $200
Bolt action. Calibers: .22 LR. or .22 WMR. Five, 6- or 10-rnd. magazine. 25-in. bbl. 43.5 in. overall. Weight: 6 lbs. Adj. rear sight, hooded bead front. Oil-finished beechwood or checkered walnut stock w/Schnabel forend. Imported 1995 and 2007.

Deluxe model	NiB $365	Ex $338	Gd $200
Varmint model	NiB $385	Ex $370	Gd $215
.22 WMR, add.			$50

American Classic (.17 HMR, .17 Mach 2, .22 LR or .22 WMR; 5-rnd. magazine, American-style walnut stock, 1999 to present) . . . . . . NiB $380 Ex $270 Gd $205
FS Mannlicher (.17 HMR, .22 LR or .22 WMR; 5-rnd. magazine, Mannlicher-style walnut stock, 2004-11) . . . . NiB $430 Ex $330 Gd $230

CZ Model ZKK 600

CZ Model ZKM 452 LUX Model

CZ 511

CZ Model ZKM 527

CZ 550 LUX Model

Scout (.22 LR, youth stock,
2000-16) . . . . NiB $250 Ex $180 Gd $140
Silhouette (.22 LR, black polymer stock,
2003-11) . . . . NiB $340 Ex $235 Gd $185
Special Military Training (.17 HMR or .22 LR, beechwood
stock, 2002-13) . . . . NiB $335 Ex $245 Gd $155
Ultra Lux (gold accents,
2006-15) . . . . NiB $370 Ex $270 Gd $205

453 . . . . NiB $455 Ex $355 Gd $270
Bolt action. Calibers: .17 HMR, .22 LR. or .22 WMR. 5-rnd.
magazine. 20.9- or 22.5-in. bbl. Made 2006 to 2012.

455 AMERICAN . . . . NiB $345 Ex $245 Gd $205
Bolt action. Calibers: .17 HMR, .22 LR. or .22 WMR. 5-rnd.
magazine. 20.5-in. bbl., interchangable bbls. w/o sights. Stock;
black polymer or checkered Turkish walnut. Made 2010-18.
FS Mannlicher (Mannlicher
style stock) . . . . NiB $430 Ex $355 Gd $300
Lux (deluxe checkered stock) . . . NiB $375 Ex $285 Gd $205
Scout (youth style stock,
16.5-in. bbl.) . . . . NiB $290 Ex $225 Gd $180
Stainless Synthetic (stainless bbl.,
black synthetic stock)** . . . . NiB $355 Ex $245 Gd $205
Suppressor Ready (16.5-in. threaded bbl.,
black synthetic stock)** . . . . NiB $350 Ex $245 Gd $205
Training Rifle (beechwood stock, adj. sights,
24.8-in. bbl.) . . . . NiB $325 Ex $245 Gd $200
Training Rifle Rustic (aged beechwood stock, adj. sights,
24.8-in. bbl.) . . . . NiB $335 Ex $255 Gd $205
Ultra Lux (deluxe beechwood stock, adj. sights,
28.6-in. bbl.) . . . . NiB $385 Ex $295 Gd $210
Varmint (walnut stock, adj. trigger, 20.5-in.
heavy bbl.). . . . . NiB $400 Ex $325 Gd $270

527 SERIES
Bolt action. Calibers: .22 Hornet, .222 Rem., .223 Rem.,
7.62x39mm. Five round magazine. 23.5-in. bbl. 42.5 in.
overall. Weight: 6.75 lbs. Adj. rear sight, hooded ramp front.
Grooved receiver. Adj. double-set triggers. Oil-finished beech-
wood or checkered walnut stock. Imported 1995-2022.
Standard model. . . . . NiB $650 Ex $465 Gd $340
Classic model . . . . NiB $655 Ex $470 Gd $338

Carbine model
(shorter configuration) . . . . . NiB $600 Ex $466 Gd $345
Deluxe model . . . . NiB $657 Ex $572 Gd $373

537 SPORTER SERIES
Bolt action. Calibers: .243 Win., .270 Win., 7x57mm, .308
Win., .30-06. Four or 5-rnd. magazine. 19- or 23.5-in. bbl.
40.25 or 44.75 in. overall. Weight: 7 to 7.5 lbs. Adj. folding
leaf rear sight, hooded ramp front. Shrouded bolt. Standard or
Mannlicher-style checkered walnut stock. Imported 1995.
Standard model. . . . . NiB $529 Ex $460 Gd $345
Mountain Carbine model . . . . . NiB $555 Ex $439 Gd $326

511 SERIES . . . . NiB $355 Ex $252 Gd $155
Semiauto. Caliber: .22 LR. 8-rnd. magazine. 22- in. bbl., 38.6
in. overall. Weight: 5.39 lbs. Receiver top fitted for telescop-
ic sight mounts. Walnut wood-lacquered checkering stock.
Imported 1996, 1998 to 2001, 2005 to 2006.
Mannlicher model . . . . add $126

550 SERIES
Bolt action. Calibers: .243 Win., 6.5x55mm, .270 Win., 7mm
Mag., 7x57, 7x64, .30-06, .300 Win Mag., .375 H&H, .416
Rem., .416 Rigby, .458 Win. Mag., 9.3x62. Four or 5-rnd.
detachable magazine. 20.5- or 23.6-in. bbl. Weight: 7.25 to 8
lbs. No sights or Express sights on magnum models. Receiver
drilled and tapped for scope mount. Standard or Mannlicher-
style checkered walnut stock w/buttpad. Imported 1995 to
2018.
Standard (imported 1995 to 2000). .NiB $510 Ex $423 Gd $326
Magnum . . . . NiB $855 Ex $633 Gd $465
Lux . . . . NiB $530 Ex $456 Gd $355
Battue Lux (1998) . . . . NiB $500 Ex $426 Gd $325
Mannlicher . . . . NiB $817 Ex $579 Gd $370
Calibers .416 Rem., .416 Rigby, .458 Win. Mag., add. . . . $100
Carbine (20.6-in. brrl.) . . . . NiB $960 Ex $710 Gd $510
Varmint . . . . NiB $760 Ex $520 Gd $410
Magnum H.E.T. (28-in. bbl., Kevlar stock,
2009–13) . . . . NiB $3510 Ex $3130 Gd $1955
H.E.T. II (.338 LM, 25-in. bbl., adj. composite stock,
2014–date) . . . . NiB $3510 Ex $3130 Gd $1955
Badland Western Series (.338 LM, 25-in. bbl., kevalr stock,
2014–date) . . . . NiB $2330 Ex $2055 Gd $1280
Sonoran Western Series (standard calibers,
24- or 26-in. bbl., Manners stock,
2014–date) . . . . NiB $2880 Ex $2530 Gd $1580
Ultimate Hunting Rifle (.300 Win.
Mag., 23.6-in. heavy bbl.,
various stock, 2009–date). . NiB $1210 Ex $1030 Gd $630
Urban Counter Sniper (.308 Win.,
16-in. bbl., Kevlar stock,
2010–13) . . . . NiB $2280 Ex $2010 Gd $1255

550 AMERICAN SAFARI FIELD MAGNUM SERIES
Mauser style bolt action. Calibers: .375 H&H, .416 Rigby,
.458 Win. Mag., .458 Lott or .505 Gibbs. 3-, 4- or 5-rnd. fixed
magazine. 24- or 25-in. bbl. Weight: 9.9 lbs. Express sights.
Stock: checkered walnut. Imported 2004–22.
Standard model. . . . . NiB $1000 Ex $855 Gd $510
.505 Gibbs caliber, add. $2000
Fancy model (fancy grade
walnut) . . . . NiB $1755 Ex $1580 Gd $1055
Deluxe model (fancy grade walnut,
2004–11) . . . . NiB $1705 Ex $1480 Gd $930
Composite stock (Kevlar or Aramid
composite) . . . . NiB $1505 Ex $1330 Gd $1055
Laminate stock . . . . NiB $1150 Ex $955 Gd $655

RIFLES

555 SPORTER SERIES . . . . **NiB $800 Ex $730 Gd $505**
Push-feed bolt action. Calibers: .308 Win. or .30-06. 3-rnd. detachable magazine. 24-in. bbl. w/sights. Weight: 7.2 lbs. Stock: checkered walnut. Imported 2006–disc.

557 SPORTER SERIES . . . . **NiB $730 Ex $655 Gd $470**
Push-feed bolt action. Calibers: .234 Win., .270 Win., 6.6x55, .308 Win. or .30-06. 4-rnd. internal magazine. 20.5-in. bbl. Weight: 7.1 lbs. Stock: checkered walnut or Manners. Imported 2014–22.
Manners stock, add **$400**
synthetic stock, deduct **$125**
Carbine model (20.5-in. bbl. w/sights,
   walnut stock, 2014–16) . . . . . **NiB $730 Ex $630 Gd $455**
Varmint model (25.6-in. heavy bbl.,
   walnut stock, 2016–date) . . . . **NiB $755 Ex $680 Gd $480**

600 SERIES
Push-feed bolt action. Calibers: .223 Rem., .224 Valkrie, 6mm Creedmoor, 6.5 Creedmoor, 7.62x39mm, .308 Win., .30-06, or .300 Win. Mag.; 3-, 5- or 10-rnd. detachable magazine. 16.5- to 24-in. bbl. Weight: 6.6-7.9 lbs. Sights: Iron and/or optic ready. Stock: Wood or polymer. Adj. trigger. Imported 2022–date.
Alpha model (20- or 24-in. bbl.,
   black polymer stock) . . . . **NiB $750 Ex $680 Gd $755**
Lux model (20 or 24-in. bbl., iron sights,
   walnut Bavarian style stock) . . . **NiB $850 Ex $790 Gd $710**
Range model (24-in. heavy bbl., optic ready,
   laminate precision stock) . . . **NiB $1199 Ex $1000 Gd $990**
Trail model (16.5-in. bbl., optic
   ready, PDW adj. stock) . . . . . **NiB $1155 Ex $1000 Gd $700**

750 SNIPER . . . . **NiB $1780 Ex $1555 Gd $930**
Mauser style bolt action. Calibers: .308 Win., 10-rnd. detachable magazine. 26-in. bbl. w/muzzle brake. Weight: 12.8 lbs. Express sights. Stock: adj. composite. Imported 2006–19.

CZECHOSLOVAKIAN MILITARY — Brno, Czechoslovakia

Manufactured by Ceska Zbrojovka.

MODEL 1924 (VZ24) MAUSER
MILITARY RIFLE . . . . **NiB $600 Ex $580 Gd $455**
Similar to German Kar., 98k and F.N. (Belgian Model 1924.) Caliber: 7.9mm Mauser. Five round box magazine. 23.25-in. bbl. Weight: 8.5 lbs. Sights: Adj. rear; blade front w/guards. of Belgian-type military stock, full handguard. Made 1924 thru WWII. Many of these rifles were made for export. As produced during the German occupation, this model was known as Gewehr 24t.

Daewood Precision Industries DR200

Daisy V/L Standard

MODEL 1933 (VZ33) MAUSER
MILITARY CARBINE . . . . **NiB $600 Ex $555 Gd $455**
Modification of German M/98 action w/smaller receiver ring. Caliber: 7.9mm Mauser. 19.25-in. bbl. Weight: 7.5 lbs. Sights: Adj. rear; blade front w/guards. Military-type full stock. Mfd. 1933 thru WWII. A similar model, produced during the German occupation, was designated Gew. 33/40.

DAEWOO PRECISION INDUSTRIES — Korea
Manufactured in Korea, previously imported by Kimber of America; Daewoo Precision Industries; Nationwide Sports and KBI, Inc.

DR200 SA SEMIAUTO SPORTER
Caliber: .223 Rem. (5.56mm). Six or 10-rnd. magazine. 18.4-in. bbl. 39.25 in. overall. Weight: .9 lbs. Protected post front sight, fully-adj. aperture rear. Forged aluminum receiver w/rotating locking bolt assembly. Synthetic sporterized thumbhole stock. Imported from 1994 to 1996.
Sporter model . . . . **NiB $679 Ex $545 Gd $459**
Varmint model . . . . **NiB $650 Ex $579 Gd $356**

DR300 SA SEMIAUTO
SPORTER . . . . **NiB $670 Ex $602 Gd $421**
Similar to Model Daewoo DR200 except chambered for 7.62x39mm. Imported from 1994 to 1996.

DAISY — Rogers, AR

Daisy V/L rifles carry the first and only commercial caseless cartridge system. These rifles are expected to appreciate considerably in future years. The cartridge, no longer made, is also a collector's item. Production was discontinued following BATF ruling the V/L model to be a firearm.

COLLECTOR'S KIT . . . . **NiB $590 Ex $427 Gd $304**
Presentation-grade rifle w/gold plate inscribed w/owner's name and gun serial number mounted on the stock. Also includes a special gun case, pair of brass gun cradles for wall-hanging, 300 rnd. of 22 V/L ammunition and a certificate signed by Daisy president Cass S. Hough. Approx. 1,000 manufactured from 1968 to 1969.

PRESENTATION GRADE . . . . . . **NiB $347 Ex $296 Gd $245**
Same specifications as standard model except w/walnut stock. Approx. 4,000 manufactured from 1968 to 1969.

STANDARD RIFLE . . . . **NiB $269 Ex $224 Gd $175**
Single-shot under-lever action. Caliber: .22 V/L (caseless cartridge, propellant ignited by jet of hot air). 18-in. bbl. Weight: 5 lbs. Sights: Adj. open rear, ramp w/blade front. Wood-grained Lustran stock (foam-filled). About 19,000 manufactured 1968 to 1969.

DAKOTA ARMS, INC. — Sturgis, SD
Currently owned by Freedom Arms Inc.

MODEL 10
Falling block action. Single shot. Chambered for most commercially-loaded calibers. 23-in. bbl. 39.5 in. overall. Weight: 5.5 lbs. Top tang safety. No sights. Checkered pistol-grip buttstock and semi-beavertail forearm, QD swivels, rubber recoil pad. Made 1992 to date.
Standard calibers . . . . **NiB $4679 Ex $3066 Gd $1977**
Deluxe model, add **$1380**

MODEL 22 . . . . **NiB $2655 Ex $2330 Gd $1455**
Bolt action. Calibers: .17 HMR, .22 LR, .22 WMR, .22 Hornet. Five round magazine. 22-in. bbl. Weight: 6.5 lbs.

Dakota Model 10 Single-Shot Rifle

Dakota Arms Model 76 African Grade

Adj. trigger. Checkered classic-style Claro or English walnut stock w/black recoil pad. Made 1992–98, reintro. 2003 to 2004.

MODEL 76 AFRICAN . . . . . **NiB $7998 Ex $4056 Gd $2597**
Same general specifications as Model 76 Safari. Calibers: .404 Jeffery, .416 Rigby, .416 Dakota, .450 Dakota. 24-in. bbl. Weight: 8 lbs. Checkered select walnut stock w/two cross bolts. "R" prefix on ser. nos. Intro. 1989.

MODEL 76 ALPINE . . . . **NiB $5634 Ex $2789 Gd $2009**
Same general specifications as Model 76 Classic except short action w/blind magazine. Calibers: .22-250, .243, 6mm Rem., .250-3000, 7mm-08, .308. 21-in. bbl. Weight: 7.5 lbs. Made 1989-92.

MODEL 76 CLASSIC . . . . . . **NiB $5629 Ex $3467 Gd $2240**
Calibers: .257 Roberts, .270 Win., .280 Rem., .30-06, 7mm Rem. Mag., .300 Win. Mag., .338 Win. Mag., .375 H&H Mag., .458 Win. Mag. 21- or 23-in. bbl. Weight: 7.5 lbs. Receiver drilled and tapped for sights. Adj. trigger. Classic-style checkered walnut stock w/steel grip cap and solid recoil pad. Right- and left-hand models. Made 1987 to date.
Deluxe model, add **$2100**
Professional Hunter modell (magnum calibers, fiberglass
  stock, 2013–date) . . . . . **NiB $7510 Ex $6855 Gd $1255**

MODEL 76 LONGBOW TACTICAL
BOLT-ACTION RIFLE . . . . . **NiB $4466 Ex $3459 Gd $2390**
Calibers: .300 Dakota Mag., .330 Dakota Mag., .338 Lapua Mag. Blind magazine. Ported 28-in. bbl. 50 to 51 in. overall. Weight: 13.7 lbs. Black or oliver green fiberglass stock w/adj. cheekpiece and buttplate. Receiver drilled and tapped w/one-piece rail mount and no sights. Made 1997-2009.

MODEL 76 SAFARI . . . . . . **NiB $7533 Ex $5416 Gd $2307**
Calibers: .300 Win. Mag., .338 Win. Mag., .375 H&H Mag. .458 Win. Mag. 23-in. bbl. w/bbl. band swivel. Weight: 8.5 lbs. Ramp front sight, standing leaf rear. Checkered fancy walnut stock w/ebony forend tip and solid recoil pad. Made 1987 to date.

MODEL 76 TRAVELER SERIES
Threadless take-down action w/interchangeable bbl. capability based on the Dakota 76 design. Calibers: .257 through .458 Win (Standard-Classic & Safari) and .416 Dakota, .404 Jeffery, .416 Rigby, .338 Lapua and .450 Dakota Mag. (E/F Family-African Grade). 23- to 24- in. bbl. Weight: 7.5 to 9.5 lbs. Right or left-hand action. X grade (Classic) or XXX grade (Safari or African) oil finish English Bastogne or Claro walnut stock. Made 1999 to date.
Classic Grade . . . . **NiB $6644 Ex $5428 Gd $2380**
Safari Grade . . . . **NiB $8577 Ex $6502 Gd $2866**
African Grade . . . . **NiB $9233 Ex $7544 Gd $3209**

Interchangeable bbl. assemblies
  Standard calibers, add **$2500**
  Safari calibers, add **$2700**
  African calibers, add **$2970**

MODEL 76 VARMINT . . . . . **NiB $2280 Ex $1988 Gd $1165**
Similar to Model 76 Classic except single-shot action w/ heavy bbl. chambered for .17 Rem. to 6mm PPC. Weight: 13.7 lbs. Checkered walnut or synthetic stock. Receiver drilled and tapped for scope mounts and no sights. Made 1994-98.

MODEL 97 HUNTER SERIES
Bolt action. Calibers: .22-250 Rem. to .330 Dakota Mag. (Lightweight), .25-06 to .375 Dakota Mag. (Long Range). 22-, 24- or 26-in. bbl. 43 to 46 in. overall. Weight: 6.16 lbs. to 7.7 lbs.
Black composite fiberglass stock w/recoil pad. Fully adj. match trigger. Made 1997-2004.
Lightweight model . . . . **NiB $1930 Ex $1675 Gd $944**
Long Range model . . . . **NiB $3355 Ex $2810 Gd $1755**
Classic Grade . . . . **NiB $6644 Ex $5428 Gd $2380**
Outfitter Takedown . . . . **NiB $4955 Ex $4280 Gd $3310**

MODEL 97 VARMINT . . . . . **NiB $3734 Ex $2566 Gd $1896**
Similar to Model 97 Hunter except single-shot action w/ heavy bbl. chambered .22-250 Rem. to .308 Win. Checkered walnut stock. Receiver drilled and tapped for scope mounts and no sights. Made 1998-2004.

DOUBLE RIFLE. . **NiB $25,500 Ex $21,250 Gd $11,250**
Side-by-side. Round boxlock break action. Calibers: .470 NE, .500 NE or .570 NE. Made 2001–05.

CHARLES DALY — Harrisburg, PA
Imported by K.B.I., Inc., Harrisburg, PA; previously by Outdoor Sports Headquarters, Inc.

EMPIRE GRADE BOLT-ACTION RIFLE (RF)
Similar to Superior Grade except w/checkered California walnut stock w/rosewood grip cap and forearm cap. High polished blued finish and damascened bolt. Made 1998. Disc.
Empire Grade (.22 LR) . . . . **NiB $370 Ex $324 Gd $223**
Empire Grade (.22WMR) . . . . . **NiB $406 Ex $322 Gd $235**
Empire Grade (.22 Hornet) . . . . **NiB $556 Ex $444 Gd $320**

FIELD GRADE BOLT-ACTION RIFLE (RF)
Caliber: .22 LR. 16.25-, 17.5- or 22.63-in. bbl. 32 to 41 in. overall. Single-shot (True Youth) and 6- or 10-rnd. magazine. Plain walnut-finished hardwood or checkered polymer stock. Blue or stainless finish. Imported from 1998. Disc.
Field Grade (Standard w/22.63-in.
  bbl.) . . . . **NiB $157 Ex $128 Gd $95**
Field Grade
  (Youth w/17.5-in. bbl.) . . . . **NiB $170 Ex $139 Gd $99**
Field Grade (True Youth
  w/16.25-in. bbl.) . . . . **NiB $188 Ex $155 Gd $131**
Field Grade (Polymer w/stainless
  action) . . . . **NiB $158 Ex $130 Gd $100**

FIELD GRADE HUNTER BOLT-ACTION RIFLE
Calibers: .22 Hornet, .223 Rem., .243 Win., .270 Win., 7mm Rem. Mag. .308 Win., .30-06, .300 Win. Mag., .300 Rem. Ultra Mag., .338 Win. Mag. Three, 4-, or 5-rnd. magazine. 22- or 24-in. bbl. w/o sights. Weight: 7.2 to 7.4 lbs. Checkered walnut or black polymer stock. Receiver drilled and tapped. Blue or stainless finish. Imported from 1998. Disc.

RIFLES

Field Grade Hunter (walnut stock) .... NiB $572 Ex $457 Gd $339
Field Grade Hunter (polymer stock) ... NiB $589 Ex $478 Gd $339
w/Left-hand model, add $35

HAMMERLESS DRILLING
See listing under Charles Daly shotguns.

HORNET RIFLE........... NiB $1299 Ex $1088 Gd $759
Same as Herold Rifle. See listing of that rifle for specifications. imported during the 1930s. Disc.

MAUSER 98
Calibers: .243 Win., .270 Win., 7mm Rem. Mag. .308 Win., .30-06, .300 Win. Mag., .375 H&H, or .458 Win. Mag. Three, 4-, or 5-rnd. magazine. 23-in. bbl. 44.5 in. overall. Weight: 7.5 lbs. Checkered European walnut (Superior) or fiberglass/ graphic (Field) stock w/recoil pad. Ramped front sight, adj. rear. Receiver drilled and tapped w/side saftey. Imported from 1998. Disc.
standard calibers Disc........ NiB $466 Ex $423 Gd $155
375 H&H and 458 Win. Mag... NiB $669 Ex $572 Gd $354
Superior Grade (standard calibers)
   Disc.....................NiB $669 Ex $572 Gd $454
Superior Grade (magnum calibers)
   Disc.....................NiB $903 Ex $766 Gd $641

MINI-MAUSER 98
Similar to Mauser 98 except w/19.25-in. bbl. chambered for .22 Hornet, .22-250 Rem., .223 Rem., or 7.62x39mm. Five round magazine. Imported from 1998. Disc.
Field Grade................ NiB $409 Ex $358 Gd $233
Superior Grade............. NiB $533 Ex $447 Gd $259

SUPERIOR GRADE BOLT-ACTION RIFLE
Calibers: .22 LR. .22 WMR, .22 Hornet. 20.25- to 22.63-in. bbl. 40.5 to 41.25 in. overall. Five, 6-, or 10-rnd. magazine. Ramped front sight, adj. rear w/grooved receiver. Checkered walnut stock. Made 1998. Disc.
Superior Grade (.22 LR) .... NiB $179 Ex $150 Gd $100
Superior Grade (.22WMR) .... NiB $244 Ex $190 Gd $145
Superior Grade (.22 Hornet)...NiB $399 Ex $345 Gd $239

SEMIAUTO RIFLE
Caliber: .22 LR. 20.75-in. bbl. 40.5 in. overall. 10-rnd. magazine. Ramped front sight, adj. rear w/grooved receiver. Plain walnut-finished hardwood stock (Field), checkered walnut (Superior), checkered polymer stock or checkered California walnut stock w/rosewood grip cap and forearm cap (Empire). Blue or stainless finish. Imported from 1998. Disc.
Field Grade................ NiB $145 Ex $126 Gd $85
Field Grade (Polymer
   w/stainless action) .... NiB $161 Ex $136 Gd $92
Superior Grade............. NiB $215 Ex $188 Gd $132
Empire Grade .... NiB $355 Ex $290 Gd $200

BOLT ACTION RIFLE .... NiB $922 Ex $659 Gd $560

Calibers: .22 Hornet. Bbl.: 24 in. Five round box magazine, hinged floorplate. Sights: Ramp front, leaf rear. Walnut stock, checkered grip and forearm. Early version rifle, introduced 1931 by Franz Jaeger Co. Discontinued 1939. Imported by Charles Daly but same model was imported by A. F. Stoeger as Herold Rifle.

SUPERIOR
COMBINATION GUN .... NiB $1354 Ex $1149 Gd $1013
Calibers: 12-guage shotgun over .22 Hornet, .223 Remington, .22-250, .243 Win., .270 Win., or .30-06. Barrels: 23 1/2 in.

Shotgun choked Imp. Cyl. Weight: About 7.5 pounds. Checkered walnut, pistol grip, semi-beavertail forend. Silvered, engraved receiver. Chrome-moly steel barrels, double triggers, extractors. Gold bead front sight. Introduced 1997, imported by K.B.I.

EMPIRE COMBINATION GUN...NiB $1743 Ex $1540 Gd $1179
Similar to Superior Combination Gun but with fancy grade wood, European style comb and cheekpiece, slimmer forend. Introduced 1997, imported by K.B.I.

FIELD GRADE AUTO RIFLE .... NiB $167 Ex $109 Gd $94
Calibers: .22 LR. Semiauto, 10-rnd. magazine, shell deflector. Bbl.: 20 3/4 in. Weight: 6.5 pounds. Overall length: 40.5 in. Stock: Hardwood, walnut-finished, Monte Carlo style. Sights: Hooded front, adjustable open rear. Grooved for scope mounting. Blued finish. Introduced 1998. Imported by K. B. I.

EMPIRE GRADE AUTO RIFLE .. NiB $210 Ex $166 Gd $135
Similar to Field Grade Auto Rifle but with select California walnut stock, hand checkering. Contrasting forend and grip caps. Damascened bolt, high-polish blued finish. Introduced 1998; discontinued.

TRUE YOUTH BOLT-ACTION RIFLE... NiB $156 Ex $100 Gd $75
Caliber: .22 LR. Single-shot., bolt-action. Bbl.: 16.25 in. Weight: 3 pounds. Overall length: 32 in. Walnut-finished hardwood stock. Sights: Blade front, adjustable rear. Blued finish. Introduced 1998. Imported by K. B. I.

DANIEL DEFENSE — Savannah, GA

DD SERIES
Similar to DDM4 series except with mil-spec buttstock. Made 2010 to date.
DDXV (5.56 NATO) .... NiB $1280 Ex $960 Gd $710
DDV6.8 (6.8 SPC, 2010-11).... NiB $1380 Ex $980 Gd $730

DDM4 SERIES
Semiauto AR15 platform. Action: gas impingement system. Caliber: 5.56 NATO, 30-rnd. magazine. 16-in. bbl. w/A2 birdcage flash hider. Sights: BUIS. Furniture: A2 pistol grip, Magpul adj. Made 2010 to date.
DDM4V1 (original model) ... NiB $1600 Ex $1130 Gd $830
DDM4V2 (Omega X 7.0
   rail, 2011-13) .... NiB $1580 Ex $1130 Gd $810
DDM4V3 (5.56 NATO or 6.8 SPC, mid-length
   gas system) .... NiB $1600 Ex $1130 Gd $830
DDM4V4 (Omega X 9.0 rail,
   dicont. 2013) .... NiB $1480 Ex $1030 Gd $710
DDM4V5 (5.56 NATO or 300 BLK,
   Omega X 12.0 rail)...... NiB $1530 Ex $1130 Gd $830
DDM4V7 (5.56 NATO w/16-in. brrl. or
   6.8 SPC w18-in. brrl.).... NiB $1400 Ex $1060 Gd $760

DELTA 5 .... NiB $2199 Ex $2100 Gd $2000
Bolt action. Calibers: .308 Win. Bbl.: 20-in. heavy Palma profile, threaded, interchangeable. 5-rnd. detachable magazine. Sights: Picatinny scope base. Stock: Carbon fiber reinforced

Daniel Defense DDM4V7

DPMS Panther REPR

DSA Para Congo

polymer, adj. LOP and riser. 3-lug bolt w/60 degreased bolt throw. Made 2019-20.

DPMS FIREARMS — St. Cloud, MN

Previously in Becker, MN; previously called DPMS, Inc. (Defense Procurement Manufacturing Facilities); currently owned by The Freedom Group. Mfg. discontinued 2020. Part of Remington bankruptcy in 2020; purchased by JJE Capital Holdings.

PANTHER CARBINE . . . . **NiB $830 Ex $450 Gd $410**
Semiauto AR15 platform. Caliber: .223 Rem. 30-rnd. magazine. 16-in. heavy bbl. w/A2 flash hider, A3 flat top upper, A2 pistol grip, Pardus collapsible buttstock. Weight: 7.1 lbs. Made 1993-2020.
6.8mm Carbine (2006-11) . . . . **NiB $880 Ex $600 Gd $520**
6.8mm SPCII Hunter
 (2011-12) . . . . **NiB $1050 Ex $730 Gd $630**
7.62x39mm Carbine
 (2000-11) . . . . **NiB $730 Ex $480 Gd $430**
A2 "The Agency" (16-in. bbl., Surefire flashlight, EOTech
 sight, 2007-12) . . . . **NiB $1730 Ex $650 Gd $580**
A2 Tactical (16-in. heavy bbl., A2 handguard,
 2004-13) . . . . **NiB $740 Ex $480 Gd $430**
AP4 (16-in. M4 contour bbl., fixed M4 buttstock
 2004-12) . . . . **NiB $630 Ex $480 Gd $380**
DCM (20-in. heavy stainless bbl.,
 1998-2003; 2006-12) . . . . . . **NiB $970 Ex $600 Gd $520**
Lo-Pro Classic (16-in. heavy bbl., A2 buttstock,
 flat top upper, 2002-12) . . . . **NiB $650 Ex $450 Gd $400**
Pardus (16-in. heavy stainless bbl., aluminum free
 float handguard, adj. stock,
 2006-08) . . . . **NiB $1350 Ex $800 Gd $680**
Race Gun (24-in. stainless bbl., Hot Rod handguard, IronStone
 stock, 2001-08) . . . . **NiB $1450 Ex $950 Gd $840**
SDM-R (20-in. heavy bbl., aluminum free float handguard,
 Harris bipod, 2007-08) . . . . **NiB $1180 Ex $830 Gd $730**
Tuber (16-in. heavy bbl., aluminum free float handguard,
 flat top upper, 2002-08) . . . . **NiB $650 Ex $450 Gd $400**

PANTHER .22 . . . . **NiB $780 Ex $550 Gd $480**
Similar to Panther model except chambered in .22 LR w/16-in. heavy bbl. Weight: 7.85 lbs. Made 2003-08.
AP4 (16-in. M4 contour bbl.,
 2004-08) . . . . **NiB $750 Ex $500 Gd $470**
DCM (20-in. fluted bbl.,
 2004-08) . . . . **NiB $850 Ex $550 Gd $480**

PANTHER LR-.308 . . . . **NiB $1200 Ex $650 Gd $580**
Similar to Panther model except chambered in .308 Win. w/24-in. free float heavy bbl. Weight: 11.25 lbs. Made 2003-20.
LR-.308B (18-in. bbl., 2003-12) . . .**NiB $995 Ex $650 Gd $580**
LR-.308T (24-in. bbl., 7.62x51mm NATO,
 2004-12) . . . . **NiB $995 Ex $650 Gd $580**
LR-.308 AP4 (20-in. bbl., 7.62x51mm NATO,
 2003-12) . . . . **NiB $1100 Ex $730 Gd $600**
LR-.308C (20-in. bbl., 7.62x51mm NATO, A3 flat top w/
 handle 2003-12) . . . . **NiB $1050 Ex $730 Gd $600**

PANTHER LR-30S . . . . **NiB $1050 Ex $730 Gd $600**
Similar to Panther LR-.308 model except chambered in .300 RSUM w/20-in. free float heavy bbl. Made 2004-08.

PANTHER LR-243 . . . . **NiB $1280 Ex $730 Gd $600**
Similar to Panther LR-.308 model except chambered in .243 Win. w/20-in. free float heavy bbl. Made 2006-13.

PANTHER CSAT TACTICAL . . **NiB $1500 Ex $830 Gd $730**
Similar to Panther model except chambered in 5.56x45mm NATO. w/16-in. bbl., Magpul buttstock and psitol grip. Weight: 7.8 lbs. Made 2010-12.

PANTHER RAPTR . . . . **NiB $1400 Ex $850 Gd $730**
Similar to Panther model except chambered in 5.56x45mm NATO. w/16-in. bbl., Crimson Trace laser, Ergo Z-Rail, AP4 buttstock Weight: 8.2 lbs. Made 2010-11.

PANTHER REPR . . . . **NiB $2590 Ex $1400 Gd $1200**
Similar to Panther LR-.308 model except w/18- or 20-in. free float fluted heavy bbl., Magpul stock, Hogue rubber pistol grip, Gem Tech flash hider. Made 2009 to date.

PRAIRIE PANTHER . . . . **NiB $1240 Ex $750 Gd $580**
Similar to Panther model except w/20-in. heavy fluted free floated bbl. Weight: 8.75 lbs. Made 1993-99; 2010-20.

DSA — Barrington, IL

DA-AR SERIES . . . . **NiB $880 Ex $780 Gd $500**
Semiauto AR15 platform. Caliber: .223 Rem. 30-rnd. magazine. 16-in. heavy or standard bbl. Made 2006–08.
CV1 Carbine
 (flattop receiver, 2004–05) . . . **NiB $780 Ex $710 Gd $510**
LE4 Carbine (2004–12) . . . . **NiB $780 Ex $710 Gd $510**
S1 (2004–05) . . . . **NiB $830 Ex $755 Gd $430**

SA58 SERIES
FAL and SA58 style platform. Gas piston system. Semiauto. Caliber: .308 Win., 10- or 20-rnd. magazine. Furniture: Black polymer buttstock, pistols grip. 16- to 24-in. bbl. w/flash hider. Weight: 8.7 to 11 lbs. Made 2001 to date.
Carbine (16.25- or 18-in. brrl.,
 2011 to date) . . . . **NiB $1500 Ex $1060 Gd $880**
Congo (2003-10) . . . . **NiB $1970 Ex $1890 Gd $1500**
G1 (2003-10) . . . . **NiB $2000 Ex $1980 Gd $1600**
Gray Wolf (.300 WSM or .308 Win., 21-in. bull brrl., gray
 furniture, 2003-10) . . . . . . **NiB $1960 Ex $1460 Gd $1060**
Imbel 58 (Imbell parts,
 2011–12) . . . . **NiB $880 Ex $780 Gd $455**
Para (folding stock, 2011
 to date) . . . . **NiB $1780 Ex $1360 Gd $960**
Para Congo (folding stock,
 2003-10) . . . . **NiB $2220 Ex $1990 Gd $1770**
Predator (.243 Win., .260 Rem. or .308 Win.; 16- or 19-in.
 brrl., green furniture,
 2003-12) . . . . **NiB $1530 Ex $1060 Gd $780**
Spartan (16- or 18-in. brrl., OD green furniture, case, 2009
 to date) . . . . **NiB $2300 Ex $1760 Gd $1330**

RIFLES

**SPR (19-in. fluted brrl., case, bipod,
2009 to date)** . . . . **NiB $4380 Ex $3510 Gd $2760**
Standard (21-in. brrl.). . . . . **NiB $1500 Ex $1060 Gd $880**
Tactical Carbine (16.25-in. brrl., 1999-12) . . . . **NiB $1500 Ex
$1060 Gd $880**

STG58 . . . . **NiB $1000 Ex $810 Gd $610**
Austrian FAL platform. Gas piston system. Semiauto. Caliber:
.308 Win., 10- or 20-rnd. magazine. Weight: 10 lbs. Imported
2006-08 and 2011-12.

EAGLE ARMS INC. — Geneseo, IL

*Previously Coal Valley, Illinois. In 1995, Eagle Arms Inc.,
became a division of ArmaLite and reintroduced that logo. For
current ArmaLite production see models under that listing.*

MODEL EA-15 CARBINE
Caliber: .223 Rem. (5.56mm). 30-rnd. magazine. 16-in. bbl.
and collapsible buttstock. Weight: 5.75 lbs. (E1); 6.25 lbs. (E2
w/heavy bbl. & National Match sights). Made 1990 to 1995;
reintro. 2002 to 2005.
E1 Carbine . . . . **NiB $976 Ex $739 Gd $510**
E2 Carbine . . . . **NiB $976 Ex $739 Gd $510**

MODEL EA-15 GOLDEN
EAGLE MATCH RIFLE . . . . **NiB $1244 Ex $977 Gd $657**
Same general specifications as EA-15 Standard, except w/
E2-style National Match sights. 20-in. Douglas Heavy Match
bbl. NM trigger and bolt-carrier group. Weight: 12.75 lbs.
Made 1991 to 1995, reintro. 2002.

MODEL EA-15 . . . . **NiB $1221 Ex $722 Gd $504**
Same as EA-15 Carbine except 20-in. bbl., 39 in. overall and
weighs 7 lbs. Made 1990-93; reintro. 2002 to 2005.

EMF COMPANY, INC. — Santa Ana, CA

*Importer, distributor and retailer of numerous reproduction
rifles. See Davide Pedersoli & Co., F.A.P F.LLI. Pietta, Armi
Sport, and Uberti for values on reproduction rifles and deduct
10%.*

**MODEL AP-74 SEMIAUTO
CARBINE.** . . . . **NiB $397 Ex $300 Gd $221**
Calibers: .22 LR or .32 ACP, 15-rnd. magazine. 20-in. bbl.
w/flash reducer. 38 in. overall. Weight: 6.75 lbs. Protected

pin front sight; protected rear peep sight. Lightweight plastic
buttstock; ventilated snap-out forend. Importation disc. 1989.

**MODEL AP74-W SPORTER
CARBINE.** . . . . **NiB $419 Ex $321 Gd $213**
Sporterized version of AP-74 w/wood buttstock and forend.
Importation disc. 1989.

MODEL AP74 PARATROOPER . . . **NiB $433 Ex $260 Gd $242**
Same general specifications as Model AP74-W except w/
folding tubular buttstock. Made in .22 LR. only. Importation
disc. 1987.

ERMA-WERKE — Dachau, Germany

*Previously imported by Precision Sales International; Nygord
Precision Products; Mandall's Shooting Supplies.*

**MODEL EG72 PUMP-ACTION
REPEATER** . . . . **NiB $158 Ex $110 Gd $98**
Visible hammer. Caliber: .22 LR. 15-rnd. magazine. 18.5-in.
bbl. Weight: 5.25 lbs. Sights: open rear; hooded front.
Receiver grooved for scope mounting. Straight-grip stock,
grooved slide handle. Imported from 1970 to 1976.

MODEL EG73 . . . . **NiB $288 Ex $223 Gd $172**
Same as Model EG712 except chambered for .22 WMR w/12-
rnd. tubular magazine, 19.3-in. bbl. Imported from 1973 to
1997.

**MODEL EG712 LEVER-ACTION
REPEATING CARBINE.** . . . . **NiB $297 Ex $229 Gd $167**
Styled after Winchester Model 94. Caliber: .22 LR. Long, Short.
Tubul33 magazine holds 15 LR, 17 Long, 21 Short. 18.5-in.
bbl. Weight: 5.5 lbs. Sights: Open rear; hooded ramp front.
Receiver grooved for scope mounting. Western carbine-style
stock and forearm w/bbl. band. Imported 1976 to 1997. Note:
A similar carbine by Erma was marketed in U.S. as Ithaca
Model 72 Saddle Gun.

MODEL EGM1 . . . . **NiB $290 Ex $247 Gd $180**
Same as Model EM1 except w/unslotted buttstock, ramp front
sight, 5-rnd. magazine standard. Imported from 1970 to 1995.

**MODEL EM1 .22 SEMIAUTO
CARBINE.** . . . . **NiB $387 Ex $320 Gd $222**
Styled after U.S. Carbine cal. 30 M1. Caliber: .22 LR. 10- or
15-rnd. magazine. 18-in. bbl. Weight: 5.5 lbs. Carbine-type

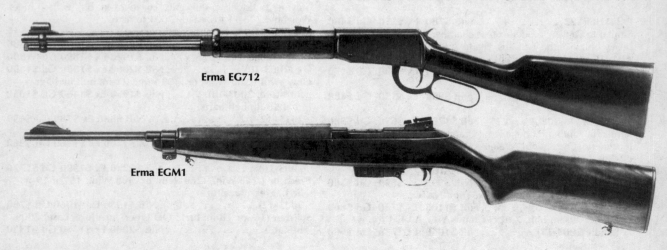

Erma EG712

Erma EGM1

sights. Receiver grooved for scope mounting. Military stock/handguard. Imported 1966 to 1997.

EUROPEAN AMERICAN ARMORY — Sharpes, FL

MODEL HW 660 BOLT-ACTION
SINGLE-SHOT RIFLE . . . . NiB $909 Ex $745 Gd $495
Caliber: .22 LR. 26.8-in. bbl., 45.7 in. overall. Weight: 10.8 lbs. Match-type aperture rear sight; Hooded ramp front. Stippled walnut stock. Imported from 1992 to 1996.

MODEL HW BOLT-ACTION SINGLE-SHOT
TARGET RIFLE . . . . NiB $895 Ex $740 Gd $485
Same general specification as Model HW 660 except equipped w/ target stock. Imported from 1995 to 1996.

MODEL SABITTI SP1822
Caliber: .22 LR. 10-rnd. detachable magazine. 18.5 in. bbl. 37.5 in. overall. Weight: 5.25 to 7.15 lbs. No sights. Hammer-forged heavy non-tapered bbl. Scope-mounted rail. Flush-mounted magazine release. Alloy receiver w/non-glare finish. Manual bolt lock. Wide claw extractor. Blowback action. Cross-trigger safety. Imported 1994 to 1996.
Traditional Sporter model . . . . . NiB $259 Ex $206 Gd $149
Thumbhole Sporter
**   model (synthetic stock) . . . . . NiB $379 Ex $312 Gd $221**

FABRIQUE NATIONALE HERSTAL — Herstal & Liege, Belgium
Formerly Fabrique Nationale d'Armes de Guerre.

MODELS 1924, 1934/30 AND 1930
MAUSER MILITARY RIFLES . . . NiB $445 Ex $337 Gd $241
Similar to German Kar. 98k w/straight bolt handle. Calibers: 7mm, 7.65mm and 7.9mm Mauser. Five round box magazine. 23.5-in. bbl. Weight: 8.5 lbs. Sights: Adj. rear; blade front. Military stock of M/98 pattern w/slight modification. Model differences are minor. Also produced in a short carbine model w/17.25-in. bbl. Note: These rifles were manufactured under contract for Abyssinia, Argentina, Belgium, Bolivia, Brazil, Chile, China, Colombia, Ecuador, Iran, Luxembourg, Mexico, Peru, Turkey, Uruguay and Yugoslavia. Such arms usually bear the coat of arms of the country for which they were made together with the contractor's name and date of manufacture. Also sold commercially and exported to all parts of the world.

MODEL 1949 SEMIAUTO
MILITARY RIFLE . . . . NiB $799 Ex $647 Gd $328
Gas-operated. Calibers: 7mm, 7.65mm, 7.92mm, .30-06. 10-rnd. box magazine, clip fed or loaded singly. 23.2-in. bbl. Weight: 9.5 lbs. Sights: Tangent rear-shielded post front. Pistol-grip stock, handguard. Note: Adopted by Belgium in 1949; also by Belgian Congo, Brazil, Colombia, Luxembourg, Netherlands, East Indies, and Venezuela. Approx. 160,000 were made.

MODEL 1950 MAUSER
MILITARY RIFLE . . . . NiB $533 Ex $360 Gd $287
Same as previous F.N. models of Kar. 98k type except chambered for .30-06.

DELUXE MAUSER BOLT-ACTION
SPORTING RIFLE . . . . NiB $799 Ex $689 Gd $443
American calibers: .220 Swift, .243 Win., .244 Rem., .250/3000, .257 Roberts, .270 Win., 7mm, .300 Sav., .308 Win. .30-06. European calibers: 7x57, 8x57JS, 8x60S, 9.3x62, 9.5x57, 10.75x68mm. Five round box magazine. 24-in. bbl. Weight: 7.5-8.25 lbs. American model is standard w/hooded ramp front sight and Tri-Range rear; Continental model w/two-leaf rear. Checkered stock w/cheekpiece, pistol-grip, swivels. Made 1947-63.

DELUXE MAUSER PRESENTATION
GRADE . . . . NiB $1337 Ex $1096 Gd $752
Same as regular model except w/select grade stock; engraving on receiver, trigger guard, floorplate and bbl. breech. Disc. 1963.

FAL/FNC/LAR SEMIAUTO
Same as standard FAL military rifle except w/o provision for automatic firing. Gas-operated. Calibers: 7.62mm NATO (.308 Win.) or 5.56mm (.223 Rem.). 10- or 20-rnd. box magazine. 25.5-in. bbl. (including flash hider). Weight: 9 lbs. Sights: Post front; aperture rear. Fixed wood or folding buttstock, pistol-grip, forearm/handguard w/carrying handle and sling swivels. Disc. 1988.
F.N. FAL/LAR model (Light
**   Automatic Rifle) . . . . NiB $2594 Ex $2216 Gd $1402**
F.N. FAL/HB model (h. bbl.) . NiB $2955 Ex $2343 Gd $1644
F.N. FAL/PARA (Paratrpr) . . NiB $3566 Ex $2886 Gd $1854
F.N. FNC Carbine
**   model (.223 cal.) . . . . . . NiB $2715 Ex $1954 Gd $1294**
F.N. FNC Carbine model w/flash
**   suppresser (.223 cal.) . . . NiB $2790 Ex $2033 Gd $1387**

SUPREME MAUSER BOLT-ACTION
SPORTING RIFLE . . . . NiB $808 Ex $865 Gd $443
Calibers: .243, .270, 7mm, .308, .30-06. Four round magazine in .243 and .308; 5-rnd. in other calibers. 22-in. bbl. in .308; 24-in. in other calibers. Sights: Hooded ramp front, Tri-Range peep rear. Checkered stock w/ Monte Carlo cheekpiece, pistol-grip, swivels. Weight: 7.75 lbs. Made 1957-75.

SUPREME MAGNUM MAUSER NiB $865 Ex $689 Gd $474
Calibers: .264 Mag., 7mm Mag., .300 Win. Mag. Similar as standard caliber model except 3-rnd. magazine capacity.

FN AMERICA (FNH USA) — Liege, Belgium
Current FN production shown below. NOTE: FNH USA imports and manufactures in U.S. for the commercial, law enforcement and military markets. Below are products for commercial/civilian market.

– Semiauto Models –

FN15 SERIES
Semiauto. AR15 platform. Action: direct gas impingement. Caliber: 5.56 NATO, 30-rnd. magazine.
16-in. bbl. w/A2 flash hider, optic ready. Stock: adj. 6-position, pistol grip. Weight: 6.6 lbs. Made 2014–date.
1776 model (2015-date) . . . . . . NiB $780 Ex $690 Gd $490
Carbine model (M4 carry handle,
**   2014-date) . . . . NiB $980 Ex $890 Gd $580**

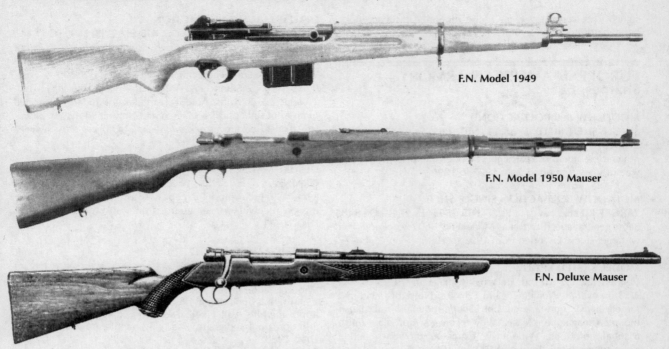

F.N. Model 1949

F.N. Model 1950 Mauser

F.N. Deluxe Mauser

Competition model (18-in. bbl.,
 Timney trigger, 2016-date) NiB $1920 Ex $1690 Gd $1040
DMR model (18-in. free float bbl.,
 Timney trigger, 2015-date) . . NiB $1630 Ex $1430 Gd $930
MOE SLG model (Magpul furniture,
 2015-date) . . . . NiB $1490 Ex $1320 Gd $880
Patrol Carbine model (Midwest
 Industries rail, 2016-date) . . NiB $1030 Ex $980 Gd $580
Rifle model (20-in. bbl., removable
 carry handle, 2014-date) . . . . . NiB $980 Ex $890 Gd $580
Sporting model (18-in. match bbl., Magpul
 CTR stock, 2015-date) . . . . . NiB $1490 Ex $1320 Gd $880
Tactical model (Magpul
 MBUS stock, Midwest
 Industries rail, 2015-date) . NiB $1255 Ex $1110 Gd $730
Tactical .300 BLK model (.300 BLK,
 2015-date) . . . . NiB $1255 Ex $1110 Gd $730

MILITARY COLLECTOR SERIES
Similar to FN15 series except replicas of iconic M16 style rifles.
M4 model (M4 style,
 2015-date) . . . . NiB $1490 Ex $1320 Gd $880
M16 model (M16A2 style,
 2015-date) . . . . NiB $1490 Ex $1320 Gd $880
M249S model (semi auto version of M249
 SAW light machine gun, 5.56 NATO w/200-rnd.
 belt or 30-rnd. magazine). . NiB $7255 Ex $6510 Gd $4255

FN SCAR SERIES
Short stroke gas system. Semiauto. SA. Caliber: 5.56 NATO or
7.62 NATO. 10- or 20-rnd. magazines. 16.25-in. bbl. Finish:
matte black. Sights: BUIS. Weight: 7.25 lbs. Made 2009 to
date.
SCAR 16S (5.56 NATO). . . . NiB $2700 Ex $2060 Gd $1580
SCAR 17S (7.62 NATO). . . . NiB $2930 Ex $2180 Gd $1580

FNAR . . . . NiB $1560 Ex $1200 Gd $860
Short stroke gas system. Semiauto. SA. Caliber: 7.62 NATO.
10- or 20-rnd. magazines. 16- or 20-in. bbl. Finish: matte
black. Weight: 9 lbs. Made 2009-13.
Competition (20-in. fluted brrl.,
 2013 to date) . . . . NiB $1767 Ex $1130 Gd $830

FS2000 . . . . NiB $2430 Ex $1830 Gd $1460
Bullpup style. Semiauto. SA. Caliber: .223 Rem., 10- or 30-rnd.
uses AR15 style magazines. 17.4-in. bbl. Receiver: Polymer.
Sights: BUIS. Finish: black or OD green. Weight: 7.6 lbs. Mfg.
from 2006 to 2013.

PS90 . . . . NiB $1930 Ex $1460 Gd $1080
Bullpup style. Semiauto. SA. Caliber: 5.7x28mm, 10- or
30-rnd. 16 in. bbl. Receiver: Polymer. Sights: non-magnifying
optic. Finish: black or OD green. Weight: 6 lbs. Made 2005-11.

– Bolt Action Models –
BALLISTA . . . . NiB $6955 Ex $6410 Gd $4510
Bolt action, modular, multi-caliber. Caliber: .308 Win., .300
Win. Mag. or .338 LM; 5- or 8-rnd. detachable magazine.
Heavy 26-in. fluted bbl. Stock: ambidextrous, folding, fully adj.
aluminum chassis. Finish: FDE. Weight: 15.1 lbs.

PBR. . . . . NiB $1080 Ex $830 Gd $630
Bolt action. Caliber: .300 WSM or .308 Win. 4-rnd. fixed
or detachable magazine. Heavy 22-in.bbl. Stock: Hogue
Overmold. Finish: black. Weight: 9.5 lbs.

PSR SERIES
Bolt action. Caliber: .300 WSM or .308 Win. 3-, 4- or 5-rnd.
fixed or detachable magazine. Heavy 22-in. bbl. Stock:
McMillian fiberglass. Finish: black. Weight: 8 to 9 lbs.
PSR I (.308 Win.,
 disc. 2009) . . . . NiB $2000 Ex $1500 Gd $1100

FN M249S

FN Ballista

**PSR II (.300 WSM,
 disc. 2009)** . . . . NiB $2000 Ex $1500 Gd $1100
**PSR III (4-rnd. magazine,
 disc. 2009)** . . . . NiB $2000 Ex $1500 Gd $1100

SPR SERIES
Winchester Model 70–style bolt action. Caliber: .308 Win.;
4-rnd. detachable magazine. 20-in. fluted or non-fluted bbl.
Stock: McMillan fiberglass. Finish: matte black. Weight: 11.8-
12.4 lbs.
A1a model (fluted bbl.) . . . . NiB $2010 Ex $1780 Gd $1180
**A1 model (non-fluted bbl.),
 deduct** $250
**A2 model (20-in. fluted or 24-in. non-fluted
 bbl., disc. 2009)** . . . . NiB $2510 Ex $2190 Gd $1380
**A3 G model (24-in. fluted bbl.,
 fiberglass stock, 14.3 lbs.)** . NiB $3180 Ex $2755 Gd $1710
**A5M model (.308 Win. or .300 WSM,
 20- or 24-in. bbl., McMillan fiberglass stock,
 11.3-11.8 lbs.)** . . . . NiB $2630 Ex $2330 Gd $1480
**A5M XP model (.308 Win., 20- or 24-in.
 bbl., adj. McMillan fiberglass stock,
 11.5-11.8 lbs.)** . . . . NiB $2630 Ex $2330 Gd $1480

TSR XP/XP USA . . . . NiB $1055 Ex $930 Gd $610
Winchester Model 70 short (XP model) or ultra short (XP USA)
bolt action. Caliber: .223 Rem., 7.62x39mm, .308 Win., or
.300 WSM; 3-, 4-, 5- or 6-rnd. fixed or detachable magazine.
20-in. fluted or 24-in. non-fluted bbl. Stock: Hogue synthetic.
Finish: matte black. Weight: 11.8-12.4 lbs.

FEATHER INDUSTRIES, INC. — Boulder, CO

See MITCHELL ARMS for current production.

MODEL AT-9 SEMIAUTO RIFLE
Caliber: 9mm Parabellum. 10-, 25-, 32-, or 100-rnd. magazine.
17-in. bbl. 35 in. overall (extended). Hooded post front sight,
adj. aperture rear. Weight: 5 lbs. Telescoping wire stock w/
composition pistol-grip and barrel-shroud handguard. Matte
black finish. Made 1988-95.
Model AT-9 . . . . NiB $898 Ex $714 Gd $479
w/32-rnd. magazine, add $100
w/100-rnd. drum magazine, add $300

MODEL AT-22 . . . . NiB $355 Ex $232 Gd $171
Caliber: .22 LR. 20-rnd. magazine. 17-in. bbl. 35 in. overall
(extended). Hooded post front sight; adj. aperture rear. Weight:
3.25 lbs. Telescoping wire stock w/composition pistol-grip and
barrel shroud handguard. Matte black finish.

MODEL F2 SA CARBINE . . . . . . NiB $331 Ex $258 Gd $149
Similar to AT-22, except w/fixed Polymer stock and pistol-grip.
Made 1992-95.

MODEL F9 SA CARBINE . . . . . . NiB $758 Ex $599 Gd $400
Similar to AT-9, except w/fixed Polymer stock and pistol-grip.
Made 1992-95.

FINNISH LION — Jyväkylylä, Finland
Manufactured by Valmet Oy, Tourula Works.

CHAMPION FREE RIFLE . . . . . . NiB $688 Ex $545 Gd $390
Bolt-action single-shot target rifle. Double-set trigger.
Caliber: .22 LR. 28.75-in. heavy bbl. Weight: 16 lbs. Sights:
Extension rear peep; aperture front. Walnut free-rifle stock
w/full pistol-grip, thumbhole, beavertail forend, hook butt-
plate, palm rest, hand stop, swivel. Made 1965-72.

STANDARD ISU TARGET RIFLE . . . NiB $421 Ex $337 Gd $213
Bolt-action, single-shot. Caliber: .22 LR. 27.5-in. bbl. Weight:
10.5 lbs. Sights: extension rear peep; aperture front. Walnut
target stock w/full pistol-grip, checkered beavertail forearm,
adj. buttplate, sling swivel. Made 1966-77.

MATCH RIFLE . . . . NiB $569 Ex $510 Gd $343
Bolt-action, single-shot. Caliber: .22 LR. 28.75-in. heavy bbl.
Weight: 14.5 lbs. Sights: Extension rear peep; aperture front.
Walnut free-rifle stock w/full pistol-grip, thumbhole, beavertail
forearm, hook buttplate, palm rest, hand stop, swivel. Made
1937-72.

STANDARD TARGET RIFLE
Bolt-action, single-shot. Caliber: .22 LR. 27.5-in. bbl. 44.5 in.
overall. Weight: 10.5 lbs. No sights; micrometer rear and globe
front International-style sights available. Select walnut stock in
target configuration. Made 1966-97.
Standard model . . . . NiB $808 Ex $679 Gd $448
Thumbhole stock model . . . . . . NiB $893 Ex $733 Gd $533
Deluxe model . . . . NiB $439 Ex $350 Gd $259

LUIGI FRANCHI, S.P.A. — Brescia, Italy

CENTENNIAL AUTOMATIC RIFLE
Commemorates Franchi's 100th anniversary (1868-1968).
Centennial seal engraved on receiver. Semiauto. Take-down.
Caliber: .22 LR. 11-rnd. magazine in buttstock. 21-in. bbl.
Weight: 5.13 lbs. Sights: Open rear; gold bead front on ramp.

RIFLES

Checkered walnut stock and forend. Deluxe model w/fully engraved receiver, premium grade wood. Made in 1968.
Standard model . . . . NiB $433 Ex $321 Gd $224
Engraved model . . . . NiB $478 Ex $379 Gd $270

MOMENTUM SERIES
Bolt-action. 60 degree bolt lift. Caliber: .22-250, .243, 6.5 Creedmoor, .270, .308, .30-06, 350 Bushmaster, or .300 Win. Mag.; 4-rnd. magazine. Barrel: 22- or 24-in. threaded or non-threaded. Weight: 6.6-7.8 lbs. Sights: Optic ready. Black synthetic stock. Made 2018-date.
Standard model . . . . NiB $555 Ex $500 Gd $405
Elite model (.223 Rem., 6.5 Creedmoor,
   or .308; Cerakote bronze or
   cobalt finish, muzzle brake) . . . NiB $730 Ex $640 Gd $500
Elite Varmint model
   (.22-250, 2022-date) . . . . NiB $999 Ex $790 Gd $690

FRANCOTTE — Leige, Belgium
Imported by Armes de Chasse, Hertford, NC; previously by Abercrombie & Fitch.

BOLT-ACTION RIFLE
Custom rifle built on Mauser style bolt action. Available in three action lengths. Calibers: .17 Bee to .505 Gibbs. Barrel length: 21- to 24.5-in. Weight: 8 to 12 lbs. Stock dimensions, wood type and style to customer's specifications. Engraving, appointments and finish to customer's preference. Note: Deduct 25% for models w/o engraving.
Short action . . . . NiB $9770 Ex $7725 Gd $4690
Standard action . . . . NiB $7859 Ex $6233 Gd $3834
Magnum Francotte action . . NiB $14,000 Ex $11,770 Gd $7690

BOXLOCK MOUNTAIN RIFLE
Custom single-shot rifle built on Anson & Deeley style boxlock or Holland & Holland style sidelock action. 23- to 26-in. barrels chambered to customer's specification. Stock dimensions, wood type and style to customer's specifications. Engraving, appointments and finish to customer's preference. Note: Deduct 30% for models w/o engraving.
Boxlock . . . . NiB $14,299 Ex $12,200 Gd $7800
Sidelock . . . . NiB $22,438 Ex $17,950 Gd $12,206

DOUBLE RIFLE
Custom side-by-side rifle. Built on Francotte system boxlock or back-action sidelock. 23.5- to 26-in. barrels chambered to customer's specification. Stock dimensions, wood type and style to customer's specifications. Engraving, appointments and finish to customer's preference. Note: Deduct 30% for models w/o engraving.
Boxlock . . . . NiB $26,750 Ex $16,875 Gd $10,270
Sidelock . . . . NiB $31,760 Ex $26,900 Gd $16,975

FRENCH MILITARY — Saint Etienne, France

MODEL 1936 MAS MILITARY RIFLE . . NiB $209 Ex $170 Gd $103
Bolt-action. Caliber: 7.5mm MAS. Five-rnd. box magazine. 22.5-in. bbl. Weight: 8.25 lbs. Sights: Adj. rear; blade front. Two-piece military-type stock. Bayonet carried in forend tube. Made 1936-40 by Manufacture Francaise d'Armes et de Cycles de St. Etienne (MAS).

GALIL — Israel
Manufactured by Israel Military Industries, Israel. Not currently imported, previously imported by UZI America Inc., North Haven, CT; previously by Action Arms, Springfield Armory and Magnum Research, Inc.

AR SERIES
Semiautomatic. Calibers: .308 Win. (7.62 NATO), .223 Rem. (5.56mm). 25-rnd. (.308) or 35-rnd. (.223) magazine. 16-in. (.223) or 18.5-in. (.308) bbl. w/flash suppressor. Weight: 9.5 lbs. Folding aperture rear sight, post front. Folding metal stock w/ carrying handle. Imported 1982 to 1994. Currently select fire models available to law enforcement only.
Model .223 AR . . . . NiB $3233 Ex $1998 Gd $1200
Model .308 AR . . . . NiB $3233 Ex $1998 Gd $1200
Model .223 ARM. . . . . NiB $3227 Ex $2290 Gd $1669
Model .308 ARM. . . . . NiB $3227 Ex $2290 Gd $1669

SPORTER . . . . NiB $1723 Ex $1009 Gd $707
Same general specifications as AR Model except w/hardwood thumbhole stock and 5-rnd. magazine. Weight: 8.5 lbs. Imported 1991 to 1994.

French Military 1936 MAS Military Rifle

Finnish Lion Match

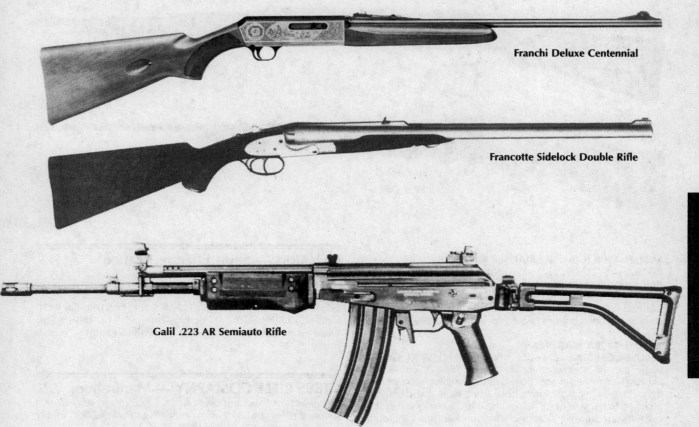

Franchi Deluxe Centennial

Francotte Sidelock Double Rifle

Galil .223 AR Semiauto Rifle

GARCIA CORPORATION — Teaneck, NJ

BRONCO 22 SINGLE-SHOT RIFLE . . NiB $151 Ex $112 Gd $88
Swing-out action. Takedown. Caliber: .22 LR, Long, Short. 16.5-in. bbl. Weight: 3 lbs. Sights: Open rear-blade front. One-piece stock and receiver, crackle finish. Intro. 1967. Discontinued.

GERMAN MILITARY — Germany
Manufactured by Ludwig Loewe & Co., Berlin, other contractors and by German arsenals and various plants under German government control.

MODEL 24T (GEW. 24T) . . . . . NiB $875 Ex $800 Gd $610
Same general specifications as Czech Model 24 (VZ24) Mauser Rifle w/minor modification and laminated wood stock. Weight: 9.25 lbs. Made in Czechoslovakia during German occupation; adopted 1940.

MODEL 29/40 (GEW. 29/40). . . NiB $1000 Ex $900 Gd $680
Same general specifications as Kar. 98K w/minor differences. Made in Poland during German occupation; adopted 1940.

MODEL 33/40 (GEW. 33/40)
MAUSER RIFLE . . . . NiB $2500 Ex $2010 Gd $1510
Same general specifications as Czech Model 33 (VZ33) Mauser Carbine w/minor modifications and laminated wood stock as found in war-time Model 98K carbines. Made in Czechoslovakia during German occupation; adopted 1940.

MODELS 41 AND 41-W (GEW. 41, GEW. 41-W)
Gas-operated, muzzle cone system. Caliber: 7.9mm Mauser. Ten-rnd. box magazine. 22.5-in. bbl. Weight: 10.25 lbs. Sights: Adj. leaf rear; blade front. Military-type stock w/semi-pistol grip, plastic handguard. Note: Model 41 lacks bolt release found on Model 41-W; otherwise, the models are the same. These early models were mfd. in Walther's Zella-Mehlis plant. Made c.1941 to 1943.
Model 41 . . . . NiB $20,000 Ex $18,750 Gd $12,000
Model 41-W . . . . NiB $8000 Ex $7000 Gd $5000

MODEL 43 (GEW. 43, KAR. 43)
RIFLES. . . . . NiB $3500 Ex $3000 Gd $5000
Gas-operated, bbl. vented as in Russian Tokarev. Caliber: 7.9mm Mauser. 10-rnd. detachable box magazine. 22- or 24-in. bbl. Weight: 9 lbs. Sights: Adj. rear; hooded front. Military-type stock w/semi-pistol-grip, wooden handguard. Note: These rifles are alike except for minor details, have characteristic late WWII mfg. short cuts: cast receiver and bolt cover, stamped steel parts, etc. Gew. 43 may have either 22- or 24-in. bbl. The former length was standardized in late 1944, when weapon designation was changed to "Kar. 43." Made 1943-45.

MODEL 1888 (GEW. 88) MAUSER-MANNLICHER
SERVICE RIFLE . . . . NiB $900 Ex $850 Gd $605
Bolt-action w/straight bolt handle. Caliber: 7.9mm Mauser (8x57mm). Five round Mannlicher box magazine. 29-in. bbl. w/jacket. Weight: 8.5 lbs. Fixed front sight, adj. rear. Military-type full stock. Mfd. by Ludwig Loewe & Co., Haenel, Schilling and other contractors.

German Military Mauser Kar. 98k

Golden Eagle Model 7000

MODEL 1898 (GEW. 98) MAUSER MILITARY
RIFLE . . . . NiB $900 Ex $800 Gd $605
Bolt action with straight bolt handle. Caliber: 7.9mm Mauser (8x57mm). Five round box magazine. 29-in. stepped bbl. Weight: 9 lbs. Sights: Blade front; adj. rear. Military-type full stock w/rounded bottom pistol grip. Adopted 1898.

MODEL 1898A (KAR. 98A)
MAUSER CARBINE . . . . NiB $800 Ex $730 Gd $605
Same general specifications as Model 1898 (Gew.98) Rifle except has turned-down bolt handle, smaller receiver ring, light 23.5-inch straight taper bbl., front sight guards, sling is attached to left side of stock, weight: 8 lbs. Note: Some of these carbines are marked "Kar. 98;" the true Kar. 98 is the earlier original M/98 carbine w/17-in. bbl. and is rarely encountered.

MODEL 1898B (KAR. 98B)
MAUSER CARBINE . . . . NiB $1000 Ex $955 Gd $605
Same general specifications as Model 1898 (Gew.98) Rifle except has turned-down bolt handle and sling attached to left side of stock. This is post-WWI model.

MODEL 1898K (KAR. 98K)
MAUSER CARBINE . . . . NiB $2500 Ex $2000 Gd $1500
Same general specifications as Model 1898 (Gew.98) Rifle except has turned-down bolt handle, 23.5-in. bbl., may have hooded front sight, sling attached to left side of stock, weighs about 8.5 lbs. Adopted in 1935, this was the standard German service rifle of WWII. Note: Late-war models had stamped sheet steel trigger guards and many of the Model 98K carbines made during WWII had laminated wood stocks These weigh .5 to .75 pound more than the previous Model 98K. Value shown is for earlier type.

MODEL VK 98 PEOPLE'S RIFLE
("VOLKSGEWEHR") . . . . . . NiB $2500 Ex $2000 Gd $1500
Kar. 98K-type action. Caliber: 7.9mm. Single-shot or repeater (latter w/rough hole-in-the-stock 5-rnd. "magazine" or fitted w/10-rnd. clip of German Model 43 semi-auto rifle). 20.9-in. bbl. Weight: 7 lbs. Fixed V-notch rear sight dovetailed into front receiver ring; front blade welded to bbl. Crude, unfinished, half-length stock w/o buttplate. Last ditch weapon made in 1945 for issue to German civilians. Note: Of value only as a military arms collector's item, this hastily-made rifle should be regarded as unsafe to shoot.

GÉVARM — Saint Etienne, France
Manufactured by Gevelot.

E-1 AUTOLOADING RIFLE . . . . NiB $234 Ex $190 Gd $150
Caliber: .22 LR. 8-rnd. clip magazine. 19.5-in. bbl. Sights: Open rear; post front. Pistol-grip stock and forearm of French walnut.

GIBBS RIFLE COMAPNY — Martinsburg, WV
Manufacturer and importer of U.S., German, and British military rifles and sidearms as well as Parker-Hale sniper rifles. See separate rifle listings.

GOLDEN EAGLE — Houston, TX
Manufactured by Nikko Firearms Ltd., Tochigi, Japan.

MODEL 7000 GRADE I
AFRICAN . . . . NiB $743 Ex $578 Gd $468
Same as Grade I Big Game except: Caliber: .375 H&H Mag. and .458 Win. Mag. Two-rnd. magazine in .458, weight: 8.75 lbs. in .375 and 10.5 lbs. in .458, furnished w/sights. Imported 1976–81.

MODEL 7000 BIG GAME SERIES
Bolt action. Calibers: .22-250, .243 Win., .25-06, .270 Win., Weatherby Mag., 7mm Rem. Mag., .30-06, .300 Weatherby Mag., .300 Win. Mag., .338 Win. Mag. Magazine capacity: 4 rnd. in .22-250, 3 rnd. in other calibers. 24- or 26-in. bbl. (26-in. only in 338). Weight: 7 lbs., .22-250; 8.75, lbs., other calibers. Furnished w/o sights. Fancy American walnut stock, skip checkered, contrasting wood forend tip and grip cap w/gold eagle head, recoil pad. Imported 1976 to 1981.
Grade I . . . . NiB $722 Ex $630 Gd $455
Grade II . . . . NiB $755 Ex $689 Gd $479

GREIFELT & CO. — Suhl, Germany

SPORT MODEL 22 HORNET BOLT-ACTION
RIFLE . . . . NiB $2388 Ex $1907 Gd $1412
Caliber: .22 Hornet. Five round box magazine. 22-in. Krupp steel bbl. Weight: 6 lbs. Sights: Two-leaf rear; ramp front.

Carl Gustaf Deluxe

Carl Gustaf Grand Prix

Walnut stock, checkered pistol-grip and forearm. Made before WWII.

GRENDEL, INC. — Rockledge, FL

R31 . . . . **NiB $500 Ex $455 Gd $340**
Semiauto. Caliber: .22 WMR. 30-rnd. detachable magazine in pistol grip. 16-in. bbl. Weight: 64 oz. Stock: telescoping steel wire. Made 1991–95.

CARL GUSTAF — Eskilstuna, Sweden
Manufactured by Carl Gustaf Stads Gevärsfaktori.

MODEL 2000 BOLT-ACTION RIFLE
Calibers: .243, 6.5x55, 7x64, .270, .308 Win., .30-06, 7mm Rem. Mag., .300 Win. Mag. Three round magazine. 24-in. bbl. 44 in. overall. Weight: 7.5 lbs. Receiver drilled and tapped. Hooded ramp front sight, open rear. Adj. trigger. Checkered European walnut stock w/Monte Carlo cheekpiece and Wundhammer palmswell grip. Imported 1991 to 1995
w/o sights . . . . **NiB $1443 Ex $1235 Gd $879**
w/sights. . . . . **NiB $1790 Ex $1390 Gd $1009**
LUXE. . . . . **NiB $1744 Ex $1689 Gd $1035**

DELUXE . . . . **NiB $707 Ex $579 Gd $522**
Same specifications as Monte Carlo Standard. Calibers: 6.5x55, 308 Win., .30-06, 9.3x62. Four round magazine in 9.3x62. Jeweled bolt. Engraved floorplate and trigger guard. Deluxe French walnut stock w/rosewood forend tip. Imported 1970 to 1977.

GRAND PRIX SINGLE-SHOT
TARGET RIFLE . . . . **NiB $577 Ex $459 Gd $202**
Special bolt action with "world's shortest lock time." Single-stage trigger adjusts down to 18 oz. Caliber: .22 LR. 26.75-in. heavy bbl. w/adj. trim weight. Weight: 9.75 lbs. Furnished w/o sights. Target-type Monte Carlo stock of French walnut, adj. cork buttplate. Imported from 1970 to 1977.

MONTE CARLO STANDARD BOLT-ACTION
SPORTING RIFLE . . . . **NiB $507 Ex $422 Gd $370**
Carl Gustaf 1900 action. Calibers: 6.5x55, 7x64, .270 Win., 7mm Rem. Mag., .308 Win., .30-06, 9.3x62. Five round magazine, except 4-rnd. in 9.3x62 and 3-rnd. in 7mm Rem. Mag. 23.5-in. bbl. Weight: 7 lbs. Sights: Folding leaf rear; hooded ramp front. French walnut Monte Carlo stock w/ cheekpiece, checkered forearm and pistol grip, sling swivels. Also available in left-hand model. Imported from 1970 to 1977.

SPECIAL . . . . **NiB $575 Ex $401 Gd $376**
Also designated "Grade II" in U.S. and "Model 9000" in Canada. Same specifications as Monte Carlo Standard. Calibers: .22-250, .243 Win., .25-06, .270 Win., 7mm Rem. Mag., .308 Win., .30-06, .300 Win. Mag. Three round magazine in magnum calibers. Select wood stock w/rosewood forend tip. Left-hand model avail. Imported from 1970 to 1977.

SPORTER. . . . . **NiB $512 Ex $355 Gd $291**
Also designated "Varmint-Target" in U.S. Fast bolt action w/large Bakelite bolt knob. Trigger pull adjusts down to 18 oz. Calibers: .222 Rem., .22-250, .243 Win., 6.5x55. Five round magazine except 6-rnd. in .222 Rem. 26.75-in. heavy bbl. Weight: 9.5 lbs. Furnished w/o sights. Target-type Monte Carlo stock of French walnut. Imported from 1970 to 1977.

STANDARD. . . . . **NiB $512 Ex $355 Gd $291**
Same specifications as Monte Carlo Standard. Calibers: 6.5x55, 7x64, .270 Win., .308 Win., .30-06, 9.3x62. Classic-style stock w/o Monte Carlo. Imported from 1970 to 1977.

TROFÉ. . . . . **NiB $588 Ex $479 Gd $382**
Also designated "Grade III" in U.S. and "Model 8000" in Canada. Same specifications as Monte Carlo Standard. Calibers: .22-250, .25-06, 6.5x55, .270 Win., 7mm Rem. Mag., .308 Win., .30-06, .300 Win. Mag. Three round magazine in magnum calibers. Furnished w/o sights. Fancy wood stock w/ rosewood forend tip, high-gloss lacquer finish. Imported from 1970 to 1977.

C.G. HAENEL — Suhl, Germany

'88 MAUSER SPORTER . . . . **NiB $813 Ex $508 Gd $380**
Same general specifications as Haenel Mauser-Mannlicher except w/Mauser 5-rnd. box magazine.

GRADING: **NiB** = New in Box   **Ex** = Excellent or NRA 95%   **Gd** = Good or NRA 68%

Hammerli-Tanner 300M

Harrington & Richardson Model 60 Reising

MAUSER-MANNLICHER BOLT-ACTION
SPORTING RIFLE . . . . NiB $821 Ex $572 Gd $400
Mauser M/88-type action. Calibers: 7x57, 8x57, 9x57mm. Mannlicher clip-loading box magazine, 5-round. 22- or 24-in. half or full octagon bbl. w/raised matted rib. Double-set trigger. Weight: 7.5 lbs. Sights: Leaf-type open rear; ramp front. Sporting stock w/cheekpiece, checkered pistol-grip, raised side-panels, Schnabel tip, swivels.

HÄMMERLI AG JAGD-UND-SPORTWAFFENFABRIK — Lenzburg, Switzerland

Imported by Sigarms, Exeter, NH; previously by Hammerli USA; Mandall Shooting Supplies, Inc. & Beeman Precision Arms.

MODEL 45 SMALLBORE BOLT-ACTION SINGLE-SHOT
MATCH RIFLE . . . . NiB $765 Ex $654 Gd $453
Calibers: .22 LR. 22 Extra Long. 27.5-in. heavy bbl. Weight: 15.5 lbs. Sights: Micrometer peep rear; globe front. Free-rifle stock w/cheekpiece, full pistol-grip, thumbhole, beavertail forearm, palmrest, Swiss-type buttplate, swivels. Made 1945-57.

MODEL 54 SMALLBORE
MATCH RIFLE . . . . NiB $709 Ex $544 Gd $423
Bolt-action, single-shot. Caliber: .22 LR. 27.5-in. heavy bbl. Weight: 15 lbs. Sights: Micrometer peep rear; globe front. Free-rifle stock w/cheekpiece, thumbhole, adj. hook buttplate, palm rest, swivel. Made 1954-57.

MODEL 508 FREE RIFLE . . . . . . NiB $707 Ex $546 Gd $413
Bolt-action, single-shot. Caliber: .22 LR. 27.5-in. heavy bbl. Weight: 15 lbs. Sights: Micrometer peep rear; globe front. Free-rifle stock w/cheekpiece, thumbhole, adj. hook buttplate, palm rest, swivel. Made 1957-62.

MODEL 506 SMALLBORE
MATCH RIFLE . . . . NiB $769 Ex $650 Gd $439
Bolt-action, single-shot. Caliber: .22 LR. 26.75-in. heavy bbl. Weight: 16.5 lbs. Sights: Micrometer peep rear; globe front. Free-rifle stock w/cheekpiece, thumbhole adj. hook buttplate, palmrest, swivel. Made 1963-66.

MODEL OLYMPIC 300 METER BOLT-ACTION SINGLE-SHOT
FREE RIFLE . . . . NiB $905 Ex $755 Gd $556
Calibers: .30-06, .300 H&H Magnum for U.S.A.; ordinarily produced in 7.5mm, other calibers available on special order. 29.5-in. heavy bbl. Double-pull or double-set trigger. Sights: Micrometer peep rear, globe front. Free-rifle stock w/cheekpiece, full pistol grip, thumbhole, beavertail forend, palmrest, Swiss-type buttplate, swivels. Made 1945-59.

TANNER 300 METER FREE RIFLE . . . NiB $937 Ex $740 Gd $534
Bolt-action, single-shot. Caliber: 7.5mm standard, available in most popular centerfire calibers. 29.5-in. heavy bbl. Weight: 16.75 lbs. Sights: Micrometer peep rear; globe front. Free-rifle stock w/cheekpiece, thumbhole, adj. hook buttplate, palmrest, swivel. Intro. 1962.

HARRINGTON & RICHARDSON, INC. (H&R, H&R 1871) — Gardner, MA

Currently H&R 1872, formerly Harrington & Richardson Arms Co. of Worcester, Mass. One of the oldest and most distinguished manufacturers of handguns, rifles and shotguns, H&R suspended operations on January 24, 1986. In 1987, New England Firearms was established as an independent company producing selected H&R models under the NEF logo. In 1991, H&R 1871, Inc. was formed from the residual of the parent company and that took over the New England Firearms facility. H&R 1871 produced firearms under both its logo and the NEF brand name until 1999, when the Marlin Firearms Company acquired the assets of H&R 1871. Marlin was purchased by the Freedom Group Inc. in 2008. Part of Remington bankruptcy in 2020; purchased by JJE Capital Holdings.

MODEL 60 REISING . . . . NiB $1266 Ex $899 Gd $598
Semiauto. Caliber: .45 Automatic. 12- and 20-rnd. detachable box magazines. 18.25-in. bbl. Weight: 7.5 lbs. Sights: Open rear; blade front. Plain pistol-grip stock. Made 1944-46.

MODEL 65 MILITARY
AUTOLOADING RIFLE . . . . . . NiB $496 Ex $322 Gd $208
Also called "General." Caliber: .22 LR. 10-rnd. detachable box magazine. 23-in. heavy bbl. Weight: 9 lbs. Sights: Redfield 70 rear peep, blade front w/protecting "ears." Plain

Harrington & Richardson
Model 65 Military

Harrington & Richardson
Model 150 Leatherneck

Harrington & Richardson
Model 155

Harrington & Richardson
Model 158 Topper Jet

Harrington & Richardson
Model 171

pistol-grip stock, "Garand" dimensions. Made 1944-46. Note: This model was used as a training rifle by the U.S. Marine Corps.

MODEL 150 LEATHERNECK
AUTOLOADER . . . . **NiB $338 Ex $234 Gd $110**
Caliber: .22 LR. only. Five round detachable box magazine. 22-in. bbl. Weight: 7.25 lbs. Sights: Open rear; blade front, on ramp. Plain pistol-grip stock. Made 1949-53.

MODEL 151 . . . . NiB $338 Ex $234 Gd $110
Same as Model 150 except w/Redfield 70 rear peep sight.

MODEL 155 SINGLE-SHOT
RIFLE . . . . **NiB $279 Ex $178 Gd $126**
Model 158 action. Calibers: .44 Rem. Mag., .45-70 Govt. 24- or 28-in. bbl. (latter in .44 only). Weight: 7 or 7.5 lbs. Sights: Folding leaf rear; blade front. Straight-grip stock, forearm w/bbl. band, brass cleaning rod. Made 1972-82.

MODEL 157 SINGLE-SHOT
RIFLE . . . . **NiB $333 Ex $154 Gd $121**
Model 158 action. Calibers: .22 WMR, .22 Hornet, .30-30. 22-in. bbl. Weight: 6.25 lbs. Sights: Folding leaf rear; blade front. Pistol-grip stock, full-length forearm, swivels. Made 1976-86.

MODEL 158 TOPPER JET SINGLE-SHOT COMBINATION
Shotgun-type action w/visible hammer, side lever, auto ejector. Caliber: .22 Rem. Jet. 22-in. bbl. (interchanges with .30-30, .410 ga., 20 ga. bbls.). Weight: 5 lbs. Sights: Lyman

folding adj. open rear; ramp front. Plain pistol-grip stock and forearm, recoil pad. Made 1963-67.
Rifle only . . . . **NiB $250 Ex $171 Gd $126**
Interchangeable bbl. .30-30, shotgun, add **$75**

MODEL 158C . . . . NiB $250 Ex $171 Gd $126
Same as Model 158 Topper Jet except calibers .22 Hornet, .30-30, .357 Mag., .357 Mag., .44 Mag. Straight-grip stock. Made 1963-86.

MODEL 163 MUSTANG . . . . . NiB $250 Ex $168 Gd $124
Same as Model 158 Topper except w/gold-plated hammer and trigger, straight-grip stock and contoured forearm. Made 1964-67.

MODEL 165 LEATHERNECK . . . . NiB $250 Ex $170 Gd $126
Semiauto. Caliber: .22 LR. 10-rnd. detachable box magazine. 23-in. bbl. Weight: 7.5 lbs. Sights: Redfield 70 rear peep; blade front, on ramp. Plain pistol-grip stock, swivels, web sling. Made 1945-61.

MODEL 171 . . . . NiB $633 Ex $466 Gd $257
Model 1873 Springfield Cavalry Carbine replica. Caliber: .45-70. 22-in. bbl. Weight: 7 lbs. Sights: Leaf rear; blade front. Plain walnut stock. Made 1972-81.

MODEL 171 DELUXE . . . . NiB $776 Ex $523 Gd $309
Same as Model 171 except engraved action and different sights. Made 1972-86.

MODEL 172 . . . . NiB $759 Ex $588 Gd $454
Same as Model 171 Deluxe except silver-plated, w/fancy walnut stock, checkered, w/grip adapter; tang-mounted aperture sight. Made 1972-86.

GRADING: **NiB** = New in Box   **Ex** = Excellent or NRA 95%   **Gd** = Good or NRA 68%

MODEL 173 . . . . **NiB $1663 Ex $963 Gd $538**
Model 1873 Springfield Officer's Model replica, same as 100th Anniversary Commemorative except w/o plaque on stock. Made 1972-86.

MODEL 174 . . . . **NiB $1266 Ex $1009 Gd $633**
Little Big Horn Commemorative Carbine. Same as Model 171 Deluxe except w/tang-mounted aperture sight, grip adapter. Made 1972-84.

MODEL 178 . . . . **NiB $735 Ex $422 Gd $328**
Model 1873 Springfield Infantry Rifle replica. Caliber: .45-70. 32-in. bbl. Weight: 8 lbs. 10 oz. Sights: Leaf rear; blade front. Full-length stock w/bbl. bands, swivels, ramrod. Made 1973-86.

MODEL 250 SPORTSTER . . . . . . **NiB $220 Ex $111 Gd $80**
Bolt-action. Caliber: .22 LR. Five-rnd. detachable box magazine. 23-in. bbl. Weight: 6.5 lbs. Sights: Open rear; blade front, on ramp. Plain pistol-grip stock. Made 1948-61.

MODEL 251 . . . . **NiB $255 Ex $128 Gd $90**
Same as Model 250 except w/Lyman No. 55H rear sight.

MODEL 265 "REG'LAR" . . . . . . **NiB $337 Ex $140 Gd $98**
Bolt-action. Caliber: .22 LR. 10-rnd. detachable box magazine. 22-in. bbl. Weight: 6.5 lbs. Sights: Lyman No. 55 rear peep; blade front, on ramp. Plain pistol-grip stock. Made 1946-49.

MODEL 300 ULTRA . . . . **NiB $572 Ex $521 Gd $302**
Mauser-type action. Calibers: .22-250, .243 Win., .270 Win., .30-06, .308 Win., 7mm Rem. Mag., .300 Win. Mag. Three round magazine in 7mm and .300 Mag. calibers, 5-rnd. in others. 22- or 24-in. bbl. Sights: Open rear; ramp front. Checkered stock w/rollover cheekpiece and full pistol grip, contrasting wood forearm tip and pistol grip, rubber buttplate, sling swivels. Weight: 7.25 lbs. Made 1965-82.

MODEL 301 CARBINE . . . . **NiB $523 Ex $412 Gd $287**
Same as Model 300 except w/18-in. bbl., Mannlicher-style stock, weighs 7.25 lbs.; not available in caliber .22-250. Made 1967-82.

MODEL 308 AUTOMATIC RIFLE . . . **NiB $531 Ex $390 Gd $277**
Original designation of the Model 360 Ultra. Made 1965-67.

MODEL 317 ULTRA WILDCAT
BOLT-ACTION RIFLE . . . . **NiB $650 Ex $495 Gd $380**
Sako short action. Calibers: .17 Rem. 17/.223 (handload), .222 Rem., .223 Rem. Six round magazine. 20-in. bbl. No sights, receiver dovetailed for scope mounts. Checkered stock w/ cheekpiece and full pistol grip, contrasting wood forearm tip and pistol-grip cap, rubber buttplate. Weight: 5.25 lbs. Made 1968-76.

MODEL 317P PRESENTATION
GRADE . . . . **NiB $710 Ex $546 Gd $488**
Same as Model 317 except w/select grade fancy walnut stock w/basket weave carving on forearm and pistol-grip. Made 1968-76.

MODEL 330 HUNTER'S RIFLE . . . **NiB $439 Ex $326 Gd $244**
Similar to Model 300, but w/plainer stock. Calibers: .243 Win., .270 Win., .30-06, .308 Win., 7mm Rem. Mag., .300 Win. Mag. Weight: 7.13 lbs. Made 1967-72.

MODEL 333 . . . . **NiB $439 Ex $326 Gd $244**
Plainer version of Model 300 w/uncheckered walnut-finished hardwood stock. Calibers: 7mm Rem. Mag. and .30-06. 22-in. bbl. Weight: 7.25 lbs. No sights. Made in 1974.

MODEL 340 . . . . **NiB $450 Ex $341 Gd $259**
Mauser-type action. Calibers: .243 Win., .308 Win., .270 Win., .30-06, 7x57. 22-in. bbl. Weight: 7.25 lbs. Hand-checkered American walnut stock. Made 1982-84.

MODEL 360 ULTRA . . . . **NiB $534 Ex $380 Gd $300**
Gas-operated Semiauto. Calibers: .243 Win., .308 Win. Three round detachable box magazine. 22-in. bbl. Sights: Open rear; ramp front. Checkered stock w/rollover cheekpiece, full pistol grip, contrasting wood forearm tip and pistol-grip cap, rubber buttplate, sling swivels. Weight: 7.25 lbs. Made 1967-78.

MODEL 361 . . . . **NiB $556 Ex $439 Gd $333**
Same as Model 360 except w/full rollover cheekpiece for right- or left-hand shooters. Made 1970-73.

MODEL 369 ACE BOLT-ACTION
SINGLE-SHOT RIFLE . . . . **NiB $178 Ex $140 Gd $96**
Caliber: .22 LR. 22-in. bbl. Weight: 6.5 lbs. Sights: Lyman No. 55 rear peep, blade front, on ramp. Plain pistol-grip stock. Made 1946 to 1947.

MODEL 370 ULTRA MEDALIST **NiB $555 Ex $423 Gd $320**
Varmint and target rifle based on Model 300. Calibers: .22-250, .243 Win., 6mm Rem. Three round magazine. 24-in. varmint weight bbl. No sights. Target-style stock w/semibea-vertail forearm. Weight: 9.5 lbs. Made 1968-73.

MODEL 422 SLIDE-ACTION
REPEATER . . . . **NiB $375 Ex $234 Gd $141**
Caliber: .22 LR. Long, Short. Tubular magazine holds 21 Short, 17 Long, 15 LR. 24-in. bbl. Weight: 6 lbs. Sights: Open rear; ramp front. Plain pistol-grip stock grooved slide handle. Made 1956–58.

MODEL 450 . . . . **NiB $403 Ex $221 Gd $130**
Same as Model 451 except w/o front and rear sights.

MODEL 451 MEDALIST BOLT-ACTION
TARGET RIFLE . . . . **NiB $433 Ex $222 Gd $130**
Caliber: .22 LR. Five round detachable box magazine. 26-in. bbl. Weight: 10.5 lbs. Sights: Lyman No. 524F extension rear; Lyman No. 77 front, scope bases. Target stock w/full pistol-grip and forearm, swivels and sling. Made 1948-61.

MODEL 465 TARGETEER SPECIAL
BOLT-ACTION REPEATER . . . . . **NiB $423 Ex $233 Gd $144**
Caliber: .22 LR. 10-rnd. detachable box magazine. 25-in. bbl. Weight: 9 lbs. Sights: Lyman No. 57 rear peep; blade front, on ramp. Plain pistol-grip stock, swivels, web sling strap. Made 1946-47.

MODEL 707 AUTOLOADER . . . **NiB $456 Ex $321 Gd $188**
Caliber: .22 WMR. Five-rnd. magazine. 22-in. bbl. Weight: 6.5 lbs. Sights: Folding leaf rear; blade front, on ramp. Monte Carlo-style stock of American walnut. Made 1977-86.

MODEL 707 DELUXE . . . . **NiB $508 Ex $381 Gd $285**
Same as Model 707 Standard except w/select custom polished and blued finish, select walnut stock, hand checkering, and no iron sights. Fitted w/H&R Model 432 4x scope. Made 1980-86.

Harrington & Richardson
Model 300

Harrington & Richardson
Model 360 Ultra

Harrington & Richardson
Model 700 Deluxe

Harrington & Richardson
Model 750 Pioneer

Harrington & Richardson
Ultra Varmint

RIFLES

MODEL 750 PIONEER BOLT-ACTION
SINGLE-SHOT RIFLE . . . . NiB $145 Ex $104 Gd $80
Caliber: .22 LR, Long, Short. 22- or 24-in. bbl. Weight: 5 lbs. Sights: Open rear; bead front. Plain pistol-grip stock. Made 1954-81; redesigned 1982; disc. 1985.

MODEL 751 SINGLE-SHOT RIFLE . . NiB $170 Ex $95 Gd $77
Same as Model 750 except w/Mannlicher-style stock. Made in 1971.

MODEL 755 SAHARA SINGLE-SHOT
RIFLE . . . . NiB $166 Ex $90 Gd $67
Blow-back action, automatic ejection. Caliber: .22 LR, Long, Short. 18-in. bbl. Weight: 4 lbs. Sights: Open rear; military-type front. Mannlicher-style stock. Made 1963-71.

MODEL 760 SINGLE-SHOT . . . . NiB $188 Ex $100 Gd $80
Same as Model 755 except w/conventional sporter stock. Made 1965-70.

MODEL 765 PIONEER BOLT-ACTION
SINGLE-SHOT RIFLE . . . . NiB $188 Ex $97 Gd $66
Caliber: .22 LR, Long, Short. 24-in. bbl. Weight: 5 lbs. Sights: Open rear; hooded bead front. Plain pistol-grip stock. Made 1948-54.

MODEL 800 LYNX AUTOLOADING
RIFLE . . . . NiB $407 Ex $224 Gd $119
Caliber: .22 LR. Five or 10-rnd. clip magazine. 22-in. bbl. Open sights. Weight: 6 lbs. Plain pistol-grip stock. Made 1958-60.

MODEL 852 FIELDSMAN BOLT-ACTION
REPEATER . . . . NiB $198 Ex $101 Gd $89
Caliber: .22 LR, Long, Short. Tubular magazine holds 21 Short, 17 Long, 15 LR. 24-in. bbl. Weight: 5.5 lbs. Sights: Open rear; bead front. Plain pistol-grip stock. Made 1952-53.

MODEL 865 PLAINSMAN BOLT-ACTION
REPEATER . . . . NiB $167 Ex $115 Gd $80
Caliber .22 LR, Long, Short. Five round detachable box magazine. 22- or 24-in. bbl. Weight: 5.25 lbs. Sights: Open rear, bead front. Plain pistol-grip stock. Made 1949-86.

MODEL 866
BOLT-ACTION REPEATER . . . . . . NiB $197 Ex $115 Gd $80
Same as Model 865, except w/Mannlicher-style stock. Made 1971.

MODEL 1873 100TH ANNIVERSARY (1871-1971)
COMMEMORATIVE OFFICER'S SPRINGFIELD
REPLICA . . . . NiB $866 Ex $659 Gd $475
Model 1873 "trap door" single-shot action. Engraved breech block, receiver, hammer, lock, band and buttplate. Caliber: .45-70. 26-in. bbl. Sights: Peep rear; blade front. Checkered walnut stock w/anniversary plaque. Ramrod. Weight: 8 lbs. 10,000 made in 1971.

MODEL 5200 SPORTER . . . . . . NiB $677 Ex $376 Gd $277
Turn-bolt repeater. Caliber: .22 LR. 24-in. bbl. Classic-style American walnut stock. Adj. trigger. Sights: Peep receiver; hooded ramp front. Weight: 6.5 lbs. Disc. 1983.

MODEL 5200 MATCH RIFLE . . NiB $590 Ex $495 Gd $368
Same action as 5200 Sporter. Caliber: .22 LR. 28-in. target weight bbl. Target stock of American walnut. Weight: 11 lbs. Made 1982-86.

CUSTER MEMORIAL ISSUE
Limited Edition Model 1873 Springfield Carbine replica, richly engraved and inlaid w/gold, fancy walnut stock, in mahogany display case. Made in 1973.
Officers' Model
    Limited to 25 pieces . . . NiB $4125 Ex $2990 Gd $12423
Enlisted Men's model,
    limited to 243 pieces . . . . NiB $2033 Ex $1021 Gd $690

TARGETEER JR. BOLT-ACTION
RIFLE . . . . NiB $227 Ex $177 Gd $145
Caliber: .22 LR. Five-rnd. detachable box magazine. 20-in. bbl. Weight: 7 lbs. Sights: Redfield 70 rear peep; Lyman No. 17A front. Target stock, junior-size w/pistol grip, swivels and sling. Made 1948-51.

NOTE: *The following models are manufactured and distributed by the reorganized company of H&R 1871, Inc.*

BUFFALO CLASSIC . . . . NIB $425 EX $370 GD $270
Similar to Handi-Rifle except .45 LC or .45-70. Barrel: 20- or 32-in. Sights: William rear, Lyman front. Finish: Color case hardened. Stock: Checkered walnut. Mfg. 1995-2018.

HANDI-GUN COMBINATION NIB $340 EX $300 GD $220
Similar to Handi-Rifle except w/rifle and shotgun barrels. Caliber: .22 Hornet, .223, .243, .30-30, .30-06 or .45-70 and 12 or 20 ga. Barrel: 22-in. Finish: Blue or nickel. Stock: Hardwood or synthetic. Mfg. 2008-13.

HANDI-RIFLE SERIES . . . . NIB $275 EX $240 GD $170
Side lever. Single shot. Automatic ejector. Caliber: .204 Ruger, .22-250, .223, .243, .25-06, .270, .280, 7mm-08, .30-30, .308, .30-06, .35 Whelen, .444 Marlin, .45-70 or .500 S&W. Barrel: 22- or 26-in., regular or heavy. Sights: Adj. iron, optic-ready. Weight: 7 lbs. Finish: Blued. Stock: Plain comb or Monte Carlo hardwood. Mfg. 2008-13.
Combo model (.243, .270 or .30-06 and 12
    or 20 ga.; 20-, 24- or 26-in. bbl., black
    synthetic stock, 2009-11) . . . . NiB $285 Ex $245 Gd $170
Compact model (.243 or 7mm-08, 22-in.
    bbl., hardwood stock, no sights,
    2008-13) . . . . NiB $275 Ex $240 Gd $170
Superlight model (.223 or .243,
    20- or 22-in. bbl., black
    synthetic stock, 2008-12) . . . . NiB $285 Ex $245 Gd $170
Synthetic model (.22 Hornet, .223, .243, .270,
    .30-06, .35 Whelen, .357 Mag., .44 Mag.,
    .444 Marlin, or .45-70, 22-in. bbl., black
    synthetic stock, 2008-14) . . . . NiB $285 Ex $245 Gd $170
Synthetic Compact model (.223 or .243,
    20- or 22-in. bbl., black synthetic stock,
    2008-14) . . . . NiB $285 Ex $245 Gd $170
Synthetic Hand-Grip model (.204 Ruger, .22-250,
    .223, .243, .25-06, .308 or .45-70; 22-, 24- or
    26-in. bbl., black synthetic thumbhole
    stock, 2010-13) . . . . NiB $295 Ex $250 Gd $175

Synthetic Stainless model
    (.270, 7mm Rem. Mag., .30-06 or
    .300 Win. Mag., 22- or 26-in.
    bbl., black synthetic stock,
    stainless finish, 2008) . . . . NiB $260 Ex $205 Gd $125

SPORTSTER . . . . NIB $180 EX $150 GD $105
Similar to Handi-Rifle except in .17 HMR, .17 Mach 2, .22 LR or .22 WMR. Barrel: Mid weight or heavy 20- or 22-in. Finish: Blue. Stock: Synthetic. Mfg. 1999-2013.

SURVIVOR . . . . NIB $280 EX $240 GD $405
Similar to Survivor shotgun except in .223 or .308. Barrel: Heavy 22- or 24-in. Finish: Blue. Stock: Synthetic thumbhole w/ammo storage compartment. Mfg. 2008-14.

TARGET RIFLE . . . . NIB $350 EX $285 GD $185
Similar to Handi-Rifle except .38-55 w/ 28-in. heavy bbl. Sights: Adj. target. Mfg. 1998-2007.

ULTRA HUNTER SERIES
Side-lever single-shot. Calibers: .22 WMR up to .45-70 Govt. Barrel: 22-, 24-, or 26-in. Weight: 7-8 lbs. Curly maple or laminated stock. Barrel-mounted scope mount, no sights. Made 1993-2013.
Standard model. . . . . NiB $330 Ex $280 Gd $260
Standard model (.45-70 Govt.) . . NiB $450 Ex $380 Gd $270
Comp model (.270 or .30-06, 23-in.
    bbl. w/compensator, laminate
    stock, 1997-2003) . . . . NiB $315 Ex $245 Gd $155
Rocky Mountain Elk Foundation 1st Edition
    (.280, 26-in. bbl., 1995-96) . . NiB $225 Ex $180 Gd $135
Rocky Mountain Elk Foundation
    2nd Edition (.35 Whelen,
    26-in. bbl., 1996-97) . . . . NiB $270 Ex $220 Gd $165
Varmint model (.204 Ruger,
    .22-250, .223, .243, .25-06 or .308;
    24-in. heavy fluted bbl., cinnamon laminate
    Monte Carlo or thumbhole or black synthetic
    stock, 1998-2013) . . . . NiB $335 Ex $280 Gd $215

HARRIS GUNWORKS — Englewood, CO
Formerly McMillan Gun Works in Phoenix, AZ. Sporting line of firearms discontinued, now specializes in custom competition and tactical arms.

BENCHREST COMPETITOR . . . NiB $2680 Ex $2430 Gd $1430
Bolt action. Various benchrest calibers. Made 1993–2000.

NATIONAL MATCH
COMPETITOR . . . . NiB $3130 Ex $2680 Gd $1655
Bolt action. Calibers: .308 Win. or 7mm-08. Made 1993–2000.

SIGNATURE ALASKAN . . . . NiB $3510 Ex $3108 Gd $2110
Same general specifications as Classic Sporter except w/match-grade bbl. Made 1990–2000.

SIGNATURE CLASSIC SPORTER
The prototype for Harris' Signature Series, this bolt-action rifle is available in three lengths: SA (standard/ short) — from .22-250 to .350 Rem Mag.; LA (long) — .25-06 to .30-06; MA (Magnum) — 7mm STW to .416 Rem. Mag. Four-rnd. or 3-rnd. (Magnum) magazine. Bbl. lengths: 22, 24 or 26 in. Weight: 7 lbs. (short action). No sights; rings and bases provided. Harris fiberglass stock, Fibergrain or wood stock optional. Stainless, matte black or black chrome sulfide finish. Available in right- and left-hand models.

Heckler & Koch
Model HK91 A-2

Heckler & Koch
Model HK940 Carbine

Heckler & Koch
Model HK PSG-1

Heckler & Koch
Model USC Carbine

Made 1988-2000. Disc. Has pre-64 Model 70-style action for dangerous game.

Classic Sporter, standard. . . NiB $2565 Ex $2347 Gd $1424
Classic Sporter, stainless . . . NiB $2565 Ex $2347 Gd $1424
Talon Sporter . . . . NiB $2613 Ex $2092 Gd $1474

**SIGNATURE TITANIUM MOUNTAIN
RIFLE. . . . .** NiB $3037 Ex $2977 Gd $1609
Same general specifications as Harris (McMillan) Classic Sporter except w/titanium action and graphite-reinforced fiberglass stock. Made 1995-2000.

**SIGNATURE
VARMINTER . . . .** NiB $2512 Ex $2233 Gd $1429
Same general specifications as Harris (McMillan) Classic Sporter except w/heavy, contoured bbl., adj. trigger, fiberglass stock and field bipod. Made 1988-2000.

TALON SAFARI
Same general specifications as Harris (McMillan) Classic Sporter except w/Harris Safari-grade action, match-grade bbl. and "Safari" fiberglass stock. Made 1988-2000.

Safari Magnum . . . . NiB $3809 Ex $3166 Gd $2179
Safari Super Magnum . . . . . NiB $4322 Ex $3561 Gd $2574

HECKLER & KOCH, GMBH — Oberndorf am Neckar, Germany.
Imported by Heckler & Koch, Inc., Sterling, VA.

G3. . . . . NiB $1970 Ex $1723 Gd $1019
Semiauto. Delayed roller block action. Commercial version of select-fire rifle Caliber: .308 (7.62mm). 20-rnd. magazine. 17.7-in. bbl. 40.4 in. overall. Sights: Hooded post front; adj. rotary diopter rear. Weight: 9 lbs. Stock: polymer. Imported 1962–1998.

**MODEL 911 SEMIAUTO
RIFLE. . . . .** NiB $1970 Ex $1723 Gd $1019
Caliber: .308 (7.62mm). Five-rnd. magazine. 19.7-in. bull bbl. 42.4 in. overall. Sights: Hooded post front; adj. aperture rear. Weight: 11 lbs. Kevlar-reinforced fiberglass thumbhole-stock. Imported 1989 to 1993.

GRADING: **NiB** = New in Box **Ex** = Excellent or NRA 95% **Gd** = Good or NRA 68%

MODEL HK91 A-2
SEMIAUTO . . . . **NiB $2634 Ex $2133 Gd $1388**
Delayed roller-locked blow-back action. Caliber: 7.62mmx51 NATO (308 Win.) 5- or 20-rnd. box magazine. 19-in. bbl. Weight: W/o magazine, 9.37 lbs. Sights L "V" and aperture rear, post front. Plastic buttstock and forearm. Disc. 1991.

MODEL HK91 A-3 . . . . **NiB $2721 Ex $2490 Gd $1665**
Same as Model HK91 A-2 except w/retractable metal buttstock, weighs 10.56 lbs. Disc. 1991.

MODEL HK93 SEMIAUTO
Delayed roller-locked blow-back action. Caliber: 5.56mmx45 (.223 Rem.). 5- or 20-rnd. magazine. 16.13-in. bbl. Weight: W/o magazine, 7.6 lbs. Sights: "V" and aperture rear; post front. Plastic buttstock and forearm. Disc. 1991.
HK93 A-2 . . . . **NiB $2835 Ex $2177 Gd $1198**
HK93 A-3 w/
retractable stock. . . . . **NiB $3590 Ex $2816 Gd $2021**

MODEL HK94
Semiauto. Caliber: 9mm Para. 15-rnd. magazine. 16-in. bbl. Weight: 6.75 lbs. Aperture rear sight, front post. Plastic buttstock and forend or retractable metal stock. Imported 1983 to 1991.
HK94-A2 w/standard stock NiB $4054 Ex $3209 Gd $2775
HK94-A3 w/retractable stock, add **20%**

MODEL HK300 . . . . **NiB $1423 Ex $955 Gd $600**
Semiauto. Caliber: .22 WMR. Five- or 15-rnd. box magazine. 19.7-in. bbl. w/polygonal rifling. Weight: 5.75 lbs. Sights: V-notch rear; ramp front. High-luster polishing and bluing. European walnut stock w/cheekpiece, checkered forearm and pistol-grip. Disc. 1989.

MODEL HK630 . . . . **NiB $1733 Ex $1277 Gd $1009**
Semiauto. Caliber: .223 Rem. Four- or 10-rnd. magazine. 24-in. bbl. Overall length: 42 in. Weight: 7 lbs. Sights: Open rear; ramp front. European walnut stock w/Monte Carlo cheekpiece. Imported from 1983 to 1990.

MODEL HK770 . . . . **NiB $2244 Ex $1703 Gd $1099**
Semiauto. Caliber: .308 Win. Three- or 10-rnd. magazine. Overall length: 44.5 in. Weight: 7.92 lbs. Sights: Open rear; ramp front. European walnut stock w/Monte Carlo cheekpiece. Imported from 1983 to 1986.

MODEL HK940 . . . . **NiB $2055 Ex $1833 Gd $1079**
Semiauto. Caliber: .30-06 Springfield. Three- or 10-rnd. magazine. Overall length: 47 in. Weight: 8.8 lbs. Sights: Open rear; ramp front. European walnut stock w/Monte Carlo cheekpiece. Imported from 1983 to 1986.

MODEL HK PSG-1
MARKSMAN'S RIFLE . . . **NiB $13,955 Ex $12,510 Gd $8510**
Caliber: .308 (7.62mm). Five- and 20-rnd. magazine. 25.6-in. bbl. 47.5 in. overall. Hensoldt 6x42 telescopic sight. Weight: 17.8 lbs. Matte black composite stock w/pistol-grip. Imported from 1988 to 1998.

MR556A1 . . . . **NiB $3000 Ex $2310 Gd $1710**
Semiauto AR15 platform. Action: gas piston system. Caliber: 5.56 NATO, 30-rnd. magazine. Heavy 16.5-in. bbl. w/muzzle brake. Sights: diopter. Finish: black anodized. Made 2009 to date.
Competition model (Magpul CTR stock,
2014-date) . . . . **NiB $2900 Ex $2555 Gd $1710**

MR762A1 . . . . **NiB $3600 Ex $2700 Gd $1950**
Semiauto AR15 platform. Action: gas piston system. Caliber: 7.62 NATO, 10- or 20-rnd. magazine. 16.5-in. bbl. w/muzzle brake. Sights: BUIS. Finish: black anodized. Made 2009 to date.

Long Range Package (Leupold 3-9x VX-R scope, adj. stock, LaRue bipod, 2009 to date), add **$2000**
Long Range Package II (Leupold 3-9x VX-R scope, adj. stock, LaRue bipod, 2009–date) . . . . **NiB $5755 Ex $5155 Gd $3510**

MODEL SL8-1 RIFLE . . . . **NiB $2006 Ex $1409 Gd $987**
Caliber: .223 Win. Ten-rnd. magazine. 20.80- in. bbl. 38.58 in. overall. Weight: 8.6 lbs. Gas-operated, short-stroke piston w/rotary locking bolt. Rear adjustable sight w/ambidextrous safety selector lever. Polymer receiver w/adjustable buttstock. Introduced in 1999.

SLB 2000 . . . . **NiB $1160 Ex $900 Gd $780**
Short stroke gas system. Semiauto. SA. Caliber: .308 Win. or .30-06, 2- 5- or 10-rnd. magazines. 19.68-in. bbl. Finish: matte black. Stock: checkered walnut. Weight: 7.25 lbs. Imp. from 2001 to 2003.

MODEL SR-9 . . . . **NiB $2130 Ex $1850 Gd $1044**
Semiauto. Caliber: .308 (7.62mm). Five round magazine. 19.7-in. bull bbl. 42.4 in. overall. Hooded post front sight; adj. aperture rear. Weight: 11 lbs. Kevlar-reinforced fiberglass thumbhole-stock w/wood grain finish. Imported from 1989 to 1993.

MODEL SR-9 TARGET RIFLE . . **NiB $2844 Ex $2166 Gd $1482**
Same general specifications as standard SR-9 except w/ PSG-1 trigger group and adj. buttstock. Imported from 1992 to 1994.

MODEL USC CARBINE RIFLE . . . **NiB $1675 Ex $1133 Gd $790**
Caliber: 45 ACP. 10-rnd. magazine. 16- in. bbl., 35.43 in. overall. Weight: 6 lbs. Blow-back operating system. Polymer receiver w/integral grips. Rear adjustable sight w/ambidextrous safety selector lever. Introduced in 1999.

HENRY REPEATING ARMS — Bayonne, NJ

MINI BOLT . . . . **NiB $260 Ex $215 Gd $90**
Caliber: .22 Short, LR. Single shot. 16.25-in. bbl. Stainless steel receiver, synthetic stock. Made 2002 to date.

ACU-BOLT . . . . **NiB $335 Ex $225 Gd $120**
Caliber: .17 HMR, .22 LR or .22 WMR. Single shot. 20-in. bbl. Stainless steel receiver, synthetic stock. Made 2004 to date.

LEVER ACTION . . . . **NiB $335 Ex $225 Gd $120**
Caliber: .17 HMR, .22 Short, Long, LR or .22 WMR. Lever action, 15-rnd. (.22 LR) tube magazine. 16.12-, 18.25-, 19.25-, or 20-in. rnd. or octagon bbl. Blued receiver, American walnut stock. Made 1997 to date.
Carbine Large Loop. . . . . **NiB $290 Ex $186 Gd $130**
Golden Boy (brass receiver) . . . **NiB $455 Ex $390 Gd $265**

"BIG BOY" LEVER ACTION . . . **NiB $790 Ex $655 Gd $405**
Caliber: .38 Special/.357 Mag., 17 HMR, .44 Special/.44 Mag. or .45 LC. Lever action, 10-rnd. tube magazine. 20-in. octagon bbl. Brass receiver, American walnut stock. Made 2003 to date. In 2020, steel frame rifles transitioned to both a tube loading port and side loading gate.
Deluxe II (hand engraved) . . **NiB $1725 Ex $1230 Gd $710**
All Weather model (matte chrome), add **$70**
Carbine model (16.5-in. bbl.,
2015–date) . . . . **NiB $790 Ex $655 Gd $405**
Deluxe Engraved 3rd Ed. model
(hand engraved, 2015–date) NiB $1655 Ex $1455 Gd $930
Silver model (aluminum receiver,
2016–date) . . . . **NiB $855 Ex $755 Gd $480**

Henry Repeating Arms Big Boy

**Heym
Model SR-20 Standard**

RIFLES

**Silver Deluxe Engraved model
(engraved aluminum receiver,
1,000 mfg., 2016–date)** . . . . **NiB $1610 Ex $1410 Gd $885**
**Steel model (matte blue steel receiver,
2015–date)** . . . . **NiB $755 Ex $680 Gd $480**
**X model (black polymer pistol grip stock,
fiber optic sights, 2019–date)** . **NiB $870 Ex $810 Gd $650**

.30-30 LEVER ACTION . . . . **NiB $750 Ex $680 Gd $480**
Caliber: .30-30 Win. Lever action, 6-rnd. tube magazine.
20-in. rnd. or octagon bbl. Blued receiver, American walnut
stock. Made 2008 to date.
Brass receiver/octagon bbl., add. **$100**
case hardened model, add **$100**
All Weather model (matte chrome), add **$100**

LONG RANGER . . . . **NiB $980 Ex $860 Gd $680**
Lever action w/6-lug rotary head. Caliber: .223 Rem., .243
Win., 6.5 Creedmoor or .308 Win.; 4- or 5-rnd. detachable
magazine. Barrel: 20- or 22-in. free float w/ or w/o sights.
Finish: Blued. Stock: American walnut straight pistol grip w/
rubber butt pad. Made 2016–date.
**Deluxe Engraved model (engraved
receiver, 2018-date)** . . . . . . **NiB $1680 Ex $1470 Gd $1145**
**Express model (5.56 NATO, 16.5-in.
threaded bbl., 2022-date)** . . . **NiB $1235 Ex $1000 Gd $890**

NEW ORIGINAL HENRY . . . . . . **NiB $2055 Ex $1780 Gd $1130**
Similar to lever action Henry Model 1860. Caliber: .44-40 or
.45 LC; 13-rnd. tubular magazine. Barrel: 24-in. w/ folding
ladder rear, blade front sights. Finish: Blued bbl., brass receiver.
Stock: American walnut straight pistol grip w/brass crescent
butt pad. Weight: 9 lbs. Made 2014–date.
**Deluxe Engraved 1st Ed. model
(scroll engraved receiver, 1,000 mfg. 2014)** **NiB $3155 Ex
$2755 Gd $1755**
**Deluxe Engraved 2nd Ed. model (scroll engraved receiver,
1,000 mfg. 2017)** . . . . **NiB $3155 Ex $2755 Gd $1755**
**Deluxe Engraved 3rd Ed. model (scroll engraved receiver,
1,000 mfg. 2019)** . . . **NiB $3155 Ex $2755 Gd $1755**
Iron Frame model (steel receiver, .44-40, 2016–date) . . . **NiB
$2355 Ex $2010 Gd $1310**
**Rare Carbine model (brass receiver, .44-40, 20.5-in. bbl.,
2016–date)** . . . . **NiB $2010 Ex $1780 Gd $1130**
**Silver Deluxe Engraved model (scroll engraved nickel receiv-
er, 1,000 mfg. 2019)** . . . . **NiB $3155 Ex $2755 Gd $1755**

.45-70 LEVER ACTION . . . . **NiB $755 EX $680 GD $480**
Caliber: .45-70. Barrel: 18.5 in., optic ready w'sights; 4-rnd. tube
magazine. Blued receiver. Stock: pistol grip American walnut stock.
Brass receiver/octagon bbl., add. **$75**
case hardened model, add **$100**
All Weather model (matte chrome), add **$100**

PUMP ACTION. . . . . **NiB $335 Ex $225 Gd $120**
Caliber: .22 Short, Long, LR or .22 WMR. Pump action, 16-rnd.
(.22 LR) tube magazine. 18.25- or 20.5-in. rnd. bbl. Blued
receiver, American walnut stock. Made 1999 to date.

SIDE GATE SERIES . . . . **NiB $977 Ex $880 Gd $730**
Similar to .30-30 and .45-70 series of lever action rifles except w/
side loading gate in addition to tube loading slot. Caliber: .38-55,
.30-30, .35 Rem. or .45-70; 4- or 5-rnd. tubular magazine. Barrel:
20-in. rnd. Finish: Blued bbl., brass receiver. Stock: American
walnut straight pistol grip w/brass butt pad. Made 2019–date.
**X model (black polymer pistol grip stock, fiber optic sights,
2019-date)** . . . . **NiB $870 Ex $810 Gd $650**

SINGLE SHOT SERIES . . . . **NiB $380 Ex $340 Gd $240**
Break action with exposed manual hammer. Caliber: .223 Rem.,
.243 Win., .44 Mag., .30-30, .357 Mag., .45-70 or .308 Win.
Barrel: 22-in. rnd. Finish: Blued bbl., brass or blued receiver.
Stock: American walnut straight or pistol grip w/brass or rubber
butt pad. Sights: open and optic ready. Made 2017–date.

U.S. SURVIVAL .22 . . . . **NiB $225 Ex $170 Gd $115**
Similar to Armalite AR-7 takedown rifle. Caliber: .22 LR.
Semiauto action, 8-rnd. magazine. Made 1997 to date.

HEROLD — Suhl, Germany

Made by Franz Jaeger & Company.

**BOLT-ACTION REPEATING
SPORTING RIFLE** . . . . **NiB $1044 Ex $800 Gd $634**
"Herold-Repetierbüchse." Miniature Mauser-type action w/
unique 5-rnd. box magazine on hinged floorplate. Double-set
triggers. Caliber: .22 Hornet. 24-in. bbl. Sights: Leaf rear; ramp
front. Weight: 7.75 lbs. Fancy checkered stock. Made before
WWII. Note: These rifles were imported by Charles Daly and
A.F. Stoeger Inc. of New York City and sold under their names.

HEYM RIFLES AMERICA, INC. — Germany

*Manufactured by Heym, GmbH & Co JAGWAFFEN KD.,
Gleichamberg, Germany (previously imported by Heym
America, Inc.; Heckler & Koch; JagerSport, Ltd.)*

MODEL 55B DOUBLE RIFLE
Kersten boxlock action w/double cross bolt and cocking indica-
tors. Calibers: .308 Win., .30-06, .375 H&H, .458 Win. Mag.,
.470 N.E. 25-in. bbl. 42 in. overall. Weight: 8.25 lbs. Sights: fixed
V-type rear; front ramp w/silver bead. Engraved receiver w/option-
al sidelocks, interchangeable bbls. and claw mounts. Checkered
European walnut stock. Imported from Germany.
Model 55 (boxlock) . . . . . . **NiB $6677 Ex $6488 Gd $5745**
Model 55 (sidelock) . . . . . . **NiB $9544 Ex $7890 Gd $6791**
w/extra rifle bbls., add **$6000**

w/extra shotgun bbls., add $3000

MODEL 88B DOUBLE RIFLE
Modified Anson & Deeley boxlock action w/standing gears, double underlocking lugs and Greener extension w/crossbolt. Calibers: 8x57 JRS, 9.3x74R, .30-06, .375 H&H, .458 Win. Mag., .470 Nitro Express, .500 Nitro Express. Other calibers available on special order. Weight: 8 to 10 lbs. Top tang safety and cocking indicators. Double triggers w/front set. Fixed or 3-leaf express rear sight, front ramp w/silver bead. Engraved receiver w/optional sidelocks. Checkered French walnut stock. Imported from Germany.
Model 88B Boxlock . . . . . **NiB $11,669 Ex $8875 Gd $6067**
Model 88B/SS Sidelock . . . **NiB $15,538 Ex $10,850 Gd $7410**
Model 88B Safari (Magnum) . . . **NiB $15,038 Ex $12,050 Gd $8226**

EXPRESS BOLT-ACTION RIFLE
Same general specifications as Model SR-20 Safari except w/modified magnum Mauser action. Checkered AAA-grade European walnut stock w/cheekpiece, solid rubber recoil pad, rosewood forend tip and grip cap. Calibers: .338 Lapua Magnum, .375 H&H, .378 Wby. Mag., .416 Rigby .450 Ackley, .460 Wby. Mag., .500 A-Square, .500 Nitro Express, .600 Nitro Express. Other calibers available on special order, but no change in used gun value. Imported from Germany 1989 to 1995.
Standard Express Magnum . **NiB $5644 Ex $4490 Gd $3230**
600 Nitro Express . . . . **NiB $5895 Ex $5133 Gd $3190**
Left-hand models, add $750

SR-20 BOLT-ACTION RIFLE
Calibers: .243 Win., .270 Win., .308 Win., .30-06, 7mm Rem. Mag., .300 Win. Mag., .375 H&H. Five round (standard) or 3-rnd. (Magnum) magazine. Bbl. length: 20.5-in. (SR-20L); 24-in. (SR-20N); 26-in. (SR-20G). Weight: 7.75 lbs. Adj. rear sight, blade front. Checkered French walnut stock in Monte Carlo style (N&G Series) or full Mannlicher (L Series). Imported from Germany. Disc. 1992.
SR-20L . . . . **NiB $2316 Ex $1832 Gd $1209**
SR-20N . . . . **NiB $2279 Ex $1856 Gd $1200**
SR-20G . . . . **NiB $2865 Ex $2379 Gd $1600**

SR-20 CLASSIC BOLT-ACTION RIFLES
Same as SR-20 except w/.22-250 and .338 Win. Mag. plus metric calibers on request. 24-in. (standard) or 25-in. (Magnum) bbl. Checkered French walnut stock. Left-hand models. Imported from Germany since 1985; Sporter version 1989 to 1993.
Classic (Standard) . . . . **NiB $1860 Ex $1875 Gd $1423**
Classic (Magnum) . . . . **NiB $2355 Ex $2216 Gd $1466**
Classic Sporter (Std.
   w/22-in. bbl.) . . . . **NiB $2556 Ex $2203 Gd $1499**
Classic Sporter (Mag.
   w/24-in. bbl.) . . . . **NiB $1899 Ex $2288 Gd $1633**
Left-hand models, add $350

SR-20 ALPINE, SAFARI AND TROPHY SERIES
Same general specifications as Model SR-20 Classic Sporter except Alpine Series w/20-in. bbl., Mannlicher stock, chambered in standard calibers only; Safari Series w/24-in. bbl., 3-leaf express sights and magnum action in calibers .375 H & H, .404 Jeffrey, .425 Express, .458 Win. Mag.; Trophy Series w/Krupp-Special tapered octagon bbl. w/quarter rib and open sights, standard and Magnum calibers. Imported from Germany from 1989 to 1993.
Alpine Series . . . . **NiB $1969 Ex $1812 Gd $1492**
Safari Series . . . . **NiB $2308 Ex $2177 Gd $1545**
Trophy Series (Stand. calibers) . . **NiB $2589 Ex $2115 Gd $1904**
Trophy Series
   (Magnum calibers) . . . . **NiB $2733 Ex $2118 Gd $1944**

J.C. HIGGINS RIFLES
See Sears, Roebuck & Company.

HI-POINT FIREARMS — Dayton, OH

CARBINE SERIES
Semiauto recoil-operated carbine. Calibers: 9mm Parabellum or 40 S&W. 10-rnd. magazine. 16.5-in. bbl. 31.5 in. overall. Protected post front sight, aperture rear w/integral scope mount. Matte blue, chrome or Parkerized finish. Checkered polymer grip/frame. Made 1996 to date.
Model 995 TS, 9mm
   (blue or Parkerized) . . . . **NiB $290 Ex $255 Gd $205**
Model 409TS, .40 S&W
   (blue or Parkerized) . . . . **NiB $295 Ex $265 Gd $215**
w/laser sights, add $50
Model 459TS, (.45 Auto,
   black, 2011-date) . . . . **NiB $300 Ex $275 Gd $225**
Model 389TS, (.380 Auto,
   black, 2016-date) . . . . **NiB $290 Ex $255 Gd $205**
Model 1095TS, (.45 Auto,
   black, 2011-date) . . . . **NiB $300 Ex $275 Gd $225**
w/camo finish, add $25

Hi-Point Model 995 TS

HIGH STANDARD SPORTING FIREARMS — East Hartford, CT
Formerly High Standard Mfg. Co., Hamden, CT. A long-standing producer of sporting arms, High Standard discontinued its operations in 1984.

SPORT-KING PUMP RIFLE . . . . . **NiB $207 Ex $144 Gd $98**
Hammerless slide-action. Caliber: .22 LR, .22 Long, .22 Short. Tubular mag. holds 17 LR, 19 Long, or 24 Short. 24-in. bbl. Weight: 5.5 lbs. Sights: Partridge rear; bead front. Monte Carlo stock w/pistol grip, serrated semibeavertail forearm. Made 1963-76.

HI-POWER DELUXE RIFLE . . . . **NiB $475 Ex $315 Gd $221**
Mauser-type bolt action, sliding safety. Calibers: .270, .30-06. Four round magazine. 22-in. bbl. Weight: 7 lbs. Sights: Folding open rear; ramp front. Walnut stock w/checkered pistol-grip and forearm, Monte Carlo comb, QD swivels. Made 1962-65.

HI-POWER FIELD . . . . **NiB $255 Ex $179 Gd $126**
Same as Hi-Power Deluxe except w/plain field style stock. Made 1962-66.

SPORT-KING CARBINE . . . . **NiB $379 Ex $318 Gd $200**
Same as Sport-King Field Autoloader except w/18.25-in. bbl., Western-style straight-grip stock w/bbl. band, sling and swivels. Made 1964-73.

SPORT-KING DELUXE
AUTOLOADER . . . . **NiB $280 Ex $213 Gd $100**
Same as Sport-King Special Autoloader except w/checkered stock. Made 1966-75.

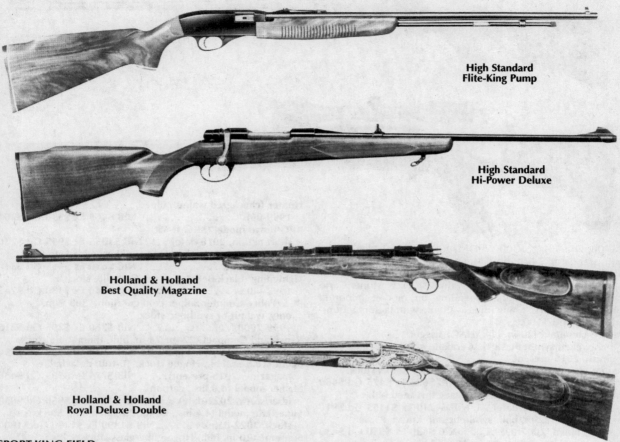

High Standard
Flite-King Pump

High Standard
Hi-Power Deluxe

Holland & Holland
Best Quality Magazine

Holland & Holland
Royal Deluxe Double

SPORT-KING FIELD
AUTOLOADER . . . . **NiB $229 Ex $130 Gd $90**
Calibers: .22 LR, .22 Long, .22 Short (high speed). Tubular magazine holds 15 LR, 17 Long, or 21 Short. 22.25-in. bbl. Weight: 5.5 lbs. Sights: Open rear; beaded post front. Plain pistol-grip stock. Made 1960-66.

SPORT-KING SPECIAL
AUTOLOADER . . . . **NiB $210 Ex $166 Gd $106**
Same as Sport-King Field except stock w/Monte Carlo comb and semibeavertail forearm. Made 1960-66.

HOLLAND & HOLLAND, LTD. — London, England
Imported by Holland & Holland, New York, NY.

NO. 2 MODEL HAMMERLESS EJECTOR
DOUBLE RIFLE . . . . . **NiB $15,650 Ex $12,800 Gd $10,770**
Same general specifications as Royal Model except plainer finish. Disc. 1960.

BEST QUALITY MAGAZINE
RIFLE . . . . **NiB $15,300 Ex $12,000 Gd $9890**
Mauser or Enfield action. Calibers: .240 Apex, .300 H&H Mag., .375 H&H Magnum. Four round box magazine. 24-in. bbl. Weight: 7.25 lbs., 240 Apex; 8.25 lbs., .300 Mag. and .375 Mag. Sights: Folding leaf rear; hooded ramp front. Detachable French walnut stock w/cheekpiece, checkered pistol-grip and forearm, swivels. Currently mfd. Specifications given apply to most models.

DE LUXE MAGAZINE
RIFLE . . . . **NiB $16,780 Ex $13,966 Gd $9566**
Same specifications as Best Quality except w/exhibition-grade stock and special engraving. Currently mfd.

ROYAL HAMMERLESS
EJECTOR RIFLE . . . . . **NiB $43,000 Ex $33,900 Gd $24,775**
Sidelock. Calibers: .240 Apex, 7mm H&H Mag., .300 H&H Mag., .300 Win. Mag., .30-06, .375 H&H Mag., .458 Win. Mag., .465 H&H Mag. 24- to 28-in. bbls. Weight: From 7.5 lbs. Sights: Folding leaf rear, ramp front. Cheekpiece stock of select French walnut, checkered pistol-grip and forearm. Currently mfd. Same general specifications apply to prewar model.

ROYAL DELUXE DOUBLE
RIFLE . . . . **NiB $57,956 Ex $47,888 Gd $32,600**
Formerly designated "Modele Deluxe." Same specifications as Royal Model except w/exhibition-grade stock and special engraving. Currently mfd.

HOWA — Tokyo, Japan
Imported by Legacy Sports Int., Reno, NV. See also Mossberg (1500) Smith & Wesson (1500 & 1707) and Weatherby (Vanguard).

MODEL 1500 SERIES
Bolt action. Calibers: .22-250, .204 Ruger, .223, .243 Win., 6.5 Creedmoor, 6.5x55mm, .25-06, .270 Win., .308 Win.,

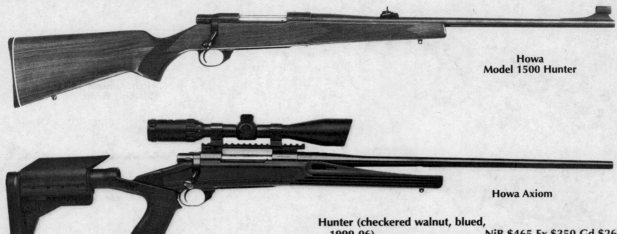

Howa Model 1500 Hunter

Howa Axiom

.30-06, 7mm Mag., .300 Win. Mag.,. .338 Win. Mag. 22-in. bbl. (standard); 24-in. bbl. (Magnum). 42.5 in. overall (standard). Weight: 7.5 lbs. Adj. rear sight hooded ramp front or optic ready. Stock: Checkered walnut stock w/Monte Carlo cheekpiece or synthetic depending on model. Imported since 1988. NOTE: Many rifles available with factory mounted scope, add $100.

Alpine Mountain (20-in. bbl., HACT trigger, lightweight synthetic stock, Cerakote gray finish, 2015-present. . . . . . . NiB $1000 Ex $730 Gd $530

Axiom Standard (22-in. bbl., synthetic adj. Knoxx stock, blued or stainless, 2007-09) . . NiB $630 Ex $475 Gd $480

APC model (aluminum chassis, heavy threaded bbl., 10.5-12 lbs., 2018-date) . . . NiB $1310 Ex $1155 Gd $910

Axiom model (22-in. bbl., synthetic adj. Knoxx stock, blued, 2007-09) . . . . . . NiB $630 Ex $550 Gd $430

Axiom Varminter (20- or 24-in. heavy bbl., synthetic adj. Knoxx stock, blued or stainless, 2007-14) . . . . NiB $775 Ex $585 Gd $430

Classic Laminate Varminter (laminate standard or thumbhole stock, 24-in. bbl., 2012-16) . . . NiB $730 Ex $530 Gd $380

Custom (22- or 24-in. bbl.,synthetic or laminate stock, blued or stainless, 2002-04) . . NiB $775 Ex $585 Gd $430

Elevate model (4.3 lbs., carbon fiber wrapped bbl./stock, 2022-date) . . . . NiB $1640 Ex $1570 Gd $1000

Foxy Woods model (pink camo synthetic stock, 2015-17) . . . . NiB $565 Ex $495 Gd $385

Full Dip model (full camo finish, 2019-date) . . . . NiB $770 Ex $680 Gd $530

Gameking model (short or long action, disc. 2018). . . . . NiB $600 Ex $530 Gd $410

GRS model (GRS Berserk stock, disc. 2018) . . . . NiB $1155 Ex $930 Gd $710

HCR (short action, aluminum chassis stock, HACT trigger, various Cerakote finishes, 2016-present) . . . . NiB $1155 Ex $805 Gd $605

HS Precision model (kevlar/fiberglass stock, short or long action, 2018-date) . . . NiB $930 Ex $830 Gd $630

Hogue (Hogue Overmold stock, various stock finishes, 2007-present) . . . . NiB $530 Ex $400 Gd $285

Hogue Heavy Barrel Varminter (Hogue Overmold stock, various stock finishes) . . . . NiB $600 Ex $455 Gd $330

Hogue Kryptek (Hogue Overmold stock w/Kryptek camo, 2014-present) . . . . NiB $610 Ex $465 Gd $340

Hogue Stainless (Hogue Overmold stock, various stock finishes, 2007-15) . . . . NiB $600 Ex $455 Gd $330

Hogue Youth (Hogue Overmold youth stock, various stock finishes, 2009-present) . . . . . . NiB $565 Ex $455 Gd $330

Hunter (checkered walnut, blued, 1999-06) . . . . NiB $465 Ex $350 Gd $260

KRG Bravo model (KRG stock, short action, 2018-date) . . . . NiB $1055 Ex $955 Gd $730

Kuiu (short or long action, Hogue pillar bedded stock, 2017-present) . . . . NiB $610 Ex $465 Gd $340

Lightening (black Bell & Carlson Carbelite stock, 1993-08) . . . . NiB $440 Ex $330 Gd $245

PCS (Police Counter Sniper configuration, .308 Win. only, walnut or synthetic stock, 1999-2000) . . . . NiB $380 Ex $295 Gd $215

Ranchland Compact (22- or 24-in. bbl., thumbhole stock, blued or stainless, 2003-present) . NiB $520 Ex $390 Gd $290

Scout (18.5-in. bbl., Hogue stock, 10-rnd. detachable magazine, 2016-present) . . . . . NiB $775 Ex $585 Gd $430

Stalker model (4.6 lbs., carbon fiber stock, 2022-date) . . . . . NiB $1030 Ex $960 Gd $850

Super Lite model (4.4 lbs., 20-in. threaded bbl., Stocky's stock, 2022-date). . . . . . . NiB $1399 Ex $1290 Gd $1000

Supreme (20-in. bbl., Hogue fiberglass stock, 7 lbs., 2008-present) . . . . NiB $565 Ex $425 Gd $315

Texas Safari (recountoured bolt sleeve, brown laminated stock, blue teflon finish, 2002-03) . . . . NiB $1355 Ex $1015 Gd $745

Talon Thumbhole Varminter (20-, 22- or 24-in. standard or heavy bbl., synthetic Axiom stock, 2010-16) . . . . NiB $715 Ex $530 Gd $380

Trophy (22- or 24-in. bbl., adj. sights, Monte Carlo stock, 1988-92) . . . . NiB $530 Ex $400 Gd $295

Ultralight (laminated wood stock, blued or stainless, 2002-08) . . . . NiB $490 Ex $370 Gd $270

Varmint (24-in. heavy bbl., synthetic or wood stock, blued or stainless, 2001-06) . . NiB $455 Ex $340 Gd $250

Magnum calibers, add. $20

Stainless models, add $30

Full dip camo models, add $100

MODEL 1500 MINI ACTION SERIES

Same general specifications as Model 1500 rifles, except w/ chambered in 6MM ARC, .223 Rem., 6.5 Grendel, .330 BLK, 7.62×39, or 350 Legend; 5- or 10-rnd detachable magazine. Bbl.: 16.5 or 20-in. threaded. Stock: HTI synthetic, pillar-bedded or aluminum chassis. Made 2015 to date.

HTI stock . . . . NiB $455 Ex $380 Gd $310

chassis stock . . . . NiB $1010 Ex $870 Gd $655

EXCL Light model (EXCL Lite chassis, Luth-AR adj. stock, 2019-date) . . NiB $500 Ex $455 Gd $360

Lightweight model (20-in. lightweight bbl., 5.7 lbs., 2015-date). . . . . . . NiB $500 Ex $455 Gd $360

Lightweight model (20-in. heavy bbl., 7.1 lbs., 2015-date). . . . . . . NiB $545 Ex $480 Gd $380

H-S PRECISION — Rapid City, SD

PRO-SERIES
Custom rifle built on Remington 707 bolt action. Calibers: .22 to .416, 24- or 26-in. bbl. w/fluted option. Aluminum bedding block system w/take-down option. Kevlar/carbon fiber stock to customer's specifications. Appointments and options to customer's preference. Made 1990 to date.

Sporter model . . . . NiB $2180 Ex $1830 Gd $1100
Pro-Hunter model (PHR) . . NiB $2866 Ex $2033 Gd $1108
Long-Range Model . . . . NiB $4597 Ex $3766 Gd $2080
Long-Range takedown
  model . . . . NiB $2355 Ex $1944 Gd $1390
Marksman model . . . . NiB $2966 Ex $1830 Gd $1106
Marksman takedown model NiB $2977 Ex $2133 Gd $1490
Varmint takedown model
  (VTD) . . . . NiB $4369 Ex $2835 Gd $2000
Left-hand models, add $227

HUNGARIAN MILITARY — Budapest, Hungary
Manufactured at government arsenal.

MODEL 1935M MANNLICHER
MILITARY RIFLE . . . . NiB $370 Ex $287 Gd $186
Caliber: 8x52mm Hungarian. Bolt action, straight handle. Five round projecting box magazine. 24-in. bbl. Weight: 9 lbs. Adj. leaf rear sight, hooded front blade. Two-piece military-type stock. Made 1935-40.

MODEL 1943M (GERMAN GEW 98/40) MANNLICHER
MILITARY RIFLE . . . . NiB $388 Ex $322 Gd $200
Modification, during German occupation, of Model 1935M. Caliber: 7.9mm Mauser. Turned-down bolt handle and Mauser M/98-type box magazine; other differences are minor. Made 1940 to end of war in Europe.

HUSQVARNA VAPENFABRIK A.B. — Husqvarna, Sweden

MODEL 456 LIGHTWEIGHT
FULL-STOCK SPORTER . . . . NiB $713 Ex $466 Gd $339
Same as Series 4000/4100 except w/sporting style full stock w/ slope-away cheekrest. Weight: 6.5 lbs. Made 1959-70.

SERIES 1000 SUPER GRADE . . . NiB $572 Ex $479 Gd $339
Same as 1951 Hi-Power except w/European walnut sporter stock w/Monte Carlo comb and cheekpiece. Made 1952-56.

SERIES 1100 DELUXE MODEL HI-POWER BOLT-ACTION
SPORTING RIFLE . . . . NiB $557 Ex $468 Gd $339
Same as 1951 Hi-Power, except w/jeweled bolt, European walnut stock. Made 1952-56.

1950 HI-POWER SPORTING RIFLE . . . NiB $554 Ex $415 Gd $300
Mauser-type bolt action. Calibers: .220 Swift, .270 Win. .30-06 (see note below), 5-rnd. box magazine. 23.75-in. bbl. Weight: 7.75 lbs. Sights: Open rear; hooded ramp front. Sporting stock of Arctic beech, checkered pistol grip and forearm, swivels. Note: Husqvarna sporters were first intro. in U.S. about 1948; earlier models were also available in calibers 6.5x55, 8x57 and 9.3x57. Made 1946-51.

1951 HI-POWER RIFLE . . . . NiB $554 Ex $415 Gd $300
Same as 1950 Hi-Power except w/high-comb stock, low safety.

SERIES 3000 CROWN GRADE . NiB $643 Ex $455 Gd $300
Same as Series 3100, except w/Monte Carlo comb stock.

SERIES 3100 CROWN GRADE . NiB $643 Ex $455 Gd $300
HVA improved Mauser action. Calibers: .243, .270, 7mm, .30-06, .308 Win. Five round box magazine. 23.75-in. bbl. Weight: 7.75 lbs. Sights: Open rear; hooded ramp front. European walnut stock, checkered, cheekpiece, pistol-grip cap, black forend tip, swivels. Made 1954-72.

SERIES 4000 LIGHTWEIGHT RIFLE . . . NiB $699 Ex $433 Gd $297
Same as Series 4100 except w/Monte Carlo comb stock and no rear sight.

SERIES 4100 LIGHTWEIGHT RIFLE . . NiB $616 Ex $423 Gd $260
HVA improved Mauser action. Calibers: .243, .270, 7mm, .30-06, .308 Win. Five round box magazine. 20.5-in. bbl. Weight: 6.25 lbs. Sights: Open rear; hooded ramp front. Lightweight walnut stock w/cheekpiece, pistol grip, Schnabel forend tip, checkered, swivels. Made 1954-72.

SERIES 6000 IMPERIAL CUSTOM
GRADE . . . . NiB $877 Ex $633 Gd $409
Same as Series 3100 except fancy-grade stock, 3-leaf folding rear sight, adj. trigger. Calibers: .243, .270, 7mm Rem. Mag. .308, .30-06. Made 1968-70.

SERIES 7070 IMPERIAL MONTE
CARLO LIGHTWEIGHT . . . . . . NiB $920 Ex $577 Gd $400
Same as Series 4000 Lightweight except fancy-grade stock, 3-leaf folding rear sight, adj. trigger. Calibers: .243, .270, .308, .30-06. Made 1968-70.

SERIES 8000 IMPERIAL GRADE . . . . NiB $831 Ex $569 Gd $389
Same as Model 9000 except w/jeweled bolt, engraved floorplate, deluxe French walnut checkered stock, no sights. Made 1971-72.

SERIES 9000 CROWN GRADE . . . . NiB $633 Ex $459 Gd $348
New design Husqvarna bolt action. Adj. trigger. Calibers: .270, 7mm Rem. Mag., .30-06, .300 Win. Mag. Five round box magazine, hinged floorplate. 23.75-in. bbl. Sights: Folding leaf rear; hooded ramp front. Checkered walnut stock w/Monte Carlo cheekpiece, rosewood forend tip and pistol-grip cap. Weight: 7 lbs. 3 oz. Made 1971-72.

SERIES P-3000 PRESENTATION . . . NiB $1179 Ex $889 Gd $627
Same as Crown Grade Series 3000 except w/selected stock, engraved action, adj. trigger. Calibers: .243, .270, 7mm Rem. Mag., .30-06. Made 1968-70.

INLAND MANUFACTURING — Dayton, OH

M1 CARBINE
Similar to U.S. M1 Carbine. Caliber: .30 U.S. Carbine. 15- or 30-rnd. magazine. 18-in. bbl. 35.75 in. overall. Weight: 5.2 lbs. Sights: blade front, w/guards; adj. peep rear. Parkerized finish. Made 2014 to present.
1944 model (low wood walnut stock,
  no bayonet lug) . . . . NiB $1139 Ex $900 Gd $800
1944 model (low wood walnut stock,
  w/bayonet lug) . . . . NiB $1139 Ex $900 Gd $800

RIFLES

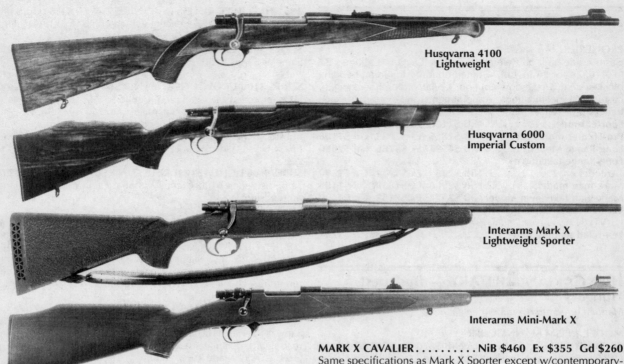

Husqvarna 4100
Lightweight

Husqvarna 6000
Imperial Custom

Interarms Mark X
Lightweight Sporter

Interarms Mini-Mark X

Jungle model (low wood walnut stock, no bayonet lug,
   flash hider) . . . . NiB $1159 Ex $905 Gd $805
Scout model (polymer/textured wood stock,
   aluminum picatinny handguard,
   flash hider) . . . . NiB $1295 Ex $1000 Gd $900
M1A Paratrooper (collapsible wire stock,
   no bayonet lug) . . . . NiB $1279 Ex $1000 Gd $900

INTERARMS — Alexandria, VA

The following Mark X rifles are manufactured by Zavodi Crvena Zastava, Belgrade, Yugoslavia.

MARK X ALASKAN . . . . NiB $708 Ex $447 Gd $321
Same specs as Mark X Sporter, except chambered for .375 H&H Mag. and .458 Win. Mag. w/3-rnd. magazine. Stock w/ recoil-absorbing cross bolt and heavy duty recoil pad. Weighs 8.25 lbs. Made 1976-84.

MARK X BOLT-ACTION SPORTER SERIES
Mauser-type action. Calibers: .22-250, .243, .25-06, .270, 7x57, 7mm Rem. Mag., .308, .30-06, .300 Win. Mag. Five round magazine (3-rnd. in magnum calibers). 24-in. bbl. Weight: 7.5 lbs. Sights: Adj. leaf rear; ramp front, w/hood. Classic-style stock of European walnut w/Monte Carlo comb and cheekpiece, checkered pistol grip and forearm, black forend tip, QD swivels. Made 1972-97.
Mark X Standard . . . . NiB $479 Ex $355 Gd $260
Mark X Camo (Realtree) . . . . . . NiB $499 Ex $440 Gd $327
American Field, std.
   (rubber recoil pad) . . . . NiB $570 Ex $460 Gd $368
American Field, Magnum
   (rubber recoil pad) . . . . NiB $689 Ex $572 Gd $408

MARK X CAVALIER . . . . NiB $460 Ex $355 Gd $260
Same specifications as Mark X Sporter except w/contemporary-style stock w/rollover cheekpiece, rosewood forend tip/grip cap, recoil pad. Intro. 1974; Disc.

**MARK X CONTINENTAL MANNLICHER
STYLE CARBINE** . . . . NiB $643 Ex $412 Gd $277
Same specifications as Mark X Sporter except straight European-style comb stock w/sculptured cheekpiece. Precise double-set triggers and classic "butterknife" bolt handle. French checkering. Weight: 7.25 lbs. Disc.

MARK X LIGHTWEIGHT SPORTER . . . NiB $445 Ex $355 Gd $260
Calibers: .22-250 Rem., .270 Win., 7mm Rem. Mag., .30-06 or 7mm Mag. Four- or 5-rnd. magazine. 20-in. bbl. Synthetic Carbolite stock. Weight: 7 lbs. Imported from 1988-90. Reintro. 1994-97.

**MARK X MARQUIS MANNLICHER-STYLE
CARBINE** . . . . NiB $575 Ex $408 Gd $290
Same specifications as Mark X Sporter except w/20-in. bbl., full-length Mannlicher-type stock w/metal forend/muzzle cap. Calibers: .270, 7x57, .308, .30-06. Imported 1976 to 1984.

MINI-MARK X BOLT-ACTION RIFLE . . . NiB $448 Ex $359 Gd $260
Miniature M98 Mauser action. Caliber: .223 Rem. Five round magazine. 20-in. bbl. 39.75 in. overall. Weight: 6.25 lbs. Adj. rear sight, hooded ramp front. Checkered hardwood stock. Imported from 1987 to 1994.

MARK X VISCOUNT . . . . NiB $440 Ex $368 Gd $258
Same specifications as Mark X Sporter except w/plainer field grade stock. Imported from 1974 to 1987.

WHITWORTH EXPRESS SERIES . . . . . NiB $1035 Ex $603 Gd $422
Mauser-type bolt-action. Calibers: .375 H&H Mag., .458 Win. Mag. Three round magazine. 24-in. bbl. Weight: 8 lbs. Sights: 3-leaf express open rear, ramp front w/hood. English-style stock of European walnut, w/cheekpiece, black forend tip, checkered pistol grip and forearm, recoil pad, QD swivels. Imported from 1974 to 1996 by Whitworth Rifle Co., England.

ITALIAN MILITARY — Italy

Manufactured by government plants at Brescia, Gardone, Terni, and Turin, Italy.

MODEL 38 MILITARY RIFLE.... NiB $167 Ex $120 Gd $85
Modification of Italian Model 1891 Mannlicher-Carcano Military Rifle w/turned-down bolt handle, detachable folding bayonet. Caliber: 7.35mm Italian Service (many arms of this model were later converted to the old 6.5mm caliber). Six round box magazine. 21.25-in. bbl. Weight: 7.5 lbs. Sights: Adj. rear-blade front. Military straight-grip stock. Adopted 1938.

ITHACA GUN COMPANY, INC. — King Ferry, NY

Formerly Ithaca, New York.

**MODEL 49 SADDLEGUN LEVER ACTION
SINGLE-SHOT RIFLE......... NiB $166 Ex $135 Gd $96**
Martini-type action. Hand-operated rebounding hammer. Caliber: .22 LR, Long, Short. 18-in. bbl. Open sights. Western carbine-style stock. Weight: 5.5 lbs. Made 1961-78.

**MODEL 49 SADDLEGUN—
DELUXE .... NiB $220 Ex $167 Gd $121**
Same as standard Model 49 except w/gold-plated hammer and trigger, figured walnut stock, sling swivels. Made 1962-75.

**MODEL 49 SADDLEGUN—
MAGNUM................. NiB $205 Ex $188 Gd $130**
Same as standard Model 49 except chambered for .22 WMR cartridge. Made 1962-78.

**MODEL 49 SADDLEGUN—
PRESENTATION .... NiB $333 Ex $239 Gd $166**
Same as standard Model 49 Saddlegun except w/gold-plated hammer and trigger, engraved receiver, full fancy-figured walnut stock w/gold nameplate. Available in .22 LR or .22 WMR. Made 1962-74.

**MODEL 49 SADDLEGUN—
ST. LOUIS BICENTENNIAL.... NiB $370 Ex $333 Gd $169**
Same as Model 49 Deluxe except w/commemorative inscription. 200 made in 1964. Top value is for rifle in new, unfired condition.

**MODEL 49R SADDLEGUN
REPEATING RIFLE........... NiB $298 Ex $243 Gd $154**
Similar in appearance to Model 49 Single-Shot. Caliber: .22 LR, Long, Short. Tubular magazine holds 15 LR, 17 Long, 21 Short. 20-in. bbl. Weight: 5.5 lbs. Sights: Open rear-bead front. Western-style stock, checkered grip. Made 1968-71.

MODEL 49 YOUTH SADDLEGUN .. NiB $177 Ex $138 Gd $105
Same as standard Model 49 except shorter stock for young shooters. Made 1961-78.

REPEATING CARBINE........ NiB $379 Ex $300 Gd $208
Caliber: .22 LR, Long, Short. Tubular magazine holds 15 LR, 17 Long, 21 Short. 18.5-in. bbl. Weight: 5.5 lbs. Sights: Open rear; hooded ramp front. Receiver grooved for scope mounting. Western carbine stock and forearm of American walnut. Made 1973-78.

**MODEL 72 SADDLEGUN—
DELUXE .... NiB $443 Ex $370 Gd $250**
Same as standard Model 72 except w/silver-finished and engraved receiver, octagon bbl., higher grade walnut stock and forearm. Made 1974-76.

**MODEL LSA-65 BOLT ACTION
STANDARD GRADE .... NiB $479 Ex $443 Gd $337**
Same as Model LSA-55 Standard Grade except calibers .25-06, .270, .30-06; 4-rnd. magazine, 23-in. bbl., weight: 7 lbs. Made 1969-77.

MODEL LSA-65 DELUXE ..... NiB $590 Ex $531 Gd $355
Same as Model LSA-65 Standard Grade except w/special features of Model LSA-55 Deluxe. Made 1969-77.

**MODEL X5-C LIGHTNING
AUTOLOADER .... NiB $222 Ex $177 Gd $123**
Takedown. Caliber: .22 LR. Seven round clip magazine. 22-in. bbl. Weight: 6 lbs. Sights: Open rear; Ray-bar front. Pistol-grip stock, grooved forearm. Made 1958-64.

**MODEL X5-T LIGHTNING AUTOLOADER
TUBULAR REPEATING RIFLE .. NiB $222 Ex $177 Gd $123**
Same as Model X5-C except w/16-rnd. tubular magazine, stock w/plain forearm.

**MODEL X-15 LIGHTNING
AUTOLOADER .... NiB $222 Ex $177 Gd $123**
Same general specifications as Model X5-C except forend is not grooved. Made 1964-67.

**BSA CF-2 BOLT-ACTION REPEATING
RIFLE.................... NiB $510 Ex $370 Gd $277**
Mauser-type action. Calibers: 7mm Rem. Mag., .300 Win. Mag. Three round magazine. 23.6-in. bbl. Weight: 8 lbs. Sights: Adj. rear; hooded ramp front. Checkered walnut stock w/ Monte Carlo comb, rollover cheekpiece, rosewood forend tip, recoil pad, sling swivels. Imported from 1976 to 1977. Mfd. by BSA Guns Ltd., Birmingham, England.

JAPANESE MILITARY — Tokyo, Japan

Manufactured by government plant.

MODEL 38 ARISAKA SERVICE RIFLE... NiB $656 Ex $390 Gd $220
Mauser-type bolt action. Caliber: 6.5mm Japanese. Five round box magazine. Bbl. lengths: 25.38 and 31.25 in. Weight: 9.25 lbs. w/long bbl. Sights: fixed front, adj. rear. Military-type full stock. Adopted in 1905, the 38th year of the Meiji reign hence, the designation "Model 38."

MODEL 38 ARISAKA CARBINE ... NiB $656 Ex $390 Gd $220
Same general specifications as Model 38 Rifle except w/19-in. bbl., heavy folding bayonet, weight 7.25 lbs.

MODEL 44 CAVALRY CARBINE... NiB $1190 Ex $690 Gd $355
Same general specifications as Model 38 Rifle except w/19-in. bbl., heavy folding bayonet, weight 8.5 lbs. Adopted in 1911, the 44th year of the Meiji reign, hence the designation, "Model 44."

MODEL 99 SERVICE RIFLE .... NiB $577 Ex $255 Gd $200
Modified Model 38. Caliber: 7.7mm Japanese. Five round box magazine. 25.75-in. bbl. Weight: 8.75 lbs. Sights: Fixed front; adj. aperture rear; anti-aircraft sighting bars on some early models; fixed rear sight on some late WWII rifles. Military-type full stock, may have bipod. Takedown paratroop model was also made during WWII. Adopted in 1939, (Japanese year 2599) from which the designation "Model 99" is taken. Note: The last Model 99 rifles made were of poor quality; some with cast steel receivers. Value shown is for earlier type.
**Sniper Rifle (w/4x
  scope)................ NiB $3900 Ex $3431 Gd $1817**

GRADING: **NiB** = New in Box   **Ex** = Excellent or NRA 95%   **Gd** = Good or NRA 68%

Italian Model 38 Military Rifle

Ithaca Model 49

Ithaca Model 72
Saddlegun Deluxe

Ithaca
Model LSA-65 Standard

Ithaca
Model X5-T

Japanese Military Model 38 Arisaka

JARRETT CUSTOM RIFLES — Jackson, SC

MODEL NO. 2 WALK ABOUT
BOLT-ACTION RIFLE. . . . . .NiB $4788 Ex $3077 Gd $2043
Custom lightweight rifle built on Remington M707 action. Jarrett match- grade barrel cut and chambered to customer's specification in short action calibers only. McMillan fiberglass stock pillar-bedded to action. Made 1995-2003.

MODEL NO. 3 CUSTOM
BOLT-ACTION RIFLE. . . . . NiB $4800 Ex $3147 Gd $2090
Custom rifle built on Remington M707 action. Jarrett match grade barrel cut and chambered to customer's specification. McMillan classic fiberglass stock pillar-bedded to action and finished to customer's preference. Made 1989 to date.

MODEL NO. 4 PROFESSIONAL HUNTER
BOLT-ACTION RIFLE. . . . . NiB $6988 Ex $5876 Gd $4490
Custom magnum rifle built on Winchester M70 "controlled feed" action. Jarrett match grade barrel cut and chambered

Ithaca
Model X-15

Ithaca
BSA CF-2

Johnston Automatics 1941
Military Model

Johnson Sporting Rifle

Iver Johnson Model M-1

to customer's specification in magnum calibers only. Quarter rib w/iron sights and two Leupold scopes w/Q-D rings and mounts. McMillan classic fiberglass stock fitted and finished to customer's preference.

JOHNSON AUTOMATICS, INC. — Providence, RI

MODEL 1941 SEMIAUTO MILITARY RIFLE . . . . **NiB $7433 Ex $5740 Gd $3328**
Short-recoil operated. Removable, air-cooled, 22-in. bbl. Caliber: .30-06, 7mm Mauser. 10-rnd. rotary magazine. Two-piece wood stock, pistol grip, perforated metal radiator sleeve over rear half of bbl. Sights: Receiver peep; protected post front. Weight: 9.5 lbs. Note: The Johnson M/1941 was adopted by the Netherlands government in 1940-41 and the major portion of the production of this rifle, 1941-43, was on Dutch orders. A quantity was also bought by the U.S. government for use by Marine Corps parachute troops (1943) and for Lend Lease. All these rifles were caliber .30-06; the 7mm Johnson rifles were made for the South American government.

SPORTING RIFLE
PROTOTYPE . . . . **NiB $14,000 Ex $11,500 Gd $7595**
Same general specifications as military rifle except fitted w/ sporting stock, checkered grip and forend. Blade front sight; receiver peep sight. Less than a dozen made prior to World War II.

IVER JOHNSON ARMS, INC. — Jacksonville, AR
(formerly of Fitchburg, Massachusetts, and Middlesex, New Jersey)

LI'L CHAMP. . . . . **NiB $227 Ex $146 Gd $90**
Bolt action. Caliber: .22 Short, Long, LR. Single-shot. 16.25-in. bbl. 32.5 in. overall. Weight: 3.25 lbs. Adj. rear sight, blade front. Synthetic composition stock. Made 1986-88.

MODEL M-1 SEMIAUTO CARBINE
Similar to U.S. M-1 Carbine. Calibers: 9mm Parabellum 30 U.S. Carbine. 15- or 30-rnd. magazine. 18-in. bbl. 35.5 in. overall. Weight: 6.5 lbs. Sights: blade front, w/guards; adj. peep rear. Walnut, hardwood or collapsible wire stock. Parkerized finish.
(30 cal. w/hardwood) . . . . NiB $460 Ex $340 Gd $220
(30 cal. w/walnut) . . . . NiB $506 Ex $374 Gd $242
(30 cal. w/wire) . . . . NiB $469 Ex $388 Gd $222
5.7mm or 9mm, add 30%

GRADING: **NiB** = New in Box   **Ex** = Excellent or NRA 95%   **Gd** = Good or NRA 68%

283

Iver Johnson Model SC30FS

Iver Johnson Trailblazer

MODEL PM30. . . . . .NiB $413 Ex $320 Gd $190
Similar to U.S. Carbine, Cal. 30 M1. 18-in. bbl. Weight: 5.5
lbs. 15- or 30-rnd. detachable magazine. Both hardwood and
walnut stock.

MODEL SC30FS . . . . .NiB $466 Ex $390 Gd $233
Similar to Survival Carbine except w/folding stock. Made
1983-89.

SURVIVAL . . . . .NiB $433 Ex $399 Gd $230
Similar to Model PM30 except in stainless steel. Made 1983-
89. W/folding high-impact plastic stock add $35.

TRAILBLAZER . . . . .NiB $277 Ex $160 Gd $126
Semiauto. Caliber: .22 LR. 18-in. bbl. Weight: 5.5 lbs. Sights: Adj.
rear, blade front. Hardwood stock. Made 1983-85.

MODEL X BOLT-ACTION RIFLE . . . NiB $270 Ex $189 Gd $115
Takedown, Single-shot. Caliber: .22 Short, Long and LR. 22-in.
bbl. Weight: 4 lbs. Sights: Open rear; blade front. Pistol-grip
stock w/knob forend tip. Made 1928-32.

MODEL XX (2X) . . . . .NiB $323 Ex $170 Gd $100
Improved version of Model X w/heavier 24-in. bbl. larger stock
(w/o knob tip), weight: 4.5 lbs. Made 1932-55.

K.B.I., INC. — Harrisburg, PA

See listing under Armscor; Charles Daly; FEG; Liberty and I.M.I.

SUPER CLASSIC
Calibers: .22 LR, .22 Mag., RF, .22 Hornet. Five- or 10-rnd.
capacity. Bolt and semiauto action. 22.6- or 20.75-in. bbl.
41.25 or 40.5 in. overall. Weight: 6.4 to 6.7 lbs. Blue finish.
Oil-finished American walnut stock w/hardwood grip cap and
forend tip. Checkered Monte Carlo comb and cheekpiece. High
polish blued barreled action w/damascened bolt. Dovetailed
receiver and iron sights. Recoil pad. QD swivel posts.
M-1500 SC, .22 LR . . . . .NiB $482 Ex $223 Gd $170
M-1500SC, .22 WMR . . . . .NiB $289 Ex $233 Gd $177
M-1800-S, .22 Hornet. . . . . . . .NiB $455 Ex $380 Gd $256
M-2000 SC, semiauto, .22 LR . . NiB $290 Ex $244 Gd $179

K.D.F. INC. — Sequin, TX

MODEL K15 BOLT-ACTION RIFLE
Calibers: (Standard) .22-250, .243 Win., 6mm Rem., .25-
06, .270 Win., .280 Rem., 7mm Mag., .30-60; (Magnum)
.300 Wby., .300 Win., .338 Win., .340 Wby., .375 H&H,
.411 KDF, .416 Rem., .458 Win. Four round magazine
(standard), 3-shot (magnum). 22-in. (standard) or 24-in.
(magnum) bbl. 44.5 to 46.5 in. overall. Weight: 8 lbs.
Sights optional. Kevlar composite or checkered walnut
stock in Classic, European or thumbhole-style. Note: U.S.
Manufacture limited to 25 prototypes and pre-production
variations.
Standard model. . . . . .NiB $1796 Ex $1721 Gd $977
Magnum model. . . . . .NiB $1834 Ex $1597 Gd $1106

KEL-TEC CNC INDUSTRIES, INC. — Cocoa, FL

CMR30 . . . . NiB $555 Ex $480 Gd $300
Semiauto. Caliber: .22 WMR; 30-rnd. detachable magazine.
Receiver: polymer w/picatinny rail. Sights: open, flip up. Stock:
collapsable stock. 16.1-in. bbl. Weight: 3.8 lbs. Mfg. 2015–date.

M43 BULLPUP . . . . .NiB $1610 Ex $1400 Gd $880
Semiauto, bullpup design. Caliber: .223 Rem.; 30-rnd. AR style
detachable magazine. Wood furniture. Sights: open. 17.4-in.
bbl. Weight: 7 lbs. Mfg. 2014–15.

RDB SERIES
Semiauto, bullpup design w/short stroke action. Caliber:
.223 Rem. or .300 BLK; 30-rnd. AR style detachable
magazine. Polymer furniture w/pistol grip. Sights: optic
ready. 17.3-, 20- or 24-in. bbl. Weight: 7 lbs. Mfg.
2014–date.
RDB17 (17.3-in. bbl., pistol grip) . .NiB $1055 Ex $955 Gd $630
Hunter model (20.5-in. bbl.,
    straight stock) . . . . .NiB $1055 Ex $955 Gd $630
Survival model (16.1-in. bbl.,
    straight stock) . . . . .NiB $1055 Ex $955 Gd $630

RFB SERIES
Semiauto, bullpup design w/short stroke action. Caliber:
.308 Win.; 10- or 20-rnd. detachable magazine. Polymer
furniture w/pistol grip. Sights: optic ready. 18- or 20-in.
bbl. Weight: 9.1 lbs. Finish: black, OD green, FDE. Mfg.
2016–date.
RFB (18-in. bbl. w/muzzle
  brake) . . . . NiB $1630 Ex $1410 Gd $900
Hunter model (24-in. bbl.), add $200

**Kel-Tec
Sub-Series Semiauto Rifle shown
expanded and folded**

Kel Tec RFB

RMR30 . . . . **NiB $505 Ex $405 Gd $280**
Semiauto. Caliber: .22 WMR; 30-rnd. detachable magazine. Receiver: polymer w/picatinny rail. Sights: open, flip up. Stock: collapsable stock. 16.1-in. bbl. Weight: 3.8 lbs. Mfg. 2011–14.

SUB-SERIES
Semiauto blow-back action w/pivoting bbl., takedown. 9mm Parabellum or 40 S&W. Interchangeable grip assembly accepts most double column, high capacity handgun magazines. 16.1-in. bbl. 31.5 in. overall. Weight: 4.6 lbs. Hooded post front sight, flip-up rear. Matte black finish. Tubular buttstock w/grooved polymer buttplate and vented handguard. Made 1997-2000.
Sub-9 model (9mm) . . . .**NiB $395 Ex $333 Gd $265**
Sub-40 model (.40 S&W) . . . . .**NiB $395 Ex $333 Gd $265**

SUB-2000 . . . .**NiB $380 Ex $300 Gd $200**
Similar to Sub-9 and Sub-40. Accepts Glock, Beretta, S&W or SIG pistol magazines. Made 2001 to 2015.

SUB-2000 GEN 2 . . . .**NiB $455 Ex $400 Gd $255**
Similar to SUB-2000 except w/metal sights. Accepts Glock, Beretta, or S&W pistol magazines. Made 2016–date.

SU-16 SERIES
Semiauto w/pivoting bbl. Caliber: 5.56 NATO. Compatibale with AR-style magazines. 16- or 18.5-in. bbl. Weight: 4.7 lbs. Matte black, OD green or tan finish. Polymer stock. Made 2003 to date.
Sub-9 model (9mm) . . . .**NiB $395 Ex $333 Gd $265**
**Sub-40 model
  (.40 S&W)** . . . .**NiB $395 Ex $333 Gd $265**
**SU-16A (18-in. bbl.,
  full stock)** . . . .**NiB $580 Ex $420 Gd $355**
**SU-16B (16-in. bbl.,
  full stock)** . . . .**NiB $645 Ex $670 Gd $380**
**SU-16C (.300 BLK or 5.56
  NATO, 16-in. bbl.,
  folding stock)** . . . .**NiB $680 Ex $585 Gd $390**
**SU-16CA (5.56 NATO, 16-in. bbl.,
  folding stock)** . . . .**NiB $680 Ex $585 Gd $390**
**SU-16E (5.56 NATO, 16-in. bbl.,
  AR style stock)** . . . .**NiB $830 Ex $730 Gd $390**

SU-22 SERIES
Similar to SU-16 except chambered in .22 LR; 26-rnd. magazine. Stock: adj. fixed or folding. 16-in. bbl. Weight: 4 lbs. Mfg. 2008–date.
Fixed stock . . . .**NiB $480 Ex $420 Gd $265**
Folding stock (disc. 2019), add **$20**

KIMBER MANUFACTURING, INC. — Troy, AL

Manufactured by Kimber Manufacturing, Inc., Yonkers, NY, formerly Kimber of America, Inc.; Kimber of Oregon, Inc.

Note: *From 1980-91, Kimber of Oregon produced Kimber firearms. A redesigned action designated by serialization with a "B" suffix was introduced 1986. Pre-1986 production is recognized as the "A" series but is not so marked. These early models in rare configurations and limited-run calibers command premium prices from collectors. Kimber of America, in Clackamas, Oregon, acquired the Kimber trademark and resumed manufactured of Kimber rifles. During this transition, Nationwide Sports Distributors, Inc. in Pennsylvania and Nevada became exclusive distributors of Kimber products. In 1997, Kimber Manufacturing acquired the trademark with manufacturing rights and expanded production to include a 1911-A1-style Semiauto pistol, the Kimber Classic 45. Rifle production resumed in late 1998 with the announcement of an all-new Kimber .22 rifle and a refined Model 84 in both single-shot and repeater configurations.*

MODEL 82 BOLT-ACTION RIFLE
Small action based on Kimber's "A" Model 82 rimfire receiver w/twin rear locking lugs. Calibers: .22 LR, .22 WRF, .22 Hornet, .218 Bee, .25-20. 5- or 10-rnd. magazine (.22 LR); 5-rnd. magazine (22WRF); 3-rnd. magazine (.22 Hornet). .218 Bee and .25-20 are single-shot. 18- to 25-in. bbl. 37.63 to 42.5 in. overall. Weight: 6 lbs. (Light Sporter), 6.5 lbs. (Sporter), 7.5 lbs. (Varmint); 10.75 lbs. (Target). Right- and left-hand actions are available in distinctive stock styles.
Cascade (disc. 1987) . . . .**NiB $890 Ex $674 Gd $388**
Classic (disc. 1988) . . . .**NiB $885 Ex $674 Gd $388**
Continental . . . .**NiB $1482 Ex $1197 Gd $823**
Custom Classic (disc. 1988) . .**NiB $1041 Ex $833 Gd $579**
Mini Classic . . . .**NiB $679 Ex $555 Gd $389**

GRADING: **NiB** = New in Box   **Ex** = Excellent or NRA 95%   **Gd** = Good or NRA 68%   **285**

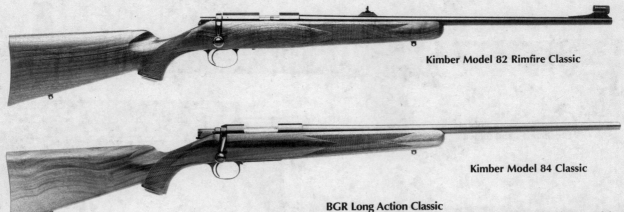

Kimber Model 82 Rimfire Classic

Kimber Model 84 Classic

Super America . . . . NiB $1307 Ex $1165 Gd $909
Super Continental . . . . NiB $2220 Ex $1390 Gd $925
All-American Match . . . . NiB $1978 Ex $1165 Gd $789
Deluxe Grade (disc. 1990). . NiB $1388 Ex $1097 Gd $898
Hunter (w/laminated stock) . . . NiB $912 Ex $833 Gd $523
Government Target . . . . NiB $660 Ex $550 Gd $330

MODEL 82C CLASSIC BOLT-ACTION RIFLE
Caliber: .22 LR. Four- or 10-rnd. magazine. 21-in. air-gauged bbl. 40.5 in. overall. Weight: 6.5 lbs. Receiver drilled and tapped for Warne scope mounts; no sights. Single-set trigger. Checkered Claro walnut stock w/red buttpad and polished steel grip cap. Reintroduced 1993.

Classic model . . . . NiB $833 Ex $688 Gd $495
Left-hand model, add $100

MODEL 84 BOLT-ACTION RIFLE
Classic (disc. 1988) Compact-medium action based on a scaled-down Mauser-type receiver, designed to accept small base centerfire cartridges. Calibers: .17 Rem., .221 Fireball, .222 Rem., .223 Rem. Five round magazine. Same general barrel and stock specifications as Model 82.

Classic (disc. 1988) . . . . NiB $1100 Ex $821 Gd $577
Continental . . . . NiB $1400 Ex $1098 Gd $769
Custom Classic (disc. 1988) . . NiB $1410 Ex $978 Gd $713
Super America (disc. 1988) . . NiB $1925 Ex $1078 Gd $757
Super Continental I
   (disc. 1988) . . . . NiB $2100 Ex $1170 Gd $844
1990 Classifications
   Deluxe Grade (disc. 1990) . . .NiB $1310 Ex $1044 Gd $733
Hunter/Sporter
   (laminated stock) . . . . NiB $1010 Ex $943 Gd $665
Super America (disc. 1991). . NiB $1988 Ex $1146 Gd $825
Super Varmint (disc. 1991) . . NiB $1137 Ex $1187 Gd $825
Ultra Varmint (disc. 1991) . . NiB $1189 Ex $1123 Gd $779

MODEL 89 BGR (BIG GAME RIFLE)
Large action combining the best features of the pre-64 Model 70 Winchester and the Mauser 98. Three action lengths are offered in three stock styles. Calibers: .257 Roberts, .25-06, 7x57, .270 Win., .280 Win., .30-06, 7mm Rem. Mag., .300 Win. Mag., .300 H&H, .338 Win., 35 Whelen, .375 H&H, .404 Jeffrey, .416 Rigby, .460 Wby., .505 Gibbs (.308 cartridge family to follow). Five round magazine (standard calibers); 3-rnd. magazine (Magnum calibers). 22- to 24-in. bbl. 42 to 44 in. overall. Weight: 7.5 to 10.5 lbs. Model 89 African features express sights on contoured quarter rib, banded front sight. Barrel-mounted recoil lug w/integral receiver lug and twin recoil crosspins in stock.

BGR Long Action Classic
   (disc. 1988) . . . . NiB $944 Ex $844 Gd $588
Custom Classic (disc. 1988). . . NiB $1288 Ex $1044 Gd $745
Super America . . . . NiB $1548 Ex $1270 Gd $926
1990 Classifications Deluxe Grade:
   Featherweight . . . . NiB $1995 Ex $1490 Gd $1044
Medium. . . . . NiB $1866 Ex $1566 Gd $1135
.375 H&H. . . . . NiB $1956 Ex $1577 Gd $1145
Hunter Grade (laminated stock)
   .270 and .30-06 . . . . NiB $1370 Ex $1105 Gd $800
.375 H&H . . . . NiB $1676 Ex $1356 Gd $944
Super America: Featherweight . . . NiB $2088 Ex $1703 Gd $1213
Medium. . . . . NiB $2189 Ex $1760 Gd $1217
.375 H&H . . . . NiB $2788 Ex $2274 Gd $1590
African — All calibers. . . . . NiB $5635 Ex $3955 Gd $2766

MODEL 84M SERIES
Bolt-action Mauser style. Improved version of Model 84C. Calibers: .22-250 Rem., .204 Ruger, .223 Rem., .243 Win., .260 Rem., .308 Win., or 7mm-08. Model 70 style safety. Stock: walnut or laminate. Intro. 2001.

Adirondack (synthetic stock, satin stainless finish, 18-in.
   brrl., 2014 to date) . . . . NiB $1510 Ex $1130 Gd $830
Classic (checkered walnut stock, 2001
   to date) . . . . NiB $1030 Ex $760 Gd $560
Classic LongMaster Classic (24-in. heavy brrl.,
   2002 to date) . . . . NiB $1130 Ex $880 Gd $660
Classic LongMaster VT (26-in. heavy brrl.,
   2001 to date) . . . . NiB $1180 Ex $860 Gd $610
Classic Pro Varmint (24-in. heavy brrl.,
   2004 to date) . . . . NiB $1180 Ex $860 Gd $610
Classic Select Grade (Claro or French walnut stock, 2006 to
   date) . . . . NiB $1030 Ex $760 Gd $560
Classic Stainless (checkered walnut stock,
   2001 to date) . . . . NiB $1030 Ex $760 Gd $560
Classic Stainless Select Grade (Claro or French walnut stock,
   2012-16). . . . . NiB $1300 Ex $930 Gd $730
Classic SVT (short brrl. version of LongMaster VT, 2001 to
   date) . . . . NiB $1130 Ex $880 Gd $660
Classic Varmint (26-in. heavy brrl.,
   2001 to date) . . . . NiB $1130 Ex $880 Gd $660
LPT (24-in. brrl., synthetic stock,
   2008 to date) . . . . NiB $1300 Ex $1180 Gd $730
Montana (synthetic stock, satin stainless finish,
   2003 to date) . . . . NiB $1180 Ex $880 Gd $680
Mountain Ascent (synthetic stock, 22-in. fluted brrl., 2012 to
   date) . . . . NiB $1995 Ex $1410 Gd $1100
Superamerica (fancy walnut stock, high luster blue finish,
   2003 to date) . . . . NiB $1930 Ex $1460 Gd $1030

MODEL 8400 SERIES
Bolt-action Mauser style. Calibers: .25-06 Rem., .270 WSM, .270 Win., 7mm WSM, 7mm Rem. Mag., .30-06, .300 WSM, .300 Win. Mag., .325 WSM, or .338 Win. Mag. Model 70

Kimber Model 89 Super America

style safety. 24-in. bbl. Stock: checkered walnut. Finish: blued. Intro. 2003.

Advanced Tactical II (Manners MCS-TF4 stock,
2014 to date) . . . . NiB $3700 Ex $2830 Gd $2030
Caprivi (dangerous game calibers, checkered AA walnut
stock, 2008 to date) . . . . . NiB $3110 Ex $2130 Gd $1510
Caprivi Special Edition (.375 H&H Mag., checkered AAA
walnut stock, 2011-12). . . NiB $4510 Ex $3610 Gd $3200
Classic (checkered walnut stock,
2003 to date) . . . . NiB $1030 Ex $760 Gd $650
Classic Select Grade (Claro or French walnut stock,
2006 to date) . . . . NiB $1260 Ex $910 Gd $710
Classic Stainless (checkered walnut stock,
stainless, 2001-11) . . . . . . NiB $1030 Ex $760 Gd $650
Classic Stainless Select Grade (Claro or French
walnut stock, 2012-16). . . . . NiB $1300 Ex $930 Gd $730
Montana (synthetic stock, satin stainless finish,
2003 to date) . . . . NiB $1180 Ex $880 Gd $680
Patrol/Police Tactical (McMillian stock, 24- or 26-in. brrl.,
2009-13). . . . . NiB $1170 Ex $1000 Gd $730
Patrol Tactical (Manners stock,
2014 to date) . . . . NiB $2080 Ex $2130 Gd $1810
Sonora (brown laminate stock, flutes stainless brrl.,
2008-11). . . . . NiB $1110 Ex $830 Gd $610
Superamerica (fancy walnut
stock, high luster blue finish,
2003 to date) . . . . NiB $1930 Ex $1460 Gd $1030
Tactical Series (synthetic stock, 24-in. brrl.,
2007-13). . . . . NiB $1680 Ex $1260 Gd $910
Talkeetna (.375 H&H Mag., carbon fiber stock,
2008 to date) . . . . NiB $1830 Ex $1360 Gd $1000

KNIGHT'S ARMAMENT COMPANY — Titusville, FL

Formerly, Vero Beach, FL.

SR-15 SEMIAUTO MATCH
RIFLE. . . . . NiB $1733 Ex $1544 Gd $1103
AR-15 configuration. Caliber: .223 Rem. (5.56mm). Five- or 10-rnd. magazine. 20-in. w/free-floating, match-grade bbl., 38 in. overall. Weight: 7.9 lbs. Integral Weaver-style rail. Two-stage target trigger. Matte black oxide finish. Black synthetic AR-15A2-style stock and forearm. Made 1997-2008.

M-4 SEMIAUTO CARBINE
Similar to SR-15 rifle except w/16-in. bbl. Sights and mounts optional. Fixed synthetic or collapsible buttstock. Made 1997-2008.
w/collapsible stock . . . . . . NiB $1520 Ex $1388 Gd $1077

SR-15 M-5. . . . . NiB $1765 Ex $1488 Gd $1165
Semiauto. Caliber: .223 Rem. (5.56mm). Five- or 10-rnd. magazine. 20-in. bbl. 38 in. overall. Weight: 7.6 lbs. Integral

Weaver-style rail. Two-stage target trigger. Matte black oxide finish. Black synthetic AR-15A2-style stock and forearm. Made 1997-2008.

SR-25 MATCH RIFLE
Similar to SR-25 Sporter except w/free floating 20- or 24-in. match bbl. 39.5-43.5 in. overall. Weight: 9.25 and 10.75 lbs., respectively. Integral Weaver-style rail. Sights and mounts optional. 1 MOA guaranteed. Made 1993-2008.
Model SR-25 LW Match
(w/20-in. bbl.) . . . . NiB $5744 Ex $3289 Gd $2665
W/RAS (Rail Adapter
System), add $350

SR-25 SEMIAUTO CARBINE
Similar to SR-25 Sporter except w/free floating 16-in. bbl. 35.75 in. overall. Weight: 7.75 lbs. Integral Weaver-style rail. Sights and mounts optional. Made 1995-2008.
Carbine (w/o sights) . . . . NiB $6000 Ex $3927 Gd $1949
w/RAS (Rail Adapter
System), add $300

SR-25 . . . . NiB $2784 Ex $2409 Gd $1709
AR-15 configuration. Caliber: .308 Win. (7.62 NATO). Five, 10- or 20-rnd. magazine. 20-in. bbl. 39.5 in. overall. Weight: 8.75 lbs. Integral Weaver-style rail. Protected post front sight adjustable for elevation, detachable rear adjustable for windage. Two-stage target trigger. Matte black oxide finish. Black synthetic AR-15A2-style stock and forearm. Made 1993-97.

SR-50 . . . . NiB $6833 Ex $6096 Gd $3597
Gas-operated Semiauto action. Caliber: .50 BMG. 10-rnd. magazine. 35.5-in. bbl. 58.5 in. overall. Weight: 31.75 lbs. Integral Weaver-style rail. Two-stage target trigger. Matte black oxide finish. Tubular-style stock. Limited production from 1996 to 2008.

KONGSBERG — Kongsberg, Norway

Imported by Kongsberg America L.L.C., Fairfield, CT.

MODEL 393 CLASSIC SPORTER
Calibers: .22-250 Rem., .243 Win., 6.5x55, .270 Win., 7mm Rem. Mag., .30-06, .308 Win. .300 Win. Mag., .338 Win. Mag. Three- or 4-rnd. rotary magazine. 23-in. bbl. (Standard) or 26-in. bbl. (magnum). Weight: 7.5 to 8 lbs. 44 to 47 in. overall. No sights w/ dovetailed receiver or optional hooded blade front sight, adjustable rear. Blue finish. Checkered European walnut stock w/rubber buttplate. Imported from 1994 to 1998.
Standard calibers . . . . NiB $957 Ex $779 Gd $597
Magnum calibers . . . . NiB $1289 Ex $1100 Gd $800
Left-hand model, add $150
w/optional sights, add. $75

RIFLES

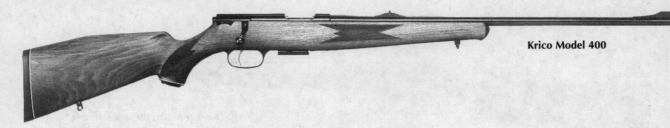

Krico Model 400

MODEL 393 DELUXE SPORTER
Similar to Classic Model except w/deluxe European walnut stock. Imported from 1994 to 1998.
Standard calibers . . . . **NiB $1017 Ex $909 Gd $599**
Magnum calibers . . . . **NiB $1347 Ex $1117 Gd $809**
Left-hand model, add **$150**
w/optional sights, add. **$75**

MODEL 393 THUMBHOLE SPORTER
Calibers: 22-250 Rem. or 308 Win. Four round rotary magazine. 23-in. heavy bbl. Weight: 8.5 lbs. 44 in. overall. No sights, dovetailed receiver. Blue finish. Stippled American walnut thumbhole stock w/adjustable cheekpiece. Imported from 1993 to 1998.
Right-hand model . . . . **NiB $1453 Ex $1347 Gd $650**
Left-hand model . . . . **NiB $1533 Ex $1377 Gd $800**

KRICO — Stuttgart-Hedelfingen, Germany
Manufactured by Sportwaffenfabrik, Kriegeskorte GmbH; imported by Northeast Arms, LLC, Ft. Fairfield, Maine; previously by Beeman Precision Arms, Inc. and Mandell Shooting Supplies.

MODEL 260
SEMIAUTO RIFLE . . . . **NiB $744 Ex $656 Gd $459**
Caliber: .22 LR. 10-rnd. magazine. 20-in. bbl. 38.9 in. overall. Weight: 6.6 lbs. Hooded blade front sight; adj. rear. Grooved receiver. Beech stock. Blued finish. Introduced 1989. Disc.

MODEL 300 BOLT-ACTION RIFLE
Calibers: .22 LR. .22 WMR, .22 Hornet. 19.6-in. bbl. (22 LR), 23.6-in. (22 Hornet). 38.5 in. overall. Weight: 6.3 lbs. Double-set triggers. Sights: Ramped blade front, adj. open rear. Checkered walnut-finished hardwood stock. Blued finish. Introduced 1989. Disc.
Model 300 Standard . . . . **NiB $735 Ex $568 Gd $445**
Model 300 Deluxe . . . . **NiB $779 Ex $589 Gd $455**
Model 300 SA (Monte Carlo walnut
stock) . . . . **NiB $897 Ex $744 Gd $553**
Model 300 Stutzen (full-length walnut
stock) . . . . **NiB $1023 Ex $864 Gd $654**

MODEL 311 SMALL-BORE RIFLE
Bolt action. Caliber: .22 LR. 5- or 10-rnd. clip magazine. 22-in. bbl. Weight: 6 lbs. Single- or double-set trigger. Sights: Open rear; hooded ramp front; available w/factory-fitted Kaps 2.5x scope. Checkered stock w/cheekpiece, pistol-grip and swivels. Disc. 1962.
w/scope sight . . . . **NiB $376 Ex $347 Gd $233**
w/iron sights only . . . . **NiB $355 Ex $333 Gd $270**

MODEL 320 BOLT-ACTION
SPORTER. . . . . **NiB $920 Ex $622 Gd $423**
Caliber: .22 LR. Five round detachable box magazine. 19.5-in. bbl. 38.5 in. overall. Weight: 6 lbs. Adj. rear sight, blade ramp front. Checkered European walnut Mannlicher-style stock w/low comb and cheekpiece. Single or double-set triggers. Imported from 1986 to 1988.

MODEL 340 METALLIC SILHOUETTE
BOLT-ACTION RIFLE. . . . . **NiB $788 Ex $658 Gd $466**
Caliber: .22 LR. Five round magazine. 21-in. heavy, bull bbl. 39.5 in. overall. Weight: 7.5 lbs. No sights. Grooved receiver for scope mounts. European walnut stock in off-hand, match-style configuration. Match or double-set triggers. Imported from 1983 to 1988. Disc.

MODEL 360S BIATHLON
RIFLE . . . . **NiB $1455 Ex $1188 Gd $687**
Caliber: .22 LR. Five 5-rnd. magazines. 21.25-in. bbl. w/snow cap. 40.5 in. overall. Weight: 9.25 lbs. Straight-pull action. Match trigger w/17-oz. pull. Sights: Globe front, adj. match peep rear. Biathlon-style walnut stock w/high comb and adj. butt-plate. Imported from 1991. Disc.

MODEL 360 S2 BIATHLON
RIFLE. . . . . **NiB $1423 Ex $1189 Gd $655**
Similar to Model 360S except w/pistol-grip activated action. Biathlon-style walnut stock w/black epoxy finish. Imported from 1991. Disc.

MODEL 400 BOLT-ACTION
RIFLE. . . . . **NiB $889 Ex $766 Gd $544**
Caliber: .22 Hornet. Five round detachable box magazine. 23.5-in. bbl. Weight: 6.75 lbs. Adj. open rear sight, ramp front. European walnut stock. Disc. 1990.

MODEL 420 BOLT-ACTION
RIFLE. . . . . **NiB $1043 Ex $833 Gd $568**
Same as Model 400 except w/full-length Mannlicher-style stock and double-set triggers. Scope optional, extra. Disc. 1989.

MODEL 440 S BOLT-ACTION
RIFLE . . . . **NiB $889 Ex $745 Gd $540**
Caliber: .22 Hornet. Detachable box magazine. 20-in. bbl. 36.5 in. overall. Weight: 7.5 lbs. No sights. French walnut stock w/ventilated forend. Disc. 1988.

MODEL 500 MATCH RIFLE NiB $3633 Ex $2988 Gd $1077
Caliber: .22 LR. Single-shot. 23.6-in. bbl. 42 in. overall. Weight: 9.4 lbs. Kricotronic electronic ignition system. Sights: Globe front; match micrometer aperture rear. Match-style European walnut stock w/adj. butt.

MODEL 600 BOLT-ACTION
RIFLE. . . . . **NiB $1177 Ex $1055 Gd $733**
Same general specifications as Model 707 except w/short action. Calibers: .17 Rem., .222, .223, .22-250, .243, 5.6x50 Mag. and 308. Introduced 1983. Disc.

MODEL 620 . . . . **NiB $1206 Ex $1119 Gd $726**
Same as Model 600 except w/short-action-chambered for .308 Win. only and full-length Mannlicher-style stock w/Schnabel forend tip. 20.75-in. bbl. Weight: 6.5 lbs. No longer imported.

MODEL 640 SUPER SNIPER BOLT-ACTION
REPEATING RIFLE. . . . . **NiB $1863 Ex $1277 Gd $905**
Calibers: .223 Rem., .308 Win. Three round magazine. 26-in. bbl. 44.25 in. overall. Weight: 9.5 lbs. No sights drilled and

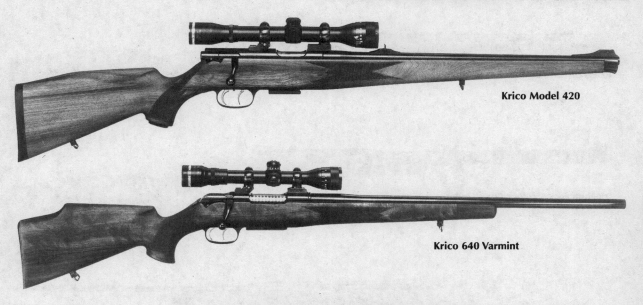

Krico Model 420

Krico 640 Varmint

RIFLES

tapped for scope mounts. Single or double-set triggers. Select walnut stock w/adj. cheekpiece and recoil pad. Disc. 1989.

MODEL 640 VARMINT RIFLE . . NiB $997 Ex $844 Gd $638
Caliber: .222 Rem. Four round magazine. 23.75-in. bbl. Weight: 9.5 lbs. No sights. European walnut stock. No longer imported.

MODEL 707 BOLT-ACTION RIFLE
Calibers: .17 Rem., .222, .222 Rem. Mag., .223, .22-250, 5.6x50 Mag., .243, 5.6x57 RSW, 6x62, 6.5x55, 6.5x57, 6.5x68 .270 Win., 7x64, 7.5 Swiss, 7mm Mag., .30-06, .300 Win., 8x68S, 9.3x64. 24-in. (standard) or 26-in. (magnum) bbl. 44 in. overall (standard). Weight: 7.5 lbs. Adj. rear sight; hooded ramp front. Checkered European-style walnut stock w/Bavarian cheekpiece and rosewood Schnabel forend tip. Imported from 1983 to date.
Hunter . . . . NiB $1146 Ex $896 Gd $790
Deluxe . . . . NiB $1244 Ex $1043 Gd $733
Deluxe R . . . . NiB $1096 Ex $790 Gd $695
Deluxe Stutzen . . . . NiB $1290 Ex $770 Gd $655

MODEL 720 BOLT-ACTION RIFLE
Same general specifications as Model 707 except in calibers .270 Win. and .30-06 w/full-length Mannlicher-style stock and Schnabel forend tip. 20.75-in. bbl. Weight: 6.75 lbs. Disc. importing 1990.
Sporter Model . . . . NiB $1144 Ex $1043 Gd $728
Ltd. Edition . . . . NiB $2419 Ex $2179 Gd $1188

BOLT-ACTION SPORTING
RIFLE . . . . NiB $733 Ex $634 Gd $438
Miniature Mauser action. Single- or double-set trigger. Calibers: .22 Hornet, .222 Rem. Four round clip magazine. 22-24- or 26-in. bbl. Weight: 6.25 lbs. Sights: Open rear; hooded ramp front. Checkered stock w/cheekpiece, pistol-grip, black forend tip, sling swivels. Imported from 1956 to 1962. Disc.

CARBINE . . . . NiB $743 Ex $637 Gd $440
Same as Krico Sporting Rifle except w/20- or 22-in. bbl., full-length Mannlicher-type stock. Disc. 1962.

SPECIAL VARMINT RIFLE . . . . . NiB $743 Ex $637 Gd $440
Same as Krico Rifle except w/heavy bbl., no sights, weight: 7.25 lbs. Caliber: .222 Rem. only. Disc. 1962.

KRIEGHOFF — Ulm (Donau), Germany
Manufactured by H. Krieghoff Jagd und Sportwaffenfabrik. See also Combination Guns under Krieghoff shotgun listings.

TECK OVER/UNDER RIFLE
Kersten action, double crossbolt, double underlugs. Boxlock. Calibers: 7x57r5, 7x64, 7x65r5, .30-30, .308 Win. .30-06, .300 Win. Mag., 9.3x74r5, .375 H&H Mag. .458 Win. Mag. 25-in. bbls. Weight: 8 to 9.5 lbs. Sights: Express rear; ramp front. Checkered walnut stock and forearm. Made 1967. Disc.
Standard calibers . . . . NiB $8843 Ex $6953 Gd $5442
.375 H&H Mag. (Disc. 1988) and
    .458 Win. Mag . . . . NiB $10650 Ex $7566 Gd $6831

ULM OVER/ UNDER
RIFLE . . . . NiB $14,790 Ex $11,110 Gd $6990
Same general specifications as Teck model except w/side-locks w/leaf Arabesque engraving. Made 1963. Disc.

ULM-PRIMUS OVER/UNDER
RIFLE . . . . NiB $20,244 Ex $16,277 Gd $10,550
Delux version of Ulm model, w/detachable sidelocks, higher grade engraving and stock wood. Made 1963. Disc.

L.A.R. MANUFACTURING, INC. — West Jordan, UT

BIG BOAR COMPETITOR . . NiB $2230 Ex $1966 Gd $1429
Bolt-action. Single-shot, bull-pup action. Caliber: .50 BMG. 36-in. bbl. 45.5 in. overall. Weight: 28.4 lbs. Made 1994-2011.

T-50 . . . . NiB $3000 Ex $2810 Gd $2650
Bolt-action. Single-shot. Caliber: .50 BMG. 32 to 36-in. bbl. Weight: 30.5 to 32 lbs. Made 2009-12.

LAKEFIELD ARMS LTD. — Ontario, Canada
See also listing under Savage for production since 1994.

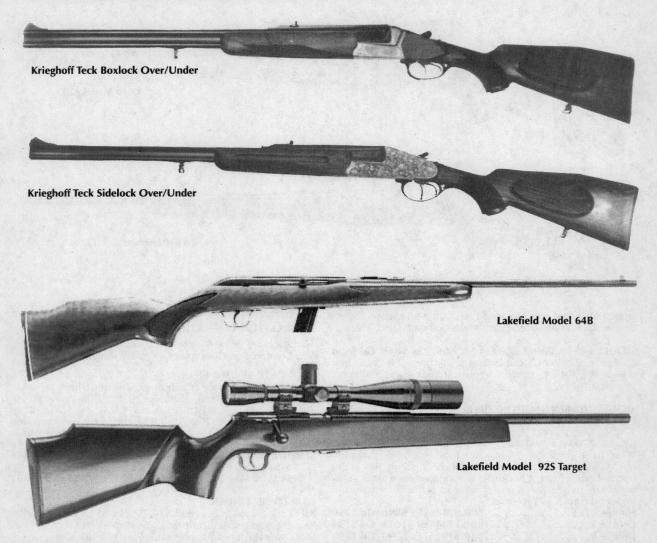

Krieghoff Teck Boxlock Over/Under

Krieghoff Teck Sidelock Over/Under

Lakefield Model 64B

Lakefield Model 92S Target

**MODEL 64B SEMIAUTO
RIFLE. NiB $150 Ex $110 Gd $85**
Caliber: .22 LR. 10-rnd. magazine. 20-in. bbl. Weight: 5.5 lbs. 40 in. overall. Bead front sight, adj. rear. Grooved receiver for scope mounts. Stamped checkering on walnut-finished hardwood stock w/Monte Carlo cheekpiece. Imported from 1990 to 1994.

**MODEL 90B BOLT-ACTION
TARGET RIFLE. . . . . NiB $476 Ex $359 Gd $232**
Caliber: .22 LR. Five round magazine. 21-in. bbl. w/snow cap. 39.63 in. overall. Weight: 8.25 lbs. Adj. receiver peep sight; globe front w/colored inserts. Receiver drilled and tapped for scope mounts. Biathlon-style natural finished hardwood stock w/shooting rails, hand stop and butthook. Made 1991-94.

MODEL 91T/91TR BOLT-ACTION TARGET RIFLE
Calibers: .22 Short, Long, LR. 25-in. bbl. 43.63 in. overall. Weight: 8 lbs. Adj. rear peep sight; globe front w/inserts. Receiver drilled and tapped for scope mounts. Walnut-finished hardwood stock w/shooting rails and hand stop. Model 91TR is a 5-rnd. clip-fed repeater. Made 1991-94.
Model 91T single-shot. . . . . . . NiB $378 Ex $299 Gd $148
Model 91TR repeater
** (.22 LR only). . . . . NiB $416 Ex $266 Gd $171**

MODEL 92S TARGET RIFLE . . . NiB $300 Ex $257 Gd $184
Same general specifications as Model 90B except w/conventional target-style stock. 8 lbs. No sights, but drilled and tapped for scope mounts. Made 1993-95.

MODEL 93M BOLT ACTION . . NiB $188 Ex $157 Gd $110
Caliber: .22 WMR. 5-rnd. magazine. 20.75-in. bbl. 39.5 in. overall. Weight: 5.75 lbs. Bead front sight, adj. open rear. Receiver grooved for scope mount. Thumb-operated rotary safety. Checkered walnut-finished hardwood stock. Blued finish. Made in 1995.

MARK I BOLT-ACTION RIFLE. . . . NiB $133 Ex $98 Gd $77
Calibers: .22 Short, Long, LR. Single-shot. 20.5-in. bbl. (19-in. Youth Model); available in smoothbore. Weight: 5.5 lbs. 39.5 in. overall. Bead front sight; adj. rear. Grooved receiver for scope mounts. Checkered walnut-finished hardwood stock w/Monte Carlo and pistol-grip. Blued finish. Made 1990-94.

MARK II BOLT-ACTION RIFLE
Same general specifications as Mark I except has repeating action w/10-rnd. detachable box magazine. .22 LR. only. Made 1992-94.
Mark II standard model . . . . NiB $137 Ex $120 Gd $80

Mark II Youth model
(w/19-in. bbl.) . . . . NiB $132 Ex $111 Gd $83
Mark II left-hand model . . . . . . NiB $169 Ex $137 Gd $100

LAURONA — Eibar, Spain

Manufactured in Eibar, Spain; imported by Galaxy Imports, Victoria, TX.

MODEL 2000X O/U EXPRESS RIFLE
Calibers: .30-06, 8x57 JRS, 8x75 JR, .375 H&H, 9.3x74R Five round magazine. 24-in. separated bbls. Weight: 8.5 lbs. Quarter rib drilled and tapped for scope mount. Open sights. Matte black chrome finish. Monte Carlo-style checkered walnut buttstock; tulip forearm. Custom orders only. Imported from 1993 to date.
Standard calibers . . . . NiB $3166 Ex $2480 Gd $1723
Magnum calibers . . . . NiB $3790 Ex $3044 Gd 2133

LUNA — Mehlis, Germany
Manufactured by Ernst Friedr. Büchel.

SINGLE-SHOT TARGET RIFLE NiB $1043 Ex $788 Gd $558
Falling block action. Calibers: .22 LR. .22 Hornet. 29-in. bbl. Weight: 8.25 lbs. Sights: Micrometer peep rear tang; open rear; ramp front. Cheekpiece stock w/full pistol-grip, semibeavertail forearm, checkered, swivels. Made before WWII.

MAGNUM RESEARCH, INC. — Minneapolis, MN

MOUNTAIN EAGLE BOLT-ACTION RIFLE SERIES
Calibers: .222 Rem., .223 Rem., .270 Win., .280 Rem., 7mm Rem. Mag., 7mm STW, .30-06, .300 Win. Mag., .338 Win. Mag., .340 Wby. Mag., .375 H&H, .416 Rem. Mag. Five round (std.) or 4-rnd. (Mag.). 24- or 26-in. bbl. 44 to 46 in. overall. Weight: 7.75 to 9.75 lbs. Receiver drilled and tapped for scope mount; no sights. Blued finish. Fiberglass composite stock. Made 1994-2000.
Standard model. . . . . NiB $1379 Ex $1209 Gd $744
Magnum model. . . . . NiB $1997 Ex $1202 Gd $931
Varmint model (Intro. 1996) NiB $1498 Ex $1216 Gd $938
Calibers .375 H&H, .416 Rem. Mag., add $325
Left-hand model, add $110

MAGTECH — Las Vegas, NV
Manufactured by CBC, Brazil.

MODEL MT 122.2/S BOLT-ACTION
RIFLE. . . . . NiB $135 Ex $121 Gd $75
Calibers: .22 Short, Long, Long Rifle. Six- or 10-rnd. clip. Bolt action. 25-in. free-floating bbl. 43 in. overall. Weight: 6.5 lbs. Double locking bolt. Red cocking indicator. Safety lever. Brazilian hardwood finish. Double extractors. Beavertail forearm. Sling swivels. Imported from 1994. Disc.

MODEL MT 122.2/R . . . . NiB $140 Ex $116 Gd $88
Same as Model MT 122.2/S except adj. rear sight and post front sight. Introduced 1994. Disc.

MODEL MT 122.2/T . . . . NiB $151 Ex $122 Gd $93
Same as Model MT 122.2/S except w/adj. micrometer-type rear sight and ramp front sight. Introduced 1994. Disc.

MANNLICHER-SCHOENAUER SPORTING RIFLES — Austria
Manufactured by Steyr-Daimler-Puch, A.-G.

NOTE: *Certain Mannlicher-Schoenauer models were produced before WWII. Manufacture of sporting rifles and carbines was resumed at the Steyr-Daimler-Puch plant in Austria in 1950 during which time the Model 1950 rifles and carbines were introduced.*

In 1967, Steyr-Daimler-Puch introduced a series of sporting rifles with a bolt action that is a departure from the Mannlicher-Schoenauer system of earlier models. In the latter, the action is locked by lugs symmetrically arranged behind the bolt head as well as by placing the bolt handle ahead of the right flank of the receiver, the rear section of which is open on top for backward movement of the bolt handle. The current action, made in four lengths to accommodate different ranges of cartridges, has a closed-top receiver; the bolt locking lugs are located toward the rear of the bolt (behind the magazine). The Mannlicher-Schoenauer rotary magazine has been redesigned as a detachable box type made of Makrolon. Previously imported by Gun South, Inc. Trussville, AL.

— PRE-WWII PRODUCTION —

MODEL 1903 BOLT-ACTION SPORTING
CARBINE. . . . . NiB $2790 Ex $2133 Gd $1500
Caliber: 6.5x53mm (referred to in some European gun catalogs as 6.7x53mm, following the Austrian practice of designating calibers by bullet diameter). Five round rotary magazine. 450mm (17.7-in.) bbl. Weight: 6.5 lbs. Double-set trigger. Sights: Two-leaf rear; ramp front. Full-length sporting stock w/ cheekpiece, pistol-grip, trap buttplate, swivels. Pre-WWII.

MODEL 1905 CARBINE . . . . . NiB $1966 Ex $904 Gd $633
Same as Model 1903 except w/19.7-in. bbl.chambered 9x56mm and weight: 6.75 lbs. Pre-WWII.

MODEL 1908 CARBINE . . . . . NiB $1910 Ex $909 Gd $640
Same as Model 1905 except calibers 7x57mm and 8x56mm Pre-WWII.

MODEL 1910 CARBINE . . . . NiB $1823 Ex $1535 Gd $870
Same as Model 1905 except in 9.5x57mm. Pre-WWII.

MODEL 1924 CARBINE . . . NiB $1767 Ex $1543 Gd $1067
Same as Model 1905 except caliber .30-06 (7.62x63mm). Pre-WWII.

— POST-WWII PRODUCTION —

MODEL 1950 BOLT-ACTION
SPORTING RIFLE . . . . NiB $1947 Ex $1466 Gd $590
Calibers: .257 Roberts, .270 Win., .30-06. Five round rotary magazine. 24-in. bbl. Weight: 7.25 lbs. Single trigger or double-set trigger. Redesigned low bolt handle, shotgun-type safety. Sights: Folding leaf open rear; hooded ramp front. Improved half-length stock w/cheekpiece, pistol grip, checkered, ebony forend tip, swivels. Made 1950-52.

MODEL 1950 CARBINE . . . . NiB $2065 Ex $1567 Gd $997
Same general specifications as Model 1950 Rifle except w/20-in. bbl., full-length stock, weighs 7 lbs. Made 1950-52.

MODEL 1950 6.5 CARBINE NiB $2060 Ex $1550 Gd $990
Same as other Model 1950 Carbines except caliber 6.5x53mm, w/18.25-in. bbl., weighs 6.75 lbs. Made 1950-52.

RIFLES

GRADING: **NiB** = New in Box   **Ex** = Excellent or NRA 95%   **Gd** = Good or NRA 68%

Magnum Research Mountain Eagle Bolt-Action Rifle

Mannlicher Model L Rifle

Mannlicher Model M Carbine

Mannlicher Model M Professional

MODEL 1952 IMPROVED CARBINE . . . . **NiB $1866 Ex $1444 Gd $905**
Same as Model 1950 Carbine except w/swept-back bolt handle, redesigned stock. Calibers: .257, .270, 7mm, .30-06. Made 1952-56.

MODEL 1952 IMPROVED 6.5 CARBINE. . . . . **NiB $2088 Ex $1091 Gd $623**
Same as Model 1952 Carbine except caliber 6.5x53mm, w/18.25-in. bbl. Made 1952-56.

MODEL 1952 IMPROVED SPORTING RIFLE . . . . **NiB $1847 Ex $1350 Gd $896**
Same as Model 1950 except w/swept-back bolt handle, redesigned stock. Calibers: .257, .270, .30-06, 9.3x62mm. Made 1952-56 and imported exclusively by Stoeger Arms Corp.

MODEL 1956 CUSTOM CARBINE . . . **NiB $2055 Ex $831 Gd $567**
Same general specifications as Models 1950 and 1952 Carbines except w/redesigned stock w/high comb. Drilled and tapped

for scope mounts. Calibers: .243, 6.5mm, .257, .270, 7mm, .30-06, .308. Made 1956-60.

CARBINE, MODEL 1961-MCA . . . **NiB $1867 Ex $1278 Gd $990**
Same as Model 1956 Carbine except w/universal Monte Carlo design stock. Calibers: .243 Win., 6.5mm, .270, .308, .30-06. Made 1961-71.

RIFLE, MODEL 1961-MCA . . **NiB $2159 Ex $1389 Gd $997**
Same as Model 1956 Rifle except w/universal Monte Carlo design stock. Calibers: .243, .270, .30-06. Made 1961-71.

HIGH VELOCITY BOLT-ACTION SPORTING RIFLE . . . . **NiB $2650 Ex $1630 Gd $1190**
Calibers: 7x64 Brenneke, .30-06 (7.62x63), 8x60 Magnum, 9.3x62, 10.75x68mm. 23.6-in. bbl. Weight: 7.5 lbs. Sights: British-style 3-leaf open rear; ramp front. Half-length sporting stock w/cheek-piece, pistol grip, checkered, trap buttplate, swivels. Also produced in a takedown model. Pre-WWII.
10.75x68mm, add **105%**

Mannlicher-Schoenauer
Model 1950 Sporting Rifle

Mannlicher-Schoenauer
Model 1950 Carbine

Mannlicher-Schoenauer
Model 1950 Carbine

Mannlicher-Schoenauer Model
1950 Sporting Rifle

Mannlicher-Schoenauer Model
1950 Improved Carbine

Mannlicher Schoenauer
High Velocity Bolt-Action Sporting Rifle

— RECENT PRODUCTION UNDER STEYR MANNLICHER —

MODEL L CARBINE . . . . NiB $1666 Ex $1189 Gd $835
Same general specifications as Model SL Carbine except w/
type "L" action, weight: 6.2 lbs. Calibers same as for Model L
Rifle. Imported 1968 to 1996.

MODEL L RIFLE . . . . NiB $2177 Ex $1508 Gd $1009
Same general specifications as Model SL Rifle except w/type "L"
action, weighs 6.3 lbs. Calibers: .22-250, 5.6x57 (disc. 1991),
.243 Win., 6mm Rem. .308 Win. Imported 1968 to 1996.

MODEL L VARMINT RIFLE . . NiB $2107 Ex $1600 Gd $977
Same general specs as Model SL Varmint Rifle except w/type "L"
action. Calibers: .22-250, .243 Win., .308 Win. Imported 1969–96.

MODEL LUXUS BOLT-ACTION RIFLE
Same general specifications as Models L and M except w/3-
rnd. detachable box magazine and single-set trigger. Full
or half-stock w/low-luster oil or high-gloss lacquer finish.
Disc. 1996.
Full stock. . . . . NiB $2133 Ex $1790 Gd $1305
Half stock . . . . NiB $2733 Ex $1966 Gd $928

MODEL M CARBINE
Same general specifications as Model SL Carbine except w/
type "M" action, stock w/recoil pad, weighs 6.8 lbs. Left-hand
version w/additional 6.5x55 and 9.3x62 calibers intro. 1977.
Imported 1969 to 1996.
Right-hand carbine . . . . NiB $1688 Ex $1570 Gd $909
Left-hand carbine . . . . NiB $2088 Ex $1964 Gd $1507

GRADING: **NiB** = New in Box   **Ex** = Excellent or NRA 95%   **Gd** = Good or NRA 68%

RIFLES

MODEL M PROFESSIONAL RIFLE .. **NiB $1079 Ex $800 Gd $633**
Same as standard Model M Rifle except w/synthetic (Cycolac) stock, weighs 7.5 lbs. Calibers: 6.5x55, 6.5x57, .270 Win., 7x57, 7x64, 7.5 Swiss, .30-06, 8x57JS, 9.3x62. Imported 1977 to 1993.

MODEL M RIFLE
Same general specifications as Model SL Rifle except w/type "M" action, stock w/forend tip and recoil pad; weighs 6.9 lbs. Calibers: 6.5x57, .270 Win., 7x57, 7x64, .30-06, 8x57JS, 9.3x62. Made 1969 to date. Left-hand version also in calibers 6.5x55 and 7.5 Swiss. Imported 1977 to 1996.
Right-hand rifle . . . . **NiB $1667 Ex $1188 Gd $832**
Left-hand rifle . . . . **NiB $2317 Ex $1951 Gd $1489**

MODEL S RIFLE . . . . **NiB $1674 Ex $1203 Gd $855**
Same general specs as Model SL Rifle except w/type "S" action, 4-rnd. magazine, 25.63-in. bbl., stock w/forend tip and recoil pad, weighs 8.4 lbs. Calibers: 6.5x68, .257 Weatherby Mag., .264 Win. Mag., 7mm Rem. Mag., .300 Win. Mag., .300 H&H Mag., .308 Norma Mag., 8x68S, .338 Win. Mag., 9.3x64, .375 H&H Mag. Imported 1970 to 1996.

MODEL SL CARBINE . . . . . . **NiB $1664 Ex $1176 Gd $815**
Same general specifications as Model SL Rifle except w/20-in. bbl. and full-length stock, weight: 6 lbs. Imported 1968 to 1996.

MODEL SL RIFLE . . . . **NiB $1744 Ex $1278 Gd $823**
Steyr-Mannlicher SL bolt action. Calibers: .222 Rem., .222 Rem., .222 Rem. Mag., .223 Rem. Five round rotary magazine, detachable. 23.63-in. bbl. Weight: 6 lbs. Single- or double-set trigger (mechanisms interchangeable). Sights: Open rear; hooded ramp front. Half stock of European walnut w/Monte Carlo comb and cheekpiece, skip-checkered forearm and pistol grip, rubber buttpad, QD swivels. Imported 1967 to 1996.

MODEL SL VARMINT RIFLE . . . **NiB $1233 Ex $1198 Gd $854**
Same general specifications as Model SL Rifle except caliber .222 Rem. only, w/25.63-in. heavy bbl., no sights, weighs 7.92 lbs. Imported 1969 to 1996.

MODEL SSG MATCH TARGET RIFLE
Type "L" action. Caliber: .308 Win. (7.62x51 NATO). Five- or 10-rnd. magazine, single-shot plug. 25.5-in. heavy bbl. Weight: 10.25 lbs. Single trigger. Sights: Micrometer peep rear; globe front. Target stock, European walnut or synthetic, w/full pistol-grip, wide forearm w/swivel rail, adj. rubber buttplate. Imported 1969 to date.
w/walnut stock . . . . **NiB $2388 Ex $1956 Gd $1267**
w/synthetic stock . . . . **NiB $1488 Ex $1131 Gd $709**

MODEL S/T RIFLE . . . . **NiB $1278 Ex $1564 Gd $931**
Same as Model S Rifle except w/heavy 25.63-in. bbl., weight: 9 lbs. Calibers: 9.3x64, .375 H&H Mag., .458 Win. Mag. Option of 23.63-in. bbl. in latter caliber. Imported 1975 to 1996.

M72 MODEL L/M CARBINE . . **NiB $1043 Ex $762 Gd $513**
Similar to M72 Model L/M Rifle except w/20-in. bbl. and full-length stock, weight: 7.2 lbs. Imported from 1972 to date.

M72 MODEL L/M RIFLE . . . . . . **NiB $906 Ex $821 Gd $600**
M72 bolt-action, type L/M receiver front-locking bolt internal rotary magazine (5-rnd.). Calibers: .22-250, 5.6x57, 6mm Rem., .243 Win., 6.5x57, .270 Win., 7x57, 7x64, .308 Win., .30-06. 23.63-in. bbl. Weight: 7.3 lbs. Single- or double-set trigger (mechanisms interchangeable). Sights: Open rear; hooded ramp front. Half stock of European walnut, checkered forearm and pistol-grip, Monte Carlo cheekpiece, rosewood forend tip, recoil pad QD swivels. Imported 1972 to 1981.

M72 MODEL S RIFLE . . . . **NiB $876 Ex $756 Gd $544**
Same general specifications as M72 Model L/M Rifle except w/magnum action, 4-rnd. magazine, 25.63-in. bbl., weighs 8.6 lbs. Calibers: 6.5x68, 7mm Rem. Mag., 8x68S, 9.3x64, .375 H&H Mag. Imported from 1972 to 1981.

M72 MODEL S/T RIFLE . . . . **NiB $1755 Ex $1461 Gd $999**
Same as M72 Model S Rifle except w/heavy 25.63-in. bbl., weighs 9.3 lbs. Calibers: .300 Win. Mag. 9.3x64, .375 H&H Mag., .458 Win. Mag. Option of 23.63-in. bbl. in latter caliber. Imported from 1975 to 1981.

MODEL SBS FORESTER SERIES
Calibers: .243 Win., .25-06 Rem., .270 Win., .6.5x55mm, 6.5x57mm, 7x64mm, 7mm-08 Rem., .30-06, .308 Win. 9.3x64mm. Four round detachable magazine. 23.6-in. bbl. 44.5 in. overall. Weight: 7.5 lbs. No sights w/drilled and tapped for Browning A-Bolt configuration. Checkered American walnut stock w/Monte Carlo cheekpiece and Pachmayr swivels. Polished or matte blue finish. Imported from 1997 to 2002; reintro. 2005.
Standard calibers . . . . **NiB $955 Ex $823 Gd $595**
Mountain Rifle (w/20-in. bbl.) . . . . **NiB $975 Ex $805 Gd $555**
For magnum calibers, add. **$50**
For metric calibers, add **$126**

MODEL SBS PRO-HUNTER SERIES
Similar to the Forester Model, except w/ASB black synthetic stock. Matte blue finish. Imported from 1997 to date.
Standard calibers . . . . **NiB $1000 Ex $879 Gd $467**
Mountain Rifle (w/20-in. bbl.) . **NiB $897 Ex $689 Gd $523**
.376 Steyr . . . . **NiB $887 Ex $679 Gd $513**
Youth/Ladies rifle . . . . **NiB $720 Ex $689 Gd $523**
For magnum calibers, add. **$50**
For metric calibers, add **$150**
w/walnut stock . . . . **NiB $2307 Ex $1896 Gd $1371**
w/synthetic stock, add **$150**

MARLIN FIREARMS CO. — Ilion, NY

Formerly manufactured in North Haven, Connecticut, acquired by Freedom Group Inc. in 2007 and manufactured in Ilion, New York. In 2000 Marlin acquired H&R 1871 including Harrington & Richardson (H&R) New England Firearms, and Wesson & Harrington. See Shotgun section for L. C. Smith listings. In the 2020 Remington bankruptcy, Ruger purchased all Marlin assets. To facilitate locating Marlin rifles, models are grouped into categories: Centerfire Bolt-action Rifles, Centerfire Lever-Action Rifles, Centerfire Semiauto Rifles, Rimfire Bolt-action Rifles, Rimfire Lever-action Rifles, Rimfire Semiauto Rifles, Slide-action (pump) Rifles. For a complete listing, please refer to the index.

Note: *In 1960 Marlin began marketing inexpensive rifles and shotguns under the Glenfield name.*

- CENTERFIRE BOLT-ACTION MODELS -

MODEL 322 BOLT-ACTION
VARMINT RIFLE . . . . **NiB $597 Ex $390 Gd $278**
Sako short Mauser action. Caliber: .222 Rem. Three round clip magazine. 24-in. medium weight bbl. Checkered stock. Sights: Two-position peep rear; hooded ramp front. Weight: 7.5 lbs. Made 1954-57.

MODEL 455 BOLT-ACTION SPORTER
FN Mauser action w/Sako trigger. Calibers: .30-06 or .308. Five round box magazine. 24-in. medium weight stainless-steel bbl. Monte Carlo stock w/cheekpiece, checkered pistol grip and forearm. Lyman No. 48 receiver sight; hooded ramp front. Weight: 8.5 lbs. Made 1957-59.
.30-06 Spfd., 1079 produced . . **NiB $707 Ex $535 Gd $325**
.308 Win., 59 produced . . . . . . **NiB $800 Ex $610 Gd $475**

Marlin Model 9 9mm Carbine

Marlin Model 455 Sporter

Marlin-Glenfield Model 30A

MODEL MR-7 . . . . **NiB $555 Ex $380 Gd $277**
Bolt action. Calibers: .25-06 Rem., .270 Win., .280 Rem., .308 Win. or .30-06. Four round magazine. 22-in. bbl. w/ or w/o sights. 43.31 in. overall. Weight: 7.5 lbs. Checkered American walnut or birch stock w/recoil pad and sling-swivel studs. Jeweled bolt w/cocking indicator and 3-position safety. Made 1996-99.
w/birch stock, intro. 1998 . . . . NiB $460 Ex $379 Gd $255
w/open sights, add **$50**

MODEL X-7 . . . . **NiB $403 Ex $355 Gd $305**
Bolt action, short or long action. Calibers: .223 Rem., .243 Win., .25-06 Rem., .270 Win., 7mm-08, .308 Win. or .30-06. Four round internal magazine. 22-in. bbl. w/o sights. 43.31 in. overall. Weight: 6.5 lbs. Black synthetic stock. Two-position safety. Scope bases. Blued finish. Made 2008-15.
X7C (camo stock), add **$20**
X7W (wood stock), add **$110**

- CENTERFIRE LEVER-ACTION MODELS -

MODEL 30/30A & 30AS LEVER-ACTION
Caliber: .30/30 Win. Six-rnd. tubular magazine. 20-in. bbl. w/ Micro-Groove rifling. 38.25 in. overall. Weight: 7 lbs. Brass bead front sight, adj. rear. Solid top receiver, offset hammer spur for scope use. Walnut-finished hardwood stock w/pistol-grip. Mar-Shield finish. Made 1964-2000.
Model 30/30A . . . . **NiB $290 Ex $198 Gd $160**
Model 30AS . . . . **NiB $290 Ex $198 Gd $160**
Model 30AS w/4x scope, add **$25**

MODEL 30 . . . . **NiB $280 Ex $133 Gd $100**
Lever action. Same as Marlin Model 336C except chambered for .30-30 only, w/4-rnd. magazine, plainer stock and forearm of walnut-finished hardwood. Made 1966-68.

MODEL 30A . . . . **NiB $279 Ex $190 Gd $139**
Lever action. Same as Model 336C but chambered for .30-30 only, w/checkered walnut-finished hardwood stock. Made 1969-83.

MODEL 36G . . . . **NiB $879 Ex $633 Gd $260**
Same as Marlin Model 336C except chambered for .30-30 only, w/5-rnd. magazine, plainer stock. Made 1960-65.

MODEL 36 LEVER-ACTION REPEATING CARBINE
Calibers: .30-30, .32 Special. Seven-rnd. tubular magazine. 20-in. bbl. Weight: 6.5 lbs. Sights: Open rear; bead front. Pistol-grip stock, semibeavertail forearm w/carbine bbl. band. Early production w/receiver, lever and hammer color casehardened and the remaining metal blued. Late production w/blued receiver. Made 1936 to 1948. Note: In 1936, this was designated "Model 1936" and was so marked on the upper tang. In 1937, the model designation was shortened to "36". An "RC" serial number suffix identifies a "Regular/Carbine".
Model 1936 CC receiver
  (w/long tang, no SN prefix) . **NiB $909 Ex $744 Gd $500**
Model 1936 CC receiver
  (w/short tang, no SN prefix) **NiB $645 Ex $531 Gd $390**
Model 1936 CC receiver
  (w/SN prefix) . . . . **NiB $534 Ex $488 Gd $345**
Model 36, CC receiver
  (w/SN prefix) . . . . **NiB $508 Ex $433 Gd $300**
Model 36, blued receiver
  (w/SN prefix) . . . . **NiB $482 Ex $390 Gd $289**

MODEL 36 SPORTING CARBINE
Same as M36 carbine except w/6-rnd., (2/3 magazine) and weighs 6.25 lbs.
Model 1936, CC receiver
  (w/long tang, no SN prefix) . **NiB $860 Ex $707 Gd $499**
Model 1936, CC receiver
  (w/short tang, no SN prefix) **NiB $656 Ex $567 Gd $380**
Model 1936, CC receiver
  (w/SN prefix) . . . . **NiB $588 Ex $497 Gd $355**

GRADING: **NiB** = New in Box   **Ex** = Excellent or NRA 95%   **Gd** = Good or NRA 68%

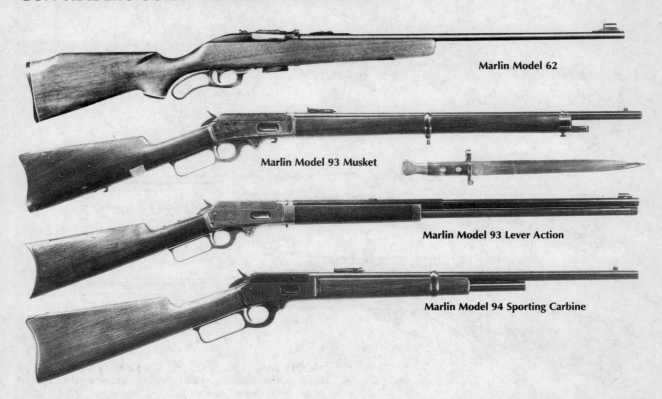

Marlin Model 62

Marlin Model 93 Musket

Marlin Model 93 Lever Action

Marlin Model 94 Sporting Carbine

Model 36, CC receiver
(w/SN prefix) . . . . NiB $555 Ex $457 Gd $339
Model 36, blued receiver
(w/SN prefix) . . . . NiB $480 Ex $413 Gd $303

MODEL 36A/36A-DL LEVER-ACTION REPEATING RIFLE
Same as Model 36 Carbine except has 24-in. bbl. w/hooded front sight and 2/3 magazine holding 6 cartridges. Weight: 6.75 lbs. Note: An "A" serial number suffix identifies a Rifle while an "A-DL" suffix designates a Deluxe Model w/checkered stock, semibeavertail forearm, swivels and sling. Made 1936-48.
Model 1936, CC receiver (w/long tang,
no SN prefix) . . . . NiB $1180 Ex $1077 Gd $790
Model 1936, CC receiver
(w/short, tang, no SN prefix) NiB $795 Ex $556 Gd $378
Model 1936, CC receiver
(w/SN prefix) . . . . NiB $845 Ex $589 Gd $465
Model 36, CC receiver,
(w/SN prefix) . . . . NiB $775 Ex $451 Gd $348
Model 36, blued receiver
(w/SN prefix) . . . . NiB $744 Ex $440 Gd $332
ADL model, add $25%

MODEL 62 LEVERMATIC RIFLE NiB $555 Ex $440 Gd $190
Lever-action. Calibers: .256 Magnum, .30 Carbine. Four round clip magazine. 23-in. bbl. Weight: 7 lbs. Sights: Open rear; hooded ramp front. Monte Carlo-style stock w/pistol-grip, swivels and sling. Made in .256 Magnum 1963 to 1966; in .30 Carbine 1963 to 1969.

MODEL 92 LEVER-ACTION REPEATING RIFLE
Calibers: .22 Short, Long, LR. .32 Short, Long (rimfire or centerfire by changing firing pin). Tubular magazines holding 25 Short, 20 Long, 18 LR (.22); or 17 Short, 14 Long (.32); 16-in. bbl. model w/shorter magazine holding 15 Short, 12 Long, 10 LR. Bbl. lengths: 16 (.22 cal. only) 24, 26, 28 in. Weight: 5.5

lbs. w/24-in. bbl. Sights: open rear; blade front. Plain straight-grip stock and forearm. Made 1892 to 1916. Note: Originally designated "Model 1892."
Model 92 (.22 caliber) . . . . . NiB $1598 Ex $1400 Gd $883
Model 92 (.32 caliber) . . . . . NiB $1554 Ex $1268 Gd $956

MODEL 93/93SC CARBINE
Same as Standard Model 93 Rifle except in calibers .30-30 and .32 Special only. Model 93 w/7-rnd. magazine. 20-in. rnd. bbl., carbine sights, weight: 6.75 lbs. Model 93SC magazine capacity 5 rnd., weight 6.5 lbs.
Model 93 Carbine
(w/saddle ring) . . . . NiB $1689 Ex $1423 Gd $1108
Model 93 Carbine "Bull's-Eye"
(w/o saddle ring) . . . . NiB $1449 Ex $1188 Gd $976
Model 93SC Sporting
Carbine . . . . NiB $1377 Ex $1087 Gd $915

MODEL 1893/93 LEVER-ACTION
REPEATING RIFLE . . . . NiB $2833 Ex $2022 Gd $1370
Solid frame or takedown. Calibers: .25-36 Marlin, .30-30, .32 Special, .32-40, .38-55. Tubular magazine holds 10 cartridges. 26-in. rnd. or octagon bbl. standard; also made w/28-, 30- and 32-in. bbls. Weight: 7.25 lbs. Sights: Open rear; bead front. Plain straight-grip stock and forearm. Made 1893-1936. Note: Before 1915 designated "Model 1893."

MODEL 93 MUSKET . . . . . NiB $5610 Ex $ 3766 Gd $2833
Same as Standard Model 93 except w/30-in. bbl., angular bayonet, ramrod under bbl., musket stock, full-length military-style forearm. Weight: 8 lbs. Made 1893-1915.

MODEL 94 . . . . NiB $2655 Ex $1840 Gd $989
Lever action. Solid frame or takedown. Calibers: .25-20, .32-20, .38-40, .44-40. 10-rnd. tubular magazine. 24-in. rnd. or octagon bbl. Weight: 7 lbs. Sights open rear; bead front. Plain straight-grip stock and forearm (also available w/pistol-

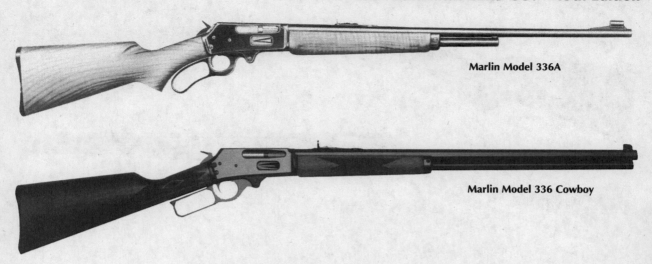

Marlin Model 336A

Marlin Model 336 Cowboy

grip stock). Made 1894-1934. Note: Before 1906 designated "Model 1894."

MODEL 94 LEVER-ACTION COWBOY SERIES
Calibers: .357 Mag., .44-40, .44 Mag., .45 LC. 10-rnd. magazine. 24-in. tapered octagon bbl. Weight: 7.5 lbs. 41.5 in. overall. Marble carbine front sight, adjustable semi-buckhorn rear. Blue finish. Checkered, straight-grip American black walnut stock w/hard rubber buttplate. Made 1996 to date. Cowboy II introduced in 1997.
Cowboy model (.45 LC) . . . . . . **NiB $833 Ex $650 Gd $466**
**Cowboy II model (.357 Mag., .44-40,
    .44 Mag.)** . . . . **NiB $854 Ex $659 Gd $572**

MODEL 308MX . . . . **NiB $686 Ex $2022 Gd $1370**
Lever action. Calibers: .308 Marlin Express. 5-rnd. tube magazine. 22-in. bbl. Weight: 7.25 lbs. Blue finish. Checkered, pistol-grip American black walnut stock w/rubber butt pad. Made 2007 to date.
308MXLR (stainless, 24-in. bbl.), add **$200**

MODEL 336A . . . . **NiB $570 Ex $400 Gd $338**
Lever action. Improved version of Model 36A Rifle w/same general specifications except w/improved action w/rnd. breech bolt. Calibers: .30-30, .32 Special (disc. 1963), .35 Rem. (intro. 1952). Made 1948-63; reintroduced 1973, disc. 1980.

MODEL 336A-DL . . . . **NiB $665 Ex $544 Gd $351**
Same as Model 336A Rifle except w/deluxe checkered stock and forearm, swivels and sling. Made 1948-63.

MODEL 336AS . . . . **NiB $475 Ex $291 Gd $139**
Lever action. Similar to Model 30AS. Caliber: .30-30 Win., Six round tubular magazine. 20- in. Micro-Groove bbl. 38.25 in. overall. Weight: 7 lbs. Maine birch pistol grip stock w/swivel studs and hard rubber butt plate. Tapped for scope mount and receiver sight. Screw-adjustable open rear and ramp front sight. Checkered walnut finish. Made 1999-2020.

MODEL 336C . . . . **NiB $559 Ex $398 Gd $290**
Improved version of Model 36 Carbine w/same general specifications except w/improved action w/rnd. breech bolt. Original calibers: .30-30 and .32 Win. Spec. Made 1948-83. Note: Caliber .35 Rem. intro. 1953. Caliber .32 Winchester Special disc. 1963.

MODEL 336 COWBOY
LEVER-ACTION RIFLE . . . . **NiB $600 Ex $445 Gd $380**
Calibers: .30-30 Win., or .38-55 Win., 6- rnd. tubular magazine. 24- in. tapered octagon bbl. 42.5 in. overall. Weight: 7.5 lbs. American black walnut checkering stock. Marble carbine front sight w/solid top receiver drilled and tapped for scope mount. Mar-Shield finish. Made 1998-2020.

MODEL 336CS W/SCOPE . . . . . **NiB $479 Ex $338 Gd $266**
Lever-action w/hammer block safety. Caliber: .30/30 Win. or .35 Rem. Six round tubular magazine. 20-in. rnd. bbl. w/ Micro-Groove rifling. 38.5 in. overall. Weight: 7 lbs. Ramp front sight w/hood, adj. semi-buckhorn folding rear. Solid top receiver drilled and tapped for scope mount or receiver sight; offset hammer spur for scope use. American black walnut stock w/pistol-grip, fluted comb. Mar-Shield finish. Made 1984-2020.

MODEL 336DT DELUXE TEXAN . . **NiB $500 Ex $466 Gd $359**
Same as Model 336T except w/select walnut stock and forearm, hand-carved longhorn steer and map of Texas on buttstock. Made 1962-64.

MODEL 336M LEVER-ACTION
RIFLE . . . . **NiB $590 Ex $495 Gd $359**
Calibers: .30-30 Win., 6- rnd. tubular magazine. 20- in. stainless steel Micro Groove bbl., 38.5 in. overall. Weight: 7 lbs. American black walnut w/checkered pistol-grip stock. Adjustable folding semi-buckhorn rear and ramp front sight w/brass bead and removable Wide-Scan hood. Tapped for receiver sight and scope mount. Mar-Shield finish. Made 1999-2020.

MODEL 336 MARAUDER . . . . . **NiB $600 Ex $485 Gd $300**
Same as Model 336 Texan Carbine except w/16.25-in. bbl., weight: 6.25 lbs. Made 1963-64.

MODEL 336-MICRO
GROOVE ZIPPER . . . . **NiB $845 Ex $633 Gd $390**
General specifications same as Model 336 Sporting Carbine except caliber .219 Zipper. Made 1955-61.

MODEL 336 OCTAGON . . . . . . **NiB $570 Ex $498 Gd $300**
Same as Model 336T except chambered for .30-30 only w/22-in. octagon bbl. Made in 1973.

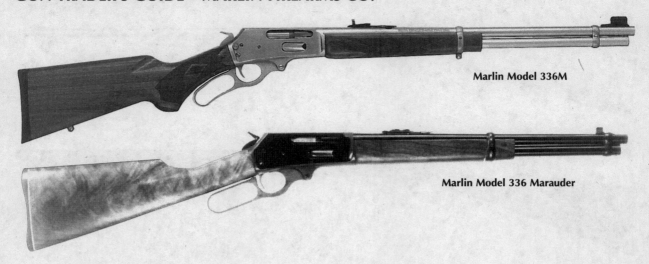

Marlin Model 336M

Marlin Model 336 Marauder

MODEL 336 SPORTING
CARBINE . . . . **NiB $845 Ex $589 Gd $445**
Same as Model 336A rifle except w/20-in. bbl., weight: 6.25 lbs. Made 1948-63.

MODEL 336T TEXAN CARBINE . . . **NiB $369 Ex $277 Gd $228**
Same as Model 336 Carbine except w/straight-grip stock and is not available in caliber .32 Special. Made 1953-83. Caliber .44 Magnum made 1963-67.

MODEL 336TS . . . . **NiB $400 Ex $333 Gd $190**
Lever-action w/hammer-block safety. Caliber: .30-30 Win. Six round tubular magazine. 18.5-in. Micro-Groove bbl. 37 in. overall. Weight: 6.5 lbs. Ramp front sight, adj. semi-buckhorn folding rear. Straight-grip American black walnut stock. Made 1983–87.

MODEL 336 ZANE GREY
CENTURY . . . . **NiB $488 Ex $439 Gd $300**
Similar to Model 336A except w/22-in. octagonal bbl., caliber .30-30, Zane Grey Centennial 1872-1972 medallion inlaid in receiver; select walnut stock w/classic pistol-grip and forearm; brass buttplate, forend cap. Weight: 7 lbs. 10,000 produced (numbered ZG1 through ZG10,000). Made in 1972.

MODEL 338MX . . . . **NiB $685 Ex $545 Gd $380**
Simialr to the 308MX except chambered in .338 Marlin Express. Made 2014–20.
338MXLR (stainless, 24-in. bbl.), add **$200**

MODEL 375 . . . . **NiB $845 Ex $589 Gd $445**
Same as Model 336CS except chambered in .375 Win. Made 1980-83.

MODEL 444 LEVER-ACTION . . **NiB $482 Ex $390 Gd $235**
Action similar to Model 336. Caliber: .444 Marlin. Four round tubular magazine. 24-in. bbl. Weigh: 7.5 lbs. Sights: Open rear; hooded ramp front. Monte Carlo stock w/straight grip, recoil pad. Carbine-style forearm w/bbl. band. Swivels, sling. Made 1965-71.

MARLIN MODEL 444 SPORTER . . **NiB $576 Ex $445 Gd $235**
Same as Model 444 Rifle except w/22-in. bbl., pistol-grip stock and forearm as on Model 336A, recoil pad, QD swivels and sling. Made 1972-83.

MODEL 444P (OUTFITTER) . . . **NiB $559 Ex $447 Gd $255**
Lever action. Caliber: .444 Marlin. Five round tubular magazine. 18.5-in. ported bbl., 37 in. overall. Weight: 6.75 lbs. Ramp front and adjustable folding rear sights. Black walnut straight grip stock w/cut checkering and Mar-Shield finish. Made 1999-2002.

MODEL 444SS . . . . **NiB $570 Ex $449 Gd $240**
Same general specifications as Model 444 except w/hammer safety. Made 1984-2002. (Changed to M444 in 2001.)

MODEL 1894 LEVER-ACTION RIFLE
See Marlin Model 94 listed previously under this section.

MODEL 1894 CARBINE . . . . . . **NiB $415 Ex $300 Gd $245**
Replica of original Model 94. Caliber: .44 Rem. 10-rnd. magazine. 20-in. rnd. bbl. Weight: 6 lbs. Sight: Open rear; ramp front. Straight-grip stock. Made 1969-84.
Octagon bbl. (made 1973) . . . . **NiB $525 Ex $390 Gd $239**
Sporter model (w/22-in. bbl.)
   made 1973) . . . . **NiB $585 Ex $369 Gd $345**

MODEL 1894C . . . . **NiB $605 Ex $555 Gd $405**
Reproduction of original 1894. Calibers: .357 Mag.; 8-rnd. tubular magazine. 18.5-in. octagon bbl. Weight: 6 lbs. Sights: adj. semibuckhorn folding rear sight, brass bead front w/ or w/o hood. Stock: straight grip wood w/ or w/o checkering. Made 1984–2015.
1894CP model (16.2-in. ported bbl.,
   2001-02), add **$75**
1894CL model (.32-20, 22-in. bbl.,
   2005-07), add **$100**

MODEL 1894CB COWBOY . . . . **NiB $965 Ex $780 Gd $610**
Lever action. Calibers: .32 H&R Mag., .357 Mag., .44-40, .44 Mag. or .45 LC; 10-rnd. tubular magazine. 20- or 24-in. octagon bbl. Weight: 7.5 lbs. Sights: Marbles adj. semibuckhorn rear sight, brass bead front. Stock: smooth straight grip wood. Made 1996–2015, reintro. 2017–20.
.357 Mag., .44-40, .44 Mag. calibers, add **$55**
Competition model (.38 Spl.
   or .45 LC, 22-in. tapered bbl., 2002-05), add **$100**

MODEL 1894CL CLASSIC . . . . . **NiB $743 Ex $545 Gd $355**
Lever action. Calibers: .218 Bee, .25-20 Win., .32-20 Win. Six round tubular magazine. 22-in. bbl. 38.75 in. overall. Weight: 6.25 lbs. Adj. semibuckhorn folding rear sight, brass

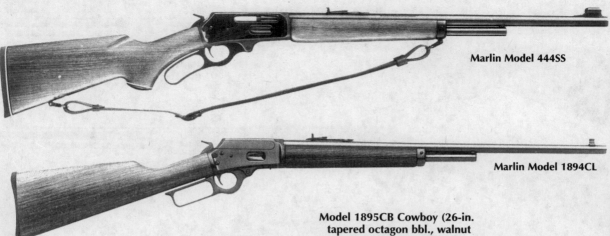

Marlin Model 444SS

Marlin Model 1894CL

bead front. Receiver tapped for scope mounts. Straight-grip American black walnut stock w/Mar-Shield finish. Made 1988-94.

MODEL 1894CS . . . . **NiB $779 Ex $545 Gd $369**
Lever action. Caliber: .357 Magnum, .38 Special. Nine round tubular magazine. 18.5-in. bbl. 36 in. overall. Weight: 6 lbs. Side ejection. Hammer block safety. Square finger lever. Bead front sight, adj. semi-buckhorn folding rear. Offset hammer spur for scope use. Two-piece straight grip American black walnut stock w/white buttplate spacer. Mar-Shield finish. Made 1984-2002.
Model 1894C Dark (18.5-in. rnd. bbl., .357 Mag., black painted wood stock, 2020 only) . . . . . . **NiB $830 Ex $810 Gd $795**

MODEL 1894CSBL . . . . **NiB $1180 Ex $1030 Gd $655**
Caliber: .357 Mag. or .44 Mag; 8-rnd. tubular magazine. 16.5-in. bbl. Weight: 6.6 lbs. Side ejection. Hammer block safety. Big loop lever. Sights: XS Sights Lever Rail w/ghost ring. Stock: black/gray laminate w/rubber butt plate. Finish: matte stainless. Made 2011-20.

MODEL 1894CST . . . . **NiB $999 Ex $900 Gd $700**
Caliber: .357 Mag.; 8-rnd. tubular magazine. 16.5-in. bbl. w/threaded muzzle. Weight: 6.6 lbs. Side ejection. Hammer block safety. Big loop lever. Sights: XS ghost ring. Stock: black hardwood w/rubber butt plate. Finish: matte stainless. Made 2011-20.

MODEL 1894S LEVER-ACTION NiB $522 Ex $347 Gd $245
Calibers: .41 Mag., .44 Rem. Mag., .44 S&W Special, .45 Colt.10-shot tubular magazine. 20-in. bbl. 37.5 in. overall. Weight: 6 lbs. Sights and stock same as Model 1894M. Made 1984-2002.

MODEL 1895 . . . . **NiB $445 Ex $390 Gd $235**
Model 336-type action. Caliber: .45-70 Government. Four round magazine. 22-in. bbl. Weight: 7 lbs. Sights: Open rear; bead front. Straight-grip stock, forearm w/metal end cap, QD swivels, leather sling. Made 1972-84. NOTE: Early models had 8-groove rifling, later models had 12-groove Micro Groove rifling. Add 10% for 8-grroove models. Early stocks were straight then changed to pistol grip. Later models have cross-bolt safety and have less value.
Model 1895SS (Mar-Shield finish, walnut pistol grip stock, 1983–2020) . . . . . . **NiB $675 Ex $580 Gd $430**

Model 1895CB Cowboy (26-in. tapered octagon bbl., walnut straight grip stock, 2001-11, reintro. 2014–20) . . . . **NiB $815 Ex $680 Gd $480**
Model 1895CBA (18.5-in. tapered octagon bbl., walnut straight grip stock, 2015-16, reintro. 2018–20) . . . **NiB $815 Ex $680 Gd $480**
Model 1895XLR (24-in. bbl., black/gray laminate stock, 2006–11) . . . . . **NiB $810 Ex $710 Gd $555**

MODEL OF 1895 . . . . **NiB $5555 Ex $3555 Gd $2360**
Lever-action repeater. Solid frame or takedown. Calibers: .33 WCF, .38-56, .40-65, .40-70, .40-82, .45-70. Nine round tubular magazine. 24-in. rnd. or octagongon bbl. standard (other lengths available). Weight: 8 lbs. Sights: Open rear; bead front. Plain stock and forearm (also available w/pistol-grip stock). Made 1895 to 1915.

MODEL 1895G GUIDE GUN. . . . . **NiB $590 Ex $389 Gd $280**
Lever action. Caliber: .45-70 Govt., 4- rnd. magazine. 18.5-in. ported bbl., 37 in. overall. Weight: 6.75 lbs. Ramp front and adjustable folding rear sights. Black walnut straight grip stock w/cut checkering and Mar-Shield finish. 2,500 made starting in 1998. Ported bbl. disc. 2002.
Model 1895GS (stainless finish, 2001–20) . . . . **NiB $780 Ex $610 Gd $330**
Model 1895GBL (6-rnd. magazine, big loop, Marshield finish, brown laminate stock, 2010–20) . . . . . **NiB $705 Ex $580 Gd $430**
Model 1895GSBL (6-rnd. magazine, big loop, Marshield finish, green laminate stock, 2015–20) . . . . **NiB $1030 Ex $910 Gd $680**

MODEL 1895M. . . . . **NiB $448 Ex $290 Gd $144**
Lever action. Caliber: .450 Marlin. Four round tubular magazine, 18.5- in. ported bbl. w/Ballard-type rifling. 37 in. overall. Weight: 6.75 lbs. Genuine American black walnut straight-grip stock w/checkering. Ventilated recoil pad. Adjustable folding semi-buckhorn rear and ramp front sights. Mar-Shield finish. Made 2000-20.
Model 1895MR (22-in. bbl., 2003–04) . . . . **NiB $680 Ex $600 Gd $430**
Model 1895MXLR (24-in. bbl., black/gray laminate stock, 2006–09) . . . . . **NiB $680 Ex $600 Gd $430**

MODEL 1894S. . . . . **NiB $522 Ex $347 Gd $245**
Calibers: .41 Mag., .44 Rem. Mag., .44 S&W Special, .45. Colt.10-shot tubular magazine. 20-in. bbl.37.5 in. overall. Weight: 6 lbs. Sights and stock same as Model 1894M. Made 1984-2002.

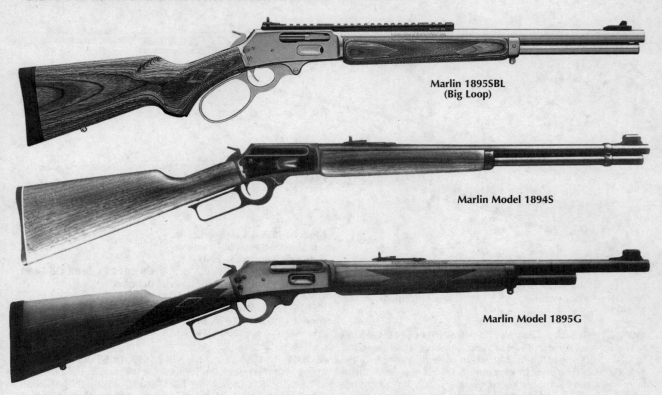

Marlin 1895SBL
(Big Loop)

Marlin Model 1894S

Marlin Model 1895G

MODEL 1895SBL BIG LOOP SERIES

Caliber: .45-70; 6-rnd. tubular magazine. 18.5-in. bbl. Weight: 8 lbs. Side ejection. Hammer block safety. Big loop lever. Sights: XS Lever Rail w/ghost ring. Stock: black/gray laminate w/rubber butt plate. Finish: matte stainless or matte blue. Made 2010–20.

1895SBL (matte stainless,
 Marlin mfg.) . . . . NiB $1240 Ex $1030 Gd $655
1895GBL (matte blue, semibuckhorn
 sights) . . . . NiB $800 Ex $710 Gd $655
Trapper model (16.5-in. bbl., matte stainless,
 Skinner peep sight, black hardwood
 stock, Marlin mfg.) . . . . NiB $1220 Ex $1010 Gd $655
Dark Series model (16.25-in. threaded bbl.,
 matte black, XS Lever Rail sight,
 black hardwood stock) . . . . . . NiB $810 Ex $655 Gd $455

MODEL 1894CB SERIES

Caliber: .45-70; 6-rnd. tubular magazine. 18.5- or 26-in. tapered octagon bbl. Weight: 6-7 lbs. Side ejection. Hammer block safety. Square loop lever. Sights: adj. Marbles. Stock: straight grip walnut w/plastic butt plate. Finish: blue. Made 2001–11, reintro. 2014–20.

1895CB (26-IN. BBL.) . . . . NIB $780 EX $605 GD $330
1895CBA (18.5-IN. BBL.) . . . . . NIB $780 EX $605 GD $330

MODEL 1895SS . . . . NiB $609 Ex $448 Gd $356

Lever action. Caliber: .45-70 Govt. Four round tubular magazine. 22-in. bbl. w/Micro-Groove rifling. 40.5 in. overall. Weight: 7.5 lbs. Ramp front sight w/brass bead and Wide-Scan hood; adj. semi-buckhorn folding rear. Solid top receiver tapped for scope mount or receiver sight. Off-set hammer spur for scope use. Two-piece American black walnut stock w/fluted comb, pistol-grip, sling swivels. Made 1984 to 2020. (Changed to M1895 in 2001.)

MODEL 1936 LEVER-ACTION CARBINE

See Marlin Model 36 listed previously under this section.

NOTE: *In 2022 Ruger reintroduced the Model 1895 SBL and 1895 Trapper with modifications. All new Ruger manufactured rifles have an RM serial number prefix. Made in Mayodan, NC.*

- RECENT MANUFACTURE (2022 TO DATE) -

MODEL 1895 SBL . . . . NiB $1399 Ex $1300 Gd $1200

Caliber: .45-70 Gov't; 6-rnd. tubular magazine. 18.5-in. bbl. Weight: 7.3 lbs. Sights: Ghost ring rear, tritium fiber optic front, Picatinny rail. Stock: Gray laminate w/rubber butt pad and checkered grip areas, red/white Marlin bullseye logo, laser engraved horse/rider Marlin logo in grip, sling studs. Finish: Polished stainless. Side ejection, nickel plated bolt w/ spiral flutes. Hammer block safety. Big loop lever. Made 2022–date.

Trapper model (16-in. bbl.,
 Ruger mfg.) . . . . NiB $1340 Ex $1200 Gd $700

- CENTERFIRE SEMIAUTO MODELS -

MODEL 9 SEMIAUTO CARBINE

Calibers: 9mm Parabellum. 12-rnd. magazine. 16.5-in. bbl. 35.5 in. overall. Weight: 6.75 lbs. Manual bolt hold-open. Sights: Hooded post front; adj. open rear. Walnut-finished hardwood stock w/rubber buttpad. Blued or nickel-Teflon finish. Made 1985-99.

Model 9 . . . . NiB $525 Ex $387 Gd $213
Model 9N, nickel-Teflon
 (disc. 1994) . . . . NiB $475 Ex $390 Gd $146

MODEL 45 . . . . NiB $390 Ex $290 Gd $198

Semiauto action. Caliber: .45 Auto. Seven round clip.16.5-in. bbl. 35.5 in. overall. Weight: 6.75 lbs. Manual bolt hold-open. Sights: Ramp front sight w/brass bead, adj. folding rear.

Marlin-Glenfield Model 10

Marlin Model 15YN

Marlin Model 20

Receiver drilled and tapped for scope mount. Walnut-finished hardwood stock. Made 1986-99.

- RIMFIRE BOLT-ACTION MODELS -

MODEL 10 . . . . **NiB $140 Ex $110 Gd $85**
Bolt-action. Same as Marlin Model 101 except w/walnut-finished hardwood stock. Made 1966-79. Note: Later production featuring hot-ironstamped wood pistol grip to simulate checkering/carving; plain forend.

MODEL 15Y/15YN
Bolt-action, single-shot "Little Buckaroo" rifle. Caliber: .22 Short, Long or LR. 16.25-in. bbl. Weight: 4.25 lbs. Thumb safety. Ramp front sight; adj. open rear. One-piece walnut Monte Carlo stock w/full pistol-grip. Made 1984-88. Reintroduced in 1989–2020 as Model 15YN.
Model 15Y . . . . **NiB $200 Ex $130 Gd $98**
Model 15YN . . . .**NiB $215 Ex $140 Gd $110**

MODEL 20 . . . . **NiB $779 Ex $439 Gd $310**
Bolt-action. Same as Marlin Model 80/780 except w/bead front sight, walnut-finished hardwood stock. Made 1966 to 1982. Note: Recent production has stamped pistol grip; plain forend.

MODEL 25MB . . . . **NiB $179 Ex $110 Gd $95**
Caliber: .22 Short, Long or LR; 7-rnd. clip. 22-in. bbl. Weight: 5.5 lbs. Ramp front sight, adj. open rear. One-piece walnut Monte Carlo stock w/full pistol-grip Mar-Shield finish. Made 1984-88.

MODEL 25M . . . . **NiB $167 Ex $119 Gd $95**
Caliber: .22 WMR. 7-rnd. clip. 22-in. bbl. Weight: 6 lbs. Ramp front sight w/brass bead, adj. open rear. Walnut-finished stock w/Monte Carlo styling and full pistol-grip. Sling swivels. Made 1986-88.

MODEL 25MB MIDGET MAGNUM. . . . . **NiB $190 Ex $126 Gd $99**
Bolt action. Caliber: .22 WMR. Seven round capacity.16.25-in. bbl. Weight: 4.75 lbs. Walnut-finished Monte Carlo-style stock w/full pistol grip and abbreviated forend. Sights: Ramp front w/ brass bead, adj. open rear. Thumb safety. Made 1986-88.

MODEL 25MG/25MN/25N/25NC
Caliber: .22 WMR (Model 25MN) or .22 LR. (Model 25N). Seven round clip magazine. 22-in. bbl. 41 in. overall. Weight: 5.5 to 6 lbs. Adj. open rear sight, ramp front; receiver grooved for scope mounts. One piece walnut-finished hardwood Monte Carlo stock w/pistol grip. Made 1989-2003.
Model 25MG (Garden Gun) . . . **NiB $218 Ex $179 Gd $126**
Model 25MN . . . .**NiB $200 Ex $167 Gd $110**
Model 25N . . . .**NiB $177 Ex $155 Gd $109**
Model 25 NC (camo stock), add. **$50**

MODEL 65 SINGLE-SHOT . . . . . . **NiB $139 Ex $93 Gd $70**
Takedown. Caliber: .22 LR, Long, Short. 24-in. bbl. Weight: 5 lbs. Sights: Open rear; bead front. Plain pistol-grip stock w/grooved forearm. Made 1932-38. Model 65E is same as Model 65 except w/rear peep sight and hooded front sight.

MODEL 70 . . . . **NiB $188 Ex $95 Gd $65**
Bolt-action. Same as Marlin Model 989M2 except w/walnut-finished hardwood stock; no handguard. Made 1966-69.

MODEL 80 BOLT-ACTION REPEATING RIFLE
Takedown. Caliber: .22 LR, Long, Short. Eight round detachable box magazine. 24-in. bbl. Weight: 6 lbs. Sights: Open rear; bead front. Plain pistol-grip stock. Made 1934-39. Model 80E, w/peep rear sight; hooded front, made 1934-40.
Model 80 Standard . . . . **NiB $190 Ex $135 Gd $95**
Model 80E. . . . .**NiB $175 Ex $110 Gd $85**

MODEL 80C/80DL BOLT-ACTION REPEATER
Improved version of Model 80. Model 80C w/bead from sight, semibeavertail forearm; made 1940-70. Model 80DL w/peep rear sight; hooded blade front sight on ramp, swivels; made 1940-65.
Model 80C . . . . **NiB $200 Ex $155 Gd $100**
Model 80DL . . . .**NiB $167 Ex $110 Gd $90**

MODEL 80G. . . . .**NiB $100 Ex $65 Gd $45**
Bolt action. Same as Marlin Model 80C except w/plain stock, bead front sight. Made 1960-65.

MODEL 81/81E BOLT-ACTION REPEATER

Takedown. .22 LR, Long, Short. Tubular magazine holds 24 Short, 20 Long, 18 LR. 24-in. bbl. Weight: 6.25 lbs. Sights: Open rear, bead front. Plain pistol-grip stock. Made 1937-40. Model 81E w/peep rear sight; hooded front w/ramp.

Model 81 . . . . NiB $220 Ex $176 Gd $110
Model 81E. . . . . NiB $245 Ex $195 Gd $139

MODEL 81C/81DL BOLT-ACTION REPEATER

Improved version of Model 81 w/same general specifications. Model 81C w/bead front sight, semibeavertail forearm; made 1940-70. Model 81 DL w/peep rear sight, hooded front, swivels; disc. 1965.

Model 81C . . . . NiB $239 Ex $188 Gd $100
Model 81DL . . . . NiB $220 Ex $199 Gd $110

MODEL 81G . . . . NiB $110 Ex $78 Gd $66

Bolt action. Same as Marlin Model 81C except w/plain stock, bead front sight. Made 1960-65.

MODEL 100 . . . . NiB $200 Ex $123 Gd $90

Single-shot. Takedown. Caliber: .22 LR, Long, Short. 24-in. bbl. Weight: 4.5 lbs. Sights: Open rear; bead front. Plain pistol-grip stock. Made 1936-60.

MODEL 100SB . . . . NiB $120 Ex $90 Gd $65

Same as Model 100 except smoothbore for use w/22 shot cartridges, shotgun sight. Made 1936-41.

MODEL 100 TOM MIX

SPECIAL . . . . NiB $315 Ex $200 Gd $146
Same as Model 100 except w/peep rear sight; hooded front; sling. Made 1936-46.

MODEL 101 . . . . NiB $100 Ex $75 Gd $55

Improved version of Model 100 w/same general specifications, except w/stock w/beavertail forearm, weighs 5 lbs. Intro. 1951. Disc.

MODEL 101 DL . . . . NiB $119 Ex $85 Gd $70

Same as Model 101 except has peep rear sight; hooded front, swivels. Disc.

MODEL 101G . . . . NiB $110 Ex $79 Gd $55

Bolt action. Same as Marlin Model 101 except w/plain stock. Made 1960 to 1965.

MODEL 122 SINGLE-SHOT JUNIOR

TARGET RIFLE. . . . . NiB $135 Ex $95 Gd $75
Bolt action. Caliber: .22 LR, .22 Long, .22 Short. 22-in. bbl. Weight: 5 lbs. Sights: Open rear; hooded ramp front. Monte Carlo stock w/pistol-grip, swivels, sling. Made 1961-65.

MODEL 780/781/782/783 BOLT-ACTION REPEATER SERIES

Bolt action. Caliber: .22 LR, Long, Short. Seven round clip magazine. 22-in. bbl. Weight: 5.5 to 6 lbs. Sights: Open rear; hooded ramp front. Receiver grooved for scope mounting. Monte Carlo stock w/checkered pistol-grip and forearm. Made 1971-88.

Standard model. . . . . NiB $145 Ex $100 Gd $85
w/17-rnd. tubular mag. . . . . NiB $145 Ex $100 Gd $85
.22 WMR w/swivels, sling. . . . . . . NiB $145 Ex $100 Gd $85
w/12-rnd. tubular mag. . . . . NiB $145 Ex $100 Gd $85

MODEL 880/881/882/883 BOLT-ACTION REPEATER SERIES

Caliber: .22 rimfire. Seven round magazine. 22-in. bbl. 41 in. overall. Weight: 5.5 to 6 lbs. Hooded ramp front sight; adj. folding rear. Grooved receiver for scope mounts. Checkered Monte Carlo-style walnut stock w/QD studs and rubber recoil pad. Made 1989-97.

.22 LR . . . . NiB $220 Ex $177 Gd $115
Stainless .22 LR. . . . . NiB $269 Ex $200 Gd $150
Squirrel .22 LR . . . . NiB $269 Ex $223 Gd $160
Model 881 w/7-rd. tub. mag. NiB $244 Ex $175 Gd $110
Model 882 (.22 WMR) . . . . NiB $235 Ex $189 Gd $115
w/laminated hardwood stock . . NiB $277 Ex $189 Gd $120
Stainless w/Fire sights. . . . . NiB $290 Ex $222 Gd $167
Stainless .22 LR. . . . . NiB $195 Ex $227 Gd $170
Model 883
    (.22 WMR w/12-rnd.
    tubular mag.) . . . . NiB $235 Ex $179 Gd $120
w/nickel-Teflon finish . . . . NiB $279 Ex $226 Gd $180
Stainless w/laminated stock . . . NiB $297 Ex $200 Gd $177

MODEL 915/917/925/980/981/982/983 SERIES

Bolt action w/T-900 fire control system. Caliber: .17 Mach 2, .17 HMR, .22 Short/Long/LR, .22 WMR. Single-shot or 4- or 7-rnd. detachable or tube magazine. 22-in. bbl. Weight: 4.5-5.5 lbs. Sights: adj. rear, ramp front; optic ready. Stock: Checkered Monte Carlo-style walnut or black synthetic. Made 2004-10.

915Y Little Buckaroo (youth model,
    single shot, 15.25-in. bbl.) . . . . NiB $170 Ex $150 Gd $80
917 (.17 HMR, black synthetic
    stock, 4- or 7-rnd.
    magazine). . . . . NiB $205 Ex $175 Gd $115
917M2 (.17 Mach 2) . . . . NiB $190 Ex $165 Gd $105
917V (.17 HMR, wood stock,
    no sights/optic ready). . . . . . . NiB $230 Ex $195 Gd $125
917VR (.17 HMR, wood stock,
    no sights/optic ready,
    heavy bbl.) . . . . NiB $215 Ex $180 Gd $120
917VRS (.17 HMR,
    wood stock, no sights/
    optic ready, stainless) . . . . NiB $320 Ex $270 Gd $140
917VRT (.17 HMR,
    laminate thumbhole
    stock, no sights/optic ready) . . NiB $330 Ex $270 Gd $140
917VST (.17 HMR, laminate
    thumbhole stock, no
    sights/optic ready, stainless) . . . NiB $370 Ex $280 Gd $155
922 (.22 WMR, hardwood
    stock, open sights/ optic
    ready, disc.) . . . . NiB $420 Ex $360 Gd $280 925
(.22 LR, hardwood stock,
    open sights/optic ready). . . . . . NiB $180 Ex $145 Gd $80
925C (.22 LR, camo stock,
    open sights/optic ready) . . . . . NiB $205 Ex $165 Gd $80
925SR (.22 LR, synthetic stock,
    open sights/optic ready) . . . . . NiB $205 Ex $165 Gd $80
925M (.22 WMR, wood stock,
    open sights/optic ready) . . . . . . NiB $205 Ex $165 Gd $80
925RM (.22 WMR,
    synthetic stock,
    open sights/optic ready) . . . . . NiB $200 Ex $160 Gd $80
980S (.22 LR, wood stock,
    open sights/optic
    ready, stainless) . . . . NiB $255 Ex $205 Gd $115
980V (.22 LR, wood stock,
    open sights/optic ready,
    stainless, heavy bbl.) . . . . NiB $270 Ex $215 Gd $125
981T (.22 Short/Long/LR,
    synthetic stock, open sights/
    optic ready, tube magazine) . . . . NiB $185 Ex $150 Gd $85
982 (.22 WMR, wood stock,
    open sights/optic ready) . . . . . NiB $260 Ex $215 Gd $125

Marlin-Glenfield Model 70

Marlin-Glenfield Model 80G

Marlin Model 80C

Marlin Model 81DL

Marlin Model 780

982L (.22 WMR, laminate
   stock, open sights/optic
   ready) . . . . NiB $280 Ex $235 Gd $140
982S (.22 WMR, wood
   stock, open sights/
   optic ready, stainless) . . . . . . NiB $285 Ex $240 Gd $145
983 (.22 WMR, wood
   stock, open sights/
   optic ready, tube magazine) . NiB $270 Ex $215 Gd $125
983T (.22 WMR, synthetic
   stock, open sights/
   optic ready, tube magazine) . . NiB $215 Ex $180 Gd $115
983S (.22 WMR, synthetic

stock, open sights/optic
   ready, tube magazine, stainless) . . NiB $215 Ex $180 Gd $115

MODEL 2000 TARGET RIFLE . . NiB $590 Ex $479 Gd $338
Bolt-action single-shot. Caliber: .22 LR. Optional 5-rnd.
adapter kit available. 22-in. bbl. 41 in. overall. Weight: 8 lbs.
Globe front sight, adj. peep or aperture rear. two-stage target
trigger. Textured composite Kevlar or black/gray laminated
stock. Made 1991-95.
w/adj. comb
   (made 1994 only) . . . . NiB $643 Ex $522 Gd $355
w/laminated stock
   (intro. 1996) . . . . NiB $654 Ex $535 Gd $429

XT SERIES

Bolt action w/Pro-Fire adj. trigger. Caliber: .17 HMR, .22 S/L/LR or .22 WMR; 4- or 7-rnd. detachable or 17-, 19- 20-rnd. tube magazine. 16.25- or 22-in. bbl. Weight: 3-7 lbs. Sights: adj. rear, ramp front; optic ready. Stock: Smooth Monte Carlo-style hardwood or black synthetic. Finish: blue or stainless. Made 2011-20.

XT-17R (.17 HMR, black synthetic stock, 22-in. bbl., blue) . . . . NiB $220 Ex $190 Gd $135

XT-17SR (.17 HMR, black synthetic stock, 22-in. bbl., stainless) . . . . NiB $255 Ex $225 Gd $155

XT-17V (.17 HMR, wood stock, 22-in. heavy bbl., blue) . . . . NiB $235 Ex $200 Gd $135

XT-17VR (.17 HMR, black synthetic stock, 22-in. heavy bbl., blue) . . . . NiB $235 Ex $200 Gd $135

XT-17VSL (.17 HMR, black synthetic stock, 22-in. heavy bbl., stainless) . . . NiB $345 Ex $290 Gd $185

XT-17VLB (.17 HMR, brown laminate thumbhole stock, 22-in. heavy bbl., blue) . . . . NiB $340 Ex $290 Gd $185

XT-17VSLB (.17 HMR, gray laminate thumbhole stock, 22-in. heavy bbl., stainless) . . . NiB $400 Ex $330 Gd $205

XT-22 (.22 LR, 7-rnd. magazine, wood stock, 22-in. bbl., blue) . . . . NiB $185 Ex $150 Gd $90

XT-22R (.22 LR, 7-rnd. magazine, synthetic stock, 22-in. bbl., blue) . . . . . . NiB $180 Ex $150 Gd $90

XT-22RC (.22 LR, 7-rnd. magazine, synthetic camo stock, 22-in. bbl., blue) . . . . . . NiB $205 Ex $160 Gd $90

XT-22RZ (.22 LR, 7-rnd. magazine, synthetic stock, 22-in. threaded bbl., blue) . . . . . NiB $205 Ex $160 Gd $90

XT-22SR (.22 LR, 7-rnd. magazine, synthetic stock, 22-in. bbl., stainless) . . . . NiB $280 Ex $230 Gd $155

XT-22TR (.22 S/L/LR, synthetic stock, tube magazine, blue) . . . . NiB $180 Ex $150 Gd $90

XT-22TSR (.22 S/L/LR, synthetic stock, tube magazine, stainless) . . . . NiB $235 Ex $200 Gd $135

XT-22VR (.22 LR, 7-rnd. magazine, synthetic stock, 22-in. heavy bbl., blue) . . . NiB $185 Ex $150 Gd $90

XT-22Y1 (.22 S/L/LR, single shot, youth wood stock, 16.25-in. bbl., blue) . . . . . . NiB $180 Ex $150 Gd $90

XT-22YS1 (.22 S/L/LR, single shot, youth wood stock, 16.25-in. bbl., stainless) . . . . NiB $190 Ex $155 Gd $90

XT-22YR (.22 S/L/LR, 7-rnd. magazine, synthetic stock, 16.25-in. bbl., blue) . . . . . NiB $190 Ex $155 Gd $90

XT-22YSR (.22 S/L/LR, 7-rnd. magazine, synthetic stock, 16.25-in. bbl., stainless) . . . NiB $200 Ex $160 Gd $90

XT-22M (.22 WMR, 7-rnd. magazine, wood stock, 22-in. bbl., blue) . . . . NiB $205 Ex $160 Gd $90

XT-22MR (.22 WMR, 4- and 7-rnd. magazine, synthetic stock, 22-in. bbl., blue) . . NiB $200 Ex $160 Gd $90

XT-22MTR (.22 WMR, 12-rnd. tube magazine, synthetic stock, 22-in. bbl., blue) . . . . NiB $205 Ex $160 Gd $90

XT-22MTSL (.22 WMR, 12-rnd. tube magazine, brown laminate stock, 22-in. bbl., stainless, 2011–14) . . . . NiB $300 Ex $255 Gd $175

XT-22MTW (.22 WMR, 12-rnd. tube magazine, walnut stock, 22-in. bbl., blue, 2011-15) . . . . NiB $280 Ex $235 Gd $155

XT-22MVSR (.22 WMR, synthetic stock, 22-in. bbl., stainless, 2011–14) . . . . NiB $280 Ex $235 Gd $155

- RIMFIRE LEVER-ACTION MODELS -

MODEL 1892 . . . . NIB $2155 EX $1655 GD $1130
Lever action. Caliber: .22 S/l/lr or .32 S/l. Barrel: 16-, 24-, 26- or 28-in., Full tube magazine. Stock: smooth straight grip. Mfg. 1892-1916.

MODEL 39 CARBINE . . . . NiB $556 Ex $355 Gd $298
Same as 39M except w/lightweight bbl., 3/4 magazine (capacity: 18 Short, 14 Long, 12 LR), slimmer forearm. Weight: 5.25 lbs. Made 1963-67.

MODEL 39 CENTURY LTD. . . . NiB $755 Ex $655 Gd $580
Commemorative version of Model 39A. Receiver inlaid w/ brass medallion, "Marlin Centennial 1870-1970." Square lever. 20-in. octagon bbl. Fancy walnut straight-grip stock and forearm; brass forend cap, buttplate, nameplate in buttstock. 35,388 made in 1970.

MODEL 39 LEVER-ACTION
REPEATER . . . . NiB $4955 Ex $3510 Gd $1720
Takedown. Casehardened receiver. Caliber: .22 LR, Long, Short. Tubular magazine holds 25 Short, 20 Long, 18 LR. 24-in. octagon bbl. Weight: 5.75 lbs. Sights: Open rear; bead front. Plain pistol-grip stock and forearm. Made 1922-38.

MODEL 39A
General specifications same as Model 39 except w/blued receiver, rnd. bbl., heavier stock w/semibeavertail forearm, weight 6.5 lbs. Made 1939-60.

1st model (no prefix, 1939) . . . . NiB $2210 Ex $1710 Gd $955
2nd model ("B" prefix,1940) . . . . NiB $955 Ex $1380 Gd $905
3rd model, 1st variation (blue receiver, 1946–50) . . . . NiB $755 Ex $580 Gd $480
3rd model, 2nd variation (white spacer stock, 1951–53) . . . . NiB $555 Ex $455 Gd $305
3rd model, 3rd variation (Micro-Groove rifling, 1954–57) . . . . NiB $455 Ex $380 Gd $305

MODEL 39A 90TH
ANNIVERSARY RIFLE . . . . . . NiB $1555 Ex $1410 Gd $505
Commemorates Marlin's 90th anniversary. Same general specifications as Golden 39A except w/chrome-plated bbl. and action, stock and forearm of select walnut-finely checkered, carved figure of a squirrel on right side of buttstock. 500 made in 1960. Top value is for rifle in new, unfired condition.
Carbine model (500 produced, 1960 only) . . . . NiB $1555 Ex $1410 Gd $505

Marlin Model 781

Marlin Model 882L

Marlin Model 883N

Marlin Model 2000

MODEL 39A ARTICLE II RIFLE . . . NiB $580 Ex $500 Gd $380
Commemorates National Rifle Association Centennial 1871-1971. "The Right to Bear Arms" medallion inlaid in receiver. Similar to Model 39A. Magazine capacity: 26 Short, 21 Long, 19 LR. 24-in. octagon bbl. Fancy walnut pistol-grip stock and forearm; brass forend cap, buttplate. 6,244 made in 1971. Golden 39A/39AS Rifle Same as Model 39A except w/gold-plated trigger, hooded ramp front sight, sling swivels. Made 1960-87 (39A); Model 39AS from 1988 to 2020.
Golden 39A . . . . NiB $620 Ex $480 Gd $255
Golden 39AS (w/hammer
   block safety) . . . . NiB $620 Ex $480 Gd $255

MODEL 39A "MOUNTIE" . . . . NiB $479 Ex $300 Gd $190
Same as Model 39A except w/lighter, straight-grip stock, slimmer forearm. Weight: 6.25 lbs. Made 1953-60.
Carbine . . . . NiB $495 Ex $300 Gd $190

MODEL 39A OCTAGON . . . . . NiB $700 Ex $600 Gd $430
Same as Golden 39A except w/oct. bbl., plain bead front sight, slimmer stock and forearm, no pistol-grip cap or swivels. Made in1973. (2551 produced).

MODEL 39D . . . . NiB $440 Ex $280 Gd $200
Same as Model 39M except w/pistol-grip stock, forearm w/bbl. band. Made 1970-74.

39M ARTICLE II CARBINE . . . . NiB $580 Ex $500 Gd $130
Same as 39A Article II Rifle except w/straight-grip buttstock, square lever, 20-in. octagon bbl., reduced magazine capacity. 3,824 units, made in 1971.

GOLDEN 39A . . . . NIB $480 EX $380 GD $205
Calibers: .22 Short, Long and LR. Tubular magazine holds 21 Short, 16 Long or 15 LR cartridges. 20-in. bbl. 36 in. overall. Weight: 6 lbs. Gold-plated trigger. Hooded ramp front sight, adj. folding semi-buckhorn rear. Two-piece, straight-grip American black walnut stock. Sling swivels. Mar-Shield finish. Made 1957-87.

NOTE: *Currently the model 39A is available through Marlin's custom shop in a Fancy configuration w/checkered walnut stock w/ an MSRP of $3495.*

GOLDEN 39M
   (carbine, 1972-87) . . . . NiB $555 Ex $430 Gd $255
octagonal bbl. (1973 only) . . . NiB $495 Ex $469 Gd $390
Current production. . . . . NiB $480 Ex $380 Gd $205

MODEL 39M "MOUNTIE" CARBINE
Same as Model 39A "Mountie" Rifle except w/20-in. bbl. Weight: 6 lbs. 500 made in 1960. (For values See Marlin 39 90th Anniversary Carbine)

MODEL 39TDS CARBINE . . . . . NiB $545 Ex $369 Gd $290
Same general specifications as Model 39M except takedown style w/16.5-in. bbl. and reduced magazine capacity. 32.63 in. overall. Weight: 5.25 lbs. Made 1988-95.

MODEL 56 LEVERMATIC RIFLE . . . NiB $345 Ex $250 Gd $149
Same as Model 57 except clip-loading. Magazine holds eight rounds. Weight: 5.75 lbs. Made 1955-64.

GRADING: **NiB** = New in Box   **Ex** = Excellent or NRA 95%   **Gd** = Good or NRA 68%

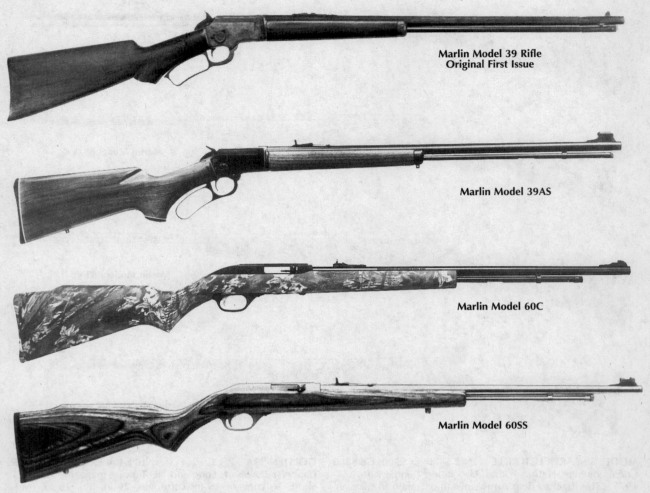

Marlin Model 39 Rifle Original First Issue

Marlin Model 39AS

Marlin Model 60C

Marlin Model 60SS

MODEL 57 LEVERMATIC RIFLE . . . NiB $375 Ex $227 Gd $132
Lever-action. Cal: .22 LR, 22 Long, 22 Short. Tubular mag. holds 19 LR, 21 Long, 27 Short. 22 in. bbl. Wt: 6.25 lbs. Sights: Open rear, adj. for windage and elevation; hooded ramp front. Monte Carlo-style stock w/pistol-grip. Made 1959-65.

MODEL 57M LEVERMATIC. . . . NiB $415 Ex $255 Gd $148
Same as Model 57 except chambered for 22 WMR cartridge, w/24-in. bbl., 15-rnd. magazine. Made 1960-69.

MODEL 97 . . . . NiB $2590 Ex $2066 Gd $1269
Lever action. Takedown. Caliber: .22 LR, Long, Short. Tubular magazine; full length holds 25 Short, 20 Long, 18 LR; half length holds 16 Short, 12 Long and 10 LR. Bbl. lengths: 16, 24, 26, 28 in. Weight: 6 lbs. Sights: Open rear; bead front. Plain, straight-grip stock and forearm (also avail. w/pistol-grip stock). Made 1897-1922. Note: Before 1905 designated "Model 1897."

MODEL 1870-1970 CENTENNIAL MATCHED PAIR,
MODELS 336 AND 39 . . . . NiB $2230 Ex $1766 Gd $1180
Presentation-grade rifles in luggage-style case. Matching serial numbers. Fancy walnut straight-grip buttstock and forearm brass buttplate and forend cap. Engraved receiver w/inlaid medallion; square lever. 20-in. octagon bbl. Model

336: .30-30, 7-rnd. capacity; weight: 7 lbs. Model 39: .22 Short, Long, LR, tubular magazine holds 21 Short, 16 Long, 15 LR. 1,000 sets produced. Made in 1970. Top value is for rifles in new, unfired condition.

MODEL 1894M. . . . . NiB $495 Ex $443 Gd $233
Lever action. Caliber: .22 WMR.11-rnd. tubular magazine. 20-in. bbl. Weight: 6.25 lbs. Sights: Ramp front w/brass bead and Wide-Scan hood; adj. semi-buckhorn folding rear. Offset hammer spur for scope use. Straight-grip American black walnut stock w/white buttplate spacer. Squared finger lever. Made 1986-88.

MODEL 1897 COWBOY . . . . . NiB $643 Ex $489 Gd $369
Lever action. Caliber: .22 LR., capacity: 19 LR, 21 L, or 26 S, tubular magazine. 24-in. tapered octagon bbl., 40 in. overall. Weight: 6.5 lbs. Marble front and adjustable rear sight, tapped for scope mount. Black walnut straight grip stock w/ cut checkering and Mar-Shield finish. Made 1999-2001.

- RIMFIRE SEMIAUTO MODELS -

MODEL 49/49DL AUTOLOADING RIFLE
Same as Model 99C except w/two-piece stock, checkered after 1970. Made 1968-71. Model 49DL w/scrollwork on sides of receiver, checkered stock and forearm; made 1971-78.
Model 49 . . . . NiB $200 Ex $190 Gd $145
Model 49DL . . . . NiB $227 Ex $179 Gd $144

Marlin Model 56

Marlin Model 57

Marlin Model 70HC

Marlin Model 70P Papoose

MODEL 50/50E AUTOLOADING RIFLE

Takedown. Cal: .22 LR. Six round detachable box mag. 22 in. bbl. Wt: 6 lbs. Sights: Open rear; bead front; Mdl. 50E w/peep rear sight, hooded front. Plain pistol-grip stock, forearm w/ finger grooves. Made 1931-34.

Model 50 . . . . NiB $227 Ex $190 Gd $124
Model 50E. . . . . NiB $235 Ex $200 Gd $130

MODEL 60 SEMIAUTO RIFLE. . . . . NiB $227 Ex $145 Gd $90

Caliber: .22 LR. 14-rnd. tubular magazine. 22-in. bbl. 40.5 in. overall. Weight: 5.5 lbs. Grooved receiver. Ramp front sight w/ removable hood; adj. open rear. Anodized receiver w/blued bbl. Monte Carlo-style walnut-finished hardwood stock w/Mar-Shield finish. Made 1981 to date. Note: Marketed 1960 to 1980 under Glenfield promotion logo and w/slightly different stock configuration.

MODEL 60C SELF-LOADING

RIFLE . . . . NiB $198 Ex $130 Gd $107
Caliber: .22 LR. 14- rnd. tubular mag. 22 in. Micro-Groove bbl., 40.5 in. overall. Wt: 5.5 lbs. Screw-adjustable open rear and ramp front sights. Aluminum receiver, grooved for scope mount. Hardwood Monte Carlo stock w/Mossy Oak "Break-Up" camouflage pattern. Made 2000-20.

MODEL 60SS SEMIAUTO RIFLE

Same general specifications as Model 60 except w/stainless bbl. and magazine tube. Synthetic, uncheckered birch or laminated black/gray birch stock w/nickel-plated swivel studs. Made 1993-2020.

w/uncheckered birch stock. . . . NiB $278 Ex $200 Gd $135
w/laminated birch stock . . . . . . NiB $270 Ex $197 Gd $126
w/fiberglass stock . . . . NiB $260 Ex $188 Gd $126

MODEL 70HC SEMIAUTO

Caliber: .22 LR. Seven and 15-rnd. magazine. 18-in. bbl. Weight: 5.5 lbs. 36.75 in. overall. Ramp front sight; adj. open rear. Grooved receiver for scope mounts. Walnut-finished hardwood stock w/ Monte Carlo and pistol-grip. Made 1988-96.

Marlin model . . . . NiB $200 Ex $155 Gd $124
Glenfield model . . . . NiB $155 Ex $126 Gd $100

MODEL 70P SEMIAUTO. . . . . NiB $290 Ex $189 Gd $100

"Papoose" takedown. Caliber: .22 LR. Seven round clip. 16.25-in. bbl. 35.25 in. overall. Weight: 3.75 lbs. Sights: Ramp front, adj. open rear. Side ejection, manual bolt hold-open. Cross-bolt safety. Walnut-finished hard-wood stock w/abbreviated forend, pistol-grip. Made 1984-94.

MODEL 70PSS . . . . NiB $338 Ex $200 Gd $175

Semiauto "Papoose" takedown carbine. Caliber: .22 LR. Seven round clip. 16.25- in. bbl., 35.25 in. overall. Weight: 3.25 lbs. Ramp front and adjustable open rear sights. Automatic last-shot hold open (1996). Black fiberglass synthetic stock. Made 1995-2020.

MODEL 75C

SEMIAUTO . . . . NiB $233 Ex $158 Gd $109
Caliber: .22 LR. 13-rnd. tubular magazine.18-in. bbl. 36.5 in. overall. Weight: 5 lbs. Side ejection. Cross-bolt safety. Sights:

Ramp-mounted blade front; adj. open rear. Monte Carlo-style walnut-finished hardwood stock w/pistol-grip. Made 1975-92.

MODEL 88-C/88-DL TAKEDOWN RIFLE
Takedown. Caliber: .22 LR. Tubular magazine in buttstock holds 14 cartridges. 24-in. bbl. Weight: 6.75 lbs. Sights: Open rear; hooded front. Plain pistol-grip stock. Made 1947-56. Model 88-DL w/received peep sight, checkered stock and sling swivels, made 1953-56.

Model 88-C. . . . . NiB $200 Ex $145 Gd $100
Model 88-DL. . . . . NiB $200 Ex $145 Gd $100

MODEL 89C/89DL AUTOLOADING RIFLE
Clip magazine version of Model 88-C. Seven round clip (12-rnd. in later models); other specifications same. Made 1950-61. Model 89-DL w/receiver peep sight, sling swivels.

Model 89-C. . . . . NiB $200 Ex $145 Gd $100
Model 89-DL. . . . . NiB $210 Ex $150 Gd $105

MODEL 98. . . . . NiB $255 Ex $138 Gd $100
Semiauto. Solid frame. Caliber: .22 LR. Tubular magazine holds 15 cartridges. 22-in. bbl. Weight: 6.75 lbs. Sights: Open rear; hooded ramp front. Monte Carlo stock w/cheekpiece. Made 1950-61.

MODEL 99. . . . . NiB $255 Ex $138 Gd $100
Semiauto. Caliber: .22 LR. Tubular magazine holds 18 cartridges. 22-in. bbl. Weight: 5.5 lbs. Sights: Open rear; hooded ramp front. Plain pistol-grip stock. Made 1959-61.

MODEL 99C. . . . . NiB $209 Ex $177 Gd $119
Same as Model 99 except w/gold-plated trigger, receiver grooved for tip-off scope mounts, Monte Carlo stock (checkered in later production). Made 1962-78.

MODEL 99DL. . . . . NiB $266 Ex $255 Gd $144
Same as Model 99 except w/gold-plated trigger, jeweled breech bolt, Monte Carlo stock w/pistol-grip, swivels and sling. Made 1960-65.

MODEL 99M1 CARBINE. . . . . NiB $200 Ex $99 Gd $80
Same as Model 99C except styled after U.S. .30 M1 Carbine; 9-rnd. tubular magazine, 18-in. bbl. Sights: Open rear; military-style ramp front; carbine stock w/handguard and bbl. band, sling swivels. Weight: 4.5 lbs. Made 1966-79.

MODEL 795. . . . . NiB $167 Ex $130 Gd $115
Semiauto. Caliber: .22 LR. 10- rnd. clip. 18- in. Micro-Groove bbl., 37 in. overall. Weight: 5 lbs. Screw-adjustable open rear and ramp front sight. Monte Carlo synthetic stock with checkering swivel studs. Made 1999-2020.

MODEL 922 MAGNUM . . . . . . NiB $390 Ex $244 Gd $160
Similar to Model 9 except chambered for .22 WMR. Seven round magazine. 20.5-in. bbl. 39.5 in. overall. Weight: 6.5 lbs. American black walnut stock w/Monte Carlo. Blued finish. Made 1993-2001.

MODEL 989. . . . . NiB $210 Ex $144 Gd $110
Semiauto. Caliber: .22 LR. Seven round clip magazine. 22-in. bbl. Weight: 5.5 lbs. Sights: Open rear; hooded ramp front. Monte Carlo walnut stock w/pistol grip. Made 1962-66.

MODEL 989M2 CARBINE. . . . . NiB $250 Ex $145 Gd $100
Semiauto. Same as Model 99M1 except clip-loading, 7-rnd. magazine. Made 1966-99.

MODEL 990
Semiauto. Caliber: .22 LR. 17-rnd. tubular magazine. 22-in. bbl. 40.75 in. overall. Weight: 5.5 lbs. Side ejection. Cross-bolt safety. Ramp front sight w/brass bead; adj. semi-buckhorn folding rear. Receiver grooved for scope mount. Monte Carlo-style American black walnut stock w/checkered pistol grip and forend. Made 1979-87.

Model 990 . . . . NiB $135 Ex $100 Gd $85
w/14-rnd. mag, laminated
    hardwood stock, QD swivels,
    blackrecoil pad. Made
    1992–2020) . . . . NiB $208 Ex $155 Gd $110

MODEL 995 . . . . NiB $233 Ex $167 Gd $110
Semiauto. Caliber: .22 LR. Seven round clip magazine.18-in. bbl. 36.75 in. overall. Weight: 5 lbs. Cross-bolt safety. Sights: Ramp front w/brass bead; adj. folding semi-buckhorn rear. Monte Carlo-style American black walnut stock w/checkered pistol grip and forend. Made 1979-94.

MODEL 7000 . . . . NiB $255 Ex $190 Gd $146
Semiauto. Caliber: .22 LR. 10-rnd. magazine. 18-in. bbl. Weight: 5.5 lbs. Synthetic stocks. No sights; receiver grooved for scope. Semiauto. Side ejection. Manual bolt hold-open. Cross-bolt safety. Matte finish. Made 1997-2001.
Model 7000T . . . . NiB $390 Ex $290 Gd $220

MODEL A-1 . . . . NiB $185 Ex $110 Gd $90
Semiauto. Takedown. Caliber: .22 LR. Six round detachable box magazine. 24-in. bbl. Weight: 6 lbs. Open rear sight. Plain pistol-grip stock. Made 1935-46.

MODEL A-1C . . . . NiB $185 Ex $110 Gd $90
Improved version of Model A-1 w/same general specifications, stock w/semibeavertail forend. Made 1940-46.

MODEL A-1DL . . . . NiB $185 Ex $110 Gd $90
Same as Model A-1C above, except w/peep rear sight; hooded front, swivels.

MODEL A-1E . . . . NiB $190 Ex $126 Gd $95
Same as Model A-1 except w/peep rear sight; hooded front.

MODEL 99G. . . . . NiB $170 Ex $75 Gd $65
Semiauto. Same as Marlin Model 99C except w/plain stock, bead front sight. Made 1960-65.

MODEL 989G. . . . . NiB $179 Ex $110 Gd $79
Semiauto. Same as Marlin Model 989 except w/plain stock, bead front sight. Made 1962-64.

- SLIDE-ACTION MODELS (CENTERFIRE AND RIMFIRE)-

MODEL 18 BABY . . . . NiB $1405 Ex $1105 Gd $610
Slide-action repeater. Exposed hammer. Solid frame. Caliber: .22 Short, Long, LR. Tubular magazine holds 14 Short cartridges. 20-in. bbl., rnd. or octagon. Weight: 3.75 lbs. Sights: Open rear; bead front. Plain straight-grip stock and slide handle. Made 1906-09.

MODEL 20 SLIDE-ACTION . . . NiB $1405 Ex $1105 Gd $605
Exposed hammer. Takedown. Caliber: .22 LR, Long, Short. Tubular magazine: Half-length holds 15 Short, 12 Long, 10 LR; full-length holds 25 Short, 20 Long, 18 LR. 24-in. octagon bbl.

Weight: 5 lbs. Sights: Open rear; bead front. Plain straight-grip stock, grooved slide handle. Made 1907-22. Note: After 1920 was designated "Model 20-S."

MODEL 25 SLIDE-ACTION
REPEATER . . . .**NiB $879 Ex $540 Gd $431**
Exposed hammer. Takedown. Caliber: .22 Short (also handles 22 CB caps). Tubular magazine holds 15 Short. 23-in. bbl. Weight: 4 lbs. Sights: Open rear; beaded front. Plain straight-grip stock and slide handle. Made 1909-10.

MODEL 27 . . . . .NiB $1159 Ex $909 Gd $650
Slide-action repeater. Exposed hammer. Takedown. Calibers: .25-20, .32-20. Magazine (tubular) holds 7 rnd. 24-in. octagon bbl. Weight: 5.75 lbs. Sights: Open rear; bead front. Plain, straight-grip stock, grooved slide handle. Made 1910-16.

MODEL 27S . . . . .NiB $909 Ex $579 Gd $388
Same as Model 27 except w/rnd. bbl., also chambered for .25 Stevens rimfire Made 1920-32.

MODEL 29 SLIDE-ACTION
REPEATER . . . .**NiB $660 Ex $388 Gd $290**
Similar to Model 20 w/23-in. rnd. bbl., half magazine only, weight 5.75 lbs. Made 1913-16.

MODEL 32 SLIDE-ACTION
REPEATER . . . .**NiB $1154 Ex $690 Gd $533**
Hammerless. Takedown. Caliber: .22 LR, Long, Short. Tubular magazine holds 15 Short, 12 Long, 10 LR; full magazine, 25 Short, 20 Long, 18 LR. 24-in. octagon bbl. Weight: 5.5 lbs. Sights: Open rear; bead front. Plain pistol-grip stock, grooved slide handle. Made 1914-15.

MODEL 37 . . . . .NiB $650 Ex $442 Gd $237
Slide action. Similar to Model 29 except w/24-in. bbl. and full magazine. Weight: 5.25 lbs. Made 1913-16.

MODEL 38 . . . . .NiB $744 Ex $418 Gd $339
Slide action. Hammerless. Takedown. Caliber: .22 LR, Long, Short. 2/3 magazine (tubular) holds 15 Short, 12 Long, 10 LR. 24-in. octagon or rnd. bbls. Weight: 5.5 lbs. Sights: Open rear; bead front. Plain shotgun-type pistol-grip buttstock w/ hard rubber buttplate, grooved slide handle. Ivory bead front sight; adj. rear. About 20,000 Model 38 rifles were made 1920-30.

MAUSER SPORTING RIFLES — Oberndorf am Neckar, Germany

Manufactured by Mauser-Werke GmbH. Imported by Blaser USA in San Antoinio; previously by Brolin Arms, Pomona, CA; Gun South, Inc.; Gibbs Rifle Co.; Precision Imports, Inc. and KDF, Inc.

Before the end of WWI the name of the Mauser firm was "Waffenfabrik Mauser A.-G." Shortly after WWI it was changed to "Mauser-Werke A.-G." This information may be used to determine the age of genuine original Mauser sporting rifles made before WWII because all bear either of these firm names as well as the Mauser banner trademark. The first four rifles listed were manufactured before WWI. Those that follow were produced between World Wars I and II. The early Mauser models can generally be identified by the pistol grip, which is rounded instead of capped, and the M/98 military-type magazine floorplate and catch. The
later models have hinged magazine floorplates with lever or button release.

NOTE: *The "B" series of Mauser .22 rifles (Model ES340B, MS350B, etc.) were improved versions of their corresponding models and were introduced about 1935.*

- PRE-WORLD WAR I PRODUCTION -

BOLT-ACTION SPORTING CARBINE
Calibers: 6.5x54, 6.5x58, 7x57, 8x57, 957mm. 19.75-in. bbl. Weight: 7 lbs. Full-stocked to muzzle. Other specifications same as for standard rifle.
W/20-in. bbl. (Type M) . . . .**NiB $2489 Ex $2066 Gd $1445**
**W/20- or 24-in.
bbl. (Type S)** . . . .**NiB $2566 Ex $2155 Gd $1486**

BOLT-ACTION SPORTING RIFLE
Calibers: 6.5x55, 6.5x58, 7x57, 8x57, 9x57, 9.3x62 10.75x68. Five-rnd. box magazine, 23.5-in. bbl. Weight: 7 to 7.5 lbs. Pear-shaped bolt handle. Double-set or single trigger. Sights: Tangent curve rear; ramp front. Pistol-grip stock, forearm w/Schnabel tip and swivels.
Type A, English export . . . .**NiB $2669 Ex $2276 Gd $1559**
Type B . . . .**NiB $1790 Ex $1466 Gd $1080**

BOLT-ACTION SPORTING RIFLE,
MILITARY MODEL TYPE C . . .**NiB $3854 Ex $3165 Gd $2189**
So called because of stepped M/98-type bbl., military front sight and double-pull trigger. Calibers: 7x57, 8x57, 9x57mm. Other specifications same as for standard rifle.

BOLT-ACTION SPORTING RIFLE
SHORT MODEL TYPE K . . .**NiB $3856 Ex $3169 Gd $2190**
Calibers: 6.5x54, 8x51mm. 19.75-in. bbl. Weight: 6.25 lbs. Other specifications same as for standard rifle.

- PRE-WORLD WAR II PRODUCTION -

MODEL DSM34 BOLT-ACTION SINGLE-SHOT
SPORTING RIFLE . . . .**NiB $670 Ex $445 Gd $338**
Also called "Sport-model." Caliber: .22 LR. 26-in. bbl. Weight: 7.75 lbs. Sights: Tangent curve open rear; Barleycorn front. M/98 military-type stock, swivels. Intro. c. 1935.

MODEL EL320 BOLT-ACTION SINGLE-SHOT
SPORTING RIFLE . . . .**NiB $556 Ex $449 Gd $339**
Caliber: .22 LR. 23.5-in. bbl. Weight: 4.25 lbs. Sights: Adj. open rear; bead front. Sporting stock w/checkered pistol grip, swivels.

MODEL EN310 BOLT-ACTION SINGLE-SHOT
SPORTING RIFLE . . . .**NiB $499 Ex $420 Gd $298**
Caliber: .22 LR. ("22 Lang fur Buchsen.") 19.75-in. bbl. Weight: 4 lbs. Sights: Fixed open rear, blade front. Plain pistol-grip stock.

MODEL ES340 BOLT-ACTION SINGLE-SHOT
TARGET RIFLE . . . .**NiB $765 Ex $455 Gd $338**
Caliber: .22 LR. 25.5-in. bbl. Weight: 6.5 lbs. Sights: Tangent curve rear; ramp front. Sporting stock w/checkered pistol-grip and grooved forearm, swivels.

MODEL ES340B BOLT-ACTION SINGLE-SHOT
TARGET RIFLE. . . . .**NiB $765 Ex $445 Gd $356**
Caliber: .22 LR. 26.75-in. bbl. Weight: 8 lbs. Sights: Tangent curve open rear; ramp front. Plain pistol-grip stock, swivels.

RIFLES

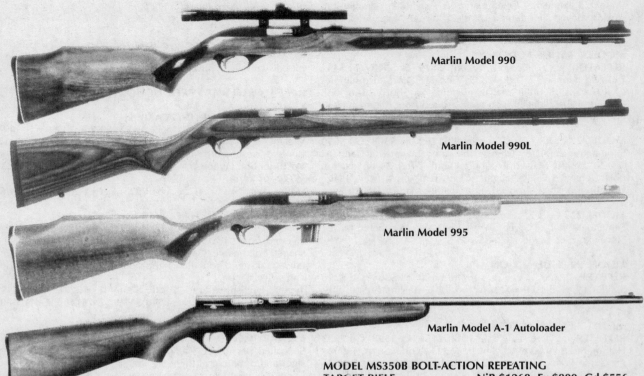

Marlin Model 990

Marlin Model 990L

Marlin Model 995

Marlin Model A-1 Autoloader

**MODEL ES350 BOLT-ACTION SINGLE-SHOT
TARGET RIFLE** . . . . **NiB $977 Ex $775 Gd $558**
"Meistershaftsbuchse" (Championship Rifle). Caliber: .22 LR. 27.5-in. bbl. Weight: 7.75 lbs. Sights: Open micrometer rear; ramp front. Target stock w/checkered pistol-grip and forearm, grip cap, swivels.

**MODEL ES350B BOLT-ACTION SINGLE-SHOT
TARGET RIFLE** . . . . **NiB $970 Ex $668 Gd $495**
Same general specifications as Model MS350B except single-shot, weight: 8.25 lbs.

**MODEL KKW BOLT-ACTION SINGLE-SHOT
TARGET RIFLE** . . . . **NiB $944 Ex $667 Gd $544**
Caliber: .22 LR. 26-in. bbl. Weight: 8.75 lbs. Sights: Tangent curve open rear; Barleycorn front. M/98 military-type stock, swivels. Note: This rifle has an improved design Mauser 22 action w/separate nonrotating bolt head. In addition to being produced for commercial sale, this model was used as a training rifle by the German armed forces; it was also made by Walther and Gustoff. Intro. just before WWII.

**MODEL MM410 BOLT-ACTION REPEATING
SPORTING RIFLE** . . . . **NiB $2166 Ex $1590 Gd $955**
Caliber: .22 LR. Five round detachable box magazine. 23.5-in. bbl. Weight: 5 lbs. Sights: Tangent curve open rear; ramp front. Sporting stock w/checkered pistol-grip, swivels.

**MODEL MM410B BOLT-ACTION REPEATING
SPORTING RIFLE** . . . . **NiB $2166 Ex $1590 Gd $955**
Caliber: .22 LR. Five round detachable box magazine. 23.5-in. bbl. Weight: 6.25 lbs. Sights: Tangent curve open rear; ramp front. Lightweight sporting stock w/checkered pistol-grip, swivels.

**MODEL MS350B BOLT-ACTION REPEATING
TARGET RIFLE** . . . . **NiB $1268 Ex $800 Gd $556**
Caliber: .22 LR. Five round detachable box magazine. Receiver and bbl. grooved for detachable rear sight or scope. 26.75-in. bbl. Weight: 8.5 lbs. Sights: Micrometer open rear; ramp front. Target stock w/checkered pistol grip and forearm, grip cap, sling swivels.

**MODEL MS420 BOLT-ACTION REPEATING
SPORTING RIFLE** . . . . **NiB $1145 Ex $879 Gd $606**
Caliber: .22 LR. Five round detachable box magazine. 25.5-in. bbl. Weight: 6.5 lbs. Sights: Tangent curve open rear; ramp front. Sporting stock w/checkered pistol grip, grooved forearm swivels.

**MODEL MS420B BOLT-ACTION REPEATING
TARGET RIFLE** . . . . **NiB $1156 Ex $922 Gd $633**
Caliber: .22 LR. Five round detachable box magazine. 26.75-in. bbl. Weight: 8 lbs. Sights: Tangent curve open rear; ramp front. Target stock w/checkered pistol grip, grooved forearm, swivels.

STANDARD MODEL RIFLE . . . . **NiB $339 Ex $210 Gd $159**
Refined version of German Service Kar. 98k. Straight bolt handle. Calibers: 7mm Mauser (7x57mm), 7.9mm Mauser (8x57mm). Five round box magazine. 23.5-in. bbl. Weight: 8.5 lbs. Sights: Blade front; adj. rear. Walnut stock of M/98 military-type. Note: These rifles were made for commercial sale and are of the high quality found in the Oberndorf Mauser sporters. They bear the Mauser trademark on the receiver ring.

**TYPE "A" BOLT-ACTION SPORTING
RIFLE** . . . . **NiB $7000 Ex $6200 Gd $3005**
Special British Model. 7x57, 30-06 (7.62x63), 8x60, 9x57, 9.3x62mm. Five round box mag. 23.5-in. rnd. bbl. Weight: 7.25 lbs. Mil.-type single trigger. Sights: Express rear; hooded ramp front. Circassian walnut sporting stock w/checkered pistol-grip and forearm, w/ or w/o cheekpiece, buffalo horn forend tip and grip cap, detachable swivels. Variations: Octagon bbl., double-set trigger, shotgun-type safety, folding peep rear sight, tangent curve rear sight, three-leaf rear sight.

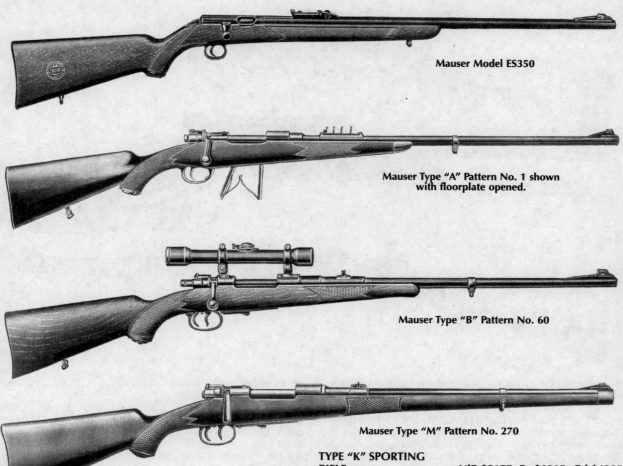

Mauser Model ES350

Mauser Type "A" Pattern No. 1 shown with floorplate opened.

Mauser Type "B" Pattern No. 60

Mauser Type "M" Pattern No. 270

TYPE "A" BOLT-ACTION SPORTING RIFLE, MAGNUM MODEL . . . . NiB $5598 Ex $3473 Gd $2745

Same general specifications as standard Type "A" except w/ Magnum action, weighs 7.5 to 8.5 lbs. Calibers: .280 Ross, .318 Westley Richards Express, 10.75x68mm, .404 Nitro Express.

TYPE "A" BOLT-ACTION SPORTING RIFLE, SHORT MODEL . . . . NiB $6149 Ex $4144 Gd $2448

Same as standard Type "A" except w/short action, 21.5-in. rnd. bbl., weight 6 lbs. Calibers: .250-3000, 6.5x54, 8x51mm.

TYPE "B" BOLT-ACTION SPORTING RIFLE . . . . NiB $5005 Ex $4885 Gd $2544

Normal Model. Calibers: 7x57, .30-06 (7.62x63), 8x57, 8x60, 9x57, 9.3x62, 10.7568mm. Five round box magazine. 23.5-in. rnd. bbl. Weight: 7.25 lbs. Double-set trigger. Sights: Three-leaf rear, ramp front. Fine walnut stock w/checkered pistol-grip, Schnabel forend tip, cheekpiece, grip cap, swivels. Variations: Octagon or half-octagon bbl., military-type single trigger, shotgun-type safety, folding peep rear sight, tangent curve rear sight, telescopic sight.

TYPE "K" SPORTING RIFLE . . . . NiB $8177 Ex $6805 Gd $4285

Light Short Model. Same specifications as Normal Type "B" model except w/short action, 21.5-in. rnd. bbl., weight: 6 lbs. Calibers: .250-3000, 6.5x54, 8x51mm.

TYPE "M" BOLT-ACTION SPORTING CARBINE . . . . . NiB $6000 Ex $5133 Gd $3200

Calibers: 6.5x54, 7x57, .30-06 (7.62x63), 8x51, 8x60, 9x57mm. Five round box magazine. 19.75-in. rnd. bbl. Weight: 6 to 6.75 lbs. Double-set trigger, flat bolt handle. Sights: Three-leaf rear; ramp front. Stocked to muzzle, cheekpiece, checkered pistol-grip and forearm, grip cap, steel forend cap, swivels. Variations: Military-type single trigger, shotgun-type trigger, shotgun-type safety, tangent curve rear sight, telescopic sight.

TYPE "S" BOLT-ACTION SPORTING CARBINE . . . . NiB $6000 Ex $5009 Gd $3005

Calibers: 6.5x54 7x57, 8x51, 8x60, 9x57mm. Five-rnd. box magazine. 19.75-in. rnd. bbl. Weight: 6 to 6.75 lbs. Double-set trigger. Sights: Three-leaf rear; ramp front. Stocked to muzzle, Schnabel forend tip, cheekpiece, checkered pistol-grip w/cap, swivels. Variations: Same as listed for Normal Model Type "B."

- POST-WORLD WAR II PRODUCTION -

NOTE: *Production of original Mauser sporting rifles (66 series) resumed at the Oberndorf plant in 1965 by Mauser-Jagdwaffen GmbH, now Mauser-Werke Oberndorf GmbH. The Series 2000-3000-4000 rifles, however, were made*

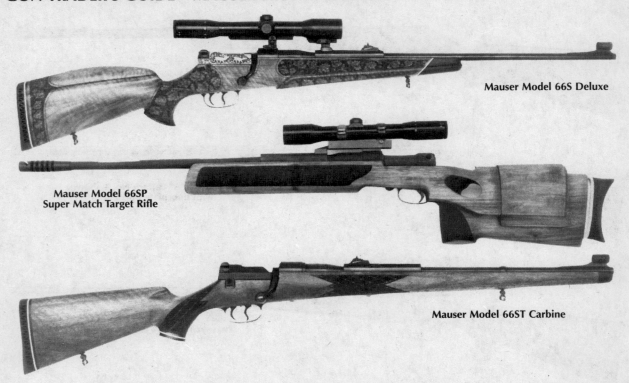

Mauser Model 66S Deluxe

Mauser Model 66SP Super Match Target Rifle

Mauser Model 66ST Carbine

for Mauser by Friedrich Wilhelm Heym Gewehrfabrik, Muennerstadt, West Germany.

MODEL 66S BOLT-ACTION STANDARD SPORTING RIFLE
Telescopic short action. Bbls. interchangeable within cal. group. Single- or double-set trigger (interchangeable). Cal: .243 Win., 6.5x57, .270 Win., 7x64, .308 Win., .30-06. Three round mag. 23.6 in. bbl. (25.6 in. in 7x64). Wt: 7.3 lbs. (7.5 lbs. in 7x64). Sights: Adj. open rear, hooded ramp front. Select Eur. walnut stock, Monte Carlo w/cheekpiece, rosewood forend tip and pistol-grip cap, skip checkering, recoil pad, sling swivels. Made 1974 to 1995, export to U.S. disc. 1974. Note: U.S. designation, 1971 to 1973, was "Model 660."
Model 66S. . . . . NiB $4739 Ex $3054 Gd $2044
w/extra bbl. assembly, add $600

MODEL 66S DELUXE SPORTER
Limited production special order. Model 66S rifles and carbines are available with elaborate engraving, gold and silver inlays and carved select walnut stocks. Added value is upward of $4500.

MODEL 66S ULTRA
Same general specifications as Model 66S Standard except w/20.9-in. bbl., weight: 6.8 lbs.
Model 66S Ultra . . . . NiB $1754 Ex $1644 Gd $1097
w/extra bbl. assembly, add $600

MODEL 77 SERIES . . . . NiB $1135 Ex $955 Gd $755
Calibers: .243 Win., .270 Win., 6.5x57, 7x64, .308 Win., or .30-06; detachable magazine. Set trigger. Barrel: 24-in. Weight: 7.25 lbs. Sights: open; optic ready. Stock: walnut w/European cheekpiece. Disc.

MODEL 66SG BIG GAME. . NiB $3077 Ex $2100 Gd $1388
Same general specifications as Model 66S Standard except w/25.6-in. bbl., weight 9.3 lbs. Calibers: .375 H&H Mag., .458 Win. Mag. Note: U.S. designation, 1971-73, was "Model 660 Safari."

w/ extra bbl. assembly, add $600

MODEL 66SH HIGH PERFORMANCE . . . . NiB $1706 Ex $1530 Gd $1109
Same general specifications as Model 66S Standard except w/25.6-in. bbl., weighs 7.5 lbs. (9.3 lbs. in 9.3x64). Calibers: 6.5x68, 7mm Rem. Mag., 7mm S.E.v. Hoffe, .300 Win. Mag., 8x68S, 9.3x64.

MODEL 66SP SUPER MATCH BOLT-ACTION TARGET RIFLE. . . . . NiB $4198 Ex $3707 Gd $2033
Telescopic short action. Adj. single-stage trigger. Caliber: .308 Win. (chambering for other cartridges available on special order). Three round magazine. 27.6-in. heavy bbl. w/muzzle brake, dovetail rib for special scope mount. Weight: 12 lbs. Target stock w/wide and deep forearm, full pistol-grip, thumbhole adj. cheekpiece, adj. rubber buttplate.

MODEL 66ST CARBINE. . . . NiB $2635 Ex $1710 Gd $1277
Same general specifications as Model 66S Standard except w/20.9-in. bbl., full-length stock, weight: 7 lbs.
w/extra bbl. assembly, add $600

MODEL 83 . . . . NiB $2215 Ex $2188 Gd $1360
Centerfire single-shot, bolt-action rifle for 300-meter competition. Caliber: .308 Win. 25.5-in. fluted bbl. Weight: 10.5 lbs. Adj. micrometer rear sight globe front. Fully adj. competition stock. Disc. 1988.

MODEL 96 . . . . NiB $677 Ex $633 Gd $455
Calibers: .25-06, .270 Win., 7x64, .308 Win., .30-06, 7mm Rem. Mag., .300 Win. Mag. 22-in. bbl.; magnums 24-in. Weight: 6.25 lbs. No sights; drilled and tapped for scope. Walnut stock. Five-rnd. top-loading magazine. 3-position safety.

MODEL 99 CLASSIC BOLT-ACTION RIFLE
Calibers: .243 Win., .25-06, .270 Win., .30-06, .308 Win., .257 Wby., .270 Wby., 7mm Rem. Mag., .300 Win., .300 Wby.

Mauser Model 99

Mauser Model 201

Mauser Model 3000

Mauser Model 4000

.375 H&H. Four round magazine (standard), 3-rnd. (Magnum). Bbl.: 24-in. (standard) or 26-in. (Magnum). 44 in. overall (standard). Weight: 8 lbs. No sights. Checkered European walnut stock w/rosewood grip cap available in Classic and Monte Carlo styles w/High-Luster or oil finish. Disc. importing 1994.

Standard Classic or
 Monte Carlo (oil finish) . . NiB $1156 Ex $1077 Gd $710
Magnum Classic or
 Monte Carlo (oil finish) . . NiB $1266 Ex $1109 Gd $800
Standard Classic or
 Monte Carlo (H-L finish) . NiB $1188 Ex $1098 Gd $775
Magnum Classic or
 Monte Carlo (H-L finish) . NiB $1347 Ex $1109 Gd $790

MODEL 107 RIFLE . . . . NiB $369 Ex $277 Gd $210
Bolt-action. Caliber: .22 LR. Mag. Five round magazine. 21.5-in. bbl. 40 in. overall. Weight: 5 lbs. Receiver drilled and tapped for rail scope mounts. Hooded front sight, adj. rear. Disc. importing 1994.

MODEL 201/201 LUXUS BOLT-ACTION RIFLE
Calibers: .22 LR. .22 Win. Mag. Five round magazine. 21-in. bbl. 40 in. overall. Weight: 6.5 lbs. Receiver drilled and tapped for scope mounts. Sights optional. Checkered walnut-stained beech stock w/Monte Carlo. Model 201 Luxus w/ checkered European walnut stock QD swivels, rosewood forend and rubber recoil pad. Made 1989-97.

Standard model. . . . . NiB $670 Ex $555 Gd $400
Magnum . . . . NiB $722 Ex $569 Gd $440
Luxus Standard model. . . . . . . NiB $756 Ex $544 Gd $468
Luxus Magnum model. . . . . . . NiB $844 Ex $633 Gd $560

MODEL 2000 BOLT-ACTION
SPORTING RIFLE . . . . NiB $539 Ex $355 Gd $290
Modified Mauser-type action. Calibers: .270 Win., .308 Win., .30-06. Five-rnd. magazine. 24-in. bbl. Weight: 7.5 lbs. Sights: Folding leaf rear; hooded ramp front. Checkered walnut stock w/Monte Carlo comb and cheekpiece, forend tip, sling swivels. Made 1969-71. Note: Model 2000 is similar in appearance to Model 3000.

MODEL 2000 CLASSIC BOLT-ACTION SPORTING RIFLE
Calibers: .22-250 Rem., .234 Win., .270 Win., 7mm Mag., .308 Win., .30-06, .300 Win. Mag. Three or 5-rnd. magazine. 24-in. bbl. Weight: 7.5 lbs. Sights: Folding leaf rear; hooded ramp front. Checkered walnut stock w/Monte Carlo comb and cheekpiece, forend tip, sling swivels. Imported 1998. Note: The Model 2000 Classic is designed to interchange bbl. assemblies within a given caliber group.

Classic model . . . . NiB $1696 Ex $ 1377 Gd $1044
Professional model . . . . NiB $3228 Ex $2709 Gd $1995
w/recoil compensator. . . . . NiB $3245 Ex $2730 Gd $1100
Sniper model. . . . . NiB $2010 Ex $1544 Gd $1120
Varmint model . . . . NiB $1996 Ex $1528 Gd $965
Extra bbl. assembly, add $950

MODEL 3000 BOLT-ACTION
SPORTING RIFLE . . . . NiB $570 Ex $440 Gd $400
Modified Mauser-type action. Calibers: .243 Win., .270 Win., .308 Win., .30-06. Five round magazine. 22-in. bbl. Weight: 7 lbs. No sights. Select European walnut stock, Monte Carlo style w/cheekpiece, rosewood forend tip and pistol-grip cap, skip checkering, recoil pad, sling swivels. Made 1971-74.

MODEL 3000 MAGNUM . . . . . NiB $641 Ex $486 Gd $379
Same general specifications as standard Model 3000, except w/3-rnd. magazine, 26-in. bbl., weight: 8 lbs. Calibers: 7mm Rem. Mag., .300 Win. Mag., .375 H&H Mag.

Midland Model 2707 Bolt-Action Rifle

MODEL 4000 VARMINT RIFLE. . NiB $466 Ex $380 Gd $269
Same general specifications as standard Model 3000, except w/smaller action, folding leaf rear sight; hooded ramp front, rubber buttplate instead of recoil pad, weight 6.75 lbs. Calibers: .222 Rem., .223 Rem. 22-in. bbl. Select European walnut stock w/rosewood forend tip and pistol-grip cap. French checkering and sling swivels.

McMILLAN GUN WORKS — Phoenix, AZ

See Harris Gunworks.

GEBRÜDER MERKEL — Suhl, Germany

For Merkel combination guns and drillings, see listings under Merkel shotguns.

OVER/UNDER RIFLES ("BOCK-DOPPELBÜCHSEN")
Calibers: 5.6x35 Vierling, 6.5x58r5, 7x57r5, 8x57JR, 8x60R Magnum, 9.3x53r5, 9.3x72r5, 9.3x74r5, 10.3x60R as well as most of the British calibers for African and Indian big game. Various bbl. lengths, weights. In general, specifications correspond to those of Merkel over/under shotguns. Values of these over/under rifles (in calibers for which ammunition is obtainable) are about the same as those of comparable shotgun models currently manufactured. For more specific data, see Merkel shotgun models indicated below.

Model 210	NiB $5766	Ex $4470	Gd $3210
Model 210E	NiB $6630	Ex $4950	Gd $3765
Model 213	NiB $13,760	Ex $10,550	Gd $7330
Model 240E1	NiB $7113	Ex $4966	Gd $3412
Model 313E	NiB $19,670	Ex $16,750	Gd $10,355
Model 320E	NiB $15,770	Ex $12,559	Gd $9220
Model 321	NiB $17,210	Ex $13,880	Gd $9155
Model 321E	NiB $17,998	Ex $14,760	Gd $9970
Model 322	NiB $12,550	Ex $14,770	Gd $10,049
Model 323E	NiB $23,760	Ex $19,210	Gd $12,960
Model 324	NiB $27,650	Ex $21,880	Gd $15,330

MEXICAN MILITARY — Mexico

Manufactured by Government Arsenal, Mexico, D.F.

MODEL 1936 MAUSER
MILITARY RIFLE . . . . NiB $221 Ex $169 Gd $95
Same as German Kar.98k w/minor variations and U.S. M/1903 Springfield-type knurled cocking piece.

MIDLAND RIFLES — Martinsburg, WV

Manufactured by Gibbs Rifle Company, Inc., Martinsburg, West Virginia.

MODEL 2100 . . . . NiB $413 Ex $338 Gd $228
Bolt-action. Calibers: .22-250, .243 Win., 6mm Rem., .270 Win., 6.5x55, 7x57, 7x64, .308 Win., and .30-06. Springfield 1903 action. Four-rnd. magazine. 22-in. bbl. 43 in. overall. Weight: 7 lbs. Flip-up rear sight; hooded ramp front. Finely finished and checkered walnut stock w/pistol-grip cap and sling swivels. Steel recoil bar. Action drilled and tapped for scope mounts. Production disc.1997.

MODEL 2600 . . . . NiB $445 Ex $370 Gd $220
Same general specifications as Model 2100 except no pistol-grip cap, and stock is walnut-finished hardwood. Made 1992 to 1997.

MODEL 2707 . . . . NiB $443 Ex $284 Gd $220
Same general specifications as Model 2100 except the weight of this rifle as been reduced by utilizing a tapered bbl., anodized aluminum trigger housing and lightened stock. Weight: 6.5 lbs. Disc.

MODEL 2800 LIGHTWEIGHT . . . . NiB $466 Ex $355 Gd $269
Same general specifications as Model 2100 except w/laminated birch stock. Made 1992-94 and from 1996-97.

MITCHELL ARMS, INC. — Fountain Valley, CA

Formerly Santa Ana, California.

MODEL 15/22 SEMIAUTO
High Standard-style action. Caliber: .22 LR. 15-rnd. magazine (10-rnd. after 10/13/94). 20.5-in. bbl. 37.5 in. overall. Weight: 6.25 lbs. Ramp front sight; adj. open rear. Blued finish. Mahogany stock; Monte Carlo-style American walnut stock on Deluxe model. Made 1994-96.
NiB $300 Ex $233 Gd $179 . . NiB $300 Ex $233 Gd $179
Carbine . . . . NiB $300 Ex $233 Gd $179
Deluxe . . . . NiB $259 Ex $166 Gd $126

MODEL 9300 SERIES
Bolt-action. Calibers: .22 LR. .22 Mag. Five or 10-rnd. magazine. 22.5-in. bbl. 40.75 in. overall. Weight: 6.5 lbs. Beaded ramp front sight; adj. open rear. Blued finish. American walnut stock. Made 1994-95.
Model 9302 (.22 LR w/checkered
    stock, rosewood caps) . . . . . NiB $319 Ex $239 Gd $177
Model 9302 (.22 Mag., checkered
    stock, rosewood caps) . . . . . NiB $317 Ex $237 Gd $175
Model 9303 (.22 LR, plain stock) . . NiB $317 Ex $237 Gd $175
Model 9304 (.22 Mag.,
    checkered stock) . . . . NiB $266 Ex $201 Gd $177
Model 9305 (.22 LR,
    special stock) . . . . NiB $221 Ex $179 Gd $235

AK-22 SEMIAUTO RIFLE . . . . NiB $359 Ex $248 Gd $189
Replica of AK-47 rifle. .22 LR. .22 WMR., 20-rnd. magazine (.22 LR), 10-rnd. (.22 WMR). 18-in. bbl. 36 in. overall. Weight: 6.5 lbs. Sights: Post front; open adj. rear. European walnut stock and forend. Matte black finish. Made 1985-94.

CAR-15 . . . . **NiB $525 Ex $355 Gd $283**
Replica of AR-15 CAR rifle. Caliber: .22 LR. 15-rnd. magazine.16.25-in. bbl. 32 in. overall. Sights: Adj. post front; adj. aperture rear. Telescoping buttstock and ventilated forend. Matte black finish. Made 1990-94.

GALIL 22 SEMIAUTO RIFLE . . . . **NiB $439 Ex $289 Gd $198**
Replica of Israeli Galil rifle. Calibers: .22 LR. .22 WMR., 20-rnd. magazine (.22 LR), 10-rnd. (.22 WMR). 18-in. bbl. 36 in. overall. Weight: 6.5 lbs. Sights: Adj. post front; rear adj. for windage. Folding metal stock w/European walnut grip and forend. Matte black finish. Made 1987-93.

M-16A 22 SEMIAUTO RIFLE . . . . **NiB $479 Ex $266 Gd $179**
Replica of AR-15 rifle. Caliber: .22 LR. 15-rnd. magazine. 20.5-in. bbl. 38.5 in. overall. Weight: 7 lbs. Sights: Adj. post front, adj. aperture rear. Black composite stock and forend. Matte black finish. Made 1990-94.

MAS 22 SEMIAUTO RIFLE . . . . **NiB $439 Ex $290 Gd $221**
Replica of French MAS bullpup rifle. Caliber: .22 LR. 20-rnd. magazine. 18-in. bbl. 28 in. overall. Weight: 7.5 lbs. Sights: Adj. post front, folding aperture rear. European walnut buttstock and forend. Matte black finish. Made 1987-93.

PPS SEMIAUTO RIFLE
Caliber: .22 LR. 20-rnd. magazine, 50-rnd. drum. 16.5-in. bbl. 33.5 in. overall. Weight: 5.5 lbs. Sights: Blade front; adj. rear. European walnut stock w/ventilated bbl. shroud. Matte black finish. Made 1989-94.
Model PPS (20-rnd.
    magazine) . . . . **NiB $370 Ex $259 Gd $188**
Model PPS/50 (50-rnd.
    drum) . . . . **NiB $522 Ex $402 Gd $300**

MONTGOMERY WARD — Chicago, IL

NOTE: *Firearms under the "private label" names of Western Field and Hercules are manufactured by such firms as Mossberg, Stevens, Marlin, and Savage for distribution and sale by Montgomery Ward.*

MODEL 14M-497B WESTERN FIELD
BOLT-ACTION RIFLE . . . . **NiB $160 Ex $121 Gd $90**
Caliber: .22 RF. Seven round detachable box magazine. 24-in. bbl. Weight: 5 lbs. Sights: Receiver peep; open rear; hooded ramp front. Pistol-grip stock. Mfg. by Mossberg.

MODEL M771 WESTERN FIELD
LEVER-ACTION RIFLE . . . . **NiB $221 Ex $177 Gd $135**
Calibers: .30-30, .35 Rem. Six round tubular magazine. 20-in. bbl. Weight: 6.75 lbs. Sights: Open rear; ramp front. Pistol-grip or straight stock, forearm w/bbl. band. Mfg. by Mossberg.

MODEL M772 WESTERN FIELD
LEVER-ACTION RIFLE . . . . **NiB $235 Ex $190 Gd $131**
Calibers: .30-30, .35 Rem. Six round tubular magazine. 20-in. bbl. Weight: 6.75 lbs. Sights: Open rear; ramp front. Pistol-grip or straight stock, forearm w/bbl. band. Mfg. by Mossberg.

MODEL M775
BOLT-ACTION RIFLE . . . . **NiB $158 Ex $139 Gd $99**
Calibers: .222 Rem., .22-250, .243 Win., .308 Win. Four round magazine. Weight: 7.5 lbs. Sights: Folding leaf rear; ramp front. Monte Carlo stock w/cheekpiece, pistol-grip. Mfg by Mossberg.

MODEL M776 BOLT-ACTION
RIFLE . . . . **NiB $260 Ex $227 Gd $159**
Calibers: .222 Rem., .22-250, .243 Win., .308 Win. Four round magazine. Weight: 7.5 lbs. Sights: Folding leaf rear; ramp front. Monte Carlo stock w/cheekpiece, pistol-grip. Mfg. by Mossberg.

MODEL M778 LEVER-ACTION NiB $255 Ex $188 Gd $138
Calibers: .30-30, .35 Rem. Six round tubular magazine. 20-in. bbl. Weight: 6.75 lbs. Sights: Open rear; ramp front. Pistol-grip or straight stock, forearm w/bbl. band. Mfg. by Mossberg.

MODEL M780 BOLT-ACTION
RIFLE . . . . **NiB $265 Ex $237 Gd $168**
Calibers: .222 Rem., .22-250, .243 Win., .308 Win. Four round magazine. Weight: 7.5 lbs. Sights: Folding leaf rear; ramp front. Monte Carlo stock w/cheekpiece, pistol grip. Mfg. by Mossberg.

MODEL M782 . . . . **NiB $259 Ex $233 Gd $177**
Same general specifications as Model M780.

MODEL M808 . . . . **NiB $155 Ex $133 Gd $90**
Takedown. Caliber: .22RF. Fifteen round tubular magazine. Bbls.: 20- and 24-in. Weight: 6 lbs. Sights: Open rear; bead front. Pistol-grip stock. Mfg. by Stevens.

MODEL M832 . . . . **NiB $166 Ex $144 Gd $90**
Bolt-action. Caliber: .22 RF. Seven round clip magazine. 24-in. bbl. Weight: 6.5 lbs. Sights: Open rear; ramp front. Mfg. by Mossberg.

MODEL M836 . . . . **NiB $169 Ex $122 Gd $95**
Takedown. Caliber: .22RF. Fifteen round tubular magazine. Bbls.: 20- and 24-in. Weight: 6 lbs. Sights: Open rear; bead front. Pistol-grip stock. Mfg. by Stevens.

MODEL M865 CARBINE . . . . . . **NiB $188 Ex $146 Gd $144**
Lever-action. Hammerless. Caliber: .22RF. Tubular magazine. Made w/both 18.5-in. and 20-in. bbls., forearm w/bbl. band, swivels. Weight: 5 lbs. Mfg. by Mossberg.

MODEL M894 CARBINE . . . . . . **NiB $198 Ex $137 Gd $105**
Semiauto. Caliber: .22 RF. Fifteen round tubular magazine. 20-in. bbl. Weight: 6 lbs. Sights: Open rear; ramp front. Monte Carlo stock w/pistol-grip. Mfg. by Mossberg.

MODEL M-SD57 . . . . **NiB $178 Ex $133 Gd $95**
Takedown. Caliber: .22RF. 15-rnd. tubular magazine. Bbls.: 20- and 24-in. Weight: 6 lbs. Sights: Open rear; bead front. Pistol-grip stock. Mfg. by Stevens.

O.F. MOSSBERG & SONS, INC. — North Haven, CT

Formerly New Haven, CT.

4X4 CENTERFIRE RIFLE . . . . . . **NiB $485 Ex $410 Gd $380**
Bolt-action. Calibers: .22-250, .25-06, .243, .270, .30-06, .270 WSM, 7mm-08, 7mm Rem., .300 Win. Mag., .300 WSM, or .338 Win. Mag. 4- or 5-rnd detacable magazine. Bbl: 22- or 24-in. (fluted). Weight: 6.7-7.8 lbs. Finish: blue or Marinecote. Stock: wood or polymer w/vent forearm. Sights: open sights (.30-06, .300 Win. Mag., or 338 Win. Mag. only), Weaver base. Sling swivel studs. Made 2007-15.

MODEL 10 BOLT-ACTION SINGLE-SHOT
RIFLE . . . . NiB $338 Ex $190 Gd $120
Takedown. Caliber: .22 LR, Long, Short. 22-in. bbl. Weight:
4 lbs. Sights: Open rear; bead front. Plain pistol-grip stock w/
swivels, sling. Made 1933-35.

MODEL 14 SINGLE-SHOT
RIFLE . . . . NiB $338 Ex $190 Gd $120
Bolt-action. Takedown. Caliber: .22 LR, Long, Short. 24-in. bbl.
Weight: 5.25 lbs. Sights: Peep rear; hooded ramp front. Plain
pistol-grip stock w/semi-beavertail forearm, 1.25-in. swivels.
Made 1934-35.

MODEL 20 BOLT-ACTION SINGLE-SHOT
RIFLE . . . . NiB $338 Ex $190 Gd $120
Takedown. Caliber: .22 LR, Long, Short. 24-in. bbl. Weight: 4.5
lbs. Sights: Open rear; bead front. Plain pistol-grip stock and
forearm w/finger grooves, sling and swivels. Made 1933-35.

MODEL 25/25A BOLT-ACTION SINGLE-SHOT RIFLE
Takedown. Caliber: .22 LR, Long, Short. 24-in. bbl. Weight: 5
lbs. Sights: Peep rear; hooded ramp front. Plain pistol-grip stock
w/semibeavertail forearm. 1.25-in. swivels. Made 1935-36.
Model 25 . . . . NiB $338 Ex $190 Gd $120
Model 25A (Improved Model 25,
   1936-38) . . . . NiB $325 Ex $190 Gd $120

MODEL 26B/26C SINGLE-SHOT
Bolt-action. Takedown. Caliber: .22 LR, Long, Short. 26-in.
bbl. Weight: 5.5 lbs. Sights; Rear, micrometer click peep or
open; hooded ramp front. Plain pistol-grip stock swivels. Made
1938-41.
Model 26B . . . . NiB $338 Ex $190 Gd $120
Model 26C (No rear
   sights or sling swivels) . . . . . . NiB $250 Ex $132 Gd $91

MODEL 30 SINGLE-SHOT
RIFLE . . . . NiB $338 Ex $190 Gd $120
Bolt-action. Takedown. Caliber: .22 LR, Long, Short. 24-in.
bbl. Weight: 4.5 lbs. Sights: Peep rear; bead front, on hooded
ramp. Plain pistol-grip stock, forearm w/finger grooves. Made
1933-35.

MODEL 34 SINGLE-SHOT
RIFLE . . . . NiB $338 Ex $190 Gd $120
Bolt-action. Takedown. Caliber: .22 LR, Long, Short. 24-in. bbl.
Weight: 5.5 lbs. Sights: Peep rear; hooded ramp front. Plain
pistol-grip stock w/semibeavertail forearm, 1.25-in. swivels.
Made 1934-35.

MODEL 35 TARGET GRADE BOLT-ACTION
SINGLE-SHOT RIFLE . . . . NiB $440 Ex $300 Gd $166
Caliber: .22 LR. 26-in. heavy bbl. Weight: 8.25 lbs. Sights:
Micrometer click rear peep; hooded ramp front. Large target
stock w/full pistol grip. cheekpiece, full beavertail forearm,
1.25-in. swivels. Made 1935-37.

MODEL 35A BOLT-ACTION SINGLE-SHOT
RIFLE . . . . NiB $440 Ex $300 Gd $166
Caliber: .22 LR. 26-in. heavy bbl. Weight: 8.25 lbs. Sights:
Micrometer click peep rear; hooded front. Target stock w/
cheekpiece full pistol grip and forearm, 1.25-in. sling swivels.
Made 1937-38.

MODEL 35A-LS . . . . NiB $440 Ex $300 Gd $166
Caliber .22 LR. Same as Model 35A but w/Lyman No. 57 rear
sight, 17A front. Target stock w/checkpiece, full pistol-grip
and forearm.

MODEL 35B . . . . NiB $440 Ex $300 Gd $166
Same specifications as Model 44B except single-shot. Made
1938-40.

MODEL 40 BOLT-ACTION
REPEATER . . . . NiB $222 Ex $140 Gd $100
Takedown. Caliber: .22 LR. Long, Short, 16-rnd. tubular maga-
zine. 24-in. bbl. Weight: 5 lbs. Sights: Peep rear; bead front, on
hooded ramp. Plain pistol-grip stock, forearm w/finger grooves.
Made 1933-35.

MODEL 42 BOLT-ACTION
REPEATER . . . . NiB $278 Ex $155 Gd $110
Takedown. Caliber: .22 LR. Long, Short. Seven-rnd. detachable box magazine. 24-in. bbl. Weight: 5 lbs. Sights: Receiver
peep, open rear; hooded ramp front. Pistol-grip stock. 1.25-in.
swivels. Made 1935-37.

MODEL 42A/L42A BOLT-ACTION REPEATERS
Takedown. Caliber: .22 LR. Long, Short. Seven-rnd. detachable
box magazine. 24-in. bbl. Weight: 5 lbs. Sights: Receiver peep,
open rear; ramp front. Plain pistol-grip stock. Made 1937-38.
Model L42A (left-hand action) made 1937-41.
Model 42A . . . . NiB $279 Ex $169 Gd $120
Model L42A . . . . NiB $288 Ex $179 Gd $130

MODEL 42B/42C REPEATERS
Bolt-action. Takedown. Caliber: .22 LR. Long, Short. Five-rnd.
detachable box magazine. 24-in. bbl. Weight: 6 lbs. Sights:
Micrometer click receiver peep, open rear hooded ramp front.
Plain pistol-grip stock, swivels. Made 1938-41.
Model 42B . . . . NiB $289 Ex $190 Gd $100
Model 42C (No rear peep sight) . . . NiB $235 Ex $155 Gd $110

MODEL 42M
REPEATER . . . . NiB $345 Ex $233 Gd $135
Bolt-action. Caliber: .22 LR, Long, Short. Seven-rnd. detachable
box magazine. 23-in. bbl. Weight: 6.75 lbs. Sights: Microclick
receiver peep, open rear; hooded ramp front. Two-piece
Mannlicher-type stock w/cheekpiece and pistol-grip, swivels.
Made 1940-50.

MODEL 43/L43
REPEATERS . . . . NiB $376 Ex $256 Gd $198
Bolt-action. Speedlock, adj. trigger pull. Caliber: .22 LR. Seven-
rnd. detachable box magazine. 26-in. heavy bbl. Weight: 8.25
lbs. Sights: Lyman No. 57 rear; selective aperture front. Target
stock w/cheekpiece, full pistol-grip, beavertail forearm, adj.
front swivel. Made 1937-38. Model L43 is same as Model 43
except w/left-hand action.

MODEL 43B . . . . NiB $390 Ex $300 Gd $170
Same as Model 44B except w/Lyman No. 57 receiver sight and
No. 17A front sight. Made 1938-39.

MODEL 44 BOLT-ACTION
REPEATER . . . . NiB $397 Ex $276 Gd $160
Takedown. Caliber: .22 LR, Long, Short. Tubular magazine holds
16 LR. 24-in. bbl. Weight: 6 lbs. Sights: Peep rear; hooded ramp
front. Plain pistol-grip stock w/semi-beavertail forearm, 1.25-in.
swivels. Made 1934-35. **Note:** Do not confuse this rifle w/later
Models 44B and 44US, which are clip repeaters.

MODEL 44B
TARGET RIFLE . . . . NiB $389 Ex $266 Gd $160
Bolt-action. Caliber: .22 LR. Seven-rnd. detachable box maga-
zine. Made 1938-41.

Mossberg Model 25

Mossberg Model 35A

Mossberg Model 40

Mossberg Model L42A

Mossberg Model 42C

Mossberg Model L-43

MODEL 44US

Bolt-action. Caliber: .22 LR. Seven round detachable box magazine. 26-in. heavy bbl. Weight: 8.5 lbs. Sights: Micrometer click receiver peep, hooded front. Target stock, swivels. Made 1943-48. Note: This model was used as a training rifle by the U.S. Armed Forces during WWII.

Model 44US . . . . NiB $395 Ex $279 Gd $145
Model 44US (marked
   U.S. Property) . . . . NiB $395 Ex $279 Gd $145

MODEL 45 . . . . NiB $254 Ex $178 Gd $117

Bolt-action. Takedown. Caliber: .22 LR, Long, Short. Tubular magazine holds 15 LR, 18 Long, 22 Short. 24-in. bbl. Weight: 6.75 lbs. Sights: Rear peep; hooded ramp front. Plain pistol-grip stock, 1.25-in. swivels. Made 1935-37.

MODEL 45A, L45A, 45AC BOLT-ACTION REPEATERS

Takedown. Caliber: .22 LR, Long, Short. Tubular magazine holds 15 LR, 18 Long, 22 Short. 24-in. bbl. Weight: 6.75 lbs. Sights: Receiver peep, open rear; hooded blade front sight mounted on ramp. Plain pistol-grip stock, 1.25-in. sling swivels. Made 1937-38.

Model 45A. . . . . NiB $300 Ex $190 Gd $145
Model L45A (Left-hand action) NiB $655 Ex $355 Gd $279
Model 45AC
   (No receiver peep sight) . . . . NiB $249 Ex $177 Gd $123

MODEL 45B/45C BOLT-ACTION REPEATERS

Takedown. Caliber: .22 LR, Long, Short. Tubular magazine holds 15 LR, 18 Long, 22 Short. 24-in. bbl. Weight: 6.25 lbs. Open rear sight; hooded blade front sight mounted on ramp. Plain pistol-grip stock w/sling swivels. Made 1938-40.

GRADING: **NiB** = New in Box   **Ex** = Excellent or NRA 95%   **Gd** = Good or NRA 68%

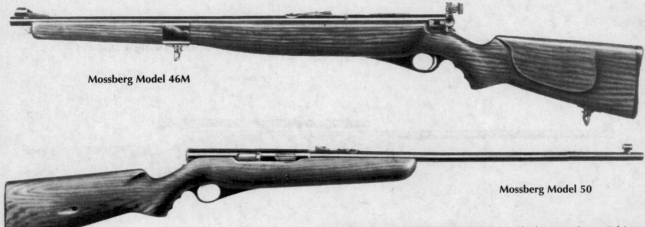

Mossberg Model 46M

Mossberg Model 50

Model 45B . . . . **NiB $338 Ex $233 Gd $138**
Model 45C (No sights, made 1935
  to 1937) . . . . **NiB $338 Ex $233 Gd $138**

MODEL 46 BOLT-ACTION
REPEATER . . . . **NiB $338 Ex $233 Gd $138**
Takedown. Caliber: .22 LR, Long, Short. Tubular magazine holds
15 LR, 18 Long, 22 Short. 26-in. bbl. Weight: 7.5 lbs. Sights:
Micrometer click rear peep; hooded ramp front. Pistol-grip stock
w/cheekpiece, full beavertail forearm, 1.25-in. swivels. Made
1935-37.

MODEL 46A, 46A-LS, L46A-LS BOLT-ACTION REPEATERS
Takedown. Caliber: .22 LR, Long, Short. Tubular magazine
holds 15 LR, 18 Long, 22 Short. 26-in. bbl. Weight: 7.25 lbs.
Sights: Micrometer click receiver peep, open rear; hooded
ramp front. Pistol-grip stock w/cheekpiece and beavertail fore-
arm, quick-detachable swivels. Made 1937-38.
Model 46A . . . . **NiB $338 Ex $233 Gd $138**
Mdl. 46A-LS (w/Lyman No. 57
  receiver sight) . . . . **NiB $386 Ex $276 Gd $189**
Model L46A-LS
  (Left-hand action) . . . . **NiB $650 Ex $355 Gd $269**

MODEL 46B BOLT-ACTION
REPEATER . . . . **NiB $290 Ex $167 Gd $133**
Takedown. Caliber: .22 LR, Long, Short. Tubular magazine
holds 15 LR, 18 Long, 22 Short. 26-in. bbl. Weight: 7 lbs.
Sights: Micrometer click receiver peep, open rear, hooded
front. Plain pistol-grip stock w/cheekpiece, swivels. Note:
Postwar version of this model has full magazine holding 20 LR,
23 Long, 30 Short. Made 1938-50.

MODEL 46BT . . . . **NiB $347 Ex $229 Gd $176**
Same as Model 46B except w/heavier bbl. and stock. Weight:
7.75 lbs. Made 1938-39.

MODEL 46C . . . . **NiB $347 Ex $229 Gd $176**
Same as Model 46 except w/a heavier bbl. and stock than that
model. Weight: 8.5 lbs. Made 1936-37.

MODEL 46M BOLT-ACTION
REPEATER . . . . **NiB $347 Ex $229 Gd $176**
Caliber: .22 LR, Long, Short. Tubular magazine holds 22 Short, 18
Long, 15 LR. 23-in. bbl. Weight: 7 lbs. Sights: Microclick receiver
peep, open rear; hooded ramp front. Two-piece Mannlicher-type
stock w/cheekpiece and pistol-grip, swivels. Made 1940-52.

MODEL 50 AUTOLOADING RIFLE. . **NiB $298 Ex $213 Gd $139**
Same as Model 51 except w/plain stock w/o beavertail cheekpiece, swivels or receiver peep sight. Made 1939-42.

MODEL 51 AUTOLOADING RIFLE. . **NiB $298 Ex $213 Gd $139**
Takedown. Caliber: .22 LR. Fifteen-rnd. tubular magazine in
buttstock. 24-in. bbl. Weight: 7.25 lbs. Sights: Micrometer
click receiver peep, open rear; hooded ramp front. Cheekpiece
stock w/full pistol grip and beavertail forearm, swivels. Made
in 1939 only.

MODEL 51M. . . . . **NiB $278 Ex $154 Gd $123**
Semiauto. Caliber: .22 LR. Fifteen-rnd. tubular magazine. 20-in.
bbl. Weight: 7 lbs. Sights: Microclick receiver peep, open rear;
hooded ramp front. Two-piece Mannlicher-type stock w/pistol-
grip and cheekpiece, hard-rubber buttplate and sling swivels.
Made 1939-46.

MODEL 140B SPORTER-TARGET
RIFLE. . . . . **NiB $254 Ex $186 Gd $134**
Same as Model 140K except w/peep rear sight, hooded ramp
front sight. Made 1957-58.

MODEL 140K BOLT-ACTION
REPEATER . . . . **NiB $248 Ex $197 Gd $123**
Caliber: .22 LR, .22 Long, .22 Short. Seven-rnd. clip magazine.
24.5-in. bbl. Weight: 5.75 lbs. Sights: Open rear; bead front.
Monte Carlo stock w/cheekpiece and pistol-grip, sling swivels.
Made 1955-58.

MODEL 142-A BOLT-ACTION
REPEATING CARBINE. . . . . **NiB $277 Ex $233 Gd $166**
Caliber: .22 Short Long, LR. Seven-rnd. detachable box magazine. 18-in. bbl. Weight: 6 lbs. Sights: Peep rear, military-type
front. Monte Carlo stock w/pistol-grip, hinged forearm pulls
down to form hand grip; sling swivels mounted on left side of
stock. Made 1949-57.

MODEL 142K . . . . **NiB $244 Ex $152 Gd $109**
Same as Model 142 except w/open rear sight. Made 1953-57.

MODEL 144 BOLT-ACTION
TARGET RIFLE . . . . **NiB $390 Ex $288 Gd $215**
Caliber: .22 LR. Seven-rnd. detachable box magazine. 26-in.
heavy bbl. Weight: 8 lbs. Sights: Microclick receiver peep;
hooded front. Pistol-grip target stock w/beavertail forearm, adj.
hand stop, swivels. Made 1949-54. Note: This model designation was resumed c.1973 to replace Model 144LS, and then
disc. again in 1985.

MODEL 144LS . . . . NiB $385 Ex $277 Gd $205
Same as Model 144 except w/Lyman No. 57MS or Mossberg S331 receiver sight and Lyman 17A front sight. Made 1954 to date. Note: Since 1973, this model has been marketed as Model 144.

**MODEL 146B BOLT-ACTION
REPEATER** . . . . NiB $347 Ex $190 Gd $139
Takedown. Caliber: .22 LR, Long, Short. Tubular magazine holds 30 Short, 23 Long, 20 LR. 26-in. bbl. Weight: 7 lbs. Sights: Micrometer click rear peep, open rear; hooded front. Plain stock w/pistol-grip, Monte Carlo comb and cheekpiece, knob forend tip, swivels. Made 1949-54.

MODEL 151K . . . . NiB $290 Ex $193 Gd $130
Same as Model 151M except w/24-in. bbl., weight: 6 lbs., w/o peep sight, plain stock w/Monte Carlo comb and cheekpiece, pistol-grip knob, forend tip, w/o swivels. Made 1950-51.

MODEL 151M. . . . . NiB $370 Ex $199 Gd $138
Improved version of Model 51M w/same general specifications, complete action is instantly removable w/o use of tools. Made 1946-58.

MODEL 152 CARBINE . . . . NiB $276 Ex $197 Gd $135
Semiauto. Caliber: .22 LR. Seven-rnd. detachable box magazine. 18-in. bbl. Weight: 5 lbs. Sights: Peep rear; military-type front. Monte Carlo stock w/pistol-grip, hinged forearm pulls down to form hand grip, sling mounted on swivels on left side of stock. Made 1948–57.

MODEL 152K. . . . . NiB $233 Ex $176 Gd $121
Same as Model 152 except w/open instead of peep rear sight. Made 1950-57.

**MODEL 320B BOY SCOUT TARGET
RIFLE.** . . . . NiB $233 Ex $176 Gd $121
Same as Model 340K except single-shot w/auto. safety. Made 1960 to 1971.

**MODEL 320K HAMMERLESS
BOLT-ACTION SINGLE-SHOT** . . NiB $200 Ex $123 Gd $90
Same as Model 346K except single-shot, w/drop-in loading platform, automatic safety. Weight: 5.75 lbs. Made 1958-60.

MODEL 321B . . . . NiB $347 Ex $190 Gd $139
Same as Model 321K except w/receiver peep sight. Made 1972-75.

**MODEL 321K BOLT-ACTION
SINGLE-SHOT.** . . . . NiB $347 Ex $190 Gd $139
Same as Model 341 except single-shot. Made 1972-80.

**MODEL 333 AUTOLOADING
CARBINE.** . . . . NiB $266 Ex $180 Gd $145
Caliber: .22 LR. 15-rnd. tubular magazine. 20-in. bbl. Weight: 6.25 lbs. Sights: Open rear; ramp front. Monte Carlo stock w/ checkered pistol grip and forearm, bbl. band, swivels. Made 1972-73.

**MODEL 340B TARGET
SPORTER.** . . . . NiB $231 Ex $188 Gd $133
Same as Model 340K except w/peep rear sight, hooded ramp front sight. Made 1958-81.

**MODEL 340K HAMMERLESS BOLT-ACTION
REPEATER** . . . . NiB $231 Ex $188 Gd $133
Same as Model 346K except clip type, 7-rnd. magazine. Made 1958-71.

MODEL 340M. . . . . NiB $650 Ex $390 Gd $238
Same as Model 340K except w/18.5-in. bbl., Mannlicher-style stock w/swivels and sling. Weight: 5.25 lbs. Made 1970-71.

**MODEL 341 BOLT-ACTION
REPEATER** . . . . NiB $290 Ex $144 Gd $110
Caliber: .22 Short. Long, LR. Seven-rnd. clip magazine. 24-in. bbl. Weight: 6.5 lbs. Sights: Open rear, ramp front. Monte Carlo stock w/checkered pistol-grip and forearm, sling swivels. Made 1972-85.

**MODEL 342K HAMMERLESS BOLT-ACTION
CARBINE.** . . . . NiB $240 Ex $150 Gd $113
Same as Model 340K except w/18-in. bbl., stock w/no cheek-piece, extension forend is hinged, pulls down to form hand grip; sling swivels and web strap on left side of stock. Weight: 5 lbs. Made 1958-74.

MODEL 346B . . . . NiB $240 Ex $180 Gd $113
Same as Model 346K except w/peep rear sight, hooded ramp front sight. Made 1958-67.

**MODEL 346K HAMMERLESS BOLT-ACTION
REPEATER** . . . . NiB $240 Ex $150 Gd $113
Caliber: .22 Short. Long, LR. Tubular magazine holds 25 Short, 20 Long, 18 LR. 24-in. bbl. Weight: 6.5 lbs. Sights: Open rear; bead front. Walnut stock w/Monte Carlo comb, cheekpiece, pistol-grip, sling swivels. Made 1958-71.

**MODEL 350K AUTOLOADING
RIFLE — CLIP TYPE.** . . . . NiB $240 Ex $150 Gd $113
Caliber: .22 Short (High Speed), Long, LR. Seven-rnd. clip magazine. 23.5-in. bbl. Weight: 6 lbs. Sights: Open rear; bead front. Monte Carlo stock w/pistol-grip. Made 1958-71.

**MODEL 351C AUTOLOADING
CARBINE.** . . . . NiB $240 Ex $150 Gd $113
Same as Model 351K except w/18.5-in. bbl., Western carbine-style stock w/bbl. band and sling swivels. Weight: 5.5 lbs. Made 1965-71.

**MODEL 351K AUTOLOADING
SPORTER.** . . . . NiB $240 Ex $150 Gd $113
Caliber: .22 LR. Fifteen-rnd. tubular magazine in buttstock. 24-in. bbl. Weight: 6 lbs. Sights: Open rear; bead front. Monte Carlo stock w/pistol-grip. Made 1960-71.

**MODEL 352K AUTOLOADING
CARBINE.** . . . . NiB $240 Ex $150 Gd $113
Caliber: .22 Short, Long, LR. Seven-rnd. clip magazine. 18-in. bbl. Weight: 5 lbs. Sights: Open rear; bead front. Monte Carlo stock w/pistol grip; extension forend of Tenite is hinged, pulls down to form hand grip; sling swivels, web strap. Made 1958-71.

**MODEL 353 AUTOLOADING
CARBINE.** . . . . NiB $240 Ex $150 Gd $113
Caliber: .22 LR. Seven round clip magazine. 18-in. bbl. Weight: 5 lbs. Sights: Open rear; ramp front. Monte Carlo stock w/checkered pistol-grip and forearm; black Tenite extension forend pulls down to form hand grip. Made 1972-85.

RIFLES

Mossberg Model 144LS

Mossberg Model 146B

Mossberg Model 151M

Mossberg Model 152

MODEL 377 PLINKSTER
AUTOLOADER . . . . **NiB $278 Ex $200 Gd $155**
Caliber: .22 LR. Fifteen-rnd. tubular magazine. 20-in. bbl.
Weight: 6.25 lbs. 4x scope sight. Thumbhole stock w/rollover
cheekpiece, Monte Carlo comb, checkered forearm; molded of
modified polystyrene foam in walnut-finish; sling swivel studs.
Made 1977-79.

MODEL 380 . . . . NiB $278 Ex $200 Gd $155
Semiauto. Caliber: .22 LR. Fifteen-rnd. buttstock magazine.
20-in. bbl. Weight: 5.5 lbs. Sights: Open rear; bead front.
Made 1980-85.

MODEL 400 PALOMINO
LEVER-ACTION. . . . . **NiB $390 Ex $242 Gd $161**
Hammerless. Caliber: .22 Short, Long, LR. Tubular magazine
holds 20 Short, 17 Long, 15 LR. 24-in. bbl. Weight: 5.5 lbs.
Sights: Open rear; bead front. Monte Carlo stock w/checkered
pistol-grip; beavertail forearm. Made 1959-64.

MODEL 402 PALOMINO CARBINE. . NiB $390 Ex $242 Gd $161
Same as Model 400 except w/18.5-in. (1961-64) or 20-in.
bbl. (1964-71), forearm w/bbl. band, swivels; magazine
holds two fewer rounds. Weight: 4.75 lbs. Made 1961-71.

MODEL 430 AUTOLOADING RIFLE. . NiB $340 Ex $180 Gd $135
Caliber: .22 LR. Eighteen-rnd. tubular magazine. 24-in. bbl.
Weight: 6.25 lbs. Sights: Open rear; bead front. Monte Carlo
stock w/checkered pistol grip; checkered forearm. Made
1970-71.

MODEL 432 WESTERN-STYLE
AUTO . . . . **NiB $340 Ex $180 Gd $135**
Same as Model 430 except w/plain straight-grip carbine-type
stock and forearm, bbl. band, sling swivels. Magazine capacity: 15 cartridges. Weight: 6 lbs. Made 1970-71.

MODEL 464 . . . . NiB $530 Ex $440 Gd $385
Lever-action. Caliber: .22 LR or .30-30, 7- or 14-rnd. magazine. 18- or 20-in. bbl. Stock: hardwood straight- or pistol-grip
stock, smooth or checkered. Sights: adj. open, drilled and
tapped. Top tang safety. Weight: 6.75 lbs. Caliber: .30-30.
Made 2008–21.
.22 LR, subtract **$35**
w/pistol-grip stock, add **$45**
SPX (polymer adj. stock), add **$30**
ZMB (polymer adj. stock, flash hider), add **$10**

MODEL 472 BRUSH GUN . . . . NiB $340 Ex $180 Gd $135
Same as Model 472 Carbine w/straight-grip stock except w/18-
in. bbl., weight: 6.5 lbs. Caliber: .30-30. Magazine capacity: 5
rnd. Made 1974-76.

MODEL 472
CARBINE. . . . . **NiB $340 Ex $180 Gd $135**
Lever action. Calibers: .30-30, .35 Rem. Six round tubular
magazine. 20-in. bbl. Weight: 6.75 to 7 lbs. Sights: Open rear;
ramp front. Pistol-grip or straight-grip stock, forearm w/bbl.
band; sling swivels on pistol-grip model saddle ring on straight-
grip model. Made 1972-79.

MODEL 472 ONE IN
FIVE THOUSAND . . . . **NiB $705 Ex $455 Gd $170**
Same as Model 472 Brush Gun except w/Indian scenes etched
on receiver; brass buttplate, saddle ring and bbl. bands,

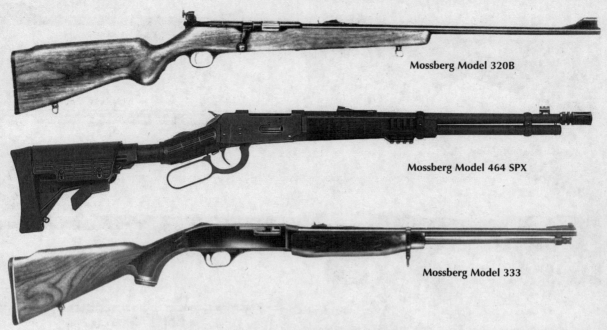

Mossberg Model 320B

Mossberg Model 464 SPX

Mossberg Model 333

gold-plated trigger, bright blued finish, select walnut stock and forearm. Limited edition of 5,000; serial numbered 1 to 5,000. Made in 1974.

MODEL 472 RIFLE . . . . NiB $340 Ex $180 Gd $135
Same as Model 472 Carbine w/pistol-grip stock except w/24-in. bbl., 5-rnd. magazine, weight: 7 lbs. Made 1974-76.

MODEL 479
Caliber: .30-30. Six-rnd. tubular magazine. 20-in. bbl. Weight: 6.75 to 7 lbs. Sights: Open rear; ramp front. Made 1983-85.

Model 479 Rifle . . . . NiB $340 Ex $180 Gd $135
Model 479PCA
  (carbine w/20-in. bbl.) . . . . . NiB $340 Ex $180 Gd $135
Model 479RR (Roy Rogers model,
  5000 Ltd. Ed.) . . . . NiB $665 Ex $423 Gd $240

MODEL 620K HAMMERLESS SINGLE-SHOT
BOLT-ACTION RIFLE . . . . NiB $290 Ex $179 Gd $133
Single shot. Caliber: .22 WMR. 24-in. bbl. Weight: 6 lbs. Sights: Open rear; bead front. Monte Carlo stock w/cheek-piece, pistol-grip, sling swivels. Made 1959-60.

MODEL 620K-A . . . . NiB $290 Ex $179 Gd $133
Same as Model 640K except w/sight modification. Made 1960-68.

MODEL 640K CHUCKSTER HAMMERLESS
BOLT-ACTION RIFLE . . . . NiB $338 Ex $228 Gd $136
Caliber: .22 WMR. Five-rnd. detachable clip magazine. 24-in. bbl. Weight: 6 lbs. Sights: Open rear; bead front. Monte Carlo stock w/cheekpiece, pistol grip, sling swivels. Made 1959-84.

MODEL 640KS . . . . NiB $338 Ex $ 228 Gd $136
Deluxe version of Model 640K w/select walnut stock hand checkering; gold-plated front sight, rear sight elevator, and trigger. Made 1960-64.

MODEL 640M . . . . NiB $665 Ex $423 Gd $240
Similar to Model 640K except w/heavy receiver and jeweled bolt. 20-in. bbl., full length Mannlicher-style stock w/Monte Carlo comb and cheekpiece, swivels and leather sling. 40.75 in. overall. Weight: 6 lbs. Made 1971-73.

MODEL 642K CARBINE . . . . . . NiB $396 Ex $277 Gd $194
Caliber: .22 WMR. Five-rnd. detachable clip magazine. 18-in. bbl. Weight: 5 lbs. 38.25 in. overall. Sights: Open rear; bead front. Monte Carlo walnut stock w/black Tenite forearm extension that pulls down to form hand grip. Made 1961-68.

MODEL 702 PLINKSTER . . . . NiB $187 Ex $100 Gd $85
Semiauto. Caliber: .22 LR, 10- or 20-rnd. magazine. 18- or 21-in. bbl. Weight: 4 lbs. Sights: Leaf rear; ramp front. Stock: wood, polymer sporter (black, camo, pink) or thumbhole (black). Made 2006 to present.
Bantam, subtract $10
Duck Commander, add $50

MODEL 715T . . . . NiB $375 Ex $330 Gd $300
Semiauto, AR-style. Caliber: .22 LR, 10- or 25-rnd. magazine. 16.25-in. bbl. Weight: 5-5.5 lbs. Sights: open/rail or rail onlt. Stock: polymer (black, camo, pink). Made 2012 to present.
Duck Commander, add $100
Tatctcal Carry (18-in. bbl.), subtract $60

MODEL 800 BOLT-ACTION
CENTERFIRE RIFLE . . . . NiB $455 Ex $307 Gd $200
.222 Rem., .22-250, .243 Win., .308 Win. Four-rnd. mag., 3-rnd. in .222. 22-in. bbl. Weight: 7.5 lbs. Sights: Folding leaf rear; ramp front. Monte Carlo stock w/cheekpiece, checkered pistol-grip and forearm, sling swivels. Made 1967-79.

MODEL 800D SUPER GRADE . NiB $455 Ex $307 Gd $200
Deluxe version of Model 800 except w/stock w/rollover comb and cheekpiece, rosewood forend tip and pistol-grip cap. Weight: 6.75 lbs. Chambered for all calibers listed for the Model 800 except for .222 Rem. Sling swivels. Made 1970-73.

Mossberg 702 Plinkster

Mossberg Model 346K

Mossberg MVP Precision

Mossberg Model 352K Carbine

Mossberg Model 377 Plinkster

Mossberg Model 400

MODEL 800M. . . . . **NiB $650 Ex $315 Gd $209**
Same as Model 800 except w/flat bolt handle, 20-in. bbl., Mannlicher-style stock. Weight: 6.5 lbs. Calibers: .22-250, .243 Win., .308 Win. Made 1969-72.

MODEL 800VT
VARMINT/TARGET . . . . **NiB $455 Ex $307 Gd $200**
Similar to Model 800 except w/24-in. heavy bbl., no sights. Weight: 9.5 lbs. Calibers: .222 Rem., .22-250, .243 Win. Made 1968-79.

MODEL 801 HALF-PINT
PLINKSTER . . . . **NiB $230 Ex $200 Gd $175**
Bolt-action, single shot. Caliber: .22 LR. 16-in. bbl. Weight: 4 lbs. Sights: Leaf rear; ramp front. Stock: hardwood (12.25 LOP). Made 2008 to present.

MODEL 802 PLINKSTER . . . . . **NiB $230 Ex $200 Gd $175**
Bolt-action. Caliber: .22 LR. 18- or 20-in. bbl. 10-rnd. magazine. Weight: 4 lbs. Sights: Leaf rear; ramp front. Stock: hardwood, or polymer thumbhole (black or pink). Finish: blued or chrome. Made 2006 to present.
Bantam (18-in. bbl., wood stock) . . . **NiB $230 Ex $200 Gd $175**
Varmint (21-in. bull bbl.) . . . . . **NiB $230 Ex $200 Gd $175**

MODEL 810 BOLT-ACTION CENTERFIRE RIFLE
Calibers: .270 Win., .30-06, 7mm Rem. Mag., .338 Win. Mag. Detachable box magazine (1970-75) or internal magazine w/ hinged floorplate (1972 to date). Capacity: Four-rnd. in .270 and .30-06, 3-rnd. in Magnums. 22-in. bbl. in .270 and .30-06, 24-in. in Magnums. Weight: 7.5 to 8 lbs. Sights: Leaf rear; ramp front. Stock w/Monte Carlo comb and cheekpiece, checkered pistol-grip and forearm, grip cap, sling swivels. Made 1970-79.
Standard calibers . . . . **NiB $390 Ex $333 Gd $232**
Magnum calibers . . . . **NiB $370 Ex $316 Gd $226**

MODEL 817 . . . . **NiB $219 Ex $190 Gd $155**
Bolt-action. Caliber: .17 HMR. 21-in. bbl. 6-rnd. magazine. Weight: 4 lbs. Sights: Leaf rear; ramp front. Stock: Polymer

Mossberg Model 472 Brush Gun

Mossberg Model 640KS

Mossberg Patriot Night Train

Mossberg Model 642K shown w/forearm extension pulled down

Mossberg MVP Varmint

RIFLES

thumbhole (black). Finish: blued or brushed chrome. Made 2007 to present.
Varmint (21-in. bull bbl.) . . . . . NiB $261 Ex $220 Gd $185

MODEL 1500 MOUNTAINEER GRADE I
CENTERFIRE RIFLE . . . . NiB $441 Ex $338 Gd $288
Calibers: .223, .243, .270, .30-06, 7mm Mag. 22-in. or 24-in. (7mm Mag.) bbl. Weight: 7 lbs. 10 oz. Hardwood walnut-finished checkered stock. Sights: Hooded ramp front w/gold bead; fully adj. rear. Drilled and tapped for scope mounts. Sling swivel studs. Imported from 1986 to 1987.Model 1500 Varmint Bolt-Action Rifle Same as Model 1500 Grade I except w/22-in. heavy bbl. Chambered in .222, .22-250, .223 only. High-luster blued finish or Parkerized satin finished stock. Imported from Japan 1986 to 1987.
High-luster blue . . . . NiB $440 Ex $328 Gd $288
Parkerized satin finish. . . . . NiB $455 Ex $338 Gd $298

MODEL 1707LS CLASSIC HUNTER
BOLT-ACTION RIFLE. . . . . NiB $479 Ex $369 Gd $266
Same as Model 1500 Grade I except w/checkered classic-style stock and Schnabel forend. Chambered in 243, 270, 30-06 only. Imported from Japan 1986 to 1987.

MODEL ATR. . . . . NiB $375 Ex $310 Gd $270
Bolt-action. Calibers: .243, .270, 7mm-08, .308 or .30-06. 3-rnd interbal magazine. Bbl. 22-in. fluted or non-fluted. Weight: 7 lbs. Finish: blue or Marinecote. Stock: walnut, Dura-wood or polymer. Sights: open sights or Weaver base. Sling swivel studs. LBA adj. trigger standard in 2009. Made 2005-15.

w/camo stock, add $50
Bantam . . . . NiB $375 Ex $310 Gd $270
Deer Thug (scoped combo). . . . NiB $485 Ex $380 Gd $330
Night Train Special (.308, w/scope) NiB $620 Ex $520 Gd $460

MODEL B BOLT-ACTION RIFLE. . .NiB $340 Ex $205 Gd $113
Takedown. Caliber: .22 LR, Long, Short. Single-shot. 22-in. bbl. Sights: Open rear; bead front. Plain pistol-grip stock. Made 1930-32.

MODEL BLAZE . . . . NiB $187 Ex $160 Gd $100
Semiauto. Caliber: .22 LR, 10- or 25-rnd. magazine. 16.5-in. bbl. Weight: 3.5 lbs. Stock: polymer. Length: 35.75 in. Sights: open sights. Finish: blued. Made 2014 to present.
Camo finish, add. $90
Combo (w/Dead Ringer green dot sight), add $65

MODEL BLAZE-47 . . . . NiB $375 Ex $340 Gd $300
Similar to Blaze except styled like an AK-47 w/wood stock and furniture. Adj. fiber optic sights. Finish: blued. Made 2014–20.
Polymer stock and furniture, subtract. $46

MODEL K SLIDE-ACTION
REPEATER . . . . NiB $545 Ex $390 Gd $233
Hammerless. Takedown. Caliber: .22 LR, Long, Short. Tubular magazine holds 20 Short, 16 Long, 14 LR. 22-in. bbl. Weight: 5 lbs. Sights: Open rear; bead front. Plain, straight-grip stock. Grooved slide handle. Made 1922-31.

Mossberg Model 800D

Mossberg ATR

Mossberg Model 810

Mossberg Model L

Mossberg Model R

MODELS L42A/L43/L45A/L46A-LS
See Models 42A, 43, 45A and 46A-LS respectively; "L" refers to a left-hand version of those rifles.

MODEL L SINGLE-SHOT RIFLE . . . NiB $850 Ex $535 Gd $429
Martini-type falling-block lever-action. Takedown. Caliber: .22 LR, Long, Short. 24-in. bbl. Weight: 5 lbs. Sights: Open rear; bead front. Plain pistol-grip stock and forearm. Made 1929-32.

MODEL M REPEATER . . . . NiB $550 Ex $340 Gd $227
Specifications same as for Model K except w/24-in. octagon bbl., pistol-grip stock, weighs 5.5 lbs. Made 1928-31.

MODEL MMR HUNTER . . . . . NiB $1028 Ex $980 Gd $800
Semiauto, AR15 style. Calibers: 5.56mm NATO, 5-rnd. magazine, compatiable with AR15 magazines. 20-in.free floated bbl. Weight: 7 lbs. Stock: A2 style polymer. Length: 39 in. Sights: none, rail. Finish: Matte black, Mossy Oak Treestand or Mossy Oak Brush. Made 2011-16.
Camo finish, add. $100

MODEL MMR TACTICAL . . . . NiB $1028 Ex $980 Gd $800
Simialr to MMR Hunter model except w/matte balck finish only, 10- or 30-rnd. magazine, adj. stock, Sights: adj/rail or rail only. Made 2011-16.
w/rail only, subtract $40

MODEL MVP FLEX . . . . NiB $996 Ex $900 Gd $875
Simialr to MVP Predator except FLEX system 6-position stock. Made 2013 to present.
Scoped combo . . . . NiB $1177 Ex $995 Gd $875

MODEL MVP-LC . . . . NiB $1438 Ex $1200 Gd $1000
Bolt-action. Calibers: 5.56mm NATO or 7.62mm NATO, 10-rnd. magazine, compatiable with AR15 magazines. 16.25- or 18.5-in. (7.62mm NATO) fluted bbl. w/threaded muzzle. Weight: 8-10 lbs. Stock: light weight aluminum chassis. Length: 35.5-37.75 in. Sights: none, rail. Bipod. LBA adj. trigger. Made 2015 to present.
Combo (Voretx scope) . . . . NiB $2102 Ex $2000 Gd $1988

MODEL MVP-LR . . . . NiB $996 Ex $900 Gd $875
Similar to MVP-LC except long range variant w/20-in. medium bull bbl., threaded muzzle. Weight: 7-8 lbs. Stock: Green textured w/adj comb, benchrest style. Length: 39-39.5 in. Sights: rail. Made 2015 to present.
LR-T Tactical (16.25-in. bbl., sights) . . . NiB $996 Ex $900 Gd $875

MODEL MVP PATROL . . . . NiB $748 Ex $700 Gd $685
Simialr to MVP Predator except available also in .300 ACC BLK, 16.25-in. medium bull, fluted bbl. w/flash suppressor. Weight: 9.25-10 lbs. Stock: textured (tan or black). Length: 35.25-37.5 in. Sights: iron and rail. Made 2013 to present.
Scoped combo, add $100
Thunder Ranch (green stock) . . NiB $771 Ex $710 Gd $695

MODEL MVP PREDATOR . . . . . NiB $732 Ex $600 Gd $520
Bolt-action. Calibers: 5.56mm NATO or 7.62mm NATO, 10-rnd. magazine, compatiable with AR15 magazines. 18.5- or 20-in.medium bull, fluted bbl. w/threaded muzzle. Weight: 8-8.5 lbs. Stock: laminated wood sporter style. Length: 37.5-40 in. Sights: none, rail. LBA adj. trigger. Made 2011 to present.
Scoped combo, add $50

MODEL MVP SCOUT . . . . NiB $777 Ex $700 Gd $685
Simialr to MVP Predator except available only in 7.62mm NATO, 16.25-in. medium bull, bbl. w/flash suppressor. Weight: 6.75 lbs. Stock: synthetic (black). Length: 37.5 in. Sights: rail. Made 2015 to present.

Musgrave RSA NR1

Musgrave Valiant NR6

Musketeer Mauser Sporter

Scoped combo, add $170

MODEL MVP VARMINT . . . . . . NiB $732 Ex $600 Gd $520
Simialr to MVP Predator except available also in .204 Ruger, 24-in.medium bull, fluted bbl. w/threaded muzzle. Weight: 9.25-10 lbs. Stock: laminated wood bench rest style. Length: 43-44 in. Sights: none, rail. Made 2011 to present.
Scoped combo w/bipod, add $170

MODEL PATRIOT . . . . NiB $438 Ex $400 Gd $370
Bolt-action. Calibers: .22-250, .243, .25-06, .270, 7mm-08, .308 or .30-06, 7mm Rem. Mag., .300 Win. Mag., .338 Win. Mag., or .375 Ruger. 4- or 5-rnd magazine. Bbl: 22-in. fluted or sporter style. Weight: 6.5-7.25 lbs. Finish: blue or Marinecote. Stock: walnut or sythetic. Sights: open sights or Weaver base. LBA adj. trigger. Sling swivel studs. Made 2015 to present.
w/synthetic stock, subtract $50
Night Train I (scope, bipod) . . . NiB $811 Ex $795 Gd $700
Night Train II (fluted threaded bbl.,
scope, bipod) . . . . NiB $680 Ex $515 Gd $390
Predator model (varmint calibers, Vortex
scope) . . . . NiB $380 Ex $285 Gd $205
Youth/Bantam model
(12-in. LOP) . . . . NiB $455 Ex $345 Gd $255

MODEL R BOLT-ACTION
REPEATER . . . . NiB $379 Ex $265 Gd $190
Takedown. Caliber: .22 LR, Long, Short. Tubular magazine. 24-in. bbl. Sights: Open rear; bead front. Plain pistol-grip stock. Made 1930-32.

MODEL SSI . . . . NiB $480 Ex $400 Gd $370
Lever-action, single shot. Calibers: .22-250, .223, .243, .270, .308, .30-06 or 12 gauge. Interchangable bbls., 24-in. Weight: 8-10 lbs. Finish: blued or camo. Stock: checkered walnut. Sights: drilled and tapped. Made 2001-04.

MUSGRAVE MFRS. & DIST. (PTY) LTD. — Bloemfontein, South Africa

PREMIER NR5 BOLT- ACTION
HUNTING RIFLE . . . . NiB $460 Ex $375 Gd $288
Calibers: .243 Win., .270 Win., .30-06, .308 Win., 7mm Rem. Mag. Five-rnd. magazine. 25.5-in. bbl. Weight: 8.25 lbs. Furnished w/o sights, but drilled and tapped for scope mount.

Select walnut Monte Carlo stock w/cheekpiece, checkered pistol-grip and forearm, contrasting pistol-grip cap and forend tip, recoil pad, swivel studs. Musgrave or Mauser action. Made 1971-76.

RSA NR1 BOLT-ACTION SINGLE-SHOT
TARGET RIFLE . . . . NiB $449 Ex $420 Gd $300
Caliber: .308 Win. (7.62mm NATO). 26.4-in. heavy bbl. Weight: 10 lbs. Sights: Aperture receiver; tunnel front. Walnut target stock w/beavertail forearm, handguard, bbl. band, rubber buttplate, sling swivels. Made 1971-76.

VALIANT NR6 HUNTING
RIFLE . . . . NiB $415 Ex $369 Gd $255
Similar to Premier except w/24-in. bbl.; stock w/straight comb, skip French-style checkering, no grip cap or forend tip. Sights: Leaf rear; hooded ramp front bead sight. Weight: 7.7 lbs. Made 1971-76.

MUSKETEER RIFLES — Washington, D.C.

Manufactured by Firearms International Corp.

MAUSER SPORTER
FN Mauser bolt action. .243, .25-06, .270, .264 Mag., .308, .30-06, 7mm Mag., .300 Win. Mag. Magazine holds 5 standard, 3 Magnum cartridges. 24-in. bbl. Weight: 7.25 lbs. No sights. Monte Carlo stock w/checkered pistol-grip and forearm, swivels. Made 1963-72.
Standard Sporter . . . . NiB $415 Ex $295 Gd $255
Deluxe Sporter . . . . NiB $459 Ex $380 Gd $276
Standard Carbine . . . . NiB $415 Ex $295 Gd $255

NAVY ARMS — Martinsburg, WV

Importer of reproduction firearms. A division of Forgett Trading LLC which also owns Gibbs Rifle Company. Previously Union City, NJ and Ridgefield, NJ.

.45-70 MAUSER CARBINE . . . . NiB $333 Ex $227 Gd $160
Same as .45-70 Mauser Rifle except w/18-in. bbl., straight-grip stock w/low comb, weight: 7.5 lbs. Disc.

.45-70 MAUSER RIFLE . . . . NiB $260 Ex $221 Gd $155
Siamese Mauser bolt action. Caliber: .45-70 Govt. Three-rnd. magazine. 24- or 26-in. bbl. Weight: 8.5 lbs. w/26-in. bbl. Sights: Open rear; ramp front: Checkered stock w/Monte Carlo comb. Intoduced 1973. Disc.

GRADING: **NiB** = New in Box   **Ex** = Excellent or NRA 95%   **Gd** = Good or NRA 68%

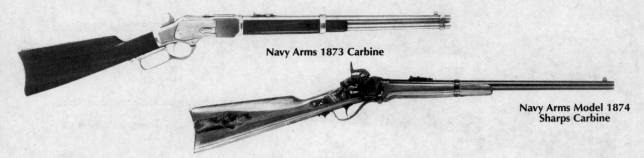

Navy Arms 1873 Carbine

Navy Arms Model 1874 Sharps Carbine

MODEL 1873 WINCHESTER
BORDER RIFLE . . . . NiB $1077 Ex $869 Gd $378
Replica of Winchester Model 1873 Short Rifle. Calibers: .357 Mag., .44-40, and .45 Colt. 20- in. bbl., 39.25 in. overall. Weight: 7.6 lbs. Blued full octagonal barrel, color casehardened receiver w/walnut stocks. Made 1999-2009.

MODEL 1873 CARBINE . . . . . NiB $1043 Ex $756 Gd $399
Similar to Model 1873 Rifle except w/blued receiver, 10-rnd. magazine, 19-in. rnd. bbl. carbine-style forearm w/bbl. band, weighs 6.75 lbs. Disc. Reissued in 1991 in .44-40 or .45 Colt.

MODEL 1873 LEVER-ACTION
RIFLE. . . . . NiB $1043 Ex $756 Gd $399
Replica of Winchester Model 1873. Casehardened receiver. Calibers: .22 LR, .357 Magnum, .44-40. 15-rnd. magazine. 24-in. octagon bbl. Weight: 8 lbs. Sights: Open rear; blade front. Straight-grip stock, forearm w/end cap. Disc. Reissued in 1991 in .44-40 or .45 Colt w/12-rnd. magazine. Disc. 1994.

MODEL 1873 TRAPPER . . . . . . NiB $744 Ex $560 Gd $425
Same as Model 1873 Carbine, except w/16.5-in. bbl., 8-rnd. magazine, weighs 6.25 lbs. Disc.

MODEL 1873 SPORTING CARBINE/RIFLE
Replica of Winchester Model 1873 Sporting Rifle. Calibers: .357 Mag. (24.25- in. bbl. only), .44-40 and .45 Colt. 24.25-in. bbl. (Carbine) or 30-in. bbl. (Rifle). 48.75 to 53 in. overall. Weight: 8.14 to 9.3 lbs. Octagonal barrel, casehardened receiver and checkered walnut pistol-grip. Made 1999-2003.
Carbine model . . . . NiB $970 Ex $844 Gd $630
Rifle model . . . . NiB $1035 Ex $928 Gd $670

MODEL 1874 SHARPS CAVALRY
CARBINE. . . . . NiB $1010 Ex $733 Gd $580
Replica of Sharps 1874 Cavalry Carbine. Similar to Sniper Model, except w/22-in. bbl. and carbine stock. Caliber: .45-70. Imported from 1997 to 2009.

MODEL 1874 SHARPS SNIPER RIFLE
Replica of Sharps 1874 Sharpshooter's Rifle. Caliber: .45-70. Falling breech, single-shot. 30-in. bbl. 46.75 in. overall. Weight: 8.5 lbs. Double-set triggers. Color casehardened receiver. Blade front sight; rear sight w/elevation leaf. Polished blued bbl. Military three-band stock w/patch box. Imported from 1994 to 2000.
Infantry model (single trigger) . NiB $933 Ex $790 Gd $630
Sniper model (double set trigger) . . NiB $2013 Ex $1118 Gd $956

ENGRAVED MODELS
Yellowboy and Model 1873 rifles are available in deluxe models w/select walnut stocks and forearms and engraving in three grades. Grade "A" has delicate scrollwork in limited areas. Grade "B" is more elaborate w/40 percent coverage. Grade "C" has highest grade engraving. Add to value:

Grade "A" . . . . NiB $1023 Ex $779 Gd $615
Grade "B" . . . . NiB $1126 Ex $986 Gd $813
Grade "C" . . . . NiB $1568 Ex $995 Gd $723

HENRY LEVER-ACTION RIFLE
Replica of the Winchester Model 1860 Henry Rifle. Caliber: .44-40. Twelve round magazine. 16.5-, 22- or 24.25-in. octagon bbl. Weight: 7.5 to 9 lbs. 35.4 to 43.25 in. overall. Sights: Blade front, adjustable ladder rear. European walnut straight grip buttstock w/bbl. and side stock swivels. Imported from 1985 to date. Brass or steel receiver. Blued or color casehardened metal.
Carbine w/22-in. bbl.
   (introduced 1992) . . . . NiB $735 Ex $479 Gd $376
Military rifle model
   (w/brass frame) . . . . NiB $989 Ex $688 Gd $482
Trapper model
   (w/brass frame) . . . . NiB $735 Ex $479 Gd $376
Trapper model
   (w/iron frame) . . . . NiB $1055 Ex $800 Gd $479
w/"A" engraving, add $325
w/"B" engraving, add $550
w/"C" engraving, add $950

MARTINI TARGET RIFLE . . . . . . NiB $556 Ex $379 Gd $333
Martini single-shot action. Calibers: .444 Marlin, .45-70. 26- or 30-in. half-octagon or full-octagon bbl. Weight: 9 lbs. w/26-in. bbl. Sights: Creedmoor tang peep, open middle, blade front. Stock w/cheekpiece and pistol-grip, forearm w/Schnabel tip, both checkered. Intro. 1972. Disc.

REVOLVING CARBINE . . . . NiB $641 Ex $540 Gd $400
Action resembles that of Remington Model 1875 Revolver. Casehardened frame. Calibers: .357 Magnum, .44-40, .45 Colt. Six round cylinder. 20-in. bbl. Weight: 5 lbs. Sights: Open rear; blade front. Straight-grip stock brass trigger guard and buttplate. Intro. 1968. Disc.

ROLLING BLOCK BABY
CARBINE. . . . . NiB $255 Ex $190 Gd $155
Replica of small Remington Rolling Block single-shot action. Casehardened frame, brass trigger guard. Calibers: .22 LR, .22 Hornet, .357 Magnum, .44-40. 20-in. octagon or 22-in. rnd. bbl. Weight: 5 lbs. Sights: Open rear; blade front. Straight-grip stock, plain forearm, brass buttplate. Imported from 1968 to 1981.

ROLLING BLOCK BUFFALO
CARBINE. . . . . NiB $439 Ex $333 Gd $227
Same as Buffalo Rifle except w/18-in. bbl., weight: 10 lbs

ROLLING BLOCK BUFFALO
RIFLE. . . . . NiB $720 Ex $572 Gd $338
Replica Remington Rolling Block single-shot action. Casehardened frame, brass trigger guard. Calibers: .444 Marlin, .45-70, .50-70. 26- or 30-in. heavy half-octagon or full-

Navy Arms Martini
Target Rifle

Navy Arms
Yellowboy Carbine
.22 LR

Navy Arms
Revolving Carbine

Navy Arms
Rolling Block Buffalo Rifle

New England Arms (H&R 1871) Handi-Rifle

H&R 1871 Survivor

RIFLES

octagon bbl. Weight: 11 to 12 lbs. Sights: Open rear; blade front. Straight-grip stock w/brass buttplate, forearm w/brass bbl. band. Made 1971-2003.

ROLLING BLOCK CREEDMOOR RIFLE
Same as Buffalo Rifle except calibers .45-70 and .50-70 only, 28- or 30-in. heavy half-octagon or full-octagon bbl., Creedmoor tang peep sight.
Target model . . . . NiB $1530 Ex $1109 Gd $775
Deluxe target model (disc. 1998) NiB $1677 Ex $1330 Gd $190

YELLOWBOY CARBINE . . . . . . NiB $865 Ex $590 Gd $443
Similar to Yellowboy Rifle except w/19-in. bbl., 10-rnd. magazine (14-rnd. in 22 Long Rifle), carbine-style forearm. Weight: 6.75 lbs. Disc. Reissued 1991 in .44-40 only.

YELLOWBOY LEVER-ACTION
REPEATER . . . . NiB $1035 Ex $567 Gd $359
Replica of Winchester Model 1866. Calibers: .38 Special, .44-40. 15-rnd. magazine. 24-in. octagon bbl. Weight: 8 lbs. Sights: Folding leaf rear; blade front. Straight-grip stock, forearm w/end cap. Intro. 1966. Disc. Reissued 1991 in .44-40 only w/12-rnd. magazine and adj. ladder-style rear sight.

YELLOWBOY TRAPPER'S . . . . . . NiB $723 Ex $500 Gd $379
Same as Yellowboy Carbine except w/16.5-in. bbl., 8-rnd. magazine, weighs 6.25 lbs. Disc.

NEW ENGLAND FIREARMS — Gardner, MA
In 1987, New England Firearms was established as an independent company producing selected H&R models under the NEF logo.

In 1991, H&R 1871, Inc. was formed from the residual of the parent company and that took over the New England Firearms facility. H&R 1871 produced firearms under both its logo and the NEF brand name until 1999, when the Marlin Firearms Company acquired the assets of H&R 1871.

HANDI-RIFLE . . . . **NiB $245 Ex $190 Gd $137**
Single-shot, break-open action w/side-lever release. Calibers: .22 Hornet, .22-250, .223, .243, .270, .30-30, .30-06, .45-70. 22-in. bbl. Weight: 7 lbs. Sights: Ramp front; folding rear. Drilled and tapped for scope mounts. Walnut-finished hardwood or synthetic stock. Blued finish. Made 1989-2008.
Synthetic . . . . **NiB $290 Ex $200 Gd $128**
Synthetic/Stainless . . . . **NiB $325 Ex $266 Gd $159**
Youth model . . . . **NiB $300 Ex $233 Gd $144**
10th Anniversary model . . . . . **NiB $822 Ex $555 Gd $375**
Trapper's Edition . . . . **NiB $337 Ex $265 Gd $190**

SUPER LIGHT HANDI-RIFLE . . **NiB $378 Ex $229 Gd $145**
Cal.: .22 Hornet, .223 Rem., .243 Win. Same as Handi Rifle but with black synthetic stock and forearm, recoil pad. Bbl.: 20-in. special contour w/rebated muzzle. .223 Rem. model includes scope base and hammer extension. Weight: 5.5 lbs. Made 1997 to 2008.

SPORTSTER . . . . **NiB $218 Ex $144 Gd $90**
Cal.: .17 HMR, .17 Mach 2, .22 LR, .22 Mag. Bbl.: 20 or 22 in., Weaver-style rail, no sights. Adult or youth (.22 LR only) dimensions. Stock and forearm: Black polymer. Made 1999-2008.

SURVIVOR . . . . **NiB $297 Ex $195 Gd $115**
Cal.: .223 Rem., .308 Win., .357 Mag., .410/.45 Long Colt. Similar to Survivor series shotgun but with removable forearm and thumbhole stock (both with ammo compartments). Bbl.: 20 or 22 in., blue or nickel finish. Weight: 6 lbs. Made 1996-2008.

NEWTON SPORTING RIFLES — Buffalo, NY
Manufactured by Newton Arms Co., Charles Newton Rifles Corp. and Buffalo Newton Rifle Co.

BUFFALO SPORTING RIFLE NiB $2590 Ex $1800 Gd $970
Same general specifications as Standard Model, Second Type. Made c. 1922 to 1932 by Buffalo Newton Rifle Co.

MAUSER SPORTING RIFLE NiB $2125 Ex $1633 Gd $1110
Mauser (Oberndorf) action. Caliber: .256 Newton. Five round box magazine, hinged floorplate. Double-set triggers. 24-in. bbl. Open rear sight, ramp front sight. Sporting stock w/checkered pistol-grip. Weight: 7 lbs. Made c. 1914 by Newton Arms Co.

**STANDARD MODEL SPORTING RIFLE,
FIRST TYPE** . . . . **NiB $3597 Ex $2044 Gd $1035**
Newton bolt action, interrupted screw-type breech-locking mechanism, double-set triggers. Calibers: .22, .256, .280, .30, .33, .35 Newton, .30-06. 24-in. bbl. Sights: Open rear or cocking-piece peep; ramp front. Checkered pistol-grip stock. Weight: 7 to 8 lbs., depending on caliber. Made c. 1916 to 1918 by Newton Arms Co. Second type was prototype only; never manufactured.

NEWTON SPRINGFIELD . . . **NiB $1568 Ex $1105 Gd $890**
Kit including a Marlin-built sporting stock with .256 Newton barrel. Springfield 1903 action and sights provided by customer. Original has square-cut barrels marked "Newton Arms Co. Buffalo, NY." Mfg. 1914 to 1917.

NIKKO FIREARMS, LTD. — Tochiga, Japan
See listings under Golden Eagle Rifles.

NOBLE MFG. CO. — Haydenville, MA

**MODEL 10 BOLT-ACTION
SINGLE-SHOT RIFLE** . . . . **NiB $121 Ex $89 Gd $73**
Caliber: .22 LR, Long, Short. 24-in. bbl. Plain pistol-grip stock. Sights: Open rear, bead front. Weight: 4 lbs. Made 1955-58.

**MODEL 20 BOLT-ACTION
SINGLE-SHOT RIFLE** . . . . **NiB $126 Ex $92 Gd $75**
Manually cocked. Caliber: .22 LR, Long, Short. 22-in. bbl. Weight: 5 lbs. Sights: Open rear; bead front. Walnut stock w/ pistol grip. Made 1958-63.

**MODEL 33 SLIDE-ACTION
REPEATER** . . . . **NiB $230 Ex $110 Gd $80**
Hammerless. Caliber: .22 LR, Long, Short. Tubular magazine holds 21 Short, 17 Long, 15 LR. 24-in. bbl. Weight: 6 lbs. Sights: Open rear; bead front. Tenite stock and slide handle. Made 1949-53.

MODEL 33A . . . . **NiB $115 Ex $89 Gd $69**
Same general specifications as Model 33 except w/wood stock and slide handle. Made 1953-55.

**MODEL 222 BOLT-ACTION
SINGLE-SHOT RIFLE** . . . . **NiB $240 Ex $120 Gd $80**
Manually cocked. Caliber: .22 LR, Long, Short. Barrel integral w/receiver. Overall length: 38 in. Weight: 5 lbs. Sights: Interchangeable V-notch and peep rear; ramp front. Scope mounting base. Pistol-grip stock. Made 1958-71.

**MODEL 236 SLIDE-ACTION
REPEATING RIFLE** . . . . **NiB $159 Ex $140 Gd $97**
Hammerless. Caliber: .22 Short, Long, LR. Tubular magazine holds 21 Short, 17 Long, 15 LR. 24-in. bbl. Weight: 5.5 lbs. Sights: Open rear; ramp front. Pistol-grip stock, grooved slide handle. Made 1951-71.

MODEL 278 LEVER-ACTION RIFLE . . . **NiB $227 Ex $139 Gd $110**
Hammerless. Caliber: .22 Short, Long, LR. Tubular magazine holds 21 Short, 17 Long, 15 LR. 24-in. bbl. Weight: 5.5 lbs. Sights: Open rear; ramp front. Stock w/semipistol-grip. Made 1958-71.

NORINCO — Beijing, China
Manufactured by Northern China Industries Corp., Beijing, China. Imported by Century International Arms; Interarms; KBI and others.

Nornico SKS Carbine

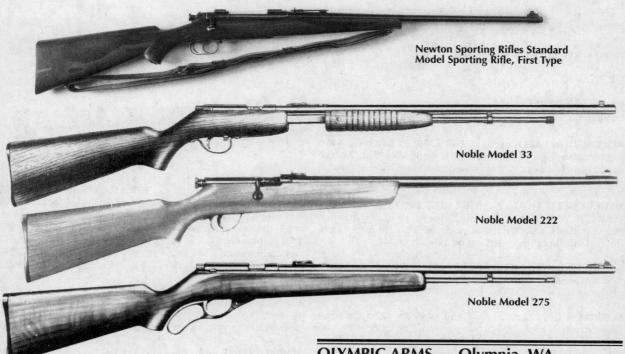

Newton Sporting Rifles Standard
Model Sporting Rifle, First Type

Noble Model 33

Noble Model 222

Noble Model 275

MODEL 81S/AK SEMIAUTO RIFLE

Semiauto Kalashnikov style AK-47 action. Caliber: 7.62x39mm. Five, 30- or 40-rnd. magazine. 17.5-in. bbl. 36.75 in. overall. Weight: 8.5 lbs. Hooded post front sight, 500 meters leaf rear sight. Oil-finished hardwood (military style) buttstock, pistol grip, forearm and handguard or folding metal stock. Black oxide finish. Imported 1988 to 1989.

w/wood stock . . . . NiB $1244 Ex $965 Gd $733
w/folding metal stock . . . . . . NiB $1266 Ex $1002 Gd $753

MODEL 84S/AK SEMIAUTO RIFLE

Similar to 81S except chambered in: .223 (5.56mm). Imported from 1988 to 1989.

w/wood stock . . . . NiB $1479 Ex $1032 Gd $678
Model 84S-3 (w/folding
  metal stock) . . . . NiB $1688 Ex $954 Gd $669
Model 84S-3 (w/composite
  stock) . . . . NiB $1337 Ex $1043 Gd $645

MODEL AK-47 THUMBHOLE SPORTER

Similar to 81S except w/Walnut-finished thumbhole stock w/ recoil pad. Imported from 1991 to 1993.

5.56mm. . . . . NiB $775 Ex $466 Gd $337
7.62x39mm. . . . . NiB $564 Ex $466 Gd $339

MODEL MAK 90/01 SPORT . . . NiB $733 Ex $455 Gd $337

Similar to Model AK-47 Thumbhole Sporter except w/minor modifications implemented to meet importation requirements. Imported from 1994 to 1995.

SKS . . . . NiB $320 Ex $300 Gd $250

Licensed copy of the Soviet made-SKS. Semiauto. Caliber: 7.62x39mm w/10-rnd. integral magazine fed by a stripper clip. Rifle. Bbl.: 20.5 in. Stock: wood. Overall length: 41.375 in. All SKS models are surplus-grade weapons. Imported 1988-89.

OLYMPIC ARMS — Olympia, WA

Began as Schuetzen Gun Works (SGW) in Colorado Springs in 1956 moved to Washington in 1975. Closed in 2017.

PCR SERIES Gas-operated semiauto action. Calibers: .17 Rem., .223, 7.62x39, 6x45, 6PPC or 9mm, .40 S&W, 4.5ACP (in carbine version only). Ten-rnd. magazine. 16-, 20- or 24-in. bbl. Weight: 7 to 10.2 lbs. Black composite stocks. Post front, rear adj. sights; scope ready flattop. Barrel fluting. William set trigger. Made 1994-2004.

PCR-1 Ultra Match . . . . NiB $981 Ex $760 Gd $583
PCR-2 Mult-iMatch ML-1 . . . . NiB $1032 Ex $915 Gd $633
PCR-3 Multi-Match ML-2 . . . . NiB $1070 Ex $959 Gd $654
PCR-4 AR-15 Match . . . . NiB $877 Ex $808 Gd $521
MCR-5 CAR-15 (.223 Rem.) . . . NiB $977 Ex $803 Gd $522
PCR5 CAR-15
  (9mm, 40 S&W, .45 ACP) . . . NiB $903 Ex $794 Gd $538
PCR-5 CAR (.223 Rem.) . . . . . . NiB $955 Ex $731 Gd $510
PCR-6/A-2 (7.62x39mm) . . . . . NiB $895 Ex $692 Gd $486
PCR-7 Eliminator (.223 Rem., 16.5-in.
  bbl., 1999–2004) . . . . NiB $755 Ex $680 Gd $505
PCR-8 (.223 Rem., 20-in. bbl.,
  2001–04) . . . . NiB $730 Ex $655 Gd $505
PCR-9/10/40/45 (9mm, 10mm, .40 Auto
  or .45 Auto; 16-in. bbl., 2001–04) . . . . NiB $780 Ex $700 Gd $505
PCR-16 (.223 Rem., 16-in. match bbl.,
  2003–04) . . . . NiB $755 Ex $680 Gd $505
PCR-30 (.30 Carbine,
  mfg. 2004 only) . . . . NiB $830 Ex $730 Gd $530

PLINKER SERIES . . . . NiB $1135 Ex $955 Gd $755
Similar to PCR-5 except w/ 16-in. bbl. Made 2001-04.
Plinker Plus (16-in. bbl. w/A2 flash suppressor,
  2005–15) . . . . NiB $640 Ex $565 Gd $370
Plinker Plus Compact (Fiberlite handguard,
  2015–17) . . . . NiB $595 Ex $505 Gd $330
Plinker Plus Flat Top (flat top upper,
  2012–17) . . . . NiB $620 Ex $545 Gd $390

Olympic Arms LTF Tactical Rifle

Olympic Arms K4B

Olympic Arms K7 Eliminator

Plinker Plus 20 (20-in. bbl., 2012–17) . . . . **NiB $655 Ex $580 Gd $390**

BOLT-ACTION SAKO . . . . **NiB $755 Ex $575 Gd $456**
Cal.: Various from .17 Rem. to .416 Rem. Mag. Bbl.: Fluted; various stock options. Value is for base model without custom options.

ULTRA CSR TACTICAL . . . . **NiB $1877 Ex $1355 Gd $1043**
Cal.: .308 Win. Sako action. Bbl.: Heavy, 26 in., broach cut. Stock: Bell & Carlson black or synthetic with aluminum bedding. Harris bipod included. Made 1996-2000.

COUNTER SNIPER RIFLE . . **NiB $1490 Ex $1266 Gd $1079**
Bolt action. Cal.: .308 Win. Bbl.: Heavy, 26-in. Stock: Camo fiberglass. Weight: 10.5 lbs. Disc. 1987.

SURVIVOR 1 . . . . **NiB $455 Ex $276 Gd $264**
Converts M1911 into bolt-action carbine. Cal.: .223 Rem., .45 ACP. Bbl.: 16.25 in. Collapsible stock. Available for S&W and Browning Hi-Power. Weight: 5 lbs.

CAR 97 . . . . **NiB $909 Ex $693 Gd $633**
Cal.: .223 Rem., 9mm Para., 10mm, .40 S&W, .45 ACP. Similar to PCR-5 but w/ 16-in. button-rifled barrel. A2 sights, fixed CAR stock, post-ban muzzle brake. Weight: 7 lbs. Made 1997-2004.
M-4 version (disc. 2004), add **$75**

FAR-15 . . . . **NiB $1035 Ex $780 Gd $669**
Featherweight model. Cal.: .223 Rem. Bbl.: 16 in., lightweight, button-rifled, collapsible stock. Weight: 9.2 lbs. Made 2001-04.

GI-16 . . . . **NiB $989 Ex $760 Gd $590**
Cal.: .223 Rem. Forged aluminum receiver, matte finish. Bbl.: Match grade, 16 in., button rifled. Collapsible stock. Weight: 7 lbs. Made 2004 and 2006.

GI-20 . . . . **NiB $877 Ex $698 Gd $549**
Cal. .223 Rem. Similar to GI-16 except w/20-in. heavy bbl., A-2 lower. Weight: 8.4 lbs. Made 2004.

OA-93 Carbine . . . . **NiB $1390 Ex $1133 Gd $976**
Based on OA-93 pistol. Cal.: .223 Rem. Bbl.: 16 in. Flattop receiver. Aluminum side folding stock, round aluminum handguard, Vortex flash supp. Weight: 7.5 lbs. Made 1998 and 2004-07.

OA-93PT . . . . **NiB $1077 Ex $976 Gd $692**
Similar to OA-93 carbine but with aluminum receiver, black matte anodized finish. Bbl.: 16 in., match grade chromemoly steel with removable muzzle brake, push-button removable stock. Weight: 7 lbs. Made 2006-07.

LTF TACTICAL RIFLE . . . . . . **NiB $1338 Ex $1056 Gd $777**
Cal. .223 Rem. Bbl.: 16 in., fluted or non-fluted w/flash supp. Black matte anodized receiver. Firsh-type forearm, Picatinny rails, Parkerized steel parts. Tube-style stock. Weight: 6.4 lbs.
Fluted bbl., add **10%**

K3B CARBINE . . . . **NiB $1189 Ex $873 Gd $689**
Cal. .223 Rem. Bbl.: 16 in., match grade chromemoly steel w/ flash supp. A2 rear sight and buttstock; adj. front post sight.
A3 Flattop receiver, add **$75**
FAR carbine, add **$75**
M4 carbine, add **$75**
A3-TC carbine, add **$250**

K4B/K4B68 . . . . **NiB $1087 Ex $764 Gd $590**
Cal.: .223 Rem., 6.8 SPC. Bbl.: 20 in., match grade, chromemoly steel, button rifled; flash supp. Adj. A2 rear sight and front post; A2 buttstock, upper receiver and hand guard. Weight: 8.5 lbs.
Flattop receiver, add **$150**

K4B-A4 . . . . **NiB $1034 Ex $766 Gd $588**
Cal.: .223 Rem. Bbl.: 20 in. w/A2 flash supp.; bayonet lug. Flattop receiver. Adj. post front sight. Firsh handguard, Picatinny rails. Made 2006-08.

K7 ELIMINATOR . . . . **NiB $1087 Ex $800 Gd $633**
Cal.: .223 Rem. Bbl.: 16 in., stainless steel w/flash supp.; adj. A2 rear sight and front post; A2 buttstock. Weight: 7.8 lbs.

K8 TARGET MATCH . . . . **NiB $1087 Ex $723 Gd $572**
Cal.: .223 Rem. Bbl.: 20-in. bull bbl., stainless, button rifling; Picatinny flattop upper, A2 buttstock. Weight: 8.5 lbs.

K8-MAG . . . . **NiB $1423 Ex $1150 Gd $976**
Similar to Target Match model. Cal.: .223 WSSM, .243 WSSM, .25 WSSM, .300 WSM. 24-in. bbl. Weight: 9.4 lbs.

K9/K10/K40/K45 . . . . **NiB $1132 Ex $955 Gd $780**
Cal.: 9mm Para., 10mm Norma, .40 S&W, .45 ACP. Blowback action. Bbl.: 16 in. w/flash suppressor and bayonet lug. Adj. A2 rear sight. Collapsible stock. Weight: 6.7 lbs.

K9GL/K40GL . . . . **NiB $1188 Ex $992 Gd $694**
Similar to K9 series. Cal.: 9mm Para., .40 S&W. Lower designed to accept Glock magazines. Bbl.: 16 in.; flash suppressor. Collapsible stock. No magazine furnished.
A3 upper, add **$126**

K16 . . . . **NiB $962 Ex $710 Gd $577**
Cal.: .223 Rem. Bbl.: 16 in., free-floating, button rifled. Picatinny flattop upper; A2 buttstock. Weight: 7.5 lbs.
K30R . . . . **NiB $1077 Ex $879 Gd $683**
w/A3 upper, add **$126**

K-30 . . . . **NiB $978 Ex $668 Gd $533**
Cal.: 7.62x39mm. Bbl.: 16-in. stainless steel, adj. rear sight. Parkerized steel parts. Six-point collapsible stock.

K68 . . . . NiB $1198 Ex $978 Gd $645
Cal.: 6.8 Rem. SPC. Bbl.: 16-in. stainless steel, A2 upper with adj. rear sight and flash suppressor. Matte black anodized receiver, Parkerized steel parts. Six-position collapsible A2 stock w/pistol grip.
w/A3 upper, add $126

K74 . . . . NiB $1027 Ex $903 Gd $645
Cal.: 5.45x39mm. Bbl.: 16-in. button rifling; flash suppressor and adj. front sight. Six-position collapsible stock. Weight: 6.75 lbs.

PARKER-HALE LIMITED — Birmingham, England

MODEL 81 AFRICAN . . . . NiB $909 Ex $789 Gd $533
Same general specifications as Model 81 Classic except in caliber .375 H&H only. Sights: African Express rear; hooded blade front. Barrel-band swivel. All-steel trigger guard. Checkered European walnut stock w/pistol grip and recoil pad. Engraved receiver. Imported from 1986 to 1991.

MODEL 81 CLASSIC BOLT-ACTION
RIFLE. NiB $745 Ex $627 Gd $439
Calibers: .22-250, .243 Win., .270 Win., 6mm Rem., 6.5x55, 7x57, 7x64, .308 Win., .30-06, .300 Win. Mag., 7mm Rem. Mag. Four round magazine. 24-in. bbl. Weight: 7.75 lbs. Sights: Adj. open rear, hooded ramp front. Checkered pistol-grip stock of European walnut. Imported from 1984 to 1991.

MODEL 85 SNIPER RIFLE . NiB $2730 Ex $2161 Gd $1578
Caliber: .308 Win. Ten or 20-rnd. M-14-type magazine. 24.25-in. bbl. 45 in. overall. Weight: 12.5 lbs. Blade front sight, folding aperture rear. McMillan fiberglass stock w/detachable bipod. Imported from 1989 to 1991.

MODEL 87 BOLT-ACTION REPEATING
TARGET RIFLE. . . . . NiB $1425 Ex $1233 Gd $757
Calibers: .243 Win., 6.5x55, .308 Win., .30-06 Springfield, .300 Win. Mag. Five-rnd. detachable box magazine. 26-in. bbl. 45 in. overall. Weight: 10 lbs. No sights; grooved for target-style scope mounts. Stippled walnut stock w/adj. buttplate. Sling swivel studs. Parkerized finish. Folding bipod. Imported 1988–91.

MODEL 1000 STANDARD RIFLE . . . NiB $460 Ex $359 Gd $248
Calibers: .22-250, .243 Win., .270 Win., 6mm Rem., .308 Win., .30-06. Four-rnd. magazine. Bolt action. 22-in. or 24-in. (22-250) bbl. 43 in. overall. 7.25 lbs. Checkered walnut Monte Carlo-style stock w/satin finish. Imported from 1984 to 1988.

MODEL 1100 LIGHTWEIGHT BOLT-ACTION
RIFLE. NiB $535 Ex $443 Gd $337
Same general specifications as Model 1000 Standard except w/22-in. lightweight profile bbl., hollow bolt handle, alloy trigger guard and floorplate, 6.5 lbs., Schnabel forend. Imported 1984 to 1991.

MODEL 1100M AFRICAN MAGNUM
RIFLE. NiB $858 Ex $745 Gd $500
Same as Model 1000 Standard except w/24-in. bbl. in calibers .404 Jeffery, .458 Win. Mag. Weight: 9.5 lbs. Sights: Adj. rear; hooded post front. Imported from 1984 to 1991.

RIFLES

MODEL 1200 SUPER CLIP BOLT-ACTION
RIFLE. NiB $763 Ex $555 Gd $423
Same as Model 1200 Super except w/detachable box magazine in calibers .243 Win., 6mm Rem., .270 Win. .30-06 and .308 Win., .300 Win. Mag., 7mm Rem. Mag. Imported from 1984 to 1991.

MODEL 1200 SUPER BOLT-ACTION
SPORTING RIFLE . . . . NiB $586 Ex $480 Gd $355
Mauser-type bolt action. Calibers: .22-250, .243 Win., 6mm Rem., .25-06, .270 Win., .30-06, .308 Win. Four round magazine. 24-in. bbl. Weight: 7.25 lbs. Sights: Folding open rear, hooded ramp front. European walnut stock w/rollover Monte Carlo cheekpiece, rosewood forend tip and pistol-grip cap, skip checkering, recoil pad, sling swivels. Imported from 1968 to 1991.

MODEL 1200 SUPER MAGNUM . . . NiB $556 Ex $550 Gd $369
Same general specifications as 1200 Super except calibers 7mm Rem. Mag. and .300 Win. Mag., 3-rnd. magazine. Imported 1988 to 1991.

MODEL 1200P PRESENTATION NiB $580 Ex $459 Gd $347
Same general specifications as 1200 Super except w/scroll-engraved action, trigger guard and floorplate, no sights. QD swivels. Calibers: .243 Win. and .30-06. Imported from 1969 to 1975.

MODEL 1200V VARMINT. . . . . NiB $557 Ex $498 Gd $425
Same general specifications as 1200 Super, except w/24-in. heavy bbl., no sights, weight: 9.5 lbs. Calibers: .22-250, 6mm Rem., .25-06, .243 Win. Imported from 1969-89.

MODEL 1300C SCOUT . . . . . . NiB $733 Ex $689 Gd $550
Calibers: .243, .308 Win. 10-rnd. magazine. 20-in. bbl. w/ muzzle brake. 41 in. overall. Weight: 8.5 lbs. No sights, drilled and tapped for scope. Checkered laminated birch stock w/QD swivels. Imported in 1991.

MODEL 2100 MIDLAND
RIFLE. NiB $380 Ex $321 Gd $244
Bolt-action. Calibers: .22-250, .243 Win., 6mm Rem., .270 Win., 6.5x55, 7x57, 7x64, .308 Win., .30-06. Four-rnd. box magazine. 22-in. or 24-in. (22-250) bbl. 43-in. overall. Weight: 7 lbs. Sights: Adj. folding rear; hooded ramp front. Checkered European walnut Monte Carlo stock w/pistol-grip. Imported from 1984 to 1991.

MODEL 2707 LIGHTWEIGHT . NiB $370 Ex $329 Gd $237
Same general specifications as Model 2100 Midland except w/ tapered lightweight bbl. and aluminum trigger guard. Weight: 6.5 lbs. Imported in 1991.

MODEL 2800 MIDLAND . . . . . NiB $375 Ex $319 Gd $245
Same general specifications as model 2100 except w/laminated birch stock. Imported in 1991.

PEDERSEN CUSTOM GUNS — North Haven, CT
Division of O.F. Mossberg & Sons, Inc.

MODEL 3000 GRADE I BOLT-ACTION
RIFLE. NiB $1034 Ex $809 Gd $544
Richly engraved w/silver inlays, full-fancy American black walnut stock. Mossberg Model 810 action. Calibers: .270 Win., .30-06, 7mm Rem. Mag., .338 Win. Mag. Three-rnd. magazine, hinged floorplate. 22-in. bbl. in .270 and .30-

**Parker-Hale
Model 81 Classic**

**Parker-Hale
Model 87**

06, 24-in. in Magnums. Weight: 7 to 8 lbs. Sights: Open rear; hooded ramp front. Monte Carlo stock w/roll-over cheekpiece, wraparound hand checkering on pistol grip and forearm, rosewood pistol-grip cap and forend tip, recoil pad or steel buttplate w/trap, detachable swivels. Imported 1973 to 1975.

MODEL 3000 GRADE II . . . . . . NiB $733 Ex $480 Gd $380
Same as Model 3000 Grade I except less elaborate engraving, no inlays, fancy grade walnut stock w/recoil pad. Imported 1973 to 1975.

MODEL 3000 GRADE III . . . . . NiB $579 Ex $380 Gd $299
Same as Model 3000 Grade I except no engraving or inlays, select grade walnut stock w/recoil pad. Imported from 1973 to 1974.

**MODEL 4700 CUSTOM DELUXE
LEVER-ACTION RIFLE** . . . . NiB $279 Ex $238 Gd $175
On Mossberg Model .472 action. Calibers: .30-30, 35 Rem. Five-rnd. tubular magazine. 24-in. bbl. Weight: 7.5 lbs. Sights: Open rear, hooded ramp front. Hand-finished black walnut stock and beavertail forearm, barrel band swivels. Imported in 1975.

PEDERSOLI, DAVIDE — Brescia, Italy
Founded 1957. Manufacturer of high-quality replica firearms frequently marked with importer's or retailer's name, e.g., Cabela's, Cimarron F.A. Co., E.M.F. Company Inc., Taylor's & Co., etc. See those importers or retailers for current values.

J.C. PENNEY CO., INC. — Dallas, TX
Firearms sold under the J.C. Penney label were mfd. by Marlin, High Standard, Stevens, Savage and Springfield.

**MODEL 2025 BOLT-ACTION
REPEATER** . . . . NiB $100 Ex $65 Gd $55
Takedown. Caliber: .22 RF. Eight round detachable box magazine. 24-in. bbl. Weight: 6 lbs. Sights: Open rear; bead front. Plain pistol-grip stock. Manufactured by Marlin.

**MODEL 2035 BOLT-ACTION
REPEATER** . . . . NiB $100 Ex $65 Gd $55
Takedown. Caliber: .22 RF. Eight round detachable box magazine. 24-in. bbl. Weight: 6 lbs. Sights: Open rear; bead front. Plain pistol-grip stock. Manufactured by Marlin.

MODEL 2935 LEVER-ACTION . . . NiB $210 Ex $170 Gd $121
Same general specifications as Marlin Model 336.

**MODEL 6400 BOLT-ACTION
CENTERFIRE RIFLE** . . . . NiB $210 Ex $170 Gd $110
Same general specifications as Savage Model 340.

MODEL 6660 AUTOLOADING RIFLE . . . NiB $115 Ex $90 Gd $75
Caliber: .22 RF. Tubular magazine. 22-in. bbl. Weight: 5.5 lbs. Sights: Open rear; hooded ramp front. Plain pistol-grip stock. Manufactured by Marlin.

PLAINFIELD MACHINE COMPANY — Dunellen, NJ

M-1 CARBINE . . . . NiB $227 Ex $166 Gd $135
Same as U.S. Carbine, Cal. .30, M-1 except also available in caliber 5.7mm (.22 caliber w/necked-down .30 Carbine cartridge case). Current production w/ventilated metal handguard and barrel band w/o bayonet lug; earlier models have standard military-type fittings. Made 1960-77.

**M-1 CARBINE, COMMANDO
MODEL** . . . . NiB $232 Ex $171 Gd $145
Same as M-1 Carbine except w/paratrooper-type stock w/telescoping wire shoulderpiece. Made 1960-77.

M-1 CARBINE, MILITARY SPORTER . . . NiB $227 Ex $166 Gd $135
Same as M-1 Carbine except w/unslotted buttstock and wood handguard. Made 1960-77.

M-1 DELUXE SPORTER . . . . NiB $232 Ex $171 Gd $145
Same as M-1 Carbine except w/Monte Carlo sporting stock Made 1960-73.

POLISH MILITARY — Poland
Manufactured by Government Arsenals at Radom and Warsaw, Poland.

Pedersen Model 3000
Grade III

Plainfield M-1 Carbine

MODEL 1898 (KARABIN 98, K98) MAUSER
MILITARY CARBINE . . . . NiB $331 Ex $210 Gd $166
Same as German Kar. 98A except for minor details. First manufactured during early 1920s.

MODEL 1898 (KARABIN 98, WZ98A) MAUSER
MILITARY RIFLE . . . . NiB $289 Ex $180 Gd $145
Same as German Kar. 98 used in WWI except for minor details. Manufacture began c. 1921.

MODEL 1929 (KARABIN 29, WZ29) MAUSER
MILITARY RIFLE . . . . NiB $331 Ex $210 Gd $166
Same as Czech Model 24, mfd. 1929 thru WWII except for minor details. A similar model produced during German occupation was designated Gew. 29/40.

WILLIAM POWELL & SON LTD. — Birmingham, England

DOUBLE-BARREL
RIFLE. . . . . NiB $32,278 Ex $26,900 Gd $18,900
Boxlock. Made to order in any caliber during the time that rifle was manufactured. Bbls.: Made to order in any legal length, but 26 in. recommended. Highest grade French walnut buttstock and forearm w/fine checkering. Metal is elaborately engraved. Imported by Stoeger from 1938 to 1951.

BOLT-ACTION RIFLE. . . . . . NiB $2888 Ex $2367 Gd $1699
Mauser-type bolt action. Calibers: 6x54 through .375 H&H Magnum. Three and 4-shot magazine, depending upon chambering. 24-in. bbl. Weight: 7.5 to 8.75 lbs. Sights: Folding leaf rear; hooded ramp front. Cheekpiece stock, checkered forearm and pistol grip, swivels. Imported by Stoeger from 1938 to 1951.

Purdey Double Rifle

Purdey Bolt-Action Rifle

Polish Model 1929 Mauser

PTR 91, INC. — Aynor, SC
Previously Bristol, CT and Farmington, CT.

MODEL PTR-91F . . . . NiB $1150 Ex $900 Gd $600
Delayed roller-locked blow-back action similar to H&K G3. Caliber: .308 Win. 20-rnd. magazine. 18-in. bbl. H&K Navy type polymer trigger group. Sights: H&K style front post and rear adj. diopter. Plastic buttstock. Matte black finish. and forearm. Made 2005 to date.
PTR-91 AI (match grade bbl.,
2005-08) . . . . NiB $1170 Ex $730 Gd $570
PTR-91 Classic (black or wood
stock, 2012) . . . . NiB $880 Ex $650 Gd $460
PTR-91 KC (16-in. bbl.). . . . . NiB $1160 Ex $910 Gd $600
PTR-91T (green furniture). . . . . NiB $900 Ex $850 Gd $550
PTR-MSG 91 Sniper (18-in. fluted
target bbl.) . . . . NiB $1980 Ex $1600 Gd $900

PUMA — Brescia, Italy
Manufactured by Armisport Chiappa in Brescia, Italy, and imported by Legacy Sports Int'l., Reno, NV.

MODEL 1886 LEVER ACTION NiB $1260 Ex $880 Gd $625
Reproduction of Winchester 1886 lever action. Caliber: .45-70. 7- or 8-rnd. tube magazine. 22- or 26-in. rnd. or octagon bbl. Case colored receiver, Italian walnut stock. Made 2009 to 2014.

MODEL M92 LEVER ACTION. . NiB $925 Ex $710 Gd $460
Similar to Winchester Model 1892. Caliber: .38 Special/.357 Mag., .44 Special/.44 Mag., .45 LC, .454 Casull or .480 Ruger. 9- or 10-rnd. tube magazine. 20-in. rnd. or octagon bbl. Blue, brass or case colored receiver, walnut stock. Made 2001 to 2014.

PPS/22 . . . . NiB $480 Ex $330 Gd $280
Styled after Soviet "Burp Gun." Caliber: .22 LR. Semiauto. 16-in. bbl., 10- or 50-rnd. (drum) magazine. Made 2009-10.

JAMES PURDEY & SONS LTD. — London, England

BOLT-ACTION RIFLE. NiB $22,800 Ex $19,970 Gd $12,770
Mauser-type bolt action. Calibers: 7x57, .300 H&H Magnum, .375 H&H Magnum, 10.75x73. Three round magazine. 24-in. bbl. Weight: 7.5 to 8.75 lbs. Sights: Folding leaf rear; hooded ramp front. Cheekpiece stock, checkered forearm and

GRADING: **NiB** = New in Box   **Ex** = Excellent or NRA 95%   **Gd** = Good or NRA 68%

333

Puma M92

pistol-grip, swivels. Currently manufactured; same general specifications apply to pre-WWII model.

DOUBLE RIFLE

Sidelock action, hammerless, ejectors. Almost any caliber is available but the following are the most popular: .375 Flanged Magnum Nitro Express, .500/465 Nitro Express .470 Nitro Express, .577 Nitro Express. 25.5-in. bbls. (25-in. in .375). Weight: 9.5 to 12.75 lbs. Sights: Folding leaf rear; ramp front. Cheekpiece stock, checkered forearm and pistol-grip, recoil pad, swivels. Currently manufactured to individual measurements and specifications; same general specifications apply to pre-WWII model.

H&H calibers	NiB $72,665	Ex $57,550	Gd $38,750
NE calibers	NiB $85,000	Ex $56,000	Gd $39,000

RAPTOR ARMS COMPANY, INC. — Newport, NH

BOLT-ACTION RIFLE

Calibers: .243 Win., .270 Win., .30-06 or .308 Win. Four round magazine. 22-in. sporter or heavy bbl. Weight: 7.3 to 8 lbs. 42.5 in. overall. No sights w/drilled and tapped receiver or optional blade front, adjustable rear. Blue, stainless or "Taloncote" rust-resistant finish. Checkered black synthetic stock w/Monte Carlo cheepiece and vented recoil pad. Imported from 1997 to 1999.

Raptor Sporter model	NiB $255	Ex $190	Gd $155
Raptor Deluxe Peregrine model (disc. 1998)	NiB $258	Ex $195	Gd $159
Raptor heavy bbl. model	NiB $277	Ex $222	Gd $195
Raptor stainless bbl. model	NiB $299	Ex $257	Gd $213
w/optional sights, add			$40

REMINGTON ARMS COMPANY — Madison, NC

Manufacturing locations in Ilion, New York, Lonoke, AR, and Mayfield, Kentucky. Acquired by Freedom Group Inc. in 2007. In 2020 bankruptcy all Remington firearm assets were purchase by Roundhill Group.

To facilitate locating Remington firearms, models are grouped into four categories: Single-shot rifles, bolt-action repeating rifles, slide-action (pump) rifles, and Semiauto rifles. For a complete listing, please refer to the index.

- SINGLE-SHOT MODELS -

NO. 1 SPORTING RIFLE . . . NiB $6223 Ex $3856 Gd $2210

Single-Shot, rolling-block action. Calibers: .40-50, .40-70, .44-77, .50-45, .50-70 Gov't. centerfire and .44 Long, .44 Extra Long, .45-70, .46 Long, .46 Extra Long, .50-70 rimfire. Bbl. lengths: 28- or 30-in. part octagon. Weight: 5 to 7.5 lbs. Sights: Folding leaf rear sight; sporting front, dovetail bases. Plain walnut straight stock; flanged-top, semicarbine buttplate. Plain walnut forend with thin, rounded front end. Made 1868-1902.

NO. 1 1/2 SPORTING RIFLE . . . NiB $4190 Ex $1200 Gd $1888

Single-Shot, rolling-block action. Calibers: .22 Short, Long, or Extra Long. 25 Stevens, .32, and .38 rimfire cartridges. .32-20, .38-40 and .44-40 centerfire. Bbl. lengths: 24-, 26-, 28- or 30-in. part octagon. Remaining features similar to Remington No. 1. Made 1869-1902.

NO. 2 SPORTING RIFLE

Single-shot, rolling-block action. Calibers: .22, .25, .32, .38, .44 rimfire or centerfire. Bbl. lengths: 24, 26, 28 or 30 in. Weight: 5 to 6 lbs. Sights: Open rear; bead front. Straight-grip sporting stock and knobtip forearm of walnut. Made 1873-1909.

Calibers: .22, .25, .32	NiB $3575	Ex $2040	Gd $989
Calibers: .38, .44	NiB $9650	Ex $8129	Gd $5450

NO. 3 CREEDMOOR AND SCHUETZEN

RIFLES . . . . NiB $16,187 Ex $12,750 Gd $10,510
Produced in a variety of styles and calibers, these are collector's items and bring far higher prices than the sporting types. The Schuetzen Special, which has an under-lever action, is especially rare — perhaps fewer than 100 have been made.

NO. 3 HIGH POWER RIFLE

Single-shot, Hepburn falling-block action w/side lever. Calibers: .30-30, .30-40, .32 Special, .32-40, .38-55, .38-72 (high-power cartridges). Bbl. lengths: 26-, 28-, 30-in. Weight: About 8 lbs. Open sporting sights. Checkered pistol-grip stock and forearm. Made 1893-1907.

Calibers: .30-30, .30-40, .32 Special, .32-40	NiB $9775	Ex $7956	Gd $5110
Calibers: .38-55, .38-72	NiB $9688	Ex $8154	Gd $6422

NO. 3 SPORTING RIFLE . . . NiB $9775 Ex $7279 Gd $6788

Single-shot, Hepburn falling-block action w/side lever. Calibers: .22 WCF, .22 Extra Long, .25-20 Stevens, .25-21 Stevens, .25-25 Stevens, .32 WCF, .32-40 Ballard & Marlin, .32-40 Rem., .38 WCF, .38-40 Rem., 38-.38-50 Rem., .38-55 Ballard & Marlin, .40-60 Ballard & Marlin, .40-60 WCF, .40-65 Rem. Straight, .40-82 WCF, .45-70 Gov't., .45-90 WCF, also was supplied on special order in bottle-necked .40-50, .40-70, .40-90, .44-77, .44-90, .44-105, .50-70 Gov., .50-90 Sharps Straight. Bbl. lengths: 26-in. (22, 25, 32 cal. only), 28-in., 30-in.; half-octagon or full-octagon. Weight: 8 to 10 lbs. Sights: Open rear; blade front. Checkered pistol-grip stock and forearm. Made 1880 to c. 1911.

NO. 4 SINGLE-SHOT RIFLE . . NiB $1630 EX $944 Gd $755

Rolling-block action. Solid frame or takedown. Calibers: .22 Short and Long, .22 LR, .25 Stevens R.F., .32 Short and Long R.F. 22.5-in. octagon bbl., 24-in. available in .32 caliber only. Weight: About 4.5 lbs. Sights: Open rear; blade front. Plain walnut stock and forearm. Made 1890-1933.

NO. 4S MILITARY MODEL 22 SINGLE-SHOT

RIFLE . . . . NiB $2650 Ex $2033 Gd $997
Rolling-block action. Calibers: .22 Short, Long LR. 28-in. bbl. Weight: About 5 lbs. Sights: Military-type rear; blade

front. Military-type stock w/handguard, stacking swivel, sling. Has a bayonet stud on the barrel; bayonet and scabbard were regularly supplied. Note: At one time the Military Model was the official rifle of the Boy Scouts of America and was called the Boy Scout Rifle. Made 1913-33.

NO. 5 SPECIAL SINGLE-SHOT RIFLE

Single-shot, rolling-block action. Calibers: 7mm Mauser, .30-30, .30-40 Krag, .303 British, .32-40, .32 Special, .38-55 (high-power cartridges). Bbl. lengths: 24, 26 and 28 in. Weight: About 7 lbs. Open sporting sights. Plain straight-grip stock and forearm. Made 1902 to 1918. Note: Models 1897 and 1902 Military Rifles, intended for the export market, are almost identical with the No. 5, except for 30-in. bbl. full military stock and weight (about 8.5 lbs.); a carbine was also supplied. The military rifles were produced in caliber 8mm Lebel for France, 7.62mm Russian for Russia and 7mm Mauser for the Central and South American government trade. Also offered to retail buyers.

Sporting model . . . . NiB $934 Ex $733 Gd $530
Military model . . . . NiB $731 Ex $554 Gd $400

NO. 6 TAKEDOWN RIFLE. . . . . NiB $675 Ex $535 Gd $459

Single-shot, rolling-block action. Calibers: .22 Short, Long, LR; .32 Short, Long RF. 20-in. bbl. Weight: Avg. 4 lbs. Sights: Open front and rear; tang peep. Plain straight-grip stock, forearm. Made 1901-33.

NO. 7 TARGET AND SPORTING

RIFLE. . . . . .NiB $9707 Ex $7235 Gd $6755
Single-shot. Rolling-block Army Pistol frame. Calibers: .22 Short, .22 LR. 25-10 Stevens R.F. (other calibers available on special order). Half-octagon bbls.: 24-, 26-, 28-in. Weight: About 6 lbs. Sights: Lyman combination rear; Beach combination front. Fancy walnut stock, Swiss buttplate available. Made 1903-11.

MODEL 33 SERIES

Bolt action. Single shot. Caliber: .22 S/L/LR. 24-in. bbl. Weight: About 4.5 lbs. Sights: Open rear, bead front. Plain, pistol-grip stock, forearm with grasping grooves. Made 1931-36.

33 . . . . NiB $255 Ex $230 Gd $155
33 NRA. . . . . NiB $230 Ex $480 Gd $280
33-P . . . . NiB $330 Ex $310 Gd $195
33 SB . . . . NiB $405 Ex $355 Gd $255

MODEL 40X CENTERFIRE

RIFLE . . . . .NiB $2690 Ex $2044 Gd $1107
Specifications same as for Model 40X Rimfire (heavy weight). Calibers: .222 Rem., .222 Rem. Mag., 7.62mm NATO, .30-06 (others were available on special order). Made 1961-64. Value shown is for rifle w/o sights.

MODEL 40X HEAVYWEIGHT BOLT-ACTION TARGET RIFLE (RIMFIRE)

Caliber: .22 LR. Single shot. Action similar to Model 722. Click adj. trigger. 28-in. heavy bbl. Redfield Olympic sights. Scope bases. High-comb target stock bedding device, adj. swivel, rubber buttplate. Weight: 12.75 lbs. Made 1955-64.

w/ sights . . . . NiB $3370 Ex $2133 Gd $1320
w/o sights . . . . NiB $2390 Ex $1096 Gd $675

MODEL 40X SPORTER . . . . . NiB $3000 Ex $1947 Gd $944

Same general specifications as Model 707 C Custom (see that listing in this section) except in caliber .22 LR. Made 1972-77.

MODEL 40X STANDARD BARREL

Same as Model 40X Heavyweight except has lighter barrel. Weight: 10.75 lbs.

w/ sights . . . . NiB $579 Ex $416 Gd $322
w/o sights . . . . NiB $495 Ex $338 Gd $256

MODEL 40-XB CENTERFIRE

MATCH RIFLE. . . . . NiB $2055 Ex $2010 Gd $1960
Bolt-action, single-shot. Calibers: .222 Rem., .222 Rem. Mag., .223 Rem., .22-250, 6x47mm, 6mm Rem., .243 Win., .25-06, 7mm Rem. Mag., .30-06, .308 Win. (7.62mm NATO), .30-338, (7.62mm NATO), .30-338, .300 Win. Mag. 27 25-in. standard or heavy bbl. Target stock w/adj. front swivel block on guide rail, rubber buttplate. Weight w/o sights: Standard bbl., 9.25 lbs.; heavy bbl., 11.25 lbs. Value shown is for rifle without sights. Made 1964-2020.

MODEL 40-XB RANGEMASTER CENTERFIRE RIFLE

Single-shot target rifle with same basic specifications as Model 40-XB Centerfire Match. Additional calibers in .220 Swift, 6mm BR Rem. and 7mm BR Rem., and stainless bbl. only. American walnut or Kevlar (weighs 1 lb. less) target stock with forend stop. Discontinued 1994.

right-hand model . . . . NiB $2130 Ex $1810 Gd $1000
left-hand model, add.. . . . . $300
Kevlar stock, right-hand model . . . NiB $2430 Ex $2055 Gd $1210
Kevlar stock, Repeater, add $150
w/2 oz. trigger, add $300
Repeater model, add. $150

MODEL 40-XB RANGEMASTER RIMFIRE

MATCH RIFLE. . . . . NiB $1380 Ex $1255 Gd $805
Bolt-action, single-shot. Caliber: .22 LR. 28-in. standard or heavy bbl. Target stock with adj. front swivel block on guide rail, rubber buttplate. Weight w/o sights: Standard bbl., 10 lbs.; heavy bbl., 11.25 lbs. Value shown is for rifle without sights. Made 1964-74.

MODEL 40-XB VARMINT SPECIAL

RIFLE. . . . . NiB $2160 Ex $2050 Gd $900
Same general specifications as Model 40-XB Repeater except has synthetic stock (Kevlar). Made 1987-94.

MODEL 40-XBBR BENCH REST RIFLE

Bolt action, single shot. Calibers: .222 Rem., .222 Rem. Mag., .223 Rem., 6x47mm, .308 Win. (7.62mm NATO). 20- or 26-in. unblued stainless-steel bbl. Supplied w/o sights. Weight: w/ 20-in. bbl., 9.25 lbs., w/ 26-in. bbl.,12 lbs. (Heavy Varmint class; 7.25 lbs. w/Kevlar stock (Light Varmint class). Made 1974-2004; reintroduced 2007-20.

Model 40-XBBR (disc.) . . . . NiB $3550 Ex $2896 Gd $1600
Model 40-XBBR KS
  (Kevlar stock) . . . . NiB $3504 Ex $2973 Gd $1679

MODEL 40-XC NATIONAL MATCH COURSE RIFLE

Bolt-action repeater. Caliber: .308 Win. (7.62mm NATO). Five round magazine, clip slot in receiver. 24-in. bbl. Supplied w/o sights. Weight: 11 lbs. Thumb groove stock w/adj. hand stop and sling swivel, adj. buttplate. Disc 2004, reintroduced 2006–20.

wood stock (disc. 1989) . . . NiB $2510 Ex $2120 Gd $1300
Kevlar stock (disc. 2014). . . NiB $2630 Ex $2230 Gd $1410

MODEL 40-XR CUSTOM SPORTER RIFLE

Caliber: .22 LR or .22 WMR. 24-in. contoured bbl. Supplied w/o sights. Made in four grades of checkering, engraving and other custom features. Made 1987-91.

Grade I . . . . NiB $1505 Ex $1355 Gd $820
Grade II . . . . NiB $2755 Ex $2255 Gd $1230

RIFLES

**Remington No. 7
Target and Sporting Rifle**

**Remington
Model 40X Standard Rimfire**

**Remington
Model 40-XB Centerfire**

**Remington
Model 40-XBR**

**Remington
Model 40-XR Custom Sporter Grade II**

**Remington
Model 40-XR Rimfire Position Rifle**

**Remington
Model 580**

Grade III . . . . NiB $3505 Ex $2910 Gd $1545
Grade IV . . . . NiB $4880 Ex $4110 Gd $2966

MODEL 40-XR RIMFIRE POSITION RIFLE
Bolt action, single shot. Caliber: .22 LR. 24-in. heavy bbl. Supplied w/o sights. Weight: 10 lbs. Position-style stock w/ thumb groove, adj. hand stop and sling swivel on guide rail, adj. buttplate. Made 1974-2004, reintro. 2007-11.
KS model (w/Kevlar stock). . . . NiB $2555 Ex $2210 Gd $1210
wood stock, deduct. $500

MODEL 41 TARGETMASTER SERIES
Bolt action. Single shot. Caliber: .22 Short, Long, LR. 27-in. bbl. Weight: About 5.5 lbs. Sights: Open rear; bead front. Plain pistol-grip stock. Made 1936-40.

41 A . . . . NiB $255 Ex $230 Gd $145
41 AS (.22 Rem. Spl.) . . . . NiB $405 Ex $385 Gd $255
41 P (peep sight) . . . . NiB $305 Ex $265 Gd $175
41 SB (smooth bore) . . . . NiB $405 Ex $350 Gd $225

MODEL 510 TARGETMASTER SERIES
Takedown. Single shot. Caliber: 22 S/L/LR. 25-in. bbl. Weight: about 5.5 lbs. Sights: Open rear; bead front. Stock: Plain pistol-grip. Made 1939-62.
510 A . . . . NiB $255 Ex $170 Gd $130
510 C (carbine) . . . . NiB $380 Ex $330 Gd $205
510 P (peep rear sight, Patridge
  front on ramp) . . . . NiB $285 Ex $255 Gd $170
510 Routledge (smooth bore) . . . . . NiB $255 Ex $170 Gd $130
510-X SB (smoothbore for use w/
  shot cartridges, bead front sight,
  no rear sight) . . . . NiB $400 Ex $330 Gd $200
510-X . . . . NiB $400 Ex $330 Gd $200

Remington
International Match

Remington
Nylon 10

Remington Model Seven

Remington Model Seven FS

Remington Model Seven
KS Custom Rifle

RIFLES

MODEL 514 SERIES

Takedown. Single shot. Caliber: .22 S/L/LR. 24-in. bbl. Weight: 4.75 lbs. Sights: Open rear; bead front. Plain pistol-grip stock.
514 (mfg. 1948–70) . . . . NiB $180 Ex $157 Gd $126
514 P (receiver peep sight,
  mfg. 1952–72) . . . . NiB $230 Ex $200 Gd $129
514 BC Boy's Carbine (21-in. bbl., 1-in.
  shorter stock, mfg. 1961–70) . . NiB $230 Ex $205 Gd $125
514 Routledge (smooth bore) . . . NiB $305 Ex $270 Gd $180

MODEL 514 SERIES

Takedown. Single shot. Caliber: .22 S/L/LR. 24-in. bbl. Weight: 4.75 lbs. Sights: Open rear; bead front. Plain pistol-grip stock.

514 (mfg. 1948–70) . . . . NiB $180 Ex $157 Gd $126
514 P (receiver peep sight,
  mfg. 1952–72) . . . . NiB $230 Ex $200 Gd $129
514 BC Boy's Carbine (21-in. bbl., 1-in. shorter
  stock, mfg. 1961–70) . . . . NiB $230 Ex $205 Gd $125
514 Routledge (smooth bore) . . . NiB $305 Ex $270 Gd $180

540-X RIMFIRE SERIES

Bolt-action, single-shot, target rifle. Caliber: .22 LR. 26-in. heavy bbl. Supplied w/o sights. Weight: About 8 lbs. Target stock w/Monte Carlo cheekpiece and thumb groove, guide rail for hand stop and swivel, adj. buttplate. Made 1969-74.
540-X . . . . NiB $455 Ex $300 Gd $141

GRADING: **NiB** = New in Box   **Ex** = Excellent or NRA 95%   **Gd** = Good or NRA 68%

Remington Model 30A

Remington Model 34

**540-XR (position style stock, mfg.
1974–84)** . . . . NiB $505 Ex $455 Gd $330
**540-XRJR (1.75-in. shorter stock.
mfg. 1974–84)** . . . . NiB $480 Ex $430 Gd $305

MODEL 580 SERIES
Bolt action. Single shot. Caliber: .22 S/L/LR. 24-in. bbl. Weight:
4.75 lbs. Sights: Bead front; U-notch rear. Monte Carlo stock.
Made 1967–78.
580 . . . . NiB $200 Ex $155 Gd $120
**580 BR Boy's Rifle (1-in. shorter stock,
mfg. 1971-78).** . . . . NiB $200 EX $155 Gd $120
**580 SB (smooth bore for .22 LR shot
cartridges, mfg. 1967-78)** . . . . . NiB $300 Ex $210 Gd $149

INTERNATIONAL FREE RIFLE. . .NiB $1100 Ex $824 Gd $482
Same as Model 40-XB rimfire and centerfire except has free
rifle-type stock with adj. buttplate and hook, adj. palm rest,
movable front sling swivel, 2-oz. trigger. Weight: About 15 lbs.
Made 1964-74. Value shown is for rifle with professionally
finished stock, no sights.

INTERNATIONAL MATCH FREE
RIFLE. . . . . .NiB $1133 Ex $1055 Gd $677
Calibers: .22 LR, .222 Rem., .222 Rem. Mag., 7.62mm
NATO, .30-06 (others were available on special order). Model
40X-type bolt- action, single-shot. 2-oz. adj. trigger. 28-in.
heavy bbl. Weight: About 15.5 lbs. Free rifle-style stock with
thumbhole (furnished semifinished by mfr.); interchangeable
and adj. rubber buttplate and hook buttplate, adj. palm rest,
sling swivel. Made 1961 to 1964. Value shown is for rifle with
professionally-finished stock, no sights.

NYLON 10 . . . . .NiB $580 Ex $475 Gd $280
Caliber: .22 Short, Long, LR. 19.13-or 24-in. bbl. Weight: 4.25
lbs. Open rear sight; ramped blade front. Receiver grooved for
scope mount. Brown nylon stock. Made 1962-66.
24-in. bbl., add **50%**

XR-100 RANGEMASTER . . . . NiB $880 Ex $730 Gd $455
XP-100 pistol action. Single shot. Calibers: .204 Ruger, .223
Rem. or .22-250 Rem. 26-in. bbl. Stock: laminate thumbhole.
Weight: 9.1 lbs. Adj. trigger. Made 2005-07.

- BOLT-ACTION REPEATING MODELS -

MODEL FIVE . . . . NiB $185 Ex $165 Gd $125
Bolt action. Calibers: .22 LR or .22 WMR; 5-rnd. magazine.
22-in. bbl. Weight: 6.75 lbs. Stock: brown laminate. Finish:
blue. Made in Serbia, 2006-09.
Youth model (16.5-in. bbl.) . . . . NiB $155 Ex $130 Gd $80

MODEL SEVEN
Calibers: .17 Rem., .222 Rem., .223 Rem., .243 Win., 6mm
Rem., 7mm-08 Rem., .308 Win. Magazine capacity: 5-rnd.
in .17 Rem., .222 Rem., .223 Rem., 4-rnd. in other calibers.
18.5-in. bbl. 37.5 in. overall. Weight: 6.5 lbs. Walnut stock
checkering, and recoil pad. Made 1983-99. .223 Rem. added
in 1984. Disc. 2020.
Standard calibers. . . . . NiB $525 Ex $459 Gd $325
.17 Rem & .222 Rem. . . . . NiB $577 Ex $485 Gd $350

MODEL SEVEN AWR . . . . . . NiB $2500 Ex $2155 Gd $1255
Custom Shop model w/fiberglass stock, stainless, magnum
calibers, detachable magazine. Made 2002-08.
**AWR II model (Bell and Carlson stock,
2008-11), add** **$75**

MODEL SEVEN CDL. . . . . NiB $820 Ex $655 Gd $355
Calibers: .17 Rem. Fireball, .204 Ruger, .223 Rem., .22-250,
.243 Win., .260 Rem. 6.8mm SPC, 7mm-08 Rem. or .308
Win.; fixed capacity: 4-rnd. magazine. Barrel: 20- or 22-in.
Stock: checkered walnut w/R3 or SuperCell recoil pad. Adj.
X-Mark Pro trigger. Finish: satin blue. Weight: 6.5 lbs. Made
2006-20.
**CDL Magnum model (.270 WSM, 7mm RSAUM,
.300 RSAUM, .300 WSM or .350 Rem. Mag.,
2006-11), add** **$50**

MODEL SEVEN FS RIFLE. . . . . . NiB $559 Ex $495 Gd $356
Calibers: .243, 7mm-08 Rem. or .308 Win. Weight: 5.25 lbs.
Fiberglass stock, reinforced with DuPont Kevlar at points of bed-
ding and stress. Made 1987-89.

MODEL SEVEN KS . . . . NiB $2269 Ex $1090 Gd $789
Calibers: .223 Rem., 7mm-08, .308, .35 Rem. and .350 Rem.
Mag. 20-in. bbl. Custom-made in Remington's Custom Shop
with Kevlar stock. Made 1987-2020.

MODEL SEVEN LS RIFLE. . . . . . NiB $654 Ex $495 Gd $338
Calibers: .223 Rem., .243 Win., .260 Rem., 7mm-08 and
308 Win. 20-in. matte bbl. Laminated hardwood stock w/
matte brown finish. Weight: 6.5 lbs. Made 2000 to 2005.
**LS Magnum model (7mm RSAUM or .300
RSAUM, 2002-05), add** **$25**
**LSS model (.22-250, .243 Win. or 7mm-08;
2000-03), add** **$20**

MODEL SEVEN
CUSTOM MS . . . . NiB $2230 Ex $2205 Gd $1155
Custom Shop model fitted with a laminated full Mannlicher-
style stock. Weight: 6.75 lbs. Various calibers available. Made
1993-99.

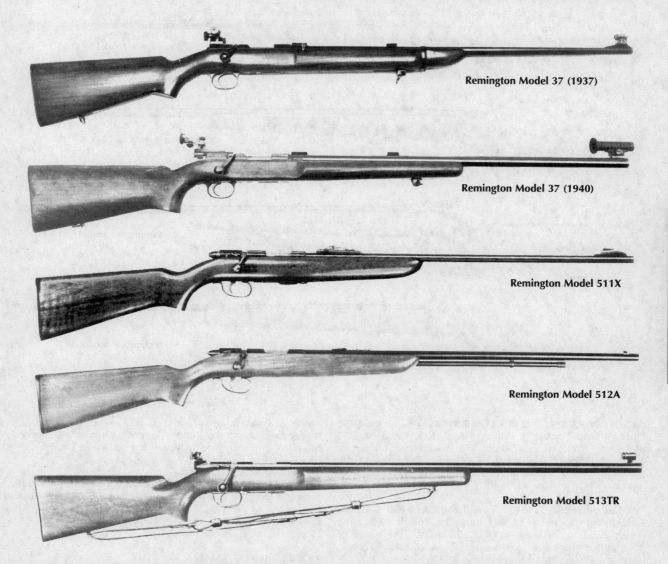

Remington Model 37 (1937)

Remington Model 37 (1940)

Remington Model 511X

Remington Model 512A

Remington Model 513TR

MODEL SEVEN SS RIFLE. . . . . .NiB $650 Ex $445 Gd $316
Same as Model Seven except 20-in. stainless bbl., receiver and bolt; black synthetic stock. Calibers: .243, 7mm-08 or .308. Made 1994-2006.
SS Magnum model (7mm RSAUM or .300
RSAUM, 2002-06), add $25

MODEL SEVEN XCR CAMO . . . .NiB $930 Ex $830 Gd $555
Fluted stainless 20-in. bbl., camo synthetic stock, Made 2007 only.

MODEL SEVEN PREDATOR . . . .NiB $770 Ex $680 Gd $405
Calibers: .17 Rem. Fireball, .204 Ruger, .223 Rem., .22-250, or .243 Win. Fluted stainless 22-in. bbl., camo synthetic stock, Made 2008-15.

MODEL SEVEN LAMINATE. . . . .NiB $770 Ex $680 Gd $405
Calibers: .223 Rem., .243 Win. or .308 Win. Stock: laminate. Open sights. Made 2015-20.

MODEL SEVEN SYNTHETIC . . . .NiB $590 Ex $490 Gd $355
Calibers: .223 Rem., .243 Win., 7mm-08 or .308 Win. Stock: black synthetic. Made 2011-date.

Synthetic Stainless model (stainless, 2015–20), add $130

MODEL SEVEN YOUTH RIFLE . NiB $575 Ex $370 Gd $279
Similar to the standard Model Seven except fitted with hardwood stock with a 12.19-in. pull. Calibers: .243, 6mm, 7mm-08 only. Made 1993-2007.

MODEL 30A BOLT-ACTION
EXPRESS RIFLE . . . . .NiB $705 Ex $650 Gd $405
Standard Grade. Modified M/1917 Enfield Action. Calibers: .25, .30, .32 and .35 Rem., 7mm Mauser, .30-06. Five round box magazine. 22-in. bbl. Weight: About 7.25 lbs. Sights: Open rear; bead front. Walnut stock w/checkered pistol grip and forearm. Made 1921 to 1940. Note: Early Model 30s had a slender forend with Schnabel tip, military-type double-pull trigger.

MODEL 30R CARBINE . . . . . . .NiB $755 Ex $630 Gd $405
Same as Model 30A except has 20-in. bbl., plain stock weight about 7 lbs.

GRADING: **NiB** = New in Box   **Ex** = Excellent or NRA 95%   **Gd** = Good or NRA 68%

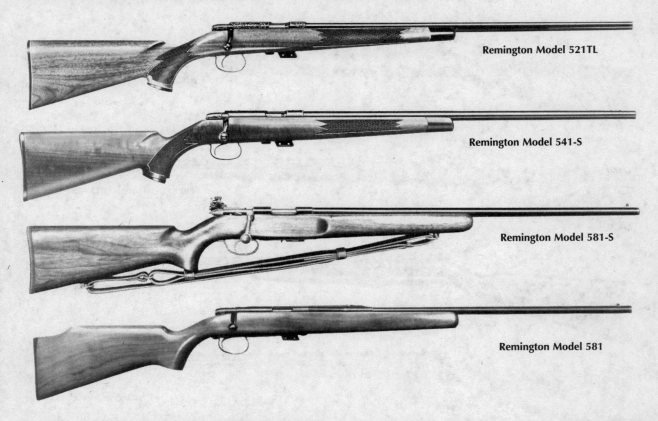

Remington Model 521TL

Remington Model 541-S

Remington Model 581-S

Remington Model 581

MODEL 30S SPORTING RIFLE NiB $790 Ex $650 Gd $455
Special Grade. Same action as Model 30A. Calibers: .257 Roberts, 7mm Mauser, .30-06. Five round box magazine. 24-in. bbl. Weight: About 8 lbs. Lyman No. 48 Receiver sight, bead front sight. Special high comb stock with long, full forearm, checkered. Made 1930-40.

MODEL 34 SERIES . . . . NiB $805 Ex $730 Gd $505
Takedown. Caliber: .22 Short, Long, LR. Tubular magazine holds 22 Short, 17 Long or 15 LR. 24-in. bbl. Weight: 5.25 lbs. Sights: Open rear; bead front. Plain, pistol-grip stock, forearm w/grasping grooves. Made 1932-36.
34 NRA (Lyman peep sight) . . . . NiB $505 Ex $480 Gd $300
34-P . . . . NiB $380 Ex $330 Gd $215

MODEL 34 NRA TARGET RIFLE NiB $553 Ex $390 Gd $256
Same as Model 34 Standard except has Lyman peep rear sight, Partridge-type front sight, .88-in. sling and swivels, weight: About 5.75 lbs.

MODEL 37 RANGEMASTER TARGET RIFLE
Model of 1937. Caliber: .22 LR. 5-rnd. box magazine, single shot adapter also supplied as standard equipment. 28-in. heavy bbl. Weight: About 12 lbs. Remington front and rear sights, scope bases. Target stock, swivels, sling. Note: Original 1937 model had a stock with outside bbl. band similar in appearance to that of the old-style Winchester Model 52, forearm design was modified and bbl. band eliminated in 1938. Made 1937-40.
w/factory sights . . . . NiB $2210 Ex $1210 Gd $710
w/out sights . . . . NiB $1310 Ex $1210 Gd $710

MODEL 37 RANGEMASTER
TARGET RIFLE . . . . NiB $1210 EX $1055 GD $710

Model of 1940. Same as Model of 1937 except has "Miracle" trigger mechanism and Randle-design stock with high comb, full pistol-grip and wide beavertail forend. Made 1940-54.

MODEL 40-XB CENTERFIRE
REPEATER . . . . NiB $2430 Ex $2055 Gd $1000
Same as Model 40-XB Centerfire except 5-rnd. repeater. Calibers: .222 Rem., .222 Rem. Mag., .223 Rem., .22-250, 6x47mm, 6mm Rem., .243 Win., .308 Win. (7.62mm NATO). Heavy bbl. only. Discontinued.

MODEL 78 SPORTSMAN
BOLT-ACTION RIFLE. . . . . NiB $496 Ex $390 Gd $322
Calibers: .223 Rem., .243 Win., .270 Win., .30-06 Springfield and .308 Win.; 4-rnd. magazine. 22-in. bbl. Weight: 7 lbs. Adj. sights. Stock: smooth hardwood. Made 1984-89.

MODEL 341 SPORTSMASTER SERIES
Caliber: .22 S/L/LR. Tubular magazine holds 22 Short, 17 Long, 15 LR. 27-in. bbl. Weight: About 6 lbs. Sights: Open rear; bead front. Plain pistol-grip stock. Made 1936-40.
341 A . . . . NiB $305 Ex $280 Gd $165
341 P (peep sight) . . . . NiB $355 Ex $305 Gd $205
341 SB (smooth bore) . . . . NiB $505 Ex $445 Gd $280

MODEL 511 SCOREMASTER SERIES
Takedown. Caliber: 22 S/L/LR. 6-rnd. detachable box magazine. 25-in. bbl. Weight: About 5.5 lbs. Sights: Open rear; bead front. Plain pistol-grip stock. Made 1939-62.
511 A . . . . NiB $266 Ex $188 Gd $145
511 P (peep rear sight,
Partridge-type blade front,
mfg. 1939–62) . . . . NiB $290 Ex $260 Gd $165
511-X (mfg. 1964–66) . . . . NiB $259 Ex $210 Gd $155

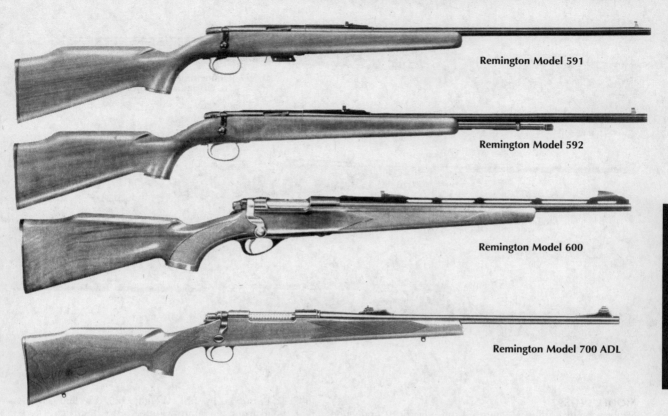

Remington Model 591

Remington Model 592

Remington Model 600

Remington Model 700 ADL

MODEL 512 SPORTSMASTER SERIES
Takedown. Caliber: .22 S/L/LR. Tubular magazine holds 22 Short, 17 Long, 15 LR. 25-in. bbl. Weight: About 5.75 lbs. Sights: Open rear; bead front. Plain pistol-grip stock w/semi-beavertail forend. Made 1940-62.

512 A . . . . NiB $269 EX $179 Gd $139
512P (peep rear sight, blade front,
  on ramp, mfg. 1940–62). . . . . . NiB $300 Ex $260 Gd $165
512-X (Tubular magazine, mfg.
  1964–66) . . . . NiB $300 Ex $260 Gd $165

MODEL 513 MATCHMASTER SERIES
Caliber: .22 LR. 6-rnd. detachable box magazine. 27-in. bbl. Weight: About 6.75 lbs. Sights: Marble open rear, Partridge type front. Stock: checkered wood sporter. Made 1941-56.

513S/513SA (mfg. 1940–57) . . . NiB $854 Ex $492 Gd $312
513P (Remington Point-Crometer sights,
  mfg. 1942–50) . . . . NiB $930 Ex $780 Gd $505
513TR(Redfield No. 75 rear; globe front,
  target stock, sling and swivels, mfg.
  1941–69) . . . . NiB $450 Ex $299 Gd $211

MODEL 521TL JUNIOR
TARGET. . . . . NiB $398 Ex $269 Gd $191
Takedown. Caliber: .22 LR. 6-rnd. detachable box magazine. 25-in. bbl. Weight: About 7 lbs. Sights: Lyman No. 57RS rear; dovetailed blade front. Target stock. Sling and swivels. Made 1947-69.

MODEL 522 VIPER . . . . NiB $129 Ex $128 Gd $102
Calibers: .22 LR. 10-rnd. magazine. 20-in. bbl. 40 in. overall. Weight: 4.63 lbs. Checkered black PET resin stock with beavertail forend. Dupont high-tech synthetic lightweight receiver. Matte black finish on all exposed metal. Made 1993-2020.

MODEL 541-S CUSTOM SERIES
Bolt-action repeater. Scroll engraving on receiver and trigger guard. Caliber: .22 S/L/LR. 5-rnd. clip magazine. 24-in. bbl. Weight: 5.5 lbs. Supplied w/o sights. Checkered walnut stock w/ rosewood-finished forend tip, pistol-grip cap and buttplate. Made 1972-84.

Sporter . . . . NiB $855 Ex $805 Gd $555
541-T (checkered walnut stock,
  mfg. 1986-99). . . . . NiB $500 Ex $311 Gd $193
541-T-HB (heavy bbl. mfg.
  1993-99). . . . . NiB $550 Ex $360 Gd $250

MODEL 547 CUSTOM CLASSIC SERIES
Model 700 style action. Caliber: .17 HMR, .22 LR or .22 WMR; 5-rnd. magazine. 22-in. Shilen custom bbl. Supplied w/o sights. Smooth walnut stock. 3 lb. trigger. Custom shop. Made 2008-15.

547 . . . . NiB $1130 Ex $955 Gd $630
541-C (18.5-in. bbl., mfg.
  2009-15) . . . . NiB $1355 Ex $1080 Gd $705
547-T (22-in. med. contour bbl.,
  mfg. 2009-15). . . . . NiB $1755 Ex $1510 Gd $905

MODEL 581/582 SERIES
Similar as Model 580 except has 5-rnd. box or tube magazine. 24-in. bbl. Smooth hardwood stock. Made 1967–84.

581 (box magazine) . . . . NiB $230 Ex $205 Gd $130
Smooth bore model, add $60
581 Sportsman model (box magazine,
  mfg. 1986–99) . . . . NiB $230 Ex $205 Gd $130
582 (tube magazine, mfg.
  1967–84) . . . . NiB $230 Ex $205 Gd $130

GRADING: NiB = New in Box   Ex = Excellent or NRA 95%   Gd = Good or NRA 68%

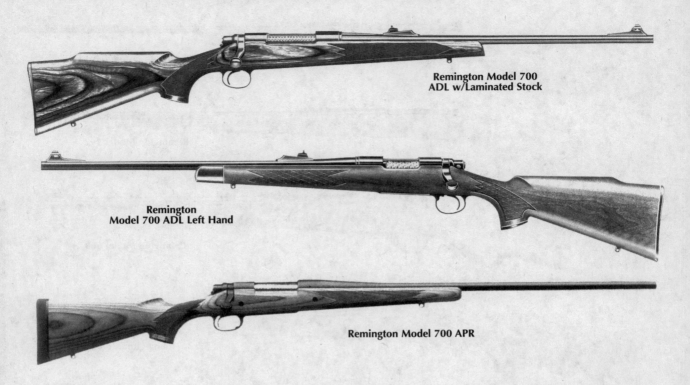

Remington Model 700 ADL w/Laminated Stock

Remington Model 700 ADL Left Hand

Remington Model 700 APR

MODEL 591/592
Caliber: 5mm Rimfire Magnum. 4-rnd. clip or 10-rnd. tube magazine. 24-in. bbl. Weight: 5 lbs. Sights: Bead front; U-notch rear. Monte Carlo stock. Weight: 5-5.5 lbs. Made 1970-74.
591 (detachable magazine) .... NiB $355 Ex $315 Gd $205
592 (tubular magazine)....... NiB $355 Ex $315 Gd $205

MODEL 600 SERIES
Bolt action, dog-leg bolt handle. Calibers: .222 Rem., .223 Rem., .243 Win., 6mm Rem., .308 Win., .35 Rem., 5-rnd. magazine (6-rnd. in .222 Rem.) 18.5-in. bbl. with ventilated rib. Weight: 6 lbs. Sights: Open rear; blade ramp front. Monte Carlo stock w/pistol-grip. Made 1964-67.
.222 Rem.................... NiB $550 Ex $445 Gd $333
.223 Rem............... NiB $1505 Ex $1210 Gd $555
.35 Rem.................. NiB $641 Ex $540 Gd $499
standard calibers........... NiB $510 Ex $390 Gd $338
Mohawk model (no VR,
   1971–79) .... NiB $1055 Ex $930 Gd $605

MODEL 600 MAGNUM ..... NiB $1044 Ex $800 Gd $645
Same as Model 600 except calibers 6.5mm Mag. and .350 Rem. Mag., 4-rnd. magazine, special Magnum-type bbl. with bracket for scope back-up, laminated walnut and beech stock w/recoil pad. QD swivels and sling; weight: About 6.5 lbs. Made 1965-67.

MODEL 600 MONTANA
TERRITORIAL CENTENNIAL... NiB $990 Ex $755 Gd $559
Same as Model 600 except has commemorative medallion embedded in buttstock. Made in 1964. Value is for rifle in new, unfired condition.

MODEL 660 SERIES
Bolt action w/dog-leg bolt handle. Calibers: .222 Rem., 6mm Rem., .243 Win., .308 Win., 5-rnd. magazine. (6-rnd. in .222 Rem.) 20-in. bbl. Weight: 6.5 lbs. Sights: Open rear; bead front on ramp. Monte Carlo stock, checkered, black pistol-grip cap and forend tip. Made 1968-71.
.222 Rem .... NiB $610 Ex $480 Gd $390
Other calibers.............. NiB $560 Ex $443 Gd $355

MODEL 660 MAGNUM ..... NiB $1110 Ex $955 Gd $605
Same as Model 660 except calibers 6.5mm Rem. Mag. and .350 Rem. Mag., 4-rnd. magazine, laminated walnut-and-beech stock with recoil pad. QD swivels and sling. Made 1968-71.

MODEL 673 GUIDE RIFLE ... NiB $805 Ex $680 Gd $455
Patterned after Model 600 but w/Model Seven action. Calibers: .243 Win., .300 Rem. Ultra Mag., .350 Rem. Mag., .308 Win. or 6.5mm Rem. Mag.; 3-rnd. fixed magazine. Barrel: 22-in. VB w/open sights, optic ready. Stock: laminate. Finish: blue. Made 2003-06.

MODEL 700 ADL .... NiB $535 Ex $369 Gd $266
Calibers: .22-250, .222 Rem., .25-06, 6mm Rem., .243 Win., .270 Win., .30-06, .308 Win., 7mm Rem. Mag. Magazine capacity: 6-rnd. in .222 Rem.; 4-rnd. in 7mm Rem. Mag. Five round in other calibers. Bbl. lengths: 24-in. in .22-250, .222 Rem., .25-06, 7mm Rem. Mag.; 22-in. in other calibers. Weight: 7 lbs. standard; 7.5 lbs. in 7mm Rem. Mag. Sights: Ramp front; sliding ramp open rear. Monte Carlo stock w/cheekpiece, skip checkering, recoil pad on Magnum. Laminated stock also avail. Made 1962-2005.

MODEL 700 APR .... NiB $2900 Ex $2290 Gd $1998
Acronym for African Plains Rifle. Calibers: 7mm Rem. Mag., 7mm STW, 300 Win. Mag., 300 Wby. Mag., 300 Rem. Ultra Mag., 338 Win. Mag., 375 H&H. Three round magazine. 26-in. bbl. on a magnum action. 46.5 in. overall.

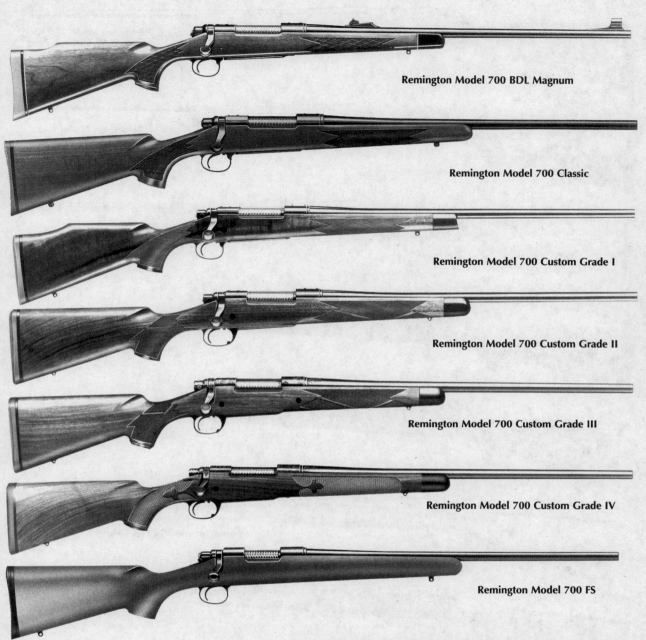

Remington Model 700 BDL Magnum

Remington Model 700 Classic

Remington Model 700 Custom Grade I

Remington Model 700 Custom Grade II

Remington Model 700 Custom Grade III

Remington Model 700 Custom Grade IV

Remington Model 700 FS

Weight: 7.75 lbs. Matte blue finish. Checkered classic-style laminated wood stock w/black magnum recoil pad. Made 1994-2004.

MODEL 700 AS BOLT-ACTION RIFLE
Similar to the Model 700 BDL except with non-reflective matte black metal finish, including the bolt body. Weight: 6.5 lbs. Straight comb synthetic stock made of Arylon, a fiberglass-reinforced thermoplastic resin with non-reflective matte finish. Made 1988-92.

Standard caliber . . . . NiB $555 Ex $440 Gd $339
Magnum caliber . . . . NiB $579 Ex $466 Gd $340

MODEL 700 AWR BOLT-ACTION
RIFLE. . . . . NiB $1566 Ex $1264 Gd $1090
Acronym for Alaskan Wilderness Rifle, similar to Model 700 APR except w/24-in. stainless bbl. and black chromed action. Matte gray or black Kevlar stock w/straight comb and raised cheekpiece fitted w/black magnum recoil pad. Made 1994-2004.

MODEL 700 BDL CENTERFIRE RIFLE
Same as Model 700 ADL except has hinged floorplate hooded ramp front sight, stock w/black forend tip and pistol-grip cap, cut checkering, QD swivels and sling. Additional calibers: .17 Rem., .223 Rem., .264 Win. Mag., 7mm-08, .280, .300 Sav., .300 Win. Mag., 8mm Rem. Mag., .338 Win. Mag., .35

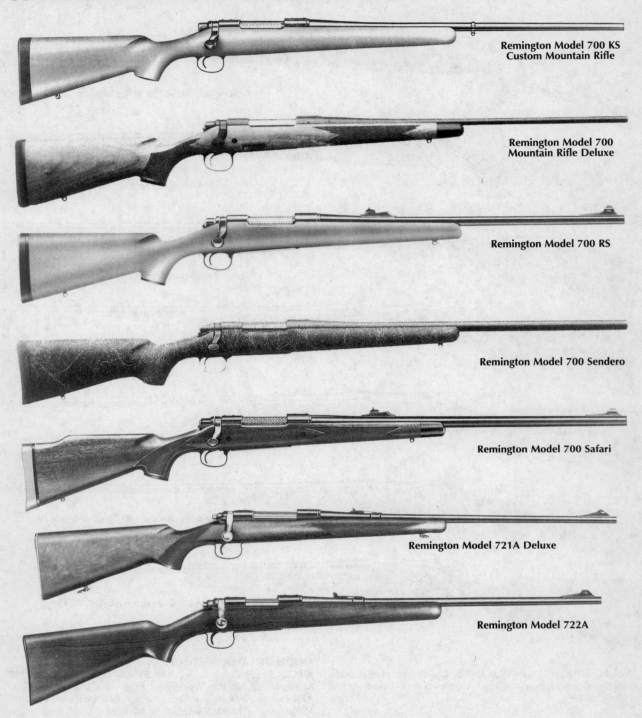

Remington Model 700 KS
Custom Mountain Rifle

Remington Model 700
Mountain Rifle Deluxe

Remington Model 700 RS

Remington Model 700 Sendero

Remington Model 700 Safari

Remington Model 721A Deluxe

Remington Model 722A

Whelen. All have 24-in. bbls. Magnums have 4-rnd. magazine, recoil pad, weighs 7.5 lbs; .17 Rem. has 6-rnd. magazine, weighs 7 lbs. Made 1962 to date. Made 1973-2004.

Standard calibers . . . . NiB $810 Ex $466 Gd $333
Magnum calibers and .17
Rem. . . . . NiB $855 Ex $555 Gd $380
Left-hand, .270 Win. A
nd .30-06 . . . . NiB $855 Ex $469 Gd $343
Left hand, 7mm Rem. Mag. & .222
Rem. . . . . NiB $788 Ex $559 Gd $495

MODEL 700 BDL EUROPEAN RIFLE
Same general specifications as Model 700 BDL, except has oil-finished walnut stock. Calibers: .243, .270, 7mm-08, 7mm Mag., .280 Rem., .30-06. Made 1993-95.
Standard calibers . . . . NiB $495 Ex $422 Gd $370
Magnum calibers . . . . NiB $579 Ex $466 Gd $357

MODEL 700 BDL SS BOLT-ACTION RIFLE
Same as Model 700 BDL except w/24-in. stainless bbl., receiver and bolt plus black synthetic stock. Calibers: .223 Rem., .243

Remington Nylon 11

Remington Model 783

Win., 6mm Rem., .25-06 Rem., .270 Win. .280 Rem., 7mm-08, 7mm Rem. Mag., 7mm Wby. Mag., .30-06, .300 Win., .308 Win., .338 Win. Mag. 375 H&H. Made 1992-2004.

Standard calibers	NiB $625	Ex $509	Gd $347
Magnum calibers, add.			$100
DM (detachable magazine), add.			$50
DM-B (w/muzzle brake), add			$126

MODEL 700 BDL VARMINT
SPECIAL . . . . **NiB $695 Ex $449 Gd $315**
Same as Model 700 BDL except has 24-in. heavy bbl., no sights, weighs 9 lbs. (8.75 lbs. in 308 Win.). Calibers: .22-250, .222 Rem., .223 Rem., .25-06, 6mm Rem., .243 Win., .308 Win. Made 1967-94.

MODEL 700 CS BOLT-ACTION RIFLE
Similar to Model 700 BDL except with nonreflective matte black metal finish, including the bolt body. Straight comb synthetic stock camouflaged in Mossy Oak Bottomland pattern. Made 1992–94.

Standard calibers	NiB $590	Ex $495	Gd $369
Magnum calibers	NiB $641	Ex $500	Gd $370

MODEL 700 CLASSIC
Same general specifications as Model 700 BDL except has "Classic" stock of high-quality walnut with full-pattern cut-checkering, special satin wood finish; Schnabel forend. Brown rubber buttpad. Hinged floorplate. No sights. Weight: 7 lbs. Also chambered for "Classic" cartridges such as .257 Roberts and .250-3000. Introduced in 1981–2020.

Standard calibers	NiB $916	Ex $588	Gd $369
Magnum calibers	NiB $977	Ex $588	Gd $369

MODEL 700 CUSTOM BOLT-ACTION RIFLE
Same general specifications as Model 700 BDL except custom-built; available in choice of grades, each with higher quality wood, different checkering patterns, engraving, high-gloss blued finish. Introduced in 1965–2020.

C Grade I	NiB $1965	Ex $1110	Gd $800
C Grade II	NiB $2490	Ex $1854	Gd $1354
C Grade III	NiB $2988	Ex $2360	Gd $1635
C Grade IV	NiB $4955	Ex $3290	Gd $2990
D Peerless Grade	NiB $2855	Ex $1590	Gd $1122
F Premier Grade	NiB $3634	Ex $2989	Gd $2190

MODEL 700 FS BOLT-ACTION RIFLE
Similar to Model 700 ADL except with straight comb fiberglass stock reinforced with DuPont Kevlar, finished in gray or gray camo with Old English-style recoil pad. Made 1987-89.

Standard calibers	NiB $600	Ex $479	Gd $259
Magnum calibers	NiB $720	Ex $590	Gd $433

MODEL 700 KS CUSTOM MOUNTAIN RIFLE
Similar to standard Model 700 MTN Rifle, except with custom Kevlar reinforced resin synthetic stock with standard or wood-grain finish. Calibers: .270 Win., .280 Rem., 7mm Rem Mag., .30-06, .300 Win. Mag., .300 Wby. Mag., 8mm Rem. Mag., .338 Win. Mag., .35 Whelen, .375 H&H. Four round magazine. 24-in. bbl. Weight: 6.75 lbs. Made 1986-2008.

Standard KS stock (disc. 1993)	NiB $1899	Ex $1380	Gd $1079
Wood-grain KS stock	NiB $1139	Ex $899	Gd $655
Stainless synthetic (1995-97)	NiB $2090	Ex $1421	Gd $1008
Left-hand model, add			$100

MODEL 700 LS BOLT-ACTION RIFLE
Similar to Model 700 ADL except with checkered Monte Carlo-style laminated wood stock with alternating grain and wood color, impregnated with phenolic resin and finished with a low satin luster. Made 1988-93.

Standard calibers	NiB $690	Ex $550	Gd $395
Magnum calibers	NiB $779	Ex $598	Gd $443

MODEL 700 LSS BOLT-ACTION RIFLE
Similar to Model 700 BDL except with stainless steel barrel and action. Checkered Monte Carlo-style laminated wood stock with alternating grain and gray tinted color impregnated with phenolic resin and finished with a low satin luster. Made 1996-2004.

Standard calibers	NiB $510	Ex $440	Gd $290
Magnum calibers	NiB $588	Ex $479	Gd $466

MODEL 700 MOUNTAIN RIFLE
Lightweight version of Model 700. Calibers: .243 Win., .25-06, .257 Roberts, .270 Win., 7x57, 7mm-08 Rem., .280 Rem., .30-06 and .308 Win. Four round magazine. 22-in. bbl. Weight: 6.75 lbs. Satin blue or stainless finish. Checkered walnut stock and redesigned pistol grip, straight comb, contoured cheekpiece, Old English-style recoil pad and satin oil finish or black synthetic stock with pressed checkering and blind magazine. Made 1986-94.

DM model (intro. 1995)	NiB $755	Ex $488	Gd $367
SS model (stainless synthetic, disc. 1993)	NiB $500	Ex $443	Gd $309
DM Model (New 1995)	NiB $685	Ex $443	Gd $339
SS Model stainless synthetic (disc. 1993)	NiB $450	Ex $390	Gd $287

MODEL 700 RS BOLT-ACTION RIFLE
Similar to the Model 700 BDL except with straight comb DuPont Rynite stock finished in gray or gray camo with Old English style recoil pad. Made 1987-90.

Standard calibers	NiB $600	Ex $433	Gd $380
Magnum calibers	NiB $677	Ex $535	Gd $390
.280 Rem. (Limited prod.)	NiB $739	Ex $596	Gd $415

MODEL 700 SAFARI GRADE
Big game heavy magnum version of the Model 700 BDL. 8mm Rem. Mag., .375 H&H Mag., .416 Rem. Mag. and .458 Win. Mag. 24-in. heavy bbl. Weight: 9 lbs. Blued or stainless finish. Checkered walnut stock in synthetic/Kevlar stock with standard matte or wood-grain finish with old English style recoil pad. Made 1962-2000.

Safari Classic/Monte Carlo	NiB $1498	Ex $1044	Gd $610
Safari KS (Kevlar stock, intro. 1989)	NiB $1335	Ex $1155	Gd $927
Safari KS (wood-grain stock, intro. 1992)	NiB $1296	Ex $1133	Gd $909
Safari KS SS (stainless, intro. 1993)	NiB $1577	Ex $1326	Gd $1055
Safari model, left-hand, add			$126

RIFLES

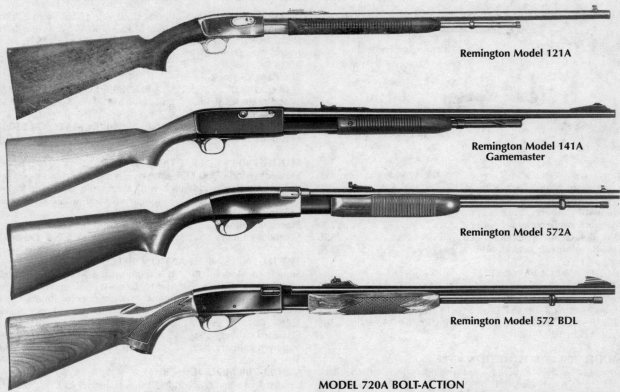

Remington Model 121A

Remington Model 141A Gamemaster

Remington Model 572A

Remington Model 572 BDL

MODEL 700 SENDERO BOLT-ACTION RIFLE
Same as Model 700 VS except chambered in long action and magnum .25-06 Rem., .270 Win., .280 Rem., 7mm Rem. Mag., .300 Win. Made 1994-2002.

Standard calibers . . . . **NiB $707 Ex $589 Gd $390**
Magnum calibers, add. **$50**
SF model (stainless, fluted bbl.), add **$150**

MODEL 700 VLS (VARMINT LAMINATED STOCK)
BOLT-ACTION RIFLE. . . . . **NiB $899 Ex $555 Gd $390**
Same as Model 700 BDL Varmint Special except w/ 26-in. polished blue barrel. Laminated wood stock with alternating grain and wood color impregnated with phenolic resin and finished with a satin luster. Calibers: .222 Rem., .223 Rem., .22-250 Rem., .243 Win., 7mm-08 Rem., .308 Win. Weight: 9.4 lbs. Made 1995-2020.

MODEL 700 VS BOLT-ACTION RIFLE
Same as Model 700 BDL Varmint Special except w/26-in. matte blue or fluted stainless barrel. Textured black or gray synthetic stock reinforced with Kevlar, fiberglass and graphite with full length aluminum bedding block. Calibers: .22-250 Rem., .220 Swift, .223 Rem., .308 Win. Made 1992-2020.

Model 700 VS . . . . **NiB $888 Ex $559 Gd $444**
Model SF (fluted bbl.). . . . . **NiB $790 Ex $677 Gd $535**
Model 700 VS SF/SF-P
  (fluted & ported bbl.) . . . . . **NiB $1043 Ex $866 Gd $657**

MODEL 710 SPORTSMAN . . . . . **NiB $430 Ex $380 Gd $270**
Bolt action, 3 lug bolt, polymer or steel receiver extension. Calibers: .243 Win., .270 Win., 7mm Rem. Mag., .30-06 or .300 Win.; 3- or 4-rnd. detachable magazine. Barrel: 22-in., optic ready. Stock: synthetic. Finish: matte blue. Made 2001-06.

MODEL 720A BOLT-ACTION
HIGH . . . . **NiB $1610 Ex $1410 Gd $710**
Modified M/1917 Enfield action. .257 Roberts, .270 Win., .30-06. Five round box magazine. 22-in. bbl. Weight: About 8 lbs. Sights: Open rear; bead front, on ramp. Pistol-grip stock, checkered. Model 720R has 20-in. bbl.; Model 720S has 24-in. bbl. Made in 1941.

MODEL 721 STANDARD GRADE BOLT-ACTION
HIGH-POWER RIFLE . . . . **NiB $505 Ex $455 Gd $280**
Calibers: .270 Win., .30-06. Four round box magazine. 24-in. bbl. Weight: About 7.25 lbs. Sights: Open rear; bead front, on ramp. Plain sporting stock. Made 1948-62. **NOTE:** *ADL and BDL models in standard and magnum calibers are not marked but have checkered and deluxe wood, respectively. For ADL models add $25, BDL models add $100.*
Magnum model
(.264 Win. Mag. or .300
H&H Mag.; 26-in. bbl.) . . . . . . **NiB $705 Ex $605 Gd $455**

MODEL 722A STANDARD GRADE SPORTER
Same as Model 721A bolt-action except shorter action. .222 Rem. mag., .243 Win., .257 Roberts, .308 Win., .300 Savage. Four or 5-rnd. magazine. Weight: 7-8 lbs. .222 Rem. introduced 1950; .244 Rem. introduced 1955. Made 1948-62. **NOTE:** *ADL and BDL models have checkered and deluxe wood, respectively. For BDL models add $260.*
.257 Roberts & .308 Win., add **20%**
.222 Rem. Mag. & .243 Win, add **25%**
Other calibers. . . . . **NiB $530 Ex $480 Gd $305**

MODEL 725 KODIAK . . . . **NiB $6010 Ex $4010 Gd $2210**
Similar to Model 725ADL. Calibers: .375 H&H Mag., .458 Win. Mag. Three round magazine. 26-in. bbl. with recoil reducer built into muzzle. Weight: About 9 lbs. Deluxe, reinforced Monte Carlo stock with recoil pad, black forend tip swivels, sling. Fewer than 100 made in 1961.

**Remington Model 760
Gamemaster**

MODEL 725ADL BOLT-ACTION REPEATING RIFLE

Calibers: .222, .243, .244, .270, .280, .30-06. Four round box mag. (5-rnd. in 222). 22-in. bbl. (24-in. in .222). Weight: About 7 lbs. Sights: Open rear, hooded ramp front. Monte Carlo comb stock w/pistol-grip, checkered, swivels. Made 1958-61.

.222 Rem., .243 Win., .244 Rem, add			$300
.270 Win. . . . . NiB $767	Ex $659	Gd $467
.280 Rem. . . . . NiB $1055	Ex $905	Gd $405
.30-06 . . . . NiB $655	Ex $605	Gd $405

MODEL 770 SERIES

Model 700 based bolt action w/60 degree bolt lift. Calibers: .243 Win., .270 Win., 7mm-08, .308 Win., .30-06, .300 Win. Mag. or 7mm Rem. Mag.; 3- or 4-rnd detachable magazine. Bbl.: 22- or 24-in. Stock: black synthetic. Weight: 8.5 lbs. Finish: Matte blue. Made 2007-14.

Blue model . . . . NiB $335	Ex $265	Gd $190
Stainless model, add			$60

MODEL 783 SERIES

Bolt action. Calibers: .22-250, .223 Rem., .243 Win., .270 Win., .308 Win., .30-06, .300 Win. Mag., 7mm Rem. Mag. 3- or 4-rnd detachable magazine. Bbl.: 22- or 24-in. free floated w/o sights. Stock: Pillar bedded black synthetic. Weight: 7.25-8.5 lbs. Finish: Matte blue. Crossfire adj. trigger. Made 2013-20.

w/synthetic stock . . . . NiB $400	Ex $330	Gd $255
Camo model (Mossy Oak finish, disc.			
2014) . . . . NiB $430	Ex $355	Gd $290
Compact model (12.3-in. LOP). . NiB $400	Ex $330	Gd $255
Walnut model (checkered walnut			
stock) . . . . NiB $455	Ex $340	Gd $280

MODEL 788 . . . . NiB $655 Ex $555 Gd $355

Calibers: .222 Rem., .22-250, .223 Rem., 6mm Rem., .243 Win., 7mm-08 Rem., .308 Win., .30-30, .44 Rem. Mag. Three round clip magazine (4-rnd. in .222 and .223 Rem.). 24-in. bbl. in .22s, 22-in. in other calibers. Weight: 7.5 lbs. w/ 24-in. bbl.; 7.25 lbs. w/ 22-in. bbl. Sights: Blade front on ramp; U-notch rear. Plain Monte Carlo stock. Made 1967-84.

.30-30 Win, add		10%
7mm-08 Rem, add		15%
.44 Mag, add.		30%

MODEL 798 SERIES

Bolt action. Square bridge Mauser-style action. Calibers: .243 Win.-.458 Win. Mag. 3- or 4-rnd box magazine. Bbl.: 22- or 24-in. w/o sights. Stock: Synthetic, laminate or walnut. Weight: 7.25-8.5 lbs. Finish: Polished blue. Mfg. by Zastava. Imported 2006 to 2009.

Standard calibers . . . . NiB $455	Ex $340	Gd $280
Magnum calibers . . . . NiB $495	Ex $370	Gd $295
Safari Grade model			
(.375 H&H or .458 Win.			
Mag., laminated stock) . . . . . . NiB $955	Ex $755	Gd $580

MODEL 799 . . . . NiB $550 Ex $430 Gd $340

Bolt action. Mauser-style short action. Calibers: .22 Hornet, .22-250 Rem., .22 Rem., .223 Rem. or 7.62x39mm. 4-rnd box magazine. Bbl.: 20-in. w/o sights. Stock: Synthetic, laminate, or walnut. Finish: Polished blue. Mfg. by Zastava. Imported 2006 to 2008.

NYLON 11 . . . . NiB $605 Ex $530 Gd $280

Clip type. Caliber: .22 Short, Long, LR. Six- or 10-rnd. clip mag. 19.63- or 24-in. bbl. Weight: 4.5 lbs. Sights: Open rear; blade front. Nylon stock. Made 1962-66.

24-in. bbl., add		50%

NYLON 12 . . . . NiB $555 Ex $505 Gd $275

Same as Nylon 11 except has tubular magazine holding 22 Short, 17 Long, 15 LR. Made 1962-66.

- SLIDE AND LEVER-ACTION RIFLES -

MODEL SIX. . . . . NiB $705 Ex $605 Gd $280

Slide action. Hammerless. Calibers: 6mm Rem., .243 Win., .270 Win. 7mm Express Rem., .30-06, .308 Win. 22-in. bbl. Weight: 7.5 lbs. Checkered Monte Carlo stock and forearm. Made 1981-88.

MODEL 12 SEIES SLIDE-ACTION REPEATERS

Standard Grade. Hammerless. Takedown. Caliber: .22 Short, Long or LR. Tubular magazine holds 15 Short, 12 Long or 10 LR cartridges. 22- or 24-in. rnd. or octagonal bbl. Open rear sight, bead front. Plain, half-pistol-grip stock and grooved slide handle of walnut. Made 1909-36.

Model 12A . . . . NiB $1355	Ex $1155	Gd $705
Model 12B (22 Short only			
w/octagon bbl.) . . . . NiB $2205	Ex $1910	Gd $855
Model 12C			
(w/24-in. octagon bbl.). . . NiB $1710	Ex $1455	Gd $810
Model 12CS (22 WRF w/24-in.			
octagon bbl.) . . . . NiB $1655	Ex $1430	Gd $855

MODEL 14 SERIES SLIDE-ACTION
REPEATING RIFLE. . . . . NiB $955 Ex $810 Gd $510

Standard grade. Hammerless. Takedown. Calibers: .25 Rem., .30 Rem., .32 Rem. and .35 Rem. Five round tubular magazine. 22-in. bbl. Weight: About 6.75 lbs. Sights: Open rear; bead front. Plain half-pistol-grip stock and grooved slide handle of walnut. Made 1912-35.

14R Carbine (18.5-in. bbl., straight			
grip stock) . . . . NiB $1380	Ex $1210	Gd $610

MODEL 14 1/2 RIFLE . . . . . . NiB $1755 Ex $1510 Gd $955

Similar to Model 14A except calibers: .38-40 and .44-40, 1 full magazine. 22.5-in. bbl. Made 1913-34.

14 1/2 Carbine			
(18.5-in. bbl., pistol			
grip stock) . . . . NiB $2410	Ex $2110	Gd $1210

RIFLES

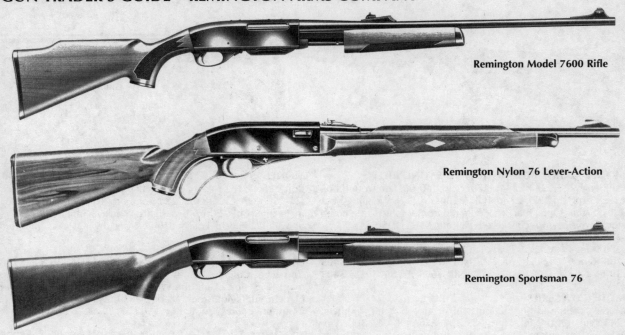

Remington Model 7600 Rifle

Remington Nylon 76 Lever-Action

Remington Sportsman 76

MODEL 25A SLIDE-ACTION
REPEATER . . . . **NiB $1355 Ex $1155 Gd $755**
Standard Grade. Hammerless. Takedown. Calibers: .25-20, .32-20. 10-rnd. tubular magazine. 24-in. bbl. Weight: About 5.5 lbs. Sights: Open rear; bead front. Plain, pistol-grip stock, grooved slide handle. Made 1923-36.
25R Carbine (18-in. bbl., straight grip
  stock, 6-rnd. magazine) . . . NiB $2755 Ex $2455 Gd $2010

MODEL 121 FIELDMASTER SERIES
Slide action. Standard Grade. Hammerless. Takedown. Caliber: .22 S/L/LR. Tubular magazine holds 20 Short, 15 Long or 14 LR cartridges. 24-in. rnd. bbl. Weight: 6 lbs. Plain, pistol-grip stock and grooved semi-beavertail slide handle. Made 1936-54.
121A . . . . NIB $1180 EX $1000 GD $555
121S (.22 REMINGTON SPECIAL,
  12-RND. MAGAZINE,) . . . NIB $1555 EX $1310 GD $710
121SB (SMOOTHBORE) . . . . NIB $1880 EX $1610 GD $910

MODEL 141 GAMEMASTER SERIES
Standard Grade. Hammerless. Takedown. Calibers: .30 Rem., .32 Rem. or .35 Rem.; 5-rnd. tubular magazine. 24-in. bbl. Weight: About 7.75 lbs. Open sights. Stock: Plain, pistol-grip stock. Made 1935-50.
141A . . . . NiB $855 Ex $730 Gd $455
141R Carbine (18.5-in. bbl., mfg.
  1935–42) . . . . NiB $1610 Ex $1410 Gd $960

MODEL 572 FIELDMASTER SERIES
Hammerless. Caliber: .22 S/L/LR. Tubular magazine holds 20 Short, 17 Long, 15 LR. 23-in. bbl. Weight: About 5.5 lbs. Sights: Open rear; ramp front. Pistol-grip stock, grooved forearm. Made 1958–62.
572 A Lightweight (4 lbs.) . . . . . NiB $455 Ex $430 Gd $305
572 BDL Deluxe (checkered stock, blade ramp front sight,
  mfg. 1966–date) . . . . NiB $555 Ex $400 Gd $195
572 Fieldmaster (mfg.
  1955–88) . . . . NiB $330 Ex $305 Gd $180
572 SB (smoothbore for .22 LR shot cartridges,
  mfg. 1961–2009) . . . . NiB $640 Ex $460 Gd $195

MODEL 760 BICENTENNIAL
COMMEMORATIVE . . . . **NiB $800 Ex $650 Gd $280**
Same as Model 760 except has commemorative inscription on receiver. Made in 1976.

MODEL 760 GAMEMASTER SERIES
Slide action. Hammerless. Calibers: .223 Rem., 6mm Rem., .243 Win., .257 Roberts, .270 Win. .280 Rem., .30-06, .300 Sav., .308 Win., .35 Rem. 22-in. bbl. Weight: About 7.5 lbs. Sights: Open rear; bead front, on ramp. Plain pistol-grip stock, grooved slide handle on early models; recent production has checkered stock and slide handle. Made 1952-80.
.222 Rem . . . . NiB $1195 Ex $1021 Gd $744
.223 Rem . . . . NiB $1409 Ex $1135 Gd $739
.257 Roberts . . . . NiB $933 Ex $779 Gd $489
Other calibers . . . . NiB $505 Ex $405 Gd $280
760 ADL (deluxe checkered stock,
  standard or high comb, grip cap,
  sling swivels, mfg. 1953-63) . . . NiB $702 Ex $605 Gd $280
760 BDL Deluxe (.270 Win., .30-06 or .308 Win., Monte
  Carlo cheekpiece stock forearm w/black tip, basket-weave
  checkering, mfg. 1953-80) . . . . NiB $605 Ex $455 Gd $280
760 C Carbine (.270, .280, .30-06, .35 Rem.
  or .308 only, 18.5-in. bbl., 7.25 lbs., mfg.
  1961–80) . . . . NiB $905 Ex $805 Gd $405

MODEL 7600 SERIES
Similar to Model 76. Calibers: 6mm Rem., .243 Win., .270 Win., .280 Rem., .308 Win., .30-06 or .35 Whelen; 4-rnd. detachable magazine. 22-in. bbl. Stock: pressed checkering, straight or Monte Carlo comb in high gloss or satin. Finish: blue. Weight: 7.5 lbs. Made 1981-2020.
7600 . . . . NiB $715 Ex $555 Gd $330
7600 Carbine (18.5-in. bbl.,
  7.25 lbs.) . . . . NiB $715 Ex $555 Gd $330
7600 Special Purpose (.270 Win. or .30-06,
  matte black finish, smooth American walnut
  stock, mfg. 1993–94) . . . . NiB $430 Ex $355 Gd $240

Remington Model 7400

7600 Synthetic (.243 Win., .270 Win., .280 Rem., .308 Win. or .30-06; matte black finish, black synthetic stock, mfg. 1998–2016) . . . . **NiB $615 Ex $480 Gd $270**
7600 Synthetic Carbine (.30-06; matte black finish, black synthetic stock, mfg. 1998-2016) . . . . **NiB $615 Ex $480 Gd $270**

NYLON 76 . . . . **NiB $899 Ex $677 Gd $468**
Short-throw lever action. Caliber: .22 LR. 14-rnd. buttstock tubular magazine. Weight: 4 lbs. Black (add $707) or brown nylon stock and forend. Made 1962-64. Remington's only lever-action rifle.

SPORTSMAN 76 SLIDE-ACTION RIFLE. . . . . **NiB $375 Ex $300 Gd $200**
Caliber: .30-06, 4-rnd. magazine. 22-in. bbl. Weight: 7.5 lbs. Open rear sight; front blade mounted on ramp. Uncheckered hardwood stock and forend. Made 1985-87.

- SEMIAUTO RIFLES -

MODEL FOUR
Autoloading. Hammerless. Calibers: 6mm Rem., .243 Win., .270 Win. 7mm Express Rem.; .30-06, .308 Win. 22-in. bbl. Weight: 7.5 lbs. Sights: Open rear; bead front, on ramp. Monte Carlo checkered stock and forearm. Made 1981-87.
Standard model. . . . . **NiB $722 Ex $465 Gd $369**

MODEL FOUR DIAMOND ANNIVERSARY LTD. EDITION. . . . . **NiB $1377 EX $1088 Gd $976**
Same as Model Four Standard except has engraved receiver w/inscription, checkered high-grade walnut stock and forend. Only 1,500 produced. Made in 1981 only. (Value for new condition.)

MODEL 8 AUTOLOADING RIFLE. . . . . **NiB $1510 Ex $1310 Gd $955**
Standard Grade. Takedown. Calibers: .25, .30, .32 and .35 Rem. Five-round, clip-loaded magazine. 22-in. bbl. Weight: 7.75 lbs. Sights: Adj. and dovetailed open rear; dovetailed bead front. Half-moon metal buttplate on plain straight-grip walnut stock; plain walnut forearm with thin curved end. Made 1906-36.

MODEL 16 AUTOLOADING RIFLE. . . . . **NiB $1710 Ex $1480 Gd $755**
Takedown. Closely resembles the Winchester Model 03 Semiauto rifle. Calibers: .22 Short, .22 LR, 22 Rem. Auto. 15-rnd. tubular magazine in buttstock. 22-in. bbl. Weight: 5.75 lbs. Sights: Open rear; dovetailed bead front. Plain straight-grip stock and forearm. Made 1914-28. Note: In 1918 this model was discontinued in all calibers except .22 Rem. Auto; specifications are for that model.

MODEL 24A AUTOLOADING RIFLE . . . . **NiB $1410 Ex $1255 Gd $605**
Standard Grade. Takedown. Calibers: .22 Short only, .22 LR. only. Tubular magazine in buttstock, holds 15 Short or 10 LR. 21-in. bbl. Weight: About 5 lbs. Sights: Dovetailed adj. open rear; dovetailed bead front. Plain walnut straight-grip buttstock; plain walnut forearm. Made 1922-35.

NYLON 66 APACHE BLACK . . . **NiB $580 Ex $530 Gd $355**
Same as Nylon 66 Mohawk Brown listed below except bbl. and receiver cover chrome-plated, black stock. Made 1962 -84.

NYLON 66 BICENTENNIAL COMMEMORATIVE . . . . **NiB $597 Ex $433 Gd $259**
Same as Nylon 66 Mohawk Brown listed below except has commemorative inscription on receiver. Made 1976 only.

NYLON 66 BLACK DIAMOND RIFLE. . . . . **NiB $500 Ex $325 Gd $244**
Similar to Nylon 66 Black Apache except with blued bbl. and receiver cover. Made 1978-87.

NYLON 66 MOHAWK BROWN AUTOLOADER . . . . **NiB $450 Ex $278 Gd $230**
Caliber: .22 LR. Tubular magazine in buttstock holds 14 rnd. 19.5-in. bbl. Weight: About 4 lbs. Sights: Open rear; blade front. Brown nylon stock and forearm. Made 1959-87.
Seneca Green model (green stock and forearm, mfg. 1959-90) . . . . . . **NiB $630 Ex $555 Gd $355**

NYLON 77 . . . . **NiB $400 Ex $295 Gd $220**
Same as Nylon 66 except w/5-rnd. clip magazine. Made 1970-71.

SPORTSMAN 74 . . . . **NiB $405 Ex $355 Gd $240**
Caliber: .280 Rem. or .30-06, 4-rnd. magazine. 22-in. bbl. Uncheckered buttstock and forend. Open rear sight; ramped blade front sight. Made 1984-87.

MODEL 81 WOODSMASTER AUTOLOADER . . . . **NiB $1355 Ex $1210 Gd $710**
Standard Grade. Takedown. Calibers: .30 Rem., .32 Rem. and .35 Rem., .300 Sav. Five round box magazine (not detachable). 22-in. bbl. Weight: 8.25 lbs. Sights: Open rear; bead front. Plain walnut pistol-grip stock, forearm. Made 1936-50.

MODEL 241A SPEEDMASTER AUTOLOADER . . . . **NiB $1355 Ex $880 Gd $605**
Standard Grade. Takedown. Calibers: .22 Short only, .22 LR. only. Tubular magazine in buttstock, holds 15 Short or 10 LR. 24-in. bbl. Weight: About 6 lbs. Sights: Open rear, bead front. Plain walnut stock and forearm. Made 1935-51.

MODEL 550 SERIES
"Power Piston" or floating chamber, which permits interchangeable use of 22 Short, Long or LR cartridges. Dual extractors. Tubular magazine holds 22 Short, 17 Long, 15 LR. 24-in. bbl. Weight: About 6.25 lbs. Sights: Open rear; bead front. Plain, one-piece pistol-grip stock. Made 1941-71.
550 A . . . . **NiB $280 Ex $245 Gd $155**
550 P (peep rear sight, blade front) . . . . **NiB $355 Ex $330 Gd $205**
550-1 (single extractor, 1946–70) . . . . **NiB $355 Ex $330 Gd $205**
550-2G (Gallery Special, 22-in. bbl., screw eye for counter chain and fired shell deflector) . . . . **NiB $355 Ex $330 Gd $205**

RIFLES

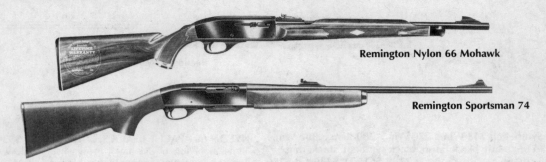

Remington Nylon 66 Mohawk

Remington Sportsman 74

MODEL 522 VIPER . . . . NiB $129 Ex $128 Gd $102
Calibers: .22 LR. 10-rnd. magazine. 20-in. bbl. 40 in. overall. Weight: 4.63 lbs. Checkered black PET resin stock with beavertail forend. Dupont high-tech synthetic lightweight receiver. Matte black finish on all exposed metal. Made 1993-97.

MODEL 552 SPEEDMASTER SERIES
Semiauto. Caliber: .22 S/L/LR. Tubular magazine holds 20 Short, 17 Long, 15 LR. 25-in. bbl. Weight: About 5.5 lbs. Sights: Open rear; bead front. Synthetic stock. Made 1997-98.
552A . . . . NiB $280 Ex $245 Gd $155
552 BDL DELUXE (checkered walnut
  stock, mfg. 1966 to date) . . . . . NiB $555 Ex $405 Gd $215
552 C (21-in. bbl., mfg.
  1961-77) . . . . NiB $280 Ex $245 Gd $155

MODEL 597 SERIES
Semiauto. Caliber: .17 HMR, .22 LR or .22 WMR; 8- or 10-rnd. magazine. 20-in. free float bbl. Weight: About 5.5 lbs. Sights: Open rear; bead front. Pistol-grip stock, semi-beavertail forearm. Made 1997-2020.
597 . . . . NiB $170 Ex $135 Gd $95
597 AAC-SD (synthetic stock,
  16.5-in. threaded bbl., mfg.
  2011–14) . . . . NiB $205 Ex $165 Gd $105
597 Camo (camo synthetic stock,
  mfg. 2008–date) . . . . NiB $245 Ex $200 Gd $125
597 Custom Target (green laminate
  stock, mfg. 1998–2000). . . . . NiB $505 Ex $445 Gd $280
597 Custom Target (.22 WMR,
  green laminate stock, mfg.
  1998–2000) . . . . NiB $605 Ex $530 Gd $335
597 FLX (FLX camo synthetic stock,
  mfg. 2009–14) . . . . NiB $245 Ex $200 Gd $125
597 Heavy Barrel (synthetic stock,
  16.5-in. heavy bbl., mfg.
  2012–date) . . . . NiB $205 Ex $165 Gd $105
597 Magnum Synthetic (.17 HMR,
  synthetic stock, mfg.
  1997–2014) . . . . NiB $420 Ex $335 Gd $180
597 Magnum Synthetic LS (.17 HMR
  or .22 WMR, brown laminate stock,
  mfg. 1998–2003) . . . . NiB $320 Ex $280 Gd $180
597 Magnum Synthetic LS Heavy
  Barrel(.17 HMR or .22 WMR, heavy bbl.,
  brown laminate stock, mfg.
  1998–2003) . . . . NiB $500 Ex $415 Gd $250
597 Sporter (hardwood stock, mfg.
  1998–2000) . . . . NiB $165 Ex $145 Gd $90
597 Stainless Sporter
  (hardwood stock,
  stainless, mfg. 2000 only). . . . NiB $195 Ex $170 Gd $110
597 HB LS (stainless, laminate stock,
  heavy bbl., mfg. 1997–2007) . . NiB $290 Ex $255 Gd $160

597 LSS (stainless, laminate stock,
  mfg. 2001-07). . . . . NiB $280 Ex $245 Gd $155
597 SS (stainless, mfg.
  1998–2000) . . . . NiB $225 Ex $200 Gd $125
597 TVP (stainless, green laminate stock,
  mfg. 2008–14) . . . . NiB $480 Ex $385 Gd $220
597 VTR (.22 LR or .22 WMR, 16-in.
  heavy bbl., As or Pardus stock,
  mfg. 2010–11) . . . . NiB $520 Ex $380 Gd $280

MODEL 740 WOODSMASTER NiB $330 Ex $280 Gd $205
Standard Grade. Gas-operated. Calibers: .30-06 or .308. Four round detachable box magazine. 22-in. bbl. Weight: About 7.5 lbs. Plain pistol-grip stock, semibeavertail forend with finger grooves. Sights: Open rear; ramp front. Made 1955-59.
ADL model (checkered stock). . NiB $380 Ex $330 Gd $230
BDL model (select wood) . . . . . NiB $400 Ex $345 Gd $230

**MODEL 742 BICENTENNIAL
COMMEMORATIVE** . . . . NiB $588 Ex $380 Gd $355
Same as Model 742 Woodsmaster rifle except has commemorative inscription on receiver. Made in 1976. (Value for new condition.)

**MODEL 742 WOODSMASTER
AUTOMATIC.** . . . . NiB $405 Ex $330 Gd $240
Gas-operated Semiauto. Calibers: 6mm Rem., .243 Win., .280 Rem., .30-06, .308 Win. Four round clip magazine. 22-in. bbl. Weight: 7.5 lbs. Sights: Open rear; bead front, on ramp. Checkered pistol-grip stock and forearm. Made 1960-80.
742 ADL DELUXE (checkered walnut stock,
  engraved receiver) . . . . NiB $455 Ex $355 Gd $240
742 BDL DELUXE (Monte Carlo basket weave checkered
  walnut stock) . . . . NiB $405 Ex $355 Gd $240
742 C (carbine, 18.5-in.bbl.,
  1961-80) . . . . NiB $455 Ex $355 Gd $240
742 CDL (carbine, 18.5-in.bbl., checkered
  walnut stock, 1961-63) . . . . . . NiB $480 Ex $430 Gd $305

**MODEL 742D PEERLESS
GRADE.** . . . . NiB $4010 Ex $3010 Gd $2110
Same as Model 742 except scroll engraved, fancy wood. Made 1961-80.

**MODEL 742F PREMIER
GRADE.** . . . . NiB $8200 Ex $6500 Gd $4000
Same as Model 742 except extensively engraved with game scenes and scroll, finest grade wood. Also available with receiver inlaid with gold; adds 50 percent to value. Made 1961-80.

MODEL 7400 SERIES
Similar to Model 742. Calibers: 6mm Rem., .234 Win., .270 Win., 7mm Express, .280 Rem., .308 Win., .30-06 or 35 Whelen. Stock: press checkered Monte Carlo. Made 1981–2005.
7400 (22-in. bbl.) . . . . NiB $520 Ex $415 Gd $235

7400 Carbine (18.5-in. bbl.) .. NiB $520 Ex $415 Gd $235
7400 SP (.270 or .30-06, Special Purpose
   matte black finish, satin American walnut
   stock, mfg. 1993–94) . . . . NiB $440 Ex $375 Gd $235
7400 Synthetic (synthetic stock, matte
   black receiver, 2003–04) . . . . . NiB $470 Ex $390 Gd $270
7400 Synthetic Carbine (synthetic
   stock, matte black receiver, 18.5-in. bbl., 1998–2006) . NiB
   $470 Ex $390 Gd $270
7400 Weathermaster (synthetic stock, matte
   nickel receiver, 2003–04) . . . . . NiB $500 Ex $405 Gd $270

MODEL R-15 . . . . NiB $1380 Ex $1010 Gd $730
Semiauto AR15 platform. Action: direct gas impingement
system. Caliber: .450 Bushmaster, 4-rnd. magazine. 18-in.
bbl. fluted. Stock: fixed. Finish: Mossy Oak Break-Up. Made
2010-15.
Hunter (.30 Rem., 2009–15) . . . NiB $1150 Ex $900 Gd $730
VTR Predator (.204 Ruger
   or .223 Rem., 18- or
   20-in. bbl., 2008–13) . . . . . . NiB $1160 Ex $910 Gd $710

MODEL R-25 . . . . NiB $1500 Ex $1080 Gd $860
Semiauto AR10 platform. Action: direct gas impingement system. Caliber: .243 Win., 7mm-08 or .308 Win., 4-rnd. magazine. 20-in.bbl. Stock: fixed. Finish: Mossy Oak Treestand.
Weight: 7.75 lbs. Made 2009-14.
R-25 GII (20-in. fluted
   stainless bbl., 2015–16) . . . . NiB $1500 Ex $1230 Gd $855

JOHN RIGBY & CO. — Paso Robles, CA

MODEL 278 MAGAZINE SPORTING
RIFLE. . . . . .NiB $6475 Ex $5144 Gd $3576
Mauser action. Caliber: .278 High Velocity or 7x57mm; 5-rnd.
box magazine. 25-in. bbl. Weight: about 7.5 lbs. Sights:
Folding leaf rear; bead front. Sporting stock w/half-pistol-grip,
checkered. Specifications given are those of current model;
however, in general, they apply also to prewar model.

MODEL 278 LIGHTWEIGHT MAGAZINE
RIFLE. . . . . .NiB $5110 Ex $4122 Gd $2833
Same as standard .278 rifle except has 21-in. bbl. Weight: 6.75
lbs.

MODEL 350 MAGNUM MAGAZINE
SPORTING RIFLE . . . . .NiB $4332 Ex $3633 Gd $2490
Mauser action. Caliber: .350 Magnum. Five round box magazine. 24-in. bbl. Weight: About 7.75 lbs. Sights: Folding leaf
rear; bead front. Sporting stock with full pistol-grip, checkered. Currently mfd.

MODEL 416 BIG GAME MAGAZINE
SPORTING RIFLE . . . . .NiB $7688 Ex $6133 Gd $4286
Mauser action. Caliber: .416 Big Game. Four round box maga-
zine. 24-in. bbl. Weight: 9 to 9.25 lbs. Sights: Folding leaf rear;
bead front. Sporting stock with full pistol-grip, checkered.
Currently mfd.

BEST QUALITY HAMMERLESS EJECTOR
DOUBLE RIFLE . . . . . NiB $73,675 Ex $62,000 Gd $38,550
Sidelocks. Calibers: .278 Magnum, .350 Magnum, .470 Nitro
Express. 24- to 28-in. bbls. Weight: 7.5 to 10.5 lbs. Sights:
Folding leaf rear; bead front. Checkered pistol-grip stock and
forearm.

SECOND QUALITY HAMMERLESS EJECTOR
DOUBLE RIFLE . . . . . NiB $13,600 Ex $11,290 Gd $10,375
Same general specifications as Best Quality double rifle except
boxlock.

THIRD QUALITY HAMMERLESS EJECTOR
DOUBLE RIFLE . . . . . . NiB $11,689 Ex $10,450 Gd $7,800
Same as Second Quality double rifle except plainer finish and
not of as high quality.

ROCK ISLAND AROMORY (RIA) — Manila, Philippines
Armscor brand, imports and mfg. in Pahrump, NV since 2016.

M14Y . . . . NiB $149 Ex $100 Gd $80
Bolt-action. Caliber: .22 LR, 10-rnd. magazine. Bbl.: 18-in.
Sights: adj. rear, hooded ramp front. Stock: Monte Carlo wood.
Weight: 5 lbs. Youth size stock. Made 2016 to date.

M11600 SA. . . . . NiB $199 Ex $185 Gd $130
Semiauto. Caliber: .22 LR, 10-rnd. magazine. Bbl.: 18-in.
Sights: peep rear, post front. Stock: Black wood. Weight: 6.5
lbs. AR style. Made 2016 to date.

MAK22 SA . . . . NiB $199 Ex $185 Gd $130
Semiauto. Caliber: .22 LR, 10-rnd. magazine. Bbl.: 18-in.
Sights: adj. rear, post front. Stock: Wood. Weight: 7 lbs. AK-47
style. Made 2016 to date.

M20P SA. . . . . NiB $159 Ex $140 Gd $110
Semiauto. Caliber: .22 LR, 10-rnd. magazine. Bbl.: 21-in.
Sights: adj. rear, hooded bead front. Stock: Wood. Weight: 6.5
lbs. Made 2016 to date.

TM22 . . . . NiB $280 Ex $275 Gd $220
Semiauto. Caliber: .22 LR, 10-, 15-, or 25-rnd. magazine.
Bbl.: 18-in. Sights: Optic ready. Stock: Skeleton, AR pistol grip.
Weight: 6.5 lbs. AR style, aluminum rail. Made 2020 to date.
Feather model (M4 style) ... NiB $250 Ex $235 Gd $210

ROSS RIFLE CO. — Quebec, Canada

MODEL 1910 BOLT-ACTION SPORTING RIFLE
Straight-pull bolt-action with interrupted screw-type lugs.
Calibers: .280 Ross, .303 British. Four round or 5-rnd. maga-
zine. Bbl. lengths: 22, 24, 26 in. Sights: Two-leaf open rear;
bead front. Checkered sporting stock. Weight: About 7 lbs.
Made c. 1910 to end of World War I. Note: Most firearm
authorities agree that this and other Ross models with inter-
rupted screw-type lugs are unsafe to fire.
Military model . . . . NiB $2175 Ex $1370 Gd $989
Military Match Target model . NiB $10,300 Ex $7227 Gd $3590

ROSSI — Sao Leopoldo, Brazil
*Currently imported exclusively by BrazTech Int'l. in Miami, FL
since 1998; previously by Interarms in Alexandria. VA.*

CIRCUIT JUDGE. . . . . NiB $625 Ex $470 Gd $345
Revolver. DA/SA. Calibers: .22 LR/.22 WMR or .44 Mag. Bbl.:
18.5-in. Sights: adj. rear, fiber optic front. Stock: Monte Carlo
wood. Weight: 5.5 lbs. Made 2011-15.
.44 Mag., deduct. $100

RIO GRANDE. . . . . NiB $555 Ex $420 Gd $305
Lever action. Calibers: .30-30 or .45-70. Bbl.: 20-in. Sights:
adj. buckhorn rear, post front. Stock: smooth wood. Weight: 7
lbs. Made 2010-14.
stainless, add. $25

SINGLE SHOT RIFLE. . . . . NiB $180 Ex $130 Gd $105
Break action. Caliber: .243 Win. or .270 Win. 23-in. bbl. Stock:
Black synthetic. Finish: matte blue. Weight: 6.25 lbs. Made
2017-date.

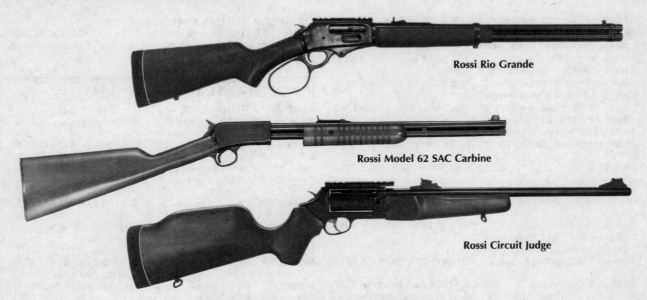

Rossi Rio Grande

Rossi Model 62 SAC Carbine

Rossi Circuit Judge

WIZARD . . . . **NiB $310 Ex $230 Gd $170**
Break action. Single shot. Calibers: .22-250, .223 Rem., .243 Win., .270 Win., .308 Win., .30-06. Bbl.: 22 in. Stock: Monte Carlo wood. Sights: adj. rear, post front. Weight: 6.25-7 lbs. Made 2010-15.

62 GALLERY MODEL . . . . **NiB $215 Ex $159 Gd $126**
Similar to Winchester Model 62. Calibers: .22 LR, Long, Short or .22 WMR. Tubular magazine holds 13 LR, 16 Long, 20 Short. 23-in. bbl. 39.25 in. overall. Weight: 5.75 lbs. Sights: Open rear; bead front. Straight-grip stock, grooved slide handle. Blued, nickel or stainless finish. Imported 1970 to 1998. Values same as SAC Model.
Carbine . . . . **NiB $215 Ex $159 Gd $126**
.22 WMR, add **$20**
Nickel or stainless finish, add **$50**

MODEL 65/92 . . . . **NiB $338 Ex $250 Gd $190**
Similar to Winchester Model 92. Caliber: .38 Special/.357 Mag., .44 Mag., .44-40, .45 LC. 8- or 10-rnd. magazine. 16-, 20- or 24-in. rnd. or half-octagonal bbl. Weight: 5.5 to 6 lbs. 33.5- to 41.5-in. overall. Satin blue, chrome or stainless finish. Brazilian hardwood buttstock and forearm. Made 1978-98 reintro. 2010-date.
W/octagon bbl . . . . **NiB $400 Ex $329 Gd $278**
LL Lever model . . . . **NiB $510 Ex $396 Gd $280**
Engraved, add **$100**
Chrome or stainless, add **$50**

RUGER — Southport, CT

Manufacturing facilities in Newport, NH, and Prescott, AZ; previously manufactured in Southport, CT. To facilitate locating Ruger firearms, models are grouped into three categories: Single-shot/Lever-action Rifles (below), Semiauto Rifles and Bolt-action Rifles. For a complete listing, please refer to the index.

- SINGLE-SHOT RIFLES / LEVER-ACTION RIFLES -

NO. 1-A LIGHT SPORTER . . . **NiB $1255 Ex $905 Gd $655**
Same as No.1 Standard except has 22-in. bbl., folding leaf rear sight on quarter-rib and ramp front sight, Alexander Henry pattern forearm. Made 1966 to date.
**No.1-AB (semi-beavertail
  forend, 1997-date)** . . . . **NiB $1010 Ex $755 Gd $510**

**NO. 1-S MEDIUM
  SPORTER** . . . . **NiB $1155 Ex $840 Gd $480**
Same as No. 1 Light Sporter except has 26-in. bbl. 22-in. in 45-70); weight: 8 lbs (7.25 lbs. in .45-70). Calibers: 7mm Rem. Mag., .300 Win. Mag., .45-70. Made 1966-2014.
**No. 1 K1-S-BBZ (matte stainless finish, grey laminated
  stock, 2001–10)** . . . . **NiB $980 Ex $480 Gd $400**
**.450 Bushmaster (matte stainless finish, grey
  laminated stock, 20-in. bbl. w/muzzle
  brake, 2018-19)** . . . . **NiB $1580 Ex $1280 Gd $830**
**.450 Marlin (matte stainless finish, grey laminated
  stock, 20-in. bbl. w/muzzle
  brake, 2018-19)** . . . . **NiB $1580 Ex $1280 Gd $830**

NO. 1-RSI INTERNATIONAL . . **NiB $1110 Ex $840 Gd $510**
Similar to the No. 1 Light Sporter except with lightweight 20-in. bbl. and full Mannlicher-style forend, in calibers .243 Win., .270 Win., 7x57mm, .30-06. Weight: 7.25 lbs. Disc. 2014.

NO. 1-V VARMINTER . . . . **NiB $1110 Ex $840 Gd $480**
Same as No. 1 Standard except has heavy 24-in. bbl. with target scope bases, no quarter-rib. Weight: 9 lbs. Calibers: .22-250, .25-06, 7mm Rem. Mag., .300 Win. Mag. Made 1966-2014.
**No. 1 K1-V-BBZ (matte stainless finish, grey laminated stock,
  2001–10)** . . . . **NiB $930 Ex $430 Gd $360**

NO.1-B STANDARD RIFLE . . . **NiB $1010 Ex $710 Gd $430**
Falling-block single-shot action with Farquharson-type lever. Calibers: .22-250, .243 Win., 6mm Rem., .25-06, .270 Win., .30-06, 7mm Rem. Mag., .300 Win. Mag. 26-in. medium bbl. Weight: 8 lbs. No sights, has quarter-rib for scope mounting. Checkered pistol-grip buttstock and semibeavertail forearm, QD swivels, rubber buttplate. Made 1966-2010.
**No. 1 K1-B-BBZ (matte stainless finish, grey laminated
  stock, 2001–10)** . . . . **NiB $980 Ex $480 Gd $400**

NO.1 TROPICAL RIFLE . . . . . . **NiB $1055 Ex $655 Gd $380**
Same as No. 1 Light Sporter except has heavy 24-in. bbl.; calibers are .375 H&H .404 Jeffery, .416 Rigby, and .458 Win. Mag. Weight: 8.25 to 9 lbs. Made 1966 to date.
**No. 1 K1-H-BBZ (matte stainless
  finish, grey laminated stock,
  2001–10)** . . . . **NiB $930 Ex $430 Gd $360**

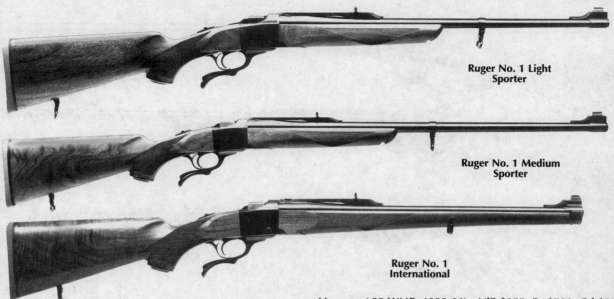

Ruger No. 1 Light Sporter

Ruger No. 1 Medium Sporter

Ruger No. 1 International

NO.3 CARBINE.............NiB $905 Ex $805 Gd $555
Falling-block action with American-style lever. Calibers: .22 Hornet, .223 Rem., .30-40 Krag, .357 Win., .44 Mag., .45-70. 22-in. bbl. Weight: 6 lbs. Sights: Folding leaf rear; gold bead front. Carbine-style stock w/curved buttplate, forearm with bbl. band. Made 1972-87.

MODEL 96
Caliber: .22 LR, .22 Mag., .44 Mag. Detachable 10-, 9- or 4-rnd. magazine. 18.5-in. bbl. Weight: 5.25 lbs. Front gold bead sights.   Drilled and tapped for scope. American hardwood stock. Made 1996-2008.
.22 LR or .22 WMR..........NiB $805 Ex $530 Gd $355
.44 Mag...................NiB $1005 Ex $730 Gd $555

- SEMIAUTO RIFLES -

MODEL 10/22 CARBINE
Caliber: .22 LR. Detachable 10-rnd. rotary magazine. 18.5-in. bbl. Weight: 5 lbs. Sights: Folding leaf rear; bead front. Carbine-style stock with bbl. band and curved buttplate (walnut stock discontinued 1980). Blued finish. Made 1964 to date. International and Sporter versions discontinued 1971.
Standard (hardwood stock)....NiB $279 Ex $120 Gd $100
Standard (synthetic stock).....NiB $279 Ex $120 Gd $100
Standard (synthetic stock, LaserMax sight), add.......$100
Standard (stainless finish).....NiB $310 Ex $130 Gd $110
**Standard Sporter (checkered
    wood stock)**.............NiB $455 Ex $330 Gd $235
**Compact (16.1-in. bbl., hardwood stock, fiber
    optic sights, 2005-17)**......NiB $305 Ex $270 Gd $205
**Compact (16.1-in. bbl., black synthetic stock, fiber
    optic sights, 2018-date)**.....NiB $270 Ex $235 Gd $185
**Competition (16.1-in. fluted bull bbl.,
    laminated stock w/adj. cheek riser,
    Picatinny rail, 2018-date)**....NiB $780 Ex $680 Gd $530
**Fingergroove Sporter (monte carlo wood stock,
    1966-71)**...............NiB $855 Ex $655 Gd $455
Fingergroove Sporter (checkered stock), add.........30%
**International (Mannlicher-style
    stock, 1966-69)**...........NiB $810 Ex $655 Gd $455
**K-10/22 RB (birch stock, stainless
    finish)**..................NiB $260 Ex $178 Gd $144

Magnum (.22 WMR, 1999-06) . NiB $955 Ex $780 Gd $555
RB (birch stock, blued finish) .. NiB $260 Ex $178 Gd $144
**RBI International (blued, Mannlicher-style
    stock, 1994-2003)**.........NiB $260 Ex $120 Gd $110
**RBI International (stainless, Mannlicher-style
    stock, 1994-2003)**.........NiB $330 Ex $130 Gd $120
Rifle (20-in. bbl, 2004-06) ....NiB $220 Ex $110 Gd $100
SP Deluxe Sporter (intro. 1966)... NiB $260 Ex $178 Gd $144
**Tactical (synthetic stock, flash
    hider 2010-date)**..........NiB $320 Ex $275 Gd $215
**Tactical Target (16.1-in. heavy bbl. w/spiral design, Hogue
    stock 2010-16)** ....NiB $505 Ex $400 Gd $280
**Takedown Backpacker (stainless,
    Magpul stock, 2020-date)** .. NiB $455 Ex $405 Gd $305
**Takedown TD (synthetic stock, backpack,
    stainless, 2010-date)**........NiB $375 Ex $325 Gd $255
**Takedown TDT (w/flash suppressor,
    blued, 2013-date)** ....NiB $395 Ex $345 Gd $270
**Takedown Threaded (threaded
    fluted heavy bbl., blued, Ruger
    modular stock, 2016-date)** ...NiB $540 Ex $480 Gd $370
**Target (20-in. heavy bbl. w/spiral
    design, blued finish, brownlaminated
    stock, 1996-2017)**.........NiB $475 Ex $390 Gd $265
**Target (20-in. heavy bbl. w/spiral design,
    stainless finish, black laminated
    stock, 1996-08, 2010-17)**......NiB $530 Ex $455 Gd $360
**Target (thumbhole stock,
    2001-02),** ....NiB $530 Ex $455 Gd $330
**Target Lite (threaded bbl., matte black, laminated
    thumbhole stock, 2017-date)** . NiB $555 Ex $485 Gd $375

MODEL 44
Gas-operated. Caliber: .44 Magnum. Four round tubular magazine (with magazine release button since 1967). 18.5-in. bbl. Weight: 5.75 lbs. Sights: Folding leaf rear; gold bead front. Carbine-style stock w/bbl. band and curved buttplate. Made 1961-86. International and Sporter versions discontinued 1971.
Standard ....NiB $955 Ex $855 Gd $455
**International (Mannlicher-style
    stock)**...................NiB $1360 Ex $955 Gd $710
**Sporter (MC stock w/finger
    groove, disc. 1971))** ......NiB $1360 Ex $955 Gd $655
RS (peep rear sight, disc. 1978) ..NiB $1210 Ex $1010 Gd $655

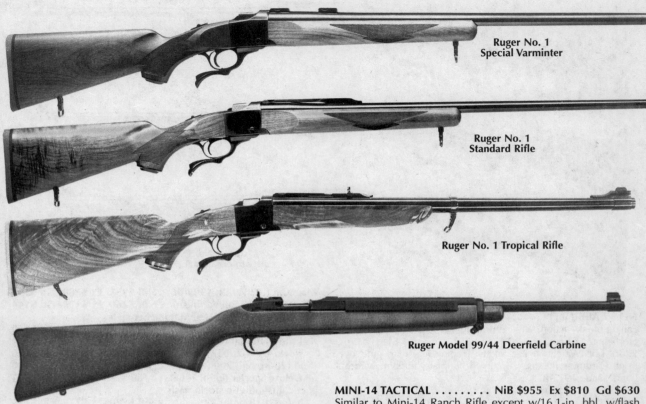

Ruger No. 1 Special Varminter

Ruger No. 1 Standard Rifle

Ruger No. 1 Tropical Rifle

Ruger Model 99/44 Deerfield Carbine

MODEL 99/44 DEERFIELD ... NiB $855 Ex $755 Gd $510
Similar to Model 44 except w/four-rnd. rotary detachable box magazine, rotating bolt w/dual front locking lugs, integral scope mount. Made 2000-06.

MINI-14
Gas-operated. Caliber: .223 Rem. 5-, 10- or 20-rnd. box magazine. 18.5-in. bbl. Weight: About 6.5 lbs. Sights: Peep rear; blade front mounted on removable barrel band. Pistol-grip stock w/curved buttplate, handguard. Made 1974-2004.
Blued finish. . . . . NiB $725 Ex $579 Gd $375
K-Mini-14/S stainless steel . . . . NiB $815 Ex $580 Gd $444
Mini-14/5F w/blued finish,
    folding stock. . . . . NiB $1144 Ex $995 Gd $790
K-Mini-14/SF w/stainless finish,
    folding stock. . . . . NiB $855 Ex $690 Gd $545

MINI-14 RANCH RIFLE
Similar to Mini-14 except w/receiver machined for scope mounts. Recent manufacture chambered in 5.56mm NATO. Weight: 7 lbs. Made 1982 to date.
Blued finish. . . . . NiB $939 Ex $630 Gd $550
Blued finish (polymer stock), add. $15
Stainless finish. . . . . NiB $979 Ex $680 Gd $580
Stainless finish (folding stock), add. $350
Stainless finish (polymer stock) NiB $979 Ex $680 Gd $580
Stainless finish (6.8SPC,
    2007-11). . . . . NiB $979 Ex $680 Gd $580

MINI-14 TARGET . . . . NiB $1100 Ex $940 Gd $740
Similar to Mini-14 Ranch Rifle except w/22-in. stainless heavy bbl. w/harmonic stabilizer, thumbhole stock. Made 2007-16.
w/Hogue synthetic stock . . . . NiB $1100 Ex $940 Gd $740

MINI-14 TACTICAL . . . . NiB $955 Ex $810 Gd $630
Similar to Mini-14 Ranch Rifle except w/16.1-in. bbl. w/flash hider, synthetic stock. Weight: 6.75 lbs. Made 2009 to date.
w/collapsible stock . . . . NiB $955 Ex $810 Gd $630

MINI-THIRTY
Similar to Mini-14 except chambered in 7.62 x 39mm. 5-rnd. detachable magazine. 18.5-in. bbl. 37.25 in. overall. Weight: 7 lbs. 3 oz. Designed for use with telescopic sights. Walnut stained stock. Sights: Peep rear; blade front mounted on bbl. band. Blued or stainless finish. Made 1987-2004.
Blued finish. . . . . NiB $655 Ex $455 Gd $380
Stainless finish. . . . . NiB $955 Ex $800 Gd $630
Stainless finish (polymer stock,
    1990 to date) . . . . NiB $979 Ex $730 Gd $580
Tactical model (polymer stock, flash
    suppressor, 1990 to date) . . . . NiB $960 Ex $810 Gd $630

PC SERIES SEMIAUTO CARBINES
Calibers: 9mm Parabellum (PC9) or .40 S&W (PC40). 10-rnd. magazine. 15.25-in. bbl. Weight: 6.25 lbs. Integral Ruger scope mounts with or without sights. Optional blade front sight, adjustable open rear. Matte black oxide finish. Matte black Zytel stock w/checkered pistol-grip and forearm. Made 1998-2006.
w/no sights . . . . NiB $580 Ex $390 Gd $270
w/adjust. sights, add. $30

PC CARBINE (NEW MFG.) . . . . . NiB $555 Ex $490 Gd $380
Semiauto. Blow-back action. Calibers: 9mm w/modular magazine wells for Ruger and Glock pistol magazines. Bbl.: 16.12-in. fluted and threaded. Stock: textured polymer w/adj. LOP. Sights: Ghost ring and Picatinny rail. Finish: Matte black. Takedown. Made 2018 to date.
w/aluminum handguard, add $50
w/aluminum handguard, pistol grip
    and AR style stock, add. $150

AR-556 . . . . **NiB $680 Ex $610 Gd $460**
Semiauto. Stripped down version of the SR-556 model. Calibers: 5.56mm NATO. Bbl.: 16.1-in. w/muzzle brake. Stock: Six-position, telescoping, M4-style. Sights: Ruger Rapid Deploy adj. rear, adj. post. and Picatinny rail. Finish: Matte black. Takedown. Made 2015 to date.

**MPR (up graded features and calibers,
    2019 to date). . . . . NiB $780 Ex $680 Gd $530**
Optics (no sights, 2019-20) . . . NiB $610 Ex $480 Gd $380

SR-556/SR-556 CARBINE. . . NiB $1530 Ex $1230 Gd $955
Semiauto AR15 platform w/gas piston system. Caliber: 5.56mm NATO or 6.8 SPC. 10-, 25- or 30-rnd. magazine. 16.1-in. bbl., adj. gas block, Troy folding sights, fixed or collapsible butt-stock. Weight: 7.9 lbs. Made 2009-19.

**SR-556E (vented aluminum rail,
    m4 stock, 2011-14). . . . . . . NiB $1030 Ex $830 Gd $655**
**SR-556VT (20-in. bbl., A2 buttstock, Mappul
    grip 2013-14) . . . . NiB $1510 Ex $1180 Gd $930**
**Takedown model (takedown, Elite 452 trigger,
    KeyMod handguard, Magpul grip, adj. stock,
    2015–18) . . . . NiB $1655 Ex $1310 Gd $1030**

SR-762 CARBINE . . . . NiB $1755 Ex $1410 Gd $1110
Semiauto AR15 platform w/gas piston system. Caliber: 7.62mm NATO. 20-rnd. magazine. 16.1-in. bbl., adj. gas block, adj. folding sights, collapsible buttstock. Weight: 8.6 lbs. Made 2013-19.

- BOLT-ACTION RIFLES -

MODEL 77 SERIES
Bolt action. Mauser style, 2-lug bolt. Receiver with integral scope mount base or with round top. Short stroke or magnum length action (depending on caliber) in the former type receiver, magnum only in the latter. .22-250, .220 Swift, 6mm Rem., .243 Win., .250-3000, .25-06, .257 Roberts, 6.5 Rem. Mag., .270 Win., 7x57mm, 7mm-08 7mm Rem. Mag., .280 Rem., .284 Win., .308 Win., .30-06, .300 Win. Mag. .338 Win. Mag., .350 Rem. Mag., .458 Win. Mag. Five round magazine standard, 4-rnd. in .220 Swift, 3-rnd. in magnum calibers. 22   24- or 26-in. bbl. (depending on caliber). Weight: About 7 lbs.; .458 Mag. model, 8.75 lbs. Round-top model furnished w/folding leaf rear sight and ramp front; integral base model furnished w/scope rings, with or w/o open sights. Stock w/checkered pistol grip and forearm, pistol-grip cap, rubber recoil pad, QD swivel studs. Made 1968-92.

w/integral base, no sights . . . . NiB $605 Ex $500 Gd $330
6.5 Rem. Mag., add. $100
.284 Win., add $50
.338 Win. Mag., add. $75
.350 Rem. Mag., add. $75
**Model 77PL (w/round
    top receiver). . . . . NiB $555 Ex $455 Gd $305**
**Model 77RL (ultra light,
    no sights, disc. 1992). . . . . . . NiB $555 Ex $455 Gd $330**
**Model 77RS (ultra light,
    w/sights, disc. 1992). . . . . . . NiB $605 Ex $480 Gd $330**
**Model 77RS African (.458 Win.
    Mag., disc. 1991) . . . . NiB $655 Ex $555 Gd $405**
**Model 77RSC African (.458 Win. Mag., Circassian
    walnut stock, 1976-78) . . . . . . NiB $855 Ex $655 Gd $455**
**Model 77RSC, .458 Win. Mag.,
    w/walnut stock, add. $126**
w/fancy grade Circassian walnut stock, add. $707
**Model 77RSI International w/Mannlicher stock,
    short action, 18.5-in. bbl . . . NiB $675 Ex $466 Gd $339**
**Model 77ST (w/round top, open
    sights) . . . . NiB $630 Ex $555 Gd $400**

.338 Win. Mag., add $75
**Model 77V Varmint (w/integral base, heavy
    bbl., no sights 1968-92) . . . . NiB $630 Ex $555 Gd $400**

MODEL 77 MARK II SERIES
Revised Model 77 action. Same general specifications as Model 77 except with new 3-position safety and fixed blade ejector system. Calibers .22 PPC, .223 Rem., 6mm PPC, 6.5x55 Swedish, .375 H&H, .404 Jeffery and .416 Rigby also available. Weight: 6 to 10.25 lbs. Made 1989-2012.

**Compact Magnum (.330 RUM, .308 Win., or .338 RCM, walnut
    stock, blued, 2008-12) . . . . NiB $580 Ex $505 Gd $400**
**Compact Magnum (.330 RUM, .308 Win., or .338 RCM, syn-
    thetic stock, stainless, 2008-12). NiB $755 Ex $620 Gd $430**
**LR (left-hand, integral base,
    no sights, 1991-07). . . . . NiB $530 Ex $480 Gd $370**
**R (integral base, no sights,
    disc. 2006). . . . . NiB $505 Ex $455 Gd $350**
RL (ultralight, no sights, 1990-08) . NiB $655 Ex $580 Gd $430
**LFP (ultralight , 20-in. bbl., black
    synthetic stock, 1999-08) . . . . . NiB $655 Ex $580 Gd $430**
**RFP All-Weather (stainless bbl./action, Zytel injection-molded
    stock, 1990-06) . . . . NiB $535 Ex $430 Gd $315**
**RLS (ultralight, open sights,
    disc. 1990). . . . . NiB $505 Ex $455 Gd $350**
**RS (integral base,
    open sights, 1990-04) . . . . NiB $555 Ex $430 Gd $280**
**RS Express (fancy grade French walnut stock,
    integral base, open sights) . . . NiB $1255 Ex $880 Gd $755**
**RSFP All-Weather (stainless bbl./action, Zytel injection-molded
    stock, disc. 2004) . . . . NiB $580 Ex $505 Gd $400**
**RSM (.375 H&H, .416 Rigby, or .458
    Lott; Circassian walnut stock;
    express sights, 1990-2010) . . NiB $1955 Ex $1430 Gd $980**
**RBZ (stainless bbl./action, brown
    laminate stock, 1997-08). . . . . . NiB $580 Ex $505 Gd $400**
**RSBZ (stainless bbl./action, brown
    laminate stock, disc. 2004) . . . . NiB $530 Ex $480 Gd $370**
**VBS/RVT(heavy 26- or 28-in. bbl., stainless, black
    laminated stock, 1993-2012). . . NiB $755 Ex $620 Gd $430**
**RVTBBZ Target (heavy 26- or 28-in. bbl., stainless, black
    laminated stock, disc. 2004) . . . . NiB $800 Ex $655 Gd $48**

MODEL 77 GUNSITE SCOUT SERIES
Similar to Model 77 Mark II except w/16.5-in. bbl. w/flash hider, 10-shot detacable box magazine, 5.56 NATO, .308 Win., .350 Legend, or .450 Bushmaster, forward scope mount, blued or stainless finish, laminated or composite stock w/spacers. Weight: 7 lbs. Made 2011 to date.

blued . . . . NiB $1010 Ex $855 Gd $680
stainless . . . . NiB $1055 Ex $905 Gd $705

MODEL 77/17 SERIES
Similar to 77/22 series except in .17 Mach 2, .17 HMR, .17 WSM or .17 Hornet; 6-rnd rotary magazine. Bbl.: 18.5- or 20-in. Stock: Checkered American walnut or Green Mountain laminate. Finish: Stainless or blued. Made 1984 to date.

**.17 Mach 2 or .17 HMR
    (2002-16) . . . . NiB $830 Ex $7305 Gd $455**
**.17 WSM or .17 Hornet
    (2018-date). . . . . NiB $855 Ex $755 Gd $580**
stainless. . . . . NiB $805 Ex $550 Gd $355

MODEL 77/22 HORNET . . . . . NiB $556 EX $445 Gd $339
Mini-Sporter built on the 77/22 action in caliber .22 Hornet. Six round rotary magazine. 20- in. bbl. 40 in. overall. Weight: 6 lbs. Receiver machined for Ruger rings (included). Beaded front sight and open adj. rear, or no sights. Blued

---

GRADING: **NiB** = New in Box   **Ex** = Excellent or NRA 95%   **Gd** = Good or NRA 68%

RIFLES

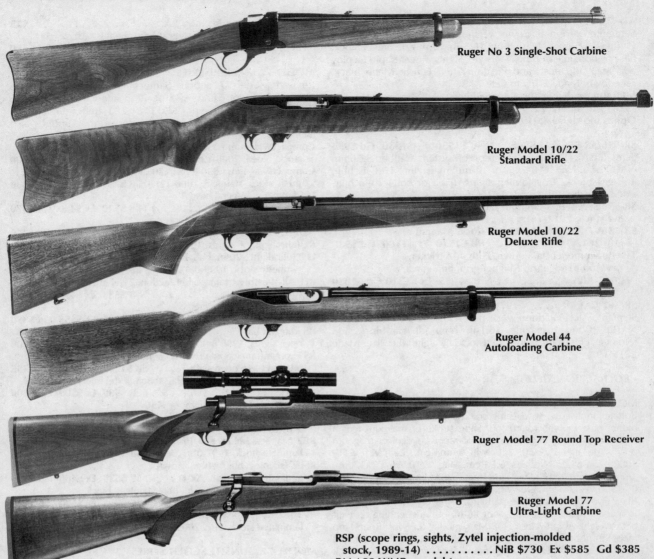

Ruger No 3 Single-Shot Carbine

Ruger Model 10/22
Standard Rifle

Ruger Model 10/22
Deluxe Rifle

Ruger Model 44
Autoloading Carbine

Ruger Model 77 Round Top Receiver

Ruger Model 77
Ultra-Light Carbine

or stainless finish. Checkered American walnut stock. Made 1994 to date.

RH (rings, no sights, 1994-19) . . . . . . NiB $625 Ex $470 Gd $369
RSH (rings & sights, 1994-19) . . . . . NiB $625 Ex $470 Gd $369
**VHZ (stainless finish, laminated
    wood stock, 1995-date)** . . . . NiB $735 Ex $544 Gd $390

MODEL 77/22 SERIES
Bolt action. Push feed 2-lug bolt. Calibers: .22 LR or .22 WMR. 10-shot (.22 LR) or 9-shot (.22 WMR) rotary magazine. 20-in. bbl. 39.75 in. overall. Weight: 5.75 lbs. Integral scope bases; with or w/o sights. Checkered American walnut or Zytel injection-molded stock. Stainless or blued finish. Made 1983 to date. (Blued); stainless. Introduced 1989.
**R (no sights, walnut stock,
    blued, 1984-16)** . . . . NiB $755 Ex $630 Gd $455
**RS (sights, walnut stock,
    blued, 1984-16)** . . . . NiB $785 Ex $660 Gd $485
**RP (scope rings, no sights, Zytel injection-molded
    stock, 1989-14)** . . . . NiB $700 Ex $555 Gd $355

**RSP (scope rings, sights, Zytel injection-molded
    stock, 1989-14)** . . . . NiB $730 Ex $585 Gd $385
**RM (.22 WMR, no sights,
    walnut stock, 1990-16)** . . . . . . NiB $755 Ex $630 Gd $455
**RSM (.22 WMR, sights,
    walnut stock, 1990-16)** . . . . . . NiB $765 Ex $660 Gd $485
**RMP (.22 WMR, no sights, Zytel injection-molded
    stock, 1990-14)** . . . . NiB $700 Ex $555 Gd $355
**RSMP (.22 WMR, sights, Zytel injection-molded
    stock, 1990-14)** . . . . NiB $730 Ex $585 Gd $385
**VBZ (no sights, stainless,
    laminated stock, 1995-16)** . . . NiB $790 Ex $680 Gd $500
**VMBZ (.22 WMR, sights, stainless,
    laminated stock, 1993-16)** . . . NiB $790 Ex $680 Gd $500

MODEL 77/357 SERIES
similar to the 77/44 except in .357 Mag. Made 2017 to date.
blued finish . . . . NiB $940 Ex $600 Gd $640
stainless finish . . . . NiB $855 Ex $755 Gd $580

MODEL 77/44 SERIES
Bolt action. 2-lug push feed bolt. Similar to the 77/22RH. Chambered .44 Rem. Mag. Four round rotary magazine. 18.5-in. bbl. 38.25 in. overall. Weight: 6 lbs. Gold bead front sight, folding adjustable rear w/integral scope base and Ruger rings. Blue or stainless finish. Synthetic or checkered American

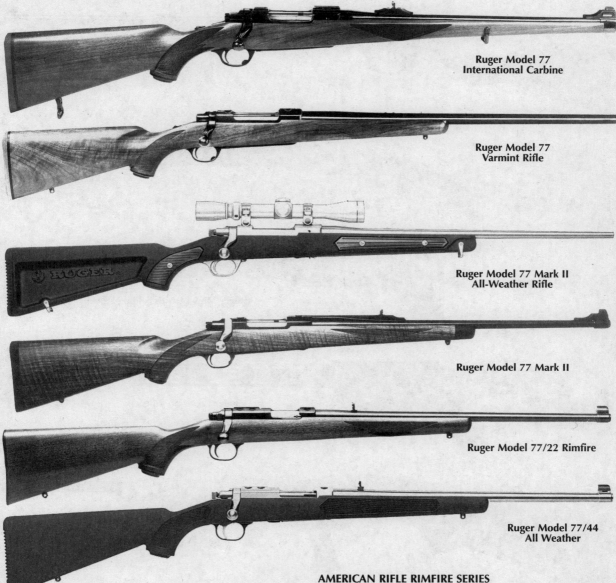

Ruger Model 77 International Carbine

Ruger Model 77 Varmint Rifle

Ruger Model 77 Mark II All-Weather Rifle

Ruger Model 77 Mark II

Ruger Model 77/22 Rimfire

Ruger Model 77/44 All Weather

walnut stock w/rubber buttpad and swivels. Made 1997-04, 2009-16, reintro. 2017.

blued/synthetic stock . . . . .NiB $805 Ex $705 Gd $550
blued/walnut stock . . . . .NiB $875 Ex $775 Gd $620
stainless/synthetic stock . . . . . .NiB $855 Ex $755 Gd $580

AMERICAN RIFLE SERIES
Three-lug push-feed bolt w/70-degree bolt lift, short or long action, integral scope mount, adj. trigger, black polymer stock, flush-fit rotary magzine, no sights. Calibers: .223 Rem., .22-250, .243 Win., .270 Win., 7mm-08, .308 Win., or .30-06. 22-in. bbl. (depending on caliber). Weight: 6.1 to 6.4 lbs. Made 2012 to date.
Standard (blued finish) . . . . . . .NiB $459 Ex $280 Gd $250
All-Weather (22-in. bbl., stainless
   finish) . . . . .NiB $595 Ex $320 Gd $280
All-Weather Compact (18-in. bbl.,
   stainless finish) . . . . .NiB $595 Ex $320 Gd $280
Compact (18-in. bbl., blued finish) . . .NiB $459 Ex $280 Gd $250

AMERICAN RIFLE RIMFIRE SERIES
Push-feed bolt w/60-degree bolt lift, integral scope mount, adj. trigger, black modular polymer stock w/adj. LOP, 22-in. bbl., 9- or 10-rnd. flush-fit rotary magazine, no sights, blued finish. Calibers: .17 HMR, .22 LR, .22 Mag. Weight: 5.5 to 6 lbs. Made 2013 to date.
Standard . . . . .NiB $339 Ex $190 Gd $150
Compact (18-in. bbl.) . . . . .NiB $339 Ex $190 Gd $150
w/threaded bbl., add $30

MODEL HAWKEYE SERIES
Revised Model 77 Mark II action w/same general specifications except w/Mauser style controlled feed, LC6 trigger, one-piece stainless bolt, integral scope base. no sights. Weight: 7 to 8.25 lbs. Made 2007 to date.
HM77R (blued finish) . . . . .NiB $830 Ex $730 Gd $570
African (adj. sights, wood stock w/ebony tip, blued finish,
   2007-12) . . . . .NiB $1030 Ex $880 Gd $655
African (muzzle brake, adj. sights,
   wood stock w/ebony tip
   blued finish, 2013-date) . .NiB $1110 Ex $1000 Gd $730

Ruger Model 96/44

Ruger Mini-14

Ruger Mini-14 with Folding Stock

Ruger Precision Rifle

Ruger Model PC9

Ruger AR-55 MPR (Multi Purpose Rifle)

Ruger American Rifle Predator Model

**Russian Military Model 91/30
Mosin-Nagant Sniper Rifle**

Alaskan (adj. sights, Hogue overmold stock stainless finish,
2007-12) . . . . NiB $955 Ex $905 Gd $755
Alaskan (adj. sights, Hogue overmold stock, matte
stainless, 2019-date) . . . . . NiB $1110 Ex $1010 Gd $730
All-Weather (synthetic stock stainless
finish) . . . . NiB $680 Ex $530 Gd $320
All-Weather Ultra Light (6.5 lbs., synthetic stock stainless
finish, 2009 only) . . . . NiB $580 Ex $330 Gd $280
Compact (walnut stock, 16.5-in. bbl., blue finish,
2009-17, 2020-date) . . . . . . NiB $835 Ex $730 Gd $570
Compact Laminate (laminate stock, 16.5-in. bbl., stainless
finish, 2009-date) . . . . NiB $915 Ex $800 Gd $620
Hunter (optic ready, walnut stock, matte stainless,
2019-date) . . . . NiB $955 Ex $830 Gd $730
Hunter FTW (optic ready, hardwood camo stock,
muzzle brake, matte stainless,
2016-date) . . . . NiB $1105 Ex $1000 Gd $730
International (adj. sights, Mannlicher checkered stock matet
blue finish, 2009-10) . . . . . . NiB $755 Ex $430 Gd $350
Guide Gun (20-in. bbl. w/muzzle brake, express sights,
Green Mountain laminated stock, matte
stainless, 2013-date) . . . . . NiB $1110 Ex $960 Gd $730
Laminated (laminated stock, stainless finish,
2008-10) . . . . NiB $680 Ex $580 Gd $405
Long-Range Hunter (optic ready, laminated stock, muzzle
brake, matte stainless, detachable
magazine, 2018-date) . . . . NiB $1110 Ex $1000 Gd $730
Magnum Hunter (Hogue green overmold stock, stainless
finish, 24-in. bbl. w/muzzle brake, .300 Win. Mag. only,
2013-15) . . . . NiB $905 Ex $795 Gd $530
Predator (22- or 24-in. heavy bbl., laminated stock, stainless
finish,2009-date) . . . . NiB $980 Ex $855 Gd $680
Sporter (22- or 24-in. bbl., brown or black laminate stock matte
stainless finish, 2009-13) . . . NiB $765 Ex $320 Gd $270
Tactical (22-in. heavy bbl., Hogue black
overmold stock, Harris bipod,matte
blue finish, 2009-13) . . . . . NiB $1050 Ex $650 Gd $580
Ultra Light (6.5 lbs., 20-in. bbl., no sights, walnut stock blue
finish, 2009-10) . . . . NiB $695 Ex $410 Gd $360

PRECISION RIFLE SERIES
Bolt-action. Calibers: .243 Win., .300 PRC, .308 Win., 6mm
Creedmoor, 6.5 Creedmoor, 6.5 PRC, .300 Win. Mag., or .338
Lapua Mag. Bbl.: 20-, 24- or 26-in. w/muzzle device, free
floated. Magazine: 10-rnd. detachable Magpul PMAG. Stock:
w/adj. LOP and riser. Sights: Picatinny rail. Finish: Matte black.
Made 2015 to date.
non-magnum calibers . . . . NiB $1280 Ex $955 Gd $730
magnum calibers. . . . . NiB $1780 Ex $1455 Gd $1230

RUSSIAN MILITARY — Tula, Russia
Principal U.S.S.R. Arms Plant, Tula.

MODEL 1891 MOSIN. . . . . NiB $400 Ex $300 Gd $130
Nagant system bolt action. Caliber: 7.62mm Russian. Five
round box magazine. 31.5-in. bbl. Weight: About 9 lbs. Sights:
Open rear; blade front. Full stock w/straight grip. Specifications
given are for WWII version; earlier types differ slightly. Note:
In 1916, Remington Arms Co. and New England Westinghouse
Co. produced 250,000 of these rifles on a contract from the
Imperial Russian Government. Few were delivered to Russia
and the balance bought by the U.S. Government for train-
ing in 1918. Eventually, many of these rifles were sold to
N.R.A. members for about $3 each by the Director of Civilian
Marksmanship.
Sniper model ("PU" style scope,
turned bolt handle) . . . . . . NiB $1600 Ex $1400 Gd $1000

TOKAREV MODEL 40 SEMIAUTO
MILITARY RIFLE . . . . NiB $1800 Ex $1200 Gd $800
Gas-operated. Caliber: 7.62mm Russian. 10-rnd. detachable
box magazine. 24.5-in. bbl. Muzzle brake. Weight: About 9
lbs. Sights: Leaf rear, hooded post front. Full stock w/pistol grip.
Differences among Models 1938,1940 and 1941 are minor.

SAKO — Riihimaki, Finland
*Manufactured by Sako L.T.D. Formerly imported by Stoeger
Industries, Wayne NJ (formerly by Garcia Corp.) until 2000.
Imported by Beretta USA 2001 to date.*

MODEL 72 . . . . NiB $1090 Ex $865 Gd $660
Single model designation replacing Vixen Sporter, Vixen Carbine,
Vixen Heavy Barrel, Forester Sporter, Forester Carbine, Forester
Heavy Barrel, Finnbear Sporter, and Finnbear Carbine, with same
specifications, except all but heavy barrel models fitted with
open rear sight. Values same as for corresponding earlier models.
Imported from 1972 to 1974.

MODEL 74 SERIES
Bolt action. Long-action calibers: .25-06, .270 Win. 7mm Rem.
Mag., .30-06, .300 Win. Mag., .338 Win. Mag., .375 H&H Mag.
Medium-action calibers: .220 Swift, .22-250, .243 Win., .308 Win.
Short-action calibers: .222 Rem., .223 Rem. Magazine: Fixed box.
Barrel: 18-, 23- or 24-in. Stock: Standard wood or Mannlicher-type
stock. Imported from 1974 to 1978.
Carbine model (.30-06, 18-in. bbl.,
Mannlicher-type stock) . . . . . . NiB $700 Ex $600 Gd $400
Heavy Bbl. model, all action lengths
(target-style checkered European walnut
stock w/beavertail forearm) . . NiB $655 Ex $580 Gd $380
Super Sporter model, all action lengths (24-in. bbl.,
checkered European walnut stock w/Monte
Carlo cheekpiece) . . . . NiB $700 Ex $600 Gd $400

MODEL 75 SERIES
Bolt action available in 5 action lengths (Short, Medium, Short
Magnum, Long and Magnum) depending on caliber. Three
locking lugs, 70 degree bolt lift, push feed. Caliber: .17 Rem.,
.222 Rem., .223 Rem., .22-250, .243, .25-06, .260 Rem., .270
Win., .270 WSM, .270 Wby. Mag., .280 Rem., 6.5x55mm,
7mm-08, 7mm Rem. Mag., 7mm RUM, 7mm Wby. Mag.,
7mm STW, 7mm WSM, .308 Win, .30-06, .300 WSM, .300
Win Mag., .300 Wby. Mag., .300 RUM, .338 Win. Mag., .340
Wby. Mag., .375 H&H and .416 Rem. Mag.; detachable or
fixed box 4- to 6-rnd. magazine. Stock: Wood or synthetic w/

RIFLES

rubber recoil pad. Barrel: 22- or 24.37-in. Weight: 6.5-9 lbs. depending on caliber. Sights: Drilled/tapped, w/ or w/o sights. 3-position tang safety. Mfg. 1997-2007.

Custom Deluxe model (oil finish checkered walnut
w/rosewood tip stock) . . . NiB $3755 Ex $3255 Gd $2180
Deluxe model (gloss checkered walnut
w/rosewood tip stock) . . . . NiB $1705 Ex $1455 Gd $930
Grey Wold model (stainless steel bbl., no sights, gray stock
laminated and checkered
stock, 2005-07). . . . . NiB $1230 Ex $930 Gd $705
Hunter model (checkered walnut stock,
no sights) . . . . NiB $1130 Ex $905 Gd $630
King Ranch model (similar to Deluxe model,
2006-07). . . . . NiB $2055 Ex $1655 Gd $1055
Single Shot model (stainless heavy bbl., no
sights, 2004-07) . . . . NiB $2855 Ex $2380 Gd $1855
Stainless Synthetic model (matte stainless,
black composite stock) . . . . . NiB $1155 Ex $905 Gd $645
Stainless Varmint Laminate model (23.6-in.
heavy bbl., matte stainless, no sights, brown
laminated stock, 1999-05) . NiB $1480 Ex $1180 Gd $770
Stainless Varmint Laminate w/set trigger
model (23.6-in. heavy bbl., matte stainless,
no sights, brown laminated stock,
1999-05). . . . . NiB $1680 Ex $1380 Gd $855
Stainless Walnut model (matte stainless, checkered
walnut stock, 1992-02) . . . . . NiB $1055 Ex $845 Gd $580
Varmint model (23.6-in. heavy bbl.,
no sights, beavertail forend stock,
1998-08). . . . . NiB $1405 Ex $1005 Gd $730
Varmint w/set trigger model (23.6-in.
heavy bbl., no sights, beavertail forend
stock, 2005-07). . . . . NiB $1580 Ex $1280 Gd $805

MODEL 78 SERIES

Bolt action. Caliber: .22 LR or .22 WMR; 5-rnd. magazine. 22.5-in. bbl. Weight, 6.75 lbs. No sights. Checkered European walnut stock, Monte Carlo cheekpiece. Imported from 1977–86.

Super Rimfire model . . . . . . NiB $1255 Ex $1105 Gd $855
Super Hornet model (.22 Hornet, 4-rnd.
magazine, 1977-87) . . . . . NiB $1255 Ex $1105 Gd $855

MODEL 85 SERIES

Bolt action available in 6 action lengths (Extra Small, Small, Samll-Medium, Medium, Large and Extra Large) depending on caliber. Three locking lugs, 70 degree bolt lift, control feed. Caliber: .22-250 thru .338 Lapua Mag.; detachable 4-, 5- or 6-rnd. magazine. Stock: Wood or synthetic w/rubber recoil pad. Barrel: 20.25- to 26-in. Weight: 7-9.5 lbs. depending on caliber. Sights: Drilled/tapped, w/ or w/o sights. Mfg. 2009-date.

Bavarian model (Bavarian cheek
piece stock w/rosewood tip,
w/sights, set trigger) . . . . . NiB $2000 Ex $1755 Gd $1355
Black Wolf model (wood stock
w/adj. LOP and cheekpiece,
2018-19). . . . . NiB $2030 Ex $1780 Gd $1380
Carbon Stainless model (matte stainless,
black carbon fiber stock, adj.
trigger, 2015-date) . . . . . . NiB $2805 Ex $2455 Gd $1905
Carbon Wolf model (carbon
fiber stock w/adj. LOP and
cheekpiece, 2018-date) . . NiB $3190 Ex $2790 Gd $2170
Classic model (checkered walnut
stock w/rosewood tip,
w/sights, 2009-date) . . . . . NiB $2045 Ex $1790 Gd $1390
Finn Bear model (Monte Carlo walnut stock,
optic ready, 2015) . . . . NiB $2040 Ex $1680 Gd $1005

Finnlight Stainless model (stainless,
black synthetic stock, optic
ready, 2001-date) . . . . NiB $1625 Ex $1425 Gd $1105
Finnlight II Stainless model (Cerakote
stainless finish, composite stock,
optic ready, 2018-date). . . NiB $2190 Ex $1915 Gd $1490
Grey Wolf model (checkered grey laminate
stock, 2007-date) . . . . NiB $1530 Ex $1355 Gd $1055
Hunter model (checkered walnut stock,
blued, 2006-08) . . . . NiB $1405 Ex $1105 Gd $780
Kodiak model (grey laminate stock, blued,
sights, 2009-date) . . . . NiB $1745 Ex $1530 Gd $1190
Long Range model (checkered laminate
stock, muzzle brake, no sights,
2016-date) . . . . NiB $2600 Ex $2280 Gd $1780
Stainless Synthetic model
(matte stainless, black synthetic
stock, 2007-08). . . . . NiB $1280 Ex $980 Gd $680
Synthetic model (blued, black synthetic
stock, 2014-15). . . . . NiB $1490 Ex $1180 Gd $805
Varmint model (no sights, uncheckered
walnut or brown laminated
stock, 2008-date) . . . . NiB $1830 Ex $1600 Gd $1245

MODEL A7 SERIES

Similar to the Model 85 and Tikka T3. Two action lengths (Short and Medium) depending on caliber. Caliber: .22-250 Rem. thru .300 Win. Mag.; detachable magazine. Stock: Synthetic w/ recoil pad. Barrel: 22.4- or 24.3-in. Weight: 7-8 lbs. depending on caliber. Sights: Weaver style base. Finish: Blue. Mfg. 2009-11.

Blue model . . . . NiB $830 Ex $705 Gd $555
Stainless . . . . NiB $1205 Ex $1055 Gd $755
Big Game Roughtech model
(synthetic Roughneck pistol
grip stock, 2014-17) . . . . . . NiB $1105 Ex $955 Gd $730
Coyote Roughtech model
(synthetic Roughneck pistol
grip stock, 2016-17) . . . . . . NiB $1055 Ex $930 Gd $705
Long Range Roughtech model
(synthetic Roughneck pistol
grip stock, 2016-17) . . . . . . NiB $1280 Ex $1055 Gd $805

SUPER DELUXE SERIES . . . . NIB $2410 EX $1830 GD $1255
Same specifications as Standard Grade except w/22 lines to the in. French checkering, rosewood grip cap and forend tip, semibeavertail forend. Grade AI (short action), Grade AII (medium action), Grade AIII (long action). Disc. 1997.

DELUXE LIGHTWEIGHT BOLT-ACTION

RIFLE. . . . . NiB $1190 Ex $1021 Gd $699
Same general specifications as Hunter Lightweight except w/ beautifully grained French walnut stock; superb high-gloss finish, fine hand-cut checkering, rosewood forend tip and grip cap. Imported from 1985-97.

FIBERCLASS . . . . NiB $1137 Ex $1077 Gd $650
Bolt action. All-weather fiberglass stock version of Sako barreled long action. Calibers: .25-06, .270, .30-06, 7mm Rem. Mag., .300 Win. Mag., .338 Win. Mag., .375 H&H Mag. Bbl. length: 22.5 in. Overall length: 44.25 in. Weight: 7.25 lbs. Imported 1984 to 1996.

Carbine model (18.5-in. bbl.,
1986–91) . . . . NiB $1000 Ex $900 Gd $730

FINNBEAR SERIES

Long Mauser-type bolt action. Calibers: .25-06, .264 Mag. .270, .30-06, .300 Win. Mag., .338 Mag., 7mm Mag., .375 H&H

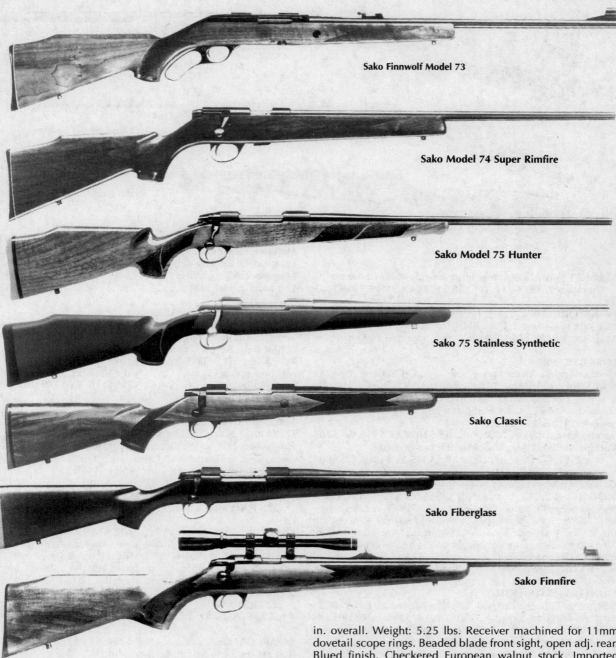

Sako Finnwolf Model 73

Sako Model 74 Super Rimfire

Sako Model 75 Hunter

Sako 75 Stainless Synthetic

Sako Classic

Sako Fiberglass

Sako Finnfire

Mag.; 5-rnd. standard caliber or 4-rnd. magnum caliber. 24-in. bbl. Weight: 7 lbs. Hooded ramp front sight. Sporter stock w/ Monte Carlo cheekpiece, checkered pistol-grip and forearm, recoil pad, swivels. Imported 1961-71.

Sporter model . . . . NiB $1105 Ex $980 Gd $730
Carbine model (20-in. bbl., Mannlicher-type
   full stock) . . . . NiB $1305 Ex $1105 Gd $805
Deluxe model (skipline checkered
   walnut w/rosewood tip stock,
   engraved floorplate) . . . . NiB $1655 Ex $1405 Gd $1000

FINNFIRE/FINNFIRE II SERIES
Mini-Sporter built for rimfires on a scaled-down Sako design. Caliber: .22 LR. 5- or 10-rnd. magazine. 22-in. bbl. 39.5 in. overall. Weight: 5.25 lbs. Receiver machined for 11mm dovetail scope rings. Beaded blade front sight, open adj. rear. Blued finish. Checkered European walnut stock. Imported from 1994 to 2005.

Hunter model . . . . NiB $855 Ex $730 Gd $530
Varmint model . . . . NiB $900 Ex $775 Gd $575
Sporter model . . . . NiB $980 Ex $855 Gd $655
Finnfire II (.17 HMR or .22 LR,
   oil finish wood stock, 22-in.
   bbl., 2014-17) . . . . NiB $955 Ex $830 Gd $655

FINNWOLF
(MODEL 73) SERIES . . . . . . NIB $1755 EX $1505 GD $1305
Lever action. Hammerless. Calibers: .243 Win., .308 Win. Four round clip magazine. 23-in. bbl. Weight: 6.75 lbs. Hooded ramp front sight. Sporter stock w/Monte Carlo cheekpiece, checkered pistol-grip and forearm, swivels (available w/right- or left-hand stock). Imported 1963 to 1972.

Sako Finnfire Heavy Barrel

Sako Forester Sporter

Sako Golden Anniversary

Model 73 (3-rnd. magazine, flush floorplate, stock has no cheekpiece, 1973-75) . . . . NiB $1755 Ex $1505 Gd $1305

FINNSPORT 2707 . . . . NiB $808 Ex $597 Gd $466
Bolt-action. Calibers: .270, .30-06, 7mm Rem. Mag., .300 Win. Mag. Bbl. length: 24 in. Weight: 8 lbs. Imported 1984 to 1986.

FORESTER SERIES
Medium-length Mauser-type bolt action. Calibers: .22-250, .243 Win., .308 Win.; 5-rnd. magazine. 23-in. bbl. Weight: 6.5 lbs. Hooded ramp front sight. Sporter stock w/Monte Carlo cheekpiece, checkered pistol grip and forearm, swivels. Imported 1957–71.
Sporter model . . . . NiB $1055 Ex $930 Gd $705
**Carbine model (20-in. bbl., Mannl icher-type full
   stock, 1958-71)** . . . . NiB $1305 Ex $1105 Gd $805

GOLDEN ANNIVERSARY
MODEL . . . . NiB $2866 Ex $2210 Gd $1570
Special presentation-grade rifle issued in 1973 to commemorate Sako's 50th anniversary. 1,000 (numbered 1 to 1,000) made. Same specifications as Deluxe Sporter: Long action, 7mm Rem. Mag. receiver, trigger guard and floorplate decorated w/gold oak leaf and acorn motif. Stock of select European walnut, checkering bordered w/hand-carved oak leaf pattern.

HUNTER LIGHTWEIGHT
Bolt action. Calibers: AI (Short Action) .17 Rem., .222 Rem., .223 Rem.; AII (Medium Action) .22-250 Rem., .243 Win., .308 Win.; AIII (Long Action) .25-06 Rem., .270 Win., .30-06, .338 Win. Mag., and .375 H&H Mag. 5- or 6-rnd. magazine. Bbl. length: 21.5 in., AI; 22 in., AII; 22.5 in., AIII. Overall length: 42.25-44.5 in. Weight: 5.75 lbs., AI; 6.75 lbs. AII; 7.25 lbs., AIII. Monte Carlo-style European walnut stock, oil finished. Hand-checkered pistol-grip and forend. Imported from 1985-97. Left-hand version intro. 1987.
AI (Short Action) models . . . . . . NiB $855 Ex $690 Gd $495
AII (Medium Action) models. . . . NiB $855 Ex $690 Gd $495
AII (Long Action) models . . . . . . NiB $895 Ex $730 Gd $535
magnum calibers, add. $60
Left-hand model, add $80
Carbine model (18.5-in. bbl.) . . . NiB $730 Ex $655 Gd $495

LAMINATED
Similar in style and specifications to Hunter Grade except w/ stock of resin-bonded hardwood veneers. Available 18 calibers in AI (Short), AII (Medium) or AV action, left-hand version in 10 calibers, AV only. Imported from 1987 to 1995.

Short Action models . . . . NiB $1030 Ex $835 Gd $595
Medium Action models. . . . . . . NiB $990 Ex $795 Gd $555
Long Action models . . . . NiB $1050 Ex $855 Gd $615
Magnum calibers, add. $85
Left-hand model, add $100

MANNLICHER-STYLE CARBINE
Similar to Hunter Model except w/full Mannlicher-style stock and 18.5-in. bbl. Weighs 7.5 lbs. Chambered in .243, .25-06, .270, .308, .30-06, 7mm Rem. Mag., .300 Win. Mag., .338 Win. Mag., .375 H&H. Imported 1977–96.
Medium action . . . . NiB $1055 Ex $830 Gd $555
Long action . . . . NiB $1110 Ex $870 Gd $580
Magnum calibers, add. $65

MAUSER ACTION . . . . NiB $700 Ex $505 Gd $350
FN Mauser action. Calibers: .270, .30-06. Five round magazine. 24-in. bbl. Sights: Open rear leaf; Partridge front; hooded ramp. Checkered stock w/Monte Carlo comb and cheekpiece. Weight: 7.5 lbs. Imported from 1950 to 1957.
**Magnum Mauser action
   (w/recoil pad, .300 H&H Mag.,
   .375 H&H Mag.)** . . . . NiB $750 Ex $640 Gd $500

QUAD. . . . . NIB $765 EX $655 GD $505
Bolt-action. 50 degree bolt lift. Interchangeable barrels in four different rimfire calibers: .17 HMR; .17 Mach 2, .22 LR, and .22 WMR. Barrel: 22-in. Finish: Blued Weight: 5.75 lbs. Stock: Black synthetic w/adj. buttpad. Imported 2005–07
**2 bbl. set (.17 HMR or
   .22 LR, 2008)** . . . . NiB $1505 Ex $1255 Gd $880
4 bbl. set (2005–11) . . . . NiB $1480 Ex $1280 Gd $905

SAFARI GRADE . . . . NiB $2240 Ex $1790 Gd $1255
Bolt action. Long action. Calibers: .300 Win. Mag., .338 Win. Mag., .375 H&H. Oil-finished European walnut stock w/hand-checkering. Barrel band swivel, express-type sight rib; satin or matte blue finish. Imported from 1980 to 1996.

SPORTER DELUXE . . . . NiB $1290 Ex $1045 Gd $687
Same as Vixen, Forester, Finnbear and Model 74 except w/ fancy French walnut stock w/skip checkering, rosewood forend tip and pistol-grip cap, recoil pad, inlaid trigger guard and floorplate. Disc.

STANDARD GRADE AI . . . . . . NiB $1077 Ex $823 Gd $440
Short bolt-action. Calibers: .17 Rem., .222 Rem., .223 Rem. Five round magazine. 23.5-in. bbl. Weight: 6.5 lbs. No sights. Checkered European walnut stock w/Monte Carlo cheekpiece, QD swivel studs. Imported 1978 to 1985.

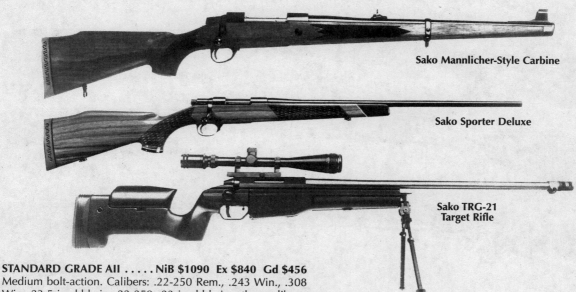

Sako Mannlicher-Style Carbine

Sako Sporter Deluxe

Sako TRG-21 Target Rifle

STANDARD GRADE AII . . . . . NiB $1090 Ex $840 Gd $456
Medium bolt-action. Calibers: .22-250 Rem., .243 Win., .308 Win. 23.5-in. bbl. in .22-250; 23-in. bbl. in other calibers. Five round magazine. Weight: 7.25 lbs. Checkered European walnut stock w/Monte Carlo cheekpiece, QD swivel studs. Imported from 1978 to 1985.

STANDARD GRADE AIII . . . . . NiB $1178 Ex $843 Gd $545
Long bolt action. Calibers: .25-06 Rem., .270 Win., .30-06, 7mm Rem. Mag., .300 Win. Mag., .338 Win. Mag., .375 H&H. 24-in. bbl. 4-rnd. magazine. Weight: 8 lbs. Imported from 1978 to 1984.

TRG BOLT-ACTION TARGET RIFLE
Caliber: .308 Win., .330 Win. or .338 Lapua Mag. Detachable 10-rnd. magazine. 25.75- or 27.2-in. bbl. Weight: 10.5 to 11 lbs. Blued action w/stainless barrel. Adjustable two-stage trigger. modular reinforced polyurethane target stock w/adj. cheekpiece and buttplate. Options: Muzzle break; detachable bipod; QD sling swivels and scope mounts w/1-in. or 30mm rings. Imported from 1993 to 2004.
TRG 21 .308 Win . . . . NiB $2376 Ex $2099 Gd $1545
TRG 22 .308 Win . . . . NiB $2459 Ex $2288 Gd $1590
TRG 41 .338 Lapua . . . . NiB $2788 Ex $2690 Gd $1877
TRG-42 (.300 Win Mag. or .338
Lapua) . . . . NiB $3154 Ex $2651 Gd $1835

TRG-S BOLT-ACTION RIFLE
Calibers: .243, 7mm-08, .270, .30-06, 7mm Rem. Mag., .300 Win. Mag., .338 Win. Mag. Five shot magazine (standard calibers), 4-shot (magnum), 22- or 24-in. bbl. 45.5 in. overall. Weight: 7.75 lbs. No sights. Reinforced polyurethane stock w/ Monte Carlo. Imported 1993–2004.
Standard calibers . . . . NiB $823 Ex $707 Gd $466
Magnum calibers . . . . NiB $880 Ex $844 Gd $545

VARMINT RIFLE . . . . NiB $1030 Ex $800 Gd $550
Available in short and medium action w/ heavy 22.75-in. bbl. Caliber: .17 Rem., .222 Rem., .223 Rem., .22-250 Rem., .243 Win., 7mm-08 or .308 Win. Disc. 1997.

VIXEN SERIES
Short Mauser-type bolt-action. Cal.: .218 Bee, .22 Hornet, .222 Rem., .222 Rem. Mag., .223 Rem.; 5-rnd. magazine. 23.5-in. bbl. Weight: 6.5 lbs. Hooded ramp front sight. Sporter stock w/ Monte Carlo cheekpiece, checkered pistol-grip and forearm, swivels. Imported 1946-71.

Sporter model . . . . NiB $1055 Ex $930 Gd $705
Carbine model (20-in. bbl., Mannlicher-type
full stock) . . . . NiB $1305 Ex $1105 Gd $805
Heavy Barrel model (heavy bbl., target-style stock
w/beavertail forearm) . . . . . . NiB $1055 Ex $930 Gd $705

J. P. SAUER & SOHN — Eckernforde, Germany
Formerly Suhl, Germany. Imported by Sigarms Exeter, NH, previously by Paul Company Inc. and G.U. Inc.

MAUSER BOLT-ACTION SPORTING
RIFLE. . . . . NiB $1457 Ex $1089 Gd $777
Calibers: 7x57 and 8x57mm most common, but these rifles were produced in a variety of calibers including most of the popular Continental calibers as well as our .30-06. Five round box magazine. 22- or 24-in. Krupp steel bbl., half-octagon w/ raised matted rib. Double-set trigger. Weight: 7.5 lbs. Sights: Three-leaf open rear; ramp front. Sporting stock w/cheek-piece, checkered pistol grip, raised side-panels, Schnabel tip, swivels. Also made w/20-in. bbl. and full-length stock. Mfd. before WWII.

MODEL S-90 BOLT-ACTION RIFLES
Calibers: .243 Win., .308 Win. (Short action); .25-06, .270 Win., .30-06 (Medium action); 7mm Rem. Mag., .300 Win. Mag., .300 Wby., .338 Win., .375 H&H (Magnum action). Four round (standard) or 3-rnd. magazine (magnum). Bbl. length: 20-in. (Stutzen), 24-in. Weight: 7.6 to 10.75 lbs. Adjustable (Supreme) checkered Monte Carlo style stock. contrasting forend and pistol grip cap w/high-gloss finish or European (Lux) checkered Classic-style European walnut stock w/satin oil finish. Imported from 1983 to 1989.
S-90 Standard . . . . NiB $1154 Ex $990 Gd $587
S-90 Lux . . . . NiB $1389 Ex $1100 Gd $654
S-90 Safari. . . . . NiB $1411 Ex $1127 Gd $665
S-90 Stutzen . . . . NiB $1144 Ex $994 Gd $482
S-90 Supreme . . . . NiB $1490 Ex $1167 Gd $800
Grade I engraving, add $650
Grade II engraving, add $850
Grade III engraving add $1200
Grade IV engraving, add. $1717

GRADING: **NiB** = New in Box   **Ex** = Excellent or NRA 95%   **Gd** = Good or NRA 68%

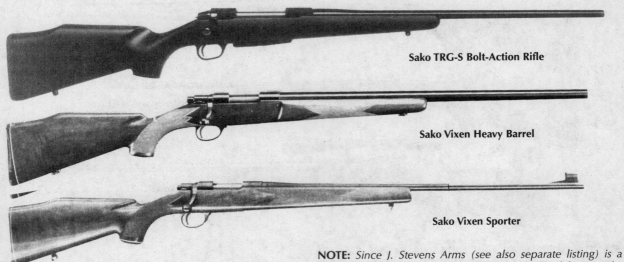

Sako TRG-S Bolt-Action Rifle

Sako Vixen Heavy Barrel

Sako Vixen Sporter

MODEL 200 BOLT-ACTION RIFLES

Calibers: .243 Win., .25-06, .270 Win., 7mm Rem Mag., .30-06, .308 Win., .300 Win. Mag., Detachable box magazine. 24-in. (American) or 26-in. (European) interchangeable bbl. Standard (steel) or lightweight (alloy) action. Weight: 6.6 to 7.75 lbs. 44 in. overall. Stock options: American Model w/checkered Monte Carlo style 2-piece stock contrasting forend and pistol grip cap w/high gloss finish and no sights. European walnut stock w/Schnabel forend, satin oil finish and iron sights. Contemporary Model w/synthetic carbon fiber stock. Imported from 1986 to 1993.

Standard model	NiB $1266	Ex $1093	Gd $707
Lightweight model	NiB $1278	Ex $1043	Gd $580
Contemporary model	NiB $1260	Ex $1017	Gd $565
American model	NiB $1260	Ex $1017	Gd $565
European model	NiB $1395	Ex $1070	Gd $532
Left-hand model, add			$200
Magnum calibers, add			$130
Interchangeable bbl. assembly, add			$325

MODEL 202 BOLT-ACTION RIFLES

Calibers: .243 Win., 6.5x55, 6.5x57, 6.6x68, .25-06, .270 Win., .280 7x64, .308, .30-06, Springfield, 7mm Rem. Mag., .300 Win. Mag., .300 Wby. Mag., 8x68S, .338 Win. Mag., .375 H&H Mag. Removable 3-rnd. box magazine. 23.6- and 26-in. interchangable bbl. 44.3 and 46 in. overall. Modular receiver drilled and tapped for scope bases. Adjustable two-stage trigger w/dual release safety. Weight: 7.7 to 8.4 lbs. Stock options: Checkered Monte Carlo-style select American walnut two-piece stock; Euro-classic French walnut two-piece stock w/semi Schnabel forend and satin oil finish; Super Grade Claro walnut two-piece stock fitted w/rosewood forend and grip cap w/high-gloss epoxy finish. Imported from 1994 to 2004.

Standard model	NiB $2660	Ex $1848	Gd $983
Euro-Classic model	NiB $1369	Ex $897	Gd $633
Super Grade model	NiB $1119	Ex $888	Gd $603
Left-hand model, add			$150
Magnum calibers, add			$126
Interchangeable bbl. assembly, add			$295

SAVAGE ARMS — Westfield, MA

Formerly Chicopee Falls, MA, and Utica, NY. Acquired by ATK in 2013.

NOTE: *Since J. Stevens Arms (see also separate listing) is a division of Savage Industries, certain Savage models carry the "Stevens" name.*

To facilitate locating Savage rifles, discontinued and current models are grouped into five categories: Bolt-action Rifles (below), Break-action Rifles, Lever-action Rifles, Semiauto Rifles, and Slide-Action Rifles. For complete model listings, please refer to the index.

- BOLT-ACTION RIFLES -

MODEL 1904 . . . . NiB $228 Ex $140 Gd $90
Bolt-action, single-shot. Takedown. .22 Short, Long, LR. 18-in. bbl. Weight: About 3 lbs. Sights: Open rear; bead front. Plain, straight-grip, one-piece stock. Made 1904-17.

MODEL 1905 . . . . NiB $220 Ex $138 Gd $85
Bolt-action, single-shot. Takedown. .22 Short, Long, LR. 22-in. bbl. Weight: About 5 lbs. Sights: Open rear; bead front. Plain, straight-grip one-piece stock. Made 1905-19.

MODEL 3 SERIES

BOLT ACTION. SINGLE SHOT. . . NiB $100 Ex $61 Gd $59
Takedown. Caliber: .22 Short, Long, LR. 26-in. bbl. on prewar rifles, postwar production w/24-in. bbl. Weight: 5 lbs. Sights: Open rear; bead front. Plain pistol-grip stock. Made 1933 to 1952.
3S (peep rear sight, hooded front,
1933–42) . . . . NiB $116 Ex $89 Gd $59
3ST (fitted w/swivels and sling,
1933–42) . . . . NiB $120 Ex $85 Gd $50

MODEL 4 SERIES . . . . NiB $149 Ex $90 Gd $59
Takedown. Caliber: .22 Short, Long, LR. Five round detachable box magazine. 24-in. bbl. Weight: 5.5 lbs. Sights: Open rear; bead front. Checkered pistol-grip stock on prewar models, early production had grooved forearm; postwar rifles have plain stocks. Made 1933-65.
4M (.22 WMR, 1933–42) . . . . NiB $110 Ex $95 Gd $60
4S (peep rear sight, hooded front,
1933–42) . . . . NiB $120 Ex $105 Gd $70

MODEL 5 SERIES . . . . NiB $126 Ex $78 Gd $57
Same as Model 4 except w/tubular magazine (holds 21 Short, 17 Long, 15 LR), weight: 6 lbs. Made 1936-61.
5S (peep rear sight, hooded front,
1936–42) . . . . NiB $120 Ex $105 Gd $70

MODEL 19
TARGET RIFLE SERIES . . . . NiB $325 Ex $270 Gd $209
Model of 1933. Speed lock. Caliber: .22 LR. Five round detachable box magazine. 25-in. bbl. Weight: 8 lbs. Adj. rear peep sight, blade front on early models, later production equipped w/extension rear sight, hooded front. Target stock w/full pistol-grip and beavertail forearm. Made 1933-46.

19 NRA (full military stock w/pistol-grip,
1919–33) . . . . NiB $300 Ex $205 Gd $126
19H (.22 Hornet, w/Model 23D-type bolt mechanism, loading
port, magazine, 1933–42) . . . . . NiB $575 Ex $340 Gd $265
19L (Lyman No. 48Y receiver sight, 17A front sight,
1933–42) . . . . NiB $348 Ex $290 Gd $185
19M (heavy 28-in.bbl. w/scope bases, 9.25 lbs.,
1933–42) . . . . NiB $356 Ex $465 Gd $227

MODEL 20-1926 HI-POWER . . NiB $944 Ex $725 Gd $420
Same as Model 1920, except w/24-in. medium weight bbl., improved stock, Lyman 54 rear peep sight, weight: 7 lbs. Made 1926-29.

MODEL 23 SERIES
Bolt-action. Caliber: 22 LR. 5-rnd. detachable box magazine. 23-in. bbl. Weight: 6 lbs. Sights: Open rear, blade or bead front. Plain pistol-grip stock w/slender forearm and Schnabel tip. Made 1923–33.

23A . . . . NiB $270 Ex $208 Gd $177
23AA (speed lock, improved stock,
6.5 lbs., 1933–42) . . . . NiB $370 Ex $278 Gd $200
23B (.25-20, 25-in. bbl., improved
stock w/full forearm, 6.5 lbs.,
1923–42) . . . . NiB $333 Ex $235 Gd $179
23C (.32-20, 1923–42) . . . . NiB $389 Ex $290 Gd $175
23D (.22 Hornet, 1933–47) . . . . NiB $415 Ex $300 Gd $220

MODEL 25 VARMINTER SERIES
Lightweight Varminter Series. Calibers: .17 Hornet, .22 Hornet, .204 Ruger or .223 Rem., 4-rnd detachable magazine. 22- or 24-in. bbl. No sights, optic ready. Stock: laminate wood. Finish: matte blue. Weight: 8.25 lbs. Length: 43.75 in. Accutrigger. Made 2008 to date.

Lightweight Varminter . . . . NiB $665 Ex $585 Gd $370
Classic (22-in. bbl., 2008–10) . . . NiB $690 Ex $580 Gd $380
Varminter-T (thumbhole stock) . . NiB $690 Ex $580 Gd $380
Walking Varminter (black
synthetic stock, 2011–date) . . NiB $505 Ex $405 Gd $240
Walking Varminter Camo
(RealTree Extra or Realtree Max 1 stock), add $50

MODEL 35
MODEL 35 . . . . NiB $90 Ex $80 Gd $70
Bolt-action. Caliber: .22 LR, 5-rnd. magazine. 22-in. bbl. Discontinued 1985.

MODEL 36
MODEL 36 . . . . NiB $90 Ex $80 Gd $70
Simialr to Model 35 except single-shot. 22-in. bbl. Made 1983-84.

MODEL 40
MODEL 40 . . . . NiB $379 Ex $280 Gd $227
Bolt-action. Standard Grade. Calibers: .250-3000, .300 Sav., .30-30, .30-06. Four round detachable box magazine. 22-in. bbl. in calibers .250-3000 and .30-30; 24-in. in .300 Sav. and .30-06. Weight: 7.5 lbs. Sights: Open rear; bead front, on ramp. Plain pistol-grip stock w/tapered forearm and Schnabel tip. Made 1928-40.

MODEL 45 SUPER SPORTER
MODEL 45 SUPER SPORTER . . NiB $423 Ex $265 Gd $220
Special Grade. Same as Model 40 except w/checkered pistol-grip and forearm, Lyman No. 40 receiver sight. Made 1928-40.

MODEL 46
MODEL 46 . . . . NiB $90 Ex $80 Gd $70
Simialr to Model 35 except w/tubular magazine. Made 1969-73.

MODEL 63K KEY LOCK
MODEL 63K KEY LOCK . . . . NiB $120 Ex $90 Gd $60
Bolt action, single shot. Trigger locked w/key. Caliber: .22 Short, Long, LR. 18-in. bbl. Weight: 4 lbs. Sights: Open rear; hooded ramp front. Full-length stock w/pistol grip, swivels. Made 1970-72.

63KM (.22 WMR, 1970-72) . . . . NiB $125 Ex $100 Gd $65

MODEL 1920 HI-POWER BOLT-ACTION RIFLE
Short Mauser-type action. Calibers: .250/3000, .300 Sav. Five round box magazine. 22-in. bbl. in .250 cal.; 24-in. in .300 cal. Weight: About 6 lbs. Sights: Open rear; bead front. Checkered pistol-grip stock w/slender forearm and Schnabel tip. Made 1920-26.

.250-3000 Savage . . . . NiB $1029 Ex $833 Gd $690
.300 Savage . . . . NiB $969 Ex $755 Gd $588

NOTE: *Anschutz In 1965, Savage began the importation of rifles manufactured by J. G. Anschutz GmbH, Ulm, West Germany. Models designated "Savage/Anschutz" are listed in this section, those marketed in the U.S. under the "Anschutz" name are included in that firm's listings. Anschutz rifles are now distributed in the U.S. by Precision Sales Int'l., Westfield, Mass. See "Anschutz" for detailed specifications.*

MARK 10 BOLT-ACTION
TARGET RIFLE. . . . . NiB $534 Ex $359 Gd $265
Single shot. Caliber: .22 LR. 26-in. bbl. Weight: 8.5 lbs. Sights: Anschutz micrometer rear; globe front. Target stock w/full pistol-grip and cheekpiece, adj. hand stop and swivel. Made 1967-72.

MARK 10D. . . . . NiB $544 Ex $369 Gd $259
Same as Mark 10 except has redesigned stock with Monte Carlo comb, different rear sight. Weight: 7.75 lbs. Made in 1972.

MODEL 54 CUSTOM SPORTER NiB $766 Ex $639 Gd $400
Same as Anschutz Model 1422D.

MODEL 54M. . . . . NiB $945 Ex $670 Gd $439
Same as Anschutz Model 1522D.

MODEL 64 BOLT-ACTION
TARGET. . . . . NiB $655 Ex $512 Gd $338
Same as Anschutz Model 1403.

MODEL 153 BOLT-ACTION
SPORTER. . . . . NiB $697 Ex $488 Gd $349
Caliber: .222 Rem. Three round clip magazine. 24-in. bbl. Sights: Folding leaf open rear; hooded ramp front. Weight: 6.75 lbs. French walnut stock w/cheekpiece, skip checkering, rosewood forend tip and grip cap, swivels. Made 1964-67.

MODEL 153S . . . . NiB $770 Ex $556 Gd $390
Same as Model 153 except has double-set trigger. Made 1965-67.

MODEL 164 CUST. SPORTER. NiB $775 Ex $561 Gd $195
Same as Anschutz Model 1416.

MODEL 164M. . . . . NiB $660 Ex $454 Gd $300
Same as Anschutz Model 1516.

RIFLES

MODEL 184 SPORTER . . . . NiB $638 Ex $484 Gd $288
Same as Anschutz Model 1441.

**MODEL 34 BOLT-ACTION
REPEATER.** . . . . NiB $190 Ex $126 Gd $88
Caliber: .22 Short, Long, LR. 20-in. bbl. Weight: 4.75 lbs.
Sights: Open rear; bead front. Plain pistol-grip stock. Made
1965-80.

MODEL 34M. . . . . NiB $190 Ex $146 Gd $98
Same as Model 34 except chambered for 22 WMR. Made
1969-73.

MODEL 35 . . . . NiB $190 Ex $146 Gd $98
Bolt-action repeater. Caliber: 22 LR. Six round clip magazine.
22-in. bbl. Weight: About 5 lbs. Sights: Open rear; ramp front.
Monte Carlo stock w/checkered pistol grip and forearm. Made
1982-85.

MODEL 35M . . . . NiB $219 Ex $140 Gd $100
Same as Model 35 except chambered for .22 WMR. Made
1982-85.

MODEL 36 . . . . NiB $90 Ex $80 Gd $70
Same as Model 35 except single shot. Made 1983-84.

MODEL 46 . . . . NiB $190 Ex $136 Gd $100
Bolt-action. Caliber: .22 Short, Long, LR. Tubular magazine
holds 22 Short, 17 Long, 15 LR. 20-in. bbl. Weight: 5 lbs. Plain
pistol-grip stock on early production; later models have Monte
Carlo stock w/checkering. Made 1969-73.

MODEL 65 . . . . NiB $219 Ex $138 Gd $99
Bolt-action. Caliber: .22 Short, Long, LR. Five round clip magazine. 20-in. bbl. Weight: 5 lbs. Sights: Open rear; ramp front.
Monte Carlo stock w/checkered pistol grip and forearm. Made
1969-73.

MODEL 65M. . . . . NiB $200 Ex $134 Gd $90
Same as Model 65 except chambered for .22 WMR, has 22-in.
bbl., weighs 5.25 lbs. Made 1969-81.

**MODEL 73 BOLT-ACTION
SINGLE-SHOT.** . . . . NiB $159 Ex $138 Gd $89
Caliber: .22 Short, Long, LR. 20-in. bbl. Weight: 4.75 lbs. Sights:
Open rear; bead front. Plain pistol-grip stock. Made 1965-80.

MODEL 73Y YOUTH MODEL. . . NiB $150 Ex $110 Gd $90
Same as Model 73 except has 18-in. bbl., 1.5-in. shorter buttstock, weight: 4.5 lbs. Made 1965-80.

MODEL 74 LITTLE FAVORITE. . . NiB $167 Ex $115 Gd $98
Same as Model 72 Crackshot except has black-finished frame,
22-in. round bbl., walnut-finished hardwood stock. Weight:
4.75 lbs. Made 1972-74.

MODEL 93 SERIES
Bolt-action. Caliber: .17 HMR or .22 WMR, 5-rnd. magazine.
21-in. bbl. Weight: 5 lbs. Sights: optic ready. Stock: black synthetic or wood. AccuTrigger added 2006. Made 1996–date.
93 Classic (24-in. standard or heavy bbl., w/ or
  w/o aperture sight, 2008-10) . . NiB $490 Ex $430 Gd $335
93 BRJ (21-in. heavy bbl. w/spiral
  flutes, Royal Jacarnada wood
  laminate stock, 2010-date). . . . NiB $490 Ex $430 Gd $335
93 BSEV (21-in. heavy bbl. w/spiral
  flutes, Evolution thumbhole wood
  laminate stock, 2010-date). . . . NiB $590 Ex $530 Gd $435

93 BTVSS (21-in. heavy stainless
  bbl. w/spiral flutes, Boyd's
  thumbhole stock, 2007-date) . . NiB $480 Ex $420 Gd $330
93 G (wood stock, open sights) . NiB $255 Ex $225 Gd $175
93 F. . . . . NiB $259 Ex $230 Gd $185
93 F Camo (synthetic
  stock, 2002-04) . . . . NiB $185 Ex $165 Gd $125
93 FSS (stainless, new 1997). . . . NiB $346 Ex $320 Gd $190
93 FV (heavy varmint bbl.), add $70
93 FV-SR (16.5-in. heavy bbl., suppressor ready,
  optic ready, no sights, new 2014) NiB $368 Ex
  $340 Gd $310 93 FV-SR Landry (gator camo
  stock, new 2015) . . . . NiB $424 Ex $400 Gd $385
93 FVSS (heavy varmint bbl., stainless), add. $100
93 Minimalist (.22 WMR, wood laminate green or brown
  stock, blued, 18-in. bbl.). . . . . .NiB $360 Ex $300 Gd $250
93 G (adj. sights, checkered walnut-finished
  hardwood stock w/Monte Carlo
  cheekpiece, 1996-date) . . . . .NiB $346 Ex $320 Gd $190
93R17 F (.17 HMR, 2003–date) . . . . .NiB $268 Ex $240 Gd $195
93R17 FSS (.17 HMR, stainless) . . NiB $334 Ex $310 Gd $300
93R17 FV (.17 HMR, heavy varmint bbl.), add $40
93R17 FV-SR (.17 HMR, 16.5-in.
  heavy bbl., suppressor ready, optic
  ready, no sights). . . . . NiB $368 Ex $340 Gd $310
93R17 FVSS (.17 HMR, heavy varmint bbl.,
  stainless), add. $100
93R17 GV (.17 HMR, high luster wood stock,
  2003 to date). . . . . NiB $299 Ex $240 Gd $200
93R17 GLV (.17 HMR, left hand), add $10
93R17 TR (.17 HMR, 22-in. fluted bbl.,
  wood tactical style, 7.5 lbs., 2010 to
  date). . . . . NiB $558 Ex $540 Gd $500
93R17 TRR-SR (.17 HMR, additional Picatinny
  rails), add $100
93R17 Minimalist (.17 HMR, wood laminate green or brown
  stock, blued, 18-in. bbl.) . . . . . NiB $370 Ex $310 Gd $260

NOTE: *The Model 110 series was first produced in 1958 and
continues production to date with a variety of engineering
and cosmetic changes along the way. The series uses a two lug
push-feed bolt. Recent changes include Savage logo etched on
bolt (1994), pillar bedded stocks (1996), AccuTrigger (2003),
left-hand ejection port with target actions (2007), Accustock
(2009), dual port action (2009), stainless steel only target
actions (2010). Model 10 rifles are short action rifles, Model
110 are long actions rifles. The Model 10/110 action is used
with Model 11/111, 12/112, 14/114 and 16/116 models
with differences as noted. Numerous Package models are fitted with factory mounted scopes. Left hand variants for some
models.*

MODEL 10BA . . . . NiB $2010 Ex $1770 Gd $1400
Law Enforcement Series. Calibers: .308 only, 10-rnd. detachable magazine. 24-in. bbl. w/muzzle brake. Weight: 13.4 lbs.
Sights: optic ready. Stock: aluminum chassis w/Magpul PRS-G3
stock. Made 2009-16.
10BAT/S-K (adj. tactical stock, made 2009
  to 2013) . . . . NiB $1750 Ex $1500 Gd $1200
10BAT/S-K (adj. tactical stock, made
2009–13) . . . . NiB $1750 Ex $1500 Gd $1200

MODEL 10 BA STEALTH. . . . . . NIB $1055 EX $930 GD $720
Similar to 10BA/BAS except w/aluminum chassis Calibers: 6.5
Creedmoor or .308 Win. Mag. Bbl.: 20- or 24-in. w/threaded
muzzle. Finish: Matte black or bronze. 2016-19.
**Evolution (FAB Defense buttstock, monolithic aluminum
  chassis, FDE, 2018-20)** . . . . NiB $1560 Ex $1360 Gd $1060

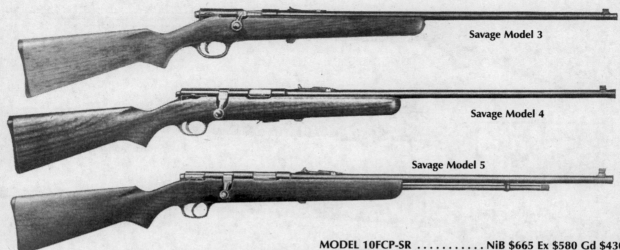

Savage Model 3

Savage Model 4

Savage Model 5

MODEL 10 GRS . . . . **NiB $1315 Ex $1155 Gd $895**
Cal.: 6mm Creedmoor, 6.5 Creedmoor, 6.5 PRC or .308 Win.; detachable 10-rnd. AI-style magazine. Bbl.: 20-, 24- or 26-in. heavy fluted. Weight: 8.9-9.2 lbs. Sights: Optic ready. Stock: GRS adj. fiberglass. Finish: Matte black. AccuTrigger. Made 2007-date.

MODEL 10 GY . . . . **NiB $560 Ex $365 Gd $245**
Cal.: .223 Rem., .243 Win., or .308 Win. Bbl.: 22-in. Sights: Optic ready and open. Stock: Checkered hardwood w/shorter LOP. Disc. 2007.

MODEL 10FCM . . . . **NiB $480 Ex $410 Gd $330**
Cal.: .243 Win., .270 WSM, .300 WSM, .308 Win. or 7mm-08; detachable magazine. 20-in. bbl. 41.5 in. overall. Weight: 6.25 lbs. No sights, drilled and tapped. Black graphite/fiberglass composition stock. Non-glare matte blue finish. Made 2005-06.

MODEL 10FCM SCOUT . . . . **NiB $730 Ex $580 Gd $460**
Cal.: 7.62x39mm, .308 or 7mm-08, 4-rnd. detachable magazine. 20-in.bbl. Weight: 6.1 lbs. Sights: ghost ring/optic ready. Stock: black synthetic. Matte blue finish. AccuStock standard in 2009. Made 1999-03, reintro. 2007-13.

MODEL 10FCP CHOATE . . . . . . **NiB $705 Ex $580 Gd $430**
Law Enforcement Series. Cal.: .308 Win.; 4-rnd detachable magazine. 24-in. bbl. Stock: Choate synthetic. Matte black finish. Disc. 2007.

MODEL 10FCP H-S PRECISION **NiB $725 Ex $590 Gd $430**
Law Enforcement Series. Cal.: .308 Win.; 4-rnd detachable magazine. 24- or 26-in. bbl. w/muzzle brake. 44.5-49.5 in. overall. Weight: 9-10.7 lbs. Stock: H-S Precision fiberglass. Matte black finish. Disc. 2016.

MODEL 10FCP MCMILLAN . . **NiB $1330 Ex $1035 Gd $760**
Law Enforcement Series. Similar to Model 10FCP H-S Precision except .308 Win. only and McMillian fiberglass stock. Made 2007-16.

MODEL 10FCP-K . . . . **NiB $850 Ex $730 Gd $600**
Law Enforcement Series. Similar to Model 10FCP H-S Precision except .223 Rem. or .308 Win. only. Bbl.: 24-in. heavy w/ muzzle brake. Stock: AccuStock. Made 2009-13.

MODEL 10FCP-SR . . . . **NiB $665 Ex $580 Gd $430**
Cal.: .308 Win., 10-rnd detachable magazine. Bbl.: 20- or 24-in. heavy fluted, suppressor ready. Stock: AccuStock. Oversized bolt handle. Made 2015-16.

MODEL 10FP . . . . **NiB $630 Ex $445 Gd $370**
Law Enforcement Series. Cal.: .223 Rem. or .308 Win.; 4-rnd. magazine. Bbl.: 20- or 24-in. heavy. Stock: Black synthetic McMillian. Weight: 6.2 lbs. Oversized bolt handle. Made 1998-2010.
LE1 model (.223 Rem., 20-in.
 heavy bbl., 2002-10) . . . . **NiB $850 Ex $640 Gd $430**
LE1A model (.308 Win., 20-in. heavy
 bbl., Choate stock, 2002-10) . . **NiB $870 Ex $700 Gd $480**
LE2 model (.223 Rem., 26-in.
 heavy bbl., 2002-06) . . . . **NiB $630 Ex $510 Gd $360**
LE2A model (.308 Win., 26-in.
 heavy bbl., 2002-06) . . . . **NiB $630 Ex $510 Gd $360**
Duty model (open sights,
 2002 only) . . . . **NiB $440 Ex $360 Gd $570**
SR model (supressor
 ready, 2011-13) . . . . **NiB $630 Ex $510 Gd $430**
FPCPXP model (Burris or Leupold scope,
 Harris bipod, 2002-09) . . . . **NiB $2280 Ex $1855 Gd $1310**

MODEL 10FP H-S PRECISION . . **NiB $725 Ex $590 Gd $430**
Law Enforcement Series. Cal.: .308 Win.; 4-rnd detachable magazine. 24- or 26-in. bbl. w/muzzle brake. 44.5-49.5 in. overall. Weight: 9-10.7 lbs. Stock: H-S Precision fiberglass. Matte black finish. Disc. 2006.

MODEL 10FP MCMILLAN . . . . . **NiB $865 Ex $735 Gd $535**
Law Enforcement Series. Cal.: .308 Win.; 4-rnd. magazine. Bbl.: 26-in. heavy. Stock: McMillian tactical fiberglass. Made 2003-06.

MODEL 10FP-SR . . . . **NiB $630 Ex $445 Gd $370**
Law Enforcement Series. Cal.: .223 Rem. or .308 Win.; 4-rnd. magazine. Bbl.: 20- or 24-in. heavy. Stock: Black synthetic McMillian. Weight: 6.2 lbs. Oversized bolt handle. AccuTrigger. Made 2011-13.

MODEL 10
PRECISION CARBINE . . . . **NiB $820 Ex $680 Gd $440**
Cal.: .223 Rem., .308 Win. or .300 AAC BLK., 4-rnd. detachable magazine. Bbl.: 20-in. w/ or w/o threaded muzzle. Weight: 7 lbs. Sights: Optic ready. Stock: camo AccuStock. Oversized bolt handle. Made 2009-15.

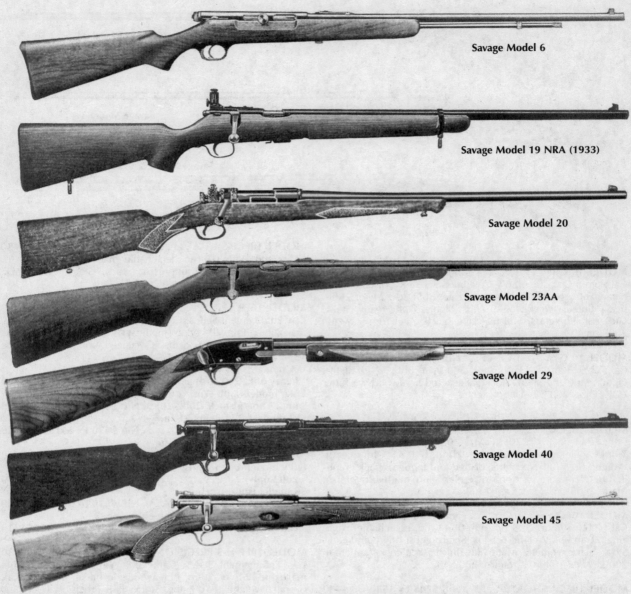

Savage Model 6

Savage Model 19 NRA (1933)

Savage Model 20

Savage Model 23AA

Savage Model 29

Savage Model 40

Savage Model 45

MODEL 10 PREDATOR
HUNTER . . . . NiB $835 Ex $680 Gd $455
Cal.: .204 Ruger, .22-250 Rem., .223 Rem., .243 Win., .260 Rem., 6.5 Creedmoor, or 6.5x285 Norma; detachable magazine. 22- or 24-in. bbl. Weight: 7.25 lbs. Optic ready. Stock: laminate or AccuStock. Finish: Mossy Oak Brush, Snow or RealTree Max 1. Made 2007-18.

MODEL 10 TROPHY
HUNTER XP PACKAGE . . . . NiB $630 Ex $550 Gd $430
Cal.: .22-250 Rem., .223 Rem., .243 Win., .308 Win.; detachable 4-rnd. magazine. 22-in. bbl. Weight: 8.3 lbs. Factory mounted Weaver 3-9x40 scope. Stock: Satin wood. Finish: Matte black. Mfg. 2012-date.

MODEL 10 SAVAGE
ASHBURY PRECISION . . . . . NiB $1530 Ex $1355 Gd $1055
Cal.: 6.5 Creedmoor or .308 Win.; detachable AICS 5-rnd. magazine. 24-in. bbl. Weight: 10.5 lbs. Stock: Saber modular chassis system w/folding stock. AccuTrigger. Mfg. 2017-18.

MODEL 11BTH HUNTER . . . . . NiB $820 Ex $680 Gd $460
Cal.: .204 Ruger, .22-250 Rem., .223 Rem., .243 Win., or .308 Win.; 4-rnd. hinged floor plate magazine. Bbl.: 22-in. Sights: None. Finish: Blued. Stock: Brown laminate wood thumbhole. Weight: 6.7 lbs. AccuTrigger. Mfg. 2008-18.

MODEL 11 DOA HUNTER XP . NiB $630 Ex $480 Gd $330
Cal.: .243 Win., .260 Rem., .270 WSM, 6.5 Creedmoor, .308 Win., .300 WSM, or 7mm-08; 2- or 4-rnd. detachable magazine. Bbl.: 22- or 24-in. Sights: None. Finish: Blued. Stock: Black synthetic. AccuTrigger, factory mounted scope. Mfg. 2017-18.
WSW calibers . . . . NiB $660 Ex $510 Gd $360

MODEL 11F . . . . NiB $630 Ex $480 Gd $330
Cal.: .204 Ruger, .22-250 Rem., .223 Rem., .243 Win., .260 Rem., .270 WSM, 7.62x39mm, .308 Win., .300 RSUM, .300 WSM, 7mm RSUM, 7mm WSM, 7mm-08; fixed, detachable or hinged floor plate magazine. Bbl.: 22- or 24-in. Sights: None. Finish: Blued. Stock: Black syn-

thetic. AccuTrigger and AccuStock on later variants. Mfg. 1999-01, reintro. 2003-17.

11FNS (non-WSM calibers) . . . . NiB $630 Ex $480 Gd $330

MODEL 11FCNS . . . . NiB $630 Ex $480 Gd $330
Similar to Model 11F except w/AccuStock or pillar bedded synthetic stock, AccuTrigger. Made 1999-01, reintro. 2003-15.

MODEL 11FCXP3 PACKAGE . . . NiB $430 Ex $355 Gd $280
Cal.: .243 Win. or .308 Win.; detachable magazine. 22-in. bbl. Factory mounted scope. Stock: Black synthetic. Finish: Matte black. Disc. 2011.

MODEL 11FYXP3 PACKAGE . . . NiB $530 Ex $455 Gd $380
Youth model. Cal.: .223 Rem., .243 Win., 7mm-8, or .308 Win.; detachable magazine. 22-in. bbl. Factory mounted scope. Stock: Black synthetic w/12.5-in. LOP. AccuTrigger. Finish: Matte black. Disc. 2002-11.

MODEL 11FYCAK . . . . NiB $590 Ex $440 Gd $310
Youth model. Cal.: .243 Win., 7mm-8, or .308 Win.; detachable magazine. 22-in. bbl. Stock: Black synthetic w/12.5-in. LOP. Finish: Matte black. Disc. 2006-10.

MODEL 11FXP3 . . . . NiB $630 Ex $480 Gd $330
Cal.: .204 Ruger, .22-250 Rem., .223 Rem., .243 Win., .260 Rem., .270 WSM, 7.62x39mm, .308 Win., .300 RSUM, .300 WSM, 7mm RSUM, 7mm WSM, 7mm-08. Bbl.:22- or 24-in. Sights: None. Finish: Matte black. Stock: Black graphite/fiberglass. Factory mounted scope. Mfg. 1994-11.

MODEL 11G . . . . NiB $510 Ex $420 Gd $255
Similar to models 11F except wood stock w/pressed checkering. Blued finish. Made 1998-11.
11GNS (no sights) . . . . NiB $500 Ex $410 Gd $245

MODEL 11GC . . . . NiB $510 Ex $420 Gd $255
Cal.: .22-250 Rem., .243 Win., .260 Rem., .308 Win., or 7mm-08. Bbl.: 22-in. Finish: Blued. Stock: Hardwood. Sights: Open. Made 1999-01.

MODEL 11 HOG HUNTER . . . . NiB $490 Ex $430 Gd $340
Specialty Series. Cal.: .223 Rem., .308 Win., or .338 Fed.; 4-rnd. internal magazine. Bbl.: 20-in. threaded. Weight: 7.2 lbs. Sights: no sights, optic ready. Stock: OD green synthetic. Finish: Matte black. AccuTrigger. Made 2012-17.

MODEL 11 HUNTER XP . . . . . . NiB $630 Ex $480 Gd $330
Cal.: .22-250 Rem., .223 Rem., .243 Win. or .308 Win.; 4-rnd. detachable magazine. Bbl.: 22-in. Sights: None. Finish: Blued. Stock: Black synthetic. Factory mounted scope. Mfg. 2012-14.

MODEL 11 LADY HUNTER . . . . NiB $815 Ex $715 Gd $555
Specialty Series. Cal.: .223 Rem., .243 Win., 6.5 Creedmoor, .308 Win., 7mm-08 or .30-06; 4-rnd. detachable magazine. 20-in. Weight: 6 lbs. Sights: Optic ready. Stock: Satin pressed checkered Monte Carlo w/ shorter LOP. Finish: Matte black. AccuTrigger. Made 2012 to date.

MODEL 11 LIGHTWEIGHT
HUNTER . . . . NiB $890 Ex $780 Gd $610
Specialty Series. Cal.: .223 Rem., .243 Win., .260 Rem., 6.5 Creedmoor, .308 Win., 7mm-08 or .30-06; 4-rnd. detachable magazine. 20-in. bbl. Weight: 5.5 lbs. Sights: no sights, optic ready. Stock: Wood sporter. Finish: Matte black. AccuTrigger. Spiral fluted bolt, lightening cuts in receiver and stock. Made 2011 to date.

MODEL 11 LONG
RANGE HUNTER . . . . NiB $1136 Ex $960 Gd $780
Specialty Series. Cal.: .260 Rem., 6.5 Creedmoor, .308 Win., .300 WSM, or .338 Fed.; 2- or 3-rnd. detachable magazine. Bbl.: 26-in. w/muzzle brake. Weight: 8.4 lbs. Sights: No sights, optic ready. Stock: Karsten w/adj. cheek riser. Finish: Matte black. AccuTrigger. Made 2011-17.

MODEL 11 SCOUT . . . . NiB $730 Ex $580 Gd $460
Cal.: .308 Win., 10-rnd. detachable magazine. Bbl.: 18-in. w/muzzle brake. Weight: 7.8 lbs. Sights: Open, Scout style scope mount. Stock: FDE AccuStock. Matte blue finish. AccuTrigger. Made 2015-17.

MODEL 11 TROPHY
HUNTER XP . . . . NiB $630 Ex $480 Gd $330
Cal.: .204 Ruger, .22-250 Rem., .223 Rem., .243 Win., 6.5 Creedmoor, .260 Rem., .270 WSM, 7mm-08, .300 WSM, .308 Win., or .338 Fed.; 4-rnd. detachable magazine. Bbl.: 22- or 24-in. Sights: None. Finish: Blued. Stock: Black synthetic. AccuTrigger. Factory mounted scope. Mfg. 2012-20.
Youth (shorter LOP, 2014-20) . . NiB $630 Ex $480 Gd $330

MODEL 11 TROPHY
PREDATOR HUNTER XP . . . . . . NiB $610 Ex $535 Gd $425
Cal.: .22-250 Rem., .223 Win., .243 Win., or 6.5 Creedmoor; 4-rnd. detachable magazine. Bbl.: 22-in. medium. Sights: None. Finish: Matte black. Stock: Snow Camo or Mossy Oak Brush camo, synthetic. Weight: 9 lbs. AccuTrigger. Factory mounted scope. Disc. 2018.

MODEL 12BTCSS . . . . NiB $1180 Ex $1030 Gd $810
Cal.: .204 Ruger, .22-250 Rem., or .223 Rem.; 4-rnd. magazine. Bbl.: 26-in. fluted heavy stainless. Sights: None. Stock: Brown laminate thumbhole. Weight: 10 lbs. AccuTrigger. Oversized bolt knob. Mfg. 2008-date.

MODEL 12BVSS . . . . NiB $1040 Ex $915 Gd $705
Dual port action. Cal.: .204 Ruger, .22-250 Rem., .223 Rem., .243 Win., .300 WSM, or .308 Win. Bbl.: 26-in. fluted heavy stainless. Sights: None. Stock: Brown laminate w/flat beavertail forend. Weight: 9 lbs. w/ or w/o AccuTrigger. Mfg. 1998-date.

MODEL 12 BENCHREST . . . NiB $1520 Ex $1330 Gd $1030
Target Series. Dual port action. Cal.: 6 Norma BR, 6.5x284 Norma or .308 Win.; single shot. Bbl.: 29-in. heavy stainless steel. Wood laminate stock. Matte stainless finish. No sights, optic ready. AccuTrigger. Weight: 12.75 lbs. Length: 49 in. Made 2009 to date.

MODEL 12 F CLASS . . . . NiB $1480 Ex $1300 Gd $1010
Target Series. Similar to Model 12 Benchrest except in 6 Norma BR or 6.5x284 Norma only. 30-in. heavy bbl. Weight: 13.3 lbs. Length: 50 in. Left load port, right eject action. Made 2007 to date.

MODEL 12 F/TR . . . . NiB $1390 Ex $1220 Gd $955
Target Series. Similar to Model 12 Benchrest except in .223 Rem. or .308 Win. only. 30-in. heavy bbl. Weight: 12.65 lbs. Length: 50 in. Made 2007 to date.

MODEL 12FCV . . . . NiB $670 Ex $580 Gd $455
Cal.: .204 Ruger, .22-250 Rem., or .223 Rem.; 4-rnd. detachable magazine. Bbl.: 26-in. heavy. Sights: None. Finish: Blued. Stock: Black synthetic AccuStock. AccuTrigger. Mfg. 2010-18.

RIFLES

Savage Model 60

MODEL 12FV/12FVY . . . . .NiB $615 Ex $480 Gd $370
Dual port action. Cal.: .204 Ruger, .22-250 Rem., .223 Rem., .243 Win. or .308 Win.; 4-rnd. detachable magazine. Bbl.: 26-in. Sights: None. Finish: Blued. Stock: Black synthetic. w/ or w/o AccuTrigger. FVY youth model w/shorter LOP. Mfg. 1998-14.

MODEL 12FVSS . . . . .NiB $670 Ex $580 Gd $455
Dual port action. Cal.: .22-250 Rem., .223 Rem., .270 WSM, .300 WSM, or .308 Win. Bbl.: 26-in. fluted heavy stainless. Sights: None. Stock: Black synthetic. w/ or w/o AccuTrigger. Mfg. 1998-12.

**MODEL 12 LONG
RANGE PRECISION** . . . . . . .NiB $1180 Ex $1030 Gd $810
Target Series. Cal.: .243 Win., .260 Rem. or 6.5 Creedmoor, 4-rnd. detachable magazine. 26-in. heavy, fluted bbl. H-S Precision fiberglass stock. Blued. No sights, optic ready. AccuTrigger. Weight: 11 lbs. Length: 46.25 in. Made 2011 to date.

**MODEL 12 LONG RANGE
PRECISION VARMINTER** . . . .NiB $1410 Ex $1230 Gd $955
Target Series. Single-shot. Cal.: .204 Ruger, .22-250 Rem., .223 Rem. or 6mm Norma; detachable magazine. 26-in. bbl. No sights, optic ready. AccuTrigger. Made 2008-10.

**MODEL 12 LONG RANGE PRECISION
VARMINTER REPEATER** . . . . .NiB $1090 Ex $930 Gd $730
Target Series. Cal.: .204 Ruger, .22-250 Rem., .223 Rem. or 6mm Norma; detachable magazine. 26-in. bbl. No sights, optic ready. AccuTrigger. Made 2008-10.

MODEL 12 PALMA. . . . . . . .NiB $1935 Ex $1690 Gd $1315
Target Series. Similar to Model 12 Benchrest except in .308 Win. only. 30-in. heavy bbl. Weight: 12.65 lbs. Length: 49.75 in. Stock: laminated wood, veted forend, adj. comb and LOP. Made 2009 to date.

**MODEL 12 VARMINT
LOW PROFILE** . . . . .NiB $1070 Ex $1030 Gd $810
Varmint Series. Similar to Model 12BVSS except w/smaller left-side ejection port. Made 2004 to date.

**MODEL 14 CLASSIC/AMERICAN
CLASSIC**. . . . . NiB $815 Ex $680 Gd $480
Classic Series. Various short-action calibers. 22- or 24-in. bbl. Weight: 7 lbs. Detachable 3- or 4-rnd. magazine. No sights, drilled and tapped. AccuTrigger. Right- or left-hand actions. Stock: Checkered walnut w/black forend tip. Finish: High luster blue. Made 2005-18.

MODEL 14 EURO CLASSIC . . . . NiB $755 Ex $600 Gd $450
Classic Series. Similar to the Model 14 American Classic/Classic except in .22-250, .243 or .308 and checkered walnut w/black forend tip and cheek rest. Made 2006-10.

MODEL 16 BEAR HUNTER. . . . . NiB $945 Ex $755 Gd $555
Specialty Series. Calibers: .300 WSM, .338 Fed., or .325 WSM; internal magazine w/hinged floorplate. 23-in. bbl. w/muzzle brake. Stock: Synthetic AccuStock. AccuTrigger Weight: 7.5 lbs. Made 2011-18.

**MODEL 16 TROPHY
HUNTER XP PACKAGE** . . . . .NiB $655 Ex $580 Gd $455
Package Series. Cal.: .204 Ruger, .22-250 Rem., .223 Rem., .243 Win., 6.5 Creedmoor, .260 Rem., .270 WSM, 7mm-08, .308 Win., .300 WSM or .33 Fed.; 4-rnd. detachable magazine. 22- or 24-in. bbl. Black synthetic stock, AccuTrigger. Weight: 7.25 lbs. Factory mounted Nikon 3-9x40mm scope. Made 2012-20.

**MODELS 16BSS
WEATHER WARRIOR** . . . . NiB $565 Ex $400 Gd $270
Similar to the Model 16FSS except w/brown laminated checkered wood stock. Weight: 7.75 lbs. Mfg. 2002-03.

**MODELS 16FCSAK
WEATHER WARRIOR** . . . . NiB $565 Ex $400 Gd $270
Similar to the Model 16BSS Weather Warrior except chambered in .243 Win., .270 WSM, .308 Win., .300 WSM, or 7mm-08; detachable magazine. Bbl.: Fluted 22-in. stainless w/ adj. muzzle brake. Weight: 6.5 lbs. Disc. 2005.

**MODELS 16FCSS
WEATHER WARRIOR** . . . . NiB $465 Ex $400 Gd $270
Similar to the Model 16BSS Weather Warrior except w/stainless bbl./action. Weight: 6.75 lbs. Mfg. 1999-01.

**MODELS 16FCSAK
WEATHER WARRIOR** . . . . NiB $565 Ex $400 Gd $270
Similar to the Model 16BSS Weather Warrior except chambered in .243 Win., .270 WSM, .308 Win., .300 WSM, or 7mm-08; detachable magazine. Bbl.: Fluted 22-in. stainless w/ adj. muzzle brake. Weight: 6.5 lbs. Disc. 2005.

MODELS 16FHSS . . . . NiB $730 Ex $630 Gd $455
Cal.: .204 Ruger, .22-250 Rem., .223 Rem., .243 Win., .260 Rem., .270 WSM, .308 Win., .300 WSM, .300 RSUM, 7mm-08, 7mm WSM, 7mm RSUM. Bbl.: 22- or 24-in. Stock: Black checkered synthetic. Finish: Stainless. Sights: None. Made 1998-11.

MODELS 16FSS. . . . . NiB $585 Ex $480 Gd $335
Cal.: .22-250 Rem., .223 Rem., .243 Win., .250 Savage, .270 WSM, .308 Win., .300 WSM, or 7mm-08; 2- or 4-rnd. magazine. Bbl.: 22- or 24-in. Stock: Black checkered synthetic or AccuStock. Finish: Stainless. Sights: None. AccuTrigger. Made 2006-13.

MODELS 16FHSAK. . . . . NiB $720 Ex $455 Gd $415
Similar to the Model 16FSS except w/adj. muzzle brake. Mfg. 2006-10.

MODEL 16FXP3 PACKAGE . . . . . NiB $630 Ex $500 Gd $365
Similar to the Model 16 Trophy Hunter XP Package except w/ factory mounted nickel-finish scope. Mfg. 2002-11.

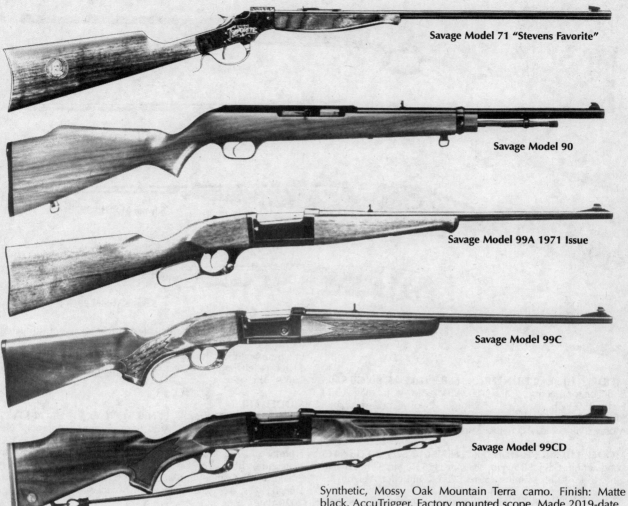

Savage Model 71 "Stevens Favorite"

Savage Model 90

Savage Model 99A 1971 Issue

Savage Model 99C

Savage Model 99CD

MODEL 16
LIGHTWEIGHT HUNTER . . . . . . **NiB $890 Ex $780 Gd $610**
Cal.: .223 Rem., .243 Win., .308 Win., or 7mm-08; 4-rnd. detachable magazine. Sights: no sights, optic ready. Stock: Black synthetic. Finish: Matte black. Weight: 5.5 lbs. AccuTrigger. Made 2016-18.

MODEL 110
APEX HUNTER XP . . . . **NiB $570 Ex $505 Gd $420**
Cal.: .204 Ruger, .22-250 Rem., .223 Rem., .243 Win., .25-06, 6.5 Creedmoor, 6.5 PRC, 6.5x284 Norma, .260 Rem., .270 WSM, .270 Win., .308 Win., .300 WSM, 7mm-08, 7mm WSM, .350 Legend, .30-06, 7mm Rem. Mag., .300 Win. Mag., or .338 Win Mag.; 2-, 3- or 4-rnd. magazine. Bbl.: 20-, 22- or 24-in. Weight: 9.0 lbs. Stock: Black synthetic. AccuTrigger. Factory mounted scope. Made 2019-date.
Muddy Girl camo . . . . **NiB $620 Ex $545 Gd $430**

MODEL 110
APEX PREDATOR XP . . . . **NiB $655 Ex $580 Gd $455**
Cal.: .204 Ruger, .22-250 Rem., .223 Rem., .243 Win., 6.5 Creedmoor, or .308 Win.; 4-rnd. detachable magazine. Bbl.: 20- or 24-in. threaded. Weight: 8.4-9.9 lbs. Stock:

Synthetic, Mossy Oak Mountain Terra camo. Finish: Matte black. AccuTrigger. Factory mounted scope. Made 2019-date.

MODEL 110 APEX STORM . . . . . **NiB $660 Ex $580 Gd $450**
Cal.: .204 Ruger, .22-250 Rem., .223 Rem., .243 Win., .25-06, 6.5 Creedmoor, 6.5 PRC, .270 Win., 7mm-08, .260 Rem., .308 Win., .350 Legend, .30-06, .270 WSM, .300 WSM, 7mm Rem. Mag., .300 Win. Mag., .338 Win. Mag.; 3- or 4-rnd. detachable magazine. Bbl.: 20-, 22-, or 24-in. stainless. Weight: 8-9 lbs. Stock: Synthetic, black. Finish: Matte stainless. AccuTrigger. Factory mounted scope. Made 2019-date.

MODEL 110BA/BAS . . . . **NiB $2180 Ex $1910 Gd $1455**
Law Enforcement Series. Similar to 10BA except in .300 Win. Mag. or .338 Lapua Mag. 26-in.bbl. w/muzzle brake. Weight: 15.75 lbs. Made 2010-17.

MODEL 110 BA STEALTH . . . **NiB $1555 Ex $1355 Gd $1055**
Similar to 110BA/BAS except w/aluminum chassis. Cal.: .300 Win. Mag. or .338 Lapua Mag.; 10-rnd. magazine. Bbl.: 26-in. w/muzzle brake. Stock: FAB Defense GLR-SHOCK. Weight: 11.5 lbs. Finish: Matte black or bronze. AccuTrigger. Mfg. 2016-19.

MODEL 110 BA
STEALTH EVOLUTION . . . . . **NiB $1790 Ex $1560 Gd $1210**
Similar to 110BA Stealth except w/24-in. heavy fluted bbl., monolithic aluminum chassis. Stock: Adj. FAB Defense. Weight: 11.3 lbs. Finish: FDE. AccuTrigger. Mfg. 2018-19.

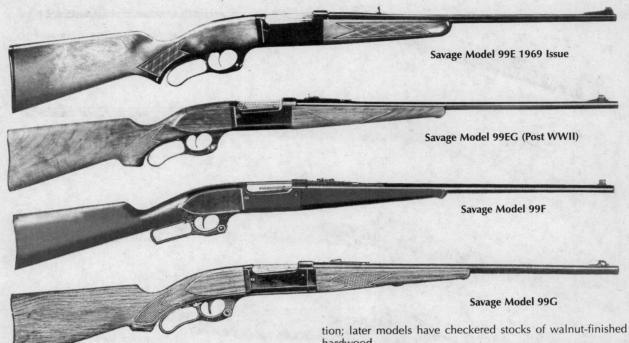

Savage Model 99E 1969 Issue

Savage Model 99EG (Post WWII)

Savage Model 99F

Savage Model 99G

MODEL 110 BEAR HUNTER. . . . NiB $910 Ex $790 Gd $605
Short or long action. Cal.: .300 WSM, .300 Win. Mag., .338 Fed., .338 Win. Mag., or .375 Ruger; 2- or 4-rnd. magazine. Bbl.: 23-in. stainless w/muzzle brake. Weight: 7.5 lbs. Finish: Mossy Oak camo. AccuStock. AccuTrigger. Mfg. 2018-date.

MODEL 110 BRUSH HUNTER . . NiB $610 Ex $530 Gd $415
Long action. Cal.: .338 Win. Mag. or .375 Ruger; 3-rnd. magazine. Bbl.: 20-in. stainless. Stock: Gray synthetic. Weight: 7.3 lbs. AccuTrigger. Mfg. 2018-date.

MODEL 110C . . . . NiB $455 Ex $400 Gd $315
Cal.: .22-250, .243, .25-06, .270, .308, .30-06, 7mm Rem. Mag., .300 Win. Mag.; 4-rnd. detachable magazine (3-rnd. magnum calibers). 22-in. bbl. (24-in. in magnum calibers). Weight: 6.7-8lbs. Sights: Open rear; ramp front. Stock: Checkered Monte Carlo-style walnut (magnum calibers has recoil pad). Model 110CL is left hand variant. Made 1966-85.

MODEL 110 CLASSIC. . . . . NiB $880 Ex $770 Gd $600
Short or long action. Cal.: .243 Win., .270 Win., 6.5 Creedmoor, .308 Win., .30-06, 7mm Rem. Mag., .300 Win. Mag.; 4-rnd. detachable magazine. Bbl.: 22- or 24-in. threaded. Weight: 8 lbs. Sights: Optic ready. Stock: Classic brown walnut. AccuTrigger. Made 2020 to date.

MODEL 110D . . . . NiB $355 Ex $310 Gd $245
Similar to Model 110C except has internal magazine with hinged floorplate. Cal.: .243 Win., .270 Win., .30-06, 7mm Rem. Mag., .300 Win. Mag. Model 110DL is left hand variant. Made 1972-88.

MODEL 110E . . . . NiB $355 Ex $310 Gd $245
Cal.: .22-250, .223 Rem., .243 Win., .270 Win., .308 Win., 7mm Rem. Mag., or .30-06; 4-rnd. box magazine (3-rnd. in magnum calibers). 20- or 22-in. bbl. (24-in. stainless steel in magnum calibers). Weight: 6.75-7.75 lbs. Sights: Open rear; ramp front. Stock: Plain Monte Carlo on early produc-

tion; later models have checkered stocks of walnut-finished hardwood
(magnum calibers have recoil pad). Made 1963-88. Model 110EL is left hand variant (.30-06 or 7mm Rem. Mag.; mfg. 1969-73).

MODEL 110
ELITE PRECISION . . . . NiB $1710 Ex $1510 Gd $1155
Short or long action. Cal.: .223 Rem., 6mm Creedmoor, 6.5 Creedmoor, .308 Win., .300 Win. Mag., .300 PRC, .300 Norma, or .338 Lapua Mag.; 5- or 10rnd. AICS detachable magazine. Bbl.: 26- or 30-in. stainless w/muzzle brake. Stock: CORE Competition aluminum chassis, MDT pistol grip. Weight: 12.2-15 lbs. Finish: Matte black. AccuTrigger. Mfg. 2020-date.

MODEL 110
ENGAGE HUNTER XP . . . . NiB $530 Ex $465 Gd $360
Short or long action. Cal.: .25-06, .260 Rem., .243 Win., 6.5 Creedmoor, 6.5 PRC, 6.5x284 Norma, .270 WSM, .270 Win., .280 Ackley Imp., .308 Win., 7mm-08, 7mm Rem. Mag., or .30-06, .300 WSM, .300 Win. Mag., .338 Fed., .350 Legend, or .450 Bushmaster; 2- or 4-rnd. detachable magazine. Bbl.: 22- or 24-in. stainless. Weight: 7.2-8.2 lbs. Sights: Factory mounted scope. Stock: Gray synthetic. AccuTrigger. Made 2018-date.

MODEL 110F . . . . NiB $355 Ex $310 Gd $245
Same as Model 110E except w/black Rynite synthetic stock, swivel studs. Made 1988-93.

MODEL 110FCP . . . . NiB $730 Ex $605 Gd $430
Law Enforcement Series. Cal.: .25-06 or .300 Win. Mag.; 4-rnd detachable magazine. 24-in. heavy bbl. w/muzzle brake. 44.5-49.5 in. overall. Weight: 9 lbs. Stock: Black synthetic. Matte black finish. Oversized bolt knob. Disc. 2000 .

MODEL 110FCP
H-S PRECISION . . . . NiB $1145 Ex $1010 Gd $780
Law Enforcement Series. Cal.: .300 Win. Mag. or .338 Lapua Mag.; 4-rnd detachable magazine. 24- or 26-in. bbl. w/muzzle brake. 44.5-49.5 in. overall. Weight: 9-10.7 lbs. Stock: H-S Precision fiberglass. Matte black finish. Made 2012-19.

Savage Model 99R (Pre-WWII)

Savage Model 99R (Post-WWII)

Savage Model 99RS (Pre-WWII)

Savage Model 99T

Savage Model 110B

MODEL 110FM
SIERRA ULTRA LIGHT . . . . **NiB $430 Ex $375 Gd $295**
Cal.: .243 Win., .270 Win., .30-06, .308 Win.; 5-rnd. magazine. 20-in. bbl. 41.5 inc. overall. Weight: 6.25 lbs. No sights w/drilled and tapped receiver. Black graphite/ fiberglass composition stock. Non-glare matte blue finish. Made 1996-2000.

MODEL 110FNS . . . . **NiB $355 Ex $310 Gd $245**
Same as Model 110F except w/o sight. Made 1991-93.

MODEL 110FP
TACTICAL POLICE . . . . **NiB $580 Ex $470 Gd $315**
Law Enforcement Series. Cal.: .26-06, .30-06, .300 Win. Mag. or 7mm Rem. Mag.; 4-rnd. internal magazine. 24-in. bbl. 45.5 in. overall. Weight: 8.5 lbs. Stock: Black Rynite composite. Finish: Matte blue. w/ or w/o AccuTrigger. Made 1990-01 and 2003-08.

MODEL 110FXP3 . . . . **NiB $430 Ex $355 Gd $295**
Same as Model 110F except w/factory mounted scope. Made 1989-93.

MODEL 110G . . . . **NiB $355 Ex $310 Gd $245**
Cal.: .22-250, .223 Rem., .243 Win., .25-06, .250 Savage, .300 Savage, .270 Win., .308 Win., 7mm Rem. Mag., .300 Win. Mag., or .30-06; internal box magazine. Bbl.: 20- or 22-in. Weight: 7-7.2 lbs. Sights: Open rear; ramp front. Stock: Checkered hardwood w/walnut finished. Made 1989-93.
110GC (4-rnd. detachable
   magazine, 1992-93) . . . . **NiB $430 Ex $375 Gd $295**
110GL (left hand variant; .270 Win., .30-06 or .300 Win..
   Mag.; mfg. 1989-93) . . . . **NiB $355 Ex $310 Gd $245**
110GCXP3 Package (factory
   mounted scope, Disc. 2001) . . **NiB $455 Ex $400 Gd $305**

MODEL 110GV . . . . **NiB $355 Ex $310 Gd $245**
Varmint model. Cal.: .22-250 or .223 Rem.; 5-rnd. magazine. Bbl.: 24-in. medium. Weight: 8.2 lbs. Stock: Checkered harg-wood. Sights: None. Mfg. 1989-93.

MODEL 110GY
YOUTH/LADIES . . . . **NiB $405 Ex $355 Gd $275**
Same as Model 110G except w/walnut-finished hardwood stock and 12.5-in. LOP. Cal.: .243 Win. and .300 Savage. Made 1991-2000.

MODEL 110
HAYMAKER (WOLVERINE) . . . . . **NiB $810 Ex $710 Gd $550**
Short action. Cal.: .450 Bushmaster; 4-rnd. AICS magazine. Bbl.: 18-in. heavy w/muzzle brake. Finish: Matte black.

Weight: 8 lbs. AccuTrigger, AccuStock. Intro. as Wolverine and renamed Haymaker. Mfg. 2018-date.

MODEL 110 HIGH COUNTRY. . NiB $990 Ex $855 Gd $680
Short or long action. Cal.: .243 Win., 6.5 Creedmoor, 6.5 PRC, .270 Win., .280 Ackley Imp., .280 Nosler, .308 Win., 7mm Rem. Mag., .30-06, or .300 Win. Mag.; 3- or 4-rnd. detachable magazine. Bbl.: 22- or 24-in. fluted medium, threaded w/muzzle brake. Weight: 8-8.5 lbs. Sights: Optic ready. Finish: True Timber Strata camo. AccuTrigger, AccuStock. Made 2019-date.

MODEL 110 HOG HUNTER. . . . NiB $540 Ex $480 Gd $370
Short action. Cal.: .223 Rem., .308 Win., .350 Legend, or .338 Fed.; 4-rnd. detachable magazine. Bbl.: 18- or 20-in. threaded. Finish: Matte black. Sights: Open. Stock: OD green synthetic. Weight: 7.2 lbs. AccuTrigger. Mfg. 2018-date.

MODEL 110 HUNTER . . . . NiB $680 Ex $610 Gd $455
Short or long action. Cal.: .204 Ruger, .22-250 Rem., .223 Rem., .243 Win., .25-06, 6.5 Creedmoor, .270 Win., .308 Win., .280 Ackley Imp., .30-06, 7mm Rem. Mag., or .300 Win. Mag.; 3- or 4-rnd. detachable magazine. Bbl.: 22- or 24-in. Weight: 7.2 lbs. AccuTrigger, gray AccuStock. Made 2018-date.

MODEL 110K . . . . NiB $355 Ex $310 Gd $245
Same as Model 110E except w/laminated camouflage stock. Made 1986-88.

MODEL 110
LIGHTWEIGHT STORM . . . . . . NiB $680 Ex $610 Gd $455
Short or long action. Cal.: .223 Rem., .243 Win., 6.5 Creedmoor, .270 Win., .308 Win., or 7mm-08; 4-rnd. detachable magazine. Bbl.: 20-in. stainless. Weight: 6.5 lbs. Stock: Black synthetic. AccuTrigger. Made 2018-date.

MODEL 110
LONG RANGE HUNTER. . . . . . NiB $1000 Ex $875 Gd $680
Similar to Model 100 Hunter except w/26-in. bbl. w/muzzle brake, gray AccuStock. Made 2018-date.

MODEL 110M. . . . . NiB $405 Ex $355 Gd $275
Same as Model 110MC except chambered in 7mm Rem. Mag. .264, .300 win. Mag., or .338 Win. Mag. 24-in. bbl. Stock with recoil pad. Weight: 7.75 to 8 lbs. Made 1963-69.

MODEL 110MC . . . . NiB $430 Ex $275 Gd $295
Same as Model 110 except w/Monte Carlo-style stock. Made 1959-69.

MODEL 110
MAGPUL HUNTER. . . . . NiB $900 Ex $790 Gd $610
Short action. Cal.: .308 Win. or 6.5 Creedmoor; 5-rnd. AICS detachable magazine. Bbl.: 18- in. heavy threaded. Finish: Tungsten Cerakote. Sights: Optic ready. Stock: Magpul Hunter. Weight: 9 lbs. AccuTrigger. Oversized bolt handle. Mfg. 2021-date.

MODEL 110P PREMIER GRADE
Cal.: .243 Win., 7mm Rem. Mag., .30-06; 3- or 4-rnd. magazine. Bbl.: 22- or 24-in. Weight: 7-7.75 lbs. Sights: Open rear folding leaf; ramp front. Stock: French walnut w/Monte Carlo comb and cheekpiece, rosewood forend tip/pistol-grip cap, skip checkering, sling swivels, magnum calibers w/recoil pad. Made 1964-70.
.243 Win. and .30-06 . . . . NiB $455 Ex $400 Gd $315
7mm Rem. Mag. . . . . NiB $505 Ex $445 Gd $345

MODEL 110PE
PRESENTATION GRADE. . . . . . . NiB $705 Ex $605 Gd $455
Same as Model 110P except w/engraved receiver/floorplate/trigger guard. Made 1968-70.

MODEL 110
PRAIRIE HUNTER. . . . . NiB $655 Ex $580 Gd $455
Short action. Cal.: .224 Valkyrie; detachable magazine. Bbl.: 22-in. threaded. Finish: Matte black. Sights: Optic ready. Weight: 8.7 lbs. AccuTrigger, gray AccuStaock. Disc. 2021.

MODEL 110 PRECISION . . . . NiB $1325 Ex $1160 Gd $910
Short or long action. Cal.: 6.5 Creedmoor, .300 PRC, .308 Win., .300 Win. Mag. or .338 Lapua Mag.; 5- or 8-rnd. AICS detachable magazine. Bbl.: 20- or 24-in.bbl. heavy w/BA muzzle brake. Stock: MDT aluminum chassis w/adj. buttstock. Finish: FDE Cerakote. Sights: Optic ready. Weight: 9-11 lbs. Made 2010-date.

MODEL 110 PREDATOR. . . . . . . NiB $805 Ex $705 Gd $555
Short action. Cal.: .204 Ruger, .22-250 Rem., .223 Rem., .243 Win., .260 Rem., 6.5 Creedmoor, or .308 Win.; 4-rnd. detachable magazine. Bbl.: 22- or 24-in. heavy threaded. Weight: 8.5 lbs. AccuTrigger, RealTree Max 1 camo AccuStock. Made 2018-date.

MODEL 110
PREDATOR HUNTER . . . . NiB $820 Ex $705 Gd $555
Same as Model 110 Predator except in 6.5x284 Norma, 24-in. bbl. Made 2011-14.

MODEL 110
RIDGE WARRIOR. . . . . NiB $840 Ex $730 Gd $570
Short action. Cal.: 6.5 Creedmoor or .308 Win.; 10-rnd. detachable magazine. Bbl.: 24-in.bbl. heavy fluted threaded. Stock: Mossy Oak Overwatch camo synthetic. Finish: Gray PVD. Sights: Optic ready. Weight: 8.8 lbs. AccuTrigger. Made 2010-date.

MODEL 110S . . . . NiB $355 Ex $310 Gd $245
Silhouette model. Cal.: .308 Win. or 7mm-08; 4-rnd magazine. 22-in. heavy bbl. Weight: 8.6 lbs. Stock: Wundhammer pistol grip. Sights: None. Disc. 1989.

MODEL 110 SCOUT. . . . . NiB $745 Ex $655 Gd $505
Short action. Cal.: .223 Rem., .308 Win., .338 Fed., or .450 Bushmaster; 10-rnd. detachable magazine. Bbl.: 18-in.bbl. w/muzzle brake. Finish: Matte black. Sights: Optic ready. Weight: 8.8 lbs. AccuTrigger, FDE AccuStock. Made 2018-date.

MODEL 110 STORM. . . . . NiB $770 Ex $675 Gd $525
Short or long action. Cal.: .223 rem., .22-250, .243 Win., .25-06, 6.5 Creedmoor, 6.5 PRC, 6.5x284 Norma, .270 win., .270 WSM, .280 Ackley Imp., 7mm-08, 7mm Rem. Mag., .30-06, .300 WSM, .300 Win. Mag., or .338 Fed.; 2- or 4-rnd. magazine. Bbl.: 22- or 24-in. stainless. Weight: 7.2 lbs. Sights: optic ready. Accutrigger, gray AccuStock. Made 2018-date.

MODEL 110 TACTICAL. . . . . NiB $705 Ex $675 Gd $525
Short or long action. Cal.: .223 rem., .22-250, .243 Win., .25-06, 6.5 Creedmoor, 6.5 PRC, 6.5x284 Norma, .270 win., .270 WSM, .280 Ackley Imp., 7mm-08, 7mm Rem. Mag., .30-06, .300 WSM, .300 Win. Mag., or .338 Fed.; 2- or 4-rnd. magazine. Bbl.: 22- or 24-in. fluted, threaded. Finish: Matte balck. Weight: 7.2 lbs. Sights: optic ready. Accutrigger, gray AccuStock. Oversized bolt handle. Made 2018-date.

MODEL 110
TACTICAL DESERT . . . . **NiB $700 Ex $670 Gd $520**
Similar to Model 110 Tactical except w/FDE AccuStock. Made 2018-date.

MODEL 110 TIMBERLINE . . . . . . **NiB $995 Ex $855 Gd $680**
Similar to Model 110 STORM except w/RealTree Escape camo AccuStock, blue printed action, threaded bbl. Made 2020-date.

MODEL 110 ULTRALITE . . . . . **NiB $1320 Ex $1155 Gd $895**
Similar to Model 110 STORM except w/PROOF Research carbon fiber wrapped bbl., 6 lbs. Made 2020-date.

MODEL 110
ULTRALITE CAMO . . . . **NiB $1320 Ex $1155 Gd $895**
Similar to Model 110 ULTRALITE except w/KUIU Verde 2.0 camo. Made 2020-date.

MODEL 110V . . . . **NiB $355 Ex $310 Gd $245**
Varmint model. Cal.: .22-250 or .223 Rem.; 5-rnd. magazine. Bbl.: 26-in. medium. Weight: 9.2 lbs. Stock: Wundhammer pistol grip. Sights: None. Disc. 1989.

MODEL 110WLE . . . . **NiB $455 Ex $400 Gd $305**
Cal.: .250-3000 Savage, .300 Savage, or 7x57mm Mauser. Mfg. 1991-93.

MODEL 110 TROPHY
HUNTER XP PACKAGE . . . . **NiB $630 Ex $550 Gd $430**
Cal.: .270 Win., .30-06, .300 Win. Mag. or 7mm Rem. Mag., detachable magazine. 22- or 24-in. bbl. Weight: 9.3 lbs. Factory mounted scope. Stock: Satin wood. Finish: Matte black. AccuTrigger. Mfg. 2012-19.

MODEL 111 B HUNTER . . . . **NiB $630 Ex $530 Gd $405**
Long action. Cal.: .25-06, .270 Win., or .30-06; hinged floorlate internal magazine. Bbl.: 22-in. Disc. 2008.

MODEL 111 BT HUNTER . . . . . . **NiB $630 Ex $530 Gd $405**
Similar to Model 111 B Hunter except w/brown laminate thumbhole stock. Made 2010-18.

MODEL 111 CHIEFTAIN
Calibers: .243 Win., .270 Win., 7x57mm, 7mm Rem. Mag. .30-06. 3- or 4-rnd. clip magazine. Bbl.: 22- or 24-in. Weight: 7.5-8.25 lbs. Sights: Leaf rear; hooded ramp front. Stock: Select walnut stock w/Monte Carlo comb and cheekpiece, checkered, pistol-grip cap, QD swivels and sling. Made 1974-79.
standard calibers. . . . . **NiB $405 Ex $355 Gd $275**
magnum calibers. . . . . **NiB $455 Ex $400 Gd $310**

MODEL 111
DOA HUNTER XP . . . . **NiB $580 Ex $405 Gd $335**
Long action. Cal.: .25-06, .270 Win., 6.5x284 Norma, .30-06, 7mm Rem. Mag., .300 Win. Mag., .338 Win. Mag.; 3- or 4-rnd. detachable magazine. 22- or 24-in. bbl. Weight: 8 lbs. Sights: Factory mounted scope. Stock: Black synthetic. Disc. 2017.

MODEL 111F . . . . **NiB $408 Ex $405 Gd $290**
Similar to the Model 111G except with graphite/fiberglass composite stock. Weight: 6.25 lbs. Made 1994-11.
Model 111FC (detachable
magazine, 1994-03) . . . . **NiB $455 Ex $400 Gd $370**
Model 111FHNS (detachable magazine,
AccuTrigger, synthetic or
AccuStock, 2006-12) . . . . **NiB $580 Ex $500 Gd $370**
Model 111FYCAKS
(youth stock, 2006-09) . . . . . . **NiB $530 Ex $405 Gd $305**

MODEL 111FAK EXPRESS . . . . . . **NiB $430 Ex $375 Gd $295**
Long action. Cal.: .270 Win., .30-06, .300 Win. Mag., .338 Win. Mag. or 7mm Rem. Mag. Bbl.: 22-in. w/adj. muzzle brake. Sights: None. Stock: Black graphite fiberglass. Made 1996-98.

MODEL 111FCNS . . . . **NiB $630 Ex $505 Gd $370**
Long action. Cal.: .25-06, .270 Win., .30-06, .300 Win. Mag., .338 Win. Mag. or .375 Ruger; 4-rnd. detachable magazine. Bbl.: 22- or 24-in. Sights: None. Stock: Black synthetic stock or AccuStock. Accutrigger. Made 2005-17.

MODEL 1111G . . . . **NiB $700 Ex $510 Gd $420**
Long action. Cal.: .22-250, .223 Rem., .243 Win., .250 Savage, .25-06, .270 Win., .300 Savage, 7mm-08, .308 Win., .30-06, 7mm Rem. Mag., 7mm RUM., .300 Win. Mag., .300 RUM, or .338 Win. Mag. Bbl.: 20-, 22-, or 24-in. Weight: 7 lbs. Sights: Open or no sights, drilled/tapped. Stock: Walnut finish hardwood w/checkereing, vent recoil pad. Made 1994-2010.
Model 111GC (detachable
magazine, 1994-01) . . . . **NiB $430 Ex $375 Gd $295**
Model 111GCNS (detachable magazine,
no sights, 2005-12) . . . . **NiB $505 Ex $420 Gd $255**

MODEL 111 HOG HUNTER. . . . **NiB $480 Ex $430 Gd $340**
Specialty Series. Long action. Cal.: .338 Win. Mag.; 4-rnd. internal magazine. 20-in. threaded bbl. Weight: 6 lbs. Sights: Open. Stock: OD green synthetic. Finish: Matte black. AccuTrigger. Made 2012-16.

MODEL 111
HUNTER XP PACKAGE . . . . **NiB $470 Ex $405 Gd $335**
Similar to Model 111 DOA HUNTER XP but in .270 Win., .30-06, 7mm Rem. Mag., or .300 Win. Mag.; 4-rnd. detachable magazine. 22- or 24-in. bbl. Weight: 8 lbs. Sights: Factory mounted scope. Stock: Black synthetic. Finish: Matte black. Disc. 2012-14.

MODEL 111 LADY HUNTER . . . **NiB $815 Ex $715 Gd $555**
Long action. Cal.: .270 Win. or .30-06; 4-rnd. magazine. Bbl.: 20-in. Weight: 6 lbs. Sights: None, optic ready. Stock: Walnut finish hardwood w/pressed checkering, Monte Carlo style comb. Finish: Matte black. Accutrigger. Made 2012-date.

MODEL 111
LIGHTWEIGHT HUNTER . . . . . . **NiB $900 Ex $780 Gd $610**
Long action. Cal.: .270 Win., 6.5x284 Norma, or .30-06; 4-rnd. detachable magazine hinged floorplate. Bbl.: 20-in. Weight: 6 lbs. Sights: no sights, optic ready. Stock: Walnut finish hardwood. Finish: Blued. Accutrigger. Mfg. 2011 to date.

MODEL 111 LONG
RANGE HUNTER . . . . **NiB $980 Ex $670 Gd $530**
Long action. Cal.: .25-06 Rem., 6.5x284 Norma, .300 Win. Mag., 7mm Rem. Mag., or .338 Lapua Mag.; 3-rnd. internal or detachable magazine. 26-in. bbl. w/ muzzle brake. Weight: 8.4-9.25 lbs. Sights: no sights, optic ready. Matte black finish. AccuTrigger, black AccuStock. Made 2011-17.
.338 Lapua Mag . . . . **NiB $1210 Ex $1055 Gd $820**

MODEL 111 TROPHY
HUNTER XP PACKAGE . . . . **NiB $630 Ex $550 Gd $430**
Long action. Cal.: .25-06, .270 Win., 6.5x284 Norma, .30-06, .300 Win. Mag., 7mm Rem. Mag. .338 Win. Mag.; 4-rnd. detachable magazine. 22- or 24-in. bbl. Weight: 7.2 lbs. Factory mounted scope. Stock: Black synthetic. Finish: Matte black. AccuTrigger. Mfg. 2012-20.

RIFLES

MODEL 112BV . . . . **NiB $520 Ex $378 Gd $266**
Varmint Series. Long action. Cal.: .22-250 Rem..223 Rem.; 4-rnd. magazine. Bbl.: 26-in. heavy fluted bbl. Stock: Brown laminate w/Wundhammer grip. Disc. 1980.
Model 112BVSS (w/fluted stainless bbl., w/ or
w/o AccuTrigger, 1994-05) . . . **NiB $605 Ex $530 Gd $415**
Model 12BVSS-S (stainless finish,
single-shot, 2002-05) . . . . **NiB $555 Ex $485 Gd $380**

MODEL 112BT . . . . **NiB $955 Ex $830 Gd $655**
Competition grade. Cal.: .223 Rem. or .308 Win., 5-rnd. internal magazine. Bbl.: 26-in. heavy. Stock: Wood laminate w/ Wundhammer grip, adj. cheek riser. Sights: None. Weight: 11 lbs. Made 1994-2001.
Model 12BTS (stainless finish, .300 Win. Mag.,
single shot, 1995-2001) . . . . . **NiB $905 Ex $780 Gd $605**

MODEL 112FV . . . . **NiB $405 Ex $355 Gd $275**
Varmint Series. Similar to models 112BV except w/blued finish, black synthetic stock, 9 lbs. Made 1991-98 date.
Model 12FVS (single shot,
1992-93) . . . . **NiB $380 Ex $335 Gd $260**
Model 12FVSS-S (stainless finish,
single-shot, 1993-2002) . . . . . **NiB $505 Ex $445 Gd $345**

MODEL 112
MAGNUM TARGET . . . . **NiB $890 Ex $780 Gd $605**
Competition grade. Cal.: .338 Lapua Mag., single shot. Bbl.: 26-in. heavy w/muzzle brake. Stock: Wood gray laminate. Finish: Matte black. Sights: None. Weight: 12 lbs. Made 2015-date.

MODEL 112V VARMINT . . . . . . **NiB $405 Ex $355 Gd $275**
Single shot. Cal.: .220 Swift, .222 Rem., .223 Rem., .22-250, .243 Win., or .25-06. Bbl.: 26-in. heavy. Sights: Scope bases, w/o sights. Weight: 9.25 lbs. Stock: Select walnut varmint style w/checkered pistol-grip, high comb, QD sling swivels. Made 1975-79.

MODEL 112 VARMINTER
LOW PROFILE . . . . **NiB $670 Ex $550 Gd $375**
Long action. Cal.: .25-06 Rem. or .300 Win. Mag.; 4-rnd. internal magazine. Bbl.: 26-in. heavy fluted stainless. Sights: Scope bases, w/o sights. Weight: 10 lbs. Stock: Brown laminated w/ flat beavertail forend. Disc. 2006.

MODEL 114 AMERICAN
CLASSIC/CLASSIC. . . . . **NIB $815 EX $680 GD $480**
Long action. Cal.: .270 Win., 7mm Rem. Mag., .30-06, or .300 Win. Mag.; American Classic w/detachable magazine, Classic w/hinged floorplate magazine. Bbl.: 22- or 24-in. Sights: None, drilled/tapped. Stock: Checkered walnut w/black forend tip. Finish: high luster blue. Made 2005-18.
stainless. . . . . **NiB $880 Ex $755 Gd $580**

MODEL 114 EURO CLASSIC . . . . . **NIB $755 EX $600 GD $530**
Similar to Model 114 American Classic/Classic except in .270 Win. or .30-06 and checkered Monte Carlo walnut stock w/oil finish. Made 2006-10. CE (Classic European) made 1996-2001.
Model 114CE (7x64mm
Brenneke, adj. sights) . . . . **NiB $505 Ex $445 Gd $345**

MODEL 114C CLASSIC. . . . . . . **NIB $755 EX $600 GD $530**
Long action. Cal.: .270 Win., 7mm Rem. Mag., .30-06, or .300 Win. Mag.; 3- or 4-rnd. detachable magazine. Bbl.: 22- or 24-in. Sights: Drilled/tapped. Stock: High gloss checkered walnut w/black forend tip. Finish: high luster blue. Made 1991-2000. CU (Classic Ultra) disc. 1995.

Model 114CU (adj. sights) . . . . . **NiB $755 Ex $600 Gd $530**

MODEL 114U. . . . . **NIB $505 EX $445 GD $345**
Similar to Model 114C except in 7mm STW. Made 1996-2001.

MODEL 116 ALASKA
BRUSH HUNTER . . . . **NIB $640 EX $505 GD $400**
Specialty Series. Long action. Cal.: .338 Win. Mag. or .375 Ruger, internal magazine. 20-in. bbl. w/open sights. Synthetic stock, AccuTrigger. Weight: 7.6 lbs. Length: 41.5 in. Made 2012-18.

MODEL 116 BEAR HUNTER . . . **NIB $945 EX $755 GD $555**
Specialty Series. Long action. Cal.: .300 Win. Mag., .338 Win. Mag. or .375 Ruger, internal magazine. 23-in. bbl. w/muzzle brake. Synthetic black or camo AccuStock, AccuTrigger. Weight: 7.75 lbs. Made 2011-16.

MODELS 116BSS
WEATHER WARRIOR. . . . . **NIB $565 EX $485 GD $350**
Similar to the Model 116FSS except w/brown laminated checkered wood stock. Weight: 7.75 lbs. Mfg. 2001-02.

MODEL 116 TROPHY
HUNTER XP PACKAGE . . . . **NIB $655 EX $580 GD $455**
Long action. Various calibers. 22- or 24-in. bbl. Black synthetic stock, AccuTrigger. Finish: stainless. Weight: 7.25 lbs. Factory mounted Nikon 3-9x40mm scope. Made 2012 to date.

MODELS 116FSAK. . . . . **NIB $535 EX $470 GD $345**
Long action. Cal.: .270 Win., .30-06, 7mm Mag., .300 Win. Mag., .338 Win. Mag. Bbl.: Fluted 22-in. stainless w/adj. muzzle brake. Weight: 6.5 lbs. Made 1994-04.
Model 116FCSAK (detachable
magazine; 1994-2000) . . . . **NiB $565 Ex $500 Gd $355**

MODELS 116FSS . . . . **NIB $580 EX $480 GD $335**
Satin stainless action and bbl. Cal.: .22-250, .223 Rem., .243 Win., .270 Win., .308 Win., .30-06, 7mm Rem. Mag., 7mm STW, 7mm RUM, .300 Win. Mag., .300 RUM, .338 Win. Mag., or .375 Ruger; 3- or 4-rnd. magazine. 22-, 24- or 26-in. bbl. Weight: About 6.7 lbs. Black Rynite stock w/recoil pad and swivel studs. Receiver drilled and tapped, no sights. Made 1991-2011.
Model 116FCSS (AccuTrigger,
2005-17). . . . . **NiB $755 Ex $630 Gd $455**
Model 116FHSS (AccuTrigger,
muzzle brake, 2006-13) . . . . . . **NiB $730 Ex $630 Gd $455**
MODEL 116FSK KODIAK (22-in. bbl., "Shock Suppressor"
recoil reducer, 1994-2000) . . . **NiB $500 Ex $435 Gd $330**

MODEL 116FXP3 PACKAGE . . . **NIB $630 EX $500 GD $365**
Similar to the Model 116 Trophy Hunter XP Package except w/ factory mounted nickel finish scope. Made 2002-11.

MODEL 116
LIGHTWEIGHT HUNTER . . . . . **NiB $655 Ex $580 Gd $455**
Long action. Cal.: .270 Win.; 4-rnd. detachable magazine. Bbl.: 20-in. Weight: 6 lbs. Sights: no sights, optic ready. Stock: Black synthetic. Finish: Blued. AccuTrigger. Disc. 2016.

MODEL 116SE
(SAFARI EXPRESS) . . . . **NIB $900 EX $780 GD $630**
Long action. Cal.:.300 Win. Mag., .300 RUM, .338 Win. mag., .375 H&H, .425 Express, or .458 Win. Mag. 24-in. stainless bbl. w/muzzle brake. Stock: Checkered walnut w/ebony forend tip, recoil pad. Weight: 6.5 lbs. Made 1994-2004.

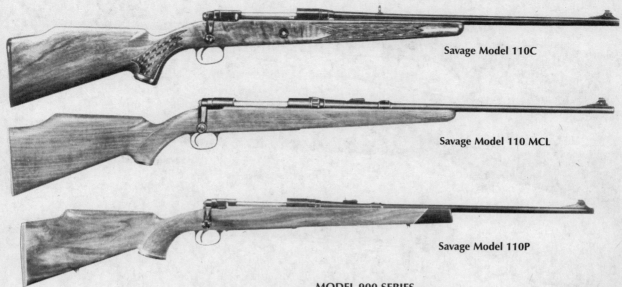

Savage Model 110C

Savage Model 110 MCL

Savage Model 110P

MODEL 116US

(ULTRA STAINLESS) . . . . .NiB $630 EX $555 GD $450
Long action. Cal.: .270 Win., 7mm Rem Mag., .30-06, .300 Win. Mag. 34-in. stainless bbl. Stock: Checkered walnut w/ ebony forend tip. Weight: 7.8 lbs. Made 1995-98.

MODEL 16/116FXP3 PACKAGE . . .NiB $782 Ex $630 Gd $500
Similar to the Model 16/116 Trophy Hunter XP Package except w/factory mounted nickel finish scope. Made 2002-11.

MODEL 116-SE, 116-US RIFLES
Calibers: .270 Win., 7mm Rem Mag., .30-06, .300 Win. Mag. (116US); .300 Win. Mag., .338 Win. mag., .425 Express, .458 Win. Mag. (116SE). 24-in. stainless barrel (with muzzle brake 116SE only). 45.5 in. overall. Weight: 7.2 to 8.5 lbs. Three round magazine. 3-leaf Express sights 116SE only. Checkered Classic style select walnut stock with ebony forend tip. Stainless finish. Made 1994-2004.
Model 116SE (Safari Express) . .NiB $947 Ex $788 Gd $556
Model 116US (Ultra Stainless) . NiB $660 Ex $498 Gd $400

MODEL 340 BOLT-ACTION REPEATER
Calibers: .22 Hornet, .222 Rem., .223 Rem., .227 Win., .30-30. Clip magazine; 4-rnd. capacity (3-rnd. in 30-30). Bbl. lengths: Originally 20-in. in .30-30, 22-in. in .22 Hornet; later 22-in. in .30-30, 24-in. in other calibers. Weight: 6.5 to 7.5 lbs. depending on caliber and vintage. Sights: Open rear (folding leaf on recent production); ramp front. Early models had plain pistol-grip stock, checkered since 1965. Made 1950-85. (Note: Those rifles produced between 1947-50 were .22 Hornet Stevens Model .322 and .30-30 Model .325. The Savage model, however, was designated Model .340 for all calibers.)
Pre-1965 w/plain stock. . . . . .NiB $266 Ex $190 Gd $105
Savage Model 340C Carbine. . .NiB $278 Ex $228 Gd $140

MODEL 340S DELUXE . . . . . . .NiB $345 Ex $298 Gd $218
Same as Model 340 except has checkered stock, screw eyes for sling, peep rear sight, hooded front. Made 1955-60.

MODEL 342 . . . . .NiB $345 Ex $298 Gd $218
Designation, 1950 to 1955, of Model 340 .22 Hornet.

MODEL 342S DELUXE . . . . . . .NiB $355 Ex $325 Gd $227
Designation, 1950 to 1955, of Model 340S .22 Hornet.

MODEL 900 SERIES
Bolt action. Caliber .22 LR; single shot or 5-rnd. magazine. Stock: smooth hardwood. Barrel: 21- or 25-in. Weight: 8-8.25 lbs.
900B Biathlon (repeater, carrying and shooting rails, butt hook/hand stop, 21-in. bbl. w/snow cover, peep sights, 1996–2001) . . . . .NiB $450 Ex $395 Gd $250
900S Silhoutte (single shot, shooting rail/hand stop, no sights, 21-in. bbl., 1996–97) . . . . .NiB $305 Ex $270 Gd $170
900TR Target (single shot, shooting rail/hand stop, front sight has 7 aperture inserts, 25-in. bbl., 1996–2001) . . . . .NiB $400 Ex $350 Gd $220

AXIS SERIES
Bolt action. Calibers: .223 Rem., .243 Win., .25-06 Rem., .270 Win., 6.5 Creedmoor, .308 Win., or .30-06. Bbl: 22-in. Stock: black synthetic. Weight: 6.3 lbs. Finish: matte black. Magazine: 4-rnd. detachable box. Made 2011–date.
blued. .NiB $330 Ex $290 Gd $225
camo (Mossy Oak
  Break Up, disc. 2014) . . . . . . .NiB $390 Ex $340 Gd $285
stainless (2011-13) . . . . .NiB $360 Ex $330 Gd $280
Heavy Barrel, add. $20
SR (suppressor ready, 2012-18.) . .NiB $355 Ex $305 Gd $250
XP (scope combo), add. $40
XP Camo (scope combo), add. $110
XP Stainless (scope combo), add. $160

AXIS II SERIES
Similar to Axis XP except w/Accutrigger. Made 2014 to date.
blued. . . . . .NiB $385 Ex $340 Gd $265
300 Blackout (.300 BLK,
  Picatinny rail) . . . . .NiB $385 Ex $340 Gd $265
Compact . . . . .NiB $385 Ex $340 Gd $265
Overwatch (Mossy Oak Overwatch
  camo, Picatinny rail) . . . . .NiB $475 Ex $420 Gd $335
Precision (22-in. bbl., 10-rnd. mag., MDT
  aluminum chassis, 2020-22) . .NiB $845 Ex $735 Gd $560
XP (synthetic stock, factory
  mounted scope, blued) . . . . . .NiB $430 Ex $380 Gd $300
XP Hardwood (wood stock,
  factory mounted scope) . . . . .NiB $530 Ex $480 Gd $400
XP Stainless (synthetic stock, factory
  mounted scope, stainless) . . . .NiB $505 Ex $450 Gd $345
XP Youth (black synthetic or pink camo stock, factory
  mounted scope, blued) . . . . . .NiB $430 Ex $380 Gd $300

GRADING: **NiB** = New in Box   **Ex** = Excellent or NRA 95%   **Gd** = Good or NRA 68%

Savage Model 111 Chieftain

Savage Model 111F

Savage Model 112V

Savage Model 116FCSAK

Savage Model 116 Bear Hunter

B SERIES

Bolt action. Cal.: .17 HMR, .22 LR or .22 WMR; 10-rnd. detachable rotary magazine. Bbl.: 16.5-, 18-, or 21-in. Sights: Iron or optic ready. Stock: Black synthetic or wood. Finish: Blued, stainless steel, or camo. Accu-Trigger. Mfg. 2017-19, reintro. 2022.

B17 BNS-SR (.17 HMR, laminated wood
   stock, blued, 18-in. bbl.) . . . . . NiB $540 Ex $490 Gd $420
B17 F (.17 HRM, synthetic
   stock, blued). . . . . NiB $380 Ex $310 Gd $270
B17 F Compact (.17 HMR, synthetic
   stock, blued, 18-in. bbl.) . . . . . NiB $330 Ex $265 Gd $215
B17 FV (.17 HMR, synthetic stock,
   blued, 21-in. heavy bbl.) . . . . . NiB $360 Ex $300 Gd $260
B17 FV Stainless (.17 HMR, synthetic stock,
   stainless, 21-in. heavy bbl.) . . . NiB $440 Ex $400 Gd $360
B17 FV-SR (.17 HMR, synthetic stock, stainless,
   16.2-in. threaded bbl.) . . . . NiB $370 Ex $310 Gd $290
B17 FV-SR Overwatch (.17 HMR,
   camo synthetic stock, stainless,
   16.2-in. threaded bbl.) . . . . NiB $430 Ex $400 Gd $360
B17 Precision (.17 HMR, MDT aluminum chassis, black,
   18-in. threaded bbl.) . . . . NiB $650 Ex $610 Gd $590
B17 Precision Lite (.17 HMR, MDT aluminum
   chassis, black, 18-in. carbon fiber
   wrap threaded bbl.) . . . . NiB $940 Ex $900 Gd $860
B22 BNS-SR (.22 LR, laminated wood
   stock, blued, 18-in. bbl.) . . . . . NiB $520 Ex $470 Gd $400
B22 F (.22 LR, synthetic
   stock, blued). . . . . NiB $320 Ex $255 Gd $205
B22 F Compact (.22 LR, synthetic stock,
   blued, 18-in. bbl., sights) . . . . . NiB $320 Ex $255 Gd $205
B22 FV (.22 LR, synthetic stock,
   blued, 21-in. heavy bbl.) . . . . . NiB $340 Ex $300 Gd $260
B22 FV Stainless (.22 LR, synthetic stock,
   stainless, 21-in. heavy bbl.) . . . NiB $440 Ex $400 Gd $360
B22 FV-SR (.22 LR, synthetic stock, stainless, 16.2-in.
   threaded bbl.). . . . . NiB $360 Ex $300 Gd $280
B22 FV-SR Overwatch (.22 LR, camo synthetic stock, stainless, 16.2-in. threaded bbl.) . . . NiB $390 Ex $330 Gd $310
B22 G (.22 LR, wood stock,
   stainless, 21-in. bbl., sights) . . . NiB $490 Ex $410 Gd $390
B22 Precision (.22 LR, MDT aluminum chassis, black, 18-in.
   threaded bbl.). . . . . NiB $650 Ex $610 Gd $590
B22 Precision Lite (.22 LR, MDT aluminum
   chassis, black, 18-in. carbon fiber
   wrap threaded bbl.) . . . . NiB $940 Ex $900 Gd $860
B22 Magnum BNS-SR (.22 WMR, laminated wood stock,
   blued, 18-in. bbl.). . . . . NiB $540 Ex $490 Gd $420
B22 Magnum F (.22 WMR,
   synthetic stock, blued) . . . . NiB $340 Ex $275 Gd $225
B22 Magnum F Compact (.22 WMR, synthetic stock, blued,
   18-in. bbl.). . . . . NiB $330 Ex $265 Gd $215
B22 Magnum FV (.22 WMR, synthetic stock, blued, 21-in.
   heavy bbl.) . . . . NiB $360 Ex $320 Gd $280
B22 Magnum FV Stainless (.22 WMR, synthetic stock, stainless, 21-in. heavy bbl.) . . . . NiB $440 Ex $400 Gd $360
B22 Magnum FV-SR (.22 WMR, synthetic stock, stainless,
   16.2-in. threaded bbl.) . . . . NiB $370 Ex $310 Gd $290
B22 Magnum G (.22 WMR, wood stock,
   stainless, 21-in. bbl., sights) . . . NiB $510 Ex $490 Gd $390

Savage Edge

Savage Model 219

Savage Mark II BV

B22 Magnum Precision (.22 WMR, MDT aluminum chassis, black, 18-in. threaded bbl.) . . . **NiB $650 Ex $610 Gd $590**
B22 Magnum Precision Lite (.22 WMR, MDT aluminum chassis, black, 18-in. carbon fiber wrap threaded bbl.) . . . . **NiB $940 Ex $900 Gd $860**

MODEL B.MAG SERIES
Bolt-action. Caliber: .17 WSM, 8-rnd. rotary magazine. 22-in. bbl. Weight: 4.5 lbs. Sights: optic ready. Stock: black synthetic. AccuTrigger. Made 2013 to date.
Blued . . . . **NiB $345 Ex $305 Gd $235**
Blued Heavy Barrel . . . . **NiB $365 Ex $320 Gd $250**
Sporter (stainless or blued heavy bbl.) . . . . . **NiB $460 Ex $410 Gd $320**
Stainless Heavy Barrel . . . . **NiB $395 Ex $345 Gd $260**
Target (stainless) . . . . **NiB $525 Ex $460 Gd $360**

CUB . . . . **NiB $227 Ex $180 Gd $160**
Bolt-action, single-shot. Calibers: .17 Mach 2 or .22 LR. 16-in. bbl. Weight: 4.5 lbs. Sights: Open rear; ramp front. Stock: hardwood or polymer (pink). AccuTrigger added 2006. Made 2003-11.
Target (thumbhole stock), add **$100**

EDGE . . . . **NiB $330 Ex $340 Gd $300**
Bolt-action. Caliber: .223., .22-250, .243, .25-06, .270, .308, .30-06 or 7mm-08, 4-rnd. detachable magazine. 22-in. bbl. Weight: 6.5 lbs. Drilled and tapped. Stock: black synthetic. Blued finish. Made 2010-11.
XP (scope combo), add **$50**

IMPULSE SERIES
Straight pull bolt-action. Cal.: .22-250 Rem., .243, 6mm Creedmoor, 6.5 Creedmoor, 6.5 PRC, .300 PRC, .308 Win., .30-06, .300 WSM, .300 Win. Mag., .338 Lapua Mag.; 2-,3- or 4-rnd. detachable magazine. Bbl.: 22-in. fluted, threaded. Weight: 8.5-9 lbs. Optic ready. AccuTrigger, AccuStock. Matte black or stainless finish. Made 2021-date.
Big Game (KUIU Verde 2.0 camo stock, hazel green Cerakote finish) . . . . **NiB $1235 Ex $1080 Gd $840**
Elite Precision (26-in. stainless bbl.; MDT ACC adj. chassis, gray Cerakote finish) . . . . . **NiB $2499 Ex $2390 Gd $1390**
Hog Hunter (18-, 20-, or 24-in. heavy bbl.; OD green stock, matte black finish) . . . . **NiB $1180 Ex $1030 Gd $810**
Predator (20-in. bbl.; Mossy Oak Terra Gila camo stock, matte black finish) . . . . **NiB $1180 Ex $1030 Gd $810**

MODEL MARK I G . . . . **NiB $272 Ex $240 Gd $190**
Bolt-action, single-shot. Calibers: .22 Short, Long, LR. 18- or 20.75-in. bbl. Weight: 5 lbs. Sights: Open rear; ramp front. Stock: hardwood. AccuTrigger added 2006. Made 1996 to date.
Mark I FVT (synthetic stock, new 2005), add **$10**
Mark I GY (youth model), subtract **$40**

MODEL MARK II SERIES
Bolt-action. Calibers: .17 Mach 2 or .22 LR, 10-rnd. magazine. Bbl.: 21-in. Weight: 5 lbs. Sights: Open rear; ramp front. Stock: black polymer. Blued finish. AccuTrigger added 2006. Mark II B models in .22 LR only, w/ 21-in. heavy spiral fluted bbl., and laminated wood stock. Add $50 for left hand models. Made 1998 to date.
Camo (synthetic stock, new 2002), subtract **$30**
Mark II F . . . . **NiB $308 Ex $290 Gd $230**
Mark II BRJ (blued) . . . . **NiB $475 Ex $415 Gd $330**
Mark II BSEV (stainless, laminate thumbhole stock) . . . **NiB $560 Ex $485 Gd $380**
Mark II BTV (blued, laminate thumbhole stock) . . . . **NiB $355 Ex $305 Gd $245**
Mark II BTVSS (stainless, laminate thumbhole stock) . . . . **NiB $430 Ex $380 Gd $300**
Mark II BV (heavy bbl., laminate stock) . . . . **NiB $315 Ex $275 Gd $210**
Mark II Camo (synthetic stock, 2002-22) . . . . **NiB $235 Ex $205 Gd $160**
Mark II FSS (stainless) . . . . **NiB $336 Ex $300 Gd $265**
Mark II FV (heavy varmint bbl.) . . **NiB $344 Ex $310 Gd $280**
Mark II FVT (heavy varmint bbl., target sights) . . . . **NiB $471 Ex $440 Gd $400**
Mark II FV-SR (.22 LR only, 16.5-in. heavy bbl., suppressor ready, optic ready, no sights, new 2011) . . . . **NiB $471 Ex $440 Gd $400**
Mark II FV-SR Landry (gator camo stock, new 2015) . . . . **NiB $461 Ex $430 Gd $390**
Mark II FXP (.22 LR only, satin blue finish, optic ready, no sights, OD gren stock, new 2014) . . . . **NiB $461 Ex $430 Gd $390**
Mark II G (wood stock) . . . . **NiB $230 Ex $205 Gd $160**
Mark II GY (youth size stock) . . . **NiB $230 Ex $205 Gd $160**
Mark II Minimalist (.22 LR, wood laminate green or brown stock, blued, 18-in. bbl.) . . . . . **NiB $370 Ex $310 Gd $260**
Mark II TR (22-in. fluted bbl., wood tactical style stock) . . . . **NiB $480 Ex $420 Gd $330**
Mark II TRR-SR (Picatinny rails) . . **NiB $555 Ex $485 Gd $380**

RASCAL SERIES
Bolt-action, single-shot. Caliber: .22 S/L/LR. 16-in. bbl. Weight: 4.5 lbs. Sights: Open rear; ramp front. Stock: hardwood or

RIFLES

Savage Model 340

Savage Axis XP

Savage/Anschutz Mark 10D

Savage-Stevens Model 34

polymer (various colors). Weight: 2.6 lbs. AccuTrigger. Made 2102 to date.

synthetic stock . . . . NiB $180 Ex $160 Gd $140
hardwood stock . . . . NiB $220 Ex $200 Gd $180
FV-SR (heavy threaded bbl.,
    polymer stock) . . . . NiB $200 Ex $175 Gd $140
Minimalist (Gator Camo
    synthetic stock) . . . . NiB $205 Ex $175 Gd $140
Landry (Boyd's laminated
    stock, threaded bbl.) . . . . NiB $245 Ex $215 Gd $170
Red, White & Blue (American
    flag stock) . . . . NiB $205 Ex $175 Gd $140
Target (heavy threaded bbl.,
    hardwood stock) . . . . NiB $285 Ex $250 Gd $195
Target XP (heavy threaded bbl., hardwood stock,
    factory mounted scope) . . . . . NiB $365 Ex $320 Gd $250

- BREAK-ACTION RIFLES -

MODEL 219 . . . . NiB $227 Ex $119 Gd $67
Single-shot. Hammerless. Takedown. Shotgun-type action with top lever. Calibers: .22 Hornet, .25-20, .32-20, .30-30. 26-in. bbl. Weight: about 6 lbs. Sights: Open rear; bead front. Plain pistol-grip stock and forearm. Made 1938-65.
Model 219L (w/side lever,
    made 1965-67) . . . . NiB $155 Ex $100 Gd $70

MODEL 221-229 UTILITY GUNS
Same as Model 219 except in various calibers, supplied in combination with an interchangeable shotgun bbl. All versions discontinued.
Model 221 (.30-30, 12-ga.
    30-in. bbl.) . . . . NiB $155 Ex $80 Gd $55

Model 222 (.30-30, 16-ga.
    28-in. bbl.) . . . . NiB $155 Ex $80 Gd $55
Model 223 (.30-30, 20-ga.
    28-in. bbl.) . . . . NiB $155 Ex $80 Gd $55
Model 227 (.22 Hornet, 12-ga.
    30-in. bbl.) . . . . NiB $155 Ex $80 Gd $55
Model 228 (.22 Hornet, 16-ga.
    28-in. bbl.) . . . . NiB $155 Ex $80 Gd $55
Model 229 (.22 Hornet, 20-ga.
    28-in. bbl.) . . . . NiB $155 Ex $80 Gd $55

- LEVER-ACTION RIFLES -

MODEL 71 "STEVENS FAVORITE" SINGLE-SHOT LEVER-ACTION RIFLE . . . . NiB $229 Ex $114 Gd $98
Replica of original Stevens Favorite issued as a tribute to Joshua Stevens, "Father of .22 Hunting." Caliber: .22 LR. 22-in. full-octagon bbl. Brass-plated hammer and lever. Sights: Open rear; brass blade front. Weight: 4.5 lbs. Plain straight-grip buttstock and Schnabel forend; brass commemorative medallion inlaid in buttstock, brass crescent-shaped buttplate. 10,000 produced. Made in 1971 only. Top value is for new, unfired gun.

NOTE: *The Model 72 is a "Favorite"-type single-shot unlike the smaller, original "Crackshot" made by Stevens from 1913 to 1939. See "Stevens" for additional models.*

MODEL 72 CRACKSHOT SINGLE-SHOT
LEVER-ACTION RIFLE . . . . NiB $190 Ex $109 Gd $79
Falling-block action. Casehardened frame. Caliber: .22 Short, Long, LR. 22-in. octagon bbl. Weight: 4.5lbs. Sights: Open rear; bead front. Plain straight-grip stock and forend of walnut. Made 1972-89.

Savage-Stevens Model 46

Savage Rascal

Savage-Stevens Model 72 — Crackshot

Savage-Stevens Model 73

Savage A17

MODEL 89 SINGLE-SHOT LEVER-ACTION CARBINE. . . . . NiB $121 Ex $90 Gd $66
Martini-type action. Caliber: .22 Short, Long, LR. 18.5-in. bbl. Weight: 5 lbs. Sights: Open rear; bead front. Western-style carbine stock w/straight grip, forearm with bbl. band. Made 1976-89.

MODEL 1899 SERIES
Lever action, hammerless. Caliber: .303 Savage, .30-30 Win., .25-35 WCF, .32-40 WCF, .38-55 WCF, or .250-3000. Internal box magazine. Stock: wood with straight grip, crescent or flat buttplate. Mfg. 1899–1921.
1899A (22- or 26-in. bbl.) . . . . NiB $1310 Ex $1055 Gd $680
1899B (26-in. octagon bbl.). . . . NiB $1410 Ex $1210 Gd $710
**1899C (26-in. half octagon
    bbl.)** . . . . NiB $1710 Ex $1555 Gd $910
**1899D (30-in. bbl., musket length
    stock)** . . . . NiB $1710 Ex $1555 Gd $910
**1899H (20-in. bbl.,
    1905-15)** . . . . NiB $1355 Ex $1155 Gd $630
**1899 .250-3000 (takedown frame, pistol grip stock,
    1914-21)** . . . . NiB $1510 Ex $1280 Gd $695

NOTE: *Introduced in 1899, the Model 99 has been produced in a variety of styles and calibers. Original designation "Model 1899" was changed to "Model 99" c.1920. Earlier rifles and carbines—similar to Models 99A, 99B and 99H— were available in calibers .25-35, .30-30, .303 Sav., .32-40 and .38-55. Post-WWII Models 99A, 99C, 99CD, 99DE, 99DL, 99F and 99PE have top tang safety other 99s have slide safety on right side of trigger guard. Models 99C and*

99CD have detachable box magazine instead of traditional rotary magazine.

MODEL 99A (I). . . . . NiB $1015 Ex $768 Gd $545
Hammerless. Solid frame. Calibers: .30-30, .300 Sav., .303 Sav. Five-rnd. rotary magazine. 24-in. bbl. Weight: 7.25 lbs. Sights: Open rear; bead front, on ramp. Plain straight-grip stock, tapered forearm. Made 1920-36.

MODEL 99A (II) . . . . NiB $915 Ex $668 Gd $445
Current model. Similar to original Model 99A except w/top tang safety, 22-in. bbl., folding leaf rear sight, no crescent buttplate. Calibers: .243 Win., .250 Sav., .300 Sav., .308 Win. Made 1971-82.

MODEL 99B . . . . NiB $1245 Ex $938 Gd $577
Takedown. Otherwise same as Model 99A except weight: 7.5 lbs. Made 1920-36.

MODEL 99C . . . . NiB $560 Ex $488 Gd $399
Current model. Same as Model 99F except w/clip magazine instead of rotary. Calibers: .243 Win., .284 Win., .308 Win. Four round detachable magazine holds one round less in .284. Weight: 6.75 lbs. Made 1965-98.

MODEL 99CD. . . . . NiB $698 Ex $599 Gd $389
Deluxe version of Model 99C. Calibers: .243 Win., .250 Sav., .308 Win. Hooded ramp front sight. Weight: 8.25 lbs. Stock w/Monte Carlo comb and cheekpiece, checkered pistol-grip, grooved forearm, swivels and sling. Made 1975-81.

**MODEL 99DE CITATION
GRADE** . . . . NiB $955 Ex $679 Gd $495
Same as Model 99PE except w/less elaborate engraving. Made 1968-70.

Savage-Stevens Model 89

Savage-Stevens Model 987-T

MODEL 99DL DELUXE.......NiB $745 Ex $576 Gd $359
Postwar model. Calibers: .243 Win., .308 Win. Same as Model 99F, except w/high comb Monte Carlo stock, sling swivels. Weight: 6.75 lbs. Made 1960-73.

MODEL 99E CARBINE (I).....NiB $656 Ex $500 Gd $439
Pre-WWII type. Solid frame. Calibers: .22 Hi-Power, .250/3000, .30/30, .300 Sav., .303 Sav. w/22-in. bbl.; .300 Sav. 24-in. Weight: 7 lbs. Other specifications same as Model 99A. Made 1920-36.

MODEL 99E CARBINE (II) ....NiB $709 Ex $505 Gd $457
Current model. Solid frame. Calibers: .250 Sav., .243 Win., .300 Sav., .308 Win. 20- or 22-in. bbl. Checkered pistol-grip stock and forearm. Made 1960-89.

MODEL 99EG (I)...........NiB $877 Ex $687 Gd $476
Pre-WWII type. Solid frame. Plain pistol-grip stock and forearm. Otherwise same as Model G. Made 1936-41.

MODEL 99EG (II) ....NiB $1023 Ex $799 Gd $600
Post-WWII type. Same as prewar model except w/checkered stock and forearm. Calibers: .250 Sav., .300 Sav., .308 Win. (intro. 1955), .243 Win., and .358 Win. Made 1946-60.

MODEL 99F
FEATHERWEIGHT (I) ....NiB $813 Ex $707 Gd $514
Pre-WWII type. Takedown. Specifications same as Model 99E, except weight: 6.5 lbs. Made 1920-42. Some marked 99M.

MODEL 99F
FEATHERWEIGHT (II) ....NiB $945 Ex $735 Gd $567
Postwar model. Solid frame. Calibers: .243 Win., .300 Sav., .308 Win. 22-in. bbl. Checkered pistol-grip stock and forearm. Weight: 6.5 lbs. Made 195-73.

MODEL 99G..............NiB $1290 Ex $933 Gd $707
Takedown. Checkered pistol-grip stock and forearm. Weight: 7.25 lbs. Other specifications same as Model 99E. Made 1920-42.

MODEL 99H CARBINE......NiB $926 Ex $577 Gd $4455
Solid frame. Calibers: .250/3000, .30/30, .300 Sav. 20-in. special weight bbl. Walnut carbine stock w/metal buttplate; walnut forearm w/bbl. band. Weight: 6.5 lbs. Open rear sights; ramped blade front sight. Other specifications same as Model 99A. Made 1931-42.

MODEL 99K ....NiB $3854 Ex $2650 Gd $2128
Deluxe version of Model G w/similar specifications except w/ fancy stock and engraving on receiver and bbl. Lyman peep rear sight and folding middle. Made 1931-42.

MODEL 99PE PRESENTATION
GRADE ....NiB $2055 Ex $1717 Gd $854
Same as Model 99DL except w/engraved receiver (game scenes on sides), tang and lever, fancy walnut Monte Carlo stock and forearm w/hand checkering, QD swivels. Calibers: .243, .284, .308. Made 1968 to 1970.

MODEL 99R (I)............NiB $735 Ex $588 Gd $499
Pre-WWII type. Solid frame. Calibers: .250-3000 (22-in. bbl.), .300 Sav. (24-in. bbl.). Weight: 7.5 lbs. Special large pistol-grip stock and forearm, checkered. General specifications same as other Model 99 rifles. Made 1936-42.

MODEL 99R (II) ....NiB $689 Ex $498 Gd $356
Post-WWII type. Same as prewar mod except w/24-in. bbl. only, w/screw eyes for sling swivels. Calibers: .250 Sav., .300 Sav., .308 Win., .243 Win. and .358 Win. Made 1946-60.

MODEL 99RS (I)...........NiB $944 Ex $650 Gd $489
Pre-WWII type. Same as prewar Model 99R except equipped w/Lyman rear peep sight and folding middle sight, quick detachable swivels and sling. Made 1932-42.

MODEL 99RS (II) ....NiB $756 Ex $600 Gd $467
Post-WWII type. Same as postwar Model 99RS except equipped w/Redfield 70LH receiver sight, blank in middle sight slot. Made 1946-60.

MODEL 99T ....NiB $1707 Ex $1032 Gd $744
Featherweight. Solid frame. Calibers: .22 Hi-Power, .30/30, .303 Sav. w/20-in. bbl.; .300 Sav. w/22-in. bbl. Checkered pistol-grip stock and beavertail forearm. Weight: 7 lbs. General specifications same as other Model 99 rifles. Made 1936-42.

MODEL 99-358............NiB $1156 Ex $903 Gd $657
Similar to current Model 99A except caliber .358 Win. has grooved forearm, recoil pad, swivel studs. Made 1977-80.

ANNIVERSARY MODEL 1895
LEVER-ACTION..........NiB $6235 Ex $4589 Gd $2240
Replica of Savage Model 1895 Hammerless Lever-Action Rifle issued to commemorate the 75th anniversary (1895-1970) of Savage Arms. Caliber: .308 Win. Five round rotary magazine. 24-in. full-octagon bbl. Engraved receiver. Brass-plated lever. Sights: Open rear; brass blade front. Plain straight-grip buttstock, Schnabel-type forend; brass medallion inlaid in buttstock, brass

crescent-shaped buttplate. 9,999 produced. Made in 1970 only. Top value is for new, unfired specimen.

- SEMIAUTO RIFLES -

MODEL 1912 . . . . NiB $800 Ex $533 Gd $337
Takedown. Caliber: 22 LR. only. Seven round detachable box magazine. 20-in. bbl., plain stock and forearm. Made 1912-16.

MODEL 6 AUTOLOADING RIFLE . . . NiB $169 Ex $94 Gd $57
Takedown. Caliber: .22 Short, Long, LR. Tubular magazine holds 21 Short, 17 Long, 15 LR. 24-in. bbl. Weight: 6 lbs. Sights: Open rear; bead front. Checkered pistol-grip stock on prewar models, postwar rifles have plain stocks. Made 1938-68.
**6S (peep rear sight/hooded
    front, 1938-42)** . . . . NiB $170 Ex $95 Gd $50

MODEL 7 . . . . NiB $167 Ex $105 Gd $59
Same general specifications as Model 6 except w/5-rnd. detachable box magazine. Made 1939-51.
**7S (peep rear sight/hooded
    front, 1938-42)** . . . . NiB $167 Ex $105 Gd $62

MODEL 60 . . . . NiB $115 Ex $80 Gd $48
Caliber: .22 LR. 15-rnd. tubular magazine. 20-in. bbl. Weight: 6 lbs. Sights: Open rear, ramp front. Monte Carlo stock of walnut w/checkered pistol-grip and forearm. Made 1969-72.

MODEL 64 SERIES
Semiauto. Blow back action. Cal.: .22 LR; 10-rnd. detachable steel magazine. Bbl.: 20.2- or 21-in. Sights: Adj. open. Stock: Black or synthetic or wood. Finish: Blued, stainless steel. Add $50 for XP models w/factory mounted scope. Mfg. 1996-date.
**64 BTV (21-in. heavy bbl., thumbhole
    wood stock, 2008-12)** . . . . . . NiB $330 Ex $290 Gd $230
**64 Camo (synthetic stock, 21-in.
    bbl., 2003-date)** . . . . NiB $180 Ex $160 Gd $125
**64 G (checkered wood stock,
    open sights)** . . . . NiB $205 Ex $185 Gd $145
64 F (black polymer stock) . . . . . NiB $130 Ex $115 Gd $90
**64 FSS (stainless,
    synthetic stock)** . . . . NiB $195 Ex $170 Gd $135
**64 F Takedown (black polymer
    stock, 16.5-in bbl.)** . . . . NiB $220 Ex $195 Gd $150
**64 FV (black polymer stock,
    heavy bbl., disc. 2004)** . . . . . . NiB $180 Ex $165 Gd $140
**64 FVSS (stainless, synthetic
    stock, heavy bbl.)** . . . . NiB $195 Ex $170 Gd $135
**64 FV-SR (black polymer stock,
    heavy threaded bbl.)** . . . . NiB $160 Ex $145 Gd $120
**64 TRR-SR (Picatinny rail,
    16.5-in. heavy fluted bbl.,
    wood tactical style stock)** . . . . NiB $330 Ex $290 Gd $225

MODEL 80 . . . . NiB $215 Ex $170 Gd $126
Semiauto. Caliber: 22 LR. 15-rnd. tubular magazine. 20-in. bbl. Weight: 6 lbs. Sights: Open rear, bead front. Monte Carlo stock of walnut w/checkered pistol-grip and forearm. Made 1976 to date. (Note: This rifle is essentially the same as the Model 60 of 1969 to 1972 except for a different style of checkering, side instead of top safety and plain bead instead of ramp front sight.)

MODEL 88 . . . . NiB $190 Ex $110 Gd $88
Similar to Model 80 except has walnut-finished hardwood stock, plain bead front sight. Weight: 5.75 lbs. Made 1969-72.

MODEL 90 . . . . NiB $194 Ex $161 Gd $126
Similar to Model 60 except w/16.5-in. bbl. w/folding leaf rear sight, bead front. 10-rnd. tubular magazine. Uncheckered, carbine style walnut stock w/bbl. Band and sling swivels. Weight: 5.75 lbs. Made 1969-72.

MODEL 987-T. . . . . NiB $217 Ex $166 Gd $129
Semiauto. Caliber: .22 LR. 15-rnd. tubular magazine. 20-in. bbl. Weight: 6 lbs. Sights: Open rear; ramp front. Monte Carlo stock w/checkered pistol grip and forearm. Made 1981-89.

A SERIES
Semiauto. Delayed blow back action. Cal.: .17 HMR, .22 LR or .22 WMR; 10-rnd. detachable rotary magazine. Bbl.: 16.5-, 18-, or 21-in. Sights: Optic ready. Stock: Black or camo synthetic, aluminum chassis or laminated wood. Finish: Blued, stainless steel. Accu-Trigger. Mfg. 2015-date.
**A17 (.17 HMR, black synthetic
    stock, blued, 22-in. bbl.)** . . . . NiB $430 Ex $380 Gd $300
**A17 HM2 (.17 HMR, black synthetic
    stock, blued, 22-in. bbl.)** . . . . NiB $330 Ex $290 Gd $230
**A17 Heavy Barrel (.17 HMR, wood stock,
    blued, 22-in. heavy bbl.)** . . . . NiB $550 Ex $490 Gd $370
**A17 Overwatch (.17 HMR, camo
    synthetic stock, blued)** . . . . . . NiB $590 Ex $480 Gd $420
**A17 Pro Varmint (.17 HMR, wood stock,
    blued, 22-in. heavy bbl.)** . . . . NiB $730 Ex $590 Gd $520
**A17 Sporter (.17 HMR, wood laminate
    stock, blued, 22-in. bbl.)** . . . . NiB $610 Ex $500 Gd $450
**A17 Target Sporter Laminate (.17 HMR, wood laminate
    stock, blued, 22-in. bbl.)** . . . . NiB $520 Ex $455 Gd $355
**A17 Target Thumbhole (.17 HMR,
    wood laminate thumbhole
    stock, blued, 22-in. bbl.)** . . . . NiB $700 Ex $600 Gd $470
**A22 (.22 LR, black synthetic
    stock, blued, 22-in. bbl.)** . . . . NiB $300 Ex $290 Gd $200
**A22 BNS-SR (.22 LR, laminated wood
    stock, blued, 18-in. bbl.)** . . . . NiB $520 Ex $470 Gd $400
**A22 FSS (.22 LR, black synthetic
    stock, stainless, 22-in. bbl.)** . . NiB $380 Ex $330 Gd $250
**A22 FV-SR (.22 LR, synthetic stock, stainless,
    16.2-in. threaded bbl.)** . . . . . . NiB $380 Ex $320 Gd $300
**A22 FV-SR Overwatch (.22 LR,
    camo synthetic stock, stainless,
    16.2-in. threaded bbl.)** . . . . . . NiB $420 Ex $390 Gd $300
**A22 Precision (.22 LR, MDT aluminum chassis,
    black, 18-in. threaded bbl.)** . . NiB $650 Ex $610 Gd $590
**A22 Precision Lite (.22 WMR, MDT aluminum
    chassis, black, 18-in. carbon
    fiber wrap threaded bbl.)** . . . . NiB $940 Ex $900 Gd $860
**A22 Pro Varmint (.22 LR, wood stock,
    blued, 22-in. heavy bbl.)** . . . . NiB $560 Ex $500 Gd $480
**A22 Target Thumbhole (.22 LR, wood laminate thumbhole
    stock, blued, 22-in. bbl.)** . . . . NiB $490 Ex $410 Gd $370
**A22 Magnum (.22 WMR, black synthetic
    stock, blued, 22-in. bbl.)** . . . . NiB $530 Ex $500 Gd $480
**A22 Magnum Pro Varmint (.22 HMR, wood stock,
    blued, 22-in. heavy bbl.)** . . . . NiB $730 Ex $700 Gd $580
**A22 Magnum Target Thumbhole (.22 WMR,
    wood laminate thumbhole
    stock, blued, 22-in. bbl.)** . . . . NiB $700 Ex $680 Gd $550

MSR 10 SERIES
AR15-style. Semi-auto. Calibers: .308 Win. or 6.5 Creedmoor. Muzzle brake, adj. gas block. Stock: Six-position, telescoping, Sights: optic-ready Picatinny rail. Finish: Matte black. Made 2017 to date.

RIFLES

Competition HD model (.308 Win., 18-in. Proof
Research carbon fiber wrapped bbl., Magpul
CTR stock, Hogue grip) . . NiB $3355 Ex $2980 Gd $2280
Hunter model (16- or 18-in.
bbl.) . . . . NiB $1455 Ex $1280 Gd $1010
Hunter Overwatch model (Mossy
Oak Overwatch camo) . . NiB $1155 Ex $1380 Gd $1055
Long Range model (20- or 21-in.
bbl.) . . . . NiB $2230 Ex $1980 Gd $1530
Precision model (22.5-in. stainless heavy
bbl., Magpul PSR stock, TangoDown
Battlegrip Flip grip) . . . . . NiB $2380 Ex $2130 Gd $1630

MSR 15 SERIES
AR15-style. Semi-auto. Calibers: 5.56mm/.223 Rem. Wylde
chamber, .224 Valkyrie, .22 Nosler, or 6.8 SPC. Bbl.: 16.13-in.
w/muzzle brake. Stock: Blackhawk Six-position, telescoping,
M4-style. Finish: Matte black. Takedown. Made 2017 to date.
Competition model (.223 Rem. or .224 Valkyrie, 18-in. Proof
Research carbon fiber wrapped bbl., Magpul CTR stock,
Hogue grip) . . . . NiB $2810 Ex $2480 Gd $1910
Long Range model (.224 Valkyrie, 22-in.
stainless bbl.) . . . . NiB $1680 Ex $1480 Gd $1155
Patrol model (A2 style
front sight). . . . . NiB $830 Ex $730 Gd $555
Recon model (Blackhawk
flip-up sights) . . . . NiB $910 Ex $810 Gd $630
Recon 2.0 Overwatch model (Mossy Oak Overwatch camo,
Magpul MOE stock/grip) . . . . NiB $1055 Ex $955 Gd $730
Recon LPR model (.224 Valkyrie, .22 Nosler,
6.8 SPC or .223 Rem.) . . . . . NiB $1230 Ex $1080 Gd $830
Valkyrie model (.224 Valkyrie, 18-in. heavy
bbl., Magpul URB stock) . . NiB $1455 Ex $1310 Gd $1010

- SLIDE-ACTION RIFLES -

MODEL 1903 . . . . NiB $733 Ex $549 Gd $370
Hammerless. Takedown. Caliber: .22 Short, Long, LR.
Detachable box magazine. 24-in. octagon bbl. Weight: About
5 lbs. Sights: Open rear; bead front. Pistol-grip stock, grooved
slide handle. Made 1903-21.

MODEL 1909 . . . . NiB $800 Ex $533 Gd $337
Hammerless. Takedown. Similar to Model 1903 except
has 20-in. round bbl., plain stock and forearm, weight:
Approximately 4.75 lbs. Made 1909-15.

MODEL 1914 . . . . NiB $520 Ex $347 Gd $239
Hammerless. Takedown. Caliber: .22 Short, Long, LR, Tubular
magazine holds 20 Short, 17 Long, 15 LR. 24-in. octagon bbl.
Weight: About 5.75 lbs. Sights: Open rear; bead front. Plain
pistol-grip stock, grooved slide handle. Made 1914-24.

MODEL 25 . . . . NiB $346 Ex $391 Gd $237
Takedown. Hammerless. Caliber: .22 Short, Long, LR.
Tubular magazine holds 20 Short, 17 Long, 15 LR. 24-in.
octagon bbl. Weight: 5.75 lbs. Sights: Open rear; blade
front. Plain pistol-grip stock, grooved slide handle. Made
1925-29.

MODEL 29 . . . . NiB $500 Ex $380 Gd $265
Takedown. Hammerless. Caliber: .22 Short, Long, LR.
Tubular magazine holds 20 Short, 17 Long, 15 LR. 24-in.
bbl., octagon on prewar, round on postwar production.
Weight: 5.5 lbs. Sights: Open rear; bead front. Stock w/
checkered pistol grip and slide handle on prewar, plain
stock and grooved forearm on postwar production. Made
1929-67.

MODEL 170 . . . . NiB $249 Ex $190 Gd $106
Calibers: .30-30, .35 Rem. Three round tubular magazine.
22-in. bbl. Weight: 6.75 lbs. Sights: Folding leaf rear; ramp
front. Select walnut stock w/checkered pistol-grip Monte
Carlo comb, grooved slide handle. Made 1970-81.
Model 170C (18.5-in. bbl., straight comb,
.30-30 only, 1974-81) . . . . . . NiB $355 Ex $310 Gd $245

V.C. SCHILLING — Suhl, Germany

MAUSER-MANNLICHER BOLT ACTION
SPORTING RIFLE . . . . NiB $938 Ex $744 Gd $539
Same general specifications as given for the Haenel Mauser-
Mannlicher Sporter. See separate listing.

'88 MAUSER SPORTER . . . . NiB $909 Ex $722 Gd $515
Same general specifications as Haenel '88 Mauser Sporter. See
separate listing.

SCHULTZ & LARSEN GEVAERFABRIK — Otterup, Denmark

MATCH RIFLE NO. 47 . . . . NiB $690 Ex $555 Gd $360
Caliber: .22 LR. Bolt-action, single-shot, set trigger. 28.5-
in. heavy bbl. Weight: 14 lbs. Sights: Micrometer receiver,
globe front. Free-rifle stock w/cheekpiece, thumbhole, adj.
Schuetzen-type buttplate, swivels, palmrest.

FREE RIFLE MODEL 54 . . . . NiB $866 Ex $780 Gd $598
Calibers: 6.5x55mm or any standard American centerfire
caliber. Schultz & Larsen M54 bolt-action, single-shot,
set trigger. 27.5-in. heavy bbl. Weight: 15.5 lbs. Sights:
Micrometer receiver; globe front. Free-rifle stock w/cheek-
piece, thumbhole, adj. Schuetzen-type buttplate, swivels,
palm rest.

MODEL 54J
SPORTING RIFLE . . . . NiB $684 Ex $528 Gd $430
Calibers: .270 Win., .30-06, 7x61 Sharpe & Hart. Schultz &
Larsen bolt action. Three-rnd. magazine. 24-in. bbl. in .270
and .30-06, 26-in. in 7x61 S&H. Checkered stock w/Monte
Carlo comb and cheekpiece. Value shown is for rifle less
sights.

SEARS, ROEBUCK & COMPANY — Chicago, IL

*The most encountered brands or model designations used by
Sears are J. C. Higgins and Ted Williams. Firearms sold under
these designations have been mfd. by various firms including
Winchester, Marlin, Savage, Mossberg, etc.*

MODEL 2C BOLT-ACTION
RIFLE. . . . . NiB $159 Ex $119 Gd $95
Caliber: .22RF. Seven round clip mag. 21-in. bbl. Weight: 5
lbs. Sights: Open rear; ramp front. Plain Monte Carlo stock.
Mfd. by Win.

MODEL 42 BOLT-ACTION
REPEATER. . . . . NiB $159 Ex $119 Gd $95
Takedown. Caliber: .22RF. Eight round detachable box maga-
zine. 24-in. bbl. Weight: 6 lbs. Sights: Open rear; bead front.
Plain pistol-grip stock. Mfd. by Marlin.

MODEL 42DL
BOLT-ACTION REPEATER . . . . . . NiB $159 Ex $119 Gd $95
Same general specifications as Model 42 except fancier grade w/peep sight, hooded front sight and swivels.

MODEL 44DL LEVER-ACTION
RIFLE . . . . .NiB $239 Ex $179 Gd $130
Caliber: .22RF. Tubular magazine holds 19 LR cartridges. 22-in. bbl. Weight: 6.25 lbs. Sights: Open rear; hooded ramp front. Monte Carlo-style stock w/pistol grip. Mfd. by Marlin.

MODEL 53 BOLT-ACTION
RIFLE. . . . . .NiB $289 Ex $198 Gd $155
Calibers: .243, .270, .308, .30-06. Four-rnd. magazine. 22-in. bbl. Weight: 6.75 lbs. Sights: Open rear; ramp front. Standard sporter stock w/pistol-grip, checkered. Mfd. by Savage.

MODEL 54 LEVER-ACTION
RIFLE. . . . . .NiB $222 Ex $188 Gd $135
Similar general specifications as Winchester Model 94 carbine. Made in .30-30 caliber only. Mfd. by Winchester.

MODEL 103 SERIES BOLT-ACTION
REPEATER . . . . .NiB $229 EX $121 Gd $98
Same general specifications as Model 103.2 w/minor changes. Mfd. by Marlin.

MODEL 103.2 BOLT-ACTION
REPEATER . . . . .NiB $145 Ex $100 Gd $90
Takedown. Caliber: .22RF. Eight-rnd. detachable box magazine. 24-in. bbl. Weight: 6 lbs. Sights: Open rear; bead front. Plain pistol-grip stock. Mfd. by Marlin.

R. F. SEDGLEY, INC. — Philadelphia, PA

SPRINGFIELD SPORTER . . . . NiB $1290 Ex $1189 Gd $633
Springfield '03 bolt action. Calibers: .220 Swift, .218 Bee, .22-3000, R, .22-4000, .22 Hornet, .25-35, .250-3000, .257 Roberts, .270 Win., 7mm, .30-06. 24-in. bbl. Weight: 7.5 lbs. Sights: Lyman No. 48 receiver; bead front on matted ramp. Checkered walnut stock, grip cap, sling swivels. Disc. 1941.

SPRINGFIELD LEFT-HAND
SPORTER. . . . . .NiB $1674 Ex $1412 Gd $954
Bolt-action reversed for left-handed shooter; otherwise the same as standard Sedgley Springfield Sporter. Disc. 1941.

SPRINGFIELD MANNLICHER-TYPE
SPORTER. . . . . .NiB $1515 Ex $1479 Gd $1088
Same as standard Sedgley Springfield Sporter except w/20-in. bbl., Mannlicher-type full stock w/cheekpiece, weight: 7.75 lbs. Disc. 1941.

SHILEN RIFLES, INC. — Enis, TX

DGA BENCHREST RIFLE. . . . NiB $1529 Ex $1244 Gd $977
DGA single-shot bolt-action. Calibers as listed for Sporter. 26-in. medium-heavy or heavy bbl. Weight: From 10.5 lbs. No sights. Fiberglass or walnut stock, classic or thumbhole pattern. Currently manufactured.

DGA SPORTER . . . . .NiB $1567 Ex $1189 Gd $843
DGA bolt action. Calibers: .17 Rem., .222 Rem., .223 Rem. .22-250, .220 Swift, 6mm Rem., .243 Win., .250 Sav., .257 Roberts, .284 Win., .308 Win., .358 Win. Three round blind

R.F. Sedgley Springfield Sporter

magazine. 24-in. bbl. Average weight: 7.5 lbs. No sights. Select Claro walnut stock w/cheekpiece, pistol grip, sling swivel studs. Currently manufactured.

DGA VARMINTER. . . . . . . .NiB $1455 Ex $1209 Gd $1155
Same as Sporter except w/25-in. medium-heavy bbl. Weight: 9 lbs.

SHILOH RIFLE MFG. CO. — Big Timber, MT

SHARPS MODEL 1874
BUSINESS RIFLE . . . . NiB $1149 Ex $1072 Gd $698
Replica of 1874 Sharps similar to No. 3 Sporting Rifle. .32-40, .38-55, .40-50 BN, .40-70 BN, .40-90 BN, .45-70 ST, .45-90 ST, .50-70 ST, .50-100 ST. 28-in. round heavy bbl. Blade front sight, buckhorn rear. Double-set triggers. Straight-grip walnut stock w/steel crescent buttplate. Made 1986 to date.

SHARPS MODEL 1874 LONG RANGE
EXPRESS RIFLE . . . . NiB $1798 Ex $1703 Gd $1166
Replica of 1874 Sharps w/single-shot falling breech action. .32-40, .38-55, .40-50 BN, .40-70 BN, .40-90 BN, .45-70 ST, .45-90 ST, .45-110 ST, .50-70 ST, .50-90 ST, .50-110 ST. 34-in. tapered octagon bbl. 51 in. overall. Weight: 10.75 lbs. Globe front sight, sporting tang peep rear. Walnut buttstock w/pistol-grip and Schnabel-style forend. Color casehardened action w/double-set triggers Made 1986 to date.

SHARPS MODEL 1874 SADDLE
RIFLE. . . . . .NiB $1267 Ex $1133 Gd $723
Similar to 1874 Express Rifle except w/30-in. bbl., blade front sight and buckhorn rear. Made 1986 to date.

SHARPS MODEL 1874 SPORTING
RIFLE NO. 1 . . . . .NiB $1355 Ex $1187 Gd $745
Similar to 1874 Express Rifle except w/30-in. bbl., blade front sight and buckhorn rear. Made 1986 to date.

SHARPS MODEL 1874 SPORTING
RIFLE NO. 3 . . . . .NiB $1150 Ex $1007 Gd $688
Similar to 1874 Sporting Rifle No. 1 except w/straight-grip stock w/steel crescent buttplate. Made 1986 to date.

SHARPS MODEL 1874 MONTANA ROUGHRIDER
Similar to 1874 Sporting Rifle No. 1 except w/24- to 34-in. half-octagon or full-octagon bbl. Standard or deluxe walnut stock w/pistol-grip or military-style buttstock. Made 1989 to date.
Standard model. . . . . .NiB $1154 Ex $715 Gd $646
Deluxe model . . . . .NiB $1300 Ex $990 Gd $615

SIG SWISS INDUSTRIAL COMPANY — Neuhausen-Rhine Falls, Switzerland

AMT SEMIAUTO. . . . . . . .NiB $4798 Ex $3270 Gd $2775
.308 Win.(7.62 NATO). Five, 10, or 20-rnd. magazine. 18.5-in. bbl. w/flash suppressor. Weight: 9.5 lbs. Sights: Adj. aperture rear, post front. Walnut buttstock and forend w/synthetic pistol grip. Imported 1980 to 1988.

GRADING: **NiB** = New in Box   **Ex** = Excellent or NRA 95%   **Gd** = Good or NRA 68%

Shilen DGA Benchrest Rifle

Shiloh Rifle Mfg. Co. Model 1874 Long Range Express

AMT SPORTING RIFLE . . . . NiB $4876 Ex $3129 Gd $2210
Semiauto version of SG510-4 automatic assault rifle based on Swiss Army SIGW57. Roller-delayed blowback action. Caliber: 7.62x51mm NATO (.308 Win.). Five, 10- and 20-rnd. magazines. 19-in. bbl. Weight: 10 lbs. Sights, aperture rear, post front. Wood buttstock and forearm, folding bipod. Imported from 1960 to 1988.

PE-57 SEMIAUTO RIFLE . . . NiB $6596 Ex $4348 Gd $3100
Caliber: 7.5 Swiss. 24-rnd. magazine. 23.75-in. bbl. Weight: 12.5 lbs. Sights: Adj. aperture rear; post front. High-impact synthetic stock. Imported from Switzerland during the 1980s.

SIG SAUER — Neuhausen, Switzerland
Manufactured and imported by SIG Sauer USA in Exeter, NH. To facilitate locating SIG Sauer rifles, models are grouped into two categories: bolt-action rifles (below) and Semiauto rifles. For a complete listing, please refer to the index.

- BOLT-ACTION RIFLES -

TACTICAL 2 . . . . NiB $4171 Ex $2400 Gd $1900
Push-feed, straight pull action. Calibers: .223 Rem., .308 Win., .300 Win. Mag. or .338 Lapua. 4- or 5-rnd. detachable box magazine. 24.7-, 25.6-, or 27-in. fluted bbl. w/muzzle brake. Aluminum chassis, adj. trigger, ambidextrous Blaser stock w/ adj. LOP and cheekpiece. Made 2007-15.

SIG50 . . . . NiB $9825 Ex $5100 Gd $4900
Push-feed action. .50 BMG only. 5-rnd. detachable box magazine. 29-in. fluted bbl. w/muzzle brake. McMillan stock. Made 2011-12; 2014-15.

SSG 3000 . . . . NiB $2400 Ex $1500 Gd $1250
Push-feed action, .308 Win. only, 5-rnd. detachable box magazine, 23.4-in. heavy bbl. w/muzzle brake, adj. McMillan stock. Made 2000-12.
Patrol (18-in. bbl.). . . . . NiB $1499 Ex $830 Gd $700

- SEMIAUTO RIFLES -

SIG M400 . . . . NiB $1313 Ex $874 Gd $750
Semiauto AR15 platform w/gas impingment system. Caliber: 5.56mm NATO. 30-rnd. magazine. 16-in. bbl., removable adj. sights. Weight: 6.5 lbs. Overall: 39.5 in. Made 2012 to date.
B5 (16-in. bbl., SOPMOD 6-pos. stock,
mfg. 2015). . . . . NiB $1140 Ex $890 Gd $680
Carbon Fiber (16-in. bbl., carbon fiber handguard,
2014-15) . . . . NiB $1850 Ex $1355 Gd $1005
Classic (16-in. bbl., M4 style handguard,
2014-15) . . . . NiB $1070 Ex $820 Gd $650
Elite (16-in. bbl., M-LOK
handguard) . . . . NiB $1030 Ex $805 Gd $600
Enhanced Carbine (16-in. bbl., MOE furniture,
2012-14) . . . . NiB $1050 Ex $805 Gd $600
Enhanced Patrol (16-in. bbl.,
2014-16) . . . . NiB $1205 Ex $955 Gd $705
Hunting (20-in. bbl., 2012 only) . . . NiB $975 Ex $680 Gd $600
Predator (18-in. heavy bbl., Geissele two-stage
trigger) . . . . NiB $1350 Ex $1055 Gd $790
SWAT (16-in. bbl., quad rail) . . NiB $1110 Ex $880 Gd $650
Varminter (22-in. bbl., 2013-15) . . NiB $1395 Ex $820 Gd $650

SIG516 SERIES
Semiauto AR-15 style platform. Short-stroke gas piston system. Caliber: 5.56mm NATO. Bbl.: 16- or 18in. w/4-pos. gas regulator. Sights: Picatinny rail. Stock: Magpul adj. Weight: 7.1-7.4 lbs. Finish: Matte black. Overall: 36.5 in. Made 2011 to date.
Basic Patrol (polymer handguard) . . . NiB $1100 Ex $820 Gd $630
Carbon Fiber (16-in. bbl., carbon fiber handguard,
2014-15) . . . . NiB $1705 Ex $1255 Gd $955
Patrol (Magpul MOE furniture, black or FDE
finish) . . . . NiB $1605 Ex $1190 Gd $920
Precision Marksman (18-in. free float bbl., Magpul PRS
stock, 2011-13) . . . . NiB $2055 Ex $1505 Gd $1080
Sight Ready Platform (16-in. bbl., alum. handguard,
mfg. 2015). . . . . NiB $1455 Ex $1080 Gd $855
Sport Configuration Model (16-in. bbl., fixed stock,
2011-12) . . . . NiB $1355 Ex $1080 Gd $820

SIG522 SERIES
Semiauto AR-15 style platform. Blow back system. Caliber: .22 LR w/10- or 25-rnd. mag. Bbl.: 16-in. Stock: Folding or adj. Weight: 6.5 lbs. Finish: Matte black. Made 2009-15.

SIG SSG 3000 Patrol

SIG Tactical 2

SIG556 Patrol

**Smith & Wesson
Model 1707 LS Classic Hunter**

Classic (polymer handguard) . . . NiB $500 Ex $370 Gd $280
Classic SWAT (alum. handguard). . . NiB $670 Ex $515 Gd $390
Commando (training suppressor). . . NiB $580 Ex $440 Gd $330
Commando SWAT (training suppressor, quad rail
   handguard) . . . . NiB $620 Ex $475 Gd $355
Field (20-in. bbl., polymer
   handguard) . . . . NiB $470 Ex $335 Gd $255
Target (20-in. bbl., Hogue
   handguard) . . . . NiB $730 Ex $585 Gd $455

SIG551-A1 . . . . NiB $1599 Ex $930 Gd $800
Semiauto w/gas piston system. Caliber: 5.56mm NATO. 20- or
30-rnd. Swiss 550-style clear magazine. 16-in. bbl., adj. sights,
folding polymer stock. Weight: 7 lbs. Overall: 34.6 in. Made
2012-15.

SIG556 CLASSIC . . . . NiB $1299 Ex $850 Gd $700
Similar to gas piston system SG550 military rifle except
Semiauto. Caliber: 5.56mm NATO. 30-rnd. AR51-style magazine. 16-in. bbl., adj. sights, folding polymer stock. Weight: 8.2
lbs. Overall: 35.8 in. Made 2007 to 2013.
DMR (Magpul PRS stock,18-in.
   heavy bbl., optic ready
   2008-13) . . . . NiB $1732 Ex $930 Gd $800
Holo (M4-style stock, red dot
   holographic sight) . . . . NiB $1832 Ex $1030 Gd $900
Patrol (polymer handguard,
   2010-13) . . . . NiB $1266 Ex $850 Gd $700
Patrol SWAT (aluminum handguard,
   2010-13) . . . . NiB $1266 Ex $850 Gd $700
SWAT (quad-rail handguard), add $140
xi model (5.56mm NATO,
   300 BLK or 7.62x39mm,
   polymer handguard, folding stock,
   2014-16) . . . . NiB $1300 Ex $1040 Gd $765
xi SWAT model (5.56mm NATO or 7.62x39mm, alum.
   handguard, folding stock,
   2015-16) . . . . NiB $1405 Ex $1105 Gd $835

SIG556R . . . . NiB $1332 Ex $900 Gd $760
Similar to SG556 except chambered in 7.62x39mm. 30-rnd.
AK-style magazine, red dot optic. Weight: 7 lbs. Made 2011-13.

SIG716 SERIES
Semiauto AR-15 style platform. Short stroke piston system.
Caliber: 7.62mm NATO w/20-rnd. mag. Bbl.: 16-in. Weight:
11 lbs. Finish: Matte black. Made 2011 to 2013, G2 series
2015 to date.

G2 Patrol (6-pos. adj. stock, black or FDE finish,
   2017 to date) . . . . NiB $2030 Ex $1480 Gd $1065
G2 Designated Marksman (Magpul UBR stock,
   2015 to date) . . . . NiB $2630 Ex $1880 Gd $1330
Patrol (Magpul ACS stock, black, OD green or FDE finish,
   2011-16) . . . . NiB $1970 Ex $1530 Gd $1155
Precision Marksman (18-in. free float bbl., Magpul PRS
   stock, mfg. 2013) . . . . NiB $2255 Ex $1630 Gd $1145

SIG SCM . . . . NiB $1030 Ex $805 Gd $600
Semiauto AR-15 style platform. Direct gas impingement system
system. Caliber: 5.56mm NATO w/10-rnd. mag. Bbl.: 16-in.
Weight: 8 lbs. Stock: A2 style fixed. Finish: Matte black. Made
2010-11.
SCM 22 model (.22 LR, 18-in. bbl., polymer handguard,
   fixed stock, mfg. 2011) . . . . NiB $1530 Ex $1105 Gd $835

SIG MCX SERIES
Semiauto. Short stroke piston system. Caliber: 5.56mm NATO
or 300 BLK w/30-rnd. mag. Bbl.: 16-in. Stock: Folding and adj.
Weight: 5.8-6 lbs. Overall: 29-in. collapsed, 35.7 extended.
Finish: Matte black or FDE. Made 2015 to date.
Carbine (2015-16) . . . . NiB $500 Ex $370 Gd $280
Virtus Patrol (internal recoil system, Sig Matchlite
   Duo Trigger, modular handguard and bbl. system,
   2017 to date) . . . . NiB $2230 Ex $2210 Gd $2100

SIG MPX . . . . NiB $1715 Ex $1255 Gd $955
Semiauto. Short stroke piston system. Caliber: 9mm w/30-rnd.
mag. Bbl.: 16-in. Stock: Folding and adj. Weight: 6.63 lbs.
Overall: 35.25-in. extended. Finish: Matte black or FDE. Made
2013 to date.

SIG TREAD . . . . NiB $950 Ex $900 Gd $800
Semiauto AR-15 style platform. Direct gas impingement system
system. Caliber: 5.56mm NATO w/30-rnd. mag. Bbl.: 16-in.
Sights: Picatinny rail. Weight: 7 lbs. Stock: Magpul SL-K adj.
Handguard: M-LOK. Finish: Matte black. Made 2019 to date.

SMITH & WESSON — Springfield, MA
*Manufactured by Husqvarna, Vapenfabrik A.B., Huskvarna,
Sweden, & Howa Machinery LTD., Shinkawa-Chonear, Nagota
452, Japan.*

MODEL 1500 . . . . NiB $410 Ex $339 Gd $269
Bolt-action. .243 Win., .270 Win., .30-06, 7mm Rem. Mag.
22-in. bbl. (24-in. in 7mm Rem. Mag.). Weight: 7.5 lbs.
American walnut stock w/Monte Carlo comb and cheekpiece,
cut checkering. Sights: Open rear, hooded ramp, gold bead-
front. This model was also imported by Mossberg (see separate
listings); Imported from 1979 to 1984.

MODEL 1500DL DELUXE . . . . NiB $410 Ex $339 Gd $269
Same as standard model, except w/o sights; w/engine-turned
bolt, decorative scroll on floorplate, French checkering.
Imported from 1983 to 1984.

**MODEL 1707 LS "CLASSIC
HUNTER"** . . . . NiB $460 Ex $388 Gd $318
Bolt action. Calibers: .243 Win., .270 Win., .30-06, 5-rnd.
magazine. 22-in. bbl. Weight: 7.5 lbs. Solid recoil pad, no
sights, Schnabel forend, checkered walnut stock. Imported
1983 to 1984.

RIFLES

GRADING: **NiB** = New in Box   **Ex** = Excellent or NRA 95%   **Gd** = Good or NRA 68%

MODEL A BOLT-ACTION . . . . . NiB $443 Ex $329 Gd $290
Similar to Husqvarna Model 9000 Crown Grade. Mauser-type bolt action. Calibers: .22-250, .243 Win., .270 Win., .308 Win., .30-06, 7mm Rem. Mag., .300 Win. Mag. Five round magazine except 3-rnd. capacity in latter two calibers. 23.75-in. bbl. Weight: 7 lbs. Sights: Folding leaf rear; hooded ramp front. Checkered walnut stock w/Monte Carlo cheek-piece, rosewood forend tip and pistol-grip cap, swivels. Made 1969-72.

MODEL B . . . . NiB $460 Ex $367 Gd $238
Same as Model A except w/20.25-in. extra-light bbl., Monte Carlo cheekpiece w/Schnabel-style forearm, weight: 6 lbs., 10 oz. Calibers: .243 Win., .30-06.

MODEL C . . . . NiB $460 Ex $367 Gd $238
Same as Model B except w/cheekpiece stock w/straight comb.

MODEL D . . . . NiB $588 Ex $469 Gd $240
Same as Model C except w/full-length Mannlicher-style forearm.

MODEL E . . . . NiB $588 Ex $469 Gd $240
Same as Model B except w/full-length Mannlicher-style forearm.

M&P10 SERIES
Semiauto AR10 platform. Action: direct gas impingement system. Caliber: .308 Win., 20-rnd. magazine. 18-in. bbl. w/flash hider. Ambidextrous controls. Finish: matte black. Made 2013 to date.
Standard (adj. stock) . . . . NiB $1480 Ex $1060 Gd $760
Magpul (Magpul furniture) . . NiB $1795 Ex $1396 Gd $1095
**Optic Ready Camo (Magpul furniture,
  camo finish)** . . . . NiB $1729 Ex $1210 Gd $915

M&P15 SERIES
Semiauto AR15 platform. Action: direct gas impingement system. Caliber: .223 Rem./5.56 NATO, 30-rnd. magazine. 16-in. bbl. w/flash hider. Finish: matte black. Numerous model configurations. Made 2006 to date.
Standard (adj. stock) . . . . NiB $1260 Ex $960 Gd $860
Magpul MOE furniture, add $100
VTAC II (VLTOR buttstock), add $200

M&P15-22 SERIES
Semiauto AR15 style platform. Action: Blowback system. Caliber: .22 LR, 10- or 25-rnd. magazine. 16.5-in. bbl. Finish: numerous. Numerous model configurations. Made 2009 to date.
Standard (adj. stock) . . . . NiB $430 Ex $360 Gd $310
Magpul MOE furniture, add $100

SPRINGFIELD ARMORY INC. — Colona, IL
Formerly of Geneseo, IL. This is a private firm not to be confused with the former U.S. Government facility in Springfield, Mass.

BM-59 SEMIAUTO RIFLE
Gas-operated. Caliber: .308 Win. (7.62mm NATO). 20-rnd. detachable box magazine. 19.3-in. bbl. w/flash suppressor. About 43 in. overall. Weight: 9.25 lbs. Adj. military aperture rear sight, square post front; direct and indirect grenade launcher sights. European walnut stock w/handguard or folding buttstock (Alpine Paratrooper). Made 1981-90.
Standard model . . . . NiB $1844 Ex $1329 Gd $911
Paratrooper model . . . . NiB $2136 Ex $1779 Gd $1533

HELLION . . . . NIB $1990 EX $1890 GD $1600
Semiauto. Based on VHS-2 bullpup. Cal.: 5.56 NATO. Bbl.: 16-in. w/muzzle device and adj. gas system. Stock: 5-position

**Springfield Armory
BM-59**

**Springfield Armory
SAR-8 Sporter Rifle**

adj. w/cheek riser. Sights: Optic ready, flip up sights. Length: 28.2-29.7 ins. Weight: 8 lbs. Mfg. 2022-date.

M-1 GARAND SEMIAUTO RIFLE
Gas-operated. Calibers: .30-06 or .308 Win. (7.62 NATO), .30-06. Eight round stripper clip. 24-in. bbl. 43.5 in. overall. Weight: 9.5 lbs. Adj. aperture rear sight, military square blade front. Standard "Issue-grade" walnut stock or folding buttstock. Made 1979-90.
Standard model . . . . NiB $779 Ex $588 Gd $353
National Match model . . . . NiB $909 Ex $799 Gd $489
Ultra Match model . . . . NiB $1000 Ex $808 Gd $589
Sniper model . . . . NiB $1264 Ex $876 Gd $665
Tanker model . . . . NiB $954 Ex $677 Gd $498

MATCH M1A
Same as Standard M1A except w/National Match-grade bbl. w/modified flash suppressor, National Match sights, turned trigger pull, gas system assembly in one unit, modified mainspring guide glass-bedded walnut stock. Super Match M1A w/premium-grade heavy bbl. (weight: 10 lbs).
National Match model . . . . NiB $2155 Ex $1870 Gd $1270
Super Match model . . . . . . NiB $2695 Ex $1899 Gd $1721

STANDARD M1A SEMIAUTO
Gas-operated. Similar to U.S. M14 service rifle except w/o provision for automatic firing. Caliber: 7.65mm NATO (.308 Win.). Five, 10- or 20-rnd. detachable box magazine. 25.13-in. bbl w/flash suppressor. Weight: 9 lbs. Sights: Adj. aperture rear; blade front. Fiberglass, birch or walnut stock, fiberglass handguard, sling swivels. Made 1996-2000.
w/fiberglass or birch stock . . . NiB $1198 Ex $694 Gd $645
w/walnut stock . . . . NiB $1412 Ex $1100 Gd $833

M1A LOADED . . . . NiB $1660 Ex $1230 Gd $880
Similar to M1A Standard except in .308 Win. only, 22-in. National Match or stainless bbl. Stock: black or green polymer or smooth walnut. Finish: blued. Weight: 9.5 lbs. Made 1999 to date.
Green polymer stock, add $20
Stainless bbl., add $100
Walnut stock, add $115

M1A SCOUT SQUAD . . . . . . NiB $1680 Ex $1410 Gd $1055
Similar to M1A Standard except in .308 Win. only, 18-in. bbl. Stock: black or green fiberglass or smooth walnut. Finish: blued. Weight: 9 lbs. Made 1997 to date.

M1A SOCOM 16 SERIES
Similar to Scout Squad except 16.25-in. bbl. Stock: black or green fiberglass. Sights: Tritium front. Weight: 8.7 lbs. Made 2004 to date.
Standard model . . . . NiB $1810 Ex $1530 Gd $1155

SOCOM 16 II model (Picatinny
rail, composite stock)........NiB $2110 Ex $1880 Gd $1455
SOCOM 16 CQB model (adj.
CQB composite stock).......NiB $1910 Ex $1630 Gd $1230
SOCOM 16 Tanker model
(walnut stock)..............NiB $1810 Ex $1530 Gd $1155

M1A/M21 TACTICAL SERIES
Similar to M1A Super National Match except 22-in. bbl., adj.
walnut stock. Weight: 11.5 lbs. Made 1990-2010.
White Feather model
(fiberglass M3A McMillian
stock, Harris bipod,
2001-09).................NiB $4755 Ex $4160 Gd $3235

M6 SCOUT RIFLE/SHOTGUN COMBO
Similar to (14-in.) short-barrel Survival Gun provided as
backup weapon to U.S. combat pilots. Calibers: .22 LR/.410
and .22 Hornet/.410. 18.5-in. bbl. 32 in. overall. Weight: 4 lbs.
Parkerized or stainless steel finish. Folding detachable stock w/
storage for fifteen .22 LR cartridges and four .410 shells. Drilled
and tapped for scope mounts. Intro. 1982 and imported from
Czech Republic 1995 to 2004.
First Issue (no trigger guard) .... NiB $340 Ex $340 Gd $280
Second Issue (w/trigger guard) ...... NiB $430 Ex $340 Gd $280
.22 Hornet models .... NiB $780 Ex $655 Gd $480

SAR-8 SPORTER RIFLE
Similar to H&K 911 Semiauto rifle. Calibers: .308 Win.,
(7.62x51 mm NATO). Detachable 5- 10- or 20-rnd. magazine.
18- or 20-in. bbl. 38.25 or 45.3 in. overall. Weight: 8.7 to 9.5
lbs. Protected front post and rotary adj. rear sight. Delayed
roller-locked blow-back action w/fluted chamber. Kevlar-
reinforced fiberglass thumb-hole style wood stock. Imported
from 1990 to 1998.
w/wood stock (disc. 1994) ...NiB $1077 Ex $877 Gd $658
w/thumb-hole stock ....NiB $1127 Ex $976 Gd $679

SAR-48 AND SAR-4800
Similar to Browning FN FAL/LAR Semiauto rifle. Calibers: .233
Rem. (5.56x45) and 3.08 Win. (7.62x51) NATO. Detachable
5- 10- or 20-rnd. magazine. 18- or 21-in. chrome-lined bbl.
38.25 or 45.3 in. overall. Weight: 9.5 to 13.25 lbs. Protected
post front and adj. rear sight. Forged receiver and bolt w/adj.
gas system. Pistol-grip or thumb-hole style; synthetic or wood
stock. Imported 1985; reintroduced 1995.
w/pistol-grip stock,
disc. 1989..............NiB $1788 Ex $1289 Gd $990
w/wood stock,
disc. 1989..............NiB $2577 Ex $2066 Gd $1500
w/folding stock,
disc. 1989............NiB $2854 Ex $2310 Gd $1669
w/thumb-hole stock ....NiB $1329 Ex $1100 Gd $796

SAINT SERIES
Semiauto AR-15 platform w/gas impingement system. Caliber:
5.56mm NATO. 30-rnd. Magpul PMAG magazine. Bbl.: 16-in.
Sights: Flip-up rear, A2 style front. Stock: BCM adj. 6-pos.
Handguard: Bravo Company, KeyMod, PKMR. Weight: 6.7 lbs.
Made 2016 to date.
Standard model............. NiB $780 Ex $750 Gd $550
Edge model (match trigger, Bravo Company
Mod 0 SOPMOD stock, M-LOK handgard,
2019 to date)........... NiB $1299 Ex $1180 Gd $990
Edge ATC model (flat match trigger,
B5 Systems Enhanced SopMod
stock, 18-in. Ballistic Advantage
bbl., 2022-date)........ NiB $1540 Ex $1400 Gd $1110
Victor model (M-LOK handgard, 2019
to date) .... NiB $1070 Ex $900 Gd $860

SQUIRES BINGHAM CO., INC. — Makati, Rizal, Philippines

MODEL 14D DELUXE.........NiB $159 Ex $123 Gd $88
Bolt action. Caliber: .22 LR. Five round box magazine. 24-in. bbl.
Sights: V-notch rear; hooded ramp front. Receiver grooved for
scope mounting. Pulong Dalaga stock w/contrasting forend tip and
grip cap, checkered forearm and pistol-grip. Weight: 6 lbs. Disc.

MODEL 15 ....NiB $189 Ex $127 Gd $115
Same as Model 14D except chambered for .22 WMR.
Importation. Disc.

MODEL M16...............NiB $190 Ex $166 Gd $126
Styled after U.S. M16 military rifle. Caliber: .22 LR. 15-rnd.
box magazine. 19.5-in. bbl. w/muzzle brake/flash hider. Rear
sight in carrying handle, post front on high ramp. Black-painted
mahogany buttstock and forearm. Weight: 6.5 lbs. Importation
disc.

MODEL M20D DELUXE ......NiB $277 Ex $227 Gd $131
Caliber: .22 LR. 15-rnd. box magazine. 19.5-in. bbl. w/muzzle
brake/flash hider. Sights: V-notch rear; blade front. Receiver
grooved for scope mounting. Pulong Dalaga stock w/contrast-
ing forend tip and grip cap, checkered forearm/pistol-grip.
Weight: 6 lbs. Importation disc.

STAG ARMS, LLC — Cheyenne, WY
Formerly New Britain, CT

NOTE: *Left hand model values are $25 to $50 higher.*

MODEL 1................. NiB $949 Ex $600 Gd $500
Semiauto AR15 platform w/gas impingement system. Caliber:
5.56mm NATO. 30-rnd. magazine. 16-in. bbl., mil-spec
collapsible buttstock, A2 flashhider, sights and pistol grip.
Removeable carry handle. Weight: 7 lbs. Made 2003-18

MODEL 2................. NiB $940 Ex $590 Gd $490
Similar to Model 1 except w/folding rear sight. Weight: 6.5 lbs.
Made 2003-18.
Model 2T (quad rail handguard), add $190

MODEL 3................. NiB $895 Ex $550 Gd $480
Similar to Model 1 except optic ready, Diamondhead VRS
handguard. Weight: 6.1 lbs. Made 2011-18.
Model 3G (18-in. bbl. w/3G
compensator, Magpul stock and
pistols grip, Samson Evolution
handguard, 6.1 lbs.,
2011-18)...............NiB $1459 Ex $900 Gd $780
Model 3T (Diamondhead folding
sights and handguard,
7.4 lbs., 2014-18).........NiB $999 Ex $600 Gd $530
Model 3T-M (Diamondhead folding sights and
handguard, Magpul stock and pistol grip, 7.4 lbs.,
2014-18)...............NiB $1160 Ex $700 Gd $580

MODEL 4................. NiB $1015 Ex $630 Gd $560
Similar to Model 1 except w/20-in. bbl., A2 buttstock, 5-rnd.
magazine. Weight: 8.5 lbs. Made 2003-18.
Model 4L (left-hand variant), add $50

MODEL 5................. NiB $895 Ex $550 Gd $480
Similar to Model 1 except w/o rear sight, chambered in 6.8SPC
II. Weight: 6.4 lbs. Made 2011-18.

RIFLES

MODEL 6 . . . . **NiB $1055 Ex $650 Gd $530**
Similar to Model 1 except w/o sights, 24.1-in. heavy bbl., Hogue aluminum handguard. Weight: 10 lbs. Made 2011-18.

MODEL 7 . . . . **NiB $1055 Ex $650 Gd $530**
Similar to Model 6 except w/20.8-in. heavy bbl., chambered in 6.8SPC II. Weight: 10 lbs. Made 2003-18.

MODEL 8 . . . . **NiB $1055 Ex $650 Gd $530**
Similar to Model 1 except w/gas piston system, Diamondhead flip-up sights. Weight: 6.9 lbs. Made 2011-18.
Model 8T (Diamondhead
    folding sights and handguard,
    7.2 lbs., 2013-18) . . . . **NiB $1275 Ex $730 Gd 600**

MODEL 9 . . . . **NiB $990 Ex $580 Gd $500**
Semiauto AR15 platform w/blowback system. Caliber: 9mm. 32-rnd. magazine. 16-in. bbl., mil-spec collapsible buttstock, A2 flashhider and pistol grip, optic ready. Weight: 6.8 lbs. Made 2015-18.
Model 9T (Diamondhead folding sights and free float
    handguard, 7.9 lbs., 2015-18) . . . . **NiB $1275 Ex $730 Gd 600**

MODEL STAG 15 SERIES
Semiauto AR15 platform w/gas impingement system. Caliber: 5.56mm NATO or 6.8 SPC. 30-rnd. magazine. 16-, 20- or 24-in. bbl. w/ or w/o A2 flashhider. Stock: fixed or mil-spec collapsible buttstock. Sights: A2 style or optic ready. Removeable carry handle or flat top. Weight: 6.2-10 lbs. Made 2018-date.
3Gun Elite (Magpul ACS stock, 16.5-in.
    Stag 15 M-LOK SL handguard) . . . **NiB $895 Ex $550 Gd $485**
LEO (mil-spec stock, quad rail handguard) . . . **NiB $895 Ex $550 Gd $485**
M4 (M4 style, 16-in. bbl.) . . . . . . **NiB $895 Ex $550 Gd $485**
O.R.C. (optic ready, flat tip) . . . **NiB $895 Ex $550 Gd $485**
Retro (M16A2 style, 20-in. bbl.) NiB $999 Ex $600 Gd $530
Tactical (Magpul CTR stock, 13.5-in. Stag 15
    M-LOK SL handguard) . . . . **NiB $999 Ex $600 Gd $530**
Super Varminter (6.8 SPC, Magpul fixed stock,
    Hogue free float handguard, 22-in. bbl.) . . . . **NiB $1055 Ex $650 Gd $530**
Varminter (Magpul fixed stock, Hogue free
    float handguard, 24-in. bbl.) NiB $1055 Ex $650 Gd $530

MODEL STAG 10 SERIES
Semiauto AR10 platform w/gas impingement system. Caliber: 6.5 Creedmoor or 7.62 NATO. 10-rnd. magazine. 16-, 18- or 24-in. bbl. w/VG6 Gamma muzzle device. Stock: Magpul PSR or ACS. Sights: optic ready, flat top. Weight: 8.2-8.6 lbs. Made 2018-date.
10S M-LOK (Magpul ACS stock, 16-in. bbl.,
    13.5-in. Stag 15 M-LOK SL handguard) NiB $895 Ex $550 Gd $485
10 M-LOK (7.62 NATO, Magpul ACR stock,
    24-in. bbl., 16.5-in. Stag 15 M-LOK
    SL handguard) . . . . **NiB $895 Ex $550 Gd $485**
10 M-LOK (6.5 Creedmoor, Magpul PRS
    stock, 24-in. bbl., 16.5-in. Stag 15 M-LOK
    SL handguard) . . . . **NiB $999 Ex $600 Gd $530**

STANDARD ARMS COMPANY — Wilmington, DE

MODEL G AUTOMATIC RIFLE NiB $815 Ex $569 Gd $355
Gas-operated. Autoloading. Hammerless. Takedown. .25-35, .30-30, .25 Rem., .30 Rem., .35 Rem. Magazine capacity: 4 rounds in .35 Rem., 5 rounds in other calibers. 22.38-in. bbl. Weight: 7.75 lbs. Sights: Open sporting rear; ivory bead front. Shotgun-type stock. Made c. 1910. Note: This was the first gas-operated rifle manufactured in the U.S. While essentially an autoloader, the gas port can be closed and the rifle may be operated as a slide-action repeater.

MODEL M HAND-OPERATED
RIFLE . . . . **NiB $737 Ex $543 Gd $431**
Slide-action repeater w/same general specifications as Model G except lacks autoloading feature. Weight: 7 lbs.

STAR — Eibar, Spain
Manufactured by Bonifacio Echeverria, S.A.

ROLLING BLOCK CARBINE . . . **NiB $500 Ex $337 Gd $178**
Single-shot, similar to Remington Rolling Block. .30-30, .357 Mag., .44 Mag. 20-in. bbl. Weight: 6 lbs. Sights: Folding leaf rear; ramp front. Walnut straight-grip stock w/ crescent buttplate, forearm w/bbl. band. Imported 1934 to 1975.

STERLING ARMAMENT, LTD. — Essex, England
Imported by Lanchester U.S.A., Inc., Dallas, Texas.

MARK 6 SEMIAUTO
CARBINE . . . . **NiB $1822 Ex $1177 Gd $987**
Caliber: 9mm Para 34-rnd. magazine. Bbl.: 16.1 in. Weight: 7.5 lbs. Flip-type rear peep sight, ramp front. Folding metal skeleton stock. Made 1983-94.

J. STEVENS ARMS CO. — Chicopee Falls, MA
A division of Savage Industries, Westfield, Massachusetts, owned by ATK since 2013. J. Stevens Arms eventually became a division of Savage Industries. Consequently, the "Stevens" brand name is used for some rifles by Savage; see separate Savage-Stevens listings under Savage.

NO. 12 MARKSMAN SINGLE-SHOT
RIFLE . . . . **NiB $456 Ex $324 Gd $189**
Lever-action, tip-up. Takedown. Calibers: .22 LR, .25 R.F., .32 R.F. 22-in. bbl. Plain straight-grip stock, small tapered forearm.

NO. 14 LITTLE SCOUT SINGLE-SHOT
RIFLE . . . . **NiB $455 Ex $310 Gd $180**
Caliber: .22 RF. 18-in. bbl. One-piece slab stock readily distinguishes it from the No. 14X that follows. Made 1906-10.

NO. 14 1/2 LITTLE SCOUT SINGLE-SHOT
RIFLE . . . . **NiB $455 Ex $309 Gd $200**
Rolling block. Takedown. Caliber: .22 LR. 18- or 20-in. bbl. Weight: 2.75 lbs. Sights: open rear; blade front. Plain straight-grip stock, small tapered forearm.

MODEL 15 . . . . **NiB $227 Ex $150 Gd $144**
Same as Stevens-Springfield Model 15 except w/24-in. bbl., weight: 5 lbs., w/redesigned stock. Made 1948-65.

MODEL 15Y YOUTH'S RIFLE . . **NiB $221 Ex $155 Gd $127**
Same as Model 15 except w/21-in. bbl., short buttstock, weight: 4.75 lbs. Made 1958-65.

Stevens No. 14.5 Little Scout

Stevens No. 44 Ideal

Stevens Ideal Schuetzen Rifle

Stevens Model 87

NO. 44 IDEAL SINGLE-SHOT

RIFLE . . . . **NiB $689 Ex $466 Gd $380**
Rolling block. Lever-action. Takedown. Calibers: .22 LR, .25 R.F., .32 R.F., .25-20 S.S., .32-20, .32-40, .38-40, .38-55, .44-40. Bbl. lengths: 24-in., 26-in. (round, half-octagon, full-octagon). Weight: 7 lbs w/26-in. round bbl. Sights: Open rear; Rocky Mountain front. Plain straight-grip stock and forearm. Made 1894-1932.

NO. 44 1/2 IDEAL SINGLE-SHOT

RIFLE. . . . . **NiB $990 Ex $848 Gd $578**
Falling-block. Lever-action rifle. Aside from the new design action intro. 1903, specifications of this model are the same as those of Model 44. Model 44X disc. 1916.

NOS. 45-54 IDEAL SINGLE-SHOT RIFLES
These are higher-grade models, differing from the standard No. 44 and 44.5 chiefly in finish, engraving, set triggers, levers, bbls., stock, etc. The Schuetzen types (including the Stevens-Pope models) are in this series. Model Nos. 45 to 54 were intro. 1896 and originally had the No. 44-type rolling-block action, which was superseded in 1903 by the No. 44.5-type falling-block action. These models were all disc. about 1916. Generally speaking, the 45-54 series rifles, particularly the Stevens Pope and higher grade Schuetzen models are collector's items, bringing much higher prices than the ordinary No. 44 and 44.5.

MODEL 66 BOLT-ACTION REPEATING

RIFLE. . . . . **NiB $255 Ex $140 Gd $121**
Takedown. Caliber: .22 Short, Long, LR. Tubular magazine holds 13 LR, 15 Long, 19 Short. 24-in. bbl. Weight: 5 lbs. Sights: Open rear, bead front. Plain pistol-grip stock w/grooved forearm. Made 1931-35.

NO. 70 VISIBLE LOADING

SLIDE-ACTION . . . . **NiB $579 Ex $398 Gd $255**
Exposed hammer. Caliber: .22 LR, Long, Short. Tubular magazine holds 11 LR., 13 Long, 15 Short. 22-in. bbl. Weight: 4.5 lbs. Sights: Open rear; bead front. Plain straight-grip stock, grooved slide handle. Made 1907-34. Note: Nos. 702, 71, 712, 72, 722 essentially the same as No. 70, differing chiefly in bbl. length or sight tooling.

MODEL 87 AUTOLOADING

RIFLE. . . . . **NiB $167 Ex $121 Gd $90**
Takedown. Caliber: .22 LR. 15-rnd. tubular magazine. 24-in. bbl. (20-in. on current model). Weight: 6 lbs. Sights: Open rear, bead front. Pistol-grip stock. Made 1938 to date. Note: This model originally bore the "Springfield" brand name, disc. in 1948.

MODEL 200 . . . . **NiB $420 Ex $370 Gd $330**
Bolt action. Calibers: .22-250 Rem., .223 Rem., .243 Win., .25-06, .270 Win., 7mm-08, .308 Win., .30-06 or .300 Win. Mag. 3- or 4-rnd. internal magazine. 22- or 24-in. bbl. Weight: 6.5 lbs. No sights. Stock: synthetic. Made 2005-13.

MODEL 300 . . . . **NiB $205 Ex $180 Gd $160**
Bolt action. Caliber: .22 LR, 10-rnd. magazine. 20.75-in. bbl. Weight: 5 lbs. Adj. sights. Stock: synthetic. Made 2006-13.

MODEL 305 . . . . **NiB $205 Ex $180 Gd $160**
Similar to Model 300 except in .22 WMR. Made 2006 to 2013.

MODEL 322 HI-POWER BOLT-ACTION

CARBINE. . . . . **NiB $487 Ex $333 Gd $202**
Caliber: .22 Hornet. 4-rnd. detachable magazine. 21-in. bbl. Weight: 6.75 lbs. Sights: Open rear; ramp front. Pistol-grip stock. Made 1947 to 1950 (See Savage models 340, 342.)

GRADING: **NiB** = New in Box   **Ex** = Excellent or NRA 95%   **Gd** = Good or NRA 68%

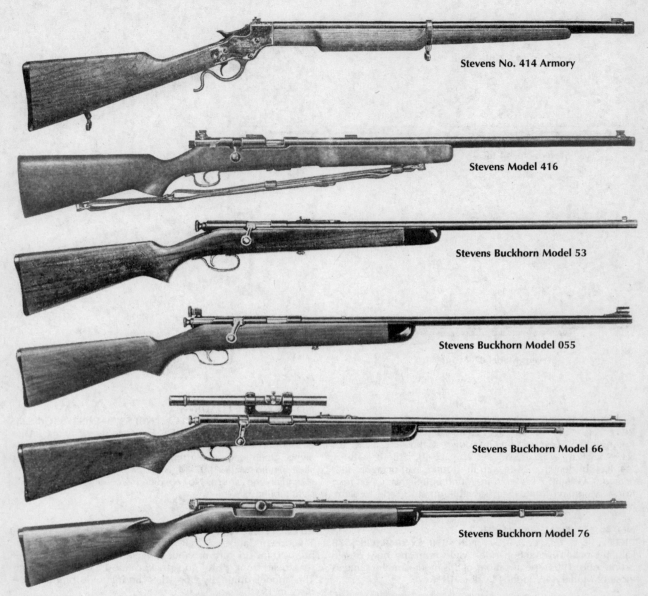

Stevens No. 414 Armory

Stevens Model 416

Stevens Buckhorn Model 53

Stevens Buckhorn Model 055

Stevens Buckhorn Model 66

Stevens Buckhorn Model 76

MODEL 322-S . . . . **NiB $479 Ex $338 Gd $200**
Same as Model 325 except w/peep rear sight. (See Savage models 340S, 342S.)

**MODEL 325 HI-POWER BOLT-ACTION
CARBINE.** . . . . **NiB $479 Ex $338 Gd $200**
Caliber: .30-30. Three round detachable box magazine. 21-in. bbl. Weight: 6.75 lbs. Sights: Open rear; bead front. Plain pistol-grip stock. Made 1947-50. (See Savage Model 340.)

MODEL 325-S . . . . **NiB $479 Ex $338 Gd $200**
Same as Model 325 except w/peep rear sight. (See Savage Model 340S.)

**NO. 414 ARMORY MODEL SINGLE-SHOT
RIFLE.** . . . . **NiB $488 Ex $398 Gd $316**
No. 44-type lever-action. Calibers: .22 LR only, .22 Short only. 26-in. bbl. Weight: 8 lbs. Sights: Lyman receiver peep; blade front. Plain straight-grip stock, military-type forearm, swivels. Made 1912-32.

**MODEL 416 BOLT-ACTION TARGET
RIFLE.** . . . . **NiB $159 Ex $100 Gd $77**
Caliber: .22 LR. Five round detachable box magazine. 26-in. heavy bbl. Weight: 9.5 lbs. Sights: Receiver peep; hooded front. Target stock, swivels, sling. Made 1937-49.

**NO. 419 JUNIOR TARGET MODEL BOLT-ACTION
SINGLE-SHOT RIFLE.** . . . . **NiB $433 Ex $325 Gd $255**
Takedown. Caliber: .22 LR. 26-in. bbl. Weight: 5.5 lbs. Sights: Lyman No. 55 rear peep; blade front. Plain junior target stock w/pistol grip and grooved forearm, swivels, sling. Made 1932-36.

**BUCKHORN MODEL 053 BOLT-ACTION
SINGLE-SHOT RIFLE.** . . . . **NiB $200 Ex $148 Gd $110**
Takedown. Calibers: .22 Short, Long, LR., .22 WRF. .25 Stevens R.F. 24-in. bbl. Weight: 5.5 lbs. Sights: Receiver peep; open middle; hooded front. Sporting stock w/pistol-grip and black forend tip. Made 1935-48.

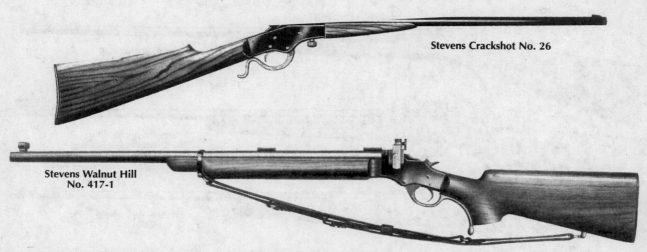

Stevens Crackshot No. 26

Stevens Walnut Hill
No. 417-1

BUCKHORN MODEL 53 . . . . . NiB $220 Ex $179 Gd $122
Same as Buckhorn Model 053 except w/open rear sight and plain bead front sight.

BUCKHORN 055 . . . . NiB $233 Ex $188 Gd $126
Takedown. Same as Model 056 except in single-shot configuration. Weight: 5.5 lbs. Caliber: .22 LR, Long, Short. 24-in. bbl. Weight: 6 lbs. Sights: Receiver peep, open middle, hooded front. Made 1935-48.

BUCKHORN MODEL 056 . . . . NiB $230 Ex $190 Gd $131
Takedown. Bolt action. Caliber: .22 LR, Long, Short. Five round detachable box magazine. 24-in. bbl. Weight: 6 lbs. Sights: Receiver peep, open middle, hooded front. Sporting stock w/ pistol grip and black forend tip. Made 1935-48.

BUCKHORN MODEL 56 . . . . . NiB $230 Ex $190 Gd $131
Same as Buckhorn Model 056 except w/open rear sight and plain bead front sight.

BUCKHORN NO. 057 . . . . NiB $233 Ex $155 Gd $120
Same as Buckhorn Model 076 except w/5-rnd. detachable box magazine. Made 1939-48.

BUCKHORN NO. 57 . . . . NiB $230 Ex $155 Gd $120
Same as Buckhorn Model 76 except w/5-rnd. detachable box magazine. Made 1939-48.

BUCKHORN MODEL 066 . . . NiB $290 Ex $227 Gd $130
Takedown. Bolt action. Caliber: .22 LR, Long, Short. Tubular magazine holds 21 Short, 17 Long, 15 LR. 24-in. bbl. Weight: 6 lbs. Sights: Receiver peep; open middle; hooded front. Sporting stock w/pistol grip and black forend tip. Made 1935-48.

BUCKHORN MODEL 66 . . . . . NiB $219 Ex $133 Gd $210
Same as Buckhorn Model 066 except w/open rear sight, plain bead front sight.

**BUCKHORN NO. 076 AUTOLOADING
RIFLE. NiB $227 Ex $188 Gd $135**
Takedown. Caliber: .22 LR. 15-rnd. tubular magazine. 24-in. bbl. Weight: 6 lbs. Sights: Receiver peep; open middle; hooded front. Sporting stock w/pistol grip, black forend tip. Made 1938-48.

BUCKHORN NO. 76 . . . . NiB $227 Ex $188 Gd $135
Same as Buckhorn No. 076 except w/open rear sight, plain bead front sight.

**CRACKSHOT NO. 26 SINGLE-SHOT
RIFLE. NiB $338 Ex $229 Gd $170**
Lever-action. Takedown. Calibers: .22 LR, .32 R.F. 18-in. or 22-in. bbl. Weight: 3.25 lbs. Sights: Open rear; blade front. Plain straight-grip stock, small tapered forearm. Made 1913-39.

CRACKSHOT NO. 26.5 . . . . . . NiB $325 Ex $220 Gd $195
Same as Crackshot No. 26 except w/smoothbore bbl. for shot cartridges.

"STEVENS FAVORITE"
Also see Savage Model 71.

**FAVORITE NO. 17 SINGLE-SHOT
RIFLE. NiB $333 Ex $227 Gd $200**
Lever-action. Takedown. Calibers: .22 LR, .25 R.F., .32 R.F. 24-in. round bbl; other lengths were available. Weight: 4.5 lbs. Sights: Open rear; Rocky Mountain front. Plain straight-grip stock, small tapered forearm. Made 1894-1935.

FAVORITE NO. 18 . . . . NiB $422 Ex $300 Gd $179
Same as Favorite No. 17 except w/Vernier peep rear sight, leaf middle sight, Beach combination front sight.

FAVORITE NO. 19 . . . . NiB $439 Ex $333 Gd $220
Same as Favorite No. 17 except w/Lyman combination rear sight, leaf middle sight, Lyman front sight.

FAVORITE NO. 20 . . . . NiB $420 Ex $325 Gd $215
Same as Favorite No. 17 except w/smoothbore barrel.

FAVORITE NO. 27 . . . . NiB $439 Ex $333 Gd $220
Same as Favorite No. 17 except w/octagon bbl.

FAVORITE NO. 28 . . . . NiB $439 Ex $333 Gd $220
Same as Favorite No. 18 except w/octagon bbl.

FAVORITE NO. 29 . . . . NiB $439 Ex $333 Gd $220
Same as Favorite No. 19 except w/octagon bbl.

**WALNUT HILL NO. 417-0 SINGLE-SHOT
TARGET RIFLE. . . . . NiB $909 Ex $777 Gd $530**
Lever-action. Calibers: .22 LR only, .22 Short only, .22 Hornet. 28-in. heavy bbl. (extra heavy 29-in. bbl. also available). Weight: 10.5 lbs. Sights: Lyman No. 52L extension rear; 17A front, scope bases mounted on bbl. Target stock w/ full pistol-grip, beavertail forearm, bbl. band, swivels, sling. Made 1932-47.

GRADING: **NiB** = New in Box   **Ex** = Excellent or NRA 95%   **Gd** = Good or NRA 68%

Stevens-Springfield
Model 82

Stevens-Springfield
Model 83

Stevens-Springfield
Model 84

Stevens-Springfield
Model 85

Stevens-Springfield
Model 86-S

WALNUT HILL NO. 417-1 . . . . NiB $909 Ex $750 Gd $521
Same as No. 417-0 except w/Lyman No. 48L receiver sight.

WALNUT HILL NO. 417-2 . . . . NiB $909 Ex $750 Gd $521
Same as No. 417-0 except w/Lyman No. 144 tang sight.

WALNUT HILL NO. 417-3 . . . . NiB $909 Ex $750 Gd $521
Same as No. 417-0 except w/o sights.

**WALNUT HILL NO. 417.5
SINGLE-SHOT RIFLE** . . . . NiB $909 Ex $750 Gd $521
Lever-action. Calibers: .22 LR, .22 WMR, .25 R.F., .22 Hornet.
28-in. bbl. Weight: 8.5 lbs. Sights: Lyman No. 144 tang peep,
folding middle; bead front. Sporting stock w/pistol-grip, semi-
beavertail forearm, swivels, sling. Made 1932-40.

**WALNUT HILL NO. 418 SINGLE-SHOT
RIFLE** . . . . NiB $988 Ex $768 Gd $589
Lever-action. Takedown. Calibers: .22 LR only, .22 Short only.
26-in. bbl. Weight: 6.5 lbs. Sights: Lyman No. 144 tang peep;
blade front. Pistol-grip stock, semi-beavertail forearm, swivels,
sling. Made 1932-40.

WALNUT HILL NO. 418-5 . . . . NiB $988 Ex $768 Gd $589
Same as No. 418 except also available in calibers .22 WRF
and .25 Stevens R.F., w/Lyman No. 2A tang peep sight, bead
front sight.

STEVENS-SPRINGFIELD

**MODEL 82 BOLT-ACTION SINGLE-SHOT
RIFLE** . . . . NiB $178 Ex $144 Gd $115
Takedown. Caliber: .22 LR, Long, Short. 22-in. bbl. Weight: 4
lbs. Sights: Open rear; gold bead front. Plain pistol-grip stock
w/grooved forearm. Made 1935-39.

**MODEL 83 BOLT-ACTION SINGLE-SHOT
RIFLE** . . . . NiB $200 Ex $155 Gd $110
Takedown. Calibers: .22 LR, Long, Short; .22 WRF, .25 Stevens
R.F. 24-in. bbl. Weight: 4.5 lbs. Sights: Peep rear; open middle;
hooded front. Plain pistol-grip stock w/grooved forearm. Made
1935-39.

MODEL 84 . . . . NiB $220 Ex $190 Gd $128
Same as Model 86 except w/5-rnd. detachable box magazine.
Pre-1948 rifles of this model were designated Springfield
Model 84, later known as Stevens Model 84. Made 1940-65.

MODEL 84-S (084) . . . . NiB $220 Ex $190 Gd $128
Same as Model 84 except w/peep rear sight and hooded front
sight. Pre-1948 rifles of this model were designated Springfield
Model 084, later known as Stevens Model 84-S. Disc.

MODEL 85 . . . . NiB $244 Ex $199 Gd $139
Same as Stevens Model 87 except w/5-rnd. detachable
box magazine. Made 1939 to date. Pre-1948 rifles of this
model were designated Springfield Model 85, currently
known as Stevens Model 85. Earlier models command
slight premiums.

MODEL 85-S (085) . . . . NiB $224 Ex $167 Gd $126
Same as Model 85 except w/peep rear sight and hooded front sight. Pre-1948 models were designated Springfield Model 085; also known as Stevens Model 85-S.

MODEL 86 BOLT-ACTION . . . . NiB $224 Ex $167 Gd $126
Takedown. Caliber: .22 LR, Long, Short. Tubular magazine holds 15 LR, 17 Long, 21 Short. 24-in. bbl. Weight: 6 lbs. Sights: Open rear, gold bead front. Pistol-grip stock, black forend tip on later production. Made 1935 to 1965. Note: The Springfield brand name was disc. in 1948.

MODEL 86-S (086) . . . . NiB $230 Ex $172 Gd $128
Same as Model 86 except w/peep rear sight and hooded front sight. Pre-1948 rifles of this model were designated as Springfield Model 086, later known as Stevens Model 86-S. Disc.

MODEL 87-S (087) . . . . NiB $233 Ex $215 Gd $156
Same as Stevens Model 87 except w/peep rear sight and hooded front sight. Pre-1948 rifles of this model were designated as Springfield Model 087, later known as Stevens Model 87-S. Disc.

STEYR ARMS — Austria

Formerly Steyr Daimer Puch A.G. from 1911 to 1960 in Steyr, Austria. Currently imported by Steyr Arms Inc., Bessemer, AL. See also listings under Mannlicher-Schoenauer.

AUG SA A3 M1 . . . . NiB $4220 Ex $3370 Gd $2340
Bull-pup. Gas-operated, Semiauto. Caliber: .223 Rem. (5.56mm). Thirty or 40-rnd. magazine. 20-in. bbl. standard; optional 16-in. or 24-in. heavy bbl. w/folding bipod. 31 in. overall. Weight: 8.5 lbs. Sights: Integral 1.5x scope and mount. Black high-impact synthetic stock w/folding vertical grip. Imported 2006 to date.
Green finish . . . . NiB $3400 Ex $2980 Gd $2710
Grey finish . . . . NiB $3100 Ex $2380 Gd $2410
1.5x or 3x optic, add $400
42-rnd. magazine, add $100

SCOUT . . . . NiB $2099 Ex $1855 Gd $1580
Designed by Jeff Cooper. Bolt-action repeater. Caliber: .223 Rem., .243 Win., .308 Win., 7mm-08 or .376 Steyr; 5-rnd. detachable box magazine. 19-in. bbl. Sights: picatinny rail. Stock: grey, black or camo polymer. Made 1998 to date.

STOEGER — New York, NY

Manufactured by Franz Jaeger & Co., Suhl, Germany; dist. in the U.S. by A. F. Stoeger, Inc., New York, NY.

HORNET RIFLE . . . . NiB $1388 Ex $1008 Gd $659
Same specifications as Herold Rifle, designed and built on a Miniature Mauser-type action. See listing under Herold Bolt-Action Repeating Sporting Rifle for additional specifications. Imported during the 1930s.

SURVIVAL ARMS — Orange, CT

AR-7 EXPLORER . . . . NiB $180 Ex $155 Gd $98
Caliber: .22 LR. Eight round magazine. Weight: 3 lbs. Polymer stocks. Drift adj. sights. Disassembles into five separate elements, allowing barrel, action and magazine to fit into butt-stock; assembles quickly w/o tools. Choice of camo, silvertone or black matte finishes. Made 1992-95.

SWISS MILITARY

MODEL 1911 RIFLE . . . . NiB $755 Ex $570 Gd $515
Straight pull bolt action. Caliber: 7.5x55mm Swiss. 6-rnd. magazine. Weight: 8.8 lbs. Stock: smooth wood. Sights: adj. rear. Manufactured by Schmidt Rubin. Surplus firearms.
K1911 Carbine (23.3-in. bbl.) . . . NiB $755 Ex $570 Gd $515

THOMPSON

See Auto Ordnance.

THOMPSON/CENTER ARMS —
Springfield, MA

Acquired by Smith & Wesson in 2007; formerly in Rochester, NH.

To facilitate locating Thompson/Center rifles, models are grouped into three categories: single-shot rifles (below), Semiauto and bolt-action rifles. For a complete listing, please refer to the index.

- SINGLE-SHOT RIFLES -

CONTENDER CARBINE
Calibers: .22 LR, .22 Hornet, .222 Rem., .223 Rem., 7mm T.C.U., 7x30 Waters, .30-30 Win., .35 Rem., .44 Mag., .357 Rem. Max. and .410 bore. 21-in. interchangeable bbls. 35 in. overall. Adj. iron sights. Checkered American walnut or Rynite stock and forend. Made 1986-2000.
Standard model (rifle calibers) NiB $466 Ex $287 Gd $198
Standard model (.410 bore) . . . NiB $459 Ex $280 Gd $210
Rynite stock model (rifle
  calibers) . . . . NiB $390 Ex $290 Gd $245
Rynite stock model (.410 bore) NiB $390 Ex $300 Gd $244
Youth model (all calibers) . . . . . NiB $495 Ex $320 Gd $235
Extra bbl. (rifle calibers), add $25
Extra bbl. (.410 bore), add $35

CONTENDER CARBINE
SURVIVAL SYSTEM . . . . NiB $655 Ex $488 Gd $370
Similar to standard Contender Carbine w/Rynite stock and forend. Comes w/two 16.25-in. bbls. chambered in .223 and .45/.410 bore. Camo Cordura case.

STAINLESS CONTENDER CARBINE
Same as standard Contender Carbine Model, except stainless steel w/blued sights. Calibers: .22 LR, .22 Hornet, .223 Rem., 7-30 Waters, .30-30 Win., .410. Walnut or Rynite stock and forend. Made 1993-2000.
Walnut stock model . . . . NiB $445 Ex $390 Gd $325
Rynite stock model . . . . NiB $495 Ex $425 Gd $300
Youth stock model . . . . NiB $467 Ex $388 Gd $287
Extra bbls. (rifle calibers), add $25

ENCORE RIFLE . . . . NiB $788 Ex $521 Gd $379
Single-shot, break-action. Cal.: Rimfire and centerfire from .17 Mach 2 to .45-70 Gov't. Bbl.: 24 to 16 in., interchangeable. Hammer block safety, trigger guard opening lever. Stock: Synthetic black, Realtree camo or American walnut; smooth forearm, Monte Carlo stock w/pistol grip.; adj. rear sight.

RIFLES

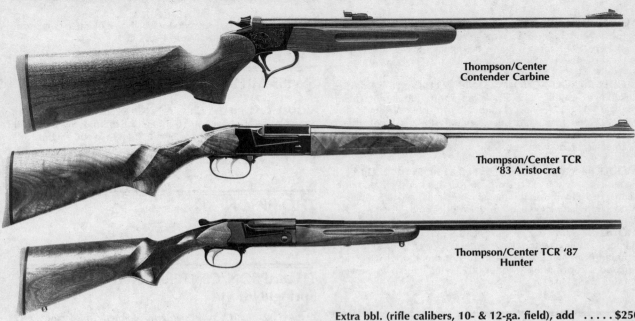

Thompson/Center Contender Carbine

Thompson/Center TCR '83 Aristocrat

Thompson/Center TCR '87 Hunter

w/extra blued bbls., add $245
Camo models, add $150
w/thumbhole stock, add $227
.17 Mach 2, add $75
w/stainless bbl., add $400
Hunter pkg. (scope, bases, case), add $300

ENCORE KATAHDIN . . . . **NiB $633 Ex $467 Gd $379**
Same as Encore but w/ 18-in. blued bbl. Cal.: .444 Marlin, .450 Marlin or .45-70 Gov't. Stock: Black composite. Fiber optic sights, drilled and tapped for scope. Weight: 6.6 lbs. Made 2002-05.

PRO HUNTER RIFLE . . . . **NiB $944 Ex $670 Gd $433**
Cal.: Various. Bbl.: 28 in., stainless steel. Recoil reducing Flex-Tech stock (thumbhole option) in black or camo.
w/camo stock, add $100
w/ extra bbl., add $400

HOTSHOT (CAMO STOCK) . . **NiB $395 Ex $299 Gd $214**
Youth model. Cal.: 22 LR. Bbl.: 19 in. Stock: Black synthetic, Realtree AP camo or AP pink camo. Auto safety; drilled and tapped for scope. Weight: 3 lbs.
w/pink camo stock, add $25

TCR '83/ARISTOCRAT MODEL . . .**NiB $497 Ex $445 Gd $277**
Break frame, overlever action. Calibers: .223 Rem., .22/250 Rem., .243 Win., 7mm Rem. Mag., .30-06 Springfield. Interchangeable bbls.: 23 in. in length. Weight: 6 lbs., 14 oz. American walnut stock and forearm, checkered, black rubber recoil pad, cheekpiece. Made 1983-87.
Aristocrat model . . . . **NiB $569 Ex $439 Gd $280**
Extra bbl. (rifle calibers), add $278

TCR '87 HUNTER RIFLE . . . . . . **NiB $544 Ex $345 Gd $200**
Similar to TCR '83 except in calibers .22 Hornet, .222 Rem., 223 Rem., .22-250 Rem., .243 Win., .270 Win., 7mm-08, .308 Win., .30-06, .32-40 Win. Also 12-ga. slug and 10- and 12-ga. field bbls. 23-in. standard or 25.88-in. heavy bbl. interchangeable. 39.5 to 43.38 in. overall. Weight: 6 lbs., 14 oz. to 7.5 lbs. Iron sights optional. Checkered American black walnut buttstock w/fluted end. Disc. 1992.

Extra bbl. (rifle calibers, 10- & 12-ga. field), add $250
Extra bbl. (12-ga. slug), add $300

- BOLT-ACTION RIFLES -

COMPASS . . . . **NiB $355 Ex $300 Gd $255**
Bolt action. Cal.: .204 Ruger, .22-250 Rem., .223 Rem., .243 Win., .270 Win., .30-06, .300 Win. Mag., .308 Win., 6.5 Creedmoor or 7mm Rem. Mag. Bbl.: 20- or 24-in. threaded. Three lug, 60-degree bolt. Stock: Composite w/textured inserts. 4- or 5-rnd. rotary magazine. Adj. trigger. No sights. Weight: 7.5 pounds. Made 2016-19.

COMPASS II SERIES . . . . **NiB $370 Ex $330 Gd $255**
Updated version of Compass rifle. Similar calibers. Generation II trigger. Stock: Black composite. No sights. Weight: 7-8.5 pounds. Made 2020 to date.
Compact model (16.5-in.
    threaded bbl.) . . . . **NiB $370 Ex $330 Gd $255**
Utility model (21.6-in. bbl.) . . . . **NiB $330 Ex $290 Gd $230**

DIMENSION . . . . **NiB $689 Ex $380 Gd $300**
Push-feed, short or long action, interchangeable barrels. Calibers.: .204 Ruger, .22-250 Rem., .223 Rem., .243 Win., .270 Win., .308 Win., .30-06, .300 Win. Mag., 7mm-08, 7mm Rem. Mag. Bbl.: 22 or 24 in., 3-rnd. detachable box magazine, black synthetic stock w/adj. LOP, Weaver style mounts. Made 2012-18.

ICON SERIES . . . . **NiB $1167 Ex $855 Gd $766**
Bolt action. Cal.: .22-250 Rem., .270 Win., .30-06, .300 Win. Mag., .308 Win., .30 TC, 6.5 Creedmoor, 7mm Mag. Bbl.: 24 in. Medium or long action, hinged floor plate (on long action). Stock: Black synthetic or RealTree camo, checkered American walnut, classic walnut or Ultra Wood; pistol grip and forearm. Adj. trigger, cocking indicator, three-shot magazine (on medium action). Jeweled bolt handle. Weaver-style bases. Weight: 7.5 pounds. Made 2007-12.
Walnut stock, add $75
Precision Hunter model (.204 Ruger, .223 Rem., .22-250
    Rem., .243 Win., 6.5 Creedmoor, .308 Win.; 22-in. fluted
    bbl. w/5R button rifling; tactical-style bolt handle;
    brown synthetic stock w/cheekpiece and beavertail
    fore end; 2009-12) . . . . **NiB $905 Ex $780 Gd $580**

Thompson/Center Icon Warlord

Thompson/Center Dimension RH Scoped

Thompson/Center Model R-55 Classic

Thompson/Center Encore Katahdin

Warlord model (.308 Win. or .338 Lapua; 5- or 10-rnd. magazine; fluted, stainless steel bbl., carbon fiber tactical style stock w/adj. cheek piece, flat black or desert sand, 2010-11) . . . . **NiB $3000 Ex $2600 Gd $1810**

VENTURE. . . . . **NiB $632 Ex $495 Gd $375**
Bolt action. Cal.: 270 Win., .30-06, 7 mm Rem. Mag., .300 Win. Mag. Bbl.: 24 in., tapered match grade w/ 5R button rifling. Stock: Black synthetic, sporter design, textured grip. Adj. trigger, two-position safety. Made 2009-19.
Predator model (.204 Ruger, .223 Rem., .22-250 Rem. or .308 Win.; 22-in. fluted bbl.; composite stock w/100% Realtree Max-1 camo; Weather Shield bolt handle; 6.75 lbs.). . . . . . . **NiB $545 Ex $480 Gd $370**

VENTURE II SERIES . . . . **NiB $480 Ex $420 Gd $330**
Updated version of Venture rifle. Similar calibers. Generation II trigger. Stock: Black composite. No sights. Weight: 7.3-8.5 pounds. Made 2020 to date.

- SEMIAUTO RIFLES -

SILVER LYNX . . . . **NiB $488 Ex $390 Gd $300**
Semiauto. Cal.: .22 LR. Bbl.: 20 in., match grade; 5-rnd. magazine, stainless steel action and bbl. Stock: Black composite with Monte Carlo cheek piece. Weight: 5.5 lbs. Made 2004-05.

R22 SERIES. . . . . **NiB $355 Ex $320 Gd $265**
Semiauto. Cal.: .22 LR; 10-rnd. rotary magazine. Bbl.: 17 in. button rifled. Sights: Green fiber optic front/adj. peep rear. Stock: Composite or hardwood, various colors. Weight: 4.4 lbs. Made 2019-date.
Hardwood stock, add **$50**
Camo finish, add. **$20**

MODEL R-55 CLASSIC. . . . . . . **NiB $629 Ex $428 Gd $326**
Semiauto. Cal.: .17 Mach 2, .22 LR. Bbl.: 22 in., match grade; adj. rear sight; blue finish. Blow-back action. Smooth Monte Carlo walnut stock. Weight: 5.5 lbs. Made 2000-09.
R-55 Target. . . . . **NiB $677 Ex $466 Gd $389**
R-55 Sporter . . . . **NiB $519 Ex $405 Gd $310**

TIKKA — Riihimaki, Finland
Manufactured by Sako, Ltd. of Riihimaki, Finland and Armi Marocchi in Italy. Acquired by Beretta Holdings in 2000.

NOTE: *Tikka New Generation, Battue and Continental series bolt action rifles are being manufactured by Sako, Ltd., in Finland. Tikka O/U rifles (previously Valmet) are being manufactured in Italy by Armi Marocchi. For earlier importation see additional listings under Ithaca LSA and Valmet 412S models.*

—COMBINATION, O/U MODELS—

MODEL 412S . . . . **NiB $1135 Ex $944 Gd $725**
Break action, double bbl. O/U. Calibers: .308 Win., .30-06, 9.3x74R. 24-in. bbl. w/quarter rib machined for scope mounts; automatic ejectors (9.3x74R only). 40 in. overall. Weight: 8.5 lbs. Ramp front and folding adj. rear sight. Barrel selector on trigger. European walnut buttstock and forearm. Model 412S was replaced by the 512S version in 1994. Imported from 1989–93.
w/extra bbl. assembly (O/U shotgun), add. **$707**
w/extra bbl. assembly (O/U Combo), add **$800**
w/extra bbl. assembly (OU/rifle), add **$1050**

MODEL 512S. . . . . **NiB $1559 Ex $1440 Gd $1100**
Formerly Valmet 412S. In 1994, following the joint venture of 1989, the model designation was changed to 512S. Imported from 1994–97.
w/extra bbl. assembly (O/U rifle), add. **$800**

—BOLT ACTION MODELS—

LSA55 SERIES
Mauser-type action. Calibers: .222 Rem., .22-250, 6mm Rem. Mag., .243 Win., .308 Win. Three round clip magazine. 22.8-in. bbl. Weight: 6.8 lbs. Sights: Folding leaf rear; hooded ramp front. Checkered walnut stock w/Monte Carlo cheekpiece, swivels. Made 1965-88.
Standard model. . . . . **NiB $555 Ex $389 Gd $244**
Sporter model (22.8-in. heavy bbl., no sights, beavertail forearm stock, 9 lbs.) . . . . **NiB $580 Ex $482 Gd $369**
Deluxe model (w/rollover cheekpiece, rosewood grip cap and forend tip, skip checkering, high-luster blue) . . . . **NiB $590 Ex $534 Gd $450**

LSA65 SERIES
Same as LSA55 Standard except calibers: .25-06, 6.5x55 .270 Win., .30-06. Five-rnd. magazine, 22-in. bbl., weight: 7.5 lbs. Imported 1970-88.
Standard model. . . . . **NiB $495 Ex $398 Gd $277**
Deluxe model . . . . **NiB $598 Ex $522 Gd $369**

MODEL M55 SERIES
Bolt action. Calibers: .222 Rem., .22-250 Rem., .223 Rem. .243 Win., .308 Win. (6mm Rem. and 17 Rem. available in Standard and Deluxe models only). 23.2-in. bbl. (24.8-in. Sporter and Heavy Barrel models). 42.8 in. overall (44-in. Sporter and Heavy Barrel models). Weight: 7.25-9 lbs. Monte Carlo-style stock w/pistol-grip. Sling swivels. Imported 1965–88.
Continental . . . . **NiB $745 Ex $560 Gd $420**
Deluxe model . . . . **NiB $808 Ex $579 Gd $443**
Sporter . . . . **NiB $733 Ex $577 Gd $400**
Sporter w/sights . . . . **NiB $755 Ex $572 Gd $390**
Standard . . . . **NiB $669 Ex $544 Gd $367**
Super Sporter . . . . **NiB $833 Ex $466 Gd $398**
Super Sporter w/sights . . . . **NiB $909 Ex $478 Gd $514**
Trapper . . . . **NiB $755 Ex $556 Gd $443**

RIFLES

M65 SERIES

Bolt action. Calibers: .25-06, .270 Win., .308 Win., .30-06, 7mm Rem. Mag., .300 Win. Mag. (Sporter and Heavy Bbl. models in .270 Win., .308 Win. and .30-06 only). 22.4-in. bbl. (24.8-in. in Sporter and Heavy Bbl. models). 43.2 in. overall (44 in. in Sporter, 44.8 in. in Heavy Bbl.). Weight: 7.5 to 9.9 lbs. Monte Carlo-style stock w/pistol-grip. Disc. 1989.

Continental	NiB $755	Ex $572	Gd $439
Deluxe Magnum	NiB $800	Ex $677	Gd $495
Deluxe model	NiB $770	Ex $587	Gd $467
Magnum	NiB $709	Ex $540	Gd $440
Sporter	NiB $579	Ex $555	Gd $398
Sporter w/sights	NiB $789	Ex $645	Gd $445
Standard	NiB $670	Ex $690	Gd $479
Super Sporter	NiB $898	Ex $690	Gd $489
Super Sporter w/sights	NiB $909	Ex $695	Gd $494
Super Sporter Master	NiB $1143	Ex $944	Gd $643
Wild Boar model (20.8-in. bbl., 41.6 in. length, 7.5 lbs.)	NiB $790	Ex $650	Gd $469

BATTUE MODEL

BATTUE MODEL	NiB $568	Ex $466	Gd $388

Similar to Hunter Model except designed for snapshooting w/ hooded front and open rear sights on quarter rib. Blued finish. Checkered select walnut stock w/matt lacquered finish. Imported 1991-97.

Magnum calibers, add. $50

CONTINENTAL MODEL

Similar to Hunter Model except w/prone-style stock w/wider forearm and 26-in. heavy bbl. chambered for 17 Rem., .22-250 Rem., .223 Rem., .308 Win. (Varmint); .25-06 Rem., .270 Win., 7mm Rem. Mag., .300 Win. Mag. (Long Range). Weight: 8.6 lbs. Imported 1991–2003.

Continental Long-Range model	NiB $690	Ex $558	Gd $390
Continental Varmint model	NiB $640	Ex $500	Gd $355
Magnum calibers, add. 40%			

NEW GENERATION RIFLES (MODELS 595/695)

Short-throw bolt available in three action lengths. Calibers: .22-250 Rem., .223 Rem., .243 Win., .308 Win., (medium action) .25-06 Rem., .270 Win., .30.06, (Long Action) 7mm Rem. Mag., .300 Win. Mag., .338 Win.

Standard calibers	NiB $769	Ex $688	Gd $487
Magnum calibers, add. $50			

PREMIUM GRADE RIFLE

Similar to New Generation rifles except w/hand-checkered deluxe wood stock w/roll-over check-piece and rosewood grip cap and forend tip. High polished blued finish. Imported from 1989 to 1994.

Standard calibers	NiB $923	Ex $755	Gd $488
Magnum calibers, add. $50			

SPORTER MODEL

SPORTER MODEL	NiB $909	Ex $779	Gd $633

Similar to Hunter Model except 23.5-in. bbl., 5-rnd. detachable mazigine. Caliber: .22-250 Rem., .223 Rem., .308 Win. Weight: 8.6 lbs. Adj. buttplate and cheekpiece w/stippled pistol grip and forend. Imported 1998-2003.

T3 SERIES

Bolt action, dual lugs, 90 degree bolt lift. Calibers: .223, .22-250, .243Win., .308 Win., .25-06, .270 Win., 6.5x55, 270 WSM, 7mm Rem. Mag., .30-06, .300 WSM, .300 Win. Mag., .338 Win. Mag.; 3-, 4-, 5- or 6-rnd. single stack or 10-rnd. double stack detachable box magazine. Bbl: 22 7/16 in.; 24.37-in. magnum calibers. Weight: 6.75 pounds. No sights. Stock: checkered walnut or black synthetic w/butt pad. Imported 2003-15.

Big Boar Synthetic model

(19-in. bbl., black synthetic stock, 6.1 lbs., 2006-07)	NiB $655	Ex $580	Gd $430

Camo Stainless model (stainless bbl. and action, synthetic stock w/Realtree HD hardwoods

finish, 6.2 lbs., 2006-07)	NiB $655	Ex $580	Gd $430

CTR model (20-in. heavy bbl., synthetic stock w/adj. cheekpiece, 7.5 lbs., 10-rnd.

steel magazine, 2014-15)	NiB $955	Ex $830	Gd $655

CTR Stainless model (20-in. heavy stainless bbl., synthetic stock w/adj. cheekpiece, 7.5 lbs., 10-rnd.

steel magazine, 2015)	NiB $1055	Ex $955	Gd $755

Deluxe model (oil finish walnut stock w/rosewood

tip, 2006-07)	NiB $900	Ex $730	Gd $555

Forest model (blued, Monte Carlo

oil finish walnut stock).	NiB $855	Ex $755	Gd $555

Hunter model	NiB $695	Ex $585	Gd $420

Laminated Stainless model (stainless bbl. and action,

grey laminated stock).	NiB $880	Ex $755	Gd $555
left-hand models, add $70			

Lite model (synthetic stock;

6.2 lbs.)	NiB $555	Ex $489	Gd $410

Lite Compact model (synthetic stock w/12.5in.

LOP, 6.2 lbs.)	NiB $555	Ex $489	Gd $410

Lite Stainless model (stainless bbl. and action,

synthetic stock, 6.2 lbs.)	NiB $685	Ex $570	Gd $420

Scout CTR model (20-in. heavy bbl., synthetic stock,

2010-12)	NiB $830	Ex $730	Gd $530

Super Varmint model (stainless heavy bbl., synthetic

stock, adjustable trigger) . .	NiB $1255	Ex $1005	Gd $700

Tactical model (20-in. bbl. w/muzzle brake, black phosphate finish, synthetic stock

w/adj. comb)	NiB $1555	Ex $1230	Gd $880

Varmint model (heavy bbl., synthetic stock,

adj. trigger)	NiB $800	Ex $705	Gd $505

T3X SERIES

Imported version of the T3, left- and right-hand actions, widened angular ejection port. Note: T3x parts are compatible with T3 models. Calibers: .204 Ruger to .300 WSM.; 3-, 4-, 5- or 6-rnd. single stack detachable box magazine. Bbl: 22.4 or 24.3 in., fluted or non-fluted. Weight: 6.6-7 lbs. Sights: Optic ready. Stock: Checkered walnut, black synthetic or laminate w/ butt pad. Imported 2016-date.

Arctic model (Canadian Ranger model, 20-in. stainless bbl., laminated stock,

open sights)	NiB $2000	Ex $1950	Gd $1750

CTR model (20- or 24-in. bbl., black modular synthetic

stock, 7.4 lbs.)	NiB $980	Ex $855	Gd $680

CTR Stainless model (20- or
24-in. stainless bbl.,
black modular synthetic
stock, 7.4 lbs.) . . . . NiB $1080 Ex $955 Gd $730
Forest model (walnut stock) . . . . NiB $955 Ex $830 Gd $655
Hunter model (checkered
walnut stock) . . . . NiB $790 Ex $690 Gd $540
Hunter Stainless model
(stainless bbl./action,
checkered walnut stock) . . NiB $1000 Ex $880 Gd $680
Laminated Stainless model
(stainless bbl./action,
grey laminated stock) . . . . . NiB $1000 Ex $880 Gd $680
left-hand models, add $100
Lite model (black
synthetic modular
stock; 5.9-7 lbs.) . . . . NiB $655 Ex $580 Gd $455
Lite Compact model (black
synthetic modular stock
w/12.5in. LOP, 5.9 lbs.) . . . . NiB $655 Ex $580 Gd $455
Lite Stainless model (stainless
bbl./action, black synthetic
modular stock, 6.2 lbs.) . . . . NiB $780 Ex $685 Gd $530
TACT model (synthetic
stock w/adj. cheekpiece,
heavy threaded bbl.,
Picatinny rail) . . . . NiB $1710 Ex $1510 Gd $1110
TACT A1 model (fully adj.
aluminum chassis stock
w/vertical grip, heavy bbl.,
Picatinny rail) . . . . NiB $1710 Ex $1510 Gd $1110
Varmint model (heavy bbl.,
black synthetic stock) . . . . . NiB $855 Ex $755 Gd $580

WHITETAIL SERIES
Calibers: .22-250 Rem., .223 Rem., .243 Win., .25-06
Rem., .270 Win., 7mm Rem. Mag., .308 Win .30.06, .300
Win. Mag., .338 Win. Mag. Three or 5-rnd. detachable box
magazine. 20.5- to 24.5-in. bbl. with no sights. 42 to 44.5
in. overall. Weight: 7 to 7.5 lbs. Adj. single-stage or single-
set trigger. Blued or stainless finish. All-Weather synthetic
or checkered select walnut stock w/matt lacquered finish.
Imported 1991-02.
Hunter model . . . . NiB $633 Ex $523 Gd $389
Deluxe model . . . . NiB $689 Ex $534 Gd $445
Synthetic model . . . . NiB $689 Ex $534 Gd $445
Stainless model . . . . NiB $689 Ex $534 Gd $445
Magnum calibers, add. $50
Left-hand model, add $100

UBERTI — Accokeek, MD
*Formerly in Lakeville, Connecticut. Manufactured By Aldo
Uberti, Ponte Zanano, Italy. Imported by Stoeger Industries,
Accokeek, MD. Division of Beretta Holdings.*

1866 YELLOW BOY
Replica of Winchester Model 1866 lever-action repeater.
Calibers: .22 LR, .22 WMR, .38 Spec., .44-40, .45 LC. 24.25-
in. octagonal bbl. 43.25 in. overall. Weight: 8.25 lbs. Blade
front sight,rear elevation leaf. Brass frame and buttplate. Bbl.,
magazine tube, other metal parts blued. Walnut buttstock and
forearm.
Rifle . . . . NiB $976 Ex $667 Gd $390

Carbine (19-in.
round bbl.). . . . . NiB $944 Ex $600 Gd $409
Trapper (16-in. bbl.,
Disc. 1989. . . . . NiB $1145 Ex $855 Gd $600
Rimfire (Indian Rifle) . . . . NiB $744 Ex $523 Gd $379
Rimfire (Indian Carbine). . . . . . NiB $744 Ex $523 Gd $379

1873 SPORTING RIFLE
Replica of Winchester Model 1873 lever-action repeater.
Calibers: .22 LR, .22 WMR, .38 Spl., .357 Mag., .44-40, .45
LC. 24.25- or 30-in. octagonal bbl. 43.25 in. overall. Weight:
8 lbs. Blade front sight; adj. open rear. Color case-hardened
frame. Bbl., magazine tube, hammer, lever and buttplate blued.
Walnut buttstock and forearm.
Sporting Rifle model . . . . NiB $1095 Ex $809 Gd $572
Carbine (19-in.
round bbl.). . . . . NiB $790 Ex $666 Gd $445
Competition model
(octagon bbl.,
rubber butt pad) . . . . NiB $1280 Ex $1120 Gd $955
Musket model (30-in. rnd. bbl.,
1999-02) . . . . NiB $880 Ex $705 Gd $580
Special Sporting model
(half rnd. half
octagon bbl.) . . . . NiB $1240 Ex $1085 Gd $930
Trapper (16-in. bbl.,
disc. 1990) . . . . NiB $1095 Ex $809 Gd $572

1860 HENRY RIFLE
Replica of Henry lever-action repeating rifle. Calibers: .44-
40, .45 LC. 24.5-in. half-octagon bbl. 43.75 in. overall.
Weight: 9.25 lbs. Blade front sight; rear sight adj. for eleva-
tion. Brass frame, buttplate and magazine follower. Bbl.,
magazine tube and remaining parts blued. Walnut buttstock.
Rifle . . . . NiB $1177 Ex $808 Gd $590
Carbine (22.5-in. bbl.) . . . . . . NiB $1177 Ex $808 Gd $590
Trapper (16- or
18-in. bbl.). . . . . NiB $1177 Ex $808 Gd $590
Steel frame, add $100

1871 ROLLING BLOCK BABY
CARBINE. . . . . NiB $450 Ex $380 Gd $319
Calibers: .22 LR, .22WMR, .22 Hornet, .357 Mag. Bbl.: 22
in. Overall length: 35 1/2 in. Weight: 4 3/4 pounds. Copy of
Remington New Model No. 4 carbine featuring brass butt plate
and trigger guard; blued barrel; color case-hardened frame.
Introduced in 1986.

1874 SHARPS RIFLE
Reproduction of 1874 Sharps. Caliber: .45-70 Govt. Bbl.: 22-,
32-, or 34-in. Weight: 10.25-11 lbs. Stock: Checkered walnut,
straight or pistol grip. Finish: blued barrel; color case-hardened
frame. Imported since 2006.
Adobe Walls model (32-in. bbl.,
disc. 2009) . . . . NiB $2090 Ex $1900 Gd $1700
Buffalo Hunter model
(32-in. bbl.) . . . . NiB $2610 Ex $2280 Gd $1955
Cavalry Carbine model
(20-in. bbl., disc. 2009) . . . NiB $1690 Ex $1500 Gd $1300
Deluxe model (34-in. bbl.,
gold inlay) . . . . NiB $3255 Ex $2855 Gd $2455
Down Under model
(34-in. bbl.) . . . . NiB $2700 Ex $2365 Gd $2030
Extra Deluxe model (32-in.
bbl., gold inlay,
engraving). . . . . NiB $4380 Ex $3830 Gd $3310

RIFLES

Long Range model (34-in. bbl. half rnd. half octagon, disc. 2009) . . . . NiB $2390 Ex $2200 Gd $2000
Special model (32-in. bbl., pistol grip stock) . . . . NiB $2070 Ex $1805 Gd $1555

1876 CENTENNIAL RIFLE. . . NiB $1440 Ex $1255 Gd $1080
Reproduction of Winchester Model 1876 lever action. Calibers: .40-60 WCF, .45-60 WCF, .45-75 WCF, or .50-90 WCF. Bbl.: 28-in. octagon. Weight: 10 lbs. Stock: Smooth walnut, straight grip. Finish: blued barrel; color case-hardened frame. Imported since 2008.

1883 BURGESS RIFLE . . . . NiB $1280 Ex $1120 Gd $955
Reproduction of Burgess lever action. Caliber: .45 LC. Bbl.: 20- or 25.5-in. octagon. Stock: Smooth walnut, straight grip. Finish: blued barrel; color case-hardened frame. Imported 2010-16.

1885 WINCHESTER HIGH WALL. . . NiB $970 Ex $845 Gd $720
Reproduction of Winchester Model 1885 single shot. Calibers: .22 Hornet, .30-30, .38-55, .40-60, .44 Mag., .44-40, .45 LC, .45-70, .45-90 or .45-120. Bbl.: 28-, 30-, or 32-in. octagon. Weight: 7-9 lbs. Stock: Smooth walnut, straight grip. Finish: blued barrel; color case-hardened frame. Imported since 1999.

1886 WINCHESTER SPORTING NiB $1870 Ex $1635 Gd $1410
Reproduction of Winchester Model 1886 lever action. Calibers: .45-70 Govt. Bbl.: 26-in. octagon. Weight: 9 lbs. Stock: Checkered walnut, straight grip. Finish: blued barrel; color case-hardened frame. Imported since 2017.
Hunter Lite model (22-in. rnd. bbl.) . . . . NiB $1805 Ex $1580 Gd $1355

SPRINGFIELD TRAPDOOR CARBINE. . . . . NiB $1780 Ex $1555 Gd $1330
Calibers: .45-70 Govt. Bbl.: 22 in. Overall length: 41.3 in. Weight: 7.3 lbs. Copy of Springfield carbine/rifle. Stock: smooth walnut. Finish: blued barrel; color case-hardened frame. Introduced in 2006.
Rifle model (32-in. bbl.) . . . . NiB $1780 Ex $1555 Gd $1330

ULTRA-HI PRODUCTS COMPANY — Hawthorne, NJ

MODEL 2200 SINGLE-SHOT BOLT-ACTION RIFLE. . . . . NiB $235 Ex $166 Gd $120
Caliber: .22 LR, Long, Short. .23-in. bbl. Weight: 5 lbs. Sights: Open rear; blade front. Monte Carlo stock w/pistol grip. Made in Japan. Intro. 1977; Disc.

ULTRA LIGHT ARMS COMPANY — Granville, WA

MODEL 20 BOLT-ACTION RIFLE
Calibers: .22-250 Rem., .243 Win., 6mm Rem., .250-3000 Savage, .257 Roberts, .257 Ack., 7mm Mauser, 7mm Ack., 7mm-08 Rem., .284 Win., .300 Savage, .308 Win., .358 Win. Box magazine. 22-in. ultra light bbl. Weight: 4.75 lbs. No sights. Synthetic stock of Kevlar or graphite finished, seven different colors. Nonglare matte or bright metal finish. Medium-length action available L.H. models. Made 1985-99.
Standard model. . . . . NiB $2270 Ex $2056 Gd $1190
Left-hand model, add $150

MODEL 20S BOLT-ACTION RIFLE
Same general specifications as Model 20 except w/short action in calibers 17 Rem., .222 Rem., .223 Rem., .22 Hornet only.
Standard model . . . . NiB $2467 Ex $2144 Gd $1180
Left-hand model, add $126

MODEL 24 BOLT-ACTION RIFLE
Same general specifications as Model 20 except w/long action in calibers .25-06, .270 Win., .30-06 and 7mm Express only.
Standard model. . . . . NiB $2350 Ex $2123 Gd $1179
Left-hand model, add $126

MODEL 28 BOLT-ACTION RIFLE. . . . . NiB $2709 Ex $2033 Gd $1190
Same as Model 20 except w/long magnum action in calibers .264 Win. Mag., 7mm Rem. Mag., .300 Win. Mag., .338 Win. Mag. only. Offered w/recoil arrester. Left-hand model available.

MODEL 40 BOLT-ACTION RIFLE
Similar to Model 28 except in calibers .300 Wby. and .416 Rigby. Weight: 5.5 lbs. Made 1994-99.
Standard model. . . . . NiB $2770 Ex $2055 Gd $1290
Left-hand, model, add. $126

UNIQUE — Hendaye, France

Manufactured by Manufacture d'Armes des Pyrénées Francaises.

T66 MATCH RIFLE . . . . NiB $469 Ex $388 Gd $289
Single-shot bolt-action rifle. Caliber: .22 LR. 25.5-in. bbl. Weight: 10.5 lbs. Sights: Micrometer aperture rear; globe front. French walnut target stock w/Monte Carlo comb, bull pistol-grip, wide and deep forearm, stippled grip surfaces, adj. swivel on accessory track, adj. rubber buttplate. Made in 1966. Disc.

U.S. MILITARY — Springfield, MA

Manufactured by Springfield Armory, Remington Arms Co., Winchester Repeating Arms Co., Inland Mfg. Div. of G.M.C., and other contractors. Unless otherwise indicated, the following U.S. military rifles were mfg. at Springfield Armory, Springfield, Mass.

MODEL 1898 KRAG-JORGENSEN CARBINE. . . . . NiB $5000 Ex $3500 Gd $1100
Same general specifications as Model 1898 Rifle except w/22-in. bbl., weight: 8 lbs., carbine-type stock. Note: The foregoing specifications apply, in general, to Carbine models 1896 and 1899, which differed from Model 1898 only in minor details.

MODEL 1898 KRAG-JORGENSEN MILITARY RIFLE . . . . NiB $3000 Ex $1010 Gd $610
Bolt action. Caliber: .30-40 Krag. Five round hinged box magazine. 30-in. bbl. Weight: 9 lbs. Sights: Adj. rear; blade front. Military-type stock, straight grip. Note: The foregoing specifications apply, in general, to Rifle models 1892 and 1896, which differed from Model 1898.

MODEL 1903 MARK I SPRINGFIELD . . . . NiB $4950 Ex $3500 Gd $1200
Same as Standard Model 1903 except altered to permit use of the Pedersen Device. This device, officially designated "U.S. Automatic Pistol Model 1918," converted the M/1903 to a Semiauto weapon firing a .30 caliber cartridge similar to .32 automatic pistol ammunition. Mark I rifles have a slot

milled in the left side of the receiver to serve as an ejection port when the Pedersen Device was in use; these rifles were also fitted w/a special sear and cut-off. Some 65,000 of these devices were manufactured and, presumably, a like number of M/1903 rifles were converted to handle them. During the early 1930s, all Pedersen Devices were ordered destroyed and the Mark I rifles were reconverted by replacement of the special sear and cut-off w/standard components. Some 20-odd specimens are known to have escaped destruction and are in government museums and private collections. Probably more are extant. Rarely is a Pedersen Device offered for sale, so a current value cannot be assigned. However, many of the altered rifles were bought by members of the National Rifle Association through the Director of Civilian Marksmanship. Value shown is for the Mark I rifle w/o the Pedersen Device.

MODEL 1903 NATIONAL MATCH
SPRINGFIELD . . . . NiB $5000 Ex $3500 Gd $1500
Same general specifications as Standard Model 1903 except specially selected w/star-gauged bbl., Type C pistol-grip U.S. Model 1903 National Match Springfield (Con't) stock, polished bolt assembly; early types have headless firing pin assembly and reversed safety lock. Produced especially for target shooting.

MODEL 1903 SPRINGFIELD MILITARY RIFLE
Modified Mauser-type bolt action. Caliber: .30-06. Five round box magazine. 23.79-in. bbl. Weight: 8.75 lbs. Sights: Adj. rear; blade front. Military-type stock straight grip. Note: M/1903 rifles of Springfield manufacture w/serial numbers under 800,000 (1903 to 1918) have casehardened receivers; those between 800,000 and 1,278,767 (1918 to 1927) were double heat-treated; rifles numbered over 1,278,767 have nickle steel bolts and receivers. Rock Island production from No. 1 to 285,507 have case-hardened receivers. Improved heat treatment was adopted in May 1918 with No. 285,207; about three months later, with No. 319,921, the use of nickel steel was begun, but the production of some double-heat-treated carbon-steel receivers and bolts continued. Made 1903 to 1930 at Springfield Armory during WWI, M/1903 rifles were also made at Rock Island Arsenal, Rock Island, Ill.
w/case-hardened
  receiver . . . . NiB $7500 Ex $5000 Gd $3000
w/double heat-
  treated receiver . . . . NiB $4950 Ex $3300 Gd $2500
w/nickel steel receiver . . . . NiB $4950 Ex $3300 Gd $2500
Marine Sniper model . . . NiB $20,000 Ex $12,000 Gd $5000

MODEL 1903 SPRINGFIELD
SPORTER. . . . . NiB $6000 Ex $3500 Gd $1500
Same general specifications as National Match except w/sporting design stock, Lyman No. 48 receiver sight.

MODEL 1903 STYLE T SPRINGFIELD
MATCH RIFLE. . . . . NiB $9000 Ex $8500 Gd $7000
Similar to Springfield Sporter except w/heavy bbl. (26-, 28- or 30-in.), scope bases, globe front sight, weight: 12.5 lbs. w/26-in. bbl.

MODEL 1903 TYPE A SPRINGFIELD
FREE RIFLE . . . . NiB $9000 Ex $8000 Gd $7000
Same as Style T except made w/28-in. bbl. only, w/Swiss buttplate, weight: 13.25 lbs.

MODEL 1903 TYPE B SPRINGFIELD
FREE RIFLE . . . . NiB $9000 Ex $8000 Gd $7000
Same as Type A, except w/cheekpiece stock, palm rest, Woodie double-set triggers, Garand fast firing pin, weight: 14.75 lbs.

MODEL 1903-A1 SPRINGFIELD
Same general specifications as Model 1903 except may have Type C pistol-grip stock adopted in 1930. The last Springfields produced at the Springfield Armory were of this type; final serial number was 1,532,878, made in 1939. Note: Late in 1941, Remington Arms Co., Ilion, N.Y., began production, under government contract, of Springfield rifles of this type w/a few minor modifications. These rifles are numbered 3,000,001-3,348,085 and were manufactured before the adoption of Model 1903-A3.
Springfield manufacture . . . NiB $4500 Ex $3500 Gd $1200
Remington manufacture . . . NiB $4500 Ex $3500 Gd $1200

MODEL 1903-A3
SPRINGFIELD . . . . NiB $1260 Ex $710 Gd $410
Same general specifications as Model 1903-A1, except modified to permit increased production and lower cost; may have either straight-grip or pistol-grip stock, bolt is not interchangeable w/earlier types, w/receiver peep sight, many parts are stamped sheet steel, including the trigger guard and magazine assembly. Quality of these rifles, lower than that of other 1903 Springfields, reflects the emergency conditions under which they were produced. Mfd. during WWII by Remington Arms Co. and L. C. Smith Corona Typewriters, Inc.
Smith Corona mfg., add 25%

MODEL 1903-A4
SPRINGFIELD SNIPER . . . . . NiB $5000 Ex $3800 Gd $1800
Same general specifications as Model 1903-A3, except w/ M73B1 or M84 scope in Redfield mount. No front sight.

MODEL 1922-M1 22 SPRINGFIELD
TARGET RIFLE. . . . . NiB $3500 Ex $2000 Gd $1000
Modified Model 1903. Caliber: .22 LR. Five round detachable box magazine. 24.5-in. bbl. Weight: 9 lbs. Sights: Lyman No. 48C receiver, blade front. Sporting-type stock similar to that of Model 1903 Springfield Sporter. Issued 1927. Note: The earlier Model 1922, which is seldom encountered, differs from the foregoing chiefly in the bolt mechanism and magazine.

M2 22 SPRINGFIELD TARGET
RIFLE. . . . . NiB $1800 Ex $1200 Gd $700
Same general specifications as Model 1922-M1 except w/ speedlock, improved bolt assembly adj. for headspace. Note: These improvements were later incorporated in many rifles of the preceding models (M1922, M1922MI) and arms so converted were marked "M1922M2" or "M1922MII."

CALIBER .30, M1 (GARAND) MIL.
RIFLE. . . . . NiB $1260 Ex $1050 Gd $710
Clip-fed, gas-operated, air-cooled Semiauto. Uses a clip containing 8 rounds. 24-in. bbl. Weight: W/o bayonet, 9.5 lbs. Sights: Adj. peep rear; blade front w/guards. Pistol-grip stock, handguards. Made 1937-57. Note: Garand rifles have also been produced by Winchester Repeating Arms Co., Harrington & Richardson Arms Co. and International Harvester Co. Deduct 25% for arsenal-assembled mismatches.
M1-C Sniper . . . . NiB $5000 Ex $3660 Gd $2860
M1-D Sniper . . . . NiB $4500 Ex $2800 Gd $1730

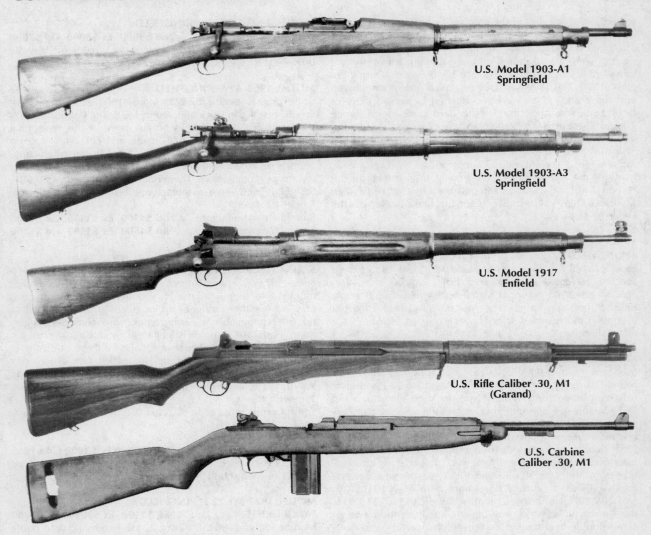

U.S. Model 1903-A1
Springfield

U.S. Model 1903-A3
Springfield

U.S. Model 1917
Enfield

U.S. Rifle Caliber .30, M1
(Garand)

U.S. Carbine
Caliber .30, M1

CALIBER .30, M1, NATIONAL MATCH . . . . **NiB $2800 Ex $1810 Gd $1010**
Accurized target version of the Garand. Glass-bedded stock; match grade bbl., sights, gas cylinder. "NM" stamped on bbl. forward of handguard.

NOTE: *The U.S. Model 1917 Enfield was mfd. 1917 to 1918 by Remington Arms Co. of Delaware (later Midvale Steel & Ordnance Co., Eddystone, PA); Remington Arms Co., Ilion, NY; Winchester Repeating Arms Co., New Haven, CT.*

MODEL 1917 ENFIELD MILITARY RIFLE . . . . **NiB $1895 Ex $1430 Gd $530**
Modified Mauser-type bolt action. Caliber: .30-06. Five round box magazine. 26-in. bbl. Weight: 9.25 lbs. Sights: Adj. rear; blade front w/guards. Military-type stock w/semi-pistol-grip. This design originated in Great Britain as the, "Pattern 14" and was mfd. in caliber .303 for the British Government in three U.S. plants. In 1917, the U.S. Government contracted w/these firms to produce the same rifle in caliber .30-06; over two million of these Model 1917 Enfields were mfd. While no more were produced after WWI, the U.S. supplied over a million of them to Great Britain during WWII. Reworked w/matte blue or parkerized finish, subtract....30%

NOTE: *The WWII-vintage .30-caliber U.S. Carbine was mfd. by Inland Mfg. Div. of G.M.C., Dayton, OH; Winchester Repeating Arms Co., New Haven, CT, and other contractors: International Business Machines Corp., Poughkeepsie, NY; National Postal Meter Co., Rochester, NY; Quality Hardware & Machine Co., and Rock-Ola Co., Chicago, IL; Saginaw Steering Gear Div. of G.M.C., Saginaw, M1; Standard Products Co., Port Clinton, OH; Underwood-Elliott-Fisher Co., Hartford, CT.*

CARBINE, CALIBER .30, M1 . . . **NiB $860 Ex $500 Gd $360**
Gas-operated (short-stroke piston), Semiauto. 15- or 30-rnd. detachable box magazine. 18-in. bbl. Weight: 5.5 lbs. Sights: adj. rear; blade front sight w/guards. Pistol-grip stock w/handguard, side-mounted web sling. Made 1942 to 1945. In 1963, 150,000 surplus M1 Carbines were sold at $20 each to members of the National Rifle Assn. by the Dept. of the Army. Note: For Winchester and Rock-Ola, add 30%; for Irwin Pedersen, add 80%. Quality Hardware did not complete its production run. Guns produced by other manufacturers were marked "Unquality" & command premium prices.
M1 A1 Paratrooper Type 1 (folding wire stock, flip-up sight, no bayonet lug) . . . . **Nib $5510 Ex $3260 Gd $2160**

M1 A1 Paratrooper Type 2 (folding wire stock, adj. rear sight, bayonet lug) . . . . Nib $5510 Ex $2710 Gd $1760
M1 A1 Paratrooper Type 3 (folding wire stock, adj. rear sight, bayonet lug) . . . . Nib $3210 Ex $2160 Gd $1510

U.S. REPEATING ARMS CO.

See Winchester rifle listings.

UNIVERSAL FIREARMS, INC. — Miami, FL

STANDARD M-1 CARBINE . . . NiB $375 Ex $246 Gd $175
Same as U.S. Carbine, Cal. .30, M1 except may have either wood or metal handguard, bbl. band w/ or w/o bayonet lug; 5-rnd. magazine standard. Made 1964-87.
Deluxe (caliber .256, deluxe walnut
  Monte Carlo stock) . . . . NiB $466 Ex $348 Gd $210

UZI — Ramat HaSharon, Israel

Manufactured by Israel Military Industries.

MODEL B CARBINE
Semiauto. Calibers: 9mm Parabellum, .41 Action Express, .45 ACP. 20- to 50-rnd. magazine. 16.1-in. bbl. Weight: 8.4 lbs. Metal folding stock. Front post-type sight, open rear, both adj. Imported by Action Arms 1983 to 1989. NFA (Selective Fire) models imported by UZI America, INC., 1983 to 1994.
Model B Carbine (9mm or .45
  ACP) . . . . NiB $1500 Ex $1149 Gd $963
Model B Carbine (.41 AE) . . . NiB $1500 Ex $1149 Gd $963
Centerfire conversion unit, add $215
Rimfire conversion unit, add. $150

MINI CARBINE . . . . NiB $2375 Ex $2153 Gd $1535
Similar to Uzi Model B except w/ 19.75-in. bbl.and chambered 9mm Parabellum only. 20-rnd. magazine. Weight: 7.2 lbs. Imported in 1989.

VALMET — Jyväskylä, Finland

M-62S SEMIAUTO
RIFLE. . . . . NiB $2590 Ex $2088 Gd $1675
Semiauto version of Finnish M-62 automatic assault rifle based on Russian AK-47. Gas-operated rotating bolt action.

Caliber: 7.62mmX39 Russian. 15- and 30-rnd. magazines. 16.63-in. bbl. Weight: 8 lbs. w/metal stock. Sights: Tangent aperture rear; hooded blade front w/luminous flip-up post for low-light use. Tubular steel or wood stock. Intro. 1962. Disc.

M-71S . . . . NiB $1988 Ex $1766 Gd $1064
Same specifications as M-62S except caliber 5.56mmx45 (.223 Rem.), w/open rear sight, reinforced resin or wood stock, weight: 7.75 lbs. w/former. Made 1971-89.

M-76 SEMIAUTO RIFLE
Semiauto assault rifle. Gas-operated, rotating bolt action. Caliber: 223 Rem. 15- and 30-rnd. magazines. Made 1984-89.
Wood stock. . . . . NiB $1788 Ex $1373 Gd $1055
Folding stock. . . . . NiB $1947 Ex $1522 Gd $1140

M-78 SEMIAUTO
RIFLE. . . . . NiB $1865 Ex $1492 Gd $1170
Caliber: 7.62x51 (NATO). 24.13-in. bbl. Overall length: 43.25 in. Weight: 10.5 lbs.

M-82 SEMIAUTO
CARBINE. . . . . NiB $1748 Ex $1399 Gd $1180
Caliber: .223 Rem. 15- or 30-rnd. magazine. 17-in. bbl. 27 in. overall. Weight: 7.75 lbs.

MODEL 412 S DOUBLE
RIFLE. . . . . NiB $1095 Ex $1077 Gd $933
Boxlock. Manual or automatic extraction. Calibers: .243, .308, .30-06, .375 Win., 9.3x74R. Bbls.: 24-in. over/under. Weight: 8.63 lbs. American walnut checkered stock and forend.

HUNTER . . . . NiB $955 Ex $755 Gd $639
Similar to M-78 except in calibers .223 Rem. (5.56mm), .243 Win., .308 Win. (7.62 NATO) and .30-06. Five, 9- or 15-rnd. magazine. 20.5-in. plain bbl. 42 in. overall. Weight: 8 lbs. Sights: Adj. combination scope mount/rear; blade front, mounted on gas tube. Checkered European walnut buttstock and extended checkered forend and handguard. Imported from 1986 to 1989.

VICKERS LTD. — Crayford, Kent, England

JUBILEE MODEL SINGLE-SHOT-
TARGET RIFLE. . . . . NiB $545 Ex $390 Gd $265
Round-receiver Martini-type action. Caliber: .22 LR. 28-in. heavy bbl. Weight: 9.5 lbs. Sights: Parker-Hale No. 2 front;

Uzi Semiauto Model B Carbine

RIFLES

Valmet M-62S

Valmet Hunter

**Vickers Jubilee
Single-Shot Target Rifle**

Perfection rear peep. One-piece target stock w/full forearm and pistol-grip. Made before WWII.

EMPIRE MODEL . . . . NiB $569 Ex $439 Gd $287
Similar to Jubilee Model except w/27- or 30-in. bbl., straight-grip stock, weight: 9.25 lbs. w/30-in. bbl. Made before WWII.

VOERE — Vohrenvach, Germany

**VEC-91 LIGHTNING BOLT-ACTION
RIFLE**. . . . . NiB $2765 Ex $2165 Gd $1540
Features unique electronic ignition system to activate or fire caseless ammunition. Calibers: 5.56 UCC (.222 Cal.), 6mm UCC caseless. Five round magazine. 20-in. bbl. 39 in. overall. Weight: 6 lbs. Open adj. rear sight. Drilled and tapped for scope mounts. European walnut stock w/cheekpiece. Twin forward locking lugs. Imported from 1992 to date.

VOERE, VOELTER & COMPANY — Vaehrenbach, Germany

Mauser-Werke acquired Voere in 1987 and all models are now marketed under new designations.

**MODEL 1007 BIATHLON
REPEATER** . . . . NiB $466 Ex $350 Gd $254
Caliber: 22 LR. Five round magazine. 19.5-in. bbl. 39 in. overall. Weight: 5.5 lb. Sights: Adj. rear, blade front. Plain beechwood stock. Imported from 1984 to 1986.

**MODEL 1013 BOLT-ACTION
REPEATER** . . . . NiB $766 Ex $544 Gd $389
Same as Model 1007 except w/military-style stock in 22 WMR caliber. Double-set triggers optional. Imported 1984 to 1986 by KDF, Inc.

MODEL 2107 BOLT-ACTION REPEATER
Caliber: 22 LR. Five or 8-rnd. magazine. 19.5-in. bbl. 41 in. overall. Weight: 6 lbs. Sights: Adj. rear sight, hooded front. European hardwood Monte Carlo-style stock. Imported 1986 by KDF, Inc.
Standard model. . . . . NiB $439 Ex $278 Gd $255
Deluxe model . . . . NiB $469 Ex $347 Gd $266

WALTHER — Ulm and Arnsberg, Germany
Manufactured by the German firms of Waffenfabrik Walther and Carl Walther Sportwaffenfabrik.

NOTE: *The following Walther rifles were mfd. before WWII by Waffenfabrik Walther, Zella-Mehlis (Thür.), Germany.*

**MODEL 1 AUTOLOADING RIFLE
(LIGHT)**. . . . . NiB $976 Ex $723 Gd $500
Similar to Standard Model 2 but w/20-in. bbl., lighter stock, weight: 4.5 lbs.

**MODEL 2 AUTOLOADING
RIFLE**. . . . . NiB $1045 Ex $690 Gd $533
Bolt-action, may be used as autoloader, manually operated repeater or single-shot. Caliber: .22 LR. Five or 9-rnd. detachable box magazine. 24.5-in. bbl. Weight: 7 lbs. Sights: Tangent-curve rear; ramp front. Sporting stock w/checkered pistol grip, grooved forearm, swivels. Disc.

**OLYMPIC BOLT-ACTION
MATCH RIFLE**. . . . . NiB $1354 Ex $1095 Gd $800
Single-shot. Caliber: .22 LR. 26-in. heavy bbl. Weight: 13 lbs. Sights: Micrometer extension rear; interchangeable front. Target stock w/checkered pistol-grip, thumbhole, full beavertail forearm covered w/corrugated rubber, palm rest, adj. Swiss-type buttplate, swivels. Disc.

Walther Model 1

Walther Model 2

**MODEL V BOLT-ACTION
SINGLE-SHOT RIFLE** . . . . **NiB $645 Ex $544 Gd $368**
Caliber: .22 LR. 26-in. bbl. Weight: 7 lbs. Sights: Open rear;
ramp front. Plain pistol-grip stock w/grooved forearm. Disc.

**MODEL V MEISTERBÜCHSE
(CHAMPION)** . . . . **NiB $675 Ex $494 Gd $338**
Same as standard Model V except w/micrometer open rear
sight and checkered pistol-grip. Disc.

— POST WWII PRODUCTION —

NOTE: *The Walther rifles listed below have been manufactured
since WWII by Carl Walther Sportwaffenfabrik, Ulm (Donau),
Germany.*

MODEL GX-1 FREE RIFLE . . . **NiB $1985 Ex $1544 Gd $933**
Bolt-action, single-shot. Caliber: .22 LR. 25.5-in. heavy bbl.
Weight: 15.9 lbs. Sights: Micrometer aperture rear; globe
front. Thumbhole stock w/adj. cheekpiece and buttplate w/
removable hook, accessory rail. Left-hand stock available.
Accessories furnished include hand stop and sling swivel,
palm rest, counterweight assembly.

MODEL KKJ SPORTER . . . . . **NiB $1355 Ex $1108 Gd $650**
Bolt action. Caliber: .22 LR. Five round box magazine. 22.5-
in. bbl. Weight: 5.5 lbs. Sights: Open rear; hooded ramp front.
Stock w/cheekpiece, checkered pistol-grip and forearm, sling
swivels. Disc.

MODEL KKJ-HO . . . . **NiB $1543 Ex $1337 Gd $1110**
Same as Model KKJ except chambered for .22 Hornet. Disc.

MODEL KKJ-MA . . . . **NiB $1321 Ex $1231 Gd $650**
Same as Model KKJ except chambered for .22 WMR. Disc.

**MODEL KKM INTERNATIONAL
MATCH RIFLE** . . . . **NiB $944 Ex $669 Gd $609**
Bolt-action, single-shot. Caliber: .22 LR. 28-in. heavy bbl.
Weight: 15.5 lbs. Sights: Micrometer aperture rear; globe front.
Thumbhole stock w/high comb, adj. hook buttplate, accessory
rail. Left-hand stock available. Disc.

MODEL KKM-S . . . . **NiB $1000 Ex $877 Gd $641**
Same specifications as Model KKM, except w/adj. cheekpiece.
Disc.

**MOVING TARGET MATCH
RIFLE** . . . . **NiB $1067 Ex $833 Gd $554**
Bolt-action, single-shot. Caliber: .22 LR. 23.6-in. bbl. w/
weight. Weight: 8.6 lbs. Supplied w/o sights. Thumbhole
stock w/adj. cheekpiece and buttplate. Left-hand stock
available.

PRONE 400 TARGET RIFLE . . . . **NiB $833 Ex $715 Gd $500**
Bolt-action, single-shot. Caliber: .22 LR. 25.5-in. heavy bbl.
Weight: 10.25 lbs. Supplied w/o sights. Prone stock w/adj.
cheekpiece and buttplate, accessory rail. Left-hand stock available. Disc.

MODEL SSV VARMINT RIFLE . . **NiB $770 Ex $697 Gd $488**
Bolt-action, single-shot. Calibers: .22 LR, .22 Hornet. 25.5-in.
bbl. Weight: 6.75 lbs. Supplied w/o sights. Monte Carlo stock
w/high cheekpiece, full pistol grip and forearm. Disc.

**MODEL U.I.T. SPECIAL MATCH
RIFLE** . . . . **NiB $1187 Ex $1070 Gd $833**
Bolt-action, single-shot. Caliber: .22 LR. 25.5-in. bbl. Weight:
10.2 lbs. Sights: Micrometer aperture rear; globe front. Target
stock w/high comb, adj. buttplate, accessory rail. Left-hand
stock avail. Disc. 1993.

**MODEL U.I.T. SUPER MATCH
RIFLE** . . . . **NiB $1169 Ex $1966 Gd $788**
Bolt-action, single-shot. Caliber: .22 LR. 25.5-in. heavy bbl.
Weight: 10.2 lbs. Micrometer aperture rear; globe front. Target
stock w/support for off-hand shooting, high comb, adj. butt-
plate and swivel. Left-hand stock available. Disc. 1993.

WEATHERBY, INC. — Sheridan, WY
Formerly Atascadero, CA, and South Gate, CA.

NOTE: *The Mark V action went into mass production in
1958 South Gate, CA. From 1959 to 1973 the Mark V was
manufactured by J.P. Sauer in Germany; from 1973 to 1995
manufacturing was done by Howa in Japan. Since 1995, Mark
V manufacturing has been in the U.S. Mark V rifles manufactured in Germany are valued at 20%-30% more. Mark V rifles
w/ 26-in. bbl. add $25. Mark V rifles have been produced in
a variety of standard and magnum calibers. Typically proprietary Weatherby calibers have a higher value; .30-378 Wby.,
.378 Wby., .416 Wby., and .460 Wby. are valued at 25%-38%
more. All Vanguard series rifles are manufactured by Howa
in Japan.*

CROWN CUSTOM RIFLE . . **NiB $8260 Ex $6298 Gd $4470**
Calibers: .240, .30-06, .257, .270, 7mm, .300, and .340.
Bbl.: Made to order. Super fancy walnut stock. Also available
w/engraved barreled action including gold animal overlay.
Custom Shop rifle. Disc. 2010.

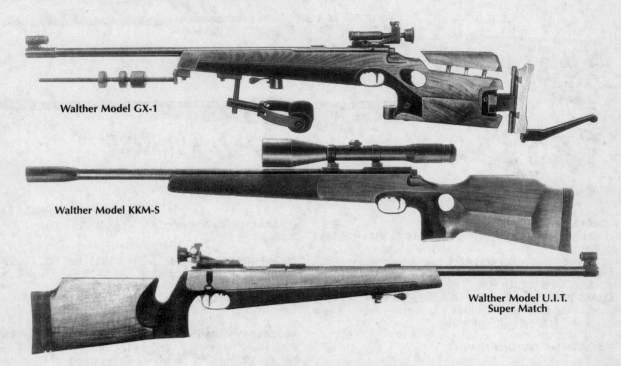

Walther Model GX-1

Walther Model KKM-S

Walther Model U.I.T.
Super Match

DELUXE .378 MAGNUM
RIFLE. . . . . .NiB $2233 Ex $2148 Gd $1490
Bolt-action. South Gate production. Same general specifications as Deluxe Magnum in other calibers except caliber .378 W. M. Schultz & Larsen action; 26-in. bbl. Disc. 1958.

DELUXE . . . . NiB $2000 Ex $1500 Gd $1000
Bolt-action. South Gate production. Calibers: .220 Rocket, .257 Weatherby Mag., .270 Wby. Mag, 7mm Wby. Mag., .300 Wby. Mag., .375 Wby. Mag. Specially processed FN Mauser action. 24-in. bbl. (26-in. in .375 cal.). Monte Carlo-style stock w/cheekpiece, black forend tip, grip cap, checkered pistol-grip and forearm, quick-detachable sling swivels. Value shown is for rifle w/o sights. Disc. 1958.

DELUXE RIFLE . . . . NiB $1844 Ex $1623 Gd $1189
Same general specifications as Deluxe Magnum except chambered for standard calibers such as .270, .30-06, etc. Disc. 1958.

MARK V ARROYO. . . . . NiB $2370 Ex $1700 Gd $1200
Similar to Mark V Deluxe except w/laminated Monte Carlo composite stock. Calibers: various standards and Wby. Mag. BBl.: 24-, 26- or 28-in. w/Accubrake and fluted. LXX trigger, Finish: Kuiu Cias camo Cerakote. Weight: 8.75 lbs. Made 2014 to present.
RC (range certified, sub-MOA guarantee), add. $400
.338 Lapua Mag., .30-378 Wby. Mag.
  or .338-378 Wby. Mag., add $200

MARK V DANGEROUS
GAME RIFLE . . . . NiB $3055 Ex $2125 Gd $1555
Similar to Mark V Deluxe except w/adj. sights, fiberglass Monte Carlo stock. Calibers: various standard mag. and Wby. Mag. BBl.: 24- or 26-in. w/Accubrake. LXX trigger. Finish: black oxide. Weight: 8.75-9.5 lbs. Made 2001 to present.
RC (range certified, sub-MOA guarantee), add. $400
.378 Wby. Mag. or .416 Wby. Mag., add $200
.460 Wby. Mag., add. $400

MARK V EUROMARK . . . . NiB $1820 Ex $1270 Gd $970
Similar to Mark V Deluxe except w/oil finished Monte Carlo wood or American Claro stock. Calibers: various standard mag. and Wby. Mag. Bbl.: 24-, 26- or 28-in. Finish: satin blue. Made 1986-92, reintro. 1995-02, reintro. 2010-15.
**.378 Wby. Mag. or
  .416 Wby. Mag., add $300
.460 Wby. Mag. (muzzle brake,
  disc. 2002) . . . . NiB $2155 Ex $1620 Gd $600**

MARK V FIBERMARK . . . . . . NiB $2633 Ex $1845 Gd $1579
Similar to Mark V Deluxe except w/fiberglass stock and in .30-06, .240 Wby. Mag., .257 Wby. Mag., .270 Wby. Mag., 7mm Wby. Mag., .300 Wby. Mag. or .340 Wby. Mag. 24- or 26-in. bbl. Right or left hand actions. Made 1983-92.
**Fibermark (2001-15), add. $10
Stainless (2001-04), deduct. $200**

MARK V LAZERMARK. . . . . . NiB $2385 Ex $1810 Gd $1330
Similar to Mark V Deluxe except w/laser carved oak leaf pattern in wood stock and in .257 Wby. Mag., .270 Wby. Mag., 7mm Wby. Mag., .300 Wby. Mag. or .340 Wby. Mag. 24- or 26-in. bbl. Bright blued. Weight: 8.5 lbs. Made 1985-2016.
**Varmintmaster (.22-250 or .224 Varminmaster,
  disc. 1991) . . . . NiB $1090 Ex $820 Gd $600
.378 Wby. Mag. or .416
  Wby. Mag. (muzzle brake,
  disc. 2002) . . . . NiB $1855 Ex $1400 Gd $1025
.460 Wby. Mag. (muzzle brake,
  disc. 2002) . . . . NiB $2155 Ex $1620 Gd $600**

MARK V OUTFITTER . . . . . . NiB $2300 Ex $1670 Gd $1190
Similar to Mark V Accumark except w/laminated Monte Carlo carbon fiber stock. Calibers: various standards and Wby. Mag. BBl.: 22-, 24-, 26- or 28-in. fluted. LXX trigger, Finish: desert camo Cerakote. Weight: 5.5-6.75 lbs. Made 2015 to present.
RC (range certified, sub-MOA guarantee), add. $400
6.5-300 Wby. Mag. or .300 Wby. Mag., add. $200

MARK V SAFARI
GRADE CUSTOM . . . . **NiB $6110 Ex $4350 Gd $3010**
Similar to Mark V Deluxe except w/adj. express sights, satin finish French walnut Monte Carlo stock. Calibers: various standard mag. and Wby. Mag. BBl.: 26- or 28-in. w/Accubrake. LXX trigger. Weight: 8.75-9.5 lbs. Made 2001 to present.
RC (range certified, sub-MOA guarantee), add **$400**
.378 Wby. Mag. or .416 Wby. Mag., add **$200**
.460 Wby. Mag., add **$400**

MARK V SPECIAL VARMINT RIFLE . . **NiB $920 Ex $690 Gd $510**
Similar to Mark V Deluxe except w/Monte Carlo composite stock. Calibers: .22-250 or .223 Rem. Bbl.: 22-in. bbl. Weight: 7.5 lbs. Made 2003-05.
Special Varmint Rifle
   (2007-08) . . . . **NiB $1020 Ex $770 Gd $560**

MARK V SPORTER . . . . **NiB $1450 Ex $770 Gd $720**
Similar to Mark V Deluxe except w/high gloss or satin wood stock. Calibers: various standard mag. and Wby. Mag. BBl.: 24- or 26-in. Finish: matte blue. Weight: 8 lbs. Made 1993 to present.

MARK V SUPER
PREDATORMASTER . . . . **NiB $1370 Ex $1030 Gd $750**
Similar to Mark V Accumark except w/26-in. fluted bbl. Calibers: .220 Swift, .22-250, .223 Rem., .243 Win., 7mm-08, or .308 Win. Weight: 6.5 lbs. Made 2001-04.

MARK V SUPER
VARMINTMASTER . . . . **NiB $1600 Ex $1200 Gd $880**
Similar to Mark V Accumark except w/24-in. fluted bbl. Calibers: .22-250, .223 Rem., .243 Win., 7mm-08, or .308 Win. Weight: 8.5 lbs. Made 2000-09.

MARK V SYNTHETIC . . . . . . **NiB $3055 Ex $2125 Gd $1555**
Similar to Mark V Deluxe except w/aluminum chassis stock. Calibers: various standard mag. and Wby. Mag. Bbl.: 24- or 26- or 28-in. Finish: matte black. Weight: 8 lbs. Made 1997-2012.
fluted bbl., deduct **$290**

MARK V TACMARK . . . . **NiB $1070 Ex $770 Gd $600**
Similar to Mark V Deluxe except w/black synthetic stock. Calibers: .338 Lapua Mag., .30-378 Wby. Mag. or .338-378 Wby. Mag. BBl.: 28-in. Finish: matte black. Weight: 11.25 lbs. Made 2016 to present.
Elite (LXX trigger, camo finish,
   sub-MOA guarantee), add **$1500**

MARK V TERRAMARK . . . . . . **NiB $2385 Ex $1810 Gd $1330**
Similar to Mark V Deluxe except w/laminated Monte Carlo stock. Calibers: various standards and Wby. Mag. BBl.: 26-in.

w/muzzle brake. LXX trigger, Finish: FDE Cerakote. Weight: 8.75 lbs. Made 2014 to present.
RC (range certified, sub-MOA guarantee), add **$400**
.338 Lapua Mag., .30-378 Wby. Mag.
   or .338-378 Wby. Mag., add **$200**

MARK V THREAT RESPONSE
RIFLE . . . . **NiB $2385 Ex $1810 Gd $1330**
Similar to Mark V Deluxe exc

MARK V ACCUMARK SERIES
Bolt-action. Japan, and U.S. production. Weatherby Mark V magnum action. Calibers: .257 Wby., .270 Wby., 7mm Rem. Mag., 7mm Wby., 7mm STW, .300 Win. Mag., .300 Wby. Mag., .30-338 Wby., .30-378 Wby. and .340 Wby. 26- or 28-in. stainless bbl. w/black oxide flutes. 46.5 or 48.5 in. overall. Weight: 8 to 8.5 lbs. No sights, drilled and tapped for scope. Stainless finish w/blued receiver. H-S Precision black synthetic stock w/aluminum bedding plate, recoil pad and sling swivels. Imported from 1996 to date.
.30-338 & .30-378 Wby. Mag, add **$300**
All other calibers . . . . **NiB $1900 Ex $1300 Gd $930**
Left-hand model, add **$100**
RC model (range certified, magnum
   calibers) . . . . **NiB $2110 Ex $1655 Gd $1010**
RC model (range certified, standard
   calibers) . . . . **NiB $1955 Ex $1555 Gd $975**

MARK V CLASSICMARK I
Same general specifications as Mark V Deluxe except w/ checkered select American Claro walnut stock w/oil finish and presentation recoil pad. Satin metal finish. Imported from 1992 to 1993.
standard calibers . . . . **NiB $1100 Ex $884 Gd $572**
.300 Wby. or .340 Wby., add **$20**
Caliber .378 Wby., add **$50**
Caliber .416 Wby., add **$75**
Caliber .460 Wby., add **$100**

MARK V CLASSICMARK LL RIFLE
Same general specifications as Classicmark I except w/checkered select American walnut stock w/oil finish steel grip cap and Old English recoil pad. Satin metal finish. Right-hand only. Imported from 1992 to 1993.
standard calibers . . . . **NiB $1530 Ex $1043 Gd $844**
.378 Wby., add **$25**
.416 Wby., add **$200**
.460 Wby., add **$400**
Safari Classic (adj. sights, disc. 1992), add **$775**

MARK V DELUXE RIFLE . . . **NiB $2633 Ex $1845 Gd $1579**
Similar to Mark V Sporter except w/Lightweight Mark V action designed for standard calibers w/sixlocking lugs rather than

Weatherby Mark V Classicmark I

Weatherby Fiberguard

Weatherby Crown Custom

Weatherby Fibermark

Weatherby Mark V Safari Grade

Weatherby Mark XXII Deluxe

Weatherby Vanguard I VGL

Westley Richards & Co. Best Quality Double Rifle

nine, 4- or 5-rnd. magazine. 24-in. bbl. 44 in. overall. Weight: 6.75 lbs. Checkered Monte Carlo American walnut stock w/ rosewood forend and pistol grip and diamond inlay. Imported from 1957 to date.

MARK V DELUXE
Bolt action. Mark V action, right or left hand. Calibers: .22-250, .30-06- .224 Weatherby Varmintmaster; .240, .257, .270, 7mm, .300, .340, .375, .378, .416, .460 Weatherby Magnums. Box magazine holds 2 to 5 cartridges depending on caliber. 24- or 26-in. bbl. Weight: 6.5 to 10.5 lbs. Monte Carlo-style stock w/cheekpiece, skip checkering, forend tip, pistol-grip cap, recoil pad, QD swivels. Values shown are for rifles w/o sights. Made in Germany 1958 to 1969; in Japan 1970 to 1994, 1995 to present U.S. Values shown for Japanese and U.S. production.
Standard and Wby. calibers . NiB $2000 Ex $1408 Gd $956
.30-378 Wby. Mag. or .378 Wby. Mag., add $500
.416 Wby. Mag., add. $520
.460 Wby. Mag., add. $775

MARK XXII DELUXE .22 AUTOMATIC
SPORTER, CLIP-FED MODEL . . NiB $846 Ex $547 Gd $397
Semiauto w/single-shot selector. Caliber: .22 LR. Five and 10-rnd. clip magazines. 24-in. bbl. Weight: 6 lbs. Sights: Folding leaf open rear; ramp front. Monte Carlo-type stock w/ cheekpiece, pistol-grip, forend tip, grip cap, skip checkering, QD swivels. Intro. 1964. Made in Italy from 1964 to 1969; in Japan, from 1970 to 191981; in the U.S., from 1982 to 1990.

MARK XXII, TUBULAR MAGAZINE
MODEL. . . . . NiB $844 Ex $546 Gd $397
Same as Mark XXII, clip-fed model except w/15-rnd. tubular magazine. Made in Japan from 1973-81; in the U.S., from 1982-90.

VANGUARD I SERIES
Bolt action. Calibers: .243 Win., .25-06, .270 Win., 7mm Rem. Mag., .30-06, .300 Win. Mag. Five round magazine; (3-rnd. in Magnum calibers). 24-in. bbl. Weight: 7 lbs. 14 oz. No sights. Monte Carlo-type stock w/cheekpiece, rosewood forend tip and pistol-grip cap, checkering, rubber buttpad, QD swivels. Imported from 1970 to 1984.
Alaskan (nickel plating, 1993-94). . . NiB $630 Ex $475 Gd $350
Back Country Custom (stainless, fluted bbl.,
   composite stock, 2008-09) . . . NiB $900 Ex $680 Gd $500
Carbine (20-in. bbl., composite stock,
   2009-11) . . . . NiB $450 Ex $340 Gd $250
Classic I (checkered classic style stock,
   1989-94) . . . . NiB $555 Ex $439 Gd $231

Classic II (custom checkered classic style stock,
   1989-92) . . . . NiB $675 Ex $500 Gd $375
Compact (20-in. bbl., youth style stock,
   2005-09) . . . . NiB $570 Ex $435 Gd $320
Deluxe (gloss Monye Carlo stock w/rosewood tip,
   2006-09) . . . . NiB $840 Ex $630 Gd $465
Fiberguard (green fiberglass stock, blued,
   disc. 1988) . . . . NiB $500 Ex $370 Gd $270
Predator (injection molded stock, adj. trigger,
   2009-11) . . . . NiB $740 Ex $555 Gd $405
Sage Country Custom (composite stock,
   2008-09) . . . . NiB $570 Ex $435 Gd $320
Sporter (checkered walnut stock, matte blue,
   2005-11) . . . . NiB $600 Ex $440 Gd $320
Sub-MOA (Monte Carlo synthetic stock, satin stainless,
   2005-11) . . . . NiB $865 Ex $655 Gd $480
Sub-MOA Varmint (laminate stock,
   2006-11) . . . . NiB $920 Ex $700 Gd $500
Synthetic (synthetic stock, matte blue or satin stainless,
   1997-11) . . . . NiB $450 Ex $340 Gd $250
Thumbhole Laminate (laminate thumbhole stock,
   2006-08) . . . . NiB $600 Ex $440 Gd $320
Varmint Special (laminate Monte Carlo stock,
   2009-10) . . . . NiB $720 Ex $540 Gd $400
Youth (youth size synthetic stock,
   2010-11) . . . . NiB $450 Ex $340 Gd $250
VGL model (w/20-in. bbl., plain checkered stock,
   matte finish) . . . . NiB $650 Ex $533 Gd $400
VGS model (w/24-in. bbl.) . . . . . NiB $440 Ex $388 Gd $338
VGX model (w/higher
   grade finish) . . . . .NiB $655 Ex $493 Gd $339
VGX Deluxe model (custom checkered classic-style
   stock, 1989-94) . . . . NiB $720 Ex $587 Gd $340
Weatherguard (synthetic stock,
   1989-93) . . . . NiB $445 Ex $335 Gd $245

VANGUARD II SERIES
Same general specifications as Vanguard I series except 3-position safety, two-stage trigger, synthetic stock, and Sub-MOA guarantee. Made 2016 to present.
Accuguard (laminated Monte Carlo stock w/spider web
   finish, stainless fluted bbl.) . . . NiB $950 Ex $705 Gd $480
Back Country (blued, fluted bbl., synthetic Monte
   Carlo stock). . . . . NiB $1230 Ex $905 Gd $705
Camilla (20-in. bbl., wood stock). . . NiB $730 Ex $580 Gd $430
Carbine (20-in. bbl., composite
   stock). . . . . NiB $525 Ex $375 Gd $300
Deluxe (gloss Monte Carlo stock
   w/rosewood tip) . . . . NiB $995 Ex $730 Gd $505

Dangerous Game Rifle (laminate Monte Carlo stock, adj. sights) . . . . NiB $1100 Ex $800 Gd $500

H-Bar RC (laminate Monte Carlo stock w/beaver tail forend, Range Certified) . . . . NiB $1100 Ex $800 Gd $500

Lazerguard (gloss Monte Carlo wood stock, blued) . . . . NiB $1050 Ex $755 Gd $505

Modular Chassis (aluminum chassis stock, 10-rnd. detachable magazine) . . . . . . NiB $1330 Ex $920 Gd $700

RC (composite Monte Carlo stock, Range Certified) . . . . NiB $990 Ex $720 Gd $500

Select (black Monte Carlo stock, matte blue) . . . . NiB $490 Ex $380 Gd $270

Sporter (checkered walnut stock, matte blue) . . . . NiB $720 Ex $570 Gd $420

Synthetic (synthetic stock, matte blue or matte stainless) . . . . NiB $525 Ex $375 Gd $300

Synthetic Compact (synthetic youth stock, matte blue) . . . . NiB $490 Ex $380 Gd $270

TRR RC (laminate Monte Carlo stock w/beaver tail forend, Range Certified) . . . . NiB $1020 Ex $750 Gd $520

Varmint RC (composite Monte Carlo stock w/beaver tail forend, Range Certified) . . . . NiB $1020 Ex $750 Gd $520

Varmint Special (laminate Monte Carlo stock) . . . . NiB $720 Ex $540 Gd $400

Weatherguard DBM (detachable magazine, synthetic stock, gray Cerakote) . . . . NiB $650 Ex $533 Gd $400

Weatherguard Carbine (20-in. bbl., synthetic stock, gray Cerakote) . . . . NiB $650 Ex $533 Gd $400

Weatherguard H-Bar (22-in. heavy bbl., synthetic stock, gray Cerakote) . . . . NiB $670 Ex $500 Gd $330

Wilderness DBM (detachable magazine, composite stock) . . . . NiB $870 Ex $670 Gd $520

WBY-X SERIES . . . . NiB $645 Ex $495 Gd $330
Similar to Vanguard II series except w/20-, 22- or 24-in. bbl. Calibers: various standard calibers. Finish: matte blue. Stock: composite Monte Carlo. Weight: 6.5-8.5 lbs. Finish: various camo. Made 2014-16.

WEIHRAUCH — Melrichstadt, Germany
Imported by European American Armory, Sharpes, FL.

MODEL HW 60 TARGET RIFLE NiB $677 Ex $559 Gd $445
Single-shot. Caliber: .22 LR. 26.75-in. bbl. Walnut stock. Adj. buttplate and trigger. Hooded ramp front sight. Push button safety. Imported 1995 to 1997.

MODEL HW 66 BOLT-ACTION RIFLE. . . . . NiB $645 Ex $482 Gd $338
Caliber: .22 Hornet. 22.75-in. bbl. 41.75 in. overall. Weight: 6.5 lbs. Walnut stock w/cheekpiece. Hooded blade ramp front sight. Checkered pistol grip and forend. Imported from1989 to 1990.

MODEL HW 660 MATCH BOLT-ACTION RIFLE. . . . . NiB $942 Ex $745 Gd $500
Caliber: .22 LR. 26-in. bbl. 45.33 in. overall. Weight: 10.75 lbs. Walnut or laminated stock w/adj. cheekpiece and buttplate. Checkered pistol grip and forend. Adj. trigger. Imported 1991 to 2005.

WESTERN FIELD RIFLES
See listings under "W" for Montgomery Ward.

WESTLEY RICHARDS & CO., LTD. — London, England

BEST QUALITY DOUBLE RIFLE. . . NiB $35,000 Ex $28,900 Gd $19,670
Boxlock, hammerless, ejector. Hand-detachable locks. Calibers: .30-06, .318 Accelerated Express, .375 Mag., .425 Mag. Express, .465 Nitro Express, .470 Nitro Express. 25-in. bbls. Weight: 8.5 to 11 lbs. Sights: leaf rear; hooded front. French walnut stock w/cheekpiece, checkered pistol grip and forend.

BEST QUALITY MAGAZINE RIFLE
Mauser or Magnum Mauser action. Calibers: 7mm High Velocity, .30-06, .318 Accelerated Express, .375 Mag., .404 Nitro Express, .425 Mag. Bbl. lengths: 24-in.; 7mm, 22-in.; .425 caliber, 25-in. Weight 7.25 to 9.25 lbs. Sights: Leaf rear; hooded front.
Standard action . . . . NiB $11,970 Ex $7295 Gd $5790
Magnum action . . . . NiB $13,888 Ex $11,679 Gd $8957

WICHITA ARMS — Wichita, KS

MODEL WCR CLASSIC BOLT-ACTION RIFLE
Single-shot. Calibers: .17 Rem through .308 Win. 21-in. octagon bbl. Hand-checkered walnut stock. Drilled and tapped for scope w/no sights. Right or left-hand action w/Canjar trigger. Non-glare blued finish. Made 1978 to date.
Right-hand model . . . . NiB $2578 Ex $2044 Gd $1760
Left-hand model . . . . NiB $3544 Ex $2967 Gd $2178

MODEL WMR STAINLESS MAGNUM BOLT-ACTION RIFLE . . . . . NiB $2275 Ex $1938 Gd $1179
Single-shot or w/blind magazine action chambered .270 Win. through .458 Win. Mag. Drilled and tapped for scope with no sights. Fully adj. trigger. 22- or 24-in. bbl. Hand-checkered select walnut stock. Made 1980-84.

MODEL WSR SILHOUETTE BOLT-ACTION RIFLE
Single-shot, bolt action, chambered in most standard calibers. Right or left-hand action w/fluted bolt. Drilled and tapped for scope mount with no sights. 24-in. bbl. Canjar trigger. Metallic gray Fiberthane stock w/vented rubber recoil pad. Made 1983-95.
Right-hand model . . . . NiB $2588 Ex $2066 Gd $1449
Left-hand model . . . . NiB $2744 Ex $2190 Gd $1633

MODEL WVR VARMINT RIFLE
Calibers: .17 Rem through .308 Win. Three round magazine. Right or left-hand action w/jeweled bolt. 21-in. bbl. w/o sights. Drilled and tapped for scope. Hand-checkered American walnut pistol-grip stock. Made 1978-97.
Right-hand model . . . . NiB $2577 Ex $2038 Gd $1289
Left-hand model . . . . NiB $2798 Ex $2260 Gd $1678

WICKLIFFE RIFLES — Wickliffe, OH
Manufactured by Triple S Development Co., Inc.

'76 COMMEMORATIVE MODEL. . . . . NiB $1169 Ex $1044 Gd $939
Limited edition of 100. Same as Deluxe Model except w/filled etching on receiver sidewalls, U.S. silver dollar inlaid in stock, 26-in. bbl. only, comes in presentation case. Made in 1976 only.

RIFLES

Wickliffe Rifles Model 76

Winchester Model 1873
Lever-Action Rifle

'76 DELUXE MODEL. . . . . NiB $522 Ex $415 Gd $331
Same as Standard Model except w/22-in. bbl. in .30-06 only;
high-luster blued finish, fancy-grade figured American walnut
stock w/nickel silver grip cap.

**'76 STANDARD MODEL SINGLE-SHOT
RIFLE.** . . . . NiB $443 Ex $300 Gd $217
Falling-block action. Calibers: .22 Hornet, .223 Rem., .22-250,
.243 Win., .25-06, .308 Win., .30-06, .45-70. 22-in. light-
weight bbl. (.243 and .308 only) or 26-in. heavy sporter bbl.
Weight: 6.75 or 8.5 lbs., depending on bbl. No sights. Select
American walnut Monte Carlo stock w/right or left cheekpiece
and pistol-grip, semi-beavertail forearm. Intro. 1976. Disc.

STINGER MODEL . . . . NiB $433 Ex $300 Gd $217
Falling block, single-shot. Calibers: .22 Hornet and .223 Rem.
.22-in. bbl. w/no sights. American walnut Monte Carlo stock w/
continental-type forend. Made 1979-80.

TRADITIONALIST MODEL . . . . NiB $441 Ex $339 Gd $200
Falling block single-shot. Calibers: .30-06, .45-70. 24-in. bbl.
w/open sights. Hand-checkered. American walnut classic-style
buttstock and forearm. Made 1979-80.

WILKINSON ARMS CO. — Covina, CA

TERRY CARBINE . . . . NiB $551 Ex $408 Gd $354
Caliber: 9mm Para. Semiauto. Thirty round magazine. 16-in.
bbl. 30 in. overall. Weight: 6 lbs. Dovetailed receiver for scope
mounting. Bolt-type safety. Ejection port w/automatic trap door.
Blowback action. Fires from closed bolt. Made 1975. Disc.

TED WILLIAMS RIFLES

See Sears, Roebuck and Company.

WINCHESTER — Morgan, UT

*Formerly New Haven, Connecticut. In 1987 Fabrique
Nationale d'Armes de Guerre (FN) acquired U.S.
Repeating Arms Company, including the license to manufacture Winchester-brand firearms. Winchester has gone
through numerous restructuring and slight name changes
since 1866 when it first started production. Formerly
known as Winchester Repeating Arms Co., and then mfd.*

Close-up barrel engraving on Winchester
Model 1873 One of One Thousand.

*by Winchester-Western Div., Olin Corp., later by U.S.
Repeating Arms Company. In 1999, production rights
were acquired by Browning Arms Company. FN acquired
Browning in 1977.*

MODEL 1866 RIFLES & CARBINES (RECENT MFG.)
Similar to Standard Model 1866 "Yellow Boy" rifle w/brass
receiver. Caliber: .38 Spl. or .44-40. Barrel: 20-in. octagon bbl.
Sights: folding ladder rear sight. Stock: walnut, straight grip.
Finish: Blued. Mfg. 2017–19.
Short Rifle . . . . NiB $1155 Ex $1000 Gd $630
Deluxe Octagon
  (24-in. octagon bbl.) . . NiB $1755 Ex $1600 Gd $830

EARLY MODELS 1873 (MFG. 1873 – 1918)
NOTE: *Most Winchester rifles manufactured prior to 1918 used
the date of approximate manufacture as the model number.
For example, the Model 1894 repeating rifle was manufactured
from 1894 to 1937. When Winchester started using two-digit
model numbers after 1918, the "18" was dropped and the
rifle was then called the Model 94. The Model 1892 was
called the Model 92, etc. Serial numbers for the Model 1973s
manufactured from 1873-1918 include 1 to 700734. There are
numerous reproductions of the following models: Model 1873,
Model 1885, Model 1886, Model 1892, Model 1895, Model
53 and Model 71*

**MODEL 1873 LEVER-ACTION
CARBINE.** . . . . NiB $4820 Ex $3933 Gd $2577
Same as Standard Model 1873 Rifle except w/20-in. bbl.,
12-rnd. magazine, weight: 7.25 lbs.

MODEL 1873 LEVER-ACTION

RIFLE. . . . . .NiB $5088 Ex $3482 Gd $2100
Calibers: .32-20, .38-40, .44-40; a few were chambered for .22 rimfire. Fifteen round magazine, also made w/6-rnd. half magazine. 24-in. bbl. (round, half-octagon, octagon). Weight: 8.5 lbs. Sights: Open rear; bead or blade front. Plain straight-grip stock and forearm. Made 1873-1924. 720,610 rifles of this model were mfd.

MODEL 1873 — ONE OF

ONE THOUSAND NiB $196,000+ Ex $150,000 Gd $90,000
During the late 1870s, Winchester offered Model 1873 rifles of superior accuracy and extra finish, designated "One of One Thousand" grade, at $100. These rifles are marked "1 of 1000" or "One of One Thousand." Only 136 of this model are known to have been manufactured. This is one of the rarest of rifles and, because so few have been sold in recent years, it is extremely difficult to assign a value, however, an "excellent" specimen would probably bring a price upward of $200,000.

MODEL 1873 SPECIAL SPORTING

RIFLE. . . . . NiB $11,375 Ex $10,450 Gd $7,707
Same as Standard Model 1873 Rifle except this type has receiver casehardened in colors, pistol-grip stock of select walnut, octagon bbl. only.

MODEL 1873 RIFLES & CARBINES (RECENT MFG.)

Similar to Standard Model 1873 Rifle except .357 Mag/.38 Spl., .44-40 or .45 LC. 20-in. round bbl. Straight grip. Blued. Reintroduced 2013 to present.
Short Rifle. . . . . .NiB $1300 Ex $1150 Gd $995
Short Rifle Case Hardened .NiB $1580 Ex $1179 Gd $1100
Sporter Octagon (straight grip; 24-in. bbl.; case hardened
  finish) . . . . .NiB $1740 Ex $1279 Gd $1200
Sporter Octagon (pistol grip; 24-in. bbl.; case hardened
  finish) . . . . .NiB $1740 Ex $1279 Gd $1200
Sporter Octagon (pistol grip; 24-in. bbl.;
  blued finish) . . . . NiB $1740 Ex $1279 Gd $1200

Carbine (straight grip; 20-in. rnd. bbl.;
  saddle ring) . . . . NiB $1210 Ex $1100 Gd $800
Deluxe Sporter (checkered straight grip;
  24-in. half octagon/half rnd. bbl.; case
  hardened) . . . . NiB $1300 Ex $1080 Gd $710
Deluxe Sporting (checkered pistol grip;
  24-in. half octagon/half rnd. bbl.; case
  hardened) . . . . NiB $1560 Ex $1350 Gd $970

MODEL 1885 SINGLE-SHOT RIFLE

Designed by John M. Browning, this falling-block, lever-action rifle was manufactured from 1885 to 1920 in a variety of models and chambered for most of the popular cartridges of the period — both rimfire and centerfire from .22 to .50 caliber. There are two basic styles of frames, low-wall and high-wall. The low-wall was chambered only for the lower-powered cartridges, while the high-wall was supplied in all calibers and made in three basic types. The standard model for No. 3 and heavier barrels is the type commonly encountered; the thin-walled version was supplied with No. 1 and No. 2 light barrels and the thick-walled action in the heavier calibers. Made in both solid frame and takedown versions. Barrels were available in five weights ranging from the lightweight No. 1 to the extra-heavy No. 5 in round, half-octagon and full-octagon styles. Many other variations were also offered.

MODEL 1885 HIGH-WALL SINGLE-SHOT

SPORTING RIFLE . . . . .NiB $5335 Ex $3100 Gd $2066
Solid frame or takedown. No. 3, 30-in. bbl., standard. Weight: 9.5 lbs. Standard trigger and lever. Open rear sights; blade front sight. Plain stock and forend.

MODEL 1885 LOW-WALL SINGLE-SHOT

SPORTING RIFLE . . . . .NiB $1550 Ex $1466 Gd $1000
Solid frame. No. 1, 28-in. round or octagon bbl. Weight: 7 lbs. Open rear sight; blade front sight. Plain stock and forend.

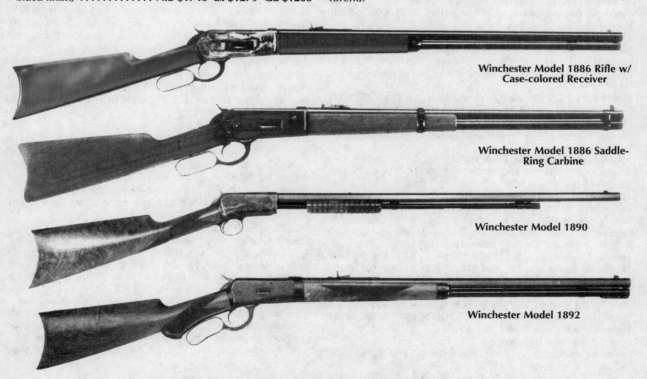

Winchester Model 1886 Rifle w/
Case-colored Receiver

Winchester Model 1886 Saddle-
Ring Carbine

Winchester Model 1890

Winchester Model 1892

GRADING: **NiB** = New in Box   **Ex** = Excellent or NRA 95%   **Gd** = Good or NRA 68%

MODEL 1885 SINGLE-SHOT SCHUETZEN
RIFLE . . . . NiB $10,000 Ex $7860 Gd $5779
Solid frame or takedown. High-wall action. Schuetzen double-set trigger. Spur finger lever. No. 3, 30-in. octagon bbl. Weight: 12 lbs. Vernier rear peep sight; wind-gauge front sight. Fancy walnut Schuetzen stock with checkered pistol-grip and forend. Schuetzen buttplate; adj. palm rest.

MODEL 1885 SINGLE-SHOT SPECIAL
SPORTING RIFLE . . . . NiB $7335 Ex $5550 Gd $5090
Same general specifications as the standard high-wall model except with checkered fancy walnut stock and forend.

MODEL 1885
SINGLE-SHOT MUSKET . . . . NiB $1590 Ex $1171 Gd $878
Solid frame. Low-wall. .22 Short and Long Rifle. 28-in. round bbl. Weight: 8.6 lbs. Lyman rear peep sight; blade front sight. Military-type stock and forend. Note: The U.S. Government purchased a large quantity of these muskets during World War I for training purposes.

MODEL 1885 SINGLE-SHOT "WINDER"
MUSKET . . . . NiB $1488 Ex $1203 Gd $1037
Solid frame or takedown. High-wall. Plain trigger. 28-in. round bbl. Weight: 8.5 lbs. Musket rear sight; blade front sight. Military-type stock and forend w/bbl. band and sling stud/rings.

MODEL 1885 HIGH-WALL SINGLE-SHOT (RECENT MFG.)
Solid frame. 28-in., oct. bbl.; Calibers: .223 Rem., .22-250 Rem., .270 WSM, .300 WSM, or 7mm WSM. Weight: 8.5 lbs. No sights. Checkered stock. Adj. trigger. Blued finish. Made 2005-06.
Hunter . . . . NiB $1090 Ex $1000 Gd $800
BPCR (.45-70; 30-in. half-rnd., half-oct. bbl.; 10 lbs.;
   case hardened) . . . . . . NiB $10,270 Ex $7668 Gd $5790
Cenntenial Hunter (.30-06) NiB $1620 Ex $1530 Gd $1300
Standard model . . . . NiB $1090 Ex $1000 Gd $800
Traditional Hunter (crescent buttplate, 28-in.
   octagon bbl. w/sights) . . . . . NiB $1090 Ex $1000 Gd $800

MODEL 1885 LOW-WALL SINGLE-SHOT (RECENT MFG.)
Solid frame. 24- or 24.5-in. half-rnd., half-oct. or oct. bbl.; Calibers: .17HMR, .22 LR, .22 Hornet, .223 Rem., .22-250 Rem., or .243 Win. Weight: 8 lbs. Smooth or checkered stock. Blued finish.
Grade I .22 LR (1999-2001) . . . NiB $828 Ex $740 Gd $630
High Grade .22 LR (1999-2001)NiB $1180 Ex $1060 Gd $880
Low Wall 1885 (2003-06) . . . . NiB $1070 Ex $880 Gd $720
Hunter Rimfire (2014-present)NiB $1470 Ex $1330 Gd $1100

MODEL 1886 LEVER-ACTION RIFLE
Solid frame or takedown. .33 Win., .38-56, .38-70, .40-65, .40-70, .40-82, .45-70, .45-90, .50-100, .50-110. The .33 Win. and .45-70 were the last calibers in which this model was supplied. Eight round tubular magaine; also 4-rnd. half-magazine. 26-in. bbl. (round, half-octagon, octagon). Weight: 7.5 lbs. Sights: Open rear; bead or blade front. Plain straight-grip stock and forend or standard models. Made 1886-1935.
Standard model . . . . NiB $8288 Ex $6399 Gd $5100
Takedown model . . . . NiB $10,270 Ex $7668 Gd $5790
Deluxe model (checkered pistol grip and high-quality
   walnut stock) . . . . NiB $17,689 Ex $13,790 Gd $10,777
Lightweight model (.45-70, .33 WCF; tapered round bbl.; half
   magazine; shotgun butt) . . . NiB $7689 Ex $5790 Gd $4999
Lightweight Deluxe model (checkered
   pistol grip and high-quality
   walnut stock) . . . . NiB 19,600 Ex $17,000 Gd $13,300

MODEL 1886 SADDLE-RING
CARBINE . . . . NiB $19,690 Ex $16,660 Gd $13,750
Same as standard rifle except w/ 22-in. bbl., carbine buttstock and forend. Saddle ring on left side of receiver. Made 1886-1935.

MODEL 1886 LEVER-ACTION RIFLE (RECENT MFG.)
Newr mfg., simialr to 1886 rifle except .45-70 only. 26-in. octagon bbl.; Weight: 7.5 lbs. Sights: Open rear; blade front. Straight-grip stock and forend. Blued finish. Made 1997-98.
High Grade (gold inlays,
   checkered wood) . . . . . . NiB $1625 Ex $1325 Gd $1060
Takedown model . . . . NiB $1200 Ex $1060 Gd $900
Extra Light Grade I (22-in. rnd. tapered bbl.; weight:
   7.25 lbs.; made 2000–01 and
   2010–12) . . . . NiB $1270 Ex $1180 Gd $950
Extra Light High Grade (gold inlays, checkered wood; made
   2000-01) . . . . NiB $1270 Ex $1180 Gd $950
Short Rifle (24-in. rnd. bbl.; weight: 8.37 lbs.; plain wood;
   made 2011-present) . . . . . NiB $1270 Ex $1180 Gd $950
Deluxe Case Hardened (24-in. octagon bbl.;
   weight: 9.75 lbs.; checkered wood; made
   2015-present) . . . . NiB $1740 Ex $1180 Gd $950

MODEL 1890 SLIDE-ACTION RIFLE
Visible hammer. Calibers: .22 Short, Long, LR; .22 WRF (not interchangeable). Tubular magazine holds 15 Short, 12 Long, 11 LR; 12 WRF. 24-in. octagon bbl. Weight: 5.75 lbs. Sights: Open rear; bead front. Plain straight-grip stock, grooved slide handle. Originally solid frame; after No. 15,499, all rifles of this model were takedown-type. Fancy checkered pistol-grip stock, nickel-steel bbl. supplied at extra cost, which can also increase the value by 100% or more. Made 1890-1932.
.22 WRF, blued model . . . . . NiB $2079 Ex $1754 Gd $1166
.22 LR, blued model . . . . . . NiB $2148 Ex $2066 Gd $1180
Color casehardened receiverNiB $6689 Ex $5349 Gd $3730

MODEL 1892 . . . . NiB $3482 Ex $2210 Gd $1588
Lever action. Solid frame or takedown. Calibers: .25-20, .32-20, .38-40, .44-40. Thirteen round tubular magazine; also 7-rnd. half-magazine. 24-in. bbl. (round, octagon, half-octagon). Weight: from 6.75 lbs. up. Sights: Open rear; bead front. Plain straight-grip stock and forend. Made 1892-1941.
Deluxe (pistol-grip stock) NiB $15,300 Ex $13,600 Gd $11,700
Musket (full length stock) NiB $21,800 Ex $18,200 Gd $14,600

MODEL 1892 SADDLE-RING
CARBINE . . . . NiB $5321 Ex $2549 Gd $1266
Same general specifications as the Model 1892 rifle except carbine buttstock, forend and sights. 20-in. bbl. Saddle ring on left side of receiver.
Trapper (12-, 14-, 15-, 16-, or 18-in. bbl.; most common
   15-in.,) . . . . NiB $21,800 Ex $18,200 Gd $14,600

MODEL 1892 CARBINES & RIFLES (RECENT MFG.)
Similar to the original Model 1892. Calibers: .357 Mag., .44-40, .44 Mag. or .45 LC; 10-rnd. tube magazine. 16-, 20- or 24-in. rnd. or octagon bbl. Weight: 6.25 lbs. 41.25 in. overall. Sights: Bead front, adj. buckhorn rear. Blue finish. Stock: smooth straight-grip walnut. Made 1997–99.
Button Magazine (crescent buttplate, forearm cap and but-
   ton magazine; 20-in. half round/
   octagon bbl.; disc.) . . . . NiB $1300 Ex $1250 Gd $800
Carbine (20-in. rnd. bbl., saddle ring, 2011–13, reintro.
   2014–date) . . . . NiB $900 Ex $860 Gd $650

Winchester Model 1894

Winchester Model 1894
Fancy-Grade Takedown

Winchester Model 1894 Saddle-
Ring Carbine

Winchester Model 1895 Rifle

Winchester Model 1895
Carbine

Large Loop Carbine (large loop lever, 20-in. rnd. bbl., saddle ring, 2011–12, reintro. 2014–date) . . . . NiB $1100 Ex $980 Gd $670
Short Rifle (20-in. tapered octagon bbl., disc) . . . . NiB $900 Ex $860 Gd $650
Short Rifle Case Hardened (20-in. tapered octagon bbl., case hardened finish, 2011–12) . . . . NiB $950 Ex $880 Gd $750
Short Rifle (20-in. rnd. bbl., 2014–date) . . . . NiB $900 Ex $860 Gd $650
Trapper Takedown (takedown, pistol grip checkered stock, crescent buttplate, forearm cap, 16-in. octagon bbl., 2011–12) . . . NiB $1400 Ex $1350 Gd $850
Trapper (straight grip smooth stock, 16-in. rnd. bbl., 2011–12) . . . . NiB $1000 Ex $950 Gd $850
Grade II (gold appointments and receiver game scene, .45 LC only, production of 1,000 in 1997) . . . . NiB $1388 Ex $1167 Gd $828

NOTE: *Winchester Model 1894 and Model 94 rifles are divided by dates of manufacture. Early Model 1894 rifles were manufactured from 1894 to 1898 (serial number range: 1-147684), those made from 1898 to 1929 (serial numbers continues to 1077097). Starting in 1929 only carbines were manufactured. Model 94 Saddle Ring models made from 1929 to late 1930s.*

MODEL 1894 . . . . NiB $6530 Ex $4739 Gd $3220
Lever action. Solid frame or takedown. .25-35, .30-30, .32-40, .32 Special, .38-55. Seven round tubular magazine or 4-rnd. half-magazine. 26-in. bbl. (round, octagon, half-octagon). Weight: about 7.35 lbs. Sights: Open rear; bead front. Plain straight-grip stock and forearm on standard model; crescent-shaped or shotgun-style buttplate. Made 1894-1937. See also Winchester Model 94 for later variations of this model.

MODEL 1894 DELUXE . . .NiB $12,890 Ex $10,669 Gd $8777
Same general specifications as the standard rifle except checkered pistol-grip buttstock and forend using high-grade walnut. Engraved versions are considerably higher in value.

MODEL 1894 SADDLE-RING CARBINE. . . . . .NiB $2866 Ex $1806 Gd $1100
Same general specifications as the Model 1894 standard rifle except 20-in. bbl., carbine buttstock, forend, and sights. Saddle ring on left side of receiver. Weight: about 6.5 lbs.

MODEL 1894 STANDARD CARBINE. . . . . .NiB $6798 Ex $4890 Gd $3855
Same general specifications as Saddle-Ringle Carbine except shotgun type buttstock and plate, no saddle ring, standard open rear sight. Sometimes called "Eastern Carbine." See also Winchester Model 94 carbine.

1895 CARBINE . . . . .NiB $4297 Ex $3037 Gd $1971
Same as Model 95 Standard Rifle except has 22-in. bbl., carbine-style buttstock and forend, weight: About 8 lbs., calibers .30-40 Krag, .30-03, .30-06 and .303, solid frame only.

MODEL 1895 . . . . .NiB $3364 Ex $2130 Gd $1266
Lever action. Calibers: .30-40 Krag, .30-03, .30-60, .303 British, 7.62mm Russian, .35 Win., .38-72, .40-72, .405 Win. Four round box magazine except .30-40 and .303, which have 5-rnd. magazines. Bbl. lengths: 24-, 26-, 28-in. (round, half-octagon, octagon). Weight: About 8.5 lbs. Sights: Open rear; bead or blade front. Plain straight-grip stock and forend (standard). Both solid frame and takedown models were made from1897 to 1931.

MODEL 1895 GRADE 1 (RECENT MFG.)
Similar to the original Model 1895. Calibers: .270 Win., .30-06, .30-40 Krag, or .405 Win. 4-rnd. magazine. 24-in. round bbl. Weight: 8 lbs. Bead front sight, adjustable buckhorn rear. Top tang safety. Blue finish. Smooth straight-grip walnut stock and forewarm. Made 1997-2004.
Grade I model. . . . . .NiB $1180 Ex $1060 Gd $900
Limited Edition (.30-06 only, 1995-97) . . . . .NiB $980 Ex $700 Gd $580
Limited Edition High Grdae (.30-06, 1995-2002) . . . .NiB $1760 Ex $1300 Gd $1000

MODEL 1895 THEODORE ROOSEVELT SERIES (RECENT MFG.)
Similar to Model 1895 Grade 1 except .405 Win. only, high polish blue, gold inlays, engraved receiver.

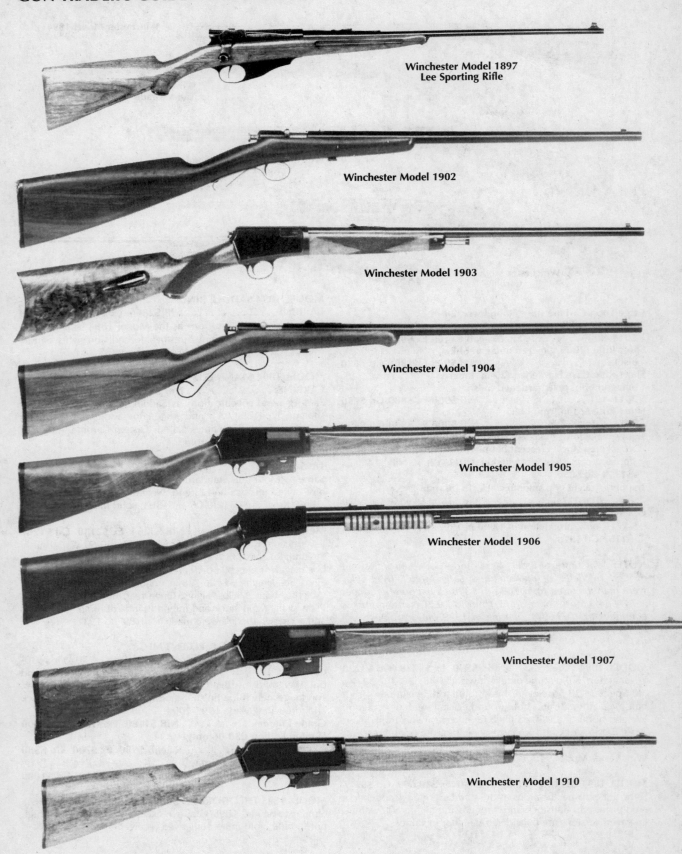

**Winchester Model 1897
Lee Sporting Rifle**

Winchester Model 1902

Winchester Model 1903

Winchester Model 1904

Winchester Model 1905

Winchester Model 1906

Winchester Model 1907

Winchester Model 1910

150th Anniversary Custom Grade
  (2008). . . . . NiB $2760 Ex $2360 Gd $1900
150th Anniversary High Grade
  (2008). . . . . NiB $1500 Ex $1300 Gd $1060
Safari High Grade (2009) . . NiB $1580 Ex $1360 Gd $1100
Safari Custom Grade
  (2 gun set, 2009) . . . . . . NiB $3360 Ex $2960 Gd $2500

MODEL (1897) LEE BOLT-ACTION RIFLE
Straight-pull bolt-action. .236 U.S. Navy, 5-rnd. box magazine, clip loaded. 24- and 28-in. bbl. Weight: 7.5 to 8.5 lbs. Sights: Folding leaf rear sight on musket; open sporting sight on sporting rifle.
Musket model . . . . NiB $1939 Ex $1777 Gd $1129
Sporting rifle. . . . . NiB $2000 Ex $1808 Gd $1110

MODEL 1900 BOLT-ACTION SINGLE-SHOT
RIFLE. . . . . NiB $628 Ex $499 Gd $356
Takedown. Caliber: .22 Short and Long. 18-in. bbl. Weight: 2.75 lbs. Open rear sight; blade front sight. One-piece, straight-grip stock. Made 1899-1902.

MODEL 1902 BOLT-ACTION SINGLE-SHOT
RIFLE. . . . . NiB $495 Ex $369 Gd $269
Takedown. Basically the same as Model 1900 with minor improvements. Calibers: .22 Short and Long, .22 Extra Long, .22 LR. Weight: 3 lbs. Made 1902-31.

MODEL 1903 SELF-LOADING
RIFLE. . . . . NiB $1133 Ex $909 Gd $577
Takedown. Caliber: .22 Win. Auto. Ten round tubular magazine in buttstock. 20-in. bbl. Weight: 5.75 lbs. Sights: Open rear; bead front. Plain straight-grip stock and forearm (fancy grade illustrated). Made 1903-36.

MODEL (1904) 99 THUMB-TRIGGER BOLT-ACTION
SINGLE-SHOT RIFLE. . . . . NiB $833 Ex $707 Gd $510
Takedown. Same as Model 1902 except fired by pressing a button behind the cocking piece. Made 1904-23.

MODEL 1904 BOLT-ACTION SINGLE-SHOT
RIFLE. . . . . NiB $469 Ex $388 Gd $269
Similar to Model 1902. Takedown. Caliber: 22 Short, Long Extra Long, LR. 21-in. bbl. Weight: 4 lbs. Made 1904-31.

MODEL 1905
SELF-LOADING RIFLE. . . . . NiB $768 Ex $580 Gd $500
Takedown. Calibers: .32 Win. SL or .35 Win. SL. Five or 10-rnd. detachable box magazine. 22-in. bbl. Weight: 7.5 lbs. Sights: Open rear; bead front. Plain pistol-grip stock and forearm. Made 1905-20.

MODEL 1906
SLIDE-ACTION REPEATER . . NiB $1590 Ex $1077 Gd $733
Takedown. Visible hammer. Caliber: .22 Short, Long, LR. Tubular magazine holds 20 Short, 16 Long or 14 LR. 20-in. bbl. Weight: 5 lbs. Sights: Open rear; bead front. Straight-grip stock and grooved forearm. Made 1906-32.

MODEL 1907
SELF-LOADING RIFLE. . . . . NiB $733 Ex $589 Gd $421
Takedown. Caliber: .351 Win. SL. Five or 10-rnd. detachable box magazine. 20-in. bbl. Weight: 7.75 lbs. Sights: Open rear; bead front. Plain pistol-grip stock and forearm. Made 1907-57.

MODEL 1910 SELF-LOADING RIFLE. . . NiB $910 Ex $707 Gd $533
Takedown. Caliber: .401 Win. SL. Four round detachable box magazine. 20-in. bbl. Weight: 8.5 lbs. Sights: Open rear; bead front. Plain pistol-grip stock and forearm. Made 1910-36.

MODEL 43 BOLT-ACTION
SPORTING RIFLE . . . . NiB $855 Ex $679 Gd $480
Standard Grade. Calibers: .218 Bee, .22 Hornet, .25-20, .32-20 (latter two discontinued 1950). Three round detachable box magazine. 24-in. bbl. Weight: 6 lbs. Sights: Open rear, bead front on hooded ramp. Plain pistol-grip stock with swivels. Made 1949-57.

MODEL 43 SPECIAL GRADE . . NiB $855 Ex $679 Gd $480
Same as Standard Model 43 except has checkered pistol-grip and forearm, grip cap.

MODEL 47 BOLT-ACTION SINGLE-SHOT
RIFLE. . . . . NiB $466 Ex $370 Gd $245
Caliber: .22 Short, Long, LR. 25-in. bbl. Weight: 5.5 lbs. Sights: Peep or open rear; bead front. Plain pistol-grip stock. Made 1949-54.

MODEL 52 BOLT-ACTION TARGET RIFLE
Standard bbl. First type. .22 LR. Five round box magazine. 28-in. bbl. Weight: 8.75 lbs. Sights: Folding leaf peep rear; blade front sight; standard sights various other combinations available. Scope bases. Semi-military-type target stock w/pistol grip; original model has grasping grooves in forearm; higher comb and semi-beavertail forearm on later models. Numerous changes were made in this model; the most important was the adoption of the speed lock in 1929. Model 52 rifles produced before this change are generally referred to as "slow lock" models. Last arms of this type bore serial numbers followed by the letter "A." Made 1919 to 1937.
Slow Lock model. . . . . NiB $909 Ex $622 Gd $370
Speed Lock model. . . . . NiB $733 Ex $466 Gd $379

MODEL 52 HEAVY BARREL . . . NiB $1379 Ex $1008 Gd $798
First type speed lock. Same general specifications as Standard Model 52 of this type except has heavier bbl., Lyman No. 17G front sight, weight: 10 lbs.

MODEL 52 INTERNATIONAL MATCH RIFLE
Similar to Model 52-D Heavy Barrel except has special lead-lapped bbl., laminated "free rifle"-style stock with high comb, thumbhole, hook buttplate, accessory rail, handstop/swivel assembly, palm rest. Weight: 13.5 lbs. Made 1969-78.
With standard trigger . . . . . . NiB $1577 Ex $1103 Gd $922
With Kenyon or I.S.U. trigger, add $350

MODEL 52 INTERNATIONAL
PRONE . . . . NiB $1470 Ex $1133 Gd $909
Similar to Model 52-D Heavy Barrel except has special lead-lapped bbl., prone stock with full pistol-grip, rollover cheekpiece removable for bore-cleaning. Weight 11.5 lbs. Made 1975-80.

MODEL 52 SPORTING RIFLE
First type. Same as Standard Model 52 of this type except has lightweight 24-in. bbl., Lyman No. 48 receiver sight and gold bead front sight on hooded ramp, deluxe checkered sporting stock with cheekpiece, black forend tip, etc. Weight: 7.75 lbs. Made 1934 to 1958. Reintroduced 1993.
Model 52 Sporter . . . . NiB $4677 Ex $3200 Gd $1590

Winchester Model 47

Winchester Model 52
Standard Barrel

Winchester Model 52
International Match

Winchester Model 52
International Prone Target

Winchester Model 52-B
Standard Barrel

Winchester Model 52-B
Sporter

Winchester Model 52-C
Heavy Barrel

Model 52A Sporter . . . . NiB $3290 Ex $2733 Gd $1266
Model 52B Sporter . . . . NiB $4633 Ex $2479 Gd $1790
Model 52C Sporter . . . . NiB $5125 Ex $4120 Gd $2798
Model 52 C Sporter
  (1993 BAC re-issue) . . . . NiB $650 Ex $500 Gd $433

MODEL 52-B BOLT-ACTION RIFLE
Standard bbl. Extensively redesigned action. Supplied with choice of "Target" stock, an improved version of the previous Model 52 stock, or "Marksman" stock with high comb, full pistol grip and beavertail forearm. Weight: 9 lbs. Offered with a wide choice of target sight combinations (Lyman, Marble-Goss,

Redfield, Vaver, Winchester), value shown is for rifle less sight equipment. Other specifications as shown for first type. Made 1935-47. Reintroduced 1997.

Target model . . . . NiB $1270 Ex $968 Gd $755
BAC model (1997 BAC re-issue) . . NiB $1270 Ex $968 Gd $755
USRAC Sporting model . . . . . . NiB $768 Ex $600 Gd $455

MODEL 52-B BULL GUN HEAVY
BARREL . . . . NiB $1880 Ex $1144 Gd $600
Same specifications as Standard Model 52-B except Bull Gun has extra heavy bbl., Marksman stock only, weight: 12 lbs. Heavy Bbl. model weight: 11 lbs. Made 1940-47.

MODEL 52-C BOLT-ACTION RIFLE

Improved action with "Micro-Motion" trigger mechanism and new-type "Marksman" stock. General specifications same as shown for previous models. Made 1947-61, Bull Gun from 1952. Value shown is for rifle less sights.

Bull Gun (w/extra heavy bbl.,
   wt. 12 lbs.) . . . . NiB $1877 Ex $976 Gd $694
w/standard bbl.
   (wt. 9.75 lbs.) . . . . NiB $1466 Ex $800 Gd $659
Target model (w/heavy bbl.) . . NiB $1455 Ex $909 Gd $689

NOTE: *Following WWI, Winchester had financial difficulties and, like many other firearm firms of the day, failed. However, Winchester continued to operate in the hands of receivers. Then, in 1931, The Western Cartridge Co.—under the leadership of John Olin—purchased all assets of the firm. After that, Winchester leaped ahead of all other firms of the day in firearm and ammunition development. The first sporting firearm to come out of the Winchester plant after WWI was the Model 20 shotgun, but this was quickly followed by the famous Model 52 bolt-action rifle. This was also a time when Winchester dropped the four-digit model numbers and began using two-digit numbers instead. This model-numbering procedure, with one exception (Model 677), continued for the next several years.*

MODEL 52-D BOLT-ACTION

TARGET RIFLE. . . . . NiB $1377 Ex $976 Gd $488
Redesigned Model 52 action, Single-Shot. Caliber: .22 LR. 28-in. standard or heavy bbl., free-floating, with blocks for standard target scopes. Weight: With standard bbl., 9.75 lbs., with heavy barrel, 11 lbs. Restyled Marksman stock with accessory channel and forend stop, rubber buttplate. Made 1961 to 1978. Value shown is for rifle without sights.

MODEL 53 LEVER-ACTION

REPEATER . . . . NiB $2343 Ex $1869 Gd $1333
Modification of Model 92. Solid frame or takedown. Calibers: .25-20, .32-20, .44-40. Six round tubular half-magazine in solid frame model. Seven round in takedown. 22-in. nickel steel bbl. Weight: 5.5 to 6.5 lbs. Sights: Open rear; bead front. Redesigned straight-grip stock and forearm. Made 1924-32.

MODEL 54 BOLT-ACTION HIGH POWER

SPORTING RIFLE (I) . . . . NiB $1570 Ex $933 Gd $667
First type. Calibers: .270 Win., 7x57mm, .30-30, .30-06, 7.65x53mm, 9x57mm. Five round box magazine. 24-in. bbl. Weight: 7.75 lbs. Sights: Open rear; bead front. Checkered stock w/pistol grip, tapered forearm w/Schnabel tip. This type has two-piece firing pin. Made 1925-30.

MODEL 54 BOLT-ACTION HIGH POWER

SPORTING RIFLE (II) . . . . NiB $1180 Ex $922 Gd $744
Standard Grade. Improved type with speed lock and one-piece firing pin. Calibers: .22 Hornet, .220 Swift, .250/3000, .257 Roberts, .270 Win., 7x57mm, .30-06. Five round box magazine. 24-in. bbl., 26-in. in cal. .220 Swift. Weight: About 8 lbs. Sights: Open rear, bead front on ramp. NRA-type stock w/ checkered pistol-grip and forearm. Made 1930 to 1936. Add $200 for .22 Hornet caliber.

MODEL 54 CARBINE (I) . . . . . NiB $1495 Ex $884 Gd $601

First type. Same as Model 54 rifle except has 20-in. bbl., plain lightweight stock with grasping grooves in forearm. Weight: 7.25 lbs.

MODEL 54 CARBINE (II) . . . . NiB $1566 Ex $912 Gd $648

Improved type. Same as Model 54 Standard Grade Sporting Rifle of this type except has 20-in. bbl. Weight: About 7.5 lbs. This model may have either NRA-type stock or the lightweight stock found on the first-type Model 54 Carbine.

MODEL 54 NATIONAL MATCH

RIFLE. . . . . NiB $1722 Ex $967 Gd $679
Same as Standard Model 54 except has Lyman sights, scope bases, Marksman-type target stock, weighs 9.5 lbs. Same calibers as Standard Model.

MODEL 54 SNIPER'S MATCH

RIFLE. . . . . NiB $2489 Ex $1388 Gd $633
Similar to the earlier Model 54 Sniper's Rifle except has Marksman-type target stock, scope bases, weight: 12.5 lbs. Available in same calibers as Model 54 Standard Grade.

MODEL 54 SNIPER'S RIFLE. . . NiB $2566 Ex $1534 Gd $770

Same as Standard Model 54 except has heavy 26-in. bbl., Lyman No. 48 rear peep sight and blade front sight semi-military stock, weight: 11.75 pounds, cal. .30-06 only.

MODEL 54 SUPER GRADE. . . NiB $3144 Ex $2057 Gd $1166

Same as Standard Model 54 Sporter except has deluxe stock with cheekpiece, black forend tip, pistol-grip cap, quick detachable swivels, 1-in. sling strap.

MODEL 54 TARGET RIFLE . . . . NiB $888 Ex $572 Gd $390

Same as Standard Model 54 except has 24-in. medium-weight bbl. (26-in. in cal. .220 Swift), Lyman sights, scope bases, Marksman-type target stock, weight: 10.5 lbs., same calibers as Standard Model.

MODEL 55 "AUTOMATIC"

SINGLE-SHOT. . . . . NiB $379 Ex $290 Gd $210
Caliber: .22 Short, Long, LR. 22-in. bbl. Sights: Open rear, bead front. One-piece walnut stock. Weight: About 5.5 lbs. Made 1958-60.

MODEL 55 LEVER-ACTION REPEATER

Modification of Model 94. Solid frame or takedown. Calibers: .25-35, .30-30, .32 Win. Special. Three round tubular half magazine. 24-in. nickel steel bbl. Weight: About 7 lbs. Sights: Open rear; bead front. Made 1924-32.
Standard model
   (straight grip). . . . . NiB $2133 Ex $1670 Gd $1006
Deluxe model (pistol grip) . NiB $2287 Ex $1744 Gd $1140

MODEL 56 BOLT-ACTION SPORTING

RIFLE. . . . . NiB $1179 Ex $1143 Gd $707
Solid frame. Caliber: .22 LR., .22 Short. Five or 10-rnd. detachable box magazine. 22-in. bbl. Weight: 4.75 lbs. Sights: Open rear; bead front. Plain pistol-grip with Schnabel forend. Made 1926-29.

MODEL 57 BOLT-ACTION RIFLE

Solid frame. Same as Model 56 except available (until 1929) in .22 Short as well as LR w/ 5- or 10-rnd. magazine. Has semi-military style target stock, bbl. band on forend, swivels and web sling, Lyman peep rear sight, weight: 5 lbs. Made 1926-36.
Sporter model. . . . . NiB $888 Ex $654 Gd $500
Target model. . . . . NiB $733 Ex $679 Gd $500

GRADING: NiB = New in Box   Ex = Excellent or NRA 95%   Gd = Good or NRA 68%

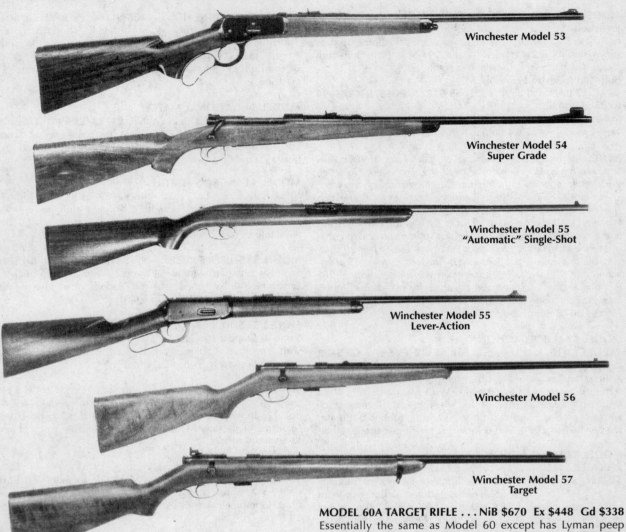

Winchester Model 53

Winchester Model 54
Super Grade

Winchester Model 55
"Automatic" Single-Shot

Winchester Model 55
Lever-Action

Winchester Model 56

Winchester Model 57
Target

MODEL 58 BOLT-ACTION
SINGLE-SHOT . . . . NiB $1056 Ex $800 Gd $598
Similar to Model 52. Takedown. Caliber. .22 Short, Long LR.
18-in. bbl. Weight: 3 lbs. Sights, Open rear; blade front. Plain,
flat, straight-grip hardwood stock. Not serial numbered. Made
1928-31.

MODEL 59 BOLT-ACTION
SINGLE-SHOT . . . . NiB $1268 Ex $1009 Gd $756
Improved version of Model 58, has 23-in. bbl., redesigned
stock w/pistol grip, weight: 4.5 lbs. Made in 1930.

MODEL 60/60A BOLT-ACTION SINGLE-SHOT
Redesign of Model 59. Caliber: .22 Short, Long, LR. 23-in. bbl.
(27-in. after 1933). Weight: 4.25 lbs. Sights: Open rear, blade
front. Plain pistol-grip stock. Made 1930-34 (60), 1932-39
(60A).
Model 60 . . . . NiB $445 Ex $276 Gd $200
Model 60A . . . . NiB $556 Ex $380 Gd $338

MODEL 60A TARGET RIFLE . . . NiB $670 Ex $448 Gd $338
Essentially the same as Model 60 except has Lyman peep
rear sight and square top front sight, semi-military target
stock and web sling, weight: 5.5 lbs. Made 1932-39.

MODEL 61 HAMMERLESS SLIDE-ACTION REPEATER
Takedown. Caliber: .22 Short, Long, LR. Tubular magazine
holds 20 Short, 16 Long, 14 LR. 24-in. round bbl. Weight:
5.5 lbs. Sights: Open rear; bead front. Plain pistol-grip stock,
grooved semi-beavertail slide handle. Also available w/ 24-in.
full-octagon bbl. and only calibers .22 Short, .22 LR or .22
WRF. Note: Octagon barrel model discontinued 1943 to 1944;
assembled 1948.
w/round bbl. . . . . NiB $1330 Ex $987 Gd $478
w/grooved receiver . . . . NiB $1268 Ex $1160 Gd $800
w/octagon bbl. . . . . NiB $1766 Ex $1447 Gd $1006

MODEL 61 MAGNUM . . . . NiB $2650 Ex $1854 Gd $1000
Same as Standard Model 61 except chambered for .22 WMR;
magazine holds 12 rounds. Made 1960-63.

MODEL 62 VISIBLE
HAMMER . . . . NiB $1560 Ex $1288 Gd $1043
Modernized version of Model 1890. Caliber: .22 Short, Long,
LR. 23-in. bbl. Weight: 5.5 lbs. Plain straight-grip stock,
grooved semibeavertail slide handle. Also available in Gallery

Winchester Model 58

Winchester Model 59

Winchester Model 60A

Winchester Model 61

Model chambered for .22 Short only. Made 1932-59. Note: Pre-WWII model (small forearm) commands 25% higher price.

MODEL 63 SELF-LOADING RIFLE
Takedown. Caliber: .22 LR High Speed only. Ten round tubular magazine in buttstock. 23-in. bbl. Weight: 5.5 lbs. Sights: Open rear, bead front. Plain pistol-grip stock and forearm. Originally available w/ 20-in. bbl. as well as 23-in. Made 1933-59. Reintroduced in 1997.

w/23-in. bbl. . . . . NiB $1144 Ex $996 Gd $573
w/20-in. bbl. . . . . NiB $2690 Ex $1877 Gd $1133
w/grooved receiver . . . . NiB $2711 Ex $1912 Gd $995
Grade I (1997 BAC re-issue) . . . NiB $707 Ex $576 Gd $488
High Grade (1997 BAC re-issue) NiB $705 Ex $579 Gd $495

MODEL 64 . . . . NiB $1355 Ex $100 Gd $900
Evolution of the Model 55. Calibers: .219 Zipper, .25-35, .30-30 (most common), or .32 Win. Special. 5-rnd. tubular half magazine. 20-, 24-, or 26-in. (standard) bbl. Weight: About 7 lbs. Stock: pistol grip. Finish: Blued. Made 1933–57 and 1972–72.
Carbine variant (20-in. brl.) . . . . **add, 150%**
.219 Zipper caliber . . . . **add, 500%**
.25-35 WCF caliber . . . . **add, 300%**

MODEL 65 . . . . NiB $5450 Ex $4000 Gd $3450
Evolution of the Model 53. Calibers: .218 Bee, .25-20, or .32-20. 7-rnd. tubular half magazine. 22-in. bbl. Weight: About 7 lbs. Stock: pistol grip. Finish: Blued. Made 1933–47, about 5,704 mfg'd.
Deluxe variant (checkered
stock) . . . . NiB $8750 Ex $6850 Gd $6000

MODEL 67 BOLT-ACTION
SINGLE-SHOT RIFLE . . . . NiB $345 Ex $259 Gd $200
Takedown. Calibers: .22 Short, Long, LR, .22 LR round (smoothbore), .22 WRF. 27-in. bbl. Weight: 5 lbs. Sights: Open rear, bead front. Plain pistol-grip stock (original model had grasping grooves in forearm). Made 1934-63.

MODEL 67 BOY'S RIFLE . . . . . . NiB $345 Ex $259 Gd $200
Same as Standard Model 67 except has shorter stock, 20-in. bbl., weighs 4.25 lbs.

MODEL 68 BOLT-ACTION
SINGLE-SHOT . . . . NiB $345 Ex $259 Gd $200
Same as Model 67 except has rear peep sight. Made 1934-46.

MODEL 69 BOLT- ACTION
RIFLE'S . . . . NiB $450 Ex $370 Gd $200
Takedown. Caliber: .22 Short, Long, LR. Five or 10-rnd. box magazine. 25-in. bbl. Weight: 5.5 lbs. Peep or open rear sight. Plain pistol-grip stock. Rifle cocks on closing motion of the bolt. Made 1935-37.

MODEL 69A BOLT-ACTION RIFLE
Same as the Model 69 except cocking mechanism was changed to cock the rifle by the opening motion of the bolt. Made 1937-63. Note: Models with grooved receivers command 20% higher prices.
Model 69A standard . . . . NiB $489 Ex $397 Gd $290
Match model w/Lyman No. 57E
receiver sight . . . . NiB $546 Ex $444 Gd $314
Target model w/Winchester
peep rear sight, swivels, sling NiB $690 Ex $567 Gd $389

MODEL 70
Introduced in 1937, the Model 70 Bolt-Action Repeating Rifle was offered in several styles and calibers. Only minor design changes were made over a period of 27 years and more than 500,000 of these rifles were sold. The original model was dubbed "The Rifleman's Rifle." In 1964, the original Model 70 was superseded by a revised version with redesigned action, improved bolt, swaged (free-floating) barrel, restyled stock. This model again underwent major changes in 1972. Most visible: New stock with contrasting forend tip and grip cap, cut checkering (instead of impressed as in

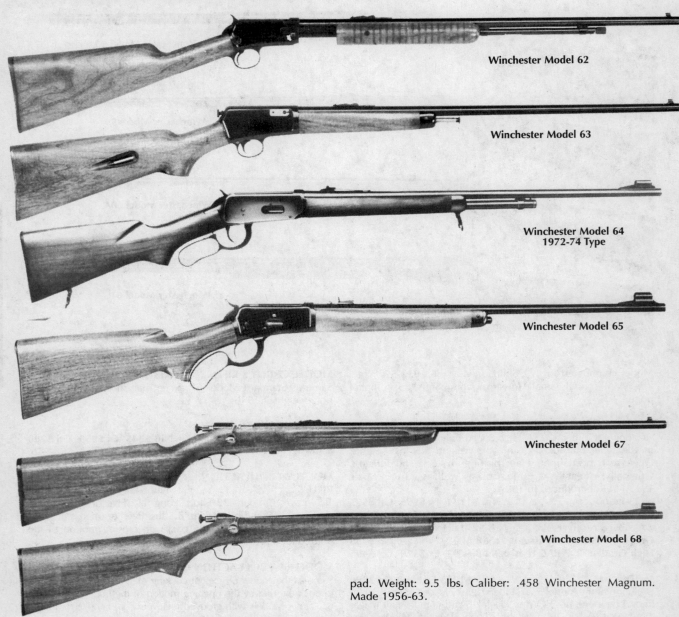

Winchester Model 62

Winchester Model 63

Winchester Model 64
1972-74 Type

Winchester Model 65

Winchester Model 67

Winchester Model 68

predecessor) knurled bolt handle. The action was machined from a solid block of steel with barrels made from chrome molybdenum steel. Other changes in the design and style of the Model 70 continued. The XTR models were added in 1978 along with the Model 70A, the latter omitting the white liners, forend caps and floor plates. In 1981, an XTR Featherweight Model was added to the line, beginning with serial number G1,440,000. This version featured lighter barrels, fancy-checkered stocks with Schnabel forend. After U.S. Repeating Arms took over the Winchester plant, the Model 70 went through even more changes as described under that section of Winchester rifles.

PRE-1964 MODEL 70

MODEL 70 AFRICAN RIFLE NiB $8000 Ex $5600 Gd $3809
Same general specifications as Super Grade Model 70 except w/25-in. bbl., 3-rnd. magazine, Monte Carlo stock w/recoil

pad. Weight: 9.5 lbs. Caliber: .458 Winchester Magnum. Made 1956-63.

MODEL 70 ALASKAN
Same as Standard Model 70 except calibers .338 Win. Mag., .375 H&H Mag.; 3-rnd. magazine in .338, 4-rnd. in .375 caliber; 25-in. bbl.; stock w/recoil pad. Weight: 8 lbs. in .338; 8.75 lbs. in .375 caliber. Made 1960-63.

.338 Win. Mag. . . . . NiB $4135 Ex $2170 Gd $1166
.375 H&H Mag. . . . . NiB $4395 Ex $2100 Gd $1189

MODEL 70 BULL GUN. . . . NiB $4467 Ex $3889 Gd $2356
Same as Standard Model 70 except w/heavy 28-in. bbl., scope bases, Marksman stock, weighs 13.25 lbs., caliber .300 H&H Magnum and .30-06 only. Disc. in 1963.

MODEL 70 FEATHERWEIGHT SPORTER
Same as Standard Model 70 except w/redesigned stock and 22-in. bbl., aluminum trigger guard, floorplate and buttplate. Calibers: .243 Win., .264 Win. Mag., .270 Win., .308 Win., .30-06, .358 Win. Weight: 6.5 lbs. Made 1952-63.

Winchester Model 69

.243 Win.	NiB $1790	Ex $1019	Gd $707
.264 Win. Mag	NiB $2164	Ex $1443	Gd $998
.270 Win.	NiB $1869	Ex $1233	Gd $854
.30-06 Springfield	NiB $1043	Ex $888	Gd $596
.308 Win.	NiB $1278	Ex $866	Gd $658
.358 Win.	NiB $4566	Ex $3000	Gd $2043

MODEL 70 NATIONAL MATCH

RIFLE . . . . NiB $3376 Ex $1943 Gd $1723
Same as Standard Model 70 except w/scope bases, Marksman-type target stock, weight: 9.5 lbs. caliber .30-06 only. Disc. 1960.

MODEL 70 STANDARD GRADE
Calibers: .22 Hornet, .220 Swift, .243 Win., .250-3000, .257 Roberts, .270 Win., 7x57mm, .30-06, .308 Win., .300 H&H Mag., .375 H&H Mag. Five round box magazine (4-rnd. in Magnum calibers). 24-in. bbl. standard; 26-in. in .220 Swift and .300 Mag.; 25-in. in .375 Mag.; at one time a 20-in. bbl. was available. Sights: Open rear; hooded ramp front. Checkered walnut stock; Monte Carlo comb standard on later production. Weight: From 7.75 lbs. depending on caliber and bbl. length. Made 1937-63.

.22 Hornet (1937-58)	NiB $3466	Ex $2033	Gd $1266
.220 Swift (1937-63)	NiB $1497	Ex $1266	Gd $879
.243 Win. (1955-63)	NiB $2145	Ex $1077	Gd $910
.250-3000 Sav. (1937-49)	NiB $5433	Ex $3810	Gd $2244
.257 Roberts (1937-59)	NiB $3809	Ex $2088	Gd $1110
.264 Win. Mag. (1959-63, ltd pr)	NiB $1988	Ex $1154	Gd $877
.270 Win. (1937-63)	NiB $2588	Ex $2000	Gd $1165
7x57mm Mauser (1937-49)	NiB $6970	Ex $4650	Gd $4077

7.65 Argentine (1937, limited prod.) Very Rare

.30-06 Springfield (1937-63)	NiB $3466	Ex $1880	Gd $1299

.308 Win. (1952-63, special order) Very Rare

.300 H&H (1937-63)	NiB $3598	Ex $2079	Gd $1599

.300 Sav. (1944-50, limited prod.) Rare

.300 Win. Mag. (1962-63)	NiB $2244	Ex $1867	Gd $1265
.338 Win. Mag. (1959-63, special order only)	NiB $2144	Ex $1675	Gd $1197

.35 Rem. (1941-47, limited prod.) Very Rare
.358 Win. (1955-58) Very Rare

.375 H&H (1937-63)	NiB $4676	Ex $4054	Gd $2354
.458 Win. Mag. (1956-63) Super Grade only	NiB $4000	Ex $2978	Gd $2369

9x57 Mauser (1937 only, limited prod.) Very Rare

MODEL 70 SUPER GRADE
Same as Standard Grade Model 70 except w/deluxe stock w/cheekpiece, black forend tip, pistol-grip cap, quick detachable swivels, sling. Disc. 1960. Prices for Super Grade models also reflect rarity in both production and caliber. Values are generally twice that of standard models of similar configuration.

MODEL 70 SUPER GRADE FEATHERWEIGHT
Same as Standard Grade Featherweight except w/deluxe stock w/cheekpiece, black forend tip, pistol-grip cap, quick detachable swivels, sling. Disc. 1960. Note: SG-FWs are very rare, but unless properly documented will not command premium prices. Prices for authenticated Super Grades Featherweight models are generally 4 to 5 times that of a standard production Featherweight model w/similar chambering.

MODEL 70 TARGET RIFLE
Same as Standard Model 70 except w/24-in. medium-weight bbl., scope bases, Marksman stock, weight 10.5 lbs. Originally offered in all of the Model 70 calibers, this rifle was available later in calibers .243 Win. and .30-06. Disc. 1963. Values are generally twice that of standard models of similar configuration.

MODEL 70 TARGET HEAVY

WEIGHT . . . . NiB $3160 Ex $2244 Gd $1590
Same general specifications as Standard Model 70 except w/ either 24- or 26-in. heavy weight bbl. weight: 10.5 lbs. No checkering. .243 and .30-06 calibers.

MODEL 70 TARGET BULL

BARREL . . . . NiB $4466 Ex $2587 Gd $1964
Same general specifications as Standard Model 70 except 28-in. heavy weight bbl. and chambered for either .30-06 or .300 H&H Mag. Drilled and tapped for front sight base. Receiver slotted for clip loading. Weight: 13.25 lbs.

MODEL 70 VARMINT . . . . . NiB $2388 Ex $1454 Gd $1145
Same general specifications as Standard Model 70 except w/26-in. heavy bbl., scope bases, special varminter stock. Calibers: .220 Swift, .243 Win. Made 1956-63.

MODEL 70 WESTERNER . . . . . . NiB $707 Ex $569 Gd $355
Same as Standard Model 70 except calibers .264 Win. Mag., .300 Win. Mag.; 3-rnd. magazine; 26-in. bbl. in former caliber, 24-in. in latter. Weight: 8.25 lbs. Made 1960-63.

1964-TYPE MODEL 70

MODEL 70 AFRICAN . . . . NiB $595 Ex $397 Gd $338
Caliber: .458 Win. Mag. Three round magazine. 22-in. bbl. Weight: 8.5 lbs. Special "African" sights. Monte Carlo stock w/ebony forend tip, hand-checkering, twin stock-reinforcing bolts, recoil pad, QD swivels. Made 1964-71.

MODEL 70 DELUXE . . . . NiB $790 Ex $588 Gd $445
Calibers: .243, .270 Win., .30-06, .300 Win. Mag. Five round box magazine (3-rnd. in Magnum). 22-in. bbl. (24-in. in Magnum). Weight: 7.5 lbs. Sights: Open rear; hooded ramp front. Monte Carlo stock w/ebony forend tip, hand-checkering, QD swivels, recoil pad on Magnum. Made 1964-71.

MODEL 70 INTERNATIONAL ARMY
MATCH RIFLE . . . . NiB $1198 Ex $955 Gd $744
Caliber: .308 Win. (7.62 NATO). Five round box magazine. 24-in. heavy barrel. Externally adj. trigger. Weight: 11 lbs. ISU

RIFLES

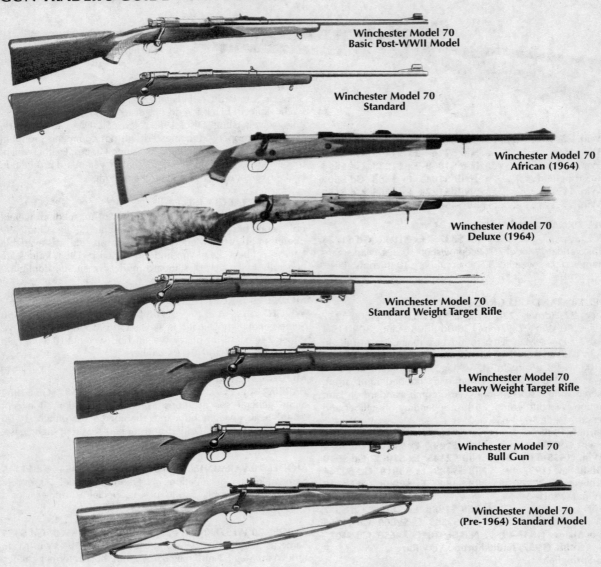

Winchester Model 70
Basic Post-WWII Model

Winchester Model 70
Standard

Winchester Model 70
African (1964)

Winchester Model 70
Deluxe (1964)

Winchester Model 70
Standard Weight Target Rifle

Winchester Model 70
Heavy Weight Target Rifle

Winchester Model 70
Bull Gun

Winchester Model 70
(Pre-1964) Standard Model

stock w/military oil finish, forearm rail for standard accessories, vertically adj. buttplate. Made in 1971. Value shown is for rifle w/o sights.

MODEL 70 MAGNUM

Calibers: 7mm Rem. Mag.; .264, .300, .338 Win. Mag.; .375 H&H Mag. Three round magazine. 24-in. bbl. Weight: 7.75 to 8.5 lbs. Sights: Open rear; hooded ramp front. Monte Carlo stock w/cheekpiece, checkering, twin stock-reinforcing bolts, recoil pad, swivels. Made 1964-71.

375 H&H Mag. . . . . **NiB $1043 Ex $787 Gd $678**
Other calibers. . . . . **NiB $800 Ex $687 Gd $473**

MODEL 70 MANNLICHER . . **NiB $1266 Ex $1090 Gd $789**

Calibers: .243, .270, .308 Win., .30-06. Five round box magazine. 19-in. bbl. Sights: open rear; hooded ramp front. Weight: 7.5 lbs. Mannlicher-style stock w/Monte Carlo comb and cheekpiece, checkering, steel forend cap, QD sling swivels. Made 1969-71.

MODEL 70 STANDARD . . . . . . NiB $788 Ex $577 Gd $400

Calibers: .22-250, .222 Rem., .227, .243, .270, .308 Win., .30-06. Five round box magazine. 22-in. bbl. Weight: 7.5 lbs. Sights: Open rear; hooded ramp front. Monte Carlo stock w/ cheekpiece, checkering, swivels. Made 1964-71.

MODEL 70 TARGET . . . . . . NiB $4200 Ex $2765 Gd $1489

Calibers: .308 Win. (7.62 NATO) and .30-06. Five round box magazine. 24-in. heavy bbl. Blocks for target scope. No factory sights installed, but drilled and tapped for front and rear sights. Weight: 10.25 lbs. High-comb Marksman-style stock, aluminum hand stop, swivels. Straight-grain, one-piece stock w/sling swivels, but no checkering. Made 1964-71.

MODEL 70 VARMINT . . . . . NiB $2160 Ex $1576 Gd $1009

Same as Model 70 Standard except w/24-in. target weight bbl., blocks for target scope. No factory sights installed, but drilled and tapped for front and rear sights. Available in calibers .22-250, .222 Rem., and .243 Win. only. Weight: 9.75 lbs. Made 1964-71.

1972-TYPE MODEL 70

MODEL 70 AFRICAN . . . . NiB $909 Ex $733 Gd $523
Similar to Model 70 Magnum except w/22-in. bbl. caliber .458 Win. Mag. w/special African open rear sight, reinforced stock w/ebony forend tip, detachable swivels and sling; front sling swivel stud attached to bbl. Weight: 8.5 lbs. Made 1972-92.

MODEL 70 CLASSIC SM
Similar to Model 70 Classic Sporter except w/checkered black composite stock and matte metal finish. Made 1994-96.

MODEL 70 CLASSIC SM	NiB $765	Ex $595	Gd $355
.375 H&H	NiB $944	Ex $765	Gd $535
w/BOSS, add			$150
w/open sights, add			$50

MODEL 70 CLASSIC SPORTER
Similar to Model 70 Sporter except w/pre-64-style action w/ controlled round feeding, classic-style stock. Optional open sights. Made 1994-2006.

Standard model	NiB $835	Ex $599	Gd $456
w/BOSS, add			$150
w/open sights, add			$50

MODEL 70 CLASSIC SPORTER STAINLESS
Similar to Model 70 Classic Sporter except w/matte stainless steel finish. Weight: 7.5 lbs. No sights. Made 1994-2006.

Standard model	NiB $875	Ex $679	Gd $369
Magnum model	NiB $845	Ex $743	Gd $498
w/BOSS, add			$126

MODEL 70 CUSTOM SHARPSHOOTER
Calibers: .22-250, .223, .308 Win., .300 Win. Mag. 24- or 26-in. bbl. 44.5 in. overall (24-in. bbl.). Weight: 11 lbs. Custom-fitted, hand-honed action. McMillan A-2 target-style stock. Matte blue or stainless finish. Made 1992-96.

Blued model	NiB $2145	Ex $1598	Gd $1195
NiB $2145 Ex $1598 Gd $1195	NiB $2167	Ex $1620	Gd $2125

MODEL 70 CUSTOM SPORTING SHARPSHOOTER
Similar to Custom Sharpshooter Model except w/sporter-style gray composite stock. Stainless 24- or 26-in. bbl. w/blued receiver. Calibers: .270, 7mm STW, .300 Win. Mag. Made 1993-2006.

Blued model (disc. 1995)	NiB $2155	Ex $1635	Gd $1266
Stainless model	NiB $2260	Ex $1723	Gd $1319

MODEL 70 GOLDEN 50TH ANNIVERSARY EDITION
BOLT-ACTION RIFLE . . . . . . NiB $1693 Ex $1279 Gd $1039
Caliber: .300 Win. Three round magazine. 24-in. bbl. 44.5 in. overall. Weight: 7.75 lbs. Checkered American walnut stock. Hand-engraved American scroll pattern on bbl., receiver, magazine cover, trigger guard and pistol-grip cap. Sights: Adj. rear; hooded front ramp. Inscription on bbl. reads "The Rifleman's Rifle 1937 to 1987." Only 500 made 1986-87. (Value for guns in new condition.)

MODEL 70 FEATHERWEIGHT
CLASSIC . . . . NiB $735 Ex $520 Gd $449
Similar to Model 70 XTR Featherweight except w/controlled-rnd. feeding system. Calibers: .270, .280 and .30-06. Made 1992-2006.

MODEL 70 INTERNATIONAL
ARMY MATCH . . . . NiB $1095 Ex $944 Gd $654
Caliber: .308 Win. (7.62mm NATO). Five round magazine, clip slot in receiver bridge. 24-in. heavy barrel. Weight: 11 lbs. No sights, but drilled and tapped for front and rear iron sights, and/ or scope mounts. ISU target stock. Intro. 1973; disc.

MODEL 70 LIGHTWEIGHT . . . NiB $679 Ex $449 Gd $227
Calibers: .22-250 and .223 Rem.; .243, .270 and .308 Win.; .30-06 Springfield. Five round mag. capacity (6-rnd. .223 Rem.). 22-in. barrel. 42 to 42.5 in. overall. Weight: 6 to 6.25 lbs. Checkered classic straight stock. Sling swivel studs. Made 1986-95.

MODEL 70 MAGNUM
Same as Model 70 except w/3-rnd. magazine, 24-in. bbl., reinforced stock w/recoil pad. Weight: 7.75 lbs. (except 8.5 lbs. in .375 H&H Mag.). Calibers: .264 Win. Mag., 7mm Rem. Mag., .300 Win. Mag., .338 Win. Mag., .375 H&H Mag. Made 197-80.

.375 H&H Magnum	NiB $655	Ex $533	Gd $400
Other magnum calibers	NiB $554	Ex $495	Gd $388

MODEL 70 STANDARD . . . . . . NiB $677 Ex $439 Gd $331
Same as Model 70A except w/5-rnd. magazine, Monte Carlo stock w/cheekpiece, black forend tip and pistol-grip cap w/ white spacers, checkered pistol grip and forearm, detachable sling swivels. Same calibers plus .227 Win. Made 1972-80.

MODEL 70 STANDARD
CARBINE . . . . NiB $596 Ex $437 Gd $369
Same general specifications as Standard Model 70 except 19-in. bbl. and weight: 7.25 lbs. Shallow recoil pad. Walnut stock and forend w/traditional Model 70 checkering. Swivel studs. No sights, but drilled and tapped for scope mount.

MODEL 70 SPORTER DBM . . . . NiB $755 Ex $585 Gd $359
Same general specifications as Model 70 Sporter SSM except w/ detachable box magazine. Calibers: .22-250 (disc. 1994), .223 (disc. 1994), .243 (disc. 1994), .270, 7mm Rem. Mag., .308 (disc. 1994), .30-06, .300 Win. Mag. Made 1992-94.

S-model (w/iron sights) . . . . NiB $589 Ex $496 Gd $369

MODEL 70 STAINLESS
SPORTER SSM . . . . NiB $688 Ex $495 Gd $390
Same general specifications as Model 70 XTR Sporter except w/checkered black composite stock and matte finished receiver, bbl. and other metal parts. Calibers: .270, 7mm Rem. Mag., .30-06, .300 Win. Mag., .338 Win. Mag. Weight: 7.75 lbs. Made 1992 to 1994.

MODEL 70 CLASSIC
SUPER GRADE . . . . NiB $977 Ex $857 Gd $590
Calibers: .270, 7mm Rem. Mag., .30-06, .300 Win. Mag., .338 Win. Mag. Five round magazine (standard), 3-rnd. (magnum). 24-in. bbl. 44.5 in. overall. Weight: 7.75 lbs. Checkered walnut stock w/sculptured cheekpiece and tapered forend. Scope bases and rings, no sights. Controlled-rnd. feeding system. Made 1990-95. Improved in 1999. Disc. 2006.

MODEL 70 TARGET . . . . NiB $976 Ex $945 Gd $588
Calibers: .30-06 and .308 Win. (7.62mm NATO). Five round magazine. 26-in. heavy bbl. Weight: 10.5 lbs. No sights, but drilled and tapped for scope mount and open sights. High-comb

RIFLES

Winchester Model 70
International Army Match (1964)

Winchester Model 70
Mannlicher (1964)

Winchester Model 70
Standard (1964)

Winchester Model 70
Target (1964)

Winchester Model 70 African (1964)

Marksman-style target stock, aluminum hand stop and swivels. Intro. 1972. Disc.

MODEL 70 ULTRA MATCH . . NiB $1099 Ex $976 Gd $569
Similar to Model 70 Target but custom grade w/26-in. heavy bbl. w/deep counterbore, glass bedding, externally adj. trigger. Intro. 1972. Disc.

MODEL 70 VARMINT (HEAVY BARREL)
Same as Model 70 Standard except w/medium-heavy, counter-bored 26-in. bbl., no sights, stock w/less drop. Weight: 9 lbs. Calibers: .22-250 Rem., .223 Rem., .243 Win., .308 Win. Made 1972-93. Model 70 SHB, in .308 Win. only w/black synthetic stock and matte blue receiver/bbl. Made 1992-93.
Model 70 Varmint . . . . NiB $699 Ex $633 Gd $390
Model 70 SHB (synthetic stock,
   heavy bbl.) . . . . NiB $745 Ex $641 Gd $440

MODEL 70 WIN-CAM RIFLE . . NiB $576 Ex $488 Gd $338
Caliber: .270 Win. and .30-06 Springfield. 24-in. barrel. Camouflage one-piece laminated stock. Recoil pad. Drilled and tapped for scope. Made 1986-87.

MODEL 70 WINLITE
BOLT-ACTION RIFLE . . . . NiB $855 Ex $570 Gd $448
Calibers: .270 Win., .280 Rem., .30-06 Springfield, 7mm Rem., .300 Win. Mag., and .338 Win. Mag. Five round magazine; 3-rnd. for Magnum calibers. 22-in. bbl.; 24-in. for Magnum calibers. 42.5 in. overall; 44.5, Magnum calibers. Weight: 6.25 to 7 lbs. Fiberglass stock w/rubber recoil pad, sling swivel studs. Made 1986-90.

MODEL 70 WIN-TUFF BOLT-ACTION RIFLE
Calibers: .22-250, .223, .243, .270, .308 and .30-06 Springfield. 22-in. bbl. Weight: 6.25–7 lbs. Laminated dye-shaded brown wood stock w/recoil pad. Barrel drilled and tapped for scope. Swivel studs. FWT Model made from 1986 to 1994. LW Model intro. 1992.
Featherweight model . . . . NiB $590 Ex $470 Gd $388
Lightweight model
   (Made 1992–93) . . . . NiB $590 Ex $470 Gd $388

MODEL 70 XTR
FEATHERWEIGHT. . . . . NiB $590 Ex $470 Gd $388
Similar to Standard Win. Model 70 except lightweight American walnut stock w/classic Schnabel forend, checkered. 22-in. bbl., hooded blade front sight, folding leaf rear sight. Stainless-steel magazine follower. Weight: 6.75 lbs. Made 1984-94.

MODEL 70 XTR SPORTER
RIFLE. NiB $744 Ex $545 Gd $376
Calibers: .264 Win. Mag., 7mm Rem. Mag., .300 Win. Mag., .200 Weatherby Mag., and .338 Win. Mag. Three round maga-zine. 24-in. barrel. 44.5 in. overall. Weight: 7.75 lbs. Walnut Monte Carlo stock. Rubber buttpad. Receiver tapped and drilled for scope mounting. Made 1986-94.

MODEL 70 XTR SPORTER
MAGNUM. . . . . NiB $598 Ex $482 Gd $369
Calibers: .264 Win. Mag., 7mm Rem. Mag., .300 Win. Mag., .338 Win. Mag. Three round magazine. 24-in. bbl. 44.5 in. overall. Weight: 7.75 lbs. No sights furnished, optional adj. folding leaf rear; hooded ramp. Receiver drilled and tapped for scope. Checkered American walnut Monte Carlo-style stock w/ satin finish. Made 1986-94.

MODEL 70 XTR SPORTER
VARMINT . . . . NiB $707 Ex $420 Gd $268
Same general specifications as Model 70 XTR Sporter, except in calibers .223, .22-250, .243 only. Checkered American walnut Monte Carlo-style stock w/cheekpiece. Made 1986-94.

MODEL 70A . . . . NiB $450 Ex $316 Gd $231
Calibers: .222 Rem., .22-250, .243 Win., .25-06, .270 Win., .30-06, .308 Win. Four round magazine. 22-in. bbl. (except 24- or 26-in. in 25-06). Weight: 7.5 lbs. Sights: Open rear; hooded ramp front. Monte Carlo stock w/checkered pistol grip and forearm, sling swivels. Made 1972-78.

MODEL 70A MAGNUM . . . . . . NiB $476 Ex $316 Gd $236
Same as Model 70A except w/3-rnd. magazine, 24-in. bbl., recoil pad. Weight: 7.75 lbs. Calibers: .264 Win. Mag., 7mm Rem. Mag., .300 Win. Mag. Made 1972-78.

MODEL 70 ULTIMATE CLASSIC BOLT-ACTION RIFLE
Calibers: .25-06 Rem., .264 Win., .270 Win., .270 Wby. Mag., .280 Rem., 7mm Rem. Mag., 7mm STW, .30-06, Mag., .300 Win. Mag., .300 Wby. Mag., .300 H&H Mag., .338 Win. Mag., .340 Wby. Mag., .35 Whelen, .375 H&H Mag., .416 Rem. Mag. and .458 Win. Mag. Three, 4- or 5-rnd. magazine. 22- 24- 26-in. stainless bbl. in various configurations including: full-fluted tapered round, half round and half octagonal or tapered full octagonal. Weight: 7.75 to 9.25 lbs. Checkered fancy walnut stock. Made in 1995.
Model 70 Ultimate Classic . NiB $2153 Ex $1999 Gd $1098
Magnum calibers (.375 H&H, .416 and .458), add. $250

MODEL 70 LAMINATED STAINLESS BOLT-ACTION
RIFLE. . . . . NiB $2150 Ex $1792 Gd $952
Calibers: .270 Win., .30-06 Spfld., 7mm Rem. Mag., .300 Win. Mag., and .338 Win. Mag. Five round magazine. 24-in. bbl. 44.75 in. overall. Weight: 8 to 8.525 lbs. Gray/Black laminated stock. Made 1998-99.

MODEL 70 CHARACTERISTICS

MODEL 70 FIRST MODEL (SERIAL NUMBERS 1 – 80,000)
First manufactured in 1936; first sold in 1937. Receiver drilled for Lyman No. 57W or No. 48WJS receiver peep sights. Also drilled and tapped for Lyman or Fecker scope sight block. Weight w/24-in. bbl. in all calibers except .375 H&H Mag.: 8.25 lbs. 9 lbs. in H&H Mag. Early type safety located on bolt top. Production of this model ended in 1942 near serial number 80,000 due to World War II. Cross-sectional view of the pre-1964 Winchester Model 70's speed lock action. This action cocks on the opening movement of the bolt with polished, smooth-functioning cams and guide lug, ensuring fast and smooth operation.

MODEL 70 SECOND MODEL
(SERIAL NUMBERS 80,000–350,000)
All civilian production of Winchester Model 70 rifles halted during World War II. Production resumed in 1947 w/ improved safety and integral front-sight ramp. Serial numbers started at around 80,000. This model type was produced until 1954, ending around serial number 350,000.

MODEL 70 THIRD MODEL (SERIAL NUMBERS 350,000 – 400,000)
This variety was manufactured from 1954 to 1960 and retained many features of the Second Model except that a folding rear sight replaced the earlier type and front-sight ramps were brazed onto the bbl. rather than being an integral part of the bbl. The Model 70 Featherweight Rifle was intro. in 1954 in .308 WCF caliber. It was fitted w/light 22-in. bbl. and was also available w/either a Monte Carlo or Standard stock. The .243 Win. cartridge was added in 1955 in all grades of the Winchester Model 70 except the National Match and Bull Gun models. The .358 Win. cartridge was also intro. in 1955, along w/new Varmint Model chambered in .243 caliber only.

MODEL 70 FOURTH MODEL (SERIAL NUMBERS 400,000 – 500,000)
Different markings were inscribed on the barrels of these models and new magnum calibers were added; that is, .264 Win Mag., .338 Win. Mag, and .458 Win. Mag. All bbls. of this variation were about 0.13 in. shorter than previous ones. The .22 Hornet and .257 Roberts were disc. in 1962; the .358 Win. caliber in 1963.

MODEL 70 FIFTH MODEL (SERIAL NUMBERS 500,000 TO ABOUT 570,000)
These rifles may be recognized by slightly smaller checkering patterns and slightly smaller lightweight stocks. Featherweight bbls. were marked "Featherweight." Webbed recoil pads were furnished on magnum calibers.

POST-1964 MODEL 70 RIFLES

In 1964, the Winchester-Western Division of Olin Industries claimed that they were losing money on every Model 70 they produced. Both labor and material costs had increased to a level that could no longer be ignored. Other models followed suit. Consequently, sweeping changes were made to the entire Winchester line. Many of the older, less popular models were discontinued. Models that were to remain in production were modified for lower production costs.

1964 WINCHESTER MODEL 70 RIFLES SERIAL NUMBERS 570,000 TO ABOUT 707,000)
The first version of the "New Model 70s" utilized a free-floating barrel, swaged rifle bore, new stock and sights, new type of bolt and receiver, and a different finish throughout on both the wood and metal parts. The featherweight grade was dropped, but six other grades were available in this new line:
Standard
Deluxe (Replaced Previous Super Grade)
Magnum
Varmint
Target
African

1966 MODEL 70 RIFLES (SERIAL NUMBERS 707,000-G TO ABOUT 1,005,000)
In general, this group of Model 70s had fancier wood checkering, cross-bolt stock reinforcement, improved wood finish and improved action. One cross-bolt reinforcement was used on standard guns. Magnum calibers, however, used an additional forward cross-bolt and red recoil pad. The free-floating barrel clearance forward of the breech taper was reduced in thickness. Impressed checkering was used on the Deluxe models until 1968. Hand checkering was once again used on Deluxe and Carbine models in 1969; the big, red "W" was removed from all grip caps. A new, red safety-indicator and undercut cheekpiece was introduced in 1971.

RIFLES

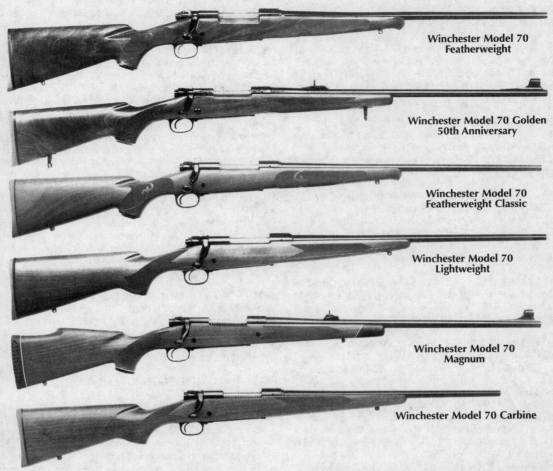

Winchester Model 70
Featherweight

Winchester Model 70 Golden
50th Anniversary

Winchester Model 70
Featherweight Classic

Winchester Model 70
Lightweight

Winchester Model 70
Magnum

Winchester Model 70 Carbine

1972 MODEL 70 RIFLES
(SERIAL NUMBERS G1,005,000 TO ABOUT G1,360,000)

Both the barrels and receivers for this variety of Model 70s were made from chrome molybdenum (C-M) steel. The barrels were tapered w/spiral rifling, ranging in length from 22 to 24 in. Calibers .222 Rem., .227 Win. .22-250, .243 Win., .25-06, .270, .308 Win., .30-06 and .458 WM used the 22-in. length, while the following calibers used the 24-in. length: .222 Rem., .22-250, .243 Win., .264 Win. Mag., 7mm Mag., .300 and .375 H&H Mag. The .227 Win caliber was dropped in 1973; Mannlicher stocks were also disc. in 1973. The receiver for this variety of Model 70s was machined from a block of C-M steel. A new improved anti-bind bolt was introduced along with a new type of ejector. Other improvements included hand-cut checkering, pistol-grip stocks with pistol-grip and dark forend caps. An improved satin wood finish was also utilized.

1978 MODEL 70 RIFLES (SERIAL NUMBERS BEGAN
AROUND G1,360,000)

This variety of Model 70 was similar to the 1972 version except that a new XTR style was added which featured high-luster wood and metal finishes, fine-cut checkering, and similar embellishments. All Model 70 rifles made during this period used the XTR style; no standard models were available. In 1981, beginning with serial number G1,440,000 (approximately), a Featherweight version of the Model 70 XTR was introduced. The receiver was identical to the 1978 XTR, but lighter barrels were fitted. Stocks were changed to a lighter design with larger scroll checkering patterns and a Schnabel forend with no Monte Carlo

comb. A satin sheen stock finish on the featherweight version replaced the high-luster finish used on the other XTR models. A new-style red buttplate with thick, black rubber liner was used on the Featherweight models. The grip cap was also redesigned for this model. 2006 – U.S. Repeating Arms Model 70 RIFLES

In the early 1980s, negotiations began between Olin Industries and an employee-based corporation. The result of these negotiations ended with Olin selling all tools, machinery, supplies, etc. at the New Haven plant to the newly-formed corporation which was eventually named U.S. Repeating Arms Company. Furthermore, U.S. Repeating Arms Company purchased the right to use the Winchester name and logo. Winchester Model 70s went through very few changes the first two years after the transition. However, in 1984, the Featherweight Model 70 XTR rifles were offered in a new short action for .22-250 Rem., .223 Rem., .243 Win. and .308 Win. calibers, in addition to their standard action which was used for the longer cartridges. A new Model 70 lightweight carbine was also introduced this same year. Two additional models were introduced in 1985 — the Model 70 Lightweight Mini-Carbine Short Action and the Model 70 XTR Sporter Varmint. The Model 70 Winlite appeared in the 1986 "Winchester" catalog, along with two economy versions of the Model 70 — the Winchester Ranger and the Ranger Youth Carbine. Five or six different versions of the Winchester Model 70 had been sufficient for 28 years (1937 to 1964). Now, changes in design and the addition of new models each year seemed to be necessary to keep the rifle alive. New models were added, old models dropped, changed in design, etc., on a regular basis. Still, the Winchester Model 70 Bolt-Action Repeating Rifle — in any of its variations — is the most popular bolt-action rifle ever built.

**Winchester Model 70
XTR Sporter**

Winchester Model 70A

1992 through 2006 Model 70 Rifles

By 1992 Winchester decided to bring back the control round feed system, naming it the Classic model series. Models include the Classic Featherweight, Classic Sporter, Classic Laminate, and Classic DBM. Winchester during this period also introduced stainless steel models, like the Classic Stainless, Classic Laminate Stainless, and Coyote Stainless Laminate. Economy models include the Ranger and Ranger Compact. Varmint and hunting models were now being equipped with composite stocks like the Stealth, Super Shadow, Ultimate Shadow, and Pro Shadow. In 1997, Belgian Wallon Region government purchased U.S. Repeating Arms along with Browning Arms and Fabrique Nationale (FN). On March 31, 2006, Winchester closed the U.S Repeating Arms plant. A sad day in New Haven, Connecticut.

MODEL 70 BLACK SHADOW . NiB $556 Ex $379 Gd $300
Calibers: .243 Win., .270 Win., .300 Win. Mag., .308 Win., .338 Win. Mag., .30-06 Spfld., 7mm STW., 7mm Rem. Mag. and 7mm-08 Rem. Three, 4- or 5-rnd. magazine. 20- 24- 25- or 26-in. bbls. 39.5 to 46.75 in. overall.Weight: 6.5 to 8.25 lbs. Composite, Walnut or Gray/Black laminated stocks. Made 1998-2006.

**MODEL 70 CLASSIC CAMO BOLT-ACTION
RIFLE . . . . NiB $990 Ex $887 Gd $554**
Calibers: .270 Win., 30-06 Spfld., 7mm Rem. Mag., .300 Win. Mag. Three or 5-rnd. magazine. 24- or 26-in. bbl. 44.75 to 46.75 in. overall. Weight; 7.25 to 7.5 lbs. Mossy Oak finish and composite stock. Made 1998-2006.

**MODEL 70 CLASSIC COMPACT
BOLT-ACTION RIFLE . . . . . NiB $3329 Ex $2221 Gd $2069**
Calibers: .243 Win., .308 Win., and 7mm-08 Rem. Three round magazine. 20-in. bbl., 39.5 in. overall. Weight: 6.5 lbs. Walnut stock. Made 1998-2006.

**MODEL 70 CLASSIC LAREDO RANGE
HUNTER BOLT-ACTION RIFLE**
Calibers: 7mm STW, 7mm Rem. mag., .300 Win. Mag. Three round magazine. 26-in. bbl. 46.75 in. overall. Weight: 9.5 lbs. Composite stock. Made 1996-99.
Classic Laredo . . . . NiB $788 Ex $675 Gd $500
w/fluted bbl. (intro. 1998) . . . . NiB $833 Ex $733 Gd $513
Bossa Classic model . . . . NiB $800 Ex $689 Gd $466

MODEL 70 COYOTE . . . . NiB $875 Ex $612 Gd $432
Calibers: .22-250 Rem., .223 Rem., and .243 Win. Five or 6-rnd. magazine. 24- in. bbl., 44 in. overall. Weight: 9 lbs. Medium-heavy stainless steel barrel w/laminated stock. Reverse taper forend. Made 1999. Disc.

**MODEL 70 RANGER COMPACT
RIFLE . . . . NiB $555 Ex $369 Gd $257**
Calibers: .22-250 Rem., .223 Rem., .243 Win., 7mm-08 Rem., Mag., and .308 Win. Five or 6-rnd. magazine. 20- or 22-in. bbl. 41 in. overall. Weight: 6.5 lbs. Adjustable TRUGLO front and rear fiber optic sights. Push-feed action. Made 1999-2000.

MODEL 70 STEALTH RIFLE . . . . NiB $920 Ex $707 Gd $449
Varminter style bolt-action rifle. Calibers: .22-250 Rem., .223 Rem., and .308 Win. Five or 6-rnd. magazine. 26- in. bbl. 46 in. overall. Weight: 10.75 lbs. Black synthetic stock w/Pillar

Plus Accu Block and full-length aluminum bedding block. Matte blue finish. Made 1999. Disc.

2006 through Present Model 70 Rifles

By August 2006, Olin Corporation, owner of the Winchester trademarks, signed a license agreement with Browning to produce Winchester brand rifles and shotguns. Browning and the former licensee, U.S. Repeating Arms Company, are both subsidiaries of FN Herstal. In 2008, Winchester reintroduced the Model 70 control round feed system and manufactured the rifles in the FN factory in Columbia, South Carolina. In 2013 FN relocated Model 70 assembly to Portugal. Since 2015 the barrel stamp on a Model 70 reads: "Imported by BACO, Inc., Morgan, Utah – Made in Portugal by Browning Viana."

MODEL 71 LEVER-ACTION REPEATER
Solid frame. Caliber: .348 Win. Four round tubular magazine. 20- or 24-in. bbl. Weight: 8 lbs. Sights: Open or peep rear; bead front on ramp w/hood. Walnut stock. Made 1935-57.
**Standard Grade
(no checkering, grip cap,
sling or swivels) . . . . NiB $1370 Ex $1167 Gd $789**
**Special Grade (checkered pistol
grip and forearm, grip cap,
QD swivels and sling) . . NiB $2144 Ex $1798 Gd $1129**
**Special Grade carbine (w/20-in. bbl.,
disc. 1940) . . . . NiB $2695 Ex $2155 Gd $1769**
**Standard Grade carbine
(20-in. bbl., disc. 1940) . NiB $2266 Ex $1880 Gd $1249**

**MODEL 72 BOLT-ACTION
REPEATER . . . . NiB $525 Ex $266 Gd $189**
Tubular magazine. Takedown. Caliber: .22 Short, Long, LR. Magazine holds 20 Short, 16 Long or 15 LR. 25-in. bbl. Weight: 5.75 lbs. Sights: Peep or open rear; bead front. Plain pistol-grip stock. Made 1938-59.

MODEL 73 LEVER-ACTION REPEATER
See Model 1873 rifles, carbines, "One of One Thousand" and other variations of this model at the beginning of Winchester Rifle Section. Note: The Winchester Model 1873 was the first lever-action repeating rifle bearing the Winchester name.

**MODEL 74 SELF-LOADING
RIFLE . . . . NiB $389 Ex $290 Gd $198**
Takedown. Calibers: .22 Short only, .22 LR only. Tubular magazine in buttstock holds 20 Short, 14 LR. 24-in. bbl. Weight: 6.25 lbs. Sights: Open rear; bead front. Plain pistol-grip stock, one-piece. Made 1939-55.

MODEL 75 SPORTING RIFLE . . NiB $600 Ex $299 Gd $210
Same as Model 75 Target except has 24-in. bbl., checkered sporter stock, open rear sight; bead front on hooded ramp, weight: 5.5 lbs.

MODEL 75 TARGET RIFLE . . . . NiB $600 Ex $299 Gd $210
Caliber: .22 LR. 5- or 10-rnd. box magazine. 28-in. bbl. Weight: 8.75 lbs. Target sights (Lyman, Redfield or Winchester). Target stock w/pistol grip and semi-beavertail forearm, swivels and sling. Made 1938-59.

RIFLES

MODEL 77 SEMIAUTO RIFLE,
CLIP TYPE . . . . **NiB $322 Ex $190 Gd $133**
Solid frame. Caliber: .22 LR. Eight round clip magazine. 22-in. bbl. Weight: About 5.5 lbs. Sights: Open rear; bead front. Plain, one-piece pistol-grip stock. Made 1955-63.

MODEL 77, TUBULAR
MAGAZINE . . . . **NiB $379 Ex $269 Gd $200**
Same as Model 77. Clip type except has tubular magazine holding 15 rounds. Made 1955-63.

MODEL 86 CARBINE AND RIFLE
See Model 1886 at beginning of Winchester Rifle section.

MODEL 88 CARBINE
Same as Model 88 Rifle except has 19-in. bbl., plain carbine-style stock and forearm with bbl. band. Weight: 7 lbs. Made 1968 to 1973.
Standard calibers . . . . **NiB $1335 Ex $1098 Gd $866**
.284 Win. . . . . **NiB $2095 Ex $1788 Gd $1077**

MODEL 88 LEVER-ACTION RIFLE
Hammerless. Calibers: .243 Win., .284 Win., .308 Win., .358 Win. Four round box magazine. Three round in pre-1963 models and in .284. 22-in. bbl. Weight: About 7.25 lbs. One-piece walnut stock with pistol-grip, swivels (1965 and later models have basket-weave ornamentation instead of checkering). Made 1955-73. Note: .243 and .358 introduced 1956, later discontinued 1964; .284 introduced 1963.
Model 88 (checkered stock) . . **NiB $1045 Ex $744 Gd $469**
w/basketweave checkering . . . **NiB $1045 Ex $744 Gd $469**
.243 Win. . . . . **NiB $1269 Ex $1088 Gd $899**
.284 Win. . . . . **NiB $2300 Ex $1969 Gd $1675**

MODEL 94 PRE WWII, POST-'64 TO 2006
NOTE: *Post-'64 Model 94 rifles began with serial number 2700000. In 1992 a crossbolt safety was added except for "100th Anniversary" models made in 1994. Manufacturing ceased in New Haven, CT, in 2006.*

MODEL 94 ANTIQUE CARBINE NiB $588 Ex $448 Gd $290
Same as standard Post-64 Model 94 Carbine except has decorative scrollwork and casehardened receiver, brass-plated loading gate, saddle ring; caliber .30-30 only. Made 1964-84.

MODEL 94 CARBINE
Same as Model 1894 Rifle except 20-in. round bbl., 6-rnd. full-length magazine. Weight: About 6.5 lbs. Originally made in calibers .25-35, .30-30, .32 Special and .38-55. From 1940 to 1964 barrels were rollmarked "Model 94" These models are all considerd "pre-'64" models and demand a premium. Original version discontinued 1964.
Pre WWII (under
  No. 1,300,000) . . . . **NiB $7250 Ex $5988 Gd $3866**
Postwar, pre-1964
  (under No. 2,707,000) . . . . . **NiB $865 Ex $707 Gd $530**

MODEL 94 CLASSIC CARBINE . . NiB $655 Ex $443 Gd $400
Same as Canadian Centennial '67 Commemorative Carbine except without commemorative details; has scroll-engraved receiver, gold-plated loading gate. Made 1967-70.

MODEL 94 CLASSIC RIFLE . . NiB $6744 Ex $5467 Gd $4388
Same as Centennial '67 Commemorative Rifle except without commemorative details; has scroll-engraved receiver, gold-plated loading gate. Made 1968-70.

MODEL 94 DELUXE CARBINE . . NiB $845 Ex $600 Gd $400
Caliber: .30-30 Win. Six round magazine. 20-in. bbl. 37.75 in. overall. Weight: 6.5 lbs. Semi-fancy American walnut stock with rubber buttpad, long forearm and specially cut checkering. Engraved with "Deluxe" script. Made 1987-2006.

MODEL 94 LONG BARREL
RIFLE. . . . . **NiB $707 Ex $449 Gd $370**
Caliber: .30-30 Win. Seven round magazine. 24-in. bbl. 41.75 in. overall. Weight: 7 lbs. American walnut stock. Blade front sight. Made 1987-2006.

MODEL 94 TRAPPER
Same as Model 94 Carbine except w/16-in. bbl. and weighs 6 lbs. 2 oz. Angle Eject introduced in 1985 also chambered for .357 Mag., .44 Mag. and .45 LC. Made 1980-2006.
Top eject (disc. 1984) . . . . **NiB $755 Ex $573 Gd $388**
Angle eject (.30-30) . . . . **NiB $445 Ex $306 Gd $200**
.357 Mag., .44 mag., .45 LC, add **$50**

MODEL 94 WIN-TUFF RIFLE . . NiB $556 Ex $400 Gd $297
Caliber: .30-30 Win. Six round magazine. 20-in. bbl. 37.75 in. overall. Weight: 6.5 lbs. Brown laminated wood stock. Made 198 to -2006.

MODEL 94 WRANGLER CARBINE
Same as standard Model 94 Carbine except has 16-in. bbl., engraved receiver and chambered for .32 Special & .38-55 Win.
Top-eject model (disc. 1984) . . **NiB $623 Ex $414 Gd $331**
Wranger II, angle-eject model
  (disc. 1985) . . . . **NiB $544 Ex $387 Gd $244**

MODEL 94 XTR BIG BORE
Modified Model 94 action for added strength. Calibers: .307 Win., .356 Win., .375 Win. or .444 Marlin. 20-in. bbl. Six round magazine. Rubber buttpad. Checkered stock and forearm. Weight: 6.5 lbs. Made 1978-2006.
Top eject (disc. 1984) . . . . **NiB $755 Ex $577 Gd $488**
Angle eject (intro. 1985) . . . . . . **NiB $441 Ex $379 Gd $255**
.356 Win. or .375 Win., add **$200**

MODEL 94 XTR LEVER-ACTION RIFLE
Same general specifications as standard M94 and Angle Eject M94 except chambered for .30-30 Win. and 7-30 Waters and has 20- or 24-in. bbl. Weight: 6.5 to 7 lbs. Made 1978-88 by U.S. Repeating Arms.
Top eject (disc. 1984) . . . . **NiB $744 Ex $ 533 Gd $445**
Angle eject (.30-30) . . . . **NiB $744 Ex $533 Gd $445**
Deluxe angle eject (.30-30) . . . **NiB $744 Ex $533 Gd $445**
7-30 Waters, add **$100**

NOTE: *In 2010 production of Model 94 rifles resumed with manufacturing done by Miroku in Japan and continues to date.*

MODEL 94 CARBINE . . . . . . **NiB $1199 EX $1000 Gd $930**
Similar to Post-'64 Model 94. Calibers: .30-30 and .38-55. 20-in. bbl. 7-rnd. magazine. Top tang safety. Rebounding hammer. Plain walnut stock and forearm. Weight: 6.5 lbs. Made 2013 to present.
Short Rifle (2012-present) . . . . **NiB $1229 Ex $990 Gd $900**
Sporter (half round, half octagon bbl., checkered stock,
  2011-present) . . . . **NiB $1399 Ex $1280 Gd $955**
Trails End Takedown
  (.30-30, .38-55, .450 Marlin;
  round bbl.; checkered stock;
  2012-present) . . . . **NiB $1495 Ex $1379 Gd $1055**

Winchester Model 70 Black Shadow

Winchester Model 72

Winchester Model 74

MODEL 94 COMMEMORATIVES

MODEL 94 ANTLERED GAME . NiB $775 Ex $639 Gd $482
Standard Model 94 action. Gold-colored medallion inlaid in stock. Antique gold-plated receiver, lever tang and bbl. bands. Medallion and receiver engraved with elk, moose, deer and caribou. 20.5-in. bbl. Curved steel buttplate. In .30-30 caliber. 19,999 made in 1978.

MODEL 94 BICENTENNIAL
'76 CARBINE. . . . . NiB $944 Ex $812 Gd $654
Same as Standard Model 94 Carbine except caliber .30-30 Win. only; antique silver-finished, engraved receiver; stock and forearm of fancy walnut, checkered, Bicentennial medallion embedded in buttstock, curved buttplate. 20,000 made in 1976.

MODEL 94 BUFFALO BILL COMMEMORATIVE
Same as Centennial '66 Rifle except receiver is black-chromed, scroll-engraved and bears name "Buffalo Bill"; hammer, trigger, loading gate, saddle ring, forearm cap, and buttplate are nickel-plated; Buffalo Bill Memorial Assn. commemorative medallion embedded in buttstock; "Buffalo Bill Commemorative" inscribed on bbl., facsimile signature "W.F. Cody, Chief of Scouts" on tang. Carbine has 20-in. bbl., 6-rnd. magazine, 7-lb. weight. 112,923 made in 1968.
Carbine. . . . . NiB $733 Ex $597 Gd $433
Rifle . . . . NiB $778 Ex $650 Gd $469
Matched carbine/rifle set . . NiB $1590 Ex $1370 Gd $1007

CANADIAN CENTENNIAL '67 COMMEMORATIVE
Same as Centennial '66 Rifle except receiver engraved with maple leaves and forearm cap is black-chromed, buttplate is blued, commemorative inscription in gold on barrel and top tang: "Canadian Centennial 1867–1967." Carbine has 20-in. bbl., 6-rnd. magazine, weight: 7 lb., 90,398 made in 1967.
Carbine. . . . . NiB $667 Ex $498 Gd $300
Rifle . . . . NiB $667 Ex $498 Gd $300
Matched carbine/rifle set . . . . . NiB $725 Ex $535 Gd $350

CENTENNIAL '66 COMMEMORATIVE
Commemorates Winchester's 100th anniversary. Standard Model 94 action. Caliber: .30-30. Full-length magazine holds 8 rounds. 26-in. octagon bbl. Weight: 8 lbs. Gold-plated receiver and forearm cap. Sights: Open rear; post front. Saddle ring.

Walnut buttstock and forearm with high-gloss finish, solid brass buttplate. Commemorative inscription on bbl. and top tang of receiver. 100,478 made in 1966.
Carbine . . . . NiB $727 Ex $537 Gd $353
Rifle . . . . NiB $727 Ex $537 Gd $353
Matched carbine/rifle set . . . NiB $1579 Ex $1355 Gd $954

MODEL 94 CHEYENNE
COMMEMORATIVE . . . . NiB $976 Ex $755 Gd $642
Available in Canada only. Same as Standard Model 94 Carbine except chambered for .44-40. 11,227 made in 1977.

MODEL 94 CHIEF CRAZY HORSE
COMMEMORATIVE . . . . NiB $888 Ex $733 Gd $521
Cailber: .38-55, 7-rnd. tubular magazine. 24-in. bbl., 41.75 in. overall. Walnut stock with medallion of the United Sioux Tribes; buttstock and forend also decorated with brass tacks. Engraved receiver. Open rear sights; bead front sight. 19,999 made in 1983.

MODEL 94 COLT COMMEMORATIVE
CARBINE SET . . . . NiB $2689 Ex $2077 Gd $1370
Standard Model 94 action. Caliber: .44-40 Win. 20-in. bbl. Weight: 6.25 lbs. Features the horse-and-rider trademark and distinctive WC monogram in gold etching on left side of receiver. Sold in set with Colt Single Action Revolver chambered for same caliber.

MODEL 94 COWBOY COMMEMORATIVE CARBINE
Same as Standard Model 94 Carbine except caliber .30-30 only; nickel-plated receiver, tangs, lever, bbl. bands; engraved receiver, "Cowboy Commemorative" on bbl., commemorative medallion embedded in buttstock; curved buttplate. 20,915 made in 1970. Nickel-silver medallion inlaid in stock. Antique silver-plated receiver engraved with scenes of the old frontier. Checkered walnut stock and forearm. 19,999 made in 1970.
Cowboy carbine . . . . NiB $744 Ex $588 Gd $414
1 of 300 model . . . . NiB $3278 Ex $2966 Gd $2288

MODEL 94 GOLDEN SPIKE COMMEMORATIVE
CARBINE. . . . . NiB $855 Ex $670 Gd $495
Same as Standard Model 94 Carbine except caliber .30-30 only; gold-plated receiver, tangs and bbl. bands; engraved receiver, commemorative medallion embedded in stock. 64,758 made in 1969.

MODEL 94 ILLINOIS SESQUICENTENNIAL
COMMEMORATIVE CARBINE... NiB $622 Ex $398 Gd $287

Same as Standard Model 94 Carbine except caliber .30-30 only; gold-plated buttplate, trigger, loading gate, and saddle ring; receiver engraved with profile of Lincoln, commemorative inscription on receiver, bbl.; souvenir medallion embedded in stock. 31,124 made in 1968.

MODEL 94 LEGENDARY FRONTIERSMEN
COMMEMORATIVE .... NiB $769 Ex $655 Gd $488

Standard Model 94 action. Caliber: .39-55. 24-in. round bbl. Nickel-silver medallion inlaid in stock. Antique silver-plated receiver engraved with scenes of the old frontier. Checkered walnut stock and forearm. 19,999 made in 1979.

MODEL 94 LEGENDARY LAWMEN
COMMEMORATIVE .... NiB $769 Ex $655 Gd $488

Same as Standard Model 94 Carbine except .30-30 Win. only; antique silver-plated receiver engraved with action law-enforcement scenes. 16-in. Trapper bbl., antique silver-plated bbl. bands. 19,999 made in 1978.

MODEL 94 LONE STAR COMMEMORATIVE
Same as Theodore Roosevelt Rifle except yellow-gold plating; "Lone Star" engraving on receiver and bbl., commemorative medallion embedded in buttstock. 30,669 made in 1970.

Rifle or carbine............. NiB $754 Ex $598 Gd $449
Matched carbine/rifle set ... NiB $1499 Ex $1288 Gd $955

MODEL 94 NRA CENTENNIAL
MUSKET .... NiB $707 Ex $597 Gd $479

Commemorates 100th anniversary of National Rifle Association of America. Standard Model 94 action. Caliber: .30-30. Seven round magazine. 26-in. bbl. Sights: Military folding rear; blade front. Black chrome-finished receiver engraved "NRA 1871–1971" plus scrollwork. Barrel inscribed "NRA Centennial Musket." Musket-style buttstock and full-length forearm; commemorative medallion embedded in buttstock. Weight: 7.13 lbs. Made in 1971.

MODEL 94 NRA CENTENNIAL
RIFLE.................... NiB $715 Ex $609 Gd $520

Same as Model 94 Rifle except has commemorative details as in NRA Centennial Musket (barrel inscribed "NRA Centennial Rifle"); caliber .30-30, 24-in. bbl., QD sling swivels. Made in 1971.

MODEL 94 NRA CENTENNIAL
MATCHED SET .... NiB $1400 Ex $1266 Gd $1077

Rifle and musket were offered in sets with consecutive serial numbers. Note: Production figures not available. These rifles offered in Winchester's 1972 catalog.

MODEL 94 NEBRASKA CENTENNIAL
COMMEMORATIVE CARBINE NiB $1133 Ex $933 Gd $633

Same as Standard Model 94 Carbine except caliber .30-30 only; gold-plated hammer, loading gate, bbl. band, and buttplate; souvenir medallion embedded in stock, commemorative inscription on bbl. 2,500 made in 1966.

MODEL 94 THEODORE ROOSEVELT
COMMEMORATIVE RIFLE/CARBINE

Standard Model 94 action. Caliber: .30-30. Rifle has 6-rnd. half-magazine, 26-in. octagon bbl., weight: 7.5-lb. Carbine has 6-rnd. full magazine, 20-in. bbl., weight: 7-lb. White gold-plated receiver, upper tang, and forend cap; receiver engraved with American Eagle, "26th President 1901–

1909," and Roosevelt's signature. Commemorative medallion embedded in buttstock. Saddle ring. Half pistol-grip, contoured lever. 49,505 made in 1969.

Carbine.................. NiB $733 Ex $560 Gd $398
Rifle .... NiB $733 Ex $560 Gd $398
Matched set .... NiB $1415 Ex $1153 Gd $805

MODEL 94 TEXAS RANGER ASSOCIATION
CARBINE................. NiB $769 Ex $654 Gd $498

Same as Texas Ranger Commemorative Model 94 except special edition of 150 carbines, numbered 1 through 150, with hand-checkered full-fancy walnut stock and forearm. Sold only through Texas Ranger Association. Made in 1973.

MODEL 94 TEXAS RANGER
COMMEMORATIVE CARBINE . NiB $655 Ex $496 Gd $400

Same as Standard Model 94 Carbine except caliber .30-30 Win. only, stock and forearm of semi-fancy walnut, replica of Texas Ranger star embedded in buttstock, curved buttplate. 5,000 made in 1973.

MODEL 94 JOHN WAYNE COMMEMORATIVE
CARBINE............... NiB $1597 Ex $1166 Gd $769

Standard Model 94 action. Caliber: .32-40. 18.5-in. bbl. Receiver is pewter-plated with engraving of Indian attack and cattle drive scenes. Oversized bow on lever. Nickel-silver medallion in buttstock bears a bas-relief portrait of Wayne. Selected American walnut stock with deep-cut checkering. Introduced by U.S. Repeating Arms in 1981.

MODEL 94 WELLS FARGO & CO. COMMEMORATIVE
CARBINE.................. NiB $770 Ex $544 Gd $339

Same as Standard Model 94 Carbine except .30-30 Win. only; antique silver-finished, engraved receiver; stock and forearm of fancy walnut, checkered, curved buttplate. Nickel-silver stage-coach medallion (inscribed "Wells Fargo & Co. —1852–1977—125 Years") embedded in buttstock. 20,000 made in 1977.

MODEL 94 O. F. WINCHESTER COMMEMORATIVE
RIFLE.................... NiB $854 Ex $650 Gd $599

Standard Model 94 action. Caliber: .38-55. 24-in. octagonal bbl. Receiver is satin gold-plated with distinctive engravings. Stock and forearm semi-fancy American walnut with high grade checkering.

MODEL 94 WRANGLER CARBINE
Same as standard Model 94 Carbine except w/16-in. bbl., engraved receiver and chambered for .32 Special and .38-55 Win. Angle Eject introduced in 1985 as Wrangler II, also chambered for .30-30 Win., .44 Mag. and .45 LC. Made 1980 to 1986. Re-introduced in 1992.

Top eject (disc. 1984) .... NiB $398 Ex $290 Gd $200
Wrangler II, angle eject (.30-30)NiB $390 Ex $285 Gd $195
.44 Mag or .45 LC, add.......................... $50

MODEL 94 WYOMING DIAMOND JUBILEE
COMMEMORATIVE
CARBINE............... NiB $2166 Ex $1812 Gd $1347

Same as Standard Model 94 Carbine except caliber .30-30 Win. only, receiver engraved and casehardened in colors, brass saddle ring and loading gate, souvenir medallion embedded in buttstock, commemorative inscription on bbl. 1,500 made in 1964.

MODEL 94 ALASKAN PURCHASE CENTENNIAL
COMMEMORATIVE CARBINE... NiB $2379 Ex $2006 Gd $1339

Same as Wyoming issue except different medallion and inscription. 1,501 made in 1967.

Winchester Model 75
Sporting

Winchester Model 88
Pre-1965

Winchester Model 70
Coyote

Winchester Model 70
Ranger Compact

Winchester Model 70
Stealth

Winchester Model 94
Traditional

MODEL 94 OLIVER WINCHESTER 200TH ANNIVERSARY CUSTOM GRADE RIFLE . . . NiB $1959 Ex $1880 Gd $1630
Reintroduction of Model 94, similar as Post-'64 models except .30-30, 8-rnd. magazine. Bbl.: 26-in. half octagon, half round. Weight: 8 lbs. Sights: buckhorn rear; Marbles front. Finish: blued, engraved. High grade walnut stock. Made 2010.
High Grade (silver
   nitride finish) . . . . NiB $1469 Ex $1400 Gd $1055

MODEL 100 AUTOLOADING
RIFLE . . . . NiB $675 Ex $559 Gd $466
Gas-operated Semiauto. Calibers: .243, .284, .308 Win. Four round clip magazine (3-rnd. in .284). 22-in. bbl. Weight: 7.25 lbs. Sights: Open rear; hooded ramp front. One-piece stock w/ pistol grip, basket-weave checkering, grip cap, sling swivels. Made 1961-73.

MODEL 100 CARBINE . . . . NiB $800 Ex $622 Gd $482
Same as Model 100 Rifle except has 19-in. bbl., plain carbine-style stock and forearm with bbl. band. Weight: 7 lbs. Made 1967 to 1973.

MODEL 121 DELUXE . . . . NiB $200 Ex $126 Gd $90
Same as Model 121 Standard except has ramp front sight, stock with fluted comb and sling swivels. Made 1967-73.

MODEL 121 STANDARD BOLT-ACTION
SINGLE SHOT. . . . . NiB $167 Ex $100 Gd $80
Caliber: .22 Short, Long, LR. 20.75-in. bbl. Weight: 5 lbs. Sights: Open rear; bead front. Monte Carlo-style stock. Made 1967 to 1973.

MODEL 121 YOUTH . . . . NiB $200 Ex $126 Gd $90
Same as Model 121 Standard except has 1.25-in. shorter stock. Made 1967-73.

MODEL 131 BOLT-ACTION
REPEATER . . . . NiB $269 Ex $227 Gd $178
Caliber: .22 Short, Long or LR. Seven round clip magazine. 20.75-in. bbl. Weight: 5 lbs. Sights: Open rear; ramp front. Plain Monte Carlo stock. Made 1967-73.

MODEL 135 . . . . NiB $244 Ex $169 Gd $155
Same as Model 131 except chambered for .22 WMR cartridge. Magazine holds 5 rounds. Made in 1967.

MODEL 141 BOLT-ACTION TUBULAR
REPEATER . . . . NiB $279 Ex $216 Gd $155
Same as Model 131 except has tubular magazine in butt-stock; holds 19 Short, 15 Long, 13 LR. Made 1967-73.

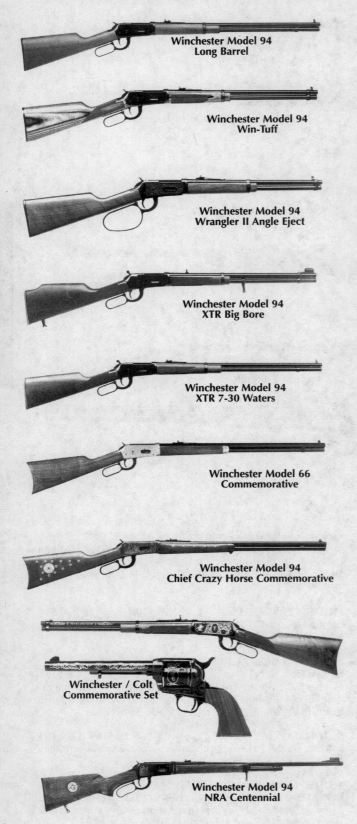

Winchester Model 94
Long Barrel

Winchester Model 94
Win-Tuff

Winchester Model 94
Wrangler II Angle Eject

Winchester Model 94
XTR Big Bore

Winchester Model 94
XTR 7-30 Waters

Winchester Model 66
Commemorative

Winchester Model 94
Chief Crazy Horse Commemorative

Winchester / Colt
Commemorative Set

Winchester Model 94
NRA Centennial

MODEL 145 . . . . **NiB $256 Ex $200 Gd $145**
Same as Model 141 except chambered for .22 WMR; magazine holds 9 rounds. Made in 1967.

**MODEL 150 LEVER-ACTION
CARBINE** . . . . **NiB $244 Ex $180 Gd $126**
Same as Model 250 except has straight loop lever, plain carbine-style straight-grip stock and forearm with bbl. band. Made 1967-73.

MODEL 190 CARBINE . . . . **NiB $255 Ex $195 Gd $135**
Same as Model 190 rifle except has carbine-style forearm with bbl. band. Made 1967-73.

**MODEL 190 SEMIAUTO
RIFLE** . . . . **NiB $265 Ex $210 Gd $145**
Same as current Model 290 except has plain stock and forearm. Made 1966-78.

MODEL 250 DELUXE RIFLE . . . **NiB $300 Ex $233 Gd $150**
Same as Model 250 Standard Rifle except has fancy walnut Monte Carlo stock and forearm, sling swivels. Made 1965-71.

**MODEL 250 STANDARD LEVER-ACTION
RIFLE** . . . . **NiB $249 Ex $175 Gd $126**
Hammerless. Caliber: .22 Short, Long or LR. Tubular magazine holds 21 Short, 17 Long, 15 LR. 20.5-in. bbl. Sights: Open rear; ramp front. Weight: About 5 lbs. Plain stock and forearm on early production; later model has checkering. Made 1963-73.

MODEL 255 DELUXE RIFLE . . . **NiB $338 Ex $265 Gd $175**
Same as Model 250 Deluxe Rifle except chambered for .22 WMR cartridge. Magazine holds 11 rounds. Made 1965-73.

MODEL 255 STANDARD RIFLE . . . **NiB $265 Ex $198 Gd $144**
Same as Model 250 Standard Rifle except chambered for .22 WMR cartridge. Magazine holds 11 rounds. Made 1964-70.

MODEL 270 DELUXE RIFLE . . . **NiB $288 Ex $149 Gd $145**
Same as Model 270 Standard Rifle except has fancy walnut Monte Carlo stock and forearm. Made 1965-73.

**MODEL 270 STANDARD
SLIDE-ACTION RIFLE** . . . . **NiB $200 Ex $137 Gd $110**
Hammerless. Caliber: .22 Short, Long or LR. Tubular magazine holds 21 Short, 17 Long, 15 LR. 20.5-in. bbl. Sights: Open rear; ramp front. Weight: About 5 lbs. Early production had plain walnut stock and forearm (slide handle); latter also furnished in plastic (Cycolac); last model has checkering. Made 1963-73.

MODEL 278 DELUXE RIFLE . . . **NiB $322 Ex $268 Gd $144**
Same as Model 270 Deluxe Rifle except chambered for .22 WMR cartridge. Tubular magazine holds 11 rounds. Made 1965-70.

MODEL 278 STANDARD RIFLE . . . **NiB $266 Ex $190 Gd $133**
Same as Model 270 Standard Rifle except chambered for .22 WMR cartridge. Magazine holds 11 rounds. Made 1964-70.

MODEL 290 DELUXE RIFLE . . . **NiB $325 Ex $278 Gd $175**
Same as Model 290 Standard Rifle except has fancy walnut Monte Carlo stock and forearm. Made 1965-73.

MODEL 290 STANDARD SEMIAUTO RIFLE
Caliber: .22 Long or LR. Tubular magazine holds 17 Long, 15 LR. 20.5-in. bbl. Sights: Open rear; ramp front. Weight: About

Winchester Model 100

Winchester Model 250 Deluxe

Winchester Model 270 Deluxe

Winchester Model 310

Winchester Model 320

Winchester Model 490 Rifle

Winchester Model 670 Bolt-Action Rifle

Winchester Model 670 Magnum

Winchester Model 9422 Boy Scouts of America Commemorative

Winchester Model 9422 Eagle Scout Limited Edtion

Winchester Model 9422 WinCam

Winchester Model 9422 XTR Classic

Winchester XPR standard model

5 lbs. Plain stock and forearm on early production; current model has checkering. Made 1963-77.

w/plain stock/forearm . . . . NiB $286 Ex $227 Gd $133
w/checkered stock/forearm . . . NiB $300 Ex $255 Gd $156

**MODEL 310 BOLT-ACTION
SINGLE SHOT** . . . . NiB $370 Ex $300 Gd $210
Caliber: .22 Short, Long, LR. 22-in. bbl. Weight: 5.63 lbs. Sights: Open rear; ramp front. Monte Carlo stock w/checkered pistol-grip and forearm, sling swivels. Made 1972-75.

**MODEL 320 BOLT-ACTION
REPEATER** . . . . NiB $370 Ex $300 Gd $210
Same as Model 310 except has 5-rnd. clip magazine. Made 1972-74.

MODEL 490 . . . . NiB $388 Ex $298 Gd $234
Caliber: .22 LR. Five round clip magazine. 22-in. bbl. Weight: 6 lbs. Sights: Folding leaf rear; hooded ramp front. One-piece walnut stock w/checkered pistol grip and forearm. Made 1975-77.

**MODEL 670 BOLT-ACTION
SPORTING RIFLE** . . . . NiB $386 Ex $308 Gd $231
Calibers: .227 Win., .243 Win., .270 Win., .30-06, .308 Win. Four round magazine. 22-in. bbl. Weight: 7 lbs. Sights: Open rear; ramp front. Monte Carlo stock w/checkered pistol-grip and forearm. Made 1967-73.

MODEL 670 CARBINE . . . . NiB $356 Ex $338 Gd $244
Same as Model 670 Rifle except has 19-in. bbl. Weight: 6.75 lbs. Calibers: .243 Win., .270 Win., .30-06. Made 1967-70.

MODEL 670 MAGNUM . . . . . . NiB $410 Ex $356 Gd $281
Same as Model 670 Rifle except has 24-in. bbl., reinforced stock with recoil pad with slightly different checkering pattern. Weight: 7.25 lbs. Calibers: .264 Win. Mag., 7mm Rem. Mag., .300 Win. Mag. Open rear sight; ramp front sight with hood. Made 1967-70.

**MODEL 770 BOLT-ACTION
SPORTING RIFLE** . . . . NiB $443 Ex $321 Gd $277
Model 70-type action. Calibers: .22-250, .222 Rem., .243, .270 Win., .30-06. Four round box magazine. 22-in. bbl. Sights: Open rear; hooded ramp front. Weight: 7.13 lbs. Monte Carlo stock, checkered pistol-grip and forend; sling swivels. Made 1969-71.

MODEL 770 MAGNUM . . . . . . NiB $443 Ex $318 Gd $233
Same as Standard Model 770 except 24-in. bbl., weight: 7.25 lbs., recoil pad. Calibers: 7mm Rem. Mag., .264 and .300 Win. Mag. Made 1969-71.

MODEL 9422 LEVER-ACTION RIMFIRE RIFLES
Similar to the standard Model 94 except chambered for .22 Rimfire. Calibers: .22 Short, Long, LR. (9422) or .22 WMR (9422M). Tubular magazine holds 21 or 15 Short.17 or 12 Long, 15 or 11 LR (9422 or Trapper) or 11 or 8 WRM (9422M or Trapper M). 16.5- or 20.5 in. bbl. 33.125- to 37.125 in. overall. Weight: 5.75 to 6.25 lbs. Open rear sight; hooded ramp front. Carbine-style stock and barrel-band forearm. Stock options: Walnut (Standard), laminated brown (WinTuff), laminated green (WinCam). Made 1972. Disc.
Standard model . . . . NiB $655 Ex $368 Gd $265
WinCam model . . . . NiB $690 Ex $376 Gd $254
WinTuff model . . . . NiB $533 Ex $337 Gd $233
Legacy model . . . . NiB $844 Ex $577 Gd $300
Trapper model (16.5-in. bbl.) . . NiB $765 Ex $456 Gd $268

XTR Classic model . . . . NiB $800 Ex $587 Gd $370
High Grade Series I . . . . NiB $1389 Ex $1085 Gd $770
High Grade Series II . . . . NiB $1389 Ex $1985 Gd $770
25th Anniversary Edition
   Grade (1 of 2,500) . . . . NiB $860 Ex $569 Gd $447
25th Anniversary Edition
   High Grade (1 of 250) . . NiB $1688 Ex $1233 Gd $1044
25th Anniversary Edition
   High Grade (1 of 250) . . . . . NiB $843 Ex $667 Gd $495
Eagle Scout Commemorative
   (1 of 1,000) . . . . NiB $1448 Ex $1177 Gd $988
.22 WRM, add 10%

DOUBLE XPRESS RIFLE . . . NiB $4889 Ex $4550 Gd $3000
Over/under double rifle. Calibers: .257 Roberts, .270 Win.,
.30-06, 7x57mm, 7x57mmR, 7x65mmR or 9.3x74mmR. 23.5-
in. bbl. Weight: 8.5 lbs. Manufactured for Olin Corp. by Olin-
Kodensha in Japan. Made 1984-85.

**RANGER YOUTH BOLT-ACTION
CARBINE** . . . . NiB $499 Ex $338 Gd $270
Calibers: .223 (discontinued 1989), .243 Win., and .308 Win.
Four and 5-rnd. magazine. Bbl.: 20-in. Weight: 5.75 lbs.
American hardwood stock. Open rear sight. Made 1985-2006
by U.S. Repeating Arms.

**RANGER LEVER-ACTION
CARBINE** . . . . NiB $655 Ex $398 Gd $290
Caliber: .30-30. Five round tubular magazine. Bbl.: 20-in. rnd.
Weight: 6.5 lbs. American hardwood stock. Economy version of
Model 94. Made 1985-2006 by U.S. Repeating Arms.

RANGER BOLT-ACTION CARBINE . . NiB $470 Ex $388 Gd $243
Calibers: .223 Rem., .243 Win., .270, .30-06, 7mm Rem. (discontinued 1985), Mag. Three and 4-rnd. magazine. Bbl.: 24-in.
in 7mm; 22-in. in .270 and .30-06. Open sights. American
hardwood stock. Made 1985-99 by U.S. Repeating Arms.

SUPER X (SXR)
Semiauto. Caliber: .270 WSM, .30-06, .300 WSM, .300 Win.
Mag., 3- or 4-rnd. magazine, 22- or 24-in. bbl., no sights,
checkered walnut stock. Blued finish. Made 2006-09.
Grade I . . . . NiB $790 Ex $600 Gd $450

WILDCAT
Bolt action. Caliber: .22 LR, 5- or 10-rnd. magazine, 21-in.
regular or heavy bbl., fixed sights, checkered hardwood stock.
Blued finish. 4.5 to 5.5 lbs. Imported from Russia 2007-09.
Standard bbl. . . . . NiB $215 Ex $150 Gd $115
Heavy bbl. . . . . NiB $255 Ex $200 Gd $165

XPR SERIES
Bolt action. Cal.: .243 Win., .270 Win., .30-06, .300 Win.
Mag., .308 Win., 6.5 Creedmoor, 7mm-08, 7mm Rem. Mag.,
.338 Win. Mag., .300 WSM, .325 WSM. Bbl.: 22-, 24- or 26-in.
Stock: Composite w/textured inserts. 3-rnd. detachable maga-
zine. No sights. Weight: 6.75-7.25 pounds. Made 2015 to date.
standard model . . . . NiB $480 Ex $380 Gd $330
Compact model (13-in. LOP) . . . NiB $480 Ex $380 Gd $330
Hunter Camo model (various camo
   finishes) . . . . NiB $530 Ex $400 Gd $335
Hunter Camo Compact model (various camo
   finishes, 13-in. LOP) . . . . NiB $530 Ex $400 Gd $335

Winslow Commander Grade

Winslow Crown Grade

**Winslow Regent Grade
Bushmaster Stock**

WINSLOW ARMS COMPANY — Camden, SC

BOLT-ACTION SPORTING RIFLE
Action: FN Supreme Mauser, Mark X Mauser, Remington 707
and 788, Sako, Winchester 70. Standard calibers: .17-222,
.17-223, .222 Rem., .22-250, .243 Win., 6mm Rem., .25-06,
.257 Roberts, .270 Win., 7x57, .280 Rem., .284 Win., .308
Win., .30-06, .358 Win. Magnum calibers: .17-222 Mag.,
.257 Wby., .264 Win., .270 Wby., 7mm Rem., 7mm Wby.,
.300 H&H, .300 Wby., .300 Win., .308 Norma, 8mm Rem.,
.338 Win., .358 Norma, .375 H&H, .375 Wby., .458 Win.
Three-rnd. magazine in standard calibers, 2-rnd. in magnum.
24-in. barrel in standard calibers, 26-in. in magnum. Weight:
w/ 24-in. bbl., 7 to 7.5 lbs.; w/ 26-in. bbl., 8 to 9 lbs. No
sights. Stocks: "Bushmaster" with slender pistol-grip and beavertail forearm, "Plainsmaster" with full curl pistol-grip and
flat forearm; both styles have Monte Carlo cheekpiece. Values
shown are for basic rifle in each grade; extras such as special
fancy wood, more elaborate carving, inlays and engraving
can increase these figures considerably. Made 1962-89.
Commander Grade . . . . . . NiB $1897 Ex $1565 Gd $1177
Regal Grade . . . . NiB $2066 Ex $1590 Gd $1322
Regent Grade . . . . NiB $2175 Ex $1698 Gd $1443
Regimental Grade . . . . NiB $2966 Ex $2490 Gd $1788
Crown Grade . . . . NiB $3228 Ex $2579 Gd $2188
Royal Grade . . . . NiB $3590 Ex $2666 Gd $2077
Imperial Grade . . . . NiB $4100 Ex $3695 Gd $3000
Emperor Grade . . . . NiB $7070 Ex $5266 Gd $4590

ZEPHYR — U.S.
*Manufactured by Victor Sarasqueta Company, Eibar, Spain;
imported by Stoeger.*

DOUBLE RIFLE . . . . . NiB $22,656 Ex $18,622 Gd $12,799
Boxlock. Double barrels. Calibers: Available in practically
every caliber from .22 Hornet to .505 Gibbs. Bbls.: 22 to 28
in. standard, but any lengths were available on special order.
Weight: 7 lbs. for the smaller calibers up to 12 or more lbs.
for the larger calibers. Imported by Stoeger from about 1938
to 1951.

SHOTGUNS

ADAMY, GEBR. JAGDWAFFEN — Suhl, Germany

NOTE: *Custom gunmaker established 1820; currently from 1921. Previously imported by New England Custom Gun service, Claremont, NH. Specializes in custom break-action shotguns (S/S, O/U) drillings, vierlings, single-shot rifles. Models and grades are numerous, contact factory for specific information.*

ALDENS — Chicago, IL

MODEL 670 CHIEFTAIN. . . . . . **NiB $331 Ex $239 Gd $190**
Slide-action. Hammerless. Gauges: 12, 20 and others. Three round tubular magazine. Bbl.: 26- to 30-in.; various chokes. Weight: 6.25 to 7.5 lbs. depending on bbl. length and ga. Walnut-finished hardwood stock.

AMERICAN ARMS — N. Kansas City, MO

See also Franchi Shotguns.

BRISTOL (STERLING) O/U . . . . **NiB $853 Ex $621 Gd $500**
Boxlock w/Greener crossbolt and engraved sideplates. Single selective trigger. Selective automatic ejectors. Gauges: 12, 20; 3-in. chambers. 26-, 28-, 30-, or 32-in. VR bbls. w/screw-in choke tubes (Improved Cylinder/Modified/Full). Weight: 7 lbs. Antique-silver receiver w/game scene or scroll engraving. Checkered full pistol-grip-style buttstock and forearm w/high-gloss finish. Imported 1986-88 designated Bristol; redesignated Sterling 1989 to 1990.

**BRITTANY HAMMERLESS
DOUBLE**. . . . . **NiB $863 Ex $744 Gd $508**
Boxlock w/engraved case-colored receiver. Single selective trigger. Selective automatic ejectors. Gauges: 12, 20. 3-in. chambers. Bbls.: 25- or 27-in. w/screw-in choke tubes (IC/M/F). Weight: 6.5 lbs. (20 ga.). Checkered English-style walnut stock w/semi-beavertail forearm or pistol-grip stock w/high-gloss finish. Imported 1989 to 2000.

CAMPER SPECIAL. . . . . **NiB $217 Ex $166 Gd $90**
Similar to the Single Barrel except takedown model w/21-in. bbl., M choke and pistol-grip stock. Made in 1989.

COMBO . . . . **NiB $292 Ex $200 Gd $156**
Similar to the Single-Barrel model except available w/interchangeable rifle and shotgun bbls. .22 LR/20-ga. shotgun or .22 Hornet/12-ga. shotgun. Rifle bbl. has adj. rear sights; blade-type front sight. Made in 1989.

DERBY HAMMERLESS DOUBLE
Sidelock w/engraved sideplates. Single non-selective or double triggers. Selective automatic ejectors. Gauges: 12, 20, 28 and .410. 3 in. chambers. Bbls.: 26-in. (IC/M) or 28-in. (M/F). Weight: 6 lbs. (20 ga.). Checkered English-style walnut stock and splinter forearm w/hand-rubbed oil finish. Engraved frame/sideplates w/antique silver finish. Imported 1986 to 1994.
12 or 20 ga. . . . . **NiB $1254 Ex $907 Gd $677**
28 ga. or .410 (disc. 1991) . . . **NiB $1377 Ex $979 Gd $855**

F.S. SERIES O/U
Greener crossbolt in Trap and Skeet configuration. Single selective trigger. Selective automatic ejectors. 12 gauge only. 26-, 28-, 30-, or 32-in. separated bbls. Weight: 6.5 to 7.25 lbs. Black or chrome receiver. Checkered walnut buttstock and forearm. Imported 1986 to 1987.
Model F.S. 200 Boxlock. . . . . . **NiB $867 Ex $677 Gd $490**
Model F.S. 300 Boxlock. . . . . **NiB $1099 Ex $827 Gd $568**
Model F.S. 400 Sidelock . . . . **NiB $1386 Ex $1197 Gd $871**
Model F.S. 500 Sidelock . . . . **NiB $1386 Ex $1197 Gd $871**

GENTRY/YORK HAMMERLESS DOUBLE
Chrome, coin-silver or color casehardened boxlock receiver w/scroll engraving. Double triggers. Extractors. Gauges: 12, 16, 20, 28, .410. 3-in. chambers (16 and 28 have 2.75-in.). Bbls.: 26-in. (IC/M) or 28-in. (M/F, 12, 16 and 20). Weight: 6.75 lbs. (12 ga.). Checkered walnut buttstock w/pistol-grip and beavertail forearm; both w/semi-gloss oil finish. Imported as York from 1986 to 1988, redesignated Gentry 1989 to 2000.
Gentry 12, or 16 or 20 ga. . . . . **NiB $733 Ex $577 Gd $428**
Gentry 28 ga. or .410. . . . . **NiB $755 Ex $590 Gd $488**
York 12, 16 or 20 ga. (disc. 1988). . . . **NiB $690 Ex $577 Gd $433**
York 20 ga. or .410 . . . . **NiB $690 Ex $577 Gd $433**

GRULLA #2 HAMMERLESS DOUBLE
True sidelock w/engraved detachable sideplates. Double triggers. Extractors and cocking indicators. Gauges: 12, 20, .410 w/3-in. chambers; 28 w/2.75-in. 26-in. bbl. Imported 1989 to 2000.
Standard model. . . . . **NiB $3798 Ex $2886 Gd $2166**
Two-bbl. set (disc. 1995). . . . **NiB $3876 Ex $3688 Gd $2544**

SILVER I O/U
Boxlock. Single selective trigger. Extractors. Gauges: 12, 20 and .410 w/3-in. chambers; 28 w/2.75 in. Bbls.: 26-in. (IC/M), 28-in. (M/F, 12 and 20 ga. only). Weight: 6.75 lbs. (12 ga.). Checkered walnut stock and forearm. Antique-silver receiver w/scroll engraving. Imported 1987 to 2000.
12 or 20 ga. . . . . **NiB $622 Ex $535 Gd $368**
28 ga. or .410. . . . . **NiB $663 Ex $590 Gd $477**

SILVER II O/U
Similar to Model Silver I except w/selective automatic ejectors and 26-in. bbls. w/screw-in tubes (12 and 20 ga.). Fixed chokes (28 and .410). Made 1987 to 2000.
12 or 20 ga. . . . . **NiB $735 Ex $600 Gd $489**
28 ga or .410 . . . . **NiB $730 Ex $652 Gd $464**
Upland Lite II . . . . **NiB $1254 Ex $1066 Gd $855**
Two-bbl. set . . . . **NiB $1293 Ex $1088 Gd $867**

SILVER LITE O/U
Similar to Model Silver II except w/blued, engraved alloy receiver. Available in 12 and 20 ga. only. Imported from 1990 to 1992.
Standard Model . . . . **NiB $922 Ex $655 Gd $477**

American Arms
Bristol (Sterling) Over/Under

American Arms
Derby Hammerless Double

American Arms
Gentry/York Hammerless Double

American Arms
Silver Over/Under

American Arms
WS/SS Hammerless Double

Two-bbl. Set . . . . **NiB $1169 Ex $908 Gd $733**

SILVER SKEET/TRAP . . . . **NiB $855 Ex $640 Gd $569**
Similar to the Silver II Model except has 28-in. (Skeet) or
30-in. (Trap) ported bbls. w/target-style rib and mid-bead sight.
Imported 1992 to 1994.

SILVER SPORTING O/U . . . . . **NiB $966 Ex $768 Gd $633**
Boxlock. Single selective trigger. Selective automatic ejectors.
Gauges: 12, 2.75-in. chambers. 28-in. bbls.w/Franchoke tubes
(SK, IC, M and F). Weight: 7.5 lbs. Checkered walnut stock and
forearm. Special broadway rib and vented side ribs. Engraved
receiver w/chrome-nickel finish. Imported from 1990 to 2000.

SINGLE-SHOT SHOTGUN
Break-open action. Gauges: 10 (3.5), 12, 20, .410, 3-in. chamber. Weight: about 6.5 lbs. Bead front sight. Walnut-finished
hardwood stock w/checkered grip and forend. Made 1988-90.
10 ga. (3.5-in.) . . . . **NiB $198 Ex $117 Gd $75**
12 & 20 ga., .410 . . . . **NiB $200 Ex $99 Gd $66**
Multi-choke bbl., add **$50**
Slugger (12 or 20 ga., 24-in. slug bbl.
   w/ sights, 1989). . . . . **NiB $105 Ex $80 Gd $60**

TS/OU 12 SHOTGUN . . . . **NiB $744 Ex $555 Gd $490**
Turkey Special. Boxlock. Single selective trigger. Selective
automatic ejectors. Gauge: 12, 3.5-in. chambers. Bbls.: 24-in.
O/U w/screw-in choke tubes (IC, M, F). Weight: 6 lbs. 15 oz.
Checkered European walnut stock and beavertail forearm.
Matte blue finish. Imported 1987 to 2000.

TS/SS 10 . . . . **NiB $700 Ex $533 Gd $400**
Turkey Special. Same general specifications as Model WS/ SS
10, except w/26-in. side-by-side bbls., screw-in choke tubes
(F/F) and chambered for 10-ga. 3.5-in. shells. Weight: 10 lbs.,
13 oz. Imported 1987 to 1993.

TS/SS 12 . . . . **NiB $766 Ex $533 Gd $421**
Same general specifications as Model WS/SS 10 except in 12
ga. w/26-in. side-by-side bbls. and 3 screw-in choke tubes
(IC/M/F). Weight: 7 lbs., 6 oz. Imported 1987 to 2000.

WS O/U 12 SHOTGUN . . . . . . **NiB $644 Ex $538 Gd $377**
Waterfowl Special. Boxlock. Single selective trigger. Selective
automatic ejectors. Gauge: 12; 3.5-in. chambers. Bbls.: 28-in.
O/U w/screw-in tubes (IC/M/F). Weight: 7 lbs. Checkered
European walnut stock and beavertail forearm. Matte blue
metal finish. Imported 1987-2000.

WS/SS 10 . . . . **NiB $883 Ex $671 Gd $428**
Waterfowl Special. Boxlock. Double triggers. Extractors.
Gauge: 10; 3.5-in. chambers. Bbls.: 32-in. side/side choked
F/F. Weight: About 11 lbs. Checkered walnut stock and bea-
vertail forearm w/satin finish. Parkerized metal finish. Imported
from 1987 to 1995.

WT O/U SHOTGUN . . . . **NiB $844 Ex $657 Gd $533**
Same general specifications as Model WS/OU 12 except chambered for 10-ga. 3.5-in. shells. Extractors. Satin wood finish and
matte blue metal. Imported 1987 to 2000.

ARMALITE, INC. — Costa Mesa, CA

AR-17 GOLDEN GUN . . . . **NiB $863 Ex $643 Gd $559**
Recoil-operated Semiautomatic. High-test aluminum bbl.
and receiver housing. 12 ga. only. Two round capacity. 24-in.
bbl. w/interchangeable choke tubes: IC/M/F. Weight: 5.6 lbs.
Polycarbonate stock and forearm recoil pad. Gold-anodized
finish standard, also made w/black finish. Made 1964-1965.
Fewer than 2,000 produced.

ARMSCOR (Arms Corp.) — Manila, Philippines

*Imported until 1991 by Armscor Precision, San Mateo, CA;
1991–95 by Ruko Products, Inc., Buffalo NY.*

MODEL M-30 FIELD PUMP SHOTGUN
Double slide-action bars w/damascened bolt. Gauge: 12 only
w/3-in. chamber. Bbl.: 28-in. w/fixed chokes or choke tubes.
Weight: 7.6 lbs. Walnut or walnut finished hardwood stock.
Disc. 2013.
w/hard wood stock, fixed
   choke or choke tubes . . . . . . **NiB $288 Ex $212 Gd $149**
w/walnut
   stock and choke tubes . . . . . **NiB $366 Ex $247 Gd $169**
Model M-30DG (Deer Gun) . . . . **NiB $266 Ex $198 Gd $137**

Armalite AR-17
Golden Gun

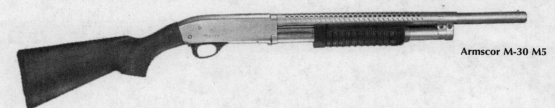

Armscor M-30 M5

Model M-30SAS (Special
  Air Services) . . . . NiB $277 Ex $218 Gd $125
Model M-30 M5 (matte chrome
  finish) . . . . NiB $199 Ex $180 Gd $110

MODEL M-30 RIOT PUMP
Double-action slide bar w/damascened bolt. Gauge: 12 only
w/3-in. chamber. Bbls: 18.5 and 20-in. w/IC bore. Five- or 7-rnd.
magazine. Weight: 7 lbs, 2 oz. Walnut finished hardwood stock.
Disc. 1999, reintro. 2001 to 2008.
5-rnd. magazine . . . . NiB $190 Ex $121 Gd $90
W/7-rnd. magazine . . . . NiB $219 Ex $135 Gd $100

MODEL M-30 SPECIAL COMBO
Simlar to Special Purpose Model except has detachable syn-
thetic stock that removes to convert to pistol-grip configuration.
Model M-30C (disc. 1995) . . . . NiB $210 Ex $200 Gd $155
Model M-30RP (disc. 1995) . . . NiB $210 Ex $200 Gd $155

ARMSPORT, INC. — Miami, FL

1000 SERIES HAMMERLESS DOUBLES
Side-by-side w/engraved receiver, double triggers and extrac-
tors. Gauges: 10 (3.5), 12, 20, .410- 3-in. chambers. Model
1033: 10 ga., 32-in. bbl. Model 1050/51: 12 ga., 28-in. bbl.,
M/F choke. Model 1052/53: 20 ga., 26-in. bbl., I/M choke.
Model 1054/57: .410 ga., 26-in. bbl., I/M. Model 1055: 28
ga., Weight: 5.75 to 7.25 lbs. European walnut buttstock and
forend. Made in Italy. Importation disc. 1993.
Model 1033 (10 ga., disc. 1989) . . NiB $844 Ex $690 Gd $497
Model 1050 (12 ga., disc. 1993) . . NiB $766 Ex $692 Gd $477
Model 1051 (12 ga., disc. 1985) . . NiB $503 Ex $412 Gd $326
Model 1052 (20 ga., disc. 1985) . . NiB $477 Ex $390 Gd $288
Model 1053 (20 ga., disc. 1993) . . NiB $790 Ex $666 Gd $459
Model 1054 (.410, disc. 1992) . . . NiB $888 Ex $739 Gd $522
Model 1055 (28 ga., disc. 1992) . . NiB $554 Ex $448 Gd $336
Model 1057 (.410, disc. 1985) . . . NiB $569 Ex $481 Gd $357

MODEL 1125 SINGLE-SHOT
SHOTGUN . . . . NiB $196 Ex $139 Gd $98
Bottom-opening lever. Gauges: 12, 20. 3-in. chambers. Bead
front sight. Plain stock and forend. Imported 1987-89.

MODEL 2700 GOOSE GUN
Similar to the 2700 Standard Model except 10 ga. w/3.5-
in. chambers. Double triggers w/28-in. bbl. choked IC/M
or 32-in. bbl., F/F. 12mm wide VR. Weight: 9.5 lbs. Canada
geese engraved on receiver. Antiqued silver-finished action.
Checkered European walnut stock w/rubber recoil pad.
Imported from Italy 1986 to 1993.
W/fixed choke . . . . NiB $1167 Ex $933 Gd $676
W/choke tubes . . . . NiB $1433 Ex $979 Gd $724

MODEL 2700 OVER/UNDER SERIES
Hammerless, takedown shotgun w/engraved receiver. Selective
single or double triggers. Gauges: 10, 12, 20, 28 and .410.
Bbl.: 26-or 28-in. w/fixed chokes or choke tubes. Weight: 8
lbs. Checkered European walnut buttstock and forend. Made
in Italy. Importation disc. 1993.

Model 2701 12 ga. (disc. 1985) . . . NiB $613 Ex $500 Gd $357
Model 2702 12 ga. . . . . NiB $635 Ex $525 Gd $378
Model 2703 20 ga. (disc. 1985) . . . NiB $668 Ex $544 Gd $365
Model 2704 20 ga. . . . . NiB $655 Ex $548 Gd $400
Model 2705 (.410, DT, fixed
  chokes) . . . . NiB $775 Ex $638 Gd $454
Model 2730/31 (BOSS-style
  action, SST Choke tubes) . . . NiB $868 Ex $733 Gd $538
Model 2733/35 (Boss-style
  action, extractors) . . . . NiB $790 Ex $644 Gd $466
Model 2741 (Boss-style
  action, ejectors) . . . . NiB $678 Ex $566 Gd $412
Model 2742 Sporting Clays
  (12 ga./choke tubes) . . . . NiB $835 Ex $679 Gd $555
Model 2744 Sporting Clays
  (20 ga./choke tubes) . . . . NiB $855 Ex $677 Gd $499
Model 2750 Sporting Clays
  (12 ga./sideplates) . . . . NiB $955 Ex $723 Gd $528
Model 2751 Sporting Clays
  (20 ga./sideplates) . . . . NiB $943 Ex $759 Gd $544

MODEL 2755 SLIDE-ACTION SHOTGUN
Gauge: 12 w/3-in. chamber. Tubular magazine. Bbls.: 28- or
30-in. w/fixed choke or choke tubes. Weight: 7 lbs. European
walnut stock. Made in Italy 1986 to 1987.
Standard model, fixed choke . . NiB $444 Ex $366 Gd $270
Standard model, choke tubes. . . . NiB $579 Ex $489 Gd $355
Police model, 20-in. bbl. . . . . . NiB $390 Ex $333 Gd $244

MODEL 2900 TRI-BARREL (TRILLING) SHOTGUN
Boxlock. Double triggers w/top-tang bbl. selector. Extractors.
Gauge: 12; 3-in. chambers. Bbls.: 28-in. (IC, M and F). Weight:
7.75 lbs. Checkered European walnut stock and forearm. Engraved
silver receiver. Imported 1986 to 1987 and 1990 to 1993.
Model 2900 (W/fixed chokes) . . NiB $2288 Ex $1844 Gd $1307
Model 2900 (choke tubes) . . . . NiB $2945 Ex $2385 Gd $1669
Deluxe grades, add $600

ARRIETA, S.L. — Elgoibar, Spain
*Imported by New England Arms Corp., Wingshooting
Adventures Quality Arms, Griffin & Howe and Orvis. Custom
double-barreled shotguns with frames scaled to individual
gauges. Standard gauges are 12 and 16. Add: 5% for small
gauges (20, 24, 28, 32 and .410 bore) on currently manufactured models; $900 for single trigger (most actions); 5% for
matched pairs; 10% for rounded action on standard models;
extra bbls., add $2,500 to $3,800 per set.*

MODEL 557 STANDARD . . . . . . NiB $6500 Ex $3966 Gd $2044
Gauges: 12, 16 or 20. Demi-Bloc steel barrels, detachable
engraved sidelocks, double triggers, ejectors.

MODEL 570 LIEJA . . . . NiB $6955 Ex $4820 Gd $2588
Gauges: 12, 16 or 20. Non-detachable sidelocks.

MODEL 578 VICTORIA . . . . NiB $11,000 Ex $8500 Gd $6000
Gauges: 12, 16 or 20. Similar to Model 570 but with fine
English scrollwork.

SHOTGUNS

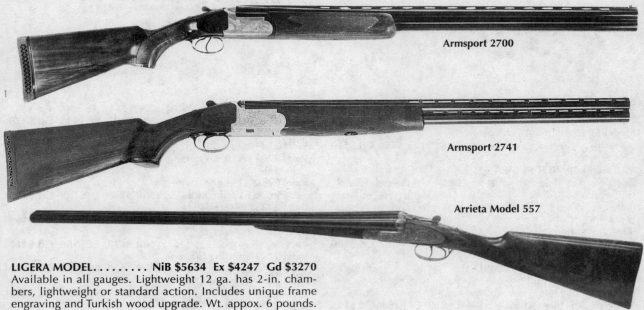

Armsport 2700

Armsport 2741

Arrieta Model 557

LIGERA MODEL . . . . **NiB $5634 Ex $4247 Gd $3270**
Available in all gauges. Lightweight 12 ga. has 2-in. chambers, lightweight or standard action. Includes unique frame engraving and Turkish wood upgrade. Wt. appox. 6 pounds.

MODEL 590 REGINA . . . . . . **NiB $4250 Ex $3177 Gd $2229**
Gauges: 12, 16 or 20. Similar to Model 570 but has more elaborate engraving.

MODEL 595 PRINCIPE . . . **NiB $5579 Ex $4367 Gd $3410**
Available in all gauges, sidelock, engraved hunting scenes, ejectors,double triggers.

MODEL 600 IMPERIAL . . .**NiB $13,250 Ex $9500 Gd $7010**
Gauges: 12, 16 or 20. Self-opening action, very ornate engraving throughout.

**MODEL 601 IMPERIAL
TYRO** . . . . **NiB $9110 Ex $6005 Gd $4337**
Available in all gauges, sidelock, nickel plating, ejectors, single selective trigger, border engraving.

MODEL 801 . . . . **NiB $12,870 Ex $11,665 Gd $10,644**
All gauges, detachable sidelocks, ejectors,coin-wash finish, Churchill-style engraving.

MODEL 802 . . . . **NiB $12,760 Ex $11,544 Gd $8534**
Gauges: 12, 16 or 20. Similar to Model 801 except with nondetachable sidelocks, finest Holland-style engraving.

BOSS ROUND BODY . . . . **NiB $8260 Ex $7733 Gd $6477**
Available in all gauges, Boss pattern best quality engraving, wood upgrade.

MODEL 803 . . . . **NiB $15,510 Ex $11,100 Gd $8010**
Available in all gauges. Similar to Model 801 except finest Purdey-style engraving.

MODEL 871 . . . . **NiB $6010 Ex $4144 Gd $2608**
Available in all gauges. Rounded frame sidelock action with Demi-Bloc barrels, scroll engraving, ejectors, double trigger.

MODEL 871 EXTRA FINISH . . . **NiB $7555 Ex $4759 Gd $3977**
Similar to Model 871 except with standard game scene engraving with woodcock and ruffed grouse.

MODEL 872 . . . . **NiB $16,110 Ex $13,690 Gd $11,550**
Available in all gauges, rounded frame sidelock action, Demi-Bloc barrels, elaborate scroll engraving with third lever fastener.

MODEL 873 . . . . **NiB $16,760 Ex $14,788 Gd $11,766**
Available in all gauges. Sidelock, gold line engraved action, ejectors, single selective trigger.

MODEL 874 . . . . **NiB $12,980 Ex $11,887 Gd $6,777**
Available in all gauges. Sidelock, gold line engraved action, Demi-Bloc barrels.

MODEL 875 . . . . **NiB $18,760 Ex $14,449 Gd $11,733**
Available in all gauges. Custom model built to individual specifications only, elaborate engraving, gold inlays

MODEL 931 . . . . **NiB $36,000 Ex $26,000 Gd $16,000**
Available in all gauges. Self-opening action, elaborate engraving, H&H selective ejectors.

ASTRA — Guernica, Spain
Manufactured by Unceta y Compania.

MODEL 650 O/U SHOTGUN
Hammerless, takedown w/double triggers. 12 ga. w/.75-in. chambers. Bbls.: 28-in. (M/F or SK/SK); 30-in. (M/F). Weight: 6.75 lbs. Checkered European walnut buttstock and forend. Disc. 1987.
w/extractors . . . . .NiB $733 Ex $579 Gd $454
w/ejectors . . . . .NiB $844 Ex $685 Gd $477

MODEL 750 O/U SHOTGUN
Similar to the Model 650 except w/selective single trigger and ejectors. Made in field, skeet and trap configurations from 1980. Disc. 1987.
Field model w/extractors . . . . .NiB $779 Ex $637 Gd $500
Field model w/ejectors . . . . . . .NiB $888 Ex $755 Gd $566
Trap or Skeet model . . . . .NiB $1099 Ex $867 Gd $559

AyA Model 53E

AYA (AGUIRRE Y ARANZABAL) — Eibar, Spain

Previously manufactured by Diarm. Imported by Armes De Chasse, Hertford, NC.

MODEL 1 HAMMERLESS DOUBLE
A Holland & Holland sidelock similar to the Model 2 except in 12 and 20 ga. only, w/special engraving and exhibition-grade wood. Weight: 5-8 lbs., depending on ga. Imported by Diarm until 1987, since 1992 by Armes de Chasse.
Model 1 Standard . . . . . . NiB $11,500 Ex $8700 Gd $6780
Model 1 Deluxe . . . . . . NiB $15,610 Ex $11,600 Gd $8360
w/extra set of bbls., add $750

MODEL 2 . . . . NiB $5760 Ex $4380 Gd $3410
Side-by-side. Sidelock action w/selective single or double triggers automatic ejectors and safety. Gauges: 12, 20, 28, (2.75-in. chambers), .410 (3-in. chambers). Bbls.: 26- or 28-in. w/various fixed choke combinations. Weight: 7 lbs. (12 ga.). English-style straight walnut buttstock and splinter forend. Imported by Diarm until 1987, since 1992 by Armes de Chasse.
Deluxe . . . . .NiB $7300 Ex $5510 Gd $3760
Bill Haus Dreamgun (2003-07) . . NiB $5510 Ex $4130 Gd $3030
w/extra set of bbls., add $1450

MODEL 4 . . . . NiB $2010 Ex $1510 Gd $1110
Lightweight Anson & Deely boxlock, scalloped frame. Gauges: 12, 16, 20, 28, and .410. Bbls.: 25- to 28-in. w/concave rib. Importation disc. 1987 and resumed 1991 to 2008 by Armes de Chasse.
Deluxe . . . . .NiB $5960 Ex $4480 Gd $3210

MODEL 37 SUPER . . . . . . .NiB $3266 Ex $2279 Gd $2099
O/U. Sidelock. automatic ejectors. Selective single trigger. Made in all gauges, bbl. lengths and chokes. VR bbls. Elaborately engraved. Checkered stock (w/straight or pistol grip) and forend. Disc. 1995.

MODEL 37 SUPER A . . . . NiB $14,000 Ex $10,100 Gd $6260
Similar to the Standard Model 37 Super except has nickel steel frame and is fitted w/detachable sidelocks engraved w/game scenes. Importation disc. 1987 and resumed 1992 by Armes de Chasse. Disc.

MODEL 53 . . . . .NiB $8210 Ex $6010 Gd $4630
Same general specifications as Model 117 except more elaborate engraving and select figured wood. Importation disc. 1987 and resumed in 1992 by Armes de Chasse.

MODEL 56 HAMMERLESS DOUBLE
Pigeon weight Holland & Holland sidelock w/Purdey-style third lug and sideclips. Gauges: 12, 16, 20. Receiver has fine-line scroll and rosette engraving; gold-plated locks. Importation disc. 1987 and resumed 1992 by Armes de Chasse.
12 ga. . . . . NiB $13,760 Ex $8980 Gd $4610
16 ga. (early importation), add 20%
20 ga. (early importation), add 20%

MODEL 76 HAMMERLESS
DOUBLE . . . . .NiB $955 Ex $838 Gd $529
Anson & Deeley boxlock. Auto ejectors. Selective single trigger. Gauges: 12, 20 (3-in.). Bbls.: 26-, 28-, 30-in. (latter in 12 ga. only), any standard choke combination. Checkered pistol-grip stock/beavertail forend. Disc.

MODEL 76 .410 . . . . .NiB $1099 Ex $877 Gd $669
Same general specifications as 12 and 20 ga. Model 76 except chambered for 3-in. shells in .410, has extractors, double triggers, 26-in. bbls. only, English-style stock w/straight grip and small forend. Disc.

MODEL 117 . . . . NiB $1887 Ex $1077 Gd $868
Side-by-side. Holland & Holland-type sidelocks, hand-detachable. Engraved action. Automatic ejectors. Selective single trigger. Gauges: 12, 20 (3-in.). Bbls.: 26-, 27-, 28-, 30-in.; 27- and 30-in. in 12 ga. only; any standard choke combination. Checkered pistol-grip stock and beavertail forend of select walnut. Manufactured in 1985.

ADARRA . . . . NiB $4960 Ex $3600 Gd $2660
S/S. Boxlock. Gauge: 12, 16, 20 or 28. Double triggers. Fixed chokes. Stock: Straight grip. Finish: case hardened, silver or in the white. Introduced 2013.

ARRATE . . . . NiB $5960 Ex $4550 Gd $3010
O/U. Boxlock or side plates. Fixed chokes. Ejectors. Stock: Grade 2 Wood. Finish: matte black or silver. Introduced 2013.

BILL HANUS BIRDGUN . . . . NiB $2660 Ex $1990 Gd $1470
S/S. Similar to Model 53. Anson & Deeley boxlock. Gauge: 16, 20 or 28. Fixed chokes. Frames proportioned to gauge. 1997-2007.

BOLERO . . . . .NiB $455 Ex $400 Gd $255
Same general specifications as Matador except non-selective single trigger and extractors. Gauges: 12 16, 20, 20 Magnum (3-in.), .410 (3-in.). Note: This model, prior to 1956, was designated F. I. Model 400 by the importer. Made 1955-63, reintro. disc 1984.

CENTENARY . . . . NiB $9500 Ex $7160 Gd $5360
S/S. Sidelock. Gauge: 12, 16, 20 or 28. Introduced 2016.

CONTENTO OVER/UNDER SHOTGUN
Boxlock w/Woodward side lugs and double internal bolts. Gauge: 12 (2.75-in. chambers). Bbls.: 26-, 28-in. field; 30-, 32-in. trap; fixed chokes as required or screw-in choke tubes. Hand-checkered European walnut stock and forend. Single selective trigger and automatic ejectors.
M.K.2 . . . . .NiB $1155 Ex $897 Gd $655
M.K.3 . . . . .NiB $1887 Ex $1533 Gd $1095
W/extra bbl., add $500

CORAL SERIES
O/U. Boxlock w/Kersten cross bolt. Gauge 12 or 16. Ejectors. Disc. 1985.
selective trigger and automatic ejectors.
"A" Model . . . . NiB $1280 Ex $880 Gd $700
"B" Model (engraved receiver) NiB $1400 Ex $930 Gd $730

GRADING: NiB = New in Box   Ex = Excellent or NRA 95%   Gd = Good or NRA 68%

SHOTGUNS

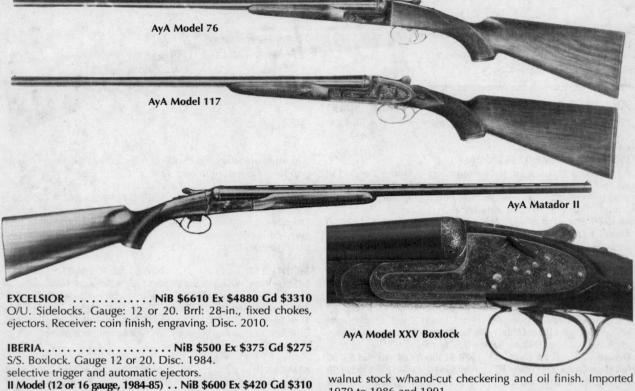

AyA Model 76

AyA Model 117

AyA Matador II

AyA Model XXV Boxlock

EXCELSIOR . . . . **NiB $6610 Ex $4880 Gd $3310**
O/U. Sidelocks. Gauge: 12 or 20. Brrl: 28-in., fixed chokes,
ejectors. Receiver: coin finish, engraving. Disc. 2010.

IBERIA. . . . . **NiB $500 Ex $375 Gd $275**
S/S. Boxlock. Gauge 12 or 20. Disc. 1984.
selective trigger and automatic ejectors.
II Model (12 or 16 gauge, 1984-85) . . **NiB $600 Ex $420 Gd $310**

MATADOR SERIES . . . . **NiB $555 Ex $490 Gd $339**
S/S. Anson & Deeley boxlock. Selective automatic ejectors.
Selective single trigger. Gauges: 12, 16, 20, 20 Magnum
(3-in.). Bbls: 26-, 28-, 30-in.; any standard choke combination. Weight: 6.5 to 7.5 lbs., depending on ga. and bbl. length.
Checkered pistol-grip stock and beavertail forend. Note: This
model, prior to 1956, was designated F. I. Model 400E by the
U.S. importer, Firearms Int'l. Corp. of Washington, D.C. Made
1955-63.
II Model (12 or 20 gauge,
   1964-69) . . . . **NiB $680 Ex $510 Gd $375**
III Model (12 or 20 gauge, disc.
   1970-85) . . . . **NiB $800 Ex $600 Gd $440**

PREMIUM . . . . **NiB $8260 Ex $6760 Gd $5360**
S/S. Sidelock. Gauge: 12, 16, 20 or 28. Introduced 2016.

MODEL XXV BOXLOCK
Anson & Deeley boxlock w/double locking lugs. Gauges: 12
and 20. 25-in. chopper lump, satin blued bbls. w/Churchill rib.
Weight: 5 to 7 lbs. Double triggers. Automatic safety and ejectors. Color-casehardened receiver w/Continental-style scroll
and floral engraving. European walnut stock. Imported 1979
to 1986 and 1991.
12 or 20 ga. . . . . **NiB $3255 Ex $2688 Gd $2100**
w/extra set of bbls., add **$1250**

MODEL XXV SIDELOCK
Holland & Holland-type sidelock. Gauges: 12, 20, 28 and
.410; 25-, 26-, 27- 28-, 29-, and 32-in. bbls. Chopper lump,
satin blued bbls. w/Churchill rib. Weight: 5 to 7 lbs. Double
triggers standard or selective or non-selective single trigger
optional. Automatic safety and ejectors. Cocking indicators. Color-casehardened or coin-silver-finished receiver w/
Continental-style scroll and floral engraving. Select European

walnut stock w/hand-cut checkering and oil finish. Imported
1979 to 1986 and 1991.
12 or 20 ga. . . . . **NiB $6110 Ex $4220 Gd $3188**
28 ga. or .410 bore (disc. 1997), add **$500**

BAIKAL — Izhevsk and Tula, Russia

MODEL IZH-18M SINGLE SHOT . . . **NiB $130 Ex $80 Gd $65**
Hammerless w/cocking indicator. Automatic ejector. Manual
safety. Gauges: 12 , 20, 16 w/2.75-in. chamber or .410 w/3-in.
chamber. Bbls.: 26-, 28-in. w/fixed chokes (IC, M, F). Weight: 5.5
to 6 lbs. Made in Russia. Imported 1998-04 and 2011.

MODEL IZH-27 FIELD O/U . . . **NiB $400 Ex $341 Gd $244**
Boxlock. Double triggers w/extractors. 12 ga.; 2.75-in. chambers. Bbls.: 26-in., IC/M; 28-in., M/F w/fixed chokes. Weight:
6.75 lbs. Imported 1999-04.

MODEL IZH-43 SERIES
Side-by-side. Boxlock. Gauges: 12, 16, 20 or .410 w/2.75- or
3-in. chambers. Bbls.: 20-, 24-, 26- or 28-in. w/fixed chokes or
choke tubes. Single selective or double triggers. Weight: 6.75
lbs. Checkered hardwood (standard on Hunter II Model) or
walnut stock and forend (standard on Hunter Model). Blued,
engraved receiver. Imported 1994 to 2004.
Traditional Hunting model . . . . **NiB $350 Ex $260 Gd $190**
Field model (20, 26 or 28-in. bbls., Disc.
   1996). . . . . **NiB $235 Ex $180 Gd $135**
Hunter (IZH-43K) model (12 or 20 ga. w/external)
   hammers) . . . . **NiB $340 Ex $245 Gd $185**
2 bbl. sets, add . . . **$175** . . . . **NiB $477 Ex $366 Gd $257**
Bounty Hunter model (20-in. bbrls,
   2001-02) . . . . **NiB $240 Ex $210 Gd $160**
Bounty Hunter (external hammers) model
   (20-in. bbrls, 2000-04) . . . . **NiB $290 Ex $220 Gd $160**

MODEL MP94 (IZH-94) . . . . . . NiB $560 Ex $350 Gd $220

O/U combination shotgun over rifle. Boxlock. Gauges/calibers: 12 or 20 ga./.223 Rem., .30-06, .308 Win. or 7.62x39mm. Double triggers w/extractors. Bbls.: 19.5- or 23.5-in. w/ choke tubes or fixed choke. Weight: 8.5 lbs. Blued. Checkered walnut stock and forearm. Made in Russia. Made 2009 to date. Also sold as Model SPR94.

.410/.22 LR or .22 Mag. . . . . . NiB $562 Ex $300 Gd $170

MODEL MP210. . . . . NiB $460 Ex $350 Gd $260

S/S. Boxlock. Gauges: 12, 16, 20, 28 or .410. Bbls.: 20-, 26- or 28-in., ejectors or extractors. Blued. Stock: Checkered walnut. Imported 2009.

MODEL MP213. . . . . NiB $800 Ex $600 Gd $440

S/S. Boxlock. Gauges: 12 only. Bbls.: 20-, 26- or 28-in. Removable trigger assembly. Blued. Stock: Checkered walnut.

MODEL MP220 . . . . NiB $330 Ex $260 Gd $180

S/S. Boxlock. Gauges: 12 or 20. Bbls.: 20-, 26- or 28-in. Blued. Stock: Uncheckered walnut. Imported 2009.

MODEL MP233 Sporting . . . . . . NiB $780 Ex $585 Gd $430

O/U. Boxlock. Gauges: 12 only. Bbls.: 26-, 28- or 29.5-in. w/ or w/o porting, ejectors. Blued. Removable trigger assembly. Stock: Checkered walnut. Imported 1999 to 2004.

MODEL MP310. . . . . NiB $545 Ex $410 Gd $300

O/U. Boxlock. Gauges: 12, 16, 20, 28 or .410. Bbls.: 26- or 28-in., ejectors. Blued. Stock: Checkered walnut. Imported 2009.
Sporting model (engraved nickel receiver, 2009), add . . $100

THE BAKER GUN & FORGING CO. — Batavia, NY

Made 1903–1933 by Baker Gun Company

BATAVIA LEADER HAMMERLESS DOUBLE

Side-by-side. Sidelock. Plain extractors. Double triggers. Gauges: 12, 16, 20. Bbls.: 26- to 32-in.; any standard boring. Weight: About 7.75 lbs. (12 ga. w/30-in. bbls.). Checkered pistol-grip stock and forearm.
w/extractors . . . . NiB $2000 Ex $1400 Gd $500
Bativa Ejector (w/ejectors), add $200
Bativa Damascus (w/damascus brrls), add $300

BATAVIA SPECIAL. . . . . NiB $1510 Ex $1230 Gd $500

Same general specifications as the Batavia Leader except 12 and 16 ga. only; extractors, Homotensile steel bbls.

BLACK BEAUTY

Similar to Batavia Special except higher quality and finer finish throughout; has line engraving, special steel bbls., select walnut stock w/straight, full or half-pistol-grip.
w/extractors . . . . NiB $1510 Ex $1200 Gd $444
w/ejectors. . . . . NiB $1810 Ex $1790 Gd $577
Special (w/ejectors) . . . . NiB $1810 Ex $1360 Gd $544

GRADE R . . . . NiB $3210 Ex $2833 Gd $1106

High-grade gun w/same general specifications as the Batavia Leader except has fine Damascus or Krupp fluid steel bbls., engraving in line, scroll and game scene designs, checkered stock and forearm of fancy European walnut; 12 and 16 ga. only. Deduct 60% for Damascus bbls.

GRADE S . . . . NiB $2210 Ex $2013 Gd $1077

Same general specifications as the Batavia Leader except higher quality and finer finish throughout; has Flui-tempered steel bbls., line and scroll engraving, checkered stock w/half-pistol-grip and forearm of semi-fancy imported walnut; 10, 12 and 16 ga.
w/ejectors, add $300

PARAGON, EXPERT AND DELUXE GRADES

Made to order only, these are the higher grades of Baker hammerless sidelock double-bbl. shotguns. After 1909, the Paragon Grade, as well as the Expert and Deluxe intro. that year, had a crossbolt in addition to the regular Baker system taper wedge fastening. There are early Paragon guns w/Damascus bbls. and some are non-ejector, but this grade was also produced w/ automatic ejectors and w/the finest fluid steel bbls., in lengths to 34 in., standard on Expert and Deluxe guns. Differences among the three models are in overall quality, finish, engraving and grade of fancy figured walnut in the stock and forearm; Expert and Deluxe wood may be carved as well as checkered. Choice of straight, full or half-pistol grip was offered. A single trigger was available in the two higher grades. The Paragon was available in 10 ga (Damascus bbls. only), and the other two models were regularly produced in 12, 16 and 20 ga.
Paragon grade . . . . NiB $5010 Ex $4010 Gd $2033
Paragon grade w/auto ejector . . . . NiB $4455 Ex $2978 Gd $2270
Expert grade . . . . NiB $8010 Ex $6510 Gd $2844
Deluxe grade . . . . NiB $17,000 Ex $12,000 Gd $7133
w/ejectors, add. $550

BARRET FIREARMS MFG. — Murfreesboto, TN

SOVEREIGN SERIES

O/U. Boxlock w/ornamental sideplates. Gauge 12, 20 or 28. Brrls.: 26-, 28- or 30-in., choke tubes, ejectors. Stock: Prince of Wales grip, checkered walnut. Receiver: coin finish, engraved. Made 2016-20.
Albany model . . . . NiB $5255 Ex $4010 Gd $3010
BxPRO Model (12 gauge only, 30
** or 32-in. brrls.) . . . . NiB $2800 Ex $2300 Gd $2010**
Rutherford Model (12, 16, 20 or 28 gauge;
** 26- or 28-in. brrls.). . . . . . . NiB $2010 Ex $1610 Gd $1210**
Beltrami (SxS; 12, 20 or 28;
** ejectors; 2016-20) . . . . NiB $5510 Ex $4455 Gd $3355**

BELKNAP SHOTGUNS — Louisville, KY

Belknap was a hardware distributor from 1840 thru 1986 that had shotguns made and marked with their own name by Savage and Stevens.

MODEL B-63 SINGLE-SHOT. . . NiB $229 Ex $135 Gd $105

Takedown. Visible hammer. Automatic ejector. Gauges: 12, 20 and .410. Bbls.: 26- to 36-in., F choke. Weight: Average 6 lbs. Plain pistol-grip stock and forearm.

MODEL B-63E SINGLE-SHOT . . . NiB $209 Ex $133 Gd $95

Same general specifications as Model B-68 except has side lever opening instead of top lever.

MODEL B-64
SLIDE-ACTION SHOTGUN . . . NiB $339 Ex $244 Gd $225

Hammerless. Gauges: 12, 16, 20 and .410. Three round tubular magazine. Various bbl. lengths and chokes from 26-in. to 30-in. Weight: 6.25 to 7.5 lbs. Walnut-finished hardwood stock.

GRADING: **NiB** = New in Box   **Ex** = Excellent or NRA 95%   **Gd** = Good or NRA 68%

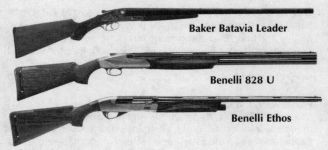

Baker Batavia Leader

Benelli 828 U

Benelli Ethos

MODEL B-65C
AUTOLOADING SHOTGUN... NiB $533 Ex $400 Gd $290
Browning-type lightweight alloy receiver. 12 ga. only. Four round tubular magazine. Bbl.: plain, 28-in. Weight: About 8.25 lbs. Disc. 1949.

MODEL B-68 SINGLE-SHOT ... NiB $199 Ex $144 Gd $100
Takedown. Visible hammer. Automatic ejector. Gauges: 12, 16, 20 and .410. Bbls.: 26-in. to 36-in.; F choke. Weight: 6 lbs. Plain pistol-grip stock and forearm.

BENELLI — Urbino, Italy

Imported by Benelli USA, Accokeek, MD. Benelli's interia recoil models have been imported since the 1960s.

828 U . . . . NiB $2250 Ex $1760 Gd $1380
O/U. Break action. Gauge: 12. Brrls; 26- or 28-in. w/ 5 choke tubes. Weight: 6.5 lbs. Finish: Matte black or polished aluminum. Stock: Grade AA walnut, w/Progressive Comfort System buttstock. Removable trigger assembly. Patented Steel Locking System. Imported 2015.
20 gauge . . . . NiB $3000 Ex $2900 Gd $1500
Sport model (12 gauge, extended choke tubes, 32-in. bbl.,
  matte blue receiver) . . . . NiB $4000 Ex $3890 Gd $1800
Upland model (12 gauge, extended choke tubes, 24-in. bbl.,
  matte blue receiver) . . . . NiB $3000 Ex $2900 Gd $1500

SL-80 SERIES
Semiautomatic. Gauge: 12 only. 2.75-in. chamber. Bbl.: 26 or 28-in., fixed choke, ventrib. Finish: semi-gloss black. Weight: 7.4 lbs. Matte black finish and European hardwood stock. Disc. 1985.
Model 80 Special Skeet/Trap (12 gauge, fixed choke,
  28-in. bbl., nickel receiver) . . . NiB $900 Ex $700 Gd $580
Model 201 Field Grade (20 gauge, 26-in. bbl.,
  5.8 lbs.) . . . . NiB $830 Ex $700 Gd $510
Model 121 M1 MILITARY/POLICE (7-rnd.
  magazine, 19.75-in. bbl. 39.75 in. overall, cylinder
  choke, Post front sight, fixed buckhorn rear
  sight.) . . . . NiB $680 Ex $555 Gd $335
Model 121 Slug (21-in. bbl., iron
  sights) . . . . NiB $880 Ex $710 Gd $50
Model 121V field grade . . . . NiB $780 Ex $630 Gd $430
Model 123V field grade (Ergal aluminum alloy
  receiver photo engraved) . . . . . NiB $880 Ex $710 Gd $50

BIMILLIONAIRE . . . . NiB $2480 Ex $1555 Gd $1110
Semiauto. Gauge: 12 or 20, 4-rnd. magazine. Brrls: 26-in. Weight: 6-7.3 lbs. Finish: coin receiver with elaborate engraving. Stock: Grade AA walnut. Removable trigger assembly. Imported 2010-12.

BLACK EAGLE SERIES
Semiauto. Two-piece aluminum and steel receiver. Ga: 12; 3-in. chamber. Four round magazine. Screw-in choke tubes

(SK, IC, M, IM, F). Bbls.: Ventilated rib; 21, 24, 26 or 28 in. w/bead front sight; 24-in. rifled slug. 42.5 to 49.5 in. overall. Weight: 7.25 lbs. (28-in. bbl.). Matte black lower receiver w/blued upper receiver and bbl. Checkered walnut stock w/high-gloss finish and drop adjustment. Imported from 1989 to 1990 and 1997 to 1998.
Limited edition . . . . NiB $1587 Ex $1090 Gd $965
Competition model . . . . NiB $953 Ex $755 Gd $523
Slug model (disc. 1992) . . . . . NiB $815 Ex $608 Gd $466
Standard model (disc. 1990) . . NiB $879 Ex $770 Gd $505

CORDOBA . . . . NiB $1800 Ex $1230 Gd $760
Interia-operated semiauto. Gauges: 12 or 20 gauge w/3-in. chamber. 28- or 30-in. bbl. 49.7 to 51.7 in. overall. Weight: 6.3 to 7.3 lbs. Four round magazine. Five screw-in choke tubes (C, IC, M, IM, F). ComfortTech stock. Matte black finish. Imported 2005 to date.

ETHOS . . . . NiB $1780 Ex $1355 Gd $980
Interia-operated semiauto. Gauge: 12, 20 or 28 gauge w/3-in. chamber, 4-rnd. magazine; 26- or 28-in. bbl.; Weight: 6.5 lbs.; Stock: AA Grade satin walnut w/Progressive Comfort recoil system; Finish: Black or nickel receiver. Four round magazine. Imported 2014 to date.
BE.S.T. model (Benelli Surface Treatment,
  black anodized receiver, black polymer
  stock, 2020-date) . . . . NiB $1955 Ex $1655 Gd $1280
BE.S.T. Cordoba model (Benelli Surface Treatment,
  ported bbl., black anodized receiver, black polymer
  stock, 2021-date) . . . . NiB $2000 Ex $1755 Gd $1355
Sport model (ported bbl., engraved nickel
  receiver, 2018-date) . . . . . . NiB $2000 Ex $1685 Gd $1280
Supersport model (ported bbl., nickel receiver, carbon
  fiber stock, 2021-date) . . . . NiB $1965 Ex $1710 Gd $1410

EXECUTIVE SERIES
Semiauto. Montefeltro-style rotating bolt w/three locking lugs. All-steel lower receiver engraved, gold inlay by Bottega Incisione di Cesare Giovanelli. 12 ga. only. 21-, 24-, 26-, or 28-in. VR bbl. w/5 screw-in choke tubes or fixed chokes. Custom deluxe walnut stock and forend. Built to customer specifications on special order from 1996-2012.
Grade I . . . . NiB $6500 Ex $4100 Gd $3010
Grade II . . . . NiB $7355 Ex $4755 Gd $3355
Grade III . . . . NiB $8510 Ex $5255 Gd $3655

LEGACY . . . . NiB $1625 Ex $1255 Gd $780
Semiauto. Gauges: 12 and 20 ga. w/3-in. chambers. 24-26- or 28-in. bbl. 47.63 to 49.62 in. overall. Weight: 5.8 to 7.5 lbs. Four round magazine. Five screw-in choke tubes. Lower alloy receiver and upper steel reciever cover. Features Benelli's inertia recoil operating system. Imported 1998 to date.
Sporting model (12 gauge only, 28- or 30-in. brrl., grey
  medallion on receiver) . . NiB $2180 Ex $1580 Gd $1110
Limited Edition (engraved receiver, only
  2000 mfg.) . . . . NiB $1755 Ex $1255 Gd $910

M1 SUPER 90 PRACTICAL . . . . . NiB $930 Ex $680 Gd $455
Interia-operated Semiauto. Gauge: 12. Chambers: 3-in. Bbl. 26 -in. w/muzzle brake. Stock: Synthetic, black. Weight: 7.6 lbs. Includes set of 3 choke tubes. Oversized controls. Imported 1998-2004.

M1 SUPER 90 TACTICAL. . . . . . NiB $730 Ex $530 Gd $340
Interia-operated Semiauto. Gauge: 12, 3-in. chamber. 5-rnd. magazine. Cylinder choke. 18.5-in. bbl. Weight: 6.7 to 7 lbs. Matte black finish. Stock: Synthetic, traditional or pistol grip.

Benelli Legacy Limited Edition (Only 250 Made)

Benelli M1 – Super 90 w/Pistol Grip

Sights: Post front, fixed buckhorn rear, drift adj. Imported 1993-2004.

M1 SUPER 90 DEFENSE . . . . . NiB $1093 Ex $966 Gd $509
Same general specifications as Model Super 90 except w/pistol-grip stock. Available w/Ghost-Ring sight option. Imported 1986 to 1998.

M1 SUPER 90 FIELD . . . . NIB $855 EX $680 GD $430
Inertia-recoil Semiauto shotgun. Gauge: 12; 3-in. chamber. Three round magazine. Bbl.: 21, 24, 26 or 28 in. 42.5 to 49.5 in. overall. Choke: SK, IC, M, IM, F. Matte receiver. Standard polymer stock or satin walnut (26- or 28-in. bbl. only). Bead front sight. Imported from 1990 to 2006.
w/Realtree camo stock . . . . . . NiB $1066 Ex $743 Gd $488
w/polymer stock . . . . NiB $766 Ex $563 Gd $447
w/walnut stock . . . . NiB $1031 Ex $660 Gd $458

M1 SUPER 90
Same general specifications as M1 Super 90 Field except w/5-rnd. magazine. 18.5-in. bbl. Cylinder bore. 39.75 in. overall. Weight: 6.5 lbs. Polymer standard stock. Rifle or Ghost-Ring sights. Imported 1986 to 1998.
w/rifle sights . . . . NiB $988 Ex $677 Gd $549
w/ghost-ring sights . . . . NiB $1096 Ex $786 Gd $659
w/Realtree camo finish, add $150

M1 SUPER 90 SPORTING
SPECIAL . . . . NiB $877 Ex $655 Gd $589
Same general specifications as M1 Super 90 Field except w/18.5-in. bbl. 39.75 in. overall. Weight: 6.5 lbs. Ghost-ring sights. Polymer stock. Imported from 1993 to 1997.

M2 SERIES
Redesign of M1 w/ new receiver, trigger guard, safety. Guage: 12 or 20, 3-in. chamber. Bbl.: 21-, 24-, 26- or 28-in. ventrib w/chokes, Crio treatment. Stock: Synthetic or satin wood, Comfort Tech system. Finish: matte black or camo. Weight: 6.9 to 7.2 lbs. Interia-operated Semiauto. Imported 2004 to date.
American Series model (12 gauge, 26- or
28-in. VR bbl., synthetic stock, black
or camo, 2010-11) . . . . NiB $990 Ex $880 Gd $680
Field . . . . NiB $1300 Ex $1000 Gd $730
Field camo finish, add. $100
Field Compact (13-in. LOP) . . NiB $1300 Ex $1000 Gd $730
Field Rifled Slug (24-in. rilfed bbl., adj.
iron sights) . . . . NiB $1310 Ex $1000 Gd $730
Field Rifled Slug camo finish, add. $100
Field Turkey (21-, 24- or 26-in. bbl., optic ready,
disc. 2015) . . . . NiB $1310 Ex $900 Gd $600
American Series (12 gauge, 26- or 28-in. bbl., black or
camo finish, 2010-11) . . . . . . NiB $1000 Ex $755 Gd $630
Three Gun (21-in. bbl., mfg.
2012-15) . . . . NiB $2350 Ex $1800 Gd $1000
Practical (26-in. bbl., 2005) . . NiB $1196 Ex $970 Gd $480
Tacical (18.5-in. bbl., traditional or pistol grip stock,
imported 2005) . . . . NiB $1230 Ex $900 Gd $510

M3 SUPER 90 PUMP/AUTOLOADER
Inertia-recoil Semiauto and/or pump action. Gauge: 12. Seven round magazine. Cylinder choke. 19.75-in. bbl. 41 in. overall (31 in. folded). Weight: 7 to 7.5 lbs. Matte black finish. Stock: standard synthetic, pistol-grip or folding tubular steel. Standard rifle or Ghost-Ring sights. Imported 1989 to 2015. Caution: Increasing the magazine capacity to more than 5 rounds in M3 shotguns w/pistol-grip stocks violates provisions of the 1994 Crime Bill. This model may be used legally only by the military and law-enforcement agencies.
Standard model. . . . . NiB $1477 Ex $1067 Gd $799
Pistol-grip model . . . . NiB $1644 Ex $1133 Gd $990
w/folding stock . . . . NiB $1190 Ex $955 Gd $944
w/laser sight . . . . NiB $1766 Ex $1388 Gd $1100
w/ghost-ring sights, add $100

M4 TACTICAL . . . . NiB $1755 Ex $1255 Gd $930
Gas-operated Semiauto. Civilian version of U.S. military M4, gas regulating system. Gauge: 12; 3-in. chamber. Four round magazine. Bbl.: 18.5 in. 40 in. overall. Choke: M. Matte receiver. Standard or pistol grip sythetic stock. Ghost ring rear, post front sights. Imported from 2003 to date.
M1040 Limited Edition (2,500 mfg.,
2003-04) . . . . NiB $1380 Ex $960 Gd $660
Cerakote Tactical (Carakote finish, 2016 only), add $200
H20 Tactical (H20 Carakote finish), add. $200

MONTEFELTRO (SUPER 90)
Semiauto. Gauges: 12 or 20 gauge w/3-in. chamber. 21- 24- 26- or 28-in. bbl. 43.7 to 49.5 in. overall. Weight: 5.3 to 7.5 lbs. Four round magazine. Five screw-in choke tubes (C, IC, M, IM, F). High gloss or satin walnut or Realtree Camo stock. Blued metal finish. Imported 1988 to 2011.
Silver model (nickel/blue engraved receiver,
2007). . . . . NiB $1590 Ex $1330 Gd $830
Standard Hunter model . . . . . NiB $1155 Ex $865 Gd $490
Slug model (disc. 1992) . . . . . . NiB $744 Ex $639 Gd $440
Turkey model . . . . NiB $744 Ex $639 Gd $440
Uplander model . . . . NiB $744 Ex $639 Gd $440
Limited Edition (1995-96) . . . NiB $2077 Ex $1688 Gd $1176
Grade II (upgraded wood stock,
gold accents) . . . . NiB $1000 Ex $780 Gd $610

MONTEFELTRO . . . . NiB $1010 Ex $755 Gd $410
Semiauto. Gauges: 12 or 20 gauge w/3-in. chamber. 24- 26- or 28-in. ventrib bbl. Stock: Satin walnut. Blued metal finish. Imported 2012 to date.
Compact model (13-in. LOP) . . NiB $1010 Ex $755 Gd $410
Left Hnaded model, add. $90
Sporting model (30-in. bbl.) . . . NiB $1230 Ex $910 Gd $660
Synthetic Stock model (black
finish) . . . . NiB $1010 Ex $755 Gd $410

NOVA. NiB $410 Ex $310 Gd $210
Pump-action. Gauge: 12 or 20. Chambers: 2.75 or 3 in. Four-round magazine. Bbl. 24, 26 or 28 in.; red bar sights. Stock: Synthetic,(Xtra Brown in 12 gauge or Timber HD in 20 gauge).

GRADING: **NiB** = New in Box   **Ex** = Excellent or NRA 95%   **Gd** = Good or NRA 68%

SHOTGUNS

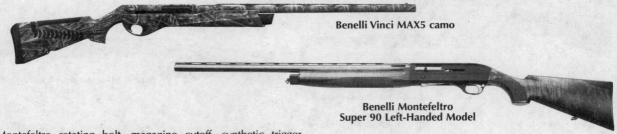

Benelli Vinci MAX5 camo

**Benelli Montefeltro
Super 90 Left-Handed Model**

Montefeltro rotating bolt, magazine cutoff, synthetic trigger assembly. Introduced 1999. Imported from Italy.

H20 model (matte nickel finish)   NiB $605 Ex $510 Gd $355
Slug model (24-in. rifled bbl.,
   open sights) . . . . NiB $450 Ex $360 Gd $290
Slug and Field Combo model (24-in. rifled bbl. and 26-in.
   smooth bore bbl.) . . . . NiB $465 Ex $370 Gd $300
Tactical model (18.5-in. bbl.,
   open sights) . . . . NiB $405 Ex $355 Gd $275
camo finish, add $100

RAFFAELLO SERIES
Semiauto. Gauge: 12, 3-in. chamber w/4-rnd. magazine. 26-in. ventrib bbl. Stock: Satin walnut. Blued metal finish. Imported 2005 to 2012.

Standard model . . . . NiB $1630 Ex $1155 Gd $810
Deluxe model (engraved
   receiver) . . . . NiB $2000 Ex $1555 Gd $1110
Limited Edition Deluxe Legacy model (engraved receiver,
   gold inlay) . . . . NiB $2480 Ex $1555 Gd $1110
Crio 28 model (28 gauge) . . . NiB $1755 Ex $1355 Gd $1000
Executive Limited Edition model (20 gauge, silver "E" inset
   in pistol grip, 2007-12) . . . NiB $2480 Ex $1555 Gd $1110

SPORT . . . . NiB $1266 Ex $999 Gd $654
Similar to the Black Eagle Competition model except has one-piece matte-finished alloy receiver w/inscribed red Benelli logo. 26 or 28 in. bbl. w/2 inchangable carbon fiber VRs. Oil-finished checkered walnut stock w/adjustable buttpad and buttstock. Imported 1997 to 2002.

SPORT II . . . . NiB $1700 Ex $1280 Gd $810
Semiauto. Gauge: 12 or 20, 3-in. chamber.. Bbl.: 26-, 28- or 30-in. w/ventrib, ported w/5 extended choke tubes. Stock: Checkered walnut. Weight 8 lbs. Imported 2003 to date.

SUPER BLACK EAGLE SERIES
Interia-operated Semiauto. Same general specifications as Black Eagle except w/3.5-in. chamber that accepts 2.75-, 3- and 3.5-in. shells. Two round magazine (3.5-in.), 3-rnd. magazine (2.75- or 3-in.). High-gloss, satin finish or camo stock. Realtree camo, matte black or blued metal finish. Imported 1991 to 2005.

Standard model . . . . NiB $1096 Ex $933 Gd $766
Realtree camo model . . . . . . NiB $1221 Ex $1099 Gd $866
Slug model . . . . NiB $1254 Ex $958 Gd $744
Limited edition . . . . NiB $1979 Ex $1654 Gd $1177
w/wood stock, add $40
Left-hand model, add $100

SUPER BLACK EAGLE I SERIES
Similar to Super Black Eagle but updated design. Finish: Realtree camo, matte black or blued metal finish. Stock: wood or synthetic, traditional or Steady Grip pistol grip. Disc. 2005.
wood stock model . . . . NiB $1110 Ex $810 Gd $555
camo finish, add $100
Steady Grip model, add $200

SUPER BLACK EAGLE II SERIES
Similar to Super Black Eagle I but updated design. Bbl.: 24-, 26- or 28-in., ventrib, Crio treatment. Finish: Various camo, matte black or blued metal finish. Stock: ComforTech wood or synthetic, traditional or Steady Grip pistol grip. Imported 2004 to date.

wood stock model . . . . NiB $1110 Ex $810 Gd $555
camo finish, add $100
Slug model (24-in. rifled bbl. w/open sights,
   2004-16) . . . . NiB $1755 Ex $1280 Gd $855
SteadyGrip Turkey model (24-in. bbl., optic ready,
   pistol grip stock, full camo finish,
   disc. 2016) . . . . NiB $1810 Ex $1310 Gd $860

SUPER BLACK EAGLE III . . . . NiB $1700 Ex $1280 Gd $810
Similar to Super Black Eagle II but updated design. Bbl.: 26- or 28-in., VR, Crio treatment. Finish: Various camo or black. Stock: ComforTech synthetic. Weight: 5.9-7 lbs. Imported 2017 to date.
Camo finish, ... add $90
Rifled Slug model (12 gauge, 24-in.
   bbl. w/iron sights, black synthetic
   stock, 2018-date) . . . . . . NiB $1755 Ex $1530 Gd $1210
Turkey Performance Shop model (12 gauge,
   24-in. bbl., synthetic SteadyGrip
   camo stock, 2019) . . . . . . NiB $2655 Ex $2330 Gd $1810
Water Performance Shop model
   (12 gauge, 28-in. bbl., synthetic
   camo stock, 2019) . . . . NiB $2730 Ex $2390 Gd $1855
BE.S.T. model (Benelli Surface Treatment,
   black anodized receiver, black polymer
   Tech3 stock, 2020-date) . . NiB $1955 Ex $1655 Gd $1280

SUPER VINCI . . . . NiB $1600 Ex $1180 Gd $780
Similar to Vinci series except 12 gauge only, 3.5-in. chamber. Bbl.: 26-, 28- or 30-in. w/ventrib, Crio treatment, choke tubes. Stock: Synthetic ComforTech. Finish: Matte black or various camo. Weight 7 lbs. Imported 2011 to date.
Turkey model (full camo finish) . . NiB $1680 Ex $1230 Gd $930

SUPERNOVA . . . . NiB $490 Ex $355 Gd $255
Pump action. Gauge: 12, 3.5-in. chamber. Bbl.: 24-, 26-, or 28-in. w/ventrib, choke tubes. Stock: Synthetic ComforTech. Finish: Matte black or various camo. Weight 8 lbs. Imported 2006 to date.
Slug model (24-in. rifled bbl. w/sights,
   optic ready) . . . . NiB $710 Ex $455 Gd $330
SteadyGrip Turkey model (pistol grip stock, full camo,
   24-in. bbl.) . . . . NiB $610 Ex $455 Gd $355
Tactical model (traditional or pistol grip stock,
   black or full camo finish, 18.5-in. bbl.,
   rifle or ghost ring sights) . . . . . NiB $455 Ex $335 Gd $255

SUPERSPORT . . . . NiB $1910 Ex $1500 Gd $1080
Semiauto. Gauge: 12 or 20, 3-in. chamber, 4-rnd. magazine. Bbl.: 28- or 30-in. w/ventrib, ported w/5 extended choke

Beretta Model 682 Over/Under Sporting

Beretta Model 682 Over/Under Trap

tubes. Stock: Black carbon fiber. Finish: Satin nickel receiver w/Supersport on side. Weight 7.9 lbs. Magazine window 20 gauge only. Imported 2004 to date.

ULTRA LIGHT . . . . **NiB $1500 Ex $1010 Gd $710**
Interia-operated Semiauto. Gauges: 12, 20 or 28 gauge w/3-in. chamber. 24- or 26-in. bbl. 45.5 to 47.5 in. overall. Weight: 5.0 to 6.1 lbs. Two round magazine. Five screw-in choke tubes (C, IC, M, IM, F). High gloss WeatherCoat stock. Blued metal finish. Imported 2006 to date.

VINCI SERIES
Interia-operated Semiauto. 3-piece modular construction. Gauges: 12 gauge w/3-in. chamber. 26- or 28-in. bbl. 45.7 to 49.7 in. overall. Weight: 6.7 to 6.9 lbs. Three round magazine. Five screw-in choke tubes (C, IC, M, IM, F). ComfortTech stock. Matte black finish. Imported 2009 to date.
black finish . . . . **NiB $1280 Ex $955 Gd $710**
full camo finish, add **$100**
Slug model (24-in. rifled bbl. w/rifle sights), add **$100**
Cordoba model (28- or 30-in. ventrib bbl.,
   2011-15) . . . . **NiB $1800 Ex $1310 Gd $755**
Speed Bolt model (tungsten speed bolt for faster
   cycling, 2013-15) . . . . **NiB $1430 Ex $1080 Gd $780**
Supersport model (28- or 30-in. ported bbl.,
   2011-15) . . . . **NiB $1955 Ex $1410 Gd $955**
Tactical model (12 gauge, 18.5-in. bbl., synthetic pistol
   grip stock, 2014-20) . . . . . . **NiB $1310 Ex $1110 Gd $855**

BERETTA USA CORP. — Accokeek, MD.

Manufactured by Fabbrica D'Armi Pietro Beretta S.P.A. in Gardone Val Trompia (Brescia), Italy. Imported by Beretta USA. Previously by Garcia Corp.

MODEL 409PB
HAMMERLESS DOUBLE . . . . **NiB $1555 Ex $1310 Gd $855**
SxS. Boxlock. Double triggers. Plain extractors. Gauges: 12, 16, 20, 28. Bbls.: 27.5-, 28.5- and 30-in., IC/M choke or M/F choke. Weight: from 5.5 to 7.75 lbs., depending on ga. and bbl. length. Straight or pistol-grip stock and beavertail forearm, checkered. Imported 1934 to 1964.

MODEL 410E
SxS. Same general specifications as Model 409PB except has automatic ejectors and is of higher quality throughout. Imported 1934 to 1964.
12 ga. . . . . **NiB $1510 Ex $1280 Gd $810**
20 ga. . . . . **NiB $2882 Ex $2096 Gd $1377**
28 ga. . . . . **NiB $3881 Ex $3036 Gd $2456**

MODEL 410 10-GA.
MAGNUM. . . . . **NiB $1555 Ex $1310 Gd $855**
SxS. Same as Model 410E except heavier construction. Plain extractors. Double triggers. 10-ga. Magnum, 3.5-in. chambers. 32-in. bbls., both F choke. Weight: about 10 lbs. Checkered pistol-grip stock and forearm, recoil pad. Imported 1934 to 1984.

MODEL 411E
SxS. Same general specifications as Model 409PB except has sideplates, automatic ejectors and is of higher quality throughout. Imported 1934 to 1964.
12 ga. . . . . **NiB $2077 Ex $1700 Gd $1179**
20 ga. . . . . **NiB $2866 Ex $2234 Gd $1590**
28 ga. . . . . **NiB $4339 Ex $3977 Gd $2766**

MODEL 424 HAMMERLESS
DOUBLE . . . . **NiB $1288 Ex $1292 Gd $957**
SxS. Boxlock. Light border engraving. Plain extractors. Gauges: 12, 20; chambers 2.75-in. in former, 3-in. in latter. Bbls.: 28-in. M/F choke, 26-in. IC/M choke. Weight: 5 lbs. 14 oz. to 6 lbs. 10 oz., depending on ga. and bbl. length. English-style straight-grip stock and forearm, checkered. Imported 1977 to 1984.

MODEL 426E . . . . **NiB $1588 Ex $1233 Gd $1067**
Same as Model 424 except action body is finely engraved, silver pigeon inlaid in top lever; has selective automatic ejectors and selective single trigger, stock and forearm of select European walnut. Imported 1977-84.

MODEL 450, 451 AND 452 SERIES
SxS. Custom English-style sidelock. Single, non-selective trigger or double triggers. Manual safety. Selective automatic ejectors. Gauge: 12; 2.75- or 3-in. chambers. Bbls.: 26, 28 or 30 in. choked to customers' specifications. Weight: 6.75 lbs. Checkered high-grade walnut stock. Receiver w/coin-silver finish. Imported 1948. Disc.
Model 450 EL (disc. 1982) . . . **NiB $8334 Ex $6688 Gd $4731**
Model 450 EELL (disc.
   1982) . . . . **NiB $10,655 Ex $6798 Gd $4880**
Model 451 (disc. 1987) . . . . **NiB $6443 Ex $5670 Gd $3990**
Model 451 E (disc. 1989) . . **NiB $7125 Ex $6225 Gd $4350**
Model 451 EL (disc.
   1985) . . . . **NiB $17,787 Ex $14,866 Gd $11,700**
Model 451 EELL (disc.
   1990) . . . . **NiB $15,788 Ex $12,877 Gd $10,777**
Model 452 (Intro.
   1990) . . . . **NiB $29,988 Ex $21,980 Gd $18,799**
Model 452 EELL
   (intro. 1992) . . . . . **NiB $41,665 Ex $35,000 Gd $27,889**
w/extra bbls, add **30%**

MODEL 470 AND 471 SILVER HAWK SERIES
SxS. Gauge: 12 and 20 ga. w/3-in. chambers. 26- or 28-in. bbl. Weight: 5.9 to 6.5 lbs. Low profile, improved box lock action w/single selective trigger. Selected walnut, checkered stock and forend. Metal front bead sight. Scroll-engraved receiver w/gold inlay and silver chrome finish. Imported 1999 to date.
Model 470 Silver Hawk
   (12 gauge, 1998-02) . . . . . **NiB $2355 Ex $1710 Gd $1230**
20 gauge model, add **15%**
Model 470 EL (12 or 20 gauge,
   2002-06) . . . . **NiB $4510 Ex $4010 Gd $3555**

SHOTGUNS

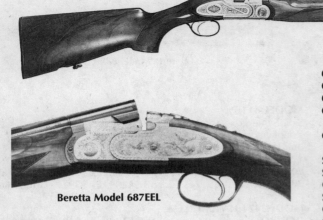

Beretta Model 687EL

Beretta Model 687EEL

Model 471 Silver Hawk
(2003-13) . . . . NiB $3660 Ex $2710 Gd $1810
Model 471 EL (2005-10) . . . NiB $7510 Ex $5510 Gd $3755
w/extra bbls., add. 30%

MODEL 486 PARALLELO . . . NiB $4655 Ex $2610 Gd $1855
Side-by-side. Rounded boxlock. Gauges: 12, 20 or 28. Bbls.: 28- or 30-in. w/fixed choke or choke tubes. Stock: Checkered pistol-grip buttstock and forend. Ejectors and extractors. Weight: 7.2 lbs. Imported 2014 to date.

MODEL 625
Side-by-side. Boxlock. Gauges: 12 or 20. Bbls.: 26-, 28- or 30-in. w/fixed choke combinations. Single selective or double triggers w/extractors. Checkered English-style buttstock and forend. Imported 1984 to 1986.
w/double triggers . . . . NiB $1591 Ex $900 Gd $667
w/single selective trigger . . . NiB $1880 Ex $1067 Gd $700
20 ga., add $200

MODEL 626 SERIES
Field Grade side-by-side. Boxlock action w/single selective trigger, extractors and automatic safety. Gauges: 12 (2.75-in. chambers); 20 (3-in. chambers). Bbls.: 26- or 28-in. w/ Mobilchoke or various fixed-choke combinations. Weight: 6.75 lbs. (12 ga.). Bright chrome finish. Checkered European walnut buttstock and forend in straight English style. Imported 1985 to 1994.
Field (disc. 1988) . . . . NiB $1500 Ex $1190 Gd $700
Onyx . . . . NiB $1779 Ex $1288 Gd $1006
Onyx Magnum (3.5-in.,
       disc. 1993) . . . . NiB $1798 Ex $1388 Gd $1098
20 ga., add 50%

MODEL 627
Same as Model 626 S/S except w/engraved sideplates and pistol-grip or straight English-style stock. Imported 1985 to 1994.
Model 627 EL Field . . . . NiB $2370 Ex $2090 Gd $1550
Model 627 EL Sport . . . . . . NiB $2592 Ex $2210 Gd $1776
Model 627 EELL . . . . NiB $4460 Ex $3978 Gd $2666

MODEL 682 SERIES
O/U. Hammerless takedown w/single selective trigger. Gauges: 12, 20, 28, .410. Bbls.: 26- to 34-in. w/fixed chokes or Mobilchoke tubes. Checkered European walnut buttstock/forend in various grades and configurations. Imported 1984 to 2000.

Comp Skeet model . . . . NiB $1566 Ex $1160 Gd $1004
Comp Skeet Deluxe model NiB $1789 Ex $1440 Gd $1166
Comp Super Skeet . . . . NiB $2599 Ex $2055 Gd $1490
Comp Skeet model, 2-bbl.
    set (disc. 1989) . . . . NiB $5100 Ex $4256 Gd $2920
Comp Skeet, 4 bbl. set
    (disc. 1996). . . . . NiB $5786 Ex $4670 Gd $3241
Sporting Continental . . . . . . NiB $1589 Ex $1170 Gd $1097
Sporting Combo . . . . NiB $1778 Ex $1566 Gd $1180
Gold Sporting . . . . NiB $1788 Ex $1266 Gd $1011
Super Sporting . . . . NiB $1566 Ex $1365 Gd $1291
Comp Trap Gold X . . . . NiB $2269 Ex $1775 Gd $1231
Comp Trap Top Single
    (1986-95) . . . . NiB $2177 Ex $1688 Gd $1166
Comp Trap Live Pigeon
    (1990-98) . . . . NiB $2769 Ex $2255 Gd $1568
Comp Mono/Combo Trap
    Gold X . . . . NiB $2977 Ex $2510 Gd $1765
Comp Mono Trap (1985-88) . . NiB $1867 Ex $1588 Gd $1100
Super Trap Gold X
    (1991-95) . . . . NiB $2267 Ex $1880 Gd $1266
Super Trap Combo Gold X
    (1991-97) . . . . NiB $3166 Ex $2478 Gd $1776
Super Trap Top Single Gold X
    (1991-95) . . . . NiB $2265 Ex $2099 Gd $1369
Super Trap Unsingle
    (1992-94) . . . . NiB $2210 Ex $2050 Gd $1319

MODEL 686 SERIES
O/U. Low-profile improved boxlock action. Single selective trigger. Selective automatic ejectors. Gauges: 12, 20, 28 w/3.5-3- or 2.75-in. chambers, depending upon ga. Bbls.: 26-, 28-, 30-in. w/fixed chokes or Mobilchoke tubes. Weight: 5.75 to 7.5 lbs. Checkered American walnut stock and forearm of various qualities, depending upon model. Receiver finishes also vary, but all have blued bbls. Sideplates to simulate sidelock action on EL models. Imported 1988 to 1995.
Field Onyx . . . . NiB $1335 Ex $1108 Gd $733
(3.5-in. Mag., disc.
    1993 & reintro.1996) . . NiB $4370 Ex $2888 Gd $2280
EL Gold Perdiz (1992-97) . . NiB $2077 Ex $1576 Gd $1200
Essential (1994-96) . . . . NiB $1009 Ex $808 Gd $635
Silver Essential (1997-98) . . . . NiB $1180 Ex $966 Gd $680
Silver Pigeon Onyx
    (intro. 1996) . . . . NiB $1566 Ex $1254 Gd $870
Silver Perdiz Onyx
    (disc. 1996) . . . . NiB $1488 Ex $1155 Gd $866
Silver Pigeon/Perdiz Onyx Combo . . NiB $1133 Ex $866 Gd $633
L Silver Perdiz (disc. 1994) . . NiB $1288 Ex $1007 Gd $766
Skeet Silver Pigeon (1996-98) NiB $1276 Ex $988 Gd $766
Skeet Silver Perdiz
    (1994-96) . . . . NiB $1570 Ex $1288 Gd $944
Skeet Silver Pigeon/Perdiz
    Combo . . . . NiB $1570 Ex $1288 Gd $944
Sporting Special (1987-93) NiB $1798 Ex $1369 Gd $1100
Sporting English (1991-92) . NiB $1820 Ex $1400 Gd $1188
Sporting Onyx
    w/fixed chokes (1991-92) NiB $1743 Ex $1388 Gd $1014
Sporting Onyx w/ choke
    tubes (intro. 1992) . . . . . . NiB $1344 Ex $1130 Gd $966

Beretta Model A-303

Sporting Onyx Gold
(disc. 1993) . . . . NiB $1879 Ex $1577 Gd $1188
Sporting Silver Pigeon
(intro. 1996) . . . . NiB $1598 Ex $1266 Gd $1005
Sporting Silver Perdiz
(1993-96) . . . . NiB $1612 Ex $1288 Gd $1130
Sporting Collection Sport
(1996-97) . . . . NiB $1188 Ex $1033 Gd $892
Sporting Combo . . . . NiB $2667 Ex $2174 Gd $1545
Trap International (1994-95) . . NiB $1144 Ex $967 Gd $755
Trap Silver Pigeon
(intro. 1997) . . . . NiB $1266 Ex $1057 Gd $798
Trap Top Mono (intro. 1998) . . NiB $1279 Ex $1088 Gd $800
Ultralight Onyx (intro. 1992). . NiB $1599 Ex $1366 Gd $968
Ultralight Del. Onyx
(intro. 1998). . . . . NiB $2056 Ex $1665 Gd $1156

MODEL 687 SERIES
O/U. Same as Model 686 except w/decorative sideplates and varying grades of engraving and game-scene motifs.
L Onyx (disc. 1991) . . . . NiB $1460 Ex $1233 Gd $865
L Onyx Gold Field (1988-89). . . . NiB $1688 Ex $1344 Gd $966
L Onyx Silver Pigeon. . . . . . NiB $1288 Ex $1668 Gd $1208
EL Onyx (disc. 1990) . . . . . . NiB $2855 Ex $2344 Gd $1629
EL Gold Pigeon . . . . NiB $3266 Ex $2688 Gd $1863
EL Gold Pigeon small
frame . . . . NiB $3090 Ex $2451 Gd $1761
EL Gold Pigeon Sporting
(intro 1993) . . . . NiB $4388 Ex $3571 Gd $2510
EELL Diamond Pigeon . . . . NiB $4416 Ex $3620 Gd $2560
EELL Diamond Pigeon Skeet . . NiB $4233 Ex $3548 Gd $2480
EELL Diamond Pigeon
Sporting . . . . NiB $4416 Ex $3578 Gd $2560
EELL Diamond Pigeon
X Trap . . . . NiB $3966 Ex $3133 Gd $2190
EELL Diamond Pigeon
Mono Trap . . . . NiB $4088 Ex $3310 Gd $2366
EELL Diamond Pigeon
Trap Combo . . . . NiB $5480 Ex $4766 Gd $3266
EELL Field Combo. . . . . NiB $4570 Ex $3775 Gd $2760
EELL Skeet 4-bbl. set . . . . . NiB $7588 Ex $5977 Gd $3554
EELL Gallery Special . . . . . . NiB $7233 Ex $5610 Gd $3798
EELL Gallery Special
Combo . . . . NiB $8235 Ex $6799 Gd $4571
EELL Gallery Special
pairs . . . . NiB $17,844 Ex $14,560 Gd $10,134
Sporting English (1991-92). . . NiB $2247 Ex $1867 Gd $1359
Sporting Silver Pigeon
(intro. 1996). . . . . NiB $2079 Ex $1677 Gd $1261
Sporting Silver Perdiz
(1993-96) . . . . NiB $2255 Ex $1767 Gd $1388

MODEL 690 SERIES
O/U. Boxlock. Gauge: 20 or 12; 3-in. chmbr. Barrel: 26- or 28-in. VR. w/Optima choke tubes. Imported 2017–date.
Field I (satin nickel receiver
w/etching, satin stock) . . NiB $2310 Ex $2055 Gd $1655
Field III (satin nickel receiver w/rollmark engraving, satin
stock) . . . . NiB $2255 Ex $1880 Gd $1130

Sporting (orange receiver
accents) . . . . NiB $2255 Ex $1910 Gd $1310

MODEL 692 SERIES
O/U. Boxlock. Gauge: 12; 3-in. chmbr. Barrel: 30- or 32-in. VR. w/OBSP-HP tubes. Imported 2014–date.
Sporting . . . . NiB $3320 Ex $2610 Gd $1810
US Trap (Monte Carlo
style stock) . . . . NiB $4190 Ex $3590 Gd $2630

MODEL 1200 SERIES
Semiauto. Short recoil action. Gauge: 12; 2.75- or 3-in. chamber. Six round magazine. 24-, 26- or 28-in. VR bbl. w/fixed chokes or Mobilchoke tubes. Weight: 7.25 lbs. Matte black finish. Adj. technopolymer stock and forend. Imported 1988 to 1990.
w/fixed choke (disc. 1989) . . . NiB $466 Ex $359 Gd $266
Riot (disc. 1994) . . . . NiB $476 Ex $368 Gd $277
w/Mobilchoke (disc. 1994). . . . NiB $741 Ex $577 Gd $400
Riot model . . . . NiB $805 Ex $633 Gd $451
w/Pistol-grip stock, add $65
w/Tritium sights, add $100

MODEL A300 OUTLANDER SERIES
Semiauto, gas system. Gauge: 12, 3-in. chamber. Bbl.: 28-in. ventrib, 5 choke tubes. Stock: black synthetic, oiled wood or full camo. Weight: 7.1 lbs. From 2012 to date.
synthetic stock . . . . NiB $675 Ex $500 Gd $380
wood stock, add $100
full camo finish, add $70
Turkey Camo model (100% Realtree Xtra Green
camo finish . . . . NiB $700 Ex $655 Gd $530

MODEL A-301 SERIES
Semiauto. Gas-operated. Scroll-decorated receiver. Gauge: 12 or 20; 2.75-in. chamber in former, 3-in. in latter. Three round magazine. Bbl.: Ventilated rib; 28-in. F or M choke, 26-in. IC. Weight: 6 lbs., 5 oz. – 6 lbs., 14 oz., depending on gauge and bbl. length. Checkered pistol-grip stock/forearm. Imported 1968 to 1982.
Field model . . . . NiB $400 Ex $335 Gd $245
Magnum model . . . . NiB $400 Ex $335 Gd $245
Skeet model (26-in. bbl., gold plated
trigger) . . . . NiB $400 Ex $335 Gd $245
Slug model (22-in. bbl. w/slug choke,
rifle sights). . . . . NiB $400 Ex $335 Gd $245
Trap model (30-in. bbil., Monte Carlo wood stock, gold
plated trigger) . . . . NiB $400 Ex $335 Gd $245

MODEL A-302 SERIES
Similar to gas-operated Model 301. Hammerless, takedown shotgun w/tubular magazine and Mag-Action that handles both 2.75- and 3-in. Magnum shells. Gauge: 12 or 20; 2.75- or 3-in. Mag. chambers. Bbl.: Vent or plain; 22-in./Slug (12 ga.); 26-in./IC (12 or 20) 28-in./M (20 ga.), 28-in./Multi-choke (12 or 20 ga.) 30-in./F (12 ga.). Weight: 6.5 lbs., 20 ga.; 7.25.lbs., 12 ga. Blued/black finish. Checkered European walnut, pistol-grip stock and forend. Imported from 1983 to c. 1987.
Standard model w/fixed choke . NiB $466 Ex $338 Gd $254
Standard model w/multi-choke . . NiB $490 Ex $345 Gd $258
Super Lusso model (hand engraved,
custom wood) . . . . NiB $1710 Ex $1255 Gd $910

GRADING: **NiB** = New in Box   **Ex** = Excellent or NRA 95%   **Gd** = Good or NRA 68%

447

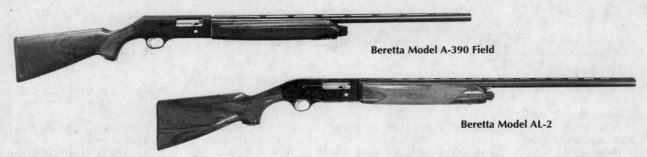

Beretta Model A-390 Field

Beretta Model AL-2

MODEL A-303 SERIES
Semiauto. Similar to Model 302, except w/target specifications in Trap, Skeet and Youth configurations, and weighs 6.5 to 8 lbs. Imported from 1983 to 1996.

Field and Upland models	NiB $523	Ex $400	Gd $288
Skeet and Trap (disc. 1994)	NiB $488	Ex $366	Gd $257
Slug model (disc. 1992)	NiB $453	Ex $377	Gd $260
Sporting Clays	NiB $600	Ex $453	Gd $279
Super Skeet	NiB $500	Ex $433	Gd $318
Super Trap	NiB $643	Ex $494	Gd $388
Waterfowl/Turkey model (disc. 1992)	NiB $525	Ex $460	Gd $354
Youth	NiB $405	Ex $376	Gd $277
w/Mobil choke, add			$75

MODEL AL-390 SERIES
Semiauto. Gas-operated, self-regulating action designed to handle any size load. Gauges: 12 or 20 w/ 3-in. chamber. Three round magazine. Bbl.: 24, 26, 28 or 30 in. w/VR and Mobilchoke tubes. Weight: 7.5 lbs. Select walnut stock w/ adj. comb. Blued or matte black finish. Imported 1992-96. Superseded by AL-390 series.

Standard/Slug models	NiB $525	Ex $377	Gd $296
Field/Silver Mallard models	NiB $525	Ex $377	Gd $296
Deluxe/Gold Mallard models	NiB $485	Ex $335	Gd $250
Turkey/Waterfowl model (w/matte finish)	NiB $577	Ex $366	Gd $300
20 ga., add			$75

MODEL AL-390 TARGET SERIES
Similar to the Model 390 Field except w/2.75-in. chamber. Skeet: 28-in. ported bbl. w/wide VR and fixed choke (SK). Trap: 30- or 32-in. w/Mobilchoke tubes. Weight: 7.5 lbs. Fully adj. buttstock. Imported from 1993 to 1996.

Sport Trap model	NiB $599	Ex $367	Gd $290
Sport Skeet model	NiB $479	Ex $345	Gd $266
Sporting Clays model (unported)	NiB $700	Ex $579	Gd $421
Super Trap model (ported)	NiB $577	Ex $367	Gd $292
Super Skeet model (ported)	NiB $569	Ex $355	Gd $307
w/ported bbl., add			$100
20 ga., add			$75

MODEL AL-1 FIELD GUN.... NiB $566 Ex $349 Gd $279
Same as Model AL-2 gas-operated Field Gun except has bbl. w/o rib, no engraving on receiver. Imported from 1971 to 1973.

MODEL AL-2 FIELD
Semiauto. Field Gun. Gas-operated. Engraved receiver (1968 version, 12 ga. only, had no engraving). Gauge: 12 or 20. 2.75-in. chamber. Three round magazine. Bbls.: VR; 30-in. F choke, 28-in. F or M choke, 26-in. IC. Weight: 6.5 to 7.25 lbs, depending on ga. and bbl. length. Checkered pistol-grip stock and forearm. Imported from 1968 to 1975.

w/Plain receiver	NiB $435	Ex $315	Gd $229
w/Engraved receiver	NiB $633	Ex $500	Gd $378

MODEL AL-2 MAGNUM ..... NiB $515 Ex $377 Gd $255
Same as Model AL-2 Field Gun except chambered for 12 ga. 3-in. Magnum shells; 30-in. F or 28-in. M choke bbl. only. Weight: About 8 lbs. Imported from 1973 to 1975.

MODEL AL-2 SKEET GUN .... NiB $466 Ex $321 Gd $234
Same as Model AL-2 Field Gun except has wide rib, 26-in. bbl. in SK choke only, checkered pistol-grip stock and beavertail forearm. Imported 1973 to 1975.

MODEL AL-2 TRAP GUN ..... NiB $445 Ex $341 Gd $246
Same as Model AL-2 Field Gun except has wide rib, 30 in. bbl. in F choke only, beavertail forearm. Monte Carlo stock w/recoil pad. Weight: About 7.75 lbs. Imported 1973 to 75.

MODEL AL-3
Similar to corresponding AL-2 models in design and general specifications. Imported from 1975 to 1976.

Field model	NiB $466	Ex $331	Gd $244
Magnum model	NiB $475	Ex $350	Gd $266
Skeet model	NiB $486	Ex $351	Gd $264
Trap model	NiB $453	Ex $335	Gd $266
Deluxe Trap (fully engraved receiver, glod trigger, premium grade wood stock, 1975-76)	NiB $605	Ex $566	Gd $339

AL390 FIELD SHOTGUN
Lightweight version of A-390 series. Gauges: 12 or 20 ga. 22-24-, 26-, 28-, or 30-in. bbl. 41.7 to 47.6 in. overall. Weight: 6.4 to 7.5 lbs. Imported 1992 to 1999.

Field/Silver Mallard model (12 or 20 ga.)	NiB $655	Ex $465	Gd $300
Field/Silver Mallard Youth model (20 ga.)	NiB $500	Ex $355	Gd $245
Field/Slug (12 ga. only)	NiB $525	Ex $433	Gd $266
Silver Mallard camo model	NiB $533	Ex $379	Gd $295
Silver Mallard model, synthetic stock	NiB $566	Ex $430	Gd $349
Gold Mallard (12 or 20 ga.)	NiB $800	Ex $656	Gd $445
NWTF Special model, camo	NiB $645	Ex $355	Gd $339
NTWF Special model, synthetic	NiB $600	Ex $440	Gd $322
NWTF Special Youth model	NiB $590	Ex $367	Gd $292

AL390 SPORT SPORTING SHOTGUN
Similar to Model AL-390 Sport Skeet. Gauges: 12 or 20 ga., 28- or 30-in. bbls. Weight: 6.8 to 8 lbs. Imported from 1995-99.

Sport Sporting	NiB $566	Ex $396	Gd $300
Sport Sporting Collection	NiB $590	Ex $433	Gd $335
Sport Sporting Youth (20 ga. only)	NiB $590	Ex $454	Gd $397
Sport Gold Sporting	NiB $823	Ex $577	Gd $446
EELL Sport Diamond Sporting	NiB $2166	Ex $1488	Gd $1094
w/ported bbl., add			$100

**Beretta Model AL-391
Urika Gold Sporting**

Beretta Model BL-1

AL390 SPORT SKEET SHOTGUN
Gauges: 12 ga. only. 26- or 28-in. bbl. w/3-rnd. mqagazine. Weight: 7.6 to 8 lbs. Matte finish wood and metal. Imported 1995 to 1999.
Sport Skeet . . . . NiB $498 Ex $366 Gd $279
Sport Super Skeet . . . . NiB $576 Ex $377 Gd $301
w/ported bbl., add $125

AL390 SPORT TRAP SHOTGUN
Gauges: 12 ga. only. 30- or 32-in. bbl. w/3-rnd. chamber. Weight: 7.8 to 8.25 lbs. Matte finish wood and metal. Black recoil rubber pad. Imported from 1995 to 1999.
Sport Trap . . . . NiB $564 Ex $379 Gd $288
Sport Super Trap . . . . NiB $688 Ex $512 Gd $360
Multi-choke bbl. (30-in. only), add $65
w/Ported bbl., add $125

AL391 URIKA SERIES
Semiauto. Gauge: 12 and 20 ga. w/3-in. chambers. 28- 30- or 32-in. bbl. Weight: 6.6 to 7.7 lbs. Self-compensating gas valve. Adjustable synthetic and walnut stocks w/ five interchangeable chokes. Imported from 2001 to 2006.
Urika. NiB $923 Ex $800 Gd $655
Urika synthetic . . . . NiB $865 Ex $758 Gd $600
Urika camo
  w/Realtree Hardwoods . . . . . NiB $977 Ex $844 Gd $654
Urika Gold w/black receiver . . . NiB $896 Ex $588 Gd $464
Urika Gold w/silver receiver . . . NiB $1196 Ex $974 Gd $799
Urika Youth . . . . NiB $900 Ex $779 Gd $698
Urika Sporting . . . . NiB $1088 Ex $965 Gd $600
Urika Gold
  Sporting w/black receiver . . . NiB $859 Ex $655 Gd $488
Urika Gold Sporting
  w/silver receiver . . . . NiB $1256 Ex $1011 Gd $733
Urika Trap . . . . NiB $1047 Ex $798 Gd $633
Urika Gold Trap . . . . NiB $1066 Ex $881 Gd $700
Parallel Target . . . . NiB $1066 Ex $881 Gd $700

AL391 URIKA 2 SERIES
Similar to Urika series except w/improved gas operating system. Imported from 2007 to present.
Urika 2 (X-Tra wood stock, Disc.
  2013) . . . . NiB $1305 Ex $930 Gd $680
Urika 2 Synthetic (black synthetic stock,
  Disc. 2013) . . . . NiB $980 Ex $680 Gd $480
Urika 2 Camo (Realtree Hardwoods or Advantage Max-4,
  disc. 2013) . . . . NiB $1055 Ex $780 Gd $580
Urika 2 Gold (wild finish wood stock, engraved receiver,
  disc. 2009) . . . . NiB $896 Ex $588 Gd $464
Urika 2 Sporting (28- or 30-in. bbl., X-Tra wood stock, Disc.
  2012) . . . . NiB $1305 Ex $930 Gd $705
Urika 2 Parallel (28-, 30- or 32-in. bbl., X-Tra wood stock,
  Disc. 2011) . . . . NiB $1305 Ex $930 Gd $705

AL391 TEKNYS SERIES
Semiauto. Gauge: 12 and 20 ga. w/3-in. chambers. Bbl.: 26- or 28-in. Receiver: colored w/pattern. Stock:X-tra wood, Gel-Tek pad. Weight: 5.9 or 7.3 lbs. Five interchangeable chokes. Imported from 2003 to 2005.
Teknys . . . . NiB $1055 Ex $780 Gd $530
Teknys Gold (engraved receiver, jeweled bolt,
  deluxe wood, 2003-10) . . . NiB $1680 Ex $1210 Gd $880
Teknys Gold King Ranch (King Ranch engraved
  receiver, 2006-11) . . . . . . NiB $2080 Ex $1610 Gd $1045
Teknys Gold Sporting (28- or 30-in. bbl., two-tone receiver,
  2003-13) . . . . NiB $1900 Ex $1260 Gd $930
Teknys Gold Target (30- or 32-in. bbl., gold trigger, satin
  wood stock, 2004-10) . . . . NiB $1980 Ex $1230 Gd $880
Teknys Gold Trap (30-in. bbl., nickel receiver, deluxe walnut
  stock, 2007-13) . . . . NiB $2080 Ex $1430 Gd $1055

AL391 XTREMA AND XTREMA2 SERIES
Semiauto. Gauge: 12 ga. w/3.5-in. chamber. Bbl.: 24-, 26- or 28-in. Stock: black synthetic, Gel-Tek pad. Weight: 7.8 lbs. OptimaChoke Plus choke tubes. Imported from 2002 to 2011.
Xtrema/Xtrema2 . . . . NiB $1155 Ex $855 Gd $630
Xtrema/Xtrema2 Camo (cammo receiver/bbl./stock, 2002-
  12), add $200
Kick-off reduction stock, add $250

A400 XPLOR SERIES
Semiauto. Gauge: 12, 20 and 28 ga. w/3-in. chambers. Bbl.: 26-, 28- or 30-in. VR w/Optima-Bore choke tubes. Receiver: bronze finish. Stock: X-Tra Grain wood. Weight: 5.5 or 6.5 lbs. Imported from 2014 to present.
Xplor Action . . . . NiB $1450 Ex $980 Gd $705
Xplor Unico (2.75-, 3- or 3.5-in.
  Unico chamber) . . . . NiB $1580 Ex $1030 Gd $755
Xplor Lite Synthetic (black synthetic stock, 6.6 lbs.) . . . . NiB
  $1455 Ex $980 Gd $730
Xplor Lite (12 ga. only, 26-, 28- or
  30-in. bbl.) . . . . NiB $1300 Ex $905 Gd $705
Xplor Action (Blink gas
  system) . . . . NiB $1500 Ex $1055 Gd $755
Extreme Kick-Off (Blink gas system,
  Kick-off stock) . . . . NiB $1580 Ex $1030 Gd $755

A400 XCEL SERIES
Semiauto. Blink gas system. Gun Pod is a digital display. Gauge: 12 or 20 ga. w/3-in. chambers. Bbl.: 28-, 30- or 32-in. VR w/Optima-Bore HP choke tubes. Receiver: light blue finish. Stock: X-Tra Grain wood. Weight: 7.7 lbs. Imported from 2011 to present.
Xcel Sporting (3 interchangeable
  weights) . . . . NiB $1580 Ex $1030 Gd $755
Xcel Parallel Target Kick-Off (28-, 30- or 32-in.
  bbl., X-Tra Grain Monte Carlo wood
  stock) . . . . NiB $1630 Ex $1100 Gd $855

MODEL ASE 90 O/U SHOTGUN
Competition-style receiver w/coin-silver finish and gold inlay featuring drop-out trigger group. Gauge: 12; 2.75-in. chamber. Bbls.: 28- or 30-in. w/fixed or Mobilchoke tubes; VR. Weight:

SHOTGUNS

Beretta Model BL-3

Beretta A400 Xplor Action

Beretta FS-1 Folding

Beretta Mark II Trap Gun

Beretta S55B

Beretta S682 Gold E Trap

8.5 lbs. (30-in. bbl.). Checkered high-grade walnut stock. Imported 1992 to 1994.

Pigeon, Skeet, Trap models NiB $3719 Ex $2466 Gd $1967
Sporting Clays model . . . . . NiB $8171 Ex $6559 Gd $4577
Trap Combo model . . . . NiB $13,878 Ex $10,798 Gd $8657
Deluxe model (introduced
    1996) . . . . NiB $17,366 Ex $12,988 Gd $9853

MODEL ASE SERIES O/U SHOTGUN
Boxlock. Single non-selective trigger. Selective automatic ejectors. gauges: 12 and 20. Bbls. 26-, 28-, 30-in.; IC and M choke or M and F choke. Weight: about 5.75-7 lbs. Checkered pistolgrip stock and forearm. Receiver w/various grades of engraving. Imported 1947 to 1964.

Model ASE (light scroll
    engraving) . . . . NiB $2366 Ex $1971 Gd $1388
Model ASEL (half coverage
    engraving) . . . . NiB $3341 Ex $2679 Gd $1882
Model ASEELL (full coverage
    engraving) . . . . NiB $4966 Ex $4054 Gd $2866
For 20 ga. models, add **95%**

MODEL BL-1/BL-2 O/U
Boxlock. Plain extractors. Double triggers.12 gauge, 2.75-in. chambers only. Bbls.: 30-and 28-in. M/F choke, 26-in. IC/M choke. Weight: 6.75-7 lbs., depending on bbl. length. Checkered pistol-grip stock and forearm. Imported 1968 to 1973.

Model BL-1 . . . . NiB $478 Ex $339 Gd $227
Model BL-2 (single selective
    trigger) . . . . NiB $596 Ex $487 Gd $356

MODEL BL-2/S . . . . NiB $554 Ex $451 Gd $307
Similar to Model BL-1, except has selective "Speed-Trigger," VR bbls., 2.75- or 3-in. chambers. Weight: 7-7.5 lbs. Imported 1974 to 1976.

MODEL BL-3 . . . . NiB $690 Ex $579 Gd $491
Same as Model BL-1, except has deluxe engraved receiver, selective single trigger, VR bbls., 12 or 20 ga., 2.75-in. or 3-in.

chambers in former, 3-in. in latter. Weight: 6-7.5 lbs. depending on ga. and bbl. length. Imported 1968 to 1976.

MODELS BL-4/BL-6
Higher grade versions of Model BL-3 w/more elaborate engraving and fancier wood; Model BL-6 has sideplates. Selective automatic ejectors standard. Imported 1968-76.
Model BL-4 . . . . NiB $966 Ex $779 Gd $633
Model BL-5 . . . . NiB $996 Ex $800 Gd $671
Model BL-6 (1973-76) . . . . . . NiB $1287 Ex $1108 Gd $977

SERIES BL SKEET GUNS
Models BL-3, BL-4, BL-5 and BL-6 w/standard features of their respective grades plus wider rib and skeet-style stock, 26-in. bbls. SK choked. Weight: 6-7.25 lbs. depending on ga.
Model BL-3 skeet gun . . . . . . NiB $1166 Ex $877 Gd $588
Model BL-4 skeet gun . . . . NiB $822 Ex $658 Gd $433
Model BL-5 skeet gun . . . . NiB $966 Ex $700 Gd $582
Model BL-6 skeet gun . . . . . NiB $1139 Ex $1076 Gd $755

SERIES BL TRAP GUNS
Models BL-3, BL-4, BL-5 and BL-6 w/standard features of their respective grades plus wider rib and Monte Carlo stock w/ recoil pad; 30-in. bbls., improved M/F or both F choke. Weight: About 7.5 lbs.
Model BL-3 . . . . NiB $679 Ex $466 Gd $388
Model BL-4 . . . . NiB $733 Ex $566 Gd $452
Model BL-5 . . . . NiB $966 Ex $753 Gd $521
Model BL-6 . . . . NiB $1166 Ex $893 Gd $600

D10 TRIDENT TRAP
GUNS . . . . NiB $7520 Ex $5000 Gd $2510
Removeable trigger group. 12 gauge, 3-in. chambers. Bbls.: 30-and 32-in. Optima choke tubes. Weight: 8.8 lbs., depending on bbl. length. Wlanut stock and forearm. Imported 2000 to 2008.
Top Single . . . . NiB $7520 Ex $5000 Gd $2510
Bottom Single . . . . NiB $7520 Ex $5000 Gd $2510
Combo . . . . NiB $9060 Ex $7200 Gd $4000
Model BL-6 . . . . NiB $1166 Ex $893 Gd $600

MODEL FS-1
FOLDING SINGLE . . . . NiB $238 Ex $167 Gd $95
Formerly "Companion." Folds to length of bbl. Hammerless. Underlever. Gauge: 12, 16, 20, 28 or .410. Bbl.: 30-in. in 12 ga., 28-in. in 16 and 20 ga.; 26-in. in 28 and .410 ga.; all F choke. Checkered semipistol-grip stock/forearm. Weight: 4.5-5.5 lbs. depending on ga. Disc. 1971.

MODEL GR-2 HAMMERLESS
DOUBLE . . . . NiB $956 Ex $788 Gd $641
Boxlock. Plain extractors. Double triggers. Gauges: 12, 20; 2.75-in. chambers in former, 3-in. in latter. Bbls.: VR; 30-in. M/F choke (12 ga. only); 28-in. M/F choke, 26-in. IC/M choke. Weight: 6.5 to 7.5 lbs. depending on ga. and bbl. length. Checkered pistol-grip stock and forearm. Imported 1968 to 1976.

MODEL GR-3 . . . . NiB $1174 Ex $1021 Gd $751
Same as Model GR-2 except has selective single trigger chambered for 12-ga. Three inch or 2.75-in. shells. Magnum model has 30-in. M/F choke bbl., recoil pad. Weight: about 8 lbs. Imported 1968 to 1976.

MODEL GR-4 . . . . NiB $1359 Ex $1165 Gd $943
Same as Model GR-2 except has automatic ejectors and selective single trigger, higher grade engraving and wood. 12 ga., 2.75-in. chambers only. Imported 1968 to 1976.

Beretta S682 Gold E Double Trap

Beretta Model SO-2

Beretta Model SO-3

Beretta Model SO-4

Beretta Model SO-5

Beretta Model SO-7

GRADE 100 O/U

SHOTGUN . . . . **NiB $2134 Ex $1741 Gd $1288**
Sidelock. Double triggers. Automatic ejectors. 12 ga. only. Bbls.:
26-, 28-, 30-in., any standard boring. Weight: About 7.5 lbs.
Checkered stock and forend, straight or pistol grip. Disc.

GRADE 200 . . . . **NiB $2780 Ex $2284 Gd $1633**
Same general specifications as Grade 00 except higher quality;
bores and action parts hard chrome plated. Disc.

MARK II SINGLE-BARREL

TRAP GUN . . . . **NiB $774 Ex $623 Gd $441**
Boxlock action similar to that of Series "BL" over-and-unders.
Engraved receiver. Automatic ejector. 12 ga. only. 32- or 34-in.
bbl. w/wide VR. Weight: About 8.5 lbs. Monte Carlo stock w/
pistol grip and recoil pad, beavertail forearm. Imported 1972
to 1976.

MODEL S55B O/U

SHOTGUN . . . . **NiB $672 Ex $490 Gd $336**
Boxlock. Plain extractors. Selective single trigger. Gauges: 12,
20; 2.75- or 3-in. chambers in former, 3-in. in latter. Bbls. VR;
30-in. M/F choke or both F choke in 12-ga. Three inch Magnum
only; 28-in. M/F choke; 26 in. IC/M choke. Weight: 6.5 to 7.5
lbs. depending on ga. and bbl. length. Checkered pistol-grip
stock and forearm. Introduced in 1977. Disc.

MODEL S56E

. . . . **NiB $853 Ex $567 Gd $356**
Same as Model S55B except has scroll-engraved receiver selective automatic ejectors. Introduced in 1977. Disc.

MODEL S58 SKEET GUN

. . . . . **NiB $855 Ex $621 Gd $443**
Same as Model S56E except has 26-in. bbls. of Boehler Antinit
Anticorro steel, SK choked, w/wide VR; skeet-style stock and
forearm. Weight: 7.5 lbs. Introduced in 1977.

MODEL S58 TRAP GUN

. . . . . . **NiB $620 Ex $494 Gd $368**
Same as Model S58 Skeet Gun except has 30-in. bbls. bored
IM/F Trap, Monte Carlo stock w/recoil pad. Weight: 7 lbs. 10
oz. Introduced in 1977. Disc.

SILVER HAWK FEATHERWEIGHT HAMMERLESS DOUBLE-BARREL SHOTGUN
Boxlock. Double triggers or non-selective single trigger. Plain
extractor. Gauges: 12, 16, 20, 28, 12 Mag. Bbls.: 26- to 32-in.
w/high matted rib, all standard choke combinations. Weight: 7
lbs. (12 ga. w/26-in. bbls.). Checkered walnut stock w/beaver-
tail forearm. Disc. 1967.
w/double triggers . . . . **NiB $1133 Ex $844 Gd $521**
w/single trigger, add **$200**

SILVER SNIPE O/U SHOTGUN
Boxlock. Non-selective or selective single trigger. Plain extractor. Gauges: 12, 20, 12 Mag., 20 Mag. Bbls.: 26-, 28-, 30-in.;
plain or VR; chokes IC/M, M/F, SK number 1 and number 2, F/F.
Weight: From about 6 lbs. in 20 ga. to 8.5 lbs. in 12 ga. (Trap
gun). Checkered walnut pistol-grip stock, forearm. Imported
1955 to 1967.
w/plain bbl., non-selective
   trigger . . . . **NiB $779 Ex $643 Gd $448**
w/VR bbl., non-selective
   single trigger . . . . **NiB $779 Ex $643 Gd $448**
w/selective single trigger, add **$100**

GOLDEN SNIPE O/U
Same as Silver Snipe except has automatic ejectors, VR is
standard feature. Imported 1959 to 1967.
w/non-selective single trigger . . .**NiB $1256 Ex $1065 Gd $645**

MODEL 57E O/U
Same general specifications as Golden Snipe, but higher quality throughout. Imported 1955 to 1967.
w/non-selective single trigger . . . **NiB $977 Ex $765 Gd $545**
w/selective single trigger . . . . **NiB $1165 Ex $996 Gd $703**

MODEL SL-2 PIGEON SERIES SHOTGUN
Hammerless. Takedown.12 ga. only. Three round magazine.
Bbls.: VR; 30-in. F choke, 28-in. M, 26-in. IC. Weight: 7-7.25
lbs., depending on bbl. length. Receiver w/various grades of
engraving. Checkered pistol-grip stock and forearm. Imported
1968 to 1971.
Pump shotgun . . . . **NiB $553 Ex $442 Gd $308**
Silver Pigeon . . . . **NiB $466 Ex $367 Gd $377**
Gold Pigeon . . . . **NiB $663 Ex $507 Gd $464**
Ruby Pigeon . . . . **NiB $863 Ex $638 Gd $477**

"SO" SERIES SHOTGUNS
O/U. Jubilee Series introduced in 1998. The Beretta Boxlock
is made with mechanical works from a single block of hot
forged, high-resistance steel. The gun is richly engraved in
scroll and game scenes. All engraving is signed by master
engravers. High-quality finishing on the inside with high
polishing of all internal points. Sidelock. Selective automatic
ejectors. Selective single trigger or double triggers. 12 ga. only,
2.75- or 3-in. chambers. Bbls.: VR (wide type on skeet and
trap guns); 26-, 27-, 29-, 30-in.; any combination of standard
chokes. Weight: 7 to 7.75 lbs., depending on bbl. length, style
of stock and density of wood. Stock and forearm of select
walnut, finely checkered; straight or pistol-grip, field, skeet
and trap guns have appropriate styles of stock and forearm.
Models differ chiefly in quality of wood and grade of engraving. Models SO-3EL, SO-3EELL, SO4 and SO-5 have hand-
detachable locks. "SO-4" is used to designate skeet and trap
models derived from Model SO-3EL, but with less elaborate
engraving. Models SO3EL and SO-3EELL are similar to the
earlier SO-4 and SO-5, respectively. Imported 1933 to date.
Jubilee (.410, 12, 16,
  20, 28 ga.) . . . . **NiB $15,000 Ex $9000 Gd $6155**

SHOTGUNS

Model SO-1 (imported 1934,
    disc.) . . . . NiB $4000 Ex $3000 Gd $2255
Model SO-2 . . . . .NiB $3995 Ex $2355 Gd $1680
Model SO-3 . . . . .NiB $4550 Ex $3210 Gd $2410
Model SO-3EL . . . . NiB $10,000 Ex $4255 Gd $3055
Model SO-3EELL . . . . NiB $14,755 Ex $8550 Gd $6510
Model SO-4 Field, Skeet
    or Trap gun . . . . NiB $6500 Ex $4750 Gd $3655
Model SO-5 Sporting,
    Skeet or Trap model. NiB $22,000 Ex $10,250 Gd $6410
w/extra bbl. set, add 25%

MODELS SO-6 AND SO-9 PREMIUM
GRADE SHOTGUNS

High-grade over/unders in the SO series. Gauges: 12 ga. only (SO-6); 12, 20, 28 and .410 (SO-9). Fixed or Mobilchoke (12 ga. only). Sidelock action. Silver or casehardened receiver (SO-6); English custom hand-engraved scroll or game scenes (SO-9). Supplied w/leather case and accessories. Imported 1990 to date.
SO-6 EL Field grade . . .NiB $24,255 Ex $15,010 Gd $9755
Model SO-6 EELL . . . NiB $65,000 Ex $45,000 Gd $25,000
Model SO-9 . . . . . . NiB $35,000 Ex $20,510 Gd $12,210
Model SO-9EELL Special (w/custom
    engraving) . . . . custom starting at $125,000 to $320,000
w/extra bbl. set, add 25%

MODEL SO-6/SO-7 SIDE-BY-SIDE MODELS

S/S w/same general specifications as SO Series over/unders except higher grade w/more elaborate engraving, fancier wood.
Model SO-6 (imported
    1948-93) . . . . .NiB $17,500 Ex $11,250 Gd $7255
Model SO-7 (imported
    1948-90) . . . . NiB $45,000 Ex $30,000 Gd $19,950

MODEL SV10 SERIES

O/U. Boxlock. Gauge: 20 or 12; 3-in. chmbr. Barrel: 26- or 28-in. VR. w/Optima tubes. Receiver: satin finish w/floral engraving. Imported 2012–14.
Perennia I . . . . NiB $2110 Ex $1830 Gd $1410
Perennia III (w/ or w/o Kick-Off stock,
    removable trigger group,
    2008–14) . . . . NiB $2710 Ex $2255 Gd $1580
Prevail I Sporting (30- or 32-in. bbl.,
    w/ or w/o Kick-Off stock,
    2012–13) . . . . NiB $1910 Ex $1755 Gd $1410
Prevail III Sporting (26-, 28-, 30- or 32-in. bbl.,
    w/ or w/o Kick-Off stock,
    2012–13) . . . . NiB $1910 Ex $1755 Gd $1410
Prevail I Trap (12 gauge, 30- or 32-in. bbl., w/ or
    w/o Kick-Off stock, 2012–13) . . . NiB $2130 Ex $1810 Gd
    $1555 Model TR-1 Single-Shot

TRAP GUN . . . . .NiB $355 Ex $279 Gd $125
Hammerless. Underlever action. Engraved frame.12 ga. only. 32-in. bbl. w/VR. Weight: About 8.25 lbs. Monte Carlo stock w/pistol grip and recoil pad, beavertail forearm. Imported 1968 to 1971.

MODEL TR-2. . . . . .NiB $364 Ex $231 Gd $156
Same as Model TR-1 except has extended ventilated rib. Imported 1969-73.

VICTORIA PINTAIL (ES100)

Semiauto. Short Montefeltro-type recoil action. Gauge: 12 w/3-in. chamber. Bbl.: 24-in. slug, 24-, 26- or 28-in. VR w/ Mobilchoke tubes. Weight: 7 lbs. to 7 lbs., 5 oz. Checkered synthetic or walnut buttstock and forend. Matte finish on both metal and stock. Imported 1993 and 2005.
Field model w/synthetic
    stock (intro. 1998) . . . . .NiB $522 Ex $320 Gd $244
Field model w/walnut
    stock (disc. 1998) . . . . .NiB $733 Ex $535 Gd $431
Rifled slug model w/synthetic
    stock (intro. 1998) . . . . .NiB $544 Ex $378 Gd $296
Stndard slug model
    w/walnut stock (disc. 1998) NiB $544 Ex $378 Gd $296
Wetland Camo model
    (intro. 2000) . . . . .NiB $677 Ex $460 Gd $339

BERNARDELLI, VINCENZO —
Gardone V.T. (Brescia), Italy

Previously imported by Armsport, Miam, FL (formerly by Magnum Research, Inc., Quality Arms, Stoeger Industries, Inc. & Action Arms, LTD).

115 SERIES O/U SHOTGUNS

Boxlock w/single trigger and ejectors. 12 ga. only. 25.5-, 26.75-, and 29.5-in. bbls. Concave top and vented middle rib. Anatomical grip stock. Blued or coin-silver finish w/various grades of engraving. Imported 1985 to 1997.
Standard Model . . . . NiB $1844 Ex $1532 Gd $1176
Hunting Model 115E
    (disc. 1990) . . . . .NiB $2247 Ex $1993 Gd $1612
Hunting Model 115L
    (disc. 1990) . . . . .NiB $2788 Ex $2391 Gd $2095
Hunting Model 115S
    (disc. 1990) . . . . .NiB $3712 Ex $3122 Gd $2210
Target Model 115
    (disc. 1992) . . . . .NiB $1977 Ex $1678 Gd $1440
Target Model 115E
    (disc. 1992) . . . . .NiB $6108 Ex $5388 Gd $3789
Target Model 115L
    (disc. 1992) . . . . .NiB $3855 Ex $3410 Gd $2377
Target Model 115S
    (disc. 1992) . . . . .NiB $6077 Ex $4129 Gd $3755
Trap/Skeet Model 115S
    (imported 1996-97) . . . .NiB $3366 Ex $2581 Gd $1786
Sporting Clays Model 115S
    (imported 1995-97) . . . .NiB $3944 Ex $3216 Gd $2533

Bernardelli Gamecock

Bernardelli Standard Gamecock

BRESCIA
HAMMER DOUBLE . . . . **NiB $1564 Ex $1096 Gd $839**
Back-action sidelock. Plain extractors. Double triggers. Gauges: 12, 20. Bbls.: 27.5 or 29.5-in. M/F choke in 12 ga. 25.5-in. IC/M choke in 20 ga. Weight: From 5.75 to 7 lbs., depending on ga. and bbl. length. English-style stock and forearm, checkered. No longer imported.

ELIO . . . . **NiB $1232 Ex $1006 Gd $781**
Lightweight game gun, 12 ga. only, w/same general specifications as Standard Gamecock (S. Uberto 1) except weight: About 6 to 6.25 lbs.; has automatic ejectors, fine English-pattern scroll engraving. No longer imported.

GAMECOCK, PREMIER (ROME 3)
Same general specifications as Standard Gamecock (S. Uberto 1) except has sideplates, auto ejectors, single trigger. No longer imported.
Roma 3 (disc. 1989,
   reintroduced 1993-97) . . **NiB $1790 Ex $1435 Gd $1108**
Roma 3E (disc. 1950) . . . . . **NiB $1956 Ex $1600 Gd $1119**
Roma 3M w/single trigger
   (disc. 1997). . . . . **NiB $1956 Ex $1600 Gd $1119**

GAMECOCK, STANDARD (S. UBERTO 1) HAMMERLESS
DOUBLE-BARREL SHOTGUN. . NiB $900 Ex $766 Gd $563
Boxlock. Plain extractors. Double triggers. Gauges: 12, 16, 20; 2.75-in. chambers in 12 and 16, 3-in. in 20 ga. Bbls. 25.5-in. IC/M choke; 27.5-in. M/F choke. Weight: 5.75-6.5 lbs., depending on ga. and bbl. length. English-style straight-grip stock and forearm, checkered. No longer imported.

GARDONE HAMMER
DOUBLE. . . . . **NiB $2766 Ex $2261 Gd $1600**
Same general specifications as Brescia except for higher grade engraving and wood, but not as high as the Italia. Half-cock safety. Disc. 1956.

HEMINGWAY HAMMERLESS DOUBLE
Boxlock. Single or double triggers w/hinged front. Selective automatic ejectors. Gauges: 12 and 20 w/2.75- or 3-in. chambers, 16 and 28 w/2.75-in. Bbls.: 23.5- to 28-in. w/fixed chokes. Weight: 6.25 lbs. Checkered English-style European walnut stock. Silvered and engraved receiver.
Standard model . . . . **NiB $2288 Ex $1866 Gd $1383**
Deluxe model
   w/sideplates (disc. 1993) **NiB $2698 Ex $2210 Gd $1679**
w/single trigger, add $125

ITALIA. . . . . **NiB $1866 Ex $1044 Gd $623**
Same general specifications as Brescia except higher grade engraving and wood. Disc. 1986.

ROMA 4 AND ROMA 6
Same as Premier Gamecock (Rome 3) except higher grade engraving and wood, double triggers. Disc. 1997.
Roma 4 (disc. 1989) . . . . . . **NiB $1847 Ex $1412 Gd $1095**
Roma 4E (disc. 1997) . . . . . **NiB $1796 Ex $1370 Gd $1060**
Roma 6 (disc. 1989) . . . . . . **NiB $1488 Ex $1233 Gd $1000**
Roma 6E (disc. 1997) . . . . . **NiB $2533 Ex $2000 Gd $1277**

ROMA 7, 8, AND 9
Side-by-side. Anson & Deeley boxlock; hammerless. Ejectors; double triggers. 12 ga. Barrels: 27.5-or 29.5-in. M/F chokes. Fancy hand-checkered European walnut straight or pistol-grip stock, forearm. Elaborately engraved, silver-finished sideplates. Imported 1994 to 1997.

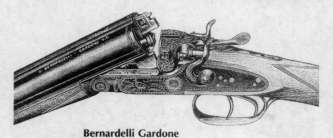

Bernardelli Gardone

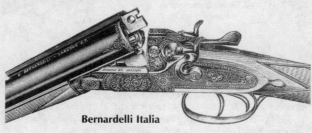

Bernardelli Italia

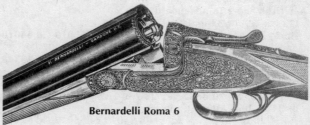

Bernardelli Roma 6

Roma 7 . . . . **NiB $3366 Ex $2160 Gd $1500**
Roma 8 . . . . **NiB $3866 Ex $2571 Gd $1880**
Roma 9 . . . . **NiB $4665 Ex $3748 Gd $2977**

S. UBERTO 2. . . . . **NiB $1460 Ex $1277 Gd $898**
Same as Standard Gamecock (S. Uberto 1) except higher grade engraving and wood. Currently imported.

S. UBERTO F.S.
Same as Standard Gamecock except w/higher grade engraving, wood and has auto-ejectors. Disc. 1989, reintro. 1993 to 1997.
Model FS. . . . . **NiB $1746 Ex $1544 Gd $1100**
Model V.B. Incisio . . . . **NiB $2169 Ex $1754 Gd $1239**
w/single trigger, add $100

HOLLAND V.B. SERIES SHOTGUNS
Holland & Holland-type sidelock action. Auto-ejectors. Double triggers. 12 ga. only. Bbl. length or choke to custom specification. Silver-finish receiver (Liscio) or engraved coin finish receiver (Incisio). Extra-select wood and game scene engraving (Lusso). Checkered stock (straight or pistol-grip). Imported 1992 to 1997.
Model V.B. Liscio. . . . . . **NiB $11,650 Ex $10,500 Gd $8675**
Model V.B. Incisio . . . . . . **NiB $12,200 Ex $9779 Gd $6755**
Model V.B. Lusso. . . . . **NiB $9465 Ex $8119 Gd $5231**
Model V.B. Extra . . . . . . **NiB $14,766 Ex $10,877 Gd $8669**
Model V.B. Gold . . . . **NiB $49,600 Ex $44,688 Gd $37,789**
w/Engraving Pattern No. 4, add $1250
w/Engraving Pattern No. 12, add $5000
w/Engraving Pattern No. 20, add $9500
w/Single trigger, add. $700

BLASER — Isny im Allgäu, Germany
Since 2006 imported and distributed by Blaser USA in San Antonio, TX. Previously imported by SIG Arms (2002—06) and Autumn Sales Inc. (1988–2002).

SHOTGUNS

**Boss Hammerless
Side-By-Side**

F3 SERIES
O/U. Boxlock. .410, 28 20 or 12 gauge; 3-in. chamber w/ejectors. Barrel: 27-, 28- or 29-in. VR w/Briley tubes. Add $2555 to $3500 for extra barrel assembly. NOTE: Values given for standard models, higher grades available.

**American Super Trap Standard
(12 ga., 30- or 32-in. bbl., Monte Carlo
stock, 2007 to date)** .... NiB $7010 Ex $6010 Gd $4010
**Game Standard (20 or 12 ga., Schnabel forend, 2007-09,
reintro. 2014)**.......... NiB $5330 Ex $4530 Gd $3330
**Competition Sporting Standard (.410, 28 20 or 12 ga., 28-, 30-,
32- or 34-in. bbl., 2005 to date)** NiB $6010 Ex $5010 Gd $3355
**Skeet (.410, 28, 20 or 12 ga., 28-, 30-, 32-
or 34-in. bbl., Monte Carlo
stock, 2007-13)** .... NiB $6010 Ex $5010 Gd $3355
**Super Skeet Standard (12 ga., 30- or 32-in. bbl., Monte Carlo
stock, 2014 to date)** .... NiB $6960 Ex $6010 Gd $4010
**SuperSport Standard (12 ga., 30- or 32-in. bbl.,
2011 to date)** .... NiB $7010 Ex $6010 Gd $4010
**Vantage (.410, 28, 20 or 12 ga., 30-, 32- or 34-in. raised VR
bbl., 2015 to date)** .... NiB $6610 Ex $5610 Gd $3810

BOSS & COMPANY — London, England
Custom built shotguns considered some of the world's finest. Extremely expensive. Values given are approximate.

HAMMERLESS
SIDE-BY-SIDE ...... NiB $89,762 Ex $79,260 Gd $56,142
Sidelock. Automatic ejectors. Double triggers, non-selective or selective single trigger. Made in all gauges, bbl. lengths and chokes. Checkered stock and forend, straight or pistol-grip.

HAMMERLESS O/U ..NiB $116,182 Ex $105,680 Gd $79,260
Sidelock. Automatic ejectors. Selective single trigger. Made in all gauges, bbl. lengths and chokes. Checkered stock and forend, straight or pistol-grip. Disc.

BREDA MECCANICA BRESCIANA — Brescia, Italy
Formerly ERNESTO BREDA, Milan, Italy. Previously imported by Tristar (Kansas City, MO), Gryphon International (Kansas City, MO) and Diana Imports Co., (San Francisco, CA).

ANDROMEDA SPECIAL ...... NiB $755 Ex $665 Gd $525
Side-by-side.12 gauge, single trigger; ejectors, select checkered walnut stock; satin finish on receiver with elaborate engraving.

PEGASO SERIES
O/U. Boxlock. Gauge: 12 or 20, 3-in. chamber. Bbl.: 26-, 28- or 30-in. w/choke tubes. Single trigger. Ejectors. Stock: wood. Finish: silver receiver, engraving. From 2004 to date.
Hunter model .... NiB $2000 Ex $1630 Gd $1325

SIRIO STANDARD .... NiB $2176 Ex $1788 Gd $1354
12 or 20 gauge. Engraved box lock action. Bbl. 26 or 28 in.; single trigger; ejectors. Blue only. Also available in skeet model.

VEGA SERIES
O/U. Boxlock. Gauge: 12 or 20, 3-in. chamber. Bbl.: 26- or 28-in. Single trigger. Ejectors. Stock: wood. Finish: Blued. From 2000 to date.
Special model .... NiB $580 Ex $465 Gd $405
**Special Trap model (30- or
32-in. bbl.)** .... NiB $890 Ex $765 Gd $680
**Lusso model (engraving, deluxe
wood stock** .... NiB $1700 Ex $1110 Gd $855

GOLD SERIES
12 or (lightweight) 20 gauge, 2.75-in. chamber. Bbl. 25 or 27 in.; ventilated rib standard. Recoil operated
**Antares Standard
Model** .... NiB $543 Ex $421 Gd $336
Argus Model .... NiB $521 Ex $390 Gd $266
Aries Model .... NiB $521 Ex $390 Gd $266

STANDARD. .... NiB $377 Ex $290 Gd $245
12 gauge, 2-3/4-in. chamber. Recoil operated. Bbl. 25 or 27 in. Light engraving. Disc.

GRADE 1 .... NiB $644 Ex $500 Gd $336
Similar to Standard model but with fancier wood and engraving.

GRADE 2 .... NiB $756 Ex $644 Gd $500
Similar to Grade 1 but with more engraving, etc.

GRADE 3 .... NiB $966 Ex $771 Gd $654
Same as Grade 1 but with custom-quality embellishments.

MAGNUM MODEL .... NiB $546 Ex $400 Gd $297
Similar to Standard Grade but w/ 3-in. chambers.

ALTAIR SPECIAL .... NiB $533 Ex $400 Gd $336
Semiauto. 12 gauge, 2.75-in. chamber. Gas-operated. Bbl. 25 or 27 in., ventilated rib standard. Alloy construction, blue or chrome receiver.

ASTRO .... NiB $1126 Ex $853 Gd $700
Semiauto. Inertia action. 12 gauge (disc. 2002) or 20 gauge, 3-in. chamber. Inertia action. Bbl. 22 (slug), 24, 26, 28 or 30 in.; ventilated rib. Black synthetic, Advantage camo, or Circassian walnut stock and forearm. Imported 2001.
Advantage camo model, add. $125

ASTROLUX .... NiB $1588 Ex $1344 Gd $1033
Similar to Astro model except has two-tone receiver with engraving and deluxe checkered Circassian walnut stock and forearm. Imported 2001 to 2002.

ERMES SERIES .... NiB $1044 Ex $788 Gd $648
12 gauge, 3-in. chamber. Semiauto. Inertia recoil operating system, aluminum alloy receiver, nickeel plated or blue finish on lower receiver. Bbl. 24, 26, or 28 in. Deluxe checkered Circassian walnut stock and forearm. Imported 2001.

Ermes Silver . . . . NiB $1287 Ex $1095 Gd $869
Ermes Gold . . . . NiB $1452 Ex $1138 Gd $1009

MIRA . . . . NiB $880 Ex $622 Gd $500
12 gauge, 3-in. chamber. Semiauto, gas-operated. Aluminum alloy receiver; black or Advantage camo finish. Bbl. 22 (slug), 24, 26, 28 or 30 in., ventilated rib. Circassian walnut or black synthetic stock and forearm. Imported 2001.
Sporting Clays model, add $50
w/black synthetic stock & forearm, deduct 10%

ARIES 2 . . . . NiB $879 Ex $793 Gd $649
12 gauge, 2-3/4-in. chamber. Semiauto, gas-operated. Engraved two-tone receiver. Bbl. 20 or 30 in., ventilated rib. Deluxe checkered Circassian walnut or black synthetic stock and forearm. Imported 2001 only.

CHIRON . . . . NiB $1500 Ex $1055 Gd $805
Semiauto, inertia-operated action. Gauge: 12, 3-in. chamber. Stock: Synthetic. Finish: Matte black or camo. Weight: 7.5 lbs. Imported 2007–08.

ECHO . . . . NiB $1555 Ex $1055 Gd $805
Semiauto, inertia-operated action. Gauge: 12 or 20, 3-in. chamber. Stock: Checkered walnut. Finish: Blued, bronze, or nickel. Weight: 6-6.5 lbs. Imported 2007–08.

GRIZZLY . . . . NiB $1500 Ex $1055 Gd $805
Semiauto, inertia-operated action. Gauge: 12, 3.5-in. chamber. Stock: Synthetic. Finish: Matte black or camo. Weight: 7.5 lbs. Imported 2007–08.

XANTHOS . . . . NiB $1999 Ex $1505 Gd $1000
Semiauto, inertia-operated action. Gauge: 12, 3-in. chamber. Bbl.: 28-in. ventricle, 3 choke tube. Stock: Deluxe checkered walnut. Finish: Blue, gray, or chrome. Weight: 7.5 lbs. Imported 2007–08.

BRETTON-GAUCHER — St. Etienne, France

BABY STANDARD
SPRINT O/U . . . . NiB $1088 Ex $855 Gd $687
Inline sliding breech action. 12 or 20 gauge w/2.75-in. chambers. 27.5-in. separated bbls. w/VR and choke tubes. Weight: 4.8 to 5 lbs. Engraved alloy receiver. Checkered walnut buttstock and forearm w/satin oil finish. Limited import.

SPRINT DELUXE O/U . . . . . . NiB $1077 Ex $863 Gd $700
Similar to the Standard Model except w/engraved coin-finished receiver and chambered 12, 16 and 20 ga. Limited import.

FAIR PLAY O/U . . . . NiB $1088 Ex $863 Gd $600
Lightweight action similar to the Sprint Model except w/hinged action that pivots open and is chambered 12 or 20 gauge only. Limited import.

BRNO — Brno and Uherski Brod, Czech Republic (formerly Czechoslovakia)

ZH 300 SERIES SHOTGUNS
O/U. Hammerless boxlock w/double triggers. Gauge: 12 or 16 w/2.75- or 3-in. chambers. Bbls.: 26, 27.5 or 30 in.; choked M/F. Weight: 7 lbs. Skip-line checkered walnut stock w/classic-style cheekpiece. Imported from 1986-93.
Model 300 (disc. 1993) . . . . NiB $786 Ex $547 Gd $408

Model 301 Field (disc. 1991) . . NiB $667 Ex $582 Gd $400
Model 302 Skeet (disc. 1992) . NiB $745 Ex $557 Gd $442
Model 303 Trap (disc. 1992) . . NiB $749 Ex $566 Gd $449

ZH 300 SERIES COMBINATION GUNS
O/U. Similar to the 300 Series over/under shotgun except lower bbl. chambered in rifle calibers.
Model 300 Combo
   8-bbl. Set (disc. 1991) . . NiB $3375 Ex $2977 Gd $2500
Model 304 12 ga./7x57R
   (disc. 1995) . . . . NiB $846 Ex $698 Gd $535
Model 305 12 ga./5.6x52R
   (disc. 1993) . . . . NiB $921 Ex $769 Gd $544
Model 306 12 ga./5.6x50R
   (disc. 1993) . . . . NiB $965 Ex $798 Gd $579
Model 307 12 ga./.22 Hornet
   (Imported since 1995) . . . . . NiB $843 Ex $755 Gd $507
Model 324 16 ga./7x57R
   (disc. 1987) . . . . NiB $880 Ex $742 Gd $509

MODEL 500 SHOTGUN . . . . NiB $900 Ex $777 Gd $568
O/U. Hammerless boxlock w/double triggers and ejectors. 12 ga. w/2.75-in. chambers. 27.5-in. bbls. choked M/F. 44 in. overall. Weight: 7 lbs. Etched receiver. Checkered walnut stock w/classic style cheekpiece. Imported from 1987 to 1991.

500 SERIES COMBINATION GUNS
O/U. Similar to the 500 Series over/under shotgun above, except w/lower bbl. chambered in rifle calibers and set trigger option. Imported from 1987 to 1995.
Model 502 12 ga./.222 or .243
   (disc. 1991) . . . . NiB $2088 Ex $1256 Gd $1077
Model 502 12 ga. .308 or .30-06
   (disc. 1991) . . . . NiB $1164 Ex $1038 Gd $772
Model 571 12 ga./6x65R
   (disc. 1993) . . . . NiB $853 Ex $709 Gd $587
Model 572 12 ga./7x65R
   (imported since 1992) . . . . . NiB $881 Ex $733 Gd $600
Model 584 12 ga./7x57R
   (imported since 1992) . . . NiB $1264 Ex $1033 Gd $800
Sport Series 4-bbl. set
   (disc. 1991) . . . . NiB $3153 Ex $2571 Gd $1863

571 SUPER SERIES
O/U. Hammerless sidelock w/selective single or double triggers and ejectors. 12 ga. w/2.75- or 3-in. chambers. 27.5-in. bbls. choked M/F. 44.5 in. overall. Weight: 7.25 lbs. Etched or engraved side plates. Checkered European walnut stock w/ classic-style cheekpiece. Imported from 1987 to 1991.
shotgun (disc. 1992) . . . . NiB $866 Ex $731 Gd $577
Combo (disc. 1992) . . . . NiB $2021 Ex $1190 Gd $977
3-bbl. set (disc. 1990) . . . . NiB $1993 Ex $1578 Gd $1266
engraving, add $1350

581 SOLO O/U SHOTGUN . . . . NIB $966 EX $738 GD $561
Hammerless boxlock w/double triggers, ejectors and automatic safety. 12 ga. w/2.75- or 3-in. chambers. 28-in. bbls. choked M/F. Weight: 7.5 lbs. Checkered walnut stock. Disc. 1996.

ZP 149 HAMMERLESS DOUBLE
Sidelock action w/double triggers, automatic ejectors and automatic safety. 12 ga. w/2.75- or 3-in. chambers. 28.5-in. bbls. choked M/F. Weight: 7.25 lbs. Checkered walnut buttstock with cheekpiece.
Standard model . . . . NiB $669 Ex $458 Gd $388
Engraved model . . . . NiB $700 Ex $477 Gd $421

SHOTGUNS

GRADING: NiB = New in Box   Ex = Excellent or NRA 95%   Gd = Good or NRA 68%

BROLIN ARMS, INC. — Pomona, CA

FIELD SERIES PUMP SHOTGUN
Slide-action. Gauge: 12 ga. w/3-in. chamber. 24-, 26-, 28- or 30-in. bbl. 44 and 50 in. overall. Weight: 7.3 to 7.6 lbs. Cross-bolt safety. VR bbl. w/screw-in choke tube and bead sights. Non- reflective metal finish. Synthetic or oil-finished wood stock w/swivel studs. Made 1997-98.

Synthetic stock model . . . . NiB $254 Ex $188 Gd $95
Wood stock model . . . . NiB $200 Ex $129 Gd $75

COMBO MODEL PUMP SHOTGUN
Similar to the Field Model except w/extra 18.5- or 22-in. bbl. w/bead or rifle sight. Made 1997-98.

Synthetic stock model . . . . NiB $279 Ex $200 Gd $115
Wood stock model . . . . NiB $331 Ex $240 Gd $193

LAWMAN MODEL PUMP SHOTGUN
Similar to the Field Model except has 18.5-in. bbl. w/cylinder bore fixed choke. Weight: 7 lbs. Dual operating bars. Bead, rifle or ghost ring sights. Black synthetic or wood stock. Matte chrome or satin nickel finish. Made 1997-99.

Synthetic stock model . . . . NiB $217 Ex $151 Gd $90
Wood stock model . . . . NiB $217 Ex $151 Gd $90
w/rifle sights, add $35
w/ghost ring sights, add $50
w/satin nickel finish (disc. 1997), add $50

SLUG MODEL PUMP SHOTGUN
Similar to the Field Model except has 18.5- or 22-in. bbl. w/IC fixed choke or 4-in. extended rifled choke. Rifle or ghost ring sights or optional cantilevered scope mount. Black synthetic or wood stock. Matte blued finish. Made 1998-99.

Synthetic stock model . . . . NiB $288 Ex $202 Gd $166
Wood stock model . . . . NiB $300 Ex $221 Gd $180
w/rifled bbl., add $25
w/cantilevered scope mount, add $50

TURKEY SPECIAL PUMP SHOTGUN
Similar to the Field Model except has 22-in. VR bbl. w/extended extra-full choke. Rifle or ghost ring sights or optional cantilevered scope mount. Black synthetic or wood stock. Matte blued finish. Made 1998-99.

Synthetic stock model . . . . NiB $266 Ex $190 Gd $125
Wood stock model . . . . NiB $305 Ex $237 Gd $154
w/cantileveredscope mount, add $50

BROWNING — Morgan, UT

AMERICAN BROWNING SHOTGUNS

Designated "American" Browning because they were produced in Ilion, New York, the following Remington-made Brownings are almost identical to the Remington Model 11A and Sportsman and the Browning Auto-5. They are the only Browning shotguns manufactured in the U.S. during the 20th century and were made for Browning Arms when production was suspended in Belgium because of WW II.

NOTE: *Fabrique Nationale Herstal (formerly Fabrique Nationale d'Armes de Guerre) of Herstal, Belgium, is the long-time manufacturer of Browning shotguns dating back to 1900. Miroku Firearms Mfg. Co. of Tokyo, Japan, bought into the Browning company and has, since the early 1970s, undertaken*

American Browning Grade I

American Browning Special

Browning Model 12 Limited Editon Grade I

Browning Model 12 Limited Editon Grade V

Browning Model 42 Limited Editon Grade V

Browning B-2000

Browning Model A-500

Browning Automatic-5 Buck Special

Browning Automatic-5 Classic

some of the production. The following shotguns were manufactured for Browning by these two firms.

SPECIAL 441
Same general specifications as Grade I except supplied w/ raised matted rib or VR. Disc. 1949.

w/raised matted rib . . . . NiB $894 Ex $756 Gd $435
w/VR. . . . . NiB $925 Ex $790 Gd $466
20 ga., add 20%

SPECIAL SKEET MODEL . . . . . . NiB $815 Ex $645 Gd $477
Same general specifications as Grade I except has 26-in. bbl. w/VR and Cutts Compensator. Disc. 1949.

UTILITY FIELD GUN . . . . NiB $608 Ex $458 Gd $339
Same general specifications as Grade I except has 28-in. plain bbl. w/Poly Choke. Disc. 1949.

MODEL 12 LIMITED EDITION
Special limited edition similar to Winchester Model 12 slide/pump action. Gauge: 20 or 28. Five-rnd. tubular magazine. 26-in. bbl., M choke. 45 in. overall. Weight: about 7 lbs. Grade I has blued receiver, checkered walnut stock w/matte finish. Grade V has engraved receiver, checkered deluxe walnut stock w/high-gloss finish. Made 1988-92.

Browning Automatic-5 Gold Classic

Grade I, 20 ga. 8600 prod..... NiB $780 Ex $655 Gd $530
Grade I, 28 ga. .... NiB $1055 Ex $880 Gd $710
Grade V, 20 ga 4000 prod. . . NiB $1355 Ex $1130 Gd $910
Grade V, 28 ga .... NiB $1680 Ex $1355 Gd $1010

MODEL 42 LIMITED EDITION

Special limited edition similar to Winchester Model 42 pump shotgun. Same general specifications as Model 12 except w/smaller frame in .410 ga. and 3-in. chamber. Made 1991-93.
Grade I (6000 produced) ..... NiB $900 Ex $780 Gd $555
Grade V (6000 produced)... NiB $1510 Ex $1230 Gd $930

A-500G GAS-OPERATED SEMIAUTO

Same general specifications as Browning Model A-500R except gas-operated. Made 1990-93.
Buck Special .... NiB $590 Ex $466 Gd $339
Hunting model .... NiB $688 Ex $491 Gd $388

A-500G SPORTING CLAYS.... NiB $663 Ex $490 Gd $388

Same general specifications as Model A-500G except has matte blued receiver w/"Sporting Clays" logo. 28- or 30-in. bbl. w/Invector choke tubes. Made 1992-93.

A-500R SEMIAUTO

Recoil-operated. Gauge: 12. 26- to 30-in. VR bbls. 24-in. Buck Special. Invector choke tube system. 2.75- or 3-in. Magnum cartridges. Weight: 7 lbs., 3 oz.-8 lbs., 2 oz. Crossbolt safety. Gold-plated trigger. Scroll-engraved receiver. Gloss-finished walnut stock and forend. Made by FN from 1987 to 1993.
Hunting model .... NiB $677 Ex $476 Gd $388
Buck Special .... NiB $692 Ex $490 Gd $433

A-BOLT SERIES

Bolt-action repeating single-barrel shotgun. 12 ga. only w/3-in. chambers, 2-rnd. magazine. 22- or 23-in. rifled bbl., w/ or w/o a rifled invector tube. Receiver drilled and tapped for scope mounts. Bbl. w/ or w/o open sights. Checkered walnut or graphite/fiberglass composite stock. Matte black metal finish. Imported 1995 to 1998, reintro. 2011–15.
Stalker (composite stock) ..... NiB $830 Ex $700 Gd $600
Hunter (walnut stock)............ NiB $830 Ex $710 Gd $600
w/rifled bbl., add $155
w/open sights, add $50

GRADE I AUTOLOADER (AUTO-5)

Recoil-operated autoloader. Similar to the Remington Model 11A except w/different style engraving and identified w/the Browning logo. Gauges: 12, 16 or 20. Plain 26- to 32-in. bbl. w/any standard boring. Two or four shell tubular magazine w/ magazine cut-off. Weight: About 6.88 lbs. (20 ga.) to 8 lbs. (12 ga.). Checkered pistol-grip stock and forearm. Made 1940-49.
American Browning Grade I
 Auto-5, 12 or 16 ga........ NiB $856 Ex $744 Gd $400
20 ga., add 20%

AUTOLOADING SHOTGUNS, GRADES II, III & IV

These higher grade models differ from the Standard or Grade I in general quality, grade of wood, checkering, engraving, etc., otherwise specifications are the same. Grade IV guns, sometimes called Midas Grade, are inlaid w/yellow and green gold. Disc. in 1940.
Grade II, plain bbl........... NiB $1698 Ex $1390 Gd $976
Grade III, plain bbl......... NiB $1580 Ex $1176 Gd $833
Grade IV, plain bbl........ NiB $4469 Ex $3865 Gd $3033
w/raised, matted rib bbl., add 15%
w/VR bbl., add 30%

AUTO-5, LIGHT 20

Same general specifications as Standard Model except lightweight and 20 ga. Bbl.: 26- or 28-in.; plain or VR. Weight: About 6.25-6.5 lbs. depending on bbl. Made 1958-1976 by FN, since then by Miroku.
FN manu., plain bbl.......... NiB $844 Ex $633 Gd $429
FN manu., VR bbl.......... NiB $1267 Ex $988 Gd $687
Miroku manu., VR,
 fixed choke .... NiB $965 Ex $743 Gd $846
Miroku manu., VR,
 invectors .... NiB $1065 Ex $844 Gd $600

AUTO-5, BUCK SPECIAL MODELS

Same as Light 12, Magnum 12, Light 20, Magnum 20, in respective gauges, except 24-in. plain bbl. bored for rifled slug and buckshot, fitted w/rifle sights (open rear, ramp front). Weight: 6.13-8.25 lbs. depending on ga. Made 1964-1976 by FN, since then by Miroku.
FN manu., w/plain bbl....... NiB $1276 Ex $889 Gd $567
Miroku manu., ... NiB $966 Ex $843 Gd $544
w/3-in. mag. rec., add $10%

AUTO-5 CLASSIC .... NiB $1186 Ex $983 Gd $889

Gauge: 12. 5-rnd. capacity. 28-in. VR bbl./M choke. 2.75-in. chamber. Engraved silver-gray receiver. Gold-plated trigger. Crossbolt safety. High-grade, hand-checkered select American walnut stock w/rounded pistol grip. 5,000 issued; made in Japan in 1984, engraved in Belgium.

AUTO-5 GOLD CLASSIC . . NiB $9887 Ex $6690 Gd $4690

Same general specifications as Automatic-5 Classic except engraved receiver inlaid w/gold. Pearl border on stock and forend plus fine-line hand-checkering. Each gun numbered "One of Five Hundred," etc. 500 issued in 1984; made in Belgium.

AUTO-5, LIGHT 12

12 ga. only. Same general specifications as Standard Model except lightweight (about 7.25 lbs.), has gold-plated trigger. Guns w/rib have striped matting on top of bbl. Fixed chokes or Invector tubes. Made 1948-1976 by FN, since then by Miroku.
FN manu., plain bbl. .... NiB $889 Ex $655 Gd $498
FN manu., w/raised matte rib . NiB $954 Ex $777 Gd $675
FN manu., VR .... NiB $1098 Ex $966 Gd $676
Miroku manu., VR,
 fixed choke.............. NiB $889 Ex $667 Gd $487
Miroku manu., VR,
 Invectors .... NiB $1099 Ex $776 Gd $566

AUTO-5, MAGNUM 12 GAUGE

Same general specifications as Standard Model. Chambered for 3-in. Magnum 12-ga. shells. Bbl.: 28-in. M/F, 30- or 32-in. F/F, plain or VR. Weight: 8.5-9 lbs. depending on bbl. Buttstock has recoil pad. Made 1958-1976 by FN, since then by Miroku. Fixed chokes or Invector tubes.
FN manu., plain bbl. .... NiB $954 Ex $779 Gd $549
FN manu., VR bbl. .... NiB $1288 Ex $977 Gd $765
Miroku manu., VR, fixed
 chokes.................. NiB $888 Ex $645 Gd $455
Miroku manu., VR,
 Invectors .... NiB $1066 Ex $707 Gd $500

AUTO-5, MAGNUM 20 GAUGE

Same general specifications as Standard Model except chambered for 3-in. Magnum 20-ga. shell. Bbl.: 26- or 28-in., plain or VR. Weight: 7 lbs., 5 oz.-7 lbs., 7 oz. depending on bbl. Made 1967-1976 by FN, since then by Miroku.

SHOTGUNS

GRADING: NiB = New in Box Ex = Excellent or NRA 95% Gd = Good or NRA 68%

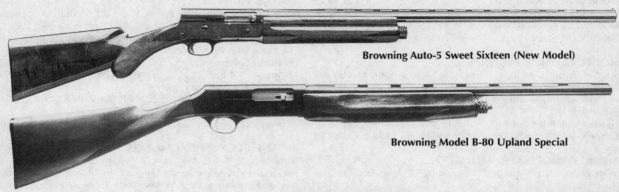

Browning Auto-5 Sweet Sixteen (New Model)

Browning Model B-80 Upland Special

FN manu., plain bbl. . . . . NiB $944 Ex $768 Gd $567
FN manu., VR bbl. . . . . NiB $1333 Ex $989 Gd $779
Miroku manu., VR, Invectors . . . . . . NiB $989 Ex $766 Gd $590

AUTO-5, SKEET MODEL
12 ga. only. Same general specifications as Light 12. Bbl.: 26-or 28-in., plain or VR, SK choke. Weight: 7 lbs., 5 oz.-7 lbs., 10 oz. depending on bbl. Made by FN prior to 1976, since then by Miroku.
FN manu., plain bbl. . . . . . NiB $1177 Ex $956 Gd $654
FN manu., VR bbl. . . . . NiB $1769 Ex $1166 Gd $956
Miroku manu., VR bbl. . . . . NiB $987 Ex $766 Gd $554

AUTO-5 STALKER
Similar to Automatic-5 Light and Magnum models except w/ matte blue finish and black graphite fiberglass stock and forearm. Mfg. Miroku. Made 1992-97.
Light model . . . . NiB $980 Ex $680 Gd $555
Magnum model . . . . NiB $1080 Ex $780 Gd $655

AUTO-5, STANDARD (GRADE I)
Recoil-operated. Gauge: 12 or 16 (16-gauge guns made prior to WW II were chambered for 2-in. shells; standard 16 disc. 1964). Four shell magazine in 5-rnd. model, prewar guns were also available in 3-rnd. model. Bbls.: 26- to 32-in.; plain, raised matted or VR; choice of standard chokes. Weight: About 8 lbs., in 12 ga., 7.5 lbs., in 16 ga. Checkered pistol-grip stock and forearm. (Note: Browning Special, disc. about 1940.) Made 1900-73 by FN.
Grade I (plain bbl.) . . . . NiB $844 Ex $677 Gd $544
Grade I (or Browning Special),
   w/raised matted rib . . . . . . NiB $977 Ex $778 Gd $580
Grade I (or Browning Special),
   w/vent. s rib . . . . NiB $977 Ex $778 Gd $580

AUTO-5, SWEET 16
16 ga. Same general specifications as Standard Model except lightweight (about 6.75 lbs.), has gold plated trigger. Guns w/o VR have striped matting on top of bbl. Made 1937-76 by FN.
w/plain bbl. . . . . NiB $1189 Ex $793 Gd $555
w/raised matted or VR . . . . NiB $1769 Ex $1388 Gd $1012

AUTO-5, SWEET SIXTEEN
NEW MODEL. . . . . NiB $1399 Ex $1156 Gd $922
Reissue of popular 16-gauge Hunting Model w/5-rnd. capacity, 2.75-in. chamber, scroll-engraved blued receiver, high-gloss French walnut stock w/rounded pistol grip. 26- or 28-in. VR bbl. F choke tube. Weight: 7 lbs., 5 oz. Reintro. 1987 to 1993. Mfg. by Miroku.

AUTO-5, TRAP MODEL . . . . NiB $1277 Ex $965 Gd $777
12 ga. only. Same general specifications as Standard Model except has trap-style stock, 30-in. VR bbl. F choke. Weight: 8.5 lbs. Disc. 1971.

A5 SERIES
Inertia-operated Semiauto. 12 ga., 3- or 3.5-in. chamber. Barrel: 26-, 28- or 30-in., VR, 3 Invector choke tubes. Aluminum receiver. Stock: Walnut, checkered. Weight: 6.75 lbs. Made 2012 to present.
Camo model . . . . NiB $1280 Ex $1030 Gd $780
Hunter model . . . . NiB $1310 Ex $1110 Gd $830
Hunter High Grade model, add $200
Sweet Sixteen (16 ga., walnut stock), deduct $70
Stalker model (black synthetic stock), deduct $90
Ultimate model (etched receiver, grade
   III wood stock), add $300
Wicked Wing model (bronze finish), add $175

MODEL B-80 SERIES
Semiauto, gas operation. Gauge: 12 or 20; 2.75- or 3-in. chmbr., 4-rnd. magazine. Bbl.: 26-, 28- or 30-in. VR, any standard fixed choke or Invector tubes. Weight: 6-8 lbs. depending on ga. and bbl. Checkered pistol-grip stock and forearm. Receiver: steel or aluminum. Made 1981–88. Mfg. by Beretta.
Standard . . . . NiB $455 Ex $380 Gd $280
Plus (3-in. camber.), add $20
Superlight (aluminum receiver), add $40
Upland Special (22-in. VR bbl., Invector tubes, 5 lbs., check-
   ered walnut straight-grip
   stock, 1986–88) . . . . NiB $530 Ex $455 Gd $330
Invector tubes, add. 10%

B-2000 SERIES
Semiauto. Gas-operated. Gauge: 12 or 20, 2.75-in. chamber. 4-rnd. magazine. Bbl.: 26-, 28-, 30-in., any standard fixed choke, plain matted bbl. (12 ga. only) or VR. Weight: 6 lbs. 11 oz.-7 lbs. 12 oz. depending on ga. and bbl. length. Stock: Checkered wood pistol-grip stock/forearm. Made 1974-81 by FN; assembled in Portugal.
Buck Special model (24-in. bbl.
   w/rifle sights) . . . . NiB $455 Ex $355 Gd $310
Magnum model (3-in. chamber) NiB $500 Ex $380 Gd $330
Skeet model (26-in. VR bbl.) . . . . NiB $455 Ex $355 Gd $310
Trap model (30- or 32-in. VR bbl., Monte
   Carlo stock) . . . . NiB $455 Ex $355 Gd $310

BPS MAGNUM STALKER . . . . . NiB $680 Ex $530 Gd $330
Same general specifications as BPS series except in 10 or 12 ga. w/Invector choke system , 3.5-in. chmbr.; 22-, 26-, 28- or 30-in. bbls.; matte blue metal finish w/matte black stock. Made 1987-2016.

Browning BPS Hunter

Browning BPS Youth & Ladies Model

**Browning BPS
Waterfowl – Mossy Oak Shadow Grass**

Browning BPS Stalker

Browning B-SS 20 Gauge Sporter

camo finish (1999–2015), add $100
Waterfowl model (10 ga., 28- or 30-in. bbl.
  w/Invector tubes, 1993–98) . . . NiB $620 Ex $510 Gd $355
Buck Special model (10 or 12 ga., 24-in. bbl.,
  1990–97) . . . . NiB $510 Ex $530 Gd $340

BPS SERIES
Slide/pump action. Gauges: 12, 16, 20 or .410 w/3-in. of 2.75-in. chamber.; Bbls.: 22-, 24-, 26-, 28-, 30-, or 32-in. VR; fixed choke or Invector/Invector Plus tubes. Weight: 7.5 lbs. (w/28-in. bbl.). Stock: Checkered select walnut pistol-grip and semi-beavertail forearm or composite, recoil pad. Finish: blued, matte blue, or camo. 1977 to date. Mfg. by Miroku. **NOTE:** Invector or Standard Invector choke tube system was introduced in 1983. In 1989, Invector-Plus chokes were introduced to fit the then new back-bored shotgun barrels. These two choke tubes are not interchangeable.
Hunter (wood stock, blued) . . . NiB $600 Ex $470 Gd $235
Pigeon Grade (12 ga., high grade wood,
  1992–98) . . . . NiB $555 Ex $470 Gd $315
Upland Special (straight grip wood,
  1985–2008) . . . . NiB $600 Ex $470 Gd $235
Stalker (matte blue, composite stock,
  1987–date) . . . . NiB $566 Ex $477 Gd $375
Camo (various camo finishes,
  1999-date) . . . . NiB $680 Ex $570 Gd $305
Turkey Special (12 or 20 ga., matte finish,
  20.5-in. bbl., 1992–2001) . . . . NiB $410 Ex $345 Gd $220

All Purpose (12 or 20 ga., 26- or 28-in. bbl.,
  composite stock, camo finish,
  2013–14) . . . . NiB $800 Ex $700 Gd $440
Micro (20 ga., 22-in. bbl., wood stock,
  2001–13) . . . . NiB $570 Ex $485 Gd $235
Micro Midas (22-, 24- or 26-in. bbl.,
  wood stock, bright blue,
  2013–date) . . . . NiB $600 Ex $485 Gd $235
Micro Youth (20 ga., 22-in. bbl., 13.25-in.
  LOP wood stock, bright blue,
  1986–2002) . . . . NiB $600 Ex $485 Gd $235
Buck Special (12 or 20 ga., 20.5- or 22-in. rifled bbl. or
  rifled choke tube, wood stock, cantilever mount, 1988–
  date) . . . . NiB $710 Ex $600 Gd $330
Rifled Deer Camo (12 or 20 ga., 22-in.
  rifled bbl., composite stock, cantilever
  mount, various camo finishes,
  2007–date) . . . . NiB $730 Ex $620 Gd $310
Trap (12 ga. w/2.75-in. chmbr., 30-in.
  VR bbl., wood Monte Carlo stock,
  2007–date) . . . . NiB $720 Ex $610 Gd $310
16, 20 or .410 ga. models, add $35
w/fixed choke, deduct 20%
w/Invector tubes, deduct 10%

BSA 10 SEMIAUTO SHOTGUN
Gas-operated short-stroke action. 10 ga.; 3.5-in. chamber. Five round magazine. Bbls.: 26-, 28-or 30-in. w/Invector tubes and VR. Weight: 10.5 lbs. Checkered select walnut buttstock and forend. Blued finish. Made 1993 to date.

Browning BT-99

Browning Citori Lightning

Browning Citori Skeet Gun

Note: Although as the BSA 10, this model is now marketed as the Gold Series. See separate listing for pricing.

B-SS SIDE-BY-SIDE

Boxlock. Automatic ejectors. Non-selective single trigger (early production) or selective-single trigger (late production). Gauges: 12 or 20 w/3-in. chambers. Bbls.: 26-, 28-, or 30-in.; IC/M, M/F, or F/F chokes; matte solid rib. Weight: 7 to 7.5 lbs. Checkered straight-grip stock and beavertail forearm. Made 1972-88 by Miroku.

Standard model (early/NSST) . NiB $1276 Ex $956 Gd $835
Standard model (late/SST) . . . NiB $1276 Ex $956 Gd $835
Grade II (antique
  silver receiver) . . . . NiB $3365 Ex $2990 Gd $2455
20 ga. models, add $650

B-SS SIDE-BY-SIDE SIDELOCK

Same general specifications as B-SS boxlock models except sidelock version available in 26- or 28-in. bbl. lengths. 26-in. choked IC/M; 28-in., M/F. Double triggers. Satin-grayed receiver engraved w/rosettes and scrolls. German nickel-silver sight bead. Weight: 6.25 lbs. to 6 lbs., 11 oz. 12 ga. made in 1983; 20 ga. Made in 1984. Disc. 1988.

12 ga. model . . . . NiB $3865 Ex $3077 Gd $2027
20 ga. model . . . . NiB $5277 Ex $3388 Gd $2879

B-SS S/S 20 GAUGE

SPORTER. . . . . NiB $3241 Ex $2766 Gd $1547
Same as standard B-SS 20 ga. except has selective single trigger, straight-grip stock. Introduced 1977. Disc. 1987.

NOTE: *The BT-99 trap gun series was introduced in 1969 and has become a popular with trap shooters. Early BT-99 models had fixed chokes. The BT-99 Plus with adjustable stock replaced the BT-99 and in 1995 the BT-100 replaced the BT-99 Plus. The main differenced between the BT-100 and BT-99/BT-99 Plus was BT-100 had a higher rib, a drop out trigger group, and was available in either blued steel or stainless steel. Sales dropped on the BT-100 so Browning reintroduced the BT-99 in 2000 in a similar configuration as the early 1969 models with a true beaver tail forend. The reintroduced BT-99 also only features extractors, no ejectors. The BT-100 was discontinued in 2001.*

BT-99 SERIES

Single-shot. Boxlock. Automatic ejector. 12 ga. only. 32- or 34-in. VR bbl. w/M, IM or F fixed choke or Invector tubes or Invector Plus tubes. Weight: 8 lbs. Stock: Checkered pistol-grip stock and beavertail forearm, recoil pad. Made 1968-94, mfg. Miroku.

w/Invector Plus tubes . . . . NiB $905 Ex $705 Gd $555
w/fixed choke, subtract $130
w/Invector tubes, subtract $100
two bbl. set, add $200
Pigeon Grade model (satin gray gold accent receiver, high grade
  walnut, mfg. 1978-85). . . . . NiB $1700 Ex $1200 Gd $655
Pigeon Grade model (gold accent receiver, high grade
  walnut, mfg. 1986-94). . . . . . NiB $1400 Ex $880 Gd $530
Signature Painted model (painted red/black stock,
  1993-94) . . . . NiB $1255 Ex $905 Gd $605
Stainless model (1993-94). . . . NiB $1505 Ex $1005 Gd $780

BT-99 (RECENT MFG.)

Reintroduction of BT-99. Made 2001 to date.
w/fixed stock . . . . NiB $1235 Ex $905 Gd $605
w/adj. stock, add $400
Golden Clays model (gold accent receiver
  w/engraving) . . . . NiB $3745 Ex $2705 Gd $1855
Grade II model (silver nitride receiver w/gold accents,
  2008-14) . . . . NiB $2445 Ex $1755 Gd $1180
Micro model (30- or 32-in. VR bbl., 7.7 lbs.,
  13.75-in. LOP). . . . . NiB $1080 Ex $780 Gd $605
Micro model w/adj. stock, add $400
Midas model (28- or 30-in. VR bbl., 7.7 lbs.,
  13-in. LOP) . . . . NiB $1080 Ex $780 Gd $605

BT-99 MAX

Boxlock. 12 ga. only w/ejector selector and no safety. 32- or 34-in. ported bbl. w/high post VR. Checkered select walnut buttstock and finger-grooved forend w/high luster finish. Engraved receiver w/blued or stainless metal finish. Made 1995-96.

Blued. . . . . NiB $1398 Ex $1110 Gd $790
Stainless . . . . NiB $1941 Ex $1590 Gd $1166

BT-99 PLUS

Similar to the BT-99 Competition except w/Browning Recoil Reduction System. Made 1989-95.

Grade I . . . . NiB $1869 Ex $1275 Gd $1013
Pigeon grade . . . . NiB $1977 Ex $1276 Gd $912
Signature grade . . . . NiB $1877 Ex $1233 Gd $888
Stainless model . . . . NiB $2106 Ex $1433 Gd $1133
Golden Clays. . . . . NiB $2926 Ex $2474 Gd $2310

BT-99 PLUS (RECENT MFG.) . . . NiB $2500 Ex $1805 Gd $1355
Reintroduction of BT-99 Plus Bbl.: 32- or 34-in. high post ported VR. Stock: Gloss checkered walnut w/adj. comb. Finish: blue w/engraving. Weight: 8.5 lbs. Made 2015 to date.

BT-100 SINGLE-SHOT TRAP

Similar to the BT-99 Max, except w/additional stock options and removable trigger group. Made 1995 to 2002.

w/Invector Plus tubes . . . . . . NiB $1910 Ex $1310 Gd $580
Stainless model . . . . NiB $2215 Ex $1605 Gd $820
Satin model . . . . NiB $1410 Ex $755 Gd $655
w/adj. comb, add $150
w/thumbhole stock, add $350
w/replacement trigger assembly, add $550
w/fixed choke, deduct $100

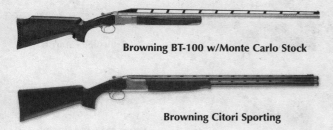

Browning BT-100 w/Monte Carlo Stock

Browning Citori Sporting

NOTE: *The Citori has been the basic, classic U/O platform for Browning from 1973 to the present. The line has evolved over the years: 325 (intro. 1993), 425 (intro. 1995), XS (intro. 2000) 525 (into. 2001), 625 (intro. 2008) and the 725 (intro. 2011). For the most part the differences between the generations is cosmetic. For example, the 525 target models have a ventilated side rib, while the 425 models have solid side ribs. The 525 has a more pronounced pistol grip radius than the 425and the 525 target models also have a palm swell; the 425 target models do not. The 725 is true update being a much lighter and trimmer version than previous Citori models.*

CITORI HUNTING MODELS

O/U. Boxlock. Gauges: 12, 16 (disc. 1989), 20, 28 (disc. 1992) and .410 bore (disc. 1989). Bbl. lengths: 24-, 26-, 28-, or 30-in. w/VR. Chambered 2.75-, 3- or 3.5-in. mag. Chokes: IC/M, M/F (Fixed Chokes); Standard Invector, or Invector plus choke systems. Overall length ranges from 41-47 in. 2.75-, 3- or 3-in. Mag. loads, depending on ga. Weight: 5.75 lbs. to 7 lbs. 13 oz. Single selective, gold-plated trigger. Medium raised German nickel-silver sight bead. Checkered, rounded pistol-grip walnut stock w/beavertail forend. Invector Chokes and Invector Plus became standard in 1988 and 1995, respectively. Made from 1973 to date by Miroku.

Grade I (disc. 1994) . . . . NiB $1076 Ex $792 Gd $566
Grade I - 3.5-in. Mag.
  (1989 to date). . . . . NiB $1155 Ex $830 Gd $655
Grade II (disc. 1983). . . . . . . NiB $1288 Ex $1079 Gd $721
Grade III (1985-95) . . . . NiB $1910 Ex $1310 Gd $900
Grade V (disc. 1984). . . . . . NiB $4955 Ex $4010 Gd $3010
Grade VI (1985-95). . . . . . . NiB $2888 Ex $2069 Gd $1277
Sporting Hunter model (12 and 20 ga.,
  1998 to date) . . . . NiB $1255 Ex $1176 Gd $700
Satin Hunter model
(12 ga. only, 1998 to date) . . NiB $1155 Ex $1006 Gd $744
Upland Hunter (12 or 20 ga. only, straght grip,
  1984-2000). . . . . NiB $1200 Ex $730 Gd $505
White Upland Hunter Special (12 or 20 ga.
  only, silver nitride receiver, straght grip,
  2000-01) . . . . NiB $1255 Ex $880 Gd $655
w/o Invector choke system, deduct $150
3.5-in. mag., add. $120
For disc. gauges (16, 28 and .410), add 15%

CITORI LIGHTNING MODELS

O/U. Same general specifications as the Citori Hunting models except w/classic Browning rounded pistol-grip stock. Made from 1988 to date by Miroku.

Classic Grade I (Invector Plus choke tubes,
  2005-07) . . . . NiB $1610 Ex $1110 Gd $730
Classic Feather Grade I (Invector Plus choke tubes,
  2005-06) . . . . NiB $1655 Ex $1110 Gd $730
Super Grade I (Invector Plus choke tubes,
  2005-07) . . . . NiB $1600 Ex $1000 Gd $710

Grade I (w/o Invector choke
  tubes) . . . . NiB $1210 Ex $955 Gd $612
Grade I (w/Invector choke tubes) . . . NiB $1730 Ex $1210 Gd $880
Grade III. . . . . NiB $2010 Ex $1455 Gd $1010
Grade IV. . . . . NiB $3035 Ex $1955 Gd $1255
Grade VI . . . . NiB $2830 Ex $2010 Gd $1455
Grade VII . . . . NiB $4810 Ex $3310 Gd $2230
Gran Lightning model . . . . NiB $2010 Ex $1455 Gd $1010
Feather model (alloy
  receiver) . . . . NiB $1880 Ex $1230 Gd $855
Feather Combo model
  (2-bbl. set) . . . . NiB $3155 Ex $2110 Gd $1510
Privilege model (w/engraved
  sideplates) . . . . NiB $4855 Ex $3966 Gd $2767
Micro Grade I (1991-01) . . . . . NiB $1255 Ex $855 Gd $655
Micro Grade III (Invector choke tubes,
  disc. 1993) . . . . NiB $1610 Ex $1180 Gd $830
Micro Grade VI (Invector choke tubes,
  1993-94). . . . . NiB $2030 Ex $1510 Gd $1030
White Lightning (Isilver nitride receiver w/scroll and rosette engraving. Satin wood finish w/round pistol grip. Made 1998 to 2001.
12. 20 ga. models . . . . NiB $1769 Ex $1213 Gd $879
28 ga., .410 models
  (Intro. 2000) . . . . NiB $1887 Ex $1369 Gd $1228
w/o Invector choke system, deduct $250
28 ga. and .410, add. 15%

CITORI SKEET MODELS

Same as Hunting model except has skeet-style stock and forearm, 26- or 28-in. bbls., both bored SK choke. Available w/ either standard VR or special target-type, high-post, wide VR. Weight (w/26-in. bbls.): 12 ga., 8 lbs., 20 ga., 7 lbs. Made 1974 to date by Miroku.

Grade I . . . . NiB $1390 Ex $1166 Gd $990
Grade II . . . . NiB $1690 Ex $1345 Gd $1125
Grade III. . . . . NiB $1789 Ex $1433 Gd $1093
Grade V (disc. 1984). . . . . . . NiB $2500 Ex $1810 Gd $1255
Grade VI (disc. 1995) . . . . . NiB $2345 Ex $1765 Gd $1299
Golden Clays. . . . . NiB $2866 Ex $1889 Gd $1465
28 ga. and .410, add. 15%
Grade I, 3-bbl. set (disc. 1996). . NiB $2465 Ex $2079 Gd $1500
Grade III, 3-bbl. set
  (disc. 1996). . . . . NiB $3577 Ex $2260 Gd $1545
Grade VI, 3-bbl. set
  (disc. 1994). . . . . NiB $3781 Ex $2477 Gd $2053
Golden Clays, 3-bbl. set
  (disc. 1995). . . . . NiB $4376 Ex $3069 Gd $2210
Grade I, 4-bbl. set. . . . . NiB $3588 Ex $3066 Gd $2754
Grade III, 4-bbl. set . . . . . . NiB $4361 Ex $3276 Gd $2390
Grade VI, 4-bbl. set
  (disc. 1994). . . . . NiB $4733 Ex $3489 Gd $2466
Golden Clays, 4-bbl. set
  (disc. 1995). . . . . NiB $5656 Ex $3892 Gd $2721
XS Skeet/Ultra XS Skeet (12 or 20 gauge,
  2000-13). . . . . NiB $2755 Ex $2010 Gd $1455
725 Skeet (12 gauge, 2014
  to date) . . . . NiB $2730 Ex $2010 Gd $1510

CITORI SPORTER MODELS

Similar to Citori Superlight models except w/26-in. brrls. and straight grip stock. Disc. 1983.

standard model. . . . . NiB $1455 Ex $1055 Gd $755
Grade II model . . . . NiB $1610 Ex $1210 Gd $855
Grade V model . . . . NiB $2755 Ex $1810 Gd $1455

SHOTGUNS

Browning Citori Superlight Field Shotgun

Browning Citori White Lightning Over/Under

Browning Liége Over/Under Shotgun

Browning Citori Trap

Browning Gold Hunter

CITORI SPORTING CLAYS MODELS

Similar to the standard Citori Lightning model except Classic-style stock with rounded pistol-grip. 30-in. back-bored bbls. with Invector Plus tubes. Receiver with "Lightning Sporting Clays Edition" logo. Made from 1989 to date.

GTI model (1989-94) . . . . . . NiB $1167 Ex $1058 Gd $821
GTI Golden Clays model
  (1993-94) . . . . NiB $2455 Ex $1749 Gd $1256
Lightning model (intro. 1989) . . . NiB $1440 Ex $1102 Gd $866
Lightning Golden Clays
  (1993-98) . . . . NiB $2736 Ex $1871 Gd $1319
Lightning Pigeon Grade
  (1993-94) . . . . NiB $1622 Ex $1188 Gd $887
Micro Citori Lightning model
  (w/low rib) . . . . NiB $1588 Ex $1266 Gd $1006
Special Sporting model
  (intro. 1989) . . . . NiB $1590 Ex $1268 Gd $1010
Special Sporting
Golden Clays (1993-98) . . . NiB $3231 Ex $3110 Gd $2127
Special Sporting Pigeon Grade
  (1993-94) . . . . NiB $1454 Ex $1167 Gd $944
Ultra model (intro. 1995) . . . NiB $1661 Ex $1288 Gd $937
Ultra Golden Clays
  (intro. 1995) . . . . NiB $2134 Ex $1822 Gd $1645
Model 325 (1993-94) . . . . NiB $1310 Ex $955 Gd $710
Model 325 Golden Clays
  (1993-94) . . . . NiB $2545 Ex $1889 Gd $1438
Model 425 Grade I
  (1995-01) . . . . NiB $1761 Ex $1216 Gd $1022
Model 425 Golden Clays
  (1995-01) . . . . NiB $2730 Ex $2255 Gd $1650
Model 425 WSSF
  (1995-99) . . . . NiB $1896 Ex $1459 Gd $1256
525 Sporting (12, 20, 28 or 410 gauge,
  2002-08) . . . . NiB $2430 Ex $1750 Gd $1010
525 Sporting Grade I (sliver nitride receiver,
  2005-07) . . . . NiB $1955 Ex $1430 Gd $810
525 Golden Clays (gold inlays,
  2002-07) . . . . NiB $3780 Ex $2310 Gd $1510
625 Sporting (silver nitride receiver w/gold inlays,
  2008-13) . . . . NiB $3280 Ex $2110 Gd $1455
725 Sporting (lower profile receiver,
  2012 to date) . . . . NiB $2780 Ex $1955 Gd $1380
725 Sporting Golden Clays (lower profile receiver,
  2017 to date) . . . . NiB $4655 Ex $3555 Gd $2510

725 Sporting Grade V (lower profile receiver w/deep relief
  engraving, 2015 only) . . . . NiB $4555 Ex $3110 Gd $2355
725 Sporting Grade VII (lower profile receiver w/deep relief
  engraving, 2015 only) . . . . NiB $5555 Ex $4010 Gd $3010
725 Sporting Adj. Comb (lower
  profile receiver, adj. comb
  stock, 2015 to date) . . . . . NiB $3510 Ex $3110 Gd $2010
Model 802 Sporter (ES) Extended
  Swing (intro. 1996) . . . . . NiB $1488 Ex $1299 Gd $993
w/2 bbl. set, add $1000
w/adj. stock, add $250
w/high rib, add $125
w/ported bbl., add $100

CITORI SUPERLIGHT MODELS

Similar to the Citori Hunting model except w/straight-grip stock and Schnabel forend tip. Made by Miroku 1982 to date.

Feather (1999 to date) . . . . . NiB $2055 Ex $1410 Gd $1010
Grade I . . . . NiB $1150 Ex $850 Gd $625
Grade III (1986-02) . . . . . . NiB $2100 Ex $1510 Gd $1010
Grade V (disc. 1985) . . . . . . NiB $2955 Ex $1910 Gd $1255
Grade VI (1983-02) . . . . NiB $2955 Ex $2010 Gd $1455
Grade VI (w/sideplate, disc.) . . . NiB $3350 Ex $2255 Gd $1830
w/o Invectors, deduct $300
28 ga. and .410, add 10%

CITORI TRAP MODELS

Same as Hunting model except 12 ga. only, has Monte Carlo or fully adjustable stock and beavertail forend, trap-style recoil pad; 20- or 32-in. bbls.; M/F, IM/F, or F/F. Available with either standard VR or special target-type, high-post, wide VR. Weight: 8 lbs. Made 1974-2001 by Miroku.

Grade I Trap . . . . NiB $1035 Ex $888 Gd $698
Grade I Trap Pigeon grade
  (disc. 1994) . . . . NiB $1857 Ex $1589 Gd $1134
Grade I Trap Signature grade
  (disc. 1994) . . . . NiB $1756 Ex $1477 Gd $1234
Grade I Plus Trap (disc. 1994) . . . NiB $2878 Ex $2330 Gd $2099
Grade I Plus Trap w/ported bbls.
  (disc. 1994) . . . . NiB $1979 Ex $1488 Gd $1253
Grade I Plus Trap
  Combo (disc. 1994) . . . . NiB $2773 Ex $2078 Gd $1760
Grade I Plus Trap Golden Clays
  (disc. 1994) . . . . NiB $3176 Ex $2465 Gd $2200
Grade II w/HP rib
  (disc. 1984) . . . . NiB $1989 Ex $1423 Gd $1166
Grade III Trap . . . . NiB $1958 Ex $1688 Gd $1290
Grade V Trap (disc. 1984) . . NiB $1890 Ex $1656 Gd $1388
Grade VI Trap (disc. 1994) . NiB $2066 Ex $1879 Gd $1488
Grade VI Trap Golden Clays
  (disc. 1994) . . . . NiB $3000 Ex $2698 Gd $2365

CITORI UPLAND SPECIAL MODELS

A shortened version of the Hunting model fitted w/ 24-in. bbls. and straight-grip stock.

12, 20 ga. models . . . . NiB $1277 Ex $1097 Gd $900
16 ga. (disc. 1989) . . . . NiB $1426 Ex $1266 Gd $954
w/o Inv. Chokes, deduct $150

CITORI WHITE LIGHTNING O/U SHOTGUN
Similar to the standard Citori Lightning model except w/silver
nitride receiver w/scroll and rosette engraving. Satin wood finish w/round pistol grip. Made 1998-2001.
12. 20 ga. models . . . . NiB $1769 Ex $1213 Gd $879
28 ga., .410 models
   (Intro. 2000) . . . . NiB $1887 Ex $1369 Gd $1228

CITORI WHITE UPLAND
SPECIAL . . . . NiB $1389 Ex $1168 Gd $879
Similar to the standard Citori Upland model except w/silver
nitride receiver w/scroll and rosette engraving. Satin wood finish w/round pistol grip. Made 2000-01.

CYNERY SERIES
Monolock hinge system. Gauges: 12, 20, 28 or .410 bore.
Bbl. lengths: 26-, or 28-in. w/VR. Chambered 3-in. Chokes:
Invector Plus choke tubes. Overall length ranges from 43-45 in.
Weight: 5 to 6 lbs. Single selective, gold-plated trigger. Wood
or composite stock. Silver nitride finish. Made from 2004 to
date.
Field grade (2004-07) . . . . NiB $1580 Ex $955 Gd $780
Field grade (2010-14) . . . . . . NiB $2430 Ex $1810 Gd $930
Field grade (current mfg.) . . . NiB $1575 Ex $1110 Gd $830
Classic Field grade . . . . NiB $2360 Ex $1000 Gd $720
Classic Field Grade III (upgraded wood, engraved
   receiver, 2007-13) . . . . . NiB $3410 Ex $2455 Gd $1780
Classic Field Grade VI (upgraded wood, engraved receiver,
   gold inlays, 2007-13) . . . NiB $5185 Ex $3810 Gd $2755
Classic Sporting (2006-13) . . . NiB $3110 Ex $2380 Gd $1610
Classic Trap (2007-14) . . . NiB $3340 Ex $2555 Gd $1790
Classic Trap Unsingle Combo
   (2008-14) . . . . NiB $5185 Ex $3690 Gd $2670
Classic Trap Unsingle Combo
   (current mfg.) . . . . NiB $3630 Ex $2810 Gd $2010
Composite Ultimate Turkey (100% Mossy
   Oak Break-Up Country camo, synthetic stock,
   2017 to date) . . . . . NiB $1930 Ex $1480 Gd $1055
CX (reverse striker system, 2017
   to date) . . . . NiB $1430 Ex $1010 Gd $755
CX Composite (reverse striker system, synthetic stock,
   2017 to date) . . . . NiB $1380 Ex $955 Gd $655
Euro Field grade . . . . NiB $2300 Ex $1500 Gd $760
Feather (2007-14) . . . . NiB $2530 Ex $1655 Gd $960
Feather (current mfg.) . . . . . . NiB $1800 Ex $1330 Gd $930
Feather Composite (synthetic
   stock) . . . . NiB $1755 Ex $1310 Gd $910
Micro Midas (deluxe wood and engraving,
   2015 to date) . . . . NiB $1580 Ex $1110 Gd $830
Sporting (made 2004-07) . . . . NiB $1900 Ex $1410 Gd $840
Sporting (current mfg) . . . . . NiB $2000 Ex $1530 Gd $1130

DOUBLE AUTOMATIC (STEEL RECEIVER)
Short recoil system. Takedown. 12 ga. only. Two round capacity. Bbls.: 26-, 28-, 30-in.; any standard choke. Checkered
pistol-grip stock and forend. Weight: About 7.75 lbs. Made
1955-61.
w/plain bbl. . . . . NiB $889 Ex $679 Gd $453
w/recessed-rib bbl. . . . . NiB $1167 Ex $1090 Gd $756

GOLD HUNTER SERIES
Semiauto. Self-cleaning, gas-operated, short-stroke action.
Gauges: 10 or 12 (3.5-in. chamber); 12 or 20, 3-or 3.5 in. cham-
ber. 26-, 28-, or 30-in. bbl. w/Invector or Invector Plus choke

tubes. Checkered walnut stock. Polished or matte black metal
finish. Made 1994-2005. Mfg. in Belgium, assembled in Portulag.

Hunter (Light 10 ga. 3.5-in.
   w/walnut stock) . . . . NiB $1499 Ex $1277 Gd $1108
Hunter (12 ga. 3.5-in.) . . . . NiB $977 Ex $790 Gd $559
Hunter (12 or 20 ga.
   3-in.) . . . . NiB $1067 Ex $880 Gd $670
Hunter Classic model
   (12 or 20 ga., 3-in.) . . . . . . NiB $921 Ex $787 Gd $600
Hunter High Grade Classic
   (12 or 20 ga., 3-in.) . . . . NiB $1690 Ex $1225 Gd $1098
Deer Hunter (12 ga. w/22-in. smooth or rifled
   bbl., cantilevered scope mount,
   1997-05) . . . . NiB $910 Ex $884 Gd $643
Deer Hunter (Mossy Oak Camo, 2006-08), add $50
Evolve (12 ga. only, engraved receiver, shim adj.
   stock, 2004-07) . . . . NiB $910 Ex $530 Gd $340
Evolve Sporting (12 ga. only, engraved receiver gold accents,
   shim adj. stock, 2006-07) . . . . NiB $955 Ex $555 Gd $355
Fusion (12 or 20 ga., shim adj. stock,
   2001-07) . . . . NiB $910 Ex $555 Gd $355
Fusion High Grade (silver nitride receiver w/gold inlays,
   2005-07) . . . . NiB $1830 Ex $1130 Gd $855
Golden Clays (12 ga. only,
   coin finish receiver, satin
   finish stock, 1999-08) . . . . . . NiB $1655 Ex $955 Gd $755
Micro (20 ga. only, 13.8-in. LOP,
   2001-05) . . . . NiB $780 Ex $455 Gd $310
Sporting Clays (12 ga. only, 28- or 30-in. bbl., gloss finish
   stock, 1996-08) . . . . NiB $1010 Ex $705 Gd $505
Superlight Micro (20 ga. only, 13.8-in. LOP, 6.1 lbs.,
   2006-07) . . . . NiB $855 Ex $530 Gd $310
Turkey Hunter Camo
   (12 ga. /24-in. bbl.) . . . . NiB $987 Ex $699 Gd $534
Upland Special (12 or 20 ga., 24- or 26-in. bbl.,
   7 lbs., 2001-05) . . . . NiB $780 Ex $455 Gd $310
Waterfowl Hunter Camo
   (12 ga. w/24-in. bbl.) . . . . . . NiB $987 Ex $699 Gd $534

GOLD STALKER SERIES
Similar to Hunter series except w/black composite stock.
Invector or Invector Plus choke tubes. Graphite/fiberglass com-
posite stock. Polished or matte black finish. Made 1998-2007.
Light (10 ga., 3.5-in. . . . . NiB $1487 Ex $1269 Gd $1109
Field model (12 ga. 3.5-in.) . . . . NiB $1048 Ex $911 Gd $500
Field model (12 or 20 ga.,
   3-in.) . . . . NiB $898 Ex $654 Gd $521
Classic Model
   (21 or 20 ga., 3-in.) . . . . NiB $1754 Ex $1228 Gd $1067
Deer model
   (12 ga. w/22-in. bbl.) . . . . . . NiB $855 Ex $529 Gd $380
Turkey Camo model
   (12 ga. w/24-in. bbl.) . . . . . . NiB $799 Ex $482 Gd $355
Waterfowl Camo model
   (12 ga. w/24-in. bbl.) . . . . . . NiB $943 Ex $667 Gd $543

GOLD SPORTING CLAYS SERIES
Similar to Gold Hunter Series except w/2.75-in. chamber
and 28- or 30-in. ported bbl. w/Invector Plus chokes. Made
1996-2008.

Standard model. . . . . NiB $1132 Ex $821 Gd $677
Youth or Ladies models. . . . NiB $1677 Ex $1265 Gd $1071
w/engraved nickel receiver . . . NiB $1793 Ex $1277 Gd $1056

LIEGE O/U SHOTGUN (B26/27)
Boxlock. Automatic ejectors. Non-selective single trigger. 12 ga.
only. Bbls.: 26.5-, 28-, or 30-in.; 2.75-in. chambers in 26.5- and
28-in., 3-in. in 30-in., IC/M, M/F, or F/F chokes; VR. Weight:

SHOTGUNS

Browning Over/Under Gold Classic

7 lbs., 4 oz.to 7 lbs., 14 oz., depending on bbls. Checkered pistol-grip stock and forearm. Made 1973-1975 by FN.

Liège (B-26 BAC production)...NiB $1488 Ex $1161 Gd $988

Liège (B-27 FN prod.,
Standard Game model)... NiB $1488 Ex $1161 Gd $988
Deluxe Game model...... NiB $1522 Ex $1269 Gd $1043
Grand Delux Game model . NiB $1687 Ex $1438 Gd $1210
Deluxe Skeet model .... NiB $1488 Ex $1161 Gd $988
Deluxe Trap model .... NiB $1488 Ex $1161 Gd $988
NRA Sporting .... NiB $1067 Ex $700 Gd $5254

LIGHT SPORTING 802ES ... NiB $1476 Ex $1211 Gd $989
Over/under. Invector-plus choke tubes. 12 ga. only w/ 28-in. bbl. Weight: 7 lbs., 5 oz.

LIGHTNING SPORTING CLAYS
Similar to the standard Citori Lightning model except Classic-style stock with rounded pistol grip. 30-in. back-bored bbls. with Invector Plus tubes. Receiver with "Lightning Sporting Clays Edition" logo. Made 1989-94.

Standard model .... NiB $1396 Ex $1178 Gd $909
Pigeon grade .... NiB $1378 Ex $1161 Gd $882

MAXUS SERIES
Semiauto. Power Driven gas system. Gauge: 12, 3- or 3.5-in. chamber. Bbl.: 26-, 28-, 30-in., VR bbl. w/Invector Plus tubes Vector Pro forcing cone. Weight: 7 lbs. Stock: Checkered walnut. Removable Lightning trigger group. Made from 2009 to date.

All Purpose model (26-in. bbl., Mossy Oak finish, synthetic
stock, 2014 only) .... NiB $1430 Ex $1080 Gd $790
All Purpose Hunter model (3.5-in. chamber,
26-in. bbl., Mossy Oak finish, synthetic
stock, 2015 to date) ..... NiB $1430 Ex $1080 Gd $790
Camo model (various Mossy Oak camo finishes,
composite stock)......... NiB $1305 Ex $880 Gd $630
Camo model w/3.5-in. chamber, add $90
Hunter model (satin nickel receiver receiver w/engraving,
2010 to date) .... NiB $1330 Ex $930 Gd $680
Hunter model w/3.5-in. chamber, add $100
Rifled Deer Stalker model (12 ga. only, 3-in. chamber, 22-in.
rifled bbl. w/cantilever scope mount, matte black finish,
2011 to date) .... NiB $1305 Ex $930 Gd $680
Rifled Deer Camo model (12 ga., 3-in. chamber, 22-in. rifled
bbl. w/cantilever scope mount, Mossy Oak camo finish,
2011 to date) .... NiB $1400 Ex $980 Gd $705
Stalker model (12 ga., 3-in. chamber, 26-
or 28-in. VR bbl., matte black finish receiver,
2009 to date) .... NiB $1180 Ex $805 Gd $605
Stalker model w/3.5-in. chamber, add $125
Sporting model (12 ga. only, 3-in. chamber,
28- or 30-in. VR bbl., satin silver finish receiver,
2011 to date) .... NiB $1530 Ex $1055 Gd $755
Sporting Carbon Fiber model (12 ga. only, 3-in. chamber,
28- or 30-in. VR carbon fiber bbl., carbon fiber finish
receiver, 2010 to date) .... NiB $1330 Ex $955 Gd $680
Sporting Golden Clays model (12 ga. only, 3-in.

chamber, 26-, 28- or 30-in. VR bbl., satin nickel finish
receiver w/engraving, checkered gloss walnut stock,
2013 to date) .... NiB $1730 Ex $1205 Gd $855
Ultimate model (12 ga. only, 3-in. chamber,
26-, 28- or 30-in. VR bbl., receiver w/game
bird engraving, checkered satin walnut stock,
2013 to date) .... NiB $1605 Ex $1130 Gd $805
Wicked Wings model (12 ga. only, 3-in. chamber, 26- or
28-in. VR bbl., cerakote bronze
receiver/Mossy Oak bbl., composite
stock, 2017 to date) ..... NiB $1430 Ex $880 Gd $680
Wicked Wings model w/3.5-in. chamber, add $125

MAXUS II SERIES
Semiauto. Similar to Maxus series but sleeker design w/new Inflex Technology recoil pad and SoftFlex cheek pad combine to reduce recoil, rubber overmolded grip, and oversized controls. Gauge: 12, 3- or 3.5-in. chamber. Bbl.: 26-, 28-, 30-in., VR bbl. w/Invector Plus tubes Vector Pro forcing cone. Weight: 7 lbs. Stock: Composite. Made from 2020 to date.

All-Purpose Hunter model (12 ga. only,
3-in. chamber, 26- or 28-in. VR bbl.,
carbon fiber finish)..... NiB $1900 Ex $1850 Gd $1100
Mossy Oak Shadow Grass Habitat model (12 ga.
only, 3-in. chamber, 26- or 28-in. VR bbl.,
camo receiver/bbl.) .... NiB $1800 Ex $1750 Gd $1000
Sporting Carbon Fiber model (12 ga. only, 3-in. chamber,
26- or 28-in. VR bbl., Mossy Oak Break-Up Country
camo receiver/bbl.) .... NiB $1900 Ex $1850 Gd $1100
Stalker model (12 ga. only, 3-in. chamber, 26- or 28-in. VR
bbl., black receiver/bbl.) . NiB $1600 Ex $1550 Gd $900
Wicked Wing model (12 ga. only, 3-in.
chamber, 26- or 28-in. VR bbl., cerakote
bronze receiver/bbl.) ... NiB $1900 Ex $1850 Gd $1100

O/U CLASSIC .... NiB $2359 Ex $2091 Gd $1389
Gauge: 20, 2.75-in. chambers. 26-in. blued bbls. choked IC/M. Gold-plated, single selective trigger. Manual, top-tang-mounted safety. Engraved receiver. High grade, select American walnut straight-grip stock with Schnabel forend. Fine-line checkering with pearl borders. High-gloss finish. 5,000 issued in 1986; made in Japan, engraved in Belgium.

O/U GOLD CLASSIC ..... NiB $6245 Ex $4890 Gd $3179
Same general specifications as Over/Under Classic except more elaborate engravings, enhanced in gold, including profile of John M. Browning. Fine oil finish. 500 issued; made in 1986 in Belgium.

RECOILLESS TRAP SHOTGUN
The action and bbl. are driven forward when firing to achieve 72 percent less recoil. 12 ga, 2.75-in. chamber. 30-in. bbl. with Invector Plus tubes; adjustable VR. 51.63 in. overall. Weight: 9 lbs. Adj. checkered walnut buttstock and forend. Blued finish. Made 1993-96.

Standard model............ NiB $1088 Ex $865 Gd $644
Micro model (27-in. bbl.) ... NiB $1088 Ex $865 Gd $644
Signature model (27-in. bbl.) ....NiB $1088 Ex $865 Gd $644

SILVER SERIES
Semiauto. Active value gas-operated. Gauge: 12 or 20, 3- or 3.5-in. chamber. Bbl.: 26-, 28-, 30-in., VR bbl. w/Invector Plus tubes. Finish: Gloss blue semi-humpback receiver and bbl. Weight: 6.25 lbs. -7.5 lbs. 12 oz. depending on ga. and bbl. length. Stock: Satin checkered wood. Made from 2006 to date.

Black Lightning (3-in.
chamber, gloss blue finish,
2017 to date)............ NiB $1080 Ex $780 Gd $580

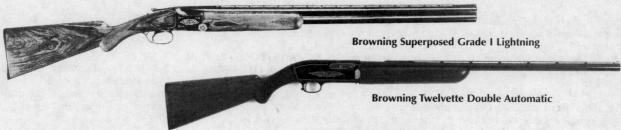

Browning Superposed Grade I Lightning

Browning Twelvette Double Automatic

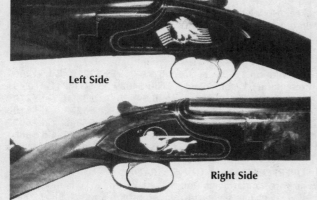

Left Side

Right Side

Browning Superposed Bicentennial

Browning Superposed Grade IV Diana (Postwar)

Browning Superposed Grade V Midas (Postwar)

Camo w/3.5-in. chamber (various camo finishes receiver, 2006 to date) . . . . NiB $1170 Ex $830 Gd $630
Hunter (silver finish receiver, 2006 to date) . . . . NiB $1055 Ex $655 Gd $580
Hunter w/3.5-in. chamber (silver finish receiver, 2006 to date), add $160
Lightning (12 ga. only, 26- or 18-in. VR bbl., silver receiver), add $120
Lightning w/3.5-in. chamber (12 ga. only, 26- or 18-in. VR bbl., silver receiver) . . . . . . NiB $1045 Ex $655 Gd $500
Matte Hunter (3-in. chamber, matte black finish, 2017 to date) . . . . NiB $1000 Ex $630 Gd $480

Matte Hunter Micro Midas (silver/matte black receiver, 2017 to date) . . . . NiB $1000 Ex $630 Gd $480
Micro (20 ga. only, 26-in. VR bbl., 6.2 lbs., 13-in. LOP) . . . . NiB $1030 Ex $655 Gd $500
NWTF Camo (12 ga. only, 24-in. bbl., Mossy Oak camo finishes, 2008-14) . . . . NiB $1180 Ex $955 Gd $680
NWTF Camo w/3.5-in. chamber (12 ga. only, 24-in. bbl., Mossy Oak camo finishes, 2008 to date), add $175
Rifled Deer Camo (12 or 20 ga., 3-in. chamber, 22-in. rifled bbl. w/cantilever scope mount, various camo finishes, 2008 to date) . . . . NiB $1255 Ex $905 Gd $605
Rifled Deer Matte (20 ga. only, 3-in. chamber, 22-in. rifled bbl. w/cantilever scope mount, satin finish walnut stock, 2017 to date) . . . . NiB $1155 Ex $830 Gd $630
Rifled Deer Satin (12 or 20 ga., 3-in. chamber, 22-in. rifled bbl. w/cantilever scope mount, satin finish walnut stock, 2008 to date) . . . . NiB $1170 Ex $830 Gd $630
Rifled Deer Stalker (12 ga. only, 3-in. chamber, 22-in. rifled bbl. w/cantilever scope mount, matte black finish, 2018 to date) . . . . NiB $1130 Ex $755 Gd $530
Sporting (12 ga. only, 2.75-in. chamber, 28- or 30-in. VR ported bbl., silver finish receiver, 2009 to date) . . . . NiB $1120 Ex $780 Gd $580
Sporting Micro (12 ga. only, 2.75-in. chamber, 28- or 30-in. VR ported bbl., silver finish receiver, 13.75-in. LOP, 2009 to date) . . . . NiB $1120 Ex $780 Gd $580
Stalker (12 ga. only, 3.5-in. chamber, 26- or 28-in. VR bbl., matte black finish receiver, 2006 to date) . . . . NiB $1080 Ex $730 Gd $530

SUPERPOSED BICENTENNIAL COMMEMORATIVE . . . NiB $13,650 Ex $12,790 Gd $9779
Special limited edition issued to commemorate U.S. Bicentennial. 51 guns, one for each state in the Union plus one for Washington, D.C. Receiver with sideplates has engraved and gold-inlaid hunter and wild turkey on right side, U.S. flag and bald eagle on left side, together with state markings inlaid in gold, on blued background. Checkered straight-grip stock and Schnabel-style forearm of highly- figured American walnut. Velvet-lined wood presentation case. Made in 1976 by FN. Value shown is for gun in new, unfired condition. See illustration.

SUPERPOSED BROADWAY 12 TRAP . . . . . NiB $2084 Ex $1766 Gd $1460
Same as Standard Trap Gun except has 30- or 32-in. bbls. with wider Broadway rib. Disc. 1976.

SUPERPOSED SHOTGUNS, HUNTING MODELS
Over/under boxlock. Selective automatic ejectors. Selective single trigger; earlier models (worth 25% less) supplied w/ double triggers, twin selective triggers or non-selective single trigger. Gauges: 12, 20 (intro. 1949, 3-in. chambers in later production), 28, .410 (latter two ga. intro. 1960). Bbls.: 26.5-, 28-, 30-, 32-in., raised matted or VR, prewar Lightning Model

SHOTGUNS

made w/ribbed bbl., postwar version supplied only w/VR; any combination of standard chokes. Weight (w/26.5-in. VR bbls.): Standard 12, 7 lbs., 11 oz., Lightning 12, 7 lbs., 6 oz.; Standard 20, 6 lbs., 8 oz.; Lightning 20, 6 lbs., 4 oz.; Lightning 28, 6 lbs., 7 oz.; Lightning .410, 6 lbs., 10 oz. Checkered pistol-grip stock/forearm.

Higher grades (Pigeon, Pointer, Diana, Midas, Grade VI) differ from standard Grade I models in overall quality, engraving, wood and checkering; otherwise, specifications are the same. Midas Grade and Grade VI guns are richly gold inlaid. Made by FN 1928-76. Prewar models may be considered as disc. in 1940 when Belgium was occupied by Germany. Grade VI offered 1955-60. Pointer Grade disc. in 1966, Grade I Standard in 1973, Pigeon Grade in 1974. Lightning Grade I, Diana and Midas Grades were not offered after 1976.

Grade I standard weight	NiB $2390	Ex $1979	Gd $1749
Grade I Lightning	NiB $2209	Ex $1867	Gd $1428
Grade I Lightning, pre-war, matted bbl., no rib	NiB $2979	Ex $2255	Gd $1217
Grade II - Pigeon	NiB $4400	Ex $2790	Gd $1966
Grade III - Pointer	NiB $5000	Ex $4155	Gd $3860
Grade IV - Diana	NiB $8250	Ex $6300	Gd $3760
Grade V - Midas	NiB $7300	Ex $5012	Gd $3690
Grade VI	NiB $10,000	Ex $8292	Gd $6659
For 20 ga., add			20%
For 28 ga., add			75%
For .410, add			50%
Values shown are for models w/VR.			
w/raised matted rib, deduct			10%

SUPERPOSED LIGHTNING AND SUPERLIGHT MODELS (REISSUE B-25)

Reissue of popular 12-and 20-ga. Superposed shotguns. Lightning models available in 26.5- and 28-in. bbl. lengths w/2.75- or 3-in. chambering, full pistol grip. Superlight models available in 26.5-in. bbl. lengths w/2.75-in. chambering only, and straight-grip stock w/Schnabel forend. Both have hand-engraved receivers, fine-line checkering, gold-plated single selective trigger, automatic selective ejectors, manual safety. Weight: 6 to 7.5 lbs. Reintroduced 1985.

Grade I, Standard	NiB $2377	Ex $1898	Gd $1344
Grade II, Pigeon	NiB $5696	Ex $3863	Gd $3000
Grade III, Pointer	NiB $8879	Ex $5770	Gd $3760
Grade IV, Diana	NiB $8009	Ex $5679	Gd $3698
Grade V, Midas	NiB $13,750	Ex $11,299	Gd $10,650
w/extra bbls., add			50%

SUPERPOSED MAGNUM . . NiB $1988 Ex $1572 Gd $1189

Same as Grade I except chambered for 12-ga. 3-in. shells, 30-in. VR bbls., stock w/recoil pad. Weight: About 8.25 lbs. Disc. 1976.

SUPERPOSED BLACK

DUCK LTD. ISSUE. . . . . . NiB $10,390 Ex $8977 Gd $5640
Gauge: 12. Superposed Lightning action. 28-in. VR bbls. Choked M/F. 2.75-in. chambers. Weight: 7 lbs., 6 oz. Gold-inlaid receiver and trigger guard engraved w/black duck scenes. Gold-plated, single selective trigger. Top-tang mounted manual safety. Automatic, selective ejectors. Front and center ivory sights. High-grade, hand-checkered, hand-oiled select walnut stock and forend. 500 issued in 1983.

SUPERPOSED MALLARD

DUCK LTD. ISSUE. . . . . . NiB $10,768 Ex $7322 Gd $5680
Same general specifications as Ltd. Black Duck issue except mallard duck scenes engraved on receiver and trigger guard,

dark French walnut stock w/rounded pistol-grip. 500 issued in 1981.

SUPERPOSED PINTAIL

DUCK LTD. ISSUE. . . . . . NiB $10,766 Ex $7298 Gd $5660
Same general specifications as Ltd. Black Duck issue except pintail duck scenes engraved on receiver and trigger guard. Stock is of dark French walnut w/rounded pistol-grip. 500 issued in 1982.

SUPERPOSED, PRESENTATION GRADES

Custom versions of Super-Light, Lightning Hunting, Trap and Skeet Models, w/same general specifications as those of standard guns, but of higher overall quality. The four Presentation grades differ in receiver finish (grayed or blued), engraving gold inlays, wood and checkering. Presentation 4 has sideplates. Made by FN, these models were Intro. in 1977.

Presentation 1	NiB $3475	Ex $2770	Gd $12967
Presentation 1, gold-inlaid	NiB $4889	Ex $3388	Gd $2491
Presentation 2	NiB $4956	Ex $3860	Gd $2709
Presentation 2, gold-inlaid	NiB $7900	Ex $5275	Gd $4100
Presentation 3, gold-inlaid	NiB $9975	Ex $7866	Gd $6077
Presentation 4	NiB $9106	Ex $7320	Gd $5863
Presentation 4, gold-inlaid	NiB $13,675	Ex $11,960	Gd $9989

SUPERPOSED SKEET GUNS, GRADE I

Same as standard Lightning 12, 20, 28 and .410 Hunting models, except has skeet-style stock and forearm, 26.5- or 28-in. VR bbls. w/SK choke. Available also in All Gauge Skeet Set: Lightning 12 w/one removable forearm and three extra sets of bbls. in 20, 28 and .410 ga. in fitted luggage case. Disc. 1976. (For higher grades see listings for comparable Hunting models)

12 or 20 ga.	NiB $2170	Ex $1690	Gd $1167
28 ga. or .410	NiB $2566	Ex $2278	Gd $1489
Combo skeet set (all gauges)	NiB $6549	Ex $6000	Gd $5489

SUPERPOSED SUPER

LIGHT MODEL . . . . NiB $7101 Ex $4877 Gd $4128
Ultralight field gun version of Standard Lightning Model has classic straight-grip stock and slimmer forearm. Available only in 12 and 20 gauges (2.75-in. chambers), w/26.5-in. VR bbls. Weight: 6.5 lbs., (12 ga.); 6 lbs., (20 ga.). Made 1967-76.

SUPERPOSED TRAP GUN . . NiB $5321 Ex $3867 Gd $2998

Same as Grade I except has trap-style stock, beavertail forearm, 30-in. VR bbls., 12 ga. only. Disc. 1976. (For higher grades see listings for comparable hunting models)

TWELVETTE DOUBLE AUTOMATIC

Lightweight version of Double Automatic w/same general specifications except aluminum receiver. Bbl. w/plain matted top or VR. Weight: 6.75 to 7 lbs., depending on bbl. Receiver is finished in black w/gold engraving; 1956-61 receivers were also anodized in gray, brown and green w/silver engraving. Made 1955-71

w/plain bbl.	NiB $900	Ex $600	Gd $380
w/VR bbl.	NiB $1000	Ex $750	Gd $476

CZ (CESKA ZBROJOVKA), INC. — Uhersky Brod, Czech Republic

Imported by CZ-USA, Kansas City, KS.

581 SOLO. . . . . NiB $740 Ex $575 Gd $430
O/U boxlock action with double triggers and ejectors. 12 ga. 2-3/4-in. chambers. Disc. 1995, resumed 1999 to 2005.

CZ USA Woodcock Deluxe

ALL-AMERICAN SERIES . . . . . . **NiB $2110 Ex $755 Gd $555**
O/U boxlock action with single trigger and ejectors. 12 ga. 2.75-in. chamber. Bbl.: 30- or 32-in. VR extended choke tubes. Finish: Gloss black receiver. Stock: Checkered walnut adj. butt-stock. Weight: 8.5 lbs. Made 2017 to date.
Trap Combo model (single bbl. w/dual adj. rib and O/U bbl. w/stepped rib,
2005-13) . . . . **NiB $2890 Ex $2180 Gd $1590**
Single Trap model (single 30-, 32-, or 34-in. bbl. w/stepped rib) . . . . **NiB $1360 Ex $1250 Gd $900**

ARMARILLO . . . . **NiB $625 Ex $430 Gd $210**
Similar to Durago S/S, double triggers. Made 2005 to 2006.

BOBWHITE . . . . **NiB $778 Ex $500 Gd $260**
S/S hammerless boxlock action with double trigger and extractors. 12, 16 or 20 ga. 3-in. chambers. Bbl.: 26 or 28 in. Finish: case hardened. Stock: straight English grip, walnut. Weight: 6 to 7 lbs. Made 2005-15, reintroduced 2019.

CZ 612/620 SERIES
Pump action. Gauge: 12 (612) or 20 (620), 3-in. chamber. Bbl.: 28-in. VR w/3 choke tubes. Finish: Matte chrome. Stock: Walnut. Weight: 5.4 to 6.2 lbs. Made 2014 to date.
612 Field model . . . . **NiB $345 Ex $135 Gd $220**
612 HC-P model (tactical polymer pistol grip stock, ghost ring sights, 2013-15) . . . . **NiB $315 Ex $255 Gd $220**
612 Home Defense model (polymer stock, ghost ring sights, 2013-15) . . . . **NiB $270 Ex $215 Gd $175**
612 Magnum Turkey model (3.5-in. chamber, Realtree camo polymer stock, 26-in. bbl.) . . . **NiB $370 Ex $280 Gd $200**
612 Magnum Waterfowl model (3.5-in. chamber, Realtree camo polymer stock, 28-in. bbl.) . . . . **NiB $370 Ex $280 Gd $200**
612 Target model (3-in. chamber, Monte Carlo wood stock, 28-in. bbl. w/3 extended choke tubes) . . . . **NiB $475 Ex $355 Gd $265**
612 Trap model (3-in. chamber, Monte Carlo wood stock, 32-in. ported bbl. w/3 extended choke tubes, disc. 2017) . . . . **NiB $425 Ex $325 Gd $240**
612 Wildfowl Magnum model (3.5-in. chamber, 26-in. VR bbl. w/2 choke tubes, 2013-14) . . . . **NiB $375 Ex $305 Gd $240**
620 Big Game model (3-in. chamber, 22-in. bbl. w/Weaver rail extended rifled choke tube, synthetic stock, disc. 2017) . . **NiB $345 Ex $280 Gd $220**
620 Youth model (shorter LOP, disc. 2017) . . . . **NiB $285 Ex $230 Gd $190**
620/628 Field Select model (20 or 28 ga., 28-in. bbl. w/3 choke tube, walnut stock) . . **NiB $365 Ex $280 Gd $205**

CZ 712/720 SERIES . . . . **NiB $420 Ex $305 Gd $235**
Semiauto. Gas-operated action. Gauge: 12 (712) or 20 (720), 3-in. chamber. Bbl.: 26- or 28-in. VR w/choke tubes. Finish: Matte black chrome. Stock: Laser cut walnut. Weight: 6.3 to 7.3 lbs. Made 2008 to date.
NOTE: 720 is 20 gauge model name, add $90.
712/720 ALS G2 model (ATI polymer stock, disc. 2018) . . . . **NiB $490 Ex $370 Gd $305**

712 G2 Green model (green anodized receiver, disc. 2019) . . . . **NiB $420 Ex $305 Gd $235**
712 3-Gun G2 model (22-in. bbl., w/9-rnd. extended magazine, black synthetic stock, over sized controls, disc. 2016) . . . . **NiB $545 Ex $405 Gd $305**
712 Practical G2 model (22-in. bbl. w/9-rnd. extended magazine, 2014-15) . . . . **NiB $600 Ex $500 Gd $420**
712 Synthetic G2 model (28-in. bbl., black synthetic stock, disc. 2018) . . **NiB $430 Ex $330 Gd $270**
712 Synthetic G2 Camo model (28-in. bbl., Mossy Oak synthetic stock, disc. 2018) . . **NiB $595 Ex $430 Gd $355**
712 Target G2 model (30-in. bbl. w/stepped VR, disc. 2019) . . . **NiB $595 Ex $430 Gd $355**
712 Utility G2 model (black synthetic stock, 20-in. bbl.) . . . . **NiB $430 Ex $330 Gd $270**
712 Magnum model (3.5-in. chamber, 24- or 28-in. bbl.) . . . . **NiB $430 Ex $330 Gd $270**

CZ 812 WATERFOWL . . . . **NiB $600 Ex $525 Gd $405**
Semiauto. Recoil-operated action. Gauge: 12, 3-in. chamber. Bbl.: 28-in. VR w/extended choke tubes. Finish: Camo. Stock: Polymer. Weight: 6.7 lbs. Disc. 2015.

CZ 912/920 SERIES . . . . **NiB $480 Ex $420 Gd $230**
Semiauto. Gas-operated action. Gauge: 12 (912) or 20 (920), 3-in. chamber. Bbl.: 28-in. VR w/choke tubes. Finish: High gloss black. Stock: High gloss walnut. Weight: 6.4 to lbs. Made 2011-20.

CZ 1012 SERIES . . . . **NiB $545 Ex $480 Gd $370**
Semiauto. Inertia-operated action. Gauge: 12, 2-3/4-in. chamber. Bbl.: 26- or 28-in. VR w/choke tubes. Finish: Matte black. Stock: Walnut. Weight: 6.4 to lbs. Made 2019-date.
Synthetic model (polymer stock, Bottomlands or Oak Shadow camo) . . . . **NiB $545 Ex $480 Gd $370**

CANVASBACK (103 D) . . . . **NiB $670 Ex $460 Gd $275**
O/U boxlock action with single trigger and extractors. 12, 20 28 ga. 3-in. chambers. Bbl.: 26 or 28 in., VR, 5 choke tubes, black chrome finish, light engraving. Stock: pistol grip, checkered walnut. Weight: 6.3 to 7.5 lbs. Made 2005-13.
Gold (gold inlays). . . . . **NiB $830 Ex $480 Gd $300**
Gold (28 or .410) . . . .**add 20%**

DRAKE . . . . **NiB $545 Ex $405 Gd $305**
O/U boxlock action with single trigger and extractors. 12 or 20 ga. 3-in. chamber. Bbl.: 28-in. VR 5 choke tubes. Finish: gloss black receiver. Stock: Checkered walnut. Weight: 7.4 lbs. Made 2016 to date.
All-Terrain model (28-in. bbls., walnut stock, OD green Cerakote finish) . . . . . . **NiB $705 Ex $620 Gd $480**

DURANGO . . . . **NiB $725 Ex $530 Gd $245**
S/S hammerless boxlock action with single trigger and extractors. 12 or 20 ga. 3-in. chambers. Bbl.: 20 in. Stock: round knob pistol grip, walnut. Weight: 6 to 6.7 lbs. Made 2005-06.

GRADING: **NiB** = New in Box **Ex** = Excellent or NRA 95% **Gd** = Good or NRA 68%

HAMMER COACH . . . . NiB $778 Ex $500 Gd $260
S/S boxlock action with double trigger, exposed hammers and extractors. 12 ga. 3-in. chambers. Bbl.: 20 in., fixed choke. Finish: case hardened. Stock: pistol grip. Weight: 6.7 lbs. Made 2006 to date.
Classic (12, 30-in. bbl.,
2010-date) . . . . NiB $963 Ex $580 Gd $300

LIMITED EDITION . . . . NiB $1980 Ex $1520 Gd $800
O/U w/ engraved boxlock action with single gold trigger and ejectors. 12 ga. 3-in. chambers. Bbl.: 28 in., VR. Stock: Cicassin walnut. 50 mfg. Made 2006-09.

MALLARD . . . . NiB $583 Ex $360 Gd $230
O/U boxlock action with dual triggers and extractors. 12 or 20 ga. 3-in. chambers. Bbl.: 28 in., VR, 5 choke tubes, coin finish receiver, black chrom bbl. Stock: prince of whales grip, Turkish walnut. Weight: 6.5 to 7.5 lbs. Made 2005-15.

REDHEAD DELUXE (103E) . . . . . NiB $820 Ex $630 Gd $400
O/U boxlock action with single trigger and ejectors. 12 or 20 ga. Bbl.: 26- or 28-in. VR 5 choke tubes. Finish: Coin finish receiver. Stock: pistol grip w/round knob checkered walnut. Weight: 6.7 to 7.9 lbs. Made 2005-14.
Mini (28 or .410, 2005-13) . . . . . NiB $800 Ex $630 Gd $400

REDHEAD PREMIER . . . . NiB $959 Ex $630 Gd $400
O/U boxlock action with single trigger and ejectors. 12 or 20 ga. 3-in. chambers. Bbl.: 26 or 28 in., VR, 5 choke tubes, black chrome bbl. coin finish receiver. Stock: pistol grip, checkered walnut. Weight: 6.7 to 7.9 lbs. Made 2015.
Mini (28 or .410, 2005-13) . . . NiB $800 Ex $630 Gd $400
Target (12 ga., 30-in. bbl.) . . . NiB $1389 Ex $830 Gd $440
All-Terrain model (28- or 30-in. bbls.,
walnut stock, OD green
Cerakote finish, 2020-date) . . NiB $990 Ex $855 Gd $680

RINGNECK . . . . NiB $900 Ex $790 Gd $580
S/S boxlock action w/ engraved sideplates, single trigger and extractors. 12, 16 or 20 ga. 3-in. chambers. Bbl.: 26 or 28 in., 5 choke tubes. Finish: black chrome bbl., case hardened receiver. Stock: pistol grip, checkered walnut. Weight: 6.3 to 7.1 lbs. Made 2005-14.
16 ga., add $200
Mini (28 or .410) . . . . NiB $1229 Ex $800 Gd $410
Target (12 ga., 30-in. bbl.) . . . NiB $1298 Ex $810 Gd $430
Deluxe Custom (20 ga., 28-in. bbl.,
2006-12) . . . . NiB $1700 Ex $1260 Gd $630
Competition (12 ga., 28-in. ported bbl.,
2010-11) . . . . NiB $2730 Ex $1830 Gd $1000

SHARP TAIL TARGET . . . . NiB $1130 Ex $905 Gd $655
O/U boxlock action with single trigger and ejectors. 12 ga. 3-in. chamber. Bbl.: 30-in. VR w/6 Kicks choke tubes. Finish: Color casehardened receiver. Stock: Checkered walnut w/beaver tail forend. Weight: 7.5 lbs. Made 2015 to date.

SPORTER . . . . NiB $2120 Ex $1830 Gd $1330
O/U boxlock action with single trigger and ejectors. 12 ga. 3-in. chambers. Bbl.: 30 or 32 in., VR, 6 extended choke tubes, black chrome bbl., matte black receiver. Stock: pistol grip w/ palm swell, adj. comb, Grade II Turkish walnut. Weight: 8.7 lbs. Made 2008-16.
Standard Grade G2 (Monte Carlo stock,
2013-16) . . . . NiB $1680 Ex $1205 Gd $880
Standard Grade G2 w/adj. VR (2014-15), add $1200

STERLING SERIES
O/U boxlock action with single trigger and ejectors. Gauge: 12 3-in. chamber. Bbl.: 28-in. VR w/5 choke tubes. Stock: Checkered walnut. Weight: 7.5 lbs. Made 2013 to date.
Lady model (fixed or
adj. stock, two-tone
receiver) . . . . NiB $1155 Ex $905 Gd $705
Southpaw model
(designed for left-handed
shooters) . . . . NiB $890 Ex $705 Gd $505
Upland model
(stippled walnut stock,
two-tone receiver) . . . . NiB $890 Ex $705 Gd $505

SUPREME FIELD . . . . NiB $1570 Ex $1375 Gd $1070
O/U boxlock action with single trigger and ejectors. Gauge: 12, 20, or 28 3-in. chamber. Bbl.: 28-in. VR w/5 extended choke tubes. Finish: Polished nickel chrome. Stock: Grade III checkered walnut. Weight: 7 to 7.9 lbs. Made 2018 to date.

SWAMP MAGNUM. . . . . NiB $940 Ex $830 Gd $640
O/U boxlock action with single trigger and ejectors. Gauge: 12, 3.5-in. chamber. Bbl.: 30-in. VR w/5 extended choke tubes. Finish: Camo. Stock: Synthetic camo. Weight: 7.1 lbs. Made 2017 to date.
Reaper model (26-in. bbls., Synthetic camo stock,
camo finish, Picatinny rail) . . . NiB $870 Ex $755 Gd $595

UPLAND ULTRALIGHT . . . . NiB $890 Ex $705 Gd $505
O/U boxlock action with single trigger and ejectors. Gauge: 12 or 20 3-in. chamber. Bbl.: 26- or 28-in. VR w/5 choke tubes. Finish: Matte black or green. Stock: Checkered walnut. Weight: 6 lbs. Made 2010 to date.

WINGSHOOTER. . . . . NiB $880 Ex $630 Gd $500
O/U boxlock action with single trigger and ejectors or extractors. Gauge: 12, 20, 28 or .410 3-in. chamber. Bbl.: 28-in. VR w/5 choke tubes. Finish: Black sideplates w/gold accents. Stock: Checkered walnut. Weight: 6 to 7.9 lbs. Made 2011-14.
Elite model (single bbl. w/dual adj. rib and O/U bbl.
w/stepped rib, 2005-13) . . . . NiB $2890 Ex $2180 Gd $1590
Single Trap model (12 or 20 ga., engraved side plates,
2015 to date) . . . . NiB $905 Ex $680 Gd $505

WOODCOCK DELUXE. . . . . . . NiB $1080 Ex $730 Gd $400
O/U boxlock action with single trigger and ejectors. 12 or 20 ga. 3-in. chambers. Bbl.: 26 or 28 in., VR, 5 choke tubes, black chrome bbl. case hardened receiver w/ sideplates. Stock: prince of whales pistol grip, schnabel forend, walnut. Weight: 6.8 to 7.8 lbs. Made 2005-10.
Custom (20, 2006-10) . . . . . . NiB $1900 Ex $1330 Gd $710
Target (12 ga., 30-in. bbls.) . . . NiB $1389 Ex $830 Gd $440

CENTURY ARMS — St. Albans, VT, and Boca Raton, FL
Formerly Century International Arms, Inc.

ARTHEMIS . . . . NiB $522 Ex $390 Gd $259
O/U boxlock action with double triggers and extractors. 12, 20, 28 ga. or .410 bore. 3-in. chambers. 28-in. bbls. Single set trigger, extractors. Checkered wood stock and forearm. Weight: 5.3 to 7.4 lbs. Mfg. in Turkey by Khan. Disc.

ARTHEMIS O/U . . . . NiB $475 Ex $310 Gd $245
Gauge: 12, 20, 28, .410. Bbl.: 28 in., VR, 3-in. chamber. Single selective trigger, extractors. Stock: Checkered walnut.

Weight: 5.3 to 7.4 lbs. Mfg. by PAR. Imported from 2002 to 2009.

CATAMOUNT FURY I . . . . **NiB $675 Ex $430 Gd $275**
Gas-operated adj. piston, Semiauto w/ detchable 5- or 10-rnd. magazine. Gauge: 12. Bbl.: 20.1 in., choke tubes. Stock: standard style checkered synthetic. Mfg. in China. Imported 2013 to date.

CATAMOUNT FURY II . . . . **NiB $695 Ex $450 Gd $295**
Similar specs as Fury I except synthetic thumbhole stock. Mfg. in China. Imported 2013 to date.

COACH MODEL . . . . **NiB $325 Ex $200 Gd $140**
Side-by-side. Gauge: 12, 20, .410. Bbl.: 20 in., exposed hammers, double trigger. Stock: Checkered walnut. Sling swivels. Mfg. in China.

MODEL IJ2 . . . . **NiB $220 Ex $155 Gd $100**
Slide-action. Gauge: 12; 2.75-in. or 3-in. chamber. Bbl.: 19 in., fixed choke. Ghost ring rear or fiber optic sights. Weight: 7 lbs. Mfg. in China.

PHANTOM . . . . **NiB $295 Ex $240 Gd $190**
Semiauto. Gauge: 12. 3-in. chamber. Bbl.: 24, 26 or 28 in.; VR. Three choke tubes. Stock: Black synthetic. Mfg. in Turkey. Disc.

PW87 . . . . **NiB $390 Ex $325 Gd $160**
Repro. of Winchester 1887 lever-action. Gauge: 12. 2-3/4-in. chamber. Bbl.: 19 in. w/ brass bead M choke. Stock: smooth hardwood. Mfg. in China. Imported from 2013 to date.

SAS-12 . . . . **NiB $250 Ex $185 Gd $100**
Semiauto. Gauge: 12. 2.75-in. chamber. Bbl.: 22 or 23.5 in. Detachable 3- or 5-rnd. mag.
Ghost ring rear sight, add **$25**

ULTRA 87 . . . . **NiB $255 Ex $180 Gd $110**
Slide-action. Gauge: 12. Bbl.: 19 in. Optional heat shield and pistol grip. Side folding stock. Includes extra 28-in. bbl. Weight: 8.2 lbs.

CHARLES DALY, INC. — New York, NY

The pre-WWII Charles Daly shotguns, w/the exception of the Commander, were manufactured by various firms in Suhl, Germany. The postwar guns, except for the Novamatic series, were produced by Miroku Firearms Mfg. Co., Tokyo. Miroku ceased production in 1976 and the Daly trademark was acquired by Outdoor Sports Headquarters, in Dayton, Ohio. OSHI continued to market O/U shotguns from both Italy and Spain under the Daly logo. Automatic models were produced in Japan for distribution in the USA. In 1996, KBI, Inc. in Harrisburg, PA acquired the Daly trademark and currently imports firearms under that logo.

COMMANDER O/U SHOTGUN
Daly-pattern Anson & Deeley system boxlock action. Automatic ejectors. Double triggers or Miller selective single trigger. Gauges: 12, 16,20, 28, .410. Bbls.: 26- to 30-in., IC/M or M/F choke. Weight: 5.25 to 7.25 lbs. depending on ga. and bbl. length. Checkered stock and forend, straight or pistol grip. The two models, 100 and 200, differ in general quality, grade of wood, checkering, engraving, etc.; otherwise specs are the same. Made in Belgium c. 1939.
Model 100 . . . . **NiB $665 Ex $500 Gd $397**

Charles Daly Over/Under
Field Grade (Postwar)

Charles Daly
Field Semiauto

Model 200 . . . . **NiB $866 Ex $703 Gd $511**
w/Miller single trigger, add **$150**

HAMMERLESS DOUBLE-BARREL SHOTGUN
Daly-pattern Anson & Deeley system boxlock action. Automatic ejectors except "Superior Quality" is non-ejector. Double triggers. Gauges: 10, 12, 16, 20, 28, .410. Bbls.: 26- to 32-in., any combination of chokes. Weight: from 4 to 8.5 lbs. depending on ga. and bbl. length. Checkered pistol-grip stock and forend. The four grades—Regent Diamond, Diamond, Empire, Superior—differ in general quality, grade of wood, checkering, engraving, etc.; otherwise specifications are the same. Disc. about 1933.
Diamond quality . . . . . **NiB $12,677 Ex $10,445 Gd $7869**
Empire quality . . . . **NiB $6133 Ex $4632 Gd $3144**
Regent Diamond quality . . **NiB $14,878 Ex $12,966 Gd $10,077**
Superior quality . . . . **NiB $1522 Ex $1292 Gd $1000**

HAMMERLESS DRILLING
Daly pattern Anson & Deeley system boxlock action. Plain extractors. Double triggers, front single set for rifle bbl. Gauges: 12, 16, 20, .25-20, .25-35, .30-30 rifle bbl. Supplied in various bbl. lengths and weights. Checkered pistol-grip stock and forend. Auto rear sight operated by rifle bbl. selector. The three grades — Regent Diamond, Diamond, Superior—differ in general quality, grade of wood, checkering, engraving, etc.; otherwise, specifications are the same. Disc. 1933.
Diamond quality . . . . **NiB $7235 Ex $5530 Gd $4200**
Regent Diamond quality . . **NiB $14,866 Ex $11,977 Gd $9977**
Superior quality . . . . **NiB $3733 Ex $2988 Gd $2036**

HAMMERLESS DOUBLE
EMPIRE GRADE . . . . **NiB $1887 Ex $1352 Gd $1091**
Boxlock. Plain extractors. Non-selective single trigger. Gauges: 12, 16, 20; 3-in. chambers in 12 and 20, 2.75-in. in 16 ga. Bbls.: VR; 26-, 28-, 30-in. (latter in 12 ga. only); IC/M, M/F, F/F. Weight: 6 to 7.75 lbs., depending on ga. and bbls. Checkered pistol-grip stock and beavertail forearm. Made 1968-71.

1974 WILDLIFE
COMMEMORATIVE . . . . . . **NiB $2466 Ex $2167 Gd $1477**
Limited issue of 500 guns. Similar to Diamond Grade over/under. 12-ga. trap and skeet models only. Duck scene engraved on right side of receiver, fine scroll on left side. Made in 1974.

NOVAMATIC LIGHTWEIGHT AUTOLOADER
Same as Breda. Recoil-operated. Takedown. 12 ga., 2.75-in. chamber. Four-round tubular magazine. Bbls.: Plain VR; 26-in. IC or Quick-Choke w/three interchangeable tubes, 28-in. M or F choke. Weight (w/26-in. VR bbl.): 7 lbs., 6 oz. Checkered pistol-grip stock and forearm. Made 1968 by Ernesto Breda, Milan, Italy.
w/plain bbl. . . . . **NiB $398 Ex $277 Gd $198**

SHOTGUNS

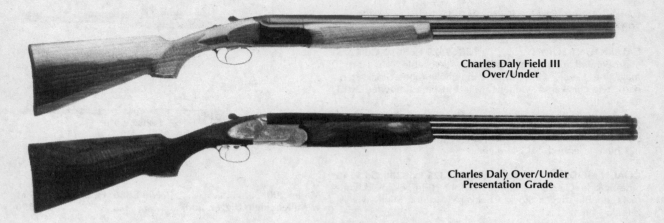

**Charles Daly Field III
Over/Under**

**Charles Daly Over/Under
Presentation Grade**

w/VR bbl. . . . . NiB $397 Ex $260 Gd $200
w/Quick-Choke, add $50

NOVAMATIC SUPER LIGHTWEIGHT
Lighter version of Novamatic Lightweight. Gauges: 12, 20. Weight (w/26-in. VR bbl.): 12 ga., 6 lbs., 10 oz., 20 ga., 6 lbs. SK choke available in 26-in. VR bbl. 28-in. bbls. in 12 ga. only. Quick-Choke in 20 ga. w/plain bbl. Made 1968 by Ernesto Breda, Milan, Italy.
12 ga., plain bbl.. . . . . NiB $387 Ex $288 Gd $198
12 ga., VR bbl. . . . . NiB $387 Ex $288 Gd $198
20 ga., plain bbl. . . . . NiB $543 Ex $433 Gd $315
20 ga., plain bbl. w/Quick-Choke NiB $388 Ex $335 Gd $217
20 ga., VR bbl. . . . . NiB $433 Ex $290 Gd $200

NOVAMATIC SUPER LIGHTWEIGHT
20 GA. MAGNUM . . . . NiB $377 Ex $296 Gd $200
Same as Novamatic Super Lightweight 2, except 3-in. chamber, has 3-rnd. magazine, 28-in. VR bbl., F choke.

NOVAMATIC
12 GA. MAGNUM . . . . NiB $377 Ex $296 Gd $200
Same as Novamatic Lightweight, except chambered for 12-ga. Magnum 3-in. shell. Has 3-rnd. magazine, 30-in. VR bbl., F choke, and stock w/recoil pad. Weight: 7.75 lbs.

NOTE: *Post-War Charles Daly shotguns were imported by Sloan's Sporting Goods trading as Charles Daly in New York. In 1976, Outdoor Sports Headquarters acquired the Daly trademark and continued to import European-made shotguns under that logo. In 1996, KBI, Inc., in Harrisburg, PA, acquired the Daly trademark and currently imports firearms under that logo.*

NOVAMATIC TRAP GUN . . . . . NiB $643 Ex $500 Gd $355
Same as Novamatic Lightweight except has 30-in. VR bbl., F choke and Monte Carlo stock w/recoil pad. Weight: 7.75 lbs.

O/U SHOTGUNS (PRE-WWII)
Daly-pattern Anson & Deeley-system boxlock action. Sideplates. Auto ejectors. Double triggers. Gauges: 12, 16, 20. Supplied in various bbl. lengths and weights. Checkered pistol-grip stock and forend. The two grades — Diamond and Empire — differ in general quality, grade of wood, checkering, engraving, etc.; otherwise specifications are the same. Disc. about 1933.

Diamond Quality . . . . NiB $6133 Ex $4965 Gd $3476
Empire Quality . . . . NiB $4771 Ex $3865 Gd $2700

O/U SHOTGUNS (POST-WWII)
Boxlock. Auto ejectors or selective auto/manual ejection. Selective single trigger. Gauges: 12, 12 Magnum (3-in. chambers), 20 (3-in. chambers), 28, .410. Bbls.: VR; 26-, 28-, 30-in.; standard choke combinations. Weight: 6 to 8 lbs. depending on ga. and bbls. Select walnut stock w/pistol grip, fluted forearm checkered; Monte Carlo comb on trap guns; recoil pad on 12-ga. mag. and trap models. The various grades differ in quality of engraving and wood. Made 1963-76.
Diamond grade . . . . NiB $1588 Ex $1266 Gd $990
Field grade . . . . NiB $933 Ex $800 Gd $576
Superior grade . . . . NiB $1139 Ex $1008 Gd $853
Venture grade . . . . NiB $900 Ex $773 Gd $525

SEXTUPLE MODEL SINGLE-BARREL TRAP GUN
Daly-pattern Anson & Deeley system boxlock action. Six locking bolts. Auto ejector. 12 ga. only. Bbls.: 30-, 32-, 34-in., VR. Weight: 7.5 to 8.25 lbs. Checkered pistol-grip stock and forend. The two models made Empire and Regent Diamond differ in general quality, grade of wood, checkering, engraving, etc., otherwise specifications are the same. Disc. about 1933.
**Regent Diamond
quality (Linder)** . . . . NiB $2788 Ex $2188 Gd $1886
**Empire quality
(Linder)** . . . . NiB $5300 Ex $4260 Gd $3143
**Regent Diamond quality
(Sauer)** . . . . NiB $3921 Ex $3288 Gd $2876
Empire quality (Sauer) . . . . NiB $2966 Ex $2377 Gd $1677

SINGLE-SHOT TRAP GUN
Daly-pattern Anson & Deeley system boxlock action. Auto ejector. 12 ga. only. Bbls.: 30-, 32-, 34-in., VR. Weight: 7.5 to 8.25 lbs. Checkered pistol-grip stock and forend. This model was made in Empire Quality only. Disc. about 1933.
Empire grade (Linder) . . . . . NiB $4765 Ex $3966 Gd $2960
Empire grade (Sauer) . . . . . NiB $2477 Ex $2099 Gd $1776

SUPERIOR GRADE
SINGLE-SHOT TRAP . . . . NiB $954 Ex $833 Gd $700
Boxlock. Automatic ejector. 12 ga. only. 32- or 34-in. VR bbl. F choke. Weight: About 8 lbs. Monte Carlo stock w/pistol grip and recoil pad, beavertail forearm, checkered. Made 1968-76.

DIAMOND GRADE O/U
Boxlock. Single selective trigger. Selective automatic ejectors. Gauges: 12 and 20, 3-in. chambers (2.75 target grade). Bbls.: 26, 27- or 30-in. w/fixed chokes or screw-in tubes. Weight:

7 lbs. Checkered European walnut stock and forearm w/oil finish. Engraved antique silver receiver and blued bbls. Made 1984-90.

Standard model	NiB $1088	Ex $900	Gd $670
Skeet model	NiB $1155	Ex $966	Gd $733
Trap model	NiB $1155	Ex $966	Gd $733

DIAMOND GTX DL HUNTER O/U SERIES
Sidelock. Single selective trigger and selective auto ejectors. Gauges: 12, 20, 28 ga. or .410 bore. 26-, 28- and 30-in. bbls w/3-in. chambers (2.75-in. 28 ga.). Choke tubes (12 and 20 ga.), Fixed chokes (28 and 410). Weight: 5-8 lbs. Checkered European walnut stock w/hand-rubbed oil finish and recoil pad. Made 1997-2001.

Diamond GTX DL Hunter	NiB $11,977	Ex $9478	Gd $5800
Diamond GTX EDL Hunter	NiB $13,778	Ex $10,771	Gd $8987
Diamond GTX Sporting (12 or 20 ga.)	NiB $5921	Ex $4771	Gd $3380
Diamond GTX Skeet (12 or 20 ga.)	NiB $5540	Ex $4380	Gd $3100
Diamond GTX Trap (12 ga. only)	NiB $6144	Ex $4766	Gd $3200

EMPIRE DL HUNTER O/U . . NiB $1456 Ex $1277 Gd $956
Boxlock. Ejectors. Single selective trigger. Gauges:12, 20, 28 ga. and .410 bore. 26- or 28- in. bbls. w/3-in. chambers (2.75-in. 28 ga.). Choke tubes (12 and 20 ga.), Fixed chokes (28 and .410). Engraved coin-silver receiver w/game scene. Imported from 1997 to 1998.

EMPIRE EDL HUNTER SERIES
Similar to Empire DL Hunter except engraved sideplates. Made 1998 to date.

Hunter model	NiB $1477	Ex $1133	Gd $890
Sporting model	NiB $1371	Ex $1108	Gd $870
Skeet model	NiB $1388	Ex $1170	Gd $880
Trap model	NiB $1366	Ex $1109	Gd $853
28 ga., add			$110
.410 ga, add			$150
Multi-chokes w/Monte Carlo stock, add			$175

DSS HAMMERLESS DOUBLE . . NiB $885 Ex $744 Gd $561
Boxlock. Single selective trigger. Selective automatic ejectors. Gauges: 12 and 20; 3-in. chambers. 26-in. bbls. w/screw-in choke tubes. Weight: 6.75 lbs. Checkered walnut pistol-grip stock and semi-beavertail forearm w/recoil pad. Engraved antique silver receiver and blued bbls. Made from 1990. Disc.

FIELD GRADE O/U . . . . NiB $675 Ex $570 Gd $449
Boxlock. Single selective trigger. Extractors. Gauges: 12 and 20; 3-in. chambers. Bbls.: 26-in., IC/M; 28-in., M/F. Weight: 6.75 lbs. (12 ga.). Checkered walnut stock and forearm w/semi-gloss finish and recoil pad. Engraved color-casehardened receiver and blued bbls. Made from 1989. Disc.

FIELD SEMIAUTO SHOTGUN . NiB $622 Ex $476 Gd $377
Recoil-operated. Takedown. 12-ga. and 12-ga. Magnum. Bbls.: 27- and 30-in.; VR. Made 1982-88.

FIELD III O/U SHOTGUN . . . . NiB $679 Ex $580 Gd $445
Boxlock. Plain extractors. Non-selective single trigger. Gauges: 12 or 20. Bbls.: VR; 26- and 28-in.; IC/M, M/F. Weight: 6 to 7.75 lbs. depending on ga. and bbls. Chrome-molybdenum

steel bbls. Checkered pistol-grip stock and forearm. Made from 1982. Disc.

LUXIE O/U . . . . NiB $900 Ex $733 Gd $529
Similar to the Field Grade except w/selective automatic ejectors and choke tubes. Gauges: 12, 20, 28 and .410. Receiver w/antique silver finish and blued bbls. Made 1989-94.

MULTI-XII SELF-LOADING
SHOTGUN . . . . NiB $656 Ex $490 Gd $387
Similar to the gas-operated field semiauto except w/new Multi-Action gas system designed to shoot all loads w/o adjustment. 12 ga. w/3-in. chamber. 27-in. bbl. w/Invector choke tubes, VR. Made in Japan from 1987 to 1988.

PRESENTATION GRADE O/U . . . NiB $1254 Ex $1009 Gd $770
Purdey boxlock w/double cross-bolt. Gauges: 12 or 20. Engraved receiver w/single selective trigger and auto-ejectors. 27-in. chrome-molybdenum steel, rectified, honed and internally chromed, VR bbls. Hand-checkered deluxe European walnut stock. Made 1982-86.

SUPERIOR II SHOTGUN O/U . . . NiB $1064 Ex $880 Gd $602
Boxlock. Plain extractors. Non-selective single trigger. Gauges: 12 or 20. Bbls.: chrome-molybdenum VR 26-, 28-, 30-in., latter in magnum only, assorted chokes. Silver engraved receiver. Checkered pistol-grip stock and forearm. Made 1982-88

SPORTING CLAYS O/U . . . . . . NiB $833 Ex $644 Gd $535
Similar to the Field Grade except in 12 ga. only w/ported bbls. and internal choke tubes. Made 1990-96.

CHIAPPA FIREARMS LTD., — DAYTON, OH

Chiappa owns ARMI SPORT REPLICA FIREARMS MFG. and manufactures Cimarron, Legacy Sports, Taylor's & Co. Imported currently, manufactured in Italy.

MODEL 1887 . . . . NiB $1363 Ex $1295 Gd $400
Lever action. Gauge: 12 ga., 18.5, 22, 24 or 28-in. bbl., choke tubes. Color-casehardened or chrome receiver. Weight: 6.6 lbs. Stock: oil finished smooth walnut. Made from 2009 to date.

CHURCHILL — Italy and Spain

Imported by Ellett Brothers, Inc., Chapin, SC; previously by Kassnar Imports, Inc., Harrisburg, PA

AUTOMATIC SHOTGUN
Gas-operated. Gauge: 12, 2.75- or 3-in. chambers. Five round magazine w/cutoff. Bbl.: 24-, 25-, 26-, 28-in. w/ICT choke tubes. Checkered walnut stock w/satin finish. Imported from 1990 to 1994.

Standard model	NiB $657	Ex $571	Gd $455
Turkey model	NiB $697	Ex $586	Gd $434

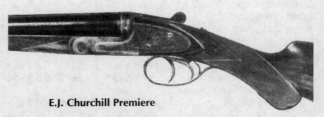

E.J. Churchill Premiere

SHOTGUNS

Churchill Automatic Shotgun

Churchill Windsor Grade Side-by-Side Shotgun

MONARCH O/U SHOTGUN
Hammerless, takedown w/engraved receiver. Selective single or double triggers. Gauges: 12, 20, 28, .410; 3-in. chambers. Bbls.: 25- or 26-in. (IC/M); 28-in. (M/F). Weight: 6.5-7.5 lbs. Checkered European walnut buttstock and forend. Made in Italy from 1986 to 1993.
w/double triggers . . . . NiB $490 Ex $378 Gd $225
w/single trigger . . . . NiB $588 Ex $466 Gd $321

REGENT O/U SHOTGUNS
Gauges: 12 or 20; 2.75-in. chambers. 27-in. bbls. w/interchangeable choke tubes and wide VR. Single selective trigger, selective automatic ejectors. Checkered pistol-grip stock in fancy walnut. Imported from Italy 1984 to 1988 and 1990 to 1994.
Regent V(disc. 1988) . . . . NiB $987 Ex $680 Gd $590
Regent VII w/sideplates (disc. 1994) . . . . . NiB $873 Ex $779 Gd $544

REGENT SKEET . . . . NiB $873 Ex $779 Gd $544
12 or 20 ga. w/2.75-in. chambers. Selective automatic ejectors, single-selective trigger. 26-in. over/under bbls. w/VR. Weight: 7 lbs. Made in Italy from 1984 to 1988.

REGENT TRAP . . . . NiB $876 Ex $654 Gd $490
12-ga. competition shotgun w/2.75-in. chambers. 30-in. over/under bbls. choked IM/F, vent side ribs. Weight: 8 lbs. Selective automatic ejectors, single selective trigger. Checkered Monte Carlo stock w/Supercushion recoil pad. Made in Italy 1984 to 1988.

SPORTING CLAYS O/U . . . . . . NiB $945 Ex $800 Gd $575
Same general specifications as Windsor IV except in 12 ga. only w/28-in. ported bbls. and choke tubes. Selective automatic ejectors. Weight: 7.5 lbs. Made 1992-94.

WINDSOR O/U SHOTGUNS
Hammerless, boxlock w/engraved receiver, selective single trigger. Extractors or ejectors. Gauges: 12, 20, 28 or .410; 3-in. chambers. Bbls.: 24 to 30 in. w/fixed chokes or choke tubes. Weight: 6 lbs., 3 oz. (Flyweight) to 7 lbs., 10 oz. (12 ga.). Checkered straight (Flyweight) or pistol-grip stock and forend of European walnut. Imported from Italy 1984 to 1993.
Windsor III w/fixed chokes. . . . NiB $668 Ex $544 Gd $455
Windsor III w/choke tubes . . . . NiB $798 Ex $670 Gd $555
Windsor IV w/fixed chokes
   (disc. 1993) . . . . NiB $768 Ex $659 Gd $455
Windsor IV w/choke tubes . . . . NiB $833 Ex $754 Gd $500

WINDSOR SIDE-BY-SIDE SHOTGUNS
Boxlock action w/double triggers, ejectors or extractors and automatic safety. Gauges: 10, (3.5-in. chambers); 12, 20, 28, .410 (3-in. chambers), 16 (2.75-in. chambers). Bbls.: 23 to 32 in. w/various fixed choke or choke tube combinations. Weight: 5 lbs., 12 oz. (Flyweight) to 11.5 lbs. (10 ga.). European walnut buttstock and forend. Imported from Spain 1984 to 1990.
Windsor I 10 ga. . . . . NiB $569 Ex $400 Gd $327
Windsor I 12 ga. thru .410. . . . NiB $569 Ex $400 Gd $327
Windsor II 12 or 20 ga. . . . . . . NiB $569 Ex $400 Gd $327
Windsor VI 12 or 20 ga. . . . . . . NiB $569 Ex $400 Gd $327

E.J. CHURCHILL, LTD. —
Surrey (previously London), England

The E.J. Churchill shotguns listed below are no longer imported.

PREMIERE QUALITY HAMMERLESS DOUBLE
Sidelock. Automatic ejectors. Double triggers or selective single trigger. Gauges: 12, 16, 20, 28. Bbls.: 25-, 28- 30-, 32-in.; any degree of boring. Weight: 5-8 lbs. depending on ga. and bbl. length. Checkered stock and forend, straight or pistol-grip.
w/double triggers . . . NiB $46,775 Ex $36,950 Gd $30,000
w/single selective trigger, add. $10%

FIELD MODEL HAMMERLESS DOUBLE
Sidelock Hammerless ejector gun w/same general specifications as Premiere Model but of lower quality.
w/double triggers . . . . . . NiB $10,667 Ex $9260 Gd $8110
w/single selective trigger, add. 10%

PREMIERE QUALITY O/U SHOTGUN
Sidelock. Automatic ejectors. Double triggers or selective single trigger. Gauges: 12, 16, 20, 28. Bbls.: 25-, 28-, 30-, 32-in., any degree of boring. Weight: 5-8 lbs. depending on ga. and bbl. length. Checkered stock and forend, straight or pistol-grip.
w/double triggers . . . NiB $55,000 Ex $38,000 Gd $25,000
w/selective single trigger, add. 10%
w/raised VR, add. 15%

UTILITY MODEL HAMMERLESS DOUBLE-BARREL
Anson & Deeley boxlock action. Double triggers or single trigger. Gauges: 12, 16, 20, 28, .410. Bbls.: 25-, 28-, 30-, 32-in., any degree of boring. Weight: 4.5-8 lbs. depending on ga. and bbl. length. Checkered stock and forend, straight or pistol-grip.
w/double triggers . . . . NiB $7340 Ex $6077 Gd $4340
w/single selective trigger, add. 10%

XXV PREMIERE HAMMERLESS
DOUBLE.......... **NiB $47,000 Ex $40,000 Gd $35,000**
Sidelock. Assisted opening. Automatic ejectors. Double triggers. Gauges: 12, 20. 25-in. bbls. w/narrow, quick-sighting rib; any standard choke combination. English-style straight-grip stock and forearm, checkered.

XXV IMPERIAL .... NiB $14,775 Ex $12,700 Gd $9775
Similar to XXV Premiere but no assisted opening feature.

XXV HERCULES .... NiB $10,750 Ex $9450 Gd $6680
Boxlock, otherwise specifications same as for XXV Premiere.

XXV REGAL............NiB $6277 Ex $4988 Gd $3500
Similar to XXV Hercules but w/o assisted opening feature. Gauges: 12, 20, 28, .410.

CIMARRON ARMS — Fredericksburg, TX

Importer of reproductions and replicas manufactured by Armi-Sport and Polytech.

1878 COACH GUN SERIES
SxS. Exposed hammers, double triggers. Ga.: 20 or 12, 3-in. chamber. Bbl.: 20- or 26-in. Stock: Smooth wood w/pistol grip. Finish: Blued or antique. Mfg. by Polytech, imported 2007-date.
Field Grade model .... **NiB $545 Ex $480 Gd $370**
Deluxe model
   (checkered stock) .... **NiB $645 Ex $580 Gd $470**

1881 HAMMERLESS COACH GUN SERIES
SxS. Hammerless, double triggers. Ga.: 20 or 12, 2-3/4-in. chamber. Bbl.: 20- to 30-in. w/choke tubes. Stock: Smooth wood w/straight grip. Finish: Blued. Mfg. by Polytech, imported 2010-15.
Field Grade model .... **NiB $610 Ex $530 Gd $410**
Deluxe model (checkered stock) **NiB $660 Ex $580 Gd $460**

1883 DOUBLE
BARREL SHOTGUN .... **NiB $755 Ex $655 Gd $515**
SxS. Ga.: .410 or 12, 2-3/4-in. chamber. Bbl.: 18- to 28-in. Stock: Wood. Finish: Blued. Imported 2015-19.

1887 LEVER ACTION SERIES
Reproduction of Winchester Model 1887 lever-action repeater shotgun. Exposed hammer. Ga.: 12, 2-3/4-in. chamber. Bbl.: 20-, 22- or 24-in. Stock: Smooth wood w/pistol grip. Finish: Blued or antique. Mfg. by Armi-Sport, imported 2010-18.
Standard model............ **NiB $1220 Ex $1070 Gd $830**
w/choke tubes (20- or
   30-in. bbl., 2019-date) ...... **NiB $525 Ex $430 Gd $330**
Terminator model
   (12 ga., 20- or 22-in.
   bbl., pistol grip, 2010-18).. **NiB $1220 Ex $1070 Gd $830**

1889 DOUBLE
BARREL SHOTGUN .... **NiB $755 Ex $655 Gd $515**
SxS. Ga.: .410 or 12, 2-3/4-in. chamber. Bbl.: 18-, 20- or 22-in. Stock: Wood, beavertail or splinter forend. Finish: Blued. Imported 2015-20.

1897 PUMP ACTION SERIES
Reproduction of Winchester Model 1897 slide-action repeater shotgun. Exposed hammer. Ga.: 12, 2-3/4-in. chamber. Bbl.: 20-in. w/choke tubes. Stock: Smooth wood w/pistol grip.

Finish: Blued or antique. Mfg. by Polytech, imported 2007-14, reintro. 2017-date.
Standard model............. **NiB $400 Ex $350 Gd $280**
Trench model (heat shield,
   bayonet lug, 2019-21) ...... **NiB $440 Ex $390 Gd $300**

DOC HOLLIDAY DOUBLE
BARREL SHOTGUN .... **NiB $1385 Ex $1215 Gd $945**
SxS. Exposed hammers, double triggers. Ga.: 12, 2-3/4-in. chamber. Bbl.: 20-in. Stock: Checkered wood pistol grip, splinter forend. Finish: Blued/case hardened. "Doc Holliday" engraved side plate. Imported 2015-date.

WYATT EARP DOUBLE
BARREL SHOTGUN .... **NiB $1385 Ex $1215 Gd $945**
SxS. Exposed hammers, double triggers. Ga.: 12, 2-3/4-in. chamber. Bbl.: 20-in. Stock: Checkered wood pistol grip, splinter forend. Finish: Blued/case hardened. "Wyatt Earp" engraved side plate. Imported 2013-14.

CLASSIC DOUBLES — Tochigi, Japan

Imported by Classic Doubles International, St. Louis, MO, and previously by Olin as Winchester Models 101 and 23.

MODEL 101 O/U SHOTGUN
Boxlock. Engraved receiver w/single selective trigger, auto ejectors and combination bbl. selector and safety. Gauges: 12, 20, 28 or .410, 2.75-, 3-in. chambers, 25.5- 28- or 30-in. VR bbls. Weight: 6.25 – 7.75 lbs. Checkered French walnut stock. Imported from 1987 to 1990.
Classic I Field .... **NiB $1590 Ex $1488 Gd $1033**
Classic II Field........... **NiB $1879 Ex $1540 Gd $1133**
Classic Sporter .... **NiB $2066 Ex $1788 Gd $1233**
Classic Sporter combo .... **NiB $3475 Ex $2870 Gd $2035**
Classic Trap.............. **NiB $1380 Ex $1166 Gd $990**
Classic Trap Single....... **NiB $1435 Ex $1140 Gd $1089**
Classic Trap combo....... **NiB $2560 Ex $2053 Gd $1498**
Classic Skeet .... **NiB $1765 Ex $1600 Gd $1179**
Classic Skeet 2-bbl. set .... **NiB $2867 Ex $2374 Gd $1790**
Classic Skeet 4-bbl. set .... **NiB $4488 Ex $3972 Gd $2633**
ClassicWaterfowler....... **NiB $1554 Ex $1266 Gd $1031**
For Grade II (28 ga.), add...................... **$900**
For Grade II (.410), add **$300**

MODEL 201 SIDE-BY-SIDE SHOTGUN
Boxlock. Single selective trigger, automatic safety, selective ejectors. Gauges: 12 or 20; 3-in. chambers. 26- or 28-in. VR bbl., fixed chokes or internal tubes. Weight: 6 to 7 lbs. Checkered French walnut stock and forearm. Imported 1987 to 1990.
Field model............. **NiB $2687 Ex $1490 Gd $1264**
Skeet model .... **NiB $2687 Ex $1490 Gd $1264**
With internal choke tubes, add.................... **$100**

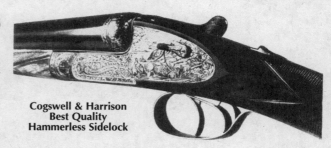

**Cogswell & Harrison
Best Quality
Hammerless Sidelock**

SHOTGUNS

MODEL 201
SMALL BORE SET . . . . NiB $4650 Ex $3751 Gd $2975
Same general specifications as the Classic Model 201 except w/smaller frame, in 28 ga. (IC/M) and .410 (F/M). Weight: 6-6.5 lbs. Imported from 1987 to 1990.

COGSWELL & HARRISON, LTD. —
London, England

AMBASSADOR HAMMERLESS DOUBLE-BARREL
SHOTGUN . . . . NiB $6056 Ex $4533 Gd $3718
Boxlock. Sideplates w/game scene or rose scroll engraving. Automatic ejectors. Double triggers. Gauges: 12, 16, 20. Bbls.: 26-28-, 30-in.; any choke combination. Checkered straight-grip stock and forearm. Disc.

AVANT TOUT SERIES HAMMERLESS DOUBLE-BARREL
SHOTGUNS . . . . NiB $2688 Ex $2133 Gd $1954
Boxlock. Sideplates (except Avant Tout III Grade). Automatic ejectors. Double triggers or single trigger (selective or non-selective). Gauges: 12, 16, 20. Bbls.: 25-, 27.5-, 30-in., any choke combination. Checkered stock and forend, straight grip standard. Made in three models (Avant Tout I or Konor, Avant Tout II or Sandhurst. Avant Tout III or Rex) which differ chiefly in overall quality of engraving, grade of wood, checkering, etc. General specifications are the same. Disc.
Avant Tout I. . . . . NiB $3544 Ex $3160 Gd $2477
Avant Tout II . . . . NiB $2983 Ex $2786 Gd $1966
Avant Tout III . . . . NiB $2254 Ex $2090 Gd $1760
w/non-selective single trigger, add $250
w/selective single trigger, add $425

BEST QUALITY HAMMERLESS
SIDELOCK DOUBLE-BARREL SHOTGUN
Hand-detachable locks. Automatic ejectors. Double triggers or single trigger (selective or non-selective). Gauges: 12, 16, 20. Bbls.: 25-, 26-, 28-, 30-in., any choke combination. Checkered stock and forend, straight grip standard.
Victor model. . . . . NiB $6570 Ex $5461 Gd $4130
Primic model (disc.) . . . . . . NiB $6640 Ex $5521 Gd $4200
w/non-selective single trigger, add $250
w/selective single trigger, add. $450

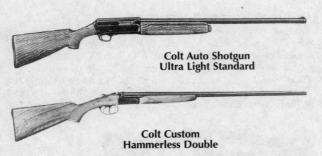

**Colt Auto Shotgun
Ultra Light Standard**

**Colt Custom
Hammerless Double**

HUNTIC MODEL HAMMERLESS DOUBLE
Sidelock. Automatic ejectors. Double triggers or single trigger (selective or non-selective). Gauges: 12, 16, 20. Bbls.: 25-, 27.5-, 30-in.; any choke combination. Checkered stock and forend, straight grip standard. Disc.
w/double triggers . . . . NiB $4077 Ex $2986 Gd $1769
w/non-selective single trigger, add $250
w/selective single trigger, add. $400

MARKOR HAMMERLESS DOUBLE
Boxlock. Non-ejector or ejector. Double triggers. Gauges: 12, 16, 20. Bbls.: 27.5 or 30-in.; any choke combination. Checkered stock and forend, straight grip standard. Disc.
Non-ejector . . . . NiB $1784 Ex $1599 Gd $1188
Ejector model, add 20%

REGENCY HAMMERLESS
DOUBLE. . . . . NiB $4395 Ex $3667 Gd $2971
Anson & Deeley boxlock action. Automatic ejectors. Double triggers. Gauges: 12, 16, 20. Bbls.: 26-, 28-, 30-in., any choke combination. Checkered straight-grip stock and forearm. Introduced in 1970 to commemorate the firm's bicentennial, this model has deep scroll engraving and the name "Regency" inlaid in gold on the rib. Disc.

COLT'S MFG. CO., INC. — Hartford, CT

Auto Shotguns were made by Franchi and are similar to corresponding models of that manufacturer.

AUTO SHOTGUN — ULTRA LIGHT STANDARD
Recoil-operated. Takedown. Alloy receiver. Gauges: 12, 20. Mag. holds 4 rounds. Bbls.: plain, solid or VR, chrome-lined; 26-in. IC or M choke, 28-in. M or F choke, 30-in. F choke, 32-in. F choke. Weight: 12 ga., about 6.25 lbs. Checkered pistol-grip stock and forearm. Made 1964-66.
w/plain bbl. . . . . NiB $400 Ex $297 Gd $200
w/solid rib bbl. . . . . NiB $450 Ex $344 Gd $250
w/VR bbl. . . . . NiB $450 Ex $344 Gd $250

AUTO SHOTGUN — MAGNUM CUSTOM
Same as Magnum except has engraved receiver, select walnut stock and forearm. Made 1964-66.
w/Solid-rib bbl. . . . . NiB $544 Ex $422 Gd $300
w/VR bbl. . . . . NiB $600 Ex $470 Gd $351

AUTO SHOTGUN — ULTRA LIGHT CUSTOM
Same as Standard Auto except has engraved receiver, select walnut stock and forearm. Made 1964-66.
w/solid-rib bbl. . . . . NiB $544 Ex $470 Gd $366
w/VR bbl. . . . . NiB $600 Ex $495 Gd $379

AUTO SHOTGUN — MAGNUM
Same as Standard Auto except steel receiver, chambered for 3-in. Magnum shells, 30- and 32-in. bbls. in 12 ga., 28-in. in 20 ga. Weight: 12 ga., about 8.25 lbs. Made 1964-66.

Colt Standard Pump

Colt-Sauer Drilling

Grade I	NiB $2788	Ex $2308	Gd $1683
Grade II	NiB $3166	Ex $2521	Gd $1790
Grade III	NiB $3767	Ex $2866	Gd $1946
Waterfowler	NiB $2581	Ex $2264	Gd $1598

CONNENTO/VENTUR — Formerly imported by Ventura, Seal Beach, CA

MODEL 51 . . . . **NiB $456 Ex $361 Gd $295**
Gauge: 12, 16, 20, 28 and .410. Double-barrel, box-lock action. Barrels: 26, 28, 30 and 32 in.; various chokes; extractors; and double triggers. Checkered walnut stock. Introduced in 1980, discontinued 1985.

MODEL 52 . . . . **NiB $610 Ex $433 Gd $329**
Same as Model 51 except in 10 gauge.

MODEL 53 . . . . **NiB $538 Ex $449 Gd $300**
Same as Model 51 except with scalloped receiver, automatic ejectors and optional single selective trigger. Discontinued in 1985.

W/single trigger, add **25%**

MODEL 62 . . . . **NiB $1132 Ex $990 Gd $760**
Holland & Holland-design sidelock shotgun with various barrel lengths and chokes; automatic ejectors; cocking indicators. Floral engraved receiver, checkered walnut stock. Discontinued in 1982.

MODEL 64 . . . . **NiB $1388 Ex $1054 Gd $877**
Same as Model 62 except deluxe finish. Discontinued.

GRADE I . . . . **NiB $1259 Ex $988 Gd $844**
Gauge: 12. Over/under shotgun. Barrels: 32 in.; screw-in choke tubes; high ventilated rib; automatic ejectors; single selective trigger standard. Checkered Monte Carlo walnut stock.

MARK II . . . . **NiB $1569 Ex $1236 Gd $1006**
Same as Mark I model but with an extra single barrel and fitted leather case.

MARK III . . . . **NiB $1788 Ex $1469 Gd $1100**
Same as Mark I model but with finely figured walnut stock and engraved metal.

MARK III Combo . . . . **NiB $2877 Ex $2243 Gd $2071**
Same as Mark III model above but with extra single barrel and fitted leather case.

---

w/plain bbl.	NiB $552	Ex $447	Gd $332
w/solid-rib bbl.	NiB $622	Ex $470	Gd $356
w/VR bbl.	NiB $644	Ex $500	Gd $371

CUSTOM HAMMERLESS
DOUBLE . . . . **NiB $766 Ex $509 Gd $446**
Boxlock. Double triggers. Auto ejectors. Gauges: 12 Mag., 16. Bbls.: 26-in. IC/M; 28-in. M/F; 30-in. F/F. Weight: 12 ga., about 7.5 lbs. Checkered pistol-grip stock and beavertail forearm. Made in 1961.

COLTSMAN PUMP SHOTGUN . . **NiB $489 Ex $355 Gd $269**
Takedown. Gauges: 12, 16, 20. Magazine holds 4 rounds. Bbls.: 26-in. IC; 28-in. M or F choke; 30-in. F choke. Weight: About 6 lbs. Plain pistol-grip stock and forearm. Made 1961-1965 by Manufrance.

CUSTOM PUMP . . . . **NiB $500 Ex $377 Gd $286**
Same as Standard Pump shotgun except has checkered stock, VR bbl. Weight: About 6.5 lbs. Made 1961-1963 by Manufrance.

SAUER DRILLING . . . . **NiB $4466 Ex $3778 Gd $2360**
Three-bbl. combination gun. Boxlock. Set rifle trigger. Tang bbl. selector, automatic rear sight positioner. 12 ga. over .30-06 or .243 rifle bbl. 25-in. bbls., F and M choke. Weight: About 8 lbs. Folding leaf rear sight, blade front w/brass bead. Checkered pistol-grip stock and beavertail forearm, recoil pad. Made 1974-1985 by J. P. Sauer & Sohn, Eckernförde, Germany.

CONNECTICUT VALLEY CLASSICS — Westport, CT

SPORTER 101 O/U
Gauge: 12; 3-in. chamber. Bbls.: 28-, 30- or 32-in. w/ screw-in tubes. Weight: 7.75 lbs. Engraved stainless or nitrided receiver; blued bbls. Checkered American black walnut buttstock and forend w/low-luster satin finish. Made 1993-98.

Classic Sporter	NiB $1966	Ex $1634	Gd $1388
Stainless Classic Sporter	NiB $2764	Ex $2259	Gd $1744

FIELD O/U
Similar to the standard Classic Sporter over/under model except w/30-in. bbls. only and non-reflective matte blued finish on both bbls. and receiver for Waterfowler; other grades w/different degrees of embellishment; Grade I the lowest and Grade III the highest. Made 1993-1998.

DAKOTA ARMS, INC. — Sturgis, SD

CLASSIC FIELD GRADE
S/S SHOTGUN . . . . **NiB $7566 Ex $6548 Gd $4456**
Boxlock. Gauge: 20 ga. 27-in. bbl. w/fixed chokes. Double triggers. Selective ejectors. Color-casehardened receiver. Weight: 6 lbs. Checkered English walnut stock and splinter forearm w/ hand-rubbed oil finish. Made 1996-98.

Grade II (engraving,
2004-07) . . . . **NiB $5200 Ex $4500 Gd $3500**
Grade III (gold engraving,
2004-07) . . . . **NiB $6200 Ex $5500 Gd $4500**

PREMIER GRADE
S/S SHOTGUN . . . . **NiB $14,765 Ex $11,466 Gd $9224**
Similar to Classic Field Grade model except w/50% engraving coverage. Exhibition grade English walnut stock. Made from 1996 to date.

SHOTGUNS

AMERICAN LEGEND
S/S SHOTGUN . . . . . **NiB $16,750 Ex $15,000 Gd $11,550**
Limited edition built to customer's specifications. Gauge: 20 ga. 27-in. bbl. Double triggers. Selective ejectors. Fully engraved, coin-silver finished receiver w/gold inlays. Weight: 6 lbs. Hand checkered special-selection English walnut stock and forearm. Made 1996-2005.

DARNE S.A. — Saint-Etienne, France

HAMMERLESS DOUBLE-BARREL SHOTGUNS
Sliding-breech action w/fixed bbls. Auto ejectors. Double triggers. Gauges: 12, 16, 20, 28; also 12 and 20 Magnum w/3-in. chambers. Bbls.: 27.5-in. standard, 25.5- to 31.5-in. lengths available; any standard choke combination. Weight: 5.5 to 7 lbs. depending on ga. and bbl. length. Checkered straight-grip or pistol-grip stock and forearm. The various models differ in grade of engraving and wood. Manufactured from 1881 to 1979.

Model R11 (Bird Hunter) . . **NiB $7044 Ex $4698 Gd $2677**
Model R15 (Pheasant
   Hunter) . . . . **NiB $14,900 Ex $12,785 Gd $10,000**
Model R16 (Magnum) . . . . . **NiB $3775 Ex $2730 Gd $2167**
Model V19 (Quail
   Hunter) . . . . **NiB $22,000 Ex $17,500 Gd $14,275**
Model V22 . . . . **NiB $31,000 Ex $26,800 Gd $22,975**
Model V Hors Série No. 1 . . . . **NiB $77,000 Ex $58,650 Gd $46,790**

DAVIDSON GUNS — Greensboro, SC
Manufactured by Fabrica de Armas ILJA, Eibar, Spain; distributed by Davidson Firearms Co., Greensboro, NC

MODEL 63B DOUBLE-BARREL
SHOTGUN . . . .**NiB $433 Ex $279 Gd $200**
Anson & Deeley boxlock action. Frame engraved and nickel plated. Plain extractors. Auto safety. Double triggers. Gauges: 12, 16, 20, 28, .410. Bbl. lengths: 25 (.410 only), 26, 28, 30 in. (latter 12 ga. only). Chokes: IC/ M, M/F, F/F. Weight: 5 lbs., 11 oz. (.410) to 7 lbs. (12 ga.). Checkered pistol-grip stock and forearm of European walnut. Made in 1963. Disc.

MODEL 63B MAGNUM
Similar to standard Model 63B except chambered for 10 ga. 3.5-in., 12 and 20 ga. 3-in. Magnum shells; 10 ga. has 32-in. bbls., choked F/F. Weight: 10 lb., 10 oz. Made from 1963. Disc.
12-and 20 ga. magnum . . . . . .**NiB $455 Ex $300 Gd $210**
10 ga. magnum . . . .**NiB $477 Ex $369 Gd $230**

MODEL 69SL DOUBLE-BARREL
SHOTGUN . . . .**NiB $455 Ex $400 Gd $270**
Sidelock action w/detachable sideplates, engraved and nickel plated. Plain extractors. Auto safety. Double triggers. 12 and 20 ga. Bbls.: 26-in. IC/M, 28-in. M/F. Weight: 12 ga., 7 lbs., 20 ga., 6.5 lbs. Pistol-grip stock and forearm of European walnut, checkered. Made 1963-76.

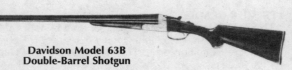

**Davidson Model 63B
Double-Barrel Shotgun**

MODEL 73 STAGECOACH
HAMMER DOUBLE . . . .**NiB $331 Ex $229 Gd $130**
Sidelock action w/detachable sideplates and exposed hammers. Plain extractors. Double triggers. Gauges: 12, 20, 3-in. chambers. 20-in. bbls, M/F chokes. Weight: 7 lbs., 12 ga.; 6.5 lbs., 20 ga. Checkered pistol-grip stock and forearm. Made from 1976. Disc.

DIAMOND SHOTGUNS
Currently imported by ADCO Sales, Inc, Woburn, MA. Established circa 1981, all guns manufactured in Turkey.

GOLD SERIES
(SEMIAUTO) . . . .**NiB $354 Ex $280 Gd $175**
12 gauge, 3-in. chamber. Gas operated. Bbl. 24 (slug) or 28 in. Ventilated rib with three choke tubes. Semi-humpback design, anodized alloy frame, gold etching. Rotary bolt. Black synthetic or checkered Turkish walnut forearm and stock with recoil pad. Value $50 less for slug version.

IMPERIAL SERIES
. . . .**NiB $475 Ex $345 Gd $265**
Gauge: 12 (3.5-in.) or 20 (3-in.). Bbl.: 24 (12 ga. slug), 26 (20 ga.) or 28 in.; VR, rotary bi-lateral bolt, deluxe checkered stock and forearm. Imported 2003.

ELITE SERIES
. . . .**NiB $445 Ex $323 Gd $200**
Gauge: 12, 3-in. Bbl.: 22 (slug), 24, 26 or 28 in.; ventilated rib, deluxe checkered walnut stock and forearm. Imported 2001. Deduct $50 for slug model.

PANTHER SERIES
. . . .**NiB $415 Ex $338 Gd $200**
Gauge: 12, 3-in. Gas-operated. Black synthetic stock and forearm. Bbl.: 20 (slug or regular) or 28 in. Imported 2002.
Walnut stock and forearm, add **$75**
Slug version . . . .**deduct $50**

MARINER
. . . .**NiB $338 Ex $198 Gd $110**
Gauge: 12, 3-in. Gas operated. Bbl.: 20 (slug) or 22 in. VR. Anodized alloy frame and receiver, satin silver finish. Checkered walnut stock and forearm. Imported 2002.
Slug model, deduct **$50**

GOLD ELITE SERIES
(SLIDE-ACTION) . . . .**NiB $354 Ex $260 Gd $200**
12 gauge, 3-in. chamber. Bbl. 24 (slug with open sights), or 28 in.; ventilated rib. Semi-humpback design. Anodized alloy frame, synthetic black or Turkish walnut stock and forearm. Weight: 7 lbs. Imported 2001. Value $40 less for synthetic stock.

DICKINSON, LLC — Huglu, Turkey
Manufactured by Akdas in Turkey and imported by Dickinson, LLC in Moorpark, CA.

O/U MODELS
Boxlock action. Gauge: 12, 20, 28 ga. or .410 bore, Bbl.: 24-, 26-, 28- or 30-in. VR w/choke tubes (12 or 20 ga. models only), ejectors or extractors. Single trigger. Stock: checkered wood. Finish: white or black steel receiver. Weight: 6 1/2 to 7 lbs.
Hunter model . . . .**NiB $675 Ex $555 Gd $455**
Hunter Deluxe model (case hardened
   receiver) . . . .**NiB $1100 Ex $880 Gd $655**
Hunter Light model (black, engraved receiver,
   6 lbs.) . . . .**NiB $700 Ex $580 Gd $455**
w/sideplates, add **15%**

Osso L2 model (trigger plate action, blued
receiver, 28- or 30-in. VR bbl., walnut
stock) . . . . NiB $1795 Ex $1330 Gd $1000
Osso M1 model (trigger plate action, nickel engraved
receiver w/sideplates, 28- or 30-in. VR bbl.,
walnut stock) . . . . NiB $2160 Ex $1555 Gd $1130
Osso X1 model (side lock action, nickel engraved
receiver, 28- or 30-in. VR bbl., adj. walnut
stock) . . . . NiB $3950 Ex $2930 Gd $2030

PUMP/SLIDE MODELS
Pump/slide action. Gauge: 12. Bbl.: 18.5- or 28-in. w/fixed
or choke tubes. Stock: Synthetic black tradition. Finish: Matte
black. Weight: 6 lbs.
XX3B Field model (28-in. bbl.,
choke tubes) . . . . NiB $240 Ex $205 Gd $175
XX3B Combo model (18.5- and
28-in. bbl.) . . . . NiB $295 Ex $240 Gd $195
XX3B-2 Tactical model (18.5-in. bbl., fixed choke,
front rifle sight) . . . . NiB $200 Ex $175 Gd $155

S/S MODELS
Trigger plate, boxlock or side lock action. Gauge: 12, 16, 20,
28 ga. or .410 bore, Bbl.: 24-, 26-, 28- or 30-in. w/fixed or
choke tubes (12, 16, or 20 ga. only), ejectors. Single or double
triggers. Stock: Walnut English, Prince of Wales, or pistol grip
stock, w/ or w/o checkering. Finish: Color case hardened,
French grey, or gold inlaid receiver. Weight: 5 1/2 to 7 lbs.
Estate model (trigger plate
action) . . . . NiB $1625 Ex $1280 Gd $955
Estate Combo model (trigger plate action,
extra bbl. set), add $600
Plantation model (boxlock
action) . . . . NiB $1875 Ex $1405 Gd $1000
Prestige model (sidelock
action) . . . . NiB $4125 Ex $3205 Gd $2404

SEMIAUTO MODELS
Inertia action. Gauge: 12. Bbl.: 18.5-, 20-, 22- or 24-in. w/fixed
or choke tubes. Rifle sights. Stock: Synthetic black tradition or
pistol grip. Finish: Matte black. Weight: 6 lbs.
AK212T model
(tradition stock) . . . . NiB $350 Ex $290 Gd $230
AK212TP model (pistol grip
stock) . . . . NiB $390 Ex $320 Gd $270

EXCEL ARMS OF AMERICA — Gardner, MA

SERIES 100 O/U SHOTGUN
Gauge: 12. Single selective trigger. Selective auto ejectors.
Hand-checkered European walnut stock w/full pistol grip,
tulip forend. Black metal finish. Chambered for 2.75-in. shells
(Model 103 for 3-in.). Weight: 6. 88 to 7.88 lbs. Disc 1988.
Model 101 w/26-in. bbl., IC/M NiB $465 Ex $367 Gd $266
Model 102 w/28-in. bbl., IC/M NiB $465 Ex $367 Gd $266
Model 103 w/30-in. bbl., M/F . NiB $465 Ex $367 Gd $266
Model 104 w/28-in.
bbl., IC/M. . . . . NiB $465 Ex $367 Gd $266
Model 105, w/28-in. bbl.,
5 choke tubes . . . . NiB $645 Ex $480 Gd $387

Model 106, w/28-in. bbl.,
5 choke tubes . . . . NiB $776 Ex $689 Gd $558
Model 107 Trap, w/30-in. bbl.,
Full or 5 tubes . . . . NiB $776 Ex $689 Gd $558

SERIES 200 SIDE-BY-SIDE
SHOTGUN . . . . NiB $667 Ex $496 Gd $368
Gauges: 12, 20, 28 and .410. Bbls.: 26-, 27- and 28-in.; various choke combinations. Weight: 7 lbs. average. American or
European-style stock and forend. Made 1985-87.

SERIES 300 O/U
SHOTGUN . . . . NiB $1328 Ex $1133 Gd $1033
Gauge: 12. Bbls.: 26-, 28- and 29-in. Non-glare black-chrome
matte finish. Weight: 7 lbs. average. Selective auto ejectors,
engraved receiver. Hand-checkered European walnut stock and
forend. Made 1985-86.

FABARM — Brescia, Italy

*Last imported by Heckler & Koch, Inc., of Sterling, VA
(previously by Ithaca Acquisition Corp., St. Lawrence Sales,
Inc. and Beeman Precision Arms, Inc.) See listings under
Heckler & Koch.*

FIAS — Fabrica Italiana Armi Sabatti
Gardone Val Trompia, Italy

GRADE I O/U
Boxlock. Single selective trigger. Gauges: 12, 20, 28, .410;
3-in. chambers. Bbls.: 26-in. IC/M; 28-in. M/F; screw-in
choke tubes. Weight: 6.5 to 7.5 lbs. Checkered European
walnut stock and forearm. Engraved receiver and blued
finish.
12 ga. model. . . . . NiB $587 Ex $480 Gd $355
20 ga. model. . . . . NiB $633 Ex $512 Gd $367
28 ga. and .410. . . . . NiB $800 Ex $665 Gd $457

FOX — New Britain, CT

*Made by A. H. Fox Gun Co., Philadelphia, PA, 1903 to 1930,
and since then by Savage Arms, originally of Utica, NY, now of
Westfield, MA. In 1993, Connecticut Shotgun Manufacturing
Co. (CSMC) of New Britain, CT reintroduced selected models.
CSMC currently makes the Fox A Grade shotgun for Savage.*

NOTE: *Values shown are for 12 and 16 ga. doubles made by A.
H. Fox. Twenty gauge guns often are valued up to 75% higher.
Savage-made Fox models generally bring prices 25% lower.
With the exception of Model B, production of Fox shotguns was
discontinued about 1942.*

MODEL B HAMMERLESS
DOUBLE . . . . NiB $523 Ex $387 Gd $244
Boxlock. Double triggers. Plain extractor. Gauges: 12, 16, 20,
.410. 24- to 30-in. bbls., VR on current production; chokes: M/F,
C/M, F/F (.410 only). Weight: About 7.5 lbs., 12 ga. Checkered
pistol-grip stock and forend. Made about 1940 to 1985.

Fox Model B

SHOTGUNS

MODEL B-ST . . . . NiB $644 Ex $475 Gd $350
Same as Model B except has non-selective single trigger. Made 1955-66.

MODEL B-DE . . . . NiB $645 Ex $476 Gd $351
Same as Model B-ST except frame finished in satin chrome, select walnut buttstock w/checkered pistol grip and beavertail forearm. Made 1965-66.

MODEL B-DL . . . . NiB $678 Ex $558 Gd $421
Same as Model B-ST except frame finished in satin chrome, select walnut buttstock w/checkered pistol grip side panels, beavertail forearm. Made 1962-66.

MODEL B-SE . . . . NiB $922 Ex $700 Gd $531
Same as Model B except has selective ejectors and single trigger. Made 1966-89.

HAMMERLESS DOUBLE-BARREL SHOTGUNS
The higher grades have the same general specifications as the standard Sterlingworth model, w/differences chiefly in workmanship and materials. Higher grade models are stocked in fine select walnut; quantity and quality of engraving increases w/grade and price. Except for Grade A, all other grades have auto ejectors.
Grade A . . . . NiB $3160 Ex $1641 Gd $1895
Grade AE . . . . NiB $3598 Ex $2977 Gd $2110
Grade BE . . . . NiB $4962 Ex $3988 Gd $2860
Grade CE . . . . NiB $6200 Ex $5110 Gd $3628
Grade DE . . . . NiB $12,779 Ex $11,360 Gd $10,475
Grade FE . . . . NiB $22,679 Ex $18,960 Gd $13,000
Grade XE . . . . NiB $8634 Ex $7321 Gd $4208
w/Kautzy selective single trigger, add $400
w/VR, add $500
w/beavertail forearm, add $300
20 ga. model, add 60%

SINGLE-BARREL TRAP GUNS
Boxlock. Auto ejector.12 ga. only. 30- or 32-in. VR bbl. Weight: 7.5 to 8 lbs. Trap-style stock and forearm of select walnut, checkered, recoil pad optional. The four grades differ chiefly in quality of wood and engraving; Grade M guns, built to order, have finest Circassian walnut. Stock and receiver are elaborately engraved and inlaid w/gold. Disc. 1942. Note: In 1932, the Fox Trap Gun was redesigned and those manufactured after that date have a stock w/full pistol grip and Monte Carlo comb; at the same time frame was changed to permit the rib line to extend across it to the rear.
Grade JE . . . . NiB $3990 Ex $2367 Gd $2031
Grade KE . . . . NiB $5366 Ex $4979 Gd $4000
Grade LE . . . . NiB $6778 Ex $4789 Gd $3760
Grade ME . . . . NiB $15,975 Ex $12,880
Gd $9355

"SKEETER" DOUBLE-BARREL
SHOTGUN . . . . NiB $4990 Ex $4078 Gd $2855
Boxlock. Gauge: 12 or 20. Bbls.: 28 in. w/full-length VR. Weight: Approx. 7 lbs. Buttstock and beavertail forend of select American walnut, finely checkered. Soft rubber recoil pad and ivory bead sights. Made in early 1930s.

STERLINGWORTH DELUXE
Same general specifications as Sterlingworth except 32-in. bbl. also available, recoil pad, ivory bead sights.
w/extractors . . . . NiB $2187 Ex $1654 Gd $1100
w/ejectors . . . . NiB $2370 Ex $1979 Gd $1466
20 ga., add $45%

STERLINGWORTH HAMMERLESS DOUBLE
Boxlock. Double triggers (Fox-Kautzky selective single trigger extra). Plain extractors (auto ejectors extra). Gauges: 12,16, 20. Bbl. lengths: 26-, 28-, 30-in.; chokes F/F, M/F, C/M (any combination of C to F choke borings was available at no extra cost). Weight: 12 ga., 6.88 to 8.25 lbs.; 16 ga., 6 to 7 lbs.; 20 ga., 5.75 to 6.75 lbs. Checkered pistol-grip stock and forearm.
w/extractors . . . . NiB $1800 Ex $1489 Gd $1000
w/ejectors . . . . NiB $2170 Ex $1770 Gd $1254
w/selective single trigger, add 25%

STERLINGWORTH SKEET AND UPLAND GUN
Same general specifications as the standard Sterlingworth except has 26- or 28-in. bbls. w/skeet boring only, straight-grip stock. Weight: 7 lbs. (12 ga.).
w/extractors . . . . NiB $2588 Ex $2066 Gd $1489
w/ejectors . . . . NiB $3000 Ex $2469 Gd $1785
20 ga., add 45%

SUPER HE GRADE . . . . NiB $5863 Ex $4791 Gd $3310
Long-range gun made in 12 ga. only (chambered for 3-in. shells on order), 30- or 32-in. full choke bbls., auto ejectors standard. Weight: 8.75 to 9.75 lbs. General specifications same as standard Sterlingworth.

— *Current MFG.* —

CSMC HAMMERLESS DOUBLE-BARREL SHOTGUNS
High-grade doubles similar to the original Fox models. 20 ga. only. 26- 28- or 30-in. bbls. Double triggers automatic safety and ejectors. Weight: 5.5 to 7 lbs. Custom Circassian walnut stock w/hand-rubbed oil finish. Custom stock configuration: straight, semi- or full pistol-grip stock w/traditional pad, hard rubber plate checkered or skeleton butt; Schnabel, splinter or beavertail forend. Made 1993 to date.
CE grade . . . . NiB $19,500 Ex $14,000 Gd $10,500
XE grade . . . . NiB $22,000 Ex $15,500 Gd $11,300
DE grade . . . . NiB $25,000 Ex $17,500 Gd $13,250
FE grade . . . . NiB $30,000 Ex $25,500 Gd $19,130

FOX A GRADE . . . . NiB $4500 Ex $3850 Gd $2955
Break action. Anson Deeley-style box lock action, side-by-side. Holland & Holland-style ejectors. Gauge: 12. Barrels: 26- or 28-in. w/solid rib and choke tubes. Double triggers. Automatic safety. Front brass bead sight. Finish: Bone and charcoal case color-receiver. Stock: American black walnut w/oil finish, checkering, straight grip, splinter fore-end. Mfg. by CSMC for Savage, 2017-date.

FRANCHI (LUIGI FRANCHI S.P.A.) — Brescia, Italy

Imported by Benelli USA since 1998. Previously imported by FIE.

MODEL 48/AL ULTRA LIGHT
Recoil-operated, semi-auto, takedown, hammerless shotgun w/ tubular magazine. Gauges: 12 or 20 (2.75-in.); 12-ga. Magnum (3-in. chamber). Bbls.: 24- to 32-in. w/various choke combinations. Weight: 5 lbs., 2 oz. (20 ga.) to 6.25 lbs. (12 ga.). Checkered pistol-grip walnut stock and forend w/high-gloss finish. Made1950-2016.
Field model . . . . NiB $850 Ex $655 Gd $555
Field Model Deluxe model (English or Prince
of Wales stock, high gloss blued receiver,
2000-16) . . . . NiB $995 Ex $655 Gd $430
Hunter or magnum models . . . NiB $977 Ex $580 Gd $476

Franchi Model 500
Standard Autoloader

Franchi Model 520 Deluxe

Franchi Model 520
Eldorado Gold

Franchi Aspire

Franchi 612 Variopress Sporting

SHOTGUNS

MODEL 500 STANDARD
AUTOLOADER . . . . **NiB $400 Ex $288 Gd $190**
Gas-operated. 12 gauge. Four round magazine. Bbls.: 26-, 28-in.; VR; IC, M, IM, F chokes. Weight: About 7 lbs. Checkered pistol-grip stock and forearm. Made 1976-80.

MODEL 520 DELUXE
MODEL 520 DELUXE . . . . **NiB $478 Ex $355 Gd $279**
Same as Model 500 except higher grade w/engraved receiver. Made 1975-79.

MODEL 520 ELDORADO
GOLD . . . . **NiB $1088 Ex $877 Gd $743**
Same as Model 520 except custom grade w/engraved and gold-inlaid receiver, finer quality wood. Intro. 1977.

MODEL 610VS
Semiauto. Gas-operated Variopress system adjustable to function w/2.75- or 3- in. shells. 12 gauge. Four round magazine. 26- or 28-in. VR bbls. w/Franchoke tubes. Weight: 7 lbs., 2 oz. 47.5 in. overall. Alloy receiver w/four-lug rotating bolt and loaded chamber indicator. Checkered European walnut butt-stock and forearm w/satin finish. Imported from 1997.
Standard model. . . . . **NiB $766 Ex $600 Gd $445**
Engraved model . . . . **NiB $800 Ex $655 Gd $500**

MODEL 612 SERIES
Semiauto, VarioSystem/Vaiomax gas operating action. Gauge: 12 ga. Only. 24- to 28-in. bbl. 45 to 49-in. overall. Weight: 6.8 to 7 lbs. Five round magazine. Bead type sights with C, IC, M chokes. Blued, matte or Advantage camo finish. Imported from 1999 to 2004.
w/satin walnut stock,
blued finish. . . . . **NiB $645 Ex $559 Gd $369**
w/synthetic stock, matte finish NiB $665 Ex $590 Gd $400
w/Advantage camo finish . . . . . **NiB $800 Ex $645 Gd $449**
Defense model . . . . **NiB $600 Ex $469 Gd $360**
Sporting model . . . . **NiB $966 Ex $733 Gd $544**

MODEL 620 VARIOPRESS
Semiauto. Gauge: 20 ga. Only. 24- 26- or 28-in. bbl. 45 to 49-in. overall. Weight: 5.9 to 6.1 lbs. Five round magazine. Bead type sights with C, IC, M chokes. Satin walnut or Advantage camo stock. Imported from 1999 to 2004.
w/satin walnut stock, matte finish. . . **NiB $655 Ex $498 Gd $367**
w/Advantage camo finish . . . . . **NiB $790 Ex $554 Gd $421**
Youth model w/short stock . . . . **NiB $615 Ex $490 Gd $379**

MODEL 712 SERIES
Semiauto. Benelli Inertia system action. Gauge: 12 only, 3-in. chamber. Bbl.: 24-, 26- or 28-in. VR w/choke tubes. Stock: Weathercoat walnut or camo. Weight: 7 lbs. Imported 2004.
w/Weathercoat walnut stock . . . **NiB $715 Ex $570 Gd $450**
w/camo stock, add **$40**
Raptor model (30-in. ported bbl., nickel receiver
w/green logo, 2005-07). . . . . . . **NiB $845 Ex $580 Gd $445**

MODEL 720 SERIES
Similar to Model 712 except 20 gauge and wood stock only. Imported 2004-11.
w/wood stock . . . . **NiB $875 Ex $605 Gd $430**
Competition model (28-in. bbl. w/extended choke tubes,
2008-11). . . . . **NiB $845 Ex $580 Gd $445**
Raptor model (28-in. bbl., blued receiver,
2005-07). . . . . **NiB $845 Ex $580 Gd $445**

MODEL 912
MODEL 912 . . . . **NiB $670 Ex $505 Gd $530**
Semiauto. VarioSyste/Variomax gas-operated action. Gauge: 12 only, 3.5-in. chamber. Bbl.: 24-, 26-, 28- or 30-in. VR w/3 choke tubes. Stock: nation walnut, black or camo composite. Weight: 7.5 to 7.8 lbs. Imported from 2001 to 2005.
w/satin walnut stock, matte finish . . . **NiB $655 Ex $498 Gd $367**
w/camo finish, add **$100**
Youth model w/short stock . . . . **NiB $615 Ex $490 Gd $379**

MODEL 2003 TRAP O/U . . **NiB $1355 Ex $1109 Gd $1005**
Boxlock. Auto ejectors. Selective single trigger. 12 ga. Bbls.: 30-, 32-in. IM/F, F/F, high-VR. Weight (w/30-in. bbl.): 8.25 lbs. Checkered walnut beavertail forearm and stock w/straight or

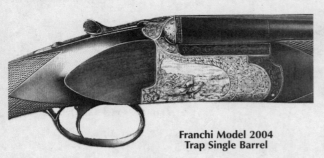

Franchi Model 2004
Trap Single Barrel

Monte Carlo comb, recoil pad. Luggage-type carrying case. Introduced 1976. Disc.

MODEL 2004 TRAP SINGLE
BARREL TRAP . . . . NiB $1366 Ex $1288 Gd $915
Same as Model 2003 except single bbl., 32- or 34-in. Full choke. Weight (w/32-in. bbl.): 8.25 lbs. Introduced 1976. Disc.

MODEL 2005 COMBINATION
TRAP . . . . NiB $1977 Ex $1760 Gd $1233
Model 2004/2005 type gun w/two sets of bbls., single and over/under. Introduced 1976. Disc.

MODEL 2005/3 COMBINATION
TRAP . . . . NiB $2660 Ex $2175 Gd $1648
Model 2004/2005 type gun w/three sets of bbls., any combination of single and over/under. Introduced 1976. Disc.

MODEL 3000/2 COMBINATION
TRAP . . . . NiB $2876 Ex $2599 Gd $1879
Boxlock. Automatic ejectors. Selective single trigger. 12 ga. only. Bbls.: 32-in. over/under choked F/IM, 34-in. underbarrel M choke; high VR. Weight (w/32-in. bbls.): 8 lbs., 6 oz. Choice of six different castoff buttstocks. Introduced 1979. Disc.

AFFINITY 3 SERIES
Semiauto. Inertia system action. Gauge: 12 or 20 w/3-in. chamber. Bbl.: 26- or 28-in. VR w/3 choke tubes. Stock: walnut or black synthetic, shim kit. Finish: Matte black or various camo patterns. Weight: 5.6-6.5 lbs. Imported 2012 to date.
w/synthetic stock . . . . NiB $730 Ex $580 Gd $480
w/wood stock . . . . NiB $830 Ex $680 Gd $580
w/camo finish, add $100
3.5 model (3.5-in. chamber), add $150
Catalyst model (28-in. VR bbl., designed for
     female shooter) . . . . NiB $855 Ex $655 Gd $555
Compact model (24- or 26-in. VR bbl., 12.3-13.3-in.
     LOP) . . . . NiB $1030 Ex $755 Gd $555
Elite model (Cerakote grey receiver, various camo
     synthetic stock) . . . . NiB $1419 Ex $1200 Gd $900
Sporting model (28- or 30-in. VR bbl., nickel receiver,
     synthetic stock, 2013-16) . . NiB $1030 Ex $755 Gd $555

ALCIONE SERIES
O/U. Boxlock. Anson & Deeley system action. Auto ejectors. Double triggers. Gauge: 12 ga. w/3-in. chambers. Bbl.: 26- or 28-in. w/fixed or Franchoke tubes. Stock: Checkered straight-grip stock and forearm.
standard model (1940-50) . . . . . NiB $675 Ex $225 Gd $170
Classic model (blue non-engraved receiver, Franchoke
     tubes, 2004-05) . . . . NiB $1125 Ex $880 Gd $655
Field model (nickel-finished receiver, Franchoke tubes,
     1998-05) . . . . NiB $1125 Ex $880 Gd $655

SL Sport model (sideplates, 30-in. ported bbl.,
     disc. 2005) . . . . NiB $1435 Ex $955 Gd $730
SP model (engraved sideplates w/gold accents, 28-in. VR
     bbl., 2003-05) . . . . NiB $2325 Ex $1755 Gd $1280
SX model (removable engraved sideplates, 26- or 28-in. VR
     bbl., 2001-05) . . . . NiB $1535 Ex $1055 Gd $805
Titanium model (12 or 20 ga. 26- or 28-in. VR bbls., alumi-
     num alloy receiver w/titanium inserts, removable side-
     plates, 2002-05) . . . . NiB $1260 Ex $955 Gd $805

ARISTOCRAT SERIES
O/U. Boxlock action. Selective auto ejectors. Selective single trigger. Gauge: 12. Bbls.: 26-in. IC/M; 28- and 30-in. M/F choke, VR, ejectors. Weight: 7 lbs. Stock: Checkered pistol-grip stock and forearm. Made 1960-69.
Field model . . . . NiB $660 Ex $440 Gd $380
Deluxe grade (Higher quality, w/stock and forearm
     of select walnut, elaborate relief engraving
     on receiver, trigger guard, tang and top lever.
     1960-66.) . . . . NiB $990 Ex $840 Gd $775
Imperial and Monte Carlo models (Custom guns made
     in Field, Skeet and Trap models w/the same general
     specifications as standard for these types. Imperial and
     Monte Carlo grades are of highest quality w/stock and
     forearm of select walnut, fine engraving — elaborate on
     latter grade. 1967-69) . . NiB $2640 Ex $2095 Gd $1820
Magnum model (32-in. VR bbls. choked F/F,
     1962-65) . . . . NiB $660 Ex $445 Gd $380
Silver King model (stock and forearm of select
     walnut, elaborately engraved silver-finished receiver,
     1962-69) . . . . NiB $750 Ex $540 Gd $475
Skeet model (26-in. VR bbls. w/SK chokes No. 1 and No. 2,
     skeetstyle stock and forearm, 7.5 lbs., later production had
     wider (10mm) rib, 1960-69) . NiB $715 Ex $500 Gd $435
Supreme grade (game birds inlaid in gold on receiver.
     1960-66) . . . . NiB $1430 Ex $1160 Gd $995
Trap model (30-in. VR bbls., M/F choke, trap-style
     stock w/recoil pad, beavertail forearm. Later
     production had Monte Carlo comb, 10mm rib.
     1960-69) . . . . NiB $745 Ex $530 Gd $455

AIRONE . . . . NiB $1320 Ex $940 Gd $750
S/S. Boxlock. Anson & Deeley system action. Ejectors. Double triggers. 12 ga. Engraved receiver. Stock: Checkered straight English-grip stock and forearm. Made 1940-50.

ASTORE SERIES
S/S. Boxlock. Anson & Deeley system action. Similar to Airone model except less engraving. Plain extractors. Made 1937-60.
Standard model . . . . NiB $990 Ex $775 Gd $640
5 model (higher grade wood, fine engraving. automatic
     ejectors, single trigger, 28-in. bbl. M/F
     or IM/F chokes are standard on current production.
     Disc.) . . . . NiB $2200 Ex $1650 Gd $1465

Franchi Astore 5

II model (not as high grade, w/either extractors or auto ejectors, double triggers, pistol-grip stock. 27-in. bbl. IC/IM; 28-in. M/F chokes. Mfg. in Spain.) . . . . NiB $1210 Ex $940 Gd $805

ASPIRE . . . . NiB $1950 Ex $1480 Gd $1080
O/U. Boxlock round action. Gauge: 28 or 410. Bbl.: 28-in. VR w/5 choke tubes, Finish: case hardened receiver. Stock: oil finish checkered pistol-grip stock. Automatic safety. Made 2013-15.

BLACK MAGIC ASPIRE . . . . . NiB $1950 Ex $1480 Gd $1080
O/U. Boxlock round action. Gauge: 28 or 410. Bbl.: 28-in. VR w/5 choke tubes, Finish: case hardened receiver. Stock: oil finish checkered pistol-grip stock. Automatic safety. Made 2013-15.
Game model . . . . NiB $550 Ex $400 Gd $305
Skeet model (26-in. VR ported bbl.
   w/fixed choke) . . . . NiB $580 Ex $430 Gd $466
Trap model (30-in. VR bbl. w/Franchoke
   tubes) . . . . NiB $615 Ex $435 Gd $330

BLACK MAGIC SPORTING HUNTER . . NiB $995 Ex $805 Gd $655
O/U. Boxlock action. Gauge: 12. Bbl.: 28-in. VR w/Franchoke tubes, ejectors. Finish: Black receiver w/gold accents. Stock: Checkered walnut. Imported 1989 to 1991
Lightweight model (6 lbs.), subtract $20

DE LUXE MODEL PRITI O/U . . NiB $400 Ex $320 Gd $210
Boxlock. 12 or 20 ga. only. 26- or 28-in. VR bbls. w/ choke tubes. Single trigger. Weight: 7.4 lbs. Imported 1988 to 1989.

ELITE . . . . NiB $600 Ex $430 Gd $325
Similar Prestige model except w/engraved receiver. Imported 1985-89.

FENICE . . . . NiB $1245 Ex $910 Gd $660
Semiauto. Similar action as 48 AL. Gauge: 20 or 28. Bbl.: 26- or 28-in. VR w/choke tubes, Finish: Silver receiver w/engraving and gold accents. Stock: oil finish checkered walnut. Weight: 5.4-5.7 lbs. Imported 2007 to 2016.

HIGHLANDER . . . . NiB $1195 Ex $880 Gd $680
S/S. Scalloped boxlock action. Gauge: 12 or 20. Bbl.: 26-in. VR w/choke tubes, Finish: blued or case hardened. Stock: oil finish checkered walnut. Weight: 6.1-6.4 lbs. Imported 2007 to 2009.

I-12 INERTIA . . . . NiB $700 Ex $480 Gd $355
Semiauto. Benelli Inertia system action. Gauge: 12 only, 3-in. chamber. Bbl.: 24-, 26- or 28-in. VR w/choke tubes. Stock: Walnut or synthetic camo. Finish: Blued. Weight: 7.5 lbs. Imported 2005-11.
w/camo finish, add $100
Limited White Gold (higher grade walnut, engraved matte
   nickel receiver, 2006-11) . . NiB $1430 Ex $805 Gd $730
Sporting (30-in. VR bbl. w/extended choke tube, satin walnut
   stock, 2008-11). . . . . NiB $1180 Ex $455 Gd $355
Upland Hunter (26-in. VR bbl. w/choke tube, satin walnut
   stock, 2008-09) . . . . NiB $1080 Ex $805 Gd $605

INSTINCT L . . . . NiB $1195 Ex $880 Gd $680
O/U. Boxlock action. Gauge: 12, 20, or 28. Bbl.: 28-in. VR w/5 choke tubes, Finish: case hardened receiver. Stock: oil finish checkered walnut w/straight English grip. Weight: 5.7-6.4 lbs. Made 2012 to date.
Catalyst (12 ga., 28-in. VR bbl., designed for female shoot-
   ers) . . . . NiB $1375 Ex $1005 Gd $1305
SL (12 or 20 ga., 26- or 28-in. VR bbl. w/extended
   tubes) . . . . NiB $1475 Ex $1055 Gd $805

Sporting (12 ga., 30-in. VR bbl. w/extended tubes,
   nickel finish receiver) . . . . NiB $1675 Ex $1180 Gd $855

PRESTIGE . . . . NiB $580 Ex $400 Gd $315
Semiauto. Gas-operated action. Gauge: 12 only. Various bbl. lengths. Imported 1985-89.

RENAISSANCE FIELD O/U . . NiB $1430 Ex $1240 Gd $680
O/U. Boxlock. Blued receiver. 12, 20 or 28 ga. 26- or 28-in. VR bbls. w/ choke tubes. Oil finish walnut stock w/ Twin Shock recoil pad. Weight: 5.5 to 6.2 lbs. Imported from 2006 to 2010.
Field model . . . . NiB $1425 Ex $1010 Gd $755
Classic (gold trigger & inlays) . . NiB $1575 Ex $1230 Gd $800
Classic Combo (two bbl. set) . NiB $2330 Ex $1700 Gd $1200
Elite (engraved w/ gold inlays) . . NiB $2000 Ex $1500 Gd $830
Sporting (30-in. ported bbls.) . . NiB $1930 Ex $1460 Gd $830

VELOCE O/U . . . . NiB $1260 Ex $1000 Gd $740
Aluminum engraved receiver w/ gold inlays. 20 or 28 ga. 26- or 28-in. VR bbls. w/ choke tubes. Pistol or straight deluxe oil finish stock. Weight: 5.5 to 5.8 lbs. Imported 2001–05.
Grade II (semi pistol grip) . . NiB $1760 Ex $1240 Gd $900
Squire (two bbl. set) . . . . . . NiB $2070 Ex $1500 Gd $910

STANDARD MODEL AUTOLOADER
Recoil operated. Light alloy receiver. Gauges: 12, 20. Four round magazine. Bbls.: 26-, 28-, 30-in.; plain, solid or VR, IC/M, F chokes. Weight: 12 ga., about 6.25 lbs. 20 ga., 5.13 lbs. Checkered pistol-grip stock and forearm. Made from 1950. Disc.
w/plain bbl. . . . . NiB $490 Ex $335 Gd $260
w/solid rib . . . . NiB $550 Ex $512 Gd $339
w/VR . . . . NiB $560 Ex $489 Gd $368

CROWN, DIAMOND AND IMPERIAL GRADE
Same general specifications as Standard Model except these are custom guns of the highest quality. Crown Grade has hunting scene engraving, Diamond Grade has silver-inlaid scroll engraving; Imperial Grade has elaborately engraved hunting scenes w/figures inlaid in gold. Stock and forearm of fancy walnut. Made 1954-75.
Crown grade . . . . NiB $1670 Ex $1496 Gd $1212
Diamond grade . . . . NiB $2044 Ex $1760 Gd $1233
Imperial grade . . . . NiB $2480 Ex $2239 Gd $1799

STANDARD MODEL MAGNUM
Same general specifications as Standard model except has 3-in. chamber, 32-in. (12 ga.) or 28-in. (20 ga.) F choke bbl., recoil pad. Weight: 12 ga., 8.25 lbs.; 20 ga., 6 lbs. Formerly designated "Superange Model." Made 1954-88.
w/plain bbl. . . . . NiB $500 Ex $412 Gd $286
w/VR . . . . NiB $577 Ex $468 Gd $360

DYNAMIC-12
Same general specifications and appearance as Standard Model, except 12 ga. only, has heavier steel receiver. Weight: About 7.25 lbs. Made 1965-72.
W/plain bbl. . . . . NiB $522 Ex $430 Gd $331
W/VR . . . . NiB $550 Ex $433 Gd $330

DYNAMIC-12 SLUG GUN . . . . NiB $578 Ex $490 Gd $354
Same as standard gun except 12 ga. only, has heavier steel receiver. Made 1965-1972.

DYNAMIC-12 SKEET GUN . . . . NiB $677 Ex $549 Gd $456
Same general specifications and appearance as Standard model except has heavier steel receiver, made only in 12 ga. w/26-in. VR bbl., SK choke, stock and forearm of extra fancy walnut. Made 1965-72.

Franchi Falconet Over/Under Buckskin

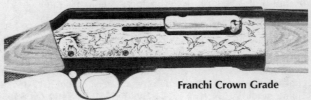

Franchi Crown Grade

Franchi Diamond Grade

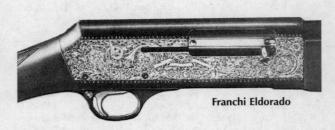

Franchi Eldorado

ELDORADO MODEL . . . . NiB $588 Ex $370 Gd $355
Same general specifications as Standard model except highest grade w/gold-filled engraving, stock and forearm of select walnut, VR bbl. only. Made 1954-75.

**FALCONET INTERNATIONAL
SKEET MODEL** . . . . NiB $1163 Ex $977 Gd $800
Similar to Standard Skeet model but higher grade. Made 1970-74.

**FALCONET INTERNATIONAL
TRAP MODEL** . . . . NiB $1165 Ex $980 Gd $803
Similar to Standard model but higher grade; w/straight or Monte Carlo comb stock. Made 1970-74.

FALCONET O/U FIELD MODELS
Boxlock. Auto ejectors. Selective single trigger. Gauges: 12, 16, 20, 28, .410. Bbls.: 24-, 26-, 28-, 30-in.; VR. Chokes: C/IC, IC/M, M/F. Weight: from about 6 lbs. Engraved lightweight alloy receiver, light-colored in Buckskin model, blued in Ebony model, pickled silver in Silver model. Checkered walnut stock and forearm. Made 1968-75.
Buckskin or Ebony model . . . . NiB $655 Ex $460 Gd $449
Silver model . . . . NiB $655 Ex $460 Gd $449

**FALCONET STANDARD SKEET
MODEL** . . . . NiB $1055 Ex $876 Gd $690
Same general specifications as Field models except made only w/26-in. bbls. w/SK chokes No. 1 and No. 2, wide VR, color-casehardened receiver skeet-style stock and forearm. Weight: 12 ga., about 7.75 lbs. Made 1970-74.

**FALCONET STANDARD
TRAP MODEL** . . . . NiB $1366 Ex $965 Gd $744
Same general specifications as Field models except made only in 12 ga. w/30-in. bbls., choked M/F, wide VR, color-casehardened receiver, Monte Carlo trap style stock and forearm, recoil pad. Weight: About 8 lbs. Made 1970-74.

GAS-OPERATED SEMIAUTO SHOTGUN
Gas-operated, takedown, hammerless shotgun w/tubular magazine. 12 ga. w/2.75-in. chamber. Five round magazine. Bbls.: 24 to 30 in. w/VR. Weight: 7.5 lbs. Gold-plated trigger. Checkered pistol-grip stock and forend of European walnut. Imported from Italy 1985 to 1990.
Prestige model . . . . NiB $677 Ex $456 Gd $449
Elite model . . . . NiB $688 Ex $571 Gd $388

HAMMERLESS SIDELOCK DOUBLES
Hand-detachable locks. Self-opening action. Auto ejectors. Double triggers or single trigger. Gauges: 12,16, 20. Bbl. lengths, chokes, weights according to customer's specifications. Checkered stock and forend, straight or pistol grip. Made in six grades — Condor, Imperiale, Imperiale S, Imperiale Montecarlo No. 5, Imperiale Montecarlo No.11, Imperiale Montecarlo Extra — which differ chiefly in overall quality, engraving, grade of wood, checkering, etc.; general specifications are the same. Only the Imperial Montecarlo Extra Grade is currently manufactured.

Condor grade . . . . NiB $7897 Ex $6200 Gd $4978
**Imperial, Imperiales
grades** . . . . NiB $11,776 Ex $9899 Gd $7217
**Imperial Monte Carlo grades
No. 5, 11** . . . . NiB $32,766 Ex $25,777 Gd $21,989
**Imperial Monte Carlo
Extra grade** . . . . Custom only. Prices start at $110,000
HUNTER MODEL
Same general specifications as Standard Model except higher grade w/engraved receiver; w/ribbed bbl. only. Made 1950-90.
w/solid rib . . . . NiB $500 Ex $390 Gd $322
w/VR. . . . . NiB $616 Ex $488 Gd $400

HUNTER MODEL MAGNUM . . NiB $544 Ex $454 Gd $330
Same as Standard Model Magnum except higher grade w/engraved receiver, VR bbl. only. Formerly designated "Wildfowler Model." Made 1954-73.

PEREGRINE MODEL 400 . . . . . NiB $733 Ex $544 Gd $400
Same general specifications as Model 451 except has steel receiver. Weight (w/26.5-in. bbl.): 6 lbs., 15 oz. Made 1975-78.

PEREGRINE MODEL 451 O/U . NiB $605 Ex $451 Gd $267
Boxlock. Lightweight alloy receiver. Automatic ejectors. Selective single trigger. 12 ga. Bbls.: 26.5-, 28-in.; choked C/IC, IC/M, M/F; VR. Weight (w/26.5-in. bbls.): 6 lbs., 1 oz. Checkered pistol-grip stock and forearm. Made 1975-78.

Franchi Hunter Model w/Ventilated Rib

Franchi Black Magic

Franchi LAW-12

Franchi SPAS-12

Franchi Sporting 2000

SHOTGUNS

SKEET GUN . . . . **NiB $450 Ex $320 Gd $228**
Same general specifications and appearance as Standard Model except made only w/26-in. VR bbl., SK choke. Stock and fore-arm of extra fancy walnut. Made 1972-74.

SLUG GUN . . . . **NiB $435 Ex $288 Gd $190**
Same as Standard Model except has 22-in. plain bbl., Cyl. bore, folding leaf open rear sight, gold bead front sight. Made 1960-90. Disc.

TURKEY GUN . . . . **NiB $556 Ex $377 Gd $298**
Same as Standard Model Magnum except higher grade w/ turkey scene engraved receiver, 12 ga. only, 36-in. matted-rib bbl., Extra Full choke. Made 1963-65.

FALCONET 2000 . . . . **NiB $1355 Ex $1121 Gd $967**
O/U. Boxlock. Single selective trigger. Selective automatic ejectors. Gauge: 12, 2.75-in. chambers. Bbls.: 26-in. w/ Franchoke tubes; IC/M/F. Weight: 6 lbs. Checkered walnut stock and forearm. Engraved silver receiver w/gold-plated game scene. Imported from 1992 to 1993.

Francotte
Model 8446

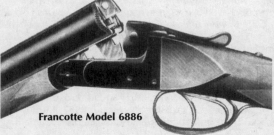

Francotte Model 6886

GRADING: **NiB** = New in Box   **Ex** = Excellent or NRA 95%   **Gd** = Good or NRA 68%

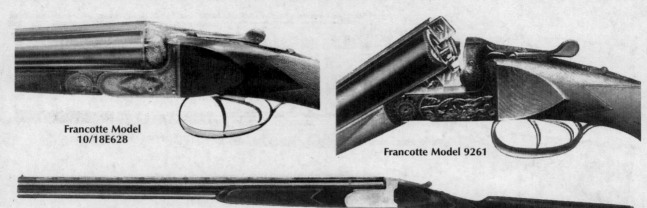

Francotte Model
10/18E628

Francotte Model 9261

Galef Silver Snipe Over/Under Shotgun

LAW-12 . . . . **NiB $689 Ex $454 Gd $377**
Similar to the SPAS-12 Model except gas-operated Semiauto action only, ambidextrous safety, decocking lever and adj. sights. Made 1983-94.

SPAS-12
Selective operating system functions as a gas-operated Semiauto or pump action. Gauge: 12, 2.75-in. chamber. Seven round magazine. Bbl.: 21.5 in. w/cylinder bore and muzzle protector or optional screw-in choke tubes, matte finish. 41 in. overall w/fixed stock. Weight: 8.75 lbs. Blade front sight, aperture rear sight. Folding or black nylon buttstock w/pistol grip and forend, non-reflective anodized finish. Made 1983-94. Limited importation.
Fixed stock . . . . **NiB $1510 Ex $1180 Gd $910**
Folding stock, add $220
w/choke tubes, add $150

SPAS-15 . . . . **NiB $5000 Ex $4500 Gd $2390**
Similar to SPAS-12 model except w/6-rnd. detachable magazine, folding wire stock, carry handle. Weight: 11 lbs. Limited importation in 1989 and very rare due the BATF ban.

SPORTING 2000 . . . . **NiB $1376 Ex $1125 Gd $966**
Similar to the Falconet 2000. Boxlock. Single selective trigger. Selective automatic ejectors. Gauge: 12; 2.75-in. chambers. Ported (1992-93) or unported 28-in. bbls., w/VR. Weight: 7.75 lbs. Blued receiver. Bead front sight. Checkered walnut stock and forearm; plastic composition buttplate. Imported from 1992-93 and 1997-98.

AUGUSTE FRANCOTTE & CIE., S.A. — Liège, Belgium

Francotte shotguns for many years were distributed in the U.S. by Abercrombie & Fitch of New York City. This firm has used a series of model designations for Francotte guns which do not correspond to those of the manufacturer. Because so many Francotte owners refer to their guns by the A & F model names and numbers, the A & F series is included in a listing separate from that of the standard Francotte numbers.

BOXLOCK HAMMERLESS DOUBLES
Anson & Deeley system. Side clips. Greener crossbolt on models 6886, 8446, 4996 and 9261; square crossbolt on Model 6930, Greener-Scott crossbolt on Model 8537, Purdey bolt on Models 11/18E and 10/18E/628. Auto ejectors. Double triggers.

Made in all standard gauges, barrel lengths, chokes, weights. Checkered stock and forend, straight or pistol-grip. The eight models listed vary chiefly in fastenings as described above, finish and engraving, etc.; custom options increase value. Disc.
Model 6886 . . . . . . **NiB $14,688 Ex $13,879 Gd $11,776**
Model 8446 (Francotte Special),
 6930, 4996 . . . . . . **NiB $15,889 Ex $14,799 Gd $14,776**
Model 8537, 9261 (Francotte Original),
11/18E . . . . **NiB $17,345 Ex $16,221 Gd $14,998**
Model 10/18E/628 . . **NiB $17,998 Ex $16,789 Gd $15,900**

BOXLOCK HAMMERLESS DOUBLES – A & F SERIES
Boxlock, Anson & Deeley type. Crossbolt. Sideplate on all except Knockabout Model. Side clips. Auto ejectors. Double triggers. Gauges: 12, 16, 20, 28, .410. Bbls.: 26- to 32-in. in 12 ga., 26- and 28-in. in other ga.; any boring. Weight: 4.75 to 8 lbs. depending on gauge and barrel length. Checkered stock and forend; straight, half or full pistol grip. The seven grades (No. 45 Eagle Grade, No. 30, No. 25, No. 20, No. 14, Jubilee Model, Knockabout Model) differ chiefly in overall quality, engraving, grade of wood, checkering, etc.; general specifications are the same. Disc.
Jubilee model No. 14 . . . . . **NiB $4200 Ex $2633 Gd $1470**
Jubilee model No. 18 . . . . . **NiB $4687 Ex $3577 Gd $1890**
Jubilee model No. 20 . . . . . **NiB $5670 Ex $4122 Gd $2250**
Jubilee model No. 25 . . . . . **NiB $6245 Ex $4738 Gd $2290**
Jubilee model No. 30 . . . . . **NiB $7832 Ex $6110 Gd $3580**
Eagle grade No. 45 . . . . **NiB $11,100 Ex $8854 Gd $5220**
Knockabout model . . . . **NiB $3377 Ex $2688 Gd $1769**
20 ga., add 125%
28 ga. or .410, add 300%

BOXLOCK HAMMERLESS DOUBLES (W/SIDEPLATES)
Anson & Deeley system. Reinforced frame w/side clips. Purdey-type bolt except on Model 8535, which has Greener crossbolt. Auto ejectors. Double triggers. Made in all standard gauges, bbl. lengths, chokes, weights. Checkered stock and forend, straight or pistol grip. Models 10594, 8535 and 6982 are of equal quality, differing chiefly in style of engraving; Model 9/40E/38321 is a higher grade gun in all details and has fine English-style engraving. Built to customer specifications.
Models 10594, 8535, 6982 NiB $6044 Ex $4566 Gd $3177
Model 9/40E/3831 . . . . **NiB $6588 Ex $5344 Gd $3889**

Galef Companion Folding Single-Barrel Shotgun

FINE O/U SHOTGUN .. NiB $10,566 Ex $8978 Gd $6450
Model 9/40.SE. Boxlock, Anson & Deeley system. Auto ejectors. Double triggers. Made in all standard gauges; bbl. length, boring to order. Weight: About 6.75 lbs. 12 ga. Checkered stock and forend, straight or pistol grip. Manufactured to customer specifications. Disc 1990.

FINE SIDELOCK HAMMERLESS
DOUBLE . . . . NiB $26,350 Ex $21,789 Gd $15,680
Model 120.HE/328. Automatic ejectors. Double triggers. Made in all standard ga.; bbl. length, boring, weight to order. Checkered stock and forend, straight or pistol-grip. Manufactured to customer specifications. Disc. 1990.

HALF-FINE O/U
SHOTGUN . . . . NiB $11,656 Ex $9377 Gd $6275
Model SOB.E/11082. Boxlock, Anson & Deeley system. Auto ejectors. Double triggers. Made in all standard gauges; barrel length, boring to order. Checkered stock and forend, straight or pistol grip. Note: This model is similar to No. 9/40.SE except general quality lower. Disc. 1990.

GALEF SHOTGUNS — New York, NY

Manufactured for J. L. Galef & Son, Inc., New York, NY; by M. A. V. I., Gardone F. T., Italy; by Zabala Hermanos, Eiquetta, Spain; and by Antonio Zoli, Gardone V. T., Italy

SILVER SNIPE OVER/UNDER
SHOTGUN . . . . NiB $699 Ex $598 Gd $445
Boxlock. Plain extractors. Single trigger. Gauges: 12, 20; 3-in. chambers. Bbls: 26-, 28-, 30-in. (latter in 12 ga. only); IC/M, M/F chokes; VR. Weight: 12 ga. w/28-in. bbls., 6.5 lbs. Checkered walnut pistol-grip stock and forearm. Introduced by Antonio Zoli in 1968. Disc.

GOLDEN SNIPE . . . . NiB $689 Ex $570 Gd $455
Same as Silver Snipe, except has selective automatic ejectors. Made by Antonio Zoli 1968 to date.

MONTE CARLO TRAP
SINGLE-BARREL SHOTGUN. . . NiB $356 Ex $221 Gd $177
Hammerless. Underlever. Plain extractor. 12 ga. 32-in. bbl., F choke, VR.
Weight: About 8.25 lbs. Checkered pistol-grip stock w/Monte Carlo comb and recoil pad, beavertail forearm. Introduced by M. A. V. I. in 1968. Disc.

Galef Zabala Hammerless Double-Barrel Shotgun

SILVER HAWK HAMMERLESS
DOUBLE . . . . NiB $565 Ex $455 Gd $300
Boxlock. Plain extractors. Double triggers. Gauges: 12, 20; 3-in. chambers. Bbls.: 26-, 28-, 30-in. (latter in 12 ga. only); IC/M, M/F chokes. Weight: 12 ga. w/26-in. bbls., 6 lbs. 6 oz. Checkered walnut pistol-grip stock and beavertail forearm. Made by Angelo Zoli 1968 to 1972.

COMPANION FOLDING SINGLE-BARREL SHOTGUN
Hammerless. Underlever. Gauges: 12 Mag., 16, 20 Mag., 28, .410. Bbls.: 26-in. (.410 only), 28-in. (12, 16, 20, 28), 30-in. (12-ga. only); F choke; plain or VR. Weight: 4.5 lbs. for .410 to 5 lbs., 9 oz. for 12 ga. Checkered pistol-grip stock and forearm. Made by M. A. V. I. from 1968-83.
w/plain bbl. . . . . NiB $245 Ex $179 Gd $95
w/ventilated rib . . . . NiB $270 Ex $196 Gd $110

ZABALA HAMMERLESS DOUBLE-BARREL SHOTGUN
Boxlock. Plain extractors. Double triggers. Gauges: 10 Mag., 12 Mag., 16, 20 Mag., 28, .410. Bbls.: 22-, 26-, 28-, 30-, 32-in.; IC/IC, IC/M, M/F chokes. Weight: 12 ga. w/28-in. bbls., 7.75 lbs. Checkered walnut pistol-grip stock and beavertail forearm, recoil pad. Made by Zabala from 1972-83.
10 ga. NiB $355 Ex $270 Gd $200
Other ga. . . . . NiB $244 Ex $179 Gd $115

GAMBA — Gardone V. T. (Brescia), Italy

DAYTONA COMPETITION O/U
Boxlock w/Boss-style locking system. Anatomical single trigger; optional adj., single-selective release trigger. Selective automatic ejectors. Gauge: 12 or 20; 2.75- or 3-in. chambers. Bbls.: 26.75-, 28-, 30- or 32-in. choked SK/SK, IM/F or M/F. Weight: 7.5 to 8.5 lbs. Black or chrome receiver w/blued bbls. Checkered select walnut stock and forearm w/oil finish. Imported by Heckler & Koch until 1992.
American Trap model . . . . . NiB $2240 Ex $1680 Gd $1021
Pigeon, Skeet, Trap models . . NiB $1323 Ex $1078 Gd $877
Sporting model . . . . NiB $5678 Ex $4498 Gd $3123
Sideplate model . . . . NiB $11,789 Ex $9809 Gd $5977
Engraved models . . . . . . NiB $13,788 Ex $10,666 Gd $7477
Sidelock model . . . . . . NiB $28,560 Ex $23,778 Gd $19,580

ARMAS GARBI — Eibar, Spain

MODEL 100
SIDELOCK SHOTGUN . . . . NiB $5700 Ex $3433 Gd $2433
Gauges: 12, 16, 20 and 28. Bbls.: 25-, 28-, 30-in. Action: Holland & Holland pattern sidelock; automatic ejectors and double trigger. Weight: 5 lbs., 6 oz. to 7 lbs. 7 oz. English-style straight grip stock w/fine-line hand-checkered butt; classic forend. Made from 1985 to date.

MODEL 101
SIDELOCK SHOTGUN . . . . NiB $6788 Ex $4331 Gd $3000
Same general specifications as Model 100 above, except the sidelocks are handcrafted w/hand-engraved receiver; select walnut straight-grip stock.

SHOTGUNS

Golden Eagle Model 5000 Grade II Field

Gorosabel Model 504 Shotgun

Greener Empire Model Hammerless

Greener Far-Killer

MODEL 102
SIDELOCK SHOTGUN . . . . NiB $7175 Ex $4576 Gd $3177
Similar to the Model 101 except w/large scroll engraving. Made 1985-93.

MODEL 103
HAMMERLESS DOUBLE
Similar to Model 100 except w/Purdey-type, higher grade engraving.
Model 103A Standard. . NiB $14,675 Ex $11,650 Gd $9967
Model 103A Royal Deluxe . . . NiB $11,870 Ex $9443 Gd $7655
Model 103B . . . . NiB $21,660 Ex $17,707 Gd $15,990
Model 103B Royal Deluxe . . NiB $25,677 Ex $22,770 Gd $18,989

MODEL 200 HAMMERLESS
DOUBLE . . . . NiB $17,766 Ex $15,221 Gd $11,488
Similar to Model 100 except w/double heavy-duty locks. Continental-style floral and scroll engraving. Checkered deluxe walnut stock and forearm.

GARCIA CORPORATION — Teaneck, NJ

BRONCO 22/.410
O/U COMBO . . . . NiB $300 Ex $197 Gd $100
Swing-out action. Takedown. 18.5-in. bbls.; .22 LR over, .410 ga. under. Weight: 4.5 lbs. One-piece stock and receiver, crackle finish. Intro. In 1976. Disc.

BRONCO .410 SINGLE SHOT . . NiB $233 Ex $120 Gd $90
Swing-out action. Takedown. .410 ga. 18.5-in. bbl. Weight: 3.5 lbs. One-piece stock and receiver, crackle finish. Intro. In 1967. Disc.

GOLDEN EAGLE FIREARMS INC. — Houston, TX.
Manufactured by Nikko Firearms Ltd., Tochigi, Japan

EAGLE MODEL 5000
GRADE I FIELD O/U . . . . NiB $989 Ex $844 Gd $659
Receiver engraved and inlaid w/gold eagle head. Boxlock. Auto ejectors. Selective single trigger. 12, 20 ga.; 2.75- or 3-in. chambers, 12 ga., 3-in.; 20 ga. Bbls.: 26-, 28-, 30-in. (latter only in 12-ga. 3-in. Mag.); IC/M, M/F chokes; VR. Weight: 6.25 lbs., 20 ga.; 7.25 lbs., 12 ga.; 8 lbs., 12-ga. Mag. Checkered pistol-grip stock and semi-beavertail forearm. Imported 1975-82. Note: Guns marketed 1975 to 1976 under the Nikko brand name have white receivers; guns made since 1976 are blued.

EAGLE MODEL 5000
GRADE I SKEET . . . . NiB $954 Ex $743 Gd $522
Same as Field model except has 26- or 28-in. bbls. w/wide (11 mm) VR, SK choked. Imported from 1975 to 1982.

EAGLE MODEL 5000
GRADE I TRAP . . . . NiB $954 Ex $755 Gd $569
Same as Field model except has 30-, or 32-in. bbls. w/wide (11 mm) VR (M/F, IM/F, F/F chokes), trap-style stock w/recoil pad. Imported from 1975 to 1982.

EAGLE MODEL 5000
GRADE II FIELD . . . . NiB $1077 Ex $890 Gd $776
Same as Grade I Field model except higher grade w/fancier wood, more elaborate engraving and "screaming eagle" inlaid in gold. Imported from 1975 to 1982.

EAGLE MODEL 5000
GRADE II SKEET . . . . NiB $1100 Ex $940 Gd $800
Same as Grade I Skeet model except higher grade w/fancier wood, more elaborate engraving and "screaming eagle" inlaid in gold; inertia trigger, vent side ribs. Imported from 1975-82.

EAGLE MODEL 5000
GRADE II TRAP . . . . NiB $1100 Ex $940 Gd $800
Same as Grade I Trap model except higher grade w/fancier wood, more elaborate engraving and "screaming eagle" inlaid in gold; inertia trigger, vent side ribs. Imported from 1975 to 1982.

EAGLE MODEL 5000
GRADE III GRANDEE . . . . . NiB $2760 Ex $2255 Gd $1798
Best grade, available in Field, Skeet and Trap models w/same general specifications as lower grades. Has sideplates w/game scene engraving, scroll on frame and bbls., fancy wood (Monte Carlo comb, full pistol-grip and recoil pad on Trap model). Made 1976-82.

GOROSABEL — Spain

MODEL 503 SHOTGUN . . . . . NiB $1088 Ex $866 Gd $735
Gauges: 12, 16, 20 and .410. Action: Anson & Deely-style boxlock. Bbls.: 26-, 27-, and 28-in. Select European walnut, English or pistol grip, sliver or beavertail forend, hand-checkering. Scalloped frame and scroll engraving. Intro. 1985; disc.

MODEL 504 SHOTGUN . . . . . NiB $1167 Ex $953 Gd $655
Gauge: 12 or 20. Action: Holland & Holland-style sidelock. Bbl.: 26-, 27-, or 28-in. Select European walnut, English or pistol grip, sliver or beavertail forend, hand-checkering. Holland-style large scroll engraving. Inro. 1985; disc.

MODEL 505 SHOTGUN . . . . NiB $1590 Ex $1266 Gd $965
Gauge: 12 or 20. Action: Holland & Holland-style sidelock. Bbls.: 26-, 27-, or 28-in. Select European walnut, English or pistol grip, silver or beavertail forend, hand-checkering. Purdey-style fine scroll and rose engraving. Intro. 1985; disc.

STEPHEN GRANT — Hertfordshire, England

BEST QUALITY SELF-OPENER DOUBLE-BARREL
SHOTGUN . . . . NiB $19,870 Ex $16,920 Gd $12,612
Sidelock, self-opener. Gauges: 12, 16 and 20. Bbls.: 25 to 30 in. standard. Highest-grade English or European walnut straight-grip buttstock and forearm w/Greener type lever. Imported by Stoeger in the 1950s.

BEST QUALITY SIDE-LEVER DOUBLE-BARREL
SHOTGUN . . . . NiB $13,657 Ex $11,770 Gd $9879
Sidelock, self-lever. Gauges: 12, 16 and 20. Bbls.: 25 to 30 in. standard. Highest-grade English or European walnut straight-grip buttstock and forearm w/Greener type lever. Imported by Stoeger in the 1950s.

W. W. GREENER, LTD. — Birmingham, England

EMPIRE MODEL HAMMERLESS DOUBLES
Boxlock. Non-ejector or w/automatic ejectors. Double triggers. 12 ga. only (2.75-in. or 3-in. chamber). Bbls.: 28- to 32-in.; any choke combination. Weight: from 7.25 to 7.75 lbs. depending on bbl. length. Checkered stock and forend, straight- or half-pistol grip. Also furnished in "Empire Deluxe Grade," this model has same general specs, but deluxe finish.
Empire model, non-ejector NiB $1887 Ex $1671 Gd $1388
Empire model, ejector. . . . . NiB $1955 Ex $1771 Gd $1480

Empire Deluxe model,
   non-ejector . . . . NiB $2088 Ex $1933 Gd $1387
Empire Deluxe model,
   ejector . . . . NiB $2677 Ex $2200 Gd $1588

FARKILLER MODEL GRADE F35
HAMMERLESS DOUBLE-BARREL SHOTGUN
Boxlock. Non-ejector or w/automatic ejectors. Double triggers. Gauges: 12 (2.75-in. or 3-in.), 10, 8. Bbls.: 28-, 30- or 32-in. Weight: 7.5 to 9 lbs. in 12 ga. Checkered stock, forend; straight or half-pistol grip.
Non-ejector, 12 ga. . . . . NiB $1577 Ex $1122 Gd $909
Ejector, 12 ga. . . . . NiB $3897 Ex $3138 Gd $2217
Non-ejector, 10 or 8 ga. . . . NiB $2886 Ex $2231 Gd $1977
Ejector, 10 or 8 ga. . . . . NiB $5500 Ex $4230 Gd $3110

G. P. (GENERAL PURPOSE)
SINGLE BARREL . . . . NiB $444 Ex $358 Gd $229
Greener Improved Martini Lever Action. Takedown. Ejector. 12 ga. only. Bbl. lengths: 26-, 30-, 32-in. M or F choke. Weight: 6.25 to 6.75 lbs. depending on bbl. length. Checkered straight-grip stock and forearm.

HAMMERLESS EJECTOR DOUBLE-BARREL SHOTGUNS
Boxlock. Auto ejectors. Double triggers, non-selective or selective single trigger. Gauges: 12, 16, 20, 28, .410 (two latter gauges not supplied in Grades DH40 and DH35). Bbls.: 26-, 28-, 30-in.; any choke combination. Weight: From 4.75 to 8 lbs. Depending on ga. and bbl. length. Checkered stock and forend, straight- or half-pistol grip. The Royal, Crown, Sovereign and Jubilee models differ in quality, engraving, grade of wood, checkering, etc. General specifications are the same.
Royal Model Grade DH75 . . . . . . NiB $4170 Ex $3008 Gd $2166
Crown Model Grade DH55 . . . . . NiB $5166 Ex $3188 Gd $2270
Sovereign Model Grade DH40 . . NiB $5277 Ex $4866 Gd $3900
Jubilee Model Grade DH35 . . . . . NiB $4197 Ex $3145 Gd $2176
w/selective single trigger, add $400
w/non-selective single trigger, add $300
w/VR, add $425
w/single trigger, add $455

**Greifelt Grade No. 1
Over-and-Under Shotgun**

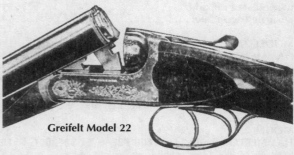

Greifelt Model 22

GRADING: **NiB** = New in Box   **Ex** = Excellent or NRA 95%   **Gd** = Good or NRA 68%

Greifelt Model 103E

Greifelt Model 103

GREIFELT & COMPANY — Suhl, German

GRADE NO. 1 O/U SHOTGUN
Anson & Deeley boxlock, Kersten fastening. Auto ejectors. Double triggers or single trigger. Elaborately engraved. Gauges: 12, 16, 20, 28, .410. Bbls.: 26- to 32-in., any combination of chokes, vent or solid matted rib. Weight: 4.25 to 8.25 lbs. depending on ga. and bbl. length. Straight- or pistol-grip stock, Purdey-type forend, both checkered. Manufactured prior to World War II.
w/solid matted-rib bbl.,
   except .410 & 28 ga. . . . NiB $3797 Ex $3166 Gd $2280
w/solid matted-rib bbl.,
   .410 & 28 ga. . . . . NiB $3844 Ex $3208 Gd $2300
w/ventilated rib, add $125
w/single trigger, add $550

GRADE NO. 3 O/U SHOTGUN
Same general specifications as Grade No. 1 except less fancy engraving. Manufactured prior to World War II.
w/solid matted-rib bbl.,
   except .410 & 28 ga. . . . NiB $2987 Ex $2379 Gd $1979
w/solid matted-rib bbl.,
   .410 & 28 ga. . . . . NiB $5187 Ex $4156 Gd $3110
w/ventilated rib, add $125
w/single trigger, add $450

MODEL 22
HAMMERLESS DOUBLE . . . NiB $2288 Ex $1843 Gd $1244
Anson & Deeley boxlock. Plain extractors. Double triggers. Gauges: 12 and 16. Bbls.: 28- or 30-in., M/F choke. Checkered stock and forend, pistol grip and cheekpiece standard, English-style stock also supplied. Manufactured since World War II.

MODEL 22E
HAMMERLESS DOUBLE . . . NiB $2866 Ex $2430 Gd $1832
Same as Model 22 except has automatic ejectors.

MODEL 103
HAMMLERLESS DOUBLE . . NiB $2100 Ex $1821 Gd $1292
Anson & Deeley boxlock. Plain extractors. Double triggers. Gauges: 12 and 16. Bbls.: 28- or 30-in., M and F choke. Checkered stock and forend, pistol grip and cheekpiece standard, English-style stock also supplied. Manufactured since World War II.

MODEL 103E
HAMMERLESS DOUBLE . . . NiB $2200 Ex $1727 Gd $1224
Same as Model 103 except has automatic ejectors.

MODEL 143E O/U SHOTGUN
General specifications same as pre-war Grade No. 1 Over-and-Under, except this model is not supplied in 28 and .410 ga. or w/32-in. bbls. Model 143E is not as high quality as the Grade No. 1 gun. Mfd. Since World War II.
w/raised matted rib,
   double triggers . . . . NiB $2571 Ex $2068 Gd $1563
w/VR, single
   selective trigger . . . . NiB $2860 Ex $2276 Gd $1865

HAMMERLESS DRILLING (THREE-BARREL
COMBINATION GUN) . . . . NiB $3677 Ex $3220 Gd $2179
Boxlock. Plain extractors. Double triggers, front single set for rifle bbl. Gauges: 12, 16, 20; rifle bbl. in any caliber adapted to this type of gun. 26-in. bbls. Weight: About 7.5 lbs. Auto rear sight operated by rifle bbl. selector. Checkered stock and forearm, pistol-grip and cheekpiece standard. Manufactured prior to WW II. Note: Value shown is for guns chambered for cartridges readily obtainable. If rifle bbl. is an odd foreign caliber, value will be considerably less.

O/U COMBINATION GUN
Similar in design to this maker's over-and-under shotguns. Gauges: 12, 16, 20, 28, .410; rifle bbl. in any caliber adapted to this type of gun. Bbls.: 24- or 26-in., solid matted rib. Weight: From 4.75 to 7.25 lbs. Folding rear sight. Manufactured prior to WWII. Note: Values shown are for gauges other than .410 w/ rifle bbl. Chambered for a cartridge readily obtainable; if in an odd foreign caliber, value will be considerably less. .410 ga. increases in value by about 50%.
w/non-automatic ejector . . NiB $5477 Ex $4651 Gd $3822
w/automatic ejector . . . . . . NiB $6055 Ex $5310 Gd $4430

HARRINGTON & RICHARDSON ARMS
now H&R 1871, Inc. —Gardner, MA

Formerly Harrington & Richardson Arms Co. of Worcester, Mass. One of the oldest and most distinguished manufacturers of handguns, rifles and shotguns, H&R suspended operations on January 24, 1986. In 1987, New England Firearms was established as an independent company producing selected H&R models under the NEF logo. In 1991, H&R 1871, Inc. was formed from the residual of the parent company and then took over the New England Firearms facility. H&R 1871 produced firearms under both their logo and the NEF brand name until 1999, when the Marlin Firearms Company acquired the assets of H&R 1871. Production ceased in 2015. Purchased by JJE Capital Holdings, as part of Remington bankruptcy in 2020.

NO. 3 HAMMERLESS
SINGLE-SHOT SHOTGUN . . . . . NiB $230 Ex $115 Gd $85
Takedown. Automatic ejector. Gauges: 12, 16, 20, .410. Bbls.: plain, 26- to 32-in., F choke. Weight: 6.5 to 7.25 lbs. depending on ga. and bbl. length. Plain pistol-grip stock and forend. Discontinued 1942.

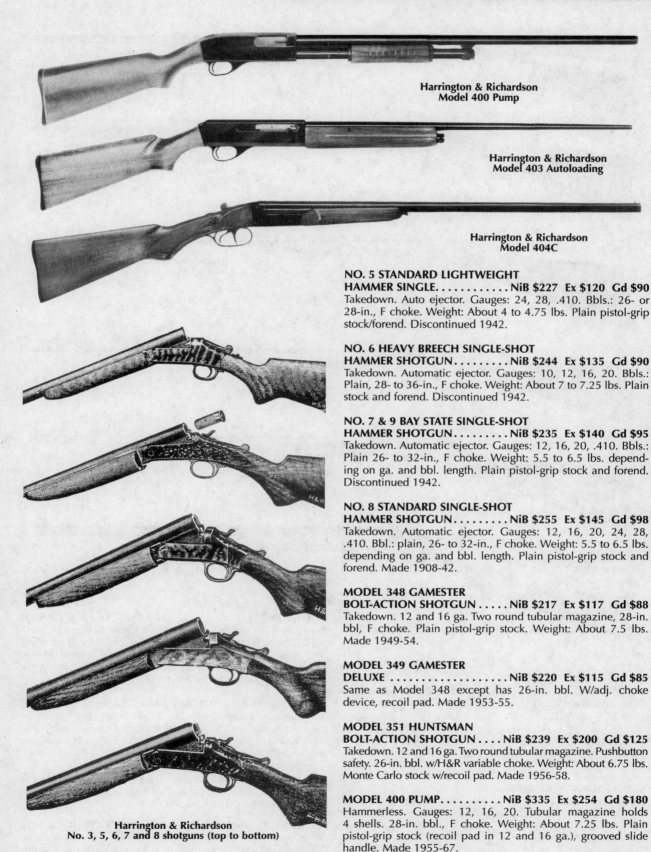

**Harrington & Richardson
Model 400 Pump**

**Harrington & Richardson
Model 403 Autoloading**

**Harrington & Richardson
Model 404C**

Harrington & Richardson
No. 3, 5, 6, 7 and 8 shotguns (top to bottom)

NO. 5 STANDARD LIGHTWEIGHT
HAMMER SINGLE. . . . . NiB $227 Ex $120 Gd $90
Takedown. Auto ejector. Gauges: 24, 28, .410. Bbls.: 26- or 28-in., F choke. Weight: About 4 to 4.75 lbs. Plain pistol-grip stock/forend. Discontinued 1942.

NO. 6 HEAVY BREECH SINGLE-SHOT
HAMMER SHOTGUN. . . . . NiB $244 Ex $135 Gd $90
Takedown. Automatic ejector. Gauges: 10, 12, 16, 20. Bbls.: Plain, 28- to 36-in., F choke. Weight: About 7 to 7.25 lbs. Plain stock and forend. Discontinued 1942.

NO. 7 & 9 BAY STATE SINGLE-SHOT
HAMMER SHOTGUN. . . . . NiB $235 Ex $140 Gd $95
Takedown. Automatic ejector. Gauges: 12, 16, 20, .410. Bbls.: Plain 26- to 32-in., F choke. Weight: 5.5 to 6.5 lbs. depending on ga. and bbl. length. Plain pistol-grip stock and forend. Discontinued 1942.

NO. 8 STANDARD SINGLE-SHOT
HAMMER SHOTGUN. . . . . NiB $255 Ex $145 Gd $98
Takedown. Automatic ejector. Gauges: 12, 16, 20, 24, 28, .410. Bbl.: plain, 26- to 32-in., F choke. Weight: 5.5 to 6.5 lbs. depending on ga. and bbl. length. Plain pistol-grip stock and forend. Made 1908-42.

MODEL 348 GAMESTER
BOLT-ACTION SHOTGUN . . . . . NiB $217 Ex $117 Gd $88
Takedown. 12 and 16 ga. Two round tubular magazine, 28-in. bbl, F choke. Plain pistol-grip stock. Weight: About 7.5 lbs. Made 1949-54.

MODEL 349 GAMESTER
DELUXE . . . . NiB $220 Ex $115 Gd $85
Same as Model 348 except has 26-in. bbl. W/adj. choke device, recoil pad. Made 1953-55.

MODEL 351 HUNTSMAN
BOLT-ACTION SHOTGUN . . . . NiB $239 Ex $200 Gd $125
Takedown. 12 and 16 ga. Two round tubular magazine. Pushbutton safety. 26-in. bbl. w/H&R variable choke. Weight: About 6.75 lbs. Monte Carlo stock w/recoil pad. Made 1956-58.

MODEL 400 PUMP. . . . . NiB $335 Ex $254 Gd $180
Hammerless. Gauges: 12, 16, 20. Tubular magazine holds 4 shells. 28-in. bbl., F choke. Weight: About 7.25 lbs. Plain pistol-grip stock (recoil pad in 12 and 16 ga.), grooved slide handle. Made 1955-67.

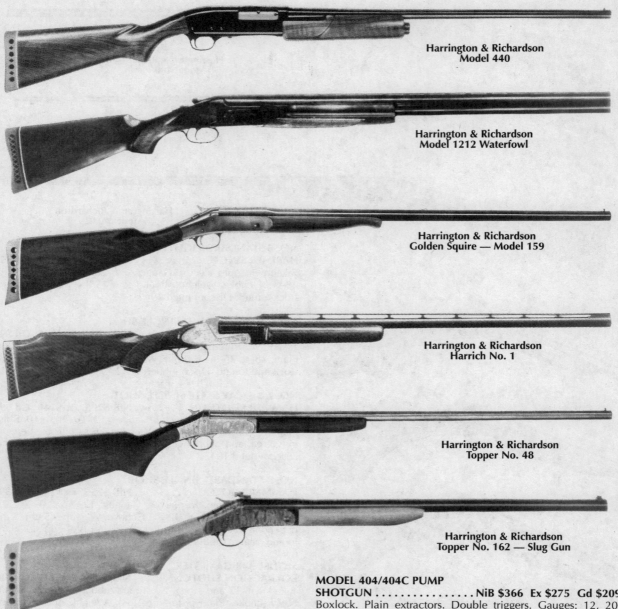

Harrington & Richardson
Model 440

Harrington & Richardson
Model 1212 Waterfowl

Harrington & Richardson
Golden Squire — Model 159

Harrington & Richardson
Harrich No. 1

Harrington & Richardson
Topper No. 48

Harrington & Richardson
Topper No. 162 — Slug Gun

MODEL 401 . . . . NiB $335 Ex $240 Gd $190
Same as Model 400, except has H&R variable choke. Made 1956-63.

MODEL 402 . . . . NiB $315 Ex $220 Gd $170
Similar to Model 400 except .410 ga., weight: About 5.5 lbs. Made 1959-67.

**MODEL 403 AUTOLOADING
SHOTGUN** . . . . NiB $338 Ex $300 Gd $210
Takedown. .410 ga. Tubular magazine holds four shells. 26-in. bbl., F choke. Weight: About 5.75 lbs. Plain pistol-grip stock and forearm. Made in 1964.

**MODEL 404/404C PUMP
SHOTGUN** . . . . NiB $366 Ex $275 Gd $209
Boxlock. Plain extractors. Double triggers. Gauges: 12, 20, .410. Bbls.: 28-in. in 12 ga. (M/F choke), 26-in. in 20 ga. (IC/M and .410 (F/F). Weight: 5.5 to 7.25 lbs. Plain walnut-finished hardwood stock and forend on Model 404; 404C checkered. Made in Brazil by Amadeo Rossi from 1969-72.

MODEL 440 PUMP SHOTGUN . . NiB $255 Ex $194 Gd $145
Hammerless. Gauges: 12, 16, 20. 2.75-in. chamber in 16 ga., 3-in. in 12 and 20 ga. Three round magazine. Bbls.: 26-, 28-, 30-in.; IC, M, F choke. Weight: 6.25 lbs. Plain pistol-grip stock and slide handle, recoil pad. Made 1968-73.

MODEL 442 PUMP SHOTGUN . . NiB $320 Ex $254 Gd $188
Same as Model 440 except has VR bbl., checkered stock and forearm, weight: 6.75 lbs. Made 1969-73.

ULTRA SLUG SERIES. . . . . NiB $287 Ex $220 Gd $175
Singel shot 12 or 20 ga w/3-in. chamber w/heavy-wall 24-in. fully rifled bbl. w/scope . Weight: 9 lbs. Walnut-stained Monte

Carlo stock, sling swivels, black nylon sling. Made from 1995 to date.

MODEL 1212 FIELD . . . . NiB $435 Ex $321 Gd $250
Boxlock. Plain extractors. Selective single trigger. 12 ga., 2.75-in. chambers. 28-in. bbls., IC/IM, VR. Weight: 7 lbs. Checkered walnut pistol-gip stock and fluted forearm. Made 1976-80 by Lanber Arms S. A., Zaldibar (Vizcaya), Spain.

**MODEL 1212
WATERFOWL GUN** . . . . NiB $544 Ex $368 Gd $277
Same as Field Gun except chambered for 12-ga, 3-in. mag. shells, has 30-in. bbls., M/F chokes, stock and recoil pad, weight: 7.5 lbs. Made 1976-80.

**MODEL 1908
SINGLE-SHOT SHOTGUN** . . . . NiB $244 Ex $177 Gd $100
Takedown. Automatic ejector. Gauges: 12, 16, 24 and 28. Bbls.: 26- to 32-in., F choke. Weight: 5.25 to 6.5 lbs. depending on ga. and bbl. length. Casehardened receiver. Plain pistol-grip stock. Bead front sight. Made 1908-34.

**MODEL 1908 .410 (12MM)
SINGLE-SHOT SHOTGUN** . . . . NiB $233 Ex $177 Gd $120
Same general specifications as standard Model 1908 except chambered for .410 or 12mm shot cartridge w/bbl. milled down at receiver to give a more pleasing contour.

MODEL 1915 SINGLE-SHOT SHOTGUN
Takedown. Both non-auto and auto-ejectors available. Gauges: 24, 28, .410, 14mm and 12mm. Bbls.: 26- or 28-in., F choke. Weight: 4 to 4.75 lbs. depending on ga. and bbl. length. Plain black walnut stock w/semi pistol-grip.
24 ga. . . . . NiB $390 Ex $275 Gd $190
28, .410 ga.. . . . . NiB $390 Ex $275 Gd $190

FOLDING GUN . . . . NiB $320 Ex $210 Gd $165
Single bbl. hammer shotgun hinged at the front of the frame, the bbl. folds down against the stock. Light Frame model: gauges — 28, 14mm, .410; 22-in. bbl.; weighs about 4.5 lbs. Heavy Frame model: gauges — 12, 16, 20, 28, .410; 26-in. bbl.; weighs from 5.75 to 6.5 lbs. Plain pistol-grip stock and forend. Disc. 1942.

**GOLDEN SQUIRE MODEL 159 SINGLE-BARREL
HAMMER SHOTGUN** . . . . NiB $265 Ex $170 Gd $121
Hammerless. Side lever. Automatic ejection. Gauges: 12, 20. Bbls: 30-in. in 12 ga., 28-in. in 20 ga., both F choke. Weight: About 6.5 lbs. Straight-grip stock w/recoil pad, forearm w/Schnabel. Made 1964-66.

**GOLDEN SQUIRE JR.
MODEL 459** . . . . NiB $255 Ex $170 Gd $125
Same as Model 159 except gauges 20 and .410, 26-in. bbl., youth stock. Made in 1964.

**HARRICH NO. 1 SINGLE-BARREL
TRAP GUN** . . . . NiB $1733 Ex $1456 Gd $974
Anson & Deeley-type locking system w/Kersten top locks and double underlocking lugs. Sideplates engraved w/hunting scenes. 12 ga. Bbls.: 32-, 34-in.; F choke; high VR. Weight: 8.5 lbs. Checkered Monte Carlo stock w/pistol-grip and recoil pad, beavertail forearm, of select walnut. Made in Austria 1971 to 1975.

**"TOP RIB"
SINGLE-BARREL SHOTGUN**. . . NiB $335 Ex $265 Gd $190
Takedown. Auto ejector. Gauges: 12, 16 and 20. Bbls.: 28- to 30-in., F choke w/full-length matted top rib. Weight: 6.5 to 7 lbs. depending on ga. and bbl. length. Black walnut pistol-grip stock (capped) and forend; both checkered. Flexible rubber buttplate. Made during 1930s.

**TOPPER NO. 48 SINGLE-BARREL
HAMMER SHOTGUN**. . . . . NiB $280 Ex $195 Gd $145
Similar to old Model 8 Standard. Takedown. Top lever. Auto ejector. Gauges: 12, 16, 20, .410. Bbls.: plain; 26- to 30-in.; M or F choke. Weight: 5.5 to 6.5 lbs. depending on ga. and bbl. length. Plain pistol-grip stock and forend. Made 1946-57.

TOPPER MODEL 099 DELUXE . . . NiB $244 Ex $155 Gd $110
Same as Model 158 except has matte nickel finish, semipistol grip walnut-finished American hardwood stock; semibeavertail forearm; 12, 16, 20, and .410 ga. Made 1982-86.

**TOPPER MODEL 148 SINGLE-SHOT
HAMMER SHOTGUN**. . . . . NiB $200 Ex $177 Gd $120
Takedown. Side lever. Auto-ejection. Gauges: 12, 16, 20, .410. Bbls.: 12 ga.,30-, 32- and 36-in.; 16 ga., 28- and 30-in.; 20 and .410 ga., 28-in.; F choke. Weight: 5 to 6.5 lbs. Plain pistol-grip stock and forend, recoil pad. Made 1958-61.

**TOPPER MODEL 158 (058) SINGLE-SHOT
HAMMER SHOTGUN**. . . . . NiB $245 Ex $165 Gd $120
Takedown. Side lever. Automatic ejection. Gauges: 12, 20, .410 (2.75-in. and 3-in. shells); 16 (2.75-in.). bbl. length and choke combinations: 12 ga., 36-in./F, 32-in./F, 30-in./F, 28-in./F or M; .410, 28-in./F. Weight: about 5.5 lbs. Plain pistol-grip stock and forend, recoil pad. Made 1962-81. Note: Designation changed to 058 in 1974.

**TOPPER MODEL 162
SLUG GUN**. . . . . NiB $300 Ex $221 Gd $165
Same as Topper Model 158 except has 24-in. bbl., Cyl. bore, w/rifle sights. Made 1968-86.

**TOPPER MODEL 176 10 GA.
MAGNUM.** . . . . NiB $280 Ex $185 Gd $145
Similar to Model 158, but has 36-in. heavy bbl. chambered for 3.5-in. 10- ga. Mag. shells, weight: 10 lbs.; stock w/Monte Carlo comb and recoil pad, longer and fuller forearm. Made 1977-86.

TOPPER MODEL 188 DELUXE . . NiB $265 Ex $200 Gd $145
Same as standard Topper Model 148 except has chromed frame, stock and forend in black, red, yellow, blue, green, pink, or purple colored finish. .410 ga. only. Made 1958-61.

**TOPPER MODEL 198 (098)
DELUXE** . . . . NiB $244 Ex $180 Gd $130
Same as Model 158 except has chrome-plated frame, black finished stock and forend; 12, 20 and .410 ga. Made 1962-1981. Note: Designation changed to 098 in 1974.

TOPPER JR. MODEL 480 . . . . . NiB $236 Ex $165 Gd $100
Similar to No. 48 Topper except has youth-size stock, 26-in. bbl, .410 ga. only. Made 1958-61.

TOPPER NO. 488 DELUXE . . . . NiB $254 Ex $179 Gd $115
Same as standard No. 48 Topper except chrome-plated frame, black lacquered stock and forend, recoil pad. Disc. 1957.

TOPPER MODEL 490 . . . . NiB $245 Ex $185 Gd $135
Same as Model 158 except has youth-size stock (3 in. shorter), 26-in. bbl.; 20 and 28 ga. (M choke), .410 (F). Made 1962-1986.

SHOTGUNS

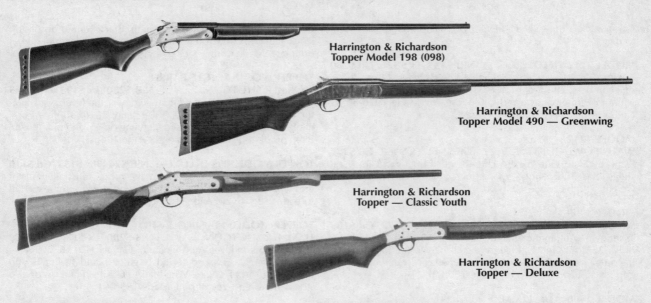

Harrington & Richardson
Topper Model 198 (098)

Harrington & Richardson
Topper Model 490 — Greenwing

Harrington & Richardson
Topper — Classic Youth

Harrington & Richardson
Topper — Deluxe

TOPPER MODEL 490
GREENWING . . . . NiB $266 Ex $190 Gd $140
Same as the Model 490 except has a special high-polished finish. Made 1981-86.

TOPPER JR. MODEL 580 . . . . . NiB $210 Ex $166 Gd $100
Same as Model 480 except has colored stocks as on Model 188. Made 1958-61.

TOPPER MODEL 590 . . . . NiB $210 Ex $166 Gd $100
Same as Model 490 except has chrome-plated frame, black finished stock and forend. Made 1962-63.

NOTE: *The following models are manufactured and distributed by the reorganized company of H&R 1871, Inc.*

EXCELL AUTO SERIES . . . . NIB $455 EX $400 GD $305
Semiauto. Gas operated action. Gauges: 12; 3-in. chamber. Barrel: 28- VR w/screw-in choke tubes. Weight: 7 lbs. Finish: Matte black. Stock: Black synthetic. Mfg. 2014–15.
Tactical model (18.5-in. bbl., black synthetic stock,
 2014-15) . . . . NiB $455 Ex $400 Gd $305
Turkey model (12 ga., 22-in. VR bbl.,
 100% RealTree Hardwoods camo, fiber optic
 front sight, 2014-15) . . . . NiB $530 Ex $505 Gd $405
Waterfowl model (12 ga., 28-in. VR bbl.,
 100% RealTree Advantage Wetlands camo, bead
 front sight, 2014-15) . . . . NiB $530 Ex $505 Gd $405

EXCELL AUTO 5 SERIES . . . . . . NIB $305 EX $255 GD $185
Semiauto. Gas operated action. Gauges: 12; 3-in. chamber. Capacity: 5 rnds. Barrel: 28- VR w/screw-in choke tubes. Weight: 7 lbs. Finish: Matte black, camo. Stock: Black synthetic, walnut or camo. Mfg. 2005-07.
Turkey model (22-in. VR bbl., RealTree Advantage
 Hardwoods camo) . . . . NiB $530 Ex $505 Gd $405
Combo model (12 ga., 28-in. VR and
 24-in. rifled bbls.) . . . . NiB $430 Ex $385 Gd $295

PARDNER PUMP SERIES . . . . . . NIB $190 EX $170 GD $135
Slide/pump action. Gauges: 12 or 20; 3-in. chamber. Barrel: 26- or 28- VR w/screw-in choke tubes. Weight: 7.5 lbs. Finish: Matte black. Stock: Walnut or synthetic. Mfg. 2008–14.
Compact model (20 ga., 21-in. VR bbl.,
 youth size stock, 2008-14) . . . NiB $180 Ex $170 Gd $135

Pump Protector model (12 ga., 18.5-in. bbl.,
 cylinder bore, black synthetic
 stock, 2008-14) . . . . NiB $180 Ex $170 Gd $135

PARDNER SERIES . . . . NiB $180 EX $155 GD $125
Side lever. Single shot. Automatic ejector. Gauges: 12, 20, 28 or .410; 2.75- or 3-in. chamber. Barrel: 26-, 28- or 32-in.; fixed or screw-in choke. Weight: 5 to 6 lbs. Finish: Color case hardened receiver, blued bbl. Stock: Hardwood or synthetic. Mfg. 2008–14.
Compact model (20 or 28 ga.
 or .410., 22- or 24-in. bbl.,
 youth size stock, 2008-14) . . . NiB $195 Ex $170 Gd $165
Turkey Gun model (10, 12 or 20 ga., 22- or 24-in. bbl.,
 fixed or tubes, Realtree Hardwood camo or
 matte black, 2008–14) . . . . . . NiB $240 Ex $210 Gd $165
Waterfowl model (10 ga., 30- or 32-in. bbl.,
 Mossy Oak Break Up camo or blued,
 2008-09) . . . . NiB $190 Ex $155 Gd $105

MODEL 098 TOPPER SERIES . . . . NiB $145 Ex $115 Gd $85
Side lever. Single shot. Automatic ejector. Gauges: 12, 16, 20, 28 or .410; 2.75- or 3-in. chamber. Barrel: 26- or 28-in.; fixed or screw-in choke tubes. Weight: 5-6 lbs. Finish: Satin nickel receiver, blued bbl. Stock: Plain pistol-grip stock and semi-beavertail forend w/black finish. Mfg. 1991-2011.
W/screw-in choke tube, add. $25
3.5-in. chamber model (12 ga.) . . NiB $130 Ex $115 Gd $90
Deluxe Classic model (12 or 20 ga., VR bbl.,
 walnut stock, 2004-11) . . . . . . NiB $205 Ex $180 Gd $125
Deluxe Slug model (12 ga., 24-in. rifled bbl.,
 hardwood stock, 1996-99) . . . . NiB $155 Ex $120 Gd $90
Jr. model (20 ga or .410., 22-in. bbl., youth size
 hardwood stock, 1991-2011) . . NiB $150 Ex $125 Gd $85
Jr. Classic model (20 ga. or .410., 22-in. bbl., youth size
 walnut stock, 1991-2011) . . . . NiB $180 Ex $155 Gd $105
N.W.T.F. Turkey Mag model (10 or 12 ga., 24-in. bbl.,
 Mossy Oak camo, 1991-96) . . . NiB $150 Ex $125 Gd $85
N.W.T.F. 1994 Youth model (20 ga., 22-in. bbl.,
 Mossy Oak camo, 1994-95) . . . NiB $150 Ex $125 Gd $85
N.W.T.F. 2000 Youth model (12 or 20 ga., 22-in. bbl.,
 Mossy Oak camo, 2000-04) . . NiB $180 Ex $155 Gd $105
Trap model (12 ga., 30-in. VR bbl.,
 walnut stock, 2008-11) . . . . . . NiB $370 Ex $320 Gd $230

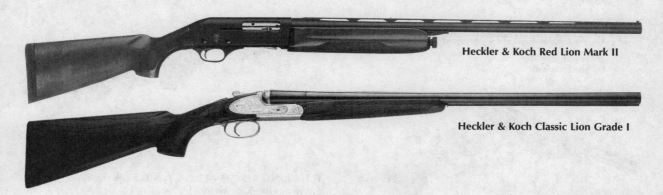

Heckler & Koch Red Lion Mark II

Heckler & Koch Classic Lion Grade I

SURVIVOR . . . . **NIB $255 EX $215 GD $165**
Similar to Topper series except .410/.45 LC; 3-in. chamber, 20-in. bbl. w/screw-in choke tube. Weight: 6 lbs. Finish: Blue or nickel. Stock: Synthetic thumbhole. Mfg. 1994–2014.

THE TAMER. . . . . **NIB $190 EX $155 GD $105**
Similar to Topper series except 20 ga. or .410; 3-in. chamber. Barrel: 19- or 20-in.; fixed full choke. Weight: 6 lbs. Finish: Satin nickel. Stock: Synthetic thumbhole, stores 3-4 shells. Mfg. 1994–2014.

TRACKER II SLUG GUN . . . . . . **NIB $245 EX $200 GD $135**
Similar to Topper series except 12 or 20 ga.; 3-in. chamber. 24-in. rifled bbl. Weight: 5.25 lbs. Finish: Blued. Stock: Hardwood. Sights: Adj. Mfg. 2008–14.

ULTRA SLUG HUNTER SERIES
Similar to Topper series except 12 or 20 ga.; fully rifled 22- or 24-in. bbl. and hardwood Monte Carlo stock.
SB1-920 model (20 ga. built on
   12-ga. receiver, 1996-2011) . . **NiB $195 Ex $160 Gd $105**
Standard model (1995-2014) . . . **NiB $255 Ex $220 Gd $210**
Deluxe model (checkered laminate stock,
   1997-2014) . . . . **NiB $325 Ex $285 Gd $210**
Light model (hardwood stock,
   5.25 lbs., 2008-14) . . . . **NiB $245 Ex $200 Gd $155**
Thumbhole model (laminate thumbhole
   stock, 8.5 lbs., 2008-14) . . . . . **NiB $360 Ex $300 Gd $235**

WHITETAILS UNLIMITED
SLUG GUN. . . . . **NIB $225 EX $190 GD $130**
Similar to Tracker II Slug Gun except 12 ga.; 3-in. chamber. 24-in. rifled bbl. Weight: 5.25 lbs. Stock: Checkered laminated Monte Carlo. Sights: Adj. Mfg. 1998-99.

HECKLER & KOCH (FABARM) — Oberndorf am Neckar, Germany, and Sterling, VA

CLASSIC LION SIDE-BY-SIDE SHOTGUN
12 ga. only. 28- or 30-in. non-ported Tribor bbl. w/3-in. chamber. 46.5 to 48.5-in. overall. Weight: 7 to 7.2 lbs. Five choke tubes; C, IC, M, IM, F. Traditional boxlock design. Oil-finished walnut forearms and stocks w/diamond-cut checkering. Imported from 1999 to date.
Classic Lion Grade I . . . . **NiB $1456 Ex $1288 Gd $890**
Classic Lion Grade II. . . . . **NiB $2177 Ex $1766 Gd $1292**

CAMO LION SEMIAUTO
SHOTGUN . . . . **NiB $988 Ex $853 Gd $679**
12 ga. Only. 24 to 28-in. Tribor bbl. 44.25-48.25-in. overall. Weight: 7-7.2 lbs. 3 in. chamber w/5 choke tubes - C, IC, M, IM, F. Two round mag. Camo covered walnut stock w/rear front bar sights. Imp. 1999 to date.

MAX LION O/U
SHOTGUN . . . . **NiB $1977 Ex $1660 Gd $1000**
12 or 20 ga. 26- 28- or 30-in. TriBore system bbls. 42.5-47.25-in. overall. Weight: 6.8-7.8 lbs. 3-in. chamber w/5 choke tubes - C, IC, M, IM, F. Single selective adj. trigger and auto ejectors. Side plates w/high-grade stock and rubber recoil pad. Made from 1999 to date.

RED LION MARK II SEMIAUTO
SHOTGUN . . . . **NiB $954 Ex $700 Gd $544**
12 ga. Only. 24- 26- or 28-in. TriBore system bbls. 44.25 to 48.25-in. overall. Weight: 7 to 7.2 lbs. 3-in. chamber w/five choke tubes- C, IC, M, IM, F. Two round magazine. Matte finish w/walnut wood stock. Rubber vented recoil pad w/leather cover. Made from 1999 to date.

SILVER LION O/U
SHOTGUN . . . . **NiB $1388 Ex $1097 Gd $766**
12 or 20 ga. 26- 28- or 30-in. TriBore system bbls. 43.25-47.25 in.overall. 3-in. chamber w/5 choke tubes - C, IC, M, IM, F. Single selective trig. and auto ejectors. Wal. stock w/rubber recoil pad. Made from 1999 to date.

SPORTING CLAY LION
SEMIAUTO SHOTGUN. . . . . . **NiB $1087 Ex $944 Gd $644**
12 ga. only. 28- or 30-in. bbl. w/3-in. chamber and ported Tribore system barrel. Matte finish w/gold plated trigger and carrier release button. Made from 1999 to date.

HENRY REPEATING ARMS — Bayonne, NJ

SINGLE SHOT SERIES
Break action. Gauge: 12, 20 or 410. Bbl.: 26- or 28-in.w/ fixed (410) or choke tubes (12 and 20). Finish: Blued or brass. Stock: smooth walnut. Made 2017 to date.
blued finish. . . . . **NiB $370 Ex $270 Gd $185**
brass finish, add **$100**

LEVER ACTION SERIES
Lever action. Gauge: .410. Bbl.: 20- or 24-in. w/fixed choke. Finish: Blued. Stock: Checkered walnut. Made 2017 to date.
w/24-in. bbl.. . . . . **NiB $830 Ex $655 Gd $530**
w/20-in. bbl., add. **$50**

HERCULES SHOTGUNS

See Listings under "W" for Montgomery Ward.

SHOTGUNS

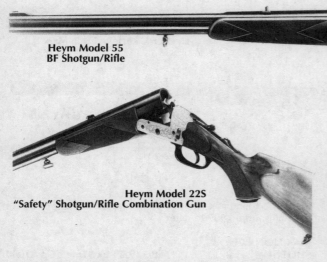

Heym Model 55
BF Shotgun/Rifle

Heym Model 22S
"Safety" Shotgun/Rifle Combination Gun

HEYM — Münnerstadt, Germany

**MODEL 22S "SAFETY" SHOTGUN/
RIFLE COMBINATION . . . . NiB $3798 Ex $2889 Gd $2250**
16 and 20 ga. Cal: .22 Mag., .22 Hornet, .222 Rem., .222
Rem. Mag., 5.6x50R Mag., 6.5x57R, 7x57R, .243 Win.
24-in. bbls. 40 in. overall. Weight: About 5.5 lbs. Single-
set trigger. Left-side bbl. selector. Integral dovetail base for
scope mounting. Arabesque engraving. Walnut stock. Disc.
1993.

**MODEL 55 BF SHOTGUN/
RIFLE COMBO . . . . NiB $7045 Ex $5370 Gd $4398**
12, 16 and 20 ga. Calibers: 5.6x50R Mag., 6.5x57R, 7x57R,
7x65R, .243 Win., .308 Win., .30-06. 25-in. bbls., 42 in. overall. Weight: About 6.75 lbs. Black satin-finished, corrosion-
resistant bbls. of Krupp special steel. Hand-checkered walnut
stock w/long pistol-grip. Hand-engraved leaf scroll. German
cheekpiece. Disc. 1988.

J. C. HIGGINS

See Sears, Roebuck & Company.

HIGH STANDARD SPORTING ARMS —
East Hartford, CT; formerly High Standard
Mfg. Corp. of Hamden, CT

*In 1966, High Standard introduced new series of Flite-King
Pumps and Supermatic autoloaders, both readily identifiable
by the damascened bolt and restyled checkering. To avoid
confusion, these models are designated "Series II" in this text.
This is not an official factory designation. Operation of this
firm was discontinued in 1984.*

**FLITE-KING FIELD
PUMP—12 GA. . . . . NiB $256 Ex $180 Gd $110**
Hammerless. Magazine holds five rounds. Bbls.: 26-in. IC,
28-in. M or F, 30-in. F choke. Weight: 7.25 lbs. Plain pistol-grip
stock and slide handle. Made 1960-66.

FLITE-KING BRUSH—12 GA. . . NiB $285 Ex $245 Gd $170
Same as Flite-King Field 2 except has 18- or 20-in. bbl. (cylinder bore) w/rifle sights. Made 1962-64.

FLITE-KING BRUSH DELUXE . . NiB $275 Ex $190 Gd $120
Same as Flite-King Brush except has adj. peep rear sight,
checkered pistol grip, recoil pad, fluted slide handle, swivels
and sling. Not available w/18-in. bbl. Made 1964-1966.

FLITE-KING BRUSH (SERIES II) . . . NiB $275 Ex $190 Gd $120
Same as Flite-King Deluxe 12 (II) except has 20-in. bbl., cylinder bore, w/rifle sights. Weight: 7 lbs. Made 1966-75.

**FLITE-KING BRUSH
DELUXE (II) . . . . NiB $290 Ex $200 Gd $135**
Same as Flite-King Brush (II) except has adj. peep rear sight,
swivels and sling. Made 1966-75.

FLITE-KING DELUXE 12 GA. (SERIES II)
Hammerless. Five round magazine. 27-in. plain bbls.w/adj.
choke. 26-in. IC, 28-in. M or F. 30-in. F choke. Weight: About
7.25 lbs. Checkered pistol-grip stock and forearm, recoil pad.
Made 1966-75.
w/adj. choke . . . . NiB $245 Ex $170 Gd $110
w/fixed choke . . . . NiB $245 Ex $170 Gd $110

**FLITE-KING DELUXE
20, 28, .410 GA. (SERIES II) . . . NiB $255 Ex $178 Gd $120**
Same as Flite-King Deluxe 12 (II) except chambered for 20 and
.410 ga. 3-in. shell, 28 ga. 2.75-in. shell w/20- or 28-in. plain
bbl. Weight: About 6 lbs. Made 1966-75.

**FLITE-KING DELUXE RIB
12 GA. . . . . NiB $280 Ex $200 Gd $155**
Same as Flite-King Field 12 except VR bbl. (28-in. M or F. 30-in.
F). Checkered stock and forearm. Made 1961-66.

FLITE-KING DELUXE RIB 12 GA. (II)
Same as Flite-King Deluxe 12 (II) except has VR bbl., available
in 27-in. w/adj. choke, 28-in. M or F, 30-in. F choke. Made
1966-75.
w/adj. choke . . . . NiB $292 Ex $217 Gd $175
w/fixed choke . . . . NiB $292 Ex $217 Gd $175
FLITE-KING DELUXE RIB 20 GA. . . NiB $265 Ex $198 Gd $125
Same as Flite-King Field 20 except VR bbl. (28 in. M or F),
checkered stock and slide handle. Made 1962-66.

FLITE-KING DELUXE RIB 20, 28, .410 GA. (SERIES II)
Same as Flite-King Deluxe 20, 28, .410 (II) except 20 ga. available w/27-in. adj. choke, 28-in. M or F choke. Weight: about
6.25 lbs. Made 1966-75.
w/adj. choke . . . . NiB $265 Ex $198 Gd $125
w/o adj. choke . . . . NiB $265 Ex $198 Gd $125

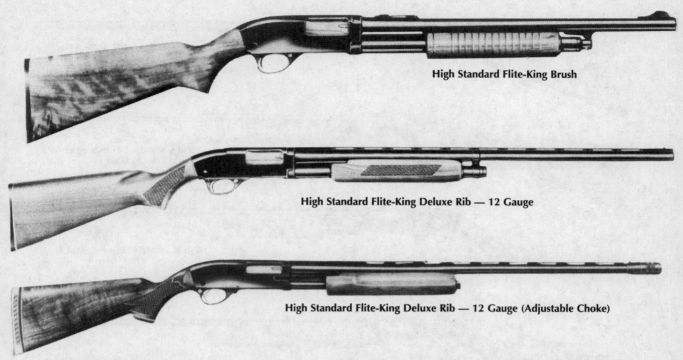

High Standard Flite-King Brush

High Standard Flite-King Deluxe Rib — 12 Gauge

High Standard Flite-King Deluxe Rib — 12 Gauge (Adjustable Choke)

FLITE-KING DELUXE SKEET GUN
12 GA. (SERIES II). . . . . **NiB $544 Ex $423 Gd $318**
Same as Flite-King Deluxe Rib 12 (II) except available only w/26-in. VR bbl., SK choke, recoil pad optional. Made 1966-75.

FLITE-KING DELUXE SKEET GUN
20, 28, .410 GA. (SERIES II) . . . . **NiB $454 Ex $39 Gd $243**
Same as Flite-King Deluxe Rib 20, 28, .410 (II) except available only w/26-in. VR bbl., SK choke. Made 1966-1975.

FLITE-KING DELUXE TRAP
GUN (SERIES II)) . . . . **NiB $338 Ex $265 Gd $129**
Same as Flite-King Deluxe Rib 12 (II) except available only w/30-in. VR bbl., F choke; trap-style stock. Made 1966-1975.

FLITE-KING FIELD PUMP
20 GA. . . . . **NiB $250 Ex $175 Gd $135**
Hammerless. Chambered for 3-in. Magnum shells, also handles 2.75-in. Magazine holds four rounds. Bbls.: 26-in. IC, 28-in. M or F choke. Weight: About 6 lbs. Plain pistol-grip stock and slide handle. Made 1961-66.

FLITE-KING FIELD PUMP
SHOTGUN 16 GA . . . . **NiB $250 Ex $175 Gd $135**
Same general specifications as Flite-King 12 except not available in Brush, Skeet and Trap Models or 30-in. bbl. Values same as for 12-ga. guns. Made 1961-65.

FLITE-KING PUMP
SHOTGUN (.410) . . . . **NiB $350 Ex $275 Gd $235**
Same general specifications as Flite-King 20 except not available in Special and Trophy Models, or w/other than 26-in. choke bbl. Add $100 to 20 gauge price. Made 1962-66.

FLITE-KING SKEET 12 GA. . . . . **NiB $330 Ex $225 Gd $170**
Same as Flite-King Deluxe Rib except 26-in. VR bbl., w/SK choke. Made 1962-66.

FLITE-KING SPECIAL 12 GA. . . . **NiB $250 Ex $175 Gd $135**
Same as Flite-King Field 12 except has 27-in. bbl. w/adj. choke. Made 1960-66.

FLITE-KING SPECIAL 20 GA. . . . **NiB $250 Ex $175 Gd $135**
Same as Flite-King Field 20 except has 27-in. bbl. w/adj. choke. Made 1961-66.

FLITE-KING TRAP 12 GA. . . . . . . **NiB $330 Ex $225 Gd $140**
Same as Flite-King Deluxe Rib 12 except 30-in. VR bbl., F choke, special trap stock w/recoil pad. Made 1962-66.

FLITE-KING TROPHY 12 GA. . . . **NiB $290 Ex $200 Gd $105**
Same as Flite-King Deluxe Rib 12 except has 27-in. VR bbl. w/adj. choke. Made 1960-66.

FLITE-KING TROPHY 20 GA. . . . **NiB $290 Ex $200 Gd $105**
Same as Flite-King Deluxe Rib 20 except has 27-in. VR bbl. w/adj. choke. Made 1962-66.

SUPERMATIC DEER GUN. . . . . **NiB $345 Ex $165 Gd $100**
Same as Supermatic Field 12 except has 22-in. bbl. (cylinder bore) w/rifle sights, checkered stock and forearm, recoil pad. Weight: 7.75 lbs. Made in 1965.

SUPERMATIC DELUXE 12 GA. (SERIES II)
Gas-operated autoloader. Four round magazine. Bbls.: Plain; 27-in. w/adj. choke (disc. about 1970); 26-in. IC, 28-in. M or F. 30-in. F choke. Weight: About 7.5 lbs. Checkered pistol-grip stock and forearm, recoil pad. Made 1966-75.
w/adj. choke . . . . **NiB $375 Ex $195 Gd $120**
w/VR, add. **$40**

SUPERMATIC DELUXE 20 GA. (SERIES II)
Same as Supermatic Deluxe 12 (II) except chambered for 20 ga. Three inch shell; bbls. available in 27-in. w/adj. choke

SHOTGUNS

GRADING: **NiB** = New in Box   **Ex** = Excellent or NRA 95%   **Gd** = Good or NRA 68%

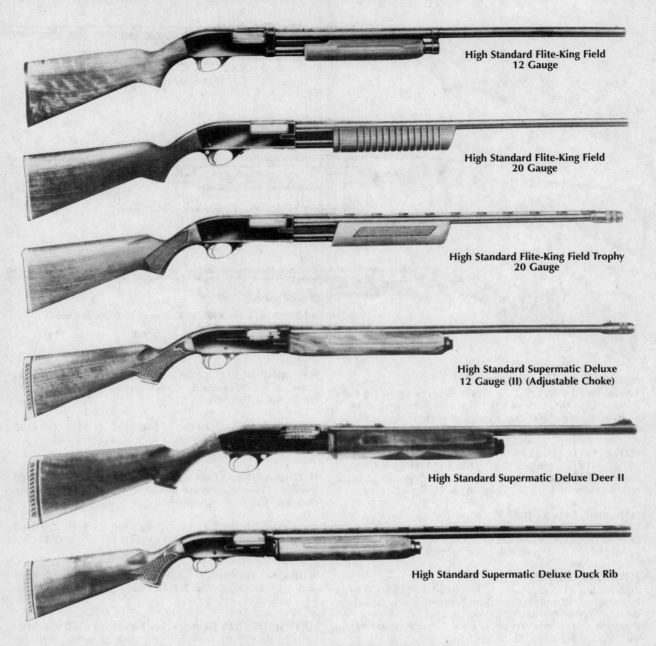

High Standard Flite-King Field 12 Gauge

High Standard Flite-King Field 20 Gauge

High Standard Flite-King Field Trophy 20 Gauge

High Standard Supermatic Deluxe 12 Gauge (II) (Adjustable Choke)

High Standard Supermatic Deluxe Deer II

High Standard Supermatic Deluxe Duck Rib

(disc. about 1970), 26-in. IC, 28-in. M or F choke. Weight: About 7 lbs. Made 1966-75.

w/adj. choke . . . . NiB $315 Ex $199 Gd $99
VR, add $20

SUPERMATIC DELUXE DEER GUN
(SERIES II). . . . . NiB $345 Ex $165 Gd $100
Same as Supermatic Deluxe 12 (II) except has 22-in. bbl., cylinder bore, w/rifle sights. Weight: 7.75 lbs. Made 1966-74.

SUPERMATIC DELUXE DUCK
12 GA. MAGNUM (SERIES II). . NiB $335 Ex $227 Gd $140
Same as Supermatic Deluxe 12 (II) except chambered for 3-in. magnum shells, 3-rnd. magazine, 30-in. plain bbl., F choke. Weight: 8 lbs. Made 1966-74.

SUPERMATIC DELUXE RIB
12 GA. . . . . NiB $335 Ex $227 Gd $140
Same as Supermatic Field 12 except VR bbl. (28-in. M or F, 30-in. F), checkered stock and forearm. Made 1961-66.

SUPERMATIC DELUXE RIB 12 GA. (II)
Same as Supermatic Deluxe 12 (II) except has VR bbl.; available in 27-in. w/adj. choke, 28-in. M or F, 30-in. F choke. Made 1966-75.

w/adj. choke . . . . NiB $335 Ex $227 Gd $140
w/VR, add $50

SUPERMATIC DELUXE RIB
20 GA. . . . . NiB $377 Ex $265 Gd $180
Same as Supermatic Field 20 except VR bbl. (28-in. M or F), checkered stock and forearm. Made 1963-66.

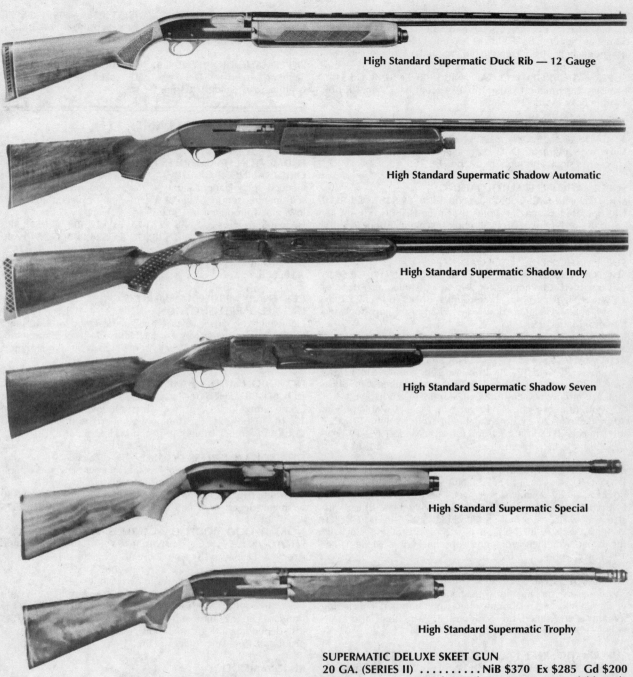

High Standard Supermatic Duck Rib — 12 Gauge

High Standard Supermatic Shadow Automatic

High Standard Supermatic Shadow Indy

High Standard Supermatic Shadow Seven

High Standard Supermatic Special

High Standard Supermatic Trophy

SHOTGUNS

SUPERMATIC DELUXE RIB 20 GA. (II)
Same as Supermatic Deluxe 20 (II) except has VR bbl. Made 1966-75.
w/adj. choke . . . . NiB $377 Ex $265 Gd $180
w/VR, add. $50

SUPERMATIC DELUXE SKEET GUN
12 GA. (SERIES II). . . . . NiB $380 Ex $275 Gd $190
Same as Supermatic Deluxe Rib 12 (II) except available only w/26-in. VR bbl., SK choke. Made 1966-75.

SUPERMATIC DELUXE SKEET GUN
20 GA. (SERIES II) . . . . NiB $370 Ex $285 Gd $200
Same as Supermatic Deluxe Rib 20 (II) except available only w/26-in. VR bbl., SK choke. Made 1966-75.

SUPERMATIC DELUXE
TRAP GUN (SERIES II) . . . . NiB $315 Ex $239 Gd $177
Same as Supermatic Deluxe Rib 12 (II) except available only w/30-in. VR bbl., full choke; trap-style stock. Made 1966-1975.

SUPERMATIC DELUXE DUCK RIB
12 GA. MAG. (SERIES II) . . . . . NiB $375 Ex $265 Gd $180
Same as Supermatic Deluxe Rib 12 (II) except chambered for 3-in. magnum shells, 3-rnd. magazine; 30-in. VR bbl., F choke. Weight: 8 lbs. Made 1966-75.

GRADING: **NiB** = New in Box   **Ex** = Excellent or NRA 95%   **Gd** = Good or NRA 68%   **497**

SUPERMATIC DUCK
12 GA. MAG. . . . . NiB $355 Ex $241 Gd $188
Same as Supermatic Field 12 except chambered for 3-in. Magnum shell, 30-in. F choke bbl., recoil pad. Made 1961-66.

SUPERMATIC TROPHY 12 GA. . . . NiB $300 Ex $198 Gd $140
Same as Supermatic Deluxe Rib 12 except has 27-in. VR bbl. w/adj. choke. Made 1961-66.

SUPERMATIC DUCK RIB
12 GA. MAG. . . . . NiB $355 Ex $241 Gd $188
Same as Supermatic Duck 12 Magnum except has VR bbl., checkered stock and forearm. Made 1961-66.

SUPERMATIC FIELD AUTOLOADING
SHOTGUN 12 GA. . . . . NiB $270 Ex $197 Gd $110
Gas-operated. Magazine holds four rounds. Bbls.: 26-in. IC, 28-in. M or F choke, 30-in. F choke. Weight: About 7.5 lbs. Plain pistol-grip stock and forearm. Made 1960-66.

SUPERMATIC FIELD AUTOLOADING
SHOTGUN 20 GA . . . . NiB $290 Ex $217 Gd $156
Gas-operated. Chambered for 3-in. mag. shells, also handles 2.75-in. Magazine holds three rounds. Bbls.: 26-in. IC, 28-in. M or F choke. Weight: About 7 lbs. Plain pistol-grip stock and forearm. Made 1963-66.

SUPERMATIC SHADOW
AUTOMATIC. . . . . NiB $455 Ex $265 Gd $200
Gas-operated. Ga.: 12, 20, 2.75- or 3-in. chamber in 12 ga., 3-in. in 20 ga. Mag. holds four 2.75-in. shells, three 3-in. Bbls.: Full-size airflow rib; 26-in. (IC or SK choke), 28-in. (M, IM or F), 30-in. (trap or F choke), 12-ga. 3-in. Mag. available only in 30-in. F choke; 20 ga. not available in 30-in. Weight: 12 ga., 7 lbs. Checkered walnut stock and forearm. Made 1974-1975 by Caspoll Int'l., Inc., Tokyo.

SUPERMATIC SHADOW
INDY O/U. . . . . NiB $935 Ex $770 Gd $500
Boxlock. Fully engraved receiver. Selective auto ejectors. Selective single trigger. 12 ga. 2.75-in. chambers. Bbls.: Full-size airflow rib; 27.5 in. both SK choke, 29.75-in. IM/F or F/F. Weight: W/29.75-in. bbls., 8 lbs. 2 oz. Pistol-grip stock w/ recoil pad, ventilated forearm, skip checkering. Made 1974-1975 by Caspoll Int'l., Inc., Tokyo.

SUPERMATIC SHADOW SEVEN . . NiB $755 Ex $533 Gd $400
Same general specifications as Shadow Indy except has conventional VR, less elaborate engraving, standard checkering forearm is not vented, no recoil pad. 27.5-in. bbls.; also available in IC/M, M/F choke. Made 1974-75.

SUPERMATIC SKEET 12 GA. . . . NiB $344 Ex $245 Gd $177
Same as Supermatic Deluxe Rib 12 except 26-in. VR bbl. w/SK choke. Made 1962-66.
SUPERMATIC SKEET 20 GA. . . . NiB $390 Ex $277 Gd $217
Same as Supermatic Deluxe Rib 20 except 26-in. VR bbl. w/SK choke. Made 1964-66.

SUPERMATIC SPECIAL 12 GA. NiB $290 Ex $190 Gd $145
Same as Supermatic Field 12 except has 27-in. bbl. w/adj. choke. Made 1960-66.

SUPERMATIC SPECIAL 20 GA. NiB $315 Ex $220 Gd $145
Same as Supermatic Field 20 except has 27-in. bbl. w/adj. choke. Made 1963-66.

SUPERMATIC TRAP 12 GA. . . . NiB $330 Ex $245 Gd $170
Same as Supermatic Deluxe Rib 12 except 30-in. VR bbl., F choke, special trap stock w/recoil pad. Made 1962-66.

SUPERMATIC TROPHY 20 GA. NiB $360 Ex $275 Gd $190
Same as Supermatic Deluxe Rib 20 except has 27-in. VR bbl. w/adj. choke. Made 1963-66.

HOLLAND & HOLLAND, LTD. —
London, England

BADMINTON HAMMERLESS DOUBLE-BARREL SHOTGUN, ORIGINAL NO. 2 GRADE
General specifications same as Royal Model except without self-opening action. Made as a game gun or pigeon and wildfowl gun. Introduced in 1902. Disc.
w/double triggers . . . NiB $27,875 Ex $22,500 Gd $18,975
w/single trigger . . . . . NiB $28,875 Ex $24,000 Gd $19,600
20 ga., add 25%
28 ga., add 40%
.410, add 65%

CENTENARY MODEL HAMMERLESS DOUBLE-BARREL SHOTGUN
Lightweight (5.5 lbs.). 12 ga. game gun designed for 2-in. shell. Made in four grades — Model Deluxe, Royal, Badminton, Dominion. Values: Add 35% to prices shown for standard guns in those grades. Disc. 1962.

DOMINION MODEL HAMMERLESS
DOUBLE-BBL. SHOTGUN . . . NiB $7355 Ex $6121 Gd $3896
Game Gun. Sidelock. Auto ejectors. Double triggers. Gauges: 12, 16, 20. bbls. 25- to 30-in., any standard boring. Checkered stock and forend, straight grip standard. Disc. 1967.

DELUXE HAMMERLESS DOUBLE
Same as Royal Model except has special engraving and exhibition grade stock and forearm. Currently manufactured.
w/double triggers . . . NiB $44,579 Ex $41,960 Gd $34,590
w/single trigger . . . . NiB $66,800 Ex $53,980 Gd $40,676

NORTHWOOD MODEL HAMMERLESS DOUBLE-BARREL
SHOTGUN . . . . NiB $6154 Ex $4944 Gd $4000
Anson & Deeley system boxlock. Auto ejectors. Double triggers. Gauges: 12, 16, 20, 28 in Game Model; 28 ga. not offered in Pigeon Model; Wildfowl Model in 12 ga. only (3-in. chambers available). Bbls.: 28-in. standard in Game and Pigeon Models, 30-in. in Wildfowl Model; other lengths, any standard choke combination available. Weight: From 5 to 7.75 lbs. depending on ga. and bbls. Checkered straight-grip or pistol-grip stock and forearm. Disc. 1990.

RIVIERA MODEL
PIGEON GUN . . . . . NiB $32,877 Ex $25,788 Gd $19,900
Same as Badminton Model but supplied w/two sets of bbls., double triggers. Disc. 1967.

ROYAL MODEL HAMMERLESS DOUBLE
Self-opening. Sidelocks hand-detachable. Auto ejectors. Double triggers or single trigger. Gauges: 12, 16, 20, 28 .410. Built to customer's specifications as to bbl. length, chokes, etc. Made as a Game Gun or Pigeon and Wildfowl Gun, the latter having treble-grip action and side clips. Checkered stock and forend, straight grip standard. Made from 1885, disc. 1951.

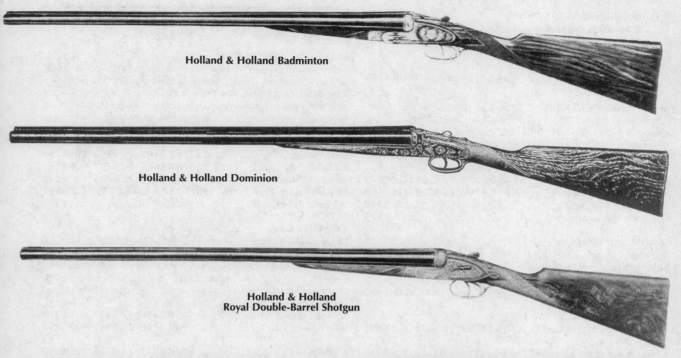

Holland & Holland Badminton

Holland & Holland Dominion

Holland & Holland
Royal Double-Barrel Shotgun

w/double triggers . . . **NiB $39,900 Ex $31,676 Gd $28,800**
w/single trigger . . . . **NiB $44,980 Ex $42,600 Gd $36,700**

ROYAL MODEL O/U
Sidelocks, hand-detachable. Auto-ejectors. Double triggers or single trigger. 12 ga. Built to customer's specifications as to bbl. length, chokes, etc. Made as a Game Gun or Pigeon and Wildfowl Gun. Checkered stock and forend, straight grip standard. Note: In 1951 Holland & Holland introduced its New Model Under/Over w/an improved, narrower action body. Disc. 1960.
New model
   (double triggers) . **NiB $40,770 Ex $32,550 Gd $21,900**
New model
   (single trigger) . . . **NiB $41,800 Ex $33,750 Gd $22,500**
Old model
   (double triggers) . **NiB $33,970 Ex $27,600 Gd $20,550**
Old model
   (single trigger) . . . **NiB $36,975 Ex $29,500 Gd $21,880**

SINGLE-SHOT SUPER TRAP GUN
Anson & Deeley system boxlock. Auto-ejector. No safety. 12 ga. Bbls.: Wide VR, 30- or 32-in., w/Extra Full choke. Weight: About 8.75 lbs. Monte Carlo stock w/pistol grip and recoil pad, full beavertail forearm. Models differ in grade of engraving and wood used. Disc.
Standard grade . . . . **NiB $4890 Ex $2988 Gd $1598**
Deluxe grade . . . . **NiB $7355 Ex $6355 Gd $3559**
Exhibition grade . . . . **NiB $9677 Ex $7355 Gd $4977**

SPORTING O/U . . . . **NiB $31,750 Ex $24,776 Gd $17,870**
Blitz action. Auto ejectors; single selective trigger. Gauges: 12 or 20 w/2.75-in. chambers. Barrels: 28- to 32-in. w/screw-in choke tubes. Hand-checkered European walnut straight-grip or pistol grip stock, forearm. Made 1993-2003.

SPORTING O/U
DELUXE . . . . **NiB $38,875 Ex $32,669 Gd $23,670**
Same general specs as Sporting O/U except better engraving and select wood. Made from 1993 to date.

HUGLU — Huglu, Turkey
Imported by Turkish Firearms Corp.

MODEL 101 B 12 SERIES
O/U. Boxlock action. Gauge: 12 w/3-in. chambers. Combination 30- or 32-in. top single & O/U bbls. w/fixed chokes or choke tubes. Weight: 8 lbs. Automatic ejectors or extractors. Single selective trigger. Manual safety. Circassian walnut Monte Carlo trap stock w/palm-swell grip and recoil pad. Silvered frame w/engraving. Imported from 1993 to 1997.
AT-DT COMBO O/U TRAP
   model . . . . **NiB $2387 Ex $1885 Gd $1444**
ST O/U TRAP (32-in.
   O/U configuration only,
   1994-96) . . . . **NiB $1577 Ex $1377 Gd $937**

MODEL 103 SERIES
Gauges: 12, 16, 20, 28 or .410. 28-in. bbls. w/ fixed chokes. Engraved action w/inlaid game scene and dummy sideplates. Double triggers, extractors and manual safety. Weight: 7.5 lbs. Circassian walnut stock. Imported 1995-96.
B 12 model . . . . **NiB $2387 Ex $1885 Gd $1444**
28 ga. and .410, add **$125**
C 12 model (ejectors, 12 or 20, black
   receiver w/50% engraving coverage,
   1995-97) . . . . **NiB $979 Ex $766 Gd $634**
C 12 model (extractors, 12 or 20, black
   receiver w/50% engraving coverage,
   1995-97) . . . . **NiB $920 Ex $733 Gd $578**
D 12 model (extractors, 12 or
   20, w/80% engraving
   coverage, 1995-97) . . . . **NiB $920 Ex $733 Gd $578**
D 12 model (ejectors, 12 or
   20, w/80% engraving
   coverage, 1995-97) . . . . **NiB $979 Ex $766 Gd $634**

SHOTGUNS

F 12 model (extractors, 12 or
20, w/100% engraving
coverage, 1996-97)...... NiB $1000 Ex $835 Gd $657
F 12 model (ejectors, 12 or
20, w/100% engraving
coverage, 1996-97).... NiB $1154 Ex $1010 Gd $745

MODEL 104 A 12 ST O/U
Boxlock. Gauges: 12, 20, 28 or .410. 28-in. bbls. w/fixed
chokes or choke tubes. Silvered, engraved receiver w/15%
engraving coverage. Double triggers, manual safety and extractors or ejectors. Weight: 7.5 lbs. Circassian walnut stock w/field
dimensions. Imported from 1995 to 1997.
Model 104A w/extractors .... NiB $777 Ex $688 Gd $545
Model 104A w/ejectors ...... NiB $790 Ex $700 Gd $600
28 ga. and .410, add $150
w/Choke Tubes, add $75

MODEL 200 SERIES DOUBLE
Boxlock. Gauges: 12, 20, 28, or .410 w/3-in. chambers. 28-in.
bbls. w/fixed chokes. Silvered, engraved receiver. Extractors,
manual safety, single selective trigger or double triggers.
Weight: 7.5 lbs. Circassion walnut stock. Imported from 1995
to 1997.
Model 200 (w/15%
engraving coverage, SST) .. NiB $1033 Ex $878 Gd $633
Model 201 (w/30%
engraving coverage, SST) . NiB $1277 Ex $1100 Gd $955
Model 202 (w/Greener
cross bolt, DT) .... NiB $888 Ex $645 Gd $469
28 ga. and .410, add......................... $125

HUNTER ARMS COMPANY — Fulton, NY

FULTON HAMMERLESS DOUBLE-BARREL SHOTGUN
Boxlock. Plain extractors. Double triggers or non-selective
single trigger. Gauges: 12 16, 20. Bbls.: 26- to 32-in. various
choke combinations. Weight: about 7 lbs. Checkered pistol-
grip stock and forearm. Disc. 1948.
w/double triggers .... NiB $775 Ex $450 Gd $375
w/single trigger .... NiB $990 Ex $700 Gd $555

SPECIAL HAMMERLESS DOUBLE-BARREL SHOTGUN
Boxlock. Plain extractors. Double triggers or non-selective
single trigger. Gauges: 12,16, 20. Bbls.: 26- to 30-in. various
choke combinations. Weight: 6.5 to 7.25 lbs. depending on
bbl. length and ga. Checkered full pistol-grip stock and forearm.
Disc. 1948.
w/double triggers .... NiB $933 Ex $655 Gd $500
w/single trigger .... NiB $1155 Ex $820 Gd $600

IGA — Veranopolis, Brazil
Imported by Stoeger Industries, Inc., Accokeek, MD.

STANDARD COACH GUN
Side-by-side double. Gauges: 12, 20 and .410. 20-in. bbls.
w/3-in. chambers. Fixed chokes (standard model) or screw-in
tubes (deluxe model). Weight: 6.5 lbs. Double triggers. Ejector
and automatic safety. Blued or nickel finish. Hand-rubbed
oil-finished pistol grip stock and forend w/hand checkering
(hardwood on standard model or Brazilian walnut (deluxe).
Imported from 1983 to 2000.
blued finish................ NiB $400 Ex $295 Gd $200
nickel finish............... NiB $465 Ex $377 Gd $259
engraved stock .... NiB $445 Ex $335 Gd $225
Deluxe Coach Gun (intro. 1997) NiB $400 Ex $290 Gd $195
w/choke tubes, add.............................. $75

CONDOR I
O/U, single trigger; Gauges: 12 or 20. 26- or 28-in. bbls. of
chrome-molybdenum steel. Chokes: Fixed — M/F or IC/M;
screw-in choke tubes (12 and 20 ga.). Three inch chambers.
Weight: 6.75 to 7 lbs. Sighting rib w/anti-glare surface. Hand-
checkered hardwood pistol-grip stock and forend. Imported
from 1983 to 1985.
w/fixed choke.............. NiB $420 Ex $377 Gd $210
w/screw-in tubes .... NiB $510 Ex $441 Gd $350

CONDOR II .... NiB $477 Ex $365 Gd $290
Same general specifications as the Condor I O/U except w/
double triggers and fixed chokes only; 26-in. bbls., IC/M;
28-in. bbls., M/F.

CONDOR OUTBACK .... NiB $499 Ex $370 Gd $290
Same general specifications as the Condor I O/U except w/ 20-in.
bbls., IC/M choke tubes, rifle-style sights. Made 2007 to date.

CONDOR SUPREME......... NiB $655 Ex $545 Gd $477
Same general specifications as Condor I except upgraded
w/fine-checkered Brazilian walnut buttstock and forend, a
matte-laquered finish, and a massive monoblock that joins
the bbls. in a solid one-piece assembly at the breech end.
Bbls. w/recessed interchangeable choke tubes formulated for
use w/steel shot. Automatic ejectors. Imported from 1995 to
2000.

CONDOR TURKEY .... NiB $755 Ex $600 Gd $445
12 gauge only. 26-in. VR bbls. w/3-in. chambers fitted w/
recessed interchangeable choke tubes. Weight: 8 lbs.
Mechanical single trigger. Ejectors and automatic safety.
Advantage camouflage on stock and bbls. Made 1997-2000.

CONDOR WATERFOWL ..... NiB $770 Ex $605 Gd $475
Similar to Condor Turkey-Advantage camo model except w/30-
in. bbls. Made 1998-2000.

IGA Turkey S/S Shotgun

Inland Manufacturing M37 Trench Gun

DELUXE HUNTER CLAYS . . . . . **NiB $700 Ex $552 Gd $435**
Same general specifications and values as IGA Condor
Supreme. Imported from 1997 to 1999.

DOUBLE DEFENSE . . . . **NiB $499 Ex $280 Gd $135**
Similar to Coach S/S box lock. Gauges: 12 or 20 ga., 20-in.
ported bbls. w/ Picatinny rails. Fixed IC choke; 3-in. chambers.
Weight: 6.4 to 7.1 lbs. Single trigger. Matte black finish receiver
and pistol-grip wood stock. Imported from 2009 to date.
Non-ported bbl. . . . . **NiB $479 Ex $275 Gd $120**

ERA MODEL 2000 . . . . **NiB $500 Ex $379 Gd $290**
Gauge: 12 w/3-in. chambers. 26- or 28-in. bbls. of chrome-
molybdenum steel w/screw-in choke tubes. Extractors. Manual
safety. (Mechanical triggers.) Weight: 7 lbs. Checkered Brazilian
hardwood stock w/oil finish. Imported from 1992 to 1995.

REUNA SINGLE-SHOT
Visible hammer. Under-lever release. Gauges: 12, 20 and .410;
3-in. chambers. 26- or 28-in. bbls. w/fixed chokes or screw-in
choke tubes (12 ga. only). Extractors. Weight: 5.25 to 6.5 lbs.
Plain Brazilian hardwood stock and semi-beavertail forend.
Imported from 1992 to1998.
w/fixed choke . . . . **NiB $210 Ex $155 Gd $90**
w/choke tubes. . . . . **NiB $275 Ex $190 Gd $145**

UPLANDER
S/S box lock; Gauges: 12, 20, 28 and .410. 26- or 28-in. bbls.
of chrome-molybdenum steel. Various fixed-choke combinations; screw-in choke tubes (12 and 20 ga.). Three inch
chambers (2.75-in. in 28 ga.). Weight: 6.25 to 7 lbs. Double
triggers. Automatic safety. Matte-finished solid sighting rib.
Hand checkered pistol-grip or straight stock and forend w/
hand-rubbed, oil-finish. Imported from 1997 to 2000.
Upland w/fixed chokes. . . . . . . **NiB $390 Ex $275 Gd $225**
Upland w/screw-in tubes . . . . . **NiB $420 Ex $345 Gd $290**
English model (straight grip) . . . **NiB $500 Ex $395 Gd $290**
Ladies model . . . . **NiB $477 Ex $365 Gd $300**
Supreme model. . . . . **NiB $610 Ex $477 Gd $325**
Youth model . . . . **NiB $477 Ex $345 Gd $270**

UPLANDER TURKEY MODEL . **NiB $588 Ex $440 Gd $379**
12 gauge only. 24-in. solid rib bbls. w/3-in. chambers choked
F&F. Weight: 6.75 lbs. Double triggers. Automatic safety.
Advantage camouflage on stock and bbls. Made 1997-2000.

INLAND MANUFACTURING — Dayton, OH

M37 TRENCH GUN . . . . **NiB $1279 EX $1000 GD $900**
Similar to U.S. M37 pump-action. Gauge: 12, 4+1 capacity. 20-in. bbl. 38.5 in. overall. Weight: 6.7 lbs. Sights: front.
Finish: Parkerized. Stock: oil finished wood. Heat shield and
bayonet lug. Made from 2016 to present.

ITHACA GUN COMPANY — Upper Sandusky, OH
*Formerly Ithaca Gun Company in Ithaca, NY (1883-1986) and
King Ferry, NY (1989-2005). In 2007 the company was pur-
chased and relocated to Upper Sandusky, OH.*

—NEW MANUFACTURE (2006-PRESENT)—

MODEL 37 SERIES
Similar to old Model 37 except chambered in 28, 20 or 12 gauge
w/2.75-in. chamber. Bbl: 24-, 26- or 28-in. VR w/3 choke tubes.
Gold plated trigger. Stock: fancy AAA walnut w/ Pachmayr recoil
pad. Finish: matte blue or hard chrome. Weight: 6 lbs.
Classic Featherweight . . . . **NiB $1030 Ex $910 Gd $710**
28 gauge, add **$260**
hard chrome, add **$310**
Classic Featherweight Trap (30-in. VR bbl., 12 gauge w/3-in.
chamber, disc. 2023) . . . . **NiB $895 Ex $620 Gd $405**
Classic Featherweight Trap Combo
(w/Deerslayer bbl.), add **$120**
Classic Featherweight Ladies Stock (w/special
LOP and cast stock) . . . . **NiB $1030 Ex $910 Gd $710**
Classic Featherweight Trap Youth
(w/youth stock), deduct **$20**
Defense (18.5- or 20-in. bbl., 5- or 8-rnd. capacity, walnut
or synthetic stock) . . . . **NiB $855 Ex $755 Gd $580**
Hog Slayer (12 gauge, 20-in. rifled bbl. w/sights, synthetic tock,
camo or blued, disc. 2016) . . **NiB $780 Ex $555 Gd $405**
Tactical (12 gauge, 18.5- or 20-in. bbl., 5- or 8-rnd. capacity,
synthetic pistol grip stock,
blued) . . . . **NiB $700 Ex $530 Gd $355**
Turkey Slayer (20 or 12 gauge w/3-in. chamber,
23-in. bbl. w/extended full choke tube and fiber optic
sights) . . . . **NiB $740 Ex $555 Gd $380**
Waterfowler (20 or 12 gauge w/3-in. chamber,
28- or 30-in. VR bbl., synthetic stock,
camo finish) . . . . **NiB $855 Ex $755 Gd $580**

MODEL 37 DEERSLAYER SERIES
Similar to the Classic Featherweight except 20 or 12 gauge
w/3-in. chamber. Bbl.: fixed, 24-in. w/rifle sights. Stock: wood,
traditional or thumbhole.
Deerslayer II . . . . **NiB $1030 Ex $910 Gd $710**
Deerslayer III (26-in. fluted fixed bbl.,
w/Weaver base.) . . . . **NiB $1195 Ex $1055 Gd $820**

- MANUFACTURED 1959-96 -

MODEL 37 BICENTENNIAL
COMMEMORATIVE . . . . **NiB $645 Ex $553 Gd $445**
Limited to issue of 1976. Similar to Model 37 Supreme except
has special Bicentennial design etched on receiver, fancy
walnut stock and slide handle. Serial numbers U.S.A. 0001

SHOTGUNS

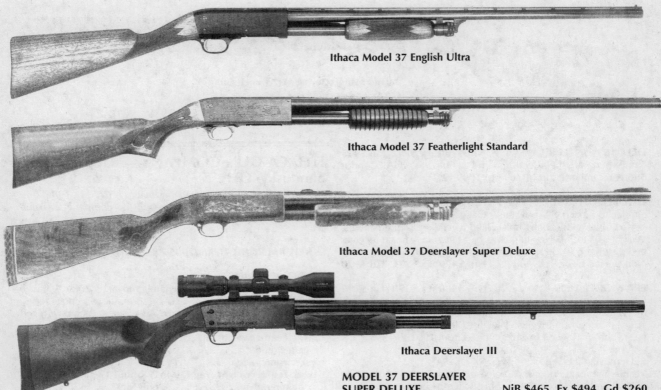

Ithaca Model 37 English Ultra

Ithaca Model 37 Featherlight Standard

Ithaca Model 37 Deerslayer Super Deluxe

Ithaca Deerslayer III

to U.S.A. 1976. Originally issued w/presentation case w/cast-pewter belt buckle. Made in 1976. Best value is for gun in new, unfired condition.

MODEL 37 DEERSLAYER DELUXE
Formerly "Model 87 Deerslayer Deluxe" reintroduced under the original Model 37 designation w/the same specifications. Available w/smooth bore or rifled bbl. Made 1959-2005.
w/smoothbore bbl. . . . . NiB $555 Ex $480 Gd $355
w/rifled bbl. . . . . NiB $575 Ex $490 Gd $335

MODEL 37 DEERSLAYER II. . . . NiB $530 Ex $395 Gd $240
Gauges: 12 or 20 ga. 5-rnd. capacity. 20- or 25-in. rifled free floating bbl. Weight: 7 lbs. Monte Carlo checkered walnut stock and forearm. Receiver drilled and tapped for scope mount. Made 1996-2005.
Storm (synthetic
   stock, 2003-04). . . . . NiB $355 Ex $320 Gd $300
Guide Series (laminated
   stock, disc. 2005) . . . . NiB $510 Ex $420 Gd $300

MODEL 37 DEERSLAYER III . . . NiB $760 Ex $680 Gd $530
Similar to Deerslayer II except 12 ga. only, 26-in. smoothbore bbl., 11 lbs. Made 2003-04.

MODEL 37 DEERSLAYER . . . . . NiB $410 Ex $355 Gd $270
Same as Model 37R except has 20- or 26-in. bbl. smoothbore for rifled slugs, rifle-type sights. Made 1959-86.

MODEL 37 DELUXE VR
SUPER DELUXE. . . . . NIB $465 EX $344 GD $220
Same general specifications as Model 37 Featherlight except w/ deluxe high gloss stock with checkering, 26-, 28-, or 30-in. VR bbl., gold trigger, 3 choke tubes. Made 1996-2005.

MODEL 37 DEERSLAYER
SUPER DELUXE . . . . NiB $465 Ex $494 Gd $260
Formerly "Deluxe Deerslayer." Same as Model 37 Standard Deerslayer except has stock and slide handle of fancy walnut. Made 1962-86.

MODEL 37 ENGLISH
ULTRALIGHT . . . . NiB $530 Ex $490 Gd $260
Same general specifications as Model 37 Ultralite except straight grip stock, 25-in. VR bbl. 12, 16, or 20 gauge. Made 1984-87.
Deluxe Classic model (16 or 20 ga.;
   24-, 26-, or 28-in. VR bbl., straight
   or pistol grip stock) . . . . NiB $710 Ex $560 Gd $380

MODEL 37 FEATHERLIGHT
Similar to Model 37R except w/aluminum receiver. Gauges: 12, 16, 20. 4-rnd. magazine. Bbl. lengths: 26-, 28-, 30-in. (the latter in 12 ga. only); standard fixed chokes. Weight: From 5.75 to 7.5 lbs. depending on ga. and bbl. length. Checkered pistol-grip stock and slide handle. Some guns made in the 1950s and 1960s have grooved slide handle; plain or checkered pistol-grip. Made 1937-85.
Standard model w/checkered
   pistol grip . . . . NiB $675 Ex $390 Gd $300
w/plain stock . . . . NiB $325 Ex $229 Gd $190
Model 37D Deluxe (1954-77). . NiB $675 Ex $390 Gd $300
Model 37DV Deluxe
   VR (1962-84) . . . . NiB $675 Ex $390 Gd $300
Model 37R Deluxe
   solid rib (1955-61) . . . . NiB $675 Ex $390 Gd $300
Model 37V Standard
   VR (1962-84) . . . . NiB $315 Ex $244 Gd $148

MODEL 37 FIELD GRADE
MAGNUM. . . . . NiB $355 Ex $298 Gd $199
Same general specifications as Model 37 Featherlight except w/ detachable choke tubes. VR bbl. Made 1984-87.

Ithaca Model 51 Deluxe Trap

MODEL 37 CLASSIC . . . . **NiB $685 Ex $555 Gd $465**
Ggs: 12 or 20 ga. 20- or 28-in. VR bbl. w/choke tubes. Knuckle-cut receiver and orig. style "ring-tail" forend. Lim. prod. Made 1998-2005.

MODEL 37 $1000 GRADE
Custom built, elaborately engraved and inlaid w/gold, hand-finished working parts, stock and forend of select figured walnut. General specifications same as standard Model 37. Note: Designated The $1000 Grade prior to World War II. Made 1937-67.
$1000 grade . . . . **NiB $5750 Ex $5210 Gd $4255**
$5000 grade . . . . **NiB $5255 Ex $4855 Gd $3855**

MODEL 37 SUPREME GRADE . . **NiB $955 Ex $588 Gd $535**
Available in Skeet or Trap Gun, similar to Model 37T. Made 1967-86 and 1997. Subtract $225 for newer models.

MODEL 37 ULTRALITE
Same general specifications as Model 37 Featherlight except streamlined forend, gold trigger, Sid Bell grip cap and VR. Weight: 5 to 5.75 lbs. Made 1978-87.
Standard . . . . **NiB $500 Ex $400 Gd $363**
W/choke tubes, add $150

MODEL 37R SOLID RIB
Adaptation of the earlier Remington Model 17, a Browning design patented in 1915. Hammerless. Takedown. Steel receiver. Gauges: 12, 16 (disc. 1973), 20. 4-rnd. magazine. Bbl.: 26-, 28-, 30-in. (the latter in 12 ga. only); standard fixed chokes. Weight: 5.75 to 7.5 lbs. depending on ga. and bbl. length. Checkered pistol-grip stock and slide handle. Some guns made in the 1950s and 1960s have grooved slide handle; plain or checkered pistol-grip. Made 1937-1952.
w/checkered pistol grip . . . . . . **NiB $440 Ex $330 Gd $180**
w/plain stock . . . . **NiB $400 Ex $280 Gd $150**

MODEL 37S SKEET GRADE . . . **NiB $565 Ex $455 Gd $335**
Same general specifications as the Model 37 Featherlight except has VR and large extension-type forend; weight: About .5 lb. more. Made 1937-55.

MODEL 37T TARGET GRADE . . **NiB $545 Ex $376 Gd $255**
Same general specifications as Model 37 Featherlight except has VR bbl., checkered stock and slide handle of fancy walnut (choice of skeet- or trap-style stock). Note: This model replaced Model 37S Skeet and Model 37T Trap. Made 1955-91.

MODEL 37T TRAP GRADE . . . . **NiB $545 Ex $376 Gd $255**
Same gen. specs. as Mdl. 37S except has straighter trap-style stock of select walnut, recoil pad; weight: About .5 lb. more. Made 1937-55.

MODEL 37 TURKEYSLAYER
Gauges: 12 ga. (Standard) or 20 ga. (youth). Slide action. 22-in. bbl. Extended choke tube. Weight: 7 lbs. Advantage camouflage or Realtree pattern. Made 1996-2005.
Standard model . . . . **NiB $425 Ex $260 Gd $190**
Youth model (intro. 1998). . . . **NiB $555 Ex $456 Gd $345**

MODEL 37 WATERFOWLER . . . **NiB $490 Ex $375 Gd $260**
12 ga. only w/28-in. bbl. Wetlands camouflage. Made 1998-2005.

MODEL 51 DEERSLAYER . . . . . **NiB $400 Ex $279 Gd $200**
Same as Model 51 Standard except has 24-in. plain bbl. w/ slug boring, rifle sights, recoil pad. Weight: About 7.25 lbs. Made 1972-84.

MODEL 51 SUPREME SKEET
GRADE . . . . **NiB $525 Ex $390 Gd $270**
Same as Model 51 Standard except 26-in. VR bbl. only, SK choke, skeet-style stock, semi-fancy wood. Weight: About 8 lbs. Made 1970-87.

MODEL 51 SUPREME TRAP
Same as Model 51 Standard except 12 ga. only, 30-in. bbl. w/ broad floating rib, F choke, trap-style stock w/straight or Monte Carlo comb, semifancy wood, recoil pad. Weight: About 8 lbs. Made 1970-87.
w/straight stock . . . . **NiB $544 Ex $390 Gd $295**
w/Monte Carlo stock, add $75

MODEL 51 FEATHERLITE STANDARD
Gas-operated. Gauges: 12, 20. Three round. Bbls.: Plain or VR, 30-in. F choke (12 ga. only), 28-in. F or M, 26-in. IC. Weight: 7.25-7.75 lbs. depending on ga. and bbl. Checkered pistol-grip stock, forearm. Made 1970-1980. Avail. in 12 and 20 ga., 28-in. M choke only.
w/plain bbl. . . . . **NiB $300 Ex $197 Gd $121**
w/VR, add $65

MODEL 51A STANDARD MAGNUM
Same as Model 51 Standard except has 3-in. chamber, handles Magnum shells only; 30-in. bbl. in 12 ga., 28-in. in 20 ga., F or M choke, stock w/recoil pad. Weight: 7.75-8 lbs. Made 1972-82.
w/plain bbl. (disc. 1976). . . . . . **NiB $375 Ex $290 Gd $200**
w/camo finish, add $65

MODEL 51A TURKEY GUN . . . **NiB $455 Ex $300 Gd $217**
Same general specifications as standard Model 51 Magnum except 26-in. bbl. and matte finish. Disc. 1986.

MODEL 66 LONG TOM . . . . . . **NiB $210 Ex $155 Gd $100**
Same as Model 66 Standard except has 36-in. F choke bbl., 12 ga. only, checkered stock and recoil pad standard. Made 1969-74.

MODEL 66 STANDARD SUPER SINGLE LEVER
Single shot. Hand-cocked hammer. Gauges: 12 (disc. 1974), 20, .410, 3-in. chambers. Bbls.: 12 ga., 30-in. F choke, 28-in. F or M; 20 ga., 28-in. F or M; .410, 26-in. F. Weight: About 7 lbs. Plain or checkered straight-grip stock, plain forend. Made 1963-78.
Standard model . . . . **NiB $220 Ex $115 Gd $90**
VR model (20 ga.,
    1969-74) . . . . **NiB $225 Ex $159 Gd $135**
Youth model (1965-78) . . . . **NiB $250 Ex $179 Gd $130**

SHOTGUNS

Ithaca Model 66RS Buckbuster

MODEL 66RS BUCKBUSTER . . NiB $279 Ex $200 Gd $155
Same as Model 66 Standard except has 22-in. bbl. cylinder bore w/rifle sights, later version has recoil pad. Originally offered in 12 and 20 ga.; the former was disc. in 1970. Made 1967-78.

NOTE: Previously issued as the Ithaca Model 37, the Model 87 guns listed below were made available through the Ithaca Acquisition Corp. From 1986-95. Production of the Model 37 resumed under the original logo in 1996.

MODEL 87 DEERLSLAYER SHOTGUN
Gauges: 12 or 20, 3-in. chamber. Bbls.: 18.5-, 20- or 25-in. (w/special or rifled bore). Weight: 6 to 6.75 lbs. Ramp blade front sight, adj. rear. Receiver grooved for scope. Checkered American walnut pistol-grip stock and forearm. Made 1988-96.

Basic model . . . . NiB $445 Ex $355 Gd $225
Basic Field Combo
(w/extra 28-in. bbl.) . . . . NiB $475 Ex $390 Gd $280
Deluxe model . . . . NiB $480 Ex $395 Gd $290
Deluxe Combo
(w/extra 28-in. bbl.) . . . . NiB $635 Ex $460 Gd $339
DSPS (8-rnd. model) . . . . NiB $554 Ex $400 Gd $290
Field model . . . . NiB $433 Ex $330 Gd $287
Monte Carlo model . . . . NiB $448 Ex $356 Gd $255
Ultra model (disc. 1991) . . . . . NiB $500 Ex $398 Gd $325

MODEL 87 DEERSLAYER II
RIFLED SHOTGUN . . . . NiB $600 Ex $433 Gd $310
Similar to Standard Deerslayer except w/solid frame construction and 25-in. rifled bbl. Monte Carlo stock. Made 1988-96.

MODEL 87 ULTRALITE
FIELD PUMP SHOTGUN . . . . . NiB $490 Ex $387 Gd $260
Gauges: 12 and 20; 2.75-in. chambers. 25-in. bbl. w/choke tube. Weight: 5 to 6 lbs. Made 1988-90.

MODEL 87 FIELD GRADE
Gauge: 12 or 20.; 3-in. chamber. Five round magazine. Fixed chokes or screw-in choke tubes (IC, M, F). Bbls.: 18.5-in. (M&P); 20- and 25-in. (Combo); 26-, 28-, 30-in. VR. Weight: 5 to 7 lbs. Made 1988-96.

Basic field model (disc. 1993) . . NiB $446 Ex $270 Gd $210
Camo model . . . . NiB $490 Ex $339 Gd $260
Deluxe model . . . . NiB $505 Ex $340 Gd $280
Deluxe Combo model . . . . NiB $590 Ex $493 Gd $377
English model . . . . NiB $490 Ex $339 Gd $260
Hand grip model
(w/polymer pistol-grip) . . . . NiB $533 Ex $425 Gd $315
M&P model (disc. 1995) . . . . . . NiB $466 Ex $380 Gd $279
Supreme model . . . . NiB $720 Ex $589 Gd $400
Turkey model . . . . NiB $445 Ex $365 Gd $256
Ultra Deluxe model
(disc. 1992) . . . . NiB $400 Ex $356 Gd $260

HAMMERLESS DOUBLE-BARREL SHOTGUNS
Boxlock. Plain extractors, auto ejectors standard on the "E" grades. Double triggers, non-selective or selective single trig-ger extra. Gauges: Magnum 10, 12; 12, 16, 20, 28, .410. Bbls.: 26- to 32-in., any standard boring. Weight: 5.75 (.410) to 10.5 lbs. (Magnum 10). Checkered pistol-grip stock and forearm standard. Higher grades differ from Field Grade in quality of workmanship, grade of wood, checkering, engraving, etc.; general specifications are the same. Ithaca doubles made before 1925 (serial number 425,000) the rotary bolt and a stronger frame were adopted. Values shown are for this latter type; earlier models valued about 50% lower. Smaller gauge guns may command up to 75% higher. Disc. 1948.

Field grade . . . . NiB $1088 Ex $900 Gd $677
No. 1 grade . . . . NiB $1377 Ex $1099 Gd $890
No. 2 grade . . . . NiB $2480 Ex $2077 Gd $1100
No. 3 grade . . . . NiB $2456 Ex $1866 Gd $1376
No. 4E grade (ejector) . . . . . NiB $6225 Ex $3688 Gd $2977
No. 5E grade (ejector) . . . . . NiB $5235 Ex $3767 Gd $4400
Extras:
Magnum 10 or 12 ga.
(in other than the four highest grades), add 20%
Automatic ejectors (grades No. 1, 2, 3,
w/ejectors designated No. 1E, 2E, 3E), add 35%
Selective single trigger, add $250
Non-selective single trigger, add $200
Beavertail forend (Field No. 1 or 2), add $200
Beavertail forend (No. 3 or 4), add $200
Beavertail forend (No. 5, 7 or $2000 grade), add $200
Ventilated rib (No. 4, 5, 7 or $2000 grade), add $400
Ventilated rib (lower grades), add $250

LSA-55 TURKEY GUN . . . . NiB $935 Ex $700 Gd $590
Over/under shotgun/rifle combination. Boxlock. Exposed hammer. Plain extractor. Single trigger. 12 ga./222 Rem. 24.5-in. ribbed bbls. (rifle bbl. has muzzle brake). Weight: About 7 lbs. Folding leaf rear sight, bead front sight. Checkered Monte Carlo stock and forearm. Made 1970-1977 by Oy Tikkakoski AB, Finland.

MAG-10 AUTOMATIC SHOTGUN
Gas-operated. 10 ga. 3.5-in. Magnum. Three round capacity. 32-in. plain (Standard Grade only) or VR bbl. F choke. Weight: 11 lbs., plain bbl.; 11.5 lbs., VR. Standard grade has plain stock and forearm. Deluxe and Supreme Grades have checkering, semi-fancy and fancy wood respectively, and stud swivel. All have recoil pad. Deluxe and Supreme grades made 1974 to 191982. Standard Grade intro. in 1977. All grades disc. 1986.

Camo model . . . . NiB $735 Ex $555 Gd $379
Deluxe grade . . . . NiB $890 Ex $774 Gd $522
Roadblocker . . . . NiB $855 Ex $740 Gd $533
Standard grade, plain bbl. . . . . NiB $744 Ex $610 Gd $477
Standard grade w/VR . . . . NiB $844 Ex $633 Gd $530
Standard grade, w/choke tubes NiB $988 Ex $755 Gd $544
Supreme grade . . . . NiB $1044 Ex $856 Gd $600

SINGLE-SHOT TRAP, FLUES AND KNICK MODELS
Boxlock. Hammerless. Ejector. 12 ga. only. Bbl. lengths: 30-, 32-, 34-in. (32-in. only in Victory grade). VR. Weight: About 8 lbs. Checkered pistol-grip stock and forend. Grades differ only in quality of workmanship, engraving, checkering, wood, etc. Flues Model, serial numbers under 400,000, made 1908 to 1921. Triple-bolted Knick Model, serial numbers above 400,000, made since 1921. Victory Model disc. in 1938, No.

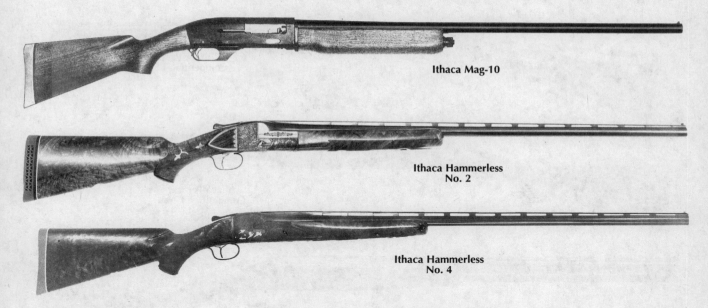

Ithaca Mag-10

Ithaca Hammerless
No. 2

Ithaca Hammerless
No. 4

7-E in 1964, No. 4-E in 1976, No. 5-E in 1986, Dollar Grade in 1991. Values shown are for Knick Model; Flues models about 50% lower.

Victory grade . . . . NiB $1379 Ex $1100 Gd $925
No. 4-E . . . . NiB $3766 Ex $3470 Gd $1790
No. 5-E . . . . NiB $5000 Ex $4766 Gd $2128
No. 6-E (rare) . . . . . . NiB $16,980 Ex $14,700 Gd $10,000
No. 7-E (rare) . . . . NiB $7445 Ex $6000 Gd $4655
$2,000 grade . . . . NiB $9,500 Ex $8500 Gd $6650
Pre-war $1000 grade . . NiB $10,000 Ex $9577 Gd $6650
Sousa grade (rare) . . .NiB $14,500+ Ex $12,700+ Gd $9000+

NOTE: *The following Ithaca-Perazzi shotguns were manufactured by Manifattura Armi Perazzi, Brescia, Italy. See also separate Perazzi listings.*

**PERAZZI COMPETITION
I SKEET** . . . . **NiB $14,877 Ex $13,900 Gd $11,270**
Boxlock. Auto ejectors. Single trigger. 12 ga. 26.75-in. VR bbls. SK choke w/integral muzzle brake. Weight: About 7.75 lbs. Checkered skeet-style pistol-grip buttstock and forearm; recoil pad. Made 1969-74.

**PERAZZI COMPETITION
TRAP I O/U** . . . . **NiB $14,889 Ex $13,679 Gd $11,650**
Boxlock. Auto ejectors. Single trigger. 12 ga. 30- or 32-in. VR bbls. IM/F choke. Weight: About 8.5 lbs. Checkered pistol-grip stock, forearm; recoil pad. Made 1969-74.

**PERAZZI COMPETITION I
TRAP SINGLE BARREL** . . **NiB $11,770 Ex $9455 Gd $7655**
Boxlock. Auto ejection. 12 ga. 32- or 34-in. bbl., VR, F choke. Weight: 8.5 lbs. Checkered Monte Carlo stock and beavertail forearm, recoil pad. Made 1973-78.

**PERAZZI COMPETITION IV
TRAP GUN** . . . . **NiB $13,890 Ex $11,870 Gd $10,000**
Boxlock. Auto ejection. 12 ga. 32- or 34-in. bbl. With high, wide VR, four interchangeable choke tubes (Extra Full, F, IM, M). Weight: About 8.75 lbs. Checkered Monte Carlo stock and beavertail forearm, recoil pad. Fitted case. Made 1977-78.

**PERAZZI LIGHT GAME
O/U FIELD** . . . . **NiB $15,800 Ex $14,790 Gd $13,955**
Boxlock. Auto ejectors. Single trigger. 12 ga. 27.5-in. VR bbls., M/F or IC/M choke. Weight: 6.75 lbs. Checkered field-style stock and forearm. Made 1972-74.

PERAZZI MIRAGE . . . . **NiB $6987 Ex $4677 Gd $2700**
Same as Mirage Trap except has 28-in. bbls., M and Extra Full choke, special stock and forearm for live bird shooting. Weight: About 8 lbs. Made 1973-78.

PERAZZI MIRAGE SKEET . . **NiB $4350 Ex $3866 Gd $2789**
Same as Mirage Trap except has 28-in. bbls. w/integral muzzle brakes, SK choke, skeet-stype stock and forearm. Weight: About 8 lbs. Made 1973-78.

PERAZZI MIRAGE TRAP . . . **NiB $4365 Ex $3900 Gd $2820**
Same general specifications as MX-8 Trap except has tapered rib. Made 1973-78.

Ithaca Hammerless
Field Grade

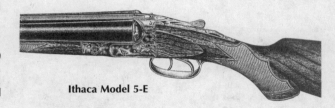

Ithaca Model 5-E

SHOTGUNS

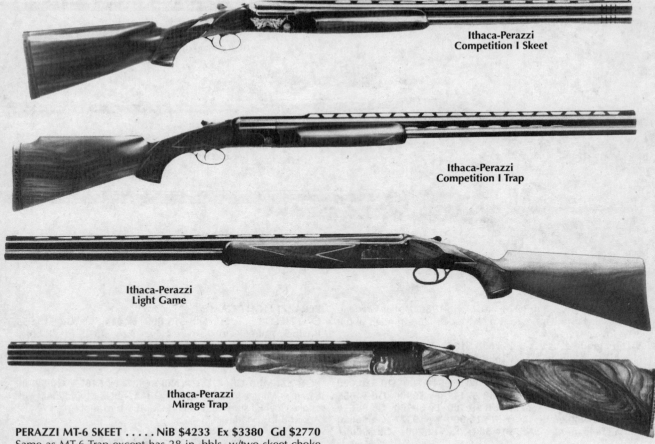

Ithaca-Perazzi
Competition I Skeet

Ithaca-Perazzi
Competition I Trap

Ithaca-Perazzi
Light Game

Ithaca-Perazzi
Mirage Trap

PERAZZI MT-6 SKEET . . . . . NiB $4233 Ex $3380 Gd $2770
Same as MT-6 Trap except has 28-in. bbls. w/two skeet choke tubes instead of Extra Full and F, skeet-style stock and forearm. Weight: About 8 lbs. Made 1976-78.

PERAZZI MT-6 TRAP
COMBO . . . . NiB $5377 Ex $4260 Gd $3100
MT-6 w/extra single under bbl. w/high-rise aluminum VR, 32- or 34-in.; seven interchanageable choke tubes (IC through Extra Full). Fitted case. Made 1977-78.

PERAZZI MT-6 TRAP O/U . . . NiB $3700 Ex $2566 Gd $2044
Boxlock. Auto selective ejectors. Non-selective single trigger. 12 ga. Barrels separated, wide VR, 30-or 32-in., five interchangeable choke tubes (Extra full, F, IM, M, IC). Weight: About 8.5 lbs. Checkered pistol-grip stock/forearm, recoil pad. Fitted case. Made 1976-78.

PERAZZI MX
8 TRAP COMBO . . . . NiB $5688 Ex $4355 Gd $2460
MX-8 w/extra single bbl., VR, 32- or 34-in., F choke, forearm; two trigger groups included. Made 1973-78.

Ithaca Single-Shot Trap
"Dollar Grade"

PERAZZI MX-8 TRAP O/U . . . NiB $4356 Ex $3879 Gd $2889
Boxlock. Auto selective ejectors. Non-selective single trigger. 12 ga. Bbls.: High VR; 30- or 32-in., IM/F choke. Weight: 8.25 to 8.5 lbs. Checkered Monte Carlo stock and forearm, recoil pad. Made 1969-78.

PERAZZI SINGLE-BARREL
TRAP GUN . . . . NiB $3350 Ex $2459 Gd $2000
Boxlock. Auto ejection. 12 ga. 34-in. VR bbl., F choke. Weight: Abaout 8.5 lbs. Checkered pistol-grip stock, forearm; recoil pad. Made 1971-72.

NOTE: *The following Ithaca-SKB shotguns, manufactured by SKB Arms Company, Tokyo, Japan, were distributed in the U.S. by Ithaca Gun Company from 1966-76. See also listings under SKB.*

SKB MODEL 100 SIDE-BY-SIDE . . . NiB $779 Ex $580 Gd $490
Boxlock. Plain extractors. Selective single trigger. Auto safety. Gauges: 12 and 20; 2.75-in. and 3-in. chambers respectively. Bbls.: 30-in., F/F (12 ga. only); 28-in., F/M; 26-in., IC/M (12 ga. only); 25-in., IC/M (20 ga. only). Weight: 12 ga., about 7 lbs.; 20 ga., about 6 lbs. Checkered stock and forend. Made 1966-1976.

SKB MODEL 150 FIELD GRADE . . . NiB $770 Ex $600 Gd $488
Same as Model 100 except has fancier scroll engraving, beavertail forearm. Made 1972-74.

SKB 200E FIELD GRADE S/S . . . NiB $1077 Ex $767 Gd $580
Same as Model 100 except auto selective ejectors, engraved and silver-plated frame, gold-plated nameplate and trigger, beavertail forearm. Made 1966-76.

SKB MODEL 200E SKEET GUN. . . . NiB $995 Ex $687 Gd $485
Same as Model 200E Field Grade except 26-in. (12 ga.) and 25-in. (20 ga./2.75-in. chambers) bbls., SK choke; nonautomatic safety and recoil pad. Made 1966-76.

SKB MODEL 200 ENGLISH . . NiB $1154 Ex $990 Gd $759
Same as Model 200E except has scrolled game scene engraving on frame, English-style straight-grip stock; 30-in. bbls. not available; special quail gun in 20 ga. has 25-in. bbls., both bored IC. Made 1971-76.

SKB MODEL 300 STANDARD AUTOMATIC SHOTGUN
Recoil-operated. Gauges: 12, 20 (3-in.). Five round capacity. Bbls.: plain or VR; 30-in. F choke (12 ga. only), 28-in. F or M, 26-in. IC. Weight: about 7 lbs. Checkered pistol-grip stock and forearm. Made 1968-72.
w/plain bbl. . . . . NiB $1088 Ex $765 Gd $490
20 ga, add. 30%

SKB MODEL 500
FIELD GRADE O/U. . . . . NiB $665 Ex $455 Gd $323
Boxlock. Auto selective ejectors. Selective single trigger. Non-automatic safety. Gauges: 12 and 20; 2.75-in. and 3-in. chambers respectively. VR bbls.: 30-in. M/F (12 ga. only); 28-in. M/F; 26-in. IC/M. Weight: 12 ga., about 7.5 lbs; 20 ga., about 6.5 lbs. Checkered stock and forearm. Made 1966-76.

SKB MODEL 500 MAGNUM. . . . NiB $639 Ex $455 Gd $344
Same as Model 500 Field Grade except chambered for 3-in. 12 ga. shells, has 30-in. bbls., IM/F choke. Weight: About 8 lbs. Made 1973-1976.

SKB MODEL 600 DOUBLES
GUN. . . . . NiB $1096 Ex $766 Gd $500
Same as Model 600 Trap Grade except specially choked for 21-yard first target, 30-yard second. Made 1973-75.

SKB MODEL 600 FIELD
GRADE . . . . NiB $1100 Ex $775 Gd $525
Same as Model 500 except has silver-plated frame, higher grade wood. Made 1969-76.

SKB MODEL 600 MAGNUM . . . NiB $1125 Ex $800 Gd $550
Same as Model 600 Field Grade except chambered for 3-in. 12 ga. shells; has 30-in. bbls., IM/F choke. Weight: 8.5 lbs. Made 1969-72.

SKB MODEL 600 SKEET GRADE
Same as Model 500 except also available in 28 and .410 ga., has silver-plated frame, higher grade wood, recoil pad, 26- or 28-in. bbls. (28-in. only in 28 and .410), SK choke. Weight: 7 to 7.75 lbs. depending on ga. and bbl. length. Made 1966-76.

12 or 20 ga. . . . . NiB $1155 Ex $830 Gd $575
28 ga. or .410. . . . . NiB $1500 Ex $1266 Gd $1077

SKB MODEL 600 SKEET SET. . . NiB $2866 Ex $2249 Gd $1545
Model 600 Skeet Grade w/matched set of 20, 28 and .410 ga. bbls., 28-in., fitted case. Made 1970-76.

SKB MODEL 600
TRAP GRADE O/U . . . . NiB $1055 Ex $700 Gd $533
Same as Model 500 except 12 ga. only, has silver-plated frame, 30- or 32-in. bbls. choked F/F or F/IM, choice of Monte Carlo or straight stock of higher grade wood, recoil pad. Weight: About 8 lbs. Made 1966-76.

SKB MODEL 680 ENGLISH. . . . NiB $1388 Ex $1055 Gd $775
Same as Model 600 Field Grade except has intricate scroll engraving, English-style straight-grip stock and forearm of extra-fine walnut; 30-in. bbls. not available. Made 1973-76.

SKB MODEL 700
SKEET COMBO SET . . . . . . NiB $3988 Ex $2970 Gd $2175
Model 700 Skeet Grade w/matched set of 20, 28 and .410 ga. bbls., 28-in. fitted case. Made 1970-71.

SKB MODEL 700 SKEET
GRADE . . . . NiB $955 Ex $779 Gd $575
Same as Model 600 Skeet Grade except not available in 28 and .410 ga., has more elaborate scroll engraving, extra-wide rib, higher grade wood. Made 1969-75.

SKB MODEL 700 TRAP GRADE . . .NiB $945 Ex $665 Gd $544
Same as Model 600 Trap Grade except has more elaborate scroll engraving, extra-wide rib, higher grade wood. Made 1969-1975.

SKB MODEL 700
DOUBLES GUN . . . . NiB $866 Ex $744 Gd $559
Same as Model 700 Trap Grade except choked for 21-yard first target, 30-yard second target. Made 1973-75.

SKB MODEL 900
DELUXE AUTOMATIC. . . . . . . NiB $475 Ex $359 Gd $255
Same as Model 30 except has game scene etched and gold-filled on receiver, VR standard. Made 1968-72.

SKB MODEL 900 SLUG GUN. . NiB $350 Ex $264 Gd $190
Same as Model 900 Deluxe except has 24-in. plain bbl. w/ slug boring, rifle sights. Weight: About 6.5 lbs. Made 1970-72.

SKB CENTURY SINGLE-SHOT
TRAP GUN . . . . NiB $689 Ex $500 Gd $356
Boxlock. Auto ejector. 12 ga. Bbls.: 32- or 34-in., VR, F choke. Weight: About 8 lbs. Checkered walnut stock w/pistol grip, straight or Monte Carlo comb, recoil pad, beavertail forearm. Made 1973-74.

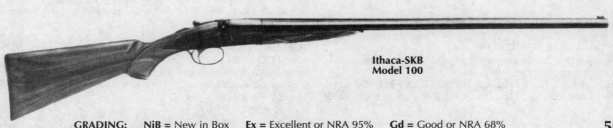

Ithaca-SKB
Model 100

SHOTGUNS

Ithaca-SKB Model 280 English

Ithaca-SKB Model 700 Skeet Grade

Ithaca-SKB Model 900 Deluxe

Ithaca-SKB Century Trap

Ithaca-SKB Century II Trap

Ithaca-SKB Model XL300

SKB CENTURY II TRAP . . . .**NiB $700 Ex $495 Gd $400**
Boxlock. Auto ejector. 12 ga. Bbls: 32- or 34-in., VR, F choke. Weight: 8.25 lbs. Improved version of Century. Same general specifications except has higher comb on checkered stock stock, reverse-taper beavertail forearm w/redesigned locking iron. Made 1975-76.

SKB MODEL XL300 STANDARD AUTOMATIC
Gas-operated. Gauges: 12, 20 (3-in.). Five round capacity. Bbls.: Plain or VR; 30-in. F choke (12 ga. only), 28-in. F or M, 26-in. IC. Weight: 6 to 7.5 lbs. depending on ga. and bbl. Checkered pistol-grip stock, forearm. Made 1972-76.
w/plain bbl. . . . .**NiB $389 Ex $296 Gd $210**
w/ventilated rib . . . .**NiB $365 Ex $283 Gd $205**

SKB MODEL XL900
DELUXE AUTOMATIC. . . . .**NiB $379 Ex $335 Gd $260**
Same as Model XL300 except has game scene finished in silver on receiver, VR standard. Made 1972-76.

SKB MODEL XL
900 SKEET GRADE . . . .**NiB $490 Ex $377 Gd $315**
Gas-operated. Gauges: 12, 20 (3-in.). Five round tubular magazine. Same as Model XL900 Deluxe except has scrolled receiver finished in black chrome, 26-in. bbl. only, SK choke, skeet-style stock. Weight: 7 or 7.5 lbs. depending on ga. Made 1972-76.

SKB MODEL XL
900 SLUG GUN . . . .**NiB $445 Ex $377 Gd $290**
Same as Model XL900 Deluxe except has 24-in. plain bbl. w/ slug boring, rifle sights. Weight: 6.5 or 7 lbs. depending on ga. Made 1972-76.

Kel-Tec KSG

SKB MODEL
XL900 TRAP GRADE. . . . . **NiB $488 Ex $358 Gd $290**
Same as Model XL900 Deluxe except 12 ga. only, has scrolled
receiver finished in black chrome, 30-in. bbl. only, IM or F
choke, trap style w/straight or Monte Carlo comb, recoil pad.
Weight: About 7.75 lbs. Made 1972-76.

IVER JOHNSON ARMS & CYCLE WORKS — Jacksonville, AR

*Fitchburg, MA; currently a division of the American Military
Arms Corp., Jacksonville, AR*

CHAMPION GRADE TOP SNAP
Auto ejector. Gauges: 12,16, 20, 28 and .410. Bbls.: 26- to 36-in.,
F choke. Weight: 5.75 to 7.5 lbs. depending on ga. and bbl.length.
Plain pistol-grip stock and forend. Extras include checkered stock
and forend, pistol-grip cap and knob forend. Known as Model 36.
Also made in a Semi-Octagon Breech, Top Matted and Jacketed
Breech (extra heavy) models. Made in Champion Lightweight as
Model 39 in gauges 24, 28, 32 and .410, .44 and .45 caliber, 12
and 14mm w/same extras. $200; add $100 in the smaller and
obsolete gauges. Made 1909-73.

Standard model. . . . . **NiB $377 Ex $290 Gd $100**
Semi-octagon breech . . . . **NiB $466 Ex $351 Gd $229**
Top matted rib (disc. 1948). . . . **NiB $398 Ex $297 Gd $195**

HERCULES GRADE HAMMERLESS DOUBLE
Boxlock. (Some made w/false sideplates.) Plain extractors and
auto ejectors. Double or Miller single triggers (both selective
or non-selective). Gauges: 12, 16, 20 and .410. Bbl. lengths:
26- to 32-in., all chokes. Weight: 5.75 to 7.75 lbs. depending
on ga. and bbl. length. Checkered stock and forend. Straight
grip in .410 ga. w/both 2.5- and 3-in. chambers. Extras include
Miller single trigger, Jostam Anti-Flinch recoil pad and Lyman
ivory sights at extra cost. Disc. 1946.

w/double triggers, extractors . . . .**NiB $1166 Ex $955 Gd $760**
w/double triggers, ejectors, add **30%**
w/non-selective single trigger, add **$50**
w/selective single trigger, add. **$50**
.410 ga., add **100%**

MATTED RIB SINGLE-SHOT HAMMER SHOTGUN
IN SMALLER GAUGES. . . . . **NiB $400 Ex $355 Gd $210**
Same general specifications as Champion Grade except has
solid matted top rib, checkered stock and forend. Weight: 6 to
6.75 lbs. Disc. 1948.

MODEL 412/422 SILVER SHADOW O/U SHOTGUN
Boxlock. Plain extractors. Double triggers or non-selective single
trigger. 12 ga., 3-in. chambers. Bbls.: 26-in. IC/M; 28-in. IC/M,
28-in. M/F; 30-in. both F choke; VR. Weight: w/28-in. bbls., 7.5
lbs. Checkered pistol-grip stock/forearm. Made by F. Marocchi,
Brescia, Italy from 1973 to 1977.

Model 412 w/double triggers . **NiB $590 Ex $455 Gd $387**
Model 422 w/single trigger . . .**NiB $754 Ex $600 Gd $445**

SKEETER MODEL HAMMERLESS DOUBLE
Boxlock. Plain extractors or selective auto ejectors. Double triggers or Miller single trigger (selective or non-selective). Gauges:
12, 16, 20, 28 and .410. 26- or 28-in. bbls., skeet boring standard. Weight: About 7.5 lbs.; less in smaller gauges. Pistol- or
straight-grip stock and beavertail forend, both checkered, of
select fancy-figured black walnut. Extras include Miller single
trigger, selective or non-selective, Jostam Anti-Flinch recoil pad
and Lyman ivory rear sight at additional cost. Disc. 1942.

w/dbl triggers, plain extr . . . **NiB $2298 Ex $1987 Gd $1133**
w/double triggers, automatic ejectors, add **20%**
w/non-selective single trigger, add **20%**
w/selective single trigger, add. **50%**
20 ga,add **30%**
28 ga., add **90%**
.410 ga., add **100%**

SPECIAL TRAP SINGLE-SHOT
HAMMER SHOTGUN . . . . . . **NiB $500 Ex $365 Gd $298**
Auto ejector. 12 ga. only. 32-in. bbl. w/VR, F choke. Checkered
pistol-grip stock and forend. Weight: about 7.5 lbs. Disc. 1942.

SUPER TRAP HAMMERLESS DOUBLE
Boxlock. Plain extractors. Double trigger or Miller single trigger
(selective or non-selective), 12 ga. only, F choke 32-in. bbl.,
VR. Weight: 8.5 lbs. Checkered pistol-grip stock and beavertail
forend, recoil pad, Disc. 1942.

w/double triggers . . . . **NiB $1756 Ex $1170 Gd $990**
w/non-selective single trigger, add **$150**
w/selective single trigger, add. **$150**

KBI INC.
See listings under Armscor, Baikal, Charles Daly, Fias, & Omega.

KEL-TEC — Cocoa, FL

KSG SERIES
Pump/slide action in bullpup configuration w/twin magazine
tubes, 10-rnd. capacity. Gauge: 12, 3-in. chamber. Bbl.: 18.5-
in. w/fixed cyl. bore choke. Stock: textured polymer w/pistol
grip. Length: 26.1 in. Weight: 6.9 lbs. Made 2011 to date.

black finish . . . . **NiB $880 Ex $680 Gd $505**
Tan or OD green finish, add **$50**
NR model (folding forend grip) NiB $1110 Ex $880 Gd $655
25 model (30.5-in. bbl.) . . . . . . **NiB $1225 Ex $955 Gd $805**

SHOTGUNS

Kimber Augusta

KESSLER ARMS CORP. — Silver Creek, NY

LEVER-MATIC REPEATING
SHOTGUN . . . . NiB $335 Ex $227 Gd $179
Lever action. Takedown. Gauges: 12, 16, 20; three-round magazine. Bbls.: 26-, 28-, 30-in.; F choke. Plain pistol-grip stock, recoil pad. Weight: 7 to 7.75 lbs. Disc. 1953.

THREE SHOT BOLT REPEATER . . . . NiB $200 Ex $138 Gd $90
Takedown. Gauges: 12, 16, 20. Two-round detachable box magazine. Bbls.: 28-in. in 12 and 16 ga.; 26-in. in 20 ga.; F choke. Weight: 6.25 to 7.25 lbs. depending on ga. and bbl. length. Plain one-piece pistol-grip stock recoil pad. Made 1951-53.

KIMBER — Yonkers, NY

AUGUSTA SERIES . . . . NiB $4755 Ex $3755 Gd $2755
O/U. Boss type action. Gauges: 12, 2.75- or 3-in. chambers. Bbls.: 26 to 34-in. VR. Finish: polished blue. Stock: Checkered wood. Weight: 7 to 7.75 lbs. Note: Available in Field, Sporting, Skeet and Trap variants w/limited numbers produced. Mfg. by Investarm in Italy. Imported 2003-05.

MARIAS SERIES . . . . NiB $4995 Ex $3755 Gd $2755
O/U. Boss type action. Gauges: 12 or 20, 2.75- or 3-in. chambers. Bbls.: 26-, 28- or 30-in. VR, w/5 choke tubes. Finish: charcoal blue receiver w/engraved detachable sideplates. Stock: High grade checkered walnut. Mfg. in Turkey. Imported 2006-08.

VALIER SERIES . . . . NiB $3530 Ex $2680 Gd $2210
S/S. Seven pin sidelock action. Gauges: 16 or 20. Bbls.: 26- or 28-in. VR, w/fixed chokes and extractors. Finish: Blued, case hardened or bone charcoal blue receiver w/engraving. Stock: High grade checkered walnut w/straight English-grip. Weight: 6.5 lbs. Mfg. in Turkey. Imported 2005-07.
Grade II model (ejectors,
2005-08) . . . . NiB $4500 Ex $3055 Gd $2210

H. KRIEGHOFF JAGD UND SPORTWAFFENFABRIK — Ulm (Donau), Germany

MODEL 32 FOUR-BARREL SKEET SET
Over/under w/four sets of matched bbls.: 12, 20, 28 and .410 ga., in fitted case. Available in six grades that differ in quality of engraving and wood. Disc. 1979.
Standard grade . . . . NiB $9344 Ex $7120 Gd $4688
München grade . . . . NiB $10,077 Ex $8767 Gd $6233

San Remo grade . . . . NiB $13,876 Ex $11,990 Gd $10,550
Monte Carlo grade . . NiB $20,000 Ex $17,890 Gd $14,650
Crown grade . . . . NiB $27,700 Ex $22,800 Gd $15,660
Super Crown grade . . NiB $29,000 Ex $24,770 Gd $17,600
Exhibition grade . . . . NiB $32,000 Ex $28,900 Gd $23,750

MODEL 32 STANDARD GRADE O/U
Similar to prewar Remington Model 23. Boxlock. Auto ejector. Single trigger. Gauges: 12, 20, 28, .410. Bbls.: VR, 26.5- to 32-in., any chokes. Weight: 12 ga. Field gun w/28-in. bbls., about 7.5 lbs. Checkered pistol-grip stock and forearm of select walnut; available in field, skeet and trap styles. Made 1958-81.
w/one set of bbls. . . . . NiB $3125 Ex $2460 Gd $2099
Low-rib two-bbl. trap combo . . . NiB $4166 Ex $3550 Gd $2779
Vandalia (high-rib) two- bbl.
   trap combo . . . . NiB $5355 Ex $4288 Gd $3150

MODEL 32 STANDARD GRADE
SINGLE-SHOT TRAP GUN . NiB $4160 Ex $3277 Gd $3080
Same action as over/under. 28 ga. or .410 bore w/low VR on bbl.; M, IM, or F choke. Checkered Monte Carlo buttstock w/ thick cushioned recoil pad, beavertail forearm. Disc. 1979.

MODEL K-80
Refined and enhanced version of the Mdl. 32. Single selective mech. trig., adj. for position; release trigger optional. Fixed chokes or screw-in choke tubes. Interchangeable front bbl. Hangers to adjust point of impact. Quick-removable stock. Color casehardened or satin grey fin. rec.; alum. alloy rec. on lightweight models. Avail. in stand. plus 5 engraved grades. Made from 1980 to date. Standard grade shown except where noted.

SKEET MODELS
Skeet International . . . . NiB $9160 Ex $5375 Gd $3853
Skeet Special . . . . NiB $9277 Ex $6659 Gd $4390
Skeet standard model . . . . . NiB $9000 Ex $4788 Gd $3360
Skeet w/choke tubes. . . . NiB $12,776 Ex $9879 Gd $5780
SKEET SETS - Disc.
  1999. Standard grade
    2-bbl. set . . . . NiB $12,769 Ex $10,000 Gd $6690
Standard grade
    4-bbl. set . . . . NiB $14,879 Ex $11,890 Gd $9877
Bavaria grade 4-bbl. set . . . NiB $11,900 Ex $9388 Gd $7710
Danube grade
    4-bbl. set . . . . NiB $23,998 Ex $20,600 Gd $17,000
Gold Target grade
    4-bbl. set . . . . NiB $31,800 Ex $24,800 Gd $17,955

SPORTING MODELS
Pigeon . . . . NiB $9980 Ex $6654 Gd $4135
Sporting Clays . . . . NiB $9566 Ex $5760 Gd $4400

TRAP MODELS
Trap Combo, add 30%
Trap Single, add $600
Trap Standard . . . . NiB $10,550 Ex $7677 Gd $4612
Trap Unsingle . . . . NiB $11,880 Ex $9678 Gd $6389
RT models (removable trigger), add $1500

MODEL KS-5 SINGLE-BARREL TRAP
Boxlock w/no sliding top-latch. Adjustable or optional release trigger. Gauge: 12; 2.75-in. chamber. Bbl.: 32-, 34-in. w/fixed choke or screw-in tubes. Weight: 8.5 lbs. Adjustable or Monte Carlo European walnut stock. Blued or nickel receiver. Made 1985-99. Redesigned and streamlined in 1993.

**Krieghoff Model 32
Standard Field Gun**

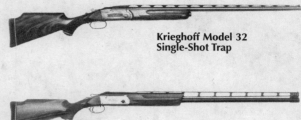

**Krieghoff Model 32
Single-Shot Trap**

**Krieghoff K-80
w/Screw-in Choke Tubes**

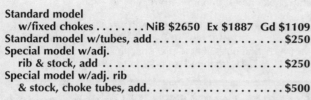

**Krieghoff K-80
Trap Unsingle**

Standard model
w/fixed chokes . . . . NiB $2650 Ex $1887 Gd $1109
Standard model w/tubes, add $250
Special model w/adj.
rib & stock, add $250
Special model w/adj. rib
& stock, choke tubes, add. $500

TRUMPF DRILLING. . . NiB $14,987 Ex $13,677 Gd $10,880
Boxlock. Steel or Dural receiver. Split extractor or ejector
for shotgun bbls. Double triggers. Gauges: 12, 16, 20; latter
w/either 2.75- or 3-in. chambers. Calibers: .243, 6.5x57r5,
7x57r5, 7x65r5, .30-06; other calibers available. 25-in. bbls.
w/solid rib, folding leaf rear sight, post or bead front sight; rifle
bbl. soldered or free floating. Weight: 6.6 to 7.5 lbs. depending
on type of receiver, ga. and caliber. Checkered pistol-grip stock
w/cheekpiece and forearm of figured walnut, sling swivels.
Made 1953-2003.

NEPTUN DRILLING . . . NiB $14,988 Ex $11,987 Gd $9000
Same general specifications as Trumpf model except has sidelocks w/hunting scene engraving. Disc. 2003.

**NEPTUN-PRIMUS
DRILLING. . . . . NiB $19,800 Ex $16,779 Gd $13,980**
Deluxe version of Neptun model; has detachable sidelocks,
higher grade engraving and fancier wood. Disc. 2003.

**TECK O/U
RIFLE-SHOTGUN . . . . NiB $9788 Ex $5780 Gd $4466**
Boxlock. Kersten dble. crossbolt system. Steel or Dural receiver. Split extractor or eject. for shotgun bbl. Single or double
triggers. Gauges: 12, 16, 20; latter w/either 2.75- or 3-in.
chamber. Cal.: .22 Hornet, .222 Rem., .222 Rem. Mag., 7x57r5,
7x64, 7x65r5, .30-30, .300 Win. Mag., .30-06, .308, 9.3x74R.
25-in. bbls. With solid rib, folding leaf rear sight, post or bead
front sight; over bbl. is shotgun, under bbl. rifle (later fixed or
interchangeable; ext. rifle bbl., $175). Wt: 7.9-9.5 lbs. depend-
ing on type of rec. and caliber. Checkered pistol-grip stock w/
cheekpiece and semi-beavertail forearm of fig. walnut, sling
swivels. Made 1967-2004. Note: This comb. gun is similar in
appearance to the same model shotgun.

TECK O/U SHOTGUN . . . . NiB $7354 Ex $5678 Gd $4000
Boxlock. Kersten double crossbolt system. Auto ejector. Single
or double triggers. Gauges: 12, 16, 20; latter w/either 2.75- or
3-in. chambers. 28-in. VR bbl., M/F choke. Weight: About 7
lbs. Checkered walnut pistol-grip stock and forearm. Made
1967-1989.

**ULM O/U
RIFLE-SHOTGUN . . . NiB $16,228 Ex $12,876 Gd $10,336**
Same general specifications as Teck model except has sidelocks
w/leaf Arabesque engraving. Made 1963-2004. Note: This
combination gun is similar in appearance to the same model
shotgun.

ULM O/U SHOTGUN . NiB $13,899 Ex $11,679 Gd $8445
Same general specifications as Teck model except has sidelocks
w/leaf Arabesque engraving. Made 1958-2004.

ULM-P LIVE PIGEON GUN
Sidelock. Gauge: 12. 28- and 30-in. bbls. Chokes: F/IM.
Weight: 8 lbs. Oil-finished, fancy English walnut stock w/semi-
beavertail forearm. Light scrollwork engraving. Tapered, VR.
Made 1983-2004.
Standard . . . . NiB $19,577 Ex $15,890 Gd $11,088
Dural. . . . . NiB $13,776 Ex $11,087 Gd $9459

ULM-PRIMUS O/U . . NiB $19,779 Ex $17,888 Gd $13,090
Deluxe version of Ulm model; detachable sidelocks, higher
grade engraving and fancier wood. Made 1958-2004.

**ULM-PRIMUS O/U
RIFLE-SHOTGUN . . . NiB $21,870 Ex $18,744 Gd $15,877**
Deluxe version of Ulm model; has detachable sidelocks, higher
grade engraving and fancier wood. Made 1963 to 2004. Note:
This combination gun is similar in appearance to the same
model shotgun.

ULM-S SKEET GUN
Sidelock. Gauge: 12. Bbl.: 28-in. Chokes: Skeet/skeet. Other
specifications similar to the Model ULM-P. Made 1983-86.
Bavaria . . . . NiB $13,789 Ex $11,132 Gd $9000
Standard . . . . NiB $1188 Ex $9131 Gd $7330

ULM-P O/U LIVE TRAP GUN
Over/under sidelock. Gauge: 12. 30-in. bbl. Tapered VR.
Chokes: IM/F; optional screw-in choke. Custom grade versions
command a higher price. Disc. 1986.
Bavaria . . . . NiB $18,966 Ex $15,980 Gd $12,776
Standard . . . . NiB $15,660 Ex $13,000 Gd $10,100

**Krieghoff
Neptun Drilling**

SHOTGUNS

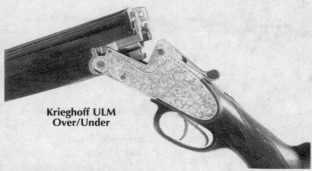

**Krieghoff ULM
Over/Under**

ULTRA TS RIFLE-SHOTGUN
Deluxe Over/Under combination w/25-in. VR bbls. Chambered 12 ga. only and various rifle calibers for lower bbl. Kickspanner design permits cocking w/thumb safety. Satin receiver. Weight: 6 lbs. Made 1985-95 Disc.
Ultra O/U combination . . . NiB $4220 Ex $3670 Gd $2800
Ultra B w/selective front triggerNiB $5589 Ex $4498 Gd $4000

LANBER — Zaldibar, Spain

MODEL 82 O/U SHOTGUN. . . NiB $577 Ex $459 Gd $390
Boxlock. Gauge: 12 or 20; 3-in. chambers. 26- or 28-in. VR bbls. w/ejectors and fixed chokes. Weight: 7 lbs., 2 oz. Double or single-selective trigger. Engraved silvered receiver. Checkered European walnut stock and forearm. Imported 1994.

MODEL 87 DELUXE . . . . NiB $875 Ex $760 Gd $555
Over/Under; boxlock. Single selective trigger. 12 or 20 gauge w/3-in. chambers. Barrels: 26- or 28-in. w/choke tubes. Silvered engraved receiver. Imported 1994 only.

MODEL 97 SPORTING CLAYS . NiB $998 Ex $790 Gd $566
Over/Under; boxlock. Single selective trigger. 12 ga. w/2.75-in. chambers. Bbls: 28-in. w/choke tubes. European walnut stock, forend. Engraved receiver. Imported 1994 only.

**MODEL 844 MST
MAGNUM O/U . . . . NiB $533 Ex $448 Gd $360**
Field grade. Gauge: 12. 3-in. Mag. chambers. 30-in. flat VR bbls. Chokes: M/F. Weight: 7 lbs., 7 oz. Single selective trigger. Blued bbls. and engraved receiver. European walnut stock w/

hand-checkered pistol grip and forend. Imported from 1984 to 1986.

MODEL 2004 LCH O/U . . . . . . NiB $669 Ex $490 Gd $370
Field grade. Gauge: 12. 2.75-in. chambers. 28-in. flat VR bbls. 5 interchangeable choke tubes: Cyl, IC, M, IM, F. Weight: About 7 lbs. Single selective trigger. Engraved silver receiver w/fine-line scroll. Walnut stock w/checkered pistol-grip and forend. Rubber recoil pad. Imported from 1984 to 1986.

MODEL 2004 LCH O/U SKEET. . . NiB $855 Ex $659 Gd $544
Same as Model 2004 LCH except 28-in. bbls. w/5 interchangeable choke tubes. Imported from 1984 to 1986.

MODEL 2004 LCH O/U TRAP. . . NiB $764 Ex $520 Gd $413
Gauge: 12. 30-in. VR bbls. Three interchangeable choke tubes: M, IM, F. Manual safety. Other specifications same as Model 2004 LCH O/U. Imported from 1984 to 1986.

CHARLES LANCASTER — London, England

**"TWELVE-TWENTY" DOUBLE-BARREL
SHOTGUN . . . . NiB $16,788 Ex $14,990 Gd $10,880**
Sidelock, self-opener. Gauge: 12. Bbls.: 24 to 30 in. standard. Weight: About 5.75 lbs. Elaborate metal engraving. Highest quality English or French walnut buttstock and forearm. Imported by Stoeger in the 1950s.

JOSEPH LANG & SONS — London, England

**HIGHEST QUALITY
O/U SHOTGUN . . . . NiB $31,900 Ex $27,678 Gd $20,980**
Sidelock. Gauges: 12, 16, 20, 28 and .410. Bbls.: 25 to 30 in. standard. Highest grade English or French walnut buttstock and forearm. Selective single trigger. Imported by Stoeger in 1950s.

LAURONA — Eibar, Spain

MODEL 300 SERIES
Same general specifications as Model 300 Super Series except supplied w/29-in. over/under bbls. and beavertail forearms. Disc. 1992.
Trap model . . . . NiB $1377 Ex $1190 Gd $921
Sporting Clays model . . . . . NiB $1389 Ex $1440 Gd $1000

**Lanber Model 82
Field Grade**

**Laurona Grand
Trap — GTO**

SILHOUETTE 300 O/U
Boxlock. Single selective trigger. Selective automatic ejectors. Gauge: 12; 2.75-, 3- or 3.5-in. chambers. 28- or 29-in. VR bbls. w/flush or knurled choke tubes. Weight: 7.75 to 8 lbs. Checkered pistol-grip European walnut stock and beavertail forend. Engraved receiver w/silvered finish and black chrome bbls. Made 1988-92.
Model 300 Sporting Clays...NiB $1498 Ex $1277 Gd $900
Model 300 Trap, single.....NiB $1577 Ex $1264 Gd $900
Model 300 Ultra-Magnum .NiB $1599 Ex $1300 Gd $1055

SUPER MODEL O/U SHOTGUNS
Boxlock. Single selective or twin single triggers. Selective automatic ejectors. Gauges: 12 or 20; 2.75- or 3-in. chambers. 26-, 28- or 29-in. VR bbls. w/fixed chokes or screw-in choke tubes. Weight: 7 to 7.25 lbs. Checkered pistol-grip European walnut stock. Engraved receiver w/silvered finish and black chrome bbls. Made 1985-89.
Model 82 Super Game (disc.)..NiB $688 Ex $500 Gd $395
Model 83 MG Super Game...NiB $1090 Ex $800 Gd $707
Model 84 S Super Trap.....NiB $1366 Ex $1150 Gd $986
Model 85 MS Super Game...NiB $1098 Ex $833 Gd $727
Model 85 MS 2-bbl. set....NiB $2200 Ex $1789 Gd $1340
Model 85 MS Special Sporting
** (disc.)................NiB $1390 Ex $1173 Gd $999**
Model 85 MS Super Trap....NiB $1386 Ex $1160 Gd $974
Model 85 MS Pigeon......NiB $1409 Ex $1190 Gd $1034
Model 85 MS Super Skeet..NiB $1409 Ex $1190 Gd $1034

LEBEAU-COURALLY — Liege, Belgium

BOXLOCK SIDE BY-SIDE...NiB $19,000 Ex $15,870 Gd $10,477
Gauges: 12, 16, 20 and 28. 26- to 30-in. bbls. Weight: 6.5 lbs. average. Checkered, hand-rubbed, oil-finished, straight-grip stock of French walnut. Classic forend. Made 1986-88 and 1993.

LEFEVER ARMS COMPANY — Syracuse and Ithaca, NY

NOTE: *Lefever sidelock hammerless double-barrel shotguns were made by Lefever Arms Company of Syracuse, New York from about 1885-1915 (serial numbers 1 to 70,000) when the firm was sold to Ithaca Gun Company of Ithaca, New York. Production of these models was continued at the Ithaca plant until 1919 (serial numbers 70,001 to 72,000). Grades listed are those that appear in the last catalog of the Lefever Gun Company, Syracuse. In 1921, Ithaca introduced the boxlock Lefever Nitro Special double, followed in 1934 by the Lefever Grade A; there also were two single-barrel Lefevers made from 1927-42. Manufacture of Lefever brand shotguns was disc. in 1948. Note: "New Lefever" boxlock shotguns made circa 1904 to 1906 by D. M. Lefever Company, Bowling Green, Ohio, are included in a separate listing.*

GRADE A HAMMERLESS DOUBLE-BARREL SHOTGUN
Boxlock. Plain extractors or auto ejector. Single or double triggers. Gauges: 12, 16, 20, .410. Bbls.: 26-32 in., standard chokes. Weight: About 7 lbs. in 12 ga. Checkered pistol-grip stock and forearm. Made 1934-42.
w/plain extractors,
** double triggers..........NiB $1198 Ex $955 Gd $773**
w/automatic ejector, add......................33%

w/single trigger, add.............................10%
w/Beavertail Forearm, add.......................$100
16 ga., add.....................................25%
20 ga., add.....................................80%
.410 ga., add..................................200%

GRADE A SKEET MODEL
Same as A Grade except standard features include auto ejector, single trigger, beavertail forearm; 26-in. bbls., skeet boring. Disc. 1942.
A Grade Skeet model, 12 ga...NiB $1699 Ex $1188 Gd $880
16 ga., add.....................................40%
20 ga., add.....................................80%
.410 ga., add..................................200%

HAMMERLESS SINGLE-SHOT
TRAP GUN.................NiB $766 Ex $600 Gd $477
Boxlock. Ejector. 12 ga. only. 26- or 32-in. bbl.; Full choke. Weight: About 8 lbs. Checkered pistol-grip stock. Auto ejector; boxlock. Made 1904-06. Rare.

LONG RANGE HAMMERLESS
SINGLE-BARREL FIELD GUN..NiB $500 Ex $394 Gd $277
Boxlock. Plain extractor. Gauges: 12, 16, 20, .410. Bbl. lengths: 26-32 in. Weight: 5.5 to 7 lbs. depending on ga. and bbl. length. Checkered pistol-grip stock and forend. Made 1927-42.

NITRO SPECIAL HAMMERLESS DOUBLE
Boxlock. Plain extractors. Single or double triggers. Gauges: 12, 16, 20, .410. Bbls.: 26- to 32-in., standard chokes. Weight: about 7 lbs. in 12 ga. Checkered pistol-grip stock and forend. Made 1921-48.
Nitro Special w/double triggers...NiB $855 Ex $522 Gd $377
Nitro Special W/single trigger .NiB $933 Ex $654 Gd $433
16 ga., add.....................................25%
20 ga., add.....................................50%
.410 ga., add..................................200%

SIDELOCK HAMMERLESS DOUBLES
Plain extractors or auto ejectors. Boxlock. Double triggers or selective single trigger. Gauges: 10, 12, 16, 20. Bbls.: 26-32 in.; standard choke combinations. Weight: 5.75 to 10.5 lbs. depending on ga. and bbl. length. Checkered walnut straight-grip or pistol-grip stock and forearm. Grades differ chiefly in quality of workmanship, engraving, wood, checkering, etc.; general specifications are the same. DS and DSE Grade guns lack the cocking indicators found on all other models. Suffix "E" means model has auto ejector; also standard on A, AA, Optimus, and Thousand Dollar Grade guns.
H grade.................NiB $2266 Ex $1770 Gd $1480
HE grade ....NiB $3270 Ex $2266 Gd $1780
G grade ....NiB $2288 Ex $1998 Gd $1440
GE grade ....NiB $3388 Ex $2771 Gd $1880
F grade ....NiB $2566 Ex $1966 Gd $1276
FE grade ....NiB $3360 Ex $2770 Gd $1866
E grade ....NiB $3790 Ex $2690 Gd $2210
EE grade ....NiB $5750 Ex $3880 Gd $2547
D grade.................NiB $4980 Ex $3777 Gd $2869
DE grade................NiB $7132 Ex $4971 Gd $4111
DS grade................NiB $1754 Ex $1530 Gd $1129
DSE grade...............NiB $2184 Ex $1788 Gd $1290
C grade.................NiB $7443 Ex $4270 Gd $2988
CE grade................NiB $9112 Ex $8445 Gd $6110
B grade ....NiB $10,500 Ex $8667 Gd $6330
BE grade ....NiB $10,580 Ex $8777 Gd $6580
A grade.............. NiB $19,880 Ex $17,900 Gd $16,888

SHOTGUNS

**Lefever A Grade
Hammerless Double-Barrel Shotgun**

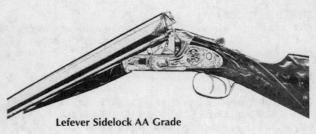

Lefever Sidelock AA Grade

AA grade. . . . . NiB $28,566 Ex $23,667 Gd $21,876
Optimus grade . . . . . NiB $47,900 Ex $42,870 Gd $37,980
Thousand Dollar gradeNiB $78,980 Ex $46,888 Gd $36,890
w/single trigger, add. 10%
10 ga., add 15%
16 ga., add 45%
20 ga., add 90%

D. M. LEFEVER COMPANY — Bowling Green, OH

NOTE: *In 1901, D. M. "Uncle Dan" Lefever, founder of the Lefever Arms Company, withdrew from that firm to organize D. M. Lefever, Sons & Company (later D. M. Lefever Company) to manufacture the "New Lefever" boxlock double- and single-barrel shotguns. These were produced at Bowling Green, Ohio, from about 1904-06, when Dan Lefever died and the factory closed permanently. Grades listed are those that appear in the last catalog of D. M. Lefever Co.*

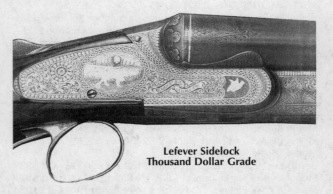

**Lefever Sidelock
Thousand Dollar Grade**

HAMMERLESS DOUBLE-BARREL SHOTGUNS

"New Lefever." Boxlock. Auto ejector standard on all grades except O Excelsior, which was regularly supplied w/plain extractors (auto ejector offered as an extra). Double triggers or selective single trigger (latter standard on Uncle Dan Grade, extra on all others). Gauges: 12, 16, 20. Bbls.: Any length and choke combination. Weight: 5.5 to 8 lbs. depending on ga. and bbl. length. Checkered walnut straight-grip or pistol-grip stock and forearm. Grades differ chiefly in quality of workmanship, engraving, wood, checkering, etc. General specifications are the same.

O Excelsior grade w/plain
    extractors . . . . NiB $2889 Ex $2255 Gd $1989
O Excelsior grade w/automatic
    ejectors. . . . . NiB $3244 Ex $2990 Gd $2469
No. 9, F grade. . . . . NiB $3277 Ex $2929 Gd $2240
No. 8, E grade. . . . . NiB $4240 Ex $3888 Gd $2377
No. 7, D grade . . . . NiB $5277 Ex $4766 Gd $3698
No. 6, C grade . . . . NiB $7000 Ex $4590 Gd $3667
No. 5, B grade . . . . NiB $6722 Ex $4588 Gd $3292
No. 4, AA grade . . . . NiB $10,770 Ex $8857 Gd $5497
Uncle Dan grade. . . . . Very rare: $165,000+
w/single trigger, add. 10%
16 ga., add 45%
20 ga., add 15%

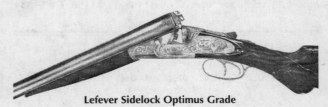

Lefever Sidelock Optimus Grade

D. M. LEFEVER SINGLE-BARREL TRAP GUN

Boxlock. Auto ejector. 12 ga. only. Bbls.: 26- to 32 in., F choke. Weight: 6.5 to 8 lbs. depending on bbl. length. Checkered walnut pistol-grip stock and forearm. Made 1904-06. Extremely rare.

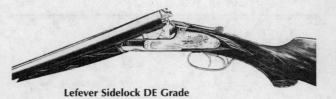

Lefever Sidelock DE Grade

LEGACY SPORTS — Reno, NV

Importer of a variety of shotgun brands including Escort (mfg. Hatsan Arms Co., in Izmir, Turkey), Pointer, Verona (mfg. F.A.I.R., Faust or Piette in Italy).

Lefever Sidelock Sideplate BE Grade

Lefever Sidelock Sideplate CE Grade

**Magtech Model 586.2
Slide-Action**

ESCORT O/U SERIES.

O/U. Boxlock action. Gauge: 12 only. Bbl.: 28-in. VR w/5 choke tubes and extractors. Stock: Walnut or synthetic. Imported 2007 to 2015.

w/synthetic stock . . . . NiB $555 Ex $430 Gd $320
w/wood stock . . . . NiB $655 Ex $530 Gd $420
**Shorty Home Defense (18-in. bbl.; synthetic stock,
    2011-15)**. . . . . NiB $580 Ex $455 Gd $330

ESCORT PUMP/SLIDE ACTION SERIES.

Pump/slide action. Gauge: 12 or 20, 3-in. chamber. Bbl.: 26- or 28-in. VR w/3 choke tubes. Stock: Walnut or synthetic. Imported 2015 to date.

M87 (walnut stock) . . . . NiB $305 Ex $230 Gd $180
**Aimguard (18-in. bbl. w/fixed cyl. bore choke, synthetic
    stock)** . . . . NiB $270 Ex $200 Gd $155
**Field Hunter (black synthetic stock, black or camo finish,
    disc. 2015)** . . . . NiB $330 Ex $255 Gd $205
**Gladius Home Defense (20 ga., 18-in. bbl.
    w/muzzle brake, ghost ring sights, synthetic
    pistol-grip stock)**. . . . . NiB $440 Ex $280 Gd $230
**Marine Guard (18-in. bbl. w/fixed cyl. bore choke, synthetic
    stock, nickel receiver)**. . . . . . NiB $340 Ex $270 Gd $220
**MP Tactical (18-in. bbl. w/fixed cyl. bore choke, synthetic
    pistol-grip stock)** . . . . NiB $355 Ex $280 Gd $230
**Standard Magnum (3.5-in. chamber, synthetic stock w/shim
    system)** . . . . NiB $340 Ex $270 Gd $220

ESCORT SEMIAUTOMATIC SERIES.

Semiauto. Gas-operated action. Gauge: 12 or 20, 3-in. chamber. Bbl.: 20-, 22-, 24-, 26- or 28-in. VR w/3 choke tubes. Stock: Walnut or synthetic. Finish: blued or various camo patterns. Imported 2002 to 2013.

w/synthetic stock . . . . NiB $405 Ex $320 Gd $255
w/wood stock . . . . NiB $505 Ex $420 Gd $355
**Aimguard (18- or 20-in. bbl., synthetic stock, black chrome
    finish, 2004-07)** . . . . NiB $345 Ex $280 Gd $235
**Extreme Magnum (28-in. VR bbl. w/5 Hevi-Shot choke tubes,
    black synthetic stock, SMART value self regulating gas
    system)** . . . . NiB $505 Ex $390 Gd $300
**Extreme Magnum 3.5-in. (12 ga., 3.5-in.
    chamber)** . . . . NiB $595 Ex $470 Gd $360
**Gladius Home Defense model (12 or 20 ga., 18-in. bbl. w/
    fixed cal. bore, ghost ring sights, synthetic pistol-grip
    stock)** . . . . NiB $530 Ex $410 Gd $320
**MP Tactical (12 or 20 ga., 3-in. chamber, synthetic
    pistol-grip stock)**. . . . . NiB $480 Ex $370 Gd $280
**Standard Magnum (26- or 28-in. VR bbl. w/3 tubes,
    black synthetic stock, FAST loading
    system)** . . . . NiB $430 Ex $330 Gd $255
**Supreme Magnum (26- or 28-in. VR bbl. w/5 choke
    tubes, black synthetic stock, SMART value
    self regulating gas system, FAST loading
    system)** . . . . NiB $570 Ex $450 Gd $340
**Turkey/Coyote Tactical (24-in. VR bbl. w/full choke tube,
    camo synthetic pistol grip stock, FAST loading system,
    2013-15)**. . . . . NiB $600 Ex $470 Gd $360

**Waterfowl/Turkey Combo (24-in. VR bbl. w/TriViz sights and
    28-in. VR bbl. w/HiViz sight, synthetic stock, 2003-08
    and 2010-11)** . . . . NiB $570 Ex $450 Gd $340
**Yote (12 or 20 a., 22-in. VR bbl. w/3 choke tubes,
    camo synthetic stock, SMART value self regulating
    gas system)** . . . . NiB $505 Ex $390 Gd $300

POINTER O/U SERIES

O/U. Boxlock action. Gauge: 12, 20, 28 or 410. Stock: Checkered walnut. Single trigger. Extractors or ejectors. Finish: blue or nickel engraved.

**1000 Field (wood stock,
    blue finish)** . . . . NiB $580 Ex $430 Gd $330
**Clays (28- or 30-in. bbl. walnut
    stock)** . . . . NiB $865 Ex $645 Gd $475
**Italian Sporting/Field (nickel receiver,
    2007-08)**. . . . . NiB $1155 Ex $880 Gd $630

POINTER PUMP/SLIDE ACTION SERIES.

Pump/slide action. Gauge: 12 or 20, 3-in. chamber. Bbl.: 28-in. VR w/3 choke tubes. Stock: Black synthetic.

**Slug Combo (24-in. rifled bbl. and 28-in.
    VR bbl., black synthetic stock, matte
    black finish)** . . . . NiB $530 Ex $400 Gd $300
**Standard (28-in. VR bbl., black synthetic stock, matte black
    finish, disc. 2015)** . . . . NiB $355 Ex $270 Gd $200

POINTER SEMIAUTO SERIES.

Semiauto. Gas-operated action. Gauge: 12, 20 or 28. Bbl.: 28-in. VR w/5 choke tubes. Magazine cutoff. Stock: Walnut, laminate or synthetic. Finish: blued or various camo patterns.

w/laminate stock . . . . NiB $700 Ex $550 Gd $430
w/synthetic stock . . . . NiB $530 Ex $400 Gd $300
w/wood stock . . . . NiB $600 Ex $450 Gd $330
Camo (camo finish). . . . . NiB $580 Ex $430 Gd $320
**Deluxe (matte black or camo
    finish)** . . . . NiB $580 Ex $430 Gd $320
**Slug Combo (24-in. rifled bbl. and 28-in. VR bbl.,
    black synthetic stock, matte black
    finish)** . . . . NiB $650 Ex $490 Gd $360

POINTER SINGLE SHOT. . . . . . . NiB $165 Ex $125 Gd $95
Break action. Gauge: 12, 20 or 410. Stock: black synthetic. Exposed hammer. Finish: Matte black.

MAGTECH — San Antonio, TX

Manufactured by CBC in Brazil.

MODEL 586-2 SLIDE-ACTION SHOTGUN

Gauge: 12; 3-in. chamber. 19-, 26- or 28-in. bbl.; fixed chokes or integral tubes. 46.5 in. overall. Weight: 8.5 lbs. Double-action slide bars. Brazilian hardwood stock. Polished blued finish. Imported 1992 to 1995.

**Model 586.2F (28-in. bbl.,
    fixed choke)** . . . . NiB $288 Ex $147 Gd $100
**Model 586.2P (19-in. plain
    bbl., cyl. bore)** . . . . NiB $244 Ex $165 Gd $99

GRADING: **NiB** = New in Box   **Ex** = Excellent or NRA 95%   **Gd** = Good or NRA 68%

SHOTGUNS

Model 586.2 S (24-in. bbl.,
rifle sights, cyl. bore) . . . . NiB $290 Ex $155 Gd $125
Model 586.2 VR (VR w/tubes) . . . . . . NiB $275 Ex $198 Gd $135

MARLIN FIREARMS CO. — North Haven, CT

*Formerly New Haven, CT. In 2000 Marlin purchase H&R
1871 (New England Firearms), in 2007 Marlin was purchased
by the Freedom Group and in 2010. Currently no shotguns
are manufactured nor branded Marlin.*

MODEL 16 VISIBLE HAMMER SLIDE-ACTION REPEATER
Takedown. 16 ga. Five round tubular magazine. Bbls.: 26- or
28-in., standard chokes. Weight: About 6.25 lbs. Pistol-grip
stock, grooved slide handle; checkering on higher grades.
Difference among grades is in quality of wood, engraving on
Grades C and D. Made 1904-10.
Grade A . . . . NiB $400 Ex $322 Gd $297
Grade B . . . . NiB $590 Ex $477 Gd $388
Grade C . . . . NiB $722 Ex $466 Gd $388
Grade D . . . . NiB $1496 Ex $1377 Gd $947

MODEL 17 BRUSH GUN . . . . . NiB $389 Ex $297 Gd $190
Same as Model 17 Standard except has 26-in. bbl., cylinder
bore. Weight: About 7 lbs. Made 1906-1908.

MODEL 17 RIOT GUN. . . . . . . NiB $480 Ex $308 Gd $200
Same as Model 17 Standard except has 20-in. bbl., cylinder
bore. Weight: About 6.88 lbs. Made 1906-08.

MODEL 17 STANDARD VISIBLE HAMMER
SLIDE-ACTION REPEATER . . . . NiB $422 Ex $290 Gd $188
Solid frame.12 ga. Five round tubular magazine. Bbls.: 30- or
32-in., F choke. Weight: About 7.5 lbs. Straight-grip stock,
grooved slide handle. Made 1906-08.

MODEL 19 VISIBLE HAMMER SLIDE-ACTION REPEATER
Similar to Model 1898 but improved, lighter weight, w/two
extractors, matted sighting groove on receiver top. Weight:
About 7 lbs. Made 1906-07.
Grade A . . . . NiB $466 Ex $390 Gd $277
Grade B . . . . NiB $566 Ex $448 Gd $339
Grade C . . . . NiB $744 Ex $390 Gd $244
Grade D . . . . NiB $1396 Ex $1087 Gd $944

MODEL 21 TRAP VISIBLE HAMMER
SLIDE-ACTION REPEATER
Similar to Model 19 w/same general specifications except has
straight-grip stock. Made 1907-09.
Grade A . . . . NiB $433 Ex $290 Gd $197
Grade B . . . . NiB $580 Ex $450 Gd $344
Grade C . . . . NiB $788 Ex $590 Gd $445
Grade D . . . . NiB $1488 Ex $1116 Gd $977

MODEL 24 VISIBLE HAMMER SLIDE-ACTION REPEATER
Similar to Model 19 but has improved takedown system and
auto recoil safety lock, solid matted rib on frame. Weight:
About 7.5 lbs. Made 1908-15.
Grade A . . . . NiB $376 Ex $190 Gd $112
Grade B . . . . NiB $448 Ex $277 Gd $156
Grade C . . . . NiB $766 Ex $500 Gd $410
Grade D . . . . NiB $1500 Ex $1399 Gd $1177

MODEL 26
BRUSH GUN . . . . NiB $388 Ex $270 Gd $135
Same as Model 26 Standard except has 26-in. bbl., cylinder
bore. Weight: About 7 lbs. Made 1909-15.

MODEL 26 RIOT GUN. . . . . . . NiB $360 Ex $266 Gd $131
Same as Model 26 Standard except has 20-in. bbl., cylinder bore. Weight: About 6.88 lbs. Made 1909-15.

MODEL 26 STANDARD VISIBLE HAMMER
SLIDE-ACTION REPEATER . . . . NiB $366 Ex $298 Gd $199
Similar to Model 24 Grade A except solid frame and straight-
grip stock. 30- or 32-in. full choke bbl. Weight: About 7.13 lbs.
Made 1909-15.

MODEL 28 HAMMERLESS SLIDE-ACTION REPEATER
Takedown. 12 ga. Five round tubular magazine. Bbls.: 26-, 28-,
30-, 32-in., standard chokes; matted-top bbl. except on Model
28D, which has solid matted rib. Weight: About 8 lbs. Pistol-
grip stock, grooved slide handle; checkering on higher grades.
Grades differ in quality of wood, engraving on Models 28C and
28D. Made 1913-22; all but Model 28A disc. in 1915.
Model 28A . . . . NiB $433 Ex $288 Gd $165
Model 28B . . . . NiB $577 Ex $458 Gd $313
Model 28C . . . . NiB $755 Ex $544 Gd $340
Model 28D . . . . NiB $1480 Ex $1198 Gd $955

MODEL 28T TRAP GUN. . . . . . NiB $789 Ex $566 Gd $449
Same as Model 28 except has 30-in. matted-rib bbl., Full
choke, straight-grip stock w/high-fluted comb of fancy walnut,
checkered. Made in 1915.

MODEL 28TS TRAP GUN. . . . . NiB $588 Ex $400 Gd $378
Same as Model 28T except has matted-top bbl., plainer stock.
Made in 1915.

MODEL 30 FIELD GUN . . . . . . NiB $466 Ex $355 Gd $245
Same as Model 30 Grade B except has 25-in. bbl., M choke,
straight-grip stock. Made 1913-14.

MODEL 30 VISIBLE HAMMER SLIDE-ACTION REPEATER
Similar to Model 16 but w/Model 24 improvements. Made
1910-14. See illustration next page.
Grade A . . . . NiB $460 Ex $388 Gd $210
Grade B . . . . NiB $660 Ex $433 Gd $309
Grade C . . . . NiB $777 Ex $566 Gd $363
Grade D . . . . NiB $1488 Ex $1177 Gd $1065

MODELS 30A, 30B, 30C, 30D
Same as Model 30; designations were changed in 1915. Also
available in 20 ga. w/25- or 28-in. bbl., matted-top bbl. on all
grades. Suffixes "A," "B," "C" and "D" correspond to former
grades. Made in 1915.
Model 30A . . . . NiB $412 Ex $290 Gd $188
Model 30B . . . . NiB $576 Ex $445 Gd $310
Model 30C . . . . NiB $756 Ex $554 Gd $39
Model 30D . . . . NiB $1421 Ex $1131 Gd $1070

MODEL 31 STANDARD VISIBLE HAMMER
SLIDE-ACTION REPEATER . . . . NiB $366 Ex $298 Gd $199
Similar to Model 24 Grade A except solid frame and straight-
grip stock. 30- or 32-in. full choke bbl. Weight: About 7.13 lbs.
Made 1909-15.
Model 31A . . . . NiB $476 Ex $355 Gd $254
Model 31B . . . . NiB $598 Ex $455 Gd $389
Model 31C . . . . NiB $766 Ex $644 Gd $490
Model 31D . . . . NiB $1498 Ex $1154 Gd $990

MODEL 31F FIELD GUN . . . . . NiB $488 Ex $366 Gd $271
Same as Model 31B except has 25-in. bbl., M choke, straight-
or pistol-grip stock. Made 1915-17.

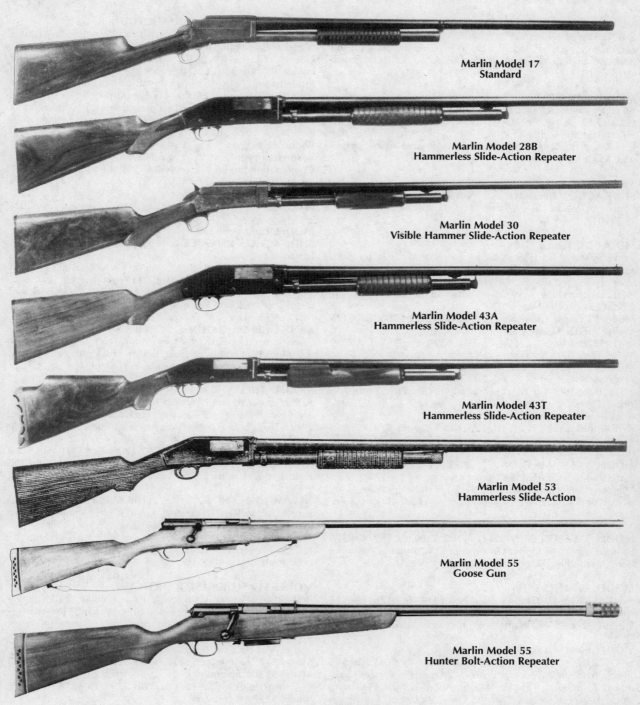

Marlin Model 17
Standard

Marlin Model 28B
Hammerless Slide-Action Repeater

Marlin Model 30
Visible Hammer Slide-Action Repeater

Marlin Model 43A
Hammerless Slide-Action Repeater

Marlin Model 43T
Hammerless Slide-Action Repeater

Marlin Model 53
Hammerless Slide-Action

Marlin Model 55
Goose Gun

Marlin Model 55
Hunter Bolt-Action Repeater

SHOTGUNS

**MODEL 42A VISIBLE HAMMER
SLIDE-ACTION REPEATER . . . . NiB $498 Ex $366 Gd $288**
Similar to pre-World War I Model 24 Grade A w/same general
specifications but not as high quality. Made 1922-34.

MODEL 43 HAMMERLESS SLIDE-ACTION REPEATER
Similar to pre-World War I Models 28A, 28T and 28TS, w/same
general specifications but not as high quality. Made 1923-30.

Model 43A . . . . NiB $355 Ex $200 Gd $144
Model 43TS . . . . NiB $665 Ex $400 Gd $228

MODEL 44 HAMMERLESS SLIDE-ACTION REPEATER
Similar to pre-World War I Model 31A w/same general specifications but not as high quality. 20 ga. only. Model 44A is a
standardgrade field gun. Model 44S Special Grade has checkered stock and slide handle of fancy walnut. Made 1923-35.

Model 44A . . . . NiB $466 Ex $381 Gd $222
Model 44S . . . . NiB $622 Ex $476 Gd $338

GRADING: **NiB** = New in Box   **Ex** = Excellent or NRA 95%   **Gd** = Good or NRA 68%

MODEL 49 VISIBLE HAMMER SLIDE-ACTION REPEATING
SHOTGUN . . . . **NiB $566 Ex $449 Gd $367**
Economy version of Model 42A, offered as a bonus on the purchase of four shares of Marlin stock. About 3000 made 1925 to 1928.

MODEL 50DL BOLT
ACTION SHOTGUN . . . . **NiB $388 Ex $229 Gd $131**
Gauge: 12 w/3-in. chamber. Two round magazine. 28-in. bbl. w/modified choke. 48.75 in. overall. Weight: 7.5 lbs. Checkered black synthetic stocks w/ventilated rubber recoil pad. Made 1997-1999.

MODEL 53 HAMMERLESS
SLIDE-ACTION REPEATER . . . . **NiB $480 Ex $200 Gd $144**
Similar to Model 43A w/same general specifications. Made 1929-30.

MODEL 55 GOOSE GUN
Same as Model 55 Hunter except chambered for 12-ga. 3-in. Magnum shell, has 36-in. bbl., F choke, swivels and sling. Weight: About 8 lbs. Walnut stock (standard model) or checkered black synthetic stock w/ventilated rubber recoil pad (GDL model). Made 1962-96.
Model 55 Goose Gun . . . . NiB $335 Ex $266 Gd $195
Model 55GDL Goose Gun
   (1997-2000)) . . . . NiB $398 Ex $297 Gd $239

MODEL 55 HUNTER BOLT-ACTION REPEATER
Takedown. Gauges: 12, 16, 20. Two round clip magazine. 28-in. bbl. (26-in. in 20 ga.), F or adj. choke. Plain pistol-grip stock; 12 ga. has recoil pad. Weight: About 7.25 lbs.; 20 ga., 6.5 lbs. Made 1954-65.
w/plain bbl. . . . . NiB $120 Ex $70 Gd $50
w/adj. choke . . . . NiB $155 Ex $99 Gd $75

MODEL 55 SWAMP GUN . . . . . NiB $225 Ex $179 Gd $90
Same as Model 55 Hunter except chambered for 12-ga. 3-in. Magnum shell, has shorter 20.5-in. bbl. w/adj. choke, sling swivels and slightly better-quality stock. Weight: About 6.5 lbs. Made 1963-65.

MODEL 55S SLUG GUN . . . . NiB $200 Ex $99 Gd $75
Same as Model 55 Goose Gun except has 24-in. bbl., cylinder bore, rifle sights. Weight: About 7.5 lbs. Made 1974-79.

MODEL 59 AUTO-SAFE
BOLT-ACTION SINGLE . . . . **NiB $244 Ex $176 Gd $95**
Takedown. Auto thumb safety, .410 ga. 24-in. bbl., F choke. Weight: About 5 lbs. Plain pistol-grip stock. Made 1959-1961.

MODEL 60 SINGLE-SHOT
SHOTGUN . . . . **NiB $210 Ex $145 Gd $95**
Visible hammer. Takedown. Boxlock. Automatic ejector. 12 ga. 30- or 32-in. bbl., F choke. Weight: About 6.5 lbs. Pistol-grip stock, beavertail forearm. Note: Only about 600 were produced in 1923.

MODEL 63 HAMMERLESS SLIDE-ACTION REPEATER
Similar to Models 43A and 43T w/same general specifications. Model 63TS Trap Special is same as Model 63T Trap Gun except stock style and dimensions to order. Made 1931-35.
Model 63A . . . . NiB $466 Ex $355 Gd $200
Model 63T or 63TS . . . . NiB $484 Ex $355 Gd $241

MODEL 90 STANDARD O/U SHOTGUN
Hammerless. Boxlock. Double triggers; non-selective single trigger was available as an extra on pre-war guns except .410. Gauges: 12, 16, 20, .410. Bbls.: Plain; 26-, 28- or 30-in.; chokes IC/M or M/F; bbl. designchanged in 1949, eliminating full-length rib between bbls. Weight: 12 ga., about 7.5 lbs.; 16 and 20 ga., about 6.25 lbs. Checkered pistol-grip stock and forearm, recoil pad standard on prewar guns. Postwar production: Model 90-DT (double trigger), Model 90-ST (single trigger). Made 1937-58.
w/double triggers . . . . NiB $566 Ex $400 Gd $245
w/single trigger . . . . NiB $670 Ex $555 Gd $435
Combination model . . . . . . NiB $2879 Ex $1976 Gd $1777
16 ga., deduct 10%
20 ga., add 15%
.410, add 30%

MODEL 120 MAGNUM
SLIDE-ACTION REPEATER . . . . **NiB $354 Ex $230 Gd $155**
Hammerless. Takedown. 12 ga. (3-in.). Four round tubular magazine. Bbls.: 26-in. VR, IC; 28-in. VR M choke; 30-in. VR, F choke; 38-in. plain, F choke; 40-in. plain, F choke; 26-in. slug bbl. w/rifle sights, IC. Weight: About 7.75 lbs. Checkered pistol-grip stock and forearm, recoil pad. Made 1971-85.

MODEL 120 SLUG GUN . . . . . NiB $344 Ex $265 Gd $175
Same general specifications as Model 120 Magnum except w/20-in. bbl. and about .5 lb. lighter in weight. No VR. Adj. rear rifle sights; hooded front sight. Disc. 1990.

MODEL .410 LEVER-ACTION REPEATER
Action similar to that of Marlin Model 93 rifle. Visible hammer. Solid frame. .410 ga. (2.5-in. shell). Five round tubular magazine. 22- or 26-in. bbl., F choke. Weight: About 6 lbs. Plain pistol-grip stock and grooved beavertail forearm. Made 1929-32.
w/22-in. bbl. . . . . NiB $2200 Ex $1310 Gd $890
w/26-in. bbl. . . . . NiB $1800 Ex $1110 Gd $750
Deluxe model, add 30%

NEW MODEL .410 . . . . NiB $550 Ex $405 Gd $340
Similar to Model .410 Lever Action. Visible hammer w/ hammer block safety. Solid frame. .410 ga. (2.5-in. shell). 4- or 5-rnd. tubular magazine. 22-in. bbl. w/ full choke. Weight: 9.5 lbs. Stock: checkered black American walnut. Sight: green fiber optic front. Made 2004-05.

MODEL 512 SLUGMASTER SHOTGUN
Bolt-action repeater. Gauge: 12; 3-in. chamber, 2-rnd. magazine. 21-in. rifled bbl. w/adj. open sight. Weight: 8 lbs. Walnut-finished birch stock (standard model) or checkered black synthetic stock w/ventilated rubber recoil pad (GDL model). Made 1994-99.
Model 512 Slugmaster . . . . NiB $466 Ex $338 Gd $243
Model 512DL Slugmaster
   (intro. 1998) . . . . NiB $390 Ex $278 Gd $176
Model 512P Slugmaster
   w/ported bbl. (intro. 1999) . NiB $447 Ex $366 Gd $260

MODEL 1898 VISIBLE HAMMER REPEATER
Slide/pump action. Takedown. 12 ga. Five shell tubular magazine. Bbls.: 26-, 28-, 30-, 32-in.; standard chokes. Weight: About 7.25 lbs. Pistol-grip stock, grooved slide handle; checkering on higher grades. Difference among grades is in quality of wood, engraving on Grades C and D. Made 1898-1905. Note: This was the first Marlin shotgun.

Marlin Model 55
Swap Gun

Marlin Model 59
Bolt-Action Single

Marlin Model 60
Single Shot

Marlin Model 90
Standard Over-and-Under

SHOTGUNS

Marlin Model 120
Magnum Slide-Action Repeater

Marlin Model 410
Lever-Action Repeater

Marlin Model 512
Slugmaster

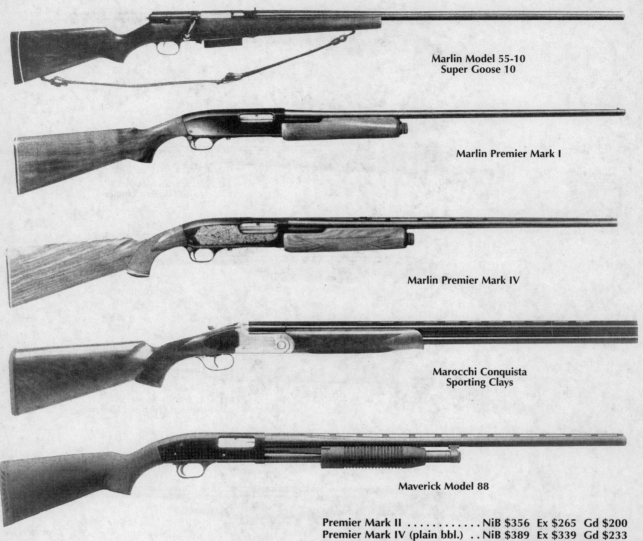

Marlin Model 55-10
Super Goose 10

Marlin Premier Mark I

Marlin Premier Mark IV

Marocchi Conquista
Sporting Clays

Maverick Model 88

Premier Mark II . . . . NiB $356 Ex $265 Gd $200
Premier Mark IV (plain bbl.) . . NiB $389 Ex $339 Gd $233
Premier Mark IV (VR bbl.) . . . . NiB $400 Ex $370 Gd $280

Grade A (Field) . . . . NiB $387 Ex $270 Gd $190
Grade B . . . . NiB $558 Ex $400 Gd $294
Grade C . . . . NiB $700 Ex $554 Gd $449
Grade D . . . . NiB $2170 Ex $1799 Gd $954

MODEL 55-10 SUPER
GOOSE . . . . NiB $292 Ex $225 Gd $179
Similar to Model 55 Goose Gun except chambered for 10 ga.
3.5-in. Magnum shell, has 34-in. heavy bbl., F choke. Weight:
About 10.5 lbs. Made 1976-85.

PREMIER MARK I
SLIDE-ACTION REPEATER . . . . NiB $255 Ex $198 Gd $110
Hammerless. Takedown. 12 ga. Magazine holds 3 shells. Bbls.:
30-in. F choke, 28-in. M, 26-in. IC or SK choke. Weight: About
6 lbs. Plain pistol-grip stock and forearm. Made in France from
1960-63.

PREMIER MARK II & IV
Same action and mechanism as Premier Mark except engraved
receiver (Mark IV is more elaborate), checkered stock and
forearm, fancier wood, VR and similar refinements. Made
1960-63.

NOTE: *In 1960 Marlin began marketing inexpensive rifles and
shotguns under the Glenfield name.*

GLENFIELD MODEL 50
BOLT-ACTION REPEATER . . . . . NiB $320 Ex $255 Gd $175
Similar to Model 55 Hunter except chambered for 12-or
20-ga., 3-in. Magnum shell; has 28-in. bbl. in 12 ga., 26-in. in
20 ga., F choke. Made 1966-74.

GLENFIELD 778 SLIDE-ACTION
REPEATER . . . . NiB $325 Ex $255 Gd $180
Hammerless. 12 ga. 2.75-in. or 3-in. Four round tubular
magazine. Bbls.: 26-in. IC, 28-in. M, 30-in. F, 38-in. MXR,
20-in. slug bbl. Weight: 7.75 lbs. Checkered pistol-grip. Made
1979-84.

MAROCCHI — Brescia, Italy
Imported by Precision Sales International of Westfield, MA.

CONQUISTA MODEL O/U SHOTGUN
Boxlock. Gauge: 12; 2.75-in. chambers. 28-, 30- or 32-in.
VR bbl. Fixed choke or internal tubes. 44.38 to 48 in. over-

all. Weight: 7.5 to 8.25 lbs. Adj. single-selective trigger. Checkered American walnut stock w/recoil pad. Imported 1994 to 2003.

Lady Sport Grade I	NiB $1978	Ex $1754	Gd $1288
Lady Sport Grade II	NiB $2144	Ex $1788	Gd $1488
Lady Sport Grade III	NiB $3577	Ex $2875	Gd $2290
Skeet Model Grade I	NiB $1895	Ex $1544	Gd $1154
Skeet Model Grade II	NiB $2250	Ex $1863	Gd $1455
Skeet Model Grade III	NiB $3598	Ex $3210	Gd $2240
Sporting Clays Grade I	NiB $1890	Ex $1669	Gd $1275
Sporting Clays Grade II	NiB $2200	Ex $1790	Gd $1376
Sporting Clays Grade III	NiB $3550	Ex $2977	Gd $2169
Trap Model Grade I	NiB $1890	Ex $1588	Gd $1300
Trap Model Grade II	NiB $2170	Ex $1877	Gd $1470
Trap Model Grade III	NiB $3588	Ex $3120	Gd $2260
Left-handed model, add			10%

MAVERICK ARMS, INC. — Eagle Pass, TX
Ditrubuted by O.F. Mossberg.

MODEL 88 BULLPUP . . . . NiB $265 Ex $190 Gd $110
Gauge: 12; 3-in. chamber. Bbl.: 18.5-in. w/fixed choke, blued. Weight: 9.5 lbs. Dual safeties: Grip style and crossbolt. Fixed sights in carrying handle. High-impact black synthetic stock; trigger-forward bullpup configuration w/twin pistol-grip design. Made 1990-95.

MODEL 88 DEER GUN. . . . . . NiB $377 Ex $241 Gd $176
Crossbolt safety and dual slide bars. Cylinder bore choke. Gauge: 12 only w/3-in. chamber. Bbl.: 24-in. Weight: 7 lbs. Synthetic stock and forearm. Disc. 1995.

MODEL 88 PUMP SHOTGUN
Gauge: 12; 2.75- or 3-in. chamber. Bbl.: 28 in./M or 30 in./F w/fixed choke or screw-in integral tubes; plain or VR, blued. Weight: 7.25 lbs. Bead front sight. Black synthetic or wood buttstock and forend; forend grooved. Made from 1989 to date.
Synthetic stock w/plain bbl.	NiB $287	Ex $228	Gd $175
Synthetic stock w/VR bbl.	NiB $300	Ex $238	Gd $195
Synthetic Combo w/18.5- in. bbl.	NiB $321	Ex $220	Gd $184
Wood stock w/VR bbl./tubes	NiB $300	Ex $225	Gd $179
Wood Combo w/VR bbl./tubes	NiB $255	Ex $200	Gd $162

MODEL 88 SECURITY . . . . NiB $275 Ex $190 Gd $145
Crossbolt safety and dual slide bars. Optional heat shield. Cylinder bore choke. Gauge: 12 only w/3-in. chamber. Bbl.: 18.5-in. Weight: 6 lbs., 8 oz. Synthetic stock and forearm. Made from 1993 to date.

MODEL 91 PUMP SHOTGUN
Same as Model 88, except w/2.75-, 3- or 3.5-in. chamber, 28-in. bbl. W/ACCU-F choke, crossbolt safety and synthetic stock only. Made 1991-95.
Synthetic stock w/plain bbl.	NiB $330	Ex $256	Gd $180
Synthetic stock w/VR bbl.	NiB $335	Ex $270	Gd $195

MODEL 95 BOLT-ACTION . . . . NiB $255 Ex $190 Gd $140
Modified, fixed choke. Built-in two round magazine. Gauge: 12 only. Bbl.: 25-in. Weight: 6.75 lbs. Bead sight. Synthetic stock and rubber recoil pad. Made 1995-97.

MODEL HS12 TACTICAL . . . . . NiB $582 Ex $350 Gd $150
O/U boxlock. C or IM choke. Single trigger w/ extractors. Gauge: 12 only. Bbl.: 18.5-in. Weight: 6.25 lbs. Fiber optic

sight. Synthetic stock w/ rubber recoil pad. Picatinny rails. Made from 2011 to date.
Thunder Ranch. . . . . NiB $583 Ex $360 Gd $160

MODEL HUNTER FIELD. . . . . NiB $518 Ex $275 Gd $130
O/U boxlock. C or IM choke. Single trigger w/ extractors. Gauge: 12 only. Bbl.: 28-in. Weight: 7 lbs. Front bead sight. Synthetic stock w/ rubber recoil pad. Made from 2010 to date.

GEBRÜDER MERKEL — Suhl, Germany
Manufactured by Suhler Jagd-und Sportwaffen GmbH. Imported by GSI, Inc., Trussville, AL, previously by Ames de Chasse.

MODEL 8 HAMMERLESS DOUBLE . . . . NiB $1522 Ex $1190 Gd $955
Anson & Deeley boxlock action w/Greener double-bbl. hook lock. Double triggers. Extractors. Automatic safety. Gauges: 12, 16, 20; 2.75- or 3-in. chambers. 26-or 28-in. bbls. w/fixed standard chokes. Checkered European walnut stock, pistol-grip or English-style w/or w/o cheekpiece. Scroll-engraved receiver w/tinted marble finish.

MODEL 47E SIDE-BY-SIDE . . .NiB $4000 Ex $3200 Gd $1890
Hammerless boxlock similar to Model 8 except w/automatic ejectors and cocking indicators. Double hook bolting. Single selective or double triggers. 12, 16 or 20 ga. w/2.75-in. chambers. Standard bbl lengths, choke combos. Hand-checkered European walnut stock, forearm; pistol-grip and cheekpiece or straight English style; sling swivels.

MODEL 47LSC SPORTING CLAYS S/S . . . . NiB $3100 Ex $2500 Gd $1789
Anson & Deeley boxlock action w/single-selective adj. trigger, cocking indicators and manual safety. Gauge: 12; 3-in. chambers. 28-in. bbls.w/Briley choke tubes and H&H-style ejectors. Weight: 7.25 lbs. Color case-hardened receiver w/Arabesque engraving. Checkered select-grade walnut stock, beavertail forearm. Imported from 1993 to 1994.

MODELS 47SL/147SL/247SL/347S/447S HAMMERLESS SIDELOCKS
Same general specifications as Model 147E except has side-locks engraved w/Arabesques, borders, scrolls or game scenes in varying degrees of elaborateness.
Model 47SL	NiB $8350	Ex $5780	Gd $4200
Model 147SL	NiB $10,099	Ex $7988	Gd $6754
Model 147SSL	NiB $9655	Ex $6130	Gd $4200
Model 247SL	NiB $8360	Ex $5110	Gd $3966
Model 347SL	NiB $7229	Ex $5263	Gd $3800
Model 447SL	NiB $10,450	Ex $8550	Gd $5110
28 ga. .410, add			20%

NOTE: *Merkel over/under guns were often supplied with accessory barrels, interchangeable to convert the gun into an arm of another type; for example, a set might consist of one pair each of shotgun, rifle and combination gun barrels. Each pair of interchangeable barrels has a value of approximately one-third that of the gun with which they are supplied.*

MODEL 100 O/U SHOTGUN
Hammerless. Boxlock. Greener crossbolt. Plain extractor. Double triggers. Gauges: 12, 16, 20. Made w/plain or ribbed bbls. in various lengths and chokes. Plain finish, no engraving. Checkered forend and stock w/pistol grip and cheekpiece or English-style. Made prior to WWII.

SHOTGUNS

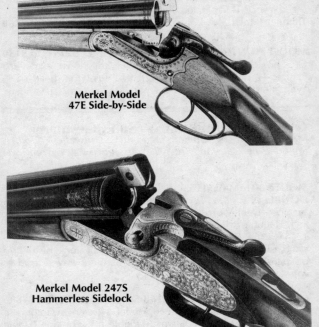

**Merkel Model
47E Side-by-Side**

**Merkel Model 247S
Hammerless Sidelock**

**Merkel Model 347S
Hammerless Sidelock**

**Merkel Model 122
Hammerless Double**

w/plain bbl. . . . . NiB $1964 Ex $1771 Gd $1333
w/ribbed bbl. . . . . NiB $2175 Ex $1890 Gd $1377

MODELS 101 AND 101E O/U
Same as Model 100 except ribbed bbl. standard, has separate extractors (ejectors on Model 101E), English engraving. Made prior to World War II.

Model 101 . . . . NiB $2210 Ex $1879 Gd $1360
Model 101E . . . . NiB $2330 Ex $1968 Gd $1466

MODEL 122
HAMMERLESS DOUBLE . . . NiB $3965 Ex $3177 Gd $2300
Similar to the Model 147S except w/nonremovable sidelocks in gauges 12, 16 or 20. Imported since 1993.

MODEL 122E HAMMERLESS
SIDELOCK. . . . . NiB $4865 Ex $3850 Gd $2700
Similar to the Model 122 except w/removable sidelocks and cocking indicators. Importation disc. 1992.

MODEL 126E HAMMERLESS
SIDELOCK. . . . . NiB $25,788 Ex $22,650 Gd $18,700
Holland & Holland system, hand-detachable locks. Auto ejectors. Double triggers. 12, 16 or 20 gauge w/standard bbl. lengths and chokes. Checkered forend and pistol-grip stock; available w/cheekpiece or English-style buttstock. Elaborate game scenes and engraving. Made prior to WW II.

MODEL 127E HAMMERLESS
SIDELOCK. . . . . NiB $24,849 Ex $21,939 Gd $16,374
Similar to the Model 126E except w/elaborate scroll engraving on removable sidelocks w/cocking indicators. Made prior to WW II.

MODEL 128E HAMMERLESS
BOXLOCK DOUBLE . NiB $28,679 Ex $22,167 Gd $16,954
Scalloped Anson & Deeley action w/hinged floorplate and removable sideplates. Auto-ejectors. Double triggers. Elaborate hunting scene or Arabesque engraving. 12, 16 or 20 gauge w/various bbl. lengths and chokes. Checkered forend and stock w/pistol grip and cheekpiece or English-style. Made prior to WW II.

MODEL 130 HAMMERLESS
BOXLOCK DOUBLE . . . NiB $21,400 Ex $18,560 Gd $16,450
Similar to Model 128E except w/fixed sideplates. Auto ejectors. Double triggers. Elaborate hunting scene or Arabesque engraving. Made prior to WW II.

MODELS 147/147E HAMMERLESS
BOXLOCK DOUBLE-BARREL
Anson & Deeley system w/extractors or auto ejectors. Single selective or double triggers. Gauges: 12, 16, 20 or 28 ga. (Three-in. chambers available in 12 and 20 ga.). Bbls.: 26-in. standard, other lengths available w/any standard choke combination. Weight: 6.5 lbs. Checkered straight-grip stock and forearm. Disc. 1998.
Model 147 w/extractors . . . NiB $2588 Ex $2254 Gd $1899
Model 147E w/ejectors . . . . NiB $5540 Ex $3770 Gd $2840

MODELS 200/200E/201/201E/202/202E/202EL
O/U SHOTGUNS
Hammerless. Boxlock. Kersten double crossbolt. Scalloped frame. Sideplates on Models 202 and 202E. Arabesque or hunting engraving supplied on all except Models 200 and 200E. "E" models have ejectors, others have separate extractors, signal pins, double triggers. Gauges: 12, 16, 20, 24, 28, 32 (last three not available in postwar guns). Ribbed bbls. in various lengths and chokes. Weight: 5.75 to 7.5 lbs. depending on bbl. length and gauge. Checkered forend and stock w/pistol grip and cheekpiece or English-style. The 200, 201, and 202 differ in overall quality, engraving, wood, checkering, etc.; aside from the faux sideplates on Models 202 and 202E, general specifications are the same. Models 200, 201, 202, and 202E, all made before WW II, are disc. Models 201E &202E in production w/revised 2000 series nomenclature.

Merkel Model 147E
Hammerless Boxlock Double-Barrel Shotgun

Merkel Model 200E
O/U Shotgun

Merkel Model 203E
Sidelock O/U Shotgun

Model 200	NiB $2920	Ex $2255	Gd $1730
Model 200E.	NiB $3688	Ex $2987	Gd $2116
Model 200 ES Skeet	NiB $4760	Ex $4200	Gd $2977
Model 200ET Trap.	NiB $4660	Ex $4189	Gd $3255
Model 200 SC Sporting Clays. . .	NiB $6930	Ex $4599	Gd $3238
Model 201 (disc.)	NiB $3400	Ex $2566	Gd $1888
Model 201E (Pre-WW II) .	NiB $7335	Ex $4990	Gd $3288
Model 201E (Post-WW II). .	NiB $5100	Ex $3991	Gd $2977
Model 201 ES Skeet	NiB $8100	Ex $6655	Gd $5133
Model 201 ET Trap	NiB $7661	Ex $6255	Gd $4409
Model 202 (disc.)	NiB $8255	Ex $5588	Gd $3577
Model 202E (Pre-WW II). .	NiB $8255	Ex $4967	Gd $3886
Model 202E (Post-WWII & 202EL).	NiB $7091	Ex $5897	Gd $3994

MODEL 203E SIDELOCK O/U SHOTGUNS
Hammerless action w/hand-detachable sidelocks. Kersten double cross bolt, auto ejectors and double triggers. Gauges: 12 or 20 (16, 24, 28 and 32 disc.). 26.75- or 28-in. VR bbls. Arabesque engraving standard or hunting engraving optional on coin-finished receiver. Checkered English or pistol-grip stock and forend.
Model 203E sidelock
   (disc. 1998). . . . . NiB $10,335 Ex $8556 Gd $5830
Model 203ES skeet (imported
   1993-97). . . . . . . NiB $12,450 Ex $12,330 Gd $10,245
Model 203ET trap
   (disc. 1997). . . . . NiB $13,770 Ex $12,560 Gd $10,665

MODEL 204E O/U . . . . NiB $8843 Ex $6751 Gd $4766
Similar to Model 203E; has Merkel sidelocks, fine English engraving. Made prior to World War II.

MODEL 210E SIDE-LOCK
O/U . . . . NiB $7239 Ex $5340 Gd $3882
Kersten double cross-bolt, scroll-engraved, casehardened receiver. 12, 16 or 20 ga. Double-triggers; pistol-grip stock w/ cheekpiece.

MODEL 211E SIDE-LOCK
O/U . . . . NiB $6865 Ex $5388 Gd $4488
Same specifications as Model 210E except w/engraved hunting scenes on silver-gray receiver.

MODELS 300/300E/301/301E/302 O/U
Merkel-Anson system boxlock. Kersten double crossbolt, two underlugs, scalloped frame, sideplates on Model 302. Arabesque or hunting engraving. "E" models and Model 302 have auto ejectors, others have separate extractors. Signal pins. Double triggers. Gauges: 12, 16, 20, 24, 28, 32. Ribbed bbls. in various lengths and chokes. Checkered forend and stock w/pistol grip and cheekpiece or English-style. Grades 300, 301 and 302 differ in overall quality, engraving, wood, checkering, etc.; aside from the dummy sideplates on Model 302, general specifications are the same. Manufactured prior to World War II.

Model 300	NiB $5865	Ex $3579	Gd $2988
Model 300E	NiB $8155	Ex $6888	Gd $5224
Model 301	NiB $6960	Ex $4977	Gd $3200
Model 301E	NiB $8235	Ex $6276	Gd $5004
Model 302	NiB $14,998	Ex $12,688	Gd $10,097

MODEL 303E SIDELOCK O/U
Hammerless action w/hand-detachable sidelocks. Kersten double cross bolt, auto ejectors and double triggers. Gauges: 12 or 20 (16, 24, 28 and 32 disc.). 26.75- or 28-in. VR bbls. Arabesque engraving standard or hunting engraving optional on coin-finished receiver. Checkered English or pistol-grip stock and forend.
Model 203E sidelock (disc.
   1998) . . . . NiB $10,335 Ex $8556 Gd $5830

MODEL 304E O/U . . NiB $24,770 Ex $19,760 Gd $13,010
Special version of the Model 303E-type, but higher quality throughout. This is the top grade Merkel over/under. Currently manufactured. Special order items.

MODELS 400/400E/401/401E O/U
Similar to Model 101 except have Kersten double crossbolt, Arabesque engraving on Models 400 and 400E, hunting engraving on Models 401 and 401E, finer general quality. "E"

SHOTGUNS

**Merkel Model 303E
O/U Shotgun**

models have Merkel ejectors, others have separate extractors. Made prior to World War II.

Model 400	NiB $2190	Ex $1993	Gd $1465
Model 400E	NiB $2433	Ex $2254	Gd $1934
Model 401	NiB $2798	Ex $2170	Gd $1588
Model 401E	NiB $4366	Ex $3757	Gd $2486

O/U COMBINATION GUNS ("BOCKBÜCHSFLINTEN")

Shotgun bbl. over, rifle bbl. under. Gauges: 12, 16, 20; calibers: 5.6x35 Vierling, 7x57r5, 8x57JR, 8x60R Mag., 9.3x53r5, 9.3x72r5, 9.3x74R and others including domestic calibers from .22 Hornet to .375 H&H. Various bbl. lengths, chokes and weights. Other specifications and values correspond to those of Merkel over/under shotguns listed below. Currently manufactured. Model 210 & 211 series disc. 1992.
Models 410, 410E, 411E (see shotgun models 400, 400E, 401, 401E)
Models 210, 210E, 211, 211E, 212, 212E
(see shotgun models 200, 200E, 201, 201E, 202, 202E)

MODEL 2000EL O/U

Kersten double cross-bolt. Gauges: 12 and 20. 26.75- or 28-in. bbls. Weight: 6.4 to 7.28 lbs. Scroll engraved silver-gray receiver. Automatic ejectors and single selective or double triggers. Checkered forend and stock w/pistol grip and cheekpiece or English-style stock w/luxury grade wood. Imported from 1998 to 2005.

Model 2000EL Standard	NiB $5733	Ex $4560	Gd $3288
Model 2000EL Sporter	NiB $5980	Ex $4677	Gd $3455

MODEL 2001EL O/U

Gauges: 12, 16, 20 and 28; Kersten double cross-bolt lock receiver. 26.75- or 28-in. IC/mod, mod/full bbls. Weight: 6.4 to 7.28 lbs. Three-piece forearm, automatic ejectors and single selective or double triggers. Imported from 1993 to 2005.

Model 2001EL 12 ga.	NiB $6566	Ex $5270	Gd $3880
Model 2001EL 16 ga. (disc. 1997)	NiB $6400	Ex $5277	Gd $3760
Model 2001EL 20 ga.	NiB $6400	Ex $5277	Gd $3760
Model 2001EL 28 ga. (made 1995)	NiB $7200	Ex $5933	Gd $4200

MODEL 2002EL . . . . NiB $11,990 Ex $8530 Gd $6177
Same specifications as Model 2000EL except hunting scenes w/Arabesque engraving.

ANSON DRILLINGS

Three-bbl. combination guns; usually made w/double shotgun bbls., over rifle bbl., although "Doppelbüchsdrillingen" were made w/two rifle bbls. over and shotgun bbl. under. Hammerless.Boxlock. Anson & Deeley system. Side clips. Plain extractors. Double triggers. Gauges: 12, 16, 20; rifle calibers: 7x57r5, 8x57JR and 9.3x74R are most common, but other calibers from 5.6mm to 10.75mm available. Bbls.: standard drilling 25.6 in.; short drilling, 21.6 in. Checkered pistol-grip stock and forend. The three models listed differ chiefly in overall quality, grade of wood, etc.; general specifications are the same. Made prior to WW II.

Model 142 Engraved	NiB $5698	Ex $4887	Gd $3366
Model 142 Standard	NiB $4880	Ex $3688	Gd $2588
Model 145 Field	NiB $3865	Ex $3200	Gd $2365

MIIDA — Tochigi, Japan

Manufactured for Marubeni America Corp., New York, by Olin-Kodensha Co., Tochigi, Japan

MODEL 612 FIELD

GRADE O/U . . . . NiB $863 Ex $665 Gd $400
Boxlock. Auto ejectors. Selective single trigger. 12 ga. Bbls.: VR; 26-in., IC/M; 28-in., M/F choke. Weight: W/26-in. bbl., 6 lbs., 11 oz. Checkered pistol-grip stock and forearm. Made 1972-74.

MODEL 2100 SKEET GUN . . . . NiB $954 Ex $749 Gd $488
Similar to Model 612 except has more elaborate engraving on frame (50 percent coverage), skeet-style stock and forearm of select grade wood; 27-in. VR bbls., SK choke. Weight: 7 lbs., 11 oz. Made 1972-74.

MODEL 2200T TRAP GUN,

MODEL 2200S SKEET GUN . . . NiB $925 Ex $691 Gd $541
Similar to Model 612 except more elaborate engraving on frame (60 percent coverage), trap- or skeet-style stock and semi-beavertail forearm of fancy walnut, recoil pad on trap stock. Bbls.: Wide VR; 29.75-in., IM/F choke on Trap Gun; 27-in., SK choke on Skeet Gun. Weight: Trap, 7 lbs., 14 oz.; Skeet, 7 lbs., 11 oz. Made 1972-74.

MODEL 2200 TRAP

& SKEET MODELS . . . . NiB $1088 Ex $766 Gd $594
Same as models 2200T and 2200S except more elaborate engraving on frame (70% coverage). Made 1972-74.

GRANDEE MODEL GRT/IRS

TRAP/SKEET GUN . . . . NiB $2655 Ex $2390 Gd $1866
Boxlock w/sideplates. Frame, breech ends of bbls., trigger guard and locking lever fully engraved and gold inlaid. Auto ejectors. Selective single trigger. 12 ga. Bbls.: Wide VR; 29-in., F choke on Trap Gun; 27-in., SK choke on Skeet Gun. Weight: Trap, 7 lbs., 14 oz.; Skeet, 7 lbs., 11 oz.

**Miida Model 612
Field Grade O/U**

Trap- or skeet-style stock and semi-beavertail forearm of extra fancy wood, recoil pad on trap stock. Made 1972-74.

MITCHELL ARMS — Santa Ana, CA

MODEL 9104/9105 PUMP SHOTGUNS
Slide action in Field/Riot configuration. Gauge: 12; 5-rnd. tubular magazine. 20-in. bbl.; fixed choke or screw-in tubes. Weight: 6.5 lbs. Plain walnut stock. Made 1994-96.
Model 9104 (w/plain bbl.) .... NiB $299 Ex $288 Gd $188
Model 9105 (w/rifle sight) .... NiB $299 Ex $288 Gd $188
w/choke tubes, add. $40

MODEL 9108/9109 PUMP SHOTGUN
Slide action in Military/Police/Riot configuration. Gauge: 12; 7-rnd. tubular magazine. 20-in. bbl.; fixed choke or screw-in tubes. Weight: 6.5 lbs. Plain walnut stock and grooved slide handle w/brown, green or black finish. Blued metal. Made 1994-96.
Model 9108 (w/plain bbl.) .... NiB $292 Ex $225 Gd $196
Model 9109 (w/rifle sights). . . . NiB $292 Ex $225 Gd $196
w/choke tubes, add. $40

MODEL 9111/9113 PUMP SHOTGUN
Slide action in Military/Police/Riot configuration. Gauge: 12; 6-rnd. tubular magazine. 18.5-in. bbl.; fixed choke or screw-in tubes. Weight: 6.5 lbs. Synthetic or plain walnut stock and grooved slide handle w/brown, green or black finish. Blued metal. Made 1994-96.
Model 9111 (w/plain bbl.) .... NiB $292 Ex $225 Gd $196
Model 9113 (w/rifle sights). . . . NiB $292 Ex $225 Gd $196
w/choke tubes, add. $40

MODEL 9114/9114FS
Slide action in Military/Police/Riot configuration. Gauge: 12; 7-rnd. tubular magazine. 20-in. bbl.; fixed choke or screw-in tubes. Weight: 6.5-7 lbs. Synthetic pistol-grip or folding stock. Blued metal. Made 1994-96.
Model 9114 . . . . NiB $345 Ex $245 Gd $169
Model 9114FS. . . . . NiB $345 Ex $245 Gd $169

MODEL 9115/9115FS
PUMP SHOTGUN. . . . . NiB $366 Ex $240 Gd $159
Slide action in Military/Police/Riot configuration. Gauge: 12; 6-rnd. tubular magazine. 18.5-in. bbl. w/heat-shield handguard. Weight: 7 lbs. Gray synthetic stock and slide handle. Parkerized metal. Made 1994-96.

MOLOT-ORUZHIE LTD. — Vyatskiye Polyany, Russia

VEPR-12 . . . . NiB $1000 Ex $900 Gd $800
Semiauto. Patterned after AK-47 rifle and RPK light machine gun. Gauge: 12; 5-, 8- or 10-rnd. detachable box magazine. Barrel: 19-in., threaded for choke tubes. Weight: 7 lbs. Stock: fixed wood or synthetic, folding metal; pistol grip. Sights: adj. RPK style w/ Picatinny rail. Imported by Izhmash in 2004 and 2015 by FIME Group. Importation banned since 2014 due to US sanctions.
Fixed wood/synthetic stock, deduct $200
SBS (12-in. bbl.), add $400

MONTGOMERY WARD
See shotgun listings under Ward, Montgomery.

MORRONE SHOTGUN — Hope Valley, RI
Manufactured by Rhode Island Arms Company, Hope Valley, RI

STANDARD MODEL 46 O/U . NiB $1366 Ex $890 Gd $677
Boxlock. Plain extractors. Non-selective single trigger. Gauges: 12, 20. Bbls.: Plain, VR; 26-in. IC/M; 28-in. M/F choke. Weight: About 7 lbs., 12 ga.; 6 lbs., 20 ga. Checkered straight- or pistol-grip stock and forearm. Made 1949-53. Note: Fewer than 500 of these guns were produced, about 50 in 20 ga. A few had VR bbls. Value shown is for 12 ga. w/ plain bbls. The rare 20 ga. and VR types should bring considerably more.

O.F. MOSSBERG & SONS, INC. — North Haven, CT

Formerly New Haven, Connecticut. Current manufacturing in Eagle Pass, TX.

MODEL G4/70/73/73B. . . . . NiB $150 Ex $85 Gd $50
Single shot. .410 ga. only. Made 1932-40.

MODEL 83D & 183D . . . . NiB $217 Ex $121 Gd $95
Bolt action, 3-rnd.. Takedown. .410 ga. only. Two shell fixed top-loading magazine. 23-in. bbl. w/two interchangeable choke tubes (M/F). Later production had 24-in. bbl. Plain one-piece pistol-grip stock. Weight: about 5.5 lbs. Originally designated Model 83D, changed in 1947 to Model 183D. Made 1940-71.

MODEL 85D & 185D BOLT-ACTION
REPEATING SHOTGUN . . . . NiB $217 Ex $121 Gd $95
Bolt action. Takedown. 3-rnd.. 20 ga. only. Two-shell detachable box magazine. 25-in. bbl., three interchangeable choke tubes (F, M, IC). Later production had 26-in. bbl. w/F/IC choke tubes. Weight: About 6.25 lbs. Plain one-piece, pistol-grip stock. Originally designated Model 85D, changed in 1947 to Model 185D. Made 1940-71.

MODEL 183K . . . . NiB $240 Ex $131 Gd $100
Same as Model 183D except has 25-in. bbl. w/variable C-Lect-Choke instead of interchangeable choke tubes. Made 1953-1986.

MODEL 185K . . . . NiB $240 Ex $131 Gd $100
Same as Model 185D except has variable C-Lect-Choke instead of interchangeable choke tubes. Made 1950-63.

MODEL 190D. . . . . NiB $240 Ex $131 Gd $100
Same as Model 185D except in 16 ga. Weight: About 6 lbs. Made 1955-71.

MODEL 190K . . . . NiB $240 Ex $131 Gd $100
Same as Model 185K except in 16 ga. Takedown. Three round capacity; 2-rnd. magazine. Weight: About 6.75 lbs. Made 1956-63.

MODEL 195D. . . . . NiB $240 Ex $131 Gd $100
Same as Model 185D except in 12 ga. Takedown. Three round capacity; 2-rnd. magazine. Weight: About 6.75 lbs. Made 1955-71.

MODEL 195K . . . . NiB $240 Ex $131 Gd $100
Same as Model 185K except in 12 ga. Takedown. Three round capacity; 2-rnd. magazine. Weight: About 7.5 lbs. Made 1956-63.

SHOTGUNS

Mossberg Model 83D

Mossberg Model 85D
Bolt-Action Repeating Shotgun

Mossberg Model 183K

MODEL 200D . . . . NiB $355 Ex $240 Gd $125
Same as Model 200K except w/two interchangeable choke tubes instead of C-Lect choke. Made 1955-59.

MODEL 200K
SLIDE-ACTION REPEATER . . . . NiB $355 Ex $190 Gd $120
12 ga. 3-rnd. detachable box magazine. 28-in. bbl. C-Lect choke. Plain pistol-grip stock. Black nylon slide handle. Weight: About 7.5 lbs. Made 1955-59.

MODEL 395K BOLT-ACTION
REPEATER . . . . NiB $255 Ex $155 Gd $120
Takedown. Three round (detachable-clip magazine holds two rounds).12 ga. (3-in. chamber). 28-in. bbl. w/C-Lect-Choke. Weight: About 7.5 lbs. Monte Carlo stock w/recoil pad. Made 1963-83.

MODEL 385K . . . . NiB $240 Ex $131 Gd $100
Same as Model 395K except 20 ga. (3-in.), 26-in. bbl. w/C-Lect-Choke. Weight: About 6.25 lbs.

MODEL 390K . . . . NiB $240 Ex $131 Gd $100
Same as Model 395K except 16 ga. (2.75-in.). Made 1963-74.

MODEL 395S SLUGSTER . . . . . NiB $240 Ex $131 Gd $100
Same as Model 395K except has 24-in. bbl., cylinder bore, rifle sights, swivels and web sling. Weight: About 7 lbs. Made 1968-81.

NOTE: *The Model 500 has been in continuous production since 1960 with numerous variations and configurations produced over the years.*

MODEL 500 ACCU-CHOKE
SHOTGUN . . . . NiB $290 Ex $231 Gd $125
Pump-action. Gauge: 12. 24- or 28-in. bbl. Weight: 7.25 lbs. Checkered walnut-finished wood stock w/ventilated recoil pad. Available w/synthetic field or Speed-Feed stocks. Drilled and tapped receivers, swivels and camo sling on camo models. Made from 1987 to date.

MODEL 500 ATI MODELS
Similar to Model 500 Persuader series except w/18.5-in. bbl., 12 gauge only, adj. synthetic stock. 2016 to date.
ATI Tactical (ATI Akita adj. stock, 18.5-in. bbl.,
   gray/black finish). . . . . NiB $585 Ex $515 Gd $400
ATI Tactical Cruiser (ATI
   6-position adj. stock,
   18.5-in. bbl., shell holder). . . NiB $585 Ex $515 Gd $400

MODEL 500 BANTAM SHOTGUN
Same as Model 500 Sporting Pump except 12, 20, or .410 22-in. bbl. w/ACCU-Choke tubes or 24-in. w/F choke; VR.

Scaled-down checkered hardwood or synthetic stock w/standard or Realtree camo finish. Made 1990-96, 1998 to 1999, and 2001 to date.
w/wood stock. . . . . NiB $405 Ex $355 Gd $270
w/synthetic stock . . . . NiB $405 Ex $355 Gd $270
Bantum Combo (extra bbl.) . . . . . . NiB $445 Ex $395 Gd $310

MODEL 500 BULLPUP
SHOTGUN . . . . NiB $722 Ex $486 Gd $344
Pump. Gauge: 12. Six or 8-rnd. capacity. Bbl.: 18.5 to 20 in. 26.5 and 28.5 in. overall. Weight: About 9.5 lbs. Multiple independent safety systems. Dual pistol grips, rubber recoil pad. Fully enclosed rifle-type sights. Synthetic stock. Ventilated bbl. heat shield. Made 1987-90.

MODEL 500 CAMO
Same as Model 500 Sporting Pump except 12 ga. only. Receiver drilled and tapped. QD swivels and camo sling. Special camouflage finish. Made from 1986 to date.
Standard model . . . . NiB $390 Ex $255 Gd $200
Combo model (w/ext.
   Slugster bbl., 1994-98) . . . . . NiB $409 Ex $270 Gd $220

MODEL 500 CAMPER . . . . NiB $290 Ex $210 Gd $175
Same general specifications as Model 500 Field Grade except .410 bore, 6-rnd. magazine, 18.5-in. plain cylinder bore bbl. Synthetic pistol grip and camo carrying case. Made 1986-90.

MODEL 500 COMBO MODELS
Similar to Model 500 Hunting All Purpose except w/extra bbl.
Combo Field/Deer (blue finish, wood stock, VR and rifle
   sight bbls.) . . . . NiB $570 Ex $520 Gd $490
Combo Field/Deer (blue finish, wood
   stock w/rubber comb, VR and
   cantilever mount bbls.). . . . . NiB $600 Ex $570 Gd $520
Combo Field/Deer (blue finish, synthetic stock w/rubber
   comb, VR and cantilever mount bbls., factory mounted
   scope) . . . . NiB $540 Ex $500 Gd $480
Combo Field/Deer (full camo finish,
   wood stock w/rubber comb,
   VR and rifle sight bbls.) . . . . NiB $640 Ex $600 Gd $580
Combo Field/Security (blue finish, wood stock and pistol
   grip, VR and defense bbls.). . NiB $550 Ex $500 Gd $480
Combo Turkey/Deer (full camo
   finish, synthetic stock, VR and
   rifle sight bbls.) . . . . NiB $690 Ex $650 Gd $600

MODEL 500 CRUISER MODELS
.410, 20, or 12 gauge; 6- or 7-rnd. magazine. Bbl.: 18.5-, 20-, or 21-in. plain w/fixed Cylinder Bore choke. Sights: Bead front. Stock: Black polymer pistol grip. 1989 to 2019.
Cruiser (6-rnd., 18.5-in. bbl.) . . NiB $400 Ex $350 Gd $275
w/heat shield . . . . NiB $420 Ex $370 Gd $295

Mossberg Mode 500 Accu-Choke

Mossberg Model 500 Bullpup Shotgun

Mossberg Model 500 Camo Pump

Mossberg Model 500 Mariner w/pistol grip configuration

Mossberg Model 500 Persuader Law Enforcement w/ Speedfeed stock

Cruiser Blackwater Series (ported off the door breacher, 12 gauge, 2011-14) . . . . NiB $430 Ex $380 Gd $300
Cruiser Mil-Spec (20-in. bbl., 12 gauge, disc. 1997) . . . . . NiB $400 Ex $350 Gd $275
Cruiser Road Blocker (18.5-in. heavy wall bbl., 12 gauge, 2009-14) . . . . NiB $480 Ex $420 Gd $330
Cruiser Rolling Thunder (23-in. heavy wall bbl., 12 gauge, 2009-14) . . . . NiB $480 Ex $420 Gd $330
Cruiser Tactical Light Forend (18.5-in. bbl., tactical light forend, 12 gauge, 2008-15) . NiB $565 Ex $480 Gd $380
Cruiser Tactical Tri-Rail (18.5-in. bbl., LaserLyte lase forend, 12 gauge, 2014-15) . . . . NiB $590 Ex $505 Gd $400

MODEL 500 FIELD GRADE HAMMERLESS SLIDE-ACTION REPEATER

Pre-1977 type. Takedown. Gauges: 12, 16, 20, .410. Three inch chamber (2.75-in. in 16 ga.). Tubular magazine holds five 2.75-in. rounds or four three-in. Bbls.: Plain- 30-in. regular or heavy Magnum, F choke (12 ga. only); 28-in., M or F; 26-in., IC or adj. C-Lect-Choke; 24-in. Slugster, cylinder bore, w/rifle sights. Weight: 5.75 to lbs. Plain pistol-grip stock w/recoil pad, grooved slide handle. After 1973, these guns have checkered stock and slide handles; Models 500AM and 500AS have receivers etched w/game scenes. The latter has swivels and sling. Made 1962-76.

Model 500A, 12 ga., ... NiB $310 Ex $225 Gd $170
Model 500AM, 12 ga., hvy. Mag. bbl. . . . . NiB $310 Ex $225 Gd $170
Model 500AK, 12 ga., C-Lect-Choke . . . . NiB $335 Ex $250 Gd $190
Model 500AS, 12 ga., Slugster . . . . NiB $359 Ex $250 Gd $195
Model 500B 16 ga., ... NiB $369 Ex $275 Gd $205
Model 500BK, 16 ga., C-Lect-Choke . . . . NiB $300 Ex $220 Gd $145
Model 500BS, 16 ga., Slugster . . . NiB $359 Ex $250 Gd $195
Model 500C 20 ga., ... NiB $360 Ex $275 Gd $160
Model 500CK, 20 ga., C-Lect-Choke . . . . NiB $335 Ex $250 Gd $190
Model 500CS, 20 ga., Slugster NiB $330 Ex $239 Gd $180
Model 500E, .410 ga., ... NiB $300 Ex $220 Gd $140
Model 500EK, .410 ga., C-Lect-Choke . . . . NiB $350 Ex $275 Gd $165

MODEL 500 "L" SERIES

"L" in model designation. Same as pre-1977 Model 500 Field Grade except not available in 16 ga., has receiver etched w/ different game scenes; Accu-Choke w/three interchangeable

tubes (IC, M, F) standard, restyled stock and slide handle. Bbls.: plain or VR; 30- or 32-in., heavy, F choke (12 ga. Magnum and VR only); 28-in., Accu-Choke (12 and 20 ga.); 26-in. F choke (.410 bore only); 18.5-in. (12 ga. only), 24-in. (12 and 20 ga.) Slugster w/rifle sights, cylinder bore. Weight: 6 to 8.5 lbs. Intro. 1977.

Model 500ALD, 12 ga., plain bbl. (disc. 1980) . . . . . NiB $275 Ex $195 Gd $110
Model 500ALDR, 12 ga., VR . . . . NiB $300 Ex $220 Gd $131
Model 500ALMR, 12 ga., Heavy Duck Gun (disc. 1980) . . . . NiB $325 Ex $240 Gd $165
Model 500CLD, 20 ga., plain bbl. (disc. 1980) . . . . . NiB $355 Ex $265 Gd $185
Model 500CLDR, 20 ga., VR . . . . NiB $310 Ex $235 Gd $135
Model 500CLS, 20 ga., Slugster (disc. 1980) . . . . . . NiB $355 Ex $265 Gd $185
Model 500EL, .410 ga., plain bbl. (disc. 1980) . . . . . NiB $295 Ex $200 Gd $125
Model 500ELR, .410 ga., VR. . . . . NiB $325 Ex $240 Gd $135

MODEL 500 MARINER . . . . . . NiB $500 Ex $390 Gd $277
Slide action. Gauge: 12. 18.5 or 20-in. bbl. Six round and 8-rnd. respectively. Weight: 7.25 lbs. High-strength synthetic buttstock and forend. Available in extra round-carrying Speed Feed synthetic buttstock. All metal treated for protection against saltwater corrosion. Intro. 1987.

MODEL 500 MUZZLELOADER

COMBO. . . . . NiB $390 Ex $275 Gd $190
Same as Model 500 Sporting Pump except w/extra 24-in. rifled .50-caliber muzzleloading bbl. w/ramrod. Made 1991-1996.

MODEL 500 PERSUADER LAW ENFORCEMENT

Similar to pre-1977 Model 500 Field Grade except 12 ga. only, 6- or 8-rnd. capacity, has 18.5- or 20-in. plain bbl., cylinder bore, either shotgun or rifle sights, plain pistol-grip stock and grooved slide handle, sling swivels. Special Model 500ATP8-SP has bayonet lug, Parkerized finish. Intro. 1995.

Model 500ATP6, 6-rnd., 18.5-in. bbl., shotgun sights . . . . NiB $410 Ex $275 Gd $190
Model 500ATP6CN, 6-rnd., nickle finish "Cruiser" pistol-grip. . . . . . NiB $440 Ex $300 Gd $225
Model 500ATP6N, 6-rnd., nickel finish, 2.75- or 3-in. Mag. shells . . . . NiB $410 Ex $275 Gd $190
Model 500ATP6S, 6-rnd., 18.5-in. bbl., rifle sights . . . . NiB $410 Ex $275 Gd $190
Model 500ATP8, 8-rnd., 20-in. bbl., shotgun sights . . . . NiB $440 Ex $300 Gd $225
Model 500ATP8S, 8-rnd., 20-in. bbl., rifle sights . . . . . . NiB $450 Ex $315 Gd $240
Model 500ATP8-SP Spec. Enforcement . . . . NiB $391 Ex $313 Gd $226
Model 500 Bullpup . . . . NiB $690 Ex $500 Gd $345

GRADING: **NiB** = New in Box **Ex** = Excellent or NRA 95% **Gd** = Good or NRA 68%

**Mossberg Model 500
Camper with carry case**

**Mossberg Model 500
Turkey/Deer Combo**

**Model 500 Intimidator w/laser
sight, blued** . . . . NiB $644 Ex $470 Gd $329
**Model 500 Intimidator w/laser sight,
parkerized** . . . . NiB $425 Ex $320 Gd $190
**Model 500 Security
combo pack** . . . . NiB $345 Ex $270 Gd $185
**Model 500 Cruiser w/pistol
grip** . . . . NiB $440 Ex $325 Gd $220
**Model 500 Chainsaw (chainsaw style forend grip,
2011-19)** . . . . NiB $550 Ex $350 Gd $250

MODEL 500 PIGEON GRADE
Same as Model 500 Super Grade except higher quality w/
fancy wood, floating VR; field gun hunting dog etching, trap
and skeet guns have scroll etching. Bbls.: 30-in., F choke (12
ga. only); 28-in., M choke; 26-in., SK choke or C-Lect-Choke.
Made 1971-75.
**Model 500APR, 12 ga., field,
trap or skeet** . . . . NiB $510 Ex $409 Gd $320
**Model 500APKR, 12 ga.
field gun, C-Lect-Choke** . . . . NiB $455 Ex $279 Gd $144
**Model 500 APTR, 12 ga., Trap gun,
Monte Carlo stock** . . . . NiB $475 Ex $300 Gd $165
**Model 500CPR, 20 ga., field
or skeet gun** . . . . NiB $365 Ex $279 Gd $180
**Model 500EPR, .410 ga.
field or skeet gun** . . . . NiB $345 Ex $292 Gd $190

MODEL 500 CAMO COMBO . . . NiB $440 Ex $335 Gd $255
Gauges: 12 and 20. 24- and 28-in. bbl. w/adj. rifle sights.
Weight: 7 to 7.25 lbs. Available w/blued or camo finish. Drilled
and tapped receiver w/sling swivels and camo web sling. Made
1987-98.

MODEL 500 SLUGSTER
Pump. Gauges: 12 or 20 w/3-in. chamber. 24-in. smoothbore or rifled bbl. w/adj. rifle sights or intregral scope mount
and optional muzzle break (1997 porting became standard).
Weight: 7 to 7.25 lbs. Wood or synthetic stock w/standard
or Woodland Camo finish. Blued, matte black or Marinecote
metal finish. Drilled and tapped receiver w/camo sling and
swivels. Made 1987-2018.
Slugster (w/cyl. bore, rifle sights) . . . NiB $335 Ex $245 Gd $190
Slugster (w/rifled bore, ported) . . . NiB $415 Ex $335 Gd $240
Slugster (w/rifled bore, unported) . . . . NiB $320 Ex $219 Gd $190
**Slugster (w/rifled bore, ported,
integral scope mount)** . . . . . NiB $320 Ex $219 Gd $190
Slugster (w/Marinecote and synthetic stock), add $100
Slugster (w/Truglo fiber optics), add $50

MODEL 500 REGAL
Similar to regular Model 500 except higher quality workmanship throughout. Gauges: 12 and 20. Bbls.: 26- and 28-in.
w/various chokes, or Accu-Choke. Weight: 6.75 to 7.5 lbs.
Checkered walnut stock and forearm. Made 1985-87.

Model 500 w/Accu-Choke . . . . NiB $320 Ex $219 Gd $190
Model 500 w/fixed choke . . . . NiB $300 Ex $200 Gd $165

MODEL 500 SPORTING PUMP
Gauges: 12, 20 or .410, 2.75- or 3-in. chamber. Bbls.: 22 to 28
in. w/fixed choke or screw-in tubes; plain or VR. Weight: 6.25
to 7.25 lbs. White bead front sight, brass mid-bead. Checkered
hardwood buttstock and forend w/walnut finish.
Standard model . . . . NiB $345 Ex $275 Gd $190
Field combo (w/extra Slugster bbl.) . . NiB $440 Ex $325 Gd $240

MODEL 500 SUPER GRADE
Same as pre-1977 Model 500 Field Grade except not made
in 16 ga., has VR bbl., checkered pistol grip and slide handle.
Made 1965-1976.
Model 500AR, 12 ga. . . . . NiB $400 Ex $299 Gd $221
**Model 500AMR, 12 ga.,
heavy magnum bbl.** . . . . NiB $400 Ex $299 Gd $221
**Model 500AKR, 12 ga.,
C-Lect-Choke** . . . . NiB $425 Ex $315 Gd $235
Model 500CR 20 ga. . . . . NiB $400 Ex $299 Gd $221
**Model 500CKk, 20 ga.,
C-Lect-Choke** . . . . NiB $425 Ex $315 Gd $235
Model 500ER, .410 ga. . . . . NiB $400 Ex $299 Gd $221
**Model 500EKR, .410 ga.,
C-Lect-Choke** . . . . NiB $425 Ex $315 Gd $235

MODEL 500 TURKEY/DEER
COMBO . . . . NiB $425 Ex $315 Gd $235
Pump (slide action). Gauge: 12. 20- and 24-in. bbls. Weight: 7.25
lbs. Drilled and tapped receiver, camo sling and swivels. Adj. rifle
sights and camo finish. VR. Made 1987-97.

MODEL 500 TURKEY GUN . . . NiB $465 Ex $325 Gd $254
Same as Model 500 Camo except w/24-in. ACCU-Choke bbl.
w/extra full choke tube and ghost ring sights. Made 1992-1997,
reintroduced from 2020 to date.
**Turkey (22-in. VR bbl. w/extended choke
tube, fiber optic front sight, optic ready,
12 gauge, 2023-date)** . . . . . . NiB $645 Ex $600 Gd $560
**Turkey (24-in. VR bbl. w/fixed or extended
choke tube, fiber optic front sight, optic
ready, .410, 2020-date)** . . . . . NiB $645 Ex $600 Gd $560
**Turkey (20-in. VR bbl. w/extended
choke tube, fiber optic front sight,
12 gauge, 2023-date)** . . . . . . NiB $600 Ex $580 Gd $540
**Tactical Turkey (20 or 12 ga., 20-in. VR bbl. w/extended
choke tube, fiber optic front sight, adj. stuck w/pistol
grip, 2016-date)** . . . . NiB $605 Ex $540 Gd $420

MODEL 500 VIKING PUMP SHOTGUN
Gauges: 12 or 20 w/3-in. chamber. 24-, 26- or 28-in. bbls.
available in smoothbore w/Accu-Choke and VR or rifled bore
w/iron sights and optional muzzle brake (1997 porting became
standard). Optional optics: Slug Shooting System (SSS). Weight:
6.9 to 7.2 lbs. Moss-green synthetic stock. Matte black metal
finish. Made 1996-98.
**Mdl. 500 Viking (w/VR &
choke tubes, unported)** . . . . . NiB $300 Ex $225 Gd $144
**Mdl. 500 Viking (w/rifled
bore, ported)** . . . . NiB $390 Ex $295 Gd $240

**Mdl. 500 Viking (w/rifled
bore, SSS & ported)** . . . . NiB $390 Ex $295 Gd $240
**Mdl. 500 Viking
(w/rifled bore, unported)** . . . NiB $300 Ex $225 Gd $144
**Mdl. 500 Viking Turkey
(w/VR, tubes, ported)** . . . . . . NiB $300 Ex $225 Gd $144

MODEL 500 WATERFOWL/DEER

COMBO . . . . NiB $455 Ex $350 Gd $285
Same general specifications as the Turkey/Deer combo except
w/either 28- or 30-in. bbl. along w/the 24-in. bbl. Made from
1987 to date.

MODEL 500 ATR SUPER

GRADE TRAP . . . . NiB $400 Ex $310 Gd $225
Same as pre-1977 Model 500 Field Grade except 12 ga. only
w/VR bbl.; 30-in. F choke, checkered Monte Carlo stock w/
recoil pad, beavertail slide handle. Made 1968-71.

MODEL 500 DSPR DUCK STAMP

COMMEMORATIVE . . . . NiB $600 Ex $465 Gd $300
Limited edition of 1000 to commemorate the Migratory Bird
Hunting Stamp program. Same as Model 500DSPR Pigeon
Grade 12-Gauge Magnum Heavy Duck Gun w/heavy 30-in.
VR bbl., F choke; receiver has special wood duck etching. Gun
accompanied by a special wall plaque. Made in 1975.

MODEL 500 FLEX SERIES
Similar to Model 500 except with FLEX TLS System which
allows swapping of pistol grips, butt-stocks, forends, and recoil
pads without tools. Made from 2012 to date.
All Purpose model. . . . . NiB $420 Ex $315 Gd $235
Deer/Security Combo model . . . NiB $680 Ex $445 Gd $380
**Field/Security
Combo model (2017-18)** . . . . . NiB $500 Ex $445 Gd $380
Hunting model (2012-18) . . . . . . NiB $587 Ex $475 Gd $410
Hunting model (20 ga., 2014-17) . . NiB $420 Ex $315 Gd $235
Tactical model (2012-16) . . . . . . NiB $535 Ex $475 Gd $400
Tactical Cruiser model (2014-22) . . NiB $500 Ex $445 Gd $380
**Turkey/Security
Combo model (2015-18)** . . . . . . NiB $585 Ex $515 Gd $440
**Waterfowl/Security Combo
model (2015-18)** . . . . NiB $565 Ex $500 Gd $420

MODEL 500 BULLPUP . . . . NiB $745 Ex $449 Gd $335
Same general specifications as the Model 500 Bullpup except
20-in. bbl. and 9-rnd. magazine. Made 1989-90.

Note: The primary differences between the Model 500 and Model
590/Model 535 is the magazine tube design. The Model 500
magazine tube is sealed with a threaded hole at the end to hold
the barrel in place. The Model 590/Model 535 magazine tube is
opened at the end and the barrel is attached via a magazine cap.

MODEL 505 BANTAM . . . . NiB $500 Ex $480 Gd $410
Similar to Model 500 Bantam except .410 or 20 gauge only;
4-rnd. magazine. Bbl.: 20-in. VR w/Accu-Choke choke tubes.
Sights: Bead front. Stock: Wood youth size stock.

MODEL 510 MIN SUPER BANTAM . . NiB $400 Ex $355 Gd $275
Similar to Model 505 Bantam except .410 or 20 gauge only;
3- or 2-rnd. magazine. Bbl.: 18.5-in. VR w//fixed choke. Sights:
Bead front. Stock: Synthetic stock with LOP spacers. Blued or
camo finish. 2010 to date.

MODEL 535 ATS SERIES
Pump/slide action. Gauge: 12, 3.5-in. chamber. Bbls.: 28-in. VR w/
Accu-set choke tubes. Finish: Matte blue. Stock: Checkered walnut

or synthetic. Bead front sight. Weight: 6.5-7 lbs. ATS (All Terrain
Shotgun). Later model had LPA trigger. Made 2005-19.
**All Purpose Field model
(walnut stock)** . . . . NiB $380 Ex $285 Gd $205
**Deer/Field Combo model (24-in. rifled bbl. w/rifle sights and
28-in. VR bbl., wood stock)** . NiB $425 Ex $320 Gd $235
**Slugster model (24-in. fluted or non-fluted rifled
bbl. w/rifle sights, camo or blue finish,
2005-14)** . . . . NiB $380 Ex $280 Gd $205
**Thumbhole Turkey model (20-in. VR bbl., fiber optic sights,
synthetic thumb-hole stock, Mossy Oak or Realtree
finishes, 2007-14)** . . . . NiB $555 Ex $420 Gd $305
**Turkey model (22-in. VR bbl., fiber optic sights,
synthetic traditional stock, Mossy Oak or Realtree
finishes)** . . . . NiB $445 Ex $335 Gd $245
**Turkey/Deer Combo model (24-in. rifled bbl.
w/rifle sights and 24-in. VR bbl., synthetic
stock)** . . . . NiB $490 Ex $370 Gd $270
**Turkey/Deer Combo model (24-in. rifled bbl.
w/rifle sights and 24-in. VR bbl., synthetic stock,
LPA trigger)** . . . . NiB $525 Ex $395 Gd $290
**Turkey/Waterfowl Combo model (22-in. VR bbl.
w/fiber optic sights and 28-in. VR bbl., synthetic
stock)** . . . . NiB $490 Ex $370 Gd $270
**Turkey Recoil Reduction System model (22-in. VR bbl., fiber
optic sights, synthetic traditional stock w/Mathews
Harmonic Damper technology, Mossy Oak or Realtree
finishes, 2013-15)** . . . . NiB $495 Ex $365 Gd $270
**Turkey Tactical model (22-in. VR bbl., fiber optic sights,
synthetic pistol-grip stock, Mossy Oak or Realtree
finishes)** . . . . NiB $555 Ex $420 Gd $305
**Turkey Thug model (20-in. VR bbl., fiber optic sights,
synthetic pistol-grip stock, Mossy Oak finish,
LPA trigger)** . . . . NiB $640 Ex $480 Gd $355
**Waterfowl model (26- or 28-in. VR bbl.,
camo synthetic stock, matte blue or
camo finish)** . . . . NiB $385 Ex $290 Gd $215
**Waterfowl Recoil Reduction System model (22-in. VR bbl.,
fiber optic sights, synthetic traditional stock w/Mathews
Harmonic Damper technology, Mossy Oak or Realtree
finishes, 2013-15)** . . . . NiB $495 Ex $365 Gd $270

MODEL 500 JUST IN CASE . . . . . NiB $485 Ex $425 Gd $330
Similar to Model 500 Cruiser except w/impact resistant storage
tube. 2013 to 2016.

MODEL 500 THUNDER RANCH . . NiB $445 Ex $390 Gd $305
Similar to Model 500 Persuader series except w/18.5-in. bbl.,
12 gauge only, Picatinny forend, black synthetic stock. Thunder
Ranch logo engraved on receiver. 2011 to 2018.

MODEL 590 SERIES
Pump/slide action. Gauge: 12, 3-in. chamber. Bbl.: 20-in. fixed cyl.
bore choke w/ or w/o heat shield. 9-rnd. magazine. Sights: bead or
ghost ring. Stock: black synthetic. Finish: matte blue or parkerized.
Weight: 7.25 lbs. Made 1987 to date unless noted below.
Special Purpose model . . . . NiB $480 Ex $340 Gd $265
**7 Shot model (18.5-in. bbl., 7-rnd magazine, bead sight,
matte blue)** . . . . NiB $390 Ex $290 Gd $215
**9 Shot model (20-in. bbl., ghost ring
sights, synthetic stock)** . . . . . NiB $475 Ex $415 Gd $330
**Bullpup model (similar to Model 500 Bullpup
except 9-rnd. capacity and 20-in. bbl.,
1989-90)** . . . . NiB $655 Ex $455 Gd $330
**Chainsaw (18.5-in. bbl., pistol grip, railed forend with top
handle, 2020-date)** . . . . NiB $530 Ex $465 Gd $355
**Cruiser (18.5-in. bbl.,
pistol grip, 2020-date)** . . . . . NiB $445 Ex $390 Gd $305

Mossberg Model 590 A1

Mossberg Model 595

Double Action model (18.5- or 20-in. bbl., double action trigger pull, parkerized, 2000-03). . . . . NiB $455 Ex $340 Gd $250
Flex Tactical model (20-in. bbl., bead sight, 9-rnd. capacity, Flex system stock). . . . . NiB $580 Ex $435 Gd $320
Line Launcher model (line dispensing canister, blaze orange stock, parkerized). . . . . NiB $455 Ex $340 Gd $250
Mag-Fed (18.5-in. bbl., 5-rnd. detachable magazine, synthetic stock, 2018-date) . . . . . NiB $530 Ex $465 Gd $355
Mariner model (20-in. bbl., 9-rnd magazine, Marinecote finish, 1989-93 and 2009-18). . NiB $600 Ex $450 Gd $330
Persuader (20-in. bbl., synthetic stock, w/ or w/o heat shield, 2020-date). . . . . NiB $480 Ex $420 Gd $330
Retrograde (matte blue finish, wood stock/corncob forend, 18.5- or 20-in. plain bbl. w/heat shield, 2020-date). . . . . NiB $525 Ex $490 Gd $360
Shockwave model (14-in. bbl., bead sight, 6-rnd. capacity, Shockwave Raptor pistol grip) . . . . NiB $390 Ex $290 Gd $215
Special Purpose (20-in. bbl., 9-rnd. magazine, synthetic stock, w/ or w/o heat shield, bead or ghost ring sights, 1987-2019). . . . . NiB $480 Ex $420 Gd $330
Special Purpose Double Action (double action trigger, 18.5- or 20-in. bbl., 6- or 9-rnd. magazine, synthetic stock, bead or ghost ring sights, 2000-03) . . . . . . NiB $445 Ex $390 Gd $305
Tactical Light Forend model (20-in. bbl. w/heatshield, bead sight, 9-rnd. capacity, Insight tactical light forend, disc. 2015) . . . . NiB $600 Ex $450 Gd $330
Tactical Tri-Rail model (20-in. bbl. w/heatshield, bead sight, 9-rnd. capacity, tri-rail forend, 2011-15). . . . . NiB $580 Ex $430 Gd $315
Tactical XS Express Sights model (20-in. bbl. w/heatshield, 9-rnd. capacity, XS Express sights, disc. 2015) . . . . NiB $630 Ex $430 Gd $355

MODEL 590 SHOCKWAVE SERIES
Based on Model 590 action except w/14-in. cylinder bore bbl. and bird's-head pistol-grip. Gauge: 12- or 20-gauge or .410 bore. 6-rnd. magazine. Bureau of Alcohol, Tobacco, Firearms & Explosives has defines the 590 Shockwave as a "firearm" per the Gun Control Act, but not a Class 3/NFA firearm. Mfg. 2017-date.
Standard model. . . . . NiB $405 Ex $355 Gd $280
Box magazine model
(11-rnd. box magazine) . . . . NiB $405 Ex $355 Gd $280
w/Crimson Trace Lasersaddle, add $140
Nightstick model
(wood grip/forend). . . . . . . NiB $500 Ex $440 Gd $340
Shock 'N Saw model
(chainsaw style forend). . . . NiB $500 Ex $440 Gd $340
SPX model (breacher muzzle device, 5-rnd. shell holder, heat shield). . . . NiB $500 Ex $440 Gd $340

Note: *There are differences between the Model 500/Model 590/Model 535 and the Model 590A1. The Model 500/Model 590/Model 535 have a polymer trigger guard and safety but-*

ton. The Model 590A1 has an aluminum trigger guard and safety, a heavy-wall barrel and a bayonet lug.

MODEL 590A1 SERIES
Pump/slide action. Gauge: 12, 3-in. chamber. Bbl.: 18.5- or 20-in. have wall fixed cyl. bore choke w/ or w/o heat shield bayonet lug. 7- or 9-rnd. magazine. Sights: bead, 3-dot or ghost ring. Aluminum trigger guard and safety button. Stock: black synthetic or Speedfeed stock. Finish: matte blue or parkerized. Weight: 7-7.5 lbs. Made 2009 to date unless noted below.
w/7-rnd. magazine, traditional
stock. . . . . NiB $520 Ex $390 Gd $290
w/Speedfeed stock . . . . NiB $770 Ex $440 Gd $340
Adjustable Stock model (20-in. bbl., 3-dot sights, 6- or 9-rnd. capacity, 6-position adj. pistol-grip stock, 2009-15). . . . . NiB $705 Ex $530 Gd $380
Bantam model (18.5-in. bbl., ghost ring sights, 6-rnd. capacity, 13-in. LOP, 2009-15) . . . . . . NiB $600 Ex $455 Gd $330
Kryptek Typhon Camo model (18.5-in. bbl., ghost ring sights, 6- or 7-rnd. capacity, Kryptek Typhon Camo finish). . . . . NiB $600 Ex $455 Gd $330
LPA Trigger model (18.5-in. fluted bbl., 3-dot sights, 6-rnd. capacity, LPA adj. trigger, 2011-14) . . NiB $555 Ex $420 Gd $305
Mariner model (18.5-in. bbl., 6- or 7-rnd magazine, Marinecote finish) . . . . NiB $650 Ex $490 Gd $355
Retrograde (matte blue finish, wood stock/corncob forend, 20-in. plain bbl. w/heat shield, 2020-date). . . NiB $870 Ex $755 Gd $600
Special Purpose model (engraved receiver, ghost ring sights, disc. 1997). . . . . NiB $555 Ex $415 Gd $305
Special Purpose Blackwater Series model (20-in. bbl., 9-rnd magazine, ghost ring sights, Speedfeed stock, Blackwater logo on receiver, 2011-14) . . NiB $655 Ex $505 Gd $380
SPX model (20-in. bbl., 9-rnd magazine, ghost ring sights, M9 bayonet/scabbard) . . . . . NiB $770 Ex $580 Gd $480
Tactical Light Forend model (18.5-in. bbl., bead sight, 6-rnd. capacity, Insight tactical light forend, disc. 2015) . . . . NiB $640 Ex $480 Gd $355
Tactical Tri-Rail model (20-in. bbl., bead sight, 9-rnd. capacity, tri-rail forend, 6-position adj. pistol-grip stock) . . . . NiB $755 Ex $585 Gd $455
Tactical XS Express Sights model (20-in. bbl., 9-rnd. capacity, XS Express sights) . . . . NiB $580 Ex $440 Gd $330
U.S. Service model (20-in. bbl., bead sight, 9-rnd. capacity, parkerized finish, USSM engraved on receiver, 2013-15). . . . . NiB $530 Ex $400 Gd $305

MODEL 590S MODELS
Similar to Model 590 series except cycles 1.75", 2.75", or 3" shells, 12 gauge only, 18.5-in. or 20-in. bbl., synthetic stock. 2021 to date.
Optic Ready (red dot
optic mount). . . . . NiB $700 Ex $680 Gd $610
w/M-LOK forend. . . . . NiB $800 Ex $780 Gd $710
Shockwave (18.5-in. bbl., Shockwave Raptor grip, 2021-date) . . . . NiB $530 Ex $465 Gd $355

MODEL 595/595K
BOLT-ACTION REPEATER . . . . . NiB $425 Ex $260 Gd $159
12 ga. only. Four round detachable magazine. 18.5-in. bbl. Weight: About 7 lbs. Walnut finished stock w/recoil pad and sling swivels. Made 1985-86.

MODEL 695 BOLT-ACTION SLUGSTER
Gauge: 12 w/3-in. chamber. Two round detachable magazine. 22-in. fully rifled and ported bbl. w/blade front and folding leaf rear sights. Receiver drilled and tapped for Weaver style scope bases. Available w/1.5x-4.5x scope or fiber optics installed.

Mossberg Model 500 Chainsaw

Weight: 7.5 lbs. Black synthetic stock w/swivel studs and recoil pad. Made 1996-2002.

Model 695 (w/ACCU-choke
   bbl.) . . . . NiB $300 Ex $220 Gd $175
Model 695 (w/open sights) . . . . NiB $380 Ex $296 Gd $207
Model 695 (w/1.5x-4.5x
   Bushnell scope) . . . . NiB $390 Ex $310 Gd $219
Model 695 (w/Truglo
   fiber optics) . . . . NiB $385 Ex $305 Gd $210
Model 695 OFM Camo . . . . . . NiB $355 Ex $280 Gd $196

MODEL 695 BOLT-ACTION
TURKEY GUN. . . . . NiB $375 Ex $265 Gd $195
Similar to 695 Slugster Model except has smoothbore 22-in. bbl. w/extra-full turkey Accu-choke tube. Bead front and U-notch rear sights. Full OFM camo finish. Made 1996-2002.

MODEL 712 AUTOLOADING SHOTGUN
Gas-operated, takedown, hammerless shotgun w/5-rnd. (4-rnd. w/3-in. chamber) tubular magazine. 12 ga. Bbls.: 28-in. VR or 24-in. plain bbl. Slugster w/rifle sights. Fixed choke or ACCU-choke tube system. Weight: 7.5 lbs. Plain alloy receiver w/top-mounted ambidextrous safety. Checkered. stained hardwood stock w/recoil pad. Imported from Japan 1986 to 1990.

w/fixed chokes . . . . NiB $450 Ex $340 Gd $250
w/ACCU-Choke tube
   system, add. $25
Regal (ACCU-choke, deluxe checkered stock,
   gold trigger, 1986-87) . . . . NiB $450 Ex $340 Gd $250

MODEL 835 ULTI-MAG SERIES
Pump/slide action. Gauge: 12, 3.5-in. chamber. Bbls.: 20-, 24-, 26- or 28-in. VR w/Accu-mag choke tubes. 6-rnd. magazine. Finish: Matte blue or various camo. Stock: Checkered walnut, synthetic thumbhole, pistol-grip or traditional. Sights: Bead, fiber optic or scope mount. Weight: 7.5-7.75 lbs. Some model equipped w/LPA trigger. Made 1988 to date unless note below.

w/synthetic stock (disc. 1991) . . NiB $410 Ex $315 Gd $235
w/wood stock (disc. 1991) . . . . . NiB $380 Ex $285 Gd $205
Field model (24- or 28-in. VR bbl., checkered walnut stock,
   blued finish, disc. 1998) . . . . NiB $275 Ex $205 Gd $155
Field Crown Grade model (gold trigger, ported to unproved
   bbl., checkered walnut stock, blued or camo finish,
   1994-05) . . . . NiB $320 Ex $340 Gd $180
Field Turkey model (24-in. VR ported bbl.,
   wood stock, parkerized finish,
   1997-2000) . . . . NiB $325 Ex $245 Gd $180
Field New Turkey model (24-in. VR ported bbl.,
   synthetic stock, fiber optic sights, various camo finishes,
   1999-01) . . . . NiB $455 Ex $340 Gd $250
NWTF (National Wild Turkey Federation) Limited
   Edition model (24-in. VR bbl. w/ACCU-MAG chokes.
   Realtree camo finish. QD swivel and post, disc.
   1989) . . . . NiB $430 Ex $325 Gd $240
NWTF Special Edition model
   (disc. 1991) . . . . NiB $400 Ex $325 Gd $225
Special Hunter model (24- or 26-in. VR ported bbl.,
   black synthetic stock, parkerized finish,
   1998-05) . . . . NiB $320 Ex $240 Gd $180

Slugster model (24-in. fluted or non-fluted ported
   rifled bbl. w/rifle sights or scope mount, camo or blue
   finish, 2007-14) . . . . NiB $540 Ex $400 Gd $300
Turkey model (24-in. VR ported bbl., fiber optic
   sights, synthetic stock, various camo
   finishes) . . . . NiB $520 Ex $390 Gd $290
Turkey Grand Slam Series model (20-in. VR ported bbl. w/X-
   Factor choke tube, fiber optic sights, synthetic stock,
   various camo finishes) . . . . . NiB $535 Ex $405 Gd $295
Turkey Recoil Reduction System model (24-in. VR
   ported bbl. w/Ulti-Full choke tube, fiber optic sights,
   synthetic traditional stock w/Mathews Harmonic
   Damper technology, Mossy Oak
   camo finishes). . . . . NiB $560 Ex $420 Gd $305
Turkey Tactical model (20-in. VR bbl. w/X-Factor choke tube,
   fiber optic sights, adj. synthetic stock, Mossy Oak camo
   finishes, 2006-15) . . . . NiB $680 Ex $505 Gd $365
Turkey Thugs model (20-in. VR bbl. w/X-Factor choke tube,
   fiber optic sights and TruGlo red dot optic, synthetic pistol-
   grip stock, Mossy Oak finish, LPA trigger, engraved w/
   Turkey Thugs logo, 2011-15) . . NiB $615 Ex $455 Gd $330
Turkey Thumbhole model (20-in. VR bbl. w/X-Factor choke
   tube, fiber optic sights, synthetic thumb-hole stock,
   standard or LPA trigger, Mossy Oak or Realtree camo
   finishes, 2007-14) . . . . NiB $580 Ex $430 Gd $330
Turkey Thumbhole Laminated model (20-in. VR bbl. w/X-
   Factor choke tube, fiber optic sights, laminated wood
   thumb-hole stock, Mossy Oak or Realtree camo finishes,
   disc. 2008) . . . . NiB $555 Ex $420 Gd $305
Turkey/Deer Combo model (24-in. ported rifled bbl. w/scope
   mount and 24-in. VR ported bbl., synthetic stock w/dual
   comb, various camo finishes). . . NiB $565 Ex $425 Gd $295
Turkey/Deer Combo model (24-in. ported rifled bbl.
   w/scope mount and 24-in. VR ported bbl.,
   synthetic stock w/dual comb, various camo finishes,
   LPA trigger). . . . . NiB $600 Ex $450 Gd $330
Turkey/Waterfowl Combo model (24-in. VR ported bbl. w/
   fiber optic sights and 28-in. VR bbl., synthetic stock,
   various camo finishes) . . . . . NiB $565 Ex $425 Gd $315
Waterfowl model (26- or 28-in. VR bbl., bead or
   fiber optic sights, synthetic stock, various camo
   finishes) . . . . NiB $445 Ex $335 Gd $245
Waterfowl Duck Commander model (28-in. VR bbl.
   w/Accu-mag choke tube, fiber optic sights, synthetic
   traditional stock, Realtree Max-5 camo finish, American
   flag bandana, 2014-15) . . . . NiB $640 Ex $365 Gd $270
Waterfowl Duck Commander Recoil Reduction System model
   (28-in. VR bbl., fiber optic sights, synthetic traditional
   stock w/Mathews Harmonic Damper technology, various
   camo finishes, 2013-15). . . NiB $665 Ex $530 Gd $430
Waterfowl Flyway Series model (28-in. VR bbl.
   w/X-Factor choke tube, fiber optic sights, synthetic
   traditional stock, Advantage Max-4 camo finish,
   2005-15). . . . . NiB $475 Ex $345 Gd $255
Waterfowl Recoil Reduction System model (28-in. VR bbl.,
   fiber optic sights, synthetic traditional stock w/Mathews
   Harmonic Damper technology, various camo finishes,
   2013-15) . . . . NiB $495 Ex $365 Gd $270
Viking model (28-in. bbl. w/Accu-Choke and optional
   muzzle brake porting became standard in 1997,
   7.7 lbs., green synthetic stock, matte black metal
   finish, 1996-98) . . . . NiB $265 Ex $200 Gd $150

MODEL 930 SERIES
Semiauto. Gas-operated action. Gauges: 12 only, 3-in. chamber. Bbls.: 18.5 to 28-in. w/VR except 18.5-in.. Finish: Matte blue or camo. Stock: Checkered walnut or synthetic. White bead or fiber optic front sight. Made 2005 to date unless noted below.

SHOTGUNS

Mossberg Model 1000
Junior Autoloading

Mossberg Model 5500
Guardian

Waterfowl (26- or 28-in. ported VR bbl., camo wood stock,
matte blue receiver) . . . . NiB $600 Ex $455 Gd $340

— HUNTING/SPORTING VARIANTS—

All Purpose Field (28-in. ported bbl., wood
stock) . . . . NiB $580 Ex $460 Gd $365
All Purpose Field (28-in. ported bbl.,
synthetic stock). . . . . NiB $480 Ex $360 Gd $265
Deer/Field Combo (24-in. ported rifled bbl. and 26-in. VR
bbl., synthetic stock) . . . . . . NiB $670 Ex $485 Gd $370
Deer/Waterfowl Combo (24-in.
ported rifled bbl. and 28-in.
VR bbl., synthetic stock). . . . NiB $645 Ex $485 Gd $355
Duck Commander Signature (26-in. VR bbl. w/ACCU-Set
choke tubes, Realtree camo finish, synthetic stock,
Duck Commander engraving,
2014-16) . . . . NiB $830 Ex $630 Gd $385
Duck Commander Waterfowl (26-in. VR bbl. w/ACCU-Set
choke tubes, Realtree camo finish, synthetic stock,
American flag bandana,
2014-16). . . . . NiB $770 Ex $555 Gd $430
Patrick Flanigan Rhythm Series (28-in. VR bbl.,
blue/yellow synthetic stock, 12-rnd magazine,
2012-13). . . . . NiB $700 Ex $530 Gd $390
Pro Series Sporting (28-in. ported VR bbl. w/extended
choke tubes, Cerakote tungsten finish, walnut stock,
tune action) . . . . NiB $905 Ex $680 Gd $500
Pro Series Waterfowl (28-in. ported VR bbl.
w/ACCU-Set choke tubes, camo finish, synthetic
stock, tuned action) . . . . NiB $755 Ex $670 Gd $420
JM Pro Series (22- or 24-in. VR bbl., 9- or 10-rnd. extended
magazine, engraved receiver, synthetic stock, tuned action
per Jerry Miculek's specs) . . . NiB $700 Ex $525 Gd $385
Slugster (24-in. ported rifled bbl., camo
synthetic stock). . . . . NiB $640 Ex $495 Gd $380
Slugster (24-in. ported rifled bbl., synthetic
stock) . . . . NiB $580 Ex $435 Gd $320
Slugster (24-in. ported rifled bbl.,
wood stock) . . . . NiB $600 Ex $455 Gd $340
Snow Goose (28-in. VR bbl., 13-rnd. extend magazine, blued
finish, synthetic stock) . . . . . NiB $825 Ex $620 Gd $355
Snow Goose (28-in. VR bbl., 13-rnd. extend
magazine, Kryptek Yeti camo finish, synthetic
stock) . . . . NiB $875 Ex $675 Gd $425
Turkey model (24-in. ported VR bbl., camo synthetic pistol-
grip stock). . . . . NiB $790 Ex $595 Gd $435
Turkey (24-in. ported VR bbl., camo synthetic
stock) . . . . NiB $705 Ex $530 Gd $390
Turkey (24-in. ported VR bbl., wood
stock) . . . . NiB $605 Ex $430 Gd $290
Waterfowl (26- or 28-in. ported VR bbl., camo synthetic
stock) . . . . NiB $580 Ex $435 Gd $320

—TACTICAL/DEFENSE VARIANTS—

Field/Security Combo (18.5-in. bbl. and 28-in. VR bbl., black
synthetic stock, black finish) . .NiB $645 Ex $420 Gd $305
Special Purpose Home Security (18.5-in. bbl.
w/fixed cyln. bore and bead sight, black synthetic stock,
2007-16) . . . . NiB $555 Ex $405 Gd $355
Special Purpose Roadblocker (18.5-in. bbl. w/muzzle
brake, black synthetic stock,
2009-11). . . . . NiB $580 Ex $570 Gd $305
Special Purpose SPX (18.5-in. bbl., ghost ring sights, black
synthetic traditional stock) . . NiB $755 Ex $570 Gd $420
Special Purpose SPX (18.5-in. bbl., ghost ring sights, black
synthetic pistol-grip stock) . . NiB $855 Ex $670 Gd $520
Special Purpose SPX (18.5-in. bbl., ghost ring sights, coyote tan
synthetic pistol-grip stock) . . NiB $875 Ex $690 Gd $540
Special Purpose SPX Blackwater Series (18.5-in. bbl., ghost ring
sights, 8-rnd. capacity, black synthetic pistol-grip stock,
oversized controls, 2011-14) . .NiB $755 Ex $580 Gd $420
Special Purpose SPX Typhoon (18.5-in. bbl., ghost
ring sights, Kryptex Typhoon camo synthetic pistol-grip
stock) . . . . NiB $890 Ex $670 Gd $490
Tactical (18.5-in. bbl. w/heatshield, white dot sights,
5-rnd. capacity, black synthetic traditional stock,
2011-16). . . . . NiB $605 Ex $525 Gd $340
Tactical (18.5-in. bbl. w/o heatshield, white dot sights,
5-rnd. capacity, black synthetic traditional stock,
2008-16). . . . . NiB $590 Ex $430 Gd $320
Tactical 8-Shot (18.5-in. bbl., bead sights, 8-rnd. capacity,
black synthetic traditional stock) . .NiB $525 Ex $395 Gd $290

MODEL 935 SERIES
Similar to Model 930 series except w/3.5-in. chamber. Made
2004 to date unless noted below.
Magnum Combo (24-in. ported rifled bbl. and 24-in. VR bbl.,
synthetic stock). . . . . NiB $855 Ex $645 Gd $475
Magnum Slugster (24-in. rifled bbl., rifle sights
or scope mount, camo synthetic stock, disc.
2011) . . . . NiB $655 Ex $505 Gd $400
Magnum Turkey (24-in. ported VR bbl., camo synthetic traditional stock) . . . . NiB $745 Ex $555 Gd $405
Magnum Turkey (24-in. ported VR bbl., camo synthetic
pistol-grip stock). . . . . NiB $880 Ex $655 Gd $485
Magnum Waterfowl (26- or 28-in. VR bbl.
w/ACCU-Set choke tubes, camo finish,
synthetic stock). . . . . NiB $655 Ex $490 Gd $355

MODEL 940 PRO SERIES
Semiauto w/cleaner running gas operated system. Ga.: 12,
3-in. chamber; 4-rnd. magazine. Bbl.: 28-in. VR w/choke tubes.
Stock: Black synthetic; adj. LOP, cast, drop. Sights: Fiber optic.

Weight: 7.7 lbs. Finish: Matte black. Enlarged/beveled loading port, oversized controls, elongated elevator. Made 2020 to date.

JM Pro model (24-in. VR bbl., 5- or 9-rnd.
magazine, gold accents) . . . . NiB $920 Ex $810 Gd $700
Pro Field model. . . . . NiB $900 Ex $810 Gd $700
Pro Snow Goose model (28-in. VR bbl., 12-rnd.
magazine, Truetimber Vipe Snow camo/gary
Cerakote finish) . . . . NiB $1090 Ex $920 Gd $810
Pro Tactical model (18.5-in. VR bbl., 7-rnd.
magazine, optic ready) . . . . NiB $1120 Ex $920 Gd $810
Pro Turkey model (18.5- or 24-in.
VR bbl., MO Camo finish) . . NiB $1120 Ex $920 Gd $810
Pro Waterfowl model (28-in. VR bbl., Truetimber Prairie
camo/brown Cerakote finish) . .NiB $1090 Ex $920 Gd $810

MODEL 950S SERIES
Pump action. Based on Model 500 except capable of cycling 1.75, 2.75 and 3-in. shotshells interchangeably. Stock: Black synthetic. Made 2022 to date.
Standard model. . . . . NiB $620 Ex $560 Gd $470
w/ghost ring sights . . . . NiB $730 Ex $780 Gd $600
Shockwave model (18.5-in.) . . . . NiB $620 Ex $560 Gd $470
Shockwave heavy wall model
(14.5-in.) . . . . NiB $620 Ex $560 Gd $470

MODEL 1000 AUTOLOADING SHOTGUN
Gas-operated, takedown, hammerless shotgun w/tubular magazine. Gauges: 12, 20; 2.75- or 3-in. chamber. Bbls.: 22- to 30-in. VR w/fixed choke or ACCU-Choke tubes; or 22-in. plain bbl, Slugster w/rifle sights. Weight: 6.5 to 7.5 lbs. Scroll-engraved alloy receiver, crossbolt-type safety. Checkered walnut buttstock and forend. Imported from Japan 1986 to 1987.
Junior model, 20 ga., 22-in. bbl. . . . NiB $555 Ex $435 Gd $320
Standard model w/fixed choke . . . NiB $555 Ex $435 Gd $320
Standard model w/choke tubes . . . NiB $555 Ex $435 Gd $320

MODEL 1000 SUPER AUTOLOADING SHOTGUN
Similar to Model 1000, but in 12 ga. only w/3-in. chamber and new gas metering system. Bbls.: 26-, 28- or 30-in. VR w/ ACCU-Choke tubes.
Standard model w/choke tubes . . NiB $555 Ex $435 Gd $320
Waterfowler model (Parkerized) . . NiB $590 Ex $466 Gd $380

MODEL 1000S SUPER SKEET . . NiB $655 Ex $500 Gd $422
Similar to Model 1000 in 12 or 20 ga., except w/all-steel receiver and vented jug-type choke for reduced muzzle jump. Bright-point front sight and brass mid-bead. 1 and 2 oz. forend cap weights.

MODEL 5500 AUTOLOADING SHOTGUN
Gas-operated. Takedown. 12 ga. only. Four round magazine (3-rnd. w/3-in. shells). Bbls.: 18.5- to 30-in.; various chokes. Checkered walnut finished hardwood. Made 1985-86.
Model 5500 w/ACCU-Choke . . NiB $300 Ex $210 Gd $148
Model 5500 modified junior . . NiB $300 Ex $210 Gd $148
Model 5500 Slugster . . . . NiB $355 Ex $209 Gd $155
Model 5500 12 ga. Mag . . . . . . NiB $335 Ex $254 Gd $190
Model 5500 Guardian . . . . NiB $330 Ex $250 Gd $180

MODEL 5500 MKII AUTOLOADING SHOTGUN
Same as Model 5500 except equipped w/two Accu-Choke bbls.: 26-in. ported for non-Magnum 2.75-in. shells; 28-in. for magnum loads. Made 1988-93.
Standard model . . . . NiB $330 Ex $209 Gd $135
Camo model . . . . NiB $366 Ex $270 Gd $198
NWTF Mossy Oak model . . . . . NiB $415 Ex $330 Gd $225
USST model (1991-92) . . . . NiB $370 Ex $292 Gd $217

MODEL 6000 AUTO
SHOTGUN . . . . NiB $320 Ex $231 Gd $198
Similar to the Model 9200 Regal except has 28-in. VR bbl. w/M ACCU-Choke tube only. Made 1993 only.

MODEL 9200 CAMO SHOTGUN
Similar to the Model 9200 Regal except has synthetic stock and forend and is completely finished in camouflage pattern (incl. bbl.). Made from 1993 to date.
Standard model
(OFM camo) . . . . NiB $500 Ex $415 Gd $306
Turkey model
(Mossy Oak camo) . . . . NiB $475 Ex $429 Gd $360
Turkey model
(Shadow Branch
camo) . . . . NiB $615 Ex $490 Gd $376
Comb. model
(24 & 28-in. bbls.
w/OFM camo) . . . . NiB $635 Ex $515 Gd $390

MODEL 9200 CROWN (REGAL) AUTOLOADER
Gauge: 12; 3-in. chamber. Bbls.: 18.5- to 28-in. w/ACCU-Choke tubes; plain or VR. Weight: 7.25 to 7.5 lbs. Checkered hardwood buttstock and forend w/walnut finish. Made 1992-2001.
Model 9200 Bantam (w/1-in.
shorter stock) . . . . NiB $500 Ex $433 Gd $329
Model 9200 w/ACCU-Choke . . . NiB $500 Ex $433 Gd $329
Model 9200 w/rifled bbl. . . . . NiB $500 Ex $433 Gd $329
Model 9200 Combo (w/extra
Slugster bbl.) . . . . NiB $550 Ex $493 Gd $379
Model 9200 SP (w/matte blue finish,
18.5-in. bbl.) . . . . NiB $500 Ex $433 Gd $329

MODEL 9200 PERSUADER. . . . NiB $500 Ex $443 Gd $329
Similar to the Model 9200 Regal except has 18.5-in. plain bbl. w/fixed M choke. Parkerized finish. Black synthetic stock w/ sling swivels. Made 1996-2001.

MODEL 9200 A1
JUNGLE GUN . . . . NiB $665 Ex $533 Gd $347
Similar to the Model 9200 Persuader except has mil-spec heavy wall 18.5-in. plain bbl. w/cyl. bore designed for 00 Buck shot. 12 ga. w/2.75-in. chamber. Five round magazine. 38.5 in. overall. Weight: 7 lbs. Black synthetic stock. Parkerized finish. Made 1998-2001.

MODEL 9200
SPECIAL HUNTER . . . . NiB $555 Ex $435 Gd $365
Similar to the Model 9200 Regal except has 28-in. VR bbl. w/ ACCU-Choke tubes. Parkerized finish. Black synthetic stock. Made 1998-2001.

MODEL 9200 TROPHY
Similar to the Model 9200 Regal except w/24-in. rifled bbl. or 24- or 28-in. VR bbl. w/ACCU-Choke tubes. Checkered walnut stock w/sling swivels. Made 1992-98.
Trophy (w/VR bbl.) . . . . NiB $650 Ex $583 Gd $479
Trophy (w/rifled bbl. & cantilever
scope mount) . . . . NiB $675 Ex $609 Gd $495
Trophy (w/rifled bbl. & rifle sights) . . . NiB $635 Ex $570 Gd $460

MODEL 9200 USST
AUTOLOADER . . . . NiB $525 Ex $390 Gd $295
Similar to the Model 9200 Regal except has 26-in. VR bbl. w/ ACCU-Choke tubes. "United States Shooting Team" engraved on receiver. Made from 1993 to date.

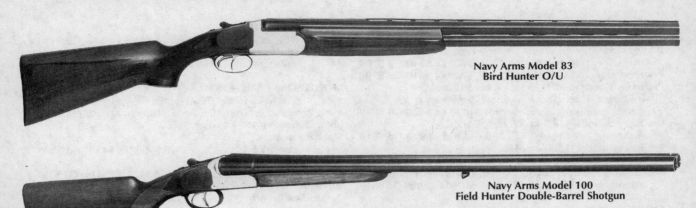

Navy Arms Model 83
Bird Hunter O/U

Navy Arms Model 100
Field Hunter Double-Barrel Shotgun

MODEL 9200
VIKING AUTOLOADER . . . . . . **NiB $425 Ex $330 Gd $290**
Gauge: 12 w/3-in. chamber. 28-in. smoothbore bbl. W/Accu-Choke and VR. Weight: 7.7 lbs. Green synthetic stock. Matte black metal finish. Made 1996-98.

MODEL HS410
HOME SECURITY PUMP SHOTGUN
Gauge: .410; 3-in. chamber. Bbl.: 18.5-in. w/muzzle brake; blued. Weight: 6.25 lbs. Synthetic stock and pistol-grip slide. Optional laser sight. Made from 1990 to date. A similar version of this gun is marketed by Maverick Arms under the same model designation.
Standard model . . . . **NiB $345 Ex $270 Gd $195**
Laser model . . . . **NiB $544 Ex $396 Gd $277**

MODEL SA-20 SERIES
Semiauto. Gas-operated action. Gauge: 20 or 28, 3-in. chamber. Bbls.: 26-in. VR w/choke tubes. Finish: Matte blue. Stock: Checkered walnut or synthetic. Bead front sight. Made 2008 to date unless noted below.
w/synthetic stock . . . . **NiB $480 Ex $405 Gd $265**
All Purpose Field (walnut stock) NiB $545 Ex $405 Gd $305
Bantam All Purpose (synthetic stock w/13-in.
** LOP)** . . . . **NiB $480 Ex $360 Gd $265**
Muddy Girl All Purpose (synthetic stock w/Muddy Girl camo
** finish)** . . . . **NiB $505 Ex $380 Gd $280**
Tactical/Railed (20-in. bbl., ghost ring sights, synthetic traditional stock) . . . . **NiB $480 Ex $360 Gd $265**
Tactical/Railed (20-in. bbl., ghost ring sights, synthetic pistol-grip stock) . . . . **NiB $490 Ex $370 Gd $275**
Turkey (22-in. VR bbl., 3-dot sights, synthetic traditional stock, Mossy Oak finish) . . . . **NiB $540 Ex $405 Gd $305**
Turkey Thugs Series (22-in. VR bbl., 3-dot sights,
** synthetic traditional stock, Mossy Oak finish,**
** engraved receiver)** . . . . **NiB $540 Ex $405 Gd $305**

LINE LAUNCHER . . . . **NiB $1066 Ex $833 Gd $545**
Gauge: 12 w/blank cartridge. Projectile travels from 250 to 275 feet.

"NEW HAVEN BRAND" SHOTGUNS
Promotional models, similar to their standard guns but plainer in finish, are marketed by Mossberg under the "New Haven" brand name. Values generally are about 20 percent lower than for corresponding standard models.

ONYX RESERVE SPORTING . . . **NiB $760 Ex $580 Gd $370**
O/U boxlock, blued engraved receiver. Gauges: 12 only; 3-in. chambers. Bbls.: 28-in. ported VR. Checkered walnut stock and forearm. Made 2010 to 2012.

SILVER RESERVE FIELD . . . . . . **NiB $600 Ex $460 Gd $340**
O/U boxlock, gold inlay silver receiver. Gauges: 12, 20, 28 or .410. Bbls.: 26- or 28-in. VR. Checkered walnut stock and forearm. Extractors. Mfg. in Turkey. Imported from 2005 to 2012.
Sporting . . . . **NiB $755 Ex $585 Gd $400**

SILVER RESERVE II FIELD . . . . . **NiB $736 Ex $470 Gd $300**
O/U boxlock, silver receiver w/ engraving. Gauges: 12, 20, 28 or .410. Bbls.: 26- or 28-in. VR. Checkered black walnut stock and forearm. Extractors or ejectors. Imported from 2012 to date.
Sporting (ported 28-in. bbl.) . . **NiB $1253 Ex $580 Gd $350**
Super Sport (ported 30- or
** 32-in. bbl.)** . . . . **NiB $1253 Ex $580 Gd $350**

SILVER RESERVE FIELD . . . . **NiB $860 Ex $640 Gd $370**
S/S boxlock, blued or silver w/ scroll engrved receiver, extractors. Gauges: 12, 20, 28 or .410. Bbls.: 26- or 28-in. Checkered black walnut stock and forearm. Extractors. Made 2008-12.
Onyx (12 ga., onyx finish) . . . . **NiB $860 Ex $640 Gd $380**

SILVER RESERVE II FIELD . . . . . **NiB $1100 Ex $690 Gd $420**
S/S boxlock, blued or silver w/ scroll engrved receiver. Gauges: 12, 20 or 28. Bbls.: 26- or 28-in. Checkered black walnut stock and forearm. Weight: 6.5 to 7.5 lbs. Made from 2012 to date.

NAVY ARMS —Ridgefield, NJ

MODEL 83/93 BIRD HUNTER O/U
Hammerless. Boxlock, engraved receiver. Gauges: 12 and 20; 3-in. chambers. Bbls.: 28-in. chrome lined w/double VR construction. Checkered European walnut stock and forearm. Gold plated triggers. Imported 1984 to 1990.
Model 83 w/extractors . . . . . . **NiB $355 Ex $285 Gd $200**
Model 93 w/ejectors . . . . **NiB $379 Ex $339 Gd $255**

MODEL 95/96 O/U
Same as the Model 83/93 except w/five interchangeable choke tubes. Imported 1984 to 1990.
Model 95 w/extractors . . . . . . **NiB $448 Ex $355 Gd $210**
Model 96 w/ejectors . . . . **NiB $555 Ex $376 Gd $280**

MODEL 100/150 FIELD HUNTER DOUBLE-BARREL
Boxlock. Gauges: 12 and 20. Bbls.: 28-in. chrome lined. Checkered European walnut stock and forearm. Imported 1984 to 1990.

Model 100 . . . . NiB $460 Ex $390 Gd $288
Model 150 (auto ejectors) . . . . NiB $510 Ex $355 Gd $290

MODEL 100 O/U . . . . NiB $277 Ex $169 Gd $109
Hammerless, takedown shotgun w/engraved chrome receiver. Single trigger. 12, 20, 28, or .410 ga. w/3-in. chambers. Bbls.: 26-in. (F/F or SK/SK); VR. Weight: 6.25 lbs. Checkered European walnut buttstock and forend. Imported 1986 to 1990.

NEW ENGLAND FIREARMS —
Gardner, MA

In 1987, New England Firearms was established as an independent company producing selected H&R models under the NEF logo after Harrington & Richardson suspended operations on January 24, 1986. In 1991, H&R 1871, Inc. was formed from the residual of the parent H&R company and then took over the New England Firearms facility. H&R 1871 produced firearms under both their logo and the NEF brand name until 1999, when the Marlin Firearms Company acquired the assets of H&R 1871.

NEW ENGLAND FIREARMS NWTF TURKEY SPECIAL
Similar to Turkey and Goose models except 10 or 20 gauge w/22- or 24-in. plain bbl. w/screw-in full-choke tube. Mossy Oak camo finish on entire gun. Made 1992-96.
Turkey Special 10 ga. . . . . . NiB $265 Ex $177 Gd $98
Turkey Special 20 ga. . . . . NiB $335 Ex $219 Gd $189

NRA FOUNDATION YOUTH . . NiB $190 Ex $155 Gd $100
Smaller scale version of Pardner Model chambered for 20, 28 or .410 w/22- in. plain bbl. High luster blue finish. NRA Foundation logo laser etched on stock. Made 1999-2002.

PARDNER SHOTGUN
Takedown. Side lever. Single bbl. Gauges: 12, 20 and .410 w/3-in. chamber; 16 and 28 w/2.75-in. chamber. 26-, 28- or 32-in., plain bbl. w/fixed choke. Weight: 5-6 lbs. Bead front sight. Pistol grip-style hardwood stock w/walnut finish. Made from 1988 to date.

Standard model . . . . NiB $255 Ex $185 Gd $99
Youth model . . . . NiB $255 Ex $185 Gd $99
Turkey model . . . . NiB $323 Ex $217 Gd $110
w/32-in. bbl., add $40

PARDNER SPECIAL PURPOSE 10-GA SHOTGUN
Similar to the standard Pardner model except chambered 10 ga. only w/3.5-in. chamber. 24- or 28-in., plain bbl. w/full choke tube or fixed choke. Weight: 9.5 lbs. Bead front sight. Pistol-grip-style hardwood stock w/camo or matte black finish. Made from 1989 to date.
Special Purpose model w/fixed
  choke . . . . NiB $315 Ex $220 Gd $125
w/camo finish, add $40
w/choke tube, add $25
w/24-in. bbl. turkey option, add $50

PARDNER SPECIAL PURPOSE
WATERFOWL SINGLE-SHOT . . NiB $255 Ex $190 Gd $129
Similar to Special Purpose 10 Ga. model except w/32-in. bbl. Mossy Oak camo stock w/swivel and sling. Made from 1988 to date.

PARDNER TURKEY GUN
Similar to Pardner model except chambered in 12 ga. w/3.0- or 3.5-in. chamber. 24-in. plain bbl. W/turkey full-choke tube or fixed choke. Weight: 9.5 lbs. American hardwood stock w/ camo or matte black finish. Made from 1999 to date.
Standard Turkey model . . . . NiB $200 Ex $110 Gd $85
Camo Turkey model . . . . NiB $200 Ex $110 Gd $85

SURVIVOR SERIES
Takedown single bbl. shotgun w/side lever release, Automatic ejector and patented transfer-bar safety. Gauges: 12, 20, and .410/.45 ACP w/3-in. chamber. 22-in. bbl. w/modified choke and bead sight. Weight: 6 lbs. Polymer stock and forend w/hollow cavity for storage. Made 1992-93 and 1995 to date.
12 or 20 ga. w/blued finish. . . . . NiB $220 Ex $144 Gd $98
12 or 20 ga.
  w/nickel finish . . . . NiB $260 Ex $177 Gd $120
.410/.45 LC add $75

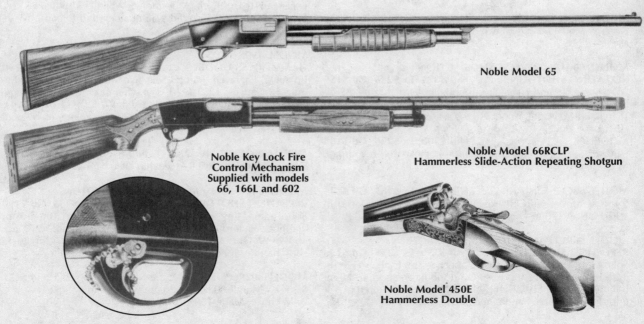

Noble Model 65

Noble Key Lock Fire
Control Mechanism
Supplied with models
66, 166L and 602

Noble Model 66RCLP
Hammerless Slide-Action Repeating Shotgun

Noble Model 450E
Hammerless Double

GRADING: **NiB** = New in Box   **Ex** = Excellent or NRA 95%   **Gd** = Good or NRA 68%

SHOTGUNS

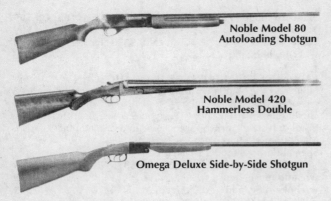

Noble Model 80
Autoloading Shotgun

Noble Model 420
Hammerless Double

Omega Deluxe Side-by-Side Shotgun

TRACKER SLUG GUN
Similar to Pardner model except in 10, 12 or 20 ga. w/24-in. w/cylinder choke or rifled slug bbl. (Tracker II). Weight: 6 lbs. American hardwood stock w/walnut or camo finish, Schnabel forend, sling swivel studs. Made 1992-2001.

Tracker Slug (10 ga.) . . . . NiB $180 Ex $110 Gd $79
Tracker Slug (12 or 20 ga.) . . . . NiB $219 Ex $120 Gd $85
Tracker II (rifled bore) . . . . NiB $219 Ex $120 Gd $85

NIKKO FIREARMS LTD. — Tochigi, Japan

See listings under Golden Eagle Firearms, Inc.

NOBLE MANUFACTURING COMPANY — Haydenville, MA

Series 602 and 70 are similar in appearance to the corresponding Model 66 guns.

MODEL 40 HAMMERLESS SLIDE-ACTION
REPEATING SHOTGUN . . . . . . NiB $255 Ex $190 Gd $130
Solid frame. 12 ga. only. Five round tubular magazine. 28-in. bbl. w/ventilated Multi-Choke. Weight: About 7.5 lbs. Plain pistol-grip stock, grooved slide handle. Made 1950-55.

MODEL 50 SLIDE-ACTION . . . NiB $266 Ex $190 Gd $125
Same as Model 40 except w/o Multi-Choke. M or F choke bbl. Made 1953-55.

MODEL 60 HAMMERLESS SLIDE-ACTION
REPEATING SHOTGUN . . . . . . NiB $325 Ex $255 Gd $159
Solid frame. 12 and 16 ga. Five round tubular magazine. 28-in. bbl. w/adj. choke. Plain pistol-grip stock w/recoil pad, grooved slide handle. Weight: About 7.5 lbs. Made 1955-66.

MODEL 65 . . . . NiB $300 Ex $225 Gd $165
Same as Model 60 except without adj. choke and recoil pad. M or F choke bbl. Made 1955-66.

MODEL 66CLP . . . . NiB $235 Ex $185 Gd $135
Same as Model 66RCLP except has plain bbl. Introduced in 1967. Disc.

MODEL 66RCLP HAMMERLESS SLIDE-ACTION
REPEATING SHOTGUN . . . . . . NiB $339 Ex $235 Gd $176
Solid frame. Key lock fire control mechanism. Gauges: 12, 16. 3-in. chamber in 12 ga. Five round tubular magazine. 28-in. bbl., VR, adj. choke. Weight: About 7.5 lbs. Checkered pistol-grip stock and slide handle, recoil pad. Made 1967-70.

MODEL 66RLP . . . . NiB $329 Ex $225 Gd $165
Same as Model 66RCLP except w/F or M choke. Made 1967-70.

MODEL 66XL . . . . NiB $245 Ex $185 Gd $129
Same as Model 66RCL except has plain bbl., F or M choke, slide handle only checkered, no recoil pad. Made 1967-70.

MODEL 70CLP HAMMERLESS SLIDE-ACTION
REPEATING SHOTGUN . . . . . . NiB $277 Ex $198 Gd $145
Solid frame. .410 gauge. Magazine holds 5 rounds. 26-in. bbl. w/adj. choke. Weight: About 6 lbs. Checkered buttstock and forearm, recoil pad. Made 1958-70.

MODEL 70RCLP . . . . NiB $280 Ex $199 Gd $149
Same as Model 70CLP except has VR. Made 1967-70.

MODEL 70RLP . . . . NiB $278 Ex $199 Gd $145
Same as Model 70CLP except has VR and no adj. choke. Made 1967-70.

MODEL 70XL . . . . NiB $255 Ex $160 Gd $110
Same as Model 70CLP except without adj. choke and checkering on buttstock. Made 1958-70.

MODEL 80 . . . . NiB $344 Ex $265 Gd $196
Recoil-operated. .410 ga. Magazine holds three 3-in. shells, four 2.5-in. shells. 26-in. bbl., full choke. Weight: About 6 lbs. Plain pistol-grip stock and fluted forearm. Made 1964-66.

MODEL 166L DEER GUN . . . . . NiB $355 Ex $270 Gd $199
Solid frame. Key lock fire control mechanism. 12 ga. 2.75-in. chamber. Five round tubular magazine. 24-in. plain bbl., specially bored for rifled slug. Lyman peep rear sight, post ramp front sight. Receiver dovetailed for scope mounting. Weight: About 7.25 lbs. Checkered pistol-grip stock and slide handle, swivels and carrying strap. Made 1967-70.

MODEL 420
HAMMERLESS DOUBLE . . . . . NiB $466 Ex $361 Gd $255
Boxlock. Plain extractors. Double triggers. Gauges: 12 ga. 3-in. mag.; 16 ga.; 20 ga. 3-in. mag.; .410 ga. Bbls.: 28-in., except .410 in 26-in., M/F choke. Weight: About 6.75 lbs. Engraved frame. Checkered walnut stock and forearm. Made 1958-70.

MODEL 450E
HAMMERLESS DOUBLE . . . . . NiB $490 Ex $376 Gd $290
Boxlock. Engraved frame. Selective auto ejectors. Double triggers. Gauges: 12, 16, 20. 3-in. chambers in 12 and 20 ga. 28-in. bbls., M/F choke. Weight: About 6 lbs., 14 oz., 12 ga. Checkered pistol-grip stock and beavertail forearm, recoil pad. Made 1967-70.

MODEL 602CLP . . . . NiB $366 Ex $255 Gd $235
Same as Model 602RCLP except has plain barrel. Made 1958-70.

MODEL 602RCLP HAMMERLESS SLIDE-ACTION
REPEATING SHOTGUN . . . . . . NiB $355 Ex $255 Gd $190
Solid frame. Key lock fire control mechanism. 20 ga. 3-in. chamber. Five round tubular magazine. 28-in. bbl., VR, adj. choke. Weight: About 6.5 lbs. Checkered pistol-grip stock/ slide handle, recoil pad. Made 1967-70.

MODEL 602RLP . . . . NiB $315 Ex $233 Gd $157
Same as Model 602RCLP except without adj. choke, bored F or M choke. Made 1967-70.

MODEL 602XL . . . . **NiB $285 Ex $177 Gd $145**
Same as Model 602RCL except has plain bbl., F or M choke, slide handle only checkered, no recoil pad. Made 1958-70.

MODEL 662 . . . . **NiB $308 Ex $244 Gd $165**
Same as Model 602CLP except has aluminum receiver and bbl. Weight: About 4.5 lbs. Made 1966-70.

OMEGA — Brescia, Italy, and Korea

FOLDING OVER/UNDER STANDARD SHOTGUN
Hammerless Boxlock. Gauges: 12, 20, 28 w/2.75-in. chambers or .410 w/3-in. chambers. Bbls.: 26- or 28-in. VR w/ fixed chokes (IC/M, M/F or F/F (.410). Automatic safety. Single trigger. 40.5 in. overall (42.5 in., 20 ga., 28-in. bbl.). Weight: 6 to 7.5 lbs. Checkered European walnut stock and forearm. Imported from 1984 to 1994.
Standard model (12 ga.) . . . . . . **NiB $475 Ex $355 Gd $298**
Standard model (20 ga.) . . . . . . **NiB $475 Ex $355 Gd $298**
**Standard model
  (28 ga. & .410)** . . . . **NiB $475 Ex $355 Gd $298**

O/U DELUXE SHOTGUN . . . . . **NiB $390 Ex $287 Gd $200**
Gauges: 20, 28 and .410. 26- or 28-in. VR bbls. 40.5 in. overall (42.5 in., 20 ga., 28-in. bbl.). Chokes: IC/M, M/F or F/F (.410). Weight: About 5.5-6 lbs. Single trigger. Automatic safety. European walnut stock w/checkered pistol grip and tulip forend. Imported from Italy 1984 to 1990.

DELUXE SIDE-BY-SIDE . . . . **NiB $290 Ex $225 Gd $165**
Same general specifications as the Standard Side-by-Side except has checkered European walnut stock and low bbl. rib. Made in Italy from 1984 to 1989.

STANDARD SIDE-BY-SIDE . . . . . **NiB $245 Ex $135 Gd $90**
Gauge: .410. 26-in. bbl. 40.5 in. overall. Choked F/F. Weight: 5.5 lbs. Double trigger. Manual safety. Checkered beechwood stock and semi-pistol grip. Imported from Italy 1984 to 1989.

STANDARD SINGLE-SHOT SHOTGUN
Gauges: 12, 16, 20, 28 and .410. Bbl. lengths: 26-, 28- or 30-in. Weight: 5 lbs., 4 oz. to 5 lbs., 11 oz. Indonesian walnut stock. Matte-chromed receiver and top lever break. Imported from 1984 to 1987.
Standard fixed . . . . **NiB $155 Ex $90 Gd $65**
Standard folding . . . . **NiB $175 Ex $110 Gd $75**
Deluxe folding . . . . **NiB $255 Ex $185 Gd $95**

DELUXE SINGLE-SHOT . . . . **NiB $229 Ex $145 Gd $99**
Same general specifications as the Standard single bbl. except has checkered walnut stock, top lever break, fully-blued receiver, VR. Imported from Korea 1984 to 1987.

PARKER BROTHERS — Meriden, CT
This firm was taken over by Remington Arms Company in 1934 and its production facilities moved to Remington's Ilion, New York, plant. In 1984, Winchester took over production until 1999.

HAMMERLESS DOUBLE-BARREL SHOTGUNS
Grades V.H. through A-1 Special. Boxlock. Auto ejectors. Double triggers or selective single trigger. Gauges: 10, 12, 16, 20, 28, .410. Bbls.: 26- to 32-in., any standard boring. Weight:

6.88-8.5 lbs.,12 ga. Stock and forearm of select walnut, checkered; straight, half-or full-pistol grip.
Grades differ only in quality of workmanship, grade of wood, engraving, checkering, etc. General specifications are the same for all. Disc. about 1940.
**V.H. grade, 12 or
  16 ga.** . . . . **NiB $5733 Ex $4187 Gd $2266**
V.H. grade, 20 ga. . . . . **NiB $9455 Ex $6077 Gd $3145**
V.H. grade, 28 ga. . . . . **NiB $28,998 Ex $27,966 Gd $26,778**
V.H. grade, .410 . . . . **NiB $34,669 Ex $25,766 Gd $21,560**
G.H. grade, 12 ga. . . . . **NiB $7566 Ex $3998 Gd $2779**
G.H. grade, 16 ga. . . . . **NiB $8120 Ex $4233 Gd $2988**
G.H. grade, 20 ga. . . . . **NiB $12,960 Ex $10,679 Gd $7789**
G.H. grade, 28 ga. . . **NiB $33,790 Ex $29,645 Gd $27,889**
G.H. grade, .410. . . . . **NiB $45,890 Ex $39,955 Gd $27,987**
**D.H. grade, 12 or
  16 ga.** . . . . **NiB $10,440 Ex $7866 Gd $4350**
D.H. grade, 20 ga. . . **NiB $16,777 Ex $13,790 Gd $11,556**
D.H. grade, 28 ga. . . **NiB $43,088 Ex $39,655 Gd $32,200**
D.H. grade, .410. . . . **NiB $72,799 Ex $48,950 Gd $37,788**
C.H. grade, 12 or 16 ga. . . . . **NiB $17,300 Ex $13,988 Gd $10,996**
C.H. grade, 20 ga. . . **NiB $25,779 Ex $20,099 Gd $17,376**
C.H. grade, 28 ga. . . **NiB $73,588 Ex $60,977 Gd $52,411**
B.H. grade, 12 or 16 ga. . . . **NiB $21,689 Ex $18,933 Gd $16,900**
B.H. grade, 20 ga. . . . . **NiB $31,889 Ex $22,765 Gd $17,766**
B.H. grade, 28 ga. . . **NiB $40,550 Ex $33,980 Gd $24,665**
A.H. grade, 12 or 16 ga. . . . **NiB $92,778 Ex $80,000 Gd $66,789**
A.H. grade, 20 ga. . . . **NiB $57,778 Ex $40,099 Gd $30,277**
A.H. grade, 28 ga. . . **NiB $104,000 Ex $88,987 Gd $67,033**
A.A.H. grade, 12 or 16 ga. . . . **NiB $57,980 Ex $52,077 Gd $37,773**
A.A.H. grade, 20 ga. . . . . **NiB $83,672 Ex $62,955 Gd $43,900**
A.A.H. grade, 28 ga. . . . . **NiB $200,000 Ex $175,000 Gd $155,000**
**A-1 Special grade,
  12 or 16 ga.** . . . . . **NiB $100,000 Ex $80,000 Gd $60,000**
A-1 Special grade, 20 ga. . . **NiB $82,000 Ex $65,000 Gd $45,000**
**A-1 Special grade,
  28 ga.** . . . . **NiB $200,000 Ex $165,000 Gd $110,000**
w/selective-single trigger, add **20%**
w/VR, add. **35%**
Non-ejector models, deduct **30%**

SINGLE-SHOT TRAP GUNS
Hammerless. Boxlock. Ejector. 12 ga. only. Bbl. lengths: 30-, 32-, 34-in., any boring, VR. Weight: 7.5-8.5 lbs. Stock and forearm of select walnut, checkered; straight, half-or full-pistol grip. The five grades differ only in quality of workmanship, grade of wood, checkering, engraving, etc. General specifications same for all. Disc. about 1940.
S.C. grade . . . . **NiB $9355 Ex $7088 Gd $5167**
S.B. grade . . . . **NiB $11,870 Ex $7279 Gd $6344**
S.A. grade . . . . **NiB $17,500 Ex $14,223 Gd $11,989**
S.A.1 Special (rare) . . **NiB $42,000 Ex $31,000 Gd $27,000**

SKEET GUN
Same as other Parker doubles from Grade V.H.E. up except selective single trigger and beavertail forearm are standard on this model, as are 26-in. bbls., SK choke. Discontinued about 1940. Values are 35 percent higher.

TROJAN HAMMERLESS DOUBLE-BARREL SHOTGUN
Boxlock. Plain extractors. Double trigger or single trigger. Gauges: 12, 16, 20. Bbls.: 30-in. both F choke (12 ga. only), 26- or 28-in. M and F choke. Weight: 6.25-7.75 lbs. Checkered pistol-grip stock and forearm. Disc. 1939.
12 ga. . . . . **NiB $5444 Ex $4249 Gd $2677**
16 ga. . . . . **NiB $6077 Ex $4488 Gd $3210**
20 ga. . . . . **NiB $6898 Ex $4539 Gd $3556**

SHOTGUNS

Parker B.H. Grade

Parker C.H. Grade

Parker A-1 Special Grade

Parker A.H. Grade

Parker S.C. Grade

Parker D.H. Grade

Parker G.H. Grade

Parker Trojan Hammerless Double-Barrel Shotgun

PARKER REPRODUCTIONS — Middlesex, NJ

NOTE: *Previous located in Webb City, MO and mfg. at Olin-Kodensha (Winchester) factory in Japan to original Parkers specs; production ended 1989. Starting in 2006, Remington and Connecticut Shotgun produced an AAHE in 28 ga., which has since been discontinued. JJE Capital Holdings bought Parker during the 2020 Remington bankruptcy.*

HAMMERLESS DOUBLE-BARREL SHOTGUNS

Reproduction of the original Parker boxlock. Single selective trigger or double triggers. Selective automatic ejectors. Automatic safety. Gauges: 12, 16, 20, 28 or .410 w/2.75- or 3-in. chambers. Bbls.: 26- or 28-in. w/fixed or internal screw choke tubes SK/SK, IC/M, M/F. Weight: 5.5-7 lbs. Checkered English-style or pistol-grip American walnut stock w/beavertail or splinter forend and checkered skeleton buttplate. Color casehardened receiver with game scenes and scroll engraving. Produced in Japan by Olin Kodensha from 1984-88.

DHE grade, 12 ga. . . . . NiB $4500 Ex $3400 Gd $2910
DHE grade, 20 ga . . . . NiB $5010 Ex $4855 Gd $3310
DHE grade, 28 ga . . . . NiB $6510 Ex $5510 Gd $3610
Sporting Clay model (choke tubes,
   2-bbl. set), add $700

w/beavertail forend, add $150
w/extra bbls., add $1000
DHE grade 2-bbl. set
   (16 & 20 ga.) . . . . NiB $8510 Ex $7510 Gd $5155
DHE grade 2-bbl. set
   (28 & .410) . . . . NiB $16500 Ex $14010 Gd $9020
DHE grade 3-bbl. set . . . . NiB $20,000 Ex $18000 Gd $14000
BHE Grade Lim. Ed., 12 ga. . . NiB $9000 Ex $8500 Gd $6130
20 ga. . . . . NiB $11000 Ex $9500 Gd $6500
28 ga. . . . . NiB $20,000 Ex $17500 Gd $13000
.410 ga. . . . . NiB $22,000 Ex $19,000 Gd $13,500

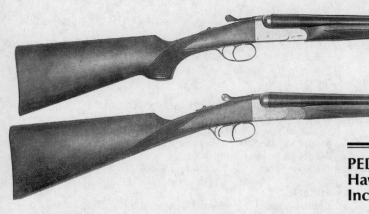

Parker-Hale Model 545A

Parker-Hale Model 645E

28 ga. and
.410 2 bbl. set. . . . . NiB $32,500 Ex $27,000 Gd $20,000
A-1 Special Grade
12 ga. . . . . NiB $16,000 Ex $13,500 Gd $10,500
20 ga. . . . . NiB $20,000 Ex $18,500 Gd $12,000
28 ga./.410 bore
2 bbl. set. . . . . . . NiB $35,000 Ex $30,000 Gd $20,0000
16/20 ga. 2 bbl. set. . NiB $30,000 Ex $28,000 Gd $20,0000
3-bbl. set. . . . . NiB $58,000 Ex $48,000 Gd $35,000
Custom Engraved model (all custom and value varies)
AAHE . . . . NiB $49,995 EX $45,000 GD $43,000
Recent reproduction of Parker with extensive graving and select wood stock and in 28 ga.

PARKER-HALE LIMITED — Manufactured by Ignacio Ugartechea, Spain

MODEL 645A (AMERICAN)
SIDE-BY-SIDE SHOTGUN . . . NiB $1344 Ex $1116 Gd $844
Gauges: 12, 16 and 20. Boxlock action. 26- and 28-in. bbls. Chokes: IC/M, M/F. Weight: 6 lbs. average. Single non-selective trigger. Automatic safety. Hand-checkered pistol grip walnut stock w/beavertail forend. Raised matted rib. English scroll-design engraved receiver. Disc. 1990.

MODEL 645E (ENGLISH) SIDE-BY-SIDE SHOTGUN
Same general specifications as the Model 645A except double triggers, straight grip, splinter forend, checkered butt and concave rib. Disc. 1990.
12, 16, 20 ga. w/ 26- or 28-in.
bbl. NiB $1388 Ex $1166 Gd $898
28, .410 ga. w/ 27-in.
bbl. . . . . NiB $1800 Ex $1490 Gd $1128

MODEL 645E-XXV
12, 16, 20 ga. w/ 25-in. bbl. NiB $1288 Ex $1189 Gd $900
28, .410 ga. w/ 25-in. bbl. . . . . . . NiB $1698 Ex $1377 Gd $1110

PEDERSEN CUSTOM GUNS — North Haven, CT; div. of O.F. Mossberg & Sons, Inc.

MODEL 1000 O/U HUNTING SHOTGUN
Boxlock. Auto ejectors. Selective single trigger. Gauges: 12, 20. 2.75-in. chambers in 12 ga., 3-in. in 20 ga. Bbls.: VR; 30-in. M/F (12 ga. only); 28-in. IC/M (12 ga. only), M/F; 26-in. IC/M. Checkered pistol-grip stock and forearm. Grade I is the higher quality gun with custom stock dimensions, fancier wood, more elaborate engraving, silver inlays. Made 1973-75.
Grade I . . . . NiB $2366 Ex $1969 Gd $1449
Grade II . . . . NiB $2210 Ex $1781 Gd $1290

MODEL 1000 MAGNUM
Same as Model 1000 Hunting Gun except chambered for 12-ga. Magnum 3-in. shells, 30-in. bbls., IM/F choke. Made 1973-75.
Grade I . . . . NiB $2809 Ex $2277 Gd $1677
Grade II . . . . NiB $2400 Ex $1900 Gd $1378

MODEL 1000 SKEET GUN
Same as Model 1000 Hunting Gun except has skeet-style stock; 26- and 28-in. bbls. (12 ga. only), SK choke. Made 1973-75.
Grade I . . . . NiB $2433 Ex $1977 Gd $1698
Grade II . . . . NiB $1998 Ex $1569 Gd $1062

MODEL 1000 TRAP GUN
Same as Model 1000 Hunting Gun except 12 ga. only, has Monte Carlo trap-style stock, 30- or 32-in. bbls., M/F or IM/F choke. Made 1973-75.
Grade I . . . . NiB $2287 Ex $1862 Gd $1300
Grade II . . . . NiB $1844 Ex $1477 Gd $1106

MODEL 1500 O/U
HUNTING SHOTGUN . . . . NiB $790 Ex $676 Gd $478
Boxlock. Auto ejectors. Selective single trigger. 12 ga. 2.75- or 3-in. chambers. Bbls.: VR; 26-in. IC/M; 28- and 30-in. M/F; Magnum has 30-in., IM/F choke. Weight: 7-7.5 lbs., depending on bbl. length. Checkered pistol-grip stock and forearm. Made 1973-75.

MODEL 1500 SKEET GUN . . . . NiB $833 Ex $690 Gd $569
Same as Model 1500 Hunting Gun except has skeet-style stock, 27-in. bbls., SK choke. Made 1973-75.

SHOTGUNS

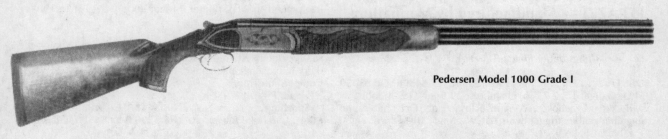

Pedersen Model 1000 Grade I

MODEL 1500 TRAP GUN.....NiB $788 Ex $648 Gd $520
Same as Model 1500 Hunting Gun except has Monte Carlo trap-style stock, 30- or 32-in. bbls., M/F or IM/F chokes. Made 1973-75.

MODEL 2000 HAMMERLESS DOUBLE
Boxlock. Auto ejectors. Selective single trigger. Gauges: 12, 20. 2.75-in. chambers in 12 ga., 3-in. in 20 ga. Bbls.: VR; 30-in. M/F (12 ga. only); 28-in. M/F, 26-in. IC/M choke. Checkered pistol-grip stock and forearm. Grade I is the higher quality gun w/custom dimensions, fancier wood, more elaborate engraving, silver inlays. Made 1973-74.
Grade I ....NiB $2887 Ex $2260 Gd $1740
Grade II ....NiB $2389 Ex $2276 Gd $1578

MODEL 2500
HAMMERLESS DOUBLE......NiB $780 Ex $655 Gd $356
Boxlock. Auto ejectors. Selective single trigger. Gauges: 12, 20. 2.75-in. chambers in 12 ga., 3-in. in 20 ga. Bbls.: VR; 28-in. M/F; 26-in. IC/M choke. Checkered pistol-grip stock and forearm. Made 1973-74.

MODEL 4000 HAMMERLESS SLIDE-ACTION
REPEATING SHOTGUN ......NiB $597 Ex $440 Gd $375
Custom version of Mossberg Model 500. Full-coverage floral engraving on receiver. Gauges: 12, 20, .410. Three-in. chamber. Bbls.: VR; 26-in. IC or SK choke; 28-in. F or M; 30-in. F. Weight: 6-8 lbs. depending on ga. and bbl. Checkered stock and slide handle of select wood. Made in 1975.

MODEL 4000 TRAP GUN.....NiB $590 Ex $466 Gd $265
Same as standard Model 4000 except 12 ga. only, has 30-in. F choke bbl., Monte Carlo trap-style stock w/recoil pad. Made in 1975.

MODEL 4500 ....NiB $500 Ex $390 Gd $335
Same as Model 4000 except has simpler scroll engraving. Made in 1975.

MODEL 4500 TRAP GUN.....NiB $525 Ex $420 Gd $366
Same as Model 4000 Trap Gun except has simpler scroll engraving. Made in 1975.

J. C. PENNEY CO., INC. — Dallas, TX

Savage, Springfield and Glenfield manufactured shotguns under the J.C. Penny name and model numbers.

MODEL 4011 - *See High Standard, Flight King model for specs. and value.*
MODEL 6610 - *See Savage, model 340 for specs. and value.*
MODEL 6630 - *See Glenfield, model 50 for specs. and value.*
MODEL 6670 - *See Springfield, model 67H for specs. and value.*
MODEL 6870 - *See Savage, Model 30 for specs. and value.*

PERAZZI — Manufactured by Manifattura Armi Perazzi, Brescia, Italy

See also listings under Ithaca-Perazzi.

DB81.................NiB $5266 Ex $4300 Gd $3450
O/U. Gauge: 12; 2.75-in. chambers. 29.5- or 31.5-in. bbls. w/ wide VR; M/F chokes. Weight: 8 lbs., 6 oz. Detachable and interchangeable trigger with flat V-springs. Bead front sight. Interchangeable and custom-made checkered stock; beavertail forend. Imported 1988 to 1994.

DB81 SINGLE-SHOT TRAP...NiB $5850 Ex $4700 Gd $3110
Same general specifications as the DB81 over/under except in single bbl. version w/32- or 34-in. wide VR bbl., F choke. Imported 1988 to 1994.

GRAND AMERICAN 88 SPECIAL SINGLE TRAP
Same general specifications as MX8 Special Single Trap except w/high ramped rib. Fixed choke or screw-in choke tubes.
Model 88 standard ....NiB $4988 Ex $3988 Gd $2777
Model 88 w/interchangeable
    choke tubes ....NiB $4990 Ex $4100 Gd $3099

MIRAGE
O/U. Gauge: 12; 2.75-in. chambers. Bbls.: 27.63-, 29.5- or 31.5-in. VR w/fixed chokes or screw-in choke tubes. Single selective trigger. Weight: 7 to 7.75 lbs. Interchangeable and custom-made checkered buttstock and forend.
Competition Trap,
    Skeet, Pigeon, Sporting ...NiB $6400 Ex $5440 Gd $3200
Skeet 4-bbl. sets .....NiB $14,680 Ex $12,890 Gd $9800
Competition Special (w/adj. 4-position
    trigger) add...................................$500

MX-1
O/U. Similar to Model MX8 except w/ramp-style, tapered rib and modified stock configuration.
Competition Trap, Skeet,
    Pigeon & Sporting .....NiB $7280 Ex $5010 Gd $3110
w/fixed chokes, subtract.........................20%
w/choke tubes, add................................$300

MX-2
O/U. Similar to Model MX-1 except w/broad high-ramped competition rib. Disc. 1996.
Competition-Trap, Skeet,
    Pigeon & Sporting .....NiB $7280 Ex $5010 Gd $3110
w/choke tubes, add.............................$300

MX-3
O/U. Similar to Model MX-8 model except w/ramp-style, tapered rib and modified stock configuration.
Competition Trap, Skeet,
    Pigeon & Sporting. NiB $48,988 Ex $42,998 Gd $35,999
Competition Special (w/adj. 4-position trigger) add ...$400
Game models ....NiB $4478 Ex $3659 Gd $2699
Combo O/U plus SB .....NiB $5563 Ex $4478 Gd $3380
SB Trap 32- or 34-in. .....NiB $3987 Ex $3166 Gd $2267
Skeet 4-bbl. sets ......NiB $12,888 Ex $10,099 Gd $7789
Skeet Special 4-bbl. sets ... NiB $13,066 Ex $11,288 Gd $8,996

MX-3 SPECIAL PIGEON ...NiB $5344 Ex $4276 Gd $3110
Gauge: 12; 2.75-in. chambers. 29.5- or 31.5-in. VR bbl.; IC/M and extra full chokes. Weight: 8 lbs., 6 oz. Detachable and interchangeable trigger group w/flat V-springs. Bead front sight. Interchangeable and custom-made checkered stock for live pigeon shoots; splinter forend. Imported 1991 to 1992.

MX-4
O/U. Similar to Model MX-3 in appearance and shares the MX8 locking system. Detachable, adj. 4-position trigger standard. Interchangeable choke tubes optional.
Competition Trap,
    Skeet, Pigeon &
    Sporting ....NiB $4487 Ex $4089 Gd $3124
MX4C (w/choke tubes) ...NiB $5388 Ex $4500 Gd $3787

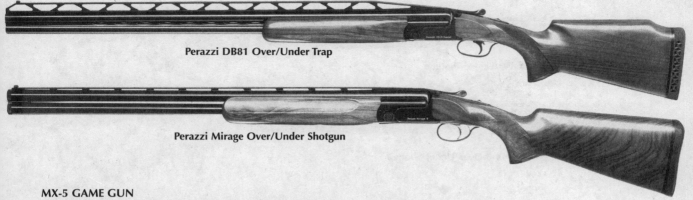

Perazzi DB81 Over/Under Trap

Perazzi Mirage Over/Under Shotgun

MX-5 GAME GUN

O/U. Similar to Model MX-8 except in hunting configuration, chambered in 12 or 20 ga. Non-detachable single selective trigger.

MX5 Standard . . . . NiB $4000 Ex $2886 Gd $2066
MX5C (w/choke tubes) . . . NiB $4264 Ex $3188 Gd $2200

MX-6 AMER.

TRAP SINGLE-BARREL . . . . NiB $4302 Ex $2677 Gd $1988
Single shot. Removable trigger group. 12 ga. Barrels: 32- or 34-in. with fixed or choke tubes. Raised VR. Checkered European walnut Monte Carlo stock, beavertail forend. Imported 1995 to 1998.

MX-6 SKEET . . . . NiB $4410 Ex $3410 Gd $2410
Same general specs as MX-6 American Trap single barrel except over/under; boxlock. Barrels: 26.75- or 27.50-in. Imported 1995 to 1998.

MX-6 SPORTING . . . . NiB $4277 Ex $3100 Gd $2250
Same specs as MX-6 American Trap single barrel except over/under; boxlock. Single selective trigger; external selector. Barrels: 28.38-, 29.50-, or 31.50-in. Imported 1995 to 1998.

MX-6 TRAP . . . . NiB $4350 Ex $2929 Gd $1877
Same general specs as MX-6 American Trap single barrel except over/under; boxlock. Barrels: 29.50-, 30.75-, or 31.50-in. Imported 1995 to 1998.

MX-7 . . . . NiB $4188 Ex $3755 Gd $2690
O/U. Similar to Model MX-12 except w/MX-3-style receiver and top-mounted trigger selector. Bbls.: 28.73-, 2.5-, 31.5-in. w/VR; screw-in choke tubes. Imported 1992 to 1998.

MX-8

O/U. Gauge: 12, 2.75-in. chambers. Bbls.: 27.63-, 29.5- or 31.5-in. VR w/fixed chokes or screw-in choke tubes. Weight: 7 to 8.5 lbs. Interchangeable and custom-made checkered stock; beavertail forend. Special models have detachable and interchangeable 4-position trigger group w/flat V-springs. Imported 1968 to date.

MX-8 Standard . . . . NiB $8099 Ex $4133 Gd $2377
MX-8 Special (adj. 4-pos.
   trigger) . . . . NiB $4229 Ex $3378 Gd $2490
MX-8 Special single
   (32-or 34-in. bbl.) . . . . NiB $8380 Ex $7121 Gd $4365
MX-8 Special combo . . . . . NiB $8009 Ex $6355 Gd $4682

MX-8/20 . . . . NiB $4155 Ex $3370 Gd $2499
Similar to the Model MX-8 except w/smaller frame and custom stock. Available in sporting or game configurations with fixed chokes or screw-in tubes. Imported 1993 to date.

MX-9 . . . . NiB $6880 Ex $5672 Gd $4200
Gauge: 12; 2.75-in. chambers. Bbls.: 29.5- or 30.5-in. w/choke tubes and vent side rib. Selective trigger. Checkered walnut stock w/adj. cheekpiece. Available in single bbl., combo, O/U trap, skeet, pigeon and sporting models. Imported 1993 to 1994.

MX-10 O/U SHOTGUN . . . NiB $8355 Ex $6270 Gd $5600
Similar to the Model MX-9 except w/fixed chokes and different rib configuration. Imported 1993.

MX-10 PIGEON-

ELECTROCIBLES . . . . NiB $8996 Ex $6133 Gd $4400
O/U. boxlock. Removable trigger group; external selector. 12 gauge. Barrels: 27.50- or 29.50-in. Checkered European walnut adjustable stock, beavertail forend. Imported 1995 to date.

MX–11 AMERICAN

TRAP COMBO . . . . NiB $5440 Ex $4688 Gd $3277
Over/Under; boxlock. External selector. Removable trigger group; single selective trigger. 12 ga. Bbls: 29-1/2- to 34-in. with fixed or choke tubes; VR. European walnut Monte Carlo adjustable stock, beavertail forend. Imported 1995 to date.

MX-11 AMERICAN TRAP

SINGLE BARREL . . . . NiB $5155 Ex $4309 Gd $2879
Same general specs as MX11 American Trap combo except 32- or 34-in. single bbl. Imported 1995 to 1996.

MX-11 PIGEON-ELECTROCIBLES

O/U . . . . NiB $5331 Ex $4277 Gd $3100
Same specs as MX11 American Trap combo except 27.50 O/U bbls. Checkered European walnut pistol grip adjustable stock, beavertail forend. Imported 1995 to 1996.

MX-11 SKEET O/U . . . . NiB $5390 Ex $4369 Gd $3122
Same general specs as MX11 American Trap combo except 26.75 or 27.50-in. O/U bbls. Checkered European walnut pistol-grip adjustable stock, beavertail forend. Imported 1995 to 1996.

MX-11 SPORTING O/U . . . NiB $5344 Ex $4766 Gd $3409
Same general specs as MX11 American Trap combo except 28.38, 29.50-, or 31.50-in. O/U bbls. Checkered European walnut pistol-grip adjustable stock, beavertail forend. Imported 1995 to 1996.

MX-11 TRAP O/U . . . . NiB $5293 Ex $4266 Gd $3109
Same general specs as MX11 American Trap combo except 29.50,- 30.75, or 31.50-in. O/U bbls. Checkered European

GRADING: **NiB** = New in Box   **Ex** = Excellent or NRA 95%   **Gd** = Good or NRA 68%   **541**

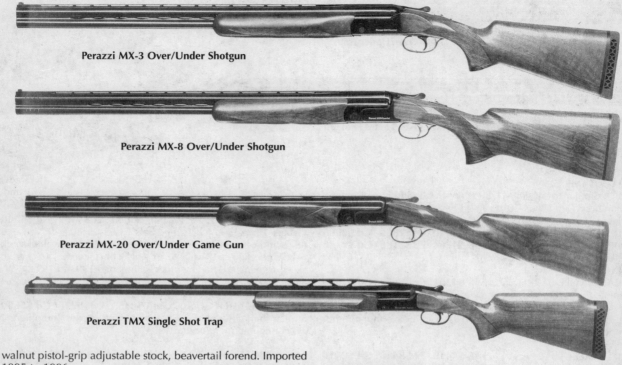

Perazzi MX-3 Over/Under Shotgun

Perazzi MX-8 Over/Under Shotgun

Perazzi MX-20 Over/Under Game Gun

Perazzi TMX Single Shot Trap

walnut pistol-grip adjustable stock, beavertail forend. Imported 1995 to 1996.

MX-12 O/U GAME GUN
Gauge: 12, 2.75-in. chambers. Bbls.: 26-, 27.63-, 28.38- or 29.5-in., VR, fixed chokes or screw-in choke tubes. Non-detachable single selective trigger group w/coil springs. Weight: 7.25 lbs. Interchangeable and custom-made checkered stock; Schnabel forend.
Standard . . . . NiB $8600 Ex $5855 Gd $4110
w/choke tubes, add. $400

MX-14 AMERICAN TRAP
SINGLE-BARREL . . . . NiB $10,955 Ex $8000 Gd $5455
Single shot. Removable trigger group; unsingle configuration. 12 ga. Bbl: 34-in. with fixed or choke tubes; VR. Checkered European walnut Monte Carlo adjustable stock, beavertail forend. Imported 1995 to 1996.

MX-15 AMERICAN TRAP
SINGLE-BARREL . . . . NiB $6810 Ex $4855 Gd $3310
Full choke. Detachable trigger group. Gauge: 12 only w/ 2.75-in. chamber. Bbls: 32 and 34-in. Weight: 8 lbs., 6 oz.

MX-20 GAME GUN
O/U. Gauges: 20, 28 and .410; 2.75- or 3-in. chambers. 26-in. VR bbls., M/F chokes or screw-in chokes. Auto selective ejectors. Selective single trigger. Weight: 6 lbs., 6 oz. Non-detachable coil-spring trigger. Bead front sight. Interchangeable and custom-made checkered stock w/Schnabel forend. Imported from 1988 to date.
Standard grade . . . . NiB $8610 Ex $5855 Gd $4110
MX20C w/choke tubes, add $450

MX-28 GAME GUN
. . . . NiB $16,500 Ex $9,555 Gd $7010
Similar to the Model MX-12 except chambered in 28 ga. w/26-in. bbls. fitted to smaller frame. Imported from 1993 to date.

w/choke tubes, add. $400

MX-410 GAME GUN
. . . . . NiB $16,555 Ex $9,555 Gd $7,010
O/U. Similar to the Model MX-12 except in .410 bore w/3-in. chambers, 26-in. bbls. fitted to smaller frame. Imported from 1993 to date.

TM1 SPECIAL
SINGLE-SHOT TRAP . . . . . . NiB $3150 Ex $2770 Gd $2000
Gauge: 12- 2.75-in. chambers. 32- or 34-in. bbl. w/wide VR; full choke. Weight: 8 lbs., 6 oz. Detachable and interchangeable trigger group with coil springs. Bead front sight. Interchangeable and custom-made stock w/checkered pistol grip and beavertail forend. Imported from 1988 to 1995.

TMX SPECIAL
SINGLE-SHOT TRAP . . . . . . NiB $3890 Ex $2553 Gd $1966
Same general specifications as Model TM1 Special except w/ ultra-high rib. Interchangeable choke tubes optional.

PIOTTI — Brescia, Italy

BOSS O/U . . . . NiB $58,998 Ex $50,000 Gd $35,965
Over/Under; sidelock. Gauges: 12 or 20. Barrels: 26- to 32-in. Standard chokes. Best quality walnut. Custom-made to customer's specifications. Imported from 1993 to date.

KING NO. 1 SIDELOCK . . . NiB $35,866 Ex $29,821 Gd $19,670
Gauges: 10, 12, 16, 20, 28 and .410. 25- to 30-in. bbls. (12 ga.), 25- to 28-in. (other ga.). Weight: About 5 lbs. (.410) to 8 lbs. (12 ga.) Holland & Holland pattern sidelock. Double triggers standard. Coin finish or color casehardened. Level file-cut rib. Full-coverage scroll engraving, gold inlays. Hand-rubbed, oil-finished, straight-grip stock with checkered butt, splinter forend.

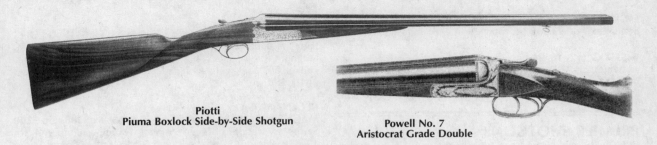

Piotti
Piuma Boxlock Side-by-Side Shotgun

Powell No. 7
Aristocrat Grade Double

KING EXTRA SIDE-BY-SIDE

SHOTGUN . . . . NiB $77,850 Ex $52,290 Gd $42,777
Same general specifications as the Piotti King No. 1 except has choice of engraving, gold inlays, plus stock is of exhibition-grade wood.

LUNIK SIDE-LOCK

SHOTGUN . . . . NiB $35,660 Ex $31,299 Gd $26,000
Same general specifications as the Monte Carlo model except has level, file-cut rib. Renaissance-style, large scroll engraving in relief, gold crown in top lever, gold name, and gold crest in forearm, finely figured wood.

MONTE CARLO

SIDE-LOCK SHOTGUN . NiB $11,488 Ex $9889 Gd $7577
Gauges: 10, 12, 16, 20, 28 or .410. Bbls.: 25- to 30-in. Holland & Holland pattern sidelock. Weight: 5-8 lbs. Automatic ejectors. Double triggers. Hand-rubbed oil-finished straight-grip stock with checkered butt. Choice of Purdey-style scroll and rosette or Holland & Holland-style large scroll engraving.

PIUMA BOXLOCK SIDE-BY-SIDE

SHOTGUN . . . . NiB $18,667 Ex $12,933 Gd $10,011
Same general specifications as the Monte Carlo model except has Anson & Deeley boxlock action w/demi-bloc bbls., scalloped frame. Standard scroll and rosette engraving. Hand-rubbed, oil-finished straight-grip stock.

WILLIAM POWELL & SON, LTD. — Birmingham, England

NO. 1 BEST GRADE DOUBLE-BARREL

SHOTGUN . . . . NiB $42,777 Ex $38,698 Gd $31,033
Sidelock. Gauges: Made to order w/ 12, 16 and 20 the most common. Bbls.: Made to order in any length but 28 in. was recommended. Highest grade French walnut buttstock and forearm with fine checkering. Metal elaborately engraved. Imported by Stoeger from about 1938 to 1951.

NO. 2 BEST GRADE

DOUBLE-BARREL . . NiB $29,766 Ex $24,761 Gd $16,888
Same general specifications as the Powell No. 1 except plain finish without engraving. Imported by Stoeger from about 1938 to 1951.

NO. 6 CROWN GRADE

DOUBLE-BARREL . . NiB $15,999 Ex $12,733 Gd $10,111
Boxlock. Gauges: Made to order w/ 12, 16 and 20 the most common. Bbls.: Made to order, but 28 in. was recommended. Highest grade French walnut buttstock and forearm with fine checkering. Metal elaborately engraved. Uses Anson & Deeley locks. Imported by Stoeger from about 1938 to 1951.

NO. 7 ARISTOCRAT GRADE DOUBLE-BARREL

SHOTGUN . . . . NiB $9022 Ex $6988 Gd $4766
Same general specifications as the Powell No. 6 Crown Grade Double-Barrel above, except with lower quality wood and metal engraving.

PRECISION SPORTS SHOTGUNS

Importer located in Cortland, NY; manufactured by Ignacio Ugartechea, Spain.

600 SERIES AMERICAN HAMMERLESS DOUBLES

Boxlock. Single selective trigger. Selective automatic ejectors. Automatic safety. Gauges: 12, 16, 20, 28, .410; 2.75- or 3-in. chambers. Bbls.: 26-,27- or 28-in. w/raised matte rib; choked IC/M or M/F. Weight: 5.75-7 lbs. Checkered pistol-grip walnut buttstock with beavertail forend. Engraved silvered receiver with blued bbls. Imported from 1986 to 1994.

640A (12, 16, 20 ga. w/extractors) . . . NiB $1177 Ex $909 Gd $677
640A (28 ga., .410 w/extractors) . . . NiB $1288 Ex $1067 Gd $779
640 Slug Gun (12 ga.
   w/extractors) . . . . NiB $1277 Ex $1059 Gd $723
645A (12, 16, 20 ga.
   w/ejectors) . . . . NiB $1177 Ex $909 Gd $677
645A (28 ga., .410, two-bbl. set) . . . NiB $1488 Ex $1176 Gd $877
645A (20/28 ga. two-bbl. set) . . . NiB $1563 Ex $1253 Gd $919
650A (12 ga. w/extractors,
   choke tubes) . . . . NiB $1165 Ex $977 Gd $710
655A (12 ga. w/ejectors,
   choke tubes) . . . . NiB $1288 Ex $1022 Gd $766

600 SERIES ENGLISH HAMMERLESS DOUBLES

Boxlock. Same general specifications as American 600 series except w/double triggers and concave rib. Checkered English-style walnut stock w/splinter forend, straight grip and oil finish.

640E (12, 16, 20 ga. w/extractors) . . . NiB $956 Ex $790 Gd $622
640E (28 ga., .410 w/extractors) . . . . NiB $1088 Ex $900 Gd $644
640 Slug Gun (12 ga.
   w/extractors) . . . . NiB $1297 Ex $1044 Gd $780
645E (12, 16, 20 ga. w/ejectors) . . . NiB $1300 Ex $1066 Gd $800
645E (28 ga., .410 w/ejectors) . . . . . NiB $1266 Ex $1022 Gd $776
645E (20/28 ga. two-bbl. set) . . . . . NiB $1545 Ex $1296 Gd $1000
650E (12 ga. w/extractors,
   choke tubes) . . . . NiB $1178 Ex $938 Gd $715
655E (12 ga. w/ejectors,
   choke tubes) . . . . NiB $1190 Ex $980 Gd $750

MODEL 640M MAGNUM 10 HAMMERLESS DOUBLE

Similar to Model 640E except in 10 ga. w/3.5-in. Mag. chambers. Bbls.: 26-, 30-, 32-in. choked F/F.
Model 640M Big Ten, Turkey   NiB $1106 Ex $933 Gd $700
Model 640M Goose Gun . . . . NiB $1133 Ex $955 Gd $735

GRADING: **NiB** = New in Box   **Ex** = Excellent or NRA 95%   **Gd** = Good or NRA 68%

MODEL 645E-XXV HAMMERLESS DOUBLE
Similar to Model 645E except w/25-in. bbl. and Churchill-style rib.

645E-XXV (12, 16, 20 ga.
 w/ejectors) . . . . NiB $1160 Ex $982 Gd $755
645E-XXV (28, .410 ga.
 w/ejectors) . . . . NiB $1366 Ex $1093 Gd $835

PREMIER SHOTGUNS
Premier shotguns have been produced by various gunmakers in Europe.

AMBASSADOR MODEL FIELD GRADE HAMMERLESS
DOUBLE-BARREL SHOTGUN. . NiB $544 Ex $466 Gd $377
Sidelock. Plain extractors. Double triggers. Gauges: 12, 16, 20, .410. 3-in. chambers in 20 and .410 ga., 2.75- in. in 12 and 16 ga. Bbls.: 26-in. in .410 ga., 28 in. in other ga.; choked M/F. Weight: 6 lbs., 3 oz.-7 lbs., 3 oz. depending on gauge. Checkered pistol-grip stock and beavertail forearm. Intro. in 1957; disc.

BRUSH KING . . . . NiB $440 Ex $330 Gd $255
Same as standard Regent model except chambered for 12 (2.75-in.) and 20 ga. (3-in.) only; has 22-in. bbls., IC/M choke, straight-grip stock. Weight: 6 lbs., 3 oz. in 12 ga.; 5 lbs., 12 oz. in 20 ga. Introduced in 1959; disc.

CONTINENTAL MODEL FIELD GRADE HAMMER
DOUBLE-BARREL SHOTGUN. . NiB $577 Ex $426 Gd $300
Sidelock. Exposed hammers. Plain extractors. Double triggers. Gauges: 12, 16, 20, .410. Three inch chambers in 20 and .410 ga., 2.75-in. in 12 and 16 ga. Bbls.: 26-in. in .410 ga.; 28-in. in other ga.; choked M/F. Weight: 6 lbs., 3 oz.-7 lbs., 3 oz. depending on gauge. Checkered pistol-grip stock and English-style forearm. Introduced in 1957; disc.

MONARCH SUPREME GRADE HAMMERLESS
DOUBLE-BARREL SHOTGUN. . NiB $667 Ex $487 Gd $367
Boxlock. Auto ejectors. Double triggers. Gauges: 12, 20. 2.75-in. chambers in 12 ga., 3-in. in 20 ga. Bbls.: 28-in. M/F; 26-in. IC/M choke. Weight: 6 lbs., 6 oz., 7 lbs., 2 oz. depending on gauge and bbl. Checkered pistol-grip stock and beavertail forearm of fancy walnut. Introduced in 1959; disc.

PRESENTATION
CUSTOM GRADE . . . . NiB $1488 Ex $1109 Gd $856
Similar to Monarch model but made to order of higher quality with hunting scene engraving, gold and silver inlay, fancier wood. Introduced in 1959; disc.

REGENT 10 GA.
MAGNUM EXPRESS . . . . NiB $665 Ex $431 Gd $345
Same as standard Regent model except chambered for 10-ga. Magnum 3.5-in. shells, has heavier construction, 32-in. bbls. choked F/F, stock with recoil pad. Weight: 11.25 lbs. Introduced in 1957; disc.

REGENT 12 GA.
MAGNUM EXPRESS . . . . NiB $465 Ex $388 Gd $290
Same as standard Regent model except chambered for 12-ga. Magnum 3-in. shells, has 30-in. bbls. choked F and F, stock with recoil pad. Weight: 7.25 lbs. Introduced in 1957; disc.

REGENT FIELD GRADE HAMMERLESS
DOUBLE-BARREL SHOTGUN. . NiB $477 Ex $355 Gd $271
Boxlock. Plain extractors. Double triggers. Gauges: 12,16, 20, 28, .410. Three inch chambers in 20 and .410 ga., 2.75-in. in other gauges. Bbls.: 26-in. IC/M, M/F (28 and .410 ga. only); 28-in. M/F; 30-in. M/F (12 ga. only). Weight: 6 lbs., 2 oz.-7 lbs., 4 oz. depending on gauge and bbl. Checkered pistol-grip stock and beavertail forearm. Introduced in 1955; disc.

JAMES PURDEY & SONS, LTD. —
London, England

HAMMERLESS DOUBLE-BARREL SHOTGUN
Sidelock. Auto ejectors. Single or double triggers. Gauges: 12, 16, 20. Bbls.: 26-, 27-, 28-, 30-in. (latter in 12 ga. only);any boring, any shape or style of rib. Weight: 5.25-5.5 lbs. depending on model, gauge and bbl length. Checkered stock and forearm, straight grip standard, pistol-grip also available. Purdey guns of this type have been made from about 1880 to date. Models include: Game Gun, Featherweight Game Gun, Two-in. Gun (chambered for 12 ga. 2-in. shells), Pigeon Gun (w/3rd fastening and side clips), values of all models are the same.
With double triggers . . NiB $62,700 Ex $54,890 Gd $44,782
With single trigger, add. $1000

OVER/UNDER SHOTGUN
Sidelock. Auto ejectors. Single or double triggers. Gauges: 12 16, 20. Bbls.: 26-, 27-, 28-, 30-in. (latter in 12 ga. only); any boring, any style rib. Weight: 6-7.5 pounds depending on gauge and bbl. length. Checkered stock and forend, straight or pistol grip. Prior to WW II, the Purdey Over/Under Gun was made with a Purdey action; since the war James Purdey & Sons have acquired the busi-ness of James Woodward & Sons and all Purdey over/under guns are now built on the Woodward principle. General specifications of both types are the same.

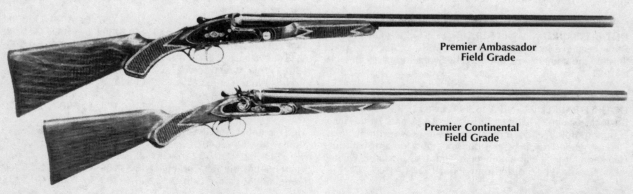

Premier Ambassador
Field Grade

Premier Continental
Field Grade

**Purdey Hammerless
Double-Barrel Shotgun**

With Purdey action,
   double triggers . . . NiB $78,880 Ex $52,609 Gd $24,655
With Woodward action, double triggers, add $3000
w/single trigger, add 10%

SINGLE-BARREL
TRAP GUN . . . . NiB $12,775 Ex $10,560 Gd $8,300
Sidelock. Mechanical features similar to those of the over/under model with Purdey action. 12 ga. only. Built to customer's specifications. Made prior to World War II.

REMINGTON ARMS CO. — Ilion, NY

NOTE: *Eliphalet Remington Jr. began making long arms with his father in 1816. In 1828 they moved their facility to Ilion, N.Y., where it remained a family-run business for decades. As the family began to diminish, other people bought controlling interests and today, still a successful gunmaking company, it is a subsidiary of the DuPont Corporation. Currently owned by the Freedom Group. Remington declared bankruptcy in 2020 and Roundhill Group purchased the Remington firearms business. Relaunched RemArms in 2023 with limited production.*

MODEL 10A STANDARD GRADE SLIDE-ACTION
REPEATING SHOTGUN . . . . . . NiB $420 Ex $335 Gd $255
Hammerless. Takedown. Six-round capacity. 12 ga. only. Five shell tubular magazine. Bbls.: Plain; 26- to 32-in.; choked F, M or Cyl. Weight: About 7.5 lbs. Plain pistol-grip stock, grooved slide handle. Made 1907-29.

MODEL 11 SPECIAL, TOURNAMENT, EXPERT AND PREMIER GRADE GUNS
These higher grade models differ from the Model 11A in general quality, grade of wood, checkering, engraving, etc. General specifications are the same.
11B Special grade . . . . NiB $788 Ex $609 Gd $466
11D Tournament grade . . . . . NiB $1388 Ex $1122 Gd $866
11E Expert grade . . . . NiB $1880 Ex $1455 Gd $1090
11F Premier grade . . . . NiB $2998 Ex $2356 Gd $1800

MODEL 11A STANDARD GRADE AUTOLOADER
Hammerless Browning type. Five round capacity. Takedown. Gauges: 12, 16, 20. Tubular magazine holds four rounds. Bbls.: Plain, solid or VR, lengths from 26-32 in., F, M, IC, Cyl., SK chokes. Weight: About 8 lbs., 12 ga.; 7.5 lbs., 16 ga.; 7.25 lbs., 20 ga. Checkered pistol grip and forend. Made 1905-49.
w/plain bbl. . . . . NiB $355 Ex $260 Gd $229
w/solid-rib bbl. . . . . NiB $477 Ex $339 Gd $366
w/ventilated-rib bbl. . . . . .NiB $544 Ex $420 Gd $367

MODEL 11R RIOT GUN . . . . . . NiB $445 Ex $300 Gd $195
Same as Model 11A Standard grade except has 20-in. plain bbl., 12 ga. only. Remington Model 11-48. (See Remington Sportsman-48 Series.)

NOTE: *Model 11-87 bbls. are not interchangable w/ Model 1100 bbls.*

MODEL 11-87 PREMIER AUTOLOADER
Gas-operated. Gauge: 12; 3-in. chamber. Bbl.: 26-, 28- or 30-in. with REMChoke. Weight: 8.13- 8.38 lbs., depending on bbl. length. Checkered walnut w/ satin finish. Made 1987-2006.
Deer Gun w/cant. scope mt. . . . NiB $855 Ex $654 Gd $477
Premier Skeet (1987-99) . . . . . NiB $740 Ex $535 Gd $420
Premier Standard . . . . NiB $766 Ex $598 Gd $455
Premier Trap (1987-99) . . . . NiB $844 Ex $707 Gd $510
Left-hand models, add $125

MODEL 11-87 PREMIER SUPER MAGNUM
Gas-operated. Gauge: 12 only, 3-1/2-in. chamber. Bbl.: 28-in. only with extended REMChoke. Weight: 8.4 lbs. Checkered gloss finish walnut stock and forend. Made 2001-06.
standard . . . . NiB $760 Ex $622 Gd $479
Camo (disc. 2004) . . . . NiB $836 Ex $684 Gd $489

MODEL 11-87 SP (SPECIAL PURPOSE)
Same general specifications as Model 11-87 Premier except with non-reflective wood finish and Parkerized metal. 26-, 28- or 30-in. VR bbl. with REMChoke tubes. Made 1987-93.
standard . . . . NiB $600 Ex $400 Gd $280
Deer Gun (21-in. bbl., rifle sights) NiB $690 Ex $445 Gd $295
Magnum (3-1/2-in. chamber) . . NiB $730 Ex $450 Gd $300

MODEL 11-87 SPS (SPECIAL PURPOSE SYNTHETIC)
Same general specifications as Model 11-87 SP except with synthetic buttstock and forend. 21-, 26- or 28-in. VR bbl. with REMChoke tubes. Matte black or Mossy Oak camo finish (except NWTF turkey gun). Made 1990-2007.
Deer Gun (21-in. bbl., rifle
   sights) . . . . NiB $696 Ex $494 Gd $358
Magnum (3-in., matte black,
   disc. 2004) . . . . NiB $733 Ex $643 Gd $471
Camo (Mossy Oak camo) . . . . NiB $760 Ex $622 Gd $479
Deer Gun w/cant. scope mt.
   (1987-2005) . . . . NiB $859 Ex $633 Gd $490
NWTF Turkey Gun
   (Brown Trebark, disc. 1993) NiB $775 Ex $690 Gd $510
NWTF Turkey Gun
   (Greenleaf, disc. 1996) . . . . . NiB $725 Ex $650 Gd $479
NWTF Turkey
   Gun (Mossy Oak, disc. 1996) NiB $730 Ex $655 Gd $485
NWTF Turkey Gun (Mossy Oak Breakup,
   introduced 1999) . . . . NiB $730 Ex $655 Gd $485
NWTF 20 ga. Turkey Gun (Mossy Oak
   Breakup, 1998 only) . . . . NiB $730 Ex $655 Gd $485
Thumbhole Deer Gun
   (2006-07) . . . . NiB $730 Ex $655 Gd $485
SPST Turkey Gun (matte bl.) . . NiB $730 Ex $655 Gd $485
Super Magnum (3-1/2-in.,
   matte black, disc. 2007) . . . . NiB $950 Ex $730 Gd $300
Super Magnum Turkey Camo (3-1/2-in., Mossy
   Oak Breakup, disc. 2007) . . . NiB $950 Ex $730 Gd $300
Waterfowl (Mossy Oak Shadow
   Grass) . . . . NiB $1010 Ex $780 Gd $530

GRADING: NiB = New in Box   Ex = Excellent or NRA 95%   Gd = Good or NRA 68%

SHOTGUNS

Purdey Over and Under

Purdey Single-Shot Trap

MODEL 11-87 SPORTING
CLAYS . . . . **NiB $866 Ex $700 Gd $509**
Gas-operated. Gauge: 12 only. Bbl.: 26-in. only with extended REMChoke. Weight: 7.5 lbs. Checkered satin finish walnut stock and forend. Made 1929-99.
NP (nickel plated receiver) . . . . NiB $890 Ex $735 Gd $533

MODEL 11-87 SPORTSMAN
Same general specifications as Model 11-87 Premier except with matte metal finish. 12 or 20 ga. Bbl.: 20- or 21-in. rifled or 26- or 28-in. w/ REMChoke. Weight: 7.3-8.3 lbs. Made 2005-20.
Camo (Mossy Oak New Breakup) . . . NiB $915 Ex $570 Gd $370
Field (wood stock). . . . . NiB $845 Ex $470 Gd $270
ShurShot (synthetic thumbhole stock, cantilever
   scope mount) . . . . NiB $1012 Ex $680 Gd $430
Synthetic (synthetic stock) . . . NiB $804 Ex $460 Gd $260
Synthetic Deer (synthetic stock,
   cantilever. scope mount) . . NiB $929 Ex $585 Gd $385

MODEL 11-96 EURO LIGHTWEIGHT
AUTOLOADING SHOTGUN . . NiB $800 Ex $644 Gd $500
Lightweight version of Model 11-87 w/reprofiled receiver. 12 ga. only w/3-in. chamber. 26- or 28-in. bbl. w/6mm VR and RemChoke tubes. Semi-fancy Monte Carlo walnut buttstock and forearm. Weight: 6.8 lbs. w/26-in. bbl. Made in 1996 only.

MODEL 17A STANDARD GRADE SLIDE-ACTION REPEATING SHOTGUN
Hammerless. Takedown. Five round capacity. 20 ga. only. Four round tubular magazine. Bbls.: plain; 26- to 32-in.; choked F, M or Cyl. Weight: About 5.75 lbs. Plain pistol-grip stock, grooved slide handle. Made 1921-33. Note: The present Ithaca Model 37 is an adaptation of this Browning design.
Plain bbl.. . . . . NiB $422 Ex $292 Gd $190
Solid rib . . . . NiB $490 Ex $400 Gd $290

MODEL 29A STANDARD GRADE SLIDE-ACTION
REPEATING SHOTGUN . . . . . . NiB $390 Ex $300 Gd $287
Hammerless. Takedown. Six round capacity. 12 ga. only. Five round tubular magazine. Bbls.: plain- 26- to 32-in., choked F, M or Cyl. Weight: About 7.5 lbs. Checkered pistol-grip stock and slide handle. Made 1929-33.

MODEL 29T TARGET GRADE . . NiB $600 Ex $490 Gd $377
Same general specifications as Model 29A except has trap-style stock with straight grip, extension slide handle, VR bbl. Disc. 1933.

MODEL 31/31L SKEET GRADE
Same general specifications as Model 31A except has 26-in. bbl. with raised solid or VR, SK choke, checkered pistol-grip stock and beavertail forend. Weight: About 8 lbs., 12 ga. Made 1932-39.
Model 31 Standard w/raised
   solid rib . . . . NiB $477 Ex $290 Gd $200
Model 31 Standard w/ventilated
   rib . . . . NiB $566 Ex $408 Gd $335
Model 31L Lightweight w/raised
   solid rib . . . . NiB $455 Ex $330 Gd $245
Model 31L Lightweight w/ventilated
   rib . . . . NiB $555 Ex $350 Gd $287

MODEL 31A MODELS
Pump action. Hammerless. Takedown. 3- or 5-rnd. capacity. Gauges: 12, 16, 20. Tubular magazine. Bbls.: Plain, solid or VR; lengths from 26 -32 in.; F, M, IC, C or SK choke. Weight: About 7.5 lbs., 12 ga.; 6.75 lbs., 16 ga.; 6.5 lbs., 20 ga. Earlier models have checkered pistol-grip stock and slide handle; later models have plain stock and grooved slide handle. Made 1931-49.
Model 31A w/ plain bbl. . . . . . . NiB 410 Ex $360 Gd $270
Model 31A w/ solid rib bbl. . . . . . NiB $480 Ex $410 Gd $310
Model 31A w/ VR bbl. . . . . NiB $510 Ex $430 Gd $330
Model 31H Hunter
   (sporting-style stock) . . . . . . NiB $430 Ex $360 Gd $280
Model 31R Riot Gun (20-in.
   plain bbl., 12 ga.) . . . . NiB $510 Ex $450 Gd $330
Model 31B Special (high grade
   wood stock) . . . . NiB $660 Ex $560 Gd $400
Model 31D Tournament
   (high grade wood stock,
   scroll engraving) . . . . NiB $1610 Ex $1360 Gd $890
Model 31E Expert (high grade wood stock, game scene
   engraving). . . . . NiB $1760 Ex $1510 Gd $1110
Model 31F Premier (high grade wood stock, game scene
   engraving). . . . . NiB $2960 Ex $2560 Gd $1880

MODEL 31/31L SKEET GRADE
Same general specifications as Model 31A except has 26-in. bbl. with raised solid or VR, SK choke, checkered pistol-grip stock and beavertail forend. Weight: About 8 lbs., 12 ga. Made 1932-39.
Model 31 Standard w/raised
   solid rib . . . . NiB $500 Ex $455 Gd $370
Model 31 Standard w/ventilated
   rib. . . . . NiB $660 Ex $555 Gd $430
Model 31L (lightweight receiver), add 10%

MODEL 31S TRAP SPECIAL/31TC TRAP GRADE
Same general specifications as Model 31A except 12 ga. only, has 30- or 32-in. VR bbl., F choke, checkered trap stock with full pistol grip and recoil pad, checkered extension beavertail

Remington Model 31

Remington Model 11-87 SPS

Remington Model SP-10 Magnum Camo

forend. Weight: About 8 lbs. (Trap Special has solid-rib bbl., half pistol-grip stock with standard walnut forend).

Model 31S Trap Special ...... **NiB $560 Ex $510 Gd $410**
Model 31TC Trap grade ...... **NiB $880 Ex $810 Gd $580**
w/lightweight receiver, add **10%**

MODEL 32A STANDARD GRADE

O/U. Hammerless. Takedown. Auto ejectors. Early model had double triggers, later built with selective single trigger only. 12 ga. only. Bbls.: Plain, raised matted solid or VR; 26-, 28-, 30-, 32-in.; F/M choke standard, option of any combination of F, M, IC, C, SK choke. Weight: About 7.75 lbs. Checkered pistol-grip stock and forend. Made 1932-42.

w/double triggers .... **NiB $2165 Ex $1800 Gd $1287**
w/selective single
  trigger .... **NiB $2466 Ex $2100 Gd $1533**
w/raised solid rib, add **10%**
w/ventilated rib, add **20%**

MODEL 32 TOURNAMENT, EXPERT AND PREMIER GRADE GUNS

These higher-grade models differ from the Model 32A in general quality, grade of wood, checkering, engraving, etc. General specifications are the same. Made 1932-42.

Model 32D Tournament
  grade .... **NiB $3755 Ex $3310 Gd $2560**
Model 32E Expert grade ... **NiB $4555 Ex $4166 Gd $3000**
Model 32F Premier
  grade .... **NiB $6555 Ex $5809 Gd $3976**

MODEL 32 SKEET GRADE .. **NiB $2200 Ex $1798 Gd $1433**
Same general specifications as Model 32A except 26- or 28-in. bbl., SK choke, beavertail forend, selective single trigger only. Weight: About 7.5 lbs. Made 1932-42.

MODEL 32TC

TARGET (TRAP) GRADE .. **NiB $3233 Ex $2866 Gd $1974**
Same general specifications as Model 32A except 30- or 32-in. VR bbl., F choke, trap-style stock with checkered pistol-grip and beavertail forend. Weight: About 8 lbs. Made l932-42.

MODEL 89 (1889) .... **NiB $2133 Ex $1788 Gd $1141**
Hammers. Circular action. Gauges: 10, 12, 16, 28- to 32-in. bls.; steel or Damascus twist. Weight 7-10 lbs. Made 1889-08.

MODEL 90-T SINGLE-SHOT

TRAP................ **NiB $1988 Ex $1790 Gd $1377**
Gauge: 12; 2.75-in. chambers. 30-, 32- or 34-in. VR bbl. with fixed chokes or screw-in REMChokes; ported or non-ported. Weight: 8.25 lbs. Checkered American walnut standard or Monte Carlo stock with low-luster finish. Engraved sideplates and drop-out trigger group optional. Made 1990-97.

MODEL 105 CTI .... **NiB $1230 Ex $880 Gd $600**
Gas-operated, Semiauto. Titanium and carbon fiber receiver. Gauge: 12; 3-in. chamber. Bbl.: 26- or 28-in. with REMChoke. Weight: 7 lbs., depending on bbl. length. Checkered walnut stock and forend in satin finish. Made 2006-08.
105 CTi-II (2009 only) ...... **NiB $1230 Ex $880 Gd $600**

MODEL 300 IDEAL.......... **NiB $1155 Ex $880 Gd $755**
O/U. Boxlock action. Gauge: 12, 3-in. chamber. Bbls.: 26-, 28- or 30-in. VR w/3 RemChoke tubes. Finish: Gloss blue. Stock: Checkered satin walnut. Sights: two beads. Weight: 7.3-7.7 lbs. Engraved receiver. Made 2000-01.

MODEL 332 SERIES

O/U. Underlock boxlock action. Gauge: 12, 3-in. chamber. Bbls.: 26-, 28- or 30-in. VR w/3 RemChoke tubes. Finish: matte black. Stock: Checkered high gloss walnut. Sights: two beads. Weight: 7.5-8 lbs. Engraved receiver. Made 2001-06.
standard model............. **NiB $1430 Ex $930 Gd $630**
Peerless D Grade model .... **NiB $3155 Ex $1510 Gd $1400**
Premier F Grade model..... **NiB $6300 Ex $2980 Gd $2800**

MODEL 396 O/U

Boxlock. 12 ga. only w/2.75-in. chamber. 28- and 30-in. blued bbls. w/Rem chokes. Weight: 7.50 lbs. Nitride-grayed, engraved receiver, trigger guard, tang, hinge pins and forend metal. Engraved sideplates. Checkered satin-finished American walnut stock w/target style forend. Made 1996-98.
Sporting Clays........... **NiB $1933 Ex $1658 Gd $1277**
Skeet.................. **NiB $1855 Ex $1544 Gd $1153**

NOTE: *The Model 870 was introduced in 1950. Over 11 million have been built to date. Early models featured fixed chokes. In 1986, the screw-in RemChoke choke tube system was introduced. In 1969, Remington introduced 28 gauge and*

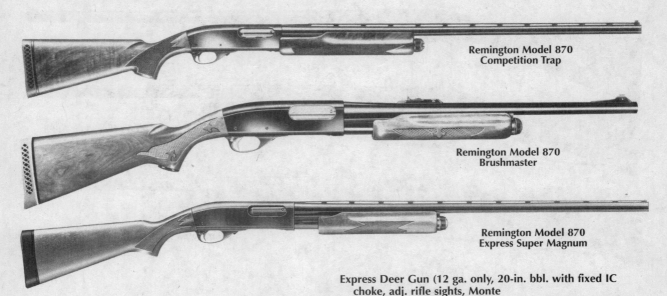

**Remington Model 870
Competition Trap**

**Remington Model 870
Brushmaster**

**Remington Model 870
Express Super Magnum**

.410 bore models with a scaled down receiver size. In 1972, a 20-gauge lightweight version was introduced on the same sized receiver. Currently, all of the smaller gauge variants are produced on that size receiver; 16-gauge models used a 12-gauge receiver. In 2023, RemArms reintroduced the Model 870 with the Fieldmaster and Wingmaster.

MODEL 870 BRUSHMASTER. . .NIB $405 EX $355 GD $270
Same as Model 870 Standard except in 20 or 12 gauge, 20-in. bbl., blued, satin finish stock. Right and left hand models. Disc. 1994.

MODEL 870 DM MODELS
Same general specifications Model 870 except w/6-rnd. detachable magazine. 12 gauge only. Bbl.: 18.5-in. with REMChoke or fixed choke. Matte blue finish. Made 2018-20.
w/hardwood stock . . . . NiB $455 Ex $400 Gd $305
DM Magpul (REMChoke,
    Magpul stock) . . . . NiB $690 Ex $605 Gd $470
DM Predator (REMChoke, ShurShot stock, XS ghost ring
    sights) . . . . NiB $690 Ex $605 Gd $470
DM Tactical (REMChoke, black pistol grip stock, XS ghost
    ring sights) . . . . NiB $690 Ex $605 Gd $470

MODEL 870 EXPRESS MODELS
Same general specifications as Model 870 Wingmaster except has low-luster walnut-finished hardwood stock with pressed checkering and black recoil pad. Gauges: 12, 16, 20, or .410, 3-in. chambers. Bbls.: 26- or 28-in. VR with REMChoke; 25-in. VR with fixed choke (.410 only). Black oxide metal finish. Made 1987-2020.
12 or 20 ga. . . . . NiB $355 Ex $290 Gd $200
.410 (w/fixed choke) . . . . NiB $455 Ex $300 Gd $225
Express Combo (w/extra
    20-in. deer bbl.) . . . . NiB $465 Ex $387 Gd $290
Express Compact Camo (20 ga. only, 21-in. bbl., camo synthetic stock, 2009–20) . . . . . . NiB $360 Ex $315 Gd $245
Express Compact Laminate (20 ga. only, 21-in. VR bbl., laminate stock, 2008–14) . . . . NiB $340 Ex $275 Gd $195
Express Compact Synthetic (20 ga. only, 21-in. VR bbl., black synthetic stock, 2009–20) . . . . NiB $360 Ex $315 Gd $245
Express Compact Youth (16 or 20 ga., 21-in. VR bbl., camo synthetic stock, 2009–12) . . . . NiB $340 Ex $275 Gd $195

Express Deer Gun (12 ga. only, 20-in. bbl. with fixed IC choke, adj. rifle sights, Monte
    Carlo stock,1991-2020) . . . . . NiB $433 Ex $297 Gd $200
w/rifled bbl. . . . . NiB $450 Ex $310 Gd $220
Express Hardwoods Home Defense (12 ga. only. 18.5-in. bbl. w/fixed cylinder choke, bead front sight, hardwood stock, matte blue finish, 2016-20) . . NiB $360 Ex $315 Gd $270
Express Junior (20 ga. only, 18.7-in. VR bbl., camo synthetic stock, 2006–08) . . . . NiB $365 Ex $335 Gd $240
Express Junior Compact (20 ga. only, 18.7-in. VR bbl., black synthetic stock, 2009–20) . . . . NiB $360 Ex $315 Gd $270
Express Magnum ShurShot Deer (20 or 12 ga., 23-in. rifled bbl., cantilever mount, black thumbhole stock, 2008–14) . . . . NiB $480 Ex $420 Gd $330
Express Magnum ShurShot Turkey (12 ga. only, 21-in. bbl., camo thumbhole
    stock, 2008–20) . . . . NiB $465 Ex $405 Gd $320
Express Synthetic (12 ga. only. 18-in. bbl. w/cylinder choke, bead front sight, checkered synthetic stock, non-reflective black finish, 1995-2020) . . . . . NiB $422 Ex $300 Gd $200
Express Synthetic Home Defense (12 ga. only. 18-in. bbl. w/cylinder choke, bead front sight, checkered synthetic stock, non-reflective black
    finish, 1995-2020) . . . . NiB $422 Ex $300 Gd $200
Express Synthetic Tactical (12 or 20 ga., 7-rnd. magazine, 18.5-in. bbl. w/fixed cylinder choke, bead front sight, black synthetic stock, black oxide finish, 1991-2020) . . . . NiB $380 Ex $335 Gd $260
Express Synthetic Youth Combo (21-in. VR and 20-in., 1994-2020) . . . . NiB $530 Ex $480 Gd $355
Express Tactical (12 ga., 6-rnd. magazine, 18.5-in. bbl. w/ fixed cylinder choke, bead front sight, 6-position synthetic stock, 2018-20) . . . . NiB $565 Ex $480 Gd $380
w/camo finish . . . . NiB $590 Ex $490 Gd $385
Express Tactical Knoxx (20 ga., 7-rnd. magazine, 18.5-in. bbl., Knoxx Spec-Ops synthetic stock, 2009-15) . . . . NiB $455 Ex $380 Gd $285
Express Tactical Magpul (12 ga., 6-rnd. magazine, 18.5-in. bbl., Magpul SGA synthetic stock, 2013-15) . . . . NiB $780 Ex $705 Gd $555
Express Tactical Pachmayr (12 ga., 18.5-in. bbl., Pachmayr pistol grip, 2014-15) . . . . NiB $430 Ex $380 Gd $305
Express Tactical Side Folder (20 or 12 ga., 6-rnd. magazine, 18.5-in. bbl., folding stock, 2019-20) . . . . NiB $930 Ex $815 Gd $635
Express Turkey Gun (21-in. VR bbl., Turkey Extra-Full REMChoke, 1991-2020) . . . . . NiB $448 Ex $290 Gd $210

548

**Express Youth Gun (scaled-down stock w/
12.5-in. pull and 21-in. VR bbl. with
REMChoke, 1991-2020)** . . . . . NiB $391 Ex $248 Gd $181

MODEL 870 ESM (EXPRESS SUPER MAGNUM)
Similar to Model 870 Express except chambered for 12 ga. mag. w/3.5-in. chamber. Bbls.: 23-, 26- or 28-in. VR w/ RemChoke. Checkered low-luster walnut-finished hardwood, black synthetic or camo buttstock and forearm. Matte black oxide metal finish or full camo finish. Made 1998-2020.

w/hardwood stock . . . . NiB $455 Ex $310 Gd $225
w/black synthetic stock . . . . . . NiB $455 Ex $310 Gd $225
w/camo synthetic stock . . . . . . NiB $488 Ex $395 Gd $259
**Model 870 ESM Synthetic
Turkey (w/synthetic stock)** . . NiB $488 Ex $395 Gd $259
**Model 870 ESM camo
Turkey (w/full camo)** . . . . . . NiB $488 Ex $395 Gd $259
**Model 870 ESM combo
(w/full camo, extra bbl.)** . . . NiB $509 Ex $400 Gd $323

MODEL 870 FIELDMASTER MODELS
Same general specifications as Model 870 Express except w/ walnut or black synthetic stock, sling-swivel studs, butt pad, drilled-and-tapped receiver, three choke tubes. 12 or 20 gauge. Made from 2023 to date.

w/wood stock . . . . NiB $480 Ex $460 Gd $410
**Fieldmaster Synthetic
(black polymer stock)** . . . . . . NiB $470 Ex $450 Gd $400
**Fieldmaster Deer (12 gauge, 20-in. rifled bbl.
w/rifle sights, wood stock)** . . NiB $640 Ex $560 Gd $530
**Fieldmaster Fully Rifled Cantilever
(12 gauge, 20-in. rifled bbl.
w/cantilever, wood stock)** . . . NiB $640 Ex $560 Gd $530

MODEL 870 LIGHTWEIGHT
Same as standard Model 870 but with scaled-down receiver and lightweight mahogany stock; 20 ga. only. 2.75-in. chamber. Bbls.: plain or VR; 26-in., IC; 28-in., M or F choke. REMChoke available from 1987. Weight 5.75 lbs. w/26-in. plain bbl. American walnut stock and forend with satin or Hi-gloss finish. Made 1972-94.

w/plain bbl. . . . . NiB $477 Ex $366 Gd $290
w/ventilated rib bbl. . . . . NiB $490 Ex $380 Gd $315
w/REMChoke bbl. . . . . NiB $566 Ex $435 Gd $335

MODEL 870 LIGHTWEIGHT MAGNUM
Same as Model 870 Lightweight but chambered for 20 ga. Magnum 3-in. shell; 28-in. bbl., plain or VR, F choke. Weight: 6 lbs. with plain bbl. Made 1972-94.

w/plain bbl. . . . . NiB $477 Ex $377 Gd $292
w/ventilated rib bbl. . . . . NiB $580 Ex $455 Gd $422

MODEL 870 POLICE . . . . NIB $455 EX $400 GD $305
Same as Model 870AP except 12 gauge only, 18- or 20-in. w/ fixed PC or IC choke, bead or rifle sights. 1994 to 2006.

w/parkerized finish . . . . NiB $465 Ex $410 Gd $315
w/rifle sights . . . . NiB $495 Ex $440 Gd $345

MODEL 870 POLICE . . . . NIB $455 EX $400 GD $305
Same as Model 870AP except 12 gauge only, 18- or 20-in. w/ fixed PC or IC choke, bead or rifle sights. 1994 to 2006.

w/parkerized finish . . . . NiB $465 Ex $410 Gd $315
w/rifle sights . . . . NiB $495 Ex $440 Gd $345

MODEL 870 MAGNUM DUCK GUN
Same as Model 870 Field Gun except has 3-in. chamber 12 and 20 gauge Magnum only. 28- or 30-in. bbl., plain or VR,

M or F choke, recoil pad. Weight: About 7 or 6.75 lbs. Made 1964-2020.

w/plain bbl. . . . . NiB $310 Ex $225 Gd $179
w/ventilated rib bbl. . . . . NiB $655 Ex $430 Gd $335

MODEL 870
MARINE MAGNUM . . . . NiB $735 Ex $496 Gd $359
Same general specifications as Model 870 Wingmaster except w/ 7-rnd. magazine, 18-in. plain bbl. with fixed IC choke, bead front sight and nickel finish. Made 1992-2020.

MODEL 870
SA SKEET GUN, SMALL GAUGE . . . NiB $875 Ex $677 Gd 529
Similar to Wingmaster Model 870SA except chambered for 28 and .410 ga. (2.5-in. chamber for latter); 25-in. VR bbl., SK choke. Weight: 6 lbs., 28 ga.; 6.5 lbs., .410. Made 1969-82.

MODEL 870 MISSISSIPPI
MAGNUM DUCK GUN . . . . . . NiB $865 Ex $667 Gd $520
Same as Remington Model 870 Magnum duck gun except has 32-in. bbl. "Ducks Unlimited" engraved receiver, Made in 1983.

MODEL 870
SPECIAL FIELD . . . . NiB $405 Ex $355 Gd $270
Pump action. Hammerless. Gauge: 12 or 20. 21-in. VR bbl. with REMChoke. 41.5 in. overall. Weight: 6-7 lbs. Straight-grip checkered walnut stock and forend. Made 1984-95.

MODEL 870 SPECIAL PURPOSE MODELS
Same general specifications as Model 870 Wingmaster except w/sandblasted matte blue finish, checkered oil-finished field-grade wood or synthetic stock. 12 gauge only. Bbls.: 21-, 26-, or 28-in. VR w/REMChoke. Made 1986-2020.

w/hardwood stock . . . . NiB $355 Ex $305 Gd $245
**Special Purpose Deer (23-in. rifled bbl.
w/cantilever mount, laminate
thumbhole stock, 2006-07)** . . NiB $655 Ex $580 Gd $455
**Special Purpose Super Magnum Synthetic
Camo (26- or 28-in. VR bbl., camo
stock, 1994-07)** . . . . NiB $580 Ex $480 Gd $305
**Special Purpose SPS-T Super Magnum
(23-, 26-, or 28-in. VR bbl., camo stock,
2000-07)** . . . . NiB $580 Ex $480 Gd $305
**Special Purpose SPS-BG Camo (20-in. bbl. w/rifle
sights, 1994)** . . . . NiB $355 Ex $305 Gd $245
**Special Purpose Synthetic ShurShot (23-in. rifled bbl.
w/cantilever mount, thumbhole
stock, 2008-09)** . . . . NiB $530 Ex $480 Gd $370

MODEL 870SPS MAGNUM
Same general specifications Model 870 Special Purpose Magnum except with synthetic stock and forend. 26- or 28-in. VR bbl. with REMChoke tubes. Matte black or Mossy Oak camo finish. Made 1991-2020.

70 SPS Mag. (black syn. stock) . NiB $688 Ex $455 Gd $325
870 SPS-T Camo (Mossy Oak camo) . . NiB $866 Ex $533 Gd $400

MODEL 870 TAC-14 SERIES
Based on Model 870 action except w/14-in. cylinder bore bbl. and Shockwave Raptor pistol grip. Gauge: 12- or 20-gauge. 4-rnd. magazine. Bureau of Alcohol, Tobacco, Firearms & Explosives has defines the 590 Shockwave as a "firearm" per the Gun Control Act, but not a Class 3/NFA firearm. Mfg. 2018-20.

Standard model . . . . NiB $405 Ex $370 Gd $315
**DM model (detachable 6-rnd.
magazine)** . . . . NiB $505 Ex $455 Gd $370
**Marine Magnum model
(nickel finish)** . . . . NiB $505 Ex $455 Gd $370

SHOTGUNS

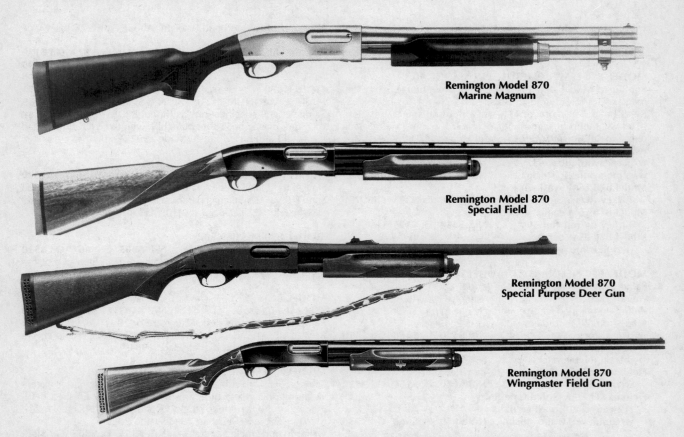

Remington Model 870
Marine Magnum

Remington Model 870
Special Field

Remington Model 870
Special Purpose Deer Gun

Remington Model 870
Wingmaster Field Gun

MODEL 870 WINGMASTER FIELD MODELS
Same general specifications as Model 870AP except checkered stock and forend. Later models have REMChoke system. Calibers: .410 or 12, 16, 20, or 28 gauge. Checkered walnut stock w/either high gloss or satin finish. Made 1964-84.
w/plain bbl. . . . . .NiB $505 Ex $430 Gd $330
w/VR bbl. . . . . .NiB $730 Ex $640 Gd $500

Wingmaster Field Small Bore (Scaled-down lightweight receivers. Gauges: 28 and .410. Plain or VR 25-in. bbl. choked IC, M or F. 5.5-6.25 lbs. depending on gauge and bbl., 1969-94)
w/plain bbl. . . . . .NiB $775 Ex $600 Gd $445
w/VR bbl. . . . . .NiB $808 Ex $625 Gd $465

MODEL 870 WINGMASTER MODELS
MODEL 870ADL WINGMASTER DELUXE GRADE
Same general specifications as Wingmaster Model 870AP except has pistol-grip stock and extension beavertail forend, both finely checkered; matted top surface or VR bbl. Made 1950-63.
w/matted top surface bbl.. . . . . .NiB $488 Ex $365 Gd $288
w/ventilated rib bbl. . . . . .NiB $509 Ex $412 Gd $300

MODEL 870AP WINGMASTER STANDARD GRADE
Hammerless. Takedown. Gauges: 12, 16, 20. Tubular magazine holds four rounds. Bbls.: Plain, matted top surface or VR; 26-in. IC, 28-in. M or F choke, 30-in. F choke (12 ga. only). Weight: About 7 lbs., 12 ga.; 6.75 lbs., 16 ga.; 6.5 lbs., 20 ga. Plain pistol-grip stock, grooved forend. Made 1950-63.
w/plain bbl. . . . . .NiB $359 Ex $300 Gd $209
w/matted surface bbl.. . . . . .NiB $435 Ex $335 Gd $225
w/ventilated rib bbl.. . . . . .NiB $466 Ex $372 Gd $260
Left-hand model . . . . .NiB $489 Ex $400 Gd $265

MODEL 870BDL WINGMASTER DELUXE SPECIAL
Same as Model 870ADL except select American walnut stock and forend. Made 1950-63.
w/matted surface bbl.. . . . . .NiB $665 Ex $445 Gd $310
w/ventilated rib bbl.. . . . . .NiB $715 Ex $477 Gd $349

MODEL 870D, 870F WINGMASTER
TOURNAMENT AND PREMIER GRADE GUNS
These higher-grade models differ from the Model 870AP in general quality, grade of wood, checkering, engraving, etc. General operating specifications are essentially the same. Made 1950-2020.
Model 870D Tournament
    grade . . . . NiB $3139 Ex $2288 Gd $1660
Model 870F Premier grade . . NiB $6445 Ex $4753 Gd $3465
Model 870F Premier gr.
    w/gold inlay . . . . NiB $10,098 Ex $7517 Gd $5237

MODEL 870R
WINGMASTER RIOT GUN. . . . .$405 EX $355 GD $270
Same as Model 870AP except 18- or 20-in. bbl., IC choke, 12 ga. only.

MODEL 870 WINGMASTER
ALL AMERICAN TRAP. . . . . NIB $800 EX $705 GD $610
Same general specifications as Model 870AP except 12 gauge, 30-in. VR bbl., engraved receiver. Made 1972-76.

MODEL 870 WINGMASTER
COMPETITION TRAP . . . . NIB $555 EX $480 GD $355
Same general specifications as Model 870AP except 12 gauge, single shot, VR bbl., recoil reducing trap-style stock. Made 1980-86.

**Remington Model 870TC
Wingmaster Trap**

MODEL 870 SC WINGMASTER SKEET GUN
Same general specifications as Model 870AP except has 26-in. VR bbl., SK choke, ivory bead front sight, metal bead rear sight, pistol-grip stock and extension beavertail forend. Weight: 6.75 to 7.5 lbs. depending on gauge. Made 1950-82.

Model 870SA Skeet grade
(disc. 1982) . . . . NiB $677 Ex $395 Gd $288
Model 870SC Skeet Target grade
(disc. 1980) . . . . NiB $795 Ex $549 Gd $400

MODEL 870TA
WINGMASTER TRAP . . . . NIB $430 EX $380 GD $280
Same general specifications as Model 870AP except 12 gauge, VR bbl., Deluxe trap-style stock and forend. Made 1978-86.

MODEL 870TB WINGMASTER
TRAP SPECIAL . . . . NIB $633 EX $500 GD $388
Same general specifications as Model 870AP Wingmaster except has 28- or 30-in. VR bbl., F choke, metal bead front sight, no rear sight. "Special" grade trap-style stock and forend, both checkered, recoil pad. Weight: About 8 lbs. Made 1950-81.

MODEL 870TC TRAP GRADE . . NIB $795 EX $554 GD $400
Same as Model 870 Wingmaster TC except has tournament-grade walnut in stock and forend w/satin finish. Over-bored 30-in. VR bbl. w/ 2.75-in. chamber and RemChoke tubes. Reissued in 1996. See separate listing for earlier model.

MODEL 870TC WINGMASTER TRAP GRADE
Same as Model 870TB except higher-grade walnut in stock and forend, has both front and rear sights. Made 1950-79. Model 870 TC reissued from 1996 to 1999. See separate listing for later model.

Model 870 TC Trap
(Standard) . . . . NiB $515 Ex $466 Gd $325
Model 870 TC Trap
(Monte Carlo) . . . . NiB $545 Ex $480 Gd $366

MODEL 870 WINGMASTER
MAGNUM DELUXE GRADE . . . NIB $667 EX $559 GD $400
Same as Model 870 Magnum standard grade except has checkered stock and extension beavertail forearm, bbl. with matted top surface. Disc. in 1963.

MODEL 870 WINGMASTER MAGNUM
STANDARD GRADE . . . . NIB $633 EX $479 GD $365
Same as Model 870AP except chambered for 12 ga. 3-in. Magnum, 30-in. F choke bbl., recoil pad. Weight: About 8.25 lbs. Made 1955-63.

MODEL 870 WINGMASTER REMCHOKE SERIES
Slide action, hammerless, takedown with blued all-steel receiver. Gauges: 12, 20; 3-in. chamber. Tubular magazine. Bbls.: 21-, 26-, 28-in. VR with REM Choke. Weight: 7.5 lbs. (12 ga.). Satin-finished, checkered walnut buttstock and forend with recoil pad. Right- or left-hand models. Made 1986-2020.
Standard model, 12 ga. . . . . NiB $500 Ex $377 Gd $266
Standard model, 20 ga. . . . . NiB $535 Ex $400 Gd $288
Youth model, 21-in. bbl. . . . . NiB $500 Ex $377 Gd $321

MODEL 870 WINGMASTER (RECENT MFG.)
Same general specifications as Model 870 Wingmaster except w/high gloss walnut stock, butt pad, three choke tubes, high gloss blue finish. .410 or 12 or 20 gauge. Made from 2023 to date.

MODEL 870 TACTICAL SERIES
Same as Model 870AP except 12 gauge only, 6- or 7-rnd. magazine. Bbls.: 18- or 20-in. w/fixed IC choke. Weight: 7.5 lbs. Stock: Black polymer or Knoxx Spec-Ops adj. w/pistol grip. Made in 2006.
w/polymer stock . . . . NiB $520 Ex $470 Gd $390
w/Knoxx stock . . . . NiB $540 Ex $490 Gd $410
TAC-2 (18-in. bbl., 2007-16) . . . . NiB $620 Ex $540 Gd $420
TAC-3 (20-in. bbl., 2007-08) . . . . NiB $620 Ex $540 Gd $420
TAC-14 (12 or 20 gauge,
 14-in. bbl., Shockwave Raptor
 Bristol grip, 2018-20) . . . . NiB $405 Ex $370 Gd $320
TAC-14 DM (12 gauge, 6-rnd.
 detachable magazine, 14-in.
 bbl., Shockwave Raptor
 Bristol grip, 2018-20) . . . . NiB $505 Ex $455 Gd $370
TAC-14 Marine Magnum
 (12 gauge, 14-in. bbl.,
 Shockwave Raptor Bristol grip,
 nickel plated, 2018-20) . . . . . . NiB $755 Ex $655 Gd $505
Tactical Blackhawk (12 gauge, 18-in. bbl., Blackhawk Spec
 Ops II adj. stock, 2012-16) . . . NiB $555 Ex $470 Gd $370
Tactical Desert Recon (12 gauge,
 18- or 20-in. bbl., Speedfeed stock,
 camo finish, 2008-09) . . . . NiB $580 Ex $505 Gd $410
Model 870F Premier grade . . . NiB $6445 Ex $4753 Gd $3465
Model 870F Premier gr.
 w/gold inlay . . . . NiB $10,098 Ex $7517 Gd $5237

MODEL 870R
WINGMASTER RIOT GUN . . . NiB $375 Ex $280 Gd $210
Same as Model 870AP except 20-in. bbl., IC choke, 12 ga. only.

MODEL 870 SA WINGMASTER SKEET GUN
Same general specifications as Model 870AP except has 26-in. VR bbl., SK choke, ivory bead front sight, metal bead rear sight, pistol-grip stock and extension beavertail forend. Weight: 6.75 to 7.5 lbs. depending on gauge. Made 1950-1982.
Model 870SA Skeet grade
 (disc. 1982) . . . . NiB $677 Ex $395 Gd $288
Model 870SC Skeet Target
 grade (disc. 1980) . . . . NiB $795 Ex $549 Gd $400

MODEL 870TB WINGMASTER
TRAP SPECIAL . . . . NiB $633 Ex $500 Gd $388
Same general specifications as Model 870AP Wingmaster except has 28- or 30-in. VR bbl., F choke, metal bead front sight, no rear sight. "Special" grade trap-style stock and forend, both checkered, recoil pad. Weight: About 8 lbs. Made 1950-81.

MODEL 870TC TRAP GRADE . . . NiB $795 Ex $554 Gd $400
Same as Model 870 Wingmaster TC except has tournament-grade walnut in stock and forend w/satin finish. Over-bored

GRADING: **NiB** = New in Box   **Ex** = Excellent or NRA 95%   **Gd** = Good or NRA 68%

SHOTGUNS

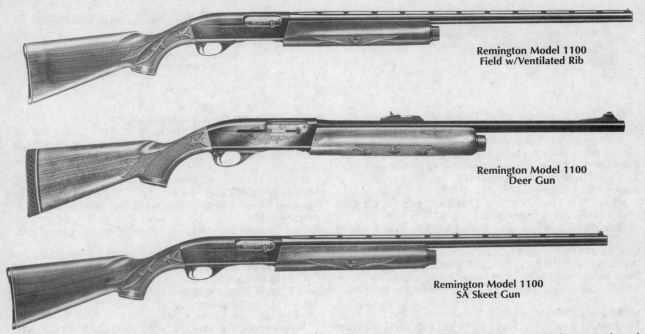

Remington Model 1100
Field w/Ventilated Rib

Remington Model 1100
Deer Gun

Remington Model 1100
SA Skeet Gun

30-in. VR bbl. w/ 2.75-in. chamber and RemChoke tubes. Reissued in 1996. See separate listing for earlier model.

MODEL 870TC WINGMASTER TRAP GRADE
Same as Model 870TB except higher-grade walnut in stock and forend, has both front and rear sights. Made 1950-79. Model 870 TC reissued in 1996. See separate listing for later model.
Model 870 TC Trap (Standard) . NiB $515 Ex $466 Gd $325
Model 870 TC Trap (Monte Carlo) NiB $545 Ex $480 Gd $366

MODEL 878A AUTOMASTER . . NiB $376 Ex $266 Gd $195
Gas-operated Autoloader. 12 ga., 3-rnd. magazine. Bbls.: 26-in. IC, 28-in. M choke, 30-in. F choke. Weight: About 7 lbs. Plain pistol-grip stock and forearm. Made 1959-62.

MODEL 887 NITRO MAG . . . NiB $445 Ex $285 Gd $200
Based on Model 870 except has Armorlokt overmolding on metal. 26- or 28-in. bbl. Finish: matte black. Stock: black synthetic. Made 2009-20.
Camo Combo . . . . NiB $728 Ex $700 Gd $300
Tactical (extended magazine, Picatinny rail, ported extended choke tube) . . . . NiB $534 Ex $340 Gd $230
Waterfowl Camo (Real Tree
   Advantage Max-4 finish . . . . NiB $594 Ex $370 Gd $270

NOTE: *The Model 1100 was introduced in 1963 with some 4 million produced to date. In 1964, 16 and 20-gauge variants were introduced. The lightweight 20-gauge variants was introduced in 1966; 28-gauge and .410 bore models were new in 1969. Initial model featured fixed chokes. New stock checkering patterns and receiver scroll markings were incorporated on all standard Model 1100 field, magnum, skeet and trap models in 1979. In 1986, the screw-in RemChoke choke tube system was introduced.*

MODEL 1100 FIELD
Semiauto. Gas-operated. Hammerless. Takedown. Gauges: 12, 16, 20. Bbls.: plain or VR; 30-in. F, 28-in. M or F, 26-in. IC; or REMChoke tubes. Weight: Average 7.25-7.5 lbs. depending on ga. and bbl. length. Checkered walnut pistol-grip stock and forearm in high-gloss finish. Made 1963-1988. 16 ga. discontinued 1980.
w/plain bbl. . . . . NiB $605 Ex $505 Gd $370
w/ventilated-rib bbl. . . . . NiB $655 Ex $555 Gd $410
w/RemChoke, add 10%
w/left-hand action, add 70%

MODEL 1100 CLASSIC FIELD . NiB $755 Ex $630 Gd $460
Similar to Model 1100 Field except 12, 16, 20 or .410 w/ light contoured REMchoke bbl. Non-engraved receiver. Made 2003-06.

MODEL 1100 DEER GUN. . . . . NiB $515 Ex $386 Gd $265
Same as Model 1100 Field Gun except has 22-in. bbl., IC, with rifle-type sights; 12 and 20 ga. only; recoil pad. Weight: About 7.25 lbs. Made 1963-98.

MODEL 1100 DUCKS UNLIMITED ATLANTIC
COMMEMORATIVE . . . . NiB $1188 Ex $987 Gd $766
Limited production for one year. Similar specifications to Model 1100 Field except w/ 32-in. F choke, VR bbl. 12-ga. Magnum only. Made in 1982.

MODEL 1100 DUCKS UNLIMITED "THE CHESAPEAKE"
COMMEMORATIVE . . . . NiB $878 Ex $753 Gd $555
Limited edition 1 to 2400. Same general specifications as Model 1100 Field except sequentially numbered with markings "The Chesapeake." 12 ga. Magnum w/ 30-in. F choke, VR bbl. Made in 1981.

MODEL 1100 SMALL GAUGE
Same as standard Model 1100 Field but scaled down. Gauges: 28, .410. 25-in. bbl., plain or VR; IC, M or F fixed choke. Weight: 6.25-7 lbs. depending on gauge. Made 1969-94.
w/plain bbl. . . . . NiB $705 Ex $605 Gd $430
w/VR bbl. . . . . NiB $755 Ex $655 Gd $480

MODEL 1100 G3 . . . . NiB $1050 Ex $800 Gd $500
Similar to Model 1100 Field except satin finish steel receiver with titanium PVD coating. 12 or 20 ga.; 3-in. chamber. Bbls.:

Remington Model 1100
Special Field

Remington Model 1100
Tournament Trap

Remington Model 3200
"One of 1000" Skeet

26- or 28-in. VR w/ ProBore choke tubes. Weight: 6.7-7.6 lbs. depending on bbl. length. Stock: RealWood fiber laminate w/ high gloss finish and checkering. Made 2006-08.

MODEL 1100 LIGHTWEIGHT
Same as standard Model 1100 but scaled-down receiver and lightweight mahogany stock; 20 ga. only, 2.75-in. chamber. Bbls.: Plain or VR; 26-in. IC; 28-in. M and F choke. Weight: 6.25 lbs. Made 1970-76.
w/plain bbl. . . . . .NiB $654 Ex $500 Gd $390
w/ventilated rib . . . . .NiB $735 Ex $566 Gd $408

MODEL 1100 LIGHTWEIGHT MAGNUM
Same as Model 1100 Lightweight but chambered for 20 gauge Magnum 3-in. shell; 28-in. bbl., plain or VR, F choke. Weight: 6.5 lbs. Made 1977-98.
w/plain bbl. . . . . .NiB $688 Ex $544 Gd $422
w/ventilated rib . . . . .NiB $788 Ex $590 Gd $466
w/choke tubes . . . . .NiB $855 Ex $598 Gd $466

MODEL 1100 LT-20 DUCKS UNLIMITED SPECIAL
COMMEMORATIVE . . . . . . .NiB $1486 Ex $1156 Gd $844
Limited edition 1 to 2400. Same general specifications as Model 1100 Field except sequentially numbered with markings, "The Chesapeake." 20 ga. only. 26-in. IC, VR bbl. Made in 1981.

MODEL 1100 LT-20 SERIES
Same as Model 1100 Field Gun except in 20 ga. with shorter 23-in. VR bbl., straight-grip stock. REMChoke series has 21-in. VR bbl., choke tubes. Weight: 6.25 lbs. Checkered grip and forearm. Made 1977-95.
LT-20 Special. . . . . .NiB $588 Ex $498 Gd $377
LT-20 Deer Gun . . . . .NiB $490 Ex $399 Gd $295
LT-20 Youth . . . . .NiB $585 Ex $444 Gd $300

MODEL 1100 MAGNUM . . . . .NiB $598 Ex $499 Gd $378
Limited production. Similar to the Model 1100 Field except w/ 26-in. F choke, VR bbl. and 3-in. chamber. Made in 1981.

MODEL 1100 MAGNUM DUCK GUN
Same as Model 1100 Field Gun except has 3-in. chamber,12 and 20 ga. Mag. only. 30-in. plain or VR bbl. in 12 ga., 28-in. in 20 ga.; M or F choke. Recoil pad. Weight: About 7.75 lbs. Made 1963-88.
w/plain bbl. . . . . .NiB $555 Ex $399 Gd $324
w/ventilated rib bbl. . . . . .NiB $575 Ex $435 Gd $355

MODEL 1100
ONE OF 3,000 FIELD . . . . . . .NiB $1110 Ex $910 Gd $510
Limited edition, numbered 1 to 3,000. Similar to Model 1100 Field except w/ fancy wood and gold-trimmed etched hunting scenes on receiver. 12 gauge w/ 28-in. M, VR bbl. Made in 1980.

MODEL 1100 SA SKEET GUN
Same as Model 1100 Field Gun, 12 and 20 ga. except has 26-in. VR bbl., SK choke or with Cutts Compensator. Weight: 7.25-7.5 lbs. Made 1963-94.
w/skeet-choked bbl. . . . . .NiB $977 Ex $644 Gd $388
w/Cutts Comp, add. $200
Left-hand action, add $75

MODEL 1100 SA
LIGHTWEIGHT SKEET . . . . . . .NiB $655 Ex $497 Gd $366
Same as Model 1100 Lightweight except has skeet-style stock and forearm, 26-in. VR bbl., SK choke. Made 1971-97.

MODEL 1100 SA
SKEET SMALL BORE . . . . .NiB $625 Ex $443 Gd $311
Similar to standard Model 1100SA except chambered for 28 and .410 ga. (2.5-in. chamber for latter); 25-in. VR bbl., SK choke. Weight: 6.75 lbs., 28 ga.; 7.25 lbs., .410. Made 1969-94.

MODEL 1100 SB
LIGHTWEIGHT SKEET . . . . . . .NiB $644 Ex $433 Gd $310
Same as Model 1100SA Lightweight except has select wood. Introduced in 1977.

MODEL 1100 SB SKEET GUN. . NiB $654 Ex $443 Gd $319
Same specifications as Model 1100SA except has select wood. Made 1963-97.

MODEL 1100
SPECIAL FIELD SHOTGUN. . . .NiB $600 Ex $492 Gd $388
Gas-operated. Five round capacity. Hammerless. Gauges: 12, 20 or .410. 21- or 23-in. VR bbl. with REMChoke. Weight: 6.5-7.25 lbs. Straight-grip checkered walnut stock and forend. Note: .410 Made 1983-99.

MODEL 1100 SP MAGNUM
Same as Model 1100 Field except 12 ga. only w/ 3-in. chambers. Bbls.: 26- or 30-in. F choke; or 26-in. with RemChoke tubes; VR. Non-reflective matte black, Parkerized bbl. and receiver. Satin-finished stock and forend. Made 1986.
w/fixed choke . . . . .NiB $475 Ex $397 Gd $321
w/REMchoke . . . . .NiB $490 Ex $417 Gd $344

MODEL 1100 SPECIAL FIELD
Similar to Model 1100 Field except 12, 20 or .410. Bbls.: 21- and 23-in. VR w/ REMChoke tubes (intro. 1987). Weight: Average 7.25-7.5 lbs. depending on ga. and bbl. length. High

SHOTGUNS

GRADING: **NiB** = New in Box   **Ex** = Excellent or NRA 95%   **Gd** = Good or NRA 68%

gloss checkered walnut straight-grip stock and forearm. Made 1983-99.

12 ga.	NiB $655	Ex $580	Gd $430
20 ga.	NiB $855	Ex $760	Gd $580
.410	NiB $1010	Ex $880	Gd $680

MODEL 1100 SYNTHETIC . . . . NiB $435 Ex $280 Gd $170
Similar to Model 1100 Field except 12, 16 or 20 ga. Bbls.: 26- or 28-in. VR w/ REMChoke tubes. Weight: Average 7-7.5 lbs. depending on ga. and bbl. length. Sythentic stock and forearm. Made 1996-2004.

Deer	NiB $500	Ex $280	Gd $170
LT 20 Youth	NiB $440	Ex $270	Gd $160

MODEL 1100 TAC-2 . . . . NiB $800 Ex $580 Gd $400
Similar to Model 1100 Field except 12 ga. only; 2-3/4-in. chamber. Bbls.: 18- or 22-in. VR w/ REMChoke tubes, HiViz sights. Weight: 7.5 lbs. depending on bbl. length. Stock: black sythentic SFIV. 6- or 8-rnd. capacity. Made 2006-20.

Tac-4 (pistol grip) . . . . NiB $870 Ex $650 Gd $240

MODEL 1100 TACTICAL . . . . . . NiB $435 Ex $280 Gd $170
Similar to Model 1100 Field except 12 ga. only; 3-in. chamber. Bbls.: 18- or 22-in. VR w/ REMChoke tubes, HiViz sights. Weight: 7.5 lbs. depending on bbl. length. Sythentic pistol grip or standard stock and forearm. 6- or 8-rnd. capacity. Disc 2006.

MODEL 1100 TOURNAMENT/PREMIER
These higher grade guns differ from standard models in overall quality, grade of wood, checkering, engraving, gold inlays, etc. General specs are the same. Made 1963-94; 1997-99; 2003–20.

1100D Tournament	NiB $966	Ex $633	Gd $577
1100F Premier	NiB $1266	Ex $1059	Gd $833
1100F Premier w/ gold inlay	NiB $10,332	Ex $7833	Gd $4460

MODEL 1100
TOURNAMENT SKEET . . . . NiB $977 Ex $738 Gd $490
Similar to Model 1100 Field except w/ 26-in. bbl. SK choke. Gauges: 12, LT-20, 28, and .410. Features select walnut stocks and new cut-checkering patterns. Made 1979-99.

MODEL 1100TA TRAP GUN. . . NiB $529 Ex $417 Gd $330
Similar to Model 1100TB Trap Gun except with regular-grade stocks. Available in both left- and right-hand versions. Made 1979-86.

MODEL 1100TB TRAP GUN
Same as Model 1100 Field Gun except has special trap stock, straight or Monte Carlo comb, recoil pad; 30-in. VR bbl., F or M trap choke; 12 ga. only. Weight: 8.25 lbs. Made 1963-79.

Straight stock	NiB $588	Ex $460	Gd $339
Monte Carlo stock	NiB $599	Ex $443	Gd $360

MODEL 1900
HAMMERLESS DOUBLE . . . NiB $1889 Ex $1366 Gd $1177
Improved version of Model 1894. Boxlock. Auto ejector. Double triggers. Gauges: 10, 12, 16. Bbls.: 28 to 32 in. Value shown is for standard grade with ordnance steel bbls. Made 1900-10.

MODEL 3200 FIELD GRADE . . . NiB $1600 Ex $1260 Gd $980
O/U, boxlock. Auto ejectors. Selective single trigger. 12 ga. 2.75-in. chambers. Bbls.: VR, 26- and 28-in. M/F; 30-in. IC/M. Weight: About 7.75 lbs. w/ 26-in. bbls. Checkered pistol-grip stock/forearm. Made 1973-78.

MODEL 3200 COMPETITION
SKEET GUN . . . . NiB $2510 Ex $2160 Gd $1630
Same as Model 3200 Skeet Gun except has gilded scrollwork on frame, engraved forend, latch plate and trigger guard, select fancy wood. Made 1973-84.

Skeet Set (four-bbl.
  set, 1973-80) . . . . NiB $6600 Ex $5600 Gd $4350

MODEL 3200
COMPETITION TRAP GUN . . NiB $2510 Ex $2155 Gd $1630
Same as Model 3200 Trap Gun except has gilded scrollwork on frame, engraved forend, latch plate and trigger guard, select fancy wood. Made 1973-84.

MODEL 3200
FIELD GRADE MAGNUM. . NiB $1810 Ex $1580 Gd $1180
Same as Model 3200 Field except chambered for 12 ga. mag. 3-in. shells 30-in. bbls., M and F or both F choke. Made 1975-77.

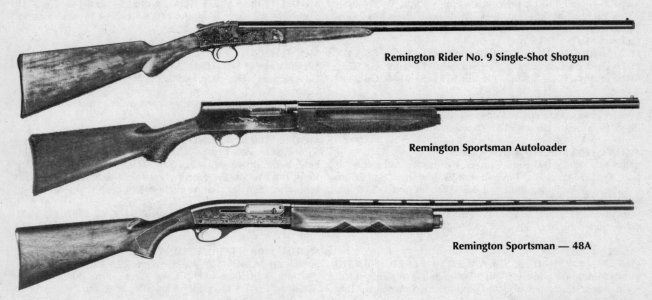

Remington Rider No. 9 Single-Shot Shotgun

Remington Sportsman Autoloader

Remington Sportsman — 48A

Remington Versa Max

Remington V3 Waterfowl

MODEL 3200 "ONE OF 1000"
Limited edition numbered 1 to 1000. Same general specifications as Model 3200 Trap Gun but has frame, trigger guard and forend latch elaborately engraved (designation "One of 1,000" on frame side), stock and forearm of high grade walnut. Supplied in carrying case.
Skeet (26- or 28-in. bbls., SK choke, skeet-style stock and
    forearm. Made in 1974) . . NiB $3255 Ex $2755 Gd $2100
Trap (Made in 1973) . . . . NiB $3255 Ex $2755 Gd $2100

MODEL 3200 SKEET GUN . . NiB $1700 Ex $1410 Gd $1110
Same as Model 3200 Field Grade except skeet-style stock and full beavertail forearm, 26- or 28-in. bbls., SK choke. Made 1973-80.

MODEL 3200
SPECIAL TRAP GUN . . . . NiB $1510 Ex $1260 Gd $980
Same as Model 3200 Trap Gun except has select fancy-grade wood and other minor refinements. Made 1973-84.

MODEL 3200 TRAP GUN . . NiB $1660 Ex $1410 Gd $1110
Same as Model 3200 Field Grade except trap-style stock w/ Monte Carlo or straight comb, select wood, beavertail forearm, 30- or 32-in. bbls. w/ventilated rib, IM/F or F/F chokes. Made 1973-77.

PEERLESS FIELD GRADE . . . . . NiB $1210 Ex $1010 Gd $710
O/U. Boxlock action. Gauge: 12, 3-in. chamber. Bbls.: 26-, 28- or 30-in. VR w/3 RemChoke tubes. Automatic safety and single selective trigger. Finish: Gloss blue. Stock: Checkered high gloss walnut. Sights: two beads. Weight: 7.5 lbs. Engraved receiver. Made 1993-98.

PREMIER FIELD GRADE SERIES
O/U. Boxlock action. Gauge: 12, 20 or 28, 3-in. chamber. Bbls.: 26- or 28-in. VR w/3 RemChoke tubes. Finish: matte black. Stock: Checkered satin walnut. Sights: two beads. Weight: 6.5-7.7 lbs. Engraved receiver. Made 2006-09, mfg. Italy.
standard model . . . . NiB $1510 Ex $1255 Gd $910
Competition STS model (titanium PVD finish, extended
    choke tubes, 2006-09) . . NiB $1855 Ex $1530 Gd $1110
Ruffed Grouse model (gold inlayed receiver,
    2006-09) . . . . NiB $1760 Ex $1460 Gd $1060
Upland Special model (case hardened receiver w/gold
    accents, 2006-10) . . . . NiB $1610 Ex $1330 Gd $955

RIDER NO. 9 SINGLE-SHOT . . NiB $555 Ex $433 Gd $335
Improved version of No. 3 Single Barrel Shotgun made in the late 1800s. Semi-hammerless. Gauges 10, 12, 16, 20, 24, 28. 30- to 32-in. plain bbl. Weight: About 6 lbs. Plain pistol-grip stock and forearm. Auto ejector. Made 1902-10.

SP-10 . . . . NiB $1610 Ex $1355 Gd $955
Autoloader. Takedown. Gas-operated with stainless steel piston. 10 ga., 3.5-in. chamber. Bbls.: 30-in. VR with REMChoke screw-in tubes. Weight: 11 lbs. Metal bead front. Checkered walnut stock with satin finish. QD swivels and camo sling. Made 1989-2010.

SP-10 MAGNUM CAMO . NiB $1755 Ex $1530 Gd $1110
Same general specifications as Model SP-10 except has 23- or 26-in. bbl. Finish: Mossy Oak, Mossy Oak BreakUp, Mossy Oak Obession, Bottomland or Duck Blind. Stock: standard or thumbhole. Made 1993-2010.
Synthetic (matte finish) . . . . . NiB $1255 Ex $1060 Gd $730
Turkey (Mossy Oak Obession) . NiB $1760 Ex $1530 Gd $1110
Turkey Combo (turkey bbl.
    and deer bbl.) . . . . NiB $1610 Ex $1180 Gd $955
Waterfowl (Mossy Oak
    Duck Blind) . . . . NiB $1760 Ex $1530 Gd $1110

SPORTSMAN A STANDARD GRADE AUTOLOADER
Same general specifications as Model 11A except magazine holds two shells. Also available in "B" Special Grade, "D" Tournament Grade, "E" Expert Grade, "F" Premier Grade. Made 1931-48. Same values as for Model 11A.
48D . . . . NiB $445 Ex $321 Gd $226

V3 FIELD SPORT SERIES
Semiauto. Versaport low-recoil gas-operated action. Gauge: 12, 3-in. chamber. Bbls.: 26- or 28-in. VR w/3 RemChoke tubes. Finish: matte black. Stock: Checkered satin walnut or black synthetic w/shim system. Sights: twin bead. Weight: 7.25 lbs. Made 2015-20.
w/synthetic stock . . . . NiB $780 Ex $655 Gd $480
w/wood stock . . . . NiB $880 Ex $755 Gd $580
Camo (various Mossy Oak camo
    finishes) . . . . NiB $880 Ex $755 Gd $580
TAC-13 Compact model (13-in. bbl., 5-rnd.
    magazine, bird's-head pistol grip,
    26.5-in. OAL, 2018-20) . . . . . . NiB $790 Ex $685 Gd $530

VERSA MAX SERIES
Gas operated Semiauto. 12 ga., 3-1/2-in. chambers only. Bbls.: 26- or 28-in. w/ VR, HiViz bead, and Pro Bore choke tubes. Finish: matte black. Stock: black synthetic w/ gray checkered insert panels. Made 2010-20.
Competition Tactical (22-in. bbl., 8-rnd.
    capacity, green cerakote,
    2014–date) . . . . NiB $1490 Ex $1280 Gd $810
Sportsman (26- or 28-in. bbl. w/ one
    choke tube, black synthetic stock,
    matte blue, 2013–date) . . . . . . NiB $915 Ex $780 Gd $555
Sportsman Camo (various camo finishes,
    2013–date) . . . . NiB $1030 Ex $830 Gd $555
Sportsman Turkey (22-in. bbl. w/ one choke tube, camo synthetic
    stock, 2013–date) . . . . NiB $1030 Ex $830 Gd $555
Synthetic (black synthetic
    stock) . . . . NiB $1230 Ex $1055 Gd $655
Tactical (22-in. VR bbl. w/ HiViz sights,
    magazine extension, Picatinny rail.
    black finish, 2012–date) . . . . . NiB $1030 Ex $830 Gd $555
Waterfowl Camo
    (camo synthetic stock,
    extended choke tubes) . . . NiB $1480 Ex $1300 Gd $805
Waterfowl Pro (camo synthetic stock,
    extended choke tubes) . . . NiB $1580 Ex $1370 Gd $855
Wood Tech (comb stock inserts, 2014–15) . . . . . . NiB $1455
Ex $1280 Gd $805Zombie
    Gargoyle Green finish
    (similar to Tactical), add $200
    Zombie Pink Explosion finish
    (similar to Tactical), add $200

SHOTGUNS

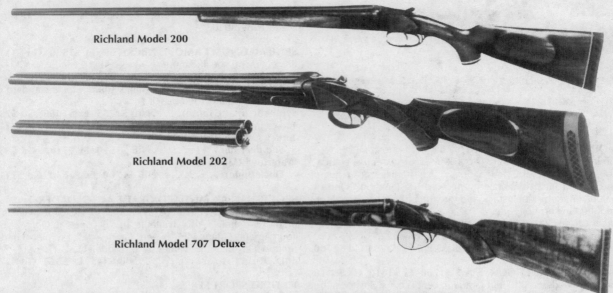

Richland Model 200

Richland Model 202

Richland Model 707 Deluxe

SPORTSMAN SKEET GUN

Same general specifications as the Sportsman A except has 26-in. bbl. (plain, solid or VR), SK choke, beavertail forend. Disc. in 1949.

Plain bbl. . . . . NiB $408 Ex $320 Gd $255
Solid-rib bbl. . . . . NiB $408 Ex $320 Gd $255
Ventilated rib bbl. . . . . NiB $475 Ex $355 Gd $290

MODEL 48 MOHAWK AUTO

Streamlined receiver. Hammerless. Takedown. Gauges: 12, 16, 20. Tubular magazine holds two rounds. Bbls.: Plain, matted top surface or VR; 26-in. IC, 28-in. M or F choke, 30-in. F choke (12 ga. only). Weight: About 7.5 lbs., 12 ga.; 6.25 lbs., 16 ga.; 6.5 lbs., 20 ga. Pistol-grip stock, grooved forend, both checkered. Made 1949-59.

Plain bbl. . . . . NiB $376 Ex $270 Gd $198
Matted top-surface bbl. . . . . . NiB $466 Ex $355 Gd $290
Ventilated rib bbl. . . . . NiB $566 Ex $477 Gd $379

MODEL 48 B, D, F SPORTSMAN
SELECT, TOURNAMENT & PREMIER GRADE GUNS

These higher grade models differ from the Sportsman-48A in general quality, grade of wood, checkering, engraving, etc. General specifications are the same. Made 1949-59.

Sportsman-48B
 Select grade . . . . NiB $490 Ex $330 Gd $225
Sportsman-48D Tournament
 grade . . . . NiB $1688 Ex $1178 Gd $988
Sportsman-48F Premier
 grade . . . . NiB $6355 Ex $3988 Gd $2500

MODEL 48SA SPORTSMAN SKEET GUN

Same general specifications as Sportsman-48A except has 26-in. bbl. with matted top surface or VR, SK choke, ivory bead front sight, metal bead rear sight. Made 1949-60.

plain bbl. . . . . NiB $377 Ex $279 Gd $200
ventilated rib bbl. . . . . NiB $466 Ex $344 Gd $229
Sportsman-48SC Skeet . . . . NiB $577 Ex $466 Gd $355
Tournament grade. . . . . NiB $1688 Ex $1299 Gd $1100
Sportsman-48SF Skeet
 Premier grade. . . . . NiB $6220 Ex $4014 Gd $2444

MODEL 11-48A RIOT GUN . . . NiB $420 Ex $322 Gd $276
Same as Model 11-48A except 20-in. plain bbl. and 12 ga. only. Disc. in 1969.

MODEL 11-48A STANDARD
GRADE 4-RND. AUTOLOADER .410 & 28 GAUGE

Same general specifications as Sportsman-48A except gauge, 3-rnd. magazine, 25-in. bbl. Weight: About 6.25 lbs. 28 ga. introduced 1952, .410 in 1954. Disc. in 1969. Values same as shown for Sportsman-48A.

MODEL 11-48A STANDARD GRADE AUTOLOADER

Same general specifications as Sportsman-48A except magazine holds four rounds, forend not grooved. Also available in Special Grade (11-48B), Tournament Grade (11-48D) and Premier Grade (11-48F). Made 1949-69. Values same as for Sportsman-48A.

MODEL 11-48SA SKEET
28 GA. AND .410 . . . . NiB $398 Ex $300 Gd $233
Same general specifications as Model 11-48A 28 gauge except has 25-in. VR bbl., SK choke. 28 ga. introduced 1952, .410 in 1954.

MODEL 58 SKEET, TARGET, TOURNAMENT
AND PREMIER GRADES

These higher grade models differ from the Sportsman-58SA in general quality, grade of wood, checkering, engraving, and other refinements. General operating and physical specifications are the same.

Sportsman-58C
 Skeet Gun . . . . NiB $544 Ex $397 Gd $322
Sportsman-58D
 Tournament . . . . NiB $1656 Ex $1267 Gd $1100
Sportsman-58SF
 Premier . . . . NiB $6222 Ex $3566 Gd $2924

SPORTSMAN-58 TOURNAMENT AND PREMIER

These higher grade models differ from the Sportsman-58ADL with VR bbl. in general quality, grade of wood, checkering, engraving, etc. General specifications are the same.

Sportsman-58D Tournament . . NiB $1099 Ex $824 Gd $590
Sportsman-58F Premier . . . NiB $1889 Ex $1488 Gd $1051

MODEL 58ADL AUTOLOADER

Deluxe grade. Gas-operated. 12 ga. Three round magazine. Bbls.: plain or VR, 26-, 28- or 30-in.; IC, M or F choke, or Remington Special Skeet choke. Weight: About 7 lbs. Checkered pistol-grip stock and forearm. Made 1956-64.

plain bbl. . . . . NiB $366 Ex $267 Gd $188 ventilated rib bbl. . . . . NiB $433 Ex $320 Gd $221

MODEL 58BDL DELUXE SPECIAL GRADE
Same as Model 58ADL except select grade wood.
plain bbl. . . . . NiB $544 Ex $422 Gd $338
ventilated rib bbl. . . . . NiB $577 Ex $476 Gd $390

MODEL 58SADL
SKEET GRADE. . . . . NiB $588 Ex $432 Gd $338
Same general specifications as Model 58ADL w/ VR bbl.
except special skeet stock and forearm.

REVELATION SHOTGUNS
See Western Auto listings.

RICHLAND ARMS COMPANY — Blissfield, MI.
Manufactured in Italy and Spain

MODEL 200
FIELD GRADE DOUBLE . . . . . . NiB $400 Ex $294 Gd $179
Hammerless, boxlock, Anson & Deeley-type. Plain extractors.
Double triggers. Gauges: 12, 16, 20, 28, .410 (3-in. chambers
in 20 and .410; others have 2.75-in.). Bbls.: 28-in. M/F choke,
26-in. IC/M; .410 w/ 26-in. M/F only; 22-in. IC/M in 20 ga.
only. Weight: 6 lbs., 2 oz. to 7 lbs., 4 oz. Checkered walnut
stock with cheekpiece, pistol grip, recoil pad; beavertail
forend. Made in Spain from 1963 to 1985.

MODEL 202
ALL-PURPOSE FIELD GUN. . . . NiB $554 Ex $348 Gd $245
Hammerless, boxlock, Anson & Deeley-type. Same as Model
200 except has two sets of barrels same gauge. 12 ga.: 30-in.
bbls. F/F, 3-in. chambers; 26-in. bbls. IC/M, 2.75-in. chambers.
20 gauge: 28-in. bbls. M/F; 22-in. bbls. IC/M, 3-in. chambers.
Made from 1963. Disc.

MODEL 707
DELUXE FIELD GUN . . . . NiB $433 Ex $266 Gd $180
Hammerless, boxlock, triple bolting system. Plain extractors.
Double triggers. Gauges: 12, 2.75-in. chambers; 20, 3-in.
chambers. Bbls.: 12 ga., 28-in. M/F, 26-in. IC/M; 20 ga., 30-in.
F/F, 28-in. M/F, 26-in. IC/M. Weight: 6 lbs., 4 oz. to 6 lbs.,
15 oz. Checkered walnut stock and forend, recoil pad. Made
1963-72.

**MODEL 711 LONG-RANGE WATERFOWL MAGNUM
DOUBLE-BARREL SHOTGUN**
Hammerless, boxlock, Anson & Deeley-type, Purdey triple
lock. Plain extractors. Double triggers. Auto safety. Gauges:
10, 3.5-in. chambers; 12, 3-in. chambers. Bbls.: 10 ga., 32-in.;
12 ga., 30-in.; F/F. Weight: 10 ga., 11 pounds; 12 ga., 7.75
lbs. Checkered walnut stock and beavertail forend; recoil pad.
Made in Spain from 1963 to 1985.
10 ga. magnum . . . . NiB $545 Ex $356 Gd $280
12 ga. magnum . . . . NiB $566 Ex $377 Gd $300

MODEL 808
O/U SHOTGUN . . . . NiB $559 Ex $394 Gd $290
Boxlock. Plain extractors. Non-selective single trigger. 12 ga.
only. Bbls. (Vickers steel): 30-in. F/F; 28-in. M/F; 26-in. IC/M.
Weight: 6 lbs., 12 oz. to 7 lbs., 3 oz. Checkered walnut stock/
forend. Made in Italy from 1963 to 1968.
Premier grade . . . . NiB $6220 Ex $4014 Gd $2444

JOHN RIGBY & CO. — London, England

HAMMERLESS BOXLOCK DOUBLE-BARREL SHOTGUN
Auto ejectors. Double triggers. Made in all gauges, barrel
lengths and chokes. Checkered stock and forend, straight grip
standard. Made in two grades: Sackville and Chatsworth. These
guns differ in general quality, engraving, etc.; specifications are
the same.
Sackville grade . . . . NiB $6450 Ex $4255 Gd $3790
Chatsworth grade . . . . NiB $4779 Ex $4109 Gd $3200

HAMMERLESS SIDELOCK DOUBLE-BARREL SHOTGUN
Auto ejectors. Double triggers. Made in all gauges, barrel
lengths and chokes. Checkered stock and forend, straight
grip standard. Made in two grades: Regal (best quality) and
Sandringham; these guns differ in general quality, engraving,
etc., specifications are the same.
Regal grade . . . . NiB $13,677 Ex $11,773 Gd $9892
Sandringham grade. . . . . NiB $11,088 Ex $9000 Gd $5698

RIZZINI, BATTISTA — Marcheno, Italy

NOTE: *Rizzini was purchased by San Swiss AG IN 2002.
Imported in the U. S. by SIB Arms, Exeter, New Hampshire;
William Larkin Moore & Co., Scottsdale, Arizona; and New
England Arms Co., Kittery, Maine.*

AURUM O/U . . . . NiB $2770 Ex $2243 Gd $2016
Gauge: 12, 16 and 20. Boxlock action, light engraving. Case
included. Introduced 1996.

AURUM LIGHT . . . . NiB $4088 Ex $2867 Gd $2390
Similaar to Aurum but 16 gauge only. Imported beginning in 2000.

ARTEMIS . . . . NiB $2733 Ex $2270 Gd $1966
Similarf to Aurum but with improved engraving and gold inlays.

ARTEMIS DELUXE . . . . NiB $6777 Ex $3861 Gd $3223
Similar to Artemis but with detailed game scene engraving.
Available in all gauges

ARTEMIS EL . . . . NiB $17,776 Ex $14,600 Gd $12,980
Same as Artemis Deluxe. Custom gun with superior quality
wood and detailed hand engraving. Disc. 2000.

MODEL 780 FIELD . . . . NiB $2140 Ex $1088 Gd $977
Gauge: 10, 12 or 16. Boxlock action, double triggers, extrac-
tors, walnut stock and forearm. Disc. 2000.
10 gauge, add $625
Ejector model (S780EL), add. $200
Single selective trigger with ejectors, add. $250
SST, ejectors and upgraded stock, add $425

MODEL S780 EMEL . NiB $14,900 Ex $13,655 Gd $11,330
Same as Model 780 Field but with special engraving and hand
finished.

MODEL 780 COMPETITION . . . NiB $1488 Ex $1276 Gd $1099
Same as Model 780 Field but with skeet, trap or sporting clays
features. Disc.1998.

**MODEL 780
SMALL GAUGE SERIES** . . . . NiB $1388 Ex $1164 Gd $889
Same as Model 780 Field but in 20, 28, or 36 gauge. Double
triggers, ejectors. Disc. 1998.

SHOTGUNS

**Rigby Regal
Side Lock**

Rizzini Aurum

MODEL 782 EM FIELD . . . NiB $1566 Ex $1275 Gd $1074
Gauge: 12 or 16. Boxlock action with sideplates, single selective trigger, ejectors and extractors, walnut stock and forearm. Disc. 1998.
Model 782 EM Slug, add $550
Model 782 EML, add. $450

MODEL S782 EMEL . NiB $14,990 Ex $11,860 Gd $10,066
Same as Model 782 EM Field but specially engraved and hand finished.

**MODEL S782 EMEL
DELUXE** . . . . NiB $13,899 Ex $11,776 Gd $10,066
Gauge: 10, 12, 16, 20, 28, 36 and .410. Barrel:28-in. ventilated rib with choke tubes (except .410); coin-finish engraving; gold inlaids; fine scroll borders; Deluxe English walnut stock. Imported 1994.

**MODEL 790
COMPETITION** . . . . NiB $1877 Ex $1687 Gd $1261
Gauge: 12 or 20. Available in trap, skeet or sporting clays models. Black frame outlined with gold line engraving. Disc. 1999.
20 ga. Sporting (sideplates and QD stock), add $1200
Trap model, 20 gauge, subtract $200

**MODEL 790 SMALL
GAUGE** . . . . NiB $1499 Ex $1179 Gd $1088
Similar to Model 790 Competition but in 20, 29, or 36 guages. Single selective trigger, ejectors. Disc. 2000.

MODEL 790 EL . . . . NiB $7088 Ex $4977 Gd $3766
Same as Model 790 but hand finished w/ 18k gold inlays, hand engraving.

**MODEL S790 EMEL
DELUXE** . . . . NiB $12,970 Ex $10,088 Gd $8990
Guages: All. Custom gun w/ 27.5-in. ventilated-rib bbls. choke tubes (except .410); color case-hardened or coin-finished receiver; ornate engraving with Rizzini crest. Stock is deluxe English walnut; leather case included.

**MODEL 792 SMALL GAUGE
MAGNUM** NiB $1791 Ex $1476 Gd $1199
Gauge: 20, 28, or 36. Magnum chambers. Single selective trigger; ejectors; engraved sideplates. Disc. 1998.

**MODEL 792 EMEL
DELUXE** . . . . NiB $9133 Ex $8093 Gd $6166
Same as Model 793 but hand finished w/ 18k gold inlays and hand engraving.

MODEL S792 EMEL. . . . NiB $14,000 Ex $11,980 Gd $10,760
Guages: All. Custom gun w/ 27.5-in. ventilated-rib bbls. choke tubes (except .410); coin-finished receiver; sideplates with fine game scene engraving and scroll borders; deluxe English walnut stock; leather case included. Imported 1994.

MODEL 2000 TRAP . . . . . . NiB $1798 Ex $1448 Gd $1190
Guage: 12 only. Nickel-finished receiver; sideplates; gold trigger; ventilated-rib bbls. Disc 1998.

**MODEL 2000
TRAP EL** . . . . NiB $5477 Ex $4100 Gd $3110
Same as Model 2000 Trap but hand finished w/ 18k gold inlays and ornate hand engraving.

MODEL 2000-SP . . . . NiB $3210 Ex $2976 Gd $2241
Guage: 12 only. Bbls.: 26, 29.5, or 32 in. Over-bored barrels with choke tubes. Engraved sideplates, semi-fancy select QD stock. Case included. Imported 1994 to 1998.

PREMIER SPORTING . . . . . NiB $2669 Ex $2280 Gd $1881
Guages: 12 or 20. Bbls.: 28, 29.5 or 32 in. five chokes per bbl. Custom built on request. Imported 1994

SPORTING EL . . . . NiB $3126 Ex $2390 Gd $2177
Same as Premier model but includes multiple chokes and fitted case. Disc. 2000.

UPLAND EL . . . . NiB $2793 Ex $2277 Gd $1965
Guages: All. Custom gun w/ 27.5-in. ventilated-rib bbls. choke tubes (except .410); case-hardened receiver; deluxe walnut stock. Hard case included. Imported 1994.

ROCK ISLAND AROMORY (RIA) —
Manila, Philippines

Armscor brand, imports and mfg. in Pahrump, NV since 2016.

ALL GENERATIONS SERIES . . . . NiB $300 Ex $280 Gd $250
Pump action. Caliber: .410 bore, 20 or 12 gauge. Bbl.: 18.5-, 26-, or 28-in. Sights: Brass bead. Stock: Polymer. Weight: 7.1-8.8 lbs. Finish: Black. Made from 2020 to date.

CARINA SERIES. . . . . NiB $300 Ex $280 Gd $250
Pump action. Caliber: 12 gauge. Bbl.: 18.5-, 26-, or 28-in. Sights: Brass bead. Stock: Polymer or wood. Weight: 7.1-8.8 lbs. Finish: Black, blued, camo. Made from 2020 to date.
camo finish . . . . NiB $350 Ex $330 Gd $300

MERIVA SERIES. . . . . NiB $200 Ex $180 Gd $150
Pump action. Caliber: 12 gauge. Bbl.: 18.5-in. Sights: Brass bead. Stock: Polymer. Weight: 6.3 lbs. Finish: Black. Made from 2019 to date.
3-1 model (2 bbls., traditional stock,
    pistol grip, 2017-date) . . . . . NiB $350 Ex $330 Gd $300

TPAS . . . . NiB $600 Ex $580 Gd $550
Pump action. Caliber: 12 gauge. Bbl.: 18.5-in. Sights: Ramp front. Stock: Wood. Weight: 8.1 lbs. Finish: Black. Heat shield. Trench style. Made from 2022 to date.

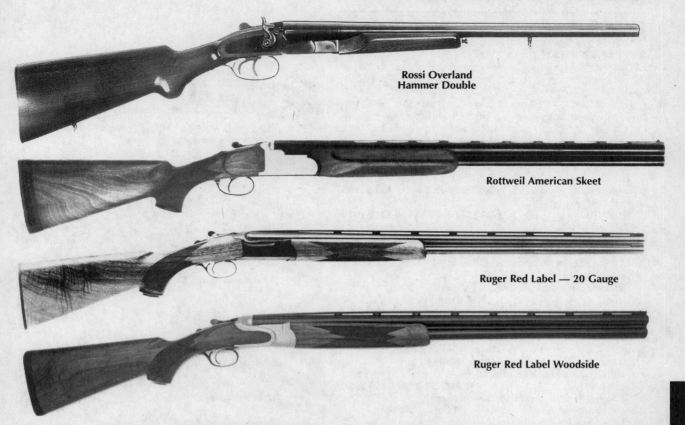

Rossi Overland Hammer Double

Rottweil American Skeet

Ruger Red Label — 20 Gauge

Ruger Red Label Woodside

TK SERIES . . . . **NiB $150 Ex $130 Gd $100**
Single Shot, break action. Caliber: .410 bore, 20 or 12 gauge. Bbl.: 20-in. VR. Sights: Brass bead. Stock: Polymer. Weight: 5.1 lbs. Exposed hammer. Made from 2019 to date.

VR SERIES
Semiauto or pump. Caliber: 20 or 12 gauge, detachable 5-rnd. magazine. Bbl.: 18- or 20-in. Sights: adj. rear/ront. Stock: Polymer. Weight: 6.9-9.5 lbs. Made from 2017 to date.
VRBP-100 (semiauto, bullpup
    design, 2019-date) . . . . **NiB $599 Ex $515 Gd $390**
VRPA40 (pump, 2019-date) . . . . **NiB $399 Ex $380 Gd $320**
VR80 (semiauto, AR style
    platform, 2019-date) . . . . . . **NiB $699 Ex $590 Gd $490**
VR82 (semiauto, 20 gauge, AR style
    platform, 2019-date) . . . . . . **NiB $730 Ex $790 Gd $720**

ROSSI — Sao Leopoldo, Brazil

SQUIRE HAMMERLESS DOUBLE-
BARREL SHOTGUN . . . . **NiB $435 Ex $333 Gd $245**
Boxlock. Plain extractors. Double triggers. 12 and 20 ga., .410. Three-in. chambers. Bbls.: 20-, 26-in. IC/M; 28-in. M/F choke. Weight: 7 to 7.5 lbs. Pistol-grip hardwood stock and beavertail forearm, unchecked. Made 1985-90.

OVERLUND
HAMMER DOUBLE . . . . **NiB $380 Ex $244 Gd $179**
Sidelock. Plain extractors. Double triggers. Gauges: 12, .410; 3-in. chambers. Bbls.: 20-in., IC/M in 12 g.; 26-in., F/F choke in .410. Weight: 7 lbs. (12 ga.); 6 lbs. (.410). Pistol-grip stock and beavertail forearm, unchecked. Note: Because of its

resemblance to the short-barreled doubles carried by guards riding shotgun on 19th-century stagecoaches, the 12 ga. version originally was called the "Coach Gun." Made 1968-89.

ROTTWEIL SHOTGUNS — Germany

MODEL 72 O/U SHOTGUN . . . **NiB $1988 Ex $1687 Gd $1277**
Hammerless, takedown with engraved receiver. 12 ga.; 2.75-in. chambers. 26.75-in. bbls. with SK/SK chokes. Weight: 7.5 lbs. Interchangeable trigger groups and buttstocks. Checkered French walnut buttstock and forend. Imported from Germany.

MODEL 650 FIELD
O/U SHOTGUN . . . . **NiB $888 Ex $675 Gd $544**
Breech action. Gauge: 12. 28-in. bbls. Six screw-in choke tubes. Automatic ejectors. Engraved receiver. Checkered pistol grip stock. Made 1984-86.

AMERICAN SKEET. . . . . **NiB $2010 Ex $1798 Gd $1288**
Boxlock action. Gauge: 12. 27-in. VR bbls. 44.5 in. overall. SK chokes. Weight: 7.5 lbs. Designed for tube sets. Hand-checkered European walnut stock with modified forend. Made 1984-87.

INTERNATIONAL
TRAP SHOTGUN . . . . **NiB $2066 Ex $1799 Gd $1263**
Box lock action. Gauge: 12. 30-in. bbls. 48.5 in. overall. Weight: 8 lbs. Choked IM/F. Selective single trigger. Metal bead front sight. Checkered European walnut stock w/pistol grip. Engraved action. Made 1984-87.

RUGER — Southport, CT

RED LABEL SERIES
O/U boxlock. Auto ejectors. Selective single trigger. 12, 20 or 28 ga. w/2.75- or 3-in. chambers. 26-in. VR bbl., IC/M or SK choke. Single selective trigger. Selective automatic ejectors. Automatic top safety. Standard gold bead front sight. Pistol-grip or English-style American walnut stock and forearm w/hand-cut checkering. The 20 ga. Model was introduced in 1977; 12 ga. version in 1982 and the stainless receiver became standard in 1985. Choke tubes were optional in 1988 and standard in 1990. Weight: 7.0 to 7.5 lbs.

w/fixed chokes . . . . NiB $1733 Ex $1388 Gd $1077
w/choke tubes. . . . . NiB $1760 Ex $1410 Gd $1100
w/engraving
  (1997-00) . . . . NiB $2210 Ex $1655 Gd $1010
w/engraving
  (2001-11) . . . . NiB $1755 Ex $1010 Gd $555
50th Anniversary model . . NiB $1355 Ex $1130 Gd $2855
All Weather Stainless model (stainless steel
  construction; 26-, 28- or 30-in.
  VR bbl. w/choke tubes, black synthetic
  stock, 1999-06). . . . . NiB $1280 Ex $810 Gd $610
English Field model (12, 20 or 28 ga.,
  straight English-style stock,
  1992-00). . . . . NiB $970 Ex $690 Gd $555
Sporting Clays model (12 or 20 ga., 30-in. VR bbl.
  w/Briley choke tubes, walnut or synthetic
  stock, twin bead, blued finish,
  1992-11). . . . . NiB $1555 Ex $905 Gd $655
All Weather Stainless model (stainless steel
  construction; 26-, 28- or 30-in. VR bbl. w/choke
  tubes, black synthetic stock,
  1999-06). . . . . NiB $1280 Ex $810 Gd $610
English Field model (12, 20 or 28 ga.,
  straight English-style stock,
  1992-00). . . . . NiB $970 Ex $690 Gd $555
Wildlife Forever Special Edition model (Limited edition
  commemorating the 50th Wildlife Forever anniversary.
  Similar to the standard Red Label model except
  chambered 12 ga. only w/engraved receiver enhanced
  w/gold mallard and pheasant inlays. 300
  produced in 1993.). . . . . NiB $1690 Ex $1655 Gd $1299
recent mfg (12 ga. only,
  disc. 2014) . . . . NiB $1255 Ex $910 Gd $655

RED LABEL WOODSIDE
Similar to the Red Label O/U except in 12 ga. only with wood sideplate extensions. Made 1995-2002.
Standard . . . . NiB $1755 Ex $1210 Gd $1110
Engraved . . . . NiB $2210 Ex $1800 Gd $1533

GOLD LABEL . . . . NiB $3650 EX $2510 GD $1500
S/S boxlock. Auto ejectors. Selective single trigger. 12 ga. w/ 3-in. chambers. 28-in. solid-rib bbl., choke tubes. Top safety. Pistol-grip or English-style American walnut stock and forearm w/hand-cut checkering. Stainless receiver. Made 2002-08.

SAIGA — Izhevsk, Russia
Mfg. by Izhmash in Izhevsk, Russia; last imported by RWC Group in Tullytown, PA.

SAIGA-12
AK-style action, gas-operated piston, Semiauto w/ detachable 5-rnd. magazine. 12 or 20 ga. w/ 3-in. chamber. Bbl.: 19- or 22-in. w/ choke tubes (12 ga. only). Stock: black synthetic.

**Sarasqueta Model 3
Hammerless Boxlock**

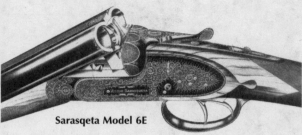

Sarasqeta Model 6E

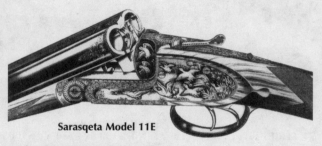

Sarasqeta Model 11E

Sarasqeta Model 12E

Finish: matte black. Weight: 6.7 to 10 lbs. Imported 2002 to 2004, reintroduced 2006 to 2014. Importation banned since 2014 due to U.S. sanctions.
12 or 20 ga. . . . . NiB $780 Ex $500 Gd $300
.410 . . . . NiB $646 Ex $415 Gd $250
Hunting Model (monte carlo style stock
  in wood or synthetic) . . . . . . NiB $885 Ex $580 Gd $360
Skeletonized Stock . . . . NiB $994 Ex $660 Gd $400
Tactical (AR15 style stock,
  10-rnd. magazine) . . . . . . NiB $1239 Ex $1115 Gd $734

VICTOR SARASQUETA, S.A. — Eibar, Spain

MODEL 3 HAMMERLESS
BOXLOCK DOUBLE-BARREL SHOTGUN
Plain extractors or auto ejectors. Double triggers. Gauges: 12, 16, 20. Made in various bbl. lengths, chokes and weights. Checkered stock and forend, straight grip standard. Imported from 1985-87.

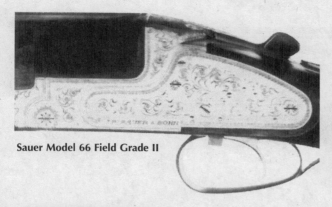

Sauer Model 66 Field Grade II

Sauer BBF 54 Combination Rifle/ Shotgun

Sauer Model 66 Field Grade III

Sauer Royal Double-Barrel Shotgun

Sauer Model 3000E Drilling

Model 3, plain extractors . . . . . NiB $599 Ex $445 Gd $329
Model 3E, automatic ejectors . NiB $655 Ex $500 Gd $435

HAMMERLESS SIDELOCK DOUBLES
Automatic ejectors (except on Models 4 and 203 which have plain extractors). Double triggers. Gauges: 12, 16, 20. Barrel lengths, chokes and weights made to order. Checkered stock and forend, straight grip standard. Models differ chiefly in overall quality, engraving, grade of wood, checkering, etc.; general specifications are the same. Imported from 1985 to 1987.
Model 4 . . . . NiB $779 Ex $643 Gd $441
Model 4E . . . . NiB $879 Ex $754 Gd $570
Model 203 . . . . NiB $744 Ex $600 Gd $435
Model 203E . . . . NiB $800 Ex $632 Gd $544

Model 6E . . . . NiB $1388 Ex $1108 Gd $700
Model 7E . . . . NiB $1443 Ex $1156 Gd $965
Model 10E . . . . NiB $2588 Ex $2188 Gd $1966
Model 11E . . . . NiB $2800 Ex $2577 Gd $2234
Model 12E . . . . NiB $3110 Ex $2770 Gd $2369

J. P. SAUER & SOHN — Eckernförde, Germany; formerly Suhl, Germany

MODEL 66 O/U FIELD GUN
Purdey-system action with Holland & Holland-type sidelocks. Selective single trigger. Selective auto ejectors. Automatic safety. Available in three grades of engraving. 12 ga. only. Krupp special steel bbls. w/VR 28-in., M/F ehoke. Weight: About 7.25 lbs. Checkered walnut stock and forend; recoil pad. Made 1966-75.
Grade I . . . . NiB $2377 Ex $2120 Gd $1798
Grade II . . . . NiB $3256 Ex $2460 Gd $2190
Grade III . . . . NiB $4100 Ex $3712 Gd $2644

MODEL 66 O/U SKEET GUN
Same as Model 66 Field Gun except 26-in. bbls. with wide VR, SK choked- skeet-style stock and ventilated beavertail forearm; non-automatic safety. Made 1966-75.
Grade I . . . . NiB $2312 Ex $2198 Gd $1655
Grade II . . . . NiB $3270 Ex $2980 Gd $2110
Grade III . . . . NiB $3988 Ex $3655 Gd $2980

MODEL 66 O/U TRAP GUN
Same as Model 66 Skeet Gun except has 30-in. bbls. choked F/F or M/F; trap-style stock. Values same as for Skeet model. Made 1966-75.

SHOTGUNS

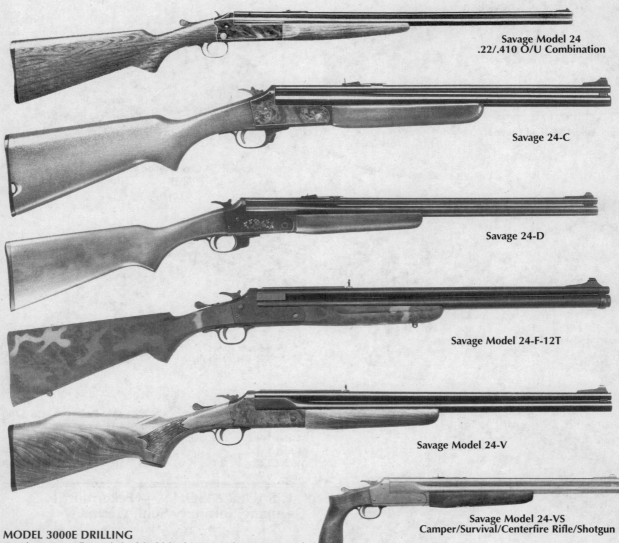

Savage Model 24
.22/.410 O/U Combination

Savage 24-C

Savage 24-D

Savage Model 24-F-12T

Savage Model 24-V

Savage Model 24-VS
Camper/Survival/Centerfire Rifle/Shotgun

MODEL 3000E DRILLING

Combination rifle and double bbl. shotgun. Blitz action with Greener crossbolt, double underlugs, separate rifle cartridge extractor, front set trigger, firing pin indicators, Greener side safety, sear slide selector locks right shotgun bbl. for firing rifle bbl. Gauge/calibers12 ga. (2.75-in. chambers); .222, .243, .30-06, 7x65R. 25-in. Krupp-Special steel bbls.; M/F choke automatic folding leaf rear rifle sight. Weight: 6.5 to 7.25 lbs. depending on rifle caliber. Checkered walnut stock and forend; pistol grip, Monte Carlo comb and cheekpiece, sling swivels. Standard model with Arabesque engraving; Deluxe model with hunting scenes engraved on action. Currently manufactured. Note: Also see listing under Colt.

Standard model . . . . NiB $4490 Ex $3891 Gd $2776
Deluxe model   . . . . NiB $5782 Ex $4669 Gd $3533

ARTEMIS DOUBLE-BARREL SHOTGUN

Holland & Holland-type sidelock with Greener crossbolt double underlugs, double sear safeties, selective single trigger, selective auto ejectors. Grade I with fine-line engraving, Grade II with full English Arabesque engraving. 12 ga. (2.75-in. chambers). Krupp special steel bbls., 28-in., M/F choke. Weight: About 6.5 lbs. Checkered walnut pistol-grip stock and beavertail forend; recoil pad. Made 1966-77.

Grade I . . . . NiB $5698 Ex $4766 Gd $4133
Grade II . . . . NiB $6880 Ex $5744 Gd $4500

BBF 54 O/U COMBINATION RIFLE/SHOTGUN

Blitz action with Kersten lock, front set trigger fires rifle bbl., slide-operated sear safety. Gauge/calibers: 16 ga.; .30-30, .30-06, 7x65R, 25-in. Krupp special steel bbls.; shotgun bbl. F choke, folding-leaf rear sight. Weight: About 6 lbs. Checkered walnut stock and forend; pistol grip, M Monte Carlo comb and cheekpiece, sling swivels. Standard model with Arabesque engraving; Deluxe model with hunting scenes engraved on action. Currently manufactured.

Standard model . . . . NiB $2977 Ex $2455 Gd $1766
Deluxe model   . . . . NiB $3566 Ex $3088 Gd $2655

ROYAL DOUBLE-BARREL SHOTGUNS

Anson & Deeley action (boxlock) with Greener crossbolt, double underlugs, signal pins, selective single trigger, selective auto ejectors, auto safety. Scalloped frame with Arabesque engraving. Krupp special steel bbls. Gauges: 12, 2.75-in. chambers, 20, 3-in. chambers. Bbls.: 30-in. (12 ga. only) and 28-in., M/F- 26-in. (20 ga. only), IC/M. Weight: 12 ga., about 6.5 lbs.; 20 ga., 6 lbs. Checkered walnut pistol-grip stock and beavertail forend; recoil pad. Made 1955-77.

Standard model . . . . NiB $1790 Ex $1533 Gd $1206
20 ga. add **20%**

SAVAGE ARMS — Westfield, MA

Formerly located in Utica, New York. Previously owned by ATK, formerly owned by Vista Outdoors. In 2019, Savage and Stevens was purchased by private investors.

MODEL 24C .22/.410 O/U
COMBINATION . . . . NiB $570 Ex $388 Gd $245
Break action combination gun. Same as Stevens No. 22-.410 with walnut stock and forearm. Made 1950-65.

MODEL 24C
CAMPER'S COMPANION . . . . . NiB $675 Ex $466 Gd $290
Same as Model 24FG except made in .22 Magnum/20 ga. only; has 20-in. bbls., shotgun tube Cyl. bore. Weight: 5.75 lbs. Trap in butt provides ammunition storage; comes with carrying case. Made 1972-89.

MODEL 24 FIELD . . . . NiB $498 Ex $277 Gd $190
Same as Models 24DL and 24MDL except frame has black or casehardened finish. Game scene decoration of frame eliminated in 1974; forearm uncheckered after 1976. Made 1970-89.

MODEL 24DL . . . . NiB $400 Ex $366 Gd $243
Same general specifications as Model 24S except top-lever opening; satin-chrome-finished frame decorated with game scenes, checkered Monte Carlo stock and forearm. Made 1962-65.

MODEL 24F-12T TURKEY GUN . . . NiB $700 Ex $488 Gd $337
12- or 20-ga. shotgun bbl./.22 Hornet, .223 or .30-30 caliber rifle. 24-in. blued bbls., 3-in. chambers, extra removable F choke tube. Hammer block safety. Color casehardened frame. DuPont Rynite camo stock. Swivel studs. Made 1989-2007.

MODEL 24FG FIELD GRADE . . . NiB $525 Ex $433 Gd $276
Same general specifications as Model 24S except top lever opening. Made 1972. Disc.

MODEL 24MDL . . . . NiB $577 Ex $400 Gd $229
Same as Model 24DL except rifle bbl. chambered for 22 WMR. Made 1962-69.

MODEL 24MS . . . . NiB $690 Ex $535 Gd $389
Same as Model 24S except rifle bbl. chambered for 22 WMR. Made 1964-71.

MODEL 24S O/U
COMBINATION . . . . NiB $477 Ex $339 Gd $225
Boxlock. Visible hammer. Side lever opening. Plain extractors. Single trigger. 20 ga. or .410 bore shotgun bbl. under 22 LR bbl., 24-in. Open rear sight, ramp front, dovetail for scope mounting. Weight: About 6.75 lbs. Plain pistol-grip stock and forearm. Made 1964-71.

MODEL 24V . . . . NiB $588 Ex $379 Gd $298
Similar to Model 24D except 20 ga. under .222 Rem., .22 Rem., .357 Mag., .22 Hornet or .30-30 rifle bbl. Made 1967-89.

MODEL 24-CS CAMPER'S COMPANION
CENTERFIRE RIFLE/SHOTGUN . . . NiB $680 Ex $389 Gd $319
Caliber: .22 LR over 20 ga. Nickel finish full-length stock and accessory pistol-grip stock. Overall length: 36 in. with full stock; 26 in. w/pistol grip. Weight: About 5.75 lbs. Made 1972-88.
.357 Mag./20 ga., add **$50**

MODEL 28A STANDARD GRADE SLIDE-ACTION
REPEATING SHOTGUN . . . . . . NiB $445 Ex $398 Gd $300
Hammerless. Takedown. 12 ga. Five round tubular magazine. Plain bbl., lengths: 26-,28-, 30-, 32-in., choked C/M/F. Weight: About 7.5 lbs. w/ 30-in. bbl. Plain pistol-grip stock, grooved slide handle. Made 1928-31.

MODEL 28B . . . . NiB $366 Ex $287 Gd $245
Raised matted rib; otherwise the same as Model 28A.

MODEL 28D TRAP GRADE. . . . NiB $366 Ex $287 Gd $245
Same general specifications as Model 28A except has 30-in. F choke bbl. w/matted rib, trap-style stock w/checkered pistol grip, checkered slide handle of select walnut.

MODEL 30 SOLID FRAME HAMMERLESS
SLIDE-ACTION SHOTGUN . . . NiB $290 Ex $221 Gd $175
Gauges: 12, 16, 20, .410. 2.75-in. chamber in 16 ga., 3- in. in other ga. Magazine holds four 2.75-in. shells or three 3-in. shells. Bbls.: VR; 26-, 28-, 30-in.; IC, M, F choke. Weight: Average 6.25 to 6.75 lbs. depending on ga. Plain pistol-grip stock (checkered on later production), grooved slide handle. Made 1958-70.

MODEL 30 TAKEDOWN
SLUG GUN. . . . . NiB $255 Ex $175 Gd $125
Same as Model 30FG except 21-in. cyl. bore bbl. with rifle sights. Made 1971-79.

MODEL 30AC SOLID FRAME. . NiB $379 Ex $288 Gd $179
Same as Model 30 Solid Frame except has 26-in. bbl. with adj. choke; 12 ga. only. Made 1959-70.

MODEL 30AC TAKEDOWN . . . NiB $366 Ex $265 Gd $160
Same as Model 30FG except has 26-in. bbl. with adj. choke; 12 and 20 ga. only. Made 1971-72.

MODEL 30D TAKEDOWN . . . . NiB $277 Ex $200 Gd $167
Deluxe Grade. Same as Model 30FG except has receiver engraved with game scene, VR bbl., recoil pad. Made from 1971. Disc.

MODEL 30FG TAKEDOWN HAMMERLESS
SLIDE-ACTION SHOTGUN . . . . NiB $265 Ex $180 Gd $95
Field Grade. Gauges: 12, 20, .410. Three-in. chamber. Magazine holds four 2.75-in. shells or three 3-in. shells. Bbls.: plain; 26-in. F choke (.410 ga. only); 28-in. M/F choke; 30-in. F choke (12 ga. only). Weight: Average 7 to 7.75 lbs. depending on gauge. Checkered pistol-grip stock, fluted slide handle. Made 1970-79.

MODEL 30L SOLID FRAME . . . NiB $300 Ex $241 Gd $176
Same as Model 30 Solid Frame except left-handed model with ejection port and safety on left side; 12 ga. only. Made 1959-70.

MODEL 30T SOLID FRAME
TRAP AND DUCK . . . . NiB $377 Ex $288 Gd $190
Same as Model 30 Solid Frame except only in 12 ga. w/30-in. F choke bbl.; has Monte Carlo stock with recoil pad, weight: About 8 lbs. Made 1963-70.

SHOTGUNS

Savage Model 30

Savage Model 30 Slug Gun

Savage Model 69-RXL

Savage Model 220

Savage Model 242

Savage Model 312 Trap

Savage Model 330

MODEL 30T TAKE DOWN
TRAP GUN . . . . **NiB $335 Ex $292 Gd $197**
Same as Model 30D except only in 12 ga. w/30-in. F choke bbl. Monte Carlo stock with recoil pad. Made 1970-73.

MODEL 42 TAKEDOWN. . . . . . . **NiB $430 Ex $340 Gd $280**
Break action combination gun w/410 bore bbl. under rife bbl. (.22 LR or .22 WMR). Exposed hammer. Single triggers. Stock: Textured black synthetic. Breaks down and stores in Uncle Mike's Go Bag. Made 2013 to date.

MODEL 69-RXL SLIDE-ACTION
SHOTGUN . . . .**NiB $366 Ex $256 Gd $190**
Similar to Model 67 (law enforcement configuration). Hammerless, side ejection top tang safe for left- or right-hand use. 12 ga. chambered for 2.75- and 3-in. magnum shells. 18.25-in. bbl. Tubular magazine holds 6 rounds (one less for 3-in. mag). Walnut finish hardwood stock with recoil pad and grooved operating handle. Weight: About 6.5 lbs. Made 1982-89.

MODEL 210F
SLUG WARRIOR. . . . .**NiB $505 Ex $405 Gd $265**
Bolt action. Built on Savage 110 action. Gauge: 12 w/3-in. chamber. Two round detachable magazine. 24-in. fully rifled bbl. Receiver drilled and tapped for scope mounts w/no sights. Weight: 7.5 lbs. Checkered black synthetic stock w/swivel studs and recoil pad. Made 1997-2000.
Camo finish, add. $40

MODEL 212 SLUG GUN . . . . . **NiB $660 Ex $585 Gd $455**
Similar to Model 210F except w/22-in. bbl. Advantage Camo or blue finish. AccuTrigger. Detachable 2-rnd. magazine. Made from 2011–date.
camo finish, add $70
Turkey model (22-in. bbl., extended choke tube,
   camo stock, 2019-date) . . . . . . **NiB $660 Ex $580 Gd $450**

MODEL 220 SINGLE BARREL SERIES
Hammerless. Break action. Auto ejector. Gauges: 12, 16, 20 or .410; single shot. Bbl.: 12 ga., 28- to 36-in., 16 ga., 28- to 32-in.; 20 ga., 26- to 32-in.; .410 bore, 26-and 28-in. Various fixed chokes. Weight: about 6 lbs. Plain pistol-grip stock and wide forearm. Made 1938–65.
Standard . . . . **NiB $130 Ex $110 Gd $70**
220AC (Savage adj. choke) . . . . . **NiB $105 Ex $90 Gd $60**
220L (side lever opening instead of top lever;
   1965–72) . . . . **NiB $95 Ex $70 Gd $45**
Same general specifications
   as Model 220 except
   has 220P (PolyChoke). . . . .**NiB $95 Ex $70 Gd $45**

MODEL 220 SLUG GUN . . . . . **NiB $605 Ex $530 Gd $415**
Built on Savage 110 bolt action. Gauge: 20 w/22-in. rifled bbl. Optic ready. 2-rnd. detachable magazine. Weight: 7.3 lbs. Synthetic black modular AccuStock. AccuTrigger. Matte black finish. Made from 2010–date.
Camo finish, add. $60
Stainless bbl./camo finish, add $180
Thumbhole model (polymer thumbhole stock, 2-rnd.
   detachable magazine). . . . .**NiB $705 Ex $620 Gd $480**
Turkey model (22-in. bbl., extended choke tube, camo stock,
   2019-date) . . . . **NiB $660 Ex $580 Gd $450**

MODEL 242 O/U SHOTGUN. . **NiB $498 Ex $376 Gd $292**
Similar to Model 24D except both bbls. .410 bore, F choke. Weight: About 7 lbs. Made 1977-80.

MODEL 312 SERIES
O/U. Boxlock action. Gauge: 12; 2.75- or 3-in. chmbrs. 26- or 28-in. VR bbls. w/F/M/IC choke tubes. 43 or 45 in. overall. Weight: 7 lbs. Top tang safety. American walnut stock with checkered pistol grip and recoil pad. Made 1990–93.
Field Grade . . . . **NiB $688 Ex $554 Gd $400**
Sporting Clays (number 1 and number 2
   Skeet tubes and 28-in.
   bbls. only) . . . . **NiB $600 Ex $535 Gd $400**
Trap (30-in. bbls. only, Monte Carlo
   buttstock) . . . . **NiB $620 Ex $555 Gd $420**

MODEL 330 O/U SHOTGUN. . **NiB $589 Ex $477 Gd $398**
Boxlock. Plain extractors. Selective single trigger. Gauges: 12, 20. 2.75-in. chambers in 12 ga., 3-in. in 20 gauge. Bbls.: 26-in. IC/M; 28-in. M/F; 30-in. M/F choke (12 ga. only). Weight: 6.25 to 7.25 lbs., depending on gauge. Checkered pistol-grip stock and forearm. Made 1969-78.

MODEL 333 O/U SHOTGUN
Boxlock. Auto ejectors. Selective single trigger. Gauges: 12, 20. 2.75-in. chambers in 12 ga., 3-in. in 20 ga. Bbls.: VR; 26-in. SK choke, IC/M; 28-in. M/F; 30-in. M/F choke (12 ga. only). Weight: Average 6.25 to 7.25 lbs. Checkered pistol-grip stock and forearm. Made 1973-79.
Model 333 12 ga. . . . .**NiB $598 Ex $467 Gd $366**
Model 333 20 ga., add 30%

MODEL 333T TRAP GUN . . . . . NiB $654 Ex $498 Gd $396
Similar to Model 330 except only in 12 ga. w/ 30-in. VR bbls., IM/F choke; Monte Carlo stock w/recoil pad. Weight: 7.75 lbs. Made 1972-79.

MODEL 389 . . . . NiB $855 Ex $680 Gd $455
Break action combination gun w/12 ga bbl. and rife bbl. (.222 Rem. or .308 Win.). Hammerless. Double triggers. Stock: Checkered walnut. Made 1988-90.

MODEL 420 O/U SHOTGUN
Boxlock. Hammerless. Takedown. Automatic safety. Double triggers or non-selective single trigger. Gauges: 12, 16, 20. Bbls.: Plain, 26- to 30-in. (the latter in 12 ga. only); choked M/F, C/IC. Weight w/ 28-in. bbls.: 12 ga., 7.75 lbs.; 16 ga., 7.5 lbs.; 20 ga., 6.75 lbs. Plain pistol-grip stock and forearm. Made 1938-42.
w/ double triggers . . . . NiB $589 Ex $477 Gd $300
w/ single trigger . . . . NiB $633 Ex $498 Gd $376

MODEL 430
Same as Model 420 except has matted top bbl., checkered stock of select walnut with recoil pad, checkered forearm. Made 1938-42.
w/ double triggers . . . . NiB $677 Ex $544 Gd $390
w/ single trigger . . . . NiB $677 Ex $559 Gd $443

MODEL 440 O/U SHOTGUN. . NiB $635 Ex $490 Gd $387
Boxlock. Plain extractors. Selective single trigger. Gauges: 12, 20. 2.75-in. chambers in 12 ga., 3-in. in 20 ga. Bbls.: VR; 26-in. SK choke, IC/M; 28-in. M/F; 30-in. M/F choke (12 ga. only). Weight: Average 6 to 6.5 lbs. depending on ga. Made 1968-72.

MODEL 440T TRAP GUN . . . . . NiB $598 Ex $488 Gd $392
Similar to Model 440 except only in 12 ga. w/ 30-in. bbls., extra-wide VR, IM/F choke. Trap-style Monte Carlo stock and semibeavertail forearm of select walnut, recoil pad. Weight: 7.5 lbs. Made 1969-72.

MODEL 444 DELUXE
O/U SHOTGUN . . . . NiB $687 Ex $500 Gd $369
Similar to Model 440 except has auto ejectors, select walnut stock and semi-beavertail forearm. Made 1969-72.

MODEL 550
HAMMERLESS DOUBLE . . . . . NiB $355 Ex $290 Gd $200
Boxlock. Auto ejectors. Non-selective single trigger. Gauges: 12, 20. 2.75-in. chamber in 12 ga., 3-in. in 20 ga. Bbls.: VR; 26-in. IC/M; 28-in. M/F; 30-in. M/F choke (12 ga. only). Weight: 7 to 8 lbs. Checkered pistol-grip stock and semi-beavertail forearm. Made 1971-73.

MODEL 720 STANDARD GRADE 5 SHOT AUTOLOADING
SHOTGUN . . . . NiB $335 Ex $269 Gd $200
Browning type. Takedown. 12 and 16 ga. Four round tubular magazine. Bbl.: plain; 26- to 32-in. (the latter in 12 ga. only); choked IC, M, F. Weight: About 8.25 lbs., 12 ga. w/ 30-in. bbl.; 16 ga., about .5 lb. lighter. Checkered pistol-grip stock and forearm. Made 1930-49.

MODEL 726 UPLAND SPORTER AUTO
SHOTGUN . . . . NiB $377 Ex $292 Gd $233
Same as Model 720 except has 2-rnd. magazine capacity. Made 1931-49.

MODEL 740C SKEET GUN . . . . NiB $410 Ex $300 Gd $237
Same as Model 726 except has special skeet stock and full beavertail forearm, equipped with Cutts Compensator. Bbl. length overall with spreader tube is about 24.5 in. Made 1936-49.

MODEL 745 LIGHTWEIGHT
AUTOLOADER . . . . NiB $377 Ex $266 Gd $198
Three- or five-round models. Same general specifications as Model 720 except has lightweight alloy receiver, 12 ga.only, 28-in. plain bbl. Weight: About 6.75 lbs. Made 1940-49.

MODEL 750 AUTO SHOTGUN . . . NiB $355 Ex $310 Gd $240
Browning-type autoloader. Takedown. 12 ga. Four round tubular magazine. Bbls.: 28-in. F or M choke; 26-in. IC. Weight: About 7.25 lbs. Checkered walnut pistol-grip stock and grooved forearm. Made 1960-67.
Model 740-AC (26-in. bbl.,
  adj. choke, 1964-67) . . . . NiB $355 Ex $310 Gd $245
Model 740-SC
  (26-in. bbl., Savage
  Super Choke, 1962-63) . . . . . . NiB $355 Ex $310 Gd $245

MODEL 755 STANDARD
GRADE AUTOLOADER. . . . . . . NiB $355 Ex $310 Gd $245
Streamlined receiver. Takedown.12 and 16 ga. Four round tubular magazine (a three-round model with magazine capacity of two rounds was also produced until 1951). Bbl.: Plain, 30-in. F choke (12 ga. only), 28-in. F or M, 26-in. IC. Weight: About 8.25 lbs., 12 ga. Checkered pistol-grip stock and forearm. Made 1949-58.
Model 750-SC (26-in. bbl.,
  recoil-reducing adj.
  Savage Super Choke.) . . . . : . . NiB $355 Ex $310 Gd $245

MODEL 775 LIGHTWEIGHT . . NiB $389 Ex $297 Gd $245
Same general specifications as Model 755 except has lightweight alloy receiver, weight: About 6.73 lbs. Made 1950-65.
Model 775-SC (26-in. bbl.,
recoil-reducing adj.
  Savage Super Choke.) . . . . NiB $355 Ex $310 Gd $245

MODEL 2400 O/U COMBINATION . . . NiB $775 Ex $577 Gd $450
Boxlock action similar to that of Model 330. Plain extractors. Selective single trigger. 12-ga. (2.75-in. chamber) shotgun bbl., F choke over .308 Win. or .222 Rem. rifle bbl.; 23.5-in.; solid matted rib with blade front sight and folding leaf rear, dovetail for scope mounting. Weight: About 7.5 lbs. Monte Carlo stock w/pistol grip and recoil pad, semibeavertail forearm, checkered. Made 1975-79 by Valmet.

FOX A-GRADE . . . . NiB $3510 Ex $3055 Gd $2410
SxS. Anson delen style boxlock action. Ga.: 20 or 12, 3 in. chambers. Bbl.: 26- or 28-in. w/solid game rib, choke tubes, ejectors. Weight: 6.5-7 lbs. Stock: Checkered walnut w/oil finish w/straight grip, splinter forend. Sights: Brass bead. Finish: Bone/charcoal case. Made 2018-20.

MILANO . . . . NiB $1355 Ex $1180 Gd $930
O/U. Boxlock action. Ga.: 28, 20 or 12 and .410 bore, 3 in. chambers. Bbl.: 28-in. VR, choke tubes. Weight: 6.2-7.5 lbs. Stock: Checkered walnut satin finish Schnabel forend. Sights: Brass bead. Finish: Satin nickel. Made 2006-08.

SHOTGUNS

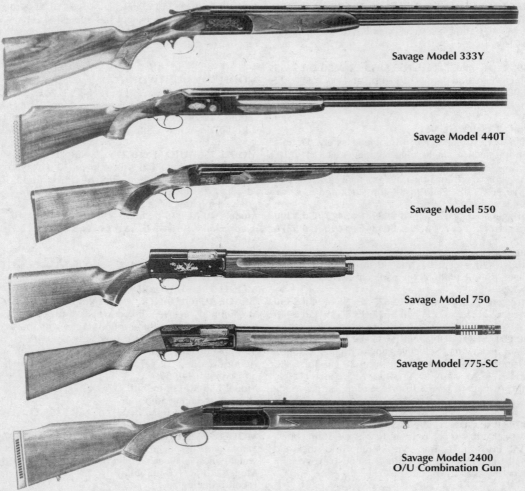

Savage Model 333Y

Savage Model 440T

Savage Model 550

Savage Model 750

Savage Model 775-SC

Savage Model 2400
O/U Combination Gun

RENEGAUGE SERIES

Semiauto. D.R.I.V. (Dual Regulating Inline Valve) gas system. Gauge: 12 ga., 3 in. Capacity: 4+1. Barrels: 26- or 28-in. VR w/3 Beretta/Benelli-style chokes (IC, M, F). Weight: 7.9-8 lbs. Length: 47.5-49.5 in. Stock: Black or camo synthetic w/rubber comb, adj. for length of pull, comb height, and drop & cast. Sights: Red fiber-optic. Oversized controls. 2020-date.

Competition model (24-in. bbl., red receiver/
   black bbl., extended magazine tube,
   black synthetic stock).... NiB $1900 Ex $1800 Gd $1600
Field model (black
   synthetic stock) .... NiB $1400 Ex $1200 Gd $900
Prairie model (TrueTimber Prairie camo stock, Cerakote
   brown sand recover/bbl.) . NiB $1500 Ex $1200 Gd $1000
Turkey Bottomland model (Mossy Oak Bottomland
   camo finish). .... NiB $1500 Ex $1200 Gd $1000
Turkey Obsession model (Mossy Oak
   Obsession camo finish) ... NiB $1500 Ex $1200 Gd $1000
Waterfowl model (Mossy Oak Shadow
   Grass Blades camo finish) NiB $1500 Ex $1200 Gd $1000

SEARS, ROEBUCK & COMPANY —
Chicago, IL

NOTE: *Although they do not correspond to specific models below, the names Ted Williams and J. C. Higgins have been used to designate various Sears shotguns at various times.*

MODEL 18
BOLT-ACTION REPEATER ..... NiB $200 Ex $125 Gd $90
Takedown. Three round top-loading magazine. Gauge: .410 only. Bbl.: 25-in. w/variable choke. Weight: About 5.75 lbs.

MODEL 20 SLIDE-ACTION
REPEATER .... NiB $300 Ex $210 Gd $155
Hammerless. Five round magazine. Bbls.: 26- to 30-in. w/ various chokes. Weight: 7.25 lbs. Plain pistol-grip stock and slide handle.

MODEL 21 SLIDE-ACTION
REPEATER .... NiB $320 Ex $235 Gd $190
Same general specifications as the Model 20 except VR and adustable choke.

MODEL 30 SLIDE-ACTION
REPEATER .... NiB $305 Ex $220 Gd $175
Hammerless. Gauges: 12, 16, 20 and .410. Four round magazine. Bbls.: 26- to 30-in., various chokes. Weight: 6.5 lbs. Plain pistol-grip stock, grooved slide handle.

MODEL 97 SINGLE-SHOT
SHOTGUN .... NiB $165 Ex $100 Gd $79
Takedown. Visible hammer. Automatic ejector. Gauges: 12, 16, 20 and .410. Bbls.: 26- to 36-in., F choke. Weight: Average 6 lbs. Plain pistol-grip stock and forearm.

MODEL 97-AC SINGLE-SHOT
SHOTGUN . . . . NiB $190 Ex $121 Gd $89
Same general specifications as Model 97 except fancier stock and forearm.

MODEL 101.7 DOUBLE-BARREL
SHOTGUN . . . . NiB $335 Ex $229 Gd $175
Boxlock. Double triggers. Gauges: 12, 16, 20, .410. Bbls.: 26- to 32-in., choked M and F. Weight: From 6 to 7.5 lbs. Plain stock and forend.

MODEL 101.7C DOUBLE-BARREL
SHOTGUN . . . . NiB $345 Ex $239 Gd $185
Same general specifications as Model 101.7 except checkered stock and forearm.

MODEL 101.25 BOLT-ACTION
SHOTGUN . . . . NiB $220 Ex $125 Gd $90
Takedown. .410 gauge. Five round tubular magazine. 24-in. bbl., F choke. Weight: About 6 lbs. Plain, one-piece pistol-grip stock.

MODEL 101.40 SINGLE-SHOT
SHOTGUN . . . . NiB $175 Ex $105 Gd $80
Takedown. Visible hammer. Automatic ejector. Gauges: 12, 16, 20 and .410. Bbls.: 26- to 36-in., F choke. Weight: Average 6 lbs. Plain pistol-grip stock and forearm.

MODEL 101.1120 BOLT-ACTION
REPEATER . . . . NiB $170 Ex $119 Gd $88
Takedown. .410 ga. 24-in. bbl., F choke. Weight: About 5 lbs. Plain one-piece pistol-grip stock.

MODEL 101.1380
BOLT-ACTION REPEATER . . . . . . NiB $195 Ex $130 Gd $95
Takedown. Gauges: 12, 16, 20. Two round detachable box magazine. 26-in. bbl., F choke. Weight: About 7 lbs. Plain one-piece pistol-grip stock.

MODEL 101.1610 DOUBLE-BARREL
SHOTGUN . . . . NiB $495 Ex $322 Gd $275
Boxlock. Double triggers. Plain extractors. Gauges: 12, 16, 20 and .410. Bbls.: 24- to 30-in. Various chokes, but mostly M and F. Weight: About 7.5 lbs, 12 ga. Checkered pistol-grip stock and forearm.

MODEL 101.1701 DOUBLE-BARREL
SHOTGUN . . . . NiB $420 Ex $335 Gd $240
Same general specifications as Model 101.1610 except satin chrome frame and select walnut stock and forearm.

MODEL 101.5350-D
BOLT-ACTION REPEATER . . . . . . NiB $229 Ex $120 Gd $89
Takedown. Gauges: 12, 16, 20. Two round detachable box magazine. 26-in. bbl., F choke. Weight: About 7.25 lbs. Plain one piece pistol-grip stock.

MODEL 101.5410
BOLT-ACTION REPEATER . . . . . . NiB $200 Ex $115 Gd $90
Same general specifications as Model 101.5350-D.

SKB ARMS COMPANY — Tokyo, Japan
Imported by G.U. Inc., Omaha, Nebraska

MODEL 385 SIDE-BY-SIDE . . . NiB $2200 Ex $1790 Gd $1176
Boxlock action w/double locking lugs. Gauges: 12, 20 and 28 w/2.75- and 3-in. chambers. 26- or 28-in. bbls. w/Inter-Choke tube system. Single selective trigger. Selective automatic ejectors and automatic safety. Weight: 6 lbs., 10 oz. Silver nitride receiver w/engraved scroll and game scene. Solid rib w/flat matte finish and metal front bead sight. Checkered American walnut English or pistol-grip stock. Imported from 1992.

MODELS 300 AND 400 SIDE-BY-SIDE SHOTGUNS
Similar to Model 200E except higher grade. Models 300 and 400 differ in that the latter has more elaborate engraving and fancier wood.
Model 300 . . . . NiB $1077 Ex $900 Gd $635
Model 400 . . . . NiB $1566 Ex $1309 Gd $1187

MODEL 400 SKEET . . . . NiB $1566 Ex $1309 Gd $1187
Similar to Model 200E Skeet except higher grade with more elaborate engraving and full fancy wood.

MODEL 480 ENGLISH . . . . NiB $1766 Ex $1510 Gd $1377
Similar to Model 280 English except higher grade with more elaborate engraving and full fancy wood.

MODEL 500 SERIES O/U SHOTGUN
Boxlock. Gauges: 12 and 20 w/2.75-or 3-in. chambers. Bbls.: 26-, 28- or 30-in. w/ VR; fixed chokes. Weight: 7.5 to 8.5 lbs. Single selective trigger. Selective automatic ejectors. Manual safety. Checkered walnut stock. Blue finish with scroll engraving. Imported 1967 to 1980.
500 Field, 12 ga. . . . . NiB $1000 Ex $750 Gd $415
500 Field, 20 ga, add 20%
500 Magnum, 12 ga, add 25%

MODEL 500 SMALL
GAUGE O/U SHOTGUN . . . . . NiB $884 Ex $652 Gd $466
Similar to Model 500 except gauges 28 and .410; has 28-in. VR bbls., M/F chokes. Weight: About 6.5 lbs.

MODEL 505 O/U SHOTGUN
Blued boxlock action. Gauge: 12, 20, 28 and .410. Bbls.: 26-, 28, 30-in.; IC/M, M/F or inner choke tubes. 45.19 in. overall. Weight: 6.6 to 7.4 lbs. Hand checkered walnut stock. Metal bead front sight, ejectors, single selective trigger and ejectors. Introduced 1988.
Standard Field, Skeet or
    Trap grade. . . . . NiB $1365 Ex $1188 Gd $765
Standard Two-bbl. Field set . . . NiB $1590 Ex $1277 Gd $1006
Skeet grade, three-bbl. set . . . NiB $1904 Ex $1888 Gd $1301
Sporting Clays . . . . NiB $1189 Ex $977 Gd $668
Trap grade two-bbl. set . . . . . . NiB $965 Ex $800 Gd $652

MODEL 585 O/U SHOTGUN
Boxlock. Gauges: 12, 20, 28 and .410; 2.75-or 3-in. chambers. Bbls.: 26-, 28-, 30-, 32- or 34-in. w/ VR; fixed chokes or Inter-choke tubes. Weight: 6.5 to 8.5 lbs. Single selective trigger. Selective automatic ejectors. Manual safety. Checkered walnut stock in standard or Monte Carlo style. Silver nitride finish with engraved game scenes. Made 1992-2008.
Field, Skeet, Trap grades . . . NiB $1477 Ex $1211 Gd $933
Field grade, two-bbl. set . . NiB $2376 Ex $1969 Gd $1387
Skeet set (20, 28, .410 ga.) . . . NiB $2933 Ex $2460 Gd $1977
Sporting Clays . . . . NiB $1700 Ex $1390 Gd $1054
Trap Combo
    (two-bbl. set) . . . . NiB $2433 Ex $1976 Gd $1366

MODEL 600 SERIES O/U SHOTGUN
Similar to 500 Series except w/silver nitride receiver. Checkered deluxe walnut stock in both Field and Target Grade configurations . Imported from 1969 to 1980.

SHOTGUNS

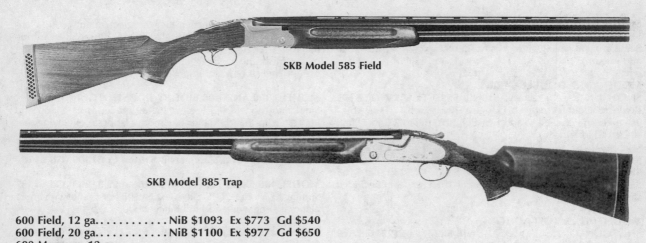

SKB Model 585 Field

SKB Model 885 Trap

600 Field, 12 ga. . . . . NiB $1093 Ex $773 Gd $540
600 Field, 20 ga. . . . . NiB $1100 Ex $977 Gd $650
600 Magnum, 12 ga.
   3-in. chambers . . . . NiB $1100 Ex $977 Gd $650
600 Skeet or Trap grade . . . . NiB $1154 Ex $1008 Gd $690
600 Trap Doubles model . . . . NiB $1154 Ex $1008 Gd $690

MODEL 600 SMALL GAUGE. . . NiB $1210 Ex $945 Gd $650
Same as Model 500 Small Gauge except higher grade with more elaborate engraving and fancier wood.

MODEL 605 SERIES O/U SHOTGUN
Similar to the Model 505 except w/engraved silver nitride receiver and deluxe wood. Introduced 1988.
Field, Skeet, Trap grade . . . . NiB $1233 Ex $1026 Gd $779
Skeet three-bbl. set . . . . . . NiB $2290 Ex $2003 Gd $1544
Sporting Clays . . . . NiB $1266 Ex $1033 Gd $780

MODEL 680 ENGLISH O/U SHOTGUN
Similar to 600 Series except w/English style select walnut stock and fine scroll engraving. Imported from 1973 to 1977.
680 English, 12 ga. . . . . NiB $1477 Ex $1179 Gd $993
680 English, 20 ga. . . . . NiB $1788 Ex $1165 Gd $1055

MODEL 685 DELUXE O/U
Similar to the 585 Deluxe except with semi-fancy American walnut stock. Gold trigger and jeweled bbl. block. Silvered receiver with fine engraving.
Field, Skeet, Trap grade . . . NiB $1477 Ex $1319 Gd $1066
Field grade, two-bbl. set . . NiB $1977 Ex $1819 Gd $1566
Skeet set . . . . NiB $1977 Ex $1819 Gd $1566
Sporting Clays . . . . NiB $1477 Ex $1319 Gd $1066
Trap Combo, two-bbl. set. NiB $2189 Ex $1844 Gd $1360

MODEL 800 SKEET/TRAP O/U
Similar to Model 700 Skeet and Trap except higher grade with more elaborate engraving and fancier wood.
Skeet model . . . . NiB $1329 Ex $1166 Gd $973
Trap model . . . . NiB $1266 Ex $1090 Gd $945

MODEL 880 SKEET/TRAP
Similar to Model 800 Skeet except has sideplates.
Skeet model . . . . NiB $1688 Ex $1470 Gd $1137
Trap model . . . . NiB $1859 Ex $1466 Gd $1123

MODEL 885 DELUXE O/U
Similar to the 685 Deluxe except with engraved sideplates.
Field, Skeet, Trap grade . . . NiB $1779 Ex $1456 Gd $1160
Field grade, two-bbl. set . . NiB $2665 Ex $2167 Gd $1800
Skeet Set . . . . NiB $1782 Ex $1693 Gd $1366
Sporting Clays. . . . . NiB $1834 Ex $1500 Gd $1220
Trap Combo . . . . NiB $2591 Ex $2277 Gd $1989

NOTE: *The following SKB shotguns were distributed by Ithaca Gun Co. from 1966-76. For specific data, see corresponding listings under Ithaca.*

CENTURY SINGLE-BARREL TRAP GUN
The SKB catalog does not differentiate between Century and Century II; however, specifications of current Century are those of Ithaca-SKB Century II.
Century (505) . . . . NiB $966 Ex $831 Gd $634
Century II (605) . . . . NiB $1190 Ex $1006 Gd $798

GAS-OPERATED AUTOMATIC SHOTGUNS
Model XL300 with plain bbl. . . . . . NiB $365 Ex $247 Gd $180
Model XL300 w/ VR . . . . NiB $400 Ex $365 Gd $217
Model XL900 . . . . NiB $449 Ex $300 Gd $198
Model XL900 Trap. . . . . NiB $487 Ex $376 Gd $221
Model XL900 Skeet. . . . . NiB $510 Ex $375 Gd $266
Model XL900 Slug. . . . . NiB $488 Ex $370 Gd $259
Model 1300 Upland, Slug. . . . . NiB $598 Ex $455 Gd $290
Model 1900 Field, Trap, Slug . . NiB $588 Ex $443 Gd $376

SKB OVER/UNDER SHOTGUNS
Model 500 Field . . . . NiB $677 Ex $489 Gd $389
Model 500 Magnum . . . . NiB $690 Ex $500 Gd $421

Sile Field Master II

Model 600 Field . . . . NiB $1070 Ex $883 Gd $600
Model 600 Magnum . . . . NiB $1165 Ex $955 Gd $690
Model 600 Trap . . . . NiB $1190 Ex $975 Gd $710
Model 600 Doubles . . . . NiB $1190 Ex $975 Gd $710
Model 600 Skeet—12 or 20 ga. . . . NiB $1190 Ex $975 Gd $710
Model 600 Skeet—28 or .410NiB $1595 Ex $1266 Gd $1065
Model 600 Skeet Combo . . NiB $2651 Ex $2210 Gd $2085
Model 600 English . . . . NiB $1190 Ex $975 Gd $710
Model 700 Trap. . . . . NiB $950 Ex $844 Gd $630
Model 700 Doubles . . . . NiB $877 Ex $600 Gd $490
Model 700 Skeet . . . . NiB $988 Ex $765 Gd $633
Model 700 Skeet Combo . . NiB $2690 Ex $2166 Gd $1650

SKB RECOIL-OPERATED AUTOMATIC SHOTGUNS
Model 300—with plain bbl. . . . . NiB $477 Ex $370 Gd $269
Model 300—w/ VR . . . . NiB $554 Ex $425 Gd $335
Model 900 . . . . NiB $559 Ex $400 Gd $298
Model 900 Slug . . . . NiB $573 Ex $455 Gd $360

SKB SIDE-BY-SIDE DOUBLE-BARREL SHOTGUNS
Model 100 . . . . NiB $795 Ex $650 Gd $425
Model 150 . . . . NiB $795 Ex $650 Gd $425
Model 200E. . . . . NiB $1179 Ex $900 Gd $808
Model 200E Skeet . . . . NiB $1179 Ex $900 Gd $808
Model 280 English . . . . NiB $1280 Ex $1006 Gd $922

SIG SAUER — (SIG) Schweizerische Industrie-Gesellschaft, Neuhausen, Switzerland

LL BEAN NEW ENGLANDER . NiB $1900 Ex $1330 Gd $955
O/U. Boxlock action. Gauge: 12, 20, 28 or 410. Imported 2001 to 2004, mfg. by Rizzini in Italy.

AURORA SERIES
O/U. Low profile boxlock action. Gauge: 12, 20, 28 or 410. Stock: Checkered walnut w/pistol grip. Imported 2000 to 2005, mfg. by Rizzini in Italy.
TR20 Field model . . . . NiB $1995 Ex $1480 Gd $1055
TR20U Field Upland model (straight English-style grip) . . . . NiB $1995 Ex $1480 Gd $1055
TR30 Field model (color case hardened receiver w/sideplates) . . . . NiB $2280 Ex $1855 Gd $1155
TR40 Gold model (color case hardened receiver w/gold inlays) . . . . NiB $2280 Ex $1855 Gd $1155
TR40 Silver model (silver receiver) . . . . NiB $2280 Ex $1855 Gd $1155
TT25 Competition model (12 or 20 ga.,28-, 30- or 32-in. bbl.) . . . . NiB $2480 Ex $1755 Gd $1305

TT45 Competition model (12, 20 or 28 ga., 28-, 30- or 32-in. bbl.) . . . . NiB $2480 Ex $1755 Gd $1305

MODEL SA3 O/U SHOTGUN
Monobloc boxlock action. Single selective trigger. Automatic ejectors. Gauges: 12 or 20 w/3- in. chambers. 26-, 28- or 30-in. VR bbls. w/choke tubes. Weight: 6.8 to 7.1 lbs. Checkered select walnut stock and forearm. Satin nickel-finished receiver w/game scene and blued bbls. Imported from 1997-98.
Field model . . . . NiB $1294 Ex $1126 Gd $966
Sporting Clays model . . . . . NiB $1500 Ex $1398 Gd $1225

MODEL SA5 O/U SHOTGUN
Similar to SA3 Model except w/detachable sideplates. Gauges: 12 or 20 w/3- in. chambers. 26.5-, 28- or 30-in. VR bbls. w/ choke tubes. Imported from 1997 to 1999.
Field model . . . . NiB $2288 Ex $2055 Gd $1530
Sporting Clays model . . . . . NiB $2455 Ex $2160 Gd $1880

SILE DISTRIBUTORS — New York, NY

FIELD MASTER II O/U
SHOTGUN . . . . NiB $735 Ex $615 Gd $479
Gauge: 12, 3-in. chambers. 28-in. bbl., IC, M, IM, F choke tubes. 45.25 in. overall. Weight: 7.25 lbs. Satin-finished walnut, checkered stock and forend. Introduced 1989.

L. C. SMITH — Fulton, NY
Made 1890–1945 by Hunter Arms Company, Fulton, NY 1946–51 and 1968–73 and 2004 by Marlin Firearms Company, New Haven, CT

L. C. SMITH DOUBLE-BARREL SHOTGUNS
NOTE: *Values shown are for L. C. Smith doubles made by Hunter. Those of 1946-51 Marlin manufacture generally bring prices about 1/3 lower. Smaller gauge models, especially in the higher grades, command premium prices: Up to 50 percent more for 20 gauge, up to 400 percent for .410.*
Crown grade, double triggers, automatic ejectors . . . NiB $11,650 Ex $9000 Gd $7750
Crown grade, selective single trigger, automatic ejectors . . NiB $12,275 Ex $10,200 Gd $9976
Deluxe grade, selective single trigger, automatic ejectors NiB $80,000 Ex $65,000 Gd $44,000
Eagle grade, double triggers, automatic ejectors . . . . . NiB $7450 Ex $6600 Gd $3540

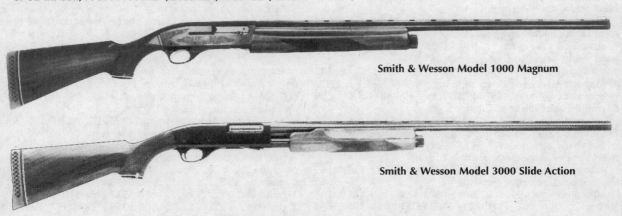

Smith & Wesson Model 1000 Magnum

Smith & Wesson Model 3000 Slide Action

SHOTGUNS

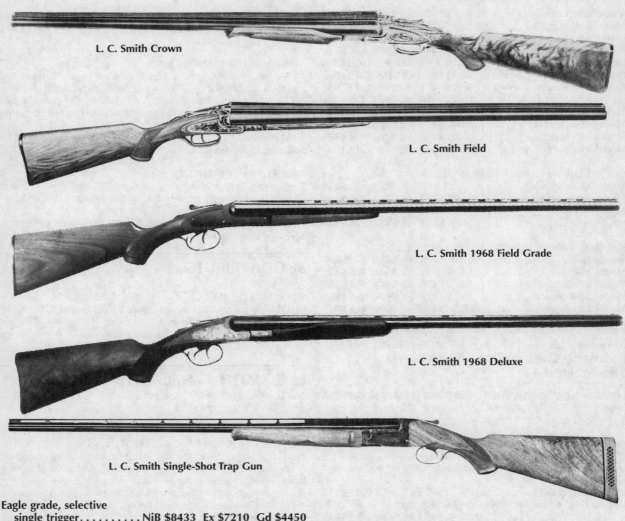

L. C. Smith Crown

L. C. Smith Field

L. C. Smith 1968 Field Grade

L. C. Smith 1968 Deluxe

L. C. Smith Single-Shot Trap Gun

Eagle grade, selective
  single trigger . . . . NiB $8433 Ex $7210 Gd $4450
Field grade, double trigger
  plain extractors . . . . NiB $1877 Ex $1659 Gd $1200
Field grade, double triggers
  auto. ej. . . . . NiB $2400 Ex $2175 Gd $1765
Field grade, non-selective single trigger,
  plain extractors . . . . NiB $1788 Ex $1489 Gd $1016
Field grade, selective single trigger,
  automatic ejectors . . . . . NiB $2276 Ex $1998 Gd $1688
Ideal grade, double triggers,
  plain extractors . . . . NiB $2698 Ex $2100 Gd $1933
Ideal grade, double triggers,
  auto. ej. . . . . NiB $3355 Ex $2288 Gd $1987
Ideal grade, selective single trigger,
  automatic ejectors . . . . . NiB $2979 Ex $2466 Gd $2132
Monogram grade, selective single trigger,
  automatic ejectors NiB $17,800 Ex $15,888 Gd $11,880
Olympic grade, selective single trigger,
  automatic ejectors . . . . NiB $7225 Ex $5179 Gd $3889
Premier grade, selective single trigger
  automatic ejectors NiB $42,975 Ex $33,670 Gd $25,000
Skeet Special, non-selective single trigger,
  automatic ejectors . . . . NiB $4055 Ex $3329 Gd $2165
Skeet Special, selective single trigger,
  auto ejectors . . . . NiB $4070 Ex $3360 Gd $2185
.410 ga. . . . . NiB $14,887 Ex $11,965 Gd $9865

Specialty grade, double triggers,
  auto ejectors . . . . NiB $4177 Ex $3688 Gd $3245
Specialty grade, selective single trigger,
  automatic ejectors . . . . . NiB $3866 Ex $3390 Gd $2788
Trap grade, sel. single trigger,
  auto ej. . . . . NiB $3687 Ex $3255 Gd $2877

L. C. SMITH HAMMERLESS DOUBLE-BARREL SHOTGUNS
Sidelock. Auto ejectors standard on higher grades, extra on Field and Ideal Grades. Double triggers or Hunter single trigger (non-selective or selective). Gauges: 12, 16, 20, .410. Bbls.: 26- to 32-in., any standard boring. Weight: 6.5 to 8.25 lbs., 12 ga. Checkered stock and forend; choice of straight, half or full pistol grip, beavertail or standard-type forend. Grades differ only in quality of workmanship, wood, checkering, engraving, etc. Same general specifications apply to all. Manufacture of these L. C. Smith guns was discontinued in 1951. Production of Field Grade 12 ga. was resumed 1968-73. **NOTE:** *L. C. Smith Shotguns manufactured by the Hunter Arms Co. 1890-13 were designated by numerals to indicate grade with the exception of Pigeon and Monogram.*

00 grade . . . . NiB $1577 Ex $1369 Gd $1100
0 grade . . . . NiB $1735 Ex $1575 Gd $1244
1 grade . . . . NiB $2170 Ex $1876 Gd $1390
2 grade . . . . NiB $3533 Ex $2177 Gd $1566

3 grade . . . . NiB $4480 Ex $3066 Gd $2200
Pigeon . . . . NiB $5250 Ex $3688 Gd $2531
4 grade . . . . NiB $6244 Ex $5187 Gd $4966
5 grade . . . . NiB $10,300 Ex $8879 Gd $6610
Monogram . . . . NiB $13,975 Ex $11,755 Gd $10,000
A1 . . . . NiB $7225 Ex $4488 Gd $3240
A2. . . . . NiB $14,779 Ex $11,960 Gd $10,066
A3 . . . . NiB $42,600 Ex $37,988 Gd $32,776

HAMMERLESS DOUBLE
MODEL 1968 FIELD GRADE . NiB $1165 Ex $980 Gd $644
Re-creation of the original L. C. Smith double. Sidelock. Plain
extractors. Double triggers. 12 ga. 28-in. VR bbls., M/F choke.
Weight: About 6.75 lbs. Checkered pistol-grip stock and forearm. Made 1968-73.

HAMMERLESS DOUBLE
MODEL 1968 DELUXE . . . . . NiB $1688 Ex $1076 Gd $884
Same as 1968 Field Grade except has Simmons floating VR,
beavertail forearm. Made 1971-73.

SINGLE-SHOT TRAP GUNS
Boxlock. Hammerless. Auto ejector.12 gauge only. Bbl. lengths:
32- or 34-in. VR. Weight: 8 to 8.25 lbs. Checkered pistol-grip
stock and forend, recoil pad. Grades vary in quality of workmanship, wood, engraving, etc.; general specifications are
the same. Disc. 1951. Note: Values shown are for L. C. Smith
single-barrel trap guns made by Hunter. Those of Marlin manu-
facture generally bring prices about one-third lower.
Olympic grade . . . . NiB $3188 Ex $2677 Gd $2190
Specialty grade . . . . NiB $3598 Ex $3200 Gd $2560
Crown grade . . . . NiB $4488 Ex $3900 Gd $2677
Monogram grade. . . . . NiB $8865 Ex $6231 Gd $4997
Premier grade . . . . . Very rare (Three or fewer manufactured)
Deluxe grade . . . . . . Very rare (Four or fewer manufactured)

NOTE: Marlin resurrected the L. C. Smith brand from 2005 to
2009 importing O/U and S/S models from manufacturers in
Italy and Spain.

MODEL LC12 . . . . NiB $860 Ex $800 Gd $560
O/U boxlock. Ejectors. !2 ga. only; 28-in. bbl., VR, choke
tubes. Stock: fluer-de-lis checkered walnut w/ pistol grip.
LC20 (20 ga.) . . . . NiB $1000 Ex $875 Gd $580

MODEL LC12 DB . . . . NiB $1400 Ex $1280 Gd $900
S/S boxlock. Ejectors. Detachable side plates. 12 ga. only;
28-in. bbl., VR, choke tubes. Stock: fluer-de-lis checkered wal-
nut w/ pistol grip, beavertail forend.
LC20 DB (20 ga.) . . . . NiB $1600 Ex $1480 Gd $1200
LC28 DB (28 ga.) . . . . NiB $1900 Ex $1695 Gd $1395
LC410 DB (.410). . . . . NiB $1900 Ex $1695 Gd $1395

SMITH & WESSON — Springfield, MA
Howa manufactured, disc. 1984.

MDEL 916 SLIDE-ACTION REPEATER
Hammerless. Solid frame. Gauges: 12, 16, 20. Three inch
chamber in 12 and 20 ga. Five round tubular magazine. Bbls.:
plain or VR; 20-in. C (12 ga., plain only); 26-in. IC- 28-in. M
or F; 30-in. F choke (12 ga. only). Weight: With 28-in. plain
bbl., 7.25 lbs. Plain pistol-grip stock, fluted slide handle. Made
1972-1981.
Plain bbl. . . . . NiB $225 Ex $170 Gd $110
Ventilated rib bbl. . . . . NiB $255 Ex $185 Gd $120

MODEL 916T
Same as Model 916 except takedown, 12 ga. only. Not avail-
able w/ 20-in. bbl. Made 1976-81.
Plain bbl. . . . . NiB $250 Ex $180 Gd $115
Ventilated rib bbl. . . . . NiB $275 Ex $200 Gd $140

MODEL 1000 AUTOLOADER. . NiB $433 Ex $355 Gd $240
Gas-operated. Takedown. Gauges: 12, 20. 2.75-in. chamber in
12 ga., 3-in. in 20 ga. Four round magazine. Bbls.: VR, 26-in.
SK choke, IC; 28-in. M or F; 30-in. F choke (12 ga. only).
Weight: With 28-in. bbl., 6.5 lbs. in 20 ga.,7.5 lbs. in 12 ga.
Checkered pistol-grip stock and forearm. Made 1972. Disc.

MODEL 3000
SLIDE ACTION . . . . NiB $425 Ex $295 Gd $190
Hammerless. 20-ga. Bbls.: 26-in. IC; 28-in. M or F. Chambered
for 3-in. magnum and 2.75-in. loads. American walnut stock
and forearm. Checkered pistol grip and forearm. Introduced
1982.

MODEL 1000 . . . . NiB $425 Ex $295 Gd $190
Same as Model 3000 but an earlier version.

MODEL 1000 MAGNUM . . . . . NiB $595 Ex $445 Gd $398
Same as standard Model 1000 except chambered for 12 ga.
magnum, 3-in. shells; 30-in. bbl. only, M or F choke; stock with
recoil pad. Weight: About 8 lbs. Introduced in 1977.

SPRINGFIELD ARMS — Built by Savage Arms Company, Utica, NY

DOUBLE-BARREL
HAMMER SHOTGUN. . . . . NiB $588 Ex $439 Gd $366
Gauges: 12 and 16. Bbls.: 28 to 32 in. In 12 ga., 32-in. model,
both bbls. have F choke. All other gauges and bbl. lengths are
left bbl., Full; right bbl., M Weight: 7.25 to 8.25 lbs., depending on gauge and bar rel length. Black walnut checkered buttstock and forend. Disc. 1934.

MODEL 67H. . . . . NiB $205 Ex $185 Gd $150
Slide/pump action. Gauges: 12, 20, 16 or.410, 3-in. chmbr.
5-rnd. magazine. Bbls.: 22- or 28-in. plain or VR w/fixed
choke. Stock: smooth wood stock, grooved forend. Finish:
blue. Weight: 6.26-7.5 lbs., depending on gauge and bbl.
length. Disc. 1989.

SQUIRES BINGHAM CO., INC. —
Makati, Rizal, Philippines

MODEL 30 PUMP. . . . . NiB $366 Ex $255 Gd $175
Hammerless. 12 ga. Five round magazine. Bbl.: 20-in. Cyl.;
28-in. M; 30-in. F choke. Weight: About 7 lbs. Pulong Dalaga
stock and slide handle. Currently manufactured.

J. STEVENS ARMS COMPANY — Chicopee Falls, MA
Founded in 1864 as J.Stevens & Co,. in Chicopee Falls, MA.
Currently owned by Savage Arms Company since 1920.

NO. 20 "FAVORITE". . . . . NiB $325 Ex $217 Gd $140
Calibers: .22 and .32 shot. Smoothbore bbl. Blade front sight;
no rear. Made 1893-1939.

SHOTGUNS

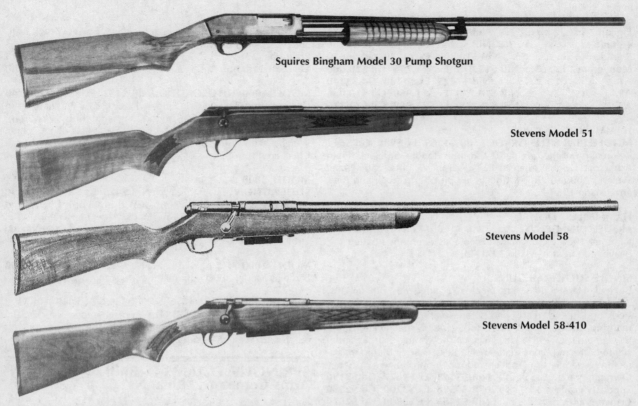

Squires Bingham Model 30 Pump Shotgun

Stevens Model 51

Stevens Model 58

Stevens Model 58-410

NO. 39 NEW MODEL POCKET. . NiB $800 Ex $605 Gd $490
Gauge: .410. Calibers: .38-40 shot, .44-40 shot. Bbls.: 10, 12, 15 or 18 in., half-octagonal smoothbore. Shotgun sights. Made 1895-1906.

NO. 22-.410 O/U COMBINATION GUN
.22 caliber rifle bbl. over .410 ga. shotgun bbl.. Visible hammer. Takedown. Single trigger. 24-in. bbls., shotgun bbl. F choke. Weight: About 6 lbs. Open rear sight and ramp front sight of sporting rifle type. Plain pistol-grip stock and forearm; originally supplied with walnut stock and forearm. "Tenite" (plastic) was used in later production. Made 1939-1950. Note: This gun is now manufactured as the Savage Model 24.
Wood stock and forearm . . . . . NiB $545 Ex $435 Gd $300
Tenite stock and forearm . . . . . NiB $525 Ex $460 Gd $345

MODEL 51 BOLT-ACTION
SHOTGUN . . . . NiB $235 Ex $154 Gd $95
Single shot. Takedown. .410 ga. 24-in. bbl., F choke. Weight: About 4.75 lbs. Plain one-piece pistol-grip stock. checkered on later models. Made 1962-71.

MODEL 58 BOLT-ACTION
REPEATER . . . . NiB $254 Ex $165 Gd $120
Takedown. Gauges: 12, 16, 20. Two round detachable box magazine. 26-in. bbl., F choke. Weight: About 7.25 lbs. Plain one piece pistol-grip stock on early models w/takedown screw on bottom of forend. Made 1933-81. Note: Later production models have 3-in. chamber in 20 ga., checkered stock with recoil pad.

MODEL 58-.410 BOLT-ACTION
REPEATER . . . . NiB $225 Ex $130 Gd $95
Takedown. .410 ga. Three round detachable box magazine. 24-in. bbl., F choke. Weight: About 5.5 lbs. Plain one piece pistol-grip stock, checkered on later production. Made 1937-81.

MODEL 59 BOLT-ACTION
REPEATER . . . . NiB $255 Ex $190 Gd $135
Takedown. .410 ga. Five round tubular magazine. 24-in. bbl., F choke. Weight: About 6 lbs. Plain, one piece pistol-grip stock, checkered on later production. Made 1934-73.

MODEL 67 PUMP SHOTGUN
Hammerless, side-ejection solid-steel receiver. Gauges: 12, 20 and .410, 2.75- or 3-in. shells. Bbls.: 21-, 26-, 28- 30-in. with fixed chokes or interchangeable choke tubes, plain or VR. Weight: 6.25 to 7.5 lbs. Optional rifle sights. Walnut-finished hardwood stock with corncob-style forend.
Standard model, plain bbl. . . . . NiB $245 Ex $195 Gd $120
Standard model, VR . . . . NiB $255 Ex $205 Gd $125
Standard model, w/choke tubes . . . NiB $275 Ex $220 Gd $155
Slug model w/rifle sights . . . . . NiB $255 Ex $205 Gd $125
Lobo model, matte finish . . . . NiB $255 Ex $205 Gd $125
Youth model, 20 ga. . . . . NiB $260 Ex $210 Gd $130
Camo model. w/choke tubes . . NiB $275 Ex $220 Gd $155

MODEL 67 WATERFOWL
SHOTGUN . . . . NiB $335 Ex $200 Gd $135
Hammerless. Gauge: 12. Three round tubular magazine. Walnut finished hardwood stock. Weight: About 7.5 lbs. Made 1972-89.

MODEL 77 SLIDE-ACTION
REPEATER . . . . NiB $225 Ex $130 Gd $95
Solid frame. Gauges: 12, 16, 20. Five round tubular magazine. Bbls.: 26-in. IC, 28-in. M or F choke. Weight: About 7.5 lbs. Plain pistol-grip stock with recoil pad, grooved slide handle. Made 1954-71.

MODEL 77-AC . . . . NiB $217 Ex $125 Gd $95
Same as Model 77 except has Savage Super Choke.

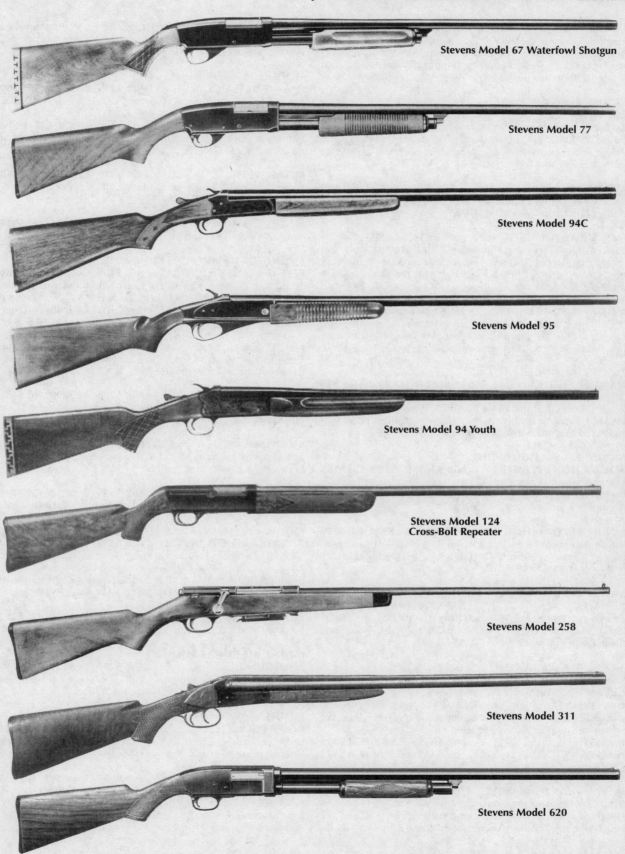

Stevens Model 67 Waterfowl Shotgun

Stevens Model 77

Stevens Model 94C

Stevens Model 95

Stevens Model 94 Youth

SHOTGUNS

Stevens Model 124
Cross-Bolt Repeater

Stevens Model 258

Stevens Model 311

Stevens Model 620

GRADING: **NiB** = New in Box   **Ex** = Excellent or NRA 95%   **Gd** = Good or NRA 68%

MODEL 79-VR SUPER VALUE.... NiB $355 Ex $265 Gd $190
Hammerless, side ejection. Bbl.: Chambered for 2.75-in. and 3-in. mag. shells. 12, 20, and .410 ga. VR. Walnut finished hardwood stock with checkering on grip. Weight: 6.75-7 lbs. Made 1979-90.

**MODEL 94 SINGLE-SHOT
SHOTGUN .... NiB $165 Ex $95 Gd $70**
Takedown. Visible hammer. Auto ejector. Gauges: 12, 16, 20, 28, .410. Bbls.: 26-, 28-, 30-, 32-, 36-in., F choke. Weight: About 6 lbs. depending on gauge and bbl.. Plain pistol-grip stock and forearm. Made 1939-61.

MODEL 94C .... NiB $165 Ex $95 Gd $70
Same as Model 94 except has checkered stock, fluted forearm on late production. Made 1965-90.

MODEL 94Y YOUTH GUN...... NiB $165 Ex $95 Gd $70
Same as Model 94 except made in 20 and .410 ga. only; has 26-in. F choke bbl., 12.5-in. buttstock with recoil pad; checkered pistol grip and fluted forend on late production. Made 1959-90.

MODEL 95 SINGLE-SHOT ..... NiB $200 Ex $140 Gd $95
Solid frame. Visible hammer. Plain extractor. 12 ga. Three-in. chamber. Bbls.: 28-in. M- 30-in. F choke. Weight: About 7.25 lbs. Plain pistol-grip stock, grooved forearm. Made 1965-1969.

**MODEL 107 SINGLE-SHOT
HAMMER SHOTGUN........ NiB $217 Ex $129 Gd $95**
Takedown. Auto ejector. Gauges: 12, 16, 20, .410. Bbl. lengths: 28- and 30-in. (12 and 16 ga.), 28-in. (20 ga.), 26-in. (.410); F choke only. Weight: About 6 lbs., 12 bore ga. Plain pistol-grip stock and forearm. Made from about 1937-53.

**MODEL 124 STRAIGHT PULL
BOLT-ACTION REPEATER ..... NiB $265 Ex $198 Gd $155**
Hammerless. Solid frame. 12 ga. only. Two round tubular magazine. 28-in. bbl.; IC, M or F choke. Weight: About 7 lbs. Tenite stock and forearm. Made 1947-52.

MODEL 240 O/U SHOTGUN... NiB $448 Ex $375 Gd $270
Visible hammer. Takedown. Double triggers. .410 ga. 26-in. bbls., F choke. Weight: 6 lbs. Tenite (plastic) pistol-grip stock and forearm. Made 1940-49.

**MODEL 258 BOLT-ACTION
REPEATER .... NiB $290 Ex $174 Gd $100**
Takedown. 20-gauge. Two round detachable box magazine. 26-in. bbl., Full choke. Weight: About 6.25 lbs. Plain, one piece pistol-grip stock. Made 1937-65.

MODEL 311 SPRINGFIELD HAMMERLESS DOUBLE
Same general specifications as Stevens Model 530 except earlier production has plain stock and forearm; checkered on current guns. Originally produced as a "Springfield" gun, this model became a part of the Stevens line in 1948 when the Springfield brand name was discontinued. Made 1931-89.
Pre-WWII .... NiB $675 Ex $450 Gd $325
Post-WWII .... NiB $335 Ex $200 Gd $125

**MODEL 311-R
HAMMERLESS DOUBLE...... NiB $300 Ex $225 Gd $145**
Same general specifications as Stevens Model 311 except compact design for law enforcement use. Bbls.: 18.25-in. 12 gauge with solid rib, chambered for 2.75 and 3-in. Mag. shells.

Double triggers and auto top tang safety. Walnut finished hardwood stock with recoil pad and semi-beavertail forend. Weight: About 6.75 lbs. Made 1982-89.

**MODEL 530
HAMMERLESS DOUBLE ..... NiB $335 Ex $245 Gd $200**
Boxlock. Double triggers. Gauges: 12, 16, 20, .410. Bbl. lengths: 26- to 32-in.; choked M/F, C/M, F/F. Weight: 6 to 7.5 pounds depending on gauge and barrel length. Checkered pistol-grip stock and forearm; some early models with recoil pad. Made 1936-54.

MODEL 530M............. NiB $339 Ex $255 Gd $210
Same as Model 530 except has Tenite (plastic) stock and forearm. Disc. about 1947.

MODEL 530ST DOUBLE GUN NiB $339 Ex $255 Gd $210
Same as Model 530 except has non-selective single trigger. Disc.

**MODEL 620 HAMMERLESS SLIDE-ACTION
REPEATING SHOTGUN ...... NiB $400 Ex $255 Gd $180**
Takedown. Gauges: 12, 16, 20. Five round tubular magazine. Bbl. lengths: 26-, 28-, 30-, 32-in.; choked F, M IC, C. Weight: About 7.75 lbs., 12 ga.; 7.25 lbs., 16 ga.- 6 lbs., 20 ga. Checkered pistol-grip stock and slide handle. Made 1927-53.

MODEL 620-C .... NiB $365 Ex $255 Gd $160
Same specifications as Model 620 except equipped with Cutts Compensator and two choke tubes.

MODEL 620-P............. NiB $288 Ex $200 Gd $155
Same specifications as Model 620 equipped with Aero-Dyne PolyChoke and 27-in. bbl.

MODEL 620-PV .... NiB $280 Ex $190 Gd $155
Same specifications as Model 620 except equipped with ventilated PolyChoke and 27-in. bbl.

MODEL 621 .... NiB $359 Ex $210 Gd $155
Same as Model 620 except has raised solid matted-rib barrel. Disc.

**MODEL 820 HAMMERLESS
REPEATING SHOTGUN ...... NiB $388 Ex $266 Gd $190**
Solid frame. 12 gauge only. Five round tubular magazine. 28-in. bbl.; IC, M or F choke. Weight: About 7.5 lbs. Plain pistol-grip stock, grooved slide handle. Early models furnished w/Tenite buttstock and forend. Made 1949-54.

MODEL 820-SC .... NiB $400 Ex $330 Gd $217
Same as Model 820 except has Savage Super Choke.

**MODEL 940 SINGLE-SHOT
SHOTGUN .... NiB $256 Ex $138 Gd $110**
Same general specifications as Model 94 except has side lever opening instead of top lever. Made 1961-70.

**MODEL 940Y
YOUTH GUN .... NiB $265 Ex $155 Gd $115**
Same general specifications as Model 94Y except has side lever opening instead of top lever. Made 1961-70.

MODEL 9478 .... NiB $145 Ex $90 Gd $65
Takedown. Visible hammer. Automatic ejector. Gauges: 12, 20, .410. Bbls.: 26-, 28-, 30-, 36-in.; Full choke. Weight: Average 6 pounds depending on gauge and barrel. Plain pistol-grip stock and forearm. Made 1978-85.

Stoeger P3000 Tactical

Stoeger M2000

MODEL 5151 SPRINGFIELD. . . NiB $556 Ex $435 Gd $300
Same specifications as the Stevens Model 311 except with checkered grip and forend; equipped with recoil pad and two ivory sights.

— *Current MFG.* —

MODEL 67 . . . . **NIB $200 EX $180 GD $160**
Slide/pump action. Gauges: 12, 20, .410; 3-in. chamber. 5-rnd. magazine. Bbls.: 20-, 22- or 28-in. w/choke tubes. Made 1986–89.
Camo finish, add. $50
Slug model (rifled 21-in.
bbl. w/sights). . . . . NiB $200 Ex $180 Gd $160

MODEL 301 . . . . **NIB $155 EX $150 GD $130**
Break action, single shot. Gauges: 12, 20, or .410; 3-in. chamber. Bbl.: 26-in, w/choke tubes. Stock: Black synthetic. Made 2017-date.
Compact model (12.5-in. LOP). . **NiB $155 Ex $150 Gd $130**
Turkey model (.410 bore, Mossy Oak Bottomland or Mossy
Oak Obsession camo). . . . . . . **NiB $180 Ex $155 Gd $130**
Turkey XP model (.410 bore, extra full extended Win. choke
tube, red dot optic, Mossy Oak Bottomland or Mossy
Oak Obsession camo). . . . . . . **NiB $205 Ex $180 Gd $150**

MODEL 320 . . . . **NIB $205 EX $180 GD $135**
Slide/pump action w/rotary bolt. Gauges: 12 or 20, 3-in. chamber. Barrel: 26- or 28-in. VR w/fixed modified choke. Finish: Blue. Stock: black synthetic. Weight: 7.5 lbs. Mfg. 2012-date.
Combo model (extra 18.5-in.
cylinder bore bbl.). . . . . **NiB $235 Ex $310 Gd $180**
Field Camo model (camo finish). . **NiB $255 Ex $205 Gd $180**
Turkey model (22-in. bbl, fiber optic sight,
camo finish). . . . . **NiB $255 Ex $205 Gd $180**
Security model (18.5-in. cylinder bore bbl.,
w/ or w/o pistol grip stock). . . **NiB $205 Ex $180 Gd $150**
Waterfowl model (28-in. bbl, fiber optic sight,
camo finish). . . . . **NiB $230 Ex $200 Gd $155**
Youth model (20 ga.,
12.5-in. LOP). . . . . **NiB $205 Ex $180 Gd $150**

MODEL 350 . . . . **NIB $255 EX $205 GD $180**
Slide/pump action w/bottom eject. Gauge: 12, 3-in. chamber. Barrel: 28-in. VR. Finish: Matte black. Stock: black synthetic. Weight: 8.2 lbs. Mfg. 2010–11.
Combo model (extra 18.5-in.
cylinder bore bbl.). . . . . **NiB $280 Ex $240 Gd $190**
Security model (18.5-in. cylinder bore bbl.,
w/pistol grip stock). . . . . **NiB $230 Ex $200 Gd $155**

MODEL 411 . . . . **NIB $155 EX $150 GD $130**
Break action, SxS. Gauges: 12, 20, or .410; 3-in. chamber. Bbl.: 28-in. w/choke tubes. Stock: Checkered walnut. Engraved side plates. Mfg. in Russia, 2004–05.

MODEL 512 GOLD WING. . . . **NiB $580 EX $480 GD $380**
Break action, boxlock, O/U. Gauges: 12, 20, 28, or .410; 3-in. chamber. Bbls.: 24-, 26- or 28-in. VR w/choke tubes. Stock: Checkered walnut. Finish: Blued w/engraved receiver w/gold inlays. Extractors. Mfg. in Turkey, 2007–15.

MODEL 555 . . . . **NIB $605 EX $505 GD $405**
Break action, boxlock, O/U. Gauges: 12, 16, 20, 28, or .410; 3-in. chamber. Bbls.: 26- or 28-in. VR w/choke tubes. Stock: Checkered walnut. Finish: Blued. Extractors. Mfg. 2015-date.
Compact model (24-in. bbls.). . . **NiB $605 Ex $505 Gd $405**
Enhanced model (auto ejectors, laser engraved
aluminum receiver). . . . . **NiB $705 Ex $605 Gd $480**
Trap model (12 or 20 ga., single 30-in. VR bbl., semi-gloss
wood stock w/adj. comb) . . . . **NiB $605 Ex $505 Gd $405**
Trap Compact model (12 or 20 ga.,
single 26-in. VR bbl., semi-gloss wood
stock w/adj. comb) . . . . **NiB $605 Ex $505 Gd $405**

MODEL 612 GOLD WING. . . . **NIB $630 EX $530 GD $380**
Break action, SxS. Gauges: 12, 20, 28, or .410; 3-in. chamber. Bbls.: 26- or 28-in. VR w/choke tubes. Stock: Checkered walnut. Engraved side plates w/gold inlays. Mfg. 2010–11.
Trail Gun model (12 or 20 ga., 20-in. bbl., checkered
wood stock, blued) . . . . **NiB $630 Ex $530 Gd $380**

MODEL 675 . . . . **NIB $255 EX $205 GD $180**
Slide/pump action. Gauge: 12, 3-in. chamber. Barrel: 24-in. VR. Finish: Matte black. Stock: Hardwood. Weight: 8.2 lbs. Mfg. 1987-88.

MODEL S1200 . . . . **NIB $490 EX $430 GD $335**
Semiauto. Inertia system action. Gauge: 12, 3-in. chamber. Barrel: 26- or 28-in. VR w/5 Beretta choke tubes. Finish: Matte black. Stock: Black synthetic or walnut. Weight: 6.4-7 lbs. Mfg. 2016-17.
Camo finish . . . . **NiB $540 Ex $480 Gd $370**

STOEGER

Current brand owned by Beretta, also see IGA (O/U Condor models and SxS Coach models) and Tikka shotguns.

MODEL 2000 SERIES
Semiauto. Benelli inertia system. 12 ga. w/3-in. chamber. 4-rnd. magazine. Bbl.: 24-, 26-, 28- or 30-in. w/5 flush choke tubes. Stock: walnut or synthetic. Finish: matte black or various camo patterns. Weight: 7.1 lbs. Imported 2001-13.
Field . . . . **NiB $440 Ex $370 Gd $235**
camo finish, add $90

MODEL 3000 SERIES
Semiauto. Benelli inertia system. 12 ga. w/3-in. chamber. 4-rnd. magazine. Bbl.: 24-, 26- or 28-in. w/3 flush choke tubes. Stock: walnut or synthetic. Finish: matte black or various camo patterns. Weight: 7.5 lbs.
Field . . . . **NiB $505 Ex $380 Gd $280**
Compact (24-in. bbl. w/fiber
optic sights) . . . . **NiB $505 Ex $380 Gd $280**
Defense (18.5-in. bbl. w/fiber optic sights,
w/ to w/o pistol grip) . . . . . . **NiB $505 Ex $380 Gd $280**
Rifled Slug (24-in. rifled bbl.) . . . **NiB $550 Ex $370 Gd $300**
Model 3020 (20 gauge). . . . . . . **NiB $505 Ex $380 Gd $280**
Model 3500 (12 gauge,
3.5-in. chamber) . . . . **NiB $580 Ex $505 Gd $330**
Model M3K 3-Gun (3-gun competition model,
12 gauge, 24-in. bbl.). . . . . . . **NiB $590 Ex $505 Gd $330**

SHOTGUNS

MODEL P3000 SERIES

Pump action. 12 ga. w2.75- and /3-in. chamber. Bbl.: 26- or 28-in. VR w/3 flush choke tubes. Stock: synthetic. Finish: matte black. Weight: 6.8 lbs.

Field . . . . NiB $255 Ex $205 Gd $155
Camo (full camo
  finish), add $90
Defense (18.5-in.
  bbl. w/sights, w/
  to w/o pistol grip) . . . . NiB $255 Ex $205 Gd $155
Model P3500 (12 gauge,
  3.5-in. chamber) . . . . NiB $340 Ex $250 Gd $180

TAR-HUNT CUSTOM RIFLES, INC. — Bloomsburg, PA

MODEL RSG-12 MATCHLESS BOLT-ACTION

SLUG GUN. . . . . NiB $2366 Ex $2165 Gd $1590
Similar to Professional model except has McMillan Fibergrain stock and deluxe blue finish. Made 1995-2004.

MODEL RSG-12 PEERLESS BOLT-ACTION

SLUG GUN. . . . . NiB $2944 Ex $2577 Gd $2320
Similar to Professional model except has McMillan Fibergrain stock and deluxe NP-3 (Nickel/Teflon) metal finish. Made 1995-2004.

MODEL RSG-12 PROFESSIONAL BOLT-ACTION SLUG GUN

Bolt action 12 ga. w/2.75-in. chamber, 2-rnd. detachable magazine, 21.5-in. fully rifled bbl. w/ or w/o muzzle brake. Receiver drilled and tapped for scope mounts w/no sights. Weight: 7.75 lbs. 41.5 in. overall. Checkered black McMillan fiberglass stock w/swivel studs and Pachmayr Deacelerator pad. Made 1991-2004.
RSG-12 model w/o muzzle
  brake (disc. 1993) . . . . . . NiB $2688 Ex $2320 Gd $1997
RSG-12 model w/muzzle
  brake . . . . NiB $2700 Ex $2375 Gd $2044

MODEL RSG-20 MOUNTAINEER BOLT ACTION

SLUG GUN. . . . . NiB $2276 Ex $1966 Gd $1433
Similar to Professional model except 20 ga. w/2.75 in. chamber. Black McMillan synthetic stock w/blind magazine. Weight: 6.5 lbs. Made 1997-2004.

TECNI-MEC SHOTGUNS — Italy

Imported by RAHN Gun Work, Inc., Hastings, MI

MODEL SPL 640 FOLDING SHOTGUN

Gauges: 12, 16, 20, 24, 28, 32 and .410 bore. 26-in. bbl. Chokes: IC/IM. Weight: 6.5 lbs. Checkered walnut pistol-grip stock and forend. Engraved receiver. Available with single or double triggers. Imported from 1988 to 1994.
w/single trigger . . . . NiB $596 Ex $477 Gd $369
w/double trigger . . . . NiB $655 Ex $498 Gd $388

THOMPSON/CENTER ARMS — Springfield, MA

Previously Rochester, NH; purchased by Smith & Wesson in 2006.

CONTENDER

.410 CARBINE. . . . . NiB $500 Ex $387 Gd $279
Gauge: .410 smoothbore. 21-in. VR bbl. 34.75 in. overall. Weight: About 5.25 lbs. Bead front sight. Rynite stock and forend. Made 1991-1997.

ENCORE 20 GA. SHOTGUN

Gauge: 20 smoothbore w/rifled slug bbl. or 26-in. VR bbl. w/three internal screw choke tubes, 38 to 40.5 in. overall. Weight: About 5.25 to 6 lbs. Bead or fiber optic sights. Walnut stock and forend. Made 1998-2009.
w/VR. . . . . NiB $485 Ex $390 Gd $275
w/rifled slug bbl. . . . . NiB $522 Ex $421 Gd $300
w/extra bbl., add $325

HUNTER SHOTGUN MODEL. . NiB $580 Ex $466 Gd $355

Single shot. Gauge: 10 or 12, 3.5-in. chamber, 25-in. field bbl. with F choke. Weight: 8 lbs. Bead front sight. American black walnut stock with recoil pad. Made 1987-92.

HUNTER SLUG MODEL . . . . . . NiB $580 Ex $466 Gd $355

Gauge: 10 (3.5-in. chamber) or 12 (3-in. chamber). Same general specifications as Model '87 Hunter Shotgun except w/ 22-in. slug (rifled) bbl. and rifle sights. Made 1987-92.

TIKKA — Finland

In 1983, purchased by Sako, Ltd. in Riihimäki, Finland. Beretta Holdings purchased Sako in 2000.

M 07 SHOTGUN/ RIFLE COMBINATION . . . . . NiB $1287 Ex $1009 Gd $766

Gauge/caliber: 12/.222 Rem. Shotgun bbl.: About 25 in.; rifled bbl.: About 22.75 in. 40.66 in. overall. Weight: About 7 lbs. Dovetailed for telescopic sight mounts Single trigger with selector between the bbls. VR. Monte Carlo-style walnut stock with checkered pistol grip and forend. Made 1965-87.

M 77 O/U SHOTGUN . . . . . NiB $1345 Ex $1265 Gd $950

Gauge: 12. 27-in. VR bbls., approx. 44 in. overall, weight: About 7.25 lbs. Bbl. selector. Ejectors. Monte Carlo-style walnut stock with checkered pistol grip and forend; rollover cheekpiece. Made 1977-87.

M 77K SHOTGUN/ RIFLE COMBINATION . . . . NiB $1733 Ex $1388 Gd $1009

Gauge: 12/70. Calibers: .222 Rem., 5.6x52r5, 6.5x55, 7x57r5, 7x65r5, .308 Win. VR bbls.: About 25 in. (shotgun); 23 in. (rifle), 42.3 in. overall. Weight: About 7.5 lbs. Double triggers. Monte Carlo-style walnut stock with checkered pistol grip and forend; rollover cheekpiece. Made 1977-86.

412S/512S SHOOTING SYSTEM

Boxlock action with both under lug and sliding top latch locking mechanism designed to accept interchangeable monobloc barrels, including O/U shotgun, combination and double rifle configurations. Blued or satin nickel receiver w/cocking indicators. Selective single trigger design w/barrel selector incorporated into the trigger (double triggers available). Blued barrels assemblies w/extractors or auto ejectors as required. Select American walnut stock with checkered pistol grip and forend. Previously produced in Finland (same as the former Valmet Model 412) but currently manufactured in Italy by joint venture arrangement with Armi Marocchi. From 1990-93, Stoeger Industries imported this model as the 412/S. In 1993 the nomenclature of this shooting system was changed to 512/S. Disc. 1997. Note: For double rifle values, see Tikka Rifles.

MODEL 412S/512S O/U SHOTGUN
Gauge: 12 w/3-in. chambers. 24-, 26-, 28- or 30-in. chrome-lined bbls. w/blued finish and integral stainless steel choke tubes. Weight: 7.25 to 7.5 lbs. Blue or matte nickel receiver. Select American walnut from stock with checkered pistol grip and forend. Imported 1990 to 1997.

Standard Field model . . . . . . NiB $1145 Ex $989 Gd $766
Standard Trap model . . . . . . NiB $1277 Ex $1050 Gd $766
Premium Field model . . . . . NiB $1688 Ex $1279 Gd $1100
Premium Trap model . . . . . NiB $1688 Ex $1279 Gd $1100
Sporting Clays model . . . . . . NiB $1233 Ex $1054 Gd $866
w/extra O/U shotgun bbl., add $700
w/extra O/U combo bbl., add $800
w/extra O/U rifle bbl., add $1025

MODEL 412S/512S OVER/UNDER COMBINATION
Gauge: 12 w/3-in. chamber. Calibers: .222 Rem., .30-06 or .308 Win. Blue or matte nickel receiver, 24-in. chrome-lined bbls. w/extractors and blued finish. Weight: 7.25 to 7.5 lbs. Select American walnut stock with checkered pistol grip and forend. Imported from 1990 to 1997.

Standard Combination
  model . . . . NiB $1598 Ex $1335 Gd $1109
Premium Combination
  model . . . . NiB $1622 Ex $1365 Gd $1135
Extra bbl. options, add $800

TRADITIONS PERFORMANCE FIREARMS —
Importers of shotguns produced by Fausti Stefano of Brescia, Italy, and ATA Firearms, Turkey.

FIELD HUNTER MODEL . . . . . . NiB $825 Ex $630 Gd $535
Same as Field I except 12 and 20 gauge, 3-in. chambers, screw-in chokes and extractors.

CLASSIC SERIES, FIELD I O/U . . NiB $853 Ex $677 Gd $545
Available in 12, 20, 28 (2 3/4-in. chamber) and .410 gauge, 26- or 28-in. VR bbls. W/fixed chokes and extractors. Weight: 6 3/4 to 7 1/4 lbs. Blued finish, silver receiver engraved with game birds. Single, selective trigger. Brass bead front sight. European walnut stock. Overall length 43 to 45 in. Intro. 2000.

FIELD II MODEL . . . . NiB $945 Ex $679 Gd $555
Same as Field I except with screw-in chokes and automatic ejectors.

FIELD III GOLD MODEL . . . NiB $1217 Ex $1109 Gd $998
Same as Field I model except 12 gauge only, high-grade, oil-finish walnut, coin-finish receiver with engraved pheasants and woodcock, deep blue finish on barrels, automatic ejectors and non-slip recoil pad.

SPORTING CLAY II MODEL . . NiB $1165 Ex $977 Gd $620
Same as Sporting Clay III model but with European walnut stocks, cut checkering and extended choke tubes. Overall length: 47 in. Weight: 7 3/4 lbs.

CLASSIC SERIES O/U
SPORTING CLAY III . . . . NiB $1200 Ex $1095 Gd $985
Available in 12 and 20 gauge, 3-in. chambers, high grade walnut stock, oil-satin finish, palm swell Schnabel forend. 28- and 30-in. bbls. w/ 3/8-in. top and middle VR, red target front bead sight. Automatic ejectors, extended choke tubes. Weight: 8 1/4 lbs. Intro. 2000.

UPLAND II MODEL . . . . NiB $1065 Ex $775 Gd $546
Same as Upland III model except with English walnut straight-grip stock and Schnabel forend, 24- and 26-in. VR bbls., floral engraving on blued receiver, automatic ejectors.

UPLAND III MODEL . . . . NiB $1187 Ex $977 Gd $755
Same as Sporting Clay III model but round pistol grip and Schnabel forend, blued receiver with engraved upland scene, weight: 7 1/2 lbs.

MAG 350 SERIES
TURKEY II O/U . . . . NiB $1144 Ex $942 Gd $700
Magnum 3 1/2-in. chambers in 12 gauge only, 24- and 26-in. bbls., screw-in flush fitting chokes: F and XF. Matte finish, engraved receiver, Mossy Oak or Realtree camo. Intro. 2000.

WATERFOWL II MODEL . . . . . NiB $1159 Ex $910 Gd $715
Same as Turkey II model except with Advantage Wetlands camo stock and barrels, weight: 8 lbs., overall length 45 in. Waterfowl model has 28-in. bbls.

MAG HUNTER II . . . . NiB $1159 Ex $910 Gd $715
Same as Turkey II model except blued engraved receiver and matte finish walnut stocks, 3 1/2-in. chambers, 28-in. bbls. with screw-in chokes.

ELITE HUNTER . . . . NiB $1256 Ex $1044 Gd $770
Same as Elite Field model except 12 and 20 gauge, European walnut stock, beavertail forend, screw-in choke tubes, extractors, three-in. chambers. Blued finish. VR, tang safety. Weight: 6 1/2 pounds.

ELITE FIELD I DT . . . . NiB $1006 Ex $853 Gd $600
Same as Elite Field I except with double triggers, fixed chokes, extractors. Available in 12, 20, 28 (2 3/4-in. chambers) and .410. Bbls: 26 in., fixed IC/M chokes. Weight: 5 1/2 to 6 1/4 lbs

ELITE FIELD I ST . . . . NiB $1118 Ex $1065 Gd $790
Same as Elite Field III except single trigger, fixed chokes, extractors; European walnut stock. Available in 12, 20, 28 (2 3/4-in. chambers) and .410 gauge; fixed IC/M chokes. Weight: 5 3/4 to 6 1/2 lbs.

ELITE FIELD III ST. . . . . NiB $1967 Ex $1689 Gd $1333
Checkered English walnut straight stock, splinter forend, fixed chokes. Available in 28 and .410 gauge, 26-in. chrome-lined bbls., Cylinder and Modified chokes. Silver trigger guard and receiver with hand-finished engraving of upland game scenes with gold inlays. Automatic ejectors. Brass front sight bead. Weight: About 6 1/2 lbs. Intro. 2000.

AL 2100 SEMIAUTO FIELD SERIES,
WALNUT MODEL . . . . NiB $366 Ex $245 Gd $190
Gas-operated, 12 and 20 gauge, 3-in. chambers, cut-checkered Turkish walnut stock and forend, blued 26- and 28-in. VR bbls., multi-choke system, chrome bore lining. Weight: About 6 lbs. Rifled barrel with cantilever mount available Intro. 2001.

SYNTHETIC STOCK MODEL . . . NiB $350 Ex $290 Gd $225
Same as the ALS 2100 Walnut model except with synthetic stock, matted finish on receiver and bbl., weight: About 6 lbs.

YOUTH MODEL . . . . NiB $344 Ex $229 Gd $175
Same as ALS 2100 Walnut model except with a shorter walnut stock (length of pull: 13 1/2 in.). Available in 12 or 20 gauge w/ 24-in. VR bbl., weight: 5 1/2 to 6 lbs.

SHOTGUNS

TriStar Tec 12

HUNTER COMBO MODEL
Same as ALS 2100 Walnut model except comes with two bbls. (28-in. VR and 24-in. slug), TruGlo adjustable sights and cantilever mount. Available with Turkish walnut or synthetic stock with matte barrel finish. Weight: 6 1/2 lbs.
Walnut stock . . . . NiB $500 Ex $377 Gd $210
Synthetic stock . . . . NiB $475 Ex $339 Gd $220

SLUG HUNTER MODEL . . . . . . NiB $355 Ex $245 Gd $190
Same as ALS 2100 Walnut except with fully-rifled barrel, choice of walnut or synthetic stocks, matte or blue finish; rifle or TruGlo adjustable sights. Weight: About 6 1/4 lbs.

TURKEY HUNTER/
WATERFOWL MODEL . . . . NiB $375 Ex $265 Gd $220
Same as ALS 2100 Walnut except with synthetic stock, 3-in. chambers, 26-in. VR bbl., screw-in chokes, Mossy Oak or Realtree camo stocks.

HOME SECURITY MODEL . . . . NiB $335 Ex $260 Gd $190
Same as ALS 2100 Walnut but w/ 20-in. cylinder-bore bbl., synthetic stock, 3-in. chambers, six-round capacity w/ 2 3/4-in. shells. Weight: About 6 lbs.

TRISTAR SPORTING ARMS —
North Kansas City, MO

Tristar imports shotguns from manufacturers in Italy, Spain and Turkey.

MODEL 1887 LEVER-ACTION
REPEATER . . . . NiB $765 Ex $580 Gd $445
Copy of John Browning's Winchester Model 1887 lever-action shotgun. 12 ga. only. 30-in. bbl. which may be cut down to any desired length of 18 in. or more. Version shown has 20-in. bbl. Imported from 1997 to 1999.

- OVER AND UNDER MODELS -

MODEL 300 O/U SHOTGUN . . NiB $465 Ex $335 Gd $199
Similar to the Model 333 except 12 ga. only w/3-in. chambers, 26- or 28-in. VR bbls. w/extractors and fixed chokes. Etched receiver w/double triggers and standard walnut stock. Imported 1994 to 1998.

MODEL 330 O/U SHOTGUN
Similar to the Model 333 except 12 ga. only w/3-in. chambers. 26-, 28- or 30-in. VR bbls w/extractors or ejectors and fixed chokes or choke tubes. Etched receiver and standard walnut stock. Imported from 1994 to 1999.
w/ extractor and fixed chokes . . NiB $545 Ex $420 Gd $300
w/ejectors and choke tubes . . . NiB $733 Ex $567 Gd $488

MODEL 333 O/U SHOTGUN
Boxlock action. 12 or 20 ga. w/3-in. chambers. 26-, 28- or 30-in. VR bbls. w/choke tubes. Single selective trigger. Selective automatic ejectors. Engraved receiver w/satin nickel finish. Checkered Turkish fancy walnut buttstock and forend. Weight: 7.5 to 7.75 lbs. Imported from 1994 to 1998.
Field model . . . . NiB $844 Ex $700 Gd $545
Sporting Clays model (1994-97) . . NiB $900 Ex $755 Gd $580
TRL Ladies Field model . . . . NiB $800 Ex $675 Gd $550

SCL Ladies Sporting Clays model
(1994-97) . . . . NiB $900 Ex $755 Gd $580

HUNTER SERIES
O/U. Boxlock action. 12 or 20 ga. w/3-in. chambers w/extractors. 26- or 28-in. VR bbls. w/choke tubes. Finish: blued. Stock: Checkered walnut. Weight: 6-7.25 lbs. Imported from 2006 to 2007.
Field Hunter (ejectors) . . . . NiB $630 Ex $455 Gd $355
Lite model (silver receiver,
5.5 lbs.) . . . . NiB $445 Ex $330 Gd $245
Gold Combo model
(2 brrl. set, 2009) . . . . NiB $880 Ex $680 Gd $530

HUNTER EX SERIES
O/U. Boxlock action. .410, 28, 20, 16 or 12 ga. w/3-in. chambers w/extractors. 26- or 28-in. VR bbls. w/choke tubes. Finish: blued. Stock: Checkered walnut. Weight: 4.7-7.25 lbs. Imported from 2008 to date.
EX model. . . . . NiB $570 Ex $430 Gd $330
EX LT model (engraved receiver, 20 or
12 gauge, 5.5-6.8 lbs.) . . . . NiB $580 Ex $455 Gd $355
Magnum model (3.5-in. chamber,
camo finish, intro. 2009) . . . . . NiB $640 Ex $455 Gd $355
Magnum model (3.5-in. chamber,
black finish, intro. 2012) . . . . NiB $570 Ex $455 Gd $355

SETTER/SETTER ST SERIES . . . . NiB $535 Ex $480 Gd $400
O/U. Boxlock action. 12 or 20 ga. w/3-in. chambers w/extractors. 26- or 28-in. VR bbls. w/choke tubes, fiber optic front sight. Etched receiver w/single gold trigger. Stock: Checkered Turkish walnut. Weight: 7 lbs. Mfg. by Arthemis in Turkey. Imported 2011, 2013 to date.

SILVER SERIES
O/U. Boxlock action. 12 or 20 ga. w/3-in. chambers w/extractors. 26- or 28-in. VR bbls. w/choke tubes. Etched receiver. Stock: Checkered Turkish walnut. Weight: 7 lbs. Imported from 2002 to 2004.
Classic (case colored receiver) . NiB $755 Ex $530 Gd $420
Hunter . . . . NiB $620 Ex $460 Gd $370
Silver II (ejectors, 2002-06) . . . NiB $745 Ex $485 Gd $370
Sporting (ported bbls.) . . . . NiB $755 Ex $530 Gd $420

SPORTING . . . . NiB $715 Ex $530 Gd $305
O/U. Greener style boxlock action. 12 ga. w/3-in. chambers w/ejectors. 28- or 30-in. VR, ported bbls. w/Beretta-style choke tubes, fiber optic front sight. Engraved receiver w/single selective trigger. Stock: Checkered Turkish walnut. Weight: 7.5 lbs. Mfg. by Arthemis in Turkey. Imported from 2008 to date.

TT SERIES
O/U. Boxlock action. 12 ga. 2.75-in. chambers. 30-in. VR bbls. w/Beretta-style choke tubes, fiber optic front sight. Stock: Checkered Turkish walnut w/adj. comb. Weight: 8.7 lbs. Imported from 2016 to date.
DTA model . . . . NiB $1310 Ex $980 Gd $720
Double Trap model (32-in. bbl.) . . NiB $1210 Ex $910 Gd $710
Combo model (32-in. bbls. and
34-in. bbls.) . . . . NiB $1555 Ex $1170 Gd $855

- PUMP/SLIDE ACTION MODELS -

COBRA SERIES . . . . NiB $290 Ex $230 Gd $190
12 ga. w/3-in. chambers. 20-, 26-, 28-in. bbl. w/choke tubes. Finish: matte black. Stock: synthetic black. Weight: 6.5 lbs. Mfg. by Armsan, Turkey. Imported from 2007 to date.
Field Camo (camo finish), add $75

![Valmet Model 412 K O/U Field Shotgun]

**Valmet Model 412 K
O/U Field Shotgun**

Force (pistol grip stock, iron sights, 18.5-in. bbl.), add. . . $50
Marine (pistol grip stock, iron sights,
    18.5-in. bbl., brushed nickel finish), add $40
Tactical (pistol grip stock, iron sights,
    18.5-in. bbl., 20 or 12 ga.), subtract $10

- SIDE BY SIDE MODELS -

MODEL 311 SIDE-BY-SIDE SHOTGUN
Boxlock action w/underlug and Greener cross bolt. 12 or 20 ga. w/3-in. chambers, 20, 28- or 30-in. bbls. w/choke tubes or fixed chokes (311R). Double triggers. Extractors. Black chrome finish. Checkered Turkish walnut buttstock and forend. Weight: 6.9 to 7.2 lbs. Imported from 1994 to 1997.
**w/extractors and
    choke tubes** . . . . **NiB $575 Ex $476 Gd $390**
**311R Model (w/20-in. bbls.
    and fixed chokes)** . . . . **NiB $445 Ex $355 Gd $235**

MODEL 411 SERIES
S/S. Boxlock action. .410, 28, 20, 16 or 12 ga. w/3-in. chambers, 26- or 28-in. bbls. w/choke tubes. Double triggers. Extractors. Finish: case colored. Stock: checkered walnut. Weight: 6.5 to 7.2 lbs. Imported from 1998 to 2005.
411 . . . . **NiB $715 Ex $580 Gd $455**
411D (16 ga.) . . . . **NiB $920 Ex $705 Gd $505**
**411F (silver engraved side
    plates)** . . . . **NiB $1430 Ex $1000 Gd $730**
411R (20-in. brrl., fixed choke) . . . **NiB $655 Ex $530 Gd $430**

BRITTANY . . . . **NiB $955 Ex $655 Gd $455**
Similar to Gentry except w/straight grip stock. Imported from 2003 to 2007.
Classic (wood upgrade, 2007-08), add $200
Sporting (sideplates, 2003-05) . . . **NiB $880 Ex $630 Gd $480**

DERBY CLASSIC . . . . **NiB $1305 Ex $905 Gd $680**
Similar to Gentry except w/straight grip stock and ejectors. Mfg. by Zabala Hermanos, Spain. Imported from 2002 to 2005.

GENTRY . . . . **NiB $780 Ex $505 Gd $385**
S/S. Boxlock action. .410, 28, 20, 16 or 12 ga. w/3-in. chambers, 26- or 28-in. bbls. w/choke tubes. Trigger: single select. Extractors. Finish: engraved. Stock: checkered pistol grip walnut. Weight: 6.5 lbs. Imported from 2003 to 2006.

PHOENIX . . . . **NiB $930 Ex $680 Gd $480**
S/S. Boxlock action. 28, 20 or 12 ga. w/3-in. chambers, 28-in. bbls. w/Beretta style choke tubes. Trigger: single select. Finish: engraved blue w/gold pheasant. Stock: checkered pistol grip walnut. Weight: 6.8 lbs. Imported from 2009 to 2010.
Combo (2 brrl. set), add $300

- SEMIAUTO MODELS -

PHANTOM SERIES . . . . **NiB $390 Ex $320 Gd $270**
12 ga. w/3- or 3.5-in. chambers, 26- or 28-in. bbls. w/choke tubes. Finish: matte black. Stock: checkered walnut or black synthetic. Weight: 6.8 lbs. Mfg. in Italy. Imported from 2001 to 2002.
3.5-in. chamber, add $75

RAPTOR SERIES . . . .**NiB $355 Ex $280 Gd $230**
20 or 12 ga. w/3-in. chambers, 26- or 28-in. bbls. w/choke tubes. Finish: matte black. Stock: black synthetic. Weight: 6.8 lbs. Mfg. by Kral Arms, Turkey. Imported from 2013 to date.
A-TAC (pistol grip stock), add $30
A-TAC Turkey (pistol grip stock, camo), add $80

TEC 12 . . . .**NiB $590 Ex $330 Gd $255**
Semiautomation or slide/pump action. Similar to Benelli M3. 12 ga. w/3-in. chambers, 20- or 28-in. bbls. w/choke tubes. Finish: matte black. Stock: black synthetic pistol grip. Sights: ghost ring/fiber optic bead. Weight: 7 lbs. Mfg. by Armsan, Turkey. Imported from 2013 to date.

TSA SERIES . . . .**NiB $345 Ex $290 Gd $230**
28, 20 or 12 ga. w/3- or 3.5-in. chambers, 26- or 28-in. VR bbls. w/choke tubes. Finish: matte blue w/gold accents or camo. Stock: checkered walnut or black synthetic. Weight: 6.8-7.5 lbs. Imported from 2003 to 2007.
3.5-in. chamber, add $200
camo finish, add $100
Marine (19-in. brrl.), add $40
Slug (24-in. rifled brrl., camo), add $30

VIPER G2 SERIES
Semiauto. gas-operated action. Gauge: 12, 20 or 28. 24-, 26- or 28-in. VR bbls. w/5 choke tubes, fiber optic front sight. Magazine cut off. Stock: Wood, black synthetic, camo or carbon fiber. Weight: 8.7 lbs. Imported from 2007 to date.
w/synthetic stock . . . . **NiB $455 Ex $340 Gd $230**
w/wood stock . . . . **NiB $500 Ex $390 Gd $305**
**Bronze (Cerakote bronze receiver, walnut
    stock)** . . . . **NiB $680 Ex $600 Gd $400**
Camo (Realtree camo finishes) . . **NiB $520 Ex $370 Gd $300**
**Max (12 ga., 3.5-in. chamber, synthetic
    stock)** . . . . **NiB $570 Ex $455 Gd $380**
**Silver (silver receiver, walnut
    stock)** . . . . **NiB $570 Ex $455 Gd $380**
Sporting (walnut stock w/adj. comb) .**NiB $705 Ex $545 Gd $400**
SR Sport (red anodized receiver) . . **NiB $525 Ex $370 Gd $280**
Tactical (12 ga., 20-in. bbl.) . . . . **NiB $400 Ex $305 Gd $240**
**Turkey (12 ga., 24-in. VR bbl.,
    camo finish)** . . . . **NiB $570 Ex $455 Gd $380**
Youth (synthetic stock) . . . . **NiB $465 Ex $340 Gd $230**
Youth (wood stock) . . . . **NiB $520 Ex $370 Gd $280**

SINGLE-BARREL BREAK-ACTION MODEL
TT-09 TRAP . . . .**NiB $755 Ex $605 Gd $480**
12 ga. w/2.75-in. chambers, 34-in. VR bbls. w/extended choke tubes. Ejectors. Receiver: etched. Stock: Monte Carlo checkered walnut. Weight: 8.5 lbs. Mfg. in Italy. Imported from 2009 to 2012.

Ward Western Field Model 50

Ward Western Field Model 52

SHOTGUNS

SHOTGUNS OF ULM — Ulm, Germany

See listings under Krieghoff.

U.S. REPEATING ARMS CO. — New Haven, CT

See Winchester shotgun listings.

VALMET — Jyväskylä, Finland

NOTE: *In 1987, Valmet and Sako merged and the Valmet production facilities were moved to Riihimaki, Finland. In 1989 a joint venture agreement was made with Armi Marocchi, and when production began in Italy, the Valmet name was changed to Tikka (Oy Tikkakoski Ab).*
See also Savage Models 330, 333T, 333 and 2400, which were produced by Valmet.

LION O/U SHOTGUN . . . . **NiB $475 Ex $388 Gd $293**
Boxlock. Selective single trigger. Plain extractors. 12 ga. only. Bbls.: 26-in. IC/M; 28-in. M/F, 30-in. M/F, F/F. Weight: About 7 lbs. Checkered pistol-grip stock and forearm. Imported 1947 to 1968.

MODEL 412 S O/U FIELD
SHOTGUN . . . . **NiB $955 Ex $744 Gd $535**
Hammerless. 12-ga., 3-in. chamber, 36-in. bbl., F/F chokes. American walnut Monte Carlo stock. Disc 1989.

MODEL 412 S SHOTGUN RIFLE
COMBINATION . . . . **NiB $1135 Ex $956 Gd $745**
Similar to model 412 K except bottom bbl. chambered for .222 Rem., .223 Rem., .243 Win., .308 Win. or .30-06. 12-ga. shotgun bbl. with IM choke. Monte Carlo American walnut stock, recoil pad.

MODEL 412 O/U
FIELD SHOTGUN . . . . **NiB $866 Ex $723 Gd $587**
12-ga. chambered for 2.75-in. shells. 26-in. bbl., IC/M chokes; 28-in. bbl., M/F chokes; 12-ga. chambered for 3-in. shells, 30-in. bbl., M/F chokes. 20-ga. (3-in. shells); 26-in. bbl., IC/M chokes; 28-in. bbl., M/ F chokes. American walnut Monte Carlo stock.

MODEL 412 ST SKEET . . . . . . **NiB $1176 Ex $922 Gd $766**
Similar to Model 412 K except skeet stock and chokes. 12 and 20 ga. Disc. 1989.

MODEL 412 SE TRAP . . . . **NiB $1176 Ex $922 Gd $766**
Similar to Model 412 K Field except trap stock, recoil pad. 30-in. bbls., IM/F chokes. Disc.1989.
w/extra bbl., add. **$500**

MONTGOMERY WARD — Chicago, IL

NOTE: *Although they do not correspond to specific models below, the names Western Field and Hercules have been used to designate various Montgomery Ward shotguns at various times.*

MODEL 25 SLIDE-ACTION
REPEATER . . . . **NiB $337 Ex $228 Gd $178**
Solid frame. 12 ga. only. Two- or 5-rnd. tubular magazine. 28-in. bbl., various chokes. Weight: About 7.5 lbs. Plain pistol-grip stock, grooved slide handle.

MODEL 40 O/U SHOTGUN. . . **NiB $866 Ex $700 Gd $522**
Hammerless. Boxlock. Double triggers. Gauges: 12, l6, 20, .410. Bbls.: Plain; 26- to 30-in., various chokes. Checkered pistol-grip stock and forearm.

MODEL 40N
SLIDE-ACTION REPEATER . . . . **NiB $329 Ex $233 Gd $179**
Same general specifications as Model 25.

(WESTERN FIELD) MODEL 50
PUMPGUN . . . . **NiB $300 Ex $244 Gd $178**
Solid frame. Gauges: 12 and 16. Two- and 5-rnd. magazine. 26-, 28- or 30-in. bbl., 48 in. overall w/28-in. bbl. Weight: 7.25 - 7.75 lbs. Metal bead front sight. Walnut stock and grooved forend.

(WESTERN FIELD) MODEL 52
DOUBLE-BARREL SHOTGUN. . **NiB $388 Ex $277 Gd $191**
Hammerless coil-spring action. Gauges: 12, 16, 20 and .410. 26-, 28-, or 30-in. bbls., 42 to 46 in. overall, depending upon bbl. length. Weight: 6 (.410 ga. w/26-in. bbl.) to 7.25 lbs. (12 ga. w/30-in. bbls.), depending upon gauge and bbl. length. Casehardened receiver; blued bbls. Plain buttstock and forend. Made circa 1954.

MODEL 172 BOLT-ACTION
SHOTGUN . . . . **NiB $217 Ex $139 Gd $95**
Takedown. Two-round detachable clip magazine.12 ga. 28-in. bbl. with variable choke. Weight: About 7.5 lbs. Monte Carlo stock with recoil pad.

MODEL 550A SLIDE-ACTION
REPEATER . . . . **NiB $367 Ex $265 Gd $190**
Takedown. Gauges: 12, 16, 20, .410. Five-round tubular magazine. Bbls.: Plain, 26- to 30-in., various chokes. Weight: 6 (.410 ga. w/26-in. bbl.) to 8 lbs. (12 ga. w/30-in. bbls.). Plain pistol-grip stock and grooved slide handle.

MODEL SB300 DOUBLE-BARREL
SHOTGUN . . . . **NiB $376 Ex $298 Gd $220**
Same general specifications as Model SD52A.

MODEL SB312 DOUBLE-BARREL
SHOTGUN . . . . **NiB $421 Ex $337 Gd $244**
Boxlock. Double triggers. Plain extractors. Gauges: 12, 16, 20, .410. Bbls.: 24- to 30-in. Various chokes. Weight: About 7.5 lbs. in 12 ga.; 6.5 lbs in .410 ga. Checkered pistol-grip stock and forearm.

MODEL SD52A DOUBLE-BARREL
SHOTGUN . . . . **NiB $344 Ex $255 Gd $200**
Boxlock. Double triggers. Plain extractors. Gauges: 12, 16, 20, .410. Bbls.: 26- to 32-in., various chokes. Plain forend and pistol-grip buttstock. Weight: 6 (.410 ga., 26-in. bbls.) to 7.5 lbs. (12 ga., 32-in. bbls.).

WEATHERBY, INC. — Sheridan, WY, formerly Pasa Robles, CA

MODEL 82 . . . . **NiB $556 Ex $435 Gd $332**
Semiauto, gas-operated. 12 ga. only. Bbls.: 22- to 30-in., various integral or fixed chokes. Weight: 7.5 lbs. Checkered walnut stock and forearm. Imported from 1982 to 1989.
BuckMaster Auto Slug
    w/rifle sights (1986-90) . . . **NiB $570 Ex $455 Gd $355**
w/fixed choke, deduct **$50**

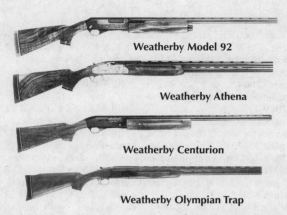

Weatherby Model 92

Weatherby Athena

Weatherby Centurion

Weatherby Olympian Trap

MODEL 92 . . . . NiB $390 Ex $288 Gd $217
Pump/slide action. Hammerless, short-stroke action. 12 ga.; 3-in. chamber. Tubular magazine. Bbls.: 22-, 26-, 28-, 30-in. with fixed choke or IMC choke tubes; plain or VR with rifle sights. Weight: 7.5 lbs. Engraved, matte black receiver and blued barrel. Checkered high-gloss buttstock and forend. Imported from Japan 1982 to 1989.
Standard Model 92 . . . . NiB $330 Ex $261 Gd $195
BuckMaster Pump Slug
    w/rifle sights, (intro. 1986) NiB $420 Ex $315 Gd $235

ATHENA
O/U. Engraved boxlock action with Greener crossbolt and sideplates. Gauges: 12, 20, 28 and .410; 2.75- or 3.5-in. chambers. Bbls.: 26-, 28-, 30- or 32-in. with fixed or IMC Multi-choke tubes. Weight: 6.75 to 7.38 lbs. Single selective trigger. Selective auto ejectors. Top tang safety. Checkered Claro walnut stock and forearm with high-luster finish. Imported from 1982 to 2002.
Field Model w/IMC multi-chokes,
    12 or 20 ga.** . . . . NiB $2177 Ex $1898 Gd $1635
Field Model W/fixed chokes,
    28 ga. or .410.** . . . . NiB $1976 Ex $1645 Gd $1389
Skeet Model w/fixed chokes,
    12 or 20 ga.** . . . . NiB $1766 Ex $1432 Gd $1255
Skeet Model w/fixed chokes,
    28 ga. or .410.** . . . . NiB $3320 Ex $2888 Gd $2366
Master Skeet tube set . . . . . NiB $3155 Ex $2776 Gd $2388
Trap Model w/IC tubes . . . . NiB $2388 Ex $1977 Gd $1677
Grade V (1993 to date) . . . . NiB $3566 Ex $3100 Gd $2665

CENTURION
Semiauto. Gas-operated. Takedown. 12 ga. 2.75-in. chamber. Three round magazine. Bbls.: VRs; 26-in. SK, IC or M 28-in. M or F; 30-in. Full choke. Weight: With 28-in. bbl., 7 lbs. 10.5 oz. Checkered pistol-grip stock and forearm, recoil pad. Made in Japan from 1972 to 1981.
Field Grade . . . . NiB $398 Ex $288 Gd $219
Trap Gun (30-in. full-choke
    bbl.)** . . . . NiB $435 Ex $377 Gd $235
Deluxe model (etched receiver,
    fancy wood stock).** . . . . NiB $525 Ex $425 Gd $265

ELEMENT SERIES
Semiauto. Inertia operated. Gauge: 12 or 20. Bbl.: 26- or 28-in. VR bbls. w/choke tubes. Stock: Walnut, black or camo synthetic. Weight: 6.25-6.75 lbs. Imported 2016 to date.
Deluxe model (28, 20 or 12 gauge, 26- or 28-in. VR bbl., walnut stock, 2015-18).....NiB $955 Ex $830 Gd $705
Synthetic model (26- or 28-in. VR bbl.,
    matte black receiver)** . . . . NiB $655 Ex $580 Gd $505
Upland model (26- or 28-in. VR bbl.,
    walnut stock)** . . . . NiB $855 Ex $755 Gd $655

Waterfowler MAX-5 model (26- or 28-in. VR bbl., camo
    finish, synthetic stock)** . . . . NiB $715 Ex $590 Gd $505

OLYMPIAN
O/U. Gauges: 12 and 20. 2.75- (12 ga.) and 3-in. (20 ga.) chambers. Bbls.: 26-, 28-, 30, and 32-in. Weight: 6.75 - 8.75 lbs. American walnut stock and forend. Disc. 1980.
Field Model. . . . . NiB $988 Ex $700 Gd $577
Skeet Model . . . . NiB $1033 Ex $800 Gd $690
Trap Model . . . . NiB $995 Ex $745 Gd $650

ORION
O/U. Boxlock with Greener crossbolt. Gauges: 12, 20, 28 and .410; 2.75- or 3-in. chambers. Bbls.: 26-, 28, 30-, 32- or 34-in. with fixed or IMC Multi-Choke tubes. Weight: 6.5 to 9 lbs. Single selective trigger. Selective auto ejectors. Top tang safety. Checkered, high-gloss pistol-grip Claro walnut stock and forearm. Finish: Grade I, plain blued receive; Grade II, engraved blued receiver; Grade III, silver gray receiver. Imported from 1982 and 2002.
Orion I Field w/IC (12 or 20 ga.) . . . NiB $1456 Ex $1188 Gd $975
Orion II Field w/IC (12 or 20 ga.) . . . NiB $1155 Ex $965 Gd $743
Orion II Classic w/IC
    (12, 20 or 28 ga.)** . . . . . . NiB $1644 Ex $1388 Gd $1166
Orion II Sporting Clays w/IC
    (12 ga.)** . . . . NiB $1997 Ex $1688 Gd $1388
Orion III Field w/IC
    (12 or 20 ga.)** . . . . NiB $1688 Ex $1397 Gd $1188
Orion III Classic w/IC
    (12 or 20 ga.)** . . . . NiB $1988 Ex $1669 Gd $1367
Orion III English Field w/IC
    (12 or 20 ga.)** . . . . NiB $1733 Ex $1448 Gd $1244
Orion Upland w/IC
    (12 or 20 ga.)** . . . . NiB $1376 Ex $1133 Gd $976
Skeet II w/fixed chokes . . . . NiB $1355 Ex $1125 Gd $950
Super Sporting Clays . . . . . NiB $1988 Ex $1743 Gd $1129

SA-08 SERIES
Semiauto. Gas operating dual valve action. Gauge: 12, 20 or 28. 18.5-, 24-, 26- or 28-in. VR bbls. w/choke tubes. Stock: Wood, black or camo synthetic. Weight: 5.25-6.75 lbs. Mfg. Turkey. Imported 2008 to date.
28 ga., add $60
Deluxe (26- or 28-in. VR bbl., matte black receiver,
    walnut stock)** . . . . NiB $715 Ex $505 Gd $380
Enter Rios (28 ga., 26- or 28-in. VR bbl., walnut stock,
    disc. 2011)** . . . . NiB $630 Ex $480 Gd $380
Kryptek Compact (24-in. VR bbl. w/choke tubes, composite
    camo stock, disc. 2014)** . . . . NiB $700 Ex $525 Gd $400
Synthetic (synthetic stock) . . . . . NiB $555 Ex $420 Gd $305
Upland (26- or 28-in. VR bbl. w/choke tubes, satin wood
    stock, matte black receiver)** . NiB $680 Ex $505 Gd $380
Waterfowl (26- or 28-in. VR bbl. w/choke tubes, synthetic
    stock, camo finish)** . . . . NiB $680 Ex $505 Gd $380
Waterfowl MAX-5 (26- or 28-in. VR bbl. w/choke
    tubes, synthetic stock, MAX-5 camo**
    finish)** . . . . NiB $680 Ex $505 Gd $380

**Westley Richards
Deluxe Sidelock**

SHOTGUNS

GRADING: **NiB** = New in Box   **Ex** = Excellent or NRA 95%   **Gd** = Good or NRA 68%

Waterfowl MAX-5 Compact (26- or 28-in. VR bbl. w/choke tubes, synthetic stock w/12-in. LOP, MAX-5 camo finish) . . . . NiB $680 Ex $505 Gd $380

WBY-X Kryptek Compact (24-in. VR bbl. w/choke tubes, composite camo stock) . . . . . NiB $680 Ex $505 Gd $380

WBY-X Kryptek GH2 (Girls Hunt 2) (24-in. VR bbl. w/choke tubes, composite camo stock w/13-in. LOP, 2014-16) . . . . NiB $655 Ex $505 Gd $355

WBY-X Kryptek Volt Compact (24-in. VR bbl. w/choke tubes, black polymer stock, 2015-16) . . . . NiB $655 Ex $505 Gd $355

SA-459 SERIES
Semiauto. Gas operating dual valve action. Gauge: 12 or 20. 18.5- or 21.25-in. bbls. w/choke tubes. Stock: Synthetic. oversized bolt handle. Weight: 6.5-7.5 lbs.

TR (18.5-in. ported bbl., black synthetic stock, 2011-16) . . . . NiB $600 Ex $455 Gd $330

Turkey (21.25-in. VR bbl. w/extended choke tubes, camo finish, 2012-14) . . . . . NiB $630 Ex $500 Gd $355

Turkey (21.25-in. VR bbl. w/extended choke tubes, camo finish) . . . . NiB $700 Ex $530 Gd $380

SAS SERIES
Semiauto. Self-compensating gas operating action. Gauge: 12. 26-, 28- or 30-in. VR bbls. w/Briley choke tubes. Stock: high grade satin walnut. Weight: 6.75-7.75 lbs. Mfg. Italy and imported 1999 to 2007.

Field (walnut stock) . . . . NiB $780 Ex $585 Gd $430

Field Camo (polymer stock w/various camo finishes) . . . . NiB $815 Ex $615 Gd $450

Field Slug (22-in. rifled bbl. w/cantilever scope mount, Monte Carlo stock, 2003-07) . . . . . . NiB $830 Ex $625 Gd $460

Field Sporting (ported bbl. w/extended choke tubes, 2002-07) . . . . NiB $855 Ex $645 Gd $475

Field Synthetic (synthetic stock) . . . NiB $750 Ex $565 Gd $415

PATRICIAN
Pump/slide action. Takedown. 12 ga. 2.75-in. chamber. Four round tubular magazine. Bbls.: VR; 26-in., SK, IC M; 28-in., M F; 30-in., F choke. Weight: With 28-in. bbl., 7 lbs., 7 oz. Checkered pistol-grip stock and slide handle, recoil pad. Made in Japan from 1972 to 1982.

Field Grade . . . . NiB $369 Ex $248 Gd $125

Deluxe model (etched receiver, fancy grade stock) . . . . NiB $455 Ex $329 Gd $260

Trap Gun (w/30-in. full-choke bbl.) . . . . NiB $399 Ex $255 Gd $190

REGENCY FIELD . . . . NiB $1387 Ex $1266 Gd $885
O/U. Boxlock with sideplates, elaborately engraved. Auto ejectors. Selective single trigger. Gauges: 12, 20. 2.75-in. chamber in 12 ga., 3-in. in 20 ga. Bbls.: VR; 26-in. SK, IC/M, M/F (20 ga. only); 28-in. SK, IC/M, M/F; 30-in. M/F (12 ga only). Weight w/ 28-in. bbls.: 7 lbs., 6 oz., 12 ga.; 6 lbs., 14 oz., 20 ga. Checkered pistol-grip stock and forearm of fancy walnut. Made in Italy from 1965 to 1982.

REGENCY TRAP GUN. . . . . . . NiB $990 Ex $823 Gd $688
Similar to Regency Field Grade except has trap-style stock with straight or Monte Carlo comb. Bbls. have vent side ribs and high, wide vent top rib; 30- or 32-in., M/F, IM/F or F/F chokes. Weight: With 32-in. bbls., 8 lbs. Made in Italy from 1965 to 1982.

PA-08 SERIES
Slide/pump action. Gauge: 12 or 20. Bbl.: 18.5-, 24-, 26- or 28-in. VR bbls. w/choke tubes. Stock: Wood, black or camo synthetic. Weight: 6-7 lbs. Mfg. in Turkey. Imported 2012 to 2017.

Knoxx HD model (18-in. VR bbl. w/fixed choke, black synthetic stock, extended magazine, disc. 2008) . . . . NiB $430 Ex $375 Gd $325

Knoxx Strutter X model (24-in. VR bbl. w/choke tubes, black or camo synthetic stock w/pistol grip, disc. 2008) . . . . NiB $430 Ex $375 Gd $325

Synthetic model (synthetic stock, 2010-17) . . . . NiB $355 Ex $315 Gd $275

Synthetic Compact model (22-in. VR bbl. w/choke tubes, synthetic stock, 2015-17) . . . . . NiB $355 Ex $315 Gd $275

Synthetic Slug Combo model (24-in. rifled bbl. and 28-in. VR bbl. w/choke tubes, synthetic stock, matte black receiver, 2012-17) . . . . . NiB $455 Ex $400 Gd $355

TR model (18.5-in. bbl. w/fixed choke, composite camo stock, 2011-16) . . . . NiB $355 Ex $315 Gd $275

Turkey model (22-in. VR bbl. w/choke tubes, synthetic camo stock, 2012-17) . . . . NiB $355 Ex $315 Gd $275

Typhon TR model (18.5-in. bbl. w/fixed choke, adj. sights, composite camo stock, 2014-15) . . . . NiB $355 Ex $315 Gd $275

Upland model (26- or 28-in. VR bbl. w/choke tubes, satin wood stock, matte black receiver, 2008-17) . . . . NiB $370 Ex $340 Gd $290

Upland Slug Combo model (24-in. rifled bbl. and 28-in. VR bbl. w/choke tubes, satin wood stock, matte black receiver, 2012-17) . . . . . . NiB $555 Ex $480 Gd $400

Waterfowl MAX-5 (26- or 28-in. VR bbl. w/choke tubes, synthetic stock w/MAX-5 camo, 2015-17) . . . . NiB $355 Ex $320 Gd $270

WBY-X Black Reaper TR (18.5-in. bbl. w/fixed choke, composite camo stock, 2014-16) . . . . NiB $400 Ex $345 Gd $300

PA-459 SERIES
Slide/pump action. Gauge: 12 or 20, 3-in. chamber. 18.5- or 21.25-in. VR bbls. w/choke tubes. Stock: Synthetic. Weight: 5.75-6.5 lbs. Mfg. in Turkey. Imported 2012 to 2016.

Black Reaper TR (18.5-in. ported bbl., black synthetic stock, adj. sights, 2014-15) . . . . NiB $470 Ex $405 Gd $355

Home Defense (19-in. ported bbl., black synthetic stock, disc. 2010) . . . . NiB $355 Ex $310 Gd $370

TR (18.5-in. ported bbl., black synthetic stock, 2011-16) . . . . NiB $480 Ex $405 Gd $345

Turkey (21.25-in. VR bbl. w/ported choke tubes, adj. sights, camo finish, 2012-16) . . . . NiB $480 Ex $405 Gd $345

Typhon TR (18.5-in. ported bbl., black synthetic stock, adj. sights, 2014-15) . . . . NiB $455 Ex $400 Gd $355

WESTERN ARMS CORP. — Ithaca, NY
A division of Ithaca Gun Company

LONG RANGE HAMMERLESS DOUBLE
Boxlock. Plain extractors. Single or double triggers. Gauges: 12, 16, 20, .410. Bbls.: 26- to 32-in., M/F choke standard. Weight: 7.5 lbs., 12 ga. Plain pistol-grip stock and forend. Made 1929-1946.

Double triggers . . . . NiB $398 Ex $244 Gd $165
Single trigger . . . . NiB $400 Ex $295 Gd $188

WESTERN AUTO — Kansas City, MO

In the 1940s Western Auto started selling shotguns manufactured by name brand manufacturers, such as O.F. Mossberg & Sons, Remington Arms, Savage Arms, Winchester Repeating Arms Company, and High Standard Manufacturing Company. Western Auto firearms sold under the "Revelation" brand name,

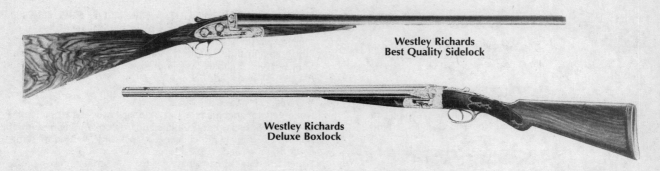

**Westley Richards
Best Quality Sidelock**

**Westley Richards
Deluxe Boxlock**

and were generally models from Savage, Marlin Firearms, or Mossberg. Other than markings, Revelation models were identical to the basic, name brand production models with bluing and plain birch or walnut stocks.

See equivalent models for specs and value.
Model 300/300AC - See Stevens/Springfield, model 30/67
Model 300A - See Savage, model 30AC
Model 300F - See Stevens, model 77C
Model 310 - See Mossberg, model 500
Model 310A/AB/B/C/E - See Mossberg, model 500A/AB/B/C/E
Model 312 - See Mossberg, model 395
Model 312AK/SB - See Mossberg, model 395K/T
Model 316 - See Mossberg, model 390
Model 316B/K - See Mossberg, model 390T/K
Model 325B - See Mossberg, model 385T
Model 325BK - See Mossberg, model 385K
Model 330 - See Mossberg, model 183
Model 330B - See Mossberg, model 183T
Model 335-3725 - See Marlin, model 59
Model 336 - See Springfield, model 951
Model 350 - See Stevens, model 94
Model 350A/M - See Savage/Stevens, model 94D/94
Model 355 - See Stevens, model 94
Model 355Y/YE - See Savage/Springfield, model 947/947YE
Model 356Y - See Springfield, model 944Y
Model 360 - See Savage, model 540
Model 360C - See Savage, model 540C
Model 400 - See Stevens, model 745
Model 400C - See Savage, model 745C
Model 460 - See Springfield, model 511
Model SD52A - See Stevens, model 311
Revelation Model 300 - See Savage, model 30D/E/F
Revelation Model R310 - See Mossberg, model 500AB
Revelation Model 360 - See Fox, model B
Revelation Model 394 Series P - See Savage/Stevens/Springfield, series 94B series P

WESTERN FIELD

See listings under Montgomery Ward. Western Field was a trademark used by Montgomery Ward.

WESTLEY RICHARDS & CO., LTD. —
Birmingham, England

NOTE: The Pigeon and Wildfowl gun, available in all of the Westley Richards models except the Ovundo, has the same general specifications as the corresponding standard field gun except has magnum action of extra strength and treble bolting, chambered for 12 gauge only (2.75- or 3-in.); 30-in. full choke barrels standard. Weight: About 8 lbs. The manufacturer warns

that 12-gauge magnum shells should not be used in their standard weight double-barrel shotguns.

**BEST QUALITY BOXLOCK HAMMERLESS
DOUBLE-BARRELSHOTGUN**
Boxlock. Hand-detachable locks and hinged cover plate. Selective ejectors. Double triggers or selective single trigger. Gauges: 12, 16, 20. Barrel lengths and boring to order. Weight: 5.5 to 6.25 lbs. depending on ga. and bbl. length. Checkered stock and forend, straight or half-pistol grip. Also supplied in Pigeon and Wildfowl models with same values. Made from 1899 to date.
Double triggers..... NiB $22,975 Ex $18,990 Gd $14,270
Selective single trigger NiB $26,790 Ex $21,998 Gd $14,880

**BEST QUALITY SIDELOCK
HAMMERLESS DOUBLE-BARREL SHOTGUN**
Hand-detachable sidelocks. Selective ejectors. Double triggers or selective single trigger. Gauges: 12, 16, 20, 28, .410. Bbl. lengths and boring to order. Weight: 4.75 to 6.75 lbs., depending on ga. and bbl. length. Checkered stock and forend, straight or half-pistol grip. Also supplied in Pigeon and Wildfowl models with same values. Currently manufactured.
Double triggers..... NiB $29,669 Ex $26,766 Gd $22,880
Selective single trigger.... NiB $30,000 Ex $27,898 Gd $24,550

**DELUXE MODEL BOXLOCK
HAMMERLESS DOUBLE-BARREL SHOTGUN**
Same general specifications as standard Best Quality gun except higher quality throughout. Has Westley Richards top-projection and treble-bite lever-work, hand-detachable locks. Also supplied in Pigeon and Wildfowl models with same values. Currently manufactured.
w/double trigger...... NiB $12,767 Ex $10,433 Gd $8998
w/selective single trigger.. NiB $32,880 Ex $30,880 Gd $13,990

DELUXE MODEL SIDELOCK
Same as Best Quality Sidelock except higher grade engraving and wood. Currently manufactured.
w/double triggers ... NiB $27,889 Ex $22,999 Gd $14,887
w/single trigger..... NiB $31,998 Ex $26,999 Gd $18,998

MODEL E HAMMERLESS DOUBLE
Anson & Deeley-type boxlock action. Selective ejector or non-ejector. Double triggers. Gauges: 12, 16, 20. Barrel lengths and boring to order. Weight: 5.5 to 7.25 lbs. depending on type, ga. and bbl. length. Checkered stock and forend, straight or half-pistol grip. Also supplied in Pigeon and Wildfowl models with same values. Currently manufactured.
Ejector model .... NiB $5388 Ex $4378 Gd $2990
Non-ejector model .... NiB $4998 Ex $3788 Gd $3277

OVUNDO (O/U) ... NiB $19,677 Ex $16,999 Gd $12,998
Hammerless. Boxlock. Hand-detachable locks. Dummy sideplates. Selective ejectors. Selective single trigger. 12 ga. Barrel

SHOTGUNS

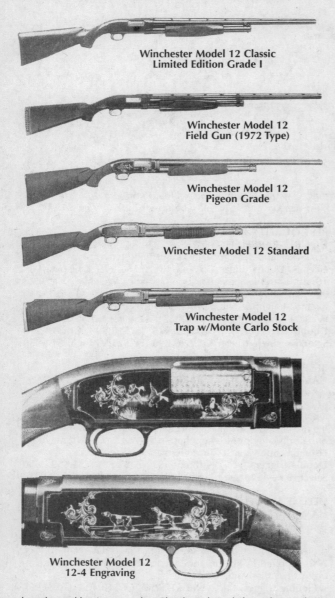

Winchester Model 12 Classic
Limited Edition Grade I

Winchester Model 12
Field Gun (1972 Type)

Winchester Model 12
Pigeon Grade

Winchester Model 12 Standard

Winchester Model 12
Trap w/Monte Carlo Stock

Winchester Model 12
12-4 Engraving

lengths and boring to order. Checkered stock/forend, straight or half-pistol grip. Mfd. before WW II.

TED WILLIAMS
See listings under Sears, Roebuck and Company shotguns.

WINCHESTER —New Haven, CT
Formerly Winchester Repeating Arms Co., and then mfd. by Winchester-Western Div., Olin Corp., later by U.S. Repeating Arms Company. In 1999, production rights were acquired by Browning Arms Company.

MODEL 12 LIMITED EDITION
Gauge: 20; 2.75-in. chamber. Bbl.: 26-in. VR; IC. Weight: 7 lbs. Checkered walnut buttstock and forend. Polished blue finish (Grade I) or engraved with gold inlays (Grade IV). Made 1993-95.
Grade I (4000) . . . . NiB $1000 Ex $840 Gd $660
Grade IV (1000) . . . . NiB $1600 Ex $1310 Gd $1000

MODEL 12 FEATHERWEIGHT. . . NiB $830 Ex $605 Gd $380
Same as Model 12 Standard w/plain barrel except has alloy trigger guard. Modified takedown w/redesigned magazine tube, cap and slide handle. 12 ga. only. Bbls.: 26-in. IC; 28-in. M or F; 30-in. F choke. Serial numbers with "F" prefix. Weight: About 6.75 lbs. Made 1959-62.

MODEL 12 "Y" SERIES
Same general specifications as Standard Model 12 but 12 ga. only, 26- 28- or 30-in. VR bbl., standard chokes. Engine-turned bolt and carrier. Hand-checkered stock/slide handle of semi-fancy walnut. Made 1972-75.
Note: This later version has a letter "Y" serial number prefix and is referred to as the "Y" Series.
Super Pigeon model Note: This later version has a letter "Y" serial number prefix and is referred to as the "Y" Series.
Field Grade model . . . . NiB $800 Ex $685 Gd $522
Limited Edition Grade I model (20 ga. only, 26-in. VR bbl.,
1993-95) . . . . NiB $1000 Ex $830 Gd $655
Limited Edition Grade IV model (20 ga. only, 26-in.
VR bbl., engraved receiver,
1993-95) . . . . NiB $1505 Ex $1255 Gd $1000
Pigeon model (rare only 480 mfg.) . . NiB $1430 Ex $1030 Gd $790
Pigeon Grade 1 variants (trap, skeet and field
models, few mfg.) . . . . NiB $1510 Ex $1010 Gd $810
Pigeon Grade 2 model (engraved receiver, mfg.
1985) . . . . NiB $1880 Ex $1510 Gd $1160
Pigeon Grade 3 model (engraved receiver, mfg.
1985) . . . . NiB $1880 Ex $1510 Gd $1160
Pigeon Grade 4 model (engraved receiver, mfg.
1985) . . . . NiB $2210 Ex $1610 Gd $1210
Pigeon Grade 5 model (engraved receiver, mfg.
1985) . . . . NiB $2755 Ex $1910 Gd $1355
Skeet Grade model (26-in. VR bbl. w/fixed skeet choke,
1972-75) . . . . NiB $1200 Ex $900 Gd $655
Super Pigeon model (tuned action, engraved receiver, high
grade wood, 1964-72) . . . NiB $3755 Ex $2655 Gd $505
Trap Grade model (30-in. VR bbl. w/fixed full choke,
1972-80) . . . . NiB $1100 Ex $855 Gd $655

MODEL 12 HEAVY DUCK GUN
Same general specifications as Standard Grade except 12 ga. only chambered for 3-in. shells. 30- or 32-in. plain, solid or VR bbl. w/full choke only. Three round magazine. Checkered slide handle and pistol-grip walnut buttstock w/recoil pad. Weight: 8.5 to 8.75 lbs. Made 1935-63.
Plain bbl. ` . . . . NiB $1366 Ex $890 Gd $644
Solid rib (disc. 1959) . . . . . . NiB $1977 Ex $1288 Gd $876
VR. . . . . NiB $3288 Ex $2810 Gd $2466

MODEL 12 PIGEON GRADE
Deluxe versions of the regular Model 12 Standard or Field Gun, Duck Gun, Skeet Gun and Trap Gun made on special order. This grade has finer finish throughout, hand-smoothed action, engine-turned breech bolt and carrier, stock and extension slide handle of high grade walnut, fancy checkering, stock dimensions to individual specifications. Engraving and carving available at extra cost ranging from about $135 to over $1000. Disc. 1965.
Field Gun, plain bbl. . . . . . NiB $4233 Ex $3698 Gd $3166
Field Gun, VR . . . . NiB $2255 Ex $1987 Gd $1459
Skeet Gun, matted rib. . . . . NiB $2255 Ex $1987 Gd $1459
Skeet Gun, VR. . . . . NiB $3889 Ex $3350 Gd $3180
Skeet Gun, Cutts Compensator . . . NiB $1755 Ex $1398 Gd $1100
Trap Gun, matted rib . . . . . NiB $2233 Ex $1966 Gd $1399
Trap Gun, VR . . . . NiB $2288 Ex $2190 Gd $2008
16 ga. (Field), add 100%
16 ga. (Skeet), add 100%
20 ga. (Field), add 175%

Winchester Model 21 Custom Grade

Winchester Model 21 Pigeon Grade

Winchester Model 23

Winchester Model 24

Winchester Model 25

Winchester Model 36

20 ga. (Skeet), add **175%**
28 ga. (Skeet), add **550%**

MODEL 12 RIOT GUN . . . . . NiB $2010 Ex $1900 Gd $810
Same general specifications as plain barrel Model 12 Standard except has 20-in. cylinder bore bbl.,12 gauge only. Made 1918-63.

MODEL 12 SKEET GUN . . . NiB $2350 Ex $1830 Gd $1155
Gauges: 12, 16, 20, 28. Five round tubular magazine. 26-in. matted rib bbl., SK choke. Weight: About 7.75 lbs., 12 ga.; 6.75 lbs., other gauges. Bradley red or ivory bead front sight. Winchester 94B middle sight. Checkered pistol-grip stock and extension slide handle. Made 1933-1976.
16 ga., add **35%**
20 ga., add **85%%**
28 ga., add **120%**
w/Cutts Compensator (non-factory fitted), subtract **50%**
w/VR bbl., add **20%**
w/milled VR bbl., add **50%**

MODEL 12 STANDARD
Pump/slide action. Hammerless. Takedown. Gauges: 12, 16, 20, 28. Six round tubular magazine. Plain bbl. Lengths: 26- to 32-in.; choked F to Cyl. Weight: About 7.5 lbs., 12 ga. 30-in., 6.5 lbs. in other ga. w/ 28-in. bbl. Plain pistol-grip stock, grooved slide handle. Made 1912-64.
12 ga., 28-in. bbl., Full choke . . . . . NiB $660 Ex $530 Gd $360
16 ga. . . . . NiB $900 Ex $710 Gd $480
20 ga. . . . . NiB $1120 Ex $910 Gd $630
28 ga. . . . . NiB $5755 Ex $4630 Gd $3580
w/Cutts Compensator (non-factory fitted), subtract **50%**
w/VR bbl., add **20%**
w/milled VR bbl., add **50%**

MODEL 12 SUPER PIGEON
GRADE . . . . NiB $4100 Ex $3850 Gd $2120
Custom version of Model 12 with same general specifications as standard models. 12 ga. only. 26-, 28- or 30-in. VR bbl., any standard choke. Engraved receiver. Hand-smoothed and fitted action. Full fancy walnut stock and forearm made to individual order. Made 1965-72.

MODEL 12 TRAP GUN
Same general specifications as Standard Model 12 except has straighter stock, checkered pistol grip and extension slide handle, recoil pad, 30-in. matted-rib bbl., F choke, 12 ga. only. Disc. after World War II; VR model disc. 1965.
w/milled VR bbl. . . . . NiB $2000 Ex $1550 Gd $1080
w/Hydrocoil stock, add **20%**

MODEL 20 . . . . NiB $1205 Ex $805 Gd $505
Single-shot break action w/manual hammer. Takedown. .410 bore. 2.5-in. chamber. 26-in. bbl., F choke. Checkered pistol-grip stock and forearm. Weight: About 6 lbs. Made 1919-24.

ORIGINAL MODEL 21 DOUBLE-BARREL SHOTGUNS (ORIGINAL PRODUCTION SERIES - 1930 to 1959)
Hammerless. Boxlock. Automatic safety. Double triggers or selective single trigger, selective or non-selective ejection (all postwar Model 21 shotguns have selective single trigger and selective ejection). Gauges: 12, 16, 20, 28 and .410 bore. Bbls.: Raised matted rib or VR; 26-, 28-, 30-, 32-in., the latter in 12 ga. only; F, IM, M, IC, SK chokes. Weight: 7.5 lbs., 12 ga. w/30-in. bbl.; about 6.5 lbs. 16 or 20 ga. w/28-in. bbl. Checkered pistol- or straight-grip stock, regular or beavertail forend. Made 1930-59.
Standard Grade, 12 ga. . . . NiB $7755 Ex $5755 Gd $4500
Standard Grade, 16. Ga. . . . NiB $9755 Ex $7755 Gd $6000
Standard Grade, 20 ga. . . . NiB $11,000 Ex $8000 Gd $6500
Tournament Grade, 12 ga.
(1933-34) . . . . NiB $5733 Ex $5000 Gd $3889
Tournament Grade, 16 ga.
(1933-34) . . . . NiB $6893 Ex $6324 Gd $4388
Tournament Grade, 20 ga.
(1933-34) . . . . NiB $8244 Ex $6887 Gd $4632
Trap Grade, 12 ga.
(1940-59) . . . . NiB $5689 Ex $5000 Gd $4277
Trap Grade, 16 ga.
(1940-59) . . . . NiB $6044 Ex $4988 Gd $3776
Trap Grade, 20 ga.
(1940-59) . . . . NiB $7768 Ex $6322 Gd $3200
Skeet Grade, 12 ga.
(1936-59) . . . . NiB $5463 Ex $4465 Gd $3100
Skeet Grade, 16 ga.
(1936-59) . . . . NiB $6200 Ex $4988 Gd $3677
Skeet Grade, 20 ga.
(1936-59) . . . . NiB $7100 Ex $5998 Gd $4325
Duck Gun, 12 ga., 3-in.
(1940-52) . . . . NiB $5980 Ex $4966 Gd $3544
Magnum, 12 ga., 3-in.)
(1953-59) . . . . NiB $5688 Ex $4765 Gd $3300
Magnum, 20 ga., 3-in.
(1953-59) . . . . NiB $6900 Ex $5779 Gd $4200
Cust. Deluxe grade,
12 ga. (1993-59) . . . . NiB $8634 Ex $6892 Gd $4855
Cust. Deluxe grade,
16 ga., (1933-59) . . . . NiB $10,339 Ex $8833 Gd $6450
Cust. Deluxe grade,
20 ga. (1933-59) . . . . . NiB $11,880 Ex $9893 Gd $6588
Cust. Deluxe grade, 28 ga.
(1933-59) Very Rare . . . . NiB $30,000+
Cust. Deluxe grade, .410 (1933-59)
Very Rare . . . . NiB $35,000+
Fewer than 100 sm. bore models (28 ga. and .410) were built, which precludes accurate pricing, but projected values could exceed $30,000. Such rare specimens should be authenticated by factory letter and/or independent appraisals.

SHOTGUNS

w/VR,12 ga. models, add $900
w/VR, 16 ga. models, add. $1825
w/VR, 20 ga. models, add. $1375
w/double triggers & extractors, deduct 30%
w/double triggers, selective ejection, deduct 20%

With Custom Engraving:
No.1 pattern, add 25%
No. 2 pattern, add 35%
No. 3 pattern, add 50%
No. 4 pattern, add 35%
No. 5 pattern, add 65%
No. 6 pattern, add 75%

MODEL 21 CUSTOM, PIGEON, GRAND AMERICAN (CUSTOM SHOP SERIES - PRODUCTION 1959 TO 1981)

Since 1959 the Model 21 has been offered through the Custom Shop in deluxe models. (Custom, Pigeon, Grand American) on special order. General specifications same as for Model 21 standard models except these custom guns have full fancy American walnut stock and forearm with fancy checkering, finely polished and hand-smoothed working parts, etc.; engraving inlays, carved stocks and other extras are available at additional cost. Made 1959-1981.
Custom grade, 12 ga. . . . NiB $11,980 Ex $9876 Gd $6759
Custom grade, 16 ga.. . NiB $17,544 Ex $13,977 Gd $10,655
Custom grade, 20 ga. . .NiB $14,677 Ex $11,877 Gd $8321
Pigeon grade, 12 ga. NiB $17,889 Ex $14,670 Gd $10,300
Pigeon grade, 16 ga. NiB $22,889 Ex $18,987 Gd $13,770

Pigeon grade, 20 ga. NiB $21,800 Ex $19,880 Gd $14,800
Grand American, 12 ga. NiB $25,700 Ex $19,900 Gd $14,600
Grand American, 16 ga. NiB $39,600 Ex $31,877 Gd $22,955
Grand American, 20 ga. NiB $30,888 Ex $27,888 Gd $20,556
Grand American 3-barrel Set . . NiB $42,750 Ex $35,799 Gd $25,799
Small Bore Models
   28 ga. and .410 (fewer than 20 made), ... $35,000+
Fewer than 20 Small Bore models (28 ga. and .410) were built during this period, which precludes accurate pricing, but projected values could exceed $35,000. Such rare specimens should be authenticated by factory letter and/or independent appraisals.

For Custom Shop Engraving from this period:
#1 Pattern, add 10%
#2 Pattern, add 15%
#3 Pattern, add 25%
#4 Pattern, add 35%
#5 Pattern, add 45%
#6 Pattern, add 50%

MODEL 21 U.S.R.A. CUSTOM SERIES (CUSTOM SHOP PRODUCTION 1982 TO DATE*)

Individual model designations for the Model 21 (made from 1931 to 1982) were changed when U.S. Repeating Arms Company assumed production. The new model nomenclature for the Custom/Built catagory, includes: Standard Custom, Special Custom and Grand American — all of which are available on special order through the Custom Shop. General specifications remained the same on these consolidated model variations and included the addition of a Small Bore 2-Barrel Set (28/.410) and a 3-Barrel Set (20/28/.410). Made 1982 to date *Winchester stopped cataloging the Model 21 after 1987. Current manufacture is by Connecticut Shotgun Manufacturing Company with guns marked Model 21.
Standard custom model . . . NiB $6988 Ex $5570 Gd $4000
Special Custom model . . . . NiB $8000 Ex $6500 Gd $4666
Grand American
   model . . . . NiB $14,880 Ex $12,980 Gd $9660

Grand American model,
   2-bb. set . . . . NiB $48,900 Ex $38,790 Gd $26,998
Grand American, 3-bbl.
   set. . . . . NiB $72,877 Ex $59,988 Gd $26,800

NOTE: *The values shown above represent the basic model in each catagory. Since many customers took advantage of the custom built options, individual gun appointments vary and values will need to be adjusted accordingly. For this reason, individual appraisals should be obtained on all subject firearms.*

MODEL 23 SIDE-BY-SIDE SHOTGUN

Boxlock. Single trigger. Automatic safety. Gauges: 12, 20, 28, .410. Bbls.: 25.5-, 26-, 28-in. with fixed chokes or Winchoke tubes. Weight: 5.88 to 7 lbs. Checkered American walnut buttstock and forend. Made in 1979 for Olin at its Olin-Kodensha facility, Japan.
Classic 23 (gold inlay,
   engraved) . . . . .NiB $2779 Ex $2466 Gd $2365
Custom 23 (plain receiver,
   Winchoke) . . . . .NiB $1477 Ex $1155 Gd $966
Heavy Duck 23, Standard . NiB $2768 Ex $2398 Gd $2077
Lightweight 23, Classic. . . . NiB $2188 Ex $1808 Gd $1266
Light Duck 23, Standard. . . NiB $2987 Ex $2665 Gd $2240
Light Duck 23, 12 ga. Golden
   Quail. . . . . NiB $2877 Ex $2549 Gd $2266
Light Duck 23, .410 Golden
   Quail. . . . . NiB $4577 Ex $4328 Gd $3972
Custom Set 23, 20 & 28 ga. . . . NiB $6988 Ex $5100 Gd $3766

MODEL 24 HAMMERLESS DOUBLE

S/S. Boxlock. Double triggers. Plain extractors. Auto safety. Gauges: 12, 16, 20. Bbls.: 26-in. IC/M; 28-in. M/F (also IC/M in 12 ga. only); 30-in. M and F in 12 ga. only. Weight: About 7.5 lbs., 12 ga. Metal bead front sight. Plain pistol-grip stock, semi-beavertail forearm. Made 1939-57.
12 ga. model. . . . . .NiB $830 Ex $630 Gd $355
16 ga. model. . . . . .NiB $955 Ex $680 Gd $400
20 ga. model. . . . . NiB $1000 Ex $810 Gd $555

MODEL 25 RIOT GUN. . . . . . . NiB $677 Ex $455 Gd $390
Same as Model 25 Standard except has 20-in. cylinder bore bbl., 12 ga. only. Made 1949-55.

MODEL 25 . . . . NiB $555 Ex $405 Gd $305
Pump/slide action. Hammerless. Solid frame. 12 ga. only. Four round tubular magazine. 28-in. Plain bbl.; IC, M or F choke. Weight: About 7.5 lbs. Metal bead front sight. Plain pistol-grip stock, grooved slide handle. Made 1949-55.

MODEL 36 SINGLE-SHOT
BOLT ACTION . . . . NiB $1893 Ex $1688 Gd $1477
Takedown. Uses 9mm Short or Long shot or ball cartridges interchangeably. 18-in. bbl. Plain stock. Weight: About 3 lbs. Made 1920-27.

MODEL 37 SINGLE-SHOT SHOTGUN

Semi-hammerless. Auto ejection. Takedown. Gauges: 12, 16, 20, 28, .410. Bbl. lengths: 28-, 30-, 32-in. in all gauges except .410; 26- or 28-in. in .410; all barrels plain with F choke. Weight: About 6.5 pounds, 12 ga. Made 1937-63.
12, 16, 20 ga. models . . . . NiB $559 Ex $438 Gd $315
Youth model (20 ga.
   w/red dot indicator) . . . . . . .NiB $559 Ex $438 Gd $315
.410 model . . . . .NiB $769 Ex $588 Gd $437
28 ga. model ("Red Letter"
   version) . . . . NiB $2687 Ex $2531 Gd $2033
Other "Red Letter" models, add. 20%
W/32-in. bbl., add 15%

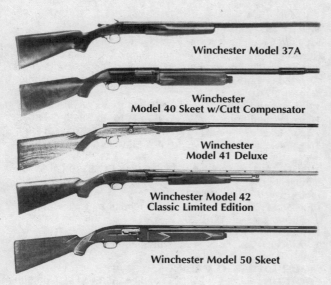

Winchester Model 37A

Winchester Model 40 Skeet w/Cutt Compensator

Winchester Model 41 Deluxe

Winchester Model 42 Classic Limited Edition

Winchester Model 50 Skeet

MODEL 37A SINGLE-SHOT SHOTGUN
Similar to Model 370 except has engraved receiver and gold trigger, checkered pistol-grip stock, fluted forearm; 16 ga. available w/ 30-in. bbl. only. Made 1973-80.
12, 16 or 20 ga. models . . . . . NiB $579 Ex $300 Gd $219
28 ga. model . . . . NiB $2590 Ex $2331 Gd $2268
.410 model . . . . NiB $754 Ex $559 Gd $366
w/32-in. bbl., add $50

MODEL 37A YOUTH . . . . NiB $566 Ex $397 Gd $244
Similar to Model 370 Youth except has engraved receiver and gold trigger, checkered pistol-grip stock, fluted forearm. Made 1973-1980.

MODEL 40 . . . . NiB $830 Ex $555 Gd $400
Semiauto. Long recoil action. 12 ga. only. Four round tubular magazine. 28- or 30-in. bbl.; M or F choke. Weight: About 8 lbs. Bead sight on ramp. Plain pistol-grip stock, semi-beavertail forearm. Made 1940-41.
Skeet model . . . . NiB $970 Ex $720 Gd $530

MODEL 41 . . . . NiB $730 Ex $555 Gd $430
Single-shot. Bolt action. Takedown. .410 bore. 2.5-in. chamber (chambered for 3-in. shells after 1932). 24-in. bbl., F choke. Plain straight stock standard. Also made in deluxe version. Made 1920-34.

MODEL 42 STANDARD GRADE
First pump/slide action designed for .410 bore. Hammerless. Takedown. .410 bore (3- or 2.5-in. shell). Tubular magazine holds five 3-in. or six 2.5-in. shells. 26- or 28-in. plain or solid-rib bbl.; cylinder bore, M or F choke. Weight: 5.8 to 6.5 lbs. Plain pistol-grip stock; grooved slide handle. Made 1933-63.
w/plain bbl. . . . . NiB $2210 Ex $1930 Gd $1380
w/solid rib . . . . NiB $3660 Ex $3160 Gd $2160

MODEL 42
CLASSIC LTD. EDITION . . . NiB $1886 Ex $1599 Gd $1179
Gauge: .410 w/ 2.75-in. chamber. Bbl.: 26-in. VR; F choke. Weight: 7 lbs. Checkered walnut buttstock and forend. Engraved blue with gold inlays. Limited production of 850. Made from 1993.

MODEL 42 DELUXE . . . NiB $15,200 Ex $12,700 Gd $9100
Same general specifications as the Model 42 Trap Grade except available w/VR after 1955. Finer finish throughout w/hand-smoothed action, engine-turned breech bolt and carrier, stock and extension slide handle of high grade walnut, fancy checkering, stock dimensions to individual specifications. Engraving and carving were offered at extra cost. Made 1940-63.

NOTE: *Exercise caution on VR models not marked "DELUXE" on the bottom of the receiver. A factory letter will insure that the rib was installed during the initial manufacturing process. Unfortunately, factory authentication is not always possible due to missing or destroyed records. To further complicate this matter, not all VR ribs were installed by Winchester. From 1955-63, both Deluxe and Skeet Grade models were available with Simmons style ribs. After-market rib installations are common.*

MODEL 42 PIGEON GRADE
This higher-grade designation is similar to the Deluxe grade and is available in all configurations. May be identified by engraved Pigeon located at the base of the magazine tube. Most production occurred in the late 1940's. **NOTE:** *To determine the value of any Model 42 Pigeon Grade, add 50% to value listed under the specified Model 42 configuration.*

MODEL 42 SKEET GUN
Same general specifications as Model 42 Standard except has checkered straight or pistol-grip stock and extension slide handle, 26- or 28-in. plain, solid-rib or VR bbl. May be choked F., M, Imp. Cyl. or Skeet. Note: Some Model 42 Skeet Guns are chambered for 2.5-in. shells only. Made 1933-63.
w/plain bbl. . . . . NiB $4160 Ex $3760 Gd $3110
w/solid rib . . . . NiB $6010 Ex $5300 Gd $3760
w/VR. . . . . NiB $7160 Ex $6260 Gd $4510
w/ 2.5-in. chamber, add 35%

MODEL 42 TRAP GRADE
This higher grade designation was available in both field and skeet configurations and is fitted w/deluxe wood w/trap grade checkering pattern and marked "TRAP" on bottom of receiver. Made 1934-1939. Superseded by the Deluxe model in 1940.
w/plain bbl. . . . . NiB $15,200 Ex $12,600 Gd $9000

MODEL 50 STANDARD GRADE . . NiB $655 Ex $455 Gd $355
Non-recoiling bbl. and independent chamber. Gauges: 12 and 20. Two round tubular magazine. Bbl.: 12 ga. — 26-, 28-, 30-in.; 20 ga. — 26-, 28-in.; IC, SK, M, F choke. Checkered pistol-grip stock and forearm. Weight: About 7.75 lbs. Made 1954-61.
w/VR bbl., add $100
Skeet model (26-in. VR bbl.,
 walnut stock) . . . . NiB $1310 Ex $955 Gd $705
Trap model (30-in. VR bbl., Monte Carlo
 wood stock) . . . . NiB $1310 Ex $955 Gd $705

MODEL 59. . . . . NiB $755 Ex $505 Gd $305
Semiauto. Short-recoil action. Gauge: 12. Magazine holds two rounds. Alloy receiver. Win-Lite steel and fiberglass bbl.: 26-in. IC, 28-in. M or F choke, 30-in. F choke; also furnished w/ 26-in. bbl. with Versalite choke (interchangeable F, M, IC tubes; one supplied with gun). Weight: About 6.5 lbs. Checkered pistol-grip stock and forearm. Made 1959-1965.

MODEL 1885 SINGLE-SHOT
SHOTGUN . . . . NiB $4377 Ex $3554 Gd $2566
Falling-block action, same as Model 1885 Rifle. Highwall receiver. Solid frame or takedown. 20 ga. 3-in. chamber. 26-in. bbl.; plain, matted or mattmaed rib; Cyl. bore, M or F choke. Weight: About 5.5 lbs. Straight-grip stock and forearm. Made 1914-16.

SHOTGUNS

Winchester Model 1897 Riot Gun

Winchester Model 101

Winchester Model 370

Winchester Model 1001 Sporting Clays

MODEL 1887 LEVER-ACTION SHOTGUN
First of John Browning's patent shotgun designs produced by Winchester. 10 or 12 ga. on casehardened frame fitted w/20-in. blued, cylinder bore or full choke 30- or 32-in. bbl. Plain or checkered walnut stock and forend. Made 1887-1901.

10 or 12 ga. Standard model	NiB $4188	Ex $3765	Gd $3287
10 or 12 ga. Deluxe model	NiB $9233	Ex $8977	Gd $6450
10 or 12 ga. Riot Gun	NiB $2770	Ex $2256	Gd $1656

w/.70-150 Ratchet rifled bbl. .70 cal.
rifle/87 produced) . . . . . NiB $4350 Ex $3000 Gd $2275
w/3 or 4 blade Del. Damascus bbl., add 20%

MODEL 1893 . . . . NiB $1155 Ex $930 Gd $600
First pump-action shotgun manufactured by Winchester. Standard Grade. Solid frame. Gauges: 12 black powder shells only. Five-round tubular magazine. Bbl.: Plain; 30 or 32 in., F choked. Plain pistol-grip stock, grooved slide handle. Appox. 34,000 mfg.Made 1893-97.

MODEL 1897 BUSH GUN
Takedown or solid frame. Same general specifications as standard Model 1897 except w/ 26-in. cylinder bore bbl. Made 1897-1931.

w/solid frame	NiB $995	Ex $700	Gd $554
Takedown model	NiB $1299	Ex $1056	Gd $800

MODEL 1897 RIOT GUN
Takedown or solid frame. Same general specifications as standard Model 1897 except 12 ga. only, 20-in. cylinder bore bbl. Made 1898-1935.

w/solid frame	NiB $1544	Ex $1187	Gd $900
Takedown model	NiB $1390	Ex $1055	Gd $773

MODEL 1897 TRAP, TOURNAMENT & PIGEON GRADES
These higher grade models offer higher overall quality than the standard grade. Made 1897-1939.

Standard Trap grade	NiB $2600	Ex $2208	Gd $1188
Special Trap grade	NiB $2755	Ex $2320	Gd $1755
Tournament grade (Black Diamond)	NiB $2971	Ex $2387	Gd $1698
Pigeon grade	NiB $12,755	Ex $9533	Gd $4950

MODEL 1897 TRENCH GUN . . NiB $4800 Ex $3693 Gd $2138
Solid frame. Same as Model 1897 Riot Gun except has handguard and is equipped with a bayonet. World War I government issue, from 1917 to 1918.
w/military markings, add 20%

MODEL 1897 SLIDE-ACTION REPEATER
Standard Grade. Takedown or solid frame. Gauges: 12 and 16. Five-round tubular magazine. Bbl.: Plain; 26 to 32 in., the latter in 12 ga. only; choked F to Cyl. Weight: About 7.75 lbs. (12 ga. w/28-in. bbl.). Plain pistol-grip stock, grooved slide handle. Made 1897-1957.

12 ga. w/solid frame	NiB $1110	Ex $855	Gd $675
16 ga. w/solid frame	NiB $1110	Ex $855	Gd $675
12 ga., takedown model	NiB $1356	Ex $1108	Gd $888
16 ga., takedown model	NiB $1356	Ex $1108	Gd $888

MODEL 1901 . . . . NiB $3855 Ex $3510 Gd $2755
Similar to Model 1887 lever-action shotgun except with more rugged action for 10 ga.. Bbl.: 32-in. plain bbl. Finish: Blue. Stock: Smooth walnut. 5-rnd. tubular magazine. Appox. 13,500 mfg. Made 1901-20.
Deluxe model)checkered walnut
stock) . . . . NiB $5780 Ex $5265 Gd $4130

MODEL 1911 AUTOLOADING
SHOTGUN . . . . NiB $755 Ex $655 Gd $500
Hammerless. Takedown. 12 gauge only. Four round tubular magazine. Bbl.: plain, 26- to 32-in., standard borings. Weight: About 8.5 lbs. Plain or checkered pistol-grip stock and forearm. Made 1911-25.

MODEL 96 XPRT SERIES
O/U. Boxlock action similar to Model 101. Plain receiver. Auto ejectors. Selective single trigger. Gauges: 12, 20. 3-in. chambers. Bbl.: VR; 26-in. IC/M; 28-in. M/F, 30-in. F/F choke (12 ga. only). Weight: 6.25 to 8.25 lbs. depending on ga. and bbls. Checkered pistol-grip stock and forearm. Made 1976-82 for Olin Corp. at its Olin-Kodensha facility in Japan.

Field Grade model	NiB $880	Ex $655	Gd $480
Skeet Grade model	NiB $930	Ex $730	Gd $500
Trap Grade model	NiB $880	Ex $655	Gd $480

MODEL 101 SERIES
Boxlock. O/U. Engraved receiver. Auto ejectors. Single selective trigger. Combination bbl. selector and safety. Gauges: 12 and 28, 2.75-in. chambers; 20 and .410, 3-in. chambers. VR bbls.: 30- (12 ga. only) and 26.5-in., IC/M. Weight: 6.25 to 7.75 lbs. depending on gauge and bbl. length. Hand-checkered French walnut and forearm. Made 1963-81. Gauges other than 12 introduced in 1966. NOTE: All Winchester Model 101s are mfd. for Olin Corp. at its Olin-Kodensha facility in Tochigi, Japan. Production for Olin Corp. stopped in Nov. 1987. Importation of Model 101s was continued by Classic Doubles under that logo until 1990. See separate heading for additional data.

Field 12	NiB $1110	Ex $930	Gd $655
Field 28 and .410 ga., add	. . . . 50%		
Field 20 ga., add	. . . . 20%		

Field recent mfg. (12 ga., 26- or 28-in. VR bbls. w/Invector
choke tubes, high gloss stock, blued engraved
receiver, 2007-date) . . . . . NiB $1740 Ex $1530 Gd $1190
Magnum (30-in. bbl., 12 or 20 ga.
w/ 3-in. chambers w/F/M or
F/F choke, 1966-81) . . . . . . NiB $1310 Ex $1110 Gd $810
Quail Special 12 ga. (small-frame Model 101, 25.5-in. bbls.
W/Winchoke tubes, straight grip stock, imported from
Japan in 1984 to 1987). . . NiB $2910 Ex $2500 Gd $2000

Quail Special 20 ga.	NiB $3510	Ex $3110	Gd $2210
Quail Special 28 ga.	NiB $5260	Ex $4510	Gd $3610
Quail Special .410	NiB $4510	Ex $3860	Gd $2810

Skeet (26.5-in. bbl., 12 or 20 ga., 28-in. bbl., 28 ga. or .410,
1966-84) . . . . NiB $1200 Ex $1010 Gd $775

Winchester Model 1300 Deer Series — Advantage Full Camo Pattern

Winchester Model 1300 Defender Series — Stainless Marine Synthetic Stock

Winchester Model 1300 Defender 5-Shot Combo

Winchester Model 1300 Lady Defender — Synthetic Pistol Grip Stock

Skeet Three Gauge
Set (1974-84) . . . . NiB $3800 Ex $3480 Gd $2855
Trap (30- or 32-in. bbl., 12 ga. only, standard or wide VR,
1966-84) . . . . NiB $1330 Ex $1110 Gd $830
Single Barrel Trap (32- or 34-in. bbl., 12 ga. only, Monte
Carlo stock, 1967-71) . . . . . . NiB $885 Ex $665 Gd $500

MODEL 101 DIAMOND GRADE
Similar to Model 101 Pigeon Grade except Skeet and Trap
models only w/silvered receiver, Winchoke choke tubes. Made
1981-90.
Standard Skeet (27.5-in. VR bbl.,
12 ga., disc. 1987) . . . . . . NiB $1730 Ex $1530 Gd $1980
Standard Skeet (27.5-in. VR bbl.,
20 ga., disc. 1987), add 20%
Standard Skeet (27.5-in. VR bbl., 28 ga.
or .410, disc. 1987), add 30%
Four Gauge Skeet Set . . . . . . NiB $4600 Ex $4100 Gd $3100
Standard Trap (30- or 32-in. VR bbl.,
12 ga. only, disc. 1987) . . NiB $1710 Ex $1510 Gd $1110
Unsingle Trap (32- or 34-in. VR bbl.,
12 ga. only, disc. 1986) . . NiB $1910 Ex $1680 Gd $1210
Oversingle Trap (34-in. VR bbl.,
12 ga. only, 1986-87) . . . . NiB $2110 Ex $1800 Gd $1430
Oversingle Combo (oversingle bbl. and O/U bbls.,12 ga.
only, disc. 1987) . . . . NiB $2955 Ex $2730 Gd $2255
Sporting recent mfg. (12 ga. only w/28-, 30-, or
32-in. ported VR bbls. w/Invector choke tubes,
silver nitride receiver, high grade walnut
stock, 2007-22) . . . . NiB $2180 Ex $1910 Gd $1480
Trap Combo (two sets 30- or 34-in. VR O/U bbls.,12 ga.
only, disc. 1987) . . . . NiB $2955 Ex $2730 Gd $2255

MODEL 101 PIGEON GRADE XTR
Similar to Model 101 Field except engraved silvered frame and
select wood. Winchoke tubes. Made 1974-87.
12 ga. model . . . . NiB $2260 Ex $2010 Gd $1455
20 ga. model . . . . NiB $2710 Ex $2355 Gd $1810
28 ga. model . . . . NiB $3760 Ex $3310 Gd $2510
.410 model . . . . NiB $3510 Ex $3260 Gd $2510

Featherweight (12 or 20 ga., w/25.5-in. bbl. w/fixed IC/IM
chokes or Winchokes, English straight grip stock, 6.5 lb.,
disc. 1987) . . . . NiB $1955 Ex $1755 Gd $1280
Lightweight (20 ga. only w/ 27-in. bbl.,
receiver engraved w/gold, Limited
production, 1995-96) . . . . NiB $2500 Ex $2210 Gd $1810
Lightweight Two Barrel Set
(28 ga./.410) . . . . NiB $3600 Ex $3355 Gd $2760
Skeet 12 ga. . . . . NiB $1855 Ex $1655 Gd $1230
Skeet 20 ga., add 25%
Skeet 28 ga. or .410, add 50%
Sporting (12 ga. only w/30- or 32-in. ported, wide
VR bbl., silver nitride receiver, adj. high grade
walnut stock, 2009-10) . . NiB $2280 Ex $1855 Gd $1380
Super (12 ga. only, gold inlay engraved
receiver, 1985-87) . . . . . . NiB $5100 Ex $4900 Gd $3900
Trap (12 ga. only, coin finished engraved
receiver, disc. 1985) . . . . . . NiB $1555 Ex $1355 Gd $930
Trap recent mfg. (12 ga. only, 30- or 32-in. bbls.
w/Invector choke tubes, TruGlo fiber optic front
bead, high gloss wood stock, nickel-plated
receiver, 2008-20) . . . . . . NiB $2300 Ex $2030 Gd $1580

MODEL 370 . . . . NiB $245 Ex $200 Gd $99
Single-shot. Visible hammer. Auto ejector. Takedown. Gauges:
12, 16, 20, 28, .410. 2.75-in. chambers in 16 and 28 ga.,
3-in. in other ga. Bbls.: 12 ga., 30-, 32- or 36-in.,16 ga; 30- or
32-in.; 20 and 28 ga., 28-in.; .410 bore, 26-in., all F choke.
Weight: 5.5-6.25 lbs. Plain pistol-grip stock and forearm. Made
1968-73.
Youth (26-in. bbl., 12.5-in.
LOP stock, 1968-73) . . . . NiB $180 Ex $150 Gd $100

MODEL 1001
O/U. Boxlock. 12 ga., 2.75- or 3-in. chambers. Bbls.: 28- or
30-in. VR; WinPlus choke tubes. Weight: 7-7.75 lbs. Checkered
walnut buttstock and forend. Blued finish with scroll engraved
receiver. Made 1993-98.
Field model (28-in. bbl., 3-in.) . . . . . . NiB $1133 Ex $978 Gd $726
Sporting Clays model . . . . . . NiB $1166 Ex $1044 Gd $863
Sporting Clays Lite model . . . . NiB $1187 Ex $990 Gd $734

MODEL 1200 SERIES
Slide-action. Front-locking rotary bolt. Takedown. 4-rnd. magazine. Gauges: 12, 16, 20 (2.75-in. chamber). Bbl.: Plain or
VR; 26-, 28-, 30-in.; IC, M, F choke or with Winchoke (interchangeable tubes IC-M-F). Weight: 6.5 to 7.25 lbs. Checkered
pistol-grip stock and fore arm (slide handle), recoil pad; also
available from 1966 to 1970 w/Winchester recoil reduction
system (Cycolac stock). Made 1964-83.

NOTE: *Even though the 1200 series was introduced in 1964
and was supplanted by the Model 1300 in 1978, the Security
series (including the Defender model) was marketed under 1200
series alpha-numeric product codes (G1200DM2R) until 1989.
In 1990, the same Defender model was marketed under a 4-digit
code (7715) and was then advertised in the 1300 series.*
Field w/plain bbl. . . . . NiB $305 Ex $255 Gd $185
Field w/VR bbl . . . . NiB $330 Ex $280 Gd $200
Field w/recoil reduction system, add $100
Field w/Winchoke, add $50
Deer Gun (22-in. bbl. w/rifle-type sights; 12 ga. only, 6.5
lbs., 1965-74) . . . . NiB $355 Ex $305 Gd $215
Defender (12 ga. w/3-in. chamber. 18-in. bbl. w/cylinder
bore and metal front bead or rifle sights. 4- or 7-rnd.
magazine, 5.5 to 6.75 lbs. 25.6 in. (PG Model) or 38.6 in.

SHOTGUNS

overall. Matte blue finish. Synthetic pistol grip or walnut finished hardwood stock) . . . . NiB $355 Ex $305 Gd $215

Magnum Field (3-in. 12 and 20 ga.; plain or VR bbl., 28- or 30-in., F choke. Weight: 7.38 to 7.88 lbs. 1964-83) . . . . NiB $350 Ex $300 Gd $200

Ranger (hardwood stock/ribbed forend, 28-in. VR bbl. w/Winchoke, made from 1982 to 1990 by U. S. Repeating Arms) . . . . NiB $225 Ex $195 Gd $145

Skeet Gun (12 or 20 ga.; 2-rnd. magazine, tuned trigger, 26-in. VR bbl. w/SK choke, semi-fancy walnut stock, 7.25 to 7.5 lbs., 1965-73) . . . . NiB $405 Ex $330 Gd $240

Stainless Police (6-rnd. magazine. 18-in. bbl. w/cylinder bore choke, rifle sights, 7 lbs., bright chrome finish, synthetic pistol grip or walnut finished hardwood stock, 1984-90) . . . . NiB $355 Ex $305 Gd $215

Trap Gun (12 or 20 ga.; 2-rnd. magazine, tuned trigger, 30-in. VR bbl. w/SK choke or 28-in. w/Winchoke, semi-fancy walnut stock, 7.25 to 7.5 lbs., 1965-73) . . . . NiB $405 Ex $330 Gd $240

MODEL 1300 CAMOPACK . . . . NiB $465 Ex $390 Gd $279
Gauge: 12.3-in. Magnum. Four round magazine. Bbls.: 30-and 22-in. with Winchoke system. Weight: 7 lbs. Laminated stock with Win-Cam camouflage green, cut checkering, recoil pad, swivels and sling. Made 1987-88.

MODEL 1300 DEER SERIES
Similar to standard Model 1300 except 12 or 20 ga. only w/ special 22-in. cyl. bore or rifled bbl. and rifle-type sights. Weight: 6.5 lbs. Checkered walnut or synthetic stock w/satin walnut, black or Advantage Full Camo Pattern finish. Matte blue or full-camo metal finish. Made 1994-2006.
w/walnut stock (intro. 1994) . . NiB $425 Ex $360 Gd $265
Black Shadow Deer model w/synthetic stock
 (intro. 1994) . . . . NiB $400 Ex $298 Gd $220
Advantage Camo model
 (1995-98) . . . . NiB $445 Ex $377 Gd $280
Deer Combo
Deer Combo w/22- and 28-in. bbls.
 (1994-98) . . . . NiB $515 Ex $455 Gd $390
W/rifled bbl. (intro. 1996), add $75

MODEL 1300 DEFENDER SERIES
Gauges: 12 or 20 ga. 18- 24- 28-in. VR bbl. w/3-in. chamber. Four-, 7- or 8- round magazine. Weight: 5.6 to 7.4 lbs. Blued, chrome or matte stainless finish. Wood or synthetic stock. Made 1985-2006.
Combo model . . . . NiB $490 Ex $375 Gd $277
Hardwood stock model. . . . . . . NiB $365 Ex $299 Gd $200
Synthetic pistol-grip model. . . . NiB $270 Ex $283 Gd $203
Synthetic stock model. . . . . NiB $335 Ex $279 Gd $225
Lady Defender synthetic
 stock (made 1996) . . . . NiB $320 Ex $255 Gd $210
Lady Defender synthetic
 Pistol-grip (made 1996) . . . . NiB $320 Ex $255 Gd $210
Stainless marine
 model w/synthetic stock. . . . NiB $555 Ex $435 Gd $290

MODEL 1300 DELUXE
Gauges: 12 and 20 w/3-in. chamber. Four round magazine. Bbl.:22, 26 or 28 in. VR bbl. w/Winchoke tubes. Weight: 6.5 lbs. Checkered walnut buttstock and forend w/high luster finish. Polished blue metal finish with roll-engraved receiver. Made 1984-2006.
Model 1300 Deluxe
 w/high gloss finish . . . . NiB $500 Ex $390 Gd $292

Model 1300 Ladies/Youth model
 w/22-in. bbl., (disc. 1992) . . . . . NiB $455 Ex $360 Gd $258

MODEL 1300 FEATHERWEIGHT
Hammerless. Takedown. Four round magazine. Gauges: 12 and 20 (3-in. chambers). Bbls.: 22, 26 or 28 in. w/plain or VR w/Winchoke tubes. Weight: 6.38 to 7 lbs. Checkered walnut buttstock, grooved slide handle. Made 1978-94.
w/plain bbl. . . . . NiB $400 Ex $365 Gd $290
w/VR . . . . NiB $400 Ex $365 Gd $290
XTR model . . . . NiB $400 Ex $365 Gd $290

MODEL 1300 RANGER SERIES
Gauges: 12 or 20 ga. w/3-in. chamber. Five round magazine. 22- (Rifled), 26- or 28-in. VR bbl. w/Winchoke tubes. Weight: 7.25 lbs. Blued finish. Walnut-finished hardwood buttstock and forend. Made 1984-2006.
Standard model . . . . NiB $377 Ex $366 Gd $270
Combo model . . . . NiB $465 Ex $399 Gd $280
Ranger Deer combo
 (D&T w/rings & bases) . . . . . NiB $455 Ex $380 Gd $265
Ranger Ladies/Youth . . . . NiB $366 Ex $255 Gd $190

MODEL 1300 FIELD GUN
Slide-action. Takedown w/front-locking rotary bolt. Gauges: 12, 20 w/3-in. chamber. Four round magazine. Bbl.: VR; 26-, 28-, 30-in. w/ Win-choke tubes IC-M-F). Weight: 7.25 lbs. Checkered walnut or synthetic stock w/standard, black or Advantage Full Camo Pattern finish. Matte blue or full-camo metal finish. Made 1994-2006.
Standard Field w/walnut stock . NiB $445 Ex $320 Gd $266
Black Shadow w/black
 synthetic stock . . . . NiB $365 Ex $275 Gd $200
Advantage Camo model . . . . . . NiB $455 Ex $375 Gd $290

MODEL 1300 SLUG HUNTER SERIES
Similar to standard Model 1300 except chambered 12 ga. only w/special 22-in. smoothbore w/sabot-rifled choke tube or fully rifled bbl. w/rifle-type sights. Weight: 6.5 lbs. Checkered walnut, hardwood or laminated stock w/satin walnut or WinTuff finish. Matte blue metal finish. Made 1988-94.
w/hardwood stock . . . . NiB $465 Ex $365 Gd $250
w/laminated stock. . . . . NiB $515 Ex $400 Gd $290
w/walnut stock . . . . NiB $500 Ex $380 Gd $265
Whitetails Unlimited model
 w/beavertail forend . . . . NiB $475 Ex $396 Gd $300
w/sabot-rifled choke tubes, add $50

MODEL 1300 TURKEY SERIES
Gauges: 12 or 20 ga. 22-in. bbl. w/3-in. chamber. Four round magazine. 43 in. overall. Weight: 6.4 to 6.75 lbs. Buttstock and magazine cap, sling studs w/Cordura sling. Drilled and tapped to accept scope base. Checkered walnut, synthetic or laminated wood stock w/low luster finish. Matte blue or full camo finish. Made 1985-2006.
w/Advantage camo . . . . NiB $390 Ex $285 Gd $216
w/Realtree All-Purpose camo . . NiB $488 Ex $369 Gd $275
w/Realtre Gray All-Purpose
 camo. . . . . NiB $500 Ex $405 Gd $325
w/Realtree All-Purpose
 camo (matte finish). . . . . NiB $525 Ex $420 Gd $355
w/Black Shadow synthetic stock NiB $355 Ex $285 Gd $190
w/Win-Cam green
 laminate stock . . . . NiB $445 Ex $365 Gd $225
Win-Cam combo
 (22- or 30-in. bbl.) . . . . NiB $465 Ex $420 Gd $350
Win-Cam NWTF model
 (22- or 30-in. bbl.) . . . . NiB $525 Ex $375 Gd $285

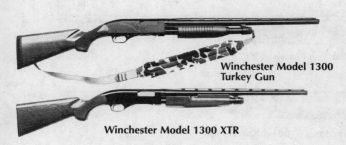

Winchester Model 1300 Turkey Gun

Winchester Model 1300 XTR

Win-Cam Youth/Ladies
model (20 ga.) . . . . NiB $565 Ex $435 Gd $310
Win-Tuf model w/brown
laminated wood stock . . . . NiB $490 Ex $388 Gd $265

MODEL 1300 WATERFOWL
Pump-action. Similar to 1300 Standard model except has 28- or 30-in. VR bbl. w/Winchoke tubes. Weight: 7 lbs. Matte blue metal finish. Checkered walnut finished hardwood or brown laminated Win-Tuffwood stock w/camo sling, swivels and recoil pad. Made 1984-92.
w/hardwood stock . . . . NiB $435 Ex $300 Gd $220
w/laminated stock. . . . . NiB $435 Ex $300 Gd $220

MODEL 1300 XTR . . . . NiB $550 Ex $455 Gd $3209
Pump-action. Hammerless. Takedown. Four shot magazine. Gauges: 12 and 20 (3-in. chambers). Bbl.: Plain or VR; 28-in. bbls.; Winchoke (interchangeable tubes IC-M-F). Weight: About 7 lbs. Disc. 2006.

MODEL 1400 SERIES
Semiauto. Gas-operated. Front-locking rotary bolt. Takedown. 2-rnd. magazine. Gauges: 12, 16, 20 (2.75-in. chamber). Bbl.: Plain or VR; 26-, 28-, 30-in.; IC, M, F choke, or with Winchoke (interchangeable tubes IC-M-F). Weight: 6.5 to 7.25 lbs. Checkered pistol-grip stock and forearm, recoil pad, also available with Winchester recoil reduction system (Cycolac stock). Made 1964-68.
Field w/plain bbl . . . . NiB $455 Ex $380 Gd $280
Field w/VR bbl . . . . NiB $505 Ex $430 Gd $305
Field w/recoil reduction system, add $130
Field w/Winchoke, add $50
Deer Gun (22-in. bbl. w/ rifle-type sights, 12 ga. only, 6.25 lbs., 1965-68) . . . . NiB $405 Ex $330 Gd $240
Ranger (12 or 20 ga., 28-in. VR bbl. w/ F choke.
   Overall length: 48.63 in. Weight: 7 to 7.25 lbs. Walnut finish, hardwood stock and forearm with cut checkering. Made 1984-90 by
   U. S. Repeating Arms) . . . . NiB $405 Ex $330 Gd $240
Ranger Deer Combo (24-in. plain bbl. w/ rifle sights and 26- or 28-in. VR bbl.) . . . . NiB $455 Ex $380 Gd $290
Skeet Gun (12 and 20 ga. only, 26-in. VR bbl., SK choke, semi-fancy walnut stock and forearm.
   Weight: 7.25 to 7.5 lbs. Made 1965-68.
   Also available with Winchester recoil reduction system add $50) . . . NiB $505 Ex $430 Gd $310
Trap Gun (12 ga. only w/ 30-in. VR bbl., F choke. Semi-fancy walnut stock, straight or Monte Carlo trap style. Also available with Winchester recoil reduction system. Weight: About 8.25 lbs., 1965-68) . . . . NiB $505 Ex $430 Gd $310

MODEL 1400 MARK II SERIES
Similar to Model 1400 Field Gun, except not chambered for 16 gauge; Winchester Recoil Reduction System not available after 1970. Only 28-in. bbl. w/Winchoke offered after 1973. Made 1968-78.

Field w/plain bbl . . . . NiB $450 Ex $365 Gd $287
Field w/plain bbl.
   and Winchoke . . . . NiB $475 Ex $388 Gd $315
Field w/VR bbl . . . . NiB $544 Ex $390 Gd $290
Field w/VR bbl. and Winchoke . . . NiB $566 Ex $445 Gd $390
w/Winchester recoil reduction system, add $150
Deer Gun (22-in. bbl. w/ rifle-type sights, 12 ga. only, 6.25 lbs., 1968-73) . . . . . NiB $405 Ex $330 Gd $240
Skeet Gun (Made 1968-73) . . . . . . NiB $505 Ex $430 Gd $310
Trap Gun (28-in. bbl. w/Winchoke, Winchester recoil reduction system not available after 1970. Made 1968-73) . . . . NiB $505 Ex $430 Gd $310
Utility Skeet Gun (field grade wood stock, 1968-73) . . . . NiB $490 Ex $400 Gd $300
Utility Trap Gun (field grade wood stock, 1970-73) . . . . NiB $490 Ex $400 Gd $300

MODEL 1500 XTR . . . . NiB $465 Ex $300 Gd $290
Semiauto. Gas-operated. Gauges: 12 and 20 (2.75-in. chambers). Bbl.: Plain or VR; 28-in.; WinChoke (interchangeable tubes IC-M-F). American walnut stock and forend; checkered grip and forend. Weight: 7.25 lbs. Made 1978-82.

MODEL 9410 TRADITIONAL SERIES
Lever action based on the Model 94 design. .410 bore, 2.5-in. chamber. Bbl.: 24-in. w/Invector choke tubes and TruGlo sights. Stock: Walnut. Top tang safety. Made 2001 to 2006.
standard model . . . . NiB $1000 Ex $680 Gd $400
Semi Fancy model (better wood) . . . NiB $1355 Ex $880 Gd $580
Packer model (20-in. bbl.) . . . NiB $1000 Ex $680 Gd $400
Ranger model (fixed choke) . . . . NiB $830 Ex $530 Gd $330

MODEL SXP (SUPER X PUMP) SERIES
Pump/slide action. Gauge: 12 or 20, 3-in. chamber. Bbl.: 26- or 28-in. VR w/3 Invector Plus choke tubes and brass bead sight. Stock: wood or synthetic. Weight: 6.75-7.1 lbs. Made 2013 to date.
Black Shadow Deer model (22-in. rifled bbl. w/TruGlo sights and scope mount, black synthetic stock) . . . . NiB $455 Ex $355 Gd $270
Black Shadow Field model (24-, 26- or 28-in. VR w/3 Invector Plus choke tubes, black synthetic stock) . . . . NiB $330 Ex $245 Gd $190
Defender model (12 or 20 ga., 18-in. bbl. w/fixed choke, black synthetic stock) . . . . . . NiB $300 Ex $235 Gd $180
Extreme Deer model (22-in. rifled bbl. w/fiber optic sights and scope mount, black synthetic stock w/modular comb) . . . . NiB $480 Ex $365 Gd $270
Extreme Deer Hunter model (12 ga., 22-in. rifled bbl. w/fiber optic sights and scope mount, black synthetic pistol-grip stock w/modular comb) . . . . NiB $530 Ex $400 Gd $305
Field model (checkered wood stock) . . . . NiB $355 Ex $290 Gd $225
Long Beard model (12 ga., 24-in. VR bbl. w/Invector Plus tubes and fiber optic sights, camo synthetic pistol-grip stock w/modular comb) . . . . NiB $455 Ex $355 Gd $270
Marine Defender model (12 or 20 ga., 18-in. bbl. w/Invector Plus tubes, matte chrome finish, black synthetic stock) . . . . . . NiB $355 Ex $290 Gd $225
Shadow Defender model (12 or 20 ga., 18-in. bbl. w/fixed choke, black synthetic pistol-grip stock) . . . . NiB $380 Ex $305 Gd $255
Shadow Marine Defender model (12 or 20 ga., 18-in. bbl. w/ Invector Plus tubes, matte chrome finish, black synthetic pistol-grip stock) . . . . NiB $430 Ex $320 Gd $240
Trap model (12 ga., 30- or 32-in. VR bbl. w/Invector Plus tubes, Monte Carlo stock) . . . . NiB $430 Ex $320 Gd $240

SHOTGUNS

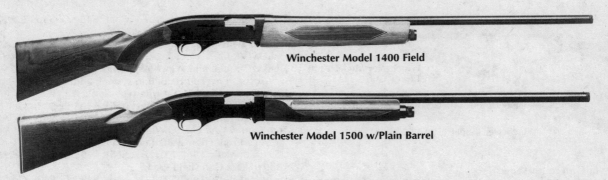

Winchester Model 1400 Field

Winchester Model 1500 w/Plain Barrel

Turkey model (12 or 20 ga., 24-in. VR bbl. w/fiber optic sights, black synthetic stock) . . . . . NiB $390 Ex $305 Gd $255

Turkey Hunter model (12 or 20 ga., 24-in. VR bbl. w/fiber optic sights, camo synthetic stock) . . . NiB $455 Ex $355 Gd $270

Ultimate Defender model (12 ga., 18-in. bbl. w/extended breeches tube, matte chrome finish, black synthetic stock, 2015-16) . . . . NiB $430 Ex $320 Gd $240

Ultimate Marine Defender model (12 ga., 18-in. bbl. w/extended breeches tube, black synthetic stock) . . . . NiB $470 Ex $380 Gd $305

Universal Hunter model (black synthetic stock, 3- or 3.5-in. chamber, fiber optic front sight) . . . . NiB $355 Ex $290 Gd $225

Waterfowl Hunter model (camo synthetic stock, 3- or 3.5-in. chamber, fiber optic front sight) . . . . NiB $400 Ex $305 Gd $205

SUPER-X MODEL I SERIES

Semiauto. Gas-operated. Takedown.12 ga. 2.75-in. chamber Four round magazine. Bbl.: VR 26-in. IC; 28-in. M or F; 30-in. F choke. Weight: About 7 lbs. Checkered pistol-grip stock. Made 1974-81.

Field model . . . . NiB $555 Ex $480 Gd $330

Skeet model (26-in. bbl., skeet style stock) . . . . NiB $755 Ex $630 Gd $455

Trap model (30-in. bbl., straight or Monte Carlo style stock) . . . . NiB $655 Ex $555 Gd $405

SUPER-X MODEL I

CUSTOM SKEET OR TRAP . . . . . . NiB $1355 Ex $1110 Gd $900
Same as Super-X Field Gun except Skeet has 26-in. bbl., SK choke, skeet-style stock and forearm of select walnut; Trap has 30-in. bbl., IM or F choke, trap-style stock (straight or Monte Carlo comb) of select walnut, recoil pad. Made 1974-84.

MODEL SUPER X2 MAGNUM SERIES

Semiauto. self-adjusting gas operated action. Gauge: 12, 3- or 3.5-in. chamber. Bbl.: 26- or 28-in. VR w/3 Invector Plus choke tubes and brass bead sight. 5-rnd. magazine. Stock: walnut or synthetic. Weight: 7.25-8 lbs. Made 1999-2006.

Field (checkered walnut stock, 1999-04) . . . . NiB $755 Ex $580 Gd $470

Field Composite (black synthetic stock, 2004-05) . . . . NiB $780 Ex $590 Gd $470

Field Light (checkered walnut stock, 6.25-6.75 lbs., 2005-06) . . . . NiB $840 Ex $605 Gd $505

Field Practical MK I (22-in. bbl. w/Invector tubes and TruGlo sights, black synthetic stock, 2003-07) . . . . NiB $965 Ex $680 Gd $505

Field Practical MK II (22-in. bbl. w/Invector tubes and ghost ring sights, 8-rnd. extended magazine, black synthetic stock, 2002-06) . . . . NiB $1080 Ex $720 Gd $555

Field Rifled Deer (22-in. rifled bbl. w/cantilever base, black synthetic stock, 2002-05) . . . NiB $800 Ex $590 Gd $460

Field Sporting Clays (28- or 30-in. VR w/3 Invector Plus choke tubes, checkered walnut or red Dura Touch stock, 2001-07) . . . . NiB $880 Ex $615 Gd $505

Field Sporting Clays Signature II (28- or 30-in. VR w/3 Invector Plus choke tubes, red anodized receiver, checkered walnut or red Dura Touch stock, 2005-06) . . . . NiB $890 Ex $630 Gd $505

Composite (3.5-in. chamber, black synthetic stock, 1999-05) . . . . NiB $890 Ex $630 Gd $505

Composite Greenhead (3.5-in. chamber, green Dura Touch stock, 2002-05) . . . . NiB $900 Ex $625 Gd $500

Composite Camo Turkey (3.5-in. chamber, 24-in. VR bbl., camo finish, 2000-07) . . . . NiB $1040 Ex $705 Gd $500

Composite Camo Waterfowl (3.5-in. chamber, 28-in. VR bbl., camo finish, 1999-05) . . . . NiB $1000 Ex $690 Gd $500

Composite Turkey (3.5-in. chamber, 24-in. VR bbl., matte finish, 1999-02) . . . . NiB $885 Ex $620 Gd $500

Composite Universal Hunter (3.5-in. chamber, camo synthetic stock, fiber optic front sight, 2002-07) . . . . NiB $1055 Ex $705 Gd $520

MODEL SX3 (SUPER X3) MAGNUM SERIES

Semiauto. self-adjusting Active Valve gas operated action. Gauge: 12 or 20, 3- or 3.5-in. chamber. Bbl.: 24-, 26- or 28-in. VR w/3 Invector Plus choke tubes and brass bead sight. 4-rnd. magazine. Stock: walnut or synthetic, adj. LOP. Weight: 6.6-7 lbs. Made 2006 to 2017 and as noted below.

Black Shadow (12 or 20 ga., black synthetic stock, matte black receiver w/red accents) . . . . NiB $900 Ex $700 Gd $530

Black Shadow model (12 ga. 3.5-in. chamber, black synthetic stock, 2012-16) . . . . NiB $930 Ex $705 Gd $505

Cantilever Buck (12 or 20 ga., 22-in. rifled bbl., checkered synthetic stock) . . . . NiB $1000 Ex $755 Gd $580

Cantilever Extreme Turkey (12 or 20 ga. 3.5-in. chamber, 24-in. VR bbl. w/cantilever optic mount, camo synthetic stock) . . . . NiB $1055 Ex $780 Gd $580

Classic Field (checkered walnut stock non-adj., 2008-09) . . . . NiB $980 Ex $755 Gd $580

Composite (3.5-in. chamber, black synthetic stock, 2006-11) . . . . NiB $1050 Ex $805 Gd $580

Composite All Purpose Field (12 or 20 ga., 3.5-in. chamber, camo synthetic stock, 2006-11) . . . . NiB $1230 Ex $830 Gd $630

Composite Cantilever Extreme Turkey model (12 ga. 3.5-in. chamber, 24-in. VR bbl. w/cantilever optic mount, camo synthetic stock, 2006-11) . . NiB $1230 Ex $830 Gd $630

Composite Sporting (28-, 30- or 32-in. VR bbl. w/extended Briley choke tubes, black synthetic stock, matte nickel receiver, fiber optic front sight, 2002-07) . . . . NiB $1455 Ex $1005 Gd $755

Composite Waterfowl (12 or 20 ga., 3.5-in. chamber, camo synthetic stock, 2006-11) . . NiB $1230 Ex $830 Gd $630

Field model (12 or 20 ga., checkered satin walnut stock) . . . . NiB $1000 Ex $755 Gd $580

Field Cantilever (12 or 20 ga., 22-in. rifled bbl., checkered synthetic stock, 2006-11) . . NiB $1030 Ex $755 Gd $580

Field Composite (12 or 20 ga., checkered synthetic stock, 2006-11). . . . . NiB $980 Ex $755 Gd $580
Gray Shadow (12 ga. 3.5-in. chamber, 26- or 28-in. VR bbl., gray receiver, gray synthetic stock, disc. 2009) . . . . NiB $1055 Ex $780 Gd $580
Long Beard (12 ga. 3.5-in. chamber, 24-in. VR bbl., camo synthetic stock). . . . . NiB $1080 Ex $830 Gd $605
Sporting model (12 ga., 28-, 30- or 32-in. VR ported bbl. w/extended Invector Plus choke tubes, matte gray receiver, satin checkered walnut stock w/adj. comb) . . . . NiB $1455 Ex $1005 Gd $755
Ultimate Sporting (12 ga., 28-, 30- or 32-in. VR bbl. w/extended Invector Plus choke tubes, matte nickel finish, satin checkered walnut stock w/adj. comb). . . . . NiB $1580 Ex $1055 Gd $805
Universal Hunter (12 or 20 ga., camo synthetic stock, TruGlo fiber optic front sight, 2012-16). .NiB $1055 Ex $780 Gd $580
Universal Hunter (3.5-in. chamber, camo synthetic stock, fiber optic front sight, 2012-16) . . . NiB $1030 Ex $755 Gd $605
Walnut Field (checkered walnut stock, 2006-14). . . . . NiB $1030 Ex $755 Gd $580
Waterfowl Hunter (camo synthetic stock, fiber optic front sight). . . . . NiB $1030 Ex $755 Gd $580
Waterfowl Hunter (12 ga. 3.5-in. chamber, camo synthetic stock, 2012-16). . . . . NiB $1055 Ex $780 Gd $580

Winchester SX4

MODEL SX4 (SUPER X4) MAGNUM SERIES
Semiauto. Self-adjusting Active Valve gas operated action. Gauge: 12 or 20, 3- or 3.5-in. chamber. Bbl.: 24-, 26- or 28-in. VR w/3 Invector Plus choke tubes and TruGlo fiber optic sight. 3- or 4-rnd. magazine. Stock: walnut or synthetic w/LOP spacers. Weight: 6.5-6.75 lbs. Made 2107 to date and as noted below.
Cantilever Buck (12 ga., 22-in. rifled bbl., checkered synthetic stock, Weaver rail) . . NiB $820 Ex $705 Gd $630
Compact model (black synthetic stock w/13-in. LOP) . . . . NiB $690 Ex $630 Gd $555
Field model (12 or 20 ga., checkered satin walnut stock) . . . . NiB $805 Ex $705 Gd $630
Field Compact model (walnut stock w/13-in. LOP). . . . . NiB $805 Ex $705 Gd $630
NWTF Cantilever Turkey (12 ga. 3.5-in. chamber, 24-in. VR bbl. w/cantilever optic mount, camo synthetic stock) . . . . NiB $905 Ex $805 Gd $700
SX4 (Super X4) model (Quadra-Vent ported bbl., black stock) . . . . NiB $690 Ex $630 Gd $555
Universal Hunter (12 or 20 ga., camo synthetic stock, TruGlo fiber optic front sight) . . . . NiB $905 Ex $805 Gd $700
Upland Field (checkered walnut stock) . . . . NiB $955 Ex $830 Gd $720
Waterfowl Hunter (20 or 12 ga. 3- or 3.5-in. chamber, camo synthetic stock) . . . . NiB $805 Ex $705 Gd $630
Waterfowl Hunter Compact model (13-in. LOP) . . . . NiB $805 Ex $705 Gd $630

JAMES WOODWARD & SONS —
London, England

James Woodward & Sons was acquired by James Purdey & Sons after World War II.

BEST QUALITY HAMMERLESS DOUBLE
Sidelock. Automatic ejectors. Double triggers or single trigger. Built to order in all standard gauges, bbl. lengths, boring

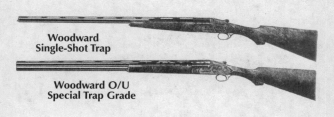

Woodward Single-Shot Trap

Woodward O/U Special Trap Grade

and other specifications. Made as a field gun, pigeon and wildfowl gun, skeet gun or trap gun. Manufactured prior to World War II.
12 ga. w/double triggers . . . .NiB $30,000 Ex $22,700 Gd $18,900
20 ga. w/double triggers . . . .NiB $33,000 Ex $26,890 Gd $18,700
28 ga. w/double triggers . . . .NiB $40,600 Ex $33,560 Gd $25,000
.410 ga. w/double triggers . . .NiB $45,000 Ex $36,900 Gd $25,000
w/selective single trigger, add 10%

BEST QUALITY O/U SHOTGUN
Sidelock. Automatic ejectors. Double triggers or single trigger. Built to order in all standard gauges, bbl. lengths, boring and other specifications, including Special Trap Grade w/ VR. Woodward introduced this type of gun in 1908. Made until World War II.
12 ga. w/double triggers . . . .NiB $31,660 Ex $25,850 Gd $20,000
20 ga. w/double triggers . . . .NiB $42,500 Ex $35,980 Gd $25,500
28 ga. w/double triggers . . . .NiB $55,000 Ex $44,900 Gd $32,000
.410 ga. .410 w/double triggers . . .NiB $63,000 Ex $49,800 Gd $35,000
w/single trigger, add 10%

BEST QUALITY
SINGLE-SHOT TRAP . NiB $14,860 Ex $12,790 Gd $10,000
Sidelock. Mechanical features of the O/U gun. VR bbl. 12 ga. only. Built to customer's specifications and measurements, including type and amount of checkering, carving and engraving. Made prior to World War II.

ZEPHYR — Manufactured by Victor Sarasqueta Company, Eibar, Spain

MODEL 1
O/U SHOTGUN . . . . .NiB $1341 Ex $1083 Gd $778
Same general specifications as Field Model O/U except with more elaborate engraving, finer wood and checkering. Imported by Stoeger 1930s- to 1951.

MODEL 2
O/U SHOTGUN . . . . .NiB $1746 Ex $1393 Gd $994
Sidelock. Auto ejectors. Gauges: 12, 16, 20, 28 and .410. Bbls.: 25 to 30 in. most common. Modest scroll engraving on receiver and sideplates. Checkered, straight-grain select walnut buttstock and forend. Imported by Stoeger 1930s to 1951.

MODEL 3
O/U SHOTGUN . . . . .NiB $2369 Ex $1888 Gd $1337
Same general specifications as Zephyr Model 2 O/U except with more elaborate engraving, finer wood and checkering. Imported by Stoeger 1930s to 1951.

MODEL 400E FIELD GRADE DOUBLE-BARREL SHOTGUN
Anson & Deeley boxlock system. Gauges: 12 16, 20, 28 and .410. Bbls.: 25 to 30 in. Weight: 4.5 lbs. (.410) to 6.25 lbs. (12 ga.). Checkered French walnut buttstock and forearm. Modest scroll engraving on bbls., receiver and trigger guard. Imported by Stoeger 1930s to 1950s.

SHOTGUNS

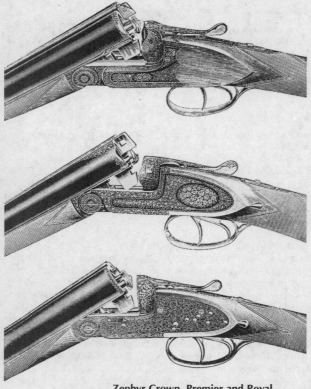

Zephyr Crown, Premier and Royal Grades (top to bottom)

12, 16 or 20 ga. . . . . NiB $2166 Ex $1388 Gd $1000
28 ga. or .410 . . . . NiB $1877 Ex $1497 Gd $1000
w/selective single
   trigger, add $250

MODEL 401 E SKEET GRADE DOUBLE-BARREL SHOTGUN
Same general specifications as Field Grade except with beavertail forearm. Bbls.: 25 to 28 in. Imported by Stoeger 1930s
to 1950s.
12, 16 or 20 ga. . . . . NiB $1954 Ex $1600 Gd $1216
28 ga., or .410 . . . . NiB $2144 Ex $1698 Gd $1277
w/selective single trigger, add $450
w/non-selective single trigger, add $300

MODEL 402E DELUXE DOUBLE-BARREL
SHOTGUN . . . . NiB $2455 Ex $2089 Gd $1466
Same general specifications as Model 400E Field Grade except
for custom refinements. The action was carefully hand-honed
for smoother operation; finer, elaborate engraving throughout,
plus higher quality wood in stock and forearm. Imported by
Stoeger 1930s to 1950s.

CROWN GRADE. . . . . NiB $1800 Ex $1498 Gd $1056
Boxlock. Gauges: 12, 16, 20, 28 and .410. Bbls.: 25 to 30 in.
standard but any lengths could be ordered. Weight: 6 lbs., 4 oz.
(.410) to 7 lbs., 4 oz. (12 ga.). Checkered Spanish walnut stock
and beavertail forearm. Receiver engraved with scroll patterns.
Imported by Stoeger 1938 to 1951.

FIELD MODEL O/U SHOTGUN . . NiB $988 Ex $745 Gd $566
Anson & Deeley boxlock. Auto ejectors. Gauges: 12, 16 and
20. Bbls.: 25 to 30 in. standard- full-length matt rib. Double

triggers. Checkered buttstock and forend. Light scroll engraving
on receiver. Imported by Stoeger 1930s to 1951.

HONKER SINGLE-SHOT
SHOTGUN . . . . NiB $676 Ex $580 Gd $390
Sidelock. Gauge: 10; 3.5-in. magnum. 36-in. VR barrel w/F
choke. Weight: 10.5 lbs. Checkered select Spanish walnut buttstock and beavertail forend; recoil pad. Imported by Stoeger
1950s to 1972.

PINEHURST DOUBLE-BARREL
SHOTGUN . . . . NiB $1388 Ex $1190 Gd $800
Boxlock. Gauges: 12, 16, 20, 28 and .410. Bbls.: 25 to 28 in.
most common. Checkered, select walnut buttstock and forend.
Selective single trigger and auto ejectors. Imported by Stoeger
1950s to 1972.

PREMIER GRADE DOUBLE-BARREL
SHOTGUN . . . . NiB $2870 Ex $2300 Gd $1560
Sidelock. Gauges: 12, 16, 20, 28 and .410. Bbls.: Any length,
but 25 to 30 in. most popular. Weight: 4.5 lbs. (.410) to 7 lbs.
(12 ga.). Checkered high-grade French walnut buttstock and
forend. Imported by Stoeger 1930s to 1951.

ROYAL GRADE DOUBLE-BARREL
SHOTGUN . . . . NiB $4388 Ex $2287 Gd $2077
Same general specifications as the Premier Grade except
with more elaborate engraving, finer checkering and wood.
Imported by Stoeger 1930s to 1951.

STERLINGWORTH II DOUBLE-BARREL
SHOTGUN . . . . NiB $1000 Ex $790 Gd $678
Genuine sidelocks with color-casehardened sideplates.
Gauges: 12, 16, 20 and .410. Bbls.: 25 to 30 in. Weight: 6 lbs.,
4 oz. (.410) to 7 lbs., 4 oz. (12 ga.). Select Spanish walnut butt-
stock and beavertail forearm. Light scroll engraving on receiver
and sideplates. Automatic, sliding-tang safety. Imported by
Stoeger 1950s to 1972.

THUNDERBIRD DOUBLE-BARREL
SHOTGUN . . . . NiB $1221 Ex $900 Gd $755
Sidelock. Gauges: 12 and 10 Magnum. Bbls.: 32-in., both F
choke. Weight: 8 lbs., 8 oz. (12 ga.), 12 lbs. (10 ga.). Receiver
elaborately engraved with waterfowl scenes. Checkered select
Spanish walnut buttstock and beavertail forend. Plain extractors, double triggers. Imported by Stoeger 1950 to 1972.

UPLAND KING DOUBLE-BARREL
SHOTGUN . . . . NiB $1290 Ex $1066 Gd $886
Sidelock. Gauges: 12, 16, 20, 28 and .410. Bbls.: 25 to 28 in.
most popular. Checkered buttstock and forend of select walnut.
Selective single trigger and auto ejectors. Imported by Stoeger
1950 to 1972.

UPLANDER 4E DOUBLE-BARREL
SHOTGUN . . . . NiB $900 Ex $688 Gd $525
Same general specifications as the Zephyr Sterlingworth II
except with selective auto ejectors and highly polished sideplates. Imported by Stoeger 1951 to 1972.

WOODLANDER II DOUBLE-BARREL
SHOTGUN . . . . NiB $645 Ex $465 Gd $377
Boxlock. Gauges: 12, 20 and .410. Bbls.: 25 to 30 in. Weight:
6 lbs., 4 oz. (.410) to 7 lbs., 4 oz. (12 ga.). Checkered
Spanish walnut stock and beavertail forearm. Engraved receiv-
er. Imported by Stoeger 1950 to 1972.

Index

GRADING: **NiB** = New in Box **Ex** = Excellent or NRA 95% **Gd** = Good or NRA 68%

INDEX

Notes